# READER'S DIGEST

# 1981

# ALMANAC

## AND YEARBOOK

PUBLISHED ANNUALLY BY
THE READER'S DIGEST ASSOCIATION, INC.
PLEASANTVILLE, NEW YORK 10570

**Reader's Digest**

# 1981

# ALMANAC
## AND YEARBOOK

A specially commissioned work
prepared by
David C. Whitney Associates, Inc.
with the editors of
The Reader's Digest Association, Inc.

# CONTENTS

The main sections of the *Reader's Digest 1981 Almanac and Yearbook* are listed below along with the contents of each. To find specific information on persons, places, or subjects, turn to the alphabetical *Index* with its more than 9,000 references on pages 978–1024.

# MAJOR NEWS DEVELOPMENTS: 1980

For the convenience of the reader who seeks the entire year's news at a glance, following is a listing of some of 1980's major events and developments with references to the page numbers on which they are reviewed in words and pictures.

The multitude of events and developments that affected the United States and the world in 1980 are examined in detail throughout the *Reader's Digest 1981 Almanac and Yearbook.*

For the reader who wishes to review the events of the year in the order in which they happened, pages 8–30 provide a month-by-month, day-by-day chronology.

Facing each monthly summary of events is a FOCUS page providing details of a major event or development.

The main body of the *Almanac* contains 38 sections arranged alphabetically from *Acci-* *dents and Disasters* to *Women's Rights.* Within these sections other articles examine additional important happenings of 1980. Each section also contains the latest facts and statistics on thousands of persons, places, and events.

To find a specific fact the reader should consult the alphabetical *Index* on pages 987–1024.

QUICK QUIZ questions at the bottom of pages in the sections *History* and *Nations of the World* guide the curious reader to interesting and unusual information throughout the *Reader's Digest 1981 Almanac and Yearbook.*

# JANUARY

**1   New U.S. minimum wage of $3.10 per hour** takes effect.

**1   Fire in social club kills 45:** New Year's Eve party in Chapais, Quebec, ends in disaster.

**1   Earthquake in Azores kills 52:** Measures 7.0 on Richter scale; Terceira Is. hardest hit.

**3–6  Gandhi wins landslide election in India:** Former prime minister's Congress-I party wins 351 of 542 seats in lower house of parliament, over two-thirds majority; takes office Jan. 14.

**4   Grain shipments to Soviet Union barred:** President Carter also suspends sale of technology equipment, curtails Soviet fishing in U.S. waters, and considers U.S. boycott of summer Olympics in Moscow, in retaliation for Soviet invasion of Afghanistan in December 1979.

**4   Mauritanian president ousted in coup:** Mohammed Mahmoud Ould Luly replaced after 6 months in office by former prime minister Mohammed Khouna Ould Haidalla.

**6   Futures trading in grain suspended:** Government acts to prevent disarray in U.S. markets after embargo of grain shipments to Soviets.

**8   Dow Jones average jumps 19.71 points:** Largest advance in stock prices since Nov. 1, 1978.

**8   "Test-tube baby" clinic approved in Virginia:** State health authorities approve laboratory at Eastern Virginia Medical School in Norfolk to help women unable to conceive normally.

**9   Saudi Arabia executes 63 for mosque attack:** Beheaded for participation in November 1979 raid on Grand Mosque in Mecca.

**11   Sextuplets born in Florence, Italy:** Rosanna Giannini gives birth to four boys and two girls.

**14   UN resolution condemns Soviets:** General Assembly votes, 104–18, to approve resolution deploring Soviet invasion of Afghanistan; does not mention Soviet Union by name but asks immediate withdrawal of foreign troops from Afghanistan.

**14   American newsmen expelled from Iran:** Ouster due to "biased reporting."

**14   Marshall Islands granted self-rule:** Agreement with U.S. allows people to be autonomous in domestic and foreign affairs except in defense and security matters; U.S. to supply economic assistance in exchange for military rights for minimum of 15 years.

**14   Lung cancer in women rising:** U.S. surgeon general reports that death rate from lung cancer could become higher than from breast cancer in women by 1983.

**16   Workers to be warned against carcinogens:** Labor Department announces first comprehensive rules to protect workers against exposure to cancer-causing substances.

**16   N.Y. Stock Exchange has 2d-busiest day ever:** Volume soars to 67.7 million shares traded.

**17   Price of gold rises above $800 per ounce:** Closes in New York at $802; hits $835 on London market Jan. 18.

**19   Former Supreme Court Justice dies at 81:** William O. Douglas served on Court longer than any other justice, from 1939 to 1975.

**20   Pro football Super Bowl XIV:** Won by Pittsburgh Steelers, 31–19, over Los Angeles Rams at Pasadena, Calif.

**20   Bullring collapses in Colombia, killing 222:** More than 500 injured in town of Sincelejo.

**21   Iran air crash kills 128:** All aboard Iran Air Boeing 727 perish as plane crashes in Elburz Mountains near Teheran.

**21   Carter asks support of Olympic boycott:** Sends personal messages to more than 100 heads of government seeking support for proposal to boycott summer games in Moscow unless Soviet Union withdraws troops from Afghanistan.

**21   Carter, Bush win in Iowa precinct caucuses:** President Carter beats Sen. Edward Kennedy (D-Mass.) by 2–1 margin; George Bush upsets Ronald Reagan in Republican caucus.

**22   Andrei Sakharov expelled from Moscow:** Nobel laureate and leading dissident stripped of honors and exiled to industrial city of Gorky following call for Soviet Union to withdraw from Afghanistan.

**23   State of the Union message presented:** President Carter warns that U.S. would use military force to repel any threat to Persian Gulf, calls for renewal of draft registration, vows aid to Pakistan to resist outside aggression, asks for energy conservation and comprehensive energy policy.

**23–25  Oil companies announce record 1979 profits:** Exxon Corp. net profit is $4.295 billion with 55% net increase over 1978; Mobil Corp. reports net profit of $2.01 billion, a 78% increase; Texaco Inc. shows net profit of $1.76 billion, 106% more than 1978.

**24   Earthquake rocks San Francisco area:** Little damage reported; measures 5.5 on Richter scale.

**24   Air crash in Burma kills 42 soldiers:** Transport plane crashes near Mandalay.

**24   Congress approves trade pact with China:** Senate votes, 74–8, House votes, 294–88, to give China most-favored-nation status, putting into effect pact signed in July 1979.

**25   Iran elects first president:** Finance minister Aholhassan Bani-Sadr receives 75% of vote.

**28   Ship collision kills 23 in Tampa Bay:** Coast Guard vessel *Blackthorn* collides with oil tanker *Capricorn* near St. Petersburg, Fla.

**28   President Carter sends budget to Congress:** Offers $615.8 billion budget for fiscal year 1981; deficit of $15.8 billion would be lowest in seven years; mild recession forecast.

**28   Canadians spirit 6 Americans out of Iran:** U.S. citizens, not among 50 known hostages, fly out of Iran on Canadian diplomatic passports with forged Iranian visas after being hidden in embassy for 3 months; Canada closes embassy as its diplomats leave with Americans.

**29   Islamic nations denounce Soviet Union, Iran:** Foreign ministers gathered in Islamabad, Pakistan, condemn Soviet Union for Afghanistan invasion and rebuke Iran for holding American hostages.

**29   Trade deficit decreased in 1979:** Commerce Department announces deficit fell by $3.7 billion to $24.7 billion despite $17.2 billion increase in cost of imported oil.

**29   U.S. Steel Corp. reports big loss:** $561.7 million in fourth quarter of 1979 is largest quarterly loss to date in U.S. corporate history.

**31   Queen Juliana to abdicate:** Will step down from Netherlands throne on 71st birthday, April 30, in favor of eldest daughter Princess Beatrix.

# AFGHANS RESIST SOVIET INVASION

FOCUS

Afghan rebels set out on horseback for raid on Soviet troops near Herat, the nation's third-largest city. Taking advantage of the rugged, mountainous countryside, Afghan guerrillas effectively use hit-and-run tactics.

United Press Int'l.

Defying world opinion, the Soviet Union escalated its military intervention in Afghanistan in 1980, killing thousands of Muslim guerrillas with air and tank attacks against Afghan villages.

But the Muslim guerrillas fought back and by midyear had inflicted casualties on about 10% of the 85,000 Soviet invasion troops.

The Soviet invasion of its southern neighbor began on Christmas 1979 because Moscow's leaders were angered at the independence exhibited by the country's communist president, Hafizullah Amin. Two days later Soviet forces captured and executed Amin, replacing him with pro-Moscow puppet Babrak Karmel.

Denouncing the Soviet action and calling for a withdrawal of Soviet troops, President Carter on Jan. 4, 1980, embargoed sales of grain and high-technology equipment to the Soviet Union. He delayed Senate consideration of ratification of the SALT II agreement. In the following months, about 55 other nations joined the U.S. in protest by boycotting the Olympic Games held in Moscow (see pages 836–837).

When the UN Security Council voted 12–2 on Jan. 7, calling for withdrawal of Soviet troops, the Soviet Union vetoed the measure. Soviet leaders then ignored a similar resolution adopted 104–18 by the UN General Assembly on Jan. 14.

# FEBRUARY

**1    Unemployment up to 6.2% in January:** Level is highest since July 1978, Labor Department reports; increase from 5.9% in December 1979.

**2–3    FBI "Abscam" probe revealed:** TV and press reports uncover 2-year bribery and corruption investigation against members of Congress (see opposite page).

**2–3    New Mexico prison riot leaves 33 dead:** Nearly 1,000 inmates of New Mexico State Penitentiary in Santa Fe go on 36-hour rampage; many fires begun; National Guard and police recapture prison on Feb. 3.

**4    U.S. issues dietary guidelines:** Departments of Agriculture and Health and Human Services jointly recommend avoidance of too much fat, cholesterol, sugar, salt, and alcohol; guidelines aimed at establishing national nutrition policy.

**5    State Department issues human-rights study:** Annual report includes communist countries for first time; accuses Soviet Union of total "disregard for basic human rights" in Afghanistan.

**6    Bolshoi dancers defect:** Sulamith Messerer, 71, a teacher, and son Mikhail Messerer, 31, a dancer with Soviet Union's Bolshoi Ballet, request asylum at U.S. Embassy in Tokyo, Japan.

**7    Chrysler Corp. reports record loss:** Company's $375.8 million fourth-quarter loss brings total 1979 loss to $1.1 billion, believed largest yearly deficit in U.S. corporate history.

**8    President Carter asks new draft plan:** Urges program in which both men and women whose 19th and 20th birthdays fall in 1980 be required to register; congressional opposition expected.

**10    Maine Democratic caucuses go for Carter:** President wins 44% of vote, Sen. Edward Kennedy 40%, and Calif. Gov. Jerry Brown 14%.

**11    Chicago schools reopen after strike:** Schools in nation's third-largest school district had been closed two weeks in teachers' strike.

**12    Alaska lands designated wildlife refuges:** Interior Secretary Cecil D. Andrus orders 40 million acres of federal landholdings made into wildlife refuges after Senate delays action on 1978 bill to protect acreage; bars new oil, gas, and mineral development for at least 20 years.

**12    IOC reaffirms Moscow as Olympic site:** International Olympic Committee backs summer games in Moscow as scheduled, despite U.S. request they be moved or postponed.

**13    Stock market reaches 17-month high:** Dow Jones average closes at 903.84, highest since Sept. 12, 1978.

**13–22    Storms paralyze California, Arizona:** Pacific storms cause widespread flooding, leave 36 dead in Southern California and Arizona; damage estimated at more than $300 million.

**13–24    Winter Olympic Games held at Lake Placid:** Athletes from 38 nations compete in upstate New York; East Germany wins 23 medals, Soviet Union is second with 22, U.S. third with 12.

**14    Amoco settles suit, agrees to pay $700 million:** Standard Oil Company (Indiana) settles Energy Department charges of price violations; does not admit guilt but will make $300 million worth of reimbursements to customers, price cuts, and payments to government; will spend $400 million in accelerated investment in production.

**15    Polish prime minister replaced:** Piotr Jaroszewicz replaced by Edward Babiuch after politburo shakeup.

**17    George Bush wins Puerto Rican primary:** Defeats Sen. Howard Baker (R-Tenn.) in first Republican primary of 1980 presidential race.

**18    Trudeau wins in Canada:** Voters return Pierre Trudeau and his Liberal Party to office 9 months after losing to Progressive Party and Joe Clark; Liberals win 146 seats, Progressives acquire only 103; Trudeau sworn in March 3.

**21    Congressman resigns post in Abscam scandal:** Rep. Richard Kelly (R-Fla.) resigns from House Republican Conference to avoid possible expulsion for allegations in Abscam investigation; remains member of House.

**21–27    General strike in Afghanistan:** Begins in Kabul in response to Muslim rebel call for protest against Soviet military presence; over 300 killed in street fighting.

**22    Consumer Price Index soared 1.4% in January:** Labor Department reports steepest monthly increase since August 1973; shows 16.8% annual inflation rate.

**25    Military coup staged in Surinam:** Government of Premier Henck A. E. Arron toppled, had been in power since independence in 1975; nation to be controlled by military council.

**26    Reagan, Carter win New Hampshire primary:** President Carter wins clear 49% to 38% victory over Sen. Edward Kennedy; Ronald Reagan defeats George Bush, 50% to 23%.

**26    Radioactive water spills at reactor:** Crystal River power plant in Redlevel, Fla., shuts down automatically after valve ruptures; no radiation is released outside plant.

**26    Supreme Court backs hazardous work refusals:** Rules that employers cannot take reprisals against workers who refuse in good faith to work in unsafe areas or at dangerous tasks.

**26    Israel and Egypt exchange ambassadors:** Israeli Ambassador Eliahu Ben-Elissar presents credentials to Egyptian President Anwar al-Sadat in Cairo; simultaneously Ambassador Saad Mortada presents credentials to Israeli President Yitzhak Navon in Jerusalem.

**27    Court upholds testimony by spouse:** Supreme Court rules unanimously that a person can voluntarily testify against his or her spouse in federal criminal trials.

**27    Leftists seize embassy in Colombia:** Guerrillas capture embassy of Dominican Republic in Bogotá during diplomatic reception; hold diplomats from 17 nations, including U.S. Ambassador Diego C. Asencio; release 13 hostages on Feb. 28 and 5 more on Feb. 29; demand ransom and release of political prisoners.

**27–29    Robert Mugabe wins Zimbabwe Rhodesia election:** Former guerrilla leader's ZANU-Patriotic Front party wins 62.9% of popular vote and captures 57 of 80 seats reserved for blacks in 100-member parliament.

**28    Most autos fail safety test:** Department of Transportation says all 1979 foreign cars and most domestic autos failed to provide protection to occupants during 35-mile-an-hour crash test; Chevrolet Citation, Plymouth Horizon, and Ford Mustang performed especially well.

# FBI'S ABSCAM SNARES CONGRESSMEN

FOCUS

Newspapers revealed in February that the FBI had been conducting an investigation of corrupt members of the U.S. Congress and other public officials for two years in an operation called *Abscam*. FBI undercover agents posing as Arab sheiks and businessmen had paid out hundreds of thousands of dollars in bribes, while pretending to obtain favors from the officials.

During the next several months the Justice Department obtained indictments of six U.S. representatives, one U.S. senator, and 13 other public officials and businessmen on such charges as bribery, conspiracy, and extortion.

The members of Congress who were indicted included: Sen. Harrison A. Williams Jr. (D-N.J.), chairman of the Senate Committee on Labor and Human Resources; Rep. Frank Thompson Jr. (D-N.J.), chairman of the House Committee on Administration; Rep. John M. Murphy (D-N.Y.), chairman of the House Committee on Merchant Marine and Fisheries; Rep. Michael O. Myers (D-Pa.), Rep. Raymond F. Lederer (D-Pa.), Rep. John W. Jenrette Jr. (D-S.C.), and Rep. Richard Kelly (R-Fla.), the only Republican congressman to be charged in the investigation.

By mid-December juries had convicted Thompson, Murphy, Myers, and Jenrette.

Of the six members of the U.S. House of Representatives indicted in the scandal, only Lederer won reelection in the November election. Myers was ousted from Congress (see page 156) and Jenrette resigned his seat. Sen. Williams is not up for election again until 1982, and did not indicate whether he will try to run for another term in the U.S. Senate.

Other public officials indicted in the Abscam investigation included Angelo J. Errichetti, mayor of Camden, N.J.; George X. Schwartz, president of Philadelphia's city council; and Philadelphia councilmen Harry P. Janotti and Louis C. Johanson.

FBI used concealed TV cameras to record congressmen and others performing criminal acts. This shows Rep. Michael Myers (D-Pa.), *second from left*, taking envelope containing $50,000 from FBI undercover agent.

08-22-79    12:43:25

Wide World

# MARCH

**1    UN Security Council rebukes Israel:** Adopts resolution calling for dismantling of settlements in West Bank; U.S. joins 14 other nations in unanimous vote; President Carter disavows vote on March 3 (see opposite page).

**1    Kidnap victim found after 7 years:** Steven Stayner, 14, found in Ukiah, Calif., along with another kidnap victim, Timothy Lee White, 5; Stayner, abducted on his way from school in Merced, Calif., Dec. 4, 1972, lived with Kenneth Parnell, 48, believing Parnell's story that his parents didn't want him.

**2–3    Spring snowstorms kill 36:** Record low temperatures reported in southeastern states.

**3    Kissinger wins Supreme Court decision:** Court rules, 5–2, that former secretary of state Henry Kissinger does not have to return transcripts of telephone conversations made in office.

**4    Massachusetts, Vermont hold primaries:** Sen. Edward Kennedy defeats President Carter, 65% to 29% in Mass., while Anderson squeaks by Bush with 32% on Republican side; in Vermont Anderson polls 33% to Reagan's 30% in GOP vote; Carter outdraws Kennedy, 75% to 25%.

**5    Channel Islands become 40th National Park:** Nation's newest national park includes Santa Rosa, Santa Cruz, San Miguel, Anacap, Santa Barbara, and Prince islands in California.

**6    Supermarket chains freeze some prices:** A & P and Safeway Stores announce 30-day price-freeze on own brand products.

**7    Producer Price Index increased 1.5% in February,** Labor Department reports; annual rate before compounding is 18%.

**7    Two million tires recalled:** Uniroyal Tire Co. announces recall of 1975–77 steel-belted radials because of tread and belt separations.

**7    Unemployment down in February:** Labor Department reports drop of 0.2%.

**8    Reagan wins landslide in South Carolina primary:** Sweeps Republican race with 54%; Connally receives 29% and Bush, 16%.

**10    UN commission fails to see hostages:** 5-member panel leaves Iran after Ayatollah Khomeini overrules efforts to visit captives.

**11    Primaries held in Florida, Georgia, and Alabama:** Ronald Reagan wins all three GOP contests; President Carter is victor in Democratic contests.

**12    Illinois man found guilty of 33 murders:** John Wayne Gacy, 37, sentenced March 13 to electric chair for most murders in U.S. history.

**13    Ford acquitted in auto-crash trial:** Jury in Winamac, Ind., finds Ford Motor Co. not guilty on 3 charges of reckless homicide in connection with deaths of 3 young women in fiery crash of their 1973 Pinto auto; first case in which a U.S. corporation stood trial on criminal charges in case involving product defect.

**14    Air crash near Warsaw, Poland, kills 87:** Passengers on Polish jetliner include 22 boxers and officials of U.S. amateur boxing team.

**14    President unveils new anti-inflation program:** Plans to cut federal spending $13 billion to balance budget, curb consumer credit, impose immediate fee on imported oil.

**15    Ford announces he will not enter GOP race:** Former President Gerald Ford says he will not enter 1980 presidential race.

**15    Dole quits GOP race:** Sen. Robert Dole (R-Kan.) withdraws from presidential contest.

**17    Stock market dips 23.04 points:** Dow Jones average closes at 788.65; biggest one-day loss since Oct. 9, 1979.

**17    President Carter signs new Refugee Act of 1980:** First major overhaul of immigration laws since 1965 raises number allowed to enter U.S. to 320,000 from 290,000 per year.

**18    Major banks raise prime lending rate:** Cost to best business customers reaches 19%.

**18    Carter, Reagan win Illinois primaries:** On Democratic side, President Carter wins 65% of vote against Kennedy's 31%; Ronald Reagan polls 48%, while John Anderson gets 38%.

**23    Shah leaves Panama:** Deposed Shah of Iran leaves exile in Panama; arrives in Cairo March 24 and is granted permanent asylum.

**24    Stock prices move to 2-year low:** Dow Jones average falls 19.71 points to 765.44; lowest since April 6, 1978.

**24    Westerners evacuated from Chad:** All American personnel at U.S. Embassy in Ndjamena among 400 whites to leave because of civil war.

**24    Archbishop assassinated in El Salvador:** Archbishop Oscar Arnulfo Romero killed while officiating mass in San Salvador.

**25    Consumer Price Index rose 1.4% in Feb.,** Labor Department reports; annual inflation rate stands at 16.8%.

**25    New York, Connecticut hold primaries:** Sen. Edward Kennedy wins 59% of vote in New York, against Carter's 41%; Kennedy gets 47% in Connecticut to Carter's 41%; on GOP side, Bush wins Connecticut poll with 39% to Reagan's 34%; Reagan wins 75% of New York vote to Bush's 6%.

**27    Oil platform capsizes in North Sea:** 128 killed off coast of Stavanger, Norway.

**27    Gold-mine accident kills 31:** Cable of mineshaft at Vaal Reefs mine in South Africa snaps, plunging 31 miners to death.

**27    Dormant volcano erupts in Washington:** Mount St. Helens in Cascade Mountains, spews clouds of steam and ash; residents evacuated.

**27    U.S. posts largest trade deficit in history:** Value of imports exceeded exports in February by $5.6 billion, Commerce Department reports.

**27    Silver price plunges:** Hits $10.80 after 15 consecutive days of decline; due to huge sell-off March 26 by Bache Halsey Stuart Shields Inc. when clients, the Hunt brothers, could not put up needed $100 million to cover futures position.

**29    Confusion over Iran relations:** Iran announces receipt of letter from President Carter to Ayatollah Khomeini apologizing for U.S. policy; White House denies message even though Iranians release text; Iran president Bani-Sadr acknowledges, March 30, receipt of letter from Carter that White House does not deny.

**29    U.S., Turkey sign agreement:** Allows U.S. continuing use of 12 military bases in Turkey in exchange for economic and military aid.

**31    New banking law signed:** President Carter signs bill establishing universal system of banking reserves and gradually raising ceilings on interest paid to small savers.

# MOUNT ST. HELENS VOLCANO ERUPTS

A plume of steam and ash rises from Mount St. Helens volcano in the state of Washington as it erupts on May 18. Eruption of the volcano caused devastation over large areas of Washington and Oregon. Volcanic ash blanketed areas as far as 500 miles away and drifted even farther eastward. The eruption set off mud flows, floods, and landslides, causing damage estimated at more than $2.7 billion. Thirty-four bodies were recovered by the end of September, with 32 other persons still missing.

United Press Int'l.

On March 27, 1980, Mount St. Helens volcano, dormant for 123 years, spewed forth clouds of steam and ash, following a week of earthquakes that had rumbled through the mountain and surrounding countryside. Scientists, believing it to be the first stages of a major eruption, recommended evacuation of the surrounding area.

Located in the Cascade Range in southwest Washington, the volcano had its most recent previous eruption in 1857.

The mountain continued to spray steam and ash for weeks until May 18, when it erupted with giant force, sending clouds of ash 60,000 feet high. About 1,500 feet of the cap atop the 9,671-foot mountain was completely blown away. Towns as far as 500 miles away were showered with the volcanic ash. Two earthquakes, measuring 5.0 on the Richter scale, were recorded just before the giant explosion. The resultant mudslides and floods brought death to 66 persons, although the toll would have been much higher had the area not been evacuated earlier. Property damage was estimated at nearly $3 billion.

Additional major eruptions occurred on May 25, June 12, July 22, Aug. 7, and Oct. 17–18.

New earthquakes in late December brought fears of another major eruption.

Data from the U.S. Geological Survey predicted that ash fallout from the erupting volcano could cause serious flooding in 1981 in southwestern Washington, along the Cowlitz River, which was clogged by mud flows after the May 18 eruption.

# APRIL

**1   Carter, Reagan win Wisconsin, Kansas primaries:** Carter gets 56% of Wisconsin vote and 57% of Kansas votes; Reagan wins 40% of Wisconsin vote and 63% in Kansas.

**1   British steel strike settled:** Tentative agreement reached in London to settle 13-week strike at British Steel Corporation; longest countrywide walkout since World War II; pact provides 15.5% pay increase.

**1–11   New York City transit strike affects millions:** 33,000 mass-transit workers strike, forcing New Yorkers to find other means of getting to work; many walk, bicycle, skateboard, and roller skate. Settlement includes 17% pay increase over two years and cost-of-living adjustments.

**2   Brown drops out of Democratic race:** Gov. Edmund G. Brown Jr. returns to California after winning only 5% of vote in Wisconsin primary.

**2   Windfall profits tax on oil signed:** President Carter signs Crude Oil Windfall Profit Tax Act of 1980, designed to bring U.S. government more than $220 billion in revenues by 1990.

**2   Prime interest rate hits 20% at major banks.**

**4   Producer Price Index rose 1.4% in March,** Labor Department reports; annual rate before compounding is 16.8%.

**4   Unemployment up in March:** Labor Department reports 6.2% of work force unemployed; up from 6.0% in February.

**4   New government formed in Italy:** Francesco Cossiga, a Christian-Democrat, forms Italy's 39th government since World War II; first to include socialists since 1974.

**5   Record price paid for postage stamp:** Crudely printed magenta British Guiana 1856 stamp sold at auction in New York for $850,000.

**5   Carter, Reagan win Louisiana primary:** President wins 56% of vote; Reagan's total is 75%.

**6   Cubans jam Peruvian embassy in Havana:** Crowd estimated at 10,000 seeking refuge and passage out of Cuba; authorities begin supplying food and water April 7; refugees begin fleeing to U.S. April 17.

**7–9   Tornadoes hit 12 states in Midwest:** 4 killed.

**7   U.S. severs diplomatic ties with Iran:** Action taken after Ayatollah Khomeini rules that hostages in U.S. embassy must remain in custody of Islamic militants until yet-to-be-elected parliament decides their fate; Iranian diplomats ousted from U.S. and U.S. exports to Iran banned.

**9   Residents return to Enewetak Atoll:** 175 persons officially resettle at site of first U.S. hydrogen bomb explosion in 1952; radiation cleanup began in 1976.

**11   Government bans sexual harassment on job:** Equal Employment Opportunity Commission publishes regulations explicitly forbidding sexual harassment of employees by supervisors, whether in private industry or government.

**11   Chrysler agrees to repair 200,000 defects:** Federal Trade Commission announces agreement to replace rusted front fenders on 1976 and 1977 Aspens and Volares.

**12   U.S. Olympic Committee endorses boycott:** Votes by 2–1 margin to support President Carter.

**12   Liberian president killed in coup:** President William R. Tolbert Jr. and 27 others killed in predawn assault staged by army enlisted men; Sgt. Samuel K. Doe, 28, assumes leadership, vows end to corruption.

**12–14   Heavy rains, flooding hit south central U.S.:** 5 killed in Louisiana, Mississippi.

**13   Brazilian airliner crash kills 54:** Country's worst air disaster in 20 years occurs near Florianópolis, Brazil, during tropical rainstorm.

**14   Red Cross officials visit Tehran hostages:** Report all hostages they saw appeared in generally good condition.

**15   Alaska ends state income tax:** Gov. Hammond signs law abolishing state income tax and giving residents cash dividends from oil profits.

**18   Figures show recession slowdown:** Commerce Department reports growth of nation's economy slowed in first quarter; real gross national product grew at seasonally adjusted annual rate of 1.1%, below 2% annual rate for fourth quarter of 1979.

**18   Zimbabwe becomes fully independent:** British flag lowered in capital of Harare (Salisbury), ending long struggle for black majority rule.

**18   Mother of hostage flies to Iran:** Mrs. Barbara Timm, mother of Sgt. Kevin Hermening, and her husband defy President Carter's ban on travel to Iran; allowed to see son on April 21.

**22   Stock prices hit 2-year low:** Dow Jones average drops 4.27 points to 759.13, lowest level since April 4, 1978; rebounds more than 30 points April 23 in best advance since Nov. 1, 1978.

**22   Kennedy, Bush win Pennsylvania primary:** Kennedy defeats Carter 49% to 44%; Bush wins 53% of vote against Reagan's 45%.

**24   Rep. Anderson declares independent candidacy:** John B. Anderson (R-Ill.) withdraws from Republican race for president and declares he will run as independent.

**24   UN Security Council rebukes Israel:** 12–0 vote deplores Israel's earlier 5-day occupation of southern Lebanon; U.S., Soviet Union, and East Germany abstain.

**24–25   U.S. fails in attempt to rescue hostages in Iran:** See opposite page.

**25   British jetliner crashes in Canary Islands:** Chartered jet hits mountain on Tenerife just prior to landing; 146 killed.

**26   Iranian militants move hostages:** Announce dispersal to thwart rescue attempts by U.S.

**26   Kennedy wins Michigan caucuses:** Edges President Carter by less than 300 votes; only 40% of eligible voters participated.

**27   Colombian embassy siege ends:** 61-day occupation of Dominican Republic's embassy in Bogotá ends peacefully; left-wing guerrillas and 12 remaining hostages are flown to Cuba where hostages are freed; guerrillas remain in Cuba.

**28   Secretary of State Cyrus Vance resigns:** Opposed President Carter for Iran rescue attempt; Sen. Edmund Muskie (D-Maine) named new secretary of state April 29.

**30   Iranian embassy in London seized:** Five Arab Iranians threaten to blow up embassy and 20 hostages unless Iran gives in to demands to release 91 political prisoners.

**30   Bert Lance acquitted of fraud charges:** Former federal budget director cleared by Atlanta jury on nine counts of bank fraud.

# U.S. FAILS TO RESCUE HOSTAGES FROM IRAN

United Press Int'l.

Bodies of U.S. military personnel lie amid wreckage of aircraft lost in failed attempt to rescue hostages in Iran.

A secret U.S. military mission to rescue the American hostages held in Iran failed on April 24–25. Eight U.S. servicemen were killed, and five others were injured.

First news about the mission and its failure came in an announcement by President Carter in a radio and TV broadcast at 7 A.M. EST on April 25, while most of the nation was sleeping. In the broadcast the President took responsibility for canceling the operation because of "equipment failure" after the task force had landed at a remote desert location in Iran. The servicemen were killed when a helicopter and a transport plane collided during the hasty withdrawal that the President ordered.

The operation had been intended to send 90 U.S. combat troops into Teheran to rescue the 53 hostages held there since Nov. 4, 1979.

Eight helicopters took part, being launched from the U.S. aircraft carrier *Nimitz*. One turned back. One was forced down in the desert before reaching the rendezvous point in Iran. A third failed after reaching the desert site.

The President ordered the mission aborted at 4:57 P.M. EST on April 24.

U.S. Secretary of State Cyrus Vance resigned on principle three days later, on April 28, having opposed the raid (see page 421).

Iran displayed the bodies of the eight U.S. servicemen at the captured U.S. embassy in Teheran as "documents of the crimes of America." Later the bodies were returned to the U.S.

An official Defense Department report on the mission was released on Aug. 23. Prepared under the chairmanship of retired Adm. James L. Holloway 3d, the report criticized both the planning and execution of the mission, pointing out in part that a full-scale dress rehearsal had not been conducted.

# MAY

**1    U.S., Japan sign technology pact:** Agreement calls for five years of cooperation in broad range of scientific research.

**2    April unemployment soars:** Bureau of Labor Statistics announces rate at 7%, up from March total of 6.2%.

**3    Carter, Reagan win Texas primaries:** Carter wins 56% of Democratic tally; Reagan gets 51.7% in Republican contest.

**4    President Tito of Yugoslavia dies:** 87-year-old leader of Communist Party succumbs to illness.

**5    Iran's London embassy stormed, hostages freed:** British commando team frees 19 persons held hostage since April 30; 3 Iranian Arab terrorists are killed; 2 hostages had been killed before military action.

**5    President Carter to admit Cuban refugees:** Pledges U.S. will provide "open heart and open arms" to fleeing Cubans (see opposite page).

**5    Karamanlis elected president of Greece:** Premier Constantine Karamanlis wins on third ballot; George Rallis selected May 8 as new premier.

**6    Carter, Reagan win landslides in 3 primaries:** Trounce opponents in Indiana, North Carolina, and Tennessee; Kennedy and Bush win in Washington, D.C.

**7    Two new cabinet departments become official:** 27-year-old Department of Health, Education, and Welfare splits into Department of Health and Human Services and new Department of Education in White House ceremonies.

**7    Edmund Muskie confirmed as secretary of state:** Sworn in on May 8.

**7    Record first-quarter trade deficit announced:** Commerce Department reports $12.2 billion deficit for first 3 months of 1980.

**8    UN condemns Israel:** UN Security Council deplores Israel's deportation of three West Bank leaders May 3 after terrorist attack; vote is 14–0 with U.S. abstaining.

**9    Ship collides with bridge in Tampa Bay:** 35 killed; phosphate carrier *Summit Venture* hits Sunshine Skyway Bridge in St. Petersburg, Fla., tearing away 1,000-foot section; bus, truck, and several cars drop into Tampa Bay.

**11    Nationwide strike ends in Sweden:** Labor and management accept pact providing wage increases of 7% after 1 million workers are idle for nearly 2 weeks.

**11    Military seizes power in Uganda:** President Geoffrey Binaisa ousted.

**12    Balloon flight across North America completed:** Maxie L. Anderson, 45, and son Kris, 23, land near Matane, Quebec, Canada, 4 days and 2,817 miles from launching near San Francisco.

**13    Oil import fee blocked:** Federal judge in Washington rules that President Carter lacks legal authority to impose fee on imported oil that would have raised gasoline prices 10¢ per gallon.

**13    Maryland, Nebraska primaries held:** President Carter wins with 47% of vote in both; Reagan gets 78% in Nebraska, 48% in Maryland.

**16    Ruling party defeated in Japan:** Prime Minister Masayoshi Ohira's Liberal Democratic Party suffers stunning defeat in no-confidence motion; general elections called for June.

**17    Toxic waste dump linked to chromosome damage:** Study of residents of Love Canal area near Niagara Falls, N.Y., reports 30% have suffered some chromosome damage; emergency declared May 21 as plans are made to evacuate more than 700 families from contaminated area.

**17–19    Miami riots cause $100 million damage:** Racial rioting erupts after all-white jury in Tampa acquits former Miami police officers of murder of black Miami business man; 18 people die as result of riots.

**17–22    Islamic Conference meets in Pakistan:** Foreign ministers adopt 7-point resolution proposing to mediate Afghanistan crisis; call for immediate withdrawal of Soviet troops; condemn U.S. for Iran hostage rescue attempt.

**18    Total martial law imposed in South Korea:** Rioting causes government of Premier Shin Hyon Hwack to resign May 20; new cabinet formed May 21 with Park Choong Hoon as premier.

**18    Mount St. Helens' volcano erupts in Washington:** 66 killed or missing as giant blast blows volcanic ash across Northwest, causing mudslides and floods (see page 13).

**18    Peruvian voters reelect former president:** Fernando Belaunde Terry, ousted in 1968, captures 43% of vote to become new president.

**20    Quebec voters reject separatist government:** 58.2% of voters reject referendum calling for Quebec province to become independent from Canada; Prime Minister Trudeau calls for period of national healing and new constitution.

**20    Fire in Jamaica kills 157:** Home for poor and elderly burns in Kingston; arson blamed.

**20    Michigan, Oregon primaries held:** George Bush defeats Ronald Reagan 57% to 32% in Michigan, while Gov. Edmund G. Brown Jr. defeats Lyndon H. LaRouche Jr.; Carter, Reagan win resounding victories in Oregon.

**22    Egyptians vote for constitutional changes:** Overwhelmingly approve referendum allowing unlimited term of office for President Anwar al-Sadat, affirming Islamic justice as major source of law, and establishing multiparty system.

**23    Consumer Price Index rose 0.9% in May:** Labor Department reports 10.8% annual rate before compounding.

**24    World Court demands release of hostages:** Orders immediate release of all 53 Americans held in Iran, calls for reparation payments, and warns against putting any hostage on trial; Iran calls verdict "meaningless."

**25    Israeli defense minister quits:** Ezer Weizman resigns in opposition to government's policy of settlement in occupied territories.

**26    Bush quits Republican presidential race:** Will support Ronald Reagan.

**27    Arkansas, Idaho, Kentucky, Nevada vote:** President Carter wins all Democratic primaries, while Ronald Reagan wins all Republican polls.

**27    Consumption of cholesterol controversy:** Report by Food and Nutrition Board of National Academy of Sciences says clinical studies show no concrete evidence that reducing levels of cholesterol in diet would prevent heart disease; sparks controversy in medical field.

**30    Government index indicates recession:** Index of leading economic indicators dropped 4.8% in April, Commerce Department reports; sharpest drop in 32-year history of index.

# CUBAN REFUGEES FLEE TO U.S.

Thousands of Cubans crowded onto small boats in 1980 to escape from the communist regime in their country.

In January 1980 Peru and Venezuela granted a handful of Cubans asylum in their embassies in Cuba, rejecting demands by the Cuban government that they be returned as "criminals." Cuba posted guards to prevent more Cubans from entering the embassies.

On April 1 six Cubans crashed a bus through the Peruvian embassy gates, killing one of the Cuban guards. Cuba withdrew its embassy guards on April 4, and about 7,000 Cubans flooded into the Peruvian embassy compound during the next few days. On April 6, Cuba's President Fidel Castro announced that the refugees would be granted safe passage out of the country.

The U.S. State Department on April 10 declared that the U.S. would accept "a fair share" of the refugees. And on April 14 President Carter authorized admittance to the U.S. of 3,500 of the refugees.

On April 20, Castro announced that Cubans wishing to go to the U.S. would be free to do so by boarding boats at the port of Mariel, about 20 miles from Havana. Within a few hours scores of small boats put to sea from Florida to pick up the refugees.

As the flood of Cuban refugees was joined by additional thousands of Haitians escaping from their country, President Carter said on May 6 that the U.S. would welcome them with "an open heart and open arms."

However, eight days later, on May 14, the President announced plans to stem the influx. He ordered the Coast Guard to seize boats being used to carry the refugees, saying the U.S. henceforth would only accept Cuban immigrants prescreened in Cuba.

Many boat owners ignored the order, and in the next several months the Coast Guard confiscated more than 1,000 boats.

However, the tide of refugees mounted to more than 125,000 before Cuba announced on Sept. 25 that refugee boats no longer could use the port of Mariel.

Refugees were housed and processed at several U.S. relocation centers. Some riots broke out as refugees became impatient at restrictions on their freedom. Some decided to return to Cuba, and a few hijacked airliners to accomplish the purpose.

The U.S. imprisoned about 2,000 of the refugees who admitted having committed various crimes in Cuba. Court hearings were planned for each case.

# JUNE

**1    Cuban refugees riot:** About 200 burst through gate at Fort Chaffee, Ark., processing center, then rampage, injuring 40; 35 arrested June 2 as army troops are called in.

**2–5    Iran holds anti-U.S. conference:** Delegation of 10 Americans, headed by former Attorney General Ramsey Clark, attends in defiance of President Carter's ban on travel to Iran.

**3    Final primary elections held:** President Carter gains delegate majority but Edward Kennedy wins 5 of 8 primaries; takes California, New Jersey, New Mexico, Rhode Island, South Dakota as Carter wins Montana, Ohio, West Virginia; Ronald Reagan wins all GOP primaries.

**3    Tornadoes rip through Nebraska:** Series of 7 tornadoes destroy much of Grand Island, Neb., killing 5, injuring 134; more than 550 buildings destroyed.

**5–6    Congress overrides Carter veto on oil:** House votes, 335–34, to bar 10¢-a-gallon fee on imported oil; Senate votes, 73–16; first override of Democratic president's veto since 1952.

**6    Producer price rise reduced in May:** 0.3% is smallest monthly rise in 32 months, signaling slowdown of inflation, Labor Department reports.

**6    Unemployment rate soars in May:** 7.8% rate is highest since November 1976.

**7    Freight train hits bus in South Africa:** At least 45 killed in Empageni, South Africa.

**7–8    Bangladesh immigrants massacred:** Tribal residents of Tripura state in India kill 350 Bengali residents of village of Mandai.

**10    Cambodian rebels ambush train:** Followers of deposed Prime Minister Pol Pot kill between 150 and 200 people northwest of Phnom Penh.

**10    House censures Rep. Charles Wilson (D-Calif.):** Violated House rules by converting campaign funds to personal use and accepting funds from person with direct interest in legislation before Congress; third member of House to be censured in 20th century.

**11    Carter appoints new chief of staff:** Jack H. Watson Jr. replaces Hamilton Jordan, who joins Carter's reelection campaign.

**11    Israel and Egypt agree to resume talks:** Negotiations on Palestinian autonomy to begin in Washington at end of June.

**12    Japanese prime minister dies:** Premier Masayoshi Ohira felled by heart attack, leaving governing Liberal Democratic Party without a leader 10 days before parliamentary elections.

**12    Congress approves 1981 budget:** Senate votes, 61–26, and House votes, 205–95, to approve resolution calling for $613.6 billion in spending with $200 million surplus.

**13    European Community nations agree on Mideast:** 9-member organization meeting in Venice, backs full self-determination for Palestinians, declares Palestine Liberation Organization (PLO) should be involved in peace negotiations.

**13    AT&T loses antitrust case:** MCI Communications Corp. awarded $600 million in suit charging AT&T prevented MCI's growth by its dominance in local telephone services; award by federal district court jury in Chicago automatically triples to record $1.8 billion under provisions of Sherman Antitrust Act.

**16    Court upholds patents on life forms:** Supreme Court rules, 5–4, that new forms of life created in laboratories are eligible for patents under current law.

**16–18    Clashes in South Africa leave 30 dead:** 174 injured in Cape Town when mixed-race demonstrators clash with police..

**17    May housing starts lowest in 5 years:** Commerce Department reports new-home construction at annually adjusted rate of 920,000 in May, lowest level since February 1975.

**20    "Boat people" can stay for 6 months:** Carter administration says 114,000 Cubans and 15,000 Haitians who have arrived in U.S. by boat can remain for 6 months and may become permanent residents after 2 years if Congress enacts appropriate legislation.

**22–23    President Carter attends Venice summit:** Meets with leaders of Germany, Japan, Britain, Canada, France, and Italy; statesmen pledge development of energy alternatives; denounce Soviet invasion of Afghanistan.

**24    Joblessness in Britain at record high:** Unemployment totals 1,467,400, highest since World War II.

**24    Consumer prices up 0.9% in May,** Labor Department reports.

**25    Court broadens right to sue states:** Supreme Court votes, 6–3, that private citizens can collect damages from state or local governments when they violate federal laws.

**26    France announces neutron bomb development:** President Valéry Giscard d'Estaing says prototype of neutron bomb has been tested and could be ready in 2–3 years for decision on whether or not to produce it.

**27    Carter signs draft registration measure:** President signs funding bill authorizing $13.3 million to put into effect program to register 4 million young men aged 19 or 20 for the draft.

**27    Trade deficit increased in May:** Value of imports exceeded exports by $3.96 billion, Commerce Department reports.

**28    Italian air crash kills 81:** DC-9 crashes into Tyrrhenian Sea on flight from Bologna, Italy, to Palermo, Sicily.

**29    Elections held in Bolivia:** Former president Hernán Siles Zuazo wins popular vote but falls short of majority needed; election to be settled by Congress Aug. 4.

**30    Woman becomes Iceland's president:** Vigdis Finnbogadottir, leftist opponent of Iceland's membership in NATO, becomes first female head of state in Iceland.

**30    Supreme Court upholds abortion funding limits:** Rules, 5–4, that neither local nor federal government is required to provide funds for abortions for poor women; decision upholds 1976 Hyde Amendment, which prohibited use of Medicaid funds for abortions in most instances; estimated 250,000–300,000 women a year will lose abortion funding.

**30    Sioux Nation wins $122.5 million lawsuit:** Supreme Court rules, 8–1, that Sioux Indians are entitled to $122.5 million in compensation and interest for 1877 illegal seizure of Black Hills of South Dakota; decision upholds 1979 U.S. Court of Claims ruling, which was largest ever made by Court of Claims.

# PRESIDENTIAL PRIMARY BATTLES

Sen. Edward Kennedy (D–Mass.) became the main contender against President Jimmy Carter for the Democratic presidential nomination in 1980. Although Kennedy repeatedly challenged Carter to debate with him on the issues, the President refused to do so on the basis that national affairs, especially the problem of the hostages held in Iran, made it impossible for him to leave the White House to participate in the primary elections campaign. Because of his strong showing in the primaries, Kennedy was expected to be a leading candidate for the Democratic presidential nomination in 1984.

United Press Int'l.

The largest number of presidential primaries in the nation's history stretched the tolerance of voters for political campaigning to the limit in 1980. Many believed that a better way to select a President had to be found—otherwise the length and the expense of such campaigns would prevent worthy candidates from participation in future years.

In all, 34 states as well as Puerto Rico and the District of Columbia held presidential preference primaries in 1980 to determine which candidates their delegates to national political conventions should support.

In the Republican primaries, Ronald Reagan amassed a clear majority of the convention delegates, winning more than 7.6 million votes or about 60% of the total. Among the eight other major contenders for the GOP nomination, George Bush led with about 3 million votes, or about 24%. Rep. John B. Anderson (R–Ill.) was third with 1.5 million votes, or about 12%. Others who sought the Republican nomination, splitting only 4% of the vote, included (in order of the number of votes they received): Sen. Howard Baker of Tennessee, Rep. Philip Crane of Illinois, former Secretary of the Treasury John Connally, businessman Benjamin Fernandez, perennial candidate Harold Stassen, and Sen. Robert Dole of Kansas.

The contest for the Democratic presidential nomination was much more of a horse race. Sen. Edward Kennedy of Massachusetts, representing the liberal wing of the party, was rebuffed by Carter in demands for a face-to-face debate. Appealing to liberal and minority voters, Kennedy won more than 7.3 million votes in the primaries, or about 37%, to Carter's bare majority of 10 million votes, or 51%. More importantly, Kennedy won the states with the largest number of electoral votes, California and New York, as well as Pennsylvania, New Jersey, Connecticut, and, of course, Massachusetts.

# JULY

**1   Trucking deregulation bill signed:** President Carter signs Motor Carrier Act of 1980, which deregulates U.S. trucking industry; could save consumers $8 billion a year.

**1–4   OAU summit held in Sierra Leone:** Organization of African Unity, meeting in Freetown, denounces U.S. base on Indian Ocean island of Diego Garcia, calls for withdrawal of Western investment in South Africa, condemns Israel's new settlements on West Bank and its pending incorporation of East Jerusalem as part of Israel.

**2   Supreme Court backs open criminal trials:** Rules, 7–1, that public access to criminal trials is guaranteed by First Amendment.

**2   Court upholds racial quotas:** Rules, 6–3, backing constitutionality of federal public-works program requiring 10% of funding to be spent on minority contractors; first time Court specifically endorses use of federal benefits based on race of recipients.

**3   June unemployment drops to 7.7%:** Decrease from May's 7.8% announced by Labor Department.

**6   Reports say 70 killed on Chinese oil rig:** Offshore rig, in Bo Hai Gulf, collapses during storm.

**7   Soviet air crash kills 163:** TU–154 jetliner crashes in Kazakhstan, Central Asia.

**10   Drug manufacturers agree on warnings:** Food and Drug Administration announces makers of Valium, Librium, and other tranquilizers have agreed to warn doctors that the drugs should not be used to relieve "everyday" stress.

**11   Iranian hostage freed:** Richard I. Queen, 28, is released by captors because of deteriorating health, after being held in U.S. Embassy in Teheran since Nov. 4, 1979; had been hospitalized in Teheran since July 7; diagnosed on July 15 by doctors at U.S. hospital in Wiesbaden, West Germany, as having multiple sclerosis.

**13   President of Botswana dies:** Seretse Khama, 59, president since nation's independence from Britain in 1966, dies in Gaborone of cancer; Vice President Quett Masire is elected on July 18 to succeed Khama as president.

**14–17   Republicans choose Reagan, Bush:** Delegates to Republican National Convention, in Detroit, Mich., formally nominate Ronald Reagan as candidate for presidency, with George Bush as running mate. See page 21.

**14–30   Conference on women held in Copenhagen:** Delegates from more than 100 nations meet for second world conference of the United Nations Decade for Women; meeting ends in discord when U.S. and 21 other nations refuse because of political disagreements to sign document, outlining 5-year plan to improve status of women.

**17   Military stages coup in Bolivia:** Action taken to head off expected August election by congress of Hernan Siles Zuazo, a leftist, as president; U.S. suspends all military aid to Bolivia and recalls ambassador.

**17   Prime Minister of Japan elected:** Zenko Suzuki chosen; forms cabinet carefully balanced between three rival factions of his party.

**18   Satellite orbited by India:** First successful launch by that nation; two earlier Indian satellites had been put into orbit by Soviet rockets.

**19–Aug. 3   Summer Olympic Games held in Moscow:** Athletes from 81 nations participate; U.S., West Germany, Japan and about 55 other nations boycott because of Soviet invasion of Afghanistan. See page 9.

**21–Aug. 2   Draft registration proceeds:** Nearly 4 million 19- and 20-year-old men register at post offices; some protests occur but are generally peaceful; registration began as scheduled after Supreme Court Justice William F. Brennan Jr., (July 19) lifted July 18 ruling by three-judge panel in Philadelphia, proclaiming Selective Service Act unconstitutional for excluding women.

**22   British unemployment soars:** Reaches post-World War II high of 7.8%, or 1.9 million persons; Prime Minister Margaret Thatcher defeats July 29 vote of no-confidence by 333–274 margin.

**22   Doctors revise code of ethics:** American Medical Association adopts new code at Chicago convention, permitting doctors to advertise fees and to refer patients to chiropractors.

**23   Consumer Price Index up 1% in June,** Labor Department reports; unexpectedly large annual rate of 12% shocks economists.

**24   Prime lending rate falls to $10^{3}/_{4}$%:** Two major banks slice prime rate $1/4$% below Federal Reserve discount rate for first time since February 1972; Fed lowers discount rate to 10% on July 25.

**24   Special panel to probe Billy Carter activities:** Sen. Birch Bayh (D-Ind.) named chairman of Senate committee to investigate activities of President Carter's brother as paid agent for Libya; probe requested after disclosure on July 22 that Billy Carter was used as liaison in effort to enlist Libya's aid in freeing Iran hostages.

**24   U.S. automakers report 2d quarter losses:** General Motors shows record $412 million loss; American Motors reports $84.9 million, its largest quarterly loss; Ford announces (July 29) record quarterly loss of $467.9 million; Chrysler reports (July 31) $536.1 million loss, largest quarterly deficit by U.S. automaker.

**26   New Jersey hotel fire kills 24:** Mostly elderly and retarded trapped inside Bradley Beach wood and stucco structure.

**27   Shah of Iran dies in Cairo, Egypt:** Deposed leader of Iran dies of cancer; state funeral held on July 29; no foreign heads of state invited.

**28   Democratic government returns to Peru:** President Fernando Belaunde Terry inaugurated for 5-year term; return to constitutional government ends 12 years of military rule.

**29   Stock market at highest level in 3 years:** Dow Jones average closes at 931.91, highest close since May 19, 1977.

**29   UN calls for formation of Palestinian state:** General Assembly votes, 112–7, asking for establishment of Palestinian state and withdrawal of Israel from all occupied lands by Nov. 15.

**30   Jerusalem affirmed as capital of Israel:** Israeli parliament approves, 69–15, bill formalizing present status; Prime Minister Begin announces intention to move office to East Jerusalem.

**30   New nation of Vanuatu proclaimed:** Territory formerly known as New Hebrides ends 74 years of joint French and British rule; Anglican priest, Walter Lini, sworn in as first prime minister of independent nation.

# GOP CHOOSES REAGAN–BUSH TICKET

Balloons scattered over GOP delegates in Detroit as Ronald Reagan was nominated for the presidency on July 16.

Because former California governor Ronald Reagan had locked up the Republican presidential nomination by winning 28 of the party's 34 presidential primaries, delegates attending the Republican National Convention in Detroit on July 14–17 expected little excitement.

As expected, Reagan was awarded the nomination on the first ballot on July 16, receiving the support of 1,939 of the convention's 1,994 delegates.

Even while the votes were being tabulated for Reagan's nomination, excitement began to build on the floor of the convention as word circulated that Reagan had chosen former President Gerald Ford as his running mate. Ford himself confirmed he was open to the possibility in two TV interviews that night. Some newspapers went to press announcing the Reagan-Ford ticket as an accomplished fact (see page 682).

However, at the last minute the arrangement collapsed because Reagan, Ford, and their advisers could not agree on the specific "meaningful" duties to be assigned the former President.

To allay rumors, Reagan then made an unprecedented post-midnight appearance before the convention to confirm that his discussions with Ford had broken down and that his choice as a running mate was former CIA director George Bush, who had been his leading challenger for the nomination in the primary races.

After his choice of Bush had been ratified by the convention on the night of July 17, Reagan made his formal acceptance speech, calling for "a new consensus with all those across the land who share a community of values embodied in these words: family, work, neighborhood, peace, and freedom."

He asserted his readiness to unify the country in the face of "three grave threats" that he specified as "a disintegrating economy, a weakened defense, and an energy policy based on the sharing of scarcity."

# AUGUST

**2  Explosion in Bologna, Italy, kills 81:** Terrorist bomb rips through wing of central train station during prime vacation period.

**4–11  Hurricane hits Caribbean and Gulf Coast:** Hurricane Allen batters Barbados, St. Lucia, Haiti, Jamaica, and Cuba, before ripping through Mexico's Yucatán peninsula and then Texas-Mexico coastline; 272 persons killed.

**5  Regional autonomy approved in Belgium:** Belgian parliament votes, 156–19, for plan to give more autonomy to Dutch area of Flanders and French area of Wallonia.

**5  Acid rain pact signed by U.S., Canada:** Agreement calls for more stringent enforcement of antipollution laws on both sides of border.

**6  Zimbabwe minister held on murder charge:** Edgar Z. Tekere, minister of manpower planning and development, charged with Aug. 4 murder of elderly white farmer, reportedly in retaliation for earlier altercation with black soldiers.

**11  Iranian premier appointed:** Parliament approves Mohammed Ali Rajai, former education minister.

**11–14  Democratic convention renominates Carter:** Delegates to Democratic National Convention in New York City renominate Jimmy Carter, with Mondale as running mate. See page 23.

**13  ICC deregulates railroad freight rates:** Interstate Commerce Commission votes, 5–2, to curb power of nation's railroads to collectively set freight rates; effective Oct. 1.

**13  Military coup in Suriname ousts president:** Johan Ferrier, president since 1975, is replaced by Prime Minister Chin A. Sen.

**13  Riot near mosque kills 86 in India:** Riot erupts near Moradabad after some worshipers believed police had allowed pigs to wander into mosque area.

**14  Holy war against Israel asked:** Crown Prince Fahd of Saudi Arabia urges *jihad* (holy war) against Israel by all Muslim nations because of annexation of East Jerusalem.

**14  Fire in Iraq kills 59:** Electrical fire sweeps through movie theater in Baghdad.

**14–31  Poland paralyzed by strikes:** Labor unrest causes strikes throughout country, beginning in Gdansk, then spreading; causes ouster on Aug. 24 of Premier Edward Babiuch and three other members of ruling Politboro; new premier is Josef Pinkowski; strike leaders and government sign agreements on Aug. 31, allowing right to form independent labor unions and to strike.

**15  Stock market soars:** Dow Jones average hits 966.72, highest close since Nov. 16, 1977.

**15  Drought death toll reaches 1,272:** Heat wave, begun June 23, over 20 states in U.S. Midwest and South, causing extensive agricultural damage; losses expected to exceed $12 billion.

**16  London fire kills 37:** Arson suspected in blaze in two social clubs in Soho district.

**16  South Korean president resigns:** Choi Kyu Hah quits to pave way for Gen. Chon Too Hwan's nomination, which occurs on Aug. 18; is formally elected on Aug. 27.

**18  Stock prices take nose dive:** Dow Jones average plunges 18.09 points to close at 948.63; largest drop since March 24, 1980.

**18  Plane crash in Saudi Arabia kills 301:** Saudi Arabian Lockheed L-1011 jet lands in flames at Riyadh airport after fire starts in passenger cabin.

**20  UN condemns Israel on Jerusalem policy:** Security Council votes, 14–0, for resolution to ignore Israel's declaration that Jerusalem is undivided capital; asks countries with embassies in Jerusalem to remove them; U.S. abstains in vote.

**21  U.S. and Somalia sign arms agreement:** U.S. to have access to military facilities in Somalia in exchange for $25 million in military aid in 1981.

**21–22  Billy Carter testifies in probe:** President's brother says under oath that he never attempted to influence U.S. policy toward Libya, nor had he been urged to do so by Libyan government.

**22  Consumer prices did not rise in July:** Consumer Price Index shows no monthly increase for first time since March 1967, Labor Department reports.

**22  Ferryboat sinks in Mexico, killing 50:** Ferry carrying bus, passenger cars, and trucks sinks near Ciudad Del Carmen, Mexico.

**24  New canal to be dug in Israel:** Israeli cabinet authorizes canal to be built between Mediterranean and Dead Seas; to be 65 miles long and cost approximately $700 million.

**25  Zimbabwe becomes 153d UN member.**

**25  Anderson names running mate:** John B. Anderson chooses Patrick J. Lucey, Democratic governor of Wisconsin in 1971–77, to be vice-presidential candidate on his independent ticket.

**26  Air crash in Indonesia kills 31:** Indonesian Viscount turboprop crashes on approach to airport in Jakarta after part of tail falls off.

**26  Carter veto overridden by Congress:** Senate votes, 85–0, to strike down veto of salary increase for doctors and dentists at veterans hospitals; House of Representatives had earlier voted to override veto.

**27  New prime minister named in Zaire:** Nguza Karl-i-Bond had been sentenced to death for treason in 1977, but was pardoned and released by President Mobuto Sese Seko in 1979.

**27  British unemployment tops 2 million:** British government reports 2,001,208 unemployed in August, highest level in 45 years.

**27  U.S. trade deficit narrowed in July:** $1.85 billion deficit is smallest since March 1979, Commerce Department announces.

**28  Carter outlines new economic plan:** Proposes "economic program for the eighties," which includes tax reductions for individuals and businesses, extension of eligibility for unemployment benefits to maximum of 52 weeks, and passage of $1 billion of extra revenue sharing for cities; Reagan denounces program as "political."

**29  Federal employees to get 9.1% pay raise:** President Carter approves increase to 1.4 million government workers; effective Oct. 1.

**29  Economic indicators surged in July:** Commerce Department announces record increase of 4.6% in its index of leading economic indicators.

**30  ABSCAM co-defendants convicted:** Rep. Michael J. Myers (D-Pa.); Camden, N.J., mayor Angelo J. Errichetti; Philadelphia city councilman Louis C. Johanson; and Philadelphia attorney Howard L. Criden are convicted of bribery and conspiracy in first of trials dealing with bribe-taking from agents posing as Arab sheiks.

# CARTER WINS DEMOCRATIC NOMINATION

Delegates at the Democratic National Convention in New York City set off a demonstration on Aug. 13 as President Carter won the party's nomination to seek a second term in the White House. However, those who had supported Sen. Edward Kennedy (D-Mass.) for the nomination were only lukewarm in their enthusiasm. Many saw it as an unpromising omen that most of the red, white, and blue balloons that were supposed to shower down during the convention's finale remained stuck in nets on the ceiling of Madison Square Garden.

When Democrats convened at their national convention in New York City on Aug. 11, public-opinion polls showed President Carter trailing Republican presidential candidate Ronald Reagan by a considerable margin.

Although the President claimed to have a majority of the 3,331 delegates pledged to support his nomination, many believed he should be dumped in favor of Sen. Edward Kennedy, Vice President Walter Mondale, or Secretary of State Edmund Muskie. Their only hope for doing so lay in overturning a convention rule requiring delegates to vote on the first ballot for the candidate they had been elected to support.

Other than Kennedy, the most prominent supporter of an "open convention" was New York's Gov. Hugh L. Carey. Shortly after the convention convened on Aug. 11, the key issue came to a vote. Carter forces held firm, defeating the rule change by a vote of 1,936.42 to 1,390.58. Immediately afterward, Kennedy announced his withdrawal from the race for the presidential nomination.

Observers universally agreed that the high-light of the convention was the speech by Kennedy on the following night, Aug. 12, in which he called on Democrats to revitalize "the glory and the greatness of our tradition to speak for those who have no voice, to remember those who are forgotten, to respond to the frustrations and fulfill the aspirations of all Americans seeking a better life in a better land." His words touched off a wild 40-minute demonstration.

As foreordained by the rules fight, Carter won the nomination on the first ballot on Aug. 13 by a vote of 2,123 to Kennedy's 1,150.5.

After the convention nominated Mondale for a second term as Vice President on Aug. 14, President Carter made his acceptance speech, setting the tone for the ensuing campaign with a no-holds-barred attack on GOP nominee Reagan as the supporter of "an all-out nuclear arms race" and an advocate of "abandoning arms control policies" whose "radical and irresponsible course would threaten our security—and could put the whole world in peril."

# SEPTEMBER

**4  New moon of Jupiter discovered:** National Aeronautics and Space Administration (NASA) announces discovery of 16th Jovian satellite by Dr. Stephen P. Synnott of Voyager Project.

**5  World's longest road tunnel opens:** Construction of 10.01-mile-long St. Gotthard tunnel, from Göschenen to Airolo, Switzerland, took 11 years; cost $420 million and 19 lives.

**5  Unemployment rate declined in August:** Labor Department announces drop to 7.6%.

**7  Chinese premier resigns:** Prime Minister Hua Guofeng formally steps down at session of National People's Congress, but retains post as chairman of Communist Party; replaced as premier by Zhao Ziyang on Sept. 10.

**8  Combat divisions "not ready":** Confidential Defense Department report reveals six overseas-based divisions are "combat ready," but 6 of 10 army divisions in U.S. were each rated in December 1979 as needing six weeks to fully train and equip for combat.

**10  Syria and Libya announce merger:** Proclamation issued in Damascus and Tripoli unifying two countries with aim of more effectively fighting Israel; to have one Congress and one executive authority.

**11  Voters in Chile approve new constitution:** Charter to allow extension of military rule until 1989; victory for Gen. Augusto Pinochet Ugarte wins approval to stay in power until 1989.

**11  Fifteen nations sign sea-life pact:** Convention on the Conservation of Antarctic Living Marine Resources signed in Australia provides for establishment of quotas for harvesting different forms of marine life in the Antarctic Ocean.

**12  Turkish government ousted in military coup:** Armed forces commander Gen. Kenan Everen heads government to halt widespread terrorism; Bulent Ulusu appointed prime minister Sept. 20.

**12  Carter approves grain credits for Poland:** President approves $670 million new credit guarantees for purchase of grain by Poland as expression of "solidarity" with Polish people.

**12  U.S. aide says recession has ended:** Chief economist in Commerce Department says recession ended in July; sees slow growth ahead.

**12  Middle class pays more tax, says IRS:** Internal Revenue Service reports that American middle class pays 60.1% of Federal income taxes although middle-income earners comprise only 38.2% of taxpayers; middle-Americans defined as families earning $15,000–$50,000 per year.

**12  Air crash in Bahamas kills 34:** Chartered DC-3 crashes into Atlantic Ocean in storm.

**15  UN General Assembly opens 35th session.**

**15  Railroads file merger plans:** Union Pacific, Missouri Pacific, and Western Pacific railroads announce merger plans to create 22,800-mile rail system, spanning 21 western states.

**16  St. Vincent becomes 154th member of UN.**

**17  Iraq cancels border agreement with Iran:** Iraqi President Saddam Hussein declares 1975 border pact "null and void."

**17  Ousted president of Nicaragua assassinated:** Anastasio Somoza Debayle slain in Asunción, Paraguay, where he had lived in exile after being ousted as leader of Nicaragua in July 1979.

**17  Trade agreement with China signed:** U.S. and China sign pact covering textiles, shipping, airline service, and consular services.

**18  World's largest airport terminal opens:** New $500 million terminal dedicated in Atlanta, Ga., 2.2 million square feet in area; equipped to handle 55 million passengers a year.

**19  Missile silo blast near Damascus, Ark.:** Explosion rocks underground Titan 2 missile silo, killing 1 serviceman and injuring 22; 1,400 residents in 5-mile radius evacuated for 12 hours; officials declare no evidence of radioactive debris or damage to nuclear warhead itself.

**21  Reagan-Anderson debate:** President Carter refuses to join televised debate sponsored by League of Women Voters.

**22  Iran, Iraq border dispute becomes war:** Iraq launches heavy attack on Iran with bombing planes, rockets, and artillery. See page 25.

**22  Stocks at highest level in 3¹/₂ years:** Dow Jones average closes at 974.57, highest level since Jan. 13, 1977.

**22  Gold prices surge past $700 an ounce,** for first time since February.

**23  Food and beverage prices jumped 1.7% in** August for annual rate of 20.4%, Labor Department reports; largest rise since July 1975.

**24  Income tax repealed in Alaska:** Gov. Jay S. Hammond signs bill abolishing state income tax for all residents, refunding $185.5 million to taxpayers for 1979 and 1980.

**22  Colombia accused of torturing prisoners:** Amnesty International says government uses beating, drugs, shock, and rape on prisoners.

**24  Anderson ruled eligible for campaign funds:** Federal Election Commission says he will receive retroactive federal campaign financing if he receives at least 5% of popular vote.

**25  Judge bars release of census data:** U.S. District Judge Horace Gilmore of Detroit invalidates 1980 census count because of undercount of minorities; orders figures adjusted upward before release of data.

**26  Trade deficit narrowed in August:** Deficit of $1.1 billion is smallest since May 1976, Commerce Department reports.

**26  Iraq ceases oil exports:** Announces suspension of shipments because of damage to oil facilities in war with Iran.

**27  Italian government collapses:** Prime Minister Francesco Cossiga resigns after 1-vote defeat in parliament over economic proposals.

**28  Panama holds first elections in 12 years:** Multiparty election held for 19 of 57 seats in national Legislative Council; majority won by government party in first national voting since military coup in 1968.

**29  Stock market plunges 18.17 points:** Dow Jones average closes at 921.23, biggest drop since March 24, 1980.

**30  U.S. sends planes to Saudi Arabia:** Four radar command planes and 300 personnel sent to Saudi Arabia in response to Saudi fears of attack in Iraq-Iran war.

**30  Arms purchases by Somalia approved:** House Appropriations Subcommittee on Foreign Operations approves sale of $20 million in weapons on condition that no Somali military forces remain in Ogaden area of neighboring Ethiopia.

# IRAQ–IRAN WAR RAGES IN MIDEAST

**FOCUS**

United Press Int'l

For about 5,000 years the peoples of what are now Iraq and Iran have battled each other for control of the vital waterway called the Shatt Al Arab that links the Tigris and Euphrates rivers of Iraq with the Persian Gulf. The war resumed in 1980, with guided missiles, tanks, and bombing planes used in place of the spears and shields of the ancients.

On Sept. 17 Saddam Hussein, the dictator-president of Iraq, abrogated a treaty his nation had signed in 1975 with the shah of Iran that provided for joint administration of the waterway. He had been incited by repeated calls for his overthrow by Ayatollah Khomeini, the fanatic revolutionary dictator of Iran.

Launching a full-scale attack on Sept. 22, Iraq bombed Iran's oil fields, and then invaded Iran with its ground forces.

Because their capitals, Baghdad and Teheran, lie only about as far apart as Kansas City and Chicago, neither Iraq nor Iran had far to go to conquer the other. At the outset, Soviet-supplied Iraq was expected to quickly overrun Iran and force Ayatollah Khomeini to sue for peace. However, the Iranians, using arms previously purchased from the U.S. by the shah, put up a surprisingly strong resistance.

By the end of the year Iraq had won control of the Iranian port of Khorramshahr and had put out of production Iran's huge refinery at Abadan.

# OCTOBER

**2   Representative expelled from House:** Rep. Michael J. Myers (D-Pa.) expelled by 376–30 vote because of Aug. 31 conviction in Abscam investigation; first expulsion of member of House of Representatives since 1861.

**3   New president named in Argentina:** Roberto Eduardo Viola named by military junta to replace Jorge Rafael Videla on March 29, 1981.

**3   Synagogue bomb kills 4 in Paris:** Explodes in car parked outside during Sabbath evening services; rally of 100,000 on Oct. 7 protests bombing and anti-Semitism.

**3   Unemployment rate dropped in September,** Labor Department reports; September jobless rate is 7.5%, down from 7.6% in August.

**4   Fire on luxury liner routs 524:** All aboard Dutch cruise ship *Prinsendam* forced by raging fire to abandon ship in stormy Gulf of Alaska; some passengers drift in lifeboats more than 13 hours before rescue.

**5   West German elections won by Schmidt:** Chancellor Helmut Schmidt's ruling coalition of Social Democrats and Free Democrats wins increased majority in lower parliament.

**5   Portuguese rightists gain in elections:** governing Democratic Alliance raises majority to 134 in 250-member parliament.

**6   Prime minister becomes president of Guyana:** Forbes Burnham, prime minister since 1964, becomes president as new constitution takes effect, giving office of president wider powers.

**7   Second congressman convicted in Abscam scheme:** Rep. John W. Jenrette (D-S.C.) found guilty of bribery and conspiracy after videotapes show him discussing payment of $100,000 for exerting influence in Congress on behalf of supposed Arab businessman.

**8   Turkey ratifies prisoner exchange with U.S.:** Treaty opens way for return to U.S. of three Americans in Turkish jails for drug smuggling.

**10   Earthquake strikes northwestern Algeria:** Most of city of Al Asnam destroyed; more than 2,950 killed; 300,000 left homeless.

**11   Cosmonauts set new space endurance mark:** Soviet astronauts return to earth after 185 days in space; Leonid Popov and Valery Ryunin broke old mark of 175 days.

**12   Government defines "natural" foods:** Federal Trade Commission says food may be advertised as natural if it contains no artificial ingredients and has no more processing than could normally be done in a home kitchen.

**13   Cuba pardons Americans in its jails:** 33 American-born citizens in Cuban prisons are released Oct. 27; three choose to remain in Cuba.

**15   Britain's Labour Party head resigns:** Former Prime Minister James Callaghan steps down after leading party since 1976; replaced by Michael Foot on Nov. 10.

**18   Australia's ruling party wins elections:** Prime Minister Malcolm Fraser's coalition of Liberal and National Country parties wins reelection with sharply reduced majority.

**18   Italy forms new government:** Christian Democrat Arnaldo Forlani heads four-party coalition; 40th government since World War II.

**19   Seventeen-year labor dispute resolved:** Textile firm J. P. Stevens & Co. and AFL-CIO Amalgamated Clothing and Textile Workers Union announce labor agreement after workers ratify first collective-bargaining contract.

**20   Yugoslavia's Communist Party names new chief:** Lazar Mojsov elected president of party's ruling presidium for one-year term.

**20   Greece returns to NATO military wing:** Had withdrawn in 1974 in protest against Turkish invasion of Cyprus.

**21   State of emergency declared in Somalia:** President Mohammed Siad Barre issues edict, claiming continuing invasion from neighboring Ethiopia.

**22   Grain pact signed by China and U.S.:** Agreement signed in Peking permits Chinese to purchase at least 6 million metric tons of wheat and corn annually in 1981–84.

**22   South Korean voters approve new constitution:** New charter, approved by 92% of electorate, limits powers of president and guarantees human rights.

**23   Soviet prime minister resigns:** Alexei N. Kosygin steps down because of illness; succeeded by first deputy, Nikolai A Tikhonov, 75.

**23   Blast destroys school in Spain:** 51 killed in explosion at elementary school in Ortuella; 49 of victims are children.

**23   TV and movie actors' 95-day strike ends:** Members of Screen Actors Guild and American Federation of Television and Radio Artists ratify 3-year contract with film and TV producers.

**24   Consumer prices rose 1% in September,** Labor Department reports; annual rate is 12.7%.

**24   Value of British pound soars:** Rises on London market to $2.464, highest in over seven years.

**25   Pope speaks out on divorced Catholics:** John Paul II, at closing of Synod of Bishops, says divorced Roman Catholics who remarry may not receive communion unless they abstain from sexual relations.

**27   Turkey's ruling junta approves charter:** Provisional constitution gives leaders unlimited powers until new constitution can be drawn up.

**27–28   Automakers announce record losses:** General Motors says it lost a record $567 million in third quarter; Ford Motor Co. announces $595 million third-quarter loss, largest ever for a U.S. corporation.

**28   Carter-Reagan debate:** Millions of viewers watch debate between presidential candidates.

**28   Two new moons orbiting Saturn discovered:** NASA officials announce presence of 13th and 14th moons, detected by *Voyager 1* satellite.

**29   Government reports huge U.S. federal budget deficit:** Deficit in fiscal year 1980 totaled $59 billion, second largest on record.

**30   President Carter names new head of World Bank:** Nominates A. W. Clausen, head of Bank of America, to succeed Robert S. McNamara.

**30   Opposition leader wins Jamaica election:** Edward P. Seaga defeats Prime Minister Michael N. Manley in landslide election; sworn in Nov. 1 as prime minister.

**30   Former Algerian president freed:** Ahmed Ben Bella, first president of Algeria, freed after 15 years of imprisonment and house arrest.

**31   Fire in Polish mental hospital kills 50:** Blaze occurs in village of Gorna Grupa.

# CARTER–REAGAN PRESIDENTIAL DEBATE

United Press Int'l.

United Press Int'l.

Throughout most of the presidential election campaign President Carter refused to participate in a three-way debate with Republican nominee Ronald Reagan and Independent candidate Rep. John B. Anderson, fearing it would enable Anderson to win liberal votes from himself.

Reagan, who approved the idea of a three-way debate, decided to debate Anderson alone under auspices of the League of Women Voters. Their televised confrontation took place on Sept. 21 in Baltimore, Md.

In the weeks that followed, public-opinion polls showed Anderson's popular support had slipped below the 15% level, causing the League of Women Voters to exclude him from their invitation for another debate.

Finally, only one week before the election, Carter and Reagan confronted each other on Oct. 28 in a nationally televised 90-minute debate broadcast from Cleveland, Ohio, on commercial networks. The program was moderated by retired ABC news commentator Howard K. Smith. The candidates responded to questions posed by a panel that included Marvin Stone, editor of *U.S. News & World Report;* Harry Ellis, national correspondent of the *Christian Science Monitor;*

William Hilliard, assistant managing editor of the *Portland Oregonian;* and Barbara Walters, correspondent for ABC News.

Simultaneously, in a program broadcast from Washington, D.C., over cable TV, Independent candidate Anderson answered the same questions asked of Carter and Reagan.

To the estimated 100 million or more TV viewers the President appeared generally grim and unsmiling as he attempted to portray his opponent as "dangerous and belligerent."

Reagan, on the other hand, appeared amiable and relaxed, protesting that Carter misrepresented his attitude on many issues. He seemed to score the most points with prospective voters in his final remarks when he asked: "Are you better off than you were four years ago? Is it easier for you to go and buy things in the stores than it was four years ago? Is there more or less unemployment in the country than there was four years ago? Is America as respected throughout the world as it was? Do you feel that our security is as safe? That we're as strong as we were four years ago? And if you answer all of those questions yes, why then I think your choice is very obvious as to who you'll vote for."

# NOVEMBER

**2   Iran states ransom demands for U.S. hostages:** Iranian parliament approves conditions required for U.S. to obtain release of hostages. See page 31.

**3   Tuna imports from Ecuador banned:** U.S. orders embargo in reprisal for seizure of U.S. fishing boats off west coast of Ecuador.

**4   Reagan elected by landslide:** Former Gov. Ronald Reagan defeats President Jimmy Carter by 489 to 49 electoral votes; election gives GOP control of U.S. Senate. See pages 29, 245–256.

**4–6   Islamic nations hold conference:** First Conference for Economic Cooperation, in Ankara, Turkey, results in 10-point plan for strengthening economic ties among Islamic states; OPEC members agree to give preference to other Muslim countries in oil sales.

**5   Stock market soars on Reagan victory:** Dow Jones average closes up 15.96 points to 953.16; volume of 84.3 million shares is largest ever for one day.

**6   Trade deficit narrowed in third quarter,** Commerce Department reports; gap of $2.7 billion is at lowest level since second quarter of 1976.

**7   Unemployment rate rose in October to 7.6%,** Labor Department reports.

**7   Producer prices rose 0.8%** in October, Labor Department reports; equal to 10.6% annual rate; Producer Price Index had declined in August and September.

**9   First elections held in Ivory Coast:** Voters elect new representatives for about two-thirds of 147-seat national assembly in first open elections since 1960 independence from France.

**9   Polish supreme court supports free trade unions:** Rules that trade-union charter does not have to refer to supremacy of Communist Party; threatened strike averted.

**10   U.S. replies to Iran:** Deputy Secretary of State Warren Christopher gives U.S. response to Iranian ransom demands for hostages' release to Algerian officials, who deliver it to Iran Nov. 12.

**10   Supreme Court rules on court costs:** Overturns decision requiring prisoner who brought unsuccessful lawsuit against prison administration to reimburse officials for legal costs; 7–2 opinion says law allowing winning side in civil-rights suits to claim reimbursement for legal fees should apply only rarely to suits by prisoners.

**10   Retail sales fell in October,** Commerce Department reports; 0.1% drop is first after four monthly increases.

**12   New rules issued on reporters' records:** Justice Department defines procedures required before government can subpoena records of news reporters or of their long-distance telephone calls.

**12   Panama wins seat on Security Council:** UN vote in General Assembly comes after Costa Rica abandons fight for vacant seat.

**15   President ousted in Guinea-Bissau coup:** Prime Minister João Bernardo Veira heads new Council of the Revolution.

**15   Palau Islands to be semiautonomous:** South Pacific islands and U.S. reach agreement to end trusteeship set up at end of World War II; Palau will manage own internal and foreign affairs while U.S. will be responsible for defense.

**16   Explosion in Thailand kills 60:** Blast occurs in Bangkok munitions factory; 400 injured.

**17   Ku Klux Klan members acquitted:** All-white jury in North Carolina frees six members of Ku Klux Klan and Nazi Party of charges of murder stemming from anti-Klan rally Nov. 3, 1979, when four white men and one black woman were killed.

**17   Penn Central settles claim with U.S.:** Three government agencies agree to pay Penn Central Corp. $2.1 billion for assets of bankrupt railroad they took over in 1976 to form Conrail; largest claims settlement by U.S. in history.

**17   Senate votes to limit school busing:** Votes 51–35 to prohibit Justice Department from using funds to bring legal cases that would result in court-ordered busing.

**18   House adopts $631 billion budget for 1981:** Representatives vote 203–191 to accept $25 million deficit for current fiscal year.

**19   Begin government narrowly wins confidence vote:** Israel's parliament supports prime minister's government with only 3-vote margin.

**20   UN urges Soviet withdrawal from Afghanistan:** General Assembly votes 111–22, asking Soviet Union to withdraw troops from Afghanistan.

**20   Stocks go over 1,000-mark:** Dow Jones average gains 9.13 points to close at 1,000.17, first time over 1,000 since Dec. 31, 1976.

**20   Japanese hotel fire kills 44:** Resort hotel in Kawaji burns.

**21   Las Vegas hotel fire kills 84:** Worst U.S. hotel fire since 1946 occurs at MGM Grand, trapping 3,500; hundreds injured; helicopters rescue trapped guests from roof.

**21   Rail crash in Italy kills 26:** Two express trains collide with uncoupled freight cars.

**23   Earthquakes in Italy kill more than 3,000:** More than 1,500 also missing after series of quakes in southern Italy; devastation widespread.

**23   Former Israeli minister ousted from party:** Former Defense Minister Ezer Weizman expelled from governing Herut Party because of vote against Prime Minister Begin in confidence test.

**24   Explosion in Turkey kills 97 women:** Were attending engagement party in Danaciobasi.

**25   Consumer prices rose 1%** in October, Labor Department reports; 12.6% above October 1979.

**25   President overthrown in Upper Volta:** Former Foreign Minister Col. Saye Zerbo leads bloodless coup; deposed President Sangoule Lamizana is arrested; new government bans all political activity.

**26   Judge dismisses Abscam convictions of two:** Federal District Judge John P. Fullam in Philadelphia says government "stretched" federal statutes and "entrapped" defendants George X. Schwartz and Harry P. Jannotti, who were convicted on Sept. 16.

**27   Soviets launch 3-man spacecraft:** Completely redesigned Soyuz-T3 is 39th in Soyuz series; completes computer-guided docking with Salyut 6 orbiting laboratory on Nov. 28; men return to Earth on Dec. 10 after repairing Salyut 6.

**28   Trade deficit rose in October,** Commerce Department reports; $1.86 billion loss is up from September total of $1.64 million.

**30   Uruguayans oppose military constitution:** In first election since 1971, Uruguayans vote 58% to 42% against continued military rule.

# REAGAN WINS WITH ELECTORAL LANDSLIDE

FOCUS

Confounding the public-opinion pollsters, who almost unanimously had forecast that the presidential election on Nov. 4 was "unpredictable" or "too close to call," Republican presidential candidate Ronald Reagan and his running mate George Bush swept to victory with an electoral landslide. President Carter's effort to win reelection to a second term was buried by a lopsided 489 to 49 electoral vote—the greatest such defeat for an incumbent President in 68 years.

The Reagan-Bush ticket also won a clear majority of the record-breaking 85 million votes cast in the election. Unofficial returns showed they had received more than 43 million votes (51%) to less than 35 million (41%) for Carter, and more than 5 million (6.5%) for Independent candidate John Anderson (see pages 245–247 and 389).

Losing every major industrial state, the President carried only the District of Columbia and six states—Georgia, Hawaii, Maryland, Minnesota, Rhode Island, and West Virginia.

Long before the polls closed in the Western states, the President phoned Reagan about 9 P.M. EST to congratulate him. About an hour later he made a public concession speech on television, declaring that his defeat "hurt."

Voter dissatisfaction with the Carter administration also was reflected in the Republicans winning control of the U.S. Senate for the first time since President Eisenhower's administration and in reducing the Democratic majority in the U.S. House of Representatives.

Most observers believed that the debate between President Carter and Reagan one week before the election had been the crucial factor that produced the Republican landslide (see page 27). In it, Reagan was able to demonstrate an amiability that overcame the President's previous efforts to portray him as a leader with "dangerous" attitudes.

President-elect Ronald Reagan and Vice President-elect George Bush held their first news conference on Nov. 6.

United Press Int'l.

# DECEMBER

**1   Dow Jones average plunges 23.89 points:** Biggest one-day loss since Oct. 9, 1979; closes at 969.45.

**2   U.S. And Turkey finalize treaty on prisoners:** Pact, effective Jan. 1, 1981, provides for exchange of prisoners and faster handling of extradition.

**2   Pope issues second encyclical:** Pope John Paul II calls on Roman Catholics to work for social justice on basis of God's mercy.

**2   President signs Alaska lands bill:** Carter signs bill creating over 104 million acres of national parks, wildlife refuges, and wilderness areas.

**3   Polish leaders plead for end to labor unrest:** Communist rulers tell nation its fate hangs in balance; U.S. voices concern about buildup of Soviet troops on border with Poland.

**3   Congressmen found guilty in Abscam trial:** Federal district court jury in Brooklyn, N.Y., convicts Rep. John M. Murphy (D-N.Y.) and Rep. Frank Thompson Jr. (D-N.J.).

**4   Connecticut governor announces resignation:** Ella T. Grasso says she will step down Dec. 31 to undergo treatment for cancer; to be replaced by Lt. Gov. William A. O'Neill.

**4   Independence voted for South African homeland:** Citizens of Ciskei ask to become fourth sovereign tribal state in South Africa.

**4   Portuguese premier dies in plane crash:** Prime Minister Francisco Sá Carneiro and Defense Minister Adelino Amaro da Costa killed with five others in crash just after takeoff from Lisbon.

**5   U.S. cuts off aid to El Salvador:** United States suspends military and economic aid until clarification of deaths of three American nuns and a lay missionary, whose bodies were discovered Dec. 4.

**5   Hijackers escape with $1.6 million:** Gunmen hijack Venezuelan DC-9 on flight from Margarita Island to Caracas; force plane to land at Higuerote, where accomplices had seized airport; escape in waiting van with $1.6 million that had been aboard plane.

**5–7   Boston mass-transit shutdown:** Financial problems cause stoppage for over two days of nation's fifth-largest mass-transit system until state legislature approves added funds.

**8   Portuguese president wins reelection:** Gen. Antonio Ramalho Eanes wins 57% of vote against right-wing challenger.

**7   Ruling party wins Taiwan elections:** Kuomintang party wins 57 of 70 seats at stake in legislature and 63 of 76 contested seats in National Assembly.

**8   Former Beatle John Lennon slain:** Member of 1960s singing group shot by former mental patient in New York City.

**10   Brezhnev proposes nonintervention in Persian Gulf:** Soviet leader invites U.S. and other nations to join in formal agreement to ban military and naval intervention in Persian Gulf area.

**10   Abscam figure resigns from House:** Rep. John W. Jenrette (D-S.C.) offers resignation to halt expulsion proceedings stemming from Oct. 8 conviction for bribery and conspiracy.

**11   First Reagan cabinet appointments announced:** See page 389.

**11   Ugandans choose Obote as president:** Election restores Milton Obote, who was deposed by dictator Idi Amin.

**12   NATO warns Soviet Union on Poland:** Communique says NATO members will retaliate if Soviet troops invade Poland.

**13   Civilian named president of El Salvador:** Ruling junta names José Napoleón Duarte first civilian president in 49 years.

**15   President reelected in Guyana:** Forbes Burnham wins 76% of vote, but international observers charge election was fraudulent.

**15   UN calls for sanctions against Israel:** General Assembly votes 98–16, calling for Security Council to cut off of trade with Israel unless it withdraws from Arab lands taken in 1967 war.

**16   OPEC raises oil prices:** Meeting in Bali, Indonesia, approves $41-a-barrel price.

**16   Suez Canal opened to supertankers:** Ceremonies mark completion of 5-year $1.3 billion project to widen and deepen canal.

**18   Ulster prisoners end hunger strike:** Seven Northern Ireland prisoners call off 7½-week strike for political status when one nears death.

**19   U.S. and Japan sign trade agreement:** Pact requires Japan to open telecommunications procurement to U.S. and other foreign suppliers.

**19   Vietnam adopts new constitution:** Charter provides for collective presidency consisting of council of state headed by a chairman.

**20   Canadian province declares tax strike:** British Colombia refuses to pay federal natural-gas excise tax as protest against Ottawa's authority to raise revenues on provincial properties.

**27   President Carter injured in ski accident:** Falls while cross-country skiing at Camp David, Md., breaking collarbone.

**31   Official U.S. Census released:** U.S. Population, 226,504,825 (see page 963).

**31   New President for Senegal:** Leopold Senghor, 74, resigns, turning over presidency to Prime Minister Abdou Diouf.

## LATE FOOTBALL RESULTS

**Dec. 14   Garden St. Bowl:** Houston 35, Navy 0.

**Dec. 14   Independence Bowl:** Southern Mississippi 16, McNeese State 14.

**Dec. 19   Holiday Bowl:** Brigham Young 46, SMU 45.

**Dec. 20   Tangerine Bowl:** Maryland 35, Fla. 20.

**Dec. 26   Fiesta Bowl:** Penn St. 31, Ohio St. 19.

**Dec. 27   Hall of Fame Game:** Arkansas 34, Tulane 15.

**Dec. 27   Liberty Bowl:** Purdue 28, Missouri 25.

**Dec. 27   Sun Bowl:** Nebraska 31, Miss. St. 17.

**Dec. 28   Pro Football AFC First Round Playoff:** Oakland 27, Houston 7.

**Dec. 28   Pro Football NFC First Round Playoff:** Dallas 34, Los Angeles 13.

**Dec. 29   Gator Bowl:** Pittsburgh 37, South Carolina 9.

**Dec. 31   Bluebonnet Bowl:** North Carolina 16, Texas 7.

### 1981

**Jan. 1   Sugar Bowl:** Georgia 17, Notre D. 10.

**Jan. 1   Rose Bowl:** Mich. 23, Washington 6.

**Jan. 1   Cotton Bowl:** Alabama 30, Baylor 2.

**Jan. 1   Orange Bowl:** Okla. 18, Florida St. 17.

**Jan. 2   Peach Bowl:** Miami (Fla.) 20, Virginia Tech 10.

# FATE OF HOSTAGES REMAINS IN DOUBT

FOCUS

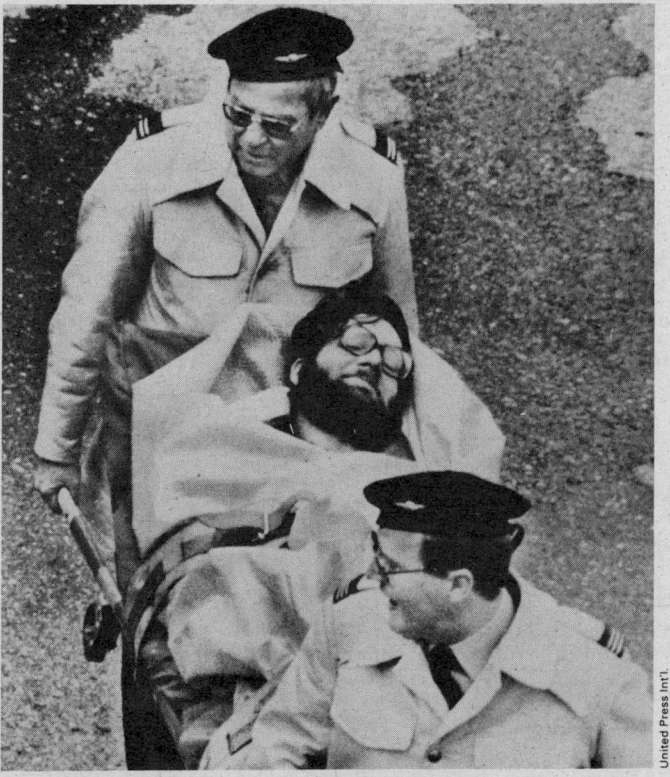

United Press Int'l.

The only one of the American hostages to be released by Iran in 1980, Richard I. Queen, 28, was carried from a Swissair plane on July 11 after arriving in Zurich, Switzerland, from Teheran. After eight months of captivity, Queen was freed so that he could receive medical treatment for multiple sclerosis that he had developed. A junior member of the U.S. foreign service, Queen said he had been well treated by his captors and had spent much of his time reading from the embassy's extensive library.

Although one U.S. hostage was freed by Iran (see above), 52 others began their second year of captivity in November 1980. Despite a bungled U.S. military effort to free them (see page 15) and exhaustive diplomatic negotiations, the U.S. government could not find a way to bring the hostages home.

Held prisoner since the U.S. embassy in Teheran was captured by Iranian militants on Nov. 4, 1979, the hostages remained the main focus of U.S. foreign policy throughout the year.

Iran's parliament on Nov. 2, 1980, set terms that the U.S. would have to meet if the hostages were to be freed. These were:

1. To pledge not to interfere politically or militarily in the affairs of Iran.

2. To unfreeze all Iranian assets, estimated at about $8 billion, that have been held under a presidential decree of Nov. 14, 1979.

3. To cancel all legal claims against Iran and to guarantee to pay any future claims made against Iran.

4. To transfer to Iran all the assets of the late shah of Iran and his close relatives.

Because the U.S. and Iran had broken diplomatic relations in April 1980, subsequent secret negotiations were carried out through a third party, Algeria. A formal "positive" U.S. reply to the Iranian demands was flown to Algeria on Nov. 10 by U.S. Deputy Secretary of State Warren M. Christopher. Algerian diplomats carried the message to Iran and then flew to Washington where they delivered an Iranian reply on Nov. 26. A second U.S. message to Iran was carried to Algeria by Christopher on Dec. 2 and was transmitted to Iran two days later. It explained that all of the demands could not be met legally by the U.S. government.

Iran replied in a note delivered on Dec. 21, demanding the U.S. deposit some $24 billion in Algeria as a "guarantee" for return of the frozen assets and the Shah's wealth.

U.S. Secretary of State Edmund Muskie termed the ransom demand "unreasonable".

# QUOTABLE QUOTES: 1980

## ON PUBLIC SERVICE

"Public service is not a chore, not a burden. It is a joy. That is happiness, that is a genuine kind of freedom, freedom with responsibility."
—**Ralph Nader,** consumer advocate, at commencement address at Colby College, Waterville, Me., in June 1980

## WHAT ELSE COULD WE DO?

"We've done what would be expected, what was normal, and what any U.S. Embassy would do for us."
—**Gilles Mathieu,** Canadian chargé d'affaires in Washington, after Canadians in Teheran helped hide and then aided the escape of six Americans from Iran, on Feb. 1, 1980

## THE LADY'S NOT FOR TURNING

"You turn if you want to. The lady's not for turning."
—**Prime Minister Margaret Thatcher** of Britain, rejecting suggestions she change her conservative economic policies, on Oct. 10, 1980

## ON INTERNATIONAL RELATIONS

"I don't think that any country is justified in entering another country."
—**Prime Minister Indira Gandhi** of India discussing Soviet invasion of Afghanistan, on Jan. 16, 1980

## TOO LATE?

"I would have spanked brother Billy a long time ago."
—**Gov. Ella Grasso** of Connecticut, referring to President Carter's brother, on July 24, 1980

## ALWAYS THE BEST

"New Yorkers are best in adversity."
—**Mayor Edward Koch** of New York City, discussing the city's transit strike, on April 1, 1980

## RARELY USED QUALITIES

"Goodwill and humility are two qualities that, as far as I know, have never really been seriously used in trying to make and keep the peace on this interdependent planet."
—**Pauline Frederick,** NBC correspondent, speaking at commencement at Fairleigh Dickinson University, Madison, N.J., in June 1980

## PAINFUL, BUT WORTH IT

"Painful? Yeah, it was."
—**Eric Heiden,** after winning a record fifth gold medal at the Winter Olympics, on Feb. 23, 1980

## NOT AGAIN!

"Every time we get to an international crisis, the farmer gets kicked in the teeth."
—**Steve Roberts,** Iowa state Republican Party chairman, on the Soviet grain embargo resulting from the Soviet invasion of Afghanistan, on Jan. 5, 1980

## EAT AND ENJOY!

"Sound nutrition is not a panacea. Good food that provides appropriate proportions of nutrients should not be regarded as a poison, a medicine, or a talisman. It should be eaten and enjoyed."
—From report issued by the **Food and Nutrition Board of the National Research Council,** on May 27, 1980

## A SOFT LANDING

"It's always a pleasure to have a soft landing."
—**Valery Ryumin,** Soviet astronaut, after returning from record 185 days in space, on Oct. 11, 1980

## MY HOUSE, YOUR HOUSE

"As from this moment Israel has its house in Egypt, and in a few days Egypt will have its house in Israel."
—**Yosef Hadass,** Israeli chargé d'affaires, discussing exchange of ambassadors by Israel and Egypt, on Feb. 18, 1980

## ALWAYS FIRST

"We'll always be first, but we're not tokens anymore."
—**Andrea Hollen,** one of West Point's first female graduates, on May 28, 1980

## ALWAYS EVIL

"Racial discrimination is evil, no matter how it is practiced, no matter who does it or why."
—**Pope John Paul II,** speaking in Nairobi, Kenya, on May 6, 1980

## THE WAY THINGS WERE

"We knew all along that if the question came down to whether people were happy with the way things had gone for the last four years, we were lost."
—**Jody Powell,** President Carter's press secretary, discussing the 1980 election results, on Nov. 8, 1980

## NOW IS THE TIME

"The time is now, my fellow Americans, to recapture our destiny, to take it into our own hands."
—**Ronald Reagan,** accepting the Republican nomination for the presidency, on July 17, 1980

# Accidents and Disasters

United Press Int'l.

Bereaved victim of Italian earthquake kneels at coffin of sister at Santomena, Italy. In background stand ruins of Church of Annunciata that was destroyed in the quake of Nov. 23, which devastated a huge area of southern Italy.

## HIGHLIGHTS: 1980

The two worst natural disasters of 1980 were earthquakes in Algeria and Italy.

The Algerian city of Al Asnam was struck by two earthquakes on Oct. 10, destroying most of the buildings and homes in the city and surrounding villages. Some 2,950 persons were killed, although early reports had estimated as many as 20,000 dead. A similar quake in the area in 1954 killed 1,600.

The U.S. and many other countries sent aid to assist Algeria with the disaster. U.S. Air Force planes flew in tons of cots, blan-

kets, tents, and other supplies. Five support ships of the U.S. Sixth Fleet brought further assistance.

A series of strong earthquakes brought havoc to southern Italy on Nov. 23. More than 3,000 persons were known to have been killed and about 1,500 were missing. Some 300,000 persons were made homeless in more than 100 towns and villages.

One of the hardest hit towns was Sant' Angelo dei Lombardi where several hundred patients were killed in the collapse of a newly

**HIGHLIGHTS: 1980** *(continued)*

constructed hospital. Dozens of young people trapped in a basement discotheque under a collapsed hotel in the town could be heard calling for help for days after the quake, but all were dead by the time enough rubble had been cleared to reach them.

Up to two weeks after the disaster, rescue workers still were finding some survivors in the wreckage of houses in outlying areas.

A huge outpouring of aid from the U.S. and other countries was sent to help the earthquake victims in Italy. The U.S. Congress passed a special appropriation of $50 million to assist in the reconstruction of buildings and roads in the area. Many Italian-Americans flew to the region to aid in relief efforts and to learn the fate of relatives.

## DISASTROUS HURRICANES AND TYPHOONS

| DATE | PLACE | DEATHS | REMARKS |
|---|---|---|---|
| 1703, Nov. 26–27 | England | 8,000 | Hurricane |
| 1864, Oct. 5 | Calcutta, India | 50,000 | Much of city stripped by cyclone |
| 1876, Oct. 31 | Bakarganj, India (now Bangladesh) | 200,000 | Storm surge inundates city |
| 1881, Oct. 8 | Indochina | 300,000 | Typhoon and storm surge |
| 1882, June 5 | Bombay, India | 100,000 | Cyclone and storm surge |
| 1899, Aug. 8 | Puerto Rico | 3,369 | San Ciriaco hurricane |
| 1900, Aug. 27–Sept. 15 | Texas | 6,000 | $25 million damage caused by storm tide that inundates Galveston island |
| 1906, Sept. 18 | Hong Kong | 10,000 | Typhoon |
| 1909, Sept. 14–21 | Louisiana and Mississippi | 350 | Wide extent of Louisiana coast inundated; $5 million damage |
| 1915, Aug. 5–25 | Texas and Louisiana | 275 | 12-foot storm tide inundates Galveston to depth of 5–6 feet; $50 million damage |
| 1915, Sept. 22–Oct. 1 | Middle Gulf Coast | 275 | 90% of buildings destroyed over large area of Louisiana south of New Orleans; $13 million damage |
| 1919, Sept. 2–15 | Florida, Louisiana, and Texas | 287 | Hurricane severe both in Florida and Texas; over 500 casualties in ships lost at sea; $22 million damage |
| 1926, Sept. 11–22 | Florida and Alabama | 243 | Very severe in Miami area and from Pensacola into southern Alabama; $73 million damage |
| 1926, Oct. 20 | Havana, Cuba | 600 | Hurricane strikes city and suburbs |
| 1928, Sept. 6–20 | Southern Florida | 1,836 | Wind-driven waters of Lake Okeechobee overflow into populated areas; $25 million damage |
| 1930, Sept. 3 | Santo Domingo, Dominican Rep. | 2,000 | Hurricane |
| 1931, Sept. 10 | British Honduras (Belize) | 1,000 | Hurricane and tidal wave destroys city of Belize |
| 1934, Sept. 21 | Honshu, Japan | 4,000 | Typhoon causes $50 million property damage |
| 1935, Aug. 29–Sept. 10 | Southern Florida | 408 | "Labor Day Storm"; barometer reading of 26.35 inches on Long Key lowest on record in Western Hemisphere; $6 million damage |
| 1935, Oct. 21 | Haiti | 2,150 | Hurricane |
| 1938, Sept. 10–22 | Long Island, New York; southern New England | 600 | Very heavy wind causes $306 million damage in New England |
| 1940, Aug. 5–15 | Georgia and Carolinas | 50 | Heavy flooding in Southeastern states as far as Tennessee from hurricane-induced rains; $2 million damage |
| 1942, Oct. 16 | Bengal India | 40,000 | Cyclone |
| 1944, Sept. 9–16 | North Carolina to New England | 46 | $102 million damage |
| 1944, Oct. 12–23 | Florida | 18 | Warnings prevent heavier casualties; $10 million damage |
| 1944, Dec. 18 | South China Sea | 800 | Three U.S. ships lost in typhoon |
| 1947, Sept. 4–21 | Florida and Middle Gulf Coast | 51 | $55 million damage on east coast of Florida and in Louisiana and Mississippi |
| 1947, Sept. 15–19 | Honshu, Japan | 1,000 | Typhoon and floods |
| 1949, Oct. 27 | Southeastern India | 1,000 | Cyclone |
| 1949, Oct. 31– Nov. 2 | Philippines | 1,000 | Typhoon |
| 1951, Dec. 9–10 | Philippines | 569 | Typhoon leaves 60,000 homeless |
| 1952, Oct. 22 | Philippines | 431 | Southern Luzon hit by typhoon |
| 1953, Sept. 26 | Vietnam | 1,000 | Typhoon and floods |
| 1954, Aug. 25–31 Carol | North Carolina to New England | 60 | $439 million property losses greatest of any single storm up to this date |
| 1954, Sept. 2–14 Edna | New Jersey to New England | 21 | $41 million damage in New England |
| 1954, Sept. 26 | Northern Japan | 1,218 | Typhoon causes train ferry to capsize |
| 1954, Oct. 5–18 Hazel | South Carolina to New York | 95 | $200 million damage in exposed North Carolina shore areas; storm retains destructive intensity through Middle Atlantic states |
| 1954, Oct. 12 | Southwestern Haiti | 410 | Hurricane Hazel leaves 250,000 homeless |

**DISASTROUS HURRICANES AND TYPHOONS** *(continued)*

| DATE | PLACE | DEATHS | REMARKS |
|---|---|---|---|
| 1955, Aug. 3–14 Connie | North Carolina | 25 | Heavy rainfall from North Carolina to New England; $46 million damage |
| 1955, Aug. 16–20 Diane | North Carolina to New England | 187 | Heavy rainfall with near-maximum runoff causes severe floods through Northeast; $714 million damage exceeds any prior storm |
| 1955, Sept. 19 | Tampico, Mexico | 300 | Hurricane Hilda |
| 1955, Sept. 22–28 | West Indies and Mexico | 712 | Hurricane Janet |
| 1956, Aug. 1 | China | 2,161 | Typhoon devastates Hopen and Honan provinces |
| 1956, Sept. 21–30 Flossy | Louisiana to Florida | 15 | $10 million damage over area from New Orleans and mouth of Mississippi to western Florida |
| 1957, June 26–29 Audrey | Texas to Alabama | 390 | Storm surge over 12 feet causes inundation of flat Louisiana coast by Gulf waters; $138 million damage |
| 1958, Sept. 27–28 | Japan | 679 | Typhoon Ida strikes central Honshu |
| 1958, Oct. 30–Nov. 5 | East Pakistan (Bangladesh) | 500 | Cyclone |
| 1959, Aug. 20 | China | 720 | Typhoon Iris strikes coast of Fukien Province |
| 1959, Sept. 17–19 | South Korea | 669 | Typhoon Sarah |
| 1959, Sept. 26–27 | Japan | 4,580 | Typhoon Vera strikes central Honshu |
| 1959, Oct. 27–28 | Mexico | 960 | Hurricane, flood, and mud slides on Pacific coast |
| 1960, Sept. 9–13 Donna | Florida to New England | 50 | $426 million damage; winds estimated near 140 mph, with gusts 175–180 mph on central Florida Keys; first storm with hurricane winds to travel up Atlantic coast in 75 years |
| 1960, Oct. 10, 31 | East Pakistan (Bangladesh) | 14,000 | Two cyclones strike Bay of Bengal area |
| 1961, May 9 | East Pakistan (Bangladesh) | 2,000 | Cyclone and storm surge |
| 1961, Sept. 11–14 Carla | Texas | 46 | Largest and most intense Gulf coast hurricane in many years; $408 million damage along wide expanse of Texas coast |
| 1961, Sept. 16–17 | Japan | 172 | Typhoon strikes Honshu and other islands |
| 1961, Oct. 31 | British Honduras (Belize) | 262 | Hurricane Hattie devastates Belize |
| 1961, Nov. 12 | Southern Mexico | 436 | Hurricane Tara |
| 1962, Sept. 1 | Hong Kong | 400 | Typhoon Wanda |
| 1962, Oct. 27 | Thailand | 769 | Cyclone |
| 1963, May 28–29 | East Pakistan (Bangladesh) | 22,000 | Cyclone and storm surge leave 1 million homeless |
| 1963, Oct. 1–9 | Caribbean Sea | 7,200 | Hurricane Flora |
| 1964, June 13–14 | West Pakistan | 250 | High winds and floods |
| 1964, Aug. 22 | Caribbean Sea | 214 | Hurricane Cleo sweeps through Guadeloupe and Haiti |
| 1964, Aug. 28– Dora Sept. 16 | Florida and Georgia | 5 | First hurricane to enter northeastern Florida during this century; $250 million damage |
| 1964, Sept. 28– Hilda Oct. 5 | Louisiana, Mississippi, Carolinas, and Georgia | 38 | Entire Louisiana coastal area evacuated (150,000 people); six closely associated tornadoes takes 27 of 38 lives; $125 million damage |
| 1964, Dec. 22 | Ceylon (Sri Lanka) | 800 | Cyclone hits east coast, principally Trincomalee |
| 1965, May 12 | East Pakistan (Bangladesh) | 13,000 | Cyclone and storm leaves 5–7 million homeless |
| 1965, Sept. 7–12 Betsy | Florida and Louisiana | 87 | Strikes Miami and devastates New Orleans and Plaquemines Parish with winds to 125 mph; damage estimated at $1.42 billion |
| 1965, Oct. 1–9 | Northern Mariana Islands | 208 | Typhoon Carmen |
| 1965, Dec. 15 | East Pakistan (Bangladesh) | 25,000 | Cyclone and storm surge |
| 1966, Sept. 25 | Japan | 318 | Typhoon Ida strikes Japan with winds to 200 mph |
| 1966, Sept. 25–Oct. 11 | West Indies, Fla., Mexico | 1,000 | Hurricane Inez carries 135–145 mph winds |
| 1967, July 9 | Southwestern Japan | 263 | Typhoon Billie causes landslides and floods |
| 1967, Sept. 5–22 Beulah | Texas | 15 | Severe flooding and 115 tornadoes; third most devastating storm in Texas history causes $208 million damage |
| 1968, April 11 | East Pakistan (Bangladesh) | 200 | Cyclone |
| 1968, May 9–10 | Burma | 1,000 | Cyclone leaves 17,200 homeless |
| 1969, May 19–20 | Andhra Pradesh, India | 608 | Cyclone leaves 20,000 homeless |
| 1969, Aug. 17–20 Camille | Mississippi and Louisiana coasts | 324 | Most destructive hurricane in U.S. history; winds up to 200 mph and tides up to 24 feet; thousands homeless; $1.42 billion damage |
| 1970, Aug. 3–5 Celia | Texas | 11 | $454 million damage caused by gusts to 161 mph; Port Aransas and Aransas Pass suffer worst destruction |
| 1970, Sept. 15 | Philippines | 300 | Typhoon strikes Luzon |
| 1970, Oct. 14 | Philippines | 575 | Typhoon strikes Luzon Island; 193 missing |
| 1970, Oct. 18 | Philippines | 631 | Typhoon strikes Mindanao Island; 284 missing |
| 1970, Nov. 12–13 | East Pakistan (Bangladesh) | 500,000 | Cyclone and storm surge devastates coastal areas |
| 1970, Nov. 20 | Philippines | 120 | Typhoon strikes Manila |
| 1971, Aug. 16–17 | Hong Kong | 100 | Typhoon Rose |
| 1971, Oct. 29–30 | India | 10,000 | Cyclone and tidal wave strike Orissa State |

**DISASTROUS HURRICANES AND TYPHOONS** (continued)

| DATE AND NAME | PLACE | DEATHS | REMARKS |
|---|---|---|---|
| 1972, June 17–23 Agnes | Florida to New York | 105 | Costliest storm in U.S. history with over $4 billion in damage; Pennsylvania is hardest hit with $1.2 billion damages and 48 deaths; New York has 24 deaths and $653 million damage |
| 1973, April–June | Bangladesh | 427 | Storms and floods leave 10,000 homeless |
| 1973, April 29–May 2 | Indonesia | 1,650 | Storm and tidal wave hit Flores and Palue islands |
| 1973, Nov. 8 | Bangladesh | 127 | Cyclone in Bay of Bengal sinks fishing fleet |
| 1974, March 25 | Bangladesh | 300 | Storm hits coast Bay of Bengal |
| 1974, June 11 | Luzon, Philippines | 71 | Typhoon Dinah strikes Luzon |
| 1974, July 6 | Japan and South Korea | 108 | Typhoon Gilda causes over $300 million damages |
| 1974, Sept. 7–8 Carmen | Louisiana | 1 | Winds up to 180 mph damage crops and coastal towns south of New Orleans; $150 million damage |
| 1974, Sept. 19–20 | Honduras | 2,000 | Hurricane Fifi leaves 115,000 homeless |
| 1974, Nov. 28 | Bangladesh | 500 | Cyclone hits Bay of Bengal coast |
| 1974, Dec. 25 | Darwin, Australia | 48 | Cyclone destroys port city; 35,000 homeless |
| 1975, May 9 | Northern Burma | 130 | Tropical storm damages 20 towns |
| 1975, Sept. 15–27 Eloise | Puerto Rico, Florida, Northeastern states | 61 | Puerto Rico hardest hit by 130 mph winds, thousands homeless; severe floods in East Coast states; $420 million damage |
| 1976, May 20–22 | Philippines | 215 | Typhoon Olga leaves 630,000 homeless |
| 1976, Aug. 9–10 Belle | Atlantic Coast, North Carolina to New England | 1 | Long Island, N.Y., hardest hit by 90 mph winds, 200,000 persons evacuated before storm; $250 million damage |
| 1976, Sept. 8–13 | Japan | 104 | Typhoon Fran causes flood; 325,000 homeless |
| 1976, Oct. 1 | Baja California, Mexico | 630 | Hurricane Liza breaks dam outside La Paz |
| 1977, July 25 | Southern Taiwan | 28 | Typhoon Thelma destroys 20,000 homes |
| 1977, July 30 | Taipei, Taiwan | 45 | Typhoon Vera hits northern Taiwan, steel bridge collapses in Taipei |
| 1977, Nov. 12 | Tamil Nadu, India | 400 | Cyclone strikes southern India |
| 1977, Nov. 14 | Philippines | 80 | Typhoon whips fire in Manila hotel, killing 47 |
| 1977, Nov. 19 | Andhra Pradesh, India | over 20,000 | Cyclone causes flooding and tidal waves |
| 1978, April 4 | Bay of Bengal | 1,000 | Storm sinks about 100 boats |
| 1978, April 16 | Eastern India | 173 | Tornado hits 10 villages; over 600 injured |
| 1978, Oct. 27 | Luzon, Philippines | 314 | Typhoon Rita leaves 50,000 homeless and estimated $85.4 million damages |
| 1978, Nov. 24 | Sri Lanka | 500 | Cyclone strikes coastal area |
| 1979, April 18 | Philippines | 29 | Typhoon causes $3 million damage |
| 1979, May 12 | Andhra Pradesh, India | 607 | Cyclone leaves 2.5 million homeless and causes $850 million in damage |
| 1979, Aug. 29– Sept. 7, David | Caribbean and eastern United States | 1,380 | Dominica and Dominican Republic hardest hit; total damage more than $1 billion |
| 1979, Sept. 12 Frederic | Florida, Alabama, Mississippi | 8 | Evacuation of 500,000 people prevents high loss of life; $1.5 billion damage |
| 1979, Oct. 19 | Japan | 52 | Typhoon Tip ravages Japan; sets off gas-tank fire at U.S. Marine base, killing 12 |
| 1980, Aug. 4–11 | Caribbean and U.S. Gulf Coast | 272 | Hurricane Allen, worst Caribbean storm in history, caused more than $1 billion damage |

# MAJOR U.S. TORNADOES SINCE 1900

Source: National Oceanic and Atmospheric Administration

| DATE | PLACE | DEATHS | INJURED | DAMAGE |
|---|---|---|---|---|
| 1900, Nov. 20 | Arkansas, Mississippi, Tennessee | 73 | many | $ 500,000 |
| 1903, June 1 | Gainesville, Georgia | 98 | 190 | $ 1,000,000 |
| 1905, May 10 | Snyder, Oklahoma | 87 | 49 | $ 20,000 |
| 1908, April 24 | Lamar and Wayne counties, Mississippi | 100 | 649 | $ 880,000 |
| 1909, March 8 | Dallas and Monroe counties, Arkansas | 64 | 671 | $ 640,000 |
| 1913, March 23 | Omaha, Nebraska | 95 | — | $ 3,500,000 |
| 1916, June 5 | Arkansas (series of tornadoes) | 83 | 400 | millions |
| 1917, March 23 | New Albany, Indiana | 45 | — | $ 2,000,000 |
| 1917, May 26 | Mattoon and Charleston, Illinois | 101 | 638 | $ 2,500,000 |
| 1917, May 27 | Tennessee and Kentucky | 70 | — | $ 2,000,000 |
| 1918, Aug. 21 | Tyler, Minnesota | 36 | — | $ 1,000,000 |
| 1919, June 22 | Fergus Falls, Minnesota | 59 | — | $ 3,500,000 |
| 1920, March 28 | Alabama and Georgia | 50 | — | $ 1,400,000 |
| 1920, March 28 | Chicago, Illinois, and vicinity | 28 | — | $ 3,000,000 |
| 1920, April 20 | Oktibbeha County, Mississippi, and Franklin County, Ala. | 87 | — | $ 1,500,000 |
| 1920, May 2 | Rogers, Mayes, and Cherokee counties in Oklahoma | 64 | — | $ 180,000 |
| 1921, April 15 | Cass County, Texas; Hempstead, Miller, Pike counties, Ark. | 61 | — | $ 1,300,000 |
| 1924, April 30 | Central South Carolina | 67 | — | $ 1,000,000 |

**MAJOR U.S. TORNADOES SINCE 1900** *(continued)*

| DATE | PLACE | DEATHS | INJURED | DAMAGE |
|---|---|---|---|---|
| 1924, June 28 | Lorain and Sandusky, Ohio | 85 | — | $ 12,000,000 |
| 1925, March 18 | Missouri, Illinois, Indiana | 689 | 1,980 | $ 17,000,000 |
| 1926, Nov. 25 | Belleville to Portland, Arkansas | 53 | — | $ 630,000 |
| 1927, April 12 | Rock Springs, Texas | 74 | — | $ 1,200,000 |
| 1927, May 9 | Randolph County, Arkansas; Poplar Bluff, Missouri | 92 | — | $ 2,300,000 |
| 1927, Sept. 29 | St. Louis, Missouri | 72 | — | $ 22,000,000 |
| 1929, April 25 | Southeastern and central Georgia | 40 | — | $ 850,000 |
| 1930, May 6 | Hill and Ellis counties, Texas | 41 | — | $ 2,100,000 |
| 1932, March 21 | Alabama (series of tornadoes) | 268 | 1,874 | $ 5,000,000 |
| 1933, May 1 | Webster and Bienville Parishes, Louisiana | 23 | 400 | $ 1,300,000 |
| 1936, April 2 | Cordele, Georgia | 23 | 500 | $ 3,000,000 |
| 1936, April 5 | Tupelo, Mississippi | 216 | 700 | $ 3,500,000 |
| 1936, April 6 | Gainesville, Georgia | 203 | 934 | $ 13,000,000 |
| 1938, Sept. 29 | Charleston, South Carolina | 32 | 150 | $ 2,000,000 |
| 1939, April 16 | Drew County, Arkansas | 27 | 62 | $ 20,000 |
| 1942, March 16 | Central to northeastern Mississippi | 75 | 525 | $ 1,400,000 |
| 1942, April 27 | Rogers and Mayes counties, Oklahoma | 52 | 181 | $ 2,000,000 |
| 1944, June 25 | Ravenna, Ohio; Pennsylvania; West Virginia; Maryland | 150 | 867 | $ 4,200,000 |
| 1945, April 12 | Oklahoma and Arkansas | 102 | 689 | $ 4,000,000 |
| 1946, Jan. 4 | Northeastern Texas | 30 | 335 | $ 2,700,000 |
| 1947, April 9 | Texas, Oklahoma, Kansas | 169 | 983 | $ 9,800,000 |
| 1948, March 19 | Bunker Hill and Gillespie, Illinois | 33 | 449 | $ 3,800,000 |
| 1949, Jan. 3 | Louisiana and Arkansas | 58 | 439 | $ 1,500,000 |
| 1949, May 21 | Cape Girardeau, Missouri | 23 | 130 | $ 3,500,000 |
| 1952, March 21–22 | Arkansas, Missouri, and Tennessee (series of tornadoes) | 208 | 1,154 | $ 14,000,000 |
| 1953, May 11 | Waco, Texas | 114 | 597 | $ 41,000,000 |
| 1953, June 8 | Flint to Lakeport, Michigan | 116 | 867 | $ 19,000,000 |
| 1953, June 9 | Central and eastern Massachusetts | 90 | 1,288 | $ 52,000,000 |
| 1953, Dec. 5 | Vicksburg, Mississippi | 38 | 270 | $ 25,000,000 |
| 1955, May 25 | Blackwell, Oklahoma | 20 | 280 | $ 8,000,000 |
| 1955, May 25 | Udall, Kansas | 80 | 270 | $ 2,200,000 |
| 1956, April 3 | Southern Michigan | 18 | 340 | $ 11,000,000 |
| 1956, April 15 | Birmingham, Alabama | 25 | 200 | $ 1,500,000 |
| 1957, May 20 | Williamsburg, Kansas, to Ruskin Heights, Missouri | 44 | 531 | millions |
| 1959, Feb. 10 | St. Louis, Missouri | 21 | 345 | millions |
| 1964, Oct. 3 | Lafourche Parish, Louisiana | 22 | 165 | $ 500,000 |
| 1965, April 11 | Illinois, Michigan, Indiana, and Ohio (series of tornadoes) | 226 | 3,000 | $620,500,000 |
| 1966, March 3 | Mississippi and western Alabama | 58 | 531 | $ 18,500,000 |
| 1967, April 21 | Boone, McHenry, and Cook counties, Ill.; Kent County, Mich. | 57 | 982 | $ 18,000,000 |
| 1968, May 15–16 | Arkansas, Illinois, Indiana, Iowa, Minnesota, Mississippi, Missouri, Nebraska, Ohio, Tennessee, and Wisconsin | 72 | 1,000 | $ 51,000,000 |
| 1969, Jan. 23 | Jefferson to Newton counties, Mississippi | 32 | 241 | $ 500,000 |
| 1969, July 4 | Northern Ohio (storm and tornadoes) | 41 | — | substantial |
| 1970, April 17 | Texas Panhandle | 25 | 200 | $ 5,000,000 |
| 1970, May 11 | Lubbock, Texas | 26 | 500 | $135,000,000 |
| 1971, Feb. 21 | Mississippi, Louisiana, Tennessee (series of tornadoes) | 121 | 1,600 | $ 19,000,000 |
| 1973, March 31 | Georgia and South Carolina | 8 | — | $100,000,000 |
| 1973, May 26–28 | 10 states in South and Midwest (series of 195 tornadoes) | 47 | — | $ 55,000,000 |
| 1974, April 3–4 | 13 states in South and Midwest (148 tornadoes) | 329 | 6,142 | $540,000,000 |
| 1974, June | Tulsa and Drumright, Okla., hit by about 20 tornadoes | 26 | 294 | $ 23,500,000 |
| 1975, Jan. 10 | Series of tornadoes in Mississippi, Alabama, and Louisana | 15 | 298 | $ 5,000,000 |
| 1975, Feb. 22 | Tornadoes, thunderstorms, and hail in Oklahoma | 4 | 91 | $ 5,000,000 |
| 1975, March 24 | Atlanta, Ga., about 500 homes, including Governor's mansion, badly damaged | 3 | 152 | $ 56,500,000 |
| 1975, March 28 | Warren, Ark., tornado hits center of city | 7 | 50 | $ 5,000,000 |
| 1975, April 24 | Neosho, Mo., tornado cuts 9-mile-long path | 3 | 22 | $ 10,500,000 |
| 1975, May 6 | Omaha, Neb., 10 or more tornadoes destroy over 1,000 homes | 3 | 133 | $400,000,000 |
| 1975, July 23 | Canton, Ill., tornado cuts ½-mile-wide path through city | 2 | 69 | $ 20,000,000 |
| 1976, March 21 | Series of 5 tornadoes strikes Michigan | 2 | 57 | $ 5,000,000 |
| 1976, March 26–29 | Arkansas and Mississippi, series of tornadoes | 8 | 249 | $ 27,000,000 |
| 1977, April 4 | Northwest of Birmingham, Alabama | 22 | 130 | $ 15,000,000 |
| 1977, Aug. 21 | Lake Mattooon, Illinois, resort area | 6 | 56 | $ 5,000,000 |
| 1978, April 18 | Series of tornadoes hits southeastern Mississippi | 4 | 31 | $ 500,000 |
| 1978, May 4 | Hits elementary school in Pinellas County, Florida | 3 | 94 | $ 3,000,000 |
| 1978, July 4–5 | Cuts 75-mile path in North Dakota and Minnesota | 9 | 73 | $ 5,000,000 |
| 1978, Sept. 16 | Destroys businesses and farms near Grinnell, Iowa | 6 | 45 | $ 5,000,000 |
| 1978, Dec. 3 | Three series of tornadoes in Arkansas and Louisiana | 4 | 250 | $100,000,000 |
| 1979, April 9–11 | Series of tornadoes in Texas and Oklahoma | 60 | 800 | $300,000,000 |
| 1980, May 12–13 | Series of tornadoes in Missouri, Pennsylvania, Michigan | 7 | — | $100,000,000 |
| 1980, June 31 | Grand Island, Neb. | 4 | 134 | $140,000,000 |

## MAJOR VOLCANIC DISASTERS

| DATE | PLACE | DEATHS | REMARKS |
|---|---|---|---|
| A.D. 79, Aug. 24–26 | Pompeii, Herculaneum, Italy ... | 16,000 | Mt. Vesuvius erupts; destroys these towns |
| 1169 | Sicily .......................... | 15,000 | Mt. Etna erupts |
| 1631, Dec. 16 | Italy .......................... | 4,000 | Mt. Vesuvius erupts; destroys five towns |
| 1669 | Sicily .......................... | 20,000 | Mt. Etna erupts for 40 days |
| 1772 | Java, Indonesia ............... | 3,000 | Mt. Papandayan erupts |
| 1783 | Iceland ....................... | 9,000 | Mt. Hekla erupts; 20 villages obliterated |
| 1815 | Sumbawo, Indonesia ......... | 12,000 | Tambora explodes, followed by tidal waves |
| 1883, Aug. 26–28 | Indonesia ..................... | 35,000 | Krakatau erupts, followed by tidal wave |
| 1902, April 8 | Guatemala .................... | 1,000 | Santa Maria erupts |
| 1902, May | Saint Vincent, West Indies .... | 2,000 | Soufrière volcano erupts |
| 1902, May 8 | Martinique, West Indies ....... | 40,000 | Mt. Pelée erupts, wiping out city of St. Pierre |
| 1911 | Philippines ................... | 1,400 | Mt. Taal, on Luzon, erupts |
| 1919 | Java, Indonesia ............... | 5,000 | Mt. Kelud erupts, 100 villages destroyed |
| 1951, Jan. 18–21 | New Guinea ................... | 3,000 | Mt. Lamington erupts |
| 1963, March | Bali, Indonesia ............... | 1,500 | Mt. Agung erupts, leaving 85,000 homeless |
| 1964, March–April | Chile ......................... | — | Villarrica erupts, routing 30,000 persons |
| 1965, Sept. 28 | Philippines ................... | 500 | Mt. Taal, on Luzon, erupts |
| 1966, April 28 | Java, Indonesia ............... | 1,000 | Mt. Kelud erupts; nine villages destroyed |
| 1968, July 29 | Costa Rica .................... | 100 | Mt. Arenal erupts for first time in 500 years |
| 1973, Jan. 23 | Heimaey, Iceland ............. | — | Kirkjufell Volcano erupts; 5,000 homeless |
| 1979, Feb. 20 | Java, Indonesia ............... | 175 | Mt. Sinila erupts; 6 villages destroyed |
| 1979, Sept. 12 | Catania, Sicily ............... | 9 | Mt. Etna erupts, 24 injured |
| 1980, May 18 | Cascade Mtns., Washington ... | 66 | Mount St. Helens erupts; $1.6 billion in damages |

## PRINCIPAL WORLD FLOODS

| DATE | PLACE | DEATHS | REMARKS |
|---|---|---|---|
| 1228 | Holland ...................... | 100,000 | Sea flood in Friesland |
| 1642 | China ........................ | 300,000 | Yellow River dikes collapse at K'ai-feng |
| 1787 | Eastern India ................ | 10,000 | Storm drives seawater inland 20 miles |
| 1861 | Sacramento, California ....... | 700 | Sacramento River overflows banks |
| 1874 | Western Pennsylvania ........ | 220 | River floods |
| 1874 | Mill River Valley, Mass. ....... | 144 | Dam bursts |
| 1881 | Mississippi and Ohio rivers .... | 138 | Rivers flood; $15,000,000 damage |
| 1887 | Honan, China ................ | 900,000 | Yellow River overflows |
| 1889, May 31 | Johnstown, Pennsylvania ..... | 2,209 | Dam bursts on South Fork Reservoir |
| 1896 | Sanriku, Japan ............... | 22,000 | Tidal wave caused by earthquake |
| 1900, Sept. 8 | Galveston, Texas ............. | 6,000 | Tidal wave caused by hurricane |
| 1903, May–June | Kansas, Missouri, Miss. rivers . | 100 | Rivers flood; $40,000,000 damage |
| 1903, June 15 | Heppner, Oregon ............. | 325 | Flash flood following cloudburst |
| 1911 | China ........................ | 100,000 | Yangtze River overflows |
| 1912, March | Bolivar County, Mississippi .... | 200 | Mississippi River floods; $70,000,000 damage |
| 1913, March 25–27 | Ohio and Indiana............. | 732 | $180,873,000 damage |
| 1913, Dec. 1–5 | Texas ........................ | 177 | Brazos River floods; $9,000,000 damage |
| 1915, Aug. 17 | Galveston, Texas ............. | 300 | Tidal wave caused by hurricane |
| 1921, June | Pueblo, Colorado ............. | 120 | Arkansas River floods |
| 1921, September | Texas ........................ | 215 | Rivers flood; $19,000,000 damage |
| 1927, Spring | Mississippi River Valley ....... | 313 | Mississippi River floods; $284,118,000 damage |
| 1927, November | New England ................. | 88 | Winooski River floods; $45,578,000 damage |
| 1928, March 13 | Santa Paula, California........ | 450 | St. Francis Dam collapses |
| 1928, Sept. 13 | Lake Okeechobee, Florida ..... | 1,836 | Flood caused by hurricane |
| 1935, May–June | Kansas ....................... | 110 | Republican and Kansas rivers flood |
| 1935, July | Pennsylvania ................. | 52 | Susquehanna River tributaries flood |
| 1936, March–April | New England, Pennsylvania ... | 107 | Rivers flood; $270,000,000 damage |
| 1937, Jan.–Feb. | Ohio and Miss. river valleys ... | 137 | 1 million homeless; $417,685,000 damage |
| 1938, March | Southern California ........... | 79 | Streams flood; $24,500,000 damage |
| 1939, July | Kentucky ..................... | 78 | Licking and Kentucky rivers flood |
| 1939 | China ........................ | 1 million | Floods in north, followed by starvation |
| 1940, August | Va., Tenn., N. and S. Carolina .. | 40 | Floods cause $12,000,000 damage |
| 1942, May | Pennsylvania ................. | 33 | Delaware and Susquehanna rivers flood |
| 1943, April–June | Midwest ...................... | 60 | Mississippi River and tributaries flood |
| 1945, Feb.–March | Ohio River Valley ............. | 18 | Ohio River floods; $30,000,000 damage |
| 1946, April 1 | Hawaii........................ | 173 | Tidal wave caused by earthquake in Alaska |
| 1947 | Honshu Island, Japan ........ | 2,000 | Flooding after typhoon |
| 1947, May–July | Middle West................... | 29 | Missouri and Upper Mississippi valleys flood; $235,000,000 damage |
| 1948, May–June | Columbia River, Washington .. | 35 | $101,725,000 damage |
| 1950, June | West Virginia ................. | 31 | Rivers flood in central part of state |
| 1951, June–July | Kansas and Missouri valleys ... | 41 | 50,000 homeless in floods; $923,224,000 damage |
| 1951, August | Manchuria .................... | 1,800 | Flood; some estimates of dead as high as 5,000 |
| 1953 | Northwest Europe ............ | 1,794 | Storm floods devastate North Sea coast |
| 1954, August | Iran .......................... | 2,000 | Flash flood |
| 1955, Aug. 18–21 | Northeastern U.S.............. | 187 | Hurricane-caused floods; $714,079,000 damage |

**PRINCIPAL WORLD FLOODS** *(continued)*

| DATE | PLACE | DEATHS | REMARKS |
|---|---|---|---|
| 1955, Oct. 7–12 | Pakistan and India | 1,700 | Flood |
| 1955, December | California, Oregon, Washington | 61 | Streams and rivers flood; $154,532,000 damage |
| 1956, August | China | 2,000 | Three provinces flood after typhoon |
| 1957 | Kyushu Island, Japan | 513 | Flood |
| 1957, April–June | Tex., Ark., Kan., La., Mo., Okla. | 18 | Floods cause $105,000,000 damage |
| 1958, July | Iowa | 19 | Flash floods on E. Nishnabotna River cause $5,850,000 damage |
| 1959, November | Western Mexico | 2,000 | Flood |
| 1959, Dec. 2 | Frejus, France | 412 | Collapse of dam and flood |
| 1960, Feb. 29 | Agadir, Morocco | 12,000 | Tidal wave caused by earthquake |
| 1960, October | East Pakistan (Bangladesh) | 10,000 | Tidal wave |
| 1961, July | Charleston, West Virginia | 22 | Flash floods on streams cause $3,238,000 damage |
| 1962, Feb. 17 | West Germany | 342 | Storm breaks North Sea dikes |
| 1963, March | Ohio River Valley | 26 | Floods cause $97,600,000 damage |
| 1963, Sept. 27 | Barcelona, Spain | 445 | Flash flood west and north of city |
| 1963, Oct. 9 | Northern Italy | 2,000 | Vaiont Dam collapses |
| 1963, Nov. 14–15 | Haiti | 500 | Flood and landslides |
| 1964, June 8–9 | Northern Montana | 31 | Floods cause $54,279,000 damage |
| 1964, December | California and Oregon | 40 | Floods cause $415,832,000 damage |
| 1965, March–May | Midwest | 16 | Missouri, Upper Mississippi, and Red River of the North flood |
| 1965, June | Nebraska | 16 | South Platte River floods; $415,076,000 damage |
| 1965, June 18–19 | Sanderson, Texas | 26 | Flash flood causes $2,715,000 damage |
| 1965, June | Kansas and Missouri | 16 | Flood causes $58,340,000 damage |
| 1966, Jan. 11–13 | Rio de Janeiro, Brazil | 405 | Floods and landslides leave 50,000 homeless |
| 1966, April–May | Texas | 14 | Sabine and Trinity rivers flood |
| 1966, Nov. 3–4 | Arno Valley, Italy | 113 | Art treasures in Florence damaged and destroyed |
| 1967, Jan.–March | Brazil | 1,200 | Heavy rains in Rio de Janeiro and São Paulo states |
| 1967, August | Alaska | — | Tanana and Chena rivers; $98,550,000 damage |
| 1967, September | Texas | — | Hurricane causes floods; $98,239,000 damage |
| 1967, Nov. 26 | Lisbon, Portugal | 464 | Record rainfall causes heavy flooding |
| 1967, Nov. 30 | Java, Indonesia | 160 | Irrigation dam collapses |
| 1968, May | Northern New Jersey | — | Floods cause $166,690,000 damage |
| 1968, Aug. 7–14 | Western India | 1,000 | Widespread flooding kills 80,000 cattle |
| 1968, Oct. 3–7 | Northeastern India | 900 | Torrential rains cause flooding |
| 1969, Jan. 18–26 | Southern California | 91 | Floods, mudslides cause $399,233,000 damage |
| 1969, March–April | Upper Midwestern states | — | Snowmelt floods cause $151,000,000 damage |
| 1969, March 16 | Northeastern Brazil | 218 | Flash floods |
| 1969, July 4 | Ohio and Michigan | 33 | Flash floods cause $87,915,000 damage |
| 1969, Aug. 20–22 | Virginia and West Virginia | 153 | Floods caused by Hurricane Camille |
| 1969, October | Tunisia | 500 | Heavy rains cause flash floods |
| 1970, January | California | 18 | Sacramento River floods |
| 1970, May–June | Romania | 215 | Danube River flood causes $500 million damages |
| 1970, July | Uttar Pradesh, India | 600 | Buses swept away by flooding of Alaknanda River |
| 1970, September | India | 600 | Floods from Bombay to Calcutta; 20,000 homeless |
| 1970, September | Arizona | 23 | Floods cause $5,000,000 damage |
| 1970, October | Puerto Rico | 50 | Floods cause $62,000,000 damage |
| 1970, October | South Vietnam | 193 | Worst floods in six years leave 200,000 homeless |
| 1970, November | Colombia | 250–750 | Heavy flooding on the Magdalena River |
| 1971, Feb. 26 | Rio de Janeiro, Brazil | 130 | Flash flood |
| 1971, April 26–28 | Salvador, Brazil | 140 | Flood from heavy rains |
| 1971, July 29 | Afghanistan | 1,000 | Flood caused by landslide into a reservoir |
| 1972, Feb. 26 | Buffalo Creek, W. Virginia | 125 | Coal-waste dam collapses |
| 1972, June 9–10 | Rapid City, South Dakota | 237 | Canyon Lake Dam collapses in flash flood |
| 1972, June 21–27 | East Coast United States | 105 | Hurricane Agnes causes $4,019,721,000 damage |
| 1972, July 1–Aug. 7 | Philippines | 454 | Floods from heavy rains |
| 1972, mid-July | Japan | 370 | Landslides and floods from heavy rains |
| 1972, Aug. 18–19 | Seoul, South Korea | 296 | Flash floods from worst rains in nation's history |
| 1973, April–May | Mississippi, Ohio, Missouri rivers | 33 | Valley floods; $1,154,770,000 damage |
| 1973, May 27–28 | North Carolina | 12 | Flash flood on French Broad River |
| 1973, June–July | New England | 11 | Floods cause $63,600,000 damage |
| 1973, Dec. 12–16 | Texas | 10 | San Jacinto River floods; $62,500,000 damage |
| 1973, Aug. 19–31 | Pakistan | 1,500 | Floods in Punjab destroys 3,000 villages |
| 1973, Oct. 19–20 | Spain | 190 | Floods and mudslides in southern Spain |
| 1974, March–May | Brazil | 2,000 | Ten states devasted by floods; 300,000 homeless |
| 1974, April 11–16 | Mississippi | 9 | Floods in Hattiesburg cause $60,000,000 damage |
| 1974, July–August | Bangladesh and India | 2,750 | Flood damage estimated at $2 billion |
| 1974, Sept. 14 | Nelson Landing, Nevada | 14 | Flash flood causes $1,000,000 damage |
| 1974, Nov. 23 | Texas | 13 | Flash floods in Travis, Hays, and Comal counties |
| 1975, April 19–20 | Lansing, Michigan | — | Grand and Red Cedar rivers; $50,000,000 damage |
| 1975, July 1–2 | North Dakota | — | Red River floods; $213,114,000 damage |
| 1975, July 15–21 | New Jersey | 4 | Floods from record rains; $125,000,000 damage |
| 1976, June | Bangladesh | 143 | Floods result from monsoon rains |

**PRINCIPAL WORLD FLOODS** (continued)

| DATE | PLACE | DEATHS | REMARKS |
|---|---|---|---|
| 1976, June 5 | Idaho | 11 | Teton River Dam bursts caused $1,000,000 damage |
| 1976, July 31–Aug. 1 | Big Thompson Canyon, Colorado | 139 | Flash flood causes $50,000,000 damage |
| 1976, July | Mexico | 120 | Floods caused by two weeks of rain in central Mexico |
| 1976, August | Pakistan | 316 | Flood waters flow from Himalayas |
| 1976, November | Indonesia | 136 | Floods caused by torrential rains in East Java |
| 1977, March 1 | Tower City, Pennsylvania | 9 | Flood traps coal miners |
| 1977, April 4–6 | Kentucky, W. Virginia, Virginia, Alabama, Mississippi, Georgia | 40 | Tornadoes cause flooding; $275,000,000 damage |
| 1977, June 30 | Karachi, Pakistan | 400 | Rains flood low-lying slum dwellings |
| 1977, July 9 | Anyang, South Korea | 188 | Heavy rains trigger floods and mudslides |
| 1977, July 19–20 | Johnstown, Pennsylvania | 74 | Rains cause dam to burst; $200,000,000 damage |
| 1977, Sept. 12–13 | Kansas City, Missouri | 25 | Flash floods cause $140,000,000 damage |
| 1977, Nov. 2–3 | Athens and Piraeus, Greece | 25 | Rivers flooded after torrential rains |
| 1977, Nov. 6 | Toccoa, Georgia | 39 | Dam bursts after 4 days of rain |
| 1978, July 6–7 | Rochester, Minnesota | 5 | Flash floods cause $100,000,000 damage |
| 1978, July 9 | Afghanistan-Pakistan border | 122 | Torrential rains cause flooding |
| 1978, Aug. 4–8 | Southern and Central Texas | 26 | Flash flood cause $50,000,000 damage |
| 1978, Aug. 8 | Swiss and Italian Alps | 23 | Torrential rains cause worst floods and mudslides in 25 years |
| 1978, Aug. 13 | Northern India | 450 | Monsoon rains cause flooding of Ganges River |
| 1978, Aug. 18 | Acajutla, El Salvador | 100 | Tidal wave strike summer resort town |
| 1978, September | Northern India | 1,500 | Heavy rains trigger floods and mudslides |
| 1978, Dec. 17–19 | Arizona | 11 | Rivers flood after heavy rain |
| 1979, April 15–17 | Jackson, Mississippi | 8 | Pearl River floods; $500,000,000 damage |
| 1979, April 28–30 | North Dakota-Minnesota | — | Red River Valley floods cause $60,000,000 damage |
| 1979, July 2 | Valdepenas, Spain | 24 | Seven-hour rainstorm causes flash flood |
| 1979, July 24–28 | Texas coast | 7 | Tropical storm Claudette causes $400,000,000 damage |
| 1979, Aug. 11 | Morvi, India | 1,335 | Rain-soaked dam collapses |
| 1979, October | Egypt | 42 | Worst floods in 25 years leaves 25,000 homeless |
| 1980, Feb. 13–22 | Southern California, Arizona | 36 | Heavy rains bring $320,000,000 damage |
| 1980, April 12–14 | South Central United States | — | Severe rains cause $400,000,000 damage |
| 1980, August | India | 987 | Floods from monsoon rains in Uttar Pradesh |
| 1980, Aug. 31 | Ibadan, Nigeria | 240 | Flood from 12-hour rainstorm |
| 1980, Sept. 17 | Orissa, India | 203 | Flash floods from overflow of Mahanadi River |

# WORLD EARTHQUAKES AND AVALANCHES

The strength of an earthquake is measured by the 9-point Richter scale developed in the 1930s by Dr. Charles Francis Richter of the California Institute of Technology. The magnitude of an earthquake is determined by the deflection it causes in the tracing needle of a seismograph at a distance of 100 kilometers (62 miles).

Each point on the Richter scale stands for a magnitude 10 times greater than the previous number. Thus an earthquake with a Richter number of 9 would be 100,000,000 times as strong as a tremor with a Richter number of 1. No earthquake has yet been recorded with a Richter number of 9.

The great San Francisco earthquake of 1906 is calculated to have had a Richter number of 8.3.

| DATE | PLACE | DEATHS | REMARKS |
|---|---|---|---|
| 526, May 20 | Antioch, Syria | 250,000 | Earthquake |
| 551, July 9 | Beirut, Lebanon | — | Destroyed by earthquake |
| 856, December | Corinth, Greece | 45,000 | Earthquake |
| 936 | Constantinople | — | Destroyed by earthquake |
| 1057 | Hopeh Province near Peking, China | 25,000 | Earthquake |
| 1268 | Cilicia, Asia Minor | 60,000 | Earthquake |
| 1290, Sept. 27 | Hopeh Province near Peking, China | 100,000 | Earthquake |
| 1293, May 20 | Kamakura, Japan | 30,000 | Earthquake |
| 1531, Jan. 26 | Lisbon, Portugal | 30,000 | Earthquake |
| 1556, Jan. 24 | Shensi, China | 830,000 | Earthquake |
| 1667, November | Shemakha, East Azerbaijan | 80,000 | Earthquake |
| 1693, Jan. 11 | Catania, Italy | 60,000 | Earthquake |
| 1703, Dec. 30 | Tokyo, Japan | 200,000 | Earthquake |
| 1737, Oct. 11 | Calcutta, India | 300,000 | Earthquake |
| 1755, June 7 | Northern Persia | 40,000 | Earthquake |
| 1755, Nov. 1 | Lisbon, Portugal | 60,000 | Earthquake destroys most of city |
| 1783, Feb. 4 | Southern Italy and Sicily | 50,000 | Wide-ranging earthquake; Messina ravaged |
| 1797, Feb. 4 | Cuzco, Peru, and Quito, Ecuador | 40,000 | Earthquakes destroy cities |
| 1811, Dec. 15 | New Madrid, Missouri | — | Heaviest recorded earthquake in North America; changes course of Mississippi River |
| 1822, Sept. 5 | Aleppo, Syria | 22,000 | Earthquake |
| 1828, Dec. 28 | Honshu, Japan | 30,000 | Earthquake |
| 1868, Aug. 13–15 | Peru and Ecuador | 25,000 | Earthquakes razes towns; $300 million loss |
| 1875, May 16 | Venezuela and Colombia | 16,000 | Earthquake |

**WORLD EARTHQUAKES AND AVALANCHES** *(continued)*

| DATE | PLACE | DEATHS | REMARKS |
|------|-------|--------|---------|
| 1886, Aug. 31 | Charleston, South Carolina | 60 | Earthquake severely damages city |
| 1896, June 15 | Sanriku coast, Japan | 22,000 | Earthquakes and seismic sea wave |
| 1906, April 18 | San Francisco, California | 700 | Earthquake followed by fire; $500 million loss |
| 1906, Aug. 16 | Chile | 1,500 | Earthquake; $100 million loss |
| 1908, Dec. 28 | Southern Italy and Sicily | 75,000 | Earthquake |
| 1915, Jan. 13 | Central Italy | 30,000 | Earthquake |
| 1918, Oct. 11 | Puerto Rico | 116 | Earthquake and tidal wave; $4 million damage |
| 1920, Dec. 16 | Kansu, China | 180,000 | Earthquake destroys 10 cities |
| 1923, Sept. 1 | Yokohama and Tokyo, Japan | 143,000 | Earthquake destroys all of Yokohama, half of Tokyo |
| 1932, Dec. 26 | Kansu, China | 70,000 | Earthquake |
| 1933, March 10 | Long Beach, California | 115 | Earthquake; about $40 million loss |
| 1935, May 31 | Quetta, Baluchistan, India | 60,000 | Earthquake |
| 1939, Jan. 24 | Chile | 30,000 | Earthquake |
| 1939, Dec. 27 | Anatolia, Turkey | 23,000 | Series of earthquakes followed by floods |
| 1946, May 31 | Eastern Turkey | 1,300 | Earthquake |
| 1946, Dec. 21 | Southern Japan | 2,000 | Earthquake and six seismic sea waves |
| 1948, June 28 | Fukui, Japan | 5,131 | Earthquake and fire destroys most of Fukui |
| 1949, Aug. 5 | Ecuador | 6,000 | Earthquake heavily damages 50 towns |
| 1950, Aug. 15 | Assam, India | 1,500 | Earthquake and widespread flooding |
| 1953, Feb. 12 | Eastern Iran | 1,000 | Earthquake destroys town of Trud |
| 1953, March 18 | Northwestern Turkey | 1,200 | Earthquake; 50,000 homeless |
| 1954, Sept. 9–12 | Algeria | 1,600 | Earthquake destroys most of Orléansville |
| 1956, June 10–17 | Northern Afghanistan | 2,000 | Series of earthquakes |
| 1957, July 2 | Iran | 2,500 | Earthquakes along shores of Caspian Sea |
| 1957, Dec. 2 | Outer Mongolia | 1,200 | Earthquake |
| 1957, Dec. 13 | Western Iran | 2,000 | Earthquake |
| 1960, Feb. 29 | Agadir, Morocco | 12,000 | Earthquake, seismic sea wave, and fire |
| 1960, May 21–30 | Chile | 5,700 | Earthquake and seismic sea waves |
| 1962, Jan. 10 | Peru | 2,000 | Avalanche on Huascarán, extinct volcano |
| 1962, Sept. 1 | Northwestern Iran | 10,000 | Earthquake |
| 1963, July 26 | Skoplje, Yugoslavia | 1,100 | Earthquake destroys most of city |
| 1964, March 27 | Alaska | 131 | Earthquake and seismic sea wave |
| 1965, March 28 | Near Santiago, Chile | 400 | Earthquake |
| 1966, Jan. 11–13 | Rio de Janeiro, Brazil | 300 | Landslide caused by record rain |
| 1966, Aug. 19 | Turkey | 2,529 | Earthquake; 100,000 homeless |
| 1967, July 29 | Venezuela | 236 | Earthquake extending from Andes to Caribbean Sea |
| 1968, Jan. 15 | Western Sicily | 224 | Series of earthquakes destroys several towns |
| 1968, Aug. 2 | Manila, Philippines | 207 | Earthquake |
| 1968, Aug. 15 | Donggala, Indonesia | 200 | Earthquake |
| 1968, Aug. 31 | Northeastern Iran | 13,000 | Earthquake, world's worst in 30 years |
| 1969, Feb. 23 | Celebes Island, Indonesia | 600 | Earthquake and seismic sea waves |
| 1970, March 28 | Western Turkey | 1,089 | Earthquakes |
| 1970, May 31 | Northern Peru | 60,000 | Earthquake and avalanche |
| 1970, Dec. 12 | Cauca Valley, Colombia | 200 | Avalanche |
| 1971, Feb. 9 | Southern California | 64 | Earthquake in San Fernando Valley |
| 1971, July 9 | North central Chile | 90 | Earthquake |
| 1972, Jan. 26 | Bogotá, Colombia | 70 | Torrential rains cause landslide |
| 1972, April 10 | Southwestern Iran | 5,374 | Earthquake |
| 1972, Dec. 23 | Managua, Nicaragua | 10,000 | Capital city destroyed by earthquake |
| 1973, Jan. 30 | Mexico | 52 | Earthquake makes 22,000 homeless |
| 1973, Aug. 28 | Mexico | 527 | Earthquake damages 67 villages |
| 1974, April 25 | Peru | 750 | Landslides destroy three villages |
| 1974, June 28 | Colombia | 200 | Landslide on eastern slope of Andes |
| 1974, Sept. 30 | Colombia | 90 | Landslide buries small town |
| 1974, Oct. 3 | Lima, Peru | 78 | Earthquake and tidal wave hit coast |
| 1974, Dec. 28 | Pakistan | 5,300 | Earthquake near Chinese border; 16,000 injured |
| 1975, Feb. 4 | Manchuria, China | Unknown | Widespread destruction by earthquake |
| 1975, July 8 | Pagan, Burma | — | Hundreds of ancient temples destroyed |
| 1975, Sept. 6 | Eastern Turkey | 2,200 | Village of Lice destroyed; 3,500 injured |
| 1976, Feb. 4 | Guatemala, Honduras | 22,934 | Earthquake leaves 1,277,000 homeless |
| 1976, May 6 | Northern Italy | 968 | Earthquake devastates Friuli area of northern Italy |
| 1976, June 26 | Western New Guinea | 443 | Earthquake results in mud and rock slides |
| 1976, July 14 | Bali, Indonesia | 500 | Earthquake |
| 1976, July 28 | China | 242,000 | Strongest earthquake since 1964 devastates Tientsin-Tangshan area of China; 164,000 injured |
| 1976, Aug. 17 | Philippines | 8,000 | Earthquake off southern island of Mindanao leaves 8,000 dead and missing |
| 1976, Oct. 29 | West Iran, Indonesia | 133 | Earthquake hits remote jungle area |
| 1976, Nov. 24 | Turkey | 3,790 | Earthquake in eastern Turkey; 50,000 homeless |
| 1977, March 4 | Bucharest, Romania | 1,541 | Earthquake almost destroys central city |
| 1977, March 22 | Southern Iran | 167 | Earthquake causes heavy damage |
| 1977, April 6 | Western Iran | 352 | Destroys mountain villages |
| 1977, Aug. 19 | Indian Ocean | 150 | Quake causes tidal waves in Bali, Lombok, and Sumbawa |

## WORLD EARTHQUAKES AND AVALANCHES (continued)

| DATE | PLACE | DEATHS | REMARKS |
|---|---|---|---|
| 1977, Nov. 23 | Western Argentina | 100 | Earthquake destroys town of Caucete |
| 1977, Dec. 20 | Southeastern Iran | 519 | Earthquake near Zarand leaves thousands homeless |
| 1978, June 20 | Salonika, Greece | 47 | Earthquake shakes northern Greece |
| 1978, Sept. 16 | Northeastern Iran | 25,000 | Earthquake destroys whole villages |
| 1979, Jan. 16 | Qaen, Iran | 199 | Earthquake strikes three villages in northeast Iran |
| 1979, March 14 | Mexico | 1 | Earthquake rocks Mexico City |
| 1979, April 15 | Yugoslavia | 235 | Earthquake jolts Adriatic coast, leaves 80,000 homeless |
| 1979, April 30 | West Sumatra, Indonesia | 82 | Landslide caused by burst of crater on Merapi volcano |
| 1979, July 9 | Jiangsu Province, China | 41 | Earthquake injures 2,000 |
| 1979, July 18 | Lomblen Island, Indonesia | 539 | Landslide on Mt. Werung causes tidal wave |
| 1979, Aug. 6 | San Francisco, Calif. | — | Strong quake jolts northern California |
| 1979, Sept. 12 | Yapen Island, Indonesia | 100 | Earthquake causes tidal wave; 10,000 homeless |
| 1979, Oct. 15 | California–Mexico border | — | Earthquake causes property damage; injures 70 |
| 1979, Nov. 14 | Northeastern Iran | 248 | Earthquake rocks 14 villages |
| 1979, Nov. 23 | Colombia | 300 | Earthquake in western Colombia causes $20 million damage |
| 1979, Dec. 12 | Colombia–Ecuador border | 133 | Six coastal towns flattened by earthquake |
| 1979, Dec. 18 | Indonesia | 27 | Earthquake on island of Bali and Lombok |
| 1980, Jan. 1 | Azores Islands | 53 | Quake jolts Terceira and St. Jorge islands |
| 1980, Jan. 24–27 | Northern California | — | Series of quakes cause $10 million damage |
| 1980, Oct. 10 | Algeria | 2,950 | Quake destroys Al Asnam; 300,000 homeless |
| 1980, Oct. 24 | South Central Mexico | 22 | Quake jolts area around Pueblo |
| 1980, Nov. 23 | Southern Italy | 3,000 | Quakes flatten 133 villages; 300,000 homeless |
| 1980, Dec. 19 | Northern Iran | 26 | Earthquakes rock Islamic holy city of Qum |

## WORLD'S WORST FIRES AND EXPLOSIONS

| DATE | PLACE | DEATHS | REMARKS |
|---|---|---|---|
| 1666, Sept. 2–6 | London, England | — | Fire destroys many public buildings, 89 churches and over 13,200 houses; 200,000 homeless |
| 1835, Dec. 16 | New York, New York | — | Nearly 700 buildings burned; $20 million loss |
| 1836, Feb. 14 | St. Petersburg, Russia | 700 | Theater fire |
| 1842, May 5–7 | Hamburg, Germany | 100 | More than 4,000 buildings destroyed |
| 1845, April 10 | Pittsburgh, Pennsylvania | — | 1,000 buildings destroyed in fire; $6 million loss |
| 1846, June 12 | Quebec, Canada | 200 | Theater fire |
| 1851, May 4 | St. Louis, Missouri | — | Much of city burned; $15 million loss |
| 1863, Dec. 8 | Santiago, Chile | 2,000 | Church burned while filled with worshipers |
| 1866, July 4 | Portland, Maine | — | City almost totally destroyed by fire; $10 million loss |
| 1866, Oct. 13 | Quebec, Canada | — | 2,500 buildings burned |
| 1871, Oct. 8–9 | Chicago, Illinois | 300 | 3½ square miles devastated by fire; 18,000 buildings lost; 100,000 homeless; $200 million loss |
| 1871, Oct. 8–14 | Michigan and Wisconsin | 1,000 | Great forest fire devastates large area |
| 1872, Nov. 9–11 | Boston, Massachusetts | — | Fire; 600 buildings ruined; $75 million loss |
| 1876, Dec. 5 | Brooklyn, New York | 295 | Conway's Theater fire |
| 1877, June 20 | St. John, New Brunswick, Canada | 100 | Fire; $12,500,000 property loss |
| 1881, Dec. 8 | Vienna, Austria | 640 | Ring Theater fire |
| 1883, Jan. 13 | Berdichev, Russia | 270 | Theater fire |
| 1887, May 25 | Paris, France | 200 | Opéra Comique fire |
| 1887, Sept. 4 | Exeter, England | 200 | Theater fire |
| 1888, May 25 | Oporto, Portugal | 200 | Baquet Theater fire |
| 1889, June 6 | Seattle, Washington | — | Fire loss about $10 million |
| 1889, Aug. 4 | Spokane, Washington | — | Fire destroys business district |
| 1894, Sept. 1 | Hinckley, Minnesota | 418 | 160,000 forest acres burned; $25 million loss |
| 1897, May 4 | Paris, France | 150 | Fire at charity bazaar |
| 1889, March 17 | New York, New York | 45 | Windsor Hotel fire |
| 1900, April 26 | Hull and Ottawa, Canada | — | Fire losses of $10 million |
| 1900, June 30 | Hoboken, New Jersey | 300 | Pier burned; property damage, $4,627,000 |
| 1902, Sept. 20 | Birmingham, Alabama | 115 | Church fire |
| 1903, Dec. 30 | Chicago, Illinois | 639 | Iroquois Theater fire |
| 1904, Feb. 7–8 | Baltimore, Maryland | — | Fire; 75 city blocks destroyed; $85 million loss |
| 1906, March 10 | Courrières, France | 1,060 | Mine explosion |
| 1906, April 18 | San Francisco, California | 700 | Following earthquake, fire devastates 4 square miles; property damage about $500 million |
| 1907, Dec. 6 | Monongah, West Virginia | 362 | Coal-mine explosion |
| 1908, Jan. 13 | Boyertown, Pennsylvania | 173 | Fire from motion-picture machine explosion |
| 1908, March 4 | Collinwood, Ohio | 161 | School fire |
| 1908, April 12 | Chelsea, Massachusetts | — | Destroyed by fire; $17 million loss |
| 1909, Feb. 15 | Acapulco, Mexico | 250 | Flores Theater fire |
| 1909, Nov. 13 | Cherry, Illinois | 259 | Coal-mine fire |
| 1911, March 25 | New York, New York | 145 | Triangle Shirtwaist Factory fire |
| 1913, Oct. 22 | Dawson, New Mexico | 263 | Mine fire |
| 1914, June 25–26 | Salem, Massachusetts | — | 1,700 buildings burned; $14 million loss |
| 1914, Dec. 15 | Fukuoka, Japan | 687 | Coal-mine disaster at Hojo Colliery |

**WORLD'S WORST FIRES AND EXPLOSIONS** (continued)

| DATE | PLACE | DEATHS | REMARKS |
|---|---|---|---|
| 1916, July 30 | Black Tom Island, Jersey City, N.J. . . . | — | German war sabotage; $220 million loss |
| 1917, April 10 | Eddystone, Pennsylvania . . . . . . . . . . | 133 | Munitions plant explosion |
| 1917, Dec. 6 | Halifax, Nova Scotia . . . . . . . . . . . . . | 1,500 | Explosion of war material causes fire; 20,000 homeless, $35 million loss |
| 1918, Oct. 4–5 | Morgan Station, New Jersey . . . . . . . | 64 | Gillespie Loading Co. explosion |
| 1918, Oct. 13–15 | Minnesota and Wisconsin . . . . . . . . . | 1,000 | Forest fires; $100 million loss |
| 1919, June 20 | San Juan, Puerto Rico . . . . . . . . . . . . | 150 | Mayaguez Theater fire |
| 1921 Sept. 21 | Oppau, Germany . . . . . . . . . . . . . . . . | 600 | Ammonium-nitrate plant explosion |
| 1922, Sept. 13 | Smyrna, Turkey . . . . . . . . . . . . . . . . . | — | City almost totally destroyed by fire; 100,000 homeless; $100 million damage; great loss of life |
| 1923, May 17 | Kershaw County, N.C. . . . . . . . . . . . . | 77 | Fire in school during presentation of play |
| 1928, May 19 | Mather, Pennsylvania . . . . . . . . . . . . | | Coal-mine explosion |
| 1929, May 15 | Cleveland, Ohio . . . . . . . . . . . . . . . . | 125 | Poisonous fumes from burning X-ray film causes mass suffocation at Crile Hospital Clinic |
| 1930, April 21 | Columbus, Ohio . . . . . . . . . . . . . . . . | 317 | Fire at Ohio State Penitentiary |
| 1934, March 22 | Hakodate, Japan . . . . . . . . . . . . . . . . | 1,500 | Fire destroys largest city north of Tokyo |
| 1934, May 19 | Chicago, Illinois . . . . . . . . . . . . . . . . | — | Union Stockyards burn; $10 million loss |
| 1934, Sept. 22 | Wrexham, Wales . . . . . . . . . . . . . . . . | 265 | Coal-mine explosion |
| 1937, Feb. 13 | Antung, Manchuria . . . . . . . . . . . . . . | 658 | Theater fire |
| 1937, March 18 | New London, Texas . . . . . . . . . . . . . . | 413 | Schoolhouse destroyed by natural-gas explosion |
| 1938, Nov. 12–16 | Changsha, China . . . . . . . . . . . . . . . . | 2,000 | Fire levels city |
| 1939, March 1 | Osaka, Japan . . . . . . . . . . . . . . . . . . | 500 | Munitions explosion destroys part of Osaka |
| 1939, July 10 | Peñaranda de Bracamonte, Spain . . | 100 | Town demolished by munitions factory explosion |
| 1939, Nov. 14 | Lagunillas, Venezuela . . . . . . . . . . . . | 500 | Oil town built on Lake Maracaibo destroyed by fire |
| 1940, April 23 | Natchez, Mississippi . . . . . . . . . . . . . | 198 | Dance-hall fire |
| 1941, May 31 | Jersey City, New Jersey . . . . . . . . . . | — | Waterfront fire; $25 million loss |
| 1941, June 8 | Smederevo, Yugoslavia . . . . . . . . . . . | 1,000 | Explosion of ammunition plant; town destroyed |
| 1942, April 26 | Honkeiko Colliery, Manchuria . . . . . . | 1,549 | Worst mine disaster in history |
| 1942, May 1 | Tessenderlo, Belgium . . . . . . . . . . . . | 250 | Chemical works explosion |
| 1942, Nov. 28 | Boston, Massachusetts . . . . . . . . . . . | 493 | Cocoanut Grove nightclub fire |
| 1942, Dec. 13 | St. John's, Newfoundland . . . . . . . . . | 100 | Knights of Columbus Hostel fire panic |
| 1943, May 7 | Sandoná, Colombia . . . . . . . . . . . . . . | 103 | Municipal Palace demolished by fire |
| 1944, April 14 | Bombay, India . . . . . . . . . . . . . . . . . . | 1,500 | Ship's fire causes explosion of ammunition |
| 1944, July 6 | Hartford, Connecticut . . . . . . . . . . . . | 168 | Audience panics in circus "Big Top" fire |
| 1944, July 17 | Port Chicago, California . . . . . . . . . . | 300 | Two ammunition-dump explosions |
| 1944, Oct. 20 | Cleveland, Ohio . . . . . . . . . . . . . . . . | 121 | Liquid-gas tanks explode; fire burns 50 blocks |
| 1946, June 5 | Chicago, Illinois . . . . . . . . . . . . . . . . | 60 | La Salle Hotel fire |
| 1946, Dec. 7 | Atlanta, Georgia . . . . . . . . . . . . . . . . | 119 | Winecoff Hotel fire |
| 1947, March 25 | Centralia, Illinois . . . . . . . . . . . . . . . | 111 | Coal-mine explosion |
| 1947, April 16 | Texas City, Texas . . . . . . . . . . . . . . . | 468 | Explosion of French ship *Grandcamp* ruins city |
| 1947, Aug. 20 | Cádiz, Spain . . . . . . . . . . . . . . . . . . . | 400 | Shipyard explosion |
| 1947, Oct. 25 | Bar Harbor, Maine . . . . . . . . . . . . . . | — | Forest fire; estimated loss at $30 million |
| 1948, March 9 | Tsingtao, China . . . . . . . . . . . . . . . . . | 200 | Ammunition storehouse explosion |
| 1948, July 28 | Ludwigshafen, Germany . . . . . . . . . . | 200 | I. G. Farben Company explosions and fire |
| 1948, Sept. 22 | Hong Kong . . . . . . . . . . . . . . . . . . . . | 135 | Fire and chemical explosion in warehouse |
| 1949, Sept. 4 | Chungking, China . . . . . . . . . . . . . . . | 1,700 | Central part of city burns; 100,000 homeless |
| 1950, May 19 | South Amboy, New Jersey . . . . . . . . | 30 | Munitions barges explode |
| 1951, May 13 | Kano, Nigeria . . . . . . . . . . . . . . . . . . | 100 | Movie house burns |
| 1951, Dec. 21 | West Frankfort, Illinois . . . . . . . . . . . | 119 | Coal-mine explosion |
| 1955, Feb. 17 | Near Yokohama, Japan . . . . . . . . . . . | 97 | Home for aged women burns |
| 1956, Aug. 7 | Cali, Colombia . . . . . . . . . . . . . . . . . | 1,100 | Seven trucks carrying dynamite explode |
| 1956, Aug. 8 | Marcinelle, Belgium . . . . . . . . . . . . . | 263 | Coal-mine fires |
| 1957, Feb. 17 | Warrenton, Missouri . . . . . . . . . . . . . | 72 | Home for aged burns |
| 1958, Feb. 19 | Near Asansol, India . . . . . . . . . . . . . | 180 | Coal-mine explosion |
| 1958, June 23 | Santo Amaro, Brazil . . . . . . . . . . . . . | 100 | Fireworks explosion |
| 1958, Dec. 1 | Chicago, Illinois . . . . . . . . . . . . . . . . | 93 | Parochial-school fire |
| 1958, Dec. 16 | Bogotá, Colombia . . . . . . . . . . . . . . . | 84 | Department-store fire |
| 1960, Jan. 21 | Coalbrook, South Africa . . . . . . . . . . | 437 | Coal-mine cave-ins and explosion |
| 1960, Feb. 22 | Zwickau, East Germany . . . . . . . . . . | 123 | Explosion in Karl Marx Mine |
| 1960, March 4 | Havana, Cuba . . . . . . . . . . . . . . . . . . | 75 | French munitions ship explodes |
| 1960, July 14 | Guatemala City, Guatemala . . . . . . . | 200 | Hospital for insane swept by fire |
| 1960, Nov. 13 | Amude, Syria . . . . . . . . . . . . . . . . . . | 152 | Movie-house fire |
| 1961, July 8 | Dolna Suce, Czechoslovakia . . . . . . | 108 | Coal-mine gas explosion |
| 1961, Dec. 17 | Niteroi, Brazil . . . . . . . . . . . . . . . . . . | 323 | Circus-tent fire |
| 1962, Feb. 7 | Saar, Germany . . . . . . . . . . . . . . . . . | 298 | Coal-mine explosion |
| 1963, May 4 | Diourbel, Senegal . . . . . . . . . . . . . . | 64 | Theater fire |
| 1963, Oct. 31 | Indianapolis, Indiana . . . . . . . . . . . . | 73 | Explosion at State Fair coliseum |
| 1963, Nov. 9 | Fukuoka, Japan . . . . . . . . . . . . . . . . | 458 | Coal-mine disaster |
| 1963, Nov. 23 | Fitchville, Ohio . . . . . . . . . . . . . . . . . | 63 | Fire burns rest home |
| 1964, July 23 | Bone, Algeria . . . . . . . . . . . . . . . . . . | 100 | Explosion aboard Egyptian munitions ship |
| 1965, May 28 | Bihar, India . . . . . . . . . . . . . . . . . . . . | 400 | Mine disaster |
| 1965, June 1 | Fukuoka, Japan . . . . . . . . . . . . . . . . | 237 | Coal-mine disaster at Yamano Colliery |
| 1965, June 8 | Kakanj, Yugoslavia . . . . . . . . . . . . . . | 108 | Mine disaster |

## WORLD'S WORST FIRES AND EXPLOSIONS *(continued)*

| DATE | PLACE | DEATHS | REMARKS |
|------|-------|--------|---------|
| 1965, Aug. 9 | Searcy, Arkansas | 53 | Explosion in a Titan 11 missile silo |
| 1967, May 22 | Brussels, Belgium | 322 | Fire in L'Innovation department store |
| 1968, April 6 | Richmond, Indiana | 43 | Explosion and fire; nearly two city blocks wrecked |
| 1968, Nov. 20 | Mannington, West Virginia | 78 | Fire and explosions in coal mine |
| 1969, March 31 | Barroteran, Mexico | 183 | Coal-mine explosion |
| 1969, Nov. 7 | Buffelstein, South Africa | 64 | Explosion in gold mine |
| 1970, Jan. 9 | Marietta, Ohio | 31 | Private nursing-home fire |
| 1970, April 9 | Osaka, Japan | 73 | Gas-leak explosions at subway construction site |
| 1970, Nov. 1 | Saint-Laurent-du-Pont, France | 144 | Fire in dance hall |
| 1970, Dec. 30 | Wooton, Kentucky | 38 | Coal-mine explosion |
| 1971, Dec. 25 | Seoul, South Korea | 163 | Hotel fire |
| 1972, March 11 | Minsk, Soviet Union | 100 | Factory fire and/or explosion |
| 1972, May 2 | Kellogg, Idaho | 91 | Sunshine silver-mine fire |
| 1972, May 13 | Osaka, Japan | 115 | Nightclub fire |
| 1972, June 6 | Wankie, Rhodesia | 427 | Coal-mine explosion |
| 1973, Feb. 10 | Staten Island, New York City | 40 | Oil storage-tank explosion |
| 1973, June 24 | New Orleans, Louisiana | 32 | Nightclub fire |
| 1973, Aug. 2 | Douglas, Isle of Man, Britain | 51 | Amusement-park fire |
| 1973, Sept. 1 | Copenhagen, Denmark | 35 | Hotel fire; 20 Americans killed |
| 1973, Nov. 29 | Kumamoto, Japan | 101 | Department-store fire; 2,500 shoppers saved |
| 1974, Feb. 1 | São Paulo, Brazil | 189 | Fire in 25-story skyscraper; 293 injured |
| 1974, June 17 | Lahore, Pakistan | 40 | Store building destroyed by fire |
| 1974, June 30 | Port Chester, New York | 24 | Nightclub fire set by arsonist; 32 injured |
| 1974, Dec. 27 | Lievin, France | 42 | Explosion and fire in coal mine |
| 1975, Jan. 22 | Manila, Philippines | 51 | Factory fire; 79 injured |
| 1975, Dec. 12 | Mecca, Saudi Arabia | 138 | Muslim pilgrims' tent-city fire; 151 injured |
| 1975, Dec. 27 | Dhanbad, India | 431 | Explosion floods coal mine |
| 1976, April 13 | Lapua, Finland | 40 | Ammunition-factory explosion |
| 1976, Oct. 24 | Bronx, New York City | 25 | Fire in social club |
| 1976, Dec. 31 | Chlebovice, Czechoslovakia | 43 | Gas explosion in coal mine |
| 1977, Feb. 25 | Moscow, Soviet Union | 45 | Fire in Rossiya Hotel, world's largest hotel |
| 1977, May 28 | Southgate, Kentucky | 164 | Nightclub fire, more than 100 injuries |
| 1977, June 9 | Abidjan, Ivory Coast | 41 | Nightclub fire |
| 1977, June 26 | Columbia, Tennessee | 42 | Maurcy County Jail fire traps inmates and visitors |
| 1977, Aug. 2 | Moatize, Mozambique | 150 | Explosion in coal mine; 9 killed in later rioting |
| 1977, Nov. 14 | Manila, Philippines | 47 | Hotel fire fanned by winds of typhoon |
| 1977, Dec. 22 | Westwego, La. | 35 | Explosion in grain elevator |
| 1978, Jan. 28 | Kansas City, Mo. | 20 | Fire in hotel |
| 1978, July 11 | Tarragona, Spain | 181 | Tank truck explodes and falls into campsite |
| 1978, Aug. 19 | Abadan, Iran | 430 | Enemies of Shah set fire in movie theater |
| 1978, Nov. 2 | Huimanguillo, Mexico | 52 | Gas pipeline explodes |
| 1978, Dec. 1 | Klerksdorp, South Africa | 41 | Gold-mine fire |
| 1978, Dec. 9 | Ellisville, Mississippi | 15 | Fire in dormitory at school for mentally retarded |
| 1979, Jan. 20 | Hoboken, N.J. | 19 | Tenement fire |
| 1979, Feb. 15 | Warsaw, Poland | 49 | Explosion in savings bank; 110 injured |
| 1979, April 2 | Farmington, Mo. | 25 | Fire in boarding house |
| 1979, April 14 | Chungsun, South Korea | 26 | Explosion in coal mine |
| 1979, July 12 | Saragossa, Spain | 71 | Oil tank explodes in luxury hotel |
| 1979, July 29 | Tuticorin, India | 104 | Fire in movie theater |
| 1979, Sept. 30 | Vienna, Austria | 25 | Fire in tourist-filled hotel |
| 1979, Oct. 10 | Bytom, Poland | 34 | Coal-mine fire |
| 1979, Oct. 27 | Munkyong, South Korea | 30 | Underground fire in coal mine |
| 1979, Oct. 31 | Czechowice-Dziedzice, Poland | 63 | Coal-mine fire |
| 1979, Nov. 5 | Bytom, Poland | 34 | Explosion in Dimitrow coal mine |
| 1979, Nov. 11 | Pioneer, Ohio | 14 | Boarding-house fire |
| 1979, Nov. 13 | Parma, Italy | 14 | Explosion destroys hospital |
| 1980, Jan. 1 | Chapais, Quebec | 45 | Fire in social club |
| 1980, Jan. 31 | Guatemala City, Guatemala | 39 | Fire in Spanish Embassy |
| 1980, April 21 | Dijon, France | 21 | Fire in home for elderly |
| 1980, May 20 | Kingston, Jamaica | 157 | Fire in home for poor and elderly |
| 1980, July 15 | Mississauga, Ontario | 21 | Nursing-home fire |
| 1980, July 26 | Bradley Beach, N.J. | 24 | Home for elderly and retarded burns |
| 1980, Aug. 2 | Bologna, Italy | 81 | Terrorist bomb explodes in railroad station |
| 1980, Aug. 15 | Baghdad, Iraq | 59 | Fire in movie theater |
| 1980, Aug. 16 | London, England | 37 | Fire in adjoining social clubs |
| 1980, Oct. 24 | Ortuella, Spain | 51 | Explosion in elementary school |
| 1980, Nov. 2 | Gorna Grupa, Poland | 50 | Fire in mental hospital |
| 1980, Nov. 16 | Bangkok, Thailand | 60 | Explosion in munitions plant |
| 1980, Nov. 19 | Kawaji, Japan | 44 | Fire in resort hotel |
| 1980, Nov. 22 | Las Vegas, Nevada | 84 | Fire in resort hotel and casino |
| 1980, Nov. 24 | Danaciobasi, Turkey | 97 | Explosion at village engagement party |
| 1980, Dec. 3 | Northern Romania | 49 | Explosion in Livezeni coal mine |
| 1980, Dec. 4 | Harrison, N.Y. | 26 | Fire in motel conference center |

# WORLD'S WORST AIRCRAFT DISASTERS

| DATE | AIRCRAFT | DEATHS | REMARKS |
|---|---|---|---|
| 1921, Aug. 24 | English dirigible R-38 (U.S. ZR-2) ... | 62 | Breaks in two over Hull, England |
| 1928, Dec. 21 | French dirigible *Dixmude* .......... | 52 | Vanishes over Mediterranean Sea or Sahara Desert |
| 1930, Oct. 5 | English dirigible R-101 ............. | 47 | Crashes near Beauvais, France |
| 1933, April 4 | U.S. dirigible *Akron II* ............. | 73 | Crashes off new Jersey coast |
| 1935, May 18 | Soviet aircraft *Maxim Gorky* ....... | 49 | Collides with a small plane over Moscow |
| 1937, May 6 | German zeppelin *Hindenburg* ....... | 36 | Burns at mooring in Lakehurst, N.J. |
| 1938, July 24 | Military stunt plane ............... | 53 | Crashes into grandstand in Bogotá, Colombia |
| 1944, Aug. 23 | U.S. bomber ...................... | 76 | Crashes into school in Freckleton, England |
| 1945, July 28 | U.S. bomber ...................... | 13 | Crashes into Empire State Building |
| 1947, May 30 | Airliner .......................... | 53 | Crashes near Port Deposit, Md. |
| 1949, Nov. 1 | P-38 fighter and DC-4 airliner ...... | 55 | Collide above airport in Washington, D.C. |
| 1950, March 12 | English airliner ................... | 80 | Crashes near Cardiff, Wales |
| 1950, June 23 | U.S. DC-4 ........................ | 58 | Crashes into Lake Michigan during storm |
| 1950, Nov. 13 | Canadian airliner ................. | 58 | Crashes on mountain near Grenoble, France |
| 1951, Dec. 16 | Nonscheduled airliner ............. | 56 | Crashes into Elizabeth River, N.J. |
| 1952, March 27 | Two Soviet planes ................. | 70 | Collide over Tula Airport, Moscow |
| 1952, Dec. 20 | U.S. Air Force plane ............... | 87 | Crashes at Larson Air Force Base, Wash. |
| 1953, June 18 | U.S. Air Force Globemaster ........ | 129 | Crashes near Tokyo, Japan |
| 1955, Oct. 6 | Airliner, DC-4 .................... | 66 | Crashes in mountains near Laramie, Wyo. |
| 1956, June 20 | Venezuelan airliner ............... | 74 | Crashes in Atlantic 40 miles south of New York City |
| 1956, June 30 | Two airliners ..................... | 128 | Collide over Grand Canyon, Ariz. |
| 1957, Aug. 11 | Chartered Canadian airliner ....... | 79 | Crashes near Quebec, Canada |
| 1958, May 18 | Belgian airliner ................... | 65 | Crashes in Casablanca, Morocco |
| 1958, Aug. 14 | Dutch airliner .................... | 99 | Crashes in ocean west of Ireland |
| 1958, Oct. 17 | Soviet jet airliner ................. | 75 | Crashes in Kanash, Soviet Union |
| 1959, Feb. 3 | U.S. turboprop airliner ............ | 65 | Crashes into East River, New York City |
| 1959, June 26 | U.S. luxury airliner ............... | 68 | Explodes near Milan, Italy |
| 1960, Feb. 25 | U.S. Navy and Brazilian planes ..... | 61 | Collide over Rio de Janeiro |
| 1960, March 17 | Turboprop airliner ................ | 63 | Mid-air explosion over Tell City, Ind. |
| 1960, Aug. 29 | French airliner ................... | 63 | Crashes into sea near Dakar, Senegal |
| 1960, Sept. 18 | U.S. DC-6AB ..................... | 80 | Crashes on takeoff from Guam |
| 1960, Oct. 4 | U.S. Electra ...................... | 62 | Crashes into harbor at takeoff in Boston, Mass. |
| 1960, Dec. 16 | U.S. DC-8 and U.S. Constellation .... | 134 | Collide over New York City |
| 1961, Feb. 15 | Belgian jet airliner ................ | 73 | Crashes near Berg, Belgium |
| 1961, May 10 | French airliner ................... | 79 | Crashes in Ghadames, Libya |
| 1961, Sept. 1 | U.S. Constellation ................ | 78 | Crashes after takeoff in Chicago, Ill. |
| 1961, Sept. 10 | U.S. charter plane ................ | 83 | Crashes in Shannon, Ireland |
| 1961, Nov. 8 | U.S. charter plane ................ | 77 | Crashes in Richmond, Va. |
| 1962, March 1 | U.S. B-707 ....................... | 95 | Explodes as it crashes into Jamaica Bay, N.Y. City |
| 1962, March 4 | English DC-7 ..................... | 111 | Crashes in jungle near Douala, Cameroon |
| 1962, March 16 | U.S. Super Constellation ........... | 107 | Crashes into western Pacific Ocean |
| 1962, June 3 | French B-707 ..................... | 130 | Crashes at takeoff in Paris, France |
| 1962, June 22 | French B-707 ..................... | 113 | Crashes near Guadeloupe, West Indies |
| 1962, July 7 | Italian DC-8 ...................... | 94 | Crashes near Bombay, India |
| 1962, Nov. 27 | Brazilian jet airliner ............... | 97 | Crashes and burns in Lima, Peru |
| 1963, Feb. 1 | British and Turkish planes ......... | 95 | Collide over Ankara, Turkey |
| 1963, June 3 | U.S. military chartered airliner ..... | 101 | Crashes in Pacific Ocean off British Columbia |
| 1963, Nov. 29 | Canadian airliner ................. | 118 | Crashes after takeoff in Montreal, Canada |
| 1963, Dec. 8 | U.S. B-707/121 ................... | 81 | Crashes near Elkton, Md. |
| 1964, Feb. 25 | U.S. DC-8 ........................ | 58 | Crashes in Lake Pontchartrain, La. |
| 1964, Feb. 29 | English Britannia ................. | 83 | Crashes near Innsbruck, Austria |
| 1964, March 1 | U.S. Constellation ................ | 85 | Crashes near Lake Tahoe, California |
| 1964, May 11 | U.S. military C-135 transport ....... | 75 | Crashes at Clark Air Force Base, the Philippines |
| 1965, Feb. 6 | Chilean DC-6B .................... | 87 | Crashes in the Andes |
| 1965, Feb. 8 | U.S. DC-7B ....................... | 84 | Plunges into Atlantic near Kennedy Airport, N.Y. City |
| 1965, May 20 | Pakistani jet airliner .............. | 119 | Crashes near Cairo, Egypt |
| 1965, June 25 | U.S. Air Force transport ........... | 84 | Crashes into mountains near Los Angeles, Calif. |
| 1965, Nov. 8 | U.S. B-727 ....................... | 58 | Crashes during landing near Cincinnati, Ohio |
| 1965, Dec. 11 | U.S. Air Force transport C-123 ..... | 85 | Crashes into mountain near Nhatrang, South Vietnam |
| 1966, Jan. 24 | Indian B-707 ..................... | 117 | Crashes into Mont Blanc, France |
| 1966, Feb. 4 | Japanese B-727 .................. | 133 | Plunges into Tokyo Bay during landing |
| 1966, March 5 | British B-707 ..................... | 124 | Catches fire above Mt. Fuji and crashes on slopes |
| 1966, April 22 | U.S. Lockheed Electra ............. | 82 | Crashes near Ardmore, Okla. |
| 1966, Sept. 1 | British turboprop ................. | 95 | Crashes during landing in Belgrade, Yugoslavia |
| 1966, Nov. 24 | TABSO Airways, Ilyushin-18........ | 82 | Crashes at Bratislava, Czechoslovakia |
| 1966, Dec. 24 | Flying Tiger CL-44 ................ | 111 | Cargo flight crashes at Danang, South Vietnam |
| 1967, April 20 | Swiss jetliner .................... | 126 | Crashes while landing at Nicosia, Cyprus |
| 1967, June 3 | British DC-6 ...................... | 88 | Crashes into Mt. Canigou in French Pyrenees |
| 1967, Nov. 20 | U.S. Convair jetliner............... | 69 | Crashes on landing near Cincinnati, Ohio |
| 1968, April 20 | South African Boeing 707 .......... | 122 | Crashes near Windhoek, South West Africa |
| 1968, May 3 | U.S. jetliner ...................... | 85 | Crashes in central Texas during thunderstorm |
| 1968, Sept. 11 | French Caravelle jetliner.......... | 95 | Catches fire and crashes off French Riviera |
| 1969, March 16 | Venezuelan DC-9 ................. | 155 | Crashes into suburb of Maracaibo, Venezuela |

## WORLD'S WORST AIRCRAFT DISASTERS (continued)

| DATE | AIRCRAFT | DEATHS | REMARKS |
|---|---|---|---|
| 1969, March 20 | Egyptian IL-18 | 91 | Crashes on landing at Aswan airport, Egypt |
| 1969, June 4 | Mexican jet | 79 | Flies into mountain near Monterrey, Mexico |
| 1969, Sept. 9 | U.S. DC-9 and Piper Cherokee | 83 | Collide over Shelbyville, Ind. |
| 1969, Sept. 20 | U.S. Phantom and Vietnamese DC-4 | 77 | Collide near Danang, South Vietnam |
| 1969, Nov. 20 | Nigerian VC-10 | 87 | Crashes near Iju, Nigeria |
| 1969, Dec. 8 | Greek DC-6B | 90 | Crashes on mountain near Athens during storm |
| 1970, Feb. 15 | Dominican Airways DC-9 | 102 | Crashes into sea after takeoff from Santo Domingo |
| 1970, July 4 | British four-engine Comet | 112 | Crashes into mountain in Spain |
| 1970, July 5 | Canadian DC-8 | 109 | Crashes near Toronto airport |
| 1970, Aug. 9 | Peruvian Electra | 101 | Crashes near Cuzco |
| 1970, Nov. 14 | U.S. DC-9 | 75 | Crashes near Kenova, W.Va. |
| 1970, Dec. 31 | Aeroflot Ilyushin-18 | 90 | Crashes at takeoff from Leningrad |
| 1971, May 23 | Yugoslav TU-134A | 78 | Crashes and burns on island off Rijeka, Yugoslavia |
| 1971, July 30 | Japanese Boeing 727 and F-86 | 162 | Collide over Morioka, Japan |
| 1971, Sept. 4 | Alaska Airlines Boeing 727 | 111 | Crashes in Tongass National Forest, Alaska |
| 1972, Jan. 7 | Iberian Airlines Caravelle | 104 | Crashes near island of Ibiza, Spain |
| 1972, March 14 | Danish Sterling Airways charter | 112 | Crashes near Gulf of Oman |
| 1972, May 6 | Alitalia DC-8 | 115 | Crashes into mountain on Sicily |
| 1972, June 18 | BEA Trident-1 | 118 | Crashes after takeoff at London |
| 1972, June | Antonov-10 | 108 | Crashes near Kharkov in the Ukraine |
| 1972, Aug. 14 | E. German Ilyushin-62 | 156 | Crashes after takeoff from Schönefeld Airport |
| 1972, Oct. 3 | Soviet Ilyushin-18 | 106 | Crashes near Black Sea resort of Sochi |
| 1972, Oct. 13 | Soviet Ilyushin-62 | 176 | Crashes near Sheremetyevo Airport |
| 1972, Dec. 3 | Spanish charter jet | 155 | Crashes in Canary Islands |
| 1972, Dec. 29 | Eastern Airlines L-1011 jet | 101 | Crashes in Everglades near Miami, Fla. |
| 1973, Jan. 22 | Royal Jordanian Airways 707 | 176 | Crashes in fog at Kano, Nigeria |
| 1973, Feb. 19 | Soviet jetliner | 77 | Crashes in landing at Prague, Czechoslovakia |
| 1973, Feb. 21 | Libyan airliner | 108 | Shot down by Israeli jets near Suez Canal |
| 1973, April 10 | British charter flight | 105 | Hits mountain near Basel, Switzerland |
| 1973, June 3 | Supersonic Soviet Tupolev 144 | 14 | First supersonic airliner crash at Paris, France |
| 1973, July 11 | Brazilian 707 jet | 122 | Burns on crashing near Paris, France |
| 1973, July 23 | Pan American 707 | 78 | After takeoff, crashes near Tahiti |
| 1973, July 31 | Delta Air Lines DC-9 | 89 | Hits seawall while landing in fog, Boston, Mass. |
| 1973, Aug. 13 | Aviaco Airline Caravelle | 85 | Hits trees while landing in fog, La Coriena, Spain |
| 1973, Dec. 22 | Charter Caravelle airliner | 106 | Crashes into mountain near Tangier, Morocco |
| 1974, Jan. 31 | Pan American 707 jet | 92 | Landing crash at Pago Pago, American Samoa |
| 1974, March 3 | Turkish Airlines DC-10 | 346 | Falls near Paris after cargo door blows off |
| 1974, April 4 | Chartered DC-4 | 77 | Takeoff crash at Francistown, Botswana |
| 1974, April 22 | Pan American 707 | 107 | Crashes into mountainside on Bali, Indonesia |
| 1974, April 27 | Soviet turboprop airliner | 118 | Takeoff crash at Leningrad |
| 1974, Sept. 8 | TWA 707 airliner | 88 | Falls in Ionian Sea off Greece in storm |
| 1974, Sept. 11 | Eastern Airlines DC-9 | 72 | Landing crash at Charlotte, N.C. |
| 1974, Dec. 1 | TWA 727 jet airliner | 92 | Crashes during landing at Washington, D.C. |
| 1974, Dec. 4 | Dutch DC-8 jet airliner | 191 | Falls during landing approach on Sri Lanka |
| 1974, Dec. 22 | Venezuelan airliner | 77 | Takeoff crash at Maturín, Venezuela |
| 1975, April 4 | Air Force C-5A Galaxy | 155 | Planeload of war orphans crashes on takeoff in South Vietnam |
| 1975, June 24 | Eastern Airlines Boeing 727 | 113 | Crashes at Kennedy Airport, New York City |
| 1975, Aug. 3 | Moroccan Boeing 707 airliner | 188 | Strikes mountain near Agadir, Morocco |
| 1975, Aug. 20 | Czechoslovak Ilyushin 62 | 126 | Landing crash near Damascus, Syria, airport |
| 1975, Oct. 25 | Bolivian Air Force Convair 440 | 70 | Hits mountain near La Paz, Bolivia |
| 1975, Oct. 30 | Yugoslav DC-9 airliner | 68 | Crashes landing in fog at Prague, Czechoslovakia |
| 1976, Jan. 1 | Lebanese Boeing 707 airliner | 82 | Explodes in storm over Arabian Desert |
| 1976, Jan. 3 | Soviet TU-134 airliner | 56 | Explodes on takeoff from airport near Moscow |
| 1976, July 28 | Czechoslovak Ilyushin 18 | 70 | Falls into lake near Bratislava, Czechoslovakia |
| 1976, Sept. 4 | Venezuelan Air Force transport | 68 | Crashes on landing at U.S. air base in Azores |
| 1976, Sept. 10 | British Trident and Yugoslav DC-9 | 176 | Collide near Zagreb, Yugoslavia |
| 1976, Sept. 19 | Turkish Boeing 727 | 155 | Strikes Karakaya Mountain in Turkey |
| 1976, Oct. 6 | Cuban DC-8 airliner | 73 | Explodes after takeoff from Barbados |
| 1976, Oct. 12 | Indian Airlines Caravelle | 95 | Crashes after takeoff from Bombay |
| 1976, Oct. 13 | Chartered Boeing 707 | 100 | Falls into downtown street in Santa Cruz, Bolivia |
| 1976, Nov. 28 | Soviet Tupolev TU-104 | 72 | Crashes after takeoff from Moscow |
| 1976, Dec. 25 | Egyptian Boeing 707 | 72 | Crashes into factory at Bangkok, Thailand |
| 1977, March 27 | Pan Am 747 and KLM 747 | 581 | Jets collide on airport runway at Santa Cruz de Tenerife, Canary Islands; aviation's worst disaster |
| 1977, April 4 | Southern Airways DC-9 | 71 | Hailstorm blamed for crash of plane at New Hope, Ga. |
| 1977, May 10 | Israeli helicopter | 54 | Crashes after takeoff near Jericho |
| 1977, May 16 | N.Y. Airways helicopter | 5 | Helicopter atop Pan Am building throws rotor blade while idling at heliport |
| 1977, May 27 | Soviet IL-62 | 66 | Crashes on landing at Havana, Cuba |
| 1977, Sept. 4 | Ecuadorian Viscount | 33 | Hits mountain peak near Cuenca, Ecuador |
| 1977, Sept. 27 | Japan Air Lines DC-8 | 34 | Crashes on hill near Kuala Lumpur, Malaysia |
| 1977, Nov. 19 | Portuguese Boeing 727 | 130 | Crashes on landing at Funchal, Madeira, airport |

## WORLD'S WORST AIRCRAFT DISASTERS (continued)

| DATE | AIRCRAFT | DEATHS | REMARKS |
|---|---|---|---|
| 1977, Dec. 4 | Malaysian jetliner | 100 | Explodes in southern Malaysia after being hijacked |
| 1978, Jan. 1 | Air India Boeing 747 | 213 | Explodes and crashes in sea near Bombay, India |
| 1978, March 16 | Bulgarian Tupolev-134 | 73 | Crashes after takeoff from Sofia, Bulgaria |
| 1978, March 25 | Burmese airliner | 48 | Explodes after leaving Rangoon, Burma |
| 1978, Sept. 25 | Boeing 727 and Cessna 172 | 144 | Collide over San Diego, Calif. |
| 1978, Nov. 15 | Icelandic Airlines DC-8 | 183 | Crashes short of runway at Colombo, Sri Lanka |
| 1978, Dec. 20 | Alitalia Airlines DC-9 | 108 | Crashes into sea short of Palermo, Italy, airport |
| 1979, Feb. 12 | Air Rhodesia Viscount | 59 | Guerrilla missile downs plane after takeoff from Kariba, Zimbabwe |
| 1979, March 14 | Jordanian Boeing 727 | 45 | Crashes while attempting to land in Doha, Qatar |
| 1979, March 18 | Soviet TU-104 | 90 | Crashes on takeoff from Moscow's Vnukovo Airport |
| 1979, May 25 | American Airline DC-10 | 273 | Crashes on takeoff from Chicago airport; worst air disaster in U.S. history |
| 1979, July 11 | Indonesian Fokker F-28 | 61 | Crashes into mountain on Sumatra, Indonesia |
| 1979, Aug. 11 | Two Soviet TU-134 jets | 173 | Collide over Ukraine in bad weather |
| 1979, Oct. 31 | Western Airlines DC-10 | 73 | Crashes on landing at Mexico City airport |
| 1979, Nov. 26 | Pakistan Int'l Airlines Boeing 707 | 156 | Crashes after takeoff from Jidda, Saudi Arabia |
| 1979, Nov. 28 | Air New Zealand DC-10 | 257 | Crashes in Antarctica during sightseeing flight |
| 1980, Jan. 21 | Iran Air Boeing 727 | 128 | Crashes in mountains near Teheran, Iran |
| 1980, March 14 | Polish IL-62 jetliner | 87 | Crashes on landing in Warsaw, Poland |
| 1980, April 12 | Transbrasil Boeing 727 | 54 | Crashes in rainstorm near Florianopolis, Brazil |
| 1980, April 25 | British Boeing 727 | 146 | Hits mountain in Tenerife, Canary Islands |
| 1980, June 28 | Itavia Airlines DC-9 | 81 | Falls into Tyrrhenian Sea on flight to Sicily |
| 1980, July 7 | Soviet TU-154 | 163 | Crashes on takeoff from Alma Ata, Soviet Union |
| 1980, July 9 | Indonesian Fokker F28 | 61 | Strikes mountain in North Sumatra |
| 1980, Aug. 19 | Saudi Arabian Lockheed Tri-star | 301 | Flames trap passengers after landing at Riyadh |
| 1980, Sept. 13 | Florida Commuter Airlines DC-3 | 34 | Crashes into Atlantic Ocean on flight to Bahamas |
| 1980, Sept. 14 | Saudi Arabian C-130 transport | 89 | Catches fire and plunges into desert near Medina |
| 1980, Dec. 21 | Colombian Caravelle Jet | 68 | Crashes in northern desert of Colombia |

## SHIPWRECKS AND MARINE DISASTERS

| DATE | CRAFT | DEATHS | REMARKS |
|---|---|---|---|
| 1831, July 19 | Lady Sherbrooke | 263 | Sinks off Cape May, N.J. |
| 1833, May 11 | Lady of the Lake | 215 | Strikes iceberg while bound for Quebec |
| 1850, March 29 | Royal Adelaide | 400 | Wrecked off Margate, England |
| 1852, March 26 | Birkenhead, troopship | 454 | Wrecked; bound for Cape of Good Hope |
| 1853, Sept. 29 | Annie Jane, immigrant vessel | 348 | Wrecked off Scotland |
| 1854, March | City of Glasgow | 450 | Vanishes; bound for Philadelphia from Liverpool |
| 1854, Sept. 27 | Arctic | 322 | Sinks near Grand Banks, off Newfoundland |
| 1857, Sept. 12 | Central America | 400 | Sinks in storm; bound for New York from Havana |
| 1858, Sept. 13 | Austria | 471 | Burns on Hamburg–New York run |
| 1859, April 27 | Pomona | 386 | Wrecked off Ireland |
| 1859, Oct. 25 | Royal Charter | 450 | Wrecked in Irish Sea |
| 1860, Sept. 8 | Lady Elgin, excursion steamer | 300 | Collides with lumber ship on Lake Michigan |
| 1865, April 27 | Sultana, river steamer | 1,450 | Explodes and sinks in Memphis, Tenn. |
| 1867, Oct. 29 | Rhone and Wye, mail boats | 1,000 | Wrecked in storm; St. Thomas, West Indies |
| 1870, Sept. 17 | Captain, English warship | 472 | Founders off Finistère, France |
| 1871, July 30 | Westfield, Staten Island (N.Y.) ferry | 104 | Boiler explosion at slip in New York City |
| 1873, April 1 | Atlantic, English steamer | 547 | Wrecked off Nova Scotia |
| 1878, Sept. 3 | Princess Alice, English steamer | 700 | Collides and sinks in River Thames |
| 1890, Sept. 19 | Ertogrul, Turkish frigate | 540 | Burns off Japanese coast |
| 1891, March 17 | Utopia, British steamer | 574 | Collides and sinks off Gibraltar |
| 1895, March 14 | Reina Regenta, Spanish cruiser | 400 | Founders in Atlantic near Gibraltar |
| 1898, Feb. 15 | Maine, U.S. battleship | 264 | Blown up in Havana Harbor |
| 1898, July 4 | Bourgogne and Cromartyshire | 560 | Collide near Sable Island off Nova Scotia |
| 1904, June 15 | General Slocum | 1,000 | Burns in East River, New York City |
| 1904, June 28 | Norge | 600 | Wrecked on Rockall Reef off Scotland |
| 1912, April 15 | Titanic | 1,502 | Strikes iceberg and sinks in the North Atlantic |
| 1912, Sept. 28 | Kichemaru | 1,000 | Sinks off coast of Japan |
| 1914, May 29 | Empress of Ireland | 1,024 | Strikes Norwegian collier in St. Lawrence River |
| 1915, May 7 | Lusitania | 1,195 | Sunk by German submarine off coast of Ireland |
| 1915, July 24 | Eastland, excursion steamer | 812 | Capsizes in Chicago River, Ill. |
| 1916, Aug. 29 | Hsin Yu | 1,000 | Sinks off coast of China |
| 1917, July 9 | Vanguard, English warship | 800 | Blown up at Scapa Flow dock off northern Scotland |
| 1918, July 12 | Kawachi, Japanese battleship | 500 | Explodes in Tokayama Bay, Japan |
| 1919, Jan. 17 | Chaonia | 460 | Wrecked in Strait of Messina, Italy |
| 1921, June 14 | Hong Kong | 1,000 | Wrecked on rocks off Swatow in South China Sea |
| 1926, Oct. 16 | Chinese troopship | 1,200 | Explodes in Yangtze River, China |
| 1927, Oct. 25 | Principessa Mafalda, Italian liner | 326 | Sinks off coast of Brazil |
| 1928, Nov. 12 | Vestris | 113 | Founders off Virginia Capes |
| 1931, June 14 | French excursion steamer | 450 | Overturns in Bay of Biscay storm off St. Nazaire |
| 1934, Sept. 8 | Morro Castle | 137 | Burns off coast of New Jersey near Asbury Park |
| 1939, May 23 | Squalus, U.S. submarine | 26 | Sinks off New Hampshire coast |

**SHIPWRECKS AND MARINE DISASTERS** *(continued)*

| DATE | CRAFT | DEATHS | REMARKS |
|---|---|---|---|
| 1939, June 1 | *Thetis*, British submarine | 99 | Sinks in Irish Sea |
| 1939, June 15 | *Phenix*, French submarine | 63 | Sinks off Indochina |
| 1941, June 16 | O-9, U.S. submarine | 33 | Sinks in test dive off Maine coast |
| 1942, Feb. 9 | *Normandie*, French liner | 1 | Burns at Hudson River pier, New York City |
| 1942, Oct. 2 | *Queen Mary* and *Curacao* | 338 | Liner rams and sinks British cruiser |
| 1942, Oct. 26 | Jewish refugee ship | 200 | Wrecked in Sea of Marmara, Turkey |
| 1944, Dec. 17–18 | Three U.S. Third Fleet destroyers | 790 | Capsize during typhoon in Philippine Sea |
| 1945, Jan. 30 | *Wilhelm Gustloff*, German ship | 6,100 | Sunk by Russian submarine in Baltic Sea |
| 1945, April 9 | U.S. Liberty ship | 360 | Explodes in harbor at Bari, Italy |
| 1945, July 29 | *Indianapolis*, U.S. cruiser | 883 | Sunk by Japanese torpedo in Pacific Ocean |
| 1946, Aug. 2 | *Vitya* | 295 | Sinks in Lake Nyasa, Tanganyika |
| 1947, Jan. 19 | *Himara* | 392 | Hits mine and sinks off Athens, Greece |
| 1947, July 17 | *Ramdas*, coastal steamer | 550 | Sinks off Bombay, India |
| 1948, Jan. 28 | *Joo Maru*, freighter | 250 | Hits mine and sinks in Inland Sea, Japan |
| 1948, Feb. 28 | Steamer | 160 | Sinks during pirate attack near Amoy, China |
| 1948, June 11 | *Kjoebenhavn*, Danish liner | 140 | Hits mine and sinks off coast of Jutland |
| 1948, Dec. 3 | Steamer | 1,140 | Explodes and sinks south of Shanghai |
| 1949, Jan. 27 | Chinese liner and collier | 600 | Collide and sink off south coast of China |
| 1949, Sept. 17 | *Noronic*, Great Lakes liner | 130 | Burns at pier in Toronto, Canada |
| 1950, Jan. 12 | *Truculent*, English submarine | 65 | Rammed by tanker in Thames Estuary |
| 1951, April 16 | *Affray*, English submarine | 75 | Sinks off Isle of Wight, near southern England |
| 1952, April 26 | *Hobson*, U.S. destroyer, and *Wasp*, aircraft carrier | 176 | Collide; *Hobson* sinks in Atlantic Ocean |
| 1953, Jan. 9 | South Korean passenger liner | 249 | Sinks in heavy seas off Pusan, South Korea |
| 1953, Jan. 31 | Ferry | 132 | Sinks in storm off Northern Ireland |
| 1953, Aug. 1 | *Monique* | 120 | Vanishes near New Caledonia in South Pacific |
| 1954, May 26 | *Bennington*, U.S. aircraft carrier | 103 | Explodes and burns off Quonset Point, R.I. |
| 1954, Sept. 26 | *Toya Maru*, Japanese ferry | 1,172 | Sinks in Tsugaru Strait, Japan |
| 1956, June 3 | Pakistani liner | 199 | Wrecked in storm in Bay of Bengal |
| 1956, July 26 | *Andrea Doria* and *Stockholm* | 50 | Collide; *Andrea Doria* sinks off Massachusetts |
| 1957, April 10 | Two pilgrimage boats | 150 | Sink in Godavari River, India |
| 1957, July 14 | Soviet ship | 270 | Runs aground in storm in Caspian Sea |
| 1958, Jan. 26 | Japanese ferry | 170 | Vanishes in Inland Sea |
| 1958, March 1 | Turkish ferry | 238 | Sinks near Istanbul, in Sea of Marmara |
| 1959, May 8 | Nile River excursion boat | 150 | Sinks north of Cairo, Egypt |
| 1960, Dec. 19 | *Constellation*, U.S. aircraft carrier | 50 | Burns in Brooklyn Navy Yard, New York |
| 1961, April 8 | *Dara*, English liner | 212 | Burns in Persian Gulf |
| 1961, July 8 | *Save* | 259 | Runs aground and explodes in Mozambique |
| 1961, Sept. 3 | *Vencedor*, excursion ship | 150 | Sinks near Buenaventura, Colombia |
| 1963, April 10 | *Thresher*, U.S. nuclear submarine | 129 | Sinks in North Atlantic |
| 1963, May 4 | Motor launch | 206 | Sinks in Upper Nile |
| 1963, Aug. 17 | *Midori Maru*, Japanese ferry | 128 | Sinks in East China Sea |
| 1963, Dec. 23 | *Lakonia*, Greek liner | 155 | Sinks after fire in Atlantic north of Madeira |
| 1964, Feb. 11 | *Voyager*, destroyer, and *Melbourne*, aircraft carrier | 85 | Collide; *Voyager* sinks near Ulladulla, Australia |
| 1965, Feb. 11 | Four fishing trawlers | 100 | Sink in Bering Sea |
| 1965, May 24 | African ferry | 150 | Capsizes in Shire River, Malawi |
| 1965, Nov. 13 | *Yarmouth Castle*, cruise ship | 90 | Catches fire and sinks in Caribbean |
| 1966, Jan. 30 | Pakistani launch and steamer | 80 | Collide at Chandpur Port, East Pakistan |
| 1966, Feb. 2 | Indonesian freighter | 89 | Sinks near Belawan |
| 1966, Oct. 26 | Indian vessel | 100 | Sinks in Kosie River, eastern India |
| 1966, Dec. 8 | *Heraklion*, Greek ferry | 217 | Sinks in storm in Sea of Crete |
| 1967, July 29 | *Forrestal*, U.S. aircraft carrier | 134 | Crippled by fire off Vietnam |
| 1968, Jan. 26 | *Dakar*, Israeli submarine | 69 | Sinks in eastern Mediterranean Sea |
| 1968, May 27 | *Scorpion*, U.S. nuclear submarine | 99 | Sinks in Atlantic Ocean southwest of Azores |
| 1969, June 2 | *Frank E. Evans*, U.S. destroyer, and *Melbourne*, aircraft carrier | 74 | Collide; *Evans* breaks in half, bow section sinks |
| 1969, June 21 | Portuguese barge | 108 | Capsizes on Zambesi River in Mozambique |
| 1970, Feb. 1 | Ceylonese ferry | 61 | Sinks at Jaffna, Ceylon |
| 1970, March 4 | *Eurydice*, French submarine | 57 | Sinks in Mediterranean near Toulon, France |
| 1970, April 12 | Soviet submarine | 88 | Sinks in Atlantic off Spain |
| 1970, July 5 | Indian launch | 150 | Capsizes in Krishna River in eastern India |
| 1970, Aug. 1 | *Christena*, motor launch | 125 | Capsizes and sinks in Caribbean off St. Kitts |
| 1970, Dec. 15 | South Korean ferry | 308 | Capsizes in Korea Strait |
| 1971, Aug. 17 | *Fatsham*, Hong Kong-Macao ferry | 88 | Capsizes during Typhoon Rose |
| 1971, Nov. 21 | *Beethoven II* | 106 | Sinks off Philippines |
| 1972, May 11 | Cargo ship and oil tanker | 83 | Collide off Buenos Aires, Argentina |
| 1973, March 22 | Two Norwegian freighters | 61 | Lost in storm off Cape May, New Jersey |
| 1973, Dec. 24 | Ecuadorian ferry | 109 | Capsizes in Pacific Ocean off Ecuador |
| 1974, Feb. 22 | South Korean tugboat | 157 | Capsizes in Chungmu harbor, South Korea |
| 1974, April 21 | Fishing schooner | 100 | Sinks southeast of Rangoon, Burma |
| 1974, May 1 | Bangladesh motor launch | 250 | Capsizes in coastal waters of Bangladesh |
| 1974, Sept. 12 | Soviet guided-missile destroyer | 350 | Explodes and sinks in Black Sea |

## SHIPWRECKS AND MARINE DISASTERS *(continued)*

| DATE | CRAFT | DEATHS | REMARKS |
|---|---|---|---|
| 1975, Jan. 25 | Bangladesh ferryboat | 100 | Sinks after collision with ferry in Buriganga River |
| 1975, Aug. 9 | Two Chinese riverboats | 500 | Collide and sink in West River, near Canton |
| 1975, Oct. 24 | Burmese ferryboat | 150 | Capsizes and sinks near Rangoon, Burma |
| 1975, Nov. 10 | U.S. ore carrier *Edmund Fitzgerald* | 29 | Sank during storm on Lake Superior |
| 1975, Dec. 18 | Burmese coastal schooner | 70 | Capsizes in storm in Andaman Sea |
| 1976, Oct. 15 | Cargo ship *Sylvia L. Ossa* | 37 | Lost; presumed sunk in Bermuda Triangle |
| 1976, Oct. 20 | Tanker and ferry *George Prince* | 77 | Collide in Mississippi River |
| 1976, Dec. 23 | Egyptian passenger ship *Patria* | 170 | 311 rescued in Red Sea sinking |
| 1976, Dec. 30 | *Grand Zenith*, Panamanian tanker | 38 | Sinks off Cape Cod, Mass. |
| 1977, Jan. 17 | U.S. Navy launch and *Urela*, Spanish freighter | 46 | Collide in Barcelona, Spain, harbor |
| 1977, Sept. 25 | Egyptian ferry | 50 | Capsizes in Nile River near Cairo |
| 1978, April 8 | Burmese coastal transport | 100 | Capsizes in Bay of Bengal |
| 1978, June 17 | Steam showboat *Whippoorwill* | 15 | Overturned by tornado on Lake Pomona, Kansas |
| 1978, Oct. 12 | Liberian tanker *Spyros* | 59 | Explodes in Singapore harbor; 90 injured |
| 1978, Dec. 2 | Vietnamese refugee boat | 143 | Sinks in rough seas off Pasir Puteh, Malaysia |
| 1979, Jan. 8 | French oil tanker *Betelgeuse* | 50 | Explodes while unloading at Bantry, Ireland |
| 1979, March 31 | Vietnamese refugee boat | 100 | Capsizes while being towed to sea off Malaysia |
| 1979, Nov. 1 | Liberian tanker *Burmah Agate* and freighter *Mimosa* | 32 | Collide near Galveston Bay, Texas |
| 1979, Nov. 15 | Romanian tanker *Independent* and Greek freighter *Evira-7* | 47 | Collide in Bosporus off Istanbul, Turkey |
| 1979, Nov. 25 | Chinese drilling rig *Bo Hai #2* | 72 | Collapses while being towed in Bohai Gulf |
| 1980, Jan. 28 | U.S. tankship *Capricorn* and U.S. Coast Guard cutter *Blackthorn* | 23 | Collide in Tampa Bay, Florida |
| 1980, Feb. 27 | Chinese ferry | 276 | Capsizes during storm in southern China river |
| 1980, March 11 | Spanish supertanker *Maria Alejandra* | 36 | Sinks off Mauritania |
| 1980, March 27 | Oil rig platform *Alexander L Kielland* | 128 | Collapses, overturns in stormy North Sea |
| 1980, April 22 | Philippine ferry and oil tanker *Tablocan City* | 300 | Collide off Mindoro Island, Philippines |
| 1980, May 9 | Freighter *Summit Venture* | 35 | Rams into bridge at Tampa Bay, Florida |
| 1980, Aug. 22 | Mexican ferry | 50 | Sinks off Ciudad del Carmen, Mexico |
| 1980, Oct. 25 | Freighter *S.S. Poet* | 34 | Disappears after leaving Philadelphia, Pa. |

## WORLD RAILROAD DISASTERS

| DATE | PLACE | DEATHS | REMARKS |
|---|---|---|---|
| 1856, July 17 | Near Philadelphia, Pennsylvania | 66 | Train wrecked |
| 1857, March 17 | Near Hamilton, Ontario, Canada | 60 | Train derailed on bridge over Desjardins Canal |
| 1864, July 15 | Near Lackawaxen, Pennsylvania | 65 | Two trains collide |
| 1876, Dec. 29 | Ashtabula, Ohio | 92 | Bridge collapses in snowstorm |
| 1879, Dec. 28 | Dundee, Scotland | 78 | Train falls from Tay Bridge |
| 1881, June 24 | Cuautla, Mexico | 200 | Train falls into river |
| 1882, July 13 | Near Tchnery, Russia | 150 | Train derailed |
| 1887, Aug. 10 | Chatsworth, Illinois | 81 | Train wrecked as burning bridge collapsed |
| 1888, Oct. 10 | Mud Run, Pennsylvania | 62 | Locomotive hits standing excursion train |
| 1889, June 12 | Near Armagh, Ireland | 80 | Train collision |
| 1891, June 14 | Near Basel, Switzerland | 100 | Train collision |
| 1896, July 30 | Atlantic City, New Jersey | 60 | Train wrecked |
| 1903, Dec. 23 | Laurel Run, Pennsylvania | 78 | Train wrecked |
| 1904, Aug. 7 | Eden, Colorado | 96 | Train wrecked |
| 1904, Sept. 24 | New Market, Tennessee | 56 | Train wrecked |
| 1906, Dec. 30 | Washington, D.C. | 53 | Train wrecked |
| 1910, March 1 | Wellington, Washington | 96 | Avalanche throws two trains into canyon |
| 1910, March 21 | Green Mountain, Iowa | 55 | Passenger train wrecked |
| 1915, May 22 | Quintinshill, near Gretna, Scotland | 227 | Troop train collides with local train |
| 1917, Dec. 12 | Modane, France | 550 | Troop train derailed near Mont Cénis tunnel |
| 1918, June 22 | Ivanhoe, Indiana | 68 | Train rams circus train |
| 1918, July 9 | Near Nashville, Tennessee | 101 | Two trains collide head-on |
| 1918, Nov. 1 | Brooklyn, New York | 92 | Five-car rapid transit train derailed |
| 1937, July 16 | Near Patna, India | 107 | Delhi–Calcutta Express derailed |
| 1938, Dec. 19 | Babacena, Minas Gerais, Brazil | 90 | Freight and passenger trains collide head-on |
| 1938, Dec. 25 | Near Kishinev, Romania | 100 | Passenger trains collide |
| 1939, Dec. 22 | Near Magdeburg, Germany | 132 | Two express trains collide |
| 1939, Dec. 22 | Near Friedrichshafen, Germany | 99 | Train wrecked |
| 1940, Jan. 29 | Osaka, Japan | 200 | Passenger trains collide and burn |
| 1943, Sept. 6 | Philadelphia, Pennsylvania | 79 | Nine cars of Congressional Limited derailed |
| 1943, Dec. 16 | Rennert, North Carolina | 72 | Two streamliners collide |
| 1944, Jan. 16 | León Province, Spain | 500 | Train wrecked inside tunnel |
| 1944, March 2 | Salerno, Italy | 521 | Train stalls in tunnel; mass suffocation |
| 1944, Dec. 31 | Near Ogden, Utah | 50 | Two sections of Pacific Limited wrecked |
| 1945, Feb. 1 | Cazadero, Mexico | 100 | Train with religious pilgrims hit by freight train |
| 1946, March 20 | Near Aracaju, Brazil | 185 | Train wrecked |

**WORLD RAILROAD DISASTERS** *(continued)*

| DATE | PLACE | DEATHS | REMARKS |
|---|---|---|---|
| 1947, Aug. 3 | Sumatra, East Indies | 400 | Train wrecked |
| 1948, March 31 | Osaka, Japan | 70 | Express hits electric train |
| 1949, April 28 | Near Johannesburg, South Africa | 73 | Three trains collide |
| 1949, Oct. 22 | Nowy Dwor, Poland | 200 | Danzig–Warsaw Express derailed |
| 1950, April 6 | Near Tanguá, Brazil | 108 | Train falls into flooded Indios River |
| 1950, May 7 | Bihar State, India | 81 | Punjab mail train crashes near Jasidih |
| 1950, Nov. 22 | Jamaica, New York | 78 | Train collides with standing commuter train |
| 1951, Feb. 6 | Woodbridge, New Jersey | 84 | Commuter train falls through temporary overpass |
| 1952, March 4 | Near Rio de Janeiro, Brazil | 119 | Two passenger trains collide |
| 1952, July 9 | Near Rzepin, Poland | 160 | Train wrecked |
| 1952, Oct. 8 | Harrow, England | 112 | Commuter train hit by two express trains |
| 1953, Dec. 24 | Near Wairoa, New Zealand | 155 | Wellington–Auckland Express falls into stream |
| 1954, Jan. 21 | North of Karachi, Pakistan | 60 | Mail express wrecked |
| 1954, Jan. 31 | Near Seoul, South Korea | 56 | Train crashes |
| 1954, Sept. 28 | East of Hyderabad, India | 137 | Express falls from flood-damaged bridge |
| 1955, April 3 | Near Guadalajara, Mexico | 300 | Train falls into canyon |
| 1956, Sept. 2 | Near Secunderabad, India | 121 | Two coaches fall into river as bridge collapses |
| 1956, Nov. 23 | Marudaiyar River, India | 143 | Express train plunges down river embankment |
| 1957, Sept. 1 | Jamaica, British West Indies | 178 | Train pitches into ravine |
| 1957, Sept. 29 | Near Montgomery, West Pakistan | 250 | Express crashes into standing oil train |
| 1957, Oct. 20 | Near Instanbul, Turkey | 89 | Two trains collide at high speed |
| 1957, Dec. 4 | Near London, England | 90 | Commuter trains collide; bridge collapses |
| 1958, March 7 | Santa Cruz, Brazil | 67 | Three commuter trains collide |
| 1958, May 8 | Near Rio de Janeiro, Brazil | 128 | Two trains collide head-on |
| 1958, Sept. 15 | Newark Bay, Elizabethport, N.J. | 48 | Train plunges through lift bridge |
| 1959, May 28 | Java, Indonesia | 92 | Train plunges into ravine |
| 1959, June 5 | São Paulo, Brazil | 60 | Two trains collide head-on |
| 1960, May 15 | Leipzig, East Germany | 59 | Local train and express collide |
| 1960, Nov. 14 | Pardubice, Czechoslovakia | 110 | Two passenger trains collide |
| 1961, Dec. 23 | Cantanzaro, Italy | 69 | Train car plummets into gorge |
| 1962, Jan. 8 | Woerden, Netherlands | 91 | Passenger trains collide |
| 1962, May 3 | Tokyo, Japan | 163 | Two commuter trains collide with freight train |
| 1962, May 31 | Voghera, Italy | 63 | Passenger train collide with freight train |
| 1962, July 21 | Dumraon, India | 69 | Passenger train and freight train collide |
| 1964, Jan. 4 | Jajinci, Yugoslavia | 66 | Commuter train hits stalled passenger train |
| 1964, Feb. 1 | Altamirano, Argentina | 70 | Express rams stalled freight train |
| 1964, July 26 | Oporto, Portugal | 94 | Train wrecked |
| 1965, Oct. 5 | Near Durban, South Africa | 100 | Passenger train derails |
| 1965, Dec. 9 | Burma | 76 | Two trains collide head-on near Toungoo |
| 1966, June 13 | Bombay, India | 60 | Two suburban trains collide |
| 1967, July 6 | Langenweddingen, East Germany | 82 | Train collides with gasoline truck |
| 1969, July 14 | Jaipur, India | 85 | Freight train collides with passenger train |
| 1970, Feb. 1 | Buenos Aires, Argentina | 139 | Two passenger trains collide |
| 1970, Feb. 16 | Northern Nigeria | 81 | Train wreck |
| 1972, June 4 | Jessore, Bangladesh | 76 | Two passenger trains collide in station |
| 1972, June 16 | Vierzy, France | 107 | Two trains collide in tunnel cave-in |
| 1972, July 21 | Lebrija, Spain | 76 | Two passenger trains collide head-on |
| 1972, Oct. 6 | Saltillo, Mexico | 208 | Speeding passenger train derails on curve |
| 1972, Oct. 30 | Chicago, Illinois | 44 | Commuter train crushed from behind by another |
| 1974, March 27 | Laurenço Marques, Mozambique | 60 | Head-on collision of two trains |
| 1974, Aug. 30 | Zagreb, Yugoslavia | 153 | Passenger train derails in station |
| 1974, Nov. 7 | Cotonou, Dahomey | 80 | Two passenger trains collide |
| 1975, Feb. 28 | London, England | 41 | Subway train crashes in blind tunnel; 70 injured |
| 1977, Jan. 18 | Granville, Australia | 82 | Commuter train derails on bridge, which collapses |
| 1977, May 30 | Assam, India | 44 | Express train falls into Beki River |
| 1977, June 27 | Near Lebus, E. Germany | 29 | Passenger train hits freight train head-on |
| 1977, Sept. 8 | Near Assuit, Egypt | 40 | Passenger train derails |
| 1977, Oct. 10 | Naini, India | 61 | Passenger train hits freight train stopped at station |
| 1977, Nov. 11 | Iri, South Korea | 57 | Freight train explodes at railroad station |
| 1978, Feb. 25 | Sa Pereya, Argentina | 37 | Train collides with truck; 100 injured |
| 1978, April 15 | Bologna, Italy | 45 | Mudslide causes collision; 120 injured |
| 1978, Dec. 21 | Salamanca, Spain | 28 | Train hits school bus; 36 injured |
| 1979, Jan. 5 | Turkey | 56 | Two express trains crash in blizzard near Ankara |
| 1979, Jan. 9 | Ankara, Turkey | 30 | Commuter train hits passenger train in fog |
| 1979, Jan. 26 | Chuadanga, Bangladesh | 70 | Express train derails |
| 1979, April 22 | Pakistan | 44 | Locomotive hits passenger train near Karachi |
| 1979, Aug. 21 | Tailing Chan, Thailand | 65 | Freight train rams commuter train |
| 1979, Sept. 13 | Stalac, Yugoslavia | 60 | Freight train crashes into express train |
| 1979, Oct. 30 | Djibouti | 50 | Train derails and crashes near Ethiopian border |
| 1980, June 7 | Empageni, South Africa | 45 | Freight train hits bus filled with shoppers |
| 1980, Aug. 19 | Northern Poland | 62 | Passenger train collides with freight train |
| 1980, Nov. 21 | Lamezia Terme, Italy | 26 | Two express passenger trains collide with freight train |
| 1980, Dec. 13 | Bihac, Yugoslavia | 23 | Freight train slams into passenger train |

# Animals in the News

Saved from death by action of the California state legislature, Sido happily cuddles in the arms of ASPCA director Richard Avanzino in San Francisco. A public outcry began when the press reported that the will of Sido's mistress, the late Mrs. Mary Murphy, instructed officials to put 10-year-old Sido to death after her own because she feared he would suffer loneliness. The legislature rushed through a new law forbidding malicious or unnecessary destruction of animals. A few hours after Gov. Jerry Brown signed the law, Superior Court Judge Jay Pfotenhauer issued an official reprieve on June 17, based on the new statute.

United Press Int'l.

## HIGHLIGHTS: 1980

### REMAINS OF LARGEST BIRD FOUND

The National Geographic Society announced in September the discovery of the fossilized remains of what is believed to be the largest bird every to fly. The creature, called a giant teratorn, had a wingspan of 25 feet, measured 11 feet from beak to tail, and weighed about 160 pounds.

The remains of the giant bird were found in Argentina by paleontologists Dr. Eduardo P. Tonni and Dr. Rosendo Pascual. They were further examined by Dr. Kenneth E. Campbell of the Natural History Museum of Los Angeles County. Dr. Campbell believes the teratorns lived by swallowing small animals whole because their long hooked beaks seemed suited for grabbing such animals quickly. The bird was tentatively dated as having lived from 5 to 8 million years ago.

### FIRST PANDA CUB BORN IN CAPTIVITY DIES

Animal lovers from around the world rejoiced when the first giant panda conceived in captivity outside China was born Aug. 10 in Mexico City. The cub, named, Xeng-Li, was the offspring of Pe-Pe and Yin-Yin, a pair of 5-year-old giant pandas presented to Mexico by the Chinese government in 1975.

However, joy turned to sadness when, eight days later, officials of the Chapultepec Zoo announced that the cub had been accidentally smothered to death by its mother, Yin-Yin.

### CONDORS RELEASED IN PERU

The first release of endangered, captive-bred Andean condors into a wild habitat was an apparent success, the U.S. Fish and Wildlife Service announced in August. Shortly after six young vultures were set free in July, they joined a small existing population in the coastal mountains of Peru, soaring alongside the older birds and adopting their feeding habits.

The Andean condor program began in late 1966 when nine immature wild birds were captured in the Argentinian highlands and brought to the Fish and Wildlife Service's Patuxent Wildlife Research Center near Laurel,

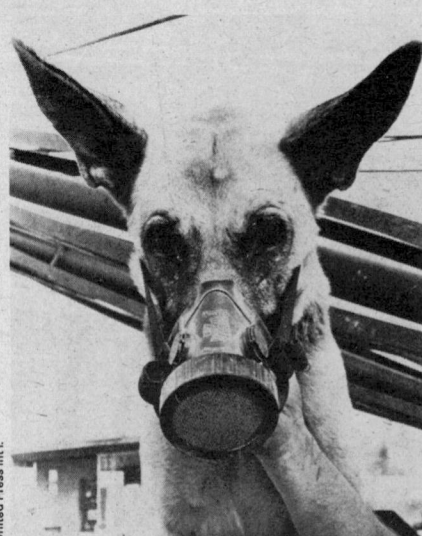

United Press Int'l.

A German Shepherd in Moses Lake, Wash., seems unhappy on May 24, as respirator mask is adjusted over his muzzle. Fallout from nearby Mt. St. Helens volcanic eruption covered the ground in Moses Lake with up to 6 inches of ash.

**HIGHLIGHTS: 1980** *(continued)*

Md. Eventually, after the condors paired off, scientists discovered ways to double, and in some cases even quadruple, normal egg production. The resulting chicks became part of a small, self-sustaining captive population from which the six juveniles were selected for the reintroduction effort.

On July 11, the young condors were flown from Dulles International Airport, Va., to Lima, Peru, accompanied by Dr. James Carpenter, endangered-species research veterinarian at the Patuxent Center.

The birds were first placed temporarily in enclosures at the release sight until they became accustomed to their new surroundings. Before their release, the condors were fitted with small solar-powered radio transmitters that will enable researchers to track them through the remote mountains for up to five years. The six young condors now in Peru range in age from 1 to 3 years.

The ultimate goal of the program is to gain new information for saving the Andean condor's more critically endangered relative, the California condor.

**NEW AUSTRALIAN SHEEP BREED DEVELOPED**

A new commercial breed of sheep was developed by a rancher in Tasmania, Australia, using computer technology. Called the Cormo, the breed was developed by crossing superfine Saxon Merino ewes with Corriedale rams. The resulting Cormo combines the high yield of fine Merino wool with the generous meat production of the Corriedale.

Development was due to the efforts of Ian Downie, who took over management of family property in central Tasmania in 1959. Using computer and scientific technology, he defined the most desirable characteristics in sheep from an economic viewpoint, and tested the computer results with cross-breeding.

**UGLIEST DOG NAMED**

An 11-year-old mutt won the fifth annual Ugly Dog contest in Petaluma, Calif., on Aug. 11. Snuffy, who is part Chihuahua, topped 45 competitors to win the grand prize. He weighs about three pounds, limps with one back paw raised, and has just a few bits of multicolored fur. He is owned by 10-year-old Elaine Hibbs, of Petaluma.

**SPERM WHALES DIE IN FLORIDA COVE**

The mysterious deaths of 10 large sperm whales in northern Florida in November left scientists baffled. The carcasses were found on a beach in Comachee Cove, a narrow inlet less than a mile from the Atlantic Ocean.

Biologists theorize that the whales may have gotten lost, trying to find their way back to the open sea. None of the scientists, however, can discover why they decided to enter the inlet in the first place.

**ROBIN FLIES SOUTH IN JET AIRCRAFT**

A tiny robin was saved from death in Kennebunk, Me., in November, and transported to a warmer climate by commercial jetliner. It was discovered, freezing and starving, in the middle of a road by Christine Panek, 55, as she was driving home from work. She rescued the tiny bird and nursed it back to health.

After two weeks of special care, Ms. Panek

## PREGNANCY PERIOD OF ANIMALS

| ANIMAL | PREGNANCY | AVERAGE IN LITTER | ANIMAL | PREGNANCY | AVERAGE IN LITTER | ANIMAL | PREGNANCY | AVERAGE IN LITTER |
|---|---|---|---|---|---|---|---|---|
| Baboon | 6 months | 1 | Fox | 51 days | 4–10 | Mouse | 19–21 days | 1–9 |
| Cat | 9 weeks | 1–6 | Goat | 151 days | 1–3 | Pig | 113 days | 4–6 |
| Cow | 280 days | 1–2 | Gorilla | 8½ months | 1–2 | Rabbit | 1 month | 4 |
| Chimpanzee | 226 days | 1 | Horse | 330 days | 1 | Sheep | 148 days | 2 |
| Dog | 61 days | 1–4 | Kangaroo | 38–40 days | 1 | Squirrel | 44 days | 4 |
| Dolphin | 8–9 months | 1 | Lion | 108 days | 4 | Tiger | 100 days | 2–4 |
| Elephant | 21 months | 1 | Mink | 6 weeks | 4–8 | Zebra | 12 months | 1 |

arranged for the bird to be taken to Florida in the cockpit of a Delta Airlines jetliner. After examination at the Ft. Myers, Fla., Nature Center, the robin was judged to be healthy enough to be set free, and then was released.

### NEW RULES FOR PET BIRDS SET
New rules for bringing pet birds into the U.S. from trips abroad became effective on Feb. 19 by order of the U.S. Department of Agriculture. Under the regulations, travelers returning to the U.S. with pet birds they took with them abroad do not have to place the birds in quarantine facilities if their birds are accompanied by U.S. health certificates, are identified by leg bands or tattoos, and have remained separate from all other birds and poultry while out of the U.S.

Pet birds returning to the U.S. after more than 60 days abroad still must be isolated by the owner for 30 days at a specified location (usually the owner's residence) and examined by a veterinarian of the Department of Agriculture's Animal and Plant Health Inspection Service (APHIS) before being cleared for entry.

Personally owned pet birds may enter the U.S. at nine specified ports of entry if the birds are accompanied by a health certificate from the nation of origin and are quarantined for 30 days in Department of Agriculture facilities. Quarantine is not required for birds from Canada, which may be brought in with a Canadian government health certificate or by certification by the owners that the birds are healthy and have been kept separate from all other birds.

The import rules are designed to keep contagious poultry diseases out of the U.S.

### ILLINOIS CREATES A SNAKE CROSSING
Snakes have the right of way in the Shawnee National Forest in southwestern Illinois twice a year, when the U.S. Forest Service closes a two-mile stretch of road. Because the biannual snake migration in the LaRue Pine Hills Ecological Area in the forest occurs regularly in April and September, officials decided it was easier to close the road than to caution motorists.

Hundreds of snakes, including poisonous species, must slither 500 feet from their winter homes in the bluffs of the area to one of several swamps created by the backwaters of the Mississippi and Big Muddy rivers in the spring. They return to their winter homes in the autumn.

### NEW BEETLE SPECIES DISCOVERED
Plant pathologist Dr. Bhisham Singh, a scientist with the U.S. Department of Agriculture's Animal and Plant Health Inspection Service (APHIS) discovered a previously unknown species of beetle during a routine collection

A gorilla enjoys a relaxing stretch on the lawn in a cageless, natural setting at the Columbus (Ohio) Zoo in August. After a garden-supply company provided bluegrass sod for the outdoor quarters, keepers reported an immediate improvement in the animals' dispositions, eating habits, and digestion. Because the animals played more, the zoo put up bleachers so visitors could watch them frolicking from spring through fall.

**HIGHLIGHTS: 1980** *(continued)*
of diseased wheat from a field in Clare County, Mich., in March.

The tiny, dark creature, about four-hundredths of an inch long, feeds on ergot, a common fungus of grain. The fungus is poisonous to warm-blooded animals, including humans, and is a problem to farmers.

Dr. Singh and other scientists began experiments to see whether the insect helped carry the dangerous fungus, or whether it could be used to control the spread of ergot.

The beetle, an obscure species, was never before described in scientific literature. Dr. Singh placed it in the Coleoptera order, the Phalacridae family, and the *Acylomus* genus.

### INFANT KILLED BY PET PYTHON

Toni Lynn Duboe, 7 months old, was bitten and crushed to death by her family's 8-foot pet python in her Dallas, Tex., home in November. The snake, due to receive its food, apparently escaped from its glass cage and crawled into her crib.

The baby's father, Robert Eugene Duboe, had owned the snake for over a year. It was fed one hamster every two weeks, and was believed to be hungry when it attacked the baby.

### BERLIN ZOO'S OLDEST RESIDENT DIES

A pike that managed to survive Allied bombings and attacks during World War II died at the Berlin Zoo in May at age 55.

The fish originally was put on display in Berlin in 1927, but was evacuated to Leipzig with other zoo residents during the final days of World War II.

The pike was returned to Berlin in 1953, when the reconstructed zoo was opened to the public.

As the oldest resident of the zoo, the pike maintained "a good appetite to the end," according to zoo officials, and showed no signs of illness.

### MIXED SPECIES TWIN CALVES PRODUCED

Australian medical researchers transplanted the embryo of a Friesian calf into the uterus of a Brahman cow, which carried the foreign offspring along with a normal fetus of her own. The result was mixed-species twins that share the same blood, although they were genetically different species of cattle. Professor Bede Morris of the Australian National University, Canberra, head of the research team, said he believed they were the first mixed-species twins born anywhere in the world.

A horse in Marietta, Ga., undergoes ancient Chinese medical treatment of acupuncture under direction of veterinarian Howard Rand, *right,* in August. Rand uses the treatment to prolong the careers of valuable race and jumping horses. Though some veterinarians question the treatment, Rand claims his acupuncture is effective.

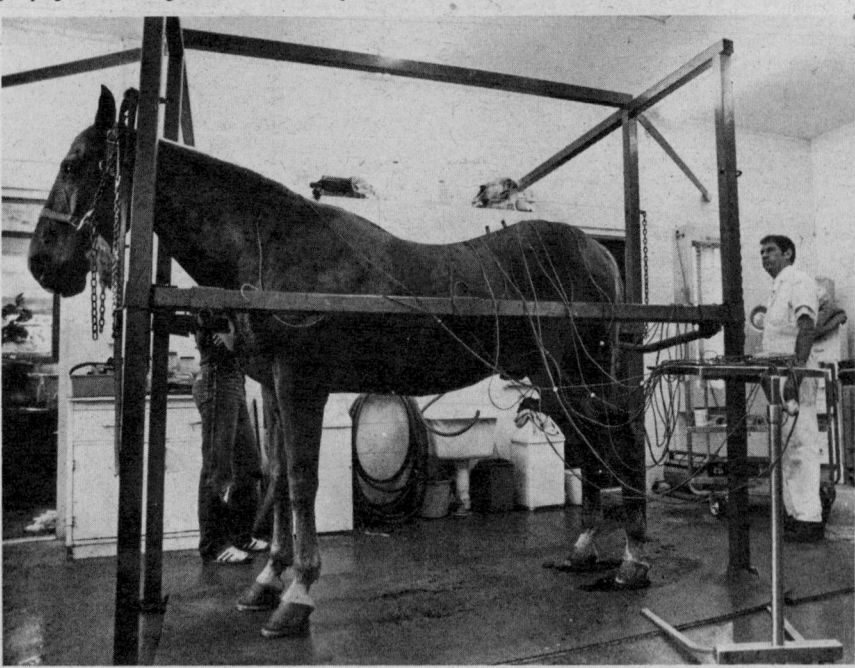

# The Arts

Wide World

Winslow Homer's *The Signal of Distress* is shown Oct. 17 at the Sotheby Parke Bernet auction house after it was purchased by Lawrence Fleischman, right, for the Kennedy Galleries for $1.7 million. It was only the second painting by an American artist to sell at auction for more than $1 million. Previously, the highest price ever paid for a Homer painting was $875,000. The 24½″-by-38½″ canvas was painted between 1892 and 1896.

## HIGHLIGHTS: 1980

### BOSTON AND WASHINGTON SHARE PAINTINGS

The famous paintings of George and Martha Washington by Gilbert Stuart will be shared by museums in both Boston and Washington, D.C. In an unusual agreement, the Smithsonian Institution's National Portrait Gallery and Boston's Museum of Fine Arts approved a plan by which the paintings will be shown in each city for three years at a time.

The portraits, owned since 1831 by the Boston Athenaeum, a private library, were offered for sale to the National Portrait Gallery in 1979 for $5 million. Bostonians protested, launching a $5 million fund-raising campaign to purchase the paintings for the city of Boston.

Under the new arrangement, the Museum of Fine Arts paid the Athenaeum $2,125,000 for its share in the paintings, and the Smithsonian paid $2,750,000, bringing the Athenaeum a total of $4.87 million.

The portraits arrived in Washington in May and will remain there until 1983, when they will be moved back to Boston Museum, where they have been on loan since 1871.

The portrait of George Washington is the one that appears on dollar bills and in reproductions in many classrooms.

### THE LAST SUPPER IN PERIL

Leonardo da Vinci's masterpiece *The Last Supper*, painted in 1494–99 on the refectory wall of the Church of Santa Maria delle Grazie, in Milan, Italy, was found to be in new danger in June. A six-foot-long crack was discovered in the wall on which the work was painted.

Leonardo used an experimental technique in painting directly on plaster, using a mixture of oil and egg tempera. However, the work began deteriorating as early as 50 years after completion. Over the centuries the wall has been exposed to wars, invasions, bombings, pollution, and restoration attempts.

The new crack appears to have begun inside the wall and is now approaching the painted surface. When it was discovered, the Italian government announced it would spend any amount needed for preservation of the work.

**HIGHLIGHTS: 1980** *(continued)*

A decision was made to install an air-conditioning or air-filter system to try to prevent further damage from pollution. Restorers performed a scientific examination of the painted surface through the use of computerized equipment. They used infrared and mass spectrometry to isolate each substance, so that solvents, fixers, and pesticides could be developed that would not harm the painting further. The solvents are to be used to remove layers of paint used by earlier restorers, that inadvertently were harmful. Restoration was expected to take four to five years, but methods must also be devised to protect the painted wall itself.

### NEW CONDUCTOR FOR BOSTON POPS

Film composer John Williams, 47, was named to replace the late Arthur Fiedler as conductor of the renowned Boston Pops Orchestra in January. Williams, composer of music for more than 60 motion pictures, is best known for his scores for *Star Wars* and *Close Encounters of the Third Kind.*

Williams planned to continue to compose music, and hoped to use the Pops to showcase some of his work as well as that of other contemporary American composers.

### STRIKE SHUTS DOWN METROPOLITAN OPERA

New York City's Metropolitan Opera on Sept. 30 postponed opening its 1980–81 season, after a month-long labor dispute centering on demands by the orchestra for a four-performance work week.

A settlement was reached at the end of October, in which the orchestra would provide four performances per week as well as four hours of rehearsal per week.

### ANOTHER RECORD YEAR IN ART MARKET

Prices for paintings and other works of art continued to skyrocket in 1980. English painter J.M.W. Turner's *Juliet and Her Nurse*, painted in 1836, fetched a record $6.4 million at the Sotheby Parke Bernet gallery in New York in May. It was the highest price ever paid for a work of art at an auction.

In December American collector Armand Hammer paid $5,126,000 for Leonardo da Vinci's notebook "Of the Nature, Weight, and Movement of Water," the highest auction price ever for a manuscript.

In May, Vincent Van Gogh's *Le Jardin du Poéte, Arles (The Garden of a Poet in Arles)* fetched $5.2 million at Christie's, New York.

In September the Whitney Museum of American Art paid $1 million for *Three Flags* by Jasper Johns. It was believed the highest price paid for the work of a living artist.

In April the world's most valuable stamp, an 1856 British Guiana 1-cent magenta, was auctioned for $850,000 in New York City.

In March a lamp designed by Louis Tiffany was auctioned at Christie's for $360,000, the highest price ever paid for an Art Nouveau object.

United Press Int'l.

Sculptor Henry Moore's *The Arch* was unveiled Oct. 17 at Kensington Gardens in London, England. The sculpture, which is executed in Roman travertine marble, weighs approximately 50 tons and stands 19 feet tall. Bronze versions of the work exist in Oslo, Norway, and Columbus, Ohio.

# AMERICAN SYMPHONY ORCHESTRAS

Source: American Symphony Orchestra League

| MAJOR ORCHESTRAS | DIRECTOR | OTHER INFORMATION |
|---|---|---|
| Atlanta Symphony Orchestra ......... | Robert Shaw | Founded 1945; Shaw became director in 1966 |
| Baltimore Symphony Orchestra ....... | Sergiu Comissiona | Founded 1916; Comissiona became director in 1968 |
| Boston Symphony Orchestra.......... | Seiji Ozawa | Founded 1881; also performs as Boston Pops, under John Williams |
| Buffalo Philharmonic Orchestra ...... | Julius Rudel | Founded 1935; Rudel became director in 1979 |
| Chicago Symphony Orchestra......... | Sir Georg Solti | Founded 1891; Solti joined orchestra in 1969 |
| Cincinnati Symphony Orchestra ....... | Michael Gielen | Founded 1895; Gielen became director in 1980 |
| Cleveland Orchestra ................. | Lorin Maazel | Founded 1918; Maazel became director in 1972 |
| Dallas Symphony Orchestra .......... | Eduarto Mata | Founded 1900; Mata became director in 1977 |
| Denver Symphony Orchestra ......... | Gaetano Delogu | Founded 1933; Delogu became director in 1979 |
| Detroit Symphony Orchestra.......... | Antal Dorati | Founded 1914; Dorati became director in 1977 |
| Honolulu Symphony Orchestra ........ | Donald Johanos | Founded 1900; Johanos became director in 1979 |
| Houston Symphony Orchestra ........ | Sergiu Comissiona | Founded 1913; Comissiona became music advisor in 1979 |
| Indianapolis Symphony Orchestra ..... | John Nelson | Founded 1930; Nelson joined orchestra in 1976 |
| Kansas City Philharmonic Orchestra ... | Maurice Peress | Founded 1933; Peress became music director in 1974 |
| Los Angeles Philharmonic ........... | Carlo Maria Giulini | Founded 1919; Giulini joined orchestra in 1977 |
| Milwaukee Symphony Orchestra ...... | Lukas Foss | Founded 1930; Foss joined orchestra in 1980 |
| Minnesota Symphony Orchestra....... | Neville Marriner | Founded 1903 as Minneapolis Symphony Orchestra; Marriner joined orchestra in 1979 |
| National Symphony Orchestra ........ | Mstislav Rostropovich | Founded 1931 as orchestra of Washington, D.C.; Rostropovich became director in 1977 |
| New Jersey Symphony Orchestra ...... | Thomas Michalak | Founded 1920; Michalak became director in 1977 |
| New Orleans Philharmonic............ | Philippe Entremont | Founded 1935; Entremont joined orchestra in 1980 |
| New York Philharmonic ............. | Zubin Mehta | America's oldest orchestra, founded in 1842; Leonard Bernstein is director emeritus; Mehta named director beginning 1978–79 season |
| North Carolina Symphony ............ | Lawrence Leighton Smith | Founded 1932; Smith became musical advisor in 1980 |
| Philadelphia Orchestra............... | Riccardo Muti | Founded 1900; Muti became director in 1980 |
| Pittsburgh Symphony ............... | André Previn | Founded 1927; Previn joined orchestra in 1975 |
| Rochester Philharmonic.............. | David Zinman | Founded 1929; Zinman named music advisor in 1973 |
| St. Louis Symphony Orchestra ........ | Leonard Slatkin | Founded 1880; Slatkin named music director in 1979 |
| San Antonio Symphony Orchestra ..... | Lawrence Leighton Smith | Founded 1937; Smith joined orchestra in 1980 |
| San Diego Symphony ................ | David Atherton | Founded 1927; became major orchestra in 1980 |
| San Francisco Symphony Orchestra ... | Edo de Waart | Founded 1911; de Waart became director in 1977 |
| Seattle Symphony Orchestra.......... | Rainer Miedel | Founded 1903; Miedel joined orchestra in 1976 |
| Syracuse Symphony Orchestra........ | Christopher Keene | Founded 1924; Keene joined orchestra in 1975 |
| Utah Symphony Orchestra............ | Varujan Kojian | Founded 1926; Kojian joined orchestra in 1980 |

# LEADING U. S. OPERA COMPANIES

Source: Central Opera Service

| MAJOR OPERAS | DIRECTOR | OTHER INFORMATION |
|---|---|---|
| Cincinnati Opera Association ......... | James de Blasis | Founded 1921; de Blasis appointed in 1973 |
| Dallas Civic Opera Company .......... | Plato Karayanis | Founded 1957; Karayanis appointed in 1977 |
| Greater Miami Opera Association...... | Robert Herman | Founded 1941; Herman appointed in 1973 |
| Houston Grand Opera ............... | David Gockley | Founded 1956; Gockley appointed in 1972 |
| Lyric Opera of Chicago .............. | Carol Fox | Founded 1954 with Fox as general manager |
| Metropolitan Opera Association (N.Y.) . | Anthony A. Bliss | Founded 1883; Bliss appointed in 1975 |
| Michigan Opera Theatre (Detroit) ..... | David Di Chiera | Founded 1966, with Di Chiera as director |
| New York City Opera Company........ | Beverly Sills | Founded 1944; Sills appointed in 1979 |
| Opera Company of Boston ........... | Sarah Caldwell | Founded 1958, with Caldwell as first director |
| Opera Company of Philadelphia ...... | Margaret Everitt | Founded 1975; Everitt appointed in 1980 |
| San Diego Opera Association ......... | Tito Capobianco | Founded 1965; Capobianco appointed in 1976 |
| San Francisco Opera Association ...... | Kurt Herbert Adler | Founded 1923; Adler appointed in 1953 |
| Santa Fe Opera Company ............ | John Crosby | Founded 1957, with Crosby as general director |
| Seattle Opera Association ........... | Glynn Ross | Founded 1962, with Ross as manager |
| Virginia Opera Association (Norfolk) ... | Peter Mark | Founded 1974, with Mark as artistic director |
| Washington Opera Company .......... | Martin Feinstein | Founded 1957; Feinstein appointed in 1979 |

# MAJOR AMERICAN BALLET COMPANIES

| | | |
|---|---|---|
| New York City Ballet ................ | George Balanchine, Jerome Robbins, and John Taras | Founded 1948; affiliated with New York State theater |
| San Francisco Ballet ................ | Lew Christensen and Michael Smuin | Founded 1937; oldest continuing American classical ballet company |

# MUSICIANS, COMPOSERS, SINGERS, DANCERS*

**Licia Albanese** (1913– ), Italian soprano who was one of the principal singers at the Metropolitan Opera after her debut in 1940.

**Marian Anderson** (1902– ), American contralto who achieved worldwide fame as a concert artist.

**Johann Christian Bach** (1735–82), German composer; J.S. Bach's 18th child. He spent much of his life in the court of England's George III, where he wrote operas and many symphonies.

**Johann Sebastian Bach** (1685–1750), German composer. A master of counterpoint, he was among the most influential composers of all time. His works include the six Brandenburg Concertos (1721), the B Minor Mass (1733–38), and many keyboard works.

**Karl Philipp Emanuel Bach** (1714–88), J.S. Bach's fifth child. With Haydn and Mozart, he helped develop the sonata form, which dominated instrumental music for two centuries.

**George Balanchine** (1904– ), Russian-American ballet dancer and choreographer; director of ballet at the Metropolitan Opera (1934–37) and the New York City Ballet (since 1948).

**Samuel Barber** (1910– ), American composer whose outstanding works include an overture to *The School for Scandal* (1931), *Adagio for Strings* (1936), and *Essays for Orchestra* (1937).

**Sir John Barbirolli** (1899–1970), English conductor who led the British National Opera (1926–27), the New York Philharmonic (1937–42), and the Houston Symphony.

**Béla Bartók** (1881–1945), Hungarian composer whose music combines folk elements with an extremely modern style. His works include three piano concertos (1926, 1931, 1945) and the *Concerto for Orchestra* (1944).

**Mikhail Baryshnikov** (1948– ), Russian ballet dancer with Kirov Ballet who defected to the West in 1974; became guest artist for world's leading ballet companies; choreographed *The Nutcracker Suite* for American Ballet Theatre in 1976; made film debut in *The Turning Point* (1976); named director of American Ballet Theatre in 1980.

**Sir Thomas Beecham** (1879–1961), English conductor who organized the London Philharmonic Orchestra in 1932 and the Royal Philharmonic in 1946.

**Ludwig van Beethoven** (1770–1827), German composer who ranks among the greatest musical geniuses of all time. His masterpieces include 9 symphonies, 32 piano sonatas, 17 string quartets, and 5 piano concertos.

**Alban Berg** (1885–1935), Austrian atonal composer and pupil of Arnold Schoenberg. His opera *Wozzeck* (1914–1920) is considered his masterpiece.

**Irving Berlin** (1888– ), American composer of popular songs, including *God Bless America.*

**Hector Berlioz** (1803–69), French composer and exponent of the Romantic movement. The *Symphonie Fantastique* (1830–31) and *Harold in Italy* (1834) are among his greatest works.

**Leonard Bernstein** (1918– ), American conductor and composer (*Jeremiah Symphony*, 1941–44; *West Side Story*, 1957) who was musical director of the New York Philharmonic Orchestra (1958–69).

**Georges Bizet** (1838–75), French composer whose *Carmen* (1873–74) is one of the world's most popular operas.

**Jussi Bjorling** (1911–60), Swedish tenor who appeared in major European and American opera houses in over 50 leading roles.

**Ernest Bloch** (1880–1959), Swiss-American composer of the opera *Macbeth* (1903–09) and the *Israel Symphony* (1912–16).

**Aleksandr Borodin** (1833–87), Russian composer of nationalistic music, including the unfinished opera *Prince Igor.*

**Johannes Brahms** (1833–97), German composer of four symphonies (1855–76, 1877, 1883, 1884–85), *The Academic Festival Overture* (1880), *The Tragic Overture* (1880–81), one violin and two piano concertos, and much chamber music.

**Alexander Brailowsky** (1896–1976), Russian-born pianist noted for his playing of Chopin.

**Benjamin Britten** (1913–76), English composer whose opera *Peter Grimes* (1945) was one of few modern operas to achieve worldwide acclaim.

**Anton Bruckner** (1824–96), Austrian composer whose works utilize romantic themes in an expanded sonata structure. He wrote nine symphonies, the last unfinished, and four masses.

**Ferruccio Busoni** (1866–1924), Italian composer whose most popular compositions are the *Comedy Overture* (1897), the *Pianoforte Concerto* (1903–04), and *Doctor Faust* (1916–24).

**William Byrd** (1543–1623), English organist and composer called the father of English music for his masses, madrigals, chamber and keyboard music.

**John Cage** (1912– ), American composer who employs random, nonmusical sounds to create highly experimental works.

**Maria Callas** (1923–77), Greek-American soprano who appeared in the major opera houses of Europe and the United States. Her greatest roles included Tosca and Norma.

**Elliott Carter** (1908– ), American composer of the ballet *Pocahontas* (1939) and the Second String Quartet (1959), for which he received the 1960 Pulitzer Prize in music.

**Enrico Caruso** (1873–1921), Italian tenor and one of the world's most celebrated opera stars. He sang with the New York Metropolitan Opera from 1903 to 1920.

**Robert Casadesus** (1899–1972), French pianist who earned a reputation as a major artist.

**Pablo Casals** (1876–1973), Spanish cellist and conductor generally regarded as the world's greatest cellist. A distinguished conductor, he formed the Orquesta Pau Casals in Barcelona in 1919.

**Feodor Chaliapin** (1873–1938), Russian basso who sang in the major European opera houses and at the Metropolitan Opera (1907–08, 1921–29).

**Lucia Chase** (1907– ), ballerina and co-director of the American Ballet Theatre (1945–80).

**Frédéric Chopin** (1810–49), Polish-French composer of highly romantic compositions for the piano. His works include 27 études, 25 preludes, 13 polonaises, and 2 concertos.

**Van Cliburn** (1934– ), American pianist, gained worldwide fame by winning 1958 International Tchaikovsky Piano Competition in Moscow.

**Aaron Copland** (1900– ), American composer whose highly successful works include *Music for the Theater* (1925), *Saga of the Prairie* (1937), *Billy the Kid* (1938), *Rodeo* (1942), *Appalachian Spring* (1944), and *Nonet* (1960).

**Franco Corelli** (1923– ), Italian tenor who made his operatic debut at the Spoleto (Italy) Festival in 1952 and debuted with the New York Metropolitan Opera in 1961.

**Henry Cowell** (1897–1965), American composer whose unconventional music includes the five *Hymn-and-Fuguing Tunes* (1941–55).

**Merce Cunningham** (1919– ), American dancer and choreographer who performed with the Martha

Graham Company (1940–45) before forming his own dance company in 1952.

**Walter Damrosch** (1862–1950), American conductor. Organized Damrosch Opera Company (1895) and led Metropolitan Opera Orchestra (1885–91, 1900–02) and New York Symphony (1903–27).

**Alexandra Danilova** (1906– ), Russian ballerina and choreographer. She was the prima ballerina with the Ballet Russe de Monte Carlo (1938–58).

**Claude Debussy** (1862–1918), French composer and founder of the impressionistic school. His best works include *L'Après-midi d'un faune* (1892–94), *La Mer* (1905), the opera *Pelléas et Mélisande* (1902), and many pieces for piano solo.

**Léo Delibes** (1836–91), French composer best known for *Sylvia* (1876) and other ballets.

**Frederick Delius** (1862–1934), English composer whose best-known compositions include *A Village Romeo and Juliet* (1900–01), *Sea Drift* (1903), and *Mass of Life* (1904–05).

**Victoria de Los Angeles** (1923– ), Spanish soprano who sang in Madrid, Milan, and Paris before joining the Metropolitan Opera in 1950.

**Agnes De Mille** (1909– ), ballerina and choreographer who created the first noteworthy American ballet, *Rodeo* (1938). She was the first to use ballet in musical comedies such as *Oklahoma!* (1943) and *Carousel* (1945).

**Sergei Diaghilev** (1872–1929), Russian ballet director who founded the famous Diaghilev's Ballet Russe in Paris in 1909.

**David Diamond** (1915– ), American composer of dissonant, rhythmic music, including *Psalm* (1936), *Rounds* (1944).

**Anton Dolin** (1904– ), English ballet dancer and choreographer who performed with Diaghilev's Ballet Russe (1921–25) and the Ballet Theater in New York. He formed several ballet companies.

**Gaetano Donizetti** (1797–1848), Italian composer of operas. *Lucia di Lammermoor* (1835) is his most popular creation.

**Anton Dvořák** (1841–1904), Czech composer whose works were strongly influenced by Bohemian folk music. He completed nine symphonies, including the New World Symphony.

**Emma Eames** (1865–1952), American soprano who starred at the Metropolitan Opera from 1891 to 1909. Her greatest performances were in *Tosca, Don Giovanni,* and *Aïda.*

**André Eglevsky** (1917–77), American ballet dancer who performed at the Ballet Russe de Monte Carlo (1939–42) and the Ballet Theater (1942–46). He was *premier danseur* at the New York City Ballet (1951–58).

**Sir Edward Elgar** (1857–1934), English composer whose distinctly British pieces include the five *Pomp and Circumstance* marches (1901–30) and *Enigma Variations* (1899).

**Duke Ellington** (1899–1974), American jazz musician and composer; best-known pieces are *Mood Indigo, Sophisticated Lady,* and *Harlem.*

**Mischa Elman** (1891–1967), Russian-American violinist who began his long and successful career at the age of twelve.

**Manuel de Falla** (1876–1946), Spanish composer whose nationalistic music includes *La Vida Breve,* (1903), *El Amor Brujo* (1915), and *Nights in the Gardens of Spain* (1916).

**Geraldine Farrar** (1882–1967), American soprano who enjoyed tremendous popularity during her career with the Metropolitan Opera (1906–22). Her most famous performances were in *Madame Butterfly* and *Carmen.*

**Eileen Farrell** (1920– ), American soprano who sang on radio and in concerts before her successful opera

debuts in San Francisco (1956) and at the Metropolitan Opera (1960).

**Suzanne Farrell** (1943– ), American ballerina with the New York City Ballet in 1961–69 and since 1975.

**Gabriel Fauré** (1845–1924), French organist and composer whose works include the lyric drama *Pénélope* (1913).

**Arthur Fiedler** (1894–1979), American conductor, who led the Boston Pops Orchestra (1930–79).

**Kirsten Flagstad** (1895–1962), Norwegian soprano hailed as one of the greatest Wagnerian sopranos of this century. She sang at the Metropolitan Opera (1935–37; 1950–52).

**Carlisle Floyd** (1926– ), American composer whose operas include *Susannah* (1953–54) and *The Passion of Jonathan Wade* (1962).

**Mikhail Fokine** (1880–1942), Russian choreographer and ballet dancer who is considered the founder of modern ballet.

**Dame Margot Fonteyn** (1919– ), English ballerina who won international acclaim. She was *prima ballerina assoluta* of the Royal Ballet.

**Lukas Foss** (1922– ), German-American composer of avant-garde music and a noted conductor.

**Stephen Foster** (1826–64), American composer of popular folk ballads, including *Oh! Susannah* (1848) and *Old Folks at Home* (1851).

**Zino Francescatti** (1905– ), French violinist who has given concerts all over the world and is considered one of the greatest living musicians.

**César Franck** (1822–90), French composer and organist whose important works include the Symphony in D minor (1886–88).

**Wilhelm Furtwängler** (1886–1954), German conductor who led virtually all the great European orchestras as well as the New York Philharmonic.

**Amelita Galli-Curci** (1882–1963), Italian soprano who won wide U.S. acclaim at the Chicago (until 1942) and Metropolitan (1926–30) operas.

**Mary Garden** (1877–1967), Scottish soprano who became a sensational star as a result of her performances throughout Europe and with the Manhattan (1907–10) and Chicago (1910–31) operas.

**George Gershwin** (1898–1937), American composer of the popular song *Swanee* (1919), *Rhapsody in Blue* (1924), *Concerto in F* for piano and orchestra (1925), *An American in Paris* (1928), and the folk opera *Porgy and Bess* (1935).

**Walter Gieseking** (1895–1956), German pianist noted for his performances of Debussy.

**Beniamino Gigli** (1890–1957), Italian tenor who was regarded as Caruso's successor at the Metropolitan Opera (1920–32; 1938–39).

**Mikhail I. Glinka** (1804–57), Russian composer regarded as father of the Russian national school. His works include *Kamarinskaya* (1848).

**Christoph Willibald von Gluck** (1714–87), German composer and influential reformer of the opera. His greatest works are *Alceste* (1767) and *Iphigénie en Tauride* (1778).

**Aleksandr Godunov** (1949– ) Russian-ballet dancer who starred with the Bolshoi Ballet of Moscow in 1971–79. He defected to the U.S. in 1979, joining the American Ballet Theatre.

**Glenn Gould** (1932– ), Canadian pianist best known as interpreter of keyboard music of Bach.

**Morton Gould** (1913– ), American composer and pianist. His works, in the traditional vein, include *Latin American Symphonette* (1940).

**Charles Gounod** (1818–93), French composer of the well-known operas *Faust* (1859) and *Romeo and Juliette* (1867).

**Martha Graham** (1894– ), American dancer, choreographer, director, and teacher of modern dance. She formed her own company in 1929.

**MUSICIANS** (continued)

**Edvard Hagerup Grieg** (1843–1907), Norwegian composer whose music was inspired by Norwegian folk tunes: the *Piano Concerto in A Minor* (1868) and the *Peer Gynt Suite* (1876).

**Oscar Hammerstein II** (1895–1960), American librettist for musicals. Wrote *The Desert Song* (1926) with Sigmund Romberg, *Show Boat* (1927) with Jerome Kern, and many with Richard Rogers, such as *Oklahoma!* (1943), *South Pacific* (1949), *The King and I* (1951), and *The Sound of Music* (1959).

**George Frideric Handel** (1685–1759), German composer of baroque music. In addition to the *Messiah* (1741) and other oratorios, he wrote operas, cantatas, and chamber music.

**Howard Hanson** (1896–   ), American composer of highly romantic works, the best known of which is the *Romantic Symphony* (1930).

**Roy Harris** (1898–1979), American composer whose best-known works are his *Third Symphony* (1939) and the *Cumberland Concerto* (1951).

**Melissa Hayden** (1923–   ), Canadian-born ballerina who starred with New York City Ballet in 1950–73.

**Franz Joseph Haydn** (1732–1809), Austrian composer who wrote the first important symphonies in the classical sonata-allegro form. He composed more than 100 symphonies and 80 string quartets.

**Jascha Heifetz** (1901–   ), Russian-American violinist and one of the foremost artists in his field. Before coming to New York (1917), he played in St. Petersburg, Kiev, Berlin, and Vienna.

**Victor Herbert** (1859–1924), Irish-American cellist, conductor, and composer best known for his operettas *Babes in Toyland* (1903), *Naughty Marietta* (1910), and *Sweethearts* (1913).

**Paul Hindemith** (1895–1963), German composer who employed highly advanced and varied methods of composition. His most important work is the symphony *Mathis der Maler* (1934).

**Arthur Honegger** (1892–1955), French composer whose best-known works include the tone poem *Pacific 231* (1923) and the oratorios *King David* (1921) and *Joan of Arc at the Stake* (1935).

**Vladimir Horowitz** (1904–   ), Russian-American pianist who has enjoyed great popularity during his career on the U.S. concert stage (since 1928).

**Engelbert Humperdinck** (1854–1921), German composer of the opera *Hansel and Gretel* (1893).

**Doris Humphrey** (1895–1958), dancer and choreographer who developed new dance approaches.

**Vincent d'Indy** (1851–1931), French composer; his masterpiece is the *Symphony Cévenole* (1886).

**Charles Ives** (1874–1954), American composer whose music captures the spirit of America. His works include the *Third Symphony* (1901–04) and the *Concord Sonata* (1909–15).

**Robert Joffrey** (1930–   ), American dancer, choreographer, and director of the Robert Joffrey Ballet Company, which he founded in 1956.

**Um Kalthoum** (1899–1975), Arab concert singer who was Egypt's most popular star from 1922 to 1972.

**Herbert von Karajan** (1908–   ), Austrian conductor who has directed the leading orchestras in Austria and Germany and has made highly successful guest appearances in the U.S.

**Jerome David Kern** (1885–1945), American composer of musicals, including *Show Boat* (1927).

**Aram Khatchaturian** (1903–78), Soviet-Armenian composer known for the lively "Sabre Dance" in his ballet *Gayane* (1924) and for his ballet *Spartacus* (1954).

**Ralph Kirkpatrick** (1911–   ), American harpsichordist and musicologist. He is an authority on the music of Domenico Scarlatti.

**Zoltán Kodály** (1882–1967), Hungarian composer whose music combines folk themes with a romantic style. His most famous works are the *Psalmus Hungaricus* (1923) for chorus, and the opera *Háry János* (1925–26).

**André Kostelanetz** (1901–80), Russian-American conductor. He directed orchestras on radio and TV for CBS and made many recordings.

**Serge Koussevitzky** (1874–1951), Russian conductor who directed the Russian State Symphony (1917–20), the Grand Opera of Moscow (1918–20), and the Boston Symphony Orchestra (1924–49).

**Fritz Kreisler** (1875–1962), Austrian-American violinist and composer who won international fame for his performances in Europe and the U.S.

**Wanda Landowska** (1877–1959), Polish-American harpsichordist, considered the greatest modern master of that instrument. She is best remembered for her recording of Bach's *Well-Tempered Clavier*.

**Leonid Lavrosky** (1905–   ), Russian choreographer who directed the Leningrad Opera and Ballet (1938–44) and the Bolshoi Theater (1944–64).

**Lilli Lehmann** (1848–1929), German soprano and one of the foremost Wagnerian opera stars. She sang throughout Europe and with the Metropolitan Opera (1885–89; 1891–92).

**Lotte Lehmann** (1888–1976), German soprano who sang with the Hamburg (1909), the Vienna State (1914–38), and the New York Metropolitan (1934–45) operas. She later was stage director of the Metropolitan.

**Erich Leinsdorf** (1912–   ), Austrian-American conductor who led the New York Metropolitan Opera (1938–43; 1956–62), the Cleveland Orchestra (1943–44), the Rochester (N.Y.) Orchestra (1945–54), and the Boston Symphony (1962–69).

**Ruggiero Leoncavallo** (1858–1919), Italian composer whose best known work is *I Pagliacci* (1892).

**Josef Lhévinne** (1874–1944), Russian-American pianist and teacher who taught at the Moscow Conservatory (1902–06) and for many years at the Juilliard Graduate School in New York.

**José Limón** (1908–72), dancer, choreographer, and teacher who was with the Humphrey-Weidman Company and later formed his own dance group.

**Jenny Lind** (1820–87), Swedish soprano whose magnificent voice and dramatic ability made her the idol of opera lovers throughout Europe. She toured the U.S. from 1850 to 1852.

**Franz Liszt** (1811–86), Hungarian composer whose virtuosity as a pianist has never been equaled. His compositions include the *Faust Symphony* (1854–57), *Les Préludes* (1856), and 20 Hungarian rhapsodies (1851–86).

**Jean Baptiste Lully** (1632–87), French operatic composer who wrote the first French operas and founded the Paris Opera in 1672. His works include *Alceste* (1674), *Thésée* (1675), *Psyché* (1678), *Armide* (1686), and *Acis et Galatée* (1687).

**Edward MacDowell** (1861–1908), American composer whose best-known works are *Indian Suite* (1897) and the *Piano Concerto No. 2* (1890).

**Gustav Mahler** (1860–1911), Austrian composer and perhaps the last important member of the late Romantic school of symphonists. He wrote 10 great symphonies, the last unfinished, and the song cycle *Das Lied von der Erde* (1908).

**Natalia Makarova** (1940–   ), Russian ballerina who defected from Kirov Ballet in 1970; has since appeared with world's leading ballet companies.

**Gian Francesco Malipiero** (1882–   ), Italian composer of operas (*L'Orfeide*, 1918–21; *Guilio Cesare*, 1935), symphonies (*Impressions from Nature I, II, and III*, 1910–22), choral and chamber music.

**Alicia Markova** (1910–   ), English ballerina who achieved recognition for her performances with the Diaghilev Ballet Russe (1925–32); the Vic-Wells

Ballet (1932–35), where she was prima ballerina; and the Ballet Russe de Monte Carlo (1938–41).

**Giovanni Martinelli** (1885–1969), Italian tenor who made his debut in Milan (1910) and sang at the Metropolitan Opera (1913–46) in over 50 leading roles.

**Pietro Mascagni** (1863–1945), Italian composer whose best-known work is *Cavalleria rusticana* (1890).

**Jules Massenet** (1842–1912), French composer of over 20 operas, including *Manon* (1884), *Werther* (1892), *Thaïs* (1894), and *Don Quichotte* (1910).

**Léonide Massine** (1896–1979), Russian-American ballet dancer and choreographer who worked with Diaghilev's Ballet Russe (1914–20), the Ballet Russe de Monte Carlo (1932–42), and the Ballet Theater in New York (1942–44).

**Patricia McBride** (1942– ), American-born ballerina; principal dancer with New York City ballet since 1959.

**John McCormack** (1884–1945), Irish-American tenor. A major operatic star in London and New York, he confined his last years to concerts.

**Zubin Mehta** (1936– ), Indian-American conductor of the New York Philharmonic Orchestra, appointed in 1978.

**Dame Nellie Melba** (1859–1931), Australian soprano who sang with tremendous success in Brussels (1887), London (1889), Paris (1889–91), and New York (1893–96; 1907–20).

**Lauritz Melchior** (1890–1973), Danish tenor who appeared in Copenhagen (1913–21), Bayreuth (1925–26), and at the Metropolitan Opera (1926–50), where he was the leading Wagnerian tenor.

**Felix Mendelssohn** (1809–47), German composer whose beautiful music includes the Overture to *A Midsummer Night's Dream* (1826), the *Scotch Symphony* (1830–42), a violin concerto (1844), the opera *Elijah* (1846), and chamber music.

**Peter Mennin** (1923– ), American composer who has been president of the Juilliard School of Music since 1962. Among his works are seven symphonies and eight choral works.

**Gian-Carlo Menotti** (1911– ), Italian-American composer best known for his operas *Amahl and the Night Visitors* (1951) and *The Saint of Bleecker Street* (1954), which won a Pulitzer Prize in 1955.

**Yehudi Menuhin** (1916– ), American violinist who gave his first concert at the age of seven.

**Robert Merrill** (1917– ), American baritone at the Metropolitan Opera since the early 1950s.

**Giacomo Meyerbeer** (1791–1864), German composer and master of the French grand opera. Among his works are *Les Huguenots* (1836) and *L'Africaine* (1838–63).

**Darius Milhaud** (1892–1974), French composer best known for his operas *Le Pauvre Matelot* (1926) and *Christophe Colombe* (1928).

**Dimitri Mitropoulos** (1896–1960), Greek conductor who led the Paris Symphony (1932), the Minneapolis Symphony (1937–49), and the New York Philharmonic (1950–58).

**Igor Moiseyev** (1906– ), Russian dancer and choreographer who was with the Bolshoi Theatre (1924–39). In 1936 he organized the Moiseyev Dance Company.

**Pierre Monteux** (1875–1964), French conductor who directed the Metropolitan Opera (1917–19), the Boston Symphony (1919–24), the Paris Symphony (1928–35), the San Francisco Symphony (1935–52), and the London Symphony (1962–64).

**Claudio Monteverdi** (1567–1643), Italian composer credited with writing the first significant operas, including *Orfeo* (1607), *The Return of Ulysses* (1641), and *The Coronation of Poppea* (1642).

**Grace Moore** (1901–47), American soprano who sang at the Metropolitan Opera (1928–32, 1934–35, 1937–39) and made several films. She was killed in a plane crash at the height of her career.

**Wolfgang Amadeus Mozart** (1756–91), Austrian composer who epitomized the classical tradition with 41 symphonies, over 30 piano concertos, concertos for other instruments, chamber music, masses, and such operas as *Don Giovanni* (1787) and *The Magic Flute* (1791).

**Charles Münch** (1891–1968), French conductor who directed the Paris Philharmonic Orchestra (1938–46), the Boston Symphony (1949–62), and the Berkshire Music Center (1951–62).

**Patrice Munsel** (1925– ), American soprano who made her debut at the Metropolitan Opera in 1943 and has also appeared in films.

**Modest Mussorgsky** (1839–81), Russian composer whose best-known work is the opera *Boris Godunov* (1874).

**Bronislava Nijinska** (1891–1971), Russian dancer and choreographer associated with the Diaghilev Ballet Russe until 1924.

**Vaslav Nijinsky** (1890–1950), Russian ballet dancer considered by many to be the greatest of all time. He began dancing at the age of 10. He performed with the Diaghilev Ballet Russe (1909–17) until he was committed to an insane asylum.

**Birgit Nilsson** (1918– ), Swedish singer considered the greatest living Wagnerian soprano. Her triumphant debut at the Metropolitan Opera (1959) made front-page news.

**Lillian Nordica** (1857–1914), American soprano most famous for her Wagnerian roles. In addition to many appearances in Europe, she starred at the Metropolitan Opera from 1893 to 1909.

**Rudolf Nureyev** (1938– ), Russian ballet dancer who has been called a second Nijinsky. He starred with the Kirov Ballet before defecting to the West in 1961 while on a trip to London. Since then Nureyev has been the principal dancer and choreographer for the Royal Ballet.

**Jacques Offenbach** (1819–80), French composer of over 100 operettas. His masterpiece is the opera *Tales of Hoffmann* (1877–80), which was not produced until after his death.

**David Oistrakh** (1908–74), Russian violinist hailed as one of the greatest 20th century musicians.

**Carl Orff** (1895– ), German composer: best known for cantata *Carmina Burana* (1936).

**Eugene Ormandy** (1899– ), Hungarian-American conductor who came to the U.S. in 1920. He led the Minneapolis Symphony (1931–35) and the Philadelphia Orchestra (1938–79).

**Ignace Jan Paderewski** (1860–1941), Polish pianist and composer who enjoyed tremendous international popularity as a performer. His best-known composition is the *Minuet in G* for piano (1899).

**Niccolò Paganini** (1782–1840), Italian violinist considered the world's greatest violin virtuoso. He charmed audiences throughout Europe.

**Giovanni Palestrina** (1524–94), Italian composer of polyphonic sacred motets and masses and of secular madrigals. His works rank among the most important of the Italian Renaissance.

**Luciano Pavarotti**, (1935– ), Italian tenor: Made operatic debut in Reggio Emilia, Italy, in 1961; debuted with the New York Metropolitan Opera on Nov. 23, 1968.

**Anna Pavlova** (1881–1931), Russian ballerina who won international recognition for her magnificent performances in Europe and America.

**Jan Peerce** (1904– ), American tenor who sang on radio and at the Radio City Music Hall (1932–37) before joining the Metropolitan Opera in 1941.

**Roberta Peters** (1930– ), American operatic soprano: debuted with Metropolitan Opera in 1950; recorded operas; appeared in several motion pictures.

**Gregor Piatigorsky** (1903–76), Russian-born concert cellist, made his American debut in 1929. He became a U.S. citizen in 1942.

**Ezio Pinza** (1892–1957), Italian basso who sang at

**MUSICIANS** (continued)

the Metropolitan Opera (1926–48). In 1949 he was featured in the Broadway musical *South Pacific*.

**Walter Piston** (1894–1976), American composer who was awarded two Pulitzer Prizes in music for his Third (1948) and Seventh (1961) symphonies.

**Ildebrando Pizzetti** (1880–1968), Italian composer whose operas *Fedra* (1909–12) and *Debora e Jaele* (1915–21) are his most popular works.

**Lily Pons** (1904–76), French soprano who sang at the Metropolitan Opera from 1931 to 1959.

**Rosa Ponselle** (1897– ), American soprano who gave outstanding performances at the Metropolitan Opera (1918–37) and in London (1929–31).

**Cole Porter** (1893–1964), American composer of musical comedies, including *Kiss Me, Kate* (1948) and *Silk Stockings* (1955), and the songs *Night and Day* and *Begin the Beguine*.

**Francis Poulenc** (1899–1963), French composer whose works include *Concert Champêtre* (1927–28) and the Mass in G (1937).

**Leontyne Price** (1927– ), American soprano who has sung on Broadway and in major opera houses. She made her debut with the Metropolitan Opera in 1961.

**William Primrose** (1903– ), Scottish violist regarded as one of the world's finest.

**Sergei Prokofiev** (1891–1953), Russian composer and piano virtuoso. His distinctive works include the First (1916–17) and Fifth (1944) symphonies, *Peter and the Wolf* (1936), and the ballet *Romeo and Juliette* (1935–36).

**Giacomo Puccini** (1858–1924), Italian composer of the universally popular operas *La Bohème* (1896), *Tosca* (1900), and *Madame Butterfly* (1904).

**Henry Purcell** (1659–95), English composer believed by some authorities to be England's greatest. His works include the opera *Dido and Aeneas* (1689) and religious music.

**Sergei Rachmaninov** (1873–1943), Russian composer and pianist. Among his best works are the Second Piano Concerto (1901), the Second Symphony (1907), and Rhapsody on a Theme of Paganini (1934).

**Maurice Ravel** (1875–1937), French composer whose works include the ballet *Daphnis et Chloé* (1909–11) and *Rhapsodie Espagnole* (1907) and *Bolero* (1928) for orchestra.

**Fritz Reiner** (1888–1963), Hungarian conductor who directed the Cincinnati Orchestra (1922–31), the Pittsburgh Orchestra (1938–48), and the Chicago Orchestra (1953–62).

**Ottorino Respighi** (1879–1936), Italian composer known for his symphonic poems *The Fountains of Rome* (1917) and *The Pines of Rome* (1924).

**Sviatoslav Richter** (1914– ), Russian pianist acclaimed as a distinguished virtuoso.

**Wallingford Riegger** (1885–1961), American composer of highly original works, including four symphonies and Music for Brass Choir (1948–49).

**Nicholas Rimsky-Korsakov** (1844–1908), Russian nationalist composer of the *Spanish Capriccio* (1887), *Scheherazade* (1888), and *Easter Overture* (1888).

**Jerome Robbins** (1918– ), American dancer and choreographer who joined the Ballet Theater in New York (1940–44) and in 1959 became associate musical director of the New York City Ballet.

**Paul Robeson** (1898–1976), American black concert singer and actor, noted for his singing in *Showboat* (1936) and as the Moor in *Othello*.

**Richard Rodgers** (1902–79), American composer of musicals. Teamed with librettist Oscar Hammerstein II on many, including *Oklahoma!* (1943), *South Pacific* (1949), *The King and I* (1951), and *The Sound of Music* (1959).

**Sigmund Romberg** (1887–1951), American composer of operettas and musicals, including *The Student*

*Prince* (1924) and *The Desert Song* (1926).

**Gioacchino Rossini** (1792–1868), Italian composer best known for his operas *The Barber of Seville* (1816) and *William Tell* (1829).

**Anton Rubenstein** (1829–94), Russian pianist and composer whose renowned mastery of the keyboard ranked second only to that of Liszt.

**Arthur Rubinstein** (1886– ), Polish-American pianist considered one of the greatest contemporary artists.

**Ruth St. Denis** (1877–1968), American dancer, choreographer, and pioneer in the development of modern dance in the U.S.

**Charles Camille Saint-Saëns** (1835–1921), French composer of the opera *Samson et Dalila* (1868–75), three symphonies, and five piano concertos.

**Alessandro Scarlatti** (1660–1725), Italian composer of 115 operas.

**Domenico Scarlatti** (1685–1757), Italian composer and harpsichordist; son of A. Scarlatti. His roughly 500 sonatas are among the first important keyboard works written in this form.

**Alexander Schneider** (1908– ), Russian-American violinist and conductor. A member of the Budapest String Quartet (1938–68), he is also a major participant in the Casals summer music festivals.

**Arnold Schoenberg** (1874–1951), Austrian composer and creator of the 12-tone (atonal) method. His works include *Verklärte Nacht* (1899), the Variations for Orchestra (1928), and an unfinished opera, *Moses und Aron* (1932–51).

**Franz Schubert** (1797–1828), Austrian composer of over 600 songs; nine symphonies, of which the "Unfinished" (1822) is best known; and the "Trout" Quintet in A Major (1819).

**William Schuman** (1910– ), American composer; president of Lincoln Center in New York (1962–68). His works include the *American Festival Overture* (1939).

**Robert Schumann** (1810–56), German romantic composer of the Piano Concerto in A Minor (1841–45) and the Spring (1841) and Rhenish (1850) symphonies.

**Ernestine Schumann-Heink** (1861–1936), Austrian-American contralto. She appeared at the Chicago Opera (1898), the Metropolitan Opera (1899–1904), and in many concerts.

**Antonio Scotti** (1866–1936), Italian baritone who enjoyed great popularity as a member of the Metropolitan Opera (1899–1933).

**Aleksandr Scriabin** (1872–1915), Russian pianist whose notable works include *Divine Poem* (1903) and *Prometheus: A Poem of Fire* (1909–10).

**Andrés Segovia** (1893– ), Spanish guitarist noted for his interpretation of classical works.

**Marcella Sembrich** (1858–1935), Polish soprano who sang in the great European opera houses and with the Metropolitan Opera (1898–1909).

**Peter Serkin** (1947– ), American pianist and son of Rudolf Serkin. He is among the most accomplished of the younger keyboard artists.

**Rudolf Serkin** (1903– ), Austrian-American pianist who ranks among the best contemporary artists. He has toured widely and since 1951 has directed the Marlboro (Vt.) School of Music.

**Roger Sessions** (1896– ), American composer: Orchestral Suite from *The Black Maskers* (1928) and four symphonies (1927, 1946, 1957, 1958).

**Ted Shawn** (1891–1972), American dancer, choreographer, and teacher. With Ruth St. Denis he founded the influential Denishawn School for Modern Dance.

**Dimitri Shostakovich** (1906–75), Russian composer who won international acclaim with such symphonies as the Fifth (1937) and Ninth (1945).

**Jean Sibelius** (1865–1957), Finnish composer of stirring nationalist music and seven symphonies.

**Cesare Siepi** (1923– ), Italian bass and a member of the New York Metropolitan Opera since 1950.

**Beverly Sills** (1929– ), American soprano, made her debut with the New York City Opera in 1955 and with the Metropolitan Opera in 1975; appointed director of New York City Opera in 1978.

**Bedřich Smetana** (1824–84), Czech nationalist composer whose well-known works include the opera *The Bartered Bride* (1866) and the symphonic poem *My Country* (1874–79).

**Michael Somes** (1917– ), English ballet dancer who began his career with the Sadler's Wells Ballet Company in 1935 and was a leading dancer with the Royal Ballet in London.

**John Philip Sousa** (1854–1932), American band-master and composer of over 100 marches including *The Stars and Stripes Forever* (1897).

**Eleanor Steber** (1916– ), American soprano who sang with the Metropolitan Opera from 1940.

**William Steinberg** (1899–1978), German-American conductor of the Pittsburgh Symphony (1952–75) and Boston Symphony (1969–71) orchestras.

**Issac Stern** (1920– ), American violinist who has given outstanding performances throughout the world.

**Risë Stevens** (1913– ), American mezzo-soprano who sang throughout the world and with the Metropolitan Opera from the 1930s through the 1950s.

**Karlheinz Stockhausen** (1928– ), German composer whose avant-garde works include *Kontrapunkte* (1952) and *Koutackte* (1960) for electronic sounds, percussion, and piano.

**Leopold Stokowski** (1882–1977), American conductor who led the Cincinnati Symphony (1909–12), the Philadelphia Orchestra (1912–36), and the New York Philharmonic (1945–50). In 1962 he founded the American Symphony in New York.

**Johann Strauss Jr.** (1825–99), Austrian conductor and composer of more than 400 waltzes, including *The Blue Danube* (1866) and *Tales from the Vienna Woods* (1868).

**Richard Strauss** (1864–1949), German composer whose major works are the symphonic poems *Don Juan* (1888) and *Till Eulenspiegel* (1894–95) and the opera *Der Rosenkavalier* (1911).

**Igor Stravinsky** (1882–1971), Russian-French composer considered the father of modern music. Among his most important works are the ballets *The Firebird* (1910) and *The Rite of Spring (1913).*

**Sir Arthur Sullivan** (1842–1900), English composer (with W. S. Gilbert) of operettas, including *H.M.S. Pinafore* (1878) and *The Mikado* (1885).

**Joan Sutherland** (1926– ), Australian soprano. In 1961 she made a spectacular debut at the Metropolitan Opera.

**George Szell** (1897–1970), Hungarian conductor who led the Berlin State Opera (1924–30), the Metropolitan Opera (1942–45), and the Cleveland Orchestra (1946–70).

**Maria Tallchief** (1925– ), American ballerina who danced with the Ballet Russe de Monte Carlo (1942–47) and was the prima ballerina at the New York City Ballet (1954–55) and at the American Ballet Theatre (1960).

**Deems Taylor** (1885–1966), American composer: *Through the Looking Glass* (1922) for orchestra, and the opera *The King's Henchmen* (1927).

**Paul Taylor** (1930– ), American dancer and choreographer who performed with the Martha Graham Company (1955–61) and the New York City Ballet (1959–61).

**Peter Ilich Tchaikovsky** (1840–93), Russian composer. His works include six symphonies, the *Romeo and Juliet Overture* (1870), the Piano Concerto in B Flat Minor (1875), the ballet *Swan Lake* (1876), and a concerto for violin and orchestra.

**Renata Tebaldi** (1922– ), Italian soprano who has performed in Milan (1949–54, 1959), London (1950), San Francisco (1950), and at the Metropolitan Opera (since 1955).

**Twyla Tharp** (1941– ), American choreographer who uses popular and jazz music to blend ballet with modern dance.

**Virgil Thomson** (1896– ), American composer of the opera *Four Saints in Three Acts* (1928).

**Lawrence Tibbett** (1896–1960), American baritone who starred at the Metropolitan Opera (1923–50) and in several films.

**Arturo Toscanini** (1867–1957), Italian conductor renowned for his artistry. He led the orchestras at the La Scala Opera (1898–1903) and Metropolitan Opera (1908–15), and the New York Philharmonic (1927–36) and NBC Symphony (1937–54).

**Helen Traubel** (1899–1972), American soprano who excelled in Wagnerian roles at the Metropolitan Opera (1939–53) and sang with leading orchestras.

**Richard Tucker** (1914–75), American tenor who starred with the Metropolitan Opera (1945–75).

**Antony Tudor** (1909– ), English dancer and choreographer who worked with the Rambert Ballet (1930–38), Sadler's Wells Ballet (1931–36), and American Ballet Theater (1939–56). He became ballet director of the Metropolitan Opera in 1957.

**Galina Ulanova** (1910– ), Russian ballerina considered one of the greatest dancers since Anna Pavlova. She appeared with the Bolshoi Theatre from 1935, becoming prima ballerina in 1944.

**Ralph Vaughan Williams** (1872–1958), English composer: *Three Norfolk Rhapsodies* (1905–07) and the opera *Hugh the Drover* (1911–14).

**Giuseppe Verdi** (1813–1901), Italian composer of such well-known operas as *Rigoletto* (1851), *La Traviata* (1853), *Don Carlos* (1867), *Aïda* (1871), *Otello* (1886), and *Falstaff* (1893).

**Heitor Villa-Lobos** (1887–1959), Brazilian composer: *Amazonas* (1917), the *Bachiana brasiliera* (1930), and the Chorós No. 11 (1941).

**Antonio Vivaldi** (1675–1741), Italian composer of over 40 operas who is best known for his violin concertos *The Seasons* and the *Tempesta di Mare.*

**Richard Wagner** (1813–83), German romantic opera composer: *Tannhäuser* (1843–45), *Lohengrin* (1846–48), and *Die Meistersinger* (1862–67).

**Bruno Walter** (1876–1962), German conductor who directed the New York Philharmonic (1923–33, 1947–49).

**Sir William Walton** (1902– ), British composer whose works include the oratorio *Belshazzar's Feast* (1931) and the opera *Troilus and Cressida* (1954).

**Leonard Warren** (1911–60), American baritone who won acclaim at the Metropolitan Opera (1939–60), where he died onstage.

**André Watts** (1943– ), American pianist who made his debut at the age of nine and has played with numerous major orchestras.

**Carl Maria von Weber** (1786–1826), German composer who began the Romantic movement in German opera. Among his operas are *Der Freischütz* (1821) and *Oberon* (1826).

**Anton von Webern** (1883–1945), Austrian composer and pupil of Arnold Schoenberg. A leading atonal composer, he is best known for *Five Pieces for Orchestra* (1911–13) and *Variations* (1940).

**Charles Weidman** (1901–75), American dancer, choreographer, and director who helped develop modern dance; founded own company in 1941.

**Kurt Weill** (1900–50), German composer for the stage: *The Threepenny Opera* (1928), *One Touch of Venus* (1943), and *Street Scene* (1947).

**Hugo Wolf** (1860–1903), Austrian composer known for more than 250 songs composed by setting the poems of others to music.

**Igor Youskevitch** (1912– ), Russian ballet dancer with the Ballet Russe de Monte Carlo (1938) and the Ballet Theater in New York (1946–56).

# FAMOUS PAINTERS, SCULPTORS, AND ARCHITECTS

Famous artists, sculptors, architects, and painters are included in the following list. Where it was thought helpful to the reader, the artist is described according to the movement or school to which he belonged. In most cases one or more works typical of each artist's output are mentioned. See pages 981–986 for 1980 deaths.

A glossary describing the artistic movements and schools mentioned in connection with many of the artists can be found on page 68.

**Leone Battista Alberti** (1404–72), Florentine architect and a pioneer in Renaissance church design: the Church of Sant'Andrea (1470) in Mantua.

**Andrea del Sarto** (1486–1531), Florentine painter of religious frescoes: *The Birth of the Virgin* (1514).

**Fra Angelico** (c.1400–55), Florentine painter of religious subjects: *Annunciation* (c.1440–50).

**Alexander Archipenko** (1887–1964), Ukrainian-American abstract sculptor: *Boxers* (1935).

**Jean Arp** (1887–1966), French surrealist and Dadaist painter and sculptor: *Constellation According to the Laws of Chance* (1932), wood relief.

**John James Audubon** (1785?–1851), American ornithologist and artist noted for his finely detailed illustrations of American wildlife: *The Birds of America* (1827–38).

**Francis Bacon** (1910– ), English surrealist painter: *Study After Velázquez's Portrait of Pope Innocent X* (1953).

**James Barry** (1741–1806), Anglo-Irish painter: *The Progress of Human Culture* (1777–83).

**Fra Bartolommeo** (1475–1517), Italian painter of the High Renaissance: *Marriage of St. Catherine*.

**Aubrey Vincent Beardsley** (1872–98), English illustrator in black and white: *Isolde* (c.1890).

**Max Beckmann** (1884–1950), German expressionist painter: *Self-portrait with a Saxophone* (1930).

**Giovanni Bellini** (c.1430–1516), Venetian religious painter: *St. Francis in Ecstasy* (c.1485).

**George Wesley Bellows** (1882–1925), American realistic painter: *Stag at Sharkey's* (1907), *Up the Hudson* (1908).

**Thomas Hart Benton** (1889–1975), American regional painter: *Lonesome Road, Cotton Pickers.*

**Giovanni Lorenzo Bernini** (1598–1680), Italian baroque sculptor: *David* (1623), *Ecstasy of St. Teresa* (1645–52).

**George Caleb Bingham** (1811–79), American regional painter: *The County Election* (c.1851).

**Umberto Boccioni** (1882–1916), Italian futurist painter and sculptor: *The City Rises* (1910).

**Giovanni da Bologna** (1524–1608), French-born mannerist sculptor who worked in Florence: *The Rape of the Sabines* (1583).

**Pierre Bonnard** (1867–1947) French postimpressionist painter: *Man and Woman* (1900), *Nude Washing* (c.1922).

**Francesco Borromini** (1599–1677), Italian baroque architect: San Carlo alle Quattro Fontane, in Rome (begun in 1638).

**Hieronymus Bosch** or **Jerome Bos** (c.1450–1516), Flemish painter of bizarre fantasies: *The Garden of Delights* (1500).

**Sandro Botticelli** (Alessandro di Mariano dei Filipepi, c.1444–1510), Florentine religious and allegorical painter: *Primavera* (1477–78), *The Birth of Venus* (c.1480).

**Edmé Bouchardon** (1698–1762), French sculptor of religious subjects and portrait busts: *Christ Leaning on His Cross* (1745).

**François Boucher** (1703–70), French rococo painter: *The Triumph of Venus* (1740).

**Constantin Brancusi** (1876–1957), Romanian abstract sculptor: *The Kiss* (1908), *Bird in Space* (1919).

**Georges Braque** (1882–1963), French cubist painter: *Still Life, "Melody"* (1914), *The Bike* (1952).

**Il Bronzino** (Agnolo di Cosimo di Mariano, 1503–72), Florentine mannerist painter: *Eleanor de Toledo and Her Son* (c.1550).

**Pieter Bruegel the Elder** (c.1525–69), Flemish landscape painter: *The Return of the Hunters* (1565), *Peasant Wedding* (1565).

**Filippo Brunelleschi** (1377–1446), Florentine architect who produced the first important early Renaissance architecture: dome for the cathedral in Florence (1420–36).

**Bernard Buffet** (1928– ), French painter whose work derives from several modern schools: *Landscape in Provence* (1957).

**Charles Burchfield** (1893–1967), American painter of landscapes and urban scenes, especially in watercolor: *Ice Glare* (1933).

**Edward Coley Burne-Jones** (1833–98), English Pre-Raphaelite painter: *Love Among the Ruins* (1894).

**Alexander Calder** (1898–1976), American abstract sculptor who introduced the mobile and the stabile forms: *Lobster Trap and Fish Tail* (1939).

**Antonio Canova** (1757–1822), Venetian neoclassic sculptor: *Pauline Bonaparte Borghese* (1808).

**Michelangelo Merisi da Caravaggio** (1573–1610), Italian baroque painter: *Calling of St. Matthew* (1598–99).

**Jean Baptiste Carpeaux** (1827–75), French romantic sculptor: *The Dance* (in Paris Opéra, 1865–69).

**Mary Cassatt** (1845–1926), American impressionist painter: *Mother and Child at a Boating Party.*

**Andrea del Castagno** (c.1423–57), Florentine religious painter: *Last Supper* (1445–50).

**Benvenuto Cellini** (1500–71), Italian mannerist sculptor: *Perseus with the Head of Medusa* (c.1545).

**Paul Cézanne** (1839–1906), French painter who began the postimpressionist movement: *Fruit Bowl, Glass and Apples* (1879–82), *Mont Sainte-Victoire Seen from Bibemus Quarry* (1898–1900).

**Marc Chagall** (1889– ), Russian expressionist painter: *I and the Village* (1911), *The Grey House* (1917).

**Jean Baptiste Chardin** (1699–1779), French genre painter: *Return from Market* (1739).

**Giorgio de Chirico** (1888–1978), Italian surrealist painter: *The Anguish of Departure* (1913–14).

**Frederick Edwin Church** (1826–1900), American landscape painter: *Niagara Falls* (1857), *The Heart of the Andes* (1859); his *Icebergs* (1861) was sold in 1979 for record price of $2.5 million.

**Giovanni Cimabue** (Cenni di Pepo, c.1240–1302), Florentine painter of religious frescoes: *Madonna of St. Francis*, in the church at Assisi.

**Claude Lorrain** (1600–82), French landscape painter: *View of the Campagna* (c.1650).

**Clodion** (Claude Michel, 1738–1814), French rococo sculptor: *Bacchante and a Satyr, Montesquieu* (1779–83).

**Thomas Cole** (1801–48), American landscape painter and member of the Hudson River School: *The Oxbow of the Connecticut* (1836).

**John Constable** (1776–1837), English landscape painter: *Hampstead Heath* (1821).

**John Singleton Copley** (1738–1815), American painter of portraits (*Mrs. Thomas Boylston, 1766*) and romanticized historic works (*Watson and the Shark, 1778*).

**Jean Baptiste Camille Corot** (1796–1875), French romantic landscape painter: *The Bridge at Narni (1826), Homer and the Shepherds* (1845).

**Correggio** (Antonio Allegri, 1494–1534), Italian mannerist painter: *Assumption of the Virgin* (c.1525), *Jupiter and Io* (c.1532).

**Gustave Courbet** (1819–77), French realist painter: *The Stone Breakers* (1849), *Painter's Studio* (1855).

**Lucas I. Cranach** (1472–1553), German painter, etcher, and woodcut designer: Made portraits of notable contemporaries, including Martin Luther.

**John Steuart Curry** (1897–1946), American artist who painted scenes of Midwestern life: *Baptism in Kansas* (1928), *Tornado over Kansas* (1929).

**Salvador Dali** (1904– ), Spanish surrealist painter: *Persistence of Memory* (1931).

**Honoré Daumier** (1808–79), French painter, sculptor, and caricaturist of the realist school: *The Third-Class Carriage* (1862), *Don Quixote Attacking the Windmills* (1866).

**Jacques Louis David** (1748–1825), French neoclassic painter: *The Death of Marat* (1793), *The Rape of the Sabines* (1799).

**Leonardo da Vinci** (1452–1519), Italian painter, architect, and sculptor: Was influential leader of Renaissance art. Paintings include *Last Supper* (c.1495–97) and *Mona Lisa* (c.1503–05). He was also an innovator and inventor in the physical sciences and engineering.

**Stuart Davis** (1894–1964), U.S. semiabstract painter: *The Barber Shop* (1930), *Visa* (1951).

**Edgar Degas** (1834–1917), French impressionist painter: *Prima Ballerina* (1876), *Absinthe Drinkers* (1876), *Ballet Class* (c.1878).

**Willem de Kooning** (1904– ), Dutch-American abstract expressionist painter: *Woman I* (1950–52).

**Ferdinand Victor Eugène Delacroix** (1798–1863), French romantic painter: *Massacre of Scio* (1822–24), *Frédéric Chopin* (1838).

**André Derain** (1880–1954), French fauvist painter: *Seascape* and *Collioure* (both c.1905).

**Donatello** (Donato di Niccolò di Betto Bardi, c.1386–1466), Florentine sculptor of the Renaissance: statues include *St. Mark* (1411–13); panels include *St. George and the Dragon* (1415–17).

**Jean Dubuffet** (1901– ), French surrealist painter: *Landscape with Two Personages* (1952).

**Marcel Duchamp** (1887–1968), French cubist and Dadaist painter: *Nude Descending a Staircase* (1913).

**Raoul Dufy** (1877–1953), French painter influenced by the impressionists and fauvists: *Casino at Nice* (1927), *Deauville, Drying the Sails* (1933).

**Albrecht Dürer** (1471–1528), German Renaissance painter and engraver: *The Four Horsemen of the Apocalypse* (1497–98).

**Thomas Eakins** (1844–1916), American realist painter: *The Gross Clinic* (1875).

**Charles Eames** (1907-78), U.S. architect and designer: Responsible for first mass-produced molded plastic chair used in many public waiting rooms; his luxury lounge chairs regarded as ultimate in comfort.

**Sir Jacob Epstein** (1880–1959), American sculptor: the Oscar Wilde Memorial (1911), *Adam, Jacob and the Angel* (1939).

**Max Ernst** (1891–1976), German-American surrealist painter: *Two Children Are Threatened by a Nightingale* (1924), *Euclid* (1945).

**Lyonel Feininger** (1871–1956), American cubist painter: *Church in the Market Place* (1929).

**Jean Honoré Fragonard** (1732–1806), French rococo painter: *The Swing* (c.1765); *The Progress of Love* (c.1771), a series of painted panels.

**Thomas Gainsborough** (1727–88), English landscape and portrait painter: *Robert Andrews and His Wife* (c.1748–50), *The Mall* (1783).

**Paul Gauguin** (1848–1903), French postimpressionist painter: *The Yellow Christ* (1890).

**Jean Louis André Théodore Géricault** (1791–1824), French romantic painter: *Mounted Officer of the Imperial Guard* (1812), *Raft of the Medusa* (1818–19).

**Lorenzo Ghiberti** (c.1378–1455), Florentine sculptor of religious subjects: *The Sacrifice of Isaac*, (1401–02), a set of bronze doors for the Baptistery in Florence.

**Domenico Ghirlandaio** (1449–94), Florentine painter of religious subjects: *Saint Jerome* (1480).

**Alberto Giacometti** (1901–66), Swiss sculptor, mainly of the surrealist school: *The Palace at 4 A.M.* (1932–33), *Man Pointing* (1947).

**Giorgione** (c.1478–1510), Venetian painter who influenced art in Venice: *The Tempest*.

**Giotto** (di Bondone, c.1266–1337), Florentine artist generally considered one of the founders of modern, naturalist painting: religious frescoes in the Arena Chapel in Padua (1305–06).

**William James Glackens** (1870–1938), American realist painter: *Chez Mouquin* (1905).

**Arshile Gorky** (1904–48), American abstract expressionist painter: *Agony* (1947).

**Francisco José de Goya y Lucientes** (1746–1828), Spanish painter, etcher, and lithographer whose work covers a wide range, from official portraits to satire: *The Family of Charles IV* (1800), *The Third of May, 1808* (1814–15).

**El Greco** (Domenikos Theotokopoulos, c.1541–1614), Greek mannerist painter who spent most of his career in Spain: *Burial of the Count of Orgaz* (1586), *View of Toledo*.

**Juan Gris** (1887–1927), Spanish cubist painter: *Still Life Before an Open Window* (1915).

**George Grosz** (1893–1959), German-American expressionist painter: *Germany, A Winter's Tale* (1918).

**Mathias Grünewald** (c.1480–1528), German Gothic painter: *Isenheim Altarpiece* (c.1510–15).

**Francesco Guardi** (1712–93), Venetian landscape painter, especially scenes of the city: *Venice, Piazza San Marco* (1765).

**Frans Hals** (c.1580–1666), Dutch portrait and genre painter: *The Jolly Toper* (1627), *Malle Bobbe* (c.1650).

**William M. Hartnett** (1848–92), American still-life painter: *The Social Club* (1879).

**Meindert Hobbema** (1638–1709), Dutch landscape painter: *Avenue at Middelharnis* (1689).

**Hans Hofmann** (1880–1966), German-American abstract expressionist painter: *Elegy* (1950).

**William Hogarth** (1697–1764), English painter and engraver who did satiric studies of English society: *The Rake's Progress* (c.1735).

**Katsushika Hokusai** (1760–1849), Japanese painter whose work influenced Western landscape art: *Views of Famous Bridges* (1823–35), *Hundred Views of Mount Fuji* (1835).

**Hans Holbein the Younger** (c.1497–1543), German portrait painter: *Erasmus of Rotterdam* (c.1523), *Sir Thomas More* (1527), *Henry VIII* (1540).

**Winslow Homer** (1836–1910), American romantic painter, especially of seascapes: *The Gulfstream* (1889), *Breaking Storm* and *Maine Coast* (1894).

**Pieter de Hooch** (c.1629–84), Dutch genre painter: *Delft After the Explosion* (1654).

**Edward Hopper** (1882–1967), American regional painter and engraver: *Early Sunday Morning* (1930), *Night Hawks* (1942).

**Jean Antoine Houdon** (1741–1828), French neoclassic sculptor: *Morpheus* (1777), *Girl Shivering* (1783).

**Jean Auguste Dominique Ingres** (1780–1867), French neoclassic painter: *Vow of Louis XIII* (1824).

**George Inness** (1825–94), American landscape painter: *Delaware Valley* (1865), *Niagara* (1889).

**Augustus John** (1878–1961), English landscape and portrait painter: *The Marchesa Casati* (1919), *An Irish Bay* (1911–14).

**PAINTERS, SCULPTORS, AND ARCHITECTS** *(continued)*

**Jasper Johns** (1930– ), American pop artist: *Map* (1962).

**Philip Cortelyou Johnson** (1906– ), American architect who helped plan the Seagram Building and Lincoln Center, both in New York City.

**Inigo Jones** (1573–1652), English architect deeply influenced by Italian Renaissance styles: the banquet hall at Whitehall Palace (1619–22).

**Vasili Kandinsky** (1866–1944), Russian painter who originated modern abstract painting, or tachisme: *Black Patch* (1921), *Movement I* (1935).

**Rockwell Kent** (1882–1971), American illustrator and painter: illustrated *Moby Dick, Beowulf,* and *The Canterbury Tales.*

**Paul Klee** (1879–1940), Swiss painter of fantastic, often humorous subjects: *The Twittering Machine* (1922), *Park Near Lucerne* (1938).

**Franz Kline** (1910–62), American abstract expressionist painter, best known for an extensive series of paintings which he numbered rather than giving them titles.

**Oskar Kokoschka** (1886–1980), Austrian expressionist painter: *Hans Tietze and His Wife* (1909).

**Le Corbusier** (Charles Édouard Jeanneret, 1887–1965), Franco-Swiss architect who was a major influence on modern architecture: Savoye House, Poissy, France (1929–31), Secretariat Building, Chandigarh, India (1952–56).

**Doris Emrick Lee** (1905– ), American painter: *Thanksgiving* (1935).

**Fernand Léger** (1881–1955), French cubist painter: *The City* (1919), *Women in an Interior* (1922).

**Emanuel Gottlieb Leutze** (1816–68), German-American historical painter: *Washington Crossing the Delaware* (1851).

**Roy Lichtenstein** (1923– ), American pop artist: *Step-on Can with Leg,* a diptych (1961).

**Jacques Lipchitz** (1891–1973), French-Lithuanian sculptor whose works bear cubist influences: *Man with a Guitar* (1915).

**Fra Filippo Lippi** (c.1406–69), Italian painter of religious subjects: *Madonna with Saints* (c.1432).

**Richard Lippold** (1915– ), American abstract sculptor, best known for his elaborate wire constructions: *The Sun* (1953–56).

**Aristide Maillol** (1861–1944), French sculptor of the female nude: *Seated Woman* (c.1901).

**Édouard Manet** (1832–83), French painter usually associated with the impressionist movement: *Luncheon on the Grass* (1863), *The Fife Player* (1866).

**John Marin** (1870–1953), American expressionist painter best known for watercolors: *Maine Islands* (1922), *Gray Sea* (1924).

**Masaccio** (Tommaso Guidi, c.1401–28), Florentine painter of frescoes in Italian churches: *Madonna and Child* (1426).

**Henri Matisse** (1869–1954), French painter and leader of the fauvist movement: *The Joy of Life* (1905–06), *Harmony in Red* (1908–09).

**Michelangelo Buonarroti** (1475–1564), Italian painter, sculptor, and architect who was a leading figure in Renaissance art. His most famous paintings include the frescoes in the Sistine Chapel. Among his many statues are those of *David* (1501–04) and *Moses* (c.1513–15). He is generally considered the greatest sculptor and draftsman.

**Ludwig Mies van der Rohe** (1886–1969), German-American architect: Lake Shore apartments, Chicago (1950–52), Seagram Building, New York (with Philip Johnson, 1955–57).

**John Millais** (1829–96), English portrait and genre painter and, for a while, a key member of the Pre-Raphaelites: *The Carpenter's Shop* (1850).

**Jean François Millet** (1814–75), French romantic painter: *The Sower* (c.1850), *Angelus* (1859).

**Joan Miró** (1893– ), Spanish surrealist painter: *Carnival of Harlequin* (1924–25).

**Amedeo Modigliani** (1884–1920), Italian painter who lived in France, and whose work combines influences from various schools: *Boy in a Blue Jacket* (1918), *Reclining Nude* (c.1919).

**Piet Mondrian** (1872–1944), Dutch abstract expressionist painter whose canvases are painted in simple horizontal and vertical stripes: *Composition with Red, Blue, and Yellow* (1930).

**Claude Monet** (1840–1926), French painter who was among the leaders of the impressionists: *Sailboat at Argenteuil* (1875).

**Henry Moore** (1898– ), English abstract sculptor: *Recumbent Figure* (1938), *Locking Piece* (1963–65).

**Grandma Moses** (Anna Mary Robertson Moses, 1860–1961), American primitive painter of rural and domestic scenes: *Hurrah for Christmas* (1939).

**Robert Motherwell** (1915– ), American abstract expressionist painter: *Elegy for the Spanish Republic* (1953–54).

**Edvard Munch** (1863–1944), Norwegian expressionist painter: *The Scream* (1893), *Dance of Life* (1900).

**Bartolomé Esteban Murillo** (1617?–82), Spanish portrait and religious painter: *Birth of the Virgin* (c.1655), *Marriage of St. Catherine* (1682).

**Louise Nevelson** (1900– ), American sculptor in wood whose work shows cubist and surrealist influences: *Sky Cathedral* (1958).

**Georgia O'Keeffe** (1887– ), American regional painter of the Southwest: *Black Cross, New Mexico* (1929).

**Claes Oldenburg** (1929– ), American pop artist whose sculpture consists of rearranged junk and huge realistic objects, such as a giant lipstick, *Feasible Monument* (1969).

**José Clemente Orozco** (1883–1949), Mexican social-realist mural painter: *An Epic of American Civilization* (1934), at Dartmouth College.

**Charles Willson Peale** (1741–1827), American portrait painter: *George Washington* (1780).

**I.M. (Ieoh Ming) Pei** (1917– ), Chinese-born architect: John Hancock Tower, Boston; National Gallery of Art East Building, Washington, D.C.; John F. Kennedy Library, Boston.

**Claude Perrault** (1613–88), French architect who designed much of the Louvre.

**Perugino** (Pietro Vannucci, c.1445–1523), Italian painter of religious subjects, and the teacher of Raphael: *Crucifixion with Saints* (1496).

**Phidias of Athens** (c.500–432 B.C.), Greek sculptor: *Athena* (c.447–439 B.C.) in the Parthenon, a building whose construction he may have supervised.

**Pablo Picasso** (1881–1973), Spanish painter and sculptor who helped found cubism and who produced major works in styles ranging from neoclassicism to surrealism. Paintings include *Woman in White* (1923), *The Three Dancers* (1925), *Guernica* (1937). Sculptures include *Woman's Head* (1909).

**Piero della Francesca** (c.1420–92), Italian painter of religious subjects: *The Flagellation of Christ* (c.1441–51), *The Story of the True Cross* (c.1452).

**Camille Pissarro** (1830–1903), French impressionist painter: *Le Fond de l'Hermitage* (1879), *The Boulevard Montmartre* (1897).

**Jackson Pollock** (1912–56), American abstract expressionist painter noted for his "action paintings": *Convergence* (1952).

**Polycletus of Argos** (400s B.C.), Greek sculptor whose *Doryphorus* or *Spear-Bearer* (c.450–440 B.C.) was held to represent ideal human proportions.

**Nicolas Poussin** (1594–1665), French painter noted for his heroic classic style: *The Rape of the Sabine Women* (c.1636–37).

**Praxiteles** (300s B.C.), Greek sculptor: *Hermes* (c.330–320 B.C.), *Aphrodite of Cnidus* (c.330 B.C.).

**Maurice Prendergast** (1859–1924), American impressionist painter: *Ponte della Paglia* (1899).

**Pierre Proudhon** (1758–1823), French romantic painter: *Empress Josephine* (1805).

**Sir Henry Raeburn** (1756–1823), Scottish portrait painter: *The Macnab* (c.1803), *Lord Newton* (c.1806).

**Raphael Santi** or **Sanzio** (1483–1520), Italian painter and one of the greatest masters of Renaissance art: numerous *Madonnas; The School of Athens* (1509–12), a fresco in the Vatican Palace.

**Robert Rauschenberg** (1925–    ), American pop artist: *Reservoir* (1961).

**Odilon Redon** (1840–1916), French symbolist painter and lithographer: *Cyclops* (1895–1900).

**Rembrandt Harmenszoom van Rijn** (1606–69), Dutch painter and greatest of the northern European Renaissance artists: *The Supper in Emmaus* (1648), *Aristotle Contemplating the Bust of Homer* (1653), *The Polish Rider* (1655), numerous *Self-Portraits*.

**Frederic Remington** (1861–1909), American painter and sculptor of cowboys and Indians: *The Bronco Buster* (1895), *The Cheyenne* (1901).

**Pierre Auguste Renoir** (1841–1919), French impressionist painter: *Moulin de la Galette* (1876), *Luncheon of the Boating Party* (1880–81).

**Sir Joshua Reynolds** (1723–92), English portrait painter: *Garrick Between Comedy and Tragedy* (1760–61), *Dr. Beattie (The Triumph of Truth)*. He was also a writer of considerable repute.

**Diego Rivera** (1886–1957), Mexican muralist and fresco painter whose works are in such places as the National Palace, Mexico City, and the Stock Exchange, San Francisco.

**Luca della Robbia** (1400–82), Italian sculptor: *The Madonna of the Rose Garden* (c.1430).

**Norman Rockwell** (1894–1978), U.S. painter and illustrator: won popularity for realistic paintings of everyday life, many appearing as covers for *The Saturday Evening Post*.

**Auguste Rodin** (1840–1917), French impressionist sculptor: *The Thinker* (1879–89), *The Kiss* (1896–98), *Balzac* (1892–97).

**Dante Gabriel Rossetti** (1828–82), English romantic painter and poet, and leading member of the Pre-Raphaelites: *Girlhood of Mary Virgin* (1849), *Mary Magdalene* (1878).

**Mark Rothko** (1903–70), American abstract expressionist painter: *Orange, Red, Yellow* (1961), *Slate Blue and Brown on Plum* (1958) typify his studies in simple color contrasts.

**Georges Rouault** (1871–1958), French expressionist painter whose works often use dark lines to suggest stained glass: *Head of Christ* (1905), *Three Judges* (1913), *The Old King* (1916–37).

**Henri Rousseau** (1844–1910), French primitivist painter: *The Snake Charmer* (1907), *The Dream* (1910).

**Peter Paul Rubens** (1577–1640), Flemish baroque painter: *Raising of the Cross* (1609–10), *The Judgment of Paris* (1639).

**Jacob van Ruisdael** (c.1628–82), Dutch landscape painter: *The Jewish Graveyard* (c.1655).

**Charles Marion Russell** (1864–1926), American painter and sculptor of scenes of the West: *Bronc to Breakfast*.

**Albert Pinkham Ryder** (1847–1917), American painter of romantic and fantastic subjects: *Toilers of the Sea, Flying Dutchman, The Forest of Arden, The Race Track,* or *Death on a Pale Horse*.

**Eero Saarinen** (1910–61), Finnish-American architect: TWA Terminal, Kennedy Airport, New York; American Embassy, London.

**Augustus Saint-Gaudens** (1848–1907), American realist sculptor: Shaw Memorial, Boston; statue of General Sherman, New York City.

**John Singer Sargent** (1856–1925), American portrait and landscape painter: *Portrait of Madame X* (1884), *Robert Louis Stevenson* (1887).

**Georges Seurat** (1859–91), French postimpressionist painter who used tiny dots of color to create mosaiclike effects in his works: *Sunday Afternoon on the Island of La Grande Jatte* (1884–86).

**Ben Shahn** (1898–1969), American expressionist painter: *The Passion of Sacco and Vanzetti* (1931–32).

**Paul Signac** (1863–1935), French neoimpressionist painter: *The Harbor at Saint-Tropez* (1893).

**Alfred Sisley** (1839–99), Anglo-French impressionist painter: *Square at Argenteuil* (1872).

**John Sloan** (1871–1951), American realist painter of everyday life: *McSorley's Bar* (1912).

**David Smith** (1906–65), American abstract sculptor best known for his works in welded metal: *Lectern Sentinel* (1961).

**Chaim Soutine** (1894–1943), Russian-French expressionist painter: *The Madwoman* (1920).

**Jan Steen** (1626–79), Dutch genre painter: *Grace Before Meat* (c.1665).

**Philip Wilson Steer** (1860–1940), English impressionist painter: *The Bridge, Etaples* (1887), *Chepstow Castle* (1905).

**Frank Stella** (1937–    ), American modernist painter best known for his "shaped canvases": *Sinjerli II* (1969).

**Joseph Stella** (1877–1946), U.S. semiabstract painter of subjects of the Industrial Age: *The Bridge* (1922).

**Clyfford Still** (1904–80), American abstract expressionist painter: *Jamais* (1944).

**Edward Durell Stone** (1902–78), U.S. architect: John F. Kennedy center in Washington, D.C.; General Motors building in New York City; U.S. embassy in New Delhi, India.

**Gilbert Stuart** (1755–1828), American portrait painter: *George Washington, John Adams.*

**Louis Henry Sullivan** (1856–1924), American architect and a pioneer in the design of skyscrapers: Roosevelt College building, Chicago (1887–89), Chicago Stock Exchange.

**Yves Tanguy** (1900–55), French-American surrealist painter: *Mama, Papa Is Wounded* (1927).

**Albert Bertel Thorvaldsen** (1770–1844), Danish neoclassical sculptor: *Jason* (1802), *Cupid and Psyche* (1807).

**Giovanni Battista Tiepolo** (1696–1770), Venetian rococo painter of frescoes: several in Doge's Palace, Venice; Episcopal Palace, Würzburg.

**Tintoretto** (c.1518–94), Venetian mannerist painter: *Christ Before Pilate* (1566–67), *Bacchus and Ariadne* (1577), *The Last Supper* (1592–94).

**Titian** (Tiziano Vecellio, 1490?–1576), Venetian painter and one of the masters of Renaissance art: *Bacchanal* (1518), *Rape of Europa* (1559), *Christ Crowned with Thorns* (1570).

**Henri de Toulouse-Lautrec** (1864–1901), French postimpressionist painter and lithographer best known for his character studies: *Jane Avril* (1890), *At the Moulin Rouge* (1892).

**John Trumbull** (1756–1843), American painter of Revolutionary War scenes; his murals hang in U.S. Capitol.

**Joseph Mallord William Turner** (1775–1851), English romantic landscape painter: *The Grand Canal* (1835), *Rain, Steam, and Speed* (1844).

**Maurice Utrillo** (1883–1955), French painter of street scenes: *Rooftops at Sarcelle* (1909).

**Sir Anthony Van Dyck** (1599–1641), Flemish portrait and religious painter: *Portrait of Charles I Hunting* (c.1635), *The Vision of St. Augustine* and *Lamentation* (both 1634–35).

**Jan Van Eyck** (c.1390–1441), Flemish religious

**PAINTERS, SCULPTORS, AND ARCHITECTS** *(continued)*
painter: *Ghent Altarpiece* (1425–32).

**Vincent Van Gogh** (1853–90), Dutch postimpressionist painter who worked mainly in France: *The Sunflowers* (1888), *Starry Night* (1889), several self-portraits.

**Jan Van Goyen** (1596–1656), Dutch artist who was among the founders of the Dutch and Flemish school of landscape painting: *Windmill by the River* (1642).

**Diego Velázquez** (1599–1660), Spanish portrait painter: *Borrachos* (1629), *The Maids of Honor* (1656), *The Water-Carrier of Seville* (1619–21), *The Surrender of Breda* (1634–35).

**Jan Vermeer** (1632–75), Dutch genre painter: *Officer and Laughing Girl* (c.1655–60), *The Letter* (1666).

**Paolo Veronese** (1528–88), Venetian painter of religious and allegorical subjects: *Christ in the House of Levi* (1573), *The Rape of Europa* (1576), *Marriage at Cana* (1563).

**Andrea del Verrocchio** (1435–88), Florentine painter and sculptor: *Baptism of Christ* (c.1470), *Putto with a Dolphin* (c.1470).

**Maurice de Vlaminck** (1876–1958), French fauvist painter: *On the Banks of the Seine* (1906).

**Andy Warhol** (1927– ), American pop artist: *Campbell's Soup Can.*

**Antoine Watteau** (1684–1721), French baroque painter: *Gilles* (c.1716), *Pilgrimage to Cythera* (1717), *The Fatigues of War* or *Troop March* (1712–15), *Gersaint's Shop Sign* (1720).

**Max Weber** (1881–1961), American abstract and cubist painter: *Chinese Restaurant* (1915).

**Benjamin West** (1738–1820), American painter of romantic and heroic scenes: *Death of General Wolfe* (1770).

**Rogier van der Weyden** (1399–1464), Flemish painter of religious subjects: *The Last Judgment* (c.1446).

**James Abbott McNeill Whistler** (1834–1903), American painter and etcher whose work shows influences both of French impressionists and English academic painters: *Arrangement in Gray and Black*; *The Artist's Mother* (1871), *The Falling Rocket* (1874).

**Grant Wood** (1891–1942), American painter of rural Midwest scenes: *American Gothic* (1930), *Daughters of the Revolution* (1932).

**Sir Christopher Wren** (1632–1723), English architect who worked in the neoclassic style: St. Paul's Cathedral, London.

**Frank Lloyd Wright** (1869–1959), American architect who pioneered in radical designs: Johnson Wax Building, Racine, Wis. (1936–39); the Guggenheim Museum, New York City (1946–59).

**Andrew Wyeth** (1917– ), American romantic realist painter: *Winter* (1946), *Christina's World* (1948).

# MAJOR ART MOVEMENTS

**Abstract expressionism,** American painting style that reached peak in 1940s and 1950s. Form and color are emphasized for their own sake, and works seldom contain identifiable objects. Earlier European movement producing similar results (for example, Kandinsky's paintings) was called *tachisme.*

**Art nouveau,** ornate style that originated in the late 1800s. Among best-known artists in style were Louis C. Tiffany and René Lalique.

**Barbizon School,** group of French artists in mid-1800s; including Millet, who painted romantic landscapes and pastoral scenes.

**Baroque,** predominantly Italian style of art and architecture that reached peak in the mid-1600s. Baroque works are ornate and dramatic.

**Cubism,** early movement in painting and, to lesser extent, in sculpture. It reduced all shapes to simple geometric forms, or distorted objects by simultaneously presenting them from several different angles. Founders of cubism were Braque and Picasso.

**Dadaism,** movement originating in 1916 in France, expressing nihilistic protest against all previous art and culture. One of its leaders, Marcel Duchamp, attached labels to ordinary commercial products (for example, bicycle wheels, drinking fountains) and called them art.

**Expressionism,** 20th century northern European movement in painting. Usually ordinary subjects were given distorted shapes, and colors were exaggerated to produce strong emotional effects.

**Fauvism,** French movement of painters who exhibited together in Paris from about 1903 to 1905. Their use of distorted design and wild colors caused them to be called *Les fauves* (beasts) by some critics. Their leaders included Matisse and Rouault.

**Futurism,** Italian art movement of early 1900s, glorifying mechanical age, speed, and motion.

**Genre painting,** type of picture, usually of small size, that represents everyday life in unidealized manner. Examples, which are found through ages, include many peasant and tavern and household scenes depicted by Dutch painters of 1600s.

**Impressionism,** most important art movement of 1800s, mainly centered around Paris. Impressionistic painters were primarily concerned with effects of natural light in their spontaneous and undetailed portrayals of subjects in their artwork.

**Mannerism,** movement between 1520 and 1600 mainly in Italy, although probably the greatest mannerist painter was Greek-Spanish El Greco. Human figure was central subject, but it was posed in dramatically strained positions, or its shape was elongated.

**Minimal art,** kind of abstract painting developed in 1960s, eliminating emotions or symbolism.

**Neoclassicism,** movement of 1700s that arose in reaction to excesses of baroque and rococo art. Painters, and especially sculptors, consciously imitated styles and subject matter of ancient Greek and Roman art.

**New realism,** movement of 1970s, in which paintings are executed with photographic realistic detail.

**Op art,** movement of 1960s, emphasizing optical illusion through creation of complex geometric constructions or designs.

**Pop art,** New York-centered movement of 1960s, in which everyday examples of graphic design are illustrated or reproduced, often greatly enlarged. Comic strips and advertising art are favorite subjects.

**Postimpressionism,** loosely knit movement of late 1800s, mainly in rejection of impressionism. Cézanne usually considered founder of movement, although work has little in common with other postimpressionists.

**Pre-Raphaelite,** English movement of mid-1800s emphasizing purity and use of moral and religious themes. Leaders included Millais and Rossetti.

**Realism,** movement begun by Courbet in mid-1800s, depicting real people in everyday situations.

**Rococo,** movement in art and architecture that began in France in 1700s and spread to Germany and Austria. Prettiness, gaiety, and ornate delicacy characterize rococo art.

**Romanticism,** movement of early 1800s reacting against neoclassicism by combining realistic details and expression of emotions. Constable and Turner were leaders of romanticism.

**Surrealism,** essentially an outgrowth from cubism; its subject matter consists of fantastic, dreamlike objects and scenes. Surrealism reached its peak in works by Picasso, Dali, and Ernst.

# Awards and Prizes

A naturalized American, Czeslaw Milosz, 69, won the Nobel Prize for literature in 1980. A former Polish diplomat, best known as a poet, Milosz renounced communism and sought political asylum in the West in 1951. He has taught at the University of California since 1960.

United Press Int'l.

## HIGHLIGHTS: 1980

Eight Americans were among the 11 persons awarded Nobel Prizes in 1980. This brought to 166 the number of Americans who have received Nobel awards—one-third of the total presented since 1901.

The Americans who won 1980 Nobel Prizes were: George D. Snall, a scientist at the Jackson Laboratory in Bar Harbor, Me., and Venezuelan-born Baruj Benacerraf, of the Harvard Medical School, who shared in the prize for physiology or medicine; Lawrence Klein, of the University of Pennsylvania, who won the economics prize; Paul Berg, of Stanford University, and Walter Gilbert of Harvard University, who shared in the chemistry prize; James W. Cronin, of the University of Chicago, and Val L. Fitch, of Princeton University, who divided the physics prize; and Czeslaw Milosz, of the University of California, who won the literature prize.

British scientist Frederick Sanger, 62, be- came one of the few persons ever to be awarded two Nobel Prizes. He was presented half the 1980 chemistry award "for his fundamental studies of the biochemistry of nucleic acids with particular regard to recombinant DNA"—the pioneering work that enables scientists to develop new forms of life through gene-splicing. He previously won the 1958 Nobel Prize for chemistry in recognition of pioneer work in the structure of proteins, especially insulin.

The Nobel Peace Prize for 1980 was won by Argentinian Adolfo Pérez Esquivel, 48, who heads a human-rights activist organization in Latin America. In announcing the award, the Nobel committee said, "The views he represents carry a vital message to many other countries, not least in Latin America, where social and political problems, as yet unsolved, have resulted in an escalation of the use of violence."

# NOBEL PRIZES

Nobel Prizes are awarded each year to persons who have made important contributions for the good of humanity.

The awards were established in the will of Alfred Bernhard Nobel (1833–96), a Swedish chemist who became wealthy from his invention of dynamite in 1867. He regretted that dynamite had been used as an instrument of war, and left a fund of about $9 million to establish the Nobel Prizes to encourage peace and progress.

Six prizes are awarded each year in chemistry, economics, literature, peace, physics, and physiology or medicine. The first prizes were awarded in 1901. The economics prize was added in 1969. Each prize in 1980 carried a monetary award of about $212,000, divided when there was more than one recipient.

The Royal Academy of Science in Sweden picks the prizewinners in physics, chemistry, and economics. The medical faculty of Stockholm's Caroline Institute chooses the winner in the field of physiology or medicine. The Swedish Academy of Literature names the literature winner. The Norwegian parliament elects a committee of five persons to select the winner of the prize for peace.

Since the prizes first began to be awarded in 1901, a total of 166 Americans have received awards. The British are second with 80. Some 57 Germans have won Nobel Prizes, French 44, Swedes 24, Russians 14, Swiss 14, Dutch 11, Danes, 11, Italians 10, Austrians 9, Belgians 8, Norwegians 7, Japanese 5, Spanish 5, Canadians 4, Irish 4, Argentinians 4, Australians 3, and Indians 3. Two Nobel Prizes have been won by Israelis, Poles, Chileans, Hungarians, Finns, and Greeks. One each have been won by an Egyptian, an Icelander, a Czech, a Yugoslav, a Guatemalan, a South African, a Vietnamese, a Portuguese, and a Pakistani.

## NOBEL CHEMISTRY PRIZES

| YEAR | NAME AND NATIONALITY | AWARDED FOR: |
|---|---|---|
| 1901 | Jacobus H. van't Hoff, Dutch | Discovery of laws of chemical dynamics and osmotic pressure in solutions. |
| 1902 | Emil Fischer, German | Work on sugar and purine syntheses. |
| 1903 | Svante A. Arrhenius, Swedish | Electrolytic theory of dissociation. |
| 1904 | Sir William Ramsay, British | Discovery of inert gaseous elements in air and determination of their place in periodic system. |
| 1905 | Johann von Baeyer, German | Work on organic dyes and hydroaromatic compounds. |
| 1906 | Henri Moissan, French | Study and isolation of element fluorine and development of electric furnace named after him. |
| 1907 | Eduard Buchner, German | Biochemical researches and discovery of cell-free fermentation. |
| 1908 | Ernest Rutherford, British | Studies of disintegration of elements, and chemistry of radioactive substances. |
| 1909 | Wilhelm Ostwald, German | Work on catalysis and studies of fundamental principles governing chemical equilibria and rates of reaction. |
| 1910 | Otto Wallach, German | Pioneer work in field of alicyclic compounds. |
| 1911 | Marie Curie, French (Polish-born) | Discovery of elements radium and polonium, isolation of radium and study of its nature and compounds. |
| 1912 | Victor Grignard, French | Discovery of Grignard reagent. |
| | Paul Sabatier, French | Method of hydrogenating organic compounds in presence of finely disintegrated metals. |
| 1913 | Alfred Werner, Swiss (German-born) | Work on linkage of atoms in molecules. |
| 1914 | Theodore W. Richards, American | Determinations of atomic weight of many chemical elements. |
| 1915 | Richard M. Willstätter, German | Researches on plant pigments, especially chlorophyll. |
| 1916 | No award | |
| 1917 | No award | |
| 1918 | Fritz Haber, German | Synthesis of ammonia from its elements. |
| 1919 | No award | |
| 1920 | Walther H. Nernst, German | Work in thermochemistry. |
| 1921 | Frederick Soddy, British | Studies of chemistry of radioactive substances, and investigations into origin and nature of isotopes. |
| 1922 | Francis W. Aston, British | Discovery, by means of his mass spectrograph, of isotopes in a large number of nonradioactive elements. |
| 1923 | Fritz Pregl, Austrian | Invention of method of microanalysis of organic substances. |
| 1924 | No award | |
| 1925 | Richard A. Zsigmondy, German (Austrian-born) | Demonstration of heterogeneous nature of colloid solutions. |
| 1926 | Theodor Svedberg, Swedish | Work on dispersion systems and colloid chemistry. |
| 1927 | Heinrich O. Wieland, German | Studies of constitution of bile acids and related substances. |
| 1928 | Adolf O. R. Windaus, German | Research into constitution of sterols and their connection with vitamins. |
| 1929 | Arthur Harden, British | Investigations on fermentation of sugar and fermentative enzymes. |
| | Hans von Euler–Chelpin, Swedish (German-born) | |
| 1930 | Hans Fischer, German | Researches into constitution of hemin and chlorophyll. |
| 1931 | Friedrich Bergius, German | Contributions to invention and development of chemical high-pressure methods. |
| | Carl Bosch, German | |
| 1932 | Irving Langmuir, American | Discoveries and investigations in surface chemistry. |
| 1933 | No award | |

| Year | Laureate | Achievement |
|---|---|---|
| 1934 | Harold C. Urey, American | Discovery of heavy hydrogen. |
| 1935 | Frédéric Joliot-Curie, French | Synthesis of new radioactive elements. |
| | Irène Joliot-Curie, French | |
| 1936 | Peter J. W. Debye, Dutch | Knowledge of molecular structure by studies of dipole moments, diffraction of X rays, and electrons in gases. |
| 1937 | Walter N. Haworth, British | Research on carbohydrates and vitamin C. |
| | Paul Karrer, Swiss (Russian-born) | Investigations on carotenoids, flavins, and vitamins A and $B_2$. |
| 1938 | Richard Kuhn, German (Austrian-born) | Work on carotenoids and vitamins. (Prize declined.) |
| 1939 | Adolf F. J. Butenandt, German | Work on sex hormones. (Prize declined under political pressure.) |
| | Leopold Ruzička, Swiss | Work on polymethylenes and higher terpenes. |
| 1940 | No award | |
| 1941 | No award | |
| 1942 | No award | |
| 1943 | Georg de Hevesy, Hungarian | Work on use of isotopes as tracers in chemistry. |
| 1944 | Otto Hahn, German | Discovery of fission of heavy nuclei. |
| 1945 | Artturi I. Virtanen, Finnish | Research and inventions in agricultural and nutrition chemistry. |
| 1946 | James B. Sumner, American | Discovery that enzymes can be crystallized. |
| | John H. Northrop, American | Preparation of enzymes and virus proteins in pure form. |
| | Wendell M. Stanley, American | |
| 1947 | Sir Robert Robinson, British | Investigation of plant products of biological importance. |
| 1948 | Arne W. K. Tiselius, Swedish | Research on electrophoresis and adsorption analysis. |
| 1949 | William F. Giauque, American | Contributions in field of chemical thermodynamics, particularly behavior of substances at extremely low temperatures. |
| 1950 | Kurt Alder, German | Discovery and development of diene synthesis. |
| | Otto P. H. Diels, German | |
| 1951 | Edwin M. McMillan, American | Discoveries in chemistry of transuranium elements. |
| | Glenn T. Seaborg, American | |
| 1952 | Archer J. P. Martin, British | Invention of partition chromatography, method for analysis of mixtures. |
| | Richard L. M. Synge, British | |
| 1953 | Hermann Staudinger, German | Discoveries in field of macromolecular chemistry. |
| 1954 | Linus C. Pauling, American | Research into nature of chemical bond and its application. |
| 1955 | Vincent du Vigneaud, American | Work on biochemically important sulfur compounds, especially for first synthesis of polypeptide hormone. |
| 1956 | Sir Cyril N. Hinshelwood, British | Researches into mechanism of chemical reactions. |
| | Nikolai N. Semenov, Russian | |
| 1957 | Lord Todd (Alexander R. Todd), British | Work on nucleotides and nucleotide coenzymes. |
| 1958 | Frederick Sanger, British | Work on structure of proteins, especially of insulin. |
| 1959 | Jaroslav Heyrovsky, Czech | Discovery and development of polarographic methods of analysis. |
| 1960 | Willard F. Libby, American | Method to use carbon-14 for age determination in archaeology, geology, geophysics, and other branches of science. |
| 1961 | Melvin Calvin, American | Research on carbon dioxide assimilation in plants. |
| 1962 | Sir John C. Kendrew, British | Studies of structures of globular proteins. |
| | Max F. Perutz, British (Austrian-born) | |
| 1963 | Giulio Natta, Italian | Discoveries in chemistry and technology of high polymers. |
| | Karl Ziegler, German | |
| 1964 | Dorothy Crowfoot Hodgkin, British | Discovery by X-ray techniques of structure of important biochemical substances. |
| 1965 | Robert B. Woodward, American | Techniques for syntheses of complicated organic compounds. |
| 1966 | Robert S. Mulliken, American | Fundamental work on chemical bonds and electronic structure of molecules by molecular orbital method. |
| 1967 | Manfred Eigen, German | Studies of extremely fast chemical reactions effected by disturbing equilibrium by means of very short pulses of energy. |
| | Ronald G. W. Norrish, British | |
| | Sir George Porter, British | |
| 1968 | Lars Onsager, American (Norwegian-born) | Discovery of reciprocal relations that bear his name, which are fundamental to thermodynamics of irreversible processes. |
| 1969 | Derek H. R. Barton, British | Work to develop and apply concept of conformation in chemistry. |
| | Odd Hassel, Norwegian | |
| 1970 | Luis F. Leloir, Argentine (French-born) | Discovery of sugar nucleotides and their role in biosynthesis of carbohydrates. |
| 1971 | Gerhard Herzberg, Canadian (German-born) | Studies in electronic structure and geometry of molecules, particularly free radicals. |
| 1972 | Christian B. Anfinsen, American | Research relating to chemical structure and biologic reactions of protein ribonuclease. |
| | Stanford Moore, American | |
| | William H. Stein, American | |
| 1973 | Ernest Otto Fischer, German | Research on merging of organic and metallic compounds, seeking solution to automobile exhaust pollution. |
| | Geoffrey Wilkinson, British | |
| 1974 | Paul J. Flory, American | Pioneering analytical methods for studying long-chain molecules, leading to development of many plastics and synthetic materials. |
| 1975 | John Warcus Cornforth, British (Australian-born) | Research in field of stereochemistry, study of how properties of chemical compounds are affected by arrangement of their atoms. |
| | Vladimir Prelog, Swiss (Yugoslav-born) | |
| 1976 | William N. Lipscomb, American | Studies on structure and bonding of compounds called boranes, providing new insight into nature of chemical bonding. |
| 1977 | Ilya Prigogine, Belgian (Russian-born) | Lifetime contributions to nonequilibrium thermodynamics, particularly theory of dissipative structures that helps explain how living organisms use energy and how life originated. |
| 1978 | Peter Mitchell, British | Research on energy transformations in living cells and formulation of the chemiosmotic theory of how cells convert food into metabolic energy. |
| 1979 | Herbert C. Brown, American (British-born) | Development of boron and phosphorus compounds linking large molecules, enabling mass production of many pharmaceuticals and industrial chemicals. |
| | Georg Wittig, West German | |
| 1980 | Paul Berg, American | Pioneering work in gene-splicing or genetic engineering. |
| | Walter Gilbert, American | Determining the chemical structure of nucleic acids in regard to DNA used in gene-splicing. |
| | Frederick Sanger, British | |

## NOBEL ECONOMICS PRIZES

| | | |
|---|---|---|
| 1969 | Ragnar Frisch, Norwegian ........... Jan Tinbergen, Dutch | Development of mathematical models for analyzing economic activity. |
| 1970 | Paul A. Samuelson, American ......... | Raising level of scientific analysis in economic theory. |
| 1971 | Simon Kuznets, American ............. | Working out methods to determine country's gross national product. |
| 1972 | Kenneth J. Arrow, American .......... Sir John R. Hicks, British | Pioneering studies in theory of general economic equilibrium. |
| 1973 | Wassily Leontief, American (Russian-born) | Development of "input-output" method of economic analysis used by most industrial nations. |
| 1974 | Gunnar Myrdal, Swedish ............. Friedrich A. von Hayek, Austrian | Pioneering work in theory of money and economic fluctuations. |
| 1975 | Leonid V. Kantorovich, Russian ........ Tjalling C. Koopmans, American (Dutch-born) | Contributions to theory of optimum allocation of resources. |
| 1976 | Milton Friedman, American ........... | Achievements in consumption analysis, monetary history and theory, and demonstration of complexity of stabilization policy. |
| 1977 | Bertil Ohlin, Swedish ................ James Edward Meade, British | For pathbreaking contributions to theory of international trade and international capital movement. |
| 1978 | Herbert Simon, American ............. | Pioneering research into how businesses and other organizations make economic decisions. |
| 1979 | Sir Arthur Lewis, British.............. (St. Lucian-born) Theodore W. Schultz, American | For efforts to solve economic problems of need and poverty in world and to find solutions for developing nations. |
| 1980 | Lawrence Klein, American ............ | For development of econometric models to analyze economic fluctuations. |

## NOBEL LITERATURE PRIZES

| | | | |
|---|---|---|---|
| 1901 | Scully-Prudhomme (René Prudhomme), French | 1941 | No award |
| 1902 | C. M. T. Mommsen, German | 1942 | No award |
| 1903 | Björnstijerne Björnson, Norwegian | 1943 | No award |
| 1904 | Frédéric Mistral, French | 1944 | Johannes V. Jensen, Danish |
| | José Echegaray, Spanish | 1945 | Gabriela Mistral, Chilean |
| 1905 | Henryk Sienkiewicz, Polish | 1946 | Hermann Hesse, Swiss (German-born) |
| 1906 | Giosuè Carducci, Italian | 1947 | André Gide, French |
| 1907 | Rudyard Kipling, British | 1948 | T. S. Eliot, British (American-born) |
| 1908 | Rudolf C. Eucken, German | 1949 | William Faulkner, American |
| 1909 | Selma Lagerlöf, Swedish | 1950 | Bertrand Russell, British |
| 1910 | Paul J. L. Heyse, German | 1951 | Pär F. Lagerkvist, Swedish |
| 1911 | Count Maurice Maeterlinck, Belgian | 1952 | François Mauriac, French |
| 1912 | Gerhart Hauptmann, German | 1953 | Sir Winston Churchill, British |
| 1913 | Rabindranath Tagore, Indian | 1954 | Ernest Hemingway, American |
| 1914 | No award | 1955 | Halldór K. Laxness, Icelandic |
| 1915 | Romain Rolland, French | 1956 | Juan Ramón Jiménez, Spanish |
| 1916 | Carl G. von Heidenstam, Swedish | 1957 | Albert Camus, French |
| 1917 | Karl A. Gjellerup, Danish | 1958 | Boris L. Pasternak, Russian (Prize declined) |
| | Henrik Pontoppidan, Danish | 1959 | Salvatore Quasimodo, Italian |
| 1918 | No award | 1960 | Saint-John Perse, French |
| 1919 | Carl F. G. Spitteler, Swiss | 1961 | Ivo Andrić, Yugoslavian |
| 1920 | Knut Hamsun, Norwegian | 1962 | John Steinbeck, American |
| 1921 | Anatole France, French | 1963 | George Seferis, Greek |
| 1922 | Jacinto Benavente, Spanish | 1964 | Jean-Paul Sartre, French (Prize declined) |
| 1923 | William Butler Yeats, Irish | 1965 | Mikhail Sholokhov, Russian |
| 1924 | Wladyslaw S. Reymont, Polish | 1966 | Shmuel Yosef Agnon, Israeli (Austrian-born) |
| 1925 | George Bernard Shaw, British (Irish-born) | | Nelly Sachs, Swedish (German-born) |
| 1926 | Grazia Deledda, Italian | 1967 | Miguel Angel Asturias, Guatemalan |
| 1927 | Henri Bergson, French | 1968 | Yasunari Kawabata, Japanese |
| 1928 | Sigrid Undset, Norwegian (Danish-born) | 1969 | Samuel Beckett, Irish |
| 1929 | Thomas Mann, German | 1970 | Aleksandr I. Solzhenitsyn, Russian |
| 1930 | Sinclair Lewis, American | 1971 | Pablo Neruda, Chilean |
| 1931 | Erik A. Karlfeldt, Swedish | 1972 | Heinrich Böll, German |
| 1932 | John Galsworthy, British | 1973 | Patrick White, Australian |
| 1933 | Ivan A. Bunin, French (Russian-born) | 1974 | Eyvind Johnson, Swedish |
| 1934 | Luigi Pirandello, Italian | | Harry Edmund Martinson, Swedish |
| 1935 | No award | 1975 | Eugenio Montale, Italian |
| 1936 | Eugene O'Neill, American | 1976 | Saul Bellow, American |
| 1937 | Roger Martin du Gard, French | 1977 | Vicente Aleixandre, Spanish |
| 1938 | Pearl S. Buck, American | 1978 | Isaac Bashevis Singer, American (Polish-born) |
| 1939 | Frans E. Sillanpää, Finnish | 1979 | Odysseus Elytis, Greek |
| 1940 | No award | 1980 | Czeslaw Milosz, American (Polish-born) |

## NOBEL PEACE PRIZES

| | | | |
|---|---|---|---|
| 1901 | Jean H. Dunant, Swiss | 1945 | Cordell Hull, American |
| | Frédéric Passy, French | 1946 | Emily G. Balch, American |
| 1902 | Élie Ducommun, Swiss | | John R. Mott, American |
| | Charles A. Gobat, Swiss | 1947 | Friends Service Council, British |
| 1903 | Sir William R. Cremer, British | | American Friends Service Committee |
| 1904 | Institute of International Law | 1948 | No award |
| 1905 | Baroness Bertha von Suttner, Austrian | 1949 | Lord John Boyd Orr of Brechin, British |
| 1906 | Theodore Roosevelt, American | 1950 | Ralph J. Bunche, American |
| 1907 | Ernesto T. Moneta, Italian | 1951 | Léon Jouhaux, French |
| | Louis Renault, French | 1952 | Albert Schweitzer, French (German-born) |
| 1908 | Klas P. Arnoldson, Swedish | 1953 | George C. Marshall, American |
| | Fredrik Bajer, Danish | 1954 | Office of UN High Commissioner for Refugees |
| 1909 | Auguste M. F. Beernaert, Belgian | 1955 | No award |
| | Paul H. B. B. d'Estournelles de Constant, French | 1956 | No award |
| | | 1957 | Lester B. Pearson, Canadian |
| 1910 | Permanent International Peace Bureau | 1958 | Georges Pire, Belgian |
| 1911 | Tobias M. C. Asser, Dutch | 1959 | Philip J. Noel-Baker, British |
| | Alfred H. Fried, Austrian | 1960 | Albert J. Luthuli, South African |
| 1912 | Elihu Root, American | 1961 | Dag Hammarskjöld, Swedish (posthumous) |
| 1913 | Henri Lafontaine, Belgian | 1962 | Linus C. Pauling, American |
| 1914–16 | No award | 1963 | International Committee of the Red Cross |
| 1917 | International Committee of the Red Cross | | Red Cross Societies League |
| 1918 | No award | 1964 | Martin Luther King Jr., American |
| 1919 | Woodrow Wilson, American | 1965 | United Nations Children's Fund (UNICEF) |
| 1920 | Léon V. A. Bourgeois, French | 1966 | No award |
| 1921 | Karl H. Branting, Swedish | 1967 | No award |
| | Christian L. Lange, Norwegian | 1968 | René Cassin, French |
| 1922 | Fridtjof Nansen, Norwegian | 1969 | International Labor Organization (ILO) |
| 1923 | No award | 1970 | Norman E. Borlaug, American |
| 1924 | No award | 1971 | Willy Brandt, German |
| 1925 | Sir J. Austen Chamberlain, British | 1972 | No award |
| | Charles G. Dawes, American | 1973 | Henry A. Kissinger, American (German-born) |
| 1926 | Aristide Briand, French | | Le Duc Tho, North Vietnamese |
| | Gustav Stresemann, German | 1974 | Eisaku Sato, Japanese |
| 1927 | Ferdinand Buisson, French | | Sean MacBride, Irish |
| | Ludwig Quidde, German | 1975 | Andrei D. Sakharov, Russian |
| 1928 | No award | 1976 | Betty Williams and Mairead Corrigan, organiz- |
| 1929 | Frank B. Kellogg, American | | ers of peace movement to resist terrorist |
| 1930 | Lars O. N. Söderblom, Swedish | | violence in Northern Ireland |
| 1931 | Jane Addams, American | 1977 | Amnesty International, organization that |
| | Nicholas Murray Butler, American | | exposes governmental violations of human |
| 1932 | No award | | rights |
| 1933 | Sir Norman Angell, British | 1978 | Anwar el-Sadat, president of Egypt, and |
| 1934 | Arthur Henderson, British | | Menachem Begin, prime minister of Israel, |
| 1935 | Carl von Ossietzky, German | | for Mideast peace initiative to end |
| 1936 | Carlos Saavedra Lamas, Argentinian | | three decades of conflict |
| 1937 | Viscount Cecil of Chelwood, British | 1979 | Mother Teresa, Indian (Albanian-born), for |
| 1938 | International Office for Refugees | | charitable work in helping poor of Calcutta. |
| 1939–43 | No award | 1980 | Adolfo Pérez Esquivel, Argentinian, |
| 1944 | International Committee of the Red Cross | | a leading human-rights advocate. |

## NOBEL PHYSICS PRIZES

| | | |
|---|---|---|
| 1901 | Wilhelm C. Roentgen, German | Discovery of Roentgen rays (X rays). |
| 1902 | Hendrik A. Lorentz, Dutch | Researches into influence of magnetism upon radiation |
| | Pieter Zeeman, Dutch | phenomena. |
| 1903 | Antoine Henri Becquerel, French | Discovery of spontaneous radioactivity. |
| | Marie Curie, French (Polish-born) | Joint researches on radiation phenomena discovered by |
| | Pierre Curie, French | A. Henri Becquerel. |
| 1904 | Lord Rayleigh (John W. Strutt), British | Investigations of densities of most important gases and discovery of argon. |
| 1905 | Philipp E. A. von Lenard, German (Hungarian-born) | Work on cathode rays. |
| 1906 | Sir Joseph John Thomson, British | Theoretical and experimental investigations on conduction of electricity by gases. |
| 1907 | Albert A. Michelson, American (German-born) | Optical precision instruments for spectroscopic and meteorological investigations. |
| 1908 | Gabriel Lippmann, French (Luxembourgian-born) | Method of reproducing colors photographically based on phenomenon of interference. |
| 1909 | Guglielmo Marconi, Italian | Development of radio (wireless telegraphy). |
| | Carl F. Braun, German | |
| 1910 | Johannes D. van der Waals, Dutch | Work on equation of state for gases and liquids. |
| 1911 | Wilhelm Wien, German | Discoveries regarding laws of heat radiation. |
| 1912 | Nils G. Dalén, Swedish | Invention of automatic regulators to be used with gas accumulators for illuminating lighthouses and buoys. |

**NOBEL PHYSICS PRIZES** (continued)

| | | |
|---|---|---|
| 1913 | Heike Kamerlingh-Onnes, Dutch ....... | Investigations on properties of matter at lower temperatures, which led to production of liquid helium. |
| 1914 | Max von Laue, German .............. | Discovery of diffraction of X rays by crystals. |
| 1915 | Sir William H. Bragg, British .......... | The analysis of crystal structure by means of X rays. |
| | Sir William L. Bragg, British | |
| 1916 | No award | |
| 1917 | Charles G. Barkla, British............. | Discovery of characteristic Roentgen radiation of elements. |
| 1918 | Max K. E. L. Planck, German ......... | Discovery of energy quanta. |
| 1919 | Johannes Stark, German.............. | Discovery of Doppler effect in canal rays and splitting of spectral lines in electric fields. |
| 1920 | Charles E. Guillaume, French .......... (Swiss-born) | Discovery of anomalies in nickel-steel alloys. |
| 1921 | Albert Einstein, American ............ (German-born) | Studies in theoretical physics, and especially for discovery of law of photoelectric effect. |
| 1922 | Niels Bohr, Danish .................. | Investigation of atomic structure and radiation. |
| 1923 | Robert A. Millikan, American ......... | Work on elementary charge of electricity and on photoelectric effect. |
| 1924 | Karl M. G. Siegbahn, Swedish ........ | Discoveries and research in field of X-ray spectroscopy. |
| 1925 | James Franck, German ............... | Discovery of laws governing impact of electron upon |
| | Gustav Hertz, German | atom. |
| 1926 | Jean B. Perrin, French .............. | Work on discontinuous structure of matter, and especially for discovery of sedimentation equillibrium. |
| 1927 | Arthur H. Compton, American ......... | Discovery of Compton effect concerning increase in wave-length of X rays and gamma rays scattered by electrons. |
| | Charles T. R. Wilson, British .......... (Scottish-born) | Method of making paths of electrically charged particles visible by condensation of vapor. |
| 1928 | Owen W. Richardson, British ......... | Work on thermionics, phenomena associated with emission of electrically charged particles by heated body, and for discovery of Richardson's law. |
| 1929 | Prince Louis-Victor de Broglie, French...................... | Discovery of wave nature of electrons. |
| 1930 | Sir Chandrasekhara V. Raman, Indian............................ | Work on scattering of light and discovery of Raman effect. |
| 1931 | No award | |
| 1932 | Werner Heisenberg, German .......... | Creation of quantum mechanics, which led to discovery of allotropic forms of hydrogen. |
| 1933 | Paul A. M. Dirac, British ............. | Extensions of atomic theory. |
| | Erwin Schrödinger, Austrian | |
| 1934 | No award | |
| 1935 | Sir James Chadwick, British .......... | Discovery of neutron. |
| 1936 | Carl D. Anderson, American ......... | Discovery of positron. |
| | Victor F. Hess, Austrian .............. | Discovery of cosmic radiation. |
| 1937 | Clinton J. Davisson, American ........ | Experimental discovery of diffraction of electrons by crystals. |
| | George P. Thomson, British | |
| 1938 | Enrico Fermi, American .............. (Italian-born) | Demonstrations of existence of new radioactive elements produced by neutron irradiation, and discovery of nuclear reactions caused by slow neutrons. |
| 1939 | Ernest O. Lawrence, American ........ | Invention and development of cyclotron and results obtained from its use in investigation of artificial radioactive elements. |
| 1940 | No award | |
| 1941 | No award | |
| 1942 | No award | |
| 1943 | Otto Stern, American (German-born) .. | Contribution to development of molecular-ray method and discovery of magnetic moment of proton. |
| 1944 | Isidor Isaac Rabi, American .......... | Resonance method for recording magnetism of atomic nuclei. |
| 1945 | Wolfgang Pauli, American ............ | Discovery of exclusion, or Pauli, principle in quantum physics. |
| 1946 | Percy Williams Bridgman, American ... | Invention of apparatus to produce extremely high pressures, and resulting discoveries in field of high-pressure physics. |
| 1947 | Sir Edward V. Appleton, British ....... | Investigations of physics of upper atmosphere and discovery of Appleton layer of ionosphere. |
| 1948 | Patrick M. S. Blackett, British......... | Development of Wilson cloud-chamber method and resulting discoveries in fields of nuclear physics and cosmic radiation. |
| 1949 | Hideki Yukawa, Japanese ............. | Theoretical prediction of existence of mesons. |
| 1950 | Cecil F. Powell, British ............... | Development of photographic method of studying nuclear processes and resulting discoveries regarding mesons. |
| 1951 | Sir John D. Cockcroft, British ........ | Research on transmutation of atomic nuclei by artificially |
| | Ernest T. S. Walton, Irish | accelerated atomic particles. |
| 1952 | Felix Bloch, American ............... (Swiss-born) | Development of new methods for nuclear-magnetic precision measurements and related discoveries. |
| | Edward M. Purcell, American | |
| 1953 | Frits Zernike, Dutch ................. | Demonstration of phase-contrast method, and invention of phase-contrast microscope. |
| 1954 | Max Born, British (German-born) ..... | Fundamental research in quantum mechanics. |
| | Walther Bothe, German .............. | Coincidence method of counting, used in nuclear and cosmic-ray research. |
| 1955 | Polykarp Kusch, American ............ (German-born) | Precise determination of magnetic moment of electron. |
| | Willis E. Lamb, American ............ | Discoveries concerning fine structure of hydrogen spectrum. |

| 1956 | John Bardeen, American<br>Walter H. Brattain, American<br>William Shockley, American | Research on semiconductors and discovery of transistor. |
|---|---|---|
| 1957 | Tsung-Dao Lee, American<br>(Chinese-born)<br>Chen Ning Yang, American<br>(Chinese-born) | Investigation of parity laws, which led to important discoveries regarding elementary particles. |
| 1958 | Paval A. Cherenkov, Russian<br>Ilya M. Frank, Russian<br>Igor J. Tamm, Russian | Discovery and interpretation of Cherenkov effect. |
| 1959 | Owen Chamberlain, American<br>Emilio G. Segrè, American (Italian-born) | Discovery of antiproton. |
| 1960 | Donald A. Glaser, American | Invention of bubble chamber. |
| 1961 | Robert Hofstadter, American<br><br>Rudolf L. Mössbauer, German | Studies of electron scattering with resulting discoveries concerning structure of nucleons.<br>Studies of resonance absorption of gamma radiation and resulting discovery of Mössbauer effect. |
| 1962 | Lev D. Landau, Russian | Theories of condensed matter, especially liquid helium. |
| 1963 | Maria Goeppert-Mayer, American<br>J. Hans D. Jensen, German<br>Eugene P. Wigner, American | Discoveries concerning nuclear shell structures.<br><br>Contribution to theory of atomic nucleus and elementary particles. |
| 1964 | Nikolai G. Basov, Russian<br>Aleksandr M. Prokhorov, Russian<br>Charles H. Townes, American | Fundamental work in field of quantum electronics, leading to construction of maser-laser oscillators and amplifiers. |
| 1965 | Richard P. Feynman, American<br>Julian S. Schwinger, American<br>Sin-itiro Tomonaga, Japanese | Research in quantum electrodynamics, which contributed to understanding of elementary particles in high-energy physics. |
| 1966 | Alfred Kastler, French | Discovery and development of optical methods for studying Herzian resonances in atoms. |
| 1967 | Hans A. Bethe, American<br>(German-born) | Contributions to theory of nuclear reaction, especially discoveries concerning energy production of stars. |
| 1968 | Luis W. Alvarez, American | Contributions to physics of subatomic particles, in particular discovery of large number of resonance states. |
| 1969 | Murray Gell-Mann, American | Contributions and discoveries concerning classification of elementary particles and their interactions. |
| 1970 | Hannes O. G. Alfvén, Swedish<br><br>Louis E. F. Néel, French | Contributions and discoveries in magnetohydrodynamics with applications in plasma physics.<br>Discoveries and work in ferromagnetism and antiferromagnetism with applications in solid-state physics. |
| 1971 | Dennis Gabor, British<br>(Hungarian-born) | Invention of system of three-dimensional photography known as holography. |
| 1972 | John Bardeen, American<br>Leon N. Cooper, American<br>John R. Schrieffer, American | Development of superconductivity theory of certain metals at very low temperatures. |
| 1973 | Ivar Giaever, American<br>(Norwegian-born)<br>Leo Esaki, Japanese<br>Brian D. Josephson, British | Developments relating to miniature electronic semiconductors and superconductors.<br><br>Discovery of "Josephson effects" of electric supercurrent. |
| 1974 | Antony Hewish, British<br>Sir Martin Ryle, British | Studies of universe using radiotelescopes; Dr. Hewish discovered pulsars in 1967. |
| 1975 | L. James Rainwater, American<br>Aage Bohr, Danish<br>Ben Roy Mottelson, Danish<br>(American-born) | Discovery and explanation of fact that nuclei of some atoms are not spherical and discovery of connection between collective motion and particle motion in atomic nucleus. |
| 1976 | Burton Richter, American<br>Samuel C. C. Ting, American | Independent discoveries of Psi or J particle, heavy elementary particle believed smallest building block of matter. |
| 1977 | John H. Van Vleck, American<br><br>Philip W. Anderson, American<br>Sir Nevill F. Mott, British | Founding modern magnetism by explaining magnetic properties of solids and how foreign ion or atom behaves in crystal.<br>Discoveries made separately in sold-state physics that led to use of amorphous material, such as glass, in electronic switching and memory devices. |
| 1978 | Robert W. Wilson, American<br>Arno A. Penzias, American<br>(German-born)<br>Pyotr Leontevitch Kapitsa, Russian | Discovery of cosmic microwave background radiation, confirming "big bang" theory of creation of universe.<br><br>Basic research in low-temperature physics. |
| 1979 | Steven Weinberg, American<br>Abdus Salam, Pakistani<br>Sheldon L. Glashow, American | Development of theory of weak interactions, regarded as a major step toward unifying knowledge of four major forces of nature: gravity, electromagnetism, force that holds together atomic nuclei, and weak force that causes radioactive decay in some atomic nuclei. |
| 1980 | James W. Cronin, American<br>Val L. Fitch, American | Discovery in 1964 of asymmetry in behavior of subatomic particles, later used to explain "big bang" theory of birth of universe. |

## NOBEL PHYSIOLOGY OR MEDICINE PRIZES

| Year | Recipient | Contribution |
|---|---|---|
| 1901 | Emil A. von Behring, German | Work on serum therapy, especially for use against diphtheria. |
| 1902 | Sir Ronald Ross, British | Investigation of how malaria parasites enter the body. |
| 1903 | Niels R. Finsen, Danish | Contribution to treatment of tuberculous skin diseases, especially lupus vulgaris, with concentrated light radiation. |
| 1904 | Ivan P. Pavlov, Russian | Work on physiology of digestion. |
| 1905 | Robert Koch, German | Investigations and discoveries in relation to tuberculosis. |
| 1906 | Camillo Golgi, Italian | Work on structure of nervous system. |
| | Santiago Ramón y Cajal, Spanish | |
| 1907 | Charles L. A. Laveran, French | Work on role played by protozoa in causing diseases. |
| 1908 | Paul Ehrlich, German | Work on immunity. |
| | Elie Metchnikoff, French (Russian-born) | |
| 1909 | Emil T. Kocher, Swiss | Work on physiology, pathology, and surgery of thyroid gland. |
| 1910 | Albrecht Kossel, German | Contributions to knowledge of cell chemistry made through his work on proteins, including nucleic substances. |
| 1911 | Allvar Gullstrand, Swedish | Work on dioptrics of eye. |
| 1912 | Alexis Carrel, American | Work on vascular suture and transplantation of blood vessels and organs. |
| 1913 | Charles R. Richet, French | Work on anaphylaxis and allergies. |
| 1914 | Robert Bárány, Hungarian | Work on physiology and pathology of inner ear. |
| 1915–18 | No award | |
| 1919 | Jules Bordet, Belgian | Discoveries relating to immunity. |
| 1920 | Schack A. S. Krogh, Danish | Discovery of capillary motor-regulating mechanism. |
| 1921 | No award | |
| 1922 | Archibald V. Hill, British | Discovery relating to production of heat in muscle. |
| | Otto F. Meyerhof, German | Discovery of fixed relationship between consumption of oxygen and metabolism of lactic acid in muscle. |
| 1923 | Frederick G. Banting, Canadian | Discovery of insulin. |
| | John J. R. Macleod, Canadian | |
| 1924 | Willem Einthoven, Dutch | Discovery of mechanism of electrocardiogram. |
| 1925 | No award | |
| 1926 | Johannes A. G. Fibiger, Danish | Experimental production of cancerlike growth in rats. |
| 1927 | Julius Wagner-Jauregg, Austrian | Use of malaria inoculation to treat paralysis and mental deterioration associated with syphilis. |
| 1928 | Charles J. H. Nicolle, French | Work on typhus. |
| 1929 | Christiaan Eijkman, Dutch | Discovery of health defects due to vitamin $B_1$ deficiency. |
| | Sir Frederick G. Hopkins, British | Discovery of growth-stimulating vitamins. |
| 1930 | Karl Landsteiner, American (Austrian-born) | Discovery of human blood groups. |
| 1931 | Otto H. Warburg, German | Discovery of nature and mode of action of respiratory enzyme. |
| 1932 | Edgar D. Adrian, British | Discoveries regarding functions of nerve cells. |
| | Sir Charles S. Sherrington, British | |
| 1933 | Thomas H. Morgan, American | Discoveries concerning role of chromosome in heredity. |
| 1934 | George R. Minot, American | Discoveries concerning liver therapy in cases of anemia. |
| | William P. Murphy, American | |
| | George H. Whipple, American | |
| 1935 | Hans Spemann, German | Discovery of organizer effect in embryonic development. |
| 1936 | Sir Henry H. Dale, British | Discoveries relating to chemical transmission of nerve impulses. |
| | Otto Loewi, American (Austrian-born) | |
| 1937 | Albert Szent-Györgyi von Nagyrapolt, American (Hungarian-born) | Studies in body metabolism with special reference to role of vitamin C and fumaric acid. |
| 1938 | Corneille J. F. Heymans, Belgian | Discovery of role played by sinus and aortic mechanisms in regulation of respiration. |
| 1939 | Gerhard Domagk, German | Discovery of antibacterial effects of drug prontosil. (Prize declined under political pressure; awarded later.) |
| 1940 | No award | |
| 1941 | No award | |
| 1942 | No award | |
| 1943 | Henrik C. P. Dam, Danish | Discovery of vitamin K. |
| | Edward A. Doisy, American | Discovery of chemical nature of vitamin K. |
| 1944 | Joseph Erlanger, American | Discoveries relating to highly differentiated functions of single nerve fibers. |
| | Herbert S. Gasser, American | |
| 1945 | Sir Alexander Fleming, British | Discovery of penicillin and its curative effect in various infectious diseases. |
| | Ernst B. Chain, British (German-born) | |
| | Sir Howard W. Florey, British (Australian-born) | |
| 1946 | Hermann J. Muller, American | Discovery of production of mutations by means of X rays. |
| 1947 | Carl F. Cori, American (Czech-born) | Discovery of course of catalytic conversion of glycogen. |
| | Gerty T. Cori, American (Czech-born) | |
| | Bernardo A. Houssay, Argentine | Discovery of part played by hormone of anterior pituitary lobe in metabolism of sugar. |
| 1948 | Paul H. Müller, Swiss | Discovery of high efficiency of DDT as insecticide. |
| 1949 | Walter R. Hess, Swiss | Discovery of functional organization of interbrain as coordinator of activities of internal organs. |
| | Antonio Moniz, Portuguese | Discovery of value of prefrontal lobotomy in certain psychoses. |
| 1950 | Philip S. Hench, American | Discoveries relating to hormones of adrenal cortex, their structure and biological effects. |
| | Edward C. Kendall, American | |
| | Tadeus Reichstein, Swiss (Polish-born) | |
| 1951 | Max Theiler, American (S. African-born) | Discoveries concerning yellow fever and how to combat it. |
| 1952 | Selman A. Waksman, American | Discovery of streptomycin, first antibiotic effective against TB. |
| 1953 | Hans A. Krebs, British (German-born) | Discovery of citric acid cycle. |
| | Fritz A. Lipmann, American (German-born) | Discovery of coenzyme A and its importance for intermediary metabolism. |

| 1954 | John F. Enders, American<br>Federick C. Robbins, American<br>Thomas H. Weller, American | Discovery of ability of poliomyelitis viruses to grow in cultures of various types of tissue. |
|---|---|---|
| 1955 | Alex H. T. Theorell, Swedish | Discoveries concerning oxidation enzymes. |
| 1956 | André F. Cournand, American (French-born)<br>Werner Forssmann, German<br>Dickinson W. Richards Jr., American | Discoveries concerning heart catheterization and pathological changes in circulatory system. |
| 1957 | Daniel Bovet, Italian (Swiss-born) | Discoveries relating to synthetic compounds that inhibit action of certain body substances. |
| 1958 | George W. Beadle, American<br>Edward L. Tatum, American<br>Joshua Lederberg, American | Discovery that genes act by regulating definite chemical events.<br>Discoveries concerning genetic recombination and organization of genetic material of bacteria. |
| 1959 | Arthur Kornberg, American<br>Severo Ochoa, American (Spanish-born) | Discovery of mechanisms in biological synthesis of RNA and DNA. |
| 1960 | Sir F. Macfarlane Burnet, Australian<br>Peter B. Medawar, British (Brazilian-born) | Discovery of acquired immunological tolerance. |
| 1961 | Georg von Békésy, American (Hungarian-born) | Discoveries of physical mechanism of stimulation within cochlea of inner ear. |
| 1962 | Francis H. C. Crick, British<br>James D. Watson, American<br>Maurice H. F. Wilkins, British | Discoveries concerning molecular structure of nuclear acids and its significance for information transfer in living material. |
| 1963 | Sir John C. Eccles, Australian<br>Alan L. Hodgkin, British<br>Andrew F. Huxley, British | Discoveries concerning nerve-cell membrane. |
| 1964 | Konrad E. Bloch, American<br>Feodor Lynen, German | Discoveries concerning mechanism and regulation of cholesterol and fatty-acid metabolism. |
| 1965 | François Jacob, French<br>André Lwoff, French<br>Jacques Monod, French | Discovery of regulatory processes in body cells that contribute to genetic control of enzymes and virus synthesis. |
| 1966 | Charles B. Huggins, American<br><br>Francis Peyton Rous, American | Discoveries concerning hormonal treatment of cancer of prostate gland.<br>Discovery of tumor-inducing viruses in chickens. |
| 1967 | Ragnar Granit, Swedish (Finnish-born)<br>Haldan Keffer Hartline, American<br>George Wald, American | Discoveries concerning primary chemical and physiological visual processes in eye. |
| 1968 | Robert W. Holley, American<br>Har Gobind Khorana, American (Indian-born)<br>Marshall W. Nirenberg, American | Explanation of genetic code that determines function of cells. |
| 1969 | Max Delbrück, American (German-born)<br>Alfred D. Hershey, American<br>Salvador D. Luria, American (Italian-born) | Discoveries concerning reproductive mechanism and genetic structure of viruses. |
| 1970 | Julius Axelrod, American<br>Ulf von Euler, Swedish<br>Bernard Katz, British | Basic research in chemistry of nerve transmission. |
| 1971 | Earl W. Sutherland Jr., American | Discoveries concerning mechanisms of action of hormones. |
| 1972 | Gerald M. Edelman, American<br>Rodney Porter, British | Determination of antibody's exact chemical structure. |
| 1973 | Karl von Frisch, Austrian<br>Konrad Lorenz, Austrian<br>Nikolaas Tinbergen, British (Dutch-born) | Discoveries in individual and social behavior patterns of birds and bees in relation to natural selection and survival of species. |
| 1974 | Albert Claude, American (Luxembourgian-born)<br>Christian Rene de Duve, Belgian<br>George Emil Palade, American (Romanian-born) | Founding science of cell biology, pioneering in use of electron microscope to study living cells, and discovering such cell parts as ribosomes and lysosomes. |
| 1975 | David Baltimore, American<br>Howard Martin Temin, American<br>Renato Dulbecco, American (Italian-born) | Research discoveries concerning interaction between tumor viruses and genetic material of living cell. |
| 1976 | Baruch S. Blumberg, American<br><br>D. Carleton Gajdusek, American | Research that led to test for hepatitis virus in donated blood and to experimental vaccine against hepatitis.<br>Discovery of virus causing kuru disease among cannibals in New Guinea, transmitted through eating of human brains. |
| 1977 | Rosalyn S. Yalow, American<br><br>Roger C. L. Guillemin, American (French-born)<br>Andrew V. Schally, American (Polish-born) | Development of radioimmunoassay, use of radioactive materials to measure hormones and other substances in blood and tissues.<br>Discovery and synthesis of peptide hormones produced by hypothalmus in brain, providing greater understanding of brain's control of body's chemistry. |
| 1978 | Daniel Nathans, American<br>Hamilton O. Smith, American<br>Werner Arber, Swiss | Research that made possible gene splicing or recombinant DNA to create mutant life forms by discovering and using enzymes called *restriction endonucleases*. |
| 1979 | Allan McLeod Cormack, American<br>Godfrey Newbold Hounsfield, British | Development of computed axial tomography (CAT), an X-ray scanning technique used in medical diagnosis of patients. |
| 1980 | George D. Snell, American<br>Baruj Benacerraf, American (Venezuelan-born)<br>Jean Dausset, French | Identification of the HLA antigens, or histocompatability system, in human cells, leading to more successful surgical transplants of human organs. |

# PULITZER PRIZES

The Pulitzer Prizes are the most prestigious awards made each year in the United States for journalism, literature, and music. The prizes were established under terms of the will of Joseph Pulitzer (1847–1911), a Hungarian immigrant who in 1878 founded one of America's great newspapers, the *St. Louis* (Mo.) *Post-Dispatch*, and then in 1883 purchased New York City's *The World*, making it into a crusading newspaper with the largest circulation in the United States.

Upon his death in 1911, Pulitzer left $2 million to found a graduate school of journalism at Columbia University in New York City with the provision that after the school had operated for at least three years prizes should be awarded annually for the advancement of journalism, literature, music, and public service. The Columbia University School of Journalism was founded in 1912. The first Pulitzer Prizes began to be awarded in 1917.

Each prize carries an award of $1,000 except for the gold medal award to a newspaper for meritorious public service.

Prizes in journalism are awarded in 12 categories. Prizes in literature, drama, and music are awarded in seven areas. In addition, special awards are made from time to time.

## LOCAL INVESTIGATIVE REPORTING

1953 Edward J. Mowery, *New York World-Telegram & Sun*
1954 Alvin S. McCoy, *Kansas City* (Mo.) *Star*
1955 Roland K. Towery, *Cuero* (Tex.) *Record*
1956 Arthur Daley, *New York Times*
1957 Wallace Turner and William Lambert, *Portland Oregonian*
1958 George Beveridge, *Washington Evening Star*
1959 John Harold Brislin, *Scranton* (Pa.) *Tribune and Scrantonian*
1960 Mariam Ottenberg, *Washington Evening Star*
1961 Edgar May, *Buffalo Evening News*
1962 George Bliss, *Chicago Tribune*
1963 Oscar O'Neal Griffin Jr., *Pecos* (Tex.) *Independent and Enterprise*
1964 James V. Magee, Albert V. Gaudiosi, and Frederick A. Meyer, *Philadelphia Bulletin*
1965 Gene Goltz, *Houston Post*
1966 John A. Frasca, *Tampa* (Fla.) *Tribune*
1967 Gene Miller, *Miami Herald*
1968 J. Anthony Lukas, *New York Times*
1969 Albert Delugach and Denny Walsh, *St. Louis Globe-Democrat*
1970 Harold E. Martin, *Montgomery* (Ala.) *Advertiser*
1971 William Hugh Jones, *Chicago Tribune*
1972 Ann DeSantis, S. A. Kurkjian, T. Leland, and G. M. O'Neill, *Boston Globe*
1973 *Sun* Newspapers, Omaha, Nebr.
1974 William Sherman, *New York Daily News*
1975 *Indianapolis Star*
1976 Staff of *Chicago Tribune*
1977 Acel Moore and Wendell Rawls Jr., *Philadelphia Inquirer*, for investigation of state mental hospital
1978 Anthony R. Dolan, *Stamford* (Conn.) *Advocate*, for reports on city corruption
1979 Gilbert M. Paul and Elliot G. Jaspin, *Pottsville* (Pa.) *Republican*, for investigation of destruction of coal company by organized crime
1980 Stephen A. Kurkjian, Alexander B. Hawes Jr., Nils J. Bruzelius, Joan Vennochi, and Robert Porterfield, *Boston Globe*, for investigation of Boston's transit system

## LOCAL GENERAL REPORTING

1953 *Providence* (R.I.) *Journal and Evening Bulletin*
1954 *Vicksburg* (Miss.) *Sunday Post-Herald*
1955 Caro Brown, *Alice* (Tex.) *Daily Echo*
1956 Lee Hills, *Detroit Free Press*
1957 *Salt Lake Tribune*
1958 *Fargo* (N.D.) *Forum*
1959 Mary Lou Werner, *Washington Evening Star*
1960 Jack Nelson, *Atlanta Constitution*
1961 Sanche de Gramont, *New York Herald Tribune*
1962 Robert D. Mullins, *Deseret News*, Salt Lake City, Utah

1963 Sylvan Fox, Anthony Shannon, and William Longgood, *New York World-Telegram & Sun*
1964 Norman C. Miller, *Wall Street Journal*
1965 Melvin H. Ruder, *Hungry Horse* (Mont.) *News*
1966 Staff, *Los Angeles Times*
1967 Robert V. Cox, *Chambersburg* (Pa.) *Public Opinion*
1968 *Detroit Free Press*
1969 John Fretterman, *Louisville Courier-Journal*
1970 Thomas Fitzpatrick, *Chicago Sun-Times*
1971 *Akron* (Ohio) *Beacon Journal*
1972 R. I. Cooper and J. W. Machacek, *Rochester* (N.Y.) *Times-Union*
1973 *Chicago Tribune*
1974 Arthur M. Petacque and Hugh F. Hough, *Chicago Sun-Times*
1975 *Xenia* (Ohio) *Daily Gazette*
1976 Gene Miller, *Miami Herald*, who dug up evidence that freed two men convicted of murder
1977 Margo Huston, *Milwaukee Journal*
1978 Richard Whitt, *Louisville* (Ky.) *Courier-Journal*, for coverage of nightclub fire
1979 Staff of *San Diego* (Calif.) *Evening Tribune* for coverage of midair collision
1980 Staff of *Philadelphia Inquirer* for coverage of Three Mile Island nuclear plant accident

## NATIONAL REPORTING

1942 Louis Stark, *New York Times*
1943 No award
1944 Dewey L. Fleming, *Sun*, Baltimore
1945 James B. Reston, *New York Times*
1946 Edward A. Harris, *St. Louis Post-Dispatch*
1947 Edward T. Folliard, *Washington Post*
1948 Bert Andrews, *New York Herald Tribune*, and Nat S. Finney, *Minneapolis Tribune*
1949 Charles P. Trussell, *New York Times*
1950 Edwin O. Guthman, *Seattle Times*
1951 No award
1952 Anthony Leviero, *New York Times*
1953 Don Whitehead, Associated Press
1954 Richard Wilson, Cowles Newspapers
1955 Anthony Lewis, *Washington Daily News*
1956 Charles Bartlett, *Chattanooga* (Tenn.) *Times*
1957 James Reston, *New York Times*
1958 Relman Morin, Associated Press
1959 Howard Van Smith, *Miami News*
1960 Vance Trimble, Scripps-Howard
1961 Edward R. Cony, *Wall Street Journal*
1962 Nathan G. Caldwell and Gene S. Graham, *Nashville Tennessean*
1963 Anthony Lewis, *New York Times*
1964 Merriman Smith, United Press International
1965 Louis Kohlmeier, *Wall Street Journal*
1966 Haynes Johnson, *Washington Evening Star*
1967 Monroe W. Karmin and Stanley W. Penn, *Wall Street Journal*

1968   Howard James, *Christian Science Monitor*, and Nathan Kotz, *Register*, Des Moines, Iowa
1969   Robert Cahn, *Christian Science Monitor*
1970   William J. Seton, *Chicago Daily News*
1971   Lucinda Franks and Thomas Powers, United Press International
1972   Jack Anderson, syndicated columnist
1973   Robert Boyd and Clark Hoyt, the Knight Newspapers
1974   James R. Polk, *Washington Star-News*, and Jack White, *Providence* (R.I.) *Journal-Bulletin*
1975   Donald L. Barlett and James B. Steel, *Philadelphia Inquirer*
1976   James Risser, *Register*, Des Moines, Iowa
1977   Walter Mears, Associated Press
1978   Gaylord Shaw, *Los Angeles Times*, for investigation of unsafe dams
1979   James Risser, *Register*, Des Moines, Iowa, for series on pollution caused by farmers
1980   Bette Swenson Orsini and Charles Stafford, *St. Petersburg* (Fla.) *Times* for investigation of Church of Scientology

## INTERNATIONAL CORRESPONDENCE

1942   Laurence E. Allen, Associated Press
1943   Ira Wolfert, North American Newspaper Alliance
1944   Daniel DeLuce, Associated Press
1945   Mark S. Watson, *Sun*, Baltimore
1946   Homer W. Bigart, *New York Herald Tribune*
1947   Eddy Gilmore, Associated Press
1948   Paul W. Ward, *Sun*, Baltimore
1949   Price Day, *Sun*, Baltimore
1950   Edmund Stevens, *Christian Science Monitor*
1951   Keyes Beech and Fred Sparks, *Chicago Daily News*, Homer Bigart and Marguerite Higgins, *New York Herald Tribune*, Relman Morin and Don Whitehead, Associated Press
1952   John M. Hightower, Associated Press
1953   Austin Wehrwein, *Milwaukee Journal*
1954   Jim G. Lucas, Scripps-Howard Newspapers
1955   Harrison Salisbury, *New York Times*
1956   William Randolph Hearst Jr., Kingsbury Smith, and Frank Conniff, International News Service
1957   Russell Jones, United Press
1958   *New York Times*
1959   Joseph Martin and Philip Santora, *New York Daily News*
1960   A.M. Rosenthal, *New York Times*
1961   Lynn Heinzerling, Associated Press
1962   Walter Lippmann, New York Herald Tribune Syndicate
1963   Hal Hendrix, *Miami News*
1964   Malcolm W. Browne, Associated Press David Halberstam, *New York Times*
1965   J.A. Livingston, *Philadelphia Bulletin*
1966   Peter Arnett, Associated Press
1967   R.J. Hughes, *Christian Science Monitor*
1968   Alfred Friendly, *Washington Post*
1969   William Tuohy, *Los Angeles Times*
1970   Seymour M. Hersh, Dispatch News Service
1971   Jimmie Lee Hoagland, *Washington Post*
1972   Peter R. Kann, *Wall Street Journal*
1973   Max Frankel, *New York Times*
1974   Hedrick Smith, *New York Times*
1975   William Mullen and Ovie Carter, *Chicago Tribune*
1976   Sydney H. Schanberg, *New York Times*
1977   No award
1978   Henry Kamm, *New York Times*, for reports on Indochinese refugee "boat people"
1979   Richard Ben Cramer, *Philadelphia Inquirer*, for dispatches on war in Middle East

1980   Joel Brinkley and Jay Mather, *Louisville* (Ky.) *Courier-Journal* for Cambodia coverage

## FEATURE WRITING

1979   Jon D. Franklin, *Baltimore Evening Sun*, for two-part report on brain operation
1980   Madeline Blais, *Miami Herald*

## EDITORIAL WRITING

1917   *New York Tribune*
1918   *Courier-Journal*, Louisville, Ky.
1919   No award
1920   Harvey E. Newbranch, *Evening World-Herald*, Omaha
1921   No award
1922   Frank M. O'Brien, *New York Herald*
1923   William Allen White, *Emporia* (Kans.) *Gazette*
1924   *Boston Herald*
       Special award: Frank I. Cobb, *New York World*
1925   *Charleston* (S.C.) *News and Courier*
1926   Edward M. Kingsbury, *New York Times*
1927   F.L. Bullard, *Boston Herald*
1928   Grover Cleveland Hall, *Montgomery* (Ala.) *Advertiser*
1929   Louis I. Jaffee, *Norfolk Virginian-Pilot*
1930   No award
1931   Charles S. Ryckman, *Fremont* (Nebr.) *Tribune*
1932   No award
1933   *Kansas City Star*
1934   E.P. Chase, *Atlantic* (Iowa) *News-Telegraph*
1935   No award
1936   Felix Morley, *Washington Post*
       George B. Parker, Scripps-Howard
1937   John W. Owens, *Baltimore Sun*
1938   W.W. Waymack, *Register and Tribune*, Des Moines, Iowa
1939   Ronald G. Callvert, *Portland Oregonian*
1940   Bart Howard, *St. Louis Post-Dispatch*
1941   Reuben Maury, *New York Daily News*
1942   Geoffrey Parsons, *New York Herald Tribune*
1943   Forrest W. Seymour, *Register and Tribune*, Des Moines, Iowa
1944   Henry J. Haskell, *Kansas City Star*
1945   George W. Potter, *Providence* (R.I.) *Journal-Bulletin*
1946   Hodding Carter, *Delta Democrat-Times*, Greenville, Miss.
1947   William Grimes, *Wall Street Journal*
1948   Virginius Dabney, *Richmond* (Va.) *Times-Dispatch*
1949   John H. Crider, *Boston Herald*
       Herbert Elliston, *Washington Post*
1950   Carl M. Saunders, *Jackson* (Mich.) *Citizen Patriot*
1951   William Fitzpatrick, *New Orleans States*
1952   Louis LaCoss, *St. Louis Globe-Democrat*
1953   Vermont Royster, *Wall Street Journal*
1954   Don Murray, *Boston Herald*
1955   Royce Howes, *Detroit Free Press*
1956   Lauren K. Soth, *Register and Tribune*, Des Moines, Iowa
1957   Buford Boone, *Tuscaloosa* (Ala.) *News*
1958   Harry S. Ashmore, *Arkansas Gazette*, Little Rock
1959   Ralph McGill, *Atlanta Constitution*
1960   Lenoir Chambers, *Norfolk Virginian-Pilot*
1961   William J. Dorvillier, *San Juan* (P.R.) *Star*
1962   Thomas M. Storke, *Santa Barbara* (Calif.) *News-Press*
1963   Ira B. Harkey Jr., *Pascagoula* (Miss.) *Chronicle*
1964   Hazel Smith, *Lexington* (Miss.) *Advertiser*
1965   John R. Harrison, *Gainesville* (Fla.) *Sun*

**PULITZER PRIZES** (continued)

1966    Robert Lasch, *St. Louis Post-Dispatch*
1967    Eugene C. Patterson, *Atlanta Constitution*
1968    John S. Knight, Knight Newspapers
1969    Paul Greenberg, *Pine Bluff* (Ark.) *Commercial*
1970    Philip Geyelin, *Washington Post*
1971    Horance G. Davis Jr., *Gainesville* (Fla.) *Sun*
1972    J. Strohmeyer, *Bethlehem* (Pa.) *Globe-Times*
1973    Roger B. Linscott, *Berkshire Eagle,* Pittsfield, Mass.
1974    F. Gilman Spencer, *Trenton Trentonian*
1975    John Daniell Maurice, *Charleston* (W.Va.) *Daily Mail*
1976    Philip P. Kerby, *Los Angeles Times*
1977    Warren L. Lerude, Foster Church, Norman F. Cardoza, *Reno Evening Gazette* and *Nevada State Journal*
1978    Meg Greenfield, *Washington Post*
1979    Edwin M. Yoder Jr., *Washington Star*
1980    Robert L. Bartley, *Wall Street Journal*

## CARTOON PULITZER PRIZES

1922    Rollin Kirby, *New York World*
1923    No award
1924    Jay Norwood Darling, *New York Tribune*
1925    Rollin Kirby, *New York World*
1926    Daniel R. Fitzpatrick, *St. Louis Post-Dispatch*
1927    Nelson Harding, *Brooklyn Daily Eagle*
1928    Nelson Harding, *Brooklyn Daily Eagle*
1929    Rollin Kirby, *New York World*
1930    Charles R. Macauley, *Brooklyn Daily Eagle*
1931    Edmund Duffy, *Baltimore Sun*
1932    John McCutcheon, *Chicago Tribune*
1933    Harold Morton Talburt, *Washington Daily News*
1934    Edmund Duffy, *Baltimore Sun*
1935    Ross A. Lewis, *Milwaukee Journal*
1936    No award
1937    Clarence Daniel Batchelor, *New York Daily News*
1938    Vaughn Shoemaker, *Chicago Daily News*
1939    Charles G. Werner, *Daily Oklahoman,* Oklahoma City
1940    Edmund Duffy, *Baltimore Sun*
1941    Jacob Burck, *Chicago Times*
1942    Herbert L. Block (Herblock), Newspaper Enterprise Association Service
1943    Jay Norwood Darling, *New York Herald Tribune*
1944    Clifford K. Berryman, *Washington Evening Star*
1945    William (Bill) Mauldin, United Features Syndicate, Inc.
1946    Bruce Russell, *Los Angeles Times*
1947    V. Shoemaker, *Chicago Daily News*
1948    Reuben L. (Rube) Goldberg, *New York Sun*
1949    Lute Pease, *Newark,* (N.J.) *Evening News*
1950    James T. Berryman, *Washington Evening Star*
1951    Reginald W. Manning, *Arizona Republic,* Phoenix, Ariz.
1952    Fred L. Packer, *New York Mirror*
1953    Edward D. Kuekes, *Cleveland Plain Dealer*
1954    Herbert L. Block (Herblock), *Washington Post & Times-Herald*
1955    Daniel R. Fitzpatrick, *St. Louis Post-Dispatch*
1956    Robert York, *Louisville Times*
1957    Tom Little, *Nashville Tennessean*
1958    Bruce M. Shanks, *Buffalo Evening News*
1959    William (Bill) Mauldin, *St. Louis Post-Dispatch*
1960    No award
1961    Carey Orr, *Chicago Tribune*
1962    E.S. Valtman, *Hartford* (Conn.) *Times*
1963    Frank Miller, *Des Moines Register*
1964    Paul Conrad, *Denver Post*

1965    No award
1966    Don Wright, *Miami News*
1967    Patrick B. Oliphant, *Denver Post*
1968    E. G. Payne, *Charlotte* (N.C.) *Observer*
1969    John Fischetti, *Chicago Daily News*
1970    Thomas Darcy, *Newsday,* Garden City, N.Y.
1971    Paul Conrad, *Los Angeles Times*
1972    J. K. MacNelly, *Richmond* (Va.) *News Leader*
1973    No award
1974    Paul Szep, *Boston Globe*
1975    Garry Trudeau, creator of "Doonesbury"
1976    Tony Auth, political cartoonist, *Philadelphia Inquirer*
1977    Paul Szep, *Boston Globe*
1978    J. K. MacNelly, *Richmond* (Va.) *News Leader*
1979    Herbert L. Block (Herblock), *Washington Post*
1980    Don Wright, *Miami News*

## NEWS PHOTOGRAPHY PULITZER PRIZES

1942    Milton Brooks, *Detroit News*
1943    Frank Noel, Associated Press
1944    Frank Filan, Associated Press
1945    Joe Rosenthal, Associated Press
1946    No award
1947    Arnold Hardy, amateur photographer
1948    Frank Cushing, *Boston Traveler*
1949    Nathaniel Fein, *New York Herald Tribune*
1950    Bill Crouch, *Oakland* (Calif.) *Tribune*
1951    Max Desfor, Associated Press
1952    John Robinson and Don Ultang, *Des Moines Register and Tribune*
1953    William M. Gallagher, *Flint* (Mich.) *Journal*
1954    Mrs. Walter M. Schau, photographer
1955    John L. Gaunt Jr., *Los Angeles Times*
1956    *New York Daily News*
1957    Harry A. Trask, *Boston Traveler*
1958    William C. Beall, *Washington Daily News*
1959    William Seaman, *Minneapolis Star*
1960    Andrew Lopez, United Press International
1961    Yasushi Nagao, Mainichi Newspapers, Tokyo, Japan
1962    Paul Vathis, Associated Press
1963    Hector Rondon, *La Republica,* Caracas, Venezuela
1964    Robert H. Jackson, *Dallas Times Herald*
1965    Horst Faas, Associated Press
1966    Kyoichi Sawada, United Press International
1967    Jack R. Thornell, Associated Press
1968    Rocco Morabito, *Jacksonville* (Fla.) *Journal*
1969    Edward T. Adams, Associated Press
1970    Steve Starr, Associated Press
1971    John Paul Filo, amateur photographer
1972    H. Faas, M. Laurent, Associated Press
1973    Huynh Cong Ut, Associated Press
1974    Anthony K. Roberts, freelance
1975    Gerald H. Gay, *Seattle Times*
1976    Stanley Forman, *Boston Herald-American*
1977    Stanley Forman, *Boston Herald-American,* and Neal Ulevich, Associated Press
1978    John W. Blair, freelance
1979    Thomas J. Kelley III, *Pottstown* (Pa.) *Mercury*
1980    Unidentified photographer of Iranian firing squad.

## FEATURE PHOTOGRAPHY PULITZER PRIZES

1968    Toshio Sakai, United Press International
1969    Moneta Sleet Jr., *Ebony* magazine
1970    Dallas Kinney, *Palm Beach* (Fla.) *Post*
1971    Jack Dykinga, *Chicago Sun-Times*
1972    Dave Kennerly, United Press International
1973    B. Lanker, *Topeka* (Kans.) *Capital-Journal*
1974    Slava Veder, Associated Press
1975    Matthew Lewis, *Washington Post*

1976 Photographic staff of *Louisville Courier-Journal and Times*
1977 Robin Hood, *News-Free Press*, Chattanooga, Tenn.
1978 J. Ross Baughman, freelance
1979 Staff of *The Boston Herald-American*
1980 Erwin H. Hagler, *Dallas Times Herald*

## MERITORIOUS PUBLIC SERVICE

1917 No award
1918 *New York Times*
1919 *Milwaukee Journal*
1920 No award
1921 *Boston Post*
1922 *World,* New York
1923 *Memphis Commercial Appeal*
1924 *World,* New York
1925 No award
1926 *Enquirer Sun,* Columbus, Ga.
1927 *Canton (Ohio) Daily News*
1928 *Indianapolis Times*
1929 *Evening World,* New York
1930 No award
1931 *Atlanta Constitution*
1932 *Indianapolis News*
1933 *New York World-Telegram*
1934 *Medford (Oreg.) Mail Tribune*
1935 *Sacramento (Calif.) Bee*
1936 *Cedar Rapids (Iowa) Gazette*
1937 *St. Louis Post-Dispatch*
1938 *Bismarck (N.D.) Tribune*
1939 *Miami Daily News*
1940 *Waterbury (Conn.) Republican and American*
1941 *St. Louis Post-Dispatch*
1942 *Los Angeles Times*
1943 *World-Herald,* Omaha, Nebr.
1944 *New York Times*
1945 *Detroit Free Press*
1946 *Scranton (Pa.) Times*
1947 *Baltimore Sun*
1948 *St. Louis Post-Dispatch*
1949 *Nebraska State Journal*
1950 *Chicago Daily News; St. Louis Post-Dispatch*
1951 *Miami Herald; Brooklyn Eagle*
1952 *St. Louis Post-Dispatch*
1953 *News Reporter,* Whiteville, N.C. *Tabor City (N.C.) Tribune*
1954 Newsday, Garden City, N.Y.
1955 *Columbus (Ga.) Ledger and Sunday Ledger-Enquirer*
1956 *Watsonville (Calif.) Register-Pajaronian*
1957 *Chicago Daily News*
1958 *Arkansas Gazette,* Little Rock
1959 *Utica (N.Y.) Observer-Dispatch Utica (N.Y.) Daily Press*
1960 *Los Angeles Times*
1961 *Amarillo (Tex.) Globe-Times*
1962 *Panama City (Fla.) News-Herald*
1963 *Chicago Daily News*
1964 *St. Petersburg (Fla.) Times*
1965 *Hutchinson (Kans.) News*
1966 *Boston Globe*
1967 *Louisville Courier-Journal; Milwaukee Journal*
1968 *Riverside (Calif.) Press*
1969 *Los Angeles Times*
1970 Newsday, Garden City, N.Y.
1971 *Winston-Salem (N.C.) Journal and Sentinel*
1972 *New York Times*
1973 *Washington Post*
1974 Newsday, Garden City, N.Y.
1975 *Boston Globe*
1976 *Anchorage (Alaska) Daily News*
1977 *Lufkin (Tex.) News*
1978 *Philadelphia Inquirer*

1979 *Point Reyes (Calif.) Light,* for Synanon exposé
1980 Gannett News Service, for exposing mismanagement of funds of Pauline Fathers

## CRITICISM PULITZER PRIZES

1970 Ada Louise Huxtable, *New York Times*
1971 Harold C. Schonberg, *New York Times*
1972 Frank L. Peters Jr., *St. Louis Post-Dispatch*
1973 Ronald Powers, *Chicago Sun-Times*
1974 Emily Genauer, *Newsday* syndicate
1975 Roger Ebert, *Chicago Sun-Times*
1976 Alan M. Kriegsman, *Washington Post*
1977 William McPherson, *Washington Post*
1978 Walter Kerr, *New York Times*
1979 Paul Gapp, *Chicago Tribune*
1980 William A. Henry III, TV critic, *Boston Globe*

## COMMENTARY PULITZER PRIZES

1970 Marquis Childs, *St. Louis Post-Dispatch*
1971 William A. Caldwell, *Record,* Hackensack, N.J.
1972 Mike Royko, *Chicago Daily News*
1973 David S. Broder, *Washington Post*
1974 Edwin A. Roberts Jr., *National Observer*
1975 Mary McGrory, *Washington Star*
1976 Walter W. (Red) Smith, sports columnist, *New York Times*
1977 George F. Will, syndicated columnist, Washington Post Writers Group
1978 William Safire, columnist, *New York Times*
1979 Russell Baker, columnist, *New York Times*
1980 Ellen H. Goodman, columnist, *Boston Globe*

## REPORTING PULITZER PRIZES: 1917–1952

1917 Herbert B. Swope, *World,* New York
1918 Harold A. Littledale, *New York Evening Post*
1919 No award
1920 John J. Leary Jr., *World,* New York
1921 Louis Seibold, *World,* New York
1922 Kirke L. Simpson, Associated Press
1923 Alva Johnston, *New York Times*
1924 Magner White, *San Diego Sun*
1925 James W. Mulroy, Alvin H. Goldstein, *Chicago Daily News*
1926 William B. Miller, *Courier-Journal,* Louisville
1927 John T. Rogers, *St. Louis Post-Dispatch*
1928 No award
1929 Paul Y. Anderson, *St. Louis Post-Dispatch*
1930 Russell D. Owen, *New York Times*
1931 A. B. MacDonald, *Kansas City Star*
1932 W. C. Richards, D. D. Martin, J. S. Pooler, F. D. Webb, J. N. W. Sloan, *Detroit Free Press*
1933 Francis A. Jamieson, Associated Press
1934 Royce Brier, *San Francisco Chronicle*
1935 William H. Taylor, *New York Herald Tribune*
1936 Lauren D. Lyman, *New York Times*
1937 John J. O'Neill, *New York Herald Tribune,* William L. Laurence, *New York Times,* Howard W. Blakeslee, Associated Press, Gobind Behari Lal, Universal Service, David Dietz, Scripps-Howard newspapers
1938 Raymond Sprigle, *Pittsburgh Post-Gazette*
1939 Thomas L. Stokes, Scripps-Howard
1940 S. Burton Heath, *New York World-Telegram*
1941 Westbrook Pegler, *New York World-Telegram*
1942 Stanton Delaplane, *San Francisco Chronicle*
1943 George Weller, *Chicago Daily News*
1944 Paul Schoenstein and associates, *New York Journal-American*
1945 Jack S. McDowell, *Call-Bulletin,* San Francisco
1946 William L. Laurence, *New York Times*
1947 Frederick Woltman, *New York World-Telegram*
1948 George E. Goodwin, *Atlanta Journal*
1949 Malcolm Johnson, *Sun,* New York
1950 Meyer Berger, *New York Times*

**PULITZER PRIZES** (continued)

1951    Edward Montgomery, *San Francisco Examiner*
1952    George de Carvalho, *San Francisco Chronicle*

## NEWSPAPER HISTORY PULITZER AWARD

1918    Minna Lewinson and Henry Beetle Hough, for their history of services rendered to the public by the American press during 1917.

## SPECIAL PULITZER PRIZE CITATIONS

1938    *Edmonton Journal*, for defending freedom of the press in Alberta, Canada.
1941    *New York Times*, for the public educational value of its foreign news reporting, exemplified by its scope, excellence of writing and presentation, and supplementary background information and interpretation.
1944    To Mrs. William Allen White, for interest and services during previous seven years as member of Advisory Board of the Graduate School of Journalism, Columbia University.
        Byron Price, Director of the Office of Censorship, for the creation and administration of the newspaper and radio codes.
1945    The cartographers of the American press, whose maps of the war fronts helped notably to clarify and increase public information on the progress of the armies and navies engaged in World War II.
1947    (Pulitzer Centennial year)
        Columbia University and the Graduate School of Journalism, for their efforts to maintain and advance the high standards governing the Pulitzer Prize awards.
1948    To Dr. Frank Diehl Fackenthal, a scroll indicating appreciation of his interest and service during the preceding years.
1951    Cyrus L. Sulzberger, of *New York Times*, for his exclusive interview with Archbishop Aloysius Stepinac of Yugoslavia.
1952    *Kansas City Star*, for the news coverage of the great regional flood of 1951 in Kansas and northwestern Missouri.
        Max Case, of *New York Journal-American*, for his exposures of corruption in basketball.
1953    *New York Times*, for the section of its Sunday edition headed *Review of the Week*, which for 17 years brought enlightened commentary to its readers.
1958    Walter Lippmann, nationally syndicated columnist of *New York Herald Tribune*, for the wisdom, perception, and high sense of responsibility with which he commented on national and international affairs.
1964    Gannett Newspapers, Rochester, N.Y., for their program *The Road to Integration*, a distinguished example of the use of a newspaper group's resources to complement the work of its individual newspapers.
1973    James T. Flexner, for *George Washington*, a four-volume biography.
1976    Scott Joplin (1868–1917), special Bicentennial year award for his contributions to American music with such compositions as *Maple Leaf Rag*.
1976    John Hohenberg, for 22 years of service as administrator of the Pulitzer Prizes.
1977    Alex Haley, for *Roots*, an "important contribution to the literature of slavery."
1978    E. B. White, for contributions to literature; Richard L. Strout, for contributions to journalism.

## FICTION PULITZER PRIZES

1917    No award
1918    *His Family*, by Ernest Poole
1919    *The Magnificent Ambersons*, by Booth Tarkington
1920    No award
1921    *The Age of Innocence*, by Edith Wharton
1922    *Alice Adams*, by Booth Tarkington
1923    *One of Ours*, by Willa Cather
1924    *The Able McLaughlins*, by Margaret Wilson
1925    *So Big*, by Edna Ferber
1926    *Arrowsmith*, by Sinclair Lewis
1927    *Early Autumn*, by Louis Bromfield
1928    *The Bridge of San Luis Rey*, by Thornton Wilder
1929    *Scarlet Sister Mary*, by Julia Peterkin
1930    *Laughing Boy*, by Oliver LaFarge
1931    *Years of Grace*, by Margaret Ayer Barnes
1932    *The Good Earth*, by Pearl S. Buck
1933    *The Store*, by T.S. Stribling
1934    *Lamb in His Bosom*, by Caroline Miller
1935    *Now in November*, by Josephine Winslow Johnson
1936    *Honey in the Horn*, by Harold L. Davis
1937    *Gone with the Wind*, by Margaret Mitchell
1938    *The Late George Apley*, by John Phillips Marquand
1939    *The Yearling*, by Marjorie Kinnan Rawlings
1940    *The Grapes of Wrath*, by John Steinbeck
1941    No award
1942    *In This Our Life*, by Ellen Glasgow
1943    *Dragon's Teeth*, by Upton Sinclair
1944    *Journey in the Dark*, By Martin Flavin
1945    *A Bell for Adano*, by John Hersey
1946    No award
1947    *All the King's Men*, by Robert Penn Warren
1948    *Tales of the South Pacific*, by James Michener
1949    *Guard of Honor*, by James Gould Cozzens
1950    *The Way West*, by A. B. Guthrie Jr.
1951    *The Town*, by Conrad Richter
1952    *The Caine Mutiny*, by Herman Wouk
1953    *The Old Man and the Sea*, by Ernest Hemingway
1954    No Award
1955    *A Fable*, by William Faulkner
1956    *Andersonville*, by MacKinlay Kantor
1957    No award
1958    *A Death in the Family*, by James Agee
1959    *The Travels of Jaimie McPheeters*, by Robert Lewis Taylor
1960    *Advise and Consent*, by Allen Drury
1961    *To Kill a Mockingbird*, by Harper Lee
1962    *The Edge of Sadness*, by Edwin O'Connor
1963    *The Reivers*, by William Faulkner
1964    No award
1965    *The Keepers of the House*, by Shirley Ann Grau
1966    *The Collected Stories of Katherine Anne Porter*, by Katherine Anne Porter
1967    *The Fixer*, by Bernard Malamud
1968    *The Confessions of Nat Turner*, by William Styron
1969    *House Made of Dawn*, by N. Scott Momaday
1970    *Collected Stories*, by Jean Stafford
1971    No award
1972    *Angle of Repose*, by Wallace Stegner
1973    *The Optimist's Daughter*, by Eudora Welty
1974    No award
1975    *The Killer Angels*, by Michael Shaara
1976    *Humboldt's Gift*, by Saul Bellow
1977    No award
1978    *Elbow Room*, by James Alan McPherson
1979    *The Stories of John Cheever*, by John Cheever
1980    *The Executioner's Song*, by Norman Mailer

## DRAMA PULITZER PRIZES

1917  No award
1918  *Why Marry?*, by Jesse L. Williams
1919  No award
1920  *Beyond the Horizon*, By Eugene O'Neill
1921  *Miss Lulu Bett*, by Zona Gale
1922  *Anna Christie*, by Eugene O'Neill
1923  *Icebound*, by Owen Davis
1924  *Hell-Bent for Heaven*, by Hatcher Hughes
1925  *They Knew What They Wanted*,
      by Sidney Howard
1926  *Craig's Wife*, by George Kelly
1927  *In Abraham's Bosom*, by Paul Green
1928  *Strange Interlude*, by Eugene O'Neill
1929  *Street Scene*, by Elmer L. Rice
1930  *The Green Pastures*, by Marc Connelly
1931  *Alison's House*, by Susan Glaspell
1932  *Of Thee I Sing*, by George S. Kaufman, Ira
      Gershwin, and Morris Ryskind
1933  *Both Your Houses*, by Maxwell Anderson
1934  *Men in White*, by Sidney Kingsley
1935  *The Old Maid*, by Zoe Akins
1936  *Idiot's Delight*, by Robert E. Sherwood
1937  *You Can't Take It with You*, by Moss Hart
      and George S. Kaufman
1938  *Our Town*, by Thornton Wilder
1939  *Abe Lincoln in Illinois*, by Robert E. Sherwood
1940  *The Time of Your Life*, by William Saroyan
1941  *There Shall Be No Night*,
      by Robert E. Sherwood
1942  No award
1943  *The Skin of Our Teeth*, by Thornton Wilder
1944  No award
1945  *Harvey*, by Mary Chase
1946  *State of the Union*, by Russel Crouse and
      Howard Lindsay
1947  No award
1948  *A Streetcar Named Desire*,
      by Tennessee Williams
1949  *Death of a Salesman*, by Arthur Miller
1950  *South Pacific*, by Richard Rogers, Oscar
      Hammerstein II, and Joshua Logan
1951  No award
1952  *The Shrike*, by Joseph Kramm
1953  *Picnic*, by William Inge
1954  *The Teahouse of the August Moon*,
      by John Patrick
1955  *Cat on a Hot Tin Roof*, by Tennessee Williams
1956  *Diary of Anne Frank*, by Albert Hackett and
      Frances Goodrich
1957  *Long Day's Journey Into Night*,
      by Eugene O'Neill
1958  *Look Homeward, Angel*, by Ketti Frings
1959  *J. B.*, by Archibald MacLeish
1960  *Fiorello!* by Jerome Weidman and
      George Abbott
1961  *All the Way Home*, by Tad Mosel
1962  *How to Succeed in Business Without Really
      Trying*, by Frank Loesser and Abe Burrows
1963–64  No award
1965  *The Subject Was Roses*, by Frank Gilroy
1966  No award
1967  *A Delicate Balance*, by Edward Albee
1968  No award
1969  *The Great White Hope*, by Howard Sackler
1970  *No Place to Be Somebody*, by Charles Gordone
1971  *The Effect of Gamma Rays on Man-in-the-
      Moon Marigolds*, by Paul Zindel
1972  No award
1973  *That Championship Season*, by Jason Miller
1974  No award
1975  *Seascape*, by Edward Albee
1976  *A Chorus Line*, produced by Joseph Papp
1977  *The Shadow Box*, by Michael Cristofer
1978  *The Gin Game*, by Donald L. Coburn
1979  *Buried Child*, by Sam Shepard
1980  *Talley's Folly*, by Lanford Wilson

## HISTORY PULITZER PRIZES

1917  *With Americans of Past and Present Days*,
      by J. J. Jusserand
1918  *A History of the Civil War, 1861–65*,
      by James Ford Rhodes
1919  No award
1920  *The War with Mexico*, by Justin H. Smith
1921  *The Victory at Sea*, William Sowden Sims
      and Burton J. Hendrick
1922  *The Founding of New England*,
      by James Truslow Adams
1923  *The Supreme Court in United States History*,
      by Charles Warren
1924  *The American Revolution—A Constitutional
      Interpretation*, by Charles McIlwain
1925  *A History of the American Frontier*,
      by Frederic L. Paxson
1926  *The History of the United States*,
      by Edward Channing
1927  *Pinckney's Treaty*, by Samuel Flagg Bemis
1928  *Main Currents in American Thought* (2 vols.),
      by Vernon Louis Parrington
1929  *The Organization and Administration of the
      Union Army, 1861–1865*,
      by Fred Albert Shannon
1930  *The War of Independence*,
      by Claude H. Van Tyne
1931  *The Coming of the War: 1914*,
      by Bernadotte E. Schmitt
1932  *My Experiences in the World War*,
      by John J. Pershing
1933  *The Significance of Sections in American History*,
      by Frederick J. Turner
1934  *The People's Choice*, by Herbert Agar
1935  *The Colonial Period of American History*,
      by Charles McLean Andrews
1936  *The Constitutional History of the United States*,
      by Andrew C. McLaughlin
1937  *The Flowering of New England*,
      by Van Wyck Brooks
1938  *The Road to Reunion, 1865–1900*,
      by Paul Herman Buck
1939  *A History of American Magazines*,
      by Frank Luther Mott
1940  *Abraham Lincoln: The War Years*,
      by Carl Sandburg
1941  *The Atlantic Migration, 1607–1860*,
      by Marcus Lee Hansen
1942  *Reveille in Washington*, by Margaret Leech
1943  *Paul Revere and the World He Lived In*,
      by Esther Forbes
1944  *The Growth of American Thought*,
      by Merle Curti
1945  *Unfinished Business*, by Stephen Bonsal
1946  *The Age of Jackson*,
      by Arthur M. Schlesinger Jr.
1947  *Scientists Against Time*,
      by James Phinney Baxter III
1948  *Across the Wide Missouri*, by Bernard DeVoto
1949  *The Disruption of American Democracy*,
      by Roy Franklin Nichols
1950  *Art and Life in America*, by Oliver W. Larkin
1951  *The Old Northwest: Pioneer Period, 1815–1840*,
      by R. Carlyle Buley
1952  *The Uprooted*, by Oscar Handlin
1953  *The Era of Good Feelings*,
      by George Dangerfield
1954  *A Stillness at Appomattox*, by Bruce Catton
1955  *Great River: The Rio Grande in North American
      History*, by Paul Horgan

PULITZER PRIZES (continued)

1956   *Age of Reform,* by Richard Hofstadter
1957   *Russia Leaves the War: Soviet-American Relations, 1917–1920,* by George F. Kennan
1958   *Banks and Politics in America—From the Revolution to the Civil War,* by Bray Hammond
1959   *The Republican Era: 1869–1901,* by Leonard D. White, assisted by Jean Schneider
1960   *In the Days of McKinley,* by Margaret Leech
1961   *Between War and Peace: The Potsdam Conference,* by Herbert Feis
1962   *The Triumphant Empire: Thunder-Clouds Gather in the West,* by Lawrence H. Gipson
1963   *Washington: Village and Capital, 1800–1878,* by Constance McLaughlin Green
1964   *Puritan Village: The Formation of a New England Town,* by Sumner Chilton Powell
1965   *The Greenback Era,* by Irwin Unger
1966   *Life of the Mind in America: From the Revolution to the Civil War,* by Perry Miller
1967   *Exploration and Empire: The Explorer and Scientist in the Winning of the American West,* by William H. Goetzmann
1968   *The Ideological Origins of the American Revolution,* by Bernard Bailyn
1969   *Origins of the Fifth Amendment,* by Leonard Levy
1970   *Present at the Creation: My Years in the State Department,* by Dean G. Acheson
1971   *Roosevelt: The Soldier of Freedom, 1940–1945,* by James MacGregor Burns
1972   *Neither Black Nor White,* by C. N. Degler
1973   *People of Paradox: An Inquiry Concerning the Origin of American Civilization,* by Michael Kammen
1974   *The Americans: The Democratic Experience,* by Daniel J. Boorstin
1975   *Jefferson and His Time,* by Dumas Malone
1976   *Lamy of Santa Fe,* by Paul Horgan
1977   *The Impending Crisis,* by David M. Potter
1978   *The Visible Hand: The Managerial Revolution in American Business,* by Alfred D. Chandler Jr.
1979   *The Dred Scott Case,* by Don E. Fehrenberger
1980   *Been in the Storm So Long,* by Leon F. Litwack

## BIOGRAPHY/AUTOBIOGRAPHY PULITZER PRIZES

1917   *Julia Ward Howe,* by Laura E. Richards, Maude H. Elliot, and Florence H. Hall
1918   *Benjamin Franklin, Self-Revealed,* by William Cabell Bruce
1919   *The Education of Henry Adams,* by Henry Adams
1920   *The Life of John Marshall* (4 vols.), by Albert J. Beveridge
1921   *The Americanization of Edward Bok,* by Edward Bok
1922   *A Daughter of the Middle Border,* by Hamlin Garland
1923   *The Life and Letters of Walter H. Page,* by Burton J. Hendrick
1924   *From Immigrant to Inventor,* by Michael Idvorsky Pupin
1925   *Barrett Wendell and His Letters,* by M. A. DeWolfe Howe
1926   *The Life of Sir William Osler* (2 vols.), by Harvey Cushing
1927   *Whitman,* by Emory Holloway
1928   *The American Orchestra and Theodore Thomas,* by Charles Edward Russell
1929   *The Training of an American: The Earlier Life and Letters of Walter H. Page,* by Burton J. Hendrick
1930   *The Raven,* by Marquis James
1931   *Charles W. Eliot,* by Henry James
1932   *Theodore Roosevelt,* by Henry F. Pringle
1933   *Grover Cleveland,* by Allan Nevins

1934   *John Hay,* by Tyler Dennett
1935   *R.E. Lee,* by Douglas Southall Freeman
1936   *The Thought and Character of William James,* by Ralph Barton Perry
1937   *Hamilton Fish,* by Allan Nevins
1938   *Pedlar's Progress,* by Odell Shepard
         *Andrew Jackson,* by Marquis James
1939   *Benjamin Franklin,* by Carl Van Doren
1940   *Woodrow Wilson, Life and Letters, Volumes VII and VIII,* by Ray Stannard Baker
1941   *Jonathan Edwards,* by Ola E. Winslow
1942   *Crusader in Crinoline,* by Forrest Wilson
1943   *Admiral of the Ocean Sea,* by Samuel Eliot Morison
1944   *The American Leonardo: The Life of Samuel F. B. Morse,* by Carleton Mabee
1945   *George Bancroft: Brahmin Rebel,* by Russell Blaine Nye
1946   *Son of the Wilderness,* by Linnie M. Wolfe
1947   *The Autobiography of William Allen White,* by William Allen White
1948   *Forgotten First Citizen: John Bigelow,* by Margaret Clapp
1949   *Roosevelt and Hopkins,* by Robert E. Sherwood
1950   *John Quincy Adams and the Foundations of American Foreign Policy,* by Samuel Bemis
1951   *John C. Calhoun: American Portrait,* by Margaret Louise Coit
1952   *Charles Evans Hughes,* by Merlo J. Pusey
1953   *Edmund Pendleton 1721–1803,* by David J. Mays
1954   *The Spirit of St. Louis,* by Charles A. Lindbergh
1955   *The Taft Story,* by William S. White
1956   *Benjamin Henry Latrobe,* by T. F. Hamlin
1957   *Profiles in Courage,* by John F. Kennedy
1958   *George Washington, Volumes I-VI,* by Douglas Southall Freeman; *Volume VII,* by Mary Ashworth and John Carroll
1959   *Woodrow Wilson, American Prophet,* by Arthur Walworth
1960   *John Paul Jones,* by Samuel Eliot Morison
1961   *Charles Sumner and the Coming of the Civil War,* by David Donald
1962   No award
1963   *Henry James,* by Leon Edel
1964   *John Keats,* by Walter Jackson Bate
1965   *Henry Adams,* by Ernest Samuels
1966   *A Thousand Days,* by Arthur Schlesinger Jr.
1967   *Mr. Clemens and Mark Twain,* by Justin Kaplan
1968   *Memoirs (1925–1950),* by George F. Kennan
1969   *The Man from New York: George Quinn and His Friends,* by Benjamin Reid
1970   *Huey Long,* by T. Harry Williams
1971   *Robert Frost: The Years of Triumph, 1915–1938,* by Lawrance R. Thompson
1972   *Eleanor and Franklin,* by J. P. Lash
1973   *Luce and His Empire,* by W. A. Swanberg
1974   *O'Neill, Son and Artist,* by Louis Sheaffer
1975   *The Power Broker: Robert Moses and the Fall of New York,* by Robert A. Caro
1976   *Edith Wharton: A Biography,* by Richard Warrington Baldwin Lewis
1977   *A Prince of Our Disorder* (T. E. Lawrence), by John E. Mack
1978   *Samuel Johnson,* by Walter Jackson Bate
1979   *Days of Sorrow and Pain: Leo Baeck and the Berlin Jews,* by Leonard Baker
1980   *The Rise of Theodore Roosevelt,* by Edmund Morris

## GENERAL NONFICTION PULITZER PRIZES

1962   *The Making of the President 1960,* by Theodore H. White
1963   *The Guns of August,* by Barbara Tuchman

| | |
|---|---|
| 1964 | *Anti-intellectualism in American Life,* by Richard Hofstadter |
| 1965 | *O Strange New World,* by Howard Mumford Jones |
| 1966 | *Wandering Through Winter,* by Edwin Way Teale |
| 1967 | *The Problem of Slavery in Western Culture,* by David Brion Davis |
| 1968 | *Rousseau and Revolution,* by Will and Ariel Durant |
| 1969 | *So Human an Animal: How We Are Shaped by Surroundings and Events,* by René Dubos *The Armies of the Night,* by Norman Mailer |
| 1970 | *Gandhi's Truth,* by Erik H. Erikson |
| 1971 | *The Rising Sun,* by John Toland |
| 1972 | *Stilwell and the American Experience in China, 1911–1945,* by Barbara W. Tuchman |
| 1973 | *Fire in the Lake,* by Frances FitzGerald *Children of Crisis,* by Robert Coles |
| 1974 | *The Denial of Death,* by Ernest Becker |
| 1975 | *Pilgrim at Tinker Creek,* by Annie Dillard |
| 1976 | *Why Survive? Being Old in America,* by Robert N. Butler |
| 1977 | *Beautiful Swimmers: Watermen, Crabs and the Chesapeake Bay,* by William W. Warner |
| 1978 | *The Dragons of Eden,* by Carl Sagan |
| 1979 | *On Human Nature,* by Edward O. Wilson |
| 1980 | *An Eternal Golden Braid,* by Douglas R. Hofstadter |

## POETRY PULITZER PRIZES

| | |
|---|---|
| 1918 | *Love Songs,* by Sara Teasdale |
| 1919 | *Corn Huskers,* by Carl Sandburg *Old Road to Paradise,* by Margaret Widdemer |
| 1920 | No award |
| 1921 | No award |
| 1922 | *Collected Poems,* by Edwin Arlington Robinson |
| 1923 | *The Ballad of the Harp-Weaver; A Few Figs from Thistles; eight sonnets in American Poetry, 1922, A Miscellany,* by Edna St. Vincent Millay |
| 1924 | *New Hampshire: A Poem with Notes and Grace Notes,* by Robert Frost |
| 1925 | *The Man Who Died Twice,* by Edwin Arlington Robinson |
| 1926 | *What's O'Clock,* by Amy Lowell |
| 1927 | *Fiddler's Farewell,* by Leonora Speyer |
| 1928 | *Tristram,* by Edwin Arlington Robinson |
| 1929 | *John Brown's Body,* by Stephen Vincent Benét |
| 1930 | *Selected Poems,* by Conrad Aiken |
| 1931 | *Collected Poems,* by Robert Frost |
| 1932 | *The Flowering Stone,* by George Dillon |
| 1933 | *Conquistador,* by Archibald MacLeish |
| 1934 | *Collected Verse,* by Robert Hillyer |
| 1935 | *Bright Ambush,* by Audrey Wurdemann |
| 1936 | *Strange Holiness,* by R. P. Tristram Coffin |
| 1937 | *A Further Range,* by Robert Frost |
| 1938 | *Cold Morning Sky,* by Marya Zaturenska |
| 1939 | *Selected Poems,* by John Gould Fletcher |
| 1940 | *Collected Poems,* by Mark Van Doren |
| 1941 | *Sunderland Capture,* by Leonard Bacon |
| 1942 | *The Dust Which Is God,* by William Benét |
| 1943 | *A Witness Tree,* by Robert Frost |
| 1944 | *Western Star,* by Stephen Vincent Benét |
| 1945 | *V-Letter and Other Poems,* by Karl Shapiro |
| 1946 | No award |
| 1947 | *Lord Weary's Castle,* by Robert Lowell |
| 1948 | *The Age of Anxiety,* by W. H. Auden |
| 1949 | *Terror and Decorum,* by Peter Viereck |
| 1950 | *Annie Allen,* by Gwendolyn Brooks |
| 1951 | *Complete Poems,* by Carl Sandburg |
| 1952 | *Collected Poems,* by Marianne Moore |
| 1953 | *Collected Poems 1917–1952,* by Archibald MacLeish |
| 1954 | *The Waking,* by Theodore Roethke |
| 1955 | *Collected Poems,* by Wallace Stevens |

| | |
|---|---|
| 1956 | *Poems—North & South,* by Elizabeth Bishop |
| 1957 | *Things of This World,* by Richard Wilbur |
| 1958 | *Promises: Poems 1954–56,* by Robert Penn Warren |
| 1959 | *Selected Poems 1928–1958,* by Stanley Kunitz |
| 1960 | *Heart's Needle,* by W. D. Snodgrass |
| 1961 | *Times Three: Selected Verse from Three Decades,* by Phyllis McGinley |
| 1962 | *Poems,* by Alan Dugan |
| 1963 | *Pictures from Breughel,* by William Carlos Williams |
| 1964 | *At the End of the Open Road,* by Louis Simpson |
| 1965 | *77 Dream Songs,* by John Berryman |
| 1966 | *Selected Poems,* by Richard Eberhart |
| 1967 | *Live or Die,* by Anne Sexton |
| 1968 | *The Hard Hours,* by Anthony Hecht |
| 1969 | *Of Being Numerous,* by George Oppen |
| 1970 | *Untitled Subjects,* by Richard Howard |
| 1971 | *The Carrier of Ladders,* by W. S. Merwin |
| 1972 | *Collected Poems,* by James Wright |
| 1973 | *Up Country,* by Maxine Winokur Kumin |
| 1974 | *The Dolphin,* by Robert Lowell |
| 1975 | *Turtle Island,* by Gary Snyder |
| 1976 | *Self-Portrait in a Convex Mirror,* by John Ashbery |
| 1977 | *Divine Comedies,* by James Merrill |
| 1978 | *Collected Poems,* by Howard Nemerov |
| 1979 | *Now and Then,* by Robert Penn Warren |
| 1980 | *Selected Poems,* by Donald Rodney Justice |

## MUSIC PULITZER PRIZES

| | |
|---|---|
| 1943 | *Secular Cantata No. 2,* by William Schuman |
| 1944 | *Symphony No. 4, opus 34,* by Howard Hanson |
| 1945 | *Appalachian Spring,* by Aaron Copland |
| 1946 | *The Canticle of the Sun,* by Leo Sowerby |
| 1947 | *Symphony No. 3,* by Charles Ives |
| 1948 | *Symphony No. 3,* by Walter Piston |
| 1949 | *Louisiana Story,* by Virgil Thomson |
| 1950 | *The Consul,* by Gian-Carlo Menotti |
| 1951 | *Giants in the Earth,* by Douglas S. Moore |
| 1952 | *Symphony Concertante,* by Gail Kubik |
| 1953 | No award |
| 1954 | *Concerto for Two Pianos and Orchestra,* by Quincy Porter |
| 1955 | *The Saint of Bleecker Street,* by Gian-Carlo Menotti |
| 1956 | *Symphony No. 3,* by Ernst Toch |
| 1957 | *Meditations on Ecclesiastes,* by Norman Dello Joio |
| 1958 | *The score of Vanessa,* by Samuel Barber |
| 1959 | *Concerto for Piano and Orchestra,* by John La Montaine |
| 1960 | *Second String Quartet,* by Elliott C. Carter Jr. |
| 1961 | *Symphony No. 7,* by Walter Piston |
| 1962 | *The Crucible,* by Robert Ward |
| 1963 | *Piano Concerto No. 1,* by Samuel Barber |
| 1964 | No award |
| 1965 | No award |
| 1966 | *Variations for Orchestra,* by Leslie Bassett |
| 1967 | *Quartet No. 3,* by Leon Kirchner |
| 1968 | *Echoes of Time and the River,* by George Crumb |
| 1969 | *String Quartet No. 3,* by Karel Husa |
| 1970 | *Time's Encomium,* by Charles W. Wuorinen |
| 1971 | *Synchronisms No. 6,* by Mario Davidovsky |
| 1972 | *Windows,* by Jacob Druckman |
| 1973 | *String Quartet No. 3,* by Elliott Carter |
| 1974 | *Notturno,* by Donald Martino; special citation to Roger Sessions |
| 1975 | *From the Diary of Virginia Woolf,* by Dominick Argento |
| 1976 | *Air Music,* 10 études for orchestra, by Ned Rorem |
| 1977 | *Visions of Terror and Wonder,* by Richard Wernick |
| 1978 | *Déjà Vu for Percussion Quartet and Orchestra,* by Michael Colgrass |
| 1979 | *Aftertones of Infinity,* by Joseph Schwantner |
| 1980 | *In Memory of a Summer Day,* by David Del Tredici |

## HALL OF FAME FOR GREAT AMERICANS

The Hall of Fame for Great Americans was established in 1900 by Dr. Henry Mitchell MacCracken, chancellor of New York University, to honor United States citizens.

| MEMBERS OF THE HALL OF FAME | ELECTED |
|---|---|
| Adams, John (1735–1826), 2d U.S. President | 1900 |
| Adams, John Quincy (1767–1848), 6th U.S. President | 1905 |
| Addams, Jane (1860–1935), reformer | 1965 |
| Agassiz, Louis (1807–73), naturalist | 1915 |
| Anthony, Susan B. (1820–1906), social reformer | 1950 |
| Audubon, John James (1785?–1851), ornithologist, artist | 1900 |
| Bancroft, George (1800–91), historian and diplomat | 1910 |
| Barton, Clara (1821–1912), founder of American Red Cross | 1976 |
| Beecher, Henry Ward (1813–87), theologian | 1900 |
| Bell, Alexander Graham (1847–1922), inventor | 1950 |
| Boone, Daniel (1734–1820), frontiersman | 1915 |
| Booth, Edwin (1833–93), actor | 1925 |
| Brandeis, Louis D. (1856–1941), jurist | 1973 |
| Brooks, Phillip (1835–93), theologian | 1910 |
| Bryant, William Cullen (1794–1878), writer | 1910 |
| Burbank, Luther (1849–1926), horticulturist | 1976 |
| Carnegie, Andrew (1835–1919), steelmaker and philanthropist | 1976 |
| Carver, George Washington (1859?–1943), chemist | 1973 |
| Channing, William Ellery (1780–1842), theologian | 1900 |
| Choate, Rufus (1799–1859), lawyer and legislator | 1915 |
| Clay, Henry (1777–1852), statesman | 1900 |
| Clemens, Samuel Langhorne (Mark Twain; 1835–1910), novelist | 1920 |
| Cleveland, Grover (1837–1908), 22d and 24th U.S. President | 1935 |
| Cooper, James Fenimore (1789–1851), novelist | 1910 |
| Cooper, Peter (1791–1883), philanthropist | 1900 |
| Cushman, Charlotte (1816–76), actress | 1915 |
| Eads, James (1820–87), engineer | 1920 |
| Edison, Thomas Alva (1847–1931), inventor | 1960 |
| Edwards, Jonathan (1703–58), theologian | 1900 |
| Emerson, Ralph Waldo (1803–82), poet and essayist | 1900 |
| Farragut, David Glasgow (1801–70), naval officer | 1900 |
| Foster, Stephen (1826–64), composer | 1940 |
| Franklin, Benjamin (1706–90), statesman and inventor | 1900 |
| Fulton, Robert (1765–1815), inventor | 1900 |
| Gibbs, Josiah (1839–1903), physicist | 1950 |
| Gorgas, William Crawford (1854–1920), physician | 1950 |
| Grant, Ulysses S. (1822–85), Union general and 18th U.S. President | 1900 |
| Gray, Asa (1810–88), botanist | 1900 |
| Hamilton, Alexander (1755?–1804), statesman | 1915 |
| Hawthorne, Nathaniel (1804–64), author | 1900 |
| Henry, Joseph (1797–1878), physicist | 1915 |
| Henry, Patrick (1736–99), statesman | 1920 |
| Holmes, Oliver Wendell (1809–94), writer | 1910 |
| Holmes, Oliver Wendell, Jr. (1841–1935), Supreme Court associate justice | 1965 |
| Hopkins, Mark (1802–87), educator | 1915 |
| Howe, Elias (1819–67), inventor | 1915 |
| Irving, Washington (1783–1859), author and diplomat | 1900 |
| Jackson, Andrew (1767–1845), 7th U.S. President | 1910 |
| Jackson, Stonewall (1824–63), Confederate general | 1955 |
| Jefferson, Thomas (1743–1826), 3d U.S. President | 1900 |

| MEMBERS OF THE HALL OF FAME | ELECTED |
|---|---|
| Jones, John Paul (1747–92), naval commander | 1925 |
| Kent, James (1763–1847), jurist | 1900 |
| Lanier, Sidney (1842–81), poet and musician | 1945 |
| Lee, Robert E. (1807–70), Confederate general | 1900 |
| Lincoln, Abraham (1809–65), 16th U.S. President | 1900 |
| Longfellow, Henry Wadsworth (1807–82), poet | 1900 |
| Lowell, James Russell (1819–91), poet | 1905 |
| Lyon, Mary (1797–1849), educator | 1905 |
| MacDowell, Edward Alexander (1861–1908), composer | 1960 |
| Madison, James (1751–1836), 4th U.S. President | 1905 |
| Mann, Horace (1796–1859), educator | 1900 |
| Marshall, John (1755–1835), Chief Justice of U.S. | 1900 |
| Maury, Matthew Fontaine (1806–73), naval officer and oceanographer | 1930 |
| Michelson, Albert (1852–1931), physicist | 1970 |
| Mitchell, Maria (1818–89), astronomer | 1905 |
| Monroe, James (1758–1831), 5th U.S. President | 1930 |
| Morse, Samuel F. B. (1791–1872), inventor | 1900 |
| Morton, William (1819–68), dentist | 1920 |
| Motley, John Lothrop (1814–77), historian | 1910 |
| Newcomb, Simon (1835–1909), astronomer | 1935 |
| Paine, Thomas (1737–1809), political writer | 1945 |
| Palmer, Alice (1855–1902), educator | 1920 |
| Parkman, Francis (1823–93), historian | 1915 |
| Peabody, George (1795–1869), philanthropist | 1900 |
| Penn, William (1644–1718), colonial leader | 1935 |
| Poe, Edgar Allan (1809–49), poet and author | 1910 |
| Reed, Walter (1851–1902), physician | 1945 |
| Roosevelt, Franklin Delano (1882–1945), 32d U.S. President | 1973 |
| Roosevelt, Theodore (1858–1919), 26th U.S. President | 1950 |
| Saint-Gaudens, Augustus (1848–1907), sculptor | 1920 |
| Sherman, William Tecumseh (1820–91), Union general | 1905 |
| Sousa, John Philip (1854–1932), bandleader | 1973 |
| Story, Joseph (1779–1845), Supreme Court associate justice | 1900 |
| Stowe, Harriet Beecher (1811–96), novelist | 1910 |
| Stuart, Gilbert (1755–1828), painter | 1900 |
| Thayer, Sylvanus (1785–1872), military educator | 1965 |
| Thoreau, Henry David (1817–62), essayist and poet | 1960 |
| Wald, Lillian (1867–1940), social worker | 1970 |
| Washington, Booker T. (1856–1915), educator | 1945 |
| Washington, George (1732–99), Revolutionary War general and 1st U.S. President | 1900 |
| Webster, Daniel (1782–1852), statesman | 1900 |
| Westinghouse, George (1846–1914), inventor | 1955 |
| Whistler, James A. McNeill (1834–1903), painter | 1930 |
| Whitman, Walt (1819–92), poet | 1930 |
| Whitney, Eli (1765–1825), inventor | 1900 |
| Whittier, John Greenleaf (1807–92), poet | 1905 |
| Willard, Emma (1787–1870), educator | 1905 |
| Willard, Frances Elizabeth (1839–98), reformer | 1910 |
| Williams, Roger (1603?–83), colonial leader | 1920 |
| Wilson, Woodrow (1856–1924), 28th U.S. President | 1950 |
| Wright, Orville (1871–1948), inventor | 1965 |
| Wright, Wilbur (1867–1912), inventor | 1955 |

## SPINGARN MEDAL

The highest award each year to blacks for achievement, the gold Spingarn Medal was established in 1914 by Elias Spingarn, chairman of the board of the National Association for the Advancement of Colored People (NAACP). Medals awarded by the NAACP include:

| YEAR | NAME | FIELD | YEAR | NAME | FIELD |
|---|---|---|---|---|---|
| 1960 | Langston Hughes | Literature | 1970 | Jacob Lawrence | Painting |
| 1961 | Kenneth B. Clark | Education | 1971 | Leon H. Sullivan | Economic opportunity |
| 1962 | Robert C. Weaver | Government | 1972 | Gordon Parks | The Arts |
| 1963 | Medgar W. Evers | Civil rights | 1973 | Wilson C. Riles | Education |
| 1964 | Roy Wilkins | Civil rights | 1974 | Damon J. Keith | Law |
| 1965 | Leontyne Price | Music | 1975 | Henry Aaron | Sports |
| 1966 | John H. Johnson | Publishing | 1976 | Alvin Ailey | Dance |
| 1967 | Edward W. Brooke | Government | 1977 | Alex Haley | Literature |
| 1968 | Sammy Davis Jr. | Entertainment | 1978 | Andrew Young | Government |
| 1969 | Clarence M. Mitchell Jr. | Government | 1979 | W. Rayford Logan | Education |

# Books

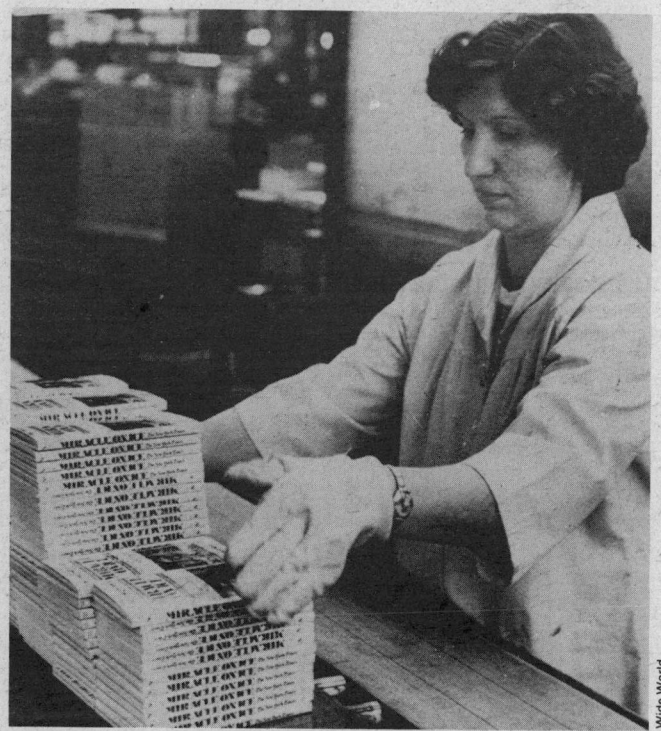

Mirella Bruno, employee of the W. F. Hall Printing Co. of Chicago, stacks first copies of *Miracle on Ice*, story of the U.S. Olympic hockey team, as books come off the assembly line Feb. 29. Bantam Publishing Co., of New York, set world record of 46 hours, 15 minutes between the time the manuscript was received to completion of the finished product. The book, by the staff of the *New York Times*, was about the unexpected gold medal win by the U.S. Olympic hockey team at the 1980 Winter Olympics at Lake Placid, N.Y.

Wide World

## HIGHLIGHTS: 1980

### BESTSELLERS IN 1980

In a special survey by *Publishers Weekly*, booksellers reported strong sales during the summer of 1980. Many dealers felt that both the heat wave, which hit much of the country, and the high cost of gasoline combined to keep people at home and reading.

*Rage of Angels* by Sidney Sheldon was the most popular hardcover fiction book. Others named as very popular in the survey were *Kane & Abel* by Jeffrey Archer, *The Bourne Identity* by Robert Ludlum, *Falling in Place* by Anne Beattie, *Bellefleur* by Joyce Carol Oates, and *Firestarter* by Stephen King.

The dealers named several nonfiction books as bestsellers. They included *Shelley Also Known as Shirley* by Shelley Winters, *Little Gloria . . . Happy at Last* by Barbara Goldsmith, and *Nothing Down* by Robert Allen.

Hardcover reprints led the paperback bestseller lists. The most popular included *So-phie's Choice* by William Styron, *Class Reunion* by Rona Jaffe, *A Woman of Substance* by Barbara Bradford Taylor, *Shibumi* by Trevanian, *War and Remembrance* by Herman Wouk, and *The Matarese Circle* by Robert Ludlum.

### *NANCY DREW* AUTHOR HONORED

Harriet Stratemeyer Adams, 87, was honored at a party given by publisher Simon & Schuster to celebrate the 50th anniversary of the publication of the first *Nancy Drew* mystery story. The series, about a teenage amateur sleuth, has been read by millions of girls.

Created in 1930 by Mrs. Adams' father, Edward Stratemeyer, Nancy Drew, who is perennially 18, is known for the blue roadster given to her by her father, Carson Drew. Her boyfriend, Ned Nickerson, and the family housekeeper, Hannah Gruen, appear in each book.

Edward Stratemeyer wrote the first three

**HIGHLIGHTS: 1980** *(continued)*

books in the series, but after his death his daughter revised those and has written all the rest. She prepared the 59th in the series in 1980.

The party also marked the publication of the series in paperback.

### FIRST PRINTING OF BOOK DESTROYED

Basic Books, subsidiary of Harper & Row, recalled its entire first edition of *Birth and Fortune, the Impact of Numbers on Personal Welfare* because of errors. The action was urged by author Richard A. Easterlin, after he discovered that four charts and tables had been accidentally transposed.

The recall of the 3,500 books already in bookstores occurred just days before the announced publication date.

It was the first such action in the history of Basic Books. The remainder of the 7,500-copy first printing was destroyed, and a new publication date was set.

### A MOVING EXPERIENCE

More than 300 persons in a 1,000-foot-long human chain spent three hours transferring the contents of the Billerica, Mass., library to a new building. The action saved an estimated $3,800 in moving fees.

## U.S. BOOK TITLES PUBLISHED

Source: *Publishers Weekly*

| CLASSIFICATION | 1950 | 1955 | 1960 | 1965 | 1970 | 1975 | 1977 | 1978 | 1979 |
|---|---|---|---|---|---|---|---|---|---|
| Agriculture | 152 | 168 | 156 | 270 | 265 | 456 | 594 | 552 | 432 |
| Art | 357 | 347 | 470 | 971 | 1,169 | 1,561 | 1,795 | 1,483 | 1,612 |
| Biography | 603 | 833 | 879 | 685 | 1,536 | 1,968 | 2,104 | 1,891 | 1,677 |
| Business | 250 | 312 | 305 | 537 | 797 | 820 | 1,077 | 1,248 | 1,172 |
| Education | 256 | 274 | 348 | 954 | 1,178 | 1,038 | 1,194 | 1,063 | 956 |
| Fiction | 1,907 | 2,073 | 2,440 | 3,241 | 3,137 | 3,805 | 3,681 | 3,693 | 2,851 |
| General Works | 345 | 387 | 282 | 634 | 846 | 1,113 | 1,448 | 1,310 | 1,138 |
| History | 516 | 665 | 865 | 1,682 | 1,995 | 1,823 | 2,022 | 2,016 | 1,747 |
| Home Economics | 193 | 255 | 197 | 300 | 321 | 728 | 795 | 845 | 716 |
| Juveniles | 1,059 | 1,485 | 1,725 | 2,895 | 2,640 | 2,292 | 2,918 | 2,909 | 2,623 |
| Language | 148 | 168 | 228 | 527 | 472 | 438 | 556 | 458 | 443 |
| Law | 298 | 305 | 394 | 436 | 604 | 915 | 948 | 1,065 | 1,000 |
| Literature | 591 | 660 | 736 | 1,686 | 3,085 | 1,904 | 1,866 | 1,800 | 1,465 |
| Medicine | 443 | 534 | 520 | 1,218 | 1,476 | 2,282 | 2,833 | 2,788 | 2,656 |
| Music | 113 | 103 | 98 | 300 | 404 | 305 | 373 | 439 | 311 |
| Philosophy, Psychology | 340 | 314 | 480 | 979 | 1,280 | 1,374 | 1,372 | 1,367 | 1,147 |
| Poetry, Drama | 531 | 493 | 492 | 994 | 1,474 | 1,501 | 1,437 | 1,217 | 1,093 |
| Religion | 727 | 849 | 1,104 | 1,855 | 1,788 | 1,778 | 2,121 | 2,180 | 1,947 |
| Science | 705 | 801 | 1,089 | 2,562 | 2,358 | 2,942 | 3,015 | 2,877 | 2,603 |
| Sociology, Economics | 515 | 520 | 754 | 3,242 | 5,912 | 6,590 | 6,814 | 6,465 | 6,234 |
| Sports, Recreation | 188 | 200 | 286 | 591 | 799 | 1,225 | 1,119 | 1,160 | 974 |
| Technology | 497 | 477 | 698 | 1,153 | 1,141 | 1,720 | 2,218 | 1,896 | 1,929 |
| Travel | 288 | 366 | 466 | 883 | 1,394 | 794 | 480 | 414 | 523 |
| TOTAL | 11,022 | 12,589 | 15,012 | 28,595 | 36,071 | 39,372 | 42,780 | 41,216 | 37,222 |

## U.S. BOOK PUBLISHING SALES

Source: Association of American Publishers

| TYPE OF SALES | 1972 | 1975 | 1978 | 1979 | Percent change from '78 |
|---|---|---|---|---|---|
| Trade (retail stores) | $ 442,000,000 | $ 549,200,000 | $ 971,400,000 | $1,016,100,000 | 14.6% |
| Adult hardbound | 251,500,000 | 313,400,000 | 586,000,000 | 608,300,000 | 13.8% |
| Adult paperback | 79,600,000 | 111,200,000 | 202,000,000 | 222,800,000 | 10.3% |
| Juvenile | 110,900,000 | 124,600,000 | 183,400,000 | 185,000,000 | 0.9% |
| Religious | 117,500,000 | 154,600,000 | 275,600,000 | 295,400,000 | 7.2% |
| Professional | 381,000,000 | 501,200,000 | 804,600,000 | 885,100,000 | 10.0% |
| Technical and scientific | 131,800,000 | 175,500,000 | 277,500,000 | 301,100,000 | 8.5% |
| Business and other | 192,200,000 | 242,300,000 | 333,300,000 | 370,000,000 | 11.0% |
| Medical | 57,000,000 | 83,400,000 | 193,800,000 | 214,000,000 | 10.4% |
| Book clubs | 240,500,000 | 303,400,000 | 463,200,000 | 501,700,000 | 8.3% |
| Mail-order books | 198,900,000 | 279,800,000 | 440,400,000 | 485,800,000 | 10.3% |
| Mass-market paperbacks | 252,800,000 | 356,200,000 | 609,000,000 | 673,300,000 | 10.6% |
| University presses | 41,400,000 | 48,800,000 | 62,200,000 | 68,000,000 | 9.3% |
| Textbooks | 872,900,000 | 1,173,700,000 | 1,569,900,000 | 1,755,700,000 | 23.7% |
| Elementary and secondary | 497,600,000 | 643,100,000 | 833,400,000 | 930,100,000 | 11.6% |
| College | 375,300,000 | 530,600,000 | 736,500,000 | 825,600,000 | 12.1% |
| Standardized tests | 26,500,000 | 36,700,000 | 51,900,000 | 61,600,000 | 18.6% |
| Subscription reference | 278,900,000 | 258,100,000 | 341,200,000 | 383,500,000 | 12.4% |
| Other | 165,400,000 | 189,000,000 | 203,100,000 | 206,000,000 | 11.8% |
| TOTAL | $3,017,800,000 | $3,810,000,000 | $5,792,500,000 | $6,332,200,000 | 9.3% |

# BESTSELLERS AND NOTEWORTHY BOOKS: 1980

Nonfiction and fiction books in the following table include most of those mentioned during 1980 on bestseller lists of the *New York Times* and *Publishers Weekly* as well as other noteworthy books published in 1980.

## NONFICTION

**All You Need to Know About the IRS: A Taxpayers Guide,** Paul N. Strassels with Robert Wool (Random House; $10.95). Guide to dealing with Internal Revenue Service.

**American Dreams: Lost and Found,** Studs Terkel (Pantheon; $14.95). Interviews with one hundred persons about their interpretation of the American dream.

**The American Establishment,** Leonard Silk and Mark Silk (Basic Books; $13.95). Look at relationship between big business and government.

**Anatomy of an Illness as Perceived by the Patient,** Norman Cousins (Norton; $9.95). Successful fight against serious illness.

**Battle of Britain,** Len Deighton (Coward, McCann & Geoghegan; $19.95). In-depth study of famous World War II battle.

**The Best Friend You'll Ever Have,** Bernard Sloan (Crown; $8.95). Family life is disrupted when author brings terminally ill mother to live in his home.

**Bittersweet,** Susan Strasberg (Putnam; $10.95). Autobiography of actress daughter of Lee and Paula Strasberg of the Actors Studio.

**The Brethren: The Supreme Court Under Chief Justice Warren E. Burger,** Bob Woodward and Scott Armstrong (Simon & Schuster; $13.95). Look at the workings of the Court in 1969–75.

**Cosmos,** Carl Sagan (Random House; $19.95). Origins of the universe are traced by author of *The Dragons of Eden.*

**Daddy's Girl,** Charlotte Vale Allen (Wyndham Books/Simon & Schuster; $10.95). Woman's account of brutal childhood including sexual abuse by her father.

**Dr. Heimlich's Guide to Emergency Medical Situations,** Henry J. Heimlich, M.D., with Lawrence Galton (Simon & Schuster; $10.95). Encyclopedia of emergency aid, by developer of Heimlich Hug to aid choking victim.

**Donahue,** Phil Donahue & Co. (Simon & Schuster; $11.95). Autobiography of talk-show host.

**Fire in the Streets: America in the 1960s,** Milton Viorst (Simon & Schuster; $14.95). Political reporter examines unrest of 1960s and main events of decade.

**The Fourth and Richest Reich,** Edwin Hartrich (Macmillan; $12.50). Look at West Germany's rise to economic power since 1945 bankruptcy.

**Free to Choose: A Personal Statement,** Milton and Rose Friedman ($9.95). Economists propose lessening of government controls on economy.

**Goodbye, Darkness: A Memoir of the Pacific War,** William Manchester (Little, Brown; $14.95). Personal account of man's war experiences in Pacific during World War II.

**Heartsounds,** Martha Weinman Lear (Simon & Schuster; $12.95). Story of five years between man's first heart attack and ultimate death.

**Helen and Teacher: The Story of Helen Keller and Anne Sullivan Macy,** Joseph P. Lash (Delacorte/Seymour Lawrence; $15). In-depth study of blind and deaf Hellen Keller and her teacher.

**Ingrid Bergman: My Story,** Ingrid Bergman and Alan Burgess (Delacorte; $14.95). Autobiography of renowned actress and film star.

**Jack: The Struggles of John F. Kennedy,** Herbert S. Parmet (Dial; $14.95). First of projected two-volume study of late president covers pre-presidential years.

**Jim Fixx's Second Book of Running,** James F. Fixx (Random House; $10). More advice about running.

**Liberty's Daughters: The Revolutionary Experience of American Women, 1750–1800,** Mary Beth Norton (Little, Brown; $17.50). Importance of women during early history of U.S.

**Little Gloria. . .Happy at Last,** Barbara Goldsmith (Knopf; $15.95). Biography of heiress and fashion designer Gloria Vanderbilt.

**Lyndon: An Oral Biography,** Merle Miller (Putnam; $17.95). Author uses interviews to describe life of late President Lyndon B. Johnson.

**A Matter of Life: The Story of a Medical Breakthrough,** Robert Edwards and Patrick Steptoe (Morrow; $9.95). Doctors responsible for first "test-tube baby" describe their achievement.

**More of Paul Harvey's the Rest of the Story,** Paul Aurandt (Morrow; $8.95). Son of famous radio, TV, and newspaper commentator reproduces some of his father's better stories.

**Music for Chameleons,** Truman Capote (Random House; $10.95). Collection of 14 short stories and essays.

**Nothing Down,** Robert Allen (Simon & Schuster; $10.95). Guide to buying real estate without putting down much money.

**Number 1,** Billy Martin and Peter Golenbock (Delacorte; $11.95). Martin tells of stormy years as manager of New York Yankees.

**The Oak and the Calf: Memoirs of a Literary Life,** Aleksandr I. Solzhenitsyn (Harper & Row; $15.95). Author's last years in Soviet Union.

**One Child,** Torey L. Hayden (Putnam; $9.95). Child, believed retarded, blossoms when treated with love and humanity.

**The Real War,** Richard Nixon (Warner Books; $12.50). Commentary by former President.

**Seems Like Yesterday,** Ann Buchwald (Putnam; $10.95). Wife of columnist Art Buchwald describes their marriage.

**Shelley Also Known as Shirley,** Shelley Winters (Morrow; $14.95). Autobiography of film star.

**Soon to Be a Major Motion Picture,** Abbie Hoffman (A Fred Jordan Book/Grosset & Dunlap; $12.95). Memoirs by well-known underground radical.

**They Call Me Assassin,** Jack Tatum with Bill Kushner (Everest House; $9.95). Hard-hitting football player discusses violence in sports.

**The Third Wave,** Alfin Toffler (Morrow; $12.95). Author of *Future Shock* looks at industrialized future of society.

**Thy Neighbor's Wife,** Gay Talese (Doubleday; $14.95). Study, researched for nine years, on sexual habits in America.

**Voices of Wisdom,** Francine Klagsbrun (Pantheon; $16.95). Jewish viewpoints, ancient and modern, on contemporary topics.

**BESTSELLERS: 1980** *(continued)*
**Walter Lippmann and the American Century,** Ronald Steel (Atlantic-Little, Brown; $19.95). Biography of late journalist and presidential adviser.
**War Within and Without: Diaries and Letters of Anne Morrow Lindbergh,** Anne Morrow Lindbergh (Harcourt Brace Jovanovich; $14.95). Account of life in Charles A. Lindbergh family in 1939–44.
**What Every Woman Needs to Know About the Law,** Martha Pomroy (Doubleday; $14.95). Reference by woman lawyer on women's legal rights.
**Will: The Autobiography of G. Gordon Liddy,** G. Gordon Liddy (St. Martin's; $13.95). One of Watergate principals tells his story.

**FICTION**

**Amazons,** Cleo Birdwell (Holt, Rinehart and Winston; $12.95). Satire about first woman to play with a National Hockey League team.
**The American Heiress,** Dorothy Eden (Coward, McCann & Geoghegan; $11.95). Young maid impersonates her former mistress and marries British aristocrat.
**Bellefleur,** Joyce Carol Oates (Dutton/A Henry Robbins Book; $12.95). Saga about family living in mythical part of United States.
**The Bleeding Heart,** Marilyn French (Summit Books/Simon & Schuster; $11.95). American man and woman, each with troubled lives, meet and love in England, by author of *The Women's Room.*
**The Bourne Identity,** Robert Ludlum (Richard Marek; $12.95). Amnesiac is stalked by terrorist across two continents.
**The Children's War,** David Bellin (Dundee Publishing/Antietam Press; $10.95). Effects of war on children in Northern Ireland.
**Circle of Love,** Syrell Rogovin Leahy (Putnam; $10.95). Love story between Jewish girl whose family has perished in Holocaust and Polish underground fighter.
**Close Relations,** Susan Isaacs (Lippincott & Crowell; $10.95). Adventures of divorced young woman who is speechwriter for a major gubernatorial candidate.
**Come Pour the Wine,** Cynthia Freeman (Arbor House; $12.95). Young woman from Kansas finds successful modeling career in New York, then marries self-centered man, by author of *Portraits.*
**The Covenant,** James A. Michener (Random House; $15.95). Saga involving 200 years of history of South Africa, by author of *Chesapeake.*
**The Cradle Will Fall,** Mary Higgins Clark (Simon & Schuster; $10.95). Famous gynecologist is found to be murderer.
**Creek Mary's Blood,** Dee Brown (Holt, Rinehart and Winston; $12.95). Lives and fortune of Indian family from 18th century to 1905.
**The Devil's Alternative,** Frederick Forsyth (Viking; $12.95). British intelligence officer obtains top-secret information concerning Soviet Union interior power struggles.
**A Dry White Season,** André Brink (Morrow; $10.95). White teacher in South Africa investigates death of black friend.
**Dynasty of Spies,** Dan Sherman (Arbor House; $11.95). Three generations of family of spies.
**Emmeline,** Judith Rossner (Simon & Schuster;

$12.95). Life of 19th century New England girl who has incestuous relationship with son she gave away at birth.
**Falling in Place,** Anne Beattie (Random House; $10.95). Violence rips apart suburban Connecticut family.
**Fanny: Being the True History of the Adventures of Fanny Hackabout-Jones,** Erica Jong (NAL Books; $12.95). 18th century heroine writes her memoirs after leading adventure-filled life, by author of *Fear of Flying.*
**The Fifth Horseman,** Larry Collins and Dominique Lapierre (Simon & Schuster; $14.95). Arab terrorists threaten to detonate hydrogen bomb in New York City unless Israel gives up territory to Palestinians.
**Firestarter,** Stephen King (Viking; $12.95). Suspense novel about young girl who can start fires by just thinking about them, by author of *Carrie.*
**Four Days,** Gloria Goldreich (Harcourt Brace Jovanovich; $10.95). Woman planning abortion reviews her life and feelings.
**The Girl in a Swing,** Richard Adams (Knopf; $10.95). Rural bachelor marries mysterious German woman.
**Green Monday,** Michael M. Thomas (Wyndham Books/Simon & Schuster; $12.95). Arab oil sheiks attempt to topple United States president.
**The Hastings Conspiracy,** Alfred Coppel (Holt, Rinehart and Winston; $12.95). Spy story involving U.S. and Britain and planned assassination.
**He/She,** Herbert Gold (Arbor House; $9.95). Young couple plans divorce.
**The Hidden Target,** Helen MacInnes (Harcourt Brace Jovanovich; $12.95). Thriller about daughter of U.S. official used as pawn in political intrigue.
**Horn of Africa,** Philip Caputo (Holt, Rinehart and Winston; $12.95) Three men must deliver weapons from CIA to Muslim band of rebels fighting in Ethiopia.
**Innocent Blood,** P.D. James (Scribners; $10.95). Adopted young women locates her birth parents with unfortunate results.
**Kane & Abel,** Jeffrey Archer (Simon & Schuster; $13.95). Lives of two men, born on same day in different places, later intersect.
**The Key to Rebecca,** Ken Follett (Morrow; $12.95). British intelligence agents try to break German code during World War II.
**Loon Lake,** E.L. Doctorow (Random House; $11.95). Life of young boy from Midwest from 1930s to 1970s.
**Man, Woman and Child,** Erich Segal (Harper & Row; $9.95). Man brings his illegitimate child into his once-peaceful household.
**Manchu,** Robert Elegant (McGraw-Hill; $12.95). Saga involving 17th century collapse of Ming dynasty in China.
**The Mask of the Enchantress,** Victoria Holt (Doubleday; $10). Illegitimate girl impersonates dead half-sister to claim share of family castle, and finds her life in danger.
**The Ninja,** Eric Van Lustbader (M. Evans; $12.95). Young man, raised in Japan, duels with ninja, one of ancient cult of Japanese assassins.
**No Love Lost,** Helen Van Slyke (Lippincott and Crowell; $10.95). Three generations of women are affected by husbands' infidelities.
**The Old Neighborhood,** Avery Corman (Simon

& Schuster; $10.95). Account of man's midlife crisis, by author of *Kramer vs. Kramer.*

**The Origin: A Biographical Novel of Charles Darwin,** Irving Stone (Doubleday; $14.95). Life of developer of theory of evolution.

**The Paladin,** Brian Garfield (Simon & Schuster; $12.95). Tale of boy who becomes "paladin" or knightly defender to Winston Churchill.

**Princess Daisy,** Judith Krantz (Crown; $12.95). Daughter of movie queen and Russian prince tries to make it on her own in world of TV.

**Rage of Angels,** Sidney Sheldon (Morrow; $12.95). Bright woman lawyer is trapped into defending Mafia hoodlums.

**Random Winds,** Belva Plain (Delacorte; $9.95). Three generations of medical family.

**The Ring,** Danielle Steel (Delacorte; $10.95) Young woman is separated from her family during Nazi era and ends up in U.S.

**The Second Coming,** Walker Percy (Farrar, Straus & Giroux; $12.95). Widower and young mental hospital escapee comfort each other.

**The Second Lady,** Irving Wallace (New American Library; $11.95). Russian actress is substituted for First Lady.

**Shaman's Daughter,** Nan F. Salerno and Rosamund M. Vanderburgh (Prentice-Hall; $12.50). Saga spanning 70 years in life of Ojibway Indian in Canada.

**Sins of the Fathers,** Susan Howatch (Simon & Schuster; $13.95). Sequel to *The Rich Are Different* focuses on Wall Street banking tyrant and his family.

**Smiley's People,** John le Carré (Knopf; $10.95). British intelligence officer follows trail of murder throughout Europe.

**Solo,** Jack Higgins (Stein and Day; $11.95). Thriller about assassin who is brilliant pianist, by author of *The Eagle has Landed.*

**The Spike,** Arnaud de Borchgrave and Robert Moss (Crown; $12.95). Russians attempt to infiltrate highest levels of U.S. government in order to misinform American public.

**Stepping,** Nancy Thayer (Doubleday; $10). Young woman becomes stepmother and fights for acceptance.

**The Tenth Commandment,** Lawrence Sanders (Putnam; $12.95). Chief investigator for law firm uncovers connection between two cases.

**The Transit of Venus,** Shirley Hazzard (Viking; $12.95). Two orphan sisters from Australia go to England to seek their fortunes.

**The Twyborn Affair,** Patrick White (Viking; $14.95). Interaction of three very diverse characters in London between two world wars.

**A Wayside Tavern,** Norah Lofts (Doubleday; $11.95). English history depicted through life of wayside tavern over the centuries.

**Who's On First,** William F. Buckley, Jr. (Doubleday; $9.95). CIA agent tries to help U.S. get satellite launched before Soviets in 1957.

**Winners,** Judith Green (Knopf; $9.95). Suburban woman, whose husband is running for governor, seeks her own identity.

## BOOK AND LITERATURE AWARDS: 1980

### AMERICAN BOOK AWARDS: 1980
In 1980 the American Book Awards, sponsored by the American Booksellers Association, replaced the National Book Awards. The winners, for books published in 1979, included:
National Medal for Literature: Eudora Welty.
**Hardcover Books**
Fiction: *Sophie's Choice,* William Styron.
General Nonfiction: *The Right Stuff,* Tom Wolfe.
History: *White House Years,* Henry A. Kissinger.
Autobiography: *By Myself,* Lauren Bacall.
Biography: *The Rise of Theodore Roosevelt,* Edmund Morris.
First novel: *Birdy,* William Wharton.
Mystery: *The Green Ripper,* John D. MacDonald.
Art: *Drawings and Digressions,* Larry Rivers with Carol Brightman.
Illustrated Art: *The Birthday of the Infanta,* Oscar Wilde.
Poetry: Ashes, Philip Levine.
Current Interest: *Julia Child and More Company,* Julia Child.
General Reference: *Congressional Quarterly's Guide to the U.S. Supreme Court,* Elder Witt.
Children's Books: *A Gathering of Days,* Joan W. Blos.
**Paperback Books**
Fiction: *The World According to Garp,* John Irving.
General Nonfiction: *The Snow Leopard,* Peter Matthiessen.
Autobiography: *And I Worked at the Writer's Trade,* Malcolm Cowley.
History: *A Distant Mirror,* Barbara W. Tuchman.
Biography: *Max Perkins,* Scott Berg.
Mystery: *Stained Glass,* William F. Buckley Jr.
Illustrated Art: *Anatomy Illustrated,* Emily Blair Chewning.
Current Interest: *The Culture of Narcissism,* Christopher Lasch.

General Reference: *The Complete Directory to Prime-Time Network TV Shows,* Tim Brooks, Earle Marsh.
Children's Books: *A Swiftly Tilting Planet,* Madeline L'Engle.

### AMERICAN LIBRARY ASSOCIATION AWARDS
The American Library Association awards, presented annually by the Children's Services Division of the American Library Association to the most distinguished books for children published in the U.S., included:
John Newbery Medal: Joan W. Blos, for *A Gathering of Days: A New England Girl's Journal, 1830–32.*
Randolph J. Caldecott Medal: Barbara Cooney, for *Ox-Cart Man.*

### BANCROFT PRIZES
The Annual Bancroft Prizes of Columbia University, recognizing books of exceptional merit and distinction in American history, included:
Robert Dallek, for *Franklin D. Roosevelt and American Foreign Policy: 1932–1945.*
Donald Worster, for *Dust Bowl: The Southern Plains in the 1930s.*
Thomas Dublin, for *Women at Work: The Transformation of Work and Community in Lowell, Massachusetts, 1826–1860.*

### EDGAR ALLAN POE AWARDS
The annual Edgar Allan Poe awards, presented by Mystery Writers of America, Inc., included:
Best Mystery Novel: *The Rheingold Route,* by Richard North Patterson.
Best Fact Crime: *The Falcon and the Snowman,* by Robert Lindsey.
Best Soft-Cover Mystery Novel: *The Hog Murders,* by Willian L. DeAndrea.
Best Juvenile Mystery: *The Kidnapping of Christina Latimore,* by Joan Lowery Nixon.

# BESTSELLERS OF THE PAST

The following were the bestselling books in the U.S. from 1921 to 1979. Sources for these lists are *70 Years of Best Sellers*, by Alice Payne Hackett (Bowker), and *Publishers Weekly*.

## FICTION BESTSELLERS

| | |
|---|---|
| 1921 | Main Street, Sinclair Lewis |
| 1922 | If Winter Comes, A.S.M. Hutchinson |
| 1923 | Black Oxen, Gertrude Atherton |
| 1924 | So Big, Edna Ferber |
| 1925 | Soundings, A. Hamilton Gibbs |
| 1926 | The Private Life of Helen of Troy, John Erskine |
| 1927 | Elmer Gantry, Sinclair Lewis |
| 1928 | The Bridge of San Luis Rey, Thornton Wilder |
| 1929 | All Quiet on the Western Front, Erich Maria Remarque |
| 1930 | Cimarron, Edna Ferber |
| 1931 | The Good Earth, Pearl S. Buck |
| 1932 | The Good Earth, Pearl S. Buck |
| 1933 | Anthony Adverse, Hervey Allen |
| 1934 | Anthony Adverse, Hervey Allen |
| 1935 | Green Light, Lloyd C. Douglas |
| 1936 | Gone with the Wind, Margaret Mitchell |
| 1937 | Gone with the Wind, Margaret Mitchell |
| 1938 | The Yearling, Marjorie K. Rawlings |
| 1939 | The Grapes of Wrath, John Steinbeck |
| 1940 | How Green Was My Valley, Richard Llewellyn |
| 1941 | The Keys of the Kingdom, A.J. Cronin |
| 1942 | The Song of Bernadette, Franz Werfel |
| 1943 | The Robe, Lloyd C. Douglas |
| 1944 | Strange Fruit, Lillian Smith |
| 1945 | Forever Amber, Kathleen Winsor |
| 1946 | The King's General, Daphne du Maurier |
| 1947 | The Miracle of the Bells, Russell Janney |
| 1948 | The Big Fisherman, Lloyd C. Douglas |
| 1949 | The Egyptian, Mika Waltari |
| 1950 | The Cardinal, Henry Morton Robinson |
| 1951 | From Here to Eternity, James Jones |
| 1952 | The Silver Chalice, Thomas B. Costain |
| 1953 | The Robe, Lloyd C. Douglas |
| 1954 | Not as a Stranger, Morton Thompson |
| 1955 | Marjorie Morningstar, Herman Wouk |
| 1956 | Don't Go Near the Water, William Brinkley |
| 1957 | By Love Possessed, James Gould Cozzens |
| 1958 | Doctor Zhivago, Boris Pasternak |
| 1959 | Exodus, Leon Uris |
| 1960 | Advise and Consent, Allen Drury |
| 1961 | The Agony and the Ecstasy, Irving Stone |
| 1962 | Ship of Fools, Katherine Anne Porter |
| 1963 | The Shoes of the Fisherman, Morris L. West |
| 1964 | The Spy Who Came in from the Cold, John Le Carré |
| 1965 | The Source, James A. Michener |
| 1966 | Valley of the Dolls, Jacqueline Susann |
| 1967 | The Arrangement, Elia Kazan |
| 1968 | Airport, Arthur Hailey |
| 1969 | Portnoy's Complaint, Philip Roth |
| 1970 | Love Story, Erich Segal |
| 1971 | Wheels, Arthur Hailey |
| 1972 | Jonathan Livingston Seagull, Richard Bach |
| 1973 | Jonathan Livingston Seagull, Richard Bach |
| 1974 | Centennial, James A. Michener |
| 1975 | Ragtime, E.L. Doctorow |
| 1976 | Trinity, Leon Uris |
| 1977 | The Silmarillion, J.R.R. Tolkien |
| 1978 | Chesapeake, James A. Michener |
| 1979 | The Matarese Circle, Robert Ludlum |

## NONFICTION BESTSELLERS

| | |
|---|---|
| 1921 | The Outline of History, H.G. Wells |
| 1922 | The Outline of History, H.G. Wells |
| 1923 | Etiquette, Emily Post |
| 1924 | Diet and Health, Lulu Hunt Peters |
| 1925 | Diet and Health, Lulu Hunt Peters |
| 1926 | The Man Nobody Knows, B. Barton |
| 1927 | The Story of Philosophy, Will Durant |
| 1928 | Disraeli, André Maurois |
| 1929 | The Art of Thinking, Ernest Dimnet |
| 1930 | The Story of San Michele, Axel Munthe |
| 1931 | Education of a Princess, Grand Duchess Marie |
| 1932 | The Epic of America, James Truslow Adams |
| 1933 | Life Begins at Forty, Walter B. Pitkin |
| 1934 | While Rome Burns, Alexander Woollcott |
| 1935 | North to the Orient, Anne Morrow Lindbergh |
| 1936 | Man the Unknown, Alexis Carrel |
| 1937 | How to Win Friends and Influence People, Dale Carnegie |
| 1938 | The Importance of Living, Lin Yutang |
| 1939 | Days of Our Years, Pierre van Paassen |
| 1940 | I Married Adventure, Osa Johnson |
| 1941 | Berlin Diary, William L. Shirer |
| 1942 | See Here, Private Hargrove, Marion Hargrove |
| 1943 | Under Cover, John Roy Carlson |
| 1944 | I Never Left Home, Bob Hope |
| 1945 | Brave Men, Ernie Pyle |
| 1946 | The Egg and I, Betty MacDonald |
| 1947 | Peace of Mind, Joshua Loth Liebman |
| 1948 | Crusade in Europe, Dwight D. Eisenhower |
| 1949 | White Collar Zoo, Clare Barnes Jr. |
| 1950 | Betty Crocker's Picture Cook Book |
| 1951 | Look Younger, Live Longer, Gaylord Hauser |
| 1952 | The Holy Bible: Revised Standard Version |
| 1953 | The Holy Bible: Revised Standard Version |
| 1954 | The Holy Bible: Revised Standard Version |
| 1955 | Gift from the Sea, Anne Morrow Lindbergh |
| 1956 | Arthritis and Common Sense, Dan Dale Alexander |
| 1957 | Kids Say the Darndest Things, Art Linkletter |
| 1958 | Kids Say the Darndest Things, Art Linkletter |
| 1959 | Twixt 12 and 20, Pat Boone |
| 1960 | Folk Medicine, D.C. Jarvis |
| 1961 | The New English Bible: The New Testament |
| 1962 | Calories Don't Count, Dr. Herman Taller |
| 1963 | Happiness Is a Warm Puppy, Charles M. Schultz |
| 1964 | Four Days, American Heritage and UPI |
| 1965 | How to Be a Jewish Mother, Dan Greenburg |
| 1966 | How to Avoid Probate, Norman F. Dacey |
| 1967 | Death of a President, William Manchester |
| 1968 | Better Homes and Gardens New Cook Book |
| 1969 | American Heritage Dictionary of the English Language, ed. William Morris |
| 1970 | Everything You Always Wanted to Know About Sex, David Reuben, M.D. |
| 1971 | The Sensuous Man, "M" |
| 1972 | The Living Bible, Kenneth Taylor |
| 1973 | The Living Bible, Kenneth Taylor |
| 1974 | The Total Woman, Marabel Morgan |
| 1975 | Angels: God's Secret Agents, Billy Graham |
| 1976 | The Final Days, Bob Woodward and Carl Bernstein |
| 1977 | Roots, Alex Haley |
| 1978 | If Life Is a Bowl of Cherries—What Am I Doing in the Pits?, Erma Bombeck |
| 1979 | Aunt Erma's Cope Book, Erma Bombeck |

# CHARACTERS IN FAMOUS BOOKS

How many of the characters listed below can you identify with the name of the book in which they appear?

You can check whether you are right by noting the number of the character and then looking to see if that number follows the title of the book you have named from the table of well-known books listed at the bottom of this page.

| | | | |
|---|---|---|---|
| 1. Roberta Alden | 33. Edward Cummings | 65. Tom Joad | 97. Nataly Rostóva |
| 2. Fern Arable | 34. Cunegonde | 66. Robert Jordan | 98. Emma Roualt |
| 3. Aunt Chloe | 35. Edmond Dantès | 67. Stanislaus Katczinsky | 99. Lady Rowena |
| 4. Aunt Em | 36. Wendy Darling | 68. Will Kennicott | 100. Evangeline St. Clare |
| 5. Aunt Polly | 37. Stephen Dedalus | 69. Kincaid | 101. Gerald Scales |
| 6. Sophia Baines | 38. Arthur Dimmesdale | 70. Elizabeth Lavenza | 102. Penrod Schofield |
| 7. David Balfour | 39. Nicole Diver | 71. Simon Legree | 103. Ebeneezer Scrooge |
| 8. Horace Benbow | 40. Temple Drake | 72. John Little | 104. Bill Sikes |
| 9. Jane Bennet | 41. Dulcinea del Toboso | 73. Prince Manfred | 105. Mattie Silver |
| 10. Bernabò of Genoa | 42. C. Auguste Dupin | 74. Jo March | 106. Julien Sorel |
| 11. Pierre Bezúkhov | 43. Léon Dupuis | 75. Mr. Micawber | 107. Willie Stark |
| 12. Leopold Bloom | 44. Tess Durbeyfield | 76. Carol Milford | 108. Alan Breck Stewart |
| 13. Raff Brinker | 45. Catherine Earnshaw | 77. Mole | 109. Becky Thatcher |
| 14. John Brooke | 46. Sondra Finchley | 78. William Morel | 110. John Thornton |
| 15. Buck | 47. Robert Fitzooth | 79. Scarlett O'Hara | 111. Tiny Tim |
| 16. Natty Bumppo | 48. Henry Fleming | 80. O-Lan | 112. Tinker Bell |
| 17. Rhett Butler | 49. Phileas Fogg | 81. Sugar-Boy O'Sheean | 113. Toad |
| 18. Mr. By-Ends | 50. Zenobia Frome | 82. Doctor Pangloss | 114. Topsy |
| 19. Philip Carey | 51. Mastro Geppetto | 83. Sancho Panza | 115. Trampas |
| 20. Eppie Cass | 52. Dr. Gibbs | 84. Passepartout | 116. Betsey Trotwood |
| 21. Holden Caulfield | 53. Joe Green | 85. Pilar | 117. Jean Valjean |
| 22. Harvey Cheyne | 54. Griffin | 86. Popeye | 118. Hilda van Gleck |
| 23. Chingachgook | 55. Clyde Griffiths | 87. Porfiry | 119. Rip Van Winkle |
| 24. Nick Chopper | 56. Griselda | 88. Hester Prynne | 120. Robert Walton |
| 25. Christian | 57. Heathcliff | 89. Queequeg | 121. Wang Lung |
| 26. Angel Clare | 58. Uriah Heep | 90. Peter Quint | 122. Mrs. Waters |
| 27. Jim Conklin | 59. Captain Hook | 91. Raskolnikov | 123. Emily Webb |
| 28. Nana Coupeau | 60. Injun Joe | 92. Rebecca | 124. Sophia Western |
| 29. Ichabod Crane | 61. Isabella | 93. Christopher Robin | 125. Wife of Bath |
| 30. Bob Cratchit | 62. Ishmael | 94. Mr. Rochester | 126. Wilbur |
| 31. Art Croft | 63. Javert | 95. Mildred Rogers | 127. Ashley Wilkes |
| 32. Sam Croft | 64. Miss Jessel | 96. Rose of Sharon | 128. George Willard |

## WELL-KNOWN BOOKS AND THEIR AUTHORS

*The Adventures of Pinocchio,* Carlo Collodi (51)
*The Adventures of Tom Sawyer,* Mark Twain (5, 60, 109)
*All Quiet on the Western Front,* Erich Remarque (67)
*All the King's Men,* Robert Penn Warren (81, 107)
*An American Tragedy,* Theodore Dreiser (1, 46, 55)
*Around the World in Eighty Days,* Jules Verne (49, 84)
*Black Beauty,* Anna Sewell (53)
*The Call of the Wild,* Jack London (15, 110)
*Candide,* François de Voltaire (34, 82)
*Canterbury Tales,* Geoffrey Chaucer (125)
*Captains Courageous,* Rudyard Kipling (22)
*The Castle of Otranto,* Horace Walpole (61, 73)
*The Catcher in the Rye,* J.D. Salinger (21)
*Charlotte's Web,* E.B. White (2, 126)
*A Christmas Carol,* Charles Dickens (30, 103, 111)
*The Count of Monte Cristo,* Alexandre Dumas (35)
*Crime and Punishment,* Feodor Dostoyevsky (87, 91)
*David Copperfield,* Charles Dickens (58, 75, 116)
*Decameron,* Giovanni Boccaccio (10)
*Don Quixote,* Miguel de Cervantes Saavedra (41, 83)
*Ethan Frome,* Edith Wharton (50, 105)
*For Whom the Bell Tolls,* Ernest Hemingway (66, 85)
*Frankenstein,* Mary Wollstonecraft Shelley (70, 120)
*Gone With the Wind,* Margaret Mitchell (17, 79, 127)
*The Good Earth,* Pearl S. Buck (80, 121)
*The Grapes of Wrath,* John Steinbeck (65, 96)
*Hans Brinker,* Mary Mapes Dodge (13, 118)
*The Invisible Man,* H.G. Wells (54)
*Ivanhoe,* Sir Walter Scott (92, 99)
*Jane Eyre,* Charlotte Brontë (94)
*Kidnapped,* Robert Louis Stevenson (7, 108)
*The Last of the Mohicans,* James Fenimore Cooper (16, 23)
*Les Misérables,* Victor Hugo (63, 117)
*Little Women,* Louisa May Alcott (14, 74)
*Madame Bovary,* Gustave Flaubert (43, 98)

*Main Street,* Sinclair Lewis (68, 76)
*The Merry Adventures of Robin Hood,* Howard Pyle (47, 72)
*The Murders in the Rue Morgue,* Edgar Allan Poe (42)
*Moby-Dick,* Herman Melville (62, 89)
*The Naked and the Dead,* Norman Mailer (32, 33)
*Nana,* Émile Zola (28)
*Of Human Bondage,* W. Somerset Maugham (19, 95)
*The Old Wives' Tale,* Arnold Bennett (6, 101)
*Oliver Twist,* Charles Dickens (104)
*Our Town,* Thornton Wilder (52, 123)
*The Ox-Bow Incident,* Walter Van Tilburg Clark (31, 69)
*Penrod and Sam,* Booth Tarkington (102)
*Peter and Wendy,* Sir James Barrie (36, 59, 112)
*The Pilgrim's Progress,* John Bunyan (18, 25)
*Pride and Prejudice,* Jane Austen (9)
*The Red and the Black,* Stendhal (106)
*The Red Badge of Courage,* Stephen Crane (27, 48)
*Sanctuary,* William Faulkner (8, 40, 86)
*The Scarlet Letter,* Nathaniel Hawthorne (38, 88)
*Silas Marner,* George Eliot (20)
*Sketchbook,* Washington Irving (29, 119)
*Sons and Lovers,* D.H. Lawrence (78)
*Tender Is the Night,* F. Scott Fitzgerald (39)
*Tess of the D'Urbervilles,* Thomas Hardy (26, 44)
*Tom Jones,* Henry Fielding (122, 124)
*The Turn of the Screw,* Henry James (64, 90)
*Ulysses,* James Joyce (12, 37)
*Uncle Tom's Cabin,* Harriet Beecher Stowe (3, 71, 100, 114)
*The Virginian,* Owen Wister (115)
*War and Peace,* Leo Tolstoy (11, 97)
*When We Were Very Young,* A.A. Milne (93)
*The Wind in the Willows,* Kenneth Grahame (77, 113)
*Winesburg, Ohio,* Sherwood Anderson (128)
*The Wizard of Oz,* Lyman Frank Baum (4, 24)
*Wuthering Heights,* Emily Brontë (45, 57)

# AUTHORS AND WRITERS

Authors, writers, poets, and dramatists whose works are of enduring interest are listed below in alphabetical order. Birth dates and nationalities are given, along with the titles of the authors' most famous works, and their major literary prizes.

See pages 981–986 for deaths of authors and writers in 1980.

**George Abbott** (1887– ), American playwright and producer: won a Pulitzer Prize as coauthor of musical comedy *Fiorello!* (1959).

**Henry Adams** (1838–1918), American historian who idealized Middle Ages and deplored materialistic modern civilization: *Mont-Saint-Michel and Chartres* (1904); *The Education of Henry Adams* (1906) won Pulitzer Prize in 1919.

**James Truslow Adams** (1878–1949), American historian: won a Pulitzer Prize for *The Founding of New England* (1921).

**Samuel Hopkins Adams** (1871–1958), American writer. His articles about fraudulent patent medicines stirred enactment in 1906 of first Pure Food and Drug Act. Wrote several biographies and novels.

**Joseph Addison** (1672–1719), English essayist. His essays in the *Tatler*, *Spectator*, and *Guardian* periodicals were noted for excellence of style.

**George Ade** (1866–1944), American humorist and playwright: *Fables in Slang* (1899), *The Sultan of Sulu* (1902), *The College Widow* (1904).

**Aeschylus** (525–456 B.C.), Greek tragic poet. Of his estimated 90 dramas, only 7 survive, including *Prometheus Bound* and *Oresteia*, a trilogy.

**James Agee** (1909–55), American essayist and novelist: *Let Us Now Praise Famous Men* (1941) is a powerful documentary on Alabama sharecroppers; *A Death in the Family* (1955), a novel, won a 1958 Pulitzer Prize.

**Conrad Aiken** (1889–1973), American poet: *Selected Poems* (1929) won a Pulitzer Prize.

**Edward Albee** (1928– ), American playwright: *Who's Afraid of Virginia Woolf?* (1962), *Tiny Alice* (1964); *A Delicate Balance* (1966) and *Seascape* (1974) both won Pulitzer Prizes.

**Louisa May Alcott** (1832–88), American children's writer: *Little Women* (1868–69), *Little Men* (1871).

**Horatio Alger** (1832–99), American author: *Ragged Dick* (1867), *Tattered Tom* (1871).

**Nelson Algren** (1909– ), American novelist: *The Man with the Golden Arm* (1949), *A Walk on the Wild Side* (1956).

**Hervey Allen** (1889–1949), American author: *Anthony Adverse* (1933).

**Hans Christian Andersen** (1805–75), Danish writer of fairy tales: *The Emperor's New Clothes*.

**Maxwell Anderson** (1888–1959), American playwright: *Elizabeth the Queen* (1930), *Winterset* (1935), *Joan of Lorraine* (1946); *Both Your Houses* (1932) won a Pulitzer Prize.

**Sherwood Anderson** (1876–1941), American novelist: *Winesburg, Ohio* (1919), short stories.

**Jean Anouilh** (1910– ), French playwright: *Waltz of the Toreadors* (1952), *Becket* (1959).

**Aristophanes** (c. 450–388 B.C.), Greek comic dramatist. Of his 40 or more plays, 11 are extant, including *Clouds*, *Lysistrata*, and *Frogs*.

**Matthew Arnold** (1822–88), English poet and critic. His romantic pessimism is expressed in such poems as "Dover Beach."

**Sholem Asch** (1880–1957), Polish-American novelist: *The Nazarene* (1939), *Moses* (1951), *The Prophet* (1955).

**Isaac Asimov** (1920– ), Russian–American author: science-fiction trilogy *Foundation* (1951–53).

**Louis Auchincloss** (1917– ), American novelist: *The Rector of Justin* (1964), *A World of Profit* (1968), *The*

*Winthrop Covenant* (1976), *The Dark Lady* (1977).

**W. H. (Wystan Hugh) Auden** (1907–73), Anglo-American poet: *The Age of Anxiety* (1947) won a Pulitzer Prize.

**Jane Austen** (1775–1817), English novelist whose books often satirize manners: *Pride and Prejudice* (1813), *Emma* (1815).

**Sir Francis Bacon** (1561–1626), English essayist and philosopher: *The Advancement of Learning* (1605), an effort to summarize all science; *Novum Organum* (1620), an inductive analysis of knowledge; *History of Henry VII* (1622); and *Maxims of the Law* (1637).

**James Baldwin** (1924– ), American novelist and essayist who portrays aspects of black problems: *Go Tell It on the Mountain* (1953), a novel.

**Honoré de Balzac** (1799–1850), French novelist and dramatist: *The Chouans* (1829), *Droll Stories* (1832–37), *Old Goriot* (1834).

**George Bancroft** (1800–91): American historian: 10-volume *History of the United States* (1834–74).

**Imamu Amiri Baraka,** formerly known as **LeRoi Jones** (1934– ), American dramatist and essayist: *Dutchman* (1964) and *The Slave* (1966).

**Sir James Matthew Barrie** (1860–1937), Scottish playwright and novelist: best-known play was *Peter Pan* (1904). Novels include *The Little Minister* (1891).

**Philip Barry** (1896–1949), American playwright: *The Philadelphia Story* (1939).

**John Barth** (1930– ), U.S. novelist: *The Sot-Weed Factor* (1960), *Giles Goat-Boy* (1966), *Letters* (1979).

**John Bartlett** (1820–1905), American bookseller and writer: *Familiar Quotations* (1855).

**Charles Baudelaire** (1821–67), French poet and leader of the French symbolist movement: *Les Fleurs du Mal* (1857).

**Samuel Beckett** (1906– ), Irish-born French novelist and playwright: *Malone Dies* (1951), a novel; *Waiting for Godot* (1952), his best-known play. He won a Nobel Prize in 1969.

**Sir Max Beerbohm** (1872–1956), English parodist and critic: *Poet's Corner* (1904), satiric essay; *Zuleika Dobson* (1912), a novel.

**S. N. Behrman** (1893–1973), American playwright: *Brief Moment* (1931), *No Time for Comedy* (1939).

**Saul Bellow** (1915– ), Canadian-born American novelist; awarded 1976 Nobel Prize: *The Adventures of Augie March* (1953), *Herzog* (1964), *Mr. Sammler's Planet* (1970), all of which won National Book Awards; *Humboldt's Gift* (1975) won 1976 Pulitzer Prize.

**Robert C. Benchley** (1889-1945), American humorist: *Inside Benchley* (1942).

**Stephen Vincent Benét** (1898–1943), American poet: *John Brown's Body* (1928) and *Western Star* (1943) won Pulitzer Prizes.

**Arnold Bennett** (1867–1931), English novelist: *The Old Wives' Tale* (1908), *Clayhanger* (1910).

**John Berryman** (1914–72), American poet: *77 Dream Songs* (1963) won a Pulitzer Prize, and *His Toy* (1968) won a National Book Award.

**Ambrose Bierce** (1842–1914?), American critic and short-story writer: *In the Midst of Life* (1898).

**Josh Billings** (real name **Henry Wheeler Shaw**, 1818–85), American humorist: *Josh Billings' Farmers' Allminax* (1869–80).

**William Blake** (1757–1827), English poet and mystic: *Songs of Innocence* (1789), *Songs of Experience* (1794).

**Robert Bly** (1926– ), American poet: *The Light*

*Around the Body* (1967) won a National Book Award.

**Giovanni Boccaccio** (1313–75), Italian poet: the *Decameron* (1348–53), the *Filostrato* (c. 1338).

**James Boswell** (1740–95), Scottish biographer and diarist: *Life of Samuel Johnson* (1791).

**Elizabeth Bowen** (1899–1973), Anglo-Irish novelist: *The Death of the Heart* (1938).

**Ray Bradbury** (1920– ), American sci-fi author: *Martian Chronicles* (1950), *Fahrenheit 451* (1953).

**Anne Bradstreet** (c. 1612–1672), American poet: *The Tenth Muse Lately Sprung Up in America* (1650).

**Bertolt Brecht** (1898–1956), German dramatist and poet. Borrowing freely from past writers, he combined polemics and lyricism in such plays as *The Threepenny Opera* (1928), *Mother Courage* (1940).

**Louis Bromfield** (1896–1956): American novelist: *Early Autumn* (1926) won a Pulitzer Prize.

**Charlotte Brontë** (1816–55), English novelist: *Jane Eyre* (1847).

**Emily Brontë** (1818–48), English novelist: *Wuthering Heights* (1847).

**Rupert Brooke** (1887–1915), English poet: his work treats the horrors of World War I.

**Gwendolyn Brooks** (1917– ), American poet: *Annie Allen* (1949) won a Pulitzer Prize.

**Van Wyck Brooks** (1886–1963), American critic and historian: *The Flowering of New England* (1936) won a Pulitzer Prize.

**Elizabeth Barrett Browning** (1806–61), English poet and translator who was the wife of Robert Browning.

**Robert Browning** (1812–89), English dramatic poet: *The Ring and the Book (1869).*

**William Cullen Bryant** (1794–1878), American poet: *Thanatopsis* (1817).

**Pearl S. Buck** (1892–1973), American novelist: *The Good Earth* (1931) won Nobel Prize and Pulitzer Prize in 1932.

**John Bunyan** (1628–88), English allegorist: *Pilgrim's Progress* (1678).

**Edmund Burke** (1729–97), English essayist and orator: *American Taxation* (1774) and *Letter to the Sheriff of Bristol* (1777) pleaded cause of American colonists.

**Robert Burns** (1759–96), Scottish lyric poet and ballad writer: "The Cotter's Saturday Night."

**Edgar Rice Burroughs** (1875–1950), American adventure and science-fiction writer, best known for his many Tarzan jungle stories.

**John Burroughs** (1837–1921), American outdoors writer: *Camping and Tramping with Roosevelt* (1907), *Under the Apple-Trees* (1916).

**George Gordon, Lord Byron** (1788–1824), English lyric poet: *Don Juan* (1819–24).

**James Branch Cabell** (1879–1958), American novelist: *Jurgen* (1919).

**Caius Julius Caesar** (100?–44 B.C.), Roman statesman and historian: *The Gallic Wars.*

**James Mallahan Cain** (1892–1977), American crime novelist: *The Postman Always Rings Twice* (1934), *Double Indemnity* (1936), *Mildred Pierce* (1941).

**Erskine Caldwell** (1903– ), American novelist: *Tobacco Road* (1932), *God's Little Acre* (1933).

**Albert Camus** (1913–60), French essayist and novelist. His *Myth of Sisyphus* (1955) was an existentialist essay. His novels include *The Stranger* (1946) and *The Plague* (1948). He won a Nobel Prize in 1957.

**Karel Capek** (1890–1938), Czech dramatist: *R.U.R.* (*Rossum's Universal Robots*, 1921).

**Truman Capote** (1924– ), American short-story writer and essayist: *Other Voices, Other Rooms* (1948); *In Cold Blood* (1965), a documentary; *Music for Chameleons* (1980).

**Thomas Carlyle** (1795–1881), Scottish critic and historical essayist: *The French Revolution* (1837).

**Lewis Carroll** (real name **Charles Lutwidge Dodgson**; 1832–98), British mathematician and author: *Alice's Adventures in Wonderland* (1865).

**Joyce Cary** (1888–1957), Anglo-Irish novelist: *The Horse's Mouth* (1944).

**Giovanni Casanova** (1752–98), Italian memoirist. His amorous and adventurous *Memoirs* were not published in their complete form until 1960–61.

**Willa Cather** (1873–1947), American novelist: *O Pioneers!* (1913), *My Antonia* (1918); *One of Ours* (1922) won a Pulitzer Prize.

**Bruce Catton** (1899–1978), American historian: *A Stillness at Appomattox* (1953) won a Pulitzer Prize.

**Caius Valerius Catullus** (84?–54 B.C.), Roman poet. Of his numerous lyric poems, 116 are extant.

**Miguel de Cervantes Saavedra** (1547?–1616), Spanish novelist: *Don Quixote* (1614).

**Raymond Chandler** (1888–1959), American mystery and detective novelist: *The Big Sleep* (1939).

**François René de Chateaubriand** (1768–1848), French essayist and novelist. Best known for his autobiography, *Mémoires d'outre-tombe (1850).*

**Geoffrey Chaucer** (1343?–1400), English poet: *Canterbury Tales* (c. 1387), *Troilus and Criseyde* (c. 1385).

**John Cheever** (1912– ), American novelist: *The Wapshot Chronicle* (1951), *Bullet Park* (1969), *Falconer* (1977); *The Stories of John Cheever* (1978) won a Pulitzer Prize.

**Anton Chekhov** (1860–1904), Russian dramatist and short-story writer. After achieving success in short fiction he produced several great plays, including *The Sea Gull* (1896) and *The Cherry Orchard* (1904).

**G. K. (Gilbert Keith) Chesterton** (1874–1936), English novelist, poet, and critic who created the "Father Brown" detective story series.

**Agatha Christie** (1891–1976), English mystery novelist: *The Murder of Roger Ackroyd* (1926) and more than 50 other crime novels.

**Sir Winston Churchill** (1874–1965), English statesman and historian: *History of the English-Speaking Peoples* (4 vols., 1956–58).

**John Ciardi** (1916– ), American poet: *As If: Poems New and Selected* (1955).

**Marcus Tullius Cicero** (106–43 B.C.), Roman statesman and orator: wrote many essays.

**Arthur C. Clarke** (1917– ), British science-fiction author: *Against the Fall of Night* (1953); coauthor of movie *2001: A Space Odyssey* (1968).

**Irvin S. Cobb** (1876–1944), American humorist and author: *Old Judge Priest* (1915).

**Jean Cocteau** (1891–1963), French dramatist, novelist, and poet: *Les Enfants Terribles* (1929), a drama.

**Robert Peter Tristram Coffin** (1892–1955), American writer: *Strange Holiness* (1935) won a Pulitzer Prize for poetry.

**Samuel Taylor Coleridge** (1772–1834), English poet and critic: collaborated with Wordsworth in the book of verse *Lyrical Ballads* (1798); *Biographia Literaria* (1817), essays on criticism.

**Colette** (full name **Sidonie Gabrielle Colette**; 1873–1954), French novelist and a leading feminist: *Chéri* (1920), *Gigi* (1945).

**Padraic Colum** (1881–1972), Irish-American novelist, dramatist, and poet. He was a leader of the Irish literary revival during the early 20th century.

**Ivy Compton-Burnett** (1892–1969), English novelist: *Brother and Sister* (1929).

**William Congreve** (1670–1729), English comic dramatist: *The Way of the World* (1700).

**Marc Connelly** (1890– ), American playwright: *Green Pastures* (1930) won a Pulitzer Prize.

**Joseph Conrad** (1857–1924), Polish-born British novelist and short-story writer: *Lord Jim* (1900), *Typhoon* (1903); *Tales of Hearsay* (1925), stories.

**James Fenimore Cooper** (1789–1851), American novelist: *The Last of the Mohicans* (1826).

**Noel Coward** (1899–1973), English playwright and

**AUTHORS AND WRITERS** *(continued)*
composer: *Private Lives (1930); Blithe Spirit* (1941).
**Malcolm Cowley** (1898–   ), American literary critic:
*Exile's Return* (1934), *The Literary Situation* (1954),
*The Faulkner-Cowley File* (1966).
**James Gould Cozzens** (1903–78), American novelist:
*Guard of Honor* (1948) won a Pulitzer Prize; *By Love
Possessed* (1957).
**Hart Crane** (1899–1932), U.S. poet: *The Bridge* (1930).
**Stephen Crane** (1871–1900), American novelist: *The
Red Badge of Courage* (1895).
**A. J. Cronin** (1896–   ), British author: *The Keys of
the Kingdom* (1941).
**Russel Crouse,** see Howard Lindsay.
**E. E. (Edward Estin) Cummings** (1894–1962), Amer-
ican poet. His books of lyric verse, including *Tulips
and Chimneys* (1923), experimented with unusual
typographical styles.
**Richard Henry Dana Jr.** (1815–1882), American au-
thor: *Two Years Before the Mast* (1840).
**Gabriele D'Annunzio** (1863–1938), Italian poet, nov-
elist, playwright: *La città morta* (1898), a play.
**Dante Alighieri** (1265–1321), Italian epic poet. His
*Divine Comedy* ranks as the most important literary
work of the Middle Ages.
**Owen Davis** (1874–1956), American playwright:
*Icebound* (1923) won a Pulitzer Prize.
**Clarence S. Day Jr.** (1874–1935), American author:
*Life with Father* (1935).
**Thomas De Quincey** (1785–1859), English author:
*Confessions of an English Opium Eater* (1821).
**Daniel Defoe** (1660–1731), English novelist and
journalist: *Robinson Crusoe* (1720), *Moll Flanders*
(1722), *Journal of the Plague Year* (1722).
**Charles Dickens** (1812–70), English novelist: *Pickwick
Papers* (1836), *Oliver Twist* (1837–39), *David Cop-
perfield* (1849–50), *Great Expectations* (1860–61).
**James Dickey** (1925–   ), American poet and novel-
ist: *Into the Stone* (1960), poetry; *Deliverance* (1970),
a novel.
**Emily Dickinson** (1830–86), American poet. Her lyric
poems reflect solitude and preoccupation with death.
**Denis Diderot** (1713–84), French encyclopedist and
novelist.
**George Dillon** (1906–68), American poet: *The Flow-
ering Stone* (1931) won a Pulitzer Prize.
**Isak Dinesen** (real name **Karen Blixen;** 1885–1962),
Danish novelist: *Seven Gothic Tales* (1934).
**E. L. (Edgar Lawrence) Doctorow** (1931–   ), American novelist: *The Book of Daniel* (1971), *Ragtime*
(1975), *Loon Lake* (1980).
**J. P. (James Patrick) Donleavy** (1926–   ), American
novelist: *The Ginger Man* (1955), *Schultz* (1979).
**John Donne** (1572–1631), English poet and preacher
noted for his metaphysical and devotional poems.
**Hilda Doolittle ("H. D.";** 1886–1961), American
poet of the American Imagist movement.
**John Dos Passos** (1896–1970), American novelist:
*U.S.A.,* a trilogy consisting of *The 42d Parallel*
(1930), *1919* (1932), and *The Big Money* (1936).
**Feodor Dostoyevsky** (1821–81), Russian novelist:
*Memoirs from the House of the Dead* (1861–62), *Crime
and Punishment* (1866), *The Idiot* (1868), *The Possessed*
(1871–72), *The Brothers Karamazov* (1879–80).
**Lloyd C. Douglas** (1877–1951), American author:
*Magnificent Obsession* (1929), *Green Light* (1935),
*The Robe* (1942), *The Big Fisherman* (1948).
**Sir Arthur Conan Doyle** (1859–1930), Scottish mys-
tery novelist and creator of Sherlock Holmes.
**Theodore Dreiser** (1871–1945), American novelist:
*Sister Carrie* (1900), *An American Tragedy* (1925).
**Allen Drury** (1918–   ), U.S. novelist: *Advise and Con-
sent* (1960) won a Pulitzer Prize; *Anna Hastings* (1977).
**John Dryden** (1631–1700), English poet, dramatist,
and critic: *Fables, Ancient and Modern* (1699).

**Alexandre Dumas, père** (1802–70), French novelist
and dramatist: *The Count of Monte Cristo* (1844) and
*The Three Musketeers* (1844).
**Alexandre Dumas, fils** (1824–95), French dramatist:
*Monsieur Alphonse* (1873), *Denise* (1885).
**Will Durant** (1885–   ), U.S. historian and philoso-
pher: *The Story of Philosophy* (1926), *The Story of
Civilization* (12 vols., begun in 1935); *Rousseau and
Revolution* (1967) won a Pulitzer Prize for nonfiction.
**Lawrence Durrell** (1912–   ), English novelist: *The
Alexandria Quartet* (1958–60), *Tunc* (1968).
**Richard Eberhart** (1904–   ), American poet: *Select-
ed Poems* (1965) won a Pulitzer Prize.
**Leon Edel** (1907–   ), American literary historian
and biographer: *Henry James* (1953–72), a 5-volume
biography. The third volume, *Henry James: The
Middle Years* (1962), won a Pulitzer Prize and a
National Book Award.
**Ilya Ehrenberg** (1891–1967), Russian novelist: *A
Street in Moscow* (1930), *Out of Chaos* (1934).
**George Eliot** (real name **Marian Evans**; 1819–80),
English novelist: *Silas Marner* (1861).
**T. S. (Thomas Stearns) Eliot** (1888–1965), Ameri-
can-born English poet and critic: *The Lovesong of J.
Alfred Prufrock* (1917), *The Wasteland* (1922). He
won a Nobel Prize in 1948.
**Ralph Ellison** (1914–   ), American novelist: *Invisible
Man* (1952).
**Ralph Waldo Emerson** (1803–82), American essayist
and poet; developed transcendentalist philosophy.
**Euripides** (485?–406 B.C.), Greek tragic dramatist.
Of about 92 plays 19 are extant, including *Medea*
(431 B.C.) and *Electra* (413 B.C.).
**James T. Farrell** (1904–79), American novelist: *Studs
Lonigan* (1932–35), a trilogy.
**William Faulkner** (1897–1962), American novelist:
*The Sound and the Fury* (1929) and *Light in August*
(1932). He won a Nobel Prize in 1949 and Pulitzer
Prizes for *A Fable* (1954) and *The Reivers* (1962).
**Edna Ferber** (1885–1968), American novelist: *So Big*
(1924) won a Pulitzer Prize; *Show Boat* (1926);
*Cimarron* (1930); *Giant* (1952).
**Lawrence Ferlinghetti** (1919–   ), American beat-
generation poet; *A Coney Island of the Mind* (1958).
**Eugene Field** (1850–95), American poet and journal-
ist: best known for children's poems "Little Boy
Blue" and "Wynken, Blynken, and Nod."
**Henry Fielding** (1707–54), English novelist and
dramatist: *Joseph Andrews* (1742), *Tom Jones* (1749).
**Edward Fitzgerald** (1809–83), English poet, translat-
ed Omar Khayyám's *Rubaiyat* in 1859.
**F. (Francis) Scott Fitzgerald** (1896–1940), American
novelist and short-story writer: *This Side of Paradise*
(1920), *The Great Gatsby* (1925).
**Gustave Flaubert** (1821–80), French novelist:
*Madame Bovary* (1857).
**Ford Madox Ford** (real name **Ford Madox Hueffer;**
1873–1939), English novelist and poet: *The Good
Soldier* (1915), *Parade's End* (1924–28), a tetralogy
published in one volume in 1950.
**E. M. (Edward Morgan) Forster** (1879–1970), English novelist and critic: *A Passage to India* (1924), a
novel; *Aspects of the Novel* (1927), criticism.
**John Fowles** (1926–   ), English novelist: *The Collector* (1963), *The Magus* (1966), *The French Lieutenant's Woman* (1970).
**Anatole France** (real name **Anatole Jacques Thibault;**
1844–1924), French novelist and satirist: *Balthasar*
(1889), short stories; won a Nobel Prize in 1921.
**Douglas Southall Freeman** (1886–1953), American
historian: *R. E. Lee,* 4 vols. (1934), and *George
Washington,* 7 vols. (1948–57) won Pulitzer Prizes.
**Robert Frost** (1874–1963), American lyric poet
captured much of the American rural spirit. He won four
Pulitzer Prizes for *New Hampshire* (1923), *Collected*

*Poems* (1930), *A Further Range* (1936), and *A Witness Tree* (1942).

**Christopher Fry** (1907– ), English dramatist and translator: *The Lady's Not for Burning* (1949).

**John Galsworthy** (1867–1933), English novelist and playwright: *The Forsyte Saga* (1922), a trilogy.

**Erle Stanley Gardner** (1889–1970), American detective-story writer: *The Case of the Velvet Claws* (1933) was his first novel featuring the lawyer Perry Mason.

**William H. Gass** (1924– ), American novelist and critic: *Omensetter's Luck* (1966), a novel; *In the Heart of the Heart of the Country* (1968).

**John Gay** (1685–1732), English dramatist and poet: *The Beggar's Opera* (1728).

**Jean Genet** (1910– ), French novelist and dramatist: *The Balcony* (1957) and *The Blacks* (1959), dramas; *Miracle of the Rose* (1951), a novel.

**Edward Gibbon** (1737–94), English historian: *The Decline and Fall of the Roman Empire* (1776–88).

**André Gide** (1869–1951), French novelist: *The Immoralist* (1902), *Straight Is the Gate* (1909).

**Allen Ginsberg** (1926– ), American poet of beat and hippie movements: *Howl and Other Poems* (1955). His *The Fall of America: Poems of These States* (1973) won a National Book Award.

**Jean Giraudoux** (1882–1944), French dramatist: *Tiger at the Gates* (1935).

**Ellen Glasgow** (1874–1945), American novelist: *In This Our Life* (1941) won a Pulitzer Prize.

**Johann Wolfgang von Goethe** (1749–1832), German poet and dramatist. His greatest work was the dramatic poem *Faust* (1808 and 1833).

**Nikolai Vasilyevich Gogol** (1809–52), Russian novelist, short-story writer, and playwright: *The Inspector General* (1836), a play; *Dead Souls* (1842), a novel.

**William Golding** (1911– ), English novelist: *Lord of the Flies* (1954) and *Darkness Visible* (1979).

**Oliver Goldsmith** (1730?–74), Irish novelist, poet, and dramatist: *The Vicar of Wakefield* (1766), a novel; *She Stoops to Conquer* (1773), a drama.

**Paul Goodman** (1911–72), American essayist and critic: *Growing Up Absurd* (1947).

**Maxim Gorki** (real name **Aleksey Maximovich Pyeshkov**; 1868–1936), Russian dramatist and novelist: *The Lower Depths* (1902), play; *Mother* (1907), novel.

**Gunter Grass** (1927– ), German novelist: *The Tin Drum* (1959), *Local Anaesthetic* (1970).

**Shirley Ann Grau** (1929– ), American novelist: *The Keepers of the House* (1964), which won a Pulitzer Prize; *The Condor Passes* (1971).

**Robert Graves** (1895– ), English poet, novelist, and critic. Besides much lyric verse, he wrote such novels as *I, Claudius* (1934) and compiled *Greek Myths* (2 vols., 1955).

**Thomas Gray** (1716–71), English poet: "Elegy Written in a Country Churchyard" (1750).

**Graham Greene** (1904– ), English novelist: *The Power and the Glory* (1940); *The End of the Affair* (1951); *The Comedians* (1966); *A Sort of Life* (1971), autobiography; *The Honorary Consul* (1973); *The Human Factor* (1978).

**Lady Augusta Gregory** (1852–1932), Irish dramatist and founder of Dublin's Abbey Theatre: her plays include *The Rising of the Moon* (1907).

**Zane Grey** (1872–1939), U.S. novelist of Old West: *The Last of The Plainsmen* (1908), *Riders of The Purple Sage* (1912).

**John Gunther** (1901–70), American author: *Inside Europe* (1936), *Inside Asia* (1939).

**A. B. Guthrie Jr.** (1901– ), American novelist: *The Big Sky* (1947); *The Way West* (1949) won a Pulitzer Prize.

**Alex Haley** (1921– ), American author: *Roots* (1976) won a special Pulitzer Prize.

**James Norman Hall**, see Charles Nordhoff.

**Dashiell Hammett** (1894–1961), U.S. detective-story writer: created Sam Spade in *The Maltese Falcon* (1930) and Nick and Nora Charles in *The Thin Man* (1934).

**Knut Hamsun** (1859–1952), Norwegian novelist: *Growth of the Soil* (1920), *Mysteries* (1927). He won a Nobel Prize in 1920.

**Lorraine Hansberry** (1930–65), American black playwright: *A Raisin in the Sun* (1959).

**Thomas Hardy** (1840–1928), English novelist, poet, and dramatist: *Tess of the D'Urbervilles* (1891) and *Jude the Obscure* (1895), novels.

**Joel Chandler Harris** (1848–1908), American novelist and short-story writer who recorded Southern dialect: *Uncle Remus: His Songs and His Sayings* (1881).

**Moss Hart** (1904–61), American playwright and stage director: co-winner of Pulitzer Prize for *You Can't Take It With You* (1936). Wrote many plays and musicals including *Lady in the Dark* (1941), *Winged Victory* (1943).

**Bret Harte** (1836–1902), American western author: *The Luck of Roaring Camp* (1870).

**Gerhart Hauptmann** (1862–1946), German dramatist, poet, and novelist: *Before Dawn* (1889), a play.

**Nathaniel Hawthorne** (1804–64), American novelist and short-story writer: *The Scarlet Letter* (1850), *The House of Seven Gables* (1851).

**Heinrich Heine** (1797–1856), German poet. Many of his romantic poems were used as lyrics in the songs of Schubert, Liszt, and Schumann.

**Robert A. Heinlein** (1907– ), American science-fiction author: *Stranger in a Strange Land* (1961), *The Past Through Tomorrow* (1967).

**Joseph Heller** (1923– ), U.S. novelist: *Catch-22* (1961), *Something Happened* (1974), *Good as Gold* (1979).

**Lillian Hellman** (1905– ), American playwright: *The Children's Hour* (1934), *The Little Foxes* (1939), *Watch on the Rhine* (1941); *An Unfinished Woman* (1969), autobiography.

**Ernest Hemingway** (1899–1961), American novelist and short-story writer: *A Farewell to Arms* (1929); *For Whom the Bell Tolls* (1940); *The Old Man and the Sea* (1952) won a Pulitzer Prize. He was awarded a Nobel Prize in 1954.

**O. Henry** (William Sydney Porter; 1862–1910), U.S. short-story writer of about 300 stories memorable for concise plotting and surprise endings.

**Herodotus** (484?–425 B.C.), Greek historian: *History of the Persian Wars*.

**Robert Herrick** (1591–1674), English poet. His highly polished verse reflects classical influences.

**John Hersey** (1914– ), American novelist and journalist: *A Bell for Adano* (1944) won a Pulitzer Prize; *Hiroshima* (1946), *The Walnut Door* (1977).

**Hermann Hesse** (1877–1962), German poet and novelist: *Steppenwolf* (1927), *Magister Ludi* (1949). He won a Nobel Prize in 1946.

**Robert Silliman Hillyer** (1895–1961), American poet: *Collected Verse* (1933) won a Pulitzer Prize.

**Laura Z. Hobson** (1900– ), U.S. novelist: *Gentleman's Agreement* (1947); *Over and Above* (1979).

**Oliver Wendell Holmes** (1809–94), American poet, essayist: "Old Ironsides" (1830), a poem; *Autocrat of the Breakfast Table* (1858), sketches.

**Homer** (c. 800–700 B.C.), Greek epic poet: the *Odyssey*, the *Iliad*.

**Gerard Manley Hopkins** (1844–89), English mystical poet: "The Windhover" (1918).

**Horace** (65–8 B.C.), Latin poet. He published three books of *Odes* and two books of *Satires*.

**Paul Horgan** (1903– ), American author: won Pulitzer Prizes for *Great River* (1954) and *Lamy of Santa Fe* (1975).

**A. E. (Alfred Edward) Housman** (1859–1936), English poet: *A Shropshire Lad* (1896).

**AUTHORS AND WRITERS** *(continued)*

**William Dean Howells** (1837–1920), American novelist and critic: *The Rise of Silas Lapham* (1885), *A Hazard of New Fortunes* (1890).

**Victor Hugo** (1802–85), French novelist, poet, and dramatist: novels include *Notre Dame de Paris* (1831) and *Les Misérables* (1862).

**Aldous Huxley** (1894–1963), English novelist and essayist: *Brave New World* (1932).

**Henrik Ibsen** (1828–1906), Norwegian dramatist. He pioneered social realism in such plays as *A Doll's House* (1879) and *Rosmersholm* (1886).

**William Inge** (1913–73), American dramatist: *Come Back, Little Sheba* (1950); *Picnic* (1952) won a Pulitzer Prize; *The Dark at the Top of the Stairs* (1958).

**Eugene Ionesco** (1912–    ), French dramatist. A pioneer in the theater of the absurd, his plays include *The Chairs* (1952) and *Rhinoceros* (1960).

**Washington Irving** (1783–1859), American editor and short-story writer: "Rip Van Winkle" and "The Legend of Sleepy Hollow" (both 1820).

**Christopher Isherwood** (1904–    ), English dramatist and novelist. His collection of sketches, *Goodbye to Berlin* (1939), was adapted for the stage in 1951 by John Van Druten as *I Am a Camera*, as was the musical *Cabaret* in 1971.

**Henry James** (1843–1916), American novelist and short-story writer: *Wings of the Dove* (1902), *The Ambassadors* (1903), *The Golden Bowl* (1904).

**Marquis James** (1891–1955), American author: won Pulitzer Prizes for biographies *The Raven* (1929) and *Andrew Jackson* (1937).

**Randall Jarrell** (1914–65), American poet: *Little Friend, Little Friend* (1945), poems of World War II.

**Robinson Jeffers** (1887–1962), American poet: *Give Your Heart to the Hawks* (1933).

**Samuel Johnson** (1709–84), English essayist, critic, poet, and lexicographer: his essays in *The Rambler* helped establish literary standards; famous for his witty *Dictionary of the English Language* (1755).

**James Jones** (1921–77), American novelist: *From Here to Eternity* (1951) won a National Book Award.

**Ben Jonson** (1573?–1637), English dramatist and poet: *Volpone* (1606), *The Alchemist* (1610).

**James Joyce** (1882–1941), Irish novelist, poet, and short-story writer. He applied poetic techniques to his novels, *A Portrait of the Artist as a Young Man* (1916), *Ulysses* (1922), and *Finnegans Wake* (1939). *Dubliners* (1914) is a short-story collection.

**Juvenal** (55?–135), Roman satirical poet.

**Franz Kafka** (1883–1924), Czech-born Austrian novelist: *Amerika* (1927), *The Castle* (1930), *The Trial* (1937).

**MacKinlay Kantor** (1904–77), American novelist, won a Pulitzer Prize for *Andersonville* (1955).

**George S. Kaufman** (1889–1961), American playwright and director: co-recipient of Pulitzer Prizes for *Of Thee I Sing* (1931) and *You Can't Take It With You* (1936).

**Nikos Kazantzakis** (1883?–1957), Greek novelist: *Zorba the Greek* (1946).

**Alfred Kazin** (1915–    ), American critic: *On Native Grounds* (1942), *The Inmost Leaf* (1955).

**John Keats** (1795–1821), English poet: "Ode on a Grecian Urn" and "To a Nightingale" (both 1820).

**George Edward Kelly** (1887–1974), American playwright: *Craig's Wife* (1925) won a Pulitzer Prize.

**Rudyard Kipling** (1865–1936), English poet, novelist, and short-story writer: *The Light That Failed* (1890), a novel; *Barrack Room Ballads* (1892); won a Nobel Prize in 1907.

**George Lyman Kittredge** (1860–1941), American literary scholar: *Shakespeare* (1916).

**Arthur Koestler** (1905–    ), British-Hungarian political novelist: *Darkness at Noon* (1941).

**Oliver La Farge** (1901–63), American author: *Laughing Boy* (1929) won a Pulitzer Prize.

**Jean de La Fontaine** (1621–95), French fabulist and poet: *Fables choisies mises en vers* (1668–94) consists of about 230 fables.

**Pär Lägerkvist** (1891–1974), Swedish Nobel Prize-winning author: *Barabas* (1951).

**Charles Lamb** (1775–1834), English essayist and critic. With his sister Mary he wrote the children's book *Tales from Shakespeare* (1807).

**Sidney Lanier** (1842–81), American poet and critic: *Poems* (1887).

**Ring Lardner** (1885–1933), American satirist and short-story writer: *You Know Me, Al* (1916).

**D. H. (David Herbert) Lawrence** (1885–1930), English novelist, poet, and critic: *Sons and Lovers* (1913), *Lady Chatterley's Lover* (1928).

**Harper Lee** (1926–    ), American novelist: *To Kill a Mockingbird* (1960) won a Pulitzer Prize.

**Cecil Day Lewis** (1904–72), English essayist and novelist: *Overtures to Death* (1938), poems. He became poet laureate of England in 1968.

**C. S. (Clive Staples) Lewis** (1898–1963), English religious essayist and poet: *The Allegory of Love* (1936), *The Screwtape Letters* (1942).

**Sinclair Lewis** (1885–1951), American novelist: *Main Street* (1920), *Babbitt* (1922), *Elmer Gantry* (1927); *Arrowsmith* (1925) won a Pulitzer Prize. He won a Nobel Prize in 1930.

**Howard Lindsay** (1889–1968) American playwright: coauthor with Russel Crouse (1893–1966) of Pulitzer Prize-winning *State of the Union* (1945) and long-running *Life with Father* (1939), in which Lindsay starred as actor.

**Vachel Lindsay** (1879–1931), American poet: *General William Booth Enters into Heaven* (1913).

**Livy** (59 B.C.–A.D. 17), Roman historian; 35 books of his 142-book *History of Rome* are extant.

**Jack London** (1876–1916), American novelist: *The Call of the Wild* (1903), *Martin Eden* (1909).

**Henry Wadsworth Longfellow** (1807–82), American poet: *Evangeline* (1847).

**Federico García Lorca** (1899–1936), Spanish poet and dramatist: *Blood Wedding* (1938).

**Amy Lowell** (1874–1925), American poet, pioneered free verse: *Sword Blades and Poppy Seeds* (1914); *What's O'Clock* (1925) won a Pulitzer Prize.

**James Russell Lowell** (1819–91), American poet and essayist: *A Fable for Critics* (1848).

**Robert Lowell** (1917–77), American poet and critic: *Lord Weary's Castle* (1946) and *The Dolphin* (1973) won Pulitzer Prizes.

**Ross Macdonald** (pseudonym of **Kenneth Millar**; 1915–    ), American mystery writer: *The Chill* (1964), *The Underground Man* (1971), *The Blue Hammer* (1976).

**Niccolò Machiavelli** (1469–1527), Italian essayist and dramatist: *The Prince* (1532).

**Archibald MacLeish** (1892–    ), American poet and dramatist. He won Pulitzer Prizes for poetry with *Conquistador* (1932) and *Collected Poems* (1952). His drama *J. B.* (1958) also won a Pulitzer Prize.

**Norman Mailer** (1923–    ), American novelist and essayist: *The Naked and the Dead* (1948), *Why Are We in Vietnam?* (1967). *The Armies of the Night* (1968) and *The Executioner's Song* (1979) won Pulitzer Prizes.

**Bernard Malamud** (1914–    ), American novelist: *The Natural* (1952), *The Assistant* (1957), *Dubin's Lives* (1979). *The Fixer* (1966) won a National Book Award and a Pulitzer Prize.

**Stéphane Mallarmé** (1842–98), French poet: *L'Après-Midi d'un faune* (1887).

**Sir Thomas Malory** (died 1471), English writer of romances: *Morte D'Arthur* (1485).

**André Malraux** (1901–76), French novelist: *Man's*

*Fate* (1933); *The Voices of Silence* (1953), essays.

**Thomas Mann** (1875–1955), German novelist: *The Magic Mountain* (1927) and *Joseph and His Brothers* (1934–44); won Nobel Prize in 1929.

**Katherine Mansfield** (1888–1923), British short-story writer: *The Garden Party* (1922).

**Edwin Markham** (1852–1940), American poet: "The Man with the Hoe" (1899).

**Christopher Marlowe** (1564–93), English dramatist and poet: *Tamburlaine the Great* (1587?), *Dr. Faustus* (1588?).

**John P. Marquand** (1893–1960), American novelist: *The Late George Apley* (1937) won a Pulitzer Prize.

**John Masefield** (1878–1967), English poet laureate (1930–67): *Salt Water Ballads* (1902).

**Edgar Lee Masters** (1869–1950), American poet: *Spoon River Anthology* (1915).

**W. Somerset Maugham** (1874–1965), English novelist and playwright: *Of Human Bondage* (1915), *The Moon and Sixpence* (1919), *The Razor's Edge* (1944).

**Guy de Maupassant** (1850–93), French novelist and short-story writer. *Une Vie* (1883) is his best novel. His 300 masterful short stories include "The Necklace" and "The Piece of String."

**François Mauriac** (1885–1970), French novelist: *The Desert of Love* (1925). He won a Nobel Prize in 1952.

**André Maurois** (1885–1967), French novelist and biographer: *Ariel* (1923), a life of Shelley; *Proust,* (1949); *Memoirs* (1970).

**Mary McCarthy** (1912– ), American novelist and essayist: *The Groves of Academe* (1952), *The Group* (1963), *Cannibals and Missionaries* (1979), novels.

**Carson McCullers** (1917–67), American novelist and playwright: *Member of the Wedding* (1946).

**Phyllis McGinley** (1905–78), American poet: *Times Three: Selected Verse from Three Decades* (1961) won a Pulitzer Prize.

**Herman Melville** (1819–91), American novelist. His allegorical *Moby-Dick,* (1851) is his masterpiece. His last great book, *Billy Budd,* was published in 1924.

**H. L. (Henry Louis) Mencken** (1880–1956), American satirist, editor, and essayist: *Prejudices* (1919–27), *Treatise on Right and Wrong* (1934), *The American Language* (1919, 1946, 1948).

**George Meredith** (1828–1909), English novelist: *The Ordeal of Richard Feverel* (1859), *The Egoist* (1879).

**W. S. Merwin** (1927– ), American poet: *The Carrier of Ladders* (1970) won a Pulitzer Prize.

**James A. Michener** (1907– ), American novelist: *Tales of the South Pacific* (1947) won a Pulitzer Prize; *The Source* (1965), *Centennial* (1974), *Chesapeake* (1978), *The Covenant* (1980).

**John Stuart Mill** (1806–73), English philosopher: *Essay on Liberty* (1859), *Utilitarianism* (1863).

**Edna St. Vincent Millay** (1892–1950), American poet best remembered for her sonnets. *The Ballad of the Harp-Weaver* (1922) won a Pulitzer Prize.

**Arthur Miller** (1915– ), American playwright: *Death of a Salesman* (1949) won a Pulitzer Prize; *The Crucible* (1953), *A View From the Bridge* (1955), *After the Fall* (1964), *The Price* (1968).

**Henry Miller** (1891–1980), American novelist: *Tropic of Cancer* (1934), *Tropic of Capricorn* (1939).

**Joaquin Miller** (1839?–1913), American poet; *Song of the Sierras* (1871), *Life Among the Modocs* (1873).

**A. A. (Alan Alexander) Milne** (1882–1956), English poet and children's writer: *Winnie-the-Pooh* (1926).

**Czeslaw Milosz** (1911– ), Polish-born American poet: *Postwar Polish Poetry* (1965), *Bells in Winter* (1978); won Nobel Prize in 1980.

**John Milton** (1608–74), English poet. His epic *Paradise Lost* (1667) is a literary landmark.

**Margaret Mitchell** (1900–49), American novelist: *Gone with the Wind* (1936) won a Pulitzer Prize.

**Jean Baptiste Molière** (1622–73), French dramatist

and one of the great comic playwrights of all time. His works include *The Miser* (1668) and *The Doctor in Spite of Himself* (1666).

**Michel Eyquem de Montaigne** (1533–92), French essayist and one of the world's great literary stylists. His essays are studies of human nature.

**Marianne Moore** (1887–1972), American poet: *Collected Poems* (1951) won a Pulitzer Prize; *O to Be a Dragon* (1959).

**Alberto Moravia** (1907– ), Italian novelist: *Two Women* (1957), *The Empty Canvas* (1961).

**Sir Thomas More** (1478–1535), English essayist: *Utopia* (1516).

**Samuel Eliot Morison** (1887–1976), American historian: *Admiral of the Ocean Sea* (1942) and *John Paul Jones* (1959) won Pulitzer Prizes.

**Christopher Morley** (1890–1957), American novelist and editor: *Kitty Foyle* (1939), a novel.

**Iris Murdoch** (1919– ), Anglo-Irish novelist: *The Bell* (1958), *A Severed Head* (1961), *The Sacred and Profane Love Machine* (1974).

**Vladimir Nabokov** (1899–1977), Russian-American novelist: *Lolita* (1955), *Pnin* (1957), *Pale Fire* (1962), *Ada* (1969).

**Ogden Nash** (1902–71), American humorous poet: *Hard Lines* (1931), *I'm a Stranger Here Myself* (1938), *You Can't Get There From Here* (1957).

**Robert Nathan** (1894– ), American author: novel *Portrait of Jennie* (1940), poetry *The Green Leaf: Collected Poems* (1950).

**Allan Nevins** (1890–1971) American historian: won Pulitzer Prizes for *Grover Cleveland* (1933) and *Hamilton Fish* (1936).

**Charles Bernard Nordhoff** (1887–1947) and **James Norman Hall** (1887–1951), American writing team: *Lafayette Flying Corps* (1920), *Mutiny on the Bounty* (1932), *The Hurricane* (1935).

**Frank Norris** (1870–1902), American novelist: *McTeague* (1899), *The Octopus* (1901), *The Pit* (1902).

**Joyce Carol Oates** (1938– ), American novelist and critic: *Them* (1969), a novel, won a National Book Award; *Childwold* (1976); *Unholy Loves* (1979); *Bellefleur* (1980).

**Sean O'Casey** (1884–1964), Irish playwright: *The Shadow of a Gunman* (1923), *Juno and the Paycock* (1924), *The Plough and the Stars* (1926).

**Edwin O'Connor** (1918–1968), American novelist: *The Last Hurrah* (1956); *The Edge of Sadness* (1961) won a Pulitzer Prize.

**Flannery O'Connor** (1925–64), American novelist and short-story writer: *Wise Blood* (1952); *The Violent Bear It Away* (1960); *Complete Stories* (1971).

**Clifford Odets** (1906–63), American playwright: *Waiting for Lefty* (1935), *Golden Boy* (1937).

**Sean O'Faoláin** (1900– ), Irish author: *King of the Beggars* (1938), biographies of Irish statesmen; *I Remember! I Remember!* (1961), short stories.

**Liam O'Flaherty** (1897– ), Irish novelist: *The Informer* (1925).

**John O'Hara** (1905–70), American novelist and short-story writer: *Appointment in Samarra* (1934), *Butterfield 8* (1935), *Pal Joey* (1940), novels.

**Omar Khayyam** (11th century), Persian poet: *The Rubaiyat.*

**Eugene O'Neill** (1888–1953), American dramatist: *Mourning Becomes Electra* (1931) and *The Iceman Cometh* (1946). Four of his plays won Pulitzer Prizes: *Beyond the Horizon* (1919), *Anna Christie* (1921), *Strange Interlude* (1927), and *Long Day's Journey Into Night* (1941); won Nobel Prize in 1936.

**José Ortega y Gasset** (1883–1955), Spanish essayist and critic: *Meditations on Quixote* (1914), *The Revolt of the Masses* (1930).

**George Orwell** (1903–50), English satirist: *Animal Farm* (1946), *Nineteen Eighty-Four* (1949).

**AUTHORS AND WRITERS** *(continued)*

**Ovid** (43 B.C.–A.D. 18), Latin poet: *Metamorphoses.*

**Thomas Paine** (1737–1809), American political essayist. His pamphlet *Common Sense* (1776) promoted America's independence from Britain.

**Dorothy Parker** (1893–1967), American poet and short-story writer: *Enough Rope* (1926), verse; *After Such Pleasures* (1933), *Here Lies* (1939), stories.

**Boris Pasternak** (1890–1960), Soviet poet, novelist, and translator of Shakespeare into Russian: *Doctor Zhivago* (1957), a novel; forced by his government to decline 1958 Nobel Prize.

**Samuel Pepys** (1633–1703), English diarist; presents vivid picture of Restoration London.

**St.-John Perse** (real name **Marie R.A.A.S. Léger;** 1887–1975), French poet who won a Nobel Prize in 1960. One of his best-known works is the long poem *Anabase* (1924).

**Francesco Petrarch** (1304–74), Italian poet of the Latin and Italian languages. He was among the first and greatest of the Renaissance poets and a popularizer of the sonnet form.

**Harold Pinter** (1930–   ), English dramatist: *The Birthday Party* (1957), *The Caretaker* (1959).

**Luigi Pirandello** (1867–1936), Italian playwright: *Six Characters in Search of an Author* (1920).

**Sylvia Plath** (1932–63), American poet and novelist: *Ariel* (1965), poems; *The Bell Jar* (1971), a novel.

**Plutarch** (45?–125), Greek biographer and essayist. His *Parallel Lives* is a collection of 46 biographies of notable Greek and Roman figures.

**Edgar Allan Poe** (1809–49), American poet and short-story writer: "The Raven" (1845) and "The Bells" (1847), poems; "The Fall of the House of Usher" (1839), and "The Gold Bug" (1843), stories.

**Alexander Pope** (1688–1744), English poet. His *Essay on Criticism* (1711) and *Essay on Man* (1734) used rhymed couplets in popularizing dominant ideas of the time; *The Rape of the Lock* (1714) is a landmark among mock-heroic poems.

**Katherine Anne Porter** (1890–1980), American short-story writer and novelist: *Pale Horse, Pale Rider* (1939), short stories; *Ship of Fools* (1962), a novel. Her *Collected Stories* (1965) won a National Book Award and a Pulitzer Prize.

**Ezra Pound** (1885–1972), American expatriate poet. He dominated the imagism and vorticism movements of early 1900s; best known for his serial poems, *Cantos* (1925–60).

**John Boynton Priestley** (1894–   ), English novelist: *The Good Companions* (1929).

**Marcel Proust** (1871–1922), French novelist. From 1913 to 1922 he produced 16-volume masterpiece, *Remembrance of Things Past.*

**Aleksandr Sergeyevich Pushkin** (1799–1837), Russian poet: *Eugene Onegin* (1828).

**Salvatore Quasimodo** (1901–68), Italian poet. His poems, philosophical interpretations of man's history, won a Nobel Prize in 1959.

**Ellery Queen,** pen name of Frederic Dannay (1905–   ) and Manfred Lee (1905–1971), American detective-story writing team: Books featured detective Ellery Queen.

**Francois Rabelais** (1494?–1553), French satirist: *Gargantua* and *Pantagruel* (both 1532).

**Jean Baptiste Racine** (1639–99), French dramatist: *Britannicus* (1669) and *Bérénice* (1670).

**Ayn Rand** (1905–   ), American novelist: *The Fountainhead* (1943), *Atlas Shrugged* (1957).

**Marjorie Kinnan Rawlings** (1896–1953), American novelist: *The Yearling* (1938) won a Pulitzer Prize.

**Erich Maria Remarque** (1897–1970), German-American novelist: *All Quiet on the Western Front* (1929), *Three Comrades* (1938).

**Kenneth Rexroth** (1905–   ), American poet and critic: *Natural Numbers* (1963), poems; *Assays* (1961), essays; *The Morning Star* (1979).

**Elmer Rice** (1892–1967), American playwright: *Street Scene* (1929) won a Pulitzer Price; *Dream Girl* (1945).

**I. A. (Ivor Armstrong) Richards** (1893–1979), Anglo-American critic, pioneer in New Criticism movement: *Principles of Literary Criticism* (1925).

**Samuel Richardson** (1689–1761), English novelist: *Pamela* (1740), *Clarissa* (1747–48).

**Conrad Richter** (1890–1968), American novelist: *The Town* (1950) won a Pulitzer Prize.

**James Whitcomb Riley** (1849–1916), American poet best-known for Indiana dialect verse: *Rhymes of Childhood* (1890).

**Rainer Maria Rilke** (1875–1926), German poet; wrote on themes of spiritual isolation.

**Arthur Rimbaud** (1854–91), French poet: *A Season in Hell* (1873), *Les Illuminations* (1886).

**Mary Roberts Rinehart** (1876–1958), American mystery novelist: *The Circular Staircase* (1908).

**Kenneth Roberts** (1885–1957), American historical novelist: *Arundel* (1930), *Northwest Passage* (1937).

**Edwin Arlington Robinson** (1869–1935), American poet: *Collected Poems* (1921), *The Man Who Died Twice* (1924), and *Tristam* (1927) won Pulitzer Prizes.

**Theodore Roethke** (1908–63), American poet: *The Waking* (1953) won a Pulitzer Prize.

**Romain Rolland** (1866–1944), French novelist and biographer: biographies of Beethoven (1903) and Tolstoy (1911); 10-volume novel *Jean-Christophe* (1904–12) won a Nobel Prize in 1915.

**Ole Edvart Rolvaag** (1876–1931), Norwegian-American novelist: *Giants in the Earth* (1927).

**Edmond Rostand** (1868–1918), French dramatist and poet: *Cyrano de Bergerac* (1897).

**Philip Roth** (1933–   ), American novelist and short-story writer: *Goodbye Columbus* (1959), *Portnoy's Complaint* (1969), *The Ghost Writer.* (1979).

**Jean Jacques Rousseau** (1712–78), French philosopher, novelist, and essayist: *The Social Contract* (1762), *Confessions* (1782).

**John Ruskin** (1819–1900), English critic and essayist: *The Seven Lamps of Architecture* (1849).

**George Russell ("A.E.";** 1867–1935), Irish poet: *Homeward: Songs by the Way* (1894).

**Saki** (real name Hector Hugh Munro; 1870–1916), English short-story writer. His stories are minor classics of satiric humor.

**J. D. (Jerome David) Salinger** (1919–   ), American novelist and short-story writer: *The Catcher in the Rye* (1951), *Franny and Zooey* (1961).

**George Sand** (real name Amandine A. L. Dupin, Baronne Dudevant; 1804–76), French novelist and playwright. She wrote about 80 novels that enjoyed wide popularity in their time.

**Carl Sandburg** (1878–1967), American poet and biographer. He wrote numerous poems celebrating America and an epic 6-volume biography of Abraham Lincoln (1926–39). *Cornhuskers* (1918), *Abraham Lincoln: The War Years* (1939), and *Complete Poems* (1950) won Pulitzer Prizes.

**George Santayana** (1863–1952), American poet and essayist. His *The Life of Reason* (1905–06) studied the development of human reason.

**William Saroyan** (1908–   ), American novelist, dramatist, and short-story writer: *My Name Is Aram* (1940), short stories; *The Human Comedy* (1943), a novel. *The Time of Your Life* (1939), a play, won a Pulitzer Prize.

**Jean Paul Sartre** (1905–80), French philosopher, novelist, and playwright: *Being and Nothingness* (1943), a treatise on existentialism; *No Exit* (1944) and *Dirty Hands* (1948), plays; declined a Nobel Prize in 1964.

**Siegfried Sassoon** (1886–1967), English poet. Much of

his work derives from bitterness about World War I: *Counterattack* (1918).

**Friedrich von Schiller** (1759–1805), German dramatist, historian, and poet: *Wallenstein* (1798–99), a dramatic trilogy. His lyric "Ode to Joy" (1785) was used by Beethoven in his Ninth Symphony.

**Delmore Schwartz** (1913–66), American poet, critic, and editor: *In Dreams Begin Responsibilities* (1938), *Shenandoah* (1941).

**Sir Walter Scott** (1771–1832), British novelist and poet: *The Lady of the Lake* (1810), a poem; *Ivanhoe* (1820), a novel.

**Lucius Annaeus Seneca** (3 B.C.?–A.D. 65), Roman dramatist: *Phaedra* and *Thyestes*.

**Robert Service** (1874–1958), Canadian poet best known for popular Yukon ballads: *Songs of a Sourdough* (1907).

**William Shakespeare** (1564–1616), English dramatist and poet. In addition to his purely poetic works such as *Venus and Adonis* (1593) and the *Sonnets* (1609), he wrote comic, tragic, and historical dramas, including *The Merchant of Venice* (1597), *Henry IV* (two parts, 1597), *Hamlet* (1600–01), and *Macbeth* (1606?).

**Karl Jay Shapiro** (1913– ), American writer: *V-Letter and Other Poems* (1944) won a Pulitzer Prize.

**George Bernard Shaw** (1856–1950), Irish-born dramatist, critic: *Man and Superman* (1903), *Major Barbara* (1905), *Pygmalion* (1912); won Nobel Prize in 1925.

**Irwin Shaw** (1913– ), American novelist: *The Young Lions* (1948), *Rich Man, Poor Man* (1970); *Beggarman, Thief* (1977); *Top of the Hill* (1979).

**Wilfrid Sheed** (1930– ), Anglo-American critic and novelist: editor of *G. K. Chesterton's Essays and Poems* (1957); *Max Jamison* (1970), a novel; *Transatlantic Blues* (1978).

**Mary Wollstonecraft Shelley** (1797–1851), English author: *Frankenstein* (1818).

**Percy Bysshe Shelley** (1792–1822), English romantic poet: *Prometheus Unbound* (1820).

**Richard Brinsley Sheridan** (1751–1816), English dramatist: *The Rivals* (1775), *The School for Scandal* (1777).

**Robert E. Sherwood** (1896–1955), American author: plays, *Waterloo Bridge* (1930), *Idiot's Delight* (1936), *Abe Lincoln in Illinois* (1938), and *There Shall Be No Night* (1940) all won Pulitzer Prizes. Biography *Roosevelt and Hopkins* (1947) also won a Pulitzer Prize.

**William L. Shirer** (1904– ), American journalist: *The Rise and Fall of the Third Reich* (1960).

**Mikhail Sholokhov** (1905– ), Russian novelist: *The Silent Don* (1941); won Nobel Prize in 1965.

**Neil Simon** (1927– ), American playwright: *Come Blow Your Horn* (1961); *Barefoot in the Park* (1963); *The Odd Couple* (1965); *Plaza Suite* (1968); *The Prisoner of Second Avenue* (1971); *California Suite* (1976); *They're Playing Our Song* (1979).

**Upton Sinclair** (1878–1968), American novelist: *The Jungle* (1906), *King Coal* (1917); *Dragon's Teeth* (1943) won a Pulitzer Prize.

**Isaac Bashevis Singer** (1904– ), Polish-American author: won National Book Awards for *A Day of Pleasure; Stories of a Boy Growing Up in Warsaw* (1969) and *A Crown of Feathers* (1973); *Shosha* (1978); won 1978 Nobel Prize for Literature.

**Dame Edith Sitwell** (1887–1964), English poet and critic: *Rustic Elegies* (1927).

**Aleksandr I. Solzhenitsyn** (1918– ), Russian novelist: *The Cancer Ward* (1968), *August 1914* (1972), *The Gulag Archipelago, 1918–1956* (1973). He won a Nobel Prize for literature in 1970.

**Susan Sontag** (1933– ), American critic and novelist: *Against Interpretation* (1966), essays; *Death Kit* (1967), a novel.

**Sophocles** (496–406 B.C.), Greek dramatist: *Oedipus Rex* and *Electra*.

**Muriel Spark** (1918– ), English novelist and short-story writer: *The Comforters* (1957), *The Prime of Miss Jean Brodie* (1961), *Territorial Rights* (1979).

**Stephen Spender** (1909– ), English poet, critic, and editor. Much of his poetry is social protest.

**Edmund Spenser** (1552–99), English poet: *The Faerie Queene*.

**Jean Stafford** (1915–79), American novelist and short-story writer: *Boston Adventure* (1944). Her *Collected Stories* won a Pulitzer Prize in 1970.

**Sir Richard Steele** (1672–1729), English essayist and dramatist. With Joseph Addison he founded and contributed essays to the *Tatler* and the *Spectator*.

**Wallace Stegner** (1909– ), American author: *Angle of Repose* (1971) won a Pulitzer Prize for fiction.

**Gertrude Stein** (1874–1946), American expatriate poet and critic: *Three Lives* (1908) and *The Autobiography of Alice B. Toklas* (1933).

**John Steinbeck** (1902–1968), American novelist: *The Grapes of Wrath* (1939) won a Pulitzer Prize; *East of Eden* (1952). He was awarded a Nobel Prize in 1962.

**Stendhal** (real name **Marie Henri Beyle;** 1783–1842), French novelist: *The Red and the Black* (1831), *The Charterhouse of Parma* (1839).

**Laurence Sterne** (1713–68), English novelist: *Tristram Shandy* (1760–67).

**Wallace Stevens** (1879–1955), American poet: *Harmonium* (1923); *Notes Toward a Supreme Fiction* (1942); *Collected Poems* (1954) won a Pulitzer Prize.

**Robert Louis Stevenson** (1850–94), Scottish novelist and poet: *Treasure Island* (1883), *A Child's Garden of Verses* (1885).

**Irving Stone** (1903– ), American author: *Lust for Life* (1934), *The Agony and the Ecstasy* (1961), *The Origin* (1980).

**Rex Todhunter Stout** (1886–1975), American detective-story writer; wrote many books around fictional fat detective Nero Wolfe.

**Harriet Beecher Stowe** (1811–96), American novelist: *Uncle Tom's Cabin* (1852).

**August Strindberg** (1849–1912), Swedish dramatist and novelist: best known for such naturalistic dramas as *The Father* (1887) and *Miss Julie* (1888).

**Jessee Hilton Stuart** (1907– ), American author: *Taps for Private Tussie* (1965).

**William Styron** (1925– ), American novelist: *Lie Down in Darkness* (1951); *The Confessions of Nat Turner* (1967), which won a Pulitzer Prize; *Sophie's Choice* (1979).

**Jacqueline Susann** (1921–74), American novelist: *Valley of the Dolls* (1966), which sold a record 17 million copies; *The Love Machine* (1969), *Once Is Not Enough* (1973), *Dolores* (1976).

**Jonathan Swift** (1667–1745), English satirist, poet, and essayist: *Tale of a Tub* (1704), *Gulliver's Travels* (1726), *A Modest Proposal* (1729).

**Algernon Charles Swinburne** (1837–1909), English poet and critic: *Songs Before Sunrise* (1871).

**John Millington Synge** (1871–1909), Irish dramatist and poet: *Riders to the Sea* (1904), *Playboy of the Western World* (1907).

**Cornelius Tacitus** (55?–117?), Roman historian who recorded contemporary history of Rome.

**Booth Tarkington** (1869–1946), American novelist: *The Magnificent Ambersons* (1918) and *Alice Adams* (1922) won Pulitzer Prizes.

**Allen Tate** (1899–1979), American poet and critic: *Mr. Pope and Other Poems* (1928).

**Sara Teasdale** (1884–1933), American poet: *Love Songs* (1917) won first Pulitzer Prize for poetry in 1918; *Flame and Shadow* (1920), *Strange Victory* (1933).

**Alfred Lord Tennyson** (1809–92), English poet: *In Memoriam* (1850), *Idylls of the King* (1859–85).

**William Makepeace Thackeray** (1811–63), English novelist: *Vanity Fair* (1847–48).

**Dylan Thomas** (1914–53), Welsh poet. A major 20th

**AUTHORS AND WRITERS** *(continued)*
century lyric poet, he also wrote a drama for voices, *Under Milk Wood* (1954).

**Henry David Thoreau** (1817–62), American essayist and poet. A champion of the individual against social organization, his best-known work is *Walden; or, Life in the Woods* (1854).

**James Thurber** (1894–1961), American humorist: *The Owl in the Attic and Other Perplexities* (1931), *My Life and Hard Times* (1934).

**Alexis de Tocqueville** (1805–59), French essayist and politician who studied and wrote extensively about the early days of the United States: *De la démocratie en Amérique* (4 vols., 1835–40).

**J. R. R. Tolkien** (1892–1973), British novelist: *The Hobbit* (1937), *Lord of the Rings* trilogy (1954–56), *The Silmarillion* (1977).

**Leo Tolstoy** (1828–1910), Russian novelist: *War and Peace* (1862–69), *Anna Karenina* (1875–77).

**Arnold Toynbee** (1889–1975), English historian. *A Study of History* (10 vols., 1934–54).

**Lionel Trilling** (1905–1975), American critic: *The Liberal Imagination* (1950).

**Anthony Trollope** (1815–82), English novelist: *The Warden* (1855), *Barchester Towers* (1857).

**Thomas Tryon** (1926– ), American novelist: *The Other* (1971), *Lady* (1974).

**Barbara Tuchman** (1912– ), American author: *The Guns of August* (1962) and *Stilwell and the American Experience in China, 1911–1945* (1971) both won Pulitzer Prizes; *A Distant Mirror: The Calamitous Fourteenth Century* (1978).

**Ivan Turgenev** (1818–83), Russian novelist and dramatist: *Fathers and Sons* (1861), a novel.

**Mark Twain** (real name **Samuel Clemens**; 1835–1910), American author: *Tom Sawyer* (1876), *Huckleberry Finn* (1884).

**Louis Untermeyer** (1885–1977), American poet and anthologist. He edited *Modern American Poetry* (1919, frequently revised).

**John Updike** (1932– ), American novelist: *The Centaur* (1963), *Couples* (1968), *Bech: A Book* (1970), and *Rabbit Redux* (1971).

**Leon Uris** (1924– ), American novelist: *Exodus* (1958), *Trinity* (1976).

**Paul Valéry** (1871–1945), French poet and critic. *Charmes* (1922) is his best verse collection.

**S. S. Van Dine** (real name **Willard Huntington Wright**; 1888–1939), American detective-story author. His books featured the amateur detective Philo Vance.

**Mark Van Doren** (1894–1972), American poet and critic: *Collected Poems* (1939) won Pulitzer Prize.

**Thorstein Veblen** (1857–1929), American essayist and social scientist: *The Theory of the Leisure Class* (1899).

**Jules Verne** (1828–1905), French novelist and a pioneer in science fiction: *Twenty Thousand Leagues Under the Sea* (1870).

**Gore Vidal** (1925– ), American author: *Visit to a Small Planet* (1956), a play for TV; *Washington, D.C.* (1967), *Burr* (1973), *1876* (1976).

**Virgil** (70–19 B.C.), Roman poet. His masterpiece is the unfinished epic *Aeneid.*

**François Marie Arouet de Voltaire** (1694–1778), French novelist, dramatist, critic, and poet. He was at his best in such short novels as *Candide* (1759).

**Kurt Vonnegut Jr.** (1922– ), American novelist: *Mother Night* (1961), *Slaughterhouse-Five* (1969), *Jailbird* (1979).

**Horace Walpole** (1717–97), English novelist: *The Castle of Otranto* (1764).

**Robert Penn Warren** (1905– ), American novelist, poet, editor, and biographer. His novel *All the King's Men* (1946) won a Pulitzer Prize, as did *Promises: Poems 1954–1956* (1957), and *Now and Then* (1978).

**Evelyn Waugh** (1903–66), English novelist: *Decline and Fall* (1928), *Brideshead Revisited* (1945), *The Loved One* (1948).

**Noah Webster** (1758–1843), American lexicographer: *An American Dictionary of the English Language* (1800–28) set standard for American lexicography.

**H. G. (Herbert George) Wells** (1866–1946), English novelist and social historian: *The Time Machine* (1895), *The War of the Worlds* (1898).

**Eudora Welty** (1909– ), American novelist and short-story writer: *Delta Wedding* (1946). *The Optimist's Daughter* (1972) won a Pulitzer Prize.

**Franz Werfel** (1890–1945), Austrian-born author: *The Song of Bernadette* (1941).

**Jessamyn West** (1907– ), American author: *The Friendly Persuasion* (1945).

**Nathanael West** (1902–40), American novelist: *The Day of the Locust* (1939).

**Rebecca West** (1892– ), English novelist and journalist: *The Return of the Soldier* (1918).

**Edith Wharton** (1862–1937), American novelist and short-story writer: *Ethan Frome* (1911); *The Age of Innocence* (1920) won a Pulitzer Prize.

**E. B. White** (1899– ), American author: *One Man's Meat* (1942), *The Points of My Compass* (1962); *Stuart Little* (1945) and *Charlotte's Web* (1952), children's classics.

**Walt Whitman** (1819–92), American poet: *Leaves of Grass* (1855).

**John Greenleaf Whittier** (1807–92), American poet: *Snowbound* (1866).

**Oscar Wilde** (1854–1900), Anglo-Irish dramatist, novelist, and poet: *The Picture of Dorian Gray* (1891), a novel; *The Importance of Being Earnest* (1899), a play; *Ballad of Reading Gaol* (1898), a poem.

**Thornton Wilder** (1897–1975), American novelist and dramatist. He won Pulitzer Prizes for the novel *The Bridge of San Luis Rey* (1927) and the plays *Our Town* (1938) and *Skin of Our Teeth* (1942).

**Tennessee Williams** (1911– ), American playwright: *The Glass Menagerie* (1944), *The Rose Tattoo* (1950); *A Streetcar Named Desire* (1947) and *Cat on a Hot Tin Roof* (1955) both won Pulitzer Prizes.

**William Carlos Williams** (1883–1963), American poet and novelist. *Paterson* (1946) is a long poem evoking the atmosphere of his native New Jersey; *Pictures from Breughel* (1962) won a Pulitzer Prize.

**Edmund Wilson** (1895–1972), American critic: *Axel's Castle* (1931), *The Scrolls from the Dead Sea* (1955; revised edition 1969).

**Thomas Wolfe** (1900–38), American novelist: *Look Homeward, Angel* (1929), *Of Time and the River* (1935), *You Can't Go Home Again* (1940).

**Virginia Woolf** (1882–1941), English novelist: *Mrs. Dalloway* (1925), *To the Lighthouse* (1927).

**William Wordsworth** (1770–1850), English poet: "Tintern Abbey" (1800); "Ode: Intimations of Immortality" (1807).

**Herman Wouk** (1915– ), American novelist: *The Caine Mutiny* (1951) won a Pulitzer Prize; *Marjorie Morningstar* (1955); *The Winds of War* (1971); *War and Remembrance* (1978).

**Richard Wright** (1908–60), American novelist: *Native Son* (1940); *Black Boy* (1945), autobiography.

**Philip Gordon Wylie** (1902–71), American author: *Generation of Vipers* (1942).

**William Butler Yeats** (1865–1939), one of Ireland's greatest poets. His works include *The Wild Swans at Coole* (1919) and *The Tower* (1928). He won a Nobel Prize in 1923.

**Yevgeny Yevtushenko** (1933– ), Russian poet. His verse deals mainly with social protest.

**Émile Zola** (1840–1902), French novelist and critic, one of the most important novelists of the naturalist school. His works include the 20-volume series *Les Rougon-Macquart* (1871–93).

# Calendars, Time and Holidays

## FEDERAL, STATE, AND RELIGIOUS HOLIDAYS AND SPECIAL DAYS: 1981

### JANUARY
1 New Year's Day (U.S. federal holiday) .... Thursday
6 Epiphany (Christian) .................... Tuesday
8 Battle of New Orleans Day (Louisiana) .. Thursday
15 Martin Luther King's Birthday (b. 1929) Thursday
19 Robert E. Lee's Birthday (born 1807) .... Monday
20 Inauguration Day (Washington, D.C.)...... Tuesday
26 Gen. Douglas MacArthur Day (Arkansas) . Monday
30 F.D. Roosevelt's Birthday (Ky.) (b. 1882) ... Friday

### FEBRUARY
1 National Freedom Day ................... Sunday
2 Groundhog Day .......................... Monday
4 Chinese New Year (Year of the Cock) .. Wednesday
12 Lincoln's 172d Birthday (born 1809) .... Monday
12 Georgia Day (Georgia).................... Monday
14 Valentine's Day ........................ Saturday
14 Admission Day (Arizona) ................ Saturday
15 Susan B. Anthony's Birthday (born 1820) . Sunday
15 Septuagesima Sunday (Christian) ......... Sunday
16 Washington's Birthday (U.S. fed. holiday) .. Monday
22 Washington's 249th Birthday (actual—born
    1732)................................... Sunday

### MARCH
1 Shrove Sunday, Quinquagesima (Christian) Sunday
2 Texas Independence Day (Texas) ........ Monday
3 Shrove Tuesday, Mardi Gras (Alabama,
    Florida, Louisiana)..................... Tuesday
3 Town Meeting Day (Vermont) ............ Tuesday
4 Ash Wednesday (Christian) ........... Wednesday
6 World Day of Prayer .................... Friday
11 Minnesota Day (Minnesota) .......... Wednesday
15 Andrew Jackson's Birthday (TN) (b. 1767) Sunday
17 St. Patrick's Day ...................... Tuesday
17 Evacuation Day (Massachusetts) ........ Tuesday
20 Spring begins at 12:03 P.M. EST ........... Friday
20 Purim (Jewish) ......................... Friday
25 Maryland Day (Maryland) ........... Wednesday
26 Kuhio Day (Hawaii) ................... Thursday
28 Seward's Day (Alaska)................... Saturday

### APRIL
1 April Fool's Day ..................... Wednesday
12 Palm Sunday (Christian) ................. Sunday
13 Thomas Jefferson's Birthday (born 1743) Monday
17 Good Friday (Christian) ................ Friday
19 Easter Sunday (Christian) ............... Sunday
19 First Day of Passover, Pesach (Jewish) ... Sunday
20 Easter Monday (North Carolina) .......... Monday
20 Patriots' Day (Massachusetts, Maine) .... Monday
21 San Jacinto Day (Texas) ............... Tuesday
22 Arbor Day (Nebraska) ............... Wednesday
24 Arbor Day (Utah) ...................... Friday
26 Daylight Saving Time begins (clocks set
    forward 1 hour at 2 A.M.)............... Sunday
26 Orthodox Easter (Orthodox) ............. Sunday
27 Fast Day (New Hampshire) ............... Monday
27 Confederate Memorial Day (Ala., Miss.) ... Monday

### MAY
1 May Day.................................. Friday
1 Loyalty Day, Law Day ................... Friday
8 Truman's Birthday (Missouri) (born 1884) .... Friday
10 Mother's Day ........................... Sunday
10 Confederate Memorial Day (S.C.)........ Sunday
16 Armed Forces Day ..................... Saturday
24 Victoria Day, Queen's Birthday (Canada).. Monday
24 Rogation Sunday (Christian) ............. Sunday
25 Memorial Day (U.S. federal holiday) ....... Monday
28 Ascension Day, Holy Thursday (Christ.) . Thursday

### JUNE
1 Jefferson Davis' Birthday (So. states) ..... Monday
3 Jefferson Davis' Birthday (actual—born
    1808) ............................. Wednesday
7 Whitsunday, Pentecost (Christian) ........ Sunday
8 Shavuot, Feast of Weeks (Jewish) ....... Monday
14 Flag Day, 204th anniversary of U.S. Flag ... Sunday
14 Trinity Sunday (Christian) ............... Sunday
18 Corpus Christi (Christian) ............... Sunday
21 Father's Day ........................... Sunday
21 Summer begins at 7:45 A.M. EDT......... Sunday

### JULY
1 Dominion Day or Canada Day (Canada) Wednesday
3 First day of Ramadan (Islamic) ........... Friday
4 Independence Day, 205th anniversary
    of U.S. Declaration of Independence....... Saturday
24 Pioneer Day (Utah) ..................... Friday

### AUGUST
3 Colorado Day (Colorado) ............... Monday
10 Victory Day (Rhode Island) (36th anniversary
    of end of World War II) ............... Monday
16 Bennington Battle Day (Vermont) ....... Sunday
21 Admission Day (Hawaii) ................. Friday
27 Lyndon B. Johnson's Birthday (Texas) .. Thursday
30 Huey P. Long's Birthday (Louisiana) ..... Sunday

### SEPTEMBER
7 Labor Day (U.S. federal holiday) ........ Monday
9 Admission Day (California) ........... Wednesday
12 Defenders' Day (Maryland) ............. Saturday
13 Grandparents Day ..................... Sunday
16 Mexico's Independence Day ........... Wednesday
17 Citizenship Day........................ Thursday
22 Autumn begins at 11:05 P.M. EDT ....... Tuesday
29 Rosh Hashana, Jewish New Year, first
    day of year 5741 of Jewish era ........ Tuesday

### OCTOBER
4 World Communion Sunday ............... Sunday
5 Child Health Day....................... Monday
8 Yom Kippur, Day of Atonement (Jewish)  Thursday
12 Columbus Day (U.S. federal holiday) ...... Monday
12 Canadian Thanksgiving Day (Canada) .... Monday
12 Pioneers' Day (South Dakota) ............ Monday
13 Sukkot, first day of Tabernacles (Jewish) .. Tuesday
25 Standard Time begins (clocks set back
    1 hour at 2 A.M.)....................... Sunday
30 Islamic New Year (Year 1402 of Islamic era) Friday
31 Halloween ............................. Saturday
31 Nevada Day (Nevada) ................... Saturday

### NOVEMBER
1 All Saints' Day (Hawaii, Louisiana) ........ Sunday
3 Election Day (in several states) .......... Tuesday
4 Will Rogers' Birthday (Okla.) (b. 1879) Wednesday
6 World Community Day ................... Friday
11 Veterans Day (U.S. federal holiday) .... Wednesday
15 Bible Sunday........................... Sunday
26 Thanksgiving Day (U.S. federal holiday) .. Thursday
27 Day after Thanksgiving (Okla., Wash.) ..... Friday
29 First Sunday in Advent (Christian) ........ Sunday

### DECEMBER
6 St. Nicholas Day (Orthodox) ............. Sunday
10 Wyoming Day (Wyoming) .............. Thursday
15 Bill of Rights Day, 190th anniversary ... Tuesday
21 Winter begins at 5:51 P.M. EST .......... Monday
21 First day of Hanukkah (Jewish) .......... Monday
25 Christmas (Christian) ................... Friday
31 New Year's Eve (Watch Night) .......... Thursday

# SPECIAL MONTHS, WEEKS, AND DAYS: 1981

The President of the United States regularly issues proclamations throughout the year designating the following months, weeks, and days for special observance.

## JANUARY
1–31    March of Dimes Birth Defects Prevention Month.
13    Stephen Foster Memorial Day.

## FEBRUARY
1    National Freedom Day, celebrates President Lincoln's signing on Feb. 1, 1865, of congressional resolution to abolish slavery.
1–28    American Heart Month.
16    Washington's Birthday (U.S. federal holiday), third Monday in February; previously on Feb. 22.

## MARCH
1–7    Save Your Vision Week, proclaimed for first week in March since 1964.
1–31    Red Cross Month, proclaimed annually for March.
15–21    National Poison Prevention Week, issued annually for third week in March since 1961.

## APRIL
1–30    Cancer Control Month, since 1938.
12–18    Pan American Week.
13    Thomas Jefferson's Birthday.
14    Pan American Day, always on April 14.

## MAY
1    Law Day, proclaimed annually since 1958.
1    Loyalty Day, proclaimed annually since 1958.
1–31    Older Americans Month, since 1963.
1–31    Steelmark Month, annually since 1967.
10    Mother's Day, second Sunday in May.
10–16    Police Week, proclaimed annually since 1963.
10–16    National Transportation Week.
15    Peace Officers Memorial Day, always proclaimed for May 15 since 1963.
15    National Defense Transportation Day, issued for third Friday in May since 1957.
16    Armed Forces Day, always on third Saturday in May since 1965.
17–23    World Trade Week, proclaimed as third week in May since 1948.
22    National Maritime Day, issued since 1933.
25    Prayer for Peace, Memorial Day, last Monday in May (U.S. federal holiday).

## JUNE
8–14    National Little League Baseball Week, proclaimed since 1959 for week beginning second Monday in June.
14    Flag Day, always on June 14; 204th anniversary of date in 1777 that Continental Congress adopted first official national flag.
14–20    National Flag Week, issued annually for week that includes June 14.
21    Father's Day, issued since 1972 for third Sunday in June.
28–
July 4    National Safe Boating Week, issued annually since 1958 for week that includes July 4.

## JULY
4    Independence Day (U.S. federal holiday), 205th anniversary of Declaration of Independence.
19–25    Captive Nations Week, issued since 1959 for the third week in July.

## AUGUST
19    National Aviation Day, issued each August 19 since 1939.
26    Women's Equality Day, 61st anniversary of ratification of 19th Amendment to U.S. Constitution.

## SEPTEMBER
7    Labor Day (U.S. federal holiday), always on first Monday in September.
13    Grandparents Day, first Sunday after Labor Day.
13–19    National Hispanic Heritage Week, proclaimed for week that includes Sept. 15–16 since 1968.
17    Citizenship Day, 194th anniversary of signing of U.S. Constitution in 1787.
17–23    Constitution Week, issued each year since 1955 for period Sept. 17–23.
26    National Hunting and Fishing Day, always fourth Saturday of September since 1979.
27    Gold Star Mother's Day, proclaimed for last Sunday in September since 1936.

## OCTOBER
4–10    National Employ the Handicapped Week, issued for first week in October since 1945.
5    Child Health Day, first Monday in October.
9    Leif Ericson Day, proclaimed for Oct. 9 since 1964.
11    General Pulaski's Memorial Day, always proclaimed for Oct. 11.
11–17    National School Lunch Week, issued for week beginning with second Sunday of October since 1963.
12    Columbus Day (U.S. federal holiday), second Monday in October since 1971; previously always on Oct. 12.
15    White Cane Safety Day, issued for Oct. 15 since 1964.
18–24    National Forest Products Week, issued annually for week beginning with third Sunday in October.
24    United Nations Day, proclaimed since 1948, always on Oct. 24.
31    National UNICEF Day, issued annually to fall on Halloween since 1967.

## NOVEMBER
11    Veterans Day (U.S. federal holiday).
27    Thanksgiving Day (U.S. federal holiday), always proclaimed for fourth Thursday in November.

## DECEMBER
2    Pan American Health Day, issued for Dec. 2, since 1940.
10    Human Rights Day, proclaimed since 1949 for every Dec. 10.
10–16    Human Rights Week, proclaimed for same period each year since 1958.
15    Bill of Rights Day, proclaimed annually for same day since 1962, commemorating 190th anniversary of date first 10 amendments to U.S. Constitution were ratified in 1791.
17    Pan American Aviation Day, proclaimed for same day each year since 1940.
17    Wright Brothers Day, celebrating their first airplane flight in 1903; issued since 1963.

## DATES OF EASTER: 1981–2004

| 1981 April 19 | 1985 April 7 | 1989 March 26 | 1993 April 11 | 1997 March 30 | 2001 April 15 |
|---|---|---|---|---|---|
| 1982 April 11 | 1986 March 30 | 1990 April 15 | 1994 April 3 | 1998 April 12 | 2002 March 31 |
| 1983 April 3 | 1987 April 19 | 1991 March 31 | 1995 April 16 | 1999 April 4 | 2003 April 20 |
| 1984 April 22 | 1988 April 3 | 1992 April 19 | 1996 April 7 | 2000 April 23 | 2004 April 11 |

# UNITED STATES TIME ZONES

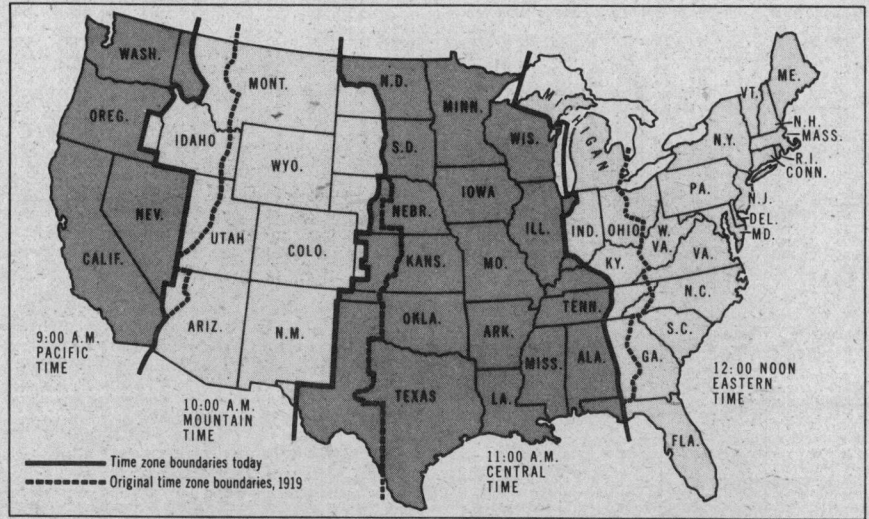

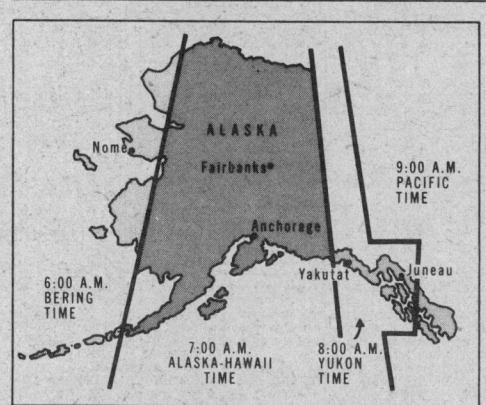

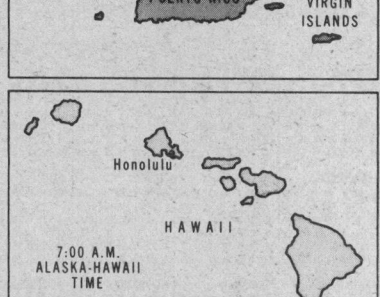

The map above shows time-zone boundaries (solid line), which in most places have moved westward somewhat from those that first went into effect on Jan. 1, 1919 (broken line).

Daylight-saving time begins at 2 A.M. on the last Sunday in April (April 26, 1981) and ends on the last Sunday in October (Oct. 25, 1981). Clocks are set ahead one hour in the spring and set back one hour in the fall.

If it had been possible to ask for the time at exactly the same moment in a number of U.S. towns in 1873, the variety of answers would have been puzzling: 12:12 P.M. in New York, 11:08 A.M. in Memphis, and so on across the nation. Yet each answer would have been right, for "Sun time" prevailed throughout much of the world until the late 1800s.

In November 1883, U.S. and Canadian rail companies agreed to set up zones for each 15 degrees of longitude with uniform time in each zone.

Most of the country went along quickly with this orderly system, but Congress did not pass a Standard Time Act until 1917. In 1966 Congress passed a Uniform Time Act urging all states to adopt daylight-saving time during half of the year from spring to fall.

As an energy conservation measure Congress passed a law in 1974 establishing year-round daylight-saving time. It was modified to eight months of daylight time in 1975, and reverted to six months in 1976.

Areas of the nation that do not observe daylight-saving time include Arizona, Hawaii, most of Indiana, Puerto Rico, the Virgin Islands, and American Samoa.

The longitudes of the standard meridians for U.S. standard time zones are Atlantic 60°W., Eastern 75°W., Central 90°W., Mountain 105°W., Pacific 120°W., Yukon 135°W., Alaska-Hawaii 150°W., and Bering 165°W.

## PAST AND FUTURE CALENDARS: 1776–2014

**Directions: Choose year you want in key below. Number opposite year is number of calendar to use for that year.**

| | | | | | |
|---|---|---|---|---|---|
| 1776. 9 | 1795. 5 | 1814. 7 | 1833. 3 | 1852. 12 | 1871. 1 |
| 1777. 4 | 1796. 13 | 1815. 1 | 1834. 4 | 1853. 7 | 1872. 9 |
| 1778. 5 | 1797. 1 | 1816. 9 | 1835. 5 | 1854. 1 | 1873. 4 |
| 1779. 6 | 1798. 2 | 1817. 4 | 1836. 13 | 1855. 2 | 1874. 5 |
| 1780. 14 | 1799. 3 | 1818. 5 | 1837. 1 | 1856. 10 | 1875. 6 |
| 1781. 2 | 1800. 4 | 1819. 6 | 1838. 2 | 1857. 5 | 1876. 14 |
| 1782. 3 | 1801. 5 | 1820. 14 | 1839. 3 | 1858. 6 | 1877. 2 |
| 1783. 4 | 1802. 6 | 1821. 2 | 1840. 11 | 1859. 7 | 1878. 3 |
| 1784. 12 | 1803. 7 | 1822. 3 | 1841. 6 | 1860. 8 | 1879. 4 |
| 1785. 7 | 1804. 8 | 1823. 4 | 1842. 7 | 1861. 3 | 1880. 12 |
| 1786. 1 | 1805. 3 | 1824. 12 | 1843. 1 | 1862. 4 | 1881. 7 |
| 1787. 2 | 1806. 4 | 1825. 7 | 1844. 9 | 1863. 5 | 1882. 1 |
| 1788. 10 | 1807. 5 | 1826. 1 | 1845. 4 | 1864. 13 | 1883. 2 |
| 1789. 5 | 1808. 13 | 1827. 2 | 1846. 5 | 1865. 1 | 1884. 10 |
| 1790. 6 | 1809. 1 | 1828. 10 | 1847. 6 | 1866. 2 | 1885. 5 |
| 1791. 7 | 1810. 2 | 1829. 5 | 1848. 14 | 1867. 3 | 1886. 6 |
| 1792. 8 | 1811. 3 | 1830. 6 | 1849. 2 | 1868. 11 | 1887. 7 |
| 1793. 3 | 1812. 11 | 1831. 7 | 1850. 3 | 1869. 6 | 1888. 8 |
| 1794. 4 | 1813. 6 | 1832. 8 | 1851. 4 | 1870. 7 | 1889. 3 |

| | | | | |
|---|---|---|---|---|
| 1890.. 4 | 1915.. 6 | 1940.. 9 | 1965.. 6 | 1990.. 2 |
| 1891.. 5 | 1916.. 14 | 1941.. 4 | 1966.. 7 | 1991.. 3 |
| 1892.. 13 | 1917.. 2 | 1942.. 5 | 1967.. 1 | 1992.. 11 |
| 1893.. 1 | 1918.. 3 | 1943.. 6 | 1968.. 9 | 1993.. 6 |
| 1894.. 2 | 1919.. 4 | 1944.. 14 | 1969.. 4 | 1994.. 7 |
| 1895.. 3 | 1920.. 12 | 1945.. 2 | 1970.. 5 | 1995.. 1 |
| 1896.. 11 | 1921.. 7 | 1946.. 3 | 1971.. 6 | 1996.. 9 |
| 1897.. 6 | 1922.. 1 | 1947.. 4 | 1972.. 14 | 1997.. 4 |
| 1898.. 7 | 1923.. 2 | 1948.. 12 | 1973.. 2 | 1998.. 5 |
| 1899.. 1 | 1924.. 10 | 1949.. 7 | 1974.. 3 | 1999.. 6 |
| 1900.. 2 | 1925.. 5 | 1950.. 1 | 1975.. 4 | 2000.. 14 |
| 1901.. 3 | 1926.. 6 | 1951.. 2 | 1976.. 12 | 2001.. 2 |
| 1902.. 4 | 1927.. 7 | 1952.. 10 | 1977.. 7 | 2002.. 3 |
| 1903.. 5 | 1928.. 8 | 1953.. 5 | 1978.. 1 | 2003.. 4 |
| 1904.. 13 | 1929.. 3 | 1954.. 6 | 1979.. 2 | 2004.. 12 |
| 1905.. 1 | 1930.. 4 | 1955.. 7 | 1980.. 10 | 2005.. 7 |
| 1906.. 2 | 1931.. 5 | 1956.. 8 | 1981.. 5 | 2006.. 1 |
| 1907.. 3 | 1932.. 13 | 1957.. 3 | 1982.. 6 | 2007.. 2 |
| 1908.. 11 | 1933.. 1 | 1958.. 4 | 1983.. 7 | 2008.. 10 |
| 1909.. 6 | 1934.. 2 | 1959.. 5 | 1984.. 8 | 2009.. 5 |
| 1910.. 7 | 1935.. 3 | 1960.. 13 | 1985.. 3 | 2010.. 6 |
| 1911.. 1 | 1936.. 11 | 1961.. 1 | 1986.. 4 | 2011.. 7 |
| 1912.. 9 | 1937.. 6 | 1962.. 2 | 1987.. 5 | 2012.. 8 |
| 1913.. 4 | 1938.. 7 | 1963.. 3 | 1988.. 13 | 2013.. 3 |
| 1914.. 5 | 1939.. 1 | 1964.. 11 | 1989.. 1 | 2014.. 4 |

## 1 1989

**JANUARY**

| S | M | T | W | T | F | S |
|---|---|---|---|---|---|---|
| 1 | 2 | 3 | 4 | 5 | 6 | 7 |
| 8 | 9 | 10 | 11 | 12 | 13 | 14 |
| 15 | 16 | 17 | 18 | 19 | 20 | 21 |
| 22 | 23 | 24 | 25 | 26 | 27 | 28 |
| 29 | 30 | 31 | | | | |

**FEBRUARY**

| S | M | T | W | T | F | S |
|---|---|---|---|---|---|---|
| | | | 1 | 2 | 3 | 4 |
| 5 | 6 | 7 | 8 | 9 | 10 | 11 |
| 12 | 13 | 14 | 15 | 16 | 17 | 18 |
| 19 | 20 | 21 | 22 | 23 | 24 | 25 |
| 26 | 27 | 28 | | | | |

**MARCH**

| S | M | T | W | T | F | S |
|---|---|---|---|---|---|---|
| | | | 1 | 2 | 3 | 4 |
| 5 | 6 | 7 | 8 | 9 | 10 | 11 |
| 12 | 13 | 14 | 15 | 16 | 17 | 18 |
| 19 | 20 | 21 | 22 | 23 | 24 | 25 |
| 26 | 27 | 28 | 29 | 30 | 31 | |

**APRIL**

| S | M | T | W | T | F | S |
|---|---|---|---|---|---|---|
| | | | | | | 1 |
| 2 | 3 | 4 | 5 | 6 | 7 | 8 |
| 9 | 10 | 11 | 12 | 13 | 14 | 15 |
| 16 | 17 | 18 | 19 | 20 | 21 | 22 |
| 23 | 24 | 25 | 26 | 27 | 28 | 29 |
| 30 | | | | | | |

**MAY**

| S | M | T | W | T | F | S |
|---|---|---|---|---|---|---|
| | 1 | 2 | 3 | 4 | 5 | 6 |
| 7 | 8 | 9 | 10 | 11 | 12 | 13 |
| 14 | 15 | 16 | 17 | 18 | 19 | 20 |
| 21 | 22 | 23 | 24 | 25 | 26 | 27 |
| 28 | 29 | 30 | 31 | | | |

**JUNE**

| S | M | T | W | T | F | S |
|---|---|---|---|---|---|---|
| | | | | 1 | 2 | 3 |
| 4 | 5 | 6 | 7 | 8 | 9 | 10 |
| 11 | 12 | 13 | 14 | 15 | 16 | 17 |
| 18 | 19 | 20 | 21 | 22 | 23 | 24 |
| 25 | 26 | 27 | 28 | 29 | 30 | |

**JULY**

| S | M | T | W | T | F | S |
|---|---|---|---|---|---|---|
| | | | | | | 1 |
| 2 | 3 | 4 | 5 | 6 | 7 | 8 |
| 9 | 10 | 11 | 12 | 13 | 14 | 15 |
| 16 | 17 | 18 | 19 | 20 | 21 | 22 |
| 23 | 24 | 25 | 26 | 27 | 28 | 29 |
| 30 | 31 | | | | | |

**AUGUST**

| S | M | T | W | T | F | S |
|---|---|---|---|---|---|---|
| | | 1 | 2 | 3 | 4 | 5 |
| 6 | 7 | 8 | 9 | 10 | 11 | 12 |
| 13 | 14 | 15 | 16 | 17 | 18 | 19 |
| 20 | 21 | 22 | 23 | 24 | 25 | 26 |
| 27 | 28 | 29 | 30 | 31 | | |

**SEPTEMBER**

| S | M | T | W | T | F | S |
|---|---|---|---|---|---|---|
| | | | | | 1 | 2 |
| 3 | 4 | 5 | 6 | 7 | 8 | 9 |
| 10 | 11 | 12 | 13 | 14 | 15 | 16 |
| 17 | 18 | 19 | 20 | 21 | 22 | 23 |
| 24 | 25 | 26 | 27 | 28 | 29 | 30 |

**OCTOBER**

| S | M | T | W | T | F | S |
|---|---|---|---|---|---|---|
| 1 | 2 | 3 | 4 | 5 | 6 | 7 |
| 8 | 9 | 10 | 11 | 12 | 13 | 14 |
| 15 | 16 | 17 | 18 | 19 | 20 | 21 |
| 22 | 23 | 24 | 25 | 26 | 27 | 28 |
| 29 | 30 | 31 | | | | |

**NOVEMBER**

| S | M | T | W | T | F | S |
|---|---|---|---|---|---|---|
| | | | 1 | 2 | 3 | 4 |
| 5 | 6 | 7 | 8 | 9 | 10 | 11 |
| 12 | 13 | 14 | 15 | 16 | 17 | 18 |
| 19 | 20 | 21 | 22 | 23 | 24 | 25 |
| 26 | 27 | 28 | 29 | 30 | | |

**DECEMBER**

| S | M | T | W | T | F | S |
|---|---|---|---|---|---|---|
| | | | | | 1 | 2 |
| 3 | 4 | 5 | 6 | 7 | 8 | 9 |
| 10 | 11 | 12 | 13 | 14 | 15 | 16 |
| 17 | 18 | 19 | 20 | 21 | 22 | 23 |
| 24 | 25 | 26 | 27 | 28 | 29 | 30 |
| 31 | | | | | | |

## 2 1990

**JANUARY**

| S | M | T | W | T | F | S |
|---|---|---|---|---|---|---|
| | 1 | 2 | 3 | 4 | 5 | 6 |
| 7 | 8 | 9 | 10 | 11 | 12 | 13 |
| 14 | 15 | 16 | 17 | 18 | 19 | 20 |
| 21 | 22 | 23 | 24 | 25 | 26 | 27 |
| 28 | 29 | 30 | 31 | | | |

**FEBRUARY**

| S | M | T | W | T | F | S |
|---|---|---|---|---|---|---|
| | | | | 1 | 2 | 3 |
| 4 | 5 | 6 | 7 | 8 | 9 | 10 |
| 11 | 12 | 13 | 14 | 15 | 16 | 17 |
| 18 | 19 | 20 | 21 | 22 | 23 | 24 |
| 25 | 26 | 27 | 28 | | | |

**MARCH**

| S | M | T | W | T | F | S |
|---|---|---|---|---|---|---|
| | | | | 1 | 2 | 3 |
| 4 | 5 | 6 | 7 | 8 | 9 | 10 |
| 11 | 12 | 13 | 14 | 15 | 16 | 17 |
| 18 | 19 | 20 | 21 | 22 | 23 | 24 |
| 25 | 26 | 27 | 28 | 29 | 30 | 31 |

**APRIL**

| S | M | T | W | T | F | S |
|---|---|---|---|---|---|---|
| 1 | 2 | 3 | 4 | 5 | 6 | 7 |
| 8 | 9 | 10 | 11 | 12 | 13 | 14 |
| 15 | 16 | 17 | 18 | 19 | 20 | 21 |
| 22 | 23 | 24 | 25 | 26 | 27 | 28 |
| 29 | 30 | | | | | |

**MAY**

| S | M | T | W | T | F | S |
|---|---|---|---|---|---|---|
| | | 1 | 2 | 3 | 4 | 5 |
| 6 | 7 | 8 | 9 | 10 | 11 | 12 |
| 13 | 14 | 15 | 16 | 17 | 18 | 19 |
| 20 | 21 | 22 | 23 | 24 | 25 | 26 |
| 27 | 28 | 29 | 30 | 31 | | |

**JUNE**

| S | M | T | W | T | F | S |
|---|---|---|---|---|---|---|
| | | | | | 1 | 2 |
| 3 | 4 | 5 | 6 | 7 | 8 | 9 |
| 10 | 11 | 12 | 13 | 14 | 15 | 16 |
| 17 | 18 | 19 | 20 | 21 | 22 | 23 |
| 24 | 25 | 26 | 27 | 28 | 29 | 30 |

**JULY**

| S | M | T | W | T | F | S |
|---|---|---|---|---|---|---|
| 1 | 2 | 3 | 4 | 5 | 6 | 7 |
| 8 | 9 | 10 | 11 | 12 | 13 | 14 |
| 15 | 16 | 17 | 18 | 19 | 20 | 21 |
| 22 | 23 | 24 | 25 | 26 | 27 | 28 |
| 29 | 30 | 31 | | | | |

**AUGUST**

| S | M | T | W | T | F | S |
|---|---|---|---|---|---|---|
| | | | 1 | 2 | 3 | 4 |
| 5 | 6 | 7 | 8 | 9 | 10 | 11 |
| 12 | 13 | 14 | 15 | 16 | 17 | 18 |
| 19 | 20 | 21 | 22 | 23 | 24 | 25 |
| 26 | 27 | 28 | 29 | 30 | 31 | |

**SEPTEMBER**

| S | M | T | W | T | F | S |
|---|---|---|---|---|---|---|
| | | | | | | 1 |
| 2 | 3 | 4 | 5 | 6 | 7 | 8 |
| 9 | 10 | 11 | 12 | 13 | 14 | 15 |
| 16 | 17 | 18 | 19 | 20 | 21 | 22 |
| 23 | 24 | 25 | 26 | 27 | 28 | 29 |
| 30 | | | | | | |

**OCTOBER**

| S | M | T | W | T | F | S |
|---|---|---|---|---|---|---|
| | 1 | 2 | 3 | 4 | 5 | 6 |
| 7 | 8 | 9 | 10 | 11 | 12 | 13 |
| 14 | 15 | 16 | 17 | 18 | 19 | 20 |
| 21 | 22 | 23 | 24 | 25 | 26 | 27 |
| 28 | 29 | 30 | 31 | | | |

**NOVEMBER**

| S | M | T | W | T | F | S |
|---|---|---|---|---|---|---|
| | | | | 1 | 2 | 3 |
| 4 | 5 | 6 | 7 | 8 | 9 | 10 |
| 11 | 12 | 13 | 14 | 15 | 16 | 17 |
| 18 | 19 | 20 | 21 | 22 | 23 | 24 |
| 25 | 26 | 27 | 28 | 29 | 30 | |

**DECEMBER**

| S | M | T | W | T | F | S |
|---|---|---|---|---|---|---|
| | | | | | | 1 |
| 2 | 3 | 4 | 5 | 6 | 7 | 8 |
| 9 | 10 | 11 | 12 | 13 | 14 | 15 |
| 16 | 17 | 18 | 19 | 20 | 21 | 22 |
| 23 | 24 | 25 | 26 | 27 | 28 | 29 |
| 30 | 31 | | | | | |

## 3 1985

**JANUARY**

| S | M | T | W | T | F | S |
|---|---|---|---|---|---|---|
| | | 1 | 2 | 3 | 4 | 5 |
| 6 | 7 | 8 | 9 | 10 | 11 | 12 |
| 13 | 14 | 15 | 16 | 17 | 18 | 19 |
| 20 | 21 | 22 | 23 | 24 | 25 | 26 |
| 27 | 28 | 29 | 30 | 31 | | |

**FEBRUARY**

| S | M | T | W | T | F | S |
|---|---|---|---|---|---|---|
| | | | | | 1 | 2 |
| 3 | 4 | 5 | 6 | 7 | 8 | 9 |
| 10 | 11 | 12 | 13 | 14 | 15 | 16 |
| 17 | 18 | 19 | 20 | 21 | 22 | 23 |
| 24 | 25 | 26 | 27 | 28 | | |

**MARCH**

| S | M | T | W | T | F | S |
|---|---|---|---|---|---|---|
| | | | | | 1 | 2 |
| 3 | 4 | 5 | 6 | 7 | 8 | 9 |
| 10 | 11 | 12 | 13 | 14 | 15 | 16 |
| 17 | 18 | 19 | 20 | 21 | 22 | 23 |
| 24 | 25 | 26 | 27 | 28 | 29 | 30 |
| 31 | | | | | | |

**APRIL**

| S | M | T | W | T | F | S |
|---|---|---|---|---|---|---|
| | 1 | 2 | 3 | 4 | 5 | 6 |
| 7 | 8 | 9 | 10 | 11 | 12 | 13 |
| 14 | 15 | 16 | 17 | 18 | 19 | 20 |
| 21 | 22 | 23 | 24 | 25 | 26 | 27 |
| 28 | 29 | 30 | | | | |

**MAY**

| S | M | T | W | T | F | S |
|---|---|---|---|---|---|---|
| | | | 1 | 2 | 3 | 4 |
| 5 | 6 | 7 | 8 | 9 | 10 | 11 |
| 12 | 13 | 14 | 15 | 16 | 17 | 18 |
| 19 | 20 | 21 | 22 | 23 | 24 | 25 |
| 26 | 27 | 28 | 29 | 30 | 31 | |

**JUNE**

| S | M | T | W | T | F | S |
|---|---|---|---|---|---|---|
| | | | | | | 1 |
| 2 | 3 | 4 | 5 | 6 | 7 | 8 |
| 9 | 10 | 11 | 12 | 13 | 14 | 15 |
| 16 | 17 | 18 | 19 | 20 | 21 | 22 |
| 23 | 24 | 25 | 26 | 27 | 28 | 29 |
| 30 | | | | | | |

**JULY**

| S | M | T | W | T | F | S |
|---|---|---|---|---|---|---|
| | 1 | 2 | 3 | 4 | 5 | 6 |
| 7 | 8 | 9 | 10 | 11 | 12 | 13 |
| 14 | 15 | 16 | 17 | 18 | 19 | 20 |
| 21 | 22 | 23 | 24 | 25 | 26 | 27 |
| 28 | 29 | 30 | 31 | | | |

**AUGUST**

| S | M | T | W | T | F | S |
|---|---|---|---|---|---|---|
| | | | | 1 | 2 | 3 |
| 4 | 5 | 6 | 7 | 8 | 9 | 10 |
| 11 | 12 | 13 | 14 | 15 | 16 | 17 |
| 18 | 19 | 20 | 21 | 22 | 23 | 24 |
| 25 | 26 | 27 | 28 | 29 | 30 | 31 |

**SEPTEMBER**

| S | M | T | W | T | F | S |
|---|---|---|---|---|---|---|
| 1 | 2 | 3 | 4 | 5 | 6 | 7 |
| 8 | 9 | 10 | 11 | 12 | 13 | 14 |
| 15 | 16 | 17 | 18 | 19 | 20 | 21 |
| 22 | 23 | 24 | 25 | 26 | 27 | 28 |
| 29 | 30 | | | | | |

**OCTOBER**

| S | M | T | W | T | F | S |
|---|---|---|---|---|---|---|
| | | 1 | 2 | 3 | 4 | 5 |
| 6 | 7 | 8 | 9 | 10 | 11 | 12 |
| 13 | 14 | 15 | 16 | 17 | 18 | 19 |
| 20 | 21 | 22 | 23 | 24 | 25 | 26 |
| 27 | 28 | 29 | 30 | 31 | | |

**NOVEMBER**

| S | M | T | W | T | F | S |
|---|---|---|---|---|---|---|
| | | | | | 1 | 2 |
| 3 | 4 | 5 | 6 | 7 | 8 | 9 |
| 10 | 11 | 12 | 13 | 14 | 15 | 16 |
| 17 | 18 | 19 | 20 | 21 | 22 | 23 |
| 24 | 25 | 26 | 27 | 28 | 29 | 30 |

**DECEMBER**

| S | M | T | W | T | F | S |
|---|---|---|---|---|---|---|
| 1 | 2 | 3 | 4 | 5 | 6 | 7 |
| 8 | 9 | 10 | 11 | 12 | 13 | 14 |
| 15 | 16 | 17 | 18 | 19 | 20 | 21 |
| 22 | 23 | 24 | 25 | 26 | 27 | 28 |
| 29 | 30 | 31 | | | | |

## 4 1986

**JANUARY**

| S | M | T | W | T | F | S |
|---|---|---|---|---|---|---|
| | | | 1 | 2 | 3 | 4 |
| 5 | 6 | 7 | 8 | 9 | 10 | 11 |
| 12 | 13 | 14 | 15 | 16 | 17 | 18 |
| 19 | 20 | 21 | 22 | 23 | 24 | 25 |
| 26 | 27 | 28 | 29 | 30 | 31 | |

**FEBRUARY**

| S | M | T | W | T | F | S |
|---|---|---|---|---|---|---|
| | | | | | | 1 |
| 2 | 3 | 4 | 5 | 6 | 7 | 8 |
| 9 | 10 | 11 | 12 | 13 | 14 | 15 |
| 16 | 17 | 18 | 19 | 20 | 21 | 22 |
| 23 | 24 | 25 | 26 | 27 | 28 | |

**MARCH**

| S | M | T | W | T | F | S |
|---|---|---|---|---|---|---|
| | | | | | | 1 |
| 2 | 3 | 4 | 5 | 6 | 7 | 8 |
| 9 | 10 | 11 | 12 | 13 | 14 | 15 |
| 16 | 17 | 18 | 19 | 20 | 21 | 22 |
| 23 | 24 | 25 | 26 | 27 | 28 | 29 |
| 30 | 31 | | | | | |

**APRIL**

| S | M | T | W | T | F | S |
|---|---|---|---|---|---|---|
| | | 1 | 2 | 3 | 4 | 5 |
| 6 | 7 | 8 | 9 | 10 | 11 | 12 |
| 13 | 14 | 15 | 16 | 17 | 18 | 19 |
| 20 | 21 | 22 | 23 | 24 | 25 | 26 |
| 27 | 28 | 29 | 30 | | | |

**MAY**

| S | M | T | W | T | F | S |
|---|---|---|---|---|---|---|
| | | | | 1 | 2 | 3 |
| 4 | 5 | 6 | 7 | 8 | 9 | 10 |
| 11 | 12 | 13 | 14 | 15 | 16 | 17 |
| 18 | 19 | 20 | 21 | 22 | 23 | 24 |
| 25 | 26 | 27 | 28 | 29 | 30 | 31 |

**JUNE**

| S | M | T | W | T | F | S |
|---|---|---|---|---|---|---|
| 1 | 2 | 3 | 4 | 5 | 6 | 7 |
| 8 | 9 | 10 | 11 | 12 | 13 | 14 |
| 15 | 16 | 17 | 18 | 19 | 20 | 21 |
| 22 | 23 | 24 | 25 | 26 | 27 | 28 |
| 29 | 30 | | | | | |

**JULY**

| S | M | T | W | T | F | S |
|---|---|---|---|---|---|---|
| | | 1 | 2 | 3 | 4 | 5 |
| 6 | 7 | 8 | 9 | 10 | 11 | 12 |
| 13 | 14 | 15 | 16 | 17 | 18 | 19 |
| 20 | 21 | 22 | 23 | 24 | 25 | 26 |
| 27 | 28 | 29 | 30 | 31 | | |

**AUGUST**

| S | M | T | W | T | F | S |
|---|---|---|---|---|---|---|
| | | | | | 1 | 2 |
| 3 | 4 | 5 | 6 | 7 | 8 | 9 |
| 10 | 11 | 12 | 13 | 14 | 15 | 16 |
| 17 | 18 | 19 | 20 | 21 | 22 | 23 |
| 24 | 25 | 26 | 27 | 28 | 29 | 30 |
| 31 | | | | | | |

**SEPTEMBER**

| S | M | T | W | T | F | S |
|---|---|---|---|---|---|---|
| | 1 | 2 | 3 | 4 | 5 | 6 |
| 7 | 8 | 9 | 10 | 11 | 12 | 13 |
| 14 | 15 | 16 | 17 | 18 | 19 | 20 |
| 21 | 22 | 23 | 24 | 25 | 26 | 27 |
| 28 | 29 | 30 | | | | |

**OCTOBER**

| S | M | T | W | T | F | S |
|---|---|---|---|---|---|---|
| | | | 1 | 2 | 3 | 4 |
| 5 | 6 | 7 | 8 | 9 | 10 | 11 |
| 12 | 13 | 14 | 15 | 16 | 17 | 18 |
| 19 | 20 | 21 | 22 | 23 | 24 | 25 |
| 26 | 27 | 28 | 29 | 30 | 31 | |

**NOVEMBER**

| S | M | T | W | T | F | S |
|---|---|---|---|---|---|---|
| | | | | | | 1 |
| 2 | 3 | 4 | 5 | 6 | 7 | 8 |
| 9 | 10 | 11 | 12 | 13 | 14 | 15 |
| 16 | 17 | 18 | 19 | 20 | 21 | 22 |
| 23 | 24 | 25 | 26 | 27 | 28 | 29 |
| 30 | | | | | | |

**DECEMBER**

| S | M | T | W | T | F | S |
|---|---|---|---|---|---|---|
| | 1 | 2 | 3 | 4 | 5 | 6 |
| 7 | 8 | 9 | 10 | 11 | 12 | 13 |
| 14 | 15 | 16 | 17 | 18 | 19 | 20 |
| 21 | 22 | 23 | 24 | 25 | 26 | 27 |
| 28 | 29 | 30 | 31 | | | |

## 5 1987

**JANUARY**

| S | M | T | W | T | F | S |
|---|---|---|---|---|---|---|
| | | | | 1 | 2 | 3 |
| 4 | 5 | 6 | 7 | 8 | 9 | 10 |
| 11 | 12 | 13 | 14 | 15 | 16 | 17 |
| 18 | 19 | 20 | 21 | 22 | 23 | 24 |
| 25 | 26 | 27 | 28 | 29 | 30 | 31 |

**FEBRUARY**

| S | M | T | W | T | F | S |
|---|---|---|---|---|---|---|
| 1 | 2 | 3 | 4 | 5 | 6 | 7 |
| 8 | 9 | 10 | 11 | 12 | 13 | 14 |
| 15 | 16 | 17 | 18 | 19 | 20 | 21 |
| 22 | 23 | 24 | 25 | 26 | 27 | 28 |

**MARCH**

| S | M | T | W | T | F | S |
|---|---|---|---|---|---|---|
| 1 | 2 | 3 | 4 | 5 | 6 | 7 |
| 8 | 9 | 10 | 11 | 12 | 13 | 14 |
| 15 | 16 | 17 | 18 | 19 | 20 | 21 |
| 22 | 23 | 24 | 25 | 26 | 27 | 28 |
| 29 | 30 | 31 | | | | |

**APRIL**

| S | M | T | W | T | F | S |
|---|---|---|---|---|---|---|
| | | | 1 | 2 | 3 | 4 |
| 5 | 6 | 7 | 8 | 9 | 10 | 11 |
| 12 | 13 | 14 | 15 | 16 | 17 | 18 |
| 19 | 20 | 21 | 22 | 23 | 24 | 25 |
| 26 | 27 | 28 | 29 | 30 | | |

**MAY**

| S | M | T | W | T | F | S |
|---|---|---|---|---|---|---|
| | | | | | 1 | 2 |
| 3 | 4 | 5 | 6 | 7 | 8 | 9 |
| 10 | 11 | 12 | 13 | 14 | 15 | 16 |
| 17 | 18 | 19 | 20 | 21 | 22 | 23 |
| 24 | 25 | 26 | 27 | 28 | 29 | 30 |
| 31 | | | | | | |

**JUNE**

| S | M | T | W | T | F | S |
|---|---|---|---|---|---|---|
| | 1 | 2 | 3 | 4 | 5 | 6 |
| 7 | 8 | 9 | 10 | 11 | 12 | 13 |
| 14 | 15 | 16 | 17 | 18 | 19 | 20 |
| 21 | 22 | 23 | 24 | 25 | 26 | 27 |
| 28 | 29 | 30 | | | | |

**JULY**

| S | M | T | W | T | F | S |
|---|---|---|---|---|---|---|
| | | | 1 | 2 | 3 | 4 |
| 5 | 6 | 7 | 8 | 9 | 10 | 11 |
| 12 | 13 | 14 | 15 | 16 | 17 | 18 |
| 19 | 20 | 21 | 22 | 23 | 24 | 25 |
| 26 | 27 | 28 | 29 | 30 | 31 | |

**AUGUST**

| S | M | T | W | T | F | S |
|---|---|---|---|---|---|---|
| | | | | | | 1 |
| 2 | 3 | 4 | 5 | 6 | 7 | 8 |
| 9 | 10 | 11 | 12 | 13 | 14 | 15 |
| 16 | 17 | 18 | 19 | 20 | 21 | 22 |
| 23 | 24 | 25 | 26 | 27 | 28 | 29 |
| 30 | 31 | | | | | |

**SEPTEMBER**

| S | M | T | W | T | F | S |
|---|---|---|---|---|---|---|
| | | 1 | 2 | 3 | 4 | 5 |
| 6 | 7 | 8 | 9 | 10 | 11 | 12 |
| 13 | 14 | 15 | 16 | 17 | 18 | 19 |
| 20 | 21 | 22 | 23 | 24 | 25 | 26 |
| 27 | 28 | 29 | 30 | | | |

**OCTOBER**

| S | M | T | W | T | F | S |
|---|---|---|---|---|---|---|
| | | | | 1 | 2 | 3 |
| 4 | 5 | 6 | 7 | 8 | 9 | 10 |
| 11 | 12 | 13 | 14 | 15 | 16 | 17 |
| 18 | 19 | 20 | 21 | 22 | 23 | 24 |
| 25 | 26 | 27 | 28 | 29 | 30 | 31 |

**NOVEMBER**

| S | M | T | W | T | F | S |
|---|---|---|---|---|---|---|
| 1 | 2 | 3 | 4 | 5 | 6 | 7 |
| 8 | 9 | 10 | 11 | 12 | 13 | 14 |
| 15 | 16 | 17 | 18 | 19 | 20 | 21 |
| 22 | 23 | 24 | 25 | 26 | 27 | 28 |
| 29 | 30 | | | | | |

**DECEMBER**

| S | M | T | W | T | F | S |
|---|---|---|---|---|---|---|
| | | 1 | 2 | 3 | 4 | 5 |
| 6 | 7 | 8 | 9 | 10 | 11 | 12 |
| 13 | 14 | 15 | 16 | 17 | 18 | 19 |
| 20 | 21 | 22 | 23 | 24 | 25 | 26 |
| 27 | 28 | 29 | 30 | 31 | | |

## 6 1982

**JANUARY**

| S | M | T | W | T | F | S |
|---|---|---|---|---|---|---|
| | | | | | 1 | 2 |
| 3 | 4 | 5 | 6 | 7 | 8 | 9 |
| 10 | 11 | 12 | 13 | 14 | 15 | 16 |
| 17 | 18 | 19 | 20 | 21 | 22 | 23 |
| 24 | 25 | 26 | 27 | 28 | 29 | 30 |
| 31 | | | | | | |

**FEBRUARY**

| S | M | T | W | T | F | S |
|---|---|---|---|---|---|---|
| | 1 | 2 | 3 | 4 | 5 | 6 |
| 7 | 8 | 9 | 10 | 11 | 12 | 13 |
| 14 | 15 | 16 | 17 | 18 | 19 | 20 |
| 21 | 22 | 23 | 24 | 25 | 26 | 27 |
| 28 | | | | | | |

**MARCH**

| S | M | T | W | T | F | S |
|---|---|---|---|---|---|---|
| | 1 | 2 | 3 | 4 | 5 | 6 |
| 7 | 8 | 9 | 10 | 11 | 12 | 13 |
| 14 | 15 | 16 | 17 | 18 | 19 | 20 |
| 21 | 22 | 23 | 24 | 25 | 26 | 27 |
| 28 | 29 | 30 | 31 | | | |

**APRIL**

| S | M | T | W | T | F | S |
|---|---|---|---|---|---|---|
| | | | | 1 | 2 | 3 |
| 4 | 5 | 6 | 7 | 8 | 9 | 10 |
| 11 | 12 | 13 | 14 | 15 | 16 | 17 |
| 18 | 19 | 20 | 21 | 22 | 23 | 24 |
| 25 | 26 | 27 | 28 | 29 | 30 | |

**MAY**

| S | M | T | W | T | F | S |
|---|---|---|---|---|---|---|
| | | | | | | 1 |
| 2 | 3 | 4 | 5 | 6 | 7 | 8 |
| 9 | 10 | 11 | 12 | 13 | 14 | 15 |
| 16 | 17 | 18 | 19 | 20 | 21 | 22 |
| 23 | 24 | 25 | 26 | 27 | 28 | 29 |
| 30 | 31 | | | | | |

**JUNE**

| S | M | T | W | T | F | S |
|---|---|---|---|---|---|---|
| | | 1 | 2 | 3 | 4 | 5 |
| 6 | 7 | 8 | 9 | 10 | 11 | 12 |
| 13 | 14 | 15 | 16 | 17 | 18 | 19 |
| 20 | 21 | 22 | 23 | 24 | 25 | 26 |
| 27 | 28 | 29 | 30 | | | |

**JULY**

| S | M | T | W | T | F | S |
|---|---|---|---|---|---|---|
| | | | | 1 | 2 | 3 |
| 4 | 5 | 6 | 7 | 8 | 9 | 10 |
| 11 | 12 | 13 | 14 | 15 | 16 | 17 |
| 18 | 19 | 20 | 21 | 22 | 23 | 24 |
| 25 | 26 | 27 | 28 | 29 | 30 | 31 |

**AUGUST**

| S | M | T | W | T | F | S |
|---|---|---|---|---|---|---|
| 1 | 2 | 3 | 4 | 5 | 6 | 7 |
| 8 | 9 | 10 | 11 | 12 | 13 | 14 |
| 15 | 16 | 17 | 18 | 19 | 20 | 21 |
| 22 | 23 | 24 | 25 | 26 | 27 | 28 |
| 29 | 30 | 31 | | | | |

**SEPTEMBER**

| S | M | T | W | T | F | S |
|---|---|---|---|---|---|---|
| | | | 1 | 2 | 3 | 4 |
| 5 | 6 | 7 | 8 | 9 | 10 | 11 |
| 12 | 13 | 14 | 15 | 16 | 17 | 18 |
| 19 | 20 | 21 | 22 | 23 | 24 | 25 |
| 26 | 27 | 28 | 29 | 30 | | |

**OCTOBER**

| S | M | T | W | T | F | S |
|---|---|---|---|---|---|---|
| | | | | | 1 | 2 |
| 3 | 4 | 5 | 6 | 7 | 8 | 9 |
| 10 | 11 | 12 | 13 | 14 | 15 | 16 |
| 17 | 18 | 19 | 20 | 21 | 22 | 23 |
| 24 | 25 | 26 | 27 | 28 | 29 | 30 |
| 31 | | | | | | |

**NOVEMBER**

| S | M | T | W | T | F | S |
|---|---|---|---|---|---|---|
| | 1 | 2 | 3 | 4 | 5 | 6 |
| 7 | 8 | 9 | 10 | 11 | 12 | 13 |
| 14 | 15 | 16 | 17 | 18 | 19 | 20 |
| 21 | 22 | 23 | 24 | 25 | 26 | 27 |
| 28 | 29 | 30 | | | | |

**DECEMBER**

| S | M | T | W | T | F | S |
|---|---|---|---|---|---|---|
| | | | 1 | 2 | 3 | 4 |
| 5 | 6 | 7 | 8 | 9 | 10 | 11 |
| 12 | 13 | 14 | 15 | 16 | 17 | 18 |
| 19 | 20 | 21 | 22 | 23 | 24 | 25 |
| 26 | 27 | 28 | 29 | 30 | 31 | |

## 7     1983

| JANUARY | FEBRUARY | MARCH | APRIL |
|---|---|---|---|
| S M T W T F S | S M T W T F S | S M T W T F S | S M T W T F S |

| MAY | JUNE | JULY | AUGUST |
|---|---|---|---|

| SEPTEMBER | OCTOBER | NOVEMBER | DECEMBER |
|---|---|---|---|

## 8     (LEAP YEAR)     1984

| JANUARY | FEBRUARY | MARCH | APRIL |
|---|---|---|---|
| S M T W T F S | S M T W T F S | S M T W T F S | S M T W T F S |

| MAY | JUNE | JULY | AUGUST |
|---|---|---|---|

| SEPTEMBER | OCTOBER | NOVEMBER | DECEMBER |
|---|---|---|---|

## 9     (LEAP YEAR)

| JANUARY | FEBRUARY | MARCH | APRIL |
|---|---|---|---|

| MAY | JUNE | JULY | AUGUST |
|---|---|---|---|

| SEPTEMBER | OCTOBER | NOVEMBER | DECEMBER |
|---|---|---|---|

## 10     (LEAP YEAR)

| JANUARY | FEBRUARY | MARCH | APRIL |
|---|---|---|---|

| MAY | JUNE | JULY | AUGUST |
|---|---|---|---|

| SEPTEMBER | OCTOBER | NOVEMBER | DECEMBER |
|---|---|---|---|

## 11     (LEAP YEAR)

| JANUARY | FEBRUARY | MARCH | APRIL |
|---|---|---|---|

| MAY | JUNE | JULY | AUGUST |
|---|---|---|---|

| SEPTEMBER | OCTOBER | NOVEMBER | DECEMBER |
|---|---|---|---|

## 12     (LEAP YEAR)

| JANUARY | FEBRUARY | MARCH | APRIL |
|---|---|---|---|

| MAY | JUNE | JULY | AUGUST |
|---|---|---|---|

| SEPTEMBER | OCTOBER | NOVEMBER | DECEMBER |
|---|---|---|---|

## 13     (LEAP YEAR)     1988

| JANUARY | FEBRUARY | MARCH | APRIL |
|---|---|---|---|

| MAY | JUNE | JULY | AUGUST |
|---|---|---|---|

| SEPTEMBER | OCTOBER | NOVEMBER | DECEMBER |
|---|---|---|---|

## 14     (LEAP YEAR)

| JANUARY | FEBRUARY | MARCH | APRIL |
|---|---|---|---|

| MAY | JUNE | JULY | AUGUST |
|---|---|---|---|

| SEPTEMBER | OCTOBER | NOVEMBER | DECEMBER |
|---|---|---|---|

# WORLD TIME ZONES

The standard time zone system is based on the division of the world into 24 zones, each 15° longitude. But as the table below shows, there are numerous variations.

The "zero" zone is centered at Greenwich, England (thus Greenwich Mean Time—GMT).

The 12th zone is divided by the 180th meridian (International Date Line) and is designated as plus 12 and minus 12 zones. When the line is crossed going west, the date is advanced one day. When it is crossed going east, the date becomes a day earlier. All other zones are designated by numbers representing how many hours the standard time of each zone differs from GMT.

The table below gives the standard time in countries around the world when it is noon (Eastern Standard Time) in New York City. An asterisk (*) indicates that it is the next day.

| COUNTRY | ZONE | TIME | COUNTRY | ZONE | TIME | COUNTRY | ZONE | TIME |
|---|---|---|---|---|---|---|---|---|
| Afghanistan | + 4:30 | 9:30 p.m. | Ghana | 0 | 5:00 p.m. | Philippines | + 8 | 1:00 a.m.* |
| Albania | + 1 | 6:00 p.m. | Greece | + 2 | 7:00 p.m. | Poland | + 1 | 6:00 p.m. |
| Algeria | 0 | 5:00 p.m. | Grenada | − 4 | 1:00 p.m. | Portugal | + 1 | 6:00 p.m. |
| Angola | + 1 | 6:00 p.m. | Guam | +10 | 3:00 a.m.* | Puerto Rico | − 4 | 1:00 p.m. |
| Argentina | − 3 | 2:00 p.m. | Guatemala | − 6 | 11:00 a.m. | Qatar | + 3 | 8:00 p.m. |
| Australia | | | Guinea | 0 | 5:00 p.m. | Romania | + 2 | 7:00 p.m. |
| Perth | + 8 | 1:00 a.m.* | Guinea-Bissau | − 1 | 4:00 p.m. | Rwanda | + 2 | 7:00 p.m. |
| Adelaide | + 9:30 | 2:30 a.m.* | Guyana | − 3:45 | 1:15 p.m. | Samoa | −11 | 6:00 a.m. |
| Sydney | +10 | 3:00 a.m.* | Haiti | − 5 | 12:00 noon | San Marino | + 1 | 6:00 p.m. |
| Austria | + 1 | 6:00 p.m. | Honduras | − 6 | 11:00 a.m. | Saudi Arabia | Sun time | c.8:00 p.m. |
| Azores | − 1 | 4:00 p.m. | Hungary | + 1 | 6:00 p.m. | Senegal | 0 | 5:00 p.m. |
| Bahamas | − 5 | 12:00 noon | Iceland | 0 | 5:00 p.m. | Seychelles | + 4 | 9:00 p.m. |
| Bahrain | + 3 | 8:00 p.m. | India | + 5:30 | 10:30 p.m. | Sierra Leone | 0 | 5:00 p.m. |
| Bangladesh | + 5:30 | 10:30 p.m. | Indonesia | + 7 | 12:00 mid. | Singapore | + 7 | 12:00 mid. |
| Barbados | − 4 | 1:00 p.m. | Iran | + 3:30 | 8:30 p.m. | Solomons | +11 | 4:00 a.m.* |
| Belgium | + 1 | 6:00 p.m. | Iraq | + 3 | 8:00 p.m. | Somalia | + 3 | 8:00 p.m. |
| Benin | + 1 | 6:00 p.m. | Ireland | 0 | 5:00 p.m. | South Africa | + 2 | 8:00 p.m. |
| Bermuda | − 4 | 1:00 p.m. | Israel | + 2 | 7:00 p.m. | Soviet Union | | |
| Bolivia | − 4 | 1:00 p.m. | Italy | + 1 | 6:00 p.m. | Moscow | + 3 | 8:00 p.m. |
| Botswana | + 2 | 7:00 p.m. | Ivory Coast | 0 | 5:00 p.m. | Gorki | + 4 | 9:00 p.m. |
| Brazil (Rio) | − 3 | 2:00 p.m. | Jamaica | − 5 | 12:00 noon | Sverdlovsk | + 5 | 10:00 p.m. |
| Britain | 0 | 5:00 p.m. | Japan | + 9 | 2:00 a.m.* | Tashkent | + 6 | 11:00 p.m. |
| Bulgaria | + 2 | 7:00 p.m. | Jordan | + 2 | 7:00 p.m. | Novosibirsk | + 7 | 12:00 mid. |
| Burma | + 6:30 | 11:30 p.m. | Kenya | + 3 | 8:00 p.m. | Irkutsk | + 8 | 1:00 a.m.* |
| Burundi | + 2 | 7:00 p.m. | Korea, North | + 9 | 2:00 a.m.* | Yakutsk | + 9 | 2:00 a.m.* |
| Cambodia | + 7 | 12:00 mid. | Korea, South | + 9 | 2:00 a.m.* | Vladivostok | +10 | 3:00 a.m.* |
| Cameroon | + 1 | 6:00 p.m. | Kuwait | + 3 | 8:00 p.m. | Spain | + 1 | 6:00 p.m. |
| Canada | | | Laos | + 7 | 12:00 mid. | Sri Lanka | + 5:30 | 10:30 p.m. |
| Victoria, B.C. | − 8 | 9:00 a.m. | Lebanon | + 2 | 7:00 p.m. | Sudan | + 2 | 7:00 p.m. |
| Edmonton, Alta. | − 7 | 10:00 a.m. | Lesotho | + 2 | 7:00 p.m. | Suriname | − 3:30 | 1:30 p.m. |
| Winnipeg, Man. | − 6 | 11:00 a.m. | Liberia | 0 | 5:00 p.m. | Swaziland | + 2 | 7:00 p.m. |
| Montreal, Que. | − 5 | 12:00 noon | Libya | + 2 | 7:00 p.m. | Sweden | + 1 | 6:00 p.m. |
| Halifax, N.S. | − 4 | 1:00 p.m. | Liechtenstein | + 1 | 6:00 p.m. | Switzerland | + 1 | 6:00 p.m. |
| St. John's, Nfld. | − 3:30 | 1:30 p.m. | Luxembourg | + 1 | 6:00 p.m. | Syria | + 2 | 7:00 p.m. |
| Canary Is. | 0 | 5:00 p.m. | Madagascar | + 3 | 8:00 p.m. | Taiwan | + 8 | 1:00 a.m.* |
| Cape Verde | − 2 | 3:00 p.m. | Malawi | + 2 | 7:00 p.m. | Tanzania | + 3 | 8:00 p.m. |
| Central Africa | + 1 | 6:00 p.m. | Malaysia | + 7:30 | 12:30 a.m.* | Thailand | + 7 | 12:00 mid. |
| Chad | + 1 | 6:00 p.m. | Maldives | + 5 | 10:00 p.m. | Togo | 0 | 5:00 p.m. |
| Chile | − 4 | 1:00 p.m. | Mali | 0 | 5:00 p.m. | Tonga | −11 | 6:00 a.m. |
| China | + 8 | 1:00 a.m.* | Malta | + 1 | 6:00 p.m. | Trinidad-Tobago | − 4 | 1:00 p.m. |
| Colombia | − 5 | 12:00 noon | Mauritania | 0 | 5:00 p.m. | Tunisia | + 1 | 6:00 p.m. |
| Comoros | + 3 | 8:00 p.m. | Mauritius | + 4 | 9:00 p.m. | Turkey | + 2 | 7:00 p.m. |
| Congo | + 1 | 6:00 p.m. | Mexico | | | Uganda | + 3 | 8:00 p.m. |
| Costa Rica | − 6 | 11:00 a.m. | (Mexico City) | − 6 | 11:00 a.m. | United Arab Em. | + 4 | 9:00 p.m. |
| Cuba | − 5 | 12:00 noon | Midway Is. | −11 | 6:00 a.m. | United States | | |
| Cyprus | + 2 | 7:00 p.m. | Mongolia | + 8 | 1:00 a.m.* | Nome, Alaska | −11 | 6:00 a.m. |
| Czechoslovakia | + 1 | 6:00 p.m. | Morocco | 0 | 5:00 p.m. | Anchorage | −10 | 7:00 a.m. |
| Denmark | + 1 | 6:00 p.m. | Mozambique | + 2 | 7:00 p.m. | Los Angeles | − 8 | 9:00 a.m. |
| Djibouti | + 3 | 8:00 p.m. | Nauru | +11:30 | 4:30 a.m.* | Denver | − 7 | 10:00 a.m. |
| Dominican Rep. | − 5 | 12:00 noon | Nepal | + 5:30 | 10:30 p.m. | Chicago | − 6 | 11:00 a.m. |
| Ecuador | − 5 | 12:00 noon | Netherlands | + 1 | 6:00 p.m. | New York | − 5 | 12:00 noon |
| Egypt | + 2 | 7:00 p.m. | New Zealand | +12 | 5:00 a.m.* | Upper Volta | 0 | 5:00 p.m. |
| El Salvador | − 6 | 11:00 a.m. | Nicaragua | − 6 | 11:00 a.m. | Uruguay | − 3 | 2:00 p.m. |
| Equatorial Guinea | + 1 | 6:00 p.m. | Niger | + 1 | 6:00 p.m. | Venezuela | − 4 | 1:00 p.m. |
| Ethiopia | + 3 | 8:00 p.m. | Nigeria | + 1 | 6:00 p.m. | Vietnam | + 7 | 12:00 mid. |
| Fiji | +12 | 5:00 a.m.* | Norway | + 1 | 6:00 p.m. | Virgin Islands | − 4 | 1:00 p.m. |
| Finland | + 2 | 7:00 p.m. | Oman | + 4 | 9:00 p.m. | Yemen, North | + 3 | 8:00 p.m. |
| France | + 1 | 6:00 p.m. | Pakistan | + 5 | 10:00 p.m. | Yemen, South | + 3 | 8:00 p.m. |
| Gabon | + 1 | 6:00 p.m. | Panama | − 5 | 12:00 noon | Yugoslavia | + 1 | 6:00 p.m. |
| Gambia | 0 | 5:00 p.m. | Papua New Guinea | +10 | 3:00 a.m.* | Zaire (Kinshasa) | + 1 | 6:00 p.m. |
| Germany, East | + 1 | 6:00 p.m. | Paraguay | − 4 | 1:00 p.m. | Zambia | + 2 | 7:00 p.m. |
| Germany, West | + 1 | 6:00 p.m. | Peru | − 5 | 12:00 noon | Zimbabwe | + 2 | 7:00 p.m. |

# Cities

Boston celebrated its 350th anniversary in May 1980 with a parade of Tall Ships in Boston Harbor. One of the most spectacular of the ships taking part was the 241-foot fully rigged *Christian Radich* of Norway.

United Press Int'l.

## HIGHLIGHTS: 1980

### CENSUS PROBLEMS

Beset by strikes of firemen, police, school teachers, and transit workers, the mayors of the nation's largest cities added a new worry in 1980—the results of the decennial U.S. Census.

Although the U.S. Census Bureau did not officially release even preliminary estimates on a nationwide basis regarding the 1980 head count, it did give local officials a preview of the figures that related to their own cities. What the mayors saw they did not like—declines in their populations that would cost them billions of dollars in federal funds and congressional seats that are allocated on the basis of census populations.

The mayors denounced the Census Bureau for giving them a low count. They and state governors initiated a rash of court suits to prevent use of the figures without a recount. As a result, no one could even estimate when the official results of the 1980 Census might be made public.

Thus, the latest figures on the populations of U.S. cities released by the Census Bureau were estimates for the year 1978, as published on pages 114–137.

Even the 1978 estimates given out by the Census Bureau in 1980 showed that 14 of the 20 largest U.S. cities had declining estimated populations. Only the Sun Belt cities showed increases.

## 20 LARGEST CITIES IN U.S.

| RANK | CITY AND STATE | POPULATION |
|------|----------------|-----------|
| 1 | New York City, N.Y. [1] ........ | 7,134,542 |
| 2 | Chicago, Ill. [1] ............... | 3,049,497 |
| 3 | Los Angeles, Calif. [1] .......... | 2,787,176 |
| 4 | Philadelphia, Pa. [1] ........... | 1,754,829 |
| 5 | Houston, Texas [1] ............. | 1,572,981 |
| 6 | Detroit, Mich. [1] ............. | 1,257,879 |
| 7 | Dallas, Texas [1] .............. | 847,420 |
| 8 | San Diego, Calif. [1] ........... | 816,659 |
| 9 | San Antonio, Texas [1] ........ | 798,195 |
| 10 | Baltimore, Md. [1] ............ | 791,857 |
| 11 | Indianapolis, Ind. [1] .......... | 704,045 |
| 12 | Phoenix, Ariz. [1] ............. | 681,355 |
| 13 | Memphis, Tenn. [1] ........... | 663,379 |
| 14 | Washington, D.C. [2] .......... | 656,000 |
| 15 | San Francisco, Calif. [1] ........ | 649,315 |
| 16 | Milwaukee, Wis. [1] ........... | 633,220 |
| 17 | Boston, Mass. [1] ............. | 597,254 |
| 18 | Cleveland, Ohio [1] ........... | 594,529 |
| 19 | San Jose, Calif. [1] ........... | 592,773 |
| 20 | New Orleans, La. [1] .......... | 556,428 |

[1] U.S. Census Bureau estimates for July 1, 1978.
[2] Estimate for July 1, 1979.

### HIGHLIGHTS: 1980 (continued)

The Census Bureau estimates indicated Baltimore had fallen from 8th place to 10th in the population rankings, being surpassed by San Diego, now 8th, and San Antonio, now 9th. Washington, D.C., the nation's capital, dropped to 14th behind Memphis. Cleveland fell to 18th, plummeting past Boston, whose population was declining at a slower rate. And New Orleans dropped to 20th behind San Jose, Calif.

### NEW NO. 2 CITY?

Perhaps the biggest controversy over the unofficial, unannounced 1980 Census figures came when Los Angeles, which was celebrating its 200th anniversary, let it be known that its preview of the figures showed the California metropolis has become second only to New York City in size of population. This news was greeted with cries of anguish in Chicago, which has held the rank of No. 2 since passing Philadelphia in 1890.

### RANKING DEPRESSED CITIES

A report prepared by Richard P. Nathan, director of Princeton University's Urban and Regional Research Center, and by James W. Fossett of the University of Michigan, said that, despite efforts by various cities to reverse their decline by elaborate building projects, most had not turned the corner.

Following are the rankings from most to least depressed in the report:
1. **Most depressed:** St. Louis, Boston, Newark, Buffalo, Pittsburgh, Cleveland, Philadelphia, Rochester, Detroit, Cincinnati, and Minneapolis.
2. Baltimore, Birmingham, Toledo, Louisville, Chicago, New Orleans, St. Paul, New York, Kansas City, Oakland, and Akron.
3. Portland, San Francisco, Milwaukee, Omaha, Columbus, Miami, Memphis, San Antonio, Seattle, and Denver.
4. Oklahoma City, Atlanta, Norfolk, Fort Worth, Baton Rouge, Los Angeles, Austin, Sacramento, Tulsa, and Wichita.
5. **Least depressed:** Charlotte, Long Beach, El Paso, Tampa, Houston, Dallas, San Diego, San Jose, Albuquerque, Phoenix, and Tucson.

### GREATEST POTENTIAL JOB MARKETS

A study for the Chase Manhattan Bank of New York predicted that the five metropolitan areas likely to show the most growth in the numbers of new jobs in the 1980s would be Tucson, Ariz.; Fort Lauderdale-Hollywood, Fla.; Houston, Texas; Las Vegas, Nev.; and Beaumont-Port Arthur, Texas.

## LARGEST U.S. METROPOLITAN AREAS

| RANK | METROPOLITAN AREA | POPULATION |
|------|-------------------|-----------|
| 1 | New York City, N.Y.-N.J. [1] ...... | 9,221,800 |
| 2 | Los Angeles-Long Beach, Calif. [1] | 7,080,900 |
| 3 | Chicago, Ill. [1] | 7,029,600 |
| 4 | Philadelphia, Pa.-N.J. [1] ........ | 4,770,400 |
| 5 | Detroit, Mich. [1] .............. | 4,386,400 |
| 6 | Boston, Mass.-N.H. [1] .......... | 3,887,800 |
| 7 | San Francisco-Oakland, Calif. [1] . | 3,183,800 |
| 8 | Washington, D.C.-Md.-Va. [1] .... | 3,016,800 |
| 9 | Dallas-Fort Worth, Texas [1] .... | 2,719,900 |
| 10 | Nassau-Suffolk, N.Y. [1] ........ | 2,690,000 |
| 11 | Houston, Texas [1] ............. | 2,595,400 |
| 12 | St. Louis, Mo.-Ill. [1] ........... | 2,385,900 |
| 13 | Pittsburgh, Pa. [1] ............. | 2,277,300 |
| 14 | Baltimore, Md. [1] ............. | 2,145,200 |
| 15 | Minneapolis-St. Paul, Minn. [1] ... | 2,063,000 |
| 16 | Newark, N.J. [1] ............... | 1,951,300 |
| 17 | Cleveland, Ohio [1] ............ | 1,938,900 |
| 18 | Atlanta, Ga. [1] ............... | 1,851,500 |
| 19 | Anaheim-Santa Ana, Calif. [1] .... | 1,833,000 |
| 20 | San Diego, Calif. [1] ............ | 1,743,600 |

## WORLD'S LARGEST METROPOLITAN AREAS

| RANK | METROPOLITAN AREA | POPULATION |
|------|-------------------|-----------|
| 1 | Mexico City, Mexico [2] .......... | 13,993,866 |
| 2 | Tokyo, Japan [2] ............... | 11,695,150 |
| 3 | Shanghai, China [2] ............ | 10,820,000 |
| 4 | Buenos Aires, Argentina [2] ...... | 9,749,000 |
| 5 | New York City, N.Y.-N.J. [1] ..... | 9,221,800 |
| 6 | Peking, China [4] .............. | 8,626,050 |
| 7 | Paris, France [2] ............... | 8,547,625 |
| 8 | Calcutta, India [2] ............. | 8,297,000 |
| 9 | Moscow, Soviet Union [2] ....... | 7,909,000 |
| 10 | Manila, Philippines [4] .......... | 7,800,000 |
| 11 | Bombay, India [2] .............. | 7,605,000 |
| 12 | Seoul, South Korea [4] .......... | 7,500,000 |
| 13 | São Paulo, Brazil [2] ............ | 7,198,608 |
| 14 | Los Angeles-Long Beach, Calif. [1] | 7,080,900 |
| 15 | Chicago, Ill. [1] ............... | 7,029,600 |
| 16 | London, Britain [2] ............. | 7,028,200 |
| 17 | Cairo, Egypt [2, 3] ............. | 5,084,463 |
| 18 | Delhi, India [2] ............... | 4,891,000 |
| 19 | Philadelphia, Pa.-N.J. [1] ........ | 4,770,400 |
| 20 | Jakarta, Indonesia [2, 3] ......... | 4,576,009 |

[1] U.S. Census Bureau estimates for July 1, 1978. [2] 1978 UN Demographic Yearbook. [3] City only. [4] Official estimate.

# LARGEST METROPOLITAN AREAS OF THE WORLD

Source: Censuses and official estimates by national governments.

Altogether 43 American metropolitan areas with populations of more than 880,000 make up slightly more than one-fifth of the world's 206 largest metropolitan areas as shown below.

| CITY | POPULATION |
|------|-----------:|
| Adana, Turkey | 1,234,735 |
| Addis Ababa, Ethiopia | 1,133,200 |
| Adelaide, Australia | 900,431 |
| Ahmedabad, India | 1,741,522 |
| Alexandria, Egypt | 2,320,000 |
| Algiers, Algeria | 2,000,000 |
| Alma-Ata, Soviet Union | 895,000 |
| Amsterdam, Neth. | 970,376 |
| Anaheim, California | 1,833,000 |
| Ankara, Turkey | 2,572,562 |
| Athens, Greece | 2,101,103 |
| Atlanta, Georgia | 1,851,500 |
| Baghdad, Iraq | 1,657,424 |
| Baku, Soviet Union | 1,460,000 |
| Baltimore, Maryland | 2,145,200 |
| Bandung, Indonesia | 1,201,730 |
| Bangalore, India | 1,653,779 |
| Bangkok, Thailand | 4,178,000 |
| Barcelona, Spain | 1,809,722 |
| Beirut, Lebanon | 938,940 |
| Belo Horizonte, Brazil | 1,557,464 |
| Berlin (East), E. Ger. | 1,101,123 |
| Berlin (West), W. Ger. | 2,984,837 |
| Birmingham, Britain | 2,358,980 |
| Bogotá, Colombia | 2,855,065 |
| Bombay, India | 7,605,000 |
| Boston, Massachusetts | 3,887,800 |
| Brisbane, Australia | 957,743 |
| Brussels, Belgium | 1,028,972 |
| Bucharest, Romania | 1,934,025 |
| Budapest, Hungary | 2,085,615 |
| Buenos Aires, Argentina | 9,749,000 |
| Buffalo, New York | 1,303,000 |
| Bursa, Turkey | 960,035 |
| Cairo, Egypt | 5,084,463 |
| Calcutta, India | 8,297,000 |
| Cali, Colombia | 990,304 |
| Canton, China | 1,840,000 |
| Cape Town, South Africa | 1,096,597 |
| Caracas, Venezuela | 2,576,000 |
| Casablanca, Morocco | 1,753,400 |
| Changchun, China | 975,000 |
| Chelyabinsk, Soviet Un. | 1,019,000 |
| Chengtu, China | 1,107,000 |
| Chicago, Illinois | 7,029,600 |
| Chittagong, Bangladesh | 889,760 |
| Chungking, China | 2,121,000 |
| Cincinnati, Ohio–Ky. | 1,389,100 |
| Cleveland, Ohio | 1,938,900 |
| Cologne, W. Germany | 1,013,771 |
| Columbus, Ohio | 1,088,900 |
| Copenhagen, Denmark | 1,327,940 |
| Dacca, Bangladesh | 1,730,253 |
| Dallas, Texas | 2,719,900 |
| Damascus, Syria | 1,142,000 |
| Delhi, India | 3,647,023 |
| Denver, Colorado | 1,504,700 |
| Detroit, Michigan | 4,386,400 |
| Dnepropetrovsk, Sov. Un. | 1,062,000 |
| Donetsk, Soviet Union | 997,000 |
| Erevan, Soviet Union | 982,000 |
| Fort Lauderdale, Florida | 881,900 |
| Fortaleza, Brazil | 1,109,839 |
| Fukuoka, Japan | 1,039,286 |
| Fushun, China | 985,000 |
| Giza, Egypt | 893,100 |
| Glasgow, Scotland | 1,727,625 |
| Gorky, Soviet Union | 1,332,000 |
| Guadalajara, Mexico | 2,343,034 |
| Hamburg, W. Germany | 1,717,383 |
| Hanoi, Vietnam | 1,000,000 |
| Harbin, China | 1,552,000 |
| Hartford, Conn. | 1,045,300 |
| Havana, Cuba | 1,861,442 |
| Houston, Texas | 2,595,400 |
| Hyderabad, India | 1,796,339 |
| Indianapolis, Indiana | 1,156,200 |
| Istanbul, Turkey | 3,864,493 |
| Izmir, Turkey | 1,660,529 |
| Jakarta, Indonesia | 4,576,009 |
| Johannesburg, So. Af. | 1,432,643 |
| Kanpur, India | 1,275,242 |
| Kansas City, Mo.–Kans. | 1,323,700 |
| Karachi, Pakistan | 3,498,634 |
| Kawasaki, Japan | 1,032,852 |
| Kazan, Soviet Union | 980,000 |
| Kharkov, Soviet Union | 1,428,000 |
| Kiev, Soviet Union | 2,131,000 |
| Kinshasa, Zaire | 2,008,352 |
| Kitakyushu, Japan | 1,067,915 |
| Kobe, Japan | 1,366,397 |
| Konya, Turkey | 1,425,910 |
| Kuibyshev, Soviet Union | 1,221,000 |
| Kunming, China | 880,000 |
| Kyoto, Japan | 1,464,964 |
| Lagos, Nigeria | 1,476,837 |
| Lahore, Pakistan | 2,165,372 |
| Leeds, Britain | 1,735,700 |
| Leningrad, Soviet Union | 4,480,000 |
| Lille, France | 934,325 |
| Lima, Peru | 3,302,523 |
| Lisbon, Portugal | 1,611,887 |
| Liverpool, Britain | 1,226,310 |
| Lodz, Poland | 1,086,700 |
| London, Britain | 7,028,200 |
| Los Angeles, California | 7,080,900 |
| Louisville, Ky.–Ind. | 887,300 |
| Lyon, France | 1,172,035 |
| Madras, India | 3,169,930 |
| Madrid, Spain | 3,520,320 |
| Manchester, Britain | 2,389,260 |
| Manila, Philippines | 7,800,000 |
| Marseille, France | 1,074,390 |
| Medellín, Colombia | 1,159,194 |
| Melbourne, Australia | 2,604,035 |
| Memphis, Tennessee | 888,800 |
| Mexico City, Mexico | 13,993,866 |
| Miami, Florida | 1,451,200 |
| Milan, Italy | 1,706,268 |
| Milwaukee, Wisconsin | 1,417,200 |
| Minneapolis, Minn.–Wis. | 2,063,000 |
| Minsk, Soviet Union | 1,273,000 |
| Monterrey, Mexico | 1,923,402 |
| Montevideo, Uruguay | 1,173,254 |
| Montreal, Canada | 2,798,000 |
| Moscow, Soviet Union | 7,909,000 |
| Munich, W. Germany | 1,314,865 |
| Nagoya, Japan | 2,083,616 |
| Nagpur, India | 930,459 |
| Nanking, China | 1,419,000 |
| Naples, Italy | 1,225,227 |
| Nassau–Suffolk, N.Y. | 2,690,000 |
| New Orleans, La. | 1,141,100 |
| New York, New York | 9,221,800 |
| Newark, New Jersey | 1,951,300 |
| Nova Ignacu, Brazil | 931,954 |
| Novosibirsk, Soviet Union | 1,324,000 |
| Odessa, Soviet Union | 1,051,000 |
| Omsk, Soviet Union | 1,042,000 |
| Osaka, Japan | 2,723,752 |
| Paris, France | 8,547,625 |
| Peking, China | 8,626,050 |
| Perm, Soviet Union | 985,000 |
| Philadelphia, Pa. | 4,770,400 |
| Phoenix, Arizona | 1,293,200 |
| Pittsburgh, Pa. | 2,277,300 |
| Poona, India | 1,135,034 |
| Port Arthur, China | 1,508,000 |
| Portland, Oreg.–Wash. | 1,140,100 |
| Porto, Portugal | 1,314,794 |
| Pôrto Alegre, Brazil | 1,043,964 |
| Prague, Czechoslovakia | 1,173,031 |
| Pusan, South Korea | 2,450,125 |
| Rangoon, Burma | 1,586,422 |
| Recife, Brazil | 1,249,821 |
| Rio de Janeiro, Brazil | 4,857,716 |
| Riverside–San Bernardino, California | 1,385,400 |
| Rochester, New York | 969,800 |
| Rome, Italy | 2,897,505 |
| Rostov-on-Don, Sov. Un. | 935,000 |
| Rotterdam, Netherlands | 1,019,924 |
| Sacramento, California | 951,000 |
| Saigon, Vietnam | 1,825,297 |
| St. Louis, Mo.–Ill. | 2,385,900 |
| Salvador, Brazil | 1,237,393 |
| Samsun, Turkey | 904,774 |
| San Antonio, Texas | 1,037,800 |
| San Diego, California | 1,743,600 |
| San Francisco, Calif. | 3,183,800 |
| San Jose, California | 1,232,200 |
| San Juan, Puerto Rico | 1,162,900 |
| Santiago, Chile | 3,691,548 |
| São Paulo, Brazil | 7,198,608 |
| Sapporo, Japan | 1,307,686 |
| Seattle–Everett, Wash. | 1,467,600 |
| Seoul, South Korea | 7,500,000 |
| Shanghai, China | 10,820,000 |
| Shenyang, China | 2,411,000 |
| Sian, China | 1,310,000 |
| Singapore, Singapore | 2,334,400 |
| Stockholm, Sweden | 1,364,175 |
| Surabaja, Indonesia | 1,556,255 |
| Sverdlovsk, Soviet Un. | 1,204,000 |
| Sydney, Australia | 3,021,982 |
| Taegu, South Korea | 1,309,131 |
| Taipei, Taiwan | 1,769,568 |
| Taiyuan, China | 1,020,000 |
| Tampa–St. Petersburg, Fla. | 1,396,300 |
| Tashkent, Soviet Union | 1,732,000 |
| Tbilisi, Soviet Union | 1,052,000 |
| Teheran, Iran | 4,496,159 |
| Tel Aviv–Yato, Israel | 1,219,900 |
| Tientsin, China | 4,280,000 |
| Tokyo, Japan | 11,695,150 |
| Torino, Italy | 1,181,567 |
| Toronto, Canada | 2,741,000 |
| Tsingtao, China | 1,121,000 |
| Turin, Italy | 1,190,621 |
| Ufa, Soviet Union | 962,000 |
| Vancouver, Canada | 1,137,000 |
| Vienna, Austria | 1,592,800 |
| Volgograd, Soviet Union | 943,000 |
| Warsaw, Poland | 2,080,200 |
| Washington, D.C. | 3,016,800 |
| Wuhan, China | 2,146,000 |
| Yokohama, Japan | 2,694,569 |

## LARGEST U.S. CITIES

Source: U.S. Census Bureau estimates for July 1, 1978, unless otherwise indicated.

New population estimates of the largest U.S. cities released by the U.S. Census Bureau in 1980 showed that three cities had topped the 100,000 mark for the first time: Eugene, Oreg.; Fullerton, Calif.; and Sterling Heights, Mich.

At the same time, three other cities had fallen below 100,000: Cambridge, Mass.; Roanoke, Va.; and Canton, Ohio.

| CITY AND STATE | POPULATION | CITY AND STATE | POPULATION | CITY AND STATE | POPULATION |
|---|---|---|---|---|---|
| Abilene, Texas | 96,573 | Garden Grove, Calif. | 121,155 | Pasadena, Texas | 104,385 |
| Akron, Ohio | 239,229 | Garland, Texas | 131,263 | Paterson, N.J. | 145,426 |
| Albany, N.Y. | 105,688 | Gary, Ind. | 156,056 | Peoria, Ill. | 122,981 |
| Albuquerque, N. Mex. | 295,150 | Glendale, Calif. | 132,235 | Philadelphia, Pa. | 1,754,829 |
| Alexandria, Va. | 104,085 | Grand Rapids, Mich. | 183,917 | Phoenix, Ariz. | 681,355 |
| Allentown, Pa. | 102,077 | Green Bay, Wis. | 91,347 | Pittsburgh, Pa. | 432,723 |
| Amarillo, Texas | 143,665 | Greensboro, N.C. | 163,493 | Ponce, Puerto Rico | 198,600 |
| Anaheim, Calif. | 207,007 | Hammond, Ind. | 101,076 | Portland, Oreg. | 364,735 |
| Anchorage, Alaska | 180,255 | Hampton, Va. | 125,116 | Portsmouth, Va. | 108,297 |
| Ann Arbor, Mich. | 105,213 | Hartford, Conn. | 127,053 | Providence, R.I. | 157,222 |
| Arlington, Texas | 132,932 | Hayward, Calif. | 95,802 | Pueblo, Colo. | 102,356 |
| Atlanta, Ga. | 405,437 | Hialeah, Fla. | 125,365 | Racine, Wis. | 92,718 |
| Aurora, Colo. | 141,548 | Hollywood, Fla. | 114,943 | Raleigh, N.C. | 138,410 |
| Austin, Texas | 319,194 | Honolulu, Hawaii | 324,871[1] | Reno, Nev. | 91,986 |
| Baltimore, Md. | 791,857 | Houston, Texas | 1,572,981 | Richmond, Va. | 219,596 |
| Baton Rouge, La. | 311,053 | Huntington Beach, Calif. | 167,897 | Riverside, Calif. | 157,087 |
| Bayamón, Puerto Rico | 208,600 | Huntsville, Ala. | 143,580 | Roanoke, Va. | 98,074 |
| Beaumont, Texas | 117,764 | Independence, Mo. | 112,544 | Rochester, N.Y. | 252,491 |
| Berkeley, Calif. | 109,898 | Indianapolis, Ind. | 704,045 | Rockford, Ill. | 139,999 |
| Birmingham, Ala. | 280,413 | Inglewood, Calif. | 88,953 | Sacramento, Calif. | 264,219 |
| Boise, Idaho | 114,033 | Irving, Texas | 105,101 | St. Louis, Mo. | 508,496 |
| Boston, Mass. | 597,254 | Jackson, Miss. | 190,791 | St. Paul, Minn. | 263,147 |
| Bridgeport, Conn. | 134,439 | Jacksonville, Fla. | 529,787 | St. Petersburg, Fla. | 230,965 |
| Brockton, Mass. | 94,130 | Jersey City, N.J. | 225,957 | Salem, Ore. | 89,770 |
| Buffalo, N.Y. | 378,617 | Kansas City, Kans. | 164,250 | Salt Lake City, Utah | 164,379 |
| Caguas, Puerto Rico | 117,600 | Kansas City, Mo. | 456,907 | San Antonio, Texas | 798,195 |
| Cambridge, Mass. | 98,187 | Knoxville, Tenn. | 185,236 | San Bernardino, Calif. | 103,982 |
| Canton, Ohio | 96,339 | Lakewood, Colo. | 126,469 | San Diego, Calif. | 816,659 |
| Carolina, Puerto Rico | 163,300 | Lansing, Mich. | 125,229 | San Francisco, Calif. | 649,315 |
| Cedar Rapids, Iowa | 107,071 | Las Vegas, Nev. | 168,932 | San Jose, Calif. | 592,773 |
| Charlotte, N.C. | 299,444 | Lexington, Ky. | 190,686 | San Juan, Puerto Rico | 516,500 |
| Chattanooga, Tenn. | 162,778 | Lincoln, Nebr. | 166,311 | Santa Ana, Calif. | 185,155 |
| Chesapeake, Va. | 113,965 | Little Rock, Ark. | 151,756 | Savannah, Ga. | 135,896 |
| Chicago, Ill. | 3,049,479 | Livonia, Mich. | 105,054 | Scranton, Pa. | 89,890 |
| Cincinnati, Ohio | 399,072 | Long Beach, Calif. | 339,629 | Seattle, Wash. | 485,487 |
| Cleveland, Ohio | 594,529 | Los Angeles, Calif. | 2,787,176 | Shreveport, La. | 201,920 |
| Colorado Springs, Colo. | 211,844 | Louisville, Ky. | 317,503 | South Bend, Ind. | 113,147 |
| Columbia, S.C. | 108,216 | Lubbock, Texas | 168,127 | Spokane, Wash. | 177,019 |
| Columbus, Ga. | 163,837 | Macon, Ga. | 121,122 | Springfield, Mass. | 161,889 |
| Columbus, Ohio | 524,304 | Madison, Wis. | 170,382 | Springfield, Mo. | 138,833 |
| Concord, Calif. | 98,974 | Mayaguez, Puerto Rico | 102,500 | Stamford, Conn. | 104,718 |
| Corpus Christi, Texas | 214,647 | Memphis, Tenn. | 663,769 | Sterling Heights, Mich. | 103,083 |
| Dallas, Texas | 847,420 | Mesa, Ariz. | 117,840 | Stockton, Calif. | 126,526 |
| Davenport, Iowa | 101,478 | Miami, Fla. | 347,862 | Sunnyvale, Calif. | 106,162 |
| Dayton, Ohio | 194,861 | Milwaukee, Wis. | 633,220 | Syracuse, N.Y. | 174,989 |
| Dearborn, Mich. | 91,652 | Minneapolis, Minn. | 353,992 | Tacoma, Wash. | 156,625 |
| Decatur, Ill. | 89,585 | Mobile, Ala. | 207,741 | Tampa, Fla. | 264,325 |
| Denver, Colo. | 474,595 | Modesto, Calif. | 97,538 | Tempe, Ariz. | 99,194 |
| Des Moines, Iowa | 192,526 | Montgomery, Ala. | 158,724 | Toledo, Ohio | 351,686 |
| Detroit, Mich. | 1,257,879 | Nashville, Tenn. | 425,424 | Topeka, Kans. | 122,100 |
| Duluth, Minn. | 93,297 | New Bedford, Mass. | 97,911 | Torrance, Calif. | 128,254 |
| Durham, N.C. | 105,060 | New Haven, Conn. | 120,561 | Trenton, N.J. | 94,772 |
| El Paso, Texas | 400,741 | New Orleans, La. | 556,428 | Tucson, Ariz. | 301,875 |
| Elizabeth, N.J. | 102,669 | New York City, N.Y. | 7,134,542 | Tulsa, Okla. | 328,684 |
| Erie, Pa. | 122,152 | Newark, N.J. | 314,412 | Virginia Beach, Va. | 245,076 |
| Eugene, Oreg. | 102,591 | Newport News, Va. | 144,023 | Waco, Texas | 103,768 |
| Evansville, Ind. | 134,388 | Norfolk, Va. | 280,568 | Warren, Mich. | 167,237 |
| Fall River, Mass. | 97,381 | Oakland, Calif. | 332,247 | Washington, D.C. | 656,000[2] |
| Flint, Mich. | 162,707 | Odessa, Tex. | 90,366 | Waterbury, Conn. | 103,810 |
| Fort Lauderdale, Fla. | 149,408 | Oklahoma City, Okla. | 372,690 | Wichita, Kans. | 267,748 |
| Fort Wayne, Ind. | 181,066 | Omaha, Nebr. | 368,347 | Wichita Falls, Texas | 94,875 |
| Fort Worth, Texas | 367,432 | Orlando, Fla. | 120,181 | Winston-Salem, N.C. | 140,438 |
| Fremont, Calif. | 122,028 | Oxnard, Calif. | 96,303 | Worcester, Mass. | 163,523 |
| Fresno, Calif. | 199,273 | Parma, Ohio | 95,862 | Yonkers, N.Y. | 190,240 |
| Fullerton, Calif. | 100,844 | Pasadena, Calif. | 106,208 | Youngstown, Ohio | 128,538 |

[1] July 1, 1977, estimate.   [2] July 1, 1979, estimate.

# LARGEST U.S. METROPOLITAN AREAS

Source: U.S. Census Bureau estimates for July 1, 1978, except Puerto Rico, which is 1976 estimate.

Among the largest metropolitan areas, those that have grown at the fastest rate since 1970 are the Florida areas of Fort Myers–Cape Coral (74.3), Sarasota (44.9%), Fort Lauderdale–Hollywood (42.2%), West Palm Beach–Boca Raton (39.5%), and Las Vegas, Nev., (37.9%).

| METROPOLITAN AREA | POPULATION | METROPOLITAN AREA | POPULATION | METROPOLITAN AREA | POPULATION |
|---|---|---|---|---|---|
| Akron, Ohio | 657,000 | Hamilton–Middletown, O. | 256,400 | Orlando, Fla. | 609,900 |
| Albany–Schenectady, N.Y. | 792,300 | Harrisburg, Pa. | 429,800 | Oxnard–Ventura–Simi Valley, Calif. | 485,500 |
| Albuquerque, N. Mex. | 408,800 | Hartford–New Britain, Ct. | 1,045,300 | Paterson–Passaic, N.J. | 444,700 |
| Allentown–Bethlehem–Easton, Pa.–N.J. | 625,700 | Honolulu, Hawaii | 719,600 | Pensacola, Fla. | 275,500 |
| Anaheim–Santa Ana–Garden Grove, Calif. | 1,833,000 | Houston, Texas | 2,595,400 | Peoria, Ill. | 360,600 |
| Anchorage, Alaska | 179,800 | Huntington–Ashland, W.Va.–Ky.–Ohio | 299,900 | Philadelphia, Pa.–N.J. | 4,770,400 |
| Ann Arbor, Mich. | 254,800 | Huntsville, Ala. | 292,700 | Phoenix, Ariz. | 1,293,200 |
| Appleton–Oshkosh, Wis. | 290,600 | Indianapolis, Ind. | 1,156,200 | Pittsburgh, Pa. | 2,277,300 |
| Atlanta, Ga. | 1,851,500 | Jackson, Miss. | 298,700 | Pittsfield, Mass. | 472,100 |
| Atlantic City, N.J. | 190,000 | Jacksonville, Fla. | 701,500 | Ponce, Puerto Rico | 260,500 |
| Augusta, Ga.–S.C. | 290,900 | Jersey City, N.J. | 554,000 | Portland, Me. | 233,500 |
| Austin, Texas | 477,900 | Johnson City–Kingsport–Bristol, Tenn.–Va. | 411,300 | Portland, Oreg.–Wash. | 1,140,100 |
| Bakersfield, Calif. | 365,300 | Johnstown, Pa. | 264,900 | Poughkeepsie, N.Y. | 233,300 |
| Baltimore, Md. | 2,145,200 | Kalamazoo, Mich. | 270,300 | Providence–Pawtucket–Warwick, R.I. | 852,800 |
| Baton Rouge, La. | 444,600 | Kansas City, Mo.–Kans. | 1,323,700 | Provo–Orem, Utah | 185,400 |
| Battle Creek, Mich. | 183,600 | Killeen–Temple, Texas | 209,100 | Raleigh–Durham, N.C. | 493,600 |
| Beaumont–Port Arthur–Orange, Texas | 364,300 | Knoxville, Tenn. | 455,700 | Reading, Pa. | 305,500 |
| Binghamton, N.Y.–Pa. | 303,400 | Lakeland–Winter Haven, Fla. | 278,200 | Richmond, Va. | 611,700 |
| Birmingham, Ala. | 818,200 | Lancaster, Pa. | 351,200 | Riverside–San Bernardino, Calif. | 1,385,400 |
| Boston, Mass.–N.H. | 3,887,800 | Lansing, Mich. | 457,700 | Roanoke, Va. | 210,800 |
| Bridgeport–Stamford–Danbury, Conn. | 808,400 | Las Vegas, Nev. | 376,800 | Rochester, N.Y. | 969,800 |
| Buffalo, N.Y. | 1,303,000 | Lexington–Fayette, Ky. | 299,800 | Rockford, Ill. | 269,300 |
| Canton, Ohio | 403,700 | Lima, Ohio | 211,600 | Sacramento, Calif. | 951,000 |
| Charleston, S.C. | 389,000 | Lincoln, Nebr. | 186,200 | Saginaw, Mich. | 227,700 |
| Charleston, W.Va. | 261,000 | Little Rock–North Little Rock, Ark. | 376,400 | St. Louis, Mo.–Ill. | 2,385,900 |
| Charlotte–Gastonia, N.C. | 605,900 | Long Branch–Asbury Park, N.J. | 499,900 | Salem, Oreg. | 225,900 |
| Chattanooga, Tenn.–Ga. | 400,900 | Lorain–Elyria, Ohio | 271,200 | Salinas–Monterey, Calif. | 275,800 |
| Chicago, Ill. | 7,029,600 | Los Angeles–Long Beach | 7,080,900 | Salt Lake City–Ogden, Ut. | 842,500 |
| Cincinnati, Ohio–Ky. | 1,389,100 | Louisville, Ky.–Ind. | 887,300 | San Antonio, Texas | 1,037,800 |
| Cleveland, Ohio | 1,938,900 | Lubbock, Texas | 200,000 | San Diego, Calif. | 1,743,600 |
| Colorado Springs, Colo. | 291,400 | Macon, Ga. | 243,100 | San Francisco–Oakland | 3,183,800 |
| Columbia, S.C. | 380,000 | Madison, Wis. | 319,000 | San Jose, Calif. | 1,232,200 |
| Columbus, Ga.–Ala. | 228,200 | Manchester–Nashua, N.H. | 260,000 | San Juan, Puerto Rico | 1,162,900 |
| Columbus, Ohio | 1,088,900 | McAllen–Pharr–Edinburg, Texas | 235,800 | Santa Barbara, Calif. | 292,000 |
| Corpus Christi, Texas | 302,100 | Melbourne–Titusville–Cocoa, Fla. | 234,400 | Santa Rosa, Calif. | 274,200 |
| Dallas–Fort Worth, Texas | 2,719,900 | Memphis, Tenn.–Ark.–Miss. | 888,800 | Savannah, Ga. | 218,500 |
| Davenport–Rock Island–Moline, Iowa–Ill. | 374,200 | Miami, Fla. | 1,451,200 | Seattle–Everett, Wash. | 1,467,600 |
| Dayton, Ohio | 834,200 | Milwaukee, Wis. | 1,417,200 | Shreveport, La. | 356,200 |
| Daytona Beach, Fla. | 217,900 | Minneapolis–St. Paul, Minn.–Wis. | 2,063,000 | South Bend, Ind. | 280,800 |
| Denver–Boulder, Colo. | 1,504,700 | Mobile, Ala. | 435,300 | Spokane, Wash. | 319,600 |
| Des Moines, Iowa | 334,100 | Modesto, Calif. | 246,100 | Springfield, Ill. | 184,600 |
| Detroit, Mich. | 4,386,400 | Montgomery, Ala. | 258,200 | Springfield, Mo. | 204,800 |
| Duluth–Superior, Minn. | 265,700 | Muskegon, Mich. | 179,800 | Springfield, Ohio | 183,200 |
| El Paso, Texas | 443,400 | Nashville–Davidson, Tenn. | 786,000 | Springfield–Chicopee–Holyoke, Mass.–Conn. | 587,200 |
| Erie, Pa. | 269,400 | Nassau–Suffolk, N.Y. | 2,690,000 | Stockton, Calif. | 313,100 |
| Eugene–Springfield, Oreg. | 257,700 | New Brunswick–Perth Amboy, N.J. | 591,100 | Syracuse, N.Y. | 649,600 |
| Evansville, Ind.–Ky. | 294,800 | New Haven–West Haven–Waterbury, Conn. | 754,600 | Tacoma, Wash. | 436,900 |
| Fayetteville, N.C. | 233,200 | New London–Norwich, Ct. | 244,500 | Tampa–St. Petersburg, Fl. | 1,396,300 |
| Flint, Mich. | 521,300 | New Orleans, La. | 1,141,100 | Toledo, Ohio–Mich. | 775,800 |
| Fort Lauderdale–Hollywood, Fla. | 881,900 | New York City, N.Y.–N.J. | 9,221,800 | Topeka, Kans. | 186,900 |
| Fort Myers, Fla. | 183,400 | Newark, N.J. | 1,951,300 | Trenton, N.J. | 317,200 |
| Fort Smith, Ark.–Okla. | 190,400 | Newport News, Va. | 361,400 | Tucson, Ariz. | 461,700 |
| Fort Wayne, Ind. | 375,700 | Norfolk–Portsmouth–Virginia Beach, Va. | 800,100 | Tulsa, Okla. | 628,500 |
| Fresno, Calif. | 479,000 | Northeast Pennsylvania | 629,200 | Utica–Rome, N.Y. | 325,500 |
| Galveston, Texas | 198,000 | Oklahoma City, Okla. | 789,400 | Vallejo–Napa, Calif. | 301,100 |
| Gary–Hammond–East Chicago, Ind. | 648,400 | Omaha, Nebr.–Iowa | 581,700 | Washington, D.C.–Md.–Va. | 3,016,800 |
| Grand Rapids, Mich. | 585,100 | | | West Palm Beach, Fla. | 486,700 |
| Greensboro–Winston Salem–High Point, N.C. | 779,300 | | | Wheeling, W.Va.–Ohio | 181,100 |
| Greenville, S.C. | 541,100 | | | Wichita, Kans. | 401,900 |
| | | | | Wilmington, Del.–N.J.–Md. | 515,500 |
| | | | | Worcester, Mass. | 645,100 |
| | | | | York, Pa. | 355,700 |
| | | | | Youngstown–Warren, O. | 545,800 |

# U.S. CITIES, ZIP CODES, AND POPULATIONS

Cities and communities with 5,000 or more people and the zip codes for these places are listed on the following pages. Population figures for cities and communities are the most recently issued Census Bureau estimates of July 1, 1978, except for those places noted.

An asterisk (*) after a zip code number indicates the place has more than one code. So you should check a zip code directory for the code for a specific street address.

| PLACE AND ZIP CODE | POP. | PLACE AND ZIP CODE | POP. | PLACE AND ZIP CODE | POP. |
|---|---|---|---|---|---|
| **ALABAMA (Ala. or AL)** | | | | | |
| Adamsville 35005 | 4,713 | Fairhope[2] 36532 | 6,268 | Opelika[2] 36801 | 21,875 |
| Alabaster[3] 35007 | 6,318 | Fayette 35555 | 4,596 | Opp[2] 36467 | 6,701 |
| Albertville[2] 35950 | 11,057 | Florence[2] 35631* | 36,507 | Oxford[2] 36203 | 11,249 |
| Alexander City[2] 35010 | 12,828 | Forestdale[1] 35214 | 6,091 | Ozark[2] 36360 | 14,580 |
| Andalusia[2] 36420 | 9,788 | Fort Payne[2] 35967 | 8,771 | Pelham[3] 35124 | 5,812 |
| Anniston[2] 36201* | 31,264 | Fultondale[2] 35068 | 7,090 | Pell City[2] 35125 | 6,417 |
| Arab[2] 35016 | 5,389 | Gadsden[2] 35901* | 48,693 | Phenix City[2] 36867 | 27,210 |
| Athens[2] 35611 | 15,592 | Gardendale[2] 35071 | 14,091 | Piedmont[2] 36272 | 5,213 |
| Atmore[2] 36502 | 8,735 | Greenville[2] 36037 | 7,540 | Pleasant Grove[2] 35127 | 6,168 |
| Attalla[2] 35954 | 7,223 | Guntersville[2] 35976 | 7,396 | Prattville[2] 36067 | 17,607 |
| Auburn[2] 36830 | 25,180 | Hartselle[2] 35640 | 8,698 | Prichard[2] 36610 | 40,265 |
| Bay Minette[2] 36507 | 7,080 | Homewood[2] 35209 | 22,445 | Rainbow City[2] 35901 | 6,023 |
| Bessemer[2] 35020 | 31,294 | Hueytown[2] 35020 | 12,745 | Roanoke[2] 36274 | 5,372 |
| Birmingham[2] 35203* | 280,413 | Huntsville[2] 35804* | 143,580 | Russellville[2] 35653 | 7,790 |
| Bluff Park[1] 35226 | 12,431 | Irondale[2] 35210 | 5,460 | Saraland[2] 36571 | 10,114 |
| Boaz[2] 35957 | 6,216 | Jackson[2] 36545 | 6,401 | Scottsboro[2] 35768 | 15,033 |
| Brewton[2] 36426 | 6,895 | Jacksonville[2] 36265 | 8,790 | Selma[2] 36701 | 24,278 |
| Center Point[1] 35215 | 15,675 | Jasper[2] 35501 | 12,256 | Sheffield[2] 35660 | 11,193 |
| Chickasaw[2] 36611 | 7,741 | Lanett[2] 36863 | 6,924 | Sylacauga[2] 35150 | 12,283 |
| Childersburg[2] 35044 | 5,162 | Leeds[2] 35094 | 9,235 | Talladega[2] 35160 | 18,271 |
| Clanton[2] 35045 | 6,643 | Midfield[2] 35228 | 6,523 | Tallassee[2] 36078 | 4,799 |
| Cullman[2] 35055 | 15,601 | Mobile[2] 36601* | 207,741 | Tarrant[2] 35217 | 7,683 |
| Decatur[2] 35602* | 40,601 | Monroeville[2] 36460 | 5,715 | Troy[2] 36081 | 12,248 |
| Demopolis[2] 36732 | 7,699 | Montgomery[2] 36116* | 158,724 | Tuscaloosa[2] 35403* | 69,263 |
| Dothan[2] 36303* | 46,868 | Mountain Brook[2] 35223 | 21,230 | Tuscumbia[2] 35674 | 8,485 |
| Enterprise[2] 36330 | 16,670 | Muscle Shoals[2] 35660 | 8,275 | Tuskegee[2] 36083 | 12,437 |
| Eufaula[2] 36027 | 10,890 | Northport[2] 35476 | 15,353 | Vestavia Hills[2] 35216 | 16,878 |
| Fairfield[2] 35064 | 12,402 | Oneonta 35121 | 4,737 | Wetumpka 36092 | 4,729 |
| | | | | | |
| **ALASKA (Alas. or AK)** | | | | | |
| Anchorage[2] 99502* | 180,255 | Fairbanks[2] 99701 | 31,994 | Juneau[2] 99801 | 19,214 |
| College 99701 | 4,511 | Fort Richardson[1] 99505 | 10,751 | Ketchikan[2] 99901 | 7,500 |
| Eielson AFB[1] 99702 | 6,149 | Fort Wainright[1] 99703 | 9,097 | Sitka[2] 99835 | 7,812 |
| | | | | | |
| **ARIZONA (Ariz. or AZ)** | | | | | |
| Ajo[4] 85321 | 6,385 | Glendale[2] 85301* | 78,188 | Prescott[2] 86301 | 18,446 |
| Apache Junction[2] 85220 | 9,606 | Globe[2] 85501 | 6,237 | Safford[2] 85546 | 6,760 |
| Avondale[2] 85323 | 6,512 | Holbrook[2] 86025 | 5,270 | Scottsdale[2] 85251* | 82,297 |
| Bisbee[2] 85603 | 10,325 | Kingman[2] 86401 | 8,383 | Sierra Vista[2] 85635 | 25,347 |
| Casa Grande[2] 85222 | 13,713 | Lake Havasu[2] 86403 | 11,972 | South Tucson[2] 85725 | 6,425 |
| Chandler[2] 85224 | 21,453 | Luke[1] 85301 | 5,047 | Sun City[1] 85351* | 13,670 |
| Clifton[2] 85533 | 5,318 | Mesa[2] 85201* | 117,840 | Superior[2] 85273 | 6,182 |
| Coolidge[2] 85228 | 6,587 | Nogales[2] 85621 | 12,526 | Tempe[2] 85282* | 99,194 |
| Douglas[2] 85607 | 13,670 | Page[2] 86040 | 4,914 | Tucson[2] 85726* | 301,875 |
| Eloy[2] 85231 | 6,193 | Paradise Valley[2] 85253 | 10,969 | West Yuma[1] 85364 | 5,552 |
| Flagstaff[2] 86001 | 32,742 | Peoria[2] 85345 | 10,184 | Winslow[2] 86047 | 7,517 |
| Fort Huachuca[1] 85613 | 6,659 | Phoenix[2] 85026* | 681,355 | Yuma[2] 85364 | 32,638 |
| | | | | | |
| **ARKANSAS (Ark. or AR)** | | | | | |
| Arkadelphia[2] 71923 | 9,761 | Fayetteville[2] 72701 | 35,349 | Malvern[2] 72104 | 10,566 |
| Batesville[2] 72501 | 8,269 | Fordyce[2] 71742 | 5,035 | Marianna[2] 72360 | 5,704 |
| Benton[2] 72015 | 18,172 | Forrest City[2] 72335 | 12,692 | McGehee[2] 71654 | 5,771 |
| Bentonville[3] 72712 | 7,832 | Fort Smith[5] 72901* | 68,432 | Monticello[2] 71655 | 7,324 |
| Blytheville[5] 72315 | 24,247 | Harrison[2] 72601 | 9,368 | Morrilton[2] 72110 | 6,462 |
| Brinkley[2] 72021 | 5,090 | Helena[2] 72342 | 8,789 | Mountain Home[2] 72653 | 6,839 |
| Camden[2] 71701 | 15,372 | Hope[2] 71801 | 9,260 | Newport[2] 72112 | 7,634 |
| Clarksville[2] 72830 | 5,313 | Hot Springs[2] 71901 | 40,603 | N. Little Rock[4] 72114* | 62,823 |
| Conway[2] 72032 | 20,109 | Jacksonville[2] 72076 | 25,546 | Osceola[2] 72370 | 8,293 |
| Crossett[2] 71635 | 6,908 | Jonesboro[2] 72401 | 31,076 | Paragould[2] 72450 | 15,199 |
| Dumas[2] 71639 | 5,241 | Little Rock[2] 72201* | 151,756 | Pine Bluff[2] 71601* | 55,857 |
| El Dorado[2] 71730 | 24,574 | Magnolia[2] 71753 | 11,656 | Pocahontas[2] 72455 | 5,845 |

[1] 1970 Census.  [2] Census Bureau estimate July 1, 1978.  [3] 1978 Special Census.  [4] 1976 estimate.

| PLACE AND ZIP CODE | | POP. |
|---|---|---|
| **ARKANSAS** *(continued)* | | |
| Rogers [2] | 72756 | 16,800 |
| Russellville [2] | 72801 | 14,753 |
| Searcy [2] | 72143 | 11,221 |
| Sherwood [3] | 72116 | 9,302 |
| **CALIFORNIA** (Calif., Cal., or CA) | | |
| Alameda [2] | 94501 | 74,348 |
| Alamo–Danville [1] | 94507 | 14,059 |
| Albany [2] | 94706 | 15,009 |
| Alhambra [2] | 91802* | 60,363 |
| Alondra Park [1] | 90249 | 12,193 |
| Altadena [1] | 91001 | 42,415 |
| Alum Rock [1] | 95116 | 18,355 |
| Anaheim [2] | 92803* | 207,007 |
| Anderson [2] | 96007 | 6,861 |
| Antioch [2] | 94509 | 37,760 |
| Apple Valley [1] | 92307 | 6,702 |
| Aptos [2] | 95003 | 8,704 |
| Arcadia [2] | 91006 | 46,587 |
| Arcata [2] | 95521 | 12,615 |
| Arden–Arcade [1] | 95825 | 82,492 |
| Arroyo Grande [2] | 93420 | 10,384 |
| Artesia [2] | 90701 | 14,679 |
| Arvin [2] | 93203 | 6,141 |
| Ashland [1] | 94577 | 14,810 |
| Atascadero [1] | 93422 | 12,611 |
| Atherton [2] | 94025 | 7,824 |
| Atwater [2] | 95301 | 15,513 |
| Auburn [2] | 95603 | 7,301 |
| Avocado Heights [1] | 91745 | 9,810 |
| Azusa [2] | 91702 | 25,401 |
| Bakersfield [2] | 93302* | 86,800 |
| Baldwin Park [2] | 91706 | 45,154 |
| Banning [2] | 92220 | 12,515 |
| Barstow [2] | 92311 | 17,020 |
| Beale East [1] | 95903 | 7,029 |
| Beaumont [2] | 92223 | 6,624 |
| Bell [2] | 90201 | 22,385 |
| Bell Gardens [2] | 90201 | 31,496 |
| Bellflower [2] | 90706 | 50,510 |
| Belmont [2] | 94002 | 25,929 |
| Benicia [2] | 94510 | 12,957 |
| Berkeley [2] | 94704* | 109,898 |
| Beverly Hills [2] | 90213* | 33,197 |
| Big Bear [1] | 92314 | 5,268 |
| Bloomington [1] | 92316 | 11,957 |
| Blythe [2] | 92225 | 7,301 |
| Brawley [2] | 92227 | 14,299 |
| Brea [2] | 92621 | 26,651 |
| Broderick–Bryte [1] | 95605 | 12,782 |
| Buena Park [2] | 90622 | 63,391 |
| Burbank [2] | 91505* | 83,856 |
| Burlingame [2] | 94010 | 27,466 |
| Calexico [2] | 92231 | 13,890 |
| Calwa [1] | 93725 | 5,191 |
| Camarillo [2] | 93010 | 30,845 |
| Camarillo Hts. [1] | 93010 | 5,892 |
| Cambrian Park [1] | 95124 | 5,316 |
| Campbell [2] | 95008 | 25,144 |
| Capitola [2] | 95010 | 8,577 |
| Cardiff–by–the–Sea [1] | 92007 | 5,724 |
| Carlsbad [2] | 92008 | 29,985 |
| Carmel–by–the–Sea [2] | 93921 | 4,780 |
| Carmichael [1] | 95608 | 37,625 |
| Carpinteria [2] | 93013 | 10,048 |
| Carson [2] | 90745 | 79,934 |
| Castro Valley [1] | 94546 | 44,760 |
| Ceres [2] | 95307 | 10,880 |
| Cerritos [2] | 90807 | 50,302 |


| PLACE AND ZIP CODE | | POP. |
|---|---|---|
| Siloam Springs [2] | 72761 | 7,605 |
| Springdale [2] | 72764 | 21,039 |
| Stuttgart [2] | 72160 | 10,399 |
| Texarkana [2] | 75501 | 19,822 |
| Trumann [2] | 72472 | 6,776 |
| Cherryland [1] | 94541 | 9,969 |
| Chico [2] | 95926 | 25,619 |
| Chico North [1] | — | 6,656 |
| China Lake [1] | 93555 | 11,105 |
| Chino [2] | 91710 | 37,106 |
| Chula Vista [2] | 92010 | 81,192 |
| Citrus Heights [1] | 95610 | 21,760 |
| Claremont [2] | 91711 | 27,843 |
| Clovis [2] | 93612 | 28,451 |
| Coachella [2] | 92236 | 8,668 |
| Coalinga [1] | 93210 | 6,253 |
| Colton [2] | 92324 | 19,215 |
| Commerce [2] | 90040 | 10,006 |
| Compton [2] | 90220* | 74,193 |
| Concord [2] | 94520* | 98,974 |
| Corcoran [2] | 93212 | 5,854 |
| Corona [2] | 91720 | 36,560 |
| Coronado [2] | 92118 | 20,969 |
| Corte Madera [2] | 94925 | 7,934 |
| Costa Mesa [2] | 92626* | 79,191 |
| Covina [2] | 91722* | 32,716 |
| Cucamonga [1] | 91730 | 5,796 |
| Cudahy [2] | 90201 | 16,612 |
| Culver City [2] | 90230 | 37,618 |
| Cypress [2] | 90630 | 40,976 |
| Daly City [2] | 94015* | 73,838 |
| Davis [2] | 95616 | 35,263 |
| Del Aire [1] | 90250 | 11,930 |
| Del Mar [2] | 92014 | 5,262 |
| Delano [2] | 93215 | 15,393 |
| Diamond Bar [1] | 91765 | 12,234 |
| Dinuba [2] | 93618 | 9,631 |
| Dixon [2] | 95620 | 6,284 |
| Dominguez [1] | 90747 | 5,980 |
| Downey [2] | 90241* | 85,158 |
| Duarte [2] | 91010 | 14,492 |
| Dublin [1] | 94566 | 13,641 |
| East Compton [1] | 90220 | 5,853 |
| East La Mirada [1] | 90638 | 12,339 |
| East Los Angeles [1] | 90022 | 105,033 |
| East Palo Alto [1] | 94303 | 17,897 |
| Edwards [1] | 93523 | 10,331 |
| El Cajon [2] | 92020* | 69,741 |
| El Centro [2] | 92243 | 23,856 |
| El Cerrito [2] | 94530 | 22,396 |
| El Encanto Hts. [1] | 93017 | 6,225 |
| El Monte [2] | 91734* | 66,597 |
| El Paso de Robles [2] | 93446 | 8,473 |
| El Rio [1] | — | 6,173 |
| El Segundo [2] | 90245 | 14,841 |
| El Toro [1] | 92630 | 8,654 |
| El Toro Station [1] | 92709 | 6,970 |
| Encinitas [1] | 92024 | 5,375 |
| Enterprise [1] | 96001 | 11,486 |
| Escondido [2] | 92025 | 59,273 |
| Eureka [2] | 95501 | 24,628 |
| Exeter [2] | 93221 | 5,386 |
| Fair Oaks [1] | 95628 | 11,256 |
| Fairfax [1] | 94930 | 7,659 |
| Fairfield [2] | 94533 | 54,605 |
| Fallbrook [1] | 92028 | 6,945 |
| Fillmore [2] | 93015 | 8,684 |
| Florence–Graham [1] | 90001 | 42,895 |


| PLACE AND ZIP CODE | | POP. |
|---|---|---|
| Van Buren [2] | 72956 | 10,796 |
| Warren [3] | 71671 | 7,031 |
| West Helena [2] | 72390 | 10,458 |
| West Memphis [2] | 72301 | 27,128 |
| Wynne [2] | 72396 | 7,605 |
| Florin [1] | 95828 | 9,646 |
| Folsom [2] | 95630 | 9,956 |
| Fontana [2] | 92335 | 28,103 |
| Fort Bragg [2] | 95437 | 5,329 |
| Fortuna [2] | 95540 | 7,974 |
| Foster City [2] | 94404 | 22,986 |
| Fountain Valley [2] | 92708 | 55,367 |
| Freedom [1] | 95019 | 5,563 |
| Fremont [2] | 94538* | 122,028 |
| Fresno [2] | 93706* | 199,273 |
| Fullerton [2] | 92631* | 100,844 |
| Galt [2] | 95632 | 5,208 |
| Garden Grove [2] | 92640* | 122,749 |
| Gardena [2] | 90247* | 44,514 |
| George [1] | 92392 | 7,404 |
| Gilroy [2] | 95020 | 18,790 |
| Glen Avon [1] | — | 5,759 |
| Glendale [2] | 91209* | 132,235 |
| Glendora [2] | 91740 | 39,855 |
| Grand Terrace [2] | 92324 | 6,785 |
| Grass Valley [2] | 95945 | 6,689 |
| Grossmont–Mount Heliz [1] | 92041 | 8,723 |
| Grover City [2] | 93433 | 8,003 |
| Hacienda Hts. [1] | 91745 | 35,969 |
| Half Moon Bay [2] | 94019 | 7,136 |
| Hanford [2] | 93230 | 19,130 |
| Hawaiian Gardens [2] | 90716 | 9,473 |
| Hawthorne [2] | 90250 | 53,798 |
| Hayward [2] | 94544* | 95,802 |
| Healdsburg [2] | 95448 | 6,726 |
| Hemet [2] | 92343 | 20,538 |
| Hemet East [1] | 92343 | 8,598 |
| Hermosa Beach [2] | 90254 | 18,674 |
| Highland [1] | 92346 | 12,669 |
| Hillsborough [2] | 94010 | 10,171 |
| Hollister [2] | 95023 | 9,620 |
| Huntington Bch. [2] | 92647* | 167,897 |
| Huntington Park [2] | 90255 | 38,546 |
| Imperial Beach [2] | 92032 | 20,197 |
| Indio [2] | 92201 | 19,351 |
| Inglewood [2] | 90311* | 88,953 |
| Irvine [2] | 92714 | 48,556 |
| Isla Vista [2] | 93017 | 13,441 |
| Kensington [1] | 94707 | 5,823 |
| La Canada–Flintridge [1] | 91011 | 19,551 |
| La Crescenta–Montrose [1] | 91214 | 19,594 |
| La Habra [2] | 90631 | 44,075 |
| La Mesa [2] | 92041 | 50,006 |
| La Mirada [2] | 90638 | 44,890 |
| La Palma [2] | 90624 | 15,246 |
| La Puente [2] | 91747* | 30,432 |
| La Verne [2] | 91750 | 20,551 |
| Ladera Heights [1] | 90045 | 6,535 |
| Lafayette [2] | 94549 | 19,572 |
| Laguna Beach [2] | 92651* | 18,188 |
| Laguna Hills [1] | 92653 | 13,676 |
| Lakeside [1] | 92040 | 11,991 |
| Lakewood [2] | 90714 | 79,520 |
| Lamont [1] | 93241 | 7,007 |
| Lancaster [2] | 93534 | 41,929 |

[1] 1970 Census.  [2] Census Bureau estimate: 1978.  [3] 1978 Special Census.

## CALIFORNIA (continued)

| PLACE AND ZIP CODE | | POP. |
|---|---|---|
| Larkspur [2] | 94939 | 12,552 |
| Lawndale [2] | 90260 | 23,389 |
| Lemon Grove [2] | 92045 | 21,086 |
| Lemoore [2] | 93245 | 8,123 |
| Lennox [1] | 90304 | 16,121 |
| Lincoln Village [1] | 95207 | 6,112 |
| Linda [1] | 95901 | 7,731 |
| Lindsay [2] | 93247 | 6,745 |
| Livermore [1] | 94550 | 49,688 |
| Lodi [2] | 95240 | 32,464 |
| Loma Linda [1] | 92354 | 9,129 |
| Lomita [2] | 90717 | 19,409 |
| Lompoc [2] | 93436 | 25,830 |
| Long Beach [2] | 90801* | 339,629 |
| Los Alamitos [2] | 90720 | 11,347 |
| Los Altos [2] | 94022 | 27,366 |
| Los Altos Hills [2] | 94022 | 7,364 |
| Los Angeles [2] | 90052* | 2,787,176 |
| Los Banos [2] | 93635 | 9,347 |
| Los Gatos [2] | 95030 | 25,452 |
| Lynwood [2] | 90262 | 39,819 |
| Madera [2] | 93637 | 19,293 |
| Manhattan Beach [2] | 90266 | 31,569 |
| Manteca [2] | 95336 | 20,762 |
| Marina [2] | 93933 | 21,070 |
| Martinez [2] | 94553 | 20,975 |
| Marysville [2] | 95901 | 9,760 |
| Mather [1] | 95655 | 7,027 |
| Maywood [2] | 90270 | 17,828 |
| Meiners Oaks-Miramonte [1] | 93641 | 7,025 |
| Menlo Park [2] | 94025 | 26,100 |
| Merced [2] | 95340 | 33,602 |
| Mill Valley [2] | 94941 | 13,486 |
| Millbrae [2] | 94030 | 20,187 |
| Milpitas [2] | 95035 | 33,885 |
| Mira Loma [1] | 91752 | 8,482 |
| Mission Viejo [1] | 92675 | 11,933 |
| Modesto [2] | 95350* | 97,538 |
| Monrovia [2] | 91016 | 29,361 |
| Montclair [2] | 91763 | 20,899 |
| Montebello [2] | 90640 | 49,271 |
| Monterey [2] | 93940* | 27,626 |
| Monterey Park [2] | 91754 | 51,125 |
| Moraga [2] | 94556 | 15,148 |
| Morgan Hill [2] | 95037 | 15,272 |
| Morro Bay [2] | 93442 | 8,759 |
| Mountain View [2] | 94042 | 55,727 |
| Muscoy [1] | 92405 | 7,091 |
| Napa [2] | 94558 | 49,398 |
| National City [2] | 92050 | 46,936 |
| Newark [2] | 94560 | 31,176 |
| Newhall [1] | 91321 | 9,651 |
| Newport Beach [2] | 92660* | 67,113 |
| Norco [2] | 91760 | 19,207 |
| North Fair Oaks [1] | 94025 | 9,740 |
| North Highlands [1] | 95660 | 31,854 |
| North Island [1] | — | 6,002 |
| Norwalk [2] | 90650 | 83,626 |
| Novato [2] | 94947 | 39,195 |
| Oakdale [2] | 95361 | 8,375 |
| Oakland [2] | 94615* | 332,247 |
| Oceanside [2] | 92054* | 68,626 |
| Oildale [1] | 93308 | 20,879 |
| Ojai [2] | 93023 | 6,253 |
| Olivehurst [1] | 95961 | 8,100 |
| Ontario [2] | 91761* | 72,534 |
| Opal Cliffs [1] | 95060 | 5,425 |
| Orange [2] | 92667 | 86,359 |
| Orangevale [1] | 95662 | 16,493 |
| Orcutt [1] | 93454 | 8,500 |
| Orinda Village [1] | 94563 | 6,790 |
| Oroville [2] | 95965* | 7,961 |
| Otay–Castle Park [1] | 92010 | 15,445 |
| Oxnard [2] | 93030 | 96,303 |
| Pacific Grove [2] | 93950 | 16,431 |
| Pacifica [2] | 94044 | 37,242 |
| Palm Desert [2] | 92260 | 11,124 |
| Palm Springs [2] | 92262 | 32,627 |
| Palmdale [2] | 93550 | 11,116 |
| Palo Alto [2] | 94303* | 54,293 |
| Palos Verdes Est. [2] | 90274 | 14,333 |
| Palos Verdes Pen. [1] | 90274 | 38,918 |
| Paradise [1] | 95969 | 14,539 |
| Paramount [2] | 90723 | 31,026 |
| Parkway–Sacramento South [1] | 95823 | 28,574 |
| Pasadena [2] | 91109* | 106,208 |
| Pendleton North [1] | 92055 | 11,803 |
| Pendleton South [1] | 92055 | 13,692 |
| Perris [2] | 92370 | 6,251 |
| Petaluma [2] | 94952 | 32,394 |
| Pico Rivera [2] | 90660 | 50,549 |
| Piedmont [2] | 94611 | 10,619 |
| Pinole [2] | 94564 | 15,164 |
| Pismo Beach [2] | 93449 | 5,035 |
| Pittsburg [2] | 94565 | 27,859 |
| Placentia [2] | 92670 | 33,876 |
| Placerville [2] | 95667 | 6,918 |
| Pleasant Hill [2] | 94523 | 24,724 |
| Pleasanton [2] | 94566 | 35,134 |
| Pomona [2] | 91766 | 85,237 |
| Port Hueneme [2] | 93041 | 18,474 |
| Porterville [2] | 93257 | 16,920 |
| Porterville West [1] | 93257 | 6,200 |
| Portola Valley [2] | 94025 | 5,152 |
| Poway [1] | 92064 | 9,422 |
| Rancho Cordova [1] | 95670 | 30,451 |
| Rancho Cucamonga [1] | — | 46,968 |
| Rancho Mirage [2] | 92270 | 6,459 |
| Rancho Palos Verdes [1] | 90274 | 38,175 |
| Rancho Rinconado [1] | 95014 | 5,149 |
| Red Bluff [2] | 96080 | 9,082 |
| Redding [2] | 96001 | 44,121 |
| Redlands [2] | 92373 | 36,566 |
| Redondo Beach [2] | 90277* | 62,469 |
| Redwood City [2] | 94064* | 54,858 |
| Reedley [2] | 93654 | 10,106 |
| Rialto [2] | 92376 | 32,104 |
| Richmond [2] | 94802* | 69,358 |
| Ridgecrest [2] | 93555 | 15,220 |
| Rio Linda [1] | 95673 | 7,524 |
| Riverbank [1] | 95367 | 5,112 |
| Riverside [2] | 92507* | 157,087 |
| Rocklin [2] | 95677 | 5,713 |
| Rodeo [1] | 94572 | 5,356 |
| Rohnert Park [2] | 94928 | 19,429 |
| Rolling Hills Est. [2] | 90274 | 7,604 |
| Rosemead [2] | 91770 | 40,165 |
| Roseville [2] | 95678 | 22,752 |
| Rossmoor [1] | 90720 | 12,922 |
| Rowland Heights [1] | 91748 | 16,881 |
| Rubidoux [1] | 92509 | 13,969 |
| Sacramento [2] | 95813* | 264,219 |
| Salinas [2] | 93901* | 78,999 |
| San Anselmo [2] | 94960 | 12,616 |
| San Bernardino [2] | 92403* | 103,982 |
| San Bruno [2] | 94066 | 37,894 |
| San Carlos [2] | 94070 | 27,091 |
| San Clemente [2] | 92672 | 25,813 |
| San Diego [2] | 92199* | 816,659 |
| San Dimas [2] | 91773 | 20,251 |
| San Fernando [2] | 91341* | 15,103 |
| San Francisco [2] | 94101* | 649,315 |
| San Gabriel [2] | 91776 | 28,902 |
| San Jacinto [2] | 92383 | 7,313 |
| San Jose [2] | 95101* | 592,773 |
| San Juan Capistrano [2] | 92690* | 17,254 |
| San Leandro [2] | 94577* | 67,829 |
| San Lorenzo [1] | 94580 | 24,633 |
| San Luis Obispo [2] | 93401 | 33,901 |
| San Marcos [2] | 92069 | 14,714 |
| San Marino [2] | 91108 | 13,465 |
| San Mateo [2] | 94402* | 79,150 |
| San Pablo [2] | 94806 | 18,507 |
| San Rafael [2] | 94901* | 45,153 |
| Sanger [2] | 93657 | 11,080 |
| Santa Ana [2] | 92711* | 185,155 |
| Santa Barbara [2] | 93102* | 73,837 |
| Santa Clara [2] | 95050* | 84,217 |
| Santa Cruz [2] | 95060* | 39,160 |
| Santa Fe Springs [2] | 90670 | 15,380 |
| Santa Maria [2] | 93454 | 36,269 |
| Santa Maria S. [1] | 93454 | 7,129 |
| Santa Monica [2] | 90406* | 88,639 |
| Santa Paula [2] | 93060 | 19,186 |
| Santa Rosa [2] | 95402* | 74,419 |
| Santee [1] | 92071 | 21,107 |
| Saratoga [2] | 95070 | 29,905 |
| Sausalito [2] | 94965 | 6,530 |
| Scotts Valley [2] | 95066 | 6,615 |
| Seal Beach [2] | 90740 | 26,927 |
| Seaside [2] | 93955 | 33,067 |
| Selma [2] | 93662 | 9,162 |
| Shafter [2] | 93263 | 6,350 |
| Sierra Madre [2] | 91024 | 11,767 |
| Signal Hill [2] | 90806 | 5,909 |
| Simi Valley [2] | 93065* | 75,245 |
| Solana Beach [1] | 92075 | 5,023 |
| Soledad [2] | 93960 | 5,719 |
| Sonoma [2] | 95476 | 5,796 |
| Soquel [1] | 95073 | 5,795 |
| South El Monte [2] | 91733 | 14,053 |
| South Gate [2] | 90280 | 60,171 |
| S. Lake Tahoe [2] | 95705 | 21,191 |
| South Modesto [1] | 95350 | 7,889 |
| South Pasadena [1] | 91030 | 22,992 |
| S. San Francisco [2] | 94080 | 49,142 |
| S. San Gabriel [1] | 91770 | 5,051 |
| South San Jose Hl. [1] | 91744 | 12,386 |
| South Whittier [1] | 90605 | 46,641 |
| South Yuba [1] | 95991 | 5,352 |
| Spring Valley [1] | 92077 | 29,742 |
| Stanford [1] | 94305 | 8,691 |
| Stanton [2] | 90680 | 23,486 |
| Stockton [2] | 95204* | 125,526 |
| Suisun City [2] | 94585 | 7,576 |
| Sun City [1] | 92381 | 5,519 |
| Sunnymead [1] | 92388 | 6,708 |
| Sunnyvale [2] | 94086* | 106,162 |
| Susanville [2] | 96130 | 7,192 |
| Temple City [2] | 91780 | 29,682 |
| Thousand Oaks [2] | 91360* | 66,411 |
| Tiburon [2] | 94920 | 7,172 |
| Torrance [2] | 90510* | 128,254 |
| Tracy [2] | 95376 | 16,306 |
| Tulare [2] | 93274 | 20,128 |
| Turlock [2] | 95380 | 21,561 |

[1] 1970 census.   [2] Census Bureau estimate July 1, 1978.   [3] 1978 Special Census.

## CALIFORNIA (continued)

| PLACE AND ZIP CODE | | POP. | PLACE AND ZIP CODE | | POP. | PLACE AND ZIP CODE | | POP. |
|---|---|---|---|---|---|---|---|---|
| Tustin [2] | 92680 | 34,612 | Villa Park [2] | 92667 | 7,417 | West Pittsburg [1] | 94565 | 5,969 |
| Tustin–Foothills [1] | 92705 | 26,598 | Visalia [2] | 93277 | 42,717 | W. Puente Valley [1] | 91746 | 20,733 |
| Twentynine Palms [1] | 92277 | 5,667 | Vista [2] | 92083 | 32,932 | W. Sacramento [1] | 95691 | 12,002 |
| Twtyn. Plms. AFB [1] | 92278 | 5,647 | Walnut [2] | 91789 | 10,229 | West Whittier– | | |
| Ukiah [2] | 95482 | 12,451 | Walnut Creek [2] | 94596* | 49,704 |   Los Nietos [1] | 90605 | 20,845 |
| Union City [2] | 94587 | 34,985 | Walnut Creek W. [1] | 94596 | 8,330 | Westminster [2] | 92683 | 70,238 |
| Upland [2] | 91786 | 42,133 | Walnut Park [1] | 90255 | 8,925 | Westmont [1] | 90047 | 29,310 |
| Vacaville [2] | 95688 | 37,686 | Wasco [2] | 93280 | 8,926 | Whittier [2] | 90605* | 69,039 |
| Valinda [1] | 91744 | 18,837 | Watsonville [2] | 95076 | 20,823 | Willowbrook [1] | 90222 | 28,705 |
| Vallejo [2] | 94590 | 71,692 | West Athens [1] | 90044 | 13,286 | Woodland [2] | 95695 | 27,485 |
| Vandenburg [1] | 93437 | 13,193 | West Carson [1] | 90502 | 15,501 | Woodside [2] | 94062 | 5,392 |
| Ventura [2] | 93001* | 68,818 | West Compton [1] | 90247 | 5,748 | Yorba Linda [2] | 92686 | 26,411 |
| Victorville [2] | 92392 | 13,211 | West Covina [2] | 91793 | 73,422 | Yreka City [2] | 96097 | 5,496 |
| View Park–Wind- | | | West Hollywood [1] | 90069 | 34,625 | Yuba City [2] | 95991 | 16,523 |
|   sor Hills [1] | 90043 | 12,268 | West Modesto [1] | 95351 | 6,135 | Yucaipa [1] | 92399 | 19,284 |

## COLORADO (Colo. or CO)

| PLACE AND ZIP CODE | | POP. | PLACE AND ZIP CODE | | POP. | PLACE AND ZIP CODE | | POP. |
|---|---|---|---|---|---|---|---|---|
| Alamosa [2] | 81101 | 8,148 | Edgewater [2] | 80214 | 5,338 | Littleton [2] | 80120* | 33,029 |
| Arvada [2] | 80001 | 83,901 | Englewood [2] | 80110* | 42,529 | Longmont [2] | 80501 | 36,958 |
| Aurora [2] | 80010* | 141,548 | Federal Heights [2] | 80221 | 6,659 | Loveland [2] | 80537 | 30,331 |
| Boulder [2] | 80302* | 76,289 | Fort Collins [2] | 80521* | 61,119 | Monte Vista [2] | 81144 | 4,976 |
| Brighton [2] | 80601 | 11,888 | Fort Morgan [2] | 80701 | 8,873 | Montrose [2] | 81401 | 7,860 |
| Broomfield [2] | 80020 | 23,701 | Fountain [2] | 80817 | 9,040 | North Glenn [2] | 80233 | 37,589 |
| Canon City [2] | 81212 | 13,115 | Golden [2] | 80401 | 14,924 | Pueblo [2] | 81003* | 102,356 |
| Cherry Hill [2] | 80206 | 6,450 | Grand Junction [5] | 81501 | 26,159 | Salida [2] | 81201 | 5,275 |
| Colorado Springs [2] | 80901* | 160,317 | Greeley [2] | 80631 | 50,472 | Sheridan [2] | 81071 | 6,454 |
| Commerce City [2] | 80022 | 15,846 | Gunnison [2] | 81230 | 5,245 | Sterling [2] | 80751 | 11,525 |
| Cortez [2] | 81321 | 6,730 | La Junta [2] | 81050 | 8,303 | Thornton [2] | 80229 | 29,928 |
| Craig [2] | 81625 | 7,323 | Lafayette [2] | 80026 | 5,416 | Trinidad [2] | 81082 | 9,793 |
| Denver [2] | 80202* | 474,595 | Lakewood [2] | 80215 | 126,469 | Westminster [2] | 80030 | 27,105 |
| Durango [2] | 81301 | 12,555 | Lamar [2] | 81052 | 8,015 | Wheat Ridge [2] | 80033 | 33,048 |

## CONNECTICUT (Conn. or CT)

| PLACE AND ZIP CODE | | POP. | PLACE AND ZIP CODE | | POP. | PLACE AND ZIP CODE | | POP. |
|---|---|---|---|---|---|---|---|---|
| Ansonia [2] | 06401 | 19,947 | Granby [3]† | 06035 | 7,564 | Old Saybrook [3]† | 06475 | 8,962 |
| Avon [3]† | 06001 | 9,847 | Greenwich [3]† | 06830 | 60,525 | Orange [3]† | 06477 | 13,949 |
| Berlin [3]† | 06037 | 15,286 | Griswold [3]† | 06351 | 8,332 | Oxford [3]† | 06483 | 6,239 |
| Bethel [3]† | 06801 | 15,136 | Groton [3]† | 06340 | 10,228 | Pawcatuck [4] | 06379 | 5,255 |
| Bloomfield [3]† | 06002 | 19,336 | Guilford [3]† | 06437 | 16,148 | Plainfield [3]† | 06374 | 13,039 |
| Branford [3]† | 06405 | 22,842 | Haddam [3]† | 06438 | 6,271 | Plainville [3]† | 06062 | 16,355 |
| Bridgeport [2] | 06602* | 144,439 | Hamden [3]† | 06514 | 50,195 | Plymouth [3]† | 06782 | 10,575 |
| Bristol [2] | 06010 | 57,334 | Hartford [2] | 06101* | 127,053 | Portland [3]† | 06480 | 8,571 |
| Brookfield [3]† | 06804 | 12,221 | Killingly [3]† | 06239 | 14,159 | Prospect [3]† | 06712 | 6,752 |
| Brooklyn [3]† | 06234 | 5,894 | Ledyard [3]† | 06339 | 18,131 | Putnam [3]† | 06260 | 6,722 |
| Burlington [3]† | 06013 | 5,681 | Litchfield [3]† | 06759 | 7,890 | Redding [3]† | 06875 | 7,288 |
| Canton [3]† | 06019 | 7,798 | Madison [3]† | 06443 | 13,575 | Ridgefield [3]† | 06877 | 21,255 |
| Cheshire [3]† | 06410 | 21,023 | Manchester [3]† | 06040 | 50,119 | Rocky Hill [3]† | 06067 | 13,887 |
| Clinton [3]† | 06413 | 11,130 | Mansfield [3]† | 06250 | 21,656 | Seymour [3]† | 06483 | 14,309 |
| Colchester [3]† | 06415 | 7,573 | Meriden [2] | 06450 | 57,001 | Shelton [2] | 06484 | 31,098 |
| Coventry [3]† | 06238 | 8,607 | Middlebury [3]† | 06762 | 6,089 | Simsbury [3]† | 06070 | 21,161 |
| Cromwell [3]† | 06416 | 9,428 | Middletown [2] | 06457 | 37,285 | Somers [3]† | 06071 | 7,615 |
| Danbury [2] | 06810 | 56,816 | Milford [2] | 06460 | 50,257 | South Windsor [3]† | 06074 | 17,042 |
| Darien [3]† | 06820 | 20,210 | Monroe [3]† | 06468 | 14,214 | Southbury [3]† | 06488 | 12,340 |
| Derby [2] | 06418 | 12,046 | Montville [3]† | 06353 | 16,898 | Southington [3]† | 06489 | 36,994 |
| Durham [3]† | 06422 | 5,333 | Naugatuck [3]† | 06770 | 26,220 | Stafford [3]† | 06075 | 8,966 |
| East Haddam [3]† | 06423 | 5,286 | New Britain [2] | 06050 | 74,192 | Stamford [2] | 06904* | 104,718 |
| East Hampton [3]† | 06424 | 8,330 | New Canaan [3]† | 06840 | 18,536 | Stonington [3]† | 06378 | 16,773 |
| East Hartford [3]† | 06108 | 53,578 | New Fairfield [3]† | 06810 | 10,740 | Storrs [1] | 06268 | 10,691 |
| East Haven [3]† | 06512 | 24,897 | New Haven [2] | 06510* | 120,561 | Stratford [3]† | 06497 | 51,463 |
| East Lyme [3]† | 06333 | 14,373 | New London [2] | 06320 | 27,789 | Suffield [2]† | 06078 | 9,634 |
| East Windsor [3]† | 06028 | 8,800 | New Milford [3]† | 06776 | 18,105 | Thomaston [3]† | 06787 | 6,277 |
| Easton [3]† | 06425 | 5,437 | Newington [3]† | 06111 | 29,478 | Thompson [3]† | 06277 | 8,247 |
| Ellington [3]† | 06029 | 9,174 | Newtown [3]† | 06470 | 19,216 | Tolland [3]† | 06084 | 10,905 |
| Enfield [3]† | 06082 | 46,417 | North Branford [3]† | 06471 | 11,928 | Torrington [3]† | 06790 | 31,320 |
| Essex [3]† | 06426 | 4,965 | North Haven [3]† | 06473 | 23,203 | Trumbull [3]† | 06611 | 34,530 |
| Fairfield [3]† | 06430 | 58,884 | Norwalk [2] | 06856* | 77,114 | Vernon [3]† | 06066 | 29,208 |
| Farmington [3]† | 06032 | 15,297 | Norwich [2] | 06360 | 39,854 | Wallingford [3]† | 06492 | 37,394 |
| Glastonbury [3]† | 06033 | 24,426 | Old Lyme [3]† | 06371 | 6,001 | Waterbury [2] | 06701* | 103,810 |

[1] 1970 Census.   [2] Census Bureau estimate July 1, 1978.   [3] 1977 estimate.   [4] 1976 estimate.
† Town or township (includes rural population).

| PLACE AND ZIP CODE | POP. | PLACE AND ZIP CODE | POP. | PLACE AND ZIP CODE | POP. |
|---|---|---|---|---|---|
| **CONNECTICUT** *(cont.)* | | | | | |
| Waterford [3] † .... 06385 | 18,156 | Wethersfield [3] † .. 06109 | 27,232 | Windsor Locks [3] † 06096 | 13,710 |
| Watertown [3] † .... 06795 | 19,314 | Willimantic [2] ...... 06226 | 14,469 | Winsted [2] ........ 06098 | 8,954 |
| West Hartford [3] † .. 06107 | 65,929 | Wilton [3] † ........ 06897 | 15,219 | Wolcott [3] † ...... 06716 | 13,275 |
| West Haven [2] .... 06516 | 52,078 | Winchester [3] † ... 06094 | 11,390 | Woodbridge [3] † .. 06525 | 8,315 |
| Weston [3] † ...... 06883 | 9,929 | Windham [3] † ...... 06280 | 20,117 | Woodbury [3] † .... 06798 | 6,908 |
| Westport [3] † .... 06880 | 27,680 | Windsor [3] † ...... 06095 | 25,098 | Woodstock [3] † ... 06281 | 5,345 |
| **DELAWARE (Del. or DE)** | | | | | |
| Brookside Park [1] . 19713 | 7,856 | Elsmere [2] ........ 19805 | 8,838 | Seaford [2] ........ 19973 | 5,443 |
| Claymont [1] ...... 19703 | 6,584 | Milford [2] ......... 19963 | 5,623 | Wilmington [2] ..... 19850* | 71,661 |
| Dover [2] ......... 19901 | 23,460 | New Castle [2] ..... 19720 | 4,877 | Wilmington Manor– | |
| Dover AFB [1] ..... 19901 | 8,106 | Newark [2] ........ 19711 | 28,413 | Chelsea–Leedon [1] 19720 | 10,134 |
| **FLORIDA (Fla. or FL)** | | | | | |
| Altamonte Springs [2] 32701 | 20,661 | Gainesville [2] ..... 32601 | 71,590 | Naples [2] ......... 33941* | 15,869 |
| Apopka [2] ........ 32703 | 5,276 | Gifford [1] ......... 32960 | 5,772 | Neptune Beach [2] . 32233 | 4,949 |
| Arcadia [2] ........ 33821 | 5,910 | Goulds [1] ......... 33170 | 6,690 | New Port Richey [2] 33552* | 9,532 |
| Atlantic Beach [2] .. 32233 | 7,889 | Greenacres [2] ..... — | 5,011 | New Smyrna Bch. [2] 32069 | 15,338 |
| Auburndale [2] ..... 33823 | 6,055 | Gulf Breeze [2] .... 32561 | 6,273 | Niceville [2] ....... 32578 | 7,322 |
| Avon Park [2] ...... 33825 | 7,203 | Gulf Gate Est. [1]... 33581 | 5,874 | N. Andrews Ter. [1]. 33308 | 7,082 |
| Azalea Park [1] .... 32807 | 7,367 | Gulfport [2] ....... 33737 | 11,436 | North Fort Myers [1] 33903 | 8,798 |
| Bartow [2] ......... 33830 | 14,518 | Haines City [2] ..... 33844 | 10,233 | North Lauderdale [2] 33068 | 15,377 |
| Bayshore Gdns. [1]. 33507 | 9,255 | Hallandale [2] ..... 33009 | 33,225 | North Miami [2] .... 33161 | 42,407 |
| Belle Glade [2] .... 33430 | 15,823 | Hialeah [2] ........ 33010* | 125,365 | N. Miami Beach [2] . 33160 | 35,991 |
| Boca Raton [2] ..... 33432 | 46,580 | Holden Heights [1] . 32805 | 6,206 | N. Palm Beach [2] .. 33408 | 11,679 |
| Boynton Beach [2] . 33435 | 32,665 | Holly Hill [2] ....... 32017 | 8,692 | Norwood [1] ....... 33169 | 14,973 |
| Bradenton [2] ...... 33506* | 27,615 | Hollywood [2] ...... 33022* | 114,943 | Oakland Park [2] ... 33334 | 21,852 |
| Brandon [1] ........ 33511 | 12,749 | Homestead [2] ..... 33030* | 20,810 | Ocala [2] .......... 32670* | 35,030 |
| Brooksville [2] ..... 33512 | 5,846 | Homestead Base [1] 33039 | 8,257 | Ocoee [2] ......... 32761 | 5,914 |
| Browardale [1] ..... 33311 | 17,444 | Indian Hbr. Bch. [2] 32937 | 6,148 | Opa–Locka [2] ..... 33054 | 13,869 |
| Browns Village [1].. 33142 | 23,442 | Jacksonville [2] .... 32203* | 529,787 | Orange Park [2] .... 32073 | 9,042 |
| Callaway [2] ....... 32401 | 6,358 | Jacksonville Bch. [2] 32250 | 14,961 | Orlando [2] ........ 32802* | 120,181 |
| Cape Canaveral [2] . 32920 | 5,108 | Jupiter [2] ......... 33458 | 7,101 | Ormond Beach [2] . 32074 | 18,653 |
| Cape Coral [2] ..... 33904 | 23,830 | Kendall [1] ........ 33156 | 35,497 | Pahokee [2] ........ 33476 | 5,690 |
| Carol City [1] ...... 33055 | 27,361 | Key West [2] ....... 33040 | 22,763 | Palatka [2] ........ 32077 | 9,409 |
| Carver Ranch Est. [1] 33209 | 5,515 | Kissimmee [2] ..... 32741 | 12,774 | Palm Bay [2] ....... 32905 | 12,394 |
| Casselberry [2] .... 32707 | 16,517 | Lake City [2] ....... 32055 | 10,537 | Palm Beach [2] .... 33480 | 9,652 |
| Chattahoochee [2] . 32324 | 4,887 | Lake Holloway [1] .. 33803 | 6,227 | Palm Beach Gds. [2] — | 11,165 |
| Clearwater [2] ..... 33515* | 77,598 | Lake Magdalene [1] 33612 | 9,266 | Palm Springs [2].... — | 8,505 |
| Clermont [2] ....... 32711 | 5,129 | Lake Park [2] ...... 33403 | 8,296 | Palmetto [2] ....... 33561 | 8,311 |
| Clewiston [2] ...... 33440 | 4,919 | Lake Wales [2] ..... 33853* | 9,235 | Panama City [2] .... 32401* | 40,918 |
| Cocoa [2] ......... 32922 | 15,679 | Lake Worth [2] ..... 33460* | 26,223 | Pembroke Pines [2] 33024 | 29,466 |
| Cocoa Beach [2] ... 32931 | 11,312 | Lakeland [2] ....... 33802* | 50,368 | Pensacola [2] ...... 32501* | 66,539 |
| Cocoa West [1] .... 32922 | 5,779 | Lantana [2] ........ 33462 | 8,117 | Perrine [1] ........ 33157 | 10,257 |
| Conway [1] ........ 32809 | 8,642 | Largo [2] .......... 33540* | 52,556 | Perry [2] .......... 32347 | 7,782 |
| Cooper City [2] .... 33328 | 6,834 | Lauderdale Lakes [2] 33313 | 23,610 | Pine Hills [1] ...... 32808 | 13,882 |
| Coral Gables [2] ... 33134 | 42,550 | Lauderhill [2] ...... 33313 | 33,288 | Pinellas Park [2] ... 33565 | 29,703 |
| Coral Springs [2] ... 33065 | 23,072 | Leesburg [2] ....... 32748 | 14,477 | Plant City [2] ...... 33566 | 15,548 |
| Crestview [2] ...... 32536 | 8,696 | Leto [1] ........... 33614 | 8,458 | Plantation [2] ...... 33317 | 42,069 |
| Cutler Ridge [1] .... 33157 | 17,441 | Lighthouse Point [2] 33064 | 12,281 | Pompano Beach [2] 33600* | 52,629 |
| Dania [1] .......... 33004 | 12,041 | Live Oak [2] ....... 32060 | 7,130 | Port Charlotte [1] .. 33952 | 10,769 |
| Davie [2] .......... 33314 | 16,188 | Lockhart [1] ....... 32860 | 5,809 | Port Orange [2] .... 32019 | 13,633 |
| Daytona Beach [2].. 32015* | 48,880 | Longboat Key [2] ... 33548 | 8,221 | Port St. Lucie [2] ... 33452 | 5,862 |
| De Funiak Spgs. [2]. 32433 | 4,924 | Longwood [2] ...... 32750 | 7,754 | Punta Gorda [2] .... 33950* | 6,904 |
| De Land [2] ........ 32720 | 13,592 | Lynn Haven [2] ..... 32444 | 5,588 | Quincy [2] ......... 32351 | 7,887 |
| Deerfield Beach [2] . 33441 | 33,103 | Maitland [2] ....... 32751 | 8,706 | Richmond Hts. [1] .. — | 6,663 |
| Delray Beach [2] ... 33444 | 32,253 | Margate [2] ........ 33063 | 30,016 | Riviera Beach [2] ... 33404 | 26,430 |
| Dunedin [2] ........ 33528 | 27,563 | Marianna [2] ....... 32446 | 7,013 | Rockledge [2] ...... 32955 | 10,776 |
| East Naples [1] .... 33940 | 6,152 | Melbourne [2] ...... 32901* | 42,307 | St. Augustine [2] ... 32084 | 12,662 |
| Edgewater [2] ...... 32032 | 5,439 | Melrose Park [1] ... 32666 | 6,111 | St. Cloud [2] ....... 32769 | 6,710 |
| Eglin [1] .......... 32542* | 7,769 | Merritt Island [1] ... 32952 | 29,233 | St. Petersburg [2] .. 33730* | 230,965 |
| Egypt Lake [1] ..... 33614 | 7,556 | Miami [2] .......... 33152* | 347,862 | St. Petersburg | |
| Englewood [1] ...... 33533 | 5,108 | Miami Beach [2] ... 33139 | 88,466 | Beach [2] ........ 33706 | 10,214 |
| Eustis [2] ......... 32726 | 7,949 | Miami Shores [2] ... 33153 | 8,855 | Sanford [2] ........ 32771 | 23,129 |
| Fernandina Bch. [2] 32034 | 8,513 | Miami Springs [2] .. 33166 | 12,282 | Sarasota [2] ....... 33578 | 50,814 |
| Florida City [2] ..... 33034 | 5,145 | Milton [2] ......... 32570 | 7,702 | Sarasota S.E. [1] ... 33579 | 6,885 |
| Fort Lauderdale [2] . 33310* | 149,408 | Mims [1] .......... 32754 | 8,309 | Satellite Beach [2].. 32937 | 7,839 |
| Fort Myers [2] ..... 33901 | 36,206 | Miramar [2] ........ 33023 | 29,772 | Sebring [2] ........ 33870 | 8,855 |
| Fort Pierce [2] ..... 33450* | 32,538 | Mount Dora [1] .... 32757 | 6,465 | South Daytona [2] .. 32021 | 11,569 |
| Ft. Walton Beach [2] 32548 | 22,760 | Myrtle Grove [1] ... 32506 | 16,186 | South Miami [2] .... 33143 | 11,314 |

[1] 1970 Census.   [2] Census Bureau estimate July 1, 1978.   [3] 1977 estimate.   [4] 1978 Special Census.   † Town or township.

| PLACE AND ZIP CODE | POP. | PLACE AND ZIP CODE | POP. | PLACE AND ZIP CODE | POP. |
|---|---|---|---|---|---|

### FLORIDA (continued)

| PLACE AND ZIP CODE | POP. | PLACE AND ZIP CODE | POP. | PLACE AND ZIP CODE | POP. |
|---|---|---|---|---|---|
| S. Miami Hts. [1] .. 33157 | 10,395 | Tampa [3] ....... 33602* | 271,365 | Warrington [1] .... 32507 | 15,848 |
| S. Patrick Shores [1] 32937 | 10,313 | Tarpon Springs [2] 33589* | 12,166 | West Miami [2] ... 33144 | 5,646 |
| Springfield [2] .... 32401 | 6,755 | Temple Terrace [2] 33617 | 10,705 | West Palm Beach [2] 33401* | 59,125 |
| Starke [2] ....... 32091 | 5,222 | Tice [1] ........ 33905 | 7,254 | West Pensacola [1] 32505 | 20,924 |
| Stuart [2] ........ 33494 | 9,245 | Titusville [2] ...... 32780 | 31,494 | W. Winter Haven [1] 33880 | 7,716 |
| Sunrise [2] ...... 33304 | 32,905 | Treasure Island [2] 33740 | 7,272 | Westwood Lakes [1] 33165 | 12,811 |
| Sweetwater [2] .... — | 7,268 | University [1] ...... 32603 | 10,039 | Wilton Manors [2] . 33305 | 13,756 |
| Sweetwater Creek [1] 33614 | 19,453 | Valparaiso [2] .... 32580 | 5,598 | Winter Garden [2] . 32787 | 6,277 |
| Tallahassee [3] ... 32301* | 85,137 | Venice [2] ...... 33595* | 12,223 | Winter Haven [2] .. 33880 | 19,647 |
| Tamarac [2] ...... 33321 | 24,609 | Vero Beach [2] ... 32960 | 16,318 | Winter Park [2] ... 32789* | 22,056 |

### GEORGIA (Ga. or GA)

| PLACE AND ZIP CODE | POP. | PLACE AND ZIP CODE | POP. | PLACE AND ZIP CODE | POP. |
|---|---|---|---|---|---|
| Acworth [2] ...... 30101 | 7,720 | Douglasville [2] ... 30134 | 12,275 | Newnan [2]....... 30263 | 12,083 |
| Adel [2] ......... 31620 | 5,036 | Dublin [2]........ 31021 | 15,490 | Norcross [2]...... 30071 | 5,410 |
| Albany [2] ....... 31706* | 77,011 | East Point [2] .... 30344 | 34,855 | Peachtree City [2]. 30269 | 5,024 |
| Alpharetta [2] .... 30201 | 5,422 | Eastman [2] ...... 31023 | 5,396 | Perry [2] ........ 31069 | 8,425 |
| Americus [2] ..... 31709 | 15,185 | Elberton [2] ..... 30635 | 6,596 | Powder Springs [2] 30073 | 5,535 |
| Athens [2] ....... 30603* | 49,185 | Fairburn [2] ..... 30213 | 5,301 | Riverdale [2] ..... 30274 | 8,540 |
| Atlanta [2] ....... 30304* | 405,437 | Fayetteville [2] ... 30214 | 5,078 | Rome [2] ........ 30161 | 28,940 |
| Augusta [2] ...... 30901* | 50,526 | Fitzgerald [2] .... 31750 | 8,100 | Roswell [2] ...... 30077 | 24,149 |
| Bainbridge [2] .... 31717 | 10,547 | Forest Park [2] ... 30050 | 19,179 | Sandersville [2] ... 31082 | 5,191 |
| Blakely [2] ....... 31723 | 5,234 | Fort Oglethorpe [2] 30742 | 5,689 | Savannah [2] ..... 31401* | 135,896 |
| Brunswick [2]..... 31520* | 18,557 | Fort Valley [2] .... 31030 | 9,593 | Smyrna [2] ....... 30080 | 21,233 |
| Buford [2] ........ 30518 | 9,083 | Gainesville [2] .... 30501 | 21,126 | Snellville [2] ..... 30278 | 12,705 |
| Cairo [2] ........ 31728 | 8,398 | Garden City [2] ... 31408 | 7,703 | Statesboro [2] .... 30458 | 16,579 |
| Calhoun [2] ...... 30701 | 5,446 | Griffin [2] ....... 30223 | 24,625 | Summerville [2].... 30747 | 5,019 |
| Carrollton [2] ..... 30117 | 14,234 | Hapeville [2] ..... 30354 | 6,614 | Swainsboro [2] .... 30401 | 7,847 |
| Cartersville [2] ... 30120 | 10,730 | Hartwell [2] ..... 30643 | 5,199 | Sylvester [2] ..... 31791 | 5,517 |
| Cedartown [2] .... 30125 | 8,649 | Hinesville [2] ..... 31313 | 8,589 | Thomaston [2].... 30286 | 10,945 |
| Chamblee [2] ..... 30341 | 7,963 | Jesup [2] ........ 31545 | 8,945 | Thomasville [2] ... 31792 | 18,288 |
| Clarkston [2] ..... 30021 | 5,784 | Jonesboro [2] .... 30236 | 6,167 | Thomson [2] ...... 30824 | 7,479 |
| College Park [2]... 30337 | 24,744 | Kennesaw [2] .... 30144 | 7,068 | Tifton [2] ........ 31794 | 12,727 |
| Columbus [2] ..... 31908* | 163,837 | La Fayette [2] .... 30728 | 5,955 | Toccoa [2] ....... 30577 | 8,495 |
| Conyers [2] ...... 30207* | 13,146 | La Grange [2] .... 30240 | 23,933 | Union City [2] .... 30291 | 4,914 |
| Cordele [2] ...... 31015 | 10,689 | Lawrenceville [2].. 30245 | 18,198 | Valdosta [2] ...... 31601* | 35,836 |
| Covington [2] ..... 30209 | 11,184 | Macon [2] ....... 31201* | 121,122 | Vidalia [2] ....... 30474 | 10,518 |
| Dalton [2] ....... 30720 | 23,533 | Marietta [2] ..... 30060 | 33,690 | Warner Robins [2] . 31093 | 40,534 |
| Dawson [2] ...... 31742 | 4,997 | Milledgeville [2] .. 31061 | 12,652 | Waycross [2] ..... 31501 | 19,233 |
| Decatur [2] ...... 30030* | 19,809 | Monroe [2] ...... 30655 | 9,173 | Waynesboro [2] ... 30830 | 5,324 |
| Doraville [2] ...... 30340 | 9,114 | Morrow [2] ....... 30260 | 5,633 | Weiser [2] ....... — | 4,865 |
| Douglas [2]....... 31533 | 10,273 | Moultrie [2] ..... 31768 | 14,109 | Winder [2] ....... 30680 | 6,592 |

### HAWAII (HI)

| PLACE AND ZIP CODE | POP. | PLACE AND ZIP CODE | POP. | PLACE AND ZIP CODE | POP. |
|---|---|---|---|---|---|
| Aiea [1] .......... 96701 | 12,560 | Kahului [1] ....... 96732 | 8,280 | Pacific Pal. [1] .... 96782 | 7,846 |
| Ewa Beach [1] .... 96706 | 7,765 | Kailua [1] ....... 96734 | 33,783 | Pearl City [1] ..... 96782 | 19,552 |
| Halawa Hts. [1] .... — | 5,809 | Kaneohe [1] ...... 96744 | 29,903 | Schofield | |
| Hickham Hsng. [1] 96818 | 7,352 | Makaha [1] ...... — | 4,644 | Barracks [1] .... 96786 | 13,516 |
| Hilo [1] .......... 96720 | 26,353 | Maunawili [1] .... — | 5,303 | Wahiawa [1] ...... 96786 | 17,598 |
| Honolulu [1] ..... 96820* | 722,689 | Mokapu [1] ...... 96734 | 7,860 | Wailuku [1] ...... 96793 | 7,979 |
| Iroquois Point [1] .. — | 4,572 | Nanakuli [1] ...... 96792 | 6,506 | Waipahu [1] ...... 96797 | 24,150 |

### IDAHO (Ida. or ID)

| PLACE AND ZIP CODE | POP. | PLACE AND ZIP CODE | POP. | PLACE AND ZIP CODE | POP. |
|---|---|---|---|---|---|
| Blackfoot [2] ..... 83221 | 10,094 | Idaho Falls [2] .... 83401 | 40,003 | Nampa [2] ....... 83651 | 28,062 |
| Boise [2] ........ 83708* | 114,033 | Jerome [2] ...... 83338 | 6,049 | Payette [2] ...... 83661 | 5,180 |
| Burley [2] ........ 83318 | 8,883 | Lewiston [2] ...... 83501 | 26,067 | Pocatello [2] ..... 83201 | 47,152 |
| Caldwell [2] ...... 83605 | 16,572 | Meridian [2] ..... 83642 | 5,713 | Rexburg [2] ...... 83440 | 11,241 |
| Chubbuck [2] .... 83201 | 6,608 | Moscow [2] ...... 83843 | 15,508 | Rupert [2]........ 83350 | 5,798 |
| Coeur D'Alene [2] . 83814 | 20,730 | Mountain Home [2] 83647 | 8,111 | Twin Falls [2] ..... 83301 | 24,129 |

### ILLINOIS (Ill. or IL)

| PLACE AND ZIP CODE | POP. | PLACE AND ZIP CODE | POP. | PLACE AND ZIP CODE | POP. |
|---|---|---|---|---|---|
| Addison [2] ...... 60101 | 29,213 | Belleville [2] ..... 62220* | 45,081 | Blue Island [2] .... 60406 | 20,181 |
| Alsip [2] ........ 60658 | 15,685 | Bellwood [2]...... 60104 | 19,537 | Bolingbrook [2] ... 60439 | 35,326 |
| Alton [2] ........ 62002 | 33,862 | Belvidere [2] ..... 61008 | 16,856 | Bourbonnais [2] .. 60914 | 12,500 |
| Arlington Hts. [2] . 60004* | 71,277 | Bensenville [2].... 60106 | 14,019 | Bradley [2] ...... 60915 | 10,828 |
| Aurora [2] ....... 60507* | 80,671 | Benton [2] ....... 62812 | 7,203 | Bridgeview [2] .... 60455 | 14,086 |
| Barrington [2]..... 60010 | 10,053 | Berkeley [2] ..... 60162 | 5,554 | Broadview [2] .... 60153 | 8,445 |
| Bartlett [2] ...... 60103 | 10,465 | Berwyn [2] ...... 60402 | 46,561 | Brookfield [2] .... 60513 | 19,742 |
| Bartonville [2] .... 61607 | 6,102 | Bethalto [2] ..... 62010 | 8,372 | Buffalo Grove [2] . 60090 | 20,712 |
| Batavia [2] ...... 60510 | 12,011 | Bloomingdale [2] . 60108 | 10,606 | Burbank [2] ...... 60459 | 29,025 |
| Beardstown [2] ... 62618 | 5,827 | Bloomington [2] .. 61701 | 41,632 | Cahokia [2] ...... 62206 | 21,091 |

[1] 1970 Census.   [2] Census Bureau estimate: 1978.   [3] 1978 Special Census.   [4] Includes county.

| PLACE AND ZIP CODE | POP. | PLACE AND ZIP CODE | POP. | PLACE AND ZIP CODE | POP. |
|---|---|---|---|---|---|
| **ILLINOIS** (*continued*) | | Granite City [2] ... 62040 | 38,699 | Murphysboro [2] .. 62966 | 9,863 |
| Cairo [2] ......... 62914 | 5,056 | Grayslake [2] .... 60030 | 5,916 | Naperville [2] .... 60540 | 37,360 |
| Calumet City [2] .. 60409 | 38,938 | Greenville [3] .... 62246 | 5,087 | Niles [2] ......... 60648 | 28,686 |
| Calumet Park [2] .. 60643 | 10,948 | Gurnee [3] ....... 60031 | 5,389 | Normal [2] ....... 61761 | 35,230 |
| Canton [2] ....... 61520 | 13,961 | Hanover Park [2] . 60103 | 25,863 | Norridge [2] ..... 60656 | 15,761 |
| Carbondale [2] ... 62901 | 23,596 | Harrisburg [2] .... 62946 | 9,471 | North Aurora [2] .. 60542 | 5,579 |
| Carlinville [2] ..... 62626 | 5,600 | Harvard [2] ...... 60033 | 5,230 | North Chicago [2] . 60064 | 41,436 |
| Carmi [2] ........ 62821 | 5,508 | Harvey [2] ....... 60426 | 32,156 | N. Riverside [2] ... 60546 | 7,090 |
| Carol Stream [2] ... — | 11,767 | Harwood Hts. [2] .. 60656 | 8,742 | Northbrook [2] ... 60062 | 30,215 |
| Carpentersville [2] 60110 | 26,313 | Hazel Crest [2] ... 60429 | 13,043 | Northfield [2] .... 60093 | 4,983 |
| Cary [2] ......... 60013 | 5,579 | Herrin [2] ....... 62948 | 10,096 | Northlake [2] ..... 60164 | 12,098 |
| Centralia [2] ..... 62801 | 15,629 | Hickory Hills [2] .. 60457 | 14,822 | Oak Brook [2] .... 60521 | 5,234 |
| Centreville [2] .... — | 11,647 | Highland [2] ..... 62249 | 6,708 | Oak Forest [2] ... 60452 | 24,429 |
| Champaign [2] ... 61820 | 57,982 | Highland Park [2] . 60035* | 32,487 | Oak Lawn [2] .... 60454* | 61,206 |
| Charleston ...... 61920 | 18,123 | Highwood [2] .... 60040 | 4,855 | Oak Park [2] ..... 60301* | 55,151 |
| Chatham [2] ..... 62629 | 5,349 | Hillside [2] ...... 60162 | 8,061 | O'Fallon [3] ..... 62269 | 11,907 |
| Chester [2] ...... 62233 | 5,296 | Hinsdale ........ 60521 | 17,015 | Olney [2] ........ 62450 | 8,715 |
| Chicago [2] ...... 60607* | 3,049,079 | Hoffman Est. [2] .. 60195 | 34,016 | Orland Park [6] ... 60462 | 18,305 |
| Chicago Hts. [2] .. 60411 | 38,530 | Hometown [2] .... 60456 | 5,846 | Ottawa [2] ...... 61350 | 17,519 |
| Chicago Ridge [2] . 60415 | 13,082 | Homewood [2] ... 60430 | 19,244 | Palatine [2] ..... 60067 | 32,003 |
| Chillicothe [2] .... 61523 | 6,072 | Hoopeston [2] ... 60942 | 6,717 | Palos Heights [2] . 60463 | 10,812 |
| Cicero [2] ....... 60650 | 58,873 | Itasca [2] ....... 60143 | 6,395 | Palos Hills [2] ... 60465 | 16,171 |
| Clarendon Hills [2] 60514 | 7,970 | Jacksonville [2] .. 62650 | 18,234 | Pana [2] ........ 62557 | 5,929 |
| Clinton [2] ....... 61727 | 7,647 | Jerseyville [2] ... 62052 | 7,252 | Paris [2] ........ 61944 | 9,614 |
| Collinsville [2] .... 62234 | 18,753 | Joliet [2] ........ 60431* | 72,372 | Park Forest [2] ... 60466 | 33,331 |
| Country Club Hls. [2] 60477 | 14,412 | Justice [2] ....... 60458 | 9,215 | Park Forest S. [2] . 60466 | 6,350 |
| Countryside [2] ... — | 5,612 | Kankakee [2] ..... 60901 | 27,988 | Park Ridge [2] ... 60068 | 40,378 |
| Crest Hill [2] ..... 60435 | 9,106 | Kewanee [2] ..... 61443 | 15,194 | Pekin [2] ........ 61554 | 32,281 |
| Crestwood [3] .... — | 9,314 | La Grange [2] .... 60525 | 16,029 | Peoria [2] ....... 61601* | 122,981 |
| Crete [2] ........ 60417 | 5,144 | La Grange Park [2] 60525 | 13,205 | Peoria Hts. [2] ... 61614 | 7,921 |
| Creve Coeur [2] .. 61611 | 7,184 | La Salle [2] ...... 61301 | 9,814 | Peru [2] ......... 61354 | 11,041 |
| Crystal Lake [2] .. 60014 | 20,018 | Lake Bluff [2] .... 60044 | 5,120 | Plano [2] ........ 60545 | 4,954 |
| Danville [2] ...... 61832 | 40,763 | Lake Forest [2] ... 60045 | 15,408 | Pontiac [2] ...... 61764 | 11,035 |
| Darien [2] ....... 60559 | 12,865 | Lake Zurich [2] ... 60047 | 7,759 | Posen [2] ........ 60469 | 5,188 |
| Decatur [2] ....... 62521* | 89,585 | Lake-in-the-Hills [2] — | 5,735 | Princeton [2] .... 61356 | 6,984 |
| Deerfield [2] ..... 60015 | 19,557 | Lansing [2] ...... 60438 | 27,609 | Prospect Hts. [2] .. 60070 | 11,288 |
| De Kalb [2] ...... 60115 | 32,830 | Lawrenceville [2] . 62439 | 5,434 | Quincy [2] ....... 62301* | 41,226 |
| Des Plaines [2] ... 60018* | 56,317 | Lemont [2] ....... 60439 | 5,141 | Rantoul [2] ...... 61866 | 23,106 |
| Dixon [2] ........ 61021 | 15,413 | Libertyville [2] ... 60048 | 16,228 | Richton Park [2] .. 60471 | 8,564 |
| Dolton [2] ....... 60419 | 25,122 | Lincoln [2] ....... 62656 | 14,565 | River Forest [2] .. 60305 | 12,749 |
| Downers Grove [2] 60515 | 41,050 | Lincolnwood [2] .. 60645 | 13,031 | River Grove [2] ... 60171 | 10,598 |
| Du Quoin [2] ..... 62832 | 6,299 | Lindenhurst [2] ... — | 15,731 | Riverdale [2] ..... 60627 | 13,888 |
| East Alton [2] .... 62024 | 7,549 | Lisle [2] ......... 60532 | 11,570 | Riverside [2] ..... 60546 | 9,371 |
| E. Chicago Hts. [2] 60411 | 5,833 | Litchfield [2] ..... 62056 | 6,804 | Robbins [2] ...... 60472 | 8,840 |
| East Moline [2] ... 61244 | 20,502 | Lockport [2] ...... 60441 | 10,424 | Robinson [2] ..... 62454 | 6,914 |
| East Peoria [2] ... 61611 | 21,697 | Lombard [2] ...... 60148 | 36,242 | Rochelle [2] ..... 61068 | 9,305 |
| East St. Louis [2] .. 62201* | 51,399 | Loves Park [2] ... 61111 | 12,091 | Rock Falls [2] .... 61071 | 10,560 |
| Edwardsville [2] .. 62025 | 13,081 | Lyons [2] ........ 60534 | 10,066 | Rock Island [2] ... 61201 | 45,992 |
| Effingham [2] ..... 62401 | 11,060 | Macomb [2] ...... 61455 | 22,084 | Rockford [3] ..... 61125* | 141,358 |
| Elgin [2] ......... 60120 | 63,132 | Madison [2] ...... 62060 | 5,371 | Rolling Mdws. [2] . 60008 | 20,176 |
| Elk Grove Vlg. [2] . 60007 | 26,039 | Marion [2] ....... 62959 | 14,058 | Romeoville [2] ... 60441 | 20,826 |
| Elmhurst [2] ..... 60126 | 44,249 | Markham [2] ..... 60426 | 15,830 | Roselle [3] ...... 60172 | 13,819 |
| Elmwood Park [2] . 60635 | 24,216 | Mascoutah [2] ... 62258 | 5,437 | Round Lake Bch. [3] 60073 | 12,148 |
| Evanston [2] ...... 60204* | 70,326 | Matteson [2] ..... 60443 | 8,916 | St. Charles [2] ... 60174 | 16,407 |
| Evergreen Park [2] 60642 | 23,320 | Mattoon [2] ...... 61938 | 17,884 | Salem [2] ........ 62881 | 7,510 |
| Fairfield [2] ...... 62837 | 5,786 | Maywood [2] ..... 60153 | 26,128 | Sandwich [2] ..... 60548 | 5,683 |
| Fairview Hts. [2] .. 62208 | 18,139 | McHenry [3] ..... 60050 | 10,059 | Sauk Village [3] ... 60411 | 10,544 |
| Flora [2] ........ 62839 | 4,994 | Melrose Park [2] .. 60160* | 19,702 | Savanna [2] ...... 61074 | 4,404 |
| Flossmoor [2] .... 60422 | 8,232 | Mendota [2] ..... 61342 | 6,874 | Schaumburg [2] .. 60194 | 50,184 |
| Forest Park [2] ... 60130 | 14,383 | Metropolis [2] .... 62960 | 6,439 | Schiller Park [2] .. 60176 | 11,483 |
| Fox Lake [2] ..... 60020 | 5,938 | Midlothian [2] .... 60445 | 13,951 | Silvis [2] ........ 61282 | 6,894 |
| Franklin Park [2] .. 60131 | 17,744 | Milan [2] ........ 61264 | 6,778 | Skokie [2] ....... 60076* | 64,696 |
| Freeport [2] ...... 61032 | 24,580 | Moline [2] ....... 61265 | 43,323 | South Elgin [2] ... 60177 | 5,508 |
| Galesburg [2] .... 61401 | 32,778 | Monmouth [2] .... 61462 | 10,193 | South Holland [2] . 60473 | 24,822 |
| Geneseo [2] ..... 61254 | 6,302 | Morris [2] ....... 60450 | 9,021 | South Stickney [1]. 60459 | 29,900 |
| Geneva [2] ...... 60134 | 10,020 | Morton [2] ....... 61550 | 15,306 | Spring Valley [2] .. 61362 | 5,528 |
| Glen Ellyn [2] .... 60137 | 24,852 | Morton Grove [2] . 60053 | 25,300 | Springfield [2] .... 62703* | 86,159 |
| Glencoe [2] ...... 60022 | 9,622 | Mount Carmel [2] . 62863 | 8,155 | Steger [2] ....... 60475 | 9,417 |
| Glendale Hts. [2] . 60137 | 21,660 | Mt. Prospect [2] .. 60056 | 52,955 | Sterling [2] ...... 61081* | 17,489 |
| Glenview [2] ..... 60025* | 31,868 | Mount Vernon [2] . 62864 | 17,208 | Stickney [2] ...... — | 6,497 |
| Glenwood [2] ..... 60425 | 10,507 | Mundelein [2] .... 60060 | 18,760 | Streamwood [2] .. 60103 | 23,077 |

[1] 1970 Census.    [2] Census Bureau estimate: 1978.    [3] 1978 Special Census.

| PLACE AND ZIP CODE | | POP. | PLACE AND ZIP CODE | | POP. | PLACE AND ZIP CODE | | POP. |
|---|---|---|---|---|---|---|---|---|
| **ILLINOIS** *(continued)* | | | Warrenville [2] .... | 60555 | 8,257 | Wheaton [2] ...... | 60187 | 40,652 |
| Streator [2] ...... | 61364* | 14,734 | Washington [2] ... | 61571 | 10,174 | Wheeling [2] ...... | 60090 | 19,555 |
| Summit [2] ...... | 60501 | 9,999 | Washington Park [2] | 62204 | 8,313 | Wilmette [2] ...... | 60091 | 30,793 |
| Swansea [2] ...... | — | 5,449 | Watseka [2] ...... | 60970 | 5,075 | Winnetka [2] ...... | 60093 | 13,800 |
| Sycamore [2] ..... | 60178 | 8,942 | Wauconda [2] .... | 60084 | 6,054 | Winthrop Hbr. [2] . | 60096 | 5,260 |
| Taylorville [2] .... | 62568 | 11,142 | Waukegan [2] .... | 60085* | 63,948 | Wood Dale [2] .... | 60191 | 11,311 |
| Tinley Park [2] .... | 60477 | 26,190 | West Chicago [2] . | 60185 | 16,273 | Wood River [2] .... | 62095 | 12,247 |
| Urbana [2] ....... | 61801 | 34,827 | West Frankfort [2] | 62896 | 8,953 | Woodridge [2] .... | 60515 | 19,926 |
| Vandalia [3] ...... | 62471 | 4,789 | Westchester [2] ... | 60153 | 17,813 | Woodstock [2] .... | 60098 | 11,512 |
| Vernon Hills [2] .. | 60061 | 6,903 | Western Spgs. [2] . | 60558 | 13,005 | Worth [2] ........ | 60482 | 12,125 |
| Villa Park [2] ..... | 60181 | 22,004 | Westmont [2] ..... | 60559 | 14,376 | Zion [2] .......... | 60099 | 18,953 |

| PLACE AND ZIP CODE | | POP. | PLACE AND ZIP CODE | | POP. | PLACE AND ZIP CODE | | POP. |
|---|---|---|---|---|---|---|---|---|
| **INDIANA (Ind. or IN)** | | | | | | | | |
| Alexandria [2] .... | 46001 | 5,814 | Gas City [2] ...... | 46933 | 6,336 | Mount Vernon [2] . | 47620 | 7,275 |
| Anderson [2] ..... | 46011* | 68,556 | Goshen [2] ...... | 46526* | 19,448 | Muncie [2] ...... | 47302* | 81,076 |
| Auburn [2] ...... | 46706 | 7,936 | Greencastle [2] ... | 46135 | 8,372 | Munster [2] ...... | 46321 | 19,984 |
| Bedford [2] ...... | 47421 | 14,166 | Greenfield [2] .... | 46140 | 12,117 | New Albany [2] ... | 47150 | 37,863 |
| Beech Grove [2] .. | 46107 | 14,198 | Greensburg [2] ... | 47240 | 8,901 | New Castle [2] .... | 47362 | 20,187 |
| Bloomington [2] .. | 47401 | 50,344 | Greenwood [2] .... | 46142 | 19,112 | New Haven [2] .... | 46774 | 6,650 |
| Bluffton [2] ...... | 46714 | 8,459 | Griffith [2] ....... | 46319 | 17,075 | New Whiteland [2] | 46184 | 4,970 |
| Boonville [2] ..... | 47601 | 5,958 | Hammond [2] ..... | 46320* | 101,076 | Noblesville [2] .... | 46060 | 11,680 |
| Brazil [2] ........ | 47834 | 7,613 | Hartford City [2] .. | 47348 | 7,721 | N. Manchester [2] . | 46962 | 5,565 |
| Brownsburg [2].. | 46112 | 9,228 | Highland [2] ...... | 46322 | 26,086 | Peru [2] ......... | 46970 | 13,397 |
| Carmel [2] ....... | 46032 | 18,050 | Hobart [2] ....... | 46342 | 22,483 | Plainfield [2] ..... | 46168 | 8,730 |
| Cedar Lake [2] ... | 46303 | 8,652 | Huntingburg [2] ... | 47542 | 5,112 | Plymouth [2] ..... | 46563 | 7,870 |
| Charlestown [2] .. | 47111 | 6,182 | Huntington [2] ... | 46750 | 15,314 | Portage [2] ...... | 46368 | 25,495 |
| Chesterton [4] ... | 46304 | 7,427 | Indianapolis [2] .. | 46206* | 704,045 | Portland [2] ...... | 47371 | 6,811 |
| Clarksville [2] .... | 47130 | 16,369 | Jasper [2] ....... | 47546 | 10,031 | Princeton [4] ..... | 47670 | 8,789 |
| Clinton [2] ....... | 47842 | 5,077 | Jeffersonville [2].. | 47130 | 22,841 | Richmond [2] ..... | 47374 | 43,440 |
| Columbia City [2] | 46725 | 5,106 | Kendallville [2] ... | 46755 | 6,547 | Rushville [2] ..... | 46173 | 7,014 |
| Columbus [2] .... | 47201 | 29,222 | Kokomo [2] ...... | 46901 | 52,153 | Salem [2] ........ | 47167 | 5,465 |
| Connersville [2] ... | 47331 | 16,959 | La Porte [2] ...... | 46350* | 22,208 | Schererville [2] ... | 46375 | 9,562 |
| Crawfordsville [2] . | 47933 | 14,153 | Lafayette [2] ..... | 47901* | 49,561 | Seymour [2] ...... | 47274 | 13,952 |
| Crown Point [4] ... | 46307 | 14,352 | Lake Station [2] ... | 46405 | 15,546 | Shelbyville [2] .... | 46176 | 13,968 |
| Danville [2] ...... | 46122 | 5,688 | Lawrence [2] ..... | 46226 | 25,955 | South Bend [2] ... | 46624* | 113,147 |
| Decatur [2] ...... | 46733 | 8,089 | Lebanon [2] ...... | 46052 | 10,112 | Speedway [2] ..... | 46224 | 14,612 |
| Dyer [2] ......... | 46311 | 10,294 | Linton [2] ....... | 47441 | 5,148 | Tell City [2] ...... | 47586 | 8,301 |
| East Chicago [2] .. | 46312 | 42,050 | Logansport [2] ... | 46947 | 17,563 | Terre Haute [2] ... | 47808* | 63,817 |
| East Gary [5] ..... | 46405 | 15,400 | Lowell [2] ....... | 46356 | 5,804 | Tipton [2] ....... | 46072 | 4,670 |
| Edinburg [2] ..... | 46124 | 5,436 | Madison [2] ...... | 47250 | 12,737 | Valparaiso [2] .... | 46383 | 23,783 |
| Elkhart [2] ....... | 46514 | 48,267 | Marion [2] ....... | 46952 | 39,710 | Vincennes [2] ..... | 47591 | 18,871 |
| Elwood [2] ....... | 46036 | 10,334 | Martinsville [2] ... | 46151 | 11,198 | Wabash [2] ...... | 46992 | 13,025 |
| Evansville [2] ..... | 47708* | 134,388 | Merrillville [4] .... | 46410 | 27,222 | Warsaw [2] ...... | 46580 | 10,320 |
| Fort Wayne [2].... | 46802* | 181,066 | Michigan City [2].. | 46360 | 41,469 | Washington [2] ... | 47501 | 10,533 |
| Frankfort [2] ..... | 46041 | 13,885 | Mishawaka [2] .... | 46544 | 39,517 | West Lafayette [2] | 47906 | 21,166 |
| Franklin [2] ...... | 46131 | 13,517 | Monticello [2] .... | 47960 | 6,257 | Whiting [2] ...... | 46394 | 6,919 |
| Gary [2] ......... | 46401* | 156,056 | Mooresville [2] ... | 46158 | 7,336 | Winchester [2] .... | 47394 | 4,977 |

| PLACE AND ZIP CODE | | POP. | PLACE AND ZIP CODE | | POP. | PLACE AND ZIP CODE | | POP. |
|---|---|---|---|---|---|---|---|---|
| **IOWA (Ia. or IA)** | | | | | | | | |
| Algona [2] ....... | 50511 | 6,603 | Denison [2] ...... | 51442 | 6,417 | Mount Pleasant [2] | 52641 | 6,822 |
| Altoona [2] ...... | 50009 | 5,454 | Des Moines [2] ... | 50318* | 192,526 | Muscatine [2] .... | 52761 | 23,545 |
| Ames [2] ......... | 50010 | 44,074 | Dubuque [2] ..... | 52001 | 60,794 | Nevada [2] ...... | 50201 | 5,333 |
| Ankeny [2] ....... | 50021 | 14,877 | Estherville [2] .... | 51334 | 7,790 | Newton [2] ....... | 50208 | 15,164 |
| Atlantic [2] ...... | 50022 | 7,600 | Evansdale [2] .... | 50707 | 5,472 | Oelwein [2] ...... | 50662 | 7,577 |
| Bettendorf [2] .... | 52722 | 27,461 | Fairfield [2] ...... | 52556 | 7,794 | Oskaloosa [2] .... | 52577 | 10,837 |
| Boone [2] ........ | 50036 | 12,147 | Fort Dodge [2] ... | 50501 | 29,744 | Ottumwa [2] ..... | 52501 | 27,285 |
| Burlington [2] .... | 52601 | 29,448 | Fort Madison [2] .. | 52627 | 13,400 | Pella [2] ......... | 50219 | 7,827 |
| Carroll [2] ....... | 51401 | 9,411 | Glenwood [2] .... | 51534 | 5,252 | Perry [2] ......... | 50220 | 6,551 |
| Cedar Falls [2].... | 50613 | 35,275 | Grinnell [2] ...... | 50112 | 8,791 | Red Oak [2] ...... | 51566 | 6,583 |
| Cedar Rapids [2].. | 52401* | 107,071 | Harlan [2] ....... | 51537 | 5,283 | Shenandoah [2] .. | 51601 | 6,318 |
| Centerville [2] .... | 52544 | 6,269 | Independence [2] . | 50644 | 6,134 | Sioux City [2] .... | 51101* | 84,394 |
| Charles City [2] ... | 50616 | 8,847 | Indianola [2] ..... | 50125 | 10,122 | Spencer [2] ...... | 51301 | 11,488 |
| Cherokee [2] ..... | 51012 | 6,772 | Iowa City [2] ..... | 52240 | 48,587 | Storm Lake [2] ... | 50588 | 8,631 |
| Clarinda [2] ...... | 51632 | 5,305 | Iowa Falls [2] .... | 50126 | 6,043 | Urbandale [2] .... | 50322 | 17,100 |
| Clear Lake City [2] | 50428 | 7,116 | Keokuk [2] ....... | 52632 | 13,862 | Vinton .......... | 52349 | 5,004 |
| Clinton [2] ....... | 52732* | 33,342 | Knoxville [2] ..... | 50138 | 7,724 | Washington [2] ... | 52353 | 5,960 |
| Coralville [2] ..... | 52241 | 7,069 | Le Mars [2] ...... | 51031 | 8,041 | Waterloo [2] ..... | 50703* | 79,613 |
| Council Bluffs [2].. | 51501 | 58,429 | Maquoketa [2] ... | 52060 | 5,885 | Waverly [2] ...... | 50677 | 7,333 |
| Creston [2] ...... | 50801 | 8,106 | Marion [2] ....... | 52302 | 19,333 | Webster City [2] .. | 50595 | 8,274 |
| Davenport [2] .... | 52802* | 101,478 | Marshalltown [2] .. | 50158 | 27,007 | W. Des Moines [2] | 50265 | 21,255 |
| Decorah [2] ...... | 52101 | 7,493 | Mason City [2] ... | 50401 | 30,165 | Windsor Hts. [2] .. | — | 7,051 |

[1] 1970 Census. [2] Census Bureau estimate: 1978. [3] 1977 estimate. [4] 1978 Special Census. [5] 1976 estimate.

| PLACE AND ZIP CODE | | POP. | PLACE AND ZIP CODE | | POP. | PLACE AND ZIP CODE | | POP. |
|---|---|---|---|---|---|---|---|---|

## KANSAS (Kan., Kans., or KS)

| Place | ZIP | POP. | Place | ZIP | POP. | Place | ZIP | POP. |
|---|---|---|---|---|---|---|---|---|
| Abilene [2] | 67410 | 6,430 | Goodland [2] | 67735 | 5,678 | Mission [2] | 66205 | 8,555 |
| Arkansas City [2] | 67005 | 12,736 | Great Bend [2] | 67530 | 16,262 | Newton [2] | 67114 | 15,634 |
| Atchison [2] | 66002 | 10,694 | Hays [2] | 67601 | 17,596 | Olathe [2] | 66061 | 33,323 |
| Augusta [2] | 67010 | 6,594 | Haysville [2] | 67060 | 8,538 | Ottawa [2] | 66067 | 10,399 |
| Bonner Springs [2] | 66012 | 7,044 | Hutchinson [2] | 67501 | 41,831 | Overland Park [2] | 66204 | 82,917 |
| Chanute [2] | 66720 | 10,058 | Independence [2] | 67301 | 10,394 | Parsons [2] | 67357 | 12,223 |
| Clay Center [2] | 67432 | 5,046 | Iola [2] | 66749 | 6,813 | Pittsburg [2] | 66762 | 18,521 |
| Coffeyville [2] | 67337 | 14,295 | Junction City [2] | 66441 | 18,684 | Prairie Village [2] | 66208 | 25,775 |
| Colby [2] | 67701 | 5,370 | Kansas City [2] | 66110* | 164,250 | Pratt [2] | 67124 | 6,811 |
| Concordia [2] | 66901 | 6,651 | Lawrence [2] | 66044 | 50,780 | Roeland Park [2] | 66203 | 12,506 |
| Derby [2] | 67037 | 9,132 | Leavenworth [2] | 66048 | 35,540 | Russell [2] | 67665 | 5,458 |
| Dodge City [2] | 67801 | 15,626 | Leawood [2] | 66206 | 12,845 | Salina [2] | 67401 | 38,798 |
| El Dorado [2] | 67042 | 12,209 | Lenexa [2] | 66215 | 13,937 | Shawnee [2] | 66202 | 25,653 |
| Emporia [2] | 66801 | 24,317 | Liberal [2] | 67901 | 15,114 | Topeka [2] | 66603* | 122,100 |
| Fairway [2] | — | 6,262 | Manhattan [2] | 66502 | 34,741 | Wellington [2] | 67152 | 7,739 |
| Fort Scott [2] | 66701 | 8,707 | McPherson [2] | 67460 | 11,114 | Wichita [2] | 67276* | 267,748 |
| Garden City [2] | 67846 | 18,653 | Merriam [2] | 66203 | 11,682 | Winfield [2] | 67156 | 11,067 |

## KENTUCKY (Ky., Ken., or KY)

| Place | ZIP | POP. | Place | ZIP | POP. | Place | ZIP | POP. |
|---|---|---|---|---|---|---|---|---|
| Ashland [2] | 41101 | 26,972 | Fort Mitchell [2] | 41017 | 7,114 | Middlesborough [2] | 40965 | 11,774 |
| Bardstown [2] | 40004 | 7,199 | Fort Thomas [2] | 41075 | 16,121 | Morehead [2] | 40351 | 7,034 |
| Bellevue [2] | 41073 | 7,791 | Fort Wright [2] | — | 5,528 | Mount Sterling [2] | 40353 | 6,149 |
| Berea [2] | 40403 | 7,868 | Frankfort [2] | 40601 | 24,831 | Murray [2] | 42071 | 13,747 |
| Bowling Green [2] | 42101 | 38,709 | Franklin [2] | 42134 | 8,019 | Newport [2] | 41071* | 21,142 |
| Campbellsville [2] | 42718 | 7,426 | Georgetown [2] | 40324 | 9,515 | Nicholasville [2] | 40356 | 10,561 |
| Central [2] | 42330 | 5,763 | Glasgow [2] | 42141 | 11,616 | Okolona [1] | 40219 | 17,643 |
| Corbin [2] | 40701 | 9,324 | Harrodsburg [2] | 40330 | 6,682 | Owensboro [2] | 42301 | 50,612 |
| Covington [2] | 41011* | 45,756 | Hazard [2] | 41701 | 5,843 | Paducah [2] | 42001 | 33,253 |
| Cynthiana [2] | 41031 | 5,921 | Henderson [2] | 42420 | 25,352 | Paris [2] | 40361 | 7,068 |
| Danville [2] | 40422 | 11,774 | Hopkinsville [2] | 42240 | 26,519 | Pikeville [2] | 41501 | 6,259 |
| Dayton [2] | 41074 | 7,401 | Independence [2] | 41051 | 6,386 | Princeton [2] | 42445 | 6,954 |
| Edgewood [2] | — | 7,947 | Jeffersontown [2] | 40299 | 11,580 | Radcliff [2] | 40160 | 14,945 |
| Elizabethtown [2] | 42701 | 15,343 | Lebanon [2] | 40033 | 5,945 | Richmond [2] | 40475 | 19,586 |
| Elsmere [2] | — | 6,158 | Lexington–Fayette [2] | 40511* | 190,686 | Russellville [2] | 42276 | 6,793 |
| Erlanger [2] | 41018 | 14,480 | Louisville [2] | 40231* | 317,503 | St. Matthews [2] | 40207 | 14,248 |
| Flatwoods [2] | 41139 | 9,808 | Ludlow [2] | 41016 | 4,882 | Shively [2] | 40216 | 18,207 |
| Florence [2] | 41042 | 16,365 | Madisonville [2] | 42431 | 17,913 | Somerset [2] | 42501 | 13,280 |
| Fort Campbell N. [1] | 42223 | 13,616 | Mayfield [2] | 42066 | 9,882 | Versailles [2] | 40383 | 7,511 |
| Fort Knox [3] | 40121 | 37,608 | Maysville [2] | 41056 | 6,864 | Winchester [2] | 40391 | 16,438 |

## LOUISIANA (La. or LA)

| Place | ZIP | POP. | Place | ZIP | POP. | Place | ZIP | POP. |
|---|---|---|---|---|---|---|---|---|
| Abbeville [2] | 70510 | 13,018 | Jeanerette [2] | 70544 | 6,782 | Patterson [2] | 70392 | 4,968 |
| Alexandria [2] | 71301 | 49,861 | Jefferson Hts. [1] | 70121 | 16,489 | Pineville [2] | 71360 | 12,381 |
| Baker [2] | 70714 | 13,324 | Jennings [2] | 70546 | 12,311 | Plaquemine [2] | 70764 | 7,598 |
| Bastrop [2] | 71220 | 14,680 | Jonesboro [2] | 71251 | 5,072 | Port Allen [2] | 70767 | 6,009 |
| Baton Rouge [2] | 70821* | 311,053 | Kaplan [2] | 70548 | 5,172 | Rayne [2] | 70578 | 9,698 |
| Bayou Cane [1] | 70360 | 9,077 | Kenner [2] | 70062 | 54,616 | Reserve [1] | 70084 | 6,381 |
| Bayou Vista [1] | 70380 | 5,121 | Lafayette [2] | 70501* | 81,127 | Ruston [2] | 71270* | 19,528 |
| Bogalusa [2] | 70427 | 17,534 | Lafayette S.W. [1] | 70501 | 5,498 | St. Martinville [2] | 70582 | 7,416 |
| Bossier City [2] | 71111 | 48,132 | Lake Charles [2] | 70601 | 79,276 | Scotlandville [1] | 70807 | 22,557 |
| Breaux Bridge [2] | 70517 | 4,949 | Lake Providence [2] | 71254 | 5,447 | Shreveport [2] | 71102* | 201,920 |
| Bunkie [2] | 71322 | 5,063 | Laplace [1] | 70068 | 5,953 | Slidell [2] | 70458 | 29,394 |
| Cooper Road [1] | 71107 | 9,034 | Leesville [2] | 71446* | 9,156 | South Fort | | |
| Covington [2] | 70433 | 9,206 | Little Farms [1] | 70123 | 15,713 | Polk [1] | 71459 | 15,600 |
| Crowley [2] | 70526 | 16,019 | Mansfield [2] | 71052 | 7,119 | Springhill [2] | 71075 | 6,343 |
| De Ridder [2] | 70634 | 11,010 | Marrero [1] | 70072 | 29,015 | Sulphur [2] | 70663 | 18,894 |
| Denham Springs [2] | 70726 | 8,997 | Metairie [1] | 70009* | 136,477 | Tallulah [2] | 71282 | 9,360 |
| Donaldsonville [2] | 70346 | 7,850 | Minden [2] | 71055 | 14,265 | Terry [1] | 71285 | 13,832 |
| Eunice [2] | 70535 | 11,917 | Monroe [2] | 71203* | 64,036 | Thibodaux [2] | 70301 | 18,276 |
| Franklin [2] | 70538 | 8,847 | Morgan City [2] | 70380 | 16,294 | Vidalia [2] | 71373 | 5,804 |
| Gonzales [2] | 70737 | 7,253 | Natchitoches [2] | 71457 | 17,793 | Ville Plate [2] | 70586 | 9,608 |
| Gretna [2] | 70053 | 30,461 | New Iberia [2] | 70560 | 34,260 | West Monroe [2] | 71291 | 16,269 |
| Hammond [2] | 70401 | 15,420 | New Orleans [2] | 70113* | 556,428 | Westwego [2] | 70094 | 13,396 |
| Harahan [2] | 70123 | 13,858 | North Fort Polk [1] | 71459 | 7,955 | Winnfield [2] | 71483 | 6,767 |
| Harvey [1] | 70058 | 6,347 | Oakdale [2] | 71463 | 6,749 | Winnsboro [2] | 71295 | 5,578 |
| Houma [2] | 70360 | 31,184 | Opelousas [2] | 70570 | 19,965 | Zachary [2] | 70791 | 7,664 |

[1] 1970 Census.  [2] Census Bureau estimate July 1, 1978.  [3] 1976 estimate.

## MAINE (Me. or ME)

| PLACE AND ZIP CODE | | POP. |
|---|---|---|
| Auburn [2] | 04210 | 23,129 |
| Augusta [2] | 04330 | 20,997 |
| Bangor [2] | 04401 | 31,124 |
| Bath [2] | 04530 | 9,855 |
| Belfast [2] | 04915 | 6,514 |
| Biddeford [2] | 04005 | 19,254 |
| Brewer [2] | 04412 | 9,090 |
| Brunswick [3]† | 04011 | 16,886 |
| Cape Elizabeth [3]† | 04107 | 7,892 |
| Caribou [2] | 04736 | 11,119 |
| Cumberland [3]† | 04021 | 5,009 |
| Ellsworth [2] | 04605 | 5,253 |
| Fairfield [3]† | 04937 | 5,988 |
| Falmouth [3]† | 04105 | 6,263 |
| Farmington [3]† | 04938 | 6,449 |
| Fort Kent [3]† | 04743 | 5,040 |
| Freeport [3]† | 04032 | 5,570 |
| Gardiner [2] | 04345 | 6,805 |
| Gorham [3]† | 04038 | 9,921 |
| Hampden [3]† | 04444 | 5,267 |
| Houlton [3]† | 04730 | 7,669 |
| Jay [3] | 04239 | 4,983 |
| Kennebunk [3]† | 04043 | 6,792 |
| Kittery [3]† | 03904 | 9,966 |
| Lewiston [2] | 04240 | 40,422 |
| Limestone [3]† | 04750 | 9,284 |
| Lincoln [3]† | 04457 | 5,196 |
| Lisbon [3]† | 04250 | 8,065 |
| Madawaska [3]† | 04756 | 6,102 |
| Millinocket [3]† | 04462 | 7,627 |
| Old Orchard Bch. [3]† | 04064 | 5,594 |
| Old Town [2] | 04468 | 8,335 |
| Orono [3]† | 04473 | 11,962 |
| Portland [2] | 04101* | 61,338 |
| Presque Isle [2] | 04769 | 11,776 |
| Rockland [2] | 04841 | 7,736 |
| Rumford [3]† | 04276 | 8,174 |
| Saco [2] | 04072 | 12,784 |
| Sanford [3]† | 04073 | 16,982 |
| Scarborough [3]† | 04074 | 10,619 |
| Skowhegan [3]† | 04976 | 7,998 |
| South Portland [2] | 04106 | 21,643 |
| Topsham [3]† | 04086 | 6,467 |
| Waterville [2] | 04901 | 16,806 |
| Wells [3]† | 04090 | 5,925 |
| Westbrook [2] | 04092 | 14,188 |
| Windham [3]† | — | 9,345 |
| Winslow [3]† | 04901 | 8,299 |
| Winthrop [2]† | 04364 | 5,044 |
| Yarmouth [3]† | 04096 | 6,134 |
| York [3]† | 03909 | 7,367 |

## MARYLAND (Md. or MD)

| PLACE AND ZIP CODE | | POP. |
|---|---|---|
| Aberdeen [2] | 21001 | 14,120 |
| Andrews [1] | 20331 | 6,418 |
| Annapolis [2] | 21401* | 33,827 |
| Arbutus [1] | 21227 | 22,745 |
| Aspen Hill [1] | 20906 | 16,799 |
| Avenel–Hillandale [1] | 20783 | 19,520 |
| Baltimore [2] | 21233* | 791,857 |
| Bel Air [2] | 21014 | 9,658 |
| Beltsville [1] | 20705 | 8,912 |
| Bethesda [1] | 20014 | 71,621 |
| Birchwood City [1] | 20021 | 9,558 |
| Bladensburg [2] | 21710 | 7,217 |
| Bowie [2] | 20715 | 37,072 |
| Brooklyn [1] | 21225 | 13,896 |
| Cambridge [2] | 21613 | 11,681 |
| Camp Springs [1] | 20031 | 22,776 |
| Capitol Hts. [2] | 20027 | 4,856 |
| Catonsville [1] | 21228 | 54,812 |
| Cheverly [2] | 20785 | 5,444 |
| Chevy Chase [1] | 20015 | 16,424 |
| Chillum [1] | 20783 | 35,656 |
| Colesville [1] | 20904 | 9,455 |
| College Park [2] | 20740 | 26,579 |
| Columbia [1] | 21045* | 8,815 |
| Coral Hills [1] | 20027 | 7,105 |
| Cumberland [2] | 21502 | 26,002 |
| District Heights [2] | 20028 | 7,200 |
| Dundalk [1] | 21222 | 85,377 |
| Easton [2] | 21601 | 7,335 |
| Edgemere [1] | 21219 | 10,352 |
| Edgewood [1] | 21040 | 8,551 |
| Elkton [2] | 21921 | 6,178 |
| Ellicott City [1] | 21043 | 9,435 |
| Essex [1] | 21221 | 38,193 |
| Ferndale [1] | 21061 | 9,929 |
| Forestville [1] | 20028 | 16,152 |
| Fort Meade [1] | 20755 | 16,699 |
| Frederick [2] | 21701 | 27,686 |
| Frostburg [2] | 21532 | 7,572 |
| Gaithersburg [2] | 20760 | 28,503 |
| Glen Burnie [1] | 21061 | 38,608 |
| Good Luck [1] | 20801 | 10,584 |
| Greenbelt [2] | 20770 | 15,775 |
| Hagerstown [2] | 21740 | 36,957 |
| Havre De Grace [2] | 21078 | 11,325 |
| Hillcrest Hts. [1] | 20031 | 24,037 |
| Hyattsville [2] | 20780* | 12,273 |
| Joppatowne [1] | 21085 | 9,092 |
| Kemp Mill [1] | 20904 | 10,037 |
| Kentland [1] | 20785 | 9,649 |
| Langley Park [1] | 20787 | 11,564 |
| Lanham–Seabr'k. [1] | 20801 | 13,244 |
| Lansdowne–Baltimore Hlds.[1] | 21227 | 17,770 |
| Laurel [2] | 20810 | 9,679 |
| Lexington Park–Patuxent River [1] | 20653 | 9,136 |
| Linthicum [1] | 21090 | 9,767 |
| Lutherville–Timonium [1] | 21093 | 24,055 |
| Maryland City [1] | — | 7,102 |
| Middle River [1] | 21220 | 19,935 |
| Mount Rainier [2] | 20822 | 6,829 |
| New Carrollton [2] | 20784 | 12,431 |
| North Potomac [1] | 20854 | 12,546 |
| N. Takoma Park[1] | 20012 | 7,373 |
| Overlea [1] | 21206 | 13,086 |
| Owings Mills [1] | 21117 | 7,360 |
| Oxon Hill [1] | 20021 | 11,974 |
| Palmer Park [1] | 20785 | 8,172 |
| Parkville [1] | 21234 | 33,589 |
| Pikesville [1] | 21208 | 25,395 |
| Pumphrey [1] | 21227 | 6,433 |
| Randallstown [1] | 21133 | 33,683 |
| Randolph [1] | 20853 | 13,233 |
| Reisterstown [1] | 21136 | 14,037 |
| Riverdale [2] | 20840 | 5,934 |
| Riverdale Hts.–East Pine [1] | 20840 | 8,941 |
| Riviera Beach [1] | 21122 | 7,464 |
| Rockville [2] | 20850* | 43,107 |
| Rosedale [1] | 21237 | 19,417 |
| Salisbury [2] | 21801 | 16,526 |
| Seat Pleasant [2] | 20027 | 7,088 |
| Severna Park [1] | 21146 | 16,358 |
| Silver Spring [1] | 20907* | 77,496 |
| South Gate [1] | 21061 | 9,356 |
| S. Kensington [1] | 20795 | 10,289 |
| South Laurel [1] | 20810 | 13,345 |
| Suitl'd.–Silver Hill [1] | 20023 | 30,355 |
| Takoma Park [2] | 20012 | 15,476 |
| Towson [1] | 21204 | 77,799 |
| Waldorf [1] | 20601 | 7,368 |
| Walker Mill [1] | 20028 | 6,322 |
| Westminster [2] | 21157 | 10,174 |
| Wheaton [1] | 20902 | 66,247 |
| White Oak [1] | 20903 | 19,769 |
| Woodlawn–Woodmoor [1] | 20901 | 28,821 |

## MASSACHUSETTS (Mass. or MA)

| PLACE AND ZIP CODE | | POP. |
|---|---|---|
| Abington [3]† | 02351 | 13,342 |
| Acton [3]† | 01720 | 18,707 |
| Acushnet [3]† | 02743 | 8,647 |
| Adams [3]† | 01220 | 10,548 |
| Agawam [3]† | 01001 | 24,955 |
| Amesbury [3]† | 01913 | 13,806 |
| Amherst [3]† | 01002 | 30,638 |
| Andover [3]† | 01810 | 27,132 |
| Arlington [3] | 02176 | 49,303 |
| Ashland [3]† | 01721 | 8,837 |
| Athol [3]† | 01331 | 10,754 |
| Attleboro [2] | 02703 | 32,834 |
| Auburn [3]† | 01501 | 15,483 |
| Avon [3]† | 02322 | 5,301 |
| Ayer [3]† | 01432* | 7,023 |
| Barnstable [3]† | 02630 | 28,830 |
| Bedford [3]† | 01730 | 13,577 |
| Belchertown [3]† | 01007 | 6,677 |
| Bellingham [3]† | 02019 | 14,776 |
| Belmont [3]† | 02178 | 26,963 |
| Beverly [2] | 01915 | 37,292 |
| Billerica [3]† | 01821 | 37,051 |
| Blackstone [3]† | 01504 | 6,581 |
| Boston [2] | 02109* | 597,254 |
| Bourne [3]† | 02532 | 11,111 |
| Braintree [3]† | 02184 | 37,236 |
| Bridgewater [3]† | 02324 | 13,904 |
| Brockton [2] | 02403 | 94,130 |
| Brookline [3]† | 02192 | 50,680 |
| Burlington [3]† | 01803 | 24,726 |
| Cambridge [3] | 02138* | 98,187 |
| Canton [3]† | 02021 | 18,299 |
| Carver [3]† | 02330 | 6,338 |
| Charlton [3]† | 01507 | 6,029 |
| Chatham [3]† | 02633 | 6,419 |
| Chelmsford [3]† | 01824 | 32,007 |
| Chelsea [2] | 02150 | 23,720 |
| Chicopee [2] | 01021* | 56,509 |
| Clinton [3]† | 01510 | 12,404 |
| Cohasset [3]† | 02025 | 7,854 |
| Concord [3]† | 01742 | 17,831 |
| Dalton [3]† | 01226 | 7,043 |
| Danvers [3]† | 01923 | 24,182 |
| Dartmouth [3]† | 02714 | 23,348 |
| Dedham [3]† | 02026 | 26,587 |
| Dennis [3]† | 02638 | 10,530 |
| Dighton [3]† | 02715 | 5,276 |
| Dracut [3]† | 01826 | 20,619 |

[1] 1970 Census.  [2] Census Bureau estimate July 1, 1978.  † Town or township.  [3] 1977 estimate.

**MASSACHUSETTS** (cont.)

| PLACE AND ZIP CODE | | POP. | PLACE AND ZIP CODE | | POP. | PLACE AND ZIP CODE | | POP. |
|---|---|---|---|---|---|---|---|---|
| Dudley [3]† | 01570 | 7,967 | Malden [2] | 02148 | 54,290 | Scituate [2]† | 02066 | 17,545 |
| Duxbury [3]† | 02332 | 10,878 | Manchester [3]† | 01944 | 5,685 | Seekonk [3]† | 02771 | 11,576 |
| E. Bridgewater [3]† | 02333 | 9,671 | Mansfield [3]† | 02048 | 13,286 | Sharon [3]† | 02067 | 13,962 |
| E. Longmeadow [3]† | 01028 | 13,334 | Marblehead [3]† | 01945 | 21,527 | Shrewsbury [3]† | 01545 | 22,267 |
| Easthampton [3]† | 01027 | 15,070 | Marlborough [2] | 01752 | 29,860 | Somerset [3]† | 02726 | 19,489 |
| Easton [3]† | 02334 | 15,055 | Marshfield [3]† | 02050 | 21,052 | Somerville [2] | 02143 | 74,873 |
| Everett [2] | 02149 | 38,447 | Mattapoisett [3]† | 02739 | 5,655 | South Hadley [3]† | 01075 | 16,290 |
| Fairhaven [3]† | 02719 | 16,093 | Maynard [3]† | 01754 | 9,845 | Southborough [3]† | 01772 | 6,481 |
| Fall River [2] | 02722* | 97,381 | Medfield [3]† | 02052 | 10,411 | Southbridge [3]† | 01550 | 16,591 |
| Falmouth [3]† | 02540* | 21,832 | Medford [2] | 02155 | 60,062 | Southwick [3]† | 01077 | 7,329 |
| Fitchburg [2] | 01420 | 37,126 | Medway [3]† | 02053 | 8,219 | Spencer [3]† | 01562 | 10,141 |
| Foxborough [3]† | 02035 | 14,115 | Melrose [2] | 02176 | 31,588 | Springfield [2] | 01101* | 161,889 |
| Framingham [3]† | 01701 | 64,079 | Methuen [3]† | 01844 | 35,401 | Sterling [3]† | 01564 | 5,043 |
| Franklin [3]† | 02038 | 18,679 | Middleborough [3]† | 02346 | 14,329 | Stoneham [3]† | 02180 | 21,575 |
| Freetown [3]† | — | 6,309 | Milford [3]† | 01757 | 23,733 | Stoughton [3]† | 02072 | 26,376 |
| Gardner [2] | 01440 | 17,815 | Millbury [3]† | 01527 | 11,929 | Stow [3]† | 01775 | 5,091 |
| Georgetown [3]† | 01833 | 5,967 | Millis [3]† | 02054 | 6,770 | Sturbridge [3]† | 01566 | 5,579 |
| Gloucester [2] | 01930 | 27,054 | Milton [3]† | 02186 | 27,281 | Sudbury [3]† | 01776 | 15,128 |
| Grafton [3]† | 01519 | 10,703 | Monson [3]† | 01057 | 7,528 | Sutton [3]† | — | 5,230 |
| Granby [3]† | 01033 | 5,446 | Montague [3]† | 01351 | 7,883 | Swampscott [3]† | 01907 | 14,216 |
| Grt. Barr'gton [3]† | 01230 | 6,662 | Nantucket [3]† | 02554 | 5,469 | Swansea [3]† | 02777 | 15,330 |
| Greenfield [3]† | 01301 | 17,937 | Natick [3]† | 01760 | 30,596 | Taunton [2] | 02780 | 41,583 |
| Groton [3]† | 01450 | 5,572 | Needham [3]† | 02192 | 29,607 | Templeton [3]† | 01468 | 6,132 |
| Groveland [3]† | 08134 | 5,087 | New Bedford [2] | 02741* | 97,911 | Tewksbury [2]† | 01876 | 24,226 |
| Halifax [3]† | 02338 | 5,304 | Newburyport [2] | 01950 | 16,133 | Topsfield [3]† | 01983 | 6,031 |
| Hamilton [3]† | 01936 | 6,825 | Newton [2] | 02158 | 87,177 | Townsend [3]† | 01469 | 5,643 |
| Hanover [3]† | 02339 | 11,101 | Norfolk [3]† | 02056 | 6,545 | Tyngsborough [3]† | 01879 | 5,190 |
| Hanson [3]† | 02341 | 8,563 | North Adams [2] | 01247 | 17,448 | Uxbridge [3]† | 01569 | 8,506 |
| Harvard [3]† | 01451 | 10,217 | North Andover [3]† | 01845 | 16,267 | Wakefield [3]† | 01880 | 25,439 |
| Harwich [3]† | 02645 | 8,395 | N. Attleborough [3]† | 02760* | 19,813 | Walpole [3]† | 02081 | 18,717 |
| Haverhill [2] | 01830 | 43,923 | North Reading [3]† | 01864 | 12,265 | Waltham [2] | 02154 | 55,092 |
| Hingham [3]† | 02043 | 19,616 | Northampton [2] | 01060 | 28,007 | Ware [3]† | 01082 | 8,424 |
| Holbrook [3]† | 02343 | 11,774 | Northborough [3]† | 01532 | 10,923 | Wareham [3]† | 02571 | 15,391 |
| Holden [3]† | 01520 | 13,861 | Northbridge [3]† | 01534 | 12,174 | Watertown [2] | 02172 | 34,927 |
| Holliston [3]† | 01746 | 13,176 | Norton [3]† | 02766 | 10,651 | Wayland [3]† | 01778 | 13,021 |
| Holyoke [2] | 01040 | 43,334 | Norwell [3]† | 02061 | 9,081 | Webster [2]† | 01570 | 14,087 |
| Hopkinton [3]† | 01748 | 6,682 | Norwood [3]† | 02062 | 30,996 | Wellesley [3]† | 02181 | 27,173 |
| Hudson [3]† | 01749 | 16,705 | Orange [3]† | 01364 | 6,022 | West Boylston [3]† | 01583 | 6,167 |
| Hull [3]† | 02045 | 10,454 | Oxford [3]† | 01540 | 11,732 | W. Bridgewater [3]† | 02379 | 6,456 |
| Hyannis [1] | 02601 | 6,847 | Palmer [3]† | 01069 | 11,702 | W. Springfield [3]† | 01089 | 28,075 |
| Ipswich [3]† | 01938 | 11,585 | Peabody [2] | 01960 | 45,204 | Westborough [3]† | 01581 | 13,914 |
| Kingston [3]† | 02364 | 6,826 | Pembroke [3]† | 02359 | 12,970 | Westfield [2]† | 01085 | 34,692 |
| Lakeville [3]† | — | 5,345 | Pepperell [3]† | 01463 | 7,053 | Westford [3]† | 01886 | 13,643 |
| Lancaster [3]† | 01523 | 6,074 | Pittsfield [2] | 01201 | 52,004 | Weston [3]† | 02193 | 11,696 |
| Lawrence [2] | 01842* | 62,488 | Plainville [3]† | 02762 | 5,469 | Westport [3]† | 02790 | 13,371 |
| Lee [3]† | 01238 | 6,166 | Plymouth [3]† | 02360 | 31,237 | Westwood [3]† | 02090 | 13,970 |
| Leicester [2]† | 01524 | 9,222 | Quincy [2] | 02169 | 88,612 | Weymouth [3]† | 02188 | 56,305 |
| Lenox [3]† | 01240 | 6,226 | Randolph [3]† | 02368 | 29,330 | Whitman [3]† | 02382 | 13,360 |
| Leominster [2] | 01453 | 35,082 | Raynham [3]† | 02767 | 8,395 | Wilbraham [3]† | 01095 | 13,080 |
| Lexington [3]† | 02173 | 32,384 | Reading [3]† | 01867 | 23,760 | Williamstown [3]† | 01267 | 8,438 |
| Lincoln [3]† | 01773 | 7,586 | Rehoboth [2]† | 02769 | 7,326 | Wilmington [3]† | 01887 | 18,167 |
| Littleton [3]† | 01460 | 6,621 | Revere [2] | 02151 | 41,368 | Winchendon [3]† | 01475 | 6,848 |
| Longmeadow [3]† | 01106 | 16,986 | Rockland [3]† | 02370 | 16,880 | Winchester [3]† | 01890 | 22,449 |
| Lowell [2] | 01853* | 87,173 | Rockport [3]† | 01966 | 6,333 | Winthrop [3]† | 02152 | 20,617 |
| Ludlow [3]† | 01056 | 18,186 | Salem [2] | 01970 | 37,684 | Woburn [2] | 01801 | 34,450 |
| Lunenburg [3]† | 01462 | 8,198 | Salisbury [3]† | 01950 | 5,220 | Worcester [2] | 01613* | 163,523 |
| Lynn [2] | 01901* | 76,229 | Sandwich [3]† | 02563 | 7,789 | Wrentham [3]† | 02093 | 7,514 |
| Lynnfield [3]† | 01940 | 12,151 | Saugus [3]† | 01906 | 24,559 | Yarmouth [3]† | 02675 | 18,575 |

**MICHIGAN (Mich. or MI)**

| PLACE AND ZIP CODE | | POP. | PLACE AND ZIP CODE | | POP. | PLACE AND ZIP CODE | | POP. |
|---|---|---|---|---|---|---|---|---|
| Adrian [2] | 49221 | 20,046 | Benton Central [1] | 49022 | 8,067 | Cheboygan [2] | 49721 | 5,518 |
| Albian [2] | 49224 | 13,347 | Benton Harbor [2] | 49022 | 15,353 | Clawson [2] | 48017 | 16,083 |
| Allegan [2] | 49010 | 5,807 | Berkley [2] | 48072 | 18,902 | Coldwater [2] | 49036 | 10,289 |
| Allen Park [2] | 48101 | 36,081 | Beverly Hills [2] | 48009 | 11,749 | Davison [2] | 48423 | 6,388 |
| Alma [2] | 48801 | 9,969 | Big Rapids [2] | 49307 | 15,075 | Dearborn [2] | 48120* | 91,652 |
| Alpena [2] | 49707 | 15,403 | Birmingham [2] | 48012* | 23,800 | Dearborn Hts. [2] | 48127 | 69,097 |
| Ann Arbor [2] | 48106* | 105,213 | Burton [2] | — | 35,033 | Detroit [2] | 48233* | 1,257,879 |
| Battle Creek [2] | 49016* | 41,328 | Cadillac [2] | 49601 | 10,659 | Dowagiac [2] | 49047 | 6,472 |
| Bay City [2] | 48706* | 45,972 | Center Line [2] | 48015 | 9,159 | East Detroit [2] | 48021 | 40,706 |
| Belding [2] | 48809 | 5,644 | Charlotte [2] | 48813 | 9,907 | E. Grand Rapids [2] | 49506 | 12,836 |

[1] 1970 Census.  [2] Census Bureau estimate: 1978.  [3] 1977 estimate.  † Town or township.

## MICHIGAN (continued)

| PLACE AND ZIP CODE | POP. | PLACE AND ZIP CODE | POP. | PLACE AND ZIP CODE | POP. |
|---|---|---|---|---|---|
| East Lansing [2].... 48823 | 50,164 | Ishpeming [2] ...... 49849 | 8,375 | Portland [2] ....... 48875 | 4,976 |
| Eaton Rapids [2] ... 48827 | 5,615 | Jackson [2] ........ 49201* | 43,057 | River Rouge [3] .... 48218 | 12,748 |
| Ecorse [2] ........ 48229 | 13,922 | Jenison [1] ........ 49428 | 11,266 | Riverview [2] ...... 48192 | 13,301 |
| Escanaba [2] ...... 49829 | 14,466 | Kalamazoo [3] ...... 49001* | 79,472 | Rochester [2] ...... 48063 | 9,511 |
| Essexville [2] ..... 48732 | 5,782 | Kentwood [2] ....... 49508 | 29,436 | Romulus [2] ....... 48174 | 24,832 |
| Farmington [2] ..... 48024 | 11,120 | Kingsford [2] ...... 49801 | 5,406 | Roseville [2] ...... 48066 | 55,819 |
| Farmington Hills [2] — | 60,818 | Lansing [3] ........ 48924* | 126,071 | Royal Oak [3] ...... 48068* | 77,380 |
| Fenton [2] ......... 48430 | 10,474 | Lapeer [2] ......... 48446 | 5,619 | Saginaw [3]........ 48605* | 84,144 |
| Ferndale [2] ....... 48220 | 26,432 | Lincoln Park [2] ... 48146 | 46,754 | St. Clair [2] ...... 48079 | 4,941 |
| Flat Rock [2]....... 48134 | 6,580 | Livonia [3]........ 48150* | 110,516 | St. Clair Shores [3] . 48080 | 85,933 |
| Flint [2] .......... 48502* | 162,707 | Ludington [2] ...... 49431 | 10,355 | St. Johns [2] ...... 48879 | 8,458 |
| Flushing [2] ....... 48433 | 8,422 | Madison Hts. [2] ... 48071 | 35,786 | St. Joseph [2] ..... 49085 | 10,718 |
| Fraser [2] ......... 48026 | 14,067 | Manistee [2] ....... 49660 | 8,098 | Saline [2].......... 48176 | 7,018 |
| Fremont [2] ........ 49412 | 5,204 | Marine City [2] .... 48039 | 5,331 | Sault Ste. Marie [2] . 49783 | 15,156 |
| Garden City [2] .... 48135 | 37,852 | Marquette [2] ...... 49855 | 24,905 | South Haven [2] .... 49090 | 5,919 |
| Grand Blanc [2]..... 48439 | 5,601 | Marshall [2] ....... 49068 | 7,449 | South Lyon [2] ..... 48178 | 4,996 |
| Grand Haven [2] .... 49417 | 12,540 | Marysville [2] ..... 48040 | 7,026 | Southfield [6] ..... 48034* | 75,085 |
| Grand Ledge [2]..... 48837 | 7,674 | Mason [2] .......... 48854 | 6,451 | Southgate [2] ...... 48195 | 32,745 |
| Grand Rapids [3]... 49501* | 185,588 | Melvindale [2] ..... 48122 | 11,659 | Springfield [2] ..... — | 5,607 |
| Grandville [2] ..... 49418 | 12,524 | Menominee [2] ...... 49858 | 10,253 | Sterling Hts. [2] ... 48077 | 103,083 |
| Greenville [2] ..... 48838 | 8,707 | Midland [2] ........ 48640 | 37,597 | Sturgis [2] ........ 49091 | 9,212 |
| Grosse Pointe [2].... 48236 | 5,971 | Milford [2] ........ 48042 | 7,884 | Swartz Creek [2] ... 48473 | 7,089 |
| Grosse Pt. Fms. [2]. 48236 | 10,218 | Monroe [2] ......... 48161 | 24,782 | Taylor [3].......... 48180 | 77,886 |
| Grosse Pointe Pk. [2] 48236 | 13,754 | Mount Clemens [2] . 48043* | 23,830 | Tecumseh [2] ...... 49286 | 8,234 |
| Grosse Pointe Wds. [2] 48236 | 19,755 | Mt. Pleasant [2] ... 48858 | 24,521 | Three Rivers [2] ... 49093 | 6,456 |
| Hamtramck [2] ...... 48212 | 22,289 | Muskegon [2] ...... 49440* | 43,237 | Traverse City [2] ... 49684 | 17,944 |
| Harper Woods [2] ... 48225 | 16,491 | Muskegon Hts. [2] .. 49444 | 15,954 | Trenton [2] ........ 48183 | 25,002 |
| Hastings [2] ....... 49058 | 7,580 | Negaunee [2] ....... 49866 | 5,568 | Troy [2] ........... 48099 | 66,478 |
| Hazel Park [2] ..... 48030 | 20,596 | New Baltimore [2] .. 48047 | 5,395 | Walker [2] ......... 49504 | 13,923 |
| Highland Park [2] .. 48203 | 28,882 | Niles [2] .......... 49120 | 13,440 | Warren [6] ......... 48089 | 170,225 |
| Hillsdale [2] ...... 49242 | 8,578 | Northville [2] ..... 48167 | 7,472 | Wayne [2] .......... 48184 | 19,365 |
| Holland [2] ....... 49423* | 28,838 | Norton Shores [2] .. 49441 | 21,160 | Westland [3] ....... 48185 | 89,270 |
| Holly [2] .......... 48442 | 5,299 | Novi [2] ........... 48050 | 17,693 | Wixom [2] .......... 48096 | 5,346 |
| Houghton [2] ...... 49931 | 6,849 | Oak Park [2] ....... 48237 | 31,820 | Wolverine Lake [2] . 49799 | 5,593 |
| Howell [2] ........ 48843 | 8,281 | Owosso [2] ......... 48867 | 18,136 | Woodhaven [2] ..... 48183 | 9,163 |
| Huntington Wds. [2] 48070 | 7,522 | Petoskey [2] ....... 49770 | 6,055 | Wyandotte [2] ...... 48192 | 35,404 |
| Inkster [2] ........ 48141 | 35,009 | Plymouth [2] ....... 48170 | 10,219 | Wyoming [2] ....... 49509 | 58,129 |
| Ionia [2] .......... 48846 | 6,580 | Pontiac [3] ....... 48056* | 79,778 | Ypsilanti [2] ...... 48197 | 27,618 |
| Iron Mountain [2].. 49801 | 8,622 | Port Huron [2] ..... 48060 | 34,662 | Zeeland [2] ........ 49464 | 5,966 |
| Ironwood [2] ....... 49938 | 7,969 | Portage [2] ........ 49081 | 36,974 | | |

## MINNESOTA (Minn. or MN)

| PLACE AND ZIP CODE | POP. | PLACE AND ZIP CODE | POP. | PLACE AND ZIP CODE | POP. |
|---|---|---|---|---|---|
| Albert Lea [2] ..... 56007 | 19,089 | East Grand Forks [2] 56721 | 8,849 | Maplewood [2] ..... 55109 | 26,606 |
| Alexandria [2] ..... 56308 | 7,470 | Eden Prairie [2].... 55344 | 10,473 | Marshall [2] ....... 56258 | 9,962 |
| Andover [2]........ — | 7,891 | Edina [2] .......... 55424 | 48,791 | Mendota Hts. [2] .. 55050 | 8,401 |
| Anoka [2] .......... 55303 | 16,219 | Elk River [2] ...... 55330 | 7,850 | Minneapolis [3] .... 55401* | 371,896 |
| Apple Valley [2] ... 55124 | 19,919 | Fairmont [2] ....... 56031 | 11,481 | Minnetonka [2] ..... 55343 | 45,390 |
| Arden Hills [2] .... — | 7,968 | Falcon Hts. [2] .... — | 5,523 | Montevideo [2]...... 56265 | 5,385 |
| Austin [2] ......... 55912 | 22,889 | Faribault [2] ...... 55021 | 15,659 | Moorhead [2] ...... 56560 | 28,901 |
| Bemidji [2] ........ 56601 | 11,251 | Farmington [2] ..... 55024 | 5,666 | Morris [2] ......... 56267 | 5,178 |
| Blaine [2] ......... 55433 | 32,439 | Fergus Falls [2] ... 56537 | 11,726 | Mound [2] .......... 55364 | 10,117 |
| Bloomington [3] .... 55420 | 78,683 | Forest Lake [2] .... 55025 | 5,466 | Mounds View [2] ... 55112 | 14,498 |
| Brainerd [2] ....... 56401 | 10,424 | Fridley [2] ........ 55432 | 36,594 | New Brighton [2] ... 55112 | 19,780 |
| Brooklyn Ctr. [2] .. 55429 | 30,969 | Golden Valley [2] .. 55427 | 22,525 | New Hope [2] ...... 55428 | 22,335 |
| Brooklyn Pk. [2] ... 55429 | 40,203 | Grand Rapids [2] ... 55744 | 9,550 | New Ulm [2] ....... 56073 | 14,024 |
| Burnsville [2] ..... 55337 | 33,890 | Ham Lake [2] ...... — | 15,387 | N. Mankato [2] ..... 56001 | 8,402 |
| Champlin [2] ....... 55316 | 8,688 | Hastings [2] ....... 55033 | 16,612 | North St. Paul [2].. 55109 | 11,351 |
| Chanhassen [2] ..... 55317 | 5,487 | Hermantown [2].... | 6,735 | Northfield [2] ...... 55057 | 11,703 |
| Chaska [2] ......... 55318 | 7,990 | Hibbing [2] ....... 55746 | 15,812 | Oakdale [2] ........ — | 11,058 |
| Chisholm [2]........ 55719 | 5,885 | Hopkins [2] ........ 55343 | 15,874 | Orono [2] .......... — | 7,096 |
| Cloquet [2] ........ 55720 | 11,184 | Hutchinson [2] ..... 55350 | 8,643 | Owatonna [2] ....... 55060 | 18,128 |
| Columbia Hts. [2] .. 55421 | 23,966 | Internat'l. Falls [2] . 56649 | 5,674 | Plymouth [2] ....... 55427 | 25,700 |
| Coon Rapids [2]..... 55433 | 32,061 | Inver Grove Hts. [2]. 55075 | 18,512 | Prior Lake [2] ..... 55372 | 7,519 |
| Cottage Grove [2] .. 55016 | 17,972 | Lake Elmo [2] ...... 55042 | 4,963 | Ramsey [2]†........ — | 7,475 |
| Crookston [2] ...... 56716* | 8,240 | Lakeville [2] ...... 55044 | 11,584 | Red Wing [2] ...... 55066 | 13,483 |
| Crystal [2]......... 55428 | 26,832 | Litchfield [2]...... 55355 | 5,294 | Redwood Falls [2] .. 56283 | 5,017 |
| Detroit Lakes [2] .. 56501 | 6,799 | Little Canada [2] ... — | 6,483 | Richfield [2] ....... 55423 | 40,465 |
| Duluth [3] ........ 55806* | 94,824 | Little Falls [2] .... 56345 | 7,614 | Robbinsdale [2] .... 55422 | 14,228 |
| Eagan [2] ......... 55121 | 19,734 | Mankato [2] ....... 56001* | 27,200 | Rochester [2] ...... 55901* | 56,732 |
| East Bethel [2] .... 55005 | 5,819 | Maple Grove [2].... — | 16,324 | Rosemount [2] ..... 55068 | 5,227 |

[1]1970 Census.   [2]Census Bureau estimate July 1, 1978.   [3]1978 Special Census.

| PLACE AND ZIP CODE | | POP. | PLACE AND ZIP CODE | | POP. | PLACE AND ZIP CODE | | POP. |
|---|---|---|---|---|---|---|---|---|
| **MINNESOTA** *(continued)* | | | Sauk Rapids [2] .... | 56379 | 5,117 | Waseca [2] ......... | 56093 | 7,938 |
| Roseville [2] ....... | 55113 | 39,331 | Shakopee [2] ...... | 55379 | 8,959 | West St. Paul [2] ... | 55118 | 18,046 |
| St. Anthony [2] ..... | 55418 | 9,372 | Shoreview [2] ...... | 55112 | 17,723 | White Bear Lake [2] | 55110 | 23,814 |
| St. Cloud [2] ....... | 56301 | 41,404 | South St. Paul [2] .. | 55075 | 20,560 | Willmar [2] ........ | 56201 | 13,889 |
| St. Louis Park [2] ... | 55426 | 44,778 | Spring L. Park [2] .. | 55432 | 9,020 | Winona [2] ........ | 55987* | 25,078 |
| St. Paul [3] ........ | 55101* | 272,465 | Stillwater [2] ....... | 55082 | 16,372 | Woodbury [2] ...... | — | 12,857 |
| St. Paul Park [2] ... | 55071 | 5,861 | Thief River Falls [2] . | 56701 | 8,926 | Worthington [2] .... | 56187 | 10,385 |
| St. Peter [2] ....... | 56082 | 8,214 | Virginia [2] ........ | 55792 | 11,058 | | | |

**MISSISSIPPI (Miss. or MS)**

| PLACE AND ZIP CODE | | POP. | PLACE AND ZIP CODE | | POP. | PLACE AND ZIP CODE | | POP. |
|---|---|---|---|---|---|---|---|---|
| Aberdeen [2] ...... | 39730 | 7,123 | Greenwood [2] ..... | 38930 | 21,497 | Ocean Springs [2] .. | 39564 | 15,612 |
| Amory [2] ......... | 38821 | 7,476 | Grenada [2] ....... | 38901 | 12,201 | Oxford [2] ......... | 38655 | 11,408 |
| Bay St. Louis [2] ... | 39520 | 7,081 | Gulfport [2] ....... | 39503* | 44,666 | Pascagoula [2] ..... | 39567 | 31,170 |
| Biloxi [2] ......... | 39530* | 43,927 | Hattiesburg [2] ..... | 39401 | 41,397 | Pass Christian [2] .. | 39571 | 5,259 |
| Booneville [2] ..... | 38829 | 5,857 | Holly Springs [2] ... | 38635 | 5,918 | Pearl [2] .......... | 39208 | 19,419 |
| Brandon [2] ....... | 39042 | 9,843 | Indianola [2] ...... | 38751 | 8,905 | Petal [2] .......... | 39465 | 9,245 |
| Brookhaven [2] .... | 39601 | 10,636 | Jackson [2] ....... | 39205* | 190,791 | Philadelphia [2] .... | 39350 | 6,263 |
| Canton [2] ........ | 39046 | 11,632 | Kosciusko [2] ...... | 39090 | 6,652 | Picayune [2] ....... | 39466 | 10,297 |
| Clarksdale [2] ..... | 38614 | 20,618 | Laurel [2] ......... | 39440 | 23,681 | Senatobia [2] ...... | 38668 | 5,246 |
| Cleveland [2] ...... | 38732 | 13,781 | Leland [2] ......... | 38756 | 5,896 | Starkville [2] ...... | 39759 | 14,128 |
| Clinton [2] ........ | 39056 | 13,379 | Long Beach [2] .... | 39560 | 8,265 | Tupelo [2] ......... | 38801 | 23,934 |
| Columbia [2] ...... | 39429 | 7,017 | Louisville [2] ...... | 39339 | 6,365 | Vicksburg [2] ...... | 39180 | 31,016 |
| Columbus [2] ...... | 39701 | 26,799 | McComb [2] ....... | 39648 | 12,364 | Waynesboro [2] .... | 39367 | 4,933 |
| Corinth [2] ........ | 38834 | 11,329 | Meridian [2] ....... | 39301 | 44,027 | West Gulfport [1] ... | 39501 | 6,996 |
| D'Iberville [1] ..... | 39532 | 7,288 | Moss Point [2] ..... | 39563 | 20,379 | West Point [2] ..... | 39773 | 8,336 |
| Ellisville [1] ...... | 39437 | 5,362 | Natchez [2] ....... | 39120 | 23,368 | Winona [2] ........ | 38967 | 5,591 |
| Greenville [2] ..... | 38701 | 42,159 | New Albany [2] .... | 38652 | 6,769 | Yazoo City [2] ..... | 39194 | 11,687 |

**MISSOURI (Mo. or MO)**

| PLACE AND ZIP CODE | | POP. | PLACE AND ZIP CODE | | POP. | PLACE AND ZIP CODE | | POP. |
|---|---|---|---|---|---|---|---|---|
| Arnold [2] ........ | 63010 | 21,503 | Frontenac [2] ...... | — | 4,709 | Nevada [2] ........ | 64772 | 9,029 |
| Aurora [2] ........ | 65605 | 6,086 | Fulton [2] ......... | 65251 | 11,418 | Normandy [2] ...... | 63121 | 6,089 |
| Ballwin [2] ........ | 63011 | 15,655 | Gladstone [2] ...... | 64118 | 31,745 | Northwoods [2] .... | — | 6,902 |
| Bellefontaine | | | Glendale [2] ....... | 63122 | 6,690 | O'Fallon [2] ....... | 63366 | 9,540 |
| Neighbors [2] .... | 63137 | 12,510 | Grandview [2] ..... | 64030 | 23,669 | Olivette [2] ....... | 63132 | 8,598 |
| Bel-Ridge [2] ...... | — | 5,302 | Hannibal [2] ....... | 63401 | 17,709 | Overland [2] ....... | 63114 | 21,667 |
| Belton [2] ......... | 64012 | 14,098 | Harrisonville [2] .... | 64701 | 6,166 | Pagedale [2] ....... | — | 4,878 |
| Berkeley [2] ....... | 63134 | 16,228 | Hazelwood [4] ..... | 63042* | 13,739 | Perryville [2] ...... | 63775 | 6,397 |
| Black Jack [2] ..... | — | 5,817 | Higginsville [2] .... | 64037 | 4,880 | Pine Lawn [2] ..... | 63120 | 5,867 |
| Blue Springs [2] ... | 64015 | 19,146 | Independence [2] ... | 64051* | 112,544 | Poplar Bluff [2] .... | 63901 | 17,189 |
| Bolivar [2] ........ | 65613 | 5,259 | Jackson [2] ....... | 63755 | 7,120 | Raytown [2] ....... | 64133 | 32,513 |
| Boonville [2] ...... | 65233 | 7,178 | Jefferson City [2] ... | 65101 | 37,749 | Richmond Hts. [2] .. | 63117 | 12,345 |
| Breckenridge Hls. [2] . | 64625 | 7,320 | Jennings [2] ...... | 63136 | 16,724 | Rock Hill [2] ...... | 63124 | 6,506 |
| Brentwood [2] ..... | 63144 | 9,493 | Joplin [2] ......... | 64801 | 41,061 | Rolla [2] .......... | 65401 | 15,563 |
| Bridgeton [2] ...... | 63044 | 17,792 | Kansas City [2] .... | 64108* | 456,907 | St. Ann [2] ........ | 63074 | 16,652 |
| Brookfield [2] ..... | 64628 | 5,066 | Kennett [2] ....... | 63857 | 10,187 | St. Charles [2] ..... | 63301 | 41,724 |
| Cape Girardeau [2] . | 63701 | 33,473 | Kinloch [2] ....... | 63140 | 5,654 | St. John [2] ....... | 63114 | 8,712 |
| Carthage [2] ...... | 64836 | 10,610 | Kirksville [2] ...... | 63501 | 15,392 | St. Joseph [2] ..... | 64501* | 76,931 |
| Caruthersville [2] .. | 63830 | 7,245 | Kirkwood [2] ...... | 63122 | 30,535 | St. Louis [2] ...... | 63155* | 508,496 |
| Chillicothe [2] ..... | 64601 | 9,491 | Ladue [2] ......... | 63124 | 10,867 | Salem [2] ......... | 65560* | 4,845 |
| Clayton [2] ........ | 63105 | 15,007 | Lebanon [2] ....... | 65536 | 8,276 | Sedalia [2] ........ | 65301 | 22,169 |
| Clinton [2] ........ | 64735 | 7,476 | Lee's Summit [2] ... | 64063 | 24,401 | Shrewsbury [2] .... | — | 5,597 |
| Columbia [2] ...... | 65201 | 65,781 | Lexington [2] ...... | 64067 | 4,776 | Sikeston [2] ....... | 63801 | 17,251 |
| Crestwood [2] ..... | 63126 | 15,305 | Liberty [2] ........ | 64068 | 15,944 | Springfield [2] ..... | 65801* | 138,833 |
| Creve Coeur [2] ... | 63141 | 10,937 | Macon [2] ........ | 63552 | 5,467 | Sullivan [2] ....... | 63080 | 5,067 |
| De Soto [2] ....... | 63020 | 5,625 | Malden [2] ........ | 63863 | 6,448 | Trenton [2] ....... | 64683 | 6,405 |
| Dellwood [2] ...... | 63136 | 6,955 | Manchester [2] .... | 63011 | 9,629 | Union [4] .......... | 63084 | 5,951 |
| Des Peres [2] ..... | 63131 | 8,355 | Maplewood [2] .... | 63143 | 10,540 | University City [2] .. | 63130 | 44,159 |
| Dexter [2] ........ | 63841 | 6,257 | Marshall [2] ....... | 65340 | 11,370 | Warrensburg [2] ... | 64093 | 15,342 |
| Ellisville [2] ...... | — | 5,152 | Maryland Hts. [1] ... | 63043 | 8,805 | Washington [2] .... | 63090 | 9,356 |
| Excelsior Spgs. [2] . | 64024 | 11,311 | Maryville [2] ...... | 64468 | 9,193 | Webb City [2] ..... | 64870 | 6,753 |
| Farmington [2] ..... | 63640 | 7,486 | Mexico [2] ........ | 65265 | 11,847 | Webster Groves [2] . | 63119 | 24,262 |
| Ferguson [2] ...... | 63135 | 25,860 | Moberly [2] ....... | 65270 | 12,917 | Wellston [2] ....... | 63112 | 6,271 |
| Festus [2] ........ | 63028 | 7,925 | Monett [2] ........ | 65708 | 5,885 | West Plains [2] .... | 65775 | 7,764 |
| Florissant [2] ...... | 63033* | 70,387 | Neosho [2] ........ | 64850 | 8,690 | Woodson Terr. [2] .. | 63134 | 5,473 |

**MONTANA (Mont. or MT)**

| PLACE AND ZIP CODE | | POP. | PLACE AND ZIP CODE | | POP. | PLACE AND ZIP CODE | | POP. |
|---|---|---|---|---|---|---|---|---|
| Anaconda–Deer | | | Butte-Silver Bow [2] | 59701 | 38,965 | Hazelwood [2] ..... | — | 13,807 |
| Lodge [2] ........ | 59711* | 13,976 | Glendive [5] ....... | 59330 | 5,872 | Helena [2] ......... | 59601* | 28,824 |
| Billings [2] ........ | 59101* | 73,086 | Great Falls [2] ..... | 59403* | 60,438 | Kalispell [2] ....... | 59901* | 16,361 |
| Bozeman [2] ....... | 59715 | 20,637 | Havre [2] ......... | 59501 | 10,612 | Laurel [2] ......... | 59044 | 5,450 |

[1] 1970 Census.   [2] Census Bureau estimate July 1, 1978.   [3] 1978 Special Censuses.   [4] 1977 estimate.

| PLACE AND ZIP CODE | POP. | PLACE AND ZIP CODE | POP. | PLACE AND ZIP CODE | POP. |
|---|---|---|---|---|---|
| **MONTANA** *(continued)* | | | | | |
| Lewiston² 59457 | 7,037 | Malmstrom¹ 59402 | 8,374 | Missoula² 59801 | 30,127 |
| Livingston² 59047 | 7,164 | Miles City² 59301 | 9,574 | Sidney⁴ 59270 | 4,937 |
| **NEBRASKA (Neb., Nebr., or NE)** | | | | | |
| Alliance² 69301 | 8,860 | Hastings² 68901 | 22,559 | Ogallala² 69153 | 5,764 |
| Beatrice² 68310 | 11,260 | Holdrege² 68949 | 5,778 | Omaha² 68108* | 368,347 |
| Bellevue² 68005 | 23,510 | Kearney² 68847 | 20,330 | Papillion² 68046 | 7,941 |
| Blair² 68008 | 6,352 | La Vista² 68128 | 11,489 | Plattsmouth² 68048 | 7,096 |
| Chadron² 69337 | 5,210 | Lexington² 68850 | 6,711 | Ralston² 68127 | 5,850 |
| Columbus² 68601 | 16,961 | Lincoln² 68501* | 166,311 | Scottsbluff² 69361 | 13,412 |
| Fairbury² 68352 | 4,913 | McCook² 69001 | 8,428 | Seward² 68434 | 5,492 |
| Falls City² 68355 | 4,974 | Nebraska City² 68410 | 7,160 | Sidney² 69162 | 6,060 |
| Fremont² 68025 | 23,626 | Norfolk² 68701 | 18,077 | South Sioux City² 68776 | 8,836 |
| Gering² 69341 | 7,288 | North Platte² 69101 | 24,547 | York² 68467 | 7,412 |
| Grand Island² 68801 | 34,751 | Offutt AFB¹ 68113 | 13,640 | | |
| **NEVADA (Nev. or NV)** | | | | | |
| Boulder City² 89005 | 7,247 | Ely² 89301 | 5,479 | North Las Vegas² 89030 | 40,358 |
| Carson City² 89701 | 29,694 | Henderson² 89015 | 21,271 | Reno² 89510* | 91,986 |
| Elko² 89801 | 8,907 | Las Vegas² 89114* | 168,932 | Sparks² 89431 | 36,953 |
| **NEW HAMPSHIRE (N.H. or NH)** | | | | | |
| Amherst³† 03031 | 8,131 | Goffstown³† 03045 | 10,103 | Merrimack³† 03054 | 16,330 |
| Bedford³† 03102 | 8,138 | Hampton³† 03842 | 9,135 | Milford³† 03055 | 8,258 |
| Berlin² 03570 | 13,888 | Hanover³† 03755 | 9,107 | Nashua² 03061 | 64,266 |
| Center Conway³† 03813 | 6,098 | Hooksett³† 03106 | 6,943 | Newport³† 03773 | 6,060 |
| Claremont² 03743 | 13,740 | Hudson³† 03051 | 12,802 | Pelham³† 03076 | 7,790 |
| Concord² 03301 | 28,809 | Keene² 03431 | 21,245 | Plaistow³† 03865 | 5,504 |
| Derry³† 03038 | 16,791 | Laconia² 03246 | 15,039 | Portsmouth² 03801 | 26,243 |
| Dover² 03820 | 22,031 | Lebanon² 03766 | 10,090 | Rochester² 03867 | 20,804 |
| Durham³† 03824 | 11,953 | Littleton³† 03561 | 5,405 | Salem³† 03079 | 23,638 |
| Exeter³† 03833 | 10,114 | Londonderry³† 03053 | 11,714 | Seabrook³† 03874 | 6,041 |
| Franklin² 03235 | 7,460 | Manchester² 03103* | 84,377 | Somersworth² 03878 | 9,301 |
| **NEW JERSEY (N.J. or NJ)** | | | | | |
| Aberdeen³ — | 18,815 | Collingswood² 08108 | 15,784 | Haddonfield² 08033 | 12,307 |
| Absecon² 08201 | 6,892 | Cresskill² 07626 | 7,801 | Haledon² 07508 | 5,963 |
| Allendale² 07401 | 6,078 | Demarest² 07627 | 5,017 | Hammonton² 08037 | 11,838 |
| Asbury Park² 07712 | 15,112 | Dover² 07801 | 13,933 | Harrison² 07029 | 11,657 |
| Atlantic City²  08401* | 41,978 | Dumont² 07628 | 18,535 | Hasbrouck Hts.² 07604 | 12,515 |
| Atlantic Hglds² 07716 | 4,991 | Dunellen² 08812 | 6,513 | Hawthorne² 07506 | 17,428 |
| Audubon² 08106 | 9,750 | East Orange² 07019* | 70,499 | Highland Park² 08904 | 13,474 |
| Barrington² 08007 | 7,820 | E. Rutherford² 07073 | 8,147 | Hightstown² 08520 | 5,183 |
| Bayonne² 07002 | 67,560 | East Windsor³† 08520 | 22,144 | Hillsdale² 07642 | 11,259 |
| Beachwood² 08722 | 7,166 | Eatontown² 07724 | 12,638 | Hoboken² 07030 | 41,942 |
| Belleville² 07109 | 36,428 | Edgewater² 07020 | 5,111 | Hopatcong² 07843 | 13,713 |
| Bellmawr² 08031 | 14,352 | Edison³† 08817* | 66,131 | Irvington² 07111 | 54,986 |
| Belmar² 07719 | 6,023 | Elizabeth² 07207* | 102,669 | Jamesburg² 08831 | 4,665 |
| Bergenfield² 07621 | 26,516 | Elmwood Park² 07407 | 19,205 | Jersey City² 07303* | 225,957 |
| Berlin² 08009 | 5,583 | Emerson² 07630 | 7,948 | Keansburg² 07734 | 9,599 |
| Bernardsville² 07924 | 6,639 | Englewood² 07631* | 23,383 | Kearny² 07032 | 35,666 |
| Bloomfield² 07003 | 49,318 | Englewood Clfs² 07632 | 5,996 | Kenilworth² 07033 | 8,592 |
| Bloomingdale² 07403 | 7,927 | Fair Haven² 07701 | 5,854 | Keyport² 07735 | 7,074 |
| Bogota² 07603 | 8,151 | Fair Lawn² 07410 | 34,951 | Kinnelon² 07405 | 8,040 |
| Boonton² 07005 | 8,697 | Fairfield³† 07006 | 7,902 | Leonia² 07605 | 8,064 |
| Bound Brook² 08805 | 9,607 | Fairview² 07022 | 10,354 | Lincoln Park² 07035 | 8,579 |
| Bridgeton² 08302 | 19,664 | Fanwood² 07023 | 8,284 | Linden² 07036 | 39,067 |
| Brigantine² 08203 | 8,501 | Florham Park² 07932 | 9,244 | Lindenwold² 08021 | 18,377 |
| Burlington² 08016 | 11,479 | Fort Lee² 07024 | 33,848 | Linwood² 08221 | 6,464 |
| Butler² 07405 | 7,697 | Franklin Lakes² 07417 | 8,363 | Little Ferry² 07643 | 9,256 |
| Caldwell² 07006 | 7,896 | Freehold² 07728 | 10,856 | Little Silver² 07739 | 5,827 |
| Camden² 08101* | 86,319 | Garfield² 07026 | 27,920 | Lodi² 07644 | 24,323 |
| Carlstadt² 07072 | 6,268 | Garwood² 07027 | 4,832 | Long Branch² 07740 | 31,829 |
| Carteret² 07008 | 20,870 | Glassboro² 08028 | 14,392 | Madison² 07940 | 16,039 |
| Chatham² 07928 | 8,962 | Glen Ridge² 07028 | 7,951 | Magnolia² 08049 | 5,617 |
| Cherry Hill²† 08034* | 67,693 | Glen Rock² 07452 | 11,923 | Manasquan² 08736 | 5,187 |
| Clayton² 08312 | 5,947 | Gloucester City² 08030 | 13,365 | Manville² 08835 | 12,012 |
| Clementon² 08021 | 5,874 | Guttenberg² 07093 | 7,975 | Margate² 08402 | 10,660 |
| Cliffside Park² 07010 | 23,277 | Hackensack² 07602* | 37,207 | Marlton¹ 08053 | 10,180 |
| Clifton² 07015* | 74,427 | Hackettstown² 07840 | 9,742 | Matawan² 07747 | 9,350 |
| Closter² 07624 | 8,331 | Haddon Hts.² 08035 | 8,828 | Maywood² 07607 | 10,093 |

¹ 1970 Census.   ² Census Bureau estimate July 1, 1978.   ³ 1977 estimate.
† Town or township (includes rural population).

| PLACE AND ZIP CODE | POP. | PLACE AND ZIP CODE | POP. | PLACE AND ZIP CODE | POP. |
|---|---|---|---|---|---|
| **NEW JERSEY** (continued) | | Paramus [2] ....... 07652 | 27,388 | Somerville [2] ...... 08876* | 13,104 |
| Medford Lakes [2] .. 08055 | 5,881 | Park Ridge [2] ..... 07656 | 8,998 | South Amboy [2] .... 08879 | 8,587 |
| Mendham [2] ...... 07945 | 4,919 | Passaic [2] ........ 07055 | 48,193 | South Orange [2] ... 07079 | 17,552 |
| Mercerville [1] ..... 08619 | 24,465 | Paterson [2] ...... 07510* | 145,426 | South Plainfield [2] . 07080 | 20,679 |
| Metuchen [2] ...... 08840 | 14,583 | Paulsboro [2] ...... 08066 | 7,204 | South River [2] ..... 08882 | 14,765 |
| Middlesex [2] ...... 08846 | 13,956 | Penns Grove [2] .... 08069 | 5,270 | Spotswood [2] ...... 08884 | 8,060 |
| Midland Park [2] ... 07432 | 7,701 | Pennsville [2][†] .... 08070 | 14,210 | Spring Lake Hts. [2] 07762 | 5,520 |
| Milltown [2] ....... 08850 | 6,741 | Perth Amboy [2] ... 08861* | 35,244 | Stratford ......... 08084 | 8,885 |
| Millville [2] ....... 08332 | 24,391 | Phillipsburg [2] .... 08865 | 17,438 | Summit [2] ........ 07901 | 22,029 |
| Montclair [2] ...... 07042* | 39,736 | Pine Hill [5] ...... 08021 | 8,241 | Tenafly [2] ........ 07670 | 13,807 |
| Montvale [2] ...... 07645 | 7,453 | Pitman [2] ........ 08071 | 9,420 | Tinton Falls [2] .... 07724 | 8,076 |
| Morris Plains [2] ... 07950 | 5,338 | Plainfield [2] ...... 07061* | 43,548 | Toms River [1] ..... 08753 | 7,303 |
| Morristown [2] ..... 07960* | 16,396 | Pleasantville [2] .... 08232 | 13,791 | Totowa [2] ........ 07512 | 11,022 |
| Mt. Ephraim [2] .... 08059 | 5,025 | Point Pleasant [2] .. 08742 | 17,380 | Trenton [2] ....... 08650* | 94,772 |
| Mountainside [2] ... 07092 | 7,068 | Pt. Pleasant Bch. [2] 08742 | 5,367 | Union Beach [2] .... 07735 | 6,195 |
| Neptune City [2] ... 07753 | 5,866 | Pompton Lakes [2] . 07442 | 10,787 | Union City [2] ..... 07087 | 51,753 |
| New Brunswick [2] . 08901* | 41,713 | Princeton [2] ...... 08540 | 12,423 | Upper Saddle R. [2]. 07458 | 8,366 |
| New Milford [2] .... 07646 | 17,423 | Prospect Park [2] .. — | 4,545 | Ventnor City [2] .... 08406 | 11,252 |
| New Providence [2]. 07974 | 13,101 | Rahway [2] ........ 07065* | 27,575 | Verona [2] ........ 07044 | 14,675 |
| New Shrewsbury [1] 07224 | 8,395 | Ramsey [2] ........ 07446 | 12,398 | Vineland [2] ....... 08360 | 52,701 |
| Newark [2] ....... 07102* | 314,412 | Raritan [2] ........ 08869 | 6,091 | Waldwick [2] ....... 07463 | 11,766 |
| Newton [2] ........ 07860 | 8,966 | Red Bank [2] ...... 07701 | 12,067 | Wallington [2] ..... 07057 | 10,371 |
| North Arlington [2]. 07032 | 16,670 | Ridgefield [2] ...... 07657 | 10,421 | Wanaque [2] ...... 07465 | 8,984 |
| North Bergen [2][†] .. 07047 | 47,468 | Ridgefield Park [2] . 07660 | 12,854 | Washington [2] ..... 07882 | 6,576 |
| North Caldwell [2] .. 07066 | 6,647 | Ridgewood [2] ..... 07451* | 25,580 | Watchung [2] ...... 07060 | 5,203 |
| North Haledon [2] .. 07508 | 7,159 | Ringwood [2] ...... 07456 | 12,497 | West Caldwell [2] ... 07006 | 11,451 |
| North Plainfield [2]. 07060 | 19,534 | River Edge [2] ..... 07661 | 11,579 | W. Long Branch [2] . 07764 | 7,108 |
| North Wildwood [2]. 08260 | 4,859 | Rockaway [2] ...... 07866 | 6,669 | West New York [2].. 07093 | 38,638 |
| Northfield [2] ...... 08225 | 7,928 | Roseland [2] ...... 07068 | 5,171 | West Orange [2] .... 07052 | 41,053 |
| Northvale [2] ...... 07647 | 5,117 | Roselle [2] ........ 07203 | 21,235 | West Paterson [2] .. 07424 | 10,603 |
| Nutley [2] ........ 07110 | 29,938 | Roselle Park [2] .... 07204 | 13,284 | Westfield [2] ...... 07091* | 32,053 |
| Oakland [2] ....... 07436 | 13,686 | Rumson [2] ........ 07760 | 7,466 | Westville [2] ...... 08093 | 4,874 |
| Ocean City [2] ..... 08226 | 12,513 | Runnemede [2] ..... 08078 | 9,470 | Westwood [2] ...... 07675 | 10,847 |
| Oceanport [2] ..... 07757 | 5,924 | Rutherford [2] ..... 07070* | 19,187 | Wharton [2] ....... 07885 | 5,605 |
| Old Bridge [1] ..... 08857 | 25,176 | Salem [2] ......... 08079 | 7,142 | White Meadow L. [1] 07886 | 8,499 |
| Oradell [2] ........ 07649 | 8,584 | Sayreville [2] ...... 08872 | 31,130 | Wood Ridge [2] .... 07075 | 8,055 |
| Orange [2] ........ 07050* | 29,846 | Secaucus [2] ...... 07094 | 14,108 | Woodbury [2] ...... 08096 | 11,386 |
| Palisades Park [2] .. 07650 | 13,133 | Somerdale [2] ..... 08083 | 6,474 | Woodcliff Lake [2].. 07675 | 5,719 |
| Palmyra [2] ....... 08065 | 7,696 | Somers Point [2] ... 08244 | 9,786 | | |

## NEW MEXICO (N.M., N. Mex., or NM)

| PLACE AND ZIP CODE | POP. | PLACE AND ZIP CODE | POP. | PLACE AND ZIP CODE | POP. |
|---|---|---|---|---|---|
| Alamogordo [2] ..... 88310 | 24,496 | Farmington [2] ..... 87401 | 31,792 | Raton [2] ......... 87740 | 7,658 |
| Albuquerque [2] ... 87101* | 295,150 | Gallup [2] ........ 87301* | 18,293 | Roswell [2] ........ 88201 | 39,511 |
| Artesia [2] ........ 88210 | 10,971 | Grants [2] ......... 87020 | 11,854 | Santa Fe [2] ...... 87501* | 46,162 |
| Aztec [2] ......... 87410 | 5,201 | Hobbs [2] ......... 88240 | 29,378 | Silver City [2] ..... 88061* | 9,858 |
| Belen [2] ......... 87002 | 6,313 | Las Cruces [2] ..... 88001* | 43,255 | Socorro [2] ........ 87801 | 6,481 |
| Carlsbad [2] ....... 88220 | 24,978 | Las Vegas [2] ...... 87701 | 14,727 | South Valley [1] .... 87105 | 29,389 |
| Clovis [2] ......... 88101 | 30,474 | Los Alamos [1] ..... 87544 | 11,310 | Truth or | |
| Deming [2] ........ 88030 | 10,433 | Lovington [2] ...... 88260 | 9,392 | Consequences [2] 87901 | 5,467 |
| Espanola [2] ...... 87532* | 7,769 | Portales [2] ........ 88130 | 10,408 | Tucumcari [2] ..... 88401* | 7,229 |

## NEW YORK (N.Y. or NY)

| PLACE AND ZIP CODE | POP. | PLACE AND ZIP CODE | POP. | PLACE AND ZIP CODE | POP. |
|---|---|---|---|---|---|
| Albany [2] ........ 12212 | 105,688 | Bethpage [1] ...... 11714 | 18,555 | Cohoes [2] ........ 12047 | 17,592 |
| Albertson [1] ...... 11507 | 6,825 | Binghamton [2] .... 13902* | 59,312 | Cold Spring Hbr. [1] 11724 | 5,450 |
| Albion [2] ........ 14411 | 5,683 | Blauvelt [1] ....... 10913 | 5,426 | Colonie [2] ........ 12212 | 8,870 |
| Alfred [2] ......... 14802 | 5,118 | Bohemia [1] ....... 11716 | 8,926 | Commack [1] ...... 11725 | 24,138 |
| Amityville [2] ...... 11701 | 8,426 | Brentwood [1] ..... 11717 | 28,327 | Congers [1] ....... 10920 | 5,928 |
| Amsterdam [2] ..... 12010 | 23,344 | Briarcliff Manor [2] . 10510 | 5,917 | Copiague [1] ...... 11726 | 19,632 |
| Arlington [1] ...... 12603 | 11,203 | Brockport [2] ...... 14420 | 12,361 | Corning [2] ....... 14830 | 13,997 |
| Auburn [2] ........ 13021 | 32,020 | Bronxville [2] ...... 10708 | 6,260 | Cortland [2] ....... 13045 | 20,238 |
| Babylon [2] ....... 11702* | 14,119 | Buffalo [3] ....... 14240* | 400,234 | Croton-on-Hudson [2] 10520 | 8,597 |
| Baldwin [1] ....... 11510 | 34,525 | Canandaigua [2] ... 14424 | 12,508 | Dansville [2] ...... 14437 | 5,148 |
| Baldwinsville [2] ... 13027 | 7,625 | Canastota [2] ...... 13032 | 5,039 | De Witt [1] ........ 13214 | 10,032 |
| Ballston Spa [2] ... 12020 | 5,694 | Canton [2] ........ 13617 | 7,363 | Deer Park [1] ..... 11729 | 32,274 |
| Batavia [2] ........ 14020 | 16,872 | Carle Place [1] .... 11514 | 6,326 | Depew [2] ........ 14043 | 26,068 |
| Bath [2] .......... 14810 | 6,255 | Catskill [2] ....... 12414 | 5,563 | Dix Hills [1] ...... 11746 | 10,050 |
| Bay Shore [1] ..... 11706* | 11,119 | Cedarhurst [2] ..... 11516 | 6,889 | Dobbs Ferry [2] ... 10522 | 11,459 |
| Bayport [1] ....... 11705 | 8,232 | Centereach [1] ..... 11720 | 9,427 | Dunkirk [2] ....... 14048 | 15,663 |
| Bayville [2] ....... 11709 | 6,735 | Central Islip [1] .... 11722 | 36,391 | East Aurora [2] .... 14052 | 7,757 |
| Beacon [2] ........ 12508 | 11,945 | Clifton Knolls [1] ... — | 5,771 | East Glenville [1] ... — | 5,898 |
| Bellmore [1] ....... 11710 | 18,431 | Cobleskill [2] ...... 12043 | 5,056 | E. Half Hollow Hls. [1] — | 9,691 |

[1] 1970 Census.    [2] Census Bureau estimate July 1, 1978.   [3] 1978 Special Census.
[†] Town or township (includes rural population).

| PLACE AND ZIP CODE | POP. | PLACE AND ZIP CODE | POP. | PLACE AND ZIP CODE | POP. |
|---|---|---|---|---|---|
| **NEW YORK** (continued) | | Johnstown [2] ..... 12095 | 9,634 | N. Tarrytown [2] ... 10591 | 8,041 |
| East Hills [1] ...... 11577 | 8,540 | Kenmore [2] ....... 14217 | 21,339 | N. Tonawanda [2] .. 14120 | 39,107 |
| East Islip [1] ....... 11730 | 6,861 | Kings Park [1] ..... 11754 | 5,555 | North Valley | |
| E. Massapequa [1] . 11758 | 15,926 | Kings Point [2] .... 11024 | 5,915 | Stream [1] ....... 11580 | 14,881 |
| East Meadow [1] ... 11554 | 46,290 | Kingston [2] ...... 12401 | 23,382 | North Wantagh [1] .. 11793 | 15,053 |
| East Neck [1] ...... — | 5,221 | Lackawanna [2] .... 14218 | 23,924 | Northport [2] ...... 11768 | 8,272 |
| East Northport [1] .. 11731 | 12,392 | Lake Grove [2] .... 11755 | 10,164 | Norwich [2] ........ 13815 | 8,238 |
| E. Patchogue [1] ... 11772 | 8,092 | Lakeview [1] ...... 14085 | 5,471 | Nyack [2] ......... 10960 | 6,185 |
| East Rochester [2] . 14445 | 8,542 | Lancaster [2] ..... 14086 | 13,446 | Oakdale [1] ........ 11769 | 7,334 |
| E. Rockaway [2] ... 11518 | 11,546 | Larchmont [2] ..... 10538 | 6,955 | Oceanside [1] ...... 11572 | 35,372 |
| East Vestal [1] ..... 13850 | 10,472 | Latham [1] ........ 12110 | 9,661 | Ogdensburg [2] .... 13669 | 12,641 |
| Eastchester [1] ..... 10709 | 23,750 | Lawrence [2] ...... 11559 | 6,643 | Old Bethpage [1] ... 11804 | 7,084 |
| Elmira [2] ........ 14901* | 34,909 | Le Roy [2] ........ 14482 | 5,330 | Olean [2] ......... 14760 | 17,766 |
| Elmont [1] ........ 11003 | 29,363 | Lindenhurst [2] .... 11757 | 29,855 | Oneida [2] ........ 13421 | 11,035 |
| Elwood [1] ........ 11731 | 15,031 | Little Falls [2] ..... 13365 | 6,484 | Oneonta [2] ....... 13820 | 14,982 |
| Endicott [2] ....... 13760 | 16,461 | Lockport [2] ...... 14094 | 27,102 | Ossining [2] ....... 10562 | 20,127 |
| Endwell [1] ....... 13760 | 15,999 | Locust Grove [1] ... 11791 | 11,626 | Oswego [2] ........ 13126 | 20,951 |
| Fairmount [1] ...... 13219 | 15,317 | Long Beach [2] .... 11561 | 32,559 | Owego [2] ........ 13827 | 4,685 |
| Fairport [2] ....... 14450 | 7,399 | Loudonville [1] ..... 12211 | 9,299 | Oyster Bay [1] ..... 11771 | 6,822 |
| Fairview [1] ....... 12601 | 8,517 | Lynbrook [2] ...... 11563 | 22,964 | Patchogue [2] ...... 11772* | 11,714 |
| Farmingdale [2] .... 11735 | 8,764 | Mahopac [1] ...... 10541 | 5,265 | Pearl River [1] ..... 10965 | 17,146 |
| Fayetteville [2] .... 13066 | 5,320 | Malone [2] ........ 12953 | 7,524 | Peekskill [2] ....... 10566 | 20,463 |
| Floral Park [1] .... 11001* | 18,192 | Malverne [2] ...... 11565 | 9,955 | Pelham [2] ........ 10803 | 7,079 |
| Franklin Square [1] . 11010 | 32,156 | Mamaroneck [2] ... 10543 | 18,031 | Pelham Manor [2] .. 10803 | 6,407 |
| Fredonia [2] ....... 14063 | 11,194 | Manhasset [1] ..... 11030 | 8,541 | Penn Yan [2] ...... 14527 | 5,119 |
| Freeport [2] ....... 11520 | 39,818 | Manlius [2] ....... 13104 | 5,050 | Plainedge [1] ...... 11714 | 10,759 |
| Fulton [2] ........ 13069 | 13,381 | Manorhaven [2] ... — | 5,697 | Plainview [1] ...... 11803 | 31,695 |
| Garden City [2] .... 11530 | 26,904 | Massapequa [1] ... 11758 | 26,821 | Plattsburgh [2] .... 12901 | 20,681 |
| Garden City Pk. [1]. 11530 | 7,488 | Massapequa Pk. [2] 11762 | 20,847 | Pleasantville [2] ... 10570 | 7,241 |
| Geneseo [2] ....... 14454 | 6,655 | Massena [2] ....... 13662 | 12,835 | Port Chester [2] ... 10573 | 22,903 |
| Geneva [2] ........ 14456 | 15,728 | Mastic Beach [1] ... 11951 | 4,870 | Port Jefferson [2] .. 11777 | 6,122 |
| Glen Cove [2] ..... 11542 | 25,305 | Mattydale [1] ..... 13211 | 8,292 | Port Jefferson | |
| Glens Falls [2] ..... 12801 | 17,088 | Mechanicville [2] .. 12118 | 5,671 | Station [1] ....... 11776 | 7,403 |
| Gloversville [2] .... 12078 | 18,322 | Medina [2] ....... 14103 | 6,441 | Port Jervis [2] ..... 12771 | 8,483 |
| Goshen [1] ........ 10924 | 5,374 | Melville [1] ....... 11747 | 6,641 | Port Washington [1] . 11050 | 15,923 |
| Gouverneur [2] .... 13642 | 4,940 | Merrick [1] ....... 11566 | 25,904 | Potsdam [2] ....... 13676 | 11,430 |
| Great Neck [2] .... 11022* | 10,760 | Middletown [2] .... 10940 | 26,277 | Poughkeepsie [2] ... 12601* | 31,200 |
| Great Neck Plz. [2]. 11021 | 6,011 | Mineola [2] ....... 11501 | 20,625 | Rensselaer [2] ..... 12144 | 9,035 |
| Greenlawn [1] ..... 11740 | 8,493 | Monroe [2] ....... 10950 | 5,177 | Riverhead [1] ...... 11901 | 7,585 |
| Half Hollow Hills [1] 11746 | 12,081 | Monsey [1] ....... 10952 | 8,797 | Rochester [2] ..... 14692* | 252,491 |
| Hamburg [2] ...... 14075 | 11,264 | Monticello [2] ..... 12701 | 6,420 | Rockville | |
| Harrison [2] ....... 10528 | 21,878 | Mount Kisco [2] ... 10549 | 8,245 | Centre [2] ....... 11570 | 27,108 |
| Hartsdale [1] ...... 10530 | 12,226 | Mount Vernon [1] .. 10551* | 73,654 | Roessleville [1] ..... 12205 | 5,476 |
| Hastings-on- | | Nanuet [1] ........ 10954 | 10,447 | Rome [2] ......... 13440 | 46,314 |
| Hudson [2] ...... 10706 | 8,580 | Nesconset [1] ..... 11767 | 10,048 | Ronkonkoma [1] ... 11779 | 7,284 |
| Hauppauge [1] ..... 11787 | 13,957 | New Cassel [1] .... 11590 | 8,721 | Roosevelt [1] ...... 11575 | 15,008 |
| Haverstraw [1] ..... 10927 | 8,930 | New Castle [1,3] ... 10514 | 15,663 | Roslyn Heights [1] .. 11577 | 7,242 |
| Hempstead [2] .... 11551* | 40,245 | New City [1] ...... 10956 | 27,344 | Rotterdam [1] ..... 12303 | 25,214 |
| Herkimer [2] ...... 13350 | 7,983 | New Hyde Park [2] . 11040 | 9,688 | Rye [2] .......... 10580 | 15,639 |
| Herricks [1] ....... 11040 | 9,112 | New Paltz [2] ..... 12561 | 6,642 | St. James [1] ...... 11780 | 10,500 |
| Hicksville [1] ..... 11802* | 49,820 | New Rochelle [2] .. 10802* | 70,861 | Salamanca [2] ..... 14779 | 7,034 |
| Hillcrest [1] ....... — | 5,357 | New Windsor [3]† .. 12550 | 19,007 | San Remo [1] ...... 11754 | 8,302 |
| Holbrook– | | New York [2] ..... 10001* | 7,134,542 | Saranac Lake [2] ... 12983 | 5,958 |
| Holtsville [1] ..... 11741 | 12,103 | Newark [2] ....... 14513 | 9,868 | Saratoga | |
| Hornell [1] ........ 14843 | 10,451 | Newburgh [2] ..... 12550 | 27,607 | Springs [2] ...... 12866 | 23,477 |
| Horseheads [2] ..... 14845 | 8,158 | Niagara Falls [2] .. 14302* | 76,925 | Sayville [1] ....... 11782 | 11,680 |
| Hudson [2] ........ 12534 | 7,725 | Niskayuna [1] ..... 12309 | 6,186 | Scarsdale [2] ...... 10583 | 18,969 |
| Hudson Falls [2] ... 12839 | 7,586 | North Amityville [1]. 11701 | 11,936 | Schenectady [2] ... 12301* | 71,676 |
| Huntington [1] ..... 11743 | 12,601 | North Babylon [1] .. 11703 | 39,526 | Scotia [2] ........ 12302 | 6,939 |
| Huntington Sta. [1]. 11746 | 28,817 | North Bellmore [1] . 11710 | 22,893 | Sea Cliff [2] ...... 11579 | 5,561 |
| Ilion [2] .......... 13357 | 9,311 | North Bellport [1] .. — | 5,903 | Seaford [1] ....... 11783 | 17,379 |
| Inwood [1] ........ 11696 | 8,433 | N. Great River [1] .. 11739 | 12,080 | Selden [1] ........ 11784 | 11,613 |
| Irvington [2] ...... 10533 | 5,817 | N. Lindenhurst [1] .. 11757 | 11,117 | Seneca Falls [2] ... 13148 | 7,203 |
| Island Park [2] ..... 11558 | 5,246 | N. Massapequa [1] . 11758 | 23,123 | Setauket–South | |
| Islip [1] .......... 11751 | 7,692 | North Merrick [1] .. 11566 | 13,650 | Setauket [1] ...... 11733 | 6,857 |
| Ithaca [2] ........ 14850 | 28,117 | North New | | Shirley [1] ........ 11967 | 6,280 |
| Jamestown [2] .... 14701 | 35,634 | Hyde Park [1] .. 11040 | 18,154 | Sloan [1] ......... — | 4,971 |
| Jefferson Valley– | | N. Patchogue [1] .. — | 5,232 | Solvay [2] ........ 13209 | 7,462 |
| Yorktown [1] .... 10535 | 9,008 | North Pelham [1] .. — | 5,184 | S. Farmingdale [1] . 11735 | 20,464 |
| Jericho [1] ........ 11753 | 14,010 | N. Syracuse [2] .... 13212 | 8,956 | S. Holbrook [1] ..... — | 6,700 |
| Johnson City [2] ... 13790 | 16,643 | | | | |

[1]1970 Census. [2]Census Bureau estimate July 1, 1978. [3]1977 estimate. † Township.

## NEW YORK (continued)

| PLACE AND ZIP CODE | | POP. | PLACE AND ZIP CODE | | POP. | PLACE AND ZIP CODE | | POP. |
|---|---|---|---|---|---|---|---|---|
| S. Huntington[1] | 11746 | 9,115 | Tuckahoe[2] | 10707 | 5,880 | Wellsville[2] | 14895 | 5,568 |
| S. Stony Brook[1] | 11790 | 15,329 | Uniondale[1] | 11553 | 22,077 | West Babylon[1] | 11704 | 12,893 |
| S. Valley Stream[1] | — | 6,595 | Utica[2] | 13503* | 78,718 | West Haverstraw[2] | 10993 | 10,054 |
| S. Westbury[1] | 11590 | 10,978 | Valley Cottage[1] | 10989 | 6,007 | West Hempstead[1] | 11552 | 20,375 |
| Southampton[2] | 11968 | 5,438 | Valley Stream[2] | 11580* | 38,924 | West Islip[1] | 11795 | 17,374 |
| Southport[1] | 14904 | 8,685 | Vernon Valley[1] | 11731 | 7,925 | West Nyack[1] | 10994 | 5,510 |
| Spring Valley[2] | 10977 | 21,378 | Vestal–Twin | | | West Sayville[1] | 11796 | 7,386 |
| Stony Brook[1] | 11790 | 6,391 | Orchards[1] | 13850 | 8,303 | Westbury[2] | 11590* | 14,666 |
| Stony Point[1] | 10980 | 8,270 | Walden[2] | 12586 | 5,596 | White Plains[2] | 10602* | 47,196 |
| Suffern[2] | 10901 | 10,110 | Wantagh[1] | 11793 | 21,873 | Whitesboro[2] | 13492 | 4,896 |
| Syosset[1] | 11791 | 10,084 | Wappingers | | | Williamsville[2] | 14221 | 7,241 |
| Syracuse[2] | 13220* | 174,899 | Falls[2] | 12590 | 6,469 | Williston Park[2] | 11596 | 9,011 |
| Tappan[1] | 10983 | 7,424 | Waterloo[2] | 13165 | 5,446 | Woodmere[1] | 11598 | 19,831 |
| Tarrytown[2] | 10591 | 11,555 | Watertown[2] | 13601 | 27,726 | Wyandanch[1] | 11798 | 15,716 |
| Thornwood[1] | 10594 | 6,874 | Watervliet[2] | 12189 | 11,693 | Yaphank[1] | 11980 | 5,460 |
| Tonawanda[2] | 14150 | 20,956 | Waverly[1] | 14892 | 4,799 | Yonkers[3] | 10701* | 191,758 |
| Troy[2] | 12180* | 58,209 | Webster[2] | 14580 | 5,610 | Yorktown Hts.[1] | 10598 | 6,805 |

## NORTH CAROLINA (N.C. or NC)

| PLACE AND ZIP CODE | | POP. | PLACE AND ZIP CODE | | POP. | PLACE AND ZIP CODE | | POP. |
|---|---|---|---|---|---|---|---|---|
| Ahoskie[2] | 27910 | 5,181 | Gastonia[2] | 28052 | 48,844 | North Belmont[1] | 28012 | 10,678 |
| Albemarle[2] | 28001 | 10,361 | Goldsboro[2] | 27530 | 35,455 | Oxford[2] | 27565 | 7,222 |
| Archdale[2] | 27263 | 6,057 | Graham[2] | 27253 | 9,475 | Raleigh[2] | 27611* | 138,410 |
| Asheboro[2] | 27203 | 16,112 | Greensboro[2] | 27420* | 163,493 | Reidsville[2] | 27320 | 12,576 |
| Asheville[2] | 28810 | 58,551 | Greenville[2] | 27834 | 32,960 | Roanoke Rapids[2] | 27870 | 14,296 |
| Belmont[2] | 28012 | 5,560 | Henderson[2] | 27536 | 13,276 | Rockingham[2] | 28379 | 7,680 |
| Bessemer City[2] | 28016 | 5,370 | Hendersonville[2] | 28739 | 8,232 | Rocky Mount[2] | 27801 | 40,627 |
| Boone[2] | 28607* | 11,905 | Hickory[2] | 28601 | 20,459 | Roxboro[2] | 27573 | 8,581 |
| Brevard[2] | 28712 | 5,807 | High Point[2] | 27260* | 68,339 | Salisbury[2] | 28144 | 24,923 |
| Burlington[2] | 27215 | 36,853 | Jacksonville[2] | 28540* | 20,891 | Sanford[2] | 27330* | 15,822 |
| Camp Le Jeune[1] | 28542 | 34,549 | Kannapolis[1] | 28081 | 36,293 | Seymour–Johnson[1] | 27530 | 8,172 |
| Canton[2] | 28716 | 4,946 | Kernersville[2] | 27284 | 6,948 | Shelby[2] | 28150 | 16,448 |
| Carrboro[2] | 27510 | 9,031 | Kings Mountain[2] | 28086 | 8,286 | Siler City[2] | 27344 | 5,340 |
| Cary[2] | 27511 | 19,032 | Kinston[2] | 28501 | 27,530 | Smithfield[2] | 27577 | 7,675 |
| Chapel Hill[2] | 27514 | 31,020 | Laurinburg[2] | 28352 | 13,316 | Southern Pines[2] | 28387 | 8,205 |
| Charlotte[2] | 28228* | 299,444 | Lenoir[2] | 28645 | 15,447 | Spring Lake[2] | 28390 | 5,921 |
| Cherry Point[1] | 28533 | 12,029 | Lexington[2] | 27292 | 16,501 | Statesville[2] | 28677 | 21,555 |
| Clinton[2] | 28328 | 8,644 | Lincolnton[2] | 28092 | 5,378 | Tarboro[2] | 27886 | 10,948 |
| Concord[2] | 28025 | 18,999 | Lumberton[2] | 28358 | 17,186 | Thomasville[2] | 27360 | 15,245 |
| Dunn[2] | 28334 | 9,149 | Monroe[2] | 28110 | 11,328 | Washington[2] | 27889 | 8,766 |
| Durham[2] | 27701* | 105,060 | Mooresville[2] | 28115 | 9,045 | Waynesville[2] | 28786 | 8,171 |
| Eden[2] | 27288 | 15,460 | Morehead City[2] | 28557 | 5,942 | West Concord[1] | 28025 | 5,347 |
| Edenton[2] | 27932 | 5,477 | Morganton[2] | 28655 | 13,745 | Whiteville[2] | 28472 | 5,065 |
| Elizabeth City[2] | 27909 | 14,337 | Mount Airy[2] | 27030 | 7,864 | Williamston[2] | 27892 | 6,101 |
| Fayetteville[2] | 28302* | 67,479 | Mount Holly[2] | 28120 | 5,262 | Wilmington[2] | 28402* | 54,867 |
| Forest City[2] | 28043 | 7,365 | New Bern[2] | 28560* | 16,984 | Wilson[2] | 27893 | 34,038 |
| Fort Bragg[1] | 28307 | 46,995 | New River–Gieger[1] | 28540 | 8,699 | Winston–Salem[2] | 27102* | 140,438 |
| Garner[2] | 27529 | 11,550 | Newton[2] | 28658 | 8,417 | | | |

## NORTH DAKOTA (N.D., or N. Dak., or ND)

| PLACE AND ZIP CODE | | POP. | PLACE AND ZIP CODE | | POP. | PLACE AND ZIP CODE | | POP. |
|---|---|---|---|---|---|---|---|---|
| Bismarck[2] | 58501* | 42,113 | Gr. Forks AFB[1] | 58201 | 10,474 | Tatman[4]† | — | 6,618 |
| Devils Lake[2] | 58301 | 7,309 | Jamestown[2] | 58401 | 15,474 | Valley City[2] | 58072 | 6,991 |
| Dickinson[2] | 58601 | 12,880 | Mandan[2] | 58554 | 14,682 | Wahpeton[2] | 58075 | 8,799 |
| Fargo[2] | 58102 | 58,256 | Mekinock[4]† | 58258 | 10,547 | Waterford[4]† | — | 5,913 |
| Grafton[2] | 58237 | 5,636 | Minot[2] | 58701 | 32,639 | West Fargo[3] | 58078 | 8,448 |
| Grand Forks[4] | 58201 | 42,052 | Minot AFB[1] | 58701 | 12,077 | Williston[2]† | 58801 | 11,823 |

## OHIO (O. or OH)

| PLACE AND ZIP CODE | | POP. | PLACE AND ZIP CODE | | POP. | PLACE AND ZIP CODE | | POP. |
|---|---|---|---|---|---|---|---|---|
| Ada[2] | 45810 | 5,830 | Beachwood[2] | 44122 | 10,892 | Brecksville[2] | 44141 | 8,746 |
| Akron[2] | 44309* | 239,229 | Bedford[2] | 44146 | 15,600 | Broadview Hts.[2] | 44147 | 13,420 |
| Alliance[2] | 44601 | 25,746 | Bedford Hts.[2] | 44146 | 12,146 | Brook Park[2] | 44142 | 29,494 |
| Amherst[2] | 44001 | 10,111 | Bellaire[2] | 43906 | 8,542 | Brooklyn[2] | 44144 | 13,257 |
| Ashland[2] | 44805 | 20,257 | Bellbrook[2] | 45305 | 5,555 | Brookville[2] | 45309 | 4,872 |
| Ashtabula[2] | 44004 | 23,400 | Bellefontaine[2] | 43311 | 11,003 | Brunswick[2] | 44212 | 27,209 |
| Athens[2] | 45701 | 21,341 | Bellevue[2] | 44811 | 9,323 | Bryan[2] | 43506 | 6,965 |
| Aurora[2] | 44202 | 9,159 | Belpre[2] | 45714 | 7,408 | Bucyrus[2] | 44820 | 13,557 |
| Avon[2] | 44011 | 7,151 | Berea[2] | 44017 | 20,158 | Cambridge[2] | 43725 | 12,660 |
| Avon Lake[2] | 44012 | 12,538 | Bexley[2] | 43209 | 14,734 | Campbell[2] | 44405 | 11,337 |
| Barberton[2] | 44203 | 26,819 | Blue Ash[2] | 45242 | 10,485 | Canfield[2] | 44406 | 6,850 |
| Bay Village[2] | 44140 | 19,089 | Bowling Green[2] | 43402 | 25,903 | Canton[2] | 44711* | 96,339 |

[1]1970 Census.  [2]Census Bureau estimate July 1, 1978.  [3]1978 Special Census.  [4]1977 estimate.
†Town or township (includes rural population).

## OHIO (continued)

| PLACE AND ZIP CODE | POP. | PLACE AND ZIP CODE | POP. | PLACE AND ZIP CODE | POP. |
|---|---|---|---|---|---|
| Celina [2] 45822 | 9,493 | Lincoln Hts. [2] — | 6,233 | Rittman [2] 44270 | 6,986 |
| Centerville [2] 45459 | 16,990 | Lockland [2] 45215 | 5,840 | Rocky River [2] 44116 | 21,898 |
| Cheviot [2] 45211 | 9,583 | Logan [2] 43138 | 6,131 | Rossford [2] 43460 | 6,070 |
| Chillicothe [2] 45601 | 24,095 | London [2] 43140 | 8,573 | St. Bernard [2] 45217 | 5,183 |
| Cincinnati [2] 45234* | 399,072 | Lorain [2] 44052* | 82,057 | St. Clairsville [2] 43950 | 5,241 |
| Circleville [2] 43113 | 14,216 | Louisville [2] 44641 | 6,913 | St. Marys [2] 45885 | 8,132 |
| Cleveland [2] 44101* | 594,529 | Loveland [2] 45140 | 9,039 | Salem [2] 44460 | 15,694 |
| Cleveland Hts. [2] 44118 | 54,097 | Lyndhurst [2] 44124 | 18,953 | Sandusky [2] 44870 | 31,088 |
| Clyde [2] 43410 | 6,094 | Macedonia [2] 44056 | 6,207 | Seven Hills [2] 44131 | 14,246 |
| Columbiana [2] 44408 | 5,607 | Madeira [2] 45243 | 10,186 | Shadyside [2] 43947 | 4,658 |
| Columbus [2] 43216* | 524,304 | Mansfield [2] 44901* | 56,704 | Shaker Heights [2] 44120 | 33,541 |
| Conneaut [2] 44030 | 14,639 | Maple Heights [2] 44137 | 31,596 | Sharonville [2] 45241 | 11,911 |
| Coshocton [2] 43812 | 13,409 | Marietta [2] 45750 | 16,400 | Sheffield Lake [2] 44054 | 10,322 |
| Crestline [2] 44827 | 5,928 | Marion [2] 43302 | 38,725 | Shelby [2] 44875 | 9,346 |
| Cuyahoga Falls [2] 44222* | 44,293 | Martins Ferry [2] 43935 | 9,837 | Sidney [2] 45365 | 18,297 |
| Dayton [2] 45401* | 194,861 | Marysville [2] 43040 | 8,374 | Silverton [2] — | 5,965 |
| Deer Park [2] 45236 | 6,456 | Mason [2] 45040 | 7,387 | Solon [2] 44139 | 13,497 |
| Defiance [2] 43512 | 16,084 | Massillon [2] 44646 | 35,214 | South Euclid [2] 44121 | 27,735 |
| Delaware [2] 43015 | 19,924 | Maumee [2] 43537 | 17,910 | Springdale [2] 45246 | 9,933 |
| Delphos [2] 45833 | 7,431 | Mayfield Hts. [2] 44124 | 20,474 | Springfield [2] 45501 | 73,376 |
| Dover [2] 44622 | 11,318 | Medina [2] 44256 | 17,284 | Steubenville [2] 43952 | 27,056 |
| East Cleveland [2] 44112 | 36,915 | Mentor [2] 44060 | 42,356 | Stow [2] 44224 | 25,354 |
| East Liverpool [2] 43920 | 21,587 | Mentor-on-Lake [2] 44060 | 8,231 | Streetsboro [2] 44240 | 8,264 |
| East Palestine [2] 44413 | 6,110 | Miamisburg [2] 45342 | 15,896 | Strongsville [2] 44136 | 26,332 |
| Eastlake [2] 44094 | 22,440 | Middleburg Hts. [2] 44017 | 15,211 | Struthers [2] 44471 | 13,269 |
| Eaton [2] 45320 | 6,838 | Middletown [2] 45042 | 47,958 | Sylvania [2] 43560 | 15,094 |
| Elyria [2] 44035* | 52,335 | Milford [2] 45150 | 4,840 | Tallmadge [2] 44278 | 15,600 |
| Englewood [2] 45322 | 11,047 | Minerva [2] 44657 | 6,014 | Tiffin [2] 44883 | 20,385 |
| Euclid [2] 44117 | 59,641 | Mingo Junction [2] 43938 | 4,844 | Tipp City [2] 45371 | 6,192 |
| Fairborn [2] 45324 | 33,259 | Mogadore [2] 44260 | 5,845 | Toledo [2] 43601* | 351,686 |
| Fairfield [2] 45014 | 26,983 | Montgomery [2] 45242 | 7,602 | Toronto [2] 43964 | 7,689 |
| Fairlawn [2] 44313 | 6,763 | Moraine [2] — | 4,863 | Trenton [2] 45067 | 6,498 |
| Fairview Park [2] 44126 | 19,853 | Mount Healthy [2] 45231 | 7,135 | Trotwood [2] 45426 | 7,921 |
| Findlay [2] 45840 | 37,570 | Mount Vernon [2] 43050 | 15,615 | Troy [2] 45373 | 18,514 |
| Forest Park [2] 45405 | 20,240 | Napoleon [2] 43545 | 8,173 | Twinsburg [2] 44087 | 7,211 |
| Fostoria [2] 44830 | 17,249 | Nelsonville [2] 45764 | 5,087 | Union [2] 45322 | 5,324 |
| Franklin [2] 45005 | 11,228 | New Carlisle [2] 45344 | 6,480 | University Hts. [3] 44118 | 16,789 |
| Fremont [2] 43420 | 19,004 | New Lexington [2] 43764 | 4,823 | Upper Arlington [2] 43221 | 37,101 |
| Gahanna [2] 43230 | 15,543 | New Philadelphia [2] 44663 | 15,357 | Upper Sandusky [2] 43351 | 5,526 |
| Galion [2] 44833 | 13,325 | Newark [2] 43055 | 39,947 | Urbana [2] 43078 | 11,967 |
| Gallipolis [2] 45631 | 7,153 | Newton Falls [2] 44444 | 5,795 | Uhrichsville [2] 44683 | 5,771 |
| Garfield Hts. [2] 44125 | 36,257 | Niles [2] 44446 | 22,911 | Van Wert [2] 45891 | 11,180 |
| Geneva [2] 44041 | 7,275 | North Canton [2] 44720 | 17,390 | Vandalia [2] 45377 | 11,894 |
| Girard [2] 44420 | 14,102 | North College Hill [2] 45239 | 11,906 | Vermilion [2] 44089 | 11,344 |
| Golf Manor [2] | 5,111 | North Olmsted [2] 44070 | 38,098 | Wadsworth [2] 44281 | 15,420 |
| Grandview Hts. [2] 43212 | 9,191 | North Ridgeville [2] 44039 | 21,219 | Wapakoneta [2] 45895 | 8,506 |
| Greenhills [2] 45218 | 5,427 | North Royalton [2] 44133 | 15,295 | Warren [2] 44481* | 59,537 |
| Greenville [2] 45331 | 12,863 | Northwood [2] — | 15,211 | Warrensville Hts. [2] 44122 | 17,313 |
| Grove City [2] 43123 | 17,993 | Norton [2] 44203 | 13,820 | Washington [2] 43160 | 13,831 |
| Hamilton [2] 45012* | 67,535 | Norwalk [2] 44857 | 14,179 | Wauseon [2] 43567 | 5,877 |
| Harrison [2] 45030 | 5,769 | Norwood [2] 45212 | 25,226 | Wellston [2] 45692 | 5,613 |
| Heath [2] 43055 | 8,319 | Oakwood [2] 45873 | 8,692 | Wellsville [2] 43968 | 6,211 |
| Highland Hts. [2] 45132 | 7,050 | Oberlin [2] 44074 | 8,353 | West Carrollton [2] 45418 | 13,134 |
| Hilliard [2] 43026 | 8,946 | Olmsted Falls [2] 44138 | 5,775 | Westerville [2] 43081 | 20,104 |
| Hillsboro [2] 45133 | 6,070 | Oregon [2] 43616 | 18,780 | Westlake [2] 44145 | 17,978 |
| Hubbard [2] 44425 | 9,191 | Orrville [2] 44667 | 8,316 | Whitehall [2] 43213 | 25,554 |
| Huron [2] 44839 | 7,604 | Oxford [2] 45056 | 20,524 | Wickliffe [2] 44092 | 17,454 |
| Independence [2] 44131 | 6,630 | Painesville [2] 44077 | 17,683 | Willard [2] 44890 | 5,416 |
| Indian Hill [2] — | 5,247 | Parma [2] 44129 | 95,862 | Willoughby [2] 44094 | 19,865 |
| Ironton [2] 45638 | 13,870 | Parma Heights [2] 44130 | 23,401 | Willoughby Hills [2] 44094 | 6,826 |
| Jackson [2] 45640 | 7,000 | Pepper Pike [2] 44124 | 6,371 | Willowick [2] 44094 | 18,599 |
| Kent [2] 44240* | 26,323 | Perrysburg [2] 43551 | 9,292 | Wilmington [2] 45177 | 9,892 |
| Kenton [2] 43326 | 8,102 | Piqua [2] 45356 | 20,030 | Wintersville [2] 43952 | 5,387 |
| Kettering [2] 45429 | 68,050 | Port Clinton [2] 43452 | 7,266 | Wooster [2] 44691 | 20,124 |
| Kirtland [2] 44094 | 6,327 | Portsmouth [2] 45662 | 23,952 | Worthington [2] 43085 | 17,470 |
| Lakewood [2] 44107 | 62,409 | Ravenna [2] 44266 | 11,898 | Wyoming [2] 45215 | 8,555 |
| Lancaster [2] 43130 | 40,021 | Reading [2] 45215 | 12,968 | Xenia [2] 45385 | 30,889 |
| Lebanon [5] 45036 | 8,438 | Reynoldsburg [2] 43068 | 19,095 | Youngstown [2] 44501* | 128,538 |
| Lima [2] 45802* | 50,602 | Richmond Hts. [2] 44143 | 10,234 | Zanesville [2] 43701 | 38,292 |

[1] 1970 Census.  [2] Census Bureau estimate July 1, 1978.  [3] 1976 estimate.

| PLACE AND ZIP CODE | POP. | PLACE AND ZIP CODE | POP. | PLACE AND ZIP CODE | POP. |
|---|---|---|---|---|---|
| **OKLAHOMA (Okla. or OK)** | | | | | |
| Ada [2] 74820 | 14,661 | Frederick [2] 73542 | 5,778 | Perry [2] 73077 | 5,610 |
| Altus [2] 73521 | 25,007 | Guthrie [2] 73044 | 10,122 | Ponca City [2] 74601 | 26,511 |
| Alva [2] 73717 | 5,848 | Guymon [2] 73942 | 8,846 | Poteau [2] 74953 | 6,200 |
| Anadarko [2] 73005 | 6,482 | Henryetta [5] 74437 | 6,167 | Pryor [2] 74361 | 7,815 |
| Ardmore [2] 73401 | 24,700 | Holdenville [2] 74848 | 5,457 | Sallisaw [2] 74955 | 6,008 |
| Bartlesville [2] 74003 | 30,329 | Hugo [2] 74743 | 6,196 | Sand Springs [2] 74063 | 12,780 |
| Bethany [2] 73008 | 21,679 | Idabel [2] 74745 | 7,164 | Sapulpa [2] 74066 | 16,480 |
| Bixby [2] 74008 | 6,352 | Jenks [2] 74037 | 5,187 | Seminole [2] 74868 | 8,024 |
| Blackwell [2] 74631 | 8,158 | Lawton [2] 73501* | 85,073 | Shawnee [2] 74801* | 26,234 |
| Broken Arrow [2] 74012 | 30,727 | Marlow [2] 73055 | 5,075 | Stillwater [2] 74074 | 34,846 |
| Chickasha [2] 73018 | 15,033 | McAlester [2] 74501 | 16,556 | Sulphur [2] 73086 | 4,849 |
| Choctaw [2] 73020 | 7,786 | Miami [2] 74354 | 13,966 | Tahlequah [2] 74464 | 8,771 |
| Claremore [2] 74017 | 10,601 | Midwest City [2] 73140 | 50,430 | Tecumseh [2] 74873 | 5,870 |
| Clinton [2] 73601 | 7,895 | Moore [2] 73153 | 30,086 | The Village [2] 73156 | 12,267 |
| Cushing [2] 74023 | 7,350 | Muskogee [2] 74401 | 41,235 | Tulsa [2] 74101* | 328,684 |
| Del City [2] 73155 | 29,625 | Mustang [2] 73064 | 6,821 | Vinita [2] 74301 | 5,100 |
| Duncan [2] 73533 | 20,724 | Nichols Hills [2] — | 4,520 | Wagoner [2] 74467 | 6,958 |
| Durant [2] 74701 | 10,607 | Norman [2] 73070* | 63,382 | Warr Acres [2] 73123 | 12,723 |
| Edmond [2] 73034 | 24,340 | Oklahoma City [2] 73125* | 372,690 | Weatherford [2] 73096 | 8,756 |
| El Reno [2] 73036 | 15,990 | Okmulgee [2] 74447 | 15,487 | Wewoka [2] 74884 | 4,573 |
| Elk City [2] 73644 | 8,373 | Owasso [2] 74055 | 5,711 | Woodward [2] 73801 | 12,273 |
| Enid [2] 73701 | 50,166 | Pauls Valley [2] 73075 | 5,366 | Yukon [2] 73099 | 19,019 |
| **OREGON (Ore., Oreg., or OR)** | | | | | |
| Albany [2] 97321 | 27,126 | Gresham [2] 97030 | 29,728 | North Bend [2] 97459 | 9,965 |
| Ashland [2] 97520 | 15,000 | Hermiston [2] 97838 | 8,226 | Ontario [2] 97914 | 8,395 |
| Astoria [2] 97103 | 10,483 | Hillsboro [2] 97123 | 24,797 | Oregon City [2] 97045 | 15,176 |
| Baker [2] 97814 | 9,556 | Hood River [2] 97031 | 5,612 | Pendleton [2] 97801 | 14,858 |
| Beaverton [2] 97005 | 26,140 | Independence [2] 97351 | 5,543 | Portland [2] 97208* | 364,735 |
| Bend [2] 97701 | 18,982 | Klamath Falls [2] 97601* | 18,228 | Prineville [2] 97754 | 5,914 |
| Canby [2] 97013 | 7,089 | La Grande [2] 97850 | 10,970 | Redmond [2] 97756 | 7,964 |
| Central Point [2] 97502 | 6,267 | Lake Oswego [2] 97034 | 21,963 | Reedsport [2] 97467 | 5,231 |
| City of the Dalles [2] 97058 | 11,229 | Lebanon [2] 97355 | 9,805 | Roseburg [2] 97470 | 19,137 |
| Coos Bay [2] 97420 | 14,609 | Lincoln City [2] 97367 | 4,919 | St. Helens [2] 97051 | 7,484 |
| Corvallis [2] 97330 | 38,823 | McMinnville [2] 97128 | 14,579 | Salem [2] 97301* | 89,770 |
| Cottage Grove [2] 97424 | 7,389 | Medford [2] 97501 | 38,072 | Seaside [2] 97138 | 4,864 |
| Dallas [2] 97338 | 9,800 | Milton-Freewater [2] 97862 | 5,215 | Silverton [2] 97381 | 5,396 |
| Eugene [2] 97401* | 102,591 | Milwaukie [2] 97222 | 19,208 | Springfield [2] 97477 | 40,913 |
| Forest Grove [2] 97116 | 11,012 | Monmouth [2] 97361 | 7,917 | Tigard [2] 97223 | 13,756 |
| Gladstone [2] 97027 | 9,607 | Newberg [2] 97132 | 9,744 | West Linn [2] 97068 | 11,929 |
| Grants Pass [2] 97526 | 15,117 | Newport [2] 97365 | 6,984 | Woodburn [2] 97071 | 11,287 |
| **PENNSYLVANIA (Pa., Penn., or PA)** | | | | | |
| Aldan [2] 19018 | 5,060 | Bridgeville [2] 15017 | 6,282 | Corry [2] 16407 | 6,820 |
| Aliquippa [2] 15001 | 20,097 | Bristol [2] 19007 | 11,224 | Crafton [2] 15205 | 7,621 |
| Allentown [2] 18101* | 102,077 | Brookhaven [2] 19015 | 7,696 | Danville [2] 17821 | 6,153 |
| Altoona [2] 16603* | 58,043 | Brownsville [2] 15417 | 5,174 | Darby [2] 19023 | 11,989 |
| Ambler [2] 19002 | 7,718 | Butler [2] 16001 | 20,818 | Dickson City [2] 18519 | 7,119 |
| Ambridge [2] 15003 | 9,352 | California [2] 15419 | 5,294 | Donora [2] 15033 | 7,404 |
| Archbald [2] 18403 | 6,334 | Camp Hill [2] 17011 | 9,185 | Dormont [2] 15216 | 10,099 |
| Arnold [2] 15068 | 6,795 | Canonsburg [2] 15317 | 11,084 | Downingtown [5] 19335 | 7,890 |
| Avalon [2] — | 6,486 | Carbondale [2] 18407 | 11,746 | Doylestown [2] 18901 | 11,557 |
| Baden [2] 15005 | 5,777 | Carlisle [2] 17013 | 19,972 | DuBois [2] 15801 | 9,447 |
| Baldwin [2] 15234 | 25,268 | Carnegie [2] 15106 | 9,815 | Dunmore [2] 18512 | 17,166 |
| Bangor [2] 18013 | 5,211 | Castle Shannon [2] 15234 | 10,627 | Duquesne [2] 15110 | 9,770 |
| Beaver [2] 15009 | 5,711 | Catasauqua [2] 18032 | 6,171 | Duryea [2] 18642 | 5,063 |
| Beaver Falls [2] 15010 | 13,670 | Chambersburg [2] 17201 | 16,541 | E. Stroudsburg [2] 18301 | 9,155 |
| Bellefonte [2] 16823 | 5,813 | Charleroi [2] 15022 | 6,377 | Easton [2] 18042 | 28,515 |
| Bellevue [2] 15202 | 9,958 | Chester [2] 19013* | 44,173 | Economy [2] — | 8,599 |
| Berwick [2] 18603 | 11,808 | Clairton [2] 15025 | 13,257 | Edinboro [2] 16412 | 5,489 |
| Bethel Park [2] 15102 | 38,362 | Clarion [2] 16214 | 7,116 | Edwardsville [2] 18704 | 5,403 |
| Bethlehem [2] 18016* | 72,550 | Clarks Summit [2] 18411 | 6,560 | Elizabethtown [2] 17022 | 8,643 |
| Blakely [2] 18447 | 6,960 | Clearfield [2] 16830 | 7,722 | Ellwood City [2] 16117 | 10,605 |
| Bloomsburg [2] 17815 | 13,177 | Clifton Heights [2] 19018 | 7,368 | Emmaus [2] 18049 | 11,880 |
| Boyertown [2] 19512 | 4,915 | Coatesville [2] 19320 | 12,204 | Ephrata [2] 17522 | 10,115 |
| Braddock [2] 15104 | 5,641 | Collingdale [2] 19023 | 10,111 | Erie [2] 16501* | 122,152 |
| Bradford [2] 16701 | 11,232 | Columbia [2] 17512 | 10,794 | Etna [2] 15223 | 5,214 |
| Brandywine Vlg. [1] 19406 | 11,411 | Connellsville [2] 15425 | 11,297 | Exeter [2] 18643 | 5,054 |
| Brentwood [2] 15227 | 12,919 | Conshohocken [2] 19428 | 8,498 | Farrell [2] 16121 | 8,734 |
| Bridgeport [2] 19405 | 4,594 | Coraopolis [2] 15108 | 7,995 | Flourtown [1] 19031 | 9,149 |

[1] 1970 Census.   [2] Census Bureau estimate July 1, 1978.   [3] 1977 estimate.

# PENNSYLVANIA (cont.)

| PLACE AND ZIP CODE | | POP. |
|---|---|---|
| Folcroft[2] | 19032 | 9,195 |
| Forest Hills[2] | 15221 | 8,491 |
| Forty Fort[2] | — | 5,314 |
| Fountain Hill[2] | — | 5,549 |
| Fox Chapel[2] | — | 4,987 |
| Frackville[2] | 17931 | 5,108 |
| Franklin[2] | 16323 | 7,818 |
| Franklin Park[2] | — | 5,547 |
| Fullerton[2] | 18052 | 7,908 |
| Gettysburg[2] | 17325 | 7,310 |
| Glassport[2] | 15045 | 6,394 |
| Glenolden[2] | 19036 | 8,119 |
| Glenside[1] | 19038 | 17,353 |
| Green Tree[2] | 15242 | 5,787 |
| Greensburg[2] | 15601 | 18,579 |
| Greenville[2] | 16125 | 9,400 |
| Grove City[2] | 16127 | 8,018 |
| Hanover[2] | 17331 | 14,313 |
| Harrisburg[2] | 17105* | 55,027 |
| Hatboro[2] | 19040 | 8,304 |
| Hatboro West[1] | 19044 | 13,542 |
| Hazleton[2] | 18201 | 28,227 |
| Hellertown[2] | 18055 | 6,716 |
| Hershey[2] | 17033 | 7,407 |
| Hollidaysburg[2] | 16648 | 6,016 |
| Homeacre–Lyndora[4] | 16045 | 8,415 |
| Homestead[2] | 15120 | 4,996 |
| Honesdale[2] | 18431 | 5,367 |
| Hummelstown[2] | 17036 | 6,159 |
| Huntingdon[2] | 16652 | 7,019 |
| Indiana[2] | 15701 | 17,480 |
| Jeannette[2] | 15644 | 13,869 |
| Jefferson[2] | 15344 | 7,634 |
| Jenkintown[2] | 19046 | 4,769 |
| Jersey Shore[2] | 17740 | 4,643 |
| Jim Thorpe[2] | 18229 | 5,332 |
| Johnstown[2] | 15901* | 37,780 |
| Kane[2] | 16735 | 4,763 |
| Kennett Square[2] | 19348 | 5,357 |
| Kingston[2] | 18704 | 15,905 |
| Kittanning[2] | 16201 | 6,203 |
| Lancaster[2] | 17604* | 56,996 |
| Lansdale[2] | 19446 | 20,430 |
| Lansdowne[2] | 19050 | 13,548 |
| Latrobe[2] | 15650 | 11,159 |
| Lebanon[2] | 17042 | 29,462 |
| Lehighton[2] | 18235 | 5,978 |
| Lewisburg[2] | 17837 | 6,056 |
| Lewistown[2] | 17044 | 9,699 |
| Lititz[2] | 17543 | 9,501 |
| Lock Haven[2] | 17745 | 9,305 |
| Lower Burrell[2] | 15068 | 14,298 |
| Mahanoy City[2] | 17948 | 6,026 |
| Manheim[2] | 17545 | 5,858 |
| McCandless[4] | — | 24,903 |
| McKees Rocks[2] | 15136 | 10,630 |
| McKeesport[2] | 15134* | 31,902 |
| Meadville[2] | 16335 | 15,656 |
| Mechanicsburg[2] | 17055 | 12,397 |
| Media[2] | 19063* | 6,221 |
| Merion[1] | 19066 | 5,686 |
| Middletown[2] | 17057 | 9,653 |
| Millersville[2] | 17551 | 7,208 |
| Millvale[2] | 15209 | 5,237 |
| Milton[2] | 17847 | 7,095 |
| Minersville[2] | 17954 | 5,504 |
| Monaca[2] | 15061 | 7,713 |
| Monessen[2] | 15062 | 12,126 |
| Monongahela[2] | 15063 | 6,098 |
| Monroeville[2] | 15146 | 31,439 |
| Montoursville[2] | 17754 | 5,910 |
| Moosic[2] | 18507 | 5,412 |
| Morrisville[2] | 19067 | 10,719 |
| Mount Carmel[2] | 17851 | 8,149 |
| Mount Joy[2] | 17552 | 5,625 |
| Mount Pleasant[2] | 15666 | 5,424 |
| Munhall[2] | 15120 | 14,670 |
| Murrysville[2] | 15668 | 15,651 |
| Nanticoke[2] | 18634 | 13,573 |
| Nazareth[2] | 18064 | 6,605 |
| New Brighton[2] | 15066 | 7,663 |
| New Castle[2] | 16101* | 35,187 |
| New Cumberland[2] | 17070 | 10,661 |
| New Kensington[2] | 15068* | 17,928 |
| Norristown[2] | 19401* | 34,626 |
| North Braddock[2] | 15104 | 8,527 |
| North East[2] | 16428 | 6,358 |
| N. Hills–Ardsley[1] | 19038 | 13,173 |
| Northampton[2] | 18067 | 8,765 |
| Norwood[2] | 19074 | 7,007 |
| Oak Lane[1] | 19126 | 6,192 |
| Oakmont[2] | 15139 | 6,789 |
| Ogontz[1] | 19001 | 5,463 |
| Oil City[2] | 16301 | 13,996 |
| Old Forge[2] | 18517 | 9,806 |
| Olyphant[2] | 18447 | 5,340 |
| Oreland[2] | 19075 | 9,114 |
| Palmerton[2] | 18071 | 5,270 |
| Palmyra[2] | 17078 | 8,073 |
| Paoli[1] | 19301 | 5,835 |
| Pencoyd[1] | — | 6,650 |
| Penn Square–Plymouth Vly.[1] | 19401 | 20,238 |
| Penn Wynn[1] | — | 6,038 |
| Perkasie[2] | 18944 | 7,488 |
| Philadelphia[2] | 19104* | 1,754,829 |
| Phoenixville[2] | 19460 | 14,688 |
| Pittsburgh[2] | 15219* | 432,723 |
| Pittston[2] | 18640* | 11,038 |
| Plains[1] | 18705 | 6,606 |
| Pleasant Hills[2] | 15236 | 10,440 |
| Plum[2] | 15239 | 25,099 |
| Plymouth[2] | 18651 | 7,659 |
| Port Vue[2] | — | 5,060 |
| Pottstown[2] | 19464 | 26,144 |
| Pottsville[2] | 17901 | 17,873 |
| Prospect Park[2] | 19076 | 6,653 |
| Punxsutawney[2] | 15767 | 7,464 |
| Quakertown[2] | 18951 | 8,989 |
| Reading[2] | 19603* | 76,742 |
| Red Lion[2] | 17356 | 5,684 |
| Ridgway[2] | 15853 | 5,475 |
| Ridley Park[2] | 19078 | 8,379 |
| Roslyn[1] | 19001 | 18,317 |
| St. Marys[2] | 15857 | 7,040 |
| Sayre[2] | 18840 | 6,803 |
| Schuylkill Haven[2] | 17972 | 6,095 |
| Scottdale[2] | 15683 | 5,730 |
| Scranton[2] | 18503* | 89,890 |
| Selinsgrove[2] | 17870 | 5,120 |
| Sewickley[2] | 15143 | 6,029 |
| Shamokin[2] | 17872 | 10,440 |
| Sharon[2] | 16146 | 20,974 |
| Sharon Hill[2] | 19079 | 7,276 |
| Sharpsburg[2] | 15215 | 4,973 |
| Sharpsville[2] | 16150 | 5,416 |
| Shenandoah[2] | 17976 | 7,179 |
| Shillington[2] | 19607 | 6,583 |
| Shippensburg[2] | 17257 | 6,992 |
| Slatington[2] | 18080 | 5,431 |
| Slippery Rock[2] | 16057 | 5,872 |
| Somerset[2] | 15501 | 6,266 |
| Souderton[2] | 18964 | 6,539 |
| S. Williamsport[2] | 17701 | 6,589 |
| State College[2] | 16801* | 38,369 |
| Steelton[2] | 17113 | 6,839 |
| Stroudsburg[2] | 18360 | 5,213 |
| Sugarcreek[2] | — | 6,104 |
| Sunbury[2] | 17801 | 11,857 |
| Swarthmore[2] | 19081 | 6,281 |
| Swissvale[2] | 15218 | 11,660 |
| Swoyersville[2] | 18704 | 5,963 |
| Tamaqua[2] | 18252 | 8,918 |
| Tarentum[2] | 15084 | 6,494 |
| Taylor[2] | 18517 | 7,775 |
| Titusville[2] | 16354 | 6,653 |
| Turtle Creek[2] | 15145 | 7,093 |
| Tyrone[2] | 16686 | 6,051 |
| Uniontown[2] | 15401 | 15,061 |
| Vandergrift[1] | 15690 | 7,008 |
| Warren[2] | 16365 | 12,054 |
| Washington[2] | 15301 | 19,851 |
| Waynesboro[2] | 17268 | 9,288 |
| West Chester[2] | 19380 | 20,721 |
| West Hazleton[2] | 18201 | 5,210 |
| West Mifflin[2] | 15122 | 26,577 |
| West Pittston[2] | 18643 | 6,481 |
| West View[1] | 15229 | 7,958 |
| West York[1] | — | 5,043 |
| Westmont[2] | — | 5,986 |
| White Oak[2] | 15131 | 10,055 |
| Whitehall[2] | 18052 | 15,984 |
| Wilkes-Barre[2] | 18701* | 53,832 |
| Wilkinsburg[2] | 15221 | 22,907 |
| Williamsport[2] | 17701 | 33,904 |
| Willow Grove[1] | 19090 | 16,494 |
| Wilson[2] | 15025 | 8,320 |
| Windber[2] | 15963 | 6,907 |
| Wyomissing[2] | 19610 | 8,337 |
| Yeadon[2] | 19050 | 11,658 |
| York[2] | 17405* | 45,622 |

# RHODE ISLAND (R.I. or RI)

| PLACE AND ZIP CODE | | POP. |
|---|---|---|
| Barrington[3]† | 02806 | 17,303 |
| Bristol[3]† | 02809 | 18,674 |
| Burrillville[3]† | 02830 | 11,826 |
| Central Falls[2] | 02863 | 14,948 |
| Coventry[3]† | 02816 | 26,108 |
| Cranston[2] | 02910 | 73,070 |
| Cumberland[3]† | 02864 | 27,702 |
| East Greenwich[3]† | 02818 | 10,710 |
| East Providence[2] | 02914 | 48,464 |
| Glocester[3]† | — | 6,989 |
| Hopkinton[3]† | 02833 | 6,363 |
| Johnston[3]† | 02919 | 24,210 |
| Kingston[2] | 02881 | 5,601 |
| Lincoln[2]† | 02865 | 17,521 |
| Middletown[3]† | 02840 | 15,851 |
| Narragansett[3]† | 02882 | 10,008 |
| Newport[2] | 02840 | 30,431 |
| N. Kingstown[3]† | 02852* | 19,774 |
| N. Providence[3]† | 02908 | 26,904 |
| N. Smithfield[3]† | 02876 | 10,211 |
| Pawtucket[2] | 02860* | 68,893 |
| Portsmouth[3]† | 02871 | 14,602 |
| Providence[2] | 02940* | 157,222 |
| Scituate[3]† | 02857 | 8,731 |

[1] 1970 Census. [2] Census Bureau estimate July 1, 1978. [3] 1977 estimate. [4] 1976 estimate. † Town or township.

### RHODE ISLAND (cont.)

| PLACE AND ZIP CODE | POP. | PLACE AND ZIP CODE | POP. | PLACE AND ZIP CODE | POP. |
|---|---|---|---|---|---|
| Smithfield [3]† 02917 | 15,655 | Wakefield [1] 02880* | 6,331 | West Warwick [3]† 02893 | 25,627 |
| S. Kingstown [3]† 02879 | 20,848 | Warren [3]† 02885 | 10,126 | Westerly [3]† 02891 | 18,008 |
| Tiverton [3]† 02878 | 13,593 | Warwick [2] 02887* | 86,722 | Woonsocket [2] 02895 | 45,837 |

### SOUTH CAROLINA (S.C. or SC)

| PLACE AND ZIP CODE | POP. | PLACE AND ZIP CODE | POP. | PLACE AND ZIP CODE | POP. |
|---|---|---|---|---|---|
| Abbeville [2] 29620 | 5,597 | Easley [2] 29640 | 13,088 | Mt. Pleasant [2] 29464 | 10,523 |
| Aiken [2] 29801 | 14,630 | Florence [2] 29501* | 32,577 | Mullins [2] 29574 | 6,042 |
| Anderson [2] 29621* | 30,420 | Forest Acres [2] 29260 | 6,755 | Myrtle Beach [2] 29577 | 20,529 |
| Barnwell [2] 29812 | 5,276 | Fort Mill [2] 29715 | 5,617 | Newberry [2] 29108 | 9,177 |
| Beaufort [2] 29902 | 8,808 | Gaffney [2] 29340 | 16,054 | North Augusta [2] 29841 | 14,251 |
| Belton [2] 29627 | 5,304 | Gantt [1] — | 11,386 | North Charleston [2] 29406 | 61,402 |
| Bennettsville [2] 29512 | 8,146 | Georgetown [2] 29440 | 11,833 | Orangeburg [2] 29115 | 17,184 |
| Berea [1] 29611 | 7,186 | Goose Creek [2] 29445 | 16,471 | Parris Island [1] 29905 | 8,868 |
| Camden [2] 29020 | 8,392 | Greenville [2] 29602* | 55,407 | Rock Hill [2] 29730 | 37,684 |
| Cayce [2] 29033 | 10,461 | Greenwood [2] 29646 | 25,720 | Seneca [2] 29678 | 8,214 |
| Charleston [2] 29401* | 59,280 | Greer [2] 29651 | 12,239 | Simpsonville [2] 29681 | 7,720 |
| Cheraw [2] 29520 | 5,309 | Hanahan [2] 29410 | 9,656 | Spartanburg [2] 29301* | 46,279 |
| Chester [2] 29706 | 7,148 | Hartsville [2] 29550 | 7,895 | Summerville [2] 29483 | 7,471 |
| Clemson [2] 29631 | 6,933 | Hilton Head Is. [5] 29928 | 6,511 | Sumter [2] 29150 | 25,086 |
| Clinton [2] 29325 | 7,687 | Lake City [2] 29560 | 6,578 | Union [2] 29379 | 10,237 |
| Columbia [2] 29201* | 108,216 | Lancaster [2] 29720 | 8,852 | Wade–Hampton [1] 29924 | 17,152 |
| Conway [2] 29526 | 9,134 | Laurens [2] 29360 | 10,010 | Walterboro [2] 29488 | 6,598 |
| Darlington [2] 29532 | 7,199 | Marion [2] 29571 | 7,839 | West Columbia [2] 29169 | 14,612 |
| Dillon [2] 29536 | 6,231 | Mauldin [2] 29662 | 7,863 | York [2] 29745 | 6,427 |

### SOUTH DAKOTA (S.D., S.Dak., or SD)

| PLACE AND ZIP CODE | POP. | PLACE AND ZIP CODE | POP. | PLACE AND ZIP CODE | POP. |
|---|---|---|---|---|---|
| Aberdeen [2] 57401 | 26,229 | Madison [2] 57042 | 5,508 | Sioux Falls [2] 57101* | 74,660 |
| Brookings [2] 57006 | 14,054 | Mitchell [2] 57301 | 13,597 | Sturgis [2] 57785 | 6,135 |
| Hot Springs [2] 57747 | 5,114 | Mobridge [2] 57601 | 4,542 | Vermillion [2] 57069 | 9,771 |
| Huron [2] 57350 | 12,825 | Pierre [2] 57501 | 12,110 | Watertown [2] 57201 | 14,444 |
| Lead [2] 57754 | 4,700 | Rapid City [2] 57701 | 52,070 | Yankton [2] 57078 | 11,698 |

### TENNESSEE (Tenn. or TN)

| PLACE AND ZIP CODE | POP. | PLACE AND ZIP CODE | POP. | PLACE AND ZIP CODE | POP. |
|---|---|---|---|---|---|
| Alcoa [2] 37701 | 6,879 | Goodlettsville [2] 37072 | 8,151 | Milan [2] 38358 | 6,666 |
| Athens [2] 37303 | 12,337 | Greeneville [2] 37743 | 14,318 | Millington [2] 38053* | 20,848 |
| Bartlett [2] 38134 | 14,358 | Harriman [2] 37748 | 9,050 | Morristown [2] 37814 | 20,479 |
| Bolivar [2] 38008 | 5,705 | Henderson [2] 38340 | 5,185 | Murfreesboro [2] 37130 | 33,400 |
| Brentwood [4] 37027 | 8,747 | Hendersonville [2] 37075 | 25,029 | Nashville– | |
| Bristol [2] 37620 | 27,048 | Humboldt [2] 38343 | 10,100 | Davidson [2] 37202 | 425,424 |
| Brownsville [2] 38012 | 8,487 | Jackson [2] 38301 | 47,532 | Newport [2] 37821 | 7,369 |
| Chattanooga [2] 37401* | 162,778 | Jefferson City [2] 37760 | 5,210 | Oak Hill [2] — | 4,757 |
| Clarksville [2] 37040 | 54,644 | Johnson City [2] 37601 | 40,288 | Oak Ridge [2] 37830 | 28,896 |
| Cleveland [2] 37311 | 31,009 | Kingsport [2] 37662* | 33,455 | Paris [2] 38242 | 10,506 |
| Clinton [2] 37716 | 5,877 | Knoxville [2] 37901* | 185,236 | Pulaski [2] 38478 | 7,355 |
| Collierville [2] 38017 | 6,983 | LaFollette [2] 37766 | 8,980 | Red Bank [2] 37415 | 15,043 |
| Columbia [2] 38401 | 23,258 | Lavergne [2] 37086 | 5,220 | Ripley [2] 38063 | 5,704 |
| Cookeville [2] 38501 | 18,526 | Lawrenceburg [2] 38464 | 10,438 | Rockwood [2] 37854 | 5,352 |
| Covington [2] 38019 | 6,275 | Lebanon [2] 37087 | 13,582 | Savannah [2] 38372 | 6,462 |
| Crossville [2] 38555 | 6,183 | Lenoir City [2] 37771 | 5,300 | Shelbyville [2] 37160 | 11,845 |
| Dickson [2] 37055 | 7,022 | Lewisburg [2] 37091 | 8,513 | Signal Mtn. [2] 37377 | 6,833 |
| Dyersburg [2] 38024 | 15,768 | Lexington [2] 38351 | 5,831 | Smyrna [2] 37167 | 8,196 |
| East Ridge [2] 37412 | 22,761 | Manchester [2] 37355 | 7,343 | Soddy–Daisy [2] 37379 | 11,011 |
| Elizabethton [2] 37643 | 12,736 | Martin [2] 38237 | 7,804 | Sparta [2] 38583 | 5,249 |
| Fayetteville [2] 37334 | 7,114 | Maryville [2] 37801 | 20,529 | Springfield [2] 37172 | 10,309 |
| Franklin [2] 37064 | 11,356 | McKenzie [2] 38201 | 4,941 | Tullahoma [2] 37388 | 15,176 |
| Gallatin [2] 37066 | 15,157 | McMinnville [2] 37110 | 10,916 | Union City [2] 38261 | 12,997 |
| Germantown [2] 38138 | 16,065 | Memphis [2] 38101* | 663,769 | Winchester [2] 37398 | 5,208 |

### TEXAS (Tex. or TX)

| PLACE AND ZIP CODE | POP. | PLACE AND ZIP CODE | POP. | PLACE AND ZIP CODE | POP. |
|---|---|---|---|---|---|
| Abilene [2] 79604* | 96,573 | Arlington [2] 76010* | 132,932 | Beeville [2] 78102 | 13,323 |
| Alamo [2] 78516 | 5,864 | Athens [2] 75751 | 9,243 | Bellaire [2] 77401 | 17,492 |
| Alamo Hts. [2] 78209 | 6,979 | Atlanta [2] 75551 | 5,783 | Bellmead [2] 76705 | 9,047 |
| Alice [2] 78332 | 20,318 | Austin [2] 78710* | 319,194 | Belton [2] 76513 | 11,302 |
| Alpine [2] 79830 | 5,814 | Azle [2] 76020 | 6,164 | Benbrook [2] 76126 | 11,649 |
| Alvin [2] 77511 | 15,980 | Balch Springs [2] 75180 | 12,938 | Big Spring [2] 79720 | 25,113 |
| Amarillo [2] 79120* | 143,665 | Bay City [2] 77414 | 16,011 | Bonham [2] 75418 | 6,810 |
| Andrews [2] 79714 | 10,332 | Baytown [2] 77520 | 53,024 | Borger [2] 79007 | 14,458 |
| Angleton [2] 77515 | 14,451 | Beaumont [2] 77704* | 117,764 | Bowie [2] 76230 | 5,489 |
| Aransas Pass [2] 78336 | 6,565 | Bedford [2] 76021 | 17,256 | Brady [2] 76825 | 5,862 |

[1] 1970 Census. [2] Census Bureau estimate July 1, 1978. [3] 1977 estimate. [4] 1978 Special Census. [5] 1975 estimate.
† Town or township.

**TEXAS** (continued)

| PLACE AND ZIP CODE | | POP. | PLACE AND ZIP CODE | | POP. | PLACE AND ZIP CODE | | POP. |
|---|---|---|---|---|---|---|---|---|
| Breckenridge [2] | 76024 | 6,144 | Graham [2] | 76046 | 8,164 | N. Richland Hills [2] | 76118 | 24,127 |
| Brenham [2] | 77833 | 10,530 | Granbury [2] | 76048 | 6,566 | Odessa [2] | 79760* | 90,366 |
| Bridge City [2] | 77611 | 8,058 | Grand Prairie [2] | 75051 | 62,855 | Orange [2] | 77630 | 26,601 |
| Brownfield [2] | 79316 | 9,704 | Grapevine [2] | 76051 | 10,804 | Palestine [2] | 75801 | 15,432 |
| Brownsville [2] | 78520 | 71,554 | Greenville [2] | 75401 | 22,665 | Pampa [2] | 79065 | 20,512 |
| Brownwood [2] | 76801 | 19,246 | Groves [2] | 77619 | 17,700 | Paris [2] | 75460 | 22,159 |
| Bryan [2] | 77801 | 37,402 | Haltom City [2] | 76117 | 29,423 | Pasadena [2] | 77501* | 104,385 |
| Burkburnett [2] | 76354 | 10,413 | Harker Heights [2] | 76541 | 9,096 | Pearland [2] | 77581 | 12,799 |
| Burleson [2] | 76028 | 12,751 | Harlingen [2] | 78550 | 41,897 | Pearsall [2] | 78061 | 6,726 |
| Cameron [2] | 76520 | 5,185 | Henderson [2] | 75652 | 11,544 | Pecos [2] | 79772 | 11,998 |
| Canyon [2] | 79015 | 8,976 | Hereford [2] | 79045 | 14,874 | Perryton [2] | 79070 | 7,636 |
| Carrizo Springs [2] | 78834 | 6,699 | Highland Park [2] | 75205 | 9,158 | Pharr [2] | 78577 | 19,767 |
| Carrollton [2] | 75006 | 29,877 | Hillsboro [2] | 76645 | 6,484 | Plainview [2] | 79072 | 19,921 |
| Carthage [2] | 75633 | 5,954 | Hitchcock [2] | 77563 | 6,824 | Plano [2] | 75074 | 53,021 |
| Castle Hills [2] | — | 5,151 | Hondo [2] | 78861 | 5,748 | Pleasanton [2] | 78064 | 6,405 |
| Cedar Hill [2] | 75104 | 5,354 | Houston [2] | 77201* | 1,572,981 | Port Arthur [2] | 77640 | 61,439 |
| Childress [2] | 79201 | 5,453 | Humble [2] | 77338* | 6,641 | Port Lavaca [2] | 77979 | 11,009 |
| Cleburne [2] | 76031 | 15,866 | Huntsville [2] | 77340 | 21,746 | Port Neches [2] | 77651 | 14,479 |
| Cleveland [2] | 77327 | 6,785 | Hurst [2] | 76053 | 30,393 | Portland [2] | 78374 | 10,896 |
| Clute City [2] | 77531 | 7,578 | Iowa Park [2] | 76367 | 6,580 | Raymondville [2] | 78580 | 9,075 |
| Coleman [2] | 76834 | 5,598 | Irving [2] | 75061* | 105,101 | Richardson [2] | 75080 | 67,518 |
| College Station [2] | 77840* | 30,539 | Jacinto City [2] | 77029 | 11,726 | Richland Hills [2] | 76118 | 9,635 |
| Colleyville [2] | 76034 | 5,439 | Jacksonville [2] | 75766 | 10,650 | Richmond [2] | 77469 | 10,043 |
| Colorado City [2] | 79512 | 5,027 | Jasper [2] | 75951 | 7,040 | River Oaks [2] | 77019 | 10,017 |
| Commerce [2] | 75428 | 7,480 | Katy [2] | 77450 | 11,912 | Robstown [2] | 78380 | 10,726 |
| Conroe [2] | 77301* | 25,741 | Kermit [2] | 79745 | 7,892 | Rockport [2] | 78382 | 5,462 |
| Copperas Cove [2] | 76522 | 22,715 | Kerrville [2] | 78028 | 15,189 | Rockwall [2] | 75087 | 5,404 |
| Corpus Christi [2] | 78408* | 214,647 | Kilgore [2] | 75662 | 11,183 | Rosenberg [2] | 77471 | 17,408 |
| Corsicana [2] | 75110 | 19,630 | Killeen [2] | 76541* | 52,236 | Round Rock [2] | 78664 | 11,033 |
| Crockett [2] | 75835 | 6,392 | Kingsville [2] | 78363 | 28,833 | Rowlett [2] | 75088 | 5,540 |
| Crowley [2] | 76036 | 6,358 | La Marque [2] | 77568 | 16,109 | San Angelo [2] | 76902* | 68,626 |
| Crystal City [2] | 78839 | 7,794 | La Porte [2] | 77571 | 9,760 | San Antonio [2] | 78284* | 798,195 |
| Cuero [2] | 77954 | 7,049 | Lake Jackson [2] | 77566 | 17,872 | San Benito [2] | 78586 | 17,293 |
| Dalhart [2] | 79022 | 6,442 | Lake Worth [2] | 76135 | 5,159 | San Juan [2] | 78589 | 7,157 |
| Dallas [2] | 75260* | 847,420 | Lamesa [2] | 79331 | 11,074 | San Marcos [2] | 78666 | 22,712 |
| Dayton [2] | 77535 | 5,653 | Lampasas [2] | 76550 | 6,641 | Sansome Pk. Vil. [2] | — | 5,729 |
| De Soto [2] | 75115 | 14,349 | Lancaster [2] | 75146 | 13,601 | Santa Fe [2] | — | 5,059 |
| Deer Park [2] | 77536 | 22,059 | Laredo [2] | 78041* | 81,383 | Schertz [2] | 78154 | 7,820 |
| Del Rio [2] | 78840 | 25,733 | League City [2] | 77573 | 15,794 | Seabrook [2] | 77586 | 5,888 |
| Denison [2] | 75020 | 23,727 | Leon Valley [2] | — | 6,327 | Seagoville [2] | 75159 | 6,003 |
| Denton [2] | 76201* | 43,571 | Levelland [2] | 79336 | 12,482 | Seguin [2] | 78155 | 17,365 |
| Dickinson [2] | 77539 | 8,411 | Lewisville [2] | 75067 | 29,192 | Sherman [2] | 75090 | 27,357 |
| Donna [2] | 78537 | 8,948 | Liberty [2] | 77575 | 6,785 | Silsbee [2] | 77656 | 9,759 |
| Dumas [2] | 79029 | 10,665 | Littlefield [2] | 79339 | 6,962 | Sinton [2] | 78387 | 5,430 |
| Duncanville [2] | 75116 | 26,729 | Live Oak [2] | — | 6,784 | Slaton [2] | 79364 | 6,931 |
| Eagle Pass [2] | 78852 | 20,799 | Livingston [2] | 77351 | 6,275 | Snyder [2] | 79549 | 12,521 |
| Edinburg [2] | 78539 | 20,666 | Lockhart [2] | 78644 | 7,189 | South Houston [2] | 77587 | 12,193 |
| Edna [2] | 77957 | 5,680 | Longview [2] | 75602* | 56,231 | Stafford [2] | 77477 | 5,824 |
| El Campo [2] | 77437 | 9,383 | Lubbock [2] | 79408* | 168,127 | Stephenville [2] | 76401 | 9,995 |
| El Paso [2] | 79910* | 400,741 | Lufkin [2] | 75901 | 30,204 | Sugar Land [2] | 77478 | 5,357 |
| Elsa [2] | 78543 | 5,350 | Mansfield [2] | 76063 | 7,729 | Sulphur Springs [2] | 75482 | 11,134 |
| Ennis [2] | 75119 | 11,516 | Marlin [2] | 76661 | 5,651 | Sweetwater [2] | 79556 | 11,916 |
| Euless [2] | 76039 | 22,601 | Marshall [3] | 75670 | 25,109 | Taylor [2] | 76574 | 10,073 |
| Everman [2] | 76140 | 6,230 | Mathis [2] | 78368 | 5,658 | Temple [2] | 76501 | 39,672 |
| Falfurrias [2] | 78355 | 5,965 | McAllen [2] | 78501 | 53,604 | Terrell [2] | 75160 | 11,864 |
| Farmers Branch [2] | 75234 | 34,761 | McKinney [2] | 75069 | 13,126 | Texarkana [2] | 75501 | 36,335 |
| Forest Hills [2] | 75702 | 10,225 | Mercedes [2] | 78570 | 10,219 | Texas City [2] | 77590 | 42,748 |
| Fort Stockton [2] | 79735 | 8,883 | Mesquite [2] | 75149* | 63,060 | Tomball [2] | 77375 | 6,489 |
| Fort Worth [2] | 76101* | 367,432 | Mexia [2] | 76667 | 6,107 | Tulia [2] | 79088 | 5,323 |
| Fredricksburg [2] | 78624 | 5,734 | Midland [2] | 79702* | 67,251 | Tyler [2] | 75702* | 66,741 |
| Freeport [2] | 77541 | 12,737 | Mineral Wells [2] | 76067 | 17,533 | Universal City [2] | 78148 | 12,198 |
| Friendswood [2] | 77546 | 16,045 | Mission [2] | 78572 | 18,839 | University Park [2] | 76308 | 23,183 |
| Gainesville [2] | 76240 | 12,882 | Missouri City [2] | 77459 | 10,870 | Uvalde [2] | 78801 | 13,035 |
| Galena Park [2] | 77547 | 9,748 | Monahans [2] | 79756 | 8,220 | Vernon [2] | 76384 | 11,162 |
| Galveston [2] | 77553* | 59,407 | Mt. Pleasant [2] | 75455 | 10,471 | Victoria [2] | 77901 | 49,394 |
| Garland [2] | 75040* | 131,263 | Nacogdoches [2] | 75961 | 26,668 | Vidor [2] | 77662 | 12,003 |
| Gatesville [2] | 76528 | 5,604 | Nassau Bay [2] | — | 7,101 | Waco [2] | 76701* | 103,768 |
| Georgetown [2] | 78626 | 10,457 | Navasota [2] | 77868 | 4,984 | Watauga [2] | 76148 | 9,535 |
| Gladewater [2] | 75647 | 6,353 | Nederland [2] | 77627 | 18,359 | Waxahachie [2] | 75165 | 13,802 |
| Gonzales [2] | 78629 | 6,318 | New Braunfels [2] | 78130 | 20,647 | Weatherford [2] | 76086 | 13,217 |

[1] 1970 Census. [2] Census Bureau estimate July 1, 1978. [3] Special Census, 1978.

| PLACE AND ZIP CODE | POP. | PLACE AND ZIP CODE | POP. | PLACE AND ZIP CODE | POP. |
|---|---|---|---|---|---|
| **TEXAS** *(continued)* | | | | | |
| Weslaco[2] 78596 | 19,823 | Wharton[2] 77488 | 8,601 | Windcrest[2] — | 7,737 |
| West Univ. Place[2] 77005 | 15,665 | White Settlement[2] 76108 | 16,914 | Woodway[2] 76710 | 5,823 |
| Westworth[2] — | 5,858 | Wichita Falls[2] 76307* | 94,875 | Yoakum[2] 77995 | 5,934 |
| **UTAH (Ut. or UT)** | | | | | |
| American Fork[2] 84003 | 12,072 | Moab[2] 84532 | 5,576 | St. George[2] 84770 | 10,262 |
| Bountiful[2] 84010 | 32,451 | Murray[2] 84107 | 27,521 | Salt Lake City[2] 84119* | 164,379 |
| Brigham City[2] 84302 | 14,691 | North Ogden[2] 84404 | 7,453 | Sandy[2] 84070 | 39,119 |
| Cedar City[2] 84720 | 11,605 | Ogden[2] 84401* | 68,624 | South Jordan[2] — | 5,822 |
| Centerville[2] 84014 | 6,921 | Orem[2] 84057 | 46,492 | South Ogden[2] 84403 | 10,666 |
| Clearfield[2] 84015* | 13,851 | Payson[2] 84651 | 8,338 | South Salt Lake[2] 84115 | 9,405 |
| East Millcreek[1] 84109 | 26,579 | Pleasant Grove[2] 84062 | 8,652 | Spanish Fork[2] 84660 | 9,373 |
| Kaysville[2] 84037 | 8,894 | Price[2] 84501 | 9,518 | Springville[2] 84663 | 11,086 |
| Kearns[1] 84118 | 17,071 | Provo[2] 84601 | 56,216 | Sunset[2] — | 6,278 |
| Layton[2] 84041 | 19,535 | Richfield[2] 84701 | 5,492 | Tooele[2] 84074 | 13,604 |
| Lehi[2] 84043 | 6,675 | Riverdale[2] — | 5,488 | Vernal[2] 84078 | 7,501 |
| Logan[2] 84321 | 24,275 | Riverton[2] 84065 | 4,872 | Washington Terr.[2] 84403 | 8,024 |
| Midvale[2] 84047 | 8,918 | Roy[2] 84067 | 18,657 | West Jordan[2] 84084 | 20,358 |
| **VERMONT (Vt. or VT)** | | | | | |
| Barre[2] 05641 | 10,004 | Essex Junction[2] 05452 | 7,700 | Rutland[2] 05701 | 18,455 |
| Bennington[3]† 05201 | 15,690 | Hartford[3]† 05047 | 7,071 | St. Albans[2] 05478 | 7,392 |
| Brattleboro[3]† 05301 | 11,608 | Middlebury[3]† 05753 | 6,892 | St. Johnsbury[3]† 05819 | 7,960 |
| Burlington[2] 05401* | 37,377 | Milton[2]† 05468 | 5,976 | S. Burlington[2] 05401 | 10,299 |
| Colchester[3]† 05446 | 11,110 | Montpelier[2] 05602 | 8,059 | Springfield[3]† 05156 | 9,770 |
| Essex[3]† 05451 | 13,616 | Rockingham[3]† — | 5,208 | Winooski[2] 05404 | 7,300 |
| **VIRGINIA (Va. or VA)** | | | | | |
| Abingdon[2] 24210 | 5,446 | Falls Church[2] 22046* | 9,016 | Norfolk[2] 23501* | 280,568 |
| Alexandria[2] 22313* | 104,085 | Farmville[2] 23901 | 6,087 | Petersburg[2] 23803* | 42,996 |
| Annandale[1] 22003 | 27,405 | Franklin[2] 23851 | 7,037 | Poquoson[2] 23662 | 9,336 |
| Arlington[4] 22210* | 152,629 | Fredericksburg[2] 22401 | 17,896 | Portsmouth[2] 23705* | 108,297 |
| Ashland[2] 23005 | 5,184 | Front Royal[2] 22630 | 10,830 | Pulaski[2] 24301 | 10,373 |
| Bedford[2] 24523 | 6,313 | Galax[2] 24333 | 6,693 | Radford[2] 24141 | 12,558 |
| Big Stone Gap[2] 24219 | 5,487 | Hampton[2] 23669* | 125,116 | Richlands[2] 24641 | 6,267 |
| Blacksburg[2] 24060 | 29,727 | Harrisonburg[2] 22801 | 18,981 | Richmond[2] 23232* | 219,596 |
| Bluefield[2] 24605 | 5,946 | Herndon[2] 22070* | 12,835 | Roanoke[2] 24022* | 98,074 |
| Bristol[2] 24201 | 20,845 | Hopewell[2] 23860 | 23,895 | Salem[2] 24153 | 24,102 |
| Buena Vista[2] 24416 | 6,724 | Jefferson[1] 22042 | 25,432 | South Boston[2] 24592 | 7,308 |
| Charlottesville[2] 22906* | 39,245 | Leesburg[2] 22075 | 8,134 | Staunton[2] 24401 | 21,523 |
| Chesapeake[2] 23320* | 113,965 | Lexington[2] 24450 | 7,661 | Suffolk[2] 23434 | 46,851 |
| Christiansburg[2] 24073 | 10,032 | Long Branch[1] 22030 | 21,634 | Tazewell[2] — | 5,451 |
| Colonial Hts.[2] 23834 | 17,317 | Lynchburg[2] 24505* | 64,466 | Vienna[2] 22180 | 20,387 |
| Covington[2] 24426 | 8,987 | Manassas[2] 22110 | 12,950 | Vinton[2] 24179 | 8,171 |
| Culpeper[2] 22701 | 8,124 | Manassas Park[2] 22110 | 8,969 | Virginia Beach[2] 23458* | 245,076 |
| Dale City[1] 22193 | 13,857 | Marion[2] 24354 | 7,373 | Waynesboro[2] 22980 | 16,244 |
| Danville[2] 24541 | 44,165 | Martinsville[2] 24112 | 17,921 | Williamsburg[2] 23185 | 11,438 |
| Emporia[2] 23847 | 5,194 | McLean[1] 22101* | 17,698 | Winchester[2] 22601 | 23,061 |
| Fairfax[2] 22030 | 20,465 | Newport News[2] 23607* | 144,023 | Wytheville[2] 24382 | 7,027 |
| **WASHINGTON (Wash. or WA)** | | | | | |
| Aberdeen[2] 98520 | 19,342 | Hoquiam[2] 98550 | 10,616 | Snohomish[2] 98290 | 5,242 |
| Anacortes[2] 98221 | 9,008 | Issaquah[2] 98027 | 5,434 | Port Townsend[2] 98368 | 6,004 |
| Auburn[2] 98002 | 24,559 | Kelso[2] 98626 | 10,659 | Pullman[2] 99163 | 21,002 |
| Bellevue[2] 98009* | 71,471 | Kennewick[2] 99336 | 28,418 | Puyallup[2] 98371 | 16,799 |
| Bellingham[2] 98225 | 44,205 | Kent[2] 98031 | 21,119 | Redmond[2] 98052 | 20,217 |
| Bothell[2] 98011 | 6,816 | Kirkland[2] 98033 | 16,712 | Renton[2] 98055 | 28,949 |
| Bremerton[2] 98310* | 41,652 | Lacey[2] 98503 | 13,382 | Richland[2] 99352 | 33,516 |
| Camas[2] 98607 | 6,179 | Longview[2] 98632 | 30,037 | Seattle[2] 98109* | 485,487 |
| Centralia[2] 98531 | 10,990 | Lynnwood[2] 98036 | 24,044 | Sedro Woolley[2] 98284 | 5,985 |
| Chehalis[2] 98532 | 6,581 | McChord AFB[1] 98438 | 6,515 | Shelton[2] 98584 | 6,958 |
| Cheney[2] 99004 | 7,164 | Mercer Island[2] 98040 | 21,318 | Spokane[2] 99210* | 177,019 |
| Clarkston[2] 99403 | 7,688 | Moses Lake[2] 98837 | 10,893 | Sunnyside[2] 98944 | 7,688 |
| College Place[2] 99324 | 5,444 | Mount Vernon[2] 98273 | 12,274 | Tacoma[2] 98413* | 156,625 |
| Des Moines[2] 98108 | 6,535 | Mountlake Terr.[2] 98043 | 16,857 | Toppenish[2] 98948 | 6,015 |
| Edmonds[2] 98020 | 28,111 | Oak Harbor[2] 98277 | 11,901 | Tumwater[2] 98502 | 6,540 |
| Ellensburg[2] 98926 | 12,609 | Olympia[2] 98501* | 29,696 | Vancouver[2] 98660* | 48,438 |
| Ephrata[2] 98823 | 5,456 | Othello[2] 99344 | 5,179 | Walla Walla[2] 99362 | 24,337 |
| Everett[2] 98201* | 52,690 | Pasco[5] 99301 | 15,599 | Wenatchee[2] 98801 | 18,136 |
| Fircrest[2] 98466 | 5,903 | Port Angeles[2] 98362 | 17,844 | Yakima[2] 98903* | 53,820 |

[1] 1970 Census. [2] Census est. July 1, 1978. [3] 1977 est. [4] Includes county. [5] 1978 Special Census. † Town or township.

| PLACE AND ZIP CODE | | POP. | PLACE AND ZIP CODE | | POP. | PLACE AND ZIP CODE | | POP. |
|---|---|---|---|---|---|---|---|---|

## WEST VIRGINIA (W. Va. or WV)

| PLACE AND ZIP CODE | | POP. | PLACE AND ZIP CODE | | POP. | PLACE AND ZIP CODE | | POP. |
|---|---|---|---|---|---|---|---|---|
| Beckley [2] | 25801 | 21,664 | Huntington [2] | 25704* | 68,261 | Parkersburg [2] | 26101 | 38,827 |
| Bluefield [2] | 24701 | 16,936 | Hurricane [2] | 25526 | 5,099 | Point Pleasant [2] | 25550 | 5,859 |
| Bridgeport [2] | 26330 | 5,599 | Kenova [2] | 25530 | 5,076 | Princeton [2] | 24740 | 7,669 |
| Buckhannon [2] | 26201 | 8,119 | Keyser [2] | 26726 | 6,642 | St. Albans [2] | 25177 | 14,485 |
| Charleston [2] | 25301* | 66,811 | Martinsburg [2] | 25401 | 13,722 | S. Charleston [2] | 25303 | 16,530 |
| Clarksburg [2] | 26301 | 22,167 | Morgantown [2] | 26505 | 31,734 | Vienna [2] | 26105 | 11,036 |
| Dunbar [2] | 25064 | 8,881 | Moundsville [2] | 26041 | 12,901 | Weirton [2] | 26062 | 25,029 |
| Elkins [2] | 26241 | 8,324 | New Martinsville [2] | 26155 | 6,889 | Weston [2] | 26452 | 6,144 |
| Fairmont [2] | 26554 | 26,136 | Nitro [2] | 25143 | 8,252 | Wheeling [2] | 26003 | 42,686 |
| Grafton [2] | 26354 | 6,464 | Oak Hill [2] | 25901 | 7,921 | Williamson [2] | 25661 | 5,157 |

## WISCONSIN (Wis., Wisc., or WI)

| PLACE AND ZIP CODE | | POP. | PLACE AND ZIP CODE | | POP. | PLACE AND ZIP CODE | | POP. |
|---|---|---|---|---|---|---|---|---|
| Antigo [2] | 54409 | 8,394 | Janesville [3] | 53545 | 50,165 | Port Washington [2] | 53074 | 8,481 |
| Appleton [2] | 54911 | 61,017 | Jefferson [2] | 53549 | 5,857 | Portage [2] | 53901 | 7,652 |
| Ashland [2] | 54806 | 9,490 | Kaukauna [2] | 54130 | 11,617 | Prairie du Chien [2] | 53821 | 5,884 |
| Ashwaubenon [2] | 54304 | 14,992 | Kenosha [2] | 53141* | 78,949 | Racine [2] | 53401* | 92,718 |
| Baraboo [2] | 53913 | 7,787 | Kimberly [2] | 54136 | 6,155 | Rhinelander [2] | 54501 | 8,365 |
| Beaver Dam [2] | 53916 | 14,482 | La Crosse [2] | 54601 | 49,231 | Rice Lake [2] | 54868 | 7,822 |
| Beloit [2] | 53511 | 33,602 | Lake Geneva [2] | 53147 | 5,455 | Richfield [3] | 53076 | 7,883 |
| Berlin [2] | 54923 | 5,286 | Little Chute [2] | 54140 | 6,956 | Ripon [2] | 54971 | 6,953 |
| Brookfield [2] | 53005 | 35,203 | Madison [2] | 53707* | 170,382 | River Falls [2] | 54022 | 8,381 |
| Brown Deer [2] | 53209 | 14,708 | Manitowoc [2] | 54220 | 33,208 | St. Francis [2] | 53207 | 10,384 |
| Burlington [2] | 53105 | 9,244 | Marinette [2] | 54143 | 12,128 | Shawano [2] | 54166 | 6,929 |
| Cedarburg [2] | 53012 | 10,371 | Marshfield [2] | 54449 | 17,258 | Sheboygan [2] | 53081 | 48,815 |
| Chippewa Falls [2] | 54729 | 12,545 | Menasha [2] | 54952 | 15,064 | Sheboygan Falls [2] | 53085 | 5,273 |
| Cudahy [2] | 53110 | 21,608 | Menomonee Falls [2] | 53051 | 31,816 | Shorewood [2] | 53211 | 14,319 |
| De Pere [2] | 54115 | 15,105 | Menomonie [2] | 54751 | 11,556 | S. Milwaukee [2] | 53172 | 23,234 |
| Delavan [2] | 53115 | 5,691 | Mequon [2] | 53092 | 16,625 | Sparta [2] | 54656 | 6,679 |
| Eau Claire [2] | 54701 | 49,336 | Merrill [2] | 54452 | 9,313 | Stevens Point [2] | 54481 | 23,708 |
| Elm Grove [2] | 53122 | 7,877 | Merton [4] | 53056 | 5,566 | Stoughton [2] | 53589 | 7,972 |
| Fond du Lac [2] | 54935 | 36,506 | Middleton [2] | 53562 | 11,583 | Sturgeon Bay [2] | 54235 | 8,241 |
| Fort Atkinson [2] | 53538 | 9,900 | Milwaukee [2] | 53201* | 633,220 | Sun Prairie [2] | 53590 | 13,757 |
| Fox Point [2] | 53217 | 8,135 | Monona [2] | 53716 | 9,512 | Superior [2] | 54880 | 29,690 |
| Franklin [2] | 53132 | 17,625 | Monroe [2] | 53566 | 9,658 | Tomah [2] | 54660 | 6,954 |
| Germantown [3] | 53022 | 9,886 | Muskego [2] | 53150 | 15,165 | Two Rivers [2] | 54241 | 12,962 |
| Glendale [2] | 53209 | 14,171 | Neenah [2] | 54956 | 23,897 | Watertown [2] | 53094 | 17,510 |
| Grafton [2] | 53024 | 8,751 | New Berlin [2] | 53151 | 32,758 | Waukesha [2] | 53186 | 50,256 |
| Green Bay [2] | 54305* | 91,347 | New London [2] | 54961 | 6,271 | Waupun [2] | 53963 | 7,935 |
| Greendale [2] | 53129 | 18,630 | Oak Creek [2] | 53154 | 16,386 | Wausau [2] | 54401 | 32,601 |
| Greenfield [2] | 53228 | 30,614 | Oconomowoc [2] | 53066 | 10,687 | Wauwatosa [2] | 53213 | 55,282 |
| Hales Corners [2] | 53130 | 8,992 | Onalaska [2] | 54650 | 9,193 | West Allis [2] | 53214 | 67,866 |
| Hartford [2] | 53027 | 7,620 | Oshkosh [2] | 54901 | 49,828 | West Bend [2] | 53095 | 22,904 |
| Hartland [2] | 53029 | 5,146 | Perry Go Place [1] | 53511 | 5,912 | Whitefish Bay [2] | 53217 | 16,339 |
| Howard [2] | 54303 | 7,418 | Platteville [2] | 53818 | 9,133 | Whitewater [2] | 53190 | 10,807 |
| Hudson [2] | 54016 | 5,855 | Plymouth [2] | 53073 | 6,127 | Wisconsin Rapids [2] | 54494 | 18,503 |

## WYOMING (Wyo. or WY)

| PLACE AND ZIP CODE | | POP. | PLACE AND ZIP CODE | | POP. | PLACE AND ZIP CODE | | POP. |
|---|---|---|---|---|---|---|---|---|
| Casper [2] | 82601* | 46,903 | Green River [2] | 82935 | 10,827 | Riverton [2] | 82501 | 9,597 |
| Cheyenne [2] | 82001 | 48,551 | Lander [2] | 82520 | 7,881 | Rock Springs [2] | 82901 | 20,646 |
| Cody [2] | 82414 | 7,265 | Laramie [2] | 82070* | 25,256 | Sheridan [2] | 82801 | 13,407 |
| Gillette [2] | 82716 | 12,483 | Rawlins [2] | 82301 | 10,641 | Worland [2] | 82401 | 5,756 |

## DIST. OF COLUMBIA (D.C. or DC)   GUAM (GU)   VIRGIN ISLANDS (V.I. or VI)

| PLACE AND ZIP CODE | | POP. | PLACE AND ZIP CODE | | POP. | PLACE AND ZIP CODE | | POP. |
|---|---|---|---|---|---|---|---|---|
| Washington [2] | 20013* | 671,001 | Tamuning [1] | 96911 | 8,230 | Charlotte Amalie [1] | 00801 | 12,220 |

## PUERTO RICO (P.R. or PR)

| PLACE AND ZIP CODE | | POP. | PLACE AND ZIP CODE | | POP. | PLACE AND ZIP CODE | | POP. |
|---|---|---|---|---|---|---|---|---|
| Aguada [4]† | 00602 | 30,900 | Fajardo [4]† | 00648 | 35,800 | Rio Grande [4]† | 00745 | 32,200 |
| Aguadilla [4]† | 00603 | 64,000 | Guayama [4]† | 00654 | 42,900 | Salinas [4]† | 00751 | 26,900 |
| Aibonito [4]† | 00609 | 23,500 | Guaynabo [4]† | 00657 | 81,300 | San German [4]† | 00753 | 34,800 |
| Arecibo [4]† | 00612 | 88,900 | Hatillo [4]† | 00659 | 27,000 | San Juan [4]† | 00936* | 522,700 |
| Barceloneta [4]† | 00617 | 24,700 | Humacao [4]† | 00661 | 49,300 | San Lorenzo [4]† | 00754 | 31,900 |
| Bayamon [4]† | 00619 | 213,600 | Isabela [4]† | 00662 | 37,200 | San Sebastian [4]† | 00755 | 36,300 |
| Cabo Rojo [4]† | 00623 | 33,100 | Juana Diaz [4]† | 00665 | 42,800 | Toa Alta [4]† | 00758 | 27,000 |
| Caguas [4]† | 00625 | 119,800 | Juncos [4]† | 00666 | 24,500 | Toa Baja [3]† | 00759 | 76,935 |
| Carolina [4]† | 00630 | 164,200 | Lares [4]† | 00669 | 20,400 | Trujillo Alto [4]† | 00760 | 48,300 |
| Catano [4]† | 00632 | 29,200 | Loiza [4]† | 00672 | 47,500 | Utuado [4]† | 00761 | 38,400 |
| Cayey [4]† | 00633 | 45,800 | Manati [4]† | 00701 | 37,400 | Vega Alta [4]† | 00762 | 25,300 |
| Cidra [4]† | 00639 | 28,100 | Mayaguez [4]† | 00708 | 106,500 | Vega Baja [4]† | 00763 | 45,300 |
| Coamo [4]† | 00640 | 31,200 | Moca [4]† | 00716 | 26,000 | Yabucoa [4]† | 00767 | 34,000 |
| Corozal [4]† | 00643 | 29,400 | Ponce [4]† | 00731 | 207,500 | Yauco [4]† | 00768 | 41,800 |

[1] 1970 Census. [2] Census Bureau estimate July 1, 1978. [3] 1978 Special Census. [4] 1977 estimate. † Includes county.

# AREAS, LATITUDES, LONGITUDES, AND ELEVATIONS OF U.S. CITIES

Sources: National Oceanic and Atmospheric Administration (elevations of weather stations); Bureau of the Census

| STATE AND CITY | AREA (sq. mi.) | LATITUDE ° | LATITUDE ' | LONGITUDE ° | LONGITUDE ' | ELEVATION (ft.) |
|---|---|---|---|---|---|---|
| **ALABAMA** | | | | | | |
| Anniston | 16.4 | 33 | 35 | 85 | 51 | 599 |
| Bessemer | 15.3 | 33 | 22 | 87 | 01 | 540 |
| Birmingham | 98.1 | 33 | 34 | 86 | 45 | 620 |
| Dothan | 72.8 | 31 | 12 | 85 | 21 | 300 |
| Florence | 21.7 | 34 | 48 | 87 | 41 | 578 |
| Gadsden | 34.8 | 34 | 02 | 86 | 00 | 565 |
| Huntsville | 114.1 | 34 | 42 | 86 | 35 | 600 |
| Mobile | 116.6 | 30 | 41 | 88 | 15 | 211 |
| Montgomery | 51.5 | 32 | 18 | 86 | 24 | 221 |
| Tuscaloosa | 43.4 | 33 | 14 | 87 | 37 | 170 |
| **ALASKA** | | | | | | |
| Anchorage | 1,699.0 | 61 | 10 | 150 | 01 | 114 |
| Fairbanks | 28.4 | 64 | 49 | 147 | 52 | 436 |
| Juneau | 3,108.0 | 58 | 22 | 134 | 35 | 12 |
| Sitka | 2,762.0 | 57 | 04 | 135 | 21 | 15 |
| **ARIZONA** | | | | | | |
| Flagstaff | 64.6 | 35 | 08 | 111 | 40 | 7,006 |
| Mesa | 49.7 | 33 | 25 | 111 | 52 | 1,230 |
| Phoenix | 275.2 | 33 | 27 | 112 | 04 | 1,083 |
| Scottsdale | 75.3 | 33 | 30 | 111 | 55 | 1,227 |
| Tempe | 37.4 | 33 | 26 | 111 | 56 | 1,150 |
| Tucson | 95.4 | 32 | 15 | 110 | 57 | 2,444 |
| Yuma | 10.4 | 32 | 44 | 114 | 37 | 240 |
| **ARKANSAS** | | | | | | |
| Fort Smith | 49.7 | 35 | 39 | 94 | 09 | 793 |
| Hot Springs | 23.4 | 34 | 31 | 93 | 03 | 680 |
| Little Rock | 60.0 | 34 | 46 | 92 | 19 | 512 |
| Pine Bluff | 17.4 | 34 | 13 | 92 | 01 | 215 |
| Texarkana | 10.8 | 33 | 27 | 94 | 00 | 361 |
| **CALIFORNIA** | | | | | | |
| Altadena | 8.8 | 34 | 11 | 118 | 08 | 1,127 |
| Bakersfield | 56.5 | 35 | 25 | 119 | 03 | 495 |
| Berkeley | 10.6 | 37 | 52 | 122 | 15 | 345 |
| Burlingame | 4.6 | 37 | 35 | 122 | 21 | 10 |
| Chula Vista | 18.6 | 32 | 36 | 117 | 06 | 9 |
| Concord | 29.4 | 37 | 58 | 121 | 59 | 195 |
| El Centro | 5.2 | 32 | 46 | 115 | 34 | -30 |
| Fairfield | 25.4 | 38 | 16 | 122 | 02 | 38 |
| Fresno | 58.6 | 36 | 46 | 119 | 43 | 328 |
| Fullerton | 22.1 | 33 | 53 | 117 | 55 | 330 |
| Hayward | 38.9 | 37 | 39 | 121 | 59 | 715 |
| Long Beach | 50.0 | 33 | 49 | 118 | 09 | 34 |
| Los Angeles | 464.6 | 34 | 03 | 118 | 14 | 270 |
| Modesto | 17.9 | 37 | 39 | 121 | 00 | 91 |
| Oakland | 54.3 | 37 | 48 | 122 | 16 | 30 |
| Oxnard | 21.9 | 34 | 12 | 119 | 11 | 49 |
| Palm Springs | 77.6 | 33 | 50 | 116 | 30 | 425 |
| Palo Alto | 25.7 | 37 | 27 | 122 | 08 | 25 |
| Pasadena | 23.1 | 34 | 09 | 118 | 09 | 864 |
| Pomona | 22.8 | 34 | 04 | 117 | 49 | 740 |
| Redwood City | 20.5 | 37 | 29 | 122 | 14 | 31 |
| Richmond | 32.1 | 37 | 56 | 122 | 21 | 55 |
| Riverside | 71.7 | 33 | 57 | 117 | 23 | 840 |
| Sacramento | 93.9 | 38 | 35 | 121 | 30 | 19 |
| Salinas | 15.1 | 36 | 40 | 121 | 36 | 85 |
| San Bernardino | 51.2 | 34 | 08 | 117 | 16 | 1,125 |
| San Diego | 323.2 | 32 | 44 | 117 | 10 | 13 |
| San Francisco | 45.4 | 37 | 47 | 122 | 25 | 52 |
| San Jose | 152.6 | 37 | 21 | 121 | 54 | 67 |
| San Mateo | 11.5 | 37 | 32 | 122 | 18 | 21 |
| Santa Ana | 27.3 | 33 | 45 | 117 | 52 | 115 |
| Santa Barbara | 21.3 | 34 | 25 | 119 | 41 | 5 |
| Santa Clara | 18.7 | 37 | 21 | 121 | 56 | 88 |
| Santa Monica | 8.3 | 34 | 00 | 118 | 30 | 15 |
| Santa Rosa | 25.9 | 38 | 27 | 122 | 42 | 167 |
| Stockton | 40.3 | 38 | 00 | 121 | 19 | 12 |
| Torrance | 20.5 | 33 | 48 | 118 | 20 | 110 |
| Ventura | 15.2 | 34 | 17 | 119 | 17 | 105 |
| Whittier | 11.7 | 33 | 58 | 118 | 02 | 340 |
| **COLORADO** | | | | | | |
| Boulder | 20.0 | 40 | 00 | 105 | 16 | 5,420 |
| Colorado Springs | 90.6 | 38 | 49 | 104 | 43 | 6,090 |
| Denver | 111.2 | 39 | 45 | 104 | 59 | 5,320 |
| Lakewood | 22.5 | 39 | 45 | 105 | 08 | 5,637 |
| Pueblo | 33.4 | 38 | 17 | 104 | 31 | 4,639 |
| **CONNECTICUT** | | | | | | |
| Bridgeport | 16.1 | 41 | 10 | 73 | 08 | 7 |
| Danbury | 43.9 | 41 | 23 | 73 | 28 | 510 |
| Hartford | 17.4 | 41 | 48 | 72 | 39 | 19 |
| Manchester | 26.9 | 41 | 46 | 72 | 29 | 420 |
| Milford | 22.3 | 41 | 12 | 73 | 05 | 30 |
| New Haven | 18.4 | 41 | 18 | 72 | 56 | 24 |
| Norwalk | 22.0 | 41 | 07 | 73 | 25 | 37 |
| Norwich | 26.1 | 41 | 32 | 72 | 04 | 20 |
| Stamford | 38.1 | 41 | 08 | 73 | 33 | 190 |
| **DELAWARE** | | | | | | |
| Wilmington | 12.9 | 39 | 40 | 75 | 36 | 74 |
| **DIST. OF COLUMBIA** | | | | | | |
| Washington | 61.4 | 38 | 56 | 77 | 02 | 10 |
| **FLORIDA** | | | | | | |
| Clearwater | 21.6 | 27 | 58 | 82 | 46 | 65 |
| Fort Lauderdale | 31.0 | 26 | 06 | 80 | 12 | 16 |
| Gainesville | 26.1 | 29 | 38 | 82 | 22 | 92 |
| Jacksonville | 750.0 | 30 | 30 | 81 | 42 | 26 |
| Key West | 4.1 | 24 | 34 | 81 | 48 | 6 |
| Miami | 34.3 | 25 | 48 | 80 | 16 | 7 |
| Orlando | 37.9 | 28 | 26 | 81 | 20 | 85 |
| Pensacola | 24.4 | 30 | 28 | 87 | 12 | 112 |
| St. Petersburg | 56.1 | 27 | 46 | 82 | 38 | 8 |
| Tampa | 84.5 | 27 | 58 | 82 | 32 | 19 |
| **GEORGIA** | | | | | | |
| Albany | 41.7 | 31 | 32 | 84 | 08 | 180 |
| Atlanta | 131.5 | 33 | 39 | 84 | 26 | 1,010 |
| Augusta | 15.2 | 33 | 22 | 81 | 58 | 148 |
| Columbus | 202.4 | 32 | 31 | 84 | 56 | 385 |
| Macon | 49.8 | 32 | 42 | 83 | 39 | 354 |
| Savannah | 27.3 | 32 | 08 | 81 | 12 | 46 |
| **HAWAII** | | | | | | |
| Hilo | 56.1 | 19 | 43 | 155 | 04 | 27 |
| Honolulu | 83.9 | 21 | 20 | 157 | 55 | 7 |
| **IDAHO** | | | | | | |
| Boise | 34.6 | 43 | 34 | 116 | 13 | 2,838 |
| Idaho Falls | 12.1 | 43 | 31 | 112 | 04 | 4,730 |
| Lewiston | 15.9 | 46 | 23 | 117 | 01 | 1,413 |
| Pocatello | 22.9 | 42 | 55 | 112 | 36 | 4,454 |
| **ILLINOIS** | | | | | | |
| Aurora | 26.7 | 41 | 45 | 88 | 21 | 690 |
| Belleville | 11.9 | 38 | 30 | 89 | 51 | 450 |
| Bloomington | 13.3 | 40 | 31 | 89 | 00 | 785 |
| Chicago | 222.8 | 41 | 47 | 87 | 45 | 607 |

| STATE AND CITY | AREA (sq. mi.) | LATITUDE ° | ' | LONGITUDE ° | ' | ELEVATION (ft.) |
|---|---|---|---|---|---|---|
| Decatur | 35.7 | 39 | 51 | 88 | 58 | 670 |
| Elgin | 19.0 | 42 | 02 | 88 | 16 | 758 |
| Joliet | 23.0 | 41 | 33 | 88 | 05 | 550 |
| Peoria | 39.4 | 40 | 40 | 89 | 41 | 652 |
| Rockford | 37.4 | 42 | 12 | 89 | 06 | 724 |
| Springfield | 39.6 | 39 | 50 | 89 | 40 | 588 |
| Waukegan | 21.8 | 42 | 21 | 87 | 53 | 700 |
| **INDIANA** | | | | | | |
| Evansville | 36.2 | 37 | 58 | 87 | 33 | 384 |
| Fort Wayne | 55.9 | 41 | 00 | 85 | 12 | 791 |
| Gary | 42.7 | 41 | 37 | 87 | 23 | 597 |
| Indianapolis | 374.2 | 39 | 44 | 86 | 17 | 792 |
| Muncie | 16.2 | 40 | 11 | 85 | 21 | 957 |
| South Bend | 31.4 | 41 | 42 | 86 | 19 | 773 |
| Terre Haute | 26.1 | 39 | 21 | 87 | 25 | 555 |
| **IOWA** | | | | | | |
| Cedar Rapids | 53.1 | 41 | 53 | 91 | 42 | 840 |
| Davenport | 60.1 | 41 | 31 | 90 | 34 | 568 |
| Des Moines | 64.4 | 41 | 32 | 93 | 39 | 938 |
| Dubuque | 17.2 | 42 | 24 | 90 | 42 | 1,056 |
| Iowa City | 21.7 | 41 | 39 | 91 | 32 | 640 |
| Sioux City | 52.2 | 42 | 24 | 96 | 23 | 1,103 |
| Waterloo | 61.4 | 42 | 33 | 92 | 24 | 868 |
| **KANSAS** | | | | | | |
| Dodge City | 10.1 | 37 | 46 | 99 | 58 | 2,582 |
| Emporia | 8.4 | 38 | 20 | 96 | 12 | 1,209 |
| Lawrence | 17.9 | 38 | 58 | 95 | 16 | 1,000 |
| Salina | 17.9 | 38 | 48 | 97 | 38 | 1,257 |
| Topeka | 58.5 | 39 | 04 | 95 | 38 | 877 |
| Wichita | 98.3 | 37 | 39 | 97 | 26 | 1,321 |
| **KENTUCKY** | | | | | | |
| Bowling Green | 21.8 | 37 | 00 | 86 | 26 | 536 |
| Covington | 13.5 | 39 | 04 | 84 | 40 | 869 |
| Lexington-Fayette | 280.2 | 38 | 02 | 84 | 36 | 966 |
| Louisville | 60.0 | 38 | 14 | 85 | 46 | 462 |
| Owensboro | 11.7 | 37 | 46 | 87 | 09 | 420 |
| **LOUISIANA** | | | | | | |
| Baton Rouge | 59.3 | 30 | 32 | 91 | 09 | 64 |
| Lafayette | 24.9 | 30 | 13 | 92 | 01 | 37 |
| Lake Charles | 26.3 | 30 | 07 | 93 | 13 | 9 |
| Monroe | 23.3 | 32 | 33 | 92 | 07 | 80 |
| New Orleans | 197.1 | 29 | 56 | 90 | 08 | 6 |
| Shreveport | 68.5 | 32 | 28 | 93 | 49 | 254 |
| **MAINE** | | | | | | |
| Bangor | 34.3 | 44 | 48 | 68 | 49 | 163 |
| Lewiston | 34.6 | 44 | 06 | 70 | 13 | 180 |
| Portland | 21.6 | 43 | 39 | 70 | 19 | 43 |
| **MARYLAND** | | | | | | |
| Baltimore | 78.3 | 39 | 17 | 76 | 37 | 14 |
| Rockville | 11.8 | 39 | 07 | 77 | 06 | 400 |
| Towson | 18.4 | 39 | 23 | 76 | 34 | 390 |
| **MASSACHUSETTS** | | | | | | |
| Boston | 46.0 | 42 | 22 | 71 | 02 | 15 |
| Brockton | 21.2 | 42 | 03 | 71 | 00 | 80 |
| Fall River | 33.0 | 41 | 43 | 71 | 08 | 190 |
| Framingham | 24.7 | 42 | 17 | 71 | 25 | 170 |
| Haverhill | 32.3 | 42 | 46 | 71 | 04 | 60 |
| Holyoke | 20.9 | 42 | 12 | 72 | 36 | 98 |
| Lawrence | 6.8 | 42 | 42 | 71 | 10 | 57 |
| New Bedford | 19.5 | 41 | 38 | 70 | 56 | 120 |
| Provincetown | 1.6 | 42 | 04 | 70 | 12 | 30 |
| Springfield | 31.7 | 42 | 07 | 72 | 35 | 190 |
| Worcester | 37.4 | 42 | 16 | 71 | 52 | 986 |
| **MICHIGAN** | | | | | | |
| Ann Arbor | 23.5 | 42 | 18 | 83 | 43 | 900 |
| Bay City | 10.7 | 43 | 37 | 83 | 52 | 590 |
| Dearborn | 24.5 | 42 | 19 | 83 | 14 | 607 |
| Detroit | 138.0 | 42 | 21 | 83 | 01 | 623 |
| Flint | 32.9 | 42 | 58 | 83 | 44 | 770 |
| Grand Rapids | 44.9 | 42 | 53 | 85 | 31 | 784 |
| Kalamazoo | 24.6 | 42 | 18 | 85 | 34 | 760 |
| Lansing | 33.7 | 42 | 47 | 84 | 36 | 841 |
| Pontiac | 19.7 | 42 | 39 | 83 | 18 | 974 |
| Saginaw | 17.4 | 43 | 32 | 84 | 05 | 662 |
| **MINNESOTA** | | | | | | |
| Duluth | 67.3 | 46 | 50 | 92 | 11 | 1,438 |
| Minneapolis | 55.5 | 44 | 53 | 93 | 13 | 834 |
| Rochester | 16.8 | 43 | 55 | 92 | 30 | 1,297 |
| **MISSISSIPPI** | | | | | | |
| Biloxi | 11.1 | 30 | 24 | 88 | 54 | 15 |
| Gulfport | 25.8 | 30 | 23 | 89 | 08 | 35 |
| Jackson | 106.1 | 32 | 19 | 90 | 05 | 330 |
| Meridian | 25.4 | 32 | 20 | 88 | 45 | 290 |
| **MISSOURI** | | | | | | |
| Columbia | 41.7 | 38 | 49 | 92 | 13 | 887 |
| Independence | 77.5 | 39 | 06 | 94 | 25 | 1,000 |
| Jefferson City | 22.4 | 38 | 34 | 92 | 11 | 640 |
| Kansas City | 316.3 | 39 | 00 | 94 | 32 | 870 |
| St. Louis | 61.2 | 38 | 37 | 90 | 11 | 446 |
| Springfield | 63.2 | 37 | 14 | 93 | 23 | 1,268 |
| **MONTANA** | | | | | | |
| Billings | 18.8 | 45 | 46 | 108 | 29 | 3,097 |
| Great Falls | 15.9 | 47 | 29 | 111 | 22 | 3,662 |
| Helena | 12.6 | 46 | 36 | 112 | 00 | 3,828 |
| **NEBRASKA** | | | | | | |
| Lincoln | 56.0 | 40 | 49 | 96 | 42 | 1,150 |
| Omaha | 86.4 | 41 | 22 | 96 | 01 | 1,309 |
| **NEVADA** | | | | | | |
| Carson City | 150.4 | 39 | 09 | 119 | 46 | 4,651 |
| Las Vegas | 54.0 | 36 | 05 | 115 | 10 | 2,162 |
| Reno | 39.5 | 39 | 30 | 119 | 47 | 4,404 |
| **NEW HAMPSHIRE** | | | | | | |
| Concord | 63.3 | 43 | 12 | 71 | 30 | 346 |
| Manchester | 32.1 | 43 | 00 | 71 | 28 | 170 |
| Nashua | 31.4 | 42 | 47 | 71 | 30 | 188 |
| **NEW JERSEY** | | | | | | |
| Atlantic City | 12.4 | 39 | 23 | 74 | 26 | 11 |
| Jersey City | 15.1 | 40 | 44 | 74 | 03 | 135 |
| Newark | 23.5 | 40 | 42 | 74 | 10 | 11 |
| Paterson | 8.4 | 40 | 54 | 74 | 09 | 100 |
| Trenton | 7.5 | 40 | 13 | 74 | 46 | 56 |
| **NEW MEXICO** | | | | | | |
| Albuquerque | 93.2 | 35 | 03 | 106 | 37 | 5,311 |
| Santa Fe | 30.7 | 35 | 39 | 105 | 58 | 6,800 |
| **NEW YORK** | | | | | | |
| Albany | 21.3 | 42 | 45 | 73 | 48 | 275 |
| Binghamton | 11.0 | 42 | 13 | 75 | 59 | 1,590 |
| Buffalo | 41.3 | 42 | 56 | 78 | 44 | 705 |
| New York | 299.7 | 40 | 47 | 73 | 58 | 132 |
| Rochester | 36.7 | 43 | 07 | 77 | 40 | 547 |
| Schenectady | 10.3 | 42 | 50 | 73 | 55 | 225 |
| Syracuse | 25.8 | 43 | 07 | 76 | 07 | 410 |
| Utica | 16.0 | 43 | 09 | 75 | 23 | 718 |
| White Plains | 9.7 | 41 | 04 | 73 | 43 | 397 |

## AREAS, LATITUDES, LONGITUDES, AND ELEVATIONS OF U.S. CITIES (continued)

| STATE AND CITY | AREA (sq. mi.) | LATITUDE ° | LATITUDE ′ | LONGITUDE ° | LONGITUDE ′ | ELEVATION (ft.) |
|---|---|---|---|---|---|---|
| **NORTH CAROLINA** | | | | | | |
| Asheville ......... | 24.8 | 35 | 36 | 82 | 32 | 2,242 |
| Charlotte ......... | 126.7 | 35 | 13 | 80 | 56 | 735 |
| Durham .......... | 39.9 | 36 | 02 | 78 | 58 | 406 |
| Fayetteville....... | 31.1 | 35 | 13 | 80 | 56 | 735 |
| Greensboro ..... | 60.5 | 36 | 05 | 79 | 57 | 897 |
| High Point ...... | 31.9 | 35 | 58 | 79 | 59 | 912 |
| Raleigh .......... | 54.5 | 35 | 47 | 78 | 42 | 400 |
| Winston-Salem ... | 61.1 | 36 | 05 | 80 | 13 | 770 |
| **NORTH DAKOTA** | | | | | | |
| Bismarck ........ | 14.8 | 46 | 51 | 100 | 33 | 1,720 |
| Fargo............ | 25.7 | 46 | 54 | 96 | 48 | 896 |
| Grand Forks ..... | 13.0 | 47 | 56 | 97 | 05 | 830 |
| Minot............ | 9.9 | 48 | 16 | 101 | 17 | 1,713 |
| **OHIO** | | | | | | |
| Akron ........... | 54.2 | 41 | 05 | 81 | 31 | 1,007 |
| Canton .......... | 19.4 | 40 | 46 | 81 | 23 | 1,020 |
| Cincinnati ....... | 78.1 | 39 | 09 | 84 | 31 | 761 |
| Cleveland ....... | 75.9 | 41 | 29 | 81 | 43 | 690 |
| Columbus........ | 173.6 | 39 | 57 | 83 | 07 | 875 |
| Dayton .......... | 45.6 | 39 | 46 | 84 | 11 | 745 |
| Hamilton ........ | 18.0 | 39 | 24 | 84 | 34 | 590 |
| Lima ............ | 12.1 | 40 | 45 | 84 | 05 | 870 |
| Mansfield ....... | 25.5 | 40 | 49 | 82 | 31 | 1,295 |
| Toledo .......... | 81.3 | 41 | 39 | 83 | 32 | 595 |
| Warren .......... | 14.8 | 41 | 09 | 80 | 49 | 900 |
| Youngstown ...... | 33.6 | 41 | 16 | 80 | 40 | 1,178 |
| **OKLAHOMA** | | | | | | |
| Lawton .......... | 40.2 | 34 | 37 | 98 | 27 | 1,150 |
| Oklahoma City ... | 629.6 | 35 | 28 | 97 | 33 | 1,200 |
| Tulsa ........... | 177.4 | 36 | 11 | 95 | 54 | 668 |
| **OREGON** | | | | | | |
| Eugene .......... | 30.7 | 44 | 07 | 123 | 13 | 364 |
| Portland ......... | 100.3 | 45 | 36 | 122 | 36 | 21 |
| Salem ........... | 35.1 | 44 | 55 | 123 | 01 | 195 |
| **PENNSYLVANIA** | | | | | | |
| Allentown ........ | 17.8 | 40 | 39 | 75 | 26 | 387 |
| Altoona .......... | 9.1 | 40 | 30 | 78 | 28 | 1,320 |
| Erie ............. | 18.9 | 42 | 05 | 80 | 11 | 732 |
| Harrisburg ....... | 7.6 | 40 | 13 | 76 | 51 | 338 |
| Lancaster ........ | 7.2 | 40 | 01 | 76 | 17 | 255 |
| Philadelphia...... | 128.5 | 39 | 57 | 75 | 09 | 35 |
| Pittsburgh ....... | 55.2 | 40 | 27 | 80 | 00 | 747 |
| Reading ......... | 9.9 | 40 | 19 | 75 | 56 | 270 |
| Scranton......... | 25.7 | 41 | 25 | 75 | 40 | 746 |
| Wilkes-Barre ..... | 6.7 | 41 | 20 | 75 | 44 | 930 |
| York ............ | 5.3 | 39 | 54 | 76 | 44 | 640 |
| **RHODE ISLAND** | | | | | | |
| Newport ......... | 7.3 | 41 | 31 | 71 | 19 | 20 |
| Providence........ | 18.1 | 41 | 44 | 71 | 26 | 51 |
| Woonsocket ...... | 7.9 | 41 | 59 | 71 | 30 | 115 |
| **SOUTH CAROLINA** | | | | | | |
| Charleston ....... | 24.2 | 32 | 47 | 79 | 56 | 9 |
| Columbia ........ | 108.9 | 33 | 59 | 81 | 01 | 242 |
| Greenville ....... | 22.4 | 34 | 52 | 82 | 24 | 1,010 |
| **SOUTH DAKOTA** | | | | | | |
| Aberdeen ....... | 6.2 | 45 | 27 | 98 | 26 | 1,296 |
| Huron .......... | 6.1 | 44 | 22 | 98 | 13 | 1,277 |
| Pierre .......... | 12.7 | 44 | 23 | 100 | 17 | 1,734 |
| Rapid City ....... | 19.2 | 44 | 04 | 103 | 16 | 3,370 |
| Sioux Falls ...... | 36.1 | 43 | 34 | 96 | 44 | 1,418 |
| **TENNESSEE** | | | | | | |
| Chattanooga ...... | 116.1 | 35 | 02 | 85 | 12 | 665 |
| Knoxville ......... | 77.3 | 35 | 57 | 83 | 55 | 895 |
| Memphis ......... | 280.8 | 35 | 09 | 90 | 03 | 205 |
| Nashville-Davidson | 479.0 | 36 | 07 | 86 | 41 | 590 |
| **TEXAS** | | | | | | |
| Abilene........... | 74.9 | 32 | 25 | 99 | 41 | 1,784 |
| Amarillo.......... | 73.8 | 35 | 14 | 101 | 42 | 3,607 |
| Arlington ......... | 85.4 | 32 | 44 | 97 | 07 | 630 |
| Austin ........... | 113.7 | 30 | 18 | 97 | 42 | 597 |
| Beaumont ........ | 71.6 | 30 | 06 | 94 | 06 | 20 |
| Brownsville ...... | 25.8 | 25 | 54 | 97 | 26 | 19 |
| Corpus Christi .... | 176.1 | 27 | 46 | 97 | 30 | 44 |
| Dallas ........... | 341.5 | 32 | 51 | 96 | 51 | 481 |
| El Paso .......... | 176.4 | 31 | 48 | 106 | 24 | 3,918 |
| Fort Worth ....... | 233.8 | 32 | 45 | 97 | 20 | 616 |
| Galveston ....... | 28.6 | 29 | 18 | 94 | 48 | 7 |
| Houston ......... | 521.1 | 29 | 45 | 95 | 22 | 96 |
| Laredo .......... | 20.5 | 27 | 30 | 99 | 28 | 396 |
| Odessa .......... | 25.1 | 31 | 53 | 102 | 24 | 2,910 |
| San Antonio ..... | 263.6 | 29 | 32 | 98 | 28 | 788 |
| Waco ........... | 72.0 | 31 | 37 | 97 | 13 | 500 |
| Wichita Falls...... | 42.9 | 33 | 58 | 98 | 29 | 994 |
| **UTAH** | | | | | | |
| Ogden .......... | 25.3 | 41 | 15 | 111 | 57 | 4,350 |
| Provo ........... | 22.6 | 40 | 13 | 111 | 40 | 4,470 |
| Salt Lake City .... | 73.5 | 40 | 46 | 111 | 53 | 4,320 |
| **VERMONT** | | | | | | |
| Burlington ........ | 10.1 | 44 | 28 | 73 | 12 | 400 |
| Montpelier ....... | 10.2 | 44 | 12 | 72 | 34 | 1,126 |
| **VIRGINIA** | | | | | | |
| Alexandria........ | 14.9 | 38 | 48 | 77 | 05 | 70 |
| Lynchburg ....... | 50.2 | 37 | 20 | 79 | 12 | 916 |
| Newport News .... | 69.1 | 37 | 01 | 76 | 27 | 50 |
| Norfolk........... | 54.2 | 36 | 54 | 76 | 12 | 22 |
| Richmond ........ | 60.3 | 37 | 30 | 77 | 20 | 164 |
| Roanoke ......... | 42.6 | 37 | 19 | 79 | 58 | 1,149 |
| **WASHINGTON** | | | | | | |
| Bellingham ....... | 21.9 | 48 | 45 | 122 | 29 | 140 |
| Everett .......... | 29.8 | 47 | 59 | 122 | 11 | 60 |
| Olympia ......... | 14.4 | 46 | 58 | 122 | 54 | 195 |
| Seattle .......... | 83.6 | 47 | 39 | 122 | 18 | 19 |
| Spokane ......... | 51.9 | 47 | 40 | 117 | 25 | 1,875 |
| Tacoma .......... | 47.8 | 47 | 15 | 122 | 26 | 267 |
| **WEST VIRGINIA** | | | | | | |
| Charleston........ | 27.5 | 38 | 21 | 81 | 39 | 600 |
| Huntington ....... | 14.7 | 38 | 25 | 82 | 27 | 565 |
| Wheeling ........ | 15.0 | 40 | 06 | 80 | 42 | 659 |
| **WISCONSIN** | | | | | | |
| Appleton ........ | 15.4 | 44 | 15 | 88 | 23 | 730 |
| Green Bay ....... | 43.0 | 44 | 29 | 88 | 08 | 682 |
| Kenosha.......... | 15.0 | 42 | 33 | 87 | 48 | 600 |
| La Crosse ....... | 15.9 | 43 | 52 | 91 | 15 | 651 |
| Madison ......... | 52.7 | 43 | 08 | 89 | 20 | 858 |
| Milwaukee ....... | 95.0 | 42 | 57 | 87 | 54 | 672 |
| Oshkosh ......... | 11.1 | 44 | 03 | 88 | 33 | 753 |
| Racine .......... | 13.9 | 42 | 43 | 87 | 52 | 695 |
| **WYOMING** | | | | | | |
| Casper .......... | 10.9 | 42 | 51 | 106 | 18 | 5,195 |
| Cheyenne ....... | 13.4 | 41 | 09 | 104 | 49 | 6,126 |
| Laramie .......... | 9.7 | 41 | 19 | 105 | 35 | 7,173 |

# Climate and Weather

United Press Int'l.

Texas rancher Hadley Wardlaw reaches down into deep crack in a watering hole near Bracketville, Texas, where lack of rain in significant amounts in 1980 severely damaged agriculture. Drought hit many other areas of the U.S. during the year. Some parts of the Midwest had less rain than in any period since the Dust Bowl of the 1930s.

## HIGHLIGHTS: 1980

### KILLER HEAT WAVE

The worst heat wave in a quarter of a century in the United States killed 1,265 persons and caused losses of about $20 billion in 1980 according to the National Oceanic and Atmospheric Administration (NOAA). The unusual weather lasted from June through most of September, affecting 26 states in the Midwest and South. Heat-related summer deaths were seven times greater than normal. Electricity usage, largely for air conditioning, set a record of 5.5% above normal. Hundreds of miles of major highways buckled, causing about $500 million in damage. Crops and

## STORMS FORECAST FOR 1981

Based on a research study of the relationship of bad storms to phases of the Moon, the worst storms in 1981 may take place in the following periods.

| | |
|---|---|
| January 7–9 | July 19–21 |
| January 23–27 | July 31–August 2 |
| February 5–7 | August 18–20 |
| February 21–23 | August 30–September 1 |
| March 7–9 | September 16–18 |
| March 23–25 | September 28–30 |
| April 5–7 | October 16–18 |
| April 22–24 | October 28–30 |
| May 4–6 | November 14–16 |
| May 21–23 | November 27–29 |
| June 3–5 | December 14–16 |
| June 20–22 | December 27–29 |
| July 2–4 | |

livestock were severely damaged. Water resources in many parts of the country were seriously jeopardized.

Most of those who died from the heat wave, according to the NOAA, were elderly or poor persons who lived in non-air-conditioned homes.

Missouri had the greatest number of heat-related fatalities—311.

The heat wave began in mid-June when temperatures soared above 100° F. in southwest Texas. By mid-July it had spread northeastward, giving the central third of the nation 100° temperatures. By September it had reached the eastern U.S., causing local officials to invoke water conservation measures.

From June 23 through Aug. 3 Dallas, Texas, registered temperatures of 100° or higher each day. From mid-June to mid-July temperatures averaged 8° above normal in Missouri, Kansas, Oklahoma, Arkansas, and north-central Texas. However, this was considerably less than the height of the Dust Bowl drought that reached its climax in July 1936 with temperatures averaging 12° above normal in the Midwest.

The drought was caused because the high altitude jet stream of air turned northward into Canada early in June instead of continuing its normal path across the north-central states. Usually the jet stream causes low-pressure areas in the Midwest to draw in moist air from the Gulf of Mexico. But the new jet-stream pattern in 1980 allowed dry westerly winds to flow across the continent, turning away the moisture-bearing air.

Climatologists have many theories about what caused the jet stream to change its pattern, including activity of sunspots, tidal forces of the Moon, dust and gases spewed into the air by volcanoes, and increasing amount of carbon dioxide in the atmosphere.

The worst known drought to affect the Midwest is believed to have taken place in the 1200s and 1300s, according to fossil evidence examined by Dr. Reid A. Bryson, director of the Institute for Environmental Studies at the University of Wisconsin. His investigation showed that during this period the American Indians were forced to leave the Great Plains because of the lack of water.

## SATELLITE MEASURES SUN'S ENERGY

The Solar Maximum Mission satellite launched by NASA on Feb. 14, 1980, has recorded fluctuations of up to 0.1% in the amount of energy being radiated by the Sun.

Scientists believe that an increase or decrease of as much as 0.5% could produce major climate changes. They say, for example, that a drop of as much as 6% in the Sun's output of radiation would be enough to cover the entire surface of the earth with ice.

Winter's first snowfall in Iowa on Oct. 27, 1980, dumped 7 inches on Des Moines and 2 inches on Ames. Iowa State University freshman Tim Schwartz brushes snow off the seat of his bicycle before tackling a slippery ride home. The surprise storm caused many auto accidents and home power outages.

# RECORD HIGH AND LOW TEMPERATURES IN U.S. STATES

Source: Environmental Data Service, NOAA, U.S. Department of Commerce

| STATE | RECORD HIGH TEMPERATURES | | | RECORD LOW TEMPERATURES | | |
|---|---|---|---|---|---|---|
| | Temp. (F.) | Date | Location | Temp. (F.) | Date | Location |
| United States | 134° | July 10, 1913 | Greenland Ranch, California | −79.8° | Jan. 23, 1971 | Prospect Creek Camp, Alaska |
| Alabama...... | 112° | Sept. 5, 1925 | Centerville | −27° | Jan. 30, 1966 | New Market |
| Alaska ...... | 100° | June 27, 1915 | Fort Yukon | −79.8° | Jan. 23, 1971 | Prospect Creek Camp |
| Arizona...... | 127° | July 7, 1905* | Parker | −40° | Jan. 7, 1971 | Hawley Lake |
| Arkansas ..... | 120° | Aug. 10, 1936 | Ozark | −29° | Feb. 13, 1905 | Pond |
| California..... | 134° | July 10, 1913 | Greenland Ranch | −45° | Jan. 20, 1937 | Boca |
| Colorado ..... | 118° | July 11, 1888 | Bennett | −60° | Feb. 1, 1951 | Taylor Park |
| Connecticut... | 105° | July 22, 1926 | Waterbury | −32° | Feb. 16, 1943 | Falls Village |
| Delaware ..... | 110° | July 21, 1930 | Millsboro | −17° | Jan. 17, 1893 | Millsboro |
| Dist. of Columbia | 106° | July 20, 1930* | Washington | −15° | Feb. 11, 1899 | Washington |
| Florida ....... | 109° | June 29, 1931 | Monticello | −2° | Feb. 13, 1899 | Tallahassee |
| Georgia ...... | 112° | July 24, 1952 | Louisville | −17° | Jan. 27, 1940 | CCC Camp F-16 |
| Hawaii ....... | 100° | Apr. 27, 1931 | Pahala | 14° | Jan. 2, 1961 | Haleakala, Maui |
| Idaho ........ | 118° | July 28, 1934 | Orofino | −60° | Jan. 16, 1943 | Island Park Dam |
| Illinois........ | 117° | July 14, 1954 | E. St. Louis | −35° | Jan. 22, 1930 | Mt. Carroll |
| Indiana ....... | 116° | July 14, 1936 | Collegeville | −35° | Feb. 2, 1951 | Greensburg |
| Iowa ......... | 118° | July 20, 1934 | Keokuk | −47° | Jan. 12, 1912 | Washta |
| Kansas ....... | 121° | July 24, 1936* | Alton (near) | −40° | Feb. 13, 1905 | Lebanon |
| Kentucky ..... | 114° | July 28, 1930 | Greensburg | −34° | Jan. 28, 1963 | Cynthiana |
| Louisiana ..... | 114° | Aug. 10, 1936 | Plain Dealing | −16° | Feb. 13, 1899 | Minden |
| Maine ........ | 105° | July 10, 1911* | North Bridgton | −48° | Jan. 19, 1925 | Van Buren |
| Maryland ..... | 109° | July 10, 1936* | Cumberland & Frederick | −40° | Jan. 13, 1912 | Oakland |
| Massachusetts | 107° | Aug. 2, 1975 | New Bedford and Chester | −34° | Jan. 18, 1957 | Birch Hill Dam |
| Michigan ..... | 112° | July 13, 1936 | Mio | −51° | Feb. 9, 1934 | Vanderbilt |
| Minnesota .... | 114° | July 6, 1936* | Moorhead | −59° | Feb. 16, 1903* | Pokegama Dam |
| Mississippi ... | 115° | July 29, 1930 | Holly Springs | −19° | Jan. 30, 1966 | Corinth 4 SW |
| Missouri...... | 118° | July 14, 1954* | Warsaw & Union | −40° | Feb. 13, 1905 | Warsaw |
| Montana...... | 117° | July 5, 1937 | Medicine Lake | −60.7° | Jan. 20, 1954 | Rogers Pass |
| Nebraska ..... | 118° | July 24, 1936* | Minden | −47° | Feb. 12, 1899 | Camp Clarke |
| Nevada....... | 122° | June 23, 1954* | Overton | −50° | Jan. 8, 1937 | San Jacinto |
| New Hampshire | 106° | July 4, 1911 | Nashua | −46° | Jan. 28, 1925 | Pittsburg |
| New Jersey ... | 110° | July 10, 1936 | Runyon | −34° | Jan. 5, 1904 | River Vale |
| New Mexico .. | 116° | July 10, 1934* | Orogrande | −50° | Feb. 1, 1951 | Gavilan |
| New York ..... | 108° | July 22, 1926 | Troy | −52° | Feb. 9, 1934 | Stillwater Reservoir |
| North Carolina | 108° | Sept. 7, 1954* | Weldon | −29° | Jan. 30, 1966 | Mt. Mitchell |
| North Dakota . | 121° | July 6, 1936 | Steele | −60° | Feb. 15, 1936 | Parshall |
| Ohio ......... | 113° | July 21, 1934* | Gallipolis (near) | −39° | Feb. 10, 1899 | Milligan |
| Oklahoma .... | 120° | July 26, 1943* | Tishomingo | −27° | Jan. 18, 1930* | Watts |
| Oregon ....... | 119° | Aug. 10, 1938* | Pendleton | −54° | Feb. 10, 1933* | Seneca |
| Pennsylvania.. | 111° | July 10, 1936* | Phoenixville | −42° | Jan. 5, 1904 | Smethport |
| Rhode Island . | 104° | Aug. 2, 1975 | Providence | −23° | Jan. 11, 1942 | Kingston |
| South Carolina | 111° | June 28, 1954* | Camden | −20° | Jan. 18, 1977 | Caesars Head |
| South Dakota . | 120° | July 5, 1936 | Gannvalley | −58° | Feb. 17, 1936 | McIntosh |
| Tennessee .... | 113° | Aug. 9, 1930* | Perryville | −32° | Dec. 30, 1917 | Mountain City |
| Texas ........ | 120° | Aug. 12, 1936 | Seymour | −23° | Feb. 8, 1933* | Seminole |
| Utah ......... | 116° | June 28, 1892 | Saint George | −50° | Jan. 5, 1913* | Strawberry Tunnel |
| Vermont...... | 105° | July 4, 1911 | Vernon | −50° | Dec. 30, 1933 | Bloomfield |
| Virginia....... | 110° | July 15, 1954 | Balcony Falls | −29° | Feb. 10, 1899 | Monterey |
| Washington ... | 118° | Aug. 5, 1961* | Ice Harbor Dam | −48° | Dec. 30, 1968 | Mazama & Winthrop |
| West Virginia . | 112° | July 10, 1936* | Martinsburg | −37° | Dec. 30, 1917 | Lewisburg |
| Wisconsin .... | 114° | July 13, 1936 | Wisconsin Dells | −54° | Jan. 24, 1922 | Danbury |
| Wyoming ..... | 114° | July 12, 1900 | Basin | −63° | Feb. 9, 1933 | Moran |

* Also on earlier dates at same or other places in the state.

## WEATHER IN U.S. STATES, CITIES, AND TERRITORIES

Source: *Local Climatological Data*, Environmental Data Service, NOAA

| PLACE | TEMPERATURE RECORDS | | | | NUMBER OF HOT AND COLD DAYS [1] | | | NUMBER OF SUNNY AND CLOUDY DAYS [1] | | | NUMBER OF STORMY DAYS [1] | | |
|---|---|---|---|---|---|---|---|---|---|---|---|---|---|
| | High | Date | Low | Date | Hot [2] | Freezing [3] | Below zero [4] | Clear | Partly cloudy | Overcast | Rain [5] | Snow [6] | Fog [7] |
| **ALABAMA** | | | | | | | | | | | | | |
| Birmingham ....... | 107° | July 1930 | -10° | Feb. 1899 | 62 | 74 | 0 | 99 | 111 | 155 | 96 | 1 | 10 |
| Huntsville ........ | 104° | July 1966 | -11° | Jan. 1966 | 51 | 75 | 0 | 111 | 93 | 161 | 102 | 1 | 21 |
| Mobile .......... | 104° | July 1952 | -1° | Feb. 1899 | 83 | 38 | 0 | 112 | 123 | 130 | 112 | 0 | 56 |
| Montgomery...... | 107° | July 1881 | -5° | Feb. 1899 | 81 | 49 | 0 | 133 | 110 | 122 | 94 | 0 | 10 |
| **ALASKA** | | | | | | | | | | | | | |
| Anchorage ....... | 86° | June 1953 | -38° | Feb. 1947 | 26 [8] | 181 | 8 | 40 | 65 | 260 | 112 | 25 | 24 |
| Barrow........... | 78° | July 1927 | -56° | Feb. 1924 | 0 | 322 | 167 | 54 | 47 | 198 | 90 | 4 | 72 |
| Fairbanks ....... | 99° | July 1919 | -66° | Jan. 1934 | 57 [8] | 212 | 98 | 72 | 96 | 197 | 113 | 22 | 7 |
| Juneau........... | 90° | July 1975 | -22° | Jan. 1972 | 23 [8] | 127 | 0 | 49 | 50 | 266 | 211 | 16 | 10 |
| Kodiak .......... | 86° | June 1953 | -12° | Feb. 1971 | 8 [8] | 95 | 0 | 53 | 62 | 250 | 220 | 17 | 13 |
| Nome............ | 86° | July 1977 | -47° | Jan. 1919 | 6 [8] | 224 | 49 | 80 | 54 | 231 | 140 | 21 | 20 |
| **ARIZONA** | | | | | | | | | | | | | |
| Flagstaff ........ | 97° | July 1973 | -30° | Jan. 1937 | 4 | 199 | 8 | 161 | 98 | 106 | 94 | 38 | 29 |
| Phoenix.......... | 118° | July 1958 | 16° | Jan. 1913 | 169 | 4 | 0 | 195 | 90 | 80 | 60 | 0 | 2 |
| Tucson .......... | 112° | June 1902 | 6° | Jan. 1913 | 150 | 13 | 0 | 186 | 95 | 84 | 75 | 0 | 1 |
| Winslow ......... | 109° | July 1971 | -19° | Dec. 1898 | 97 | 113 | 6 | 175 | 101 | 89 | 58 | 3 | 1 |
| Yuma ........... | 123° | Sept. 1950 | 22° | Jan. 1937 | 167 | 3 | 0 | 222 | 83 | 60 | 27 | 7 | 5 |
| **ARKANSAS** | | | | | | | | | | | | | |
| Fort Smith ...... | 113° | Aug. 1936 | -15° | Feb. 1899 | 90 | 92 | 0 | 131 | 90 | 144 | 97 | 9 | 16 |
| Little Rock ...... | 110° | Aug. 1936 | -13° | Feb. 1899 | 87 | 75 | 0 | 119 | 101 | 145 | 106 | 5 | 15 |
| **CALIFORNIA** | | | | | | | | | | | | | |
| Bakersfield ...... | 118° | July 1908 | 13° | Dec. 1905 | 115 | 6 | 0 | 190 | 70 | 105 | 50 | 0 | 27 |
| Fresno .......... | 115° | July 1905 | 17° | Jan. 1913 | 104 | 13 | 0 | 187 | 64 | 114 | 58 | 0 | 40 |
| Long Beach ...... | 111° | Oct. 1961 | 25° | Jan. 1963 | 27 | 2 | 0 | 167 | 106 | 92 | 59 | 0 | 21 |
| Los Angeles ..... | 110° | Sept. 1963 | 23° | Jan. 1937 | 11 | 0 | 0 | 162 | 94 | 109 | 49 | 0 | 20 |
| Sacramento ..... | 115° | June 1961 | 17° | Dec. 1932 | 68 | 19 | 0 | 194 | 69 | 102 | 60 | 0 | 26 |
| San Diego........ | 111° | Sept. 1963 | 25° | Jan. 1913 | 7 | 0 | 0 | 142 | 102 | 121 | 61 | 0 | 14 |
| San Francisco .... | 106° | June 1961 | 20° | Dec. 1932 | 4 | 3 | 0 | 157 | 92 | 116 | 50 | 0 | 11 |
| Stockton ........ | 114° | July 1972 | 19° | Jan. 1963 | 83 | 0 | 20 | 186 | 65 | 114 | 59 | 0 | 47 |
| **COLORADO** | | | | | | | | | | | | | |
| Alamosa ......... | 93° | July 1971 | -50° | Jan. 1948 | 0 | 237 | 34 | 148 | 137 | 80 | 69 | 8 | 15 |
| Colorado Springs .. | 100° | June 1954 | -32° | Jan. 1883 | 28 | 159 | 8 | 133 | 108 | 124 | 88 | 17 | 44 |
| Denver.......... | 105° | Aug. 1878 | -30° | Feb. 1936 | 52 | 146 | 7 | 126 | 115 | 124 | 74 | 21 | 20 |
| Grand Junction ... | 105° | July 1976 | -23° | Jan. 1963 | 65 | 123 | 8 | 140 | 89 | 136 | 73 | 9 | 19 |
| Pueblo.......... | 105° | July 1973 | -31° | Feb. 1951 | 72 | 151 | 7 | 142 | 110 | 113 | 71 | 8 | 6 |
| **CONNECTICUT** | | | | | | | | | | | | | |
| Bridgeport ....... | 103° | July 1957 | -20° | Feb. 1934 | 4 | 101 | 0 | 124 | 87 | 154 | 112 | 13 | 33 |
| Hartford ......... | 102° | July 1966 | -26° | Jan. 1961 | 12 | 154 | 3 | 95 | 114 | 156 | 114 | 19 | 25 |
| **DELAWARE** | | | | | | | | | | | | | |
| Wilmington....... | 107° | Aug. 1918 | -15° | Feb. 1934 | 11 | 107 | 0 | 114 | 100 | 151 | 124 | 11 | 33 |
| **DIST. OF COLUMBIA** | | | | | | | | | | | | | |
| Washington ...... | 106° | July 1930 | -15° | Feb. 1899 | 39 | 76 | 0 | 114 | 101 | 150 | 113 | 8 | 4 |
| **FLORIDA** | | | | | | | | | | | | | |
| Jacksonville ...... | 105° | July 1942 | 10° | Feb. 1899 | 64 | 28 | 0 | 93 | 125 | 147 | 105 | 0 | 55 |
| Key West ....... | 97° | Aug. 1956 | 41° | Jan. 1886 | 71 | 0 | 0 | 64 | 188 | 113 | 113 | 0 | 2 |
| Miami .......... | 100° | July 1942 | 26° | Dec. 1934 | 13 | 0 | 0 | 54 | 164 | 147 | 152 | 0 | 5 |
| Orlando.......... | 103° | Sept. 1921 | 20° | Jan. 1977 | 130 | 5 | 0 | 78 | 143 | 144 | 117 | 0 | 31 |
| Pensacola ........ | 103° | Aug. 1947 | 7° | Feb. 1899 | 61 | 27 | 0 | 117 | 114 | 134 | 100 | 0 | 44 |
| Tallahassee ...... | 104° | June 1933 | -2° | Feb. 1899 | 93 | 50 | 0 | 97 | 127 | 141 | 112 | 0 | 56 |
| Tampa.......... | 98° | June 1977 | 18° | Dec. 1962 | 81 | 6 | 0 | 75 | 136 | 154 | 100 | 0 | 21 |
| West Palm Beach . | 101° | July 1942 | 27° | Jan. 1977 | 75 | 1 | 0 | 63 | 170 | 132 | 145 | 0 | 3 |
| **GEORGIA** | | | | | | | | | | | | | |
| Athens........... | 108° | July 1930 | -3° | Feb. 1899 | 43 | 64 | 0 | 128 | 107 | 130 | 90 | 0 | 32 |
| Atlanta.......... | 103° | July 1952 | -9° | Feb. 1899 | 45 | 72 | 0 | 118 | 102 | 145 | 102 | 0 | 23 |
| Augusta.......... | 106° | July 1952 | 3° | Feb. 1899 | 84 | 64 | 0 | 118 | 106 | 141 | 90 | 1 | 30 |
| Columbus ........ | 106° | Sept. 1925 | 3° | Feb. 1899 | 93 | 58 | 0 | 126 | 105 | 134 | 93 | 0 | 11 |
| Macon .......... | 106° | June 1954 | 3° | Jan. 1966 | 96 | 56 | 0 | 117 | 110 | 138 | 85 | 0 | 18 |
| Savannah ........ | 105° | July 1879 | 8° | Feb. 1899 | 81 | 41 | 0 | 90 | 109 | 166 | 98 | 0 | 45 |
| **HAWAII** | | | | | | | | | | | | | |
| Hilo ............. | 94° | May 1966 | 51° | May 1910 | 0 | 0 | 0 | 54 | 111 | 200 | 282 | 0 | 0 |
| Honolulu ........ | 92° | Aug. 1977 | 53° | Feb. 1976 | 13 | 0 | 0 | 77 | 177 | 111 | 90 | 0 | 0 |

[1] Average per year. [2] Highest temperature 90°F. or above. [3] Lowest temperature 32°F. or below. [4] Lowest temperature 0°F. or below. [5] Rain of 0.01 inch or more. [6] Snow of 1 inch or more. [7] Visibility of 1/4 mile or less. [8] Days 70°F. and above.

## WEATHER IN U.S. STATES, CITIES, AND TERRITORIES (continued)

| PLACE | TEMPERATURE RECORDS | | | | NUMBER OF HOT AND COLD DAYS [1] | | | NUMBER OF SUNNY AND CLOUDY DAYS [1] | | | NUMBER OF STORMY DAYS [1] | | |
|---|---|---|---|---|---|---|---|---|---|---|---|---|---|
| | High | Date | Low | Date | Hot [2] | Freezing [3] | Below zero [4] | Clear | Partly cloudy | Overcast | Rain [5] | Snow [6] | Fog [7] |
| **IDAHO** | | | | | | | | | | | | | |
| Boise | 111° | July 1960 | –23° | Dec. 1972 | 32 | 99 | 3 | 99 | 99 | 167 | 86 | 3 | 21 |
| Lewiston | 117° | July 1939 | –23° | Dec. 1919 | 33 | 79 | 5 | 70 | 69 | 226 | 120 | 2 | 21 |
| Pocatello | 105° | July 1931 | –31° | Jan. 1949 | 31 | 150 | 8 | 100 | 87 | 178 | 93 | 11 | 11 |
| **ILLINOIS** | | | | | | | | | | | | | |
| Chicago | 105° | July 1934 | –23° | Dec. 1872 | 8 | 141 | 15 | 92 | 106 | 167 | 128 | 23 | 12 |
| Peoria | 113° | July 1936 | –27° | Jan. 1884 | 27 | 134 | 29 | 98 | 96 | 171 | 130 | 10 | 13 |
| Rockford | 112° | July 1936 | –25° | Jan. 1924 | 12 | 152 | 37 | 101 | 87 | 177 | 129 | 15 | 21 |
| Springfield | 112° | July 1954 | –24° | Feb. 1905 | 36 | 117 | 21 | 107 | 84 | 174 | 118 | 10 | 15 |
| **INDIANA** | | | | | | | | | | | | | |
| Evansville | 108° | July 1936 | –23° | Feb. 1951 | 50 | 98 | 9 | 116 | 100 | 149 | 117 | 8 | 19 |
| Fort Wayne | 106° | July 1936 | –24° | Jan. 1918 | 18 | 133 | 32 | 93 | 83 | 189 | 121 | 14 | 37 |
| Indianapolis | 107° | July 1934 | –25° | Jan. 1884 | 21 | 108 | 11 | 98 | 86 | 181 | 134 | 11 | 27 |
| South Bend | 109° | July 1934 | –22° | Jan. 1943 | 8 | 130 | 16 | 74 | 95 | 196 | 136 | 35 | 19 |
| **IOWA** | | | | | | | | | | | | | |
| Burlington | 111° | July 1936 | –27° | Feb. 1905 | 11 | 131 | 31 | 92 | 111 | 162 | 109 | 11 | 19 |
| Des Moines | 110° | July 1936 | –30° | Jan. 1884 | 29 | 134 | 28 | 98 | 88 | 179 | 120 | 14 | 17 |
| Sioux City | 111° | July 1939 | –35° | Jan. 1912 | 30 | 155 | 45 | 104 | 107 | 154 | 91 | 8 | 24 |
| Waterloo | 112° | Aug. 1936 | –34° | Mar. 1962 | 19 | 155 | 55 | 88 | 94 | 183 | 113 | 11 | 15 |
| **KANSAS** | | | | | | | | | | | | | |
| Concordia | 116° | Aug. 1936 | –25° | Feb. 1899 | 59 | 132 | 16 | 132 | 86 | 147 | 94 | 8 | 8 |
| Dodge City | 109° | Aug. 1936 | –26° | Feb. 1899 | 79 | 129 | 9 | 133 | 95 | 137 | 79 | 11 | 23 |
| Topeka | 114° | July 1936 | –25° | Feb. 1899 | 59 | 134 | 13 | 123 | 85 | 157 | 98 | 9 | 11 |
| Wichita | 114° | Aug. 1936 | –22° | Feb. 1899 | 86 | 120 | 5 | 131 | 100 | 134 | 93 | 8 | 17 |
| **KENTUCKY** | | | | | | | | | | | | | |
| Lexington | 108° | July 1936 | –21° | Jan. 1963 | 17 | 99 | 7 | 89 | 102 | 174 | 136 | 14 | 30 |
| Louisville | 107° | July 1901 | –20° | Jan. 1963 | 43 | 90 | 2 | 98 | 100 | 167 | 126 | 11 | 16 |
| **LOUISIANA** | | | | | | | | | | | | | |
| Baton Rouge | 110° | Aug. 1909 | 2° | Feb. 1899 | 96 | 39 | 0 | 107 | 122 | 136 | 104 | 0 | 37 |
| Lake Charles | 104° | Aug. 1951 | 12° | Jan. 1948 | 89 | 25 | 0 | 93 | 126 | 146 | 90 | 1 | 53 |
| New Orleans | 102° | June 1954 | 7° | Feb. 1899 | 89 | 17 | 0 | 105 | 110 | 150 | 118 | 0 | 32 |
| Shreveport | 110° | Aug. 1909 | – 5° | Feb. 1899 | 106 | 72 | 0 | 127 | 102 | 136 | 87 | 4 | 14 |
| **MAINE** | | | | | | | | | | | | | |
| Caribou | 96° | May 1977 | –41° | Feb. 1955 | 4 | 197 | 34 | 63 | 117 | 185 | 147 | 34 | 27 |
| Portland | 103° | Aug. 1975 | –39° | Feb. 1943 | 7 | 167 | 12 | 113 | 106 | 146 | 109 | 16 | 41 |
| **MARYLAND** | | | | | | | | | | | | | |
| Baltimore | 107° | July 1936 | – 7° | Jan. 1963 | 26 | 95 | 0 | 127 | 98 | 140 | 120 | 9 | 22 |
| **MASSACHUSETTS** | | | | | | | | | | | | | |
| Boston | 104° | July 1911 | –18° | Feb. 1934 | 9 | 109 | 0 | 124 | 103 | 138 | 116 | 16 | 20 |
| Worcester | 102° | July 1911 | –24° | Feb. 1943 | 1 | 151 | 2 | 94 | 109 | 162 | 125 | 18 | 84 |
| **MICHIGAN** | | | | | | | | | | | | | |
| Detroit | 105° | July 1934 | –24° | Dec. 1872 | 18 | 151 | 5 | 88 | 95 | 182 | 128 | 14 | 19 |
| Flint | 108° | July 1936 | –28° | Feb. 1916 | 4 | 153 | 20 | 72 | 101 | 192 | 127 | 16 | 23 |
| Grand Rapids | 108° | July 1936 | –24° | Feb. 1899 | 8 | 157 | 19 | 74 | 91 | 200 | 145 | 25 | 41 |
| Lansing | 102° | Aug. 1918 | –33° | Feb. 1875 | 11 | 160 | 27 | 72 | 94 | 199 | 144 | 18 | 25 |
| Marquette | 108° | July 1901 | –27° | Feb. 1888 | 2 | 165 | 2 | 61 | 101 | 203 | 153 | 31 | 17 |
| Sault Ste. Marie | 98° | Aug. 1947 | –37° | Feb. 1934 | 0 | 188 | 38 | 85 | 89 | 191 | 165 | 45 | 30 |
| **MINNESOTA** | | | | | | | | | | | | | |
| Duluth | 106° | July 1936 | –41° | Jan. 1885 | 2 | 182 | 60 | 81 | 112 | 172 | 115 | 20 | 50 |
| International Falls | 103° | July 1923 | –49° | Jan. 1896 | 1 | 192 | 91 | 82 | 109 | 174 | 130 | 17 | 20 |
| Minn.–St. Paul | 108° | July 1936 | –34° | Jan. 1970 | 20 | 152 | 50 | 100 | 109 | 156 | 116 | 15 | 8 |
| Rochester | 108° | July 1936 | –42° | Jan. 1887 | 7 | 169 | 63 | 95 | 101 | 169 | 126 | 17 | 24 |
| **MISSISSIPPI** | | | | | | | | | | | | | |
| Jackson | 107° | July 1930 | – 5° | Jan. 1940 | 86 | 72 | 0 | 135 | 98 | 132 | 104 | 1 | 14 |
| Meridian | 105° | Aug. 1943 | – 7° | Jan. 1940 | 86 | 78 | 0 | 104 | 122 | 139 | 103 | 1 | 28 |
| **MISSOURI** | | | | | | | | | | | | | |
| Columbia | 113° | July 1954 | –26° | Feb. 1899 | 58 | 112 | 8 | 111 | 90 | 164 | 118 | 11 | 21 |
| Kansas City | 113° | Aug. 1936 | –22° | Feb. 1899 | 53 | 115 | 18 | 123 | 87 | 155 | 103 | 10 | 24 |
| St. Louis | 115° | July 1954 | –23° | Jan. 1864 | 53 | 102 | 71 | 120 | 87 | 158 | 124 | 11 | 21 |
| Springfield | 113° | July 1954 | –29° | Feb. 1899 | 63 | 112 | 13 | 141 | 79 | 145 | 117 | 8 | 21 |

[1] Average per year. [2] Highest temperature 90°F. or above. [3] Lowest temperature 32°F. or below. [4] Lowest temperature 0°F. or below. [5] Rain of 0.01 inch or more. [6] Snow of 1 inch or more. [7] Visibility of 1/4 mile or less.

## WEATHER IN U.S. STATES, CITIES, AND TERRITORIES *(continued)*

| PLACE | TEMPERATURE RECORDS | | | | NUMBER OF HOT AND COLD DAYS [1] | | | NUMBER OF SUNNY AND CLOUDY DAYS [1] | | | NUMBER OF STORMY DAYS [1] | | |
|---|---|---|---|---|---|---|---|---|---|---|---|---|---|
| | High | Date | Low | Date | Hot [2] | Freezing [3] | Below zero [4] | Clear | Partly cloudy | Overcast | Rain [5] | Snow [6] | Fog [7] |
| **MONTANA** | | | | | | | | | | | | | |
| Billings ......... | 112° | July 1901 | -49° | Feb.1899 | 25 | 152 | 37 | 83 | 111 | 171 | 120 | 23 | 17 |
| Great Falls ...... | 107° | July 1933 | -49° | Feb.1936 | 18 | 166 | 49 | 61 | 101 | 203 | 132 | 25 | 14 |
| Helena .......... | 105° | Aug. 1969 | -42° | Jan.1957 | 24 | 170 | 32 | 69 | 111 | 185 | 112 | 23 | 5 |
| Missoula ........ | 105° | July 1973 | -33° | Jan.1957 | 16 | 188 | 11 | 64 | 82 | 219 | 127 | 24 | 21 |
| **NEBRASKA** | | | | | | | | | | | | | |
| Grand Island...... | 117° | July 1936 | -34° | Feb.1899 | 51 | 147 | 33 | 123 | 117 | 125 | 104 | 17 | 16 |
| Lincoln.......... | 115° | July 1936 | -33° | Jan.1974 | 44 | 147 | 35 | 125 | 84 | 156 | 95 | 13 | 9 |
| Omaha........... | 114° | July 1936 | -32° | Jan.1884 | 47 | 135 | 32 | 113 | 107 | 145 | 99 | 10 | 15 |
| **NEVADA** | | | | | | | | | | | | | |
| Elko ............ | 107° | July 1890 | -43° | Jan.1937 | 36 | 162 | 6 | 119 | 112 | 134 | 74 | 7 | 5 |
| Las Vegas........ | 117° | July 1942 | 8° | Jan.1963 | 145 | 22 | 0 | 225 | 64 | 76 | 45 | 0 | 1 |
| Reno ............ | 106° | July 1931 | -19° | Jan.1890 | 38 | 176 | 4 | 149 | 104 | 112 | 56 | 6 | 13 |
| **NEW HAMPSHIRE** | | | | | | | | | | | | | |
| Concord ......... | 102° | July 1966 | -37° | Feb.1943 | 27 | 199 | 32 | 95 | 116 | 154 | 113 | 22 | 53 |
| **NEW JERSEY** | | | | | | | | | | | | | |
| Atlantic City...... | 106° | June 1969 | -10° | Jan.1977 | 7 | 115 | 0 | 113 | 101 | 151 | 110 | 8 | 53 |
| Newark .......... | 105° | July 1966 | -14° | Feb.1934 | 16 | 93 | 0 | 99 | 106 | 160 | 115 | 12 | 17 |
| Trenton ......... | 106° | July 1936 | -14° | Feb.1934 | 9 | 93 | 0 | 97 | 110 | 158 | 121 | 13 | — |
| **NEW MEXICO** | | | | | | | | | | | | | |
| Albuquerque ..... | 105° | June 1974 | -17° | Jan.1971 | 71 | 99 | 0 | 178 | 92 | 95 | 74 | 7 | 10 |
| Roswell ......... | 110° | July 1958 | -29° | Feb.1905 | 92 | 85 | 2 | 162 | 105 | 98 | 70 | 5 | 3 |
| **NEW YORK** | | | | | | | | | | | | | |
| Albany .......... | 104° | July 1911 | -28° | Jan.1971 | 6 | 165 | 8 | 74 | 126 | 165 | 126 | 20 | 12 |
| Binghamton ...... | 103° | July 1936 | -28° | Jan.1893 | 1 | 154 | 3 | 51 | 115 | 199 | 159 | 29 | 50 |
| Buffalo.......... | 99° | Aug. 1948 | -21° | Feb.1934 | 2 | 145 | 3 | 50 | 84 | 231 | 162 | 27 | 17 |
| New York City .... | 107° | July 1966 | -15° | Feb.1934 | 4 | 88 | 0 | 119 | 107 | 139 | 115 | 12 | 8 |
| Rochester ....... | 102° | July 1936 | -22° | Feb.1934 | 20 | 140 | 12 | 50 | 91 | 224 | 158 | 34 | 6 |
| Syracuse ........ | 102° | July 1936 | -26° | Jan.1966 | 11 | 150 | 8 | 52 | 91 | 222 | 168 | 39 | 5 |
| **NORTH CAROLINA** | | | | | | | | | | | | | |
| Asheville ........ | 99° | July 1936 | -7° | Jan.1966 | 10 | 97 | 0 | 112 | 126 | 127 | 111 | 6 | 85 |
| Cape Hatteras .... | 97° | June 1952 | 8° | Dec.1880 | 13 | 40 | 0 | 114 | 107 | 144 | 101 | 1 | 16 |
| Charlotte ........ | 104° | Sept. 1954 | -5° | Feb.1899 | 43 | 63 | 0 | 105 | 124 | 136 | 106 | 1 | 32 |
| Greensboro ...... | 102° | July 1977 | -7° | Jan.1940 | 23 | 90 | 0 | 117 | 99 | 149 | 117 | 4 | 52 |
| Raleigh .......... | 105° | July 1952 | -2° | Feb.1899 | 55 | 83 | 0 | 122 | 97 | 146 | 111 | 4 | 38 |
| **NORTH DAKOTA** | | | | | | | | | | | | | |
| Bismarck......... | 114° | July 1936 | -45° | Feb.1936 | 21 | 178 | 70 | 98 | 108 | 159 | 116 | 17 | 11 |
| Fargo............ | 114° | July 1936 | -48° | Jan.1887 | 15 | 175 | 77 | 91 | 106 | 168 | 83 | 13 | 10 |
| **OHIO** | | | | | | | | | | | | | |
| Akron............ | 104° | Aug. 1918 | -21° | Jan.1963 | 5 | 137 | 7 | 77 | 85 | 203 | 151 | 18 | 25 |
| Cincinnati ....... | 109° | July 1934 | -25° | Jan.1977 | 14 | 115 | 13 | 100 | 77 | 188 | 130 | 12 | 38 |
| Cleveland ........ | 103° | July 1941 | -19° | Jan.1963 | 18 | 134 | 7 | 65 | 91 | 209 | 145 | 16 | 14 |
| Columbus ........ | 106° | July 1936 | -20° | Feb.1899 | 14 | 122 | 9 | 90 | 89 | 186 | 132 | 13 | 20 |
| Dayton .......... | 108° | July 1901 | -28° | Feb.1899 | 14 | 117 | 10 | 89 | 84 | 192 | 133 | 15 | 32 |
| Toledo .......... | 105° | July 1936 | -17° | Jan.1972 | 14 | 155 | 22 | 91 | 96 | 178 | 135 | 11 | 22 |
| Youngstown ...... | 100° | July 1954 | -18° | Jan.1963 | 4 | 141 | 6 | 67 | 90 | 208 | 156 | 17 | 28 |
| **OKLAHOMA** | | | | | | | | | | | | | |
| Oklahoma City.... | 113° | Aug. 1936 | -17° | Feb.1899 | 94 | 98 | 1 | 148 | 87 | 130 | 93 | 11 | 17 |
| Tulsa............ | 115° | Aug. 1936 | -16° | Jan.1930 | 96 | 94 | 1 | 144 | 81 | 140 | 87 | 7 | 9 |
| **OREGON** | | | | | | | | | | | | | |
| Astoria.......... | 101° | July 1942 | 6° | Dec.1972 | 1 | 50 | 0 | 50 | 83 | 232 | 197 | 1 | 47 |
| Eugene .......... | 106° | Aug. 1972 | -12° | Dec.1972 | 16 | 72 | 0 | 57 | 75 | 233 | 140 | 1 | 64 |
| Medford ......... | 115° | July 1946 | -10° | Dec.1919 | 37 | 76 | 0 | 108 | 72 | 185 | 102 | 0 | 50 |
| Portland ......... | 107° | July 1965 | -3° | Feb.1950 | 12 | 60 | 0 | 61 | 56 | 248 | 155 | 2 | 43 |
| Salem ........... | 108° | July 1941 | -12° | Dec.1972 | 20 | 73 | 0 | 61 | 78 | 226 | 147 | 2 | 41 |
| **PENNSYLVANIA** | | | | | | | | | | | | | |
| Allentown ........ | 105° | July 1966 | -12° | Jan.1961 | 9 | 117 | 0 | 100 | 116 | 149 | 122 | 12 | 18 |
| Erie ............. | 99° | Sept. 1953 | -16° | Feb.1875 | 3 | 150 | 8 | 59 | 106 | 200 | 154 | 29 | 16 |
| Harrisburg ....... | 107° | July 1966 | -14° | Jan.1912 | 15 | 103 | 1 | 95 | 117 | 153 | 118 | 15 | 11 |
| Philadelphia ...... | 106° | Aug. 1918 | -11° | Feb.1934 | 25 | 93 | 0 | 104 | 98 | 163 | 126 | 13 | 25 |
| Pittsburgh........ | 103° | July 1936 | -20° | Feb.1899 | 6 | 123 | 0 | 71 | 102 | 192 | 152 | 14 | 21 |

[1] Average per year. [2] Highest temperature 90°F. or above. [3] Lowest temperature 32°F. or below. [4] Lowest temperature 0°F. or below. [5] Rain of 0.01 inch or more. [6] Snow of 1 inch or more. [7] Visibility of 1/4 mile or less.

## WEATHER IN U.S. STATES, CITIES, AND TERRITORIES (continued)

| PLACE | TEMPERATURE RECORDS | | | | NUMBER OF HOT AND COLD DAYS [1] | | | NUMBER OF SUNNY AND CLOUDY DAYS [1] | | | NUMBER OF STORMY DAYS [1] | | |
|---|---|---|---|---|---|---|---|---|---|---|---|---|---|
| | High | Date | Low | Date | Hot [2] | Freezing [3] | Below zero [4] | Clear | Partly cloudy | Overcast | Rain [5] | Snow [6] | Fog [7] |
| **RHODE ISLAND** | | | | | | | | | | | | | |
| Providence ....... | 104° | Aug. 1975 | –17° | Feb. 1934 | 5 | 130 | 2 | 123 | 101 | 141 | 111 | 12 | 19 |
| **SOUTH CAROLINA** | | | | | | | | | | | | | |
| Charleston ....... | 104° | June 1944 | 7° | Feb. 1899 | 52 | 51 | 0 | 100 | 107 | 158 | 96 | 0 | 26 |
| Columbia ........ | 107° | June 1954 | – 2° | Feb. 1899 | 69 | 68 | 0 | 111 | 107 | 147 | 96 | 0 | 26 |
| Greenville ........ | 101° | July 1977 | – 6° | Jan. 1966 | 35 | 70 | 0 | 136 | 110 | 119 | 98 | 1 | 30 |
| **SOUTH DAKOTA** | | | | | | | | | | | | | |
| Aberdeen ........ | 115° | July 1936 | –46° | Jan. 1912 | 20 | 180 | 68 | 96 | 116 | 153 | 95 | 13 | 18 |
| Rapid City ....... | 110° | July 1973 | –33° | Feb. 1936 | 34 | 163 | 33 | 106 | 113 | 146 | 109 | 14 | 17 |
| Sioux Falls ....... | 110° | July 1936 | –42° | Feb. 1899 | 17 | 169 | 54 | 109 | 102 | 154 | 100 | 12 | 15 |
| **TENNESSEE** | | | | | | | | | | | | | |
| Bristol ........... | 102° | July 1952 | –15° | Jan. 1966 | 10 | 94 | 3 | 97 | 127 | 141 | 127 | 10 | 51 |
| Chattanooga...... | 106° | July 1952 | –10° | Jan. 1966 | 47 | 72 | 0 | 116 | 89 | 160 | 107 | 1 | 28 |
| Knoxville ......... | 104° | July 1930 | –16° | Jan. 1884 | 27 | 74 | 0 | 107 | 115 | 143 | 117 | 10 | 33 |
| Memphis ......... | 106° | July 1952 | –13° | Dec. 1963 | 77 | 69 | 0 | 135 | 92 | 138 | 112 | 3 | 10 |
| Nashville ......... | 107° | July 1952 | –15° | Jan. 1963 | 57 | 88 | 0 | 114 | 100 | 151 | 124 | 10 | 25 |
| **TEXAS** | | | | | | | | | | | | | |
| Abilene .......... | 111° | Aug. 1943 | – 9° | Jan. 1947 | 121 | 71 | 0 | 152 | 88 | 125 | 67 | 3 | 7 |
| Amarillo ......... | 108° | June 1953 | –16° | Feb. 1899 | 71 | 116 | 1 | 152 | 94 | 119 | 77 | 10 | 40 |
| Austin ........... | 109° | Aug. 1954 | – 2° | Jan. 1949 | 109 | 39 | 0 | 115 | 102 | 148 | 82 | 0 | 17 |
| Brownsville ...... | 104° | Sept. 1947 | 12° | Feb. 1899 | 142 | 3 | 0 | 87 | 115 | 163 | 74 | 0 | 29 |
| Dallas–Fort Worth. | 112° | Aug. 1936 | – 8° | Feb. 1899 | 115 | 64 | 0 | 146 | 81 | 138 | 69 | 5 | 15 |
| El Paso .......... | 111° | June 1978 | – 8° | Jan. 1962 | 103 | 44 | 0 | 193 | 93 | 79 | 55 | 0 | 0 |
| Galveston ........ | 101° | July 1932 | 8° | Feb. 1899 | 17 | 6 | 0 | — | — | — | 89 | 0 | — |
| Houston ......... | 108° | Aug. 1909 | 5° | Jan. 1940 | 109 | 42 | 0 | 84 | 123 | 158 | 108 | 0 | 36 |
| San Antonio ...... | 107° | Aug. 1909 | 0° | Jan. 1949 | 89 | 40 | 0 | 84 | 119 | 162 | 76 | 0 | 14 |
| **UTAH** | | | | | | | | | | | | | |
| Salt Lake City ..... | 107° | July 1960 | –30° | Feb. 1933 | 63 | 90 | 0 | 119 | 83 | 163 | 101 | 25 | 2 |
| **VERMONT** | | | | | | | | | | | | | |
| Burlington........ | 101° | Aug. 1944 | –30° | Jan. 1957 | 8 | 161 | 35 | 54 | 94 | 217 | 151 | 19 | 9 |
| **VIRGINIA** | | | | | | | | | | | | | |
| Norfolk .......... | 105° | Aug. 1918 | 2° | Feb. 1895 | 31 | 71 | 0 | 113 | 104 | 148 | 110 | 3 | 14 |
| Richmond ........ | 107° | Aug. 1918 | –12° | Jan. 1940 | 51 | 87 | 0 | 104 | 105 | 156 | 114 | 3 | 34 |
| Roanoke ......... | 105° | July 1936 | –12° | Dec. 1917 | 31 | 95 | 0 | 105 | 103 | 157 | 115 | 12 | 18 |
| **WASHINGTON** | | | | | | | | | | | | | |
| Olympia.......... | 103° | July 1941 | – 7° | Jan. 1972 | 10 | 85 | 1 | 47 | 73 | 245 | 174 | 3 | 97 |
| Seattle–Tacoma ... | 100° | June 1955 | 0° | Jan. 1957 | 4 | 28 | 0 | 63 | 79 | 223 | 146 | 2 | 34 |
| Spokane ......... | 108° | Aug. 1961 | –30° | Jan. 1888 | 18 | 145 | 9 | 66 | 77 | 222 | 112 | 19 | 52 |
| Walla Walla ...... | 113° | Aug. 1961 | –29° | Jan. 1875 | 33 | 70 | 2 | 87 | 90 | 188 | 115 | 8 | — |
| Yakima .......... | 111° | July 1928 | –25° | Feb. 1950 | 27 | 133 | 5 | 97 | 93 | 175 | 79 | 3 | 13 |
| **WEST VIRGINIA** | | | | | | | | | | | | | |
| Charleston ....... | 108° | July 1931 | –17° | Dec. 1917 | 11 | 100 | 4 | 71 | 116 | 178 | 164 | 22 | 119 |
| Huntington ...... | 108° | July 1930 | –15° | Jan. 1963 | 22 | 97 | 2 | 60 | 98 | 207 | 141 | 18 | 81 |
| Parkersburg ...... | 106° | Aug. 1918 | –27° | Feb. 1899 | 6 | 106 | 1 | — | — | — | 130 | 15 | — |
| **WISCONSIN** | | | | | | | | | | | | | |
| Green Bay ....... | 104° | July 1936 | –36° | Jan. 1888 | 2 | 171 | 39 | 84 | 111 | 170 | 115 | 16 | 14 |
| Madison ......... | 107° | July 1936 | –37° | Jan. 1951 | 15 | 174 | 39 | 84 | 114 | 167 | 116 | 14 | 16 |
| Milwaukee........ | 105° | July 1934 | –25° | Jan. 1875 | 3 | 148 | 11 | 95 | 102 | 168 | 141 | 20 | 29 |
| **WYOMING** | | | | | | | | | | | | | |
| Casper........... | 104° | July 1954 | –40° | Jan. 1972 | 26 | 185 | 36 | 94 | 105 | 166 | 110 | 31 | 13 |
| Cheyenne ........ | 100° | June 1954 | –38° | Jan. 1875 | 9 | 175 | 17 | 110 | 120 | 135 | 97 | 21 | 31 |
| Sheridan ......... | 106° | July 1954 | –41° | Dec. 1919 | 17 | 178 | 51 | 86 | 106 | 173 | 115 | 28 | 6 |
| **AMERICAN SAMOA** | | | | | | | | | | | | | |
| Pago Pago ....... | 92° | Feb. 1977 | 62° | July 1964 | 3 | 0 | 0 | 14 | 127 | 224 | 266 | 0 | 0 |
| **GUAM** | | | | | | | | | | | | | |
| Taguac .......... | 95° | Sept. 1957 | 54° | Mar. 1965 | 3 | 0 | 0 | 9 | 120 | 236 | 272 | 0 | — |
| **PACIFIC ISLANDS** | | | | | | | | | | | | | |
| Johnston Island... | 89° | Nov. 1969 | 62° | Dec. 1964 | 0 | 0 | 0 | 104 | 138 | 123 | 169 | 0 | 0 |
| Kwajalein Island .. | 97° | Oct. 1958 | 69° | Dec. 1963 | 4 | 0 | 0 | 26 | 100 | 239 | 244 | 0 | 0 |
| Wake Island ...... | 93° | Aug. 1978 | 64° | Dec. 1954 | 65 | 0 | 0 | 129 | 128 | 108 | 200 | 0 | 0 |
| **PUERTO RICO** | | | | | | | | | | | | | |
| San Juan ......... | 96° | June 1975 | 60° | Mar. 1957 | 90 | 0 | 0 | 69 | 212 | 84 | 191 | 0 | 0 |

[1] Average per year. [2] Highest temperature 90°F. or above. [3] Lowest temperature 32°F. or below. [4] Lowest temperature 0°F. or below. [5] Rain of 0.01 inch or more. [6] Snow of 1 inch or more. [7] Visibility of 1/4 mile or less.

# WEATHER IN FOREIGN COUNTRIES AND CITIES

Source: Environmental Data Service, *Climates of the World*

| COUNTRY AND CITY | TEMPERATURES (in degrees Fahrenheit) Extremes | | Daily Average Range | | | | RAINFALL (in inches) | | | | |
|---|---|---|---|---|---|---|---|---|---|---|---|
| | Low | High | Jan. | April | July | Oct. | Annual | Jan. | Apr. | July | Oct. |
| Afghanistan: Kabul | - 6 | 104 | 18–36 | 43–66 | 61–92 | 42–73 | 12.6 | 3.1 | 0.3 | 0.1 | T |
| Algeria: Algiers | 32 | 107 | 49–59 | 55–68 | 70–83 | 63–74 | 30.0 | 4.4 | 1.6 | T | 3.1 |
| Angola: Luanda | 58 | 98 | 74–83 | 75–85 | 65–74 | 71–79 | 12.7 | 1.0 | 4.6 | T | 0.2 |
| Argentina: Buenos Aires | 22 | 104 | 63–85 | 53–72 | 42–57 | 50–69 | 37.4 | 3.1 | 3.5 | 2.2 | 3.4 |
| Australia: Canberra | 14 | 109 | 55–82 | 44–67 | 33–52 | 43–68 | 23.0 | 1.9 | 1.6 | 1.8 | 2.2 |
| Austria: Vienna | -14 | 98 | 26–34 | 41–57 | 59–75 | 44–55 | 25.6 | 1.5 | 2.0 | 3.0 | 2.0 |
| Bahamas: Nassau | 41 | 94 | 65–77 | 69–81 | 75–88 | 73–85 | 46.4 | 1.4 | 2.5 | 5.8 | 6.5 |
| Bangladesh: Dacca | 43 | 108 | 56–77 | 74–92 | 79–88 | 75–88 | 73.9 | 0.3 | 5.4 | 13.0 | 5.3 |
| Barbados: Bridgetown | 61 | 95 | 70–83 | 72–86 | 74–86 | 73–86 | 50.3 | 2.6 | 1.4 | 5.8 | 7.0 |
| Bermuda: Hamilton | 40 | 99 | 58–68 | 59–71 | 73–85 | 69–79 | 57.6 | 4.4 | 4.1 | 4.5 | 5.8 |
| Bolivia: La Paz | 26 | 80 | 43–63 | 40–65 | 33–62 | 40–66 | 22.6 | 4.5 | 1.3 | 0.4 | 1.6 |
| Brazil: Brasília | 46 | 93 | 65–80 | 62–82 | 51–78 | 64–82 | 54.0 | 9.0 | 3.4 | 0.0 | 4.9 |
| Rio de Janeiro | 46 | 102 | 73–84 | 69–80 | 63–75 | 66–77 | 42.6 | 4.9 | 4.2 | 1.6 | 3.1 |
| Britain: London | 9 | 99 | 35–44 | 40–56 | 55–73 | 44–58 | 22.9 | 2.0 | 1.8 | 2.0 | 2.3 |
| Bulgaria: Sofia | -17 | 99 | 22–34 | 41–62 | 57–82 | 42–63 | 25.0 | 1.3 | 2.3 | 2.4 | 2.1 |
| Burma: Mandalay | 44 | 111 | 55–82 | 77–101 | 78–93 | 73–89 | 32.6 | 0.1 | 1.2 | 2.7 | 4.3 |
| Canada: Edmonton, Alta. | -57 | 99 | -3–16 | 28–52 | 50–74 | 30–51 | 18.0 | 0.9 | 1.0 | 3.3 | 0.8 |
| Montreal, Que. | -35 | 97 | 6–21 | 33–50 | 61–78 | 40–54 | 40.8 | 3.8 | 2.6 | 3.7 | 3.4 |
| Ottawa, Ont. | -38 | 102 | 3–21 | 31–51 | 58–81 | 37–54 | 34.3 | 2.9 | 2.7 | 3.4 | 2.9 |
| St. John, N.B. | -24 | 93 | 11–28 | 32–43 | 54–69 | 41–54 | 42.6 | 4.1 | 3.2 | 3.1 | 4.1 |
| Vancouver, B.C. | 2 | 92 | 32–41 | 40–58 | 54–74 | 44–57 | 57.4 | 8.6 | 3.3 | 1.2 | 5.8 |
| Winnipeg, Man. | -54 | 108 | -13–7 | 27–48 | 55–79 | 31–51 | 21.2 | 0.9 | 1.4 | 3.1 | 1.5 |
| Canary Islands: Las Palmas | 46 | 99 | 58–70 | 61–71 | 67–77 | 67–79 | 8.6 | 1.4 | 0.5 | T | 1.1 |
| Central Africa: Bangui | 57 | 101 | 69–90 | 71–91 | 69–85 | 69–87 | 60.8 | 1.0 | 5.3 | 8.9 | 7.9 |
| Chad: Ndjamena | 47 | 114 | 57–93 | 74–107 | 72–92 | 70–97 | 29.3 | 0.0 | 0.1 | 6.7 | 1.4 |
| Chile: Santiago | 24 | 99 | 53–85 | 45–74 | 37–59 | 45–72 | 14.2 | 0.1 | 0.5 | 3.0 | 0.6 |
| China: Canton | 31 | 101 | 49–65 | 65–77 | 77–91 | 67–85 | 63.6 | 0.9 | 6.8 | 8.1 | 3.4 |
| Shanghai | - 3 | 109 | 16–33 | 45–68 | 73–90 | 48–68 | 21.0 | 0.2 | 5.0 | 7.6 | 0.6 |
| Tientsin | -30 | 112 | -7–13 | 36–60 | 58–82 | 31–50 | 11.5 | 0.6 | 1.5 | 0.7 | 1.7 |
| Colombia: Bogotá | 30 | 75 | 48–67 | 51–67 | 50–64 | 50–66 | 41.8 | 2.3 | 5.8 | 2.0 | 6.3 |
| Congo: Brazzaville | 54 | 98 | 69–88 | 71–91 | 63–82 | 70–89 | 58.0 | 6.3 | 7.0 | T | 5.4 |
| Costa Rica: San José | 49 | 92 | 58–75 | 62–79 | 62–77 | 60–77 | 70.8 | 0.6 | 1.8 | 8.3 | 11.8 |
| Cuba: Havana | 43 | 104 | 65–79 | 69–84 | 75–89 | 73–85 | 48.2 | 2.8 | 2.3 | 4.9 | 6.8 |
| Cyprus: Nicosia | 23 | 116 | 42–58 | 50–74 | 69–97 | 58–81 | 14.6 | 2.9 | 0.8 | T | 0.9 |
| Czechoslovakia: Prague | -16 | 98 | 25–34 | 40–55 | 58–74 | 44–54 | 19.3 | 0.9 | 1.5 | 2.6 | 1.2 |
| Denmark: Copenhagen | - 3 | 91 | 29–36 | 37–50 | 55–72 | 42–53 | 23.3 | 1.6 | 1.7 | 2.2 | 3.2 |
| Dominican R.: Santo Domingo | 59 | 98 | 66–84 | 69–85 | 72–88 | 72–87 | 55.8 | 2.4 | 3.9 | 6.4 | 6.0 |
| Ecuador: Quito | 25 | 86 | 46–67 | 47–69 | 44–71 | 46–71 | 43.9 | 3.9 | 6.9 | 0.8 | 4.4 |
| Egypt: Cairo | 34 | 117 | 47–65 | 57–83 | 70–96 | 65–86 | 1.1 | 0.2 | 0.1 | 0.0 | T |
| El Salvador: San Salvador | 45 | 105 | 60–90 | 65–93 | 65–89 | 65–87 | 70.0 | 0.3 | 1.7 | 11.5 | 9.5 |
| Ethiopia: Addis Ababa | 32 | 94 | 43–75 | 50–77 | 50–69 | 45–75 | 48.7 | 0.5 | 3.4 | 11.8 | 0.6 |
| Finland: Helsinki | -23 | 89 | 17–27 | 31–43 | 57–71 | 37–45 | 27.6 | 2.2 | 1.7 | 2.3 | 2.9 |
| France: Marseille | 9 | 101 | 38–53 | 41–59 | 58–78 | 57–76 | 23.2 | 1.9 | 2.0 | 0.6 | 3.7 |
| Paris | 1 | 105 | 32–42 | 41–60 | 55–76 | 44–59 | 22.3 | 1.5 | 1.7 | 2.1 | 2.2 |
| Germany, East: Berlin | -15 | 96 | 26–35 | 38–55 | 55–74 | 41–55 | 23.1 | 1.9 | 1.7 | 3.1 | 1.7 |
| Germany, West: Hamburg | - 4 | 92 | 28–35 | 39–51 | 56–69 | 44–53 | 28.9 | 2.1 | 1.8 | 3.4 | 2.6 |
| Munich | -14 | 92 | 23–33 | 37–54 | 54–72 | 40–53 | 34.1 | 1.7 | 2.7 | 4.7 | 2.2 |
| Ghana: Accra | 59 | 100 | 73–87 | 76–88 | 73–81 | 74–85 | 28.5 | 1.3 | 3.2 | 1.8 | 2.5 |
| Greece: Athens | 20 | 109 | 42–54 | 52–67 | 72–90 | 60–74 | 15.8 | 2.2 | 0.8 | 0.2 | 1.7 |
| Guadeloupe: Basse-Terre | 54 | 92 | 64–77 | 65–79 | 68–81 | 68–81 | 140.4 | 9.2 | 7.3 | 17.6 | 12.4 |
| Guam: Agana | 54 | 95 | 72–84 | 73–86 | 72–87 | 73–86 | 88.5 | 4.6 | 3.0 | 9.0 | 13.1 |
| Guatemala: Guatemala City | 41 | 90 | 53–73 | 58–82 | 60–78 | 60–76 | 51.8 | 0.3 | 1.2 | 8.0 | 6.8 |
| Guinea: Conakry | 63 | 96 | 72–88 | 73–90 | 72–83 | 73–87 | 169.0 | 0.1 | 0.9 | 51.1 | 14.6 |
| Haiti: Port-au-Prince | 58 | 101 | 68–87 | 71–89 | 74–94 | 72–90 | 53.3 | 1.3 | 6.3 | 2.9 | 6.7 |
| Honduras: Tegucigalpa | 58 | 96 | 67–82 | 72–87 | 73–88 | 71–86 | 96.1 | 8.9 | 3.3 | 6.4 | 13.5 |
| Hong Kong: Victoria | 32 | 99 | 56–64 | 67–75 | 78–87 | 73–81 | 85.1 | 1.3 | 5.4 | 15.0 | 4.5 |
| Hungary: Budapest | -10 | 103 | 26–35 | 44–62 | 61–82 | 45–61 | 24.2 | 1.5 | 2.0 | 2.0 | 2.1 |
| Iceland: Reykjavík | 4 | 74 | 28–36 | 33–43 | 48–58 | 36–44 | 33.9 | 4.0 | 2.1 | 2.0 | 3.4 |
| India: Calcutta | 44 | 111 | 55–80 | 76–97 | 79–90 | 74–89 | 63.0 | 0.4 | 1.7 | 12.8 | 4.5 |
| New Delhi | 31 | 115 | 43–71 | 68–97 | 80–95 | 64–93 | 25.2 | 0.9 | 0.3 | 7.1 | 0.4 |
| Indonesia: Jakarta | 66 | 98 | 74–84 | 75–87 | 73–87 | 74–87 | 70.8 | 11.8 | 5.8 | 2.5 | 4.4 |
| Iran: Tehran | - 5 | 109 | 27–45 | 49–71 | 72–99 | 53–76 | 9.7 | 1.8 | 1.4 | 0.1 | 0.3 |
| Iraq: Baghdad | 18 | 121 | 39–60 | 57–85 | 76–110 | 61–92 | 5.5 | 0.9 | 0.5 | T | 0.1 |
| Ireland: Dublin | 8 | 86 | 35–47 | 38–54 | 51–67 | 43–57 | 29.7 | 2.7 | 1.9 | 2.8 | 2.7 |
| Ireland, Northern: Belfast | 14 | 82 | 34–42 | 38–53 | 52–65 | 44–55 | 38.2 | 4.2 | 2.4 | 3.5 | 3.8 |
| Israel: Jerusalem | 26 | 107 | 41–55 | 50–73 | 63–87 | 59–81 | 19.7 | 5.1 | 0.9 | 0.0 | 0.3 |
| Italy: Rome | 20 | 104 | 39–54 | 46–68 | 64–88 | 53–73 | 29.5 | 3.3 | 2.0 | 0.4 | 4.3 |

T=trace, less than 0.05 inch.  ¹Average daily minimum and maximum temperatures.

| COUNTRY AND CITY | TEMPERATURES (in degrees Fahrenheit) | | | | | | RAINFALL (in inches) | | | | |
|---|---|---|---|---|---|---|---|---|---|---|---|
| | Extremes | | Daily Average Range | | | | | | | | |
| | Low | High | Jan. | April | July | Oct. | Annual | Jan. | Apr. | July | Oct. |
| Jamaica: Kingston ............ | 56 | 97 | 67–86 | 70–87 | 73–90 | 73–88 | 31.5 | 0.9 | 1.2 | 1.5 | 7.1 |
| Japan: Tokyo ................. | 17 | 101 | 29–47 | 46–63 | 70–83 | 55–69 | 61.6 | 1.9 | 5.3 | 5.6 | 8.2 |
| Jordan: Amman............... | 21 | 109 | 39–54 | 49–73 | 65–89 | 57–81 | 10.9 | 2.7 | 0.6 | 0.0 | 0.2 |
| Kenya: Nairobi ............... | 41 | 87 | 54–77 | 58–75 | 51–69 | 55–76 | 41.8 | 1.5 | 8.3 | 0.6 | 2.1 |
| Korea, South: Seoul .......... | −12 | 99 | 15–32 | 41–62 | 70–84 | 45–67 | 49.2 | 1.2 | 3.0 | 14.8 | 1.6 |
| Lebanon: Beirut.............. | 30 | 107 | 51–62 | 58–72 | 73–87 | 69–81 | 35.1 | 7.5 | 2.2 | T | 2.0 |
| Liberia: Monrovia ............ | 62 | 97 | 71–89 | 72–90 | 72–80 | 72–86 | 174.9 | 0.2 | 11.7 | 24.2 | 25.2 |
| Libya: Tripoli ................ | 33 | 114 | 47–61 | 57–72 | 71–85 | 65–80 | 15.1 | 3.2 | 0.4 | T | 1.6 |
| Madagascar: Antananarivo ..... | 34 | 95 | 61–79 | 58–76 | 48–68 | 54–80 | 53.4 | 11.8 | 2.1 | 0.3 | 2.4 |
| Malaysia: Kuala Lumpur ....... | 64 | 99 | 72–90 | 74–91 | 72–90 | 73–89 | 96.1 | 6.2 | 11.5 | 3.9 | 9.8 |
| Mali: Bamako................. | 47 | 117 | 61–91 | 76–103 | 71–89 | 71–93 | 44.1 | T | 0.6 | 11.0 | 1.7 |
| Malta: Valletta ............... | 34 | 105 | 51–59 | 56–66 | 72–84 | 66–76 | 20.3 | 3.3 | 0.8 | T | 2.7 |
| Martinique: Fort-de-France..... | 56 | 96 | 69–83 | 71–86 | 74–86 | 73–87 | 80.4 | 4.7 | 3.9 | 9.4 | 9.7 |
| Mauritania: Nouakchott ....... | 44 | 115 | 57–85 | 64–90 | 74–89 | 71–91 | 6.2 | T | T | 0.5 | 0.4 |
| Mauritius: Port-Louis ......... | 50 | 95 | 73–86 | 70–82 | 62–75 | 64–80 | 50.6 | 8.5 | 5.0 | 2.3 | 1.6 |
| Mexico: Acapulco ............ | 60 | 97 | 70–85 | 71–87 | 75–89 | 74–88 | 55.1 | 0.3 | T | 9.1 | 6.7 |
|     Chihuahua ........... | 12 | 102 | 36–65 | 51–81 | 66–89 | 51–79 | 15.4 | 0.2 | 0.2 | 3.6 | 0.9 |
|     Mexico City .......... | 24 | 92 | 42–66 | 52–78 | 54–74 | 50–70 | 23.0 | 0.2 | 0.7 | 4.5 | 1.6 |
|     Monterrey ............ | 25 | 107 | 48–68 | 62–84 | 71–90 | 64–80 | 22.9 | 0.6 | 1.3 | 2.4 | 3.0 |
|     Veracruz ............. | 53 | 98 | 66–77 | 72–83 | 74–87 | 73–85 | 65.7 | 0.9 | 0.8 | 4.1 | 6.9 |
| Morocco: Rabat.............. | 32 | 118 | 46–63 | 52–71 | 63–82 | 58–77 | 19.8 | 2.6 | 1.7 | T | 1.9 |
| Mozambique: Maputo ......... | 45 | 114 | 71–86 | 66–83 | 55–76 | 64–82 | 29.9 | 5.1 | 2.1 | 0.5 | 1.9 |
| Netherlands: Amsterdam ...... | 3 | 95 | 34–40 | 43–52 | 59–69 | 48–56 | 25.6 | 2.0 | 1.6 | 2.6 | 2.8 |
| New Zealand: Wellington....... | 29 | 88 | 56–69 | 51–63 | 42–53 | 48–60 | 47.4 | 3.2 | 3.8 | 5.4 | 4.0 |
| Nigeria: Lagos ............... | 60 | 104 | 74–88 | 77–89 | 74–83 | 74–85 | 72.3 | 1.1 | 5.9 | 11.0 | 8.1 |
| Norway: Oslo ................ | −21 | 93 | 20–30 | 34–50 | 56–73 | 37–49 | 26.9 | 1.7 | 1.6 | 2.9 | 2.9 |
| Pakistan: Islamabad .......... | 25 | 118 | 38–62 | 59–86 | 77–98 | 57–89 | 36.5 | 2.5 | 1.9 | 8.1 | 0.6 |
| Panama: Panama City ........ | 63 | 97 | 71–88 | 74–90 | 74–87 | 73–85 | 69.7 | 1.0 | 2.9 | 7.1 | 10.1 |
| Papua N.G.: Port Moresby ..... | 64 | 98 | 76–89 | 75–87 | 73–83 | 75–86 | 39.8 | 7.0 | 4.2 | 1.1 | 1.4 |
| Paraguay: Asunción .......... | 29 | 110 | 71–95 | 65–84 | 53–74 | 62–86 | 51.8 | 5.5 | 5.2 | 2.2 | 5.5 |
| Peru: Lima .................. | 49 | 93 | 66–82 | 63–80 | 57–67 | 58–71 | 1.6 | 0.1 | T | 0.3 | 0.1 |
| Philippines: Manila ........... | 58 | 101 | 69–86 | 73–93 | 75–88 | 74–88 | 82.0 | 0.9 | 1.3 | 17.0 | 7.6 |
| Poland: Warsaw.............. | −22 | 98 | 21–30 | 38–54 | 56–75 | 41–54 | 22.0 | 1.2 | 1.5 | 3.0 | 1.7 |
| Portugal: Lisbon ............. | 29 | 103 | 46–56 | 52–64 | 63–79 | 57–69 | 27.0 | 3.3 | 2.4 | 0.2 | 3.1 |
| Puerto Rico: San Juan ........ | 60 | 94 | 67–81 | 69–84 | 74–87 | 73–87 | 64.2 | 4.7 | 3.7 | 6.3 | 5.8 |
| Romania: Bucharest.......... | −18 | 105 | 20–33 | 41–63 | 61–86 | 44–65 | 22.8 | 1.5 | 1.6 | 2.3 | 1.6 |
| Samoa, American: Pago Pago .. | 67 | 98 | 75–87 | 76–87 | 74–83 | 75–85 | 193.6 | 24.5 | 16.5 | 10.0 | 14.9 |
| Saudi Arabia: Riyadh .......... | 19 | 113 | 46–70 | 64–89 | 78–107 | 61–94 | 3.2 | 0.1 | 1.0 | 0.0 | 0.0 |
| Senegal: Dakar .............. | 53 | 109 | 64–79 | 65–81 | 76–88 | 76–89 | 21.3 | T | T | 3.5 | 1.5 |
| Seychelles: Victoria .......... | 67 | 92 | 76–83 | 77–86 | 75–81 | 75–83 | 92.5 | 15.2 | 7.2 | 3.3 | 6.1 |
| Singapore: Singapore.......... | 66 | 97 | 73–86 | 75–88 | 75–88 | 74–87 | 95.0 | 9.9 | 7.4 | 6.7 | 8.2 |
| Solomons: Tulagi ............ | 68 | 96 | 76–88 | 76–88 | 76–86 | 76–87 | 123.4 | 14.3 | 10.0 | 7.6 | 8.7 |
| Somalia: Mogadiscio ......... | 59 | 97 | 73–86 | 78–90 | 73–83 | 76–86 | 16.9 | T | 2.3 | 2.5 | 0.9 |
| South Africa: Cape Town ...... | 28 | 103 | 60–78 | 53–72 | 45–63 | 52–70 | 20.0 | 0.6 | 1.9 | 3.5 | 1.2 |
| Soviet Union: Leningrad ....... | −36 | 91 | 12–23 | 31–45 | 57–71 | 37–45 | 19.2 | 1.0 | 1.0 | 2.5 | 1.8 |
|     Moscow .......... | −49 | 96 | 9–21 | 31–47 | 55–76 | 34–46 | 24.8 | 1.5 | 1.9 | 3.0 | 2.7 |
| Spain: Madrid ............... | 14 | 102 | 33–47 | 44–64 | 62–87 | 48–66 | 16.5 | 1.1 | 1.7 | 0.4 | 1.9 |
| Sri Lanka: Colombo .......... | 59 | 99 | 72–86 | 76–88 | 77–85 | 75–85 | 92.3 | 3.5 | 9.1 | 5.3 | 13.7 |
| Sudan: Khartoum ............ | 41 | 118 | 59–90 | 72–105 | 77–101 | 75–104 | 6.2 | T | 2.1 | 0.2 |
| Surinam: Paramaribo.......... | 62 | 99 | 72–85 | 73–86 | 73–87 | 73–91 | 91.0 | 8.4 | 9.0 | 9.1 | 3.0 |
| Sweden: Stockholm .......... | −26 | 97 | 23–31 | 32–45 | 55–70 | 39–48 | 22.4 | 1.5 | 1.5 | 2.8 | 2.1 |
| Switzerland: Bern ............ | −9 | 96 | 26–35 | 39–56 | 56–74 | 42–55 | 38.5 | 1.9 | 3.0 | 4.4 | 3.5 |
| Syria: Damascus ............. | 21 | 113 | 36–53 | 49–75 | 64–96 | 54–81 | 8.6 | 1.7 | 0.5 | − T | 0.4 |
| Tahiti: Papeete .............. | 61 | 93 | 72–89 | 72–89 | 68–86 | 70–87 | 74.7 | 13.2 | 6.8 | 2.6 | 3.4 |
| Taiwan: Taipei ............... | 32 | 101 | 53–66 | 64–77 | 76–92 | 68–80 | 72.7 | 3.8 | 5.3 | 8.8 | 5.5 |
| Tanzania: Dar es Salaam ...... | 59 | 96 | 77–83 | 73–86 | 66–83 | 69–85 | 41.9 | 2.6 | 11.4 | 1.2 | 1.6 |
| Thailand: Bangkok ........... | 50 | 104 | 67–89 | 78–95 | 76–90 | 76–88 | 57.8 | 0.2 | 2.3 | 6.9 | 9.9 |
| Togo: Lomé ................. | 58 | 94 | 72–85 | 74–86 | 71–80 | 72–83 | 31.0 | 0.6 | 4.6 | 2.8 | 2.4 |
| Trinidad-Tob.: Port of Spain ... | 52 | 101 | 69–87 | 69–90 | 71–88 | 71–89 | 64.2 | 2.7 | 2.1 | 8.6 | 6.7 |
| Tunisia: Tunis ............... | 30 | 118 | 43–58 | 51–70 | 68–90 | 59–77 | 16.5 | 2.5 | 1.4 | 0.1 | 2.0 |
| Turkey: Instanbul ............ | 17 | 100 | 36–45 | 45–61 | 65–81 | 54–67 | 31.5 | 3.7 | 1.9 | 1.7 | 3.8 |
| Uganda: Kampala ............ | 53 | 97 | 65–83 | 64–79 | 62–77 | 63–81 | 46.2 | 1.8 | 6.9 | 1.8 | 3.8 |
| Upper Volta: Ouagadougou .... | 48 | 118 | 60–92 | 79–103 | 74–91 | 74–95 | 35.2 | T | 0.6 | 8.0 | 1.3 |
| Uruguay: Montevideo ......... | 25 | 109 | 62–83 | 53–71 | 43–58 | 49–68 | 37.4 | 2.9 | 3.9 | 2.9 | 2.6 |
| Venezuela: Caracas .......... | 45 | 91 | 56–75 | 60–81 | 61–78 | 61–79 | 32.9 | 0.9 | 1.3 | 4.3 | 4.3 |
| Vietnam: Hanoi .............. | 41 | 108 | 58–68 | 70–80 | 79–92 | 72–84 | 69.4 | 0.8 | 3.6 | 11.9 | 3.5 |
| Virgin Is., U.S.; Charlotte Amalie .. | 63 | 92 | 71–82 | 74–85 | 77–88 | 76–87 | 43.7 | 2.5 | 2.2 | 3.2 | 5.6 |
| Yugoslavia: Belgrade .......... | −14 | 107 | 27–37 | 45–64 | 61–84 | 47–65 | 24.6 | 1.6 | 2.2 | 1.9 | 2.7 |
| Zaire: Kinshasa .............. | 58 | 97 | 70–87 | 71–89 | 64–81 | 70–88 | 53.3 | 5.3 | 7.7 | 0.1 | 4.7 |
| Zambia: Lusaka .............. | 39 | 100 | 63–78 | 59–79 | 49–73 | 64–88 | 32.9 | 9.1 | 0.7 | T | 0.4 |
| Zimbabwe: Salisbury .......... | 32 | 95 | 60–78 | 55–78 | 44–70 | 58–83 | 32.6 | 7.7 | 1.1 | T | 1.1 |

# CAUSES OF CLIMATE AND WEATHER

Source: Environmental Data Service, U.S. Department of Commerce

The climate of a place is the long-term normal weather for a given day, month, season, or year. It is the weather we expect for spring in our hometown or for vacation time at our favorite camping grounds. These expectations are based on weather data collected over a relatively long period, usually several decades.

In contrast, weather is the current or recent state of the atmosphere. Both can be described in terms of temperature, pressure, humidity, sunshine, winds, clouds, and precipitation. For example, temperature in weather is the present temperature at a place, while temperature in climate is the average temperature for the location, determined from previous records.

The underlying causes of weather and climate are heat from the Sun and the rotation of the Earth. The radiant energy of the Sun and the constant rotation of the Earth about its axis serve to set up circulation patterns within the atmosphere. These circulation patterns carry heat and moisture from the equator to the poles, across land and sea, and over flat land and mountains. Patterns of winds, rainfall, cloudiness, and temperature tend to remain relatively steady at any given location on Earth. Weather tends to follow the same pattern year after year. These patterns determine the climate of a place.

Briefly, climate is controlled by latitude, land surfaces and sources of moisture, prevailing winds, ocean currents, elevation, and mountain barriers.

## LATITUDE

Heat from the Sun reaches the Earth after passing through approximately 93 million miles of space. The rays reaching the equator appear to come from nearly directly overhead. At points nearer the poles, the Sun appears lower in the sky. The position of the Sun causes warm climates in the equatorial regions and successively cooler climates toward the poles—thus the higher the latitude, the cooler the climate.

Seasons modify the latitude effect because of the tilt of the axis of the Earth. The Earth's axis is tilted 23.5 degrees from a line perpendicular to the plane that contains the Sun and the Earth's orbit around the Sun. Beginning about September 21 and ending about March 21, the north end of the axis points away from the Sun, so the rays from the Sun are more slanting in the Northern Hemisphere and more directly overhead in the Southern Hemisphere.

The length of daylight, hence the length of time a location receives solar heat, increases as we move from the pole to the equator during winter. During summer, the length of daylight increases north of the equator, but the more slanted rays of the Sun keep the higher latitudes cooler than the low latitudes.

## LAND SURFACES AND SOURCES OF MOISTURE

Land and water surfaces react differently to the incoming rays of the Sun. In general, land surfaces are heated rapidly by the Sun, but the heat does not penetrate deeply, so land surfaces also cool rapidly. On the other hand, water warms up slowly, holds a much larger quantity of heat than the land surface, and cools slowly.

As a result the surface layer of air over the continents is warmer in summer and colder in winter than that over the oceans. Because warm air rises, permitting air from cooler areas to flow in to replace it, there is a net inflow of cool ocean air onto continents in summer and an outflow from the continents in winter. Land and sea breezes result from a similar situation in coastal areas, where the land is colder than the water at night and early- morning but warmer later in the day.

Sources of moisture—oceans, gulfs, lakes, and other large bodies of water—have a major influence on the climate of an area. Places in the interior of continents usually tend to be hotter and drier in summer and colder in winter than coastal areas, and usually have greater differences between daily high and low temperatures.

## PREVAILING WINDS

The uneven heating of the Earth by the Sun is the main cause of wind systems. The equatorial regions receive considerably more solar heat per square mile than do the polar regions. Warm equatorial surface air rises and is replaced by cooler surface air flowing in from the poles. The unequal heating of the Earth's surface together with its rotation produces a general global movement of air.

The global air movement causes a worldwide pattern of prevailing winds. Surface winds in the Northern Hemisphere are arranged in three broad belts: the northeast trades (from the northeast) in the tropics and subtropics; the prevailing westerlies (from the west to southwest) in the middle latitudes; and the polar easterlies (from the northeast) in the polar region.

## HIGH- AND LOW-PRESSURE AREAS

The rotation of the Earth about its axis causes winds to turn to the right (clockwise) in the Northern Hemisphere. For example, a wind blowing from south to north turns toward the east. Similarly, a north wind turns toward the west. The resulting huge whirling masses of air are called high-pressure areas (also called highs or anticyclones). Between these highs are low-pressure areas (also called lows or cyclones) that rotate to the left (counterclockwise). Air tends to flow inward toward low-pressure centers and outward from high-pressure areas.

## AIR MASSES

When temperature and humidity are very much the same throughout any level in a high-pressure area, the high is called an *air mass*. Four general types of air masses are recognized in the United States: (1) cold dry air masses that move in from Canada, generally traveling south-eastward; (2) cool moist air masses that generally travel eastward across the states from the Pacific Ocean; (3) warm moist air masses that move in from the Pacific, the Gulf of Mexico, or the Atlantic; and (4) warm dry air masses that may move from the southwest.

## STORMS

Most storms and active weather occur in and around the low-pressure areas between highs.

The Canadian highs bring cool dry conditions. As they move into an area, they usually are preceded by showers along or adjacent to a cold front. The Pacific highs, also preceded by fronts, are moister and somewhat warmer than the Canadian highs.

Lows bring in warm humid air from the Pacific, the Gulf of Mexico, or the Atlantic. Lows are usually accompanied by widespread rain or snow.

The migrating highs and lows occur more frequently, are more intense, and travel faster in winter than in summer. Average motion is 750 miles per day in winter and 500 in summer.

The air masses that prevail over an area determine its climate. For example, the southeastern states are dominated in summer by a moist tropical air mass associated with a high-pressure area located offshore. The southerly winds on the west side of this high bring moist air from the Gulf of Mexico into these states. In winter the southern states are invaded by Canadian air masses that bring cold fronts across the area about once every five days.

Severe local storms, such as thunderstorms and tornadoes, and tropical cyclones up to hurricane intensity are superimposed on the general climatic pattern.

Winds in the upper atmosphere tend to "steer" moving air masses at lower levels. The jet stream, a meandering current of air at 30,000 to 50,000 feet, moves air masses in a generally eastward direction.

## SEMIPERMANENT HIGHS AND LOWS

Wind and storm patterns are strongly influenced by the locations and intensities of semipermanent high- and low-pressure areas.

The Aleutian low is the semipermanent pressure system that dominates the northern end of the North Pacific. This low intensifies and expands in winter and weakens and moves to the northwest in summer. Its average central pressure in February is 29.50 inches.

The Pacific high, another semipermanent pressure system, intensifies and expands in summer. The average summer pressure at the center of this high is 30.27 inches at its center, about 1,600 miles west of San Francisco. In its summer position, this semipermanent Pacific high effectively blocks the passage of storms into the California-Oregon-Washington coastal area, steering them instead to the coast of British Columbia. In autumn and winter this high becomes weak, and its center moves to the southwest. In this new position, it cannot block the movement of storms to the coast, so there is an increase in the frequency of storms reaching the Washington coast by September. By late November and December, storms reach the coast as far south as southern California.

The semipermanent pressure systems in the Atlantic are the Icelandic low and the Bermuda (or Azores) high. Many of the storms associated with migratory low-pressure areas in the central and eastern United States tend to drift toward the Icelandic low. The favored path of these storms is across the Great Lakes and along the valley of the St. Lawrence River.

During summer, the Bermuda high has a marked effect on the eastern states. This high is strongest in summer when it lies off the East Coast and brings a southerly flow of warm moist maritime air from the Caribbean Sea. On occasion, this warm moist air is carried into the Arizona-New Mexico area, bringing welcome rainfall.

## OCEAN CURRENTS

Well-established ocean currents have a great effect on the climates of coastal areas. Perhaps the best-known ocean current is the Gulf Stream that carries warm waters from the Florida Straits northward along the Atlantic coast and then northeastward and eastward to the British Isles. Winds blowing across this warm stream of water pick up heat and moisture and bring them over the East Coast.

The climate of the East Coast is also affected by the cold Labrador Current, which flows southward as far as Norfolk, Va. This current is responsible for frequent fogs over the coast.

The Japanese Current is the major ocean current affecting the West Coast. This current reaches the west coast of the continent at about the latitude of the United States-Canada border. Here it branches. One branch, the Alaska Current, turns northward bringing a milder warmer climate to coastal British Columbia and Alaska. The other branch, the California Current, turns southward bringing cooler water along the shore of Washington, Oregon, and California. During winter, the Davidson Current moves in from southeast of the California Current, bringing warmer weather to the coast.

## ELEVATION

Temperature in the atmosphere decreases with increasing elevation, or altitude. The usual rate of decrease is 3.3 °F. per 1,000 feet. The climatic mean temperature on a mountain generally is 3.3 °F. lower per 1,000 feet of elevation than that of nearby lower altitude stations.

## MOUNTAIN BARRIERS

Mountain ranges not only have colder temperatures at higher elevations but they also act as barriers to block the flow of prevailing winds and the movement of storms.

Air flowing upward on the slopes of a mountain barrier tends to drop much of its moisture on the windward side of the range. This is the reason deserts lie to the east of the Coast Ranges and the Cascade–Sierra Nevada ranges of California.

Because mountain ranges in the United States run north and south, they block the flow of the prevailing westerlies. Moisture-laden air from the Pacific is forced up the slopes of the Coast and Cascade–Sierra Nevada ranges where it dumps most of its moisture. In the east the Appalachian Mountains tend to block the flow of Atlantic air into the interior but permit the free passage of the cold arctic and polar air masses of Canada over the central and eastern two-thirds of the United States.

The lack of an east-west mountain barrier allows a northward flow of warm maritime tropical air far northward into the interior.

## BE YOUR OWN WEATHER FORECASTER

Source: NOAA, U.S. Department of Commerce

You can forecast weather merely by observing the direction from which the wind blows and reading the level of air pressure on a barometer.

The following table summarizes wind and barometer indications of approaching weather that are generally applicable to most U.S. regions.

| WIND DIRECTION | BAROMETER (reduced to sea level) | WEATHER FORECAST |
|---|---|---|
| SW to NW | 30.10 to 30.20 and steady | Fair, with slight temperature changes for 1 to 2 days |
| SW to NW | 30.10 to 30.20, rising rapidly | Fair, followed within 2 days by rain |
| SW to NW | 30.20 and above, stationary | Continued fair with no decided temperature change |
| SW to NW | 30.20 and above, falling slowly | Slowly rising temperature and fair for 2 days |
| S to SW | 30.00 or below, rising slowly | Clearing within a few hours and fair for several days |
| S to E | 29.80 or below, falling rapidly | Severe storm imminent, followed within 24 hours by clearing and in winter by colder temperatures |
| S to SE | 30.10 to 30.20, falling slowly | Rain within 24 hours |
| S to SE | 30.10 to 30.20, falling rapidly | Wind increasing in force; rain within 12 to 24 hours |
| SE to NE | 30.10 to 30.20, falling slowly | Rain in 12 to 18 hours |
| SE to NE | 30.10 to 30.20, falling rapidly | Increasing wind; rain within 12 hours |
| SE to NE | 30.00 or below, falling slowly | Rain will continue 1 to 2 days |
| SE to NE | 30.00 or below, falling rapidly | Rain with high wind, followed within 36 hours by clearing, and in winter by colder temperatures |
| E to NE | 30.10 and above, falling slowly | In summer, with light winds, rain may not fall for several days; in winter, rain within 24 hours |
| E to NE | 30.10 and above, falling rapidly | In summer, rain probable within 12 to 24 hours; in winter, rain or snow with increasing winds |
| E to N | 29.80 or below, falling rapidly | Severe northeast gale; in summer, heavy rain; in winter, heavy snow followed by cold wave |
| Easterly | 29.80 or below, rising rapidly | Clearing and colder |

## CLOUD FORMATIONS—AND WHAT THEY MEAN

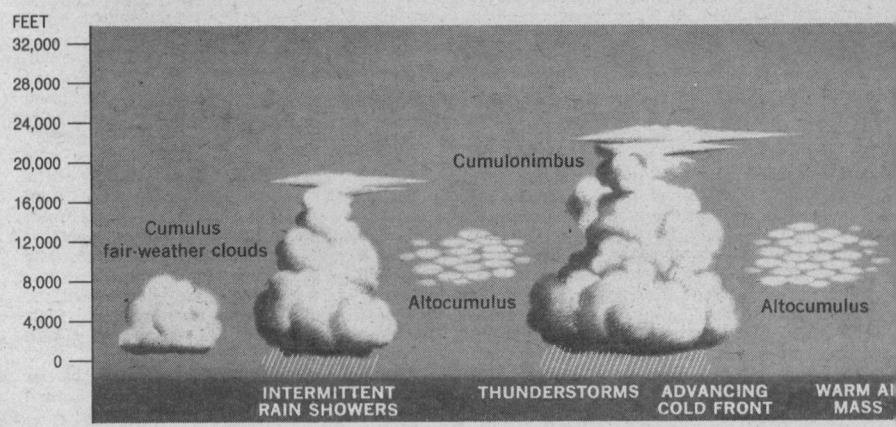

# WIND CHILL—WHY YOU FEEL COLDER THAN THE THERMOMETER

Source: Environmental Data Service, NOAA, U.S. Department of Commerce

In winter the stronger the wind the colder the weather seems. The wind causes the chill that you *feel* to be even colder than the temperature *shown* on your thermometer. The following wind-chill table prepared by the National Weather Service can help you find what the equivalent wind-chill temperature is when you know the thermometer temperature and the wind speed. For example, if the thermometer shows a temperature of 15° and you know that the wind speed is 10 mph, then look in the table and you will see that the wind-chill temperature you will feel is 3° below zero.

| WIND SPEED | THERMOMETER TEMPERATURES IN DEGREES FAHRENHEIT | | | | | | | | | | | | | |
| | 35° | 30° | 25° | 20° | 15° | 10° | 5° | 0° | −5° | −10° | −15° | −20° | −25° | −30° |
| --- | --- | --- | --- | --- | --- | --- | --- | --- | --- | --- | --- | --- | --- | --- |
| | EQUIVALENT WIND–CHILL TEMPERATURES (HOW COLD YOU SEEM TO FEEL) | | | | | | | | | | | | | |
| 5 mph | 32° | 27° | 22° | 16° | 11° | 6° | 0° | −5° | −10° | −15° | −21° | −26° | −31° | −36° |
| 10 mph | 22° | 16° | 10° | 3° | −3° | −9° | −15° | −22° | −27° | −34° | −40° | −46° | −52° | −58° |
| 15 mph | 16° | 9° | 2° | −5° | −11° | −18° | −25° | −31° | −38° | −45° | −51° | −58° | −65° | −72° |
| 20 mph | 12° | 4° | −3° | −10° | −17° | −24° | −31° | −39° | −46° | −53° | −60° | −67° | −74° | −81° |
| 25 mph | 8° | 1° | −7° | −15° | −22° | −29° | −36° | −44° | −51° | −59° | −66° | −74° | −81° | −88° |
| 30 mph | 6° | −2° | −10° | −18° | −25° | −33° | −41° | −49° | −56° | −64° | −71° | −79° | −86° | −93° |
| 35 mph | 4° | −4° | −12° | −20° | −27° | −35° | −43° | −52° | −58° | −67° | −74° | −82° | −89° | −97° |
| 40 mph | 3° | −5° | −13° | −21° | −29° | −37° | −45° | −53° | −60° | −69° | −76° | −84° | −92° | −100° |
| 45 mph | 2° | −6° | −14° | −22° | −30° | −38° | −46° | −54° | −62° | −70° | −78° | −85° | −93° | −102° |
| 50 mph | 0° | −7° | −17° | −24° | −31° | −38° | −47° | −56° | −63° | −70° | −79° | −88° | −96° | −103° |

# BEAUFORT WIND SCALE

The Beaufort wind scale indicates wind strength by a series of numbers. it was developed in 1805 by a British admiral, Sir Francis Beaufort, to help gauge wind speed without an instrument.

| BEAUFORT NUMBER | WIND NAME | SPEED (mph) | OBSERVED EFFECT OF WIND |
| --- | --- | --- | --- |
| 0 | Calm | 0–1 | Calm. Smoke rises straight up into the air. |
| 1 | Light Air | 1–3 | Weather vanes remain motionless. Smoke drifts slightly with wind. |
| 2 | Light Breeze | 4–7 | Weather vanes active. You can feel wind on your face. Leaves rustle. |
| 3 | Gentle Breeze | 8–12 | Light flags fill out with wind. Twigs on trees move. |
| 4 | Moderate Breeze | 13–18 | The wind picks up dust and loose paper. Small tree branches sway. |
| 5 | Fresh Breeze | 19–24 | Waves break on inland waters. Small trees sway in the wind. |
| 6 | Strong Breeze | 25–31 | Using an umbrella becomes difficult. Large tree branches sway. |
| 7 | Near Gale | 32–38 | Walking against the wind is difficult. Entire large trees sway. |
| 8 | Gale | 39–46 | Walking against the wind is almost impossible. Twigs break off trees. |
| 9 | Strong Gale | 47–54 | Shingles blown off house roofs. Some damage to buildings. |
| 10 | Storm | 55–63 | Entire trees blown over and uprooted. Much damage to buildings. |
| 11 | Violent Storm | 64–72 | Severe damage to crops, trees, and property. |
| 12 | Hurricane | 73–82 | Widespread violent destruction. |

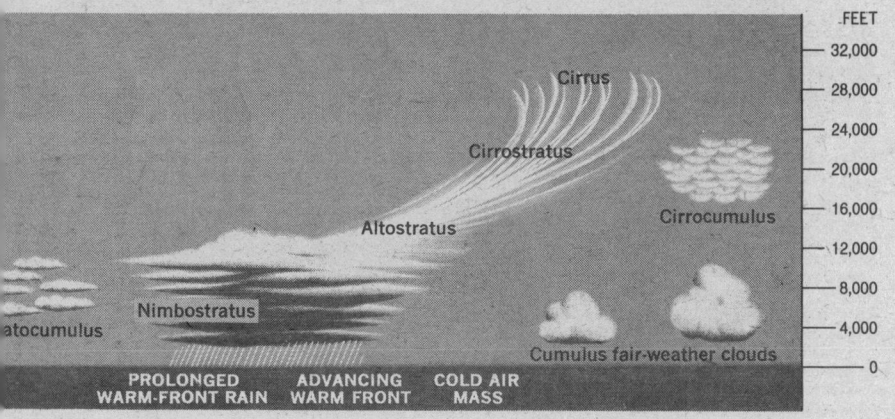

## RECORD U.S. BLIZZARDS AND SNOWSTORMS

Source: Environmental Data Service, NOAA, U.S. Department of Commerce

| DATE | PLACE | DEPTH | DESCRIPTION |
|---|---|---|---|
| 1717, Feb. 19–24 | New England | 60–72 in. | The "great snow"; drifts cover many one-story houses |
| 1888, March 11–14 | Boston, New York City, Philadelphia, Washington, D.C. | 40–50 in. | Major eastern cities paralyzed by heavy snow and winds to 70 mph; over 400 deaths |
| 1899, Feb. 11–14 | Washington, D.C. | 35.2 in. | Record snowfall in one month for capital |
| 1901, April 19–21 | Watertown, Ohio | 45 in. | Greatest 24-hour snowfall in state |
| 1911, Jan. | Tamarack, Calif. | 390 in. | Greatest U.S. snowfall in one month |
| 1921, April 14–15 | Silver Lake, Colo. | 95 in. | Snowfall of 75.8 inches in 24 hours, greatest 24-hour accumulation in U.S. history |
| 1921, Nov. 17–20 | The Dalles, Oreg. | 54 in. | Record snowfall for state |
| 1922, Jan. 27–29 | Washington, D.C. | 28 in. | Snow collapses Knickerbocker theater, killing 98 |
| 1928, April 27–28 | Bayard, W. Va. | 34 in. | Record 24-hour snowfall (34 inches) for state |
| 1933, Jan. 18–19 | Giant Forest, Calif. | 60 in. | Record 24-hour snowfall for state |
| 1935, Jan. 20–24 | Winthrop, Wash. | 52 in. | Record 24-hour snowfall for state |
| 1940, Jan. 18–22 | Watertown, N.Y. | 69 in. | Record snowfall for state |
| 1940, Jan. 23–24 | Louisville, Miss. | 15.5 in. | Record 24-hour snowfall for state |
| 1940, Nov. 11–12 | Iowa to Minnesota | — | 144 deaths; subzero temperatures; high winds |
| 1946, January | Stampede Pass, Wash. | 192.9 in. | Record snowfall in one month |
| 1946, Nov. 2–6 | New Mexico | 36 in. | Unprecedented heavy snowfall |
| 1947, March 2–5 | Readsboro, Vt. | 50 in. | Record snowfall for state |
| 1947, March 2–5 | Peru, Mass. | 47 in. | Record snowfall for state |
| 1949, Jan. 1–6 | Colorado to Dakotas | 7–30 in. | 39 deaths; severe blizzard; 70 mph winds |
| 1950, March 25–27 | Dumont, S.D. | 60 in. | Record snowfall in state |
| 1950, Nov. 23–28 | Ohio, Pa., West Virginia | 33–57 in. | Record snowfall for three states |
| 1951, March 10–14 | Iowa City, Iowa | 27.2 in. | Record snowfall for state |
| 1955, April 2–5 | Colorado to Dakotas | 30–52 in. | One of heaviest and latest spring snowstorms |
| 1956, March 16–17 | New England, New York, Pa. | 20 in. | Crippling winds and snowstorm |
| 1958, Feb. 13–19 | North Carolina to New Jersey | 36 in. | 43 deaths; damage $500 million |
| 1958, March 19–22 | Virginia to New England | 17–30 in. | Severe snowstorm; 49 deaths |
| 1959, Feb. 13–19 | Mt. Shasta Ski Bowl, Calif. | 189 in. | Greatest U.S. snowfall in one storm |
| 1959, March 11–13 | New England, New York | 20 in. | Blizzard conditions; transportation paralyzed |
| 1960, Feb. 18–20 | Maryland to New England | 20–36 in. | Damage in millions of dollars |
| 1961, Jan. 19–20 | North Carolina to New York | 10–30 in. | 37 deaths; many cities paralyzed |
| 1961, Feb. 3–5 | North Carolina to New England | 10–36 in. | 73 deaths; drifts of 15 feet |
| 1964, Feb. 2–5 | N.M., Okla., Texas | 18–36 in. | Second heaviest storm in Panhandle's history |
| 1966, Jan. 29–31 | Virginia to New England | 12–36 in. | 50 deaths; drifts to 20 feet |
| 1966, March 2–5 | Nebraska to Dakotas | 12–36 in. | 15 deaths; 100,000 cattle killed; drifts to 30 feet |
| 1967, Jan. 26–27 | Chicago and Midwest | 23 in. | Record snow and ice storms; high winds |
| 1969, Feb. 9–10 | New York and New England | 15 in. | Worst storm to hit New York City in 8 years |
| 1969, February | Mt. Washington, N.H. | 172.8 in. | State record for one-month snowfall |
| 1973, Feb. 10–11 | Georgia and Carolinas | 15–21 in. | Worst storm in South in this century |
| 1974, Dec. 1–2 | Michigan, Ohio | 17–20 in. | Record 19.2 in. of snow paralyzes Detroit |
| 1975, Jan. 10–12 | N.D., S.D., Neb., Kan., Mo., Iowa, Minn., Wis. | 8–15 in. | Winds of 80 mph drift snow to 20 feet; over 60 killed, hundreds injured; over $15 million damage |
| 1977, Jan. 1–31 | West Virginia | 104 in. | West Virginia record for one-month snowfall |
| 1977, Jan. 28–Feb. 1 | Ill., Ind., Ohio, N.Y., Pa. | 12–71 in. | Blizzard with winds to 69 mph kills 75 persons; Buffalo, N.Y., paralyzed with drifts 25 feet high |
| 1978, Jan. 26–27 | Midwestern and Eastern states | 12–34 in. | Called "worst blizzard of century"; 100 killed; winds gust to 100 mph; snow drifts to 25 feet; many roofs collapse |
| 1978, Feb. 6–7 | Middle Atlantic and New England states | 18–38 in. | Severe property damage as winds to 100 mph cause 40-foot waves to batter coast, destroying houses and driving ships ashore |
| 1979, Jan. 13–14 | Chicago and Midwest | 20.7 in. | Heavy snowfall paralyzes Chicago |
| 1980, March 2 | Middle Atlantic and Southern States | 10–28 in. | Surprise blizzard paralyzes mid-Atlantic area; Florida citrus crop damaged; 36 killed |

## U.S. AND WORLD RECORD RAINFALLS

| DURATION | DEPTH | LOCATION | DATE |
|---|---|---|---|
| 1 minute (world record) | 1.50 in. | Barst, Guadeloupe | Nov. 26, 1970 |
| 1 minute (U.S. record) | 1.23 in. | Unionville, Maryland | July, 4, 1956 |
| 15 minutes (world record) | 7.80 in. | Plumb Point, Jamaica | May 12, 1916 |
| 1 hour (U.S. record) | 12.00 in. | Holt, Missouri | June 22, 1947 |
| 1 hour (U.S. record) | 12.00 in. | Kilauea plantation, Kauai, Hawaii | Jan. 24–25, 1956 |
| 12 hours (world record) | 52.76 in. | Belouve, Réunion | Feb. 28–29, 1964 |
| 24 hours (world record) | 73.62 in. | Cilaos, Réunion | March 15–16, 1952 |
| 24 hours (U.S. record) | 38.70 in. | Yankeetown, Florida | Sept. 5–6, 1950 |
| 1 month (world record) | 366.14 in. | Cherrapunji, India | July 1861 |
| 1 month (U.S. record) | 107.00 in. | Puu Kukui, Maui, Hawaii | March 1942 |
| 1 year (world record) | 1,041.78 in. | Cherrapunji, India | Aug. 1860–July 1861 |
| 1 year (U.S. record) | 578.00 in. | Puu Kukui, Maui, Hawaii | 1950 |

# Congress of the United States

Florida Republican Paula Hawkins and her husband, Gene, express pleasure as she piles up votes in the November election to become the second woman to serve in the U.S. Senate in the 97th Congress.

## HIGHLIGHTS: 1980

When the 97th U.S. Congress convenes on Jan. 5, 1981, the U.S. Senate will be controlled by Republicans for the first time in 25 years as a result of the 1980 elections (see pages 245–256). The waning days of the lame-duck session of the 96th U.S. Congress in November and December were spent in political maneuvering as Republicans prepared to take leadership roles.

The major accomplishment of the 96th Congress in 1980 came with the establishment of a national energy policy in the adoption of modified versions of many of President Carter's proposals (see pages 257–259).

Congress was rocked by revelations of the FBI's Abscam operation and the indictment of six representatives and one senator for conspiracy and bribery (see page 11). For the first time in more than a century, the House expelled one of its members (see page 156).

President Carter's weakened leadership was demonstrated when Congress twice overrode his vetoes (see pages 157–158). However, his veto of an antibusing measure on Dec. 13, three days before Congress adjourned, was not challenged (see page 201).

Other major actions of Congress during the year are included on the following pages.

# MAJOR CONGRESSIONAL ACTIVITIES: 1980

The 96th Congress adjourned on Dec. 16, 1980, after a postelection lame-duck session more notable for what it did not accomplish than for what it did. The November-December session was necessary because Congress had delayed action on so many appropriation measures that many federal agencies would have been forced to close down for lack of funds after previous spending authorizations ran out at midnight on Dec. 15. Finally, a few hours after the deadline, an authorization bill was passed enabling departments and agencies to continue spending money at 1981 budget levels until June 5, 1981.

The funding measure was stripped of most of the sources of controversial special-interest amendments that had prolonged the session, such as an effort by congressmen to vote themselves a $10,000 annual pay raise.

## ALASKA LANDS PROTECTION

Although environmentalists believed the legislation should have been stronger, Congress approved in 1980 an Alaskan land measure that had been under congressional study for many years. Accepted by voice vote in the House on Nov. 12 and by 78 to 14 in the Senate on Aug. 19, the new law provided environmental protection for about 28% of the area of Alaska, while turning over about 38% of Alaska's land to the state government and to native Alaskans. The U.S. government retained nearly two-thirds of Alaska's area.

The measure doubled the size of the U.S. national park and wildlife refuge areas, setting aside 43.6 million acres of new national parks and 53.8 million acres of new wildlife refuges. Environmental protection restricting various types of development were imposed on 104.3 million acres of federally owned Alaskan land.

## BILLYGATE PROBE

One of the elements that contributed to President Carter's defeat for reelection was his handling of the actions of his brother Billy. After the Department of Justice revealed on July 14 that Billy had registered as an agent of Libya, the U.S. Senate created a subcommittee 10 days later to investigate the matter.

Testifying before the panel on Aug. 21–22, Billy Carter admitted that he had received $220,000 from Libya, but claimed that it merely had been a loan. He denied he had attempted to influence the President in favor of Libya. He also denied he had been tipped off by the White House that he faced prosecution for his activities unless he registered as a foreign agent.

The subcommittee issued its final 249-page report to the Senate on Oct. 2, declaring that Billy Carter's actions were "contrary to the interest of the President and the United States and merits severe criticism."

## BUDGET BOOSTED

Seeking to make good on promises to achieve a balanced federal budget, Congress wrangled for weeks in the spring of 1980 over what expenditures might be cut. It missed a May 15 deadline to set a binding budget figure for fiscal 1981, but a month later, on June 12, both houses adopted a compromise resolution calling for a spending ceiling of $613.6 billion against revenues of $613.8 billion—providing a balanced budget with a projected surplus of about $200 million.

However, when the lame-duck session of Congress convened after the November elections and after fiscal year 1981 had begun on Oct. 1, it took a new look at the budget. Final action was taken on Nov. 20, with adoption of a revised budget that boosted expenditures by $18.8 billion to a total of $632.4 billion. At the same time, estimated revenues were reduced to $605 billion, providing room, according to the resolution's sponsors, for a $39 billion tax cut in 1981. The resolution estimated the federal budget would result in a $27.4 billion deficit.

Most observers believed that the 97th Congress would seek to adopt another revised 1981 budget after convening in January 1981.

## ENVIRONMENTAL SUPERFUND

Congress gave final approval on Dec. 3 to a scaled-down proposal by President Carter for a "superfund" to pay for emergency cleanup of poisonous materials spilled or dumped in the environment. The President signed the $1.6 billion measure on Dec. 11, even though it was far less than the over $4 billion he previously had supported.

Most of the money for the fund would be derived during the next five years from special taxes on the chemical industry.

## EXPULSION OF CONGRESSMAN

Often accused of merely slapping the wrists of its members in its enforcement of ethics and morality, the House expelled one of its members on Oct. 2 for the first time in more than a century. The House voted 376 to 30 to oust Rep. Michael Myers (D-Pa.), who in August had been convicted of corruption in the Abscam scandal (see page 11).

Myers was only the fourth member of the House ever to be expelled and the first for misconduct rather than treason.

Another convicted in the Abscam scandal,

Rep. John Jenrette (D.-S.C.) resigned on Dec. 10, rather than face almost certain expulsion.

## FOREIGN AID DELAYED

Congressional disapproval of President Carter's foreign policy was expressed by its refusal for the second year in a row to approve a foreign-aid appropriation measure. However, U.S. economic and military aid to some 115 countries and territories was allowed to proceed under a continuing appropriations resolution enacted in November 1979.

On Feb. 27, 1980, a House-Senate conference committee approved a $8.1 billion foreign-aid bill for fiscal 1980, but it could not be presented to Congress for passage because the budget ceiling for the year already had been exceeded. While the measure for 1980 remained in abeyance, committees began working on a $7.1 billion foreign-aid bill for fiscal 1981.

After Congress began its lame-duck session in November, House leaders shelved the foreign-aid measure, believing it had no chance of passage.

## NEWSROOM SURPRISE RAIDS BARRED

Congress approved legislation that would prevent police from making surprise raids on newsrooms and communications organizations to search for criminal evidence.

The measure was in reaction to a 1978 Supreme Court ruling that upheld the right of police to obtain warrants to search newsrooms even when the newsmen were not suspected of criminal activity. Journalists had decried the court ruling as restricting freedom of the press.

Passed by the Senate by voice vote on Sept. 29 and by the House 357 to 2 on Oct. 1, the legislation, called the Privacy Protection Act of 1980, was signed by the President on Oct. 14. The act requires federal, state, and local authorities either to request voluntary compliance or to use subpoenas—with advance notice and the opportunity for a court hearing—instead of search warrants when they seek reporters' material as evidence.

## VETO OVERRIDE KILLS OIL IMPORT FEE

On April 2 President Carter imposed a $4.62 per barrel fee on imported oil in an effort to reduce oil consumption. The fee was to be passed on to consumers as a surcharge of 10 cents per gallon on gasoline beginning on May 15. It was estimated the levy would bring the government additional annual revenues of $12.6 billion. Although a federal district court on May 13 overturned the levy on grounds that the President had exceeded his authority, congressional opponents decided to take no chances that a higher court might reverse the decision.

By an overwhelming vote of 376 to 30, the House on June 4 approved a resolution block-

## HOW A BILL BECOMES A LAW

The process by which a bill becomes a law is long and complicated. Following is a summary of steps in the passage of legislation by Congress.

**Introduction of Bill.** The bill is introduced in the House by a representative or in the Senate by a senator. Sometimes to speed up action the same bill is introduced in both houses at the same time. All tax bills must be introduced in the House, but the Senate is free to amend them.

**First Reading.** The title of the bill is read to the House or Senate. It is given a number, and it is printed.

**Assignment to Committee.** The Speaker of the House, or the Vice President in the Senate, assigns each bill to a committee for consideration.

**Committee Consideration.** The committee may hold hearings on the bill, and then rewrite or amend it. The committee also can decide to table the bill, or kill it.

**Committee Approval.** If the committee approves the bill, it is sent to the floor to await its turn on the calendar. The bill can be pushed ahead of others in the House by the House Rules Committee or in the Senate by the majority leaders.

**Second Reading.** When the bill reaches the floor of the House or Senate, it is read in full and then debated. It may be amended or it may be returned to committee. The time for debate is limited in the House but is unlimited in the Senate unless a two-thirds majority votes to impose limits. At the end of the debate the House or Senate votes on the bill.

**Third Reading.** Only the title of the bill is read, and another vote is taken, usually by roll call.

**Consideration by Other House of Congress.** After a bill is passed by one house, it must go through the same process already described in the other house. If it is amended during the process by the other house and then is passed on third reading by a majority vote, it is returned to the house that originated the bill.

**Approval of Amendments by Originating House.** When a bill is returned to the house of Congress in which it originated, it is debated and a vote is taken to decide whether the majority approves the amended version of the bill.

**Conference Committee.** If the majority of the house in which the bill originated rejects the other house's amendments, the bill is sent to a conference committee composed of both representatives and senators. The conference committee revises the bill to reconcile the differences between its two versions.

**Final Approval by House and Senate.** After the conference committee reports out its revised version of the bill, the House and the Senate each must vote again. If a majority in each house votes to approve the bill, it then is sent to the President.

**Presidential Signature.** If the President signs the bill, it immediately becomes law.

**Becoming a Law Without Presidential Signature.** If Congress is in session the bill automatically becomes law 10 days after the President receives it, excluding Sundays, even though he does not sign it.

**Regular Veto.** The President may within 10 days veto the bill by returning it to Congress with an explanation of why he refuses to approve it.

**Pocket Veto.** If Congress adjourns within the 10-day period of presidential consideration, the bill automatically is killed if the President does not sign it.

**Overriding a Veto.** If the President vetoes a bill, Congress can make it become law if both the House and the Senate again pass the bill, each by a two-thirds majority.

**MAJOR ACTIVITIES:1980** *(continued)*

ing the levy. On that same day the Senate approved the resolution 73 to 16. The measure was tacked onto an unrelated bill raising the federal debt limit.

Defying Congress, President Carter vetoed the measure on the following day.

When a White House messenger brought the President's 22d veto message to the House a few hours later, the members hooted and jeered.

Then the House voted overwhelmingly 335 to 34 to override the veto. On the next day, June 6, the Senate followed suit with a vote of 68 to 10 against the President.

The action was the first time in 28 years that a Democratic Congress had overridden a veto by a Democratic President—the last similar override having occurred in 1952 under President Truman.

## RAILROAD DEREGULATION

President Carter on Oct. 14 approved the Staggers Rail Act of 1980 that substantially removed many federal controls from the industry.

The measure had been approved by both houses of Congress on Sept. 30, just before the congressional election recess.

The legislation gave the railroads greater flexibility in establishing freight rates. It provided that antitrust restrictions on railroad industry discussions on joint rates would be lifted by Jan. 1, 1984. However, the Interstate Commerce Commission (ICC) retained considerable regulatory power over railroads.

In signing the measure, President Carter said that it "strips away needless and costly regulations in favor of market forces." He described it as "the capstone of my own efforts to get rid of needless and burdensome federal regulations which benefit nobody and which harm all of us."

## REVENUE SHARING

Responding to appeals from governors, mayors, and local officials, Congress gave final approval on Dec. 12 to legislation extending federal revenue sharing for three years. The measure provides for $4.6 billion in annual aid to local governments in 1981–83.

Although states will not receive revenue sharing in 1981, the measure provides $2.3 billion in revenue-sharing aid to states in 1982 and again in 1983.

However, the legislation requires states to give up an equal amount of federal aid from categorical grants for any funds they accept under revenue sharing.

The revenue-sharing program had expired in September before its revival by this new legislation.

## SECOND OVERRIDE OF VETO

Demonstrating the President's weakening authority, Congress for the second time in three months overrode his veto on Aug. 26. This legislation provided a substantial pay increase for physicians and dentists working in Veterans Administration hospitals to improve health care for veterans. It also included a scholarship program that obligated recipients to work in VA hospitals after becoming doctors or nurses.

President Carter vetoed the measure on Aug. 22, stating that it would not directly help sick and disabled veterans "to give VA physicians currently earning an average of $55,000 a year up to 38% bonuses, making them by far the highest paid medical personnel in the entire government."

Only five congressmen supported the President on Aug. 26 as the House voted to override the veto 401 to 5, and the Senate followed with a unanimous vote of 85 to 0.

## TRUCKING DEREGULATION

President Carter on July 1 approved the Motor Carrier Act of 1980 that reduced federal regulation of the trucking industry. The legislation was cleared by Congress when the Senate accepted by voice vote on June 20 the measure that earlier had won overwhelming House approval.

The act gave truckers greater flexibility in setting prices and antitrust immunity from collective rate-making. It also ordered the Interstate Commerce Commission (ICC) to end many of its regulations.

In signing the legislation, President Carter said it would "eliminate the red tape and the senseless overregulation that have hampered the free growth and the development of the American trucking industry." He declared, "It will be highly anti-inflationary in effect, reducing consumer costs by as much as $8 billion a year, by ending wasteful practices and enhancing the essence of inflation."

## YOUTH EMPLOYMENT MEASURE KILLED

President Carter's main domestic social legislation introduced in 1980 proposed a new program to provide jobs and training for unemployed youth. Budget experts in Congress estimated the measure would cost about $3 billion annually. The House passed the legislation on Aug. 26 by a lopsided vote of 337 to 51. However, the Senate Labor and Human Resources Committee delayed action, reporting it out on Sept. 25, too late for Senate consideration before the election recess.

In the wake of the Democratic defeat in November, the Senate leadership decided not to bring the legislation up for debate during the lame-duck session.

# UNITED STATES SENATE IN 1981

Republicans control the U.S. Senate in the 97th Congress, with 53 members to the Democrats' 47.

The U.S. Senate with 100 members is the smaller but the more influential of the two houses of Congress.

The Senate's presiding officer is Vice President Bush.

Senate officers chosen for the 97th Congress include:

President Pro Tempore Strom Thurmond (R-S.C.), Republican Floor Leader Howard H. Baker (R-Tenn.), Democratic Floor Leader Robert C. Byrd (D-W. Va.), Republican Whip Ted Stevens (R-Alaska), and Democratic Whip Alan Cranston (D-Calif.)

Thurmond is the senior Republican senator, having served since Nov. 7, 1956.

The senior Democratic senator is John D. Stennis of Mississippi, who has served since Nov. 5, 1947.

U.S. senators are elected for terms of 6 years. A senator must be at least 30 years of age, a citizen for 9 years, and a resident of the state he represents.

Senators' salaries were raised to $60,700 on Oct. 12, 1979. Salaries of the president pro tem and majority and minority leaders were raised to $68,600.

In addition each senator receives free office space, staff salaries, travel expenses, and other allowances averaging $400,000 or more annually.

Dates in the table show when each senator took office. An asterisk (*) indicates a freshman (first-term) senator.

| State | Senators | State | Senators |
|---|---|---|---|
| Alabama | *Howell Heflin (D), Jan. 3, 1979<br>*Jeremiah Denton (R), Jan. 5, 1981 | Montana | *John Melcher (D), Jan. 3, 1977<br>*Max Baucus (D), Dec. 12, 1978 |
| Alaska | Theodore F. Stevens (R), Dec. 24, 1968<br>*Frank H. Murkowski (R), Jan. 5, 1981 | Nebraska | *Edward Zorinsky (D), Dec. 28, 1976<br>*J. J. Exon (D), Jan. 3, 1979 |
| Arizona | Barry Goldwater (R), Jan. 3, 1969<br>*Dennis DeConcini (D), Jan. 3, 1977 | Nevada | Howard W. Cannon (D), Jan. 3, 1959<br>Paul Laxalt (R), Dec. 18, 1974 |
| Arkansas | Dale Bumpers (D), Jan. 3, 1975<br>*David Pryor (D), Jan. 3, 1979 | New Hampshire | *Warren Rudman (R), Jan. 5, 1981<br>*Gordon Humphrey (R), Jan. 3, 1979 |
| California | Alan Cranston (D), Jan. 3, 1969<br>*S. I. Hayakawa (R), Jan. 2, 1977 | New Jersey | Harrison A. Williams Jr. (D), Jan. 3, 1959<br>*Bill Bradley (D), Jan. 3, 1979 |
| Colorado | Gary Hart (D), Jan. 3, 1975<br>*William L. Armstrong (R), Jan. 3, 1979 | New Mexico | Pete V. Domenici (R), Jan. 3, 1973<br>*Harrison H. Schmitt (R), Jan. 3, 1977 |
| Connecticut | *Christopher J. Dodd (D), Jan. 5, 1981<br>Lowell P. Weicker Jr. (R), Jan. 3, 1971 | New York | *Alfonse M. D'Amato (R), Jan. 5, 1981<br>*Daniel P. Moynihan (D), Jan. 3, 1977 |
| Delaware | William V. Roth Jr. (R), Jan. 1, 1971<br>Joseph R. Biden Jr. (D), Jan. 3, 1973 | North Carolina | Jesse A. Helms (R), Jan. 3, 1973<br>*John P. East (R), Jan. 5, 1981 |
| Florida | Lawton Chiles (D), Jan. 3, 1971<br>*Paula Hawkins (R), Jan. 5, 1981 | North Dakota | *Mark Andrews (R), Jan. 5, 1981<br>Quentin N. Burdick (D), Aug. 8, 1960 |
| Georgia | *Jack Mattingly (R), Jan. 5, 1981<br>Sam Nunn (D), Nov. 8, 1972 | Ohio | John H. Glenn (D), Dec. 24, 1974<br>*Howard M. Metzenbaum (D), Dec. 29, 1976 |
| Hawaii | Daniel K. Inouye (D), Jan. 3, 1963<br>*Spark M. Matsunaga (D), Jan. 3, 1977 | Oklahoma | *Don Nickles (R), Jan. 5, 1981<br>*David L. Boren (D), Jan. 3, 1979 |
| Idaho | *Steven D. Symms (R), Jan. 5, 1981<br>James A. McClure (R), Jan. 3, 1973 | Oregon | Mark O. Hatfield (R), Jan. 10, 1967<br>Robert W. Packwood (R), Jan. 3, 1969 |
| Illinois | Charles H. Percy (R), Jan. 3, 1967<br>*Alan J. Dixon (D), Jan. 5, 1981 | Pennsylvania | *Arlen Specter (R), Jan. 5, 1981<br>*H. John Heinz III (R), Jan. 3, 1977 |
| Indiana | *Dan Quayle (R), Jan. 5, 1981<br>*Richard G. Lugar (R), Jan. 3, 1977 | Rhode Island | Claiborne Pell (D), Jan. 3, 1961<br>*John H. Chafee (R), Dec. 29, 1976 |
| Iowa | *Charles E. Grassley (R), Jan. 5, 1981<br>*Roger Jepson (R), Jan. 3, 1979 | South Carolina | Strom Thurmond (R), Nov. 7, 1956<br>Ernest F. Hollings (D), Nov. 9, 1966 |
| Kansas | Robert Dole (R), Jan. 3, 1969<br>*Nancy L. Kassebaum (R), Dec. 23, 1978 | South Dakota | *James Abdnor (R), Jan. 5, 1981<br>*Larry Pressler (R), Jan. 3, 1979 |
| Kentucky | Walter (Dee) Huddleston (D), Jan. 3, 1973<br>Wendell H. Ford (D), Dec. 28, 1974 | Tennessee | Howard H. Baker Jr. (R), Jan. 3, 1967<br>*James R. Sasser (D), Jan. 3, 1977 |
| Louisiana | Russell B. Long (D), Dec. 31, 1948<br>J. Bennett Johnston Jr. (D), Nov. 14, 1972 | Texas | John G. Tower (R), June 15, 1961<br>Lloyd M. Bentsen Jr. (D), Jan. 3, 1971 |
| Maine | *George J. Mitchell (D), May 15, 1980<br>*William S. Cohen (R), Jan. 3, 1979 | Utah | Jake Garn (R), Dec. 21, 1974<br>*Orrin G. Hatch (R), Jan. 3, 1977 |
| Maryland | Charles McC. Mathias Jr. (R), Jan. 3, 1969<br>*Paul S. Sarbanes (D), Jan. 3, 1977 | Vermont | Robert T. Stafford (R), Sept. 16, 1971<br>Patrick J. Leahy (D), Jan. 3, 1975 |
| Massachusetts | Edward M. Kennedy (D), Nov. 7, 1962<br>*Paul E. Tsongas (D), Jan. 3, 1979 | Virginia | Harry F. Byrd Jr. (I-D), Nov. 12, 1965<br>*John W. Warner (R), Jan. 2, 1979 |
| Michigan | *Donald W. Riegle Jr. (D), Dec. 30, 1976<br>*Carl Levin (D), Jan. 3, 1979 | Washington | *Slade Gorton (R), Jan. 5, 1981<br>Henry M. Jackson (D), Jan. 3, 1953 |
| Minnesota | *David Durenberger (R), Nov. 8, 1978<br>*Rudy Boschwitz (R), Dec. 30, 1978 | West Virginia | Jennings Randolph (D), Nov. 5, 1958<br>Robert C. Byrd (D), Jan. 3, 1959 |
| Mississippi | John Stennis (D), Nov. 5, 1947<br>*Thad Cochran (R), Dec. 27, 1978 | Wisconsin | William Proxmire (D), Aug. 28, 1957<br>*Robert W. Kasten Jr. (R), Jan. 5, 1981 |
| Missouri | Thomas F. Eagleton (D), Dec. 28, 1968<br>*John C. Danforth (R), Dec. 27, 1976 | Wyoming | *Malcolm Wallop (R), Jan. 3, 1977<br>*Alan K. Simpson (R), Jan. 1, 1979 |

# U.S. HOUSE OF REPRESENTATIVES IN 1981

Democrats control the U.S. House of Representatives in the 97th Congress, with 243 votes to the Republicans' 192.

The chief officers of the House in the 97th Congress include: Speaker of the House Thomas P. O'Neill Jr. (D-Mass.), Democratic Floor Leader Jim Wright (D-Texas), Republican Floor Leader Robert H. Michel (R-Ill.), Democratic Whip Thomas S. Foley (D-Wash.), and Republican Whip Trent Lott (R-Miss.).

The senior Democrat is Jamie L. Whitten of Mississippi, who has served since Nov. 4, 1941. The senior Republican is John J. Rhodes of Arizona, who has served since Jan. 3, 1953.

The larger house of Congress (435 members) represents the people more directly than the Senate. Three powers are delegated exclusively to the House: (1) it originates all bills for raising revenue, (2) it elects the President if there is no electoral majority, and (3) it impeaches federal officials.

A representative must be at least 25 years of age, a citizen of the U.S. for 7 years, and a resident of the state he represents.

The salaries of representatives were raised 5.5%, to $60,700, on Oct. 12, 1979. At the same time the majority and minority leaders were raised to $68,600.

In addition each representative receives other allowances.

An asterisk (*) in the table below indicates a freshman member (one serving his first term in the House).

Congressional districts within a state are indicated by numerals. A representative-at-large is shown as AL.

**ALABAMA**
1. Jack Edwards (R)
2. William L. Dickinson (R)
3. William Nichols (D)
4. Tom Bevill (D)
5. Ronnie G. Flippo (D)
6. Albert Lee Smith Jr. (R)*
7. Richard C. Shelby (D)

**ALASKA**
AL Donald E. Young (R)

**ARIZONA**
1. John J. Rhodes (R)
2. Morris K. Udall (D)
3. Bob Stump (D)
4. Eldon D. Rudd (R)

**ARKANSAS**
1. Bill Alexander Jr. (D)
2. Ed Bethune (R)
3. John Hammerschmidt (R)
4. Beryl Anthony (D)

**CALIFORNIA**
1. Eugene A. Chappie (R)*
2. Don H. Clausen (R)
3. Robert T. Matsui (D)
4. Vic Fazio (D)
5. John L. Burton (D)
6. Phillip Burton (D)
7. George Miller III (D)
8. Ronald V. Dellums (D)
9. Fortney H. Stark (D)
10. Don Edwards (D)
11. Tom Lantos (D)*
12. Paul N. McCloskey Jr. (R)
13. Norman Y. Mineta (D)
14. Norman D. Shumway (R)
15. Tom Coelho (D)
16. Leon E. Panetta (D)
17. Charles Pashayan Jr. (R)
18. William Thomas (R)
19. R. S. Lagomarsino (R)
20. Barry Goldwater Jr. (R)
21. Bobbi Fiedler (R)*
22. Carlos J. Moorhead (R)
23. Anthony Beilenson (D)
24. Henry A. Waxman (D)
25. Edward R. Roybal (D)
26. John H. Rousselot (R)
27. Robert K. Dornan (R)
28. Julian C. Dixon (D)
29. Augustus F. Hawkins (D)
30. George E. Danielson (D)
31. Mervyn M. Dymally (D)*
32. Glenn M. Anderson (D)
33. Wayne Grisham (R)
34. Dan Lungren (R)*
35. David Dreier (R)*
36. George E. Brown Jr. (D)
37. Jerry Lewis (R)
38. Jerry M. Patterson (D)
39. William Dannemeyer (R)
40. Robert E. Badham (R)
41. Bill Lowery (R)*
42. Duncan L. Hunter (R)*
43. Clair W. Burgener (R)

**COLORADO**
1. Patricia Schroeder (D)
2. Timothy E. Wirth (D)
3. Ray Kogovsek (D)
4. Hank Brown (R)*
5. Ken Kramer (R)

**CONNECTICUT**
1. William R. Cotter (D)
2. Samuel Gejdenson (D)*
3. Lawrence J. DeNardis (R)*
4. Stewart B. McKinney (R)
5. William Ratchford (D)
6. Toby Moffett (D)

**DELAWARE**
AL Thomas B. Evans Jr. (R)

**FLORIDA**
1. Earl Hutto (D)
2. Don Fuqua (D)
3. Charles E. Bennett (D)
4. Bill Chappell Jr. (D)
5. Bill McCollum (R)*
6. C. W. Bill Young (R)
7. Sam Gibbons (D)
8. Andrew P. Ireland (D)
9. Bill Nelson (D)
10. L. A. (Skip) Bafalis (R)
11. Don Mica (D)
12. Clay Shaw (R)*
13. William Lehman (D)
14. Claude Pepper (D)
15. Dante B. Fascell (D)

**GEORGIA**
1. Ronald B. (Bo) Ginn (D)
2. Charles F. Hatcher (D)*

3. Jack T. Brinkley (D)
4. Elliott H. Levitas (D)
5. Wyche Fowler Jr. (D)
6. Newt Gingrich (R)
7. Larry P. McDonald (D)
8. Billy Lee Evans (D)
9. Ed Jenkins (D)
10. Doug Barnard (D)

**HAWAII**
1. Cecil Heftel (D)
2. Daniel Akaka (D)

**IDAHO**
1. Larry Craig (R)*
2. George V. Hansen (R)

**ILLINOIS**
1. Harold Washington (D)*
2. Gus Savage (D)*
3. Martin A. Russo (D)
4. Edward J. Derwinski (R)
5. John G. Fary (D)
6. Henry J. Hyde (R)
7. Cardiss R. Collins (D)
8. Dan Rostenkowski (D)
9. Sidney R. Yates (D)
10. John E. Porter (R)
11. Frank Annunzio (D)
12. Philip M. Crane (R)
13. Robert McClory (R)
14. John N. Erlenborn (R)
15. Tom Corcoran (R)
16. Lynn M. Martin (R)*
17. George M. O'Brien (R)
18. Robert H. Michel (R)
19. Thomas Railsback (R)
20. Paul Findley (R)
21. Edward R. Madigan (R)
22. Daniel B. Crane (R)
23. Melvin Price (D)
24. Paul Simon (D)

**INDIANA**
1. Adam Benjamin Jr. (D)
2. Floyd D. Fithian (D)
3. John P. Hiler (R)*
4. Daniel R. Coats (R)*
5. Elwood H. Hillis (R)
6. David W. Evans (D)
7. John T. Myers (R)
8. H. Joel Deckard (R)
9. Lee H. Hamilton (D)

10. Philip R. Sharp (D)
11. Andrew Jacobs Jr. (D)

**IOWA**
1. James A.S. Leach (R)
2. Tom Tauke (R)
3. Cooper Evans (R)*
4. Neal Smith (D)
5. Tom Harkin (D)
6. Berkley Bedell (D)

**KANSAS**
1. Pat Roberts (R)*
2. Jim Jeffries (R)
3. Larry Winn Jr. (R)
4. Dan Glickman (D)
5. Robert Whittaker (R)

**KENTUCKY**
1. Carroll Hubbard Jr. (D)
2. William H. Natcher (D)
3. Romano L. Mazzoli (D)
4. M. G. (Gene) Snyder (R)
5. Harold Rogers (R)*
6. Larry J. Hopkins (R)
7. Carl D. Perkins (D)

**LOUISIANA**
1. Robert L. Livingston Jr. (R)
2. Lindy Boggs (D)
3. W.J. (Billy) Tauzin (D)
4. Buddy Roemer (D)*
5. Jerry Huckaby (D)
6. W. Henson Moore III (R)
7. John B. Breaux (D)
8. Gillis W. Long (D)

**MAINE**
1. David F. Emery (R)
2. Olympia Snowe (R)

**MARYLAND**
1. Roy Dyson (D)*
2. Clarence D. Long (D)
3. Barbara A. Mikulski (D)
4. Marjorie S. Holt (R)
5. Gladys N. Spellman (D)
6. Beverly Byron (D)
7. Parren J. Mitchell (D)
8. Michael Barnes (D)

**MASSACHUSETTS**
1. Silvio O. Conte (R)
2. Edward P. Boland (D)
3. Joseph D. Early (D)

4.• Barney Frank (D)*
5. James Shannon (D)
6. Nicholas Mavroules (D)
7. Edward J. Markey (D)*
8. Thomas P. O'Neill Jr. (D)
9. John (Joe) Moakley (D)
10. Margaret M. Heckler (R)
11. Brian J. Donnelly (D)
12. Gerry E. Studds (D)

**MICHIGAN**
1. John Conyers Jr. (D)
2. Carl D. Pursell (R)
3. Harry Wolpe (D)
4. David A. Stockman (R)
5. Harold S. Sawyer (R)
6. Jim Dunn (R)*
7. Dale E. Kildee (D)
8. Bob Traxler (D)
9. Guy A. Vander Jagt (R)
10. Don Albosta (D)
11. Robert W. Davis (R)
12. David E. Bonior (D)
13. G. W. Crockett Jr. (D)*
14. Dennis M. Hertel (D)*
15. William D. Ford (D)
16. John D. Dingell (D)
17. William M. Brodhead (D)
18. James J. Blanchard (D)
19. William S. Broomfield (R)

**MINNESOTA**
1. Arlen Erdahl (R)
2. Tom Hagedorn (R)
3. Bill Frenzel (R)
4. Bruce F. Vento (D)
5. Martin O. Sabo (D)
6. Vin Weber (R)*
7. Arlan Strangeland (R)
8. James L. Oberstar (D)

**MISSISSIPPI**
1. Jamie L. Whitten (D)
2. David R. Bowen (D)
3. G. V. Montgomery (D)
4. Jon C. Hinson (R)
5. Trent Lott (R)

**MISSOURI**
1. William L. Clay (D)
2. Robert A. Young (D)
3. Richard A. Gephardt (D)
4. Ike Skelton (D)
5. Richard Bolling (D)
6. E. Thomas Coleman (R)
7. Gene Taylor (R)
8. Wendell Bailey (R)*
9. Harold L. Volkmer (D)
10. Bill Emerson (R)*

**MONTANA**
1. Pat Williams (D)
2. Ron Marlenee (R)

**NEBRASKA**
1. Douglas K. Bereuter (R)
2. Hal Daub (R)*
3. Virginia Smith (R)

**NEVADA**
AL James Santini (D)

**NEW HAMPSHIRE**
1. Norman C. D'Amours (D)
2. Judd Gregg (R)*

**NEW JERSEY**
1. James J. Florio (D)
2. William J. Hughes (D)
3. James J. Howard (D)
4. Christopher H. Smith (R)*
5. Millicent Fenwick (R)

6. Edwin B. Forsythe (R)
7. Marge Roukema (R)*
8. Robert A. Roe (D)
9. Harold C. Hollenbeck (R)
10. Peter W. Rodino Jr. (D)
11. Joseph G. Minish (D)
12. Matthew J. Rinaldo (R)
13. Jim Courter (R)
14. Frank J. Guarini (D)
15. Bernard J. Dwyer (D)*

**NEW MEXICO**
1. Manuel Lujan Jr. (R)
2. Joe Skeen (R)*

**NEW YORK**
1. William Carney (R)
2. Thomas J. Downey (D)
3. Gregory W. Carman (R)*
4. Norman F. Lent (R)
5. Raymond J. McGrath (R)*
6. John LeBoutillier (R)*
7. Joseph P. Addabbo (D)
8. B. S. Rosenthal (D)
9. Geraldine Ferraro (D)
10. Mario Biaggi (D)
11. James H. Scheuer (D)
12. Shirley A. Chisholm (D)
13. Stephen J. Solarz (D)
14. F. W. Richmond (D)
15. Leo C. Zeferetti (D)
16. Charles E. Schumer (D)*
17. Guy V. Molinari (R)*
18. S. William Green (R)
19. Charles B. Rangel (D)
20. Theodore S. Weiss (D)
21. Robert Garcia (D)
22. J. B. Bingham (D)
23. Peter A. Peyser (D)
24. Richard L. Ottinger (D)
25. Hamilton Fish Jr. (R)
26. Benjamin A. Gilman (R)
27. Matthew F. McHugh (D)
28. Samuel S. Stratton (D)
29. Gerald Solomon (R)
30. David O'B. Martin (R)*
31. Donald J. Mitchell (R)
32. George Wortley (R)
33. Gary A. Lee (R)
34. Frank Horton (R)
35. Barber B. Conable Jr. (R)
36. John J. LaFalce (D)
37. Henry J. Nowak (D)
38. Jack F. Kemp (R)
39. Stanley N. Lundine (D)

**NORTH CAROLINA**
1. Walter B. Jones (D)
2. L. H. Fountain (D)
3. Charles Whitley (D)
4. Ike F. Andrews (D)
5. Stephen L. Neal (D)
6. Eugene Johnston (R)*
7. Charles G. Rose III (D)
8. W. G. (Bill) Hefner (D)
9. James G. Martin (R)
10. James T. Broyhill (R)
11. William M. Hendon (R)*

**NORTH DAKOTA**
AL Byron L. Dorgan (D)*

**OHIO**
1. Bill Gradison (R)
2. Thomas A. Luken (D)
3. Tony P. Hall (D)
4. Tennyson Guyer (R)
5. Delbert L. Latta (R)

6. Bob McEwen (R)*
7. Clarence J. Brown (R)
8. Thomas N. Kindness (R)
9. Ed Weber (R)*
10. Clarence E. Miller (R)
11. J. William Stanton (R)
12. R. N. Shamansky (D)*
13. Donald J. Pease (D)
14. John F. Seiberling Jr. (D)
15. Chalmers P. Wylie (R)
16. Ralph S. Regula (R)
17. John M. Ashbrook (R)
18. Douglas Applegate (D)
19. Lyle Williams (R)
20. Mary Rose Oakar (D)*
21. Louis Stokes (D)
22. Dennis E. Eckart (D)*
23. Ronald M. Mottl (D)

**OKLAHOMA**
1. James R. Jones (D)
2. Mike Synar (D)
3. Wes Watkins (D)
4. Dave McCurdy (D)*
5. Mickey Edwards (R)
6. Glenn English (D)

**OREGON**
1. Les AuCoin (D)
2. Denny Smith (R)*
3. Ron Wyden (D)
4. James Weaver (D)

**PENNSYLVANIA**
1. Thomas F. Foglietta (I)*
2. William H. Gray III (D)
3. Raymond F. Lederer (D)
4. Charles Dougherty (R)
5. Richard T. Schulze (R)
6. Gus Yatron (D)
7. Robert W. Edgar (D)
8. James K. Coyne (R)*
9. E. G. (Bud) Shuster (R)
10. Joseph M. McDade (R)
11. James L. Nelligan (R)*
12. John P. Murtha (D)
13. R. L. Coughlin (R)
14. William J. Coyne (D)*
15. Donald L. Ritter (R)
16. Robert S. Walker (R)
17. Allen E. Ertel (D)
18. Doug Walgren (D)
19. William F. Goodling (R)
20. Joseph M. Gaydos (D)
21. Don Bailey (D)
22. Austin J. Murphy (D)
23. William Clinger Jr. (R)
24. Marc L. Marks (R)
25. Eugene Atkinson (D)

**RHODE ISLAND**
1. F. J. St. Germain (D)
2. Claudine Schneider (R)*

**SOUTH CAROLINA**
1. Thomas F. Hartnett (R)*
2. Floyd D. Spence (R)
3. Butler D. Derrick Jr. (D)
4. Carroll Campbell (R)
5. Kenneth L. Holland (D)
6. John L. Napier (R)*

**SOUTH DAKOTA**
1. Tom Daschle (D)
2. Clint Roberts (R)*

**TENNESSEE**
1. James H. Quillen (R)
2. John J. Duncan (R)

3. Marilyn Bouquard (D)
4. Albert Gore Jr. (D)
5. Bill Boner (D)
6. Robin L. Beard Jr. (R)
7. Ed Jones (D)
8. Harold F. Ford (D)

**TEXAS**
1. Sam B. Hall Jr. (D)
2. Charles Wilson (D)
3. James M. Collins (R)
4. Ralph M. Hall (D)*
5. Jim Mattox (D)
6. Phil Gramm (D)
7. Bill Archer (R)
8. Jack Fields (R)*
9. Jack Brooks (D)
10. J. J. Pickle (D)
11. J. Marvin Leath (D)
12. James C. Wright Jr. (D)
13. John Hightower (D)
14. William N. Patman (D)*
15. Eligio de la Garza (D)
16. Richard C. White (D)
17. Charles Stenholm (D)
18. Mickey Leland (D)
19. Kent Hance (D)
20. Henry B. Gonzalez (D)
21. Tom Loeffler (R)
22. Ron Paul (R)
23. Abraham Kazen Jr. (D)
24. Martin Frost (D)

**UTAH**
1. James V. Hanson (R)*
2. Dan Marriott (R)

**VERMONT**
AL James M. Jeffords (R)

**VIRGINIA**
1. Paul S. Trible Jr. (R)
2. G. William Whitehurst (R)
3. Thomas J. Bliley Jr. (R)*
4. Robert W. Daniel Jr. (R)
5. W. C. (Dan) Daniel (D)
6. M. Caldwell Butler (R)
7. J. Kenneth Robinson (R)
8. Stanford E. Parris (R)*
9. William C. Wampler (R)
10. Frank R. Wolf (R)*

**WASHINGTON**
1. Joel Pritchard (R)
2. Al Swift (D)
3. Don Bonker (D)
4. Sid Morrison (R)*
5. Thomas S. Foley (D)
6. Norman D. Dicks (D)
7. Mike Lowry (D)

**WEST VIRGINIA**
1. Robert H. Mollohan (D)
2. Cleve Benedict (R)*
3. Mick Staton (R)
4. Nick Joe Rahall (D)

**WISCONSIN**
1. Les Aspin (D)
2. Robert W. Kastenmeier (D)
3. Steve Gunderson (R)*
4. Clement J. Zablocki (D)
5. Henry S. Reuss (D)
6. Thomas E. Petri (R)
7. David R. Obey (D)
8. Tobias A. Roth (R)
9. F. J. Sensenbrenner Jr. (R)

**WYOMING**
AL Richard Cheney (R)

# COMMITTEES OF CONGRESS

The fate of legislation introduced in Congress depends to a large extent on what happens to it in House or Senate committees. Before a bill goes back to either house for a vote, the committee can revise it, change it beyond recognition, or simply bottle it up.

Committee chairmen, who achieve their positions largely through seniority, have considerable influence in determining which measures will or will not become law. They also can use pressure to get their favorite bills passed.

A committee's importance is determined by the kind of legislation it handles. The House Ways and Means Committee and the Senate Finance Committee are responsible for all tax, tariff, and Social Security legislation. The House Rules Committee decides which bills will go to the floor of the House. The House and Senate Appropriations Committees consider appropriation measures, and the House and Senate Budget Committees establish the federal budget for each fiscal year.

Listed below are the permanent committees, and their expected chairmen, and members by party (D-Democrat; R-Republican) during the first session of the 97th Congress in 1981.

| COMMITTEE, CHAIRMAN, AND MEMBERSHIP | JURISDICTION | COMMITTEE, CHAIRMAN, AND MEMBERSHIP |
|---|---|---|
| **SENATE** | | **HOUSE** |
| **Agriculture, Nutrition, and Forestry** Jesse A. Helms (R-N.C.) R-9, D-8 | All matters dealing with agriculture, including farm credit and security, crop insurance, soil conservation, and rural electrification; and (Senate only) forestry; human nutrition, including school nutrition programs | **Agriculture** Thomas S. Foley (D-Wash.) R-27, R-15 |
| **Appropriations** Mark O. Hatfield (R-Oreg.) R-15, D-14 | All matters pertaining to the appropriations of government revenues | **Appropriations** Jamie L. Whitten (D-Miss.) D-36, R-18 |
| **Armed Services** John G. Tower (R-Texas) R-9, D-8 | Military affairs, including aeronautical and space activities concerned with weapons systems; and (Senate only) Panama Canal and Canal Zone | **Armed Services** Melvin Price (D-Ill.) D-28, R-15 |
| **Banking, Housing, and Urban Affairs** Jake Garn (R-Utah) R-8, D-7 | All financial matters other than taxes and appropriations, particulary those concerned with banking and currency, including public and private housing matters; urban affairs | **Banking, Finance, and Urban Affairs** Ferdinand J. St. Germain (D-R.I.) D-27, R-15 |
| **Budget** Pete V. Domenici (R-N.M.) R-12, D-10 | Reviews presidential budget proposals; considers advice of congressional budget office and other committees regarding federal expenditures | **Budget** James R. Jones (D-Okla.) D-17, R-8 |
| **Commerce, Science, and Transportation** Robert W. Packwood (R-Oreg.) R-9, D-8 | Interstate transportation and communications, inland waterways, civil aeronautics; (Senate only) science; weather; (House only) foreign commerce, railroad labor, securities and exchanges, interstate oil compacts, natural gas and public health, regulation of interstate transmission of power (except between government projects) Merchant Marine, Coast Guard, Coast and Geodetic Survey, fisheries and wildlife Maintenance and operation of Panama Canal and administration of Canal Zone | **Interstate and Foreign Commerce** John D. Dingell (D-Mich.) D-27, R-15 **Merchant Marine and Fisheries** Walter B. Jones (D-N.C.) D-25, R-14 |
| **Energy and Natural Resources** James A. McClure (R-Idaho) R-11, D-9 | Energy regulation, conservation; research and development; solar energy; oil and gas; hydroelectric power; coal; naval petroleum; mining; public parks; recreation areas; public lands | **Interior and Insular Affairs** Morris K. Udall (D-Ariz.) D-26, R-14 |
| **Environment and Public Works** Robert T. Stafford (R-Vt.) R-9, D-7 | Environment in general; environmental research; fisheries and wildlife; ocean dumping; solid waste disposal; pollution; public works; dams and bridges; federal buildings | (In House split among several committees) |

| SENATE COMMITTEE, CHAIRMAN, AND MEMBERSHIP | JURISDICTION | HOUSE COMMITTEE, CHAIRMAN, AND MEMBERSHIP |
|---|---|---|
| **Select Ethics** <br> Malcolm Wallop (R-Wyo.) <br> R-3, D-3 | Standards and conduct of members and employees; recommends remedies for unethical conduct | **Standards of Official Conduct** <br> Charles E. Bennett (D-Fla.) <br> D-6, R-6 |
| **Finance** <br> Robert Dole (R-Kan.) <br> R-11, D-9 | All matters pertaining to taxes, tariffs, import quotas, social security, and social welfare | **Ways and Means** <br> Dan Rostenkowski (D-Ill.) <br> D-24, R-12 |
| **Foreign Relations** <br> Charles H. Percy (R-Ill.) <br> R-9, D-8 | Relations of the United States with foreign nations and international organizations, including the Red Cross, diplomatic service, United Nations, foreign loans, and (Senate only) treaties | **Foreign Affairs** <br> Clement J. Zablocki (D-Wis.) <br> D-22, R-12 |
| **Governmental Affairs** <br> William V. Roth Jr. (R-Del.) <br> R-9, D-8 | Reorganization of the Executive Branch, and governmental relationships between federal, state, and local governments; civil service; **and (Senate only) between U.S. and international organizations; District of Columbia** | **Government Operations** <br> Jack Brooks (D-Texas) <br> D-25, R-14 |
| **Judiciary** <br> Strom Thurmond (R-S.C.) <br> R-10, D-8 | Federal courts and judges, civil rights, civil liberties, constitutional amendments, interstate compacts, immigration and naturalization, apportionment of representatives, meetings of Congress, and members' attendance; **(Senate only)** claims against the United States; **(House only)** presidential succession and impeachment | **Judiciary** <br> Peter W. Rodino Jr. (D-N.J.) <br> D-20, R-11 |
| **Labor and Human Resources** <br> Orrin G. Hatch (R-Utah) <br> R-9, D-7 | Health, education, public welfare, labor, arts, child development, migratory labor, handicapped, health research, aging | **Education and Labor** <br> Carl D. Perkins (D-Ky.) <br> D-23, R-13 |
| **Rules and Administration** <br> Charles McC. Mathias Jr. (R-Md.) <br> R-7, D-5 | General administration of the Senate and management of the Library of Congress and the Smithsonian Institution; **(House only)** rules and orders of business of the House | **Rules** <br> Richard Bolling (D-Mo.) <br> D-11, R-5 |
| **Select Indian Affairs** <br> William S. Cohen (R-Me.) <br> R-3, D-2 | All legislation on Indian affairs; Indian problems in education, health, and other areas; Indian claims against the United States | (Indian affairs under House Interior and Insular Affairs Committee) |
| **Select Small Business** <br> Lowell P. Weicker Jr. (R-Conn.) <br> R-9, D-8 | Study and investigation of the problems of small business and of legislation affecting small business | **Small Business** <br> Parren J. Mitchell (D-Md.) <br> D-25, R-14 |
| **Veterans Affairs** <br> Alan K. Simpson (R-Wyo.) <br> R-7, D-5 | Veterans pensions, armed forces life insurance, rehabilitation, education, medical care and treatment of veterans, veterans hospitals | **Veterans Affairs** <br> G.V. Montgomery (D-Miss.) <br> D-21, R-11 |
| (see **Senate Governmental Affairs Committee**) | Operation of all municipal affairs of the District of Columbia except for the appropriation of money for its operation | **District of Columbia** <br> Ronald V. Dellums (D-Calif.) <br> D-9, R-5 |
| — | House administration; printing and correction of the Congressional Record; federal elections; and management of the Library of Congress; supervision of the Smithsonian Institution | **House Administration** <br> Augustus F. Hawkins (D-Calif.) <br> D-16, R-9 |
| — | All matters pertaining to the postal and civil services; the census; the National Archives | **Post Office and Civil Service** <br> William D. Ford (D-Mich.) <br> D-16, R-9 |
| — | Public buildings and roads; flood control, improvement of rivers and harbors; stream pollution; waterpower; and transportation | **Public Works and Transportation** <br> James J. Howard (D-N.J.) <br> D-31, R-17 |
| — | Nonmilitary scientific research, development, and administration of all matters in energy and space and aeronautical activities; National Science Foundation; National Weather Service | **Science and Technology** <br> Don Fuqua (D-Fla.) <br> D-27, R-15 |
| **Select Committee on Aging** <br> John Heinz (R-Pa.) <br> R-7, D-6 | Investigation of problems of aged.; **(Senate only) cannot send legislation to floor** | **Select Aging** <br> Claude Pepper (D-Fla.) <br> D-30, R-15 |
| **Select Intelligence** <br> Barry Goldwater (R-Ariz.) <br> R-8, D-7 | Legislation, and budgets of CIA, FBI, and other intelligence agencies of the federal government | — |

## POLITICAL MAKEUP OF CONGRESS: 1789–1981

| CONGRESS | YEARS | PRESIDENT AND PARTY | HOUSE OF REPRESENTATIVES | | | SENATE | | |
|---|---|---|---|---|---|---|---|---|
| | | | Majority Party | Minority Party | Other | Majority Party | Minority Party | Other |
| 1st | 1789–1791 | G. Washington ..... Fed | Fed-38 | AF-26 | — | Fed-17 | AF-9 | — |
| 2d | 1791–1793 | G. Washington ..... Fed | Fed-37 | DR-33 | — | Fed-16 | DR-13 | — |
| 3d | 1793–1795 | G. Washington ..... Fed | DR-57 | Fed-48 | — | Fed-17 | DR-13 | — |
| 4th | 1795–1797 | G. Washington ..... Fed | Fed-54 | DR-52 | — | Fed-19 | DR-13 | — |
| 5th | 1797–1799 | J. Adams .......... Fed | Fed-58 | DR-48 | — | Fed-20 | DR-12 | — |
| 6th | 1799–1801 | J. Adams .......... Fed | Fed-64 | DR-42 | — | Fed-19 | DR-13 | — |
| 7th | 1801–1803 | T. Jefferson ....... DR | DR-69 | Fed-36 | — | DR-18 | Fed-13 | — |
| 8th | 1803–1805 | T. Jefferson ....... DR | DR-102 | Fed-39 | — | DR-25 | Fed-9 | — |
| 9th | 1805–1807 | T. Jefferson ....... DR | DR-116 | Fed-25 | — | DR-27 | Fed-7 | — |
| 10th | 1807–1809 | T. Jefferson ....... DR | DR-118 | Fed-24 | — | DR-28 | Fed-6 | — |
| 11th | 1809–1811 | J. Madison ......... DR | DR-94 | Fed-48 | — | DR-28 | Fed-6 | — |
| 12th | 1811–1813 | J. Madison ......... DR | DR-108 | Fed-36 | — | DR-30 | Fed-6 | — |
| 13th | 1813–1815 | J. Madison ......... DR | DR-112 | Fed-68 | — | DR-27 | Fed-9 | — |
| 14th | 1815–1817 | J. Madison ......... DR | DR-117 | Fed-65 | — | DR-25 | Fed-11 | — |
| 15th | 1817–1819 | J. Monroe ......... DR | DR-141 | Fed-42 | — | DR-34 | Fed-10 | — |
| 16th | 1819–1821 | J. Monroe ......... DR | DR-156 | Fed-27 | — | DR-35 | Fed-7 | — |
| 17th | 1821–1823 | J. Monroe ......... DR | DR-158 | Fed-25 | — | DR-44 | Fed-4 | — |
| 18th | 1823–1825 | J. Monroe ......... DR | DR-187 | Fed-26 | — | DR-44 | Fed-4 | — |
| 19th | 1825–1827 | J. Q. Adams ....... Co | Co-105 | Ja-97 | — | Co-26 | Ja-20 | — |
| 20th | 1827–1829 | J. Q. Adams ....... Co | Ja-119 | Co-94 | — | Ja-28 | Co-20 | — |
| 21st | 1829–1831 | A. Jackson ......... D | D-139 | NR-74 | — | D-26 | NR-22 | — |
| 22d | 1831–1833 | A. Jackson ......... D | D-141 | NR-58 | 14 | D-25 | NR-21 | 2 |
| 23d | 1833–1835 | A. Jackson ......... D | D-147 | AM-53 | 60 | D-20 | NR-20 | 8 |
| 24th | 1835–1837 | A. Jackson ......... D | D-145 | W-98 | — | D-27 | W-25 | — |
| 25th | 1837–1839 | M. Van Buren ...... D | D-108 | W-107 | 24 | D-30 | W-18 | 4 |
| 26th | 1839–1841 | M. Van Buren ...... D | D-124 | W-118 | — | D-28 | W-22 | — |
| 27th | 1841–1843 | W. H. Harrison ..... W / J. Tyler ........... W | W-133 | D-102 | 6 | W-28 | D-22 | 2 |
| 28th | 1843–1845 | J. Tyler ........... W | D-142 | W-79 | 1 | W-28 | D-25 | 1 |
| 29th | 1845–1847 | J. K. Polk ......... D | D-143 | W-77 | 6 | D-31 | W-25 | — |
| 30th | 1847–1849 | J. K. Polk ......... D | W-115 | D-108 | 4 | D-36 | W-21 | 1 |
| 31st | 1849–1851 | Z. Taylor .......... W / M. Fillmore ....... W | D-112 | W-109 | 9 | D-35 | W-25 | 2 |
| 32d | 1851–1853 | M. Fillmore ........ W | D-140 | W-88 | 5 | D-35 | W-24 | 3 |
| 33d | 1853–1855 | F. Pierce ......... D | D-159 | W-71 | 4 | D-38 | W-22 | 2 |
| 34th | 1855–1857 | F. Pierce ......... D | R-108 | D-83 | 43 | D-40 | R-15 | 7 |
| 35th | 1857–1859 | J. Buchanan ...... D | D-118 | R-92 | 26 | D-36 | R-20 | 8 |
| 36th | 1859–1861 | J. Buchanan ...... D | R-114 | D-92 | 31 | D-36 | R-26 | 4 |
| 37th | 1861–1863 | A. Lincoln ........ R | R-105 | D-43 | 30 | R-31 | D-10 | 8 |
| 38th | 1863–1865 | A. Lincoln ........ R | R-102 | D-75 | 9 | R-36 | D-9 | 5 |
| 39th | 1865–1867 | A. Lincoln ........ U / A. Johnson ........ U | U-149 | D-42 | — | U-42 | D-10 | — |
| 40th | 1867–1869 | A. Johnson ........ U | R-143 | D-49 | — | R-42 | D-11 | — |
| 41st | 1869–1871 | U. S. Grant ....... R | R-149 | D-63 | — | R-56 | D-11 | — |
| 42d | 1871–1873 | U. S. Grant ....... R | R-134 | D-104 | 5 | R-52 | D-17 | 5 |
| 43d | 1873–1875 | U. S. Grant ....... R | R-194 | D-92 | 14 | R-49 | D-19 | 5 |
| 44th | 1875–1877 | U. S. Grant ....... R | D-169 | R-109 | 14 | R-45 | D-29 | 2 |
| 45th | 1877–1879 | R. B. Hayes ....... R | D-153 | R-140 | — | R-39 | D-36 | 1 |
| 46th | 1879–1881 | R. B. Hayes ....... R | D-149 | R-130 | 14 | D-42 | R-33 | 1 |
| 47th | 1881–1883 | J. A. Garfield ....... R / C. A. Arthur ...... R | R-147 | D-135 | 11 | R-37 | D-37 | 1 |
| 48th | 1883–1885 | C. A. Arthur ...... R | D-197 | R-118 | 10 | R-38 | D-36 | 2 |
| 49th | 1885–1887 | G. Cleveland ...... D | D-183 | R-140 | 2 | R-43 | D-34 | — |
| 50th | 1887–1889 | G. Cleveland ...... D | D-169 | R-152 | 4 | R-39 | D-37 | — |

| CONGRESS | YEARS | PRESIDENT AND PARTY | HOUSE OF REPRESENTATIVES | | | SENATE | | |
|---|---|---|---|---|---|---|---|---|
| | | | Majority Party | Minority Party | Other | Majority Party | Minority Party | Other |
| 51st | 1889–1891 | B. Harrison ........R | R-166 | D-159 | — | R-39 | D-37 | — |
| 52d | 1891–1893 | B. Harrison ........R | D-235 | R-88 | 9 | R-47 | D-39 | 2 |
| 53d | 1893–1895 | G. Cleveland ........D | D-218 | R-127 | 11 | D-44 | R-38 | 3 |
| 54th | 1895–1897 | G. Cleveland ........D | R-244 | D-105 | 7 | R-43 | D-39 | 6 |
| 55th | 1897–1899 | W. McKinley ........R | R-204 | D-113 | 40 | R-47 | D-34 | 7 |
| 56th | 1899–1901 | W. McKinley ........R | R-185 | D-163 | 9 | R-53 | D-26 | 8 |
| 57th | 1901–1903 | W. McKinley ........R / T. Roosevelt ........R | R-197 | D-151 | 9 | R-55 | D-31 | 4 |
| 58th | 1903–1905 | T. Roosevelt ........R | R-208 | D-178 | — | R-57 | D-33 | — |
| 59th | 1905–1907 | T. Roosevelt ........R | R-250 | D-136 | — | R-57 | D-33 | — |
| 60th | 1907–1909 | T. Roosevelt ........R | R-222 | D-164 | — | R-61 | D-31 | — |
| 61st | 1909–1911 | W. H. Taft .........R | R-219 | D-172 | — | R-61 | D-32 | — |
| 62d | 1911–1913 | W. H. Taft .........R | D-228 | R-161 | 1 | R-51 | D-41 | — |
| 63d | 1913–1915 | W. Wilson ..........D | D-291 | R-127 | 17 | D-51 | R-44 | 1 |
| 64th | 1915–1917 | W. Wilson ..........D | D-230 | R-196 | 9 | D-56 | R-40 | — |
| 65th | 1917–1919 | W. Wilson ..........D | D-216 | R-210 | 6 | D-53 | R-42 | — |
| 66th | 1919–1921 | W. Wilson ..........D | R-240 | D-190 | 3 | R-49 | D-47 | — |
| 67th | 1921–1923 | W. G. Harding ......R | R-301 | D-131 | 1 | R-59 | D-37 | — |
| 68th | 1923–1925 | W. G. Harding ......R / C. Coolidge .........R | R-225 | D-205 | 5 | R-51 | D-43 | 2 |
| 69th | 1925–1927 | C. Coolidge .........R | R-247 | D-183 | 4 | R-56 | D-39 | 1 |
| 70th | 1927–1929 | C. Coolidge .........R | R-237 | D-195 | 3 | R-49 | D-46 | 1 |
| 71st | 1929–1931 | H. Hoover ..........R | R-267 | D-163 | 1 | R-56 | D-39 | 1 |
| 72d | 1931–1933 | H. Hoover ..........R | D-218 | R-216 | 1 | R-48 | D-47 | 1 |
| 73d | 1933–1935 | F. D. Roosevelt .....D | D-310 | R-117 | 5 | D-60 | R-35 | 1 |
| 74th | 1935–1937 | F. D. Roosevelt .....D | D-319 | R-103 | 10 | D-69 | R-25 | 2 |
| 75th | 1937–1939 | F. D. Roosevelt .....D | D-331 | R-89 | 13 | D-76 | R-16 | 4 |
| 76th | 1939–1941 | F. D. Roosevelt .....D | D-261 | R-164 | 4 | D-69 | R-23 | 4 |
| 77th | 1941–1943 | F. D. Roosevelt .....D | D-268 | R-162 | 5 | D-66 | R-28 | 2 |
| 78th | 1943–1945 | F. D. Roosevelt .....D | D-218 | R-208 | 4 | D-58 | R-37 | 1 |
| 79th | 1945–1947 | F. D. Roosevelt .....D / Harry S. Truman ...D | D-242 | R-190 | 2 | D-56 | R-38 | 1 |
| 80th | 1947–1949 | Harry S. Truman ...D | R-245 | D-188 | 1 | R-51 | D-45 | — |
| 81st | 1949–1951 | Harry S. Truman ...D | D-263 | R-171 | 1 | D-54 | R-42 | — |
| 82d | 1951–1953 | Harry S. Truman ...D | D-234 | R-199 | 1 | D-49 | R-47 | — |
| 83d | 1953–1955 | D. D. Eisenhower ...R | R-221 | D-211 | 1 | R-48 | D-47 | 1 |
| 84th | 1955–1957 | D. D. Eisenhower ...R | D-232 | R-203 | — | D-48 | R-47 | 1 |
| 85th | 1957–1959 | D. D. Eisenhower ...R | D-233 | R-200 | — | D-49 | R-47 | — |
| 86th | 1959–1961 | D. D. Eisenhower ...R | D-283 | R-153 | — | D-64 | R-34 | — |
| 87th | 1961–1963 | John F. Kennedy ...D | D-263 | R-174 | — | D-65 | R-35 | — |
| 88th | 1963–1965 | John F. Kennedy ...D / Lyndon B. Johnson .D | D-258 | R-177 | — | D-67 | R-33 | — |
| 89th | 1965–1967 | Lyndon B. Johnson .D | D-295 | R-140 | — | D-68 | R-32 | — |
| 90th | 1967–1969 | Lyndon B. Johnson .D | D-247 | R-187 | — | D-64 | R-36 | — |
| 91st | 1969–1971 | Richard Nixon......R | D-243 | R-192 | — | D-57 | R-43 | — |
| 92d | 1971–1973 | Richard Nixon......R | D-254 | R-180 | — | D-54 | R-44 | 2 |
| 93d | 1973–1975 | Richard Nixon .....R / Gerald Ford ........R | D-243 | R-192 | — | D-56 | R-42 | 2 |
| 94th | 1975–1977 | Gerald Ford ........R | D-290 | R-145 | — | D-62 | R-38 | — |
| 95th | 1977–1979 | Jimmy Carter ......D | D-289 | R-146 | — | D-62 | R-38 | — |
| 96th | 1979–1981 | Jimmy Carter ......D | D-276 | R-159 | — | D-59 | R-41 | — |
| 97th | 1981–1983 | Ronald Reagan .....R | D-243 | R-192 | — | R-53 | D-47 | — |

Political party abbreviations: AF—Antifederalist; AM—Anti-Masonic; Co—Coalition; D—Democrat; DR—Democratic-Republican; Fed—Federalist; Ja—Jacksonian; NR—National Republican; R—Republican; U—Unionist; W—Whig.

## SPEAKERS OF THE HOUSE OF REPRESENTATIVES: 1789–1981

The speaker of the U.S. House of Representatives is the third most important position in the federal government after President and Vice President. He presides over the House and is the recognized leader of the majority party in the House of Representatives.

There are several ways in which the speaker can become President without being elected to that office, including:

If both the office of President and Vice President should become vacant as a result of the deaths or resignations of the incumbents.

If the office of Vice President is vacant and the incumbent President should die or resign

before a new Vice President is sworn in.

If the President-elect and the Vice President-elect are found not to be qualified to take office on Inauguration Day.

Rep. Thomas P. O'Neill Jr. (D-Mass.) was chosen speaker without opposition in December 1976 after the retirement of Rep. Carl Albert (D-Okla.), who had held the position since 1971. O'Neill has served in Congress since 1953 from the same district once represented by President John Kennedy.

Only one speaker ever has become President: James K. Polk of Tennessee, who served in the position in 1835–39.

| CONGRESS | SPEAKER | PARTY | CONGRESS | SPEAKER | PARTY |
|---|---|---|---|---|---|
| 1st (1789–91) | Frederick A. C. Muhlenberg | Federalist | 47th (1881–83) | J. Warren Keifer | Republican |
| 2d (1791–93) | Jonathan Trumbull | Federalist | 48th (1883–85) | John G. Carlisle | Democrat |
| 3d (1793–95) | Frederick A. C. Muhlenberg | Federalist | 49th (1885–87) | John G. Carlisle | Democrat |
| 4th (1795–97) | Jonathan Dayton | Federalist | 50th (1887–89) | John G. Carlisle | Democrat |
| 5th (1797–99) | Jonathan Dayton | Federalist | 51st (1889–91) | Thomas B. Reed | Republican |
|  | George Dent | Dem.-Rep. | 52d (1891–93) | Charles F. Crisp | Democrat |
| 6th (1799–1801) | Theodore Sedgwick | Federalist | 53d (1893–95) | Charles F. Crisp | Democrat |
| 7th (1801–03) | Nathaniel Macon | Dem.-Rep. | 54th (1895–97) | Thomas B. Reed | Republican |
| 8th (1803–05) | Nathaniel Macon | Dem.-Rep. | 55th (1897–99) | Thomas B. Reed | Republican |
| 9th (1805–07) | Nathaniel Macon | Dem.-Rep. | 56th (1899–1901) | David B. Henderson | Republican |
| 10th (1807–09) | Joseph B. Varnum | Dem.-Rep. | 57th (1901–03) | David B. Henderson | Republican |
| 11th (1809–11) | Joseph B. Varnum | Dem.-Rep. | 58th (1903–05) | Joseph G. Cannon | Republican |
| 12th (1811–13) | Henry Clay | Dem.-Rep. | 59th (1905–07) | Joseph G. Cannon | Republican |
| 13th (1813–15) | Henry Clay | Dem.-Rep. | 60th (1907–09) | Joseph G. Cannon | Republican |
|  | Langdon Cheves | Dem.-Rep. | 61st (1909–11) | Joseph G. Cannon | Republican |
| 14th (1815–17) | Henry Clay | Dem.-Rep. | 62d (1911–13) | Champ Clark | Democrat |
| 15th (1817–19) | Henry Clay | Dem.-Rep. | 63d (1913–15) | Champ Clark | Democrat |
| 16th (1819–21) | Henry Clay | Dem.-Rep. | 64th (1915–17) | Champ Clark | Democrat |
|  | John W. Taylor | Dem.-Rep. | 65th (1917–19) | Champ Clark | Democrat |
| 17th (1821–23) | Philip P. Barbour | Dem.-Rep. | 66th (1919–21) | Frederick H. Gillett | Republican |
| 18th (1823–25) | Henry Clay | Dem.-Rep. | 67th (1921–23) | Frederick H. Gillett | Republican |
| 19th (1825–27) | John W. Taylor | Dem.-Rep. | 68th (1923–25) | Frederick H. Gillett | Republican |
| 20th (1827–29) | Andrew Stevenson | Democrat | 69th (1925–27) | Nicholas Longworth | Republican |
| 21st (1829–31) | Andrew Stevenson | Democrat | 70th (1927–29) | Nicholas Longworth | Republican |
| 22d (1831–33) | Andrew Stevenson | Democrat | 71st (1929–31) | Nicholas Longworth | Republican |
| 23d (1833–35) | Andrew Stevenson | Democrat | 72d (1931–33) | John N. Garner | Democrat |
|  | John Bell | Whig | 73d (1933–35) | Henry T. Rainey | Democrat |
| 24th (1835–37) | James K. Polk | Democrat | 74th (1935–37) | Joseph W. Byrns | Democrat |
| 25th (1837–39) | James K. Polk | Democrat |  | William B. Bankhead | Democrat |
| 26th (1839–41) | Robert M. T. Hunter | Democrat | 75th (1937–39) | William B. Bankhead | Democrat |
| 27th (1841–43) | John White | Whig | 76th (1939–41) | William B. Bankhead | Democrat |
| 28th (1843–45) | John W. Jones | Democrat |  |  |  |
| 29th (1845–47) | John W. Davis | Democrat | 77th (1941–43) | Sam Rayburn | Democrat |
| 30th (1847–49) | Robert C. Winthrop | Whig | 78th (1943–45) | Sam Rayburn | Democrat |
| 31st (1849–51) | Howell Cobb | Democrat | 79th (1945–47) | Sam Rayburn | Democrat |
| 32d (1851–53) | Linn Boyd | Democrat | 80th (1947–49) | Joseph W. Martin Jr. | Republican |
| 33d (1853–55) | Linn Boyd | Democrat | 81st (1949–51) | Sam Rayburn | Democrat |
| 34th (1855–57) | Nathaniel P. Banks | American | 82d (1951–53) | Sam Rayburn | Democrat |
| 35th (1857–59) | James L. Orr | Democrat | 83d (1953–55) | Joseph W. Martin Jr. | Republican |
| 36th (1859–61) | William Pennington | Whig | 84th (1955–57) | Sam Rayburn | Democrat |
| 37th (1861–63) | Galusha A. Grow | Republican | 85th (1957–59) | Sam Rayburn | Democrat |
| 38th (1863–65) | Schuyler Colfax | Republican | 86th (1959–61) | Sam Rayburn | Democrat |
| 39th (1865–67) | Schuyler Colfax | Republican | 87th (1961–63) | Sam Rayburn | Democrat |
| 40th (1867–69) | Schuyler Colfax | Republican | 88th (1963–65) | John W. McCormack | Democrat |
|  | Theodore M. Pomeroy | Republican | 89th (1965–67) | John W. McCormack | Democrat |
| 41st (1869–71) | James G. Blaine | Republican | 90th (1967–69) | John W. McCormack | Democrat |
| 42d (1871–73) | James G. Blaine | Republican | 91st (1969–71) | John W. McCormack | Democrat |
| 43d (1873–75) | James G. Blaine | Republican | 92d (1971–73) | Carl Albert | Democrat |
| 44th (1875–77) | Michael C. Kerr | Democrat | 93d (1973–75) | Carl Albert | Democrat |
|  | Samuel S. Cox | Democrat | 94th (1975–77) | Carl Albert | Democrat |
|  | Milton Sayler | Democrat | 95th (1977–79) | Thomas P. O'Neill Jr. | Democrat |
|  | Samuel J. Randall | Democrat | 96th (1979–81) | Thomas P. O'Neill Jr. | Democrat |
| 45th (1877–79) | Samuel J. Randall | Democrat | 97th (1981–83) | Thomas P. O'Neill Jr. | Democrat |
| 46th (1879–81) | Samuel J. Randall | Democrat |  |  |  |

# Crime

Prison guard tower seen through shattered window, in New Mexico State Penitentiary at Santa Fe, site of one of the worst prison riots in history on Feb. 2–3, 1980, in which 33 inmates were killed. The official report, released in June, said an "execution squad" of prisoners tortured and killed inmates suspected of being police informants. The prison, built to accommodate 850 prisoners, actually held 1,136 at the time of the riot. The rioters did not harm prison guards held as hostages, surrendering them peacefully after the riot.

Wide World

## HIGHLIGHTS: 1980

### CRIME RATE CONTINUES TO RISE

For the third consecutive year, the rate of crime in the United States continued to soar upward in 1980. The crime rate calculated by the FBI rose 10% in the first six months of 1980. This compared with an increase of 8% in 1979 and a rise of 10.5% in 1978.

Violent crimes led the upsurge in 1980, with robberies increasing by 13% and forcible rape rising by 12%. No category of crime showed a decrease.

Crime rose at an even greater rate in rural areas—14%—than in major cities with over 1 million population, which registered a 13% increase.

Final crime statistics for 1979 showed that more than 12 million offenses were reported during the year, including more than 21,000 murders and over 466,000 robberies. Overall the crime rate for 1979 was 5,521.5 per 100,000, an increase of more than 38% since 1970 when the rate was 3,984.5 per 100,000, and an increase of 293% since 1960 when the rate was 1,887.2 per 100,000. Thus, the rate of crime has almost tripled over the past two decades.

### POLITICAL CRIMES

Corruption among public officials focused in 1980 on the Abscam trials in which several members of Congress were convicted of accepting bribes from FBI investigators (see page 11).

The Justice Department reported that in 1979 it had obtained convictions of a total of 284 corrupt federal, state, and local officials. The convictions included 102 federal officials, 31 state officials, and 151 local officials. The public integrity section of the Justice Department said that during the period it had decided not to prosecute in 16 investigations involving members of Congress.

Among officials convicted in 1980, one of the most prominent was the state attorney general of Illinois, William J. Scott. He was found guilty of tax fraud. Prosecutors

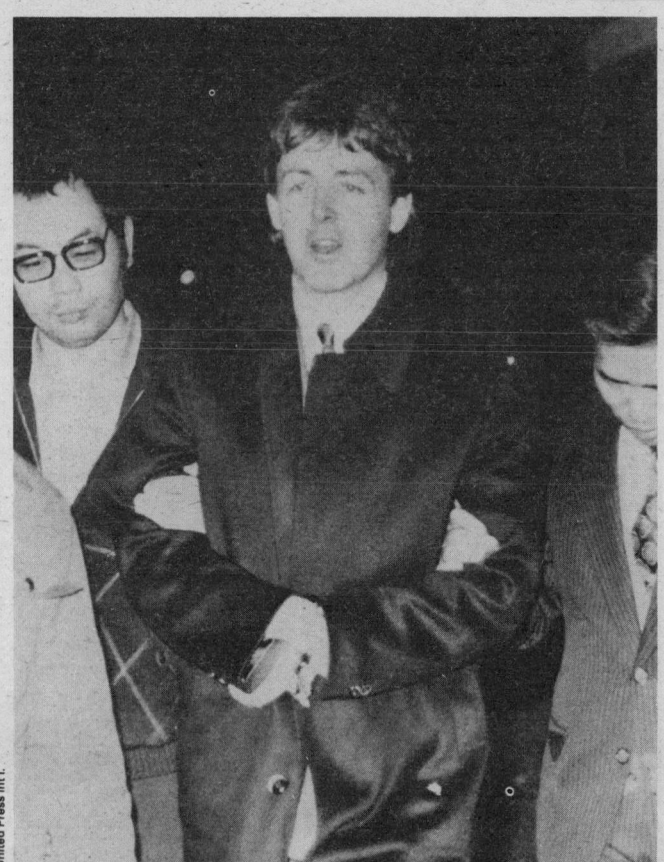

United Press Int'l.

Former Beatle superstar Paul McCartney tries to conceal handcuffs after being arrested by Japanese police in Tokyo on charges of smuggling marijuana. The 37-year-old singer was held in jail for 10 days before Japanese authorities decided to deport him.

## U.S. CRIME RATE: 1960–1979

Source: Federal Bureau of Investigation

| YEAR | REPORTED CRIMES | | VIOLENT CRIMES [2] | | PROPERTY CRIMES [3] | | MURDERS | | ROBBERIES | |
|------|-------|--------|-------|--------|-------|--------|-------|--------|-------|--------|
| | Total | Rate [1] | Total | Rate [1] | Total | Rate [1] | Total | Rate [1] | Total | Rate [1] |
| 1960 | 3,384,200 | 1,887.2 | 288,460 | 160.9 | 3,095,700 | 1,726.3 | 9,110 | 5.1 | 107,840 | 60.1 |
| 1961 | 3,488,000 | 1,906.1 | 289,390 | 158.1 | 3,198,600 | 1,747.9 | 8,740 | 4.8 | 106,670 | 58.3 |
| 1962 | 3,752,200 | 2,019.8 | 301,510 | 162.3 | 3,450,700 | 1,857.5 | 8,530 | 4.6 | 110,860 | 59.7 |
| 1963 | 4,109,500 | 2,180.3 | 316,970 | 168.2 | 3,792,500 | 2,012.1 | 8,640 | 4.6 | 116,470 | 61.8 |
| 1964 | 4,564,600 | 2,388.1 | 364,220 | 190.6 | 4,200,400 | 2,197.5 | 9,360 | 4.9 | 130,390 | 68.2 |
| 1965 | 4,739,400 | 2,449.0 | 387,390 | 200.2 | 4,352,000 | 2,248.8 | 9,960 | 5.1 | 138,690 | 71.7 |
| 1966 | 5,223,500 | 2,670.8 | 430,180 | 220.0 | 4,793,300 | 2,450.9 | 11,040 | 5.6 | 157,990 | 80.8 |
| 1967 | 5,903,400 | 2,989.7 | 499,930 | 253.2 | 5,403,500 | 2,736.5 | 12,240 | 6.2 | 202,910 | 102.8 |
| 1968 | 6,720,200 | 3,370.2 | 595,010 | 298.4 | 6,125,200 | 3,071.8 | 13,800 | 6.9 | 262,840 | 131.8 |
| 1969 | 7,410,900 | 3,680.0 | 661,870 | 328.7 | 6,749,000 | 3,351.3 | 14,760 | 7.3 | 298,850 | 148.4 |
| 1970 | 8,098,000 | 3,984.5 | 738,820 | 363.5 | 7,359,200 | 3,621.0 | 16,000 | 7.9 | 349,860 | 172.1 |
| 1971 | 8,588,200 | 4,164.7 | 816,500 | 396.0 | 7,771,700 | 3,768.8 | 17,780 | 8.6 | 387,700 | 188.0 |
| 1972 | 8,248,800 | 3,961.4 | 834,900 | 401.0 | 7,413,900 | 3,560.4 | 18,670 | 9.0 | 376,290 | 180.7 |
| 1973 | 8,718,100 | 4,154.4 | 875,910 | 417.4 | 7,842,200 | 3,737.0 | 19,640 | 9.4 | 384,220 | 183.1 |
| 1974 | 10,253,448 | 4,850.4 | 974,716 | 461.1 | 9,278,732 | 4,389.3 | 20,711 | 9.8 | 442,397 | 209.3 |
| 1975 | 11,256,566 | 5,281.7 | 1,026,284 | 481.5 | 10,230,282 | 4,800.2 | 20,505 | 9.6 | 464,973 | 218.2 |
| 1976 | 11,304,788 | 5,266.4 | 986,578 | 459.6 | 10,318,210 | 4,806.8 | 18,784 | 8.8 | 420,214 | 195.8 |
| 1977 | 10,935,777 | 5,055.1 | 1,009,499 | 466.6 | 9,926,278 | 4,588.4 | 19,121 | 8.8 | 404,847 | 187.1 |
| 1978 | 11,141,334 | 5,109.3 | 1,061,826 | 486.9 | 10,079,508 | 4,622.4 | 19,555 | 9.0 | 417,038 | 191.3 |
| 1979 | 12,152,730 | 5,521.5 | 1,178,539 | 535.5 | 10,974,191 | 4,986.0 | 21,456 | 9.7 | 466,881 | 212.1 |

[1] Crimes per 100,000 population. [2] Violent crimes include murder, forcible rape, robbery, and aggravated assault.
[3] Property crimes include burglary, larceny, and auto theft.

The public was given its first opportunity on May 28, 1980, to hear the White House tapes that implicated President Nixon in the Watergate coverup conspiracy. The National Archives in Washington, D.C., made available 31 tapes, all of which had been previously used in court cases and whose transcripts had been published. Court decisions still are pending on efforts by the former President to prevent the public from hearing the remaining thousands of hours of tapes that were secretly recorded in the White House during his administration.

United Press Int'l.

## HIGHLIGHTS: 1980 *(continued)*

charged that he had diverted political campaign funds to his personal use and had not reported them as income on his tax return.

The best-known official to begin serving time in prison in 1980 was former governor of Maryland Marvin Mandel, 60, who entered the federal prison at Eglin Air Force Base, Fla., sentenced to three years for his 1977 conviction for corruption.

Two former high-ranking FBI officials, W. Mark Felt and Edward S. Miller, were found guilty by a jury on Nov. 6, 1980, for having authorized secret break-ins of homes in 1972 and 1973 in an illegal search for evidence against the militant anti-Vietnam War group the Weather Underground.

Former President Nixon testified during the trial of Felt and Miller that he believed the director of the FBI had the authority to order such break-ins.

## CIA TURNCOAT PLEADS GUILTY

David H. Barnett, 47, a former CIA undercover agent, pleaded guilty on Oct. 29, 1980, to charges that he sold secret information to

the Soviet Union. In a statement to the court he admitted receiving $92,000 from Soviet agents for providing them with information about a CIA undercover operation he directed in Indonesia during the 1960s. Included in the information he sold were the names of 30 secret CIA agents.

Government officials said that Barnett's activities were the deepest penetration the Soviet Union was known to have accomplished in finding out secrets of the U.S. spy agency.

## INMATES OF PRISONS

Source: U.S. Law Enforcement Assistance Administration

| YEAR | STATE PRISONS | FEDERAL PRISONS | TOTAL |
|------|---------------|-----------------|-------|
| 1950 | 148,989 | 17,134 | 166,123 |
| 1955 | 165,692 | 20,088 | 185,780 |
| 1960 | 189,735 | 23,218 | 212,953 |
| 1965 | 189,855 | 21,040 | 210,895 |
| 1970 | 176,391 | 20,038 | 196,429 |
| 1971 | 177,113 | 20,948 | 198,061 |
| 1972 | 174,379 | 21,713 | 196,092 |
| 1973 | 181,396 | 22,815 | 204,211 |
| 1974 | 201,094 | 23,651 | 224,745 |
| 1975 | 225,582 | 24,134 | 249,716 |
| 1976 | 254,961 | 28,184 | 283,145 |
| 1977 | 261,405 | 30,920 | 292,325 |
| 1978 | 277,581 | 29,803 | 307,384 |
| 1979 | 287,850 | 26,233 | 314,083 |

# CRIME IN THE STATES: 1979

Source: Federal Bureau of Investigation

An estimated 12,152,730 criminal offenses were reported to law-enforcement agencies in 1979, up 9.1% from 1978. Property crimes increased 8.9%, while violent crimes increased 11.0%.

Nevada had the highest crime rate in the nation, with 8,831.6 per 100,000 population. Arizona was second with 7,857.3 and Florida

third with 7,688.1. However, California still led the nation with the largest number of crimes—1,695,108.

West Virginia had the lowest crime rate—2,325.3. North Dakota reported the fewest number of crimes—18,106. South Dakota was next to lowest with 20,393 crimes.

| STATE | REPORTED CRIMES | | VIOLENT CRIMES [2] | | PROPERTY CRIMES [3] | | MURDERS | | ROBBERIES | |
|---|---|---|---|---|---|---|---|---|---|---|
| | Total | Rate[1] | Total | Rate[1] | Total | Rate[1] | Total | Rate[1] | Total | Rate[1] |
| U.S. TOTAL .. | 12,152,730 | 5,521.5 | 1,178,539 | 535.5 | 10,974,191 | 4,986.0 | 21,456 | 9.7 | 466,881 | 212.1 |
| Alabama ..... | 159,950 | 4,243.8 | 15,578 | 413.3 | 144,372 | 3,830.5 | 496 | 13.2 | 4,127 | 109.5 |
| Alaska ....... | 25,187 | 6,203.7 | 1,994 | 491.1 | 23,193 | 5,712.6 | 54 | 13.3 | 445 | 109.6 |
| Arizona ...... | 192,505 | 7,857.3 | 14,528 | 593.0 | 177,977 | 7,264.4 | 219 | 8.9 | 4,305 | 175.7 |
| Arkansas..... | 78,933 | 3,620.8 | 7,984 | 366.2 | 70,949 | 3,254.5 | 198 | 9.1 | 1,626 | 74.6 |
| California .... | 1,695,108 | 7,468.8 | 184,087 | 811.1 | 1,511,021 | 6,657.7 | 2,952 | 13.0 | 75,767 | 333.8 |
| Colorado ..... | 195,456 | 7,051.1 | 14,472 | 522.1 | 180,984 | 6,529.0 | 161 | 5.8 | 4,353 | 157.0 |
| Connecticut .. | 180,033 | 5,779.6 | 12,902 | 414.2 | 167,131 | 5,364.4 | 131 | 4.2 | 6,021 | 193.3 |
| Delaware ..... | 37,980 | 6,525.8 | 3,127 | 537.3 | 34,853 | 5,988.5 | 33 | 5.7 | 753 | 129.4 |
| Florida ....... | 681,162 | 7,688.1 | 73,881 | 833.9 | 607,281 | 6,854.2 | 1,084 | 12.2 | 22,097 | 249.4 |
| Georgia ...... | 277,235 | 5,416.9 | 28,594 | 558.7 | 248,641 | 4,858.2 | 877 | 17.1 | 10,939 | 213.7 |
| Hawaii ....... | 66,315 | 7,247.5 | 2,651 | 289.7 | 63,664 | 6,957.8 | 66 | 7.2 | 1,688 | 184.5 |
| Idaho ........ | 38,379 | 4,240.8 | 2,613 | 288.7 | 35,766 | 3,952.0 | 49 | 5.4 | 392 | 43.3 |
| Illinois ....... | 580,504 | 5,169.2 | 54,054 | 481.3 | 526,450 | 4,687.9 | 1,203 | 10.7 | 22,235 | 198.0 |
| Indiana ...... | 248,477 | 4,601.4 | 18,254 | 338.0 | 230,223 | 4,263.4 | 448 | 8.3 | 7,167 | 132.7 |
| Iowa ......... | 124,879 | 4,301.7 | 5,259 | 181.2 | 119,620 | 4,120.6 | 65 | 2.2 | 1,457 | 50.2 |
| Kansas ....... | 115,981 | 4,895.8 | 8,376 | 353.6 | 107,605 | 4,542.2 | 130 | 5.5 | 2,423 | 102.3 |
| Kentucky ..... | 112,296 | 3,183.9 | 8,748 | 248.0 | 103,548 | 2,935.9 | 335 | 9.5 | 3,247 | 92.1 |
| Louisiana..... | 215,743 | 5,358.7 | 27,229 | 676.3 | 188,514 | 4,682.4 | 682 | 16.9 | 8,832 | 219.4 |
| Maine........ | 47,251 | 4,307.3 | 2,221 | 202.5 | 45,030 | 4,104.8 | 31 | 2.8 | 349 | 31.8 |
| Maryland ..... | 261,166 | 6,294.7 | 33,007 | 795.5 | 228,159 | 5,499.1 | 406 | 9.8 | 13,740 | 331.2 |
| Massachusetts | 341,406 | 5,917.9 | 30,650 | 531.3 | 310,756 | 5,386.7 | 212 | 3.7 | 11,724 | 203.2 |
| Michigan ..... | 566,015 | 6,147.0 | 56,558 | 614.2 | 509,457 | 5,532.8 | 834 | 9.1 | 20,218 | 219.6 |
| Minnesota .... | 178,349 | 4,392.8 | 8,973 | 221.0 | 169,376 | 4,171.8 | 93 | 2.3 | 3,754 | 92.5 |
| Mississippi ... | 71,233 | 2,960.6 | 7,786 | 323.6 | 63,447 | 2,637.0 | 302 | 12.6 | 1,702 | 70.7 |
| Missouri ..... | 240,471 | 4,939.8 | 25,662 | 527.2 | 214,809 | 4,412.7 | 543 | 11.2 | 10,267 | 210.9 |
| Montana ..... | 35,060 | 4,460.6 | 1,762 | 224.2 | 33,298 | 4,236.4 | 33 | 4.2 | 260 | 33.1 |
| Nebraska .... | 62,851 | 3,993.1 | 3,556 | 225.9 | 59,295 | 3,767.2 | 65 | 4.1 | 1,157 | 73.5 |
| Nevada ...... | 61,998 | 8,831.6 | 5,866 | 835.6 | 56,132 | 7,996.0 | 123 | 17.5 | 2,861 | 407.5 |
| New Hampshire | 40,614 | 4,578.8 | 1,241 | 139.9 | 39,373 | 4,438.9 | 21 | 2.4 | 254 | 28.6 |
| New Jersey ... | 426,765 | 5,820.6 | 36,747 | 501.2 | 390,018 | 5,319.4 | 484 | 6.6 | 18,332 | 250.0 |
| New Mexico .. | 71,835 | 5,788.5 | 7,272 | 586.0 | 64,563 | 5,202.5 | 154 | 12.4 | 1,502 | 121.0 |
| New York .... | 1,095,140 | 6,205.1 | 161,906 | 917.4 | 933,234 | 5,287.7 | 2,092 | 11.9 | 93,471 | 529.6 |
| North Carolina | 245,122 | 4,372.5 | 25,009 | 446.1 | 220,113 | 3,926.4 | 600 | 10.7 | 4,327 | 77.2 |
| North Dakota. | 18,106 | 2,755.9 | 403 | 61.3 | 17,703 | 2,694.5 | 10 | 1.5 | 65 | 9.9 |
| Ohio .......... | 550,481 | 5,129.8 | 49,092 | 457.5 | 501,389 | 4,672.3 | 865 | 8.1 | 20,909 | 194.8 |
| Oklahoma .... | 136,012 | 4,703.0 | 11,719 | 405.2 | 124,293 | 4,297.8 | 281 | 9.7 | 2,966 | 102.6 |
| Oregon ....... | 161,045 | 6,373.0 | 13,781 | 545.4 | 147,264 | 5,827.6 | 107 | 4.2 | 3,299 | 130.6 |
| Pennsylvania . | 410,047 | 3,495.4 | 39,133 | 333.6 | 370,914 | 3,161.8 | 724 | 6.2 | 17,855 | 152.2 |
| Rhode Island . | 53,599 | 5,769.5 | 3,485 | 375.1 | 50,114 | 5,394.4 | 30 | 3.2 | 1,019 | 109.7 |
| South Carolina | 148,540 | 5,066.2 | 19,889 | 678.3 | 128,651 | 4,387.8 | 368 | 12.6 | 3,156 | 107.6 |
| South Dakota. | 20,393 | 2,959.8 | 1,096 | 159.1 | 19,297 | 2,800.7 | 14 | 2.0 | 140 | 20.3 |
| Tennessee.... | 175,786 | 4,013.4 | 18,135 | 414.0 | 157,651 | 3,599.3 | 430 | 9.8 | 7,277 | 166.1 |
| Texas........ | 793,097 | 5,925.3 | 67,988 | 507.9 | 725,109 | 5,417.3 | 2,235 | 16.7 | 25,667 | 191.8 |
| Utah......... | 75,076 | 5,492.0 | 4,158 | 304.2 | 70,918 | 5,187.9 | 66 | 4.8 | 1,062 | 77.7 |
| Vermont ...... | 26,125 | 5,299.2 | 908 | 184.2 | 25,217 | 5,115.0 | 7 | 1.4 | 141 | 28.6 |
| Virginia ...... | 226,656 | 4,361.3 | 15,642 | 301.0 | 211,014 | 4,060.3 | 447 | 8.6 | 5,799 | 111.6 |
| Washington... | 256,349 | 6,529.5 | 17,064 | 434.6 | 239.285 | 6,094.9 | 187 | 4.8 | 4,739 | 120.7 |
| West Virginia . | 43,669 | 2,325.3 | 3,156 | 168.1 | 40,513 | 2,157.2 | 128 | 6.8 | 825 | 43.9 |
| Wisconsin .... | 207,112 | 4,388.0 | 7,839 | 166.1 | 199,273 | 4,221.9 | 160 | 3.4 | 2,857 | 60.5 |
| Wyoming ..... | 21,708 | 4,824.0 | 1,579 | 350.9 | 20,129 | 4,473.1 | 41 | 9.1 | 190 | 42.2 |

[1] Crimes per 100,000 population.    [2] Violent crimes include murder, forcible rape, robbery, and aggravated assault.
[3] Property crimes include burglary, larceny of $50 or more, and auto theft.

# CRIME IN U.S. METROPOLITAN AREAS: 1979

Source: Federal Bureau of Investigation

Las Vegas, Nev., remained in first place in 1979 as the metropolitan area with the highest crime rate in the United States, counting 9,982.6 crimes per 100,000 population. Daytona Beach, Fla., remained in second place with a rate of 9,656.4. Reno, Nev., was third with a rate of 9,352.9; Miami, Fla., fourth with 9,298.3; and Phoenix, Ariz., fifth with 9,013.4.

Other cities with a crime rate of more than 8,000 per 100,000 population were Bakersfield, Fresno, Sacramento, San Francisco-Oakland, and Stockton, Calif.; Fort Lauderdale, Orlando, and Tallahassee, Fla.; Tucson, Ariz.; Denver-Boulder, Colo.; and Atlantic City, N.J.

Among the nation's 10 largest metropolitan areas, San Francisco-Oakland had the highest crime rate with 8,218.0; Los Angeles-Long Beach was second with 7,806.3.

| | TOTAL CRIMES | | VIOLENT CRIMES[2] | | PROPERTY CRIMES[3] | | MURDERS | | ROBBERIES | |
|---|---|---|---|---|---|---|---|---|---|---|
| | Number | Rate[1] | Total | Rate[1] | Total | Rate[1] | Total | Rate[1] | Total | Rate[1] |
| Akron, Ohio | 34,920 | 5,324.1 | 2,750 | 419.3 | 32,170 | 4,904.8 | 28 | 4.3 | 755 | 115.1 |
| Albany-Schenectady, N.Y. | 31,068 | 3,943.2 | 1,965 | 249.4 | 29,103 | 3,693.8 | 16 | 2.0 | 545 | 69.2 |
| Albuquerque, N. Mex. | 32,723 | 7,835.3 | 3,194 | 764.8 | 29,529 | 7,070.6 | 65 | 15.6 | 895 | 214.3 |
| Allentown-Easton, Pa.-N.J. | 20,772 | 3,323.6 | 1,007 | 161.1 | 19,765 | 3,162.5 | 18 | 2.9 | 397 | 63.5 |
| Anaheim-Santa Ana, Calif. | 125,481 | 6,724.4 | 8,301 | 444.8 | 117,180 | 6,279.6 | 91 | 4.9 | 3,572 | 191.4 |
| Ann Arbor, Mich. | 18,137 | 7,087.0 | 1,433 | 559.9 | 16,704 | 6,527.1 | 8 | 3.1 | 390 | 152.4 |
| Appleton-Oshkosh, Wis. | 13,860 | 4,757.8 | 278 | 95.4 | 13,582 | 4,662.3 | 2 | 0.7 | 50 | 17.2 |
| Asheville, N.C. | 7,119 | 4,127.1 | 480 | 278.3 | 6,639 | 3,848.9 | 16 | 9.3 | 122 | 70.7 |
| Atlanta, Ga. | 145,659 | 7,811.4 | 16,386 | 878.8 | 129,273 | 6,932.7 | 376 | 20.2 | 7,551 | 404.9 |
| Atlantic City, N.J. | 16,041 | 8,436.9 | 1,236 | 650.1 | 14,805 | 7,786.8 | 15 | 7.9 | 585 | 307.7 |
| Austin, Tex. | 34,347 | 6,987.7 | 1,903 | 387.2 | 32,444 | 6,600.6 | 58 | 11.8 | 662 | 134.7 |
| Bakersfield, Calif. | 31,528 | 8,477.8 | 2,888 | 776.6 | 28,640 | 7,701.3 | 59 | 15.9 | 855 | 229.9 |
| Baltimore, Md. | 150,732 | 7,016.1 | 23,377 | 1,088.1 | 127,355 | 5,928.0 | 294 | 13.7 | 10,103 | 470.3 |
| Baton Rouge, La. | 35,543 | 7,873.5 | 3,558 | 788.2 | 31,985 | 7,085.3 | 61 | 13.5 | 677 | 150.0 |
| Battle Creek, Mich. | 9,204 | 5,002.9 | 825 | 448.4 | 8,379 | 4,554.5 | 7 | 3.8 | 223 | 121.2 |
| Beaumont-Port Arthur, Tex. | 21,296 | 5,683.6 | 2,066 | 551.4 | 19,230 | 5,132.2 | 47 | 12.5 | 615 | 164.1 |
| Binghamton, N.Y.-Pa. | 9,878 | 3,263.0 | 317 | 104.7 | 9,561 | 3,158.2 | 4 | 1.3 | 86 | 28.4 |
| Birmingham, Ala. | 51,679 | 6,270.2 | 5,136 | 623.2 | 46,543 | 5,647.1 | 137 | 16.6 | 1,909 | 231.6 |
| Boise, Idaho | 9,634 | 6,117.4 | 666 | 422.9 | 8,968 | 5,694.5 | 7 | 4.4 | 147 | 93.3 |
| Boston, Mass. | 208,342 | 6,295.3 | 21,451 | 648.2 | 186,891 | 5,647.2 | 154 | 4.7 | 9,612 | 290.4 |
| Bridgeport, Conn. | 44,646 | 5,493.7 | 2,864 | 352.4 | 41,782 | 5,141.3 | 35 | 4.3 | 1,337 | 164.5 |
| Brockton, Mass. | 23,433 | 5,926.6 | 1,673 | 423.1 | 21,760 | 5,503.5 | 4 | 1.0 | 332 | 84.0 |
| Brownsville, Tex. | 11,033 | 6,046.8 | 807 | 442.3 | 10,226 | 5,604.5 | 12 | 6.6 | 139 | 76.2 |
| Buffalo, N.Y. | 60,622 | 4,682.8 | 6,422 | 496.1 | 54,200 | 4,186.7 | 76 | 5.9 | 2,534 | 195.7 |
| Canton, Ohio | 17,883 | 4,436.2 | 1,453 | 360.4 | 16,430 | 4,075.7 | 22 | 5.5 | 563 | 139.7 |
| Cedar Rapids, Iowa | 10,646 | 6,377.9 | 481 | 288.2 | 10,165 | 6,089.8 | 4 | 2.4 | 138 | 82.7 |
| Charleston, S.C. | 25,170 | 6,439.4 | 3,329 | 851.7 | 21,841 | 5,587.7 | 38 | 9.7 | 837 | 214.1 |
| Charleston, W. Va. | 10,479 | 3,989.2 | 713 | 271.4 | 9,766 | 3,717.8 | 18 | 6.9 | 264 | 100.5 |
| Charlotte-Gastonia, N.C. | 36,566 | 6,002.8 | 4,119 | 676.2 | 32,447 | 5,326.6 | 84 | 13.8 | 874 | 143.5 |
| Chattanooga, Tenn.-Ga. | 20,168 | 4,997.1 | 1,916 | 474.7 | 18,252 | 4,522.4 | 47 | 11.6 | 568 | 140.7 |
| Chicago, Ill. | 395,989 | 5,639.5 | 39,937 | 568.8 | 356,052 | 5,070.7 | 1,001 | 14.3 | 18,476 | 263.1 |
| Cincinnati, Ohio-Ky.-Ind. | 75,860 | 5,458.1 | 6,537 | 470.3 | 69,323 | 4,987.7 | 93 | 6.7 | 2,449 | 176.2 |
| Cleveland, Ohio | 100,564 | 5,195.4 | 13,304 | 687.3 | 87,260 | 4,508.1 | 324 | 16.7 | 6,900 | 356.5 |
| Colorado Springs, Colo. | 18,389 | 6,077.5 | 1,381 | 456.4 | 17,008 | 5,621.0 | 12 | 4.0 | 405 | 133.9 |
| Columbia, S.C. | 27,627 | 7,227.6 | 3,502 | 916.2 | 24,125 | 6,311.4 | 57 | 14.9 | 736 | 192.5 |
| Columbus, Ga.-Ala. | 10,955 | 4,770.1 | 915 | 398.4 | 10,040 | 4,371.7 | 50 | 21.8 | 419 | 182.4 |
| Columbus, Ohio | 75,042 | 6,896.6 | 5,583 | 513.1 | 69,459 | 6,383.5 | 91 | 8.4 | 2,982 | 274.1 |
| Corpus Christi, Tex. | 20,955 | 6,726.6 | 1,905 | 611.5 | 19,050 | 6,115.1 | 38 | 12.2 | 530 | 170.1 |
| Dallas-Fort Worth, Tex. | 217,614 | 7,787.7 | 19,390 | 693.9 | 198,224 | 7,093.8 | 510 | 18.3 | 7,329 | 262.3 |
| Davenport, Iowa-Ill. | 21,398 | 5,716.1 | 1,598 | 426.9 | 19,800 | 5,289.2 | 18 | 4.8 | 514 | 137.3 |
| Dayton, Ohio | 58,101 | 6,971.7 | 5,341 | 640.9 | 52,760 | 6,330.8 | 90 | 10.8 | 2,737 | 328.4 |
| Daytona Beach, Fla. | 21,763 | 9,656.4 | 1,844 | 818.2 | 19,919 | 8,838.2 | 28 | 12.4 | 587 | 260.5 |
| Denver-Boulder, Colo. | 125,638 | 8,043.5 | 9,517 | 609.3 | 116,121 | 7,434.3 | 108 | 6.9 | 3,584 | 229.5 |
| Des Moines, Iowa | 24,706 | 7,376.2 | 1,461 | 436.2 | 23,245 | 6,940.0 | 17 | 5.1 | 533 | 159.1 |
| Detroit, Mich. | 277,843 | 6,776.5 | 34,562 | 786.4 | 263,281 | 5,990.2 | 605 | 13.8 | 15,449 | 351.5 |
| Duluth-Superior, Minn.-Wis. | 11,890 | 4,420.6 | 409 | 152.1 | 11,481 | 4,268.5 | 5 | 1.9 | 125 | 46.5 |
| El Paso, Tex. | 27,530 | 6,036.6 | 2,368 | 519.2 | 25,162 | 5,517.4 | 37 | 8.1 | 824 | 180.7 |
| Erie, Pa. | 11,478 | 4,267.4 | 804 | 298.9 | 10,674 | 3,968.5 | 7 | 2.6 | 299 | 111.2 |
| Eugene-Springfield, Oreg. | 18,733 | 7,030.5 | 832 | 312.3 | 17,901 | 6,718.3 | 8 | 3.0 | 303 | 113.7 |
| Evansville, Ind.-Ky. | 14,628 | 4,936.4 | 1,184 | 399.6 | 13,444 | 4,536.9 | 12 | 4.0 | 392 | 132.3 |
| Fall River, Mass. | 24,706 | 5,237.4 | 1,669 | 353.8 | 23,037 | 4,883.6 | 13 | 2.8 | 470 | 99.6 |
| Fayetteville, N.C. | 15,429 | 6,582.0 | 1,775 | 757.2 | 13,654 | 5,824.8 | 32 | 13.7 | 459 | 195.8 |
| Flint, Mich. | 38,375 | 7,346.5 | 4,536 | 868.4 | 33,839 | 6,478.1 | 48 | 9.2 | 961 | 184.0 |
| Ft. Lauderdale-Hollywood, Fla. | 80,055 | 8,776.5 | 6,678 | 732.1 | 73,377 | 8,044.4 | 129 | 14.1 | 2,938 | 322.1 |
| Fort Myers, Fla. | 10,457 | 6,494.6 | 1,238 | 768.9 | 9,219 | 5,725.7 | 19 | 11.8 | 195 | 121.1 |
| Fort Smith, Ark.-Okla. | 7,415 | 3,895.8 | 496 | 260.6 | 6,919 | 3,635.2 | 7 | 3.7 | 101 | 53.1 |

[1] Crimes per 100,000 population.    [2] Violent crimes includes murder, forcible rape, robbery, and aggravated assault.
[3] Property crimes include burglary, larceny of $50 or more, and auto theft.

## CRIME IN U.S. METROPOLITAN AREAS *(continued)*

| | TOTAL CRIMES | | VIOLENT CRIMES [2] | | PROPERTY CRIMES [3] | | MURDERS | | ROBBERIES | |
|---|---|---|---|---|---|---|---|---|---|---|
| | Number | Rate [1] | Total | Rate [1] | Total | Rate [1] | Total | Rate [1] | Total | Rate [1] |
| Fort Wayne, Ind. .......... | 17,986 | 4,764.8 | 889 | 235.5 | 17,097 | 4,529.3 | 13 | 3.4 | 391 | 103.6 |
| Fresno, Calif. ............. | 40,666 | 8,339.4 | 4,125 | 845.9 | 36,541 | 7,493.5 | 81 | 16.6 | 1,513 | 310.3 |
| Galveston-Texas City, Tex. . | 12,567 | 6,170.9 | 1,405 | 689.9 | 11,162 | 5,481.0 | 33 | 16.2 | 369 | 181.2 |
| Gary-Hammond-E. Chicago, Ind. | 37,469 | 5,750.6 | 4,179 | 641.4 | 33,290 | 5,109.2 | 120 | 18.4 | 1,964 | 301.4 |
| Grand Rapids, Mich. ...... | 29,567 | 5,010.9 | 2,228 | 377.6 | 27,339 | 4,633.3 | 19 | 3.2 | 686 | 116.3 |
| Green Bay, Wis. ........... | 7,313 | 4,072.0 | 153 | 85.2 | 7,160 | 3,986.8 | 4 | 2.2 | 32 | 17.8 |
| Greensboro-Winston-Salem-High Point, N.C.... | 40,028 | 5,102.9 | 3,539 | 451.2 | 36,489 | 4,651.7 | 77 | 9.8 | 775 | 98.8 |
| Greenville-Spartanburg,S.C. | 30,758 | 5,648.5 | 3,433 | 630.4 | 27,325 | 5,018.0 | 55 | 10.1 | 626 | 115.0 |
| Hamilton-Middletown, Ohio . | 15,774 | 6,161.2 | 812 | 317.2 | 14,962 | 5,844.1 | 13 | 5.1 | 256 | 100.0 |
| Harrisburg, Pa. ........... | 19,243 | 4,470.9 | 1,682 | 390.8 | 17,561 | 4,080.1 | 13 | 3.0 | 762 | 177.0 |
| Hartford, Conn. ........... | 58,342 | 6,302.0 | 4,664 | 503.8 | 53,678 | 5,798.2 | 43 | 4.6 | 2,285 | 246.8 |
| Honolulu, Hawaii ......... | 52,926 | 7,207.0 | 2,196 | 299.0 | 50,730 | 6,908.0 | 48 | 6.5 | 1,568 | 213.5 |
| Houston, Tex. ............ | 193,138 | 7,235.1 | 17,979 | 673.5 | 175,159 | 6,561.6 | 801 | 30.0 | 10,528 | 394.4 |
| Huntington, W.Va.-Ky.-Ohio . | 12,247 | 4,055.4 | 1,247 | 412.9 | 11,000 | 3,642.5 | 19 | 6.3 | 247 | 81.8 |
| Huntsville, Ala. ........... | 15,246 | 5,168.0 | 964 | 326.8 | 14,282 | 4,841.2 | 26 | 8.8 | 259 | 87.8 |
| Indianapolis, Ind. ......... | 64,321 | 5,534.7 | 5,632 | 484.6 | 58,689 | 5,050.1 | 126 | 10.8 | 2,587 | 222.6 |
| Jackson, Miss. ........... | 17,496 | 5,852.2 | 1,406 | 470.3 | 16,090 | 5,381.9 | 58 | 19.4 | 527 | 176.3 |
| Jacksonville, Fla. ......... | 48,748 | 6,719.6 | 5,803 | 799.9 | 42,945 | 5,919.7 | 87 | 12.0 | 1,808 | 249.2 |
| Jersey City, N.J. .......... | 34,705 | 6,260.2 | 3,387 | 611.0 | 31,318 | 5,649.2 | 66 | 11.9 | 1,869 | 337.1 |
| Johnstown, Pa. ........... | 5,354 | 2,024.4 | 512 | 193.6 | 4,842 | 1,830.8 | 6 | 2.3 | 78 | 29.5 |
| Kalamazoo, Mich. ......... | 19,336 | 7,139.0 | 1,920 | 708.9 | 17,416 | 6,430.1 | 10 | 3.7 | 427 | 157.7 |
| Kansas City, Mo.-Kans. .... | 89,286 | 6,713.0 | 10,003 | 752.1 | 79,283 | 5,960.9 | 170 | 12.8 | 3,849 | 289.4 |
| Killeen-Temple, Tex. ...... | 9,196 | 4,275.9 | 788 | 366.4 | 8,408 | 3,909.5 | 25 | 11.6 | 226 | 105.1 |
| Knoxville, Tenn. .......... | 20,398 | 4,469.5 | 1,709 | 374.5 | 18,689 | 4,095.1 | 37 | 8.1 | 639 | 140.0 |
| Lake Charles, La. ......... | 8,703 | 5,436.5 | 938 | 585.9 | 7,765 | 4,850.5 | 31 | 19.4 | 133 | 83.1 |
| Lakeland-Winter Haven, Fla. | 20,920 | 7,270.4 | 2,264 | 786.8 | 18,656 | 6,483.6 | 25 | 8.7 | 371 | 128.9 |
| Lancaster, Pa. ........... | 10,062 | 2,869.7 | 393 | 112.1 | 9,669 | 2,757.6 | 9 | 2.6 | 129 | 36.8 |
| Lansing-East Lansing, Mich. | 22,136 | 4,825.5 | 1,340 | 292.1 | 20,796 | 4,533.4 | 15 | 3.3 | 306 | 66.7 |
| Las Vegas, Nev. .......... | 39,729 | 9,982.6 | 4,077 | 1,024.4 | 35,652 | 8,958.2 | 89 | 22.4 | 2,110 | 530.2 |
| Lexington-Fayette, Ky. ..... | 15,766 | 5,217.8 | 1,022 | 338.2 | 14,744 | 4,879.6 | 25 | 8.3 | 317 | 104.9 |
| Lima, Ohio .............. | 10,482 | 4,962.1 | 671 | 317.6 | 9,811 | 4,644.4 | 10 | 4.7 | 215 | 101.8 |
| Lincoln, Nebr. ........... | 10,877 | 5,807.8 | 495 | 264.3 | 10,382 | 5,543.5 | 4 | 2.1 | 87 | 46.5 |
| Little Rock, Ark. .......... | 27,092 | 7,218.7 | 2,931 | 781.0 | 24,161 | 6,437.7 | 50 | 13.3 | 869 | 231.5 |
| Long Branch, N.J. ......... | 26,853 | 5,368.0 | 1,686 | 337.0 | 25,167 | 5,031.0 | 12 | 2.4 | 560 | 111.9 |
| Lorain-Elyria, Ohio ........ | 10,034 | 3,769.5 | 935 | 351.3 | 9,099 | 3,418.2 | 16 | 6.0 | 331 | 124.3 |
| Los Angeles-Long Beach .. | 562,725 | 7,806.3 | 86,872 | 1,205.1 | 475,853 | 6,601.2 | 1,439 | 20.0 | 38,149 | 529.2 |
| Louisville, Ky.-Ind. ........ | 45,932 | 5,137.4 | 3,816 | 426.8 | 42,116 | 4,710.6 | 104 | 11.6 | 2,054 | 229.7 |
| Lubbock, Tex. ........... | 15,141 | 7,386.5 | 1,213 | 591.8 | 13,928 | 6,794.8 | 45 | 22.0 | 239 | 116.6 |
| Lynchburg, Va. ........... | 5,616 | 3,758.7 | 398 | 266.4 | 5,218 | 3,492.4 | 13 | 8.7 | 75 | 50.2 |
| Macon, Ga. ............. | 13,108 | 5,358.2 | 1,078 | 440.7 | 12,030 | 4,917.6 | 29 | 11.9 | 385 | 157.4 |
| Madison, Wis. ........... | 21,618 | 6,716.6 | 571 | 177.4 | 21,047 | 6,539.2 | 7 | 2.2 | 233 | 72.4 |
| Manchester, N.H. ......... | 13,041 | 4,926.4 | 371 | 140.2 | 12,670 | 4,786.3 | 6 | 2.3 | 106 | 40.0 |
| McAllen-Pharr, Tex. ....... | 10,727 | 4,423.0 | 441 | 181.8 | 10,286 | 4,241.2 | 6 | 2.5 | 67 | 27.6 |
| Melbourne-Titusville, Fla.... | 16,685 | 6,882.1 | 1,359 | 560.6 | 15,326 | 6,321.6 | 21 | 8.7 | 239 | 98.6 |
| Memphis, Tenn.-Ark.-Miss. . | 51,987 | 5,823.3 | 6,648 | 744.7 | 45,339 | 5,078.6 | 116 | 13.0 | 3,505 | 392.6 |
| Miami, Fla. .............. | 139,566 | 9,298.3 | 20,602 | 1,372.6 | 118,964 | 7,925.8 | 320 | 21.3 | 8,186 | 545.4 |
| Milwaukee, Wis. .......... | 70,078 | 4,901.2 | 3,964 | 277.2 | 66,114 | 4,624.0 | 77 | 5.4 | 1,844 | 129.0 |
| Minneapolis-St. Paul, Minn. . | 118,441 | 5,668.5 | 7,438 | 356.0 | 111,003 | 5,312.5 | 66 | 3.2 | 3,446 | 164.9 |
| Mobile, Ala. ............. | 25,213 | 5,749.2 | 2,651 | 604.5 | 22,562 | 5,144.8 | 88 | 20.1 | 780 | 117.9 |
| Montgomery, Ala. ........ | 14,001 | 5,355.5 | 792 | 302.9 | 13,209 | 5,052.5 | 42 | 16.1 | 302 | 115.5 |
| Muskegon, Mich. ......... | 12,235 | 6,775.8 | 1,354 | 749.9 | 10,881 | 6,026.0 | 11 | 6.1 | 234 | 129.6 |
| Nashville, Tenn. .......... | 38,563 | 4,878.3 | 4,095 | 518.0 | 34,468 | 4,360.3 | 107 | 13.5 | 1,902 | 240.6 |
| Nassau-Suffolk, New York.. | 124,182 | 4,642.3 | 5,809 | 217.2 | 118,373 | 4,425.2 | 61 | 2.3 | 2,514 | 94.0 |
| New Brunswick, N.J. ...... | 30,332 | 5,128.0 | 2,031 | 343.4 | 28,301 | 4,784.6 | 26 | 4.4 | 654 | 110.6 |
| New Haven, Conn. ........ | 49,016 | 6,461.4 | 3,027 | 399.0 | 45,989 | 6,062.4 | 40 | 5.3 | 1,732 | 228.3 |
| New London-Norwich, Conn. ... | 14,907 | 6,064.8 | 1,241 | 504.9 | 13,666 | 5,559.9 | 8 | 3.3 | 507 | 206.3 |
| New Orleans, La. ......... | 92,283 | 7,966.7 | 12,680 | 1,094.7 | 79,603 | 6,872.0 | 308 | 26.6 | 6,500 | 561.1 |
| New York, N.Y.-N.J. ....... | 716,197 | 7,805.3 | 137,354 | 1,496.9 | 578,843 | 6,308.4 | 1,814 | 19.8 | 85,028 | 926.7 |
| Newark, N.J. ............. | 127,800 | 5,128.0 | 16,727 | 856.6 | 111,073 | 5,688.4 | 193 | 9.9 | 9,461 | 484.5 |
| Newport News-Hampton, Va. | 17,270 | 4,734.8 | 1,462 | 400.8 | 15,808 | 4,334.0 | 37 | 10.1 | 498 | 136.5 |
| Norfolk, Va.-N.C. ......... | 45,851 | 5,676.8 | 4,046 | 500.9 | 41,805 | 5,175.9 | 96 | 11.9 | 1,658 | 205.3 |
| Northeast, Pa. ........... | 16,953 | 2,698.3 | 775 | 123.4 | 16,178 | 2,574.9 | 14 | 2.2 | 256 | 40.7 |
| Oklahoma City, Okla. ...... | 53,398 | 6,736.8 | 5,018 | 633.1 | 48,380 | 6,103.7 | 101 | 12.7 | 1,440 | 181.7 |
| Omaha, Nebr.-Iowa ....... | 35,103 | 6,002.6 | 2,574 | 440.2 | 33,529 | 5,562.5 | 49 | 8.4 | 1,072 | 183.3 |
| Orlando, Fla. ............ | 54,815 | 8,689.5 | 5,731 | 908.5 | 49,084 | 7,781.0 | 61 | 9.7 | 1,344 | 213.1 |
| Oxnard, Calif. ........... | 25,950 | 5,261.2 | 2,313 | 468.9 | 23,637 | 4,792.2 | 57 | 11.6 | 779 | 157.9 |
| Parkersburg-Marietta, W.Va.-O. | 5,914 | 3,730.1 | 318 | 200.6 | 5,596 | 3,529.5 | 7 | 4.4 | 76 | 47.9 |

[1] Crimes per 100,000 population.  [2] Violent crimes includes murder, forcible rape, robbery, and aggravated assault.
[3] Property crimes include burglary, larceny of $50 or more, and auto theft.

| | TOTAL CRIMES | | VIOLENT CRIMES [2] | | PROPERTY CRIMES [3] | | MURDERS | | ROBBERIES | |
|---|---|---|---|---|---|---|---|---|---|---|
| | Number | Rate [1] | Total | Rate [1] | Total | Rate [1] | Total | Rate [1] | Total | Rate [1] |
| Paterson-Passaic, N.J. ..... | 27,864 | 6,261.5 | 2,302 | 517.3 | 25,562 | 5,744.2 | 29 | 6.5 | 1,167 | 262.2 |
| Pensacola, Fla. ............. | 20,996 | 7,368.3 | 2,056 | 721.5 | 18,940 | 6,646.8 | 31 | 10.9 | 493 | 173.0 |
| Peoria, Ill. ................. | 20,972 | 5,822.4 | 2,436 | 676.3 | 18,536 | 5,146.1 | 13 | 3.6 | 458 | 127.2 |
| Philadelphia, Pa.-N.J. ...... | 221,032 | 4,638.7 | 25,201 | 528.9 | 195,831 | 4,109.8 | 505 | 10.6 | 12,271 | 257.5 |
| Phoenix, Ariz. ............. | 121,325 | 9,013.4 | 9,071 | 673.9 | 112,254 | 8,339.5 | 137 | 10.2 | 3,072 | 228.2 |
| Pittsburgh, Pa. ............ | 74,577 | 3,281.7 | 8,240 | 362.6 | 66,337 | 2,919.1 | 118 | 5.2 | 3,894 | 171.3 |
| Portland, Maine ........... | 13,724 | 6,610.9 | 711 | 342.5 | 13,013 | 6,268.4 | 4 | 1.9 | 136 | 65.5 |
| Portland, Oreg.-Wash. ...... | 82,337 | 6,978.8 | 8,111 | 687.5 | 74,226 | 6,291.3 | 56 | 4.7 | 2,473 | 209.6 |
| Poughkeepsie, N.Y. ........ | 8,969 | 3,866.0 | 768 | 331.0 | 8,201 | 3,534.9 | 9 | 3.9 | 276 | 119.0 |
| Providence-Warwick, R.I. .... | 48,321 | 5,700.9 | 3,167 | 373.6 | 45,154 | 5,327.2 | 30 | 3.5 | 942 | 111.1 |
| Provo-Orem, Utah .......... | 7,720 | 3,982.4 | 253 | 130.5 | 7,467 | 3,851.9 | 3 | 1.5 | 43 | 22.2 |
| Pueblo, Colo. ............. | 8,260 | 6,549.6 | 1,060 | 840.5 | 7,200 | 5,709.1 | 4 | 3.2 | 97 | 76.9 |
| Racine, Wis. .............. | 10,403 | 5,821.9 | 834 | 466.7 | 9,569 | 5,355.2 | 9 | 5.0 | 223 | 124.8 |
| Raleigh-Durham, N.C. ...... | 30,678 | 6,184.4 | 2,172 | 437.9 | 28,506 | 5,746.5 | 47 | 9.5 | 567 | 114.3 |
| Reading, Pa. .............. | 9,093 | 2,981.2 | 668 | 219.0 | 8,425 | 2,762.2 | 6 | 2.0 | 288 | 94.4 |
| Reno, Nev. ............... | 16,122 | 9,352.9 | 1,140 | 661.3 | 14,982 | 8,691.5 | 21 | 12.2 | 636 | 369.0 |
| Richmond, Va. ............ | 35,995 | 5,903.1 | 2,933 | 481.0 | 33,062 | 5,422.1 | 81 | 13.3 | 1,210 | 198.4 |
| Riverside, Calif. ........... | 111,601 | 7,912.8 | 10,499 | 740.9 | 101,152 | 7,172.0 | 200 | 14.2 | 3,200 | 226.9 |
| Roanoke, Va. ............. | 13,727 | 6,450.4 | 640 | 300.7 | 13,087 | 6,149.6 | 17 | 8.0 | 278 | 130.6 |
| Rochester, N.Y. ........... | 57,990 | 6,012.5 | 3,765 | 390.4 | 54,225 | 5,622.1 | 39 | 4.0 | 1,301 | 134.9 |
| Rockford, Ill. ............. | 18,108 | 6,729.2 | 1,429 | 531.0 | 16,679 | 6,198.2 | 14 | 5.2 | 480 | 178.4 |
| Sacramento, Calif. ......... | 85,305 | 8,812.1 | 7,015 | 724.7 | 78,290 | 8,087.4 | 96 | 9.9 | 2,937 | 303.4 |
| Saginaw, Mich. ............ | 16,167 | 7,085.7 | 1,763 | 772.7 | 14,404 | 6,313.0 | 31 | 13.6 | 373 | 163.5 |
| St. Cloud, Minn. ........... | 4,223 | 2,599.0 | 102 | 62.8 | 4,121 | 2,536.2 | 4 | 2.6 | 23 | 14.2 |
| St. Louis, Mo.-Ill. .......... | 141,004 | 5,909.2 | 17,217 | 721.5 | 123,787 | 5,187.7 | 382 | 16.0 | 7,624 | 319.5 |
| Salem, Oreg. .............. | 15,503 | 6,654.4 | 734 | 315.1 | 14,769 | 6,339.3 | 12 | 5.2 | 195 | 83.7 |
| Salinas-Monterey, Calif. ..... | 16,426 | 5,850.3 | 1,553 | 553.1 | 14,873 | 5,297.2 | 33 | 11.8 | 578 | 205.9 |
| Salt Lake City-Ogden, Utah .. | 59,017 | 6,699.6 | 3,365 | 382.0 | 55,652 | 6,317.6 | 52 | 5.9 | 979 | 111.1 |
| San Antonio, Tex. .......... | 63,752 | 5,973.2 | 4,763 | 446.3 | 58,989 | 5,526.9 | 191 | 17.9 | 1,852 | 173.5 |
| San Diego, Calif. .......... | 127,455 | 7,180.4 | 10,227 | 576.2 | 117,228 | 6,604.2 | 143 | 8.1 | 4,634 | 261.1 |
| San Francisco, Calif. ....... | 266,363 | 8,218.0 | 27,951 | 862.4 | 238,412 | 7,355.6 | 357 | 11.0 | 13,812 | 426.1 |
| San Jose, Calif. ........... | 84,002 | 6,696.5 | 5,220 | 416.1 | 78,782 | 6,280.4 | 74 | 5.9 | 2,123 | 169.2 |
| Santa Barbara, Calif. ....... | 21,070 | 7,088.0 | 1,233 | 414.8 | 19,837 | 6,673.2 | 20 | 6.7 | 268 | 90.2 |
| Santa Cruz, Calif. .......... | 12,044 | 6,826.7 | 988 | 560.0 | 11,056 | 6,266.7 | 11 | 6.2 | 200 | 113.4 |
| Sarasota, Fla. ............. | 10,884 | 6,191.1 | 657 | 373.7 | 10,227 | 5,817.3 | 7 | 4.0 | 193 | 109.8 |
| Savannah, Ga. ............. | 18,498 | 8,409.3 | 2,304 | 1,047.4 | 16,194 | 7,361.9 | 30 | 13.6 | 650 | 295.5 |
| Seattle-Everett, Wash. ...... | 109,734 | 7,182.5 | 7,942 | 519.8 | 101,792 | 6,662.6 | 78 | 5.1 | 2,842 | 186.0 |
| Shreveport, La. ............ | 22,210 | 6,142.3 | 2,169 | 599.9 | 20,041 | 5,542.5 | 69 | 19.1 | 528 | 146.0 |
| Sioux City, Iowa-Nebr. ...... | 6,534 | 5,451.5 | 274 | 228.6 | 6,260 | 5,222.9 | 4 | 3.3 | 49 | 40.9 |
| South Bend, Ind. .......... | 16,035 | 5,683.6 | 1,001 | 354.8 | 15,034 | 5,328.8 | 22 | 7.8 | 477 | 169.1 |
| Spokane, Wash. ........... | 23,089 | 6,944.1 | 1,315 | 395.5 | 21,774 | 6,548.6 | 10 | 3.0 | 424 | 127.5 |
| Springfield, Ill. ............ | 13,182 | 7,152.8 | 982 | 532.9 | 12,200 | 6,620.0 | 11 | 6.0 | 330 | 179.1 |
| Springfield, Mo. ........... | 14,445 | 7,041.3 | 709 | 345.6 | 13,736 | 6,695.7 | 14 | 6.8 | 175 | 85.3 |
| Springfield, Ohio .......... | 7,298 | 3,990.4 | 499 | 272.8 | 6,799 | 3,717.5 | 5 | 2.7 | 227 | 124.1 |
| Stockton, Calif. ........... | 26,719 | 8,382.5 | 2,387 | 748.9 | 24,332 | 7,633.7 | 64 | 20.1 | 908 | 284.9 |
| Syracuse, N.Y. ............ | 33,503 | 5,183.8 | 1,786 | 276.3 | 31,717 | 4,907.4 | 17 | 2.6 | 938 | 145.1 |
| Tacoma, Wash. ............ | 29,578 | 6,507.0 | 2,248 | 494.5 | 27,330 | 6,012.5 | 23 | 5.1 | 697 | 153.3 |
| Tallahassee, Fla. ........... | 11,590 | 8,004.0 | 1,096 | 756.9 | 10,494 | 7,247.1 | 3 | 2.1 | 163 | 112.6 |
| Tampa-St. Petersburg, Fla. ... | 107,136 | 7,418.9 | 11,319 | 783.8 | 95,817 | 6,635.1 | 107 | 7.4 | 2,850 | 197.4 |
| Terre Haute, Ind. .......... | 8,312 | 4,757.3 | 268 | 153.4 | 8,044 | 4,603.9 | 10 | 5.7 | 129 | 73.8 |
| Toledo, Ohio-Mich. ........ | 50,548 | 6,537.3 | 4,238 | 548.1 | 46,310 | 5,989.2 | 60 | 7.8 | 2,026 | 262.0 |
| Topeka, Kans. ............. | 11,794 | 6,267.2 | 1,051 | 558.5 | 10,743 | 5,708.7 | 11 | 5.8 | 272 | 144.5 |
| Trenton, N.J. .............. | 21,410 | 6,745.1 | 1,739 | 547.9 | 19,671 | 6,197.2 | 31 | 9.8 | 1,007 | 317.2 |
| Tucsson, Ariz. ............. | 40,342 | 8,394.6 | 2,696 | 561.0 | 37,646 | 7,833.6 | 28 | 5.8 | 863 | 179.6 |
| Tulsa, Okla. .............. | 35,989 | 5,687.2 | 2,954 | 468.0 | 32,945 | 5,219.2 | 57 | 9.0 | 765 | 121.2 |
| Utica-Rome, N.Y. .......... | 9,760 | 3,013.9 | 498 | 153.8 | 9,262 | 2,860.1 | 9 | 2.8 | 183 | 56.5 |
| Vallejo-Fairfield-Napa, Calif. .. | 19,409 | 6,334.0 | 1,474 | 481.0 | 17,935 | 5,852.9 | 23 | 7.5 | 355 | 115.9 |
| Waco, Tex. ................ | 10,440 | 6,310.1 | 817 | 493.8 | 9,623 | 5,816.3 | 8 | 4.8 | 198 | 119.7 |
| Washington, D.C.-Md.-Va. ... | 198,384 | 6,588.2 | 20,866 | 693.0 | 177,518 | 5,895.3 | 281 | 9.3 | 11,763 | 390.6 |
| Waterloo-Cedar Falls, Iowa ... | 9,528 | 6,847.3 | 380 | 273.1 | 9,148 | 6,574.2 | 6 | 4.3 | 150 | 107.8 |
| West Palm Beach, Fla. ...... | 47,657 | 9,467.1 | 4,605 | 914.8 | 43,052 | 8,552.3 | 71 | 14.1 | 1,248 | 247.9 |
| Wheeling, W.Va.-Ohio ...... | 4,476 | 2,460.1 | 296 | 162.7 | 4,180 | 2,297.4 | 7 | 3.8 | 113 | 62.1 |
| Wichita, Kans. ............. | 25,066 | 6,228.6 | 1,766 | 438.8 | 23,300 | 5,789.8 | 39 | 9.7 | 711 | 176.7 |
| Wichita Falls, Tex. ......... | 7,578 | 5,711.4 | 896 | 675.3 | 6,682 | 5,036.1 | 6 | 4.5 | 246 | 185.4 |
| Wilmington, Del.-N.J.-Md. .... | 33,333 | 6,469.7 | 2,485 | 482.3 | 30,848 | 5,987.3 | 30 | 5.8 | 714 | 138.6 |
| Wilmington, N.C. ........... | 10,227 | 7,802.2 | 872 | 665.3 | 9,355 | 7,137.0 | 12 | 9.2 | 211 | 161.0 |
| Worcester, Mass. ........... | 28,239 | 4,381.0 | 1,858 | 288.2 | 26,381 | 4,092.7 | 26 | 4.0 | 628 | 97.4 |
| Yakima, Wash. ............. | 11,849 | 7,149.6 | 1,093 | 659.5 | 10,756 | 6,490.1 | 14 | 8.4 | 187 | 112.8 |
| York, Pa. ................. | 13,577 | 3,824.2 | 783 | 220.5 | 12,794 | 3,603.7 | 5 | 1.4 | 399 | 112.4 |
| Youngstown-Warren, Ohio .... | 21,145 | 3,880.7 | 1,942 | 356.4 | 19,203 | 3,524.3 | 44 | 8.1 | 688 | 126.3 |

[1] Crimes per 100,000 population. [2] Violent crimes includes murder, forcible rape, robbery, and aggravated assault.
[3] Property crimes include burglary, larceny of $50 or more, and auto theft.

# HISTORIC ASSASSINATIONS

**44 B.C. (March 15) Julius Caesar,** Roman general and dictator, stabbed to death in Roman Senate by Brutus, Cimber, Cassius, Casca and others.

**1792 (March 16) Gustavus III,** king of Sweden, shot at masked ball by assassin hired by nobles.

**1793 (July 13) Jean Marat,** French Revolutionary leader, stabbed by Charlotte Corday.

**1801 (March 24) Paul I,** czar of Russia, slain by Russian nobles after he refused to abdicate.

**1865 (April 14) Abraham Lincoln,** 16th U.S. President, shot by John Wilkes Booth in Ford's Theater in Washington, D.C. Died next day.

**1881 (March 13) Alexander II,** czar of Russia, assassinated by Russian terrorist.

**1881 (July 2) James A. Garfield,** 20th U.S. President, shot by disappointed job seeker Charles J. Guiteau. Died Sept. 19, 1881.

**1898 (Sept. 10) Elizabeth,** empress of Austria, assassinated in Geneva by Italian anarchist.

**1900 (July 29) Humbert I,** king of Italy, killed by Gaetano Bresci in Monza, Italy.

**1901 (Sept. 6) William McKinley,** 25th U.S. President, shot by anarchist Leon Czolgosz in Buffalo, N.Y. Died eight days later.

**1903 (June 11) Alexander I,** king of Serbia, and his wife, assassinated in Belgrade.

**1908 (Feb. 1) Carlos I,** king of Portugal, and his son, the crown prince, shot in Lisbon.

**1913 (Feb. 22) Francisco I. Madero,** president of Mexico, shot by guard after being imprisoned by Gen. Victoriano Huerta.

**1913 (March 18) George I,** king of Greece, assassinated during second Balkan War.

**1914 (June 28) Francis Ferdinand,** archduke of Austria-Hungary, and his wife, shot by Serbian nationalist in Sarajevo, starting World War I.

**1916 (Dec. 30) Grigori Rasputin,** Russian monk, poisoned, stabbed, and shot by nobles who hated his influence on Czar Nicholas II.

**1918 (July 16) Nicholas II,** czar of Russia, his wife, and children, shot in Ekaterinburg.

**1919 (April 10) Emiliano Zapata,** Mexican revolutionary and reformer, killed in ambush by agents of President Venustiano Carranza.

**1923 (July 20) Pancho Villa,** Mexican revolutionary, assassinated at his estate in Durango.

**1928 (July 17) Alvaro Obregón,** president of Mexico, killed by Roman Catholic fanatic.

**1934 (July 25) Engelbert Dollfuss,** Austrian chancellor, assassinated by Nazis.

**1934 (Oct. 9) Alexander I,** king of Yugoslavia, killed by terrorist in Marseille, France.

**1935 (Sept. 8) Huey P. Long,** U.S. senator from Louisiana and candidate for Democratic presidential nomination, shot by Dr. Carl A. Weiss. Died two days later.

**1940 (Aug. 20) Leon Trotsky,** Russian revolutionary exile, stabbed by Stalinist agent Ramón Mercader in Mexico City. Died next day.

**1948 (Jan. 30) Mohandas Gandhi,** leader of India, shot by Nathuram Godse, Hindu who blamed Gandhi for partition of India.

**1951 (July 20) Abdullah ibn Hussein,** king of Jordan, assassinated in Jerusalem.

**1955 (Jan. 2) José Antonio Remón,** president of Panama, killed by machine-gunner.

**1956 (Sept. 21) Anastasio Somoza,** president of Nicaragua, shot during election campaign dance. Died eight days later.

**1957 (July 26) Carlos Castillo Armas,** president of Guatemala, shot by a palace guard.

**1958 (July 14) Faisal II,** king of Iraq, killed in revolt by Abdul Karim Kassem.

**1959 (Sept. 25) Solomon Bandaranaike,** prime minister of Ceylon, shot by Buddhist monk.

**1960 (Aug. 29) Hazza Majali,** premier of Jordan, killed by time bomb in his office.

**1961 (May 30) Rafael L. Trujillo,** dictator and president of the Dominican Republic, slain.

**1963 (Jan. 13) Sylvanus Olympio,** president of Togo, killed by former soldiers in Lomé.

**1963 (Nov. 1-2) Ngo Dinh Diem,** president of South Vietnam, and his brother slain.

**1963 (Nov. 22) John F. Kennedy,** U.S. President, shot by Lee Harvey Oswald in Dallas.

**1966 (Sept. 6) Hendrik F. Verwoerd,** prime minister of South Africa, stabbed in parliament in Cape Town by Dimitrio Stifanos.

**1968 (April 4) Martin Luther King Jr.,** U.S. civil-rights leader, shot by ex-convict James Earl Ray in Memphis, Tenn.

**1968 (June 5) Robert F. Kennedy,** U.S. senator from New York, shot by Sirhan Sirhan in Los Angeles while celebrating California presidential primary victory. Died next day.

**1969 (Oct. 15) A. A. Shermarke,** president of Somalia, assassinated in Las Anos, Somalia.

**1973 (March 2) Cleo A. Noel Jr.,** U.S. ambassador, slain in Khartoum, Sudan, by Arab terrorists.

**1974 (Aug. 19) Rodger P. Davies,** U.S. ambassador, slain by Greek Cypriots in embassy at Nicosia, Cyprus.

**1975 (Feb. 11) Madagascar head of state** Col. Richard Ratsimandrava slain in ambush.

**1975 (March 25) King Faisal of Saudi Arabia** shot by nephew during palace reception.

**1975 (April 13) President N'Garta Tombalbaye** of Chad slain in military coup.

**1975 (Aug. 15) Bangladesh President Mujibur Rahman** killed by army officers in coup.

**1976 (Feb. 13) Nigeria's head of state, Gen. Murtala Ramat Muhammed,** killed in unsuccessful coup attempt.

**1976 (June 16) U.S. Ambassador to Lebanon Francis Meloy Jr.** assassinated by terrorists.

**1976 (July 21) British Ambassador to Ireland Christopher Biggs** slain in Ireland.

**1977 (Feb. 3) Ethiopia's chief of state Gen. Teferi Bante** assassinated in coup, reportedly by Mengistu Haile Mariam, who became dictator.

**1977 (March 18) Congo's President Marien Ngouabi** assassinated in Brazzaville.

**1977 (Oct. 11) North Yemen's President Ibrahim al-Hamdi** and his brother assassinated in Sana.

**1978 (April 27) Afghanistan's President Mohammad Daoud** slain in communist coup in Kabul.

**1978 (June 24) North Yemen's President Ahmed Hussein al-Ghashmi** assassinated by bomb carried by South Yemen envoy.

**1978 (Nov. 18) U.S. Rep. Leo J. Ryan** and 4 other Americans assassinated in Guyana by California religious sect whose members subsequently join in mass suicide-murder with 914 deaths.

**1978 (Nov. 27) San Francisco's Mayor George Moscone assassinated** by disgruntled former official Dan White.

**1979 (Feb. 14) Adolph Dubs,** U.S. Ambassador to Afghanistan, kidnapped by terrorists and killed in police shootout.

**1979 (Aug. 27) Britain's Earl Mountbatten of Burma** assassinated by remote-control bomb exploded by Irish terrorists.

**1979 (Sept 14) Afghanistan's President Noor Taraki** fatally wounded in palace coup by his prime minister, Hafizullah Amin.

**1979 (Oct. 26) South Korean President Park Chung Hee** assassinated during dinner by his intelligence chief.

# Earth

United Press Int'l.

Chinese anthropologists and local workmen conducted an extensive search in 1980 for new clues to ancient "Peking Man" near the village of Zhoukoudian, China. Remains of "Peking Man," believed to be about 500,000 years old, were discovered in the area in 1927, but were lost while being shipped to the U.S. during World War II.

## HIGHLIGHTS: 1980

### LIFE 3.5 BILLION YEARS AGO

Life has existed on the Earth for at least 3.5 billion years, according to evidence disclosed by the National Science Foundation in June 1980. The new discovery pushed back the existence of life to within about a billion years after the Earth itself is believed to have come into being.

The evidence of the earliest known form of life was found in rocks discovered in the desert area of northwestern Australia. These rocks contain the fossils of tiny bacteria consisting of strings of cells that can only be seen through the magnification of a microscope.

The findings were the result of a meticulous 3-year scientific investigation conducted by the Precambrian Paleobiology Research Group under the direction of J. William Schopf, professor of paleobiology at the University of California at Los Angeles. The investigators found five distinct types of fossil bacteria in the rocks.

### DID COMETS BRING LIFE?

As the amount of time between the origin of the Earth and the origin of life on Earth

## FACTS ABOUT THE EARTH

**Age of Earth:** 4.6 to 5 billion years.

**Area of Earth:** *Total area,* 196,940,000 square miles; *Land area,* 30%, 57,506,000 square miles; *Water area,* 70%, 139,434,000 square miles.

**Atmosphere of Earth:** Extends about 1,000 miles above surface; *Chemical composition,* nitrogen 78%, oxygen 21%, argon and other gases 1%.

**Circumference of Earth:** *Polar circumference* (distance around Earth at poles), 24,859.82 miles; *Equatorial circumference* (distance at equator), 24,901.55 mi.

**Density of Earth:** 5.52 (water has density of 1).

**Diameter of Earth:** *Polar diameter* (through Earth from pole to pole), 7,899.83 miles; *Equatorial diameter* (through Earth at equator), 7,926.41 miles.

**Distance of Moon from Earth:** *Closest distance,* 221,456 miles; *Farthest distance,* 252,711 miles; *Average distance,* 238,875 miles.

**Distance of Sun from Earth:** *Closest distance,* 91.4 million miles; *Farthest distance,* 94.5 million miles; *Average distance,* 92.9 million miles.

**Escape Velocity from Earth:** 7 miles per second.

**Inclination of Earth on Axis:** 23° 27'.

**Interior of Earth:** *Crust,* made up of igneous, sedimentary, and metamorphic rock, extends 20 miles deep under continents and about 5 miles deep under oceans; *Mantle,* layer of solid rock about 1,800 miles thick beneath Earth's crust, has temperatures of 1600° to 4400°F.; *Outer Core,* 1,400-mile thick layer of molten iron and nickel between mantle and inner core, has temperatures of 4000° to 9000°F.; *Inner Core,* ball of solid iron and nickel at Earth's center with diameter of about 1,600 miles, with temperature of about 9,000°F.

**Period of Revolution of Earth around Sun:** 1 year (or 365 days, 6 hours, 9 minutes, 9.54 seconds).

**Period of Rotation of Earth on Axis:** 1 day (or 23 hours, 56 minutes, 4.09 seconds).

**Speed of Earth in Orbit around Sun:** 18.5 miles per second.

**Volume of Earth:** 260 billion cubic miles.

**Weight or Mass of Earth:** 6,586,000,000,000,000,000,000 tons (or 6.586 sextillion tons).

## HIGHLIGHTS: 1980 *(continued)*

has diminished through new discoveries, scientists have become increasingly dissatisfied with the theory that primitive forms of life occurred spontaneously by an accidental mixing of chemicals.

A new theory of the origin of life on Earth was offered in 1980 by Dr. Chandra Wickramasinghe of University College in Cardiff, Wales.

He suggested that life was first brought to this planet by comets, which contained bacteria frozen in ice.

However, other scientists disputed the theory, arguing that even if bacteria were carried inside comets they would be unable to survive high levels of radiation in space.

### ASTEROID COLLISION WITH EARTH?

Nobel Laureate Luis Alvarez of the University of California presented evidence at a meeting of the American Association for the Advancement of Science in 1980 that an asteroid collided with the earth about 65 million years ago. The collision, Alvarez said, would have resulted in the formation of a huge dust cloud that shut off sunlight to the earth for as long as five years, killing off all the dinosaurs.

Alvarez said that evidence for his theory came from 65-million-year-old rock samples that he and his son had collected from Denmark, Italy, Spain, and from the ocean floor. The samples all showed a concentration of rare metals usually found in meteorites.

If the asteroid had crashed into the ocean, signs of its crater would long since have been eroded, Alvarez said.

### ARTIFACTS OF CLEOPATRA DISCOVERED

Underwater archaeologists reported two major discoveries in 1980 relating to Egypt's Queen Cleopatra. One group announced they

Previously unknown irrigation canals dug by the ancient Maya Indians were discovered by archaeologist Richard E. W. Adams in this radar aerial photograph of Guatemala's rain forest. The canals are not visible in ordinary photographs. The special synthetic aperture radar (SAR) was developed by NASA to map the planet Venus.

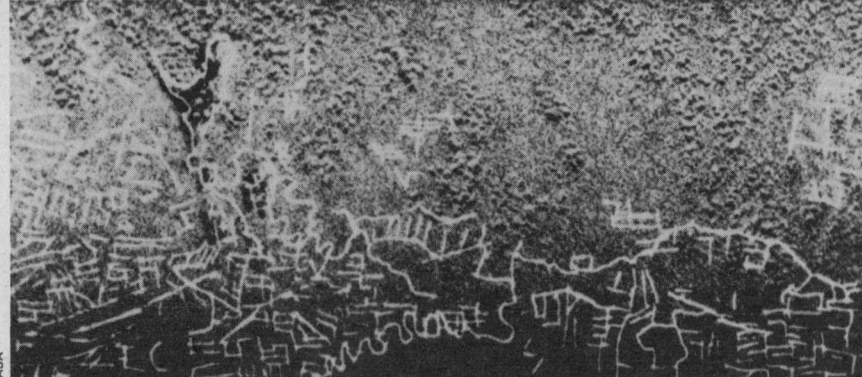

NASA

Louisiana State University geology student Winston Lancaster examines the 48-inch-long skull of a 45-million-year-old whale that was discovered on July 31, 1980, on the banks of the Red River near Montgomery, La.

Wide World

had found shipwrecks remaining from the Battle of Actium in 31 B.C. in which Cleopatra's fleet was defeated by the Romans. Another group said they had discovered her palace under the waters of the harbor of Alexandria, Egypt.

### THE SEARCH FOR ALEXANDER

Utilizing artifacts found in 1977 at the tomb of what is believed to be that of the father of Alexander the Great, a major exhibition called "The Search for Alexander" opened at the National Gallery in Washington, D.C., in November 1980. After remaining there until April 5, 1981, it will be shown at The Art Institute of Chicago from May 14 to Sept. 7, at the Museum of Fine Arts in Boston from Oct. 23, 1981, to Jan. 10, 1982, and then at the Fine Arts Museum of San Francisco from Feb. 19 to May 16, 1982.

As well as objects from the royal tomb, the exhibit contains many ancient works of art in silver and gold relating to Alexander's era that were collected from northern Greece.

## EXTREMES OF THE EARTH
Source: National Geographic Society

| | | | |
|---|---|---|---|
| Highest mountain | Mt. Everest, Nepal–China; 29,028 feet | Deepest lake | Baykal, U.S.S.R.; 5,315 ft. |
| Lowest point on surface | Dead Sea, Israel-Jordan; –1,312 feet below sea level | Driest spot | Atacama Desert, Chile; rainfall barely measurable |
| Greatest ocean depth | Mariana Trench, Pacific Ocean; 36,198 feet | Northernmost town | Ny Alesund, Spitsbergen, Norway |
| Highest volcano | Chimborazo, Ecuador; 20,561 feet | Southernmost town | Puerto Williams, Chile |
| | | Lowest town | Villages along Dead Sea; 299 feet below sea level |
| Largest desert | Sahara, North Africa; over 3 million square miles | Largest gorge | Grand Canyon, Colorado River, Arizona; 277 miles long, 1 to 20 miles wide, 1 mile deep |
| Largest island | Greenland; 840,000 square miles | | |
| Longest river | Nile, Africa; 4,145 miles | Deepest gorge | Hells Canyon, Snake River, Idaho; 7,900 feet deep |
| Highest waterfall | Angel Falls, Venezuela; 3,212 feet | Strongest wind | 231 mph; record in 1924 at Mt. Washington, New Hampshire |
| Largest lake | Caspian Sea, Asia; 143,244 square miles | Greatest tides | Bay of Fundy, Nova Scotia; 53 feet |
| Rainiest spot | Mt. Waialeale, Hawaii; average 460 inches a year | Biggest meteor crater | New Quebec, Canada; 2 miles wide |

## SEVEN CONTINENTS
Source: National Geographic Society

| NAME | AREA (in square miles) | % OF WORLD'S LAND | HIGHEST POINT (in feet) | LOWEST POINT (feet below sea level) | TEMPERATURE RECORDS HIGHEST (with date) | LOWEST (with date) |
|---|---|---|---|---|---|---|
| Asia | 16,998,000 | 29.7 | Mt. Everest Nepal–China (29,028) | Dead Sea, Israel–Jordan (1,312) | Tirat Zevi, Israel 129.0°F. (June 21, 1942) | Oymyakon, Soviet Union –89.9°F. (Feb. 6, 1933) |
| Africa | 11,682,000 | 20.4 | Mt. Kilimanjaro, Tanzania (19,340) | Lake Assal, Djibouti (512) | Al Aziziyah, Libya 136.0°F. (Sept. 13, 1922) | Ifrane, Morocco –11.2°F. (Feb. 11, 1935) |
| North America | 9,366,000 | 16.3 | Mt. McKinley, Alaska (20,320) | Death Valley, California (282) | Death Valley, California 134.0°F. (July 10, 1913) | Snag, Yukon, Canada –81.0°F. (Feb. 3, 1947) |
| South America | 6,881,000 | 12.0 | Mt. Aconcagua, Argentina (22,834) | Valdes Peninsula, Argentina (131) | Rivadavia, Argentina 120.0°F. (Dec. 11, 1905) | Sarmiento, Argentina –27.4°F. (June 1, 1907) |
| Antarctica | 5,100,000 | 8.9 | Vinson Massif (16,860) | Not known | Esperanza Station 58.3°F. (Oct. 20, 1956) | Vostok –127.0°F. (Aug. 24, 1960) |
| Europe | 4,017,000 | 7.0 | Mt. Elbrus, Soviet Union (18,510) | Caspian Sea, Soviet Union (92) | Seville, Spain 122.0°F. (Aug. 4, 1881) | Ust' Schchugor, Soviet Union –67.0°F. |
| Australia | 2,966,000 | 5.2 | Mt. Kosciusko, New South Wales (7,310) | Lake Eyre, South Australia (52) | Cloncurry, Queensland 127.6°F. (Jan. 16, 1889) | Charlotte Pass, New S. Wales –8.0°F. (July 22, 1947) |

## OCEANS OF THE EARTH AND THEIR GREATEST DEPTHS
Source: National Geographic Society

| OCEANS | AREA (in sq. mi.) | PERCENT OF WORLD'S WATER | GREATEST DEPTH IN OCEANS Location | Feet |
|---|---|---|---|---|
| Pacific Ocean | 64,186,300 | 46.0% | Mariana Trench, off the Mariana Islands | 36,198 |
| Atlantic Ocean | 33,420,000 | 23.9% | Puerto Rico Trench, off Puerto Rico | 28,374 |
| Indian Ocean | 28,350,500 | 20.3% | Java Trench, off Java | 25,344 |
| Arctic Ocean | 5,105,700 | 3.7% | Eurasia Basin | 17,880 |
| Total | 131,062,500 | 93.9% | | |

## SEAS OF THE EARTH AND THEIR AVERAGE DEPTHS

| SEAS | AREA (sq. mi.) | AVERAGE DEPTH (feet) | SEAS | AREA (sq. mi.) | AVERAGE DEPTH (feet) |
|---|---|---|---|---|---|
| South China Sea | 1,148,500 | 4,802 | East China Sea | 256,600 | 620 |
| Caribbean Sea | 971,400 | 8,448 | Andaman Sea | 218,100 | 3,667 |
| Mediterranean Sea | 969,100 | 4,926 | Black Sea | 196,100 | 3,906 |
| Bering Sea | 873,000 | 4,893 | Red Sea | 174,900 | 1,764 |
| Gulf of Mexico | 582,100 | 5,297 | North Sea | 164,900 | 308 |
| Sea of Okhotsk | 537,500 | 3,192 | Baltic Sea | 147,500 | 180 |
| Sea of Japan | 391,100 | 5,468 | Yellow Sea | 113,500 | 121 |
| Hudson Bay | 281,900 | 305 | | | |

# EARTH HISTORY

The rocks of the Earth's crust tell scientists the history of our planet. Because the rocks form layers, or *strata,* the dating of various eras and periods of Earth history relates to the age of these rocks.

## AZOIC ERA

The Earth began during this era, about 4.6 to 5 billion years ago when the solar system formed around the Sun. The oldest rocks found on the Moon, dated as 4.66 billion years old, are believed to be from this era. Meteorites, thought to have formed at the same time as the Earth, have been dated by the radioactive technique as being 4.7 billion years old. The air and the oceans formed.

## ARCHEOZOIC ERA

Beginning about 3.5 billion years ago, life originated in the warm seas in the form of bacteria and algae. Some kinds of chert, slate, and marble formed in this period contain fossils of these early types of life.

## PROTEROZOIC ERA

About 1.2 billion years ago, the first animals began to live in the oceans. These were invertebrates, or animals without backbones. They included sponges, jellyfish, and worms. Rocks that formed in this era included many metal ores, such as iron and copper. Land thrust up as continents.

## PALEOZOIC ERA

Much more is known of this era than of earlier eras because of the plentiful supply of fossils that have been found. The era is divided into six major periods.

**Cambrian Period** began about 600 million years ago and lasted about 120 million years. Most of North America was covered with seas. Mountains formed in Vermont. Fossils of small sea animals called trilobites date from this period. The first fish appeared.

**Ordovician Period** began about 500 million years ago and lasted about 45 million years. Corals and animals with shells developed in the seas.

**Silurian Period** began about 435 million years ago and lasted 30 million years. Gas, oil, and salt deposits formed. The first animals that breathed air appeared.

**Devonian Period** began about 405 million years ago and lasted 60 million years. Sharks and other large fish lived in the seas. The first amphibian animals crawled onto the land. Forests covered the swampy land.

**Carboniferous Period** began 345 million years ago and lasted about 70 million years. It is often divided into two equal-length periods called the *Mississippian* and *Pennsylvanian.* The first land animals with backbones, the reptiles, appeared. Huge coal deposits formed.

**Permian Period** began about 275 million years ago and lasted about 50 million years. The Appalachian Mountains formed in North America. The first plants with seeds developed—trees with cones.

## MESOZOIC ERA

This was the era of the dinosaurs.

**Triassic Period** began about 225 million years ago and lasted 45 million years. The first dinosaurs and turtles appeared.

**Jurassic Period** began 180 million years ago and lasted about 50 million years. The mountains of the Sierra Nevada and California Coast ranges were formed. Dinosaurs reached their biggest size. Small mammals began living on the land. Birds began to fly.

**Cretaceous Period** began about 130 million years ago and lasted about 65 million years. The Rocky Mountains formed in North America. The huge dinosaurs died out. Plants with flowers appeared.

## CENOZOIC ERA

**Tertiary Period** began about 65 million years ago and lasted about 62 million years.

*Paleocene Epoch* began 65 million years ago and lasted about 10 million years. Erosion formed soil in which flowering plants flourished. The earliest primates appeared.

*Eocene Epoch* began about 55 million years ago and lasted about 15 million years. Modern mammals appeared, including whales, camels, and monkeys.

*Oligocene Epoch* began 40 million years ago and lasted 14 million years. Large grazing animals appeared, as did primitive apes.

*Miocene Epoch* began 26 million years ago and lasted about 12 million years. Dogs, elephants, and apes became common throughout Asia and Africa.

*Pliocene Epoch* began 14 million years ago and lasted about 11 million years. The Cascade Mountains formed in North America. Most modern kinds of animals appeared, as well as the first men.

**Quaternary Period** began about 3,100,000 years ago and lasts to the present day.

*Pleistocene Epoch* lasted over 3,000,000 years. During this Ice Age, glaciers formed over most of North America and Eurasia four times. Prehistoric man hunted, made tools, tamed animals, and began farming.

*Holocene Epoch* covers the most recent 10,000 years, since the retreat of the last glaciers. Civilization developed.

## U.S. GEOGRAPHIC CENTERS AND HIGHEST AND LOWEST POINTS

Source: Geological Survey, U.S. Department of the Interior

| STATE | GEOGRAPHIC CENTER [1]<br>County and Locality | HIGHEST POINT [2]<br>Name and Altitude (in feet) | LOWEST POINT<br>Name and Altitude (in feet) |
|---|---|---|---|
| UNITED STATES | Butte Co., S.D. (West of Castle Rock) | Mt. McKinley (20,320) | Death Valley (−282) |
| Alabama | Chilton (12 mi. SW of Clanton) | Cheaha Mountain (2,407) | Gulf of Mexico [3] |
| Alaska | 63° 50′ N, 152° 00′ W, 60 miles NW of Mt. McKinley | Mt. McKinley (20,320) | Pacific Ocean [3] |
| Arizona | Yavapai (55 mi. ESE of Prescott) | Humphreys Peak (12,633) | Colorado River(70) |
| Arkansas | Pulaski (12 mi. NW of Little Rock) | Magazine Mountain (2,753) | Ouachita River (55) |
| California | Madera (38 mi. E of Madera) | Mt. Whitney (14,494) | Death Valley (−282) |
| Colorado | Park (30 mi. NW of Pikes Peak) | Mt. Elbert (14,433) | Arkansas River (3,350) |
| Connecticut | Hartford (at East Berlin) | Mt. Frissell, on south slope (2,380) | Long Island Sound [3] |
| Delaware | Kent (11 mi. S of Dover) | Ebright Road (442) | Atlantic Ocean [3] |
| District of Columbia | Near 4th and L Streets NW | Tenleytown (410) | Potomac River (1) |
| Florida | Hernando (12 mi. NNW of Brooksville) | Sec. 30, T6N, R20′W, Walton Co. (345) | Atlantic Ocean [3] |
| Georgia | Twiggs (18 mi. SE of Macon) | Brasstown Bald (4,784) | Atlantic Ocean [3] |
| Hawaii | Hawaii (20° 15′ N, 156° 20′ W, off Maui Island) | Mauna Kea (13,796) | Pacific Ocean [3] |
| Idaho | Custer (at Custer, SW of Challis) | Borah Peak (12,662) | Snake River (710) |
| Illinois | Logan (28 mi. NE of Springfield) | Charles Mound (1,235) | Mississippi River (279) |
| Indiana | Boone (14 mi. NNW of Indianapolis) | Franklin T, Wayne Co. (1,257) | Ohio River (320) |
| Iowa | Story (5 mi. NE of Ames) | Sec. 29, T100N, R41W, Osceola Co. (1,670) | Mississippi River (480) |
| Kansas | Barton (15 mi. NE of Great Bend) | Mt. Sunflower (4,039) | Verdigris River (680) |
| Kentucky | Marion (3 mi. NNW of Lebanon) | Black Mountain (4,145) | Mississippi River (257) |
| Louisiana | Avoyelles Parish (3 mi. SE of Marksville) | Driskill Mountain (535) | New Orleans (−5) |
| Maine | Piscataquis (18 mi. N of Dover) | Mt. Katahdin (5,268) | Atlantic Ocean [3] |
| Maryland | Prince Georges (4½ miles NW of Davidsonville) | Backbone Mountain (3,360) | Atlantic Ocean [3] |
| Massachusetts | Worcester (north part of city of Worcester) | Mt. Greylock (3,491) | Atlantic Ocean [3] |
| Michigan | Wexford (5 mi. NNW of Cadillac) | Mt. Curwood (1,980) | Lake Erie (572) |
| Minnesota | Crow Wing (10 mi. SW of Brainerd) | Eagle Mountain, Cook Co. (2,301) | Lake Superior (602) |
| Mississippi | Leake (9 mi. WNW of Carthage) | Woodall Mountain (806) | Gulf of Mexico [3] |
| Missouri | Miller (20 mi. SW of Jefferson City) | Taum Sauk Mountain (1,772) | St. Francis River (230) |
| Montana | Fergus (12 mi. W of Lewistown) | Granite Peak (12,799) | Kootenai River (1,800) |
| Nebraska | Custer (10 mi. NW of Broken Bow) | Johnson T. Kimball Co. (5,426) | SE corner of state (840) |
| Nevada | Lander (26 mi. SE of Austin) | Boundary Peak (13,143) | Colorado River (470) |
| New Hampshire | Belknap (3 mi. E. of Ashland) | Mt. Washington (6,288) | Atlantic Ocean [3] |
| New Jersey | Mercer (5 mi. SE of Trenton) | High Point (1,803) | Atlantic Ocean [3] |
| New Mexico | Torrance (12 mi. SSW of Willard) | Wheeler Peak (13,161) | Red.Bluff Reservoir (2,817) |
| New York | Madison (12+ mi. S of Oneida and 26+ mi. SW of Utica) | Mt. Marcy (5,344) | Atlantic Ocean [3] |
| North Carolina | Chatham (10 mi. NW of Sanford) | Mt. Mitchell (6,684) | Atlantic Ocean [3] |
| North Dakota | Sheridan (5 mi. SW of McClusky) | White Butte, Slope Co. (3,506) | Red River (750) |
| Ohio | Delaware (25 mi. NNE of Columbus) | Campbell Hill (1,550) | Ohio River (433) |
| Oklahoma | Oklahoma (8 mi. N of Oklahoma City) | Black Mesa (4,973) | Little River (287) |
| Oregon | Crook (25 mi. SSE of Prineville) | Mt. Hood (11,239) | Pacific Ocean [3] |
| Pennsylvania | Centre (2½ mi. SW of Bellefonte) | Mt. Davis (3,213) | Delaware River [3] |
| Rhode Island | Kent (1 mi. SSW of Crompton) | Jerimoth Hill (812) | Atlantic Ocean [3] |
| South Carolina | Richland (13 mi. SE of Columbia) | Sassafras Mountain (3,560) | Atlantic Ocean [3] |
| South Dakota | Hughes (8 mi. NE of Pierre) | Harney Peak (7,242) | Big Stone Lake (962) |
| Tennessee | Rutherford (5 mi. NE of Murfreesboro) | Clingmans Dome (6,643) | Mississippi River (182) |
| Texas | McCulloch (15 mi. NE of Brady) | Guadalupe Peak (8,749) | Gulf of Mexico [3] |
| Utah | Sanpete (3 mi. N of Manti) | Kings Peak (13,528) | Beaverdam Creek (2,000) |
| Vermont | Washington (3 mi. E of Roxbury) | Mt. Mansfield (4,393) | Lake Champlain (95) |
| Virginia | Buckingham (5 mi. SW of Buckingham) | Mt. Rogers (5,729) | Atlantic Ocean [3] |
| Washington | Chelan (10 mi. WSW of Wenatchee) | Mt. Rainier (14,410) | Pacific Ocean [3] |
| West Virginia | Braxton (4 mi. E of Sutton) | Spruce Knob (4,863) | Potomac River (240) |
| Wisconsin | Wood (9 mi. SE of Marshfield) | Timms Hill, Price Co. (1,952) | Lake Michigan (581) |
| Wyoming | Fremont (58 mi. ENE of Lander) | Gannett Peak (13,804) | Belle Fourche River (3,100) |

[1] Approximate   [2] Sec. = section;   T = township;   R = range;   N = north;   W = west;   S = south;   [3] Sea level.

# PREHISTORIC MAN

In the 1600s people believed that man had lived on Earth for less than 6,000 years. But with Charles Darwin's publication of the theory of evolution in 1859, anthropologists began searching for a "missing link" that might prove man had evolved from a lower primate.

The most ancient complete human skull was found by anthropologist Richard Leakey in Kenya in 1972. It has been dated as 2.9 million years old. His parents, anthropologists Louis and Mary Leakey, first proved in 1959–63 that man had lived over 1 million years ago.

Anthropologists classify prehistoric humans into several genera based largely on brain shape and size.

## HOMO SAPIENS—500,000 B.C. TO PRESENT

Two general types of prehistoric men have skulls about the size of modern men, and are classified as *Homo sapiens*.

**Cro-Magnon Man** was like modern man, standing about 6 feet tall. He was named after fossils found at Cro-Magnon, France, by Édouard Larter in 1868. The oldest remains of Cro-Magnon Man have been dated as about 35,000 years old.

**Neanderthal Man** had a brain the size of modern man's, but was somewhat shorter and had heavier bones. Fossils of Neanderthal Man were the first remains of prehistoric man to be found, creating a scientific sensation at the time of their discovery in 1856 in the Neander Valley near Düsseldorf, Germany, by Johann C. Fuhlrott.

Neanderthals are believed to have lived from about 500,000 to 25,000 B.C. in many parts of the world. Fossil remains of this type were found in Zambia (then Northern Rhodesia) in 1921 and called Rhodesian Man. Similar fossil remains found in Java, Indonesia, from 1931 to 1936 were called Solo Man. Other Neanderthaloid fossils were found by anthropologists at Steinheim, Germany, in 1933; at Swanscombe, England, in 1935–36; in caves at Mount Carmel (now in Israel) from 1929 to 1934; and at Shanidar, Iraq, in 1957.

## HOMO ERECTUS—1,700,000 TO 500,000 B.C.

*Homo erectus* was a smaller type of man about 5 feet tall with a brain about three-fourths the size of the brain of modern man.

**Heidelberg Man.** A fossil jaw discovered near Heidelberg, Germany, in 1907 by Otto Schoetensack dates to about 500,000 B.C. Identification has been difficult because no other parts of the skull were found.

**Java Man,** who made tools, hunted, and used fire, lived from about 1,000,000 to 500,000 B.C. Fossil remains of this primitive man were discovered in Java, Indonesia, by Eugène Dubois in 1891.

**Peking Man.** Several 500,000-year-old skulls were found near Peking, China, in 1927 by Davidson Black. They are believed to be of the type *Homo erectus*, although at least one skull was as large as that of a modern man.

**Kenya Man.** Richard Leakey discovered a skull identified as *Homo erectus* near Lake Turkana (Rudolf) in Kenya in 1975. It was dated as 1.5 million years old.

**Yuanmou Man.** Fossil teeth discovered in China in 1965 have been dated as 1.7 million years old.

## HOMO HABILIS—3,750,000 TO 1,500,000 B.C.

Scientists disagree as to whether certain fossils found in Africa should be classified as early man or as primates. They were called *Homo habilis* (skilled man) by their discoverers, the Leakeys, because they used stone tools.

**Olduvai Man.** The first skulls of an early type of man that used stone tools were found at Olduvai Gorge in Tanganyika in 1959–63 by the Leakeys. These remains have been dated as 1.8 million years old. The discovery provided the first evidence that man had lived more than a million years ago.

**Laetolil Man.** Jaws and teeth of 11 adults and children were discovered by Mary Leakey in the Laetolil area of Tanzania in 1975. The fossils were dated as between 3.35 and 3.75 million years old.

## HOMINOIDS—14,000,000 TO 1,300,000 B.C.

Hominoids are extinct primates that had features similar both to apes and to man.

The earliest of hominoid fossils, called *Ramapithecus,* have been found in Africa, Europe, Pakistan, and India These bones have been dated as 14 million years old.

The next known hominoid was *Australopithecus,* a small apelike creature that lived in Africa 5.5 million to 1.3 million years ago.

The *Australopithecus* stood about 4 feet tall. His brain was about one-third the size of that of modern man. The first fossils of this type were found at Taung, South Africa, in 1924 by Raymond A. Dart.

Parts of jawbones, teeth, and leg bones were found in 1973–77 by American anthropologist Donald Johanson in Ethiopia. They were dated as over 3 million years old and identified as a new species named *Australopithecus afarensis,* or Afar ape-man.

# HIGHEST MOUNTAINS

Source: National Geographic Society

Mountain ranges were formed when landmasses were pushed up. As time passed, the mountains wore away by weathering and erosion.

The Himalaya range in Asia includes Mt. Everest, the highest peak in the world.

The highest mountains in Europe lie in the Caucasus, a range in the Soviet Union that divides Europe and Asia.

In western Europe the tallest peaks are the Alps, which are located in Switzerland, Italy, France, West Germany, and Austria.

| NAME | LOCATION | FEET | NAME | LOCATION | FEET |
|---|---|---|---|---|---|
| **Highest Peaks in North America** | | | **Highest Peaks in South America** | | |
| McKinley | Alaska | 20,320 | Aconcagua | Argentina | 22,834 |
| Logan | Canada | 19,850 | Ojos del Salado | Argentina–Chile | 22,572 |
| Pico de Orizaba | Mexico | 18,700 | Bonete | Argentina | 22,546 |
| St. Elias | Alaska–Canada | 18,008 | Tupungato | Argentina–Chile | 22,310 |
| Popocatépetl | Mexico | 17,887 | Pissis | Argentina | 22,241 |
| Foraker | Alaska | 17,400 | Mercedario | Argentina | 22,211 |
| Iztaccihuatl | Mexico | 17,343 | Huascarán | Peru | 22,205 |
| Lucania | Canada | 17,147 | Llullaillaco | Argentina–Chile | 22,057 |
| King | Canada | 16,971 | El Libertador | Argentina | 22,047 |
| Steele | Canada | 16,644 | Cachi | Argentina | 22,047 |
| Bona | Alaska | 16,550 | Yerupaja | Peru | 21,709 |
| Blackburn | Alaska | 16,390 | Galán | Argentina | 21,654 |
| Kennedy | Alaska | 16,286 | El Muerto | Argentina–Chile | 21,457 |
| Sanford | Alaska | 16,237 | Sajama | Bolivia | 21,391 |
| South Buttress | Alaska | 15,885 | Nacimiento | Argentina | 21,302 |
| Wood | Canada | 15,885 | Illimani | Bolivia | 21,201 |
| Vancouver | Alaska–Canada | 15,700 | Coropuna | Peru | 21,083 |
| Churchill | Alaska | 15,638 | Laudo | Argentina | 20,997 |
| Fairweather | Alaska | 15,300 | Ancohuma | Bolivia | 20,958 |
| Zinantecatl (Toluca) | Mexico | 15,016 | Ausangate | Peru | 20,945 |
| Hubbard | Alaska–Canada | 15,015 | Toro | Argentina–Chile | 20,932 |
| Bear | Alaska | 14,831 | Illampu | Bolivia | 20,873 |
| Walsh | Canada | 14,780 | Tres Cruces | Argentina–Chile | 20,853 |
| Matlalcueyetl | Mexico | 14,636 | Huandoy | Peru | 20,852 |
| Hunter | Alaska | 14,573 | Parinacota | Bolivia–Chile | 20,768 |
| Alverstone | Alaska–Canada | 14,565 | Tórtolas | Argentina–Chile | 20,745 |
| Browne Tower | Alaska | 14,530 | Ampato | Peru | 20,702 |
| Whitney | California | 14,494 | Cóndor | Argentina | 20,669 |
| Elbert | Colorado | 14,433 | Salcantay | Peru | 20,574 |
| Massive | Colorado | 14,421 | Chimborazo | Ecuador | 20,561 |
| Harvard | Colorado | 14,420 | Huancarhuas | Peru | 20,531 |
| Rainier | Washington | 14,410 | Famatina | Argentina | 20,505 |
| Williamson | California | 14,375 | Pumasillo | Peru | 20,492 |
| Blanca Peak | Colorado | 14,345 | Solo | Argentina | 20,492 |
| La Plata Peak | Colorado | 14,336 | Polleras | Argentina | 20,456 |
| Uncompahgre Peak | Colorado | 14,309 | Pular | Chile | 20,423 |
| Crestone Peak | Colorado | 14,294 | Chañi | Argentina | 20,341 |
| Lincoln | Colorado | 14,286 | Aucanquilcha | Chile | 20,295 |
| Grays Peak | Colorado | 14,270 | Juncal | Argentina–Chile | 20,276 |
| Antero | Colorado | 14,269 | Negro | Argentina | 20,184 |
| Torreys Peak | Colorado | 14,267 | Quela | Argentina | 20,128 |
| Castle Peak | Colorado | 14,265 | Condoriri | Bolivia | 20,095 |
| Quandary Peak | Colorado | 14,265 | Palermo | Argentina | 20,079 |
| Evans | Colorado | 14,264 | Solimana | Peru | 20,068 |
| Longs Peak | Colorado | 14,256 | San Juan | Argentina–Chile | 20,049 |
| McArthur | Canada | 14,253 | Sierra Nevada | Argentina–Chile | 20,023 |
| Wilson | Colorado | 14,246 | Antofalla | Argentina | 20,013 |
| White | California | 14,246 | Marmolejo | Argentina–Chile | 20,013 |
| North Palisade | California | 14,242 | Chachani | Peru | 19,931 |
| Shavano Peak | Colorado | 14,229 | Chaupi Orko | Peru–Bolivia | 19,682 |

| NAME<br>**Highest Peaks<br>in Asia** | LOCATION | FEET | NAME<br>**Highest Peaks<br>in Europe** | LOCATION | FEET |
|---|---|---|---|---|---|
| Everest .......... | Nepal–China (Tibet) | 29,028 | Elbrus .......... | Soviet Union ... | 18,510 |
| K2 (Godwin–Austen) . | Pakistan (Kashmir) . | 28,250 | Shkara .......... | Soviet Union ........ | 17,064 |
| Kanchenjunga ....... | Nepal–India (Sikkim) | 28,208 | Dykh Tau ....... | Soviet Union ... | 17,054 |
| Lhotse I ............. | Nepal–China (Tibet) .. | 27,923 | Kashtan Tau ........ | Soviet Union ..... | 16,877 |
| Makalu I ............. | Nepal–China (Tibet) .. | 27,824 | Dzhangi Tau ........ | Soviet Union ... | 16,565 |
| Lhotse II ............ | Nepal–China (Tibet) .. | 27,560 | Kazbek .......... | Soviet Union ... | 16,558 |
| Dhaulagiri .......... | Nepal ............ | 26,810 | Mont Blanc ....... | France–Italy (Alps) ... | 15,771 |
| Manaslu I ........... | Nepal ............ | 26,760 | Monte Rosa ......... | Italy–Switzerland (Alps) | 15,203 |
| Cho Oyu ............ | Nepal–China (Tibet) .. | 26,750 | Dom ............ | Switzerland (Alps) ... | 14,911 |
| Nanga Parbat ....... | Pakistan (Kashmir) .. | 26,660 | Liskamm ......... | Switzerland (Alps) ... | 14,852 |
| Annapurna .......... | Nepal ............ | 26,504 | Weisshorn ........ | Switzerland (Alps) ... | 14,780 |
| Gasherbrum ........ | Pakistan (Kashmir) .. | 26,470 | Täschhorn ........ | Switzerland (Alps) ... | 14,733 |
| Broad .............. | Kashmir ............ | 26,400 | Matterhorn ....... | Switzerland (Alps) ... | 14,690 |
| Gosainthan ......... | China (Tibet) ....... | 26,287 | Dent Blanche ...... | Switzerland (Alps) ... | 14,293 |
| Annapurna II ....... | Nepal ............ | 26,041 | Nadelhorn ........ | Switzerland (Alps) ... | 14,196 |
| Gyachung Kang ...... | Nepal–China (Tibet) .. | 25,910 | Grand Combin ..... | Switzerland (Alps) ... | 14,154 |
| Disteghil Sar ....... | Pakistan (Kashmir) .. | 25,858 | Lenzspitze ....... | Switzerland (Alps) ... | 14,088 |
| Himalchuli ......... | Nepal ............ | 25,801 | Finsteraarhorn .... | Switzerland (Alps) ... | 14,022 |
| Nuptse ............. | Nepal–China (Tibet) . | 25,726 | Castor .......... | Switzerland (Alps) ... | 13,865 |
| Masherbrum ........ | Pakistan (Kashmir) .. | 25,660 | Zinalrothorn ...... | Switzerland (Alps) ... | 13,849 |
| Nanda Devi ......... | India ............ | 25,645 | Hohberghorn ..... | Switzerland (Alps) ... | 13,842 |
| Rakaposhi .......... | Pakistan (Kashmir) .. | 25,550 | Alphubel ......... | Switzerland (Alps) ... | 13,799 |
| Kamet ............. | India–China (Tibet) .. | 25,447 | Rimpfischhorn .... | Switzerland (Alps) ... | 13,776 |
| Namcha Barwa ...... | China (Tibet) ...... | 25,445 | Aletschhorn ...... | Switzerland (Alps) ... | 13,763 |
| Gurla Mandhata ..... | China (Tibet) ...... | 25,355 | Strahlhorn ....... | Switzerland (Alps) ... | 13,747 |
| Ulugh Muz Tagh ..... | China (Tibet–Sinkiang) | 25,340 | Dent d'Hérens .... | Switzerland (Alps) ... | 13,686 |
| Kungur ............ | China (Sinkiang) ..... | 25,325 | Breithorn ........ | Switzerland (Alps) ... | 13,665 |
| Tirich Mir .......... | Pakistan ........... | 25,230 | Bishorn .......... | Switzerland (Alps) ... | 13,645 |
| Makalu II ........... | Nepal–China (Tibet) .. | 25,120 | Jungfrau.......... | Switzerland (Alps) ... | 13,642 |
| Minya Konka ........ | China ............ | 24,900 | | | |
| Kula Gangri ........ | Bhutan–China (Tibet) | 24,784 | | | |
| Changtzu ........... | Nepal–China (Tibet) .. | 24,780 | **Highest Peaks<br>in Africa** | | |
| Muz Tagh Ata ....... | China (Sinkiang) ..... | 24,757 | | | |
| Skyang Kangri ...... | Pakistan (Kashmir) .. | 24,750 | Kilimanjaro (2 peaks): | | |
| Communism Peak .... | Soviet Union ....... | 24,590 | Kibo ............ | Tanzania ........... | 19,340 |
| Jongsang Peak ...... | Nepal–India (Sikkim) | 24,472 | Mawenzi ........ | Tanzania ........... | 16,896 |
| Pobedy Peak ........ | Soviet Union–China .. | 24,406 | Kenya .............. | Kenya .............. | 17,058 |
| Sia Kangri ......... | Pakistan (Kashmir) .. | 24,350 | Margherita .......... | Uganda–Zaire ...... | 16,763 |
| Haramosh Peak ..... | Pakistan ........... | 24,270 | Ras Dashan ......... | Ethiopia .......... | 15,158 |
| Istoro Nal ......... | Pakistan ........... | 24,240 | Meru .............. | Tanzania .......... | 14,979 |
| Tent Peak.......... | Nepal–India (Sikkim) . | 24,165 | Karisimbi .......... | Rwanda–Zaire ...... | 14,787 |
| Chomo Lhari ....... | Bhutan–China (Tibet) | 24,040 | Elgon.............. | Kenya–Uganda ...... | 14,178 |
| Chamlang .......... | Nepal ............ | 24,012 | Batu .............. | Ethiopia .......... | 14,131 |
| Kabru ............. | Nepal–India (Sikkim) | 24,002 | Gughe ............. | Ethiopia .......... | 13,780 |
| Alung Gangri ....... | China (Tibet) ........ | 24,000 | Toubkal ........... | Morocco ........... | 13,655 |
| Baltoro Kangri ...... | Pakistan (Kashmir) .. | 23,990 | Birhan ............ | Ethiopia .......... | 13,628 |
| Mussu Shan ........ | China (Sinkiang) ..... | 23,890 | | | |
| Mana............... | India ............ | 23,860 | | | |
| Baruntse .......... | Nepal ............ | 23,688 | **Highest Peaks<br>in the Pacific and<br>Southeast Asia** | | |
| Nepal Peak ........ | Nepal–India (Sikkim) . | 23,500 | | | |
| Amne Machin ...... | China ............ | 23,490 | | | |
| Gauri Sankar ....... | Nepal–China (Tibet) .. | 23,440 | Jaya .............. | Indonesia (Irian Jaya) | 16,500 |
| Badrinath .......... | India ............ | 23,420 | Pilimsit ............ | Indonesia (Irian Jaya) | 15,748 |
| Nunkun ............ | Pakistan (Kashmir) .. | 23,410 | Trikora ............ | Indonesia (Irian Jaya) | 15,585 |
| Lenina Peak ........ | Soviet Union ....... | 23,405 | Mandala ........... | Indonesia (Irian Jaya) | 15,420 |
| Pyramid ........... | Nepal–India (Sikkim) . | 23,400 | Wilhelm ........... | Papua New Guinea ... | 14,793 |
| Api................ | Nepal ............ | 23,399 | | | |
| Pauhunri .......... | India–China (Tibet) .. | 23,385 | **Highest Peaks<br>in Antarctica** | | |
| Trisul ............. | India ............ | 23,360 | | | |
| Kangto ............ | India–China (Tibet) .. | 23,260 | Vinson Massif ...... | ................... | 16,860 |
| Nyenchhen Thanglha . | China (Tibet) ....... | 23,255 | Tyree ............. | ................... | 16,290 |
| Trisuli ............. | India ............ | 23,210 | Shinn ............. | ................... | 15,750 |
| Dunagiri ........... | India ............ | 23,184 | Gardner ........... | ................... | 15,375 |
| Lombo Kangra....... | China (Tibet) ........ | 23,165 | Epperly............ | ................... | 15,100 |

# MAJOR VOLCANOES

About 600 active and 10,000 inactive or dormant volcanoes are found along three belts, closely matching the earthquake regions of the world.

The "ring of fire" includes the Pacific coasts of North and South America and Asia.

A second belt extends from the Mediterranean to the East Indies, and a third lies along the midocean ridges of the major oceans.

Volcanic activity is deceptively sporadic—brief periods of outgassing or eruption, followed by unpredictably longer dormant periods.

Many volcanoes began their eruptions on the bed of the sea. Italy's Etna and Vesuvius were submarine volcanoes originally.

Cones are inevitably modified by eruptions. Thus some heights are approximate.

See also *Major Volcanic Disasters,* page 37–38.

| NAME | LOCATION | HEIGHT |
|---|---|---|
| **AFRICA AND INDIAN OCEAN** | | |
| Kilimanjaro | Tanzania | 19,340 |
| Cameroon Mt. | Cameroon | 13,350 |
| Teide | Tenerife Island | 12,198 |
| Nyiragongo | Zaire | 11,400 |
| Nyamlagira | Zaire | 10,028 |
| Fogo | Cape Verde | 9,281 |
| Piton de la Fournaise | Réunion | 8,630 |
| Tristan da Cunha | Atlantic Ocean | 6,760 |
| **ANTARCTICA** | | |
| Erebus | Rosa Island | 12,450 |
| **ASIA AND PACIFIC OCEAN** | | |
| Klyuchevskaya | Soviet Union | 15,584 |
| Mauna Kea | Hawaii | 13,796 |
| Mauna Loa | Hawaii | 13,680 |
| Kerintji | Indonesia | 12,467 |
| Fuji | Japan | 12,388 |
| Rindjani | Indonesia | 12,224 |
| Tolbachik | Soviet Union | 12,080 |
| Semeru | Indonesia | 12,060 |
| Ichinskaya | Soviet Union | 11,880 |
| Kronotskaya | Soviet Union | 11,575 |
| Koryakskaya | Soviet Union | 11,339 |
| Slamet | Indonesia | 11,247 |
| Raung | Indonesia | 10,932 |
| Shiveluch | Soviet Union | 10,771 |
| Dempo | Indonesia | 10,364 |
| Welirang | Indonesia | 10,354 |
| Agung | Indonesia | 10,308 |
| Sundoro | Indonesia | 10,285 |
| Plosky Tolbachik | Soviet Union | 10,121 |
| Tjareme | Indonesia | 10,098 |
| Ontake | Japan | 10,049 |
| Gede | Indonesia | 9,705 |
| Merapi | Indonesia | 9,548 |
| Bezymyannaya | Soviet Union | 9,514 |
| Apo | Philippines | 9,369 |
| Tambora | Indonesia | 9,353 |
| Ruapehu | New Zealand | 9,175 |
| Peuetsagoe | Indonesia | 9,121 |
| Bromo | Indonesia | 9,088 |
| Avachinskaya | Soviet Union | 9,026 |
| Api Siau | Indonesia | 8,856 |
| Ngauruhoe | New Zealand | 7,516 |
| Sarychev | Kurile Islands | 4,910 |
| Karimsky | Soviet Union | 4,875 |
| Kilauea | Hawaii | 4,077 |
| Sakurazima | Kyushu, Japan | 3,657 |
| Suwanosezima | Ryukyus | 2,620 |
| Usu | Hokkaido, Japan | 2,385 |
| Shin-dake | Ryukyus | 2,100 |
| Taal | Philippines | 1,000 |
| **EUROPE** | | |
| Etna | Italy | 10,791 |
| Beeren Berg | Norway | 7,470 |
| Askja | Iceland | 4,954 |
| **Europe** *(continued)* | | |
| Hekla | Iceland | 4,892 |
| Vesuvius | Italy | 4,190 |
| Katla | Iceland | 3,182 |
| Stromboli | Italy | 3,038 |
| Leirhnukur | Iceland | 2,132 |
| **NORTH AMERICA** | | |
| Citlaltepec | Mexico | 18,700 |
| Popocatépetl | Mexico | 17,887 |
| Wrangell | Alaska | 14,163 |
| Colima | Mexico | 12,988 |
| Torbert | Alaska | 11,413 |
| Spurr | Alaska | 11,069 |
| Baker | Washington | 10,778 |
| Lassen | California | 10,457 |
| Redoubt | Alaska | 10,197 |
| Iliamna | Alaska | 10,016 |
| Mount St. Helens | Washington | 9,671* |
| Shishaldin | Alaska (Aleutians) | 9,387 |
| Pavlof | Alaska | 8,261 |
| Veniaminof | Alaska | 8,225 |
| Griggs | Alaska | 7,600 |
| Paricutín | Mexico | 7,451 |
| St. Augustine | Alaska | 3,969 |
| **CENTRAL AMERICA AND CARIBBEAN SEA** | | |
| Tajumulco | Guatemala | 13,845 |
| Tacaná | Guatemala | 13,428 |
| Acatenango | Guatemala | 12,992 |
| Fuego | Guatemala | 12,582 |
| Santa Maria | Guatemala | 12,372 |
| Atitlán | Guatemala | 11,565 |
| Irazú | Costa Rica | 11,260 |
| San Pedro | Guatemala | 9,921 |
| Póas | Costa Rica | 8,859 |
| Pacaya | Guatemala | 8,346 |
| San Miguel | El Salvador | 6,988 |
| San Cristóbal (El Viejo) | Nicaragua | 5,842 |
| Arenal | Costa Rica | 5,092 |
| La Soufrière | Guadeloupe | 4,812 |
| **SOUTH AMERICA** | | |
| Chimborazo | Ecuador | 20,561 |
| Guallatiri | Chile | 19,882 |
| Lascar | Chile | 19,652 |
| Cotopaxi | Ecuador | 19,347 |
| Misti | Peru | 19,098 |
| Cayambe | Ecuador | 18,996 |
| Tupungatito | Chile | 18,504 |
| Sangay | Ecuador | 17,159 |
| Tungurahua | Ecuador | 16,512 |
| Cotacachi | Ecuador | 16,204 |
| Pichincha | Ecuador | 15,696 |
| Puracé | Colombia | 15,604 |
| Reventador | Ecuador | 11,431 |
| Lautaro | Chile | 11,090 |
| Llaima | Chile | 10,239 |
| Villarrica | Chile | 9,318 |

* Estimated 1,500 feet sheared off during 1980 eruption.

## PRINCIPAL DESERTS

Once simply used for an uninhabited, or "deserted" place, the term *desert* is now commonly applied to regions that have little rainfall, scanty vegetation, and limited human use.

Of the three types of deserts commonly recognized, only a few *tropical* deserts, such as the Libyan part of the Sahara, resemble the popular image of a hot, dry, sandy expanse.

*Middle latitude* deserts lie in the "rainshadow" of a mountain barrier (as deserts in the southwestern U.S.), or deep within the moisture-starved interiors of continents (the Gobi).

*Polar* deserts occur because moisture is "locked up" as ice and snow.

Desert landscapes range from flat, sandy plains to mountainous plateaus. The rocks of deserts are typically eroded into fantastic shapes by the action of wind-driven sand.

| DESERT | LOCATION | SIZE | REMARKS |
|---|---|---|---|
| **NORTH AMERICA** | | | |
| Black Rock | Humboldt and Pershing counties, Nevada | An area of 1,000 square miles | A barren plain practically devoid of vegetation; from its surface, alkaline dust is blown into vast clouds by the summer winds. |
| Colorado | Arid region of southeastern California | 200 miles long; maximum width of 50 miles | The soil of its Imperial Valley is highly productive when irrigated. |
| Death Valley | Eastern California and Southwestern Nevada | 2,936 square miles | Yielded much borax in the 19th century. |
| Mohave | Southern California; northeast of Los Angeles extends into Mohave County, Arizona | 15,000 square miles | Needles, on the Arizona-California boundary, is one of the hottest towns in the United States. |
| Painted Desert | Coconino and Navajo counties in northern Arizona | 200 miles long; 15–30 miles wide | Within the desert are seven Hopi villages; the Painted Desert is so called because of its coloring, caused by centuries of erosion exposing brilliantly colored rock formations. |
| **SOUTH AMERICA** | | | |
| Atacama | Northern Chile | 600 miles long | An area of rich nitrate and copper deposits. |
| **AFRICA** | | | |
| Kalahari | South Africa; the Orange River marks its southern limit | 120,000 square miles | Hottentots and Bushmen inhabit the area. |
| Namib | Namibia | 800 miles long; 30–100 miles wide | Long, narrow desert plain along Atlantic coast. |
| Sahara | North Africa; on the west the desert extends to the Atlantic coast | Over 3,000,000 square miles | Nomadic herding is still an important activity in the desert, but in recent years there has been petroleum extraction; the Libyan and Nubian deserts are part of the Sahara. |
| **ASIA** | | | |
| Dasht i Kavir | Iran, from the Caspian Sea to the Persian Gulf | 300 miles long; 100 miles wide | Saline swamps and dry salt areas. |
| Gobi | Extends 1,500 miles from Manchuria to Sinkiang Province, China | 500,000 square miles | Many paleontological finds, including dinosaur eggs, have been made there. |
| Kara Kum | Asiatic Soviet Union | 110,000 square miles | The Kara Kum has a number of "old river beds" that may have been either channels or tributaries of the Amu. |
| Kizil-Kum | Asiatic Soviet Union | 370 by 220 miles | The surface is characterized by stationary sands with sparse vegetation. |
| Negev | Southern Israel | 4,700 square miles | Barren expanses of sand, now dotted with prosperous farms, orchards, and towns; has King Solomon's mines and the Dead Sea. |
| An Nafud | Northern Saudi Arabia | An average width of 200 miles | Huge area of sand dunes, populated only by a few nomads. |
| Rub al-Khali (Empty Quarter) | Southern Saudi Arabia | 300,000 square miles | Practically unexplored; it may contain large tracts of hard gravel or limestone deposits. |
| Syrian | Northernmost Saudi Arabia, extending into Jordan, Syria, and Iraq | —— | The oasis of Al Jawf has extensive palm groves and a population of more than 10,000. |
| Taklamakan | Central Asia, in the Chinese province of Sinkiang | 125,000 square miles | Ancient trade routes cross this desert, and there are reports of buried cities; the Chinese exploded their first atomic bomb there in 1964. |
| Thar (Indian) | Northwestern India, between the Gulf of Cutch and the Arabian Sea on the south | 100,000 square miles | Camel caravans still traverse the desert; parts of the Thar are disputed between India and Pakistan. |
| **AUSTRALIA** | | | |
| Great Australian | Much of central and western Australia | —— | Primitive Bushmen live in this area, which Australians prefer to call "Sparselands." |

## MAJOR ISLANDS
Source: National Geographic Society

Islands are bodies of land surrounded by water. Continents are islands in the strict sense of the word, differing from other islands only in size.

The largest islands in the world are, in square miles: Greenland (840,000); New Guinea (306,000); Borneo (280,100); Madagascar (226,658); Baffin (195,928); Sumatra (165,000); Honshu (87,805); Great Britain (84,200); Victoria (83,896); and Ellesmere (75,767).

The largest islands of the United States, in square miles, are: Hawaii (4,037); Kodiak (3,670); and Puerto Rico (3,435).

*Islands in minor waters* (in square miles): Manitoulin (Canada), Lake Huron (1,068); Singapore, Singapore Strait (224); Isle Royale, Mich., Lake Superior (209); Pinang (Malaysia), Strait of Malacca (110); Staten Island, N.Y. (58); Manhattan, N.Y. (23).

| NAME | AREA (in sq. miles) | NAME | AREA (in sq. miles) | NAME | AREA (in sq. miles) |
|---|---|---|---|---|---|
| **ARCTIC OCEAN** | | **BALTIC SEA** | | Hong Kong (Britain) ... | 29 |
| | | Aland (Finland)........ | 581 | Japan ................. | 145,809 |
| **Canadian** | | Bornholm (Denmark) .. | 227 | Hokkaido ........... | 30,144 |
| Axel Heiberg .......... | 16,671 | Gotland (Sweden) ..... | 1,164 | Honshu............. | 87,805 |
| Baffin ............... | 195,928 | | | Iwo Jima ............ | 8 |
| Banks ............... | 27,033 | **CARIBBEAN SEA** | | Kyushu ............. | 14,114 |
| Devon ............... | 21,331 | Antigua (Britain) ...... | 108 | Okinawa ............ | 459 |
| Ellesmere ........... | 75,767 | Barbados ............. | 166 | Shikoku ............ | 7,049 |
| Melville ............ | 16,274 | Cuba ................. | 44,218 | Kodiak (Alaska) ....... | 3,670 |
| Prince of Wales ....... | 12,872 | Isle of Pines ........ | 1,182 | Mariana Is. (U.S. Trust) | |
| Southampton ......... | 15,913 | Dominica ............. | 290 | Saipan ............. | 48 |
| Victoria.............. | 83,896 | Guadeloupe (France)... | 687 | Marquesas Is. (France). | 492 |
| **Soviet Union** | | Hispaniola (Haiti and | | Marshall Is. (U.S. Trust) . | 70 |
| Franz Josef Land...... | 8,000 | Dominican Republic). | 29,530 | Nauru .............. | 8 |
| Novaya Zemlya........ | 35,000 | Jamaica ............. | 4,244 | New Caledonia (France) | 6,530 |
| Wrangel .............. | 2,800 | Martinique (France).... | 425 | New Guinea (Indonesia– | |
| **Norwegian** | | Puerto Rico (U.S.) ..... | 3,435 | Papua New Guinea) . | 306,000 |
| Svalbard ............. | 23,940 | Trinidad ............. | 1,864 | New Zealand .......... | 103,883 |
| Nordaustlandet ...... | 5,410 | Virgin Is. (U.S.) ...... | 133 | North .............. | 44,204 |
| Spitsbergen ........ | 15,060 | | | South .............. | 58,304 |
| | | **INDIAN OCEAN** | | Philippines .......... | 115,831 |
| | | Andaman Is. (India) ... | 2,500 | Leyte............... | 2,787 |
| **ATLANTIC OCEAN** | | Madagascar........... | 226,658 | Luzon .............. | 40,880 |
| | | Mauritius ........... | 720 | Mindanao .......... | 36,775 |
| **British Isles** | | Pemba (Tanzania) ..... | 380 | Mindoro ........... | 3,790 |
| Great Britain, mainland | 84,200 | Réunion (France) ..... | 969 | Negros ............. | 4,907 |
| Hebrides ............. | 2,744 | Seychelles ........... | 107 | Palawan .......... | 4,554 |
| Ireland ............. | 32,599 | Sri Lanka ............ | 25,332 | Panay .............. | 4,446 |
| Man .................. | 227 | Zanzibar (Tanzania) ... | 640 | Samar .............. | 5,050 |
| Orkney Is. ........... | 390 | **Persian Gulf** | | Quemoy ............ | 56 |
| Shetland Is. ......... | 567 | Bahrain ............. | 240 | Sakhalin (Soviet Union) | 29,500 |
| Skye ................. | 670 | | | Samoa Islands ....... | 1,177 |
| **Other Atlantic Islands** | | **MEDITERRANEAN SEA** | | American Samoa .... | 76 |
| Anticosti (Canada)..... | 3,066 | Balearic Is. (Spain) .... | 1,936 | Tutuila ............ | 52 |
| Azores (Portugal) ..... | 902 | Corfu (Greece) ....... | 229 | Western Samoa ..... | 1,101 |
| Bahamas ............. | 5,380 | Corsica (France) ...... | 3,365 | Savaii ............ | 670 |
| Bermuda Is. (Britain) .. | 20 | Crete (Greece) ........ | 3,186 | Upolu ............ | 429 |
| Canary Is. (Spain) ..... | 2,808 | Cyprus .............. | 3,572 | Tahiti (France) ....... | 402 |
| Cape Breton (Canada) . | 3,981 | Elba (Italy)........... | 86 | Taiwan ............. | 13,812 |
| Cape Verde Is. ....... | 1,557 | Euboea (Greece) ...... | 1,409 | Tasmania (Australia) .. | 26,178 |
| Faeroe Is. (Denmark) .. | 540 | Malta................ | 122 | Vancouver (Canada) .. | 12,079 |
| Falkland Is. (Britain) ... | 4,700 | Rhodes (Greece) ...... | 542 | Vanuatu ............ | 5,700 |
| Fernando Po | | Sardinia (Italy) ....... | 9,262 | Viti Levu (Fiji)........ | 4,109 |
| (Equatorial Guinea) .. | 785 | Sicily (Italy) .......... | 9,822 | | |
| Greenland (Denmark) .. | 840,000 | | | **Indonesia** | |
| Iceland ............... | 39,769 | **PACIFIC OCEAN** | | Bali ................ | 2,147 |
| Long Island (New York) | 1,396 | Aleutian Is. (Alaska) ... | 6,821 | Borneo (with | |
| Madeira Is. (Portugal).. | 307 | Caroline (U.S. | | Malaysia–Britain) .... | 280,100 |
| Marajó (Brazil) ....... | 15,528 | Trust Territory) ..... | 473 | Celebes.............. | 69,255 |
| Martha's Vineyard | | Galápagos Is. (Ecuador) | 3,043 | Java ............... | 48,763 |
| (Massachusetts) ..... | 91 | Guadalcanal (Britain) .. | 2,500 | Moluccas ........... | 28,766 |
| Nantucket | | Guam (U.S.) ......... | 212 | Sumatra ............ | 165,000 |
| (Massachusetts) ..... | 46 | Hainan (China) ....... | 13,000 | Timor .............. | 11,570 |
| Newfoundland (Canada) | 42,031 | Hawaiian Is. (U.S.).... | 6,450 | | |
| Prince Edward (Canada) | 2,184 | Hawaii.............. | 4,037 | **Papua New Guinea** | |
| South Georgia (Britain) | 1,450 | Oahu ............... | 593 | New Britain .......... | 14,050 |
| Tierra del Fuego (Chile | | | | New Ireland ........... | 2,700 |
| and Argentina) ...... | 17,800 | | | | |

# LONGEST RIVERS

Source: National Geographic Society

| RIVER | EMPTIES INTO | MILES |
|---|---|---|
| **NORTH AMERICA** | | |
| Albany (Canada) | James Bay | 610 |
| Arkansas (Colo.–Ark.) | Mississippi River | 1,459 |
| Athabasca (Canada) | Lake Athabasca | 765 |
| Back (Canada) | Chantrey Inlet | 605 |
| Brazos (Texas) | Gulf of Mexico | 1,210 |
| Canadian (N.M.–Okla.) | Arkansas River | 906 |
| Churchill (Canada) | Hudson Bay | 1,000 |
| Cimarron (Colo.–Okla.) | Arkansas River | 600 |
| Colorado (Colo.–Mexico) | Gulf of California | 1,450 |
| Colorado (Texas) | Matagorda Bay | 840 |
| Columbia (U.S.–Canada) | Pacific Ocean | 1,243 |
| Cumberland (Ky.–Tenn.) | Ohio River | 720 |
| Fraser (Brit. Col.) | Strait of Georgia | 850 |
| Green (Utah–Wyo.) | Colorado River | 730 |
| James (N.D.–S.D.) | Missouri River | 710 |
| Kuskokwim (Alaska) | Kuskokwim Bay | 800 |
| Mackenzie (Canada) | Beaufort Sea | 2,635 |
| Mississippi (Minn.–La.) | Gulf of Mexico | 2,348 |
| Mississippi–Missouri–Red Rock (Mont.–La.) | Gulf of Mexico | 3,710 |
| Missouri (Mont.–Mo.) | Mississippi River | 2,315 |
| Missouri–Red Rock (Mont.–Mo.) | Mississippi River | 2,533 |
| Nelson (Canada) | Hudson Bay | 1,600 |
| North Canadian (Okla.) | Canadian River | 760 |
| North Platte (Wyo.–Nebr.) | Platte River | 680 |
| Ohio (Pa.–Ill.) | Mississippi River | 981 |
| Ohio–Allegheny (Pa.–Ill.) | Mississippi River | 1,306 |
| Ottawa (Canada) | St. Lawrence River | 790 |
| Peace (Canada) | Slave River | 1,195 |
| Pecos (N.M.–Tex.) | Rio Grande | 735 |
| Red (Okla.–Tex.–La.) | Mississippi River | 1,270 |
| Rio Grande (Colo.–Mexico) | Gulf of Mexico | 1,885 |
| Saguenay (Canada) | St. Lawrence River | 434 |
| St. Lawrence (N.Y.–Canada) | Gulf of St. Lawrence | 800 |
| Saskatchewan (Canada) | Lake Winnipeg | 1,205 |
| Snake (Wyo.–Wash.) | Columbia River | 1,038 |
| Tennessee–French Broad (N.C.–Ky.) | Ohio River | 900 |
| Trinity (Canada) | Trinity Bay | 715 |
| Usumacinta (Mexico) | Gulf of Mexico | 270 |
| White (Ark.–Mo.) | Mississippi River | 720 |
| Yukon (Alaska–Canada) | Bering Sea | 1,979 |
| **SOUTH AMERICA** | | |
| Amazon (Brazil) | Atlantic Ocean | 4,000 |
| Japura (Colombia–Brazil) | Amazon River | 1,750 |
| Madeira (Brazil) | Amazon River | 2,013 |
| Magdalena (Colombia) | Caribbean Sea | 956 |
| Negro (Brazil) | Amazon River | 1,400 |
| Orinoco (Venezuela) | Atlantic Ocean | 1,600 |
| Paraguay (Paraguay) | Paraná River | 1,584 |
| Paraná (Argentina) | Rio de la Plata | 2,485 |
| Pilcomayo (Paraguay) | Paraguay River | 1,000 |
| Purus (Peru–Brazil) | Amazon River | 2,100 |
| Rio Theodore Roosevelt (Brazil) | Aripciana River | 400 |
| São Francisco (Brazil) | Atlantic Ocean | 1,988 |
| Tocantins (Brazil) | Pará River | 1,677 |
| Uruguay (Arg.–Uruguay) | Rio de la Plata | 1,000 |

| RIVER | EMPTIES INTO | MILES |
|---|---|---|
| **EUROPE** | | |
| Bug S. (Poland–Soviet Union) | Dnieper River | 532 |
| Bug W. (Soviet Union–Poland) | Wisla River | 481 |
| Danube (W. Germany–Romania) | Black Sea | 1,776 |
| Daugava–Dvina (Soviet Union) | Gulf of Riga | 634 |
| Dnieper (Soviet Union) | Black Sea | 1,420 |
| Dniester (Soviet Union) | Black Sea | 877 |
| Don (Soviet Union) | Sea of Azov | 1,224 |
| Drava (Yugoslavia) | Danube River | 447 |
| Ebro (Spain) | Mediterranean Sea | 565 |
| Elbe (E. Germany) | North Sea | 724 |
| Loire (France) | Bay of Biscay | 634 |
| Meuse (Belgium–France) | North Sea | 580 |
| Oder (E. Germany–Poland) | Baltic Sea | 567 |
| Rhine (Switz.–Netherlands) | North Sea | 820 |
| Rhone (France–Switz.) | Mediterranean Sea | 505 |
| Seine (France) | English Channel | 482 |
| Tajo or Tagus (Spain–Port.) | Atlantic Ocean | 626 |
| Tisza (Hungary) | Danube River | 600 |
| Ural (Soviet Union) | Caspian Sea | 1,575 |
| Volga (Soviet Union) | Caspian Sea | 2,194 |
| Weser (W. Germany) | North Sea | 454 |
| Wisla (Poland) | Baltic Sea | 675 |
| **AFRICA** | | |
| Gambia (Gambia) | Atlantic Ocean | 700 |
| Niger (Nigeria) | Gulf of Guinea | 2,590 |
| Nile (Sudan–Egypt) | Mediterranean Sea | 4,145 |
| Orange (South Africa) | Atlantic Ocean | 1,300 |
| Zaire or Congo (Zaire–Congo) | Atlantic Ocean | 2,900 |
| Zambezi (Zambia–Mozambique) | Indian Ocean | 1,700 |
| **ASIA** | | |
| Amu (Soviet Union) | Aral Sea | 1,578 |
| Amur (Soviet Union) | Tatar Strait | 2,744 |
| Angara (Soviet Union) | Yenisey River | 1,151 |
| Brahmaputra | Bay of Bengal | 1,800 |
| Euphrates (Syria–Iraq) | Persian Gulf | 2,235 |
| Ganges (India–Bangladesh) | Bay of Bengal | 1,560 |
| Hsi (China) | South China Sea | 1,200 |
| Indus (Pakistan) | Arabian Sea | 1,800 |
| Irrawaddy (Burma) | Bay of Bengal | 1,300 |
| Lena (Soviet Union) | Laptev Sea | 2,734 |
| Mekong (SE Asia) | South China Sea | 2,600 |
| Ob–Irtysh (Soviet Union) | Gulf of Ob | 3,362 |
| Salween (Burma) | Gulf of Martaban | 1,500 |
| Sungari (China) | Amur River | 1,150 |
| Syr Darya (Soviet Union) | Aral Sea | 1,370 |
| Tigris (Iraq) | Euphrates River | 1,180 |
| Yangtze (China) | East China Sea | 3,964 |
| Yellow or Huang (China) | Yellow Sea | 2,903 |
| Yenisey (Soviet Union) | Kara Sea | 2,543 |
| **AUSTRALIA** | | |
| Murray–Darling | Indian Ocean | 2,310 |

# FAMOUS WATERFALLS

Source: National Geographic Society

There are tens of thousands of waterfalls scattered over the Earth, hundreds of them of considerable magnitude. The highest waterfalls in the world are: Angel (Venezuela), 3,212 feet; Yosemite (California), 2,425 feet; Southern Mardalsfossen (Norway), 2,150 feet; Tugela (South Africa), 2,014 feet; Cuquenán (Venezuela), 2,000 feet; Sutherland (New Zealand), 1,904 feet.

On the basis of annual flow combined with considerable height, Guaira, between Brazil and Paraguay, is the world's greatest waterfall; its estimated annual flow is 470,000 cusecs (cubic feet per second). A greater volume of water passes over Boyoma Falls, in Zaire, the former Democratic Republic of the Congo, but not one of its seven falls, spread over a distance of 60 miles, is higher than 10 feet.

The estimated annual flows of other great waterfalls are: Niagara (Canada and United States), 212,200 cusecs; Paulo Afonso (Brazil), 100,000; Urubupunga (Brazil), 97,000; Iguazú (Argentina and Brazil), 61,600; Patos-Maribondo (Brazil), 53,000; Victoria (Zambia and Zimbabwe), 38,400; and Kaieteur (Guyana), 23,400.

| LOCATION AND NAME | FEET HIGH [1] | LOCATION AND NAME | FEET HIGH [1] | LOCATION AND NAME | FEET HIGH [1] |
|---|---|---|---|---|---|
| **AFRICA** | | **France** | | Ribbon [5] | 1,612 |
| **Angola** | | Gavarnie [3] | 1,385 | Silver Strand [5], Meadow Br. | 1,170 |
| Duque de Braganca | 344 | **Great Britain** | | Yosemite [3],[5] | 2,425 |
| Ruacana, Cuene R. | 406 | Scotland: Glomach | 370 | Colorado | |
| **Ethiopia** | | Wales: Rhaiadr | 240 | Seven [3], S. Cheyenne Cr. | 300 |
| Dal Verme, Dorya R. | 98 | **Iceland** | | Hawaii | |
| Fincha | 508 | Detti | 144 | Akaka | 442 |
| Tesissat, Blue Nile | 140 | **Italy** | | Idaho | |
| **Lesotho** | | Frua [4], Toce R. | 470 | Shoshone [5], Snake R. | 212 |
| Maletsunyane [2] | 630 | **Norway** | | Twin, Snake R. | 120 |
| **South Africa** | | Mardalsfossen (Northern) | 1,535 | New York | |
| Aughrabies [2], Orange R. | 480 | Mardalsfossen [3] (Southern) | 2,149 | Taughannock [2] | 215 |
| Howick, Umgeni R. | 311 | Skjeggedal [3],[5], Nybuai R. | 1,378 | Oregon | |
| Tugela [3] | 2,014 | Skykkje [5] | 984 | Multnomah [3] | 620 |
| Highest single fall | 597 | Vetti | 900 | Tennessee | |
| **Tanzania–Zambia** | | Vöring, Bjoreio R. | 597 | Fall Creek | 256 |
| Kalambo [2] | 726 | **Sweden** | | Washington | |
| **Uganda** | | Handöl [3] | 427 | Mt. Rainier Natl. Park: | |
| Kabalega (Murchison) Victo- | | Tannforsen, Åre R. | 120 | Narada, Paradise R. | 168 |
| ria Nile R. | 130 | **Switzerland** | | Sluiskin, Paradise R. | 300 |
| **Zambia** | | Diesbach [3] | 394 | Palouse | 197 |
| Chirombo | 880 | Giessbach [4] | 984 | Snoqualmie [5] | 268 |
| **Zimbabwe and Zambia** | | Handegg, Aare R. | 150 | Wisconsin | |
| Victoria [2], Zambezi R. | 343 | Iffigen | 120 | Big Manitou [2],[4], Black R. | 165 |
| | | Pissevache, Salanfe R. | 213 | Wyoming | |
| **ASIA** | | Reichenbach [3] | 656 | Yellowstone Natl. Park: | |
| **India** | | Simmen [3] | 459 | Tower | 132 |
| Cauvery [2] | 330 | Staubbach [3] | 984 | Yellowstone (upper) [2] | 109 |
| Gokak [2], Ghataprabha R. | 170 | Trümmelbach [3] | 1,312 | Yellowstone (lower) [2] | 308 |
| Jog [2] (Gersoppa), Sharavathi R. | 830 | | | | |
| **Japan** | | **NORTH AMERICA** | | **SOUTH AMERICA** | |
| Kegon [2], Daiya R. | 330 | **Canada** | | **Argentina–Brazil** | |
| **Laos** | | Alberta | | Iguazú | 230 |
| Khon Cataracts [4], Mekong R. | 70 | Panther, Nigel Cr. | 600 | **Brazil** | |
| | | British Columbia | | Glass | 1,325 |
| **AUSTRALASIA** | | Della | 1,443 | Herval | 400 |
| **Australia** | | Takakkaw, Daly Glacier | 1,200 | Patos-Maribondo, Grande R. | 115 |
| New South Wales | | Northwest Territories | | Paulo Afonso, São Francisco R. | 275 |
| Wentworth [3] | 614 | Virginia, S. Nahanni R. | 294 | Urubupunga, Paraná R. | 40 |
| Wollomombi [3] | 1,100 | Quebec | | **Brazil–Paraguay** | |
| Queensland | | Montmorency | 274 | Sete Quedas (Guaira), | |
| Coomera | 210 | **Canada–United States** | | Paraná R. | 130 |
| Tully | 885 | Niagara [6] | | **Colombia** | |
| Wallaman [3] | 1,137 | American | 182 | Catarata de Candelas, | |
| New Zealand | | Horseshoe | 173 | Cusiana R. | 984 |
| Bowen | 540 | **Mexico** | | Tequendama, Bogotá R. | 427 |
| Helena | 890 | El Salto | 218 | **Guyana** | |
| Stirling | 505 | **United States** | | Kaieteur, Potaro R. | 741 |
| Sutherland [3], Arthur R. | 1,904 | California | | Great Kamarang R. | 1,600 |
| | | Feather [2], Fall R. | 640 | Marina [3], Ipobe R. | 500 |
| **EUROPE** | | Yosemite Natl. Park: | | **Venezuela** | |
| **Austria** | | Bridal Veil [2] | 620 | Angel [2],[3] | 3,212 |
| Gastein [3] | 492 | Nevada [2], Merced R. | 594 | Cuquenán | 2,000 |
| Golling [2],[3], Schwarzbach R. | 250 | | | | |
| Krimml [3] | 1,312 | | | | |

[1] Height means total drop whether in one or more leaps.   [2] Falls greatly diminish seasonally.   [3] Falls consist of more than one leap.   [4] Cascade-type falls.   [5] Falls dry part of year.   [6] Niagara's cataract is divided by Goat Island into two waterfalls.

# LARGEST LAKES IN EACH U.S. STATE

Source: National Geographic Society

| STATE | LAKE | AREA (sq. miles) | MAX. DEPTH (feet) | SHORELINE (miles) |
|---|---|---|---|---|
| Alabama | Guntersville [1,3] | 108 | 94 | 962 |
| | Walter F. George [2,3] | 71 | 90 | 640 |
| Alaska | Iliamna [1,4] | 1,150 | 1,289 | 230 |
| Arizona | Theodore Roosevelt [1,3] | 27 | 280 | 88 |
| | Powell [2,3] | 252 | 580 | 1,800 |
| Arkansas | Ouachita [1,3] | 63 | 179 | 690 |
| | Bull Shoals [2,3] | 71 | 175 | 740 |
| California | Salton Sea [1,4] | 360 | 48 | — |
| | Tahoe [2,4] | 192 | 1,644 | 71 |
| Colorado | Blue Mesa [1,3,5] | 14 | 325 | 95 |
| | Navajo [2,3,5] | 24 | 382 | 150 |
| Connecticut | Candlewood [1,3] | 8 | 85 | 75 |
| Delaware | Lum's Pond [1,3] | .34 | 22 | 5 |
| Florida | Okeechobee [1,4] | 700 | 15 | 96 |
| Georgia | Sidney Lanier [1,3] | 59 | 156 | 540 |
| | Clark Hill [2,3] | 109 | 150 | 1,200 |
| Hawaii | Waita [1,3,5] | .66 | 23 | 4 |
| Idaho | Pend Oreille [1,4] | 136 | 1,200 | 127 |
| Illinois | Carlyle [3,5] | 41 | 40 | 83 |
| | Michigan [2,4] | 22,300 | 923 | 1,660 |
| Indiana | Monroe [1,3,5] | 29 | 75 | 100 |
| | Michigan [2,4] | 22,300 | 923 | 1,660 |
| Iowa | Rathbun [1,3,5] | 18 | 55 | 180 |
| Kansas | Tuttle Creek [1,3,5] | 25 | 90 | 112 |
| Kentucky | Cumberland [1,3] | 79 | 183 | 1,255 |
| | Kentucky [2,3] | 250 | 90 | 2,380 |
| Louisiana | Pontchartrain [1,4] | 621 | 18 | 112 |
| Maine | Moosehead [1,4] | 117 | 246 | 190 |
| Maryland | Deep Creek [1,3] | 6 | 72 | 62 |
| | Conowingo [2,3,5] | 13 | 110 | 38 |
| Massachusetts | Quabbin [1,3,5] | 39 | 150 | 104 |
| Michigan | Houghton [1,4] | 31 | 20 | 30 |
| | Superior [2,4] | 31,700 | 1,330 | 2,980 |
| Minnesota | Red [1,4] | 452 | 35 | 127 |
| | Superior [2,4] | 31,700 | 1,330 | 2,980 |
| Mississippi | Grenada [1,3] | 100 | 102 | 282 |
| Missouri | Lake of the Ozarks [1,3] | 93 | 148 | 1,300 |
| Montana | Fort Peck [1,3,5] | 375 | 220 | 1,540 |
| Nebraska | McConaughy [1,3] | 50 | 130 | 105 |
| Nevada | Pyramid [1,4] | 169 | 330 | 66 |
| | Mead [2,3] | 247 | 432 | 550 |
| New Hamp. | Winnipesaukee [1,4] | 70 | 169 | 240 |
| New Jersey | Hopatcong [1,4] | 4 | 58 | 32 |
| New Mexico | Elephant Butte [1,3,5] | 57 | 176 | 201 |
| New York | Oneida [1,4] | 80 | 55 | 63 |
| | Erie [2,4] | 9,910 | 210 | 856 |
| North Carolina | Mattamuskeet | 67 | 5 | — |
| | John H. Kerr [2,3,5] | 76 | 900 | 800 |
| North Dakota | Sakakawea [1,3] | 575 | 180 | 1,600 |
| | Oahe [2,3,5] | 556 | 200 | 2,250 |
| Ohio | Lake St. Marys [1,3] | 17 | 10 | 60 |
| | Erie [2,4] | 9,910 | 210 | 856 |
| Oklahoma | Eufaula [1,3] | 160 | 87 | 600 |
| | Texoma [2,3] | 139 | 580 | 94 |
| Oregon | Klamath [1,4] | 143 | 50 | 165 |
| | Goose Lake [2,4] | 194 | 24 | 90 |
| Pennsylvania | Raystown [1,3] | 13 | 185 | 110 |
| | Erie [2,4] | 9,910 | 210 | 856 |
| Rhode Island | Scituate [1,3,5] | 5 | 94 | 38 |
| South Carolina | Marion [1,3] | 173 | 55 | 300 |
| South Dakota | Francis Case [1,3] | 159 | 140 | 540 |
| | Oahe [2,3,5] | 556 | 200 | 2,250 |
| Tennessee | Watts Bar [1,3,5] | 61 | 75 | 783 |
| | Kentucky [2,3] | 250 | 90 | 2,380 |
| Texas | Sam Rayburn [1,3,5] | 179 | 74 | 560 |
| | Toledo Bend [2,3,5] | 284 | 92 | 1,200 |
| Utah | Great Salt Lake [1,4] | 1,438 | 36 | 334 |
| Vermont | Bomoseen [1,4] | 4 | 55 | 19 |
| | Champlain [2,4] | 437 | 400 | 379 |
| Virginia | Smith Mountain [1,3] | 31 | 200 | 500 |
| | John H. Kerr [2,3,5] | 76 | 99 | 800 |
| Washington | F.D. Roosevelt [1,3] | 123 | 375 | 325 |
| West Virginia | Summersville [1,3] | 4 | 267 | 65 |
| Wisconsin | Winnebago [1,4] | 215 | 21 | 78 |
| | Superior [2,4] | 31,700 | 1,330 | 2,980 |
| Wyoming | Yellowstone [1,4] | 137 | 309 | 110 |
| | Flaming Gorge [2,3,5] | 66 | 437 | 400 |

[1] Entirely within state. [2] Shared with another state or states. [3] Man-made. [4] Natural. [5] Reservoir.

# WORLD'S LARGEST LAKES

Source: National Geographic Society

| LAKE AND LOCATION | AREA (sq. miles) | LENGTH (miles) | MAX. DEPTH (feet) |
|---|---|---|---|
| Caspian Sea (U.S.S.R.-Iran) | 143,244 | 760 | 3,360 |
| Superior (U.S.-Canada) | 31,700 | 350 | 1,330 |
| Victoria (Uganda-Tanzania-Kenya) | 26,828 | 250 | 264 |
| Aral Sea (U.S.S.R.) | 24,904 | 280 | 222 |
| Huron (U.S.-Canada) | 23,000 | 206 | 750 |
| Michigan (U.S.) | 22,300 | 307 | 923 |
| Tanganyika (Zaire-Burundi-Tanzania-Zambia) | 12,700 | 420 | 4,650 |
| Great Bear (Canada) | 12,096 | 192 | 1,463 |
| Baykal (U.S.S.R.) | 11,780 | 395 | 5,315 |
| Nyasa or Malawi (Tanzania-Mozambique-Malawi) | 11,150 | 360 | 2,280 |
| Great Slave (Canada) | 11,031 | 298 | 2,015 |
| Erie (U.S.-Canada) | 9,910 | 241 | 210 |
| Winnipeg (Canada) | 9,417 | 266 | 60 |
| Ontario (U.S.-Canada) | 7,550 | 193 | 802 |
| Balkhash (U.S.S.R.) | 7,115 | 376 | 85 |
| Ladoga (U.S.S.R.) | 6,835 | 124 | 738 |
| Chad (Chad-Niger-Nigeria) | 6,300 | 175 | 24 |
| Maracaibo (Venezuela) | 5,217 | 133 | 115 |
| Onega (U.S.S.R.) | 3,710 | 145 | 328 |
| Eyre (Australia) | 3,600 | 90 | 4 |
| Volta (Ghana) | 3,276 | 250 | — |
| Titicaca (Peru-Bolivia) | 3,200 | 122 | 922 |
| Nicaragua (Nicaragua) | 3,100 | 102 | 230 |
| Athabasca (Canada) | 3,064 | 208 | 407 |
| Reindeer (Canada) | 2,568 | 143 | — |
| Turkana (Kenya-Ethiopia) | 2,473 | 154 | 240 |
| Issyk Kul (U.S.S.R.) | 2,355 | 115 | 2,303 |
| Torrens (Australia) | 2,230 | 130 | — |
| Vänern (Sweden) | 2,156 | 91 | 328 |
| Nettilling (Canada) | 2,140 | 67 | — |
| Winnipegosis (Canada) | 2,075 | 141 | 38 |
| Mobutu Sese Seko (Zaire-Uganda) | 2,075 | 100 | 54 |
| Kariba (Zambia-Zimbabwe) | 2,050 | 175 | 390 |
| Nipigon (Canada) | 1,872 | 72 | 540 |
| Gairdner (Australia) | 1,840 | 90 | — |
| Urmia (Iran) | 1,815 | 90 | 49 |
| Manitoba (Canada) | 1,799 | 140 | 12 |
| Mweru (Zaire-Zambia) | 1,770 | 76 | 84 |

## COAST AND SHORELINE OF THE UNITED STATES

Source: National Ocean Survey, National Oceanic and Atmospheric Administration

| STATE | GENERAL COASTLINE [1] | TIDAL SHORELINE [2] | STATE | GENERAL COASTLINE [1] | TIDAL SHORELINE [2] |
|---|---|---|---|---|---|
| **United States** | **12,383** | **88,633** | South Carolina | 187 | 2,876 |
| **Atlantic Coast** | **2,069** | **28,673** | Virginia | 112 | 3,315 |
| Connecticut | — | 618 | **Gulf Coast** | **1,631** | **17,141** |
| Delaware | 28 | 381 | Alabama | 53 | 607 |
| Florida (Atlantic only) | 580 | 3,331 | Florida (Gulf only) | 770 | 5,095 |
| Georgia | 100 | 2,344 | Louisiana | 397 | 7,721 |
| Maine | 228 | 3,478 | Mississippi | 44 | 359 |
| Maryland | 31 | 3,190 | Texas | 367 | 3,359 |
| Massachusetts | 192 | 1,519 | **Pacific Coast** | **7,623** | **40,298** |
| New Hampshire | 13 | 131 | Alaska | 5,580 | 31,383 |
| New Jersey | 130 | 1,792 | California | 840 | 3,427 |
| New York | 127 | 1,850 | Hawaii | 750 | 1,052 |
| North Carolina | 301 | 3,375 | Oregon | 296 | 1,410 |
| Pennsylvania | — | 89 | Washington | 157 | 3,026 |
| Rhode Island | 40 | 384 | **Arctic Coast, Alaska** | **1,060** | **2,521** |

[1] Statute mile length of general outline of seacoast. Measurements made with unit measure of 30 minutes of latitude on charts as near scale of 1:1,200,000 as possible. [2] Statute mile length of shoreline of outer coast, offshore islands, sounds, bays, rivers, and creeks to the head of tidewater or to point where tidal waters narrow to 100 feet wide.

## TIDE RANGES IN THE UNITED STATES

Source: National Ocean Survey, National Oceanic and Atmospheric Administration

Listed below are the average tidal ranges for 1980. "Average range" is the difference in height between average high and low tides. "Spring range" is the average range occurring semimonthly due to a new or full moon. "Diurnal range" is the difference in height between average higher high tide and average lower low tide.

| EAST COAST LOCATION | AVERAGE RANGE | SPRING RANGE | WEST COAST LOCATION | AVERAGE RANGE | DIURNAL RANGE |
|---|---|---|---|---|---|
| Portland, Maine | 9.0 ft. | 10.4 ft. | Seattle, Washington | 7.6 ft. | 11.3 ft. |
| Boston, Massachusetts | 9.5 ft. | 11.0 ft. | Coos Bay, Oregon | 5.6 ft. | 7.3 ft. |
| New London, Connecticut | 2.6 ft. | 3.1 ft. | Crescent City, California | 5.1 ft. | 6.9 ft. |
| The Battery, New York City | 4.5 ft. | 5.4 ft. | San Francisco, California | 4.0 ft. | 5.7 ft. |
| Atlantic City, New Jersey | 4.1 ft. | 5.0 ft. | Santa Barbara, California | 3.6 ft. | 5.3 ft. |
| Norfolk, Virginia | 2.8 ft. | 3.4 ft. | Los Angeles, California | 3.8 ft. | 5.4 ft. |
| Charleston, South Carolina | 5.2 ft. | 6.1 ft. | San Diego, California | 4.1 ft. | 5.7 ft. |
| Savannah, Georgia | 7.4 ft. | 8.6 ft. | Honolulu, Hawaii | 1.2 ft. | 1.9 ft. |
| Miami, Fla. (E. end of causeway) | 2.0 ft. | 2.4 ft. | Cordova, Alaska | 10.1 ft. | 12.4 ft. |

## GREAT LAKES SYSTEM OF NORTH AMERICA

Source: National Ocean Survey, National Oceanic and Atmospheric Administration

| GENERAL LAKE DIMENSIONS | LAKE SUPERIOR | LAKE MICHIGAN | LAKE HURON | LAKE ST. CLAIR | LAKE ERIE | LAKE ONTARIO |
|---|---|---|---|---|---|---|
| Length in miles | 350 | 307 | 206 | 26 | 241 | 193 |
| Breadth in miles | 160 | 118 [1] | 183 [2] | 24 | 57 | 53 |
| Length of coastline in miles (including islands) | 2,730 | 1,640 | 3,830 [3] | 257 | 871 | 712 |
| Areas in square miles: | | | | | | |
| Total water surface | 31,700 [4] | 22,300 [5] | 23,000 [6] | 490 [7] | 9,910 | 7,550 [8] |
| Water surface, United States | 20,600 [4] | 22,300 [5] | 9,100 [6] | 198 [7] | 4,980 | 3,560 [8] |
| Water surface, Canada | 11,100 [4] | — | 13,900 [6] | 292 [7] | 4,930 | 3,990 [8] |
| Drainage basin (land) total | 49,300 [4] | 45,600 [5] | 51,700 [6] | 6,930 [7] | 22,700 | 27,300 [8] |
| Drainage basin land, United States | 16,900 [4] | 45,600 [5] | 16,200 [6] | 2,850 [7] | 18,000 | 15,200 [8] |
| Drainage basin land, Canada | 32,400 [4] | — | 35,500 [6] | 4,080 [7] | 4,720 | 12,100 [8] |
| Drainage basin (land and water) total | 81,000 [4] | 67,900 [5] | 74,800 [6] | 7,420 [7] | 32,600 | 34,800 [8] |
| Maximum depth, feet | 1,333 | 923 | 750 | 21 [9] | 210 | 802 |
| Average depth, feet | 489 | 279 | 195 | 10 | 62 | 283 |
| Volume of water in cubic miles | 2,930 | 1,180 | 849 | 1 | 116 | 393 |
| Length of outflow river (shown under lake from which it flows), approximate miles: | | | | | | |
| St. Marys | 70 | | | | | |
| St. Clair | | | 27 | | | |
| Detroit | | | | 32 | | |
| Niagara | | | | | 37 | |
| St. Lawrence | | | | | | 502 |

[1] Measured at wide point through Green Bay. [2] Measured at wide point through Georgian Bay. [3] Includes Georgian Bay and North Channel. [4] Including St. Marys River above Brush Point. [5] Lake Michigan including Green Bay. [6] Including St. Marys River below Brush Point, North Channel, and Georgian Bay. [7] Lake St. Clair and St. Clair and Detroit Rivers. [8] Lake Ontario including Niagara River and St. Lawrence River above Iroquois Dam. [9] Maximum natural depth; dredged navigation channel has 27.5-foot depth.

# Ecology and Environment

Gov. Richard Lamm of Colorado drops used aluminum cans into a "Golden Goat" aluminum recycling machine in a parking lot of a Denver supermarket. The machine, which operates 24 hours a day, pays users 24¢ a pound for old aluminum cans.

United Press Int'l.

## HIGHLIGHTS: 1980

### WARNING ON ACID RAIN

In its 10th annual report, the President's Council on Environmental Quality warned in 1980 that the nation faces increased danger of pollution because of acid rain. This is the name given to rain that picks up pollution by falling through air contaminated with wastes from burning fossil fuels, such as oil or coal.

The council said that dangers of acid rain had increased fiftyfold in the eastern United States during the past 25 years. Because of acid rain, the council said, "many lakes in the northeastern part of the United States and Canada now can no longer support fish and other life."

Douglas M. Costle, administrator of the Environmental Protection Agency (EPA),

further elaborated the problem, saying that acid rain has affected about 200 lakes in New York, lakes in northern Minnesota, and headwater streams from Georgia to Maine. He said that utility plants were the main culprits in giving off sulfur and nitrogen oxide pollutants.

### ENDANGERED SPECIES LIST CURBED

The U.S. Fish and Wildlife Service in 1980 withdrew proposals to list 1,876 additional species of animals and plants as endangered or threatened. The action was caused by a congressional amendment to the Endangered Species Act that required the withdrawal of all proposals not finalized within two years of their first publication. The agency explained

**HIGHLIGHTS: 1980** (continued)

that it did not have adequate personnel to complete the procedural requirements necessary to finalize the inclusion of the previously proposed endangered species.

Among the procedures now required for naming a species as endangered, the agency must provide details of the critical habitat of the species and must do an economic analysis to determine the effect of declaring an area a critical habitat.

## 250 HAZARDS TO DRINKING WATER

A subcommittee of the House of Representatives compiled a list of 250 waste-storage sites that pose a potential hazard to supplies of drinking water. The subcommittee report said that each of the sites contains potentially hazardous wastes that are not screened from penetration into the groundwater supply. Most of the sites are adjacent to industrial plants.

Illinois had the largest number of potentially dangerous sites—54. Oregon was second with 21 and South Carolina third with 20.

## PERILS OF POPULATION EXPANSION

The Environmental Fund's World Population Clock in Washington, D.C., recorded that the world's population had grown to 4.5 billion at 2:42 P.M. on March 14, 1980. The

## ENDANGERED AND THREATENED SPECIES

Source: Endangered Species Program

Twenty additional species of animals and plants were added to the lists of endangered and threatened species in 1980, bringing to 747 the number listed by the Endangered Species Program of the U.S. Fish and Wildlife Service.

| Type of Species | Endangered | | Threatened | | Species |
| | U.S. | Foreign | U.S. | Foreign | Total |
|---|---|---|---|---|---|
| Mammals ...... | 32 | 242 | 3 | 20 | 279 |
| Birds .......... | 66 | 159 | 3 | 0 | 214 |
| Reptiles ....... | 13 | 61 | 10 | 4 | 75 |
| Amphibians .... | 5 | 8 | 3 | 0 | 16 |
| Fishes ......... | 34 | 15 | 12 | 0 | 57 |
| Snails ......... | 2 | 1 | 5 | 0 | 8 |
| Clams ......... | 23 | 2 | 0 | 0 | 25 |
| Crustaceans ... | 1 | 0 | 0 | 0 | 1 |
| Insects......... | 7 | 0 | 6 | 1 | 13 |
| Plants ......... | 50 | 2 | 7 | 3 | 59 |
| Totals ......... | 233 | 490 | 49 | 28 | 747 |

clock rate is based on adding 172 persons to the world's population every minute.

Justin Blackwelder, president of the Environmental Fund, believed it was unlikely that the growth rate would continue for the next 25 years, expecting a disaster, such as three consecutive years of bad crop weather, to halt it.

Rafael M. Salas, executive director of the UN Fund for Population Activities, released statistics in 1980 predicting that by the year 2000 there will be 60 cities with populations

## STANDARD AIR POLLUTION INDEX

Source: U.S. Environmental Protection Agency

| AIR QUALITY LEVEL | INDEX VALUE | POLLUTANT LEVELS [1] | | | | | HEALTH EFFECTS AND PRECAUTIONS |
| | | Partic-ulates [2] | Sulfur dioxide | Carbon monoxide | Ozone | Nitrogen dioxide | |
|---|---|---|---|---|---|---|---|
| SIGNIFICANT HARM | 500 | 1,000 | 2,620 | 57.5 | 1,200 | 3,750 | VERY HAZARDOUS: Premature death of ill and elderly. Healthy persons experience adverse symptoms affecting normal activity. All persons should remain indoors, keeping windows and doors closed. Everyone should minimize physical exertion and avoid traffic. |
| EMERGENCY | 400 | 875 | 2,100 | 46.0 | 1,000 | 3,000 | HAZARDOUS: Premature onset of certain diseases, significant aggravation of symptoms, and decreased exercise tolerance in healthy persons. Elderly persons and those with existing diseases should stay indoors and avoid physical exertion. All persons should avoid outdoor activity. |
| WARNING | 300 | 625 | 1,600 | 34.0 | 800 | 2,260 | VERY UNHEALTHFUL: Significant aggravation of symptoms and decreased exercise tolerance in persons with heart or lung disease. Widespread symptoms in healthy population. Elderly and persons with existing heart or lung disease should stay indoors and reduce physical activity. |
| ALERT | 200 | 375 | 800 | 17.0 | 400 | 1,130 | UNHEALTHFUL: Mild aggravation of symptoms in susceptible persons. Irritation symptoms in healthy population. Persons with existing heart or respiratory ailments should reduce physical exertion and outdoor activity. |
| NAAQS [3] | 100 | 260 | 365 | 10.0 | 160 | — | MODERATE |
| 50% NAAQS | 50 | 75 | 80 | 5.0 | 80 | — | GOOD |

[1] Concentration of micrograms of pollutant per cubic meter. [2] Dust or other particles. [3] National Ambient Air Quality Standard.

Revolutionary aeroponics system of growing plants is demonstrated by worker at research facility in Moshav Sitriyya, Israel. No soil is used, so the plant roots dangle free as shown. Roots are fed every 5 to 10 minutes with an automatic spray mist of oxygen, moisture, and nutrients. Research indicates that plants grow 2 to 10 times more quickly using aeroponics instead of soil.

United Press Int'l.

of 5 million or more. He pointed out that 30 years ago, in 1950, there were only six cities of that size.

Agricultural authorities have pointed out that world consumption of grain has risen 15% since 1975, while production has gone up only 12%. The Department of Agriculture reported that U.S. grain stockpiles will be down about 39% in 1981 because of the 1980 drought that killed about one-fifth of the U.S. corn and soybean crops.

World grain reserves in 1981 were estimated by the Agriculture Department as only 19%, or about a six-week supply. Economists said that a second year of widespread drought could bring a worldwide food crisis.

## WORLD'S POPULATION GROWTH: 1975–2000
Source: U.S. Census Bureau

Estimates of how large the world's population will be by the year 2000 depend on how widely and how quickly the world's people accept family planning methods to reduce population growth.

|  | World | Africa | Asia and Oceania | Latin America | Soviet Union and Eastern Europe | Northern America, Western Europe, Japan, Australia, and New Zealand |
|---|---|---|---|---|---|---|
| **Total population (millions):** |  |  |  |  |  |  |
| 1975 | 4,090 | 399 | 2,274 | 324 | 384 | 708 |
| 2000 | 6,350 | 814 | 3,630 | 636 | 460 | 809 |
| **Net growth, 1975 to 2000:** |  |  |  |  |  |  |
| Persons (millions) | 2,260 | 415 | 1,356 | 312 | 76 | 101 |
| Percent | 55% | 104% | 60% | 96% | 20% | 14% |
| **Birthrate (per 1,000 persons):** |  |  |  |  |  |  |
| 1975 | 30.4 | 46.7 | 33.7 | 37.2 | 17.7 | 14.8 |
| 2000 | 25.6 | 38.5 | 25.9 | 28.7 | 15.9 | 14.5 |
| **Death rate (per 1,000 persons):** |  |  |  |  |  |  |
| 1975 | 12.3 | 19.0 | 13.0 | 8.9 | 9.7 | 9.6 |
| 2000 | 9.1 | 11.3 | 8.7 | 5.7 | 10.5 | 10.5 |
| **Rate of natural increase:** |  |  |  |  |  |  |
| 1975 | 1.8% | 2.8% | 2.1% | 2.8% | 0.8% | 0.5% |
| 2000 | 1.7% | 2.7% | 1.7% | 2.3% | 0.5% | 0.4% |

# WORDS IN ECOLOGY AND ENVIRONMENT

**abiotic environment**—nonliving parts of environment, including air, soil, water, climate, weather, and nonliving nutrients

**acclimatization**—way plant or animal adjusts to changes of climate

**adaptation**—way plant or animal adjusts to live in certain environment

**aerosol**—fine particles of liquids, dust, smoke, or solids that remain suspended in air for long periods of time

**air pollution**—poisoning of air by ash, bacteria, dust, gases, pollen, smoke, and other substances, both man-made and natural

**balance of nature**—stability of population of each of many kinds of animals and plants living in certain environment

**basic ingredients**—essentials needed by plants or animals to support life

**biome**—large community of animals and plants living together in specific climate and region, as in tropical rain forest

**biotic environment**—living plants, animals, and microorganisms and their interaction in certain area

**community**—animals and plants that live together and depend upon each other

**conservation**—protection and management of environment to preserve resources and basic ingredients needed for life

**decomposers**—animals, plants, microorganisms, or substances that cause materials to decompose or decay

**ecological efficiency**—relationship of amount of energy used to amount of energy passed on in ecological process, such as in food chain

**ecological pyramid**—decreased volume or number of plants or animals at each step of ecological process because of reduced ecological efficiency

**ecological succession**—gradual change or replacement in nature of elements within environment

**ecologist**—scientist who studies relationships among plants, animals, people, and their environment

**ecology**—study of relationship of plants, animals, and people to each other and to their environments

**ecosystem**—system of relationships within given community that supports life of each kind of plant and animal in area

**environment**—living and nonliving things in certain area and forces and conditions that affect them

**Environmental Protection Agency (EPA)**—federal agency responsible for protecting environment by controlling pollution

**erosion**—gradual wearing away of natural resource, such as soil being eroded by wind and floods

**fallout**—dropping to earth of dust or particles carried in air, such as radioactive fallout resulting from explosion of atomic bomb

**flood control**—building of dams, dikes, and reservoirs in effort to prevent destruction by floods and water erosion

**food chain**—series or chain of plants and animals that depend upon each other for food supply to live; for example, man eats fish, which eat shrimp, which eat algae

**habitat**—area or region in which plant or animal lives

**inversion**—condition in atmosphere that occurs when warm layer of air is trapped between two cooler layers of air, sometimes causing smog to linger over area

**life-support system**—everything needed to maintain life

**limnology**—study of lakes and other bodies of inland water and relationship of animals and plants that live in them

**mapping**—making maps to locate objects in relation to known point

**natural selection**—process that results in specific kinds of animals and plants surviving in particular environment

**net of interaction**—all living things and how they affect one another

**noise pollution**—unwanted, disagreeable sounds

**oceanography**—study of oceans and plants, animals, and resources of oceans

**pH**—symbol with scale of numbers from 0 to 14 to indicate whether water or soil is acid or alkaline; pH 7 is neutral, while pH numbers below 7 are acid and pH numbers above 7 are alkaline

**phenology**—scientific study of time that ecological events occur, such as study of hibernation of animals

**pollution**—discharge of waste materials that cause adverse and unpleasant effects to environment

**population**—all plants, animals, or people living in certain area

**population density**—relationship of total number of plants, animals, or people to area of region where they live, such as number of people per square mile

**primary consumer**—animal that eats plants and then is eaten itself by another kind of animal

**primary producer**—plant that produces energy from Sun and then provides energy to animal that eats it

**raw materials**—unprocessed materials as they come directly from land or sea

**recycling**—process to convert waste materials into useful materials, such as recycling of waste paper, glass, and aluminum

**secondary consumer**—animal that depends upon eating primary consumer for its energy; for example, fish that lives on shrimp for food is secondary consumer because shrimp is primary consumer, deriving its energy from eating algae

**soil pollution**—damage to soil, such as destruction of microscopic organisms in the soil by pesticides

**waste disposal**—process of getting rid of waste materials such as garbage or sewage

**water pollution**—discharge of waste materials into body of water

**web of life**—dependence of living things upon each other for survival

# The Economy

Recession and the slump in sales of automobiles brought long lines at unemployment offices in Detroit, Mich., throughout the year. Unemployment among auto workers caused the jobless rate in Michigan to soar to 14%.

## HIGHLIGHTS: 1980

### WORLD ECONOMIC CRISIS IN 1980s

The economic forecast for the world in the 1980s is pessimistic.

According to economic analysts, two major factors will contribute to continuing economic problems that have caused reduced production, high unemployment, and soaring inflation. These two factors are rapidly increasing population and scarce supplies of oil at continually higher prices.

U.S. government studies indicate that the population of the world will rise by about 1 billion persons during the decade—an increase of nearly 25%.

In an address to an economic conference in Austria in 1980, U.S. Undersecretary of State for Economic Affairs Richard N. Cooper pointed out that the population growth will lead to deforestation of millions of acres of land converted to agriculture, greater urbanization with increasing terrorism and anarchy in many developing countries, greatly accelerated demands for food imports to developing countries with periodic droughts and famines, and increased migration by refugees seeking to escape political repression and food shortages. He warned also that the continued increasing demand for oil by industrial countries seeking to raise production would cause higher oil prices and more consumer inflation.

Forecasts by the World Food and Agricul-

**HIGHLIGHTS: 1980** *(continued)*
tural Outlook and Situation Board indicated greater world food shortages in 1981.

**RECESSION IN THE U.S.**
Under pressure of high loan interest rates the U.S. economy slid into a recession in 1980 with a huge slump in the sales of automobiles and trucks as well as a sharp decline in the construction of housing.

Adjusted for inflation, the Gross National Product (GNP) showed a decline of 10.2% in the second quarter of 1980 compared with an increase of 1.5% in the first quarter. In the third quarter ending in September there were signs that the recession was easing as preliminary figures showed an increase of 1% in real output as reflected by the GNP.

Restrictions imposed by the Federal Reserve Board (FRB) in an effort to control inflation caused banks to raise their prime lending rates to businesses to a record 20% in April. Under political pressure in a presidential election year, the FRB eased its restric-

## U.S. EMPLOYMENT AND UNEMPLOYMENT: 1900–1980

Source: U.S. Bureau of Labor Statistics

| Year | Potential Labor Force [1] | Not in Labor Force [2] | Armed Services | Total Civil Labor Force | Employed in Agriculture | Employed in Nonfarm jobs | Unemployed | Percent Unemployed |
|---|---|---|---|---|---|---|---|---|
| 1900 | 57,950,000 | 28,877,000 | 124,000 | 28,376,000 | 11,050,000 | 15,906,000 | 1,420,000 | 5.0% |
| 1910 | 71,580,000 | 33,413,000 | 141,000 | 36,709,000 | 11,260,000 | 23,299,000 | 2,150,000 | 5.9% |
| 1920 | 82,739,000 | 41,125,000 | 380,000 | 41,340,000 | 10,440,000 | 28,768,000 | 2,132,000 | 5.2% |
| 1930 | 98,723,000 | 49,893,000 | 260,000 | 48,523,000 | 10,340,000 | 33,843,000 | 4,340,000 | 8.9% |
| 1933 | 99,150,000 | 48,019,000 | 250,000 | 50,882,000 | 10,090,000 | 27,962,000 | 12,830,000 | 25.2% |
| 1940 | 100,147,000 | 47,136,000 | 540,000 | 55,640,000 | 9,540,000 | 37,980,000 | 8,120,000 | 14.6% |
| 1947 | 103,418,000 | 42,477,000 | 1,591,000 | 59,350,000 | 7,891,000 | 49,148,000 | 2,311,000 | 3.9% |
| 1950 | 106,645,000 | 42,787,000 | 1,650,000 | 62,208,000 | 7,160,000 | 51,760,000 | 3,288,000 | 5.3% |
| 1955 | 112,732,000 | 44,660,000 | 3,049,000 | 65,023,000 | 6,449,000 | 55,724,000 | 2,852,000 | 4.4% |
| 1960 | 119,759,000 | 47,617,000 | 2,514,000 | 69,628,000 | 5,458,000 | 60,318,000 | 3,852,000 | 5.5% |
| 1965 | 129,236,000 | 52,058,000 | 2,723,000 | 74,455,000 | 4,361,000 | 66,726,000 | 3,366,000 | 4.5% |
| 1968 | 135,562,000 | 53,291,000 | 3,535,000 | 78,737,000 | 3,817,000 | 72,103,000 | 2,817,000 | 3.6% |
| 1969 | 137,841,000 | 53,602,000 | 3,506,000 | 80,733,000 | 3,606,000 | 74,296,000 | 2,831,000 | 3.5% |
| 1970 | 140,182,000 | 54,280,000 | 3,188,000 | 82,715,000 | 3,462,000 | 75,165,000 | 4,088,000 | 4.9% |
| 1971 | 142,596,000 | 55,666,000 | 2,816,000 | 84,113,000 | 3,387,000 | 75,732,000 | 4,993,000 | 5.9% |
| 1972 | 145,775,000 | 56,785,000 | 2,449,000 | 86,542,000 | 3,472,000 | 78,230,000 | 4,840,000 | 5.6% |
| 1973 | 148,263,000 | 57,222,000 | 2,327,000 | 88,714,000 | 3,452,000 | 80,957,000 | 4,304,000 | 4.9% |
| 1974 | 150,827,000 | 57,587,000 | 2,229,000 | 91,011,000 | 3,492,000 | 82,443,000 | 5,076,000 | 5.6% |
| 1975 | 153,449,000 | 58,655,000 | 2,180,000 | 92,613,000 | 3,380,000 | 81,403,000 | 7,830,000 | 8.5% |
| 1976 | 156,048,000 | 59,131,000 | 2,144,000 | 94,773,000 | 3,297,000 | 84,188,000 | 7,288,000 | 7.7% |
| 1977 | 158,559,000 | 59,025,000 | 2,133,000 | 97,401,000 | 3,244,000 | 87,302,000 | 6,855,000 | 7.0% |
| 1978 | 161,058,000 | 58,521,000 | 2,117,000 | 100,420,000 | 3,342,000 | 91,031,000 | 6,047,000 | 6.0% |
| 1979 | 163,620,000 | 58,623,000 | 2,089,000 | 102,908,000 | 3,297,000 | 93,648,000 | 5,963,000 | 5.8% |
| 1980 [3] | 166,789,000 | 59,633,000 | 2,122,000 | 105,034,000 | 3,442,000 | 93,765,000 | 7,827,000 | 7.5% |

[1] Americans 16 years and older not in institutions, such as prisons and mental hospitals. [2] Includes dependent wives and husbands, and full-time students. [3] September 1980 data.

## EMPLOYEES[1] IN U.S. INDUSTRIES: 1900–1980

Source: U.S. Bureau of Labor Statistics

| Year | Total | Mining | Construction | Manufacturing | Transportation & Public Utilities | Wholesale & Retail Trade | Finance, Insurance, and Real Estate | Services | Government Federal | Government State & Local |
|---|---|---|---|---|---|---|---|---|---|---|
| 1900 | 15,178 | 637 | 1,147 | 5,468 | 2,282 | 2,502 | 308 | 1,740 | 1,094 | |
| 1910 | 21,697 | 1,068 | 1,342 | 7,828 | 3,366 | 3,570 | 483 | 2,410 | 1,630 | |
| 1920 | 27,434 | 1,180 | 850 | 10,702 | 4,317 | 4,012 | 902 | 3,100 | 2,371 | |
| 1930 | 29,424 | 1,009 | 1,372 | 9,562 | 3,685 | 5,797 | 1,475 | 3,376 | 526 | 2,622 |
| 1932 | 23,628 | 731 | 970 | 6,931 | 2,816 | 4,683 | 1,341 | 2,931 | 559 | 2,666 |
| 1934 | 25,953 | 883 | 862 | 8,501 | 2,750 | 5,281 | 1,319 | 3,058 | 652 | 2,647 |
| 1940 | 32,376 | 925 | 1,294 | 10,985 | 3,038 | 6,750 | 1,502 | 3,681 | 996 | 3,206 |
| 1950 | 45,222 | 901 | 2,333 | 15,241 | 4,034 | 9,386 | 1,919 | 5,382 | 1,928 | 4,098 |
| 1960 | 54,234 | 712 | 2,885 | 16,796 | 4,004 | 11,391 | 2,669 | 7,423 | 2,270 | 6,083 |
| 1970 | 70,920 | 623 | 3,536 | 19,349 | 4,504 | 15,040 | 3,687 | 11,621 | 2,731 | 9,830 |
| 1973 | 76,896 | 644 | 4,015 | 20,068 | 4,644 | 16,674 | 4,091 | 13,021 | 2,663 | 11,075 |
| 1974 | 78,413 | 694 | 3,957 | 20,046 | 4,696 | 17,017 | 4,208 | 13,617 | 2,724 | 11,453 |
| 1975 | 77,051 | 745 | 3,512 | 18,347 | 4,498 | 17,000 | 4,177 | 14,006 | 2,748 | 11,973 |
| 1976 | 79,443 | 783 | 3,594 | 18,956 | 4,509 | 17,694 | 4,263 | 14,644 | 2,733 | 12,215 |
| 1977 | 82,142 | 831 | 3,844 | 19,554 | 4,589 | 18,292 | 4,508 | 15,333 | 2,727 | 12,463 |
| 1978 | 86,697 | 851 | 4,229 | 20,505 | 4,923 | 19,542 | 4,724 | 16,252 | 2,753 | 12,919 |
| 1979 | 89,886 | 960 | 4,483 | 21,062 | 5,141 | 20,269 | 4,974 | 17,078 | 2,773 | 13,147 |
| 1980 [2] | 90,664 | 1,027 | 4,685 | 20,250 | 5,163 | 20,695 | 5,173 | 17,899 | 2,780 | 12,992 |

[1] All figures in thousands (add 000). Excludes farm workers, proprietors, self-employed, domestics. [2] September 1980 data.

tions in May, letting interest rates fall. But after the November election, the FRB announced new restrictions that again sent the prime interest rate soaring to a new record of 21½% in December.

## UNEMPLOYMENT

As the recession deepened, unemployment in the U.S. rose in July to a rate of 7.8% of the work force, with about 8 million jobless. However, the rate eased to 7.6% in September and October. Hardest hit were teenagers, with more than 19% unable to find jobs in August. Black and Hispanic workers also suffered, with the black unemployment rate at 14.3% and that for Hispanics at about 11%.

Despite the high rate of unemployment, the number of persons actually employed increased 262,000 by September 1980 compared with the number working in 1979.

## INFLATION

Consumer prices continued their climb in the U.S. in 1980, reaching an annual rate of 12.7% in September, compared with a year earlier. The cost of housing and transportation increased more rapidly than other items, triggered by high interest rates for mortgages and hikes in the price of gasoline and automobiles. The annual inflation rate for housing reached 14.1% in September, and that for

## U.S. GROSS NATIONAL PRODUCT
Source: U.S. Bureau of Economic Analysis

The gross national product (GNP) is the total national output of goods and services valued at market prices. It includes all consumer purchases of goods and services, private investment expenditures, the net value of exports less imports, and government purchases of goods and services. The United States has the highest GNP of any country in the world. The following amounts are in $ billions (add 000,000,000).

| YEAR | GNP | GROWTH RATE | YEAR | GNP | GROWTH RATE |
|---|---|---|---|---|---|
| 1910 | $ 35.3 | 2.8% | 1960 | $ 506.0 | 4.0% |
| 1915 | $ 40.0 | - 0.8% | 1965 | $ 688.1 | 8.2% |
| 1920 | $ 91.5 | - 4.3% | 1970 | $ 982.4 | 5.0% |
| 1925 | $ 93.1 | 8.4% | 1972 | $1,171.1 | 10.0% |
| 1930 | $ 90.4 | - 9.8% | 1973 | $1,306.6 | 11.6% |
| 1932 | $ 58.0 | -14.7% | 1974 | $1,412.9 | 8.1% |
| 1933 | $ 55.6 | - 1.8% | 1975 | $1,528.8 | 8.2% |
| 1935 | $ 72.2 | 9.9% | 1976 | $1,706.5 | 11.6% |
| 1940 | $ 99.7 | 16.1% | 1977 | $1,877.2 | 11.0% |
| 1945 | $211.9 | - 1.7% | 1978 | $2,127.6 | 12.0% |
| 1950 | $286.2 | 10.9% | 1979 | $2,368.8 | 11.3% |
| 1955 | $399.3 | 9.0% | 1980* | $2,586.5 | 9.2% |

* Data annualized for first 9 months of 1980.

transportation was 15%.

The U.S. average price for a gallon of gasoline stood at $1.23 in September and the price for a gallon of fuel oil at $1.02.

Food prices also continued to rise with the cost of a pound of steak topping $4.

## CONSUMER AND PRODUCER PRICE INDEXES: 1955–1980
Source: U.S. Department of Labor, Bureau of Labor Statistics

| YEAR | CONSUMER PRICES (1967=100) | | | | | | PRODUCER PRICES (1967=100) | | | | | |
|---|---|---|---|---|---|---|---|---|---|---|---|---|
| | All items | | Commodities | | Services | | All commodities | | Farm products, food, and feeds | | Industrial commodities | |
| | Index | Percent change | Index | Percent change | Index | Percent change | Index | Percent change | Index | Percent change | Index | Percent change |
| 1955 | 80.2 | -0.4% | 85.1 | -0.9% | 70.9 | 2.0% | 87.8 | 0.2% | 91.2 | -4.7% | 86.9 | 2.2% |
| 1956 | 81.4 | 1.5% | 85.9 | 0.9% | 72.7 | 2.5% | 90.7 | 3.3% | 90.6 | -0.7% | 90.8 | 4.5% |
| 1957 | 84.3 | 3.6% | 88.6 | 3.1% | 75.6 | 4.0% | 93.3 | 2.9% | 93.7 | 3.4% | 93.3 | 2.8% |
| 1958 | 86.6 | 2.7% | 90.6 | 2.3% | 78.5 | 3.8% | 94.6 | 1.4% | 98.1 | 4.7% | 93.6 | 0.3% |
| 1959 | 87.3 | 0.8% | 90.7 | 0.1% | 80.8 | 2.9% | 94.8 | 0.2% | 93.5 | -4.7% | 95.3 | 1.8% |
| 1960 | 88.7 | 1.6% | 91.5 | 0.9% | 83.5 | 3.3% | 94.9 | 0.1% | 93.7 | 0.2% | 95.3 | 0% |
| 1961 | 89.6 | 1.0% | 92.0 | 0.5% | 85.2 | 2.0% | 94.5 | -0.4% | 93.7 | 0.0% | 94.8 | -0.5% |
| 1962 | 90.6 | 1.1% | 92.8 | 0.9% | 86.8 | 1.9% | 94.8 | 0.3% | 94.7 | 1.1% | 94.8 | 0% |
| 1963 | 91.7 | 1.2% | 93.6 | 0.9% | 88.5 | 2.0% | 94.5 | -0.3% | 93.8 | -1.0% | 94.7 | -0.1% |
| 1964 | 92.9 | 1.3% | 94.6 | 1.1% | 90.2 | 1.9% | 94.7 | 0.2% | 93.2 | -0.6% | 95.2 | 0.5% |
| 1965 | 94.5 | 1.7% | 95.7 | 1.2% | 92.2 | 2.2% | 96.6 | 2.0% | 97.1 | 4.2% | 96.4 | 1.3% |
| 1966 | 97.2 | 2.9% | 98.2 | 2.6% | 95.8 | 3.9% | 99.8 | 3.3% | 103.5 | 6.6% | 98.5 | 2.2% |
| 1967 | 100.0 | 2.9% | 100.0 | 1.8% | 100.0 | 4.4% | 100.0 | 0.2% | 100.0 | -3.4% | 100.0 | 1.5% |
| 1968 | 104.2 | 4.2% | 103.7 | 3.7% | 105.2 | 5.2% | 102.5 | 2.5% | 102.4 | 2.4% | 102.5 | 2.5% |
| 1969 | 109.8 | 5.4% | 108.4 | 4.5% | 112.5 | 6.9% | 106.5 | 3.9% | 108.0 | 5.5% | 106.0 | 3.4% |
| 1970 | 116.3 | 5.9% | 113.5 | 4.7% | 121.6 | 8.1% | 110.4 | 3.7% | 111.7 | 3.4% | 110.0 | 3.8% |
| 1971 | 121.3 | 4.3% | 117.4 | 3.4% | 128.4 | 5.6% | 114.0 | 3.3% | 113.9 | 2.0% | 114.1 | 3.7% |
| 1972 | 125.3 | 3.3% | 120.9 | 3.0% | 133.3 | 3.8% | 119.1 | 4.5% | 122.4 | 7.5% | 117.9 | 3.3% |
| 1973 | 133.1 | 6.2% | 129.9 | 7.4% | 139.1 | 4.4% | 134.7 | 13.1% | 159.1 | 30.0% | 125.9 | 6.8% |
| 1974 | 147.7 | 11.0% | 145.5 | 12.0% | 152.1 | 9.3% | 160.1 | 18.9% | 177.4 | 11.5% | 153.8 | 22.2% |
| 1975 | 161.2 | 9.1% | 158.4 | 8.9% | 166.6 | 9.5% | 174.9 | 9.2% | 184.2 | 3.8% | 171.5 | 11.5% |
| 1976 | 170.5 | 5.8% | 165.2 | 4.3% | 180.4 | 8.3% | 182.9 | 4.6% | 183.1 | -0.6% | 182.3 | 6.3% |
| 1977 | 181.5 | 6.5% | 174.7 | 5.8% | 194.3 | 7.7% | 194.2 | 6.1% | 188.8 | 3.1% | 195.1 | 7.0% |
| 1978 | 195.3 | 7.6% | 187.1 | 7.1% | 210.9 | 8.5% | 209.3 | 7.8% | 206.6 | 9.4% | 209.4 | 7.3% |
| 1979 | 217.7 | 11.5% | 219.4 | 17.3% | 249.3 | 18.2% | 249.7 | 19.3% | 234.6 | 13.6% | 253.1 | 20.9% |
| 1980* | 247.8 | 12.8% | 236.7 | 7.8% | 272.5 | 9.3% | 273.1 | 9.4% | 254.8 | 8.6% | 277.3 | 9.6% |

* Data for August 1980.

# WORLD TRADE BY NATIONS: 1970–1979

Source: United Nations

The value of exports and imports rose to nearly $3 trillion in 1979 as the world suffered continued inflation. U.S. exports increased to $178.6 billion and imports to $217.7 billion.

In 1979 the U.S. became the leading exporting nation in foreign trade, followed by West Germany, Japan, France, Britain, Italy, Soviet Union, Netherlands, Saudi Arabia, and Canada.

| WORLD [1] | IMPORTS [2] | | | | EXPORTS [2] | | | |
|---|---|---|---|---|---|---|---|---|
| | 1970 | 1975 | 1978 | 1979 | 1970 | 1975 | 1978 | 1979 |
| WORLD [1] | $294,100 | $800,800 | $1,213,800 | $1,521,400 | $280,100 | $788,300 | $1,176,100 | $1,475,900 |
| Afghanistan | 112 | 350 | 682 | 328 | 86 | 223 | 322 | 429 |
| Algeria | 1,257 | 5,999 | 8,682 | — | 1,009 | 4,699 | 6,322 | 9,255 |
| Argentina | 1,694 | 3,947 | 3,864 | — | 1,773 | 2,961 | 6,400 | — |
| Australia | 4,479 | 9,819 | 13,885 | 16,432 | 4,621 | 11,554 | 14,128 | 18,473 |
| Austria | 3,549 | 9,391 | 16,022 | 20,254 | 2,857 | 7,518 | 12,176 | 15,483 |
| Bahamas | 337 | 2,697 | — | — | 90 | 2,508 | — | — |
| Bahrain | 247 | 1,158 | 2,046 | — | 274 | 1,147 | 1,893 | 2,415 |
| Bangladesh | — | 874 | 1,344 | — | — | 303 | 576 | — |
| Barbados | 118 | 217 | 312 | 424 | 39 | 107 | 130 | 151 |
| Belgium-Luxembourg | 11,413 | 30,691 | 48,613 | 60,410 | 11,600 | 28,807 | 44,961 | 56,258 |
| Bolivia | 159 | 558 | 848 | 1,011 | 190 | 463 | 627 | 777 |
| Brazil | 2,849 | 12,210 | 14,538 | 19,804 | 2,739 | 8,670 | 12,527 | 15,250 |
| Britain | 21,688 | 53,487 | 78,559 | 102,969 | 19,347 | 44,113 | 71,692 | 91,030 |
| Bulgaria | 1,831 | 5,408 | 7,651 | 8,514 | 2,004 | 4,691 | 7,478 | 8,869 |
| Burma | 169 | 250 | 309 | 319 | 108 | 172 | 243 | 363 |
| Burundi | 22 | 63 | 98 | 153 | 25 | 32 | 69 | 105 |
| Cambodia | 52 | — | — | — | 38 | — | — | — |
| Cameroon | 242 | 599 | 1,057 | 1,271 | 232 | 448 | 803 | 1,129 |
| Canada | 13,360 | 34,082 | 43,434 | 52,230 | 16,119 | 32,200 | 46,065 | 55,336 |
| Central Africa | 34 | 69 | 57 | — | 31 | 48 | 72 | — |
| Chad | 61 | 133 | — | — | 30 | 48 | — | — |
| Chile | 930 | 1,535 | 2,595 | 4,219 | 1,234 | 1,661 | 2,481 | 3,766 |
| Colombia | 843 | 1,495 | 2,928 | 4,437 | 727 | 1,465 | 3,060 | 3,381 |
| Congo | 57 | 165 | 261 | — | 31 | 179 | 139 | — |
| Costa Rica | 317 | 694 | 1,184 | 1,409 | 231 | 493 | 845 | 923 |
| Cuba | 1,311 | 3,883 | 4,687 | — | 1,049 | 3,677 | 4,456 | — |
| Cyprus | 235 | 306 | 753 | 1,001 | 108 | 151 | 344 | 456 |
| Czechoslovakia | 3,695 | 9,081 | 12,565 | 14,262 | 3,792 | 8,356 | 11,747 | 13,198 |
| Denmark | 4,407 | 10,364 | 14,810 | 18,450 | 3,356 | 8,716 | 11,886 | 14,506 |
| Dominican Republic | 278 | 773 | 860 | 1,062 | 214 | 894 | 676 | 822 |
| Ecuador | 274 | 943 | 1,627 | 1,986 | 190 | 897 | 1,494 | — |
| Egypt | 787 | 3,934 | 6,727 | 3,837 | 762 | 1,402 | 1,737 | 1,840 |
| El Salvador | 214 | 598 | 1,028 | 965 | 228 | 513 | 848 | 1,052 |
| Ethiopia | 172 | 313 | 522 | 576 | 122 | 240 | 310 | 423 |
| Fiji | 104 | 268 | 356 | 470 | 68 | 159 | 199 | 249 |
| Finland | 2,636 | 7,626 | 7,863 | 11,400 | 2,306 | 5,503 | 8,570 | 11,175 |
| France | 19,114 | 54,247 | 81,805 | 106,994 | 17,935 | 52,214 | 76,609 | 98,059 |
| Gabon | 80 | 471 | 589 | — | 121 | 942 | 1,307 | — |
| Gambia | 18 | 61 | 100 | 141 | 17 | 48 | 39 | 58 |
| Germany, East | 4,847 | 11,290 | 14,572 | 16,214 | 4,581 | 10,088 | 13,267 | 15,063 |
| Germany, West | 29,814 | 74,208 | 120,668 | 157,747 | 34,189 | 90,021 | 142,090 | 171,540 |
| Ghana | 411 | 791 | — | — | 458 | 807 | — | — |
| Greece | 1,958 | 5,321 | 7,648 | 9,640 | 643 | 2,286 | 3,362 | 3,855 |
| Guatemala | 284 | 733 | 1,286 | — | 299 | 641 | 1,089 | — |
| Guyana | 134 | 344 | 279 | — | 136 | 358 | 289 | 291 |
| Haiti | 52 | 121 | 212 | — | 40 | 79 | 155 | — |
| Honduras | 221 | 404 | 696 | — | 170 | 293 | 606 | — |
| Hungary | 2,506 | 7,176 | 7,902 | 8,674 | 2,317 | 6,091 | 6,345 | 7,938 |
| Iceland | 157 | 488 | 674 | 824 | 147 | 308 | 641 | 781 |
| India | 2,124 | 6,391 | 7,955 | 8,427 | 2,026 | 4,393 | 6,614 | 6,702 |
| Indonesia | 1,002 | 4,770 | 6,690 | 7,225 | 1,108 | 7,103 | 11,643 | 15,578 |
| Iran | 1,662 | 10,343 | 16,019 | 7,261 | 2,623 | 20,212 | 22,430 | 19,000 |
| Iraq | 509 | 4,216 | 4,213 | — | 1,100 | 8,297 | 11,064 | 21,502 |
| Ireland | 1,573 | 3,779 | 7,121 | 9,858 | 1,040 | 3,192 | 5,690 | 7,175 |
| Israel | 1,422 | 4,140 | 5,582 | 7,471 | 734 | 1,835 | 3,716 | 4,553 |
| Italy | 14,970 | 38,366 | 56,445 | 77,970 | 13,206 | 34,830 | 56,051 | 72,242 |

[1] World total does not include communist nations.  [2] All figures in millions of U.S. dollars (add 000,000).

| | IMPORTS [2] | | | | EXPORTS [2] | | | |
|---|---|---|---|---|---|---|---|---|
| | 1970 | 1975 | 1978 | 1979 | 1970 | 1975 | 1978 | 1979 |
| Ivory Coast ........ | $388 | $1,127 | 2,325 | 2,493 | $469 | $1,182 | 2,323 | 2,515 |
| Jamaica .......... | 525 | 1,124 | 874 | 1,010 | 347 | 815 | 744 | 769 |
| Japan ............. | 18,881 | 57,881 | 78,732 | 110,670 | 19,318 | 55,844 | 97,503 | 103,045 |
| Jordan ............ | 184 | 731 | 1,499 | 1,949 | 34 | 153 | 297 | 402 |
| Kenya ............. | 398 | 980 | 1,709 | 1,658 | 217 | 643 | 1,022 | 1,103 |
| Korea, South ...... | 1,983 | 7,274 | 14,972 | 20,339 | 835 | 5,081 | 12,711 | 15,055 |
| Kuwait ............ | 625 | 2,388 | 4,605 | 5,368 | 1,901 | 9,184 | 10,464 | 17,498 |
| Laos .............. | 114 | — | — | — | 7 | — | — | — |
| Lebanon .......... | 567 | — | — | — | 198 | — | — | — |
| Liberia ............ | 150 | 331 | 481 | 487 | 213 | 394 | 486 | 536 |
| Libya ............. | 554 | 3,542 | 4,602 | — | 2,366 | 6,840 | 9,907 | — |
| Madagascar ....... | 170 | 367 | 443 | — | 145 | 294 | 386 | — |
| Malawi ........... | 86 | 251 | 339 | 400 | 60 | 139 | 179 | 233 |
| Malaysia .......... | 1,111 | 3,129 | 5,265 | — | 1,369 | 3,197 | 5,937 | — |
| Mali .............. | 47 | 177 | 219 | — | 33 | 53 | 107 | — |
| Malta ............. | 161 | 376 | 568 | 759 | 39 | 167 | 343 | 424 |
| Mauritania ........ | 56 | 161 | 181 | 259 | 89 | 174 | 119 | 148 |
| Mauritius ......... | 76 | 332 | 501 | 554 | 69 | 298 | 326 | 369 |
| Mexico ........... | 2,320 | 6,570 | 7,787 | 11,829 | 1,402 | 2,861 | 5,772 | 8,768 |
| Morocco .......... | 686 | 2,567 | 2,970 | 3,807 | 488 | 1,543 | 1,511 | 1,872 |
| Mozambique ...... | 324 | 417 | — | — | 156 | 202 | — | — |
| Netherlands ....... | 13,426 | 34,573 | 53,117 | 67,284 | 11,774 | 35,075 | 50,280 | 63,667 |
| New Zealand ...... | 1,245 | 3,152 | 3,500 | 4,542 | 1,225 | 2,160 | 3,752 | 4,694 |
| Nicaragua ......... | 198 | 517 | 848 | — | 175 | 375 | 774 | — |
| Niger ............. | 58 | 101 | — | — | 32 | 91 | — | — |
| Nigeria ........... | 1,031 | 6,041 | 12,763 | — | 1,225 | 7,993 | 9,865 | — |
| Norway ........... | 3,702 | 9,705 | 11,463 | 13,818 | 2,457 | 7,234 | 10,016 | 13,271 |
| Oman ............. | — | 1,047 | 1,269 | 1,387 | 206 | 1,452 | 1,598 | 2,284 |
| Pakistan .......... | 1,171 | 2,151 | 3,275 | 4,061 | 723 | 1,031 | 1,470 | 2,036 |
| Panama .......... | 357 | 892 | 942 | — | 106 | 286 | 244 | 288 |
| Papua New Guinea . | 268 | 483 | 676 | 810 | 103 | 470 | 780 | 963 |
| Paraguay ......... | 64 | 179 | 318 | 432 | 64 | 176 | 257 | 305 |
| Peru ............. | 619 | 2,629 | 1,958 | 2,022 | 1,044 | 1,315 | 1,955 | 3,533 |
| Philippines ........ | 1,286 | 3,776 | 4,732 | 6,142 | 1,142 | 2,295 | 3,425 | 4,601 |
| Poland ........... | 3,608 | 12,536 | 16,089 | 17,488 | 3,548 | 10,283 | 14,114 | 16,233 |
| Portugal .......... | 1,582 | 3,840 | 4,791 | 6,086 | 949 | 1,939 | 2,393 | 3,468 |
| Romania .......... | 1,960 | 5,342 | 8,910 | 10,916 | 1,851 | 5,341 | 8,077 | 9,724 |
| Rwanda .......... | 29 | 96 | 179 | — | 25 | 42 | 70 | — |
| Saudi Arabia ....... | 692 | 4,214 | 20,424 | — | 2,424 | 29,671 | 40,716 | 59,336 |
| Senegal ........... | 193 | 583 | — | — | 152 | 459 | — | — |
| Sierra Leone ...... | 116 | 185 | 278 | — | 101 | 131 | 161 | 146 |
| Singapore ......... | 2,461 | 8,134 | 13,049 | 17,635 | 1,554 | 5,376 | 10,134 | 14,233 |
| Somalia .......... | 45 | 162 | 241 | — | 31 | 89 | 107 | — |
| South Africa ...... | 3,556 | 7,566 | 7,193 | 8,352 | 2,142 | 4,524 | 7,182 | — |
| Soviet Union ....... | 11,732 | 36,971 | 50,550 | 57,773 | 12,800 | 33,316 | 52,216 | 64,762 |
| Spain ............ | 4,716 | 16,234 | 18,707 | 25,432 | 2,387 | 7,669 | 13,115 | 17,903 |
| Sri Lanka ......... | 389 | 751 | 939 | 1,441 | 342 | 560 | 846 | 890 |
| Sudan ............ | 325 | 956 | 1,198 | — | 294 | 438 | 533 | — |
| Suriname ......... | 115 | 262 | — | — | 135 | 277 | — | — |
| Sweden........... | 7,004 | 17,874 | 20,230 | 28,488 | 6,792 | 17,437 | 21,526 | 27,240 |
| Switzerland ....... | 6,486 | 13,305 | 23,804 | 29,354 | 5,152 | 12,957 | 23,561 | 26,507 |
| Syria ............. | 357 | 1,668 | 2,443 | 3,307 | 203 | 930 | 1,053 | 1,634 |
| Tanzania ......... | 271 | 773 | 1,142 | 1,084 | 239 | 372 | 472 | 523 |
| Thailand .......... | 1,299 | 3,280 | 5,356 | 7,156 | 710 | 2,377 | 4,085 | 5,308 |
| Togo ............. | 65 | 174 | 448 | — | 55 | 126 | 241 | — |
| Trinidad-Tobago .... | 542 | 1,471 | 1,967 | 1,946 | 480 | 1,757 | 2,039 | 2,476 |
| Tunisia ........... | 305 | 1,424 | 2,162 | 2,830 | 182 | 856 | 1,126 | 1,766 |
| Turkey ........... | 894 | 4,640 | 4,597 | 4,946 | 588 | 1,401 | 2,288 | 2,261 |
| Uganda........... | 121 | 200 | — | — | 245 | 267 | 350 | 427 |
| United Arab Emir. ... | 267 | 2,668 | 5,368 | 6,960 | 550 | 6,878 | 9,050 | 13,574 |
| UNITED STATES ... | 39,756 | 102,984 | 182,787 | 217,664 | 42,590 | 106,157 | 141,154 | 178,578 |
| Upper Volta........ | 47 | 151 | 191 | — | 18 | 44 | 42 | — |
| Uruguay .......... | 231 | 556 | 757 | 1,206 | 233 | 384 | 686 | 788 |
| Vanuatu .......... | 13 | 35 | 45 | — | 12 | 10 | 33 | — |
| Venezuela ........ | 1,641 | 5,325 | 10,614 | 9,456 | 2,599 | 8,991 | 9,126 | 13,111 |
| Vietnam .......... | 373 | — | — | — | 8 | — | — | — |
| Western Samoa .... | 14 | 37 | 53 | 73 | 5 | 7 | 11 | 18 |
| Yemen, North ..... | 32 | 294 | 1,283 | — | 3 | 11 | 7 | — |
| Yemen, South ...... | 201 | 313 | — | — | 146 | 182 | 221 | — |
| Yugoslavia ........ | 2,874 | 7,697 | 9,987 | 12,862 | 1,679 | 4,072 | 5,659 | 6,491 |
| Zaire ............. | 533 | 927 | 589 | — | 781 | 865 | 925 | — |
| Zambia ........... | 477 | 937 | 630 | — | 1,001 | 810 | 856 | — |
| Zimbabwe ........ | 329 | — | 587 | 937 | 355 | — | 876 | 1,164 |

# WORLD PRODUCTION: 1970–1979

Source: United Nations

| | 1970 | 1975 | 1976 | 1977 | 1978 | 1979 |
|---|---|---|---|---|---|---|
| **POPULATION** | | | | | | |
| World total........... | 3,610,000,000 | 4,033,000,000 | 4,107,000,000 | 4,182,000,000 | 4,258,000,000 | 4,336,000,000 |
| **AGRICULTURE** | | | | | | |
| Barley [1] | 139,426,000 | 153,000,000 | 188,000,000 | 176,000,000 | 195,000,000 | 172,000,000 |
| Cocoa beans [1] (chocolate) | 1,507,000 | 1,544,000 | 1,375,000 | 1,434,000 | 1,471,000 | 1,537,000 |
| Corn (maize) [1] ........ | 261,548,000 | 326,000,000 | 335,000,000 | 346,000,000 | 363,000,000 | 385,000,000 |
| Cotton [1] ............. | 11,738,000 | 12,294,000 | 12,097,000 | 13,913,000 | 13,133,000 | 14,042,000 |
| Eggs (hen) [1] .......... | 21,132,000 | 23,600,000 | 24,000,000 | 24,800,000 | 25,800,000 | 26,600,000 |
| Livestock | | | | | | |
| Cattle [2] ............. | 1,096,379,000 | 1,205,411,000 | 1,210,876,000 | 1,216,109,000 | 1,213,092,000 | — |
| Hogs [2] .............. | 593,758,000 | 694,209,000 | 679,411,000 | 706,926,000 | 731,799,000 | — |
| Horses [2] ............ | 67,141,000 | 62,820,000 | 62,235,000 | 62,113,000 | 61,748,000 | — |
| Sheep [2] ............. | 1,063,659,000 | 1,050,125,000 | 1,049,755,000 | 1,044,492,000 | 1,055,697,000 | — |
| Milk [1] ............... | 396,054,000 | 430,000,000 | 438,000,000 | 450,000,000 | 457,000,000 | 460,000,000 |
| Peanuts [1] ............ | 18,300,000 | 19,300,000 | 17,900,000 | 18,400,000 | 18,700,000 | 19,000,000 |
| Potatoes [1] ........... | 312,134,000 | 285,000,000 | 262,000,000 | 266,000,000 | 276,000,000 | 284,000,000 |
| Rice [1] ............... | 308,578,000 | 360,000,000 | 350,000,000 | 370,000,000 | 385,000,000 | 376,000,000 |
| Tobacco [1] ............ | 4,678,000 | 5,416,000 | 5,638,000 | 5,505,000 | 5,693,000 | 5,387,000 |
| Wheat [1] .............. | 318,319,000 | 356,000,000 | 420,000,000 | 391,000,000 | 449,000,000 | 421,000,000 |
| Wool [1] ............... | 2,768,000 | 2,638,000 | 2,596,000 | 2,580,000 | 2,603,000 | 2,675,000 |
| **FISHING** | | | | | | |
| Total catch [1] ......... | 70,000,000 | 68,600,000 | 72,100,000 | 71,200,000 | 72,400,000 | — |
| **ENERGY** | | | | | | |
| Coal [1, 3] ............. | 1,774,000,000 | 1,889,000,000 | 1,940,000,000 | 1,974,000,000 | 1,984,000,000 | 2,137,000,000 |
| Electricity [4] .......... | 4,846,000,000 | 6,331,000,000 | 6,775,000,000 | 7,066,000,000 | 7,392,000,000 | 7,519,000,000 |
| Natural gas [5] ......... | 9,567,983 | 10,943,000 | 11,393,000 | 11,655,000 | 12,093,000 | 12,464,000 |
| Petroleum [1] .......... | 2,253,000,000 | 2,575,000,000 | 2,786,000,000 | 2,901,000,000 | 2,920,000,000 | 2,999,000,000 |
| **FOOD AND BEVERAGES** | | | | | | |
| Coffee [1] ............. | 3,869,000 | 4,652,000 | 3,550,000 | 4,257,000 | 4,620,000 | 4,861,000 |
| Flour (wheat) [1] ....... | 121,450,000 | 125,700,000 | 129,100,000 | 130,100,000 | — | — |
| Meat [1] ............... | 84,567,000 | 122,800,000 | 126,500,000 | 131,300,000 | 135,500,000 | 138,100,000 |
| Sugar [1] .............. | 72,896,000 | 81,600,000 | 85,300,000 | 90,300,000 | 90,300,000 | 88,900,000 |
| Tea [1] ................ | 1,078,000 | 1,547,000 | 1,586,000 | 1,756,000 | 1,792,000 | 1,793,000 |
| **FOREST PRODUCTS** | | | | | | |
| Natural Rubber [1] ...... | 3,100,000 | 3,315,000 | 3,565,000 | 3,595,000 | 3,680,000 | 3,785,000 |
| Paper (newsprint) [1] .... | 21,535,000 | 20,948,000 | 22,489,000 | 22,708,000 | — | — |
| Sawnwood [7] ........... | 404,425 | 404,000 | 435,000 | 443,000 | — | — |
| Wood pulp [1] ........... | 104,445,000 | 81,100,000 | 89,044,000 | 90,820,000 | — | — |
| **MINERALS AND METALS** | | | | | | |
| Aluminum [1] ........... | 9,445,000 | 11,856,000 | 12,111,000 | 12,781,000 | 13,095,000 | 13,340,000 |
| Copper [1] ............. | 6,221,000 | 7,250,000 | 7,590,000 | 7,960,000 | 7,965,000 | 7,508,000 |
| Iron (pig iron) [1] ....... | 439,300,000 | 456,000,000 | 495,000,000 | 510,000,000 | 504,000,000 | 507,000,000 |
| Iron ore [1] ............. | 424,100,000 | 483,000,000 | 502,000,000 | 495,000,000 | 492,000,000 | 493,000,000 |
| Lead [1] ............... | 3,146,000 | 3,150,000 | 3,117,000 | 3,245,000 | 3,246,000 | 3,292,000 |
| Steel (crude) [1] ........ | 576,000,000 | 615,000,000 | 648,000,000 | 639,000,000 | 665,000,000 | 683,000,000 |
| Tin [1] ................. | 183,600 | 176,000 | 182,000 | 181,000 | 177,000 | 178,000 |
| Zinc [1] ................ | 4,664,000 | 4,700,000 | 4,755,000 | 4,715,000 | 4,524,000 | 4,753,000 |
| **MANUFACTURED PRODUCTS** | | | | | | |
| Automobiles [2] ......... | 22,550,000 | 25,220,000 | 28,930,000 | 30,430,000 | 32,380,000 | 31,360,000 |
| Buses and trucks [2] .... | 6,780,000 | 7,960,000 | 9,210,000 | 10,430,000 | 11,200,000 | 10,260,000 |
| Cement [1] ............. | 569,000,000 | 703,000,000 | 711,000,000 | 710,000,000 | 711,000,000 | 705,000,000 |
| Fertilizer (nitrogenous) [1] | 30,200,000 | 42,500,000 | 43,900,000 | 46,200,000 | 49,400,000 | 53,800,000 |
| Ships (merchant) [10] .... | 21,690,000 | 34,200,000 | 33,920,000 | 27,530,000 | 18,190,000 | 11,460,000 |

[1] Metric tons   [2] Units   [3] Including some brown coal and lignite.   [4] Megawatts.   [5] Teracalories.   [6] Hectoliters.
[7] Cubic meters.   [8] Metric carats.   [9] Kilograms.   [10] Gross tons launched.

# Education

Los Angeles parents and children protested in September as mandatory busing to desegregate classrooms was expanded by court order to include 153 schools. School officials released statistics showing that, since busing began in 1977, the proportion of white students in the Los Angeles school system has declined from 40% to 30% as white parents have taken their children out of the public schools. About 36,000 of the system's 510,000 students are bused under the desegregation plan.

United Press Int'l.

## HIGHLIGHTS: 1980

### FAILED ATTEMPT TO CURB BUSING

The lame-duck session of the 96th Congress approved a measure that would have curbed new court-ordered busing plans for desegregation of schools. Attached to a $9.1 billion appropriation measure for the Departments of State, Commerce, and Justice, the rider would have barred the government from bringing or joining in lawsuits calling for court-ordered school busing plans.

However, President Carter vetoed the measure, declaring it would impair the government's ability to enforce the Constitution and civil rights. Congress did not attempt to override the veto, approving a new appropriations bill without the antibusing amendment.

Opponents of busing were encouraged to believe such a measure might be approved in 1981 after President-elect Reagan declared his belief that busing had failed to achieve desegregation in schools and that it was opposed by the majority of Americans.

Because the proportion of children of racial minorities in urban school districts is now so large, proponents of educational desegregation believe that it only can be fully achieved in large cities by busing in white children from the suburbs or by busing black children to suburban schools. They cite these figures from the Department of Education's

### RISING COLLEGE AND UNIVERSITY EXPENDITURES: 1961–1981

Source: U.S. Department of Health, Education, and Welfare

| | |
|---|---|
| 1961–1962 | $ 8,500,000,000 |
| 1963–1964 | $ 11,300,000,000 |
| 1965–1966 | $ 15,200,000,000 |
| 1968–1969 | $ 22,000,000,000 |
| 1970–1971 | $ 27,100,000,000 |
| 1972–1973 | $ 31,400,000,000 |
| 1973–1974 | $ 34,300,000,000 |
| 1974–1975 | $ 38,900,000,000 |
| 1975–1976 | $ 42,700,000,000 |
| 1976–1977 | $ 46,300,000,000 |
| 1977–1978 | $ 50,400,000,000 |
| 1978–1979* | $ 54,500,000,000 |
| 1979–1980* | $ 58,000,000,000 |
| 1980–1981* | $ 65,000,000,000 |

* Estimates.

## U.S. ELEMENTARY AND SECONDARY SCHOOL ENROLLMENT: 1955-1999

Source: National Center for Educational Statistics, U.S. Department of Education

| YEAR[1] | TOTAL PUBLIC AND NONPUBLIC | | | PUBLIC | | | PRIVATE[2] | | |
|---|---|---|---|---|---|---|---|---|---|
| | K-12 | K-8 | 9-12 | K-12 | K-8 | 9-12 | K-12 | K-8 | 9-12 |
| 1955 | 35,280,000 | 27,717,000 | 7,563,000 | 30,680,000 | 23,917,000 | 6,763,000 | 4,600,000 | 3,800,000 | 800,000 |
| 1960 | 42,181,000 | 32,492,000 | 9,689,000 | 36,281,000 | 27,692,000 | 8,589,000 | 5,900,000 | 4,800,000 | 1,100,000 |
| 1965 | 48,473,000 | 35,463,000 | 13,010,000 | 42,173,000 | 30,563,000 | 11,610,000 | 6,300,000 | 4,900,000 | 1,400,000 |
| 1970 | 51,309,000 | 36,677,000 | 14,632,000 | 45,909,000 | 32,577,000 | 13,332,000 | 5,400,000 | 4,100,000 | 1,300,000 |
| 1971 | 51,181,000 | 36,065,000 | 15,116,000 | 46,081,000 | 32,265,000 | 13,816,000 | 5,100,000 | 3,200,000 | 1,300,000 |
| 1972 | 50,744,000 | 35,531,000 | 15,213,000 | 45,744,000 | 31,831,000 | 13,913,000 | 5,000,000 | 3,700,000 | 1,300,000 |
| 1973 | 50,339,000 | 34,953,000 | 15,377,000 | 45,429,000 | 31,353,000 | 14,077,000 | 4,900,000 | 3,600,000 | 1,300,000 |
| 1974 | 50,053,000 | 34,521,000 | 15,532,000 | 45,053,000 | 30,921,000 | 14,132,000 | 5,000,000 | 3,600,000 | 1,400,000 |
| 1975 | 49,791,000 | 34,027,000 | 15,704,000 | 44,791,000 | 30,487,000 | 14,304,000 | 5,000,000 | 3,600,000 | 1,400,000 |
| 1976 | 49,316,000 | 33,606,000 | 15,710,000 | 44,316,000 | 30,006,000 | 14,310,000 | 5,000,000 | 3,600,000 | 1,400,000 |
| 1977 | 48,577,000 | 32,936,000 | 15,640,000 | 43,577,000 | 29,336,000 | 14,240,000 | 5,000,000 | 3,600,000 | 1,400,000 |
| 1978 | 47,611,000 | 32,055,000 | 15,556,000 | 42,611,000 | 28,455,000 | 14,156,000 | 5,000,000 | 3,600,000 | 1,400,000 |
| 1979 | 46,657,000 | 31,442,000 | 15,235,000 | 41,577,000 | 27,822,000 | 13,735,000 | 5,100,000 | 3,600,000 | 1,500,000 |
| 1980[2] | 45,796,000 | 30,989,000 | 14,807,000 | 40,696,000 | 27,389,000 | 13,307,000 | 5,100,000 | 3,600,000 | 1,500,000 |
| 1981[2] | 44,958,000 | 30,637,000 | 14,321,000 | 39,858,000 | 27,037,000 | 12,821,000 | 5,100,000 | 3,600,000 | 1,500,000 |
| 1982[2] | 44,111,000 | 30,395,000 | 13,716,000 | 39,111,000 | 26,795,000 | 12,316,000 | 5,000,000 | 3,600,000 | 1,400,000 |
| 1983[2] | 43,766,000 | 30,301,000 | 13,465,000 | 38,666,000 | 26,601,000 | 12,065,000 | 5,100,000 | 3,700,000 | 1,400,000 |
| 1984[2] | 43,591,000 | 30,128,000 | 13,463,000 | 38,491,000 | 26,428,000 | 12,063,000 | 5,100,000 | 3,700,000 | 1,400,000 |
| 1985[2] | 43,748,000 | 30,248,000 | 13,500,000 | 38,548,000 | 26,448,000 | 12,100,000 | 5,200,000 | 3,800,000 | 1,400,000 |
| 1986[2] | 44,080,000 | 30,651,000 | 13,429,000 | 38,780,000 | 26,851,000 | 11,929,000 | 5,300,000 | 3,800,000 | 1,500,000 |
| 1988[2] | 44,974,000 | 32,259,000 | 12,715,000 | 39,374,000 | 28,257,000 | 11,115,000 | 5,600,000 | 4,000,000 | 1,600,000 |
| 1990[2] | 46,050,000 | 33,992,000 | 12,058,000 | 40,103,000 | 29,447,000 | 10,656,000 | 5,947,000 | 4,545,000 | 1,402,000 |
| 1995[2] | 50,525,000 | 37,222,000 | 13,303,000 | 43,977,000 | 32,013,000 | 11,964,000 | 6,548,000 | 5,209,000 | 1,339,000 |
| 1999[2] | 52,201,000 | 37,380,000 | 14,821,000 | 45,297,000 | 31,939,000 | 13,358,000 | 6,904,000 | 5,441,000 | 1,463,000 |

[1] Fall enrollment.   [2] Estimated.

### HIGHLIGHTS: 1980 (continued)

Office of Civil Rights on the proportion of minority students in the inner-city school districts of the six largest school districts: New York City, 71%; Los Angeles, 70%; Chicago, 78%; Philadelphia, 69%; Dade County, Fla., 62%; Detroit, 85%; and Houston, 78%.

### WIDESPREAD TEACHER STRIKES

At the beginning of the school year in September 1980 a survey by the National Education Association (NEA) showed that 60 teacher strikes were under way delaying school for some 550,000 students. The strikes affected schools in 10 states: Arizona, Illinois, Iowa, Michigan, New Jersey, New York, Ohio, Pennsylvania, Rhode Island, and Washington. The largest of the strikes in Philadelphia affected 23,000 teachers and 220,000 students. Elsewhere in Pennsylvania 3,500 teachers struck in 17 other school districts with 51,000 students.

### COURT RULINGS ON RELIGION

The U.S. Supreme Court in November ruled as unconstitutional a Kentucky state law that required display of the Ten Commandments in public-school classrooms. However, the Court let stand a ruling by a lower court that public schools could use religious materials in observing such holidays as Christmas that have "become integrated into our national culture and heritage."

### NEW COLLEGE LOANS FOR PARENTS

In legislation approved by President Carter in October, middle- and upper-income families were provided a new source of aid for sending their children to college. Under the program, parents can borrow up to $3,000 per year at 9% interest for college costs. In addition a student can borrow up to $12,500 at 9% interest. The government will subsidize the loans by paying lenders the difference between the 9% interest and the market rate.

## U.S. HIGH SCHOOL GRADUATES: 1870-1989

Source: National Center for Educational Statistics, U.S. Department of Education

| YEAR | GRADUATES | YEAR | GRADUATES | YEAR | GRADUATES | YEAR | GRADUATES |
|---|---|---|---|---|---|---|---|
| 1869-70 | 16,000 | 1949-50 | 1,199,700 | 1965-66 | 2,632,000 | 1977-78 | 3,147,000 |
| 1879-80 | 23,634 | 1951-52 | 1,196,500 | 1966-67 | 2,679,000 | 1978-79 | 3,131,000 |
| 1889-90 | 43,731 | 1953-54 | 1,276,100 | 1967-68 | 2,702,000 | 1979-80[1] | 3,078,000 |
| 1899-1900 | 94,883 | 1955-56 | 1,421,000 | 1968-69 | 2,829,000 | 1980-81[1] | 3,020,000 |
| 1909-10 | 156,429 | 1957-58 | 1,513,000 | 1969-70 | 2,896,000 | 1981-82[1] | 2,911,000 |
| 1919-20 | 311,266 | 1958-59 | 1,639,000 | 1970-71 | 2,944,000 | 1982-83[1] | 2,788,000 |
| 1929-30 | 666,904 | 1959-60 | 1,864,000 | 1971-72 | 3,008,000 | 1983-84[1] | 2,684,000 |
| 1939-40 | 1,221,475 | 1960-61 | 1,971,000 | 1972-73 | 3,043,000 | 1984-85[1] | 2,660,000 |
| 1941-42 | 1,242,375 | 1961-62 | 1,925,000 | 1973-74 | 3,080,000 | 1985-86[1] | 2,633,000 |
| 1943-44 | 1,019,233 | 1962-63 | 1,950,000 | 1974-75 | 3,140,000 | 1986-87[1] | 2,684,000 |
| 1945-46 | 1,080,033 | 1963-64 | 2,290,000 | 1975-76 | 3,155,000 | 1987-88[1] | 2,701,000 |
| 1947-48 | 1,189,909 | 1964-65 | 2,665,000 | 1976-77 | 3,161,000 | 1988-89[1] | 2,601,000 |

[1] Estimated.

# U.S. COLLEGES AND UNIVERSITIES: 1980–1981

Source: Adapted from *College Facts Chart 80–81* by National Beta Club, Box 730, Spartanburg, SC 29304

Information in the following table provides a general guide to attending more than 3,400 specific colleges and universities.

The chart includes information collected by The National Beta Club, a nonprofit leadership-service organization for high school students.

No reference to accreditation is made or implied. Inclusion of an institution does not constitute approval or endorsement of that institution.

Following are explanations of the main column headings in the table:

**Name and Address.** The schools are grouped by states to make it easier for you to locate them.

**Level.** Two-year programs—Junior **(J)**; four-year programs—Senior **(S)**; graduate program **(G)**; professional degree program **(P)**.

**Type.** Most colleges are now coordinate or coeducational **(C)**, but some are for women only **(W)** and some are for men only **(M)**.

**Affiliation.** Schools supported by taxes are **Public,** Community **(Comm)**, or **State.**

Private schools largely without church support are independent **(Ind)**. The listing of a church may indicate indirect support or direct control.

**Enrollment and Teachers** figures are for the 1979–80 school year.

**Tuition and Fees** are the average cost for the 1979–80 school year. For variations, including nonresident costs, consult the institution directly.

**Board and Room.** These are average costs for housing and food available *on the campus.* A dash (—) means room and board are *not available on the campus* or that the school did not provide this information.

**Total Cost.** These are average costs for state residents. In most cases the cost does not include laundry or other personal expenses.

| NAME | ADDRESS | FOUN-DED | AFFILI-ATION | LEVEL/TYPE | ENROLL-MENT | TEACH-ERS | TUITION & FEES | BOARD & ROOM | TOTAL COST |
|---|---|---|---|---|---|---|---|---|---|
| **ALABAMA** | | | | | | | | | |
| Alabama A.&M. University .... | Normal, AL 35762 ........ | 1875 | State | S-G/C | 4,336 | 328 | $ 490 | $1,170 | $1,660 |
| Alabama Christian College .... | Montgomery, AL 36109 ... | 1942 | C of Chr | J/C | 1,647 | 60 | $1,800 | $1,810 | $3,610 |
| Ala. Lutheran Academy & Col. | Selma, AL 36701 ........ | 1922 | Lutheran | J/C | 279 | 19 | $2,600 | $1,890 | $2,600 |
| Alabama State University ..... | Montgomery, AL 36101 .. | 1874 | S-G/C | S-G/C | 4,096 | 203 | $ 570 | $1,005 | $1,575 |
| Alexander City St. Jr. College . | Alexander City, AL 35010. | 1965 | State | J/C | 1,236 | 70 | $ 300 | — | $ 300 |
| Athens State College ........ | Athens, AL 35611 ....... | 1822 | State | S/C | 1,201 | 46 | $ 750 | $1,700 | $3,350 |
| Auburn University ........... | Auburn, AL 36830 ....... | 1856 | State | S-G/C | 18,329 | 1,488 | $ 660 | $1,425 | $2,085 |
| At Montgomery | Montgomery, AL 36117 .. | 1967 | State | S-G/C | 4,847 | 400 | $ 555 | $1,600 | $2,155 |
| Birmingham School of Law ... | Birmingham, AL 35203 ... | 1915 | Ind | G/C | 300 | 25 | $ 350 | | $ 700 |
| Birmingham-Southern College | Birmingham, AL 35204 ... | 1856 | Meth | S/C | 1,402 | 70 | $2,495 | $1,350 | $3,845 |
| Brewer State Jr. College ...... | Fayette, AL 35555 ...... | 1969 | Public | J/C | 496 | 15 | $ 406 | — | $ 406 |
| Chattahoochee Val. Comm. Col. | Phenix City, AL 36867 .... | 1973 | State | J/C | 2,276 | 99 | $ 400 | — | $ 400 |
| Daniel Payne College ........ | Birmingham, AL 35214 ... | 1889 | AME | S/C | 112 | 19 | $1,200 | $5,200 | $6,400 |
| Enterprise State Jr. College ... | Enterprise, AL 36330 .... | 1965 | State | J/C | 1,735 | 39 | $ 300 | — | $ 300 |
| Gadsden State Jr. College .... | Gadsden, AL 35901 ...... | 1965 | State | J/C | 3,538 | 107 | $ 305 | $1,050 | $1,245 |
| Geo. C. Wallace St. Comm. Col. | Dothan, AL 36303 ....... | 1965 | State | J/C | 2,953 | 90 | $ 300 | — | $ 300 |
| Geo. C. Wallace St. Comm. Col. | Selma, AL 36701 ....... | 1963 | State | J/C | 1,800 | 60 | $ 300 | — | $ 300 |
| Huntingdon College .......... | Montgomery, AL 36106 .. | 1854 | Meth | S/C | 682 | 60 | $2,250 | $1,775 | $4,025 |
| Jacksonville State University .. | Jacksonville, AL 36265 ... | 1883 | State | S-G/C | 7,183 | 326 | $ 600 | $1,100 | $1,700 |
| James H. Faulkner St. Jr. Col. . | Bay Minette, AL 36507 ... | 1965 | State | J/C | 1,405 | 91 | $ 300 | $1,215 | $1,500 |
| Jefferson Davis St. Jr. College . | Brewton, AL 36426 ...... | 1965 | State | J/C | 842 | 25 | $ 300 | — | $ 300 |
| Jefferson State Jr. College .... | Birmingham, AL 35215 ... | 1963 | State | J/C | 6,324 | 261 | $ 305 | — | $ 305 |
| John C. Calhoun St. Comm. C. | Decatur, AL 35602 ...... | 1965 | State | J/C | 5,200 | 130 | $ 300 | — | $ 300 |
| Judson College .............. | Marion, AL 36756 ....... | 1838 | Baptist | S/W | 372 | 41 | $1,800 | $1,230 | $3,030 |
| Lawson State Comm. College . | Birmingham, AL 35221 ... | 1965 | State | J/C | 1,788 | 85 | $ 307 | — | $ 307 |
| Livingston University......... | Livingston, AL 35470 .... | 1835 | State | S-G/C | 1,194 | 70 | $ 648 | $1,209 | $1,857 |
| Lomax-Hannon Jr. College .... | Greenville, AL 36037 .... | 1893 | AME | J/C | 125 | 9 | $1,105 | $1,500 | $2,605 |
| Lurleen B. Wallace St. Jr. Col. . | Andalusia, AL 36420 ..... | 1969 | State | J/C | 860 | 29 | $ 300 | — | $ 300 |
| Marion Military Institute ..... | Marion, AL 36756 ....... | 1842 | Ind | J/M | 370 | 35 | $2,812 | $1,695 | $6,000 |
| Miles College .............. | Birmingham, AL 35208 ... | 1905 | CME | S-G/C | 1,058 | 103 | $1,700 | $1,310 | $3,010 |
| Mobile College ............. | Mobile, AL 36613 ....... | 1961 | Baptist | S/C | 1,074 | 53 | $1,980 | $1,480 | $3,460 |
| Northeast Ala. St. Jr. College .. | Rainsville, AL 35686 .... | 1965 | State | J/C | 1,072 | 82 | $ 300 | — | $ 300 |
| Northwest Ala. St. Jr. College . | Phil Campbell, AL 35581 . | 1961 | State | J/C | 923 | 50 | $ 300 | — | $ 300 |
| Oakwood College ........... | Huntsville, AL 35806 .... | 1896 | 7-D Adv | S/C | 1,290 | 97 | $2,950 | $1,500 | $4,450 |
| Patrick Henry St. Jr. College .. | Monroeville, AL 36460 ... | 1965 | State | J/C | 738 | 43 | $ 300 | — | $ 300 |
| Samford University .......... | Birmingham, AL 35209 ... | 1841 | Baptist | S-G/C | 4,049 | 200 | $2,375 | $1,600 | $3,975 |
| S.D. Bishop St. Jr. College .... | Mobile, AL 36603 ....... | 1965 | State | J/C | 1,400 | 67 | $ 300 | — | $ 300 |
| Selma University ............ | Selma, AL 36701 ....... | 1878 | Baptist | J/C | 322 | 30 | $1,795 | $1,620 | $3,415 |
| Snead State Jr. College ....... | Boaz, AL 35957 ........ | 1935 | State | J/C | 967 | 35 | $ 300 | $1,110 | $1,410 |
| Southeastern Bible College ... | Birmingham, AL 35205 ... | 1935 | Ind | S-G/C | 250 | 22 | $2,200 | $1,500 | $3,700 |
| Southern Union St. Jr. College. | Wadley, AL 36276 ...... | 1922 | State | J/C | 1,439 | 54 | $ 400 | $1,220 | $1,620 |
| Spring Hill College .......... | Mobile, AL 36608 ....... | 1830 | Catholic | S/C | 900 | 70 | $3,200 | $1,800 | $5,000 |
| Stillman College ............ | Tuscaloosa, AL 35403.... | 1876 | Presby | S/C | 673 | 36 | $1,550 | $1,327 | $2,877 |
| Talladega College............ | Talladega, AL 35160 ..... | 1867 | Ind | S/C | 705 | 64 | $1,963 | $1,509 | $3,469 |
| Troy State University ........ | Troy, AL 36081 ......... | 1887 | State | S-G/C | 6,382 | 392 | $ 780 | $1,150 | $1,930 |
| Fort Rucker/Dothan ...... | Dothan, AL 36301 ....... | 1962 | State | S-G/C | 1,612 | 59 | $ 960 | — | $ 960 |
| Montgomery Branch ....... | Montgomery, AL 36104 .. | 1965 | State | S-G/C | 2,606 | 164 | $ 960 | — | $ 960 |
| Tuskegee Institute ........... | Tuskegee Inst., AL 36088 . | 1881 | Ind | S-G/C | 3,435 | 279 | $2,000 | $1,358 | $3,358 |
| University of Alabama ........ | University, AL 35486 ..... | 1831 | State | S-G/C | 17,776 | 936 | $ 765 | $1,270 | $2,035 |
| Birmingham ............. | Birmingham, AL 35294 ... | 1966 | State | S-G/C | 14,214 | 1,472 | $ 795 | — | $ 795 |
| Gadsden Center .......... | Gadsden, AL 35902 ..... | 1946 | State | G/C | 450 | 30 | $ 700 | — | $ 700 |
| Huntsville ............... | Huntsville, AL 35807 ..... | 1950 | State | S-G/C | 4,702 | 227 | $ 788 | — | $ 788 |
| University of Montevallo ..... | Montevallo, AL 35115 .... | 1896 | State | S-G/C | 2,812 | 149 | $ 560 | $1,240 | $1,800 |
| University of North Alabama . | Florence, AL 35630 ...... | 1872 | State | S-G/C | 5,189 | 233 | $ 680 | $1,374 | $2,054 |
| University of South Alabama . | Mobile, AL 36688........ | 1963 | State | S-G/C | 7,331 | 491 | $ 771 | $1,491 | $2,262 |
| Walker College .............. | Jasper, AL 35501 ....... | 1938 | Ind | J/C | 719 | 47 | $ 880 | $1,150 | $2,030 |

| NAME | ADDRESS | FOUNDED | AFFILIATION | LEVEL/TYPE | ENROLLMENT | TEACHERS | TUITION & FEES | BOARD & ROOM | TOTAL COST |
|---|---|---|---|---|---|---|---|---|---|
| **ALASKA** | | | | | | | | | |
| Alaska Bible College .......... | Glennallen, AK 99588 ...... | 1966 | Ind | S/C | 35 | 11 | $ 980 | $1,985 | $2,965 |
| Alaska Pacific University ..... | Anchorage, AK 99504 ...... | 1957 | Meth | S-G/C | 373 | 29 | $2,310 | $2,600 | $4,910 |
| Inupiat Univ. of the Arctic ..... | Barrow, AK 99723 ........ | 1975 | Ind | S/C | 37 | 15 | $2,400 | — | $2,400 |
| Sheldon Jackson College ..... | Sitka, AK 99835 .......... | 1878 | Ind | S/C | 136 | 24 | $2,440 | $2,331 | $4,771 |
| University of Alaska .......... | Anchorage, AK 99504 ...... | 1970 | State | S-G/C | 2,890 | 105 | $ 382 | — | $ 382 |
|   Anchorage Community Col. . | Anchorage, AK 99504 ...... | 1954 | State | J/C | 6,827 | 142 | $ 372 | — | $ 372 |
|   Chukchi Community College | Kotzebue, AK 99752 ...... | 1978 | State | J/C | 116 | 19 | $ 340 | — | $ 340 |
|   Fairbanks................. | Fairbanks, AK 99701 ...... | 1917 | State | S-G/C | 3,489 | 351 | $ 532 | $1,960 | $2,492 |
|   Juneau-Douglas Comm. Col. | Juneau, AK 99802 ........ | 1956 | State | J/C | 1,217 | 22 | $ 355 | — | $ 355 |
|   Kenai Peninsula Comm. Col. | Soldotna, AK 99669 ...... | 1964 | State | J/C | 830 | 60 | $ 360 | — | $ 360 |
|   Ketchikan Community Col. . | Ketchikan, AK 99901 ...... | 1954 | State | J/C | 519 | 32 | $ 340 | — | $ 340 |
|   Kodiak Community College . | Kodiak, AK 99615 ........ | 1968 | State | J/C | 503 | 36 | $ 340 | — | $ 340 |
|   Kuskokwin Community Col. . | Bethel, AK 99559 ........ | 1972 | State | J/C | 186 | 31 | $ 340 | — | $ 340 |
|   Matanuska–Susitna Comm. Col. | Palmer, AK 99645 ........ | 1957 | State | J/C | 390 | 40 | $ 340 | — | $ 340 |
|   Northwest Community Col. . | Nome, AK 99762 ........ | 1975 | State | J/C | 103 | 12 | $ 340 | — | $ 340 |
|   Prince Wm. Sound Comm. Col. | Valdez, AK 99686 ........ | 1978 | State | J/C | 628 | 5 | $ 340 | — | $ 340 |
|   Sitka Community College .. | Sitka, AK 99835 .......... | 1962 | State | J/C | 289 | 29 | $ 340 | — | $ 340 |
|   Southeastern Senior College | Juneau, AK 99802 ........ | 1972 | State | S-G/C | 2,148 | 158 | $ 340 | $1,200 | $1,540 |
|   Tanana Valley Comm. College .. | Fairbanks, AK 99701 ...... | 1974 | State | J/C | 1,916 | 142 | $ 524 | $1,960 | $2,484 |
| **ARIZONA** | | | | | | | | | |
| American Grad. Sch. Int. Man.. | Glendale, AZ 85306 ...... | 1946 | Ind | G/C | 990 | 85 | $3,470 | $1,650 | $5,120 |
| Arizona State University ...... | Temple, AZ 85281 ........ | 1885 | State | S-G/C | 37,755 | 2,177 | $ 559 | $1,300 | $1,859 |
| Arizona Western College...... | Yuma, AZ 85364 ........ | 1961 | State | J/C | 1,921 | 68 | $ 200 | $1,550 | $1,750 |
| Central Arizona College....... | Coolidge, AZ 85228 ...... | 1969 | State | J/C | 5,286 | 91 | $ 192 | $1,230 | $1,422 |
| Cochise College ............. | Douglas, AZ 85607 ...... | 1962 | State | J/C | 4,109 | 328 | $ 200 | $1,630 | $1,830 |
| College of Ganado ........... | Ganado, AZ 86505 ...... | 1970 | Ind | J/C | 420 | 25 | $1,650 | $2,550 | $4,200 |
| Devry Inst. of Technology ..... | Phoenix, AZ 85016 ...... | 1967 | Ind | S/C | 2,567 | 49 | $1,137 | — | $1,137 |
| Eastern Arizona College ...... | Thatcher, AZ 85552...... | 1888 | State | J/C | 3,467 | 272 | $ 170 | $1,374 | $1,544 |
| Embry-Riddle Aeronautical Univ. . | Prescott, AZ 86301 ...... | 1926 | Ind | S-G/C | 550 | 75 | $3,633 | $3,192 | $6,825 |
| Grand Canyon College ....... | Phoenix, AZ 85061 ...... | 1949 | Baptist | S/C | 1,150 | 54 | $1,857 | $1,404 | $3,985 |
| Maricopa County Comm. Col. . | Phoenix, AZ 85034 ...... | 1963 | County | J/C | 58,281 | 1,984 | $ 100 | — | $ 100 |
|   Glendale Comm. College ... | Glendale, AZ 85302 ...... | 1966 | County | J/C | 12,789 | 517 | $ 100 | — | $ 100 |
|   Maricopa Tech. Comm. Col. . | Phoenix, AZ 85004 ...... | 1968 | County | J/C | 3,493 | 164 | $ 100 | — | $ 100 |
|   Mesa Comm. College ....... | Mesa, AZ 85202 ........ | 1965 | County | J/C | 13,257 | 484 | $ 100 | — | $ 100 |
|   Phoenix College .......... | Phoenix, AZ 85013 ...... | 1920 | County | J/C | 13,604 | 209 | $ 100 | — | $ 100 |
|   Rio Salado Comm. College .. | Phoenix, AZ 85034 ...... | 1978 | County | J/C | 8,633 | 333 | $ 100 | — | $ 100 |
|   Scottsdale Comm. College .. | Scottsdale, AZ 85253 ...... | 1970 | County | J/C | 6,505 | 277 | $ 100 | — | $ 100 |
|   South Mountain Comm. Col. . | Phoenix, AZ 85034 ...... | 1978 | County | J/C | — | — | $ 100 | — | $ 100 |
| Mohave Comm. College....... | Kingman, AZ 86401 ...... | 1971 | Public | J/C | 3,004 | 204 | $ 120 | — | $ 120 |
| Navajo Community College ... | Tsaile, AZ 86556 ........ | 1968 | — | J/C | 1,557 | 156 | $1,230 | $1,790 | $3,020 |
| Northern Arizona University ... | Flagstaff, AZ 86011 ...... | 1899 | State | S-G/C | 11,601 | 568 | $ 600 | $1,220 | $1,820 |
| Northland Pioneer College ... | Holbrook, AZ 86025 ...... | 1972 | County | J/C | 4,323 | 330 | $ 80 | — | $ 80 |
| Ottawa University ........... | Phoenix, AZ 85015 ...... | 1865 | Baptist | S/C | — | — | — | — | — |
| Pima Community College ..... | Tucson, AZ 85709 ...... | 1967 | State | J/C | 21,769 | 1,083 | $ 140 | — | $ 140 |
| Prescott Center College ...... | Prescott, AZ 86301 ...... | 1975 | Private | S/C | 67 | 17 | $2,975 | — | $ 2,975 |
| University of Arizona ......... | Tucson, AZ 85721 ...... | 1885 | State | S-G/C | 32,000 | 1,689 | $ 550 | $1,513 | $2,063 |
| University of Phoenix ........ | Phoenix, AZ 85004 ...... | 1976 | Ind | S-G/C | 250 | 30 | $2,550 | — | $2,725 |
| Western International Univ. ... | Phoenix, AZ 85021 ...... | 1978 | Ind | S-G/C | 741 | 21 | $3,240 | — | $3,240 |
| Yavapai College ............. | Prescott, AZ 86301 ...... | 1967 | Public | J/C | 4,628 | 395 | $ 168 | $1,340 | $1,508 |
| **ARKANSAS** | | | | | | | | | |
| Arkansas Baptist College ..... | Little Rock, AR 72202 ...... | 1884 | Baptist | S/C | 445 | 21 | $ 800 | $1,125 | $1,925 |
| Arkansas College ............ | Batesville, AR 72501 ...... | 1872 | Presby | S/C | 500 | 40 | $2,150 | $1,372 | $3,522 |
| Arkansas State University .... | State Univ., AR 72467 ..... | 1909 | State | S-G/C | 7,243 | 322 | $ 600 | $1,200 | $1,800 |
|   Beebe Campus ............ | Beebe, AR 72012 ........ | 1927 | State | J/C | 779 | 34 | $ 440 | $ 925 | $1,365 |
| Arkansas Tech University ..... | Russellville, AR 72801 ..... | 1909 | State | S-G/C | 2,998 | 145 | $ 560 | $1,040 | $1,580 |
| Central Baptist College ...... | Conway, AR 72032 ...... | 1952 | Baptist | S/C | 291 | 19 | $ 540 | $1,040 | $1,580 |
| College of the Ozarks ........ | Clarksville, AR 72830 ..... | 1834 | Presby | S/C | 543 | 40 | $1,120 | $1,175 | $2,295 |
| Crowley's Ridge College ..... | Paragould, AR 72450 ..... | 1964 | C of Chr | J/C | 55 | 11 | $1,482 | $1,620 | $3,102 |
| East Arkansas Comm. College . | Forrest City, AR 72335 ... | 1973 | State | J/C | 786 | 50 | $ 180 | — | $ 180 |
| Garland County Comm. College | Hot Springs, AR 71901 ... | 1973 | State | J/C | 1,342 | 45 | $ 280 | — | $ 280 |
| Harding University ........... | Searcy, AR 72143 ........ | 1924 | C of Chr | S-G/C | 3,001 | 141 | $2,325 | $1,450 | $3,775 |
| Henderson State University ... | Arkadelphia, AR 71923 ... | 1890 | State | S-G/C | 2,785 | 175 | $ 600 | $1,000 | $1,600 |
| Hendrix College ............. | Conway, AR 72032 ...... | 1884 | Meth | S/C | 984 | 58 | $2,450 | $1,200 | $3,650 |
| John Brown University ........ | Siloam Springs, AR 72761 | 1919 | Ind | S/C | 742 | 58 | $2,100 | $1,500 | $3,600 |
| Mississippi County Comm. Col. . | Blytheville, AR 72315 ..... | 1975 | State | J/C | 1,015 | 36 | $ 288 | — | $ 288 |
| North Arkansas Comm. College | Harrison, AR 72601 ...... | 1974 | State | J/C | 857 | 130 | $ 250 | — | $ 250 |
| Ouachita Baptist University ... | Arkadelphia, AR 71923 ... | 1886 | Baptist | S-G/C | 1,578 | 110 | $1,960 | $1,320 | $3,280 |
| Philander Smith College ...... | Little Rock, AR 72202 ...... | 1877 | Meth | S/C | 596 | 52 | $1,250 | $1,225 | $2,475 |
| Phillips County Comm. College | Helena, AR 72342 ........ | 1965 | State | J/C | 3,475 | 113 | $ 348 | — | $ 348 |
| Shorter College ............. | N. Little Rock, AR 72114... | 1886 | AME | J/C | 240 | 15 | $1,139 | $1,420 | $2,559 |
| Southern Arkansas University . | Magnolia, AR 71753 ..... | 1909 | State | S-G/C | 1,932 | 116 | $ 600 | $1,096 | $1,696 |
|   El Dorado Branch .......... | El Dorado, AR 71730 ..... | 1975 | State | J/C | 514 | 19 | $ 456 | — | $ 456 |
|   Tech Branch .............. | East Camden, AR 71701.. | 1967 | State | J/C | 627 | 42 | $ 471 | $1,100 | $1,571 |
| Southern Baptist College ..... | Walnut Ridge, AR 72476.. | 1941 | Baptist | J/C | 383 | 24 | $1,550 | $1,160 | $2,710 |
| University of Arkansas ........ | Fayetteville, AR 72701 ..... | 1871 | State | S-G/C | 15,189 | 809 | $ 600 | $1,295 | $1,895 |
|   Medical Sciences Campus . | Little Rock, AR 72201 ...... | 1879 | State | G/C | 1,256 | 420 | $1,035 | — | $6,216 |
|   at Little Rock ............. | Little Rock, AR 72204 ..... | 1927 | State | S-G/C | 10,038 | 400 | $ 600 | — | $ 600 |
|   at Monticello ............. | Monticello, AR 71655 ... | 1909 | State | S/C | 1,671 | 101 | $ 600 | $1,220 | $1,820 |
|   at Pine Bluff ............. | Pine Bluff, AR 71601 ..... | 1873 | State | S/C | 2,999 | 168 | $ 600 | $ 700 | $1,300 |
| University of Central Arkansas . | Conway, AR 72032 ...... | 1907 | State | S-G/C | 5,538 | 200 | $1,200 | $ 991 | $2,191 |
| Westark Community College .. | Fort Smith, AR 72913 ..... | 1928 | State | J/C | 3,265 | 130 | $ 280 | — | $ 280 |

| NAME | ADDRESS | FOUNDED | AFFILIATION | LEVEL/TYPE | ENROLLMENT | TEACHERS | TUITION & FEES | BOARD & ROOM | TOTAL COST |
|---|---|---|---|---|---|---|---|---|---|
| **CALIFORNIA** | | | | | | | | | |
| Academy of Art College | San Francisco, CA 94108 | 1929 | Ind | S-G/C | 1,516 | 101 | $2,280 | $2,000 | $ 4,280 |
| Acad. of Arts & Humanities | Seaside, CA 93955 | 1970 | Ind | S-G/C | 68 | 14 | $1,620 | — | $ 1,620 |
| Allan Hancock College | Santa Maria, CA 93454 | 1920 | Public | J/C | 8,236 | 472 | — | — | — |
| Ambassador College | Pasadena, CA 91123 | 1947 | C of God | S/C | 409 | 34 | $1,425 | $2,100 | $ 3,525 |
| Amer. Bapt. Sem. of the West | Berkeley, CA 94704 | 1892 | Baptist | G/C | 130 | 14 | $2,400 | — | $ 2,400 |
| American College of Law | Anaheim, CA 92805 | 1972 | Ind | P/C | 120 | 14 | $1,700 | — | $ 1,700 |
| American River College | Sacramento, CA 95841 | 1955 | Public | J/C | 21,796 | 591 | — | — | — |
| Antelope Valley Comm. Col. | Lancaster, CA 93534 | 1929 | District | J/C | 6,403 | 238 | — | — | — |
| Antioch University West | San Francisco, CA 94118 | 1971 | Ind | S-G/C | 795 | 60 | $3,333 | — | $ 3,333 |
| Armstrong College | Berkeley, CA 94704 | 1918 | Ind | S-G/C | 385 | 54 | $1,890 | — | $ 1,890 |
| Art Center Col. of Design | Pasadena, CA 91103 | 1930 | Ind | S/C | 1,057 | 168 | $2,800 | — | $ 2,800 |
| Azusa Pacific College | Azusa, CA 91702 | 1899 | Ind | S-G/C | 2,751 | 130 | $3,100 | $1,580 | $ 4,680 |
| Bakersfield College | Bakersfield, CA 93305 | 1913 | Public | J/C | 11,853 | 500 | $1,680 | $1,500 | $ 3,180 |
| Barstow College | Barstow, CA 92311 | 1960 | State | J/C | 1,700 | 34 | — | — | $ 2,150 |
| Bauder College | Sacramento, CA 95825 | 1969 | Ind | J/C | 600 | 45 | $3,200 | $1,200 | $ 4,400 |
| Berean Bible College | San Diego, CA 92105 | 1970 | Ind | G/C | 210 | 20 | $ 585 | — | $ 585 |
| Bethany Bible College | Santa Cruz, CA 95066 | 1919 | A of God | S/C | 598 | 36 | $1,992 | $1,412 | $ 3,404 |
| Biola College | La Mirada, CA 90639 | 1908 | Ind | S-G/C | 2,384 | 171 | $2,766 | $1,674 | $ 4,440 |
| Brooks College | Long Beach, CA 90804 | 1970 | Ind | J/C | 1,100 | 62 | $3,380 | $2,180 | $ 5,560 |
| Brooks Institute | Santa Barbara, CA 93108 | 1946 | Private | S-G/C | 789 | 22 | $3,750 | — | $ 3,750 |
| Butte College | Oroville, CA 95965 | 1966 | Public | J/C | 8,111 | 450 | $ 59 | — | $ 59 |
| Cabrillo College | Aptos, CA 95003 | 1959 | State | J/C | 9,400 | 195 | $ 12 | — | $ 12 |
| California Baptist College | Riverside, CA 92504 | 1950 | Baptist | S/C | 746 | 61 | $2,350 | $1,330 | $ 3,680 |
| California Christian College | Fresno, CA 93703 | 1955 | Baptist | S/C | 40 | 9 | $1,000 | $1,000 | $ 2,000 |
| California Christian Univ. | Adelanto, CA 92301 | 1971 | Christian | S/C | 56 | 2 | $1,450 | — | $ 1,450 |
| Calif. Col. of Arts & Crafts | Oakland, CA 94618 | 1907 | Private | P/C | 1,101 | 68 | $3,790 | — | — |
| California Col. of Commerce | Long Beach, CA 90813 | 1921 | Ind | S/C | 186 | 22 | $1,800 | — | $ 1,800 |
| Calif. Col. of Podiatrics Med. | San Francisco, CA 94115 | 1914 | Ind | P/C | 397 | 40 | $6,200 | $1,920 | $ 8,120 |
| Calif. Graduate Institute | Los Angeles, CA 90024 | 1978 | Ind | G/C | 333 | 32 | $2,400 | — | $ 2,400 |
| Calif. Inst. of the Arts | Valencia, CA 91355 | 1962 | Ind | G/C | 750 | 140 | $4,500 | — | — |
| Calif. Inst. of Technology | Pasadena, CA 91125 | 1891 | Ind | S-G/C | 1,709 | 301 | $5,229 | $1,826 | $ 7,055 |
| Calif. International University | Los Angeles, CA 90017 | 1973 | Ind | G/C | 200 | 8 | $2,400 | $2,500 | $ 4,900 |
| Calif. Lutheran College | Thousand Oaks, CA 91360 | 1959 | Lutheran | S-G/C | 2,573 | 149 | $3,200 | $1,750 | $ 4,950 |
| Calif. Maritime Academy | Vallejo, CA 94590 | 1929 | State | S/C | 485 | 33 | $ 886 | $2,100 | $ 3,100 |
| Calif. Masonry Baptist Inst. | Bellflower, CA 90706 | 1957 | Baptist | S/C | 48 | 16 | $ 500 | — | — |
| Calif. Polytechnic St. Univ. | San Luis Obispo, CA 93407 | 1901 | State | S-G/C | 15,977 | 931 | $ 216 | $ 879 | $ 1,095 |
| Calif. Sch. of Prof. Psychology | Berkeley, CA 94704 | 1970 | Ind | G/C | 240 | 50 | $5,445 | — | $ 5,445 |
| Calif. Sch. of Prof. Psychology | Fresno, CA 93721 | 1973 | Ind | G/C | 153 | 28 | $5,445 | — | $ 5,445 |
| Calif. Sch. of Prof. Psychology | Los Angeles, CA 90004 | 1970 | Ind | G/C | 253 | 55 | $5,445 | — | $ 5,445 |
| Calif. Sch. of Prof. Psychology | San Diego, CA 92121 | 1972 | Ind | G/C | 240 | 60 | $5,445 | — | $ 5,445 |
| Calif. State College | | | | | | | | | |
| Bakersfield | Bakersfield, CA 93309 | 1965 | State | S/C | 3,000 | 145 | $ 175 | $2,000 | $ 2,175 |
| San Bernardino | San Bernardino, CA 92407 | 1962 | State | S-G/C | 4,231 | 267 | $ 201 | $1,800 | $ 2,001 |
| Stanislaus | Turlock, CA 95380 | 1957 | State | S-G/C | 3,500 | 225 | $ 200 | $1,572 | $ 1,772 |
| Calif. State Polytechnic Univ. | Pomona, CA 91768 | 1938 | State | S-G/C | 14,896 | 863 | $ 200 | $1,800 | $ 2,000 |
| Calif. State University | | | | | | | | | |
| Chico | Chico, CA 95929 | 1887 | State | S-G/C | 13,552 | 653 | $ 221 | $1,900 | $ 2,121 |
| Dominguez Hills | Carson, CA 90747 | 1962 | State | S-G/C | 7,100 | 300 | $ 210 | — | $ 210 |
| Fresno | Fresno, CA 93740 | 1911 | State | S-G/C | 14,819 | 908 | $ 205 | $1,777 | $ 1,982 |
| Fullerton | Fullerton, CA 92634 | 1959 | State | S-G/C | 21,997 | 1,232 | $ 108 | — | $ 216 |
| Hayward | Hayward, CA 94542 | 1957 | State | S-G/C | 10,604 | 582 | $ 144 | — | $ 144 |
| Long Beach | Long Beach, CA 90840 | 1949 | State | S-G/C | 30,877 | 1,851 | $ 203 | $1,900 | $ 2,103 |
| Los Angeles | Los Angeles, CA 90032 | 1947 | State | S-G/C | 24,000 | 1,200 | $ 200 | — | $ 200 |
| Northridge | Northridge, CA 91330 | 1958 | State | S-G/C | 28,152 | 1,411 | $ 190 | — | $ 190 |
| Sacramento | Sacramento, CA 95819 | 1947 | State | S-G/C | 21,222 | 920 | $ 200 | $1,660 | $ 1,860 |
| Calif. Western University | Santa Ana, CA 92701 | 1974 | Ind | S-G/C | — | — | $2,000 | — | $ 2,000 |
| Canada College | Redwood City, CA 94061 | 1968 | State | J/C | 7,960 | 270 | $ 10 | — | $ 2,400 |
| Casa Loma Inst. of Tech. | Pacoima, CA 91331 | 1966 | Ind | J/C | 105 | 8 | $3,350 | — | $ 5,400 |
| Center for Early Education | Los Angeles, CA 90048 | 1939 | Ind | S-G/C | 34 | — | — | — | — |
| Cerritos College | Norwalk, CA 90650 | 1955 | Public | J/C | 22,151 | 670 | — | — | — |
| Cerro Coso Comm. College | Ridgecrest, CA 93555 | 1974 | State | J/C | 3,938 | 80 | $ 10 | — | $ 10 |
| Chabot College | Hayward, CA 94545 | 1961 | Public | J/C | 18,826 | 683 | — | — | — |
| Chaffey College | Alta Loma, CA 91701 | 1883 | State | J/C | 11,283 | 350 | — | — | — |
| Chapman College | Orange, CA 92666 | 1861 | D of Chr | S-G/C | 1,707 | 162 | $3,400 | $1,740 | $ 5,140 |
| Christian Heritage College | El Cajon, CA 92021 | 1970 | Ind | S-G/C | 425 | 52 | $2,450 | $1,460 | $ 3,910 |
| Christian Life College | Stockton, CA 95205 | 1953 | Un Pent | P/C | 88 | 9 | $1,250 | $1,600 | $ 2,850 |
| Church Div. Sch. of Pacific | Berkeley, CA 94709 | 1893 | Episc | G/C | 83 | 13 | $2,100 | $1,452 | $ 3,552 |
| Citrus Belt Law School | Riverside, CA 92506 | 1971 | Ind | P/C | 106 | 14 | $1,228 | — | $ 1,228 |
| Citrus College | Azusa, CA 91702 | 1915 | Ind | J/C | 8,665 | 199 | $ 46 | — | $ 46 |
| City Col. of San Francisco | San Francisco, CA 94112 | 1935 | Public | J/C | 24,643 | — | — | — | — |
| City Univ. Los Angeles | Los Angeles, CA 90017 | 1974 | Ind | S-G/C | 225 | — | $2,500 | — | $ 2,500 |
| Claremont Men's College | Claremont, CA 91711 | 1946 | Ind | S/C | 849 | 94 | $4,902 | $2,050 | $ 6,952 |
| Claremont Univ. Center | Claremont, CA 91711 | 1925 | Ind | G/C | 1,509 | 150 | $3,725 | — | $ 3,725 |
| Cleveland Chiropractic Col. | Los Angeles, CA 90004 | 1911 | Ind | P/C | 285 | 28 | $3,900 | — | — |
| Coast. Sch. of Deep Sea Diving, Inc. | Oakland, CA 94601 | 1950 | Private | P/C | 250 | 6 | $1,395 | — | $ 2,000 |
| Cogswell College | San Francisco, CA 94108 | 1887 | Ind | S/C | 424 | 40 | $2,400 | — | $ 2,400 |
| Coleman College | San Diego, CA 92110 | 1963 | Ind | J-S/C | — | — | — | — | — |
| College of Alameda | Alameda, CA 94501 | 1970 | Ind | J/C | 7,088 | 204 | $ 4 | — | — |
| College of the Canyons | Valencia, CA 91355 | 1969 | State | J/C | 3,464 | 97 | $ 18 | — | $ 18 |
| College of the Desert | Palm Desert, CA 92260 | 1958 | State | J/C | 10,616 | 325 | $ 20 | — | $ 20 |
| College of Marin | Kentfield, CA 94904 | 1926 | Public | J/C | 7,000 | 260 | — | — | — |
| College of Notre Dame | Belmont, CA 94002 | 1851 | Ind | S-G/C | 1,342 | 127 | $3,200 | $2,100 | $ 5,300 |

| NAME | ADDRESS | FOUN-DED | AFFILI-ATION | LEVEL/TYPE | ENROLL-MENT | TEACH-ERS | TUITION & FEES | BOARD & ROOM | TOTAL COST |
|---|---|---|---|---|---|---|---|---|---|
| **CALIFORNIA** (continued) | | | | | | | | | |
| College of the Redwoods | Eureka, CA 95501 | 1964 | Public | J/C | 8,400 | 552 | $ 20 | $1,766 | $ 1,786 |
| College of San Mateo | San Mateo, CA 94402 | 1923 | State | J/C | 15,063 | 320 | — | — | — |
| College of the Sequoias | Visalia, CA 93277 | 1925 | State | J/C | 7,142 | 350 | $ 20 | — | $ 20 |
| College of the Siskiyous | Weed, CA 96094 | 1957 | State | J/C | 2,423 | 139 | $ 30 | $1,470 | $1,500 |
| Columbia College | Columbia, CA 95310 | 1968 | State | J/C | 2,817 | 43 | $ 50 | — | $ 50 |
| Columbia College | Hollywood, CA 90038 | 1952 | Ind | J-S/C | 300 | 36 | $2,200 | — | $2,200 |
| Columbia Pacific University | Mill Valley, CA 94941 | 1978 | Ind | S-G/C | 406 | 71 | $1,675 | — | $1,675 |
| Common College | Woodside, CA 94062 | 1971 | Ind | S/C | 15 | 40 | $3,500 | — | — |
| Compton Community College | Compton, CA 90221 | 1927 | Public | J/C | 5,265 | 84 | $ 20 | — | $ 20 |
| Contra Costa College | San Pablo, CA 94806 | 1950 | County | J/C | 8,869 | 282 | — | — | — |
| Cosumnes River College | Sacramento, CA 95823 | 1970 | Public | J/C | 4,700 | 170 | — | — | — |
| Crafton Hills College | Yucaipa, CA 92399 | 1972 | Public | J/C | 3,300 | 125 | — | — | $ 175 |
| Cuesta College | San Luis Obispo, CA 93406 | 1965 | State | J/C | 5,841 | 163 | $ 10 | — | — |
| Cuyamaca College | El Cajon, CA 92020 | 1978 | State | J/C | 2,033 | 108 | — | — | — |
| Cypress College | Cypress, CA 90630 | 1966 | Public | J/C | 12,200 | 229 | — | — | $1,750 |
| De Anza College | Cupertino, CA 95014 | 1967 | Public | J/C | 23,249 | 816 | $ 350 | — | $ 350 |
| Deep Springs College | Deep Springs, CA 89010 | 1917 | Ind | J | 22 | 7 | — | — | — |
| Diablo Valley College | Pleasant Hill, CA 94523 | 1949 | District | J/C | 18,939 | 595 | — | — | $2,620 |
| Dominican Col. of San Rafael | San Rafael, CA 94901 | 1890 | Catholic | S-G/C | 645 | 101 | $3,330 | $2,100 | $5,430 |
| Dominican Schl. of Phil. and Theol. | Berkeley, CA 94563 | 1932 | Catholic | S-G/C | 106 | 16 | $1,800 | — | — |
| Don Bosco Technical Institute | Rosemead, CA 91745 | 1969 | Catholic | J/M | 296 | 28 | $1,200 | — | $1,200 |
| D-Q University | Davis, CA 95616 | 1971 | Private | J/C | 140 | — | $1,960 | $1,845 | $3,805 |
| East Los Angeles College | Monterey Park, CA 91754 | 1945 | Public | J/C | 16,029 | 659 | — | — | — |
| El Camino College | Torrance, CA 90506 | 1947 | Public | J/C | 26,728 | 631 | $ 5 | — | $ 5 |
| Empire College | Santa Rosa, CA 95404 | 1953 | Ind | P/C | 239 | 32 | $3,300 | — | $3,300 |
| Eubanks Cons. of Music & Arts | Los Angeles, CA 90043 | 1951 | Ind | S-G/C | 30 | 43 | $1,200 | — | — |
| Evangelical Christian College | Fresno, CA 93726 | 1946 | Pent | S/C | 47 | 5 | $ 840 | $1,485 | $2,325 |
| Evergreen Valley College | San Jose, CA 95135 | 1975 | Public | J/C | 6,300 | 125 | $ 10 | — | $ 10 |
| Feather River College | Quincy, CA 95971 | 1968 | State | J/C | 1,200 | 60 | $ 15 | $3,000 | $3,015 |
| Fielding Institute | Santa Barbara, CA 93101 | 1974 | Ind | G/C | 400 | 65 | $3,800 | — | $5,000 |
| Foothill College | Los Altos Hills, CA 94022 | 1958 | State | J/C | 14,447 | 515 | $1,440 | — | $1,440 |
| Franciscan Sch. of Theology | Berkeley, CA 94709 | 1968 | Catholic | G/C | 135 | 11 | $1,050 | $2,500 | $3,550 |
| Fresno City College | Fresno, CA 93741 | 1910 | State | J/C | 14,820 | 421 | $ 20 | — | $ 20 |
| Fresno Pacific College | Fresno, CA 93702 | 1944 | Mennon | S-G/C | 733 | 50 | $2,760 | $1,625 | $4,385 |
| Fuller Theological Seminary | Pasadena, CA 91101 | 1947 | Ind | G/C | 2,394 | 198 | $2,640 | — | $2,640 |
| Fullerton College | Fullerton, CA 92634 | 1913 | State | J/C | 18,806 | 551 | $ 10 | — | $ 10 |
| Gavilan College | Gilroy, CA 95020 | 1919 | State | J/C | 2,756 | 81 | $ 18 | — | $ 18 |
| Glendale Community College | Glendale, CA 91208 | 1927 | State | J/C | 9,680 | 195 | $ 20 | — | $ 20 |
| Glendale Univ. Col. of Law | Glendale, CA 91206 | 1967 | Ind | P/C | 199 | 15 | $2,400 | — | $2,400 |
| Gold. Gate Bapt. Theol. Sem. | Mill Valley, CA 94941 | 1944 | Baptist | G/C | 563 | 25 | $ 400 | — | $4,200 |
| Golden Gate University | San Francisco, CA 94105 | 1901 | Ind | S-G/C | 9,800 | 820 | $3,500 | — | — |
| Golden State University | Pasadena, CA 91101 | 1977 | Ind | S-G/C | 841 | 43 | $1,500 | — | $1,500 |
| Grace Bible Institute | Long Beach, CA 90807 | 1974 | Brethren | S/C | 215 | 11 | $1,125 | — | $1,275 |
| Grace Col. of Disc. and Theol. | La Mesa, CA 92041 | 1970 | Ind | S-G/C | 8 | 6 | $2,000 | — | $2,000 |
| Grace Graduate School | Long Beach, CA 90807 | 1974 | Brethren | G/C | 110 | 24 | $1,800 | — | $1,950 |
| Graduate Theol. Union | Berkeley, CA 94709 | 1962 | Ind | G/C | 270 | 61 | — | — | — |
| Grantham Col. of Engineering | Los Angeles, CA 90034 | 1951 | Ind | S/C | 740 | — | — | — | — |
| Grossmont College | El Cajon, CA 92020 | 1961 | Public | J/C | 12,666 | 489 | $ 36 | — | $ 36 |
| Hartnell College | Salinas, CA 93901 | 1920 | Public | J/C | 7,000 | 285 | — | — | — |
| Harvey Mudd College | Claremont, CA 91711 | 1955 | Ind | S-G/C | 489 | 61 | $4,940 | $2,100 | $7,040 |
| Hebrew Union College | Los Angeles, CA 90007 | 1875 | Jewish | G/C | 140 | 37 | $3,000 | — | $3,000 |
| Holy Names College | Oakland, CA 94619 | 1868 | Ind | S-G/C | 628 | 98 | $2,970 | $1,800 | $4,770 |
| Humanistic Psych. Institute | San Francisco, CA 94103 | 1970 | Ind | G/C | 150 | — | $3,150 | — | $3,150 |
| Humboldt State University | Arcata, CA 95521 | 1913 | State | S-G/C | 7,761 | 550 | $ 190 | $1,800 | $1,990 |
| Humphreys College | Stockton, CA 95207 | 1896 | Ind | J/C | 300 | 17 | $1,600 | $1,100 | $2,700 |
| Humphreys Col. Sch. of Law | Fresno, CA 93721 | 1896 | Ind | P/C | 36 | 9 | $1,254 | — | $1,254 |
| Immaculate Heart College | Los Angeles, CA 90028 | 1916 | Ind | S-G/C | 543 | 86 | $3,290 | — | $3,290 |
| Imperial Valley College | Imperial, CA 92251 | 1922 | State | J/C | 4,008 | 90 | — | — | — |
| Indian Valley Colleges | Novato, CA 94947 | 1971 | Public | J/C | 3,220 | 120 | — | — | — |
| Inner City Inst. for Per. & Vis. Arts | Los Angeles, CA 90006 | 1968 | Public | S/C | 250 | 15 | $1,050 | — | $1,050 |
| Inst. of Buddhist Studies | Berkeley, CA 94704 | 1966 | Buddhist | G/C | 9 | 9 | $1,140 | — | $1,140 |
| International College | Los Angeles, CA 90024 | 1970 | Ind | S-G/C | 276 | 120 | $3,600 | — | $3,600 |
| Irvine Univ. School of Law | Santa Ana, CA 92705 | 1973 | Ind | P/C | 60 | 14 | $1,400 | — | $1,400 |
| Jesuit School of Theology | Berkeley, CA 94709 | 1934 | Catholic | P/C | 315 | 44 | $2,052 | — | $2,052 |
| John F. Kennedy University | Orinda, CA 94563 | 1964 | Ind | S-G/C | 950 | 154 | $1,200 | — | $1,200 |
| Laguna Beach School of Art | Laguna Beach, CA 92651 | 1962 | Ind | S/C | 402 | 14 | $1,250 | — | $1,250 |
| Lake Tahoe Comm. College | Lake Tahoe, CA 95702 | 1974 | State | J/C | 1,350 | 50 | $ 60 | — | $ 60 |
| Laney College | Oakland, CA 94607 | 1926 | Public | J/C | 10,000 | 340 | — | — | — |
| Lassen College | Susanville, CA 96130 | 1925 | State | J/C | 3,000 | 350 | $ 20 | $2,000 | $2,020 |
| Laurence University | Santa Barbara, CA 93101 | 1973 | Ind | G/C | 110 | 15 | $1,800 | — | $1,800 |
| L.I.F.E. Bible College | Los Angeles, CA 90026 | 1925 | 4 Square | S-G/C | 429 | 20 | $1,200 | — | $1,200 |
| Lincoln University | San Francisco, CA 94118 | 1919 | Ind | S-G/C | 600 | 55 | $1,600 | — | $1,600 |
| Linda Vista Bapt. Bible College | El Cajon, CA 92021 | 1946 | Ind | S/C | 100 | 6 | $1,650 | $1,200 | $2,850 |
| Living Word Bible College | Pasadena, CA 91107 | 1971 | Gospel | J/C | 55 | 12 | $ 570 | — | $ 570 |
| Loma Linda University | Loma Linda, CA 92354 | 1905 | 7-D Adv | G/C | 5,283 | — | $4,125 | $1,887 | $6,012 |
| Long Beach Comm. College | Long Beach, CA 90808 | 1927 | Public | J/C | 28,326 | 960 | — | — | — |
| Los Angeles Baptist College | Newhall, CA 91322 | 1927 | Baptist | S/C | 388 | 48 | $2,830 | $1,740 | $4,570 |
| Los Angeles City College | Los Angeles, CA 90029 | 1929 | Public | J/C | 18,500 | 700 | — | — | $ 650 |
| Los Ang. Col. of Chiropractic | Glendale, CA 91205 | 1911 | Ind | P/C | 714 | 40 | $5,000 | — | $5,000 |
| Los Angeles Harbor College | Wilmington, CA 90744 | 1949 | State | J/C | 11,350 | 525 | — | — | — |
| Los Angeles Pierce College | Woodland Hills, CA 91371 | 1947 | Public | J/C | 23,000 | 575 | — | — | — |
| Los Angeles Southwest College | Los Angeles, CA 90047 | 1967 | State | J/C | 7,450 | 125 | — | — | — |
| Los Angeles Trade-Tech. Col. | Los Angeles, CA 90015 | 1949 | Public | J/C | 16,500 | 710 | — | — | — |

| NAME | ADDRESS | FOUN-DED | AFFILI-ATION | LEVEL/TYPE | ENROLL-MENT | TEACH-ERS | TUITION & FEES | BOARD & ROOM | TOTAL COST |
|---|---|---|---|---|---|---|---|---|---|
| **CALIFORNIA** (continued) | | | | | | | | | |
| Los Angeles Valley College .... | Van Nuys, CA 91401 ..... | 1949 | Public | J/C | 22,055 | 700 | — | — | — |
| Los Medanos College ........ | Pittsburg, CA 94565 ..... | 1973 | Public | J/C | 5,000 | 73 | — | — | — |
| Loyola Marymount University . | Los Angeles, CA 90045 ... | 1911 | Catholic | S-G/C | 6,051 | 400 | $3,585 | $1,815 | $5,400 |
| Magna Carta University ...... | San Francisco, CA 94080 . | 1974 | Ind | P/C | 50 | 7 | $1,000 | — | $1,000 |
| Marymount Palos Verdes Col. . | Rancho Palos Verdes, CA 90274 | 1932 | Catholic | J/C | 357 | 38 | $2,950 | $2,000 | $4,950 |
| Melodyland School of Theology | Anaheim, CA 92806........ | 1973 | Ind | S-G/C | 303 | 28 | $1,991 | — | — |
| Mendocino College ........... | Ukiah, CA 95482 ......... | 1972 | State | J/C | 3,037 | 175 | — | — | — |
| Menlo College .............. | Menlo Park, CA 94025 .... | 1915 | Ind | S/C | 680 | 50 | $4,770 | $2,490 | $7,260 |
| Mennonite Brethren Bib. Sem. | Fresno, CA 93727 ........ | 1955 | Mennon | G/C | 147 | 21 | $1,600 | — | $1,600 |
| Merced Community College... | Merced, CA 95340 ....... | 1962 | Public | J/C | 7,648 | 410 | $1,124 | — | $1,124 |
| Merritt College .............. | Oakland, CA 94619 ...... | 1953 | State | J/C | 9,500 | 250 | — | — | — |
| Mills College ............... | Oakland, CA 94613 ...... | 1852 | Ind | S-G/W | 973 | 124 | $4,800 | $2,550 | $7,350 |
| Miracosta College .......... | Oceanside, CA 92054 .... | 1934 | County | J/C | 9,576 | 286 | — | — | — |
| Modesto Junior College ..... | Modesto, CA 95350 ...... | 1921 | State | J/C | 13,224 | 460 | — | — | — |
| Monterey Inst. of Inter. Stud. | Monterey, CA 93940 ..... | 1955 | Private | J-S/C | 467 | 80 | $3,800 | — | $7,225 |
| Monterey Peninsula College... | Monterey, CA 93940 ..... | 1947 | State | J/C | 8,667 | 340 | $  20 | — | $  20 |
| Moorpark College ............ | Moorpark, CA 93021 ..... | 1967 | Public | J/C | 8,557 | 345 | $  10 | — | $  10 |
| Mount St. Mary's College .... | Los Angeles, CA 90049 ... | 1925 | Catholic | S-G/W | 1,108 | 127 | $3,450 | $1,950 | $5,400 |
| Mt. San Antonio Comm. Col. .. | Walnut, CA 91789 ....... | 1946 | State | J/C | 23,245 | 726 | $  24 | —: | $  24 |
| Mt. San Jacinto Comm. College | San Jacinto, CA 92383 ... | 1963 | State | J/C | 2,750 | 41 | $  15 | — | $  15 |
| Music and Arts Inst. of S. Fran. | San Francisco, CA 94115 . | 1934 | Ind | G/C | 83 | -10 | $1,800 | — | — |
| Nairobi College.............. | E. Palo Alto, CA 94303 ... | 1969 | Ind | J/C | — | — | — | — | — |
| Napa College ............... | Napa, CA 94558 ......... | 1942 | Public | J/C | 5,691 | 249 | — | — | — |
| National Technical Schools ... | Los Angeles, CA 90037 ... | 1905 | Ind | J/C | 800 | 50 | $2,250 | — | $2,250 |
| National University ......... | San Diego, CA 92108 .... | 1971 | Ind | S-G/C | 4,626 | 450 | $3,480 | — | $3,480 |
| Naval Postgraduate School ... | Monterey, CA 93940 ..... | 1909 | Federal | G/C | 1,255 | 251 | — | — | — |
| New College of California ... | San Francisco, CA 94110 . | 1971 | Ind | S-G/C | 400 | 26 | $2,700 | $3,000 | $5,700 |
| Newport International Univ. .. | Westminister, CA 92683 . | 1976 | Ind | S-G/C | 181 | 6 | $1,850 | — | $1,850 |
| Northern Calif. Bible College | San Jose, CA 95122 ...... | 1971 | Church | S/C | 101 | 14 | $  700 | — | $  700 |
| Northrop University.......... | Inglewood, CA 90306 .... | 1942 | Ind | S-G/C | 2,009 | 110 | $3,000 | $2,547 | $5,547 |
| Nyingma Institute ........... | Berkeley, CA 94709...... | 1973 | Buddhist | G/C | — | 40 | — | — | — |
| Occidental College .......... | Los Angeles, CA 90041 ... | 1887 | Ind | S/C | 1,652 | 120 | $5,577 | $2,300 | $7,877 |
| Ohlone College .............. | Fremont, CA 94538 ...... | 1966 | Public | J/C | 8,668 | 330 | — | — | — |
| Orange Coast College ........ | Costa Mesa, CA 92626 ... | 1948 | State | J/C | 26,327 | 776 | — | — | — |
| Otis Art Institute ........... | Los Angeles, CA 90057 ... | 1897 | Ind | S-G/C | 230 | 35 | $2,900 | — | $2,900 |
| Oxnard College .............. | Oxnard, CA 93032 ....... | 1975 | Public | J/C | 5,500 | 250 | — | — | — |
| Pacific Christian College.... | Fullerton, CA 92631 ..... | 1928 | Private | S-G/C | 800 | 52 | $1,176 | $2,050 | $3,226 |
| Pacific Coast Bapt. Bible Col. | San Dimas, CA 91773 .... | 1967 | Baptist | S/C | 461 | 30 | $  700 | $1,300 | $2,000 |
| Pacific Coast University ..... | Long Beach, CA 90803 ... | 1927 | Ind | P/C | 85 | 5 | $  495 | — | — |
| Pacific Oaks College ........ | Pasadena, CA 91103 ..... | 1951 | Ind | S-G/C | 300 | 37 | $2,880 | — | $2,880 |
| Pacific School of Religion ... | Berkeley, CA 94709...... | 1866 | Int-Den | G/C | 276 | 19 | $1,965 | $1,233 | $3,198 |
| Pacific States University .... | Los Angeles, CA 90006 ... | 1928 | Ind | S-G/C | 700 | 50 | $1,880 | — | — |
| Pacific Union College ....... | Angwin, CA 94508 ....... | 1882 | 7-D Adv | S/C | 2,127 | 138 | $4,125 | $1,875 | $5,235 |
| Palomar Community College .. | San Marcos, CA 92069 ... | 1946 | Public | J/C | 14,310 | 271 | $1,530 | — | $1,530 |
| Palo Verde College........... | Blythe, CA 92225 ....... | 1947 | Public | J/C | 350 | 17 | $  12 | — | $  24 |
| Pasadena City College ....... | Pasadena, CA 91106...... | 1924 | Public | J/C | 19,100 | 850 | — | — | — |
| Pasadena Col. of Chiropractic . | Pasadena, CA 91103 ..... | 1974 | Ind | P/C | 285 | 20 | $3,000 | — | $3,000 |
| Patten Bible College ........ | Oakland, CA 94601 ...... | 1945 | Ind | S/C | 195 | 16 | $1,630 | $1,420 | $3,050 |
| Peninsula Univ. Col. of Law .. | Mountain View, CA 94043 | 1975 | Ind | P/C | 150 | 15 | $1,100 | — | $1,100 |
| Pepperdine University ....... | Malibu, CA 90265 ....... | 1937 | C of Chr | S-G/C | 7,314 | 513 | $5,100 | $2,400 | $7,500 |
|   Seaver College .......... | Malibu, CA 90265 ....... | 1972 | C of Chr | S-G/C | 2,227 | 216 | $4,290 | $2,170 | $6,460 |
| Pitzer College .............. | Claremont, CA 91711 .... | 1963 | Ind | S/C | 720 | 99 | $4,935 | $1,894 | $6,829 |
| Point Loma College ......... | San Diego, CA 92106 .... | 1902 | Nazarene | S-G/C | 1,784 | 96 | $3,214 | $1,545 | $4,759 |
| Pomona College ............. | Claremont, CA 91711 .... | 1887 | Ind | S/C | 1,342 | 130 | $4,994 | $2,060 | $7,054 |
| Porterville College .......... | Porterville, CA 93257 .... | 1927 | Public | J/C | 2,500 | 162 | — | — | — |
| Rancho Arroyo College ....... | Sacramento, CA 95826.... | 1965 | Ind | T/C | 48 | 9 | $4,000 | — | $4,000 |
| Rand Graduate Institute ..... | Santa Monica, CA 90406 . | 1970 | Ind | G/C | 42 | 29 | $3,300 | — | $3,300 |
| Reedley College ............. | Reedley, CA 93654 ...... | 1926 | State | J/C | 3,062 | 150 | $  10 | $2,240 | $2,250 |
| Relig. Sci. Sch. of Ministry .... | Los Angeles, CA 90020 ... | 1954 | Church | P/C | 120 | 10 | $1,500 | — | $1,500 |
| Rio Hondo Comm. College .... | Whittier, CA 90608 ...... | 1960 | State | J/C | 11,503 | 251 | — | — | — |
| Riverside City College ...... | Riverside, CA 92506 ..... | 1916 | State | J/C | 14,467 | 189 | — | — | — |
| Riverside University ........ | Riverside, CA 92502 ..... | 1967 | Ind | S-G/C | 1,071 | 52 | $4,500 | $4,500 | $9,000 |
| Sacramento City College ..... | Sacramento, CA 95822.... | 1916 | State | J/C | 13,274 | 462 | — | — | — |
| Saddleback College ......... | Mission Viejo, CA 92692 . | 1967 | State | J/C | 21,579 | 930 | — | — | $2,035 |
| St. Mary's College of Calif. .... | Moraga, CA 94575........ | 1863 | Catholic | S-G/C | 2,519 | 243 | $3,922 | $2,133 | $6,055 |
| St. Patrick's College ........ | Mountain View, CA 94042 | 1898 | Catholic | S/M | 49 | 13 | $1,810 | $  700 | $2,510 |
| St. Stephens Ed. Bible College . | Los Angeles, CA 90003 ... | 1952 | Baptist | S-G/C | 1,710 | 267 | $2,878 | — | $3,778 |
| San Bernardino Bible College . | Colton, CA 92324........ | 1969 | Ind | S/C | 50 | 8 | $  438 | — | $  438 |
| San Bernardino Valley College. | San Bernardino, CA 92410 | 1926 | Public | J/C | 16,000 | 230 | — | — | — |
| San Diego Bible College ..... | Chula Vista, CA 92011 ... | 1970 | Ind | S-G/C | 115 | 3 | — | — | — |
| San Diego City College ...... | San Diego, CA 92101 .... | 1914 | Public | J/C | 4,988 | 211 | — | — | — |
| San Diego Col. of Business ... | San Diego, CA 92123 .... | 1954 | Ind | J/C | 525 | 19 | $3,200 | — | $3,200 |
| San Diego Evening College ... | San Diego, CA 92108 .... | 1962 | Public | J/C | 24,000 | 1,300 | — | — | — |
| San Diego Mesa College ..... | San Diego, CA 92111 .... | 1965 | Public | J/C | 9,565 | 245 | — | — | — |
| San Diego State University .... | San Diego, CA 92182 .... | 1897 | State | S-G/C | 31,600 | 1,836 | $  192 | $1,850 | $2 042 |
|   Imperial Valley Campus ... | Calexico, CA 92231 ...... | 1960 | State | J-S/C | 432 | 45 | $  202 | — | — |
| San Fernando Val. Col. of Law . | Sepulveda, CA 91343 .... | 1962 | Ind | P/C | 385 | 22 | $2,600 | — | $2,600 |
| San Francisco Art Institute ... | San Francisco, CA 94133 . | 1874 | Ind | S/C | 555 | 46 | $3,900 | — | — |
| San Fran. Bapt. Theol. Sem. ... | San Francisco, CA 94109 . | 1958 | Baptist | G/M | 25 | 7 | $1,200 | — | — |
| San Francisco Col. of M. Sci. .. | San Francisco, CA 94109 . | 1932 | Ind | J/C | 70 | 6 | $2,100 | — | $2,100 |
| San Francisco Cons. of Music . | San Francisco, CA 94122 . | 1917 | Ind | S/C | 215 | 60 | $4,135 | — | — |
| San Francisco State Univ. .... | San Francisco, CA 94132 . | 1899 | State | S-G/C | 23,000 | 1,700 | $  200 | — | — |

| NAME | ADDRESS | FOUN-DED | AFFILI-ATION | LEVEL/TYPE | ENROLL-MENT | TEACH-ERS | TUITION & FEES | BOARD & ROOM | TOTAL COST |
|---|---|---|---|---|---|---|---|---|---|
| **CALIFORNIA** *(continued)* | | | | | | | | | |
| San Joaquin College of Law | Fresno, CA 93702 | 1969 | Ind | P/C | 81 | 22 | $2,310 | — | $2,310 |
| San Joaquin Delta College | Stockton, CA 95207 | 1935 | Public | J/C | 20,000 | 650 | $  10 | — | $  10 |
| San Jose Bible College | San Jose, CA 95108 | 1939 | Christian | S/C | 210 | 14 | $1,640 | $ 945 | $2,585 |
| San Jose City College | San Jose, CA 95128 | 1921 | Public | J/C | 13,500 | 500 | $  10 | — | $  10 |
| San Jose State University | San Jose, CA 95192 | 1857 | State | S-G/C | 26,000 | 1,685 | $ 224 | $1,900 | $2,124 |
| Santa Ana College | Santa Ana, CA 92706 | 1915 | State | J/C | 16,764 | 600 | — | — | — |
| Santa Barbara City College | Santa Barbara, CA 93109 | 1908 | Public | J/C | 8,114 | 181 | $  10 | — | $  10 |
| Santa Monica College | Santa Monica, CA 90405 | 1929 | State | J/C | 18,000 | 780 | $ 100 | — | $ 100 |
| Santa Rosa Junior College | Santa Rosa, CA 95401 | 1918 | Public | J/C | 20,000 | 700 | $  20 | $1,500 | $1,520 |
| School of Theol. at Claremont | Claremont, CA 91711 | 1885 | Meth | G/C | 398 | 32 | $3,188 | $4,000 | $7,188 |
| Scripps College | Claremont, CA 91711 | 1926 | Ind | S/W | 667 | 66 | $5,250 | $2,500 | $7,750 |
| Shasta College | Redding, CA 96001 | 1949 | State | J/C | 10,425 | 385 | $  12 | $1,639 | $1,651 |
| Shiloh Bible College | Oakland, CA 94602 | 1967 | Church | S-G/C | 423 | 23 | $  60 | — | $  60 |
| Sierra College | Rocklin, CA 95677 | 1914 | State | J/C | 8,280 | 129 | $  10 | $1,616 | $1,626 |
| Sierra College of Business | Los Angeles, CA 90013 | 1916 | Ind | J/C | 265 | 14 | $2,625 | — | $2,625 |
| Simpson College | San Francisco, CA 94134 | 1921 | Miss | S-G/C | 265 | 27 | $2,120 | $1,420 | $3,540 |
| Skadron College of Business | San Bernardino, CA 92410 | 1907 | Ind | J/C | 480 | 18 | $3,200 | — | $3,200 |
| Skyline College | San Bruno, CA 94066 | 1969 | District | J/C | 7,242 | 134 | — | — | — |
| Solano Community College | Suisun City, CA 94585 | 1945 | State | J/C | 9,000 | 400 | — | — | — |
| Sonoma State University | Rohnert Park, CA 94928 | 1960 | State | S-G/C | 5,505 | 336 | $ 200 | $2,135 | $2,335 |
| South Bay Col. of Business | Hawthorne, CA 90250 | 1965 | Ind | –/C | 300 | 12 | $3,200 | — | $3,200 |
| Southern Calif. Bible College | La Mesa, CA 92041 | 1970 | Ind | S/C | 31 | 7 | $1,020 | — | $1,020 |
| Southern Calif. College | Costa Mesa, CA 92626 | 1920 | A of God | S/C | 715 | 60 | $2,700 | $1,760 | $4,460 |
| So. Calif. Col. of Optometry | Fullerton, CA 92631 | 1904 | Ind | P/C | 414 | 84 | $4,775 | — | $4,775 |
| So. Calif. Comm. Bible College | Long Beach, CA 90805 | 1971 | Non-Den | S-G/C | 115 | 9 | $ 795 | — | $ 795 |
| So. Calif. Conserv. of Music | Sun Valley, CA 91352 | 1972 | Ind | S/C | 125 | 20 | $ 800 | — | $ 800 |
| So. Calif. Inst. of Architecture | Santa Monica, CA 90404 | 1972 | Ind | S-G/C | 300 | 45 | $2,000 | — | $2,000 |
| Southwestern College | Chula Vista, CA 92010 | 1960 | State | J/C | 11,596 | 398 | — | — | — |
| Sw. Univ. School of Law | Los Angeles, CA 90005 | 1911 | Ind | G/C | 1,674 | 87 | $4,700 | — | $9,240 |
| Stanford University | Stanford, CA 94305 | 1885 | Private | S-G/C | 12,059 | 1,020 | $6,285 | $2,354 | $8,639 |
| Starr King Sch. for Ministers | Berkeley, CA 94709 | 1904 | Unitarian | G/C | 42 | 9 | $2,250 | — | — |
| Taft College | Taft, CA 93268 | 1921 | State | J/C | 1,122 | 42 | $  20 | $1,340 | $1,360 |
| Thomas Aquinas College | Santa Paula, CA 93060 | 1969 | Catholic | S/C | 113 | 16 | $3,150 | $1,800 | $4,950 |
| Union University | Los Angeles, CA 90033 | 1972 | Private | S/C | 150 | 7 | $3,000 | — | $3,000 |
| United College of Business | Hollywood, CA 90028 | 1969 | Ind | J/C | 400 | 15 | $3,000 | — | $3,000 |
| U.S. International University | San Diego, CA 92131 | 1952 | Ind | S/C | 3,441 | 225 | $3,300 | $2,025 | $5,325 |
| University de Campesinos Libres Inc. | Fresno, CA 93728 | 1973 | Ind | S/C | — | — | — | — | — |
| University of California | | | | | | | | | |
| Berkeley Campus | Berkeley, CA 94720 | 1868 | State | S-G/C | 30,462 | 2,362 | $ 731 | $2,745 | $3,476 |
| Davis Campus | Davis, CA 95616 | 1905 | State | S-G/C | 17,981 | 1,223 | $ 786 | $1,900 | $2,686 |
| Hastings College of Law | San Francisco, CA 94102 | 1878 | State | G/C | 1,472 | 77 | $ 708 | — | $ 708 |
| Irvine Campus | Irvine, CA 92717 | 1960 | State | S-G/C | 10,033 | 685 | $ 741 | $2,300 | $3,041 |
| Los Angeles Campus | Los Angeles, CA 90024 | 1919 | State | S-G/C | 32,977 | 2,800 | $ 702 | $1,645 | $2,347 |
| Riverside Campus | Riverside, CA 92521 | 1954 | State | S-G/C | 4,617 | 453 | $ 738 | $1,900 | $2,638 |
| San Diego Campus | La Jolla, CA 92093 | 1912 | State | S-G/C | 11,183 | 830 | $ 741 | $2,100 | $2,841 |
| Santa Barbara Campus | Santa Barbara, CA 93106 | 1944 | State | S-G/C | 14,786 | 1,113 | $ 757 | $1,835 | $2,592 |
| Santa Cruz Campus | Santa Cruz, CA 95064 | 1965 | State | S-G/C | 6,093 | 346 | $ 795 | $1,950 | $2,745 |
| University of Judaism | Los Angeles, CA 90024 | 1948 | Ind | S-G/C | 210 | 50 | $2,000 | — | $2,000 |
| University of La Verne | La Verne, CA 91750 | 1891 | Brethren | S-G/C | 2,050 | 150 | $4,159 | $2,020 | $6,179 |
| Univ. of Oriental Studies | Los Angeles, CA 90006 | 1973 | Ind | S/C | 140 | 25 | $1,200 | $2,600 | $3,800 |
| University of Redlands | Redlands, CA 92373 | 1907 | Ind | S-G/C | 1,200 | 122 | $4,470 | $1,880 | $6,350 |
| University of San Diego | San Diego, CA 92110 | 1949 | Catholic | S-G/C | 4,123 | 263 | $4,100 | $2,320 | $6,420 |
| University of San Francisco | San Francisco, CA 94117 | 1855 | Catholic | S-G/C | 6,400 | 489 | $3,500 | $1,840 | $5,340 |
| University of Santa Clara | Santa Clara, CA 95053 | 1851 | Catholic | S-G/C | 7,101 | 358 | $3,990 | $2,175 | $6,175 |
| University of Southern California | Los Angeles, CA 90007 | 1880 | Ind | S-G/C | 26,902 | 2,550 | $5,390 | $2,540 | $7,930 |
| University of the Pacific | Stockton, CA 95240 | 1851 | Ind | S-G/C | 4,130 | 330 | $5,682 | $2,512 | $8,194 |
| Univ. of West Los Angeles | Culver City, CA 90230 | 1966 | Ind | P/C | 750 | 60 | $1,800 | — | — |
| Valley Commercial College | Modesto, CA 95354 | 1906 | Ind | J/C | 60 | 6 | $1,685 | — | $1,685 |
| Valley Univ. School of Law | North Hollywood, CA 91602 | 1974 | Ind | P/C | — | — | — | — | — |
| Ventura College | Ventura, CA 93003 | 1925 | State | J/C | 12,612 | 578 | — | — | — |
| Ventura College of Law | Ventura, CA 93003 | 1969 | Ind | P/C | 150 | 14 | $1,750 | — | $1,750 |
| Victor Valley College | Victorville, CA 92392 | 1960 | Public | J/C | 3,500 | 110 | $  16 | — | $  16 |
| West Coast University | Los Angeles, CA 90020 | 1909 | Ind | S-G/C | 1,400 | 250 | $2,100 | — | $2,100 |
| West Hills Community College | Coalinga, CA 93210 | 1932 | State | J/C | 2,380 | 142 | $  20 | $1,330 | $1,350 |
| West Los Angeles College | Culver City, CA 90230 | 1968 | District | J/C | 9,842 | 341 | — | — | — |
| West Valley College | Saratoga, CA 95070 | 1963 | Public | J/C | 15,700 | 502 | $  24 | — | $  24 |
| Western State Univ. Col. of Law | Fullerton, CA 92631 | 1966 | Ind | S-G/C | 1,746 | 61 | $2,656 | — | $2,656 |
| Western State Univ. Col. of Law | San Diego, CA 92101 | 1969 | Ind | P/C | 973 | 44 | $2,400 | — | $2,400 |
| Western States Col. of Engn. | Inglewood, CA 90301 | 1946 | Ind | S/C | 112 | 14 | $2,300 | — | $2,300 |
| Western University | San Diego, CA 92114 | 1922 | Ind | S-G/C | 20 | 6 | — | — | — |
| Westmont College | Santa Barbara, CA 93108 | 1940 | Ind | S-G/C | 1,028 | 54 | $3,800 | $1,800 | $5,600 |
| Whittier College | Whittier, CA 90608 | 1901 | Ind | S/C | 1,245 | 105 | $3,972 | $1,760 | $5,732 |
| Woodbury University | Los Angeles, CA 90017 | 1884 | Ind | S-G/C | 1,435 | 65 | $2,712 | — | $2,712 |
| World College West | San Rafael, CA 94902 | 1973 | Ind | S/C | 50 | 6 | $2,700 | $2,100 | $4,800 |
| Wright Institute | Berkeley, CA 94704 | 1968 | Private | G/C | 179 | 27 | $3,300 | — | $3,300 |
| Yeshiva Univ. of Los Angeles | Los Angeles, CA 90035 | 1977 | Ind | S/M | 75 | 15 | $1,825 | $3,000 | $4,800 |
| Yuba Comm. College District | Marysville, CA 95901 | 1927 | State | J/C | 8,700 | 400 | — | $1,800 | — |
| **COLORADO** | | | | | | | | | |
| Adams State College | Alamosa, CO 81102 | 1921 | State | S-G/C | 2,000 | 124 | $ 680 | $1,500 | $2,180 |
| Aims Community College | Greeley, CO 80631 | 1967 | Public | J/C | 4,713 | 267 | $ 275 | — | $ 275 |
| Arapahoe Community College | Littleton, CO 80120 | 1965 | State | J/C | 6,000 | 276 | $ 500 | — | $ 500 |

| NAME | ADDRESS | FOUN-DED | AFFILI-ATION | LEVEL/TYPE | ENROLL-MENT | TEACH-ERS | TUITION & FEES | BOARD & ROOM | TOTAL COST |
|---|---|---|---|---|---|---|---|---|---|
| **COLORADO** *(continued)* | | | | | | | | | |
| Baptist Bible Col. of Denver .. | Broomfield, CO 80020 ... | 1952 | Ind | P/C | 245 | 21 | $1,944 | $1,940 | $3,884 |
| Belleview College | Westminster, CO 80030 .. | 1921 | P/Fire | S/C | 25 | 6 | $ 634 | $1,100 | $1,950 |
| Colorado College............ | Colorado Spgs., CO 80903 | 1874 | Ind | S/C | 1,938 | 214 | $4,700 | $1,700 | $6,400 |
| Colorado Mountain College ... | Glenwood Spgs., CO 81601 | 1967 | Public | J/C | 5,500 | 110 | $ 463 | $1,717 | $2,180 |
| Colo. Northwest. Comm. College | Rangely, CO 81648 ...... | 1962 | Public | J/C | 2,950 | 129 | $ 440 | $1,300 | $1,740 |
| Colorado School of Mines .... | Golden, CO 80401 ....... | 1874 | State | S-G/C | 2,800 | 170 | $ 932 | $1,520 | $2,452 |
| Colorado State University .... | Fort Collins, CO 80523 ... | 1870 | State | S/C | 18,225 | 945 | $ 795 | $1,700 | $2,495 |
| Colorado Technical College... | Colorado Spgs., CO 80907 | 1965 | Ind | J-S/C | 385 | 38 | $1,734 | — | $1,734 |
| Colorado Women's College ... | Denver, CO 80220 ....... | 1909 | Ind | S-G/W | 467 | 90 | $3,540 | $1,950 | $5,400 |
| Community College of Denver . | Denver, CO 80218 ....... | 1968 | State | J/C | 14,308 | — | — | — | — |
| North Campus............ | Westminster, CO 80030 .. | 1968 | State | J/C | 4,900 | 119 | $ 223 | — | $ 223 |
| Red Rocks Campus ...... | Golden, CO 80401 ...... | 1969 | State | J/C | 3,860 | 220 | $ 422 | — | $ 422 |
| Conserv. Baptist Theol. Sem. . | Denver, CO 80210 ....... | 1950 | Baptist | G/C | 390 | 44 | $1,967 | $1,752 | $3,719 |
| Fort Lewis College........... | Durango, CO 81301 ...... | 1933 | State | S/C | 3,028 | 166 | $ 587 | $1,358 | $1,945 |
| Iliff School of Theology....... | Denver, CO 80210 ....... | 1892 | Meth | G/C | 350 | 17 | $1,545 | — | — |
| Lamar Community College ... | Lamar, CO 81052......... | 1937 | State | J/C | 358 | 50 | $ 533 | $1,635 | $2,168 |
| Loretto Heights College ...... | Denver, CO 80236 ....... | 1918 | Ind | S/C | 850 | 63 | $3,900 | $2,150 | $6,050 |
| Mesa College .............. | Grand Junction, CO 81501 | 1925 | State | J-S/C | 4,259 | 132 | $ 658 | $1,550 | $2,208 |
| Metropolitan State College ... | Denver, CO 80204 ....... | 1963 | State | S/C | 14,579 | 586 | $ 487 | — | $ 487 |
| Nat. Col.–Colo. Springs Ext. .. | Colorado Spgs., CO 80932 | 1974 | Private | S/C | 97 | 14 | $2,500 | — | $2,500 |
| Nat. College of Business–Ext.. | Denver, CO 80221 ....... | 1974 | Private | S/C | 100 | 10 | $2,500 | — | $2,500 |
| Nat. College of Business–Ext.. | Pueblo, CO 81004 ....... | 1975 | Private | S/C | 170 | 9 | $2,700 | — | $2,700 |
| Northeastern Junior College .. | Sterling, CO 80751 ...... | 1941 | District | J/C | 2,288 | 74 | $ 552 | $1,350 | $1,902 |
| Otero Junior College ........ | La Junta, CO 81050 ...... | 1941 | State | J/C | 785 | 45 | $ 539 | $1,641 | $2,180 |
| Pikes Peak Comm. College ... | Colorado Spgs., CO 80906 | 1967 | State | J/C | 3,659 | 558 | $ 437 | — | $ 437 |
| Regis College .............. | Denver, CO 80221 ....... | 1877 | Catholic | S/C | 1,366 | 99 | $3,500 | $1,960 | $5,460 |
| Rockmont College........... | Denver, CO 80226 ....... | 1914 | Ind. | S/C | 311 | 35 | — | — | $2,800 |
| St. Thomas Seminary ........ | Denver, CO 80210 ....... | 1907 | Catholic | S-G/M | 120 | 41 | $1,600 | $1,425 | $3,025 |
| Trinidad State Junior College . | Trinidad, CO 81082....... | 1925 | State | J/C | 1,145 | 115 | $ 643 | $1,775 | $2,418 |
| U.S. Air Force Academy ...... | USAF, CO 80840 ........ | 1954 | Federal | S/C | 4,400 | 560 | — | — | — |
| University of Colorado ....... | Boulder, CO 80309 ...... | 1876 | State | S-G/C | 20,000 | 1,725 | $ 912 | $1,600 | $2,512 |
| Colorado Springs Campus . | Colorado Spgs., CO 80907 | 1965 | State | S-G/C | 3,260 | 200 | $ 480 | — | $ 480 |
| Denver ................. | Denver, CO 80202 ...... | 1938 | State | S-G/C | 8,744 | 468 | $ 582 | — | $ 582 |
| Health Sciences Center .... | Denver, CO 80262 ...... | 1883 | State | S-G/C | 1,394 | 769 | — | — | — |
| University of Denver......... | Denver, CO 80208 ....... | 1864 | Ind | S-G/C | 7,858 | 613 | $4,530 | $1,875 | $6,405 |
| University of Northern Colo. .. | Greeley, CO 80639 ...... | 1889 | State | S-G/C | 10,982 | 614 | $ 850 | $1,800 | $2,650 |
| University of Southern Colo... | Pueblo, CO 81001 ....... | 1933 | State | S-G/C | 4,475 | 267 | $ 701 | $1,700 | $2,401 |
| Western Bible College........ | Denver, CO 80209 ...... | 1949 | Int-Den | S/C | 204 | 12 | $1,400 | $1,400 | $2,800 |
| Western Colorado University . | Grand Junction, CO 81501 | 1971 | Ind | S-G/C | 350 | 10 | $2,500 | — | $2,500 |
| Western State Col. of Colo. .... | Gunnison, CO 81230 ..... | 1911 | State | S-G/C | 3,200 | 134 | $ 473 | $1,154 | $1,627 |
| **CONNECTICUT** | | | | | | | | | |
| Albertus Magnus College..... | New Haven, CT 06511.... | 1925 | Catholic | S/W | 561 | 54 | $3,200 | $2,000 | $5,200 |
| Bridgeport Engineering Inst... | Bridgeport, CT 06606 .... | 1924 | Ind | S/C | 639 | 74 | $1,320 | — | $1,320 |
| Central Conn. State College .. | New Britain, CT 06050 ... | 1849 | State | S-G/C | 12,061 | 644 | $ 726 | $1,378 | $2,104 |
| Connecticut College .......-.. | New London, CT 06320... | 1911 | Ind | S-G/C | 1,949 | 187 | $5,900 | $2,180 | $8,080 |
| Eastern Conn. State College .. | Willimantic, CT 06226.... | 1889 | Public | S-G/C | 2,989 | 115 | $ 769 | $1,515 | $2,284 |
| Fairfield University ......... | Fairfield, CT 06430 ..... | 1942 | Catholic | S-G/C | 4,713 | 276 | $3,575 | $1,950 | $5,525 |
| Greater Hartford Comm. Col. . | Hartford, CT 06105...... | 1967 | State | J/C | 2,754 | 91 | $ 354 | — | $ 354 |
| Hartford College For Women . | Hartford, CT 06105...... | 1939 | Ind | J/W | 199 | 30 | $3,150 | $2,025 | $5,175 |
| Hartford Graduate Center.... | Hartford, CT 06120 ..... | 1955 | Ind | G/C | 1,300 | 78 | — | — | — |
| Hartford Inst. of Accounting .. | Hartford, CT 06105...... | 1940 | Ind | P/C | 75 | 10 | $1,775 | — | $2,000 |
| Hartford State Tech. College . | Hartford, CT 06106...... | 1946 | State | T/C | 881 | 47 | $ 357 | — | $ 400 |
| Holy Apostles College ...... | Cromwell, CT 06416 ..... | 1957 | Catholic | S-G/C | 94 | 18 | $1,500 | $1,500 | $3,000 |
| Housatonic Community Col... | Bridgeport, CT 06608..... | 1967 | State | J/C | 2,693 | 112 | $ 354 | — | $ 354 |
| Manchester Community Col. .. | Manchester, CT 06040 ... | 1963 | State | J/C | 5,000 | 130 | $ 354 | — | $ 354 |
| Mattatuck Community College | Waterbury, CT 06708 .... | 1967 | State | J/C | 3,275 | 148 | $ 354 | — | $ 354 |
| Middlesex Community College | Middletown, CT 06457 ... | 1966 | State | J/C | 2,500 | 65 | $ 354 | — | $ 500 |
| Mitchell College............ | New London, CT 06320... | 1938 | Ind | J/C | 867 | 52 | $3,823 | $1,900 | $5,723 |
| Morse School of Business .... | Hartford, CT 06103...... | 1860 | Ind | J/C | 780 | 36 | $2,500 | — | $2,500 |
| Mount Sacred Heart College .. | Hamden, CT 06514 ...... | 1954 | Catholic | J/W | 18 | 5 | — | — | — |
| Northwest Conn. Comm. Col. . | Winsted, CT 06098 ...... | 1965 | State | J/C | 2,269 | 62 | $ 354 | — | $ 354 |
| Norwalk Comm. College .... | Norwalk, CT 06854 ..... | 1961 | State | J/C | 2,980 | 102 | $ 354 | — | $ 354 |
| Norwalk State Tech. College . | Norwalk, CT 06854 ..... | 1961 | State | J/C | 1,625 | 45 | $ 337 | — | — |
| Post College ............... | Waterbury, CT 06708 .... | 1890 | Ind | J-S/C | 1,443 | 85 | $2,526 | $1,800 | $4,326 |
| Quinnipiac College ......... | Hamden, CT 06518 ...... | 1929 | Ind | S-G/C | 3,768 | 168 | $3,045 | $1,700 | $4,745 |
| Sacred Heart University ..... | Bridgeport, CT 06606 .... | 1963 | Ind | S-G/C | 3,656 | 200 | $2,650 | — | — |
| St. Alphonsus College ....... | Suffield, CT 06078....... | 1963 | Catholic | S/M | 80 | 24 | $3,300 | $1,500 | $4,800 |
| St. Basil's College .......... | Stamford, CT 06902 ..... | 1939 | Catholic | S/M | 9 | 9 | $1,500 | $2,600 | $4,100 |
| St. Joseph College .......... | West Hartford, CT 06117 . | 1932 | Catholic | S-G/W | 1,289 | 111 | $3,450 | $2,000 | $5,450 |
| St. Thomas Seminary ........ | Bloomfield, CT 06002 .... | 1897 | Catholic | J/M | 27 | 13 | $1,580 | $ 700 | $2,280 |
| South Central Comm. College . | New Haven, CT 06511.... | 1968 | State | J/C | 1,987 | 71 | $ 354 | — | $ 354 |
| Southern Conn. State College . | New Haven, CT 06515.... | 1893 | State | S-G/C | 11,720 | 656 | $ 716 | $1,648 | $2,364 |
| Thames Valley St. Tech. College | Norwich, CT 06360 ...... | 1963 | State | J/C | 1,100 | 45 | $ 372 | — | $ 372 |
| Trinity College ............. | Hartford, CT 06106 ..... | 1823 | Ind | S-G/C | 1,700 | 142 | $4,910 | $1,960 | $6,870 |
| Tunxis Community College ... | Farmington, CT 06032 ... | 1970 | State | J/C | 3,500 | 205 | $ 354 | — | $ 354 |
| U.S. Coast Guard Academy ... | New London, CT 06320... | 1876 | Federal | S/C | 840 | 113 | — | — | — |
| University of Bridgeport ..... | Bridgeport, CT 06602 .... | 1927 | Ind | S-G/C | 6,956 | 284 | $3,960 | $2,150 | $6,110 |
| University of Connecticut .... | Storrs, CT 06268 ........ | 1881 | State | S-G/C | 21,650 | 1,157 | $1,048 | $1,525 | $2,573 |
| Health Center ............ | Farmington, CT 06032 ... | 1961 | State | G/C | 1,107 | 298 | — | — | — |

| NAME | ADDRESS | FOUN-DED | AFFILI-ATION | LEVEL/TYPE | ENROLL-MENT | TEACH-ERS | TUITION & FEES | BOARD & ROOM | TOTAL COST |
|---|---|---|---|---|---|---|---|---|---|
| **CONNECTICUT** *(continued)* | | | | | | | | | |
| University of Hartford | Hartford, CT 06117 | 1957 | Ind | S-G/C | 10,451 | 560 | $4,050 | $2,600 | $6,650 |
| University of New Haven | West Haven, CT 06516 | 1920 | Ind | S-G/C | 7,514 | 462 | $3,194 | $1,876 | $5,070 |
| Waterbury State Tech. College | Waterbury, CT 06708 | 1964 | State | J/C | 1,567 | 44 | $ 371 | — | $ 371 |
| Wesleyan University | Middletown, CT 06457 | 1831 | Ind | S-G/C | 2,560 | 303 | $5,200 | $2,150 | $7,350 |
| Western Conn. State College | Danbury, CT 06810 | 1903 | State | S/C | 5,454 | 176 | $ 705 | $1,480 | $2,185 |
| Yale University | New Haven, CT 06520 | 1701 | Ind | S-G/C | 9,744 | 1,468 | $6,210 | $2,900 | $9,110 |
| **DELAWARE** | | | | | | | | | |
| Brandywine College | Wilmington, DE 19803 | 1965 | Private | J/C | 1,340 | 64 | $2,500 | $1,900 | $4,400 |
| Delaware Law School | Wilmington, DE 19803 | 1971 | Ind | G/C | 753 | 44 | $3,175 | — | $3,175 |
| Delaware State College | Dover, DE 19901 | 1891 | State | S/C | 2,051 | 146 | $1,150 | $1,300 | $2,450 |
| Delaware Tech. & Comm. Col. | Dover, DE 19901 | 1967 | State | T/C | 6,475 | 240 | $ 504 | — | $ 504 |
| Goldey Beacom College, Inc. | Wilmington, DE 19808 | 1886 | Ind | J-S/C | 1,490 | 27 | $2,040 | $1,275 | $3,315 |
| University of Delaware | Newark, DE 19711 | 1833 | State | S-G/C | 19,000 | 1,050 | $ 990 | $1,833 | $2,823 |
| Wesley College | Dover, DE 19901 | 1873 | Meth | S/C | 1,321 | 48 | $3,500 | $1,720 | $5,220 |
| Wilmington College | New Castle, DE 19720 | 1967 | Private | S-G/C | 814 | 75 | $2,150 | $2,000 | $4,150 |
| **DISTRICT OF COLUMBIA** | | | | | | | | | |
| American University | Washington, DC 20016 | 1893 | Meth | S-G/C | 12,824 | 842 | $4,134 | $2,126 | $6,260 |
| Antioch School of Law | Washington, DC 20009 | 1972 | Ind | G/C | 451 | 21 | $3,990 | — | $3,990 |
| Beacon College | Washington, DC 20009 | 1907 | Ind | S-G/C | 150 | — | $1,950 | — | $1,950 |
| Benjamin Franklin University | Washington, DC 20036 | 1907 | Ind | S-G/C | 850 | 60 | $2,050 | — | $2,050 |
| Catholic University of America | Washington, DC 20064 | 1887 | Catholic | S-G/C | 8,252 | 787 | $3,850 | $2,400 | $6,250 |
| Gallaudet College | Washington, DC 20002 | 1864 | Private | S-G/C | 1,480 | 203 | $ 942 | $1,725 | $2,667 |
| George Washington University | Washington, DC 20052 | 1821 | Ind | S-G/C | 23,068 | 1,571 | $3,501 | $2,500 | $6,001 |
| Georgetown University | Washington, DC 20057 | 1789 | Catholic | S-G/C | 11,922 | 1,434 | $4,970 | $2,450 | $7,420 |
| Howard University | Washington, DC 20059 | 1867 | Ind | S-G/C | 10,706 | 1,856 | $1,845 | $1,880 | $3,725 |
| Mount Vernon College | Washington, DC 20007 | 1875 | Ind | S/W | 519 | 35 | $3,700 | $2,600 | $6,300 |
| Sch. of Ad. Inter. Stud.-J.H.U. | Washington, DC 20036 | 1943 | Ind | G/C | 360 | 114 | $4,500 | $4,900 | $9,400 |
| Southeastern University | Washington, DC 20024 | 1879 | Ind | S-G/C | 1,600 | 115 | $2,250 | — | $2,250 |
| Strayer College | Washington, DC 20005 | 1898 | Ind | S/C | 1,629 | 98 | $2,160 | — | |
| Trinity College | Washington, DC 20017 | 1897 | Catholic | S-G/W | 832 | 79 | $4,050 | $2,425 | $6,475 |
| USDA Graduate School | Washington, DC 20250 | 1921 | Ind | G-C | 18,644 | 600 | $ 150 | — | $ 150 |
| Univ. of the Dist. of Columbia | Washington, DC 20008 | 1976 | Public | S-G/C | 15,096 | 651 | $ 169 | — | $ 169 |
| Washington Musical Institute | Washington, DC 20009 | 1928 | Ind | S-G/C | 168 | 6 | — | — | — |
| Wesley Theological Seminary | Washington, DC 20016 | 1882 | Meth | G/C | 336 | 39 | $2,550 | $1,250 | $3,800 |
| **FLORIDA** | | | | | | | | | |
| Ambassadors International | West Palm Beach, FL 33401 | 1964 | Ind | P/C | 150 | 2 | $ 20 | — | $ 20 |
| American Bible College | Pineland, FL 33945 | 1942 | Evang | G/C | 700 | — | — | — | — |
| Apostolic Bible School | Lakeland, FL 33810 | 1935 | Church | J/C | 12 | 8 | $ 140 | — | $ 140 |
| Baptist Bible Institute | Graceville, FL 32440 | 1943 | Baptist | S/C | 363 | 19 | $ 884 | $ 336 | $1,220 |
| Barry College | Miami, FL 33161 | 1940 | Catholic | S-G/C | 2,058 | 171 | $2,900 | $1,575 | $4,475 |
| Bauder Fashion College | Miami, FL 33131 | 1964 | Ind | T/C | 641 | 27 | $3,290 | $1,880 | $5,170 |
| Bethune-Cookman College | Daytona Beach, FL 32015 | 1904 | Meth | S/C | 1,736 | 96 | $2,725 | $1,696 | $4,421 |
| Biscayne College | Miami, FL 33054 | 1961 | Catholic | S-G/C | 2,200 | 145 | $3,065 | $1,900 | $4,965 |
| Brevard Community College | Cocoa, FL 32922 | 1960 | State | J/C | 10,000 | 200 | $ 450 | — | $ 450 |
| Broward Community College | Ft. Lauderdale, FL 33301 | 1960 | State | J/C | 23,000 | 308 | $ 450 | — | $ 450 |
| Central Florida Bible College | Orlando, FL 32856 | 1976 | Church | S/C | 126 | 9 | $1,344 | $ 700 | $2,044 |
| Central Florida Comm. College | Ocala, FL 32670 | 1957 | State | J/C | 2,505 | 106 | $ 448 | — | $ 448 |
| Chipola Junior College | Marianna, FL 32446 | 1947 | State | J/C | 1,288 | 62 | $ 192 | $1,500 | $1,692 |
| Clearwater Christian College | Clearwater, FL 33519 | 1966 | Ind | S/C | 191 | 22 | $1,248 | $1,730 | $2,978 |
| College of Boca Raton | Boca Raton, FL 33431 | 1963 | Ind | J/C | 545 | 34 | $2,900 | $1,700 | $4,600 |
| Daytona Beach Comm. College | Daytona Beach, FL 32015 | 1958 | State | J/C | 5,778 | 151 | $ 450 | — | $ 450 |
| Eckerd College | St. Petersburg, FL 33733 | 1958 | Presby | S/C | 1,062 | 87 | $3,995 | $1,625 | $5,620 |
| Edison Community College | Fort Myers, FL 33907 | 1962 | State | J/C | 4,383 | 200 | $ 448 | — | $ 448 |
| Edward Waters College | Jacksonville, FL 32209 | 1866 | AME | S/C | 703 | 53 | $1,800 | $1,600 | $3,400 |
| Embry-Riddle Aero. University | Daytona Beach, FL 32014 | 1926 | Ind | S-G/C | 4,000 | 220 | $3,633 | $2,829 | $6,462 |
| Faith Bible College | Milton, FL 32570 | 1974 | Baptist | S/C | 20 | 6 | $ 600 | — | $ 600 |
| Faith Bible Theological Sem. | Milton, FL 32570 | 1979 | Baptist | S-G/C | 75 | — | $ 600 | — | $ 600 |
| Flagler College | St. Augustine, FL 32084 | 1968 | Ind | S/C | 750 | 41 | $2,200 | $1,450 | $3,650 |
| Florida A&M University | Tallahassee, FL 32307 | 1887 | State | S-G/C | 5,536 | 289 | $ 742 | $1,600 | $2,342 |
| Florida Atlantic University | Boca Raton, FL 33431 | 1961 | State | S-G/C | 7,144 | 363 | $ 772 | $1,650 | $2,422 |
| Florida Baptist College | Lakeland, FL 33802 | 1957 | Baptist | S-G/C | 70 | 12 | $ 600 | $ 900 | $1,500 |
| Florida Beacon College | Largo, FL 33541 | 1947 | Ind | S/C | 60 | 12 | $ 990 | $1,040 | $2,030 |
| Florida Bible College | Hollywood, FL 33019 | 1962 | Ind | S/C | 400 | 33 | $1,400 | $1,806 | $3,200 |
| Florida College | Temple Terrace, FL 33617 | 1946 | Ind | J/C | 460 | 36 | $2,000 | $1,350 | $3,350 |
| Florida Inst. of Technology | Melbourne, FL 32901 | 1958 | Ind | S-G/C | 4,218 | 266 | $3,693 | $1,860 | $5,553 |
| Florida International University | Miami, FL 33199 | 1972 | State | S-G/C | 11,680 | 570 | $ 743 | — | $ 743 |
| Fla. Jr. Col. at Jacksonville | Jacksonville, FL 32202 | 1966 | State | J/C | 14,670 | 330 | $ 390 | · | $ 390 |
| Florida Keys Comm. College | Key West, FL 33040 | 1965 | Public | T-J/C | 1,700 | 40 | $ 420 | — | $ 420 |
| Florida Memorial College | Miami, FL 33054 | 1879 | Baptist | S/C | 921 | 52 | $2,800 | $1,420 | $4,300 |
| Florida School of Prof. Psy. | Miami, FL 33166 | 1978 | Ind | P/C | 129 | 25 | $4,210 | — | $4,210 |
| Florida Southern College | Lakeland, FL 33802 | 1885 | Meth | S/C | 1,677 | 131 | $2,747 | $1,850 | $4,597 |
| Florida State University | Tallahassee, FL 32306 | 1857 | State | S-G/C | 21,461 | 1,429 | $ 705 | $1,720 | $2,425 |
| Fort Lauderdale College | Fort Lauderdale, FL 33301 | 1940 | Private | S/C | 1,087 | 26 | $1,103 | — | $1,103 |
| Freedom University | Orlando, FL 32811 | 1973 | Ind | S-G/C | 1,000 | 36 | $ 825 | — | $ 825 |
| Gulf Coast Comm. College | Panama City, FL 32401 | 1957 | State | J/C | 3,967 | 150 | $ 450 | — | $ 450 |
| Heed University | Hollywood, FL 33020 | 1970 | Ind | G-P/C | 165 | 45 | $4,000 | — | $4,000 |
| Heritage College | Orlando, FL 32808 | 1976 | Baptist | S/C | 60 | 6 | $ 700 | $ 700 | $1,400 |
| Hillsborough Comm. College | Tampa, FL 33622 | 1968 | State | J/C | 11,332 | 497 | $ 420 | — | $ 420 |

| NAME | ADDRESS | FOUN-DED | AFFILI-ATION | LEVEL/TYPE | ENROLL-MENT | TEACH-ERS | TUITION & FEES | BOARD & ROOM | TOTAL COST |
|---|---|---|---|---|---|---|---|---|---|
| **FLORIDA** *(continued)* | | | | | | | | | |
| Hobe Sound Bible College .... | Hobe Sound, FL 33455 ... | 1960 | Ind | S/C | 230 | 25 | $ 938 | $ 900 | $1,838 |
| Homestead Col. of Bible ...... | Orlando, FL 32802 ....... | 1963 | Ind | S-G/C | 6,143 | 50 | $ 620 | — | $ 620 |
| Indian River Comm. College ... | Fort Pierce, FL 33450 .... | 1959 | State | J/C | 5,200 | 90 | $ 650 | — | $ 650 |
| International Fine Arts College | Miami, FL 33132 ........ | 1965 | Ind | J/C | 260 | 24 | $5,385 | $1,725 | $7,110 |
| Jacksonville University ....... | Jacksonville, FL 32211 ... | 1934 | Ind | S-G/C | 2,217 | 141 | $2,830 | $1,810 | $4,640 |
| Jones College, Fort Pierce .... | Fort Pierce, FL 33450 .... | 1918 | Ind | S/C | 160 | 12 | $1,500 | — | $1,500 |
| Jones College, Jacksonville ... | Jacksonville, FL 32211 ... | 1918 | Ind | S/C | 996 | 29 | $1,103 | — | $1,103 |
| Jones College, Orlando ....... | Orlando, FL 32802 ...... | 1918 | Ind | S/C | 1,332 | 36 | $1,103 | — | $1,103 |
| Lake City Comm. College ..... | Lake City, FL 32055 ..... | 1962 | State | J/C | 2,866 | 164 | $ 448 | $1,260 | $1,708 |
| Lakeland College ............ | Lakeland, FL 33802 ...... | 1927 | Ind | J/C | 310 | 25 | $2,473 | — | $2,473 |
| Lake-Sumter Comm. College .. | Leesburg, FL 32748 ...... | 1962 | State | J/C | 1,972 | 74 | $ 448 | — | $ 448 |
| Liberty Bible College ........ | Pensacola, FL 32506 ..... | 1965 | Charis | S-G/C | 300 | 18 | $ 845 | $1,525 | $2,370 |
| Luther Rice Seminary ........ | Jacksonville, FL 32207 ... | 1962 | Ind | P/C | 1,000 | 21 | $1,200 | — | $1,200 |
| Manatee Junior College ...... | Bradenton, FL 33506..... | 1957 | State | J/C | 5,282 | 224 | $ 238 | — | $ 238 |
| Miami Christian College ...... | Miami, FL 33167 ........ | 1949 | Int-Den | S/C | 256 | 17 | $2,090 | $1,600 | $3,690 |
| Miami-Dade Comm. College... | Miami, FL 33176 ........ | 1960 | State | J/C | 39,427 | 823 | $ 480 | — | $ 480 |
| Nassau Baptist Col. .......... | Yulee, FL 32097 ........ | 1975 | Baptist | G/C | 20 | 5 | — | — | $ 450 |
| North Florida Junior College .. | Madison, FL 32340 ...... | 1958 | State | J/C | 1,051 | 76 | $ 504 | — | $ 504 |
| Nova University ............. | Ft. Lauderdale, FL 33314 . | 1964 | Ind | S-G/C | 5,220 | 67 | — | — | — |
| Okaloosa-Walton Jr. College .. | Niceville, FL 32578 ..... | 1963 | State | J/C | 4,568 | 173 | $ 478 | — | $ 478 |
| Palm Beach Atlantic College .. | W. Palm Beach, FL 33401.. | 1968 | Baptist | S/C | 510 | 46 | $1,540 | $1,400 | $2,940 |
| Palm Beach Baptist Col. ...... | Loxahatchee, FL 33470 ... | 1975 | Baptist | S-G/C | 80 | 6 | $ 800 | $4,000 | $4,800 |
| Palm Beach Junior College.... | Lake Worth, FL 33461 .... | 1933 | State | J/C | 9,485 | 376 | $ 540 | — | $ 540 |
| Pasco-Hernando Comm. Col. .. | Dade City, FL 33525 ..... | 1972 | State | J/C | 2,279 | 164 | $ 420 | — | $ 420 |
| Pensacola Christian College... | Pensacola, FL 32503 ..... | 1974 | Ind | S-G/C | 800 | 50 | $1,600 | $1,600 | $3,200 |
| Pensacola Junior College ..... | Pensacola, FL 32504 ..... | 1948 | State | J/C | 12,718 | 534 | $ 420 | — | $ 420 |
| Polk Community College ...... | Winter Haven, FL 33880 .. | 1964 | State | J/C | 5,830 | 180 | $ 390 | — | $ 390 |
| Prospect Hall College ........ | Fort Lauderdale, FL 33301 | 1958 | Ind | S/C | 450 | 24 | $1,600 | $1,200 | $2,800 |
| Providence Christ. College ... | Riverview, FL 33569 ..... | 1965 | Baptist | S/C | 31 | 8 | $ 300 | — | $ 300 |
| Ringling School of Art ....... | Sarasota, FL 33580 ..... | 1931 | Ind | S/C | 507 | 27 | $2,100 | $1,570 | $3,670 |
| Rollins College ............. | Winter Park, FL 32789 ... | 1885 | Ind | S-G/C | 3,080 | 156 | $3,990 | $1,800 | $5,790 |
| St. John's River Comm. College | Palatka, FL 32077 ...... | 1958 | State | J/C | 1,549 | 41 | $ 416 | — | $ 416 |
| St. John Vianney Col. Sem. ... | Miami, FL 33165 ........ | 1959 | Catholic | S/M | 70 | 20 | $3,075 | — | $3,075 |
| St. Leo College ............. | Saint Leo, FL 33574 ..... | 1889 | Catholic | J/C | 1,078 | 73 | $2,670 | $1,176 | $3,846 |
| St. Petersburg Junior College . | St. Petersburg, FL 33733 . | 1927 | Public | J/C | 14,499 | 303 | $ 480 | — | $ 480 |
| Santa Fe Comm. College ..... | Gainesville, FL 32602 .... | 1965 | State | J/C | 7,369 | 245 | $ 420 | — | $ 420 |
| Sem. of St. Vincent de Paul .. | Boynton Beach, FL 33435 . | 1963 | Catholic | G/M | 72 | 13 | $1,500 | $1,500 | $3,000 |
| Seminole Community College .. | Sanford, FL 32771 ....... | 1965 | State | J/C | 4,066 | 355 | $ 420 | — | $ 420 |
| Shelton College ............ | Cape Canaveral, FL 32920 | 1891 | Ind | S/C | 40 | 15 | $1,500 | $1,150 | $2,650 |
| S: E. Col. of the Assem. of God | Lakeland, FL 33801 ..... | 1935 | A of God | S/C | 1,232 | 35 | $ 716 | $ 600 | $1,316 |
| South Florida Junior College .. | Avon Park, FL 33825 ..... | 1965 | State | J/C | 850 | 60 | $ 320 | — | $ 320 |
| Southern College ........... | Orlando, FL 32801 ...... | 1968 | Ind | S/C | 140 | 15 | $2,272 | — | $2,272 |
| Spurgeon Baptist Bible College | Mulberry, FL 33860 ..... | 1970 | Baptist | S/C | 73 | 8 | $1,116 | $1,404 | $2,520 |
| Stetson University .......... | DeLand, FL 32720 ...... | 1883 | Baptist | S-G/C | 2,946 | 146 | $3,215 | $1,654 | $4,869 |
| Tallahassee Comm. College ... | Tallahassee, FL 32304 ... | 1965 | State | J/C | 3,291 | 118 | $ 330 | — | $ 500 |
| Talmudic College of Florida .. | Miami Beach, FL 33140 ... | 1974 | Jewish | S-G/M | 85 | 6 | $1,800 | $2,000 | $3,800 |
| Tampa College ............. | Tampa, FL 33607 ....... | 1890 | Ind | S/C | 1,112 | 29 | $1,103 | — | $1,103 |
| Transylvania Bible College .... | Lakeworth, FL 33463 .... | 1975 | Int-Den | S/C | 14 | 3 | $ 450 | — | $ 450 |
| Trinity Baptist Col. .......... | Jacksonville, FL 32205 ... | 1974 | Baptist | S/C | 188 | 15 | $1,360 | $1,350 | $2,710 |
| University of Central Florida .. | Orlando, FL 32816 ...... | 1963 | State | S-G/C | 11,993 | 493 | $ 742 | $1,348 | $2,090 |
| University of Florida ........ | Gainesville, FL 32611 ... | 1853 | State | S-G/C | 32,311 | 2,600 | $ 750 | $2,300 | $3,050 |
| University of Miami ......... | Coral Gables, FL 33124 ... | 1925 | Private | S-G/C | 18,489 | 1,215 | $4,530 | $2,017 | $6,547 |
| University of North Florida .... | Jacksonville, FL 32216 ... | 1965 | State | S-G/C | 4,599 | 120 | $ 760 | — | $ 760 |
| University of Palm Beach .... | W. Palm Beach, FL 33402. | 1926 | Ind | S/C | 175 | 13 | $1,800 | — | $1,800 |
| University of Sarasota ....... | Sarasota, FL 33577 ..... | 1974 | Ind | S-G/C | 360 | 16 | $2,800 | — | $2,800 |
| University of South Florida .... | Tampa, FL 33620 ........ | 1956 | State | S-G/C | 23,581 | 808 | $ 780 | $1,490 | $2,270 |
| New College | Sarasota, FL 33580 ..... | 1960 | Public | S/C | 500 | 42 | $ 870 | $1,600 | $2,470 |
| University of Tampa ......... | Tampa, FL 33606 ....... | 1930 | Ind | S-G/C | 2,298 | 97 | $3,681 | $1,650 | $5,411 |
| University of West Florida .... | Pensacola, FL 32504 ..... | 1963 | State | S-G/C | 5,228 | 232 | $ 742 | $1,290 | $2,032 |
| Valencia Community College .. | Orlando, FL 32802 ...... | 1967 | State | J/C | 9,100 | 408 | $ 450 | — | $ 450 |
| Walden University .......... | Naples, FL 33940 ...... | 1970 | Ind | G/C | 300 | 16 | $5,385 | — | $5,385 |
| Warner Southern College ..... | Lake Wales, FL 33853 .... | 1964 | C of God | S/C | 264 | 32 | $1,920 | $1,380 | $3,300 |
| Webber College ............ | Babson Park, FL 33827... | 1927 | Ind | S/C | 150 | 17 | $2,700 | $1,500 | $4,200 |
| Yeshiva Gedolah Rabbin. Col. . | Miami Beach, FL 33139 ... | 1961 | Jewish | S/M | 42 | 2 | $1,800 | $1,500 | $3,300 |
| **GEORGIA** | | | | | | | | | |
| Abraham Baldwin Agri. College | Tifton, GA 31794 ....... | 1908 | State | J/C | 2,370 | 102 | $ 429 | $1,140 | $1,569 |
| Agnes Scott College ........ | Decatur, GA 30030 ..... | 1889 | Ind | S/W | 560 | 76 | $3,875 | $1,600 | $5,475 |
| Albany Junior College ....... | Albany, GA 31707 ...... | 1963 | State | J/C | 1,807 | 67 | $ 375 | — | $ 375 |
| Albany State College ........ | Albany, GA 31705 ...... | 1903 | State | S/C | 1,719 | 125 | $ 624 | $1,455 | $2,639 |
| Amer. Col. for Applied Arts ... | Atlanta, GA 30342 ...... | 1975 | Ind | S/C | 175 | 17 | $3,500 | $1,700 | $5,200 |
| Andrew College ............ | Cuthbert, GA 31740 ..... | 1854 | Meth | J/C | 335 | 18 | $1,620 | $1,566 | $3,186 |
| Armstrong State College ..... | Savannah, GA 31406..... | 1935 | State | S-G/C | 3,000 | 185 | $ 541 | — | $ 541 |
| Atlanta Area Tech. School .... | Atlanta, GA 30310 ...... | 1967 | Public | T/C | 1,750 | 109 | $ 108 | — | $ 108 |
| Atlanta Christian College .... | East Point, GA 30344 ... | 1937 | Christian | S/C | 207 | 21 | $1,324 | $1,220 | $2,544 |
| Atlanta College of Art ....... | Atlanta, GA 30309 ...... | 1928 | Ind | S/C | 300 | 30 | $2,600 | — | $2,600 |
| Atlanta Junior College ....... | Atlanta, GA 30310 ...... | 1974 | State | J/C | 1,396 | 87 | $ 366 | — | $ 366 |
| Atlanta Law School ......... | Atlanta, GA 30303 ...... | 1890 | Ind | G/C | 410 | 24 | $ 750 | — | $ 750 |
| Atlanta University .......... | Atlanta, GA 30314 ...... | 1867 | Ind | S-G/C | 1,363 | 139 | $2,007 | $ 630 | $2,637 |
| Augusta Area Tech. School .... | Augusta, GA 30906 ..... | 1959 | State | T/C | 1,390 | 110 | $ 110 | — | $ 110 |
| Augusta College ............ | Augusta, GA 30904 ..... | 1925 | State | S-G/C | 3,702 | 167 | $ 496 | — | $ 496 |
| Bainbridge Junior College .... | Bainbridge, GA 31717.... | 1973 | State | J/C | 500 | 51 | $ 366 | — | $ 366 |
| Berry College ............. | Mt. Berry, GA 30149 ..... | 1902 | Ind | S-G/C | 1,540 | 105 | $2,400 | $1,320 | $3,720 |
| Brenau College ............. | Gainesville, GA 30501 ... | 1878 | Private | S-G/W | 683 | 85 | $2,350 | $2,300 | $4,650 |

| NAME | ADDRESS | FOUN-DED | AFFILI-ATION | LEVEL/TYPE | ENROLL-MENT | TEACH-ERS | TUITION & FEES | BOARD & ROOM | TOTAL COST |
|---|---|---|---|---|---|---|---|---|---|
| **GEORGIA** (continued) | | | | | | | | | |
| Brewton-Parker College ..... | Mt. Vernon, GA 30445 .... | 1904 | Baptist | J/C | 799 | 24 | $1,560 | $1,350 | $2,910 |
| Brunswick Junior College ..... | Brunswick, GA 31520 ..... | 1961 | State | J/C | 1,133 | 55 | $ 488 | — | $ 488 |
| Carver Bible Inst. & College ... | Atlanta, GA 30313 ....... | 1943 | Ind | S/C | 59 | 12 | $ 673 | $1,394 | $2,067 |
| Clark College ............... | Atlanta, GA 30314 ....... | 1869 | Meth | S/C | 2,031 | 124 | $2,490 | $1,450 | $3,940 |
| Clayton Junior College ....... | Morrow, GA 30260 ....... | 1969 | State | J/C | 2,990 | 120 | $ 360 | — | $ 360 |
| Columbia Theological Sem. .. | Decatur, GA 30031 ....... | 1828 | Presby | P/C | 372 | — | $1,824 | $1,490 | $3,314 |
| Columbus College ........... | Columbus, GA 31907 ..... | 1958 | State | S-G/C | 4,655 | 266 | $ 537 | — | $ 537 |
| Covenant College ............ | Lookout Mtn., GA 37350.. | 1955 | Presby | S/C | 494 | 46 | $3,380 | $1,890 | $5,270 |
| Dalton Junior College ....... | Dalton, GA 30720 ....... | 1963 | State | J/C | 1,466 | 70 | $ 366 | — | $ 366 |
| DeKalb Community College .... | Clarkston, GA 30021 ..... | 1964 | Public | J/C | 15,236 | 72 | $ 424 | — | $ 424 |
| DeVry Inst. of Technology .... | Atlanta, GA 30341 ....... | 1969 | Ind | T/C | 1,020 | — | $3,200 | — | $3,200 |
| Draughon's Junior College .... | Savannah, GA 31401 ..... | 1899 | Ind | J/C | 537 | 35 | $1,440 | — | $1,440 |
| Emanuel County Jr. College .. | Swainsboro, GA 30401 ... | 1973 | State | J/C | 364 | 23 | $ 366 | — | $ 366 |
| Emmanuel College ........... | Franklin, GA 30639 ...... | 1919 | Pent H | J/C | 375 | 31 | $1,440 | $1,326 | $2,766 |
| Emory University ............ | Atlanta Sprys., GA 30322. | 1836 | Meth | S-G/C | 8,037 | 536 | $4,095 | $1,796 | $5,891 |
| Floyd Junior College ........ | Rome, GA 30161 ........ | 1970 | State | J/C | 1,250 | 55 | $ 348 | — | $ 348 |
| Fort Valley State College ..... | Fort Valley, GA 31030 ... | 1895 | State | S-G/C | 1,813 | 135 | $ 222 | $1,215 | $1,437 |
| Gainesville Junior College .... | Gainesville, GA 30503... | 1964 | State | J/C | 1,520 | 57 | $ 375 | — | $ 375 |
| Gammon Theological Seminary | Atlanta, GA 30314 ....... | 1883 | Meth | G/C | 131 | 35 | $1,700 | $1,100 | $2,800 |
| Georgia College ............. | Milledgeville, GA 31061 .. | 1889 | State | S-G/C | 3,368 | 179 | $ 558 | $1,119 | $1,677 |
| Georgia Inst. of Technology ... | Atlanta, GA 30332 ....... | 1885 | State | S-G/C | 11,200 | 702 | $ 875 | $1,980 | $2,855 |
| Georgia Military College ..... | Milledgeville, GA 31061 .. | 1879 | Ind | J/C | 331 | 17 | $1,275 | $2,365 | $3,640 |
| Georgia Southern College ..... | Statesboro, GA 30458.... | 1906 | State | S-G/C | 6,723 | 343 | $ 597 | $1,200 | $1,797 |
| Georgia Southwestern College | Americus, GA 31709 ..... | 1908 | State | S-G/C | 2,101 | 118 | $ 564 | $1,170 | $1,734 |
| Georgia State University ..... | Atlanta, GA 30303 ....... | 1913 | State | S-G/C | 20,338 | 681 | $ 540 | — | $ 540 |
| Gordon Junior College ....... | Barnesville, GA 30204.... | 1852 | State | J/C | 1,506 | 60 | $ 381 | $1,140 | $1,521 |
| Immanuel Baptist Schools .... | Atlanta, GA 30316 ....... | 1978 | Baptist | S-G/C | 35 | — | — | — | — |
| Interden. Theological Center .. | Atlanta, GA 30314 ....... | 1958 | Ind | G/C | 290 | 33 | $1,600 | $3,800 | $5,400 |
| John Marshall Law School .... | Atlanta, GA 30308 ....... | 1933 | Ind | P/C | 450 | 28 | $1,050 | — | $1,050 |
| Kennesaw College ........... | Marietta, GA 30061 ...... | 1966 | State | S/C | 4,135 | 125 | $ 489 | — | $3,775 |
| LaGrange College............ | LaGrange, GA 30240 .... | 1831 | Meth | S-G/C | 889 | 47 | $1,800 | $1,200 | $3,000 |
| Life Chiropractic College .... | Marietta, GA 30060 ...... | 1974 | Ind | P/C | 1,201 | 57 | $3,000 | — | $3,000 |
| Macon Junior College ....... | Macon, GA 31206 ....... | 1968 | State | J/C | 2,361 | 77 | $ 366 | — | $ 366 |
| Medical College of Georgia ... | Augusta, GA 30912 ...... | 1828 | State | S-G/C | 1,991 | 573 | $1,640 | $ 560 | $2,200 |
| Mercer University ........... | Macon, GA 31207 ....... | 1833 | Baptist | S-G/C | 4,527 | 188 | $3,066 | $1,497 | $4,503 |
| Mercer Univ. in Atlanta ...... | Atlanta, GA 30341 ....... | 1964 | Baptist | S-G/C | 1,390 | 58 | $1,641 | — | $1,641 |
| Mercer Univ. Sch. of Pharmacy | Atlanta, GA 30312 ....... | 1903 | Baptist | P/C | 364 | 35 | $3,300 | — | $3,300 |
| Middle Georgia College ...... | Cochran, GA 31014 ...... | 1884 | State | J/C | 1,514 | 77 | $ 426 | $1,275 | $1,701 |
| Morehouse College .......... | Atlanta, GA 30314 ....... | 1867 | Ind | S/M | 1,746 | 112 | $2,362 | $1,632 | $3,994 |
| Morris Brown College ........ | Atlanta, GA 30314 ....... | 1881 | AME | S/C | 1,660 | 123 | $2,565 | $1,625 | $4,840 |
| North Georgia College........ | Dahlonega, GA 30533 .... | 1873 | State | S-G/C | 1,885 | 93 | $ 585 | $1,230 | $1,815 |
| North Ga. Tech. & Voc. School | Clarkesville, GA 30523 ... | 1943 | State | T/C | 656 | 48 | $ 50 | $1,140 | $1,190 |
| Oglethorpe University ........ | Atlanta, GA 30319 ....... | 1835 | Ind | S-G/C | 1,093 | 46 | $3,100 | $1,700 | $4,800 |
| Oxford Col. of Emory Univ. ... | Oxford, GA 30267 ....... | 1836 | Meth | J/C | 525 | 30 | $3,300 | $1,635 | $4,935 |
| Paine College .............. | Augusta, GA 30901 ...... | 1882 | Meth | S/C | 828 | 60 | $2,150 | $1,350 | $3,500 |
| Phillips College............. | Augusta, GA 30902 ...... | 1948 | Ind | J/C | 500 | 30 | $1,950 | — | $1,950 |
| Phillips College............. | Columbus, GA 31901 ..... | 1951 | Ind | J/C | 415 | 20 | $3,840 | — | $3,840 |
| Piedmont College ............ | Demorest, GA 30535..... | 1897 | Ind | S/C | 400 | 30 | $1,395 | $1,725 | $3,130 |
| Reinhardt College ........... | Waleska, GA 30183 ...... | 1883 | Meth | J/C | 486 | 35 | $ 960 | $1,275 | $2,235 |
| Savannah State College ...... | Savannah, GA 31404..... | 1890 | State | S-G/C | 1,800 | 134 | $ 600 | $1,185 | $1,785 |
| Shorter College ............. | Rome, GA 30161 ........ | 1873 | Baptist | S/C | 813 | 58 | $2,150 | $1,350 | $3,500 |
| South Georgia College ....... | Douglas, GA 31533 ...... | 1906 | State | J/C | 1,252 | 60 | $ 420 | $1,200 | $1,620 |
| Southern Technical Institute .. | Marietta, GA 30060 ...... | 1948 | State | S/C | 2,385 | 100 | $ 510 | $1,700 | $2,210 |
| Spelman College ............ | Atlanta, GA 30314 ....... | 1881 | Ind | S/W | 1,250 | 110 | $2,260 | $1,750 | $4,010 |
| Thomas County Comm. Col. .. | Thomasville, GA 31792.... | 1950 | Private | J/C | 250 | 24 | $1,179 | — | $1,179 |
| Tift College ................ | Forsyth, GA 31029....... | 1847 | Baptist | S/W | 600 | 34 | $1,683 | $1,413 | $3,096 |
| Toccoa Falls College ......... | Toccoa Falls, GA 30577 .. | 1907 | Private | S/C | 582 | 29 | $1,900 | $1,500 | $3,400 |
| Truett-McConnell College ..... | Cleveland, GA 30528..... | 1946 | Baptist | J/C | 695 | 64 | $1,625 | $1,350 | $2,975 |
| University of Georgia ........ | Athens, GA 30602 ....... | 1785 | State | S-G/C | 22,046 | 1,414 | $ 753 | $1,600 | $2,353 |
| Valdosta State College ....... | Valdosta, GA 31601....... | 1906 | State | S/C | 4,852 | 250 | $ 546 | $1,029 | $1,575 |
| Wesleyan College ........... | Macon, GA 31201 ....... | 1836 | Meth | S/W | 506 | 50 | $3,370 | $1,600 | $4,970 |
| West Georgia College ........ | Carrollton, GA 30118 .... | 1933 | State | S-G/C | 5,051 | 280 | $ 597 | $1,230 | $1,827 |
| Woodrow Wilson Col. of Law .. | Atlanta, GA 30308 ....... | 1933 | Ind | G/C | 800 | 33 | $1,300 | — | $1,300 |
| Young Harris College ........ | Young Harris, GA 30582.. | 1886 | Meth | J/C | 522 | 31 | $1,785 | $1,470 | $3,255 |

**GUAM**

| University of Guam .......... | Agana, GU 96910 ...... | 1952 | State | S-G/C | 2,500 | 182 | $ 432 | $2,100 | $2,532 |

**HAWAII**

| Brig. Young U./Hawaii Camp. . | Laie, HI 96762 .......... | 1955 | Mormon | S-G/C | 1,800 | 68 | $ 760 | $1,200 | $1,960 |
| Chaminade Univ. of Honolulu . | Honolulu, HI 96816 ...... | 1955 | Catholic | S-G/C | 2,361 | 165 | $2,080 | $1,970 | $4,050 |
| Hawaii Loa College........... | Kaneohe HI 96744 ...... | 1963 | Ind | S/C | 310 | 33 | $2,100 | $2,000 | $4,100 |
| Hawaii Pacific College ....... | Honolulu, HI 96813 ...... | 1965 | Ind | S/C | 1,672 | 75 | $1,825 | — | $1,825 |
| University of Hawaii | | | | | | | | | |
|   At Manoa ............... | Honolulu, HI 96822 ...... | 1907 | State | S-G/C | 20,833 | 1,581 | $ 478 | $1,254 | $1,732 |
|   At Hilo ................. | Hilo, HI 96720 .......... | 1947 | State | S/C | 3,099 | 220 | $ 105 | $1,180 | $1,285 |
|   West Oahu College ....... | Pearl City, HI 96782 ..... | 1975 | State | S/C | 258 | 20 | $ 400 | — | $ 400 |
|   Honolulu Community College . | Honolulu, HI 96817 ..... | 1920 | State | J/C | 4,576 | 198 | $ 90 | — | $ 90 |
|   Kapiolani Community College . | Honolulu, HI 96814 ..... | 1957 | State | J/C | 4,641 | 183 | $ 90 | — | $ 90 |
|   Kauai Community College .. | Lihue, HI 96766 ........ | 1926 | State | J/C | 1,104 | 58 | $ 90 | — | $ 90 |
|   Leeward Community College | Pearl City, HI 96782 ..... | 1968 | State | J/C | 5,540 | 201 | $ 90 | — | $ 90 |
|   Maui Community College ... | Kahului, HI 96732 ...... | 1931 | State | J/C | 1,819 | 91 | $ 90 | — | $ 90 |
|   Windward Community College | Kaneohe, HI 96744 ...... | 1972 | State | J/C | 1,505 | 58 | $ 90 | — | $ 90 |

| NAME | ADDRESS | FOUN-DED | AFFILI-ATION | LEVEL/TYPE | ENROLL-MENT | TEACH-ERS | TUITION & FEES | BOARD & ROOM | TOTAL COST |
|---|---|---|---|---|---|---|---|---|---|
| **IDAHO** | | | | | | | | | |
| Boise State University | Boise, ID 83725 | 1932 | State | S-G/C | 10,728 | 455 | $ 475 | $1,500 | $1,975 |
| College of Idaho | Caldwell, ID 83605 | 1891 | Presby | S-G/C | 725 | 56 | $3,593 | $1,723 | $5,316 |
| College of Southern Idaho | Twin Falls, ID 83301 | 1965 | State | J/C | 4,550 | 104 | $ 400 | $1,600 | $2,000 |
| Idaho State University | Pocatello, ID 83209 | 1901 | State | S-G/C | 10,804 | 412 | $ 460 | $1,365 | $1,825 |
| Lewis-Clark State College | Lewiston, ID 83501 | 1893 | State | S/C | 1,499 | 93 | $ 370 | $1,550 | $1,920 |
| North Idaho College | Coeur d'Alene, ID 83814 | 1933 | Public | J-T/C | 3,206 | 109 | $ 460 | $1,395 | $1,855 |
| Northwest Nazarene College | Nampa, ID 83651 | 1913 | Nazarene | S-G/C | 1,332 | 78 | $2,325 | $1,470 | $3,795 |
| Ricks College | Rexburg, ID 83440 | 1888 | Mormon | J/C | 6,462 | 235 | $ 920 | $1,750 | $2,670 |
| University of Idaho | Moscow, ID 83843 | 1889 | State | S-G/C | 8,698 | 532 | $ 474 | $1,512 | $1,986 |
| **ILLINOIS** | | | | | | | | | |
| American Academy of Art | Chicago, IL 60604 | 1923 | Ind | J/C | 947 | 26 | $2,700 | — | $2,700 |
| American Conserv. of Music | Chicago, IL 60603 | 1886 | Ind | S-G/C | 1,781 | 135 | $2,850 | $3,900 | $6,750 |
| Augustana College | Rock Island, IL 61201 | 1860 | Lutheran | S/C | 2,404 | 149 | $3,246 | $1,572 | $4,818 |
| Aurora College | Aurora, IL 60507 | 1893 | Adv/Chr | S/C | 1,058 | 85 | $3,360 | $1,899 | $5,259 |
| Barat College | Lake Forest, IL 60045 | 1858 | Ind | S/W | 722 | 70 | $3,250 | $1,680 | $4,930 |
| Belleville Area College | Belleville, IL 62221 | 1946 | State | J/C | 11,008 | 666 | $ 444 | — | $ 444 |
| Bethany Theological Seminary | Oak Brook, IL 60521 | 1905 | Brethren | P/C | 128 | 15 | $1,800 | $ 830 | $2,630 |
| Blackburn College | Carlinville, IL 62626 | 1837 | Presby | S/C | 502 | 49 | $2,670 | $ 830 | $3,550 |
| Black Hawk College | Moline, IL 61265 | 1946 | Public | J/C | 7,949 | 206 | $ 630 | — | $ 630 |
| East Campus | Kewanee, IL 61443 | 1967 | Public | J/C | 802 | 24 | $ 630 | — | $ 630 |
| Bradley University | Peoria, IL 61625 | 1897 | Private | S-G/C | 5,006 | 369 | $3,280 | $1,530 | $4,810 |
| Carl Sandburg College | Galesburg, IL 61401 | 1966 | State | J/C | 3,552 | 108 | $ 420 | — | $ 420 |
| Catholic Theol. Union | Chicago, IL 60615 | 1967 | Catholic | G/C | 259 | 32 | $2,250 | — | $2,250 |
| Central YMCA Comm. College | Chicago, IL 60606 | 1960 | Ind | J/C | 4,401 | 297 | $2,020 | — | $2,020 |
| Chicago Acad. of Fine Arts | Chicago, IL 60601 | 1902 | — | S/C | — | — | — | — | — |
| Chicago Col. of Osteo. Med. | Chicago, IL 60615 | 1900 | Ind | P/C | 389 | 245 | $6,120 | — | $6,120 |
| Chicago State University | Chicago, IL 60628 | 1867 | State | S-G/C | 7,213 | 359 | $ 638 | — | $ 638 |
| Chicago Theol. Seminary | Chicago, IL 60637 | 1855 | C of Chr | G/C | 114 | 10 | $1,850 | $2,445 | $5,650 |
| City Colleges of Chicago | Chicago, IL 60601 | 1911 | State | J/C | 96,898 | 4,053 | $ 450 | — | $ 450 |
| Chicago City-Wide College | Chicago, IL 60601 | 1975 | State | J/C | 10,510 | 171 | $ 450 | — | $ 450 |
| Chicago Urban Skills Inst. | Chicago, IL 60609 | 1970 | State | T/C | 32,500 | 2,000 | | | |
| Daley College | Chicago, IL 60652 | 1960 | State | J/C | 6,703 | 183 | $ 450 | — | $ 450 |
| Kennedy-King College | Chicago, IL 60621 | 1934 | State | J/C | 9,387 | 352 | $ 450 | — | $ 450 |
| Loop College | Chicago, IL 60601 | 1962 | State | J/C | 7,497 | 190 | $ 450 | — | $ 450 |
| Malcolm X College | Chicago, IL 60612 | 1911 | State | J/C | 6,369 | 306 | $ 450 | — | $ 450 |
| Olive-Harvey College | Chicago, IL 60628 | 1957 | State | J/C | 5,743 | 244 | $ 450 | — | $ 450 |
| Truman College | Chicago, IL 60640 | 1956 | State | J/C | 9,022 | 254 | $ 450 | — | $ 450 |
| Wright College | Chicago, IL 60634 | 1934 | State | J/C | 9,167 | 353 | $ 450 | — | $ 450 |
| College of Dupage | Glen Ellyn, IL 60137 | 1966 | State | J/C | 22,193 | 952 | $ 540 | — | $ 540 |
| College of Lake County | Grayslake, IL 60030 | 1967 | State | J/C | 11,345 | 394 | $ 455 | — | $ 455 |
| College of St. Francis | Joliet, IL 60435 | 1930 | Catholic | S/C | 1,424 | 177 | $2,572 | $1,620 | $4,192 |
| Columbia College Chicago | Chicago, IL 60605 | 1890 | Ind | S/C | 3,327 | 350 | $2,650 | — | $2,650 |
| Concordia Teachers College | River Forest, IL 60305 | 1864 | Lutheran | S-G/C | 1,129 | 90 | $2,160 | $1,455 | $3,615 |
| Danville Area Comm. College | Danville, IL 61832 | 1946 | Public | J/C | 4,200 | 180 | $ 435 | — | $ 435 |
| De Lourdes College | Des Plaines, IL 60016 | 1927 | Catholic | S/W | 264 | 26 | $1,050 | — | $1,050 |
| DePaul University | Chicago, IL 60604 | 1898 | Ind | S-G/C | 12,857 | 676 | $3,135 | $2,323 | $5,458 |
| DeVry Institute of Technology | Chicago, IL 60618 | 1931 | Ind | J-S/C | 2,898 | 45 | $3,375 | — | $3,375 |
| Eastern Illinois University | Charleston, IL 61920 | 1895 | State | S-G/C | 9,588 | 483 | $ 790 | $1,407 | $2,197 |
| Elgin Community College | Elgin, IL 60120 | 1949 | State | J/C | 5,169 | 84 | $ 414 | — | $ 414 |
| Elmhurst College | Elmhurst, IL 60126 | 1871 | C of Chr | S/C | 3,360 | 140 | $3,500 | $1,750 | $5,250 |
| Emmaus Bible School | Oak Park, IL 60301 | 1941 | Non-Den | J/C | 170 | 12 | $ 816 | $1,800 | $2,616 |
| Eureka College | Eureka, IL 61530 | 1855 | Ind | S/C | 440 | 32 | $3,050 | $1,850 | $4,900 |
| Felician College | Chicago, IL 60659 | 1953 | Catholic | J/W | 385 | 26 | $1,400 | — | $1,400 |
| Garrett-Evang. Theol. Sem. | Evanston, IL 60201 | 1853 | Meth | G/C | 304 | 34 | $2,400 | $2,000 | $4,400 |
| George Williams College | Downers Grove, IL 60515 | 1890 | Ind | S-G/C | 1,319 | 106 | $3,183 | $1,590 | $5,173 |
| Governors State University | Park Forest S., IL 60466 | 1969 | State | S-G/C | 4,403 | 305 | $ 588 | — | $ 588 |
| Greenville College | Greenville, IL 62246 | 1892 | Meth | S/C | 879 | 68 | $3,708 | $1,720 | $5,428 |
| Hebrew Theol. College | Skokie, IL 60077 | 1922 | Jewish | S-G/C | 194 | 26 | $1,900 | $1,600 | $3,500 |
| Highland Community College | Freeport, IL 61032 | 1962 | State | J/C | 1,637 | 47 | $ 460 | — | |
| Illinois Benedictine College | Lisle, IL 60532 | 1887 | Catholic | S-G/C | 1,671 | 118 | $2,996 | $1,699 | $4,695 |
| Illinois Central College | East Peoria, IL 61635 | 1966 | State | J/C | 12,050 | 602 | $ 384 | — | $ 384 |
| Illinois College | Jacksonville, IL 62650 | 1829 | Presby | S/C | 800 | 52 | $2,305 | $1,395 | $3,700 |
| Illinois Col. of Optometry | Chicago, IL 60616 | 1872 | Ind | P/C | 596 | 73 | $5,089 | $2,418 | $7,507 |
| Ill. Col. of Podiatric Medicine | Chicago, IL 60610 | 1912 | Ind | P/C | 642 | 80 | $6,300 | — | |
| III. Eastern Comm. Colleges | | | | | | | | | |
| Frontier Comm. College | Fairfield, IL 62837 | 1977 | Public | J/C | 2,579 | 202 | $ 90 | — | $ 90 |
| Lincoln Trail College | Robinson, IL 62454 | 1969 | Public | J/C | 1,584 | 102 | $ 135 | — | $ 135 |
| Olney Central College | Olney, IL 62450 | 1963 | Public | J/C | 2,077 | 132 | $ 135 | — | $ 135 |
| Wabash Valley College | Mt. Carmel, IL 62863 | 1960 | Public | J/C | 3,235 | 128 | $ 135 | — | $ 135 |
| III. Inst. of Technology | Chicago, IL 60616 | 1892 | Ind | S-G/C | 7,058 | 575 | $3,690 | $1,800 | $5,490 |
| Chicago-Kent Col. of Law | Chicago, IL 60606 | 1888 | Ind | P/C | 911 | 65 | $3,750 | — | $3,750 |
| Illinois State University | Normal, IL 61761 | 1857 | State | S-G/C | 19,576 | 1,100 | $ 787 | $1,618 | $2,405 |
| Illinois Valley Comm. College | Oglesby, IL 61348 | 1924 | State | J/C | 3,378 | 172 | $ 350 | — | $ 350 |
| Illinois Wesleyan University | Bloomington, IL 61701 | 1850 | Meth | S/C | 1,657 | 124 | $4,380 | $1,885 | $6,265 |
| Jesuit Sch. of Theol. in Chicago | Chicago, IL 60615 | 1934 | Catholic | P/C | 98 | 18 | $2,400 | — | $2,400 |
| John A. Logan College | Carterville, IL 62918 | 1967 | State | J/C | 1,903 | 121 | $ 300 | — | $ 300 |
| John Marshall Law School | Chicago, IL 60604 | 1899 | Ind | P/C | 1,614 | 45 | $3,410 | — | $3,410 |
| Joliet Junior College | Joliet, IL 60436 | 1901 | State | J/C | 9,263 | 251 | $ 442 | — | $ 442 |
| Judson College | Elgin, IL 60120 | 1963 | Baptist | S/C | 486 | 44 | $3,482 | $2,400 | $5,882 |

| NAME | ADDRESS | FOUN-DED | AFFILI-ATION | LEVEL/TYPE | ENROLL-MENT | TEACH-ERS | TUITION & FEES | BOARD & ROOM | TOTAL COST |
|---|---|---|---|---|---|---|---|---|---|
| **ILLINOIS** (continued) | | | | | | | | | |
| Kankakee Community College . | Kankakee, IL 60901 | 1967 | State | J/C | 2,411 | 268 | $ 418 | — | $ 418 |
| Kaskaskia College | Centralia, IL 62801 | 1940 | State | J/C | 2,581 | 170 | $ 270 | — | $ 270 |
| Kendall College | Evanston, IL 60201 | 1934 | Meth | S/C | 376 | 35 | $3,230 | $1,783 | $5,013 |
| Kishwaukee College | Malta, IL 60150 | 1968 | Public | J/C | 3,600 | 185 | $ 498 | — | $ 498 |
| Knox College | Galesburg, IL 61401 | 1837 | Ind | S/C | 1,004 | 904 | $4,384 | $1,640 | $6,024 |
| Lake Forest College | Lake Forest, IL 60045 | 1857 | Presby | S/C | 1,000 | 100 | $4,807 | $1,700 | $6,507 |
| Lake Land College | Mattoon, IL 61938 | 1967 | State | J/C | 3,800 | 175 | $ 588 | — | $ 588 |
| Lewis & Clark Comm. College . | Godfrey, IL 62035 | 1971 | Public | J/C | 5,402 | 192 | $ 432 | — | $ 432 |
| Lewis University | Romeoville, IL 60441 | 1934 | Ind | S-G/C | 2,790 | 160 | $2,990 | $2,880 | $5,870 |
| Lincoln Christian College | Lincoln, IL 62656 | 1944 | Christian | S-G/C | 636 | 40 | $1,838 | $1,105 | $2,943 |
| Lincoln College | Lincoln, IL 62656 | 1865 | Ind | J/C | 491 | 48 | $3,560 | $1,600 | $5,160 |
| Lincoln Land Comm. College . | Springfield, IL 62708 | 1967 | State | J/C | 6,072 | 276 | $ 373 | — | $ 373 |
| Loyola Univ. of Chicago | Chicago, IL 60611 | 1870 | Catholic | S-G/C | 14,909 | 1,370 | $3,100 | $1,850 | $4,950 |
| Niles College | Chicago, IL 60631 | 1961 | Catholic | S/M | 140 | 25 | $2,947 | $1,000 | $3,947 |
| Lutheran Sch. of Theology | Chicago, IL 60615 | 1860 | Lutheran | P/C | 263 | 20 | $1,440 | $2,000 | $3,440 |
| McCormick Theological Sem. | Chicago, IL 60637 | 1829 | Presby | G/C | 692 | 27 | $1,850 | — | $1,850 |
| McHenry County College | Crystal Lake, IL 60014 | 1967 | State | J/C | 3,235 | 165 | $1,800 | — | $1,800 |
| McKendree College | Lebanon, IL 62254 | 1828 | Meth | S/C | 806 | 66 | $2,700 | $1,533 | $4,233 |
| MacCormac College | Chicago, IL 60604 | 1904 | Ind | J/C | 520 | 46 | $2,700 | $1,800 | $4,500 |
| MacMurray College | Jacksonville, IL 62650 | 1846 | Meth | S/C | 686 | 56 | $3,710 | $1,550 | $5,260 |
| Mallinckrodt College | Wilmette, IL 60091 | 1918 | Catholic | J/W | 250 | 25 | $1,650 | — | $1,650 |
| Meadville/Lomb. Theol. Sch. . | Chicago, IL 60637 | 1844 | Unitarian | G/C | 26 | 5 | $3,825 | — | |
| Midwest Col. of Engineering . | Lombard, IL 60148 | 1967 | Ind | S-G/C | 350 | 50 | $3,600 | — | $3,600 |
| Midwest Montessori T. Tr. Cen. | Chicago, IL 60622 | 1963 | Ind | P/C | 60 | 6 | $1,495 | — | $1,495 |
| Millikin University | Decatur, IL 62522 | 1901 | Presby | S/C | 1,568 | 125 | $3,973 | $1,655 | $5,628 |
| Monmouth College | Monmouth, IL 61462 | 1853 | Presby | S/C | 700 | 75 | $3,930 | $1,830 | $5,760 |
| Moody Bible Institute | Chicago, IL 60610 | 1886 | Ind | S/C | 1,363 | 88 | $ 230 | $2,000 | $2,230 |
| Moraine Valley Comm. College | Palos Hills, IL 60465 | 1968 | Public | J/C | 9,973 | 348 | $ 450 | — | $ 450 |
| Morton College | Cicero, IL 60650 | 1924 | State | J/C | 4,000 | 70 | $ 450 | — | $ 450 |
| Mundelein College | Chicago, IL 60660 | 1930 | Catholic | S-G/W | 1,463 | 142 | $3,405 | $1,800 | $5,205 |
| Nat. College of Chiropractic . . | Lombard, IL 60148 | 1906 | Ind | P/C | 1,008 | 70 | $3,200 | — | $3,200 |
| National Col. of Education | Evanston, IL 60201 | 1886 | Ind | S-G/C | 2,800 | 100 | $4,200 | $2,220 | $6,420 |
| Urban Campus | Chicago, IL 60603 | 1886 | Ind | S/C | 204 | 40 | $3,450 | — | $3,450 |
| Native Am. Ed. Services | Chicago, IL 60640 | 1975 | Ind | S/C | 38 | 8 | $3,000 | — | $3,000 |
| North Central College | Naperville, IL 60540 | 1861 | Meth | S/C | 1,111 | 74 | $3,360 | $1,650 | $5,010 |
| North Park College | Chicago, IL 60625 | 1891 | Evang | S/C | 1,168 | 120 | $3,387 | $1,680 | $5,067 |
| Northeastern Illinois Univ. | Chicago, IL 60625 | 1961 | State | S-G/C | 10,061 | 456 | $ 682 | — | $ 682 |
| Northern Baptist Theol. Sem. | Lombard, IL 60148 | 1913 | Baptist | G/C | 185 | 25 | $1,845 | $1,470 | $3,315 |
| Northern Illinois University | DeKalb, IL 60115 | 1895 | State | S-G/C | 25,259 | 1,268 | $ 846 | $1,640 | $2,486 |
| Northwestern University | Evanston, IL 60201 | 1851 | Ind | S-G/C | 15,429 | 1,500 | $5,985 | $2,330 | $8,315 |
| Oakton Community College | Morton Grove, IL 60053 | 1969 | Public | J/C | 6,301 | 303 | $ 400 | — | $ 400 |
| Olivet Nazarene College | Kankakee, IL 60901 | 1907 | Nazarene | S-G/C | 2,000 | 100 | $2,576 | $1,504 | $4,080 |
| Parkland College | Champaign, IL 61820 | 1966 | State | J/C | 7,200 | 145 | $ 442 | — | $ 442 |
| Parks Col. of St. Louis Univ. . | Cahokia, IL 62206 | 1927 | Catholic | S/C | 958 | 57 | $2,560 | $1,710 | $4,270 |
| Prairie State College | Chicago Hgts, IL 60411 | 1958 | State | J/C | 5,721 | 280 | $ 560 | — | $ 560 |
| Principia College | Elsah, IL 62028 | 1910 | Ind | S/C | 850 | 75 | $4,239 | $2,400 | $6,639 |
| Quincy College | Quincy, IL 62301 | 1859 | Catholic | S/C | 1,715 | 87 | $3,048 | $1,650 | $4,698 |
| Reid College of Detection | Chicago, IL 60601 | 1947 | Ind | G/C | 15 | 8 | $2,400 | — | $2,400 |
| Rend Lake College | Ina, IL 62846 | 1967 | State | J/C | 3,219 | 65 | $ 416 | — | $ 416 |
| Richland Community College . | Decatur, IL 62526 | 1971 | Public | J/C | 2,587 | 130 | $ 465 | — | $ 465 |
| Robert Morris College | Carthage, IL 62321 | 1965 | Ind | J/C | 484 | 25 | $2,935 | $2,340 | $5,275 |
| Chicago Branch | Chicago, IL 60601 | 1965 | Ind | J/C | 696 | 26 | $2,935 | — | $2,935 |
| Rock Valley College | Rockford, IL 61101 | 1964 | State | J/C | 8,008 | 549 | $ 480 | — | $ 480 |
| Rockford College | Rockford, IL 61101 | 1964 | Ind | S/C | 1,453 | 117 | $3,275 | $1,593 | $4,868 |
| Roosevelt University | Chicago, IL 60605 | 1945 | Ind | S-G/C | 6,782 | 471 | $3,000 | $2,100 | $5,100 |
| Rosary College | River Forest, IL 60305 | 1918 | Catholic | S-G/C | 1,575 | 136 | $3,440 | $2,000 | $5,440 |
| St. Xavier College | Chicago, IL 60655 | 1847 | Catholic | S-G/C | 2,133 | 168 | $2,890 | -$1,734 | $4,624 |
| Sangamon State University | Springfield, IL 62708 | 1969 | State | S-G/C | 3,518 | 207 | $ 700 | $2,330 | $3,030 |
| Sauk Valley College | Dixon, IL 61021 | 1965 | Public | J/C | 4,200 | 65 | $ 540 | — | $ 540 |
| Sch. of the Art Inst. of Chicago | Chicago, IL 60603 | 1866 | Ind | S-G/C | 1,119 | 160 | $3,816 | — | $3,956 |
| Seabury-Western Theol. Sem. . | Evanston, IL 60201 | 1933 | Episc | G/C | 65 | 11 | $2,500 | $1,600 | $4,100 |
| Sherwood Music School | Chicago, IL 60605 | 1895 | Ind | S/C | 126 | 18 | $2,200 | — | $4,500 |
| Southeastern Illinois College . . | Harrisburg, IL 62946 | 1960 | State | J/C | 1,708 | 183 | $ 224 | — | $ 224 |
| Southern Illinois University | Carbondale, IL 62901 | 1869 | State | S-G/C | 22,695 | 1,623 | $ 857 | $1,598 | $2,455 |
| So. Ill. Univ. at Edwardsville | Edwardsville, IL 62026 | 1957 | State | S-G/C | 10,475 | 582 | $ 790 | $1,800 | $2,590 |
| Spertus College of Judaica | Chicago, IL 60605 | 1925 | Ind | S-G/C | 385 | 23 | $2,710 | — | $2,710 |
| Spoon River College | Canton, IL 61520 | 1959 | Public | J/C | 2,443 | 100 | $ 640 | — | $ 640 |
| Springfield College in Illinois | Springfield, IL 62702 | 1929 | Catholic | J/C | 517 | 47 | $2,100 | — | $3,300 |
| State Community College | St. Louis, IL 62201 | 1969 | State | J/C | 1,884 | 86 | $ 275 | — | $ 275 |
| Thornton Community College . | South Holland, IL 60473 | 1927 | State | J/C | 10,000 | 182 | $ 624 | — | $ 624 |
| Trinity Christian College | Palos Heights, IL 60463 | 1959 | Ind | S/C | 389 | 34 | $2,550 | $2,250 | $4,800 |
| Trinity College | Deerfield, IL 60015 | 1897 | Ind | S/C | 780 | 59 | $3,040 | $1,560 | $4,600 |
| Triton College | River Grove, IL 60171 | 1964 | State | J/C | 22,350 | 230 | $ 470 | — | $ 470 |
| University of Chicago | Chicago, IL 60637 | 1891 | Private | S-G/C | 7,884 | 1,040 | $4,500 | $2,538 | $7,038 |
| University of Illinois | Urbana, IL 61801 | 1867 | State | S-G/C | — | — | — | — | — |
| Chicago Circle Campus | Chicago, IL 60680 | 1965 | State | S-G/C | 20,285 | 1,097 | $ 885 | — | $1,860 |
| Medical Center Campus | Chicago, IL 60680 | 1896 | State | G/C | 4,923 | 3,988 | $1,044 | $2,660 | $4,844 |
| Urbana Champaign Campus | Urbana, IL 61801 | 1867 | State | S-G/C | 34,376 | 2,416 | $ 916 | $1,898 | $3,824 |
| Vandercook College of Music . | Chicago, IL 60616 | 1928 | Ind | S-G/C | 122 | 20 | $2,500 | $1,760 | $4,260 |
| Waubonsee Community Col. . | Sugar Grove, IL 60554 | 1966 | State | J/C | 5,280 | 246 | $ 390 | — | $ 390 |
| Western Illinois University | Macomb, IL 61455 | 1899 | State | S-G/C | 13,006 | 742 | $ 756 | $1,513 | $2,269 |
| Wheaton College | Wheaton, IL 60187 | 1860 | Ind | S-G/C | 2,486 | 207 | $3,534 | $2,070 | $5,604 |
| William Rainey Harper College | Palatine, IL 60067 | 1965 | State | J/C | 20,152 | 829 | $ 549 | — | $ 549 |
| Worsham College | Chicago, IL 60610 | 1911 | Ind | T/C | 150 | 7 | $2,050 | — | $2,050 |

| NAME | ADDRESS | FOUN-DED | AFFILI-ATION | LEVEL/TYPE | ENROLL-MENT | TEACH-ERS | TUITION & FEES | BOARD & ROOM | TOTAL COST |
|---|---|---|---|---|---|---|---|---|---|
| **INDIANA** | | | | | | | | | |
| Ancilla College | Donaldson, IN 46513 | 1937 | Catholic | J/C | 303 | 23 | $ 885 | — | $ 885 |
| Anderson College | Anderson, IN 46011 | 1917 | C of God | S-G/C | 1,898 | 150 | $3,200 | $1,310 | $4,510 |
| Ball State University | Muncie, IN 47306 | 1918 | State | S-G/C | 17,557 | 890 | $ 900 | $1,350 | $2,250 |
| Bethel College | Mishawaka, IN 46544 | 1947 | Mission | S/C | 464 | 30 | $2,625 | $1,350 | $3,975 |
| Butler University | Indianapolis, IN 46208 | 1855 | Ind | S-G/C | 3,507 | 263 | $3,400 | $1,580 | $4,980 |
| Calumet College | Whiting, IN 46394 | 1951 | Catholic | S/C | 1,470 | 71 | $1,313 | — | $1,313 |
| Christian Theol. Seminary | Indianapolis, IN 46208 | 1924 | D of Chr | G/C | 299 | 17 | $1,400 | — | $1,400 |
| Concordia Theol. Seminary | Fort Wayne, IN 46825 | 1846 | Lutheran | G/M | 589 | 32 | $1,530 | $1,500 | $3,030 |
| DePauw University | Greencastle, IN 46135 | 1837 | Meth | S-G/C | 2,306 | 191 | $4,272 | $1,800 | $6,072 |
| Earlham College | Richmond, IN 47374 | 1847 | Friends | S/C | 1,015 | 109 | $4,329 | $1,610 | $5,939 |
| Elkhart Inst. of Technology | Elkhart, IN 46514 | 1882 | Ind | T/C | 125 | 5 | $1,625 | $1,400 | $3,025 |
| Fort Wayne Bible College | Fort Wayne, IN 46807 | 1904 | Mission | S/C | 473 | 36 | $2,300 | $1,500 | $3,800 |
| Franklin Col. of Indiana | Franklin, IN 46131 | 1834 | Baptist | S/C | 653 | 63 | $3,820 | $1,675 | $5,495 |
| Goshen Biblical Seminary | Elkhart, IN 46514 | 1946 | Mennon | G/C | 128 | 10 | $1,380 | $1,662 | $3,042 |
| Goshen College | Goshen, IN 46526 | 1894 | Mennon | S/C | 1,314 | 110 | $2,945 | $1,360 | $4,305 |
| Grace College | Winona Lake, IN 46590 | 1948 | Brethren | S/C | 804 | 56 | $2,480 | $1,555 | $4,035 |
| Hanover College | Hanover, IN 47243 | 1827 | Presby | S/C | 998 | 70 | $2,895 | $1,465 | $4,160 |
| Herron School of Art | Indianapolis, IN 46202 | 1902 | State | S/C | 356 | 42 | $ 780 | — | $2,630 |
| Holy Cross Junior College | Notre Dame, IN 46556 | 1966 | Catholic | J/C | 285 | 21 | $1,150 | — | $1,150 |
| Huntington College | Huntington, IN 46750 | 1897 | Brethren | S-G/C | 559 | 52 | $2,766 | $1,497 | $4,409 |
| Indiana Central University | Indianapolis, IN 46227 | 1902 | Meth | S-G/C | 3,144 | 210 | $2,880 | $1,480 | $4,360 |
| Indiana Inst. of Technology | Fort Wayne, IN 46803 | 1930 | Ind | S/C | 527 | 36 | $2,565 | $1,680 | $4,245 |
| Ind. N. Grad. Sch./Prof. Mgmt. | Marion, IN 46952 | 1963 | Ind | G/C | 55 | 10 | $1,780 | — | $1,780 |
| Indiana State University | Terre Haute, IN 47809 | 1865 | State | S-G/C | 12,056 | 667 | $ 990 | $1,325 | $2,315 |
| Ind. State Univ. Evansville | Evansville, IN 47712 | 1965 | State | S/C | 3,018 | 167 | $ 821 | — | — |
| Indiana University | Bloomington, IN 47405 | 1820 | State | S-G/C | 76,394 | 3,267 | — | — | — |
| Bloomington | Bloomington, IN 47405 | 1820 | State | S-G/C | 31,840 | 1,453 | $ 938 | $1,398 | $2,336 |
| East | Richmond, IN 47374 | 1971 | State | J/C | 1,438 | 25 | $ 780 | — | $ 780 |
| Kokomo | Kokomo, IN 46901 | 1945 | State | S/C | 2,344 | 57 | $ 780 | — | $ 780 |
| Northwest | Gary, IN 46408 | 1948 | State | S-G/C | 4,056 | 130 | $ 780 | — | $ 780 |
| Purdue Univ. at Fort Wayne | Fort Wayne, IN 46805 | 1964 | State | S-G/C | 5,402 | 148 | $ 788 | — | $ 788 |
| Purdue Univ. at Indianapolis | Indianapolis, IN 46202 | 1969 | State | S-G/C | 21,453 | 1,221 | $ 780 | — | $ 780 |
| South Bend | South Bend, IN 46615 | 1941 | State | S-G/C | 5,800 | 147 | $ 780 | — | $ 780 |
| Southeast | New Albany, IN 47150 | 1941 | State | S-G/C | 4,061 | 186 | $ 780 | — | $ 780 |
| Indiana Vocational Tech. Col. | Indianapolis, IN 46206 | 1963 | State | J/C | — | — | — | — | — |
| Central Indiana | Indianapolis, IN 46202 | 1966 | State | J/C | 2,362 | 215 | $ 795 | — | $ 795 |
| Columbus | Columbus, IN 47201 | 1967 | State | J/C | 875 | 61 | $ 795 | — | $ 795 |
| Eastcentral | Muncie, IN 47302 | 1968 | State | J/C | 1,190 | 132 | $ 795 | — | $ 795 |
| Kokomo | Kokomo, IN 46901 | 1968 | State | J/C | 962 | 90 | $ 795 | — | $ 795 |
| Lafayette | Lafayette, IN 47903 | 1968 | State | J/C | 567 | 57 | $ 795 | — | $ 795 |
| Northcentral | South Bend, IN 46619 | 1967 | State | J/C | 1,116 | 106 | $ 795 | — | $ 795 |
| Northeast | Fort Wayne, IN 46805 | 1968 | State | J/C | 1,090 | 125 | $ 795 | — | $ 795 |
| Northwest | Gary, IN 46409 | 1968 | State | J/C | 1,101 | 128 | $ 795 | — | $ 795 |
| Southcentral | Sellersburg, IN 47172 | 1968 | State | J/C | 717 | 74 | $ 795 | — | $ 795 |
| Southeast | Madison, IN 47250 | 1968 | State | J/C | 235 | 29 | $ 795 | — | $ 795 |
| Southwest | Evansville, IN 47710 | 1968 | State | J/C | 800 | 101 | $ 795 | — | $ 795 |
| Wabash Valley | Terre Haute, IN 47802 | 1966 | State | J/C | 785 | 72 | $ 795 | — | $ 795 |
| Whitewater | Richmond, IN 47374 | 1968 | State | J/C | 529 | 61 | $ 795 | — | $ 795 |
| International Business College | Fort Wayne, IN 46804 | 1889 | Ind | J/C | 400 | 20 | $2,750 | $1,900 | $4,650 |
| Manchester College | No. Manchester, IN 46962 | 1889 | Brethren | S-G/C | 1,207 | 95 | $3,145 | $1,525 | $4,670 |
| Marian College | Indianapolis, IN 46222 | 1851 | Catholic | S/C | 800 | 77 | $2,380 | $1,400 | $3,780 |
| Marion College | Marion, IN 46952 | 1920 | Wesleyan | S/C | 1,103 | 82 | $3,148 | $1,642 | $4,790 |
| Mennonite Biblical Seminary | Elkhart, IN 46514 | 1945 | Mennon | G/C | 83 | 19 | $1,380 | $1,530 | $2,910 |
| Nat. Col. of Bus.—Indianapolis | Indianapolis, IN 46205 | 1974 | Private | S/C | 36 | 6 | $2,500 | — | $2,500 |
| Northwood Inst. of Indiana | West Baden, IN 47469 | 1967 | Ind | J/C | 161 | 12 | $2,710 | $1,515 | $4,225 |
| Oakland City College | Oakland City, IN 47660 | 1885 | Baptist | S/C | 545 | 35 | $2,500 | $1,500 | $4,000 |
| Purdue University | West Lafayette, IN 47907 | 1869 | State | S-G/C | 41,948 | 2,824 | $ 933 | $1,700 | $2,633 |
| Calumet | Hammond, IN 46323 | 1869 | State | S-G/C | 6,630 | 367 | $ 926 | — | $ 926 |
| North Central Campus | Westville, IN 46391 | 1946 | State | S-G/C | 2,025 | 55 | $ 900 | — | $ 900 |
| Rose-Hulman Inst. of Tech. | Terre Haute, IN 47803 | 1874 | Ind | S/M | 1,220 | 75 | $3,216 | $1,400 | $4,616 |
| St. Francis College | Fort Wayne, IN 46808 | 1890 | Catholic | S/C | 1,364 | 85 | $1,956 | $1,600 | $3,556 |
| St. Joseph's College | Rensselaer, IN 47978 | 1889 | Catholic | S/C | 948 | 63 | $2,700 | $1,520 | $4,220 |
| St. Mary-of-The-Woods College | St. Mary/Woods, IN 47876 | 1840 | Catholic | S/W | 648 | 72 | $3,065 | $1,575 | $4,640 |
| St. Mary's College | Notre Dame, IN 46556 | 1844 | Catholic | S/W | 1,817 | 164 | $3,964 | $2,020 | $5,984 |
| St. Meinrad College | St. Meinrad, IN 47577 | 1861 | Catholic | S/M | 203 | 37 | $1,700 | $1,717 | $3,417 |
| Taylor University | Upland, IN 46989 | 1846 | Ind | S/C | 1,585 | 91 | $3,698 | $1,677 | $5,375 |
| Tri-State University | Angola, IN 46703 | 1884 | Ind | S/C | 1,281 | 69 | $2,757 | $1,440 | $4,833 |
| Union Bible Seminary | Westfield, IN 46074 | 1911 | Int-Den | S/C | 20 | 8 | $ 693 | $1,089 | $1,782 |
| University of Evansville | Evansville, IN 47702 | 1854 | Meth | S-G/C | 4,898 | 299 | $3,303 | $1,731 | $5,034 |
| University of Notre Dame | Notre Dame, IN 46556 | 1842 | Catholic | S-G/C | 8,768 | 683 | $4,175 | $1,535 | $5,710 |
| Valparaiso Technical Institute | Valparaiso, IN 46383 | 1874 | Private | T/C | 180 | 12 | $2,060 | $2,070 | $4,130 |
| Valparaiso University | Valparaiso, IN 46383 | 1859 | Lutheran | S-G/C | 4,534 | 332 | $3,672 | $1,670 | $5,342 |
| Vincennes University | Vincennes, IN 47591 | 1801 | State | J/C | 4,661 | 265 | $ 751 | $1,376 | $2,127 |
| Wabash College | Crawfordsville, IN 47933 | 1832 | Ind | S/M | 800 | 72 | $4,100 | $1,925 | $6,025 |
| **IOWA** | | | | | | | | | |
| American Institute of Business | Des Moines, IA 50321 | 1921 | Ind | J/C | 961 | 40 | $1,875 | $1,680 | $3,555 |
| Briar Cliff College | Sioux City, IA 51104 | 1930 | Catholic | S/C | 1,258 | 67 | $2,860 | $1,416 | $4,276 |
| Buena Vista College | Storm Lake, IA 50588 | 1891 | Presby | S/C | 1,283 | 48 | $3,710 | $1,470 | $5,180 |
| Central University of Iowa | Pella, IA 50219 | 1853 | Ref | S/C | 1,500 | 80 | $3,329 | $1,296 | $4,625 |
| Clarke College | Dubuque, IA 52001 | 1843 | Catholic | S-G/C | 666 | 72 | $2,735 | $1,525 | $4,270 |
| Clinton Community College | Clinton, IA 52732 | 1946 | State | J/C | 941 | 51 | $ 490 | — | $ 490 |
| Coe College | Cedar Rapids, IA 52402 | 1851 | Presby | S/C | 1,320 | 93 | $3,890 | $1,500 | $5,390 |
| Col. of Osteo. Med. & Surg. | Des Moines, IA 50312 | 1898 | Ind | P/C | 538 | 50 | $8,000 | — | — |

| NAME | ADDRESS | FOUN-DED | AFFILI-ATION | LEVEL/TYPE | ENROLL-MENT | TEACH-ERS | TUITION & FEES | BOARD & ROOM | TOTAL COST |
|---|---|---|---|---|---|---|---|---|---|
| **IOWA** *(continued)* | | | | | | | | | |
| Cornell College | Mt. Vernon, IA 52314 | 1853 | Meth | S/C | 898 | 67 | $4,040 | $1,480 | $5,520 |
| Des Moines Area Comm. Col. | Ankeny, IA 50021 | 1966 | State | J/C | 5,629 | 217 | $ 450 | — | $ 450 |
| Boone Campus | Boone, IA 50036 | 1927 | State | J/C | 605 | 45 | $ 450 | — | $2,080 |
| Divine Word College | Epworth, IA 52045 | 1912 | Catholic | S/M | 94 | 23 | $2,700 | $1,000 | $3,700 |
| Dordt College | Sioux Center, IA 51250 | 1955 | Ref | S/C | 1,218 | 70 | $2,600 | $1,130 | $3,730 |
| Drake University | Des Moines, IA 50311 | 1881 | Ind | S-G/C | 6,502 | 347 | $4,060 | $1,030 | $5,090 |
| Ellsworth Community College | Iowa Falls, IA 50126 | 1890 | State | J/C | 776 | 50 | $ 580 | $1,390 | $1,970 |
| Faith Baptist Bible College | Ankeny, IA 50021 | 1924 | Baptist | S/C | 530 | 25 | $ 846 | $ 780 | $1,626 |
| Graceland College | Lamoni, IA 50140 | 1895 | Lat. Day | S/C | 1,343 | 82 | $3,245 | $1,475 | $4,720 |
| Grand View College | Des Moines, IA 50316 | 1896 | Lutheran | S/C | 1,149 | 84 | $2,240 | $1,400 | $3,440 |
| Grinnell College | Grinnell, IA 50112 | 1846 | Private | S/C | 1,236 | 105 | $5,285 | $1,480 | $6,765 |
| Hawkeye Inst. of Technology | Waterloo, IA 50704 | 1966 | State | T/C | 1,850 | 120 | $ 507 | — | $3,500 |
| Indian Hills Comm. College | Ottumwa, IA 52501 | 1966 | State | J/C | 1,400 | 120 | $ 670 | $1,100 | $1,780 |
| Centerville Campus | Centerville, IA 52544 | 1966 | State | J/C | 2,513 | 25 | $ 670 | — | $ 670 |
| Iowa Central Comm. College | Fort Dodge, IA 50501 | 1966 | State | J/C | 2,662 | 110 | $ 500 | $1,350 | $1,850 |
| Iowa Lakes Comm. College | Estherville, IA 51334 | 1967 | State | J/C | 1,605 | 87 | $ 505 | — | $ 505 |
| Iowa State University | Ames, IA 50011 | 1858 | State | S-G/C | 23,486 | 1,814 | $ 816 | $1,467 | $2,283 |
| Iowa Wesleyan College | Mt. Pleasant, IA 52641 | 1842 | Meth | S/C | 730 | 80 | $3,257 | $1,265 | $4,522 |
| Iowa Western Comm. College | Clarinda, IA 51632 | 1966 | State | J/C | 331 | 17 | $ 740 | $1,000 | $1,740 |
| Iowa Western Comm. College | Council Bluffs, IA 51501 | 1966 | State | J/C | 2,040 | 102 | $ 740 | $1,140 | $1,880 |
| Kirkwood Comm. College | Cedar Rapids, IA 52406 | 1966 | State | J/C | 4,744 | 222 | $ 534 | — | $ 534 |
| Loras College | Dubuque, IA 52001 | 1839 | Catholic | S-G/C | 1,771 | 112 | $2,800 | $1,507 | $4,307 |
| Luther College | Decorah, IA 52101 | 1861 | Lutheran | S/C | 2,072 | 149 | $4,250 | $1,300 | $5,550 |
| Marshalltown Comm. College | Marshalltown, IA 50158 | 1927 | State | J/C | 1,096 | 55 | $ 500 | — | $ 500 |
| Marycrest College | Davenport, IA 52804 | 1939 | Catholic | S-G/C | 1,199 | 79 | $2,925 | $1,520 | $4,445 |
| Morningside College | Sioux City, IA 51106 | 1894 | Meth | S-G/C | 1,630 | 87 | $3,200 | $1,180 | $4,380 |
| Mount Mercy College | Cedar Rapids, IA 52402 | 1928 | Catholic | S/C | 1,042 | 85 | $3,115 | $1,600 | $4,715 |
| Mount St. Clare College | Clinton, IA 52732 | 1928 | Catholic | J/C | 322 | 36 | $1,650 | $1,610 | $3,260 |
| Muscatine Comm. College | Muscatine, IA 52761 | 1929 | State | J/C | 800 | 35 | $ 500 | — | $ 500 |
| North Iowa Area Comm. Col. | Mason City, IA 50401 | 1918 | State | J/C | 1,927 | 125 | $ 555 | $1,500 | $2,055 |
| Northeast Iowa Tech. Institute | Calmar, IA 52132 | 1966 | Public | T/C | 1,092 | 87 | $ 680 | $2,000 | $2,680 |
| Northwest Iowa Tech. College | Sheldon, IA 51201 | 1966 | State | T/C | 434 | 43 | $ 632 | — | — |
| Northwestern College | Orange City, IA 51041 | 1882 | Ref | S/C | 861 | 73 | $3,220 | $1,310 | $4,530 |
| Palmer Col. of Chiropractic | Davenport, IA 52803 | 1895 | Ind | P/C | 1,832 | 120 | $3,400 | — | $3,400 |
| St. Ambrose College | Davenport, IA 52803 | 1882 | Catholic | S-G/C | 1,955 | 187 | $3,300 | $1,850 | $5,150 |
| Scott Community College | Bettendorf, IA 52722 | 1966 | State | T/C | 1,812 | 100 | $ 880 | — | $ 880 |
| Palmer Campus | Davenport, IA 52803 | 1965 | State | J/C | 960 | 60 | $ 500 | — | $ 500 |
| Simpson College | Indianola, IA 50125 | 1860 | Meth | S/C | 830 | 73 | $3,985 | $1,455 | $5,440 |
| Sioux Empire College | Hawarden, IA 51023 | 1967 | Ind | J/C | 400 | 40 | $2,250 | $1,300 | $3,550 |
| Southeastern Comm. College | W. Burlington, IA 52655 | 1966 | State | J/C | 2,222 | 98 | $ 501 | — | $ 501 |
| Southwestern Comm. College | Creston, IA 50801 | 1966 | State | J/C | 535 | 41 | $ 554 | $1,400 | $1,954 |
| University of Dubuque | Dubuque, IA 52001 | 1852 | Presby | S/C | 1,039 | 45 | $3,100 | $1,800 | $4,900 |
| University of Iowa | Iowa City, IA 52242 | 1847 | State | S-G/C | 23,349 | 1,502 | $ 830 | $1,676 | $2,506 |
| University of Northern Iowa | Cedar Falls, IA 50613 | 1876 | State | S-G/C | 12,108 | 635 | $ 774 | $1,340 | $2,114 |
| Upper Iowa University | Fayette, IA 52142 | 1857 | Ind | S/C | 520 | 36 | $3,110 | $1,360 | $4,470 |
| Vennard College | University Park, IA 52595 | 1910 | Ind | S/C | 221 | 17 | $1,512 | $1,388 | $2,900 |
| Waldorf College | Forest City, IA 50436 | 1903 | Lutheran | J/C | 514 | 39 | $1,450 | $ 746 | $2,196 |
| Wartburg College | Waverly, IA 50677 | 1852 | Lutheran | S/C | 1,098 | 81 | $3,574 | $1,580 | $5,154 |
| Wartburg Theological Sem. | Dubuque, IA 52001 | 1854 | Lutheran | P/C | 267 | 20 | $ 900 | $1,295 | $2,195 |
| Western Iowa Tech. Comm. Col | Sioux City, IA 51102 | 1967 | State | J/C | 1,400 | 100 | $ 600 | — | $ 600 |
| Westmar College | LeMars, IA 51031 | 1890 | Meth | S/C | 654 | 47 | $2,870 | $1,390 | $4,260 |
| William Penn College | Oskaloosa, IA 52577 | 1873 | Friends | S/C | 583 | 43 | $4,100 | $1,380 | $5,480 |
| **KANSAS** | | | | | | | | | |
| Allen County Comm. Jr. Col. | Iola, KS 66749 | 1923 | State | J/C | 970 | 60 | $ 310 | $1,120 | $1,430 |
| Baker University | Baldwin City, KS 66006 | 1858 | Meth | S-G/C | 977 | 80 | $2,665 | $1,490 | $4,155 |
| Barton Co. Comm. College | Great Bend, KS 67530 | 1965 | State | J/C | 3,029 | 178 | $ 350 | $1,350 | $1,700 |
| Benedictine College | Atchison, KS 66002 | 1858 | Catholic | S/C | 1,045 | 85 | $2,800 | $1,600 | $4,400 |
| Bethany College | Lindsborg, KS 67456 | 1881 | Lutheran | S/C | 914 | 70 | $2,434 | $1,571 | $4,005 |
| Bethel College | North Newton, KS 67117 | 1887 | Mennon | S/C | 681 | 69 | $2,458 | $1,487 | $3,945 |
| Butler County Comm. College | El Dorado, KS 67042 | 1927 | State | J/C | 1,938 | 117 | $ 435 | $1,400 | $1,835 |
| Central Baptist Theol. Sem. | Kansas City, KS 66102 | 1901 | Baptist | P/C | 102 | 11 | $1,200 | $1,250 | $2,450 |
| Central College | McPherson, KS 67460 | 1884 | Meth | J/C | 251 | 27 | $2,550 | $1,400 | $3,950 |
| Cloud County Comm. College | Concordia, KS 66901 | 1965 | State | J/C | 1,768 | 87 | $ 375 | $1,925 | $2,500 |
| Coffeyville Comm. Jr. College | Coffeyville, KS 67337 | 1923 | State | J/C | 1,603 | 59 | $ 320 | $1,060 | $1,380 |
| Colby Community College | Colby, KS 67701 | 1964 | State | J/C | 1,975 | 77 | $ 460 | $1,300 | $1,700 |
| Cowley County Comm. College | Arkansas City, KS 67005 | 1922 | County | J/C | 1,641 | 41 | $ 360 | $1,200 | $1,560 |
| Dodge City Comm. College | Dodge City, KS 67801 | 1935 | State | J/C | 1,530 | 70 | $ 430 | $1,260 | $1,690 |
| Donnelly College | Kansas City, KS 66102 | 1949 | Catholic | J/C | 495 | 35 | $ 870 | — | $ 870 |
| Emporia State University | Emporia, KS 66801 | 1863 | State | S-G/C | 6,429 | 237 | $ 548 | $1,492 | $2,040 |
| Fort Hays State University | Hays, KS 67601 | 1902 | State | S-G/C | 5,453 | 241 | $ 638 | $1,350 | $1,988 |
| Fort Scott Comm. Jr. College | Fort Scott, KS 66701 | 1919 | State | J/C | 1,250 | 50 | $ 300 | $1,238 | $1,538 |
| Friends Bible College | Haviland, KS 67059 | 1917 | Friends | S/C | 167 | 17 | $2,650 | $1,400 | $4,050 |
| Friends University | Wichita, KS 67213 | 1898 | Ind | S/C | 909 | 72 | $2,540 | $1,295 | $3,835 |
| Garden City Comm. College | Garden City, KS 67846 | 1919 | State | J/C | 1,903 | 64 | $ 465 | $1,350 | $1,815 |
| Haskell Indian Jr. College | Lawrence, KS 66044 | 1884 | Federal | J/C | 951 | 54 | — | — | — |
| Hesston College | Hesston, KS 67062 | 1909 | Mennon | J/C | 668 | 66 | $2,640 | $1,560 | $4,200 |
| Highland Comm. Jr. College | Highland, KS 66035 | 1858 | Public | J/C | 1,489 | 51 | $ 440 | $1,150 | $1,590 |
| Hutchinson Comm. Jr. College | Hutchinson, KS 67501 | 1928 | State | J/C | 2,511 | 120 | $ 422 | $1,296 | $1,718 |
| Independence Comm. College | Independence, KS 67301 | 1925 | State | J/C | 1,103 | 71 | $ 360 | $2,100 | $2,460 |
| Johnson County Comm. Col. | Overland Park, KS 66210 | 1967 | County | J/C | 5,908 | 259 | $ 465 | — | $ 465 |
| Kansas City Kans. Comm. Col. | Kansas City, KS 66112 | 1923 | State | J/C | 2,830 | 135 | $ 400 | — | $ 400 |
| Kansas Newman College | Wichita, KS 67213 | 1933 | Catholic | S/C | 660 | 65 | $2,340 | $1,490 | $3,830 |
| Kansas State University | Manhattan, KS 66506 | 1863 | State | S-G/C | 18,619 | 1,200 | $1,396 | $ 764 | $2,160 |
| Kansas Technical Institute | Salina, KS 67401 | 1965 | State | T/C | 425 | 27 | $ 345 | $1,250 | $1,595 |

| NAME | ADDRESS | FOUN-DED | AFFILI-ATION | LEVEL/TYPE | ENROLL-MENT | TEACH-ERS | TUITION & FEES | BOARD & ROOM | TOTAL COST |
|---|---|---|---|---|---|---|---|---|---|
| **KANSAS** *(continued)* | | | | | | | | | |
| Kansas Wesleyan | Salina, KS 67401 | 1886 | Meth | S/C | 432 | 40 | $2,614 | $1,486 | $4,100 |
| Labette Comm. Jr. College | Parsons, KS 67357 | 1923 | County | J/C | 1,002 | 32 | $ 330 | — | $ 330 |
| McPherson College | McPherson, KS 67460 | 1887 | Brethren | S/C | 480 | 41 | $2,800 | $1,590 | $4,390 |
| Manhattan Christian College | Manhattan, KS 66502 | 1927 | Christian | S/C | 281 | 16 | $1,448 | $1,700 | $3,148 |
| Marymount College of Kansas | Salina, KS 67401 | 1922 | Catholic | S/C | 787 | 72 | $2,140 | $1,360 | $3,500 |
| Mid-America Nazarene College | Olathe, KS 66061 | 1966 | Nazarene | S/C | 1,292 | 70 | $1,860 | $1,450 | $3,310 |
| National College of Business | Shawnee Msn., KS 66201 | 1975 | Private | S/C | 60 | 4 | $2,500 | — | $2,500 |
| Neosho Cnty. Comm. Jr. Col. | Chanute, KS 66720 | 1936 | State | J/C | 732 | 49 | $ 310 | $1,200 | $1,510 |
| Ottawa University | Ottawa, KS 66067 | 1865 | Baptist | S/C | 550 | 45 | $2,800 | $1,100 | $3,900 |
| Pittsburg State University | Pittsburg, KS 66762 | 1903 | State | S-G/C | 5,560 | 318 | $ 510 | $1,460 | $1,970 |
| Pratt Community College | Pratt, KS 67124 | 1938 | State | J/C | 1,110 | 113 | $ 410 | $1,500 | $1,910 |
| St. John's College | Winfield, KS 67156 | 1893 | Lutheran | J/C | 223 | 26 | $2,425 | $1,500 | $3,925 |
| St. Mary College | Leavenworth, KS 66048 | 1923 | Catholic | S/W | 798 | 71 | $2,160 | $1,400 | $3,560 |
| St. Mary of the Plains College | Dodge City, KS 67801 | 1952 | Catholic | S/C | 661 | 48 | $2,270 | $1,400 | $3,670 |
| Seward County Comm. College | Liberal, KS 67901 | 1967 | Local | J/C | 1,402 | 49 | $ 360 | $1,430 | $1,790 |
| Southwestern College in Kansas | Winfield, KS 67156 | 1885 | Meth | S/C | 656 | 55 | $2,475 | $1,566 | $4,041 |
| Sterling College | Sterling, KS 67579 | 1887 | Presby | S/C | 507 | 50 | $2,770 | $1,430 | $4,200 |
| Tabor College | Hillsboro, KS 67063 | 1908 | Mennon | S/C | 445 | 45 | $2,670 | $1,670 | $4,340 |
| University of Kansas | Lawrence, KS 66045 | 1866 | State | S-G/C | 24,125 | 1,000 | $ 770 | $1,500 | $2,270 |
| Col. of Health Sciences | Kansas City, KS 66103 | 1906 | State | G/C | 2,353 | 524 | — | — | — |
| Washburn Univ. of Topeka | Topeka, KS 66621 | 1865 | City | S-G/C | 5,763 | 304 | $ 740 | $1,650 | $2,390 |
| Wichita State University | Wichita, KS 67208 | 1895 | State | S-G/C | 16,649 | 884 | $ 732 | $1,475 | $2,207 |
| **KENTUCKY** | | | | | | | | | |
| Alice Lloyd College | Pippa Passes, KY 41844 | 1923 | Ind | J-S/C | 231 | 23 | $2,015 | $1,200 | $3,215 |
| Asbury College | Wilmore, KY 40390 | 1890 | Ind | S/C | 1,248 | 107 | $2,676 | $1,454 | $4,130 |
| Ashland Comm. College | Ashland, KY 41101 | 1957 | State | J/C | 1,480 | 77 | $ 390 | — | $ 390 |
| Bellarmine College | Louisville, KY 40205 | 1950 | Catholic | S-G/C | 2,095 | 97 | $2,125 | $1,300 | $3,425 |
| Berea College | Berea, KY 40404 | 1855 | Ind | S/C | 1,434 | 125 | $ 91 | $1,377 | $1,468 |
| Brescia College | Owensboro, KY 42301 | 1950 | Catholic | S/C | 844 | 74 | $2,100 | $1,495 | $3,595 |
| Campbellsville College | Campbellsville, KY 42718 | 1906 | Baptist | S/C | 674 | 45 | $2,280 | $1,600 | $3,880 |
| Centre College of Kentucky | Danville, KY 40422 | 1819 | Ind | S/C | 750 | 65 | $4,125 | $1,825 | $5,950 |
| Cumberland College | Williamsburg, KY 40769 | 1889 | Baptist | S/C | 2,000 | 105 | $1,848 | $1,225 | $3,073 |
| Eastern Kentucky University | Richmond, KY 40475 | 1906 | State | S-G/C | 13,668 | 680 | $ 520 | $1,480 | $2,000 |
| Elizabethtown Comm. College | Elizabethtown, KY 42701 | 1964 | State | J/C | 1,768 | 39 | $ 390 | — | $ 390 |
| Georgetown College | Georgetown, KY 40324 | 1829 | Baptist | S-G/C | 1,204 | 86 | $2,440 | $1,502 | $3,942 |
| Hazard Community College | Hazard, KY 41701 | 1968 | State | J/C | 306 | 25 | $ 390 | — | $ 390 |
| Henderson Community Col. | Henderson, KY 42420 | 1960 | State | J/C | 847 | 50 | $ 390 | — | $ 390 |
| Hopkinsville Comm. College | Hopkinsville, KY 42240 | 1965 | State | J/C | 1,054 | 34 | $ 390 | — | $ 390 |
| Jefferson Comm. College | Louisville, KY 40202 | 1968 | State | J/C | 4,205 | 224 | $ 390 | — | $ 390 |
| Southwest Campus | Louisville, KY 40272 | 1972 | State | J/C | 592 | 27 | $ 390 | — | $ 390 |
| Kentucky Christian College | Grayson, KY 41143 | 1919 | Christian | S/C | 464 | 22 | $1,116 | $2,446 | $3,562 |
| Kentucky State University | Frankfort, KY 40601 | 1886 | State | S-G/C | 2,180 | 162 | $ 480 | $1,329 | $1,809 |
| Kentucky Wesleyan College | Owensboro, KY 42301 | 1858 | Meth | S/C | 816 | 51 | $2,630 | $1,460 | $4,090 |
| Lees Junior College | Jackson, KY 41339 | 1883 | Presby | J/C | 328 | 26 | $2,000 | $1,450 | $3,450 |
| Lexington Technical Institute | Lexington, KY 40506 | 1965 | State | T/C | 2,074 | 110 | $ 562 | $1,740 | $2,302 |
| Lexington Theol. Seminary | Lexington, KY 40503 | 1865 | D of Chr | P/C | 140 | 12 | $2,709 | $1,300 | $4,009 |
| Lindsey Wilson College | Columbia, KY 42728 | 1903 | Meth | J/C | 393 | 20 | $1,458 | $1,300 | $2,758 |
| Louisville Presby. Theol. Sem. | Louisville, KY 40205 | 1853 | Presby | G/C | 254 | 37 | $1,695 | $1,406 | $3,101 |
| Madisonville Community Col. | Madisonville, KY 42431 | 1968 | State | J/C | 773 | 37 | $ 390 | $1,000 | $1,390 |
| Maysville Comm. College | Maysville, KY 41056 | 1968 | State | J/C | 462 | 32 | $ 390 | — | $ 390 |
| Midway College | Midway, KY 40347 | 1847 | D of Chr | J-S/W | 330 | 36 | $2,400 | $1,500 | $3,900 |
| Morehead State University | Morehead, KY 40351 | 1922 | State | S-G/C | 7,029 | 303 | $ 480 | $1,610 | $2,090 |
| Murray State University | Murray, KY 42071 | 1922 | State | S-G/C | 7,841 | 430 | $ 540 | $1,290 | $1,830 |
| Northern Kentucky University | Highland Hgts., KY 41076 | 1968 | State | S-G/C | 7,500 | 408 | $ 650 | — | $ 650 |
| Paducah Community College | Paducah, KY 42001 | 1932 | Public | J/C | 1,591 | 76 | $ 380 | — | $ 380 |
| Pikeville College | Pikeville, KY 41501 | 1889 | Presby | S/C | 550 | 45 | $2,150 | $1,750 | $3,950 |
| Prestonsburg Comm. College | Prestonsburg, KY 41653 | 1965 | State | J/C | 522 | 27 | $ 400 | — | $ 400 |
| St. Catharine College | Springfield, KY 40061 | 1931 | Catholic | J/C | 180 | 17 | $1,450 | $1,150 | $2,600 |
| Seminary of St. Pius X | Erlanger, KY 41018 | 1955 | Catholic | S/M | 104 | 25 | $2,200 | $1,300 | $3,500 |
| Somerset Community College | Somerset, KY 42501 | 1965 | State | J/C | 885 | 70 | $ 390 | — | $ 390 |
| Southeast Community College | Cumberland, KY 40823 | 1960 | State | J/C | 487 | 20 | $ 390 | — | $ 390 |
| Southern Baptist Theol. Sem. | Louisville, KY 40206 | 1859 | Baptist | G/C | — | — | — | — | — |
| Spaulding College | Louisville, KY 40203 | 1920 | Catholic | S-G/C | 928 | 91 | $2,048 | $1,470 | $3,518 |
| Sue Bennett College | London, KY 40741 | 1896 | Meth | J/C | 273 | 31 | $1,150 | $1,290 | $2,440 |
| Thomas More College | Fort Mitchell, KY 41017 | 1921 | Catholic | S/C | 1,343 | 123 | $2,020 | $1,570 | $3,590 |
| Transylvania University | Lexington, KY 40508 | 1780 | D of Chr | S/C | 810 | 62 | $4,100 | $1,900 | $6,000 |
| Union College | Barbourville, KY 40906 | 1879 | Meth | S-G/C | 894 | 46 | $2,530 | $1,300 | $3,830 |
| University of Kentucky | Lexington, KY 40506 | 1865 | State | S-G/C | 22,515 | 1,370 | $ 562 | $1,750 | $2,312 |
| Center at Fort Knox | Fort Knox, KY 40121 | 1959 | State | S/C | 550 | 35 | $ 550 | — | $ 550 |
| University of Louisville | Louisville, KY 40208 | 1798 | State | S-G/C | 19,155 | 1,556 | $ 570 | $1,355 | $1,925 |
| Western Kentucky University | Bowling Green, KY 42101 | 1906 | State | S-G/C | 13,442 | 652 | $ 520 | $1,710 | $2,230 |
| **LOUISIANA** | | | | | | | | | |
| Baptist Christian College | Shreveport, LA 71108 | 1961 | Baptist | S/C | 245 | 12 | $1,300 | $1,200 | $2,500 |
| Bossier Parish Comm. College | Bossier City, LA 71111 | 1967 | State | J/C | 1,822 | 60 | $ 16 | — | $ 16 |
| Centenary Col. of Louisiana | Shreveport, LA 71104 | 1825 | Meth | S-G/C | 942 | 107 | $2,320 | $1,520 | $3,840 |
| Delgado College | New Orleans, LA 70119 | 1921 | State | J/C | 8,154 | 176 | $ 340 | — | $ 340 |
| Dillard University | New Orleans, LA 70122 | 1869 | Private | S-G/C | 1,248 | 91 | $2,112 | $1,550 | $3,662 |
| Grambling State University | Grambling, LA 71245 | 1901 | State | S-G/C | 3,285 | 211 | $ 544 | $1,276 | $1,820 |
| Louisiana College | Pineville, LA 71360 | 1906 | Baptist | S/C | 1,403 | 96 | $1,220 | $1,052 | $2,272 |

218   EDUCATION

| NAME | ADDRESS | FOUN-DED | AFFILI-ATION | LEVEL/TYPE | ENROLL-MENT | TEACH-ERS | TUITION & FEES | BOARD & ROOM | TOTAL COST |
|---|---|---|---|---|---|---|---|---|---|
| **LOUISIANA** (continued) | | | | | | | | | |
| Louisiana State University Agricul. and Mech. College | Baton Rouge, LA 70803 | 1860 | State | S-G/C | 25,729 | 1,216 | $ 554 | $1,356 | $1,910 |
| Alexandria | Alexandria, LA 71303 | 1960 | State | J/C | 1,288 | 87 | $ 320 | — | $ 320 |
| Eunice | Eunice, LA 70535 | 1967 | State | J/C | 1,342 | 60 | $ 300 | — | $ 300 |
| Cent. for Agri. Sci. & Rur. Dev. | | 1972 | State | — | — | — | — | — | — |
| Paul M. Herbert Law Center | Baton Rouge, LA 70803 | 1906 | State | P/C | 857 | 63 | $1,044 | $1,356 | $2,190 |
| Medical Center | New Orleans, LA 70112 | 1931 | State | S-G/C | 2,498 | 563 | $1,400 | $ 562 | $1,762 |
| Shreveport | Shreveport, LA 71105 | 1967 | State | S-G/C | 3,516 | 140 | $ 480 | — | $ 480 |
| Univ. of New Orleans | New Orleans, LA 70122 | 1958 | State | S-G/C | 14,431 | 530 | $ 524 | $ 720 | $1,244 |
| Louisiana Tech University | Ruston, LA 71272 | 1894 | State | S-G/C | 9,274 | 384 | $ 549 | $1,404 | $1,953 |
| Loyola University | New Orleans, LA 70118 | 1912 | Catholic | S-G/C | 4,535 | 298 | $2,800 | $2,015 | $4,800 |
| McNeese State University | Lake Charles, LA 70609 | 1939 | State | S-G/C | 5,156 | 256 | $ 559 | $1,400 | $1,959 |
| Nicholls State University | Thibodaux, LA 70301 | 1948 | State | S-G/C | 6,481 | 220 | $ 535 | $1,280 | $1,815 |
| Northeast Louisiana Univ. | Monroe, LA 71209 | 1931 | State | S-G/C | 9,175 | 356 | $ 426 | $1,184 | $1,610 |
| Northwest State Univ. of La. | Natchitoches, LA 71457 | 1884 | State | S-G/C | 6,500 | 255 | $ 525 | $1,351 | $1,876 |
| Notre Dame Seminary School of Theology | New Orleans, LA 70118 | 1923 | Catholic | G/C | 91 | 17 | $1,940 | $1,500 | $3,440 |
| Our Lady of Holy Cross Col. | New Orleans, LA 70114 | 1916 | Cath | S/C | 767 | 73 | $1,600 | — | $1,600 |
| St. Bernard Parish Comm. Col. | Chalmette, LA 70043 | 1968 | State | J/C | 958 | 36 | $ 55 | — | $ 55 |
| St. Joseph Seminary College | St. Benedict, LA 70457 | 1891 | Catholic | S/M | 110 | 28 | $1,800 | $1,650 | $3,450 |
| St. Mary's Dominican College | New Orleans, LA 70118 | 1910 | Catholic | S/W | 802 | 83 | $2,600 | $1,630 | $4,230 |
| Southeastern Louisiana Univ. | Hammond, LA 70402 | 1925 | State | S-G/C | 7,367 | 250 | $ 518 | $1,242 | $1,760 |
| Southern University | | | | | | | | | |
| A & M College | Baton Rouge, LA 70813 | 1880 | State | S-G/C | 8,101 | 381 | $ 450 | $1,666 | $2,116 |
| Shreveport Campus | Shreveport, LA 71107 | 1964 | State | J/C | 677 | 43 | $ 260 | — | $ 260 |
| Southern Univ. in New Orleans | New Orleans, LA 70126 | 1959 | State | S/C | 2,633 | 94 | $ 410 | — | $ 410 |
| Tulane University | New Orleans, LA 70118 | 1834 | Ind | S-G/C | 9,717 | 913 | $4,546 | $1,940 | $6,486 |
| Newcomb College | New Orleans, LA 70118 | 1886 | Ind | S/W | 1,550 | 130 | $4,600 | $1,800 | $6,400 |
| University of Southwest La. | Lafayette, LA 70503 | 1898 | State | S-G/C | 13,311 | 594 | $ 450 | $1,138 | $1,588 |
| Xavier Univ. of Louisiana | New Orleans, LA 70125 | 1915 | Catholic | S-G/C | 1,957 | 170 | $2,200 | $1,650 | $3,850 |
| **MAINE** | | | | | | | | | |
| Andover College | Portland, ME 04101 | 1966 | Ind | J/C | 350 | 20 | $1,750 | — | $1,750 |
| Bangor Theological Seminary | Bangor, ME 04401 | 1814 | C of Chr | P/C | 93 | 18 | $2,035 | $1,800 | $3,835 |
| Bates College | Lewiston, ME 04240 | 1864 | Ind | S/C | 1,470 | 126 | $4,850 | $1,535 | $6,385 |
| Beal College | Bangor, ME 04401 | 1891 | Ind | J/C | 487 | 55 | $2,425 | $1,800 | $4,225 |
| Bowdoin College | Brunswick, ME 04011 | 1794 | Ind | S/C | 1,371 | 103 | $5,885 | $2,220 | $8,105 |
| Casco Bay College | Portland, ME 04101 | 1863 | Ind | J/C | 206 | 18 | $1,960 | — | $1,960 |
| Central Maine Voc. Tech. Inst. | Auburn, ME 04210 | 1964 | State | T/C | 1,630 | 126 | $ 550 | $1,100 | $1,650 |
| Colby College | Waterville, ME 04901 | 1813 | Ind | S/C | 1,694 | 130 | $4,725 | $1,785 | $6,510 |
| College of the Atlantic | Bar Harbor, ME 04609 | 1969 | Private | S/C | 149 | 27 | $4,000 | $1,500 | $5,500 |
| Eastern Maine Voc. Tech. Inst. | Bangor, ME 04401 | 1966 | State | T/C | 460 | 50 | $ 450 | $1,400 | $1,850 |
| Husson College | Bangor, ME 04401 | 1898 | Ind | S-G/C | 811 | 40 | $2,985 | $1,840 | $4,825 |
| Kennebec Vly. Voc. Tech. Inst. | Waterville, ME 04901 | 1970 | State | T/C | 175 | 16 | $ 550 | — | $ 550 |
| Maine Maritime Academy | Castine, ME 04421 | 1941 | State | S/C | 643 | 49 | $2,555 | $1,850 | $4,405 |
| Mid-State Business School | Auburn, ME 04210 | 1916 | Ind | J/C | 120 | 8 | $1,755 | $1,200 | $2,955 |
| Augusta Campus | Augusta, ME 04330 | 1916 | Ind | J/C | 60 | 5 | $1,755 | — | $1,755 |
| Nasson College | Springvale, ME 04083 | 1912 | Ind | S/C | 615 | 45 | $3,565 | $1,650 | $5,215 |
| New England Bapt. Bible Col. | Portland, ME 04101 | 1980 | Baptist | S/C | — | 6 | $1,385 | — | $1,385 |
| North. Maine Voc. Tech. Inst. | Presque Isle, ME 04769 | 1963 | State | T/C | 504 | 42 | $ 395 | $1,150 | $1,500 |
| Portland School of Art | Portland, ME 04101 | 1882 | Ind | P/C | 230 | 20 | $3,000 | — | $3,000 |
| St. Joseph's College | North Windham, ME 04062 | 1915 | Catholic | S/C | 1,600 | 49 | $2,510 | $1,475 | $3,985 |
| South. Maine Voc. Tech. Inst. | South Portland, ME 04106 | 1946 | State | T/C | 1,466 | 84 | $ 390 | $1,136 | $1,526 |
| Thomas College | Waterville, ME 04901 | 1894 | Ind | S-G/C | 1,058 | 52 | $3,300 | $1,850 | $5,150 |
| Unity College | Unity, ME 04988 | 1965 | Ind | S/C | 427 | 40 | $3,225 | $1,750 | $4,975 |
| University of Maine | | | | | | | | | |
| Augusta | Augusta, ME 04330 | 1965 | State | J/C | 3,409 | 192 | $ 950 | — | $ 950 |
| Bangor Comm. College | Bangor, ME 04401 | 1971 | State | J/C | 557 | 55 | $ 840 | $1,700 | $2,540 |
| Farmington | Farmington, ME 04938 | 1864 | State | S/C | 1,959 | 99 | $ 805 | $1,625 | $2,430 |
| Fort Kent | Fort Kent, ME 04743 | 1878 | State | S/C | 573 | 22 | $ 800 | $1,650 | $2,450 |
| Machias | Machias, ME 04654 | 1909 | State | S/C | 729 | 39 | $ 825 | $1,650 | $2,475 |
| Orono | Orono, ME 04469 | 1865 | State | S-G/C | 11,574 | 597 | $ 935 | $1,855 | $2,790 |
| Presque Isle | Presque Isle, ME 04769 | 1903 | State | S/C | 1,408 | 78 | $ 950 | $1,887 | $2,837 |
| School of Law | Portland, ME 04102 | 1898 | State | G/C | 225 | 14 | $1,250 | — | $3,500 |
| University of New England | Biddeford, ME 04005 | 1939 | Ind | S-G/C | 460 | 40 | $3,700 | $2,160 | $5,860 |
| University of So. Maine | Gorham, ME 04038 | 1878 | State | S-G/C | 8,019 | 326 | $ 844 | $1,670 | $2,514 |
| Wash. County Voc. Tech. Inst. | Calais, ME 04619 | 1969 | State | T/C | 400 | 35 | $ 370 | $1,500 | $1,870 |
| Westbrook College | Portland, ME 04103 | 1831 | Ind | J-S/C | 935 | 88 | $3,450 | $1,750 | $5,200 |
| **MARYLAND** | | | | | | | | | |
| Allegany Community College | Cumberland, MD 21502 | 1961 | County | J/C | 1,702 | 112 | $ 500 | — | $ 500 |
| Anne Arundel Comm. College | Arnold, MD 21012 | 1961 | State | J/C | 7,300 | 400 | $ 500 | — | $ 500 |
| Antioch/George Meany Center | Silver Spring, MD 20903 | 1973 | Ind | S/C | 80 | 10 | $ 600 | $ 400 | $1,000 |
| Antioch Univ./Maryland | Baltimore, MD 21201 | 1852 | Public | S-G/C | 197 | 19 | $3,465 | — | $3,465 |
| Baltimore Hebrew College | Baltimore, MD 21215 | 1919 | Ind | G/C | 190 | 19 | $ 970 | — | $ 970 |
| Bowie State College | Bowie, MD 20715 | 1865 | State | S-G/C | 2,879 | 138 | $ 820 | $1,590 | $2,410 |
| Capitol Inst. of Technology | Kensington, MD 20795 | 1964 | Private | J-S/C | 694 | 26 | $2,160 | — | $2,160 |
| Catonsville Comm. College | Catonsville, MD 21228 | 1956 | State | J/C | 10,007 | 465 | $ 475 | — | $ 475 |
| Cecil Comm. College | North East, MD 21901 | 1968 | State | J/C | 1,168 | 84 | $ 366 | — | $ 366 |
| Charles County Comm. College | La Plata, MD 20646 | 1958 | State | J/C | 3,775 | 218 | $ 510 | — | $ 510 |
| Chesapeake College | Wye Mills, MD 21679 | 1965 | Public | J/C | 2,683 | 30 | $ 466 | — | $ 466 |

| NAME | ADDRESS | FOUN-DED | AFFILI-ATION | LEVEL/TYPE | ENROLL-MENT | TEACH-ERS | TUITION & FEES | BOARD & ROOM | TOTAL COST |
|---|---|---|---|---|---|---|---|---|---|
| **MARYLAND** *(continued)* | | | | | | | | | |
| Col. of Notre Dame of Md. | Baltimore, MD 21210 | 1896 | Ind | S/W | 544 | 79 | $3,150 | $2,000 | $5,150 |
| Columbia Union College | Takoma Park, MD 20012 | 1904 | 7-D Adv | S/C | 956 | 69 | $3,220 | $1,782 | $5,002 |
| Comm. College of Baltimore | Baltimore, MD 21215 | 1947 | City | J/C | 8,278 | 584 | $ 485 | — | $ 485 |
| Coppin State College | Baltimore, MD 21216 | 1900 | State | S-G/C | 2,825 | 182 | $ 780 | — | $ 780 |
| Dundalk Community College | Baltimore, MD 21222 | 1971 | Ind | J/C | 2,342 | 134 | $ 500 | — | $ 500 |
| Essex Community College | Baltimore Cnty., MD 21237 | 1957 | State | J/C | 9,373 | 500 | $ 540 | — | $ 540 |
| Frederick Comm. College | Frederick, MD 21701 | 1957 | State | J/C | 1,810 | 79 | $ 530 | — | $ 530 |
| Frostburg State College | Frostburg, MD 21532 | 1898 | State | S-G/C | 3,612 | 180 | $ 861 | $1,400 | $2,261 |
| Garrett Community College | McHenry, MD 21541 | 1971 | County | J/C | 666 | 50 | $ 350 | — | $ 350 |
| Goucher College | Baltimore, MD 21204 | 1885 | Ind | S-G/W | 1,009 | 136 | $4,650 | $2,600 | $7,250 |
| Hagerstown Business College | Hagerstown, MD 21740 | 1938 | Ind | J/C | 266 | 13 | $1,550 | $1,872 | $3,422 |
| Hagerstown Junior College | Hagerstown, MD 21740 | 1946 | Public | J/C | 2,141 | 65 | $ 500 | — | $ 500 |
| Harford Community College | Bel Air, MD 21014 | 1957 | Public | J/C | 3,973 | 82 | $ 534 | — | $ 534 |
| Hood College | Frederick, MD 21701 | 1893 | Ind | S-G/C | 1,775 | 154 | $3,590 | $1,880 | $5,470 |
| Howard Community College | Columbia, MD 21044 | 1966 | Ind | J/C | 2,621 | 142 | $ 506 | — | $ 506 |
| Johns Hopkins University | Baltimore, MD 21218 | 1876 | Ind | S-G/C | 3,086 | 294 | $4,500 | $2,155 | $6,655 |
| Loyola College of Maryland | Baltimore, MD 21210 | 1852 | Catholic | S-G/C | 5,217 | 330 | $2,775 | $1,750 | $4,525 |
| Maryland Inst. of Art | Baltimore, MD 21217 | 1826 | Ind | S-G/C | 942 | 98 | $3,700 | — | $3,700 |
| Montgomery College | Rockville, MD 20850 | 1946 | State | J/C | 16,321 | 800 | $ 715 | — | $ 715 |
| Morgan State University | Baltimore, MD 21239 | 1867 | State | S-G/C | 5,981 | 304 | $ 850 | $1,809 | $2,660 |
| Mount St. Mary's College | Emmitsburg, MD 21727 | 1808 | Catholic | S-G/C | 1,415 | 91 | $3,200 | $1,675 | $4,920 |
| Ner Israel Rabbinical College | Baltimore, MD 21208 | 1933 | Jewish | S-G/M | 264 | 17 | $1,500 | $1,750 | $3,250 |
| Peabody Institute J.H.U. | Baltimore, MD 21202 | 1857 | Ind | S-G/C | 448 | 101 | $4,575 | $2,362 | $6,937 |
| Prince George's Comm. Col. | Largo, MD 20870 | 1958 | Public | J/C | 13,477 | 603 | $ 555 | — | $ 555 |
| St. John's College | Annapolis, MD 21404 | 1696 | Ind | S/C | 391 | 51 | $4,750 | $1,900 | $6,550 |
| St. Mary's Col. of Maryland | St. Mary's City, MD 20686 | 1839 | State | S/C | 1,318 | 91 | $ 865 | $1,950 | $2,815 |
| St. Mary's Sem. & University | Baltimore, MD 21210 | 1791 | Catholic | P/C | 379 | 73 | $2,050 | $1,600 | $3,650 |
| Salisbury State College | Salisbury, MD 21801 | 1925 | State | S-G/C | 4,427 | 185 | $ 765 | $1,480 | $2,245 |
| Sojourner-Douglas College | Baltimore, MD 21205 | 1972 | Ind | S/C | 200 | 20 | $2,570 | — | $2,570 |
| Towson State University | Baltimore, MD 21204 | 1866 | State | S-G/C | 15,283 | 850 | $ 770 | $1,470 | $2,240 |
| United States Naval Academy | Annapolis, MD 21402 | 1845 | Fed | S/C | 4,400 | 540 | — | — | — |
| University of Baltimore | Baltimore, MD 21201 | 1925 | State | S-G/C | 5,394 | 127 | $ 800 | — | $ 800 |
| University of Maryland | | | | | | | | | |
|   Baltimore City Campus | Baltimore, MD 21201 | 1807 | State | S-G/C | 4,777 | 1,092 | $ 815 | $ 965 | $1,780 |
|   Baltimore County Campus | Baltimore, MD 21228 | 1963 | State | S-G/C | 6,393 | 271 | $ 816 | $1,766 | $2,582 |
|   College Park Campus | College Park, MD 20742 | 1856 | State | S-G/C | 37,192 | 3,227 | $ 842 | $2,090 | $2,932 |
|   Eastern Shore Campus | Princess Anne, MD 21853 | 1886 | State | S-G/C | 1,117 | 89 | $ 648 | $1,546 | $2,194 |
|   University College | College Park, MD 20740 | 1947 | State | S-G/C | 29,056 | 642 | $1,150 | $ 922 | $2,072 |
| Villa Julie College | Stevenson, MD 21153 | 1952 | Ind | J/C | 604 | 80 | $2,100 | — | $2,100 |
| Washington Bible College | Lanham, MD 20801 | 1938 | Ind | S-G/C | 589 | 35 | $1,828 | $1,694 | $3,522 |
| Washington College | Chestertown, MD 21620 | 1782 | Ind | S/C | 751 | 60 | $3,500 | $1,600 | $5,100 |
| Western Maryland College | Westminster, MD 21157 | 1867 | Ind | S-G/C | 1,300 | 117 | $3,875 | $1,750 | $5,625 |
| **MASSACHUSETTS** | | | | | | | | | |
| American International College | Springfield, MA 01109 | 1885 | Private | S-G/C | 2,061 | 130 | $3,085 | $1,700 | $4,785 |
| Amherst College | Amherst, MA 01002 | 1821 | Ind | S/C | 1,541 | 153 | $5,240 | $2,000 | $7,240 |
| Andover Newton Theol. Sch. | Newton Centre, MA 02159 | 1807 | Ind | G/C | 441 | 47 | $2,600 | $2,820 | $5,420 |
| Anna Maria College | Paxton, MA 01612 | 1946 | Catholic | S-G/C | 1,288 | 125 | $2,680 | $1,800 | $4,480 |
| Aquinas Junior College | Newton, MA 02158 | 1961 | Catholic | J/W | 305 | 28 | $1,975 | — | $1,975 |
| Aquinas Junior College | Milton, MA 02186 | 1956 | Catholic | J/W | 396 | 26 | $2,115 | — | $2,115 |
| Arthur D. Little Man. Ed. Inst. | Cambridge, MA 02140 | 1972 | Ind | G/C | 47 | 28 | $8,640 | — | $8,640 |
| Assumption College | Worcester, MA 01609 | 1904 | Catholic | S-G/C | 1,900 | 151 | $3,300 | $1,785 | $5,100 |
| Atlantic Union College | South Lancaster, MA 01561 | 1882 | 7-D Adv | S/C | 640 | 75 | $3,760 | $1,500 | $5,260 |
| Babson College | Babson Park, MA 02157 | 1919 | Ind | S-G/C | 2,971 | 124 | $4,670 | $2,220 | $6,890 |
| Bay Path Junior College | Longmeadow, MA 01106 | 1897 | Ind | J/W | 639 | 34 | $3,025 | $2,250 | $5,275 |
| Bay State Junior College | Boston, MA 02116 | 1946 | Ind | J/C | 750 | 35 | $2,200 | $2,295 | $4,495 |
| Becker Jr. Col.–Leicester | Leicester, MA 01524 | 1784 | Ind | J/C | 494 | 35 | $2,150 | $1,600 | $3,750 |
| Becker Jr. Col.–Worcester | Worcester, MA 01609 | 1887 | Ind | J/C | 647 | 40 | $2,150 | $1,500 | $3,650 |
| Bentley College | Waltham, MA 02154 | 1917 | Ind | S-G/C | 6,668 | 250 | $3,970 | $2,240 | $6,210 |
| Berklee College of Music | Boston, MA 02215 | 1945 | Ind | S/C | 2,583 | 218 | $3,000 | $1,990 | $4,990 |
| Berkshire Christian College | Lenox, MA 01240 | 1897 | Adv Chr | S/C | 150 | 22 | $2,420 | $2,200 | $4,620 |
| Berkshire Community College | Pittsfield, MA 01201 | 1960 | State | J/C | 1,600 | 70 | $ 512 | — | $ 670 |
| Blue Hills Tech. Institute | Canton, MA 02021 | 1966 | Public | T/C | 470 | 33 | $ 520 | — | $ 520 |
| Boston College | Chestnut Hill, MA 02167 | 1863 | Catholic | S-G/C | 13,969 | 930 | $4,923 | $2,586 | $7,509 |
| Boston Conserv. of Music | Boston, MA 02215 | 1867 | Ind | S-G/C | 438 | 102 | $3,100 | $1,800 | $4,900 |
| Boston State College | Boston, MA 02215 | 1852 | State | S-G/C | 5,241 | 330 | $ 677 | — | $ 677 |
| Boston University | Boston, MA 02215 | 1869 | Ind | S-G/C | 26,011 | 2,277 | $5,595 | $2,605 | $8,200 |
| Bradford College | Bradford, MA 01830 | 1803 | Ind | J-S/C | 344 | 50 | | | $6,975 |
| Brandeis University | Waltham, MA 02154 | 1948 | Ind | S-G/C | 3,523 | 340 | $5,924 | $2,600 | $8,524 |
| Bridgewater State College | Bridgewater, MA 02324 | 1840 | State | S-G/C | 4,450 | 224 | $ 815 | $1,591 | $2,406 |
| Bristol Community College | Fall River, MA 02720 | 1965 | State | J/C | 1,931 | 119 | $ 454 | — | $ 454 |
| Bunker Hill Comm. College | Charlestown, MA 02129 | 1973 | State | J/C | 2,299 | 96 | $ 470 | — | $ 470 |
| Burdett School | Boston, MA 02199 | 1879 | Ind | J/W | 657 | 28 | $2,900 | $2,400 | $5,300 |
| Cape Cod Community College | West Barnstable, MA 02668 | 1960 | State | J/C | 1,616 | 124 | $ 464 | — | $ 464 |
| Central New Eng. Col. of Tech. | Worcester, MA 01610 | 1888 | Ind | S/C | 1,219 | 87 | $2,600 | $ 900 | $3,500 |
| Chamberlayne Junior College | Boston, MA 02116 | 1892 | Ind | J/C | 1,040 | 45 | $2,370 | $2,175 | $4,545 |
| Clark University | Worcester, MA 01610 | 1887 | Ind | S-G/C | 2,425 | 129 | $4,650 | $1,655 | $6,305 |
| College of the Holy Cross | Worcester, MA 01610 | 1843 | Jesuit | S-G/C | 2,517 | 207 | $4,600 | $2,250 | $6,850 |
| Col. of Our Lady of the Elms | Chicopee, MA 01013 | 1928 | Catholic | S/W | 476 | 71 | $3,050 | $1,800 | $4,850 |
| Curry College | Milton, MA 02186 | 1879 | Ind | S/C | 1,285 | 76 | $3,900 | $2,200 | $6,100 |
| Dean Junior College | Franklin, MA 02038 | 1865 | Ind | J/C | 1,900 | 75 | $3,530 | $1,880 | $5,410 |
| Eastern Nazarene College | Quincy, MA 02170 | 1918 | Nazarene | S-G/C | 750 | 55 | $2,520 | $1,480 | $4,000 |
| Emerson College | Boston, MA 02116 | 1880 | Ind | S/C | 1,885 | 148 | $4,116 | $2,450 | $6,566 |

| NAME | ADDRESS | FOUN-DED | AFFILI-ATION | LEVEL/TYPE | ENROLL-MENT | TEACH-ERS | TUITION & FEES | BOARD & ROOM | TOTAL COST |
|---|---|---|---|---|---|---|---|---|---|
| **MASSACHUSETTS** *(continued)* | | | | | | | | | |
| Emmanuel College | Boston, MA 02115 | 1919 | Catholic | S-G/W | 1,068 | 94 | $3,410 | $1,800 | $5,210 |
| Endicott College | Beverly, MA 01915 | 1939 | Ind | J/W | 834 | 64 | $3,090 | $1,900 | $4,990 |
| Episcopal Divinity School | Cambridge, MA 02138 | 1867 | Episc | G/C | 130 | 24 | $2,700 | $1,500 | $4,200 |
| Fisher Junior College | Boston, MA 02116 | 1903 | Ind | J/W | 535 | 28 | $3,100 | $2,200 | $5,300 |
| Fitchburg State College | Fitchburg, MA 01420 | 1894 | State | S-G/C | 3,719 | 213 | $ 765 | $1,612 | $2,373 |
| Forsyth Sch. For Den. Hygienists | Boston, MA 02115 | 1916 | Ind | J/C | 200 | 25 | $4,100 | $2,500 | $6,600 |
| Framingham State College | Framingham, MA 01701 | 1839 | State | S-G/C | 3,128 | 160 | $ 655 | $1,376 | $2,031 |
| Franklin Inst. of Boston | Boston, MA 02116 | 1908 | Ind | J/C | 611 | 39 | $3,180 | — | — |
| Gordon College | Wenham, MA 01984 | 1889 | Ind | S/C | 995 | 64 | $3,390 | $1,608 | $5,070 |
| Gordon-Conwell Theol. Sem. | So. Hamilton, MA 01982 | 1884 | Ind | G/C | 663 | 53 | $2,350 | $1,500 | $3,850 |
| Grahm Junior College | Boston, MA 02215 | 1968 | Ind | J/C | — | — | — | — | — |
| Greenfield Comm. College | Greenfield, MA 01301 | 1962 | State | J/C | 1,153 | 94 | $ 480 | — | $ 480 |
| Hampshire College | Amherst, MA 01002 | 1965 | Ind | S/C | 1,210 | 124 | $5,625 | $1,800 | $7,525 |
| Harvard University | Cambridge, MA 02138 | 1636 | Ind | S-G/C | 22,269 | — | $6,000 | $3,170 | $9,170 |
| Hebrew College | Brookline, MA 02146 | 1921 | Ind | S-G/C | 177 | 11 | $ 675 | — | — |
| Hellenic College Inc. | Brookline, MA 02146 | 1937 | Orthodox | S-G/C | 185 | 31 | $2,435 | $1,500 | $3,935 |
| Holyoke Community College | Holyoke, MA 01040 | 1946 | State | J/C | 2,928 | 175 | $ 480 | — | $ 480 |
| Inst. of Open Education | Cambridge, MA 02138 | 1971 | Ind | G/C | 427 | 40 | $4,600 | — | $4,600 |
| Laboure Junior College | Boston, MA 02124 | 1971 | Catholic | J/C | 560 | 35 | $2,950 | $2,000 | $4,950 |
| Lasell Junior College | Newton, MA 02166 | 1851 | Ind | J/W | 670 | 73 | $3,590 | $2,300 | $5,890 |
| Lesley College | Cambridge, MA 02138 | 1909 | Ind | S-G/W | 1,616 | 114 | $3,740 | $2,230 | $5,970 |
| Mass. Bay Comm. College | Wellesley Hills, MA 02181 | 1961 | State | J/C | 1,928 | 131 | $ 480 | — | $ 480 |
| Mass. College of Art | Boston, MA 02215 | 1873 | State | S-G/C | 2,052 | 136 | $ 735 | — | — |
| Mass. College of Pharmacy | Boston, MA 02115 | 1823 | Ind | P/C | 1,257 | 77 | $3,100 | $3,000 | $6,100 |
| Mass. Inst. of Technology | Cambridge, MA 02139 | 1861 | Ind | S-G/C | 9,053 | 1,732 | $6,200 | $2,800 | $9,000 |
| Mass. Maritime Academy | Buzzards Bay, MA 02532 | 1891 | State | S/C | 850 | 55 | $1,100 | $3,400 | $4,500 |
| Massasoit Commmunity Col. | Brockton, MA 02402 | 1966 | State | J/C | 2,867 | 156 | $ 430 | — | $ 430 |
| Merrimack College | North Andover, MA 01845 | 1947 | Catholic | S/C | 2,168 | 128 | $3,855 | $2,382 | $6,237 |
| Middlesex Community College | Bedford, MA 01730 | 1969 | State | J/C | 6,563 | 104 | $ 508 | — | $ 508 |
| Mount Holyoke College | South Hadley, MA 01075 | 1837 | Ind | S/W | 1,850 | 206 | $5,430 | $2,570 | $8,000 |
| Mount Ida Junior College | Newton Centre, MA 02159 | 1899 | Ind | J/W | 740 | 71 | $3,200 | $2,275 | $5,475 |
| Mount Wachusett Comm. Col. | Gardner, MA 01440 | 1963 | State | J/C | 1,573 | 83 | $ 480 | — | $ 480 |
| New Eng. Col. of Optometry | Boston, MA 02115 | 1894 | Private | P/C | 362 | 36 | $4,800 | — | $4,800 |
| New Eng. Conser. of Music | Boston, MA 02115 | 1867 | Ind | S-G/C | 867 | 100 | $4,765 | $2,675 | $7,440 |
| New Eng. Inst. of App. Arts & Sci. | Boston, MA 02215 | 1907 | Ind | J/C | 135 | 18 | $2,750 | — | $2,750 |
| New England School of Law | Boston, MA 02116 | 1908 | Ind | P/C | 900 | 60 | $3,175 | — | $3,175 |
| Newbury Junior College | Boston, MA 02115 | 1962 | Private | J/C | 2,500 | 150 | $2,700 | $2,075 | $4,775 |
| Holliston Campus | Holliston, MA 01746 | 1970 | Private | J/C | 250 | 69 | $3,000 | — | $3,000 |
| Nichols College | Dudley, MA 01570 | 1815 | Ind | S-G/C | 776 | 38 | $3,490 | $2,040 | $5,530 |
| North Adams State College | North Adams, MA 01247 | 1894 | State | S-G/C | 2,100 | 110 | $ 800 | $1,650 | $2,450 |
| North Shore Comm. College | Beverly, MA 01915 | 1965 | State | J/C | 2,376 | 155 | $ 480 | — | $ 480 |
| Northeastern University | Boston, MA 02115 | 1898 | Private | S-G/C | 18,701 | 773 | $3,135 | $2,350 | $5,485 |
| Northern Essex Comm. Col. | Haverhill, MA 01830 | 1960 | State | J/C | 6,523 | 244 | $ 458 | — | $ 458 |
| Pine Manor College | Chestnut Hill, MA 02167 | 1911 | Ind | S/W | 494 | 47 | $4,900 | $3,075 | $7,975 |
| Quincy Junior College | Quincy, MA 02169 | 1958 | City | J/C | 3,780 | 200 | $ 615 | — | $ 615 |
| Quinsigamund Comm. College | Worcester, MA 01606 | 1963 | State | J/C | 5,032 | 105 | $ 475 | — | $ 475 |
| Radcliffe College | Cambridge, MA 02138 | 1879 | Ind | S/W | 2,321 | — | $5,300 | $2,840 | $9,140 |
| Regis College | Weston, MA 02193 | 1927 | Ind | S-G/W | 1,270 | 98 | $3,595 | $2,230 | $5,825 |
| Roxbury Community College | Roxbury, MA 02119 | 1973 | State | J/C | 600 | 31 | $ 456 | — | $ 456 |
| St. Hyacinth Col. Seminary | Granby, MA 01033 | 1927 | Catholic | S/M | 48 | 23 | $ 425 | $2,000 | $2,425 |
| St. John's Seminary College | Brighton, MA 02135 | 1968 | Catholic | S/M | 96 | 27 | $1,800 | $1,800 | $3,600 |
| Salem State College | Salem, MA 01970 | 1854 | State | S-G/C | 4,771 | 278 | $ 645 | $1,543 | $2,188 |
| Sch. of the Mus. of Fine Arts | Boston, MA 02115 | 1876 | Private | S-G/C | 1,200 | 81 | $3,300 | — | $3,300 |
| Sch. of the Worcester Art Mus. | Worcester, MA 01608 | 1898 | Private | P/C | 110 | 15 | $4,945 | — | $4,945 |
| Simmons College | Boston, MA 02115 | 1899 | Ind | S-G/W | 2,766 | 290 | $4,928 | $2,440 | $7,368 |
| Simon's Rock of Bard College | Gt. Barrington, MA 01230 | 1964 | Ind | S/C | 200 | 35 | $4,400 | $ 900 | $5,300 |
| Smith College | Northampton, MA 01063 | 1871 | Ind | S/W | 2,660 | 260 | $5,100 | $2,050 | $7,150 |
| Southeastern Mass. University | No. Dartmouth, MA 02747 | 1895 | State | S-G/C | 5,308 | 311 | $ 679 | $2,466 | $3,145 |
| Springfield College | Springfield, MA 01109 | 1885 | Ind | S/C | 2,433 | 127 | $3,366 | $1,683 | $4,999 |
| Springfield Tech. Comm. Col. | Springfield, MA 01105 | 1967 | State | J/C | 6,500 | 408 | $ 374 | — | $ 374 |
| Stonehill College | North Easton, MA 02356 | 1948 | Catholic | S-G/C | 2,640 | 180 | $3,300 | $1,970 | $5,270 |
| Suffolk University | Boston, MA 02114 | 1906 | Private | S-G/C | 4,707 | 277 | $2,580 | — | $2,580 |
| Swain School of Design | New Bedford, MA 02740 | 1881 | Ind | S/C | 171 | 17 | $2,700 | — | $2,700 |
| Swedenborg Sch. of Religion | Newton, MA 02158 | 1881 | Swed | G/C | 18 | 5 | $1,200 | $2,600 | $3,800 |
| Tufts University | Medford, MA 02155 | 1852 | Ind | S-G/C | 6,800 | 2,600 | $5,000 | $2,700 | $7,700 |
| Flet. Sch. of Law and Dip. | Medford, MA 02155 | 1933 | Ind | G/C | 273 | 33 | $5,480 | $3,031 | $8,511 |
| University of Lowell | Lowell, MA 01854 | 1894 | State | S-G/C | 7,689 | 510 | $ 775 | $1,650 | $2,425 |
| Univ. of Mass./Amherst | Amherst, MA 01003 | 1863 | State | S-G/C | 24,012 | 1,292 | $1,114 | $1,875 | $2,989 |
| Wellesley College | Wellesley, MA 02181 | 1875 | Ind | S/W | 2,115 | 288 | $4,360 | $2,250 | $6,610 |
| Wentworth Inst. of Tech. | Boston, MA 02115 | 1904 | Ind | T/C | 2,593 | 141 | $2,900 | $2,125 | $5,025 |
| Western New England College | Springfield, MA 01119 | 1919 | Ind | S-G/C | 2,712 | 178 | $2,820 | $1,760 | $4,580 |
| Westfield State College | Westfield, MA 01085 | 1839 | Public | S-G/C | 4,128 | 190 | $ 770 | $1,540 | $2,310 |
| Weston School of Theology | Cambridge, MA 02138 | 1922 | Catholic | P/C | 222 | 28 | $2,410 | — | $2,410 |
| Wheaton College | Norton, MA 02766 | 1834 | Ind | S/W | 1,206 | 129 | $5,285 | $2,080 | $7,365 |
| Wheelock College | Boston, MA 02215 | 1888 | Ind | S-G/C | 951 | 90 | $3,750 | $2,100 | $5,850 |
| Williams College | Williamstown, MA 01267 | 1793 | Ind | S/C | 2,013 | 169 | $5,950 | $2,330 | $8,280 |
| Woods Hole Oceanog. Inst. | Woods Hole, MA 02543 | 1930 | Private | G/C | 76 | — | $8,275 | — | $8,275 |
| Worcester Polytechnic Inst. | Worcester, MA 01609 | 1865 | Ind | S-G/C | 3,325 | 179 | $4,513 | $1,925 | $6,438 |
| Worcester State College | Worcester, MA 01602 | 1874 | State | S-G/C | 4,022 | 194 | $ 650 | $1,624 | $2,274 |
| **MICHIGAN** | | | | | | | | | |
| Adrian College | Adrian, MI 49221 | 1859 | Meth | S-G/C | 945 | 64 | $3,900 | $1,800 | $5,700 |
| Albion College | Albion, MI 49224 | 1835 | Meth | S/C | 1,783 | 116 | $4,501 | $2,014 | $6,515 |

## MICHIGAN (continued)

| NAME | ADDRESS | FOUN-DED | AFFILI-ATION | LEVEL/TYPE | ENROLL-MENT | TEACH-ERS | TUITION & FEES | BOARD & ROOM | TOTAL COST |
|---|---|---|---|---|---|---|---|---|---|
| Alma College | Alma, MI 48801 | 1886 | Ind | S/C | 1,212 | 86 | $3,716 | $1,594 | $5,310 |
| Alpena Community College | Alpena, MI 49707 | 1952 | State | J/C | 1,700 | 119 | $ 404 | $1,460 | $1,864 |
| Andrews University | Berrien Springs, MI 49104 | 1874 | 7-D Adv | S-G/C | 2,983 | 232 | $3,975 | $2,100 | $6,075 |
| Aquinas College | Grand Rapids, MI 49506 | 1922 | Catholic | S-G/C | 2,172 | 128 | $3,555 | $1,870 | $5,425 |
| Baker Jr. College of Business | Flint, MI 48507 | 1911 | Ind | J/C | 1,200 | 68 | $1,840 | $1,200 | $3,040 |
| Bay De Noc Comm. College | Escanaba, MI 49829 | 1963 | State | J/C | 1,480 | 90 | $ 435 | $ 765 | $1,200 |
| Calvin College | Grand Rapids, MI 49506 | 1876 | Ref | S-G/C | 4,024 | 202 | $2,680 | $1,380 | $4,060 |
| Calvin Theological Seminary | Grand Rapids, MI 49506 | 1876 | Ref | P/C | 210 | 18 | $1,325 | — | $1,325 |
| Center for Creative Studies | Detroit, MI 48202 | 1926 | Private | S/C | 1,034 | 113 | $2,910 | $1,230 | $4,140 |
| Central Michigan University | Mt. Pleasant, MI 48859 | 1892 | State | S-G/C | 16,281 | 982 | $ 883 | $1,600 | $2,483 |
| Cleary College | Ypsilanti, MI 48197 | 1883 | Ind | S/C | 600 | 49 | $1,550 | — | — |
| Concordia College | Ann Arbor, MI 48105 | 1963 | Lutheran | S/C | 552 | 58 | $2,278 | $1,649 | $3,927 |
| Cranbrook Academy of Art | Bloomfield Hills, MI 48013 | 1932 | Ind | P/C | 158 | 9 | $3,250 | $2,250 | $5,500 |
| Davenport College | Grand Rapids, MI 49503 | 1866 | Ind | J/C | 2,570 | 126 | $2,544 | $1,125 | $3,669 |
| Delta College | Univ. Center, MI 48710 | 1961 | Public | J/C | 9,024 | 232 | $ 555 | $1,765 | $2,320 |
| Detroit Bible College | Farmington Hills, MI 48018 | 1945 | Ind | S/C | 388 | 25 | $1,850 | — | $1,850 |
| Detroit College of Business | Dearborn, MI 48126 | 1936 | Ind | S/C | 2,198 | 133 | $2,004 | — | $2,004 |
| Detroit College of Law | Detroit, MI 48201 | 1891 | Private | P/C | 828 | 63 | $2,600 | — | $2,600 |
| Detroit Inst. of Technology | Detroit, MI 48201 | 1877 | Ind | S/C | 1,255 | 41 | $1,980 | — | $1,980 |
| Eastern Michigan University | Ypsilanti, MI 48197 | 1849 | State | S-G/C | 19,000 | 704 | $ 800 | $1,600 | $2,400 |
| Faithway Baptist College | Belleville, MI 48111 | 1974 | Baptist | S/C | 84 | 20 | $1,287 | $1,633 | $2,920 |
| Ferris State College | Big Rapids, MI 49307 | 1884 | State | S-G/C | 10,596 | 500 | $ 891 | $1,800 | $2,700 |
| General Motors Institute | Flint, MI 48502 | 1919 | Private | S/C | 2,241 | — | $1,264 | $1,090 | $2,354 |
| Glen Oaks Community College | Centreville, MI 49032 | 1965 | Public | J/C | 1,296 | 94 | $ 560 | — | $ 560 |
| Gogebic Community College | Ironwood, MI 49938 | 1932 | Public | J/C | 1,308 | 46 | $ 405 | $1,200 | $1,605 |
| Grace Bible College | Grand Rapids, MI 49509 | 1939 | Gospel | S/C | 210 | 17 | $1,455 | $1,710 | $3,915 |
| Grand Rapids Baptist College | Grand Rapids, MI 49505 | 1941 | Baptist | S/C | 934 | 52 | $2,500 | $1,770 | $4,270 |
| Grand Rapids Baptist Sem. | Grand Rapids, MI 49505 | 1941 | Baptist | G/C | 206 | 11 | $1,340 | — | $1,340 |
| Grand Rapids Junior College | Grand Rapids, MI 49503 | 1914 | Public | J/C | 5,650 | 252 | $ 527 | — | $ 527 |
| Grand Valley State Colleges | Allendale, MI 49401 | 1960 | State | S-G/C | 7,142 | 350 | $ 908 | $1,713 | $2,621 |
| Great Lakes Bible College | Lansing, MI 48901 | 1949 | C of Chr | S/C | 224 | 15 | $1,617 | $1,300 | $2,917 |
| Henry Ford Community College | Dearborn, MI 48128 | 1938 | Public | J/C | 17,364 | 711 | $ 500 | — | $ 500 |
| Highland Park Comm. College | Highland Park, MI 48203 | 1918 | State | J/C | 2,540 | 70 | $ 480 | — | $ 480 |
| Hillsdale College | Hillsdale, MI 49242 | 1844 | Ind | S/C | 1,035 | 78 | $3,840 | $1,900 | $5,740 |
| Hope College | Holland, MI 49423 | 1866 | Ref | S/C | 2,355 | 140 | $3,460 | $1,590 | $5,050 |
| Jackson Community College | Jackson, MI 49201 | 1928 | State | J/C | 1,847 | 511 | $ 620 | — | $ 620 |
| John Wesley College | Owosso, MI 48867 | 1909 | Non-Den | S/C | 80 | 6 | $3,000 | $2,350 | $5,350 |
| Jordan College | Cedar Springs, MI 49319 | 1967 | Ind | S/C | 914 | 83 | $1,745 | $1,200 | $2,945 |
| Kalamazoo College | Kalamazoo, MI 49007 | 1833 | Baptist | S/C | 1,440 | 91 | $4,794 | $1,953 | $6,747 |
| Kalamazoo Valley Comm. Col. | Kalamazoo, MI 49009 | 1967 | State | J/C | 6,814 | 230 | $ 450 | — | $ 450 |
| Kellogg Community College | Battle Creek, MI 49016 | 1956 | State | J/C | 7,000 | 251 | $ 450 | — | $ 450 |
| Kendall School of Design | Grand Rapids, MI 49503 | 1928 | Ind | P/C | 424 | 43 | $2,200 | — | $2,200 |
| Kirtland Community College | Roscommon, MI 48653 | 1966 | State | J/C | 980 | 77 | $ 400 | — | $ 400 |
| Lake Michigan College | Benton Harbor, MI 49022 | 1946 | State | J/C | 3,500 | 250 | $ 500 | — | $ 500 |
| Lake Superior State College | Sault Ste. Marie, MI 49783 | 1946 | State | S/C | 2,309 | 106 | $ 870 | $1,740 | $2,610 |
| Lansing Community College | Lansing, MI 48901 | 1957 | State | J/C | 20,129 | 987 | $ 421 | — | $ 421 |
| Lawrence Inst. of Technology | Southfield, MI 48075 | 1932 | Ind | S/C | 4,991 | 250 | $1,500 | — | $1,500 |
| Lewis College of Business | Detroit, MI 48235 | 1929 | Private | J/C | 380 | 25 | $3,200 | $2,580 | $5,780 |
| Macomb County Comm. College | Warren, MI 48093 | 1954 | State | J/C | 25,619 | 684 | $ 527 | — | $ 527 |
| Madonna College | Livonia, MI 48150 | 1947 | Catholic | S/C | 3,131 | 176 | $1,508 | $1,690 | $3,198 |
| Maryglade College Seminary | Detroit, MI 48221 | 1960 | Catholic | S/M | 9 | 1 | $2,000 | — | $2,000 |
| Marygrove College | Detroit, MI 48221 | 1927 | Catholic | S-G/C | 958 | 52 | $2,827 | $1,880 | $4,707 |
| Mercy College of Detroit | Detroit, MI 48219 | 1941 | Catholic | S/C | 2,455 | 238 | $2,340 | $1,590 | $3,930 |
| Merrill-Palmer Institute | Detroit, MI 48202 | 1920 | Ind | S-G/C | 150 | 20 | $3,250 | $1,520 | $4,770 |
| Michigan Christian College | Rochester, MI 48063 | 1959 | C of Chr | S/C | 280 | 18 | $1,846 | $1,500 | $3,346 |
| Michigan State University | East Lansing, MI 48824 | 1855 | State | S-G/C | 44,756 | 2,628 | $1,249 | $1,680 | $2,929 |
| Michigan Technical Institute | Ann Arbor, MI 48107 | 1915 | Ind | T/C | 275 | 12 | $3,100 | — | $3,100 |
| Michigan Tech. University | Houghton, MI 49931 | 1885 | State | S-G/C | 7,690 | 375 | $ 903 | $1,750 | $2,653 |
| Mid Michigan Comm. College | Harrison, MI 48625 | 1965 | State | J/C | 2,300 | 74 | $ 667 | — | $ 667 |
| Midrasha Col. of Jewish Stud. | Southfield, MI 48076 | 1948 | Ind | S/C | 232 | 18 | $ 600 | — | $ 600 |
| Midwestern Baptist College | Pontiac, MI 48053 | 1953 | Baptist | S/C | 300 | 15 | — | — | $1,630 |
| Monroe County Comm. College | Monroe, MI 48161 | 1964 | Public | J/C | 1,994 | 88 | $ 481 | — | $ 481 |
| Montcalm Community College | Sidney, MI 48885 | 1965 | State | J/C | 1,622 | 72 | $ 690 | — | $ 690 |
| Mott Community College | Flint, MI 48503 | 1923 | State | J/C | 9,800 | 440 | $ 500 | — | $ 500 |
| Muskegon Business College | Muskegon, MI 49442 | 1885 | Ind | S/C | 1,016 | 47 | $1,815 | $1,425 | $3,240 |
| Muskegon Community College | Muskegon, MI 49442 | 1926 | Public | J/C | 5,353 | 195 | $ 465 | — | $ 465 |
| Nazareth Col. at Kalamazoo | Nazareth, MI 49074 | 1924 | Catholic | S/C | 540 | 61 | $3,150 | $1,570 | $4,720 |
| North Central Michigan College | Petoskey, MI 49770 | 1958 | State | J/C | 1,836 | 80 | $ 600 | $1,600 | $2,300 |
| Northeastern Sch. of Com. | Bay City, MI 48707 | 1880 | Ind | T/C | 150 | 6 | $1,450 | — | $1,450 |
| Northern Michigan University | Marquette, MI 49855 | 1899 | State | S-G/C | 9,325 | 420 | $1,094 | $1,900 | $2,994 |
| Northwestern Michigan College | Traverse City, MI 49684 | 1951 | State | J/C | 2,971 | 99 | $ 801 | $1,550 | $2,351 |
| Northwood Institute | Midland, MI 48640 | 1959 | Private | S/C | 1,791 | 75 | $2,640 | $1,590 | $4,230 |
| Oakland Community College | Bloomfield Hills, MI 48013 | 1965 | Public | J/C | 20,683 | 300 | $ 540 | — | $ 540 |
| Oakland University | Rochester, MI 48063 | 1957 | State | S-G/C | 11,729 | 556 | $ 938 | $1,720 | $2,658 |
| Olivet College | Olivet, MI 49076 | 1844 | UC Chr | S/C | 606 | 40 | $3,420 | $1,760 | $5,180 |
| Reformed Bible College | Grand Rapids, MI 49506 | 1939 | Ind | J-S/C | 240 | 24 | $1,800 | $1,450 | $3,250 |
| Sacred Heart Seminary College | Detroit, MI 48206 | 1919 | Catholic | S/M | 120 | 20 | $1,250 | $1,250 | $2,500 |
| Saginaw Valley State College | Univ. Center, MI 48710 | 1963 | State | S-G/C | 3,855 | 204 | $ 915 | $1,759 | $2,674 |
| St. Clair County Comm. College | Port Huron, MI 48060 | 1923 | State | J/C | 3,165 | 199 | $ 426 | — | $ 426 |
| St. John's Provincial Sem. | Plymouth, MI 48170 | 1949 | Catholic | G/C | 153 | 16 | $1,600 | $1,600 | $3,200 |
| St. Mary's College | Orchard Lake, MI 48033 | 1885 | Catholic | S/C | 241 | 35 | $1,600 | $1,200 | $2,800 |
| Schoolcraft College | Livonia, MI 48152 | 1961 | Public | J/C | 9,742 | 352 | $ 530 | — | — |

| NAME | ADDRESS | FOUN-DED | AFFILI-ATION | LEVEL/TYPE | ENROLL-MENT | TEACH-ERS | TUITION & FEES | BOARD & ROOM | TOTAL COST |
|---|---|---|---|---|---|---|---|---|---|
| **MICHIGAN** *(continued)* | | | | | | | | | |
| Shaw College | Detroit, MI 48202 | 1936 | Ind | S-G/C | 603 | 47 | $2,730 | $1,270 | $4,000 |
| Siena Heights College | Adrian, MI 49221 | 1919 | Catholic | S-G/C | 1,450 | 96 | $2,650 | $1,650 | $4,300 |
| Southwestern Michigan College | Dowagiac, MI 49047 | 1964 | Public | J/C | 2,396 | 150 | $ 480 | — | $ 630 |
| Spring Arbor College | Spring Arbor, MI 49283 | 1873 | Meth | S/C | 1,048 | 97 | $3,100 | $1,450 | $4,550 |
| SS. Cyril & Methodius Sem. | Orchard Lake, MI 48033 | 1885 | Catholic | G/C | 113 | 17 | $1,500 | $1,400 | $2,900 |
| Suomi College | Hancock, MI 49930 | 1896 | Lutheran | J/C | 440 | 37 | $4,400 | $1,800 | $6,200 |
| Thomas M. Cooley Law School | Lansing, MI 48933 | 1972 | Ind | P/C | 1,020 | 84 | $2,715 | — | $2,715 |
| University of Detroit | Detroit, MI 48221 | 1877 | Ind | S-G/C | 7,267 | 254 | $3,450 | $2,000 | $5,450 |
| University of Michigan | Ann Arbor, MI 48109 | 1817 | State | S-G/C | 46,680 | 2,858 | $1,212 | $2,077 | $3,289 |
|   Dearborn Campus | Dearborn, MI 48128 | 1959 | State | S-G/C | 6,400 | 341 | $ 964 | — | $ 964 |
|   Flint Campus | Flint, MI 48503 | 1956 | State | S-G/C | 4,122 | 200 | $ 882 | — | $ 882 |
| Walsh College | Troy, MI 48084 | 1922 | Ind | S-G/C | 1,507 | 70 | $1,032 | — | — |
| Washtenaw Community College | Ann Arbor, MI 48106 | 1965 | State | J/C | 7,567 | 389 | $ 454 | — | $ 454 |
| Wayne County Comm. College | Detroit, MI 48201 | 1967 | State | J/C | 20,586 | 975 | $ 486 | — | $ 486 |
| Wayne State University | Detroit, MI 48202 | 1868 | State | S-G/C | 34,337 | 2,350 | $1,166 | — | $1,166 |
| West Shore Community College | Scottsville, MI 49454 | 1967 | State | J/C | 931 | 65 | $ 586 | — | $ 586 |
| Western Michigan University | Kalamazoo, MI 49008 | 1903 | State | S-G/C | 20,689 | 1,041 | $1,900 | $1,660 | $3,560 |
| **MINNESOTA** | | | | | | | | | |
| Anoka-Ramsey Comm. College | Coon Rapids, MN 55433 | 1965 | State | J/C | 3,360 | 136 | $ 574 | — | $ 574 |
| Augsburg College | Minneapolis, MN 55454 | 1869 | Lutheran | S/C | 1,576 | 178 | $3,660 | $1,760 | $5,420 |
| Austin Community College | Austin, MN 55912 | 1940 | State | J/C | 850 | 39 | $ 575 | — | $ 575 |
| Bemidji State University | Bemidji, MN 56601 | 1919 | State | S-G/C | 5,534 | 197 | $ 748 | $1,186 | $1,934 |
| Bethany Lutheran College | Mankato, MN 56001 | 1926 | Lutheran | J/C | 310 | 25 | $2,270 | $1,570 | $3,840 |
| Bethel College | St. Paul, MN 55112 | 1871 | Baptist | S/C | 1,989 | 140 | $3,400 | $1,575 | $4,925 |
| Bethel Theological Seminary | St. Paul, MN 55112 | 1871 | Baptist | G/C | 467 | 20 | $1,690 | — | $1,690 |
| Brainerd Community College | Brainerd, MN 56401 | 1938 | State | J/C | 691 | 28 | $ 600 | — | $ 600 |
| Carleton College | Northfield, MN 55057 | 1866 | Ind | S/C | 1,718 | 167 | $4,375 | $1,800 | $6,175 |
| College of Saint Benedict | St. Joseph, MN 56374 | 1913 | Catholic | S/W | 2,023 | 128 | $3,500 | $1,450 | $4,950 |
| College of St. Catherine | St. Paul, MN 55105 | 1905 | Catholic | S/W | 2,265 | 191 | $3,295 | $1,650 | $4,945 |
| College of St. Scholastica | Duluth, MN 55811 | 1912 | Catholic | S-G/C | 1,094 | 90 | $3,000 | $1,555 | $4,555 |
| College of St. Teresa | Winona, MN 55987 | 1907 | Catholic | S/W | 791 | 100 | $3,057 | $1,527 | $4,584 |
| College of St. Thomas | St. Paul, MN 55105 | 1885 | Catholic | S-G/C | 4,784 | 265 | $3,130 | $1,625 | $4,755 |
| Concordia College | Moorhead, MN 56560 | 1891 | ALC | S/C | 2,607 | 180 | $3,675 | $1,325 | $5,000 |
| Concordia College | St. Paul, MN 55104 | 1893 | Lutheran | S/C | 664 | 60 | $2,790 | $1,470 | $4,260 |
| Crosier Seminary Jr. College | Onamia, MN 56359 | 1922 | Catholic | J/M | 32 | 17 | $1,300 | $1,350 | $2,650 |
| Dr. Martin Luther College | New Ulm, MN 56073 | 1884 | Lutheran | S/C | 849 | 71 | $1,150 | $ 960 | $2,110 |
| E. W. Cook Inst. of Psychother. | Faribault, MN 55021 | 1971 | Ind | G/C | 14 | 11 | $ 250 | — | $ 250 |
| Fergus Falls Community College | Fergus Falls, MN 56537 | 1960 | State | J/C | 595 | 38 | $ 510 | — | $ 510 |
| Golden Valley Lutheran College | Minneapolis, MN 55422 | 1967 | Ind | J/C | 588 | 45 | $3,150 | $1,900 | $5,050 |
| Gustavus Adolphus College | St. Peter, MN 56082 | 1862 | Lutheran | S/C | 2,250 | 154 | $4,300 | $1,400 | $5,700 |
| Hamline University | St. Paul, MN 55104 | 1854 | Meth | S/C | 1,666 | 140 | $4,150 | $1,700 | $5,850 |
| Hibbing Community College | Hibbing, MN 55746 | 1916 | State | J/C | 631 | 34 | $ 600 | — | $ 600 |
| Inver Hills Comm. College | Inver Grove Hts., MN 55075 | 1970 | State | J/C | 3,700 | 185 | $ 573 | — | $ 573 |
| Itasca Community College | Grand Rapids, MN 55744 | 1922 | State | J/C | 1,073 | 100 | $ 612 | — | $ 612 |
| Lakewood Community College | White Bear La., MN 55110 | 1967 | State | J/C | 3,450 | 110 | $ 703 | — | $ 703 |
| Luther-Northwestern Sem. | St. Paul, MN 55108 | 1869 | Lutheran | P/C | 857 | 52 | $1,300 | — | $1,300 |
| Macalester College | St. Paul, MN 55105 | 1874 | Presby | S/C | 1,677 | 135 | $4,175 | $1,550 | $5,725 |
| Mankato State University | Mankato, MN 56055 | 1867 | State | S-G/C | 10,613 | 500 | $ 692 | $1,148 | $1,840 |
| Mesabi Community College | Virginia, MN 55792 | 1918 | State | J/C | 791 | 32 | $ 750 | $1,300 | $2,050 |
| Metropolitan State Univ. | St. Paul, MN 55101 | 1971 | State | S/C | 2,000 | 250 | $ 750 | — | $ 750 |
| Minneap. Col. of Art & Design | Minneapolis, MN 55404 | 1886 | Private | S/C | 630 | 55 | $3,120 | $2,000 | $5,120 |
| Minnesota Bible College | Rochester, MN 55901 | 1913 | Ind | S/C | 127 | 13 | $1,435 | $1,075 | $2,510 |
| Moorhead State University | Moorhead, MN 56560 | 1887 | State | S-G/C | 6,999 | 327 | $ 631 | $1,157 | $1,788 |
| National Col. of Bus.–Ext. | Minneapolis, MN 55416 | 1974 | Private | S/C | 133 | 10 | $2,500 | — | $2,500 |
| National Col. of Bus.–Ext. | St. Paul, MN 55109 | 1974 | Private | S/C | 120 | 10 | $2,500 | — | $2,500 |
| Normandale Community College | Bloomington, MN 55431 | 1968 | State | J/C | 4,869 | 165 | $ 574 | — | $ 574 |
| North Central Bible College | Minneapolis, MN 55404 | 1930 | A of God | J-S/C | 623 | 27 | $1,584 | $1,190 | $2,774 |
| North Hennepin Comm. College | Minneapolis, MN 55445 | 1966 | State | J/C | 4,070 | 158 | $ 574 | — | $ 574 |
| Northland Community College | Thief Riv. Falls, MN 56701 | 1965 | State | J/C | 560 | 25 | $ 600 | — | $ 600 |
| Rainy River Comm. College | Intl. Falls, MN 56649 | 1967 | State | J/C | 450 | 24 | $ 700 | — | $ 700 |
| Rochester Community College | Rochester, MN 55901 | 1915 | State | J/C | 2,911 | 145 | $ 575 | — | $ 575 |
| St. Cloud State University | St. Cloud, MN 56301 | 1869 | State | S-G/C | 11,049 | 545 | $ 678 | $1,200 | $1,878 |
| St. John's University | Collegeville, MN 56321 | 1857 | Catholic | S-G/M | 1,963 | 159 | $3,475 | $1,580 | $5,055 |
| St. Mary's College | Winona, MN 55987 | 1912 | Catholic | S-G/C | 1,354 | 100 | $3,310 | $1,660 | $4,970 |
| St. Mary's Junior College | Minneapolis, MN 55454 | 1964 | Catholic | J/C | 756 | 81 | $2,304 | — | $3,740 |
| St. Olaf College | Northfield, MN 55057 | 1874 | ALC | S/C | 3,024 | 250 | $3,925 | $1,775 | $5,700 |
| St. Paul Bible College | Bible College, MN 55375 | 1916 | C & Miss | S/C | 656 | 37 | $1,520 | $1,470 | $2,990 |
| St. Paul Seminary | St. Paul, MN 55104 | 1894 | Catholic | G/M | 119 | 19 | $2,115 | $2,160 | $4,275 |
| Southwest State University | Marshall, MN 56258 | 1963 | State | S/C | 2,040 | 104 | $ 667 | $1,200 | $1,867 |
| United Theological Seminary | New Brighton, MN 55112 | 1960 | UC Chr | G/C | 223 | 18 | $1,550 | — | $4,200 |
| University of Minnesota | | | | | | | | | |
|   Duluth Campus | Duluth, MN 55812 | 1947 | State | S-G/C | 6,855 | 492 | $1,025 | $1,750 | $2,775 |
|   Morris Campus | Morris, MN 56267 | 1960 | State | S/C | 1,450 | 92 | $1,095 | $1,425 | $2,520 |
|   Technical Col., Crookston | Crookston, MN 56716 | 1965 | State | T/C | 1,109 | 72 | $ 850 | $1,680 | $2,530 |
|   Technical Col., Waseca | Waseca, MN 56093 | 1969 | State | T/C | 1,111 | 48 | $ 906 | $1,305 | $2,211 |
|   Twin Cities Campus | Minneapolis, MN 55455 | 1851 | State | S-G/C | 56,290 | 5,455 | $1,062 | $1,800 | $2,862 |
| Vermilion Community College | Ely, MN 55731 | 1922 | State | J/C | 520 | 35 | $ 574 | — | $ 574 |
| Wm. Mitchell College of Law | St. Paul, MN 55105 | 1900 | Ind | P/C | 1,117 | 112 | $2,054 | — | $2,054 |
| Willmar Community College | Willmar, MN 56201 | 1962 | State | J/C | 848 | 48 | $ 575 | — | $ 575 |
| Winona State University | Winona, MN 55987 | 1858 | State | S-G/C | 5,064 | 256 | $ 646 | $1,170 | $1,816 |
| Worthington Comm. College | Worthington, MN 56187 | 1936 | State | J/C | 780 | 50 | $ 575 | — | $ 575 |

| NAME | ADDRESS | FOUN-DED | AFFILI-ATION | LEVEL/TYPE | ENROLL-MENT | TEACH-ERS | TUITION & FEES | BOARD & ROOM | TOTAL COST |
|---|---|---|---|---|---|---|---|---|---|
| **MISSISSIPPI** | | | | | | | | | |
| Alcorn State University ........ | Lorman, MS 39096 ...... | 1871 | State | S-G/C | 2,150 | 147 | $ 744 | $1,064 | $1,808 |
| Belhaven College ............ | Jackson, MS 39202 ...... | 1883 | Presby | S/C | 886 | 57 | $ 2,025 | $1,190 | $3,215 |
| Blue Mountain College ....... | Blue Mountain, MS 38610 | 1873 | Baptist | S/W | 371 | 34 | $ 1,460 | $1,190 | $2,650 |
| Clarke College ............. | Newton, MS 39345 ..... | 1907 | Baptist | J/C | 211 | 20 | $ 1,210 | $1,070 | $2,280 |
| Coahoma Junior College ..... | Clarksdale, MS 38614 .... | 1949 | State | J/C | 1,520 | 52 | $ 350 | $ 950 | $1,300 |
| Copiah-Lincoln Junior College . | Wesson, MS 39191 ...... | 1928 | State | J/C | 1,120 | 79 | $ 290 | $ 800 | $1,090 |
|   Natchez Campus ........... | Natchez, MS 39120 ..... | 1971 | State | J/C | 431 | 32 | $ 375 | — | $ 375 |
| Delta State University ........ | Cleveland, MS 38733 .... | 1925 | State | S-G/C | 3,250 | 200 | $ 654 | $1,066 | $1,730 |
| East Central Junior College ... | Decatur, MS 39327 ...... | 1928 | State | J/C | 806 | 53 | $ 320 | $ 794 | $1,114 |
| East Mississippi Jr. College ... | Scooba, MS 39358 ...... | 1927 | State | J/C | 1,153 | 69 | $ 300 | $ 812 | $1,112 |
| Hinds Junior College ......... | Raymond, MS 39154 ..... | 1917 | State | J/C | 6,704 | 292 | $ 310 | $ 740 | $1,050 |
| Holmes Junior College ....... | Goodman, MS 39079 ..... | 1925 | State | J/C | 875 | 54 | $ 300 | $ 800 | $1,100 |
| Itawamba Junior College ..... | Fulton, MS 38843 ...... | 1948 | Public | J/C | 2,441 | 170 | $ 340 | $1,025 | $1,365 |
| Jackson State University ...... | Jackson, MS 39217 ..... | 1877 | State | S-G/C | 7,832 | 369 | $ 620 | $1,112 | $1,732 |
| Jones County Junior College .. | Ellisville, MS 39437 ..... | 1927 | State | J/C | 2,182 | 130 | $ 250 | $ 954 | $1,204 |
| Magnolia Bible College ....... | Kosciusko, MS 39090 .... | 1976 | C of Chr | S/C | 123 | 12 | $ 500 | $ 409 | $ 905 |
| Mary Holmes College ........ | West Point, MS 39773 ... | 1892 | Presby | J/C | 472 | 34 | $ 980 | $1,198 | $2,178 |
| Meridian Junior College ...... | Meridian, MS 39301 ..... | 1937 | Public | J/C | 2,889 | 165 | $ 255 | — | $ 255 |
| Mid South Christian College... | Senatobia, MS 38668 .... | 1959 | C of Chr | S/C | 52 | 7 | $ 818 | $1,250 | $2,068 |
| Millsaps College ............ | Jackson, MS 39210 ..... | 1890 | Meth | S/C | 920 | 80 | $ 2,550 | $1,240 | $3,790 |
| Mississippi Baptist Sem. ..... | Jackson, MS 39209 ...... | 1944 | Baptist | P/C | 60 | 12 | $ 100 | — | $ 100 |
| Mississippi College ......... | Clinton, MS 39058 ...... | 1826 | Baptist | S-G/C | 3,012 | 124 | $ 1,988 | $1,270 | $3,258 |
| Mississippi Delta Jr. College .. | Moorhead, MS 38761 .... | 1926 | State | J/C | 1,441 | 94 | $ 280 | $ 788 | $1,068 |
| Miss. Gulf Coast Jr. College | | | | | | | | | |
|   Jackson County Campus ... | Gautier, MS 39553 ...... | 1965 | State | J/C | 2,234 | 84 | $ 348 | — | $ 348 |
|   Jefferson Davis Campus... | Gulfport, MS 39501 ..... | 1965 | State | J/C | 2,848 | 91 | $ 348 | — | $ 348 |
|   Perkinston Campus ....... | Perkinston, MS 39573 ... | 1911 | State | J/C | 899 | 45 | $ 304 | $ 710 | $1,014 |
| Mississippi Industrial College . | Holly Springs, MS 38635 . | 1905 | CME | S/C | 268 | 23 | $ 1,675 | $1,380 | $3,055 |
| Mississippi State University .. | Starkville, MS 39762 .... | 1878 | State | S-G/C | 11,374 | 665 | $ 867 | $1,700 | $3,600 |
| Mississippi Univ. for Women .. | Columbus, MS 39701 .... | 1884 | State | S-G/W | 2,307 | 163 | $ 674 | $1,564 | $2,238 |
| Mississippi Valley State Univ. | Itta Bena, MS 38941 ..... | 1950 | State | S-G/C | 2,734 | 156 | $ 700 | $1,133 | $1,833 |
| Natchez Junior College ...... | Natchez, MS 39120 ..... | 1885 | Baptist | J/C | 41 | 6 | $ 750 | $ 750 | $1,500 |
| Northeast Mississippi Jr. Col. . | Booneville, MS 38829 .... | 1948 | State | J/C | — | — | — | — | — |
| Northwest Mississippi Jr. Col. | Senatobia, MS 38668 .... | 1927 | State | J/C | 2,310 | 131 | $ 430 | $ 982 | $1,412 |
| Pearl River Junior College .... | Poplarville, MS 39740 ... | 1908 | State | J/C | 2,328 | 136 | $ 340 | $ 740 | $1,080 |
| Prentiss Inst. Junior College .. | Prentiss, MS 39474 ..... | 1907 | Private | J/C | — | 13 | $ 1,399 | $ 658 | $2,057 |
| Reformed Theological Sem. ... | Jackson, MS 39209 ..... | 1964 | Ind | G/C | 251 | 21 | $ 1,610 | — | $1,610 |
| Rust College .............. | Holly Springs, MS 38635. | 1866 | Meth | S/C | 723 | 34 | $ 2,468 | $1,140 | $3,608 |
| Southeastern Baptist College . | Laurel, MS 39440 ...... | 1949 | Baptist | S/C | 60 | 11 | $ 805 | $ 850 | $1,655 |
| Southwest Mississippi Jr. Col. | Summit, MS 39666 ...... | 1918 | State | J/C | 1,166 | 51 | $ 300 | $ 800 | $1,100 |
| Tougaloo College .......... | Tougaloo, MS 39174 ..... | 1869 | D of Chr | S/C | 902 | 82 | $ 1,735 | $1,215 | $2,950 |
| University of Mississippi....... | University, MS 38677 .... | 1848 | State | S-G/C | 9,635 | 494 | $ 879 | $1,314 | $2,193 |
|   Medical Center ........ | Jackson, MS 39216 ...... | 1955 | State | S-G/C | 1,512 | 412 | $ 1,600 | $3,870 | $5,470 |
| University of Southern Miss. .. | Hattiesburg, MS 39401 .. | 1910 | State | S/C | 12,298 | 612 | $ 776 | $1,330 | $2,106 |
| Utica Junior College ......... | Utica, MS 39175 ........ | 1903 | State | J/C | 854 | 58 | $ 310 | — | $ 310 |
| Wesley Biblical Seminary ..... | Jackson, MS 39206 ...... | 1974 | Tr-den | G/C | 44 | 12 | $ 1,395 | — | $1,395 |
| Wesley College ............ | Florence MS 39073 ..... | 1944 | Meth | S/C | 66 | 12 | $ 1,330 | $1,100 | $2,430 |
| Whitworth Bible College ...... | Brookhaven, MS 39601 .. | 1858 | Ind | S/C | 41 | 4 | $ 1,080 | $1,500 | $2,580 |
| William Carey College ....... | Hattiesburg, MS 39401 .. | 1906 | Baptist | S-G/C | 2,631 | 123 | $ 1,726 | $1,240 | $2,966 |
| Wood Junior College ........ | Mathiston, MS 39752 .... | 1886 | Meth | J/C | 210 | 20 | $ 550 | $ 600 | $1,150 |
| | | | | | | | | | |
| **MISSOURI** | | | | | | | | | |
| Avila College .............. | Kansas City, MO 64145 .. | 1916 | Catholic | S/C | 2,005 | 197 | $ 2,550 | $1,580 | $4,130 |
| Calvary Bible College ....... | Kansas City, MO 64111 .. | 1932 | Ind | S-G/C | 496 | 38 | $ 1,540 | $1,100 | $2,640 |
| Cardinal Glennon College .... | St. Louis, MO 63119 .... | 1900 | Catholic | S/M | 94 | 28 | $ 1,700 | $ 800 | $2,500 |
| Central Bible College ....... | Springfield, MO 65802 ... | 1922 | A of God | S/C | 1,132 | 56 | $ 1,376 | $1,380 | $2,756 |
| Central Christian Colllege..... | Moberly, MO 65270 ..... | 1957 | Christian | S/C | 140 | 13 | $ 800 | $1,300 | $2,100 |
| Central Methodist College .... | Fayette, MO 65248 ...... | 1854 | Meth | S/C | 667 | 55 | $ 3,200 | $1,500 | $4,700 |
| Central Missouri State Univ. .. | Warrensburg, MO 64093 . | 1871 | State | S-G/C | 9,905 | 550 | $ 465 | $1,560 | $2,025 |
| Cleveland Chiropractic College | Kansas City, MO 64131 .. | 1922 | Ind | P/C | 240 | 35 | $ 3,420 | — | — |
| Columbia College ........... | Columbia, MO 65216 ... | 1851 | Ind | S/C | 900 | 51 | $ 2,970 | $1,700 | $4,670 |
| Conception Seminary College . | Conception, MO 64433 .. | 1883 | Catholic | S/M | 94 | 25 | $ 1,270 | $1,830 | $3,100 |
| Concordia Seminary ......... | St. Louis, MO 63105 ..... | 1839 | Lutheran | P/M | 669 | 37 | $ 1,850 | $1,380 | $3,230 |
| Cottey College ............. | Nevada, MO 64772 ...... | 1884 | Ind | J/W | 345 | 33 | — | — | $3,800 |
| Covenant Theological Sem. .. | St. Louis, MO 63141 ..... | 1956 | Presby | P/C | 164 | 16 | $ 1,985 | $ 540 | $2,525 |
| Crowder College........... | Neosho, MO 64850 ..... | 1963 | Public | J/C | 1,146 | 45 | $ 250 | $1,050 | $1,300 |
| Culver-Stockton College ..... | Canton, MO 63435 ..... | 1853 | D of Chr | S/C | 525 | 47 | $ 2,930 | $1,730 | $4,710 |
| Drury College ............. | Springfield, MO 65802 ... | 1873 | Private | S-G/C | 2,717 | 136 | $ 2,650 | $1,387 | $4,037 |
| East Central Junior College .. | Union, MO 63084 ...... | 1968 | Public | J/C | 1,604 | 46 | $ 280 | — | $ 280 |
| Eden Theological Seminary ... | St. Louis, MO 63119 ..... | 1850 | UC Chr | G/C | 231 | 11 | $ 1,905 | $1,400 | $3,350 |
| Evangel College ............ | Springfield, MO 65802 ... | 1955 | A of God | S/C | 1,612 | 80 | $ 1,986 | $1,590 | $3,576 |
| Fontbonne College .......... | St. Louis, MO 63105 ..... | 1917 | Catholic | S-G/C | 745 | 92 | $ 2,740 | $1,520 | $4,260 |
| Hannibal-Lagrange College ... | Hannibal, MO 63401...... | 1858 | Baptist | S/C | 416 | 41 | $ 1,820 | $1,200 | $3,020 |
| Harris-Stowe College ....... | St. Louis, MO 63103 ..... | 1857 | State | S/C | 1,076 | 79 | $ 175 | — | $ 175 |
| Jefferson College........... | Hillsboro, MO 63050 ..... | 1963 | State | J/C | 2,640 | 142 | $ 300 | — | $ 300 |
| Kansas City Art Institute...... | Kansas City, MO 64111 .. | 1885 | Ind | S/C | 570 | 55 | $ 3,830 | $1,650 | $5,480 |
| Kansas City Col. of Osteo. Med. | Kansas City, MO 64124 .. | 1916 | Ind | P/C | 617 | 55 | $ 8,250 | — | $8,250 |
| Kemper Military Sch. and Col. | Boonville, MO 65233 ... | 1923 | Ind | J/C | 105 | 15 | $ 2,000 | $1,900 | $3,900 |
| Kirksville Col. of Osteo. Med. .. | Kirksville, MO 63501 .... | 1892 | Ind | P/C | 500 | 86 | $10,000 | — | — |
| Lincoln University .......... | Jefferson City, MO 65101. | 1866 | State | S-G/C | 2,415 | 200 | $ 400 | $1,170 | $1,570 |
| Lindenwood Colleges ........ | St. Charles, MO 63301 ... | 1827 | Ind | S-G/C | 1,726 | 102 | $ 3,450 | $2,500 | $5,950 |

| NAME | ADDRESS | FOUN-DED | AFFILI-ATION | LEVEL/TYPE | ENROLL-MENT | TEACH-ERS | TUITION & FEES | BOARD & ROOM | TOTAL COST |
|---|---|---|---|---|---|---|---|---|---|
| **MISSOURI** *(continued)* | | | | | | | | | |
| Logan College of Chiropractic | Chesterfield, MO 63017 | 1935 | Ind | P/C | 570 | 25 | $3,660 | — | $3,660 |
| Longview Community College | Lee's Summit, MO 64063 | 1969 | State | J/C | 4,000 | 125 | $ 685 | — | $ 685 |
| Maple Woods Comm. College | Kansas City, MO 64156 | 1969 | Public | J/C | 2,102 | 95 | $ 450 | — | $ 450 |
| Maryville College | St. Louis, MO 63141 | 1872 | Ind | S-G/C | 1,351 | 117 | $2,850 | $1,600 | $4,450 |
| Metropolitan Comm. College | Kansas City, MO 64111 | 1915 | Public | J/C | — | — | — | — | — |
| Midwestern Bapt. Theol. Sem. | Kansas City, MO 64118 | 1957 | Baptist | P/C | 438 | 20 | $ 350 | $1,350 | $1,700 |
| Mineral Area College | Flat River, MO 63601 | 1965 | State | J/C | 1,254 | 61 | $ 210 | — | $ 210 |
| Missouri Baptist College | St. Louis, MO 63141 | 1968 | Baptist | S/C | 434 | 38 | $2,100 | $1,600 | $3,700 |
| Missouri Inst. of Technology | Kansas City, MO 64114 | 1931 | Ind | T/C | 952 | 18 | $2,425 | — | $2,425 |
| Missouri School of Religion | Columbia, MO 65201 | 1895 | Int-Den | S/C | — | 7 | — | — | — |
| Missouri Southern State Col. | Joplin, MO 64801 | 1937 | State | S/C | 3,790 | 163 | $ 440 | $1,130 | $1,570 |
| Missouri Valley College | Marshall, MO 65340 | 1889 | Presby | S/C | 372 | 42 | $2,644 | $1,660 | $4,304 |
| Missouri Western St. College | St. Joseph, MO 64507 | 1915 | State | S/C | 3,777 | 182 | $ 442 | $1,016 | $1,458 |
| Moberly Junior College | Moberly, MO 65270 | 1927 | State | J/C | 850 | 48 | $ 290 | — | $ 290 |
| National College of Business | Kansas City, MO 64138 | 1975 | Private | S/C | 73 | 8 | $2,500 | — | $2,500 |
| Nazarene Theological Sem. | Kansas City, MO 64131 | 1945 | Nazarene | P/C | 464 | 28 | $ 970 | — | $ 970 |
| Northeast Missouri St. Univ. | Kirksville, MO 63501 | 1867 | State | S-G/C | 6,041 | 300 | $ 340 | $1,020 | $1,360 |
| Northwest Missouri St. Univ. | Maryville, MO 64468 | 1905 | State | S-G/C | 4,412 | 230 | $ 490 | $1,250 | $1,740 |
| Ozark Bible College | Joplin, MO 64801 | 1942 | Christian | S/C | 753 | 51 | $ 750 | $1,156 | $1,906 |
| Park College | Parkville, MO 64152 | 1875 | RLDS | S/C | 2,145 | 46 | $3,000 | $1,250 | $4,250 |
| Penn Valley Comm. College | Kansas City, MO 64111 | 1915 | State | J/C | 6,007 | 105 | $ 360 | — | $ 360 |
| Pioneer Comm. Col. | Kansas City, MO 64111 | 1976 | State | J/C | 700 | 25 | $ 400 | — | $ 400 |
| Rockhurst College | Kansas City, MO 64110 | 1910 | Catholic | S-G/C | 3,688 | 206 | $2,950 | $1,610 | $4,560 |
| St. Louis College of Pharmacy | St. Louis, MO 63110 | 1864 | Ind | S/C | 709 | 44 | $2,800 | $1,750 | $4,550 |
| St. Louis Comm. College | St. Louis, MO 63110 | 1962 | Public | J/C | 26,000 | — | $ 510 | — | $ 510 |
| Florissant Valley | Ferguson, MO 63135 | 1963 | Public | J/C | 8,800 | 300 | $ 510 | — | $ 510 |
| Forest Park | St. Louis, MO 63110 | 1962 | Public | J/C | 7,400 | 300 | $ 510 | — | $ 510 |
| Meramec | Kirkwood, MO 63122 | 1964 | Public | J/C | 9,800 | 300 | $ 510 | — | $ 510 |
| St. Louis Conserv. of Music | St. Louis, MO 63130 | 1923 | Ind | S-G/C | 103 | 33 | $2,710 | — | $2,710 |
| St. Louis University | St. Louis, MO 63103 | 1818 | Catholic | S-G/C | 10,496 | 2,162 | $3,300 | $1,712 | $5,012 |
| St. Mary's College of O'Fallon | O'Fallon, MO 63366 | 1921 | Catholic | J/C | 495 | 49 | $2,100 | — | $2,100 |
| St. Mary's Seminary College | Perryville, MO 63775 | 1818 | Catholic | S/M | 56 | 16 | $2,982 | $1,750 | $4,732 |
| St. Paul School of Theology | Kansas City, MO 64015 | 1958 | Meth | P/C | 161 | 20 | $1,660 | — | $2,560 |
| St. Paul's College | Concordia, MO 64020 | 1883 | Lutheran | J/C | 78 | 20 | $1,360 | $1,360 | $2,720 |
| School of the Ozarks | Point Lookout, MO 65726 | 1906 | Ind | S/C | ¹1,282 | 82 | — | — | — |
| Southeast Missouri State Univ. | Cape Girardeau, MO 63701 | 1873 | State | S-G/C | 8,654 | 394 | $ 360 | $1,250 | $1,610 |
| Southwest Baptist College | Bolivar, MO 65613 | 1878 | Baptist | S-G/C | 1,394 | 72 | $1,150 | $2,100 | $3,250 |
| Southwest Missouri St. Univ. | Springfield, MO 65802 | 1905 | State | S-G/C | 14,473 | 638 | $ 400 | $1,100 | $1,500 |
| State Fair Community College | Sedalia, MO 65301 | 1966 | Public | J/C | 1,400 | 56 | $ 228 | — | $ 228 |
| Stephens College | Columbia, MO 65215 | 1833 | Ind | S/W | 1,410 | 150 | $6,075 | — | $6,075 |
| Tarkio College | Tarkio, MO 64491 | 1883 | Presby | S/C | 266 | 34 | $2,825 | $1,475 | $4,300 |
| Three Rivers Comm. College | Poplar Bluff, MO 63901 | 1966 | State | J/C | 1,410 | 54 | $ 400 | — | $ 400 |
| Trenton Junior College | Trenton, MO 64683 | 1925 | Public | J/C | 516 | 34 | $ 420 | — | $ 420 |
| University of Missouri | | | | | | | | | |
| Columbia Campus | Columbia, MO 65211 | 1839 | State | S-G/C | 23,545 | 3,458 | $ 768 | $1,450 | $2,218 |
| Kansas City Campus | Kansas City, MO 64110 | 1933 | State | S-G/C | 10,824 | 962 | $ 802 | $1,568 | $2,370 |
| Rolla Campus | Rolla, MO 65401 | 1870 | State | S-G/C | 6,103 | 878 | $ 833 | $1,600 | $2,433 |
| St. Louis Campus | St. Louis, MO 63121 | 1963 | State | S-G/C | 11,357 | 670 | $ 776 | — | — |
| Washington University | St. Louis, MO 63130 | 1853 | Private | S-G/C | 10,542 | 2,261 | $4,750 | $2,363 | $7,113 |
| Webster College | St. Louis, MO 63119 | 1915 | Ind | S-G/C | 3,658 | 602 | $3,000 | $1,620 | $4,920 |
| Wentworth Mil. Acad. & Jr. Col. | Lexington, MO 64067 | 1880 | Ind | J/M | 70 | 19 | — | — | — |
| Westminster College | Fulton, MO 65251 | 1851 | Ind | S/C | 650 | 55 | $3,770 | $1,750 | $5,520 |
| William Jewell College | Liberty, MO 64068 | 1849 | Baptist | S/C | 1,400 | 83 | $2,720 | $1,410 | $4,130 |
| William Woods College | Fulton, MO 65251 | 1870 | Ind | S/W | 996 | 89 | $3,725 | $1,735 | $5,460 |
| **MONTANA** | | | | | | | | | |
| Carroll College | Helena, MT 59601 | 1909 | Catholic | S/C | 1,342 | 105 | $2,340 | $1,500 | $3,850 |
| College of Great Falls | Great Falls, MT 59405 | 1932 | Catholic | S/C | 1,132 | 88 | $2,000 | $1,240 | $3,240 |
| Dawson Community College | Glendive, MT 59330 | 1940 | State | J/C | 498 | 40 | $ 285 | $1,650 | $1,935 |
| Eastern Montana College | Billings, MT 59101 | 1927 | State | S/C | 3,610 | 144 | $ 519 | $1,650 | $2,169 |
| Flathead Valley Comm. College | Kalispell, MT 59901 | 1967 | State | J/C | 1,401 | 40 | $ 285 | — | $ 285 |
| Miles Community College | Miles City, MT 59301 | 1939 | Public | J/C | 745 | 35 | $ 300 | — | $ 300 |
| Mont. Col. of Min. Sci. & Tech. | Butte, MT 59701 | 1893 | State | S-G/C | 1,393 | 65 | $ 460 | $1,613 | $2,073 |
| Montana State University | Bozeman, MT 59717 | 1893 | State | S-G/C | 10,109 | 537 | $ 573 | $1,615 | $2,188 |
| Northern Montana College | Havre, MT 59501 | 1929 | State | S/C | 1,209 | 81 | $ 453 | $1,471 | $1,924 |
| Rocky Mountain College | Billings, MT 59102 | 1878 | Int-Den | S/C | 503 | 40 | $2,200 | $1,385 | $3,585 |
| University of Montana | Missoula, MT 59812 | 1893 | State | S-G/C | 8,376 | 396 | $ 625 | $1,706 | $2,331 |
| Western Montana College | Dillon, MT 59725 | 1893 | State | S/C | 828 | 39 | $ 486 | $1,522 | $2,008 |
| **NEBRASKA** | | | | | | | | | |
| Alliance Sch. of Prac. Nursing | Alliance, NE 69301 | 1958 | State | T/C | 30 | 7 | $ 585 | — | $3,600 |
| Bellevue College | Bellevue, NE 68005 | 1965 | Ind | S/C | 2,272 | 74 | $1,100 | — | $1,100 |
| Central Tech. Comm. Col. Area | Grand Island, NE 68801 | 1973 | Local | T/C | — | — | — | — | — |
| Central Tech. Comm. College | Hastings, NE 68901 | 1966 | Local | T/C | 2,565 | 82 | $ 418 | $ 900 | $1,318 |
| Grand Island Ed. Center | Grand Island, NE 68801 | 1975 | Local | T/C | 2,407 | 15 | $ 396 | — | $ 396 |
| Platte Technical Comm. Col. | Columbus, NE 68601 | 1967 | Local | T/C | 3,157 | 38 | $ 418 | — | $ 418 |
| Chadron State College | Chadron, NE 69337 | 1911 | State | S-G/C | 1,954 | 110 | $ 630 | $1,236 | $1,866 |
| College of Saint Mary | Omaha, NE 68124 | 1923 | Catholic | S/W | 592 | 83 | $3,222 | $1,410 | $4,632 |
| Concordia Teachers College | Seward, NE 68434 | 1894 | Lutheran | S-G/C | 1,049 | 95 | $2,670 | $1,570 | $4,240 |
| Creighton University | Omaha, NE 68178 | 1878 | Ind | S-G/C | 5,420 | 900 | $3,020 | $1,476 | $4,496 |
| Dana College | Blair, NE 68008 | 1884 | Lutheran | S/C | 502 | 48 | $2,900 | $1,285 | $4,185 |
| Doane College | Crete, NE 68333 | 1872 | UC Chr | S/C | 708 | 59 | $2,800 | $1,250 | $4,050 |

| NAME | ADDRESS | FOUN-DED | AFFILI-ATION | LEVEL/TYPE | ENROLL-MENT | TEACH-ERS | TUITION & FEES | BOARD & ROOM | TOTAL COST |
|---|---|---|---|---|---|---|---|---|---|
| **NEBRASKA** (continued) | | | | | | | | | |
| Grace College of the Bible | Omaha, NE 68108 | 1943 | Ind | S/C | 458 | 23 | $2,170 | $1,480 | $3,650 |
| Hastings College | Hastings, NE 68901 | 1882 | Presby | S/C | 785 | 65 | $2,800 | $1,480 | $4,280 |
| Kearney State College | Kearney, NE 68847 | 1903 | State | S-G/C | 6,838 | 227 | $ 570 | $1,168 | $1,738 |
| McCook Community College | McCook, NE 69001 | 1926 | State | J/C | 630 | 35 | $ 400 | $1,000 | $1,400 |
| Met. Tech. Comm. College | Omaha, NE 68103 | 1974 | Local | J/C | 5,500 | 139 | $ 517 | — | $ 517 |
| Midland Lutheran College | Fremont, NE 68025 | 1883 | Lutheran | S/C | 802 | 65 | $3,230 | $1,460 | $4,690 |
| Mid-Plains Community College | North Platte, NE 69101 | 1968 | State | J/C | 1,750 | 60 | $ 430 | — | $1,150 |
| Nebraska Christian College | Norfolk, NE 68701 | 1945 | C of Chr | S/C | 165 | 13 | $ 980 | $1,270 | $2,250 |
| Nebraska Wesleyan Univ. | Lincoln, NE 68504 | 1887 | Meth | S/C | 1,165 | 102 | $3,174 | $1,360 | $4,534 |
| Nebraska Western College | Scottsbluff, NE 69361 | 1926 | State | J/C | 1,172 | 80 | $ 465 | $1,290 | $1,965 |
| Northeast Tech. Comm. Col. | Norfolk, NE 68701 | 1928 | State | T/C | 1,537 | 95 | $ 426 | — | $ 426 |
| Peru State College | Peru, NE 68421 | 1867 | State | S/C | 766 | 48 | $ 655 | $1,392 | $2,047 |
| Platte Valley Bible College | Scottsbluff, NE 69361 | 1951 | C of Chr | S/C | 57 | 8 | $ 900 | $1,200 | $2,100 |
| Southeast Community College | | | | | | | | | |
| Fairbury/Beatrice Campus | Fairbury, NE 68352 | 1941 | Public | T/C | 430 | 25 | $ 438 | $1,160 | $1,598 |
| Lincoln Campus | Lincoln, NE 68520 | 1967 | Public | T/C | 2,585 | 85 | $ 394 | — | $ 394 |
| Milford Campus | Milford, NE 68405 | 1941 | Public | T/C | 866 | 75 | $ 588 | $1,272 | $1,860 |
| Union College | Lincoln, NE 68506 | 1891 | 7-D Adv | S/C | 885 | 102 | $3,554 | $ 700 | $4,254 |
| University of Nebraska | | | | | | | | | |
| Lincoln | Lincoln, NE 68588 | 1869 | State | S-G/C | 22,755 | 1,807 | $ 858 | $1,425 | $2,283 |
| Medical Center | Omaha, NE 68105 | 1902 | State | S-G/C | 1,912 | 559 | $2,242 | $2,242 | — |
| Omaha | Omaha, NE 68132 | 1908 | State | S-G/C | 14,718 | 471 | $ 806 | — | $ 806 |
| Sch. of Tech. Agriculture | Curtis, NE 69025 | 1965 | State | T/C | 281 | 27 | $ 768 | $1,580 | $2,348 |
| Wayne State College | Wayne, NE 68787 | 1910 | State | S-G/C | 2,400 | 120 | $ 688 | $1,266 | $1,954 |
| Western Nebraska Tech. Col. | Sidney, NE 69162 | 1965 | State | T/C | 610 | 25 | $ 450 | $ 920 | $1,370 |
| York College | York, NE 68467 | 1890 | C of Chr | J/C | 324 | 25 | $1,670 | $1,320 | $2,990 |
| | | | | | | | | | |
| **NEVADA** | | | | | | | | | |
| Northern Nevada Comm. Col. | Elko, NV 89801 | 1968 | State | J/C | 1,250 | 130 | $ 390 | — | $ 390 |
| Reno Business College | Reno, NV 89502 | 1902 | Ind | J/C | 125 | 15 | $1,800 | $1,200 | $3,000 |
| Sierra Nevada College | Incline Village, NV 89450 | 1969 | Ind | S/C | 175 | 32 | $1,500 | — | $1,500 |
| Univ. of Nevada, Las Vegas | Las Vegas, NV 89154 | 1957 | State | S-G/C | 9,447 | 385 | $ 720 | $1,875 | $2,595 |
| Univ. of Nevada, Reno | Reno, NV 89507 | 1864 | State | S-G/C | 8,642 | 348 | $1,380 | $1,596 | $2,976 |
| | | | | | | | | | |
| **NEW HAMPSHIRE** | | | | | | | | | |
| Antioch/New Eng. Grad. Cen. | Keene, NH 03431 | 1964 | Ind | G/C | 362 | 60 | $3,675 | — | $9,083 |
| Castle Junior College | Windham, NH 03087 | 1963 | Catholic | J/W | 119 | 9 | $1,400 | — | $1,400 |
| Colby-Sawyer College | New London, NH 03257 | 1837 | Ind | S/W | 647 | 60 | $4,683 | $1,992 | $6,675 |
| Daniel Webster College | Nashua, NH 03063 | 1965 | Ind | S/C | 500 | 32 | $3,350 | $1,900 | $5,250 |
| Dartmouth College | Hanover, NH 03755 | 1769 | Ind | S-G/C | 4,248 | 298 | $5,370 | $2,315 | $7,685 |
| Franklin Pierce College | Rindge, NH 03461 | 1962 | Ind | S/C | 900 | 60 | $4,040 | $3,400 | $7,440 |
| Hawthorne College | Antrim, NH 03440 | 1962 | Private | J-S/C | 530 | 50 | $3,600 | $1,400 | $5,000 |
| Hesser College | Manchester, NH 03104 | 1900 | Ind | J/C | 964 | 67 | $2,140 | $1,650 | $3,790 |
| Keene State College | Keene, NH 03431 | 1909 | Public | S/C | 2,573 | 185 | $ 800 | $1,485 | $2,285 |
| Lebanon College | Lebanon, NH 03766 | 1957 | Ind | J/C | 975 | 50 | — | — | — |
| Magdalen College | Bedford, NH 03102 | 1973 | Catholic | S/C | 75 | 8 | $2,400 | $1,600 | $4,200 |
| McIntosh College | Dover, NH 03820 | 1896 | Ind | J/C | 200 | 15 | $2,000 | — | $2,000 |
| New England College | Henniker, NH 03242 | 1946 | Ind | S/C | 1,491 | 108 | $4,680 | $1,800 | $6,480 |
| New Hampshire College | Manchester, NH 03104 | 1932 | Ind | S-G/C | 1,475 | 75 | $3,692 | $2,116 | $5,808 |
| New Hampshire Tech. Inst. | Concord, NH 03301 | 1965 | State | T/C | 667 | 58 | $ 654 | $1,326 | $1,980 |
| N.H. Voc. Tech. College | Berlin, NH 03570 | 1966 | State | T/C | 358 | 32 | $ 630 | — | $ 630 |
| N.H. Voc. Tech. College | Claremont NH 03743 | 1967 | State | T/C | 350 | 40 | $ 650 | — | $ 650 |
| N.H. Voc. Tech. College | Laconia, NH 03246 | 1967 | State | J/C | 238 | 23 | $ 625 | — | $ 625 |
| N.H. Voc. Tech. College | Manchester, NH 03102 | 1945 | State | J/C | 323 | 25 | $ 620 | — | $ 620 |
| N.H. Voc. Tech. College | Nashua, NH 03063 | 1967 | State | T/C | 1,038 | 26 | $ 625 | — | $ 625 |
| N.H. Voc. Tech. College | Portsmouth, NH 03801 | 1945 | State | T/C | 236 | 20 | $ 622 | — | $ 622 |
| Notre Dame College | Manchester, NH 03104 | 1950 | Catholic | S-G/W | 750 | 72 | $2,460 | $1,660 | $4,120 |
| Plymouth State College | Plymouth, NH 03264 | 1871 | State | S/C | 3,351 | 173 | $ 978 | $1,475 | $1,572 |
| Rivier College | Nashua, NH 03060 | 1933 | Catholic | S-G/C | 1,703 | 110 | $2,750 | $1,850 | $4,600 |
| St. Anselm's College | Manchester, NH 03102 | 1889 | Catholic | S/C | 1,923 | 146 | $3,600 | $1,880 | $5,480 |
| University of New Hampshire | Durham, NH 03824 | 1866 | State | S-G/C | 12,386 | 631 | $1,255 | $1,600 | $2,855 |
| Merrimack Valley College | Manchester, NH 03102 | 1967 | State | J/C | 364 | 15 | $ 810 | — | $ 950 |
| White Pines College | Chester, NH 03036 | 1965 | Ind | J/C | 156 | 20 | $3,000 | $2,000 | $5,000 |
| | | | | | | | | | |
| **NEW JERSEY** | | | | | | | | | |
| Alma White College | Zarephath, NJ 08890 | 1921 | Church | S/C | — | — | $1,200 | — | — |
| Assumption College for Sisters | Mendham, NJ 07945 | 1953 | Catholic | J/W | 31 | 7 | $1,200 | $ 800 | $2,000 |
| Atlantic Community College | Mays Landing, NJ 08330 | 1964 | State | J/C | 3,381 | 112 | $ 588 | — | $ 598 |
| Bergen Community College | Paramus, NJ 07652 | 1965 | Public | J/C | 10,659 | 521 | $ 575 | — | $ 575 |
| Berkeley School | Little Falls, NJ 07424 | 1931 | Ind | J/C | 432 | 17 | $2,895 | $2,400 | $5,295 |
| Berkeley School | Ridgewood, NJ 07450 | 1936 | Ind | T/C | 288 | 10 | $2,895 | — | $2,895 |
| Bloomfield College | Bloomfield, NJ 07003 | 1868 | Ind | S/C | 2,268 | 141 | $3,110 | $1,810 | $4,920 |
| Brookdale Community College | Lincroft, NJ 07738 | 1967 | County | J/C | 9,791 | 300 | $ 524 | — | $ 524 |
| Burlington County College | Pemberton, NJ 08068 | 1968 | County | J/C | 6,150 | 300 | $ 592 | — | $ 592 |
| Caldwell College | Caldwell, NJ 07006 | 1939 | Catholic | S/W | 663 | 75 | $2,750 | $1,850 | $4,600 |
| Camden County College | Blackwood, NJ 08012 | 1967 | Public | J/C | 7,761 | 335 | $ 404 | — | $ 404 |
| Centenary College | Hackettstown, NJ 07840 | 1867 | Ind | J-S/W | 689 | 74 | $3,100 | $2,550 | $5,650 |
| Col. of Med. & Dent. of N.J. | Newark, NJ 07103 | 1956 | State | G/C | 1,865 | — | $4,500 | — | $4,500 |
| Grad. Sch. of Biomedical Sci. | Newark, NJ 07103 | 1961 | State | G/C | 98 | — | $1,080 | — | — |
| New Jersey Dental School | Newark, NJ 07103 | 1956 | State | G/C | 244 | 214 | $4,000 | — | — |
| New Jersey Medical School | Newark, NJ 07103 | 1956 | State | G/C | 490 | 1,128 | $4,000 | — | — |
| N.J. Sch. of Osteopath. Med. | Piscataway, NJ 08854 | 1977 | State | G/C | 24 | 195 | $4,000 | — | — |

| NAME | ADDRESS | FOUN-DED | AFFILI-ATION | LEVEL/TYPE | ENROLL-MENT | TEACH-ERS | TUITION & FEES | BOARD & ROOM | TOTAL COST |
|---|---|---|---|---|---|---|---|---|---|
| **NEW JERSEY** (continued) | | | | | | | | | |
| College of Saint Elizabeth .... | Convent Sta., NJ 07961 .... | 1899 | Catholic | S/W | 832 | 85 | $2,990 | $1,800 | $4,790 |
| County College of Morris .... | Randolph, NJ 07869 ...... | 1965 | Public | J/C | 10,858 | 466 | $ 574 | — | $ 574 |
| Cumberland County College .. | Vineland, NJ 08360 ...... | 1965 | Public | J/C | 2,359 | 92 | $ 546 | — | $ 546 |
| Don Bosco College .......... | Newton, NJ 07860 ........ | 1928 | Catholic | S/M | 91 | 18 | $3,000 | $1,750 | $4,750 |
| Drew University ............ | Madison, NJ 07940 ....... | 1866 | Meth | S-G/C | 2,341 | 202 | $4,890 | $1,820 | $6,710 |
| Essex County College ....... | Newark, NJ 07102 ........ | 1966 | State | J/C | 6,746 | 351 | $ 564 | — | $ 564 |
| Fairleigh Dickinson Univ. | | | | | | | | | |
| Edward Williams College ... | Hackensack, NJ 07601 .... | 1942 | Ind | J/C | 884 | 45 | $2,750 | $1,699 | $4,449 |
| Florham-Madison Campus ... | Madison, NJ 07940 ....... | 1942 | Ind | S-G/C | 4,961 | 330 | $3,370 | $1,794 | $5,164 |
| Rutherford Campus ....... | Rutherford, NJ 07070 ..... | 1942 | Ind | S-G/C | 5,247 | 369 | $3,320 | $1,699 | $5,019 |
| Teaneck-Hackensack ...... | Teaneck, NJ 07666 ....... | 1942 | Ind | S-G/C | 8,704 | 853 | $3,320 | $1,699 | $5,019 |
| Felician College ............ | Lodi, NJ 07644 .......... | 1942 | Catholic | S/W | 760 | 77 | $2,415 | — | $2,415 |
| Georgian Court College ..... | Lakewood, NJ 08701 ...... | 1908 | Catholic | S-G/W | 1,258 | 108 | $2,600 | $1,600 | $4,200 |
| Glassboro State College ..... | Glassboro, NJ 08028 ..... | 1923 | State | S-G/C | 10,500 | 405 | $ 895 | $ 765 | $1,660 |
| Gloucester County College ... | Sewell, NJ 08080 ........ | 1968 | Public | J/C | 2,648 | 68 | $ 500 | — | $ 500 |
| Hudson County Comm. Col. .. | North Bergen, NJ 07047... | 1974 | County | J/C | 2,000 | 150 | $ 500 | — | $ 500 |
| Immaculate Conception Sem. . | Darlington, NJ 07430 .... | 1861 | Catholic | G/C | 217 | 34 | $1,325 | $1,375 | $2,700 |
| Jersey City State College .... | Jersey City, NJ 07305 .... | 1929 | State | S-G/C | 8,753 | 301 | $ 860 | $1,300 | $2,160 |
| Kean College of New Jersey .. | Union, NJ 07083 ......... | 1855 | State | S-G/C | 13,727 | 773 | $ 660 | $1,034 | $1,700 |
| Mercer County Comm. College | Trenton, NJ 08690........ | 1966 | County | J/C | 7,600 | 229 | $ 480 | — | $ 480 |
| Middlesex County College .... | Edison, NJ 08817........ | 1964 | County | J/C | 11,589 | 294 | $ 496 | — | $ 496 |
| Monmouth College .......... | W. Long Branch, NJ 07764 | 1933 | Ind | S-G/C | 3,803 | 220 | $3,590 | $1,000 | $4,590 |
| Montclair State College ...... | Upper Montclair, NJ 07043 | 1908 | State | S-G/C | 14,800 | 670 | $ 910 | $1,500 | $2,410 |
| New Brunswick Theol. Sem. .. | New Brunswick, NJ 08846 | 1784 | Ref | G/C | 107 | 11 | $1,650 | $ 650 | $2,300 |
| New Jersey Inst. of Tech. .... | Newark, NJ 07102 ....... | 1881 | State | S/C | 6,021 | 261 | $ 982 | $ 950 | $1,932 |
| Northeastern Bible College .. | Essex Falls, NJ 07021 .... | 1950 | Ind | S/C | 337 | 30 | $2,692 | $1,669 | $4,361 |
| Ocean County College ....... | Toms River, NJ 08753 ... | 1964 | County | J/C | 5,408 | 238 | $ 563 | — | $ 563 |
| Passaic County Comm. College | Paterson, NJ 07509 ...... | 1968 | County | J/C | 3,208 | 198 | $ 612 | — | $ 612 |
| Princeton Theol. Seminary ... | Princeton, NJ 08540 ..... | 1812 | Presby | G/C | 801 | 51 | $2,000 | $1,620 | $3,620 |
| Princeton University ........ | Princeton, NJ 08544 ..... | 1746 | Private | S-G/C | 5,939 | 1,678 | $6,300 | $2,461 | $8,761 |
| Rabbinical Col. of America ... | Morristown, NJ 07960 ... | 1956 | Jewish | S/M | 222 | 13 | $2,350 | $2,150 | $4,500 |
| Ramapo Col. of New Jersey .. | Mahwah, NJ 07430 ...... | 1969 | State | S/C | 4,300 | 190 | $ 890 | $1,125 | $2,015 |
| Rider College .............. | Lawrenceville, NJ 08648.. | 1865 | Ind | S-G/C | 5,583 | 245 | $3,250 | $1,780 | $5,030 |
| Rutgers State Univ. of N.J. | | | | | | | | | |
| Camden Col. of Arts & Sci. ... | Camden, NJ 08102 ...... | 1927 | State | S/C | 3,220 | 175 | $1,009 | — | $1,009 |
| College of Engineering .... | New Brunswick, NJ 08903 | 1864 | State | S/C | 2,307 | 99 | $1,087 | $1,872 | $2,959 |
| College of Nursing ........ | Newark, NJ 07102 ....... | 1956 | State | S/C | 564 | 49 | $1,007 | — | $1,007 |
| College of Pharmacy ...... | New Brunswick, NJ 08903 | 1927 | State | S/C | 564 | 30 | $1,087 | $1,872 | $2,959 |
| Cook College ............ | New Brunswick, NJ 08903 | 1973 | State | S/C | 2,943 | 144 | $1,080 | $1,872 | $2,952 |
| Douglass College.......... | New Brunswick, NJ 08903 | 1918 | State | S/W | 3,718 | 266 | $1,076 | $1,872 | $2,948 |
| Livingston College ........ | New Brunswick, NJ 08903 | 1969 | State | S/C | 3,717 | 242 | $1,089 | $1,872 | $2,961 |
| Mason Gross Sch. of the Arts | New Brunswick, NJ 08903 | 1976 | State | S/C | 61 | 10 | $1,076 | $1,872 | $2,948 |
| Newark Col. of Arts & Sci. .. | Newark, NJ 07102 ....... | 1946 | State | S/C | 4,085 | 255 | $1,007 | — | $1,007 |
| Rutgers College........... | New Brunswick, NJ 08903 | 1766 | State | S/C | 8,389 | 579 | $1,087 | $1,872 | $2,959 |
| University College ........ | New Brunswick, NJ 08902 | 1934 | State | S/C | 6,548 | 172 | — | — | — |
| St. Peter's College ......... | Jersey City, NJ 07306 .... | 1872 | Catholic | S-G/C | 3,973 | 367 | $3,158 | — | $3,158 |
| Salem Comm. College ...... | Penns Grove, NJ 08069 ... | 1973 | State | J/C | 1,130 | — | $ 500 | — | $ 500 |
| Seton Hall University ....... | So. Orange, NJ 07079 .... | 1856 | Catholic | S-G/C | 10,417 | 554 | $3,200 | $1,600 | $4,800 |
| Seton Hall Univ. Sch. of Law . | Newark, NJ 07102 ....... | 1951 | Catholic | P/C | 1,167 | 52 | $3,120 | — | $3,120 |
| Somerset County College .... | Somerville, NJ 08876 .... | 1966 | Public | J/C | 4,283 | 79 | $ 497 | — | $ 497 |
| Stevens Inst. of Technology .. | Hoboken, NJ 07030....... | 1870 | Ind | S-G/C | 2,550 | 200 | $4,675 | $2,470 | $7,145 |
| Stockton State College...... | Pomona, NJ 08240 ...... | 1969 | State | S/C | 4,830 | — | $ 880 | $ 864 | $1,744 |
| Trenton State College ...... | Trenton, NJ 08625....... | 1855 | State | S-G/C | 10,584 | 528 | $ 923 | $1,500 | $2,423 |
| Union College ............. | Cranford, NJ 07016....... | 1933 | Private | J/C | 5,699 | 230 | $ 575 | — | $ 575 |
| Union County Technical Inst. . | Scotch Plains, NJ 07060... | 1960 | County | T/C | 1,850 | 92 | $ 575 | — | $ 575 |
| Upsala College.............. | East Orange, NJ 07019 ... | 1893 | Lutheran | S-G/C | 1,080 | 62 | $3,794 | $1,940 | $5,734 |
| Wirths Campus .......... | Sussex, NJ 07461 ....... | 1893 | Lutheran | S-G/C | 184 | — | $3,794 | $1,940 | $5,734 |
| Westminster Choir College ... | Princeton, NJ 08540 ..... | 1926 | Ind | S-G/C | 470 | 60 | $3,625 | $1,775 | $5,400 |
| William Paterson Col. of N.J. . | Wayne, NJ 07470........ | 1855 | State | S-G/C | 12,555 | 379 | $1,000 | $ 900 | $1,900 |
| **NEW MEXICO** | | | | | | | | | |
| College of Santa Fe ......... | Santa Fe, NM 87501 ..... | 1947 | Catholic | S/C | 1,209 | 70 | $2,400 | $1,650 | $4,050 |
| College of the Southwest ..... | Hobbs, NM 88240 ....... | 1956 | Ind | S/C | 137 | 27 | $ 787 | $ 720 | $1,507 |
| Eastern New Mexico Univ. .. | Portales, NM 88130...... | 1934 | S-G/C | | 3,707 | 172 | $ 626 | $1,170 | $1,796 |
| Clovis Campus .......... | Clovis, NM 88101 ....... | 1961 | State | J/C | 600 | 93 | $ 322 | — | $ 322 |
| Eastern N.M. Univ.–Roswell | Roswell, NM 88201 ...... | 1958 | Public | J/C | 1,068 | 58 | $ 440 | $ 400 | $ 840 |
| Inst. of Amer. Indian Arts .. | Santa Fe, NM 87501 ..... | 1962 | Federal | S/C | 115 | 21 | — | — | — |
| National College of Business . | Albuquerque, NM 87125 .. | 1975 | Private | S/C | 175 | 16 | $2,500 | — | $2,500 |
| New Mexico Highlands Univ. . | Las Vegas, NM 87701 .... | 1893 | State | S-G/C | 2,275 | 135 | $ 398 | $1,240 | $1,638 |
| N. M. Inst. of Min. & Tech. .. | Socorro, NM 87801 ...... | 1889 | State | S-G/C | 1,205 | 120 | $1,398 | $1,215 | $2,613 |
| New Mexico Junior College .. | Hobbs, NM 88240 ....... | 1965 | Public | J/C | 1,459 | 99 | $ 150 | — | $ 150 |
| New Mexico Military Inst. ... | Roswell, NM 88201 ...... | 1891 | State | J/C | 467 | 50 | $ 544 | $1,010 | $1,554 |
| New Mexico State University . | Las Cruces, NM 88003 ... | 1888 | State | S-G/C | 11,864 | 696 | $ 644 | $1,176 | $1,820 |
| Alamogordo Branch ....... | Alamogordo, NM 88310 .. | 1950 | State | J/C | 1,202 | 29 | $ 404 | — | $ 404 |
| Carlsbad Branch .......... | Carlsbad, NM 88220 ..... | 1950 | State | J/C | 542 | 38 | $ 400 | — | $ 400 |
| Dona Ana Branch ......... | Las Cruces, NM 88003 ... | 1974 | State | J/C | 461 | 16 | $ 644 | $1,176 | $1,820 |
| Grants Branch ............ | Grants, NM 87020 ....... | 1968 | State | J/C | 314 | 41 | $ 356 | — | $ 356 |
| San Juan Branch .......... | Farmington, NM 87401.... | 1956 | State | J/C | 1,234 | 61 | $ 360 | — | $ 360 |
| St. John's College .......... | Santa Fe, NM 87501 ..... | 1964 | Ind | S/C | 272 | 35 | $4,750 | $1,800 | $6,550 |
| S.W. Indian Polytechnic Inst. . | Albuquerque, NM 87184 .. | 1971 | Federal | T/C | 400 | 51 | — | — | — |
| University of Albuquerque ... | Albuquerque, NM 87140 .. | 1920 | Ind | S/C | 2,089 | 74 | $1,872 | $1,500 | $3,372 |
| University of New Mexico ... | Albuquerque, NM 87131 .. | 1889 | State | S-G/C | 22,500 | 1,250 | $ 624 | $1,525 | $2,149 |
| Gallup Branch ............ | Gallup, NM 87301 ....... | 1968 | State | J/C | 1,015 | 44 | $ 348 | — | $ 348 |
| Western New Mexico Univ. ... | Silver City, NM 88061 .... | 1893 | State | S-G/C | 1,567 | 95 | $ 402 | $1,200 | $1,602 |

| NAME | ADDRESS | FOUN-DED | AFFILI-ATION | LEVEL/TYPE | ENROLL-MENT | TEACH-ERS | TUITION & FEES | BOARD & ROOM | TOTAL COST |
|---|---|---|---|---|---|---|---|---|---|
| **NEW YORK** | | | | | | | | | |
| Academy of Aeronautics | Flushing, NY 11371 | 1932 | Ind | J-T/C | 1,760 | 53 | $3,200 | — | $3,200 |
| Adelphi University | Garden City, NY 11530 | 1896 | Ind | S-G/C | 11,774 | 406 | $3,510 | $1,944 | $5,454 |
| Albany Business College | Albany, NY 12210 | 1857 | Ind | J/C | 465 | 20 | $2,150 | — | $3,000 |
| Albany College of Pharmacy | Albany, NY 12208 | 1881 | Ind | S/C | 590 | 38 | $2,197 | — | $4,947 |
| Albany Law School | Albany, NY 12208 | 1851 | Ind | G/C | 712 | 43 | $4,000 | — | — |
| Albany Medical College | Albany, NY 12208 | 1839 | Ind | P/C | 600 | 1,400 | $12,000 | — | $16,800 |
| Alfred University | Alfred, NY 14802 | 1836 | Ind | S-G/C | 2,000 | 181 | $4,900 | $2,050 | $6,950 |
| Amer. Acad. of Dramatic Arts | New York, NY 10021 | 1884 | Ind | J/C | 759 | 34 | $2,475 | $2,400 | $4,875 |
| Bank Street College of Ed. | New York, NY 10021 | 1916 | Ind | G/C | 846 | 75 | $4,800 | — | — |
| Bard College | Ann'dal.-on-Hud., NY 12504 | 1860 | Ind | S/C | 702 | 97 | $5,440 | $1,970 | $7,410 |
| Barnard College | New York, NY 10027 | 1889 | Ind | S/W | 2,450 | 238 | $5,340 | $2,340 | $7,680 |
| Berkeley-Claremont School | Hicksville, NY 11801 | 1961 | Ind | T/C | 282 | 12 | $2,895 | — | $2,895 |
| Berkeley-Claremont School | New York, NY 10017 | 1936 | Ind | T/C | 408 | 16 | $2,895 | — | $2,895 |
| Berkeley School | White Plains, NY 10604 | 1945 | Ind | T/C | 725 | 28 | $2,895 | $2,400 | $5,295 |
| Beth Israel Medical Ctr. | New York, NY 10003 | 1904 | Ind | J/C | 182 | 33 | $1,350 | $ 975 | $2,325 |
| Boricua College | New York, NY 10025 | 1974 | Ind | S/C | 685 | 46 | $3,000 | — | $3,000 |
| Bramson ORT Tech. Inst. | New York, NY 10010 | 1977 | Ind | J/C | 180 | 25 | $1,600 | — | — |
| Brooklyn Law School | Brooklyn, NY 11201 | 1901 | Ind | P/C | 1,083 | 52 | $3,800 | — | $3,800 |
| Bryant & Stratton Bus. Inst. | Buffalo, NY 14202 | 1854 | Ind | J/C | 3,800 | 120 | $2,185 | — | $2,185 |
| Bryant & Stratton Bus. Inst. | Rochester, NY 14604 | 1973 | Ind | J/C | 587 | 27 | $2,440 | — | $2,440 |
| Bryant & Stratton, Clarence Br. | Clarence, NY 14031 | 1977 | Ind | J/C | 400 | 29 | $2,050 | — | $2,050 |
| Canisius College | Buffalo, NY 14208 | 1870 | Ind | S-G/C | 3,396 | 248 | $3,175 | $1,620 | $4,795 |
| Cathedral Col. of Imm. Conc. | Douglaston, NY 11362 | 1914 | Catholic | S/M | 147 | 34 | $2,800 | $2,000 | $4,800 |
| Cazenovia College | Cazenovia, NY 13035 | 1824 | Ind | J/W | 510 | 61 | $3,670 | $1,985 | $5,655 |
| Central City Business Inst. | Syracuse, NY 13203 | 1904 | Ind | T/C | 907 | 62 | $1,855 | $1,500 | $3,355 |
| Christ the King Seminary | East Aurora, NY 14052 | 1855 | Catholic | G/M | 156 | 23 | $1,650 | $1,400 | $3,050 |
| City University of New York | | | | | | | | | |
| Bernard M. Baruch College | New York, NY 10010 | 1968 | Public | S-G/C | 14,890 | 435 | $ 925 | — | $ 925 |
| Borough of Manhat. Comm. Col. | New York, NY 10019 | 1963 | Public | J/C | 9,130 | 420 | $ 829 | — | $ 829 |
| Bronx Community College | Bronx, NY 10453 | 1957 | Public | J/C | 7,560 | 430 | $ 845 | — | $ 845 |
| Brooklyn College | Brooklyn, NY 11210 | 1930 | City | S-G/C | 14,627 | 1,467 | $1,425 | — | $1,425 |
| City College of New York | New York, NY 10031 | 1897 | City | S-G/C | 13,000 | 880 | $ 925 | — | $2,480 |
| College of Staten Island | Staten Island, NY 10301 | 1976 | City | S-G/C | 10,500 | 400 | $ 825 | — | $ 825 |
| Grad. Sch. and Univ. Center | New York, NY 10036 | 1961 | City | G/C | 2,775 | 188 | $ 953 | — | $ 953 |
| Herbert H. Lehman College | Bronx, NY 10468 | 1931 | City | S-G/C | 9,341 | 698 | $ 925 | — | $ 925 |
| Hostos Community College | Bronx, NY 10451 | 1968 | City | J/C | 2,530 | 250 | $ 925 | — | $ 925 |
| Hunter College | New York, NY 10021 | 1870 | City | S-G/C | 17,989 | 1,203 | $ 975 | — | $ 975 |
| John Jay Col. of Crim. Just. | New York, NY 10019 | 1964 | City | S-G/C | 6,394 | 418 | $ 964 | — | $ 964 |
| Kingsborough Comm. Col. | Brooklyn, NY 11235 | 1964 | City | J/C | 8,563 | 400 | $ 978 | — | $ 978 |
| LaGuardia Comm. College | L.I.C., NY 11101 | 1971 | City | J/C | 6,284 | 140 | $1,025 | — | $1,025 |
| Medgar Evers College | Brooklyn, NY 11225 | 1969 | City | S/C | 2,988 | 225 | $ 966 | — | $ 966 |
| New York City Comm. Col. | Brooklyn, NY 11201 | 1946 | City | J/C | 13,199 | 388 | $ 968 | — | $ 968 |
| Queensborough Comm. Col. | Bayside, NY 11364 | 1958 | City | J/C | 11,783 | 675 | $ 976 | — | $ 976 |
| Queens College | Flushing, NY 11367 | 1937 | City | S-G/C | 18,800 | 1,000 | $ 925 | — | $ 925 |
| York College | Jamaica, NY 11451 | 1966 | City | S/C | 3,618 | 150 | $ 935 | — | $ 935 |
| Clarkson College | Potsdam, NY 13676 | 1896 | Ind | S-G/C | 3,628 | 220 | $4,505 | $2,185 | $6,690 |
| Colg. Roch./Bexley H./Crozer | Rochester, NY 14620 | 1817 | Ecumen | G/C | 220 | 24 | $2,500 | $1,400 | $3,900 |
| Colgate University | Hamilton, NY 13346 | 1819 | Ind | S-G/C | 2,580 | 197 | $5,400 | $2,100 | $7,500 |
| College of Insurance | New York, NY 10038 | 1962 | Ind | S/C | 1,293 | 103 | $3,200 | $2,100 | $5,300 |
| College of Mt. Saint Vincent | Riverdale, NY 10471 | 1847 | Ind | S/C | 1,293 | 103 | $3,200 | $2,100 | $5,300 |
| College of New Rochelle | New Rochelle, NY 10801 | 1904 | Ind | S-G/C | 4,484 | 400 | — | — | — |
| Graduate School | New Rochelle, NY 10801 | 1904 | Ind | G/C | 815 | 42 | $1,530 | — | $1,530 |
| School of Arts & Sciences | New Rochelle, NY 10801 | 1904 | Ind | S-G/W | 932 | 75 | $3,000 | $2,150 | $5,300 |
| School of New Resources | New Rochelle, NY 10801 | 1972 | Ind | S-G/C | 2,465 | 266 | $1,500 | — | $1,500 |
| School of Nursing | New Rochelle, NY 10801 | 1976 | Ind | S/C | 272 | 16 | $3,000 | $2,150 | $5,150 |
| College of Saint Rose | Albany, NY 12203 | 1920 | Ind | S-G/C | 2,800 | 180 | $2,547 | $1,600 | $4,147 |
| Colum. Mem. Hosp. Sch. of Nur. | Staten Island, NY 10301 | 1900 | Ind | S/C | 112 | 9 | $1,420 | $ 550 | $1,970 |
| Columbia University | New York, NY 10027 | 1754 | Ind | S-G/C | 15,344 | 1,666 | $6,010 | $2,920 | $8,930 |
| Columbia College | New York, NY 10027 | 1754 | Ind | S/C | — | — | $5,172 | $2,648 | $7,820 |
| Sch. of Eng. & Ap. Science | New York, NY 10027 | 1754 | Ind | S-G/C | 1,713 | 132 | $5,256 | $2,639 | $7,895 |
| Sch. of General Studies | New York, NY 10027 | 1947 | Ind | S/C | 2,894 | 400 | $5,250 | — | $5,250 |
| Teachers College | New York, NY 10027 | 1887 | Ind | G/C | 5,333 | 252 | — | — | — |
| Concordia College | Bronxville, NY 10708 | 1881 | Lutheran | S/C | 438 | 51 | $2,645 | $1,886 | $4,531 |
| Cooper Union | New York, NY 10003 | 1859 | Ind | S/C | 857 | 143 | $ 300 | — | $ 300 |
| Cornell University | | | | | | | | | |
| Endowed Division | Ithaca, NY 14853 | 1865 | Ind | S-G/C | 10,165 | 874 | $5,860 | $2,500 | $8,360 |
| Statutory Division | Ithaca, NY 14853 | 1865 | State | S-G/C | 7,985 | 754 | $2,470 | $2,500 | $4,970 |
| Medical Center | New York, NY 10021 | 1865 | Ind | S-G/C | 568 | 437 | — | $2,450 | — |
| Culinary Inst. of America | Hyde Park, NY 12538 | 1946 | Ind | J/C | 1,600 | 80 | $4,000 | $1,000 | $5,000 |
| Daemen College | Amherst, NY 14226 | 1948 | Private | S/C | 1,436 | 139 | $3,430 | $1,750 | $6,265 |
| Dominican Col. of Blauvelt | Orangeburg, NY 10962 | 1952 | Ind | S/C | 1,231 | 68 | $1,850 | — | $1,850 |
| Dowling College | Oakdale, NY 11769 | 1959 | Ind | S-G/C | 2,210 | 67 | $3,350 | $2,000 | $5,350 |
| D'Youville College | Buffalo, NY 14201 | 1908 | Ind | S/C | 1,500 | 116 | $2,880 | $1,550 | $4,430 |
| Elizabeth Seton College | Yonkers, NY 10701 | 1960 | Ind | J/C | 1,259 | 95 | $2,450 | $1,850 | $4,300 |
| Elmira College | Elmira, NY 14901 | 1855 | Ind | S-G/C | 2,698 | 188 | $3,815 | $1,700 | $5,515 |
| Five Towns College | Merrick, NY 11566 | 1972 | Ind | J/C | 450 | 33 | $2,550 | — | $2,550 |
| Fordham University | New York, NY 10023 | 1841 | Ind | S-G/C | 6,393 | 437 | $3,750 | $2,250 | $6,060 |
| Friends World College | Huntington, NY 11743 | 1965 | Ind | S/C | 150 | 20 | $3,350 | $2,950 | $6,300 |
| General Theological Sem. | New York, NY 10011 | 1817 | Episc | G/C | 173 | 18 | $2,200 | $1,775 | $3,975 |
| Hamilton College | Clinton, NY 13323 | 1812 | Ind | S/C | 1,600 | 132 | $5,175 | $1,850 | $7,025 |
| Harriman College | Harriman, NY 10926 | 1956 | Ind | J/C | 344 | 30 | $3,080 | $2,000 | $5,080 |
| Hartwick College | Oneonta, NY 13820 | 1928 | Ind | S/C | 1,385 | 112 | $4,750 | $1,900 | $6,650 |
| Helene Fuld Sch. of Nursing | New York, NY 10035 | 1962 | Ind | J/C | 110 | 15 | $3,820 | — | $3,820 |
| Hilbert College | Hamburg, NY 14075 | 1957 | Ind | J/C | 514 | 47 | $2,050 | $1,750 | $3,800 |

| NAME | ADDRESS | FOUN-DED | AFFILI-ATION | LEVEL/TYPE | ENROLL-MENT | TEACH-ERS | TUITION & FEES | BOARD & ROOM | TOTAL COST |
|---|---|---|---|---|---|---|---|---|---|
| **NEW YORK** *(continued)* | | | | | | | | | |
| Hobart & Wm. Smith Colleges | Geneva, NY 14456 ....... | 1822 | Ind | S/C | 1,846 | 148 | $5,400 | $2,050 | $7,450 |
| Hofstra University .......... | Hempstead, NY 11550 ... | 1935 | Ind | S-G/C | 10,000 | 600 | $3,700 | $1,800 | $5,500 |
| Houghton College ......... | Houghton, NY 14744 .... | 1883 | Wesleyan | S/C | 1,205 | 98 | $3,224 | $1,700 | $4,924 |
| Buffalo Suburban Campus .. | West Seneca, NY 14224 .. | 1969 | Wesleyan | J/C | 114 | 12 | $2,839 | $1,300 | $4,139 |
| Inst. of Design and Con. .... | Brooklyn, NY 11201 ...... | 1947 | Ind | J/C | 250 | 23 | $1,520 | — | $1,520 |
| Iona College ............... | New Rochelle, NY 10801 . | 1940 | Ind | S-G/C | 5,944 | 305 | $2,980 | $1,900 | $4,880 |
| Ithaca College ............. | Ithaca, NY 14850 ........ | 1892 | Ind | S-G/C | 4,698 | 411 | $4,244 | $1,896 | $6,140 |
| Jewish Theol. Sem. of America | New York, NY 10027 ..... | 1886 | Jewish | S-G/C | 497 | 117 | $3,070 | $1,500 | $4,570 |
| Juilliard School ........... | New York, NY 10023 ..... | 1906 | Ind | S/C | 1,269 | 163 | $3,600 | — | $3,600 |
| Keuka College .............. | Keuka Park, NY 14478 ... | 1890 | Ind | S/W | 566 | 52 | $4,155 | $1,460 | $5,615 |
| King's College .............. | Briarcliff Man., NY 10510.. | 1938 | Private | S/C | 867 | 70 | $3,410 | $1,540 | $4,950 |
| Ladycliff College ........... | Highland Falls, NY 10928 . | 1933 | Ind | S/W | 490 | 51 | $2,950 | $1,850 | $4,800 |
| LeMoyne College............ | Syracuse, NY 13214 ..... | 1946 | Catholic | S/C | 1,950 | 140 | $3,089 | $1,725 | $4,814 |
| Long Island University | | | | | | | | | |
| A. & M. Schwartz Col. of Phar. | Brooklyn, NY 11201 ...... | 1886 | Ind | P/C | 950 | 43 | $3,600 | $2,750 | $6,350 |
| Brooklyn Center ......... | Brooklyn, NY 11201 ..... | 1926 | Ind | S-G/C | 7,112 | 240 | $3,260 | $2,500 | $5,760 |
| C. W. Post Center ........ | Greenvale, NY 11548 .... | 1954 | Ind | S-G/C | 12,500 | 900 | $3,400 | $2,200 | $5,600 |
| Southampton College..... | Southampton, NY 11968 . | 1963 | Ind | S-G/C | 1,422 | 68 | $3,590 | $2,090 | $5,680 |
| L.I. Col. Hosp. Sch. of Nursing | Brooklyn, NY 11201 ...... | 1883 | Ind | J/C | 87 | 10 | $1,501 | — | $3,326 |
| Manhattan College ......... | Riverdale, NY 10471 ..... | 1853 | Ind | S-G/C | 4,860 | 304 | $3,204 | $1,886 | $5,090 |
| Manhattan School of Music... | New York, NY 10027 ..... | 1917 | Ind | S-G/C | 689 | 171 | $3,430 | — | — |
| Manhattanville College....... | Purchase, NY 10577 ..... | 1841 | Ind | S-G/C | 2,130 | 167 | $4,700 | $2,350 | $7,050 |
| Mannes College of Music .... | New York, NY 10021 ..... | 1916 | Ind | S-G/C | 200 | 110 | $3,250 | — | $3,250 |
| Maria College.............. | Albany, NY 12208 ....... | 1958 | Ind | J/C | 420 | 30 | $1,900 | — | — |
| Maria Regina College ....... | Syracuse, NY 13208 ..... | 1963 | Catholic | J/W | 428 | 40 | $2,150 | $1,600 | $3,750 |
| Marist College ............. | Poughkeepsie, NY 12601 . | 1946 | Ind | S-G/C | 2,295 | 142 | $3,200 | $2,000 | $5,200 |
| Maryknoll Sch. of Theology ... | Maryknoll, NY 10545 .... | 1912 | Catholic | G/C | 232 | 35 | $1,800 | $2,400 | $4,200 |
| Marymount College ......... | Tarrytown, NY 10591 ..... | 1907 | Ind | S/W | 816 | 112 | $3,975 | $2,700 | $6,675 |
| Marymount Manhattan Col. .. | New York, NY 10021 ..... | 1936 | Ind | S/W | 2,300 | 180 | $2,800 | — | $2,800 |
| Mater Dei College .......... | Ogdensburg, NY 13669 ... | 1960 | Catholic | J/C | 341 | 31 | $1,909 | $1,610 | $3,519 |
| Medaille College ........... | Buffalo, NY 14214 ....... | 1937 | Ind | S/C | 606 | 54 | $2,425 | — | $2,425 |
| Mercy College .............. | Dobbs Ferry, NY 10522 .. | 1950 | Ind | S/C | 8,333 | 607 | $2,250 | — | $2,250 |
| Yorktown Campus ........ | Yorktown Hghts., NY 10598 | 1978 | Ind | S/C | 1,105 | — | $1,950 | — | $1,950 |
| Misericordia Hosp. Med. Cen.. | Bronx, NY 10470 ........ | 1911 | Ind | P/C | 312 | 32 | $2,500 | — | — |
| Molloy College ............. | Rockville Centre, NY 11570 | 1955 | Catholic | S/W | 1,533 | 175 | $3,000 | — | $3,000 |
| Mount Saint Alphonsus Sem.. | Esopus, NY 12429 ....... | 1907 | Catholic | G/M | 63 | 20 | $2,000 | $3,000 | $5,000 |
| Mount Saint Mary College .... | Newburgh, NY 12550 .... | 1959 | Ind | S/C | 1,072 | 74 | $3,000 | $1,850 | $4,850 |
| Nazareth Col. of Rochester ... | Rochester, NY 14610 .... | 1924 | Ind | S-G/C | 2,594 | 88 | $3,100 | $1,800 | $4,900 |
| New School for Social Res. ... | New York, NY 10011 ..... | 1919 | Ind | S-G/C | 3,013 | 300 | $4,100 | $2,800 | $6,900 |
| New York Chiropractic Col. ... | Old Brookville, NY 11545 .. | 1919 | Ind | P/C | 700 | 103 | $4,350 | — | $4,350 |
| New York Col. of Pod. Med. ... | New York, NY 10035 ..... | 1912 | Ind | P/C | 451 | 40 | $6,100 | — | $6,100 |
| New York Inst. of Finance .... | New York, NY 10005 ..... | 1922 | State | J/C | 3,880 | 38 | $1,800 | — | $1,800 |
| New York Inst. of Technology .. | Old Westbury, NY 11568 .. | 1955 | Ind | S-G/C | 10,667 | 660 | $2,560 | — | $2,560 |
| New York Law School ....... | New York, NY 10013 ..... | 1891 | Ind | G/C | 1,272 | 147 | $4,295 | — | $4,295 |
| New York Sch. of Int. Design .. | New York, NY 10022 ..... | 1924 | Ind | S/C | 925 | 38 | $2,100 | — | $2,100 |
| New York Theol. Seminary ... | New York, NY 10001 ..... | 1900 | Ind | P/C | 210 | 10 | $2,500 | — | $2,500 |
| New York University ........ | New York, NY 10003 ..... | 1831 | Ind | S-G/C | 45,320 | 5,388 | $4,520 | $2,430 | $6,950 |
| Niagara University .......... | Niagara Univ., NY 14109 .. | 1856 | Catholic | S-G/C | 3,928 | 244 | $3,120 | $1,900 | $5,020 |
| Nyack College .............. | Nyack, NY 10960 ....... | 1882 | Christian | S-G/C | 729 | 64 | $2,837 | $1,669 | $4,506 |
| Pace University | | | | | | | | | |
| College of White Plains .... | White Plains, NY 10603 .. | 1927 | Ind | S-G/C | 1,961 | 51 | $3,116 | $2,000 | — |
| New York City Campus .... | New York, NY 10038 ..... | 1906 | Ind | S-G/C | 12,849 | 513 | $3,116 | $2,075 | — |
| Plsntville/Briarcliff Cam. .. | Pleasantville, NY 10570 .. | 1906 | Ind | S-G/C | 5,022 | 380 | $3,116 | $2,225 | — |
| Paul Smith's Col. of Arts & Sci. | Paul Smith, NY 12970 .... | 1946 | Ind | J/C | 1,146 | 75 | $2,470 | $1,700 | $4,170 |
| Polytechnic Inst. of N.Y. ..... | Brooklyn, NY 11201 ...... | 1854 | Ind | S-G/C | 4,722 | 200 | $4,800 | $1,050 | $5,850 |
| Powelson Business Institute .. | Syracuse, NY 13202 .... | 1926 | Ind | J/C | 478 | 25 | $2,160 | $1,620 | $3,780 |
| Pratt Institute ............. | Brooklyn, NY 11205 ..... | 1887 | Private | S-G/C | 4,422 | 529 | $3,734 | $1,100 | $4,834 |
| Rabbi I. Elchanan Theol. Sem. | New York, NY 10033 ..... | 1886 | Jewish | P/M | 218 | 20 | $ 110 | $ 700 | $ 810 |
| Rensselaer Polytechnic Inst... | Troy, NY 12181 ......... | 1824 | Ind | S-G/C | 5,540 | 355 | $4,999 | $2,250 | $7,249 |
| Roberts Wesleyan College ... | Rochester, NY 14624 .... | 1866 | Meth | S/C | 631 | 60 | $3,200 | $1,800 | $5,000 |
| Rochester Business Institute . | Rochester, NY 14604 .... | 1863 | Ind | J/C | 156 | 11 | $2,145 | — | $2,145 |
| Rochester Inst. of Tech. ..... | Rochester, NY 14623 .... | 1829 | Ind | S-G/C | 13,999 | 1,043 | $3,537 | $2,187 | $5,724 |
| Eisenhower College ....... | Seneca Falls, NY 13148 .. | 1965 | Ind | S/C | 549 | 58 | $3,987 | $2,302 | $6,289 |
| Rockefeller University ....... | New York, NY 10021 ..... | 1901 | Ind | G/C | 100 | — | — | $ 528 | $ 528 |
| Russell Sage College ....... | Troy, NY 12180 ......... | 1916 | Ind | S-G/W | 1,576 | 165 | $3,600 | $2,090 | $5,690 |
| Junior Col. of Albany ...... | Albany, NY 12208 ....... | 1957 | Ind | J/C | 908 | 75 | $2,390 | — | $2,390 |
| St. Anthony-On-Hudson | | | | | | | | | |
| Seminary ............... | Rensselaer, NY 12144.... | 1912 | Catholic | P/M | 37 | 21 | $1,400 | $2,000 | $3,400 |
| St. Bernard's Seminary .... | Rochester, NY 14612 .... | 1893 | Catholic | P/C | 87 | 15 | $3,285 | $1,825 | $5,110 |
| St. Bonaventure University ... | St. Bonaventure, NY 14778 | 1858 | Ind | S/C | 2,781 | 167 | $3,075 | $1,765 | $4,840 |
| St. Francis College ......... | Brooklyn, NY 11201 ...... | 1884 | Private | S/C | 3,184 | 178 | $2,650 | — | $2,650 |
| St. John Fisher College ..... | Rochester, NY 14618 .... | 1948 | Ind | S/C | 3,190 | 153 | $3,475 | $1,920 | $5,395 |
| St. John's University ........ | Jamaica, NY 11439 ...... | 1870 | Catholic | S-G/C | 15,777 | 755 | $3,030 | — | $3,030 |
| Staten Island ........... | Staten Island, NY 10301 .. | 1870 | Catholic | S-G/C | 2,035 | 69 | $3,030 | — | $3,030 |
| St. Joseph's College ........ | Brooklyn, NY 11205 ..... | 1916 | Ind | S/C | 1,390 | 110 | $2,360 | — | $2,360 |
| Suffolk Campus .......... | Patchogue, NY 11772 .... | 1916 | Ind | S/C | 492 | 76 | $2,350 | — | $2,350 |
| St. Joseph's Seminary ...... | Yonkers, NY 10704 ...... | 1896 | Catholic | P/M | 73 | 27 | — | — | — |
| St. Lawrence University ..... | Canton, NY 13617 ....... | 1856 | Ind | S-G/C | 2,300 | 154 | $4,995 | $1,990 | $6,985 |
| St. Thomas Aquinas College .. | Sparkill, NY 10976........ | 1952 | Ind | S/C | 1,385 | 75 | $2,375 | $ 800 | $3,175 |
| St. Vladimir's Orth. Theol. Sem. | Tuckahoe, NY 10707 ..... | 1938 | E Orth | G/C | 104 | 18 | $1,270 | $1,290 | $2,560 |
| Sarah Lawrence College .... | Bronxville, NY 10708 ..... | 1928 | Ind | S-G/C | 1,067 | 120 | $6,250 | $2,650 | $8,900 |
| School of Visual Arts ........ | New York, NY 10010 ..... | 1947 | Ind | S/C | 2,093 | 360 | $3,100 | — | $7,000 |
| Sem. of the Immaculate | | | | | | | | | |
| Conception............. | Huntington, NY 11743 ... | 1930 | Catholic | G/C | 150 | 25 | — | — | — |
| Siena College............... | Loudonville, NY 12211 ... | 1937 | Ind | S/C | 3,016 | 171 | $3,305 | $2,070 | $5,375 |

| NAME | ADDRESS | FOUNDED | AFFILIATION | LEVEL/TYPE | ENROLLMENT | TEACHERS | TUITION & FEES | BOARD & ROOM | TOTAL COST |
|---|---|---|---|---|---|---|---|---|---|
| **NEW YORK** *(continued)* | | | | | | | | | |
| Skidmore College | Saratoga Spgs., NY 12866 | 1922 | Ind | S/C | 2,071 | 160 | $5,580 | $2,620 | $8,200 |
| State University of N.Y. | | | | | | | | | |
| Adirondack Comm. College | Glen Falls, NY 12801 | 1960 | State | J/C | 2,410 | 106 | $ 780 | — | $ 780 |
| Agricultural & Tech. College | Alfred, NY 14802 | 1908 | State | J/C | 4,226 | 214 | $1,005 | $1,750 | $2,755 |
| Agricultural & Tech. College | Canton, NY 13617 | 1907 | State | J/C | 2,605 | 120 | $1,005 | $1,680 | $2,685 |
| Agricultural & Tech. College | Cobleskill, NY 12043 | 1916 | State | J/C | 2,734 | 140 | $ 892 | $1,600 | $2,492 |
| Agricultural & Tech. College | Delhi, NY 13753 | 1913 | State | J/C | 2,630 | 130 | $ 975 | $1,620 | $2,595 |
| Agricultural & Tech. College | Farmingdale, NY 11735 | 1912 | State | J/C | 6,631 | 309 | $ 925 | $1,730 | $2,655 |
| Agricultural & Tech. College | Morrisville, NY 13408 | 1908 | State | J/C | 3,012 | 151 | $ 950 | $1,700 | $2,650 |
| Broome Community College | Birmingham, NY 13902 | 1946 | State | J/C | 5,556 | 320 | $ 805 | — | $ 805 |
| Cayuga County Comm. Col. | Auburn, NY 13021 | 1953 | State | J/C | 3,056 | 165 | $ 840 | — | $ 840 |
| Clinton Comm. College | Plattsburgh, NY 12901 | 1966 | State | J/C | 1,500 | 90 | $ 750 | — | $ 750 |
| Columbia-Greene Comm. C | Hudson, NY 12534 | 1969 | State | J/C | 1,200 | 60 | $ 795 | — | $ 795 |
| Comm. Col. of Finger Lakes | Canandaigua, NY 14424 | 1965 | State | J/C | 2,612 | 187 | $ 820 | — | $ 820 |
| Corning Community College | Corning, NY 14830 | 1956 | State | J/C | 2,500 | 135 | $ 800 | — | $ 800 |
| Downstate Medical Center | Brooklyn, NY 11203 | 1860 | State | S-G/C | 1,446 | 717 | — | — | $4,310 |
| Dutchess Community Col. | Poughkeepsie, NY 12601 | 1957 | State | J/C | 6,401 | 336 | $ 780 | — | $ 780 |
| Empire State College | Saratoga Spgs., NY 12866 | 1971 | State | S/C | 3,834 | 207 | $ 925 | — | $ 925 |
| Erie Community College | Williamsville, NY 14221 | 1946 | State | J/C | 11,791 | 750 | $ 805 | — | $ 805 |
| Fashion Institute of Tech. | New York, NY 10001 | 1944 | State | J-S/C | 10,472 | 411 | $ 900 | $2,180 | $3,080 |
| Fulton-Montgomery Comm. College | Johnstown, NY 12095 | 1963 | State | J/C | 1,500 | 85 | $ 800 | — | $ 800 |
| Genesee Comm. College | Batavia, NY 14020 | 1966 | State | J/C | 2,057 | 113 | $ 769 | — | $ 769 |
| Herkimer Co. Comm. Col. | Herkimer, NY 13350 | 1966 | State | J/C | 2,059 | 83 | $ 685 | — | $ 685 |
| Hudson Valley Comm. Col. | Troy, NY 12180 | 1953 | State | J/C | 7,147 | 331 | $1,000 | — | $1,000 |
| Jamestown Comm. College | Jamestown, NY 14701 | 1950 | State | J/C | 2,200 | 112 | $ 700 | — | $ 700 |
| Jefferson Comm. College | Watertown, NY 13601 | 1961 | State | J/C | 1,095 | 93 | $ 850 | — | $ 850 |
| Maritime College | Bronx, NY 10465 | 1874 | State | S-G/C | 1,145 | 65 | $1,005 | $2,355 | $3,360 |
| Mohawk Valley Comm. Col. | Utica, NY 13501 | 1946 | State | J/C | 3,150 | 140 | $ 750 | $1,578 | $2,328 |
| Monroe Community College | Rochester, NY 14623 | 1961 | State | J/C | 10,234 | 461 | $ 910 | — | $ 910 |
| Nassau Community College | Garden City, NY 11530 | 1959 | State | J/C | 19,805 | 1,210 | $ 976 | — | $ 976 |
| N.Y. Sch. of Indus. and L.R. at Cornell Univ. | Ithaca, NY 14853 | 1944 | State | S-G/C | 640 | 55 | $2,216 | $2,250 | $4,466 |
| N.Y. St. Col. of Agriculture & Life Sci. | Ithaca, NY 14853 | 1865 | State | S-G/C | 3,975 | 425 | $2,216 | $2,250 | $4,466 |
| N.Y. St. Col. of Ceramics | Alfred, NY 14802 | 1900 | State | S-G/C | 675 | 41 | $1,285 | $2,050 | $3,335 |
| N.Y. St. Col. of Env. Sci. & Forestry | Syracuse, NY 13210 | 1911 | State | S-G/C | 1,864 | 110 | $ 990 | $2,000 | $2,990 |
| N.Y. St. Col. of Hum. Eco. at Cornell Univ. | Ithaca, NY 14850 | 1925 | State | G/C | 1,124 | 110 | $2,470 | $2,300 | $4,770 |
| N.Y. State Col. of Optometry | New York, NY 10010 | 1971 | State | P/C | 250 | 43 | $1,540 | — | $1,540 |
| N.Y. St. Col. of Technology | Utica, NY 13502 | 1966 | State | S/C | 3,125 | 145 | $1,020 | — | $1,020 |
| N.Y. St. Col. of Vet. Med. | Ithaca, NY 14853 | 1894 | State | P/C | 384 | 105 | $4,250 | — | |
| Niagara County Comm. Col. | Sanborn, NY 14132 | 1962 | State | J/C | 3,876 | 271 | $ 800 | — | $ 800 |
| North County Comm. Col. | Saranac Lake, NY 12983 | 1967 | State | J/C | 1,426 | — | $1,500 | — | $1,500 |
| Onondaga Comm. College | Syracuse, NY 13215 | 1962 | State | J/C | 6,436 | 375 | $ 820 | — | $ 820 |
| Orange County Comm. Col. | Middletown, NY 10940 | 1950 | State | J/C | 4,877 | 145 | $ 965 | — | $ 965 |
| Rockland Comm. College | Suffern, NY 10901 | 1959 | State | J/C | 7,539 | 367 | $ 806 | — | $ 806 |
| Schenectady Co. Comm. Col. | Schenectady, NY 12305 | 1968 | State | J/C | 2,635 | 123 | $ 835 | — | $ 835 |
| State U. College | Brockport, NY 14420 | 1867 | State | S-G/C | 9,323 | 586 | $ 900 | $1,670 | $2,570 |
| State U. College | Buffalo, NY 14222 | 1867 | State | S-G/C | 10,909 | 556 | $ 900 | $1,700 | $2,600 |
| State U. College | Cortland, NY 13045 | 1868 | State | S-G/C | 5,875 | 338 | $ 925 | $1,540 | $2,465 |
| State U. College | Fredonia, NY 14063 | 1826 | State | S-G/C | 5,262 | 280 | $1,002 | $1,660 | $2,662 |
| State U. College | Geneseo, NY 14454 | 1867 | State | S-G/C | 5,551 | 316 | $1,005 | $1,680 | $2,685 |
| State U. College | Old Westbury, NY 11568 | 1966 | State | S/C | 2,892 | 167 | $ 960 | $1,200 | $2,160 |
| State U. College | Oneonta, NY 13820 | 1889 | State | S-G/C | 6,204 | 325 | $1,000 | $1,650 | $2,650 |
| State U. College | Oswego, NY 13126 | 1861 | State | S-G/C | 7,169 | 405 | $ 900 | $1,643 | $2,543 |
| State U. College | Plattsburgh, NY 12901 | 1889 | State | S-G/C | 6,155 | 365 | $1,005 | $1,670 | $2,675 |
| State U. College | Potsdam, NY 13676 | 1867 | State | S-G/C | 4,682 | 332 | $1,200 | $1,650 | $2,850 |
| State U. College | Purchase, NY 10577 | 1971 | State | S/C | 3,241 | 266 | $ 925 | $1,564 | $2,489 |
| State University of N.Y. | Albany, NY 12222 | 1844 | State | S-G/C | 15,391 | 840 | $ 997 | $1,588 | $2,585 |
| State University of N.Y. | Binghamton, NY 13901 | 1950 | State | S-G/C | 10,636 | 650 | $1,900 | $1,700 | $3,600 |
| State University of N.Y. | Buffalo, NY 14260 | 1846 | State | S-G/C | 24,683 | 1,870 | $ 998 | $1,612 | $2,610 |
| State University of N.Y. | Stony Brook, NY 11794 | 1957 | State | S-G/C | 15,984 | 1,197 | $ 925 | $1,866 | $2,791 |
| Suffolk County Comm. Col. | Selden, NY 11784 | 1959 | State | J/C | 19,638 | 750 | $ 726 | — | $ 726 |
| Sullivan County Comm. Col. | Loch Sheldrake, NY 12759 | 1962 | State | J/C | 1,559 | 84 | $ 850 | — | $ 850 |
| Tompkins Cort. Comm. Col. | Dryden, NY 13053 | 1968 | State | J/C | 2,882 | 186 | $ 800 | — | $ 800 |
| Ulster County Comm. Col. | Stone Ridge, NY 12484 | 1961 | State | J/C | 2,957 | 165 | $ 885 | — | $ 885 |
| Upstate Medical Center | Syracuse, NY 13210 | 1834 | State | P/C | 841 | 248 | $3,380 | $ 950 | $4,330 |
| Westchester Comm. College | Valhalla, NY 10595 | 1946 | State | J/C | 7,950 | 299 | $ 806 | — | $ 806 |
| Stenotype Institute | New York, NY 10019 | 1937 | Ind | J/C | 250 | 8 | $2,730 | — | $2,730 |
| Syracuse University | Syracuse, NY 13210 | 1871 | Ind | S-G/C | 20,185 | 1,000 | $4,500 | $2,300 | $6,800 |
| Utica College | Utica, NY 13502 | 1946 | Ind | S/C | 2,208 | 142 | $4,015 | $1,886 | $5,901 |
| Technical Career Inst. | New York, NY 10001 | 1909 | Ind | T/C | 1,900 | 85 | $2,800 | — | $2,800 |
| Tobe-Coburn Sch. of Fashion | New York, NY 10021 | 1937 | Ind | J/C | 195 | 20 | $2,800 | — | $7,000 |
| Touro College | New York, NY 10036 | 1970 | Ind | S-G/C | 1,852 | 236 | $3,075 | $1,300 | $4,375 |
| Trocaire College | Buffalo, NY 14220 | 1958 | Ind | J/C | 845 | 56 | $2,250 | — | $2,250 |
| Union College | Schenectady, NY 12308 | 1795 | Ind | S-G/C | 2,047 | 145 | $5,619 | $2,030 | $8,299 |
| Union Theological Seminary | New York, NY 10027 | 1836 | Ind | P/C | 430 | 47 | $3,100 | $3,200 | $6,300 |
| U.S. Merchant Marine Acad. | Kings Point, NY 11024 | 1943 | Fed | S/C | 1,100 | 83 | — | — | — |
| U.S. Military Academy | West Point, NY 10996 | 1802 | Fed | S/C | 4,218 | 562 | — | — | — |
| University of Rochester | Rochester, NY 14627 | 1850 | Ind | S-G/C | 8,100 | — | $5,560 | $2,473 | $8,033 |
| Utica School of Commerce | Utica, NY 13501 | 1896 | Ind | J/C | 287 | 16 | $2,145 | — | |
| Vassar College | Poughkeepsie, NY 12601 | 1861 | Ind | S-G/C | 2,371 | 189 | $5,375 | $2,425 | $7,800 |
| Villa Maria College of Buffalo | Buffalo, NY 14225 | 1960 | Catholic | J/C | 528 | 42 | $1,950 | — | $1,950 |
| Wadhams Hall | Ogdensburg, NY 13669 | 1924 | Catholic | S/M | 63 | 24 | $2,200 | $1,700 | $3,900 |

| NAME | ADDRESS | FOUN-DED | AFFILI-ATION | LEVEL/TYPE | ENROLL-MENT | TEACH-ERS | TUITION & FEES | BOARD & ROOM | TOTAL COST |
|---|---|---|---|---|---|---|---|---|---|
| **NEW YORK** (continued) | | | | | | | | | |
| Wagner College | Staten Island, NY 10301 | 1883 | Ind | S-G/C | 2,539 | 131 | $3,828 | $2,240 | $6,068 |
| Webb Inst. of Naval Arch. | Glen Cove, NY 11542 | 1889 | Ind | S/C | 78 | 11 | — | $2,200 | $2,600 |
| Wells College | Aurora, NY 13026 | 1868 | Ind | S/W | 500 | 55 | $4,500 | $2,000 | $6,500 |
| Westchester Business Inst. | White Plains, NY 10606 | 1915 | Ind | J/C | 549 | 18 | $2,835 | — | $2,835 |
| Wood School | New York, NY 10017 | 1879 | Ind | J/W | 452 | 20 | $2,700 | — | $2,700 |
| Yeshiva University | New York, NY 10033 | 1886 | Ind | S-G/C | 6,819 | 2,500 | $3,550 | $1,870 | $5,420 |
| **NORTH CAROLINA** | | | | | | | | | |
| Appalachian State University | Boone, NC 28608 | 1899 | State | S-G/C | 9,242 | 500 | $ 613 | $1,190 | $1,803 |
| Ashevll.-Buncombe Tech. Col. | Asheville, NC 28801 | 1959 | State | T/C | 2,250 | 145 | $ 172 | — | $ 172 |
| Atlantic Christian College | Wilson, NC 27893 | 1902 | D of Chr | S/C | 1,590 | 111 | $1,810 | $1,100 | $2,910 |
| Barber-Scotia College | Concord, NC 28025 | 1867 | Presby | S/C | 351 | 33 | $1,829 | $1,329 | $3,158 |
| Beaufort County Tech. Inst. | Washington, NC 27889 | 1967 | State | T/C | 1,250 | 36 | $ 100 | — | $ 100 |
| Belmont Abbey College | Belmont, NC 28012 | 1876 | Catholic | S/C | 777 | 56 | $2,348 | $1,420 | $3,768 |
| Bennett College | Greensboro, NC 27420 | 1873 | Meth | S/W | 622 | 54 | $2,150 | $1,180 | $3,330 |
| Brevard College | Brevard, NC 28712 | 1853 | Meth | J/C | 700 | 47 | $1,925 | $1,214 | $3,139 |
| Caldwell Community College | Hudson, NC 28638 | 1964 | State | J/C | 1,722 | 128 | $ 132 | — | $ 132 |
| Campbell College | Buies Creek, NC 27506 | 1887 | Baptist | S-G/C | 2,701 | 146 | $2,769 | $1,310 | $4,079 |
| Cape Fear Technical Inst. | Wilmington, NC 28401 | 1964 | State | T/C | 1,614 | 60 | $ 198 | — | $ 198 |
| Carteret Technical Institute | Morehead City, NC 28557 | 1963 | State | T/C | 894 | 76 | $ 117 | — | $ 117 |
| Catawba College | Salisbury, NC 28144 | 1851 | UC Chr | S/C | 983 | 60 | $2,500 | $1,440 | $5,000 |
| Catawba Valley Tech. Inst. | Hickory, NC 28601 | 1960 | State | T/C | 2,087 | 110 | $ 132 | — | $ 132 |
| Central Carolina Tech. Inst. | Sanford, NC 27330 | 1963 | State | T/C | 2,000 | 75 | $ 156 | — | $ 156 |
| Central Piedmont Comm. Col. | Charlotte, NC 28204 | 1963 | State | J/C | 24,084 | 1,171 | $ 156 | — | $ 156 |
| Chowan College | Murfreesboro, NC 27855 | 1948 | Baptist | J/C | 1,118 | 68 | $1,910 | $1,340 | $3,250 |
| Coastal Carolina Comm. Col. | Jacksonville, NC 28540 | 1964 | State | J/C | 2,157 | 91 | $ 132 | — | $ 132 |
| College of the Albemarle | Elizabeth City, NC 27909 | 1960 | State | J/C | 1,118 | 43 | $ 145 | — | $ 145 |
| Craven Community College | New Bern, NC 28560 | 1965 | State | J/C | 1,543 | 50 | $ 132 | — | $ 132 |
| Davidson College | Davidson, NC 28036 | 1837 | Presby | S/C | 1,379 | 114 | $3,600 | $1,940 | $5,540 |
| Davidson County Comm. Col. | Lexington, NC 27292 | 1958 | State | J/C | 2,000 | 130 | $ 140 | — | $ 140 |
| Duke University | Durham, NC 27706 | 1838 | Meth | S-G/C | 9,920 | 1,122 | $4,535 | $2,225 | $6,760 |
| Durham Technical Institute | Durham, NC 27703 | 1958 | State | T/C | 2,300 | 160 | $ 168 | — | $ 168 |
| East Carolina University | Greenville, NC 27834 | 1907 | State | S-G/C | 12,874 | 619 | $ 520 | $1,524 | $2,044 |
| Camp Lejeune Center | Camp Lejeune, NC 28542 | 1961 | State | S-G/C | 750 | 40 | $ 840 | — | $ 840 |
| Cherry Point Center | Cherry Point, NC 28533 | 1965 | State | S-G/C | 650 | 40 | $ 840 | — | $ 840 |
| Elizabeth City State University | Elizabeth City, NC 27909 | 1891 | State | S/C | 1,524 | 118 | $ 617 | $1,215 | $1,832 |
| Elon College | Elon College, NC 27244 | 1889 | UC Chr | S/C | 2,502 | 139 | $2,084 | $1,197 | $3,281 |
| Fayetteville State University | Fayetteville, NC 28301 | 1877 | State | S/C | 2,281 | 188 | $ 600 | $ 570 | $1,170 |
| Fort Bragg-Pope AFB Ctr. | Fort Bragg, NC 28307 | 1972 | State | S/C | 829 | 52 | $ 840 | — | $ 840 |
| Fayetteville Technical Inst. | Fayetteville, NC 28303 | 1961 | State | J/C | 5,318 | 154 | $ 121 | — | $ 121 |
| Forsyth Technical Institute | Winston-Salem, NC 27103 | 1960 | State | T/C | 2,660 | 103 | $ 126 | — | $ 126 |
| Gardner-Webb College | Boiling Springs, NC 28017 | 1907 | Baptist | S/C | 1,450 | 88 | $2,390 | $1,355 | $3,745 |
| Gaston College | Dallas, NC 28034 | 1963 | State | J/C | 3,090 | 96 | $ 156 | — | $ 156 |
| Greensboro College | Greensboro, NC 27420 | 1838 | Meth | S/C | 676 | 38 | $2,840 | $1,600 | $4,440 |
| Guilford College | Greensboro, NC 27410 | 1837 | Quaker | S/C | 1,430 | 83 | $2,995 | $1,600 | $4,595 |
| Guilford Technical Institute | Jamestown, NC 27282 | 1957 | State | T/C | 3,730 | 122 | $ 185 | — | $ 185 |
| Hamilton Jr. Col. of Business | Charlotte, NC 28202 | 1978 | Ind | J/C | 364 | 15 | $2,100 | — | $2,100 |
| Haywood Technical Institute | Clyde, NC 28721 | 1965 | State | J/C | 900 | 105 | $ 156 | — | $ 156 |
| High Point College | High Point, NC 27262 | 1924 | Meth | S/C | 1,250 | 90 | $2,225 | $1,240 | $3,465 |
| Isothermal Community College | Spindale, NC 28160 | 1966 | State | J/C | 1,650 | 50 | $ 145 | — | $ 145 |
| Johnson C. Smith University | Charlotte, NC 28216 | 1867 | Ind | S/C | 1,410 | 73 | $1,924 | $1,276 | $3,200 |
| John Wesley College | High Point, NC 27260 | 1932 | Ind | S/C | 75 | 12 | $1,359 | — | $1,359 |
| King's College | Charlotte, NC 28204 | 1901 | Private | J/W | 375 | 14 | $3,000 | $2,300 | $5,300 |
| Lees-McRae College | Banner Elk, NC 28604 | 1900 | Presby | J/C | 714 | 39 | $1,119 | $ 671 | $1,790 |
| Lenoir Community College | Kinston, NC 28501 | 1958 | State | J/C | 1,873 | 109 | $ 165 | — | $ 165 |
| Lenoir-Rhyne College | Hickory, NC 28601 | 1891 | LCA | S-G/C | 1,291 | 104 | $3,032 | $1,375 | $4,407 |
| Livingstone College | Salisbury, NC 28144 | 1879 | AME | S/C | 938 | 67 | $1,750 | $1,440 | $3,190 |
| Louisburg College | Louisburg, NC 27549 | 1787 | Meth | J/C | 710 | 45 | $2,116 | $1,400 | $3,516 |
| Mars Hill College | Mars Hill, NC 28754 | 1856 | Baptist | S/C | 1,958 | 155 | $2,585 | $1,140 | $3,725 |
| Martin Community College | Williamston, NC 27892 | 1968 | State | T/C | 680 | 50 | $ 132 | — | $ 132 |
| Meredith College | Raleigh, NC 27611 | 1891 | Baptist | S/W | 1,550 | 120 | $2,350 | $1,150 | $3,500 |
| Methodist College | Fayetteville, NC 28301 | 1956 | Meth | S/C | 943 | 48 | $2,500 | $1,650 | $4,150 |
| Mitchell Community College | Statesville, NC 28677 | 1852 | State | J/C | 1,220 | 49 | $ 144 | — | $ 144 |
| Montreat-Anderson College | Montreat, NC 28757 | 1916 | Presby | J/C | 431 | 26 | $1,800 | $1,450 | $3,250 |
| Mount Olive College | Mount Olive, NC 28365 | 1951 | Baptist | J/C | 350 | 26 | $1,550 | $1,390 | $2,940 |
| N.C. A. & T. State University | Greensboro, NC 27411 | 1891 | State | S-G/C | 5,479 | 332 | $ 682 | $1,339 | $2,021 |
| N.C. Central University | Durham, NC 27707 | 1910 | State | G/C | 4,980 | 285 | $ 545 | $1,286 | $1,831 |
| N.C. School of the Arts | Winston-Salem, NC 27107 | 1965 | State | S/C | 682 | 94 | $ 718 | $1,562 | $2,280 |
| N.C. State University | Raleigh, NC 27650 | 1889 | State | S-G/C | 19,597 | 1,249 | $ 582 | $1,540 | $2,122 |
| N.C. Wesleyan College | Rocky Mount, NC 27801 | 1956 | Meth | S/C | 850 | 44 | $2,300 | $1,390 | $3,690 |
| Peace College | Raleigh, NC 27604 | 1857 | Presby | J/W | 499 | 34 | $1,860 | $1,780 | $3,640 |
| Pembroke State University | Pembroke, NC 28372 | 1887 | State | S-G/C | 2,268 | 120 | $ 470 | $1,020 | $1,490 |
| Pfeiffer College | Misenheimer, NC 28109 | 1885 | Meth | S/C | 844 | 75 | $2,180 | $1,450 | $3,630 |
| Piedmont Bible College | Winston-Salem, NC 27101 | 1945 | Baptist | S/C | 474 | 28 | $1,600 | $1,170 | $2,770 |
| Pitt Comm. College | Greenville, NC 27834 | 1961 | State | T/C | 2,052 | 135 | $ 180 | — | $ 405 |
| Queens College | Charlotte, NC 28274 | 1857 | Presby | S-G/W | 643 | 43 | $3,175 | $1,790 | $4,965 |
| Randolph Technical Institute | Asheboro, NC 27203 | 1962 | Public | T/C | 954 | 50 | $ 171 | — | $ 171 |
| Richmond Technical Institute | Hamlet, NC 28345 | 1964 | State | T/C | 984 | 76 | $ 180 | — | $ 180 |
| Rockingham Community Col. | Wentworth, NC 27375 | 1966 | Public | J/C | 1,900 | 117 | $ 156 | — | $ 156 |
| Rowan Technical Institute | Salisbury, NC 28144 | 1963 | State | T/C | 1,770 | 160 | $ 171 | — | $ 171 |
| Sacred Heart College | Belmont, NC 28012 | 1892 | Catholic | S/W | 475 | 53 | $2,360 | $1,400 | $3,760 |
| St. Andrew's Presbyterian Col. | Laurinburg, NC 28352 | 1961 | Presby | S/C | 625 | 50 | $2,850 | $1,545 | $4,395 |
| St. Augustine's College | Raleigh, NC 27611 | 1867 | Episc | S/C | 1,765 | 71 | $1,800 | $1,100 | $2,900 |
| St. Mary's College | Raleigh, NC 27611 | 1842 | Episc | J/W | 516 | 43 | $2,598 | $1,998 | $4,596 |

| NAME | ADDRESS | FOUN-DED | AFFILI-ATION | LEVEL/TYPE | ENROLL-MENT | TEACH-ERS | TUITION & FEES | BOARD & ROOM | TOTAL COST |
|---|---|---|---|---|---|---|---|---|---|
| **NORTH CAROLINA** (continued) | | | | | | | | | |
| Salem College | Winston-Salem, NC 27108 | 1772 | Moravian | S/W | 694 | 70 | $3,100 | $1,900 | $5,000 |
| Sandhills Community College | Carthage, NC 28327 | 1963 | State | J/C | 1,568 | 87 | $ 142 | — | $ 142 |
| Shaw University | Raleigh, NC 27611 | 1865 | Baptist | S/C | 1,389 | 93 | $2,440 | $1,330 | $3,770 |
| Southeast. Bapt. Theol. Sem. | Wake Forest, NC 27587 | 1950 | Baptist | G/C | 1,055 | 35 | $ 400 | $1,500 | $2,100 |
| Southeastern Comm. College | Whiteville, NC 28472 | 1965 | State | J/C | 1,838 | 62 | $ 142 | — | $ 142 |
| Southwestern Technical Inst. | Sylva, NC 28779 | 1964 | State | T/C | 897 | 36 | $ 170 | — | $ 170 |
| Surry Community College | Dobson, NC 27017 | 1964 | State | J/C | 1,793 | 82 | $ 135 | — | $ 135 |
| Technical Inst. of Alamance | Haw River, NC 27258 | 1958 | State | T/C | 1,282 | 45 | $ 168 | — | $ 168 |
| Univ. of N.C. at Asheville | Asheville, NC 28804 | 1927 | State | S/C | 1,957 | 76 | $ 490 | $1,200 | $1,690 |
| Univ. of N.C. at Chapel Hill | Chapel Hill, NC 27514 | 1795 | State | S-G/C | 21,060 | 1,873 | $ 566 | $1,721 | $2,287 |
| Univ. of N.C. at Charlotte | Charlotte, NC 28223 | 1946 | State | S/C | 8,945 | 628 | $ 536 | $1,370 | $1,906 |
| Univ. of N.C. at Greensboro | Greensboro, NC 27412 | 1891 | State | S-G/C | 9,925 | 541 | $ 603 | $1,400 | $2,003 |
| Univ. of N.C. at Wilmington | Wilmington, NC 28406 | 1947 | State | S-G/C | 4,258 | 244 | $ 560 | $1,560 | $2,120 |
| Wake Forest University | Winston-Salem, NC 27109 | 1834 | Baptist | S-G/C | 4,736 | 614 | $3,300 | $1,500 | $4,800 |
| Wake Technical Institute | Raleigh, NC 27603 | 1958 | County | J/C | — | — | — | — | — |
| Warren Wilson College | Swannanoa, NC 28778 | 1894 | Presby | S/C | 500 | 55 | $2,800 | $1,200 | $4,000 |
| Wayne Community College | Goldsboro, NC 27530 | 1957 | State | J/C | 2,232 | 112 | $ 135 | — | $ 135 |
| Western Carolina University | Cullowhee, NC 28723 | 1889 | State | S-G/C | 6,274 | 311 | $ 578 | $1,480 | $2,058 |
| Western Piedmont Comm. Col. | Morganton, NC 28655 | 1964 | State | J/C | 1,557 | 75 | $ 135 | — | $ 135 |
| Wilkes Community College | Wilkesboro, NC 28697 | 1965 | State | J/C | 2,901 | 64 | $ 194 | — | $ 194 |
| Wilson County Tech. Institute | Wilson, NC 27893 | 1958 | State | T/C | 1,213 | 50 | $ 141 | — | $ 141 |
| Wingate College | Wingate, NC 28174 | 1896 | Baptist | S/C | 1,520 | 72 | $1,690 | $1,010 | $2,700 |
| Winston-Salem State Univ. | Winston-Salem, NC 27102 | 1892 | State | S/C | 2,224 | 140 | $ 632 | $2,107 | $2,739 |
| **NORTH DAKOTA** | | | | | | | | | |
| Bismarck Junior College | Bismarck, ND 58501 | 1939 | Ind | J/C | 2,265 | 88 | $ 630 | $1,050 | $1,680 |
| Dickinson State College | Dickinson, ND 58601 | 1918 | State | J-S/C | 1,062 | 86 | $ 609 | $1,011 | $1,620 |
| Jamestown College | Jamestown, ND 58401 | 1883 | Presby | S/C | 542 | 55 | $2,800 | $1,375 | $4,175 |
| Lake Region Junior College | Devils Lake, ND 58301 | 1941 | State | J/C | 550 | 40 | $ 650 | $1,080 | $1,730 |
| Mary College | Bismarck, ND 58501 | 1958 | Catholic | S/C | 934 | 74 | $2,000 | $1,250 | $3,250 |
| Mayville State College | Mayville, ND 58257 | 1889 | State | S/C | 746 | 59 | $ 589 | $1,071 | $1,660 |
| Minot State College | Minot, ND 58701 | 1913 | State | S-G/C | 2,277 | 135 | $ 568 | $1,333 | $1,901 |
| North Dakota State Sch. of Sci. | Wahpeton, ND 58075 | 1903 | State | J/C | 3,184 | 187 | $ 534 | $1,350 | $1,884 |
| North Dakota State University | Fargo, ND 58105 | 1890 | State | S-G/C | 7,619 | 430 | $ 522 | $1,155 | $1,677 |
| Bottineau Branch | Bottineau, ND 58318 | 1907 | State | J/C | 335 | 23 | $ 500 | $ 900 | $1,400 |
| Northwest Bible College | Minot, ND 58701 | 1934 | C of God | S/C | 213 | 9 | $1,400 | $1,400 | $2,800 |
| University of North Dakota | Grand Forks, ND 58202 | 1883 | State | S-G/C | 9,708 | 584 | $ 645 | $1,230 | $1,975 |
| Williston Center | Williston, ND 58801 | 1957 | State | J/C | 622 | 35 | $ 758 | $1,500 | $2,258 |
| Valley City State College | Valley City, ND 58072 | 1890 | State | S/C | 1,145 | 65 | $ 588 | $1,100 | $1,688 |
| **OHIO** | | | | | | | | | |
| Air Force Inst. of Technology | Wright-Pat. AFB, OH 45433 | 1921 | Federal | G/C | 577 | 104 | | | |
| Antioch College | Yellow Springs, OH 45387 | 1852 | Ind | S-G/C | 950 | 61 | $4,844 | $1,750 | $6,600 |
| Antioch International | Yellow Springs, OH 45387 | 1852 | Ind | S-G/C | — | — | $5,300 | — | $5,300 |
| Art Academy of Cincinnati | Cincinnati, OH 45227 | 1887 | Ind | S/C | 149 | 20 | $2,496 | — | $2,496 |
| Ashland College | Ashland, OH 44805 | 1878 | Brethren | S-G/C | 2,598 | 104 | $3,782 | $1,630 | $5,412 |
| Athenaeum of Ohio | Cincinnati, OH 45212 | 1829 | Catholic | S-G/M | 198 | 48 | $1,750 | $1,350 | $3,100 |
| Baldwin-Wallace College | Berea, OH 44017 | 1845 | Meth | S-G/C | 3,407 | 165 | $4,105 | $1,996 | $6,101 |
| Bliss College | Columbus, OH 43214 | 1899 | Ind | J/C | 364 | 21 | $1,800 | — | $1,800 |
| Bluffton College | Bluffton, OH 45817 | 1899 | Mennonite | S/C | 586 | 50 | $3,211 | $1,358 | $4,569 |
| Borromeo College of Ohio | Wickliffe, OH 44092 | 1954 | Catholic | S/M | 107 | 23 | $2,375 | $1,200 | $3,575 |
| Bowling Green State Univ. | Bowling Green, OH 43403 | 1910 | State | S-G/C | 16,907 | 725 | $1,086 | $1,611 | $2,697 |
| Firelands College | Huron, OH 44839 | 1965 | State | J/C | 1,139 | 66 | $ 921 | — | $ 921 |
| Capital University | Columbus, OH 43209 | 1850 | Lutheran | S-G/C | 2,598 | 204 | $4,405 | $1,830 | $6,245 |
| Case Western Reserve Univ. | Cleveland, OH 44106 | 1826 | Ind | S-G/C | 7,865 | 1,324 | $4,374 | $1,970 | $6,344 |
| Cedarville College | Cedarville, OH 45314 | 1887 | Baptist | S/C | 1,351 | 60 | $2,616 | $1,793 | $4,409 |
| Central Ohio Technical Col. | Newark, OH 43055 | 1971 | State | J/C | 1,108 | 92 | $ 830 | — | $ 830 |
| Central State University | Wilberforce, OH 45384 | 1887 | State | S/C | 2,452 | 112 | $ 873 | $1,773 | $2,646 |
| Cincinnati Bible Seminary | Cincinnati, OH 45204 | 1924 | Christian | S-G/C | 665 | 38 | $1,550 | $1,500 | $3,050 |
| Cincinnati Col. of Mort. Sci. | Cincinnati, OH 45229 | 1882 | Ind | P/C | 87 | 7 | $2,600 | $2,200 | $4,800 |
| Cincinnati Technical College | Cincinnati, OH 45238 | 1966 | State | T/C | 3,891 | 194 | $ 800 | — | $ 800 |
| Circleville Bible College | Circleville, OH 43113 | 1948 | Christian | P/C | 241 | 15 | $1,710 | $1,110 | $2,820 |
| Clark Technical College | Springfield, OH 45501 | 1962 | State | T/C | 2,497 | 60 | $ 738 | — | $ 738 |
| Cleveland Institute of Art | Cleveland, OH 44106 | 1882 | Ind | S/C | 546 | 70 | $2,840 | $2,110 | $4,950 |
| Cleveland State University | Cleveland, OH 44115 | 1964 | State | S-G/C | 17,421 | 705 | $ 960 | $1,860 | $2,820 |
| College of Mount St. Joseph | Mt. St. Joseph, OH 45051 | 1920 | Catholic | S/W | 1,480 | 134 | $2,880 | $1,875 | $4,755 |
| College of Steubenville | Steubenville, OH 43952 | 1946 | Catholic | S/C | 896 | 42 | $2,350 | $1,700 | $4,050 |
| College of Wooster | Wooster, OH 44691 | 1866 | Presby | S/C | 1,776 | 134 | $6,150 | — | $6,150 |
| Columbus Col. of Art & Design | Columbus, OH 43215 | 1879 | Ind | S/C | 857 | 82 | $2,874 | $ 800 | $3,674 |
| Columbus Tech. Institute | Columbus, OH 43215 | 1963 | State | T/C | 6,100 | 450 | $ 681 | — | $ 681 |
| Cuyahoga Community College | | | | | | | | | |
| Eastern Campus | Warrensv. Twp., OH 44122 | 1971 | County | J/C | 4,436 | 216 | $ 450 | — | $ 450 |
| Metropolitan Campus | Cleveland, OH 44115 | 1963 | County | J/C | 9,755 | 540 | $ 450 | — | $ 450 |
| Western Campus | Parma, OH 44130 | 1966 | County | J/C | 11,794 | 410 | $ 450 | — | $ 450 |
| Davis Jr. College of Business | Toledo, OH 43604 | 1858 | Ind | J/C | 260 | 25 | $1,785 | — | $1,785 |
| Defiance College | Defiance, OH 43512 | 1850 | UC Chr | S/C | 760 | 63 | $3,330 | $1,485 | $4,815 |
| Denison University | Granville, OH 43023 | 1831 | Ind | S/C | 2,056 | 158 | $5,165 | $1,895 | $7,060 |
| Dyke College | Cleveland, OH 44114 | 1848 | Ind | S/C | 1,416 | 84 | $2,125 | — | $2,125 |
| Edgecliff College | Cincinnati, OH 45206 | 1935 | Catholic | S/C | 845 | 87 | $2,176 | $1,530 | $3,706 |
| Findlay College | Findlay, OH 45840 | 1880 | C of God | S/C | 1,041 | 79 | $3,240 | $1,478 | $4,763 |
| Franklin University | Columbus, OH 43215 | 1902 | Private | S/C | 4,667 | 175 | $1,470 | — | $1,470 |
| Hebrew Union College | Cincinnati, OH 45220 | 1875 | Hebrew | G/C | 390 | 150 | $3,300 | $1,870 | $5,170 |
| Heidelberg College | Tiffin, OH 44883 | 1850 | UC Chr | S/C | 860 | 92 | $4,410 | $1,800 | $6,210 |
| Hiram College | Hiram, OH 44234 | 1850 | Ind | S/C | 1,113 | 95 | $4,657 | $1,475 | $6,182 |

| NAME | ADDRESS | FOUN-DED | AFFILI-ATION | LEVEL/TYPE | ENROLL-MENT | TEACH-ERS | TUITION & FEES | BOARD & ROOM | TOTAL COST |
|---|---|---|---|---|---|---|---|---|---|
| **OHIO** *(continued)* | | | | | | | | | |
| Hocking Technical College ... | Nelsonville, OH 45764 ... | 1968 | State | T/C | 2,800 | 148 | $ 645 | $1,800 | $2,445 |
| Jefferson Technical College .. | Steubenville, OH 43952 ... | 1966 | State | T/C | 1,596 | 127 | $ 500 | — | $ 500 |
| John Carroll University ...... | Cleveland, OH 44118 .... | 1886 | Catholic | S-G/C | 3,850 | 271 | $3,250 | $1,700 | $4,950 |
| Kent State University ........ | Kent, OH 44242 ........ | 1910 | State | S-G/C | 17,796 | 753 | $1,064 | $1,614 | $2,678 |
| Ashtabula Campus ........ | Ashtabula, OH 44004 ... | 1958 | State | J/C | 1,114 | 33 | $ 880 | — | $ 880 |
| East Liverpool Campus ... | East Liverpool, OH 43920 | 1965 | State | J/C | 603 | 17 | $ 880 | — | $ 880 |
| Geauga Campus .......... | Burton, OH 44021 ...... | 1964 | State | J/C | 306 | 9 | $ 880 | — | $ 880 |
| Salem Campus ............ | Salem, OH 44460 ........ | 1962 | State | J/C | 541 | 20 | $ 880 | — | $ 880 |
| Stark Campus ............ | Canton, OH 44720 ...... | 1946 | State | J/C | 1,833 | 62 | $ 880 | — | $ 880 |
| Trumbull Campus ......... | Warren, OH 44483 ...... | 1954 | State | J/C | 1,537 | 50 | $ 880 | — | $ 880 |
| Tuscarawas Campus ...... | New Phila., OH 44663 ... | 1962 | State | J/C | 891 | 33 | $ 880 | — | $ 880 |
| Kenyon College ............. | Gambier, OH 43022 .... | 1824 | Episc | S/C | 1,444 | 100 | $5,190 | $2,183 | $7,373 |
| Kettering Col. of Med. Arts .. | Kettering, OH 45429 .... | 1967 | Church | J/C | 365 | 50 | $2,250 | $1,150 | $3,400 |
| Lake Erie College .......... | Painesville, OH 44077 ... | 1865 | Ind | S-G/W | 1,055 | 100 | $4,532 | $1,848 | $6,380 |
| Lakeland Community College | Mentor, OH 44060 ...... | 1967 | State | J/C | 7,145 | 293 | $ 525 | — | $ 525 |
| Lima Technical College ..... | Lima, OH 45804 ........ | 1971 | State | T/C | 1,493 | 60 | $ 675 | — | $ 675 |
| Lorain County Comm. College | Elyria, OH 44035 ...... | 1964 | State | J/C | 6,051 | 312 | $ 720 | — | $ 720 |
| Lourdes College ............ | Sylvania, OH 43560 ..... | 1958 | Catholic | J/C | 516 | 32 | $1,400 | — | |
| Malone College ............. | Canton, OH 44709 ...... | 1892 | Friends | S/C | 772 | 40 | $3,361 | $1,675 | $5,036 |
| Marietta College ........... | Marietta, OH 45750 ..... | 1835 | Ind | S-G/C | 1,299 | 97 | $4,400 | $1,600 | $6,000 |
| Methodist Theol. Sch. of Ohio | Delaware, OH 43015 .... | 1958 | Meth | G/C | 235 | 32 | $1,950 | $1,500 | $3,450 |
| Miami-Jacobs Junior College | Dayton, OH 45401 ...... | 1860 | Ind | J/C | 951 | 52 | $1,995 | — | $1,995 |
| Miami University ........... | Oxford, OH 45056 ...... | 1809 | State | S-G/C | 14,758 | 718 | $1,270 | $1,590 | $2,860 |
| Hamilton Campus ........ | Hamilton, OH 45011 .... | 1968 | State | J/C | 1,772 | 37 | $1,040 | — | $1,040 |
| Middletown Campus ...... | Middletown, OH 45042 .. | 1966 | State | J/C | 1,790 | 44 | $1,040 | — | $1,040 |
| Mount Union College ....... | Alliance, OH 44601 ..... | 1846 | Meth | S/C | 1,070 | 95 | $3,690 | $1,440 | $5,130 |
| Mount Vernon Bible College .. | Mt. Vernon, OH 43050 ... | 1957 | 4 Square | S/C | 100 | 12 | $1,350 | $1,350 | $2,700 |
| Mount Vernon Nazarene Col. .. | Mt. Vernon, OH 43050 ... | 1966 | Nazarene | S/C | 1,005 | 64 | $2,140 | $1,340 | $3,480 |
| Muskingum Area Tech. Col. ... | Zanesville, OH 43701 .... | 1969 | Public | T/C | 1,338 | 74 | $ 585 | — | $ 585 |
| Muskingum College ......... | New Concord, OH 43762 | 1837 | Presby | S/C | 850 | 72 | $4,050 | $1,545 | $5,590 |
| Northwest Technical College . | Archbold, OH 43502 .... | 1968 | State | J/C | 771 | 47 | $ 700 | — | $ 850 |
| Notre Dame College of Ohio .. | Cleveland, OH 44121 .... | 1922 | Catholic | S/W | 600 | 59 | $2,375 | $1,600 | $3,975 |
| Oberlin College ............. | Oberlin, OH 44074 ...... | 1833 | Ind | S/C | 2,785 | 226 | $4,924 | $2,075 | $6,999 |
| Ohio Col. of Podiatric Med. .. | Cleveland, OH 44106 .... | 1916 | Ind | P/C | 585 | 70 | $6,387 | — | |
| Ohio Dominican College ..... | Columbus, OH 43219 .... | 1911 | Catholic | S/C | 849 | 69 | $2,980 | $1,640 | $4,620 |
| Ohio Inst. of Technology .... | Columbus, OH 43209 .... | 1952 | Ind | T/C | 2,327 | 40 | $2,345 | — | $2,345 |
| Ohio Northern University .... | Ada, OH 45810 ......... | 1871 | Church | S/C | 2,667 | 181 | $3,276 | $1,440 | $4,716 |
| Ohio State University ....... | Columbus, OH 43210 .... | 1870 | State | S-G/C | 57,938 | 5,629 | $1,005 | $1,908 | $2,913 |
| Lima Campus ............ | Lima, OH 45804 ........ | 1960 | State | S/C | 852 | 61 | $ 960 | — | $ 960 |
| Mansfield Campus ........ | Mansfield, OH 44906 .... | 1958 | State | S/C | 1,143 | 59 | $ 960 | — | $ 960 |
| Marion Campus........... | Marion, OH 43302 ...... | 1957 | State | S/C | 771 | 48 | $ 960 | — | $ 960 |
| Newark Campus .......... | Newark, OH 43055 ...... | 1957 | State | S/C | 1,071 | 60 | $ 960 | — | $ 960 |
| Ohio University ............ | Athens, OH 45701 ...... | 1804 | State | S-G/C | 13,748 | 819 | $1,056 | $1,740 | $2,796 |
| Belmont County Campus... | St. Clairsville, OH 43950.. | 1957 | State | J-S/C | 950 | 18 | $ 900 | — | $1,800 |
| Chillicothe Campus ...... | Chillicothe, OH 45601 ... | 1946 | State | J/C | 1,162 | 65 | $ 886 | — | $ 886 |
| Ironton Campus ......... | Ironton, OH 45638 ...... | 1956 | State | J/C | 1,006 | — | $ 705 | — | $ 705 |
| Lancaster Campus ........ | Lancaster, OH 43130 .... | 1968 | State | J/C | — | — | — | — | — |
| Zanesville Campus ....... | Zanesville, OH 43701 .... | 1946 | State | J/C | 1,009 | 65 | $ 885 | — | $ 885 |
| Ohio Wesleyan University .... | Delaware, OH 43015 .... | 1842 | Meth | S/C | 2,290 | 158 | $4,875 | $2,100 | $6,975 |
| Otterbein College .......... | Westerville, OH 43081 ... | 1847 | Meth | S/C | 1,480 | 115 | $3,954 | $1,542 | $5,496 |
| Owens Technical College .... | Toledo, OH 43699 ...... | 1967 | State | T/C | 3,200 | 200 | $ 660 | — | $ 660 |
| Penn-Ohio College .......... | Youngstown, OH 44507 . | 1941 | Ind | J/C | 225 | 20 | $1,280 | — | $1,280 |
| Pontifical Col. of Josephinum . | Columbus, OH 43085 .... | 1888 | Catholic | S-G/M | 162 | 35 | $2,145 | $1,687 | $3,832 |
| Ray. Walters Gen. & Tech. Col. | Cincinnati, OH 45236 ... | 1967 | State | J/C | 3,464 | 130 | $1,005 | — | $1,005 |
| Rio Grande College ......... | Rio Grande, OH 45674 ... | 1876 | Ind | S/C | 1,143 | 114 | $2,365 | $1,635 | $4,000 |
| St. Mary Seminary .......... | Cleveland, OH 44108 .... | 1848 | Catholic | G/C | 70 | 21 | — | — | — |
| Shawnee State Comm. College | Portsmouth, OH 45662... | 1975 | State | J/C | 1,900 | 170 | $ 750 | — | $ 750 |
| Sinclair Community College .. | Dayton, OH 45402 ...... | 1887 | State | J/C | 16,322 | 751 | $ 495 | — | $ 495 |
| Southern Ohio College ...... | Cincinnati, OH 45237 ... | 1927 | Ind | J/C | 1,490 | 171 | $2,012 | — | $2,400 |
| Southern State Comm. College | Wilmington, OH 45177 ... | 1975 | State | J/C | 1,300 | 95 | $ 750 | — | $ 750 |
| Tiffin University ........... | Tiffin, OH 44883 ....... | 1918 | Private | S/C | 400 | 22 | $1,850 | $1,160 | $3,010 |
| United Theological Seminary . | Dayton, OH 45406 ...... | 1871 | Meth | G/C | 301 | 21 | $1,983 | — | $1,983 |
| University of Akron ......... | Akron, OH 44325 ....... | 1870 | State | S-G/C | 23,364 | 1,219 | $ 840 | $1,650 | $2,490 |
| Wayne General & Tech. Col. | Orrville, OH 44667....... | 1972 | State | J/C | 866 | 79 | $ 840 | — | $ 840 |
| University of Cincinnati ..... | Cincinnati, OH 45221 ... | 1819 | State | S-G/C | 39,070 | 2,730 | $1,005 | $1,941 | $2,946 |
| University of Dayton ........ | Dayton, OH 45469 ...... | 1850 | Catholic | S-G/C | 10,254 | 638 | $3,044 | $1,750 | $4,844 |
| University of Toledo ........ | Toledo, OH 43606 ...... | 1872 | State | S-G/C | 18,246 | 789 | $ 972 | $1,854 | $2,826 |
| Urbana College ............ | Urbana, OH 43078 ...... | 1850 | Swed | S/C | 700 | 64 | $2,310 | $ 565 | $2,875 |
| Ursuline College ........... | Pepper Pike, OH 44124 .. | 1871 | Catholic | S/W | 970 | 84 | $2,300 | $1,400 | $3,700 |
| Walsh College ............. | Canton, OH 44720 ...... | 1958 | Catholic | S/C | 752 | 63 | $2,770 | $1,550 | $4,320 |
| Wilberforce University ...... | Wilberforce, OH 45384 .. | 1856 | AME | S/C | 1,115 | 50 | $2,360 | $1,310 | $3,670 |
| Wilmington College......... | Wilmington, OH 45177 ... | 1870 | Quaker | S/C | 700 | 68 | $3,000 | $1,545 | $4,545 |
| Wittenberg University ....... | Springfield, OH 45501 ... | 1845 | Lutheran | S/C | 2,583 | 180 | $4,077 | $1,785 | $5,862 |
| Wright State University ..... | Dayton, OH 45435 ...... | 1967 | State | S-G/C | 14,735 | 604 | $ 340 | $ 593 | $ 933 |
| Piqua Resident Cred. Cent. | Piqua, OH 45456 ....... | 1969 | State | G/C | 208 | 12 | $ 831 | — | $ 831 |
| Western Ohio Branch Cam. | Celina, OH 45822 ....... | 1969 | State | J/C | 739 | 49 | $ 885 | — | $ 885 |
| Xavier University........... | Cincinnati, OH 45207 ... | 1831 | Ind | S-G/C | 6,643 | 394 | $2,990 | $1,863 | $4,853 |
| Youngstown State University . | Youngstown, OH 44555 . | 1908 | State | S-G/C | 15,303 | 799 | $ 855 | $1,350 | $2,205 |
| **OKLAHOMA** | | | | | | | | | |
| Bacone College ............ | Muskogee, OK 74401 ... | 1880 | Baptist | J/C | 506 | 46 | $ 815 | $1,000 | $1,815 |
| Bartlesville Wesleyan College . | Bartlesville, OK 74003 ... | 1907 | Wesleyan | S/C | 662 | 59 | $2,390 | $1,660 | $4,050 |
| Bethany Nazarene College ... | Bethany, OK 73008 ..... | 1899 | Nazarene | S-G/C | 1,860 | 75 | $1,930 | $1,485 | $3,415 |
| Cameron University ......... | Lawton, OK 73505 ...... | 1908 | State | S/C | 4,700 | 196 | $ 420 | $2,572 | $2,992 |

| NAME | ADDRESS | FOUN-DED | AFFILI-ATION | LEVEL/TYPE | ENROLL-MENT | TEACH-ERS | TUITION & FEES | BOARD & ROOM | TOTAL COST |
|---|---|---|---|---|---|---|---|---|---|
| **OKLAHOMA** *(continued)* | | | | | | | | | |
| Carl Albert Junior College .... | Poteau, OK 74953 ........ | 1934 | State | J/C | 1,807 | 51 | $ 508 | — | $ 508 |
| Central State University ..... | Edmond, OK 73034 ....... | 1890 | State | S-G/C | 11,398 | 420 | $ 386 | $ 984 | $1,370 |
| Claremore College .......... | Claremore, OK 74017 ... | 1971 | State | J/C | 1,776 | 80 | $ 376 | $1,450 | $1,826 |
| Connors State College ....... | Warner, OK 74469........ | 1908 | State | J/C | 1,300 | 43 | $ 300 | $1,104 | $1,404 |
| East Central University ...... | Ada, OK 74820........... | 1909 | State | S-G/C | 3,882 | 150 | $ 448 | $ 862 | $1,310 |
| Eastern Okla. State College .. | Wilburton, OK 74578...... | 1909 | State | J/C | 1,255 | 64 | $ 350 | $1,150 | $1,500 |
| El Reno, OK 73036....... | El Reno, OK 73036....... | 1938 | State | J/C | 1,034 | 23 | $ 320 | — | $ 320 |
| Hillsdale Free Will Baptist ... | Moore, OK 73153........ | 1959 | Baptist | S/C | 150 | 20 | $1,250 | $1,400 | $2,650 |
| Langston University ......... | Langston, OK 73050 ...... | 1897 | State | S/C | 1,087 | 83 | $ 426 | $1,264 | $1,690 |
| Midwest Christian College.... | Oklahoma City, OK 73111 | 1946 | Christian | S/C | 170 | 16 | $ 960 | $1,500 | $2,460 |
| Murray State College ........ | Tishomingo, OK 73460 ... | 1908 | State | J/C | 1,344 | 37 | $ 328 | $1,380 | $1,708 |
| Northeastern Okla. A&M Col. | Miami, OK 74354 ........ | 1919 | State | J/C | 2,786 | 113 | $ 300 | $1,062 | $1,362 |
| Northeastern State University .. | Tahlequah, OK 74464..... | 1846 | State | S-G/C | 5,800 | 284 | $ 400 | $1,192 | $1,592 |
| Northern Oklahoma College .. | Tonkawa, OK 74653 ...... | 1901 | State | J/C | 1,668 | 85 | $ 324 | $1,122 | $1,446 |
| Northwestern Okla. State Univ. | Alva, OK 73717 ......... | 1897 | State | S-G/C | 2,160 | 79 | $ 430 | $1,041 | $1,471 |
| Oklahoma Baptist University | Shawnee, OK 74801 ...... | 1910 | Baptist | S/C | 1,531 | 100 | $1,800 | $1,100 | $2,900 |
| Oklahoma Christian College .. | Oklahoma City, OK 73111 | 1950 | Ind | S/C | 1,635 | 73 | $1,570 | $ 660 | $2,230 |
| Okla. City Southwestern Col. | Oklahoma City, OK 73127 | 1946 | Pent H. | S/C | 789 | 40 | $1,094 | $1,320 | $2,414 |
| Oklahoma City University ... | Oklahoma City, OK 73106 | 1904 | Meth | S-G/C | 2,583 | 94 | $2,140 | $1,690 | $3,830 |
| Okla. Missionary Baptist Col. | Marlow, OK 73055....... | 1954 | Baptist | P/C | 78 | 10 | $ 300 | — | $ 300 |
| Oklahoma School of Business | Tulsa, OK 74135 ........ | 1919 | Ind | J/C | 150 | 7 | $2,000 | — | $2,000 |
| Okla. State University ...... | Stillwater, OK 74074 ..... | 1890 | State | S-G/C | 22,003 | 1,004 | $ 427 | $1,168 | $1,595 |
| Okla. St. U. Sch. of Tech. Train. | Okmulgee, OK 74447 ..... | 1946 | State | T/C | 3,000 | 165 | $ 480 | $1,012 | $1,492 |
| Okla. State U. Tech. Institute . | Oklahoma City, OK 73107 | 1961 | State | J/C | 2,423 | 158 | $ 510 | — | $ 510 |
| Oral Roberts University ...... | Tulsa, OK 74171 ........ | 1963 | Ind | S-G/C | 4,000 | 350 | $2,950 | $2,040 | $4,950 |
| Oscar Rose Junior College ... | Midwest City, OK 73110 .. | 1970 | State | J/C | 8,000 | 275 | $ 166 | — | $ 166 |
| Panhandle State University... | Goodwell, OK 73939 ..... | 1909 | State | S/C | 976 | 67 | $ 469 | $1,066 | $1,535 |
| Phillips University ........... | Enid, OK 73701 ......... | 1906 | Christian | S-G/C | 1,284 | 73 | $2,240 | $1,560 | $3,800 |
| St. Gregory's College ........ | Shawnee, OK 74801 ...... | 1875 | Catholic | J/C | 337 | 34 | $1,650 | $1,580 | $3,230 |
| Sayre Junior College ........ | Sayre, OK 73662 ........ | 1938 | State | J/C | 288 | 24 | $ 315 | $ 980 | $1,295 |
| Seminole Junior College ..... | Seminole, OK 74868 ..... | 1931 | State | J/C | 1,650 | 52 | $ 350 | — | $ 350 |
| South Okla. City Jr. College .. | Oklahoma City, OK 73159 | 1972 | State | J/C | 6,313 | 147 | $ 228 | — | $ 328 |
| Southeastern Okla. State Univ. | Durant, OK 74701 ....... | 1909 | State | S-G/C | 4,230 | 185 | $ 440 | $1,220 | $1,660 |
| Southwestern Okla. State Univ. | Weatherford, OK 73096 .. | 1901 | State | S-G/C | 4,718 | 206 | $ 414 | $ 990 | $1,404 |
| Tulsa Junior College ........ | Tulsa, OK 74119 ........ | 1970 | State | J/C | 10,505 | 500 | $ 350 | — | $ 350 |
| University of Oklahoma ...... | Norman, OK 73019 ...... | 1890 | State | S-G/C | 21,090 | 756 | $ 508 | $1,292 | $1,800 |
| Health Sciences Center ... | Oklahoma City, OK 73190 | 1892 | State | S-G/C | 3,058 | 703 | — | — | — |
| Univ. of Sci. and Arts of Okla. | Chickasha, OK 73018 ... | 1908 | State | S/C | 1,287 | 62 | $ 400 | $1,250 | $1,650 |
| University of Tulsa ......... | Tulsa, OK 74104 ........ | 1894 | Ind | S-G/C | 6,311 | 309 | $2,440 | $1,365 | $3,805 |
| Western Okla. State College .. | Altus, OK 73521........ | 1926 | State | J/C | 1,752 | 43 | $ 375 | — | $ 375 |
| **OREGON** | | | | | | | | | |
| Blake College .............. | Eugene, OR 97402 ...... | 1961 | Ind | S/C | 14 | 2 | $3,300 | $1,700 | $5,000 |
| Blue Mountain Comm. College | Pendleton, OR 97801 ... | 1962 | State | J/C | 1,219 | 70 | $ 396 | — | $1,250 |
| Central Oregon Comm. College . | Bend, OR 97701 ........ | 1949 | Public | J/C | 4,762 | 113 | $ 432 | $1,304 | $1,736 |
| Chemeketa Comm. College .. | Salem, OR 97309 ....... | 1969 | County | J/C | 12,613 | 859 | $ 450 | — | $ 450 |
| Clackamas Comm. College .. | Oregon City, OR 97045... | 1966 | Ind | J/C | 9,339 | 484 | $ 405 | — | $ 405 |
| Clatsop Community College .. | Astoria, OR 97103....... | 1958 | State | J/C | 2,842 | 137 | $ 396 | — | $ 396 |
| Colegio Cesar Chavez ....... | Mt. Angel, OR 97362 ..... | 1973 | Ind | S/C | 110 | 20 | $1,515 | — | $3,845 |
| Columbia Christian College .. | Portland, OR 97220 ..... | 1956 | C of Chr | S/C | 333 | 23 | $2,337 | $1,518 | $4,555 |
| Concordia College .......... | Portland, OR 97211...... | 1905 | Lutheran | S/C | 325 | 32 | $2,515 | $1,800 | $4,315 |
| Eastern Oregon State College | La Grande, OR 97850 .... | 1929 | State | S-G/C | 1,591 | 84 | $ 780 | $1,710 | $2,490 |
| George Fox College ......... | Newberg, OR 97132 ..... | 1891 | Friends | S/C | 734 | 60 | $3,770 | $1,725 | $5,495 |
| Judson Baptist College ...... | The Dalles, OR 97058 .... | 1956 | Baptist | J/C | 219 | 26 | $2,600 | $1,590 | $4,190 |
| Lane Community College..... | Eugene, OR 97405....... | 1965 | Local | J/C | 8,283 | 347 | $ 429 | — | $ 429 |
| Lewis and Clark College...... | Portland, OR 97219...... | 1867 | Ind | S-G/C | 3,085 | 206 | $4,500 | $1,750 | $6,250 |
| Linfield College ............ | McMinnville, OR 97128.. | 1849 | Baptist | S/C | 1,109 | 111 | $3,885 | $1,760 | $5,645 |
| Linn-Benton Community Col. . | Albany, OR 97321 ....... | 1967 | State | J/C | 11,721 | 485 | $ 423 | — | $ 423 |
| Mount Angel Seminary ...... | St. Benedict, OR 97373... | 1887 | Catholic | S-G/M | 107 | 37 | $2,000 | $1,290 | $3,290 |
| Mt. Hood Community College | Gresham, OR 97030 ..... | 1965 | State | J/C | 10,039 | 490 | $ 390 | — | $ 390 |
| Multnomah Sch. of the Bible | Portland, OR 97220 ..... | 1936 | Ind | S-G/C | 736 | 40 | $2,190 | $1,280 | $3,470 |
| Museum Art School ......... | Portland, OR 97205...... | 1909 | Ind | S/C | 191 | 49 | $2,300 | — | $4,750 |
| Northwest Christian College .. | Eugene, OR 97401....... | 1895 | D of Chr | S/C | 291 | 20 | $2,568 | $1,555 | $4,123 |
| Oregon College of Education | Monmouth, OR 97361 ... | 1856 | State | S-G/C | 3,200 | 175 | $ 841 | $1,640 | $2,841 |
| Oregon Graduate Center .... | Beaverton, OR 97005 ... | 1963 | Ind | G/C | 42 | 21 | $4,000 | — | $4,000 |
| Oregon Inst. of Technology .. | Klamath Falls, OR 97601 | 1947 | State | S-T/C | 2,500 | 135 | $ 867 | $1,550 | $2,417 |
| Oregon State University ..... | Corvallis, OR 97331...... | 1868 | State | S-G/C | 17,206 | 2,236 | $ 846 | $1,500 | $2,346 |
| Pacific University .......... | Forest Grove, OR 97116 .. | 1849 | UC Chr | S-G/C | 1,091 | 107 | $4,300 | $1,700 | $6,000 |
| Portland Community College | Portland, OR 97219...... | 1961 | Public | J/C | 32,070 | 1,598 | $ 432 | — | $ 432 |
| Portland State University .... | Portland, OR 97207...... | 1955 | State | S-G/C | 16,841 | 1,000 | $ 890 | $2,000 | $3,110 |
| Reed College ............... | Portland, OR 97202...... | 1909 | Ind | S-G/C | 1,156 | 104 | $5,650 | $2,050 | $7,700 |
| Rogue Community College ... | Grants Pass, OR 97526 .. | 1970 | State | J/C | 3,041 | 210 | $ 432 | — | $ 432 |
| Southern Oregon State Col. .. | Ashland, OR 97520 ...... | 1926 | State | S-G/C | 4,443 | 250 | $ 858 | $1,560 | $2,418 |
| Southw. Oregon Comm. Col. . | Coos Bay, OR 97420 ..... | 1961 | Public | J/C | 5,410 | 282 | $ 420 | — | $ 420 |
| Treasure Valley Comm. Col. .. | Ontario, OR 97914....... | 1961 | State | J/C | 1,998 | 52 | $ 342 | $1,400 | $1,742 |
| Umpqua Community College | Roseburg, OR 97470 ..... | 1964 | State | J/C | 5,136 | 150 | $ 510 | — | $ 510 |
| University of Oregon ........ | Eugene, OR 97403....... | 1876 | State | S-G/C | 16,916 | 1,673 | $ 859 | $1,589 | $2,448 |
| School of Dentistry........ | Portland, OR 97201...... | 1900 | State | P/C | 400 | 175 | $2,080 | $1,009 | $2,557 |
| University of Portland ...... | Portland, OR 97203...... | 1902 | Catholic | S-G/C | 2,831 | 179 | $3,058 | $1,590 | $4,648 |
| Warner Pacific College...... | Portland, OR 97215...... | 1937 | C of Chr | S-G/C | 387 | 41 | $2,925 | $1,575 | $4,500 |
| Western Baptist College .... | Salem, OR 97302 ....... | 1935 | Baptist | S-G/C | 394 | 26 | $2,412 | $1,572 | $3,984 |
| Western Cons. Baptist Sem. . | Portland, OR 97215...... | 1927 | Baptist | G/C | 524 | 33 | $1,850 | — | $1,850 |
| Western Evangelical Sem. ... | Milwaukie, OR 97222 ... | 1945 | Int-Den | G/C | 188 | 13 | $2,445 | — | — |
| Western States Chirop. Col. . | Portland, OR 97230...... | 1908 | Ind | G/C | 480 | 41 | $3,200 | — | $3,200 |
| Willamette University ....... | Salem, OR 97301 ....... | 1842 | Meth | S-G/C | 1,775 | 175 | $3,775 | $1,695 | $5,470 |

| NAME | ADDRESS | FOUN-DED | AFFILI-ATION | LEVEL/TYPE | ENROLL-MENT | TEACH-ERS | TUITION & FEES | BOARD & ROOM | TOTAL COST |
|---|---|---|---|---|---|---|---|---|---|
| **PENNSYLVANIA** | | | | | | | | | |
| Academy of the New Church | Bryn Athyn, PA 19009 | 1876 | Swed | J-S | 147 | 31 | $1,162 | $1,227 | $2,389 |
| Albright College | Reading, PA 19604 | 1856 | Meth | S/C | 1,748 | 83 | $4,180 | $1,690 | $5,870 |
| Allegheny College | Meadville, PA 16335 | 1815 | Ind | S/C | 1,887 | 128 | $3,885 | $1,470 | $5,355 |
| Allentown Col. of St. F. De S. | Center Valley, PA 18034 | 1965 | Catholic | S/C | 750 | 50 | $3,330 | $1,980 | $6,000 |
| Alliance College | Cambrdg. Spgs., PA 16403 | 1912 | Ind | S/C | 254 | 30 | $2,400 | $1,728 | $4,128 |
| Alvernia College | Reading, PA 19607 | 1958 | Catholic | S/C | 772 | 68 | $1,950 | $1,500 | $3,450 |
| American College | Bryn Mawr, PA 19010 | 1927 | Ind | G/C | 1,400 | — | — | — | — |
| Antioch Univ., Philadelphia | Philadelphia, PA 19108 | 1968 | Ind | S-G/C | 800 | 70 | $2,750 | — | $2,800 |
| Baptist Bible College of Penn. | Clarks Summit, PA 18411 | 1932 | Baptist | S/C | 786 | 32 | $2,142 | $1,459 | $3,601 |
| Beaver College | Glenside, PA 19038 | 1853 | Presby | S-G/C | 1,925 | 130 | $4,420 | $2,050 | $6,470 |
| Biblical Theological Seminary | Hatfield, PA 19440 | 1971 | Ind | G/C | 135 | 8 | $2,012 | $1,252 | $3,264 |
| Bloomsburg State College | Bloomsburg, PA 17815 | 1839 | State | S-G/C | 6,532 | 346 | $1,040 | $1,102 | $2,142 |
| Bryn Mawr College | Bryn Mawr, PA 19010 | 1885 | Ind | S-G/W | 1,722 | 190 | $5,930 | $2,650 | $8,580 |
| Bucknell University | Lewisburg, PA 17837 | 1846 | Ind | S-G/C | 3,261 | 261 | $5,500 | $1,650 | $7,150 |
| Bucks County Comm. College | Newtown, PA 18940 | 1964 | Public | J/C | 8,789 | 191 | $ 702 | — | $ 702 |
| Butler County Comm. College | Butler, PA 16001 | 1965 | State | J/C | 959 | 54 | $ 750 | — | $ 750 |
| Cabrini College | Radnor, PA 19087 | 1957 | Catholic | S/C | 448 | 58 | $3,012 | $1,890 | $4,902 |
| California State College | California, PA 15419 | 1852 | State | S-G/C | 4,200 | 298 | $1,060 | $1,160 | $2,220 |
| Carlow College | Pittsburgh, PA 15213 | 1929 | Catholic | S/W | 959 | 88 | $3,785 | $2,000 | $5,785 |
| Carnegie-Mellon University | Pittsburgh, PA 15213 | 1900 | Private | S-G/C | 5,004 | 426 | $4,700 | $2,500 | $7,200 |
| Cedar Crest College | Allentown, PA 18104 | 1867 | UCC | S/W | 1,013 | 80 | $4,000 | $1,900 | $5,900 |
| Chatham College | Pittsburgh, PA 15232 | 1869 | Ind | S/W | 625 | 62 | $3,975 | $1,965 | $6,020 |
| Chestnut Hill College | Philadelphia, PA 19118 | 1924 | Catholic | S/W | 633 | 81 | $2,350 | $1,600 | $3,950 |
| Cheyney State College | Cheyney, PA 19319 | 1837 | State | S-G/C | 2,505 | 206 | $1,240 | $1,270 | $2,510 |
| Christ the Saviour Seminary | Johnstown, PA 15906 | 1940 | Church | S/M | 7 | 6 | $ 965 | $ 600 | $1,565 |
| Clarion State College | Clarion, PA 16214 | 1867 | State | S-G/C | 5,249 | 260 | $1,200 | $1,200 | $2,400 |
| Venango Campus | Oil City, PA 16301 | 1961 | State | J/C | 472 | 30 | $1,100 | $1,420 | $2,420 |
| College Misericordia | Dallas, PA 18612 | 1924 | Catholic | S/C | 1,000 | 97 | $2,630 | $1,650 | $4,280 |
| Combs College of Music | Philadelphia, PA 19119 | 1885 | Ind | S-G/C | 149 | 32 | $3,400 | $ 875 | $4,275 |
| Comm. Col. of Allegheny Co. | Pittsburgh, PA 15222 | 1966 | Public | J/C | | | | | |
| Allegheny Campus | Pittsburgh, PA 15212 | 1966 | Public | J/C | 6,384 | 150 | $ 630 | — | $ 630 |
| Boyce Campus | Monroeville, PA 15146 | 1966 | Public | J/C | 3,609 | 74 | $ 630 | — | $ 630 |
| College Center North | Pittsburgh, PA 15237 | 1972 | Public | J/C | 3,003 | 23 | $ 620 | — | $ 620 |
| South Campus | West Mifflin, PA 15122 | 1967 | Public | J/C | 3,231 | 81 | $ 630 | — | $ 630 |
| Comm. Col. of Beaver County | Monaca, PA 15061 | 1966 | Public | J/C | 2,000 | 83 | $ 770 | — | $ 770 |
| Comm. Col. of Philadelphia | Philadelphia, PA 19107 | 1964 | State | J/C | 12,838 | 301 | $ 650 | — | $ 650 |
| Curtis Institute of Music | Philadelphia, PA 19103 | 1924 | Ind | S/C | 129 | 62 | $ 125 | — | $ 125 |
| Delaware County Comm. Col. | Media, PA 19063 | 1967 | Public | J/C | 5,888 | 344 | $ 560 | — | $ 560 |
| Del. Val. Col. of Sci. & Agri. | Doylestown, PA 18901 | 1896 | Ind | S/C | 1,718 | 89 | $2,840 | $1,398 | $4,238 |
| Dickinson College | Carlisle, PA 17013 | 1773 | Meth | S/C | 1,685 | 120 | $4,885 | $1,970 | $6,855 |
| Dickinson School of Law | Carlisle, PA 17013 | 1834 | Ind | P/C | 480 | 36 | $2,740 | $1,650 | $4,390 |
| Drexel University | Philadelphia, PA 19104 | 1891 | Ind | S-G/C | 11,154 | 310 | $3,575 | $1,940 | $5,515 |
| Dropsie University | Philadelphia, PA 19132 | 1907 | Private | G/C | 80 | 10 | $3,500 | — | $3,500 |
| Duquesne University | Pittsburgh, PA 15219 | 1878 | Catholic | S/C | 6,825 | 458 | $3,558 | $1,605 | $5,163 |
| East Stroudsburg State Col. | E. Stroudsburg, PA 18301 | 1893 | State | S-G/C | 3,890 | 243 | $1,050 | $1,163 | $2,213 |
| Eastern Baptist Theol. Sem. | Philadelphia, PA 19151 | 1925 | Baptist | G/C | 273 | 26 | $2,000 | $2,000 | $4,000 |
| Eastern College | St. Davids, PA 19087 | 1953 | Baptist | S/C | 710 | 63 | $3,800 | $1,550 | $5,350 |
| Edinboro State College | Edinboro, PA 16444 | 1857 | State | S-G/C | 5,600 | 415 | $ 950 | $1,170 | $2,120 |
| Elizabethtown College | Elizabethtown, PA 17022 | 1899 | Brethren | S/C | 1,465 | 103 | $3,825 | $1,875 | $5,700 |
| Evangelical Sch. of Theology | Myerstown, PA 17067 | 1953 | Evang | P/C | 75 | 13 | $1,600 | — | $1,600 |
| Franklin and Marshall College | Lancaster, PA 17604 | 1787 | Ind | S/C | 1,994 | 136 | $4,950 | $1,800 | $6,750 |
| Gannon College | Erie, PA 16541 | 1944 | Catholic | S-G/C | 3,691 | 210 | $2,400 | $1,370 | $3,770 |
| Geneva College | Beaver Falls, PA 15010 | 1848 | Presby | S/C | 1,358 | 109 | $3,390 | $1,720 | $5,110 |
| Gettysburg College | Gettysburg, PA 17325 | 1832 | Lutheran | S/C | 1,900 | 165 | $4,260 | $1,450 | $5,710 |
| Gratz College | Philadelphia, PA 19141 | — | Jewish | S-G/C | 160 | 26 | $ 300 | — | $ 300 |
| Grove City College | Grove City, PA 16127 | 1876 | Presby | S/C | 2,211 | 119 | $2,230 | $1,420 | $3,650 |
| Gwynedd-Mercy College | Gwynedd Valley, PA 19437 | 1948 | Ind | J-S/C | 1,573 | 143 | $2,650 | $1,650 | $4,300 |
| Hahnemann Med. Col. & Hosp. | Philadelphia, PA 19102 | 1848 | Ind | J-P/C | 1,862 | 2,100 | — | — | — |
| Harcum Junior College | Bryn Mawr, PA 19010 | 1915 | Private | J/W | 819 | 74 | $2,370 | $1,850 | $4,220 |
| Harrisburg Area Comm. Col. | Harrisburg, PA 17110 | 1964 | State | J/C | 5,058 | — | $ 573 | — | $ 573 |
| Haverford College | Haverford, PA 19041 | 1833 | Quaker | S/C | 993 | 98 | $5,480 | $1,950 | $7,430 |
| Holy Family College | Philadelphia, PA 19114 | 1954 | Catholic | S/C | 1,185 | 102 | $2,300 | — | $2,300 |
| Immaculata College | Immaculata, PA 19345 | 1920 | Catholic | S/W | 752 | 59 | $2,550 | $1,650 | $4,200 |
| Indiana Univ. of Pennsylvania | Indiana, PA 15701 | 1875 | State | S-G/C | 12,144 | 615 | $1,072 | $1,210 | $2,282 |
| Armstrong County Campus | Kittanning, PA 16201 | 1963 | State | J/C | 476 | 15 | $1,072 | $1,210 | $2,282 |
| Punxsutawney Campus | Punxsutawney, PA 15767 | 1962 | State | J/C | 249 | 4 | $1,072 | $1,210 | $2,282 |
| Juniata College | Huntingdon, PA 16652 | 1876 | Ind | S/C | 1,274 | 69 | $4,065 | $1,845 | $5,910 |
| Keystone Junior College | La Plume, PA 18440 | 1868 | Ind | J/C | 961 | 55 | $2,650 | $1,630 | $4,280 |
| King's College | Wilkes-Barre, PA 18711 | 1946 | Catholic | S/C | 2,123 | 132 | $3,260 | $1,780 | $5,040 |
| Kutztown State College | Kutztown, PA 19530 | 1866 | State | S-G/C | 5,154 | 266 | $1,052 | $1,325 | $2,377 |
| La Roche College | Pittsburgh, PA 15237 | 1963 | Catholic | S/C | 1,300 | 135 | $2,450 | $1,800 | $4,250 |
| La Salle College | Philadelphia, PA 19141 | 1863 | Catholic | S-G/C | 4,900 | 375 | $3,300 | $2,000 | $5,300 |
| Lackawanna Junior College | Scranton, PA 18518 | 1894 | Ind | J/C | 1,115 | 86 | $1,800 | — | $1,800 |
| Lafayette College | Easton, PA 18042 | 1826 | Presby | S/C | 2,094 | 157 | $5,100 | $1,975 | $7,075 |
| Lancaster Bible College | Lancaster, PA 17601 | 1933 | Ind | S/C | 397 | 21 | $2,380 | $1,560 | $3,940 |
| Lancaster Theological Sem. | Lancaster, PA 17603 | 1825 | UC Chr | P/C | 240 | 18 | $2,400 | $1,600 | $4,000 |
| Lebanon Valley College | Annville, PA 17003 | 1866 | Meth | S/C | 970 | 100 | $4,205 | $1,970 | $6,175 |
| Lehigh County Comm. College | Schnecksville, PA 18078 | 1966 | Public | J/C | 2,940 | 68 | $ 870 | — | $ 870 |
| Lehigh University | Bethlehem, PA 18015 | 1865 | Ind | S-G/C | 6,291 | 387 | $4,550 | $1,980 | $6,530 |
| Lincoln University | Lincoln Univ., PA 19352 | 1854 | State | S-G/C | 1,261 | 103 | $1,268 | $ 775 | $2,043 |
| Lock Haven State College | Lock Haven, PA 17745 | 1870 | State | S/C | 2,416 | 168 | $1,342 | $1,192 | $2,534 |
| Lutheran Theol. Sem./Gtysbrg. | Gettysburg, PA 17325 | 1826 | Lutheran | G/C | 250 | 19 | $1,112 | $1,150 | $2,262 |
| Lutheran Theol. Sem. at Phil. | Philadelphia, PA 19119 | 1864 | Lutheran | G/C | 226 | 24 | $1,200 | $1,500 | $2,700 |
| Luzerne County Comm. Col. | Nanticoke, PA 18634 | 1967 | County | J/C | — | — | — | — | — |
| Lycoming College | Williamsport, PA 17701 | 1812 | Meth | S/C | 1,159 | 72 | $3,720 | $1,770 | $5,490 |

| NAME | ADDRESS | FOUNDED | AFFILIATION | LEVEL/TYPE | ENROLLMENT | TEACHERS | TUITION & FEES | BOARD & ROOM | TOTAL COST |
|---|---|---|---|---|---|---|---|---|---|
| **PENNSYLVANIA** (*continued*) | | | | | | | | | |
| Manor Junior College | Jenkintown, PA 19046 | 1947 | Catholic | J/W | 357 | 28 | $2,150 | $1,550 | $ 3,700 |
| Mansfield State College | Mansfield, PA 16933 | 1857 | State | S-G/C | 2,402 | 191 | $ 950 | $1,360 | $ 2,310 |
| Mary Immaculate Seminary | Northampton, PA 18067 | 1939 | Catholic | G/M | 65 | 12 | $1,560 | $1,700 | $ 3,260 |
| Marywood College | Scranton, PA 18509 | 1915 | Catholic | S-G/W | 3,141 | 210 | $2,250 | $1,700 | $ 3,950 |
| Medical Col. of Pennsylvania | Philadelphia, PA 19129 | 1850 | Ind | P/C | 453 | 223 | $7,925 | — | $ 7,925 |
| Mercyhurst College | Erie, PA 16546 | 1926 | Ind | S/C | 1,488 | 150 | $3,032 | $1,530 | $ 4,562 |
| Messiah College | Grantham, PA 17027 | 1909 | Brethren | S/C | 1,247 | 87 | $3,250 | $1,740 | $ 4,990 |
| Millersville State College | Millersville, PA 17551 | 1854 | State | S/C | 6,020 | 346 | $1,042 | $1,218 | $ 2,260 |
| Montgomery Co. Comm. Col. | Blue Bell, PA 19422 | 1964 | County | J/C | 7,129 | 366 | $ 820 | — | $ 820 |
| Moore College of Art | Philadelphia, PA 19103 | 1844 | Ind | S/W | 677 | 80 | $3,780 | $1,800 | $ 5,580 |
| Moravian College | Bethlehem, PA 18018 | 1742 | Moravian | S/C | 1,786 | 135 | $4,300 | $1,780 | $ 6,080 |
| Moravian Theological Sem. | Bethlehem, PA 18018 | 1807 | Moravian | P/C | 56 | 6 | $2,545 | $1,640 | $ 4,185 |
| Mount Aloysius Jr. College | Cresson, PA 16630 | 1939 | Catholic | J/C | 511 | 49 | $1,825 | $1,650 | $ 3,475 |
| Muhlenberg College | Allentown, PA 18104 | 1848 | Lutheran | S/C | 1,680 | 115 | $4,270 | $1,590 | $ 5,860 |
| New Castle Business College | New Castle, PA 16101 | 1894 | Ind | J/C | 150 | 7 | $2,061 | $1,485 | $ 3,546 |
| New School of Music | Philadelphia, PA 19103 | 1943 | Ind | S/C | 85 | 35 | $2,935 | — | $ 5,500 |
| Nrthmptn Co. Area Comm. Col. | Bethlehem, PA 18017 | 1966 | Public | J/C | 3,807 | 78 | $ 624 | — | $ 624 |
| Northeastern Chrstn. Jr. Col. | Villanova, PA 19085 | 1959 | C of Chr | J/C | 195 | 26 | $2,150 | $1,850 | $ 4,000 |
| Our Lady of Angels College | Aston, PA 19014 | 1965 | Catholic | S/W | 701 | 62 | $2,200 | — | $ 2,200 |
| Pierce Junior College | Philadelphia, PA 19102 | 1865 | Ind | J/C | 1,964 | 94 | $2,495 | $1,000 | $ 3,435 |
| Pendle Hill | Wallingford, PA 19086 | 1930 | Quaker | S-G/C | 34 | 7 | — | — | $ 4,400 |
| Pennco Tech. | Bristol, PA 19007 | 1961 | Ind | T/C | 500 | 26 | $2,240 | — | $ 2,240 |
| Pa. Academy of the Fine Arts | Philadelphia, PA 19102 | 1806 | Ind | P/C | 398 | 36 | $ 800 | — | $ 800 |
| Pa. College of Optometry | Philadelphia, PA 19141 | 1919 | Ind | P/C | 589 | 60 | $8,400 | — | $10,020 |
| Pa. College of Podiatric Med. | Philadelphia, PA 19107 | 1963 | Ind | P/C | 458 | 137 | $6,620 | — | $12,040 |
| Pennsylvania State Univ. | Univ. Park, PA 16802 | 1855 | State | S-G/C | 35,093 | 1,640 | $1,485 | $1,665 | $ 3,150 |
| Allentown Campus | Fogelsville, PA 18051 | 1912 | State | J/C | 414 | 20 | $1,281 | — | $ 1,281 |
| Altoona Campus | Altoona, PA 16603 | 1929 | State | J/C | 2,133 | 92 | $1,281 | $1,665 | $ 2,946 |
| Beaver Campus | Monaca, PA 15061 | 1964 | State | J/C | 1,246 | 54 | $1,281 | $1,665 | $ 2,946 |
| Behrend College | Erie, PA 16563 | 1926 | State | S-G/C | 1,830 | 102 | $1,281 | $1,665 | $ 2,946 |
| Berks Campus | Reading, PA 19608 | 1924 | State | J/C | 1,165 | 48 | $1,281 | — | $ 1,281 |
| Capitol Campus | Middletown, PA 17057 | 1966 | State | S-G/C | 2,507 | 137 | $1,440 | $1,665 | $ 3,105 |
| Delaware County Campus | Media, PA 19063 | 1966 | State | J/C | 1,380 | 62 | $1,281 | — | $ 1,281 |
| DuBois Campus | DuBois, PA 15801 | 1935 | State | J/C | 767 | 35 | $1,281 | — | $ 1,281 |
| Fayette Campus | Uniontown, PA 15401 | 1934 | State | J/C | 909 | 51 | $1,281 | — | $ 1,281 |
| Hazleton Campus | Hazleton, PA 18201 | 1934 | State | J/C | 1,105 | 44 | $1,281 | $1,665 | $ 2,946 |
| Hershey Medical Center | Hershey, PA 17033 | 1964 | State | P/C | 565 | 287 | $5,550 | — | $ 5,550 |
| McKeesport Campus | McKeesport, PA 15132 | 1947 | State | J/C | 1,282 | 54 | $1,281 | $1,665 | $ 2,946 |
| Mont Alto Campus | Mont Alto, PA 17237 | 1929 | State | J/C | 826 | 46 | $1,281 | $1,665 | $ 2,946 |
| New Kensington Campus | New Kensington, PA 15068 | 1958 | State | J/C | 1,041 | 62 | $1,281 | — | $ 1,281 |
| Ogontz Campus | Abington, PA 19001 | 1950 | State | J/C | 2,683 | 107 | $1,281 | — | $ 1,281 |
| Radnor Ctr. for Grad. Stud. | Radnor, PA 19087 | 1968 | State | G/C | 397 | 5 | $1,440 | — | $ 1,440 |
| Schuylkill Campus | Schuylkill, PA 17972 | 1934 | State | J/C | 760 | 31 | $1,281 | — | $ 1,281 |
| Shenango Valley Campus | Sharon, PA 16146 | 1965 | State | J/C | 871 | 47 | $1,281 | — | $ 1,281 |
| Wilkes-Barre Campus | Wilkes-Barre, PA 18708 | 1916 | State | J/C | 631 | 42 | $1,281 | — | $ 1,281 |
| Worthington Scrntn. Camp. | Dunmore, PA 18512 | 1923 | State | J/C | 1,082 | 55 | $1,281 | — | $ 1,281 |
| York Campus | York, PA 17403 | 1926 | State | J/C | 1,116 | 48 | $1,281 | — | $ 1,281 |
| Philadelphia Col. of Bible | Philadelphia, PA 19103 | 1913 | Ind | S/C | 526 | 40 | $2,480 | $1,730 | $ 4,210 |
| Phila. Col. of Osteo. Medicine | Philadelphia, PA 19131 | 1899 | Ind | P/C | 822 | 94 | $6,300 | — | $ 6,300 |
| Phila. Col. of Perform. Arts | Philadelphia, PA 19102 | 1870 | Ind | S-G/C | 370 | 113 | $3,600 | — | $ 3,600 |
| Phila. Col. of Pharm. and Sci. | Philadelphia, PA 19104 | 1821 | Ind | S-G/C | 1,120 | 103 | $3,500 | $1,000 | $ 4,600 |
| Phila. Col. of Textiles & Sci. | Philadelphia, PA 19144 | 1884 | Private | S-G/C | 2,827 | 179 | $2,850 | $1,750 | $ 4,600 |
| Pinebrook Junior College | Coopersburg, PA 18036 | 1969 | Fellow | J/C | 122 | 18 | $1,800 | $1,500 | $ 3,300 |
| Pittsburgh Theol. Seminary | Pittsburgh, PA 15206 | 1794 | Presby | G/C | 305 | 19 | $2,115 | — | $ 5,150 |
| Point Park College | Pittsburgh, PA 15222 | 1960 | Private | S/C | 1,511 | 128 | $3,095 | $1,560 | $ 4,655 |
| Reading Area Comm. College | Reading, PA 19603 | 1971 | Public | J/C | 1,342 | 67 | $1,140 | — | $ 1,140 |
| Reconstructionist Rab. Col. | Philadelphia, PA 19132 | 1968 | Jewish | G/C | 43 | 20 | $2,750 | — | $ 2,750 |
| Reformed Presby. Theol. Sem. | Pittsburgh, PA 15208 | 1810 | Presby | G/C | 53 | 7 | $ 915 | $ 750 | $ 1,665 |
| Robert Morris College | Coraopolis, PA 15108 | 1921 | Ind | S-G/C | 4,100 | 163 | $2,160 | $1,400 | $ 3,560 |
| Rosemont College | Rosemont, PA 19010 | 1921 | Catholic | S/W | 585 | 82 | $3,650 | $2,080 | $ 5,730 |
| St. Charles Borromeo Sem. | Philadelphia, PA 19151 | 1832 | Catholic | G/M | 235 | 37 | $2,215 | $1,800 | $ 4,015 |
| St. Francis College | Loretto, PA 15940 | 1847 | Catholic | S-G/C | 1,754 | 89 | $2,946 | $1,600 | $ 4,546 |
| St. Joseph's University | Philadelphia, PA 19131 | 1852 | Catholic | S-G/C | 5,550 | 250 | $2,875 | $1,926 | $ 4,801 |
| St. Vincent College | Latrobe, PA 15650 | 1846 | Catholic | S/M | 896 | 79 | $3,100 | $1,560 | $ 4,660 |
| Seton Hill College | Greensburg, PA 15601 | 1883 | Catholic | S/W | 922 | 77 | $3,200 | $1,740 | $ 4,940 |
| Shippensburg State College | Shippensburg, PA 17257 | 1871 | State | S-G/C | 5,915 | 277 | $3,000 | $1,204 | $ 4,204 |
| Slippery Rock State College | Slippery Rock, PA 16057 | 1889 | State | S/C | 5,694 | 341 | $ 970 | $1,210 | $ 2,180 |
| Spring Garden College | Chestnut Hill, PA 19118 | 1851 | Ind | S/C | 1,100 | 52 | $3,156 | — | $ 3,156 |
| Susquehanna University | Selinsgrove, PA 17870 | 1858 | Lutheran | S/C | 1,457 | 114 | $3,826 | $1,566 | $ 5,392 |
| Swarthmore College | Swarthmore, PA 19081 | 1864 | Quaker | S-G/C | 1,310 | 136 | $5,040 | $2,040 | $ 7,080 |
| Temple University | Philadelphia, PA 19122 | 1884 | State | S/C | 33,812 | 2,527 | $1,610 | $1,870 | $ 3,480 |
| Theol. Sem. of Ref. Epis. Ch. | Philadelphia, PA 19104 | 1886 | Episc | G/C | 65 | 7 | $ 630 | $ 500 | $ 1,130 |
| Thiel College | Greenville, PA 16125 | 1866 | Lutheran | S/C | 1,023 | 85 | $3,873 | $1,766 | $ 5,639 |
| Thomas Jefferson University | Philadelphia, PA 19107 | 1824 | Private | S/C | 753 | 82 | $4,400 | $1,800 | $ 6,200 |
| Jefferson Medical College | Philadelphia, PA 19107 | 1824 | Private | P/C | 909 | 1,792 | $8,400 | — | $13,608 |
| U.S. Army War College | Carlisle Bar, PA 17013 | 1901 | Federal | P/C | 783 | 55 | — | — | — |
| United Wesleyan College | Allentown, PA 18103 | 1921 | Wesleyan | S/C | 206 | 16 | $2,170 | $1,650 | $ 3,820 |
| Univ. Center at Harrisburg | Harrisburg, PA 17110 | 1958 | Ind | G/C | 850 | 52 | — | — | — |
| University of Pennsylvania | Philadelphia, PA 19104 | 1749 | Ind | S-G/C | 22,006 | 3,313 | $6,000 | $2,900 | $ 8,900 |
| University of Pittsburgh | Pittsburgh, PA 15260 | 1787 | State | S-G/C | 28,781 | 1,815 | $1,646 | $1,810 | $ 3,456 |
| Bradford Campus | Bradford, PA 16701 | 1963 | State | S/C | 718 | 53 | $1,520 | $1,850 | $ 3,370 |
| Greensburg Campus | Greensburg, PA 15601 | 1963 | State | S/C | 1,066 | 46 | $1,425 | — | $ 1,425 |
| Johnstown Campus | Johnstown, PA 15904 | 1927 | State | S/C | 3,040 | 155 | $1,590 | $1,800 | $ 3,390 |
| Titusville Campus | Titusville, PA 16354 | 1963 | State | J/C | 481 | 40 | $1,550 | $1,620 | $ 3,170 |

| NAME | ADDRESS | FOUN-DED | AFFILI-ATION | LEVEL/TYPE | ENROLL-MENT | TEACH-ERS | TUITION & FEES | BOARD & ROOM | TOTAL COST |
|---|---|---|---|---|---|---|---|---|---|
| **PENNSYLVANIA** *(continued)* | | | | | | | | | |
| University of Scranton | Scranton, PA 18510 | 1888 | Catholic | S-G/C | 4,440 | 230 | $2,528 | $1,600 | $4,128 |
| Ursinus College | Collegeville, PA 19426 | 1869 | C of Chr | S/C | 1,073 | 91 | $4,250 | $1,750 | $6,500 |
| Valley Forge Christian College | Phoenixville, PA 19460 | 1939 | A of God | S/C | 654 | 26 | $1,488 | $1,340 | $2,828 |
| Valley Forge Military Jr. Col. | Wayne, PA 19087 | 1938 | Ind | J/M | 128 | 23 | $2,755 | $1,530 | $4,285 |
| Villa Maria College | Erie, PA 16505 | 1925 | Catholic | S/W | 608 | 73 | $2,750 | $1,650 | $4,400 |
| Villanova University | Villanova, PA 19085 | 1842 | Catholic | S-G/C | 9,300 | 380 | $4,100 | $2,400 | $6,500 |
| Washington and Jefferson Col. | Washington, PA 15301 | 1781 | Ind | S/C | 1,053 | 95 | $4,265 | $1,625 | $5,890 |
| Waynesburg College | Waynesburg, PA 15370 | 1849 | Presby | S/C | 830 | 66 | $3,800 | $1,680 | $5,480 |
| West Chester State College | West Chester, PA 19380 | 1871 | State | S-G/C | 5,843 | 512 | $2,200 | $1,354 | $3,557 |
| Westminster College | New Wilmington, PA 16142 | 1852 | Presby | S-G/C | 1,859 | 130 | $3,730 | $1,630 | $5,360 |
| Westminster Theol. Seminary | Philadelphia, PA 19118 | 1929 | Ind | G/C | 379 | 20 | $1,890 | $1,260 | $3,150 |
| Westmoreland Co. Comm. Col. | Youngwood, PA 15697 | 1970 | County | J/C | 5,311 | 48 | $ 672 | — | $ 672 |
| Widener College | Chester, PA 19013 | 1821 | Ind | S-G/C | 4,343 | 271 | $3,760 | $1,810 | $5,570 |
| Wilkes College | Wilkes-Barre, PA 18766 | 1933 | Ind | S-G/C | 2,050 | 146 | $3,250 | $1,700 | $4,950 |
| Williamsport Area Comm. Col. | Williamsport, PA 17701 | 1965 | State | T/C | 3,061 | 134 | $ 780 | — | $ 780 |
| Wilson College | Chambersburg, PA 17201 | 1869 | Presby | S/W | 146 | 43 | $4,050 | $1,850 | $5,900 |
| York Col. of Pennsylvania | York, PA 17405 | 1776 | Ind | S-G/C | 3,628 | 196 | $2,118 | $1,428 | $3,546 |
| **PUERTO RICO** | | | | | | | | | |
| Catholic. Univ. of Puerto Rico | Ponce, PR 00731 | 1948 | Catholic | S-G/C | 11,698 | 583 | $1,750 | $1,200 | $2,950 |
| Inter Amer. Univ. of Puer. Rico | | | | | | | | | |
| Aguadilla Regional College | Aguadilla, PR 00603 | 1957 | Ind | J/C | 2,350 | 132 | $1,290 | — | $1,290 |
| Arecibo Regional College | Arecibo, PR 00612 | 1956 | Ind | J/C | 2,770 | 130 | $1,290 | — | $1,290 |
| Barranquitas Regional Col. | Barranquitas, PR 00615 | 1957 | Ind | J/C | 1,109 | 47 | $1,290 | — | $1,290 |
| Fajardo Regional College | Fajardo, PR 00648 | 1961 | Ind | J/C | 1,680 | 86 | $1,290 | — | $1,290 |
| Guayama Regional College | Guayama, PR 00854 | 1957 | Ind | J/C | 1,025 | 65 | $1,290 | — | $1,290 |
| Metropolitan Campus | San Juan, PR 00936 | 1962 | Ind | S-G/C | 12,285 | 550 | $1,290 | — | $1,290 |
| Ponce Regional College | Ponce, PR 00731 | 1962 | Ind | J/C | 1,814 | 81 | $1,290 | — | $1,290 |
| San German Campus | San German, PR 00753 | 1912 | Ind | S-G/C | 6,802 | 284 | $1,290 | $1,150 | $2,240 |
| School of Law | F. Juncos Station, PR 00910 | 1961 | Ind | G/C | 1,108 | 53 | $2,476 | — | $2,476 |
| Puerto Rico Junior College | Rio Piedras, PR 00928 | 1949 | Ind | J/C | 7,163 | 108 | $1,400 | — | $1,400 |
| University of Puerto Rico | San Juan, PR 00936 | 1903 | State | J-S-G/C | 50,667 | 3,490 | $ 200 | $1,400 | $1,600 |
| Aguadilla Regional College | Aguadilla, PR 00603 | 1972 | State | J/C | — | — | — | — | — |
| Arecibo Regional College | Arecibo, PR 00612 | 1967 | State | J/C | 2,227 | 103 | $ 194 | — | $ 194 |
| Bayamón Regional College | Bayamón, PR 00619 | 1971 | State | J/C | 2,771 | 134 | $ 80 | $ 900 | $ 980 |
| Carolina Regional College | Carolina, PR 00630 | 1974 | State | J/C | 1,091 | 67 | $ 277 | $ 540 | $ 817 |
| Cayey University College | Cayey, PR 00633 | 1967 | State | S/C | 2,601 | 105 | $ 167 | — | $1,640 |
| Humacao University | Humacao, PR 00661 | 1962 | State | J-S/C | — | — | — | — | — |
| Mayaguez Campus | Mayaguez, PR 00708 | 1911 | State | S-G/C | 8,111 | 717 | $ 210 | — | — |
| Medical Sciences Campus | Rio Piedras, PR 00936 | 1926 | State | S-G/C | — | — | — | — | — |
| La Montana Regional Col. | Utuado, PR 00672 | 1979 | State | S/C | — | — | — | — | — |
| Ponce Regional College | Ponce, PR 00732 | 1970 | State | J/C | 1,554 | 88 | $ 193 | $1,200 | $1,393 |
| Rio Piedras Campus | Rio Piedras, PR 00931 | 1903 | State | S-G/C | — | — | — | — | — |
| Univ. of the Sacred Heart | Santurce, PR 00914 | 1935 | Catholic | J-S/C | 6,425 | 280 | $1,250 | $ 800 | $2,050 |
| **RHODE ISLAND** | | | | | | | | | |
| Barrington College | Barrington, RI 02806 | 1900 | Ind | S/C | 467 | 57 | $3,049 | $1,820 | $4,869 |
| Brown University | Providence, RI 02912 | 1764 | Ind | S-G/C | 6,781 | 479 | $6,140 | $2,575 | $8,715 |
| Bryant College | Smithfield, RI 02917 | 1863 | Ind | S-G/C | 5,575 | 222 | $2,850 | $1,725 | $4,575 |
| Johnson & Wales College | Providence, RI 02903 | 1914 | Ind | S/C | 3,000 | 118 | $3,105 | $1,645 | $4,750 |
| New England Inst. of Tech. | Providence, RI 02907 | 1940 | Ind | J/C | 675 | 35 | $2,700 | — | $2,700 |
| Newport Col.-Salve Regina | Newport, RI 02840 | 1934 | Catholic | S-G/C | 1,719 | 151 | $3,350 | $2,000 | $5,350 |
| Providence College | Providence, RI 02918 | 1917 | Catholic | S-G/C | 3,488 | 244 | $3,467 | $2,310 | $5,777 |
| Rhode Island College | Providence, RI 02903 | 1854 | State | S-G/C | 7,742 | 395 | $ 775 | $2,200 | $2,975 |
| Rhode Island Junior College | Warwick, RI 02886 | 1964 | State | J/C | 11,158 | 395 | $ 464 | — | $ 464 |
| Rhode Island Sch. of Design | Providence, RI 02903 | 1877 | Ind | P/C | 1,517 | 79 | $5,260 | $2,230 | $7,490 |
| Roger Williams College | Bristol, RI 02809 | 1948 | Ind | S/C | 3,613 | 254 | $3,128 | $1,966 | $5,094 |
| University of Rhode Island | Kingston, RI 02881 | 1888 | State | S-G/C | 14,286 | 706 | $1,148 | $1,963 | $3,111 |
| **SOUTH CAROLINA** | | | | | | | | | |
| Aiken Technical College | Aiken, SC 29801 | 1972 | State | T/C | 1,489 | 97 | $ 402 | — | $ 402 |
| Allen University | Columbia, SC 29204 | 1870 | Meth | S/C | 274 | 28 | $1,760 | $1,300 | $3,060 |
| Anderson College | Anderson, SC 29621 | 1911 | Baptist | J/C | 1,117 | 58 | $1,804 | $1,350 | $3,154 |
| Baptist Col. at Charleston | Charleston, SC 29411 | 1960 | Baptist | S/C | 2,420 | 99 | $2,994 | $1,910 | $4,904 |
| Beaufort Tech. College | Beaufort, SC 29902 | 1972 | State | T/C | 1,165 | 50 | $ 480 | — | $ 480 |
| Benedict College | Columbia, SC 29204 | 1870 | Baptist | S/C | 1,613 | 111 | $2,200 | $1,600 | $3,400 |
| Bob Jones University | Greenville, SC 29614 | 1927 | Ind | S/C | 4,870 | 317 | $1,594 | $1,989 | $3,583 |
| Central Wesleyan College | Central, SC 29630 | 1906 | Wesleyan | S/C | 400 | 35 | $2,920 | $1,560 | $4,480 |
| Chesterfield-Marlb. Tech. Col. | Cheraw, SC 29520 | 1869 | State | T/C | 500 | 33 | $ 375 | — | $ 375 |
| Citadel | Charleston, SC 29409 | 1842 | State | S-G/M | 3,277 | 151 | $2,515 | $1,160 | $3,675 |
| Claflin College | Orangeburg, SC 29115 | 1869 | Meth | S/C | 866 | 62 | $2,256 | $1,094 | $3,350 |
| Clemson University | Clemson, SC 29631 | 1889 | State | S-G/C | 11,748 | 743 | $ 984 | $1,290 | $2,274 |
| Clinton Junior College | Rock Hill, SC 29720 | 1894 | Meth | J/C | 154 | 9 | $ 810 | $ 945 | $1,755 |
| Coker College | Hartsville, SC 29550 | 1908 | Ind | S/C | 321 | 37 | $2,769 | $1,487 | $4,256 |
| College of Charleston | Charleston, SC 29401 | 1770 | State | S-G/C | 5,033 | 203 | $ 750 | $1,500 | $2,250 |
| Columbia Bible College | Columbia, SC 29203 | 1923 | Ind | S-G/C | 807 | 49 | $ 600 | $ 490 | $1,090 |
| Columbia College | Columbia, SC 29203 | 1854 | Meth | S/W | 1,031 | 81 | $2,400 | $1,700 | $4,100 |
| Columbia Commercial College | Columbia, SC 29201 | 1935 | Ind | J/C | 1,017 | 49 | $1,185 | $ 810 | $1,995 |
| Converse College | Spartanburg, SC 29301 | 1889 | Ind | S-G/W | 933 | 83 | $3,560 | $1,800 | $5,360 |
| Denmark Tech. Educ. Center | Denmark, SC 29042 | 1948 | State | T/C | 600 | 32 | $ 500 | $1,400 | $1,900 |
| Erskine College | Due West, SC 29639 | 1839 | Presby | S/C | 605 | 52 | $3,015 | $1,280 | $4,295 |
| Florence-Darl. Tech. College | Florence, SC 29501 | 1963 | Public | T/C | 2,420 | 190 | $ 345 | — | $ 345 |
| Francis Marion College | Florence, SC 29501 | 1970 | State | S-G/C | 2,818 | 123 | $ 590 | $ 950 | $1,540 |
| Friendship College | Rock Hill, SC 29730 | 1891 | Baptist | J/C | 301 | 12 | $2,990 | $1,500 | $3,330 |
| Furman University | Greenville, SC 29613 | 1826 | Baptist | S-G/C | 3,069 | 192 | $3,008 | $2,000 | $5,008 |

## SOUTH CAROLINA (continued)

| NAME | ADDRESS | FOUN-DED | AFFILI-ATION | LEVEL/TYPE | ENROLL-MENT | TEACH-ERS | TUITION & FEES | BOARD & ROOM | TOTAL COST |
|------|---------|----------|--------------|------------|-------------|-----------|----------------|--------------|------------|
| Greenville Technical College .. | Greenville, SC 29606 ..... | 1962 | State | T/C | 9,852 | 510 | $ 300 | — | $ 300 |
| Holmes Col. of the Bible ..... | Greenville, SC 29601 ..... | 1898 | Ind | P/C | 120 | 13 | — | — | — |
| Horry-Georgetown Tech. Col. . | Conway, SC 29526......... | 1966 | State | T/C | 2,389 | 41 | $ 500 | — | $ 500 |
| Lander College ............. | Greenwood, SC 29646 .... | 1872 | State | S/C | 1,696 | 83 | $ 700 | $1,400 | $2,100 |
| Limestone College .......... | Gaffney, SC 29340......... | 1845 | Ind | S/C | 1,124 | 76 | $2,425 | $1,521 | $3,946 |
| Lutheran Theol. South. Sem. .. | Columbia, SC 29203 ...... | 1830 | Lutheran | P/C | 171 | 16 | $1,000 | $1,395 | $2,395 |
| Medical Univ. of S. Carolina ... | Charleston, SC 29403 ..... | 1824 | State | P/C | 2,490 | 700 | $ 788 | $1,500 | $2,288 |
| Midlands Technical College ... | Columbia, SC 29208 ...... | 1974 | State | T/C | 5,682 | 423 | $ 620 | — | $ 620 |
| Morris College ............. | Sumter, SC 29150 ........ | 1908 | Baptist | S/C | 727 | 48 | $1,792 | $1,171 | $2,963 |
| Newberry College........... | Newberry, SC 29108 ...... | 1856 | Lutheran | S/C | 883 | 76 | $3,265 | $1,480 | $4,750 |
| North Greenville College..... | Tigerville, SC 29688 ...... | 1892 | Baptist | J/C | 441 | 33 | $2,000 | $1,400 | $3,400 |
| Orangeburg-Calhoun Tech.Col. | Orangeburg, SC 29115 .... | 1966 | State | T/C | 3,242 | 119 | $ 330 | — | $1,300 |
| Piedmont Technical College ... | Greenwood, SC 29646 .... | 1966 | State | T/C | 1,459 | 50 | $ 420 | — | $ 525 |
| Presbyterian College ........ | Clinton, SC 29325 ........ | 1880 | Presby | S/C | 925 | 69 | $3,310 | $1,640 | $4,950 |
| Rutledge College ........... | Spartanburg, SC 29303 ... | 1910 | Private | J/C | 425 | 21 | $1,776 | — | $1,776 |
| Sherman Col. of Strgt. Chiro. .. | Spartanburg, SC 29304 .. | 1973 | Ind | P/C | 411 | 30 | $3,250 | — | $3,250 |
| South Carolina State Col. .... | Orangeburg, SC 29117 .... | 1896 | State | S-G/C | 3,585 | 199 | $ 640 | $1,246 | $1,886 |
| Southern Methodist College ... | Orangeburg, SC 29115 .... | 1956 | Meth | S/C | 63 | 12 | $1,110 | $1,400 | $2,510 |
| Spartanburg Tech. College.... | Spartanburg, SC 29303 ... | 1963 | State | T/C | 3,755 | 190 | $ 420 | — | $ 420 |
| Sumter Area Tech. College.... | Sumter, SC 29150 ........ | 1963 | State | T/C | 1,631 | 37 | $ 360 | — | $ 450 |
| Tri-County Tech. College .... | Pendleton, SC 29670...... | 1962 | State | T/C | 2,355 | 245 | $ 474 | — | $ 474 |
| Trident Tech. College ....... | Charleston, SC 29405 .... | 1974 | State | T/C | 5,862 | 305 | $ 440 | — | $ 440 |
| Univ. of South Carolina ...... | Columbia, SC 29208 ...... | 1801 | State | S-G/C | 25,908 | 1,173 | $ 890 | $1,500 | $2,390 |
| Aiken Campus............. | Aiken, SC 29801 ......... | 1961 | State | S/C | 1,674 | 135 | $ 710 | — | $ 710 |
| Beaufort Campus......... | Beaufort, SC 29902 ...... | 1959 | State | J/C | 656 | 41 | $ 710 | — | $ 710 |
| Coastal Carolina College .. | Conway, SC 29526........ | 1959 | State | S/C | 2,081 | 116 | $ 710 | — | $ 710 |
| Lancaster Campus........ | Lancaster, SC 29720 ..... | 1959 | State | J/C | 739 | 54 | $ 710 | — | $ 710 |
| Salkehatchie Campus ..... | Allendale, SC 29810 ...... | 1965 | State | J/C | 463 | 33 | $ 710 | — | $ 710 |
| Spartanburg Campus ..... | Spartanburg, SC 29303 .. | 1967 | State | S/C | 2,424 | 148 | $ 710 | — | $ 710 |
| Sumter Campus.......... | Sumter, SC 29150 ........ | 1966 | State | J/C | 1,106 | 60 | $ 710 | — | $ 710 |
| Union Campus ........... | Union, SC 29379 ......... | 1965 | State | J/C | 286 | 28 | $ 710 | — | $ 710 |
| Voorhees College .......... | Denmark, SC 29042....... | 1897 | Episc | S/C | 709 | 51 | $1,647 | $1,647 | $3,295 |
| Williamsburg Tech. ......... | Kingstree, SC 29556 ...... | 1969 | State | T/C | 546 | 56 | $ 320 | — | $ 320 |
| Winthrop College ........... | Rock Hill, SC 29733 ...... | 1886 | State | S-G/C | 4,979 | 245 | $ 817 | $1,156 | $1,973 |
| Wofford College ............ | Spartanburg, SC 29301 ... | 1854 | Meth | S/C | 1,078 | 63 | $3,440 | $1,910 | $5,350 |
| York Technical College ...... | Rock Hill, SC 29730 ...... | 1964 | State | T/C | 1,737 | 101 | $ 225 | — | $ 225 |

## SOUTH DAKOTA

| NAME | ADDRESS | FOUN-DED | AFFILI-ATION | LEVEL/TYPE | ENROLL-MENT | TEACH-ERS | TUITION & FEES | BOARD & ROOM | TOTAL COST |
|------|---------|----------|--------------|------------|-------------|-----------|----------------|--------------|------------|
| Augustana College........... | Sioux Falls, SD 57102 .... | 1860 | Lutheran | S-G/C | 2,243 | 130 | $3,650 | $1,345 | $4,995 |
| Black Hills State College .... | Spearfish, SD 57783 ..... | 1883 | State | S/C | 2,054 | 95 | $ 815 | $1,241 | $2,056 |
| Dakota State College ........ | Madison, SD 57042 ...... | 1881 | State | S/C | 895 | 52 | $ 753 | $1,220 | $1,973 |
| Dakota Wesleyan University... | Mitchell, SD 57301 ....... | 1885 | Meth | S/C | 526 | 60 | $2,286 | $1,405 | $3,691 |
| Freeman Junior College ...... | Freeman, SD 57029 ...... | 1900 | Men | J/C | 70 | 15 | $2,060 | $1,100 | $3,160 |
| Huron College .............. | Huron, SD 57350 ........ | 1883 | Presby | S/C | 318 | 35 | $2,560 | $1,548 | $4,108 |
| Lake Area Voc. Tech. Inst. ... | Watertown, SD 57201 .... | 1965 | Public | T/C | 657 | 54 | $ 780 | $1,800 | $2,580 |
| Mount Marty College ........ | Yankton, SD 57078 ...... | 1936 | Catholic | S/C | 590 | 58 | $2,820 | $1,440 | $4,260 |
| National College of Business .. | Rapid City, SD 57709 ..... | 1941 | Private | S/C | 1,025 | 60 | $3,000 | $1,875 | $4,875 |
| Rapid City Division .......... | Rapid City, SD 57709 ..... | 1974 | Private | S/C | 101 | 11 | $2,500 | — | $2,500 |
| National College of Business .. | Sioux Falls, SD 57101 .... | 1974 | Private | S/C | 214 | 14 | $2,500 | — | $2,500 |
| North Amer. Baptist Seminary . | Sioux Falls, SD 57105 .... | 1858 | Baptist | P/C | 179 | 16 | $1,500 | — | — |
| Northern State College ...... | Aberdeen, SD 57401 ..... | 1901 | State | S-G/C | 2,459 | 114 | $ 745 | $1,145 | $1,890 |
| Presentation College ........ | Aberdeen, SD 57401 ..... | 1951 | Catholic | J/C | 345 | 43 | $2,080 | $ 980 | $3,060 |
| Sioux Falls College ......... | Sioux Falls, SD 57101 .... | 1883 | Baptist | S/C | 774 | 57 | $2,700 | $1,390 | $4,090 |
| S. D. School of Mines & Tech. . | Rapid City, SD 57701 ..... | 1885 | State | S-G/C | 2,158 | 94 | $ 830 | $1,000 | $1,830 |
| South Dakota State University. | Brookings, SD 57007 ..... | 1881 | State | S-G/C | 6,500 | 500 | $ 838 | $1,146 | $1,984 |
| Univ. of South Dakota ....... | Vermillion, SD 57069 ..... | 1862 | State | S-G/C | 6,000 | 400 | $ 741 | $1,220 | $2,500 |
| Springfield Campus........ | Springfield, SD 57062 .... | 1881 | State | S/C | 828 | 63 | $ 692 | $1,316 | $2,008 |
| Yankton College ............ | Yankton, SD 57078 ...... | 1881 | UC Chr | S/C | 289 | 47 | $3,340 | $1,530 | $4,870 |

## TENNESSEE

| NAME | ADDRESS | FOUN-DED | AFFILI-ATION | LEVEL/TYPE | ENROLL-MENT | TEACH-ERS | TUITION & FEES | BOARD & ROOM | TOTAL COST |
|------|---------|----------|--------------|------------|-------------|-----------|----------------|--------------|------------|
| American Baptist College ..... | Nashville, TN 37207 ...... | 1924 | Baptist | S/C | 134 | 16 | $ 720 | $ 880 | $1,600 |
| Aquinas Junior College ...... | Nashville, TN 37205...... | 1961 | Catholic | J/C | 300 | 35 | $1,400 | — | $1,400 |
| Austin Peay State University .. | Clarksville, TN 37040 .... | 1927 | State | S-G/C | 5,447 | 240 | $ 498 | $1,380 | $1,878 |
| Belmont College ............ | Nashville, TN 37203 ...... | 1951 | Baptist | S/C | 1,487 | 75 | $1,850 | $1,300 | $3,150 |
| Bethel College ............. | McKenzie, TN 38201 ..... | 1842 | Presby | S/C | 394 | 24 | $1,800 | $1,440 | $3,240 |
| Bristol College ............. | Bristol, TN 37620......... | 1895 | Ind | S/C | 228 | 11 | $1,275 | — | $1,275 |
| Bryan College .............. | Dayton, TN 37321 ....... | 1930 | Ind | S/C | 645 | 51 | $2,250 | $1,950 | $4,200 |
| Carson-Newman College...... | Jefferson City, TN 37760 | 1851 | Baptist | S/C | 1,649 | 118 | $2,208 | $1,570 | $3,778 |
| Chatta. St. Tech. Comm. Col. . | Chattanooga, TN 37406 .. | 1963 | State | J/C | 4,602 | 165 | $ 273 | — | $ 273 |
| Christian Brothers College ... | Memphis, TN 38104 ..... | 1871 | Catholic | S/C | 1,330 | 114 | $2,744 | $2,040 | $4,784 |
| Cleveland State Comm. College | Cleveland, TN 37311 ..... | 1967 | State | J/C | 4,115 | 161 | $ 276 | — | $ 276 |
| Columbia State Comm. College | Columbia, TN 38401 ..... | 1966 | State | J/C | 2,351 | 118 | $ 270 | — | $ 270 |
| Cumberland Col. of Tennessee | Lebanon, TN 37087 ...... | 1842 | Ind | J/C | 470 | 30 | $1,840 | $1,350 | $3,190 |
| David Lipscomb College ..... | Nashville, TN 37203 ...... | 1891 | C of Chr | S/C | 2,293 | 120 | $2,031 | $1,500 | $3,531 |
| East Tennessee State Univ. ... | Johnson City, TN 37601 .. | 1911 | State | S-G/C | 10,195 | 576 | $ 500 | $1,500 | $2,000 |
| Emmanuel School of Religion . | Johnson City, TN 37601 .. | 1961 | Christian | G/C | 140 | 14 | $1,250 | — | $1,250 |
| Fisk University ............. | Nashville, TN 37203...... | 1866 | Ind | S-G/C | 1,101 | 81 | $2,850 | $1,635 | $4,485 |
| Freed-Hardeman College ..... | Henderson, TN 38340 .... | 1869 | C of Chr | J/C | 1,497 | 78 | $2,030 | $1,370 | $3,400 |
| Free Will Baptist Bible College. | Nashville, TN 37205...... | 1942 | Baptist | S/C | 528 | 29 | $2,440 | $1,540 | $3,980 |
| Hiwassee College .......... | Madisonville, TN 37354... | 1849 | Meth | J/C | 709 | 32 | $1,485 | $1,470 | $2,955 |
| Jackson State Comm. College . | Jackson, TN 38301 ...... | 1967 | State | J/C | 2,768 | 118 | $ 270 | — | $ 270 |
| John A. Gupton College ...... | Nashville, TN 37203...... | 1946 | Ind | J/C | 61 | 13 | $1,666 | — | $1,666 |
| Johnson Bible College ....... | Knoxville, TN 37920...... | 1893 | Christian | S/C | 412 | 25 | $1,090 | $1,720 | $2,810 |
| King College .............. | Bristol, TN 37620......... | 1867 | Presby | S/C | 235 | 35 | $2,910 | $1,670 | $4,580 |

| NAME | ADDRESS | FOUN-DED | AFFILI-ATION | LEVEL/TYPE | ENROLL-MENT | TEACH-ERS | TUITION & FEES | BOARD & ROOM | TOTAL COST |
|---|---|---|---|---|---|---|---|---|---|
| **TENNESSEE** (continued) | | | | | | | | | |
| Knoxville College | Knoxville, TN 37921 | 1875 | Presby | S/C | 698 | 39 | $2,400 | $1,635 | $4,035 |
| Lambuth College | Jackson, TN 38301 | 1843 | Meth | S/C | 764 | 70 | $2,430 | $1,350 | $3,780 |
| Lane College | Jackson, TN 38301 | 1882 | CME | S/C | 670 | 40 | $1,934 | $1,360 | $3,294 |
| Lee College | Cleveland, TN 37311 | 1918 | C of Chr | S/C | 1,442 | 55 | $1,884 | $1,425 | $3,309 |
| LeMoyne-Owen College | Memphis, TN 38126 | 1870 | UC Chr | S/C | 981 | 60 | $1,650 | — | $1,650 |
| Lincoln Memorial University | Harrogate, TN 37752 | 1897 | Private | S/C | 1,076 | 65 | $2,300 | $1,150 | $3,450 |
| Martin College | Pulaski, TN 38478 | 1870 | Meth | J/C | 240 | 22 | $1,450 | $1,350 | $2,800 |
| Maryville College | Maryville, TN 37801 | 1819 | Presby | S/C | 650 | 57 | $2,853 | $1,392 | $4,245 |
| Meharry Medical College | Nashville, TN 37208 | 1876 | Ind | P/C | 1,069 | 296 | $5,600 | $3,000 | $8,600 |
| Memphis Academy of Arts | Memphis, TN 38112 | 1936 | Ind | P/C | 220 | 26 | $1,900 | — | $1,900 |
| Memphis State University | Memphis, TN 38152 | 1912 | State | S-G/C | 21,248 | 861 | $ 478 | $2,125 | $2,603 |
| Middle Tenn. State University | Murfreesboro, TN 37132 | 1911 | State | S-G/C | 10,880 | 450 | $ 520 | $ 952 | $1,472 |
| Milligan College | Milligan Col., TN 37682 | 1881 | Christian | S/C | 775 | 48 | $2,072 | $1,868 | $3,940 |
| Morristown College | Morristown, TN 37814 | 1881 | Meth | J/C | 154 | 12 | $1,675 | $1,625 | $3,200 |
| Motlow State Community Col. | Tullahoma, TN 37388 | 1969 | State | J/C | 2,205 | 43 | $ 270 | — | $ 270 |
| Nashville State Tech. Institute | Nashville, TN 37209 | 1970 | State | J/C | 4,772 | 238 | $ 225 | — | $ 225 |
| Scarritt College | Nashville, TN 37203 | 1892 | Meth | S-G/C | 125 | 11 | $1,200 | $ 940 | $2,150 |
| Southern Col. of Optometry | Memphis, TN 38104 | 1932 | Ind | P/C | 590 | 52 | $7,800 | — | $7,800 |
| Southern Missionary College | Collegedale, TN 37315 | 1898 | 7-D Adv | S/C | 2,033 | 135 | $3,225 | $1,440 | $4,665 |
| Southwestern at Memphis | Memphis, TN 38112 | 1848 | Presby | S/C | 1,006 | 86 | $4,000 | $1,970 | $5,970 |
| State Tech. Inst. at Memphis | Memphis, TN 38134 | 1967 | State | T/C | 6,110 | 161 | $ 300 | — | $ 300 |
| Steed College | Johnson City, TN 37601 | 1940 | Private | S/C | 750 | 30 | $1,260 | — | $1,260 |
| Tennessee State University | Nashville, TN 37203 | 1912 | State | S-G/C | 8,438 | 240 | $ 504 | $1,372 | $2,000 |
| Tennessee Tech. University | Cookeville, TN 38501 | 1915 | State | S/C | 7,849 | 594 | $ 483 | $1,002 | $1,485 |
| Tennessee Temple University | Chattanooga, TN 37404 | 1946 | Baptist | S/C | 4,003 | 160 | $1,735 | $1,660 | $3,395 |
| Tennessee Wesleyan College | Athens, TN 37303 | 1857 | Meth | S/C | 467 | 37 | $2,160 | $1,560 | $3,720 |
| Tomlinson College | Cleveland, TN 37311 | 1966 | C of Chr | J/C | 297 | 19 | $1,475 | $1,500 | $2,975 |
| Trevecca Nazarene College | Nashville, TN 37210 | 1901 | Nazarene | S/C | 1,031 | 75 | $2,430 | $1,470 | $3,900 |
| Tusculum College | Greeneville, TN 37743 | 1794 | Presby | S/C | 378 | 30 | $2,430 | $1,650 | $4,080 |
| Union University | Jackson, TN 38301 | 1825 | Baptist | S/C | 1,077 | 80 | $1,720 | $ 780 | $2,700 |
| University of Tennessee | Knoxville, TN 37916 | 1794 | State | S-G/C | — | — | — | — | — |
| Center for the Health Sci. | Memphis, TN 38163 | 1850 | State | P/C | 2,095 | — | $ 800 | $ 800 | $1,600 |
| Chattanooga Campus | Chattanooga, TN 37402 | 1886 | State | S-G/C | 7,539 | 355 | $ 546 | $ 600 | $1,146 |
| Knoxville Campus | Knoxville, TN 37916 | 1794 | State | S-G/C | 30,179 | 1,374 | $ 624 | $ 750 | $1,374 |
| Martin Campus | Martin, TN 38238 | 1900 | State | S-G/C | 5,192 | 222 | $ 588 | $1,479 | $2,067 |
| Nashville Campus | Nashville, TN 37203 | 1971 | State | S-G/C | 5,629 | 156 | $ 450 | — | $ 450 |
| University of the South | Sewanee, TN 37375 | 1857 | Episc | S-G/C | 992 | 98 | $4,070 | $1,450 | $5,520 |
| Vanderbilt University | Nashville, TN 37240 | 1875 | Ind | S-G/C | 9,125 | 1,178 | $4,700 | $2,250 | $6,950 |
| Walters State Comm. College | Morristown, TN 37814 | 1970 | State | J/C | 3,870 | 75 | $ 280 | — | $ 280 |
| **TEXAS** | | | | | | | | | |
| Abilene Christian University | Abilene, TX 79699 | 1906 | C of Chr | S-G/C | 4,372 | 210 | $2,250 | $1,372 | $3,622 |
| Dallas Campus | Garland, TX 75041 | 1971 | C of Chr | S-G/C | 1,000 | 40 | $1,500 | — | $1,500 |
| Alvin Community College | Alvin, TX 77511 | 1949 | State | J/C | 3,026 | 149 | $ 116 | — | $ 116 |
| Amarillo College | Amarillo, TX 79178 | 1929 | State | J/C | 12,280 | 198 | $ 165 | — | $ 165 |
| American Technological Univ. | Killeen, TX 76541 | 1973 | Ind | S-G/C | 835 | 45 | $1,400 | — | $1,400 |
| Angelina College | Lufkin, TX 75901 | 1968 | State | J/C | 2,060 | 116 | $ 378 | $1,594 | $1,972 |
| Angelo State University | San Angelo, TX 76901 | 1928 | State | S-G/C | 5,637 | 234 | $ 420 | $1,602 | $2,022 |
| Antioch University | Austin, TX 78722 | 1852 | Ind | S-G/C | 84 | 5 | $2,225 | — | $2,225 |
| Arlington Baptist College | Arlington, TX 76012 | 1939 | Baptist | S/C | 500 | 26 | $1,200 | $1,400 | $2,600 |
| Austin College | Sherman, TX 75090 | 1849 | Presby | S-G/C | 1,130 | 93 | $3,100 | $1,400 | $4,500 |
| Austin Community College | Austin, TX 78768 | 1972 | State | J/C | 11,103 | 574 | $ 264 | — | $ 264 |
| Austin Presbyterian Theo. Sem. | Austin, TX 78705 | 1902 | Presby | G/C | 211 | 15 | $2,530 | $1,575 | $4,105 |
| Bauder Fashion College | Arlington, TX 76010 | 1967 | Ind | T/C | 540 | 42 | $3,280 | $2,280 | $5,560 |
| Baylor College of Dentistry | Dallas, TX 75246 | 1905 | Private | G/C | 528 | 214 | $ 550 | — | $2,200 |
| Baylor College of Medicine | Houston, TX 77030 | 1903 | Ind | P/C | 888 | 1,029 | $ 800 | — | $ 800 |
| Baylor University | Waco, TX 76703 | 1845 | Baptist | S-G/C | 9,594 | 500 | $2,215 | $1,729 | $3,944 |
| School of Nursing | Dallas, TX 75231 | 1909 | Baptist | S-G/C | 426 | 23 | $1,845 | $1,509 | $3,354 |
| Bee County College | Beeville, TX 78102 | 1965 | State | J/C | 1,927 | 76 | $ 322 | $1,525 | $1,847 |
| Bishop College | Dallas, TX 75241 | 1881 | Baptist | S/C | 926 | 51 | $2,140 | $1,400 | $3,540 |
| Blinn College | Brenham, TX 77833 | 1883 | County | J/C | 2,539 | 113 | $ 400 | $1,300 | $1,700 |
| Brazosport College | Lake Jackson, TX 77566 | 1968 | State | J/C | 3,641 | 173 | $ 200 | — | $ 200 |
| Central Texas College | West Killeen, TX 76541 | 1967 | State | J/C | 4,352 | 129 | $ 300 | $1,614 | $1,914 |
| Cisco Junior College | Cisco, TX 76437 | 1909 | State | J/C | 1,637 | 115 | $ 280 | $1,120 | $1,400 |
| Clarendon College | Clarendon, TX 79226 | 1898 | Public | J/C | 847 | 23 | $ 215 | $1,100 | $1,315 |
| College of the Mainland | Texas City, TX 77590 | 1967 | State | J/C | 2,500 | 69 | $ 115 | — | $ 115 |
| Commonwealth Col. of Sciences | Houston, TX 77006 | 1936 | Ind | T/C | 75 | 4 | $2,200 | — | $2,200 |
| Concordia Lutheran College | Austin, TX 78705 | 1926 | Lutheran | J-S/C | 334 | 27 | $1,750 | $1,650 | $3,400 |
| Cooke County College | Gainesville, TX 76240 | 1924 | Public | J/C | 1,508 | 63 | $ 375 | $1,500 | $1,875 |
| Corpus Christi State Univ. | Corpus Christi, TX 78412 | 1971 | State | S-G/C | 2,748 | 108 | $ 304 | $ 600 | $ 904 |
| Dallas Baptist College | Dallas, TX 75211 | 1898 | Baptist | S/C | 1,008 | 66 | $1,800 | $1,374 | $3,174 |
| Dallas Bible College | Dallas, TX 75228 | 1940 | Ind | S/C | 225 | 20 | $1,912 | $1,438 | $3,350 |
| Dallas Christian College | Dallas, TX 75234 | 1950 | Christian | S/C | 171 | 12 | $1,140 | $1,180 | $2,320 |
| Dallas Theological Seminary | Dallas, TX 75204 | 1924 | Ind | G/C | 1,188 | 55 | $2,500 | $1,775 | $4,275 |
| Del Mar College | Corpus Christi, TX 78404 | 1935 | Local | J/C | 6,955 | 503 | $ 178 | — | $ 178 |
| Devry Inst. of Technology | Dallas, TX 75235 | 1969 | Ind | T/C | 835 | 15 | $3,032 | — | $3,032 |
| East Texas Bapt. College | Marshall, TX 75670 | 1912 | Baptist | S/C | 845 | 53 | $1,519 | $1,246 | $2,765 |
| East Texas State University | Commerce, TX 75428 | 1889 | State | S-G/C | 8,752 | 430 | $ 375 | $1,464 | $1,839 |
| Texarkana | Texarkana, TX 75501 | 1972 | State | S-G/C | 1,068 | 48 | $ 428 | — | $ 428 |
| Eastfield College | Mesquite, TX 75150 | 1970 | Public | J/C | 7,600 | 130 | $ 200 | — | $ 200 |
| El Centro College | Dallas, TX 75202 | 1966 | County | J/C | 6,149 | 307 | $ 180 | — | $ 180 |
| El Paso Christian College | El Paso, TX 79902 | 1973 | Christian | J/C | 17 | 6 | $1,030 | $1,225 | $2,255 |
| El Paso County Comm. College | El Paso, TX 79998 | 1971 | State | J/C | 11,898 | 509 | $ 200 | — | $ 200 |
| Episc. Theol. Sem. of the S.W. | Austin, TX 78768 | 1951 | Episc | G/C | 75 | 8 | $2,100 | — | — |

## TEXAS (continued)

| NAME | ADDRESS | FOUNDED | AFFILIATION | LEVEL/TYPE | ENROLLMENT | TEACHERS | TUITION & FEES | BOARD & ROOM | TOTAL COST |
|---|---|---|---|---|---|---|---|---|---|
| Frank Phillips College | Borger, TX 79007 | 1948 | State | J/C | 850 | 27 | $ 250 | $ 950 | $1,200 |
| Galveston College | Galveston, TX 77550 | 1968 | State | J/C | 1,800 | 85 | $ 500 | — | $ 500 |
| Grayson County Junior College | Denison, TX 75020 | 1965 | State | J/C | 3,540 | 161 | $ 210 | $1,200 | $1,410 |
| Gulf-Coast Bible College | Houston, TX 77008 | 1953 | C of Chr | S/C | 356 | 23 | $1,890 | $1,556 | $3,446 |
| Hardin-Simmons University | Abilene, TX 79698 | 1891 | Baptist | S-G/C | 1,839 | 112 | $2,200 | $1,400 | $3,600 |
| Henderson County Jr. College | Athens, TX 75751 | 1946 | State | J/C | 2,650 | 85 | $ 218 | $1,201 | $1,419 |
| Hill Junior College | Hillsboro, TX 76645 | 1923 | State | J/C | 817 | 51 | $ 362 | $1,452 | $1,814 |
| Houston Baptist University | Houston, TX 77074 | 1960 | Baptist | S-G/C | 1,933 | 130 | $2,375 | $1,635 | $4,010 |
| Houston Comm. Col. System | Houston, TX 77007 | 1971 | State | J/C | 27,114 | 1,184 | $ 360 | — | $ 360 |
| Howard College | Big Spring, TX 79720 | 1946 | Public | J/C | 1,040 | 61 | $ 250 | $1,226 | $1,476 |
| Howard Payne University | Brownwood, TX 76801 | 1889 | Baptist | S/C | 1,173 | 74 | $1,790 | $1,360 | $3,150 |
| Huston-Tillotson College | Austin, TX 78702 | 1876 | UC Chr | S/C | 634 | 50 | $1,500 | $1,556 | $3,056 |
| Incarnate Word College | San Antonio, TX 78209 | 1881 | Catholic | S-G/C | 1,468 | 108 | $2,627 | $1,283 | $3,910 |
| Jacksonville College | Jacksonville, TX 75766 | 1899 | Baptist | J/C | 326 | 19 | $1,300 | $1,400 | $2,700 |
| Jarvis Christian College | Hawkins, TX 75765 | 1912 | Christian | S/C | 622 | 37 | $1,688 | $1,464 | $3,152 |
| Kilgore College | Kilgore, TX 75662 | 1935 | State | J/C | 3,995 | 140 | $ 330 | $1,250 | $1,580 |
| Lamar University | Beaumont, TX 77710 | 1923 | State | S-G/C | 11,800 | 613 | $ 756 | $1,750 | $2,000 |
| Orange Campus | Orange, TX 77630 | 1969 | State | J/C | 950 | 60 | $ 400 | — | $ 400 |
| Laredo Junior College | Laredo, TX 78040 | 1946 | Public | J/C | 2,981 | 106 | $ 254 | — | $ 254 |
| Laredo State University | Laredo, TX 78040 | 1969 | State | S-G/C | 770 | 40 | $ 244 | — | $ 244 |
| Lee College | Baytown, TX 77520 | 1934 | State | J/C | 4,653 | 206 | $ 250 | — | $ 250 |
| LeTourneau College | Longview, TX 75602 | 1946 | Ind | S/C | 966 | 54 | $2,536 | $1,476 | $4,012 |
| Lon Morris College | Jacksonville, TX 75766 | 1854 | Meth | J/C | 368 | 29 | $1,915 | $1,575 | $3,490 |
| Lubbock Christian College | Lubbock, TX 79407 | 1957 | C of Chr | S/C | 1,253 | 70 | $1,210 | $ 558 | $1,768 |
| McLennan Community College | Waco, TX 76708 | 1965 | State | J/C | 3,958 | 183 | $ 240 | — | $ 240 |
| McMurry College | Abilene, TX 79697 | 1923 | Meth | S/C | 1,450 | 108 | $2,145 | $1,270 | $3,415 |
| Midland College | Midland, TX 79701 | 1969 | State | J/C | 2,550 | 201 | $ 260 | — | $ 260 |
| Midwestern State University | Wichita Falls, TX 76308 | 1922 | State | S-G/C | 4,280 | 161 | $ 405 | $1,040 | $1,445 |
| Mountain View College | Dallas, TX 75211 | 1970 | Public | J/C | 5,304 | 84 | $ 90 | — | $ 90 |
| Navarro College | Corsicana, TX 75110 | 1946 | State | J/C | 1,434 | 83 | $ 350 | $1,500 | $1,850 |
| North Harris County College | Houston, TX 77073 | 1972 | State | J/C | 5,750 | 284 | $ 150 | — | $ 150 |
| North Texas State University | Denton, TX 76203 | 1890 | State | S-G/C | 17,300 | 811 | $ 440 | $1,900 | $2,340 |
| Northwood Institute of Texas | Cedar Hill, TX 75104 | 1966 | Ind | J/C | 325 | 11 | $2,800 | $1,700 | $4,500 |
| Oblate Col. of the Southwest | San Antonio, TX 78216 | 1903 | Catholic | G/C | 114 | 16 | $2,130 | — | $2,130 |
| Odessa College | Odessa, TX 79760 | 1946 | State | J/C | 4,006 | 230 | $ 245 | $1,750 | $1,995 |
| Our Lady of the Lake Univ. | San Antonio, TX 78285 | 1911 | Catholic | S-G/C | 1,744 | 100 | $2,200 | $1,830 | $4,030 |
| Pan American University | Edinburg, TX 78539 | 1927 | Public | S-G/C | 9,603 | 435 | $ 310 | $1,200 | $1,510 |
| Brownsville Campus | Brownsville, TX 78520 | 1973 | State | S-G/C | 1,154 | 61 | $ 226 | — | $ 226 |
| Panola Junior College | Carthage, TX 75633 | 1947 | State | J/C | 971 | 48 | $ 190 | $1,200 | $1,390 |
| Paris Junior College | Paris, TX 75460 | 1924 | Local | J/C | 2,294 | 115 | $ 278 | $1,436 | $1,714 |
| Paul Quinn College | Waco, TX 76704 | 1872 | AME | S/C | 412 | 38 | $1,865 | $1,600 | $3,465 |
| Prairie View A&M University | Prairie View, TX 77445 | 1878 | State | S-G/C | 5,229 | 290 | $ 430 | $1,673 | $2,103 |
| Ranger Junior College | Ranger, TX 76470 | 1926 | State | J/C | 725 | 52 | $ 300 | $ 750 | $1,050 |
| Rice University | Houston, TX 77001 | 1891 | Ind | S-G/C | 3,597 | 439 | $2,839 | $2,190 | $5,029 |
| Richland College | Dallas, TX 75243 | 1972 | State | J/C | 10,751 | 350 | $ 180 | — | $ 180 |
| St. Edward's University | Austin, TX 78704 | 1885 | Catholic | S/C | 2,180 | 140 | $2,250 | $1,750 | $4,000 |
| St. Mary's Univ. of San Antonio | San Antonio, TX 78284 | 1852 | Catholic | S-G/C | 3,374 | 108 | $2,420 | $1,520 | $3,940 |
| St. Philip's College | San Antonio, TX 78203 | 1898 | State | J/C | 7,029 | 178 | $ 440 | — | $ 440 |
| Sam Houston State University | Huntsville, TX 77341 | 1879 | State | S/C | 10,549 | 384 | $ 410 | $1,370 | $1,780 |
| San Antonio College | San Antonio, TX 78284 | 1925 | State | J/C | 20,764 | 999 | $ 160 | — | $ 160 |
| San Jacinto College, Central | Pasadena, TX 77505 | 1961 | State | J/C | 9,100 | 373 | $ 200 | — | $ 200 |
| San Jacinto College, North | Houston, TX 77049 | 1974 | State | J/C | 2,699 | 158 | $ 200 | — | $ 200 |
| Schreiner College | Kerrville, TX 78028 | 1923 | Presby | J/C | 358 | 37 | $2,410 | $1,850 | $4,260 |
| South Plains College | Levelland, TX 79336 | 1957 | State | J/C | 2,860 | 142 | $ 260 | $1,132 | $1,392 |
| South Texas College of Law | Houston, TX 77002 | 1923 | Private | P/C | 1,185 | 41 | $2,924 | — | $2,924 |
| Southern Bible College | Houston, TX 77078 | 1958 | C of Chr | J-S/C | 130 | 14 | $1,430 | $1,300 | $2,730 |
| Southern Methodist Univ. | Dallas, TX 75275 | 1911 | Meth | S/C | 8,923 | 598 | $4,340 | $2,394 | $6,734 |
| Southwest Adventist College | Keene, TX 76059 | 1893 | 7-D Adv | S/C | 731 | 41 | $3,150 | $1,580 | $4,730 |
| Southw. Assembly of God Col. | Waxahachie, TX 75165 | 1927 | A of God | S/C | 742 | 28 | $1,275 | $1,535 | $2,810 |
| Southw. Baptist Theol. Sem. | Fort Worth, TX 76122 | 1908 | Baptist | G/C | 3,564 | 176 | $ 488 | $ 938 | $1,426 |
| Southwest Christian College | Terrell, TX 75160 | 1949 | C of Chr | J/C | 337 | 18 | $1,898 | $1,300 | $3,198 |
| Southwest Texas Junior Col. | Uvalde, TX 78801 | 1946 | State | J/C | 2,083 | 114 | $ 360 | $1,080 | $1,440 |
| Southwest Texas State Univ. | San Marcos, TX 78666 | 1899 | State | S-G/C | 15,924 | 680 | $ 422 | $1,386 | $1,808 |
| Southwestern University | Georgetown, TX 78626 | 1846 | Meth | S/C | 1,001 | 70 | $2,600 | $1,700 | $4,300 |
| Stephen F. Austin State Univ. | Nacogdoches, TX 75962 | 1923 | State | S-G/C | 10,302 | 415 | $ 355 | $1,550 | $1,905 |
| Sul Ross State University | Alpine, TX 79830 | 1917 | State | S-G/C | 1,654 | 84 | $ 636 | $1,930 | $2,566 |
| Uvalde Study Center | Uvalde, TX 78801 | 1975 | State | S/C | 580 | 80 | $ 122 | — | $ 122 |
| Tarleton State University | Stephenville, TX 76402 | 1899 | State | S-G/C | 3,403 | 165 | $ 395 | $1,292 | $1,687 |
| Tarrant County Junior College | Fort Worth, TX 76102 | 1965 | State | J/C | | | | | |
| Northeast Campus | Hurst, TX 76059 | 1965 | State | J/C | 8,042 | 275 | $ 220 | — | $ 220 |
| Northwest Campus | Fort Worth, TX 76179 | 1975 | State | J/C | 3,365 | 162 | $ 250 | — | $ 250 |
| South Campus | Fort Worth, TX 76119 | 1966 | State | J/C | 8,300 | 180 | $ 220 | — | $ 220 |
| Temple Junior College | Temple, TX 76501 | 1926 | State | J/C | 2,183 | 103 | $ 266 | $1,683 | $1,949 |
| Texarkana Community College | Texarkana, TX 75501 | 1927 | State | J/C | 3,644 | 116 | $ 115 | — | $ 115 |
| Texas A&I University | Kingsville, TX 78363 | 1925 | State | S-G/C | 6,060 | 242 | $ 338 | $1,394 | $1,732 |
| Texas A&M University | College Station, TX 77843 | 1876 | State | S-G/C | 31,331 | 1,879 | $ 300 | $1,604 | $1,904 |
| Galveston Campus | Galveston, TX 77553 | 1971 | State | S/C | 641 | 72 | $ 224 | $1,700 | $1,924 |
| Texas Chiropractic College | Pasadena, TX 77505 | 1908 | Ind | P/C | 367 | 24 | $3,000 | — | $3,000 |
| Texas Christian University | Fort Worth, TX 76129 | 1873 | Christian | S/C | 5,930 | 374 | $2,892 | $1,188 | $4,080 |
| Texas College | Tyler, TX 75702 | 1892 | CME | S-G/C | 540 | 41 | $1,620 | $1,440 | $3,060 |
| Texas College of Osteo. Med. | Fort Worth, TX 76107 | 1966 | State | P/C | 312 | 120 | $ 576 | — | $6,720 |
| Texas Lutheran College | Seguin, TX 78155 | 1891 | Lutheran | S/C | 1,034 | 72 | $2,410 | $1,360 | $3,770 |
| Texas Southern University | Houston, TX 77004 | 1947 | State | S-G/C | 8,528 | 452 | $ 762 | $1,648 | $2,410 |
| Texas Southmost College | Brownsville, TX 78520 | 1926 | State | J/C | 4,860 | 125 | $ 255 | — | $ 255 |

| NAME | ADDRESS | FOUNDED | AFFILIATION | LEVEL/TYPE | ENROLLMENT | TEACHERS | TUITION & FEES | BOARD & ROOM | TOTAL COST |
|---|---|---|---|---|---|---|---|---|---|
| **TEXAS** (continued) | | | | | | | | | |
| Texas State Tech. Institute.... | Waco, TX 76705 ......... | 1969 | State | T/C | | | | | |
| Amarillo Campus .......... | Amarillo, TX 79111 ...... | 1970 | State | T/C | 713 | 57 | $ 382 | $1,540 | $1,922 |
| Harlingen Campus ......... | Harlingen, TX 78550 ..... | 1969 | State | T/C | 1,270 | 89 | $ 382 | $1,900 | $2,282 |
| Sweetwater Campus ....... | Sweetwater, TX 79556 ... | 1970 | State | T/C | 201 | 33 | $ 358 | $2,200 | $2,558 |
| Waco Campus ............ | Waco, TX 76705 ......... | 1965 | State | T/C | 3,766 | 245 | $ 382 | $2,200 | $2,582 |
| Texas Tech. University ...... | Lubbock, TX 79409 ...... | 1923 | State | S-G/C | 23,118 | 1,460 | $ 404 | $1,269 | $1,673 |
| Texas Tech. Univ. Sch. of Med. | Lubbock, TX 79430 ...... | 1969 | State | P/C | 265 | 200 | $ 619 | $3,761 | $4,380 |
| Texas Wesleyan College ...... | Fort Worth, TX 76105 .... | 1891 | Meth | S/C | 1,555 | 110 | $2,050 | $1,600 | $3,650 |
| Texas Woman's University .... | Denton, TX 76204 ....... | 1901 | State | S-G/W | 7,750 | 585 | $ 387 | $1,600 | $1,987 |
| Trinity University .......... | San Antonio, TX 78284 ... | 1869 | Ind | S-G/C | 3,285 | 282 | $3,109 | $1,565 | $4,674 |
| Tyler Junior College ........ | Tyler, TX 75701 ......... | 1926 | State | J/C | 6,420 | 307 | $ 120 | $1,403 | $1,523 |
| University of Dallas ........ | Irving, TX 75061 ........ | 1956 | Catholic | S-G/C | 2,391 | 132 | $3,002 | $1,870 | $4,672 |
| Univ. of Houston Central Camp. | Houston, TX 77004 ...... | 1927 | State | S-G/C | 28,414 | 2,245 | $ 360 | $1,680 | $2,040 |
| Clear Lake City Campus ... | Houston, TX 77058 ...... | 1971 | State | S-G/C | 5,365 | 283 | $ 360 | — | $ 360 |
| Downtown College Campus . | Houston, TX 77002 ...... | 1974 | State | S/C | 4,610 | 204 | $ 360 | — | $ 360 |
| Victoria Campus .......... | Victoria, TX 77901 ...... | 1973 | State | S-G/C | 743 | 57 | $ 360 | — | $ 360 |
| Univ. of Mary Hardin-Baylor .. | Belton, TX 76513 ....... | 1845 | Baptist | S/C | 1,077 | 68 | $1,750 | $1,360 | $3,060 |
| University of St. Thomas ..... | Houston, TX 77006 ...... | 1947 | Catholic | S-G/C | 1,765 | 150 | $2,100 | $1,400 | $3,500 |
| Univ. of Texas at Arlington .... | Arlington, TX 76019..... | 1895 | State | S-G/C | 19,135 | 1,176 | $ 450 | — | $ 450 |
| Univ. of Texas at Austin ..... | Austin, TX 78712 ....... | 1883 | State | S-G/C | 44,102 | 2,362 | $ 438 | $1,820 | $2,258 |
| Univ. of Texas at Dallas ..... | Richardson, TX 75080 ... | 1969 | State | S-G/C | 5,882 | 256 | $ 364 | — | $ 364 |
| Univ. of Texas at El Paso ..... | El Paso, TX 79968 ...... | 1913 | State | S-G/C | 15,745 | 864 | $ 385 | $1,370 | $1,755 |
| Univ. of Texas at San Antonio . | San Antonio, TX 78285 ... | 1969 | State | S-G/C | 9,453 | 422 | $ 360 | — | $ 360 |
| Univ. of Texas at Tyler ...... | Tyler, TX 75701 ........ | 1971 | State | S-G/C | 1,972 | 130 | $ 345 | — | $ 345 |
| Univ. of Tex. Health Sci. Center | Dallas, TX 75235........ | 1943 | State | S-G/C | 1,344 | 530 | $ 900 | — | $ 900 |
| Univ. of Tex. Health Sci. Center | Houston, TX 77025....... | 1973 | State | P/C | 2,466 | 595 | $ 280 | — | $ 280 |
| Dental Branch .......... | Houston, TX 77025 ...... | 1905 | State | P/C | 694 | 159 | $ 484 | — | $ 484 |
| Univ. of Tex. Health Sci. Center | San Antonio, TX 78284 ... | 1959 | State | P/C | 2,041 | 612 | $ 300 | — | $ 300 |
| Univ. of Texas Med. Branch ... | Galveston, TX 77550 ... | 1891 | State | P/C | 1,554 | 450 | $ 588 | — | $5,500 |
| Univ. of Texas of Permian Bas. | Odessa, TX 79762 ...... | 1969 | State | J-S/C | 1,597 | 84 | $1,990 | — | $2,290 |
| Vernon Regional Jr. College ... | Vernon, TX 76384 ...... | 1972 | State | J/C | 1,227 | 85 | $ 290 | $ 450 | $ 740 |
| Victoria College ........... | Victoria, TX 77901 ...... | 1925 | State | J/C | 2,340 | 85 | $ 150 | — | $ 250 |
| Wayland Baptist College...... | Plainview, TX 79072 ..... | 1908 | Baptist | S/C | 1,311 | 56 | $1,700 | $1,730 | $3,430 |
| Weatherford College ........ | Weatherford, TX 76086... | 1869 | State | J/C | 1,650 | 45 | $ 400 | $1,350 | $1,750 |
| West Texas State University .. | Canyon, TX 79016 ...... | 1910 | State | S-G/C | 6,469 | 337 | $ 412 | $1,274 | $1,686 |
| Western Texas College ...... | Snyder, TX 79549 ...... | 1969 | Public | J/C | 1,169 | 47 | $ 250 | $1,190 | $1,440 |
| Wharton County Junior College | Wharton, TX 77488 ...... | 1946 | Public | J/C | 1,906 | 90 | $ 300 | $1,140 | $1,440 |
| Wiley College ............. | Marshall, TX 75670 ..... | 1873 | Meth | S/C | 603 | 41 | $2,220 | $1,524 | $3,744 |
| **UTAH** | | | | | | | | | |
| Brigham Young University .... | Provo, UT 84602 ........ | 1875 | Mormon | S-G/C | 26,373 | 1,450 | $ 940 | $1,360 | $2,300 |
| College of Eastern Utah ...... | Price, UT 84501 ........ | 1937 | State | J/C | 851 | 45 | $ 504 | $1,365 | $1,869 |
| Dixie College .............. | St. George, UT 84770 .... | 1911 | State | J/C | 1,589 | 72 | $ 513 | $1,320 | $1,833 |
| Snow College .............. | Ephraim, UT 84627 ...... | 1888 | Ind | J/C | 1,179 | 55 | $1,221 | $ 789 | $2,010 |
| Southern Utah State College .. | Cedar City, UT 84720 .... | 1897 | State | S/C | 1,960 | 134 | $ 564 | $1,236 | $1,800 |
| Stevens Henager College ..... | Ogden, UT 84401 ....... | 1891 | Ind | J/C | 308 | 21 | $1,530 | — | $1,530 |
| University of Utah .......... | Salt Lake City, UT 84112.. | 1850 | State | S-G/C | 21,992 | 1,049 | $ 690 | $2,148 | $2,838 |
| Utah State University ....... | Logan, UT 84322 ....... | 1888 | State | S-G/C | 9,266 | 750 | $ 651 | $1,600 | $2,251 |
| Utah Technical Col. at Provo .. | Provo, UT 84601 ........ | 1941 | State | T/C | 4,031 | 140 | $ 513 | — | $ 513 |
| Utah Tech. Col. at Salt Lake ... | Salt Lake City, UT 84107... | 1948 | State | T/C | 6,679 | 169 | $ 438 | — | $ 438 |
| Weber State College ........ | Ogden, UT 84408 ....... | 1889 | State | S-G/C | 10,800 | 350 | $ 588 | $1,500 | $2,088 |
| Westminster College ........ | Salt Lake City, UT 84105.. | 1875 | Ind | S-G/C | 1,173 | 65 | $2,490 | $1,565 | $4,055 |
| **VERMONT** | | | | | | | | | |
| Bennington College ......... | Bennington, VT 05201 .... | 1925 | Private | S/C | 589 | 75 | $6,590 | $1,830 | $8,420 |
| Burlington College .......... | Burlington, VT 05401 .... | 1972 | Ind | S/C | 100 | 25 | $2,280 | — | $2,280 |
| Castleton State College....... | Castleton, VT 05735 ..... | 1787 | State | S-G/C | 1,982 | 106 | $1,124 | $1,806 | $2,930 |
| Champlain College .......... | Burlington, VT 05401 .... | 1878 | Ind | J/C | 755 | 49 | $2,850 | $2,000 | $4,850 |
| Col. of St. Joseph the Provider | Rutland, VT 05701 ...... | 1952 | Catholic | S-G/C | 373 | 50 | $2,500 | $1,525 | $4,025 |
| College of the Americas ..... | Brookfield, VT 05036 .... | 1972 | Ind | S-G/C | — | — | — | — | — |
| Community Col. of Vermont.... | Montpelier, VT 05602 .... | 1970 | State | J/C | 1,296 | 190 | $ 620 | — | $ 620 |
| Ethan Allen Community Col. ... | Manchester Ctr., VT 05255 | 1973 | Ind | J/C | 125 | 19 | $ 800 | — | $ 800 |
| Goddard College ........... | Plainfield, VT 05667 ..... | 1938 | Ind | S-G/C | 1,269 | 70 | $5,460 | $2,340 | $7,800 |
| Green Mountain College ..... | Poultney, VT 05764 ..... | 1834 | Ind | J-S/C | 475 | 39 | $3,865 | $2,200 | $6,065 |
| Johnson State College........ | Johnson, VT 05656 ..... | 1828 | State | S-G/C | 1,015 | 76 | $1,140 | $1,806 | $2,946 |
| Lyndon State College ....... | Lyndonville, VT 05851 .... | 1911 | State | S-G/C | 1,120 | 89 | $1,150 | $1,826 | $2,976 |
| Marlboro College ........... | Marlboro, VT 05344 ..... | 1946 | Ind | S/C | 232 | 34 | $5,070 | $2,290 | $7,360 |
| Middlebury College ......... | Middlebury, VT 05753 .... | 1800 | Ind | S-G/C | 1,870 | 161 | — | — | $7,800 |
| Norwich University .......... | Northfield, VT 05663 ..... | 1819 | Ind | S-G/C | 1,521 | 110 | $4,045 | $1,905 | $5,950 |
| Vermont College ........ | Montpelier, VT 05602 .... | 1834 | Ind | J-S/C | 474 | 52 | — | — | $5,270 |
| St. Michael's College ....... | Winooski, VT 05404 ..... | 1904 | Catholic | S-G/C | 1,575 | 112 | $3,715 | $1,885 | $5,600 |
| School for Int. Training ...... | Brattleboro, VT 05301.... | 1964 | Ind | S-G/C | 769 | 38 | $4,916 | $1,328 | $6,245 |
| Southern Vermont College ... | Bennington, VT 05201 .... | 1926 | Private | J-S/C | 420 | 30 | $2,550 | $2,175 | $4,725 |
| Trinity College ............ | Burlington, VT 05401 .... | 1925 | Catholic | S/W | 663 | 38 | $3,250 | $1,880 | $5,030 |
| University of Vermont ........ | Burlington, VT 05405 .... | 1791 | State | S-G/C | 10,954 | 1,146 | $1,662 | $1,887 | $3,549 |
| Vermont Law School ......... | South Royalton, VT 05068 | 1972 | Ind | P/C | 350 | 30 | $3,900 | — | $3,900 |
| Vermont Technical College ... | Randolph Ctr., VT 05061.. | 1957 | State | J/C | 700 | 50 | $1,070 | $1,826 | $2,896 |
| **VIRGINIA** | | | | | | | | | |
| Averett College............. | Danville, VA 24541 ...... | 1859 | Baptist | S-G/C | 1,047 | 52 | $2,150 | $2,050 | $4,200 |
| Bluefield College ........... | Bluefield, VA 24605 ..... | 1922 | Baptist | S/C | 391 | 35 | $1,565 | $1,515 | $3,080 |
| Bridgewater College ........ | Bridgewater, VA 22812 ... | 1880 | Church | S/C | 914 | 65 | $3,160 | $1,715 | $4,875 |
| Christopher Newport College . | Newport News, VA 23606 . | 1960 | State | S/C | 3,833 | 145 | $1,100 | — | $1,100 |
| College of William and Mary... | Williamsburg, VA 23185 .. | 1693 | State | S-G/C | 6,387 | 446 | $1,076 | $1,624 | $2,700 |

| NAME | ADDRESS | FOUN-DED | AFFILI-ATION | LEVEL/TYPE | ENROLL-MENT | TEACH-ERS | TUITION & FEES | BOARD & ROOM | TOTAL COST |
|---|---|---|---|---|---|---|---|---|---|
| **VIRGINIA** *(continued)* | | | | | | | | | |
| Eastern Mennonite College ... | Harrisonburg, VA 22801 .. | 1917 | Mennon | S/C | 1,011 | 90 | $3,360 | $1,566 | $4,926 |
| Eastern Virginia Medical Sch. . | Norfolk, VA 23501 ..... | 1973 | Ind | P/C | 255 | 100 | $5,500 | — | $6,580 |
| Emory & Henry College....... | Emory, VA 24327 ........ | 1836 | Meth | S/C | 825 | 62 | $2,535 | $1,455 | $3,990 |
| Ferrum College............. | Ferrum, VA 24088 ..... | 1913 | Meth | J-S/C | 1,558 | 75 | $2,380 | $1,110 | $3,490 |
| George Mason University ..... | Fairfax, VA 22030....... | 1957 | State | S-G/C | 12,249 | 697 | $ 888 | $2,215 | $3,103 |
| Hampden-Sydney College...... | Hampden-Sdny, VA 23943 | 1776 | Presby | S/M | 730 | 63 | $4,225 | $1,450 | $5,675 |
| Hampton Institute ........... | Hampton, VA 23668 ..... | 1868 | Ind | S-G/C | 3,169 | 222 | $2,390 | $1,340 | $3,730 |
| Hollins College .............. | Hollins Col., VA 24020 .... | 1842 | Ind | S/W | 935 | 100 | $4,800 | $2,300 | $7,100 |
| Institute of Textile Tech...... | Charlottesville, VA 22902 . | 1944 | Ind | G/C | 17 | 20 | — | — | — |
| James Madison University .... | Harrisonburg, VA 22807 .. | 1908 | State | S-G/C | 8,387 | 482 | $ 880 | $1,656 | $2,536 |
| Liberty Baptist College ....... | Lynchburg, VA 24506 .... | 1971 | Baptist | S/C | 2,537 | 130 | $1,670 | $1,900 | $3,570 |
| Longwood College ........... | Farmville, VA 23901....... | 1839 | State | S-G/C | 2,450 | 150 | $1,180 | $1,590 | $2,770 |
| Lynchburg College ........... | Lynchburg, VA 24501 ..... | 1903 | D of Chr | S/C | 2,412 | 148 | $3,450 | $1,850 | $5,300 |
| Mary Baldwin College ........ | Staunton, VA 24401...... | 1842 | Presby | S/W | 817 | 65 | $3,900 | $2,465 | $6,365 |
| Mary Washington College ..... | Fredericksburg, VA 22401 | 1908 | State | S-G/C | 2,467 | 140 | $ 870 | $1,955 | $2,825 |
| Marymount Col. of Virginia ... | Arlington, VA 22207 ..... | 1950 | Catholic | S/W | 970 | 97 | $2,850 | $1,800 | $4,650 |
| National Business College .... | Roanoke, VA 24009 ..... | 1890 | Ind | J/C | 888 | 85 | $2,008 | $1,940 | $3,948 |
| Newport News Shipbldg. Ap. Sch. | Newport News, VA 23607 . | 1919 | Ind | T/C | 645 | 12 | $ 65 | — | $ 65 |
| Norfolk College ............. | Norfolk, VA 23510 ..... | 1952 | Ind | J/C | 180 | 7 | $2,800 | — | $2,800 |
| Norfolk State University ...... | Norfolk, VA 23504 ..... | 1935 | State | S/C | 6,800 | 334 | $ 395 | $ 658 | $1,053 |
| Old Dominion University...... | Norfolk, VA 23508 ..... | 1930 | State | S-G/C | 14,647 | 483 | $ 816 | $1,690 | $2,506 |
| Presby. Sch. of Christian Ed.. | Richmond, VA 23227...... | 1914 | Presby | G/C | 104 | 14 | $1,800 | $1,654 | $3,454 |
| Protestant Episc. Theol. Sem. . | Alexandria, VA 22304 .... | 1823 | Episc | S/C | 191 | 26 | $2,500 | $1,825 | $4,325 |
| Radford University ........... | Radford, VA 24142 ..... | 1910 | State | S-G/C | 5,683 | 300 | $ 876 | $1,698 | $2,574 |
| Randolph-Macon College ..... | Ashland, VA 23005 ..... | 1830 | Meth | S/C | 959 | 72 | $3,870 | $1,620 | $5,490 |
| Randolph-Macon Woman's Col. . | Lynchburg, VA 24503 .... | 1891 | Meth | S/W | 793 | 87 | $4,500 | $2,000 | $6,500 |
| Richard Bland College........ | Petersburg, VA 23803 .... | 1961 | State | J/C | 1,071 | 31 | $ 550 | — | $ 550 |
| Roanoke College ............ | Salem, VA 24153 ........ | 1842 | Lutheran | S/C | 1,156 | 67 | $3,245 | $1,505 | $4,750 |
| St. Paul's College ........... | Lawrenceville, VA 23868 .. | 1888 | Episc | S/C | 619 | 36 | $2,125 | $1,375 | $3,497 |
| Shenandoah C. & Cons. Music. | Winchester, VA 22601 .... | 1875 | Meth | S/C | 784 | 125 | — | — | $4,250 |
| Southern Seminary Jr. College | Buena Vista, VA 24416 ... | 1867 | Ind | J/W | 216 | 27 | $3,100 | $1,800 | $4,900 |
| Sweet Briar College ......... | Sweet Briar, VA 24595 .... | 1901 | Ind | S/W | 685 | 84 | $5,000 | $1,600 | $6,600 |
| Union Theol. Sem. in Virginia . | Richmond, VA 23227 ..... | 1812 | Presby | G/C | 261 | 26 | $1,818 | $5,700 | $7,518 |
| University of Richmond ....... | Richmond, VA 23173 ..... | 1830 | Baptist | S-G/C | 4,404 | 315 | $3,410 | $1,540 | $4,950 |
| University of Virginia ........ | Charlottesville, VA 22903 . | 1819 | State | S-G/C | 16,464 | 1,579 | $ 916 | $1,852 | $2,768 |
| Clinch Valley College ....... | Wise, VA 24293 ........ | 1954 | State | S/C | 1,094 | 69 | $ 750 | $1,550 | $2,300 |
| Falls Church Regional Center | Falls Church, VA 22003 ... | 1949 | State | S-G/C | 4,000 | 225 | — | — | — |
| Virginia College ............ | Lynchburg, VA 24501 .... | 1888 | Ind | J/C | 214 | 14 | $1,410 | $1,583 | $2,993 |
| Virginia Commonwealth Univ. . | Richmond, VA 23284 ..... | 1838 | State | S-G/C | 18,674 | 1,449 | $1,127 | $1,590 | $2,717 |
| **Va. Community Col. System** | | | | | | | | | |
| Blue Ridge Comm. Col. ..... | Weyers Cave, VA 24486 .. | 1967 | State | J/C | 2,197 | 44 | $ 300 | — | $ 300 |
| Central Virginia Comm. Col. . | Lynchburg, VA 24502 ... | 1967 | State | J/C | 3,972 | 75 | $ 300 | — | $ 300 |
| Dabney S. Lancaster Com. Col. | Clifton Forge, VA 24422 .. | 1967 | State | J/C | 1,152 | 34 | $ 300 | — | $ 300 |
| Danville Comm. College ..... | Danville, VA 24541 ...... | 1968 | State | J/C | 2,236 | 72 | $ 300 | — | $ 300 |
| Eastern Shore Comm. College | Melfa, VA 23410 ........ | 1971 | State | J/C | 507 | 14 | $ 300 | — | $ 300 |
| Germanna Comm. College .. | Locust Grove, VA 22508 . | 1970 | State | J/C | 1,259 | 27 | $ 300 | — | $ 300 |
| John Tyler Comm. College ... | Chester, VA 23831....... | 1967 | State | J/C | 3,335 | 73 | $ 300 | — | $ 300 |
| J. S. Reynolds Comm. College | Richmond, VA 23241...... | 1972 | State | J-S/C | 9,006 | 171 | $ 300 | — | $ 300 |
| Lord Fairfax Comm. College . | Middletown, VA 22645 ... | 1970 | State | J/C | 1,903 | 35 | $ 300 | — | $ 300 |
| Mountain Emp. Comm. Coll. . | Big Stone Gap, VA 24219 .. | 1972 | State | J/C | 2,350 | 35 | $ 300 | — | $ 300 |
| New River Comm. College .. | Dublin, VA 24084 ....... | 1970 | State | J/C | 2,716 | 60 | $ 300 | — | $ 300 |
| Northern Va. Comm. College | Annandale, VA 22003 .... | 1966 | State | J/C | 31,447 | 495 | $ 300 | — | $ 300 |
| Patrick Henry Comm. College | Martinsville, VA 24112 ... | 1971 | State | J/C | 1,341 | 27 | $ 300 | — | $ 300 |
| Paul D. Camp Comm. College | Franklin, VA 23851 ...... | 1971 | State | J/C | 1,216 | 33 | $ 300 | — | $ 300 |
| Piedmont Va. Comm. College | Charlottesville, VA 22901 . | 1972 | State | J/C | 3,211 | 49 | $ 300 | — | $ 300 |
| Rappahannock Comm. Col. . | Glenns, VA 23149 ...... | 1970 | State | J/C | 1,270 | 27 | $ 300 | — | $ 300 |
| Southside Va. Comm. College | Alberta, VA 23821 ...... | 1970 | State | J/C | 1,957 | 43 | $ 300 | — | $ 300 |
| Southwest Va. Comm. College | Richlands, VA 24641 ..... | 1967 | State | J/C | 2,831 | 52 | $ 300 | — | $ 300 |
| Thomas Nelson Comm. Col.. | Hampton, VA 23670 ..... | 1968 | State | J/C | 6,045 | 127 | $ 300 | — | $ 300 |
| Tidewater Comm. College ... | Portsmouth, VA 23703 .... | 1968 | State | J/C | 14,950 | 239 | $ 300 | — | $ 300 |
| Va. Highlands Comm. College | Abingdon, VA 24210 ..... | 1969 | State | J/C | 1,427 | 49 | $ 300 | — | $ 300 |
| Va. Western Comm. College . | Roanoke, VA 24015 ..... | 1966 | State | J/C | 5,480 | 122 | $ 300 | — | $ 300 |
| Wytheville Comm. College .. | Wytheville, VA 24382 .... | 1967 | State | J/C | 2,028 | 52 | $ 300 | — | $ 300 |
| Virginia Intermont College .... | Bristol, VA 24201 ....... | 1884 | Baptist | S/C | 689 | 56 | $2,750 | $1,800 | $4,550 |
| Virginia Military Institute ..... | Lexington, VA 24450 ..... | 1839 | State | S/M | 1,300 | 133 | $ 600 | $1,095 | $1,695 |
| Virginia Poly. Inst. & St. Univ. . | Blacksburg, VA 24061.... | 1872 | State | S-G/C | 20,780 | 1,500 | $ 837 | $1,212 | $2,049 |
| Virginia Seminary........... | Lynchburg, VA 24501 .... | 1888 | Baptist | S-G/C | 93 | 8 | $1,410 | $1,584 | $2,994 |
| Virginia State College ....... | Petersburg, VA 23803 .... | 1882 | State | S-G/C | 4,438 | 240 | $ 979 | $1,800 | $2,779 |
| Virginia Union University ..... | Richmond, VA 23220...... | 1865 | Baptist | S-G/C | 1,178 | 85 | $2,100 | $1,535 | $3,635 |
| Virginia Wesleyan College .... | Norfolk, VA 23502 ...... | 1961 | Meth | S/C | 804 | 59 | $3,175 | $1,625 | $4,800 |
| Washington and Lee Univ. .... | Lexington, VA 24450 ..... | 1749 | Ind | S-G/M | 1,698 | 145 | $4,050 | $1,750 | $5,800 |
| **VIRGIN ISLANDS** | | | | | | | | | |
| College of the Virgin Islands | | | | | | | | | |
| St. Croix Campus .......... | St. Croix, VI 00850 ...... | 1962 | State | S-G/C | 673 | 47 | $ 397 | — | $ 397 |
| St. Thomas Campus ........ | St. Thomas, VI 00801 ..... | 1962 | State | S-G/C | 1,317 | 95 | $ 397 | $1,360 | $1,757 |
| **WASHINGTON** | | | | | | | | | |
| Bellevue Comm. College ...... | Bellevue, WA 98007 ..... | 1966 | State | J/C | 10,582 | 428 | $ 306 | — | $ 306 |
| Big Bend Comm. College ..... | Moses Lake, WA 98837 ... | 1961 | State | J/C | 2,900 | 104 | $ 306 | $1,650 | $1,956 |
| Central Washington Univ...... | Ellensburg, WA 98926 .... | 1890 | State | S-G/C | 7,909 | 310 | $ 618 | $1,810 | $2,428 |
| City College................. | Seattle, WA 98104 ....... | 1973 | Ind | S-G/C | 2,800 | 120 | $1,200 | — | $1,200 |

| NAME | ADDRESS | FOUN-DED | AFFILI-ATION | LEVEL/TYPE | ENROLL-MENT | TEACH-ERS | TUITION & FEES | BOARD & ROOM | TOTAL COST |
|---|---|---|---|---|---|---|---|---|---|
| **WASHINGTON** *(continued)* | | | | | | | | | |
| Clark Community College | Vancouver, WA 98663 | 1933 | State | J/C | 9,541 | 440 | $ 306 | — | $ 306 |
| Columbia Basin College | Pasco, WA 99301 | 1955 | State | J/C | 7,500 | 250 | $ 321 | — | — |
| Community Col. District 12 | Centralia, WA 98531 | 1967 | State | J/C | | | | | |
| Centralia College | Centralia, WA 98531 | 1925 | State | J/C | 6,635 | 248 | $ 306 | — | $ 306 |
| Olympia Technical Community College | Olympia, WA 98502 | 1967 | State | J/C | 4,133 | 169 | $ 280 | — | $ 280 |
| Cornish Inst. of Allied Arts | Seattle, WA 98102 | 1914 | Ind | S/C | 322 | 100 | $2,100 | — | $2,100 |
| Eastern Washington University | Cheney, WA 99004 | 1882 | State | S-G/C | 7,724 | 364 | $ 618 | $1,437 | $2,055 |
| Edmonds Community College | Lynnwood, WA 98036 | 1967 | State | J/C | 7,867 | 332 | $ 306 | — | $ 306 |
| Everett Community College | Everett, WA 98201 | 1941 | State | J/C | 8,837 | 326 | $ 306 | — | $ 306 |
| Evergreen State College | Olympia, WA 98505 | 1967 | State | S-G/C | 2,600 | 130 | $ 618 | $1,900 | $2,518 |
| Fort Steilacoom Comm. College | Tacoma, WA 98498 | 1967 | State | J/C | 10,041 | 395 | $ 303 | — | $ 303 |
| Fort Wright College | Spokane, WA 99204 | 1907 | Ind | S-G/C | 460 | 76 | $2,800 | $2,000 | $4,800 |
| Gonzaga University | Spokane, WA 99258 | 1887 | Catholic | S-G/C | 3,440 | 230 | $3,490 | $1,840 | $5,330 |
| Grays Harbor College | Aberdeen, WA 98520 | 1930 | State | J/C | 3,082 | 177 | $ 312 | — | $2,596 |
| Green River Comm. College | Auburn, WA 98002 | 1965 | State | J/C | 7,793 | 348 | $ 345 | — | $ 345 |
| Highline Community College | Midway, WA 98031 | 1960 | State | J/C | 9,835 | 386 | $ 306 | — | $ 306 |
| Lower Columbia Comm. College | Longview, WA 98632 | 1934 | State | J/C | 4,499 | 72 | $ 306 | — | $ 306 |
| Northwest College | Kirkland, WA 98033 | 1934 | A of God | S/C | 787 | 36 | $1,906 | $1,263 | $3,169 |
| Olympic College | Bremerton, WA 98310 | 1946 | State | J/C | 8,500 | 373 | $ 306 | — | $ 306 |
| Pacific Lutheran University | Tacoma, WA 98447 | 1890 | Lutheran | S-G/C | 3,376 | 260 | $3,552 | $1,635 | $5,187 |
| Peninsula College | Port Angeles, WA 98362 | 1961 | State | J/C | 2,761 | 190 | $ 309 | $1,610 | $1,919 |
| Puget Sound Col. of the Bible | Edmonds, WA 98020 | 1950 | Christian | S/C | 160 | 14 | $1,623 | $1,575 | $3,198 |
| St. Martin's College | Lacey, WA 98503 | 1895 | Catholic | S/C | 713 | 60 | $2,950 | $1,550 | $5,200 |
| Seattle Comm. Col. District | Seattle, WA 98109 | 1966 | State | J/C | | | | | |
| North Seattle Comm. College | Seattle, WA 98103 | 1970 | State | J/C | 8,873 | 342 | $ 288 | — | $ 288 |
| Seattle Central Comm. Col | Seattle, WA 98122 | 1967 | State | J/C | 10,633 | 481 | $ 288 | — | $ 288 |
| South Seattle Comm. College | Seattle, WA 98106 | 1970 | State | J/C | 8,119 | 297 | $ 288 | — | $ 288 |
| Seattle Pacific University | Seattle, WA 98119 | 1891 | Meth | S-G/C | 2,499 | 163 | $3,525 | $1,929 | $5,454 |
| Seattle University | Seattle, WA 98122 | 1891 | Catholic | S-G/C | 4,150 | 174 | $3,300 | $1,713 | $5,013 |
| Shoreline Comm. College | Seattle, WA 98133 | 1964 | State | J/C | 8,242 | 369 | $ 300 | — | $ 300 |
| Skagit Valley College | Mount Vernon, WA 98273 | 1926 | State | J/C | 7,606 | 77 | $ 306 | — | $ 306 |
| Spokane Community College | Spokane, WA 99207 | 1963 | State | J/C | 12,417 | 275 | $ 327 | — | $ 327 |
| Spokane Falls Comm. College | Spokane, WA 99204 | 1963 | State | J/C | 14,292 | 296 | $ 327 | — | $ 327 |
| Tacoma Comm. College | Tacoma, WA 98465 | 1965 | State | J/C | 7,114 | 351 | $ 306 | — | $ 306 |
| University of Puget Sound | Tacoma, WA 98416 | 1888 | Ind | S-G/C | 3,061 | 326 | $4,280 | $2,000 | $6,280 |
| University of Washington | Seattle, WA 98195 | 1861 | State | S-G/C | 37,037 | 2,591 | $ 687 | $2,115 | $2,802 |
| Walla Walla College | College Pl., WA 99324 | 1892 | 7-D Adv | S-G/C | 1,941 | 165 | $3,630 | $1,500 | $5,130 |
| Walla Walla Community College | Walla Walla, WA 99362 | 1967 | State | J/C | 5,800 | 132 | $ 350 | — | $ 350 |
| Washington State University | Pullman, WA 99164 | 1890 | State | S-G/C | 16,992 | 1,092 | $ 686 | $1,640 | $2,326 |
| Wenatchee Valley College | Wenatchee, WA 98801 | 1939 | State | J/C | 4,263 | 210 | $ 306 | $1,562 | $1,868 |
| Western Washington University | Bellingham, WA 98225 | 1899 | State | S-G/C | 10,104 | 435 | $ 620 | $1,880 | $2,500 |
| Whatcom Community College | Bellingham, WA 98225 | 1969 | State | J/C | 2,938 | 143 | $ 288 | — | $ 288 |
| Whitman College | Walla Walla, WA 99362 | 1859 | Ind | S/C | 1,171 | 79 | $4,510 | $1,950 | $6,460 |
| Whitworth College | Spokane, WA 99251 | 1890 | Presby | S-G/C | 1,413 | 69 | $3,950 | $1,775 | $5,725 |
| Yakima Valley College | Yakima, WA 98907 | 1928 | State | J/C | 6,300 | 325 | $ 306 | $1,775 | $2,081 |
| **WEST VIRGINIA** | | | | | | | | | |
| Alderson-Broaddus College | Philippi, WV 26416 | 1901 | Baptist | S/C | 878 | 112 | $2,993 | $1,387 | $4,380 |
| Antioch Col./Appalachia | Beckley, WV 25801 | 1971 | Ind | S/C | — | — | — | — | — |
| Appalachian Bible Institute | Bradley, WV 25818 | 1950 | Ind | S/C | 242 | 20 | $1,700 | $1,225 | $2,925 |
| Beckley College | Beckley, WV 25801 | 1933 | Ind | J/C | 1,228 | 55 | $ 792 | — | $ 792 |
| Bethany College | Bethany, WV 26032 | 1840 | D of Chr | S/C | 900 | 62 | $4,015 | $1,435 | $5,450 |
| Bluefield State College | Bluefield, WV 24701 | 1895 | State | S/C | 2,803 | 193 | $ 360 | — | $ 360 |
| Greenbriar Comm. Col. Ctr. | Lewisburg, WV 24901 | 1969 | State | J/C | 408 | 30 | $ 135 | — | $ 135 |
| Concord College | Athens, WV 24712 | 1872 | State | S/C | 2,081 | 81 | $ 368 | $1,618 | $2,986 |
| Davis & Elkins College | Elkins, WV 26241 | 1904 | Presby | S/C | 1,098 | 56 | $3,275 | $1,600 | $4,875 |
| Fairmont State College | Fairmont, WV 26554 | 1867 | State | S/C | 5,100 | 176 | $ 342 | $1,550 | $1,892 |
| Glenville State College | Glenville, WV 26351 | 1872 | State | S/C | 1,845 | 82 | $ 330 | $1,546 | $1,876 |
| Marshall University | Huntington, WV 25701 | 1837 | State | S-G/C | 11,530 | 410 | $ 375 | $1,905 | $2,280 |
| Ohio Valley College | Parkersburg, WV 26101 | 1958 | C of Chr | J/C | 233 | 20 | $1,564 | $1,280 | $2,844 |
| Parkersburg Community Col. | Parkersburg, WV 26101 | 1971 | State | J/C | 3,288 | 82 | $ 284 | — | $ 284 |
| Potomac State College | Keyser, WV 26726 | 1901 | State | J/C | 1,087 | 61 | $ 382 | $1,470 | $1,852 |
| Salem College | Salem, WV 26426 | 1888 | Ind | S-G/C | 886 | 68 | $2,890 | $1,500 | $4,390 |
| Shepherd College | Shepherdstown, WV 25443 | 1871 | State | S/C | 2,862 | 121 | $ 366 | $1,351 | $1,717 |
| Southern West Va. Comm. Col. | Logan, WV 25601 | 1971 | State | J/C | 2,059 | 56 | $ 248 | — | $ 248 |
| University of Charleston | Charleston, WV 25304 | 1888 | Ind | S/C | 1,857 | 82 | $2,150 | $1,950 | $4,100 |
| West Liberty State College | West Liberty, WV 26074 | 1837 | State | S/C | 2,631 | 165 | $ 370 | $1,557 | $1,927 |
| West Va. Col. of Grad. Studies | Institute, WV 25112 | 1972 | State | G/C | 3,227 | 140 | — | — | — |
| West Va. Inst. of Technology | Montgomery, WV 25136 | 1895 | State | S-G/C | 3,132 | 161 | $ 371 | $1,564 | $1,935 |
| West Va. Northern Comm. Col. | Wheeling, WV 26003 | 1972 | State | J/C | 3,897 | 65 | $ 284 | — | $ 284 |
| West Va. Sch. of Osteo. Med. | Lewisburg, WV 24901 | 1974 | State | P/C | 219 | 29 | $ 500 | — | $ 500 |
| West Virginia State College | Institute, WV 25112 | 1891 | State | S-T/C | 3,924 | 210 | $ 396 | $1,674 | $2,070 |
| West Virginia University | Morgantown, WV 26506 | 1867 | State | S-G/C | 21,289 | 1,347 | $ 482 | $1,730 | $2,212 |
| West Virginia Wesleyan College | Buckhannon, WV 26201 | 1890 | Meth | S-G/C | 1,714 | 122 | $2,862 | $1,841 | $4,703 |
| Wheeling College | Wheeling, WV 26003 | 1954 | Catholic | S-G/C | 1,197 | 81 | $2,845 | $1,676 | $4,521 |
| **WISCONSIN** | | | | | | | | | |
| Alverno College | Milwaukee, WI 53215 | 1936 | Ind | S-G/W | 1,340 | 107 | $2,550 | $1,250 | $3,800 |
| Beloit College | Beloit, WI 53511 | 1846 | Ind | S/C | 1,003 | 75 | $4,500 | $1,600 | $6,100 |
| Blackhawk Technical Institute | Janesville, WI 53545 | 1968 | State | T/C | 1,876 | 82 | $ 415 | — | $ 415 |
| Cardinal Stritch College | Milwaukee, WI 53217 | 1937 | Catholic | S-G/C | 1,139 | 98 | $2,900 | $1,625 | $4,525 |

| NAME | ADDRESS | FOUN-DED | AFFILI-ATION | LEVEL/TYPE | ENROLL-MENT | TEACH-ERS | TUITION & FEES | BOARD & ROOM | TOTAL COST |
|---|---|---|---|---|---|---|---|---|---|
| **WISCONSIN** (continued) | | | | | | | | | |
| Carroll College | Waukesha, WI 53186 | 1846 | Presby | S/C | 1,302 | 94 | $4,416 | $1,460 | $5,876 |
| Carthage College | Kenosha, WI 53141 | 1847 | Lutheran | S-G/C | 1,057 | 76 | $3,270 | $1,430 | $4,700 |
| Concordia College | Milwaukee, WI 53208 | 1881 | Lutheran | S/C | 413 | 47 | $2,090 | $1,670 | $3,760 |
| District One Tech. Institute | Eau Claire, WI 54701 | 1911 | Public | T/C | 2,835 | 170 | $ 450 | $1,990 | $2,440 |
| Edgewood College | Madison, WI 53711 | 1927 | Catholic | S/C | 633 | 63 | $2,600 | $1,350 | $3,950 |
| Fox Valley Technical Institute | Appleton, WI 54913 | 1967 | State | T/C | 4,627 | 184 | $ 500 | — | $ 500 |
| Gateway Technical Institute | Kenosha, WI 53142 | 1911 | Ind | T/C | 6,000 | 185 | $ 400 | — | $ 400 |
| Holy Redeemer College | Waterford, WI 53185 | 1968 | Catholic | S/M | 49 | 18 | $1,680 | $1,470 | $3,150 |
| Immanuel Lutheran College | Eau Claire, WI 54701 | 1959 | Lutheran | S/C | 52 | 11 | $ 620 | $1,075 | $1,695 |
| Institute of Paper Chemistry | Appleton, WI 54912 | 1929 | Ind | G/C | 95 | 43 | $3,000 | $1,550 | $4,550 |
| Lakeland College | Sheboygan, WI 53081 | 1862 | UC Chr | S/C | 600 | 40 | $3,220 | $2,125 | $5,345 |
| Lawrence University | Appleton, WI 54912 | 1847 | Ind | S/C | 1,113 | 108 | $5,256 | $1,569 | $6,825 |
| Madison Area Tech. College | Madison, WI 53703 | 1912 | District | J/C | 8,087 | 355 | $ 511 | — | $ 511 |
| Madison Business College | Madison, WI 53703 | 1856 | Ind | J/C | 260 | 15 | $1,600 | — | $1,600 |
| Marian College of Fond du Lac | Fond du Lac, WI 54935 | 1936 | Catholic | S/C | 499 | 62 | $2,370 | $1,400 | $3,770 |
| Marquette University | Milwaukee, WI 53233 | 1881 | Ind | S-G/C | 13,932 | 901 | $3,640 | $1,840 | $5,480 |
| Medical College of Wisconsin | Milwaukee, WI 53226 | 1913 | Ind | P/C | 760 | 660 | $5,750 | — | $5,750 |
| Mid-State Tech. Institute | Wis. Rapids, WI 54494 | 1967 | Public | T/C | 1,900 | 85 | $ 500 | — | $ 500 |
| Milton College | Milton, WI 53563 | 1844 | Ind | S/C | 750 | 40 | $2,870 | $1,570 | $4,440 |
| Milwaukee Area Tech. College | Milwaukee, WI 53203 | 1912 | State | T/C | 38,516 | 1,875 | $ 400 | — | $ 400 |
| Milwaukee Sch. of Engineering | Milwaukee, WI 53201 | 1903 | Ind | S-G/C | 2,500 | 105 | $3,100 | $1,400 | $4,500 |
| Moraine Park Tech. Institute | Fond du Lac, WI 54935 | 1911 | Ind | T/C | 2,369 | 100 | $2,000 | — | $2,000 |
| Mount Mary College | Milwaukee, WI 53222 | 1913 | Catholic | S/W | 1,126 | 123 | $2,300 | $1,400 | $3,700 |
| Mount Senario College | Ladysmith, WI 54848 | 1962 | Ind | S/C | 494 | 54 | $2,900 | $1,590 | $4,490 |
| Nashotah House | Nashotah, WI 53058 | 1842 | Episc | G/C | 85 | 7 | $2,750 | $1,650 | $4,400 |
| Nicolet Col. & Tech. Institute | Rhinelander, WI 54501 | 1968 | Public | J/C | 983 | 53 | $ 540 | — | $ 540 |
| North Central Tech. Institute | Wausau, WI 54401 | 1912 | Public | T/C | 2,300 | 120 | $ 450 | — | $ 450 |
| Northeast Wis. Tech. Institute | Green Bay, WI 54303 | 1912 | Public | T/C | 3,600 | 185 | $ 500 | — | $ 500 |
| Northland College | Ashland, WI 54806 | 1892 | UC Chr | S/C | 584 | 43 | $3,445 | $1,790 | $5,235 |
| Northwestern College | Watertown, WI 53094 | 1865 | Lutheran | S/M | 240 | 19 | $ 950 | $ 950 | $1,900 |
| Ripon College | Ripon, WI 54971 | 1851 | Ind | S/C | 950 | 75 | $4,551 | $1,525 | $6,076 |
| St. Francis De Sales College | Milwaukee, WI 53207 | 1969 | Catholic | S/M | 83 | 30 | $1,400 | $1,000 | $2,400 |
| St. Francis Sem. Sch. of Past Min. | Milwaukee, WI 53207 | 1856 | Catholic | G/C | 92 | 20 | $1,500 | $2,000 | $3,500 |
| St. Norbert College | De Pere, WI 54115 | 1898 | Catholic | S/C | 1,625 | 105 | $3,475 | $1,750 | $5,225 |
| Silver Lake College | Manitowoc, WI 54220 | 1935 | Catholic | S/C | 313 | 47 | $2,900 | $1,485 | $4,385 |
| Univ. of Wisconsin System | Madison, WI 53706 | 1971 | State | S-G/C | 150,629 | 7,036 | — | — | — |
| UW—Eau Claire | Eau Claire, WI 54701 | 1916 | State | S-G/C | 10,629 | 400 | $ 809 | $1,400 | $2,209 |
| UW—Green Bay | Green Bay, WI 54302 | 1969 | State | S-G/C | 3,842 | 153 | $ 809 | — | — |
| UW—La Crosse | La Crosse, WI 54601 | 1901 | State | S-G/C | 8,896 | 289 | $ 815 | $1,355 | $2,170 |
| UW—Madison | Madison, WI 53706 | 1849 | State | S-G/C | 40,129 | 2,100 | $ 877 | $1,635 | $2,512 |
| UW—Milwaukee | Milwaukee, WI 53201 | 1885 | State | S-G/C | 25,078 | 839 | $ 898 | $1,890 | $2,788 |
| UW—Oshkosh | Oshkosh, WI 54901 | 1871 | State | S-G/C | 10,324 | 478 | $ 830 | $1,480 | $2,310 |
| UW—Parkside | Kenosha, WI 53141 | 1969 | State | S-G/C | 5,292 | 160 | $ 803 | — | — |
| UW—Platteville | Platteville, WI 53818 | 1866 | State | S-G/C | 4,758 | 232 | $ 832 | $1,488 | $2,320 |
| UW—River Falls | River Falls, WI 54022 | 1874 | State | S-G/C | 5,128 | 236 | $ 836 | $1,604 | $2,440 |
| UW—Stevens Point | Stevens Point, WI 54481 | 1894 | State | S-G/C | 8,925 | 420 | $ 814 | $1,506 | $2,320 |
| UW—Stout | Menomonie, WI 54751 | 1893 | State | S-G/C | 7,095 | 302 | $ 810 | $1,470 | $2,280 |
| UW—Superior | Superior, WI 54880 | 1896 | State | S-G/C | 2,149 | 140 | $ 835 | $1,745 | $2,580 |
| UW—Whitewater | Whitewater, WI 53190 | 1868 | State | S-G/C | 9,679 | 375 | $ 822 | $1,490 | $2,312 |
| Univ. of Wis. Center System | Madison, WI 53706 | 1971 | State | J/C | 8,705 | 337 | — | — | — |
| Baraboo/Sauk County | Baraboo, WI 53915 | 1968 | State | J/C | 426 | 15 | $ 726 | — | — |
| Barron County | Rice Lake, WI 54868 | 1966 | State | J/C | 363 | 26 | $ 726 | — | — |
| Fond du Lac | Fond du Lac, WI 54935 | 1968 | State | J/C | 564 | 26 | $ 726 | — | — |
| Fox Valley | Menasha, WI 54952 | 1933 | State | J/C | 964 | 28 | $ 726 | — | — |
| Manitowoc County | Manitowoc, WI 54220 | 1933 | State | J/C | 391 | 13 | $ 726 | — | — |
| Marathon County | Wausau, WI 54401 | 1933 | State | J/C | 987 | 34 | $ 726 | — | — |
| Marinette County | Marinette, WI 54143 | 1936 | State | J/C | 378 | 14 | $ 726 | — | — |
| Marshfield/Wood County | Marshfield, WI 54449 | 1964 | State | J/C | 638 | 19 | $ 726 | — | — |
| Medford | Medford, WI 54451 | 1969 | State | J/C | 128 | 4 | $ 726 | — | — |
| Richland | Richland Center, WI 53581 | 1967 | State | J/C | 242 | 11 | $ 726 | — | — |
| Rock County | Janesville, WI 53545 | 1966 | State | J/C | 644 | 22 | $ 726 | — | — |
| Sheboygan County | Sheboygan, WI 53081 | 1933 | State | J/C | 636 | 26 | $ 726 | — | — |
| Washington County | West Bend, WI 53095 | 1933 | State | J/C | 616 | 22 | $ 726 | — | — |
| Waukesha County | Waukesha, WI 53186 | 1966 | State | J/C | 1,728 | 71 | $ 726 | — | — |
| Viterbo College | La Crosse, WI 54601 | 1890 | Ind | S/C | 1,074 | 114 | $3,030 | $1,600 | $4,630 |
| Waukesha County Tech. Inst. | Pewaukee, WI 53072 | 1923 | State | V-T/C | 4,347 | 210 | $ 400 | — | $ 625 |
| Western Wisconsin Tech. Inst. | La Crosse, WI 54601 | 1916 | State | T/C | 20,000 | 450 | $ 250 | $ 400 | $1,400 |
| Wisconsin Cons. of Music | Milwaukee, WI 53202 | 1899 | Ind | S-G/C | 145 | 22 | $3,000 | — | $3,000 |
| Wis. Indianhead Tech. Inst. | Rice Lake, WI 54868 | 1941 | State | T/C | 804 | 44 | $ 540 | — | — |
| Superior Campus | Superior, WI 54880 | 1912 | Public | T/C | 750 | 45 | $ 475 | $1,700 | $2,175 |
| Wisconsin Lutheran College | Milwaukee, WI 53226 | 1973 | Lutheran | J/C | 85 | 19 | $3,200 | $1,700 | $4,900 |
| Wisconsin Luth. Seminary | Mequon, WI 53092 | 1863 | Lutheran | G/M | 231 | 16 | $ 760 | $ 960 | $1,720 |
| **WYOMING** | | | | | | | | | |
| Casper College | Casper, WY 82601 | 1945 | State | J/C | 3,811 | 205 | $ 300 | $1,380 | $1,680 |
| Central Wyoming College | Riverton, WY 82501 | 1966 | State | J/C | 699 | 35 | $ 312 | $1,298 | $1,610 |
| Eastern Wyoming College | Torrington, WY 82240 | 1948 | State | J/C | 700 | 29 | $ 300 | $1,200 | $1,500 |
| Laramie County Comm. College | Cheyenne, WY 82001 | 1968 | State | J/C | 3,243 | 206 | $ 300 | — | $ 300 |
| Northwest Comm. College | Powell, WY 82435 | 1946 | State | J/C | 1,500 | 62 | $ 600 | $1,500 | $2,100 |
| Sheridan College | Sheridan, WY 82801 | 1948 | State | J/C | 1,036 | 82 | $ 340 | $1,460 | $1,800 |
| University of Wyoming | Laramie, WY 82071 | 1886 | State | S-G/C | 9,020 | 681 | $ 592 | $1,540 | $2,032 |
| Western Wyoming College | Rock Springs, WY 82901 | 1959 | State | J/C | 3,050 | 74 | $ 560 | $1,524 | $2,084 |

## ENROLLMENTS IN SCHOOLS, COLLEGES, AND UNIVERSITIES: 1979-80

Source: U.S. Office of Education, Department of Health, Education and Welfare, National Center for Education Statistics

| | ELEMENTARY AND SECONDARY SCHOOLS [1] | | COLLEGES AND UNIVERSITIES [2] | | ELEMENTARY AND SECONDARY SCHOOLS [1] | | COLLEGES AND UNIVERSITIES [2] |
|---|---|---|---|---|---|---|---|
| | K-8 | 9-12 | Total | | K-8 | 9-12 | Total |
| UNITED STATES | 27,295,750 | 13,404,859 | 11,835,898 | Missouri | 567,301 | 287,300 | 224,489 |
| Alabama | 508,176 | 230,167 | 161,542 | Montana | 103,515 | 51,371 | 32,257 |
| Alaska | 59,783 | 26,930 | 20,273 | Nebraska | 185,663 | 95,592 | 87,397 |
| Arizona | 345,986 | 152,571 | 191,054 | Nevada | 95,765 | 48,867 | 36,330 |
| Arkansas | 305,459 | 138,151 | 75,523 | New Hampshire | 109,637 | 57,327 | 42,575 |
| California | 2,672,203 | 1,290,348 | 1,717,353 | New Jersey | 829,963 | 430,802 | 315,897 |
| Colorado | 362,159 | 176,806 | 157,817 | New Mexico | 182,304 | 87,481 | 56,807 |
| Connecticut | 369,829 | 184,906 | 157,783 | New York | 1,865,374 | 1,041,489 | 980,840 |
| Delaware | 63,766 | 38,084 | 32,663 | North Carolina | 779,316 | 346,586 | 272,025 |
| Dist. of Col. | 73,601 | 30,326 | 88,821 | North Dakota | 73,956 | 41,261 | 32,255 |
| Florida | 1,009,792 | 466,870 | 399,581 | Ohio | 1,323,033 | 659,692 | 468,647 |
| Georgia | 730,242 | 325,566 | 179,975 | Oklahoma | 390,322 | 180,883 | 154,363 |
| Hawaii | 109,347 | 55,782 | 47,723 | Oregon | 310,387 | 146,931 | 156,298 |
| Idaho | 138,228 | 60,272 | 41,108 | Pennsylvania | 1,207,116 | 720,340 | 486,642 |
| Illinois | 1,338,423 | 661,908 | 619,658 | Rhode Island | 97,001 | 53,861 | 65,144 |
| Indiana | 707,880 | 353,186 | 230,909 | South Carolina | 419,917 | 191,757 | 132,905 |
| Iowa | 350,079 | 186,724 | 134,058 | South Dakota | 85,552 | 44,485 | 31,638 |
| Kansas | 281,529 | 132,464 | 134,827 | Tennessee | 597,616 | 250,313 | 201,850 |
| Kentucky | 456,411 | 206,493 | 136,666 | Texas | 1,962,135 | 850,257 | 683,484 |
| Louisiana | 543,438 | 240,188 | 155,504 | Utah | 232,877 | 93,178 | 91,392 |
| Maine | 152,608 | 70,430 | 43,384 | Vermont | 66,332 | 29,941 | 29,875 |
| Maryland | 499,544 | 261,849 | 221,151 | Virginia | 699,940 | 309,804 | 273,576 |
| Massachusetts | 668,414 | 348,983 | 400,626 | Washington | 504,438 | 244,379 | 306,807 |
| Michigan | 1,197,151 | 624,277 | 509,381 | West Virginia | 260,066 | 120,175 | 82,230 |
| Minnesota | 485,750 | 275,967 | 195,962 | Wisconsin | 532,166 | 307,674 | 258,722 |
| Mississippi | 318,811 | 153,105 | 101,375 | Wyoming | 65,398 | 28,121 | 19,704 |

[1] Public schools, Fall 1980 estimate. [2] Public and private, Fall 1980 estimates.

## LARGEST U.S. UNIVERSITY AND COLLEGE LIBRARIES

Source: U.S. Department of Health, Education, and Welfare; National Center for Education Statistics

| RANK | INSTITUTION OR BRANCH | VOLUMES | STAFF | OPERATING COSTS | | |
|---|---|---|---|---|---|---|
| | | | | Total | Salaries | Books |
| 1 | Harvard University | 9,913,992 | 913 | $16,623,983 | $9,700,694 | $4,262,774 |
| 2 | Yale University | 7,246,195 | 608 | 11,364,328 | 6,701,980 | 3,099,221 |
| 3 | University of Illinois Urbana Campus | 5,759,666 | 652 | 9,184,092 | 5,179,038 | 2,759,245 |
| 4 | University of California—Berkeley | 5,597,154 | 602 | 14,520,865 | 9,468,708 | 3,164,447 |
| 5 | University of Michigan—Ann Arbor | 5,135,952 | 584 | 9,453,606 | 6,023,018 | 2,529,438 |
| 6 | Indiana University at Bloomington | 5,029,534 | 675 | 11,334,121 | 6,424,088 | 3,714,979 |
| 7 | Columbia University | 4,924,469 | 515 | 8,701,385 | 5,555,251 | 2,163,221 |
| 8 | Stanford University | 4,577,827 | 522 | 11,418,830 | 6,418,214 | 3,681,762 |
| 9 | University of Texas at Austin | 4,406,113 | 525 | 8,591,107 | 5,173,042 | 2,620,192 |
| 10 | Cornell University Endowed Colleges | 4,207,146 | 483 | 8,478,564 | 4,897,503 | 2,499,722 |
| 11 | University of Chicago | 4,182,928 | 384 | 6,414,566 | 3,472,012 | 1,700,285 |
| 12 | University of California—Los Angeles | 4,109,146 | 540 | 11,933,620 | 7,321,908 | 3,120,650 |
| 13 | University of Washington | 3,788,788 | 488 | 9,264,753 | 5,341,686 | 2,593,683 |
| 14 | Univ. of Minnesota—Minneapolis-St. Paul | 3,702,399 | 434 | 8,387,458 | 5,527,544 | 2,062,676 |
| 15 | University of Wisconsin | 3,475,124 | 480 | 8,685,559 | 5,120,118 | 2,607,551 |
| 16 | Ohio State University | 3,446,729 | 438 | 7,242,273 | 4,534,692 | 1,676,993 |
| 17 | Princeton University | 3,172,238 | 382 | 6,867,898 | 3,964,738 | 2,199,875 |
| 18 | Duke University | 3,022,839 | 323 | 5,504,664 | 3,038,444 | 1,101,979 |
| 19 | University of Pennsylvania | 2,889,738 | 311 | 5,921,598 | 3,679,470 | 1,471,368 |
| 20 | Northwestern University | 2,714,938 | 344 | 7,348,867 | 3,847,422 | 1,652,746 |
| 21 | New York University | 2,700,261 | 319 | 5,897,484 | 3,577,711 | 1,675,404 |
| 22 | Michigan State University | 2,523,553 | 302 | 5,413,322 | 3,096,584 | 1,663,382 |
| 23 | University of North Carolina at Chapel Hill | 2,487,122 | 355 | 7,004,981 | 3,752,257 | 2,489,464 |
| 24 | University of Pittsburgh | 2,375,542 | 349 | 5,486,896 | 3,425,697 | 1,566,108 |
| 25 | University of Virginia | 2,351,842 | 321 | 6,638,975 | 3,283,426 | 2,525,724 |
| 26 | Johns Hopkins University | 2,287,058 | 219 | 4,470,213 | 2,291,206 | 1,231,659 |
| 27 | University of Iowa | 2,216,970 | 251 | 5,348,905 | 2,857,126 | 2,125,288 |
| 28 | University of Arizona | 2,184,023 | 255 | 5,378,628 | 2,384,991 | 2,481,478 |
| 29 | Rutgers University | 2,166,200 | 430 | 8,575,000 | 5,116,000 | 2,713,000 |
| 30 | Pennsylvania State University | 2,092,129 | 428 | 7,189,016 | 4,680,684 | 1,860,518 |
| 31 | University of Kansas | 2,079,434 | 262 | 4,976,223 | 2,505,646 | 1,718,395 |
| 32 | University of Florida | 2,079,344 | 287 | 7,485,554 | 2,945,462 | 3,729,602 |
| 33 | University of Missouri—Columbia | 1,984,632 | 208 | 3,670,217 | 1,897,555 | 1,401,436 |
| 34 | University of Southern California | 1,957,853 | 307 | 5,605,747 | 3,078,123 | 1,892,192 |
| 35 | University of Utah | 1,921,278 | 205 | 3,573,258 | 2,014,719 | 1,094,716 |
| 36 | University of Georgia | 1,893,897 | 264 | 5,012,116 | 2,374,684 | 2,079,431 |

# Elections

The faces of President Carter, his wife, and daughter reflect their sorrow as he concedes defeat to Ronald Reagan.

Wide World

## HIGHLIGHTS: 1980

### NATIONAL ELECTION

For the second time in four years, American voters ousted an incumbent President from the White House as Republican Ronald Reagan defeated President Jimmy Carter on Nov. 4 (see page 29 and 389). Republicans also won control of the U.S. Senate for the first time in a quarter of a century (see page 159). The GOP made substantial gains in the election of members of the U.S. House of Representatives, but Democrats managed to retain a majority as they have in every national election since 1954 (see pages 160–161). Republicans also made headway in the number of governorships and state legislative chambers under their control (see page 875).

Reagan won by a landslide, capturing 489 electoral votes to 49 for Carter. It was the first time that an incumbent President had received so few electoral votes in a reelection bid since the defeat of President William Howard Taft in 1912.

In the popular vote, Reagan received nearly 51% to Carter's 41%—the smallest percentage for an incumbent President since Herbert Hoover lost to Franklin D. Roosevelt in the midst of the Depression in 1932.

Professional politicians as well as the public were surprised by the extent of the Reagan victory because in the week before the election public-opinion pollsters had said the race was "too close to call." Yet, almost immediately after the polls closed in the Eastern states, it became apparent that Reagan would win easily. President Carter conceded the election even before the polls closed in the Western states, and subsequently was criticized by local Democratic candidates in those states who felt that his concession before everyone had voted had kept some of their supporters from the polls.

Most observers believed that the deciding factor in the Reagan landslide was his nationally televised debate with President Carter on

**HIGHLIGHTS: 1980** (continued)

Oct. 28, just one week before the election in which he asked voters to consider "Are you better off than you were four years ago?" (see page 27).

Before the election, the voters had been deluged for 10 months with campaign oratory, TV ads, debates and rallies. For the first six months attention was focused on state primaries and caucuses were held to determine which candidates the delegates to the national political conventions would support (see page 19).

In July the Republicans met in Detroit to formally nominate Reagan and endorse his choice of George Bush as his running mate (see page 21). This was followed by the Democratic national convention in New York City in August in which President Carter and Vice President Walter Mondale were nominated for a second term (see page 23).

The Republicans picked up 12 U.S. Senate seats in the November election to control that body by a margin of 53 to 47 over the Demo-

**POLITICAL PARTY ABBREVIATIONS**

In the election tables in this section, parties are designated by the following abbreviations:

| | | | |
|---|---|---|---|
| C | Conservative | L | Liberal |
| CIT | Citizens | LBT | Libertarian |
| CON | Consumers | LU | Liberty Union |
| D | Democratic | R | Republican |
| DFL | Democrat Farmer— Labor | RTL | Right to Life |
| | | ST | Statesman |
| I | Independent | SW | Socialist Workers |

crats. At the same time they gained 33 seats in the U.S. House of Representatives, reducing the Democratic majority to 243 compared with the Republicans' 192.

**PROMINENT SENATORS DEFEATED**

Among prominent Democrats defeated in U.S. Senate races were: George McGovern of South Dakota, the Democratic presidential candidate against Richard Nixon in 1972; Herman E. Talmadge of Georgia; Warren G. Magnuson of Washington; Frank Church of Idaho; Birch Bayh of Indiana; and Gaylord Nelson of Wisconsin.

Rep. John Anderson (R–Ill.), who ran as an Independent candidate, and Mary Crisp, who managed his campaign, exhibited happiness that he won a large enough vote to qualify for federal campaign funds.

United Press Int'l.

# PRESIDENTIAL ELECTION RESULTS: 1980

Unofficial returns for the 1980 presidential election showed that about 85 million Americans went to the polls, the largest number in history. But only about 53% of the nation's eligible voters cast ballots.

Independent candidate John Anderson received a substantial number of votes, more than 6.5% of all that were cast.

Other minor party candidates receiving a significant number of votes were Ed Clark (Libertarian), 881,612, and Barry Commoner (Citizens), 221,083.

| States | POPULAR VOTE | | | | | ELECTORAL VOTE | |
| --- | --- | --- | --- | --- | --- | --- | --- |
| | Reagan | Carter | Anderson | Clark | Commoner | Reagan | Carter |
| Totals | 43,201,220 | 34,913,332 | 5,581,379 | 881,612 | 221,083 | 489 | 49 |
| Alabama | 641,609 | 627,808 | 15,855 | 12,002 | 538 | 9 | |
| Alaska | 66,874 | 31,408 | 8,091 | 14,495 | — | 3 | |
| Arizona | 523,124 | 243,498 | 75,805 | 18,570 | — | 6 | |
| Arkansas | 396,689 | 392,404 | 21,057 | 8,638 | 2,237 | 6 | |
| California | 4,447,266 | 3,040,600 | 727,871 | 146,780 | 60,072 | 45 | |
| Colorado | 650,786 | 367,966 | 130,579 | 25,628 | 5,608 | 7 | |
| Connecticut | 672,648 | 537,407 | 168,260 | 8,272 | 5,956 | 8 | |
| Delaware | 111,631 | 106,650 | 16,344 | 1,986 | — | 3 | |
| Dist. of Col. | 21,765 | 124,376 | 14,971 | 1,037 | 1,686 | | 3 |
| Florida | 1,943,989 | 1,369,120 | 178,483 | 29,322 | — | 17 | |
| Georgia | 644,691 | 882,785 | 34,912 | 15,261 | — | | 12 |
| Hawaii | 130,112 | 135,879 | 32,021 | 3,269 | 1,548 | | 4 |
| Idaho | 289,789 | 109,410 | 27,142 | 8,482 | — | 4 | |
| Illinois | 2,335,806 | 1,951,073 | 344,836 | 23,604 | 4,117 | 26 | |
| Indiana | 1,232,764 | 832,213 | 107,729 | 17,776 | 4,522 | 13 | |
| Iowa | 676,556 | 508,735 | 114,589 | 12,324 | 2,191 | 8 | |
| Kansas | 562,848 | 324,974 | 67,535 | 14,089 | — | 7 | |
| Kentucky | 626,072 | 605,876 | 29,428 | 5,427 | 1,242 | 9 | |
| Louisiana | 796,240 | 707,981 | 26,198 | 8,247 | 1,698 | 10 | |
| Maine | 238,156 | 220,387 | 53,450 | 5,087 | 4,491 | 4 | |
| Maryland | 656,255 | 706,327 | 113,452 | 13,924 | — | | 10 |
| Massachusetts | 1,054,562 | 1,051,104 | 382,044 | 21,170 | 3,146 | 14 | |
| Michigan | 1,914,559 | 1,659,208 | 272,948 | 41,060 | 12,089 | 21 | |
| Minnesota | 844,459 | 924,770 | 169,960 | 30,375 | 8,202 | | 10 |
| Mississippi | 440,747 | 429,988 | 11,871 | 4,651 | — | 7 | |
| Missouri | 1,055,355 | 917,663 | 76,488 | 14,135 | — | 12 | |
| Montana | 195,108 | 111,972 | 27,919 | 9,536 | — | 4 | |
| Nebraska | 413,401 | 164,276 | 44,025 | 8,920 | — | 5 | |
| Nevada | 154,570 | 66,468 | 17,580 | 4,346 | — | 3 | |
| New Hampshire | 221,771 | 109,080 | 49,295 | 2,063 | 1,276 | 4 | |
| New Jersey | 1,506,437 | 1,119,576 | 224,173 | 20,094 | 7,765 | 17 | |
| New Mexico | 245,433 | 165,054 | 28,404 | 4,348 | 2,359 | 4 | |
| New York | 2,797,684 | 2,632,099 | 440,480 | 51,280 | 19,410 | 41 | |
| North Carolina | 913,898 | 875,776 | 52,364 | 9,866 | 2,341 | 13 | |
| North Dakota | 187,483 | 76,533 | 22,390 | 3,498 | 417 | 3 | |
| Ohio | 2,201,864 | 1,743,829 | 255,521 | 49,543 | 8,888 | 25 | |
| Oklahoma | 683,807 | 399,292 | 38,051 | 15,642 | — | 8 | |
| Oregon | 557,381 | 446,721 | 109,621 | 25,407 | 13,362 | 6 | |
| Pennsylvania | 2,252,260 | 1,932,336 | 288,704 | 31,118 | 10,760 | 27 | |
| Rhode Island | 145,576 | 185,319 | 56,213 | 2,411 | — | | 4 |
| South Carolina | 421,117 | 417,633 | 13,990 | 4,919 | — | 8 | |
| South Dakota | 198,102 | 103,909 | 21,342 | 3,839 | — | 4 | |
| Tennessee | 787,244 | 781,512 | 35,921 | 6,784 | 1,099 | 10 | |
| Texas | 2,539,144 | 1,844,349 | 109,707 | 36,825 | — | 26 | |
| Utah | 435,839 | 123,447 | 30,191 | 7,193 | 1,844 | 4 | |
| Vermont | 93,554 | 81,421 | 31,671 | 1,861 | 2,315 | 3 | |
| Virginia | 983,311 | 748,638 | 93,813 | 12,462 | 13,761 | 12 | |
| Washington | 764,393 | 583,596 | 165,443 | 25,848 | 8,442 | 9 | |
| West Virginia | 326,645 | 353,508 | 30,499 | 4,259 | — | | 6 |
| Wisconsin | 1,089,750 | 988,255 | 159,793 | 29,245 | 7,701 | 11 | |
| Wyoming | 110,096 | 49,123 | 12,350 | 4,694 | — | 3 | |

Republican Frank White, *center*, rejoices in his election as governor of Arkansas, with state's two Republican U.S. Representatives, Ed Bethune, *left*, and John Paul Hammerschmidt, *right*, both of whom won reelection.

# 1980 ELECTIONS OF STATE GOVERNORS

In the 13 races for state governor in 1980, Republicans won 7 and Democrats 6. Republicans won four governorships previously held by Democrats, bringing to 23 the statehouses they control.

In this table of unofficial results, winners are in boldface and incumbents have an asterisk(*).

| CANDIDATES AND PARTY | VOTES | PERCENT |
|---|---|---|
| **ARKANSAS** | | |
| **Frank D. White** (R) ........... | 427,818 | 52% |
| * Bill Clinton (D) ............... | 397,262 | 48% |
| **DELAWARE** | | |
| * **Pierre S. du Pont IV** (R) ...... | 159,773 | 70% |
| William J. Gordy (D) .......... | 64,903 | 29% |
| R. Lawrence Levy (LBT) ....... | 1,903 | 1% |
| **INDIANA** | | |
| **Robert D. Orr** (R) ............ | 1,231,227 | 58% |
| John A. Hillenbrand II (D) ..... | 900,433 | 42% |
| **MISSOURI** | | |
| **Christopher S. Bond** (R) ...... | 1,079,454 | 53% |
| * Joseph P. Teasdale (D) ....... | 967,757 | 47% |
| **MONTANA** | | |
| **Ted Schwinden** (D) ........... | 185,060 | 55% |
| Jack Ramirez (R) ............. | 148,732 | 45% |
| **NEW HAMPSHIRE** | | |
| * **Hugh Gallen** (D).............. | 226,285 | 59% |
| Meldrim Thomson Jr. (R)...... | 155,717 | 41% |
| James E. Pinard (LBT) ........ | 1,309 | 0% |

| CANDIDATES AND PARTY | VOTES | PERCENT |
|---|---|---|
| **NORTH CAROLINA** | | |
| * **James B. Hunt Jr.** (D) ........ | 1,128,317 | 62% |
| I. Beverly Lake Jr. (R)......... | 686,973 | 38% |
| Bobby Yates Emory (LBT) ..... | 9,879 | 0% |
| **NORTH DAKOTA** | | |
| **Allen I. Olson** (R) ............ | 145,941 | 53% |
| * Arthur A. Link (D) ............ | 127,034 | 47% |
| **RHODE ISLAND** | | |
| * **J. Joseph Garrahy** (D) ........ | 284,418 | 74% |
| Vincent A. Cianci (R).......... | 99,469 | 26% |
| **UTAH** | | |
| * **Scott M. Matheson** (D) ........ | 327,806 | 55% |
| Bob Wright (R) ............... | 264,523 | 45% |
| **VERMONT** | | |
| * **Richard A. Snelling** (R) ....... | 121,985 | 59% |
| M. Jerome Diamond (D)....... | 76,328 | 37% |
| **WASHINGTON** | | |
| **John Spellman** (R) ........... | 869,945 | 56% |
| James A. McDermott (D) ...... | 670,383 | 44% |
| **WEST VIRGINIA** | | |
| * **John D. Rockefeller IV** (D) .... | 387,806 | 54% |
| Arch A. Moore (R) ............ | 328,911 | 46% |

Wide World

# 1980 ELECTIONS OF U.S. SENATORS

In the 33 elections for U.S. senator in 1980, Republicans won 21 and Democrats 12. Having gained 12 seats previously held by Democrats, Republicans took control of the U.S. Senate in the 97th Congress in 1981 for the first time since 1955: Republicans 53, Democrats 47.

In the following tables of unofficial results, winners are set in boldface.

| CANDIDATES AND PARTY | VOTES [1] | PERCENT |
|---|---|---|
| **ALABAMA** | | |
| **Jeremiah Denton (R)** | 638,944 | 51% |
| Jim Folsom Jr. (D) | 604,083 | 48% |
| William A. Crew (LBT) | 12,043 | 1% |
| **ALASKA** | | |
| **Frank H. Murkowski (R)** | 65,924 | 55% |
| Clark S. Gruening (D) | 53,674 | 45% |
| **ARIZONA** | | |
| * **Barry Goldwater (R)** | 426,171 | 50% |
| Bill Schulz (D) | 418,371 | 49% |
| Fred R. Esser (LBT) | 11,832 | 1% |
| **ARKANSAS** | | |
| * **Dale Bumpers (D)** | 473,132 | 59% |
| Bill Clark (R) | 323,091 | 41% |
| **CALIFORNIA** | | |
| * **Alan Cranston (D)** | 4,638,488 | 59% |
| Paul Gann (R) | 3,038,180 | 39% |
| David Bergland (LBT) | 199,795 | 2% |
| **COLORADO** | | |
| * **Gary Hart (D)** | 585,928 | 51% |
| Mary Estill Buchanan (R) | 565,015 | 49% |
| **CONNECTICUT** | | |
| **Christopher J. Dodd (D)** | 765,126 | 57% |
| James L. Buckley (R) | 575,644 | 43% |
| Gerard Brennan (LBT) | 5,184 | 0 |
| **FLORIDA** | | |
| **Paula Hawkins (R)** | 1,732,828 | 51% |
| Bill Gunter (D) | 1,644,453 | 49% |
| **GEORGIA** | | |
| **Mack Mattingly (R)** | 788,757 | 51% |
| * Herman E. Talmadge (D) | 766,749 | 49% |
| **HAWAII** | | |
| * **Daniel K. Inouye (D)** | 224,485 | 78% |
| Cooper Brown (R) | 53,068 | 18% |
| H. E. Shasteen (LBT) | 10,453 | 4% |
| **IDAHO** | | |
| **Steven D. Symms (R)** | 218,793 | 50% |
| * Frank Church (D) | 214,351 | 49% |
| Larry Fullmer (LBT) | 6,645 | 1% |
| **ILLINOIS** | | |
| **Alan J. Dixon (D)** | 2,494,254 | 56% |
| David C. O'Neal (R) | 1,925,077 | 43% |
| Bruce Green (LBT) | 17,056 | 1% |
| **INDIANA** | | |
| **Dan Quayle (R)** | 1,164,678 | 54% |
| * Birch Bayh (D) | 1,000,145 | 46% |
| **IOWA** | | |
| **Charles E. Grassley (R)** | 684,701 | 54% |
| * John C. Culver (D) | 581,024 | 46% |
| **KANSAS** | | |
| * **Robert Dole (R)** | 595,194 | 64% |
| John Simpson (D) | 337,766 | 36% |
| **KENTUCKY** | | |
| * **Wendell H. Ford (D)** | 719,679 | 65% |
| Mary Louise Foust (R) | 382,434 | 35% |
| **LOUISIANA** | | |
| * **Russell B. Long (D)** | no major opposition | |
| **MISSOURI** | | |
| * **Thomas F. Eagleton (D)** | 1,057,467 | 52% |
| Gene McNary (R) | 966,897 | 48% |
| **NEVADA** | | |
| * **Paul Laxalt (R)** | 143,781 | 58% |
| Mary Gojack (D) | 92,203 | 38% |
| **NEW HAMPSHIRE** | | |
| **Warren Rudman (R)** | 195,053 | 52% |
| * John A. Durkin (D) | 178,943 | 48% |
| **NEW YORK** | | |
| **Alfonse D'Amato (R)** | 2,627,458 | 45% |
| Elizabeth Holtzman (D) | 2,538,921 | 44% |
| * Jacob K. Javits (L) | 629,468 | 11% |
| **NORTH CAROLINA** | | |
| **John P. East (R)** | 891,373 | 50% |
| * Robert Morgan (D) | 884,369 | 50% |
| **NORTH DAKOTA** | | |
| **Mark Andrews (R)** | 189,170 | 71% |
| Kent Johanneson (D) | 77,727 | 29% |
| **OHIO** | | |
| * **John Glenn (D)** | 2,731,377 | 71% |
| James E. Betts (R) | 1,129,178 | 29% |
| **OKLAHOMA** | | |
| **Don Nickles (R)** | 573,339 | 53% |
| Andy Coats (D) | 471,914 | 43% |
| Charles Nesbitt (I) | 32,545 | 3% |
| Robert Murphy (LIB) | 10,363 | 1% |
| **OREGON** | | |
| * **Bob Packwood (R)** | 578,046 | 52% |
| Ted Kulongoski (D) | 492,033 | 44% |
| Tonie Nathan (LBT) | 42,697 | 4% |
| **PENNSYLVANIA** | | |
| **Arlen Specter (R)** | 2,238,516 | 51% |
| Pete Flaherty (D) | 2,103,701 | 48% |
| David K. Walter (LBT) | 19,132 | 1% |
| **SOUTH CAROLINA** | | |
| * **Ernest F. Hollings (D)** | 595,210 | 72% |
| Marshall T. Mays (R) | 233,052 | 28% |
| **SOUTH DAKOTA** | | |
| **James Abdnor (R)** | 190,726 | 58% |
| * George McGovern (D) | 128,956 | 39% |
| Wayne Peterson (I) | 7,879 | 3% |
| **UTAH** | | |
| * **Jake Garn (R)** | 433,943 | 74% |
| Dan Berman (D) | 150,495 | 26% |
| **VERMONT** | | |
| * **Patrick J. Leahy (D)** | 103,185 | 51% |
| Stewart Ledbetter (R) | 100,722 | 49% |
| **WASHINGTON** | | |
| **Slade Gorton (R)** | 832,752 | 54% |
| * Warren G. Magnuson (D) | 702,147 | 46% |
| **WISCONSIN** | | |
| **Robert W. Kasten Jr. (R)** | 1,101,669 | 51% |
| * Gaylord Nelson (D) | 1,061,899 | 49% |

* Incumbent.   [1] Unofficial.

# 1980 ELECTIONS OF U.S. REPRESENTATIVES

In the elections of 435 U.S. representatives in 1980, Democrats won 243 seats, a loss of 33 from the previous Congress. The Republicans captured 192 seats—26 short of a majority. Democrats have controlled the House since 1955.

In the following table of unofficial election results, winners are set in boldface. Incumbents are marked with an asterisk (*).

| DIST. | CANDIDATES AND PARTY | VOTES | PERCENT |
|---|---|---|---|
| **ALABAMA** | | | |
| 1 | * **Jack Edwards** (R) | 104,395 | 88% |
| | Steve Smith (LBT) | 14,537 | 12% |
| 2 | * **William L. Dickinson** (R) | 103,556 | 61% |
| | Cecil Wyatt (D) | 62,867 | 37% |
| | Adam Hand (LBT) | 2,269 | 2% |
| 3 | * **William Nichols** (D) | no major opposition | |
| 4 | * **Tom Bevill** (D) | 130,754 | 97% |
| | A. J. Killingsworth (ST) | 3,734 | 3% |
| 5 | * **Ronnie G. Flippo** (D) | 115,101 | 94% |
| | Betty T. Benson (LBT) | 7,309 | 6% |
| 6 | * **Albert L. Smith Jr.** (R) | 89,613 | 52% |
| | W. B. Clifford (D) | 80,738 | 46% |
| 7 | * **Richard C. Shelby** (D) | 119,359 | 73% |
| | James E. Bacon (R) | 42,619 | 26% |
| **ALASKA** | | | |
| AL | * **Don Young** (R) | 87,403 | 74% |
| | Kevin Parnell (D) | 30,428 | 26% |
| **ARIZONA** | | | |
| 1 | * **John J. Rhodes** (R) | 136,781 | 74% |
| | Steve Jancek (D) | 40,000 | 22% |
| 2 | * **Morris K. Udall** (D) | 122,710 | 58% |
| | Richard H. Huff (R) | 84,364 | 40% |
| 3 | * **Bob Stump** (D) | 141,280 | 64% |
| | Bob Croff (R) | 66,311 | 30% |
| 4 | * **Eldon Rudd** (R) | 141,920 | 63% |
| | Les Miller (D) | 84,637 | 37% |
| **ARKANSAS** | | | |
| 1 | * **Bill Alexander** (D) | no major opposition | |
| 2 | * **Ed Bethune** (R) | 157,759 | 79% |
| | James G. Reid (D) | 41,976 | 21% |
| 3 | * **John Hammerschmidt** (R) | no major opposition | |
| 4 | * **Beryl Anthony Jr.** (D) | no major opposition | |
| **CALIFORNIA** | | | |
| 1 | **Eugene A. Chappie** (R) | 144,702 | 54% |
| | * Harold T. Johnson (D) | 107,388 | 40% |
| | Jim McClarin (LBT) | 17,372 | 6% |
| 2 | * **Don H. Clausen** (R) | 139,835 | 55% |
| | Norma K. Bork (D) | 108,423 | 42% |
| 3 | * **Robert T. Matsui** (D) | 168,682 | 71% |
| | Joseph Murphy (R) | 63,359 | 26% |
| 4 | * **Vic Fazio** (D) | 132,420 | 65% |
| | Albert Dehr (R) | 59,983 | 30% |
| | Robert J. Burnside (LBT) | 10,152 | 5% |
| 5 | * **John L. Burton** (D) | 100,066 | 51% |
| | Dennis McQuaid (R) | 88,287 | 45% |
| 6 | * **Phillip Burton** (D) | 91,810 | 70% |
| | Tom Spinosa (R) | 33,423 | 25% |
| | Roy Childs (LBT) | 6,617 | 5% |
| 7 | * **George Miller III** (D) | 141,565 | 65% |
| | Giles St. Clair (R) | 70,203 | 32% |
| 8 | * **Ronald V. Dellums** (D) | 107,554 | 56% |
| | Charles V. Hughes (R) | 75,972 | 39% |
| | Tom Mikuriya (LBT) | 10,386 | 5% |
| 9 | * **Fortney H. Stark** (D) | 89,589 | 55% |
| | William J. Kennedy (R) | 66,580 | 41% |
| 10 | * **Don Edwards** (D) | 100,901 | 64% |
| | John M. Lutton (R) | 45,234 | 29% |
| | Joseph Fuhrig (LBT) | 11,732 | 7% |
| 11 | **Tom Lantos** (D) | 85,203 | 51% |
| | * William H. Rover (R) | 79,586 | 47% |

| DIST. | CANDIDATES AND PARTY | VOTES | PERCENT |
|---|---|---|---|
| 12 | * **Paul N. McCloskey Jr.** (R) | 139,737 | 73% |
| | Kirsten Olsen (D) | 36,163 | 19% |
| | Bill Evers (LBT) | 14,834 | 8% |
| 13 | * **Norman Y. Mineta** (D) | 129,188 | 60% |
| | W. E. Gagne (R) | 77,576 | 36% |
| 14 | * **Norman D. Shumway** (R) | 132,516 | 61% |
| | Ann Cerney (D) | 79,260 | 36% |
| 15 | * **Tony Coelho** (D) | 106,793 | 72% |
| | Ron Schwartz (R) | 37,423 | 25% |
| 16 | * **Leon E. Panetta** (D) | 157,230 | 72% |
| | W. A. Roth (R) | 54,192 | 25% |
| 17 | * **Charles Pashayan Jr.** (R) | 127,939 | 71% |
| | Willard H. Johnson (D) | 53,320 | 29% |
| 18 | * **William M. Thomas** (R) | 122,639 | 71% |
| | Mary "Pat" Timmermans (D) | 50,029 | 29% |
| 19 | * **Robert Lagomarsino** (R) | 160,893 | 78% |
| | Carmen Lodise (D) | 36,601 | 18% |
| | Jim Trotter (LBT) | 9,674 | 4% |
| 20 | * **Barry Goldwater Jr.** (R) | 195,789 | 79% |
| | Matt Miller (D) | 42,275 | 17% |
| 21 | **Bobbi Fiedler** (R) | 73,152 | 49% |
| | * James C. Corman (D) | 72,288 | 49% |
| 22 | * **Carlos J. Moorhead** (R) | 112,533 | 64% |
| | Pierce O'Donnell (D) | 56,407 | 32% |
| 23 | * **Anthony Beilenson** (D) | 123,038 | 63% |
| | Robert Winckler (R) | 61,009 | 32% |
| | Jeffrey P. Lieb (LBT) | 10,381 | 5% |
| 24 | * **Henry A. Waxman** (D) | 91,568 | 68% |
| | Roland Cayard (R) | 38,631 | 28% |
| 25 | * **Edward R. Roybal** (D) | 48,283 | 66% |
| | Richard L. Ferraro Jr (R) | 20,665 | 28% |
| | William D. Mitchell (LBT) | 4,101 | 6% |
| 26 | * **John H. Rousselot** (R) | 113,991 | 71% |
| | Joseph L. Lisoni (D) | 39,375 | 24% |
| 27 | * **Robert K. Dornan** (R) | 106,342 | 51% |
| | Carey Peck (D) | 97,663 | 47% |
| 28 | * **Julian C. Dixon** (D) | 106,975 | 79% |
| | Robert Reid (R) | 22,638 | 17% |
| 29 | * **Augustus F. Hawkins** (D) | 79,100 | 86% |
| | Michael A. Hirt (R) | 10,094 | 11% |
| 30 | * **George E. Danielson** (D) | 72,995 | 72% |
| | J. Arthur Platten (R) | 23,683 | 24% |
| 31 | **Mervyn M. Dymally** (D) | 68,160 | 65% |
| | Don Grimshaw (R) | 37,447 | 35% |
| 32 | * **Glenn M. Anderson** (D) | 82,436 | 66% |
| | John R. Adler (R) | 38,250 | 31% |
| 33 | * **Wayne Grisham** (R) | 120,421 | 71% |
| | Fred L. Anderson (D) | 49,664 | 29% |
| 34 | * **Dan Lungren** (R) | 135,253 | 75% |
| | Simone (D) | 45,386 | 25% |
| 35 | **Dave Dreier** (R) | 99,134 | 53% |
| | * Jim Lloyd (D) | 86,728 | 47% |
| 36 | * **George E. Brown Jr.** (D) | 87,895 | 52% |
| | John P. Stark (R) | 73,096 | 44% |
| 37 | * **Jerry Lewis** (R) | 164,663 | 72% |
| | Donald M. Rusk (D) | 57,815 | 25% |
| 38 | * **Jerry M. Patterson** (D) | 90,647 | 56% |
| | Art Jacobson (R) | 65,340 | 40% |
| 39 | * **William Dannemeyer** (R) | 172,029 | 76% |
| | Leonard L. Lahtinen (D) | 53,738 | 24% |
| 40 | * **Robert E. Badham** (R) | 209,775 | 70% |
| | Michael F. Dow (D) | 65,388 | 22% |
| | Dana Mahaffey (LBT) | 24,133 | 8% |
| 41 | **Bill Lowery** (R) | 120,617 | 53% |
| | * Bob Wilson (D) | 99,102 | 43% |

| DIST. | CANDIDATES AND PARTY | VOTES | PERCENT |
|---|---|---|---|
| 42 | Duncan L. Hunter (R) | 77,819 | 53% |
|  | * Lionel Van Deerlin (D) | 68,354 | 47% |
| 43 | * Clair W. Burgener (R) | 292,039 | 86% |
|  | Tom Metzger (D) | 45,623 | 14% |

## COLORADO

| DIST. | CANDIDATES AND PARTY | VOTES | PERCENT |
|---|---|---|---|
| 1 | * Patricia Schroeder (D) | 107,332 | 59% |
|  | Naomi Bradford (R) | 67,811 | 38% |
| 2 | * Timothy E. Wirth (D) | 153,568 | 57% |
|  | John McElderry (R) | 111,792 | 41% |
| 3 | * Ray Kogovsek (D) | 105,054 | 55% |
|  | Harold McCormick (R) | 84,034 | 44% |
| 4 | Hank Brown (R) | 178,158 | 68% |
|  | Polly Baca Barragan (D) | 77,054 | 30% |
| 5 | * Ken Kramer (R) | 176,726 | 73% |
|  | Ed Schreiber (D) | 61,898 | 25% |

## CONNECTICUT

| DIST. | CANDIDATES AND PARTY | VOTES | PERCENT |
|---|---|---|---|
| 1 | * William R. Cotter (D) | 137,477 | 63% |
|  | Marjorie D. Anderson (R) | 80,873 | 37% |
| 2 | * Samuel Gejdenson (D) | 118,893 | 54% |
|  | Tony Guglielmo (R) | 102,859 | 46% |
| 3 | Lawrence J. DeNardis (R) | 108,213 | 53% |
|  | Joseph I. Lieberman (D) | 97,119 | 47% |
| 4 | * Stewart B. McKinney (R) | 122,540 | 62% |
|  | John Aristotle Phillips (D) | 73,820 | 38% |
| 5 | * William Ratchford (D) | 116,938 | 50% |
|  | Edward M. Donahue (R) | 115,059 | 50% |
| 6 | * Toby Moffett (D) | 142,980 | 59% |
|  | Nicholas Schaus (R) | 98,349 | 41% |

## DELAWARE

| DIST. | CANDIDATES AND PARTY | VOTES | PERCENT |
|---|---|---|---|
| AL | * Thomas B. Evans Jr. (R) | 133,557 | 61% |
|  | Robert L. Maxwell (D) | 81,805 | 38% |

## FLORIDA

| DIST. | CANDIDATES AND PARTY | VOTES | PERCENT |
|---|---|---|---|
| 1 | * Earl Hutto (D) | 109,541 | 62% |
|  | Warren Briggs (R) | 66,896 | 38% |
| 2 | * Don Fuqua (D) | 130,206 | 71% |
|  | John R. LaCapra (R) | 53,325 | 29% |
| 3 | * Charles E. Bennett (D) | 98,382 | 77% |
|  | Harry Radcliffe (R) | 28,837 | 23% |
| 4 | * Bill Chappell Jr. (D) | 136,301 | 66% |
|  | Barney E. Dillard Jr. (R) | 71,308 | 34% |
| 5 | Bill McCollum (R) | 172,107 | 56% |
|  | David Best (D) | 137,136 | 44% |
| 6 | * C. W. Bill Young (R) | no major opposition | |
| 7 | * Sam Gibbons (D) | 126,686 | 72% |
|  | Charles P. Jones (R) | 48,982 | 28% |
| 8 | * Andrew P. Ireland (D) | 144,200 | 72% |
|  | Scott Nicholson (R) | 56,079 | 28% |
| 9 | * Bill Nelson (D) | 130,498 | 71% |
|  | Stan Dowiat (R) | 53,330 | 29% |
| 10 | * L. A. Bafalis (R) | 260,214 | 79% |
|  | Richard D. Sparkman (D) | 69,674 | 21% |
| 11 | * Dan Mica (D) | 198,477 | 60% |
|  | Al Coogler (R) | 134,433 | 40% |
| 12 | Clay Shaw (R) | 121,465 | 54% |
|  | Alan S. Becker (D) | 103,090 | 46% |
| 13 | * William Lehman (D) | 122,555 | 75% |
|  | Alvin E. Entin (R) | 40,825 | 25% |
| 14 | * Claude Pepper (D) | 91,096 | 75% |
|  | Evelio S. Estrella (R) | 30,675 | 25% |
| 15 | * Dante B. Fascell (D) | 125,208 | 66% |
|  | Herbert J. Hoodwin (R) | 65,122 | 34% |

## GEORGIA

| DIST. | CANDIDATES AND PARTY | VOTES | PERCENT |
|---|---|---|---|
| 1 | * Ronald (Bo) Ginn (D) | no major opposition | |
| 2 | Charles F. Hatcher (D) | 89,723 | 74% |
|  | Jack E. Harrell Jr. (R) | 32,270 | 26% |
| 3 | * Jack Brinkley (D) | no major opposition | |
| 4 | * Elliott H. Levitas (D) | 98,565 | 70% |
|  | Barry E. Billington (R) | 43,013 | 30% |

| DIST. | CANDIDATES AND PARTY | VOTES | PERCENT |
|---|---|---|---|
| 5 | * Wyche Fowler Jr. (D) | 101,613 | 74% |
|  | F. William Dowda (R) | 35,664 | 26% |
| 6 | * Newt Gingrich (R) | 95,550 | 59% |
|  | Dock H. Davis (D) | 66,474 | 41% |
| 7 | * Larry P. McDonald (D) | 112,988 | 68% |
|  | Richard L. Castellucis (R) | 53,002 | 32% |
| 8 | * Billy Lee Evans (D) | 87,160 | 74% |
|  | Darwin Carter (R) | 30,898 | 26% |
| 9 | * Ed Jenkins (D) | 114,803 | 67% |
|  | David G. Ashworth (R) | 55,579 | 33% |
| 10 | * Doug Barnard (D) | 101,046 | 80% |
|  | Bruce J. Neubauer (R) | 24,888 | 20% |

## HAWAII

| DIST. | CANDIDATES AND PARTY | VOTES | PERCENT |
|---|---|---|---|
| 1 | * Cecil Heftel (D) | 98,256 | 80% |
|  | Aloma Keen Nobel (R) | 19,819 | 16% |
|  | Rockne H. Johnson (LBT) | 5,106 | 4% |
| 2 | * Daniel K. Akaka (D) | 141,477 | 90% |
|  | Don G. Smith (LBT) | 15,903 | 10% |

## IDAHO

| DIST. | CANDIDATES AND PARTY | VOTES | PERCENT |
|---|---|---|---|
| 1 | Larry Craig (R) | 116,977 | 54% |
|  | Glenn W. Nichols (D) | 100,870 | 46% |
| 2 | * George Hansen (R) | 116,123 | 59% |
|  | Diane Bilyeu (D) | 81,364 | 41% |

## ILLINOIS

| DIST. | CANDIDATES AND PARTY | VOTES | PERCENT |
|---|---|---|---|
| 1 | Harold Washington (D) | 115,617 | 95% |
|  | George Williams (R) | 6,471 | 5% |
| 2 | Gus Savage (D) | 118,148 | 88% |
|  | Marsha A. Harris (R) | 16,305 | 12% |
| 3 | * Martin A. Russo (D) | 131,683 | 69% |
|  | Lawrence C. Sarsoun (R) | 58,888 | 31% |
| 4 | * Edward J. Derwinski (R) | 146,299 | 68% |
|  | Richard S. Jalovec (D) | 70,022 | 32% |
| 5 | * John G. Fary (D) | 99,704 | 79% |
|  | Robert V. Kotowski (R) | 26,242 | 21% |
| 6 | * Henry J. Hyde (R) | 116,782 | 67% |
|  | Mario R. Reda (D) | 58,378 | 33% |
| 7 | * Cardiss Collins (D) | 75,135 | 85% |
|  | Ruth R. Hooper (R) | 13,233 | 15% |
| 8 | * Dan Rostenkowski (D) | 91,719 | 84% |
|  | Walter F. Zilke (R) | 17,067 | 16% |
| 9 | * Sidney R. Yates (D) | 98,098 | 73% |
|  | John D. Andrica (R) | 36,025 | 27% |
| 10 | * John E. Porter (R) | 132,032 | 61% |
|  | Robert A. Weinberger (D) | 85,716 | 39% |
| 11 | * Frank Annunzio (D) | 116,317 | 69% |
|  | Michael R. Zanillo (R) | 51,226 | 31% |
| 12 | * Philip M. Crane (R) | 177,594 | 74% |
|  | David McCartney (D) | 61,859 | 26% |
| 13 | * Robert McClory (R) | 131,751 | 72% |
|  | Michael Reese (D) | 52,086 | 28% |
| 14 | * John N. Erlenborn (R) | 200,934 | 77% |
|  | LeRoy E. Kennel (D) | 60,702 | 23% |
| 15 | * Tom Corcoran (R) | 150,897 | 77% |
|  | John Paul Quillin (D) | 45,722 | 23% |
| 16 | Lynn M. Martin (R) | 133,533 | 67% |
|  | Douglas R. Aurand (D) | 64,480 | 33% |
| 17 | * George M. O'Brien (R) | 131,719 | 67% |
|  | Michael A. Murer (D) | 64,869 | 33% |
| 18 | * Robert H. Michel (R) | 125,644 | 62% |
|  | John L. Knuppel (D) | 76,689 | 38% |
| 19 | * Tom Railsback (R) | 143,260 | 74% |
|  | Thomas J. Hand (D) | 51,248 | 26% |
| 20 | * Paul Findley (R) | 122,977 | 56% |
|  | David L. Robinson (D) | 96,590 | 44% |
| 21 | * Edward R. Madigan (R) | 132,174 | 68% |
|  | Penny Severns (D) | 63,474 | 32% |
| 22 | * Daniel B. Crane (R) | 144,586 | 69% |
|  | Peter M. Voelz (D) | 65,483 | 31% |
| 23 | * Melvin Price (D) | 107,106 | 64% |
|  | Ronald L. Davinroy (R) | 59,617 | 36% |

## 1980 ELECTIONS OF U.S. REPRESENTATIVES (continued)

| DIST. CANDIDATES AND PARTY | VOTES | PERCENT |
|---|---|---|
| **ILLINOIS** (continued) | | |
| 24  * Paul Simon (D) | 110,389 | 51% |
|     John T. Anderson (R) | 108,112 | 49% |
| **INDIANA** | | |
| 1  * Adam Benjamin Jr. (D) | 112,016 | 72% |
|    Joseph D. Harkin (R) | 43,537 | 28% |
| 2  * Floyd Fithian (D) | 122,192 | 54% |
|    Ernest Niemeyer (R) | 105,918 | 46% |
| 3  John P. Hiler (R) | 100,106 | 55% |
|    * John Brademas (D) | 83,140 | 45% |
| 4  Daniel R. Coats (R) | 115,351 | 60% |
|    John D. Walda (D) | 75,172 | 40% |
| 5  * Elwood Hillis (R) | 127,235 | 62% |
|    Nels J. Ackerson (D) | 79,626 | 38% |
| 6  * David W. Evans (D) | 95,999 | 50% |
|    David G. Crane (R) | 94,804 | 50% |
| 7  * John T. Myers (R) | 134,137 | 66% |
|    Patrick D. Carroll (D) | 67,619 | 33% |
| 8  * H. Joel Deckard (R) | 119,677 | 55% |
|    Kenneth C. Snider (D) | 96,963 | 45% |
| 9  * Lee H. Hamilton (D) | 136,205 | 64% |
|    George Meyers Jr. (R) | 76,708 | 36% |
| 10  * Phillip Sharp (D) | 102,696 | 53% |
|     William G. Frazier (R) | 89,980 | 47% |
| 11  * Andrew Jacobs Jr. (D) | 96,225 | 57% |
|     Sheila Suess (R) | 71,771 | 43% |
| **IOWA** | | |
| 1  * James Leach (R) | 134,248 | 64% |
|    Jim Larew (D) | 72,438 | 35% |
| 2  * Tom Tauke (R) | 116,829 | 57% |
|    Steve Sovern (D) | 87,223 | 43% |
| 3  Cooper Evans (R) | 107,830 | 51% |
|    Lynn Cutler (D) | 101,639 | 49% |
| 4  * Neal Smith (D) | 117,716 | 54% |
|    Donald C. Young (R) | 100,162 | 46% |
| 5  * Tom Harkin (D) | 128,687 | 60% |
|    Cal Hultman (R) | 85,868 | 40% |
| 6  * Berkley Bedell (D) | 128,009 | 64% |
|    Clarence S. Carney (R) | 72,049 | 36% |
| **KANSAS** | | |
| 1  Pat Roberts (R) | 119,688 | 62% |
|    Phil Martin (D) | 73,402 | 38% |
| 2  * Jim Jeffries (R) | 90,452 | 54% |
|    Sam Keys (D) | 77,464 | 46% |
| 3  * Larry Winn Jr. (R) | 109,277 | 57% |
|    Dan Watkins (D) | 82,000 | 43% |
| 4  * Dan Glickman (D) | 123,940 | 69% |
|    Clay Hunter (R) | 56,189 | 31% |
| 5  * Robert Whittaker (R) | 140,501 | 76% |
|    David L. Miller (D) | 45,283 | 24% |
| **KENTUCKY** | | |
| 1  * Carroll Hubbard Jr. (D) | no major opposition | |
| 2  * William H. Natcher (D) | 99,682 | 66% |
|    Mark T. Watson (R) | 52,123 | 34% |
| 3  * Romano L. Mazzoli (D) | 84,091 | 65% |
|    Richard Cesler (R) | 45,676 | 35% |
| 4  * M. G. (Gene) Snyder (R) | 122,794 | 67% |
|    Phil M. McGary (D) | 60,831 | 33% |
| 5  Harold Rogers (R) | 111,779 | 68% |
|    Ted R. Marcum (D) | 53,716 | 32% |
| 6  * Larry J. Hopkins (R) | 103,271 | 59% |
|    Tom Easterly (D) | 70,999 | 40% |
| 7  * Carl D. Perkins (D) | no major opposition | |
| **LOUISIANA** | | |
| 1  * Robert L. Livingston Jr. (R) | no major opposition | |
| 2  * Corrine C. Boggs (D) | no major opposition | |
| 3  * W. J. Tauzin (D) | no major opposition | |

| DIST. CANDIDATES AND PARTY | VOTES | PERCENT |
|---|---|---|
| 4  Buddy Roemer (D) | 103,511 | 64% |
|    * Claude Leach (D) | 58,641 | 36% |
| 5  * Jerry Huckaby (D) | no major opposition | |
| 6  * W. Henson Moore III (R) | no major opposition | |
| 7  * John B. Breaux (D) | no major opposition | |
| 8  * Gillis W. Long (D) | no major opposition | |
| **MAINE** | | |
| 1  * David F. Emery (R) | 186,663 | 68% |
|    Harold C. Pachios (D) | 87,367 | 32% |
| 2  * Olympia Snowe (R) | 186,083 | 79% |
|    Harold L. Silverman (D) | 50,228 | 21% |
| **MARYLAND** | | |
| 1  Roy Dyson (D) | 96,394 | 52% |
|    * Robert E. Bauman (R) | 88,736 | 48% |
| 2  * Clarence D. Long (D) | 115,846 | 57% |
|    Helen D. Bentley (R) | 88,490 | 43% |
| 3  * Barbara A. Mikulski (D) | 100,677 | 76% |
|    Russell T. Schaffer (R) | 31,346 | 24% |
| 4  * Marjorie S. Holt (R) | 116,162 | 72% |
|    James J. Riley (D) | 45,869 | 28% |
| 5  * Gladys N. Spellman (D) | 103,150 | 81% |
|    Kevin R. Igoe (R) | 24,728 | 19% |
| 6  * Beverly B. Byron (D) | 140,142 | 70% |
|    Raymond E. Beck (R) | 60,419 | 30% |
| 7  * Parren J. Mitchell (D) | 96,014 | 89% |
|    Victor Clark (R) | 12,257 | 11% |
| 8  * Michael Barnes (D) | 140,214 | 60% |
|    Newton I. Steers Jr. (R) | 94,714 | 40% |
| **MASSACHUSETTS** | | |
| 1  * Silvio O. Conte (R) | 156,167 | 75% |
|    Helen P. Doyle (D) | 52,438 | 25% |
| 2  * Edward P. Boland (D) | 120,511 | 76% |
|    Thomas P. Swank (R) | 38,675 | 24% |
| 3  * Joseph D. Early (D) | 140,632 | 72% |
|    David G. Skehan (R) | 54,409 | 28% |
| 4  Barney Frank (D) | 103,461 | 52% |
|    Richard A. Jones (R) | 95,895 | 48% |
| 5  * James M. Shannon (D) | 136,711 | 66% |
|    William C. Sawyer (R) | 70,578 | 34% |
| 6  * Nicholas Mavroules (D) | 111,344 | 52% |
|    Thomas H. Trimarco (R) | 103,120 | 48% |
| 7  * Edward J. Markey (D) | no major opposition | |
| 8  * Thomas P. O'Neill Jr. (D) | 126,425 | 78% |
|    William A. Barnstead (R) | 35,802 | 22% |
| 9  * John (Joe) Moakley (D) | no major opposition | |
| 10  * Margaret M. Heckler (R) | 131,600 | 61% |
|     Robert E. McCarthy (D) | 83,557 | 39% |
| 11  * Brian J. Donnelly (D) | no major opposition | |
| 12  * Gerry E. Studds (D) | 195,294 | 73% |
|     Paul V. Doane (R) | 71,468 | 27% |
| **MICHIGAN** | | |
| 1  * John Conyers Jr. (D) | 124,294 | 95% |
|    William M. Bell (R) | 6,374 | 5% |
| 2  * Carl D. Pursell (R) | 114,539 | 57% |
|    Kathleen F. O'Reilly (D) | 83,430 | 42% |
| 3  * Howard Wolpe (D) | 112,547 | 52% |
|    James S. Gilmore (R) | 101,988 | 47% |
| 4  * David Stockman (R) | 136,028 | 73% |
|    Lyndon G. Furst (D) | 47,656 | 26% |
| 5  * Harold S. Sawyer (R) | 117,855 | 53% |
|    Dale R. Sprik (D) | 101,664 | 46% |
| 6  Jim Dunn (R) | 113,316 | 51% |
|    * Bob Carr (D) | 109,563 | 49% |
| 7  * Dale E. Kildee (D) | 146,416 | 93% |
|    Dennis L. Barry (LBT) | 11,395 | 7% |
| 8  * Bob Traxler (D) | 123,803 | 61% |
|    Norman R. Hughes (R) | 77,066 | 38% |
| 9  * Guy Vander Jagt (R) | 160,303 | 97% |

| DIST. | CANDIDATES AND PARTY | VOTES | PERCENT |
|---|---|---|---|
| 10 | * Don Albosta (D) | 123,544 | 53% |
| | Richard J. Allen (R) | 109,104 | 46% |
| 11 | * Robert W. Davis (R) | 141,833 | 66% |
| | Dan Dorrity (D) | 73,881 | 34% |
| 12 | * David E. Bonior (D) | 113,608 | 55% |
| | Kirk Walsh (R) | 91,559 | 45% |
| 13 | George W. Crockett Jr. (D) | 79,935 | 92% |
| | M. Michael Hurd (R) | 6,521 | 7% |
| 14 | Dennis M. Hertel (D) | 89,609 | 53% |
| | Vic Caputo (R) | 77,961 | 46% |
| 15 | * William D. Ford (D) | 114,484 | 68% |
| | Gerald R. Carlson (R) | 53,570 | 32% |
| 16 | * John D. Dingell (D) | 105,669 | 70% |
| | Pamella A. Seay (R) | 42,700 | 28% |
| 17 | * William M. Brodhead (D) | 126,754 | 69% |
| | Alfred L. Patterson (R) | 44,277 | 24% |
| | William Krebaum (LBT) | 13,767 | 7% |
| 18 | * James J. Blanchard (D) | 135,587 | 65% |
| | Betty J. Suida (R) | 68,356 | 33% |
| 19 | * William S. Broomfield (R) | 165,040 | 72% |
| | Wayne E. Daniels (D) | 60,125 | 26% |

## MINNESOTA

| DIST. | CANDIDATES AND PARTY | VOTES | PERCENT |
|---|---|---|---|
| 1 | * Arlen Erdahl (R)(I) | 163,289 | 72% |
| | Russell V. Smith (DFL) | 62,777 | 28% |
| 2 | * Tom Hagedorn (R) | 151,245 | 61% |
| | Harold J. Bergquist (DFL) | 98,575 | 39% |
| 3 | * Bill Frenzel (R) | 176,964 | 76% |
| | Joel A. Saliterman (DFL) | 57,330 | 24% |
| 4 | * Bruce F. Vento (DFL) | 116,946 | 59% |
| | John Berg (I-R) | 80,664 | 41% |
| 5 | * Martin Olav Sabo (DFL) | 121,201 | 72% |
| | John Doherty (I-R) | 46,060 | 28% |
| 6 | Vin Weber (I-R) | 129,908 | 54% |
| | Archie Baumann (DFL) | 112,617 | 46% |
| 7 | * Arlan Stangeland (I-R) | 130,350 | 52% |
| | Gene Wenstrom (DFL) | 120,770 | 48% |
| 8 | * James L. Oberstar (DFL) | 175,464 | 70% |
| | Edward Fiore (R) | 69,434 | 28% |
| | Ilona Gersh (SW) | 4,000 | 2% |

## MISSISSIPPI

| DIST. | CANDIDATES AND PARTY | VOTES | PERCENT |
|---|---|---|---|
| 1 | * Jamie L. Whitten (D) | 103,988 | 63% |
| | T. K. Moffett (R) | 61,175 | 37% |
| 2 | * David R. Bowen (D) | 84,669 | 67% |
| | Frank Drake (R) | 41,783 | 33% |
| 3 | * G. V. Montgomery (D) | no major opposition | |
| 4 | * Jon C. Hinson (R) | 69,517 | 39% |
| | Leslie B. McLemore (I) | 53,288 | 30% |
| | Britt R. Singletary (D) | 52,829 | 29% |
| | John W. McInerney (I) | 3,468 | 2% |
| 5 | * Trent Lott (R) | 130,422 | 74% |
| | Jimmy McVeay (D) | 46,363 | 26% |

## MISSOURI

| DIST. | CANDIDATES AND PARTY | VOTES | PERCENT |
|---|---|---|---|
| 1 | * William Clay (D) | 89,890 | 70% |
| | Bill White (R) | 38,463 | 30% |
| 2 | * Robert A. Young (D) | 148,620 | 64% |
| | John O. Shields (R) | 82,563 | 36% |
| 3 | * Richard A. Gephardt (D) | 141,221 | 78% |
| | Robert A. Cedarburg (R) | 40,714 | 22% |
| 4 | * Ike Skelton (D) | 151,455 | 68% |
| | Bill Baker (R) | 71,868 | 32% |
| 5 | * Richard Bolling (D) | 110,952 | 70% |
| | Vincent E. Baker (R) | 47,309 | 30% |
| 6 | * E. Thomas Coleman (R) | 149,821 | 71% |
| | Vernon King (D) | 61,955 | 29% |
| 7 | * Gene Taylor (R) | 140,943 | 68% |
| | Ken Young (D) | 65,651 | 32% |
| 8 | Wendell Bailey (R) | 127,668 | 57% |
| | Steve Gardner (D) | 95,744 | 43% |
| 9 | * Harold L. Volkmer (D) | 135,618 | 56% |
| | John W. Turner (R) | 107,818 | 44% |

| DIST. | CANDIDATES AND PARTY | VOTES | PERCENT |
|---|---|---|---|
| 10 | Bill Emerson (R) | 116,715 | 55% |
| | * Bill D. Burlison (D) | 95,198 | 45% |

## MONTANA

| DIST. | CANDIDATES AND PARTY | VOTES | PERCENT |
|---|---|---|---|
| 1 | * Pat Williams (D) | 105,781 | 62% |
| | John K. McDonald (R) | 65,780 | 38% |
| 2 | * Ron Marlenee (R) | 82,966 | 59% |
| | Tom Monahan (D) | 58,440 | 41% |

## NEBRASKA

| DIST. | CANDIDATES AND PARTY | VOTES | PERCENT |
|---|---|---|---|
| 1 | * Douglas K. Bereuter (R) | 158,746 | 79% |
| | Rex S. Story (D) | 43,131 | 21% |
| 2 | * Hal Daub (R) | 105,783 | 53% |
| | Richard M. Fellman (D) | 87,674 | 44% |
| | Susan K. Putney (LBT) | 6,132 | 3% |
| 3 | * Virginia Smith (R) | 180,469 | 84% |
| | Stan Ditus (D) | 34,691 | 16% |

## NEVADA

| DIST. | CANDIDATES AND PARTY | VOTES | PERCENT |
|---|---|---|---|
| AL | * James Santini (D) | 164,714 | 68% |
| | Vince Saunders (R) | 62,920 | 26% |
| | None of the above | 8,608 | 3% |
| | Harry J. Mangrum (LBT) | 7,733 | 3% |

## NEW HAMPSHIRE

| DIST. | CANDIDATES AND PARTY | VOTES | PERCENT |
|---|---|---|---|
| 1 | * Norman D'Amours (D) | 113,840 | 61% |
| | Marshall W. Cobleigh (R) | 72,982 | 39% |
| 2 | Judd Gregg (R) | 113,091 | 64% |
| | Maurice L. Arel (D) | 63,182 | 36% |

## NEW JERSEY

| DIST. | CANDIDATES AND PARTY | VOTES | PERCENT |
|---|---|---|---|
| 1 | * James Florio (D) | 145,717 | 77% |
| | Scott L. Sibert (R) | 41,493 | 22% |
| | Ronald K. Wishart (LBT) | 1,015 | 1% |
| 2 | * William J. Hughes (D) | 131,527 | 58% |
| | Beech N. Fox (R) | 93,835 | 41% |
| | Robert Rothhouse (LBT) | 2,187 | 1% |
| 3 | * James J. Howard (D) | 106,140 | 50% |
| | Marie S. Muhler (R) | 104,119 | 49% |
| | Tom Palven (LBT) | 1,388 | 1% |
| 4 | Christopher H. Smith (R) | 88,680 | 54% |
| | * Frank Thompson Jr. (D) | 71,742 | 44% |
| | Jack Moyers (LBT) | 2,652 | 2% |
| 5 | * Millicent Fenwick (R) | 154,858 | 78% |
| | Kieran E. Pillion Jr. (D) | 40,910 | 21% |
| | Carl R. Samson (LBT) | 2,444 | 1% |
| 6 | * Edwin B. Forsythe (R) | 120,930 | 57% |
| | Lewis M. Weinstein (D) | 90,233 | 42% |
| 7 | Marge Roukema (R) | 104,033 | 52% |
| | * Andrew Maguire (D) | 95,089 | 47% |
| 8 | * Robert A. Roe (D) | 96,351 | 68% |
| | William R. Cleveland (R) | 44,666 | 31% |
| 9 | * Harold Hollenbeck (R) | 110,864 | 60% |
| | Gabriel Ambrosio (D) | 72,647 | 39% |
| 10 | * Peter W. Rodino Jr. (D) | 72,472 | 86% |
| | Everett J. Jennings (R) | 11,310 | 14% |
| 11 | * Joseph G. Minish (D) | 100,990 | 64% |
| | Robert A. Davis (R) | 55,162 | 35% |
| 12 | * Matthew J. Rinaldo (R) | 117,840 | 77% |
| | Rose Zeidwerg Monyek (D) | 33,193 | 22% |
| 13 | * Jim Courter (R) | 152,019 | 72% |
| | Dave Stickle (D) | 55,553 | 26% |
| 14 | * Frank J. Guarini (D) | 75,707 | 65% |
| | Dennis E. Teti (R) | 38,464 | 33% |
| 15 | Bernard J. Dwyer (D) | 91,349 | 54% |
| | William J. O'Sullivan Jr. (R) | 74,989 | 45% |

## NEW MEXICO

| DIST. | CANDIDATES AND PARTY | VOTES | PERCENT |
|---|---|---|---|
| 1 | * Manuel Lujan Jr. (R) | 123,049 | 51% |
| | Bill Richardson (D) | 117,152 | 49% |
| 2 | Joe Skeen (R) | 59,724 | 38% |
| | David King (D) | 54,791 | 34% |
| | Dorothy Runnels (D) | 44,804 | 28% |

## 1980 ELECTIONS OF U.S. REPRESENTATIVES (continued)

| DIST. CANDIDATES AND PARTY | VOTES | PERCENT |
|---|---|---|
| **NEW YORK** | | |
| 1 * William Carney (R)(C)(RTL) | 107,661 | 56% |
|    Thomas A. Twomey Jr. (D) | 81,695 | 42% |
|    Richard M. Cummings (L) | 3,326 | 2% |
| 2 * Thomas J. Downey (D) | 78,651 | 56% |
|    Louis J. Modica (R)(RTL) | 62,681 | 44% |
| 3   Gregory W. Carman (R)(C) | 86,842 | 53% |
|    * Jerome A. Ambro Jr. (D)(RTL) | 73,385 | 45% |
|    John T. Meehan (L) | 4,151 | 2% |
| 4 * Norman F. Lent (R)(C)(RTL) | 116,931 | 67% |
|    Charles F. Brennan (D) | 58,146 | 33% |
| 5   Raymond McGrath (R)(C)(RTL) | 104,668 | 58% |
|    Karen S. Burstein (D)(L) | 76,927 | 42% |
| 6 * John LeBoutillier (R)(C)(RTL) | 90,008 | 53% |
|    Lester L. Wolff (D)(L) | 79,701 | 47% |
| 7 * Joseph P. Addabbo (D)(R)(L) | 94,025 | 95% |
|    Francis A. Lees (C)(RTL) | 4,700 | 5% |
| 8 * B. S. Rosenthal (D)(L) | 83,445 | 76% |
|    Albert Lemishow (R)(C)(RTL) | 26,979 | 24% |
| 9 * Geraldine Ferraro (D) | 63,015 | 58% |
|    Vito P. Battista (R)(C)(RTL) | 44,086 | 41% |
|    Gertrude Geniale (L) | 1,080 | 1% |
| 10 * Mario Biaggi (D)(R)(L) | 93,451 | 94% |
|    Joseph P. Cavanna (Cons.) | 3,989 | 4% |
|    Michael F. Mari (RTL) | 1,519 | 2% |
| 11 * James H. Scheuer (D)(L) | 70,703 | 74% |
|    Andrew E. Carlan (R)(C)(RTL) | 25,173 | 26% |
| 12 * Shirley Chisholm (D)(L) | 34,431 | 85% |
|    Charles Gibbs (R) | 3,540 | 9% |
|    Ralph J. Cerrano (C) | 1,457 | 4% |
|    Joseph N. D. Caesar (RTL) | 745 | 2% |
| 13 * Stephen J. Solarz (D)(L) | 80,379 | 79% |
|    Harry DeMell (R)(C) | 19,582 | 19% |
|    Brendan J. Connolly (RTL) | 1,677 | 2% |
| 14 * Fred Richmond (D)(L) | 44,469 | 83% |
|    Christopher Lovell (R) | 8,423 | 16% |
| 15 * Leo C. Zeferetti (D) | 48,303 | 50% |
|    Paul M. Atanasio (R)(C)(RTL) | 46,107 | 47% |
|    Peter A. McNeill (L) | 2,839 | 3% |
| 16   Charles E. Schumer (D)(L) | 66,841 | 77% |
|    Theodore Silverman (R)(C) | 16,840 | 20% |
|    Mary B. Spalding (RTL) | 2,522 | 3% |
| 17   Guy V. Molinari (R)(C) | 67,663 | 48% |
|    * John M. Murphy (D)(RTL) | 49,164 | 35% |
|    Mary T. Codd (L) | 23,179 | 17% |
| 18 * S. William Green (R) | 87,540 | 56% |
|    Mark J. Green (D)(L) | 67,724 | 43% |
| 19 * Charles B. Rangel (D,R,L) | 83,507 | 97% |
|    Marjorie Garvey (C) | 2,915 | 3% |
| 20 * Theodore Weiss (D,L) | 84,661 | 83% |
|    James E. Greene (R) | 15,147 | 15% |
|    David I. Caplan (C) | 2,217 | 2% |
| 21 * Robert Garcia (D,R,L) | 31,839 | 98% |
| 22 * Jonathan Bingham (D,L) | 64,914 | 84% |
|    Robert S. Black (R) | 9,919 | 13% |
|    James J. Whalen (C) | 2,719 | 3% |
| 23 * Peter A. Peyser (D) | 67,311 | 54% |
|    Andrew Albanese (R) | 56,948 | 46% |
| 24 * Richard L. Ottinger (D) | 86,203 | 58% |
|    Joseph W. Christiana (R,C) | 60,092 | 41% |
| 25 * Hamilton Fish Jr. (R,C) | 149,666 | 80% |
|    Gunars Ozols (L) | 37,429 | 20% |
| 26 * Benjamin A. Gilman (R) | 133,508 | 73% |
|    Eugene Victor (D,L) | 38,177 | 21% |
|    Edmond W. Farrell (RTL) | 8,758 | 5% |
| 27 * Matthew F. McHugh (D) | 100,099 | 55% |
|    Neil T. Wallace (R,C) | 80,126 | 44% |
| 28 * Samuel S. Stratton (D) | 163,453 | 78% |
|    Frank Wicks (R) | 38,873 | 19% |
|    Mary A. Bradt (C, RTL) | 6,264 | 3% |
| 29 * Gerald Solomon (R,C,RTL) | 134,612 | 67% |
|    Rodger L. Hurley (D,L) | 67,808 | 33% |
| 30   David O'B. Martin (R,C) | 107,379 | 63% |
|    Mary Anne Krupsak (D,L) | 55,985 | 33% |
|    John R. Zagame (RTL) | 7,428 | 4% |
| 31 * Donald J. Mitchell (R, RTL) | 127,318 | 77% |
|    Irving A. Schwartz (D) | 36,884 | 23% |
| 32   George Wortley (R,C) | 102,983 | 61% |
|    Jeffery S. Brooks (D) | 53,557 | 31% |
|    Peter J. Del Giorno (RTL) | 11,279 | 7% |
|    John Northrup (LBT) | 2,351 | 1% |
| 33 * Gary A. Lee (R,C) | 129,122 | 76% |
|    Dolores M. Reed (D,L) | 39,240 | 22% |
|    William L. Jones (RTL) | 2,777 | 2% |
| 34 * Frank Horton (R) | 125,198 | 72% |
|    James Toole (D) | 35,351 | 21% |
|    Clyde O. Benoy (C) | 5,579 | 3% |
|    William Bastuk (RTL) | 3,472 | 2% |
|    David E. Hoesly (LBT) | 3,416 | 2% |
| 35 * Barber Conable Jr. (R) | 112,819 | 72% |
|    John M. Owens (D,C) | 40,055 | 26% |
|    Bernard M. O'Connor (RTL) | 3,287 | 2% |
| 36 * John J. LaFalce (D,L) | 118,966 | 71% |
|    H. William Feder (R,C,RTL) | 47,626 | 29% |
| 37 * Henry J. Nowak (D,L) | 91,033 | 82% |
|    Roger Heymanowski (R,C) | 16,245 | 15% |
|    Thomas A. O'Connor (RTL) | 2,807 | 3% |
| 38 * Jack F. Kemp (R,C) | 161,899 | 81% |
|    Gale A. Denn (D,L) | 37,932 | 19% |
| 39 * Stanley N. Lundine (D) | 93,123 | 55% |
|    James Abdella (R,C) | 74,173 | 44% |
|    Genevieve F. Ronan (RTL) | 2,434 | 1% |
| **NORTH CAROLINA** | | |
| 1 * Walter B. Jones (D) | no major opposition | |
| 2 * L. H. Fountain (D) | 89,878 | 71% |
|    Barry L. Gardner (R) | 36,286 | 29% |
| 3 * Charles Whitley (D) | 84,873 | 68% |
|    Larry J. Parker (R) | 40,333 | 32% |
| 4 * Ike F. Andrews (D) | 103,047 | 54% |
|    Thurman Hogan (R) | 84,685 | 45% |
|    John Cunningham (LBT) | 2,768 | 1% |
| 5 * Stephen L. Neal (D) | 99,006 | 51% |
|    Anne Bagnal (R) | 94,593 | 49% |
| 6   Eugene Johnston (R) | 80,263 | 51% |
|    * Richardson Preyer (D) | 76,916 | 49% |
| 7 * Charlie Rose III (D) | 87,904 | 69% |
|    Vivian S. Wright (R) | 40,068 | 31% |
| 8 * W. G. Hefner (D) | 94,041 | 59% |
|    L. E. Harris (R) | 66,356 | 41% |
| 9 * James G. Martin (R) | 98,288 | 58% |
|    Randall R. Kincaid (D) | 70,479 | 42% |
| 10 * James T. Broyhill (R) | 120,748 | 70% |
|    James O. Icenhour (D) | 52,518 | 30% |
| 11 * William M. Hendon (R) | 103,215 | 54% |
|    Lamar Gudger (D) | 89,330 | 46% |
| **NORTH DAKOTA** | | |
| AL  Byron L. Dorgan (D) | 165,897 | 57% |
|    Jim Smykowski (R) | 124,511 | 43% |
| **OHIO** | | |
| 1 * Bill Gradison (R) | 123,806 | 76% |
|    Donald J. Zwick (D) | 38,451 | 24% |
| 2 * Thomas A. Luken (D) | 103,366 | 59% |
|    Tom Atkins (R) | 72,721 | 41% |
| 3 * Tony P. Hall (D) | 95,426 | 59% |
|    Albert H. Sealy (R) | 66,590 | 41% |
| 4 * Tennyson Guyer (R) | 133,781 | 72% |
|    Geraldine Tebben (D) | 51,329 | 28% |
| 5 * Delbert L. Latta (R) | 136,859 | 70% |
|    James R. Sherck (D) | 57,790 | 30% |
| 6   Bob McEwen (R) | 101,226 | 55% |
|    Ted Strickland (D) | 84,231 | 45% |

| DIST. | CANDIDATES AND PARTY | VOTES | PERCENT |
|---|---|---|---|
| 7 | * Clarence J. Brown Jr. (R) | 123,917 | 76% |
| | Donald Hollister (D) | 38,964 | 24% |
| 8 | * Thomas N. Kindness (R) | 139,355 | 76% |
| | John W. Griffin (D) | 44,049 | 24% |
| 9 | Ed Weber (R) | 96,900 | 58% |
| | * Thomas L. Ashley (D) | 68,753 | 42% |
| 10 | * Clarence E. Miller (R) | 143,092 | 74% |
| | Jack E. Stecher (D) | 49,350 | 26% |
| 11 | * J. William Stanton (R) | 125,972 | 71% |
| | Patrick J. Donlin (D) | 50,553 | 29% |
| 12 | Bob Shamansky (D) | 108,598 | 53% |
| | * Samuel L. Devine (R) | 97,618 | 47% |
| 13 | * Donald J. Pease (D) | 111,968 | 64% |
| | David E. Armstrong (R) | 63,310 | 36% |
| 14 | * John F. Seiberling Jr. (D) | 103,015 | 65% |
| | Louis A. Mangels (R) | 55,794 | 35% |
| 15 | * Chalmers P. Wylie (R) | 128,333 | 73% |
| | Terry Freeman (D) | 48,361 | 27% |
| 16 | * Ralph S. Regula (R) | 149,799 | 79% |
| | Larry V. Slagle (D) | 39,194 | 21% |
| 17 | * John M. Ashbrook (R) | 128,974 | 73% |
| | Donald E. Yunker (D) | 48,486 | 27% |
| 18 | * Douglas Applegate (D) | 134,650 | 76% |
| | Gary L. Hammersley (R) | 42,301 | 24% |
| 19 | * Lyle Williams (R) | 103,866 | 57% |
| | Harry Meshel (D) | 76,944 | 43% |
| 20 | * Mary Rose Oakar (D) | no major opposition | |
| 21 | * Louis Stokes (D) | 82,288 | 88% |
| | Robert L. Woodall (R) | 11,136 | 12% |
| 22 | Dennis E. Eckart (D) | 102,383 | 54% |
| | Joseph J. Nahra (R) | 80,408 | 42% |
| | Arnold Gleisser (I) | 6,931 | 4% |
| 23 | * Ronald M. Mottl (D) | no major opposition | |

## OKLAHOMA

| DIST. | CANDIDATES AND PARTY | VOTES | PERCENT |
|---|---|---|---|
| 1 | * James R. Jones (D) | 115,381 | 58% |
| | Richard C. Freeman (R) | 82,293 | 42% |
| 2 | * Mike Synar (D) | 100,341 | 54% |
| | Gary Richardson (R) | 86,105 | 46% |
| 3 | * Wes Watkins (D) | no major opposition | |
| 4 | Dave McCurdy (D) | 74,707 | 50% |
| | Howard Rutledge (R) | 73,363 | 50% |
| 5 | * Mickey Edwards (R) | 86,518 | 68% |
| | David C. Hood (D) | 35,500 | 28% |
| | James L. Rushing (LBT) | 4,810 | 4% |
| 6 | Glenn English (D) | 110,180 | 65% |
| | Carol Ann McCurley (R) | 59,592 | 35% |

## OREGON

| DIST. | CANDIDATES AND PARTY | VOTES | PERCENT |
|---|---|---|---|
| 1 | * Les AuCoin (D) | 196,011 | 66% |
| | Lynn Engdahl (R) | 100,343 | 34% |
| 2 | Denny Smith (R) | 139,618 | 49% |
| | * Al Ullman (D) | 136,104 | 47% |
| | Lloyd King Marbet (I) | 10,674 | 4% |
| 3 | Ron Wyden (D) | 149,323 | 72% |
| | Darrell R. Conger (R) | 57,246 | 28% |
| 4 | * James Weaver (D) | 158,172 | 55% |
| | Michael Fitzgerald (R) | 130,287 | 45% |

## PENNSYLVANIA

| DIST. | CANDIDATES AND PARTY | VOTES | PERCENT |
|---|---|---|---|
| 1 | Thomas M. Foglietta (I) | 56,529 | 38% |
| | * Michael Myers (D) | 51,770 | 35% |
| | Robert R. Burke (R) | 36,919 | 25% |
| 2 | * William H. Gray III (D) | 123,020 | 97% |
| | James L. Buckman (I) | 2,217 | 2% |
| 3 | * Raymond F. Lederer (D) | 67,660 | 55% |
| | William J. Phillips (R) | 40,294 | 33% |
| | Max Weiner (CON) | 11,748 | 9% |
| | John Morris (I) | 4,005 | 3% |
| 4 | * Charles Dougherty (R) | 124,904 | 63% |
| | Thomas J. Magrann (D) | 73,892 | 37% |
| 5 | * Richard T. Schulze (R) | 157,473 | 76% |
| | Grady G. Brickhouse (D) | 47,108 | 23% |

| DIST. | CANDIDATES AND PARTY | VOTES | PERCENT |
|---|---|---|---|
| 6 | * Gus Yatron (D) | 117,559 | 67% |
| | George Hulshart (R) | 58,038 | 33% |
| 7 | * Robert W. Edgar (D) | 98,083 | 53% |
| | Dennis J. Rochford (R) | 87,618 | 47% |
| 8 | James K. Coyne (R) | 103,557 | 51% |
| | * Peter H. Kostmayer (D) | 99,588 | 49% |
| 9 | * E. G. (Bud) Shuster (R) | no major opposition | |
| 10 | * Joseph M. McDade (R) | 144,312 | 76% |
| | Gene Basalyga (D) | 42,881 | 23% |
| | Patrick Fallon (LBT) | 1,298 | 1% |
| 11 | James L. Nelligan (R) | 93,439 | 52% |
| | * Raphael Musto (D) | 86,386 | 48% |
| 12 | * John P. Murtha (D) | 107,927 | 60% |
| | Charles A. Getty (R) | 72,903 | 40% |
| 13 | * R. L. Coughlin (R) | 137,563 | 70% |
| | Pete Slawek (D) | 57,558 | 29% |
| | Jon Houser (LBT) | 1,605 | 1% |
| 14 | William J. Coyne (D) | 101,308 | 70% |
| | Stan Thomas (R) | 43,429 | 30% |
| 15 | * Donald Ritter (R) | 99,062 | 59% |
| | Jeanette Reibman (D) | 68,324 | 40% |
| 16 | * Robert S. Walker (R) | 130,584 | 78% |
| | James A. Woodcock (D) | 37,318 | 22% |
| 17 | * Allen E. Ertel (D) | 96,950 | 61% |
| | Daniel S. Seiverling (R) | 63,278 | 39% |
| 18 | * Doug Walgren (D) | 127,154 | 68% |
| | Steven R. Snyder (R) | 58,965 | 32% |
| 19 | * William Goodling (R) | 135,255 | 76% |
| | Richard P. Noll (D) | 41,544 | 23% |
| 20 | * Joseph M. Gaydos (D) | 121,260 | 72% |
| | Kathleen Meyer (R) | 46,659 | 28% |
| 21 | * Don Bailey (D) | 112,144 | 68% |
| | Dirk Matson (R) | 51,834 | 32% |
| 22 | * Austin J. Murphy (D) | 114,501 | 69% |
| | Marilyn C. Ecoff (R) | 49,579 | 30% |
| 23 | * William F. Clinger Jr. (R) | 123,171 | 75% |
| | Peter Atigan (D) | 41,079 | 25% |
| 24 | * Marc L. Marks (R) | 86,614 | 50% |
| | David C. DiCarlo (D) | 86,311 | 50% |
| 25 | * Eugene V. Atkinson (D) | 119,338 | 67% |
| | Robert H. Morris (R) | 58,708 | 33% |

## RHODE ISLAND

| DIST. | CANDIDATES AND PARTY | VOTES | PERCENT |
|---|---|---|---|
| 1 | * F. J. St. Germain (D) | 116,149 | 68% |
| | William P. Montgomery (R) | 55,559 | 32% |
| 2 | Claudine Schneider (R) | 110,175 | 56% |
| | * Edward P. Beard (D) | 88,158 | 44% |

## SOUTH CAROLINA

| DIST. | CANDIDATES AND PARTY | VOTES | PERCENT |
|---|---|---|---|
| 1 | Thomas F. Hartnett (R) | 81,093 | 51% |
| | Charles D. Ravenel (D) | 76,478 | 49% |
| 2 | * Floyd Spence (R) | 92,295 | 56% |
| | Tom Turnipseed (D) | 73,143 | 44% |
| 3 | * Butler Derrick Jr. (D) | 86,619 | 61% |
| | Marshall Parker (R) | 53,431 | 38% |
| 4 | * Carroll A. Campbell (R) | 91,391 | 93% |
| | Thomas Waldenfels (LBT) | 6,984 | 7% |
| 5 | * Kenneth Holland (D) | 99,296 | 87% |
| | Thomas Campbell (LBT) | 14,188 | 13% |
| 6 | John L. Napier (R) | 76,307 | 52% |
| | * John W. Jenrette Jr. (D) | 71,781 | 48% |

## SOUTH DAKOTA

| DIST. | CANDIDATES AND PARTY | VOTES | PERCENT |
|---|---|---|---|
| 1 | * Thomas A. Daschle (D) | 109,918 | 66% |
| | Bart Kull (R) | 57,140 | 34% |
| 2 | Clint Roberts (R) | 87,932 | 58% |
| | Kenneth D. Stofferahn (D) | 63,415 | 42% |

## TENNESSEE

| DIST. | CANDIDATES AND PARTY | VOTES | PERCENT |
|---|---|---|---|
| 1 | * James H. Quillen (R) | 130,138 | 87% |
| | John Curtis (I) | 19,985 | 13% |
| 2 | * John J. Duncan (R) | 146,983 | 76% |
| | Dave Dunaway (D) | 46,383 | 24% |

## 1980 ELECTIONS OF U.S. REPRESENTATIVES (continued)

| DIST. | CANDIDATES AND PARTY | VOTES | PERCENT |
|---|---|---|---|
| **TENNESSEE** (continued) | | | |
| 3 | * Marilyn Bouquard (D) | 117,322 | 61% |
| | Glen M. Byers (R) | 75,068 | 39% |
| 4 | * Albert Gore Jr. (D) | 136,786 | 79% |
| | James Beau Seigneur (R) | 35,687 | 21% |
| 5 | * Bill Boner (D) | 118,627 | 65% |
| | Mike Adams (R) | 62,715 | 35% |
| 6 | * Robin L. Beard Jr. (R) | no major opposition | |
| 7 | * Ed Jones (D) | 133,162 | 77% |
| | Daniel Campbell (R) | 39,470 | 23% |
| 8 | * Harold Ford (D) | no major opposition | |
| **TEXAS** | | | |
| 1 | * Sam B. Hall Jr. (D) | no major opposition | |
| 2 | * Charles Wilson (D) | 138,341 | 69% |
| | F. H. Pannill Sr. (R) | 59,001 | 30% |
| 3 | * James M. Collins (R) | 202,128 | 79% |
| | Earle S. Porter (D) | 47,433 | 18% |
| | William S. Briggs (LBT) | 6,756 | 3% |
| 4 | Ralph M. Hall (D) | 95,941 | 53% |
| | John H. Wright (R) | 86,768 | 47% |
| 5 | * Jim Mattox (D) | 69,523 | 51% |
| | Tom Pauken (R) | 66,739 | 49% |
| 6 | * Phil Gramm (D) | 133,527 | 70% |
| | Dave Haskins (R) | 57,472 | 30% |
| 7 | * Bill Archer (R) | 252,478 | 83% |
| | Robert L. Hutchings (D) | 48,600 | 16% |
| | Bill Ware (LBT) | 4,277 | 1% |
| 8 | Jack Fields (R) | 72,630 | 52% |
| | * Bob Eckhardt (D) | 67,920 | 48% |
| 9 | * Jack Brooks (D) | no major opposition | |
| 10 | * J. J. Pickle (D) | 131,738 | 59% |
| | John Biggar (R) | 86,436 | 39% |
| | Michael Grossberg (LBT) | 4,806 | 2% |
| 11 | * J. Marvin Leath (D) | no major opposition | |
| 12 | * James Wright Jr. (D) | 109,125 | 62% |
| | Jim Bradshaw (R) | 67,225 | 38% |
| 13 | * John Hightower (D) | 98,564 | 55% |
| | Ron Slover (R) | 80,789 | 45% |
| 14 | William N. Patman (D) | 89,058 | 57% |
| | Charles L. Concklin (R) | 67,540 | 43% |
| 15 | * Eligio de la Garza (D) | 102,204 | 70% |
| | Lendy McDonald (R) | 42,926 | 30% |
| 16 | * Richard C. White (D) | 104,549 | 85% |
| | Catherine A. McDivitt (LBT) | 18,983 | 15% |
| 17 | * Charles W. Stenholm (D) | no major opposition | |
| 18 | * Mickey Leland (D) | 71,986 | 80% |
| | C. L. Kennedy (R) | 16,128 | 18% |
| | Bill Fraser (LBT) | 1,983 | 2% |
| 19 | * Kent Hance (D) | 124,419 | 93% |
| | J. D. Webster (LBT) | 8,737 | 7% |
| 20 | * Henry B. Gonzalez (D) | 84,113 | 82% |
| | Merle W. Nash (R) | 17,725 | 17% |
| 21 | * Tom Loeffler (R) | 185,821 | 76% |
| | Joe Sullivan (D) | 57,800 | 23% |
| 22 | * Ron Paul (R) | 106,766 | 51% |
| | Mike Andrews (D) | 101,121 | 49% |
| 23 | * Abraham Kazen Jr. (D) | 91,148 | 71% |
| | Bobby Locke (R) | 37,109 | 29% |
| 24 | * Martin Frost (D) | 91,000 | 62% |
| | Clay Smothers (R) | 55,564 | 38% |
| **UTAH** | | | |
| 1 | James V. Hansen (R) | 156,211 | 52% |
| | * Gunn McKay (D) | 143,049 | 48% |
| 2 | * Dan Marriott (R) | 193,120 | 69% |
| | Arthur L. Monson (D) | 87,459 | 31% |
| **VERMONT** | | | |
| AL | * James M. Jeffords (R) | 153,368 | 79% |
| | Robin Lloyd (CIT) | 25,191 | 13% |
| | Peter Diamondstone (LU) | 15,189 | 8% |

| DIST. | CANDIDATES AND PARTY | VOTES | PERCENT |
|---|---|---|---|
| **VIRGINIA** | | | |
| 1 | * Paul S. Trible Jr. (R) | 130,583 | 91% |
| | Sharon D. Grant (I) | 13,585 | 9% |
| 2 | * G. William Whitehurst (R) | 95,913 | 90% |
| | Kenneth P. Morrison (LBT) | 10,820 | 10% |
| 3 | Thomas J. Bliley Jr. (R) | 96,619 | 58% |
| | John A. Mapp (D) | 60,960 | 36% |
| | James B. Turney (LBT) | 9,832 | 6% |
| 4 | * Robert W. Daniel Jr. (R) | 92,444 | 61% |
| | Cecil Y. Jenkins (D) | 59,476 | 39% |
| 5 | * W. C. (Dan) Daniel (D) | no major opposition | |
| 6 | * M. Caldwell Butler (R) | no major opposition | |
| 7 | * J. Kenneth Robinson (R) | no major opposition | |
| 8 | Stanford E. Parris (R) | 95,556 | 50% |
| | * Herbert E. Harris II (D) | 94,391 | 50% |
| 9 | * William C. Wampler (R) | 116,089 | 69% |
| | Roosevelt Ferguson (D) | 51,471 | 31% |
| 10 | Frank R. Wolf (R) | 105,606 | 52% |
| | * Joseph L. Fisher (D) | 98,673 | 48% |
| **WASHINGTON** | | | |
| 1 | * Joel Pritchard (R) | 162,298 | 78% |
| | Robin Drake (D) | 38,542 | 18% |
| | Maurice Willey (SW) | 7,603 | 4% |
| 2 | * Al Swift (D) | 146,847 | 64% |
| | Neal Snider (R) | 73,688 | 32% |
| | William L. McCord (LBT) | 8,453 | 4% |
| 3 | * Don Bonker (D) | 136,744 | 63% |
| | Rod Culp (R) | 80,122 | 37% |
| 4 | Sid Morrison (R) | 119,585 | 57% |
| | * Mike McCormack (D) | 90,133 | 43% |
| 5 | * Thomas S. Foley (D) | 108,520 | 52% |
| | John Sonneland (R) | 101,106 | 48% |
| 6 | * Norman D. Dicks (D) | 101,214 | 54% |
| | Jim Beaver (R) | 86,653 | 46% |
| 7 | * Mike Lowry (D) | 101,439 | 58% |
| | Ron Dunlap (R) | 74,650 | 42% |
| **WEST VIRGINIA** | | | |
| 1 | * Robert H. Mollohan (D) | 107,119 | 64% |
| | Joe Bartlett (R) | 61,273 | 36% |
| 2 | Cleve Benedict (R) | 102,200 | 56% |
| | Pat R. Hamilton (D) | 80,661 | 44% |
| 3 | Mick Staton (R) | 94,084 | 53% |
| | * John G. Hutchinson (D) | 84,076 | 47% |
| 4 | * Nick Joe Rahall (D) | 115,938 | 77% |
| | Winton G. Covey, Jr. (R) | 35,405 | 23% |
| **WISCONSIN** | | | |
| 1 | * Les Aspin (D) | 126,331 | 56% |
| | Kathryn H. Canary (R) | 95,960 | 43% |
| | Arthur F. Jackson (LBT) | 2,156 | 1% |
| 2 | * Robert W. Kastenmeier (D) | 142,031 | 54% |
| | James A. Wright (R) | 119,435 | 45% |
| 3 | Steven Gunderson (R) | 131,581 | 51% |
| | * Alvin Baldus (D) | 126,797 | 49% |
| 4 | * Clement J. Zablocki (D) | 144,572 | 70% |
| | Elroy C. Honadel (R) | 60,578 | 30% |
| 5 | * Henry S. Reuss (D) | 129,509 | 78% |
| | David Bathke (R) | 37,366 | 22% |
| 6 | * Thomas E. Petri (R) | 143,992 | 59% |
| | Gary R. Goyke (D) | 98,616 | 41% |
| 7 | * David R. Obey (D) | 162,010 | 65% |
| | Vinton A. Vesta (R) | 89,134 | 35% |
| 8 | * Tobias Roth (R) | 169,296 | 68% |
| | Michael R. Monfils (D) | 81,474 | 32% |
| 9 | * F. J. Sensenbrenner Jr. (R) | 204,972 | 79% |
| | Gary C. Benedict (D) | 56,040 | 21% |
| **WYOMING** | | | |
| AL | * Richard B. Cheney (R) | 116,344 | 69% |
| | Jim Rogers (D) | 53,309 | 31% |

# Energy and Resources

Row of underground earth-sheltered houses in Minneapolis, Minn., snuggles beside high-rise towers. Called the Underground Space Center, the housing was constructed under supervision of the University of Minnesota's department of civil and mineral engineering to demonstrate that such underground structures provide one of the most effective means of conserving energy.

Wide World

## HIGHLIGHTS: 1980

### DEVELOPMENT OF SYNFUELS

Called the "keystone of a national energy policy" by President Carter, the Energy Security Act was signed into law in White House ceremonies on June 30, 1980. The act creates a public corporation to encourage the development by private industry of facilities capable of producing 2 million barrels a day of synthetic fuels by the year 1992. Named the U.S. Synthetic Fuels Corporation, the body will dispense up to $88 billion in stimulating the production of oil substitutes from such resources as coal, oil shale, and tar sands.

"The Energy Security Act," President Carter said, "will launch this decade with the greatest outpouring of capital investment, technology, manpower, and resources since the space program. Its scope, in fact, is so great that it will dwarf the combined efforts expended to put Americans on the Moon and to build the entire Interstate Highway System of our country.

On Sept. 10 the President named John C. Sawhill as chairman and chief executive officer of the corporation. A former president of New York University, Sawhill had served as

**HIGHLIGHTS: 1980** *(continued)*

deputy secretary of the Department of Energy since 1979.

Because the aid to private enterprise will take the form of loans and price guarantees, much of the $88 billion may not actually be spent by the government, if the synthetic fuel plants are commercially successful.

**OIL WINDFALL PROFITS TAX**

Another major aspect of President Carter's national energy policy was signed into law on April 2, 1980, levying a tax on oil company profits that is expected to generate $227 billion in government revenues during the next decade. The tax would be phased out in the period 1988–91.

The legislation calls for taxes of 30% to 70% of the difference between the base price for producing a barrel of oil before 1979 and the higher amounts charged consumers as the result of government decontrol of oil prices. In effect, it gives the government a share in an estimated $1 trillion dollars in higher prices consumers are expected to pay because of the inflation brought by the ending of price controls on oil.

The law increased the tax credit for residential installation of energy-saving devices, allowing a credit of 40% of the first $10,000 in expenditures to a maximum of $4,000.

Revenues from the tax were earmarked to be spent with 60% going to income tax reductions, 25% to aid low-income families meet higher energy costs, and 15% for financing new energy and transportation programs.

## U.S. ENERGY PRODUCTION: 1940–2000

Source: U.S. Department of Energy

| YEAR | TOTAL [1] | COAL | OIL [2] | NATURAL GAS | OTHER [3] |
|---|---|---|---|---|---|
| 1940 | 25,088 | 53.3% | 31.3% | 11.9% | 3.5% |
| 1950 | 34,540 | 42.3% | 35.5% | 18.0% | 4.2% |
| 1960 | 41,780 | 26.6% | 39.2% | 30.3% | 3.9% |
| 1970 | 62,510 | 24.1% | 36.6% | 34.7% | 4.6% |
| 1975 | 60,060 | 25.3% | 33.5% | 32.7% | 8.5% |
| 1978 | 61,210 | 24.5% | 33.8% | 31.9% | 6.2% |
| 1979 [4] | 62,800 | 27.7% | 32.5% | 30.6% | 9.2% |
| 1985 [5] | 70,900 | 35.2% | 26.4% | 25.7% | 12.7% |
| 1990 [5] | 79,400 | 36.8% | 24.6% | 23.6% | 15.0% |
| 1995 [5] | 87,600 | 41.9% | 22.1% | 20.3% | 15.7% |
| 2000 [5] | 98,000 | 39.0% | 20.9% | 16.7% | 23.4% |

[1] In trillions of BTUs. [2] Includes natural-gas plant liquids. [3] Includes nuclear, hydropower, and geothermal energy sources. [4] Preliminary data. [5] Estimated under mid-demand/mid-supply assumptions.

In signing the windfall profits tax legislation, President Carter hailed the tax for making it possible to "divert the unearned profits of the American oil companies to our poor, to improving rapid transit, urban transit, to providing new energy sources, and to conservation of energy."

**CONTROVERSIAL SPS PROPOSAL**

One of the most controversial proposals to solve the U.S. dilemma of what to do in order to become independent of foreign sources of oil has been the suggestion for construction of a Solar Power Satellite (SPS) to generate electricity from solar power. Since 1977 the project has been under study by a special office headed by Fred Koomanoff in the Department of Energy.

## ENERGY RESERVES[1] OF THE WORLD AND OF THE UNITED STATES

Source: U.S. Department of Energy, 1980

At current rates of production, the United States' reserves of petroleum will be used up in eight years—by 1988—and natural-gas reserves will be used up in 10 years—by 1990, according to data released in 1980 by the U.S. Department of Energy.

| ENERGY SOURCES | WORLD | UNITED STATES | U.S. % OF WORLD TOTAL |
|---|---|---|---|
| **PETROLEUM[2]** (in metric tons): | | | |
| Known recoverable petroleum reserves, 1978 | 87,258,000,000 | 3,604,000,000 | 4.1% |
| Annual petroleum production | 2,974,000,000 | 432,000,000 | 14.5% |
| Years remaining that known petroleum reserves would last at present rate of consumption | 29 years | 8 years | — |
| **NATURAL GAS** (in cubic meters): | | | |
| Known recoverable natural-gas reserves, 1979 | 72,848,000,000,000 | 5,493,000,000,000 | 7.5% |
| Annual natural-gas production | 1,455,000,000,000 | 567,000,000,000 | 39.0% |
| Years remaining that known natural-gas reserves would last at present rate of production | 50 years | 10 years | — |
| **URANIUM** (in metric tons): | | | |
| Known recoverable uranium reserves, 1979 | 3,872,680 | 719,780 | 19.0% |
| Annual uranium production | 40,757 | 15,918 | 39.0% |
| Years remaining known uranium reserves would last at present rate of production | 95 years | 45 years | — |
| **COAL** (in metric tons): | | | |
| Known recoverable coal reserves, 1974 | 501,157,000,000 | 154,030,000,000 | 30.7% |
| Annual coal production | 3,018,000,000 | 515,000,000 | 17.1% |
| Years remaining known coal reserves would last at present rate of production | 166 years | 299 years | — |

[1] As of 1976. [2] Including natural-gas plant liquids.

A $200 million experimental facility to convert coal into oil was completed in 1980 at the Exxon corporation's petroleum refinery in Baytown, Texas. Constructed over a period of two years, the plant covers a 20-acre site. Coal is stored in the multistory tower, *left*, and is carried to the refinery in the overhead pipe.

United Press Int'l.

The project envisages the construction in space of a huge space station that would collect solar energy, turn it into electricity, and then beam it to Earth in the form of microwaves.

Opposition to the project is led by the Citizens' Energy Project of Washington D.C., which estimates it would cost $500 billion to $800 billion, would take 30 years to complete, would provide only 10% of U.S. energy needs and would not be cost-effective compared with generating electricity from coal or nuclear fuel.

Proponents of the SPS program are led by the L-5 Society of Tucson, Ariz., which takes its name from Lagrange Point 5, a location in space equidistant between the Earth and the Moon where a permanent space station could be located. The L-5 Society contends the system could be developed in 15 to 25 years, that the microwaves beamed to Earth would be harmless, and that such SPS systems "can supply virtually unlimited amounts of energy to any part of the globe." Proponents believe the SPS system would make it possible for the U.S. to again become an energy-exporting nation, improving its balance of payments in foreign trade that run at a deficit because of the need to import foreign oil.

### TAPPING OCEAN HEAT ENERGY

In August Congress authorized the expenditure of $75 million by the Department of Energy to begin development of pilot ocean thermal plants. Electricity would be generated by utilizing the temperature differences of the ocean, which is warm on the surface and cold at great depths.

Westinghouse Electric Corporation received patents in 1980 for the design of such a system. A mushroom-shaped structure about 300 feet wide would float on the

## U.S. CONSUMPTION OF ENERGY AND ENERGY RESOURCES: 1950–2000
Source: U.S. Department of Energy

| YEAR | COAL (tons) | NATURAL GAS (cu. ft.) | PETROLEUM (barrels)[2] | ELECTRICITY Hydro and geothermal power (megawatt hrs.) | Nuclear power (megawatt hrs.) |
|---|---|---|---|---|---|
| 1950 | 494,100,000 | 5,770,000,000,000 | 2,357,000,000 | 102,700,000 | — |
| 1955 | 447,000,000 | 8,690,000,000,000 | 3,086,000,000 | 120,400,000 | — |
| 1958 | 385,700,000 | 10,300,000,000,000 | 3,328,000,000 | 147,000,000 | — |
| 1959 | 385,100,000 | 11,320,000,000,000 | 3,467,000,000 | 144,800,000 | 200,000 |
| 1960 | 398,000,000 | 11,970,000,000,000 | 3,586,000,000 | 153,600,000 | 200,000 |
| 1961 | 390,300,000 | 12,490,000,000,000 | 3,641,000,000 | 157,500,000 | 500,000 |
| 1962 | 402,200,000 | 13,270,000,000,000 | 3,796,000,000 | 172,200,000 | 1,700,000 |
| 1963 | 423,500,000 | 13,970,000,000,000 | 3,921,000,000 | 169,000,000 | 2,300,000 |
| 1964 | 445,700,000 | 14,810,000,000,000 | 4,034,000,000 | 182,200,000 | 3,200,000 |
| 1965 | 472,000,000 | 15,280,000,000,000 | 4,202,000,000 | 197,000,000 | 3,300,000 |
| 1966 | 497,700,000 | 16,450,000,000,000 | 4,411,000,000 | 199,100,000 | 3,700,000 |
| 1967 | 491,400,000 | 17,390,000,000,000 | 4,585,000,000 | 224,900,000 | 5,500,000 |
| 1968 | 509,900,000 | 18,630,000,000,000 | 4,902,000,000 | 225,900,000 | 7,700,000 |
| 1969 | 516,400,000 | 20,060,000,000,000 | 5,106,000,000 | 254,600,000 | 12,500,000 |
| 1970 | 523,200,000 | 21,140,000,000,000 | 5,364,000,000 | 252,100,000 | 13,900,000 |
| 1971 | 501,500,000 | 21,790,000,000,000 | 5,553,000,000 | 272,800,000 | 21,800,000 |
| 1972 | 524,200,000 | 22,100,000,000,000 | 5,990,000,000 | 283,400,000 | 38,100,000 |
| 1973 | 562,600,000 | 22,050,000,000,000 | 6,317,000,000 | 289,500,000 | 54,100,000 |
| 1974 | 558,400,000 | 21,220,000,000,000 | 6,078,000,000 | 316,800,000 | 83,500,000 |
| 1975 | 562,600,000 | 19,540,000,000,000 | 5,958,000,000 | 309,100,000 | 114,000,000 |
| 1976 | 603,800,000 | 19,950,000,000,000 | 6,391,000,000 | 295,500,000 | 172,500,000 |
| 1977 | 625,300,000 | 19,520,000,000,000 | 6,727,000,000 | 241,400,000 | 191,100,000 |
| 1978 | 625,200,000 | 19,630,000,000,000 | 6,879,000,000 | 301,600,000 | 250,900,000 |
| 1979* | 680,900,000 | 19,490,000,000,000 | 6,707,000,000 | 287,800,000 | 276,400,000 |
| 1985 | 1,045,100,000 | 17,590,000,000,000 | 5,506,000,000 | 342,940,000 | 255,400,000 |
| 1990 | 1,235,300,000 | 18,840,000,000,000 | 5,566,000,000 | 365,530,000 | 507,560,000 |
| 1995 | 1,572,300,000 | 18,050,000,000,000 | 5,521,000,000 | 404,650,000 | 741,250,000 |
| 2000 | 1,700,000,000 | 16,570,000,000,000 | 5,790,000,000 | 474,800,000 | 871,370,000 |
| | | | | | 1,060,000,000 |

* Preliminary data.

## U.S. CONSUMPTION OF ENERGY IN TRILLIONS OF BTUs[1]: 1950–2000
Source: U.S. Department of Energy

| YEAR | COAL Anthracite | COAL Bituminous and Lignite | NATURAL GAS | PETROLEUM[2] | ELECTRICITY Hydro | ELECTRICITY Geothermal | ELECTRICITY Nuclear | TOTAL ENERGY USAGE Total BTUs[3] | Change From Prior Year |
|---|---|---|---|---|---|---|---|---|---|
| 1950 | 991 | 11,900 | 5,970 | 13,320 | 1,440 | — | — | 33,621 | +8.1 |
| 1955 | 579 | 10,940 | 9,000 | 17,260 | 1,410 | — | — | 39,189 | +9.3 |
| 1957 | 499 | 10,640 | 10,190 | 17,940 | 1,560 | — | — | 40,829 | +0.3 |
| 1958 | 464 | 9,370 | 10,660 | 18,540 | 1,630 | — | 2 | 40,666 | −0.4 |
| 1959 | 436 | 9,330 | 11,720 | 19,270 | 1,590 | — | 2 | 42,348 | +4.1 |
| 1960 | 426 | 9,690 | 12,390 | 19,920 | 1,650 | — | 6 | 44,082 | +4.1 |
| 1961 | 387 | 9,500 | 12,930 | 20,220 | 1,680 | — | 20 | 44,737 | +1.5 |
| 1962 | 346 | 9,830 | 13,730 | 21,050 | 1,820 | — | 27 | 46,803 | +4.7 |
| 1963 | 336 | 10,360 | 14,400 | 21,700 | 1,770 | — | 38 | 48,604 | +3.9 |
| 1964 | 344 | 10,900 | 15,290 | 22,300 | 1,910 | — | 39 | 50,783 | +4.4 |
| 1965 | 309 | 11,580 | 15,770 | 23,250 | 2,060 | — | 44 | 53,013 | +4.4 |
| 1966 | 271 | 12,210 | 17,000 | 24,130 | 2,070 | — | 64 | 55,745 | +5.1 |
| 1967 | 251 | 11,990 | 17,940 | 25,280 | 2,350 | — | 89 | 57,900 | +3.9 |
| 1968 | 234 | 12,420 | 19,210 | 26,980 | 2,350 | — | 141 | 61,335 | +5.9 |
| 1969 | 203 | 12,520 | 20,680 | 28,340 | 2,660 | — | 153 | 64,556 | +5.2 |
| 1970 | 190 | 12,470 | 21,800 | 29,520 | 2,650 | 11 | 239 | 66,880 | +3.6 |
| 1971 | 170 | 11,840 | 22,470 | 30,560 | 2,860 | 11 | 413 | 68,824 | +2.6 |
| 1972 | 136 | 12,310 | 22,700 | 32,950 | 2,940 | 31 | 584 | 71,651 | +4.1 |
| 1973 | 129 | 13,170 | 22,510 | 34,840 | 3,010 | 43 | 908 | 74,650 | +4.0 |
| 1974 | 120 | 12,760 | 21,730 | 33,050 | 3,310 | 53 | 1,270 | 72,293 | −3.1 |
| 1975 | 111 | 12,710 | 19,950 | 32,730 | 3,220 | 70 | 1,900 | 70,691 | −2.1 |
| 1976 | 112 | 13,620 | 20,350 | 34,830 | 3,070 | 78 | 2,110 | 74,150 | +4.9 |
| 1977 | 115 | 14,000 | 19,930 | 37,180 | 2,520 | 77 | 2,700 | 76,522 | +3.1 |
| 1978 | | 13,850 | 20,000 | 37,970 | 3,170 | 60 | 2,980 | 78,030 | +2.0 |
| 1979[4] | | 15,080 | 19,860 | 37,020 | 3,160 | 80 | 2,750 | 77,950 | −0.1 |
| 1985[5] | | 25,000 | 19,000 | 30,800 | 3,400 | | 5,600 | 83,880 | — |
| 1990[5] | | 29,300 | 19,500 | 31,300 | 3,700 | | 8,200 | 92,000 | — |
| 1995[5] | | 36,700 | 18,600 | 31,200 | 4,100 | | 9,600 | 100,200 | — |
| 2000[5] | | 38,200 | 17,100 | 33,600 | 11,700 | | 11,300 | 111,900 | — |

[1] One British Thermal Unit (BTU) is the quantity of heat required to raise the temperature of 1 pound of water 1 degree Fahrenheit at or near 39.2° F.   [2] Including liquids from natural-gas plants.   [3] Does not include synthetics, solar technology, and new technologies.   [4] Preliminary.   [5] Estimated under Mid Supply/Mid Demand Assumptions.

Police engaged in a tug of war with anti-nuclear activists at Seabrook, N.H., in May 1980 as some 1,000 demonstrators tried to barricade the main entrance to prevent continued construction of a $3.1 billion atomic power plant.

United Press Int'l.

surface, generating about 100 million watts of electricity with a steam turbine operating on thermal energy without additional fuel. The system also would produce large quantities of drinking water from seawater.

## REDUCED ENERGY CONSUMPTION

Energy conservation awareness, higher gasoline prices, a mild winter, and economic recession combined in 1979–80 to ease the U.S. energy problems.

In 1979 the consumption of electricity went up only 2.8% compared with an anticipated 7% rate of growth. Overall, the Department of Energy estimated that the use of all sources of energy declined by 0.1% instead of increasing by 2.3% as had been expected.

However, the Department of Energy estimates that by the year 2000 U.S. energy needs will rise 44% over the 1979 level. Much of the increased energy is expected from by a 154% greater consumption of coal during the two decades.

## HOW TO SAVE ENERGY AND MONEY ON HOME APPLIANCES

Source: U.S. Department of Energy, Offices of Conservation and Applied Analysis

If you let a single 100-watt light bulb burn steadily all year long, it would use 876 kilowatt-hours (kwh) of electricity. At a cost of 4.61¢ per kwh, this would add $40.38 to your electric bill. If you substituted a 60-watt bulb, *you would save $16.15.*

The average annual energy use and annual energy cost of home appliances in a typical American home are shown in the following table.

| ELECTRIC APPLIANCE | ANNUAL ENERGY USE | ANNUAL COST | ELECTRIC APPLIANCE | ANNUAL ENERGY USE | ANNUAL COST |
|---|---|---|---|---|---|
| Air conditioner | 1,200 kwh | $55.32 | Iron | 103 kwh | $ 4.75 |
| Can opener | 3 kwh | 0.14 | Lighting | 1,870 kwh | 86.20 |
| Clock | 20 kwh | 0.92 | Microwave oven | 100 kwh | 4.61 |
| Clothes dryer | 1,000 kwh | 46.10 | Radio | 70 kwh | 3.22 |
| Coffee maker | 118 kwh | 5.44 | Radio-phonograph | 100 kwh | 4.61 |
| Dishwasher | 1,700 kwh | 78.37 | Range | 750 kwh | 34.58 |
| Electric blanket | 138 kwh | 6.36 | Refrigerator (12 cu. ft.) | 750 kwh | 34.58 |
| Fan (attic) | 290 kwh | 13.37 | Sewing machine | 10 kwh | 0.46 |
| Fan (furnace) | 480 kwh | 22.13 | Shaver | 1 kwh | 0.05 |
| Fluorescent light | 260 kwh | 11.99 | Television (black and white) | 150 kwh | 6.92 |
| Food freezer (16 cu. ft.) | 1,600 kwh | 73.66 | Television (color) | 300 kwh | 13.83 |
| Food mixer | 10 kwh | 0.46 | Toaster | 38 kwh | 1.75 |
| Food waste disposer | 30 kwh | 1.38 | Vacuum cleaner | 45 kwh | 2.07 |
| Frying pan | 148 kwh | 6.82 | Washer (clothes) | 1,400 kwh | 64.54 |
| Hair dryer | 18 kwh | 0.83 | Water heater (all-electric) | 7,000 kwh | 322.70 |
| Hot plate | 102 kwh | 4.70 | | | |

* 4.61¢ per kwh is the 1979 national average for residential users.

## WORLD'S LARGEST HYDROELECTRIC GENERATING PLANTS

Source: *Water Power & Dam Construction;* In part, U.S. Bureau of Reclamation, Department of the Interior

| RANK | DAM | LOCATION | CAPACITY (in megawatts) Present | Ultimate | BEGAN OPERATION |
|---|---|---|---|---|---|
| 1 | Itaipu (Paraná River) | Brazil–Paraguay | — | 12,870 | UC |
| 2 | Grand Coulee (Columbia River) | Washington | 6,480 | 10,080 | 1942 |
| 3 | Guri (Caroni River) | Venezuela | 2,030 | 9,200 | 1967 |
| 4 | Tucurui | Brazil | — | 6,500 | UC |
| 5 | Sayanskaya (Yenesei River) | Soviet Union | — | 6,400 | 1980 |
| 6 | Krasnoyarsk (Yenesei River) | Soviet Union | 6,096 | 6,096 | 1968 |
| 7 | La Grande (La Grande River) | Quebec, Canada | — | 5,328 | 1979 |
| 8 | Churchill Falls (Churchill River) | Newfoundland, Canada | 5,225 | 5,225 | 1971 |
| 9 | Bratsk (Angara River) | Soviet Union | 4,600 | 4,600 | 1964 |
| 10 | Sukhovo (Sukhona River) | Soviet Union | — | 4,500 | UC |
| 11 | Ust-Ilimsk (Angara River) | Soviet Union | 720 | 4,500 | 1974 |
| 12 | Cabora Basa (Zambezi River) | Mozambique | 2,000 | 4,000 | 1975 |
| 13 | Rogunsky (Vakhsh River) | Soviet Union | — | 3,600 | UC |
| 14 | Paulo Afonso (São Francisco River) | Brazil | 1,524 | 3,409 | 1955 |
| 15 | Solteira (Paraná River) | Brazil | 3,200 | 3,200 | 1973 |
| 16 | Inga (Zaire River) | Zaire | 360 | 2,820 | 1974 |
| 17 | John Day (Columbia River) | Oregon–Washington | 2,160 | 2,700 | 1968 |
| 18 | Nurek (Vakhsh River) | Soviet Union | 1,000 | 2,700 | 1976 |
| 19 | Revelstoke (Columbia River) | British Columbia, Canada | — | 2,700 | 1983 UC |
| 20 | São Simao (Paranaba River) | Brazil | — | 2,680 | 1979 |
| 21 | Mica (Columbia River) | British Columbia, Canada | 1,736 | 2,610 | 1976 |
| 22 | Volgograd—22d Congress | Soviet Union | 2,530 | 2,530 | 1958 |
| 23 | Chiocasen (Grijalva River) | Mexico | — | 2,400 | 1980 |
| 24 | Volga–V.I. Lenin (Volga River) | Soviet Union | 2,300 | 2,300 | 1955 |
| 25 | Iron Gate S.I. (Danube River) | Romania–Yugoslavia | 2,300 | 2,300 | 1970 |
| 26 | W.A.C. Bennett (Peace River) | British Columbia, Canada | 2,416 | 2,416 | 1968 |
| 27 | Foz Do Areia | Brazil | 2,250 | 2,250 | UC |
| 28 | High Aswan (Saad–El–Aali) (Nile R.) | Egypt | 2,100 | 2,100 | 1967 |
| 29 | Tarbela (Indus River) | Pakistan | 700 | 2,100 | 1977 |
| 30 | Itumbiara (Paranaba River) | Brazil | — | 2,080 | UC |
| 31 | Chief Joseph (Columbia River) | Washington–Oregon | 1,024 | 2,069 | 1956 |
| 32 | Salto Santiago | Brazil | — | 1,998 | 1980 |
| 33 | Robert Moses—Niagara | New York | 1,950 | 1,950 | 1961 |
| 34 | Salto Grande | Argentina/Uruguay | — | 1,890 | 1981 |
| 35 | Dinorwic | Britain | — | 1,880 | 1980 |

## WORLD'S HIGHEST DAMS

Source: *Water Power & Dam Construction;* In part, U.S. Bureau of Reclamation

| RANK | NAME, LOCATION | TYPE | HEIGHT (feet) | COMPLETED |
|---|---|---|---|---|
| 1 | Rogunsky, Soviet Union | E | 1,082 | UC |
| 2 | Nurek, Soviet Union | E | 1,040 | UC |
| 3 | Grande Dixence, Switz. | G | 935 | 1962 |
| 4 | Inguri, Soviet Union | A | 892 | UC |
| 5 | Chiocasen, Mexico | R | 866 | 1980 |
| 6 | Vaiont, Italy | A | 858 | 1961 |
| 7 | Tehri, India | ER | 856 | 1989 UC |
| 8 | Mica, Canada | R | 803 | 1976 |
| 9 | Sayanskaya, Soviet Union | A | 794 | 1980 |
| 10 | Patia, Colombia | R | 787 | UC |
| 11 | Chivor, Colombia | R | 778 | 1975 |
| 12 | Mauvoisin, Switzerland | A | 777 | 1957 |
| 13 | Oroville, California | E | 770 | 1968 |
| 14 | Chirkey, Soviet Union | A | 764 | 1975 |
| 15 | Bhakra, India | G | 742 | 1963 |
| 16 | El Cajon, Honduras | A | 741 | UC |
| 17 | Hoover, Ariz.–Nev. | A-G | 726 | 1936 |
| 18 | Contra, Switzerland | A | 722 | 1965 |
| 19 | Mratinje, Yugoslavia | A | 722 | 1975 |
| 20 | Dworshak, Idaho | G | 717 | 1974 |
| 21 | Glen Canyon, Arizona | A | 710 | 1964 |
| 22 | Toktogol, Soviet Union | G | 705 | 1977 |
| 23 | Daniel Johnson, Canada | MA | 703 | 1968 |
| 24 | Luzzone, Switzerland | A | 682 | 1963 |
| 25 | Keban, Turkey | ERG | 679 | 1974 |

## WORLD'S LARGEST DAMS

Source: *Water Power & Dam Construction;* In part, U.S. Bureau of Reclamation

| RANK | NAME, LOCATION | VOLUME (cubic yds.) | COMPLETED |
|---|---|---|---|
| 1 | New Cornelia Tailings, Ariz. | 274,026,000 | 1973 |
| 2 | Tarbela, Pakistan | 186,000 | 1975 |
| 3 | Fort Peck, Montana | 125,612,000 | 1940 |
| 4 | Guri, Venezuela | 102,000 | UC |
| 5 | Oahe, South Dakota | 92,008,000 | 1963 |
| 6 | Oosterschelde, Neth. | 91,560,000 | 1980 |
| 7 | Mangla, Pakistan | 85,872,000 | 1967 |
| 8 | Gardiner, Canada | 85,600,000 | 1968 |
| 9 | Afsluitdijk, Netherlands | 82,927,000 | 1932 |
| 10 | Rogunsky, Soviet Union | 81,096,000 | UC |
| 11 | Yacyreta–Apípe, Arg.-Para. | 80,000,000 | UC |
| 12 | Oroville, California | 78,008,000 | 1968 |
| 13 | San Luis, California | 77,666,000 | 1967 |
| 14 | Nurek, Soviet Union | 75,864,000 | UC |
| 15 | Garrison, North Dakota | 66,506,000 | 1956 |
| 16 | Cochiti, New Mexico | 62,130,000 | 1975 |
| 17 | Tabka, Syria | 60,168,000 | 1975 |
| 18 | Kiev, Soviet Union | 57,552,000 | 1964 |
| 19 | W.A.C. Bennett, Canada | 57,159,000 | 1968 |
| 20 | Aswan High Dam, Egypt | 57,203,000 | 1970 |
| 21 | Tucurui, Brazil | 56,244,000 | UC |
| 22 | Dantiwada, India | 53,680,000 | 1965 |
| 23 | Saratov, Soviet Union | 52,843,000 | 1967 |
| 24 | Mission Tailings # 2, Ariz. | 52,435,000 | 1973 |
| 25 | Fort Randall, S.D. | 50,205,000 | 1956 |

E=Earth;   UC=Under Construction;   G=Gravity;   A=Arch;   R=Rockfill;   MA=Multi-arch.

## ELECTRICITY GENERATED BY ATOMIC POWER

Source: International Atomic Energy Agency

In 1980 a total of 21 countries had 238 operating reactors producing 124,403 megawatts of electricity. A total of 341 more were under construction or planned with an additional power output of 314,913 megawatts. Only 26 years earlier, in 1954, there were just two atomic reactors in the world that could generate electricity. They had a total output of 7.4 megawatts of electricity.

| RANK | COUNTRY | NUMBER OF REACTORS | ELECTRICITY OUTPUT (in megawatts) | RANK | COUNTRY | NUMBER OF REACTORS | ELECTRICITY OUTPUT (in megawatts) |
|---|---|---|---|---|---|---|---|
| 1 | United States .. | 70 | 50,900 | 12 | Belgium ....... | 4 | 1,676 |
| 2 | Japan ......... | 22 | 14,316 | 13 | Italy.......... | 4 | 1,382 |
| 3 | Soviet Union ... | 32 | 11,616 | 14 | Spain ........ | 3 | 1,073 |
| 4 | France ........ | 18 | 9,983 | 15 | Bulgaria ...... | 2 | 816 |
| 5 | West Germany . | 14 | 8,607 | 16 | Czechoslovakia. | 2 | 801 |
| 6 | Britain ........ | 32 | 6,890 | 17 | India ......... | 3 | 602 |
| 7 | Canada ....... | 10 | 5,245 | 18 | South Korea ... | 1 | 564 |
| 8 | Sweden........ | 6 | 3,700 | 19 | Netherlands ... | 2 | 499 |
| 9 | Switzerland .... | 4 | 1,940 | 20 | Argentina...... | 1 | 335 |
| 10 | Finland ....... | 3 | 1,740 | 21 | Pakistan ...... | 1 | 125 |
| 11 | East Germany .. | 5 | 1,695 | | TOTAL ........ | 238 | 124,403 |

## WORLD'S LARGEST OPERATING ATOMIC ELECTRIC POWER REACTORS

Source: International Atomic Energy Agency

| RANK | NAME | LOCATION | TYPE OF REACTOR* | ELECTRICITY NET OUTPUT (in megawatts) | BEGAN COMMERCIAL OPERATION |
|---|---|---|---|---|---|
| 1 | Biblis–B ............ | Biblis, Hesse, West Germany ............ | PWR | 1,240 | 1977 |
| 2 | KKU Unterweser ..... | Stadland, West Germany ............ | PWR | 1,230 | 1979 |
| 3 | Biblis–A ............ | Biblis, Hesse, West Germany ............ | PWR | 1,146 | 1975 |
| 4 | Ohi–1 ............. | Ohi, Fukui, Japan ............ | PWR | 1,120 | 1978 |
| 5 | Ohi–2 ............. | Ohi, Fukui, Japan ............ | PWR | 1,120 | 1979 |
| 6 | Trojan ............. | Prescott, Oregon ............ | PWR | 1,095 | 1975 |
| 7 | Salem–1 ............ | Salem, New Jersey............ | PWR | 1,090 | 1977 |
| 8 | Browns Ferry–1 ..... | Decatur, Alabama ............ | BWR | 1,067 | 1974 |
| 9 | Browns Ferry–2 ..... | Decatur, Alabama ............ | BWR | 1,067 | 1975 |
| 10 | Browns Ferry–3 ..... | Decatur, Alabama ............ | BWR | 1,067 | 1977 |
| 11 | Fukushima 1–6...... | Futaba, Fukushima, Japan ............ | BWR | 1,067 | 1979 |
| 12 | Tokai–2 ............ | Tokaimura, Ibaraki, Japan ............ | BWR | 1,056 | 1978 |
| 13 | Peach Bottom–2..... | York County, Pennsylvania ............ | BWR | 1,050 | 1974 |
| 14 | Donald C. Cook–1.... | Bridgman, Michigan ............ | PWR | 1,045 | 1975 |
| 15 | Donald C. Cook–2.... | Bridgman, Michigan ............ | PWR | 1,045 | 1978 |
| 16 | Zion–1 ............. | Zion, Illinois............ | PWR | 1,040 | 1973 |
| 17 | Zion–2 ............. | Zion, Illinois............ | PWR | 1,040 | 1974 |
| 18 | Peach Bottom–3..... | York County, Pennsylvania ............ | BWR | 1,035 | 1974 |
| 19 | Leningrad–1 ........ | Leningrad, Soviet Union ............ | LWGR | 1,000 | 1974 |
| 20 | Leningrad–2 ........ | Leningrad, Soviet Union ............ | LWGR | 1,000 | 1975 |
| 21 | Leningrad–3 ........ | Leningrad, Soviet Union ............ | LWGR | 1,000 | 1979 |
| 22 | Kursk–1 ............ | Kursk, Soviet Union ............ | LWGR | 1,000 | 1976 |
| 23 | Kursk–2 ............ | Kursk, Soviet Union ............ | LWGR | 1,000 | 1979 |
| 24 | Chernobyl–1 ........ | Chernobyl, Soviet Union ............ | LWGR | 1,000 | 1978 |
| 25 | Chernobyl–2 ........ | Chernobyl, Soviet Union ............ | LWGR | 1,000 | 1978 |
| 26 | Indian Point–3...... | Peekskill, New York ............ | PWR | 965 | 1976 |
| 27 | Bugey–2............ | St. Vulbas, France ............ | PWR | 925 | 1978 |
| 28 | Bugey–3............ | St. Vulbas, France ............ | PWR | 925 | 1978 |
| 29 | Bugey–4............ | St. Vulbas, France ............ | PWR | 925 | 1979 |
| 30 | Goesgen............ | Daeniken, Switzerland ............ | PWR | 920 | 1979 |
| 31 | Gravelines B1 ....... | Nord, France ............ | PWR | 920 | 1980 |
| 32 | Rancho Seco–1 ...... | Sacramento, California ............ | PWR | 913 | 1975 |
| 33 | Arkansas One–2 ..... | Pope, Arkansas ............ | PWR | 912 | 1980 |
| 34 | Davis-Besse–1 ...... | Ottawa, Ohio ............ | PWR | 910 | 1978 |
| 35 | Three Mile Island–2 .. | Dauphin County, Pennsylvania ............ | PWR | 905 | 1978 |
| 36 | Bugey–5............ | St. Vulbas, France ............ | PWR | 905 | 1979 |
| 37 | Dampierre–1 ........ | Dampierre, Loire, France ............ | PWR | 900 | 1980 |
| 38 | North Anna–1 ....... | Mineral, Virginia ............ | PWR | 898 | 1978 |
| 39 | Fessenheim–1 ....... | Fessenheim, France............ | PWR | 890 | 1977 |
| 40 | Fessenheim–2 ....... | Fessenheim, France............ | PWR | 890 | 1978 |
| 41 | Tihange–1 .......... | Liège, Belgium ............ | PWR | 880 | 1975 |
| 42 | Calvert Cliffs–1 ..... | Lusby, Maryland............ | PWR | 880 | 1975 |
| 43 | Calvert Cliffs–2..... | Lusby, Maryland............ | PWR | 880 | 1977 |
| 44 | KKI-Isar ............ | Ohu, Bavaria, West Germany ............ | BWR | 870 | 1978 |

\* PWR=Pressurized light-water-moderated and cooled reactor.    BWR=Boiling light-water-cooled and moderated reactor. LWGR=Light-water-cooled, graphite-moderated reactor.

# LEADING PRODUCERS OF ENERGY AND RESOURCES

Source: United Nations, *1978 Statistical Yearbook*

The 8 leading producing nations are listed for each of 24 major types of energy or resources. The U.S. ranks among the 8 top producers in 19 of the following basic resources and leads in 7.

## BAUXITE (Aluminum Ore) [1]

| Country | Amount |
| --- | --- |
| World | 79,600,000 |
| Australia | 22,806,000 |
| Jamaica | 11,420,000 |
| Guinea | 10,841,000 |
| Suriname | 4,856,000 |
| Soviet Union | 4,600,000 |
| Guyana | 3,223,000 |
| Hungary | 2,949,000 |
| Greece | 2,874,000 |

## CEMENT [1]

| Country | Amount |
| --- | --- |
| World | 759,000,000 |
| Soviet Union | 127,056,000 |
| Japan | 73,138,000 |
| United States | 72,627,000 |
| Italy | 38,204,000 |
| China | 40,000,000 |
| W. Germany | 32,163,000 |
| France | 28,956,000 |
| Spain | 27,996,000 |

## COAL [1]

| Country | Amount |
| --- | --- |
| World | 2,475,948,000 |
| United States | 603,772,000 |
| Soviet Union | 499,768,000 |
| China | 490,000,000 |
| Poland | 186,112,000 |
| Britain | 122,150,000 |
| India | 100,110,000 |
| W. Germany | 91,310,000 |
| South Africa | 85,570,000 |

## COPPER ORE [1]

| Country | Amount |
| --- | --- |
| World | 8,000,000 |
| United States | 1,364,400 |
| Soviet Union | 1,100,000 |
| Chile | 1,053,700 |
| Zambia | 819,200 |
| Canada | 780,600 |
| Zaire | 427,200 |
| Peru | 343,600 |
| Poland | 289,000 |

## DIAMONDS [2]

| Country | Amount |
| --- | --- |
| World | 40,366,000 |
| Zaire | 11,210,000 |
| Soviet Union | 9,900,000 |
| South Africa | 8,033,000 |
| Botswana | 2,660,000 |
| Ghana | 2,310,000 |
| Namibia | 2,001,000 |
| Venezuela | 833,000 |
| Sierra Leone | 771,000 |

## ELECTRICITY [3]

| Country | Amount |
| --- | --- |
| World | 7,209,682 |
| United States | 2,211,031 |
| Soviet Union | 1,150,074 |
| Japan | 532,609 |
| W. Germany | 335,320 |
| Canada | 316,549 |
| Britain | 283,280 |
| France | 210,845 |
| Italy | 166,545 |

## FISH CATCHES [1]

| Country | Amount |
| --- | --- |
| World | 73,500,000 |
| Japan | 10,733,300 |
| Soviet Union | 9,352,000 |
| China | 6,880,000 |
| Peru | 2,530,000 |
| Norway | 3,562,200 |
| United States | 3,101,500 |
| India | 2,540,000 |
| South Korea | 2,419,000 |

## FORESTRY (Roundwood) [4]

| Country | Amount |
| --- | --- |
| World | 2,538,000 |
| Soviet Union | 389,000 |
| United States | 341,400 |
| China | 195,200 |
| Brazil | 154,700 |
| Canada | 143,000 |
| Indonesia | 141,400 |
| India | 134,400 |
| Nigeria | 68,900 |

## GAS, MANUFACTURED [6]

| Country | Amount |
| --- | --- |
| World | 618,700,000 |
| Soviet Union | 148,551,000 |
| United States | 121,790,000 |
| W. Germany | 54,342,000 |
| Australia | 34,000,000 |
| Japan | 33,724,000 |
| Czechoslov. | 33,182,000 |
| Poland | 32,755,000 |
| France | 26,229,000 |

## GAS, NATURAL [6]

| Country | Amount |
| --- | --- |
| World | 11,820,600 |
| United States | 4,932,118 |
| Soviet Union | 2,889,335 |
| Netherlands | 732,594 |
| Canada | 685,899 |
| Britain | 376,701 |
| Romania | 320,900 |
| Iran | 202,201 |
| West Germany | 152,419 |

## GOLD [5]

| Country | Amount |
| --- | --- |
| World | 988,000 |
| South Africa | 699,000 |
| Canada | 52,979 |
| Japan | 37,920 |
| United States | 32,547 |
| Papua N.G. | 23,419 |
| Australia | 19,346 |
| Zimbabwe | 19,000 |
| Philippines | 17,363 |

## IRON ORE [1]

| Country | Amount |
| --- | --- |
| World | 482,800,000 |
| Soviet Union | 131,418,000 |
| Brazil | 56,600,000 |
| Australia | 60,164,000 |
| United States | 35,042,000 |
| China | 32,500,000 |
| Canada | 31,828,000 |
| India | 26,520,000 |
| South Africa | 16,576,000 |

## LEAD ORE [1]

| Country | Amount |
| --- | --- |
| World | 3,270,000 |
| United States | 537,500 |
| Soviet Union | 510,000 |
| Australia | 418,200 |
| Canada | 284,100 |
| Peru | 181,500 |
| Mexico | 163,500 |
| Yugoslavia | 130,000 |
| Bulgaria | 115,000 |

## LIGNITE (Brown Coal) [1]

| Country | Amount |
| --- | --- |
| World | 902,279,000 |
| E. Germany | 253,705,000 |
| Soviet Union | 163,513,000 |
| W. Germany | 122,948,000 |
| Czechoslov. | 93,236,000 |
| Poland | 40,780,000 |
| Yugoslavia | 36,752,000 |
| Australia | 29,262,000 |
| United States | 26,517,000 |

## NICKEL [1]

| Country | Amount |
| --- | --- |
| World | 800,600 |
| Canada | 235,361 |
| Soviet Union | 168,000 |
| New Caledonia | 115,476 |
| Australia | 81,099 |
| Cuba | 37,000 |
| Philippines | 30,666 |
| Dom. Rep. | 24,899 |
| South Africa | 21,955 |

## PAPER (Newsprint) [1]

| Country | Amount |
| --- | --- |
| World | 22,708,000 |
| Canada | 8,169,000 |
| United States | 3,188,000 |
| Japan | 2,370,000 |
| Soviet Union | 1,388,000 |
| Sweden | 1,111,000 |
| China | 1,100,000 |
| Finland | 979,000 |
| W. Germany | 544,000 |

## PETROLEUM (Crude) [1]

| Country | Amount |
| --- | --- |
| World | 2,985,879,000 |
| Soviet Union | 545,799,000 |
| Saudi Arabia | 458,460,000 |
| United States | 402,489,000 |
| Iran | 282,608,000 |
| Venezuela | 117,007,000 |
| Iraq | 122,390,000 |
| Nigeria | 102,970,000 |
| Libya | 99,503,000 |

## RUBBER, NATURAL [1]

| Country | Amount |
| --- | --- |
| World | 3,595,000 |
| Malaysia | 1,536,800 |
| Indonesia | 835,000 |
| Thailand | 426,400 |
| India | 151,600 |
| Sri Lanka | 146,200 |
| Liberia | 80,000 |
| Nigeria | 59,200 |
| Philippines | 58,200 |

## RUBBER, SYNTHETIC [1]

| Country | Amount |
| --- | --- |
| World | 6,595,000 |
| United States | 2,527,900 |
| Japan | 971,000 |
| France | 479,000 |
| W. Germany | 414,300 |
| Britain | 329,200 |
| Italy | 240,000 |
| Canada | 237,900 |
| Brazil | 188,100 |

## SILVER [1]

| Country | Amount |
| --- | --- |
| World | 10,240 |
| Mexico | 1,463 |
| Soviet Union | 1,400 |
| Canada | 1,330 |
| United States | 1,227 |
| Peru | 936 |
| Australia | 840 |
| Poland | 550 |
| Japan | 299 |

## STEEL (Crude) [1]

| Country | Amount |
| --- | --- |
| World | 667,000,000 |
| Soviet Union | 146,678,000 |
| United States | 113,701,000 |
| Japan | 102,405,000 |
| W. Germany | 38,985,000 |
| China | 27,000,000 |
| Italy | 23,334,000 |
| France | 22,094,000 |
| Britain | 20,410,000 |

## TIN CONCENTRATES [1]

| Country | Amount |
| --- | --- |
| World | 185,100 |
| Malaysia | 58,703 |
| Bolivia | 30,782 |
| Indonesia | 25,100 |
| Thailand | 24,205 |
| Australia | 10,694 |
| Brazil | 6,400 |
| Britain | 3,851 |
| Zaire | 3,560 |

## URANIUM [1]

| Country | Amount |
| --- | --- |
| World | 28,615 |
| United States | 11,200 |
| South Africa | 6,700 |
| Canada | 6,100 |
| France | 2,200 |
| Niger | 1,609 |
| Gabon | 800 |
| Australia | 400 |
| Spain | 191 |

## ZINC [1]

| Country | Amount |
| --- | --- |
| World | 5,750,000 |
| Canada | 1,054,500 |
| Soviet Union | 720,000 |
| Peru | 477,500 |
| Australia | 475,300 |
| United States | 415,500 |
| Japan | 275,700 |
| Mexico | 265,500 |
| Poland | 216,500 |

[1] In metric tons. [2] In metric carats. [3] In millions of kilowatt hours. [4] In thousands of cubic meters. [5] In kilograms. [6] In trillions of calories.

# Entertainment

United Press Int'l.

Film and TV celebrities, *from left,* Ricardo Montalban, Loretta Swit, Ralph Bellamy, and Jack Klugman join the picket lines at Burbank Studios in Hollywood, Calif., as the Screen Actors Guild and American Federation of Television and Radio Artists unions picket to support a strike that began July 21. The unions, with a combined membership of 70,000, were asking increased wages and benefits, and a share of revenues from programming for pay TV and home video cassettes. The strike affected production of most feature films and prime-time television series. It delayed the beginning of the fall television season and forced layoffs in both film and TV industries. Tentative settlement was reached Sept. 25, but the pact was not officially ratified until Oct. 23. The 95-day walkout was estimated to have cost the film and TV industries $40 million per week in lost goods and services.

## HIGHLIGHTS: 1980

Who shot J. R.? That question rebounded across the U.S. and Europe in the summer of 1980. It referred to the last episode of the spring season in which J. R. Ewing, the villainous Texas oilman of the TV show *Dallas*, was shot. Speculation centered even on J. R., played by actor Larry Hagman, who was thought not to be above shooting himself. The largest TV audience ever, some 83 million persons, watched the episode on Nov. 21 when the answer was revealed.

In the film industry, *Kramer vs. Kramer* swept most of the major awards. It received five Academy Awards, including one for best picture, and was chosen best picture by the New York Film Critics, National Society of Film Critics, and the Hollywood Foreign

Press Association, which administers the Golden Globe Awards. The film, about a man who must make a life for himself and his son after his wife walks out, starred Dustin Hoffman and Meryl Streep, both of whom won Oscars for their respective roles.

An American film, *All That Jazz*, shared the Golden Palm award for best movie at the 33d Cannes Film Festival with a Japanese film, *Kagemusha* (Shadow Warrior). *All That Jazz*, directed by Bob Fosse, was a musical depicting the last month in the life of a flamboyant choreographer-director, played by Roy Scheider. The film won four Academy Awards. A special Cannes jury prize went to French director Alain Resnais for *Mon Oncle d'Amerique* (My American Uncle.)

# MOVIES: 1980

**Airplane** (PG): Satire on series of airplane disaster movies; with Kareem Abdul-Jabbar, Lloyd Bridges; director, Jim Abrahams; Paramount.

**All That Jazz** (R): Musical drama portraying last month of choreographer's life; won four Academy Awards and Cannes Film Festival best picture award; with Roy Scheider, Ann Reinking; director, Bob Fosse; Columbia.

**American Gigolo** (R): Playboy gigolo is framed for murder; with Richard Gere, Lauren Hutton; director, Paul Schrader; Paramount.

**The Big Red One** (PG): World War II drama traces lives of five infantrymen serving together; with Lee Marvin, Mark Hamill, Robert Carradine; director, Samuel Fuller; United Artists.

**The Black Marble** (PG): Comedy about man and woman police duo who eventually fall in love; with Paula Prentiss, Robert Foxworth, Harry Dean Stanton; director, Harold Becker; Avco Embassy.

**The Blue Lagoon** (R): Young boy and girl, marooned on desert island, mature and fall in love; with Brooke Shields, Christopher Atkins; director, Randal Kleiser; Columbia.

**Blues Brothers** (R): Comedy about two men whose preoccupation with black culture and jazz lead them on wild escapades; with John Belushi, Frank Oz, Dan Aykroyd; director, John Landis; Universal.

**Bronco Billy** (PG): Comedy about cowboy traveling around old West with his Wild West Show; with Clint Eastwood, Sondra Locke, Geoffrey Lewis; director, Eastwood; Warner Bros.

**Brubaker** (R): Penologist attempts to reform corrupt prison; with Robert Redford, Jane Alexander; director, Stuart Rosenberg; 20th Century-Fox.

**Caddyshack** (R): Comedy about people at haughty country club; with Chevy Chase, Rodney Dangerfield, Ted Knight; director, Harold Ramis; Warner Bros.

**Can't Stop the Music** (PG): Musical about two friends who start singing group, The Village People; with Valerie Perrine, Bruce Jenner; director, Nancy Walker; Associated Film Distribution.

**Carny** (R): Lives of members of traveling carnival troupe; with Jodie Foster, Gary Busey, Robbie Robertson; director, Robert Kaylor; United Artists.

**The Changeling** (R): Film about mansion inhabited by ghosts; with George C. Scott, Trish Van Devere, Melvyn Douglas; director, Peter Medak; Associated Film Distribution.

**Coal Miner's Daughter** (PG): Film biography of country music singer Loretta Lynn; with Sissy Spacek, Tommy Lee Jones; director, Michael Apted; Universal.

**Cruising** (R): Drama about search for killer of homosexuals in New York City; with Al Pacino, Paul Sorvino, Karen Allen; director, William Friedkin; United Artists.

**Die Laughing** (PG): Young cab driver becomes involved in murder; with Robby Benson; director, Jeff Werner; Orion Pictures.

**Dressed to Kill** (R): Mystery thriller about psychopath who preys on attractive women; with Michael Caine, Angie Dickinson; director, Brian De Palma; Filmways.

**The Elephant Man** (PG): Life of hideously deformed man; with Anthony Hopkins, John Hurt, Anne Bancroft; director, David Lynch; Paramount.

**The Empire Strikes Back** (PG): Sequel to *Star Wars* dealing with further adventures of Luke Skywalker and friends; with Mark Hamill, Carrie Fisher, Harrison Ford; director, Irvin Kershner; 20th Century-Fox.

**Fame** (PG): Drama set at High School of Performing Arts in New York City, following group of students from first auditions to graduation; with Eddie Barth, Irene Cara, Lee Curreri; director, Alan Parker; United Artists.

**Fatso** (PG): Comedy about overweight man who unsuccessfully attempts to diet; with Dom DeLuise, Anne Bancroft, Ron Carey; director, Anne Bancroft; 20th Century-Fox.

**Ffolkes** (PG): Man foils hijacking gang that sets out to destroy oil-drilling rig; with Roger Moore, James Mason, Anthony Perkins; director, Andrew V. McLaglen; Universal.

**The Fiendish Plot of Dr. Fu Manchu** (PG): Asian master criminal seeks mystery of life's longevity; with Peter Sellers, Sid Caesar; director, Piers Haggard; Orion.

**The Final Countdown** (PG): Nuclear carrier, *USS Nimitz*, on routine trip, is transported back in time to day of Pearl Harbor attack in 1941; with Kirk Douglas, Martin Sheen; director, Don Taylor; United Artists.

**The Fog** (R): Science-fiction film about ghosts who seek revenge on northern California town; with Adrienne Barbeau, Hal Holbrook, Janet Leigh; director, John Carpenter; Avco Embassy.

**Foxes** (R): Drama about rebellious teenage girls and their relationships with their families; with Jodie Foster, Sally Kellerman; director, Adrian Lyne; United Artists.

**Gilda Live** (R): Film comedy about Gilda Radner's Broadway career; with Gilda Radner, Don Kirshner, Father Guido Sarducci; director, Mike Nichols; Warner Bros.

**Gloria** (PG): Woman protects orphaned boy whose life is threatened by mobsters; with Gena Rowlands; director, John Cassavetes; Columbia.

**The Great Santini** (PG): Drama about Marine Corps colonel; with Robert Duvall, Blythe Danner; director, Lewis John Carlino; Orion.

**The Hearse** (PG): Woman moves into ancestral home possessed by demons; with Trish Van Devere, Joseph Cotton; director, George Bowers; Crown International Pictures.

**Hero at Large** (PG): Comedy about novice actor who portrays role of Captain Avenger and takes on role in real life; with John Ritter, Bert Convy; director, Martin Davidson; United Artists.

**Hide in Plain Sight** (PG): Divorced man searches for his children after they are hidden by Justice Dept. to protect them from mob; with James Caan, Jill Eikenberry, Robert Viharo; director, James Caan; United Artists.

**Honeysuckle Rose** (PG): Comedy about traveling musician's extramarital affair and his loyal wife; with Willie Nelson, Dyan Cannon, Amy Irving; director, Jerry Schatzberg; Warner Bros.

**Hopscotch** (R): Fired CIA agent sets out to sabotage intelligence agencies of U.S., Soviet Union, Britain, and West Germany; with Walter Matthau, Glenda Jackson, Sam Waterston; director, Arthur Ibbetson; Avco Embassy.

**How to Beat the High Cost of Living** (PG): Three women attempt to cope with inflation by planning to rob shopping center; with Susan Saint James, Jessica Lange; director, Robert Scheerer; American Filmways International.

**The Human Factor** (R): Spy thriller based on Graham Greene's novel about British double agent; with Richard Attenborough, John Gielgud, Derek Jacobi; director, Otto Preminger; United Artists.

**The Hunter** (PG): Modern-day bounty hunter tracks down bail-jumping fugitives; with Steve McQueen, Eli Wallach; director, Buzz Kulik; Paramount.

**The Island** (R): Pirates plunder pleasure boats in Bermuda Triangle; with Michael Caine; director, Michael Ritchie; Universal.

**Just Tell Me What You Want** (R): Comedy about relationship between mistress and ruthless business tycoon; with Ali MacGraw, Alan King, director, Sidney Lumet; Warner Bros.

**The Kidnapping of the President** (R): Terrorist plots abduction of U.S. President; with Hal Holbrook, Van Johnson, William Shatner; director, George Mendeluk; Sefel Pictures International.

**Kramer vs. Kramer** (PG): Divorced couple battle over custody of their son; won five Academy Awards, including best picture; with Dustin Hoffman, Meryl Streep, Jane Alexander; director, Robert Benton; Columbia.

**The Last Married Couple in America** (R): Happily married pair become disillusioned when they see all their friends divorcing; with George Segal, Natalie Wood, Richard Benjamin; director, Gilbert Cates; Universal.

**Little Darlings** (R): Two teenage girls from different backgrounds meet at camp; with Tatum O'Neal, Kristy McNichol, Armand Assante; director, Ronald F. Maxwell; Paramount.

**Little Miss Marker** (PG): Six-year-old girl is left as collateral at gambling casino; with Walter Matthau, Julie Andrews, Tony Curtis; director, Walter Bernstein; Universal.

**The Long Riders** (R): Western drama portraying lives of notorious James brothers; with David Carradine, Keith Carradine, James Keach; director, Walter Hill; United Artists.

**My Bodyguard** (PG): Relationship between shrimp, bully, and very large boy in Chicago school in 1940s; with Chris Makepeace, Matt Dillon, Adam Baldwin, Ruth Gordon; director, Tony Bill; 20th Century-Fox.

**My Brilliant Career** (not rated): Strong-willed Australian woman struggles to become writer in 1890s; with Judy Davis; director, Gillian Armstrong; Analysis Film Releasing Corp.

**Night of the Juggler** (R): Former policeman's daughter is kidnapped by mistake; with James Brolin, Cliff Gorman, Richard Castellano; director, Robert Butler; Columbia.

**Nothing Personal** (PG): College professor and lawyer fight to save endangered species of Alaskan seal; with Donald Sutherland, Suzanne Somers; director, George Bloomfield; American Int'l.

**The Nude Bomb** (PG): Screen sequel to Get Smart television serial; with Don Adams, Sylvia Kristel, Rhonda Fleming; director, Clive Donner; Universal.

**One-Trick Pony** (R): Life of aging rock star; with Paul Simon, Rip Torn, Blair Brown; director, Robert M. Young; Warner Bros.

**Ordinary People** (R): Teenage boy becomes emotionally disturbed after brother's accidental death; with Mary Tyler Moore, Donald Sutherland, Judd Hirsch; director, Robert Redford; Paramount.

**Roadie** (PG): Country boy and rock groupie travel to New York to meet rock star; with Meat Loaf, Kaki Hunter, Art Carney; director, Alan Rudolph; United Artists.

**Rough Cut** (PG): Couple plans multimillion-dollar diamond robbery; with Burt Reynolds, Lesley-Anne Downe, David Niven; director, Donald Siegel; Paramount.

**Serial** (R): Comedy satirizes life-style in affluent suburb of San Francisco; with Martin Mull, Tuesday Weld, Jennifer McAlister; director, Bill Persky; Paramount.

**The Shining** (R): Horror film about destructive family relationships; with Jack Nicholson, Shelly Duvall; director, Stanley Kubrick; Warner Bros.

**Simon** (PG): Comedy about research scientists involved in government think tank; with Alan Arkin, Madeline Kahn; director, Marshall Brickman; Orion Pictures.

**Smokey and the Bandit II** (PG): Comedy about adventures of two modern-day outlaws in Texas; with Burt Reynolds, Sally Field, Jackie Gleason; director, Hall Needham; Universal.

**Stardust Memories** (PG): Comedy about life of movie director; with Woody Allen, Charlotte Rampling; director, Allen; United Artists.

**The Thirty-Nine Steps** (PG): Film remake of Alfred Hitchcock's classic about international espionage; with Robert Powell, David Warner, Eric Porter; director, Don Sharp; International Picture Show Company.

**Those Lips, Those Eyes** (R): Musical about summer stock troupe in Cleveland in early 1950s; with Frank Langella, Glynnis O'Connor; director, Michael Pressman; United Artists.

**Urban Cowboy** (PG): Young Texas farmer goes to Houston to make his fortune; with John Travolta; director, James Bridges; Paramount.

**The Watcher in the Woods** (PG): Walt Disney film about mysterious ghost who appears in English countryside; with Bette Davis, Carroll Baker, David McCallum; director, John Hough; Walt Disney Production Buena Vista.

**Wholly Moses** (PG): Parody of life of Moses; with Dudley Moore, Laraine Newman; James Coco; director, Gary Weis; Columbia.

**Willie and Phil** (R): Comedy about two men in love with same woman; with Margo Kidder, Michael Ontkean, Ray Sharkey; director, Paul Mazursky; 20th Century-Fox.

**Xanadu** (PG): Fantasy about young artist and elderly musician who fall in love with mystery woman at roller skating rink; with Olivia Newton-John, Gene Kelly, Michael Beck; director, Robert Greenwald; Universal.

# ACADEMY AWARD WINNERS

Source: American Academy of Motion Picture Arts and Sciences

| YEAR | BEST PICTURE | BEST ACTOR | BEST ACTRESS | BEST DIRECTOR |
|------|--------------|------------|--------------|---------------|
| 1927–28 | Wings | Emil Jannings, The Last Command, The Way of All Flesh | Janet Gaynor, Seventh Heaven, Street Angel, Sunrise | Frank Borzage, Seventh Heaven; Lewis Milestone, Two Arabian Knights |
| 1928–29 | Broadway Melody | Warner Baxter, In Old Arizona | Mary Pickford, Coquette | Frank Lloyd, The Divine Lady |
| 1929–30 | All Quiet on the Western Front | George Arliss, Disraeli | Norma Shearer, The Divorcee | Lewis Milestone, All Quiet on the Western Front |
| 1930–31 | Cimarron | Lionel Barrymore, A Free Soul | Marie Dressler, Min and Bill | Norman Taurog, Skippy |
| 1931–32 | Grand Hotel | Wallace Beery, The Champ Fredric March, Dr. Jekyll and Mr. Hyde | Helen Hayes, The Sin of Madelon Claudet | Frank Borzage, Bad Girl |
| 1932–33 | Cavalcade | Charles Laughton, The Private Life of Henry VIII | Katharine Hepburn, Morning Glory | Frank Lloyd, Cavalcade |
| 1934 | It Happened One Night | Clark Gable, It Happened One Night | Claudette Colbert, It Happened One Night | Frank Capra, It Happened One Night |
| 1935 | Mutiny on the Bounty | Victor McLaglen, The Informer | Bette Davis, Dangerous | John Ford, The Informer |
| 1936 | The Great Ziegfeld | Paul Muni, The Story of Louis Pasteur | Luise Rainer, The Great Ziegfeld | Frank Capra, Mr. Deeds Goes to Town |
| 1937 | The Life of Emile Zola | Spencer Tracy, Captains Courageous | Luise Rainer, The Good Earth | Leo McCarey, The Awful Truth |
| 1938 | You Can't Take It with You | Spencer Tracy, Boys Town | Bette Davis, Jezebel | Frank Capra, You Can't Take It with You |
| 1939 | Gone with the Wind | Robert Donat, Goodbye, Mr. Chips | Vivien Leigh, Gone with the Wind | Victor Fleming, Gone with the Wind |
| 1940 | Rebecca | James Stewart, The Philadelphia Story | Ginger Rogers, Kitty Foyle | John Ford, The Grapes of Wrath |
| 1941 | How Green Was My Valley | Gary Cooper, Sergeant York | Joan Fontaine, Suspicion | John Ford, How Green Was My Valley |
| 1942 | Mrs. Miniver | James Cagney, Yankee Doodle Dandy | Greer Garson, Mrs. Miniver | William Wyler, Mrs. Miniver |
| 1943 | Casablanca | Paul Lukas, Watch on the Rhine | Jennifer Jones, The Song of Bernadette | Michael Curtiz, Casablanca |
| 1944 | Going My Way | Bing Crosby, Going My Way | Ingrid Bergman, Gaslight | Leo McCarey, Going My Way |
| 1945 | The Lost Weekend | Ray Milland, The Lost Weekend | Joan Crawford, Mildred Pierce | Billy Wilder, The Lost Weekend |
| 1946 | The Best Years of Our Lives | Fredric March, The Best Years of Our Lives | Olivia de Havilland, To Each His Own | William Wyler, The Best Years of Our Lives |
| 1947 | Gentleman's Agreement | Ronald Colman, A Double Life | Loretta Young, The Farmer's Daughter | Elia Kazan, Gentleman's Agreement |
| 1948 | Hamlet | Laurence Olivier, Hamlet | Jane Wyman, Johnny Belinda | John Huston, Treasure of Sierra Madre |
| 1949 | All the King's Men | Broderick Crawford, All the King's Men | Olivia de Havilland, The Heiress | Joseph L. Mankiewicz, A Letter to Three Wives |
| 1950 | All About Eve | Jose Ferrer, Cyrano de Bergerac | Judy Holliday, Born Yesterday | Joseph L. Mankiewicz, All About Eve |
| 1951 | An American in Paris | Humphrey Bogart, The African Queen | Vivien Leigh, A Streetcar Named Desire | George Stevens, A Place in the Sun |
| 1952 | The Greatest Show on Earth | Gary Cooper, High Noon | Shirley Booth, Come Back, Little Sheba | John Ford, The Quiet Man |
| 1953 | From Here to Eternity | William Holden, Stalag 17 | Audrey Hepburn, Roman Holiday | Fred Zinnemann, From Here to Eternity |
| 1954 | On the Waterfront | Marlon Brando, On the Waterfront | Grace Kelly, The Country Girl | Elia Kazan, On the Waterfront |
| 1955 | Marty | Ernest Borgnine, Marty | Anna Magnani, The Rose Tattoo | Delbert Mann, Marty |
| 1956 | Around the World in 80 Days | Yul Brynner, The King and I | Ingrid Bergman, Anastasia | George Stevens, Giant |
| 1957 | The Bridge on the River Kwai | Alec Guinness, The Bridge on the River Kwai | Joanne Woodward, The Three Faces of Eve | David Lean, The Bridge on the River Kwai |
| 1958 | Gigi | David Niven, Separate Tables | Susan Hayward, I Want to Live | Vincente Minnelli, Gigi |
| 1959 | Ben-Hur | Charlton Heston, Ben-Hur | Simone Signoret, Room at the Top | William Wyler, Ben-Hur |
| 1960 | The Apartment | Burt Lancaster, Elmer Gantry | Elizabeth Taylor, Butterfield 8 | Billy Wilder, The Apartment |
| 1961 | West Side Story | Maximilian Schell, Judgment at Nuremberg | Sophia Loren, Two Women | Jerome Robbins, Robert Wise, West Side Story |
| 1962 | Lawrence of Arabia | Gregory Peck, To Kill a Mockingbird | Anne Bancroft, The Miracle Worker | David Lean, Lawrence of Arabia |
| 1963 | Tom Jones | Sidney Poitier, Lilies of the Field | Patricia Neal, Hud | Tony Richardson, Tom Jones |

| YEAR | BEST PICTURE | BEST ACTOR | BEST ACTRESS | BEST DIRECTOR |
|---|---|---|---|---|
| 1964 | *My Fair Lady* | Rex Harrison, *My Fair Lady* | Julie Andrews, *Mary Poppins* | George Cukor, *My Fair Lady* |
| 1965 | *Sound of Music* | Lee Marvin, *Cat Ballou* | Julie Christie, *Darling* | Robert Wise, *Sound of Music* |
| 1966 | *A Man for All Seasons* | Paul Scofield, *A Man for All Seasons* | Elizabeth Taylor, *Who's Afraid of Virginia Woolf?* | Fred Zinnemann, *A Man for All Seasons* |
| 1967 | *In the Heat of the Night* | Rod Steiger, *In the Heat of the Night* | Katharine Hepburn, *Guess Who's Coming to Dinner?* | Mike Nichols, *The Graduate* |
| 1968 | *Oliver!* | Cliff Robertson, *Charly* | Katharine Hepburn, *The Lion in Winter*; Barbra Streisand, *Funny Girl* | Sir Carol Reed, *Oliver!* |
| 1969 | *Midnight Cowboy* | John Wayne, *True Grit* | Maggie Smith, *The Prime of Miss Jean Brodie* | John Schlesinger, *Midnight Cowboy* |
| 1970 | *Patton* | George C. Scott, *Patton* | Glenda Jackson, *Women in Love* | Franklin J. Schaffner, *Patton* |
| 1971 | *The French Connection* | Gene Hackman, *The French Connection* | Jane Fonda, *Klute* | William Friedkin, *The French Connection* |
| 1972 | *The Godfather* | Marlon Brando, *The Godfather* | Liza Minnelli, *Cabaret* | Bob Fosse, *Cabaret* |
| 1973 | *The Sting* | Jack Lemmon, *Save the Tiger* | Glenda Jackson, *A Touch of Class* | George Roy Hill, *The Sting* |
| 1974 | *The Godfather, Part II* | Art Carney, *Harry and Tonto* | Ellen Burstyn, *Alice Doesn't Live Here Anymore* | Francis Ford Coppola, *The Godfather, Part II* |
| 1975 | *One Flew Over the Cuckoo's Nest* | Jack Nicholson, *One Flew Over the Cuckoo's Nest* | Louise Fletcher, *One Flew Over the Cuckoo's Nest* | Milos Forman, *One Flew Over the Cuckoo's Nest* |
| 1976 | *Rocky* | Peter Finch, *Network* | Faye Dunaway, *Network* | John Avildsen, *Rocky* |
| 1977 | *Annie Hall* | Richard Dreyfuss, *The Goodbye Girl* | Diane Keaton, *Annie Hall* | Woody Allen, *Annie Hall* |
| 1978 | *The Deer Hunter* | Jon Voight, *Coming Home* | Jane Fonda, *Coming Home* | Michael Cimino, *The Deer Hunter* |
| 1979 | *Kramer vs. Kramer* | Dustin Hoffman, *Kramer vs. Kramer* | Sally Field, *Norma Rae* | Robert Benton, *Kramer vs. Kramer* |

## OTHER ACADEMY AWARDS IN 1980:

The 52d annual Oscars for 1979 films were presented by the American Academy of Motion Picture Arts and Sciences on April 14, 1980.

**Best foreign-language film:** *The Tin Drum.*
**Best supporting actor:** Melvyn Douglas, *Being There.*
**Best supporting actress:** Meryl Streep, *Kramer vs. Kramer.*
**Best screenplay, adapted:** *Kramer vs. Kramer,* Robert Benton.
**Best screenplay, original:** *Breaking Away,* Steven Tesich.
**Best cinematography:** *Apocalypse Now,* Vittorio Storaro.
**Best film editing:** *All That Jazz,* Alan Heim.
**Best original music score:** *A Little Romance,* Georges Delerue.
**Best scoring adaptation:** *All That Jazz,* Ralph Burns.
**Best art direction:** *All That Jazz,* Philip Rosenberg, Tony Walton; set decoration, Edward Stewart, Gary Brink.
**Best costume design:** *All That Jazz,* Albert Wolsky.
**Best sound:** *Apocalypse Now,* Walter Murch, Mark Berger, Richard Beggs, Nat Boxer.
**Documentary—feature:** *Best Boy,* Ira Wohl.
**Documentary—short subject:** *Paul Robeson: Tribute to an Artist,* Janus Films, Inc.
**Short subjects—animated:** *Every Child,* Derek Lamb, producer.
**Short subjects—live:** *Board and Care,* Sarah Pillsburg and Ron Ellis, producers.
**Jean Hersholt Humanitarian Award:** Robert Benjamin (posthumously).
**Life Time Achievement Award:** Sir Alec Guinness.
**Special Awards:** Alan Splet, Hal Elias, Mark Surrerier.
**Irving Thalberg Award:** Ray Stark.

## 1980 NEW YORK FILM CRITICS AWARDS

The annual awards for 1979 film achievements presented by the New York Film Critics included:
**Best film:** *Kramer vs. Kramer.*
**Best actor:** Dustin Hoffman, *Kramer vs. Kramer.*
**Best actress:** Sally Field, *Norma Rae.*
**Best supporting actor:** Melvyn Douglas, *Being There.*
**Best supporting actress:** Meryl Streep, *Kramer vs. Kramer* and *The Seduction of Joe Tynan.*
**Best director:** Woody Allen, *Manhattan.*
**Best screenplay:** Steve Teisch, *Breaking Away.*

## 1980 NATIONAL SOCIETY OF FILM CRITICS

The 14th annual motion-picture awards by the National Society of Film Critics included:
**Best film:** *Breaking Away.*
**Best actor:** Dustin Hoffman, *Kramer vs. Kramer* and *Agatha.*
**Best actress:** Sally Field, *Norma Rae.*
**Best supporting actor:** Frederic Forrest, *Apocalypse Now* and *The Rose.*
**Best supporting actress:** Meryl Streep, *Kramer vs. Kramer, Manhattan,* and *The Seduction of Joe Tynan.*
**Best director:** Woody Allen, *Manhattan,* and Robert Benton, *Kramer vs. Kramer.*
**Best screenplay:** Steve Teisch, *Breaking Away.*

## 1980 GOLDEN GLOBE MOVIE AWARDS

The Hollywood Foreign Press Association's 37th annual Golden Globe movie awards included:
**Best dramatic film:** *Kramer vs. Kramer.*
**Best musical or comedy:** *Being There.*
**Best actor, drama:** Dustin Hoffman, *Kramer vs. Kramer.*
**Best actress, drama:** Sally Field, *Norma Rae.*
**Best actor, comedy or musical:** Peter Sellers, *Being There.*
**Best actress, comedy or musical:** Bette Midler, *The Rose.*
**Best supporting actor:** Melvyn Douglas, *Being There.*
**Best supporting actress:** Meryl Streep, *Kramer vs. Kramer.*
**Best supporting actor:** Robert Duvall, *Apocalypse Now.*
**Best director:** Francis Coppola, *Apocalypse Now.*
**Best screenplay:** Robert Benton, *Kramer vs. Kramer.*
**Best foreign film:** *La Cage Aux Folles.*
**World male film favorite:** Roger Moore.
**World female film favorite:** Jane Fonda.

# STAGE PLAYS ON AND OFF BROADWAY: 1980

**Ain't Misbehavin':** Musical based on songs associated with Fats Waller; won 3 Tony awards in 1978; conceived and directed by Richard Maltby; opened May 9, 1978.

**Annie:** Tony award-winning musical based on *Little Orphan Annie* comic strip; music and lyrics, Charles Strouse and Martin Charnin; choreography, Peter Gennaro; opened April 21, 1977.

**Barnum:** Musical about showman P.T. Barnum and life in a circus; won 2 Tony awards; with Jim Dale, Terri White; music, Cy Coleman; lyrics, Michael Stewart; book, Mark Bramble; director, Joe Layton; opened April 30, 1980.

**Bent:** Martin Sherman's drama about two homosexuals in Nazi Germany in 1934; with Richard Gere, David Marshall Grant; director, Robert Allan Ackerman; opened Dec. 2, 1979.

**The Best Little Whorehouse in Texas:** Tony award-winning musical about closing of Texas brothel; book, Larry L. King, Peter Masterson; music and lyrics, Carol Hall; director, Peter Masterson, Tommy Tune; opened April 17, 1978.

**Betrayal:** Drama, by Harold Pinter, about love triangle involving husband, wife, and husband's best friend; with Raul Julia, Blythe Danner, Roy Scheider; director, Peter Hall; opened Jan. 6, 1980.

**Billy Bishop Goes to War:** One-man musical based on World War I Canadian combat pilot who helped destroy 72 German planes; with Eric Peterson; written, composed, and directed by John Gray, Eric Peterson; opened May 29, 1980.

**Brigadoon:** Revival of 1947 musical fantasy about Scotland; book and lyrics, Alan Jay Lerner; music, Frederick Loewe; choreography, Agnes De Mille; director, Vivian Matalon; with John Curry; opened Oct. 16, 1980.

**Camelot:** Revival of popular Lerner-Loewe musical about King Arthur and Knights of Round Table; with Richard Burton, Christine Ebersole, Paxton Whitehead; director, Frank Dunlop; choreographer, Buddy Schwab; opened July 8, 1980.

**Charlie and Algernon:** Musical about retarded man who becomes genius for short time after undergoing surgery; with P.J. Benjamin, Sandy Faison; book and lyrics, David Rogers; music, Charles Strouse; director, Louis W. Scheeder; opened Sept. 14, 1980.

**Children of a Lesser God:** Drama, by Mark Medoff, about love between deaf woman and her teacher; won Tony awards for best play, best actress, best actor; with Phyllis Frelich, John Rubinstein; director, Gordon Davidson; opened March 30, 1980.

**A Chorus Line:** Highly acclaimed musical about Broadway director who must choose people for a chorus line; conceived, choreographed, directed by Michael Bennett; music, Marvin Hamlisch; lyrics, Edward Kleban; book, James Kirkwood; opened July 25, 1975.

**Dancin':** Musical show about dancing; director, choreographer, Bob Fosse; opened March 27, 1978.

**A Day in Hollywood/A Night in the Ukraine:** Musical comedy, by Dick Vosburgh, spoofing 1930s Hollywood extravanganzas and Marx Brothers; won 2 Tony awards; with Priscilla Lopez, David Garrison, Frank Lazarus; choreographers, Thommie Walsh, Tommy Tune; director, Tune; opened May 1, 1980.

**Deathtrap:** Ira Levin's thriller about playwright who writes mysteries; director, Robert Moore; opened Feb. 26, 1978.

**Division Street:** Comedy, by Steve Tesich, about former radical trying to lose his identity in Chicago; with John Lithgow, Keene Curtis; director, Tom Moore; opened Oct. 8, 1980.

**Evita:** Musical based on life of Eva Peron; won 6 Tony awards; with Patti LuPone; music, Andrew Lloyd Webber; lyrics, Tim Rice; choreography, Larry Fuller; director, Harold Prince; opened Sept. 25, 1979.

**Filumena:** Comedy, by Eduardo De Filippo, about mistress determined to marry her wealthy lover; with Joan Plowright, Frank Finlay; director Laurence Olivier; opened Feb. 10, 1980.

**42d Street:** Musical, based on 1932 film, about chorus girl who achieves stardom on Broadway; with Jerry Orbach, Tammy Grimes, Wanda Richert; director and choreographer, Gower Champion; music and lyrics, Harry Warren and Al Dubin; book, Michael Stewart and Mark Bramble; opened Aug. 25, 1980.

**Goodbye Fidel:** Drama by Howard Sackler about people living in modern-day Cuba; with Ralph Byers, Jane Alexander, Lee Richardson; director, Edwin Sherin; opened April 23, 1980.

**Harold and Maude:** Romantic comedy, by Collin Higgins, about young man in love with older woman; with Keith McDermott, Ruth Ford; director, Robert Lewis; opened Feb. 7, 1980.

**I Ought to Be in Pictures:** Neil Simon's comedy about Hollywood writer attempting to get actress daughter into movies; with Dinah Manoff, who won Tony award as best featured actress, Joyce Van Patten, Ron Leibman; director, Herbert Ross; opened April 3, 1980.

**Lunch Hour:** Romantic comedy, by Jean Kerr, set in beach house; with Sam Waterston; director, Mike Nichols; opened Nov. 6, 1980.

**The Man Who Came to Dinner:** Revival of Moss Hart and George S. Kaufman comedy about radio idol who comes to small Ohio town to lecture and stays with local family; with Patricia O'Connell, Anita Dangler, Josh Clark; director, Stephen Porter; opened June 26, 1980.

**Mister Lincoln:** Dramatic monologue, by Herbert Mitgang, touching on important moments in life of Abraham Lincoln; with Roy Dotrice; director, Peter Coe; opened Feb. 25, 1980.

**Morning's at Seven:** Paul Osborn's comedy about relationship between four elderly sisters; won 3 Tony awards including best director, with Nancy Marchand, Elizabeth Wilson, Maureen O'Sullivan, Teresa Wright, David Rounds; director, Vivian Matalon; opened April 10, 1980.

**The Music Man:** Revival of Meredith Willson's musical about good-natured, lovable con man who pretends to be music teacher; with Dick Van Dyke, Meg Bussert, Randy Morgan; director and choreographer, Michael Kidd; opened off-Broadway June 5, 1980.

**Nuts:** Drama, by Tom Topor, about woman trying to prove her mental competency to stand trial for murder; with Anne Twomey; director, Stephen Zuckerman; opened April 28, 1980.

**Of the Fields, Lately:** Drama, by David French, about reconciliation of father and estranged son; with Christopher Cooper, William Cain; director, Jamie Brown; opened May 27, 1980.

**One Night Stand:** Musical about songwriter who feels he's past his prime; with Jack Weston, Charles Kimbrough; music, Jule Styne; book, Herb Gardner; choreography, Peter Gennaro; director, John Dexter; opened Oct. 28, 1980.

**Passione:** Drama, by Albert Innaurato, about Italian-American family in Philadelphia; with Jerry Stiller, Angela Paton; director, Frank Langella; opened Sept. 23.

**Past Tense:** Drama, by Jack Zeman, about break-up of middle-aged couple; with Barbara Feldon, Laurence Luckinbill; director, Theodore Mann; opened April 24, 1980.

**The Perfect Stranger:** Comedy, by Neil Cuthbert, about improbable affair between suicidal wife and water-meter man; with Deborah Hedwall, David Rasche, Allan Wasserman; director, Jerry Zaks; opened Feb. 4, 1980.

**Peter Pan:** Musical revival of Sir James M. Barrie's story about boy who refuses to grow up; with Sandy Duncan; director and choreographer, Rob Iscove; opened Sept. 6, 1979.

**Romantic Comedy:** Comedy, by Bernard Slade, about young playwright who has affair with his associate; with Anthony Perkins, Mia Farrow; director, Joseph Hardy; opened Nov. 8, 1979.

**Sugar Babies:** Musical revue of burlesque routines; with Ann Miller, Mickey Rooney; music, Jimmy McHugh; lyrics, Dorothy Fields, Al Dubin; choreographer, Ernest Flatt; director, Ernest Flatt; opened Oct. 8, 1979.

**The Suicide:** Russian comedy, by Nikolai Erdman, about man without job contemplating suicide; with Derek Jacobi; director, Jonas Jurasas; opened Sept. 22, 1980.

**Talley's Folly:** Comedy, by Lanford Wilson, about romance between Jewish accountant and wealthy Protestant girl; won Pulitzer Prize for drama and Tony award for scenic design; with Judd Hirsch, Trish Hawkins; director, Marshall W. Mason; opened Feb. 20, 1980.

**They're Playing Our Song:** Musical about romance between two songwriters; book, Neil Simon; music, Marvin Hamlisch; lyrics, Carole Bayer Sager; opened Feb. 11, 1979.

**Tintypes:** Musical revue highlighting stereotypes from Teddy Roosevelt era; with Trey Wilson, Jerry Zaks; conceived and directed by Mary Kyte, Mel Marvin, Gary Pearle; opened off-Broadway April 21, 1980.

**Tricks of the Trade:** Thriller, by Sidney Michaels, about psychiatrist working for CIA; with George C. Scott, Trish Van Devere; opened Oct. 29, 1980.

**Watch on the Rhine:** Revival of Lillian Hellman's drama about family's reaction to Nazism in pre-World War II America; with Mary Fogarty, Jan Miner, Robert Judd; director, Arvin Brown; opened Jan. 3, 1980.

**West Side Story:** Musical revival of Jerome Robbins/Leonard Bernstein play about rivalry between white and Puerto Rican street gangs; with James J. Mellon, Ken Marshall, Mark Bove; director and choreographer, Jerome Robbins; lyrics, Stephen Sondheim; opened Feb. 14, 1980.

**Your Arms Too Short to Box with God:** Revival of Vinnette Carroll's black gospel musical dealing with crucifixion of Christ; with Adrian Bailey, Julius Richard Brown; music and lyrics, Alex Bradford; opened June 2, 1980.

## THEATER AWARDS: 1980

### TONY AWARDS: 1980

The 34th annual Antoinette Perry (Tony) awards sponsored by the American Theatre Wing and the League of N.Y. Theatres for the Broadway season May 7, 1979, through May 11, 1980:

Best play: *Children of a Lesser God,* by Mark Medoff.
Best musical: *Evita;* producer, Robert Stigwood.
Best musical book: *Evita,* by Tim Rice.
Best musical score: *Evita,* by Andrew Lloyd Webber and Tim Rice.
Best dramatic actor: John Rubinstein, *Children of a Lesser God.*
Best dramatic actress: Phyllis Frelich, *Children of a Lesser God.*
Best musical actor: Jim Dale, *Barnum.*
Best musical actress: Patti LuPone, *Evita.*
Best featured actor, comedy: David Rounds, *Morning's at Seven.*
Best featured actress, comedy: Dinah Manoff, *I Ought to Be in Pictures.*
Best featured actor, musical: Mandy Patinkin, *Evita.*
Best featured actress, musical: Priscilla Lopez, *A Day in Hollywood/A Night in the Ukraine.*
Best director, comedy: Vivian Matalon, *Morning's at Seven.*
Best director, musical: Harold Prince, *Evita.*
Best choreographer: Tommy Tune and Thommie Walsh, *A Day in Hollywood/A Night in the Ukraine.*
Best scenic designer: John Lee Beatty, *Talley's Folly;* David Mitchell, *Barnum.*
Best costume designer: Theoni V. Aldredge, *Barnum.*
Best lighting designer: David Hersey, *Evita.*

Lawrence Langner Award: Helen Hayes.
Special Tony awards: Actors Theatre of Louisville; Goodspeed Opera House; Mary Tyler Moore.
Theatre Award '80: Richard Fitzgerald, Hobe Morrison.

### NEW YORK DRAMA CRITICS CIRCLE AWARDS: 1980

Awarded annually by the drama critics of newspapers and magazines with editorial offices in New York City, the choices for the 1979–1980 season included:
Best play: *Talley's Folly,* by Lanford Wilson.
Best musical: *Evita;* directed by Harold Prince with book by Tim Rice; music and lyrics by Andrew Lloyd Webber and Tim Rice; choreography by Larry Fuller.

### OBIE AWARDS: 1980

Prizes for the best off-Broadway plays and performances are awarded annually by the newspaper *Village Voice:*
Distinguished direction: A. J. Antoon for *The Art of Dining;* Edward Cornell for *Johnny on a Spot,* Elizabeth Le Compte for *Point Judith.*
Distinguished performances: Michael Burrell in *Hess;* Michael Cristofer in *Chinchilla;* Lindsay Crouse and Michael Higgins in *Reunion;* Elizabeth Franz in *Sister Mary Ignatius Explains It All for You;* Morgan Freeman in *Mother Courage* and *Coriolanus;* John Heard in *Othello* and *Split;* Madeleine Le Roux in *La Justice;* Jon Polito for performances with Dodger Theater and BAM Theater Companies; Bill Raymond in *A Prelude to Death in Venice;* Dianne Wiest in *The Art of Dining;* Hattie Winston in *Mother Courage* and *The Michigan.*

## MOST POPULAR MADE-FOR-TV MOVIES: 1979–80 SEASON

Source: *Variety;* average Nielsen rating in millions of viewers.

| RANK | SERIES | NET-WORK | RAT-ING | RANK | SERIES | NET-WORK | RAT-ING |
|---|---|---|---|---|---|---|---|
| 1. | Guyana Tragedy: The Story of Jim Jones, Part 2 | CBS | 31.7 | 14. | And Baby Makes Six | NBC | 23.3 |
| 2. | Kenny Rogers as the Gambler | CBS | 31.3 | 15. | The Lazarus Syndrome | ABC | 23.1 |
| 3. | Scruples, Part 3 | CBS | 29.3 | 16. | If Things Were Different | CBS | 22.8 |
| 4. | Guyana Tragedy: The Story of Jim Jones, Part 1 | CBS | 28.9 | 17. | Skag | NBC | 22.7 |
| | | | | 18. | My Old Man | NBC | 22.6 |
| 5. | Carnival of Thrills | CBS | 26.0 | 19. | Breaking up Is Hard to Do, Part 1 | ABC | 22.5 |
| 6. | Scruples, Part 2 | CBS | 25.6 | 20. | When Hell Was in Session | NBC | 22.0 |
| 7. | Tenspeed and Brown Shoe | ABC | 25.4 | 21. | The Tenth Month | CBS | 21.9 |
| 8. | Aunt Mary | CBS | 25.2 | 22. | Palmerstown, U.S.A. | CBS | 21.7 |
| 9. | Nurse | CBS | 24.3 | 22. | Portrait of a Stripper | CBS | 21.7 |
| 10. | The Miracle Worker | NBC | 23.9 | 24. | Friendships, Secrets, and Lies | NBC | 21.6 |
| 10. | Scruples, Part 1 | CBS | 23.9 | 25. | Galactica Discovers Earth, Part 1 | ABC | 21.5 |
| 12. | Seizure: The Story of Kathy Morris | CBS | 23.8 | 25. | The Kid from Left Field | NBC | 21.5 |
| 13. | Once upon a Family | CBS | 23.6 | 27. | Goldie and the Boxer | NBC | 21.3 |
| | | | | 27. | The Family Man | CBS | 21.3 |

## MOST POPULAR TV SERIES: 1979–80 SEASON

Source: *Variety;* average Nielsen rating in millions of viewers.

| RANK | SERIES | NET-WORK | RAT-ING | RANK | SERIES | NET-WORK | RAT-ING |
|---|---|---|---|---|---|---|---|
| 1. | 60 Minutes | CBS | 28.2 | 51. | Tim Conway | CBS | 17.5 |
| 2. | Three's Company | ABC | 26.3 | 52. | Disney's Wonderful World | NBC | 17.3 |
| 3. | Mash | CBS | 25.4 | 53. | CBS Wednesday Movie | CBS | 17.2 |
| 4. | Alice | CBS | 25.3 | 54. | White Shadow | CBS | 17.1 |
| 5. | Dallas | CBS | 25.0 | 54. | Big Show | NBC | 17.1 |
| 6. | Flo | CBS | 24.4 | 56. | Hello, Larry | NBC | 17.0 |
| 7. | The Jeffersons | CBS | 24.3 | 57. | BJ & the Bear | NBC | 16.7 |
| 7. | Dukes of Hazzard | CBS | 24.3 | 57. | Joe's World | NBC | 16.7 |
| 9. | That's Incredible | ABC | 24.0 | 59. | The Associates | ABC | 16.4 |
| 10. | One Day at a Time | CBS | 23.0 | 59. | Hagen | CBS | 16.4 |
| 11. | Archie Bunker's Place | CBS | 22.9 | 61. | Family | ABC | 16.3 |
| 12. | Eight Is Enough | ABC | 22.7 | 61. | Buck Rogers | NBC | 16.3 |
| 13. | Taxi | ABC | 22.4 | 61. | Stockard Channing | CBS | 16.3 |
| 14. | House Calls | CBS | 22.2 | 64. | Sanford | NBC | 16.2 |
| 15. | Real People | NBC | 21.8 | 64. | Lazarus Syndrome | ABC | 16.2 |
| 15. | Happy Days | ABC | 21.8 | 66. | Bad Cats | ABC | 15.9 |
| 17. | Little House on the Prairie | NBC | 21.5 | 66. | ABC Friday Movie | ABC | 15.9 |
| 18. | Chips | NBC | 21.4 | 68. | Last Resort | CBS | 15.8 |
| 18. | Charlie's Angels | ABC | 21.4 | 68. | Rockford Files | NBC | 15.8 |
| 20. | Trapper John, M.D. | CBS | 21.2 | 68. | Facts of Life | NBC | 15.8 |
| 21. | Barney Miller | ABC | 21.1 | 71. | 240-Robert | ABC | 15.4 |
| 21. | Love Boat | ABC | 21.1 | 71. | One in a Million | ABC | 15.4 |
| 23. | Benson | ABC | 20.8 | 71. | Galactica 1980 | ABC | 15.4 |
| 24. | WKRP In Cincinnati | CBS | 20.7 | 74. | Hawaii Five-O | CBS | 15.2 |
| 24. | Soap | ABC | 20.7 | 75. | Kate Loves a Mystery | NBC | 15.1 |
| 26. | Mork & Mindy | ABC | 20.5 | 76. | Man Called Sloane | NBC | 14.9 |
| 27. | Diff'rent Strokes | NBC | 20.3 | 77. | ABC Monday Movie | ABC | 14.8 |
| 28. | Vegas | ABC | 20.1 | 78. | The Ropers | ABC | 14.4 |
| 29. | Tenspeed & Brown Shoe | ABC | 20.0 | 79. | Stone | ABC | 14.2 |
| 29. | Knots Landing | CBS | 20.0 | 80. | Here to Eternity | NBC | 14.1 |
| 29. | NBC Monday Movie | NBC | 20.0 | 81. | Best of Saturday Night Live | NBC | 14.0 |
| 32. | Angie | ABC | 19.7 | 82. | Me & Maxx | NBC | 13.9 |
| 33. | Hart to Hart | ABC | 19.6 | 83. | When the Whistle Blows | ABC | 13.8 |
| 33. | Big Event | NBC | 19.6 | 83. | CBS Saturday Movie | CBS | 13.8 |
| 33. | Lou Grant | CBS | 19.6 | 85. | The Contender | CBS | 13.7 |
| 33. | Fantasy Island | ABC | 19.6 | 85. | Shirley | NBC | 13.7 |
| 37. | NFL Football | ABC | 19.5 | 87. | Here's Boomer | NBC | 13.6 |
| 38. | Palmerstown U.S.A. | CBS | 19.3 | 88. | Young Maverick | CBS | 13.2 |
| 39. | CBS Tuesday Movie | CBS | 19.1 | 89. | Eischied | NBC | 13.2 |
| 39. | Laverne & Shirley | ABC | 19.1 | 89. | The Chisholms | CBS | 13.2 |
| 41. | Goodtime Girls | ABC | 19.0 | 91. | Detective School | ABC | 13.0 |
| 42. | The Waltons | CBS | 18.7 | 92. | Paris | CBS | 12.7 |
| 42. | Incredible Hulk | CBS | 18.7 | 93. | California Fever | CBS | 12.4 |
| 44. | 20/20 | ABC | 18.5 | 94. | Salvage 1 | ABC | 12.3 |
| 45. | ABC Sunday Movie | ABC | 18.4 | 94. | Prime Time Sunday/Saturday | NBC | 12.3 |
| 45. | Quincy | NBC | 18.4 | 96. | NBC Friday Movie | NBC | 11.6 |
| 47. | NBC Tuesday Movie | NBC | 18.1 | 96. | New Kind of Family | ABC | 11.6 |
| 48. | Barnaby Jones | CBS | 18.0 | 98. | Pink Lady | NBC | 11.3 |
| 49. | Skag | NBC | 17.8 | 98. | Out of the Blue | ABC | 11.3 |
| 50. | Sheriff Lobo | NBC | 17.6 | 100. | Beyond Westworld | CBS | 11.2 |

# TELEVISION AND RADIO AWARDS: 1980

## EMMY AWARDS: 1980

The 32d annual prime-time television Emmy Awards were presented by the Academy of Television Arts and Sciences of Hollywood, Calif., on Sept. 6, 1980. The prime-time Emmy Awards for the 1979–80 season included:

**Best dramatic series:** *Lou Grant* (CBS).
**Best actress, drama series:** Barbara Bel Geddes, for *Dallas* (CBS).
**Best actor, drama series:** Ed Asner, *Lou Grant* (CBS).
**Best supporting actress, drama series:** Nancy Marchand, *Lou Grant* (CBS).
**Best supporting actor, drama series:** Stuart Margolin, *The Rockford Files* (NBC).
**Best director, drama series:** Roger Young, *Lou Grant* (CBS).
**Best writer, drama series:** Seph Freeman, *Lou Grant* (CBS).
**Best comedy series:** *Taxi* (ABC).
**Best actress, comedy series:** Catherine Damon, *Soap* (ABC).
**Best actor, comedy series:** Richard Mulligan, *Soap* (ABC).
**Best supporting actress, comedy or variety series:** Loretta Swit, *M*A*S*H* (CBS).
**Best supporting actor, comedy or variety series:** Harry Morgan, *M*A*S*H* (CBS).
**Best director, comedy or variety series:** James Burrows, *Taxi* (ABC).
**Best writer, comedy or variety series:** Bob Colleary, *Barney Miller* (ABC).
**Best limited series:** *Edward and Mrs. Simpson* (syndicated).
**Best drama or comedy special:** *The Miracle Worker* (NBC).
**Best actress, limited series or special:** Patty Duke Astin, *The Miracle Worker* (NBC).
**Best actor, limited series or special:** Powers Boothe, *Guyana Tragedy: The Story of Jim Jones* (CBS).
**Best supporting actress, limited series or special:** Mare Winningham, *Amber Waves* (ABC).
**Best supporting actor, limited series or special:** George Grizzard, *The Oldest Living Graduate* (NBC).
**Best director, limited series or special:** Marvin Chomsky, *Attica* (ABC).
**Best writer, limited series or special:** David Chase, *Off the Minnesota Strip* (ABC).
**Best comedy-variety or music program:** *Baryshnikov on Broadway* (ABC).
**Best director, comedy-variety or music program:** Dwight Hemion, *Baryshnikov on Broadway* (ABC).
**Best informational program:** *The Body Human: The Magic Sense* (CBS).
**Best animated program:** *Carlton Your Doorman* (CBS).

## PEABODY AWARDS: 1980

The George Foster Peabody Broadcasting Awards are presented annually and administered by the School of Journalism, University of Georgia, for distinguished and meritorious public service rendered by radio and TV.

**Individual awards:** Sylvia Fine Kaye, Beverly Hills, Calif., for *Musical Comedy Tonight,* an "entertaining look at American musical comedy through four significant eras"; Robert Trout, ABC News, for "his nearly fifty years of service as a thoroughly knowledgeable and articulate commentator on national and world affairs."

**Television awards:** KTVI, St. Louis, Mo., for *The Adventures of Whistling Sam,* locally produced cartoon comments on important issues; WMAQ-TV, Chicago, for "Strip and Search," a *Unit 5 Investigative Report* which exposed practice by police of routinely strip-searching women; KOOL Television, Phoenix, Ariz., for *The Long Eyes of Kitt Peak,* which gave viewers a look at what has been called "the largest and most complex astronomical research facility on earth"; KRON-TV, San Francisco, for *Politics of Poison,* which exposed public health problems caused by herbicide sprayings in northern California; CBS News, New York City, for *CBS News Sunday Morning* and *The Boston Goes to China;* CBS-TV, New York City, for *Dummy,* about an illiterate deaf black youth who "suffered injustice after his arrest as a murder suspect because of his handicap"; ABC-TV, New York City for *Valentine,* a love story about two senior citizens, *Friendly Fire,* about a family's involvement in the Vietnam War, and *A Special Gift,* about a young boy who must choose between basketball and ballet; NBC-TV, New York City, for *When Hell was in Session,* about experiences of Vietnam prisoner of war; NBC and BBC for *Treasures of the British Crown,* a look at the paintings and jewels of the Royal Collection in Britain.

**Radio awards:** WCBS Radio, New York, for *Follow that Cab: The Great Taxi Rip-Off,* which exposed New York City cabdrivers who took advantage of unknowing passengers; WGBH Radio, Boston, for *Currer Bell, Esquire,* about the life of Charlotte Bronte; Children's Radio Theatre, Washington, D.C., for *Henny Penny Playwrighting Contest,* in which original plays, by children 5–13, were performed; Canadian Broadcasting Corporation for The *Longest Journey,* describing the nine months prior to birth; KSJN/Minnesota Public Radio, St. Paul, Minn., for *The Way to 8-A,* a study of the legal process governing commitment to mental institutions in Minnesota.

## WRITERS GUILD TV AWARDS: 1980

**Original anthology:** Millard Lampell, *Orphan Train* (CBS).
**Anthology from another source:** Fay Kanin for *Friendly Fire* (ABC).
**Comedy-episodic:** Thad Mumford and Dan Wilcox for "Are You Now, Margaret?" segment of *M*A*S*H* (CBS), and Ken Estin for "The Reluctant Fighter" espisode of *Taxi* (ABC).
**Dramatic-episodic:** Leon Tokatyan for "Vet" segment of *Lou Grant* (CBS).
**Variety:** Jerry Juhl, David Odell, Jim Henson, and Don Hinkley for *The Muppet Show* (CBS) and Dan Akroyd, Anne Beatts, James Downey, Brian Doyle-Murray, Al Franken, Tom Davis, Brian McConnachie, Lorne Michaels, Don Novello, Herb Sargent, Tom Schiller, Rosie Shuster, Walter Williams, Alan Zweibel for *Saturday Night Live* (NBC).
**Current events-documentary:** William Peters for *Death of a Family* (PBS).
**Feature documentary:** Dr. Robert E. Fuisz and Hank Whittemore for *The Body Human: The Magic Sense* (CBS).

## GOLDEN GLOBE TV AWARDS: 1980

The Hollywood Foreign Press Association's 37th annual Golden Globe TV awards included:

**Best series, drama:** *Lou Grant* (CBS).
**Best series, musical or comedy:** *Taxi* (ABC), *Alice* (CBS).
**Best motion picture made for television:** *All Quiet on the Western Front* (CBS).
**Best actor, drama:** Ed Asner, *Lou Grant* (CBS).
**Best actress, drama:** Natalie Wood, *From Here to Eternity* (NBC).
**Best actor, musical or comedy:** Alan Alda, *M*A*S*H* (CBS).
**Best actress, musical or comedy:** Linda Lavin, *Alice* (CBS).
**Best supporting actor, series:** Danny De Vito, *Taxi* (ABC).
**Best supporting actress, series:** Polly Holliday, *Alice* (CBS).

## CHRISTOPHER TV AWARDS: 1980

**To CBS for:** *. . . And Your Name is Jonah, Aunt Mary, CBS Reports: How Much for the Handicapped?, The Incredible Journey of Dr. Meg Laurel, Orphan Train, A Shining Season, Walking Through the Fire.*
**To NBC for:** *The Miracle Worker, Son-Rise: A Miracle of Love, A Man Stands Alone.*
**To ABC for:** *ABC News Closeup: The Killing Ground, Friendly Fire, The Late Great Me: Story of a Teenage Alcoholic, Which Mother Is Mine?.*
**To PBS for:** *Paul Robeson.*
**To WNET for:** *The Library of Congress: Portrait of an American Institution.*

# MUSIC AWARDS: 1980

## GRAMMY AWARDS

The 22d annual Grammy awards, presented by the National Academy of Recording Arts and Sciences, included:

**Record of the year:** *What a Fool Believes,* Doobie Bros.
**Album of the year:** *52d Street,* Billy Joel.
**Song of the year:** *What a Fool Believes,* Kenny Loggins & Michael McDonald, songwriters.
**Best new artist:** Rickie Lee Jones.
**Best instrumental arrangement:** Soulful Strut.
**Best arrangement accompanying vocalist:** *What a Fool Believes,* Doobie Brothers.
**Best album package:** *Breakfast in America,* Supertramp.
**Best female pop vocal performance:** *I'll Never Love This Way Again,* Dionne Warwick.
**Best male pop vocal performance:** *52d Street,* Billy Joel.
**Best pop vocal performance by duo, group, or chorus:** *Minute By Minute,* Doobie Brothers.
**Best pop instrumental performance:** *Rise,* Herb Alpert.
**Best rhythm and blues female vocal performance:** *Deja Vu,* Dionne Warwick.
**Best rhythm and blues male vocal performance:** *Don't Stop 'Til You Get Enough,* Michael Jackson.
**Best rhythm and blues performance by duo, group, or chorus:** *After the Love Has Gone,* Earth, Wind & Fire.
**Best rhythm and blues song:** *After the Love Has Gone,* David Foster, Jay Graydon, & Bill Champlin, songwriters.
**Best jazz vocal performance:** *Fine & Mellow,* Ella Fitzgerald.
**Best jazz solo performance:** *Jousts,* Oscar Peterson.
**Best group jazz performance:** *Duet,* Gary Burton & Chick Corea.
**Best big-band jazz performance:** *At Fargo, 1940 Live,* Duke Ellington.
**Best contemporary soul gospel performance:** *I'll Be Thinking of You,* Andrae Crouch.
**Best female country vocal performance:** *Blue Kentucky Girl,* Emmylou Harris.
**Best male country vocal performance:** *The Gambler,* Kenny Rogers.
**Best country vocal performance by a duo or group:** *The Devil Went Down to Georgia,* Charlie Daniels Band.
**Best country instrumental performance:** *Big Sandy Leather Britches,* Doc & Merle Watson.
**Best country song:** *You Decorated My Life,* Bob Morrison & Debbie Hupp, songwriters.
**Best ethnic recording:** *Muddy (Mississippi) Waters Live,* Muddy Waters, Blue Sky.
**Best recording for children:** *The Muppet Movie,* Muppets.
**Best comedy recording:** *Reality ... What a Concept,* Robin Williams.
**Best spoken word recording:** *Ages of Man (Readings from Shakespeare),* Sir John Gielgud.
**Best instrumental composition:** *Main Title Theme from "Superman,"* John Williams.
**Best original score for motion-picture or television special:** *Superman,* John Williams.
**Best cast show album:** *Sweeney Todd,* Stephen Sondheim, composer/lyricist.
**Classical album of the year:** *Brahms Symphonies (4) Complete,* Sir Georg Solti, conductor.
**Best opera recording:** *Britten: Peter Grimes,* Colin Davis conducting Royal Opera House, Covent Garden.
**Best classical choral performance:** *Brahms: A German Requiem,* Sir Georg Solti conducting; Margaret Hillis, choral director; Chicago Symphony Orchestra & Chorus, London.
**Best classical performance by soloist with orchestra:** *Bartok: Concertos for Pianos Nos. 1 & 2,* with Claudio Abbado conducting Chicago Symphony Orchestra.
**Best solo classical performance:** *The Horowitz Concerts 1978/79,* Vladimir Horowitz.
**Best classical vocal:** *O Sole Mio: Favorite Neapolitan Songs,* Luciano Pavarotti.

## NARM BESTSELLING RECORD AWARDS

The National Association of Recording Merchandisers awards for bestselling records, presented in 1980, included:

**Hit single:** *My Sharona,* The Knack.
**Film soundtrack:** *The Muppet Movie.*
**Male artist:** *The Gambler,* Kenny Rogers.
**Female artist:** *Bad Girls,* Donna Summer.
**Male soul artist:** *Off the Wall,* Michael Jackson.
**Female soul artist:** *Bad Girls,* Donna Summer.
**Soul album, group:** *Midnight Magic,* Commodores.
**Male country artist:** *The Gambler,* Kenny Rogers.
**Female country artist:** *New Kind of Feeling,* Anne Murray.
**Country album, group:** *Million Mile Reflections,* The Charlie Daniels Band.
**Comedy album:** *A Wild and Crazy Guy,* Steve Martin.
**Group album:** *Breakfast in America,* Supertramp.
**Broadway cast album:** *Annie.*
**Jazz album:** *Street Life,* Crusaders.
**Classical album:** *O Sole Mio: Favorite Neapolitan Songs,* Luciano Pavarotti.
**Children's album:** *The Muppet Movie Sound Track.*
**Bestselling album of 1979:** *Breakfast in America,* Supertramp.

## ACADEMY OF COUNTRY MUSIC AWARDS

The Academy of Country Music awards, presented in 1980, included:

**Entertainer of the year:** Willie Nelson.
**Female vocalist of the year:** Crystal Gayle.
**Male vocalist of the year:** Larry Gatlin.
**Song of the year:** *It's a Cheatin' Situation,* Moe Bandy.
**Album of the year:** *Straight Ahead,* Larry Gatlin.
**Single record of the year:** *All the Gold in California,* Larry Gatlin.
**Top vocal group:** Moe Bandy and Joe Stampley.
**Top new female vocalist:** Lacy J. Dalton.
**Top new male vocalist:** R. C. Bannon.
**Country music movie of the year:** *Electric Horseman.*
**Country artist of the decade:** Loretta Lynn.

## AMERICAN MUSIC AWARDS

Chosen by a sample of 30,000 record buyers, the 1980 American Music Awards included:

**Best soul single:** *Don't Stop 'Til You Get Enough,* Michael Jackson.
**Best pop single:** *Bad Girls,* Donna Summer.
**Best country single:** *Sleeping Single in a Double Bed,* Barbara Mandrell.
**Best soul album:** *Off the Wall,* Michael Jackson.
**Best pop album:** *Spirits Having Flown,* Bee Gees.
**Best country album:** *The Gambler,* Kenny Rogers.
**Best female soul artist:** Donna Summer.
**Best male soul artist:** Michael Jackson.
**Best female pop artist:** Donna Summer.
**Best male pop artist:** Barry Manilow.
**Best female country artist:** Crystal Gayle.
**Best male country artist:** Kenny Rogers.
**Best soul group:** Commodores.
**Best pop group:** Bee Gees.
**Best country group:** Statler Brothers.

# SHOW BUSINESS PERSONALITIES

Personalities of the theater, film, TV, and entertainment world are included in the following list. Real names follow show business names.

Members of the Theater Hall of Fame, are marked with (T). Members of the Entertainment Hall of Fame, elected by the nation's entertainment editors, are marked with (E). American

Academy of Motion Picture Arts and Sciences award winners are indicated with (A) and the year for which the Oscar was given.

See also *Musicians, Composers, Singers, Dancers,* pages 58–63; *Authors and Writers,* pages 94–102. See pages 981–986 for 1980 deaths of show business personalities.

Abbott and Costello: Bud Abbott (1895–1974), Lou Costello (1906–59), comedy team
George Abbott (1887– ), theatrical producer, T
Betty Ackerman (1928– ), actress
Roy Acuff (1903– ), country music singer
Don Adams (1927– ), actor
Edie Adams (Elizabeth Edith Enke; 1929– ), singer
Joey Adams (1911– ), comedian
Julie Adams (1927– ), actress
Maude Adams (Maude Kiskadden; 1872–1953), actress, T
Dawn Addams (1930– ), actress
Larry Adler (1914– ), musician
Luther Adler (1903– ), actor
Richard Adler (1932– ), songwriter
John Agar (1921– ), actor
Brian Aherne (1902– ), British actor
Anouk Aimee (Françoise Sorya; 1932– ), actress
Claude Akins (1918– ), actor
Anna Maria Alberghetti (1936– ), Italian-born singer
Eddie Albert (Eddie Heimberger; 1908– ), actor
Edward Albert (1951– ), actor, son of Eddie Albert
Jack Albertson (1910– ), actor, A-1968
Lola Albright (1925– ), actress
Alan Alda (1936– ), actor, son of Robert Alda
Robert Alda (Alphonso d'Abruzzo; 1914– ), actor
Fred Allen (John F. Sullivan; 1894–1956), actor, comedian
Gracie Allen (1906–64), comedienne, wife of George Burns
Mel Allen (1913– ), sportscaster
Steve Allen (1921– ), entertainer
Viola Allen (1867–1948), actress, T
Woody Allen (Allen Konigsberg; 1935– ), comedian, writer
Fran Allison (1924– ), actress
June Allyson (Ella Geisman; 1923– ), actress
Herb Alpert (1937– ), musician
Robert Altman (1925– ), film director
Don Ameche (Dominic Amici; 1908– ), actor
Ames Brothers: Joe (1924– ), Gene (1925– ), Vic (1926–78), Ed (1927– ), singing group
Leon Ames (Leon Waycoff; 1903– ), actor
Nancy Ames (1937– ), singer
Morey Amsterdam (1912– ), actor and comedian
Eddie "Rochester" Anderson (1905–77), actor
Dame Judith Anderson (Frances Margaret Anderson; 1898– ), Australian actress, T
Lynn Anderson (1947– ), country music singer
Bibi Andersson (1935– ), Swedish actress
Ursula Andress (1936– ), Swiss-born actress
Andrews Sisters: LaVerne (1913–67), Maxine (1916– ), Patty (1918– ), singing group in 1940s
Dana Andrews (Carver Daniel Andrews; 1909– ), actor
Julie Andrews (Julia Wells; 1935– ), actress and singer, A-1964
Pier Angeli (1933–71), Italian-born actress
Margaret Anglin (1876–1958), actress, T
Paul Anka (1941– ), singer and composer
Ann-Margret (Ann-Margret Olsson; 1941– ), Swedish-born actress
Michael Ansara (1922– ), actor
Michelangelo Antonioni (1912– ), Italian film director
Roscoe "Fatty" Arbuckle (1887–1933), comedian
Eve Arden (Eunice Quedens; 1912– ), actress
Alan Arkin (1935– ), actor and director
Harold Arlen (1905– ), composer
Richard Arlen (1899–1976), actor, T
George Arliss (1868–1946), British actor, A-1929–30, T
Louis Armstrong (1900–71), jazz musician and singer
Desi Arnaz (1915– ), Cuban-born actor and producer
Desi Arnaz Jr. (1953– ), actor, son of Desi
Lucie Arnaz (1951– ), actress, daughter of Desi
James Arness (James Aurness; 1923– ), actor, brother of Peter Graves
Eddie Arnold (1918– ), country music singer
Edward Arnold (1890–1956), actor
Beatrice Arthur (Bernice Frankel; 1926– ), actress
Jean Arthur (Gladys Greene; 1905– ), actress
Jane Asher (1945– ), actress
Elizabeth Ashley (1940– ), actress

Edward Asner (1929– ), actor
Fred Astaire (Frederick Austerlitz; 1899– ), dancer and actor, T, E, A-1949
John Astin (1930– ), actor
Mary Astor (1906– ), actress, A-1941
Chet Atkins (1924– ), country music singer
Richard Attenborough (1923– ), actor
Lionell Atwill (1885–1946), British actor
Mischa Auer (1905–67), Russian-born actor
Jean-Pierre Aumont (1913– ), actor
Gene Autry (1907– ), singer and cowboy actor
Frankie Avalon (1939– ), singer
John Avildsen (1942– ), director, A-1976
Lew Ayres (1908– ), actor
Charles Aznavour (1924– ), French singer, actor
Lauren Bacall (Betty Joan Perske; 1924– ), actress
Burt Bacharach (1928– ), musician and composer
Jim Backus (1913– ), actor
Buddy Baer (1915– ), actor, brother of Max
Max Baer (1909–59), boxer and actor
Joan Baez (1941– ), folk singer
Pearl Bailey (1918– ), singer
Barbara Bain (1934– ), actress
Fay Bainter (1892–1968), actress, A-1938
Bill Baird (1915– ), puppeteer
Carroll Baker (1932– ), actress
Josephine Baker (1906–75), singer
George Balanchine (1904– ), choreographer, E
Ina Balin (1937– ), actress
Lucille Ball (1910– ), comedienne
Kaye Ballard (Catherine Balotta; 1926– ), actress and comedienne
Martin Balsam (1919– ), actor, A-1965
Anne Bancroft (Anne Italiano; 1931– ), actress, A-1962
Tallulah Bankhead (1903–68), actress, T
Vilma Banky (1903– ), silent-film star
Theda Bara (1890–1955), actress, first "vamp"
Brigitte Bardot (1934– ), French actress
Lynn Bari (1917– ), actress
Phineas T. Barnum (1810–91), showman
Gene Barry (Eugene Klass; 1921– ), actor
John Barry (1933– ), British composer
Ethel Barrymore (1879–1959), actress, A-1944, T
John Barrymore (John Blythe; 1882–1942), actor, T
Lionel Barrymore (1878–1954), actor, A-1930–31, T
Richard Barthelmess (1895–1963), actor
Freddie Bartholomew (1924– ), child actor in 1930s
Eva Bartok (1926– ), actress
James Barton (1890–1962), actor
Richard Basehart (1919– ), actor
Count Basie (1904– ), musician
Shirley Bassey (1937– ), singer
Alan Bates (1930– ), British actor
Anne Baxter (1923– ), actress, A-1946
Les Baxter (1922– ), musical arranger and composer
Warner Baxter (1889–1951), actor, A-1928–29
Nora Bayes (1880–1928), vaudeville entertainer, T
Orson Bean (1928– ), actor and comedian
The Beatles: George Harrison (1943– ), John Lennon (1940– ), Paul McCartney (1942– ), Ringo Starr (1940– ), British rock group
Cecil Beaton (1904– ), British photographer, designer
Warren Beatty (1937– ), actor, brother of Shirley MacLaine
Sidney Bechet (1897–1959), jazz sax musician
Bee Gees: Barry Gibb (1946– ), Robin Gibb (1949– ), Maurice Gibb (1949– ), singers, composers
Noah Beery (1884–1946), actor
Noah Beery Jr. (1916– ), actor
Wallace Beery (1889–1949), actor, A-1931–32
Ed Begley (1901–70), actor, A-1962
Leonard Bix Beiderbecke (1903–31), jazz cornetist
Harry Belafonte (1927– ), singer and actor
David Belasco (1854–1931), impresario, T
Barbara Bel Geddes (1922– ), actress
Norman Bel Geddes (1900–58), scenic designer, T
Ralph Bellamy (1904– ), actor

## SHOW BUSINESS PERSONALITIES (continued)

Jean-Paul Belmondo (1933– ), French actor
John Belushi (1950– ), actor
Robert C. Benchley (1889–1945), humorist and author
William Bendix (1906–64), actor
Richard Benjamin (1938– ), actor
Constance Bennett (1905–65), actress, sister of Joan
Joan Bennett (1910– ), actress, sister of Constance
Michael Bennett (1943– ), director
Richard Bennett (1873–1944), actor, T, father of Constance and Joan
Tony Bennett (1926– ), singer
Jack Benny (Joseph Kubelsky; 1894–1974), comedian, E
George Benson (1943– ), blues guitarist and singer
Brook Benton (1931– ), singer
Gertrude Berg (1899–1966), actress
Candice Bergen (1946– ), actress, daughter of Edgar
Edgar Bergen (1903–78), ventriloquist
Polly Bergen (1930– ), singer
Senta Berger (1941– ), Austrian actress
Ingmar Bergman (1918– ), Swedish film director, A-1956, E
Ingrid Bergman (1915– ), Swedish actress, A-1944, 1956, 1974
Busby Berkeley (1895–1976), dance director
Milton Berle (Milton Berlinger; 1908– ), comedian
Shelley Berman (1926– ), comedian
Herschel Bernardi (1923– ), actor
Sarah Bernhardt (Rosine Bernard; 1844–1923), French actress, T
Ben Bernie (1893–1943), comedian
Chuck Berry (1926– ), rock singer and composer
Bernardo Bertolucci (1940– ), Italian film director
Richard Beymer (1939– ), actor
Charles Bickford (1889–1967), actor
Theodore Bikel (1924– ), Austrian-born actor, singer
David Birney (1940– ), actor
Joey Bishop (Joseph Gottlieb; 1919– ), comedian
Jacqueline Bisset (1944– ), actress
Bill Bixby (1934– ), actor
Cilla Black (Priscilla White; 1943– ), British singer
Karen Black (1942– ), actress
Honor Blackman (1929– ), actress
Sidney Blackmer (1895–1973), actor
Vivian Blaine (Vivienne Stapleton; 1921– ), singer, actress
Janet Blair (1921– ), actress
Linda Blair (1959– ), actress
Amanda Blake (Beverly Louise Neill; 1931– ), actress
Eubie Blake (1883– ), jazz pianist
Robert Blake (Michael Gubitosi; 1933– ), actor
Ronee Blakely (1946– ), actress
Mel Blanc (1908– ), cartoon voiceman
Joan Blondell (1909–79), actress
Claire Bloom (1931– ), British actress
Ben Blue (1900–75), comedian
Monte Blue (1890–1963), actor
Ann Blyth (1928– ), actress
Dirk Bogarde (Derek Van den Bogaerde; 1921– ), British actor
Humphrey Bogart (1899–1957), actor, A-1951, E
Peter Bogdanovich (1940– ), film director
Mary Boland (1880–1965), actress
John Boles (1895–1969), singer and actor
Ray Bolger (1904– ), dancer and actor, T
Robert Bolt (1924– ), playwright
Sonny Bono (1940– ), singer, teamed with Cher
Debby Boone (1956– ), singer, daughter of Pat Boone
Pat Boone (1934– ), singer
Richard Boone (1917– ), actor
Edwin Booth (1833–93), actor, T
Shirley Booth (1907– ), actress, A-1952, T
Victor Borge (1909– ), Danish-born pianist and comedian
Ernest Borgnine (1917– ), actor, A-1955
Frank Borzage (1893–1962), director, A-1927–28, 1931–32
Tom Bosley (1927– ), actor
Connee Boswell (1907–76), singer
Clara Bow (1905–65), actress, known as "It Girl"
David Bowie (David Jones; 1947– ), rock singer
Lee Bowman (1914– ), actor
Stephen Boyd (1928–77), Irish-born actor
William Boyd (1898–1972), cowboy actor (Hopalong Cassidy)
Charles Boyer (1899–1978), French actor
Peter Boyle (1933– ), actor
Eddie Bracken (1920– ), comedian and actor
Alice Brady (1893–1939), actress, T, A-1937
Scott Brady (Gerald Tierney; 1924– ), actor
Marlon Brando (1924– ), actor, A-1954, 1972

Keefe Brasselle (1923– ), actor
Rossano Brazzi (1916– ), Italian actor
Jacques Brel (1929–78), singer, composer
Walter Brennan (1894–1974), actor, A-1936, 1938, 1940
George Brent (1904–79), Irish-born actor
Teresa Brewer (1931– ), singer
Fanny Brice (Fannie Borach; 1891–1951), actress and singer, T
Beau Bridges (1941– ), actor, son of Lloyd Bridges
Lloyd Bridges (1913– ), actor
David Brinkley (1920– ), newscaster
Frederick Brisson (1915– ), Danish-born producer
May Britt (Maybritt Wilkins; 1936– ), Swedish-born actress
Barbara Britton (1920–80), actress
James Brolin (1942– ), actor
Charles Bronson (Charles Burchinsky; 1922– ), actor
Geraldine Brooks (Geraldine Stroock, 1925-77), actress
Mel Brooks (Melvin Kaminsky; 1926– ), comedian
James Brown (1934– ), singer
Jim Brown (1936– ), actor and football star
Joe E. Brown (1892–1973), comedian
Johnny Mack Brown (1904–74), actor
Les Brown (1912– ), bandleader
Dave Brubeck (1920– ), jazz pianist, combo leader
Lenny Bruce (1926–66), comedian
Anita Bryant (1940– ), singer
Yul Brynner (1916– ), Russian-born actor, A-1956
Edgar Buchanan (1902–79), actor
Horst Buchholz (1933– ), German actor
Genevieve Bujold (1942– ), actress
Luis Buñuel (1900– ), Spanish director
Billie Burke (1885–1970), actress, T
Carol Burnett (1934– ), comedienne
George Burns (Nathan Birnbaum, 1896– ), comedian, A-1975
Raymond Burr (1917– ), Canadian-born actor
Abe Burrows (1910– ), playwright and director
Ellen Burstyn ( Edna Gilhooley; 1932– ), actress, A-1974
Richard Burton (Richard Jenkins; 1925– ), Welsh actor
Francis X. Bushman (1883–1966), actor
Red Buttons (Aaron Schwatt; 1919– ), actor and comedian, A-1957
Ruth Buzzi (1936– ), comedienne
Edd Byrnes (1933– ), actor
James Caan (1939– ), actor
Bruce Cabot (1904–73), actor
Sebastian Cabot (1918–77), British actor
Sid Caesar (1922– ), comedian
James Cagney (1900– ), actor, A-1942, E
Jeanne Cagney (1919– ), actress, sister of James
Sammy Cahn (1913– ), composer
Michael Caine (Maurice Micklewhite; 1933– ), British actor
Zoe Caldwell (1933– ), actress
Louis Calhern (Carl Vogt; 1895–1956), actor
Michael Callan (Martin Caliniff; 1935– ), actor
Cab Calloway (1907– ), jazz musician, bandleader
Corinne Calvet (1925– ), French actress
Godfrey Cambridge (1933–76), comedian and actor
Rod Cameron (1912– ), actor
Joseph Campanella (1923– ), actor
Glen Campbell (1937– ), singer
Mrs. Patrick Campbell (1865–1940), British actress, T
Dyan Cannon (1937– ), actress
Judy Canova (1916– ), actress
Cantinflas (Mario Moreno; 1913– ), Mexican comedian
Eddie Cantor (Edward Iskowitz; 1892–1964), comedian and singer, T
Lana Cantrell (1944– ), singer
Frank Capra (1897– ), Italian-born film director, A-1934, 1936, 1938
Capucine (1935– ), French actress
Claudia Cardinale (1939– ), Italian actress
Harry Carey (1878–1947), actor
MacDonald Carey (1913– ), actor
Kitty Carlisle (Catherine Holzman; 1915– ), actress
Richard Carlson (1912– ), actor
Hoagy Carmichael (1899– ), songwriter
Judy Carne (Joyce Botterill; 1939– ), British-born comedienne, singer
Art Carney (1918– ), actor, A-1974
Karen (1950– ) and Richard (1945– ) Carpenter, singing team
Leslie Caron (1931– ), French actress and dancer
Vikki Carr (Florencia Bisenta de Casillas; 1941– ), singer
David Carradine (1940– ), actor, son of John
John Carradine (1906– ), actor

Keith Carradine (1950–  ), actor, son of John
Leo Carrillo (1880–1961), actor
Diahann Carroll (1935–  ), singer and actress
Leo G. Carroll (1892–1972), British actor
Madeleine Carroll (1906–  ), British actress
Pat Carroll (1927–  ), comedienne
Jack Carson (1910–63), comedian and actor
Johnny Carson (1925–  ), television personality
Jack Carter (1923–  ), comedian
Mrs. Leslie Carter (1862–1937), actress, T
Maybelle Carter (1909–78), country music singer
Johnny Cash (1932–  ), country music singer
Peggy Cass (1926–  ), comedienne
John Cassavetes (1929–  ), actor and director
David Cassidy (1950–  ), singer and actor
Jack Cassidy (1927–76), actor
Shaun Cassidy (1958–  ), singer and actor
Irene Castle (Irene Foote; 1893–1969) and Vernon Castle
    (Vernon Blythe; 1885–1918), wife-husband dance team
Joan Caulfield (1922–  ), actress
Dick Cavett (1936–  ), television personality
Bennett Cerf (1898–1971), television panelist, publisher
George Chakiris (1933–  ), actor, A-1961
Richard Chamberlain (1935–  ), actor
Gower Champion (1921–80), and Marge Champion
    (1925–  ), husband-wife dance team
John Chancellor (1927–  ), television commentator
Jeff Chandler (1918–61), actor
Lon Chaney (1883–1930), actor
Lon Chaney Jr. (1907–73), actor
Carol Channing (1921–  ), actress
Harry Chapin (1942–  ), singer
Sir Charles Chaplin (1889–1977), British comic actor
Geraldine Chaplin (1944–  ), actress, daughter of Charles
Sydney Chaplin (1926–  ), actor, son of Charles
Cyd Charisse (Tula Finklea; 1923–  ), actress and dancer
Ray Charles (1932–  ), musician
Charley Chase (1893–1940), comedian and director
Chevy Chase (1944–  ), comedian
Ruth Chatterton (1893–1961), actress, T
Paddy Chayefsky (1923–  ), playwright, A-1976
Chubby Checker (Ernest Evans; 1941–  ), singer
Cher (Cherilyn LaPierre; 1946–  ), singer, TV personality
Maurice Chevalier (1888–1972), French actor, A-1958
Julia Child (1912–  ), television personality
Julie Christie (1941–  ), British actress, A-1965
Jordon Christopher (1941–  ), actor and musician
Edwin P. Christy (1815–62), showman and minstrel
June Christy (1925–  ), singer
Diane Cilento (1933–  ), actress
Ina Claire (Ina Fagan; 1892–  ), actress, T
Eric Clapton (1945–  ), rock singer
Bobby Clark (1888–1960), comedian, T
Dane Clark (Bernard Zanville; 1913–  ), actor
Dick Clark (1929–  ), television personality
Petula Clark (1932–  ), British singer and actress
Roy Clark (1933–  ), country music singer
Jill Clayburgh (1945–  ), actress
Jan Clayton (1925–  ), actress
Montgomery Clift (1920–66), actor
Rosemary Clooney (1928–  ), singer
Lee J. Cobb (Leo Jacob; 1911–76), actor
Charles Coburn (1877–1961), actor, A-1943
James Coburn (1928–  ), actor
Imogene Coca (1920–  ), comedienne
Joe Cocker (John Robert Cocker; 1944–  ), singer
James Coco (1920–  ), actor and comedian
George M. Cohan (1878–1942), musician, composer, T
Myron Cohen (1902–  ), comedian
Claudette Colbert (Lily Claudette Chauchoin; 1905–  ),
    actress, A-1934
Nat King Cole (1919–65), singer and musician
Natalie Cole (1950–  ), singer, daughter of Nat King Cole
Constance Collier (1878–1955), British actress, T
Joan Collins (1933–  ), British-born actress
Judy Collins (1939–  ), singer
Bud Collyer (1908–69), actor and TV personality
Ronald Colman (1891–1958), British actor, A-1947
Jerry Colonna (1904–  ), comedian
John Coltrane (1926–67), jazz sax musician
Russ Columbo (1908–34), singer
Betty Comden (1919–  ), lyricist
Anjanette Comer (1941–  ), actress
Perry Como (1912–  ), singer
Eddie Condon (1905–73), dixieland bandleader
Ray Conniff (1916–  ), bandleader, music arranger
Chester Conklin (1886–71), silent-film comedian
Sean Connery (1930–  ), Scottish-born actor

Chuck Connors (1921–  ), actor
Robert Conrad (1935–  ), actor
William Conrad (1920–  ), actor
Hans Conreid (1917–  ), actor
Richard Conte (1915–75), Italian-born actor
Tim Conway (1933–  ), actor
Rita Coolidge (1944–  ), singer, wife of Kris Kristofferson
Jackie Coogan (1914–  ), child star in silent movies
Alistair Cooke (Alfred Alistaire; 1908–  ), British author,
    television personality
Alice Cooper (Vincent Furnier; 1948–  ), rock singer
Gary Cooper (1901–61), actor, A-1941, 1952
Jackie Cooper (1922–  ), child movie star in 1930s
Francis Ford Coppola (1939–  ), director, writer, A-1974
Ellen Corby (1913–  ), actress
Jeff Corey (1914–  ), actor
Wendell Corey (1914–68), actor
Katharine Cornell (1898–1974), stage actress, T
Charles Correll (1890–1972), radio actor, "Andy"
Bill Cosby (1938–  ), actor and comedian
Dolores Costello (1905–  ), actress, wed John Barrymore
Joseph Cotten (1905–  ), actor
Tom Courtenay (1937–  ), British actor
Noel Coward (1899–1973), British playwright, actor, and
    composer, T, A-1941
Jane Cowl (1890–1950), actress, T
Wally Cox (1924–73), comic actor
Buster Crabbe (1907–  ), actor, Olympic swim champion
Jeanne Crain (1925–  ), actress
Bob Crane (1928–78), TV star of Hogan's Heroes
Broderick Crawford (1910–  ), actor, A-1949
Joan Crawford (Lucille le Sueur; 1908–77), actress, A-1945
Michael Crawford (1942–  ), actor
Richard Crenna (1926–  ), actor
Michael Crichton (1942–  ), film director, screenwriter
Donald Crisp (1880–1974), British actor, A-1941
Linda Cristal (1936–  ), actress
Michael Cristofer (1946–  ), actor and playwright
Jim Croce (1943–73), rock singer
Walter Cronkite (1916–  ), newscaster
Hume Cronyn (1911–  ), Canadian actor, T
Bing Crosby (Harry Lillis Crosby; 1904–77), singer and
    actor, E, A-1944
Bob Crosby (1913–  ), musician, brother of Bing
David Crosby (1941–  ), rock musician
Russel Crouse (1893–1966), playwright, T
Brandon Cruz (1962–  ), actor
Xavier Cugat (1900–  ), Spanish-born bandleader
George Cukor (1899–  ), director, A-1964
Bill Cullen (1920–  ), television personality
John Cullum (1930–  ), actor
Robert Culp (1930–  ), actor
Robert Cummings (1908–  ), actor
Tony Curtis (Bernard Schwarz; 1925–  ), actor
Michael Curtiz (1888–1962), Hungarian-born director,
    A-1943
Peter Cushing (1913–  ), British actor
Charlotte Cushman (1816–75), Shakespearean actress, T
Arlene Dahl (1924–  ), actress
Dan Dailey (1915–78), actor and dancer
Abby Dalton (1935–  ), actress
Arnold Daly (1875–1927), actor
Augustin Daly (1838–99), playwright, theater manager, T
John Daly (1914–  ), newscaster, TV personality
Vic Damone (Vito Farinola; 1928–  ), singer
Bill Dana (1924–  ), comedian
Dorothy Dandridge (1923–65), actress
Rodney Dangerfield (1921–  ), comedian
Bebe Daniels (1901–71), actress, wife of Ben Lyon
Kim Darby (1948–  ), actress
Denise Darcel (1925–  ), actress
Bobby Darin (1927–73), singer
Linda Darnell (1923–65), actress
James Darren (1936–  ), actor
Danielle Darrieux (1917–  ), French actress
Jane Darwell (1880–1967), actress, A-1940
Howard Da Silva (1909–  ), actor
Jules Dassin (1911–  ), director, actor, and writer
Claude Dauphin (1905–78), French actor
John Davidson (1941–  ), singer
Marion Davies (Marion Douras; 1898–1961), actress
Ann B. Davis (1908–  ), actress
Bette Davis (1908–  ), actress, A-1935, 1938
Billy Davis Jr. (1940–  ), singer
Joan Davis (1908–61), comedienne
Mac Davis (1942–  ), songwriter
Miles Davis (1927–  ), jazz trumpet player
Ossie Davis (1917–  ), playwright and actor

**SHOW BUSINESS PERSONALITIES** (*continued*)

**Sammy Davis Jr.** (1925–    ), actor, singer, and dancer
**Anthony Dawson** (1916–    ), British actor
**Dennis Day** (1917–    ), singer
**Doris Day** (Doris Kappelhoff; 1924–    ), actress and singer
**Laraine Day** (Laraine Johnson; 1920–    ), actress
**James Dean** (1931–55), actor
**Jimmy Dean** (1928–    ), singer and entertainer
**Rosemary De Camp** (1913–    ), actress
**Yvonne De Carlo** (Peggy Middleton; 1922–    ), Canadian actress
**Frances Dee** (1907–    ), actress
**Kiki Dee** (Pauline Matthews; 1947–    ), rock singer
**Ruby Dee** (Ruby Ann Wallace; 1924–    ), actress
**Sandra Dee** (Alexandra Zuck; 1942–    ), actress
**Don Defore** (1917–    ), actor
**Gloria De Haven** (1925–    ), actress
**Olivia de Havilland** (1916–    ), British-born actress, sister of Joan Fontaine, A-1946, 1949
**Albert Dekker** (1905–68), Dutch-born actor
**Dino De Laurentiis** (1919–    ), Italian producer
**Alain Delon** (1935–    ), French actor
**Dolores Del Rio** (1905–    ), Mexican actress
**Dom DeLuise** (1933–    ), actor and comedian
**William Demarest** (1892–    ), actor
**Agnes De Mille** (1909–    ), choreographer, T
**Cecil B. De Mille** (1881–1959), director
**Carol Dempster** (1902–    ), actress
**Catherine Deneuve** (1943–    ), French actress
**Robert De Niro** (1943–    ), actor, A-1974
**Richard Denning** (1914–    ), actor
**Sandy Dennis** (1937–    ), actress, A-1966
**Bob Denver** (1935–    ), comedian
**John Denver** (Henry John Deutchendorf Jr.; 1943–    ), singer
**Bo Derek** (Mary Cathleen Collins; 1957–    ), actress
**John Derek** (Derek Harris; 1926–    ), actor
**Bruce Dern** (1936–    ), actor
**Vittorio De Sica** (1902–74), Italian actor and director
**William Devane** (1937–    ), actor
**Andy Devine** (1905–77), actor and comedian
**Colleen Dewhurst** (1926–    ), Canadian-born actress
**Brandon de Wilde** (1942–72), child actor
**Susan Dey** (1952–    ), actress
**Neil Diamond** (1941–    ), singer and songwriter
**Angie Dickinson** (Angeline Brown; 1931–    ), actress
**Bo Diddley** (1928–    ), singer and musician
**Marlene Dietrich** (Maria von Losch; 1902–    ), German-born actress
**Dudley Digges** (1879–1947), Irish actor, T
**Phyllis Diller** (Phyllis Driver; 1917–    ), comedienne
**Bradford Dillman** (1930–    ), actor
**Walt Disney** (1901–66), cartoonist and producer, E
**Richard Dix** (Ernest Brimmer; 1894–1949), actor
**Fats Domino** (1928–    ), jazz musician and composer
**Phil Donahue** (1935–    ), television personality
**Troy Donahue** (Merle Johnson; 1937–    ), actor
**James Donald** (1917–    ), British actor
**Peter Donald** (1918–    ), actor
**Robert Donat** (1905–58), British actor, A-1939
**Brian Donlevy** (1899–1972), Irish-born actor
**Diana Dors** (Diana Fluk; 1931–    ), British actress
**Jimmy Dorsey** (1904–57), bandleader, brother of Tommy
**Tommy Dorsey** (1905–56), trombonist and bandleader
**Kirk Douglas** (Issur Demsky; 1916–    ), actor
**Melvyn Douglas** (Melvyn Hesselburg; 1901–    ), actor, A-1963, 1979
**Michael Douglas** (1945–    ), actor, producer, son of Kirk
**Mike Douglas** (Michael D. Dowd, Jr.; 1925–    ), television personality
**Paul Douglas** (1907–59), actor
**Morton Downey** (1902–    ), bandleader and singer
**Hugh Downs** (1921–    ), television personality
**Alfred Drake** (Alfredo Capurro; 1914–    ), Italian-born singer and actor
**Marie Dressler** (Leila Koeber; 1869–1934), actress, A-1930–31, T
**John Drew** (1853–1927), actor, T, uncle of Barrymores
**Richard Dreyfuss** (1949–    ), actor, A-1977
**James Drury** (1934–    ), actor
**Eddy Duchin** (1905–51), musician
**Peter Duchin** (1937–    ), musician
**Howard Duff** (1917–    ), actor
**Patty Duke** (1946–    ), actress, A-1962; wed to John Astin
**Keir Dullea** (1939–    ), actor
**Faye Dunaway** (1941–    ), actress, A-1976
**Isadora Duncan** (1877–1927), dancer
**Sandy Duncan** (1946–    ), actress

**James Dunn** (1905–67), actor, A-1945
**Michael Dunn** (Gary Neil Miller; 1934–73), dwarf actor
**Irene Dunne** (1904–    ), actress
**Mildred Dunnock** (1900–    ), actress
**Jimmy Durante** (1893–1980), comedian
**Deanna Durbin** (1921–    ), Canadian actress, singer, A-1938
**Dan Duryea** (1907–68), actor
**Eleanora Duse** (1858–1924), Italian actress, T
**Bob Dylan** (Robert Zimmerman; 1941–    ), folk singer, composer
**Jeanne Eagels** (1894–1929), actress, T
**Clint Eastwood** (1930–    ), actor
**Shirley Eaton** (1936–    ), British actress
**Buddy Ebsen** (Christian Rudolph Ebsen; 1908–    ), comedian, actor
**Billy Eckstine** (1914–    ), singer
**Duane Eddy** (1938–    ), rock musician
**Nelson Eddy** (1901–67), singer and actor
**Barbara Eden** (Barbara Huffman; 1934–    ), actress
**Ralph Edwards** (1913–    ), entertainer
**Vince Edwards** (1928–    ), actor
**Richard Egan** (1921–    ), actor
**Samantha Eggar** (1940–    ), British actress
**Sergei Eisenstein** (1898–1948), Russian film director
**Anita Ekberg** (1931–    ), Swedish actress
**Britt Ekland** (1942–    ), Swedish actress
**Florence Eldridge** (Florence McKechnie; 1901–    ), actress, wed to Fredric March, T
**Yvonne Elliman** (1953–    ), rock singer
**Duke Ellington** (Edward Kennedy Ellington; 1899–1974), bandleader and composer, E
**Leif Erickson** (1914–    ), actor
**Stuart Erwin** (1903–67), comedian
**Ruth Etting** (1898–1978), dancer and singer
**Dale Evans** (Frances Butts; 1912–    ), singer, actress, wed to Roy Rogers
**Dame Edith Evans** (1888–1976), British actress
**Maurice Evans** (1901–    ), Welsh actor, T
**Chad Everett** (Raymond Cramton; 1937–    ), actor
**Everly Brothers:** Don (1937–    ) and Phil (1939–    ), country music singers
**Tom Ewell** (S. Yewell Tompkins; 1909–    ), comic actor
**Fabian** (Fabian Forte; 1942–    ), singer
**Nanette Fabray** (Nanette Fabares; 1922–    ), actress
**Douglas Fairbanks** (Julius Ullman; 1883–1939), actor, husband of Mary Pickford
**Douglas Fairbanks Jr.** (1909–    ), actor and producer
**Percy Faith** (1908–76), orchestra conductor
**Peter Falk** (1927–    ), actor
**Barry Farber** (1930–    ), radio personality
**James Farentino** (1938–    ), actor
**Donna Fargo** (1945–    ), country music singer
**Felicia Farr** (1932–    ), actress
**Geraldine Farrar** (1882–1967), opera singer and actress
**Charles Farrell** (1901–    ), actor
**Glenda Farrell** (1904–71), actress
**Mia Farrow** (1945–    ), actress, daughter of Maureen O'Sullivan
**Farrah Fawcett-Majors** (1947–    ), actress
**Alice Faye** (Alice Leppert; 1915–    ), singer, actress, wed to Phil Harris
**Marty Feldman** (1933–    ), actor
**Barbara Feldon** (1941–    ), actress
**Jose Feliciano** (1945–    ), singer
**Federico Fellini** (1920–    ), Italian writer and director
**Edith Fellows** (1923–    ), actress
**Fernandel** (1903–71), French comedian
**José Ferrer** (1912–    ), actor and director, A-1950
**Mel Ferrer** (1917–    ), actor and director
**Stepin Fetchit** (Lincoln Perry; 1902–    ), comedian
**Betty Field** (1918–73), actress
**Sally Field** (1946–    ), actress, A-1979
**Dorothy Fields** (1905–74), lyricist
**Gracie Fields** (Grace Stansfield; 1898–1979), British singer and comedienne
**Totie Fields** (1931–78), comedienne
**W. C. Fields** (William Dukinfield; 1879–1946), comedian and actor, T
**Peter Finch** (William Mitchell; 1916–77), Australian actor, A-1976
**Albert Finney** (1936–    ), British actor
**Carrie Fisher** (1956–    ), actress, daughter of Eddie Fisher and Debbie Reynolds
**Eddie Fisher** (1928–    ), singer
**Minnie Maddern Fiske** (1865–1932), actress, T
**Clyde Fitch** (1865–1932), playwright, T
**Barry Fitzgerald** (William Shields; 1888–1961), Irish actor, A-1944

Ella Fitzgerald (1918– ), singer
Geraldine Fitzgerald (1912– ), actress
Roberta Flack (1939– ), rock singer
Lester Flatt (1914–79), bluegrass musician
Peggy Fleming (1948– ), Olympic ice skater
Rhonda Fleming (Marilyn Louis; 1923– ), actress
Victor Fleming (1883–1949), director, A-1939
Louise Fletcher (1935– ), actress, A-1975
Errol Flynn (1909–59), actor
Nina Foch (1924– ), actress
Dan Fogelberg (1951– ), rock singer
Red Foley (1910–68), country music singer
Henry Fonda (1905– ), actor, T, father of Jane and Peter
Jane Fonda (1937– ), actress, A-1971, 1978
Peter Fonda (1939– ), actor
Frank Fontaine (1920–78), singer and comedian
Joan Fontaine (Joan de Havilland; 1917– ), British-born actress, A-1941, sister of Olivia de Havilland
Lynn Fontanne (1887– ), actress, T, wife of Alfred Lunt
Bryan Forbes (John Clarke; 1926– ), actor, writer, and director
Glenn Ford (Gwyllyn Ford; 1916– ), Canadian-born actor
John Ford (Sean O'Feeney; 1895–1973), director, A-1935, 1940, 1941, 1952
Paul Ford (1901–76), actor
Tennessee Ernie Ford (1919– ), country music singer
Milos Forman (1932– ), Czech-born director, A-1975
Edwin Forrest (1806–72), actor, T
John Forsythe (John Freund; 1918– ), actor
Bob Fosse (1927– ), director, A-1972, T
Jodie Foster (1962– ), actress
Preston Foster (1904–70), actor
Redd Foxx (John Sanford; 1922– ), actor
Eddie Foy Jr. (1905– ), actor and dancer
Peter Frampton (1950– ), singer
Anthony Franciosa (Anthony Papaleo; 1928– ), actor
Anne Francis (1932– ), actress
Arlene Francis (1908– ), television personality
Connie Francis (Constance Franconero; 1938– ), singer
Kay Francis (Katherine Gibbs; 1899–1968), actress
James Franciscus (1934– ), actor
Aretha Franklin (1942– ), singer
William Frawley (1887–1966), actor and comedian
Bud Freeman (1906– ), musician
Mona Freeman (Monica Freeman; 1926– ), actress
William Friedkin (1939– ), director, A-1973
Rudolf Friml (1879–1972), composer, T
Charles Frohmann (1860–1815), producer, T
Jane Froman (1911–80), singer
David Frost (1939– ), television personality
David Frye (1934– ), impressionist
Allen Funt (1914– ), television personality
Betty Furness (1916– ), television personality
Martin Gabel (1912– ), actor and producer
Jean Gabin (1904–76), French actor
Clark Gable (1901–60), actor, A-1934
Eva Gabor (1926– ), actress, sister of Zsa Zsa
Zsa Zsa Gabor (Sari Gabor; 1923– ), Hungarian-born actress
Crystal Gayle (Brenda Gayle Webb; 1951– ), country music singer
Rita Gam (1928– ), actress
Joe Garagiola (1926– ), television personality
Greta Garbo (Greta Gustafson; 1905– ), Swedish actress
Ava Gardner (Lucy Johnson; 1922– ), actress
John Garfield (Julius Garfinkle; 1913–52), actor
Art Garfunkel (1941– ), singer and composer
William Gargan (1905–79), actor
Judy Garland (Frances Gumm; 1922–69), singer and actress, E, A-1939, mother of Liza Minnelli
Erroll Garner (1923–77), pianist, composer
James Garner (James Baumgarner; 1928– ), actor
Peggy Ann Garner (1931– ), child star in 1940s, A-1945
Leif Garrett (1961– ), actor, singer
Dave Garroway (1913– ), entertainer
Greer Garson (1908– ), Irish-born actress, A-1942
John Gary (1932– ), singer
Vittorio Gassman (1922– ), Italian actor
Larry Gatlin (1949– ), country music singer
John Gavin (1935– ), actor
William Gaxton (1894–1963), actor
Marvin Gaye (1939– ), singer and songwriter
Gloria Gaynor (1949– ), singer
Janet Gaynor (Laura Gainer; 1906– ), actress, A-1927-28
Mitzi Gaynor (Francesca Mitzi von Gerber; 1930– ), actress and singer
Ben Gazzara (Biago Anthony Gazzara; 1931– ), actor
Will Geer (1902–78), actor

Judy Geeson (1950– ), British actress
Leo Genn (1905– ), British actor
Bobbie Gentry (Roberta Streeter; 1944– ), country music singer
Grace George (1879–1961), actress, T
Ira Gershwin (1896– ), lyricist, T, brother of George
Stan Getz (1927– ), saxophonist
Andy Gibb (1958– ), singer
Georgia Gibbs (1926– ), singer
Hoot Gibson (1892–1962), cowboy actor
Sir John Gielgud (1904– ), British actor, T
Billy Gilbert (1894–1971), actor and musician
John Gilbert (1897–1936), actor
Jack Gilford (1907– ), actor
Dizzy Gillespie (John Birks Gillespie; 1917– ), jazz trumpeter, developed bop
William Gillette (1855–1937), actor, T
Hermione Gingold (1897– ), British comedienne
Dorothy Gish (1898–1968), actress, sister of Lillian
Lillian Gish (Lillian de Guiche; 1896– ), actress, T
George Givot (1903– ), actor
Jackie Gleason (1916– ), comedian, actor
James Gleason (1886–1959), actor
George Gobel (1920– ), comedian
Jean Luc Godard (1930– ), French film director
Paulette Goddard (Marion Levy; 1911– ), actress
Arthur Godfrey (1903– ), radio and TV personality
John Golden (1874–1955), playwright and producer, T
Bobby Goldsboro (1942– ), country music singer
Sam Goldwyn (Samuel Goldfish; 1882–1974), director, producer, A-1946
Benny Goodman (1909– ), jazz clarinetist, bandleader
Dody Goodman (1929– ), actress
Ruth Gordon (1896– ), actress, playwright, A-1968, T
Lesley Gore (1946– ), actress
Eydie Gormé (1935– ), singer, wed to Steve Lawrence
Frank Gorshin (1932– ), actor
Marjoe Gortner (1945– ), actor
Freeman Gosden (1899– ), radio actor, "Amos"
Elliott Gould (Elliott Goldstein; 1938– ), actor
Morton Gould (1913– ), composer
Robert Goulet (1933– ), Canadian singer
Betty Grable (1916–73), actress
Martha Graham (1894– ), dancer
Gloria Grahame (Gloria Hallward; 1924– ), actress, A-1952
Farley Granger (1925– ), actor
Stewart Granger (James Stewart; 1913– ), British actor
Cary Grant (Archibald Leach; 1904– ), British-born actor
Kathryn Grant (1933– ), actress
Lee Grant (Lyova Rosenthal; 1929– ), actress, A-1975
Bonita Granville (1923– ), actress and producer
Ben Grauer (1908–77), radio and television announcer
Peter Graves (Peter Aurness; 1925– ), actor, brother of James Arness
Kathryn Grayson (Zelma Hedrick; 1922– ), actress and singer
Buddy Greco (1926– ), singer
José Greco (1918– ), Italian-born dancer
Adolph Green (1915– ), actor and lyricist
Al Green (1946– ), country music singer
Lorne Greene (1915– ), Canadian-born actor
Sidney Greenstreet (1879–1954), British-born actor
Charlotte Greenwood (1893–78), comedienne, dancer, T
Joan Greenwood (1921– ), British actress and director
Dick Gregory (1932– ), comedian
Joyce Grenfell (Joyce Phipps; 1910–79), British actress
Joel Grey (Joel Katz; 1932– ), actor, A-1972
Merv Griffin (1925– ), television entertainer
Andy Griffith (1926– ), actor
D.W. Griffith (1875–1948), 1st major U.S. film director, E
Hugh Griffith (1912–80), Welsh actor, A-1959
Tammy Grimes (1934– ), actress
Harry Guardino (1925– ), actor
Sir Alec Guinness (1914– ), British actor, A-1957
Sacha Guitry (1885–1957), French writer-director
Arlo Guthrie (1947– ), singer and actor
Sir Tyrone Guthrie (1900–71), British director, T
Woody Guthrie (1912–67), folk singer and composer
Edmund Gwenn (1875–1959), British actor, A-1947
Fred Gwynne (1924– ), actor
Buddy Hackett (Leonard Hacker; 1924– ), comedian
Joan Hackett (1942– ), actress
Gene Hackman (1930– ), actor, A-1971
Uta Hagen (1919– ), actress
Merle Haggard (1937– ), country music singer
Larry Hagman (1930– ), actor, son of Mary Martin
Alan Hale (Rufus Alan McKahan; 1892–1950), actor

**SHOW BUSINESS PERSONALITIES** (continued)

Alan Hale Jr. (1918–   ), actor, son of Alan
Bill Haley (1927–   ), singer and songwriter, said to have coined phrase "rock and roll"
Jack Haley (1902–79), comedian
Monty Hall (1923–   ), television personality
George Hamilton (1939–   ), actor
Marvin Hamlisch (1945–   ), composer and pianist
Oscar Hammerstein II (1895–1960), composer, T
Walter Hampden (1879–1955), actor, T
Susan Hampshire (1941–   ), actress
Lionel Hampton (1914–   ), jazz pianist, combo leader
W. C. Handy (1873–1958), blues composer
Otto Harbach (1873–1963), playwright, librettist, T
Ann Harding (1902–   ), actress
Sir Cedric Hardwicke (1893–1964), British actor
Oliver Hardy (1892–1957), comedian with Stan Laurel
Earl of Harewood (1923–   ), British impresario
Jean ("platinum blonde") Harlow (Harlean Carpenter; 1911–37), actress
Valerie Harper (1940–   ), actress
Barbara Harris (1937–   ), actress
Emmylou Harris (1949–   ), country music singer
Julie Harris (1925–   ), actress, T
Phil Harris (1906–   ), actor and comedian
Richard Harris (1933–   ), Irish actor
Rosemary Harris (1930–   ), British actress
Sam H. Harris (1872–1941), producer, T
George Harrison (1943–   ), singer, musician (Beatles)
Rex Harrison (Reginald Carey; 1908–   ), British actor, A-1964, T
Lorenz Hart (1895–1943), lyricist, T
William S. Hart (1870–1946), silent-screen cowboy star
David Hartman (1935–   ), television personality
Elizabeth Hartman (1945–   ), actress
Laurence Harvey (Larushka Skikne; 1928–73), Lithuanian-born actor
Signe Hasso (1910–   ), Swedish actress
Hurd Hatfield (1918–   ), actor
Donny Hathaway (1945–   ), singer
Henry Hathaway (1898–   ), director
June Haver (1926–   ), actress, wife of Fred MacMurray
June Havoc (June Hovick; 1916–   ), actress, sister of Gypsy Rose Lee
Jack Hawkins (1910–73), British actor
Howard Hawks (1896–77), director and screenwriter, A-1975
Goldie Hawn (1945–   ), comedienne, A-1969
Jill Haworth (1946–   ), British actress
Sessue Hayakawa (1890–1973), Japanese actor
Sterling Hayden (1916–   ), actor
Helen Hayes (Helen Brown; 1901–   ), actress, A-1931–32, 1970, T
Isaac Hayes (1942–   ), composer
Leland Hayward (1902–71), producer
Louis Hayward (1909–   ), South African-born actor
Susan Hayward (Edythe Marriner; 1919–75), actress, A-1958
Rita Hayworth (Marguerite Cansino; 1918–   ), actress
Edith Head (1907–   ), costume designer, A-1949, 1951, 1952, 1973
Joey Heatherton (1944–   ), actress
Eileen Heckart (1919–   ), actress
Van Heflin (Emmet Evan Heflin; 1910–71), actor, A-1942, 1972
Lillian Hellman (1905–   ), playwright, T
David Hemmings (1942–   ), British actor
Florence Henderson (1934–   ), singer and actress
Skitch Henderson (Lyle Russell Cedric; 1918–   ), musician
Jimi Hendrix (1943–70), singer
Sonja Henie (1913–69), Norwegian ice skater and actress
Paul Henreid (1907–   ), Austrian-born actor
Audrey Hepburn (1929–   ), Belgian-born actress, A-1953
Katharine Hepburn (1909–   ), actress, A-1932–33, 1967, 1968, E, T
Hugh Herbert (1897–1952), comedian
Victor Herbert (1859–1924), Irish-American composer, T
Woody Herman (1913–   ), jazz clarinetist, bandleader
James A. Herne (1839–1901), playwright and actor, T
Jean Hersholt (1886–1956), Danish-born actor
Charlton Heston (1924–   ), actor, A-1959
Eddie Heywood (1926–   ), jazz musician
Hildegarde (1906–   ), singer
George Roy Hill (1922–   ), director, A-1973
Wendy Hiller (1912–   ), British actress, A-1958
Mimi Hines (1933–   ), actress and singer
Pat Hingle (1924–   ), actor
Al Hirt (1922–   ), jazz musician

Alfred Hitchcock (1899–1980), British director, E
Raymond Hitchcock (1865–1929), actor, T
Don Ho (1930–   ), Hawaiian singer
Eddie Hodges (1947–   ), actor
John Hodiak (1914–55), actor
Dustin Hoffman (1937–   ), actor, A-1979
Hal Holbrook (1925–   ), actor and impersonator
William Holden (William Beedle; 1918–   ), actor, A-1953
Geoffrey Holder (1930–   ), choreographer
Billie Holiday (1915–59), blues singer
Judy Holliday (Judith Tuvim; 1923–65), actress, A-1950
Earl Holliman (Anthony Numkena; 1928–   ), actor
Stanley Holloway (1890–   ), British actor
Buddy Holly (1936–59), country and rock singer
Celeste Holm (1919–   ), actress, A-1947
Jack Holt (1888–1951), actor
Tim Holt (1918–73), actor, son of Jack
Oscar Homolka (1901–78), Austrian-born actor
Bob Hope (Leslie Townes Hope; 1903–   ), comedian, E, A-1940, 1944, 1952 (honorary awards)
Mary Hopkin (1950–   ), singer
Arthur Hopkins (1878–1950), producer, T
Miriam Hopkins (1902–72), actress
Dennis Hopper (1936–   ), actor
De Wolf Hopper (1858–1935), actor, T
Hedda Hopper (1890–1966), columnist, wife of De Wolf
William Hopper (1915–70), actor, son of Hedda
Lena Horne (1917–   ), singer and actress
Edward Everett Horton (1888–1970), actor
Harry Houdini (Ehrich Weiss; 1874–1926), magician
John Houseman (Jacques Haussmann; 1902–   ), actor, producer, T, A-1973
Eugene Howard (1881–1965), vaudevillian, T
Joe Howard (1867–1961), vaudevillian
Ken Howard (1944–   ), actor
Leslie Howard (Leslie Stainer; 1893–1943), British actor
Ron Howard (1954–   ), actor
Trevor Howard (1916–   ), British actor
Willie Howard (1886–1949), vaudevillian, T
Sally Ann Howes (1934–   ), actress and singer
Rock Hudson (Roy Fitzgerald; 1925–   ), actor
Howard Hughes (1905–76), movie producer, director
Henry Hull (1890–1977), actor, T
Josephine Hull (1886–1957), actress, A-1950
Engelbert Humperdinck (Arnold Dorsey; 1937–   ), singer
Marsha Hunt (1917–   ), actress
Kim Hunter (Janet Cole; 1922–   ), actress, A-1951
Tab Hunter (Art Gelian; 1931–   ), actor
Chet Huntley (1911–74), newscaster
Sol Hurok (1888–1974), impresario
Olivia Hussey (1952–   ), actress
Ruth Hussey (Ruth Carol O'Rourke; 1917–   ), actress
John Huston (1906–   ), writer, director, actor, A-1948
Walter Huston (Walter Houghston; 1884–1950), actor, T, A-1948, father of John
Betty Hutton (Betty Thornburg; 1921–   ), actress
Lauren Hutton (Mary Hutton; 1944–   ), actress
Janis Ian (1951–   ), singer
Marty Ingels (1936–   ), comedian
John Ireland (1915–   ), Canadian actor
José Iturbi (1895–1980), Spanish-born musician
Burl Ives (Burl Icle Ivanhoe; 1909–   ), actor and folk singer, A-1958
Anne Jackson (1925–   ), actress, wife of Eli Wallach
Glenda Jackson (1936–   ), British actress, A-1970, 1973
Kate Jackson (1949–   ), actress
Mahalia Jackson (1911–72), spiritual singer
Michael Jackson (1958–   ), rock singer
Sam Jaffe (1891–   ), actor
Dean Jagger (1903–   ), actor, A-1949
Mick Jagger (1944–   ), musician
Dennis James (1917–   ), television personality
Harry James (1916–   ), musician and bandleader
Joni James (1930–   ), singer
Elsie Janis (1889–1956), musical-comedy star, T
Emil Jannings (1886–1950), German actor, A-1927–28
David Janssen (David Meyer; 1930–80), actor
Renée Jeanmaire (1924–   ), French dancer and actress
Joseph Jefferson (1829–1905), actor, T
Waylon Jennings (1933–   ), country music singer
George E. Jessel (1898–   ), entertainer
Billy Joel (1949–   ), rock singer
Elton John (Reginald Dwight; 1947–   ), rock singer
Glynis Johns (1923–   ), South African-born actress
Ben Johnson (1920–   ), actor, A-1971
Celia Johnson (1908–   ), British actress
Chic Johnson (1892–1962), comedian with Ole Olsen
Rafer Johnson (1935–   ), actor, Olympic athlete

Van Johnson (1916–    ), actor
Al Jolson (Asa Yoelson; 1880–1950), singer, starred in first talking picture, T
Allan Jones (1907–    ), singer, actor
Buck Jones (1889–1942), cowboy actor
Carolyn Jones (1929–    ), singer and actress
Dean Jones (1935–    ), actor
Jack Jones (1938–    ), singer
James Earl Jones (1931–    ), actor
Jennifer Jones (Phyllis Isley; 1919–    ), actress, A-1943
Robert E. Jones (1887–1954), designer and director, T
Shirley Jones (1934–    ), actress and singer, A-1960
Spike Jones (Lindley Armstrong Jones; 1911–65), musician and comedian
Tom Jones (Thomas Jones Woodward; 1940–    ), rock singer
Janis Joplin (1943–70), singer
Scott Joplin (1868–1917), ragtime composer
Victor Jory (1902–    ), actor
Louis Jourdan (Louis Gendre; 1919–    ), French actor
Katy Jurado (1927–    ), Mexican actress
Curt Jurgens (1915–    ), German actor
Madeline Kahn (1942–    ), actress
Ida Kaminska (1899–1980), actress
Garson Kanin (1912–    ), playwright
Gabriel Kaplan (1945–    ), comedian
Boris Karloff (William Pratt; 1885–1969), British-born actor
Danny Kaye (David Kaminsky; 1913–    ), comedian and actor, A-1954
Sammy Kaye (1910–    ), musician and bandleader
Elia Kazan (1909–    ), Turkish-born director and writer, T, A-1947, 1954
Lainie Kazan (1940–    ), singer
Stacy Keach (1941–    ), actor
Buster Keaton (Joseph Francis Keaton; 1895–1966), comedian and actor, A-1959
Diane Keaton (1949–    ), actress, A-1977
Lila Kedrova (1918–    ), Russian-French actress, A-1964
Howard Keel (1919–    ), actor and singer
Ruby Keeler (Ethel Keeler; 1909–    ), actress
Laura Keene (1820–73), actress and theater manager, T
Bob Keeshan (1927–    ), TV personality (Captain Kangaroo)
Harvey Keitel (1941–    ), actor
Brian Keith (1921–    ), actor
Cecil Kellaway (1893–1973), South African-born actor
Marthe Keller (1946–    ), actress
Sally Kellerman (1937–    ), actress
Emmett Kelly (1898–79), clown
Gene Kelly (1912–    ), dancer and actor, A-1951
Grace Kelly (1928–    ), actress, A-1954
Patsy Kelly (1910–    ), comedienne
Eddie Kendricks (1940–    ), singer
Arthur Kennedy (1914–    ), actor
George Kennedy (1925–    ), actor, A-1967
Stan Kenton (Stanley Newcomb; 1912–79), jazz pianist and bandleader
Jerome Kern (1885–1945), composer, T
Deborah Kerr (1921–    ), British actress
Larry Kert (1930–    ), actor, singer
Evelyn Keyes (1919–    ), actress
Richard Kiley (1922–    ), actor and singer
Alan King (Irwin Alan Kniberg; 1927–    ), comedian
B.B. King (1925–    ), blues singer
Carole King (1941–    ), singer and composer
Dennis King (1897–1971), British-born actor
Lisa Kirk (1925–    ), actress and singer
Phyllis Kirk (Phyllis Kirkegaard; 1930–    ), actress
Dorothy Kirsten (1919–    ), singer
Eartha Kitt (1928–    ), singer
Werner Klemperer (1920–    ), German-born actor
Robert Klein (1942–    ), comedian
Jack Klugman (1922–    ), actor
Evel Knievel (Robert Craig, 1938–    ), daredevil motorcyclist
Gladys Knight (1944–    ), rock singer
Shirley Knight (1937–    ), actress, T
Don Knotts (1924–    ), actor
Sir Alexander Korda (1893–1956), Hungarian-British movie producer
Harvey Korman (1927–    ), actor
Ernie Kovacs (1919–62), comedian and comic actor
Stanley Kramer (1913–    ), director
Kris Kristofferson (1936–    ), actor and singer, husband of Rita Coolidge
Gene Krupa (1909–73), jazz drummer
Stanley Kubrick (1928–    ), producer and director
Akira Kurosawa (1910–    ), Japanese director
Kay Kyser (1905–    ), musician and bandleader

Alan Ladd (1913–64), actor
Bert Lahr (Irving Lahrheim; 1895–1967), comedian, T
Frankie Laine (Frank Paul Lo Vecchio; 1913–    ), singer
Veronica Lake (Constance Ockleman; 1919–73), actress
Hedy Lamarr (Hedwig Kiesler; 1915–    ), Austrian-born actress
Dorothy Lamour (Dorothy Kaumeyer; 1914–    ), actress
Burt Lancaster (1913–    ), actor, A-1960
Elsa Lanchester (Elizabeth Sullivan; 1902–    ), British actress
Martin Landau (1933–    ), actor
Michael Landon (Michael Orowitz; 1937–    ), actor and director
Fritz Lang (1890–1976), Austrian-born director
Walter Lang (1898–1972), director
Harry Langdon (1884–1944), comedian
Hope Lange (1931–    ), actress
Frank Langella (1940–    ), actor
Francis Langford (1914–    ), singer
Lily Langtry (Emily Charlotte Le Breton; 1856–1929), British actress, T
Angela Lansbury (1925–    ), British-born actress
Robert Lansing (Robert H. Broom; 1929–    ), actor
Mario Lanza (Alfredo Cocozza; 1921–59), singer and actor
Julius La Rosa (1930–    ), singer
Jesse L. Lasky (1880–1958), producer
Louise Lasser (1940–    ), actress
Sir Harry Lauder (Harry MacLennan; 1870–1950), Scottish comedian
Charles Laughton (1889–1962), British-American actor, A-1932–33, wed to Elsa Lanchester
Stan Laurel (Arthur Jefferson; 1890–1965), British-born comedian, teamed with Oliver Hardy
Piper Laurie (Rosetta Jacobs; 1932–    ), actress
Peter Lawford (1923–    ), British-born actor
Carol Lawrence (Carol Maria Laraia; 1935–    ), dancer and actress
Gertrude Lawrence (Gertrude Klasen; 1898–1952), British actress, singer, T
Steve Lawrence (Steve Liebowitz; 1935–    ), singer, wed to Eydie Gormé
Vicki Lawrence (1949–    ), actress, singer
Cloris Leachman (1926–    ), actress, A-1971
David Lean (1908–    ), British director, A-1957, 1962
Huddie "Lead Belly" Ledbetter (1888–1949), folk singer
Brenda Lee (1944–    ), singer
Canada Lee (1907–1952), actor
Christopher Lee (1922–    ), British actor
Gypsy Rose Lee (Louise Hovick; 1914–70), dancer, sister of June Havoc
Peggy Lee (Norma Egstrom; 1920–    ), singer
Eva Le Gallienne (1899–    ), British-born actress, T
Janet Leigh (Jeanette Morrison; 1927–    ), actress
Vivien Leigh (Vivien Hartley; 1913–67), British actress, A-1939, 1951
Margaret Leighton (1922–76), British actress
Jack Lemmon (1925–    ), actor, A-1955, 1973
Dianne Lennon (1939–    ), singer
Janet Lennon (1946–    ), singer
John Lennon (1940–80), British singer, musician (Beatles)
Kathy Lennon (1934–    ), singer
Peggy Lennon (1941–    ), singer
Lotte Lenya (Caroline Blamauer; 1900–    ), Austrian-born actress and singer
Jack E. Leonard (1911–73), comedian
Sheldon Leonard (Sheldon Bershad; 1907–    ), actor and director
Alan Jay Lerner (1918–    ), librettist and lyricist
Mervyn LeRoy (1900–    ), actor and director
Joan Leslie (1925–    ), actress
Jerry Lester (1911–    ), comedian
Oscar Levant (1906–72), musician and comedian
Sam Levene (1906–    ), actor
Sam Levenson (1911–    ), humorist
Joseph E. Levine (1905–    ), producer
Jerry Lewis (Joseph Levitch; 1926–    ), comedian, teamed with Dean Martin
Jerry Lee Lewis (1935–    ), country music artist
Joe E. Lewis (1902–71), comedian
Shari Lewis (Shari Hurwitz; 1934–    ), puppeteer
Ted Lewis (Theodore Friedman; 1891–1971), musician and vaudevillian
Wladziu Valentino Liberace (1920–    ), pianist
Beatrice Lillie (Constance Sylvia Munston; 1898–    ), British comedienne, T
Elmo Lincoln (Otto Elmo Linkenhelter; 1889–1952), actor, first film Tarzan
Jenny Lind (1820–87), Swedish singer

## SHOW BUSINESS PERSONALITIES (continued)

Hal Linden (Harold Lipshitz; 1931–   ), actor
Viveca Lindfors (1920–   ), Swedish-born actress
Pia Lindstrom (1938–   ), newscaster, daughter of Ingrid Bergman
Art Linkletter (1912–   ), entertainer
Virna Lisi (1937–   ), Italian actress
Cleavon Little (1939–   ), actor
Rich Little (1938–   ), Canadian-born comedian
Jay Livingston (1915–   ), composer
Mary Livingstone (1909–   ), comedienne, wed to Jack Benny
Frank Lloyd (1888–1960), Scottish-born director, A-1928–29, 1932–33
Harold Lloyd (1893–1971), comedian, A-1952
Gene Lockhart (1891–1957), Canadian actor
June Lockhart (1925–   ), actress, daughter of Gene
Margaret Lockwood (Margaret Day; 1916–   ), British actress
Frank Loesser (1910–69), songwriter
Ella Logan (1913–69), singer and actress
Joshua Logan (1908–   ), director and producer, T
Kenny Loggins (1948–   ), rock musician
Gina Lollobrigida (1928–   ), Italian actress
Carole Lombard (Jane Peters; 1908–42), actress, wed to Clark Gable
Guy Lombardo (1902–77), musician and bandleader
Julie London (Julie Peck; 1926–   ), singer and actress
Trini Lopez (1937–   ), singer
Jack Lord (1930–   ), actor
Pauline Lord (1890–1950), actress, T
Sophia Loren (Sophia Scicoloni; 1934–   ), Italian actress, A-1961
Peter Lorre (Laszlo Löewenstein; 1904–64), Hungarian-born actor
Dorothy Loudon (1932–   ), actress
Anita Louise (1915–70), actress
Tina Louise (1935–   ), actress
Bessie Love (1898–   ), actress
Frank Lovejoy (1912–62), actor
Edmund Lowe (1892–1971), actor
Myrna Loy (Myrna Williams; 1905–   ), actress
Ernst Lubitsch (1892–1947), German-born producer
Bela Lugosi (Arisztid Olt, 1888–1956), Hungarian-born actor
Paul Lukas (1895–1971), Hungarian-born actor, A-1943
Sidney Lumet (1924–   ), director
William Lundigan (1914–75), actor
Alfred Lunt (1893–1977), actor, wed to Lynn Fontanne, T
Ida Lupino (1918–   ), actress and director
Paul Lynde (1926–   ), comedian
Carol Lynley (1942–   ), actress
Diana Lynn (1924–71), actress
Jeffrey Lynn (1909–   ), actor
Loretta Lynn (1932–   ), country music singer
Ben Lyon (1901–79), actor, husband of Bebe Daniels
James MacArthur (1937–   ), actor, son of Helen Hayes
Jeanette MacDonald (1907–65), singer and actress
Jack MacGouran (1918–73), Irish actor
Ali MacGraw (1938–   ), actress
Ted Mack (1904–76), television personality
Gisele MacKenzie (Marie LaFeche; 1927–   ), singer
Shirley MacLaine (Shirley Beaty; 1934–   ), actress, sister of Warren Beatty
Barton MacLane (1900–69), actor
Fred MacMurray (1908–   ), actor
Patrick MacNee (1922–   ), British actor
Gordon MacRae (1921–   ), singer and actor
Sheila MacRae (1924–   ), comedienne
George Macready (1909–73), actor
Bill Macy (1922–   ), actor
Donald Madden (1933–   ), actor
Guy Madison (Robert Moseley; 1922–   ), actor
Patrick Magee (1924–   ), British actor
Anna Magnani (1908–73), Italian actress, A-1955
Marjorie Main (1890–1975), actress
Lee Majors (1940–   ), television actor
Miriam Makeba (1932–   ), singer
Karl Malden (Mladen Sekulovich; 1914–   ), actor, A-1951
Dorothy Malone (Dorothy Maloney; 1925–   ), actress, A-1956
Rouben Mamoulian (1897–   ), Russian-born director
Melissa Manchester (1951–   ), singer
Henry Mancini (1922–   ), musician and composer
Barry Manilow (1946–   ), singer and composer
Joseph L. Mankiewicz (1909–   ), director, writer, and producer, A-1949, 1950
Delbert Mann (1920–   ), director, A-1955

Jayne Mansfield (Vera Jane Palmer; 1933–67), actress
Richard Mansfield (1857–1907), German-Amer. actor, T
Robert B. Mantell (1854–1928), actor, T
Marcel Marceau (1923–   ), French pantomimist
Fredric March (Frederick Bickel; 1897–1975), actor, A-1931–32, 1946, T
Julia Marlowe (Sarah Frances Frost; 1865–1950), Shakespearean actress, T
Jean Marsh (1934–   ), actress
E. G. Marshall (1910–   ), actor
Herbert Marshall (1890–1966), British actor
Penny Marshall (1942–   ), actress
Dean Martin (Dino Crocetti; 1917–   ), singer and actor, teamed with Jerry Lewis
Dick Martin (1922–   ), television comedian
Mary Martin (1913–   ), singer and actress, T
Ross Martin (1920–   ), actor
Steve Martin (1945–   ), comedian
Tony Martin (Alvin Morris; 1913–   ), singer
Al Martino (1927–   ), singer
Lee Marvin (1924–   ), actor, A-1965
Marx Brothers: Chico (1886–1961), Harpo (1888–1964), Groucho (1890–1977), Gummo (1897–1977), Zeppo (1901–1979), comedy team
James Mason (1909–   ), British actor
Marsha Mason (1942–   ), actress
Raymond Massey (1896–   ), Canadian-born actor
Marcello Mastroianni (1924–   ), Italian actor
Johnny Mathis (1935–   ), singer
Walter Matthau (Walter Matasschanskayasky; 1920–   ), actor, A-1966
Victor Mature (1916–   ), actor
Marilyn Maxwell (Marvel Maxwell; 1922–72), actress
Elaine May (1932–   ), comedienne and writer
Louis B. Mayer (1885–1957), producer, A-1950
Curtis Mayfield (1942–   ), singer and songwriter
Virginia Mayo (Virginia Jones; 1922–   ), actress
Andrea McArdle (1964–   ), actress and singer
Mary Margaret McBride (1899–1976), radio personality
David McCallum (1933–   ), Scottish-born actor
Mercedes McCambridge (1918–   ), actress, A-1949
Leo McCarey (1898–1969), director, A-1937, 1944
Kevin McCarthy (1914–   ), actor
Paul McCartney (1942–   ), British singer (Beatles)
Doug McClure (1935–   ), actor
Marilyn McCoo (1943–   ), singer
Patty McCormack (1945–   ), actress
Myron McCormick (1907–62), actor
Tim McCoy (1891–1978), cowboy actor
Joel McCrea (1905–   ), actor
Hattie McDaniel (1895–1952), actress, A-1939
Marie McDonald (1924–65), comedienne
Roddy McDowall (1928–   ), British-born actor
Darren McGavin (1925–   ), actor
Fibber McGee (1896–   ), comedian
Molly McGee (1898–1961), comedienne
Patrick McGoohan (1928–   ), actor
Maureen McGovern (1949–   ), folk singer
Dorothy McGuire (1919–   ), actress
Frank McHugh (1899–   ), actor
Siobhan McKenna (1923–   ), Irish actress
Rod McKuen (1933–   ), singer and composer
Victor McLaglen (1883–1959), British-born actor, A-1935
Ed McMahon (1923–   ), actor and television personality
Kristy McNichol (1963–   ), actress
Steve McQueen (1932–80), actor
Audrey Meadows (1929–   ), actress
Jayne Meadows (1926–   ), actress
Anne Meara (1929–   ), comedienne
Donald Meek (1880–1946), Scottish-born actor
Ralph Meeker (Ralph Rathgeber; 1920–   ), actor
Melanie (1947–   ), singer
Sergio Mendes (1941–   ), jazz musician
Adolphe Menjou (1890–1963), actor
Helen Menken (1901–66), actress, T
Johnny Mercer (1909–76), popular-music composer
Melina Mercouri (1915–   ), Greek actress
Burgess Meredith (George Burgess; 1909–   ), actor
Una Merkel (1903–   ), actress
Ethel Merman (Ethel Zimmerman; 1908–   ), singer and actress, T
David Merrick (1911–   ), stage producer, T
Dina Merrill (Nedenia Rumbough; 1925–   ), actress
Gary Merrill (1914–   ), actor
Bette Midler (1945–   ), singer and comedienne
Jo Mielziner (1901–76), scenic designer, T
Toshiro Mifune (1920–   ), Japanese actor
Sarah Miles (1941–   ), British actress

Sylvia Miles (1932–    ), actress
Vera Miles (Vera Ralston; 1929–    ), actress
Lewis Milestone (1895–    ), director, A-1927–28, 1929–30
Ray Milland (Reginald Truscott-Jones; 1905–    ), actor, A-1945
Ann Miller (Lucy Collier; 1919–    ), dancer
Glenn Miller (1909–44), jazz trombonist and bandleader
Henry Miller (1860–1926), actor and theater manager, T
Marilyn Miller (Mary Reynolds; 1898–1936), actress, T
Mitch Miller (1911–    ), musician
Roger Miller (1936–    ), country music singer
Steve Miller (1943–    ), rock guitarist
Hayley Mills (1946–    ), actress, daughter of John
John Mills (1908–    ), British actor, A-1970
Juliet Mills (1941–    ), actress, daughter of John
Martin Milner (1927–    ), actor
Yvette Mimieux (1942–    ), actress
Sal Mineo (1939–76), actor
Liza Minnelli (1945–    ), singer and actress, A-1972, daughter of Judy Garland and Vincente Minnelli
Vincente Minnelli (1913–    ), director, A-1958
Carmen Miranda (1914–55), Portuguese-born singer
Cameron Mitchell (Cameron Mizell; 1918–    ), actor
Joni Mitchell (1943–    ), folk singer
Thomas Mitchell (1898–1962), actor, A-1939
Robert Mitchum (1917–    ), actor
Tom Mix (1880–1940), cowboy actor
Helena Modjeska (1845–1909), Polish-American actress, T
Ferenc Molnar (1878–1952), Hungarian-born playwright, T
Thelonious Monk (1918–    ), bop jazz pianist, composer
Marilyn Monroe (Norma Jean Baker; 1926–62), actress, sex symbol of 1960s
Vaughn Monroe (1911–73), musician and bandleader
Ricardo Montalban (1920–    ), Mexican actor
Yves Montand (Ivo Levi; 1921–    ), French singer, actor
Elizabeth Montgomery (1933–    ), actress
George Montgomery (George Letz; 1916–    ), actor
Robert Montgomery (1904–    ), actor, father of Elizabeth
Colleen Moore (Kathleen Morrison; 1900–    ), actress
Garry Moore (Thomas Garrison Morfit; 1915–    ), television personality
Grace Moore (1902–47), operatic singer and film actress
Mary Tyler Moore (1936–    ), actress
Melba Moore (Beatrice Moore; 1945–    , actress and singer
Roger Moore (1928–    ), British actor
Terry Moore (Helen Koford; 1932–    ), actress
Victor Moore (1876–1962), vaudeville comedian, actor, T
Agnes Moorehead (1906–74), actress
Jeanne Moreau (1928–    ), French actress
Rita Moreno (Rosita Dolores Alverio; 1931–    ), actress, A-1961
Dennis Morgan (Stanley Morner; 1910–    ), actor
Frank Morgan (Francis Wupperman; 1890–1949), actor
Helen Morgan (1900–41), actress and singer
Henry Morgan (1915–    ), comedian
Jane Morgan (Florence Currier; 1916–    ), singer
Michael Moriarty (1942–    ), actor
Robert Morley (1908–    ), British actor
Chester Morris (1901–70), actor
Robert Morse (1931–    ), actor
Jelly Roll Morton (1885–1941), jazz pianist, composer
Zero Mostel (1915–77), actor, singer, and comedian
Roger Mudd (1928–    ), newcaster
Maria Muldaur (1943–    ), folk singer
Edward Mulhare (1921–    ), British actor
Paul Muni (1896–1967), actor, A-1936, T
Patrice Munsel (1925–    ), singer
Audie Murphy (1924–71), actor, World War II hero
George Murphy (1904–    ), actor and dancer
Anne Murray (1947–    ), singer
Arthur Murray (1895–    ), dancer, husband of Kathryn
Don Murray (1929–    ), actor
Jan Murray (1917–    ), comedian
Kathryn Murray (1906–    ), dancer, wife of Arthur
Mae Murray (Marie Adrienne Koenig; 1885–1965), actress
Edward R. Murrow (1908–65), radio and TV newscaster
Jim Nabors (1933–    ), comedian and singer
Conrad Nagel (1897–1970), actor
J. Carrol Naish (1900–73), actor
Graham Nash (1942–    ), rock musician
George Jean Nathan (1882–1958), drama critic, author, T
Mildred Natwick (1908–    ), actress
Alla Nazimova (1879–1945), Russian-born actress, T
Patricia Neal (1926–    ), actress, A-1963
Pola Negri (1899–    ), Polish-born actress
Barry Nelson (Robert Neilson; 1920–    ), actor
David Nelson (1936–    ), actor, son of Ozzie

Harriet Hilliard Nelson (Peggy Lou Snyder; 1914–    ), actress, wife of Ozzie
Ozzie Nelson (1906–75), actor and bandleader
Rick Nelson (1940–    ), actor and singer, son of Ozzie
Willie Nelson (1933–    ), country music singer
Cathleen Nesbitt (1889–    ), British actress
Bob Newhart (1929–    ), comedian
Anthony Newley (1931–    ), British actor and writer
Edwin Newman (1919–    ), news commentator
Paul Newman (1925–    ), actor and director
Randy Newman (1943–    ), singer
Julie Newmar (Julia Newmeyer; 1933–    ), Swedish-born actress
Wayne Newton (1942–    ), singer
Olivia Newton-John (1948–    ), singer
Mike Nichols (Michael Peschkowsky; 1931–    ), German-born comedian and director, A-1967
Red Nichols (1905–65), jazz cornetist and combo leader
Jack Nicholson (1937–    ), actor, A-1975
Stevie Nicks (1948–    ), rock singer
Leonard Nimoy (1931–    ), actor
David Niven (1909–    ), Scottish-born actor, A-1958
Lloyd Nolan (1903–    ), actor
Nick Nolte (1940–    ), actor
Mabel Normand (Mabel Fortescue; 1894–1930), silent-movie comedienne
John Ringling North (1903–    ), circus owner
Sheree North (Dawn Bethel; 1933–    ), actress
Kim Novak (Marilyn Novak; 1933–    ), actress
Ramon Novarro (1899–1968), Mexican actor
Elliott Nugent (1900–    ), director and writer
Rudolf Nureyev (1938–    ), Russian-born dancer
Jack Oakie (Lewis D. Offield; 1903–78), comedian
Annie Oakley (1860–1926), Wild West performer, T
Warren Oates (1932–    ), actor
Merle Oberon (1911–79), British actress
Hugh O'Brian (Hugh Krampke; 1925–    ), actor
Edmond O'Brien (1915–    ), actor, A-1954
Margaret O'Brien (1937–    ), child actress, A-1944
Pat O'Brien (1899–    ), actor
Carroll O'Connor (1923–    ), actor
Donald O'Connor (1925–    ), actor and dancer
Odetta (1930–    ), folk singer and actress
Clifford Odets (1906–63), playwright, T
Maureen O'Hara (Maureen Fitzsimmons; 1920–    ), Irish-born actress
Dennis O'Keefe (1908–68), actor
Warner Oland (1880–1938), Swedish-born actor
Edna May Oliver (1883–1942), actress
Susan Oliver (1937–    ), actress
Sir Laurence Olivier (1907–    ), British actor and director, A-1944, 1948, T, E
Ole Olsen (1892–1963), vaudeville star with Chic Johnson
Ryan O'Neal (1941–    ), actor
Tatum O'Neal (1964–    ), child actress, A-1973
Eugene O'Neill (1888–1953), playwright, T, E
Jennifer O'Neill (1949–    ), Brazilian-born actress
Jerry Orbach (1935–    ), singer and actor
Roy Orbison (1936–    ), country music singer
Tony Orlando (1944–    ), singer
Donny Osmond (1957–    ), singer, brother of Marie
Marie Osmond (1959–    ), singer, sister of Donny
Maureen O'Sullivan (1911–    ), Irish-born actress
Peter O'Toole (1934–    ), Irish actor
Reginald Owen (1887–1972), British actor
Buck Owens (1929–    ), country music singer
Jack Paar (1918–    ), television personality
Al Pacino (1939–    ), actor
Geraldine Page (1924–    ), actress, T
Patti Page (Clara Anne Fowler; 1927–    ), singer
Janis Paige (1922–    ), actress
Jack Palance (Walter Palanuik; 1920–    ), actor
Betsy Palmer (1929–    ), actress
Lilli Palmer (1914–    ), German-born British actress
Franklin Pangborn (1894–1958), comedian
Irene Papas (1926–    ), Greek actress
Joseph Papp (Joseph Papirofsky; 1921–    ), producer
Charlie "Bird" Parker (1920–55), jazz sax musician
Eleanor Parker (1922–    ), singer and actress
Fess Parker (1926–    ), actor
Bert Parks (Bert Jacobson; 1914–    ), television personality
Larry Parks (1914–75), actor
Michael Parks (1938–    ), actor
Estelle Parsons (1927–    ), actress, A-1967
Dolly Parton (1946–    ), country music singer
Joseph Pasternak (1901–    ), Hungarian-born producer
Katina Paxinou (1900–73), Greek actress, A-1943
Freda Payne (1945–    ), singer

**SHOW BUSINESS PERSONALITIES** *(continued)*
John Payne (1912–  ), actor
Minnie Pearl (Sarah Ophelia Colley Cannon, 1912–  ), country music singer
Gregory Peck (1916–  ), actor, A-1962
Sam Peckinpah (1926–  ), director
Arthur Penn (1922–  ), director
George Peppard (1929–  ), actor
Anthony Perkins (1932–  ), actor
Valerie Perrine (1943–  ), actress
Bernadette Peters (1944–  ), actress
Jean Peters (1926–  ), actress
Edith Piaf (1915–63), French singer
Mary Pickford (Gladys Smith; 1893–79), Canadian-born actress, A-1928–29, 1976, wed to Douglas Fairbanks, Buddy Rogers
Molly Picon (1898–  ), actress
Walter Pidgeon (1897–  ), Canadian-born actor
Zasu Pitts (1898–1963), comedienne and actress
Donald Pleasence (1919–  ), British actor
Suzanne Pleshette (1937–  ), actress
Joan Plowright (1929–  ), actress
Christopher Plummer (1927–  ), Canadian actor
Sidney Poitier (1924–  ), actor, A-1963
Roman Polanski (1933–  ), Polish director
Michael Pollard (1939–  ), actor
Carlo Ponti (1910–  ), Italian producer, wed to Sophia Loren
Cole Porter (1893–1964), composer, T, E
Tom Poston (1927–  ), actor
Dick Powell (1904–63), actor, director, and producer
Eleanor Powell (1912–  ), dancer and actress
Jane Powell (Suzanne Burce; 1929–  ), dancer and singer
William Powell (1892–  ), actor
Tyrone Power (1913–58), actor
Stefanie Powers (Taffy Paul; 1942–  ), actress
Otto Preminger (1906–  ), Austrian-born producer
Paula Prentiss (Paula Ragusa; 1939–  ), actress
Elvis Presley (1935–77), singer, actor
Robert Preston (Robert Messervey; 1917–  ), actor
Andre Previn (1929–  ), composer and music arranger
Ray Price (1926–  ), country music singer
Vincent Price (1911–  ), actor
Charley Pride (1938–  ), country music singer
Louis Prima (1912–78), singer
Harold Prince (1928–  ), producer
Freddie Prinze (1954–77), actor
Dorothy Provine (1937–  ), actress
Juliet Prowse (1937–  ), South African-born dancer
Richard Pryor (1940–  ), comedian
Anthony Quayle (1913–  ), British actor and director
Richard Quine (1920–  ), actor and director
Anthony Quinn (1915–  ), actor, A-1952, 1956
David Rabe (1940–  ), playwright
Deborah Raffin (1953–  ), actress
George Raft (George Ranft; 1895–1980), actor
Luise Rainer (1912–  ), Austrian actress, A-1936, 1937
Ella Raines (1921–  ), actress
Bonnie Raitt (1950–  ), singer
John Raitt (1917–  ), singer
Marjorie Rambeau (1889–1970), actress
Sally Rand (1904–79), striptease fan dancer
Tony Randall (Leonard Rosenberg; 1920–  ), actor
J. Arthur Rank (1888–1972), British producer
Basil Rathbone (1892–1967), South African-born actor
Dan Rather (1931–  ), newscaster
Gregory Ratoff (1897–1961), Russian-born actor, director
Lou Rawls (1935–  ), singer
Martha Raye (Margaret Yvonne Reed; 1916–  ), actress and comedienne
Gene Raymond (1908–  ), actor
Ronald Reagan (1911–  ), actor and politician
Harry Reasoner (1923–  ), newscaster
Otis Redding (1941–67), blues singer
Helen Reddy (1942–  ), singer
Robert Redford (1936–  ), actor
Lynn Redgrave (1944–  ), British actress
Sir Michael Redgrave (1908–  ), British actor, father of Lynn and Vanessa
Vanessa Redgrave (1937–  ), British actress, A-1977
Sir Carol Reed (1906–76), British director, A-1968
Donna Reed (1921–  ), actress, A-1953
Della Reese (Deloreese Patricia Early; 1932–  ), singer
Ada Rehan (1860–1916), actress, T
Carl Reiner (1923–  ), actor, writer, and director
Robert Reiner (1947–  ), actor, son of Carl
Max Reinhardt (1873–1943), Austrian producer
Lee Remick (1935–  ), actress
Michael Rennie (1909–71), British actor

Alain Resnais (1922–  ), French director
Anne Revere (1903–  ), actress, A-1945
Burt Reynolds (1936–  ), actor
Debbie Reynolds (Mary Frances Reynolds; 1932–  ), actress, singer, and dancer
Buddy Rich (1917–  ), jazz drummer and bandleader
Charlie Rich (1932–  ), country music singer
Sir Ralph Richardson (1902–  ), British actor, T
Tony Richardson (1929–  ), British director, A-1963
Nelson Riddle (1921–  ), bandleader
Don Rickles (1928–  ), comedian
Diana Rigg (1938–  ), British actress
Ringling Bros.: Albert (1852–1916), Otto (1858–1911), Alfred (1861–1919), Charles Edward (1863–1926), John (1866–1936), circus managers
Minnie Riperton (1948–  ), singer
Cyril Ritchard (1896–1977), British actor
Tex Ritter (1907–74), country music singer
Thelma Ritter (1905–69), actress
Ritz Brothers: Al (1901–65), Jim (1903–  ), Harry (1906–  ), comedy team
Chita Rivera (1933–  ), singer and actress
Geraldo Rivera (1943–  ), newscaster
Joan Rivers (1937–  ), comedienne
Hal Roach (1892–  ), director and producer
Jason Robards Jr. (1920–  ), actor, A-1976, 1977, T
Jerome Robbins (1918–  ), dancer and choreographer, T, A-1961
Cliff Robertson (1925–  ), actor, A-1968
Dale Robertson (1923–  ), actor
Paul Robeson (1898–1976), singer and actor, T
Bill "Bojangles" Robinson (1878–1949), dancer
Edward G. Robinson (Emanuel Goldenberg; 1893–1973), actor, A-1972
Jimmie Rodgers (1897–1933), country music singer
Richard Rodgers (1902–79), composer, T, E
Buddy Rogers (1904–  ), actor, wed to Mary Pickford
Ginger Rogers (Virginia McMath; 1911–  ), actress and dancer, A-1940
Kenny Rogers (1941–  ), rock musician
Paul Rogers (1917–  ), British actor
Roy Rogers (Leonard Sly; 1912–  ), singer, cowboy actor
Will Rogers (1879–1935), humorist, T
Gilbert Roland (1905–  ), Mexican actor
Cesar Romero (1907–  ), actor
Linda Ronstadt (1946–  ), singer
Mickey Rooney (Joe Yule; 1922–  ), actor, A-1938
Pat Rooney (1880–1962), dancer and songwriter
Billy Rose (1899–1966), showman
George Rose (1920–  ), British actor, T
Diana Ross (1944–  ), singer
Katharine Ross (1943–  ), actress
Roberto Rossellini (1906–77), Italian director
Lillian Roth (1910–80), singer
Richard Roundtree (1943–  ), actor
Dan Rowan (1922–  ), television comedian
Gena Rowlands (1936–  ), actress
Charles Ruggles (1890–1970), actor
Janice Rule (1931–  ), actress
Barbara Rush (1930–  ), actress
Harold Russell (1914–  ), actor, A-1946
Jane Russell (1921–  ), actress
Lillian Russell (1861–1922), actress, T
Nipsey Russell (1924–  ), comedian
Rosalind Russell (1912–76), actress
Margaret Rutherford (1892–1972), British actress, A-1963
Irene Ryan (1903–73), actress
Robert Ryan (1913–73), actor
Bobby Rydell (1942–  ), singer
Mort Sahl (1926–  ), comedian
Eva Marie Saint (1930–  ), actress, A-1954
Susan Saint James (Susan Miller; 1946–  ), actress
Jill St. John (1940–  ), actress
Buffy Sainte-Marie (1941–  ), folk singer
Soupy Sales (Milton Hines; 1927–  ), comedian
George Sanders (1906–72), British actor, A-1950
Diana Sands (1934–73), actress
Tommy Sands (1937–  ), singer
Samantha Sang (1953–  ), singer
Michael Sarrazin (1940–  ), actor
Telly Savalas (1924–  ), actor
John Saxon (1935–  ), actor
Leo Sayer (1948–  ), rock musician
Boz Scaggs (William Royce Scaggs; 1944–  ), rock singer
Franklin Schaffner (1920–  ), director, A-1970
Dore Schary (1905–80), writer and producer
Roy Scheider (1934–  ), actor
Maria Schell (1926–  ), Austrian actress

Maximilian Schell (1930– ), Austrian actor, A-1961
Joseph M. Schenck (1878–1961), Russian-born producer, founder of 20th Century-Fox, A-1950
Joseph Schildkraut (1895–1964), Austrian actor, A-1937
John Schlesinger (1926– ), British director, A-1969
Romy Schneider (Rose-Marie Albach-Retty; 1938– ), Austrian actress
Avery Schreiber (1935– ), comedian
Paul Scofield (1922– ), British actor, A-1966
George C. Scott (1927– ), actor and director, A-1970
Lizabeth Scott (Emma Matzo; 1922– ), actress
Martha Scott (1914– ), actress
Randolph Scott (Randolph Crane; 1903– ), actor
Zachary Scott (1914–65), actor
Earl Scruggs (1924– ), country music singer
John Sebastian (1944– ), singer and composer
Jean Seberg (1938–79), actress
Neil Sedaka (1939– ), singer and composer
Pete Seeger (1919– ), folk singer
George Segal (1940– ), actor
Bob Seger (1945– ), rock musician
Peter Sellers (1925–80), British comedian and actor
David O. Selznick (1902–65), producer
Mack Sennett (1884–1960), producer, director, A-1937
Rod Serling (1924–75), writer and producer
Eric Sevareid (1912– ), television commentator
Doc Severinson (1927– ), bandleader
Ravi Shankar (1920– ), sitar player
Omar Sharif (Michael Shalhouz; 1933– ), Egyptian actor
William Shatner (1931– ), actor
Artie Shaw (Arthur Arshawsky; 1910– ), jazz clarinetist and bandleader
Robert Shaw (1927–78), actor and writer
Dick Shawn (1929– ), actor
Moira Shearer (1926– ), Scottish-born dancer
Norma Shearer (1904– ), actress, A-1929–30
George Shearing (1920– ), jazz pianist and composer
Martin Sheen (Ramon Estevez; 1940– ), actor
Cybill Shepherd (1950– ), actress
Ann Sheridan (1915–67), actress
Dinah Shore (Frances Rose Shore; 1917– ), singer and TV personality
Bobby Short (1936– ), jazz pianist
Lee Shubert (1883–1953) and J. J. Shubert (1880–1963), theater managers and producers, T
Sylvia Sidney (1910– ), actress
Simone Signoret (Simone Kaminker; 1921– ), German-born actress, A-1959
Phil Silvers (Philip Silversmith; 1912– ), actor
Alastair Sim (1900–76), Scottish actor
Jean Simmons (1929– ), British actress
Carly Simon (1945– ), singer, wife of James Taylor
Neil Simon (1927– ), playwright
Paul Simon (1940– ), singer and composer
Simone Simon (1914– ), French actress
Nina Simone (Eunice Kathleen Waymon; 1933– ), jazz vocalist
Frank Sinatra (1915– ), singer and actor, A-1953, E
Frank Sinatra Jr. (1944– ), singer, son of Frank
Nancy Sinatra (1940– ), actress, daughter of Frank
Red Skelton (1910– ), comedian
Cornelia Otis Skinner (1901–79), actress and writer
Otis Skinner (1858–1942), actor, T, father of Cornelia
Alison Skipworth (1870–1952), comedienne
Spyros Skouras (1893–1971), Greek-born film executive
Walter Slezak (1902– ), Austrian-born actor
Gracie Slick (1939– ), rock singer
Alexis Smith (1921– ), actress
Sir C. Aubrey Smith (1863–1948), British actor
Bessie Smith (1898?–1937), blues singer
Howard K. Smith (1914– ), television commentator
Kate Smith (1909– ), singer
Maggie Smith (1934– ), British actress, A-1969, 1978
Smothers Brothers: Tom (1937– ) and Dick (1939– ), comedians and singers
Carrie Snodgress (1945– ), actress
Hank Snow (1914– ), country music singer
Suzanne Somers (1948– ), actress
Elke Sommer (Elke Schletz; 1940– ), German actress
Gale Sondergaard (1899– ), actress, A-1936
Stephen Sondheim (1930– ), composer and lyricist
Ann Sothern (Harriette Lake; 1909– ), actress
E. A. Sothern (1826–81), British actor, T
E. H. Sothern (1859–1933), actor, T, son of E. A. Sothern, husband of Julia Marlowe
Sissy Spacek (1950– ), actress
Sam Spiegel (1901– ), producer
Dusty Springfield (Mary O'Brien; 1939– ), singer

Bruce Springsteen (1949– ), singer
Robert Stack (1919– ), actor
Jo Stafford (1918– ), singer
Sylvester Stallone (1946– ), actor and screenwriter
Terrence Stamp (1940– ), British actor
Arnold Stang (1925– ), comedian
Kim Stanley (Patricia Reid; 1925– ), actress
Barbara Stanwyck (Ruby Stevens; 1907– ), actress
Jean Stapleton (Jeanne Murray; 1923– ), actress
Maureen Stapleton (1925– ), actress
Kay Starr (1924– ), singer
Ringo Starr (Richard Starkey; 1940– ), British singer, musician (Beatles)
Tommy Steele (1936– ), British singer
Rod Steiger (1925– ), actor, A-1967
David Steinberg (1942– ), comedian
Jan Sterling (1923– ), actress
Cat Stevens (Steven Georgion; 1947– ), rock singer
Connie Stevens (Concetta Ingolia; 1938– ), actress and singer
George Stevens (1904–75), director, A-1951, 1956
Stella Stevens (1938– ), actress
James Stewart (1908– ), actor, A-1940
Rod Stewart (1945– ), rock singer
Stephen Stills (1945– ), rock musician
Fred Stone (1873–1959), comedian, T
Lewis Stone (1879–1953), actor
Sly Stone (1944– ), rock singer
Three Stooges: Curly Howard (1893?–1947), Shemp Howard (1895?–1955), Moe Howard (1897–75), Larry Fine (1902–75), comedy team
Larry Storch (1925– ), comedian
Gale Storm (1922– ), actress
Beatrice Straight (1918— ), actress, A-1976
Lee Strasberg (1901– ), director
Susan Strasberg (1938– ), actress, daughter of Lee
Charles E. (Tom Thumb) Stratton (1838–1883), midget
Peter Strauss (1947– ), actor
Meryl Streep (1949– ), actress, A-1979
Barbra Streisand (1942– ), singer and actress, A-1968
Elaine Stritch (1922– ), actress
Hunt Stromberg (1894–1968), producer
Sally Struthers (1948– ), actress
Preston Sturges (1898–1959), producer
Jules Styne (1905– ), British-born composer
Margaret Sullavan (1911–60), actress
Barry Sullivan (Patrick Barry; 1912– ), actor
Ed Sullivan (1902–74), columnist and TV personality
Donna Summer (1948– ), rock singer
Slim Summerville (1892–1946), comedian and director
David Susskind (1920– ), producer and TV personality
Donald Sutherland (1934– ), Canadian-born actor
Gloria Swanson (Josephine Swenson; 1899– ), actress, wed to Wallace Beery
John Cameron Swayze (1906– ), newscaster
Nita Talbot (1930– ), actress
Norma Talmadge (1897–1957), silent-film actress
William Talman (1917–68), actor
Russ Tamblyn (1935– ), actor
Akim Tamiroff (1899–1972), Russian-born actor
Jessica Tandy (1909– ), British-born actress, wed to Hume Cronyn
Norman Taurog (1899– ), director, A-1930–31
Elizabeth Taylor (1932– ), actress, A-1960, 1966
James Taylor (1948– ), singer and musician
Laurette Taylor (Laurette Cooney; 1884–1946), actress, T
Robert Taylor (Spangler Brough; 1911–69), actor
Rod Taylor (1929– ), Australian-born actor
Jack Teagarden (1905–64), jazz trombonist and singer
Shirley Temple (1928– ), child star in 1930s, A-1934
Alec Templeton (1910–63), musician
Ellen Terry (1848–1928), British actress, T
Terry-Thomas (Thomas Terry Hoar-Stevens; 1911– ), British comedian
Irving Thalberg (1899–1936), producer
Phyllis Thaxter (1921– ), actress
Danny Thomas (Amos Jacobs; 1914– ), comedian
Marlo Thomas (1938– ), actress, daughter of Danny
Richard Thomas (1951– ), actor
Sada Thompson (1929– ), actress
Dame Sybil Thorndike (1882–1976), British actress
Gene Tierney (1920– ), actress
Pamela Tiffin (1943– ), actress
Burr Tillstrom (1917– ), puppeteer
Tiny Tim (Herbert Khaury; 1923– ), singer
Ann Todd (1909– ), British actress
Michael Todd (1907–58), film producer
Richard Todd (1919– ), British actor

## SHOW BUSINESS PERSONALITIES *(continued)*

Thelma Todd (1908–35), comedienne
Lily Tomlin (1939– ), comedienne
Franchot Tone (1906–68), actor
Regis Toomey (1902– ), actor
Mel Torme (1925– ), singer
Rip Torn (1931– ), actor
Audrey Totter (1923– ), actress
Lee Tracy (1898–1968), actor
Spencer Tracy (1900–67), actor, A-1937, 1938
Mary Travers (1936– ), singer
John Travolta (1953– ), actor
Arthur Treacher (1894–1975), British actor
Sir Herbert Beerbohm Tree (1853–1917), British actor
Claire Trevor (1909– ), actress, A-1948
François Truffaut (1932– ), French director
Forrest Tucker (1919– ), actor
Sophie Tucker (Sophia Abuza; 1884–1966), singer
Sonny Tufts (Bowen Charleston Tufts; 1911–70), actor
Ike (1934– ) and Tina Turner (1941– ), singing duo
Lana Turner (Julia Turner; 1920– ), actress
Ben Turpin (1847–1940), comedian
Rita Tushingham (1940– ), British actress
Twiggy (Leslie Hornsby; 1949– ), British actress
Conway Twitty (1933– ), country music singer
Leslie Uggams (1943– ), singer and actress
Liv Ullman (1938– ), Norwegian actress
Myoshi Umeki (1929– ), Japanese actress, A-1957
Peter Ustinov (1921– ), British actor and director,
  A-1960, 1964
Brenda Vaccaro (1939– ), actress
Roger Vadim (1927– ), French director
Jerry Vale (1931– ), singer
Caterina Valente (1931– ), singer
Karen Valentine (1947– ), actress
Rudolph Valentino (Rodolpho d'Antonguolla; 1895–1926),
  Italian-born actor
Rudy Vallee (Hubert Vallee; 1901– ), singer and actor
Frankie Valli (1937– ), singer
Lee Van Cleef (1925– ), actor
Mamie Van Doren (1933– ), actress
Dick Van Dyke (1925– ), actor
Jo Van Fleet (1922– ), actress, A-1955
Vivian Vance (1912–79), actress
Trish Vandevere (1945– ), actress
Sarah Vaughan (1922– ), singer
Robert Vaughn (1933– ), actor
Gwen Verdon (1925– ), singer and dancer
Ben Vereen (1946– ), dancer
Martha Vickers (1925–71), actress
King Vidor (1895– ), director
Bobby Vinton (1935– ), singer
Jon Voight (1939– ), actor, A-1978
Joseph von Sternberg (1894–1969), Austrian-born director
Erich Von Stroheim (1885–1957), Austrian-born actor,
  director
Max Von Sydow (1929– ), Swedish actor
Lindsay Wagner (1949– ), actress
Robert Wagner (1930– ), actor, wed to Natalie Wood
Christopher Walken (1943– ), actor, A-1978
Clint Walker (1927– ), actor
Nancy Walker (Ann Swoyer; 1922– ), comedienne
Robert Walker (1919–51), actor
Mike Wallace (1918– ), television newscaster
Eli Wallach (1915– ), actor
James Wallack (1795–1864), British-American actor, T
Lester Wallack (1820–1888), actor, T, son of James
Fats Waller (1904–43), jazz pianist and singer
Hal B. Wallis (1898– ), producer
Ray Walston (1917– ), actor
Barbara Walters (1931– ), television commentator
Walter Wanger (1894–1968), producer
David Warfield (1866–1951), actor, T
Andy Warhol (1927– ), producer and director
Fred Waring (1900– ), musician and bandleader
Jack L. Warner (1892–1978), producer (Warner Brothers)
Dionne Warwick (1940– ), singer
Ethel Waters (1900–77), actress, T
Muddy Waters (McKinley Morganfield; 1915– ), country
  music singer
David Wayne (Wayne McKeekan; 1916– ), actor
John Wayne (Marion Morrison; 1907–79), actor, director,
  producer, A-1969
Dennis Weaver (1924– ), actor
Fritz Weaver (1926– ), actor
Clifton Webb (Webb Hollenbeck; 1896–1966), actor, T
Jack Webb (1920– ), actor, director, and producer
Joe Weber (1867–1942) and Lew Fields (1867–1941),

vaudeville comedians, T
Margaret Webster (1905–72), theatrical producer, T
Johnny Weissmuller (1904– ), actor (Tarzan), Olympic
  swimmer
Raquel Welch (Raquel Tejada; 1942– ), actress
Tuesday Weld (Susan Ker Weld; 1943– ), actress
Lawrence Welk (1903– ), musician and bandleader
Orson Welles (1915– ), actor, producer, director, T, E
Oskar Werner (Josef Schliessmayer; 1922– ), Austrian
  actor
Lina Wertmuller (1926– ), film director
Adam West (William Anderson; 1929– ), actor
Mae West (1892–1980), actress, T
Wheeler and Woolsey: Bert Wheeler (1895–1968), Robert
  Woolsey (1889–1938), comedy team
Barry White (1944– ), singer
Pearl White (1889–1938), actress, queen of silent serials
Paul Whiteman (1890–1967), jazz bandleader
Margaret Whiting (1924– ), singer
James Whitmore (1920– ), actor
Richard Widmark (1915– ), actor
Cornel Wilde (1918– ), actor, producer, and director
Billy Wilder (1906– ), Austrian-born producer and
  director, A-1945, 1960
Gene Wilder (Jerry Silberman; 1935– ), actor
Michael Wilding (1912–79), actor
Andy Williams (1930– ), singer
Bert Williams (1877–1922), comedian, T
Billy Dee Williams (1937– ), actor
Cindy Williams (1948– ), actress
Esther Williams (1923– ), actress, swimming champion
Hank Williams (1923–53), country music singer
Paul Williams (1940– ), songwriter
Robin Williams (1953– ), television actor, "Mork"
Nicol Williamson (1936– ), Scottish-born actor
Chill Wills (1903–78), actor
Meredith Willson (1902– ), musician
Don Wilson (1900– ), radio and television announcer
Flip Wilson (1933– ), comedian
Julie Wilson (1924– ), singer
Marie Wilson (1916–72), actress
Nancy Wilson (1937– ), singer
Paul Winchell (1924– ), ventriloquist
William Windom (1923– ), actor
Henry Winkler (1945– ), actor
Jonathan Winters (1925– ), comedian
Shelley Winters (Shirley Schrift; 1922– ), actress,
  A-1959, 1965
Robert Wise (1914– ), director, A-1961, 1965
Jane Withers (1926– ), actress, child star in 1930s
Stevie Wonder (Steveland Hardaway; 1950– ), singer and
  composer
Anna May Wong (1902–60), Chinese-American actress
Natalie Wood (Natasha Gurdin; 1938– ), actress, wed to
  Robert Wagner
Peggy Wood (1892–1978), actress, T
Joanne Woodward (1930– ), actress, A-1957
Monty Woolley (1888–1963), actor
Jo Anne Worley (1937– ), comedienne
Irene Worth (1916– ), actress, T
Fay Wray (1907– ), actress
Theresa Wright (1918– ), actress, A-1942
Earl Wrightson (1916– ), singer
Jane Wyatt (1912– ), actress
William Wyler (1902– ), director, A-1942, 1946, 1959
Jane Wyman (Sarah Jane Fulks; 1914– ), actress, A-1948
Tammy Wynette (Wynette Pugh; 1942– ), country music
  singer
Ed Wynn (Isaiah Leopold; 1886–1966), comedian, T
Keenan Wynn (1916– ), actor, son of Ed Wynn
Dana Wynter (1930– ), British actress
Glenn Yarborough (1930– ), singer
Peter Yarrow (1938– ), folk singer
Susannah York (1942– ), British actress
Alan Young (1919– ), British-born actor
Gig Young (Byron Barr; 1917–78), actor, A-1969
Loretta Young (Gretchen Belzer; 1913– ), actress, A-1947
Neil Young (1945– ), rock musician
Robert Young (1907– ), actor
Roland Young (1887–1953), British-born actor
Henny Youngman (1906– ), comedian
Darryl Zanuck (1902–79), producer
Florenz Ziegfeld (1869–1932), showman, T
Efrem Zimbalist Jr. (1923– ), actor
Fred Zinnemann (1907– ), Austrian-born director,
  A-1953, 1966
Adolph Zukor (1873–1976), Hungarian-born producer,
  brought first major movie to U.S. (1912), A-1948

# History

## HOW TIME FLIES!

Today's headlines soon become history as time slips by with frightening rapidity. In the following tables, events are recalled that happened 10, 25, 50, 100, and 200 years ago.

## EVENTS OF 10 YEARS AGO—1971

**Jury convicts Manson of murder:** Charles M. Manson and three women co-defendants found guilty of 1969 killing of actress Sharon Tate and six other persons, on *Jan. 25.*

**South Vietnamese troops invade Laos:** With U.S. air support, South Vietnamese seek to destroy Ho Chi Minh Trail supply line, on *Feb. 8.*

**Killer earthquake hits Southern California:** Earth tremors kill 64 persons and cause over $1 billion damage in Los Angeles area, on *Feb. 9.*

**Muhammad Ali defeated for boxing championship:** World heavyweight champion Joe Frazier wins 15-round decision, on *March 8.*

**Calley found guilty of My Lai massacre:** Lt. William L. Calley Jr. convicted by court-martial of 1968 slayings in Vietnam, on *March 29.*

**Mass arrests of about 10,000 war protesters in Washington, D.C.:** Hundreds of thousands of antiwar demonstrators try to shut down nation's capital, on *May 3–4.*

**Secret Pentagon Papers published:** *New York Times* begins publication of purloined secret study of Defense Department on *June 13*; government obtains injunction stopping publication on *June 15,* but Supreme Court allows publication to resume on *June 30.*

**U.S. voting age lowered to 18:** After Ohio becomes 38th state to ratify 26th Amendment to Constitution, President Nixon proclaims it on *July 5.*

**U.S. wages and prices frozen:** President Nixon orders controls on wages and prices in effort to hold inflation rate at 3% or less, on *Aug. 15.*

**Communist China admitted to UN:** After President Nixon reverses U.S. policy of opposition to communist government of China, UN admits Communist China and expels Nationalist Chinese of Taiwan, on *Oct. 25.*

**Space probe orbits Mars:** *Mariner 9* becomes first man-made satellite to circle another planet, on *Nov. 13.*

**India defeats Pakistan in 13-day war:** Indian troops invaded Pakistan to win independence for Bangladesh, on *Dec. 3–16.*

## EVENTS OF 25 YEARS AGO—1956

**Riots cause expulsion of black student in Alabama:** First black student to enter University of Alabama, Autherine Lucy, suspended on *Feb. 6* and later expelled.

**President vetoes natural-gas bill:** After evidence revealed of attempts by natural gas lobbyists to bribe members of Congress with campaign contributions, President Eisenhower vetoes bill that would have exempted independent natural-gas producers from federal rate controls, on *Feb. 17.*

**Virginia tries to evade desegregation order:** Having closed public schools to avoid integration of white and black students, state amends laws to let public funds support white students attending private schools, on *March 7.*

**$33 billion interstate highway system approved:** Federal Aid Highway Act authorizing construction of 41,000-mile network of U.S. highways to be financed by gasoline taxes signed by President Eisenhower on *June 29.*

**Hydrogen bomb tested:** Hydrogen bomb dropped from B-52 over Bikini Atoll in Pacific on *May 21.*

**Andria Doria sinking:** Swedish ocean liner *Stockholm* collides with Italian liner *Andria Doria,* which sinks off coast of Massachusetts on *July 26*; about 1,650 persons are rescued, but 50 die.

**Egypt nationalizes Suez Canal:** After U.S. withdraws promise of aid to build Aswan High Dam, Egypt's President Gamal Abdel Nasser orders nationalization of Suez Canal on *July 26*; to use tolls to finance construction of dam.

**Democrats choose Stevenson-Kefauver ticket:** At Democratic national convention in Chicago on *Aug. 13–17,* Adlai Stevenson is nominated for president on first ballot; Estes Kefauver is selected as vice-presidential candidate on second ballot, defeating contender John F. Kennedy.

**Republicans renominate Eisenhower-Nixon:** At Republican national convention in San Francisco on *Aug. 20–23,* President Eisenhower and Vice President Nixon are nominated for second term by acclamation.

**Soviet troops put down Hungarian revolution:** Revolt begins in Budapest on *Oct. 23* as anti-Marxist Imre Nagy becomes premier; Soviet troops intervene while Western nations ignore appeals for help from Hungarians; Nagy is executed; some 150,000 Hungarians flee to exile.

**Second Arab-Israeli War:** With military support by Britain and France, Israel attacks Egypt on *Oct. 29,* seizing Suez Canal; U.S. and Soviet Union oppose action, forcing acceptance of UN cease-fire on *Nov. 4,* and subsequent withdrawal of British, French, and Israeli forces.

**Eisenhower wins second term in landslide:** President Eisenhower defeats Democratic presidential nominee Adlai Stevenson in national election on *Nov. 6,* winning 57.4% of popular vote.

**Supreme Court outlaws segregation on local buses:** Rev. Martin Luther King Jr. wins his first major victory in black civil-rights movement when Supreme Court rules as unconstitutional Alabama Jim Crow law that forced blacks to sit at rear of buses, on *Dec. 13.*

QUICK QUIZ: What church was founded by John Wesley? See page 712.

## EVENTS OF 50 YEARS AGO—1931

**Congress overrides President Hoover on veterans act:** President had vetoed measure to give veterans loans on half their 1924 bonus certificates, saying it would hurt federal budget, but Congress overrides his veto on *Feb. 27.*

*Star-Spangled Banner* made national anthem: President Hoover signs congressional measure designating Francis Scott Key's song as official U.S. national anthem, on March 3.

**First electric dry razor produced:** Although patented in 1928 by Col. Jacob Schick, electric shaver is first manufactured by Schick, Inc., on *March 18.*

**Legal gambling begins in Nevada:** Casinos open on *March 20.*

**First air-conditioned trains begin service:** Air-conditioned passenger trains of Baltimore & Ohio Railroad start operation between New York City and Washington, D.C., on *May 24.*

**Moratorium on war debts initiated:** Because of worsening Great Depression around world, President Hoover proposes on *June 20* suspending payment of World War I war debts and reparations; agreement is signed by 18 nations on *Aug. 11.*

**Japan begins war with China:** Japanese troops seize control of three cities in China's northern province Manchuria on *Sept. 18* and within five months take entire region.

**Panic closes 800 banks:** Inability of U.S. banks to meet demands by depositors causes 800 banks to shut doors, in *September and October.*

**First nonstop Pacific flight:** Clyde Pangborn and Hugh Herndon land at Wenatchee, Wash., completing flight from Japan in 41 hours 13 minutes, on *Oct. 5.*

**George Washington Bridge opens:** First bridge across Hudson River between New York and New Jersey with its 3,500-foot span longest in world at time it opens on *Oct. 25.*

## EVENTS OF 100 YEARS AGO—1881

**Tuskegee Institute founded:** Established as a vocational high school for blacks called Tuskegee Normal and Industrial Institute; chartered by Alabama legislature on *Feb. 10,* 1881; opens its doors under principal Booker T. Washington, on *July 4.*

**James A. Garfield becomes 20th U.S. President:** Having narrowly defeated Democratic candidate Gen. Winfield Scott Hancock in 1880 election, Garfield is inaugurated on *March 4.*

**Russian czar assassinated:** Czar Aleksandr II is killed by terrorist bomb in St. Petersburg (now Leningrad) on *March 13,* touching off wave of persecution against Jews, many of whom emigrate to U.S. and other countries.

**Romania becomes independent kingdom:** Romania, autonomous principality of Turkey since 1866, declares its independence under King Carol I on *March 26.*

**France makes Tunisia protectorate:** French troops invade Tunis and force Turkish governor to agree to French control on *May 12.*

**American Red Cross founded:** Humanitarian Clara Barton incorporates American Association of Red Cross on *May 21.*

**President Garfield assassinated:** In railroad station in Washington, D.C., President Garfield is fatally wounded on *July 2* by disappointed government office seeker, Charles J. Guiteau, who is convicted and executed in following year; after lingering near death for many weeks, Garfield dies on *Sept. 19.*

**Sitting Bull surrenders:** Indian chief Sitting Bull, fugitive since massacre of Gen. George Custer and his troops at Battle of Little Bighorn in 1876, gives himself up to federal authorities on *July 20.*

**Chester A. Arthur becomes 21st U.S. President:** After receiving word of death of Garfield, Vice President Arthur is sworn in as President on *Sept. 20.*

**Player piano patented:** Although first completely automatic player piano is not produced until 1897, British inventor Edward H. Leveaux obtains U.S. patent for device on *Oct. 4.*

## EVENTS OF 200 YEARS AGO—1781

**Planet Uranus discovered:** 43-year-old German-born British amateur astronomer, William Herschel, reports seeing planet through telescope he had made.

*Critique of Pure Reason* published: German philosopher Immanuel Kant defends knowledge of mathematics and science derived from experiments and experience while discounting philosophy based on speculation.

**Mutiny of Pennsylvania Line:** Gen. Anthony Wayne's 2,500 troops of Continental Army rebel at lack of pay, claiming their enlistment had been only for three years, not duration of war; mutiny settled by agreement to let about 1,500 leave army; two spies that tried to get troops to desert to British are hanged, on *Jan. 1–10.*

**Americans win Battle of Cowpens:** Brig. Gen. Dan Morgan leads about 1,000 American troops defeating equal number of British soldiers under Lt. Col. Banastre Tarleton at Cowpens, S.C., killing 100 and capturing over 800, on *Jan. 17.*

**Mutiny of New Jersey troops put down:** When about 500 New Jersey troops mutiny, other American soldiers under Maj. Gen. Robert Howe capture them and execute two ringleaders, on *Jan. 20–27.*

**Articles of Confederation become effective:** First constitution for U.S. government adopted by Congress in 1777 but ratification by states not completed until Maryland signs on Feb. 27, 1781, becoming law of land on *March 1.*

**British win Battle of Guilford Court House, N.C.:** About 4,500 American troops under Maj. Gen. Nathanael Greene are defeated when attacked by British Gen. Charles Cornwallis with about 2,000 soldiers on *March 15.*

**British army surrenders at Yorktown:** In last major battle of American Revolution, Gen. George Washington, aided by French troops and warships, besieges British Gen. Charles Cornwallis and army of 8,000 troops for 10 days, forcing their surrender on *Oct. 19.*

# KEY EVENTS IN WORLD HISTORY

Many of the important events and developments in world history from the time of the first civilizations are arranged in chronological order on the following pages.

For other important events, see the tables: How Time Flies!, pages 287–288; Key Events in American History, pages 306–314; Important Dates in the History of American Women, page 980; History of the Middle East, page 420; History of the United Nations, page 422; Highlights of the Vietnam War, page 673; and World in Review, pages 7–31.

## DEVELOPMENT OF EARLY CIVILIZATIONS: 12000–550 B.C.

**c.12000 B.C.** Domestication of dogs: Evidence of dogs kept as household pets found in cave dwellings near Kirkuk, Iraq, in 1975.

**c.9000–8000 B.C.** End of Ice Age: Glaciers began receding in Europe, Asia, and North America.

**c.8000–6000 B.C.** Cultivation of grain: Wheat and barley grown for flour to make bread in Middle East; grain farming spreads to Greece about 6000 B.C.

**c.7000–6000 B.C.** Farm villages and towns develop in Middle East: Remains of villages of this period found in Iran, Turkey, and Israel.

**c.4500–3100 B.C.** Egyptians build villages along Nile River; begin to use hieroglyphics (picture writing); earliest recorded date believed 4241 B.C., marking beginning of Egyptian calendar; copper and glass come into use.

**c.4000–3000 B.C.** Sumerians build cities in valleys of Tigris and Euphrates rivers (now in Iraq); develop cuneiform writing; use wheel and bronze.

**c.3100–2890 B.C.** Egyptian kingdom formed by King Mena (or Menes) and successors of first dynasty; kings buried in stone tombs.

**c.3100–2100 B.C.** Elamites build city of Susa, now in western Iran; men ride horses.

**c.3000–1720 B.C.** Seafaring Phoenicians from city of Byblos (now in Lebanon) begin trading with Egypt and other areas around Mediterranean Sea.

**c.3000–1450 B.C.** Minoans develop city of Knossos on island of Crete; use earliest form of written Greek.

**c.2900–1460 B.C.** Hittites build city of Hattusas (now Bogazkoy) in eastern Turkey.

**c.2650–2500 B.C.** Great pyramids built by Egyptians as tombs for kings, including Great Pyramid of Giza for King Cheops.

**c.2500–1500 B.C.** Indus River valley people build cities of Harappa and Mohenjo-Daro (now in Pakistan); use script writing.

**c.2360–2305 B.C.** King Sargon I of Akkad conquers Sumerians in what is now Iraq.

**c.2130–2112 B.C.** Sumerian King Ur-Nammu builds ziggurat (tower) at city of Ur (in Iraq).

**c.1813–1783 B.C.** Assyrians rise to power with cities of Ashur, Nineveh, and Kalhu (in Iraq).

**c.1800 B.C.** Stonehenge monument of huge blocks of sandstone built in England.

**c.1800 B.C.** Father of Hebrews and Arabs, Abraham, begins journey from birthplace Ur, eventually leading his people to Egypt.

**c.1792–1750 B.C.** Babylonian King Hammurabi the Great issues code of laws; Babylonian scholars use advanced mathematics.

**c.1766–1123 B.C.** Chinese civilization develops under Shang dynasty of kings along Hwang Ho (Yellow River); script writing used; bronze tools and weapons made.

**c.1650–1125 B.C.** Mycenaean civilization in Greece centers on city of Mycenae; mythology of Greek gods develops.

**c.1531 B.C.** Hittites conquer Babylonians, destroying Babylon.

**c.1500 B.C.** Aryans from central Asia destroy Indus River valley civilization in Pakistan.

**c.1457 B.C.** Egyptians extend empire to include Syria as Thutmose III defeats Hittites.

**c.1379–1362 B.C.** Worship of single god, Aton, ordered by Egyptian Pharaoh Akhenaton; after his death, Egyptians resume worship of many gods.

**c.1375–1335 B.C.** Hittite King Suppiluliumas drives Egyptians out of Syria and Palestine; Hittites begin using some iron weapons.

**c.1350 B.C.** British Isles said to have been visited by Phoenicians, trading for tin used in making bronze.

**c.1250–1232 B.C.** Moses leads Israelites out of Egypt, giving them Ten Commandments of God; Israelites take southern Palestine from Phoenicians (Canaanites).

**c.1200–100 B.C.** Olmec civilization develops in southern Mexico; Olmecs build stone monuments, use picture writing.

**c.1194–1184 B.C.** Trojan War: Greeks of Mycenae capture city of Troy (now in Turkey).

**c.1122–256 B.C.** Chinese kings of Chou dynasty develop advanced civilization using mathematics, astronomy, silk textiles, copper coins, and some iron tools and weapons.

**c.1116–1078 B.C.** Assyrian King Tiglath-pileser I conquers Hittites; rules most of Middle East.

**c.1100 B.C.** End of Mycenaean civilization in Greece; Mycenae destroyed by invasion of Dorians from north.

**c.1078–935 B.C.** Assyria and Babylonia fall to invasion of Aramaeans and Chaldeans from north and east.

**c.1000 B.C.** Israel's first king, Saul, killed in battle with Philistines; succeeded by King David, who defeats Philistines and makes Jerusalem capital of Israel; about this time Hebrew elders begin to put Old Testament books of Bible into writing, based on oral traditions.

**c.1000–950 B.C.** Spain colonized by Phoenicians with settlement at Cádiz.

**c.961–922 B.C.** King Solomon of Israel constructs Jewish temple and palace in Jerusalem.

**c.935–913 B.C.** Assyrian King Assurdan II reestablishes dominance of Assyrians in what is now Iraq.

**c.814–750 B.C.** Phoenicians found Carthage in North Africa (now Tunisia).

**c.800–700 B.C.** Greek poet Homer believed to have composed Iliad and Odyssey.

**c.800–300 B.C.** Hinduism develops in India, with worship of many gods; society divides into caste system.

**c.776 B.C.** First Olympic Games held by Greeks to honor god Zeus.

**c.753 B.C.** Rome founded by twin brothers Romulus and Remus, according to legend.

**c.745–728 B.C.** Assyrian Empire extended to include Babylonia, Syria, and Palestine by King Tiglath-pileser III.

**c.736–715 B.C.** Greek Spartans under King Theopompus conquer Messenians of southwestern Greece.

**c.725–722 B.C.** Destruction of Israel as nation for next 2,600 years: Assyrian King Sargon II subdues rebelling Israelites, enslaving 27,000.

**c.715 B.C.** Egypt conquered by Ethiopia.

**c.683–682 B.C.** City-state Athens abolishes hereditary monarchy, establishing rule by archons chosen annually by council of nobles.

**c.680–547 B.C.** King of Lydia rules in what is now Turkey, with capital at Sardis (near present-day Izmir); first Western people to use coins as money; last king is Croesus.

**c.663 B.C.** Assyria conquers Egypt, driving out last Ethiopian pharaoh, Tanutamon.

**c.660 B.C.** Japanese Emperor Jimmu Tenno founds first dynasty, according to legend.

**c.658–675 B.C.** Byzantium (now Istanbul, Turkey) founded by Greek colonists.

**c.626–561 B.C.** Chaldeans of Babylonia conquer Assyrians; rebuild Babylon as capital of new Babylonian empire; construct hanging gardens of Babylon.

**c.600 B.C.** Southern France colonized by Greeks at Massalia (now Marseille).

**c.587–582 B.C.** Jews taken in captivity to Babylon: Babylonian King Nebuchadnezzar II captures Jerusalem; destroys Solomon's temple, ending kingdom of Judah.

**KEY EVENTS IN WORLD HISTORY** *(continued)*

**c.563–483 B.C.** Buddha (Prince Siddartha Gautama) founds Buddhism in Nepal and India.

**c.551–479 B.C.** Confucius develops philosophy-religion of Confucianism in China, providing rules of morals and ethics.

**c.550 B.C.** Taoism founded in China by Lao Tzu, according to legend.

# RISE OF ANCIENT PERSIAN EMPIRE TO FALL OF ROME: 550 B.C.–A.D. 476

**c.550–530 B.C.** Persian Empire founded by Cyrus the Great, who conquers Lydians and Babylonians to control most of Middle East.

**c.550–500 B.C.** Carthage grows as military power: Phoenician colony of Carthage in what is now Tunisia becomes major power in western Mediterranean Sea.

**c.550–100 B.C.** City of Teotihuacán develops in Mexico: City grows to cover about 3 square miles.

**c.539–516 B.C.** Jews freed from captivity as Persians conquer Babylon; Solomon's Temple rebuilt in Jerusalem with aid from Persians.

**c.530–486 B.C.** Persian Empire extended to include Egypt and Pakistan under leadership of Cambyses and Darius I.

**c.510–506 B.C.** Democracy begins in Athens with government controlled by 500-man legislative council; Athens fights off attempt by Sparta's King Cleomenes to restore aristocrats.

**c.509 B.C.** Romans establish republic; overthrow Etruscan King Tarquin the Proud.

**c.499–478 B.C.** Greeks preserve independence by defeating invasions of Persian armies of Darius I and Xerxes I.

**c.460–429 B.C.** Age of Pericles in Athens: Art, science, and democracy flourish under leadership of Pericles; Parthenon is built.

**c.447–445 B.C.** First history published in Greece: Greek historian Herodotus writes 9-volume history of known world after travel through Persian empire.

**c.431–404 B.C.** Spartans defeat Athens in Peloponnesian War; force Athens to surrender navy and tear down fortified walls.

**c404–399 B.C.** Egypt regains independence from Persia under Pharaoh Amyrtaeus of Sais.

**338 B.C.** Greece conquered by King Philip II of Macedonia, defeating allied armies of Thebes and Athens in Battle of Chaeronea.

**336–323 B.C.** Alexander the Great of Macedonia consolidates rule of Greece, destroying Thebes; conquers Persian Empire, Egypt, and Pakistan; makes Babylon his capital.

**c.321–184 B.C.** Northern India united under Maurya dynasty founded by Emperor Chandragupta.

**305–64 B.C.** Seleucid Empire rules Middle East; founded by Seleucus I, one of Alexander's generals, who builds new capital cities of Antioch in Syria and Seleucia in Iraq.

**305–30 B.C.** Egypt ruled by Greek dynasty founded by Ptolemy I, one of Alexander's generals; capital Alexandria becomes center of Greek learning with great library.

**279 B.C.** Gauls from northern Europe invade Macedonia, Greece, and found kingdom of Galatia in what is now Turkey.

**276–167 B.C.** Macedonia and Greece ruled by kings of Antigonid dynasty, descended from Antigonus, one of Alexander's generals.

**264–146 B.C.** Punic Wars fought between Roman republic and Carthage, ending with destruction of Carthage, Roman dominance of Mediterranean Sea, and establishment of Roman provinces in North Africa and Spain.

**c.250–139 B.C.** Greeks found and rule kingdom of Bactria in what is now Afghanistan; capital at Kabul.

**c.221–210 B.C.** Great Wall of China built by Chinese Emperor Shih Huang Ti, who centralizes rule of China, founds Ch'in dynasty; books written on silk scrolls.

**c.165 B.C.** Jews revolt (under leadership of Judas Maccabeus) against Seleucids; found independent kingdom of Judea.

**c.146–121 B.C.** Roman armies conquer Macedonia, Greece, Turkey, Balearic Islands, and southern France.

**c.108 B.C.** Korea conquered by China.

**c.105 B.C.** Paper invented in China.

**c.100 B.C.** India invaded by Scythians from central Asia, founding Kushana dynasty.

**c.100 B.C.–A.D.200** Mayan civilization develops in Central America.

**c.66–62 B.C.** Seleucid Empire conquered by Roman general Pompey; Syria and Judea become provinces of Rome.

**58–44 B.C.** Roman general Julius Caesar conquers all of France (Gaul); invades Germany, Britain, and Egypt; makes himself dictator of Rome until assassinated (March 15, 44 B.C.) by senators led by Cassius and Brutus.

**44–30 B.C.** Civil war among Roman generals: Won by Julius Caesar's heir Octavian (Gaius Octavius), who in Battle of Actium (Sept. 2, 31 B.C.) defeats fleet of Roman general Mark Antony and Queen Cleopatra of Egypt; Octavian makes Egypt possession of Rome, following suicides of Antony and Cleopatra.

**27 B.C.–A.D. 14** Roman Empire established and ruled by Octavian, who takes title *Emperor Augustus;* art and science flourish during reign, known as *Augustan Age;* Roman literature develops with Virgil, Horace, Ovid, Livy.

**c.5 B.C.–A.D. 30** Jesus Christ lives in Roman province of Judea, founding Christian religion; sentenced to death by crucifixion by Roman governor Pontius Pilate.

—All dates following in chronology are A.D.

**25–57** Chinese Emperor Kuang Wu Ti founds Eastern Han dynasty; Buddhism introduced to China; Vietnam conquered by Chinese army.

**43–122** England conquered by Roman army; Emperor Hadrian builds wall between England and Scotland in 122–127.

**64** Persecution of Christians begun by Roman Emperor Nero, who accuses them of starting fire that destroys much of Rome; St. Peter and St. Paul are believed to have been executed in 67 or 68.

**70** Romans destroy Jewish temple in Jerusalem; outlaw Jewish priesthood; disperse many Jews throughout Roman Empire as punishment for Jewish revolt against Roman rule.

**71–80** Colosseum built in Rome.

**c.78–96** Kushan Empire in Afghanistan and northern India ruled by King Kanishka, who sends Buddhist missionaries to China.

**98–117** Roman Emperor Trajan extends Roman Empire to include Arabia, Iraq, Armenia, and what is now Romania and Hungary.

**117–138** Roman Emperor Hadrian codifies laws of Rome; establishes postal system throughout empire; constructs many buildings, including Parthenon in Rome.

**132–135** New revolt by Jews in Jerusalem leads to final Diaspora (dispersion) of Jews.

**c.224–226** Persian Empire reestablished by Ardashir I, founding dynasty of Persian shahs called *Sassanids,* who rule until 642.

**c.250–800** Mayan civilization in Central America develops writing, astronomy, and mathematics; builds great pyramids.

**251–270** Plague kills about one-fourth of people throughout Roman Empire; German tribes invade empire from north.

**306–337** Roman Emperor Constantine I builds new capital at Constantinople (previously Byzantium, now Istanbul); becomes Christian; issues Edict of Milan (c.313), legalizing Christianity throughout Roman Empire.

**313** Koreans win independence from China.

**c.320** Gupta dynasty founded in northern India by Chandragupta I.

**c.376** Huns (Mongols) from central Asia establish Hunnic Empire in what is now Hungary.

**380** Christianity made official religion of Roman Empire by Emperor Theodosius the Great.

**395** Roman Empire permanently divided: western empire ruled from Rome; eastern empire ruled from Constantinople.

**395–476** Western Roman Empire disintegrates under series of weak emperors; Visigoths led by Alaric capture and sack Rome in 410; Huns led by Attila ravage Rome's provinces in 435–453; Rome again sacked in 455 by Vandals led by Genseric; in 476 last Roman emperor of west, Romulus Augustus, overthrown by Odoacer, leader of German Heruli.

# BYZANTINE EMPIRE, ARAB EMPIRE, AND EUROPEAN MIDDLE AGES: 481–1291

**481   Kingdom of Franks** established by Clovis I in northern France and southern Germany with capital at Paris.

**484–490   Hephthalites, or White Huns, invade Persia and India:** Asian tribesmen loot wealthy cities; dominate region until defeated in India in 528 and in Afghanistan in 557.

**493   Ostrogoth Kingdom of Italy** established by Theodoric the Great.

**c.500–542   King Arthur** and Knights of Round Table rule in England, according to legend.

**502–549   Buddhism becomes official religion in China:** Emperor Liang Wu-ti adopts Buddhism; persecutes Taoists.

**527–565   Byzantine Empire** (Eastern Roman Empire) reaches height under Macedonian Emperor Justinian I the Great; conquers North Africa, Italy, and southeastern Spain.

**c.550   Silk manufacture** begins in Byzantine Empire after Christian missionaries to China smuggle out silkworm eggs and mulberry seeds.

**568–586   Visigoths conquer Spain:** Byzantine armies driven out of Spain by Visigoth King Leovigild.

**c.587   Japanese Emperor Yomei** converts to Buddhism.

**589   Chinese Empire** reunited by armies of Sui dynasty; Great Wall of China rebuilt.

**590–640   Papal States founded in Italy:** Pope Gregory takes charge of government as well as religious affairs in central and southern Italy.

**c.597–605   English King Ethelbert I** converts to Christianity; St. Augustine becomes first archbishop of Canterbury (Ethelbert's capital).

**622–632   Mohammed founds Islamic religion;** launches holy war by Arabs on nonbelievers.

**630–648   Chinese armies** conquer Turkestan (now part of Soviet Union).

**634–644   Arab Empire** expands by conquest of Iraq, Syria, Iran, Palestine, and Egypt by Muslim armies of caliph Omar.

**661–680   Arab armies** of caliph Muawiya make new conquests, adding North Africa, Afghanistan, Pakistan, and Turkestan to Arab Empire.

**675–681   Slavic tribes** invade Balkan region.

**711–732   Spain and southern France** invaded and conquered by Arabs and Berbers from Africa.

**712–756   Chinese culture** rises to new heights under Emperor Hsuan Tsung; porcelain made; paper printed with wooden blocks; mechanical clock invented.

**768–814   Charlemagne,** king of Franks, expands empire by conquest of Germany and northern Italy; attempts to revive Western Roman Empire by having Pope Leo III crown him emperor in 800.

**c.787–794   Danish and Norse Vikings** raid England and Scotland.

**c.820–1431   Cambodia** (Khmer) rules southeast Asia from magnificent capital at Angkor Thom.

**841–856   Danish Vikings** raid France, sacking Paris in 845 and 856.

**c.855–879   Russian nation founded** by Vikings under Prince Rurik, establishing capital at Novgorod.

**867   Christianity splits** Rome and Constantinople as Eastern Orthodox Church rejects control by Roman Catholic pope.

**878   Alfred the Great** prevents Danish Vikings from conquering all of England.

**866   Normandy region of France** colonized by Viking Northmen (Normans).

**912–961   Muslim Spain** becomes Europe's main center of learning and science under caliph Abdar-Rahman III.

**962   Holy Roman Empire founded** by Otto I, king of Germany since 936, crowned by Pope John XII.

**976–1025   Byzantine Empire's power** revived by Emperor Basil II, conquering Bulgaria and Armenia.

**981   Greenland** colonized by Norse Vikings.

**987   Hugh Capet elected king of France,** founding Capetian dynasty that rules until 1328.

**c.1000   North America** discovered by Norse Vikings, who call it *Vinland.*

**1003–14   England conquered** by Denmark's King Sven.

**1055   Seljuk Turks** from central Asia under Tughril Beg capture Baghdad, capital of Arab Empire.

**1066   England invaded** by Normans led by William the Conqueror, who defeats King Harold II at Battle of Hastings (Oct. 14).

**1068–84   Southern Italy conquered** by Normans led by Robert Guiscard; Rome sacked in 1084.

**1071–85   Seljuk Turks** extend empire, conquering Asiatic Turkey and Syria.

**1096–99   First Crusade:** Answering call by Pope Urban III to rescue Holy Land from control of Muslims, about 30,000 French and Italian crusaders invade Seljuk Turkish Empire, capturing Jerusalem and Turkey; establish Latin States of the Crusaders in Middle East.

**c.1100   Timbuktu founded** in West Africa, becoming center of learning for black Muslims.

**1106   Northern France invaded and conquered** by England's King Henry I, imprisoning his brother, who had been ruler of Normandy.

**1147–49   Second Crusade:** Because Muslims had reconquered most of Asiatic Turkey, new crusade is organized by kings of France and Germany, but is defeated by Turks.

**c.1150–67   Universities of Paris and Oxford** founded in France and England.

**1167–71   Ireland claimed** by England's King Henry II as Normans colonize Ireland.

**1175–1206   Central India conquered** by Muslim ruler of Persia.

**1187   Jerusalem captured** by Saladin, Muslim sultan of Syria and Egypt.

**1189–92   Third Crusade:** Kings of England, France, and Germany lead armies in unsuccessful effort to recapture Jerusalem; however, agreement is made with Saladin to let Christians visit Jerusalem.

**c.1200–1438   Inca civilization** develops in Peru; builds great cities and road system.

**c.1200–1450   Mayan civilization** in Central America ruled from Mayapán in Yucatán, following overthrow of rulers of Chichén-Itzá.

**1202–04   Northern France recovered** by France's King Philip II from England's King John.

**1202–04   Fourth Crusade:** Setting off to invade Arab Egypt, French knights divert to attack Byzantine Empire; capture Constantinople and massacre its people; Roman Catholics replace Greeks on throne of Byzantine Empire.

**1203–23   Denmark** raids and conquers many coastal areas of Baltic Sea.

**1206–27   Genghis Khan** leads Mongols in conquest of northern China and central Asia.

**1212   Children's Crusade:** Thousands of French and German children march toward Holy Land but die or are enslaved along way.

**1215 (June 15–19)   Magna Carta** (Great Charter) agreed to by England's King John; sets first limits on monarch's absolute power by requiring assent of barons to special taxes.

**1218–21   Fifth Crusade:** Crusaders invade Egypt but are driven off.

**1228–29   Sixth Crusade:** Holy Roman Emperor Frederick II leads Teutonic Knights to Holy Land; acquires Jerusalem from sultan of Egypt, crowning himself its king.

**1230–55   Mali Empire** founded in West Africa by King Sundiata.

**1237–41   Mongol armies conquer Russia** and devastate Hungary; for next two centuries Russian princes pay tribute to Mongol Golden Horde that occupies southern Russia.

**1244   Jerusalem recaptured** by Muslims.

**1245–65   Seljuk Turkish Empire destroyed** by Mongols, who conquer Iran, Iraq, and Syria, sacking Baghdad in 1258.

**1248–54   Seventh Crusade:** France's King Louis IX leads attack on Egypt; captured by Muslims and held captive until ransom is paid.

**1260–94   Kublai Khan** rules China and Mongol Empire from Pacific Ocean to Mediterranean Sea, with capital at Peking; builds roads, canals, hospitals; encourages art and science.

**1261   Greek rule of Byzantine Empire** restored by Greek army that overthrows Roman Catholic Emperor Baldwin II.

**1265   First English parliament** meets under leader-

QUICK QUIZ:   How many U.S. representatives does your state have? See pages 160–161.

**KEY EVENTS IN WORLD HISTORY** *(continued)*
ship of Simon de Montfort.
**1269–73  Gunpowder explosives first used in war:**
Chinese defenders of cities in Yangtze River Valley use
explosives against Mongol invaders.
**1270  Eighth Crusade:** Kings of England and France
attack Carthage in North Africa; French King Louis
IX dies of plague; nothing accomplished.
**1271–95  Marco Polo** of Venice travels throughout
Mongol Empire; upon return writes book describing
wonders of Chinese civilization.
**1272–1307  Great Britain unified** for first time as English King Edward I conquers Wales and Scotland.

**1276–78  Austria** conquered by Holy Roman Emper-
or Rudolf I, founder of Hapsburg dynasty that rules
Austria until 1918.
**1281  Typhoon saves Japan from Mongol invasion;** invading army of 150,000 Mongols halted when typhoon
wrecks their fleet.
**1287  Mongols conquer Burma:** Capital city Pagan
looted; Burma made part of Kublai Khan's empire.
**1291  Last Christian crusaders** driven from Middle
East by Muslims.
**1294  First Roman Catholic missionary travels to
China:** Franciscan friar Giovanni di Monte Covino
reaches Peking; made first archbishop of China in 1307.

## RENAISSANCE, EXPLORATION, AND REFORMATION: 1300–1599

**c.1300  European Renaissance** begins in Florence, Italy, with painter Giotto and writers Dante, Petrarch,
and Boccaccio.
**1300–26  Ottoman Turkish Empire founded by Os-
man I:** Launches holy war against non-Muslims in
Middle East.
**1307–08  William Tell** helps Switzerland win independence from Austria, legend says.
**1312–37  Mali Empire** reaches height in Africa under
King Mansa Musa; said to have visited Cairo with car-
avan of 100 camels, each carrying 300 pounds of gold,
and 500 slaves, each carrying staff made of gold.
**1314  Scotland wins independence** from England as
Robert Bruce defeats English army at Battle of Bannockburn (June 24).
**1325–1519  Mexico ruled by Aztecs** from capital city
of Tenochtitlán (now Mexico City).
**1326–61  Ottoman Turkish Empire** under Sultan Or-
khan I conquers northeastern Greece.
**1337–1453  Hundred Years War:** English and French
kings fight for control of France; by 1453 England
holds only French city of Calais, but English claim
throne of France until 1801.
**1340–41  Portuguese explorers** first visit Canary Islands off coast of northwest Africa.
**1346 (Aug. 26)  England's King Edward III** wins Battle of Crécy over French, proving superiority of long-
bowmen over armored knights and crossbowmen of
France; cannon fired by gunpowder possibly introduced then.
**1347–52  Black Death** (bubonic plague) sweeps
across Europe, killing about one-fourth of estimated
100 million population.
**1361–89  Ottoman Turkish Empire expands** under
Sultan Murad I with conquest of most of what is now
Yugoslavia and Bulgaria.
**1368–98  Ming dynasty** founded in China by Emperor
Hung–wu, whose armies drive Mongols into central
Asia.
**1369–1405  Mongol ruler Tamerlane** conquers Afghanistan, Iran, Iraq, eastern Turkey, and northern India.
**c.1376–82  Bible translated into English** by John
Wycliffe and his followers.
**1378–1417  Rival popes** in Rome and at Avignon,
France, contend for control of Roman Catholic
Church.
**1381  Peasant Revolt in England** led by Wat Tyler
unsuccessfully demands end to feudal system of forced
labor and high land rents.
**1387–1412  Denmark, Norway, and Sweden united**
under Queen Margrethe of Denmark.
**1399  Revolt in England:** King Richard II imprisoned
for reasserting absolute power; parliament elects Henry
IV to throne.
**c.1400–1500  Muslim Arabs** conquer islands of Indonesia, Malaya, and southern Philippines.
**1414–17  Roman Catholics reunified** with election of
Pope Martin V; Council of Constance condemns and
executes as heretics John Huss (Jan Hus) and Jerome
of Prague for questioning validity of various church
doctrines.
**1418–60  Portugal's Prince Henry the Navigator**
sponsors exploration of Africa's coast.
**c.1422–26  Technical improvements in arts:** Oil painting developed by Flemish artist Jan Van Eyck; bronze
statues cast by Florentine sculptor Donatello; perspec-
tive used to show depth by Florentine painter Masaccio.
**1427–31  Azores Islands discovered** by Portuguese explorer Diogo de Sevilla.
**1429 (May 7)  Joan of Arc,** 17, leads French army at

Battle of Orléans, forcing English to lift siege of city;
saves France from being conquered; burned as witch by
English at Rouen on May 31, 1431.
**1453 (May 29)  Byzantine Empire comes to end** as
Ottoman Turks capture Constantinople.
**c.1454  Johann Gutenberg** invents printing with movable metal type at Mainz, Germany.
**1455–85  Wars of the Roses:** Civil war in England between rival families of York and Lancaster for throne
of England; ends with marriage of King Henry VII (of
Lancaster) to Elizabeth (of York), founding Tudor
dynasty.
**1462–1505  Ivan III the Great** rules Russia as first
czar; ends payment of tribute to Mongols; seizes part of
Lithuania from Poland.
**1479  Spain unified** by joint rule of Queen Isabella of
Castile and King Ferdinand II of Aragon; they complete conquest of Moorish Spain with capture of Granada in 1492.
**1487–88  Portuguese explorer Bartolomeu Dias** sails
around southern tip of Africa.
**1492–93  Christopher Columbus** makes first voyage of
discovery to America; lands at Bahamas island of San
Salvador on Oct. 12, 1492; discovers Cuba; establishes
settlement on Santo Domingo.
**1493  Line of Demarcation** established by Pope Alexander VI to prevent disputes between Portugal and
Spain; gives Africa and Brazil to Portugal, rest of
Americas to Spain.
**c.1495–1519  Leonardo da Vinci** paints Renaissance
masterpieces *Last Supper* and *Mona Lisa;* produces
many other works of art, science, and engineering in
Italy.
**1497–99  Portuguese explorer Vasco da Gama** sails
around Africa to India and back; gives Portugal opportunity to establish monopoly on trade in spices from
Far East to Europe.
**1501  First black slaves in America** brought to Spanish colony of Santo Domingo.
**1505–15  Portugal** fortifies India's southwest coast;
destroys Arab ships in Arabian Gulf to cut off Arab
trade with Far East; establishes Goa in India as capital
of Portuguese possessions in Asia.
**1506–1626  St. Peter's Church** built in Rome; designed and decorated by such Renaissance artists and
architects as Donato Bramante, Michelangelo, Raphael, Leonardo da Vinci, and Gian Lorenzo Bernini.
**1512–20  Ottoman Turks** conquer Syria, Arabia, and
Egypt under leadership of Sultan Selim I.
**1513 (Sept. 9)  Scotland's King James IV** invades England; defeated and killed at Battle of Flodden Field.
**1517 (Oct. 31)  Reformation** begins in Germany as
Martin Luther posts on door of church in Wittenberg
his *Ninety-Five Theses,* denouncing abuses by Roman
Catholic Church.
**1519–21  Spanish conquistador Hernándo Cortés con-
quers Mexico;** defeats Aztec Indians at their capital,
Tenochtitlán; sends back treasures of gold to Spain.
**1519–22  First voyage around world:** Begun in 1519
by Spanish explorer Ferdinand Magellan, killed in
Philippines in 1521; one of his ships, under command
of Juan Sebastián del Cano, continues around world to
Spain, arriving in 1522.
**1520–23  Sweden declares independence** from Denmark; leader of revolt takes throne as King Gustavus I.
**1520–66  Ottoman Turkish Empire** expands with conquests of Yugoslavia, Hungary, Iraq, Iran, Arabia, and
North Africa by Sultan Suleiman I the Magnificent.
**1521  Martin Luther excommunicated** by Pope Leo
X; declared outlaw punishable by death by Holy Roman Emperor Charles V; before Luther's death, in
1546, thousands in Europe turn to Protestantism.

**1526 (Aug. 29) Hungary conquered by Turks:** In Battle of Mohács, armies of Sultan Suleiman I defeat Hungarian King Lajos II; over 100,000 Hungarian Christians enslaved by Turks.

**1526–30 Mogul Empire in India** founded by Babar, descendant of Gengis Khan.

**1527–46 Mayan civilization** of Yucatán conquered by Spaniards, who burn Mayan bark-cloth books, calling them "works of the Devil."

**1529 (April 22) Portugal and Spain divide Eastern Hemisphere:** Sign Treaty of Saragossa establishing boundary between possessions in Far East, recognizing Portugal's control of Indonesia and Spain's possession of Philippines and Pacific Islands.

**1530–31 Schmalkaldic League** formed by German states and cities ruled by Protestants.

**1531 Commercial tobacco farming begun in America:** Rising demand for tobacco in Spain, where it had been introduced by Christopher Columbus, causes colonists in what is now Dominican Republic to begin raising tobacco for export.

**1531–35 Inca empire of Peru conquered** by Spanish conquistador Francisco Pizarro, who loots their gold and sends it to Spain.

**1534 Reformation begins in England** as King Henry VIII makes himself head of church after being excommunicated for divorcing Catherine of Aragon.

**1534–64 Presbyterian Protestantism,** developed by John Calvin in Switzerland, gains English Puritans and French Huguenots as adherents.

**1536–40 Denmark, Norway, and Sweden adopt Lutheranism** as national religion.

**1538 First university in Americas** founded in Santo Domingo (now Dominican Republic).

**1542 First European visits Japan;** believed to be Portuguese explorer Antonio da Mota.

**1542–51 Roman Catholicism introduced to India and Japan** by Jesuit missionary St. Francis Xavier.

**1543 Theory that Earth revolves around Sun** published by Polish scholar Nicolaus Copernicus; later suppressed by Roman Catholic Church as denial of biblical teaching.

**1546–55 Schmalkaldic War:** Holy Roman Emperor Charles V tries to force Protestant states and cities of Germany to return to Roman Catholicism; Peace of Augsburg in 1555 gives Lutherans freedom of worship.

**1547–84 Russia's Czar Ivan IV the Terrible** conquers Tatars (Mongols) to acquire Volga River region, but loses western Russia to Poland and Sweden.

**c.1550 Muskets** first developed in Spain.

**1553–58 Roman Catholicism restored in England** by Queen Mary I; about 300 Protestant leaders burned at stake, including Archbishop of Canterbury Thomas Cranmer.

**1558–1603 England ruled by Queen Elizabeth I,** who restores Protestantism, establishes Church of England (Episcopalian), and persecutes Roman Catholics, Unitarians, and radical Puritans; Renaissance reaches height in England with such writers as William Shakespeare, Edmund Spenser, and Christopher Marlowe.

**1562–68 British slave trade begins** with voyages of John Hawkins carrying slaves from Africa to Spanish colonies in Caribbean.

**1562–98 Religious wars in France** rage between Roman Catholics and Protestants (Huguenots); Roman Catholics slaughter thousands of Huguenots (Protestants) in St. Bartholomew's Day Massacre on Aug. 24, 1572; fighting ends with Edict of Nantes on April 15, 1598, giving Huguenots political rights but not full freedom of worship.

**1568–1648 Protestant Netherlands wins independence** from Catholic Spain in series of revolts; Renaissance reaches height in Netherlands with work of such Dutch masters as Peter Paul Rubens, Anthony Van Dyck, Franz Hals, and Rembrandt van Rijn.

**1568–82 Central Japan unified** by warrior-dictator Oda Nobunaga; Nagasaki becomes important port for trade with Portugal.

**1571 (Oct. 7) Turkish fleet defeated** by Spanish and Italian fleets in Mediterranean Sea in Battle of Lepanto, ending threat of further Turkish expansion.

**1571 Manila founded** by Spanish colonists in Philippines.

**1571–1603 Muslim Empire of Kanem** in central Africa reaches height of power under King Idris III, who rules from walled capital of N'gazargamu; wealth comes from slaves captured in south and sold in North Africa.

**1574 Colony of Angola** founded by Portuguese in Africa at mouth of Congo River.

**1577–80 Sir Francis Drake of England sails around world** after looting Spanish ships along South American coast.

**1580 Spain conquers Portugal,** placing Spanish Hapsburg ruler on throne.

**1587 (Feb. 8) Mary Queen of Scots beheaded** after being found guilty of plotting to kill England's Queen Elizabeth I.

**1588 (July 31–Aug. 8) Defeat of Spanish Armada:** King Philip II of Spain sends armada of 130 ships to invade England and restore Roman Catholicism; Spaniards defeated by English fleet of about 200 ships led by Adm. Lord Howard; many Spanish ships driven on Irish coast in storm.

**1589–1610 France's King Henry IV** comes to throne as Protestant but converts to Roman Catholicism in 1593 in effort to end religious wars; founds Bourbon dynasty that rules France to 1792.

**1597 Christian persecution begins in Japan;** Japan's dictator Hideyoshi executes nine Portuguese and Spanish missionaries.

**1598–1605 Serfdom established in Russia** by Czar Boris Godunov.

**c.1599 Renaissance reaches height in Spain** with work of painter El Greco, novelist Miguel de Cervantes, playwright Lope de Vega.

# EUROPE'S MONARCHS MANEUVER FOR POWER AND TERRITORY: 1600–1760

**1600 English East India Company** founded to establish English colonies and expand trade.

**1602 Dutch East India Company** established to manage Netherlands' colonization and trade.

**1605 (Nov. 5) Gunpowder plot:** In retaliation for their persecution, English Roman Catholics try to blow up England's parliament and King James I; plot uncovered and leader Guy Fawkes hanged.

**1607 First permanent English colony in North America** founded at Jamestown, Virginia.

**1608 French colony of Quebec** established in Canada by explorer Samuel de Champlain.

**1611 Protestant colony of Northern Ireland** founded by England's King James I.

**1611 King James Version of Bible** published in England after translation by group of scholars appointed by King James I.

**1611–32 Sweden becomes powerful** under Gustavus II Adolphus, winning wars with Russia, Poland, and Holy Roman Empire.

**1612 England establishes colony in India** at Surat after defeating Portuguese fleet.

**1612–14 Bermuda colonized** by English.

**1618–48 Thirty Years War:** Protestants in Holy Roman Empire rebel against oppression by Roman Catholics; Denmark, Sweden, and France invade Germany; great loss of life and property hinders Germany's development for next two centuries.

**1619–23 Dutch found Batavia** (now Jakarta) on Java as center of Far Eastern spice trade; massacre English traders in East Indies.

**1623–51 Japanese isolation** for next two centuries begun by shogun Iemitsu; foreign traders expelled, except for few Chinese and Dutch; Christianity ruthlessly stamped out.

**1627–44 Manchus invade and conquer China,** founding Manchu, or Ch'ing, dynasty that rules until 1912.

**1632–52 Taj Mahal** built in India by Shah Jahan.

**1633 Italian astronomer Galileo** tried by Roman Catholic court; forced to recant belief in Copernican theory.

**1634 Dutch capture Curaçao** in Caribbean Sea; Peter Stuyvesant becomes first governor.

**1635 French** settlers colonize Guadeloupe in Caribbean Sea.

**1637 First public opera house opened in Venice, Italy:** New art form of musical dramas had previously been performed only in palaces of nobility.

**1637 Africa's Gold Coast (Ghana)** seized by Dutch from Portugal as base for slave trade.

**1640 Portugal regains independence** in revolt against Spanish rulers.

QUICK QUIZ: Which university library has the most books? See page 244.

## KEY EVENTS IN WORLD HISTORY (continued)

**1642–49   Puritan revolution in England:** Puritan general Oliver Cromwell leads supporters of parliament in defeating royalist armies; King Charles I convicted of treason and beheaded on Jan. 30, 1649; Cromwell rules as military dictator, suppressing Church of England and decreeing Puritanical laws.

**1642–59   France attacks Spain,** taking Spain's northeastern provinces.

**1648   Bahamas settled** by British colonists from Bermuda; islands become haven for pirates.

**1650–52   Tea and coffee introduced in England:** Beverages quickly win popularity with opening of public coffeehouses.

**1652 (April 7)   Dutch establish colony in South Africa:** Settlement at Cape Town becomes supply station for Dutch ships sailing on East Indies route around Africa.

**1652–74   England and Netherlands** fight three naval wars, ending with England winning command of seas; Netherlands gives up colony of New Netherland (New York) to England in exchange for Surinam in South America.

**1655   British capture Jamaica** from Spain in Caribbean Sea.

**1656   Dutch capture Sri Lanka:** Take main Portuguese settlement at Colombo.

**1660   Monarchy restored in England** as Charles II becomes king; Church of England reestablished; other Protestant faiths and Roman Catholicism suppressed.

**1661   Palace of Versailles** construction begun by France's King Louis XIV.

**1665–66   Plague and fire** devastate London; about 75,000 persons die of plague; fire (Sept. 2–6, 1666) destroys much of London.

**1682–99   War between Austria and Ottoman Turks:** Vienna withstands 2-month siege by Turks; Austria captures Hungary from Turks.

**1685   Protestantism outlawed in France** as Edict of Nantes of 1598 is revoked; thousands of Protestants flee to other countries.

**1687 (Sept. 26)   Parthenon in Athens demolished:** In war fought in Greece between Turks and Venetians, artillery of Venetians hits ancient temple, exploding gunpowder stored there by Turks.

**1687–88   Thailand drives out foreigners:** Thai people force English traders and French missionaries to leave country, closing it to foreign influence for next two centuries.

**1688–89   Glorious Revolution in England:** Fearing King James II plans to restore Roman Catholicism, parliamentary leaders ask Dutch Prince William of Orange to protect Protestants; when William lands with army, James flees to France; monarchy given to William and his wife, who then rule as King William III and Queen Mary II; parliament adopts Bill of Rights (Dec. 16, 1689) to protect citizens from government.

**1688–97   War of the League of Augsburg** (called King William's War in America): France invades Germany, attacks English colonies in America; England, Netherlands, Spain, Sweden, and German states fight against France; Treaty of Ryswick (Sept. 30, 1697) ends war with few territorial changes.

**1689–1725   Czar Peter I the Great** rules Russia; carries out reforms to westernize nation; establishes Russia as major military power, defeating Sweden in Great Northern War in 1700–21.

**1690 (July 11)   Battle of the Boyne:** England's King William III defeats rebellion in Ireland led by former King James II.

**1698   First practical steam engine** invented by Thomas Savery in England; used to pump water from mines and to pump water supply for homes; begins era of Industrial Revolution.

**1698   Arab sultan of Oman** seizes control of east coast of Africa from Portuguese.

**1701   Kingdom of Prussia** founded in eastern Germany by King Frederick I.

**1701–14   War of the Spanish Succession** (called Queen Anne's War in America): France's King Louis XIV preserves his grandson on throne of Spain as King Philip V; fights against alliance of England, Netherlands, Austria, and Savoy (Sardinia); at war's end France and Spain promise not to unite as single monarchy; Austria wins control of Luxembourg and Belgium; France gives England northeastern Canada (Acadia); Spain gives England Gibraltar and 30-year contract to supply slaves to Spain's American colonies.

**1707 (May 1)   United Kingdom of Great Britain:** Parliaments of the Kingdom of England and Wales and of the Kingdom of Scotland each pass Act of Union, forming one government under Queen Anne.

**1717–20   War of the Quadruple Alliance:** Spain invades and captures Sardinia and Sicily; alliance of Britain, France, Netherlands, and Austria defeats Spain; Sardinia given independence under prince of Savoy.

**1721–42   British cabinet system of government** established as Sir Robert Walpole serves as chief minister of George I and George II.

**1733–35   War of the Polish Succession:** Russia and Austria fight against France, Spain, and Sardinia, winning right to place weak kings on Polish throne, paving way for partition.

**1736–39   Ottoman Turks** win most of Yugoslavia in war with Austria and Russia.

**1738–40   Persians** led by Nadir Shah invade and conquer northern India, forcing Mogul emperor to pay tribute to remain on throne.

**1740–48   War of the Austrian Succession** (called King George's War in America): Austria and Britain fight against France, Spain, Prussia, and German states that refuse to recognize Maria Theresa's claim to throne of Holy Roman Empire; at war's end she and husband, Francis I, retain throne but give up province of Silesia to Prussia.

**1741–43   Sweden attacks Russia** but is defeated; forced to give Russia control of Finland.

**1756–63   Seven Years War** (called French and Indian War in America): Britain and Prussia defeat France, Austria, Spain, and Russia; France loses colonial empire in North America and India to Britain; Prussia retains Silesia; Spain cedes Florida to Britain in exchange for Cuba.

**1757 (June 23)   Britain wins control of Bengal in India:** under leadership of Robert Clive, 3,200 troops of English East India Company defeat 50,000 Indian soldiers in Battle of Plassey.

## SOCIAL, POLITICAL, AND INDUSTRIAL REVOLUTIONS: 1760–1850

**1762   *The Social Contract*** by Jean Jacques Rousseau influences leaders of American and French revolutions with idea government requires contract between ruler and governed.

**1764–69   Machines to spin yarn invented** in England by James Hargreaves and Richard Arkwright, initiating first textile factories.

**1768–74   War between Russia and Ottoman Turks:** Russia conquers Crimean peninsula.

**1768–82   Improved steam engine** to operate machinery developed by James Watt.

**c.1770–1830   German literature and music** enriched by writers Goethe and Schiller and composers Bach, Mozart, and Beethoven.

**1772 (June 22)   Slavery ruled illegal** in Britain by Chief Justice William Lord Mansfield, but ruling does not affect status of slaves in colonies.

**1772–95   Partition of Poland:** In three steps in 1772, 1793, and 1795, Austria, Russia, and Prussia divide land and people of Poland, ending its independence.

**1775–83   American Revolutionary War:** France, Spain, and Netherlands aid Americans in defeating Britain; in Treaty of Paris, Britain recognizes U.S. independence, gives up Tobago and Senegal to France, and Minorca and Florida to Spain.

**1782   Thailand wins independence** from Burma.

**1787   Freetown, Sierra Leone, founded** by British abolitionists as haven for freed slaves.

**1788 (Jan. 26)   Sydney, Australia, settled** by British colonists.

**1789 (April 30)   George Washington** takes office as first U.S. President under Constitution.

**1789 (July 14)   Storming of Bastille:** Paris mob captures prison, symbol of royal power.

**1789–99   French Revolution:** Assembly adopts constitution limiting powers of king and nobles in 1789–90; republic declared on Sept. 21, 1792; King Louis XVI beheaded on Jan. 21, 1793; Reign of Terror with thousands guillotined in 1793–95; rule by 5-man directory in 1795–99.

**1790   First American textile factory** opened by Samuel Slater in Pawtucket, R.I.

**1791–1803   Revolt by slaves in Haiti** overthrows French rule.

**1792–97 War of the First Coalition:** In effort to restore nobility in France, coalition of Austria, Prussia, Britain, Netherlands, Spain, and Sardinia fight against France; at war's end France controls northern Italy, Netherlands, Belgium, Switzerland, and southern Germany.

**1794 Polish revolt** led by Tadeusz Kościuszko; defeated by Russia and Prussia.

**1795–96 Britain takes advantage of France's conquest of Netherlands** to take over Dutch colonies in Sri Lanka and South Africa.

**1795–99 France ruled by directory:** New constitution gives 5-man directory dictatorial power over France.

**1798 Mass production** of muskets with interchangeable parts developed by U.S. inventor Eli Whitney.

**1798 Prediction that world population would outstrip food supply** published by English economist Thomas Malthus in *Essay on the Principle of Population.*

**1798–99 Egypt invaded and conquered** by French troops led by Napoleon Bonaparte.

**1798–1800 U.S. and France fight** naval war.

**1798–1802 War of the Second Coalition:** Britain, Austria, Russia, Portugal, and Ottoman Turks fight against France; French armies win in Europe but are driven out of Egypt.

**1799 (Nov. 9) Napoleon Bonaparte** becomes dictator of France, naming himself first consul.

**1800 China bans imports of opium:** Decree by Emperor Chia-ch'ing has reverse of intended effect as corrupt officials accept bribes by foreign traders who increase flow of opium into China.

**1801 (Jan. 1) United Kingdom of Great Britain and Ireland** estalished with one monarch, one parliament, and one Protestant Episcopal Church; Catholics excluded from voting.

**1804 (Jan. 1) Haiti declares independence** from France; first black nation to gain freedom from European colonial rule.

**1804 Napoleon I becomes emperor of France,** placing crown on own head (Dec. 2).

**1804–13 Russia defeats Persia,** taking control of Georgia between Black and Caspian seas.

**1805 (Oct. 21) Battle of Trafalgar:** British fleet under Horatio Lord Nelson wins command of seas, defeating Napoleon's combined French-Spanish fleet at Strait of Gibraltar, enabling Britain to blockade Napoleonic France.

**1805–09 Napoleon I conquers continental Europe.**

**1806 (Aug. 6) Holy Roman Empire ends,** Austria having lost German states to Napoleon.

**1810–15 Unsuccessful revolutions in Mexico and Venezuela** put down by Spanish troops.

**1811 (Aug. 14) Paraguay declares independence** from Spain; becomes dictatorship in 1814 under José Rodríguez de Francia.

**1812 Napoleon meets disaster in Russia:** After occupying Moscow, which was burned, lack of supplies forces Napoleon to retreat in winter; most of army of 600,000 desert or die.

**1812–14 War of 1812:** U.S. fights Britain.

**1813–14 War of Liberation of Europe:** Allies (Britain, Austria, Russia, Prussia, Sweden, and Portugal) defeat Napoleon, capturing Paris, March 31, 1814; Napoleon abdicates and is exiled to island of Elba off coast of Italy.

**1814–24 France restores Bourbon monarchy** under King Louis XVIII.

**1815 Napoleon I escapes from Elba;** defeated by Allies led by Duke of Wellington at Battle of Waterloo in Belgium (June 18); exiled to island of St. Helena in South Atlantic.

**1815 Congress of Vienna:** Victorious Allies redraw map of Europe, returning France to pre-Napoleonic borders; Switzerland guaranteed perpetual neutrality; Sweden acquires Norway; Russia gets Poland; Netherlands obtains Belgium; Britain receives Malta, protectorate over Ionian Islands, and several French and Dutch colonies.

**1816–24 South American nations win independence** from Spain with patriot armies led by José de San Martín and Simón Bolívar.

**1820–23 Revolt in Spain:** Troops refuse to go to America to reconquer Spain's colonies; put down by intervention of French army.

**1821 (Feb. 24) Mexico declares independence** from Spain; ruled as monarchy by Gen. Agustín de Iturbide

as Emperor Agustín I (1822–23); becomes republic on Oct. 4, 1824.

**1821–31 Greece wins independence** from Ottoman Turkish Empire.

**1822 Liberia** (then called Monrovia) established in Africa by American Colonization Society as settlement for freed American slaves.

**1822 (Sept. 7) Brazil declares independence** from Portugal as constitutional monarchy under Emperor Pedro I, son of Portugal's king.

**1823 (July 1) United Provinces of Central America** declare independence from Mexico with Manuel José Arce as first president.

**1823 (Dec. 2) Monroe Doctrine** issued by U.S., warning Europe against interfering in Western Hemisphere.

**1825 (Sept. 27) First public railroad** using steam locomotive completed in England.

**1825–28 Uruguay wins independence** as result of war between Argentina and Brazil.

**1825–28 Russia defeats Persia** and wins control of Armenia and Caspian Sea.

**1828–29 Russia defeats Ottoman Turks,** occupying Bulgaria and Romania.

**1829 Britain grants Roman Catholics** right to vote and hold public office.

**1830 (July 5) France invades Algeria;** takes 40 more years to conquer interior of Algeria.

**1830 (July 28) Revolution in France:** Charles X overthrown; replaced by Louis Philippe.

**1830 (Aug. 25) Belgium begins revolt** against Netherlands; national congress chooses Leopold I as king in 1831; Dutch refuse to recognize independence until 1839.

**c.1830–1910 Russian literature and music reach golden age** with such writers as Gogol, Turgenev, Dostoyevsky, Tolstoy, and Chekhov, and such composers as Glinka, Borodin, Mussorgsky, Tchaikovsky, and Rimsky-Korsakov.

**1832–33 Egypt's ruler Mohammed Ali conquers** Syria and southern Turkey, defeating Ottoman Turkish main army; intervention by Britain, France, and Russia prevents overthrow of Ottoman Empire.

**1833 (Aug. 23) Britain abolishes slavery** in colonies; pays compensation to owners of 700,000 slaves freed.

**1837–38 Egypt captures most of Arabia** from Ottoman Turkish Empire.

**1838–40 Antarctica proven to be continent** by U.S. Navy Lt. Charles Wilkes.

**1838–41 Costa Rica, El Salvador, Guatemala, Honduras, and Nicaragua become independent.**

**1839–40 War between Egypt and Ottoman Turkish Empire:** Turks defeated in attack on Syria and forced to surrender fleet to Egypt; intervention by Britain forces Egypt to return Turkish fleet and give up claims to Syria.

**1839–42 Opium War between Britain and China:** China seizes illegally smuggled opium; Britain retaliates with attacks on cities; China forced to give Hong Kong to Britain and to open other ports to trade.

**1840 (Jan. 22) New Zealand settled** by British.

**1840 (May 6) First postage stamps** issued by Britain; U.S. follows on July 1, 1847.

**1844 (Feb. 27) Dominican Republic wins independence** in revolt from Haiti.

**1845–47 Irish potato famine** and typhus kill about 750,000; about 2 million others emigrate from Ireland to U.S. and other countries.

**1846–48 Mexican War:** U.S. defeats Mexico.

**1847 (July 26) Liberia declares independence;** first black colony in Africa to gain freedom.

**1848** *Communist Manifesto* published in Germany by Karl Marx and Friedrich Engels, calling for workers to overthrow middle class.

**1848 Switzerland becomes federal union:** New constitution provides centralized national government.

**1848 (Feb. 24) Revolution in France:** Monarchy overthrown, establishing republic; voters on Dec. 10 elect as president Prince Louis Napoleon, nephew of Napoleon I.

**1848–49 Revolutions** put down by royal troops in Austria, Hungary, Czechoslovakia, Germany, and Italy.

**1850–64 T'ai P'ing rebellion in China:** Rebel believers in Chinese form of Puritan Protestantism win control of central provinces; subdued by Manchus with aid of foreign mercenaries; about 20 million die in fighting.

QUICK QUIZ: What right does Amendment 6 to the U.S. Constitution guarantee? See page 322.

## KEY EVENTS IN WORLD HISTORY *(continued)*
## ITALIAN AND GERMAN UNIFICATION AND COLONIAL EXPANSION: 1852–1914

**1852 (Dec. 2)  France restores monarchy:** President Louis Napoleon becomes Emperor Napoleon III.

**1853  France annexes New Caledonia:** Penal colony established in Pacific island possession.

**1853–56  Crimean War:** Begins as dispute over control of Christian holy places in Jerusalem; Russia attacks Ottoman Turkish Empire; Britain and France come to aid of Turks; Russia defeated in battles on Crimean peninsula; Florence Nightingale establishes modern nursing, supervising British army hospitals; in Treaty of Paris, Russia agrees to remove forts and warships from Black Sea.

**1854  Japan forced to open two ports to trade** by U.S. Commodore Matthew C. Perry; in following two years Britain, Russia, and Netherlands obtain similar treaties.

**1854  Slavery abolished in Venezuela:** Government pays compensation to former owners; freed slaves denied civil rights.

**1855  Thailand opens ports to foreign trade:** Britain persuades King Rama IV to allow imports for first time since 1600s.

**1855–68  Ethiopia unified:** Emperor Theodore brings local chiefs under control, establishing centralized government for nation, then called Abyssinia.

**1856  Persia invades Afghanistan,** but Britain intervenes to force Persian withdrawal and recognition of Afghanistan's independence.

**1856–70  Christians persecuted in Korea** with execution of missionaries.

**1857–58  Britain takes over government of India** from British East India Company after exiling last Mogul emperior of India.

**1857–58  Second Opium War in China:** Britain and France force China to legalize opium imports and open more ports to foreign trade.

**1858  France conquers Cochin China** (South Vietnam), occupying Saigon.

**1858 (Aug. 5)  First transatlantic telegraph cable** completed by Cyrus W. Field; Britain's Queen Victoria exchanges greetings with U.S. President James Buchanan.

**1859  Theory of evolution** published by Charles Darwin in *On the Origin of Species by Means of Natural Selection.*

**1859–61  Unification of Italy:** Sardinia annexes most of northern Italy, defeating Austrian troops with aid of France in 1859–60; army of "red shirts" led by Giuseppi Garibaldi conquers Sicily and southern Italy in 1860–61, whose people vote to unite with northern Italy; on March 17, 1861, independent kingdom of Italy is proclaimed under King Victor Emmanuel II, who had ruled Sardinia since 1849.

**1860 (Oct. 12)  British and French troops capture Peking, China:** Because Chinese government reneges on observing terms of treaties, foreign troops seize capital, burning royal palace.

**1861 (March 3)  Serfdom abolished in Russia** by Czar Alexander II.

**1861–65  Civil War** in United States.

**1863  Cambodia** made French protectorate.

**1863 (June 7)  Mexico City** captured by French troops.

**1863–65  Japan's emperor orders expulsion of all foreign traders,** but bombardment of Japan by U.S., British, French, and Dutch warships forces him to approve foreign trade treaties.

**1864  Austria and Prussia fight Denmark,** taking Danish provinces.

**1864 (April 10)  Mexican monarchy** established by French with Austrian Archduke Maximilian as emperor of Mexico.

**1865–70  Paraguayan War:** Argentina, Brazil, and Uruguay invade Paraguay; about three-fourths of nation's people killed or flee to other countries; about one-fourth of Paraguay's land taken by its neighbors.

**1865–76  Russia conquers Turkestan** east of Caspian Sea.

**1866  Seven Weeks War:** Austria defeated by Prussia and Italy, both of which gain territory at Austria's expense.

**1867  Malaysian Straits Settlement** becomes British colony.

**1867 (June 19)  Mexican Emperor Maximilian** executed; Mexicans restore republic.

**1867 (July 1)  Dominion of Canada** established by Britain with confederation of Ontario, Quebec, New Brunswick, and Nova Scotia.

**1867 (Sept. 9)  Luxembourg becomes independent** neutral nation.

**1868  Japan's Emperor Mutsuhito** assumes direct rule, ending 700 years of feudal rule by shoguns (military dictators); capital moved to Tokyo.

**1869 (Nov. 17)  Suez Canal** opens.

**1870 (Oct. 2)  Italy annexes Rome** and Papal States from pope, making Rome capital of Italy.

**1870–71  Franco-Prussian War:** Prussians force surrender of Emperor Napoleon III at Battle of Sedan, Sept. 2, 1870; after four-month siege, capture Paris, Jan. 28, 1871; force France to pay indemnity of 5 billion francs; France again becomes republic.

**1871 (Jan. 18)  New German Empire** proclaimed by Kaiser Wilhelm I, who had ruled as king of Prussia since 1861.

**1873–74  France conquers Tonkin** (North Vietnam), capturing Hanoi.

**1874  Britain conquers Ashanti kingdom** in Ghana, later establishing Gold Coast colony.

**1874  Britain annexes Fiji.**

**1875–79  Egypt takes Red Sea coastal area** (Eritrea) from Ethiopia.

**1877–78  Russia attacks Ottoman Turkish Empire;** threat of British intervention prevents Russian capture of Constantinople; Turks grant independence to Romania, Montenegro, and Serbia; Russia occupies Bulgaria.

**1878  Berlin Congress** of European powers settles issues remaining from Russia's defeat of Ottoman Turks; Britain acquires Cyprus; France gains Tunisia; Austria obtains Bosnia and Herzegovina (now in Yugoslavia).

**1879–84  War of the Pacific:** Chile defeats Peru and Bolivia, taking Bolivia's entire coast and Peru's southern region.

**1880  France founds Brazzaville, Congo,** making region French protectorate.

**1881–82  Persecution of Jews begins in Russia,** forcing many to flee to other lands.

**1882  Italy invades Red Sea coast** of Ethiopia in region that later became Italian colony of Eritrea.

**1882 (May 20)  Triple Alliance** defense pact signed by Germany, Austria, and Italy.

**1882 (Sept. 13)  Britain invades Egypt:** Establishes military occupation.

**1883  Germany begins settlement of Southwest Africa.**

**1883–96  France conquers Madagascar,** exiling Queen Ranavalona III to island of Réunion.

**1884  Eastern New Guinea** divided between Britain and Germany (Dutch keep western New Guinea).

**1884–85  France forces China** to recognize French protectorate over Indochina.

**1884–88  France and Britain** take control of Somalia coast of East Africa.

**1885  Serbia attacks Bulgaria,** but is defeated as Bulgarians take eastern region of Serbia.

**1885  Germany takes Marshall and Solomon islands** in Pacific and Tanganyika in Africa.

**1885 (Jan. 26)  Massacre in Khartoum:** British Gen. Charles Gordon and his troops slain by Sudanese.

**1885 (May 2)  Congo Free State** (now Zaire) established by Belgium's King Leopold II.

**1885–86  British troops conquer Burma.**

**1885–96  Britain takes control of Kenya** in East Africa.

**1885–98  French troops gain control of most of West Africa,** defeating local rulers.

**1889  Brazil becomes republic** with overthrow of Emperor Pedro II by conservatives angered by his abolition of slavery in 1888.

**1889  Eiffel Tower** completed in Paris; at 954 feet, then highest structure in world.

**1890  Zanzibar** made British protectorate.

**1894 (Jan. 4)  France and Russia agree to defense alliance** if attacked by Germany, Austria, or Italy.

**1894  Uganda** made British protectorate.

**1894–95  War between China and Japan:** Japan wins control of Korea, Formosa (now Taiwan), and Pescadores Islands.

**1895–96  Italian troops invade Ethiopia** but are defeated, forcing Italy to recognize Ethiopia's independence.

**1896    First modern Olympic Games** held at Athens, Greece.

**1896–98    Sudan conquered** by British troops.

**1897    Germany seizes Chinese city of Tsingtao,** forcing China to sign 99-year lease on port.

**1897    Greece attacks Ottoman Turkish Empire** but is defeated, losing territory to Turks.

**1898    Spanish-American War:** U.S. ends Spanish rule of Cuba, Puerto Rico, and Philippines.

**1898 (Aug. 12)    Hawaii annexed by U.S.**

**1898–1902    Rebellion in Philippines** put down by U.S. troops, establishing American rule.

**1899    Nigeria made British protectorate.**

**1899    Persian Gulf Arab Sheikdoms made British protectorate.**

**1899    Open Door for China notes** sent to world powers by U.S. Secretary of State John Hay, obtaining assurances that leased Chinese ports would be open to U.S. trade.

**1899    First Hague Peace Conference:** Adopts rules of war and treatment of war prisoners; establishes permanent court of arbitration to settle international disputes.

**1899–1902    Boer War in South Africa:** Britain defeats Dutch settlers in South Africa to annex previously independent republics of Orange Free State and South African Republic.

**1900    Psychoanalysis** as treatment of mental disease promoted by publication of Sigmund Freud's *The Interpretation of Dreams.*

**1900–01    Boxer War in China:** China attempts to end its exploitation by killing foreigners and destroying foreign installations; U.S., Russian, British, French, and German troops subdue Chinese, capturing and looting Peking on Aug. 14, 1900, and forcing China to pay for damages to foreign property.

**1901 (Jan. 1)    Commonwealth of Australia established** by Britain.

**1902    Russia forces China** to turn over control of Manchuria (northern China).

**1902    Australia grants women right to vote** in federal elections.

**1902    Cuba gains independence** with election of first president; U.S. troops withdraw.

**1902 (Jan. 20)    Britain and Japan sign defense treaty:** Britain recognizes Japan's right to control Korea.

**1903 (Nov. 3)    Panama declares independence** from Colombia; U.S. obtains rights to Canal Zone to build Panama Canal.

**1904–05    Russo-Japanese War:** Japan attacks and defeats Russia, winning Russian ports in China, control of Korea, and southern Sakhalin Island; Russia withdraws from Manchuria.

**1905    Physics revolutionized** by Albert Einstein's theory of relativity, quantum theory, and formula for relationship of mass and energy ($E = mc^2$).

**1905    Russian czar's troops crush revolt** led by V.I. Lenin, but continued turmoil forces czar to agree to establishment of nation's first parliament, called Duma.

**1905 (June 7)    Norway declares independence** from Sweden.

**1906 (May 3)    British-controlled Egypt takes Sinai** peninsula from Ottoman Turkish Empire.

**1906–09    U.S. troops occupy Cuba** to put down rebellion by opponents of President Tomás Estrada Palma.

**1907    Second Hague Peace Conference:** World powers agree on detailed rules of war.

**1907    Morocco invaded** and occupied by French troops.

**1907    Japan makes Korea protectorate:** Japanese troops occupy nation, force abdication of Korea's emperor.

**1908    Austria annexes Bosnia and Herzogovina:** Take Balkan regions from Ottoman Turkish Empire.

**1908 (Oct. 5)    Bulgaria declares independence** from Ottoman Turkish Empire.

**1908 (Oct. 7)    Crete unites with Greece.**

**1909 (April 6)    North Pole** reached by American explorers Robert E. Peary and Matthew Henson.

**1910 (May 31)    Union of South Africa** established by Britain from former Boer states.

**1910 (Oct. 5)    Portugal becomes republic** with overthrow of monarchy.

**1911 (Dec. 16)    South Pole** first reached by Norwegian explorer Roald Amundsen.

**1911–1912    China becomes republic** with overthrow of Manchu emperor.

**1911–1912    Italy invades and takes Libya** from Ottoman Turkish Empire.

**1911–1917    Russia invades** and takes control of Persia.

**1912 (April 14–15)    British ocean liner** *Titanic* strikes iceberg and sinks in Atlantic Ocean on maiden voyage; 1,517 lives lost.

**1912 (Nov. 28)    Albania declares independence** from Ottoman Turkish Empire, becoming kingdom under Prince Wilhelm of Wied in 1914.

**1912–1913    First Balkan War:** Bulgaria, Serbia, Montenegro, and Greece join in defeating Ottoman Turkish Empire; division of spoils by great powers dissatisfies victors, leading to second Balkan War.

**1913 (June 29–Aug. 10)    Second Balkan War:** Serbia, Greece, Montenegro, Romania, and Ottoman Turks join in defeating Bulgaria, taking some of territory Bulgaria had been awarded in first Balkan War.

**1914 (April 21–Nov. 23)    U.S. Marines** occupy Veracruz, Mexico, intervening in civil war to protect American interests.

# PERIOD OF WORLD WAR I THROUGH WORLD WAR II: 1914–1945

**1914 (June 28)    Assassination** of Austria's Archduke Francis Ferdinand and his wife at Sarajevo in Austrian province of Bosnia: Austria believes Serbians responsible, issuing ultimatum to Serbia that leads to World War I.

**1914 (July 28)    World War I begins** as Austria-Hungary declares war on Serbia; Germany declares war on Russia on Aug. 1, invades Luxembourg on Aug. 2, declares war on France on Aug. 3, and invades neutral Belgium on Aug. 4, causing Britain to declare war on Germany the same day; later, Central Powers of Germany and Austria are aided by Ottoman Turkish Empire and Bulgaria, while 24 other nations join as Allies to defeat them.

**1914 (Aug. 15)    Panama Canal opens.**

**1914 (Aug. 26–30)    Battle of Tannenberg:** Germans defeat Russian army in east Prussia, eliminating threat of Russian invasion.

**1914 (Sept. 6–8)    Battle of the Marne:** Germans advance to within 15 miles of Paris, but French-British counterattack forces them to pull back; Western Front stabilizes with neither side being able to make breakthrough.

**1915 (May 7)    British ocean liner** *Lusitania* sunk by German submarine with loss of 1,198 lives.

**1915 (July 3)    U.S. Marines land in Haiti** to preserve order; remain until 1934.

**1916 (March 15)    U.S. troops invade Mexico** in pursuit of Mexican revolutionary Francisco (Pancho) Villa; withdraw on Feb. 5, 1917.

**1916 (April 24–29)    Easter Rebellion in Ireland** put down by British troops; 15 Irish leaders executed, others imprisoned.

**1916 (Nov. 29)    U.S. Marines land in Dominican Republic;** remain until 1924.

**1916–28    Civil war rages in China.**

**1917    Russian Revolution:** Riots and revolt by troops bring abdication of Czar Nicholas II on March 15; Bolsheviks (Communists) overthrow moderate provisional government on Nov. 6, making V.I. Lenin dictator.

**1917 (April 6)    U.S. declares war on Germany.**

**1917 (Dec. 6)    Finland declares independence** from Russia.

**1918 (March 3)    Russia withdraws from World War I;** signs Treaty of Brest-Litovsk with Central Powers, giving up claims to Finland, Latvia, Estonia, Lithuania, Poland, and other territories.

**1918 (July 16)    Murder of Czar Nicholas II** and his family by Bolsheviks (Communists).

**1918 (Oct. 28)    Czechoslovakia** declares independence.

**1918 (Nov. 3)    Poland** proclaims independence.

**1918 (Nov. 9)    Germany's Kaiser Wilhelm II abdicates;** flees to Netherlands.

**1918 (Nov. 11)    Armistice ends World War I;** fighting stops at 11 A.M. on Western Front.

**1918–19    Flu epidemic** around world kills estimated 5–20 million persons.

QUICK QUIZ: What was the most popular TV special in the 1979–80 season? See page 272.

## KEY EVENTS IN WORLD HISTORY *(continued)*

**1918–20   Russian Civil War:** Fighting rages across Russia between Communists (Reds) and anti-Communists (Whites); U.S., British, and French troops intervene on side of Whites but are withdrawn in 1919.

**1919 (May 16–27)   First transatlantic airplane flight:** U.S. Navy NC-4 flying boat with 5-man crew flies from Newfoundland to Lisbon, Portugal.

**1919 (June 28)   Treaty of Versailles** signed, setting peace terms with Germany and establishing League of Nations; U.S. Senate later refuses to ratify treaty or join League.

**1919 (Sept. 10)   Treaty of Saint-Germain** signed, setting peace terms for Austria and recognizing independence of Czechoslovakia, Hungary, Poland, and Yugoslavia.

**1920 (Aug. 10)   Treaty of Sèvres** signed, setting World War I peace terms with Ottoman Turkish Empire; Turkish nationalists object to severity of treaty and refuse to accept it.

**1920 (Nov. 15)   League of Nations** holds first meeting at Geneva, Switzerland.

**1920 (Dec. 17)   Japan receives mandate** over Caroline, Marshall, and Mariana islands in Pacific Ocean.

**1920 (Dec. 23)   Britain divides Ireland** into northern and southern parts, each with own parliament.

**1920–23   Greece attacks Turkish nationalists,** but is driven out of Turkey; victorious Turkish nationalists get Allies to sign Treaty of Lausanne modifying World War I penalties.

**1921 (Feb. 20)   Riza Khan Pahlevi seizes control of Iran:** After ruling as dictator for four years, makes himself shah in 1925.

**1921 (Dec. 6)   Irish Free State** formed in southern Ireland as self-governing dominion of British Empire; Northern Ireland remains part of United Kingdom.

**1922 (Feb. 6)   Washington naval arms limitation treaty** signed, setting size of navies of U.S., Britain, France, Italy, and Japan, and requiring scrapping of many warships.

**1922 (Feb. 28)   Egypt regains sovereignty** under King Fuad I as Britain ends protectorate, but British troops remain in Egypt.

**1922 (Oct. 31)   Benito Mussolini** becomes premier of Italy; *Il Duce,* as he is called by Fascist followers, becomes dictator on Nov. 25.

**1922 (Nov. 1)   End of Ottoman Turkish Empire:** Turkish nationalist leader Mustapha Kemal (Kemal Atatürk) abolishes sultanate and (in 1923) becomes first president.

**1923   French troops occupy Germany's Ruhr area:** France acts after Germany defaults on war reparations.

**1923 (Nov. 8–11)   Munich beer-hall putsch:** Unsuccessful attempt by Nazi leader Adolf Hitler to overthrow state government of Bavaria; imprisoned, Hitler writes *Mein Kampf,* blueprint for new German empire.

**1924 (Jan. 21)   Death of Lenin:** Joseph Stalin wins struggle for power, ruling as Soviet dictator until his death in 1953.

**1926 (Jan. 8)   Independent Kingdom of Hejaz and Nejd (now Saudi Arabia)** proclaimed by King Ibn Saud.

**1927 (Dec. 14)   Iraq granted independence** by Britain, but British troops remain in nation.

**1928   Nationalist government of China** established by Chiang Kai-shek with capital at Nanking after long civil war.

**1928 (April 9)   Turkey disestablishes Islam** as state religion.

**1928 (Aug. 27)   Kellogg-Briand Pact** signed, outlawing war, but provides no means of enforcement.

**1929 (June 7)   Vatican City** becomes independent nation with signing of Lateran treaties between Italy and Roman Catholic Church.

**1929–40   Worldwide Great Depression** brings severe unemployment and economic chaos.

**1930 (April 22)   London naval treaty** signed, providing further reductions in size of navies of U.S., Britain, and Japan.

**1931   British Commonwealth of Nations** established, giving dominions such as Australia and Canada complete independence with only formal allegiance to crown.

**1931 (April 14)   Spain becomes republic** with overthrow of King Alfonso XIII.

**1931–33   Japan invades and conquers Manchuria** (northern China).

**1932–35   Chaco War:** Paraguay and Bolivia fight over possession of oil-rich Chaco region; treaty in 1938 awards two-thirds of region to Paraguay.

**1933 (Jan. 30)   Adolf Hitler** becomes chancellor of Germany; *Der Führer,* as he is called by followers, becomes dictator on March 23.

**1934–36   Italian-Ethiopian War:** Italy invades and conquers Ethiopia.

**1935 (March 16)   Rearmament of Germany** ordered by Hitler, renouncing Versailles Treaty's ban on German armament.

**1936 (Oct. 27)   Berlin-Rome Axis** formed as Germany and Italy agree on working partnership; Japan later joins Axis powers with pact on Sept. 27, 1940.

**1936 (Dec. 10)   Britain's King Edward VIII** abdicates to marry American-born divorcée.

**1936–38   Soviet trials and executions** of hundreds of Communist and military leaders strengthen Stalin's hold on dictatorship.

**1936–39   Spanish Civil War:** Army revolt led by Gen. Francisco Franco restores monarchy; Italy and Germany support Franco while Soviet Union aids Spanish republicans; about 1 million die in three years of fighting; Franco establishes himself as dictator.

**1937–45   War between Japan and China:** Japan attacks China, taking most of coastal region by 1938; China's government retreats inland, continuing fight through World War II.

**1938 (March 12–13)   Austria invaded** and annexed by Germany.

**1938 (Sept. 29)   Munich agreement:** Britain, France, and Italy agree to let Germany partition Czechoslovakia.

**1938 (Oct. 1)   Germany annexes Sudetenland,** about one-third of Czechoslovakia's area.

**1939 (March 15)   Most of remainder of Czechoslovakia** taken by Germany.

**1939 (April 7)   Albania** annexed by Italy.

**1939 (Aug. 24)   Germany and Soviet Union sign** 10-year peace pact; agreement frees Hitler to start World War II.

**1939 (Sept. 1)   World War II begins** as Germany invades Poland without warning; Britain and France declare war on Germany on Sept. 3; Soviet Union invades Poland on Sept. 17; Hitler and Stalin partition Poland on Sept. 29.

**1939–40   Russo-Finnish War:** Soviet Union invades Finland, forcing nation to give up about one-tenth of its territory.

**1939–45   German slave labor and extermination of Jews:** Germany enslaves millions of conquered people, forcing them to work for German war effort; Hitler's Nazis kill about 60% of Europe's 10 million Jews.

**1940 (April 9–May 3)   Norway and Denmark** conquered by Germany.

**1940 (May 10–June 22)   German blitzkrieg conquers** Luxembourg, Netherlands, Belgium, and France; about 340,000 British and French troops escape to Britain in Dunkirk evacuation, May 28–June 4.

**1940 (July 21)   Estonia, Latvia, and Lithuania** annexed by Soviet Union.

**1940–41   Germany conquers** Romania, Bulgaria, Yugoslavia, and Greece.

**1941 (June 22)   German troops invade Soviet Union,** but meet stiff resistance and bog down in winter of 1941–42.

**1941 (Dec. 7)   Japan makes surprise air attacks** on U.S. and British bases in Pacific, bringing U.S. into World War II.

**1942–45   War in Africa and Europe:** Under command of Gen. Dwight D. Eisenhower, Allied forces defeat Axis troops in Africa by May 1943, invade Italy on Sept. 3, 1943, and land in France on June 6, 1944; Russian troops advance across eastern Europe in 1944–45, while Eisenhower's armies liberate western Europe and roll across Germany; German military leaders sign unconditional surrender on May 7, 1945; fighting ends at 12:01 A.M. on May 9.

**1942–45   War in Pacific:** U.S. Navy's defeat of Japanese fleet at Battle of Midway on June 4–7, 1942, marks turning point of war in Pacific; U.S. begins offensive with landing of Marines on Guadalcanal in Solomon Islands on Aug. 7, 1942; series of amphibious landings in 1943–45 capture Japanese island strongholds from Gilbert Islands to Okinawa; on Oct. 19, 1944, U.S. troops under Gen. Douglas MacArthur land in Philippines; atomic bombs dropped on Japan on Aug. 6 and 9, 1945, bring Japan's capitulation on Aug. 14, with formal surrender signed on Sept. 2.

# END OF COLONIAL EMPIRES, COLD WAR, AND DÉTENTE: 1945–1980

**1945–48   Communist Iron Curtain:** After World War II Soviet Union keeps its troops in eastern European nations it had "liberated" from Germany; Latvia, Estonia, and Lithuania incorporated into Soviet Union; British leader Winston Churchill warns on March 5, 1946, "an Iron Curtain has descended across Europe"; communist governments establish dictatorships In Yugoslavia, Albania, Bulgaria, Romania, Poland, East Germany, Hungary, and Czechoslovakia, all as satellites of Soviet Union.

**1945–49   Indonesian War for Independence:** Indonesian nationalists declare independence on Aug. 17, 1945; Dutch troops fight rebels in effort to reimpose colonial rule until Netherlands finally recognizes independence of Indonesia on Dec. 27, 1949.

**1945–54   Indochina War:** Nationalist leaders in 1945 declare independence in Cambodia (March), Laos (April), and Vietnam (September); France determines to reimpose colonial rule; for over eight years French troops supplied by U.S. battle guerrillas aided by Soviet Union and communist China; French will to fight breaks after Battle of Dien Bien Phu when after 55-day siege French army of 10,000 surrenders on May 7, 1954; at conference in Geneva, France agrees on July 21, 1954, to end fighting, recognizing independence of North and South Vietnam; earlier, in 1953, independence to Laos (Oct. 22) and Cambodia (Nov. 9) granted by France.

**1946 (Jan. 1)   Japan's Emperor Hirohito** disclaims his divinity, ending his worship as god.

**1946 (Jan. 10)   UN General Assembly** meets for first time; delegates of 51 nations hold meeting in London.

**1946 (March 22)   Transjordan** (now Jordan) granted independence by Britain.

**1946 (June 2)   Italy votes to become republic,** ending monarchy.

**1946 (July 4)   Philippines granted independence** by United States.

**1946 (Oct. 16)   Ten Nazi leaders hanged** as war criminals after 10-month trial at Nuremberg; chief Hitler aide Hermann Goering kills himself a few hours before execution.

**1946 (Nov. 3)   Japan adopts new constitution** under guidance of Allied Supreme Commander Gen. Douglas MacArthur, giving all emperor's power to parliament.

**1946–49   Civil War in Greece:** Greece votes to restore monarchy on Sept. 1, 1946; communist guerrillas supported by Soviet Union begin struggle to overthrow government; Truman Doctrine announced by U.S. in 1947 provides aid to Greek government, enabling it to defeat guerrillas by October 1949.

**1947 (Aug. 15)   India and Pakistan granted independence** within British Commonwealth.

**1948 (Jan. 4)   Burma granted independence.**

**1948 (Feb. 4)   Ceylon** (now Sri Lanka) given independence by Britain.

**1948 (April 3)   European Recovery Program** (Marshall Plan) enacted by U.S. at urging of President Truman to provide aid to European nations to save them from communism; over $12 billion given in four years.

**1948 (April 30)   Organization of American States (OAS)** Charter signed at Bogotá, Colombia (effective Dec. 13, 1951.)

**1948 (Dec. 23)   Seven wartime Japanese leaders hanged** for war crimes, including former Japanese prime minister Hideki Tojo.

**1948–49   First Arab-Israeli War:** Israel proclaims independence on May 14, 1948, upon withdrawal of British troops from Palestine; six Arab nations attack Israel; U.S. supports Israel with military supplies; UN mediation brings truce in 1949; over 900,000 Arabs flee Israel.

**1948–49   Berlin blockade and Berlin airlift:** Soviet Union blockades roads to West Berlin beginning on June 24; U.S. starts airlift, delivering over 2 million tons of supplies in next 16 months to prevent city from falling to communists; blockade ends on May 12, 1949.

**1949 (April 4)   NATO treaty signed** to provide military defense of western Europe.

**1949 (April 18)   Ireland declares independence** from Britain.

**1949 (Aug. 29)   Soviet Union test-explodes its first atomic bomb,** setting off fears in West that communists

would launch surprise A-bomb attack to destroy U.S. and western Europe.

**1949 (Dec. 7)   Communists win control of mainland China** after 3-year civil war.

**1950–53   Korean War:** Begins on June 25, 1950; North Korea invades South Korea; UN calls for aid to South Korea; U.S. begins sending troops on June 27; 15 other UN nations send troops; Gen. Douglas MacArthur becomes UN supreme commander; over 1 million die in war, including 54,000 U.S. servicemen; ends with truce signed on July 27, 1953.

**1950–53   Communist atomic spy ring:** Members arrested in Britain and U.S. in 1950, convicted in 1951; U.S. citizens Julius and Ethel Rosenberg executed for treason on June 19, 1953.

**1951 (Sept. 8)   Japanese peace treaty** signed in San Francisco by 49 nations: treaty goes into effect on April 28, 1952.

**1951 (Dec. 24)   Libya** becomes independent monarchy.

**1953 (June 18)   Egypt becomes republic** ruled by military junta.

**1954–62   Algerian War of Independence:** Arab nationalists attack French outposts in November 1954; over 500,000 French troops fight for 7 years to maintain colonial rule; France agrees to Algeria's independence (effective July 3, 1962).

**1955 (Feb. 12)   U.S. military aid in Vietnam War** begins as President Eisenhower sends military advisers to aid South Vietnam.

**1955 (March 25)   East Germany** granted full sovereignty by Soviet Union.

**1955 (May 5)   West Germany** becomes independent under Chancellor Konrad Adenauer.

**1955 (July 27)   Austria regains independence** as peace treaty guaranteeing its neutrality becomes effective (signed May 15).

**1956 (Oct. 23–Nov. 4)   Hungarian Revolution:** Revolt overthrows communist government but is suppressed by Soviet army; about 150,000 Hungarians flee to U.S. and other nations.

**1956 (Oct. 29–Nov. 6)   Second Arab-Israeli War:** Israel with support of France and Britain attacks Egypt; Suez Canal seized; U.S. and Soviet Union condemn action; UN arranges cease-fire on Nov. 6; British and French troops withdraw on Dec. 22; Israel withdraws from Egypt on March 1, 1957.

**1956–77   End of French colonial empire:** Begins with Indochina War of 1945–54, in which Laos, Cambodia, and Vietnam win independence, but accelerates as following nations gain independence: 1956, Morocco, Tunisia; 1958, Guinea; 1960, Cameroon, Togo, Malagasy, Dahomey, Niger, Upper Volta, Ivory Coast, Chad, Central African Republic, Congo, Gabon, Senegal, Mali, Mauritania; 1962, Algeria, after 7 years of war; 1977, Djibouti.

**1956–79   Breakup of British Empire:** Begins in 1947–48 with independence of India, Pakistan, Ceylon, and Burma, but accelerates as following nations gain independence: 1956, Sudan; 1957, Ghana, Malaysia; 1960, Somalia, Cyprus, Nigeria; 1961, Sierra Leone, South Africa, Kuwait, British Cameroons, Tanganyika; 1962, Jamaica, Trinidad and Tobago, Uganda; 1963, Zanzibar, Kenya; 1964, Malawi, Malta, Zambia; 1965, Gambia, Maldive Islands, Rhodesia; 1966, Guyana, Botswana, Lesotho, Barbados; 1967, South Yemen; 1968, Mauritius, Swaziland; 1970, Tonga, Fiji; 1971, Bahrain, Qatar, United Arab Emirates; 1973, Bahamas; 1974, Grenada; 1976, Seychelles; 1978, Solomons, Tuvalu, Dominica; 1979, St. Lucia, St. Vincent, Kiribati.

**1957 (Jan. 5)   Eisenhower Doctrine** proposed for U.S. to send troops to aid any Middle East nation to fight communist aggression; approved by U.S. Senate resolution on March 7.

**1957 (Oct. 4)   First man-made satellite** orbits Earth: *Sputnik I* launched by Soviet Union.

**1958 (Jan. 1)   European Common Market** begins, including Belgium, France, West Germany, Italy, Luxembourg, and Netherlands.

**1958 (July 15)   U.S. troops land in Lebanon** under Eisenhower Doctrine; withdraw Oct. 25.

**1958 (May 31)   France's Gen. Charles de Gaulle** becomes premier with emergency powers; becomes presi-

QUICK QUIZ: What are the four basic food groups? See page 398.

**KEY EVENTS IN WORLD HISTORY** *(continued)*
dent on Jan. 8, 1959.

**1959 (Jan. 1)** Fidel Castro overthrows Cuban dictator Fulgencio Batista after 3-year civil war.

**1959 (June 26)** St. Lawrence Seaway opens, linking Atlantic Ocean and Great Lakes.

**1960** Communist China and Soviet Union split in controversy over communist ideology.

**1960** Soviet Premier Khrushchev cancels Paris summit meeting with President Eisenhower after Soviet Union shoots down U.S. U-2 spy plane and U.S. admits sending regular spy flights over Soviet territory.

**1960** OPEC (Organization of Petroleum Exporting Countries) holds first meeting, forcing Standard Oil of New Jersey to retract an announced decrease in oil prices; OPEC's charter members were Iran, Iraq, Kuwait, Qatar, and Saudi Arabia.

**1960 (Feb. 13)** France becomes atomic power, exploding first A-bomb in desert of Algeria.

**1960 (June 23)** U.S.-Japanese mutual security treaty becomes effective.

**1960–62** Belgium ends its African colonial empire, giving independence to Belgian Congo (now Zaire) on June 30, 1960, and to Rwanda and Burundi on July 1, 1962.

**1960–67** Revolts in Congo (now Zaire): Immediately after Congo receives independence from Belgium, fighting breaks out as provinces of Katanga and Kasai seek independence; UN sends troops to aid government, 1960–64; rebellion ends in November 1967.

**1961 (Jan. 3)** U.S. breaks diplomatic relations with Cuba over refusal by Fidel Castro's government to pay for confiscated U.S. property.

**1961 (April 12)** First man orbits Earth in space: Soviet cosmonaut Maj. Yuri Gagarin.

**1961 (April 17–20)** Cuba defeats U.S.-supported Bay of Pigs invasion: Cuban troops overwhelm force of 1,600 Cuban exiles trained by U.S. CIA.

**1961 (May 31)** South Africa becomes independent republic: Severs ties with British Commonwealth of Nations because of criticism of its racial policies.

**1961 (Aug. 13)** Berlin Wall built by Soviet Union to prevent escape of East Germans to West Berlin.

**1961 (Dec. 18–19)** India seizes Portuguese colonies of Goa, Damao, and Diu.

**1962 (Jan. 1)** Western Samoa granted independence by New Zealand.

**1962 (May 31)** Israel executes Hiler aide Adolf Eichmann, convicted of directing World War II German extermination of Jews.

**1962 (Oct. 20–Nov. 22)** China invades India, but ends fighting on Nov. 22 and withdraws.

**1962 (Oct. 22–28)** Cuban missile crisis: U.S. blockades Cuba, forcing Soviet Union to withdraw nuclear missiles from island.

**1963 (Jan. 22)** France and Germany sign treaty of friendship, ending 400 years of conflict.

**1964 (March 27)** UN troops land in Cyprus to prevent fighting between Greeks and Turks.

**1964–73** U.S. intervention in Vietnam War: U.S. begins bombing of North Vietnam on Aug. 5, 1964, in retaliation for reported attack on U.S. destroyers; on Aug. 7, U.S. Congress votes President authority "to prevent further aggression"; first U.S. ground combat authorized on June 28, 1965; over 541,000 U.S. troops fighting in Vietnam by 1969; U.S. begins withdrawing in 1969; cease-fire begins on Jan. 28, 1973; last U.S. troops leave Vietnam on March 29, 1973.

**1966 (July 1)** France withdraws from NATO.

**1967 (June 5–10)** Third Arab-Israeli War: Israel launches surprise attack; captures Egypt's Sinai peninsula to east bank of Suez Canal; takes Jordan territory west of Jordan River; seizes Golan Heights from Syria; additional 750,000 Arab refugees displaced.

**1967–70** Nigerian Civil War: Attempted secession of eastern region of Biafra put down.

**1968 (Aug. 20–21)** Invasion of Czechoslovakia made by about 650,000 troops of Soviet Union and Warsaw Pact nations to oust liberal communist regime restoring civil rights.

**1968–74** African drought south of Sahara: thousands of persons and millions of cattle die.

**1970 (Sept. 4)** Chile elects communist as president, first to head any nation as result of free election; later overthrown in military revolt, Sept. 11, 1973.

**1970 (Dec. 12–20)** Riots in Poland put down by Soviet troops, but bring resignation of communist dictator Wladyslaw Gomulka.

**1971 (Feb. 11)** Seabed treaty outlawing installation of atomic weapons on ocean floor signed by U.S., Soviet Union, Britain, and others; effective on May 18, 1972.

**1971 (March 25–Dec. 16)** Bangladesh wins independence from Pakistan in civil war.

**1971 (Oct. 25)** Communist China admitted to UN as U.S. ends 22 years of opposition.

**1972 (Sept. 29)** China and Japan end state of war that began in 1937.

**1973 (Jan. 1)** European Common Market adds Britain, Denmark, and Ireland.

**1973 (June 1)** Greece ends monarchy as military dictator deposes King Constantine II.

**1973 (June 16–24)** End of Cold War between U.S. and Soviet Union seen in spirit of détente at summit meeting of President Nixon and Soviet leader Leonid I. Brezhnev in U.S.

**1973 (July 17)** Afghanistan becomes republic as military officers depose king.

**1973 (Aug. 15)** All U.S. combat operations end in Southeast Asia by congressional order.

**1973 (Oct. 6–24)** Fourth Arab-Israeli War: Egypt and Syria launch surprise attack on Israel; Israel counterattacks, crossing Suez Canal into Egypt and invading Syria; UN cease-fire ends fighting on Oct. 24.

**1973 (Oct. 17)** Oil embargo begun by Arab nations against U.S., Netherlands, and other nations in effort to force support of Arab policies against Israel; causes energy shortages; Arabs end embargo in 1974 (with U.S. on March 18).

**1974 (May 18)** India becomes sixth nuclear nation with atomic test explosion.

**1974 (July 15–Aug. 16)** War in Cyprus: Civil war begins as Greek-led national guard temporarily overthrows government; on July 20, Turkey intervenes, landing 40,000 troops, enlarging Turkish-held portion of island.

**1974 (Nov. 17)** Democracy restored in Greece with first free national election in 10 years.

**1974–76** End of Portugal's dictatorship and colonial empire in Africa: Military coup on April 25, 1974, overthrows 40-year dictatorship in Portugal; colonies given independence; socialists win parliamentary elections in 1976.

**1974–76** Worldwide inflation and recession rage when Organization of Petroleum Exporting Countries (OPEC) raises crude-oil prices nearly 500% above 1973 levels.

**1975 (April 17)** Cambodia falls to communists; red troops capture Phnom Penh.

**1975 (April 30)** South Vietnam surrenders to communists; Saigon captured by North Vietnamese troops, ending 16-year Vietnam War.

**1975 (Aug. 1)** Helsinki Pact signed by U.S., Canada, Soviet Union, and 32 European nations guaranteeing national boundaries.

**1975 (Nov. 6)** Invasion of Spanish Sahara by thousands of unarmed Moroccans; Spain agrees to give up region to Morocco and Mauritania.

**1975–76** Civil war rages in Lebanon between rightist Christians and leftist Muslims; ends when Syrian army occupies nation.

**1975–76** Communists win civil war in Angola with aid of Cuban troops and Soviet arms.

**1976 (March 23)** International Bill of Rights goes into effect with ratification by 35 nations.

**1976 (July 28)** Earthquake devastates Tientsin-Tangshan area of China; 655,237 reported dead.

**1977 (Sept. 7)** U.S. and Panama sign treaties to turn Canal over to Panama on Dec. 31, 1999.

**1977 (Nov. 19)** Egypt's President Sadat becomes first Arab national leader to visit Israel, launching drive to achieve peace in Middle East.

**1978 (Oct. 23)** China and Japan sign treaty: End 40 years of hostility with peace pact.

**1979 (Jan. 16)** Revolt overthrows shah of Iran, who flies to exile; Muslim leader Ayatollah Ruhollah Khomeini creates Islamic state with himself as ruler for life.

**1979 (March 26)** Egypt-Israel peace treaty signed at White House after mediation by President Carter; goes into effect on April 25.

**1979 (Dec. 27)** Soviet troops invade Afghanistan; overthrow communist ruler, replacing him with pro-Soviet leader.

**1979–80** U.S.-Iranian crisis: Iranians capture U.S. embassy in Teheran on Nov. 4, 1979; hold Americans hostage, demanding extradition of shah to Iran.

**1980** For events of 1980, see pages 7–31.

# KINGS, QUEENS, AND RULERS

## AUSTRIA [1]

**Hapsburg Dynasty**

| | |
|---|---|
| Franz II [2] | 1792–1835 |
| Ferdinand I | 1835–1848 |
| Franz Josef I | 1848–1916 |
| Karl I | 1916–1918 |

First Republic, 1918–1938
Part of Germany, 1938–1945
Second Republic, 1945–

## BELGIUM

**House of Coburg**

| | |
|---|---|
| Leopold I | 1831–1865 |
| Leopold II | 1865–1909 |
| Albert I | 1909–1934 |
| Leopold III | 1934–1951 |
| Baudouin | 1951– |

## BRITAIN

**Saxons and Danes**

| | |
|---|---|
| Egbert | 827–839 |
| Ethelwulf | 839–858 |
| Ethelbald | 858–860 |
| Ethelbert | 860–866 |
| Ethelred | 866–871 |
| Alfred the Great | 871–901 |
| Edward the Elder | 901–925 |
| Athelstan | 925–940 |
| Edmund | 940–946 |
| Edred | 946–955 |
| Edwy | 955–959 |
| Edgar | 959–975 |
| Edward the Martyr | 975–978 |
| Ethelred II | 978–1016 |
| Edmund Ironside | 1016 |
| Canute the Dane | 1016–1035 |
| Harold I | 1035–1040 |
| Hardicanute | 1040–1042 |
| Edward the Confessor | 1042–1066 |
| Harold II | 1066 |

**Norman**

| | |
|---|---|
| William I | 1066–1087 |
| William II | 1087–1100 |
| Henry | 1100–1135 |
| Stephen | 1135–1154 |

**Plantagenet**

| | |
|---|---|
| Henry II | 1154–1189 |
| Richard I | 1189–1199 |
| John | 1199–1216 |
| Henry III | 1216–1272 |
| Edward I | 1272–1307 |
| Edward II | 1307–1327 |
| Edward III | 1327–1377 |
| Richard II | 1377–1399 |

**Lancaster**

| | |
|---|---|
| Henry IV | 1399–1413 |
| Henry V | 1413–1422 |
| Henry VI | 1422–1461, 1470–1471 |

**York**

| | |
|---|---|
| Edward IV | 1461–1470, 1471–1483 |
| Edward V | 1483 |
| Richard III | 1483–1485 |

**Tudor**

| | |
|---|---|
| Henry VII | 1485–1509 |
| Henry VIII | 1509–1547 |
| Edward VI | 1547–1553 |
| Jane (14 days) | 1553 |
| Mary I | 1553–1558 |
| Elizabeth I | 1558–1603 |

**Stuart**

| | |
|---|---|
| James I | 1603–1625 |
| Charles I | 1625–1649 |

**Commonwealth**

| | |
|---|---|
| Long Parliament | 1649–1653 |

**Protectorate**

| | |
|---|---|
| Oliver Cromwell | 1653–1658 |
| Richard Cromwell | 1658–1659 |

**Stuart Restoration**

| | |
|---|---|
| Charles II | 1660–1685 |
| James II | 1685–1688 |

**Orange**

| | |
|---|---|
| William III | 1689–1702 |
| and Mary II | 1689–1694 |

**Stuart**

| | |
|---|---|
| Anne | 1702–1714 |

**Hanover**

| | |
|---|---|
| George I | 1714–1727 |
| George II | 1727–1760 |
| George III | 1760–1820 |
| George IV | 1820–1830 |
| William IV | 1830–1837 |
| Victoria | 1837–1901 |

**Saxe-Coburg–Gotha**

| | |
|---|---|
| Edward VII | 1901–1910 |

**Windsor**

| | |
|---|---|
| George V | 1910–1936 |
| Edward VIII (325 days) | 1936 |
| George VI | 1936–1952 |
| Elizabeth II | 1952– |

## BULGARIA

**Saxe-Coburg–Gotha**

| | |
|---|---|
| Ferdinand I [3] | 1908–1918 |
| Boris III | 1918–1943 |
| Simeon II | 1943–1946 |
| Communist state, | 1946– |

## CHINA

Hsia Dynasty, c.2200–1766 B.C.
Shang Dynasty, c.1766–1123 B.C.
Chou Dynasty, c.1122–256 B.C.
Ch'in Dynasty, 221–207 B.C.
Han Dynasty, 202 B.C.–A.D. 220
Disorder, 220–589
T'ang Dynasty, 618–907
Sung Dynasty, 960–1279
Yuan Dynasty, 1260–1368
Ming Dynasty, 1368–1644

**Manchu (Ch'ing) Dynasty**

| | |
|---|---|
| Shun-chih | 1644–1661 |
| K'ang-hsi | 1661–1722 |
| Yung-cheng | 1723–1735 |
| Chien-lung | 1736–1796 |
| Chia-ch'ing | 1796–1820 |
| Tao-kuang | 1821–1851 |
| Hsien-feng | 1851–1862 |
| T'ung-chih | 1862–1875 |
| Kuang-hsü | 1875–1908 |
| Hsüan-t'ung | 1909–1912 |
| Republic, | 1912–1949 |
| Sun Yat-sen | 1912 |
| Yüan Shih-k'ai | 1912–1916 |
| Chiang Kai-shek | 1928–1949 |
| Communist state, | 1949– |

## DENMARK

**Waldemarian Dynasty**

| | |
|---|---|
| Waldemar the Great | 1157–1182 |
| Knut VI | 1182–1202 |
| Waldemar II | 1202–1241 |
| Eric Plowpenny | 1241–1250 |
| Abel | 1250–1252 |
| Kristoffer | 1252–1259 |
| Eric V | 1259–1286 |
| Eric VI | 1286–1319 |
| Kristoffer II | 1320–1332 |
| Waldemar IV | 1340–1375 |
| Olaf [4] | 1376–1387 |
| Margrethe I [5] | 1387–1412 |
| Eric [5] | 1412–1439 |
| Kristoffer [5] | 1439–1448 |

**House of Oldenburg**

| | |
|---|---|
| Kristian I of Oldenburg [5] | 1448–1481 |
| Hans [5] | 1481–1513 |
| Kristian II [5] | 1513–1523 |
| Frederik I [6] | 1523–1533 |
| Kristian III [6] | 1534–1559 |
| Frederik II [6] | 1559–1588 |
| Kristian IV [6] | 1588–1648 |
| Frederik III [6] | 1648–1670 |
| Kristian V [6] | 1670–1699 |
| Frederik IV [6] | 1699–1730 |
| Kristian VI [6] | 1730–1746 |
| Frederik V [6] | 1746–1766 |
| Kristian VII [6] | 1766–1808 |
| Frederik VI [6] | 1808–1839 |
| Kristian VIII | 1839–1848 |
| Frederik VII | 1848–1863 |

**House of Glücksborg**

| | |
|---|---|
| Kristian IX | 1863–1906 |
| Frederik VIII | 1906–1912 |
| Kristian X | 1912–1947 |
| Frederik IX | 1947–1972 |
| Margrethe II | 1972– |

## FRANCE

**Carolingian Dynasty**

| | |
|---|---|
| Charlemagne | 768–814 |
| Louis I the Pious | 814–840 |

WEST FRANCIA

| | |
|---|---|
| Charles the Bald | 840–877 |
| Louis II | 877–879 |
| Louis III | 879–882 |
| Carloman | 879–884 |
| Eudes | 888–898 |
| Charles the Simple | 893–923 |
| Rudolph | 923–936 |
| Louis IV | 936–954 |
| Lothair | 954–986 |
| Louis V | 986–987 |

MIDDLE KINGDOMS

| | |
|---|---|
| Lothair, Emperor | 840–855 |
| Louis (Italy), Emperor | 855–875 |
| Charles (Provence), King | 855–863 |
| Lothair II (Lorraine), King | 855–869 |

**Capetian Kings**

| | |
|---|---|
| Hugh Capet | 987–996 |
| Robert II | 996–1031 |
| Henri I | 1031–1060 |
| Philippe I | 1060–1108 |

[1] From 1273 members of the Hapsburg dynasty ruled Austria as part of the German Holy Roman Empire; see list under *Germany*. [2] Franz II took title emperor of Austria in 1804 and gave up title Holy Roman emperor in 1806. [3] Ruled as prince from 1887 before proclaiming Bulgaria as independent kingdom in 1908. [4] King of Denmark and Norway after 1380. [5] Ruler of Denmark, Norway, and Sweden. [6] Ruler of Denmark and Norway.

Louis VI ...............1108–1137
Louis VII ..............1137–1180
Philippe II (August).......1180–1223
Louis VIII ..............1223–1226
Louis IX...............1226–1270
Philippe III ............1270–1285
Philippe IV ............1285–1314
Louis X ...............1314–1316
Jean I ................. 1316
Philippe V .............1316–1322
Charles IV.............1322–1328

**House of Valois**
Philippe VI .............1328–1350
Jean II ................1350–1364
Charles V .............1364–1380
Charles VI..............1380–1422
Charles VII ...........1422–1461
Louis XI ..............1461–1483
Charles VIII ...........1483–1498
Louis XII .............1498–1515
François I .............1515–1547
Henri II ..............1547–1559
François II ............1559–1560
Charles IX.............1560–1574
Henri III ..............1574–1589

**Bourbon Dynasty**
Henri IV ..............1589–1610
Louis XIII .............1610–1643
Louis XIV .............1643–1715
Louis XV ..............1715–1774
Louis XVI .............1774–1792

**First Republic, 1792–1799**

**Napoleon Bonaparte**
First Consul ............1799–1804
Napoleon I, Emperor .....1804–1814
Hundred Days .......... 1815

**Bourbon Restoration**
Louis XVIII ............1814–1824
Charles X .............1824–1830
Louis Philippe ..........1830–1848

**Second Republic, 1848–1852**
**Napoleon III, Emperor, 1852–1870**
**Third Republic, 1870–1940**
**Pétain regime, 1940–1944**
**Provisional government,
1944–1946**
**Fourth Republic, 1946–1958**
**Fifth Republic, 1958–**
Charles de Gaulle .......1958–1969
Georges Pompidou.......1969–1974
Valéry Giscard d'Estaing ..1974–

# GERMANY [1]

**Carolingian Dynasty**
Charlemagne ..........768–814
Louis (Ludwig I) the Pious ...814–840
Lothair I ..............840–855
Ludwig II the German .......843–876
Karl II the Bald ............875–877
Karl III the Fat ..........876–887
Arnulf ................887–899
Ludwig III the Child ........899–911

**Franconian House**
Konrad I ................911–918

**Saxon House**
Heinrich I the Fowler.......919–936
Otto I the Great ............936–973
Otto II ................973–983
Otto III................983–1002

Heinrich II the Saint ......1002–1024
**Franconian (Salian) House**
Konrad II ..............1024–1039
Heinrich III ............1039–1056
Heinrich IV ............1056–1106
Heinrich V ............1106–1125
Lothair II .............1125–1137

**Hohenstaufen House**
Konrad III ............1138–1152
Friedrich I Barbarossa ....1152–1190
Heinrich VI ...........1190–1197
Philipp of Swabia .......1198–1208
Otto IV of Brunswick .....1198–1215
Friedrich II ...........1215–1250
Konrad IV .............1250–1254

**Great Interregnum, 1254–1273**
**Rulers of Various Houses**
Rudolf I of Hapsburg .....1273–1291
Adolf of Nassau ........1292–1298
Albrecht I of Austria .....1298–1308
Heinrich VII of
  Luxemburg ..........1308–1313
Ludwig IV of Bavaria .....1314–1347
Friedrich of Austria .....1314–1326
Karl IV of Luxembourg .....1346–1378
Wenzel of Bohemia .......1378–1400
Ruprecht of Palatinate....1400–1410
Sigismund of
  Luxembourg ..........1411–1437

**Hapsburg Dynasty**
Albrecht II ............1438–1439
Friedrich III ...........1440–1493
Maximilian I ...........1493–1519
Karl V (of Spain) ........1519–1556
Ferdinand I............1556–1564
Maximilian II ..........1564–1576
Rudolf II .............1576–1612
Matthias ..............1612–1619
Ferdinand II ..........1619–1637
Ferdinand III .........1637–1657
Leopold I .............1657–1705
Josef I................1705–1711
Karl VI...............1711–1740
Maria Theresia .........1740–1780
Franz I................1745–1765
Josef II ..............1765–1790
Leopold II ............1790–1792
Franz II [2] ...............1792–1806

**Hohenzollern Dynasty**
Friedrich I [3] ...........1701–1713
Friedrich Wilhelm I [3] ......1713–1740
Friedrich II the Great [3] ....1740–1786
Friedrich Wilhelm II [3] .....1786–1797
Friedrich Wilhelm III [3]....1797–1840
Friedrich Wilhelm IV [3] .....1840–1861
Wilhelm I [4] ............1861–1888
Friedrich III ..........1888
Wilhelm II ............1888–1918

**Weimar Republic, 1918–1933**
**Third Reich (Nazi Dictatorship)**
Adolf Hitler ...........1933–1945
**Allied occupation, 1945–1952**
**Division into Federal Republic of
Germany (West) and German
Democratic Republic (East), 1949–**

# GREECE
**Danish House**
Otto I..................1832–1862
George I ..............1863–1913
Constantine I ..........1913–1917

Alexander I.............1917–1920
Constantine I ...........1920–1922
George II ..............1922–1923
**First Greek Republic, 1924–1935**
**Monarchy restored, 1935–1973**
George II .............1935–1947
Paul I ................1947–1964
Constantine II .........1964–1973
**Second Greek Republic, 1973–**

# HUNGARY
**Árpád Dynasty**
St. István I ............ 997–1038
Peter Orseolo ..........1038–1046
András I ..............1047–1060
Béla I ...............1061–1063
Solomon ..............1063–1074
Geza I ...............1074–1077
St. László ............1077–1095
Coloman ..............1095–1116
István II ..............1116–1131
Béla II ...............1131–1141
Geza II ..............1141–1161
István III ..............1161–1173
István IV .............1162–1163
Béla III ..............1173–1196
Emeric I .............1196–1204
László III .............1204–1205
András II .............1205–1235
Béla IV ..............1235–1270
István V .............1270–1272
László IV .............1272–1290
András III ............1290–1301
Carobert .............1308–1342
Lajos I the Great .......1342–1382
Maria ...............1382–1395
Sigismund ............1387–1437
Albrecht .............1437–1439
Ulászló I .............1439–1444
László V .............1444–1457
Mátyás Hollos .........1458–1490
Ulászló II.............1490–1516
Lajos II ..............1516–1526

**Hungary Partitioned and Ruled by
Turkey and Austria, 1526–1918**
**Revolution and Disorder,
1918–1920**
**Regency, Admiral Nicholas Horthy,
1920–1945**
**Communist state, 1945–**

# INDIA
**Mogul Emperors**
Babar ................1526–1530
Humayun .............1530–1556
Akbar the Great .......1556–1605
Jahangir ............1605–1627
Shah Jahan ..........1628–1658
Aurangzeb ...........1658–1707
Bahadur Shah I .......1707–1712
Jahandar Shah .........1712–1713
Farruk-Siar ...........1713–1719
Mohammed Shah .......1719–1748
Ahmed ...............1748–1754
Alamgir ..............1754–1759
Shah Alam ...........1759–1806
Mohammed Akbar II.....1806–1837
Bahadur Shah II .......1837–1857
**British rule, 1857–1947**
**British dominion, 1947–1950**
**Republic, 1950–**

[1] Most rulers of Germany were Holy Roman emperors from 800 through Franz II in 1792. [2] After giving up title Holy Roman emperor in 1806, he continued to rule Austria until 1835. [3] King of Prussia. [4] Emperor of Germany after 1871.

## KINGS, QUEENS, AND RULERS *(continued)*

### IRAN (PERSIA)

**Achaemenid Empire**

| | |
|---|---|
| Cyrus II | 559–530 B.C. |
| Cambyses II | 530–522 B.C. |
| Smerdis | 522 B.C. |
| Darius I | 522–486 B.C. |
| Xerxes I | 486–465 B.C. |
| Artaxerxes I | 465–424 B.C. |
| Xerxes II | 424–423 B.C. |
| Sogdianus | 424–423 B.C. |
| Darius II | 423–404 B.C. |
| Artaxerxes II | 404–359 B.C. |
| Artaxerxes III | 359–338 B.C. |
| Arses | 338–336 B.C. |
| Darius III | 336–330 B.C. |

Conquest by Alexander the Great and rule by Seleucid Greeks, 331–187 B.C.
Parthian Empire, c.171 B.C.–A.D. 224
Sasanian Empire, c.224–651
Rule by Arabs, 651–892
Samanid Dynasty, 892–999
Ghaznavid Dynasty, 999–1037
Conquest and rule by Seljuk Turks, 1037–1157
Disorder, 1157–1260
Conquest and rule by Mongol Il-khans, 1260–1353
Conquest by Mongol Timur (Tamerlane) and rule by Timurid Dynasty, 1369–1469

**Safavid Dynasty**

| | |
|---|---|
| Ismail I | 1502–1524 |
| Tahmasp I | 1524–1576 |
| Ismail II | 1576–1578 |
| Mohammed Khudabanda | 1578–1587 |
| Abbas I | 1587–1629 |
| Safi I | 1629–1642 |
| Abbas II | 1642–1667 |
| Suleiman | 1667–1694 |
| Husain | 1694–1722 |
| Tahmasp II | 1722–1731 |
| Abbas III | 1731–1736 |

Nadir Shah, 1736–1747
Zand Dynasty, 1750–1794

**Kajar Dynasty**

| | |
|---|---|
| Aga Mohammed | 1794–1797 |
| Fath Ali | 1797–1835 |
| Mohammed | 1835–1848 |
| Nasir ud-Din | 1848–1896 |
| Muzaffar ud-Din | 1896–1907 |
| Mohammed Ali | 1907–1909 |
| Ahmed Mirza | 1909–1925 |

**Pahlevi Dynasty**

| | |
|---|---|
| Riza Shah Pahlevi | 1925–1941 |
| Mohammed Riza Pahlevi | 1941–1979 |

Republic, 1979–

### ISLAMIC ARAB EMPIRE

| | |
|---|---|
| Mohammed | 622–632 |
| Abu Bakr | 632–634 |
| Omar | 634–644 |
| Othman | 644–656 |
| Ali | 656–661 |

**Omayyad Caliphate**

| | |
|---|---|
| Muawiya I | 661–680 |
| Yasid I | 680–682 |
| Muawiya II | 683 |
| Marwan I | 684–685 |
| Abdalmalik | 685–705 |
| Walid I | 705–715 |
| Sulaiman | 715–717 |
| Omar ibn Abdul-Aziz | 717–720 |
| Yazid II | 720–724 |
| Hisham | 724–743 |
| Walid II | 743–744 |
| Yazid III | 744 |
| Ibrahim | 744 |
| Marwan II | 744–750 |

**Abbasid Caliphate**

| | |
|---|---|
| Abu-l-Abbas al-Saffah | 750–754 |
| Al-Mansur | 754–775 |
| Al-Mahdi | 775–785 |
| Al-Hadi | 785–786 |
| Harun Al-Rashid | 786–809 |
| Al-Amin | 809–813 |
| Al-Mamun | 813–833 |
| Al-Mu'tasim | 833–842 |
| Al-Wathiq | 842–847 |
| Al-Mutawakkil | 847–861 |
| Al-Muntasir | 861–862 |
| Al-Musta'in | 862–866 |
| Al-Mu'tazz | 866–869 |
| Al-Muqtadi | 869–870 |
| Al-Mu'tamid | 870–892 |
| Al-Mu'tadid | 892–902 |
| Al-Mutafi | 902–908 |
| Al-Muqtadir | 908–932 |
| Al-Qahir | 932–934 |
| Al-Radi | 934–940 |
| Al-Muttaqi | 940–944 |
| Al-Mustaqfi | 944–946 |
| Al-Muti | 946–974 |
| Al-Ta'i | 974–991 |
| Al-Qadir | 991–1031 |
| Al-Qa'im | 1031–1075 |
| Al-Muqtadi | 1075–1094 |
| Al-Mustazhir | 1094–1118 |
| Al-Mustarshid | 1118–1135 |
| Al-Rashid | 1135–1136 |
| Al-Muqtafi | 1136–1160 |
| Al-Mustanjid | 1160–1170 |
| Al-Mustadi | 1170–1180 |
| Al-Nasir | 1180–1225 |
| Al-Zahir | 1225–1226 |
| Al-Mustansir | 1226–1242 |
| Al-Musta'sim | 1242–1258 |

Mongols destroy Baghdad and overthrow Arab Empire, 1258

### ITALY

| | |
|---|---|
| Vittorio Emanuele II | 1849–1878 |
| Umberto I | 1878–1900 |
| Vittorio Emanuele III | 1900–1946 |
| Umberto II | 1946 |

**Fascist Dictatorship**

| | |
|---|---|
| Benito Mussolini | 1922–1943 |

Italian Republic, 1946–

### JAPAN

Legendary period, 660 B.C.–A.D. 710
Emperor Jimmu Tenno 660–585 B.C.
Nara Period, 710–784
Heian Period, 794–1185
Kamakura Period, 1185–1333
Ashikaga Period, 1336–1568
Unification Period, 1568–1603

**Tokugawa Shoguns**

| | |
|---|---|
| Ieyasu | 1603–1605 |
| Hidetada | 1605–1623 |
| Iemitsu | 1623–1651 |
| Ietsuna | 1651–1680 |
| Tsunayoshi | 1680–1709 |
| Ienobu | 1709–1713 |
| Ietsugu | 1713–1716 |
| Yoshimune | 1716–1745 |
| Ieshige | 1745–1760 |
| Ieharu | 1760–1786 |
| Matsudaira Sadanobu | 1787–1793 |
| Ienari | 1793–1838 |
| Ieyoshi | 1838–1853 |
| Iesada | 1853–1858 |
| Iemochi | 1858–1866 |
| Yoshinobu | 1866–1867 |

**Meji Era**

| | |
|---|---|
| Emperor Mutsuhito | 1867–1912 |

**Taisho Era**

| | |
|---|---|
| Emperor Yoshihito | 1912–1926 |

**Showa Era**

| | |
|---|---|
| Emperor Hirohito | 1926– |

### JORDAN

| | |
|---|---|
| Abdullah | 1946–1951 |
| Talal | 1951–1952 |
| Hussein | 1952– |

### LIECHTENSTEIN

| | |
|---|---|
| Prince Johann II | 1858–1929 |
| Prince Franz I | 1929–1938 |
| Prince Franz Josef II | 1938– |

### LUXEMBOURG

| | |
|---|---|
| Duke Adolf of Nassau | 1890–1905 |
| William | 1905–1912 |
| Marie Adelaide | 1912–1919 |
| Charlotte | 1919–1961 |
| Prince Jean | 1961– |

### NETHERLANDS

**Houses of Orange and Nassau**

| | |
|---|---|
| Willem I (the Silent) | 1581–1584 |
| Maurice of Nassau | 1584–1625 |
| Frederik Heinrich | 1625–1647 |
| Willem II | 1647–1650 |
| Jan de Witt | 1650–1672 |
| Willem III [1] | 1672–1702 |
| Willem IV | 1711–1751 |
| Willem V | 1751–1795 |

Batavian Republic, 1795–1806

**French rule, 1806–1813**

| | |
|---|---|
| Louis Bonaparte | 1806–1810 |

**House of Orange-Nassau**

| | |
|---|---|
| Willem I | 1813–1840 |
| Willem II | 1840–1849 |
| Willem III | 1849–1890 |
| Wilhelmina | 1890–1948 |
| Juliana | 1948–1980 |
| Beatrix | 1980– |

### NORWAY

| | |
|---|---|
| Haakon VII | 1905–1957 |
| Olav V | 1957– |

### PORTUGAL

**Burgundian Dynasty**

| | |
|---|---|
| Afonso Henriques | 1139–1185 |
| Sancho I | 1185–1211 |
| Afonso II | 1211–1223 |
| Sancho II | 1223–1245 |
| Afonso III | 1245–1279 |
| Diniz | 1279–1325 |
| Afonso IV | 1325–1357 |
| Pedro I | 1357–1367 |
| Fernando I | 1367–1383 |

[1] Willem III also ruled as King William III of England and Scotland in 1689–1702.

## Avis Dynasty

| | |
|---|---|
| João I | 1385–1433 |
| Duarte I | 1433–1438 |
| Afonso V | 1438–1481 |
| João II | 1481–1495 |
| Manuel I | 1495–1521 |
| João III | 1521–1557 |
| Sebastião I | 1557–1578 |
| Henrique | 1578–1580 |

**Spanish rule, 1580–1640**

### House of Braganza

| | |
|---|---|
| João IV | 1640–1656 |
| Afonso VI | 1656–1667 |
| Pedro II | 1667–1706 |
| João V | 1706–1750 |
| José Manuel | 1750–1777 |

### House of Coburg-Braganza

| | |
|---|---|
| Maria I and Pedro III | 1777–1786 |
| Maria I | 1786–1816 |
| João VI | 1816–1826 |
| Pedro IV | 1826 |
| Maria II | 1826–1828 |
| Miguel | 1828–1833 |
| Maria II | 1833–1853 |
| Pedro V | 1853–1861 |
| Luis I | 1861–1889 |
| Carlos I | 1889–1908 |
| Manuel II | 1908–1910 |

**1st Portuguese Republic, 1910–1928**

### Fascist Dictatorship

| | |
|---|---|
| Antonio Salazar | 1928–1968 |
| Marcelo Caetano | 1968–1974 |

**2d Portuguese Republic, 1974–**

# ROMANIA

| | |
|---|---|
| Carol I | 1881–1914 |
| Ferdinand I | 1914–1927 |
| Michael | 1927–1930 |
| Carol II | 1930–1940 |
| Michael | 1940–1947 |

**Communist state, 1947–**

# RUSSIA

### Grand Princes of Moscow

| | |
|---|---|
| Vsevolod III | 1176–1212 |
| Yuri II | 1212–1216 |
| Konstantin | 1216–1219 |
| Yuri II | 1219–1238 |
| Yaroslav II | 1238–1246 |
| Andrei II | 1246–1252 |
| Aleksandr Nevski | 1252–1263 |
| Yaroslav III | 1263–1272 |
| Vasili | 1272–1277 |
| Dmitri | 1277–1294 |
| Andrei III | 1294–1304 |
| Mikhail | 1304–1319 |
| Yuri III | 1319–1325 |
| Dmitri | 1325–1326 |
| Aleksandr | 1326–1328 |
| Ivan I | 1328–1340 |
| Simeon | 1340–1353 |
| Ivan II | 1353–1359 |
| Dmitri Donskoi | 1359–1389 |
| Vasili I | 1389–1425 |
| Vasili II | 1425–1462 |

### Czars of Russia

| | |
|---|---|
| Ivan III the Great | 1462–1505 |
| Vasili III | 1505–1533 |
| Ivan IV the Terrible | 1533–1584 |
| Fedor I | 1584–1598 |
| Boris Godunov | 1598–1605 |
| Fedor II | 1605 |
| Dmitri I | 1605–1606 |
| Vasili IV | 1606–1610 |

### Romanov Dynasty

| | |
|---|---|
| Mikhail | 1613–1645 |
| Aleksei | 1645–1676 |
| Fedor III | 1676–1682 |
| Ivan V | 1682–1689 |
| Peter I the Great | 1682–1725 |
| Ekaterina Alekseevna I | 1725–1727 |
| Peter II Alekseevich | 1727–1730 |
| Anna Ioannovna | 1730–1740 |
| Ivan VI | 1740–1741 |
| Elizaveta Petrovna | 1741–1762 |
| Peter III Fedorovich | 1762 |
| Ekaterina Alekseevna II (the Great) | 1762–1796 |
| Pavel Petrovich | 1796–1801 |
| Aleksandr I Pavlovich | 1801–1825 |
| Nikolai I Pavlovich | 1825–1855 |
| Aleksandr II Nikolaevich | 1855–1881 |
| Aleksandr III Aleksandrovich | 1881–1894 |
| Nikolai II Aleksandrovich | 1894–1917 |

### Provisional Government

| | |
|---|---|
| Aleksandr Kerensky | 1917 |

**Bolshevik Revolution, 1917**

### Soviet Union, 1917–

| | |
|---|---|
| V.I. Lenin | 1917–1924 |
| Joseph Stalin | 1924–1953 |
| Georgi Malenkov | 1953–1955 |
| Nikita S. Khrushchev | 1955–1964 |
| Leonid I. Brezhnev | 1964– |

# SPAIN

### Houses of Aragon and Castile

| | |
|---|---|
| Fernando II of Aragon and Isabel I of Castile | 1479–1504 |
| Fernando II and Felipe I | 1504–1506 |
| Fernando II and Carlos II | 1506–1516 |

### Spanish Hapsburgs

| | |
|---|---|
| Carlos I (as Holy Roman Emperor, Karl V) | 1516–1556 |
| Felipe II | 1556–1598 |
| Felipe III | 1598–1621 |
| Felipe IV | 1621–1665 |
| Carlos II | 1665–1700 |

### Spanish Bourbons

| | |
|---|---|
| Felipe V | 1700–1746 |
| Fernando VI | 1746–1759 |
| Carlos III | 1759–1788 |
| Carlos IV | 1788–1808 |

### French King of Spain

| | |
|---|---|
| Joseph Bonaparte | 1808–1813 |

### 1st Bourbon Restoration

| | |
|---|---|
| Fernando VII | 1813–1833 |
| Isabel II | 1833–1868 |

### House of Savoy

| | |
|---|---|
| Amadeo I | 1868–1873 |

**1st Spanish Republic, 1873–1875**

### 2d Bourbon Restoration

| | |
|---|---|
| Alfonso XII | 1875–1885 |
| Alfonso XIII | 1886–1931 |

**2d Spanish Republic, 1931–1939**

### Fascist Dictatorship

| | |
|---|---|
| Francisco Franco | 1939–1975 |

### 3d Bourbon Restoration

| | |
|---|---|
| Juan Carlos I | 1975– |

# SWEDEN

### House of Vasa

| | |
|---|---|
| Gustaf I | 1523–1560 |
| Eric XIV | 1560–1568 |
| Johan III | 1568–1592 |
| Sigismund | 1592–1599 |

| | |
|---|---|
| Karl IX | 1604–1611 |
| Gustaf II Adolf | 1611–1632 |
| Christina | 1644–1654 |
| Karl X Gustaf | 1654–1660 |
| Karl XI | 1660–1697 |
| Karl XII | 1697–1718 |
| Ulrika Eleonora | 1718–1720 |
| Fredrik I | 1720–1751 |
| Adolf Fredrik | 1751–1771 |
| Gustaf III | 1771–1792 |
| Gustaf IV Adolf | 1792–1809 |
| Karl XIII | 1809–1818 |

### House of Bernadotte

| | |
|---|---|
| Karl XIV Johan | 1818–1844 |
| Oskar I | 1844–1859 |
| Karl XV | 1859–1872 |
| Oskar II | 1872–1907 |
| Gustaf V | 1907–1950 |
| Gustaf VI Adolf | 1950–1973 |
| Karl XVI Gustaf | 1973– |

# TURKEY

### Seljuk Sultans

| | |
|---|---|
| Tughril I | 1055–1063 |
| Alp Arslan | 1063–1072 |
| Malik Shah I | 1073–1092 |
| Mahmud | 1092–1094 |
| Barkyaruk | 1094–1104 |
| Malik Shah II | 1104 |

| | |
|---|---|
| Seljuk Turkish Empire divided | 1104 |

### Ottoman Sultans

| | |
|---|---|
| Osman | c.1299–1326 |
| Orkhan | 1326–1359 |
| Murad I | 1359–1389 |
| Bajazet I | 1389–1403 |
| Suleiman I | 1403–1411 |
| Musa | 1411–1413 |
| Mohammed I | 1413–1421 |
| Murad II | 1421–1451 |
| Mohammed II | 1451–1481 |
| Bajazet II | 1481–1512 |
| Selim I | 1512–1520 |
| Suleiman II | 1520–1566 |
| Selim II | 1566–1574 |
| Murad III | 1574–1595 |
| Mohammed III | 1595–1603 |
| Ahmed I | 1603–1617 |
| Mustafa I | 1617–1618 |
| Osman II | 1618–1622 |
| Mustafa I | 1622–1623 |
| Murad IV | 1623–1640 |
| Ibrahim | 1640–1648 |
| Mohammed IV | 1648–1687 |
| Suleiman III | 1687–1691 |
| Ahmed II | 1691–1695 |
| Mustafa II | 1695–1703 |
| Ahmed III | 1703–1730 |
| Mahmud I | 1730–1754 |
| Osman III | 1754–1757 |
| Mustafa III | 1757–1774 |
| Abdul-Hamid I | 1774–1789 |
| Selim III | 1789–1807 |
| Mustafa IV | 1807–1808 |
| Mahmud II | 1808–1839 |
| Abdul-Medjid I | 1839–1861 |
| Abdul-Aziz | 1861–1876 |
| Murad V | 1876 |
| Abdul-Hamid II | 1876–1909 |
| Mohammed V | 1909–1918 |
| Mohammed VI | 1918–1922 |

**Republic, 1923–**

# ROMAN AND BYZANTINE EMPERORS AND EMPRESSES

Octavian, the grandnephew and adopted son of Julius Caesar, founded the Roman Empire. He became emperor in 27 B.C., called himself Augustus, and took complete control of military and governmental powers. At the death of Theodosius the Great in 395, the empire was divided into east and west.

The large-scale barbarian invasions of the 400s caused the empire in the west to crumble. In 476 Odoacer, a German leader, entered Rome and forced Emperor Romulus Augustulus to abdicate.

In the east the Roman Empire continued to exist for nearly 10 more centuries under Greek rulers as the Byzantine Empire.

Where dates overlap in the following list, the title of emperor was shared.

## ROMAN EMPERORS

| | |
|---|---|
| Augustus | 27 B.C.–A.D. 14 |
| Tiberius | 14–37 |
| Caligula | 37–41 |
| Claudius | 41–54 |
| Nero | 54–68 |
| Galba | 68–69 |
| Otho | 69 |
| Vitellius | 69 |
| Vespasian | 69–79 |
| Titus | 79–81 |
| Domitian | 81–96 |
| Nerva | 96–98 |
| Trajan | 98–117 |
| Hadrian | 117–138 |
| Antoninus Pius | 138–161 |
| Marcus Aurelius | 161–180 |
| Lucius Verus | 161–169 |
| Commodus | 180–192 |
| Pertinax | 193 |
| Didius Julianus | 193 |
| Septimius Severus | 193–211 |
| Geta | 209–211 |
| Caracalla | 211–217 |
| Macrinus | 217–218 |
| Heliogabalus (Elagabalus) | 218–222 |
| Alexander Severus | 222–235 |
| Maximinus Thrax | 235–238 |
| Gordian I Africanus | 238 |
| Gordian II | 238 |
| Balbinus | 238 |
| Pupienus Maximus | 238 |
| Gordian III Pius | 238–244 |
| Philip the Arab | 244–249 |
| Decius | 249–251 |
| Hostilian | 251 |
| Gallus | 251–253 |
| Aemilian | 253 |
| Valerian | 253–259 |
| Gallienus | 259–268 |
| Claudius II Gothicus | 268–270 |
| Quintillus | 270 |
| Aurelian | 270–275 |
| Tacitus | 275–276 |
| Florian | 276 |
| Probus | 276–282 |
| Carus | 282–283 |
| Carinus | 283–285 |
| Numerian | 283–284 |
| Diocletian | 284–305 |
| Maximian | 286–305; 306–308 |
| Constantius I Chlorus | 305–306 |
| Galerius | 305–311 |
| Severus | 306–307 |
| Maxentius | 306–312 |
| Maximinus Daia | 308–313 |
| Licinius | 311–324 |
| Constantine I the Great | 311–337 |
| Constantine II | 337–340 |
| Constans | 337–350 |
| Constantius II | 337–361 |
| Julian the Apostate | 361–363 |
| Jovian | 363–364 |
| Valentinian I (in the West) | 364–375 |
| Valens (in the East) | 364–378 |
| Gratian (in the West) | 375–383 |
| Valentinian II (in the West) | 375–392 |
| Theodosius I the Great | 379–395 |
| Magnus Maximus | 383–388 |
| Eugenius | 392–394 |

## ROMAN EMPERORS IN WEST

| | |
|---|---|
| Honorius | 395–423 |
| Constantius III | 421 |
| Johannes | 423–425 |
| Valentinian III | 425–455 |
| Petronius Maximus | 455 |
| Avitus | 455–456 |
| Majorian | 457–461 |
| Libius Severus | 461–465 |
| Anthemius | 467–472 |
| Olybrius | 472 |
| Glycerius | 473 |
| Julius Nepos | 473–475 |
| Romulus Augustulus | 475–476 |

## ROMAN EMPERORS IN EAST

| | |
|---|---|
| Arcadius | 395–408 |
| Theodosius II | 408–450 |
| Marcian | 450–457 |
| Leo I | 457–474 |
| Leo II | 473–474 |
| Zeno | 474–491 |

## BYZANTINE RULERS IN EAST

| | |
|---|---|
| Anastasius I | 491–518 |
| Justin I | 518–527 |
| Justinian the Great | 527–565 |
| Justin II | 565–578 |
| Tiberius II | 578–582 |
| Maurice | 582–602 |
| Phocas I | 602–610 |
| Heraclius I | 610–641 |
| Constantine III | 641 |
| Heracleon | 641 |
| Constans II | 641–668 |
| Constantine IV | 668–685 |
| Justinian II | 685–695 |
| Leontius | 695–698 |
| Tiberius II | 698–705 |
| Justinian II | 705–711 |
| Philippicus | 711–713 |
| Anastasius II | 713–715 |
| Theodosius III | 715–717 |
| Leo III | 717–741 |
| Constantine V | 741–775 |
| Leo IV | 775–780 |
| Constantine VI | 780–797 |
| Irene | 797–802 |
| Nicephorus I | 802–811 |
| Stauracius | 811 |
| Michael I | 811–813 |
| Leo V | 813–820 |
| Michael II | 820–829 |
| Theophilus I | 829–842 |

| | |
|---|---|
| Michael III | 842–867 |
| Basil I | 867–886 |
| Leo VI | 886–912 |
| Alexander II | 912–913 |
| Constantine VII | 912–959 |
| Romanus I | 920–944 |
| Romanus II | 959–963 |
| Basil II | 963–1025 |
| Nicephorus II | 963–969 |
| John I | 969–976 |
| Constantine VIII | 1025–1028 |
| Zoë | 1028–1050 |
| Romanus III | 1028–1034 |
| Michael IV | 1034–1041 |
| Michael V | 1041–1042 |
| Constantine IX | 1042–1055 |
| Theodora | 1055–1056 |
| Michael VI | 1056–1057 |
| Isaac I | 1057–1059 |
| Constantine X | 1059–1067 |
| Romanus IV | 1068–1071 |
| Michael VII | 1071–1078 |
| Nicephorus III | 1078–1081 |
| Alexius I | 1081–1118 |
| Andronicus I | 1183–1185 |
| Isaac II | 1185–1195 |
| Alexis III | 1195–1203 |
| Isaac II | 1203–1204 |
| Alexius IV | 1203–1204 |
| Alexius V | 1204 |

## LATIN RULERS

| | |
|---|---|
| Baldwin I | 1204–1205 |
| Henry | 1205–1216 |
| Peter of Courtenay | 1216–1217 |
| Yolande | 1217–1219 |
| Robert of Courtenay | 1219–1228 |
| Baldwin II | 1228–1261 |
| John of Brienne | 1231–1237 |

## NICAEAN EMPERORS

| | |
|---|---|
| Theodore I | 1204–1222 |
| John III | 1222–1254 |
| Theodore II | 1254–1258 |
| John IV | 1258–1261 |

## PALEOLOGI EMPERORS

| | |
|---|---|
| Michael VIII | 1259–1282 |
| Andronicus II | 1282–1328 |
| Michael IX | 1295–1320 |
| Andronicus III | 1328–1341 |
| John V | 1341–1347 |
| John VI | 1347–1354 |
| John V | 1355–1376 |
| Andronicus IV | 1376–1379 |
| John V | 1379–1391 |
| John VII | 1390 |
| Manuel II | 1391–1425 |
| John VIII | 1425–1448 |
| Constantine XI | 1448–1453 |

# KEY EVENTS IN AMERICAN HISTORY

Presented here in chronological order are many of the important events in American history from the time of the early explorers to the present day. For the convenience of the reader, the table of events has been divided into 10 broad periods of history.

## PERIOD OF EXPLORATION AND COLONIZATION: 1000–1763

**c.1000   Norse Vikings** discover North America; Leif Ericson lands at Vinland (probably Newfoundland).

**1492 (Oct. 12)   Christopher Columbus** discovers America for Spain; after sailing 33 days out of sight of land, goes ashore on San Salvador (Watling) Island in Bahamas, believing he has reached East Indies.

**1492 (Dec. 26)   First Spanish settlement** in Western Hemisphere founded by Columbus at La Navidad in what is now Haiti; later destroyed by Indians.

**1496   First Permanent Spanish city** in Western Hemisphere founded by Bartholomew Columbus: Santo Domingo, now in Dominican Republic.

**1497 (June 24)   English claim for North America** established by John Cabot, landing on either Newfoundland or Nova Scotia.

**1508   First Spanish settlement in Puerto Rico** founded by Juan Ponce de León.

**1513 (April 2)   Florida discovered** and claimed for Spain by Juan Ponce de León.

**1513 (Sept. 25)   Pacific Ocean discovered** and all lands bordering it claimed for Spain by Vasco de Balboa, after crossing Isthmus of Panama.

**1524   French claim for North America** established by Giovanni da Verrazano; explored Atlantic coast and sailed into New York harbor.

**1538   First university** in Western Hemisphere, University of St. Thomas Aquinas, founded in Santo Domingo, now in Dominican Republic.

**1540–42   Francisco Vásquez de Coronado** explores American southwest, going as far north as Kansas and claiming region for Spain.

**1541 (May 8)   Mississippi River discovered** by Spanish explorer Hernando de Soto near present-day Memphis, Tenn.

**1562   First French settlement** in what is now the U.S. founded by Jean Ribaut; called Charlesfort, on Port Royal Sound in South Carolina; later abandoned.

**1564 (June)   First French colony** in Florida founded by René de Laudonnière; called Fort Caroline, near present-day Jacksonville; later destroyed by Spaniards.

**1565 (Sept. 8)   First permanent European settlement** in what is now continental U.S. established at St. Augustine, Fla., by Pedro Menéndez de Avilés of Spain.

**1585   First English colony** settled on Roanoke Island, N.C.; survived only 10 months.

**1587 (Aug. 18)   First English child,** Virginia Dare, born in what is now U.S., in second Roanoke settlement—the "Lost Colony."

**1607 (May 14)   First permanent English settlement** in what is now U.S. established at Jamestown, Va.

**1609   Hudson River explored** and claimed for Dutch by explorer Henry Hudson.

**1610   Santa Fe** established as capital of Spanish colony of New Mexico, oldest capital city in U.S.

**1614   New Netherland (New York) founded** by Dutch with building of fort at what is now Albany, N.Y.

**1619   First black slaves** in North America arrive at Jamestown in Dutch ship.

**1619 (July 30)   First legislature,** Virginia's House of Burgesses, convenes at Jamestown.

**1620 (Nov. 21)   Mayflower Compact** signed by Pilgrims aboard *Mayflower* in Provincetown, Mass., harbor.

**1620 (Dec. 26)   Pilgrims land** to found colony at Plymouth, Mass.

**1626   Manhattan Island, N.Y.,** bought by Dutch from Indians for about $24.

**1628 (Sept. 6)   Puritans land at Salem** founding Massachusetts Bay Colony (royal charter granted March 14, 1629); Boston founded in 1630.

**1634 (March 25)   Maryland founded** with landing of English Roman Catholics led by Gov. Leonard Calvert, brother of Lord Baltimore.

**1636   Providence, R.I., founded** by Roger Williams to provide religious freedom for all faiths.

**1636 (Oct 28)   Harvard College founded** in Massachusetts; first institution of higher learning in U.S.

**1638   First printing press** in English colonies set up by Stephen Day at Cambridge, Mass.; publishes first book, *Bay Psalm Book,* in 1640.

**1639 (Jan. 24)   Fundamental Orders of Connecticut** adopted; provides for elected governor and legislature.

**1649 (April 21)   Maryland's Toleration Act** passed, granting religious freedom to all Christian faiths.

**1660 (Dec. 1)   First Navigation Act** passed by British parliament to regulate colonial trade.

**1664 (Sept. 8)   New Amsterdam (now New York City)** captured by British from Dutch.

**1670 (April)   Colony of South Carolina begun** with settlement established at Charleston.

**1673 (July 17)   Père Jacques Marquette and Louis Joliet** explore Mississippi River as far south as Arkansas for France.

**1675–78   King Philip's War** fought between colonists and Indians in Massachusetts.

**1676 (Sept. 19)   Nathaniel Bacon** burns Jamestown in rebellion against Virginia's British governor.

**1677   First charter separating church and state** framed for Quaker colony of West Jersey.

**1681 (March 14)   Pennsylvania** proprietary charter granted William Penn by Charles II.

**1682 (April 9)   Sieur de La Salle** paddles down Mississippi River to its mouth, claiming Louisiana for France.

**1684 (Oct. 18)   Massachusetts Bay Colony** charter annulled by British court.

**1685–1689   Dominion of New England created** by Britain's King James II to include all New England colonies plus New York, New Jersey, and Pennsylvania; rebellions by colonists and overthrow of James II in England ends scheme.

**1689 (April 18)   Rebellion in Boston** overthrows British royal governor of New England, Sir Edmund Andros.

**1689 (Aug. 1)   Protestant rebellion in Maryland** overthrows governor of Roman Catholic proprietors; Maryland restored to Baltimore family proprietors in 1715 after their conversion to Protestantism.

**1689–1691   Rebellion in New York:** Jacob Leisler overthrows British governor and establishes elective assembly; arrested for treason and hanged in 1691.

**1689–97   King William's War** fought by British and French in New York, New England, and Canada.

**1691 (Oct. 17)   New Massachusetts royal charter** issued, incorporating Plymouth Colony and Maine into Massachusetts.

**1692   Witch trials in Salem, Mass.,** result in execution of 14 women and 6 men; 55 more plead guilty and accuse others.

**1702–13   Queen Anne's War,** in which British fight against French and Spaniards in New England, Florida, and South Carolina; France loses Hudson Bay region, Newfoundland, and Nova Scotia to Britain.

**1704 (April 24)   First successful newspaper** in colonies established: *Boston News-Letter.*

**1721 (May 29)   South Carolina** formally incorporated as royal colony.

**1729 (July 25)   North Carolina** becomes royal colony under British king.

**1732 (June 9)   Royal charter for Georgia** granted to James Edward Oglethorpe.

**1735 (Aug. 4)   Freedom of the press trial** of John Peter Zenger ends as jury acquits him of libel, asserting that truth is not libelous.

**1739–42   War of Jenkins' Ear** fought between Georgia colonists and Spaniards in Florida.

**1744–48   King George's War** fought between British and French colonists; ends with no changes in territory by either side.

**1749 (May 19)   Ohio Company** granted charter by King George II to settle Ohio Valley.

**1753   George Washington** sent to Ohio Valley by Virginia's Gov. Robert Dinwiddie to warn French to leave region.

power to move eastern Indians to land west of the Mississippi River; in next 10 years some 70,000 Indians are forced to move west to reservations.

**1831  Mechanical reaper** first demonstrated by Cyrus McCormick.

**1831 (Aug. 13–23)  Slave uprising** led by Nat Turner in Virginia; 57 whites and about 100 blacks killed; 20 blacks including Turner executed.

**1832 (April 6–Aug. 2)  Black Hawk War** fought by settlers and Indians along upper Mississippi River.

**1832 (July 10)  Recharter of U.S. Bank vetoed** by President Jackson, who detested bank.

**1832 (Dec. 10)  Nullification Proclamation** issued by President Jackson warning that any effort by South Carolina to leave Union by armed force would be treason.

**1834  Whig Party** formed to oppose President Jackson.

**1835–43  Seminole War** fought between Indians and settlers in Florida.

**1836  First state child-labor law** forbids employment of children under 15 in factories; adopted by Massachusetts.

**1836 (Feb. 23–March 6)  Siege of the Alamo:** 187 Texans and frontiersmen fight to death in San Antonio against 3,000-man Mexican army.

**1836 (March 2)  Texas declaration of independence** adopted at Washington, Texas.

**1836 (April 21)  Battle of San Jacinto:** Gen. Sam Houston defeats Mexicans and captures Mexican Gen. Santa Anna.

**1836 (June 15)  Arkansas** becomes 25th state.

**1836 (Oct. 22)  Independent Republic of Texas** installs Sam Houston as president.

**1837  Panic of 1837** strikes nation with bank closings and unemployment.

**1837 (Jan. 26)  Michigan** becomes 26th state.

**1837 (March 3)  Supreme Court membership increased to nine:** Act of Congress adds two associate justices to Court.

**1837 (March 4)  Martin Van Buren inaugurated** as 8th President of the United States.

**1837 (Oct. 6)  Samuel F. B. Morse** files patent for his invention of the telegraph.

**1837 (Nov. 7)  Murder of abolitionist editor Elijah P. Lovejoy** at Alton, Ill., by mob that also destroys his press.

**1839  Process of vulcanizing rubber** discovered by Charles Goodyear.

**1839  Mormons settle Nauvoo, Ill.:** Having been driven out of Missouri, about 10,000 Mormons travel to new home, making Nauvoo largest town in Illinois.

**1840 (July 4)  Independent Treasury Act** gives federal government right to care for own funds rather than deposit them in banks.

**1841 (March 4)  William Henry Harrison** inaugurated as 9th President of the United States.

**1841 (April 6)  John Tyler** sworn in as 10th President two days after death of Harrison.

**1841 (Aug. 13)  Repeal of Independent Treasury Act** by Whig-controlled Congress.

**1841 (Aug. 13)  Webster-Ashburton Treaty** signed, settling dispute with Britain over boundary of Maine.

**1845 (March 3)  Florida** becomes 27th state.

**1845 (March 4)  James K. Polk** inaugurated as 11th President of the United States.

**1845 (Dec. 29)  Texas** becomes 28th state.

**1846 (April 25)  Mexican troops attack U.S. soldiers** stationed on Rio Grande in Texas.

**1846 (May 13)  Congress declares war on Mexico;** House votes 174–14, Senate 40–2.

**1846 (June 15)  Oregon Treaty** settling boundary with Canada at 49th parallel approved by Senate; becomes effective Aug. 5, 1846.

**1846 (Dec. 28)  Iowa** becomes 29th state.

**1847  Mormons found Salt Lake City** and establish State of Deseret with Brigham Young as governor.

**1847 (Sept. 14)  Mexico City captured** by U.S. troops led by Gen. Winfield Scott.

**1848 (Jan. 24)  Gold discovered in California** by James W. Marshall at Sutter's Mill.

**1848 (Feb. 2)  Treaty of Guadalupe Hidalgo** ends Mexican War; California and Southwest ceded to U.S. for payment of $15 million.

**1848 (May 29)  Wisconsin** becomes 30th state.

**1848 (July 19–20)  First women's rights convention:** Held at Seneca Falls, N.Y., under leadership of Elizabeth Cady Stanton and Lucretia Coffin Mott.

**1849 (March 5)  Zachary Taylor** inaugurated as 12th President of the United States.

**1850 (July 10)  Millard Fillmore** sworn in as 13th President after death of President Taylor.

**1850 (Sept. 9)  California** becomes 31st state.

**1850 (Sept. 9–20)  Compromise of 1850** between slavery and antislavery forces in Congress admits California as free state.

**1850 (Sept. 18)  Fugitive Slave Act** requires federal government to capture runaway slaves and punish persons who aid them.

**1850 (Sept. 20)  Slave trade abolished** in District of Columbia by Congress, but slavery allowed to continue.

**1852 (March 20)  *Uncle Tom's Cabin*** by Harriet Beecher Stowe published in Boston; over 1,200,000 copies sold during first two years.

**1853 (March 4)  Franklin Pierce** inaugurated as 14th President of the United States.

**1854 (Feb. 28)  Republican Party founded** at Ripon, Wis.

**1854 (March 31)  Japan forced to open its ports** to U.S. trade by Commodore Matthew Perry.

**1854 (May 30)  Kansas-Nebraska Act** repeals Missouri Compromise; "popular sovereignty" to decide slavery issue in Kansas and Nebraska.

**1854 (June 29)  Gadsden Purchase** of southern Arizona and New Mexico for $10 million from Mexico.

**1855–56  Warfare in Kansas** between slavery and antislavery factions.

**1857 (March 4)  James Buchanan** inaugurated as 15th President of the United States.

**1858 (May 11)  Minnesota** becomes 32d state.

**1858 (Aug. 21–Oct. 15)  Lincoln-Douglas debates** in Illinois race for U.S. Senate; Lincoln loses election but becomes national figure.

**1859 (Feb. 14)  Oregon** becomes 33d state.

**1859 (Oct. 16–18)  John Brown's raid** seizes federal arsenal at Harpers Ferry, Va.

**1859 (Dec. 2)  John Brown hanged** after being found guilty of trying to incite slave revolt.

**1860 (Dec. 20)  South Carolina secedes** from Union, followed by other Southern states.

**1861 (Jan. 29)  Kansas** becomes 34th state.

**1861 (Feb. 8)  Confederate States of America organized** in convention at Montgomery, Ala.; Jefferson Davis elected provisional president on Feb. 9.

**1861 (March 4)  Abraham Lincoln** inaugurated as 16th President of the United States.

**1861 (April 12)  Civil War begins** as South Carolina troops attack federal Fort Sumter at Charleston, S.C.; fort surrenders on April 14.

**1862 (May 20)  Homestead Act** provides cheap land for settlement of West.

**1863 (Jan. 1)  Emancipation Proclamation** issued by President Lincoln freeing slaves in areas controlled by Confederacy.

**1863 (June 20)  West Virginia** becomes 35th state.

**1863 (July 1–3)  Battle of Gettysburg:** Lee's invasion of Pennsylvania turned back by General Meade's Union army.

**1864 (Oct. 31)  Nevada** becomes 36th state.

**1865 (April 9)  Lee surrenders** at Appomattox Court House, Va., ending Civil War.

**1865 (April 14)  President Lincoln shot** by John Wilkes Booth; dies on April 15.

## FROM RECONSTRUCTION TO THE 20TH CENTURY: 1865–1900

**1865 (April 15)  Andrew Johnson** sworn in as 17th President of the United States.

**1865 (Dec. 18)  Slavery abolished** by 13th Amendment to U.S. Constitution.

**1866–67  Ku Klux Klan organized;** led by ex-Confederate Gen. Nathan B. Forrest.

**1867 (March 1)  Nebraska** becomes 37th state.

**1867 (March 2)  Reconstruction Act** passed over President Johnson's veto organizes Southern states into five military districts.

**1867 (Oct. 18)  Alaska purchased** from Russia for $7.2 million.

QUICK QUIZ: Ralph Bunche was the first black American to win what prize? See page 333.

**KEY EVENTS IN AMERICAN HISTORY** *(continued)*

**1868 (Feb. 24)    President Johnson impeached** by 126–47 vote in House. After trial in Senate, key vote (May 16) is one short of two-thirds needed for conviction.
**1868 (May 30)    First Memorial Day** honors Civil War dead.
**1868 (July 28)    Citizenship granted former** slaves by 14th Amendment to U.S. Constitution.
**1869    First state board of health:** Established by act of Massachusetts legislature.
**1869 (March 4)    Ulysses S. Grant inaugurated** as 18th President of the United States.
**1869 (May 10)    First transcontinental railroad** completed with driving of golden spike at Promontory Point, Utah.
**1869 (Dec. 10)    First law giving women right to vote and hold office** in U.S. passed by Wyoming territorial legislature.
**1870    First blacks in U.S. Congress:** Black U.S. senator and black U.S. representative sworn in.
**1870    Last four Confederate States restored to Union:** Georgia, Mississippi, Virginia, and Texas readmitted; previously 1 had been readmitted in 1866 and 6 in 1868.
**1870 (March 30)    Deprivation of voting rights** because of race, color, or previous servitude prohibited by 15th Amendment to U.S. Constitution.
**1871 (Oct. 8–9)    Chicago fire** destroys 3½ square miles of city; kills 300; 100,000 made homeless.
**1873 (Sept. 18)    Panic of 1873** triggered by failure of Jay Cooke's banking firm.
**1875    Whisky Ring scandals** rock President Grant's administration with indictments of 239 persons.
**1876 (March 2)    Impeachment and resignation** of Secretary of War William W. Belknap on bribery charges; Senate later votes to acquit.
**1876 (March 10)    Telephone invented** by Alexander Graham Bell as it carries first words: "Mr. Watson, come here. I want you!"
**1876 (June 25)    Gen. George A. Custer's troops massacred** by Chief Sitting Bull's Sioux at Battle of Little Bighorn in Montana.
**1876 (Aug. 1)    Colorado** becomes 38th state.
**1876 (Nov. 7)    Disputed presidential election** causes constitutional crisis.
**1877 (March 5)    Rutherford B. Hayes inaugurated** as 19th President of the United States.
**1877 (April 10–24)    Reconstruction of South ends** as federal troops withdraw from occupation.
**1878 (Feb. 28)    Bland-Allison Act** passed over President Hayes' veto bases monetary system on gold and silver, with silver valued at ratio of 16–1.
**1879 (Oct. 19–20)    Incandescent electric light** invented by Thomas A. Edison at Menlo Park, N.J.
**1881 (March 4)    James A. Garfield inaugurated** as 20th President of the United States.
**1881 (July 2)    President Garfield shot** by assassin in Washington, D.C.; dies on Sept. 19.
**1881 (Sept. 20)    Chester A. Arthur sworn in** as 21st President of the United States.
**1882    Standard Oil Trust formed** by John D. Rockefeller, controlling 90% of nation's oil refining.
**1883 (Jan. 16)    Pendleton Act** creates basis of present federal civil service system.
**1883 (Nov.)    Standard time zones** established by U.S. and Canadian railroads.

**1885 (March 4)    Grover Cleveland inaugurated** as 22d President of the United States.
**1886 (May 4)    Haymarket Riot:** bomb thrown during anarchist-labor demonstration in Chicago kills 7 policemen, wounds 70.
**1886 (Sept. 4)    Apache Indian War** in Southwest ends with capture of Apache Chief Geronimo.
**1886 (Dec. 8)    American Federation of Labor (AFL)** organized at convention in Columbus, Ohio.
**1887 (Feb. 4)    Interstate Commerce Act** establishes federal regulation of railroads, beginning control of interstate commerce.
**1889 (March 4)    Benjamin Harrison inaugurated** as 23d President of the United States.
**1889 (April 22)    Oklahoma land rush** officially opens former Indian territory to settlement.
**1889 Nov. 2)    North Dakota and South Dakota** become 39th and 40th states.
**1889 (Nov. 8)    Montana** becomes 41st state.
**1889 (Nov. 11)    Washington** becomes 42d state.
**1890 (July 2)    Sherman Antitrust Act** prohibits industrial monopolies, called trusts; leads to "trust-busting" suits.
**1890 (July 3)    Idaho** becomes 43d state.
**1890 (July 10)    Wyoming** becomes 44th state.
**1890 (Dec. 29)    Wounded Knee, S.D., massacre** by federal troops of 300 captive Sioux Indians ends last Indian war in West.
**1892 (July 6)    Homestead Massacre:** strikers at Carnegie Steel Co. at Homestead, Pa., fire on strikebreakers, killing 7; strikes later broken after state militia called in.
**1893    Panic of 1893:** over 15,000 banks and businesses bankrupted.
**1893    First successful gasoline-powered automobile** built in U.S. by Charles and Frank Duryea at Springfield, Mass.
**1893 (March 4)    Grover Cleveland inaugurated** as 24th President of the United States.
**1894 (April 30)    Coxey's Army** of about 500 unemployed men marches on Washington, D.C., to demand relief.
**1894 (June 21–July 20)    Pullman Strike:** President Cleveland uses federal troops to restore order; federal court issues strike injunction.
**1896    Segregation of blacks** upheld by "separate but equal" doctrine of Supreme Court in *Plessy* v. *Ferguson* decision.
**1896 (Jan. 4)    Utah** becomes 45th state.
**1896 (Aug. 16)    Klondike gold rush** to Alaska begins with discovery of gold on Bonanza Creek just east of Alaska's border with Canada.
**1897 (March 4)    William McKinley inaugurated** as 25th President of the United States.
**1898 (Feb. 15)    U.S. battleship *Maine* explodes** in harbor of Havana, Cuba, killing 260 of crew.
**1898 (April 25)    U.S. declares war on Spain,** demanding independence of Cuba.
**1898 (Aug. 12)    Hawaii annexed** to U.S.
**1898 (Dec. 10)    Spanish-American War ends** with signing of treaty; Spain frees Cuba, cedes Puerto Rico and Guam islands to U.S., and sells Philippines to U.S. for $20 million.
**1899    Wake Island** claimed by U.S.
**1900 (March 14)    Gold Standard Act** establishes gold as standard for U.S. currency.

## FROM TRUST–BUSTING THROUGH WORLD WAR I: 1901–1918

**1901 (Sept. 6)    President McKinley shot** by assassin in Buffalo, N.Y.; dies on Sept. 14.
**1901 (Sept. 14)    Theodore Roosevelt sworn in** as 26th President of the United States.
**1902    First state workmen's compensation law** adopted by Maryland.
**1902 (March 10)    Trust-busting begun** by President Roosevelt with suit against J.P. Morgan's Northern Securities Co.
**1902 (June 2)    First statewide initiative and referendum law** adopted by Oregon.
**1903    First law limiting workday to 10 hours** for women adopted by Oregon.
**1903 (May 3)    First direct-primary election law** adopted by Wisconsin.
**1903 (Dec. 17)    First airplane flight** by Orville and Wilbur Wright at Kitty Hawk, N.C.
**1904 (Feb. 23)    Panama Canal Zone** control acquired by U.S. for $10 million from Panama with ratification of Hay–Bunau-Varilla Treaty.

**1906 (April 18)    San Francisco earthquake** destroys 4 square miles of city; kills 700.
**1906 (June 29)    Panama Canal Act** authorizes construction of canal with locks across Panama.
**1906 (June 30)    Pure Food and Drug Act** provides federal regulation of food and drugs.
**1906 (June 30)    Meat Inspection Act** provides federal regulation of interstate meat-packing industry.
**1907    Panic of 1907:** Stock market crash and many business failures follow collapse of Knickerbocker Trust Co. in New York.
**1907 (Feb. 20)    Immigration Act** directed against Japanese authorizes President to exclude from U.S. immigrants from any other country.
**1907 (Nov. 16)    Oklahoma** becomes 46th state.
**1909 (Jan. 11)    First inventory of U.S. natural resources** submitted to President Roosevelt by National Conservation Commission.
**1909 (March 4)    William Howard Taft inaugurated** as 27th President of the United States.

**1909** First Model T car manufactured by Henry Ford using assembly line.
**1911** First state welfare law for mothers with dependent children adopted by Illinois.
**1911 (May 15)** Standard Oil Co. of New Jersey ordered dissolved by Supreme Court in antitrust suit against Rockefeller-owned company.
**1912** First state minimum-wage law adopted by Massachusetts.
**1912 (Jan. 6)** New Mexico becomes 47th state.
**1912 (Feb. 14)** Arizona becomes 48th state.
**1913 Feb. 25)** Federal income tax authorized by 16th Amendment to U.S. Constitution.
**1913 (March 4)** Woodrow Wilson inaugurated as 28th President of the United States.
**1913 (May 31)** Popular election of U.S. senators required by 17th Amendment to U.S. Constitution.
**1913 (Dec. 23)** Federal Reserve Act reorganizes national banking system.

**1914 (Aug. 15)** Panama Canal opened to first crossing by ship.
**1914 (Sept. 26)** Federal Trade Commission established to regulate interstate commerce.
**1915** U.S. population reaches 100 million.
**1916 (March 15)** U.S. troops invade Mexico to pursue revolutionary Gen. Pancho Villa; withdraw on Feb. 5, 1917.
**1917 (Jan. 17)** Virgin Islands purchase by U.S. from Denmark for $25 million ratified; becomes effective on March 31.
**1917 (Feb. 3)** U.S. breaks relations with Germany because of its sinking of U.S. ships.
**1917 (April 6)** U.S. declares war on Germany; first U.S. troops land in France on June 26; over 2 million soldiers sent to France before armistice ends World War I on Nov. 11, 1918.
**1918** First official U.S. airmail flights: Route flown between Washington, D.C., and New York City.

## FROM PROHIBITION TO THE GREAT DEPRESSION: 1919–1932

**1919 (Jan. 29)** Prohibition of sale and manufacture of alcoholic beverages by 18th Amendment to U.S. Constitution; goes into effect Jan. 16, 1920.
**1919 (Feb. 25)** First state gasoline tax: Established by act of Oregon legislature.
**1919 (June 28)** Versailles Treaty signed embodying peace settlement for World War I and establishing League of Nations.
**1919 (Oct. 2)** President Wilson paralyzed by stroke, making him invalid for rest of life.
**1919 (Nov. 19)** Rejection of Versailles Treaty and League of Nations by U.S. Senate.
**1919–20** Mass arrests of thousands of anarchists, communists, and labor agitators by agents of U.S. Department of Justice; hundreds deported to Russia.
**1920** First commercial radio begun by KDKA in Pittsburgh and WWJ in Detroit.
**1920** U.S. becomes urban nation: For first time more than half of U.S. population lives in urban instead of rural areas.
**1920** Grand Canyon National Park established in Arizona, including much of spectacular Colorado River canyon.
**1920 (Aug. 26)** Women win right to vote with 19th Amendment to U.S. Constitution.
**1920-21** Business recession with high unemployment and some 20,000 business failures.
**1921 (March 4)** Warren G. Harding inaugurated as 29th President of the United States.
**1921 (May 19)** Immigration quotas set: Congress acts after nearly 1 million immigrate to U.S. in year.
**1921 (June 10)** Budget and Accounting Act creates General Accounting Office and Bureau of the Budget.
**1922 (Feb. 6)** Naval arms-limitation pact signed by U.S., Britain, France, Italy, and Japan, scrapping many existing warships.
**1923 (Aug. 3)** Calvin Coolidge sworn in as 30th President following death on Aug. 2 of President Warren G. Harding in San Francisco.
**1923 (Oct. 25)** Investigation of Teapot Dome scandals of Harding administration begun by U.S. Senate, leading to conviction of many former officials for bribery and conspiracy.
**1923–26** Ku Klux Klan reign of terror against minori-

ty groups reaches peak with many lynchings.
**1925** Clarence Birdseye invents quick-frozen food process to preserve food.
**1925 (July 21)** Evolution trial: John Scopes convicted in Dayton, Tenn., of teaching evolution; defended by Clarence Darrow; prosecuted by William Jennings Bryan.
**1925 (Dec. 17)** Court-martial convicts Brig. Gen. William (Billy) Mitchell of unmilitary conduct in criticizing superiors for ignoring importance of military air power.
**1926 (March 16)** First liquid-fuel rocket successfully launched by Dr. Robert H. Goddard near Auburn, Mass.; invention later makes space travel possible.
**1927 (May 21)** First solo nonstop flight across Atlantic completed by Charles A. Lindbergh; lands in Paris 33½ hours after taking off from Long Island, N.Y.
**1927 (Aug. 23)** Sacco-Vanzetti case: Anarchists Nicola Sacco and Bartolomeo Vanzetti executed in Charlestown, Mass., for 1920 murder; protesters claim conviction was on political grounds rather than on evidence.
**1928 (Aug. 27)** War outlawed by Kellogg-Briand Peace Pact; signed by U.S. and France; 62 nations eventually sign.
**1929 (Feb. 20)** American Samoa organized as territory of United States.
**1929 (March 4)** Herbert Hoover inaugurated as 31st President of the United States.
**1929 (Oct. 24)** Great Depression triggered by stock market crash; unemployed number 12 million; more than 37,000 banks, corporations, and other businesses fail by 1931.
**1932 (Feb. 2)** Reconstruction Finance Corporation (RFC) established to loan $2 billion to businesses, banks, and farm credit groups.
**1932 (March 1)** Kidnap-murder of son of aviation hero Charles A. Lindbergh at Hopewell, N.J.; after sensational trial, Bruno Richard Hauptman is convicted of crime and executed in April 1936.
**1932 (July 22)** Federal Home Loan Bank Act provides $125 million for first federal mortgage loans.
**1932 (July 28)** Bonus army of unemployed veterans, who had marched on Washington seeking immediate bonus payment, dispersed by federal troops and tanks.

## FROM THE NEW DEAL THROUGH WORLD WAR II: 1933–1945

**1933 (Feb. 6)** "Lame Duck" 20th Amendment to U.S. Constitution changes date of presidential inaugurations after 1933 to January 20.
**1933 (March 4)** Franklin Delano Roosevelt inaugurated as 32d President of the United States.
**1933 (March 6–9)** Bank holiday proclaimed by President Roosevelt with all bank operations halted; only financially sound banks allowed to open after holiday; measure taken to stop hoarding of money by persons fearing bank failures.
**1933 (March 9–June 16)** Hundred Days special session of 73d Congress passes New Deal legislation to provide relief to banks, manufacturers, farmers, labor, and unemployed.
**1933 (Dec. 5)** Prohibition repealed by 21st Amendment to U.S. Constitution.
**1934** "Dust bowl" created in Midwest by extended

drought and lack of conservation measures.
**1935 (May 27)** Supreme Court declares National Recovery Act (NRA) unconstitutional.
**1935 (Aug. 14)** Social Security Act provides first federal-state unemployment and old-age insurance.
**1935 (Aug. 31)** Neutrality Act provides measures intended to keep U.S. from becoming involved in Italian-Ethiopian War.
**1935 (Nov. 9)** CIO labor organization formed; begins organizing unions in auto and steel industries using "sit-down" strikes.
**1936 (Jan. 6)** Supreme Court rules Agricultural Adjustment Act (AAA) unconstitutional.
**1937 (May 1)** Neutrality Act adopted to prevent U.S. involvement in Spanish civil war.
**1937 (July 22)** Court-packing legislation killed by U.S. Senate; had been sought by President Roosevelt

QUICK QUIZ: What is aphasia? See page 457.

**KEY EVENTS IN AMERICAN HISTORY** *(continued)*
to liberalize Supreme Court.
**1938 (June 25)   Wages and Hours Law** provides minimum wages of 40¢ an hour and maximum workweek of 40 hours (effective in 1940); labor by children under 16 outlawed.
**1939 (April 20)   First commercial TV broadcasts** by Radio Corporation of America.
**1939 (Aug. 2)** Hatch Act forbids federal employees below policy level from taking part in political campaigns.
**1939 (Sept. 5)** Neutrality of U.S. in World War II proclaimed by President Roosevelt (Germany had invaded Poland on Sept. 1).
**1939 (Nov. 4)   New Neutrality Act** permits "cash and carry" sales of arms to belligerents.
**1940 (Sept. 3)   U.S. gives Britain 50 destroyers** in exchange for military bases in West Indies and Newfoundland.
**1940 (Sept. 16)   First U.S. peacetime draft** for compulsory military service enacted.
**1941 (March 11)   Lend-Lease Act** enables President to supply materials to Britain and Soviet Union.
**1941 (Aug. 9–12)   Atlantic Charter** of postwar goals formulated in shipboard meetings off Newfoundland by President Roosevelt and British Prime Minister Churchill.
**1941 (Dec. 7)   Japanese bomb Pearl Harbor** naval base in Hawaii.
**1941 (Dec. 8)   Declaration of war on Japan** approved by Congress with only one dissenting vote.

**1941 (Dec. 11)   Germany and Italy declare war on U.S.**
**1942 (Aug. 13)   Secret Manhattan Project** to develop atomic bomb initiated; first nuclear chain reaction achieved by Enrico Fermi in Chicago on Dec. 2.
**1944 (June 6)   D-Day** landing by U.S. troops on Normandy coast of German-occupied France.
**1944 (June 22)   GI Bill of Rights** authorizes educational and other benefits for World War II veterans.
**1945 (Feb. 4–11)   Big Three meeting** at Yalta in the Soviet Union of Roosevelt, Churchill, and Stalin sets postwar plans, including formation of United Nations.
**1945 (April 12)   Harry S. Truman sworn in** as 33d President upon death of President Roosevelt at Warm Springs, Ga.
**1945 (May 8)   V-E Day,** formal end of war in Europe; Germany had signed unconditional surrender on May 7.
**1945 (June 26)   United Nations Charter** signed in San Francisco by delegates of 50 nations.
**1945 (July 16)   First atomic bomb** successfully exploded near Alamogordo, N.M.
**1945 (July 17–Aug. 2)   Potsdam Conference** in Germany attended by Truman, Stalin, and Churchill (succeeded by Clement Attlee) decides on four-power rule of Germany and issues surrender ultimatum to Japan.
**1945 (Aug. 6)   Atomic bomb dropped on Hiroshima;** on Japan's refusal to surrender, another bomb is dropped on Nagasaki on Aug. 9.
**1945 (Aug. 14)   Japan agrees to surrender.**
**1945 (Sept. 2)   V-J Day:** formal surrender of Japan aboard battleship USS *Missouri* at Tokyo.

# FROM COLD WAR TO PRESIDENT KENNEDY'S ASSASSINATION: 1946–1963

**1946 (March 5)   Communist "Iron Curtain"** has descended across Europe, former British Prime Minister Churchill warns in commencement address at Fulton, Mo.
**1946 (July 4)   Philippines granted independence.**
**1947 (March 12)   Truman Doctrine** announced by President to resist Soviet aggression and subversion with aid for Greece and Turkey.
**1947 (June 5)   Marshall Plan** proposed by Secretary of State George C. Marshall calling for U.S. aid to rebuild Europe and preserve its freedom; aid begun with enactment of European Recovery Program on April 3, 1948.
**1947 (June 23)   Taft-Hartley Act** passed by Congress over President Truman's veto bans closed shop and places other restrictions on labor unions.
**1947 (July 18)   Pacific Islands Trust Territory** placed under U.S. administration by UN.
**1947 (July 26)   Defense Department** created to coordinate U.S. military services.
**1948 (June)   Berlin airlift** begun by U.S. and Britain, carrying 2 million tons of supplies to West Berlin in 16 months to break Soviet blockade of city.
**1949 (April 4)   North Atlantic Treaty** creating NATO defense force signed by U.S. and 11 other nations.
**1949 (Oct. 21)   U.S. Communist Party's 11 top leaders** sentenced to prison for advocating overthrow of U.S. government.
**1950 (Jan. 21)   Alger Hiss,** former State Department official, convicted of perjury for denying membership in communist spy ring.
**1950 (June 27)   Korean War:** President Truman orders U.S. forces to aid South Korea, invaded by communist North Korea on June 25.
**1950 (Aug. 1)   Guam** organized as U.S. territory.
**1950 (Aug. 27)   U.S. railroads seized** by President Truman to prevent general strike; returned to private ownership on May 23, 1952.
**1950 (Dec. 11)   Supreme Court** rules that under 5th Amendment no one can be forced to testify against himself.
**1951 (March 1)   President limited to two terms** by 22d Amendment to U.S. Constitution.
**1951 (April 11)   Gen. Douglas MacArthur** relieved of command in Korea by President Truman for disregarding orders (MacArthur had sought to extend war into communist China).
**1951 (Sept. 4)   First transcontinental TV broadcast** by President Truman at Japanese peace-treaty conference in San Francisco.
**1952 (April 8)   Nation's steel mills seized** by President Truman to prevent strike; ruled as unconstitutional by Supreme Court on June 2.
**1952 (July 25)   Puerto Rico** becomes self-governing

commonwealth of U.S.
**1952 (Nov. 1)   First hydrogen bomb** exploded by U.S. at Enewetak atoll in Pacific.
**1953 (Jan. 20)   Dwight D. Eisenhower** inaugurated as 34th President of the United States.
**1953 (June 19)   Execution of Julius and Ethel Rosenberg** at Ossining, N.Y., convicted of giving atomic secrets to Soviet Union.
**1953 (July 27)   Korean War armistice** signed at Panmunjom, Korea, ending fighting.
**1954 (Jan. 21)   First atomic-powered submarine, USS** *Nautilus,* launched at Groton, Conn.
**1954 (April 22–June 17)   Televised public hearings of charges** by Sen. Joseph McCarthy of communist subversion in U.S. Army; U.S. Senate votes to condemn McCarthy on Dec. 2.
**1954 (May 17)   Racial segregation in public schools** banned by Supreme Court.
**1954 (Sept. 8)   Southeast Asia Treaty Organization (SEATO)** defense pact signed by U.S.
**1955 (Feb. 12)   President Eisenhower** sends U.S. military advisers to train South Vietnam's army in Indochina war.
**1955 (July 18–23)   Summit meeting** of U.S., Britain, Soviet Union, and France at Geneva, Switzerland, confirms independence of East and West Germany.
**1955 (Dec. 1)   Bus boycott** in Montgomery, Ala., begun by blacks under leadership of Rev. Martin Luther King Jr.; leads to Supreme Court ruling on Nov. 13, 1956, against segregation on buses.
**1955 (Dec. 5)   AFL and CIO merge,** with George Meany becoming president.
**1956 (June 29)   Federal-Aid Highways Act** provides $32.5 billion to build 41,000-mile interstate highway system over next 13 years.
**1957 (Sept. 24)   President Eisenhower** orders federal troops to Little Rock, Ark., to protect black students desegregating high school.
**1958 (Jan. 31)   *Explorer I,*** first U.S. space satellite, launched from Cape Canaveral, Fla.
**1958 (Dec. 10)   First jet service in U.S.** begun by National Airlines on New York–Miami run.
**1959 (Jan. 3)   Alaska** becomes 49th state.
**1959 (July 21)   First atomic merchant ship,** *Savannah,* launched at Camden, N.J.
**1959 (Aug. 21)   Hawaii** becomes 50th state.
**1959 (Sept. 15–27)   Summit meeting** at Camp David, Md., between President Eisenhower and Soviet Premier Nikita Khrushchev calls for "peaceful coexistence."
**1959 (Dec. 1)   Antarctica Treaty** signed by U.S. and 11 other nations guaranteeing continent's neutrality.
**1960 (Jan. 19)   U.S. and Japan sign** mutual-defense treaty for military assistance.

1960 (May 1) U.S. U-2 spy plane shot down over Soviet Union.
1960 (May 16) Summit conference in Paris broken off by Khrushchev over U-2 incident despite apology by President Eisenhower.
1961 (Jan. 3) President Eisenhower ends diplomatic relations with communist Cuba.
1961 (Jan. 20) John F. Kennedy inaugurated as 35th President of the United States.
1961 (March 1) Peace Corps created by President Kennedy to help developing nations.
1961 (April 3) Washington, D.C., residents given vote for President by 23d Amendment.
1961 (April 17) Unsuccessful Bay of Pigs invasion of Cuba led by U.S. CIA and Cuban exiles with authorization of President Kennedy.
1961 (June 3–4) Summit meeting by Kennedy and Khrushchev at Vienna, Austria, unsuccessfully discusses reunification of Germany.
1961 (Dec. 11) U.S. provides South Vietnam with armed helicopters and crews to fight communists; U.S. forces in Vietnam total 3,200.
1962 (Feb. 20) First U.S. astronaut to orbit Earth:

Lt. Col. John H. Glenn Jr.
1962 (May 17) U.S. troops sent to Thailand to prevent possible communist invasion.
1962 (June 27) U.S. defense of Taiwan against attack by communist China pledged by President Kennedy.
1962 (Oct. 22–28) Cuban missile crisis: President Kennedy imposes naval and air blockade on Cuba, forcing Soviet Union to withdraw nuclear missiles.
1963 (June 17) Bible reading or prayers cannot be required in public schools, Supreme Court rules.
1963 (Aug. 28) Black equal-rights demonstration in Washington by 200,000 persons led by Rev. Martin Luther King Jr.
1963 (Aug. 30) Hot-line telephone set up between White House and Kremlin.
1963 (Sept. 14) First quintuplets in U.S. born to Mrs. Andrew Fischer in Aberdeen, S.D.
1963 (Oct. 10) Ban begins on atomic tests in atmosphere in treaty signed by U.S., Britain, and Soviet Union.
1963 (Nov. 22) President Kennedy assassinated in Dallas, Texas, by former U.S. marine Lee Harvey Oswald.

## ERA OF VIETNAM WAR, WATERGATE, AND ENERGY CRISIS: 1963–1980

1963 (Nov. 22) Lyndon B. Johnson sworn in as 36th President of the United States.
1964 (Feb. 4) Poll tax outlawed by 24th Amendment to U.S. Constitution.
1964 (July 2) Civil Rights Act forbids racial discrimination in hotels, motels, and restaurants, and by labor unions and businesses engaged in interstate commerce.
1964 (Aug. 7) Gulf of Tonkin Resolution gives President authority "to prevent further aggression" in Vietnam after reported North Vietnamese attack on U.S. destroyers on Aug. 2–4; first U.S. bombings of Vietnam on Aug. 5.
1964 (Aug. 20) War on Poverty program enacted.
1965 (April 28) U.S. Marines land in Dominican Republic to prevent communist takeover.
1965 (June 28) First ground combat by U.S. troops in Vietnam authorized by President Johnson; U.S. forces in Vietnam, 74,000.
1965 (Aug. 6) Voting Rights Act gives government power to force local communities to register blacks and allow them to vote.
1965 (Aug. 11–16) Riots by blacks in Watts area of Los Angeles result in 35 deaths.
1966 (May 30) First U.S. Moon landing by unmanned spaceship.
1966 (July 1) Medicare goes into effect, with medical insurance for persons 65 or older.
1967 (Jan. 27) Space Treaty signed banning military use of nuclear weapons in space.
1967 (Feb. 23) Presidential succession established by 25th Amendment to Constitution.
1967 (June 23–25) Summit meeting at Glassboro, N.J., by President Johnson and Soviet Premier Aleksei Kosygin.
1967 (July 23–30) Detroit riots by blacks put down by federal troops and National Guardsmen; 40 killed, more than 2,000 injured.
1968 U.S. population reaches 200 million.
1968 (Jan. 23) North Koreans seize USS Pueblo crew as spies; release them on Dec. 22.
1968 (April 4) Assassination of Rev. Martin Luther King Jr. in Memphis, Tenn.; followed by racial riots in more than 100 cities.
1968 (June 5) Sen. Robert F. Kennedy shot in Los Angeles; dies on June 6.
1968 (June 26) Iwo Jima and Bonin Islands returned to Japan by U.S.
1968 (July 1) Treaty on Nonproliferation of Nuclear Weapons signed by U.S., Britain, and Soviet Union; effective on March 5, 1970.
1968 (Aug. 26–30) Anti-Vietnam War demonstration during Democratic national convention in Chicago put down by police and troops.
1969 (Jan. 20) Richard M. Nixon inaugurated as 37th President of the United States.
1969 (March) U.S. troops in Vietnam reach peak level of 541,500.
1969 (June 8) Plans to reduce U.S. troops in Vietnam announced by President Nixon.
1969 (July 20) First man to walk on Moon: U.S. as-

tronaut Neil Armstrong.
1969 (Oct. 15) Vietnam Moratorium Day brings out many antiwar demonstrators across nation.
1970 (April 30) President Nixon orders U.S. troops into Cambodia.
1970 (May 4) Four Kent State University students killed in Ohio when National Guard fires into war-protest demonstration.
1971 (March 29) Lt. William L. Calley Jr. convicted by court-martial of murder of 22 Vietnamese men, women, and children in 1968 My Lai massacre (Calley freed in 1974 after federal court overturns conviction).
1971 (April 20) Busing to achieve racially balanced schools upheld by Supreme Court.
1971 (May 2–5) Over 13,400 antiwar demonstrators arrested in Washington, D.C.
1971 (June 13) Secret Pentagon Papers study of Vietnam War begins to be published in series in New York Times and Washington Post; federal government obtains injunction on June 15 against further publication, but Supreme Court on June 30 throws out injunction.
1971 (July 5) Voting age lowered to 18 by 26th Amendment to U.S. Constitution.
1971 (Aug. 15) Freeze on wages and prices to combat inflation announced by President Nixon.
1972 (Feb. 21–28) Visit to communist China by President Nixon reverses U.S. policy on China.
1972 (May 15) Okinawa and Ryukyu Islands returned to Japan after 27-year U.S. rule.
1972 (May 15) Alabama Gov. George Wallace wounded and paralyzed from waist down in attempted assassination at Laurel, Md.; Arthur H. Bremmer convicted on Aug. 4 of attempted assassination and sentenced to 63 years in prison.
1972 (May 22–30) Summit meeting in Moscow between President Nixon and Soviet leader Leonid I. Brezhnev achieves first agreement limiting production of atomic weapons; ratified by U.S. Senate on Aug. 3.
1972 (June 17) Watergate offices of Democratic National Committee in Washington, D.C., secretly wiretapped; police arrest five men in act of burglarizing offices; on June 22, Nixon tells press conference, "There is no involvement by the White House."
1972 (June 17–23) Hurricane Agnes rakes East Coast from Florida to New York; storm and floods kill 122, cause $2.1 billion in damages.
1972 (June 19) Government practice of wiretapping without court order is illegal, Supreme Court rules.
1972 (July 31) Democratic vice-presidential candidate withdraws: Sen. Thomas F. Eagleton quits as candidate after disclosure he had been treated for psychiatric problems; former Peace Corps director Sargent Shriver chosen to succeed him on Democratic ticket on Aug. 5.
1972 (Sept. 15) First Watergate indictments: Seven persons indicted for break-in at Democratic national headquarters; later, White House counsel John Dean III tells Senate committee that President Nixon congratulated him on that day for keeping indictments from reaching higher in Nixon administration.

QUICK QUIZ: What countries are members of OPEC? See page 428.

**KEY EVENTS IN AMERICAN HISTORY** *(continued)*

**1972 (Nov. 7)**  President Nixon wins election to second term by landslide 60.7% of vote.
**1973 (Jan. 28)**  Cease-fire ends U.S. participation in Vietnam War; last troops leave Vietnam on March 29.
**1973 (Jan. 30)**  Watergate burglary trial ends with conviction of seven men; two were former officials of Committee to Reelect the President and one a former White House consultant.
**1973 (Feb. 7)**  Senate Watergate investigating committee established by unanimous vote of Senate; leads to conviction of three cabinet officers and Nixon's two chief White House aides.
**1973 (Feb. 27)**  Siege of Wounded Knee, S.D., begun by Indians protesting treatment by government; two Indians killed in gunfights with federal officers; siege ends on May 8.
**1973 (April–May)**  Worst Mississippi River floods in 46 years cause $500 million damage, leave 50,000 homeless.
**1973 (May 11)**  Pentagon Papers espionage trial of Dr. Daniel Ellsberg dismissed by federal judge after disclosure that White House agents committed burglary in seeking evidence.
**1973 (June 16–24)**  Summit meeting between President Nixon and Soviet leader Brezhnev in U.S. achieves nine agreements for U.S.-Soviet cooperation.
**1973 (July 1)**  Congress orders halt to U.S. bombing of Cambodia and all U.S. military action in Indochina by Aug. 15.
**1973 (July 16)**  Existence of White House tapes revealed: Witness tells Senate Watergate hearing that conversations in White House have been taped since 1970; after long court battle, President Nixon gives up tapes to investigators; tapes show President took part in effort to cover up Watergate scandals.
**1973 (Oct. 10)**  Vice President Spiro Agnew resigns, accepts conviction for income tax evasion to avoid trial on charges of accepting bribes.
**1973 (Oct. 17)**  Arab nations cut oil exports to U.S. in retaliation for U.S. aid to Israel.
**1973 (Nov. 7)**  Limitations on President's war-making powers voted by Congress over veto.
**1973 (Nov. 25)**  Emergency restrictions on use of fuel and energy announced by President Nixon.
**1973 (Dec. 6)**  Gerald R. Ford sworn in as Vice President: first Vice President appointed under 25th Amendment to U.S. Constitution.
**1973 (Dec. 8)**  President Nixon discloses tax records; he paid less than $6,000 in income taxes for 1970–73 on income over $1 million.
**1974 (Feb. 4)**  Nation's first political kidnapping: Patricia Hearst, 19-year-old granddaughter of publisher William Randolph Hearst, taken from apartment in Berkeley, Calif.; she later joins captors in terrorist activities and eludes FBI for 19 months until surrendering on Sept. 18, 1975; jury finds her guilty of bank robbery in 1976; sentenced to 7 years in prison.
**1974 (July 24)**  U.S. Supreme Court rules President Nixon must turn over White House tapes and documents to special Watergate prosecutor.
**1974 (Aug. 9)**  President Nixon resigns to avoid impeachment and removal by Congress because of role in Watergate scandals.
**1974 (Aug. 9)**  Gerald R. Ford becomes 38th President of the United States.
**1974 (Sept. 8)**  Full pardon granted to Nixon by President Ford.
**1974 (Sept. 16)**  Conditional amnesty plan for Vietnam War draft evaders and deserters announced by President Ford.
**1974 (Oct. 15)**  Presidential election campaign public financing law signed by President Ford.
**1974 (Nov. 23–24)**  Summit meeting in Vladivostok, Soviet Union; Ford and Brezhnev agree in principle to "put cap on arms race."
**1975 (Jan. 1)**  Watergate cover-up convictions: After 3-month trial, jury finds guilty President Nixon's top aides H.R. Haldeman and John D. Ehrlichman, and former Attorney General John N. Mitchell.
**1975 (May)**  Unemployment rises to 9.2% with 8.5 million Americans out of work; highest unemployment rate since Great Depression.
**1975 (May 7)**  End of Vietnam War Era announced by President Ford one week after South Vietnam surrenders to communists.
**1975 (May 14–15)**  *Mayaguez* incident: U.S. Marines rescue U.S. freighter from Cambodians.

**1975 (July 1)**  New York City financial crisis causes layoff of 40,000 city workers.
**1975 (July 17)**  U.S. and Soviet spaceships link up for Apollo-Soyuz handshake in space.
**1975 (July 30)**  Former Teamsters Union leader James Hoffa mysteriously disappears in Michigan; believed slain by Mafia.
**1975 (Aug. 1)**  President Ford signs Helsinki pact endorsing post-World War II European boundaries and endorsing human rights.
**1975 (Sept. 5 and 22)**  Two assassination attempts on President Ford made in California.
**1975 (Dec. 20)**  Vietnam refugee program completed with resettlement of 130,000 in U.S.
**1976**  U.S. military service academies for first time admit women for officer training.
**1976 (June 5)**  300-foot-high Teton Dam collapses in Idaho; kills 69; estimated damage $1 billion.
**1976 (June 20)**  U.S. closes last military bases in Thailand at request of Thai government.
**1976 (July 4)**  U.S. celebrates 200th birthday with parades, picnics, fireworks, and prayers.
**1976 (Sept. 23)**  First face-to-face presidential public debate in history held on TV between incumbent President Ford and challenger, Democratic presidential candidate Jimmy Carter.
**1976 (Oct. 4)**  Death penalty for murder upheld by Supreme Court; lifts stay that blocked state executions for 10 years.
**1977 (Jan. 20)**  Jimmy Carter inaugurated as 39th President of the United States.
**1977 (March 1)**  U.S. extends coastal limit to 200 miles for control of fishing.
**1977 (June 20)**  Trans-Alaska $7.7 billion pipeline begins carrying oil 789 miles from Prudhoe Bay oil field to Valdez, Alaska.
**1977 (Sept. 7)**  President Carter signs Panama treaties, agreeing to turn over Panama Canal to Panama on Dec. 31, 1999; ratified April 18, 1978.
**1977 (Oct. 1)**  U.S. Department of Energy becomes 12th cabinet-level executive department, with James R. Schlesinger as first U.S. secretary of energy.
**1978 (Jan. 27)**  Nation's GNP (gross national product) reaches $2 trillion mark: economy first reached $1 trillion level in 1972.
**1978 (June 6)**  California voters begin tax revolt: Referendum approves Proposition 13, cutting local property taxes in state from $12 billion to $5 billion; sets off nationwide efforts to put lids on government spending.
**1978 (Dec. 1)**  National Park System doubled: President Carter adds 56 million acres of Alaskan land, designating 17 new national monuments.
**1979 (Jan. 1)**  U.S. and China establish diplomatic relations: For first time since communists seized power in China in 1949, U.S. and China exchange full ambassadors; at same time U.S. breaks formal relations with nationalist Chinese government on Taiwan.
**1979 (Feb. 5)**  U.S. population reaches 220 million: New mark registered by census clock in Washington, D.C.
**1979 (Feb. 12)**  President Carter asks for voluntary energy conservation: Cut-off of oil imports from Iran brings gasoline shortages to nation in next several months.
**1979 (March 28)**  First major atomic accident in U.S.: Malfunction in reactor at Three Mile Island near Harrisburg, Pa., releases radioactive steam and threatens meltdown of uranium fuel rods; thousands evacuated from area.
**1979 (June 8)**  MX missile system approved: President Carter gives go-ahead to $30 billion plan to deploy about 200 new intercontinental missiles in underground site.
**1979 (June 13)**  Sioux Indians win $100 million in land claim: Court awards compensation for land confiscated in 1877.
**1979 (Oct. 1)**  Panama Canal Zone returned to Panama: U.S. turns over control of 553-square-mile area that had been under American jurisdiction since 1904.
**1979 (Oct. 17)**  U.S. Department of Education approved in legislation signed by President Carter; becomes 13th cabinet-level department of federal government; Shirley M. Hufstedler appointed as first secretary of education.
**1979 (Oct 23)**  Emergency gasoline rationing approved: Congress gives President power to invoke rationing when necessary.
**1980 For events of 1980,** see pages 7–31.

# DECLARATION OF INDEPENDENCE

IN CONGRESS, JULY 4, 1776.

The unanimous Declaration of the thirteen united States of America,

Although the colonists had been openly fighting the British since the battles of Lexington and Concord in 1775, many members of the Continental Congress still sought a compromise. However, such patriots as John Hancock, John Adams, and Samuel Adams demanded complete independence from Britain. On June 7, 1776, Richard Henry Lee of Virginia called for a resolution on independence.

The actual drafting of the document was entrusted to Thomas Jefferson.

On July 4, 1776, Congress adopted the Declaration of Independence.

In Congress, July 4, 1776,
The unanimous Declaration of the
thirteen united States of America,

When in the Course of human events, it becomes necessary for one people to dissolve the political bands which have connected them with another, and to assume among the Powers of the earth, the separate and equal station to which the Laws of Nature and of Nature's God entitle them, a decent respect to the opinions of mankind requires that they should declare the causes which impel them to the separation.

We hold these truths to be self-evident, that all men are created equal, that they are endowed by their Creator with certain unalienable Rights, that among these are Life, Liberty and the pursuit of Happiness. That to secure these rights, Governments are instituted among Men, deriving their just powers from the consent of the governed. That whenever any Form of Government becomes destructive of these ends, it is the Right of the People to alter or to abolish it, and to institute new Government, laying its foundation on such principles and organizing its powers in such form, as to them shall seem most likely to effect their Safety and Happiness. Prudence, indeed, will dictate that Governments long established should not be changed for light and transient causes; and accordingly all experience hath shown, that mankind are more disposed to suffer, while evils are sufferable, than to right themselves by abolishing the forms to which they are accustomed. But when a long train of abuses and usurpations, pursuing invariably the same Object evinces a design to reduce them under absolute Despotism, it is their right, it is their duty, to throw off such Government, and to provide new Guards for their future security.—Such has been the patient sufferance of these Colonies; and such is now the necessity which constrains them to alter their former Systems of Government. The history of the present King of Great Britain is a history of repeated injuries and usurpations, all having in direct object the establishment of an absolute Tyranny over these States. To prove this, let Facts be submitted to a candid world.

He has refused his Assent to Laws, the most wholesome and necessary for the public good.

He has forbidden his Governors to pass Laws of immediate and pressing importance, unless suspended in their operation till his Assent should be obtained; and when so suspended, he has utterly neglected to attend to them.

He has refused to pass other Laws for the accommodation of large districts of people, unless those people would relinquish the right of Representation in the Legislature, a right inestimable to them and formidable to tyrants only.

He has called together legislative bodies at places unusual, uncomfortable, and distant from the depository of their Public Records, for the sole purpose of fatiguing them into compliance with his measures.

He has dissolved Representative Houses repeatedly, for opposing with manly firmness his invasions on the rights of the people.

He has refused for a long time, after such dissolutions, to cause others to be elected; whereby the Legislative Powers, incapable of Annihilation, have returned to the People at large for their exercise; the State remaining in the mean time exposed to all the dangers of invasion from without, and convulsions within.

He has endeavoured to prevent the population of these States; for that purpose obstructing the Laws of Naturalization of Foreigners; refusing to pass others to migration hither, and raising the conditions of new Appropriations of Lands.

He has obstructed the Administration of Justice, by refusing his Assent to Laws for establishing Judiciary Powers.

QUICK QUIZ: Who was the first UN secretary-general? See page 423.

## DECLARATION OF INDEPENDENCE *(continued)*

He has made Judges dependent on his Will alone, for the tenure of their offices, and the amount and payment of their salaries.

He has erected a multitude of New Offices, and sent hither swarms of Officers to harass our People, and eat out their substance.

He has kept among us, in times of peace, Standing Armies without the Consent of our legislatures.

He has affected to render the Military independent of and superior to the Civil Power.

He has combined with others to subject us to a jurisdiction foreign to our constitution, and unacknowledged by our laws; giving his Assent to their acts of pretended legislation:

For quartering large bodies of armed troops among us:

For protecting them, by a mock Trial, from Punishment for any Murders which they should commit on the Inhabitants of these States:

For cutting off our Trade with all parts of the world:

For imposing taxes on us without our Consent:

For depriving us in many cases, of the benefits of Trial by Jury:

For transporting us beyond Seas to be tried for pretended offences:

For abolishing the free System of English Laws in a neighbouring Province, and establishing therein an Arbitrary government, and enlarging its Boundaries so as to render it at once an example and fit instrument for introducing the same absolute rule into these Colonies:

For taking away our Charters, abolishing our most valuable Laws, and altering fundamentally the Forms of our Governments:

For suspending our own legislature, and declaring themselves invested with Power to legislate for us in all cases whatsoever.

He has abdicated Government here, by declaring us out of his Protection and waging War against us.

He has plundered our seas, ravaged our Coasts, burnt our towns, and destroyed the lives of our people.

He is at this time transporting large armies of foreign mercenaries to complete the works of death, desolation and tyranny, already begun with circumstances of Cruelty & perfidy scarcely paralleled in the most barbarous ages, and totally unworthy the Head of a civilized nation.

He has constrained our fellow Citizens taken Captive on the high Seas to bear Arms against their Country, to become the executioners of their friends and Brethren, or to fall themselves by their Hands.

He has excited domestic insurrections amongst us, and has endeavoured to bring on the inhabitants of our frontiers, the merciless Indian Savages, whose known rule of warfare, is an undistinguished destruction of all ages, sexes and conditions.

In every stage of these Oppressions We have Petitioned for Redress in the most humble terms: Our repeated Petitions have been answered only by repeated injury. A Prince, whose character is thus marked by every act which may define a Tyrant, is unfit to be the ruler of a free People.

Nor have We been wanting in attention to our British brethren. We have warned them from time to time of attempts by their legislature to extend an unwarrantable jurisdiction over us. We have reminded them of the circumstances of our emigration and settlement here. We have appealed to their native justice and magnanimity, and we have conjured them by the ties of our common kindred to disavow these usurpations, which, would inevitably interrupt our connections and correspondence. They too have been deaf to the voice of justice and of consanguinity. We must, therefore, acquiesce in the necessity, which denounces our Separation, and hold them, as we hold the rest of mankind, Enemies in War, in Peace Friends.

We, therefore, the Representatives of the United States of America, in General Congress, Assembled, appealing to the Supreme Judge of the world for the rectitude of our intentions, do, in the Name, and by Authority of the good People of these Colonies, solemnly publish and declare, That these United Colonies are, and of Right ought to be Free and Independent States; that they are Absolved from all Allegiance to the British Crown, and that all political connection between them and the State of Great Britain, is and ought to be totally dissolved; and that as Free and Independent States, they have full Power to levy War, conclude Peace, contract Alliances, establish Commerce, and to do all other Acts and Things which Independent States may of right do. And for the support of this Declaration, with a firm reliance on the protection of Divine Providence, we mutually pledge to each other our Lives, our Fortunes and our sacred Honor.                **John Hancock**

**New Hampshire**
Josiah Bartlett
Wm. Whipple
Matthew Thornton
**Massachusetts-Bay**
Saml. Adams
John Adams
Robt. Treat Paine
Elbridge Gerry
**Rhode Island**
Step. Hopkins
William Ellery
**Connecticut**
Roger Sherman
Sam'el Huntington
Wm. Williams
Oliver Wolcott
**Georgia**
Button Gwinnett
Lyman Hall
Geo. Walton
**Maryland**
Samuel Chase
Wm. Paca
Thos. Stone
Charles Carroll
of Carrollton
**Virginia**
George Wythe
Richard Henry Lee
Th. Jefferson
Benja. Harrison
Ths. Nelson, Jr.
Francis Lightfoot Lee
Carter Braxton

**New York**
Wm. Floyd
Phil. Livingston
Frans. Lewis
Lewis Morris
**Pennsylvania**
Robt. Morris
Benjamin Rush
Benja. Franklin
John Morton
Geo. Clymer
Jas. Smith
Geo. Taylor
James Wilson
Geo. Ross
**Delaware**
Caesar Rodney
Geo. Read
Tho. M'Kean
**North Carolina**
Wm. Hooper
Joseph Hewes
John Penn
**South Carolina**
Edward Rutledge
Thos. Heyward, Junr.
Thomas Lynch, Junr.
Arthur Middleton
**New Jersey**
Richd. Stockton
Jno. Witherspoon
Fras. Hopkinson
John Hart
Abra. Clark

# CONSTITUTION OF THE UNITED STATES

The Constitution of the United States embodies the fundamental principles upon which the American republic rests. A *living* instrument of government, the Constitution has been kept abreast of the times through the process of amendment, by federal laws that elaborate its clauses, and by judicial interpretation by the U.S. Supreme Court.

The original constitution of the American states, the Articles of Confederation, was ratified in 1781. Although the Articles established a kind of national unity, it did not provide for a strong central government. The individual states still held power.

When it became apparent that government under the Articles was, in the words of George Washington, "little more than the shadow without substance," agitation for a strong federal government began. This resulted in the Constitutional Convention of 1787, which met in Philadelphia to revise the Articles of Confederation.

The convention, presided over by George Washington, was torn by sharp conflict over the apportionment of power between the smaller states and the larger states.

Finally, a compromise measure won approval. This measure provided for a lower house to be elected according to population (the House of Representatives) and an upper house to be chosen by the state legislatures (the Senate). This provision for the

Senate held true until 1913, when the 17th Amendment provided for the direct popular election of senators.

After the Constitution was issued, the struggle for ratification was bitter, especially over the conferring of new powers on the central government. Alexander Hamilton, John Jay, and James Madison, in a series of newspaper essays now known as the *Federalist Papers,* did much to promote the acceptance of the Constitution. Delaware, on Dec. 7, 1787, became the first state to ratify the new Constitution. On June 21, 1788, by a vote of 57 to 46, New Hampshire became the ninth state to ratify.

By the terms of the Constitution, ratification by nine states was enough for its establishment. But the government could not succeed without the addition of New York and Virginia, neither of which had ratified. On June 25, 1788, Virginia ratified, over many objections. Finally, on July 26, 1788, New York ratified, with a recommendation that a bill of rights be appended.

With 11 states having thus ratified the Constitution, the Congress of the Confederation passed a resolution on Sept. 13, 1788, to put the new Constitution into operation. On April 1–6, 1789, the first session of the 1st U.S. Congress convened. Later, North Carolina added its ratification on Nov. 21, 1789, and Rhode Island on May 29, 1790.

## PREAMBLE

We the People of the United States, in Order to form a more perfect Union, establish Justice, insure domestic Tranquility, provide for the common defence, promote the general Welfare, and secure the Blessings of Liberty to ourselves and our Posterity, do ordain and establish this Constitution for the United States of America.

## ARTICLE I (Legislative Branch)

**Section 1.** All legislative Powers herein granted shall be vested in a Congress of the United States, which shall consist of a Senate and House of Representatives.

**Section 2.** The House of Representatives shall be composed of Members chosen every second Year by the People of the several States, and the Electors in each State shall have the Qualifications requisite for Electors of the most numerous Branch of the State Legislature.

No Person shall be a Representative who shall not have attained to the Age of twenty five Years, and been seven Years a Citizen of the United States, and who shall not, when elected, be an Inhabitant of that State in which he shall be chosen.

Representatives and direct Taxes shall be apportioned among the several States which may be included within this Union, according to their respective Numbers, [which shall be determined

by adding to the whole Number of free Persons, including those bound to Service for a Term of Years, and excluding Indians not taxed, three fifths of all other Persons.] [1] The actual Enumeration shall be made within three Years after the first Meeting of the Congress of the United States, and within every subsequent Term of ten Years, in such Manner as they shall by Law direct. The Number of Representatives shall not exceed one for every thirty Thousand, but each State shall have at Least one Representative; and until such enumeration shall be made, the State of New Hampshire shall be entitled to chuse three, Massachusetts eight, Rhode-Island and Providence Plantations one, Connecticut five, New-York six, New Jersey four, Pennsylvania eight, Delaware one, Maryland six, Virginia ten, North Carolina five, South Carolina five, and Georgia three.

When vacancies happen in the Representation from any State, the Executive Authority thereof shall issue Writs of Election to fill such Vacancies.

The House of Representatives shall chuse their speaker and other Officers; and shall have the sole Power of Impeachment.

**Section 3.** The Senate of the United States shall be composed of two Senators from each state, [chosen by the Legislature thereof,] [2] for six Years; and each Senator shall have one Vote. Immediately after they shall be assembled in

[1] Changed by 14th Amendment, section 2.   [2] Changed by 17th Amendment, section 1.

**CONSTITUTION OF U.S.** *(continued)*

Consequence of the first Election, they shall be divided as equally as may be into three Classes. The Seats of the Senators of the first Class shall be vacated at the Expiration of the second Year, of the second Class at the Expiration of the fourth Year, and of the third Class at the Expiration of the sixth Year, so that one third may be chosen every second Year; [and if Vacancies happen by Resignation, or otherwise, during the Recess of the Legislature of any State, the Executive thereof may make temporary Appointments until the next Meeting of the Legislature, which shall then fill such Vacancies.] [3]

No Person shall be a Senator who shall not have attained to the Age of thirty years, and been nine Years a Citizen of the United States, and who shall not, when elected, be an Inhabitant of that State for which he shall be chosen.

The Vice President of the United States shall be President of the Senate, but shall have no Vote, unless they be equally divided.

The Senate shall chuse their other Officers, and also a President pro tempore, in the Absence of the Vice President, or when he shall exercise the Office of President of the United States.

The Senate shall have the sole Power to try all Impeachments. When sitting for that Purpose, they shall be on Oath or Affirmation. When the President of the United States is tried, the Chief Justice shall preside: And no Person shall be convicted without the Concurrence of two thirds of the Members present.

Judgment in Cases of Impeachment shall not extend further than to removal from Office, and disqualification to hold and enjoy any Office of honor, Trust or Profit under the United States: but the Party convicted shall nevertheless be liable and subject to Indictment, Trial, Judgment and Punishment, according to Law.

**Section 4.** The Times, Places and Manner of holding Elections for Senators and Representatives, shall be prescribed in each State by the Legislature thereof; but the Congress may at any time by Law make or alter such Regulations, except as to the Places of chusing Senators.

[The Congress shall assemble at least once in every Year, and such Meeting shall be on the first Monday in December, unless they shall by Law appoint a different Day.] [4]

**Section 5.** Each House shall be the Judge of the Elections, Returns and Qualifications of its own Members, and a Majority of each shall constitute a Quorum to do Business; but a smaller Number may adjourn from day to day, and may be authorized to compel the Attendance of absent Members, in such Manner, and under such Penalties as each House may provide.

Each House may determine the Rules of its Proceedings, punish its Members for disorderly Behaviour, and, with the Concurrence of two thirds, expel a Member.

Each House shall keep a Journal of its Proceedings, and from time to time publish the same, excepting such Parts as may in their Judgment require Secrecy; and the Yeas and Nays of the Members of either House on any question shall, at the Desire of one fifth of those Present be entered on the Journal.

Neither House, during the Session of Congress, shall without the Consent of the other, adjourn for more than three days, nor to any other Place than that in which the two Houses shall be sitting.

**Section 6.** The Senators and Representatives shall receive a Compensation for their Services, to be ascertained by Law, and paid out of the Treasury of the United States. They shall in all Cases, except Treason, Felony and Breach of the Peace, be privileged from Arrest during their Attendance at the Session of their respective Houses, and in going to and returning from the same; and for any Speech or Debate in either House, they shall not be questioned in any other Place.

No Senator or Representative shall, during the Time for which he was elected, be appointed to any civil Office under the Authority of the United States, which shall have been created, or the Emoluments whereof shall have been encreased during such time; and no Person holding any Office under the United States, shall be a Member of either House during his Continuance in Office.

**Section 7.** All Bills for raising Revenue shall originate in the House of Representatives; but the Senate may propose or concur with Amendments as on other Bills.

Every Bill which shall have passed the House of Representatives and the Senate, shall, before it become a Law, be presented to the President of the United States; If he approve he shall sign it, but if not he shall return it, with his Objections to that House in which it shall have originated, who shall enter the Objections at large on their Journal, and proceed to reconsider it. If after such Reconsideration two thirds of that House shall agree to pass the Bill, it shall be sent together with the Objections, to the other House, by which it shall likewise be reconsidered, and if approved by two thirds of that House, it shall become a Law. But in all such Cases the Votes of both Houses shall be determined by Yeas and Nays, and the Names of the Persons voting for and against the Bill shall be entered on the Journal of each House respectively. If any Bill shall not be returned by the President within ten Days (Sundays excepted) after it shall have been presented to him, the Same shall be a Law, in like Manner as if he had signed it, unless the Congress by their Adjournment prevent its Return, in which Case it shall not be a Law.

Every Order, Resolution, or Vote to which the Concurrence of the Senate and House of Representatives may be necessary (except on a question of Adjournment) shall be presented to the President of the United States; and before the Same shall take Effect, shall be approved by him, or being disapproved by him, shall be repassed by two thirds of the Senate and House of Representatives, according to the Rules and Limitations prescribed in the Case of a Bill.

**Section 8.** The Congress shall have Power To lay and collect taxes, Duties, Imposts and Excises, to pay the Debts and provide for the common Defence and general Welfare of the United States; but all Duties, Imposts and Excises shall be uniform throughout the United States;

To Borrow Money on the Credit of the United States;

To regulate Commerce with foreign Nations, and among the several States, and with the

---

[3] Changed by 17th Amendment, clause 2.   [4] Changed by 20th Amendment, section 2.

Indian Tribes;

To establish an uniform Rule of Naturalization, and uniform Laws on the subject of Bankruptcies throughout the United States;

To coin Money, regulate the Value thereof, and of foreign Coin, and fix the Standard of Weights and Measures;

To provide for the Punishment of counterfeiting the Securities and current Coin of the United States;

To establish Post Offices and post Roads;

To promote the Progress of Science and useful Arts, by securing for limited Times to Authors and Inventors the exclusive Right to their respective Writings and Discoveries;

To constitute Tribunals inferior to the supreme Court;

To define and punish Piracies and Felonies committed on the high Seas, and Offences against the Law of Nations;

To declare War, grant Letters of Marque and Reprisal, and make Rules concerning Captures on Land and Water;

To raise and support Armies, but no Appropriation of Money to that Use shall be for a longer Term than two Years;

To provide and maintain a Navy;

To make Rules for the Government and Regulation of the land and naval Forces;

To provide for calling forth the Militia to execute the Laws of the Union, suppress insurrections and repel Invasions;

To provide for organizing, arming, and disciplining, the Militia, and for governing such Part of them as may be employed in the Service of the United States, reserving to the States respectively, the Appointment of the Officers, and the Authority of training the Militia according to the discipline prescribed by Congress;

To exercise exclusive Legislation in all Cases whatsoever, over such District (not exceeding ten Miles square) as may, by Cession of Particular States, and the Acceptance of Congress, become the Seat of the Government of the United States, and to exercise like Authority over all Places purchased by the Consent of the Legislature of the State in which the Same shall be for the Erection of Forts, Magazines, Arsenals, dock-Yards, and other needful Buildings;—And

To make all Laws which shall be necessary and proper for carrying into Execution the foregoing Powers, and all other Powers vested by this Constitution in the Government of the United States, or in any Department or Officer thereof.

**Section 9.** The Migration or Importation of such Persons as any of the States now existing shall think proper to admit, shall not be prohibited by the Congress prior to the Year one thousand eight hundred and eight, but a Tax or duty may be imposed on such Importation, not exceeding ten dollars for each Person.

The Privilege of the Writ of Habeas Corpus shall not be suspended, unless when in Cases of Rebellion or Invasion the public Safety may require it.

No Bill of Attainder or ex post facto Law shall be passed.

[No Capitation, or other direct Tax shall be laid, unless in Proportion to the Census or Enumeration herein before directed to be taken.] [5]

No Tax or Duty shall be laid on Articles exported from any State.

No Preference shall be given by any Regulation of Commerce or Revenue to the Ports of one State over those of another: nor shall Vessels bound to, or from, one State, be obliged to enter, clear, or pay Duties in another.

No Money shall be drawn from the Treasury, but in Consequence of Appropriations made by Law; and a regular Statement and Account of the Receipts and Expenditures of all public Money shall be published from time to time.

No Title of Nobility shall be granted by the United States: And no Person holding any Office of Profit or Trust under them, shall, without the Consent of the Congress, accept of any present, Emolument, Office, or Title, of any kind whatever, from any King, Prince, or foreign State.

**Section 10.** No State shall enter into any Treaty, Alliance, or Confederation; grant Letters of Marque and Reprisal; coin Money; emit Bills of Credit; make any Thing but gold and silver Coin a Tender in Payment of Debts; pass any Bill of Attainder, ex post facto Law, or Law impairing the Obligation of Contracts, or grant any Title of Nobility.

No State shall, without the Consent of the Congress, lay any Imposts or Duties on Imports or Exports, except what may be absolutely necessary for executing its inspection Laws: and the net Produce of all Duties and Imposts, laid by any State on Imports or Exports, shall be for the Use of the Treasury of the United States; and all such Laws shall be subject to the Revision and Controul of the Congress.

No State shall, without the Consent of Congress, lay any Duty of Tonnage, keep Troops, or Ships of War in time of Peace, enter into any Agreement or Compact with another State, or with a foreign Power, or engage in War, unless actually invaded, or in such imminent Danger as will not admit of delay.

### ARTICLE II   (Executive Branch)

**Section 1.** The executive Power shall be vested in a President of the United States of America. He shall hold his Office during the Term of four Years, and, together with the Vice President,[6] chosen for the same term, be elected, as follows

Each State shall appoint, in such Manner as the Legislature thereof may direct, a Number of Electors, equal to the whole Number of Senators and Representatives to which the State may be entitled in the Congress: but no Senator or Representative, or Person holding an Office of Trust or Profit under the United States, shall be appointed an Elector.

[The Electors shall meet in their respective States, and vote by Ballot for two Persons, of whom one at least shall be an Inhabitant of the same State with themselves. And they shall make a List of all the Persons voted for, and of the Number of Votes for each; which List they shall sign and certify, and transmit sealed to the Seat of the Government of the United States, directed to the President of the Senate. The President of the Senate shall, in the Presence of the Senate and House of Representa-

**CONSTITUTION OF U.S.** *(continued)*

tives, open all the Certificates, and the Votes shall then be counted. The Person having the greatest Number of Votes shall be the President, if such Number be a Majority of the whole Number of Electors appointed; and if there be more than one who have such Majority, and have an equal Number of Votes, then the House of Representatives shall immediately chuse by Ballot one of them for President: and if no Person have a Majority, then from the five highest on the list the said House shall in like Manner chuse the President. But in chusing the President, the Votes shall be taken by States, the Representation from each State having one Vote; a quorum for this Purpose shall consist of a Member or Members from two thirds of the States, and a Majority of all the States shall be necessary to a Choice. In every Case, after the Choice of the President, the Person having the greatest Number of Votes of the Electors shall be the Vice President. But if there should remain two or more who have equal Votes, the Senate shall chuse from them by Ballot the Vice President.] [7]

The Congress may determine the Time of chusing the Electors, and the Day on which they shall give their Votes: which Day shall be the same throughout the United States.

No Person except a natural born Citizen, or a Citizen of the United States, at the time of the Adoption of this Constitution, shall be eligible to the Office of President; neither shall any Person be eligible to that Office who shall not have attained to the Age of thirty five Years, and been fourteen Years a Resident within the United States.

In Case of the Removal of the President from Office, or of his Death, Resignation, or Inability to discharge the Powers and Duties of the said Office, the Same shall devolve on the Vice President, and the Congress may by Law provide for the Case of Removal, Death, Resignation or Inability, both of the President and Vice President, declaring what Officer shall then act as President, and such Officer shall act accordingly, until the Disability be removed, or a President shall be elected. [8]

The President shall, at stated Times, receive for his Services, a Compensation, which shall neither be encreased nor diminished during the Period for which he shall have been elected, and he shall not receive within that Period any other Emolument from the United States, or any of them.

Before he enter on the Execution of his Office, he shall take the following Oath or Affirmation:—"I do solemnly swear (or affirm) that I will faithfully execute the Office of President of the United States, and will to the best of my Ability, preserve, protect and defend the Constitution of the United States."

**Section 2.** The President shall be Commander in Chief of the Army and Navy of the United States, and of the Militia of the several States, when called into the actual Service of the United States; he may require the Opinion, in writing, of the principal Officer in each of the executive Departments, upon any Subject relating to the Duties of their respective Offices, and he shall have Power to grant Reprieves and Pardons for Offences against the United States, except in Cases of Impeachment.

He shall have Power, by and with the Advice and Consent of the Senate, to make Treaties, provided two thirds of the Senators present concur; and he shall nominate, and by and with the Advice and Consent of the Senate, shall appoint Ambassadors, other public Ministers and Consuls, Judges of the supreme Court, and all other Officers of the United States, whose Appointments are not herein otherwise provided for, and which shall be established by Law: but the Congress may by Law vest the Appointment of such inferior Officers, as they think proper, in the President alone, in the Courts of Law, or in the Heads of Departments.

The President shall have Power to fill up all Vacancies that may happen during the Recess of the Senate, by granting Commissions which shall expire at the End of their next Session.

**Section 3.** He shall from time to time give to the Congress Information of the State of the Union, and recommend to their Consideration such Measures as he shall judge necessary and expedient; he may, on extraordinary Occasions, convene both Houses, or either of them, and in Case of Disagreement between them, with Respect to the Time of Adjournment, he may adjourn them to such Time as he shall think proper; he shall receive Ambassadors and other public Ministers; he shall take Care that the Laws be faithfully executed, and shall Commission all the Officers of the United States.

**Section 4.** The President, Vice President and all civil Officers of the United States, shall be removed from Office on Impeachment for, and Conviction of, Treason, Bribery, or other High Crimes and Misdemeanors.

## ARTICLE III (Judicial Branch)

**Section 1.** The judicial Power of the United States, shall be vested in one supreme Court, and in such Inferior Courts as the Congress may from time to time ordain and establish. The Judges, both of the supreme and inferior Courts, shall hold their Offices during good Behaviour, and shall, at stated Times, receive for their Services, a Compensation, which shall not be diminished during their Continuance in Office.

**Section 2.** The judicial Power shall extend to all Cases, in Law and Equity, arising under this Constitution, the Laws of the United States, and Treaties made, or which shall be made, under their Authority;—to all Cases affecting Ambassadors, other public Ministers and Consuls;—to all Cases of admiralty and maritime Jurisdiction;—to Controversies to which the United States shall be a Party;—to Controversies between two or more States; [between a State and Citizens of another State;] [9]—between Citizens of different States;—between Citizens of the same State claiming Lands under Grants of different States, and between a State, or the Citizens thereof, and foreign States, [Citizens or Subjects] [9].

In all Cases affecting Ambassadors, other public Ministers and Consuls, and those in which a State shall be Party, the Supreme Court shall have original Jurisdiction. In all the other Cases before mentioned, the supreme Court shall have appellate Jurisdiction, both as to Law and Fact, with such Exceptions, and under such Regulations as the Congress shall make.

The Trial of all Crimes, except in Cases of Impeachment, shall be by Jury; and such Trial shall

---

[7] Superseded by 12th Amendment.    [8] Affected by 25th Amendment.    [9] Affected by 11th Amendment.

be held in the State where the said Crimes shall have been committed; but when not committed within any State, the Trial shall be at such Place or Places as the Congress may by Law have directed.
**Section 3.** Treason against the United States, shall consist only in levying War against them, or in adhering to their Enemies, giving them Aid and Comfort. No Person shall be convicted of Treason unless on the Testimony of two Witnesses to the same overt Act, or on Confession in open Court.

The Congress shall have Power to declare the Punishment of Treason, but no Attainder of Treason shall work Corruption of Blood, or Forfeiture except during the Life of the Person attainted.

## ARTICLE IV   (Relations of States)

**Section 1.** Full Faith and Credit shall be given in each State to the public Acts, Records, and judicial Proceedings of every other State. And the Congress may by general Laws prescribe the Manner in which such Acts, Records and Proceedings shall be proved, and the Effect thereof.
**Section 2.** The Citizens of each State shall be entitled to all Privileges and Immunities of Citizens in the several States.

A Person charged in any State with Treason, Felony, or other Crime, who shall flee from Justice, and be found in another State, shall on Demand of the executive Authority of the State from which he fled, be delivered up, to be removed to the State having Jurisdiction of the Crime.

No Person held to Service or Labour in one State, under the Laws thereof, escaping into another, shall in Consequence of any Law or Regulation therein, be discharged from such Service or Labour, but shall be delivered up on Claim of the Party to whom such Service or Labour may be due.
**Section 3.** New States may be admitted by the Congress into this Union; but no new State shall be formed or erected within the Jurisdiction of any other State; nor any State be formed by the Junction of two or more States, or Parts of States, without the Consent of the Legislatures of the States concerned as well as of the Congress.

The Congress shall have Power to dispose of and make all needful Rules and Regulations respecting the Territory or other Property belonging to the United States; and nothing in this Constitution shall be so construed as to Prejudice any Claims of the United States, or of any particular State.
**Section 4.** The United States shall guarantee to every State in this Union a Republican Form of Government, and shall protect each of them against invasion; and on Application of the Legislature, or of the Executive (when the Legislature cannot be convened) against domestic Violence.

## ARTICLE V   (Amending the Constitution)

The Congress, whenever two thirds of both Houses shall deem it necessary, shall propose Amendments to this Constitution, or, on the Application of the Legislatures of two thirds of the several States, shall call a convention for proposing Amendments, which, in either Case, shall be valid to all Intents and Purposes, as Part of this Constitution, when ratified by the Legislatures of three fourths of the several States, or by Conventions in three fourths thereof, as the one or the other Mode of Ratification may be proposed by the Congress; Provided that no Amendment which may be made prior to the Year One thousand eight hundred and eight shall in any Manner affect the first and fourth Clauses in the Ninth Section of the first Article: and that no State, without its Consent, shall be deprived of its equal Suffrage in the Senate.

## ARTICLE VI   (National Debts)

All Debts contracted and Engagements entered into, before the Adoption of this Constitution, shall be as valid against the United States under this Constitution, as under the Confederation.

This Constitution, and the Laws of the United States which shall be made in Pursuance thereof; and all Treaties made, or which shall be made, under the Authority of the United States, shall be the supreme Law of the Land; and the Judges in every State shall be bound thereby, any Thing in the Constitution or Laws of any State to the Contrary notwithstanding.

The Senators and Representatives before mentioned, and the Members of the several State Legislatures, and all executive and judicial Officers, both of the United States and of the several States, shall be bound by Oath or Affirmation, to support this Constitution; but no religious Test shall ever be required as a Qualification to any Office or public Trust under the United States.

## ARTICLE VII   (Ratification)

The ratification of the Conventions of nine States, shall be sufficient for the Establishment of this Constitution between the States so ratifying the Same.

**DONE** in Convention by the Unanimous Consent of the States present the Seventeenth Day of September in the Year of our Lord one thousand seven hundred and Eighty seven and of the Independence of the United States of America the Twelfth **IN WITNESS** whereof we have hereunto subscribed our Names [1]

G° Washington—Presid[t]
and deputy from Virginia

**Delaware**
Geo: Read
Gunning Bedford jun
John Dickinson
Richard Bassett
Jaco: Broom
**Maryland**
James McHenry
Dan of S[t] Tho[s] Jenifer
Danl Carroll
**Virginia**
John Blair—
James Madison Jr
**North Carolina**
W[m] Blount
Rich[d] Dobbs Spaight
Hu Williamson
**South Carolina**
J. Rutledge
Charles Cotesworth Pinckney
Charles Pinckney
Pierce Butler
**Georgia**
William Few
Abr Baldwin

**New Hampshire**
John Langdon
Nicholas Gilman
**Massachusetts**
Nathaniel Gorham
Rufus King
**Connecticut**
W[m] Sam[l] Johnson
Roger Sherman
**New York**
Alexander Hamilton
**New Jersey**
Wil: Livingston
David Brearley
W[m] Paterson
Jona: Dayton
**Pennsylvania**
B Franklin
Thomas Mifflin
Rob[t] Morris
Geo. Clymer
Tho[s] FitzSimons
Jared Ingersoll
James Wilson
Gouv Morris

[1] The order of signing was geographical, beginning in the right column with New Hampshire.

# AMENDMENTS TO THE CONSTITUTION

## BILL OF RIGHTS

The first 10 amendments to the Constitution of the United States were ratified on Dec. 15, 1791, and form what is known as the Bill of Rights.

### AMENDMENT 1 (Freedoms, Assembly, Petitions)

Congress shall make no law respecting an establishment of religion, or prohibiting the free exercise thereof; or abridging the freedom of speech, or of the press; or the right of the people peaceably to assemble, and to petition the Government for a redress of grievances.

### AMENDMENT 2 (Right to Bear Arms)

A well regulated Militia, being necessary to the security of a free State, the right of the people to keep and bear Arms, shall not be infringed.

### AMENDMENT 3 (Quartering of Soldiers)

No Soldier shall, in time of peace be quartered in any house, without the consent of the Owner, nor in time of war, but in a manner to be prescribed by law.

### AMENDMENT 4 (Search and Arrest)

The right of the people to be secure in their persons, houses, papers, and effects, against unreasonable searches and seizures, shall not be violated, and no Warrants shall issue, but upon probable cause, supported by Oath or affirmation, and particularly describing the place to be searched, and the persons or things to be seized.

### AMENDMENT 5 (Rights in Criminal Cases)

No person shall be held to answer for a capital, or otherwise infamous crime, unless on a presentment or indictment of a Grand Jury, except in cases arising in the land or naval forces, or in the Militia, when in actual service in time of War or public danger; nor shall any person be subject for the same offence to be twice put in jeopardy of life or limb; nor shall be compelled in any criminal case to be a witness against himself, nor be deprived of life, liberty, or property, without due process of law; nor shall private property be taken for public use, without just compensation.

### AMENDMENT 6 (Right to Fair Trial)

In all criminal prosecutions, the accused shall enjoy the right to a speedy and public trial, by an impartial jury of the State and district wherein the crime shall have been committed, which district shall have been previously ascertained by law, and to be informed of the nature and cause of the accusation; to be confronted with the witnesses against him; to have compulsory process for obtaining witnesses in his favor, and to have the Assistance of Counsel for his defence.

### AMENDMENT 7 (Rights in Civil Cases)

In Suits at common law, where the value in controversy shall exceed twenty dollars, the right of trial by jury shall be preserved, and no fact tried by a jury, shall be otherwise re-examined in any Court of the United States, than according to the rules of the common law.

### AMENDMENT 8 (Bail, Fines, and Punishment)

Excessive bail shall not be required, nor excessive fines imposed, nor cruel and unusual punishments inflicted.

### AMENDMENT 9 (Rights Retained by People)

The enumeration in the Constitution, of certain rights, shall not be construed to deny or disparage others retained by the people.

### AMENDMENT 10 (States' Rights)

The powers not delegated to the United States by the Constitution, nor prohibited by it to the States, are reserved to the States respectively, or to the people.

### AMENDMENT 11 (Lawsuits Against States)
(*Proclaimed Jan. 8, 1798*)

The Judicial power of the United States shall not be construed to extend to any suit in law or equity, commenced or prosecuted against one of the United States by Citizens of another State, or by Citizens or Subjects of any Foreign State.

### AMENDMENT 12 (Presidential Elections)
(*Proclaimed Sept. 25, 1804*)

The Electors shall meet in their respective states and vote by ballot for President and Vice-President, one of whom, at least, shall not be an inhabitant of the same state with themselves; they shall name in their ballots the person voted for as President, and in distinct ballots the person voted for as Vice-President, and they shall make distinct lists of all persons voted for as President, and of all persons voted for as Vice-President, and of the number of votes for each, which lists they shall sign and certify, and transmit sealed to the seat of the government of the United States, directed to the President of the Senate;—The President of the Senate shall, in the presence of the Senate and House of Representatives, open all the certificates and the votes shall then be counted;—The person having the greatest number of votes for President, shall be the President, if such number be a majority of the whole number of Electors appointed; and if no person have such majority, then from the persons having the highest numbers not exceeding three on the list of those voted for as President, the House of Representatives shall choose immediately, by ballot, the President. But in choosing the President, the votes shall be taken by states, the representation from each state having one vote; a quorum for this purpose shall consist of a member or members from two-thirds of the states, and a majority of all the states shall be necessary to a choice.

And if the House of Representatives shall not choose a President whenever the right of choice shall devolve upon them, before the fourth day of March next following, then the Vice-President shall act as President, as in the case of the death or other constitutional disability of the President.—The person having the greatest number of votes as Vice-President, shall be the Vice-President, if such number be a majority of the whole number of Electors appointed, and if no person have a majority, then from the two highest numbers on the list, the Senate shall choose the Vice-President; a quorum

for the purpose shall consist of two-thirds of the whole number of Senators, and a majority of the whole number shall be necessary to a choice. But no person constitutionally ineligible to the office of President shall be eligible to that of Vice-President of the United States.

## AMENDMENT 13 (Abolition of Slavery)
(Proclaimed Dec. 18, 1865)
**Section 1.** Neither slavery nor involuntary servitude, except as a punishment for crime whereof the party shall have been duly convicted, shall exist within the United States, or any place subject to their jurisdiction.
**Section 2.** Congress shall have power to enforce this article by appropriate legislation.

## AMENDMENT 14 (Civil Rights)
(Proclaimed July 28, 1868)
**Section 1.** All persons born or naturalized in the United States, and subject to the jurisdiction thereof, are citizens of the United States and of the State wherein they reside. No State shall make or enforce any law which shall abridge the privileges or immunities of citizens of the United States, nor shall any State deprive any person of life, liberty, or property, without due process of law; nor deny to any person within its jurisdiction the equal protection of the laws.
**Section 2.** Representatives shall be apportioned among the several States according to their respective numbers, counting the whole number of persons in each State, excluding Indians not taxed. But when the right to vote at any election for the choice of electors for President and Vice President of the United States, Representatives in Congress, the Executive and Judicial officers of a State, or the members of the Legislature thereof, is denied to any of the male inhabitants of such State, being twenty-one years of age, and citizens of the United States, or in any way abridged, except for participation in rebellion, or other crime, the basis of representation therein shall be reduced in the proportion which the number of such male citizens shall bear to the whole number of male citizens twenty-one years of age in such State.
**Section 3.** No person shall be a Senator or Representative in Congress, or elector of President and Vice President, or hold any office, civil or military, under the United States, or under any State, who, having previously taken an oath, as a member of Congress, or as an officer of the United States, or as a member of any State legislature, or as an executive or judicial officer of any State, to support the Constitution of the United States, shall have engaged in insurrection or rebellion against the same, or given aid or comfort to the enemies thereof. But Congress may by a vote of two-thirds of each House, remove such disability.
**Section 4.** The validity of the public debt of the United States, authorized by law, including debts incurred for payment of pensions and bounties for services in suppressing insurrection or rebellion, shall not be questioned. But neither the United States nor any State shall assume or pay any debt or obligation incurred in aid of insurrection or rebellion against the United States, or any claim for the loss or emancipation of any slave; but all such debts, obligations and claims shall be held illegal and void.
**Section 5.** The Congress shall have power to enforce, by appropriate legislation, the provisions of this article.

## AMENDMENT 15 (Black Suffrage)
(Proclaimed March 30, 1870)
**Section 1.** The right of citizens of the United States to vote shall not be denied or abridged by the United States or by any State on account of race, color, or previous condition of servitude.
**Section 2.** The Congress shall have power to enforce this article by appropriate legislation.

## AMENDMENT 16 (Income Taxes)
(Proclaimed Feb. 25, 1913)
The Congress shall have power to lay and collect taxes on incomes, from whatever source derived, without apportionment among the several States, and without regard to any census or enumeration.

## AMENDMENT 17 (Senatorial Election)
(Proclaimed May 31, 1913)
The Senate of the United States shall be composed of two Senators from each State, elected by the people thereof, for six years; and each Senator shall have one vote. The electors in each State shall have the qualifications requisite for electors of the most numerous branch of the State legislatures.

When vacancies happen in the representation of any State in the Senate, the executive authority of such State shall issue writs of election to fill such vacancies: Provided, That the legislature of any State may empower the executive thereof to make temporary appointments until the people fill the vacancies by election as the legislature may direct.

This amendment shall not be so construed as to affect the election or term of any Senator chosen before it becomes valid as part of the Constitution.

## AMENDMENT 18 (Prohibition of Liquor)
(Proclaimed Jan. 29, 1919)
(Repealed by 21st Amendment)
**Section 1.** After one year from the ratification of this article the manufacture, sale, or transportation of intoxicating liquors within, the importation thereof into, or the exportation thereof from the United States and all territory subject to the jurisdiction thereof for beverage purposes is hereby prohibited.
**Section 2.** The Congress and the several States shall have concurrent power to enforce this article by appropriate legislation.
**Section 3.** This article shall be inoperative unless it shall have been ratified as an amendment to the Constitution by the legislatures of the several States, as provided in the Constitution, within seven years from the date of the submission hereof to the States by the Congress.

## AMENDMENT 19 (Woman Suffrage)
(Proclaimed Aug. 26, 1920)
The right of citizens of the United States to vote shall not be denied or abridged by the United States or by any State on account of sex.

Congress shall have power to enforce this article by appropriate legislation.

## AMENDMENT 20 (Terms of Office)
(Proclaimed Feb. 6, 1933)
**Section 1.** The terms of the President and Vice-President shall end at noon on the 20th day of

## EARLY CAPITALS OF THE UNITED STATES: 1774 to 1789

The Continental Congress and its successor, the Congress of the Articles of Confederation, met in eight different cities as the seat of the national government during and after the American Revolution.

**Philadelphia, Pennsylvania:**
Sept. 5, 1774, to Oct. 26, 1774
May 10, 1775, to Dec. 12, 1776
**Baltimore, Maryland:**
Dec. 20, 1776, to March 4, 1777
**Philadelphia, Pennsylvania:**
March 5, 1777, to Sept. 18, 1777
**Lancaster, Pennsylvania:**
Sept. 27, 1777 (one day only)

**York, Pennsylvania:**
Sept. 30, 1777, to June 27, 1778
**Philadelphia, Pennsylvania:**
July 2, 1778, to June 21, 1783
**Princeton, New Jersey:**
June 30, 1783, to Nov. 4, 1783
**Annapolis, Maryland:**
Nov. 26, 1783, to June 3, 1784

**Trenton, New Jersey:**
Nov. 1, 1784, to Dec. 24, 1784

**New York City, New York:**
Jan. 11, 1785, to Nov. 4, 1785
Nov. 7, 1785, to Nov. 3, 1786
Nov. 6, 1786, to Oct. 30, 1787
Nov. 5, 1787, to Oct. 21, 1788
Nov. 3, 1788, to March 2, 1789

**AMENDMENTS** *(continued)*

January, and the terms of Senators and Representatives at noon on the 3d day of January, of the years in which such terms would have ended if this article had not been ratified; and the terms of their successors shall then begin.

**Section 2.** The Congress shall assemble at least once in every year, and such meeting shall begin at noon on the 3d day of January, unless they shall by law appoint a different day.

**Section 3.** If, at the time fixed for the beginning of the term of the President, the President-elect shall have died, the Vice-President-elect shall become President. If a President shall not have been chosen before the time fixed for the beginning of his term, or if the President-elect shall have failed to qualify, then the Vice-President-elect shall act as President until a President shall have qualified; and the Congress may by law provide for the case wherein neither a President-elect nor a Vice-President-elect shall have qualified, declaring who shall then act as President, or the manner in which one who is to act shall be selected, and such person shall act accordingly until a President or Vice-President shall have qualified.

**Section 4.** The Congress may by law provide for the case of the death of any of the persons from whom the House of Representatives may choose a President whenever the right of choice shall have devolved upon them, and for the case of the death of any of the persons from whom the Senate may choose a Vice-President whenever the right of choice shall have devolved upon them.

**Section 5.** Sections 1 and 2 shall take effect on the 15th day of October following the ratification of this article.

**Section 6.** This article shall be inoperative unless it shall have been ratified as an amendment to the Constitution by the legislatures of three-fourths of the several States within seven years from the date of its submission.

**AMENDMENT 21 (Repeal of Prohibition)**
*(Proclaimed Dec. 5, 1933)*

**Section 1.** The eighteenth article of amendment to the Constitution of the United States is hereby repealed.

**Section 2.** The transportation or importation into any State, Territory, or possession of the United States for delivery or use therein of intoxicating liquors, in violation of the laws thereof, is hereby prohibited.

**Section 3.** This article shall be inoperative unless it shall have been ratified as an amendment to the Constitution by conventions in the several States, as provided in the Constitution, within seven years from the date of the submission hereof to the States by the Congress.

**AMENDMENT 22 (Limit on Presidential Terms)**
*(Proclaimed March 1, 1951)*

**Section 1.** No person shall be elected to the office of the President more than twice, and no person who has held the office of President, or acted as President, for more than two years of a term to which some other person was elected President shall be elected to the office of the President more than once. But this Article shall not apply to any person holding the office of President when this Article was proposed by the Congress, and shall not prevent any person who may be holding the office of President, or acting as President, during the term within which this Article becomes operative from holding the office of President or acting as President during the remainder of such term.

**Section 2.** This article shall be inoperative unless it

## PRESIDENTS OF CONGRESS: 1774 to 1789

| NAME | STATE | ELECTED | REMARKS |
|---|---|---|---|
| 1. Peyton Randolph | Virginia | Sept. 5, 1774 | Resigned: Speaker of Virginia legislature 1766–75 |
| 2. Henry Middleton | South Carolina | Oct. 22, 1774 | Defected to British 1780 |
| 3. Peyton Randolph | Virginia | May 10, 1775 | Resigned because of ill health |
| 4. John Hancock | Massachusetts | May 24, 1775 | First to sign Declaration of Independence |
| 5. Henry Laurens | South Carolina | Nov. 1, 1777 | Held prisoner by British 1780–81 |
| 6. John Jay | New York | Dec. 10, 1778 | First Chief Justice of U.S. 1789–95 |
| 7. Samuel Huntington | Connecticut | Sept. 28, 1779 | Governor of Connecticut 1786–96 |
| 8. Thomas McKean | Delaware | July 10, 1781 | First President elected under Articles of Confederation |
| 9. John Hanson | Maryland | Nov. 5, 1781 | Gave Washington Congress' thanks for Yorktown victory |
| 10. Elias Boudinot | New Jersey | Nov. 4, 1782 | Signed peace treaty ending American Revolutionary War |
| 11. Thomas Mifflin | Pennsylvania | Nov. 3, 1783 | Governor of Pennsylvania 1790–99 |
| 12. Richard Henry Lee | Virginia | Nov. 30, 1784 | U.S. Senator from Virginia 1789–92 |
| 13. John Hancock | Massachusetts | Nov. 23, 1785 | Resigned without serving because of illness |
| 14. Nathaniel Gorham | Massachusetts | June 6, 1786 | Signer of U.S. Constitution |
| 15. Arthur St. Clair | Pennsylvania | Feb. 2, 1787 | Governor of Northwest Territory 1789–1802 |
| 16. Cyrus Griffin | Virginia | Jan. 22, 1788 | U.S. district judge for Virginia 1789–1810 |

shall have been ratified as an amendment to the Constitution by the legislatures of three-fourths of the several States within seven years from the date of its submission to the States by the Congress.

## AMENDMENT 23 (Washington, D.C., Suffrage)
*(Proclaimed April 3, 1961)*

**Section 1.** The District constituting the seat of Government of the United States shall appoint in such manner as the Congress may direct:

A number of electors of President and Vice President equal to the whole number of Senators and Representatives in Congress to which the District would be entitled if it were a State, but in no event more than the least populous State; they shall be in addition to those appointed by the States, but they shall be considered, for the purposes of the election of President and Vice President, to be electors appointed by a State; and they shall meet in the District and perform such duties as provided by the twelfth article of amendment.
**Section 2.** The Congress shall have power to enforce this article by appropriate legislation.

## AMENDMENT 24 (Abolition of Poll Taxes)
*(Proclaimed Feb. 4, 1964)*

**Section 1.** The right of citizens of the United States to vote in any primary or other election for President or Vice President, for electors for President or Vice President, or for Senator or Representative in Congress, shall not be denied or abridged by the United States or any State by reason of failure to pay any poll tax or other tax.
**Section 2.** The Congress shall have power to enforce this article by appropriate legislation.

## AMENDMENT 25 (Presidential Succession)
*(Proclaimed Feb. 23, 1967)*

**Section 1.** In case of the removal of the President from office or of his death or resignation, the Vice President shall become President.
**Section 2.** Whenever there is a vacancy in the office of the Vice President, the President shall nominate a Vice President who shall take office upon confirmation by a majority vote of both houses of Congress.
**Section 3.** Whenever the President transmits to the President pro tempore of the Senate and the Speaker of the House of Representatives his written

declaration that he is unable to discharge the powers and duties of his office, and until he transmits to them a written declaration to the contrary, such powers and duties shall be discharged by the Vice President as Acting President.
**Section 4.** Whenever the Vice President and a majority of either the principal officers of the executive departments or of such other body as Congress may by law provide, transmit to the President pro tempore of the Senate and the Speaker of the House of Representatives their written declaration that the President is unable to discharge the powers and duties of his office, the Vice President shall immediately assume the powers and duties of the office as Acting President.

Thereafter, when the President transmits to the President pro tempore of the Senate and the Speaker of the House of Representatives his written declaration that no inability exists, he shall resume the powers and duties of his office unless the Vice President and a majority of either the principal officers of the executive department or of such other body as Congress may by law provide, transmit within four days to the President pro tempore of the Senate and the Speaker of the House of Representatives their written declaration that the President is unable to discharge the powers and duties of his office. Thereupon Congress shall decide the issue, assembling within forty-eight hours for that purpose if not in session. If the Congress, within twenty-one days after receipt of the latter written declaration, or, if Congress is not in session, within twenty-one days after Congress is required to assemble, determines by two-thirds vote of both houses that the President is unable to discharge the powers and duties of his office, the Vice President shall continue to discharge the same as Acting President; otherwise, the President shall resume the powers and duties of his office.

## AMENDMENT 26 (18-Year-Old Suffrage)
*(Proclaimed July 5, 1971)*

**Section 1.** The right of citizens of the United States, who are eighteen years of age or older, to vote shall not be denied or abridged by the United States or by any State on account of age.
**Section 2.** The Congress shall have power to enforce this article by appropriate legislation.

# CONSTITUTIONAL AMENDMENTS NOT RATIFIED

Five amendments submitted to the states have failed to be ratified by them. In 1791, of the 12 proposed amendments to the Constitution, Articles III-XII were ratified and became the Bill of Rights, the first 10 amendments to the Constitution. But the proposed Articles I and II were not ratified.

The proposed Article I would have provided that as the population grew there could be a representative in Congress for every 50,000 people. The proposed Article II would have prevented Congress from raising its own salaries during the term in session.

The 11th Congress proposed an amendment forbidding acceptance by U.S. citizens of foreign titles "of nobility or honour."

On March 2, 1861, President James Buchan-

an signed a proposed amendment that would have forbidden any amendments to the Constitution giving Congress the power to abolish or interfere with slavery. It was not ratified. Congress approved an amendment in 1924 giving it power to regulate child labor. It was not ratified.

In 1972 an equal rights for women amendment was approved by Congress and sent to the states for ratification. It states: "Equality of rights under the law shall not be denied or abridged by the United States or any state on account of sex."

An amendment to give Washington, D.C., voting representation in Congress was approved by Congress in 1978 and sent to the states for ratification.

## U.S. TERRITORIAL EXPANSION

The total gross area (land and water) of the U.S. and its outlying areas was 3,631,407 square miles in the 1970 census. The table below outlines the nation's physical growth since independence was declared in 1776.

The area figures are precise determinations of specific territories first made by a special government committee in 1912 and subsequently adjusted to bring them into agreement with later remeasurements.

In 1979 the U.S. gave up claims to several Pacific islands including Canton and Enderbury, which became part of the nation Kiribati (formerly the Gilbert Islands).

On Oct. 1, 1979, the United States restored to Panama sovereignty over the 553-square-mile Panama Canal Zone that had been governed by the U.S. since 1904.

| DATE | ACQUISITION | GROSS AREA (in sq. miles) | HOW ACQUIRED | ACQUISITION PRICE |
|---|---|---|---|---|
| — | Original territory | 888,685 | Treaty with Britain | — |
| 1803 | Louisiana | 827,192 | Purchase from France | $15,000,000 |
| 1819 | Florida (and other areas) | 72,003 | Treaty with Spain | $ 5,000,000 |
| 1845 | Texas | 390,143 | Independent republic annexed | — |
| 1846 | Oregon | 285,580 | Treaty with Britain | — |
| 1848 | Mexican cession | 529,017 | Conquest from Mexico | $15,000,000 |
| 1853 | Gadsden Purchase | 29,640 | Purchase from Mexico | $10,000,000 |
| 1867 | Alaska | 586,412 | Purchase from Russia | $ 7,200,000 |
| 1898 | Hawaiian Islands | 6,450 | Independent republic annexed | — |
| 1898 | Puerto Rico | 3,435 | Conquest from Spain | — |
| 1898 | Guam | 212 | Conquest from Spain | — |
| 1899 | American Samoa | 76 | Division with Germany and Britain | — |
| 1917 | Virgin Islands | 133 | Purchase from Denmark | $25,000,000 |
| 1947 | Trust Territory of the Pacific Islands (Marshall and Caroline Islands) | 533 | UN Trusteeship (to be terminated in 1981, granting Micronesia independence) | — |
| 1978 | Northern Mariana Islands | 184 | Conquest from Japan in World War II (achieved Commonwealth status in 1978) | — |
| — | All other [1] | 15 | — | — |

[1] Includes following islands with gross areas (in square miles) as indicated: Midway (2); Wake (3); Palmyra (4); Navassa (2); Baker, Howland, and Jarvis (combined, 3); Johnston and Sand (combined, less than ½ sq. mi.); Kingman Reef (less than ½ sq. mi.).

## U.S. GOVERNMENT LANDHOLDINGS, BY STATE

Source: General Services Administration, Sept. 1, 1980

| STATE | TOTAL AREA Acres | FEDERALLY OWNED Acres | % | STATE | TOTAL AREA Acres | FEDERALLY OWNED Acres | % |
|---|---|---|---|---|---|---|---|
| U.S. TOTAL | 2,271,343,360 | 769,863,397.5 | 33.895 | Missouri | 44,248,320 | 2,195,583.0 | 4.962 |
| Alabama | 32,678,400 | 1,122,288.1 | 3.434 | Montana | 93,271,040 | 27,740,572.2 | 29.742 |
| Alaska | 365,481,600 | 359,133,743.3 | 98.263 | Nebraska | 49,031,680 | 712,173.0 | 1.453 |
| Arizona | 72,688,000 | 32,014,276.1 | 44.043 | Nevada | 70,264,320 | 60,506,114.1 | 86.112 |
| Arkansas | 33,599,360 | 3,358,291.1 | 9.995 | New Hamp. | 5,768,960 | 721,889.3 | 12.513 |
| California | 100,206,720 | 46,702,125.0 | 46.606 | New Jersey | 4,813,440 | 151,529.6 | 3.148 |
| Colorado | 66,485,760 | 23,607,946.5 | 35.508 | New Mexico | 77,766,400 | 25,873,744.7 | 33.271 |
| Connecticut | 3,135,360 | 9,336.9 | 0.298 | New York | 30,680,960 | 245,915.1 | 0.802 |
| Delaware | 1,265,920 | 40,851.9 | 3.227 | North Carolina | 31,402,880 | 2,050,852.1 | 6.531 |
| Dist. of Col. | 39,040 | 12,829.1 | 32.861 | North Dakota | 44,452,480 | 2,386,385.4 | 5.368 |
| Florida | 34,721,280 | 4,040,945.2 | 11.638 | Ohio | 26,222,080 | 345,308.7 | 1.317 |
| Georgia | 37,295,360 | 2,277,361.0 | 6.106 | Oklahoma | 44,087,680 | 1,589,953.2 | 3.606 |
| Hawaii | 4,105,600 | 660,620.1 | 16.091 | Oregon | 61,598,720 | 32,313,687.9 | 52.458 |
| Idaho | 52,933,120 | 33,759,571.6 | 63.778 | Pennsylvania | 28,804,480 | 732,565.3 | 2.543 |
| Illinois | 35,795,200 | 606,596.6 | 1.695 | Rhode Island | 677,120 | 8,010.8 | 1.183 |
| Indiana | 23,158,400 | 496,647.5 | 2.145 | South Carolina | 19,374,080 | 1,176,389.7 | 6.072 |
| Iowa | 35,860,480 | 227,448.3 | 0.634 | South Dakota | 48,881,920 | 3,492,308.5 | 7.144 |
| Kansas | 52,510,720 | 733,014.7 | 1.396 | Tennessee | 26,727,680 | 1,853,936.0 | 6.936 |
| Kentucky | 25,512,320 | 1,414,350.6 | 5.544 | Texas | 168,217,600 | 3,408,655.2 | 2.026 |
| Louisiana | 28,867,840 | 1,098,595.1 | 3.806 | Utah | 52,696,960 | 33,529,967.4 | 63.628 |
| Maine | 19,847,680 | 134,801.6 | 0.679 | Vermont | 5,936,640 | 295,561.9 | 4.979 |
| Maryland | 6,319,360 | 203,009.9 | 3.213 | Virginia | 25,496,320 | 2,409,747.9 | 9.451 |
| Massachusetts | 5,034,880 | 79,896.7 | 1.587 | Washington | 42,693,760 | 12,472,703.7 | 29.214 |
| Michigan | 36,492,160 | 3,467,376.2 | 9.502 | West Virginia | 15,410,560 | 1,097,058.2 | 7.119 |
| Minnesota | 51,205,760 | 3,423,003.9 | 6.685 | Wisconsin | 35,011,200 | 1,867,734.6 | 5.335 |
| Mississippi | 30,222,720 | 1,730,567.5 | 5.726 | Wyoming | 62,343,040 | 30,329,555.5 | 48.650 |

## THE STAR-SPANGLED BANNER

Oh! say, can you see, by the dawn's early light,
What so proudly we hailed at the twilight's last gleaming?
Whose broad stripes and bright stars thro' the perilous
fight,
O'er the ramparts we watched, were so gallantly
streaming?
And the rockets' red glare, the bombs bursting in air,
Gave proof thro' the night that our flag was still
there.
Oh! say, does that star-spangled banner yet wave
O'er the land of the free and the home of the brave?

On the shore, dimly seen thro' the mist of the deep,
Where the foe's haughty host in dread silence reposes,
What is that which the breeze, o'er the towering steep,
As it fitfully blows, half conceals, half discloses?
Now it catches the gleam of the morning's first beam,
In full glory reflected, now shines on the stream,
'Tis the star-spangled banner. Oh! long may it wave
O'er the land of the free and the home of the brave!

And where is that band who so vauntingly swore,
That the havoc of war and the battle's confusion
A home and a country should leave us no more?
Their blood has washed out their foul footstep's
pollution.
No refuge could save the hireling and slave
From the terror of flight or the gloom of the grave,
And the star-spangled banner in triumph doth wave
O'er the land of the free and the home of the brave.

Oh! thus be it ever when freemen shall stand
Between their loved home and the war's desolation,
Blest with vict'ry and peace may the Heav'n-rescued
land
Praise the Pow'r that hath made and preserved us a
nation.
Then conquer we must, when our cause it is just,
And this be our motto "In God is our trust."
And the star-spangled banner in triumph shall wave
O'er the land of the free and the home of the brave.

A naval bombardment during the War of 1812 led to the writing of the American national anthem.

Francis Scott Key, a successful Washington lawyer, visited the flagship of the British fleet in Chesapeake Bay, accompanying Col. John S. Skinner on an official mission to secure the release of a prisoner. Detained on board the tender on which they had come out to the flagship, the two watched the bombardment of Fort McHenry at Baltimore, Md., on the night of Sept. 13–14, 1814.

Seeing the American flag still aloft at dawn, Key was inspired to write a poem.

The poem was first printed as a broadside and then, on Sept. 20, 1814, was published in the Baltimore *Patriot.* The next day, the Baltimore *American* also printed it with the title *Defence of Fort M'Henry.*

On Oct. 19, 1814, the poem was first sung in public and for the first time given the title *The Star-Spangled Banner.* As entertainment following a performance in Baltimore of the play *Count Benyowski,* the words were sung to a tune, *Anacreon in Heaven,* then widely known in America. Key had composed his poem in obvious imitation of it. He borrowed not only the melody but meter and verse form as well.

President Wilson proclaimed *The Star-Spangled Banner* as the national anthem of the United States in 1916, but Congress did not confirm this action until 1931.

There is no official act of Congress setting the exact wording of the national anthem, and several versions—differing only in detail—remain in use today.

## PLEDGE OF ALLEGIANCE

I pledge allegiance to the flag of the United States of America and to the Republic for which it stands, one Nation under God, indivisible, with liberty and justice for all.

The Pledge of Allegiance to the flag was written by Francis Bellamy for the National Public School Celebration of Columbus Day in 1892. Bellamy was working for *The Youth's Companion,* a journal published in Boston. He had been appointed chairman of a committee to develop a program for the celebration of the 400th anniversary of the discovery of America.

Bellamy wrote the pledge in two hours on an August evening. It was published in *The Youth's Companion* on Sept. 8, 1892, and in the official program of the celebration. No one knows where the pledge was first used, although it is known to have been recited at the World's Columbian Exposition in Chicago on Oct. 21, 1892.

Originally, the pledge read: "I pledge allegiance to my flag and to the Republic for which it stands, one Nation indivisible, with liberty and justice for all."

In 1923, at the First National Flag Conference in Washington, D.C., the words "my flag" were changed to "the flag of the United States."

In the following year, at the Second National Flag Conference, the words "of America" were added to the phrase.

In 1954 the words "under God" were inserted.

Although the pledge became popular throughout the nation, it was not until 1942 that its words were included in federal legislation about flag use and customs. The pledge was given official congressional sanction in 1945.

QUICK QUIZ: Who is the governor of Ohio? See page 875.

# HISTORY OF THE AMERICAN FLAG

Banners of the American Revolution: the Moultrie, Rhode Island, Bunker Hill, and Bennington flags.

Before American independence became a reality, there were colonial or regimental flags by the score. Many local banners carried such slogans as "Don't Tread On Me."

The Moultrie flag—the first distinctive American flag displayed in the South—flew over the fort on Sullivan's Island, outside Charleston, S.C., when a British fleet attacked on June 28, 1776. The garrison, under Col. William Moultrie, forced the British to withdraw—and the flag became known by his name. The design of this blue flag with a white crescent was suggested by the garrison's blue uniforms and the silver crescents worn by the men on their caps, inscribed with *Liberty or Death*.

Rhode Island had its own flag, carried at Brandywine, Trenton, and Yorktown. It bore an anchor, 13 stars, and the word *Hope*. Its white stars in a blue field are believed to have suggested the "starry blue field" displayed on our national flag.

Among famous New England banners was the Bunker Hill. This flag—one of the first to include the pine tree—was carried by American colonial troops at the Battle of Bunker Hill on June 17, 1775.

The Bennington flag was carried by the Green Mountain Boys at the Battle of Bennington on Aug. 16, 1777.

On Jan. 1, 1776, at a ceremony at Gen. George Washington's Prospect Hill headquarters in Cambridge (now part of Somerville), Mass., the Grand Union flag was raised as the standard of the Continental Army. It was similar to the Meteor flag of Great Britain, modified by red and white stripes signifying the 13 original colonies. Retention of the British Union in the canton, with its crosses of St. George and St. Andrew, indicated continued loyalty—as the colonists saw it—to the "mother country." This flag soon became known by various names, including the Grand Union flag, the

Union flag, the Cambridge flag, and the Colours of the United Colonies.

On June 14, 1777, the Continental Congress adopted this resolution proposed by John Adams: "Resolved: that the flag of the United States be made of thirteen stripes, alternate red and white; that the Union be thirteen stars, white in a blue field representing a new constellation." Thus was born the Stars and Stripes. It appears to have been designed primarily for use at sea, not as a battle flag on land. On a voyage that began on Sept. 30, 1787, Capt. Robert Gray in the *Columbia* carried the flag around the world for the first time.

The original flag, with its 13 stripes and 13 stars, remained in use only a few years. On Dec. 26, 1793, after the admission of two new states to the Union, Stephen R. Bradley of Vermont introduced a bill in Congress "for altering the Flag of the United States." It provided, in less than four lines of print, that beginning on May 1, 1795, the Flag of the United States should be "fifteen stripes, alternate red and white, with a union of fifteen stars white in a blue field." This was passed on Jan. 13, 1794.

Peter H. Wendover, representative to Congress from New York, was responsible for the Flag Act of April 4, 1818, which is still in effect. This act specified "thirteen horizontal stripes, alternate red and white." It provided that the "union have 20 stars, white on a blue field" and "on the admission of every new state into the Union," one star would be added on the following July 4.

On June 24, 1912, President William Howard Taft issued an executive order officially prescribing the relative proportions of the flag and the arrangement of the stars.

By an executive order of President Eisenhower, dated Aug. 21, 1959, a banner with 50 stars became the official flag of the United States on July 4, 1960.

Left to right: Grand Union Flag; original Stars and Stripes; flag of 1795–1818; flag since 1960.

# HONORING THE AMERICAN FLAG

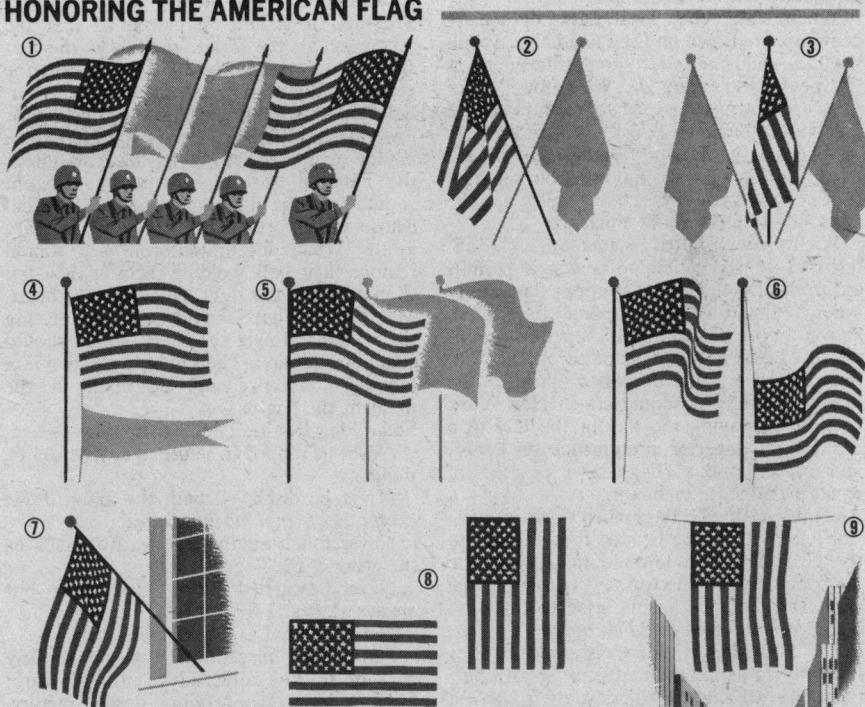

The U.S. flag code adopted by Congress provides rules for displaying and honoring the flag. The code states: "The flag represents a living country and is itself considered a living thing."

The code was amended in 1976 with Public Law 94–344 to clarify misunderstandings regarding rules that should be observed.

Below is a summary of the rules.

**Raising and Lowering:** The flag should be hoisted briskly and lowered ceremoniously.

**When to Display:** A flag made of weather-resistant material can be flown around the clock in any weather if properly illuminated.

It should be displayed especially on New Year's Day, Inauguration Day, Lincoln's Birthday, Washington's Birthday, Easter Sunday, Mother's Day, Armed Forces Day, Memorial Day, Flag Day, Independence Day, Labor Day, Constitution Day, Columbus Day, Navy Day, Veterans Day, Thanksgiving Day, Christmas Day, on other days proclaimed by the President, on the birthdays of states, and on state holidays.

**Public Buildings:** The flag should be displayed daily on or near the main administration building of every public institution, in or near every polling place on election days, and in or near every schoolhouse on school days.

**In a Procession:** When carried in a procession with another flag or flags, it should be either on the marching right (the flag's own right) or, if there is a line of other flags, in front of the center of that line (*see Figure 1 above*). It should not be carried on a parade float except flat or from a staff.

**On a Vehicle:** The flag should not be draped on or over any part of a vehicle, railroad train, or boat. When displayed on an automobile, the staff should be firmly clamped to the right front fender.

**With Other Flags:** No other flag or pennant should be placed above or, if on the same level, to the United States flag's right.

When it is displayed with another flag against a wall from crossed staffs, it should be on the right (the flag's own right) and its staff should be in front of that of the other flag (*see Figure 2*).

The U.S. flag should be at the center and at the highest point of the group when a number of flags of states or localities or society pennants are grouped and displayed from staffs (*see Figure 3*).

**HONORING THE FLAG** (continued)

When state, city, local flags, or society pennants are flown on the same halyard with the U.S. flag, the latter should always be at the peak (see Figure 4). When such other flags are flown from adjacent staffs, the U.S. flag should be hoisted first and lowered last.

When flags of two or more nations are displayed, they are to be flown from separate staffs of the same height (see Figure 5). The flags should be of about equal size.

Within the United States or any U.S. territory or possession no person is permitted to display the United Nations flag or any other national or international flag equal, above, or in a position of superior prominence or honor to, or in place of, the U.S. flag. However, this does not apply to the practice at UN headquarters in New York City of displaying the flag of the UN in a position of superior prominence or honor, and other national flags in a position of equal prominence or honor.

**At Half-Staff:** The flag, when flown at half-staff, should first be hoisted momentarily to the peak and then lowered to one-half the distance between the top and bottom of the staff. It should be again raised to the peak before it is lowered (see Figure 6).

**From a Building:** When displayed from a staff projecting horizontally or at an angle from the windowsill, balcony, or front of a building, the union (blue field) of the flag should be placed at the peak of the staff, unless the flag is at half-staff (see Figure 7).

**Not on a Staff:** When the flag is displayed other than by being flown from a staff, indoors or out, it should either be displayed flat or suspended so that its folds fall freely as though it were staffed. When displayed flat (either horizontally or vertically) against a wall or window, the union should be uppermost and to the flag's own right (to the observer's left) (see Figure 8).

**Over a Street:** When displayed over the middle of a street, the flag should be suspended vertically with the union to the north in an east-west street or to the east in a north-south street (see Figure 9).

**In an Auditorium:** When used on a speaker's platform, the flag, if displayed flat, should be above and behind the speaker. When displayed from a staff in a church or public auditorium, the flag should hold the position of superior prominence, in advance of the audience, and in the position of honor at the clergyman's or speaker's right as he faces the audience. Any other flag so displayed should be placed at the clergyman's or speaker's left or to the right of the audience.

**At an Unveiling:** The flag should never be used as covering for the statue or monument.

**At a Funeral:** When the flag is used to cover a casket, it should be placed so that the union is at the head and over the left shoulder. It should not be lowered into the grave or allowed to touch the ground.

**Saluting the Flag:** During the hoisting or lowering of the flag, when it is passing in a parade or in a review, or during rendition of the national anthem, all persons present should face the flag and stand at attention. Those in uniform should give the military salute. When not in uniform, men should remove their hats, holding them at their left shoulder with the right hand over the heart. Men without hats should salute by placing the right hand over the heart. Aliens should stand at attention. The salute to the flag in a moving column should be made at the moment the flag passes.

**Some Flag Don'ts:** The flag should:

Never be dipped in salute to any person or thing.

Never be displayed with the union down *except as a signal of dire distress.*

Never touch anything beneath it, such as the ground, the floor, or water.

Never be carried flat or horizontally, but always aloft and free.

Never be used as a ceiling covering.

Never have placed upon it, nor on any part of it, nor attached to it any mark, insignia, letter, word, figure, design, picture, or drawing of any nature.

Never be used as a receptacle for receiving, holding, carrying, or delivering anything.

Never be used as wearing apparel, bedding, or drapery.

Never be festooned, drawn back, or up, in folds, but always be allowed to fall free.

Never be fastened, displayed, used or stored in such a manner as to permit it to be easily torn, soiled, or damaged in any way.

Never be used for advertising purposes in any manner whatsoever.

Never be embroidered on such articles as cushions or handkerchiefs and the like, printed or impressed on paper napkins or boxes or anything designed for temporary use and discard.

Advertising signs should not be fastened to a staff or halyard from which the flag flies.

No part of the flag should ever be used as a costume or athletic uniform. However, a flag patch may be affixed to the uniform of military personnel, firemen, policemen, and members of patriotic organizations. The lapel flag pin, being a replica, should be worn on the left lapel near the heart.

It is a federal crime to knowingly cast contempt on the flag by "publicly mutilating, defacing, defiling, burning, or trampling upon it."

# FAMOUS PERSONS IN AMERICAN HISTORY

Brief biographies of famous persons in American history on the following pages include statesmen, political leaders, heroes, reformers, and others.

Biographies of *U.S. Presidents and First Ladies* appear on pages 343–389.

For biographical information on other famous Americans, see the following tables: *Authors and Writers*, pages 94–102; *Classi-cal Musicians, Composers, Singers, and Dancers*, pages 58–63; *Show Business Personalities*, pages 275–286; *Painters, Sculptors, and Architects*, pages 64–68; *Pioneers in Medicine*, pages 454–456; *Scientists and Inventors*, pages 729–734; *Theologians and Philosophers*, pages 710–712; and obituaries of American men and women who died in 1980, pages 981–986.

**Dean Gooderham Acheson** (1893–1971): Played major role in developing U.S. foreign policy during and after World War II under Presidents F.D. Roosevelt and Truman; served as assistant secretary of state, 1941–45, undersecretary of state, 1945–47, secretary of state, 1949–53; became target of Sen. Joseph McCarthy (R-Wis.) and his followers, who accused Acheson of being "soft on communism" and of "coddling" communists as members of State Department; born in Middletown, Conn.

**Samuel Adams** (1722–1803): Patriot leader in period of American Revolution; helped organize Sons of Liberty to oppose British Stamp Act, 1765; began committee of correspondence in Massachusetts, 1772, to inform other colonies of patriot actions; organized Boston Tea Party, 1773; delegate to Continental Congress, 1774–82; voted for and signed Declaration of Independence, 1776; lieutenant governor of Massachusetts, 1789–93; governor of Massachusetts, 1793–97; born in Boston.

**Jane Addams** (1860–1935): Founded first settlement house (or neighborhood center) in Chicago, called Hull House, with Ellen Gates Starr, 1889; became first woman president of National Conference of Charities and Corrections, 1909; as pacifist, was president of Women's International League for Peace and Freedom, 1915–29; co-recipient of Nobel Peace Prize with Nicholas Murray Butler, 1931; born in Cedarville, Ill.

**Spiro Theodore Agnew** (born 1918): 39th Vice President of U.S., 1969–73; first ever forced to resign; accepted conviction for income tax evasion, 1973, to avoid prosecution on bribery charges; Republican governor of Maryland, 1967–69; nominated Richard M. Nixon for President at national convention, 1968, and became his running mate; born in Towson, Md.

**Ethan Allen** (1738–89): Led Vermont's Green Mountain Boys in capture of British Fort Ticonderoga, May 10, 1775, in first American victory of Revolutionary War; during Battle of Montreal in September 1775, was captured and imprisoned, 1775–78; upon return, worked to achieve recognition of Vermont's independence; born in Litchfield, Conn.

**Richard Allen** (1760–1831): Founded first black religious denomination in U.S., Bethel African Methodist Episcopal Church, 1794, in Philadelphia; born a slave in Philadelphia; gained freedom, 1786.

**Susan Brownell Anthony** (1820–1906): Early advocate of women's rights, temperance, and abolition; with Elizabeth Cady Stanton founded National Woman Suffrage Association, 1869, and was its president, 1892–1900; arrested for voting in 1872; trial brought attention to women's rights movement; born in Adams, Mass.

**Johnny Appleseed** (John Chapman; 1774–1845): Legendary pioneer who planted apple trees in Ohio and Indiana along route of migrating settlers during westward movement in early 1800s; born in Leominster, Mass.

**Neil Alden Armstrong** (born 1930): First man to set foot on Moon as commander of *Apollo 11* mission, 1969, declaring: "That's one small step for a man, one giant leap for mankind"; performed first manual docking in space with astronaut David R. Scott in *Gemini 8*, 1966; flew 78 combat missions in Korean War as Navy pilot; born near Wapakoneta, Ohio.

**Benedict Arnold** (1741–1801): Revolutionary War traitor; as Continental Army major general displayed heroism in American victory at Battles of Saratoga, 1777; as military commander of Philadelphia, 1778–80, was convicted by courtmartial of using position for personal gain, but received only reprimand; as commander of West Point, N.Y., 1780, bargained with British to surrender fort for large bonus, but plot was uncovered by capture of British spy Maj. John André; Arnold escaped to British lines and fought against Americans for rest of Revolutionary War; born in Norwich, Conn.

**John Jacob Astor** (1763–1848): Became one of richest men in U.S. by monopolizing fur trade with Europe and China; established American Fur Co., 1808, and Pacific Fur Co., 1810; founded Astoria, Ore., 1811; sold fur holdings, 1834, and invested in farmland that became heart of New York City; fortune was estimated at $20 million; born in Waldorf, Germany.

**Stephen Fuller Austin** (1793–1836): Established first American settlement in Texas, on Brazos River, 1821; initiated demands for Texas independence from Mexico; became first secretary of state of independent Texas Republic, 1836; born in Wythe County, Va.

**George Bancroft** (1800–91): Historian and public official; wrote 10-volume *History of the United States*, 1834–76; as secretary of the navy, 1845–46, founded U.S. Naval Academy at Annapolis, Md.; served as U.S. minister to Britain, 1846–49, and to Germany, 1867–74; born in Worcester, Mass.

**Benjamin Banneker** (1731–1806): Black mathematician and astronomer; helped survey Dis-

QUICK QUIZ: What is the largest lake in the world? See page 331.

**FAMOUS PERSONS IN AMERICAN HISTORY** *(continued)*
trict of Columbia, 1791; published annual astronomical almanac, 1791–1802, used by abolitionists to prove blacks were as capable as whites; born in Ellicott, Md.

**Henry Barnard** (1811–1900): First U.S. commissioner of education, 1867–70; published *American Journal of Education*, 1855–82; did much to develop U.S. public-school system; born in Hartford, Conn.

**Phineas Taylor ("P.T.") Barnum** (1810–91): Showman known for his claim "There's a sucker born every minute"; opened circus *Greatest Show on Earth*, 1871; combined with major rival to form Barnum & Bailey Circus, 1881; born in Bethel, Conn.

**Clara Barton** (1821–1912): Known as "Angel of the Battlefield"; organized nursing services for Union Army during Civil War, 1861–65; served in Europe as nurse during Franco-Prussian War, 1870; founded American Red Cross, 1881, and was its first president, 1882–1904; initiated Red Cross help for peacetime disasters; born near Oxford, Mass.

**Bernard Baruch** (1870–1965): Financier and adviser to eight Presidents from Woodrow Wilson to John F. Kennedy; prepared first plan for international development and control of atomic energy as U.S. representative to UN Atomic Energy Commission, 1946; made fortune as speculator in securities; born in Camden, S.C.

**Henry Ward Beecher** (1813–87): Popular Protestant preacher and reformer; advocated women's rights, abolition of slavery, and civil-service reform; pastor of Plymouth Congregational Church in Brooklyn, N.Y., 1847–87; sought to reconcile evolution and religion; charged with adultery in sensational trial, 1874–75, but jury could not arrive at verdict; brother of Harriet Beecher Stowe; born in Litchfield, Conn.

**Thomas Hart Benton** (1782–1858): Hot-tempered Democratic U.S. senator from Missouri for 30 consecutive years, 1821–51; shot Andrew Jackson in frontier brawl in 1813 but later became Jackson's firm friend and supporter; because of personal dislike of slavery, opposed Compromise of 1850 and lost Senate seat as result; U.S. representative (D-Mo.), 1853–55; born near Hillsborough, N.C.

**Billy the Kid** (William H. Bonney; 1859–81): Western outlaw said to have killed 21 men, first when he was only 12; led cattle rustlers in series of slayings in New Mexico; sentenced to hang in 1881, killed two sheriff's deputies and escaped; tracked down and killed by Sheriff Pat Garrett, 1881; born in New York City.

**Black Hawk** (1767–1838): Indian chief of Sauk tribe; refused to honor treaty giving up lands, claiming chiefs had been made drunk before signing it; fought Black Hawk War against settlers in Illinois, 1832; Black Hawk and two sons were captured and jailed; born at Rock River, Ill.

**James Gillespie Blaine** (1830–93): U.S. secretary of state, 1881 and 1889–92; initiated first Pan American Conference, 1889; U.S. representative (R-Me.), 1863–76, speaker of the House, 1869–75; U.S. senator (R-Me.), 1876–81; as Republican candidate for President, 1884, was defeated largely because New York voters were angered by Blaine supporter labeling Democrats as party of "rum, Romanism and rebellion"; born in West Brownsville, Pa.

**Daniel Boone** (1734–1820): Pioneer frontiersman; explored Kentucky, 1767; blazed Wilderness Road through Cumberland Gap and built Boonesborough, Ky., 1775; famous as Indian fighter; born near Reading, Pa.

**John Wilkes Booth** (1838–65): Assassin of President Lincoln, 1865; a Shakespearean actor, he escaped after shooting Lincoln but was tracked down and killed 12 days later in barn near Port Royal, Va.; born in Bel Air, Md.

**James Bowie** (1796–1836): Hero of Texas War for Independence; among those who fought to death against Mexicans in Battle of the Alamo, 1836; invented frontier hunting knife, called Bowie knife; born in Burke County, Ga.

**William Bradford** (1590–1657): Pilgrim leader; came to America on *Mayflower* and helped found Plymouth Colony; elected colony's governor, 1621, he served for 30 of next 35 years; wrote *History of Plymouth Plantation*, 1651; born in Yorkshire, England.

**Omar Nelson Bradley** (born 1893): Commander of U.S. ground forces in Normandy invasion of France, 1944; then led about 1 million U.S. troops in 12th Army Group that conquered German-occupied Europe, 1944–45; U.S. Army chief of staff, 1948–49; first chairman Joint Chiefs of Staff, 1949–53; promoted to 5-star General of the Army, 1950; wrote *A Soldier's Story*, 1951; graduated from West Point, 1915; born in Clark, Mo.

**Mathew B. Brady** (c.1823–96): Photographer of U.S. Civil War; took more than 3,500 photos; born in Warren County, N.Y.

**Louis Dembitz Brandeis** (1856–1941): Associate justice of U.S. Supreme Court, 1916–39; during most of period court was controlled by conservatives, so that Brandeis often dissented from rulings, issuing his own more liberal opinions; born in Louisville, Ky.

**John Cabell Breckinridge** (1821–75): 14th Vice President of U.S., 1857–61; was unsuccessful Southern Democratic candidate for President against Lincoln, 1860; served several months in 1861 as Democratic U.S. senator from Kentucky, voting against Lincoln's war measures; escaped to South to become Confederate general and then secretary of war, 1865; after war fled to Cuba, then to England, returning home in 1868; born near Lexington, Ky.

**James Bridger** (1804–81): Frontiersman; explored Rocky Mountains as fur trapper; was first white man to discover Great Salt Lake, 1824, and one of first to describe wonders of Yellowstone region; built Fort Bridger in Wyoming, 1843, as supply station on Oregon Trail; born in Richmond, Va.

**John Brown** (1800–59): Radical abolitionist; led raid on proslavery settlers at Pottawatomie Creek in Kansas, 1856, killing five; with followers, captured federal arsenal at Harpers Ferry, Va., Oct. 16, 1859, planning to use arms to start slave revolt in South; U.S. Marines led by Col. Robert E. Lee forced Brown and followers to surrender; convicted of murder and treason against Virginia, Brown was hanged on Dec. 2,

1859; born in Torrington, Conn.

**Blanche Kelso Bruce** (1841–98): First black to serve full term as U.S. senator (R-Miss.), 1875–81; register of U.S. treasury, 1881–85, 1897–98; born in slavery near Farmville, Va.

**William Jennings Bryan** (1860–1925): Three-time loser as Democratic candidate for President, 1896, 1900, 1908; as secretary of state, 1913–15, tried to keep U.S. out of World War I, resigning when President Wilson insisted on sending strong notes of protest to Germany about submarine attacks; originally won fame with "Cross of Gold" speech at Democratic convention, 1896, calling for free coinage of silver; a believer in fundamental religion, Bryan aided prosecution at Scopes evolution trial, 1925; born in Salem, Ill.

**Ralph Johnson Bunche** (1904–71): First black American awarded Nobel Peace Prize, 1950; UN mediator in first Arab-Israeli War, 1948–49; undersecretary of state of United Nations, 1955–71; born in Detroit, Mich.

**Warren Earl Burger** (born 1907): 15th Chief Justice of U.S., appointed 1969 by President Nixon; though known as conservative, surprised many by liberal rulings favoring busing to end school segregation, 1971; overturning state laws restricting abortions during first six months of pregnancy, 1973; and denying President Nixon's claim to executive privilege in refusing to disclose White House tapes and documents in Watergate investigation, 1974; judge of U.S. Court of Appeals in Washington, D.C., 1956–69; born in St. Paul, Minn.

**Aaron Burr** (1756–1836): 3d Vice President of U.S., 1801–05; after winning tie electoral vote for President, U.S. House of Representatives decided in favor of Thomas Jefferson; killed Alexander Hamilton in duel, 1804; tried for treason for plotting independent empire in West, but acquitted, 1807; served as U.S. senator (D-R–N.Y.), 1791–97; born in Newark, N.J.

**Richard Evelyn Byrd** (1888–1957): Made first flight over North Pole, with pilot Floyd Bennett, 1926; established "Little America" base in Antarctica, 1928–30, 1933–35; made first flight over South Pole, 1929; promoted to rear admiral in U.S. Navy, 1930; born in Winchester, Va.

**Saint Frances Xavier Cabrini** (1850–1917): First U.S. citizen to be made saint by Roman Catholic Church, 1946; founded Missionary Sisters of the Sacred Heart, 1880; aided poor Italians in U.S., founding orphanages, schools, and hospitals; born in Lombardy, Italy.

**John Caldwell Calhoun** (1782–1850): 7th Vice President of U.S., 1825–32, resigning to lead nullification fight against President Jackson; as strong believer in states' rights, he felt his state, South Carolina, could nullify high federal protective tariffs that it disapproved, but Calhoun and South Carolina wilted when Jackson threatened to use force to enforce tariff; served under President Monroe as secretary of war, 1817–25, and under President Tyler as secretary of state, 1844–45; as U.S. representative (D-S.C.), 1811–17, was "war hawk" in favor of War of 1812; as U.S. senator (D-S.C.), 1832–43, 1845–50, opposed Mexican War and Compromise of 1850;

born in what is now Mount Carmel, S.C.

**Hattie Wyatt Caraway** (1878–1950): First woman elected to U.S. Senate; was appointed U.S. senator (D-Ark.) on Nov. 13, 1931, to fill vacancy caused by death of husband, Sen. Thaddeus H. Caraway; elected to U.S. Senate on Jan. 12, 1932; reelected to full terms in 1932 and 1938; born in Bakerville, Tenn.

**Benjamin Nathan Cardozo** (1870–1938): Associate justice of U.S. Supreme Court, 1932–38; on principle that Constitution was flexible to permit social change, wrote ruling upholding Social Security Act, 1937; born in New York City.

**Andrew Carnegie** (1835–1919): Industrialist and philanthropist; starting work as telegraph messenger boy at 15, he amassed fortune estimated at $500 million; developed Carnegie Steel Company, which he sold to U.S. Steel for $225 million in 1901; contributed money to build 2,500 public libraries in English-speaking countries; endowed various foundations and institutions to promote peace and education; born in Dunfermline, Scotland.

**Christopher ("Kit") Carson** (1809–68): Explored West as frontiersman and fur trapper in 1820s and 1830s; guide for John C. Frémont on expeditions to Colorado, Oregon, and California, 1842–48; organized volunteer force to check Indian raids on settlers in New Mexico during Civil War; born in Madison County, Ky.

**Salmon Portland Chase** (1808–73): 6th Chief Justice of U.S., 1864–73; presided over Senate impeachment trial of President Johnson in 1868; as Lincoln's secretary of the treasury, 1861–64, financed Union expenses in Civil War through loans and issuing "greenbacks"; as antislavery U.S. senator from Ohio, 1849–55, 1861, fought Compromise of 1850 and Kansas-Nebraska Act; first Republican governor of Ohio, 1856–60; born in Cornish, N.H.

**Cesar Estrada Chavez** (born 1927): Labor organizer of migrant farm workers, especially Mexican-Americans; formed farm workers union, 1962, now called United Farm Workers of America (UFW); a believer in nonviolence, Chavez organized nationwide boycotts against grape and lettuce growers in 1960s and 1970s to force producers to agree to union contracts; born near Yuma, Ariz.

**George Rogers Clark** (1752–1818): Frontiersman-soldier during Revolutionary War; led about 200 militia down Ohio River and across wilderness to capture British forts at Kaskaskia, Ill., 1778, and at Vincennes, Ind., 1779; destroyed Shawnee village of Chillicothe, Ohio, 1780, putting an end to Indian raids on settlers in Kentucky; born near Charlottesville, Va.

**William Clark** (1770–1838): With Meriwether Lewis, explored Missouri and Columbia rivers of new Louisiana Territory, 1804–06; governor of Missouri Territory, 1813–20; younger brother of George Rogers Clark; born in Caroline County, Va.

**Henry Clay** (1777–1852): Whig leader; three-time loser for President, 1824, 1832, 1844; mediated Missouri Compromise of 1820 and sponsored Compromise of 1850; advocated protective tariff and federal aid for internal improvements; U.S. secretary of state, 1825–29; U.S.

QUICK QUIZ: What is the highest point in the United States? See page 179.

**FAMOUS PERSONS IN AMERICAN HISTORY** *(continued)*
senator from Kentucky, 1806–07, 1810–11, 1831–42, 1849–52; U.S. representative from Kentucky, 1811–14, 1815–21, 1823–25, also serving as Speaker of the House during most of those terms; led "war hawks" in favor of War of 1812; born in Hanover County, Va.

**De Witt Clinton** (1769–1828): Father of Erie Canal, linking Hudson River with Great Lakes; private secretary to uncle, New York Gov. George Clinton, 1790–95; U.S. senator (D-R-N.Y.), 1802–03; mayor of New York City, 1803–07, 1810–11, 1813–14; unsuccessful Federalist and Peace Party candidate for President, 1812; headed commission presenting plans for Erie Canal to legislature, 1815; as governor of New York, 1817–21, 1825–28, broke ground for beginning Erie Canal, 1817, and officially opened canal, 1825; born in Napanock, N.Y.

**George Clinton** (1739–1812): 4th Vice President of U.S., 1805–12, serving under Presidents Jefferson and Madison; first state governor of New York, 1777–95, 1801–04, elected to record seven terms; as delegate to Continental Congress, 1775–76, voted for Declaration of Independence but was unable to sign it, having been called to duty as brigadier general of militia on July 8, 1776; born in Little Britain, N.Y.

**William Frederick ("Buffalo Bill") Cody** (1846–1917): Frontiersman and showman; as buffalo hunter, claimed to have killed over 4,000 in 1867–68 as food for railroad construction crews; became nationally known in 1870s as result of dime novels about him written by E.Z.C. Judson (Ned Buntline); organized traveling "Wild West" show, 1883, with which he toured U.S. and Europe for rest of life; show featured markswoman Annie Oakley and, for a while, Indian Chief Sitting Bull; born in Scott County, Iowa.

**Crazy Horse** (c.1844–77): Sioux Indian chief who helped lead Sioux War of 1876–77, protesting federal government orders that Indians remain on reservations; defeated Gen. George Crook in Battle of Rosebud; massacred Gen. George A. Custer and troops in Battle of Little Bighorn; surrendered voluntarily but was killed while being forced into prison cell.

**Davy Crockett** (1786–1836): Frontiersman and congressman; served as scout for Gen. Andrew Jackson in Creek War, 1813–14, becoming colonel in Tennessee militia; represented Tennessee in Congress, first as Democrat, 1827–31, then as Whig, 1833–35; died in Battle of the Alamo, 1836; born in Greene County, Tenn.

**George Armstrong Custer** (1839–76): Union cavalry officer whose daring and skill won him promotion to brigadier general at age 23 during Civil War; in Battle of Little Bighorn in Montana, June 25, 1876, led U.S. cavalry attack on Sioux Indians under Crazy Horse, but he and entire column of about 225 men were slain in what became known as "Custer's Last Stand"; graduated last in his class at West Point, 1861; born in New Rumley, Ohio.

**George Mifflin Dallas** (1792–1864): 11th Vice President of U.S., under President Polk, 1845–49; mayor of Philadelphia, 1829; U.S. senator (D-Pa.), 1831–33; U.S. minister to Russia, 1837–39, and to Britain, 1856–61; born in Philadelphia.

**Clarence Seward Darrow** (1857–1938): Criminal and labor lawyer noted for his defense of underdog and unpopular causes; earned first fame for defense of labor leader Eugene V. Debs in Pullman strike of 1894; initiated use of psychiatric evidence in Leopold-Loeb murder trial, saving clients from death penalty, 1924; opposed William Jennings Bryan in Scopes trial, 1925; born in Kinsman, Ohio.

**Jefferson Davis** (1808–89): President of Confederate States of America during Civil War, 1861–65; imprisoned 1865–67 on charges of treason; finally released on bond signed by Horace Greeley and others and never brought to trial; served as U.S. representative (D-Miss.), 1845–46, resigning to fight as colonel in Mexican War; won acclaim in Battles of Monterrey and Buena Vista, 1846–47; U.S. senator (D-Miss.), 1847–51, opposing Compromise of 1850; U.S. secretary of war under President Pierce, 1853–57; born in Christian (now Todd) County, Ky., on June 3, 1808.

**Charles Gates Dawes** (1865–1951): 30th Vice President of U.S., under President Coolidge, 1925–29; co-recipient of Nobel Peace Prize in 1925 for Dawes Plan, scheduling payments of $33 billion in World War I reparations by Germany; U.S. ambassador to Britain, 1929–32; first chairman of Reconstruction Finance Corporation, 1932; born in Marietta, Ohio.

**Benjamin Henry Day** (1810–89): Founded New York *Sun* in 1833 as first penny newspaper hawked on streets by newsboys; circulation of 30,000 was largest of any newspaper at that time; born in West Springfield, Mass.

**Stephen Day** (c.1594–1668): First printer in what is now U.S.; established press in Cambridge, Mass; printed first broadside, *The Freeman's Oath*, 1639; first book, *The Bay Psalm Book*, 1640; born in Cambridge, England.

**Eugene Victor Debs** (1855–1926): Socialist labor leader; established American Railway Union (ARU), 1893; jailed for disobeying federal injunction against ARU boycott on moving Pullman cars to support striking Pullman workers, 1894; ran for President five times as candidate of Social Democratic (Socialist) Party, 1900–20; jailed under wartime Espionage Act, 1918–21; born in Terre Haute, Ind.

**Stephen Decatur** (1779–1820): U.S. Navy officer; gained first fame with daring raid in harbor of Tripoli, Libya, burning U.S. frigate *Philadelphia* that had been captured by Barbary Coast Arab pirates, 1804; in War of 1812 commanded squadron that captured British warship *Macedonian;* as commodore, 1815, led squadron to Mediterranean that forced Arab pirates to give up attacks on U.S. ships; upon return gave toast: "Our country: In her intercourse with foreign nations may she always be right; but our country, right or wrong"; born in Sinepuxent, Md.

**George Dewey** (1837–1917): Admiral in Spanish-American War; destroyed Spanish Pacific fleet in Manila Bay on May 1, 1898, after giving captain of lead ship of his squadron famous command: "You may fire when you are ready, Gridley"; victory assured U.S. conquest of Philippines; graduated from Annapolis, 1858; born in Montpelier, Vt.

**John Dewey** (1859–1952): Philosopher and educator; was pragmatist, believing ideas can only be judged on basis of how well they work;

developed philosophy, called instrumentalism, that man can overcome obstacles by using experience and intelligence; taught at University of Chicago, 1894–1904, and at Columbia, 1904–30; opposed traditional memorization of facts, in favor of learning through activities to stimulate thought; born in Burlington, Vt.

**Thomas Edmund Dewey** (1902–71): Unsuccessful Republican candidate for President, 1944, 1948; three-term governor of New York, 1943–54; gained fame as district attorney and special prosecutor in New York City, convicting such gangsters as Waxey Gordon and Lucky Luciano, 1931–38; born in Owosso, Mich.

**John Dickinson** (1732–1808): Called "Penman of the Revolution" because of many important documents he wrote in early U.S. history; as Pennsylvania delegate to Stamp Act Congress, wrote *Declaration of Rights and Grievances of the Colonists of America*, 1765; published *Letters from a Farmer in Pennsylvania to Inhabitants of the British Colonies*, 1767; as delegate to Continental Congress, wrote *Petition to the King* and *Address to the Inhabitants of Quebec*, 1774, and *Declaration on the Causes and Necessity of Taking Up Arms*, 1775; opposed and refused to sign Declaration of Independence, believing colonies should remain part of British Empire; wrote Articles of Confederation, 1776, later adopted as first form of U.S. government; fought in Revolutionary War first as private, later as brigadier general, 1777–78; president of Delaware, 1781–82; president of Pennsylvania, 1782–85; presided at Annapolis Convention, 1786, that issued call for constitutional convention to revise structure of U.S. government; delegate to Constitutional Convention, 1787; born near Trappe, Md.

**Dorothea Lynde Dix** (1802–87): Devoted most of life to crusade for building of separate hospitals for mentally ill patients, who in 1840s were confined in prisons with criminals; succeeded in getting such hospitals built in 15 states, Canada, Europe, and Japan; superintendent of nurses for Union Army during Civil War; born in Hampden, Me.

**Stephen Arnold Douglas** (1813–61): Unsuccessful Democratic candidate for President against Abraham Lincoln in 1860; as U.S. senator (D-Ill.), 1847–61, helped pass Compromise of 1850 and sponsored Kansas-Nebraska Act of 1854 that replaced Missouri Compromise with "popular sovereignty" in territories on slavery issue; defeated Lincoln in Illinois Senate race in 1858, featuring seven famous Lincoln-Douglas debates; born in Brandon, Vt.

**Frederick Douglass** (1817–95): Black abolitionist; escaped from slavery in Maryland in 1838, settling in Massachusetts; published autobiography, 1845, and fled to England until friends arranged for purchase of his freedom; founded abolitionist newspaper *North Star*, 1847; recruited black troops for Union Army during Civil War, 1861–65; U.S. minister to Haiti, 1889–91; born in Tuckahoe, Md.

**W.E.B. Du Bois** (1868–1963): Black civil-rights leader and scholar; helped found National Association for the Advancement of Colored People (NAACP), 1909; edited NAACP maga-

zine *The Crisis*, 1910–34; head of sociology department, Atlanta University, 1932–44; joined Communist Party, 1961, and emigrated to Ghana, 1962; born in Great Barrington, Mass.

**John Foster Dulles** (1888–1959): U.S. secretary of state under President Eisenhower, 1953–59; in Cold War period, developed policy of "brinksmanship," going almost to point of war with communist nations, and threatened "massive retaliation" for communist aggressions; delegate to UN, 1945–50; U.S. senator (R-N.Y.), 1949; main author of Japanese peace treaty, 1951; born in Washington, D.C.

**Eleuthère Irénée du Pont de Nemours** (1771–1834): Built gunpowder plant near Wilmington, Del., 1802, providing basis for later Du Pont industrial empire developed by his descendants; learned chemistry and how to make gunpowder as student of French chemist Antoine Lavoisier; came to U.S. in 1800; born in Paris.

**Amelia Earhart** (1897–1937): First woman pilot to fly solo across Atlantic, 1932; first to fly solo from Hawaii to mainland, 1935; vanished in Pacific Ocean while attempting around-the-world flight, 1937; born in Atchison, Kan.

**Mary Baker Eddy** (1821–1910): Founded Christian Science about 1870; wrote *Science and Health*, 1875, describing belief that prayer and spiritual understanding can overcome illness; chartered Church of Christ, Scientist, 1879; established *Christian Science Monitor*, 1908; born in Bow, N.H.

**Oliver Ellsworth** (1745–1807): 3d Chief Justice of U.S., 1796–1800; as special envoy to Paris he negotiated treaty ending undeclared naval war between U.S. and France, 1800; as U.S. senator (Fed.-Conn.), 1789–96, largely responsible for drafting Federal Judiciary Act of 1789, laying basis for U.S. court system; Connecticut delegate to Continental Congress, 1777–84, and to Constitutional Convention, 1787; born in Windsor, Conn.

**James Leonard Farmer** (born 1920): Black civil-rights leader; helped found Congress of Racial Equality (CORE), 1942, to end racial discrimination by nonviolent, passive resistance; under his guidance as national director, CORE began series of lunch counter sit-ins and freedom rides in Southern states in 1960s that often touched off violent reactions and mass arrests of demonstrators; unsuccessful Republican candidate for Congress in New York City; assistant secretary of Department of Health, Education, and Welfare, in Nixon administration, 1969–70; born in Marshall, Texas.

**David Glasgow Farragut** (1801–70): U.S. Navy admiral in Civil War; best remembered for command "Damn the torpedoes. Full steam ahead!" in his victorious attack on Mobile, Ala., in August 1864; earlier became Union hero when his fleet forced surrender of New Orleans on May 1, 1862; first U.S. Navy officer to hold ranks of rear admiral (1862), vice admiral (1864), and full admiral (1866); born near Knoxville, Tenn.

**Marshall Field** (1834–1906): Merchant and philanthropist; beginning as $8-a-week sales clerk, became multimillionaire developer of largest department store in Chicago; innovated mark-

**FAMOUS PERSONS IN AMERICAN HISTORY** *(continued)*

ing products with firm prices and giving customers full exchange privileges on purchases; coined slogan "Give the Lady What She Wants"; gave land and millions of dollars to establish University of Chicago and Field Museum of Natural History; born in Conway Township, Mass.

**Benjamin Franklin** (1706–90): Helped draft and signed Declaration of Independence, 1776, alliance with France, 1778, treaty of peace with Britain, 1783, and U.S. Constitution, 1787; edited and published *Pennsylvania Gazette*, 1729–1766, and *Poor Richard's Almanack*, 1732–57; invented Franklin stove, 1740, and proved lightning was electricity, 1752; deputy postmaster of American colonies, 1753–74; wrote Albany Plan for uniting American colonies, 1754; Pennsylvania representative in London, 1757–75; member of Continental Congress and first postmaster general, 1775–76; ambassador to France, 1776–85; governor of Pennsylvania, 1785–88; born in Boston.

**John Charles Frémont** (1813–90): First Republican candidate for President, 1856; led military expeditions that explored territory from Rocky Mountains to California, 1842–44; on third expedition, 1845–47, helped capture California in Mexican War and served briefly as territory's first governor; in dispute with Maj. Gen. Stephen W. Kearny, was found guilty of insubordination by court-martial and resigned from Army; gold discovered on land he owned made him millionaire overnight; upon California's admission as state, served six months as Free-Soil Democrat U.S. senator, 1850–51; major general in Union Army in West during Civil War, 1861–64; governor of Arizona Territory, 1878–81; born in Savannah.

**Albert Gallatin** (1761–1849): U.S. secretary of the treasury under Presidents Jefferson and Madison, 1802–14; as member of War of 1812 peace commission, negotiated Treaty of Ghent, 1814; minister to France, 1815–23, and to Britain, 1826–27; born in Geneva, Switzerland.

**William Lloyd Garrison** (1805–79): Abolitionist leader; published abolitionist newspaper *Liberator*, 1831–65, promising in its first issue, "I will be heard!"; helped organize American Anti-Slavery Society, 1833, and served as president in 1840s and 1850s; burned U.S. Constitution because of clauses protecting slavery, July 4, 1854, declaring, "So perish all compromises with tyranny!"; after Civil War, crusaded for prohibition and women's rights; born in Newburyport, Mass.

**Horatio Gates** (c.1728–1806): Revolutionary War major general; commanded American army that won first major victory at Battle of Saratoga, 1777, forcing surrender of over 5,000 British troops; reputation shattered at Battle of Camden (S.C.), 1780, when his American army of 4,000 was destroyed by British General Cornwallis, and Gates fled in retreat; removed from active duty; born in Maldon, England.

**Henry George** (1839–97): Promoted "single tax" on land use to replace all other taxes to let economic laws operate freely; published ideas in *Progress and Poverty*, 1879; twice defeated as candidate for mayor of New York City, 1886, 1897; born in Philadelphia.

**Geronimo** (1829–1909): Apache Indian chief; raided settlers in Mexico, New Mexico, and Arizona; surrendered in 1886; held in confinement for rest of life but allowed to make brief appearances at St. Louis World's Fair, 1904, and in Theodore Roosevelt's inaugural procession, 1905; born in southern Arizona.

**Elbridge Gerry** (1744–1814): 5th U.S. Vice President, 1813–14, dying in office; Massachusetts delegate to Continental Congress, 1776–85, signing both Declaration of Independence and Articles of Confederation; delegate to Constitutional Convention, 1787, but refused to sign U.S. Constitution because he disagreed with some of its provisions; Antifederalist U.S. representative from Massachusetts, 1789–93; governor of Massachusetts, 1810–12; born in Marblehead, Mass.

**John Herschel Glenn Jr.** (born 1921): First U.S. astronaut to orbit Earth in space, Feb. 20, 1962; U.S. Marine fighter pilot in World War II and Korean War, flying 122 combat missions; retired as astronaut, 1964; elected U.S. senator (D-Ohio), 1974; born in Cambridge, Ohio.

**George Washington Goethals** (1858–1928): U.S. Army engineer who directed building of Panama Canal, 1907–14; governor of Panama Canal Zone, 1914–16; born in Brooklyn, N.Y.

**Barry Morris Goldwater** (born 1909): Unsuccessful Republican candidate for President, 1964; called "Mr. Conservative" because of political views; U.S. senator (R-Ariz.), 1953–65, 1969– ; born in Phoenix.

**Samuel Gompers** (1850–1924): Labor leader who helped found and was president of American Federation of Labor (AFL), 1886–94, 1896–1924; opposed formation of independent labor political party or union affiliations with political parties; established system of labor-management negotiations for written union contracts; born in London.

**Billy (William Franklin) Graham** (born 1918): Protestant evangelist; ordained as Southern Baptist minister, 1939; in four-month crusade in New York City's Madison Square Garden in 1957, nearly 2 million persons attended, resulting in more than 50,000 conversions; born near Charlotte, N.C.

**Horace Greeley** (1811–72): Unsuccessful Democratic and Liberal Republican candidate for President against U.S. Grant, 1872; founded and edited influential New York *Tribune*, 1841–72; helped Lincoln win Republican presidential nomination, 1860; supported abolition, prohibition, and protective tariffs; popularized phrase "Go west, young man" but did not originate it; born near Amherst, N.H.

**Nathanael Greene** (1742–86): Revolutionary War major general who liberated Southern states from British military occupation in series of daring battles, 1781; earlier in war, distinguished himself in Battles of Trenton, Brandywine, and Germantown; quartermaster general of Continental Army, 1778–80; born in Potowomut (now Warwick), R.I.

**Nathan Hale** (1755–76): During Revolutionary War, while on volunteer spy mission for George Washington, was captured on Long Island, N.Y., and hanged by British, Sept. 22, 1776; remembered for heroic last words: "I only regret that I have but one life to lose for my country"; born in Coventry, Conn.

**Alexander Hamilton** (c.1757–1804): Took major role in founding U.S. system of government; served in Revolutionary War as aide-de-camp to George Washington, 1777–81; commanded regiment at Battle of Yorktown, 1781; represented New York in Continental Congress, 1782–83; delegate to Constitutional Convention and signer of U.S. Constitution, 1787; wrote most essays in *The Federalist*, urging ratification of Constitution, 1787–88; as first U.S. secretary of the treasury, 1789–95, put new government on sound financial basis; helped initiate political system of two major political parties as leader of conservative Federalists in opposition to Thomas Jefferson's liberal Democratic-Republicans; appointed major general of new U.S. Army, second in command to George Washington, 1798; killed in duel with Vice President Aaron Burr, 1804; born on island of Nevis in British West Indies.

**John Hancock** (1737–93): President of Continental Congress, 1775–77, 1785–86; first signer of Declaration of Independence, 1776; was joint leader with Samuel Adams of Massachusetts colonial resistance after British seized one of his merchant ships on charges of illegal trading, 1768; first state governor of Massachusetts, 1780–85, 1787–93; born in North Braintree (now Quincy), Mass.

**Patrick Henry** (1736–99): Virginia patriot leader; best remembered for call for colonial resistance in 1775: "I know not what course others may take; but as for me, give me liberty, or give me death!"; commanded Virginia's militia, 1775–76; delegate to Continental Congress, 1774–76; first state governor of Virginia, 1776–79, 1784–86; opposed adoption of U.S. Constitution because it lacked Bill of Rights, 1787–88; born in Hanover County, Virginia.

**Oliver Wendell Holmes Jr.** (1841–1935): As associate justice of U.S. Supreme Court, 1902–32, became known as "the Great Dissenter" because he disagreed so often with conservative majority; believed court should not upset social legislation unless it specifically violated Constitution; born in Boston.

**J. Edgar Hoover** (1895–1972): Director of Federal Bureau of Investigation (FBI), 1924–72; developed FBI into efficient crime-fighting organization free of politics; initiated services to local police, such as fingerprint file for identifying criminals; born in Washington, D.C.

**Mark Hopkins** (1802–87): Educator; president of Williams College, 1836–72; gained fame when President James Garfield described his effectiveness as a teacher, saying, "Give me a log hut, with only a simple bench, Mark Hopkins on one end and I on the other"; born in Stockbridge, Mass.

**Samuel Houston** (1793–1863): Commander of army of American settlers in Texas War of Independence, 1836; defeated Mexicans in Battle of San Jacinto, April 21, 1836; president of Texas Republic, 1836–38, 1841–44; U.S. senator (D-Texas), 1846–59; as Texas governor, 1859–61, deposed for opposition to secession; U.S. representative (D-Tenn.), 1823–27; Tennessee governor, 1827–29; born near Lexington, Va.

**Charles Evans Hughes** (1862–1948): 12th Chief Justice of U.S., 1930–41; fought President

F.D. Roosevelt's effort at "court packing" to end court's reversals of New Deal legislation; associate justice of U.S. Supreme Court, 1910–16, resigning to run, unsuccessfully, as Republican candidate for President, 1916; secretary of state under Presidents Harding and Coolidge, 1921–25; born in Glens Falls, N.Y.

**Cordell Hull** (1871–1955): U.S. secretary of state, 1933–44; initiated "good neighbor" policy with Latin America, 1933; was negotiating with Japanese envoys in Washington when Pearl Harbor was bombed, 1941; developed plans for United Nations, 1944; awarded Nobel Peace Prize, 1945; U.S. representative (D-Tenn.), 1907–21, 1923–31; U.S. senator (D-Tenn.), 1931–33; born in Overton County, Tenn.

**Hubert Horatio Humphrey** (1911–78): 38th Vice President of U.S., under President L.B. Johnson, 1965–69; unsuccessful Democratic candidate for President, 1968; U.S. senator (D-Minn.), 1949–65, 1971–78; mayor of Minneapolis, Minn., 1945–49; born in Wallace, S.D.

**Thomas Jonathan ("Stonewall") Jackson** (1824–63): Confederate general; twice defeated Union Army at Bull Run, 1861, 1862; led Shenandoah Valley campaign, 1862; forced Union retreat at Chancellorsville, 1863; accidentally killed by own troops; graduated from West Point, 1846; born in Clarksburg, W.Va. (then in Va.).

**Jesse Woodson James** (1847–82): Western outlaw; led gang that included his brother Frank, Cole Younger, and others in bank and train robberies; killed by gang member Robert Ford for $5,000 reward; born in Clay County, Mo.

**John Jay** (1745–1829): 1st Chief Justice of U.S., 1790–95; New York delegate to Continental Congress, 1774–79; president of Congress, 1778–79; helped negotiate and signed treaty of peace with Britain, 1783; U.S. secretary of foreign affairs; 1784–89; authored five essays in *The Federalist*, urging ratification of U.S. Constitution, 1787–88; negotiated Jay's Treaty settling outstanding disputes with Britain, 1794; governor of New York, 1795–1801; born in New York City.

**John Paul Jones** (1747–92): U.S. naval hero in Revolutionary War; commanded *Bonhomme Richard*, forcing surrender of more heavily armed British frigate *Serapis*, 1779; during battle, reputed to have replied to British demand for surrender: "I have not yet begun to fight!"; only Continental Navy officer to receive gold medal from Congress, 1787; rear admiral in Russian Navy, 1788–89, in war with Turks; born in Kirkcudbrightshire, Scotland.

**Edward Moore ("Ted") Kennedy** (born 1932): Brother of President Kennedy; U.S. senator (D-Mass.), 1962– ; unsuccessfully opposed President Carter for Democratic presidential nomination in 1980; withdrew as candidate for Democratic presidential nomination in 1972 after receiving suspended sentence for leaving scene of fatal automobile accident on Chappaquiddick Island, Mass., 1969; born in Boston, Mass.

**Robert Francis Kennedy** (1925–68): Brother of President Kennedy; U.S. attorney general, 1961–64; U.S. senator (D-N.Y.), 1965–68; assassinated in Los Angeles while campaigning for Democratic presidential nomination, 1968; born

**FAMOUS PERSONS IN AMERICAN HISTORY** *(continued)*

in Brookline, Mass.

**Ernest Joseph King** (1878–1956): Admiral in command of U.S. fleet during World War II, 1941–45, and chief of naval operations, 1942–45; promoted to 5-star admiral of the fleet, 1944; born in Lorain, Ohio.

**Martin Luther King Jr.** (1929–68): Black civil-rights leader; awarded Nobel Peace Prize, 1964; ordained as Baptist minister, 1947; began nonviolent crusade for black rights with boycott of buses in Montgomery, Ala., to end racial discrimination in seating arrangements on buses, 1955; founder and first president of Southern Christian Leadership Conference (SCLC), 1957; at demonstration of more than 200,000 persons in Washington, D.C., 1963, made address *I Have a Dream*; assassinated by white escaped convict James Earl Ray in Memphis, Tenn., on April 4, 1968; assassination caused riots in 125 cities; born in Atlanta.

**Rufus King** (1755–1827): Unsuccessful Federalist candidate for President, 1816; Massachusetts delegate to Congress, 1784–87; signer of U.S. Constitution, 1787; U.S. senator (Fed.-N.Y.), 1789–96, 1813–25; U.S. minister to Britain, 1796–1803, 1825–26; born in Scarboro, Me. (then part of Massachusetts).

**Robert Marion La Follette** (1855–1925): Leader of Progressive movement; U.S. senator (Prog.-Wis.), 1906–25; U.S. representative (R-Wis.), 1885–91; governor of Wisconsin, 1901–05; opposed U.S. entry into World War I, 1917; opposed U.S. participation in League of Nations or World Court, 1918–19; unsuccessful Progressive candidate for President, 1924; born in Primrose, Wis.

**Alfred Mossman Landon** (born 1887): Unsuccessful Republican candidate for President, 1936; as wildcat oil prospector, became millionaire by age of 40; as governor of Kansas, 1933–37, managed state finances to maintain balanced budget while other states were going deeply into debt; born in West Middlesex, Pa.

**Richard Henry Lee** (1732–94): Virginia delegate to Continental Congress, 1774–79; introduced resolution for Declaration of Independence on June 7, 1776; as delegate to Congress, 1784–87, opposed U.S. Constitution, promoted adoption of Bill of Rights; U.S. senator (D-R-Va.), 1789–92; born in Westmoreland County, Va.

**Robert Edward Lee** (1807–70): In Civil War, commanded Confederate Army of Northern Virginia, 1862–65, after declining President Lincoln's offer to command Union Army; his master strategies gave smaller Confederate forces such victories as Seven Days Battle, Second Battle of Bull Run, Fredericksburg, and Chancellorsville; defeated at Gettysburg, 1863; appointed general in chief of Confederate armies, 1865; surrendered at Appomattox Court House, 1865; president of Washington College (now Washington and Lee University), 1865–70; born in Westmoreland County, Va.

**John Llewellyn Lewis** (1880–1969): Labor leader; president of United Mine Workers (UMW), 1920–60; organized Committee for Industrial Organizations (CIO), 1935; after CIO unions were expelled from AFL in 1938, Lewis served as CIO president until 1942; withdrew UMW from CIO in 1942 in policy dispute; born in Lucas, Iowa.

**Meriwether Lewis** (1774–1809): Leader with William Clark of expedition exploring Louisiana Purchase, 1804–06; governor of Louisiana Territory, 1807–09; born in Albemarle County, Va.

**Charles Augustus Lindbergh** (1902–74): American hero of 1920s for his courage in making first solo flight across Atlantic Ocean, on May 20–21, 1927; called "the Lone Eagle"; became semirecluse after sensational kidnap-murder of his baby son, 1932; opposed President F.D. Roosevelt's moves toward U.S. entry in World War II, but flew 50 combat missions against Japanese as civilian; born in Detroit.

**Robert R. Livingston** (1746–1813): New York delegate to Continental Congress, 1775–77, 1779–81; on committee to draft Declaration of Independence, 1776; first U.S. secretary of foreign affairs, 1781–83; as chancellor (chief judge) of New York, 1777–1801, administered presidential oath to George Washington, 1789; U.S. minister to France, 1801–04, negotiating Louisiana Purchase from France; financed Robert Fulton's steamboat development, 1803–07; born in New York City.

**Henry Cabot Lodge** (1850–1924): U.S. senator (R-Mass.), 1893–1924; pressed for U.S. entry in World War I in 1915; organized Senate opposition to Versailles Treaty and League of Nations, 1919–20; born in Boston.

**Henry Cabot Lodge Jr.** (born 1902): Unsuccessful Republican candidate for Vice President in 1960 as running mate of Richard M. Nixon; U.S. ambassador to UN, 1953–60; ambassador to South Vietnam, West Germany, and Vatican, 1963–77; U.S. senator (R-Mass.), 1937–44, 1947–53; first senator since Civil War to resign to enter U.S. Army; served in Europe in World War II, retired as major general; born in Nahant, Mass.

**Elijah Parish Lovejoy** (1802–37): Abolitionist martyr; while editor of antislavery Alton (Ill.) *Observer*, was attacked and killed by proslavery mob, 1837; born in Albion, Me.

**Mary Lyon** (1797–1849): Founded first women's college, Mount Holyoke Seminary (later College) in South Hadley, Mass., and served as its president, 1837–49; born in Buckland, Mass.

**Douglas MacArthur** (1880–1964): Commanding general of U.S. Far East forces during World War II, 1941–45; commanded occupation forces in Japan, 1945–51; supreme commander of UN forces in Korean War, 1950–51, until relieved by President Truman because of outspoken desire to invade communist China; commanded 42d Division in World War I, 1917–18; U.S. Army chief of staff, 1930–35; born in Little Rock, Ark.

**Horace Mann** (1796–1859): Led establishment of free public schools in U.S.; as secretary of new Massachusetts state board of education, 1837–48, set standards adopted by other states as well; founded first teacher-training school, in Lexington, Mass., 1839; U.S. representative (Whig-Mass.), 1848–53; president of Antioch College, 1853–59; born in Franklin, Mass.

**George Catlett Marshall** (1880–1959): Commander of all U.S. armies in World War II as chief of staff, 1939–45; as U.S. secretary of state, 1947–49, initiated Marshall Plan to rebuild Europe; awarded Nobel Peace Prize, 1953; unsuccessfully attempted to mediate civil war in

China, 1946; secretary of defense under President Truman during first years of Korean War, 1950–51; born in Uniontown, Pa.

**John Marshall** (1755–1835): 4th Chief Justice of U.S., 1801–35; established power of Supreme Court to declare laws unconstitutional in case of *Marbury* v. *Madison*, 1803; broadened scope of federal government with doctrine of implied powers, including all those necessary to carry out specific powers mentioned in U.S. Constitution; U.S. representative (Fed.-Va.), 1799–1800; U.S. secretary of state, 1800–01; born in Germantown (now Midland), Va.

**Thurgood Marshall** (born 1908): First black appointed as associate justice of U.S. Supreme Court, 1967; as head of legal services of National Association for the Advancement of Colored People (NAACP), 1940–61, won major Supreme Court decisions desegregating public schools, transportation, and housing; judge of U.S. Court of Appeals, 1961–65; U.S. solicitor general, 1965–67; born in Baltimore.

**Matthew Fontaine Maury** (1806–76): Pioneer oceanographer, called "Pathfinder of the Seas"; U.S. Navy officer, 1825–61; headed U.S. Navy's Depot of Charts and Instruments (later Naval Observatory and Hydrographic Office), 1842–61; developed uniform system of recording oceanographic data; his research on winds and currents provided basis for U.S. oceanographic charts; joined Confederate Navy during Civil War, commanding coast and harbor defenses; professor of meteorology at Virginia Military Institute, 1868–73; born near Fredericksburg, Va.

**Joseph Raymond McCarthy** (1908–57): U.S. senator (R-Wis.), 1947–57; charges that communists had infiltrated U.S. government and Army bred public hysteria; tactic of making unsupported charges came to be called *McCarthyism*; U.S. Senate censured McCarthy in 1954, ending his influence; born in Grand Chute, Wis.

**George Brinton McClellan** (1826–85): In Civil War, commanded Union Army of Potomac, 1861–62; reorganized Union forces after Bull Run defeat, 1861; directed Peninsular Campaign but failed to capture Richmond after forcing General Lee to retreat at Antietam, Md., causing Lincoln to relieve him of command, 1862; unsuccessful Democratic candidate for President, 1864; governor of New Jersey, 1878–81; graduated second in class from West Point, 1846; born in Philadelphia.

**John Cardinal McCloskey** (1810–85): First American cardinal of Roman Catholic Church, 1875–85; as archbishop of New York, 1864–85, responsible for building St. Patrick's Cathedral, opened 1879; born in Brooklyn, N.Y.

**George Stanley McGovern** (born 1922): Unsuccessful Democratic candidate for President, 1972; during campaign called Nixon administration "most corrupt in history," but majority of voters regarded this as political oratory until full extent of Watergate scandals was revealed in 1973–74; U.S. representative (D-S.D.), 1957–61; Democratic U.S. senator from South Dakota, 1963–  ; born in Avon, S.D.

**George Gordon Meade** (1815–72): In Civil War, commanded Union Army of the Potomac, 1863–65; defeated Confederate General Lee at Battle of Gettysburg, 1863, in turning point of war; graduated from West Point, 1835; born in Cádiz, Spain.

**William ("Billy") Mitchell** (1879–1936): U.S. Army general who demonstrated obsolescence of battleship by sinking several with aerial bombs in experiments in 1921–23; defying superior officers, he urged developing air force independent of U.S. Army and U.S. Navy; court-martialed and convicted of insubordination, 1925; born in Nice, France.

**Walter Frederick Mondale** (born 1928): 42d Vice President of U.S., 1977–  , elected as Democratic running mate of Jimmy Carter; U.S. senator (D-Minn.), 1964–77; attorney general of Minnesota, 1960–64; born in Ceylon, Minn.

**John Pierpont Morgan** (1837–1913): Multimillionaire banker who managed financing of many large U.S. corporations; powerful banking firm, J.P. Morgan & Company, halted gold drain on U.S. treasury by selling $62 million in bonds, 1895; organized U.S. Steel Corporation as world's largest corporation at time, 1901; helped end Panic of 1907 by loaning money to banks short of cash; born in Hartford, Conn.

**Robert Morris** (1734–1806): "Financier of the American Revolution," obtained money and supplies that made possible George Washington's achievements; as Pennsylvania delegate to Continental Congress, 1776–78, signed Declaration of Independence and Articles of Confederation; pledged personal credit to supply Washington's army for Battles of Trenton and Princeton, 1776; appointed by Congress superintendent of finance, 1781–84; as delegate to Constitutional Convention, signed U.S. Constitution, 1787; served Pennsylvania as U.S. senator, 1789–95; lost fortune and jailed for debt, 1798–1801; born in Liverpool, England.

**Lucretia Coffin Mott** (1793–1880): Abolitionist and women's rights leader; with Elizabeth Cady Stanton, organized first women's rights convention, at Seneca Falls, N.Y., 1848; aided escape of slaves through "underground railroad"; born on Nantucket, Mass.

**Carry Amelia Moore Nation** (1846–1911): Prohibitionist; conducted violent attacks on saloons in Kansas, using hatchet to smash liquor bottles and chop up furnishings; arrested many times for disturbing the peace in 1890s and early 1900s; born in Garrard County, Ky.

**Chester William Nimitz** (1885–1966): Admiral in command of U.S. Pacific Fleet in World War II, 1941–45; directed island-hopping campaign that led to Japan's surrender aboard his flagship, battleship USS *Missouri*, on Sept. 2, 1945; promoted to rank of 5-star fleet admiral, 1944; chief of naval operations, 1945–47; born in Fredericksburg, Texas.

**James Otis** (1725–83): Boston lawyer who paved way for American Revolution; his denunciation in 1761 of British writs of assistance (kind of search warrant) as illegal inspired patriots to stand up for rights; headed Massachusetts delegation to Stamp Act Congress, 1765; worked with Samuel Adams in protesting Townshend Acts and quartering of troops in Boston; born in West Barnstable, Mass.

QUICK QUIZ: What was the first capital of the United States? See page 324.

FAMOUS PERSONS IN AMERICAN HISTORY *(continued)*

**Thomas Paine** (1737–1809): Influenced adoption of Declaration of Independence by pamphlet *Common Sense,* January 1776; supported cause of freedom with series of essays, called *Crisis,* beginning in December 1776; after war, went to Europe where he wrote *The Rights of Man,* 1791–92, and *The Age of Reason,* 1794–96; returned to U.S., 1802; born in Thetford, England.

**Nathaniel Brown Palmer** (1799–1877): First explorer to sight Antarctica, on Nov. 18, 1820, while in command of 45-ton sloop *Hero;* first went to sea at age 14; commanded clipper ships trading with China, until retiring in 1850; born in Stonington, Conn.

**George Smith Patton Jr.** (1885–1945): In World War II, commanded U.S. Third Army in Europe, spearheading liberation of France, Germany, Czechoslovakia, and Austria, 1944–45; won nickname "Old Blood and Guts"; born in San Gabriel, Calif.

**Robert Edwin Peary** (1856–1920): First explorer to reach North Pole, April 6, 1909; promoted to rear admiral U.S. Navy, 1911, and retired; born in Cresson, Pa.

**William Penn** (1644–1718): Founded Pennsylvania as Quaker colony with religious freedom for other faiths, 1681; made treaty with Indians, paying for land granted to him by King Charles II, 1682; returned to England, 1684; visited Pennsylvania and wrote new constitution giving elective assembly complete lawmaking power, 1699–1701; born in London.

**Frances Perkins** (1882–1965): First woman member of presidential cabinet; U.S. secretary of labor under Presidents F.D. Roosevelt and Truman, 1933–45; U.S. civil service commissioner, 1946–53; born in Boston.

**Matthew Calbraith Perry** (1794–1858): U.S. naval officer who forced Japan to open two of its ports to U.S. trade, 1854; younger brother of Oliver Hazard Perry; born in Newport, R.I.

**Oliver Hazard Perry** (1785–1819): In War of 1812, commanded U.S. fleet on Lake Erie; after defeating British in Battle of Lake Erie, 1813, sent famous message: "We have met the enemy and they are ours"; born in South Kingston, R.I.

**John Joseph ("Black Jack") Pershing** (1860–1948): In World War I, commanding general of U.S. troops in Europe, 1917–19; U.S. Army chief of staff, 1921–24; awarded Pulitzer Prize for history in 1932 for book *My Experiences in the World War;* born near Laclede, Mo.

**Charles Cotesworth Pinckney** (1746–1825): Twice loser as Federalist candidate for President, 1804, 1808; also lost as President John Adams' running mate for Vice President, 1800; South Carolina delegate to Constitutional Convention and signer of U.S. Constitution, 1787; as special envoy to France, 1796, became famous for his reply to French official who asked for bribe: "It is no, no! Not a sixpence!"; major general in new U.S. Army, formed in 1798, third in command after Washington and Hamilton; born in Charleston, S.C.

**Pontiac** (c. 1720–69): Ottawa Indian chief who led attacks called "Pontiac's Conspiracy" on British colonial settlements west of Appalachian Mountains, 1763–66, killing hundreds of frontier families; signed peace treaty, 1766, receiving pardon by British.

**Edmund Randolph** (1753–1813): First U.S. attorney general under President Washington, 1789–94; U.S. secretary of state, 1794–95, resigning after being falsely charged with accepting bribe from France; as counsel, won acquittal for Aaron Burr in treason trial, 1807; as governor of Virginia, 1786–88, attended Constitutional Convention but refused to sign U.S. Constitution; born in Williamsburg, Va.

**Sam Rayburn** (1882–1961): Speaker of U.S. House of Representatives, 1940–47, 1949–53, 1955–61; as Texas Democrat, won election to Congress 25 consecutive times, serving 1913–61, under eight Presidents from Wilson to Kennedy; played major role in carrying out legislative programs of Presidents F.D. Roosevelt and Truman; born in Roane County, Tenn.

**Paul Revere** (1735–1818): Patriot and craftsman; on night of April 18–19, 1775, rode from Boston to Lexington, Mass., warning that the British were coming to arrest Samuel Adams and John Hancock for treason and to destroy patriot supplies; during Revolutionary War, made gunpowder, cannon, engraved and printed Continental currency, and served as lieutenant colonel of militia; designed many beautiful objects as silversmith; founded Revere Copper Co., at Canton, Mass., smelting copper and rolling it in sheets; born in Boston.

**John Davison Rockefeller** (1839–1937): Billionaire industrialist and philanthropist; made fortune in oil, founding Standard Oil Co., 1870; monopoly on oil broken by U.S. Supreme Court order, 1911; endowed University of Chicago, 1892, Rockefeller Institute of Medical Research, 1901, Rockefeller Foundation, 1913; born in Richford, N.Y.

**Nelson Aldrich Rockefeller** (1908–79): Appointed Vice President of U.S. by President Ford, serving 1974–77; governor of New York four times, 1959–73; held variety of positions in federal government, 1940–45, 1953–55; unsuccessfully sought Republican presidential nomination in 1964 and 1968; grandson of John D. Rockefeller; born in Bar Harbor, Me.

**Carl Schurz** (1829–1906): German-American editor, statesman, general; immigrated to U.S., 1852; as leader in Wisconsin Republican Party, backed Lincoln's presidential nomination, 1860; U.S. minister to Spain, 1861–62; general in Union Army, 1862–63; editor, Detroit *Post,* 1866–67; editor-founder, St. Louis *Westliche Post,* 1867–69; U.S. senator (R-Mo.), 1869–75; as U.S. secretary of the interior, 1877–81, reformed treatment of Indians and established civil-service merit system in Interior Department; editor, New York *Evening Post,* 1881–83; chief editorial writer, *Harper's Weekly,* 1892–98; born in Liblar, Prussia.

**Margaretha Meyer Schurz** (1834–76): Founded first kindergarten in U.S., in Watertown, Wis., 1856; immigrated to U.S. with husband, Carl Schurz, 1852; born in Prussia.

**Winfield Scott** (1786–1866): General and unsuccessful Whig candidate for President in 1852; became national hero for courage displayed as fighting general in War of 1812 Battles of Chippewa and Lundy's Lane, 1814; as commanding general of U.S. Army, 1841–61, became known to troops as "Old Fuss and Feathers" because of his

plumed hat; in Mexican War, commanded amphibious invasion at Veracruz, captured Mexico City, 1847; commanded Union Army at beginning of Civil War, but retired at age 75 on Nov. 1, 1861; born near Petersburg, Va.

**William Henry Seward** (1801–72): U.S. secretary of state under Presidents Lincoln and Andrew Johnson, 1861–69; arranged purchase of Alaska from Russia for $7.2 million, known at time as "Seward's Folly"; forced France to withdraw troops from Mexico after Civil War; first Whig governor of New York, 1839–42; as U.S. senator (Whig-N.Y.), 1849–55, (R-N.Y.), 1855–61, opposed slavery, Compromise of 1850, and Kansas-Nebraska Act; wounded by accomplice of John Wilkes Booth on night of Lincoln's assassination, 1865; born in Florida, N.Y.

**Philip Henry Sheridan** (1831–1888): General in Union Army in Civil War; gained fame leading successful charge on Missionary Ridge in Battle of Chattanooga, 1863; as commander of cavalry of Army of Potomac under U.S. Grant, 1864, drove Confederate troops of Gen. Jubal Early out of Virginia's Shenandoah Valley; commanding general of U.S. Army, 1884–88; believed born in Somerset, Ohio.

**William Tecumseh Sherman** (1820–91): General in Civil War; as commander of Union armies of West captured Atlanta, Sept. 1, 1864; led "March to the Sea" across Georgia with army of over 60,000, living off land and pillaging plantations and towns, capturing Savannah, Dec. 21, 1864; marching north, accepted surrender of Confederate Gen. J.E. Johnston at Durham, N.C., April 26, 1865; famed for statement "War is hell"; commanding general of U.S. Army, 1869–1884; when asked to run for President, he said, "I will not accept if nominated and will not serve if elected"; born in Lancaster, Ohio.

**Sitting Bull** (c.1834–90): Sioux Indian chief; battled U.S. Army and white settlers in 1860s and 1870s in Montana and the Dakotas; led Indians to Canada, 1877, but returned and surrendered, 1881; living on Standing Rock Reservation in South Dakota, began Ghost Dance unrest among Sioux, 1890; police and soldiers sent to arrest him killed him and his son; born in South Dakota.

**Samuel Slater** (1768–1835): Brought Industrial Revolution to U.S.; to monopolize textile industry, Britain had forbidden export of machines or emigration of persons familiar with them; having memorized details of machinery, Slater in disguise left Britain for U.S., 1789; with Moses Brown, built first successful cotton-spinning mill in U.S., in Pawtucket, R.I., 1790; opened own textile mills in New England; born in Belper, England.

**Alfred Emanuel Smith** (1873–1944): Unsuccessful Democratic presidential candidate, 1928; as first Roman Catholic to run for President, was opposed by Ku Klux Klan; also controversial because he favored repeal of prohibition; elected four times as governor of New York, serving in 1919–20; 1923–28; born in New York City.

**Jedediah Strong Smith** (c.1799–1831): Fur trader and explorer; in 1820s, mapped routes from Rockies to California and along Pacific coast; born in Bainbridge, N.Y.

**John Smith** (1580–1631): Helped found Jamestown, Va., first permanent English colony in America, 1607; captured by Indians but saved from execution by Pocahontas, daughter of chief; elected president of Virginia, 1608–09; explored and named New England, 1614; born in Willoughby, England.

**Edwin McMasters Stanton** (1814–69): U.S. secretary of war during and after Civil War, 1862–68; fired by President Andrew Johnson for harsh treatment of militarily occupied South, leading Stanton's Radical Republican supporters in Congress to bring about Johnson's impeachment and trial; U.S. attorney general, 1860–61; born in Steubenville, Ohio.

**Elizabeth Cady Stanton** (1815–1902): Leader in women's rights, abolition, and temperance movements; graduated from Troy (N.Y.) Female Seminary, 1832; married Henry B. Stanton, 1840; with Lucretia C. Mott, sponsored first U.S. women's rights convention, at Seneca Falls, N.Y., 1848; with Susan B. Anthony, organized National Woman Suffrage Association, 1869; was its first president, 1869–90; born in Johnstown, N.Y.

**Alexander Hamilton Stephens** (1812–83): Vice President of Confederate States of America during Civil War; represented Confederacy in peace conference with President Lincoln at Hampton Roads, Va., February 1865; U.S. representative (Whig-Ga.) 1843–52, (D-Ga.) 1852–59, 1873–82; imprisoned after Civil War; elected by Georgia to U.S. Senate, 1866, but not allowed to serve; governor of Georgia, 1882–83; born near Crawfordsville, Ga.

**Thaddeus Stevens** (1792–1868): Led Radical Republicans in Congress demanding harsh treatment of South after Civil War; managed impeachment of President Andrew Johnson, 1868; U.S. representative (Whig-Pa.), 1849–53, (R-Pa.), 1859–68; born in Danville, Vt.

**Adlai Ewing Stevenson** (1835–1914): Democratic Vice President of United States, 1893–97, under President Cleveland; U.S. representative (D-Ill.), 1875–77, 1879–81; unsuccessful Democratic candidate for Vice President, 1900, and for governor of Illinois, 1908; born in Christian County, Ky.

**Adlai Ewing Stevenson** (1900–65): Unsuccessful Democratic candidate for President, 1952, 1956; governor of Illinois, 1949–53; U.S. ambassador to UN, 1961–65; grandson of Vice President Adlai E. Stevenson; born in Los Angeles.

**Harlan Fiske Stone** (1872–1946): 11th Chief Justice of U.S., 1941–46; associate justice of Supreme Court, 1925–41; as U.S. attorney general, 1924–25, cleaned up Justice Department from effects of Teapot Dome scandals; supported New Deal legislation while on Supreme Court; born in Chesterfield, N.H.

**James Ewell Brown ("Jeb") Stuart** (1833–64): Confederate cavalry general in Civil War; called "eyes of the army" by General Lee; daringly circled entire Union Army to gather information; killed in battle for Richmond at Yellow Tavern, Va.; graduated from West Point, 1854; born in Patrick County, Va.

**Peter Stuyvesant** (c.1610–72): Last Dutch governor of New Netherland (now New York),

QUICK QUIZ: What were "carpetbaggers"? See page 362.

**FAMOUS PERSONS IN AMERICAN HISTORY** *(continued)*
1647–64; captured New Sweden (now Delaware, New Jersey, and part of Pennsylvania), 1655; ruled as dictator, forbidding sale of liquor to Indians, tolerating no religions other than Dutch Reformed; surrendered colony to British, Sept. 6, 1664; lost leg in military expedition against Caribbean island of St. Martin, 1644; born in Scherpenzeel, Netherlands.

**Roger Brooke Taney** (1777–1864): 5th Chief Justice of U.S., 1836–64; ruling in Dred Scott case, 1857, that Congress could not outlaw slavery in U.S. territories invalidated Missouri Compromise and Compromise of 1850, helping to bring on Civil War; served under President Jackson as attorney general, 1831–33, and as secretary of the treasury, 1833–34; because he opposed Second Bank of the U.S., Senate refused to confirm him as secretary of the treasury, 1834, and as associate justice of Supreme Court, 1835; born in Calvert County, Md.

**Samuel Jones Tilden** (1814–86): Democratic candidate for President, 1876; won majority of popular vote but Republican-controlled election commission awarded presidency to Rutherford B. Hayes; led reform group ousting corrupt Tweed ring from control of New York City government, 1872; governor of New York, 1875–76; founded New York Public Library with bequest; born in New Lebanon, N.Y.

**Harriet Tubman** (c.1820–1913): Black abolitionist; escaped slavery in Maryland, 1849; during 1850s helped hundreds of slaves escape to North on "underground railroad"; born in Dorchester County, Md.

**Nat Turner** (1800–31): Led slave uprising in Virginia in August 1831, killing about 60 whites; Turner and about 100 other blacks captured and killed; uprising led to severe slave restrictions in South; born in Southampton County, Va.

**Cornelius Vanderbilt** (1794–1877): Multimillionaire steamship and railroad magnate; quit school at 11; began operating sailboat ferry between Staten Island and New York City at 16; in 1850s began operating steamship service to Europe and San Francisco; formed New York Central Railroad, becoming its first president, 1867; donated $1 million to Central University in Nashville, Tenn., which changed its name to Vanderbilt University; fortune estimated at $100 million; born on Staten Island, N.Y.

**Lillian D. Wald** (1867–1940): Social worker; established city-wide visiting-nurse service in connection with New York City's Henry Street Settlement, which she founded and headed, 1895–1933; started first public-school nurse program, 1902; militantly campaigned against sweatshops and child labor; born in Cincinnati.

**Earl Warren** (1891–1974): 14th Chief Justice of U.S., 1953–69; liberal rulings included outlawing racial segregation in public schools (1954), liberalizing definition of obscenity (1957), banning required prayers or religious services in public schools (1962), establishing "one man, one vote" rule (1962), increasing freedom of press by limiting news media's liability for libel (1964), and improving legal protection of persons accused of crimes (1966); headed Warren Commission investigating assassination of President Kennedy, 1963–64; Republican governor of California, 1943–53; unsuccessful Republican candidate for Vice President, 1948; unsuccessful candidate for Republican presidential nomination, 1952; born in Los Angeles.

**Booker Taliaferro Washington** (1856–1915): Black educator and reformer; born a slave at Hales Ford, Va.; attended Hampton Institute, 1872–75; taught there, 1878–81; first president of Tuskegee Institute, Ala., 1881–1915; opposed political action for black civil rights; counseled blacks to work hard and acquire education; wrote *Up From Slavery,* 1901.

**Daniel Webster** (1782–1852): U.S. secretary of state, 1841–43, 1850–52; negotiated Webster-Ashburton Treaty settling Maine boundary dispute with Britain, 1842; unsuccessful Whig candidate for President, 1836; opposed War of 1812 and supported protective tariffs as Federalist U.S. representative from New Hampshire, 1813–17, and as U.S. representative from Massachusetts, 1823–27; as U.S. senator (Whig-Mass.), 1827–41, 1845–50, opposed Mexican War and supported Compromise of 1850; born in Salisbury (now Franklin), N.H.

**Charles Wilkes** (1798–1877): Discovered and named Antarctic continent on Jan. 30, 1840, while leading exploration mission for U.S. Navy; as rear admiral during Civil War, instigated Trent affair when he removed two Confederate commissioners from British ship, causing protest; born in New York City.

**Emma Hart Willard** (1787–1870): Established first college-level school for women in U.S.—Troy (N.Y.) Female Seminary, 1821; wrote poem "Rocked in the Cradle of the Deep," 1830; born in Berlin, Conn.

**Frances Elizabeth Caroline Willard** (1839–98): Educator and temperance reformer; president, Evanston (Ill.) College for Ladies, 1871–73; dean of women, Northwestern University, 1873–74; president, Woman's Christian Temperance Union (WCTU), 1879–98; founder and president of first international women's organization, World Woman's Christian Temperance Union, 1883; born in Churchville, N.Y.

**Roger Williams** (c.1603–83): Founder of Rhode Island; banished by Puritans from Massachusetts for belief in religious freedom and separation of church and state, 1635; founded first settlement at Providence, R.I., 1636; obtained charter for colony of Rhode Island, 1644; president of Rhode Island, 1654–57; born in London.

**Wendell Lewis Willkie** (1892–1944): Unsuccessful Republican candidate for President, 1940; president of electric utility company, 1933–40; wrote *One World,* 1943, promoting global unity; born in Elwood, Ind.

**John Winthrop** (1588–1649): Led Puritans to found Massachusetts Bay Colony and Boston, 1630; served as governor all but four years during 1630s and 1640s, sternly prohibiting practice of religions other than Congregationalist faith he established; born in Edwardstone, England.

**John Witherspoon** (1723–94): Only clergyman to sign Declaration of Independence; New Jersey delegate to Continental Congress, 1776–82; president, College of New Jersey (now Princeton University), 1768–94; Presbyterian pastor of Paisley, Scotland, 1757–68; born in Yester, Scotland.

# PROFILES OF OUR PRESIDENTS AND FIRST LADIES

The President and Vice President of the United States are the only officials elected by the American people as a whole.

The nation has had 40 Presidents, but only 39 men have been Chief Executive. One of them, Grover Cleveland, served nonconsecutive terms and thus was both the 22d and 24th President. Ronald Reagan became the 40th President upon taking office in 1981.

The U.S. presidency is a unique institution. Few other democratic nations have a single leader perform both the symbolic role of chief of state and at the same time the job of administering the government.

The President is simultaneously chief of state, chief executive, chief legislator, party leader, chief diplomat, and commander in chief of the armed forces. The action of the President in any one role materially affects the others, because the President is the mainspring of the governmental system.

The manner in which the President exercises his several functions generally determines his place in history.

The President may supply creative leadership and seek positively to change the shape of public opinion. Or he may assume the role of a charismatic leader by inspiring the people to greater heights of action. But the President must assume the ultimate responsibility for the nation's successes and failures during his administration.

The highlights of the Presidents' lives, including information on the women who served as First Lady, appear below and on the following pages.

## GEORGE WASHINGTON

1st President
(1789–97)

As commander of the Continental forces during the Revolutionary War and as the first President of the United States, George Washington became "father of his country."

In the eight years of his presidency the nation's basic institutions were established. Washington's personal qualities were remarkable.

Thomas Jefferson wrote that "his integrity was the most pure, his justice the most flexible, I have ever known. He was, indeed, in every sense of the word, a wise, a good and a great man."

### EARLY LIFE

Washington was the son of Augustine Washington, a moderately wealthy planter, and his second wife, Mary Ball. He was born on the family's Virginia estate (now known as Wakefield) on Feb. 22, 1732. His father died in 1743. George's half-brother Lawrence then became head of the family. George displayed an early talent for mathematics, and at the age of 15 began earning small fees by surveying. In 1748 he assisted George Fairfax in making an extensive survey of Thomas Lord Fairfax's lands in the wilderness country west of Virginia's Blue Ridge Mountains.

In 1751–52 he accompanied Lawrence, who was suffering from tuberculosis, to Barbados. There George survived a case of smallpox, becoming immune to the disease that was to plague his troops during the Revolutionary War. Lawrence died soon after returning to his Mount Vernon home. George inherited part of his estate. At 20 he obtained a commission as major in the militia.

Washington first gained public notice in 1753 when he was entrusted with a dangerous mission before the French and Indian War. He volunteered to deliver a message from Virginia Gov. Robert Dinwiddie to the French in Ohio country, warning them to leave the British-claimed territory. His two-and-a-half-month journey took him across hundreds of miles of unmapped wilderness to the shore of Lake Erie. When he returned he was commissioned lieutenant colonel.

Washington was then sent back to the frontier in command of a militia unit. In May 1754 he fought the first skirmish of the French and Indian War. He built Fort Necessity near present-day Uniontown, Pa., but was forced to surrender it to the French on July 4, 1754.

A year later, as aide-de-camp to British Gen. Edward Braddock in the disastrous expedition against Fort Duquesne, Washington established his reputation as a military leader by rallying the survivors for an orderly retreat. In 1758, commanding colonial forces supporting British regulars, he distinguished himself anew in the final capture of the French fort.

Washington, not yet 27, retired to private life when peace returned. A tall, well-built man, he was amiable, just, and immensely vital. In 1759 he married Mrs. Martha Custis, a wealthy widow with two children. He then settled down to the life of a Virginia gentleman on his plantation, Mount Vernon.

Washington was a member of the Virginia House of Burgesses (1759–74), where he became a leader in opposing British colonial policy. He served in 1774–75 as a delegate to the Continental Congress.

### COMMANDER OF THE CONTINENTAL ARMY

After the Revolution began, Washington became commander of the Continental Army, largely through the efforts of John Adams. Washington took command on July 3, 1775. His troops, unorganized and poorly disciplined, were mostly militia. Short terms of enlistment during the first years of the war kept his armies in a continuous state of disbandment and retraining.

QUICK QUIZ: When did Vietnam become a member of the UN? See page 423.

## GEORGE WASHINGTON (continued)

Congress failed to provide essential equipment, supplies, and soldiers' pay. Washington was also beset with the jealousies and intrigues of insubordinate officers.

Washington's strategy was successful in forcing the British evacuation of Boston in March 1776. He was then compelled by Congress to defend New York City. Due to the poor condition of his men and the tactical error of deploying part of his forces to Brooklyn, Washington met defeat.

But he rescued his army in a withdrawal that eventually carried them to southeastern Pennsylvania.

From there, on Christmas night 1776, he and his men crossed the Delaware, a masterful move that led to the rout of the British at Trenton and Princeton.

Washington's efforts to defend Philadelphia ended in defeat at Brandywine in September 1777 and at Germantown in October.

Washington and his 9,000 men wintered at Valley Forge, Pa., 1777–78. Seldom have a general and his army endured such extended deprivation and misery.

Washington's essential greatness matched every problem and intrigue, however, and in the spring he emerged with increased powers from Congress and a well-trained force (despite 3,000 desertions).

When the British evacuated Philadelphia to return to New York, Washington attacked the British column in the Battle of Monmouth on June 28, 1778. But the battle was lost by the cowardice of one of his officers, Maj. Gen. Charles Lee.

Three years later Charles Lord Cornwallis and his English army were trapped at Yorktown, Va., by Washington with the support of French land and sea forces. Cornwallis surrendered on Oct. 19, 1781, virtually ending the Revolutionary War.

In 1783 Washington retired from the Army and returned to Mount Vernon.

He and other patriots, becoming dissatisfied with the weakness of the government under the Articles of Confederation, joined to reorganize it. In 1787 he presided over the Constitutional Convention, which wrote the Constitution of the United States.

### FIRST PRESIDENT OF THE UNITED STATES

After the new government was organized, Washington was unanimously chosen as the first President. He took office on April 30, 1789, in New York City.

Washington's own views were Federalist. But in staffing his administration he was above partisanship. It was mainly his capacity for conciliation that kept the American Revolution free of terrorism, purges, and arbitrary seizures of power that have marked other revolutions.

He brought both Alexander Hamilton and Thomas Jefferson, leaders of opposing factions, into his cabinet.

Washington's poise, prestige, and dignity made the new government of the United States respected at home and abroad.

While President, Washington traveled extensively throughout the country.

Factions developed into political parties, and the strain put upon Washington as conciliator led to his refusal to accept a third term.

In public life Washington combined modesty with self-assurance. In his first inaugural address he acknowledged "deficiencies" in natural endowments and administrative experience. Characteristically, he set about overcoming them by study, as he had fitted himself for managing his plantations by studying agriculture.

Many precedents were set during his terms of office. The "advise and consent" role of the Senate evolved into the right of that body to approve or disapprove the President's actions but never to give him formal advice beforehand.

Chief among the vigorously debated issues of his administration were taxation and banking

## WASHINGTON'S PRESIDENTIAL ADMINISTRATION

**Congress in Session:**
1st, 2d, 3d, 4th

**Vice President:**
John Adams, 1789–97

**Secretary of the Treasury:**
Alexander Hamilton, 1789–95
Oliver Wolcott Jr., 1795–97

**Secretary of State:**
Thomas Jefferson, 1789–93
Edmund Randolph, 1794–95
Timothy Pickering, 1795–97

**Secretary of War:**
Henry Knox, 1789–95
Timothy Pickering, 1795–96
James McHenry, 1796–97

**Attorney General:**
Edmund Randolph, 1789–94
William Bradford, 1794–95
Charles Lee, 1795–97

**Postmaster General:**
Samuel Osgood, 1789–91
Timothy Pickering, 1791–95
Joseph Habersham, 1795–97

### PRESIDENTIAL ELECTION OF 1789

**Nominations:** Washington, the most popular man in the nation, was chosen by the Continental Congress. **Campaign Issues:** In this first U.S. presidential election party division was at a minimum, for only those who supported the new Constitution took part. **Remarks:** Most of the 11 states that had recently ratified the Constitution had their state legislatures choose presidential electors. New York failed to do so. Rhode Island and North Carolina had not yet ratified the new United States Constitution.

| PRESIDENTIAL CANDIDATES | PARTY | ELECTORAL VOTES |
|---|---|---|
| George Washington | None | 69 |
| John Adams | None | 34 |
| John Jay | None | 9 |
| Other candidates | None | 26 |
| Votes not cast | — | 4 |

### PRESIDENTIAL ELECTION OF 1792

**Nominations:** Washington and Adams, the incumbents, received the nomination of those who advocated a strong central government. Clinton was chosen by Antifederalist congressional leaders. **Campaign Issues:** The fiscal policy and strong centralization advocated by Alexander Hamilton, then secretary of the treasury and a staunch Federalist, provided the issues. **Remarks:** Washington's popularity could not be eclipsed. The Antifederalists had merely hoped to elect Clinton as Vice President.

| PRESIDENTIAL CANDIDATES | PARTY | ELECTORAL VOTES |
|---|---|---|
| George Washington | Federalist | 132 |
| John Adams | Federalist | 77 |
| George Clinton | Antifederalist | 50 |
| Thomas Jefferson | — | 4 |
| Aaron Burr | — | 1 |

policies, the assumption of state debts, and the jurisdiction of federal courts. During his second administration he was severely criticized by the Jeffersonians, especially for Jay's Treaty with England. In the war between England and France, Washington proclaimed neutrality and urged it as basic U.S. policy.

In his Farewell Address, he warned against "entangling alliances."

Washington died on Dec. 14, 1799. Over 178 years later, on March 13, 1978, in accord with a resolution of Congress, the U.S. Army promoted Washington to General of the Armies of the United States to preserve his seniority.

**Martha Dandridge (Custis) Washington** was born in 1731. At 18 she married Daniel Parke Custis, a wealthy plantation owner who died in 1757. She married Washington two years later.

The Washingtons had no children of their own, but Washington adopted Martha's two children, John Parke Custis and Martha Parke Custis.

Besides wealth and beauty Mrs. Washington was noted for her common sense, charm, and aristocratic graciousness She was a devoted wife. She died in 1802 and was buried beside her husband at Mount Vernon.

## JOHN ADAMS

The second President, John Adams disliked political parties and had a stormy term of office marred by factional intrigues. Although considered aloof, he was praised for his abilities even by those who disliked him.

Adams was born on Oct. 30, 1735, in Braintree (later Quincy), Mass., the son of John and Susanna (Boylston) Adams. He graduated from Harvard at 20, taught school for a time, and was admitted to the bar in 1758.

2d President
(1797–1801)

He was an outspoken opponent of the Stamp Act, arguing against the principle of taxation without representation. He gained fame as a defense attorney for the British soldiers accused of murder in the Boston Massacre of 1770.

Becoming a zealous advocate of independence, Adams was sent by Massachusetts to the Continental Congress. There he distinguished himself as a forceful leader. He proposed George Washington as commander in chief of the Continental Army and promoted adoption of the Declaration of Independence. In 1777 Adams presented the resolution establishing the design of the U.S. flag.

He next had a successful career as a diplomat for the embattled new nation. In 1777 he was sent as a commissioner to join Benjamin Franklin in France. In 1780–81 he persuaded the Netherlands to recognize the United States and lend it money. In 1782 he returned to France and helped draw up the Treaty of Paris to end the Revolutionary War. As the first U.S. envoy to Britain in 1785, Adams and his wife were met with hostility.

In 1789 he was chosen Vice President—in his opinion, "the most insignificant office that ever the invention of man contrived or his imagination conceived." A Federalist, he served under Washington for two terms.

In the 1796 presidential election, Adams won by only three electoral votes. The runner-up, Democratic-Republican leader Thomas Jefferson, became Vice President.

The United States fought an undeclared naval war with France during his administration. He did not wholeheartedly endorse the despotic Alien and Sedition Acts of 1798, but he signed them. These acts, aimed essentially at Thomas Jefferson and other critics of the Federalists, earned him the hatred of the Jeffersonians.

Defeated by Jefferson for reelection in 1800, Adams retired to Quincy, issuing political statements and writing.

Later, he carried on a long correspondence with his former rival, Jefferson.

By extraordinary coincidence, both Adams and Jefferson died on the 50th anniversary of the Republic they had done so much to establish—July 4, 1826.

**Abigail Smith Adams** (1744–1818) was the daughter of a minister. She and Adams were married in 1764. Lively and intelligent, she was one of the most distinguished First Ladies. The Adamses had two daughters and three sons—one, John Quincy Adams, became the sixth President. The Adamses in 1800 became the first presidential family to live in the White House.

## JOHN ADAMS' PRESIDENTIAL ADMINISTRATION

**Congress in Session:** 5th, 6th
**Vice President:**
  Thomas Jefferson, 1797–1801
**Secretary of State:**
  Timothy Pickering, 1797–1800
  John Marshall, 1800–01

**Secretary of the Treasury:**
  Oliver Wolcott Jr., 1797–1800
  Samuel Dexter, 1801
**Secretary of War:**
  James McHenry, 1797–1800
  Samuel Dexter, 1800

**Attorney General:**
  Charles Lee, 1797–1801
**Postmaster General:**
  Joseph Habersham, 1797–1801
**Secretary of the Navy:**
  Benjamin Stoddert, 1798–1801

## PRESIDENTIAL ELECTION OF 1796

**Nominations:** Congressional leaders of the two parties chose their respective candidates. **Campaign Issues:** Foreign policy dominated the campaign; the Federalists supported closer ties with England, while the Democratic-Republicans sought France's friendship. **Remarks:** Because of a split in the Federalist Party—between Hamilton and Adams—many Federalist electors gave their second vote to Jefferson.

| PRESIDENTIAL CANDIDATES | PARTY | ELECTORAL VOTES |
|---|---|---|
| John Adams | Federalist | 71 |
| Thomas Jefferson | Dem.–Rep. | 68 |
| Thomas Pinckney | Federalist | 59 |
| Aaron Burr | Dem.–Rep. | 30 |
| Other candidates | — | 48 |

QUICK QUIZ: Who is commandant of the Marine Corps? See page 463.

## THOMAS JEFFERSON

3d President
(1801–09)

Jefferson was rivaled among Americans only by Benjamin Franklin in the range of his interests, the quality of his intellectual contribution, and his faith in human progress.

As President he sought to curb the growing power of the U.S. Supreme Court, in which he felt the Federalists were attempting to entrench their philosophy. Jefferson believed that the federal government should be concerned mostly with foreign affairs, leaving the states free to administer local matters.

The son of Peter and Jane (Randolph) Jefferson, he was born on April 13, 1743, at Shadwell, the family estate in Virginia. His father, a tobacco plantation owner and a surveyor, died when Jefferson was 14. The boy took over management of Shadwell. He graduated from the College of William and Mary at 19 and was admitted to the bar in 1767. Five years later he married and settled at Monticello, a mansion he had personally designed.

He entered politics by winning election to Virginia's House of Burgesses in 1769 at the age of 26. There he became acquainted with Patrick Henry and other patriot leaders.

Jefferson was one of the organizers of the Virginia branch of the Committees of Correspondence, the chief medium of revolutionary agitation in the colonies.

His brilliantly written pamphlet *A Summary View of the Rights of British America* called attention to his logic, legal knowledge, and literary gifts.

He was chosen to write the Declaration of Independence in June 1776 at the Second Continental Congress, which he attended as an alternate. John Adams, who also was on the committee to write the Declaration, said he deferred to Jefferson because "I had a great opinion of the elegance of his pen."

He returned to Virginia to carry out some of his political and social principles in the newly established state. Serving in its legislature (1776–79) and as its governor (1779–81), he removed feudal vestiges from the landholding system. He framed a statute on religious freedom that became a model for the rest of the country. His proposals for public education, public libraries, and a liberal university, although not then adopted, anticipated later developments.

In 1784 Jefferson served on a special diplomatic assignment in Europe, and in 1785 he succeeded Benjamin Franklin as minister to France. His absence until October 1789 prevented him from directly participating in drafting the U.S. Constitution, but his pressure contributed to the addition of the first 10 amendments, the Bill of Rights.

Jefferson entered President Washington's cabinet as secretary of state in 1790. At first he subordinated his views to preserve the unity of the new nation, backing the trade and banking measures of Secretary of the Treasury Alexander Hamilton. However, he soon became convinced that Hamilton and his group—the Federalist Party—sought to establish a monarchy, or at least an oligarchy of wealth. Jefferson opposed this and began rallying like-minded men, who came to call themselves Republicans—a group from which the present Democratic Party traces its origin. Jefferson and Hamilton became openly antagonistic. Washington was unable to reconcile them. In 1793 Jefferson left the cabinet.

He spent the next two years remodeling his

## JEFFERSON'S PRESIDENTIAL ADMINISTRATION

**Congress in Session:**
7th, 8th, 9th, 10th

**Vice President:**
Aaron Burr, 1801–05
George Clinton, 1805–09

**Secretary of State:**
James Madison, 1801–09

**Secretary of the Treasury:**
Samuel Dexter, 1801
Albert Gallatin, 1801–09

**Secretary of War:**
Henry Dearborn, 1801–09

**Secretary of the Navy:**
Robert Smith, 1801–09

**Attorney General:**
Levi Lincoln, 1801–05
Robert Smith, 1805
John Breckinridge, 1805–07
Caesar Rodney, 1807–09

**Postmaster General:**
Joseph Habersham, 1801
Gideon Granger, 1801–09

### PRESIDENTIAL ELECTION OF 1800

**Nominations:** Jefferson and Adams were the acknowledged leaders of their parties. **Campaign Issues:** Both parties debated an undeclared naval war with France and Federalist repression of opponents through the Alien and Sedition Acts. **Remarks:** Electoral voting caused a tie between Jefferson and Burr. The House of Representatives decided the contest. On the 36th ballot Jefferson was chosen President.

| PRESIDENTIAL CANDIDATES | PARTY | ELECTORAL VOTES |
|---|---|---|
| Thomas Jefferson | Dem.–Rep. | 73 |
| Aaron Burr | Dem.–Rep. | 73 |
| John Adams | Federalist | 65 |
| Charles C. Pinckney | Federalist | 64 |
| John Jay | Federalist | 1 |

### PRESIDENTIAL ELECTION OF 1804

**Nominations:** At the first regular political caucuses, the congressional delegates of both parties unanimously nominated their respective candidates. **Campaign Issue:** Debate centered on the territorial expansion of the United States through the Louisiana Purchase, which had been achieved in the preceding year. **Remarks:** This was the first presidential election carried out under the 12th Amendment to the Constitution of the United States.

| PRESIDENTIAL CANDIDATES | PARTY | ELECTORAL VOTES |
|---|---|---|
| Thomas Jefferson | Dem.–Rep. | 162 |
| Charles C. Pinckney | Federalist | 14 |

| VICE–PRESIDENTIAL CANDIDATES | PARTY | ELECTORAL VOTES |
|---|---|---|
| George Clinton | Dem.–Rep. | 162 |
| Rufus King | Federalist | 14 |

Monticello home and experimenting with scientific agriculture. He was also active in building up the Democratic-Republican Party. He became its presidential nominee in 1796. He lost by only three electoral votes to Washington's Vice President, John Adams.

As runner-up Jefferson became Vice President in 1797 under a constitutional provision then in effect. He opposed Federalist policies, particularly the Alien and Sedition Acts that were aimed at the Antifederalists.

In protest against the repressive acts, Jefferson drafted the Kentucky Resolutions, the earliest statement of the states' rights interpretation of the Constitution.

Jefferson and his party were convinced that Adams and the Federalists wanted to go to war against the revolutionary government of France.

In 1800 the Democratic-Republicans nominated Jefferson and Aaron Burr. They easily triumphed over John Adams and the Federalists. However, Burr and Jefferson received the same number of electoral votes, and the choice of President was left to the House of Representatives. Burr tried to win the presidency. But after a long deadlock Jefferson was elected, largely because Alexander Hamilton advised Federalist congressmen to support Jefferson.

The chief foreign problem throughout Jefferson's two terms was maintaining neutrality in the conflict between England and France, both of which preyed upon U.S. shipping. Seeking to bring pressure by withholding needed goods, Jefferson sponsored acts suspending trade, especially the Embargo Act of 1807. These finally became effective, causing loss and suffering to many citizens and arousing such protest that Jefferson relaxed enforcement attempts.

One of Jefferson's major achievements was the acquisition in 1803 of the Louisiana Territory from France for $15 million. This new territory doubled the size of the U.S. In the interest of exploration and settlement, Jefferson sponsored the Lewis and Clark Expedition that blazed the pioneer trail to the Pacific Northwest.

Jefferson ordered the arrest of former Vice President Burr for treason in 1807. He regarded Burr's acquittal by Chief Justice John Marshall as a personal affront.

Jefferson retired in 1809 but remained active. He kept up a voluminous correspondence with many public figures, including his former adversary John Adams. Jefferson was instrumental in founding the University of Virginia. He also designed its buildings and served as rector in 1819–26, helping the university become one of the most advanced institutions of its time.

Jefferson died on July 4, 1826, within a few hours of his presidential predecessor and friend, John Adams—on the 50th anniversary of the Declaration of Independence. His epitaph expressed the accomplishments for which he most wanted to be remembered: "Here was buried Thomas Jefferson, author of the Declaration of American Independence, of the Statute of Virginia for Religious Freedom, and father of the University of Virginia."

**Martha Wayles (Skelton) Jefferson** (1748–82) became Jefferson's wife in 1772 but died 10 years later. He did not remarry after her death. Only two of their six children survived to maturity: Martha and Mary (Maria). Jefferson had been a widower for about 18 years when he became President. Both his daughters served as his official hostesses, aided by Dolley Madison, wife of his secretary of state.

## JAMES MADISON

Physically small and unimpressive, Madison stood about five feet six inches tall and weighed perhaps only about 100 pounds. But he was a formidable figure in the founding period of the nation.

He was the father of the Constitution, a founder of the Democratic-Republican Party, a congressman, author of the *Virginia Resolutions* and of much of the *Federalist Papers*, and the fourth President of the United States.

4th President
(1809–17)

The first of nine children of James and Nelly (Conway) Madison, he was born on March 16, 1751, in Port Conway, Va. Much of his early education was at home. He later attended the College of New Jersey (now Princeton), from which he graduated at 20. Like George Washington and others of the Virginia planter aristocracy, he supported the agitation against British colonial administration.

Madison's profound knowledge of government was first proved in 1776 when he helped draft a constitution for Virginia. In 1776 and 1777 he was a member of the executive council directing Virginia's participation in the Revolutionary War.

As a delegate to the Continental Congress for four years, Madison grew increasingly apprehensive as he watched the Congress flounder under the ineffective Articles of Confederation. After much thought he became convinced of the need for a strong national government.

In 1786 he was instrumental in the calling of a constitutional convention. At the convention in 1787 he became the leading spokesman for a strong federal government. Madison's political knowledge and persuasive logic helped secure adoption of the Constitution. The notes he kept on the sessions are the main reference source on the debates during the convention.

Madison fought for ratification of the Constitution by the states. In his own state he overcame the opposition of Patrick Henry. In the national campaign his contributions to the brilliant *Federalist Papers*, along with those of Hamilton and John Jay, had a powerful effect.

Elected to the House of Representatives in the newly established Congress (where he served for four terms), Madison led in winning passage of

**JAMES MADISON** *(continued)*
the Bill of Rights and in creation of the executive departments.

During Washington's presidency, Madison became a steadfast enemy of Hamilton and an ardent supporter of his friend Thomas Jefferson. It was during this time that he became one of the principal organizers of the opposition party, the Democratic-Republicans.

When John Adams became President in 1797, Madison retired to Montpelier, his Virginia plantation. In 1798 Madison framed the Virginia Resolutions, protesting the repressive Alien and Sedition Acts inspired by Hamilton. By asserting the right of individual states to decide on the constitutionality of the acts, these resolutions (along with the Kentucky Resolutions penned by Jefferson) became the theoretical base for the states' rights doctrine.

When Jefferson became President in 1801, Madison was named secretary of state. He worked closely with Jefferson in negotiations for the purchase of the Louisiana Territory and in keeping the United States out of the Napoleonic wars in Europe. In 1808, following the tradition of Washington, Jefferson declined a third term. Madison became the successful candidate of the Democratic-Republicans.

He began his administration by following Jefferson's policy of neutrality in the Napoleonic wars.

Finally, however, he was bullied by the "war hawks," led by John C. Calhoun and Henry Clay, into the indecisive War of 1812 against England, which began as a protest against Britain's blockade of U.S. ships trading with France.

To pay war bills and rehabilitate the economy, Madison resorted to such Federalist measures as the funding of the national debt, establishment of a national bank, and a protective tariff.

The war, which Federalist opponents called "Mr. Madison's war," went badly. New England merchants and industrialists openly opposed American participation. Even friends and supporters of his administration became discouraged by repeated setbacks suffered by American forces. Even so, Madison won reelection in 1812.

In 1814 a British fleet entered Chesapeake Bay. British troops landed in Maryland and proceeded to defeat the American militia assigned to defend Washington, D.C., at the Battle of Bladensburg on Aug. 24, 1814. The enemy set fire to the Capitol, the White House, and other public buildings, while Madison and other members of the government fled to safety. Dolley Madison saved a painting of George Washington as she hurried from the White House.

The Treaty of Ghent, signed on Dec. 24, 1814, ended the war. But because of slow communications, the Battle of New Orleans was fought two weeks later, on Jan. 8, 1815.

After the war the westward movement began in earnest. Steamboat navigation opened on the Mississippi River.

In 1817 Madison retired once more to Montpelier. Besides being a gentleman farmer, he wrote extensively, succeeded Thomas Jefferson as rector of the University of Virginia in 1826, and was a delegate to the Virginia Constitutional Convention of 1829.

Madison died at Montpelier on June 28, 1836. **Dolley Payne (Todd) Madison** (1768–1849), a 26-year-old widow and the daughter of a North Carolina planter, became Madison's wife in 1794, when he was 43. An attractive, vivacious, intelligent woman, Dolley Madison was a popular First Lady. After her husband's death she was voted an honorary seat in the House of Representatives by a unanimous congressional resolution.

## MADISON'S PRESIDENTIAL ADMINISTRATION

| Congress in Session: | Secretary of State: | Secretary of the Treasury: |
|---|---|---|
| 11th, 12th, 13th, 14th | Robert Smith, 1809–11 | Albert Gallatin, 1809–14 |
| **Vice President:** | James Monroe, 1811–17 | George Campbell, 1814 |
| George Clinton, 1809–12 | **Secretary of the Navy:** | Alexander Dallas, 1814–16 |
| Elbridge Gerry, 1813–14 | Paul Hamilton, 1809–12 | William H. Crawford, 1816–17 |
| **Secretary of War:** | William Jones, 1813–14 | |
| William Eustis, 1809–13 | Benjamin Crowninshield, 1815–17 | **Attorney General:** |
| John Armstrong, 1813–14 | **Postmaster General:** | Caesar Rodney, 1809–11 |
| James Monroe, 1814–15 | Gideon Granger, 1809–14 | William Pinkney, 1811–14 |
| William Crawford, 1815–17 | Return J. Meigs Jr., 1814–17 | Richard Rush, 1814–17 |

### PRESIDENTIAL ELECTION OF 1808

**Nominations:** Congressional caucuses nominated respective party candidates. **Campaign Issue:** Jefferson's Embargo Act.

**Remarks:** A faction of the Democratic–Republicans supported Clinton for President.

| PRESIDENTIAL CANDIDATES | PARTY | ELECTORAL VOTES | VICE–PRESIDENTIAL CANDIDATES | PARTY | ELECTORAL VOTES |
|---|---|---|---|---|---|
| James Madison | Dem.–Rep. | 122 | George Clinton | Dem.–Rep. | 113 |
| Charles C. Pinckney | Federalist | 47 | Rufus King | Federalist | 47 |
| George Clinton | Dem.–Rep. | 6 | Other candidates | — | 15 |
| Votes not cast | — | 1 | Votes not cast | — | 1 |

### PRESIDENTIAL ELECTION OF 1812

**Nominations:** A congressional caucus nominated the Democratic–Republican ticket. **Campaign Issue:** The War of 1812. **Remarks:** This was the first presidential election carried out while the nation was formally at war.

| PRESIDENTIAL CANDIDATES | PARTY | ELECTORAL VOTES | VICE–PRESIDENTIAL CANDIDATES | PARTY | ELECTORAL VOTES |
|---|---|---|---|---|---|
| James Madison | Dem.–Rep. | 128 | Elbridge Gerry | Dem.–Rep. | 131 |
| DeWitt Clinton | Federalist | 89 | Charles J. Ingersoll | Federalist | 86 |
| Votes not cast | — | 1 | Votes not cast | — | 1 |

# JAMES MONROE

5th President
(1817–25)

Although he did not rank in imagination or in brilliance with the Democratic-Republican Presidents who served before him, Monroe has been judged an abler administrator of his high office than either Jefferson or Madison.

The fourth Virginian to become Chief Executive, he was born in Westmoreland County on April 28, 1758. He was the son of Spence and Elizabeth (Jones) Monroe, landowning farmers.

Monroe left the College of William and Mary in 1776 to become a lieutenant in a Virginia regiment, saw action in several Revolutionary War battles, and achieved the rank of major. When the war ended he studied law under Thomas Jefferson.

In 1782 he was elected to the Virginia legislature. Then for three years he served in the Continental Congress, where he opposed a centralized federal government.

Under the new government Monroe served in the U.S. Senate and became a leading spokesman for Jefferson and the Democratic-Republicans.

Monroe was minister to France (1794–96) but was recalled by a dissatisfied Washington. In 1799 he was elected governor of Virginia. Jefferson sent him to assist Robert Livingston in 1803 during the Louisiana Purchase negotiations, which were virtually completed by the time he arrived. As Madison's secretary of state (1811–17) he also served a short-term appointment as secretary of war. In 1816 Monroe obtained his party's presidential nomination and was easily elected.

Because of political calm, the first years of his administration were known as the Era of Good Feelings. He made a long tour of the Northern states in 1817 and a similar journey through the Southern states in 1819. Monroe was reelected in 1820 without opposition, winning all but one electoral vote.

The good feelings, however, were only apparent. Seething dissensions erupted in North-South disputes over extension of slavery into new states to be formed from the territories. The conflict was temporarily eased in 1820 by the first Missouri Compromise. Maine was admitted as a free state and Missouri as a slave state. A boundary was drawn between future free and slave states in the Louisiana Territory.

Other events in Monroe's presidency included the acquisition of Florida (1819); recognition of the Latin American republics (1822); and promulgation of the Monroe Doctrine (1823) to protect the Western Hemisphere. In 1822 Liberia was founded in Africa as a colony for freed American slaves with its capital, Monrovia, named for Monroe.

At the end of his term Monroe retired to his home in Loudoun County, Va. He served as regent of the University of Virginia in 1826 and presided over the Virginia Constitutional Convention in 1829. He died on July 4, 1831, and was buried in New York City. In 1858 his body was removed to Richmond, Va.

**Elizabeth Kortright Monroe** (1768–1830) married Monroe in 1786. The daughter of a New York businessman, she bore him a son (who died in infancy) and two daughters.

Their home, near Jefferson's Monticello in Virginia, was called Ash Lawn.

## MONROE'S PRESIDENTIAL ADMINISTRATION

**Congress in Session:**
15th, 16th, 17th, 18th

**Vice President:**
Daniel Tompkins, 1817–25

**Secretary of State:**
John Quincy Adams, 1817–25

**Secretary of the Treasury:**
William H. Crawford, 1817–25

**Secretary of War:**
John Calhoun, 1817–25

**Attorney General:**
Richard Rush, 1817
William Wirt, 1817–25

**Secretary of the Navy:**
Benjamin Crowninshield, 1817–18
Smith Thompson, 1818–23
Samuel Southard, 1823–25

**Postmaster General:**
Return J. Meigs Jr., 1817–23
John McLean, 1823–25

## PRESIDENTIAL ELECTION OF 1816

**Nominations:** A congressional caucus nominated the Democratic–Republican ticket. **Campaign Issue:** None. The Democratic–Republican Party by this time had adopted most of the Federalist program. **Remarks:** This was the last election in which the Federalist Party nominated candidates for the offices of President and Vice President.

| PRESIDENTIAL CANDIDATES | PARTY | ELECTORAL VOTES | VICE–PRESIDENTIAL CANDIDATES | PARTY | ELECTORAL VOTES |
|---|---|---|---|---|---|
| James Monroe | Dem.–Rep. | 183 | Daniel D. Tompkins | Dem.–Rep. | 183 |
| Rufus King | Federalist | 34 | John E. Howard | Federalist | 22 |
| Votes not cast | — | 4 | Other candidates | — | 12 |
| | | | Votes not cast | — | 4 |

## PRESIDENTIAL ELECTION OF 1820

No one contested Monroe's second term because of his popularity. The Federalist Party was dead. William Plumer of New Hampshire voted against Monroe allegedly because he believed only Washington's election should be unanimous.

| PRESIDENTIAL CANDIDATES | PARTY | ELECTORAL VOTES | VICE–PRESIDENTIAL CANDIDATES | PARTY | ELECTORAL VOTES |
|---|---|---|---|---|---|
| James Monroe | Dem.–Rep. | 231 | Daniel D. Tompkins | Dem.–Rep. | 218 |
| John Quincy Adams | Independent | 1 | Other candidates | — | 14 |
| Votes not cast | — | 3 | Votes not cast | — | 3 |

QUICK QUIZ: What is the monetary unit in Greece? See page 475.

## JOHN QUINCY ADAMS

6th President
(1825–29)

A high-minded man with little popular support and no political party, John Quincy Adams entered the presidency with gloomy prospects. He was charged with stealing the White House from the popular Andrew Jackson by making a political bargain with Henry Clay.

As President, Adams alienated politicians by advocating a professional civil service free of patronage. And the one important act passed by Congress with Adams' approval—raising the protective tariff rates—angered farmers.

Born on July 11, 1767, in Braintree (now Quincy), Mass., Adams was the eldest son of President John Adams.

At the age of 10 he went to France with his father. He was educated in France and the Netherlands during his father's diplomatic service. At the age of 14 he went to Moscow where he served for two years as the private secretary of American ambassador Francis Dana. He graduated from Harvard in 1787 and was admitted to the bar in 1790.

Adams served as minister to the Netherlands (1794–97) under President Washington and as minister to Prussia (1797–1801) during his father's administration.

As a Massachusetts state senator in 1802, he demonstrated his disregard for partisan politics. Though he was the son of a Federalist President and was elected by the Federalists to the Massachusetts legislature, he did not profess any party affiliation.

Elected to the U.S. Senate in 1803, he acted so independently that the Federalists maneuvered him out of office in 1808.

In 1809 he was sent as minister to Russia, where he was held in esteem. He was in Russia during Napoleon's invasion in 1812. While there he was named and confirmed to the U.S. Supreme Court, but turned down the appointment.

In 1814 Adams negotiated the Treaty of Ghent, which ended the War of 1812.

As Monroe's secretary of state (1817–25) Adams gained great respect. He negotiated the 1819 treaty with Spain that added Florida to the United States, negotiated with Britain for the settlement of a U.S.-Canadian border dispute, and firmly dealt with Russian plans to penetrate America's West Coast. But Adams won his greatest praise as the chief architect of the Monroe Doctrine.

None of the candidates for the presidency in 1824—Adams, Jackson, William H. Crawford, Henry Clay—ran with a political party designation. Jackson received the most electoral votes but not the required majority, so the election had to be decided in the House of Representatives. Because Clay had the fewest electoral votes, he was dropped from consideration by the House. After a private meeting with Adams, Clay threw his support to Adams. In turn, Adams made Clay his secretary of state.

In 1828, running on the National Republican ticket, Adams was defeated by Andrew Jackson in his bid for reelection.

He was elected to Congress in 1830, where for 17 years he distinguished himself by his untiring and conscientious service.

In Congress, he actively opposed the extension of slavery, the annexation of Texas, and war with Mexico. He succeeded in 1844 in ending the "gag rules" in congressional debate on slavery.

Adams also sponsored the advancement of science. The Smithsonian Institution owes its development largely to him.

At the age of 80 Adams suffered a stroke while at his desk in the House of Representatives. He died two days later, on Feb. 23, 1848.

**Louisa Catherine Johnson Adams** (1775–1852), daughter of an American diplomat, married Adams in London in 1797. She made the White House a center for cultured and animated social life during his tenancy. The couple had three sons and a daughter. Their youngest son, Charles Francis Adams, served as U.S. minister to Britain during the Civil War.

## JOHN QUINCY ADAMS' PRESIDENTIAL ADMINISTRATION

**Congress in Session:**
19th, 20th

**Vice President:**
John Calhoun, 1825–29

**Secretary of State:**
Henry Clay, 1825–29

**Secretary of the Treasury:**
Richard Rush, 1825–29

**Secretary of War:**
James Barbour, 1825–28
Peter Porter, 1828–29

**Attorney General:**
William Wirt, 1825–29

**Secretary of the Navy:**
Samuel Southard, 1825–29

**Postmaster General:**
John McLean, 1825–29

## PRESIDENTIAL ELECTION OF 1824

**Nominations:** The disintegration of the Democratic-Republican Party led to presidential nominations by state legislatures. There were several "favorite son" candidates. **Campaign Issues:** The candidates supported domestic improvements and a higher protective tariff. **Remarks:** No candidate received a majority of the electoral vote. The House of Representatives finally chose Adams after Clay was eliminated because he had the fewest electoral votes. Before 1824, records of popular votes are virtually nonexistent. State legislatures usually chose the presidential electors.

| PRESIDENTIAL CANDIDATES | PARTY | ELECTORAL VOTES | POPULAR VOTE Total | Percentage | VICE-PRESIDENTIAL CANDIDATES AND ELECTORAL VOTES | | PARTY |
|---|---|---|---|---|---|---|---|
| John Quincy Adams | None | 84 | 108,740 | 30.6 | John C. Calhoun ... | 182 | None |
| Andrew Jackson | None | 99 | 153,544 | 43.1 | Nathan Sanford ... | 30 | None |
| William H. Crawford | None | 41 | 46,618 | 13.1 | Nathaniel Macon ... | 24 | None |
| Henry Clay | None | 37 | 47,136 | 13.2 | Other candidates ... | 25 | — |

# ANDREW JACKSON

7th President
(1829–37)

Although a man of personal dignity, Andrew Jackson was feared by many established citizens of his day as a dangerous upstart and the one who brought "rabble" into the White House. A leader of the movement toward increased popular participation in government, he came to symbolize the democratic sentiments of the period. Jackson's administration, which strengthened the role of the Executive Office, has been ranked as one of the most important in U.S. history.

The first "log cabin" President, Jackson was born on March 15, 1767, in Waxhaw Settlement on the border between North and South Carolina. He was the son of Irish immigrants Andrew and Elizabeth (Hutchinson) Jackson. His father died shortly before Andrew was born.

At 13 he and his brother were imprisoned by the British during the Revolutionary War. The boys caught smallpox and were released to the care of their mother. His brother and mother both died.

The orphaned Andrew Jackson lived with relatives and friends. He was admitted to the North Carolina bar in 1787 at the age of 20.

In 1788 Jackson moved west to Nashville, which later became the capital of Tennessee. He prospered in law and land speculation.

In 1797–98 Jackson served briefly in Congress, first in the House and then in the Senate. Before the War of 1812, he spent six years as a judge of the Tennessee superior court.

In 1802 Jackson was elected major general of the Tennessee state militia, a position considered next in importance to the governorship.

In the War of 1812, troops under his command crushed the Creek Indians, allies of the British, in the Battle of Horseshoe Bend in Alabama and forced them to make peace. This brought him the rank of major general in the U.S. Army. In one campaign he captured British strongholds in Florida. He then was given command of an expedition against a British army marching on New Orleans. Although outnumbered at that battle, he gained the victory that made him a national hero — even though the Battle of New Orleans was of no real military importance, having taken place a few weeks after Britain and the U.S. had signed the Treaty of Ghent, ending the War of 1812.

## JACKSON'S PRESIDENTIAL ADMINISTRATION

**Congress in Session:**
21st, 22d, 23d, 24th

**Vice President:**
John Calhoun, 1829–32
Martin Van Buren, 1833–37

**Secretary of State:**
Martin Van Buren, 1829–31
Edward Livingston, 1831–33
Louis McLane, 1833–34
John Forsyth, 1834–37

**Secretary of the Treasury:**
Samuel Ingham, 1829–31
Louis McLane, 1831–33
William J. Duane, 1833
Roger Taney, 1833–34
Levi Woodbury, 1834–37

**Attorney General:**
John Berrien, 1829–31
Roger Taney, 1831–33
Benjamin Butler, 1833–37

**Secretary of War:**
John Eaton, 1829–31
Lewis Cass, 1831–36
Benjamin Butler, 1836–37

**Secretary of the Navy:**
John Branch, 1829–31
Levi Woodbury, 1831–34
Mahlon Dickerson, 1834–37

**Postmaster General:**
John McLean, 1829
William Barry, 1829–35
Amos Kendall, 1835–37

### PRESIDENTIAL ELECTION OF 1828

**Nominations:** The Tennessee legislature nominated Jackson for the presidency. Adams was the incumbent. **Campaign Issues:** Jackson and his followers charged that the government was in the hands of an "aristocratic minority." His supporters charged the election of 1824 had been stolen from him by Adams. **Remarks:** Jackson was a popular hero.

| PRESIDENTIAL CANDIDATES | PARTY | ELECTORAL VOTES | POPULAR VOTE Total | Percentage | VICE–PRESIDENTIAL CANDIDATES AND ELECTORAL VOTES | | PARTY |
|---|---|---|---|---|---|---|---|
| Andrew Jackson.... | Democratic | 178 | 647,286 | 56.0 | John C. Calhoun... | 171 | Democratic |
| John Quincy Adams | Natl. Rep. | 83 | 508,064 | 44.0 | Richard Rush...... | 83 | Natl. Rep. |
| | | | | | William Smith ..... | 7 | Democratic |

### PRESIDENTIAL ELECTION OF 1832

**Nominations:** The modern political convention system dates from Sept. 26, 1831. Wirt was nominated on the first ballot by the Anti-Masonic Party. The National Republican Party convention met in Baltimore, Dec. 12–15, 1831, and chose Clay and Sergeant. At the Democratic Party convention in Baltimore, May 21–23, 1832, Jackson unanimously received the nomination. The Independents nominated Floyd and Lee. **Campaign Issue:** The Democrats fought the rechartering of the Second Bank of the United States. **Remarks:** The Anti-Masonic Party was the first legitimate third party.

| PRESIDENTIAL CANDIDATES | PARTY | ELECTORAL VOTES | POPULAR VOTE Total | Percentage | VICE–PRESIDENTIAL CANDIDATES AND ELECTORAL VOTES | | PARTY |
|---|---|---|---|---|---|---|---|
| Andrew Jackson.... | Democratic | 219 | 687,502 | 52.2 | Martin Van Buren... | 189 | Democratic |
| Henry Clay ........ | Natl. Rep. | 49 | 530,189 | 40.2 | John Sergeant..... | 49 | Natl. Rep. |
| John Floyd......... | Independent | 11 | — | — | Henry Lee........ | 11 | Nullifiers |
| William Wirt ....... | Anti-Masonic | 7 | 101,051 | 7.6 | Amos Ellmaker .... | 7 | Anti-Masonic |
| Votes not cast ..... | — | 2 | — | — | William Wilkins .... | 30 | Independent |
| | | | | | Votes not cast..... | 2 | — |

QUICK QUIZ: What are the symptoms of mononucleosis? See page 445.

**ANDREW JACKSON** (continued)

Jackson had acquired the reputation for personal toughness symbolized by his nickname "Old Hickory." According to some sources his duels and brawls numbered nearly 100.

In 1818 he was ordered to punish some Seminole Indians who had been raiding across the Alabama-Georgia border. He crossed over into Spanish Florida, captured Pensacola, and ordered executed two British subjects accused of inciting the raids. His unauthorized move involved the U.S. in serious trouble with both Spain and Britain, but when Florida became U.S. territory he was named its first governor— an appointment Jackson considered vindication.

The greatest popular hero of his time, a man of action, and an expansionist, Jackson by 1821 stood on the threshold of the White House. In 1824 he was nominated for that office by one of the four factions into which the ruling Democratic-Republicans had split.

Jackson won a plurality of the electoral votes, but not the required majority. The election was thrown into the House of Representatives, where supporters of one of the candidates, Henry Clay, gave their votes to John Quincy Adams, who became President. The angry Jacksonians called this "bargain and corruption."

In the election of 1828 Jackson easily defeated Adams' bid for reelection.

Jackson strengthened the authority of the presidency, taking leadership from most members of his official cabinet. His "kitchen cabinet"—an unofficial group of favorite advisers— wielded great influence. Party loyalty was intense. Members were rewarded with government posts in the spoils system.

In the nullification crisis of 1832, when South Carolina declared null and void the Tariff Act of that year, Jackson took a strong pro-Union stand. He indicated he would use troops if the state tried to secede, warning: "Our Federal Union, it must be preserved." However, he felt that the South had a real grievance and ordered a compromise tariff act.

In other respects Jackson supported the doctrine of states' rights, especially when he fought against the Bank of the United States. He finally removed the funds from this national bank and deposited them in chosen state banks.

Jackson probably could have won a third term in 1836, but instead he chose to put Vice President Martin Van Buren, a New York party politician, into the White House.

Jackson retired to The Hermitage, his Tennessee estate, but his voice was heard throughout Van Buren's administration. Because Van Buren opposed the annexation of Texas, Jackson helped James Polk win the presidency in 1844. Jackson died on June 8, 1845.

**Rachel Donelson (Robards) Jackson** (1767–1828), a divorcée, married Jackson in 1791. A mistake in her divorce proceedings made it necessary for them to be remarried three years later. This long-lived "scandal" made Jackson the butt of slurs, one of which led to a duel in which he killed his opponent. The Jacksons had no children of their own, but they adopted the son of Mrs. Jackson's brother. He was named Andrew Jackson Jr.

Mrs. Jackson died just before her husband became President. Her niece, Emily Donelson, and Jackson's daughter-in-law, Sarah Yorke Jackson, served as White House hostesses.

# MARTIN VAN BUREN

Political skill and native intelligence earned Martin Van Buren the nickname "Red Fox." As a Jacksonian Democrat he proclaimed himself a champion of the people.

But he lost popular support in the financial panic of 1837 by opposing federal aid to alleviate distress. He resisted the extension

8th President
(1837–41)

of slavery, and his stand against the annexation of Texas probably cost him the Democratic nomination in 1844.

The son of Abraham Van Buren, a farmer and innkeeper, and Maria (Hoes) Van Alen Van Buren, he was born on Dec. 5, 1782, in Kinderhook, N.Y. As a boy he waited on tables in his father's tavern. Though he never attended college, he trained in law offices and was admitted to the bar in 1803.

Van Buren's first public office was surrogate of Columbia County, N.Y., in 1808. He served as a state senator (1812–20) and during that time was state attorney general (1816–19).

As a U.S. senator (1821–28) he was inconsistent on the issues of states' rights and slavery.

Van Buren was far more important as a political leader than as a legislator. He became one of the principal figures in a powerful political clique known as the Albany Regency. He swung his support to Andrew Jackson.

He won election as governor of New York in 1828, but resigned after serving only two months to accept appointment by Jackson as U.S. secretary of state.

Probably the most influential of Jackson's advisers, Van Buren was nominated for Vice President by the Democratic Party in 1832 and was elected along with President Jackson.

In 1836, supported by Jackson, he was chosen as Democratic candidate for President and was swept into office.

To combat the Panic of 1837, Van Buren called a special session of Congress. He asked for the establishment of an independent treasury system so that the government could control the money collected from taxes rather than deposit it in private banks. He also proposed that the government issue paper money in the form of treasury notes. However, Congress did not pass the Independent Treasury Act until July 1840.

One of his most lasting contributions was installation in the White House of the first tank for hot bathwater.

Van Buren was defeated in his campaign for reelection as President in 1840. He then was denied renomination as his party's candidate in 1844,

largely because he had angered Andrew Jackson by opposing the annexation of Texas.

Running on the antislavery Free Soil Party ticket in 1848, Van Buren failed to receive a single electoral vote.

Bitterly disappointed, he retired to his home in Kinderhook, where he died on July 24, 1862.

Hannah Hoes Van Buren (1783–1819), who became his wife in 1807, was his boyhood sweetheart. They had four sons. She died while Van Buren was New York's attorney general. He never remarried. His daughter-in-law Angelica Singleton Van Buren served as White House hostess during his presidency.

## VAN BUREN'S PRESIDENTIAL ADMINISTRATION

**Congress in Session:**
25th, 26th

**Vice President:**
Richard Johnson, 1837–41

**Secretary of State:**
John Forsyth, 1837–41

**Secretary of the Treasury:**
Levi Woodbury, 1837–41

**Secretary of War:**
Joel Poinsett, 1837–41

**Secretary of the Navy:**
Mahlon Dickerson, 1837–38
James Paulding, 1838–41

**Attorney General:**
Benjamin Butler, 1837–38
Felix Grundy, 1838–40
Henry Gilpin, 1840–41

**Postmaster General:**
Amos Kendall, 1837–40
John Niles, 1840–41

### PRESIDENTIAL ELECTION OF 1836

**Nominations:** At the Democratic convention in Baltimore, May 20–22, 1836, Van Buren was backed by Jackson and was nominated unanimously. The Whigs, who held no national convention, nominated several strong sectional candidates.
**Campaign Issues:** The campaign centered on Andrew Jackson, his policies, and when Van Buren should succeed him.
**Remarks:** This was the only election in which none of the vice-presidential candidates received the required majority vote. The U.S. Senate chose Richard M. Johnson, who had been Van Buren's running mate, over Francis Granger.

| PRESIDENTIAL CANDIDATES | PARTY | ELECTORAL VOTES | POPULAR VOTE Total | Percentage | VICE–PRESIDENTIAL CANDIDATES AND ELECTORAL VOTES | PARTY |
|---|---|---|---|---|---|---|
| Martin Van Buren ... | Democratic | 170 | 765,583 | 50.9 | Richard M. Johnson. 147 | Democratic |
| William H. Harrison.. | Whig | 73 | | | Francis Granger .... 77 | Whig |
| Hugh L. White ...... | Whig | 26 | 739,795 | 49.1 | John Tyler ......... 47 | Democratic |
| Daniel Webster ...... | Whig | 14 | | | William Smith ...... 23 | Independent |
| W.P. Mangum ....... | Anti-Jackson | 11 | — | — | | |

## WILLIAM HENRY HARRISON

The Whigs in 1840 presented Harrison, their presidential candidate, as a cider-drinking, homespun, log-cabin-born, hardworking plow pusher. This was a fable, but it helped make the hero of the Battle of Tippecanoe an easy victor over Martin Van Buren.

What sort of a President Harrison would have been will never be known because of his

9th President
(1841)

early death after taking office.

Harrison's administration augured well because of the distinguished cabinet he assembled, which included Daniel Webster as secretary of state. However, Harrison died of pneumonia on April 4, 1841, a month after his inauguration—the first U.S. Chief Executive to die in the White House.

Harrison's birthplace actually was a brick mansion at "Berkeley," his family's estate in Charles City County, Va. He was born on Feb. 9, 1773, the son of Benjamin and Elizabeth (Bassett) Harrison. His father, a wealthy planter, had been one of the signers of the Declaration of Independence.

He was privately tutored and then attended

## HARRISON'S PRESIDENTIAL ADMINISTRATION

**Congress in Session:**
27th

**Vice President:**
John Tyler, 1841

**Secretary of State:**
Daniel Webster, 1841

**Secretary of the Treasury:**
Thomas Ewing, 1841

**Secretary of War:**
John Bell, 1841

**Attorney General:**
John Crittenden, 1841

**Postmaster General:**
Francis Granger, 1841

**Secretary of the Navy:**
George Badger, 1841

### PRESIDENTIAL ELECTION OF 1840

**Nominations:** The Whigs met in Harrisburg, Pa., in December 1839, choosing Harrison and Tyler. The Democrats met in Baltimore, in May 1840, and chose Van Buren without dissent. The Liberty Party met in Albany in April 1840, nominating James G. Birney and Thomas Earle—the first effort by the abolitionists to win national political power.

| PRESIDENTIAL CANDIDATES | PARTY | ELECTORAL VOTES | POPULAR VOTE Total | Percentage | VICE–PRESIDENTIAL CANDIDATES AND ELECTORAL VOTES | PARTY |
|---|---|---|---|---|---|---|
| William H. Harrison . | Whig | 234 | 1,274,624 | 53.1 | John Tyler ........ 234 | Whig |
| Martin Van Buren ... | Democratic | 60 | 1,127,781 | 46.9 | Richard Johnson... 48 | Democratic |
| James G. Birney .... | Liberty | — | 7,053 | — | Thomas Earle ..... — | Liberty |
| | | | | | L.W. Tazewell .... 11 | Independent |
| | | | | | James K. Polk..... 1 | Democratic |

QUICK QUIZ: What phone number should be called regarding a runaway child? See page 396.

**WILLIAM H. HARRISON** (*continued*)
Hampden-Sydney College. He went on to study medicine briefly in Philadelphia under Dr. Benjamin Rush, a signer of the Declaration of Independence.

In 1791 Harrison joined the Army. He resigned his commission in 1798 to become secretary of the Northwest Territory. In 1799, at the age of 26, he became its first delegate to Congress. There his proposal to divide the territory into Ohio and Indiana was approved.

As governor of Indiana Territory (1800–12), Harrison induced the Indians to cede vast tracts of land. When the Shawnee Indians attacked encroaching settlers in 1811, Harrison led an expedition that defeated the Indians in the Battle of Tippecanoe. Harrison won national fame with the battle and settled the territory's claim to 3 million acres of Indian land.

In the War of 1812 he was appointed supreme commander of the Army of the Northwest. Marching into Canada, he defeated the British and their Indian allies at the Battle of the Thames River on Oct. 5, 1813.

After resigning from the Army, he became a farmer at North Bend, Ohio. He then entered politics, winning election as a U.S. congressman (1817–19), state senator (1819–25), and U.S. senator from Ohio (1825–28). President John Quincy Adams appointed him as minister to Colombia (1828–29).

In 1834 Harrison was given the lucrative post of court clerk in Hamilton County, Ohio.

Dissident Whigs nominated Harrison for President in 1836. He came in second in a field of five, losing to Martin Van Buren.

In 1840 the Whig Party nominated him with John Tyler as his running mate. This second campaign, a successful one against Van Buren, is memorable for its slogan "Tippecanoe and Tyler too" and for its demagogy.

**Anna Tuthill Symmes Harrison** (1775–1864), the 20-year-old daughter of a well-to-do Ohio landowner, married Harrison in 1795. They had 10 children. A grandson, Benjamin Harrison, became the 23d U.S. President.

## JOHN TYLER

Tyler was the first Vice President to succeed to the presidency because of the death of the incumbent, William Henry Harrison.

Never did a President prove more disappointing to the party that had placed him in office.

An ex-Democrat and a cultured Virginian, Tyler was nominated to run on Harrison's ticket as Vice President to attract Southern votes.

10th President
(1841–45)

But when he became President, Tyler soon showed that all he had in common with Whig regulars was his antagonism to Jacksonian Democrats.

Tyler was born on March 29, 1790, in Charles City County, Va., the son of a prominent lawyer-politician. He graduated from the College of William and Mary at 17, was admitted to the bar at 19, and entered politics at 21 as a member of Virginia's state legislature. He served in Congress and as governor of Virginia before being elected Vice President. Exactly one month after taking office he succeeded Harrison, who died on April 4, 1841.

Within five months Tyler had twice vetoed a keystone measure of the Whigs—a bill to reestablish the national bank. As a result, his entire cabinet resigned, with the exception of Daniel Webster, secretary of state. Webster negotiated the Webster-Ashburton Treaty in 1842, settling a serious Canadian boundary dispute. Tyler was denounced by the Whigs and had few friends among the Democrats.

Despite strong opposition, Tyler advanced the annexation of Texas, which had won its independence from Mexico and was applying for statehood. An antislavery bloc in the Senate delayed ratification of the annexation treaty, but Tyler outmaneuvered them. Three days before his term ended, an annexation resolution was passed.

Whigs turned their backs on Tyler in 1844, choosing Clay as their presidential nominee. Tyler remained in virtual retirement for years, but in 1861 he presided over an unsuccessful Washington conference called to avert civil war. He then threw his support to the Confederacy. Tyler died on Jan. 18, 1862, in Richmond, Va.

**Letitia Christian Tyler** (1790–1842), who married Tyler in 1813, was an invalid when he became President. She died during his second year in office.

**Julia Gardiner Tyler** (1820–89), who was 30 years his junior, became his second wife in 1844. The first President to marry while in office, Tyler had 15 children, eight by his first wife. All but one lived to maturity. The last died in 1947.

## TYLER'S PRESIDENTIAL ADMINISTRATION

**Congress in Session:**
27th, 28th

**Vice President:**
After the death in office of President William Henry Harrison on April 4, 1841, and Vice President John Tyler's accession to the presidency, the vice-presidential office remained vacant. The duties of presiding over the Senate were performed by Samuel Southard and Willie Mangum, who were the presidents pro tempore of the Senate.

**Secretary of State:**
Daniel Webster, 1841–43
Abel Upshur, 1843–44
John Calhoun, 1844–45

**Secretary of the Treasury:**
Thomas Ewing, 1841
Walter Forward, 1841–43
John Spencer, 1843–44
George Bibb, 1844–45

**Secretary of War:**
John Bell, 1841
John Spencer, 1841–43
James Porter, 1843–44
Williams Wilkins, 1844–45

**Attorney General:**
John Crittenden, 1841
Hugh Legaré, 1841–43
John Nelson, 1843–45

**Secretary of the Navy:**
George Badger, 1841
Abel Upshur, 1841–43
David Henshaw, 1843–44
Thomas W. Gilmer, 1844
John Mason, 1844–45

**Postmaster General:**
Francis Granger, 1841
Charles Wickliffe, 1841–45

## JAMES KNOX POLK

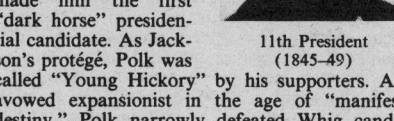

**11th President**
**(1845–49)**

At the 1844 Democratic convention a deadlock was broken when James K. Polk, supported by Andrew Jackson, was proposed as the nominee who could unite the opposing factions. His selection on the ninth ballot made him the first "dark horse" presidential candidate. As Jackson's protégé, Polk was called "Young Hickory" by his supporters. An avowed expansionist in the age of "manifest destiny," Polk narrowly defeated Whig candidate Henry Clay.

Born on Nov. 2, 1795, in Mecklenburg County, N.C., he was the son of Samuel Polk, a well-to-do farmer, and Jane Knox Polk. The family moved to Tennessee in 1806. Polk graduated from the University of North Carolina in 1818 and began to practice law in Columbia, Tenn., two years later.

He entered politics as a Jacksonian Democrat. His fiery campaigning got him elected to the Tennessee legislature.

He then served seven consecutive terms in Congress (1825–39). He became chairman of the powerful Ways and Means Committee and then majority leader of the Democratic Party. During his last four years in Congress he was Speaker of the House. In 1839 he was elected governor of Tennessee, serving until 1841.

After Polk took office as President in 1845, he sent a personal emissary, John Slidell, to Mexico to try to buy New Mexico and California. When the Mexican government refused to receive Slidell, Polk sent troops under Gen. Zachary Taylor to the disputed Rio Grande boundary. Mexican troops attacked, and Polk claimed war had begun "by act of Mexico."

Congress declared war on Mexico on May 13, 1846. A succession of American victories culminated in the capture of the Mexican capital. The war ended with the Treaty of Guadalupe Hidalgo, signed Feb. 2, 1848. Mexico accepted payment of $15 million for territory that was to become California, New Mexico, Arizona, Nevada, Utah, and parts of Colorado and Wyoming—the largest accession of territory since the Louisiana Purchase. Polk blocked the Wilmot Proviso, an attempt to exclude slavery from the new acquisitions.

In the meantime he had negotiated a Canadian boundary agreement with Britain in the Oregon Treaty of June 15, 1846. Ignoring his campaign slogan—"54°40' or Fight!"—Polk accepted the 49th parallel as the boundary with Canada.

Polk also tried to purchase Cuba from Spain for $100 million, but his offer was rejected.

Life in the White House was straitlaced during the Polk administration. Polk was a pious Methodist, and his wife was a strict Presbyterian. They banned dancing, card playing, and alcoholic beverages from the White House. And they installed the first gas lighting, replacing candles and oil lamps.

During the negotiations that led to Texas joining the Union and becoming the 28th state in 1845, Sam Houston remarked that the only thing wrong with Polk was that he drank too much water.

Former President John Quincy Adams wrote of Polk: "He has no wit, no literature, no point of argument, no gracefulness of delivery, no elegance of language, no philosophy, no pathos, no felicitous impromptus; nothing that can constitute an orator, but confidence, fluency, and labor."

Under constant harassment in Congress, not only from the Whig opposition but from resentful Northern Democrats, Polk labored strenuously to the detriment of his health. He refused renomination and died on June 15, 1849.

**Sarah Childress Polk** (1803–91) married Polk in 1824. They had no children of their own, but Mrs. Polk later adopted a daughter.

## POLK'S PRESIDENTIAL ADMINISTRATION

**Congress in Session:**
29th, 30th

**Vice President:**
George Dallas, 1845–49

**Secretary of State:**
James Buchanan, 1845–49

**Secretary of the Treasury:**
Robert Walker, 1845–49

**Secretary of War:**
William Marcy, 1845–49

**Secretary of the Navy:**
George Bancroft, 1845–46
John Mason, 1846–49

**Attorney General:**
John Mason, 1845–46
Nathan Clifford, 1846–48
Isaac Toucey, 1848–49

**Postmaster General:**
Cave Johnson, 1845–49

## PRESIDENTIAL ELECTION OF 1844

**Nominations:** At the Whig convention in Baltimore, May 1, 1844, Clay was chosen on the first ballot by acclamation. On the third ballot Frelinghuysen received 155 out of 275 votes, and then his vice-presidential nomination was made unanimous. The Democrats met in Baltimore, May 27–30, 1844. Although Van Buren had a majority of the votes, he could not obtain the necessary two-thirds majority. On the ninth ballot Polk was nominated. Dallas received the vice-presidential nomination on the second ballot, after Silas Wright had declined the nomination. The Liberty Party met in Buffalo, N. Y., Aug. 30, 1843, and unanimously nominated its candidates, Birney and Morris. **Campaign Issues:** Foreign and domestic issues included whether Texas should be annexed to the U.S. as a slave state, whether the tariff should be lowered, and what steps should be taken to settle the Oregon boundary dispute with Britain.

| PRESIDENTIAL CANDIDATES | PARTY | ELECTORAL VOTES | POPULAR VOTE Total | Percentage | VICE–PRESIDENTIAL CANDIDATES |
|---|---|---|---|---|---|
| James K. Polk | Democratic | 170 | 1,338,464 | 49.6 | George M. Dallas |
| Henry Clay | Whig | 105 | 1,300,097 | 48.1 | Theodore Frelinghuysen |
| James G. Birney | Liberty | — | 62,300 | 2.3 | Thomas Morris |

QUICK QUIZ: What newspaper was founded by Mary Baker Eddy? See page 335.

## ZACHARY TAYLOR

12th President
(1849–50)

Taylor's path to the White House was paved during the Mexican War, some two years before the 1848 Whig convention nominated him. In May 1846, soon after two victories by General Taylor's forces, it was predicted he would be elected President. Taylor scoffed at the idea, but within two years the nonpolitical hero accepted the Whig presidential nomination.

Zachary Taylor was born on Nov. 24, 1784, in Orange County, Va., while his family was on its way to a new home in Kentucky. His parents were Richard and Sarah Dabney Strother Taylor.

In 1808 he was commissioned a first lieutenant in the Army. Following his victory over the Seminoles at Lake Okeechobee, Fla., Taylor was promoted to brigadier general in 1837. He earned the nickname "Old Rough and Ready" in the Florida campaign.

In 1845 he was given command of the army in Texas. During the Mexican War he was at times defiant to the point of insubordination. An armistice Taylor granted after seizing Monterrey in 1846 created serious friction with President Polk, who thought the terms were too lenient. Taylor ignored orders to hold his position. Instead, in February 1847 he led his troops a few miles south, where he defeated numerically superior Mexican forces at Buena Vista. Taylor returned home to national acclaim.

Although a slaveholder and a conservative, Taylor was under the influence of Sen. William H. Seward (New York), leader of the antislavery Whigs. Taylor campaigned on his war record.

Taylor became the first person to win the presidency without having been previously elected to public office. Because March 4 fell on Sunday, Taylor postponed his inauguration to March 5.

Taylor's call in 1850 for admission to statehood of antislavery California alienated his Southern Whig supporters.

When Southern leaders threatened to drive federal troops from New Mexico to prevent it from becoming an antislavery state, Taylor warned he would take command of the Army.

Sen. Henry Clay offered the Compromise of 1850 in an effort to placate both North and South. President Taylor probably would have vetoed the Compromise, but he died of cholera on July 9, 1850.

**Margaret Mackall Smith Taylor** (1788–1852) married Taylor in 1810. They had six children.

## TAYLOR'S PRESIDENTIAL ADMINISTRATION

**Congress in Session:**
31st
**Vice President:**
Millard Fillmore, 1849–50
**Secretary of State:**
John Clayton, 1849–50

**Secretary of the Treasury:**
William M. Meredith, 1849–50
**Secretary of War:**
George Crawford, 1849–50
**Attorney General:**
Reverdy Johnson, 1849–50

**Postmaster General:**
Jacob Collamer, 1849–50
**Secretary of the Navy:**
William B. Preston, 1849–50
**Secretary of the Interior:**
Thomas Ewing, 1849–50

### PRESIDENTIAL ELECTION OF 1848

**Nominations:** The Democratic convention in Baltimore, May 22–26, 1848, chose Lewis Cass on the fourth ballot. Butler was chosen on the second ballot with 169 out of 253 votes cast. The Whig convention in Philadelphia, June 7–9, 1848, chose Taylor by a majority vote on the fourth ballot. Fillmore was chosen on the second ballot. The Free Soil Party convention in Buffalo, N.Y., Aug. 9–10, 1848, unanimously nominated Van Buren and Adams.

| PRESIDENTIAL CANDIDATES | PARTY | ELECTORAL VOTES | POPULAR VOTE Total | Percentage | VICE–PRESIDENTIAL CANDIDATES |
|---|---|---|---|---|---|
| Zachary Taylor ......... | Whig | 163 | 1,360,967 | 47.3 | Millard Fillmore |
| Lewis Cass ........... | Democratic | 127 | 1,222,342 | 42.5 | William O. Butler |
| Martin Van Buren ..... | Free Soil | — | 291,263 | 10.1 | Charles Francis Adams |

## MILLARD FILLMORE

13th President
(1850–53)

Fillmore took office on July 10, 1850, the day after President Taylor died. During his administration he sought to preserve the Union by conciliating the South. But the nation had become too deeply divided on the slavery issue, and his attempt to carry out the Compromise of 1850 alienated both sides. In particular, his strict enforcement of the Fugitive Slave Law of 1850 aroused the wrath of the antislavery wing of the Whig Party.

Two measures he did not initiate are also associated with Fillmore's administration. One was the dispatch of Commodore Perry to Japan to open that country's ports to U.S. trade. The other was the reorganization of the postal department to provide cheaper mail rates.

Fillmore was born on Jan. 7, 1800, in Locke, N.Y., the son of Nathaniel Fillmore, a farmer, and Phoebe Millard Fillmore.

As a youth he worked at odd jobs to earn a living, and was largely self-educated. He read law in his spare time, winning admission to the bar in 1823. After practicing briefly in East Aurora, N.Y., he moved to Buffalo.

Fillmore's political career began in 1828 when he was elected to the New York assembly. He went on to serve four terms in Congress, beginning in 1833. A Whig, he became chairman of the powerful House Ways and Means Committee when his party won control of Congress in 1841–43.

Defeated as the Whig candidate for governor

of New York in 1844, Fillmore became state comptroller.

Because of the strong stand Fillmore had taken against the extension of slavery into the territories, Henry Clay backed him for the vice presidency on the successful Whig ticket in 1848. His position was intended to offset the supposed proslavery sympathies of presidential candidate Zachary Taylor.

Fillmore lost the Whigs' support in 1852, and their presidential nomination went to Gen. Winfield Scott, who favored a more radical antislavery program.

Fillmore attempted to regain the presidency in 1856 when he accepted the presidential nomina-

tion of the anti-Catholic, antiforeigner American (Know-Nothing) Party. In the election he won only eight electoral votes. Fillmore died in Buffalo, N.Y., on March 8, 1874.

**Abigail Powers Fillmore** (1798–1853), daughter of a Baptist clergyman, married Fillmore in 1826. They had two children. She was too ill to preside at White House functions. During her tenancy the first cooking stove was installed in the White House kitchen, replacing fireplace cookery. She died a month after Fillmore completed his presidential term.

**Caroline Carmichael (McIntosh) Fillmore** (1813–81), a wealthy widow, became Fillmore's second wife in 1858.

## FILLMORE'S PRESIDENTIAL ADMINISTRATION

| | | |
|---|---|---|
| **Congress in Session:**<br>31st, 32d | **Secretary of the Treasury:**<br>Thomas Corwin, 1850–53 | **Attorney General:**<br>John J. Crittenden, 1850–53 |
| **Vice President:**<br>Vacant | **Secretary of War:**<br>Charles Conrad, 1850–53 | **Secretary of the Navy:**<br>William Graham, 1850–52<br>John Kennedy, 1852–53 |
| **Secretary of State:**<br>Daniel Webster, 1850–52<br>Edward Everett, 1852–53 | **Postmaster General:**<br>Nathan Hall, 1850–52<br>Samuel Hubbard, 1852–53 | **Secretary of the Interior:**<br>T.M.T. McKennan, 1850<br>Alexander Stuart, 1850–53 |

## FRANKLIN PIERCE

Pierce began his presidency under an emotional strain. Shortly before his term began, he and his wife saw their only surviving son killed in a train wreck. Mrs. Pierce, who disliked both Washington and her husband's involvement in politics, became withdrawn and was infrequently seen in public.

14th President
(1853–57)

A Northern Democrat, Pierce misjudged the nation's growing animosity to slavery. In the presidential election campaign, he had promised to prevent slavery from becoming a divisive political issue. But his willingness to aid Southern Democrats in the extension of slavery to new states added new fuel to the flames of the slavery controversy.

Born on Nov. 23, 1804, in Hillsboro, N.H., he was the son of Anna Kendrick Pierce and Benjamin

Pierce, a Revolutionary War general and twice New Hampshire governor. He attended Bowdoin College and was admitted to the bar in 1827.

Pierce entered politics as a Jacksonian Democrat and served two terms as a congressman in 1833–37. In 1836, at 32, he became one of the youngest men elected to the U.S. Senate. He resigned eight years later because of his wife's ill health. Pierce practiced law in Concord, N.H., and became leader of the state's Democratic Party. He served as a brigadier general of New England volunteers in the Mexican War.

Pierce was chosen president of the New Hampshire constitutional convention in 1850.

A delegate to the Democratic convention in 1852, Pierce emerged as a dark-horse presidential contender. His nomination on the 49th ballot broke a hopeless deadlock among the frontrunners. As a Northerner with pro-South sympathies, he was deemed acceptable to both sides. Pierce went on to defeat the Whig candidate, Winfield Scott, his Mexican War commander.

Believing that conciliation of the South would preserve the Union, he endorsed the Southern doctrine that the constitutional provisions on

## PIERCE'S PRESIDENTIAL ADMINISTRATION

| | | |
|---|---|---|
| **Congress in Session**<br>33d, 34th | **Secretary of the Treasury:**<br>James Guthrie, 1853–57 | **Postmaster General:**<br>James Campbell, 1853–57 |
| **Vice President:**<br>William King, 1853 | **Secretary of War:**<br>Jefferson Davis, 1853–57 | **Secretary of the Navy:**<br>James Dobbin, 1853–57 |
| **Secretary of State:**<br>William Marcy, 1853–57 | **Attorney General:**<br>Caleb Cushing, 1853–57 | **Secretary of the Interior:**<br>Robert McCleland, 1853–57 |

### PRESIDENTIAL ELECTION OF 1852

**Nominations:** At the Whig convention in Baltimore, June 17–20, 1852, Scott received a majority on the 53d ballot. The Democratic convention in Baltimore, June 1–5, 1852, deadlocked between James Buchanan and Lewis Cass. Pierce was entered as a dark horse on the 35th ballot and won on the 49th ballot. **Campaign Issues:** Personalities.

| PRESIDENTIAL CANDIDATES | PARTY | ELECTORAL VOTES | POPULAR VOTE Total | Percentage | VICE-PRESIDENTIAL CANDIDATES |
|---|---|---|---|---|---|
| Franklin Pierce ...... | Democratic | 254 | 1,601,117 | 50.9 | William R. King |
| Winfield Scott ....... | Whig | 42 | 1,385,453 | 44.1 | William A. Graham |
| John P. Hale ........ | Free Soil | — | 155,825 | 5.0 | George Julian |

QUICK QUIZ: What does a sphygmomanometer measure? See Page 460.

**FRANKLIN PIERCE** *(continued)*
property rights meant a guarantee of slavery.

He helped push through the Kansas-Nebraska Act in 1854 that repealed the Missouri Compromise of 1820, giving settlers in the Kansas Territory the opportunity to vote on the slavery issue. Guerrilla warfare broke out between opposing national forces in "Bleeding Kansas," heightening national tensions in 1855–56.

In his expansionist drive Pierce made premature and unsuccessful attempts to buy Alaska from Russia and to annex Hawaii. Another failure was the Ostend Manifesto of 1854. Issued by the American ministers to England, France, and Spain, it proposed annexation of Cuba, presumably as a slave state. Although repudiated by the State Department and the Senate, it raised protests both at home and abroad.

Pierce was more successful with two other enterprises in foreign policy. The Gadsden Purchase for $10 million from Mexico of the southern parts of Arizona and New Mexico was ratified by the Senate on June 29, 1854. That same year Commodore Matthew C. Perry signed a treaty that opened Japan's ports to shippers.

Pierce had expected to be renominated by the 1856 Democratic national convention. Instead, he was humiliatingly rejected because of his support of the Kansas-Nebraska Act.

At the end of his term Pierce toured Europe and then returned to Concord. In 1860 he supported Jefferson Davis, his former secretary of war, as the man the Democrats should nominate for President. His opposition to the Civil War and to Lincoln's administration increased his unpopularity. He died in obscurity on Oct. 8, 1869.

**Jane Means Appleton Pierce** (1806–63), Pierce's wife, was the daughter of a president of Bowdoin College. None of the couple's three sons survived to maturity. While she was First Lady, the White House was equipped for the first time with a coal-burning furnace for central heating.

## JAMES BUCHANAN

15th President
(1857–61)

Buchanan was the last President chosen because it was believed he would compromise and keep the slavery issue from tearing apart the nation.

He was born on April 23, 1791, in Cove Gap, Pa., the son of James and Elizabeth (Speer) Buchanan. After attending Dickinson College, he was admitted to the bar in 1812. He then built up a lucrative law practice in Lancaster, Pa.

Buchanan served in his state's legislature in both houses of Congress (first as a Federalist, then as a Jacksonian Democrat), as Polk's secretary of state, and as minister to England and Russia. In England he was involved in the notorious Ostend Manifesto proposing annexation of Cuba, even as a slave state. This permanently discredited Buchanan among large groups in the North.

In 1844, 1848, and 1852 Buchanan was a contender for the Democratic presidential nomination.

In 1856 he became the Democratic candidate and defeated John C. Frémont, first candidate of the new Republican Party, as well as Millard Fillmore, candidate of the Whig and American (Know-Nothing) parties. He was the fourth President to enter office with less than a majority of the popular vote.

To meet the growing North-South crisis, Buchanan could only propose preservation of the "sacred balance" between the regions. He avowed personal disapproval of slavery, yet recommended the admission of Kansas as a slave state.

He deplored secession but took no steps to check it by garrisoning federal forts in the South. Even when a U.S. ship was fired on by South Carolina shore batteries, he took no action.

Buchanan's moderate views were disliked and mistrusted by extremists both in the North and in the South. He did not seek renomination.

In the last months of his administration, seven Southern states seceded and formed the Confed-

## BUCHANAN'S PRESIDENTIAL ADMINISTRATION

**Congress in Session:**
35th, 36th

**Vice President:**
John C. Breckinridge, 1857–61

**Secretary of State:**
Lewis Cass, 1857–60
Jeremiah S. Black, 1860–61

**Secretary of the Treasury:**
Howell Cobb, 1857–60
Philip F. Thomas, 1860–61
John A. Dix, 1861

**Secretary of War:**
John Floyd, 1857–61
Joseph Holt, 1861

**Secretary of the Navy:**
Isaac Toucey, 1857–61

**Attorney General:**
Jeremiah Black, 1857–60
Edwin M. Stanton, 1860–61

**Postmaster General:**
Aaron Brown, 1857–59
Joseph Holt, 1859–61
Horatio King, 1861

**Secretary of the Interior:**
Jacob Thompson, 1857–61

## PRESIDENTIAL ELECTION OF 1856

**Nominations:** The Republican convention was held in Philadelphia, June 17–19, 1856. On the first official ballot Frémont got 520 out of 558 votes. Dayton's nomination came on the first ballot. At the Democratic convention in Cincinnati, June 2–6, 1856, Buchanan was chosen on the 17th ballot. The vice-presidential nomination of Breckinridge was unanimous. **Campaign Issue:** Slavery in the Kansas-Nebraska territories was the main issue.

| PRESIDENTIAL CANDIDATES | PARTY | ELECTORAL VOTES | POPULAR VOTE Total | Percentage | VICE–PRESIDENTIAL CANDIDATES |
|---|---|---|---|---|---|
| James Buchanan .... | Democratic | 174 | 1,832,955 | 45.3 | John C. Breckinridge |
| John C. Frémont...... | Republican | 114 | 1,339,932 | 33.1 | William L. Dayton |
| Millard Fillmore....... | American | 8 | 871,731 | 21.6 | Andrew J. Donelson |

erate States of America.

When he was 27, Buchanan had been engaged to Ann Caroline Coleman of Lancaster, but she broke the engagement because she believed he only wanted her fortune. So Buchanan became the first bachelor President.

Buchanan's niece Harriet Lane served as White House hostess during his administration.

Seven years after leaving office, Buchanan died in Lancaster on June 1, 1868.

## ABRAHAM LINCOLN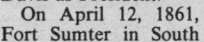

16th President
(1861–65)

When Lincoln became President, the nation was divided. In the four months between his election as President and the time he took office, seven Southern states had seceded from the Union and formed the Confederate States of America with Jefferson Davis as President.

On April 12, 1861, Fort Sumter in South Carolina was bombarded by the Confederates, and the Civil War began. Lincoln became the leader of the people of the North.

### EARLY YEARS

Lincoln's father, Thomas, was a farmer and carpenter who moved his family from Kentucky to Indiana to Illinois. Abraham was born in a log cabin in Hardin County, Ky., on Feb. 12, 1809. His mother, Nancy Hanks Lincoln, died when he was nine, and his father married Mrs. Sarah Bush Johnston, a widow.

Providing for himself at an early age, Lincoln did handyman jobs, split rails, clerked in a store, surveyed land, delivered merchandise downstream on flatboats to New Orleans, and put his hand to other tasks. In 1831 he settled in the little village of New Salem, Ill., near Springfield. There he became a partner in a grocery store that failed. His partner's death left him with a burden of debts—all of which he eventually paid.

Lincoln grew into a tall, gaunt, muscular man six feet four inches tall, with a ruggedly homely face. Possessed of great physical strength, he often put down bullies. This, along with his talent for pointed storytelling, brought him popularity in the frontier villages where he spent his young manhood.

When Lincoln answered a call for volunteers in the Black Hawk War, he was unanimously elected captain by the men of the New Salem troop. By 1834 he had gathered such a following that he was elected, as a Whig, to the Illinois legislature, where he achieved prominence during his four terms. He was admitted to the bar in 1836 and moved to nearby Springfield. He built up a prosperous law practice in a succession of partnerships, the last with William H. Herndon, who later became his biographer.

Lincoln reentered politics in 1846, again as a Whig, and was overwhelmingly elected to Congress. There his opposition to the Mexican War cost him the backing of expansionist-minded constituents. He served only one term.

In 1854, however, he was goaded out of retirement by indignation over the Kansas-Ne-

braska Act favoring the extension of slavery, which had been sponsored by Illinois Democratic Sen. Stephen A. Douglas. Lincoln ran for the Senate on the Whig ticket but was defeated. The next year he joined the newly formed Republican Party. He was among the candidates for its vice-presidential nomination, polling an impressive though not winning vote.

In 1858 Lincoln became his party's candidate for U.S. senator. One of the ringing phrases in his acceptance speech, "A house divided against itself cannot stand," helped spread his renown. His debates with Douglas, his Democratic opponent, drew nationwide attention. Lincoln asserted he was not an abolitionist, but that he regarded slavery as an injustice and an evil. He was adamantly opposed to its extension. Although Douglas won the close election, Lincoln, through his masterful exposition, had made his mark and had become widely known.

At the Republican convention in 1860, William H. Seward was the leading contender. But there was an early swing to Lincoln, who was nominated on the third ballot. With the Democrats split between Northern and Southern wings, Republican victory was inevitable. After Lincoln's election, the Southern states began seceding from the Union.

### CIVIL WAR PRESIDENT

From the beginning of hostilities Lincoln faced staggering difficulties, but he attacked the vast problems with vigor and surpassing skill. Lincoln pressed onward with the war, but even when prosecuting Southern sympathizers in the North—for which he was criticized—he sought to temper punishment with mercy.

On April 14, 1861, two days after the Confederate attack on Fort Sumter, Lincoln called for 75,000 volunteers to fight the rebels. He also ordered a blockade of Southern ports to cut them off from supplies the South needed.

Hopes by Northerners for a quick victory were dashed by the Union defeat in the First Battle of Bull Run in Virginia on July 21, 1861.

Lincoln was beset not only by the difficulties of the war but by opposition from men on his own side. Radical abolitionists condemned him as weak. Conservatives accused him of dictatorship. Jealousies and hatreds caused continual friction in his cabinet. In the midst of all this strife Lincoln continued his course with wisdom and patience, sometimes standing nearly alone.

Lincoln had offered command of the Union Army to Gen. Robert E. Lee. But Lee turned the appointment down, deciding to help his native state of Virginia by accepting command of Confederate forces. Lee inflicted a series of defeats on Northern troops while Lincoln searched for a Union general who could fight.

The dubious Northern victory at Antietam in

QUICK QUIZ: What goods are commonly on sale in April? See page 412.

## ABRAHAM LINCOLN (continued)

1862 gave Lincoln the opportunity to make a great stroke by issuing the Emancipation Proclamation, which proclaimed freedom for slaves in Confederate-controlled states.

The proclamation caused renewed enthusiasm for the war. But the fighting progressed without a decisive success until the Confederacy's defeat in 1863 at Gettysburg, Pa., where Lincoln later delivered his famous Gettysburg Address.

In 1864, after Ulysses S. Grant became commander of the Union Army and William T. Sherman took Atlanta, Lincoln's perseverance seemed vindicated.

With victory clearly in sight, the Republican Party, which had been on the point of abandoning him, rallied to Lincoln. He was renominated and reelected in 1864.

In his celebrated second inaugural address, Lincoln outlined his postwar program. He would show "malice toward none" and grant "charity for all." His policy would be based on peace without retribution.

A month after Lincoln's second inauguration Lee surrendered on April 9, 1865, to Grant at Appomattox Court House, Va.

But Lincoln's dream of restoring the Union in harmony was brought to an abrupt end on April 14, 1865, when actor John Wilkes Booth, a Southern fanatic, shot him at Ford's Theater in Washington. Lincoln died the next day.

**Mary Todd Lincoln** (1818–82) of Kentucky became Lincoln's wife in 1842 after a troubled courtship. Their marriage was not an easy one, but Mrs. Lincoln served capably as White House hostess. Because she had several relatives in the Confederate Army, her loyalty to the North was questioned.

The Lincolns had four sons: Robert Todd Lincoln (1843–1926), Edward Baker Lincoln (1846–50), William Wallace Lincoln (1850–62), and Thomas "Tad" Lincoln (1853–71).

Only one son, Robert Todd Lincoln, lived to manhood, becoming secretary of war under Presidents Garfield and Arthur.

One of their sons died at the age of four in Springfield, another in the White House at the age of 12.

The first two deaths of her sons, her husband's assassination while at her side, and the death of their youngest son at age 18 in 1871 are said to have affected Mrs. Lincoln's mind. She was temporarily committed to a private sanatorium in Batavia, Ill., in 1875.

## LINCOLN'S PRESIDENTIAL ADMINISTRATION

**Congress in Session:**
37th, 38th, 39th

**Vice President:**
Hannibal Hamlin, 1861–65
Andrew Johnson, 1865

**Secretary of State:**
William Seward, 1861–65

**Secretary of the Treasury:**
Salmon Chase, 1861–64
William Fessenden, 1864–65
Hugh McCulloch, 1865

**Secretary of War:**
Simon Cameron, 1861–62
Edwin McM. Stanton, 1862–65

**Secretary of the Navy:**
Gideon Welles, 1861–65

**Attorney General:**
Edward Bates, 1861–64
James Speed, 1864–65

**Postmaster General:**
Montgomery Blair, 1861–64
William Dennison, 1864–65

**Secretary of the Interior:**
Caleb Smith, 1861–63
John Usher, 1863–65

## PRESIDENTIAL ELECTION OF 1860

**Nominations:** The Democrats met in Charleston, S.C., April 23–May 3, 1860. They failed to choose a candidate, and many Southerners bolted the party. The convention reassembled in Baltimore on June 18 and met through June 23. Finally, after more Southerners had left, Douglas was nominated. The vice-presidential nominee, Benjamin Fitzpatrick of Alabama, declined the honor, and the party national committee chose Johnson. Many of the "bolters," who called themselves National Democrats, met in Baltimore, June 23, 1860, and chose Breckinridge and Lane. The Republicans met in Chicago, May 16–18, 1860. Sen. William H. Seward of New York was favored to win the nomination. On the third ballot Lincoln received a majority, and the nomination was then made unanimous. Hamlin was chosen on the second ballot. The Constitutional Union Party met in Baltimore, May 9–10, 1860, choosing former Secretary of War John Bell as their candidate. **Campaign Issues:** The campaign centered on slavery and the status of the Union.

| PRESIDENTIAL CANDIDATES | PARTY | ELECTORAL VOTES | POPULAR VOTE | | VICE-PRESIDENTIAL CANDIDATES |
|---|---|---|---|---|---|
| | | | Total | Percentage | |
| Abraham Lincoln ......... | Republican | 180 | 1,865,593 | 39.8 | Hannibal Hamlin |
| John C. Breckinridge ...... | Southern Democratic | 72 | 848,356 | 18.1 | Joseph Lane |
| Stephen A. Douglas ....... | Democratic | 12 | 1,382,713 | 29.5 | Herschel V. Johnson |
| John Bell ................. | Constitutional Union | 30 | 592,906 | 12.6 | Edward Everett |

## PRESIDENTIAL ELECTION OF 1864

**Nominations:** The Republicans, who had been joined by the prowar Democrats (Johnson was one), met as the National Union Party in Baltimore, June 7–8, 1864. Lincoln on a roll-call vote on the first ballot received all but 22 votes (which went to U.S. Grant), and his nomination was then made unanimous. By the end of the first ballot, after switching had taken place, Johnson had received 494 out of 500 votes and the vice-presidential nomination. The Democratic convention met in Chicago, Aug. 29–31, 1864, and McClellan, the former Union Army commanding general who had been dismissed by Lincoln, was chosen on the third ballot. Pendleton was selected as the vice-presidential candidate on the first ballot. **Campaign Issue:** Democrats criticized Lincoln's conduct of the Civil War.

| PRESIDENTIAL CANDIDATES | PARTY | ELECTORAL VOTES | POPULAR VOTE | | VICE-PRESIDENTIAL CANDIDATES |
|---|---|---|---|---|---|
| | | | Total | Percentage | |
| Abraham Lincoln ......... | Republican | 212 | 2,206,938 | 55.0 | Andrew Johnson |
| George McClellan ......... | Democratic | 21 | 1,803,787 | 45.0 | George Pendleton |
| Votes not cast............ | — | 81 | — | — | — |

# ANDREW JOHNSON

17th President
(1865–69)

Succeeding to the presidency on the death of Lincoln, Andrew Johnson was a Southerner and a Democrat. The political split that developed between Johnson and the powerful Radical Republicans led to the first effort to remove a President of the United States by impeachment.

Born on Dec. 29, 1808, in Raleigh, N.C., Johnson was the son of Jacob and Mary McDonough Johnson. His father died when Andrew was three. At the age of 13 Johnson was apprenticed to a tailor. In 1826 he moved to Greeneville, Tenn.

Unable to write or do arithmetic when he married at the age of 18, Johnson learned how with the help of his wife. He prospered as a tailor, and his shop became well known. Many other craftsmen, as well as laborers and farmers, met there to discuss community and general public affairs. The best debater in Greeneville, Johnson was frequently in the public eye.

At 19 Johnson won office as town alderman, and at 21 became mayor of Greeneville. He next served six years in the state legislature. He was elected to the U.S. House of Representatives (1843–53), governor of Tennessee (1853–57), and to the U.S. Senate (1857–62).

Although a slaveowner, Johnson vigorously opposed secession. Alone among Southern senators, he did not resign when secession began. In 1862 Lincoln appointed him military governor of Tennessee, and by 1864 Johnson had organized a loyal government there. For this achievement he was named Lincoln's running mate on the Republican ticket in 1864.

At the inauguration, March 4, 1865, when he was sworn in as Vice President, Johnson seemed to be drunk. President Lincoln cut off criticism with the remark, "He ain't no drunkard."

When he assumed the presidency on April 15, 1865, Johnson reverted to his earlier Democratic positions on tariffs, banking, internal improvements, and other issues, in opposition to the Republican Party. But the chief issue in his conflict with the Radical Republicans was their harsh Reconstruction policy.

Johnson intended to follow Lincoln's program of reconciliation with the South. He extended full amnesty to participants in the secession. But he opposed extension of full civil rights to Negroes on constitutional grounds and, in general, manifested Southern sympathies. Political attacks on Johnson became increasingly harsh.

When Congress passed a series of acts over his veto, including the Civil Rights Act of 1866, he appealed to the electorate in the congressional elections. Baited by mobs and slandered by the press, he lashed out at his political enemies in such harsh terms that he did great harm to his own cause. The Radicals won, and the conflict between Congress and the President intensified.

Although the problems of the postwar South dominated Johnson's administration, there were successes in foreign affairs, notably the 1867 purchase of Alaska from Russia negotiated by Secretary of State William Seward for the price of $7,200,000.

In 1867 Congress passed, over Johnson's veto, the Tenure of Office Act, which forbade the removal of any official appointed with the confirmation of the Senate. Johnson believed the act was unconstitutional (and 59 years later the U.S. Supreme Court upheld his judgment). He defied Congress by firing Secretary of War Edwin M. Stanton, replacing him with Gen. Ulysses S. Grant, who gave the office back to Stanton in February 1868. Johnson fired Stanton again, appointing Lorenzo Thomas to the post.

The Radical Republicans, led by Thaddeus Stevens, brought impeachment charges against Johnson for violation of the Tenure of Office Act. This first try failed, but on Feb. 24, 1868, the House passed a resolution of impeachment by a vote of 126 to 47.

On March 5, 1868, the Senate was organized as a court to hear the charges. The Senate on May 16 voted 35 to 19 against President Johnson, one vote shy of the required two-thirds majority needed to convict him. The vote that saved him was cast by Edmund G. Ross, a freshman Radical Republican senator from Kansas.

Despite a series of disappointments that might have deterred another man, Johnson continued his political activity. He sought and failed to win the nomination for President on the Democratic ticket in 1868, for U.S. senator in 1869, and for representative in 1872. But in 1874 he became the first former President to be elected to the U.S. Senate. A few months after reentering the Senate to represent Tennessee, he died on July 31, 1875.

**Eliza McCardle Johnson** (1810–76) married Andrew Johnson in 1827 when she was 16. She helped him learn to write and do arithmetic. They had three sons and two daughters. She was an invalid during her husband's term. Their daughter Martha served as the President's chief White House hostess.

## ANDREW JOHNSON'S PRESIDENTIAL ADMINISTRATION

**Congress in Session:**
39th, 40th

**Vice President:**
Vacant

**Secretary of State:**
William Seward, 1865–69

**Secretary of the Treasury:**
Hugh McCulloch, 1865–69

**Attorney General:**
James Speed, 1865–66
Henry Stanbery, 1866–68
William Evarts, 1868–69

**Postmaster General:**
William Dennison, 1865–66
Alexander Randall, 1866–69

**Secretary of the Navy:**
Gideon Welles, 1865–69

**Secretary of War:**
Edwin M. Stanton, 1865–67, 1868
Ulysses S. Grant, 1867–68
Lorenzo Thomas, 1868
John Schofield, 1868–69

**Secretary of the Interior:**
John P. Usher, 1865
James Harlan, 1865–66
Orville Browning, 1866–69

QUICK QUIZ: One pint equals how many ounces? See page 717.

## 362    HISTORY

## ULYSSES SIMPSON GRANT

18th President
(1869–77)

Grant's administrations were characterized by bitter politics and notorious corruption. A punitive Reconstruction policy gave supremacy to Northern bankers, speculators, and industrialists. It also encouraged the "carpetbaggers" who moved south to exploit both recently freed slaves and the defeated whites, helping to prolong the sectional division of the country between North and South.

Grant allowed himself to become the dupe of the "robber barons" of his time and of the shady politicians associated with them. During his two terms scandals were exposed involving cabinet members, his own secretary, and a number of congressmen. His administrations were characterized by bitter politics and corruption.

He was born on April 27, 1822, in Point Pleasant, Ohio, the son of Jesse Root and Hannah (Simpson) Grant. He switched his given names, Hiram Ulysses, when still a boy. Then "Hiram" became "Simpson" through a clerical error when he applied for admission to West Point. Grant accepted the name change. He graduated in 1843, served with distinction in the Mexican War, and was promoted twice.

In 1854 Grant was forced to resign from the Army because of excessive drinking. He tried farming, real estate, and storekeeping, all without success.

The Civil War proved his opportunity. Responding to President Lincoln's call for volunteers, he was eventually given command of a detachment of Illinois trainees. He showed outstanding ability in minor military actions and was promoted to brigadier general.

After training and mobilizing a force of 17,000 men, he conducted a bold operation against two Confederate strongholds, Fort Henry and Fort Donelson, on the Tennessee and Cumberland rivers. It was the first major Union victory. From

## GRANT'S PRESIDENTIAL ADMINISTRATION

**Congress in Session:**
41st, 42d, 43d, 44th
**Vice President:**
Schuyler Colfax, 1869–73
Henry Wilson, 1873–75
**Secretary of State:**
Elihu B. Washburne, 1869
Hamilton Fish, 1869–77
**Postmaster General:**
John Creswell, 1869–74
James W. Marshall, 1867
Marshall Jewell, 1874–76
James Tyner, 1876–77

**Secretary of the Treasury:**
Alexander T. Stewart, 1869
George Boutwell, 1869–73
William Richardson, 1873–74
Benjamin Bristow, 1874–76
Lot Morrill, 1876–77

**Attorney General:**
Ebenezer Hoar, 1869–70
Amos Akerman, 1870–71
George Williams, 1871–75
Edwards Pierrepont, 1875–76
Alphonso Taft, 1876–77

**Secretary of War:**
John Rawlins, 1869
William T. Sherman, 1869
William Belknap, 1869–76
Alphonso Taft, 1876
James Cameron, 1876–77
**Secretary of the Navy:**
Adolph Borie, 1869
George Robeson, 1869–77
**Secretary of the Interior:**
Jacob Cox, 1869–70
Columbus Delano, 1870–75
Zachariah Chandler, 1875–77

## PRESIDENTIAL ELECTION OF 1868

**Nominations:** The Republican convention met in Chicago, May 20–21, 1868, and chose Grant. The Democratic Party met in New York City, July 4–9, 1868, nominated Seymour on the 22d ballot, and declared the nomination unanimous.

**Campaign Issues:** A paramount issue was Reconstruction of the Confederate states, with the Republicans in favor of harsh measures. **Remarks:** Mississippi, Texas, and Virginia did not participate in the presidential election.

| PRESIDENTIAL CANDIDATES | PARTY | ELECTORAL VOTES | POPULAR VOTE Total | Percentage | VICE–PRESIDENTIAL CANDIDATES |
|---|---|---|---|---|---|
| Ulysses S. Grant ........ | Republican | 214 | 3,013,421 | 52.7 | Schuyler Colfax |
| Horatio Seymour ........ | Democratic | 80 | 2,703,829 | 47.3 | Francis P. Blair Jr. |
| Votes not cast .......... | — | 23 | — | — | |

## PRESIDENTIAL ELECTION OF 1872

**Nominations:** Liberal Republicans, who had defected from the Republican Party because they were dissatisfied with Grant, met in Cincinnati, May 1, 1872, and nominated Greeley and Brown on the sixth ballot. Democrats, meeting in Baltimore, July 9–10, 1872, accepted Greeley and Brown on the first ballot. The Republican convention in Philadelphia, June 5–6, 1872, chose Grant and Wilson. **Campaign Issues:** Besides Reconstruction and the "bloody shirt" (as vengeance against the South was called), other important

issues were corruption in government and the desirability of issuing paper money, which many debtors thought would aid them. Republicans ridiculed Greeley as a lifelong opponent of Democrats who now ran on their ticket. **Remarks:** Greeley died after the election but before the Electoral College met. His electoral votes went to: Thomas A. Hendricks (42); Benjamin G. Brown (18); Charles J. Jenkins (2); David Davis (1); and 3 Greeley votes were not counted. Congress rejected Greeley votes from Arkansas, Louisiana, and Georgia.

| PRESIDENTIAL CANDIDATES | PARTY | ELECTORAL VOTES | POPULAR VOTE Total | Percentage | VICE–PRESIDENTIAL CANDIDATES | ELECTORAL VOTES |
|---|---|---|---|---|---|---|
| Ulysses S. Grant ........ | Republican | 286 | 3,596,745 | 55.6 | Henry Wilson ........ | 286 |
| Horace Greeley .......... | Democratic-Liberal Rep. | — | 2,843,446 | 44.0 | Benjamin G. Brown . | 47 |
| Charles O'Connor ....... | Straight Dem. | — | 29,489 | 0.4 | John Quincy Adams . | — |
| Other candidates ........ | | 63 | — | — | Other candidates ... | — |
| Votes not cast .......... | | 17 | — | — | Votes not cast ...... | — |

that time on, his military career was an almost continuous succession of triumphs, the most brilliant being the capture of Vicksburg in 1863, which cleared the Mississippi down to the sea and split the Confederacy in two.

Satisfied that he had at last found his general, Lincoln in 1864 put Grant in supreme command of the Union armies.

Grant pushed the Confederate Army south into Virginia while Gen. William T. Sherman advanced from the west to Atlanta, Ga. On April 9, 1865, Grant accepted the surrender of Gen. Robert E. Lee at Appomattox Court House, Va. His surrender terms to Lee and his treatment of the defeated Confederates were compassionate and magnanimous.

A national hero, Grant was the Republican choice in the presidential election of 1868. He was nominated on the first ballot and easily won the presidency. At 46 he was the youngest man to become President to that time. His first term was tinged with scandal when his brother-in-law conspired with New York financier Jay Gould to corner the gold market.

In 1869 Grant approved a treaty with the Dominican Republic to annex that country. But the Senate rejected the treaty.

Grant's renomination for a second term was unanimous, and he was reelected by another landslide. His second term was wracked with scandals, leading to the resignations of two of his cabinet officers and the conviction of many government officials.

In 1880 his backers, the Stalwarts, led by Sen. Roscoe Conkling, failed to obtain Grant's nomination for a third term.

Moving to New York City, among his new financier associates, Grant invested his funds in a fraudulent banking firm. When it went bankrupt in 1884, Congress granted him some relief by reappointing him general at full pay and later by adding retirement pay.

Determined to provide for his family, Grant set to work on his memoirs. Although suffering from cancer of the throat, he kept on indomitably, finishing the two-volume book four days before his death. He died on July 23, 1885, and is interred in New York City.

**Julia Dent Grant** (1826–1902) was the daughter of a judge in St. Louis, Mo., and a sister of one of Grant's West Point classmates. She and Grant were married in 1848. They had three sons and a daughter, all surviving to maturity. As First Lady she was admired for her graces.

## RUTHERFORD BIRCHARD HAYES

The election of 1876 pitted Hayes, the Republican nominee, against Samuel J. Tilden, the Democratic candidate. It was a significant election, marking the political reentry of the South into the Union and the resurgence of the Democrats. The Republicans lost decisively in the congressional elections, and Hayes received nearly 250,000 fewer popular votes than Tilden. The electoral vote tally was disputed.

19th President
(1877–81)

A special electoral commission with a Republican majority gave the office to Hayes by a margin of only one electoral vote.

Hayes was born on Oct. 4, 1822, in Delaware, Ohio. He was the son of Rutherford Hayes, a storekeeper who died over two months before the boy was born, and Sophia Birchard Hayes. Young Hayes attended Kenyon College and Harvard.

He practiced law in Lower Sandusky and then in 1849 moved to Cincinnati. From 1858 to 1861 he served as Cincinnati solicitor.

At the outbreak of the Civil War, Hayes enlisted and was commissioned a major. He was wounded four times, rising in rank to major general. Elected to Congress in 1865 as a Republican, he supported the Radicals' Reconstruction program. In 1867 he was elected governor of Ohio and served three terms.

Facing a hostile Democratic majority in

## HAYES' PRESIDENTIAL ADMINISTRATION

**Congress in Session:**
45th, 46th
**Vice President:**
William Wheeler, 1877–81
**Secretary of War:**
George McCrary, 1877–79
Alexander Ramsey, 1879–81

**Secretary of State:**
William Evarts, 1877–81
**Secretary of the Treasury:**
John Sherman, 1877–81
**Postmaster General:**
David Key, 1877–80
Horace Maynard, 1880–81

**Attorney General:**
Charles Devens, 1877–81
**Secretary of the Navy:**
Richard Thompson, 1877–80
Nathan Goff Jr., 1881
**Secretary of the Interior:**
Carl Schurz, 1877–81

## PRESIDENTIAL ELECTION OF 1876

**Nominations:** The Republican convention in Cincinnati, June 14–16, 1876, nominated Hayes on the seventh ballot. Wheeler was nominated by acclamation. The Democrats, meeting in St. Louis, June 27–29, 1876, nominated Tilden on the second ballot. **Campaign Issues:** Reconstruction and corruption in government. **Remarks:** An electoral commission composed of eight Republicans and seven Democrats awarded disputed votes to Hayes.

| PRESIDENTIAL CANDIDATES | PARTY | ELECTORAL VOTES | POPULAR VOTE Total | Percentage | VICE–PRESIDENTIAL CANDIDATES |
|---|---|---|---|---|---|
| Rutherford B. Hayes ....... | Republican | 185 | 4,036,572 | 48.0 | William A. Wheeler |
| Samuel J. Tilden .......... | Democratic | 184 | 4,284,020 | 51.0 | Thomas A. Hendricks |
| Peter Cooper ............. | Greenback | — | 81,737 | 1.0 | Samuel F. Carey |

QUICK QUIZ: Why do tourists visit Juffure, Gambia? See page 554.

**RUTHERFORD B. HAYS** (continued)
Congress, Hayes could not obtain passage of his legislative program.

His most outstanding act, withdrawal of the last federal troops from the South, antagonized extremists in his party, and his determined efforts to reform the civil service angered Republican bosses.

The economic depression during Hayes' administration brought the first nationwide strike by rail workers in 1877. When strike riots broke out in several states, Hayes sent in federal troops.

In an effort to halt Indian wars raging in the West, Hayes banned the sale of firearms to Indians.

Hayes declined renomination and devoted his last years to education and philanthropy. He died in Fremont, Ohio, on Jan. 17, 1893.

**Lucy Ware Webb Hayes** (1831–89), who married Hayes in 1852, was the first college graduate to become First Lady.

Mrs. Hayes, a cheerful woman, was nicknamed "Lemonade Lucy" because she served only soft drinks in the White House. Both she and Hayes were total abstainers. Hayes' last executive order as President was to ban the sale of whisky on army posts. The Hayes' family life—they had eight children—was a happy one.

Hayes installed the first telephone in the White House, in 1877.

## JAMES ABRAM GARFIELD

The second U.S. President killed by an assassin, Garfield served too short a time for anyone to know what sort of Chief Executive he might have been.

Born on Nov. 19, 1831, in Orange Township, Ohio, Garfield was the son of Abram and Eliza Ballou Garfield. He was left fatherless at two and spent his early years in poverty. He worked as a

20th President
(1881)

farmer and carpenter to support his mother. At 18 he entered Western Reserve Eclectic Institute (now Hiram College). He went on to Williams College, graduating in 1856. Garfield then returned to Hiram, where he became its president. He was also a lay preacher of the Disciples of Christ. He became a state senator in 1859 and was admitted to the bar in 1860.

During the Civil War he began service as an officer of an Ohio volunteer regiment. He was promoted to the rank of major general because of his bravery at the Battle of Chickamauga.

On his election to Congress in 1863 he resigned from the Army to take his seat in the House, where he served until 1880. He was a staunch advocate of Radical Reconstruction.

Garfield was one of the members of the

electoral commission that awarded the presidential election of 1876 to Hayes. He then served as Republican minority leader of the House during Hayes' administration.

As leader of the Ohio delegation to the Republican national convention in 1880, Garfield was present at his own presidential nomination as a dark-horse candidate. Top runners at the convention that year were ex-President Grant and James G. Blaine. Up to the 34th ballot Garfield never drew more than two votes, but on the 36th ballot he won the nomination. Grant and his political sponsor, Sen. Roscoe Conkling of New York, were disgruntled. An effort was made to appease them by giving second place on the ticket to Chester Arthur, one of the Stalwarts—as Grant's supporters called themselves.

One of President Garfield's immediate problems on beginning his administration was the open break forced by Senator Conkling over the distribution of political spoils. Garfield was a brilliant orator and a man of integrity and charm. His conflict with Conkling and the political machine remained unresolved, however.

Before Garfield could make his mark as President, he was killed. Charles Guiteau, a disappointed office seeker who proclaimed himself a Stalwart, shot him on July 2, 1881. Garfield lingered until his death on Sept. 19, 1881.

**Lucretia Rudolph Garfield** (1832–1918), his wife, had been a schoolmate. They were married in 1858. The Garfields had seven children, two of whom died in childhood.

## GARFIELD'S PRESIDENTIAL ADMINISTRATION

**Congress in Session:**
47th

**Vice President:**
Chester A. Arthur, 1881

**Secretary of State:**
James Blaine, 1881

**Secretary of the Treasury:**
William Windom, 1881

**Secretary of War:**
Robert Todd Lincoln, 1881

**Attorney General:**
Wayne MacVeagh, 1881

**Postmaster General:**
Thomas James, 1881

**Secretary of the Navy:**
William Hunt, 1881

**Secretary of the Interior:**
Samuel Kirkwood, 1881

### PRESIDENTIAL ELECTION OF 1880

**Nominations:** The Republicans met in Chicago, June 2–8, 1880, and on the 36th ballot Garfield received the nomination. Arthur was chosen as the vice-presidential candidate on the first ballot. The Democrats met in Cincinnati, June 22–24, 1880, and nominated Hancock and English. **Campaign Issues:** The parties based their campaigns on the personalities of their candidates. Republicans favored high tariffs and Democrats opposed them.

| PRESIDENTIAL CANDIDATES | PARTY | ELECTORAL VOTES | POPULAR VOTE Total | Percentage | VICE–PRESIDENTIAL CANDIDATES |
|---|---|---|---|---|---|
| James A. Garfield . . . . . . | Republican | 214 | 4,453,295 | 48.5 | Chester A. Arthur |
| Winfield S. Hancock . . . . | Democratic | 155 | 4,414,082 | 48.1 | William English |
| James B. Weaver . . . . . . | Greenback | — | 308,578 | 3.4 | B. J. Chambers |
| Neal Dow . . . . . . . . . . . . | Prohibition | — | 10,305 | — | H. A. Thompson |

## CHESTER ALAN ARTHUR

Chester Arthur became President on Sept. 20, 1881, after the death of President Garfield from wounds by an assassin. A New York Republican machine politician, Arthur had been given the vice-presidential nomination in 1880 to appease supporters of ex-President Grant, who had hoped for a third-term nomination.

21st President
(1881–85)

Members of Arthur's Republican clique were called Stalwarts. Those who supported Garfield were called Half-Breeds.

Arthur was born on Oct. 5, 1829, in Fairfield, Vt., the son of William Arthur, a clergyman, and Malvina Stone Arthur. He graduated from Union College in 1848 and began teaching while studying law. Arthur was admitted to the New York bar in 1854 and developed a successful law practice. An abolitionist, Arthur took many cases defending fugitive slaves and other blacks.

He helped organize the New York militia during the Civil War and then served as quartermaster general.

In 1871 President Grant rewarded him with the post of collector of the New York Custom House, a much-sought political prize. He administered the office with personal honesty but, in the style of the time, openly dispensed political patronage to members of the powerful New York Republican machine. In 1879 President Hayes, a fellow Republican determined to reform civil service, removed Arthur from office.

As President, Arthur was stigmatized as a machine politician of dubious integrity and nicknamed "the Gentleman Boss" for his courtly manners and his taste for fine foods and expensive clothes. He had the White House redecorated in *art nouveau* style by New York designer Louis Tiffany, and he installed an elevator.

To the dismay of his political associates, Arthur's presidential administration proved honest and efficient. Arthur supported the Civil Service Reform Act of 1883, which limited the spoils system. He fought the passage of the Chinese Exclusion Act. He prosecuted corruption in the postal service, and he aided the passage of a new protective tariff.

A little more than a year after Arthur succeeded to office, his kidney trouble was diagnosed as Bright's disease. Only one or two of his closest friends were permitted to know the seriousness of his ailment. He thus lived throughout his term in the White House with the secret knowledge that he was a dying man. It is believed for this reason alone he refused to seek the 1884 nomination, to the bewilderment of his supporters.

Arthur returned to New York City and resumed his law practice. He died there on Nov. 18, 1886, a year after leaving office.

**Ellen Lewis Herndon Arthur** (1837–80) married Arthur in 1859 but died before he became President. Arthur's vivacious sister, Mary (Mrs. John McElroy), served as official White House hostess during his term.

## ARTHUR'S PRESIDENTIAL ADMINISTRATION

**Congress in Session:**
47th, 48th

**Vice President:**
Vacant

**Secretary of State:**
James G. Blaine, 1881
Frederick Frelinghuysen, 1881–85

**Secretary of War:**
Robert Todd Lincoln, 1881–85

**Secretary of the Treasury:**
William Windom, 1881
Charles Folger, 1881–84
Walter Q. Gresham, 1884
Hugh McCulloch, 1884–85

**Postmaster General:**
Thomas L. James, 1881
Timothy Howe, 1881–83
Walter Q. Gresham, 1883–84
Frank Hatton, 1884–85

**Attorney General:**
Wayne MacVeagh, 1881
Benjamin Brewster, 1881–85

**Secretary of the Navy:**
William Hunt, 1881–82
William Chandler, 1882–85

**Secretary of the Interior:**
Samuel Kirkwood, 1881–82
Henry Teller, 1882–85

## GROVER CLEVELAND

The first Democrat elected President after the Civil War, Grover Cleveland won office as a champion of honesty and reform. Cleveland became the only President to serve two nonconsecutive terms, losing a bid for reelection in 1888 and then regaining the office in the election of 1892.

22d and 24th President
(1885–89, 1893–97)

The son of Richard Falley and Ann Neal Cleveland, Stephen Grover Cleveland was born on March 18, 1837, in Caldwell, N.J. The family moved to upstate New York when Cleveland was a child. His father, a Presbyterian minister, died when the boy was 16. He worked in a store in Clinton, N.Y., and later taught school. After deciding to move west as a pioneer, he stopped in Buffalo to visit an uncle and settled there. He clerked in a law office, becoming a lawyer in 1859.

Cleveland began his political career as a Democrat. After filling minor posts, he was elected sheriff of Erie County, N.Y. (1871–73). While sheriff he sprang the trap to hang two convicted murderers, giving him the later distinction of being the only President to have hanged a man. Cleveland was elected mayor of Buffalo in 1882. Known as the "veto mayor," he drove corruption from his administration and acquired renown for honesty and efficiency.

He then was elected governor of New York (1883–84). As governor he fought the corruption of New York's Democratic Tammany

QUICK QUIZ: Who is the patron saint for mothers? See page 704.

**GROVER CLEVELAND** (continued)

machine. He cooperated with Republican reformer Theodore Roosevelt, who was then in the state legislature.

During the mud-slinging presidential campaign of 1884, opponents disclosed Cleveland had fathered an illegitimate child. Voters gave him extra points for refusing to deny the story, which was true. A further attack on the Democrats as the party of "rum, Romanism, and rebellion" boomeranged, costing Republican candidate James G. Blaine the Roman Catholic vote. Cleveland also received support from reform-minded Republicans, known as Mugwumps.

In his first term as President, Cleveland faced an unyielding Republican majority in the Senate. This opposition kept him from carrying through any planned policy.

Among the few significant acts of Cleveland's first term were his appointment of an Interstate Commerce Commission and passage of the Interstate Commerce Act of 1887.

Although he was forced to temper with expediency his own instinct for civil-service reform, he was adamant against graft, extravagance, and excessive tariffs.

In the presidential election of 1888 Cleveland won a plurality of the popular vote over Republican Benjamin Harrison, but he lost the electoral vote by a substantial margin.

During the period between his two administrations, Cleveland practiced law in New York City.

He helped the Democrats win control of Congress in the 1890 elections by his attacks on extravagant spending by the Republicans.

In 1892 Cleveland regained the White House for a second term, becoming the only defeated President ever to be reelected.

Inheriting the financial panic of 1893, he forced repeal of the Sherman Silver Purchase Act and sponsored issuance of government bonds to protect the gold reserve. By these measures he alienated the Populists and the silver advocates among the Democrats.

Determined to prevent interruption of postal service because of the 1894 strike of Pullman workers in Chicago, he sent federal troops to restore order. His action was against the wishes of the Democratic governor of Illinois and alienated organized labor.

## CLEVELAND'S ADMINISTRATION AS 22d PRESIDENT

**Congress in Session:**
49th, 50th
**Vice President:**
Thomas Hendricks, 1885
**Secretary of State:**
Thomas Bayard, 1885–89
**Secretary of War:**
William Endicott, 1885–89

**Secretary of the Treasury:**
Daniel Manning, 1885–87
Charles Fairchild, 1887–89
**Attorney General:**
Augustus Garland, 1885–89
**Secretary of the Navy:**
William Whitney, 1885–89

**Postmaster General:**
William Vilas, 1885–88
Don Dickinson, 1888–89
**Secretary of the Interior:**
Lucius Lamar, 1885–88
William Vilas, 1888–89
**Secretary of Agriculture:**
Norman Colman, 1889

## PRESIDENTIAL ELECTION OF 1884

**Nominations:** The Republicans met in Chicago, June 3–6, 1884, and Blaine was nominated on the fourth ballot, receiving 541 of 813 votes. The Democrats met in Chicago, July 8–11, 1884, and on the second ballot Cleveland received 683 of 820 votes before the nomination was made unanimous. **Campaign Issues:** Charges that Cleveland had fathered an illegitimate child and that Blaine's vote in Congress had been bought several times.

| PRESIDENTIAL CANDIDATES | PARTY | ELECTORAL VOTES | POPULAR VOTE Total | Percentage | VICE–PRESIDENTIAL CANDIDATES |
|---|---|---|---|---|---|
| Grover Cleveland....... | Democratic | 219 | 4,879,507 | 48.5 | Thomas A. Hendricks |
| James G. Blaine ....... | Republican | 182 | 4,850,293 | 48.2 | John A. Logan |
| Benjamin F. Butler ..... | Greenback | — | 175,370 | 1.7 | A.M. West |
| John P. St. John ....... | Prohibition | — | 150,369 | 1.5 | William Daniel |

## CLEVELAND'S ADMINISTRATION AS 24th PRESIDENT

**Congress in Session:**
53d, 54th
**Vice President:**
Adlai E. Stevenson, 1893–97
**Secretary of the Treasury:**
John Carlisle, 1893–97
**Secretary of War:**
Daniel Lamont, 1893–97

**Secretary of State:**
Walter Gresham, 1893–95
Richard Olney, 1895–97
**Attorney General:**
Richard Olney, 1893–95
Judson Harmon, 1895–97
**Secretary of the Navy:**
Hilary Herbert, 1893–97

**Postmaster General:**
Wilson Bissell, 1893–95
William Wilson, 1895–97
**Secretary of the Interior:**
Hoke Smith, 1893–96
David Francis, 1896–97
**Secretary of Agriculture:**
Julius Morton, 1893–97

## PRESIDENTIAL ELECTION OF 1892

**Nominations:** The Republicans met in Minneapolis, June 7–10, 1892. Harrison received $535\frac{1}{6}$ votes on the first roll call with $369\frac{1}{6}$ against him. The Democrats met in Chicago, June 21–23, 1892. Cleveland received $617\frac{1}{3}$ votes, barely more than the two-thirds necessary for the nomination. The Populists met in Omaha, July 2-5, 1892, where Weaver won the nomination on the first ballot. **Campaign Issues:** Discontent among farmers and tariff reform, the Democrats favoring a lower tariff. Populists drew off many votes from the Republicans.

| PRESIDENTIAL CANDIDATES | PARTY | ELECTORAL VOTES | POPULAR VOTE Total | Percentage | VICE–PRESIDENTIAL CANDIDATES |
|---|---|---|---|---|---|
| Grover Cleveland....... | Democratic | 277 | 5,555,426 | 46.0 | Adlai E. Stevenson |
| Benjamin Harrison ..... | Republican | 145 | 5,182,690 | 43.0 | Whitelaw Reid |
| James B. Weaver ....... | Populist | 22 | 1,029,846 | 8.5 | James G. Field |
| Other candidates....... | — | — | 285,297 | 2.5 | — |

Cleveland also felt that tendencies toward U.S. imperialism were beginning to grow. He refused to permit aid to a rebel movement in Cuba and prevented the annexation of Hawaii. Almost the only popular act of Cleveland's second term was his invocation of the Monroe Doctrine in 1895, which led Britain to arbitrate a boundary dispute with Venezuela.

Cleveland's personal fortitude was manifested by the manner with which he underwent major surgery in 1893. Stricken by a cancerous growth on his jaw, he accepted the advice of friends and was operated on in secret to prevent public alarm. The operation, necessitating removal of his upper left jaw, was performed aboard a yacht.

Blaming Cleveland for the continuing depression, voters elected a Republican majority to Congress in the 1894 elections. Cleveland was further humiliated in 1896 when the Democratic convention refused him a third term.

After leaving the White House, Cleveland retired to Princeton, N.J.. He participated little in public life. In 1901 he became a trustee of Princeton University. He later became a spokesman for insurance companies against government regulation.

Cleveland died on June 24, 1908, at his home in Princeton.

**Frances Folsom Cleveland** (1864–1947) became the bachelor President's wife in 1886. She was the 21-year-old daughter of his late law partner, as well as Cleveland's ward. Cleveland became the only President to be married in a White House wedding. Immensely popular, Mrs. Cleveland officiated at White House functions with poise and skill. The Clevelands' second child, Esther, born in 1893, was the first child of a President to be born in the White House.

# BENJAMIN HARRISON

23d President
(1889–93)

A grandson of President W. H. Harrison, Benjamin Harrison campaigned in 1888 to the tune of "Grandfather's Hat Fits Ben." The Republicans stirred anti-British sentiment against President Cleveland by tricking the British ambassador into endorsing him. Although Harrison defeated Cleveland with a majority of the electoral votes, he received 90,728 fewer popular votes.

A comparatively colorless President, Harrison followed regular Republican policies. He supported the McKinley protective tariff and the lavishly liberal Disability Pension Act. An outstanding event of his administration was the formation of what was later to become the Pan American Union. The Sherman Antitrust Act was passed to counteract popular feeling that the Republicans were the party of "big business." This proved insufficient, and the congressional elections of 1890 gave the Democrats control of the House.

Harrison was born on Aug. 20, 1833, at North Bend, Ohio. He was the son of Rep. John Scott Harrison and Edith Erwin Harrison.

He graduated from Miami (Ohio) University, passed the bar in 1853, and began law practice in Cincinnati. In 1854 he moved to Indianapolis, where he became a reporter for the Indiana supreme court.

When the Civil War began Harrison helped recruit a regiment of volunteers, of which he became a colonel in 1862. Achieving an outstanding war record, he attained the rank of brigadier general.

After the war, he built a prosperous practice as a corporation lawyer. From 1881 to 1887 Harrison served as U.S. senator from Indiana.

## HARRISON'S PRESIDENTIAL ADMINISTRATION

**Congress in Session:**
51st, 52d

**Vice President:**
Levi Morton, 1889–93

**Secretary of State:**
James Blaine, 1889–92
John Foster, 1892–93

**Secretary of the Treasury:**
William Windom, 1889–91
Charles Foster, 1891–93

**Secretary of War:**
Redfield Proctor, 1889–91
Stephen Elkins, 1891–93

**Attorney General:**
William Miller, 1889–93

**Postmaster General:**
John Wanamaker, 1889–93

**Secretary of the Navy:**
Benjamin Tracy, 1889–93

**Secretary of the Interior:**
John Noble, 1889–93

**Secretary of Agriculture:**
Jeremiah Rusk, 1889–93

## PRESIDENTIAL ELECTION OF 1888

**Nominations:** The Democrats met in St. Louis, June 5–7, 1888, and nominated Cleveland by acclamation. Thurman was a unanimous vice-presidential choice on the first roll-call vote. The Republicans met in Chicago, June 19–25, 1888. On the eighth ballot Harrison received 544 of 830 votes. Morton won the vice-presidential nomination with 592 votes on the first ballot. **Campaign:** Cleveland had approved restoring the Confederate battle flags to the South, and the Republicans made much of this. Also, a Republican politician managed to get the British ambassador to write in a letter that Cleveland would best serve the interests of Britain, arousing anti-British sentiment. **Remarks:** Opposed by New York's Tammany machine, Cleveland lost that state's 36 electoral votes, throwing the election to Harrison.

| PRESIDENTIAL CANDIDATES | PARTY | ELECTORAL VOTES | POPULAR VOTE Total | Percentage | VICE–PRESIDENTIAL CANDIDATES |
|---|---|---|---|---|---|
| Benjamin Harrison | Republican | 233 | 5,447,129 | 47.9 | Levi P. Morton |
| Grover Cleveland | Democratic | 168 | 5,537,857 | 48.6 | Allen G. Thurman |
| Clinton B. Fisk | Prohibition | — | 249,506 | 2.2 | John A. Brooks |
| Alson J. Streeter | Union Labor | — | 146,935 | 1.3 | C.E. Cunningham |

QUICK QUIZ: Which major league baseball park holds the most spectators? See page 787.

**BENJAMIN HARRISON** *(continued)*

During his administration, President Harrison installed the first electric lights in the White House, replacing gas lighting.

Defeated by Cleveland in his bid for reelection in 1892, Harrison resumed his law practice. He also served as counsel for Venezuela in the Venezuela-British boundary dispute. In 1899 he represented the U.S. at the Hague Peace Conference.

He died in Indianapolis on March 13, 1901.

**Caroline Lavinia Scott Harrison** (1832–92), his first wife, was proficient in music and painting and brought cultural distinction to her role as First Lady. The Harrisons had two children. Mrs. Harrison became ill in 1891, dying a few months before Harrison's term ended.

**Mary Scott Lord (Dimmick) Harrison** (1858–1948), was Harrison's second wife. They married in 1896 and had one child. A niece of his first wife, she had served as White House hostess during her aunt's illness.

# WILLIAM McKINLEY

McKinley's assassination in the first year of the 20th century marked the closing of an era. He was the last President to have served in the Civil War, and the last to embark on a war of territorial expansion—the Spanish-American War. The Western frontier had been tamed. A new industrial society was being created, and with it came a change from the 19th century pattern of life.

25th President
(1897–1901)

McKinley was born on Jan. 29, 1843, in Niles, Ohio, the son of William and Nancy (Allison) McKinley.

In 1861, at 18, he enlisted as a private in the Civil War. As a mess sergeant he received a battlefield commission for serving hot food to troops under fire. He later rose to major.

After the Civil War he passed the bar in 1867, establishing a law practice in Canton, Ohio.

After serving two years as a county prosecuting attorney, McKinley was elected to Congress in 1876. Except for one term, he remained there until 1891. While a House member he sponsored the restrictive McKinley Tariff Act of 1890 that pleased financial and business interests.

With the backing of Mark Hanna, a wealthy and powerful Ohio industrialist, McKinley won election and reelection as governor of Ohio (1892–96). In the panic of 1893, he gained popularity by providing free food for the Ohio unemployed.

Through Hanna's astute management, McKinley won the Republican presidential nomination in 1896. The party platform emphasized higher tariffs and an expansionist foreign policy.

## McKINLEY'S PRESIDENTIAL ADMINISTRATION

**Congress in Session:**
55th, 56th, 57th

**Vice President:**
Garret Hobart, 1897–99
Theodore Roosevelt, 1901

**Secretary of State:**
John Sherman, 1897–98
William Day, 1898
John Hay, 1898–1901

**Secretary of the Treasury:**
Lyman Gage, 1897–1901

**Secretary of War:**
Russell Alger, 1897–99
Elihu Root, 1899–1901

**Attorney General:**
Joseph McKenna, 1897–98
John Griggs, 1898–1901
Philander Knox, 1901

**Postmaster General:**
James Gary, 1897–98
Charles Smith, 1898–1901

**Secretary of the Navy:**
John Long, 1897–1901

**Secretary of the Interior:**
Cornelius Bliss, 1897–98
Ethan Hitchcock, 1898–1901

**Secretary of Agriculture:**
James Wilson, 1897–1901

## PRESIDENTIAL ELECTION OF 1896

**Nominations:** The Republicans met in St. Louis, June 16–18, 1896, and McKinley was nominated on the first ballot. The Democrats met in Chicago, July 7–11, 1896, and Bryan was nominated on the fifth ballot with 652 of 768 votes. The Populists supported Bryan. The National Democrats were so-called Gold Democrats, conservatives who opposed Bryan. **Campaign Issues:** The Democrats came out for "free and unlimited coinage of silver."

| PRESIDENTIAL CANDIDATES | PARTY | ELECTORAL VOTES | POPULAR VOTE Total | Percentage | VICE-PRESIDENTIAL CANDIDATES |
|---|---|---|---|---|---|
| William McKinley | Republican | 271 | 7,102,246 | 51.0 | Garret Hobart |
| William Jennings Bryan | Democratic | 176 | 6,492,559 | 46.7 | { Arthur Sewall |
| | | | | | { Thomas E. Watson |
| John M. Palmer | Natl. Dem. | — | 133,148 | 1.0 | Simon Buckner |
| Other candidates | — | — | 182,250 | 1.3 | — |

## PRESIDENTIAL ELECTION OF 1900

**Nominations:** The Republicans, meeting in Philadelphia, June 19–21, 1900, made McKinley's nomination unanimous. The Democrats, meeting in Kansas City, Mo., July 4–6, 1900, chose Bryan unanimously on the first ballot. **Campaign:** Democrats accused McKinley of imperialism in Cuba and the Philippines and of being the tool of big business.

| PRESIDENTIAL CANDIDATES | PARTY | ELECTORAL VOTES | POPULAR VOTE Total | Percentage | VICE-PRESIDENTIAL CANDIDATES |
|---|---|---|---|---|---|
| William McKinley | Republican | 292 | 7,218,491 | 51.7 | Theodore Roosevelt |
| William Jennings Bryan | Democratic | 155 | 6,356,734 | 45.5 | Adlai E. Stevenson |
| John G. Woolley | Prohibition | — | 208,914 | 1.5 | Henry B. Metcalf |
| Other candidates | — | — | 189,126 | 1.3 | — |

During McKinley's administration tariffs were raised and Hawaii was annexed.

The Caribbean took the spotlight after Cubans rebelled against Spain in 1895. Ruthless Spanish repression followed, and U.S. property losses on the island were substantial. An unexplained explosion on the U.S. battleship *Maine* in Havana harbor (Feb. 15, 1898) was the final push needed to bring about war.

At McKinley's request, Congress declared war on Spain on April 25, 1898. The war lasted just four months. With U.S. victory, Cuba was placed under American military rule, and Puer-

to Rico, the Philippines, and Guam became U.S. possessions.

In 1900 McKinley was reelected. Less than a year later, he was shot by Leon Czolgosz, an anarchist, in Buffalo, N.Y., on Sept. 6, 1901. He died eight days later, on Sept. 14.

**Ida Saxton McKinley** (1847–1907) married McKinley in 1871. They had two daughters, both of whom died in childhood. She was an epileptic and an invalid during her husband's administration. But she insisted on accompanying McKinley everywhere and was with him in Buffalo where he was assassinated.

## THEODORE ROOSEVELT

Roosevelt entered the White House at the age of 42—the youngest man ever to attain the presidency. His vivid personality and his enthusiasm immediately made him a popular incumbent. His intellectual interests elevated the overall tone of American politics, although his glorification of military

26th President
(1901–09)

power and force drew considerable criticism.

Neither Republican boss Mark Hanna nor President McKinley had wanted Roosevelt as the vice-presidential candidate. Hanna's reaction on learning of McKinley's death was reportedly, "Now look, that damned cowboy is President of the United States."

### EARLY LIFE

The first son of Theodore and Martha Bulloch Roosevelt, he was born on Oct. 27, 1858, in New York City. The scion of a wealthy family, he was educated by private tutors, traveled widely, graduated from Harvard (1880), and attended Columbia Law School.

As a youth Roosevelt's health was poor. His efforts to build up his physical strength by "roughing it" helped make him a sportsman, hunter, horseman, rancher, and explorer.

At the same time he retained wide cultural interests and was a prolific author, writing his first book in 1882, *The Naval War of 1812.*

### POLITICAL AND MILITARY CAREER

Throughout his life, Roosevelt's major interest was politics, which he entered as a "young insurgent" Republican advocating reforms. Roosevelt served in the New York legislature from 1881 to 1884.

At the 1884 Republican presidential convention he opposed the nomination of James G. Blaine because of Blaine's connection with a stock-rigging scandal. This cost Roosevelt the support of the New York Republican boss, Thomas Platt. In turn, when Roosevelt, a loyal Republican, campaigned for Blaine, he lost the support of the young insurgents of his party.

Considering his political career at an end, and

bereaved by the deaths of his mother and his wife on the same day in 1884, Roosevelt retired for the next two years to his North Dakota ranch. There he acquired many picturesque Western mannerisms of speech and gesture. He wrote many magazine articles about life in the West.

In 1886 Roosevelt was called back to New York City to run for mayor against powerful Democratic candidates. Although he was defeated, he attracted so much attention that President Harrison appointed him to the U.S. Civil Service Commission (1889–95), on which he became the dominant figure.

A reform mayor of New York City appointed Roosevelt head of the Board of Police Commissioners in 1895. Roosevelt proceeded vigorously to clean up the corruption-ridden police force. However, his zealous enforcement of Sunday blue laws, closing saloons, angered many of the city's residents.

In 1897 President McKinley reluctantly appointed him assistant secretary of the navy. In this post, anticipating war with Spain, he was instrumental in placing the Navy on a war footing.

At the outbreak of the Spanish-American War he resigned as assistant secretary of the navy. Then, with Leonard Wood, he organized the volunteer cavalry regiment known as the Rough Riders. On July 1, 1898, Col. Roosevelt led the Rough Riders in a charge up Cuba's San Juan Hill, an event he always continued to regard as "the great day of my life."

Roosevelt returned from Cuba a military hero. New York's "Boss" Platt, though personally averse to him, supported him for the governorship of New York. Roosevelt won and served from 1899 to 1901.

His administration as governor of New York antagonized Platt and the other Republican bosses. It was in his relations with the New York Republican political machine that he first used the term that became one of his trademarks: "Speak softly and carry a big stick, you will go far."

In 1900 New York Republican leaders decided to dispose of Roosevelt, for at least the next four years, by backing his nomination for Vice President. The McKinley-Roosevelt slate was easily elected.

### 26th PRESIDENT OF THE UNITED STATES

Roosevelt served only a few months as Vice

QUICK QUIZ: What is the driest place on the Earth? See page 178.

**THEODORE ROOSEVELT** *(continued)*
President before the assassination of McKinley made him President on Sept. 14, 1901.

This was the era of "muckraking" and reform, and Roosevelt embodied the period. He strengthened government controls over big business through a reinvigorated Interstate Commerce Commission, directed "trust-busting" actions against big corporations, and supported passage of the Meat Inspection Act and the Pure Food and Drug Act. He also advocated conservation of forestlands and irrigation of wastelands.

Roosevelt's "big stick" policy toward Latin America contributed to anti-American feeling. When Colombia refused to give him permission to build a canal across its province Panama, Roosevelt backed a revolution in Panama. He immediately recognized the rebel regime, secured from it the desired agreement, and began construction of the canal. In 1906 he visited Panama—the first President to travel outside the U.S. while in office.

Through his mediation the Russo-Japanese War was ended in 1905 at the Portsmouth (N.H.) Peace Conference.

He helped avert war between France and Germany over Morocco by sponsoring the Algeciras Conference.

His advocacy of the Hague Tribunal raised hopes for international peace.

For his activities to improve international relations, he became in 1906 the first American awarded the Nobel Peace Prize.

Roosevelt was the first President to ride in a gasoline-powered automobile (Aug. 22, 1902). He also was the first to fly in an airplane (Oct. 11, 1910), a year after leaving the White House.

## LATER ACTIVITIES

At the close of his second term Roosevelt chose as his successor William Howard Taft, his secretary of war. Roosevelt successfully backed Taft at the 1908 Republican convention and in the ensuing campaign.

After leaving the White House, Roosevelt went off on exploring and big-game expeditions and a tour of European capitals.

On his return in 1910, he broke with Taft. At the 1912 Republican convention Roosevelt sought the nomination for a third term. When Taft was selected, Roosevelt took the progressive Republicans out of the party. He organized them into a new Progressive, or "Bull Moose," Party. He then ran as the Progressive Party's presidential candidate.

During the ensuing campaign, a would-be assassin fired a shot that struck Roosevelt shortly before he was to make an address in Milwaukee, Wis., on Oct. 14, 1912. Although the bullet penetrated Roosevelt's chest, he insisted on completing his speech before going to a hospital.

The split in the Republican Party in 1912 enabled the Democratic candidate, Woodrow Wilson, to win. Roosevelt came in second, with Taft a poor third.

In addition to politics, Roosevelt engaged in what would have been separate careers for other men—exploration and writing. A former "River of Doubt" in the Brazilian jungle, which he traced to its outlet, was given the name Rio Roosevelt. He wrote nearly 40 books.

Roosevelt was deeply disappointed when President Wilson refused his offer to organize and lead a division of volunteers to fight in France in World War I.

On Jan. 6, 1919, Roosevelt died in his sleep.

**Alice Hathaway Lee Roosevelt** (1861–84) was his first wife. She died two days after the birth of their daughter, Alice.

**Edith Kermit Carow Roosevelt** (1861–1948) became Roosevelt's second wife in 1886. They had four sons and one daughter. One son died in action during World War I and two others died in World War II. As First Lady, Edith Roosevelt made the White House the social center of Washington.

## THEODORE ROOSEVELT'S PRESIDENTIAL ADMINISTRATION

**Congress in Session:**
57th, 58th, 59th, 60th
**Vice President:**
The vice-presidential office remained vacant during Roosevelt's first administration.
Charles Fairbanks, 1905–09
**Secretary of State:**
John Hay, 1901–05
Elihu Root, 1905–09
Robert Bacon, 1909
**Secretary of War:**
Elihu Root, 1901–04
William Taft, 1904–08
Luke Wright, 1908–09

**Secretary of the Treasury:**
Lyman Gage, 1901–02
Leslie Shaw, 1902–07
George Cortelyou, 1907–09
**Attorney General:**
Philander Knox, 1901–04
William Moody, 1904–06
Charles Bonaparte, 1906–09
**Secretary of the Navy:**
John Long, 1901–02
William Moody, 1902–04
Paul Morton, 1904–05
Charles Bonaparte, 1905–06
Victor Metcalf, 1906–08
Truman H. Newberry, 1908–09

**Postmaster General:**
Charles E. Smith, 1901–02
Henry Payne, 1902–04
Robert Wynne, 1904–05
George Cortelyou, 1905–07
George Meyer, 1907–09
**Secretary of the Interior:**
Ethan Hitchcock, 1901–07
James Garfield, 1907–09
**Secretary of Agriculture:**
James Wilson, 1901–09
**Secretary of Commerce and Labor:**
George Cortelyou, 1903–04
Victor Metcalf, 1904–06
Oscar Straus, 1906–09

## PRESIDENTIAL ELECTION OF 1904

**Nominations:** Republicans met in Chicago, June 21–23, 1904, and chose Roosevelt unanimously. Democrats met in St. Louis, July 6–9, 1904, and nominated Parker on the first ballot. **Remarks:** Roosevelt received a larger percentage of the popular vote than any previous President since tabulation of the vote had begun in 1824.

| PRESIDENTIAL CANDIDATES | PARTY | ELECTORAL VOTES | POPULAR VOTE Total | Percentage | VICE-PRESIDENTIAL CANDIDATES |
|---|---|---|---|---|---|
| Theodore Roosevelt ... | Republican | 336 | 7,628,461 | 56.4 | Charles W. Fairbanks |
| Alton B. Barker ....... | Democratic | 140 | 5,084,223 | 37.6 | Henry G. Davis |
| Eugene V. Debs ....... | Socialist | — | 402,283 | 3.0 | Benjamin Hanford |
| Other candidates ...... | — | — | 407,968 | 3.0 | — |

## WILLIAM HOWARD TAFT

27th President
(1909–13)

The weightiest President, William Howard Taft stood six feet two inches tall and weighed over 300 pounds. An easygoing man, Taft presided over a prosperous nation more concerned with industrial growth than world affairs. He became the only President to later serve on the Supreme Court.

Taft was born on Sept. 15, 1857, in Cincinnati, Ohio, the son of Alphonso and Louise Maria Torrey Taft. His father had served as secretary of war and attorney general under President Grant. As a youth, "Willie," as he was called, won a reputation to be feared as a wrestler and boxer. Taft graduated from Yale in 1878 and from Cincinnati Law School in 1880.

After practicing law in Cincinnati, he served successively as assistant prosecutor, assistant county solicitor, and superior court judge. He then received federal appointments as solicitor general of the U.S. (1890–92), U.S. circuit judge (1892–1900), president of the Philippine Commission (1900–01), and governor of the Philippines (1901–04).

President Roosevelt, his close friend, appointed him secretary of war (1904–08) and entrusted him with special missions to Cuba, Panama, the Philippines, and Japan.

Roosevelt chose Taft as his successor, and the Republicans nominated him as their presidential candidate in the election of 1908. Taft defeated Democrat William Jennings Bryan, who was making his third try for the White House.

Never having been elected to office before running for President, Taft had difficulty dealing with politicians and acting as leader of the Republican Party.

As President, Taft continued Roosevelt's policies, but the emphasis became more conservative. Republicans who favored progressive policies grew increasingly restive.

During his administration Arizona and New Mexico were admitted to the Union, bringing the number of U.S. states to 48.

Taft sought to conciliate the progressives by approving laws to institute postal savings and the parcel post. He also endorsed constitutional amendments authorizing direct election of senators and enactment of a federal income tax. Both were ratified by the states and were proclaimed in 1913. Taft also approved the Paine-Aldrich Act, which reduced duties on imports and opened the door to free trade with the Philippines.

These bids failed to placate the progressives, however. Led by Theodore Roosevelt, they bolted the Republican Party when it renominated Taft in 1912. They organized their own party, with Roosevelt as their candidate. The bitter split gave the election to the Democratic candidate, Gov. Woodrow Wilson of New Jersey.

Taft came in third, after Roosevelt. He was not unhappy, however, at the prospect of private life. Soon after Wilson's election he wrote, "The nearer I get to the inauguration of my successor the greater the relief I feel."

In his retirement Taft taught at Yale. During World War I he served as co-chairman of the National War Labor Board. He was among the Republicans who advocated U.S. entry into the League of Nations.

In 1921 he was appointed Chief Justice of the United States by President Harding, serving on the Supreme Court until a few weeks before his death, on March 8, 1930. He was the first President buried in Arlington National Cemetery.

**Helen Herron Taft** (1861–1943), his wife, was the daughter of a Cincinnati judge. She was a musician, and her White House musicales were highly regarded. She was ill during part of her husband's administration, so her sister, Mrs. Louise More, presided in her place.

The Tafts' children carried on the distinction of the family: Robert Alphonso was an influential senator. Charles Phelps was the first layman president of the Federal Council of Churches of Christ in America. Mrs. Helen Herron Taft Manning won note as an educator.

## TAFT'S PRESIDENTIAL ADMINISTRATION

**Congress in Session:**
61st, 62d
**Vice President:**
James Sherman, 1909–12
**Secretary of State:**
Philander Knox, 1909–13
**Secretary of the Treasury:**
Franklin MacVeagh, 1909–13

**Secretary of War:**
Jacob Dickinson, 1909–11
Henry Stimson, 1911–13
**Attorney General:**
George Wickersham, 1909–13
**Secretary of the Interior:**
Richard Ballinger, 1909–11
Walter Fisher, 1911–13

**Postmaster General:**
Frank Hitchcock, 1909–13
**Secretary of the Navy:**
George von L. Meyer, 1909–13
**Secretary of Agriculture:**
James Wilson, 1909–13
**Secretary of Com. and Labor:**
Charles Nagel, 1909–13

### PRESIDENTIAL ELECTION OF 1908

**Nominations:** Republicans met in Chicago, June 16–19, 1908, and on the first ballot ratified by acclamation Roosevelt's choice of Taft as his successor. Democrats, meeting in Denver, July 8–10, 1908, selected Bryan on the first ballot. **Campaign:** Roosevelt campaigned for Taft. Republicans promised tariff revision. Democrats called for lower tariffs, stringent antitrust enforcement, and relaxation of federal injunctions against labor strikes.

| PRESIDENTIAL CANDIDATES | PARTY | ELECTORAL VOTES | POPULAR VOTE Total | Percentage | VICE-PRESIDENTIAL CANDIDATES |
|---|---|---|---|---|---|
| William H. Taft | Republican | 321 | 7,675,320 | 51.6 | James S. Sherman |
| William Jennings Bryan | Democratic | 162 | 6,412,294 | 43.1 | John W. Kern |
| Eugene V. Debs | Socialist | — | 420,793 | 2.8 | Benjamin Hanford |
| Other candidates | — | — | 379,833 | 2.5 | |

QUICK QUIZ: What is Lauren Bacall's real name? See page 275.

## WOODROW WILSON

28th President
(1913–21)

An idealist, Wilson carried out many liberal domestic reforms, establishing new government controls on business to prevent abuses of workers. He then led the nation into World War I "to make the world safe for democracy." His greatest disappointment came when an isolationist U.S. Senate rejected U.S. participation in the postwar League of Nations he had conceived to preserve world peace.

### EARLY CAREER

Thomas Woodrow Wilson was born in Staunton, Va., on Dec. 29, 1856, the son of Joseph Ruggles Wilson, a Presbyterian minister, and Janet "Jessie" Woodrow Wilson. He graduated from the College of New Jersey (later Princeton) in 1879 and attended the University of Virginia Law School in 1881. Admitted to the Georgia bar in 1882, he practiced law for a year in Atlanta.

Deciding to become an educator, he took his Ph.D. at Johns Hopkins. Wilson then taught history and political science at Bryn Mawr and Wesleyan. In 1890 he joined Princeton's faculty. Twelve years later he became president of Princeton University, a post he held for eight years. He initiated many educational reforms and became a popular public speaker.

Wilson was nominated and elected Democratic governor of New Jersey in 1910. Despite resistance from regular Democrats, Wilson forced many progressive policies through the state legislature.

### 28th PRESIDENT OF THE UNITED STATES

At the 1912 Democratic national convention Wilson won the nomination on the 46th ballot. A split in the Republican Party was instrumental in sending him to the White House with a huge electoral-vote majority but less than 42% of the popular vote.

Wilson's first term was notable for its vigor. He became the first President to initiate frequently scheduled press conferences to keep the people informed on government activities. Liberal measures, carried out under the slogan "the New Freedom," included the Federal Reserve Act, which centralized the banking system of the country; the Keating-Owen Child Labor Act; the Farm Loan Act; the Clayton Antitrust Act; the Adamson Eight-Hour Law, reducing the working hours of trainmen; the La Follette Seamen's Act; and a lowered tariff.

## WILSON'S PRESIDENTIAL ADMINISTRATION

**Congress in Session:**
63d, 64th, 65th, 66th
**Vice President**
Thomas Marshall, 1913–21
**Secretary of State:**
William J. Bryan, 1913–15
Robert Lansing, 1915–20
Bainbridge Colby, 1920–21
**Secretary of the Treasury:**
William McAdoo, 1913–18
Carter Glass, 1918–20
David Houston, 1920–21

**Secretary of War:**
Lindley Garrison, 1913–16
Newton Baker, 1916–21
**Attorney General:**
James McReynolds, 1913–14
Thomas Gregory, 1914–19
A. Mitchell Palmer, 1919–21
**Postmaster General:**
Albert Burleson, 1913–21
**Secretary of the Navy:**
Josephus Daniels, 1913–21

**Secretary of the Interior:**
Franklin Lane, 1913–20
John Payne, 1920–21
**Secretary of Agriculture:**
David Houston, 1913–20
Edwin Meredith, 1920–21
**Secretary of Commerce:**
William Redfield, 1913–19
Joshua Alexander, 1919–21
**Secretary of Labor:**
William Wilson, 1913–21

### PRESIDENTIAL ELECTION OF 1912

**Nominations:** Republicans met in Chicago, June 18–22, 1912. Taft won, but 344 delegates did not vote. Sherman died during the campaign and was replaced by Butler. The Progressive ("Bull Moose") Party, in Chicago, Aug. 5–7, 1912, nominated Roosevelt by acclamation. The Democrats, meeting in Baltimore, June 25–July 2, 1912, took 46 ballots to decide on Wilson. **Campaign:** The Republican split between Roosevelt and Taft gave Wilson an easy victory.

| PRESIDENTIAL CANDIDATES | PARTY | ELECTORAL VOTES | POPULAR VOTE Total | Percentage | VICE-PRESIDENTIAL CANDIDATES |
|---|---|---|---|---|---|
| Woodrow Wilson .......... | Democratic | 435 | 6,296,547 | 41.9 | Thomas R. Marshall |
| Theodore Roosevelt ....... | Progressive | 88 | 4,118,571 | 27.4 | Hiram Johnson |
| William H. Taft ........... | Republican | 8 | 3,486,720 | 23.2 | James S. Sherman / Nicholas M. Butler |
| Eugene V. Debs ........... | Socialist | — | 901,255 | 6.0 | Emil Seidel |
| Other candidates.......... | — | — | 235,025 | 1.5 | — |

### PRESIDENTIAL ELECTION OF 1916

**Nominations:** The Republican convention in Chicago, June 7–10, 1916, chose Hughes on the third ballot when he received 949½ votes of 986. The Democratic convention in St. Louis, June 14–16, 1916, renominated its previous ticket by acclamation, with only one delegate opposed to Wilson. **Remarks:** Hughes went to bed before the California returns had come in, believing he had won a close election. By morning the West Coast results showed Wilson the winner.

| PRESIDENTIAL CANDIDATES | PARTY | ELECTORAL VOTES | POPULAR VOTE Total | Percentage | VICE–PRESIDENTIAL CANDIDATES |
|---|---|---|---|---|---|
| Woodrow Wilson .......... | Democratic | 277 | 9,127,695 | 49.4 | Thomas R. Marshall |
| Charles E. Hughes ........ | Republican | 254 | 8,533,507 | 46.2 | Charles W. Fairbanks |
| Allan L. Benson ........... | Socialist | — | 585,113 | 3.2 | George R. Kirkpatrick |
| Other candidates.......... | — | — | 233,909 | 1.2 | — |

To promote tariff reform, Wilson became the first President since John Adams to address Congress personally on the subject.

Wilson also favored equal rights for women. He welcomed the election in 1916 of America's first congresswoman, Jeannette Rankin of Montana. He aided the passage of the 19th Amendment, enfranchising women. Wilson also created a precedent by appointing the first woman to a subcabinet post, Annette Abbott Adams as assistant attorney general.

Opposed to prohibition, he vetoed the Volstead Act. Congress overrode his veto.

He disappointed many liberals by maintaining the "big stick" policy toward Latin America. On March 15, 1916, he sent U.S. troops into Mexico in pursuit of the revolutionary Pancho Villa. The United States purchased the Virgin Islands from Denmark in 1915 for $25 million.

The war in Europe that began in 1914 overshadowed all other foreign problems. Wilson sought to maintain U.S. neutrality, but went further in his warnings to Germany than Secretary of State William Jennings Bryan considered proper for a neutral. Bryan resigned after Wilson insisted on sending strong notes to Germany protesting the U-boat sinking of the *Lusitania* on May 7, 1915.

Under the slogan "He kept us out of war," Wilson barely won reelection in 1916 over Republican Charles Evans Hughes, who had resigned from the Supreme Court to run for the presidency.

When Germany announced in 1917 that it would resume all-out submarine operations to impose its own blockade against the Allies, Wilson took America into the world conflict with public opinion behind him. Congress declared war on Germany on April 6, 1917.

Wilson's conduct of the war was vigorous. His stated war objectives were to "make the world safe for democracy" and to promote the "ultimate peace of the world." His program was embodied in the famous "Fourteen Points" of Jan. 8, 1918. These called for open diplomacy, adjustment of colonial claims, self-determination of peoples, and formation of a "general association of nations."

After the Allies achieved victory on Nov. 11, 1918, Wilson went to France to attend the Versailles Peace Conference. There he met fierce resistance from Lloyd George, Georges Clemenceau, and other European premiers, who made secret agreements among themselves.

Wilson finally agreed to what he considered the best treaty obtainable, acceptable chiefly because it provided for the League of Nations.

Wilson had broken irreconcilably at Versailles with his longtime friend and closest adviser Col. Edward M. House, whom he had once described as his "second personality."

En route home in 1919 he became the first President to make a radio broadcast when he addressed U.S. troops from shipboard.

Wilson was dismayed upon his return home when the League was attacked by various senators. Despite opposition led by Henry Cabot Lodge, the Senate might have ratified the Versailles treaty if reservations protecting U.S. sovereignty had been incorporated. But Wilson refused to compromise.

While stumping the country to gain support for the treaty, Wilson became ill.

A stroke on Oct. 2, 1919, paralyzed Wilson's left side. For months he was seen by only a few people. Many believed Mrs. Wilson was acting in his stead.

Although repudiated at home, Wilson was eulogized abroad. In 1920 he was awarded the Nobel Peace Prize.

Nearly three years after completing his term of office, Wilson died in Washington, D.C., on Feb. 3, 1924. Entombed in the National Cathedral, he became the only President buried in Washington, D.C.

**Ellen Louise Axson Wilson** (1860–1914) married Wilson in 1885. They had three daughters. Mrs. Wilson died during her husband's second year in office.

**Edith Bolling Galt Wilson** (1872–1961), a widow, became his second wife in 1915.

## WARREN GAMALIEL HARDING

Harding was a handsome man who looked like the romantic ideal of a statesman. But he was ill equipped for the presidency. His administration is remembered for the Teapot Dome scandal and other corruption, although these did not become public until after his death.

Harding was born on Nov. 2, 1865, on a farm near what is now Blooming Grove, Ohio, the son of Dr. George Tryon and Phoebe Dickerson Harding.

29th President
(1921–23)

He graduated from Ohio Central College, worked as a teacher, and studied law.

In 1884 he and two friends invested $300 to buy the bankrupt Marion (Ohio) *Star.* As its editor and eventual full owner, he became influential in local affairs and active in Republican politics.

Harding was elected a state senator (1898–1902) and lieutenant governor (1904–06). He failed in two subsequent tries for the Ohio governorship.

Harding received national attention in 1912 when he made the address nominating President Taft for a second term at the Republican national convention.

Under the guidance of Harry M. Daugherty, an able machine politician, he was elected to the U.S. Senate in 1914.

When the Republican national convention in 1920 reached a deadlock between the two main contenders for the presidential nomination, Daugherty arranged a deal in a "smoke-filled" hotel room that won Harding the nomination.

He was elected by a landslide after a "front-

**WARREN G. HARDING** *(continued)*
porch" campaign that had "back to normalcy" as its major slogan.

During his administration the nation suffered a deep postwar depression. Taxes were reduced and tariffs were raised. Immigration was restricted for the first time with quotas.

In foreign relations, Harding called the Washington Disarmament Conference in 1921–22 that put limits on the size of navies.

While Harding was returning home from a trip to Alaska, he became ill, dying in San Francisco on Aug. 2, 1923.

Harding's wife refused to let doctors perform an autopsy, leading to later speculation that he may have been poisoned. She also burned his papers and correspondence, so no one has ever been able to learn how much Harding knew

about the corruption of his associates.

After Harding's death, Senate investigations revealed scandals of his administration in custodianship of alien property, sale of government-owned cargo ships, mismanagement of the Veterans Bureau, corruption of the Justice Department under Attorney General Daugherty, and the leasing of naval oil reserves (Teapot Dome) to private oil interests for a bribe.

Two of his cabinet members, Daugherty and Secretary of the Interior Albert B. Fall, were indicted and tried. Fall was sent to prison, but Daugherty was freed by a hung jury.

**Mrs. Florence Kling DeWolfe Harding** (1860–1924), a divorcée, became his wife in 1891. They had no children. After Harding's death, gossip alleged that he had carried on several illicit romances.

## HARDING'S PRESIDENTIAL ADMINISTRATION

**Congress in Session:**
67th, 68th

**Vice President:**
Calvin Coolidge, 1921–23

**Secretary of State:**
Charles Evans Hughes, 1921–23

**Secretary of the Interior:**
Albert Fall, 1921–23
Hubert Work, 1923

**Secretary of the Treasury:**
Andrew Mellon, 1921–23

**Secretary of War:**
John Weeks, 1921–23

**Attorney General:**
Harry Daugherty, 1921–23

**Postmaster General:**
Will Hays, 1921–22
Hubert Work, 1922–23
Harry New, 1923

**Secretary of the Navy:**
Edwin Denby, 1921–23

**Secretary of Agriculture:**
Henry C. Wallace, 1921–23

**Secretary of Commerce:**
Herbert Hoover, 1921–23

**Secretary of Labor:**
James Davis, 1921–23

### PRESIDENTIAL ELECTION OF 1920

**Nominations:** The Republican convention, in Chicago, June 8–12, 1920, deadlocked in voting on the two main contenders, Gen. Leonard Wood and Illinois Gov. Frank Lowden, but finally selected Harding on the 10th ballot. The Democrats, in San Francisco, June 28–July 6, 1920, were deadlocked until the 44th ballot. Cox then received 732½ votes, or 3½ more than the necessary 729, but a motion was carried to make the nomination unanimous. **Campaign:** Democrats attempted to make approval of the League of Nations an issue. Harding called for a return to "normalcy."

| PRESIDENTIAL CANDIDATES | PARTY | ELECTORAL VOTES | POPULAR VOTE Total | Percentage | VICE-PRESIDENTIAL CANDIDATES |
|---|---|---|---|---|---|
| Warren G. Harding | Republican | 404 | 16,143,407 | 60.4 | Calvin Coolidge |
| James M. Cox | Democratic | 127 | 9,130,328 | 34.2 | Franklin D. Roosevelt |
| Eugene V. Debs | Socialist | — | 919,799 | 3.4 | Seymour Stedman |
| Other candidates | — | — | 540,371 | 2.0 | — |

## CALVIN COOLIDGE

Coolidge had qualities and a program that appealed to the Americans of his day, a period of almost wild national prosperity. Spare of words, his nickname was "Silent Cal." He was straightforward and honest, and helped liquidate the scandals of the Harding administration. His program included economy in

30th President
(1923–29)

government, tax cuts, and reduction of the national debt.

Born on July 4, 1872, at Plymouth, Vt., he was the son of John Calvin Coolidge, a storekeeper and justice of the peace, and Victoria Josephine Moor Coolidge.

He graduated from Amherst in 1895 and was admitted to the bar two years later.

In many ways the antithesis of the back-slapping politician, Coolidge nonetheless rose swiftly in public life. He held minor offices in Nor-

thampton, Mass., where he had practiced law. He served in the state legislature (1912–15), as lieutenant governor (1916–18), and then as governor of Massachusetts (1919–20).

As governor he won national fame in 1919 when he sent state militia to break a strike by Boston police.

The 1920 Republican convention chose Coolidge as Harding's running mate. He became President on Harding's death, and in 1924 he was elected to a full term.

During Coolidge's administration speakeasies flourished in the cities despite efforts by government agents to enforce the national prohibition on sales of alcoholic beverages. Gangsters controlled the flow of illegal alcoholic beverages, leading to frequent gang wars.

Women's fashions changed drastically as "flappers" wore short skirts.

The Ku Klux Klan terrorized minority groups.

In 1927 the nation waited breathlessly as Charles A. Lindbergh made his dramatic solo flight across the Atlantic from New York to Paris.

The Kellogg-Briand Peace Pact in 1928 outlawed war (but made no provision for enforcement).

Coolidge probably could have won another term, but he refused to seek renomination in 1928 in his famous laconic message, "I do not choose to run."

On his retirement Coolidge occupied himself mainly with writing newspaper and magazine articles and with his autobiography.

The former President died on Jan. 5, 1933, in Northampton.

Grace Anna Goodhue Coolidge (1879–1957), who married Coolidge in 1905, was a graduate of the University of Vermont. She was highly regarded for her gracious and cultured manner. However, White House social activities were curtailed during Coolidge's administration by the deaths of the younger of their two sons (at 16) and of the President's father.

## COOLIDGE'S PRESIDENTIAL ADMINISTRATION

**Congress in Session:**
68th, 69th, 70th
**Vice President:**
Charles Dawes, 1925–29
**Secretary of State:**
Charles Hughes, 1923–25
Frank Kellogg, 1925–29
**Secretary of the Treasury:**
Andrew Mellon, 1923–29
**Postmaster General:**
Harry New, 1923–29

**Secretary of War:**
John Weeks, 1923–25
Dwight Davis, 1925–29
**Attorney General:**
Harry Daugherty, 1923–24
Harlan Stone, 1924–25
John Sargent, 1925–29
**Secretary of Agriculture:**
Henry C. Wallace, 1923–24
Howard M. Gore, 1924–25
William Jardine, 1925–29

**Secretary of the Navy:**
Edwin Denby, 1923–24
Curtis Wilbur, 1924–29
**Secretary of the Interior:**
Hubert Work, 1923–28
Roy O. West, 1928–29
**Secretary of Commerce:**
Herbert Hoover, 1923–28
William Whiting, 1928–29
**Secretary of Labor:**
James Davis, 1923–29

### PRESIDENTIAL ELECTION OF 1924

**Nominations:** The Republicans, meeting in Cleveland, June 10–12, 1924, chose Coolidge on the first ballot with 1,065 of 1,109 votes. Dawes was chosen after Frank Lowden had declined the vice-presidential nomination given him on the second ballot. The Democrats met in New York City in the longest of nominating conventions—it lasted from June 24 to July 9, 1924, with 60 candidates nominated for the presidency. Southern Democrats fought against the nomination of New York Gov. Al Smith, a Roman Catholic. On the 103d ballot Davis finally received the nomination. **Campaign Issues:** The main issues were the Harding administration scandals. **Remarks:** The Progressive Party was formed as a result of left-wing dissatisfaction with the major candidates as well as with the contemporary social scene.

| PRESIDENTIAL CANDIDATES | PARTY | ELECTORAL VOTES | POPULAR VOTE Total | Percentage | VICE–PRESIDENTIAL CANDIDATES |
|---|---|---|---|---|---|
| Calvin Coolidge . . . . . . . . . . . | Republican | 382 | 15,718,211 | 54.0 | Charles G. Dawes |
| John W. Davis . . . . . . . . . . . . | Democratic | 136 | 8,385,283 | 28.8 | Charles W. Bryan |
| Robert M. LaFollette . . . . . . | Progressive | 13 | 4,831,289 | 16.6 | Burton K. Wheeler |
| Other candidates . . . . . . . . . | — | — | 155,883 | 0.5 | — |

## HERBERT CLARK HOOVER

31st President
(1929–33)

While campaigning for the presidency in August 1928, Hoover said, "We are nearer to the final triumph over poverty than ever before in the history of any land. The poorhouse is vanishing from among us. We have not yet reached the goal, but we shall soon be in sight of the day when poverty will be banished from this nation." There seemed little reason then for Americans to disagree with this rosy appraisal of the nation's future, and Hoover was elected by a landslide. Less than a year later, however, the stock market crashed, beginning the Great Depression.

Hoover was born on Aug. 10, 1874, in West Branch, Iowa, the son of Jesse Clark Hoover, a blacksmith, and Hulda Randall Minthorn Hoover. He graduated from Stanford University in 1895.

Hoover became a mining engineer, prospector, and businessman, accumulating a fortune through wide-ranging operations that took him all over the world. Because of his Quaker beliefs, he worked as organizer of relief operations during World War I. His administration of relief agencies attracted worldwide attention and respect.

In 1921 Hoover was appointed secretary of commerce by President Harding. He reorganized and expanded the department, sponsored conferences on unemployment, initiated programs to conserve fisheries, and constructed public works.

Chosen the Republican presidential nominee in 1928, Hoover won election in a campaign marred by bigotry directed at the Democratic candidate, Alfred E. Smith, because of his Roman Catholic religion.

The Great Depression deepened throughout Hoover's administration. To counter it he called for an extensive public-works program to restore business and employment. He established the Reconstruction Finance Corporation, set up the Home Loan Bank, expanded the Farm Loan Bank, and supported legislation to relieve states and municipalities unable to bear the burden of the economic crisis. These measures proved ineffective, however, and Hoover's popularity waned drastically.

In foreign affairs he faced the problems of Japanese aggression in China, disarmament, and uncollected war debts.

In the presidential election of 1932, Hoover was defeated by Franklin D. Roosevelt.

In 1946 President Truman appointed Hoover

QUICK QUIZ: About how many tons of steel are produced each year? See page 200.

**HERBERT HOOVER** *(continued)*
coordinator of food supplies to dozens of countries devastated by World War II.

His long life in public service was further extended in 1947–49 and again in 1953–55, when he headed the Hoover Commission to reorganize the federal government.

Hoover died on Oct. 20, 1964, at the age of 90. **Lou Henry Hoover** (1875–1944), who was his college sweetheart, married Hoover in 1899. They had two sons. She was a charming White House hostess.

## HOOVER'S PRESIDENTIAL ADMINISTRATION

**Congress in Session:**
71st, 72d
**Vice President:**
Charles Curtis, 1929–33
**Secretary of State:**
Frank B. Kellogg, 1929
Henry Stimson, 1929–33
**Secretary of the Treasury:**
Andrew Mellon, 1929–32
Ogden Mills, 1932–33

**Secretary of War:**
James Good, 1929
Patrick Hurley, 1929–33
**Attorney General:**
William D. Mitchell, 1929–33
**Postmaster General:**
Walter Brown, 1929–33
**Secretary of the Navy:**
Charles Francis Adams, 1929–33

**Secretary of the Interior:**
Ray Lyman Wilbur, 1929–33
**Secretary of Agriculture:**
Arthur Hyde, 1929–33
**Secretary of Commerce:**
Robert Lamont, 1929–32
Roy D. Chapin, 1932–33
**Secretary of Labor:**
James Davis, 1929–30
William Doak, 1930–33

### PRESIDENTIAL ELECTION OF 1928

**Nominations:** The Republicans met in Kansas City, Mo., June 12–15, 1928. On the first ballot, Hoover received 837 of 1,089 votes. The Democrats, meeting in Houston, Texas, June 26–29, 1928, chose Smith on the first ballot with 849⅔ of 1,097½ votes. **Campaign Issues:** Smith's Catholicism, prohibition, and farm relief.

| PRESIDENTIAL CANDIDATES | PARTY | ELECTORAL VOTES | POPULAR VOTE Total | Percentage | VICE–PRESIDENTIAL CANDIDATES |
|---|---|---|---|---|---|
| Herbert C. Hoover | Republican | 444 | 21,391,993 | 58.2 | Charles Curtis |
| Alfred E. Smith | Democratic | 87 | 15,016,169 | 40.9 | Joseph T. Robinson |
| Norman M. Thomas | Socialist | — | 267,385 | 0.7 | James Maurer |
| Other candidates | — | — | 69,180 | 0.2 | — |

## FRANKLIN DELANO ROOSEVELT

Few people in the nation ever were neutral about Franklin Roosevelt. His followers loved him and his opponents hated him with remarkable vigor.

His secretary of the interior, Harold L. Ickes, said that Roosevelt seemed "either to inspire a mad devotion that can see no flaw or to kindle a hatred of an

32d President
(1933–45)

intensity that will admit of no virtue."

Roosevelt was a tradition breaker from the time he was selected as the Democrats' standard-bearer in 1932. He upset custom by flying to the national political convention to accept its nomination in person.

Taking office at the height of a national economic crisis, Roosevelt soon brought hope to a discouraged nation with his concern for the "forgotten man" and his promise of a "New Deal" for Americans.

### EARLY POLITICAL CAREER

Roosevelt was born on Jan. 30, 1882, at Hyde Park, N.Y. His parents were James and Sara Delano Roosevelt, a wealthy and socially prominent family.

He graduated from Harvard in 1904 and married his cousin Eleanor Roosevelt the following year. He attended Columbia Law School and was admitted to the bar in 1907.

After practicing law for four years, he won a Democratic seat in the New York state senate (1911–12). He established himself as leader of the reform Democrats by opposing a Tammany nominee for the U.S. Senate.

In 1912 he campaigned for Woodrow Wilson, who appointed him assistant secretary of the navy (1913–20).

The Democratic Party chose Roosevelt as their vice-presidential candidate in the unsuccessful 1920 election campaign against Harding.

In 1921 he was stricken with polio that permanently crippled him from the waist down. But by indomitable effort he learned to walk again using leg braces and crutches.

Roosevelt was urged to resume his political career by his wife and New York's Democratic Gov. Alfred E. Smith. At 46 he won election in 1928 as New York's governor, while the national Democratic ticket headed by Smith went down to defeat.

As governor, Roosevelt achieved renown for his competence. The stock market crash of 1929 brought with it the Great Depression. Roosevelt, advised by a small group of intellectuals and experts called the "Brain Trust," undertook extensive relief measures.

Roosevelt also struck at corruption in New York City politics, forcing the resignation of Mayor James J. Walker.

### 32d PRESIDENT OF THE UNITED STATES

Roosevelt was chosen by the Democrats in 1932 to oppose President Hoover, whose administration had seen the start of this period of disaster and despair. Roosevelt was elected by a wide margin and buoyantly set out to create a peaceful social revolution.

The new Congress, overwhelmed by the magnitude of the Depression and by the forceful personality of Roosevelt, surrendered much power to the President. He immediately launched a series of emergency measures to reorganize industry and agriculture—under government controls—

and to revive the faltering economy by a great expenditure of public funds.

Between March 9 and June 16, 1933, in the famous "hundred days" session, Congress enacted, under Roosevelt's guidance, more decisive legislation than in any previous congressional session in history.

This vast and many-faceted New Deal program encountered bitter opposition. Roosevelt's critics accused him of having too many radical schemes for social betterment. Among conservatives he was disparagingly referred to as "that man in the White House."

Nonetheless, in 1936 Roosevelt was reelected

## FRANKLIN D. ROOSEVELT'S PRESIDENTIAL ADMINISTRATION

**Congress in Session:**
73d, 74th, 75th, 76th,
77th, 78th, 79th
**Vice President:**
John Garner, 1933–41
Henry A. Wallace, 1941–45
Harry Truman, 1945
**Secretary of State:**
Cordell Hull, 1933–44
Edward Stettinius Jr., 1944–45
**Secretary of War:**
George Dern, 1933–36
Harry Woodring, 1936–40
Henry Stimson, 1940–45

**Secretary of the Treasury:**
William Woodin, 1933–34
Henry Morgenthau Jr., 1934–45
**Attorney General:**
Homer Cummings, 1933–39
Frank Murphy, 1939–40
Robert Jackson, 1940–41
Francis Biddle, 1941–45
**Postmaster General:**
James Farley, 1933–40
Frank Walker, 1940–45
**Secretary of Agriculture:**
Henry A. Wallace, 1933–40
Claude Wickard, 1940–45

**Secretary of Commerce:**
Daniel Roper, 1933–38
Harry Hopkins, 1938–40
Jesse Jones, 1940–45
Henry A. Wallace, 1945
**Secretary of Labor:**
Frances Perkins, 1933–45
**Secretary of the Navy:**
Claude Swanson, 1933–40
Charles Edison, 1940
Frank Knox, 1940–44
James Forrestal, 1944–45
**Secretary of the Interior:**
Harold Ickes, 1933–45

### PRESIDENTIAL ELECTION OF 1932

**Nominations:** The Republicans held their convention in Chicago, June 14–16, 1932. On the first ballot Hoover received 1,126½ of 1,150 votes. The Democrats met in Chicago, June 27–29, 1932. Roosevelt on the fourth ballot received 945 of 1,148½ votes. **Campaign Issues:** The major issues dealt with methods of meeting and alleviating the economic depression. **Remarks:** Roosevelt broke tradition by flying to Chicago to accept the nomination.

| PRESIDENTIAL CANDIDATES | PARTY | ELECTORAL VOTES | POPULAR VOTE Total | Percentage | VICE–PRESIDENTIAL CANDIDATES |
|---|---|---|---|---|---|
| Franklin D. Roosevelt ...... | Democratic | 472 | 22,809,638 | 57.4 | John Nance Garner |
| Herbert C. Hoover......... | Republican | 59 | 15,758,901 | 39.7 | Charles Curtis |
| Norman M. Thomas ....... | Socialist | — | 881,951 | 2.2 | James Maurer |
| Other candidates .......... | — | — | 278,534 | 0.7 | — |

### PRESIDENTIAL ELECTION OF 1936

**Nominations:** The Republicans convened in Cleveland, June 9–12, 1936. Landon was the only candidate placed in nomination, although 19 votes went to Senator Borah. The Democrats, meeting in Philadelphia, June 23–27, 1936, renominated Roosevelt by acclamation. **Remarks:** Roosevelt won 60.8% of the vote, a record to that time.

| PRESIDENTIAL CANDIDATES | PARTY | ELECTORAL VOTES | POPULAR VOTE Total | Percentage | VICE–PRESIDENTIAL CANDIDATES |
|---|---|---|---|---|---|
| Franklin D. Roosevelt ...... | Democratic | 523 | 27,752,869 | 60.8 | John Nance Garner |
| Alfred M. Landon.......... | Republican | 8 | 16,674,655 | 36.5 | Frank Knox |
| William Lemke ............ | Union | — | 882,479 | 1.9 | Thomas C. O'Brien |
| Other candidates .......... | — | — | 318,502 | 0.8 | — |

### PRESIDENTIAL ELECTION OF 1940

**Nominations:** The Republicans met in Philadelphia, June 24–28, 1940. Willkie won on the sixth ballot. The Democrats met in Chicago, July 15–18, 1940. Roosevelt was nominated by acclamation. **Campaign Issues:** American neutrality and the effects of New Deal reforms. **Remarks:** Roosevelt broke tradition by running for a third term.

| PRESIDENTIAL CANDIDATES | PARTY | ELECTORAL VOTES | POPULAR VOTE Total | Percentage | VICE–PRESIDENTIAL CANDIDATES |
|---|---|---|---|---|---|
| Franklin D. Roosevelt ...... | Democratic | 449 | 27,307,819 | 54.8 | Henry A. Wallace |
| Wendell L. Willkie ......... | Republican | 82 | 22,321,018 | 44.8 | Charles L. McNary |
| Other candidates .......... | — | — | 218,312 | 0.4 | — |

### PRESIDENTIAL ELECTION of 1944

**Nominations:** The Republicans convened in Chicago, June 26–28, 1944. Dewey was the only presidential candidate nominated. The Democrats, at their convention in Chicago, July 19– 21, 1944, gave Roosevelt 1,086 of 1,176 votes on first ballot. **Remarks:** Democrats campaigned on the basis that leadership should not be changed in the middle of a war.

| PRESIDENTIAL CANDIDATES | PARTY | ELECTORAL VOTES | POPULAR VOTE Total | Percentage | VICE–PRESIDENTIAL CANDIDATES |
|---|---|---|---|---|---|
| Franklin D. Roosevelt ...... | Democratic | 432 | 25,606,585 | 53.5 | Harry S. Truman |
| Thomas E. Dewey .......... | Republican | 99 | 22,014,745 | 46.0 | John W. Bricker |
| Other candidates .......... | — | — | 200,612 | 0.5 | — |

QUICK QUIZ: Who was Vice President under John Adams? See page 390.

**FRANKLIN D. ROOSEVELT** *(continued)*
by an awesome majority over his Republican opponent, Alfred M. Landon, who won only the electoral votes of Maine and Vermont.

The Supreme Court's action in declaring unconstitutional several New Deal measures slowed the pace of reform. In 1937 Roosevelt attempted to "pack the court," but was unable to reorganize it to his advantage. He failed, too, in attempting to "purge" members of Congress who had opposed New Deal measures.

By 1938 the international skies were black with the shadow of impending war. As the power of Nazi Germany grew, Roosevelt spoke out against aggression and international greed. In 1939 he personally appealed for peace to the German and Italian dictators, Hitler and Mussolini.

Roosevelt was bitterly opposed by isolationist and conservative forces. In the 1940 presidential election an acrimonious issue was made of his breaking the third-term tradition. Although Roosevelt's majority was reduced, he decisively defeated the Republican candidate, Wendell Willkie.

The history of Roosevelt's third term is that of World War II.

The Japanese attack on Pearl Harbor, Hawaii, on Dec. 7, 1941 finally drew the U.S. directly into the conflict. War production multiplied beyond the most optimistic estimates.

In the European-African theater, U.S. Gen. Dwight D. Eisenhower was made supreme commander. U.S. forces landed in North Africa and followed with the invasion of Sicily, Italy, and finally Normandy.

In the Pacific the U.S. Navy carried marines and soldiers in a series of amphibious operations against Japanese-held islands. U.S. superiority in the air brought the war to Japan itself.

In the election of 1944 Roosevelt won an unprecedented fourth term with Harry Truman as his Vice President.

Roosevelt participated in a series of conferences with Winston Churchill, Joseph Stalin, and other Allied leaders to discuss plans for the postwar world. He planned to lay the foundations of lasting peace through formation of the United Nations.

On April 12, 1945, however, Roosevelt died of a massive cerebral hemorrhage before the war had been won.

**Anna Eleanor Roosevelt Roosevelt** (1884–1962), his wife, was the niece of Theodore Roosevelt as well as a distant cousin of her husband. As a young woman she had been a volunteer social worker. She continued her civic activities after her marriage, even though she bore five sons and one daughter.

Mrs. Roosevelt also gave her husband substantial assistance in his political career. During her husband's administrations she established a precedent as a First Lady famous in her own right. In doing so, she subjected herself to controversy and criticism. She traveled widely, making numerous speeches and reporting her observations in the press. After Roosevelt's death she devoted herself to humanitarian causes. From 1949 to 1952 she was a U.S. delegate to the United Nations.

# HARRY S. TRUMAN

Unexpectedly finding himself at the helm of the world's first atomic power, President Truman used the A-bomb to bring World War II to a quick conclusion. He then magnanimously extended American help both to friends and former foes in rebuilding their war-devastated economies. Under his leadership the

33d President
(1945–53)

United States became the protector of the free world from communist subversion and aggression in the postwar years. His accomplishments were hailed in these words by British leader Winston Churchill: "You, more than any other man, have saved Western Civilization."

## EARLY LIFE

Truman was born on May 8, 1884, in Lamar, Mo., the son of John Anderson Truman, a farmer, and Martha Ellen Young Truman. He began working in a local drugstore at the age of 11 and graduated from high school at 17. He clerked and farmed until World War I, when he helped organize a field artillery unit. He rose to major by the end of the war.

Civilian life seemed bleak to Truman after the failure of his haberdashery business in Kansas City in 1921. However, he had attracted the notice of the local Democratic boss, Thomas Pendergast, who helped him win election as a Jackson County official. During this time Truman studied law.

Elected U.S. senator from Missouri in 1934, Truman served for 10 years as a sometime supporter of the New Deal. He became a national figure as chairman of the Special Senate Committee to Investigate the National Defense Program (the Truman Committee). His fair and energetic inquiry into inefficiency and bungling on war-production contracts won wide praise.

In 1944 Truman was elected Vice President as Franklin D. Roosevelt's running mate.

## 33d PRESIDENT OF THE UNITED STATES

When Roosevelt died on April 12, 1945, Truman became the first President to take office in the midst of a war.

He was immediately confronted with the problems of ending World War II and preparing for postwar readjustment. Germany surrendered in May. After Truman authorized the atomic bombing of Hiroshima and Nagasaki, Japan capitulated in August.

Nominated in 1948 as the Democratic presidential candidate, he upset all those who had forecast his certain defeat by the Republican nominee, Thomas E. Dewey. By his vigorous railroad "whistle-stop" campaigning, he not only countered a nationwide Republican swing but overcame splits in his own party. On the right, Sen. J. Strom Thurmond of South Carolina led a new States' Rights (Dixiecrat) Party of Southern Democrats antagonized by Truman's advocacy of civil rights for blacks. On the left, Henry A.

Wallace led "progressive" groups at odds with Truman's anti-Soviet stand.

In his postwar domestic policy Truman faced strong congressional opposition from a coalition of Republicans and Southern Democrats.

The conservative coalition in Congress overrode his veto of the Labor-Management Relations Act (Taft-Hartley Law), enacted the McCarran-Walter Immigration Bill over his opposition, withheld support from his efforts to initiate government-sponsored health insurance, frustrated his attempts to maintain price controls, and blocked his civil-rights program.

In domestic affairs, however, he did achieve public housing projects, an increase in the minimum wage, civilian control of nuclear energy, and desegregation of the armed forces.

In foreign affairs, threatening communist advances in 1946–47 in Europe and the Middle East resulted in the Cold War. Congress backed Truman's foreign policy, which concentrated on containing communism.

The establishment of the UN was affirmed in 1945. Congress fully supported the "Truman Doctrine" in 1947, a program of economic and military assistance to nations threatened by communism. This was expanded later in 1947 by the Marshall Plan (European Recovery Program), and was supplemented by the Point Four Program in 1949 for aid to developing nations.

A victory in the Cold War was achieved in 1948–49 when an Anglo-American airlift frustrated the communists' Berlin blockade.

To safeguard Western Europe from possible communist attack, Truman pushed through the formation in 1950 of the North Atlantic Treaty Organization (NATO), an anticommunist military alliance.

The Cold War turned hot when communist North Korea attacked South Korea in 1950. Truman sent in U.S. troops under command of World War II hero Gen. Douglas MacArthur. But their advance to the Yalu River on the Chinese border brought China into the field, and the conflict became a stalemate. In 1951 Truman raised a storm of controversy when he relieved MacArthur of his Far Eastern command for failure to obey orders.

President Truman made the first coast-to-coast TV broadcast when he opened the Japanese Peace Conference in San Francisco in 1951.

The final years of his administration were shadowed by the stalemated Korean War, unsubstantiated charges by Sen. Joseph R. McCarthy of communist infiltration in the Department of State and the U.S. Army, plus partisan claims that U.S. failure to support Gen. Chiang Kai-shek had lost China to the communists.

Refusing to consider renomination in 1952, Truman went into retirement, giving much time to writing and to the establishment of the Harry S. Truman Library at Independence, Mo., where his official papers are housed.

Truman died in his 88th year on Dec. 26, 1972, in Kansas City, Mo.

**Elizabeth Virginia "Bess" Wallace Truman,** born in 1885, was a high school classmate who married Truman in 1919. She was retiring in nature and avoided publicity. Their daughter, Margaret, was a concert singer. During most of Truman's administration, he and his wife lived in Blair House, across the street from the White House, while the Executive Mansion was completely rebuilt with a steel framework.

## TRUMAN'S PRESIDENTIAL ADMINISTRATION

**Congress in Session:**
79th, 80th, 81st, 82d
**Vice President:**
Alben Barkley, 1949–53
**Secretary of State:**
Edward R. Stettinius Jr., 1945
James Byrnes, 1945–47
George Marshall, 1947–49
Dean Acheson, 1949–53
**Secretary of the Treasury:**
Henry Morgenthau Jr., 1945
Fred Vinson, 1945–46
John Snyder, 1946–53
**Secretary of War:**
Henry L. Stimson, 1945
Robert Patterson, 1945–47
Kenneth Royal, 1947

**Secretary of Defense:**
James Forrestal, 1947–49
Louis Johnson, 1949–50
George Marshall, 1950–51
Robert Lovett, 1951–53
**Attorney General:**
Francis Biddle, 1945
Tom Clark, 1945–49
J. Howard McGrath, 1949–52
James McGranery, 1952–53
**Postmaster General:**
Frank C. Walker, 1945
Robert Hannegan, 1945–47
Jesse Donaldson, 1947–53
**Secretary of the Navy:**
James Forrestal, 1945–47

**Secretary of the Interior:**
Harold Ickes, 1945–46
Julius Krug, 1946–49
Oscar Chapman, 1949–53
**Secretary of Agriculture:**
Claude R. Wickard, 1945
Clinton Anderson, 1945–48
Charles Brannan, 1948–53
**Secretary of Commerce:**
Henry A. Wallace, 1945–46
W. Averell Harriman, 1946–48
Charles Sawyer, 1948–53
**Secretary of Labor:**
Frances Perkins, 1945
Lewis Schwellenbach, 1945–48
Maurice Tobin, 1948–53

## PRESIDENTIAL ELECTION OF 1948

**Nominations:** Republicans met in Philadelphia, June 21–25, 1948, and on the third ballot gave Dewey a unanimous vote. Democrats convened in Philadelphia, July 12–14, 1948. Truman won on the first ballot. **Campaign Issues:** Truman capitalized on attacking the "do-nothing" Republican-controlled 80th Congress, winning a surprising upset victory.

| PRESIDENTIAL CANDIDATES | PARTY | ELECTORAL VOTES | POPULAR VOTE Total | Percentage | VICE–PRESIDENTIAL CANDIDATES |
|---|---|---|---|---|---|
| Harry S. Truman .......... | Democratic | 303 | 24,105,812 | 49.5 | Alben W. Barkley |
| Thomas E. Dewey .......... | Republican | 189 | 21,970,065 | 45.1 | Earl Warren |
| J. Strom Thurmond........ | States' Rights | 39 | 1,169,063 | 2.4 | Fielding L. Wright |
| Henry A. Wallace .......... | Progressive | — | 1,157,172 | 2.4 | Glenn Taylor |
| Other candidates .......... | — | — | 285,495 | 0.6 | |

QUICK QUIZ: Which U.S. newspaper has the largest daily circulation? See page 684.

## DWIGHT DAVID EISENHOWER

34th President
(1953–61)

The victorious commander of allied forces that defeated Germany in World War II, "Ike" Eisenhower was sought as a presidential candidate by both major political parties. At first he rejected the overtures. But he finally succumbed, resigning from the Army in 1952 to become the Republican presidential nominee. He chose as his running mate Sen. Richard M. Nixon.

With the campaign slogan "I like Ike," the hero general easily defeated his Democratic opponent, Gov. Adlai E. Stevenson of Illinois, both in 1952 and 1956.

As President, Eisenhower quickly settled the Korean War. Then, after a brief recession, the nation enjoyed a high level of prosperity, clouded only by fears of a possible atomic war with the Soviet Union.

The Space Age began as the Soviets and the U.S. first launched satellites into orbit in 1957–58. Alaska and Hawaii were admitted to the Union as the 49th and 50th states in 1959.

Eisenhower was born on Oct. 14, 1890, in Denison, Texas, the son of David Jacob and Ida Elizabeth Stover Eisenhower. When he was a child his family moved to Abilene, Kan.

### MILITARY CAREER

Eisenhower graduated from West Point in 1915 as a U.S. Army second lieutenant.

In World War I, Eisenhower was commanding officer of a training camp for the new U.S. Army tank corps, near Gettysburg, Pa. After the war he was posted, successively, to the Panama Canal Zone, the office of the assistant secretary of war, and from 1935 to 1940 to the Philippines. There he learned to fly in 1939, later making him the first President to hold a pilot's license.

During World War II, Eisenhower commanded U.S. forces in the North African landings, and in 1943 became chief of Allied forces in North Africa. After directing the invasions of Sicily and Italy, he was called to England to be supreme commander of Allied Expeditionary Forces.

In 1944 Eisenhower was made a 5-star general. His genial nature helped achieve essential cooperation among the Allied forces in the Normandy invasion and in the momentous battle that won victory in Europe in 1945.

After the war, he became Army chief of staff. He wrote *Crusade in Europe* (1948), an account of World War II that became a best-seller.

Eisenhower resigned from the Army to become president of Columbia University (1948–50), but donned his uniform again to accept appointment as Supreme Commander of Allied Forces in Europe (1951–52). There he organized the NATO (North Atlantic Treaty Organization) defense forces.

## EISENHOWER'S PRESIDENTIAL ADMINISTRATION

**Congress in Session:**
83d, 84th, 85th, 86th
**Vice President:**
Richard M. Nixon, 1953–61
**Secretary of State:**
John Foster Dulles, 1953–59
Christian Herter, 1959–61
**Secretary of the Treasury:**
George Humphrey, 1953–57
Robert Anderson, 1957–61
**Postmaster General:**
Arthur Summerfield, 1953–61

**Secretary of Defense:**
Charles Wilson, 1953–57
Neil McElroy, 1957–59
Thomas Gates Jr., 1959–61
**Attorney General:**
Herbert Brownell Jr., 1953–57
William Rogers, 1957–61
**Secretary of the Interior:**
Douglas McKay, 1953–56
Frederick Seaton, 1956–61
**Secretary of Agriculture:**
Ezra Taft Benson, 1953–61

**Secretary of Commerce:**
Sinclair Weeks, 1953–58
Lewis Strauss, 1958–59
Frederick Mueller, 1959–61
**Secretary of Labor:**
Martin Durkin, 1953
James Mitchell, 1953–61
**Secretary of Health, Education, and Welfare**
Oveta Culp Hobby, 1953–55
Marion Folsom, 1955–58
Arthur Flemming, 1958–61

## PRESIDENTIAL ELECTION OF 1952

**Nominations:** The Republicans met in Chicago, July 7–11, 1952. Despite opposition from conservative Sen. Robert A. Taft (R-Ohio), Eisenhower received 845 of 1,206 votes on the first ballot, and his nomination was made unanimous. The Democrats convened in Chicago, July 21–26, 1952. Stevenson won on the third ballot. **Campaign Issues:** Conduct of the Korean War, the stalemate in the Cold War, corruption in the Democratic administration, and McCarthyism. **Remarks:** Stevenson was the first presidential nominee since Garfield to be drafted by his party.

| PRESIDENTIAL CANDIDATES | PARTY | ELECTORAL VOTES | POPULAR VOTE Total | Percentage | VICE–PRESIDENTIAL CANDIDATES |
|---|---|---|---|---|---|
| Dwight D. Eisenhower ..... | Republican | 442 | 33,936,234 | 55.1 | Richard M. Nixon |
| Adlai E. Stevenson ........ | Democratic | 89 | 27,314,992 | 44.4 | John J. Sparkman |
| Other candidates ........ | — | — | 290,959 | 0.5 | — |

## PRESIDENTIAL ELECTION OF 1956

**Nominations:** The Democrats met in Chicago, Aug. 13–17, 1956. On the first ballot Stevenson had 905½ of 1,372 votes, and his nomination was made unanimous. The Republicans, meeting in San Francisco, Aug. 20–23, 1956, renominated Eisenhower by acclamation. **Campaign Issues:** Conduct of the Cold War, atomic testing, and Eisenhower's health.

| PRESIDENTIAL CANDIDATES | PARTY | ELECTORAL VOTES | POPULAR VOTE Total | Percentage | VICE–PRESIDENTIAL CANDIDATES |
|---|---|---|---|---|---|
| Dwight D. Eisenhower ..... | Republican | 457 | 35,590,472 | 57.4 | Richard M. Nixon |
| Adlai E. Stevenson ........ | Democratic | 73 | 26,022,752 | 42.0 | Estes Kefauver |
| Other candidates ........ | — | 1 | 414,000 | 0.6 | — |

## 34th PRESIDENT OF THE UNITED STATES

During the presidential election campaign of 1952, Eisenhower had pledged to personally go to Korea to end the war there.

After winning the election, Eisenhower flew to Korea. He brought the war to an end six months after taking office.

In domestic affairs President Eisenhower restricted the role of the federal government. However, he approved extension of Social Security to millions of self-employed Americans, increased aid to farmers, and raised the minimum hourly wage to $1. He initiated construction of the 42,500-mile Interstate Highway System.

In 1956 Eisenhower refused to aid a revolt in Hungary that was crushed by Soviet troops. He also denounced an attempt by Britain, France, and Israel to seize the Suez Canal from Egypt, forcing them to withdraw their troops.

In 1957 he used federal troops to back up the Supreme Court's 1954 ruling that public schools must be racially integrated.

The President promulgated the "Eisenhower Doctrine" in 1957, promising military and economic aid to any Middle Eastern nation resisting communist subversion. The following year U.S. Marines were sent to aid Lebanon.

Late in his second term the President was embarrassed by a scandal involving his confidential aide, Sherman Adams.

President Eisenhower was frustrated in his efforts to achieve better relations with Soviet leaders by the revelation of U-2 espionage flights over the Soviet Union.

During his administration Eisenhower suffered several serious illnesses.

After leaving Washington he retired to his farm in Gettysburg, Pa., but he remained active, campaigning for Republican candidates, writing books, and commenting on national issues.

He died on March 28, 1969, and was buried in Abilene, Kan., near the Eisenhower Library and Memorial Museum.

**Mary "Mamie" Geneva Doud Eisenhower** (1896–1979) became his wife in 1916. She was a reserved and unassuming White House hostess who avoided unnecessary publicity. The Eisenhowers had two sons: Doud Dwight, who died when he was 3, and John Sheldon Doud Eisenhower, who was born in 1923.

## JOHN FITZGERALD KENNEDY

35th President
(1961–63)

The youngest elected President at 43, John F. Kennedy inspired the confidence of American youth. His inaugural address touched a national urge to aid mankind with its appeal: "Ask not what your country can do for you; ask what you can do for your country."

Before Kennedy had achieved most of his planned goals for the nation, he became the fourth U.S. President to be assassinated.

### EARLY YEARS

Kennedy was born on May 29, 1917, in Brookline, Mass., the son of Joseph P. Kennedy, a prominent and wealthy businessman, and Rose Fitzgerald Kennedy, daughter of a former mayor of Boston.

Kennedy studied briefly at Princeton and the London School of Economics. He graduated from Harvard with honors in 1940, and in the same year published his first book, the bestselling *Why England Slept*.

During World War II, Kennedy commanded a Navy PT-boat in the Pacific. In action off the Solomon Islands, his boat was sunk by an enemy destroyer. He became a hero to his crew by his courage in securing their rescue.

He was elected to Congress in 1946 and was

## KENNEDY'S PRESIDENTIAL ADMINISTRATION

**Congress in Session:**
87th, 88th

**Vice President:**
Lyndon B. Johnson, 1961–63

**Secretary of State:**
Dean Rusk, 1961–63

**Secretary of the Treasury:**
C. Douglas Dillon, 1961–63

**Secretary of Defense:**
Robert S. McNamara, 1961–63

**Attorney General:**
Robert F. Kennedy, 1961–63

**Postmaster General:**
J. Edward Day, 1961–63
John A. Gronouski Jr., 1963

**Secretary of the Interior:**
Stewart L. Udall, 1961–63

**Secretary of Agriculture:**
Orville L. Freeman, 1961–63

**Secretary of Commerce:**
Luther H. Hodges, 1961–63

**Secretary of Labor:**
Arthur J. Goldberg, 1961–62
W. Willard Wirtz, 1962–63

**Secretary of Health, Education, and Welfare:**
Abraham A. Ribicoff, 1961–62
Anthony J. Celebrezze, 1962–63

### PRESIDENTIAL ELECTION OF 1960

**Nominations:** Democrats met in Los Angeles, July 11–15, 1960. Kennedy was nominated on the first ballot. Republicans, meeting in Chicago, July 25–28, 1960, nominated Nixon on the first ballot. **Campaign Issues:** The Democrats charged there was a "missile gap," that U.S. prestige was declining abroad, and that the Soviets had forged ahead militarily. **Remarks:** Unpledged Alabama and Mississippi electors cast their votes for Sen. Harry F. Byrd (D-Va.).

| PRESIDENTIAL CANDIDATES | PARTY | ELECTORAL VOTES | POPULAR VOTE Total | Percentage | VICE–PRESIDENTIAL CANDIDATES |
|---|---|---|---|---|---|
| John F. Kennedy .......... | Democratic | 303 | 34,227,096 | 49.5 | Lyndon B. Johnson |
| Richard M. Nixon .......... | Republican | 219 | 34,108,546 | 49.4 | Henry Cabot Lodge |
| Unpledged electors ......... | — | 15 | 638,822 | 0.9 | — |
| Other candidates ......... | — | — | 138,559 | 0.2 | — |

QUICK QUIZ: What is a *stere*? See page 718.

**JOHN F. KENNEDY** (continued)

reelected with ease in 1948 and 1950. In 1952, despite the Republican landslide, Kennedy ran against and defeated the incumbent U.S. senator, Henry Cabot Lodge (R-Mass.).

In 1954–55 Kennedy underwent operations to repair a spinal injury, suffered during the war. While recuperating, he wrote *Profiles in Courage*, for which he won a 1957 Pulitzer Prize.

In 1958 Kennedy was overwhelmingly reelected to the Senate. He then began a campaign for the 1960 Democratic presidential nomination. Several important primary victories in 1960 helped ensure his nomination at the convention. Kennedy chose Sen. Lyndon B. Johnson of Texas as his running mate.

Kennedy campaigned against his Republican opponent, Richard M. Nixon, partly on the issue that the country's prestige had declined greatly during the Eisenhower administration. His cause was helped by his performance in a series of TV debates with Nixon.

Kennedy won the election in the closest presidential race of the 20th century. He became the first President who was a Roman Catholic, and the first President born in the 20th century.

## 35th PRESIDENT OF THE UNITED STATES

The Kennedy administration's program, called the New Frontier, pressed for U.S. aid to education, enlargement of civil rights, aid to economically depressed areas, medical care for the aged, and an accelerated space program. Major accomplishments in foreign affairs were the establishment of the Peace Corps, the Alliance for Progress with Latin American countries, and the nuclear test-ban treaty.

In 1961, when the CIA-led anti-Castro invasion of communist Cuba at the Bay of Pigs failed, Kennedy and the nation suffered deep humiliation.

Confidence in American power was restored in 1962 when the President's order of a naval blockade of Cuba compelled the Soviet Union to dismantle its missile bases in Cuba and remove its bombing planes from the island.

Deeply concerned with culture, Kennedy did much to foster public interest in literature and the arts. The White House guest list included many scientists, writers, artists, and musicians.

The march toward the New Frontier was brutally halted when Kennedy was assassinated in Dallas, Texas, on Nov. 22, 1963, by Lee Harvey Oswald, a former U.S. marine who believed in communism. Kennedy was buried in Arlington National Cemetery.

**Jacqueline Lee Bouvier Kennedy,** born in 1929, married Kennedy in 1953. As First Lady she redecorated the White House interior. She was noted for her charm and command of foreign languages. Widespread admiration was evoked by her courage at the time of her husband's death (she was at his side when he was killed). The Kennedys had three children: Caroline Bouvier, born in 1957; John Fitzgerald, born in 1960; and Patrick Bouvier, who died two days after his birth in 1963.

Five years after Kennedy's death, she married Greek ship-owner Aristotle Onassis in 1968. She was again widowed when Onassis died in 1975.

## LYNDON BAINES JOHNSON

36th President
(1963–69)

Within hours after Kennedy's death, Johnson was sworn in as President. He entered office with the handicap of having to take over from a man who had won adulation for himself and a new respect abroad for the nation.

Johnson's years as President increasingly filled with controversy over the Vietnam War, but both friends and foes agreed he was a persuasive man and a brilliant politician.

Johnson was born on Aug. 27, 1908, on a ranch near Stonewall, Texas, the son of Samuel Ealy Johnson, a schoolteacher and state legislator, and Rebekah Baines Johnson. He graduated from Southwest Texas State College in 1930 and then taught school. In 1932 he became secretary to a Texas congressman. An ardent New Dealer, he was named National Youth Administration director for Texas in 1935.

Johnson was elected to Congress in 1937 to fill an unexpired term, and he held the seat until 1948. He served on active duty in the U.S. Navy in 1941–42 and then returned to Congress. In 1948 he won the Democratic nomination for U.S. senator from Texas by a scant 87 votes.

In the Senate he became Democratic whip in 1951 and Senate minority leader in 1953. Democrats won control of the Senate in 1954 and Johnson, elected to a second term, became majority leader, a post he held until 1960—despite suffering a serious heart attack in 1955. As majority leader Johnson was a powerful figure.

In 1960, after a vain try for the presidential nomination, Johnson accepted second place on the Kennedy ticket. By keeping the Southern states within the party, Johnson made a major contribution in the Democrats' victory.

In filling out the remaining 14 months of Kennedy's term, President Johnson used his legislative skill to win congressional passage of his slain predecessor's program, especially in his skillful handling of the Civil Rights Act of 1964 and the Economic Opportunity Act, which declared "war on poverty."

In the 1964 election Johnson won over Sen. Barry Goldwater, the Republican candidate, by the largest percentage of the popular vote ever recorded. He strove tirelessly to push through Congress his social reform program that he called the Great Society.

Drawing on his experience as Senate leader, Johnson succeeded in getting his massive domestic program passed. In a whirlwind of activity he initiated tax cuts, gained passage of a voting rights act, instituted the Medicare plan, obtained increased federal aid for education, and approved a new immigration law.

During 1965 Johnson dispatched U.S. troops to fight communist forces trying to take over South Vietnam. At the same time he spurred intensified diplomatic efforts aimed at negotiat-

ing settlement of the war.

By 1967 President Johnson's popularity took a downward turn as the Vietnam conflict intensified. According to public-opinion polls, Americans were dissatisfied with the President's handling of the war and deeply concerned about urban riots, rising taxes, and inflation.

Discontent had grown even more intense by early 1968, and on March 31 Johnson announced he would not run for a second full term. His last year in office was one of still more tragedy: the assassination on April 4 of the respected black leader and Nobel Peace Prize-

winner Dr. Martin Luther King Jr.; the resultant city riots; the assassination of Sen. Robert F. Kennedy in June; and the strife-blemished Democratic convention in August.

After leaving the presidency in 1969, Johnson retired to his ranch near Johnson City, Texas. He died there at the age of 64 on Jan. 22, 1973. **Claudia "Lady Bird" Alta Taylor Johnson,** his wife, was born in 1912. They were married in 1934 and had two daughters: Lynda Bird (born in 1944) and Luci Baines (born in 1947). As First Lady, Mrs. Johnson spearheaded projects to beautify the national environment.

## JOHNSON'S PRESIDENTIAL ADMINISTRATION

**Congress in Session:**
88th, 89th, 90th
**Vice President:**
Hubert H. Humphrey, 1965–69
**Secretary of State:**
Dean Rusk, 1963–69
**Secretary of the Treasury:**
C. Douglas Dillon, 1963–65
Henry H. Fowler, 1965–68
Joseph W. Barr, 1968–69
**Secretary of Defense:**
Robert S. McNamara, 1963–68
Clark M. Clifford, 1968–69
**Secretary of the Interior:**
Stewart L. Udall, 1963–69

**Attorney General:**
Robert F. Kennedy, 1963–64
Nicholas deB. Katzenbach, 1964–66
Ramsey Clark, 1967–69
**Secretary of Agriculture:**
Orville L. Freeman, 1963–69
**Secretary of Commerce:**
Luther H. Hodges, 1963–64
John T. Connor, 1965–67
A. B. Trowbridge, 1967–68
C. R. Smith, 1968–69
**Secretary of Labor**
W. Willard Wirtz, 1963–69

**Postmaster General:**
John A. Gronouski Jr., 1963–65
Lawrence F. O'Brien, 1965–68
W. Marvin Watson, 1968–69
**Secretary of Health, Education, and Welfare:**
Anthony J. Celebrezze, 1963–65
John W. Gardner, 1965–68
Wilbur J. Cohen, 1968–69
**Secretary of Housing and Urban Development:**
Robert C. Weaver, 1965–68
Robert C. Wood, 1968–69
**Secretary of Transportation**
Alan S. Boyd, 1966–69

### PRESIDENTIAL ELECTION OF 1964

**Nominations:** Republicans met in San Francisco, July 13–16, 1964, and chose Goldwater on the first ballot. Democrats met in Atlantic City, N.J., Aug. 24–27, 1964, and nominated President Johnson by acclamation. **Campaign Issues:** Direct issues concerned the Vietnam War, some of the Great

Society programs of the incumbent administration, and the far right-wing support that was attracted by Goldwater. **Remarks:** President Johnson received the largest popular-vote majority and greatest percentage of the total vote than ever before won by a presidential candidate.

| PRESIDENTIAL CANDIDATES | PARTY | ELECTORAL VOTES | POPULAR VOTE Total | Percentage | VICE–PRESIDENTIAL CANDIDATES |
|---|---|---|---|---|---|
| Lyndon B. Johnson ........ | Democratic | 486 | 43,129,484 | 61.1 | Hubert H. Humphrey |
| Barry Goldwater ........... | Republican | 52 | 27,178,188 | 38.5 | William E. Miller |
| Other candidates .......... | — | — | 336,838 | 0.4 | |

## RICHARD MILHOUS NIXON

Richard Nixon became the first President to resign, giving up his administration when it became clear he was about to be impeached and convicted by Congress as a result of his misuse of presidential power in the Watergate scandals. Many of his closest associates were convicted and jailed in the affair. His administration was further stained by the resignation and conviction for income tax evasion of Vice President Spiro Agnew, who avoided trial on charges of accepting bribes.

37th President
(1969–74)

Despite Nixon's misuse of power, he was acclaimed for achievements in the area of foreign affairs. He brought an end to U.S. participation in the Vietnam War—the longest and costliest war in U.S. history. And he moved

boldly to end the Cold War with communist China and the Soviet Union.

He was born on Jan. 9, 1913, in Yorba Linda, Calif., the son of Francis Anthony and Hannah Milhous Nixon, a devout Quaker. When he was nine years old the family moved to Whittier, Calif.

Nixon graduated from Whittier College and the Duke University Law School. During World War II he worked in the Office of Price Administration and then served as a naval officer in the Pacific.

### EARLY POLITICAL CAREER

In 1946 Republicans in Nixon's California congressional district were seeking a candidate for Congress. Nixon gained their endorsement and was elected.

National fame came quickly. Serving on the House Un-American Activities Committee, Nixon pressed an investigation of charges that Alger Hiss, a former State Department official, had supplied secret documents to the Soviets. His adroit questioning discredited Hiss, who later was

QUICK QUIZ: One league equals how many nautical miles? See page 716.

**RICHARD NIXON** (continued)

convicted of perjury. The case established Nixon as an articulate foe of communism. He was elected to the Senate in 1950, but by then his use of the communist issue against political opponents was provoking criticism.

In 1952 Dwight Eisenhower chose Nixon as his running mate. During the campaign Nixon was accused of accepting large sums of money from wealthy contributors. Eisenhower told him he must come "clean as a hound's tooth," so Nixon went on TV to explain. His emotional "Checkers" speech—he referred in it to a dog of that name that he had accepted as a gift—turned the issue to his advantage, and the Eisenhower-Nixon ticket was elected.

Many Vice Presidents have languished in obscurity, but not the energetic Nixon. Eisenhower had little interest in partisan politics, and Nixon welcomed the chance to speak and campaign nationally. When Eisenhower became ill on three separate occasions, Nixon acted in his behalf with confidence and restraint.

After the Republican slate was reelected in 1956, Nixon became the almost unanimous choice of his party for the presidential nomination in 1960.

Nixon narrowly lost the 1960 presidential election to Sen. John F. Kennedy when the more articulate Kennedy gained votes in a series of TV debates with him.

He ran for governor of California in 1962 and lost. Blaming biased journalists, he announced his retirement from politics and said angrily, "You won't have Nixon to kick around anymore."

But in 1968 he was awarded the Republican presidential nomination on the first ballot. The Democrats were bitterly divided over U.S. involvement in Vietnam.

Nixon won with less than a majority of the popular vote in one of the closest elections in American history. He defeated the Democratic candidate, Vice President Hubert H. Humphrey, by less than 1% of the vote.

**FIRST TERM AS PRESIDENT**

As President, Nixon cut U.S. troop strength in Vietnam from 550,000 to 27,000 by December 1972, but he increased U.S. air and naval power in Southeast Asia. In 1972, after North Vietnam

## NIXON'S PRESIDENTIAL ADMINISTRATION

**Congresses in Session:**
91st, 92d, 93d

**Vice President:**
Spiro T. Agnew, 1969–73
Gerald R. Ford, 1973–74

**Secretary of State:**
William P. Rogers, 1969–73
Henry A. Kissinger, 1973–74

**Secretary of the Treasury:**
David M. Kennedy, 1969–71
John B. Connally Jr., 1971–72
George P. Shultz, 1972–74
William E. Simon, 1974

**Secretary of Defense:**
Melvin R. Laird, 1969–73
Elliot L. Richardson, 1973
James R. Schlesinger, 1973–74

**Attorney General:**
John N. Mitchell, 1969–72
Richard G. Kleindienst, 1972–73
Elliot L. Richardson, 1973
William B. Saxbe, 1974

**Secretary of the Interior:**
Walter J. Hickel, 1969–71
Rogers C. B. Morton, 1971–74

**Secretary of Agriculture:**
Clifford M. Hardin, 1969–71
Earl L. Butz, 1971–74

**Postmaster General:**
(abolished as cabinet post, 1971)
Winton M. Blount, 1969–71

**Secretary of Transportation:**
John A. Volpe, 1969–73
Claude S. Brinegar, 1973–74

**Secretary of Commerce:**
Maurice H. Stans, 1969–72
Peter G. Peterson, 1972–73
Frederick B. Dent, 1973–74

**Secretary of Labor:**
George P. Shultz, 1969–70
James D. Hodgson, 1970–73
Peter J. Brennan, 1973–74

**Secretary of Health, Education, and Welfare:**
Robert H. Finch, 1969–70
Elliot L. Richardson, 1970–73
Caspar W. Weinberger, 1973–74

**Secretary of Housing and Urban Development:**
George W. Romney, 1969–73
James T. Lynn, 1973–74

## PRESIDENTIAL ELECTION OF 1968

**Nominations:** Republicans in Miami Beach, Fla., Aug. 5–8, 1968, named Nixon on the first ballot. Agnew's nomination was made unanimous. The Democratic convention in Chicago, Aug. 26–29, was marred by violence both in and out of the convention hall. Humphrey and Muskie were each a first-ballot choice. **Campaign Issues:** The war in Vietnam. **Remarks:** Nixon's popular vote share—43.4%—was the lowest for a winning presidential candidate since Wilson's election in 1912. Earlier concern proved groundless that the electoral votes cast for third-party candidate Gov. George C. Wallace of Alabama might be enough to throw the election into the House of Representatives.

| PRESIDENTIAL CANDIDATES | PARTY | ELECTORAL VOTES | POPULAR VOTE Total | Percentage | VICE–PRESIDENTIAL CANDIDATES |
|---|---|---|---|---|---|
| Richard M. Nixon | Republican | 301 | 31,785,480 | 43.4 | Spiro T. Agnew |
| Hubert H. Humphrey | Democratic | 191 | 31,275,165 | 42.7 | Edmund S. Muskie |
| George C. Wallace | American | 46 | 9,906,473 | 13.5 | Curtis E. LeMay |
| Others | — | — | 244,444 | 0.4 | |

## PRESIDENTIAL ELECTION OF 1972

**Nominations:** Democrats met in Miami Beach, Fla., July 13–14, and named Sen. George McGovern of South Dakota and Sen. Thomas F. Eagleton of Missouri. When the press revealed Eagleton had received psychiatric treatment, McGovern asked him to withdraw. Sargent Shriver, brother-in-law of President Kennedy, replaced Eagleton on Aug. 8. Republicans met in Miami Beach, Aug. 22–23, nominating Nixon and Agnew for a second term. **Campaign Issues:** War in Vietnam, welfare reform. **Remarks:** One Virginia elector switched his vote from Nixon to a minor-party candidate.

| PRESIDENTIAL CANDIDATES | PARTY | ELECTORAL VOTES | POPULAR VOTE Total | Percentage | VICE–PRESIDENTIAL CANDIDATES |
|---|---|---|---|---|---|
| Richard M. Nixon | Republican | 520 | 47,169,911 | 60.7 | Spiro T. Agnew |
| George McGovern | Democratic | 17 | 29,170,383 | 37.5 | Sargent Shriver |
| John G. Schmitz | American | 0 | 1,098,482 | 1.4 | Thomas J. Anderson |
| Other candidates | — | 1 | 278,778 | 0.4 | |

invaded in force, Nixon ordered mining of the North Vietnamese ports and air attacks on land supply routes from China.

Antiwar protests were widespread but ineffective. The fatal shooting of four students by Ohio National Guardsmen during a demonstration at Kent State University in 1970 was the darkest hour of the Vietnam controversy.

The U.S. economy, plagued by government budgetary deficits, sagged in 1970. The President found it impossible to control inflation.

Many white parents opposed court-ordered busing of their children to achieve racial balance in public schools, and Nixon unsuccessfully sought a legal means of limiting such busing.

Environmentalists applauded his moves to eliminate water and air pollution, but they worked through Congress to block his plan to construct a supersonic transport plane that critics considered ecologically harmful.

President Nixon moved dramatically to end the Cold War with communist China and the Soviet Union. With U.S. support, the UN in 1971 admitted communist China and expelled the nationalist Chinese of Taiwan. In February 1972 Nixon became the first U.S. President ever to visit China while in office.

The President flew to Moscow in May 1972 for a summit meeting with leaders of the Soviet Union. Several agreements were signed, the most important being the strategic arms limitation (SALT) treaties, setting limits on the production and deployment of atomic weapons.

In the 1972 election campaign for a second term, the President sought the support of young voters going to the polls for the first time since a 1971 constitutional amendment lowered the voting age to 18. During the campaign Nixon supporters raised an unprecedented $60 million for expenses, leading to abuses later revealed in the Watergate investigations in 1973–74.

Twelve days before the election, presidential adviser Henry Kissinger, who had been conducting secret negotiations in Paris with the North Vietnamese, announced "peace is at hand."

A record of over 77 million voters cast ballots, giving the President a landslide victory over his Democratic opponent, Sen. George McGovern of South Dakota.

When Vietnam truce negotiations broke down late in 1972, Nixon ordered heavy bombing of North Vietnam until the communists returned to the talks.

## SECOND TERM AND RESIGNATION

In his inaugural address in January 1973, the President promised to work for a "peace which can endure for generations to come." A week later, on Jan. 28, 1973, a Vietnam cease-fire agreement was signed in Paris, enabling all U.S. troops to be withdrawn from Vietnam by March 29. However, U.S. planes continued to bomb communist forces in Cambodia. Despite Nixon's opposition, the Democrat-controlled Congress forced an end to all U.S. military action in Southeast Asia on Aug. 15, 1973. Two years later communist military forces took over the governments of South Vietnam, Laos, and Cambodia.

Just as President Nixon seemed about to lead the nation into a new era of peace and harmony, the Watergate scandals engulfed his administration.

The affair had begun when police on June 17, 1972, arrested five men who had broken into and installed wiretapping devices in the headquarters of the Democratic National Committee at the Watergate office building in Washington, D.C.

A Senate investigation in 1973 revealed evidence that the Watergate break-in was only part of a pattern of crimes by Nixon aides in 1972 aimed at ensuring his reelection. Nixon denied he was involved in the scandals.

On Oct. 10, 1973, Vice President Agnew resigned and accepted conviction for income tax evasion to avoid being tried on charges of accepting bribes. For the first time in the nation's history Amendment 25 to the U.S. Constitution was used as President Nixon appointed Gerald R. Ford to succeed Agnew.

President Nixon ordered the firing of special Watergate prosecutor Archibald Cox on Oct. 30, 1973, because Cox had refused to drop a court suit against the President calling for the release of White House tapes and documents relating to the Watergate scandals.

A resulting public outcry caused the House of Representatives to institute hearings to determine if Nixon should be impeached.

Nine months later, in July 1974, the House Judiciary Committee voted to recommend Nixon's impeachment on three counts: obstructing justice in covering up the Watergate scandals, violating his presidential oath of office, and defying the committee's subpoenas for evidence.

Also in July 1974 the Supreme Court by a unanimous decision ordered the President to turn over evidence subpoenaed by the new Watergate special prosecutor, Leon Jaworski.

The White House on Aug. 5, 1974, made public some of the evidence ordered released by the Supreme Court. It showed that President Nixon had obstructed the FBI investigation of the Watergate break-in to protect associates and to ensure his reelection. Republican leaders told Nixon they could not prevent his impeachment and conviction.

President Nixon resigned on Aug. 9, 1974, and retired. He was succeeded by Ford.

A month later, on Sept. 8, 1974, President Ford granted Nixon a "full, free and absolute pardon for all offenses" during his administration, thus eliminating the possibility of his indictment or trial for his role in the scandals.

In subsequent months three cabinet officers, Nixon's two top White House aides, and many other administration officials and election campaign supporters were convicted on charges growing out of the scandals.

**Thelma Catherine Patricia Ryan Nixon**, born in 1912, was a popular White House hostess. She revealed considerable skill in person-to-person diplomacy during her trips abroad. She and Nixon were married in 1940 and had two daughters. Tricia Nixon (1946–   ) married Edward Cox in the White House in 1971. Julie Nixon (1948–   ) married President Eisenhower's grandson David Eisenhower in 1968.

QUICK QUIZ: Who is prime minister of China? See page 526.

## GERALD RUDOLPH FORD

38th President
(1974–77)

The first nonelected President, Gerald R. Ford became Chief Executive when Richard Nixon resigned to avoid impeachment and conviction by Congress in the Watergate scandal. Ford had been appointed Vice President 10 months earlier, following the resignation of Spiro T. Agnew.

As President, Ford was confronted with the worst recession since the Great Depression of the 1930s. Ford served as President only 29 months, losing his bid for a full term to Democratic candidate Jimmy Carter in the 1976 election.

### EARLY LIFE

Ford was born on July 14, 1913, in Omaha, Neb. The son of Dorothy Gardner King and Leslie King, a wool trader, he was named Leslie Lynch King at birth. His parents were divorced in 1915. He and his mother returned to her parents' home in Grand Rapids, Mich., where she soon met and married Gerald Rudolf Ford, a young paint salesman. The boy was adopted by his stepfather and renamed Gerald Rudolph Ford Jr.

Ford went to the University of Michigan on an athletic scholarship, playing center on the Michigan football team.

Upon graduation he accepted an offer to become assistant football line coach and boxing coach at Yale University so that he could attend the Yale law school. After receiving his law degree in 1941 he returned to Grand Rapids.

After the United States entered World War II, Ford joined the U.S. Navy in April 1942, receiving a commission as an ensign. He served aboard the light aircraft carrier USS *Monterey* in the Pacific fighting against Japan, attaining the rank of lieutenant commander.

### CONGRESSMAN AND VICE PRESIDENT

Upon his return to Grand Rapids in 1946, Jerry Ford resumed his law practice. At the age of 35 he won election in 1948 as U.S. representative from Michigan's 5th District.

For the next quarter of a century Ford won 12 more elections to Congress, each time by a large majority. A conservative Republican, Ford followed the party line in Congress.

When Vice President Agnew resigned in October 1973 to avoid being tried on charges of bribery, President Nixon nominated Ford to fill the vacancy. After lengthy hearings, Ford was sworn in as Vice President on Dec. 6, 1973—the first to attain the office under Amendment 25 to the U.S. Constitution.

During his eight months as Vice President, Ford toured the country speaking in 40 states in an effort to preserve confidence in the national government while Congress was holding hearings to consider the possible impeachment of President Nixon in the Watergate scandals.

### PRESIDENTIAL ADMINISTRATION

Ford became President following Nixon's resignation on Aug. 9, 1974. Calling on the nation to "bind up the internal wounds of Watergate," he promised "openness and candor."

Ford's popularity took a nose dive when without consulting Congress he pardoned Nixon on Sept. 8, 1974, and eight days later announced a program of conditional amnesty for Vietnam War draft evaders and military deserters.

In the early months of Ford's administration skyrocketing inflation, caused largely by price increases for foreign oil, gripped the economy. Ford attacked inflation as "our domestic public enemy No. 1," urging consumers to buy less.

As consumers slowed their purchases, the automobile industry was hit first by a drop in sales and began closing plants in November and December 1974. The recession deepened in 1975 with unemployment soaring to more than 8.2 million persons or 8.9% of the work force in May—the highest unemployment rate since the Great Depression. To help stimulate the economy, Ford asked Congress early in 1975 to reduce income taxes. At the same time he submitted a $350 billion federal budget, and had a record deficit of more than $66 billion.

Ford asserted his conservative leadership by repeatedly vetoing spending measures passed by the Democratic-controlled Congress. Most of his 66 vetoes were upheld because of disunity in the Democratic Party. However, Congress overrode his veto 12 times—more than for any President since Andrew Johnson.

U.S. prestige in international affairs suffered in the spring of 1975 as South Vietnam and Cambodia surrendered to communist troops. When victorious Cambodian communists seized the U.S. freighter *Mayaguez* in May, President Ford moved quickly to reaffirm American power by sending U.S. Marines to recapture the ship.

## FORD'S PRESIDENTIAL ADMINISTRATION

**Congresses in Session:**
93d, 94th

**Vice President:**
Nelson A. Rockefeller, 1974–77

**Secretary of State:**
Henry A. Kissinger, 1974–77

**Secretary of Defense:**
James R. Schlesinger, 1974–75
Donald H. Rumsfeld, 1975–77

**Secretary of Commerce:**
Frederick B. Dent, 1974–75
Rogers C. B. Morton, 1975–76
Elliot L. Richardson, 1976–77

**Secretary of the Treasury:**
William E. Simon, 1974–76

**Attorney General:**
William B. Saxbe, 1974–75
Edward H. Levi, 1975–77

**Secretary of the Interior:**
Rogers C. B. Morton, 1974–75
Stanley K. Hathaway, 1975
Thomas S. Kleppe, 1975–77

**Secretary of Labor:**
Peter J. Brennan, 1974–75
John T. Dunlop, 1975–76
William J. Usery Jr., 1976–77

**Secretary of Agriculture:**
Earl L. Butz, 1974–76
John A. Knebel, 1976–77

**Secretary of Health, Education, and Welfare:**
Caspar W. Weinberger, 1974–75
F. David Mathews, 1975–77

**Secretary of Housing and Urban Development:**
James T. Lynn, 1974–75
Carla Anderson Hills, 1975–77

**Secretary of Transportation:**
Claude S. Brinegar, 1974–75
William T. Coleman Jr., 1975–77

Ford continued Nixon's policy of détente with the Soviet Union. He held his first summit meeting with Soviet leader Leonid Brezhnev at Vladivostok on Nov. 23-24, 1974, but achieved no substantive new agreements.

President Ford had further meetings with Brezhnev at Helsinki, Finland, in 1975, where he signed the Helsinki Pact that formally recognized the European border changes imposed by the Soviet Union after World War II and guaranteed human rights for the peoples of Europe.

During Ford's administration, Secretary of State Henry Kissinger used "shuttle diplomacy" involving countless jet airplane flights to cool tense international situations.

Women made two separate attempts to assassinate President Ford in September 1975. On Sept. 5, Secret Service men grabbed a pistol from the hand of Lynette Alice Fromme, 27, as she pointed it at Ford from a crowd in Sacramento, Calif. She was a follower of convicted murderer Charles Manson. On Sept. 22, Sara Jane Moore, 45, a civil-rights activist, fired a pistol at Ford as he left a San Francisco hotel, but an alert bystander deflected her aim. Both women were sentenced to life imprisonment.

At the beginning of the 1976 presidential election campaign, public opinion polls showed the Democratic nominee Jimmy Carter the clear favorite with a 10% popularity lead over Ford. To combat this advantage, Ford challenged Carter to a series of TV debates, the first in history between a President and an opponent for the office.

In the national election in November, Ford lost to Carter in a close vote.

**Elizabeth Bloomer (Warren) Ford** (1918– ), his wife, was a former professional dancer. They were married on Oct. 15, 1948, and had four children: Michael Gerald, John Gardner, Steven Meigs, and Susan Elizabeth. She strongly supported adoption of the women's equal rights amendment to the U.S. Constitution.

# JIMMY CARTER

Defeating President Ford in the closely contested 1976 election, Jimmy Carter became the first former governor of a state of the Old Confederacy to be elected President since James Polk in 1844. His achievement was possible because his advancement of civil rights won him the support of Northern liberals and blacks.

39th President
(1977–81)

Because of Carter's weak leadership as President, U.S. prestige declined abroad, while at home the nation slid into an economic recession with high rates of inflation and unemployment. As a result, he was soundly defeated by Ronald Reagan in the election of 1980, becoming the first Democratic President to lose a bid for a second term since 1888.

## EARLY LIFE

James Earl Carter Jr. was born on Oct. 1, 1924, in Plains, Ga., the first future President to be born in a hospital. He was the eldest son of James Earl and Lillian Gordy Carter. His father was a struggling farmer and storekeeper. His mother worked as a community nurse. Carter later attributed much of his success to his remarkable mother, who at the age of 68 in 1966 joined the Peace Corps and spent two years helping lepers in India.

After graduation from high school at 16 in 1941, Carter attended Georgia Southwestern College and Georgia Tech before appointment to the U.S. Naval Academy in 1943. Graduating from Annapolis in 1946, he ranked 59th in a class of 820.

As a naval officer Carter spent several years on submarine duty and did postgraduate work in nuclear physics at Union College in Schenectady, N.Y. He helped commission one of the nation's earliest atomic submarines.

After his father's death in 1953, Carter resigned from the U.S. Navy to return to his Georgia home. Over the next 10 years he became wealthy as a peanut farmer and wholesaler.

## GOVERNOR AND PRESIDENTIAL CANDIDATE

Carter won election to the Georgia senate in 1962, serving two terms until 1966 when he made an unsuccessful bid for the Democratic nomination for governor. Stung by his loss to racial segregationist Lester G. Maddox, Carter campaigned across Georgia for four years, winning election as governor in 1970.

At his inauguration as governor in January 1971, Carter became a national celebrity as the first chief executive of a Southern state to declare: "The time for racial discrimination is over." As governor he promoted civil rights for blacks and reformed the state bureaucracy, cutting state departments and agencies from 300 to 22.

Carter announced his candidacy in December 1974 for the Democratic presidential nomination. His vigorous campaign culminated in a first-ballot win at the party's national convention in New York City in July 1976.

## PRESIDENTIAL ADMINISTRATION

The 1976 election campaign was highlighted by three face-to-face TV debates with President Ford, the Republican nominee. Carter's success in the debates contributed to his victory in the November election. Perhaps of even greater importance was voter mistrust of the Republican Party because of the Watergate scandals. Voters also believed Carter would restore integrity to the federal government.

In his inaugural address on Jan. 20, 1977, the soft-spoken Carter pledged his administration to "the affirmation of our nation's continuing moral strength and our belief in an undiminished, ever-expanding American dream."

In his first major act he pardoned about 10,000 draft evaders of the Vietnam War.

To improve relations with Latin America, his

QUICK QUIZ: Name the world's 10 smallest nations. See page 469.

**JIMMY CARTER** *(continued)*

administration negotiated treaties to give up U.S. control of the Panama Canal in 1999, winning Senate ratification in 1978 despite conservative opposition.

Carter achieved his greatest triumph in international relations as a mediator with the leaders of Egypt and Israel, reconciling differences to enable them to sign a peace treaty in 1979. Later in 1979, he signed a new SALT II treaty with the Soviet Union, but failed to obtain Senate ratification.

In the 1976 presidential election campaign Carter had promised to reorganize the federal government to make it more efficient. Congress gave him the power to do so in April 1977. A major accomplishment was the reform of the Civil Service system in 1978 to allow greater latitude in the promotion and discharge of the 2.8 million federal employees. A new Department of Energy was created in 1977 and a separate Department of Education in 1980.

Confronted by a growing energy crisis from the nation's dependence on foreign oil, Carter urged strong measures to reduce the use of oil and gas as fuel. He called for a multibillion-dollar effort to develop new energy sources, financing the program with a tax on windfall profits of the major oil companies. Congress adopted much of his program in 1980. See pages 257–258.

The soaring price of oil, caused by the international OPEC cartel of oil-exporting nations, weakened the U.S. economy. A huge trade deficit caused the U.S. dollar to fall in value.

Although Carter had promised to balance the federal budget, government deficit spending grew year by year. The nation fell into recession in 1980 with high rates of unemployment and inflation.

When Soviet troops invaded Afghanistan in December 1979 to prop up a puppet communist government, President Carter sought to punish the Soviet Union with economic sanctions and a boycott of the summer Olympic Games held in Moscow (see page 9).

The nation suffered humiliation in foreign affairs after anti-American Iranian militants captured the U.S. embassy in Teheran on Nov. 4, 1979, holding more than 50 Americans prisoner for more than a year while the Carter administration was unable to free them (see page 15).

Carter had to fight for the Democratic nomination for a second term, overcoming efforts by Sen. Edward Kennedy (D-Mass.) to oust him (see pages 19 and 23).

In the 1980 election campaign he sought to portray his Republican opponent Ronald Reagan as a racist and a warmonger. But in a face-to-face TV debate with Reagan in October, viewers judged the President the loser and voted him out of office in November (see pages 27 and 29). He announced plans to retire to Plains, Ga., to write his memoirs.

**Rosalynn Smith Carter** (born Aug. 18, 1927) married Carter on July 7, 1946. They had four children: John William in 1947, James Earl III ("Chip") in 1950, D. Jeffrey in 1952, and Amy Lynn in 1967. Mrs. Carter worked tirelessly in Carter's election campaigns and aided him as a trusted adviser in public office.

## CARTER'S PRESIDENTIAL ADMINISTRATION

**Congresses in Session:**
95th, 96th
**Vice President:**
Walter F. Mondale, 1977–81
**Secretary of State:**
Cyrus R. Vance, 1977–80
Edmund S. Muskie, 1980–81
**Secretary of the Treasury:**
W. Michael Blumenthal, 1977–79
G. William Miller, 1979–81
**Secretary of Defense:**
Harold Brown, 1977–81
**Attorney General:**
Griffin B. Bell, 1977–79
Benjamin R. Civiletti, 1979–81

**Secretary of the Interior:**
Cecil D. Andrus, 1977–81
**Secretary of Agriculture:**
Robert S. Bergland, 1977–81
**Secretary of Commerce:**
Juanita M. Kreps, 1977–79
Philip Klutznick, 1979–81
**Secretary of Labor:**
F. Ray Marshall, 1977–81
**Secretary of Health, Education, and Welfare:**
Joseph A. Califano Jr., 1977–79
Patricia Roberts Harris, 1979

**Secretary of Health and Human Services:**
Patricia Roberts Harris, 1979–81
**Secretary of Housing and Urban Development:**
Patricia Roberts Harris, 1977–79
Moon Landrieu, 1979–81
**Secretary of Transportation:**
Brock Adams, 1977–79
Neil E. Goldschmidt, 1979–81
**Secretary of Energy:**
James R. Schlesinger, 1977–79
Charles W. Duncan Jr., 1979–81
**Secretary of Education:**
Shirley M. Hufstedler, 1979–81

## PRESIDENTIAL ELECTION OF 1976

**Nominations:** Democrats met in New York City on July 12–15, 1976. Carter easily won the Democratic presidential nomination on the first ballot with 2,238.5 votes to 769.5 for other candidates. Mondale received the Democratic vice-presidential nomination on the first ballot, 2,817 to 191. Republicans met in Kansas City, Mo., on Aug. 16–19, 1976. Ford narrowly won the Republican presidential nomination on the first ballot, defeating Ronald Reagan, 1,187 to 1,070. Dole was selected as the GOP vice-presidential nominee on

the first ballot, 1,921 to 338. **Campaign Issues:** Democrats denounced Ford's pardon of President Nixon and promised programs to end high levels of unemployment, to reduce taxes for low-income families, and to reorganize the federal government bureaucracy. **Remarks:** McCarthy, a liberal Democrat running as an independent, won enough votes in four states (Iowa, Maine, Oklahoma, and Oregon) to throw their 26 electoral votes to Ford. For the first time, an incumbent President debated his challenger face to face.

| PRESIDENTIAL CANDIDATES | PARTY | ELECTORAL VOTES | POPULAR VOTE Total | Percentage | VICE–PRESIDENTIAL CANDIDATES |
|---|---|---|---|---|---|
| Jimmy Carter ............ | Democratic | 297 | 40,825,839 | 50.02 | Walter F. Mondale |
| Gerald R. Ford ........... | Republican | 240 | 39,147,770 | 47.97 | Robert Dole |
| Eugene J. McCarthy ...... | Independent | 0 | 680,390 | 0.83 | — |
| Roger Lea MacBride ...... | Libertarian | 0 | 171,627 | 0.21 | David Bergland |
| Lester G. Maddox......... | American I. | 0 | 168,264 | 0.21 | William Dyke |
| Other candidates ........ | — | 1 | 609,456 | 0.75 | — |

# RONALD REAGAN

A conservative Republican, Ronald Reagan won the White House in an electoral landslide over President Jimmy Carter, promising to lift the country out of an economic recession and restore the U.S. to world leadership.

40th President
(1981–    )

A former movie actor, Reagan was only the 9th President to reach the office by defeating an incumbent Chief Executive. At 69 he was the oldest to be elected to a first term, the first who had been a labor union leader, and the first who ever had been divorced.

## EARLY LIFE

Ronald Wilson Reagan was born in Tampico, Ill., on Feb. 6, 1911. He was the second son of Nelle Wilson Reagan and John Edward Reagan. His brother Neil was two years older. The Reagans moved to Dixon, Ill., where the father earned a meager living as a shoe salesman.

The future President, nicknamed "Dutch" by his father, was popular in high school, being elected president of the student body.

Working his way through school by washing dishes, Reagan graduated in 1932 from Eureka (Ill.) College, where he played football, captained the swimming team, and acted in plays. He then was a radio sports announcer in Des Moines, Ia., until 1937.

## MOVIE STAR, GOVERNOR, AND PRESIDENT-ELECT

Having always wanted to become a professional actor, he leaped at the offer of a Hollywood movie contract in 1937. In his acting career he appeared in some 50 movies and many TV shows. An active member of the Screen Actors Guild, he headed the labor union in 1947–52 and 1959–60.

He married movie star Jane Wyman on Jan. 25, 1940. They had two children, Maureen (born 1941), and an adopted son Michael (born 1945). They were divorced in 1948.

After winning acclaim for his speeches in support of Barry Goldwater in the 1964 presidential campaign, he turned to a new career in politics.

Reagan won election as governor of California in 1966 and reelection in 1970. During his administration in 1967–75 state taxes were reformed, ending deficit spending and rebating $4.7 billion to property-tax payers. He also slowed the growth of state government and social welfare.

Reagan was an unsuccessful candidate for the Republican presidential nomination in 1968 and 1976. But in 1980 he defeated all opponents in the state primaries (see page 19) and was nominated at the GOP convention (see page 21). He then triumphed over Carter (see page 29).

Nancy Davis Reagan (born July 6, 1923), a movie actress, became Reagan's second wife on March 4, 1952. They had two children: Patricia (born 1953), a song writer, and Ronald Prescott (born 1958), a ballet dancer.

## REAGAN'S PRESIDENTIAL ADMINISTRATION

**Congress in Session:**
97th

**Vice President:**
George Bush, 1981–

**Secretary of State:**
Alexander M. Haig Jr., 1981–

**Secretary of the Treasury:**
Donald T. Regan, 1981–

**Secretary of Defense:**
Caspar W. Weinberger, 1981–

**Attorney General:**
William French Smith, 1981–

**Secretary of the Interior:**
James G. Watt, 1981–

**Secretary of Agriculture:**
John R. Block, 1981–

**Secretary of Commerce:**
Malcolm Baldrige, 1981–

**Secretary of Labor:**
Raymond J. Donovan, 1981–

**Secretary of Health and Human Services:**
Richard S. Schweiker, 1981–

**Secretary of Housing and Urban Development:**
Samuel R. Pierce Jr., 1981–

**Secretary of Transportation:**
Andrew L. Lewis Jr., 1981–

**Secretary of Energy:**
James B. Edwards, 1981–

**Secretary of Education:**
, 1981–

## PRESIDENTIAL ELECTION OF 1980

**Nominations:** Republicans met in Detroit, Mich., on July 14–17. Reagan, who had defeated nine other contenders in state primaries, received the nomination on the first ballot on July 16 with 1,939 of the convention's 1,994 votes. At the last minute Reagan failed to persuade former President Ford to join the ticket as vice-presidential candidate. He then named Bush as his choice of running mate, and the delegates ratified the decision on July 17. The Democratic National Convention met in New York City on Aug. 11–14. Carter had battled Sen. Edward Kennedy (D–Mass.) for the nomination in state primaries, winning a majority of the delegates. Although Kennedy formally withdrew as a candidate shortly after the convention opened, the party remained divided. Carter won renomination on the first ballot with 2,123 votes to Kennedy's 1,150.5. Mondale again was chosen as the vice-presidential candidate. **Campaign:** Both candidates stressed their differences in personalities rather than issues. Reagan was judged winner in a TV debate with Carter on Oct. 28, giving him momentum to win an electoral landslide a week later. **Remarks:** Rep. John B. Anderson (R–Ill.) waged a liberal independent campaign for the presidency, winning over 6% of the popular vote.

| PRESIDENTIAL CANDIDATES | PARTY | ELECTORAL VOTES | POPULAR VOTE Total | Percentage | VICE–PRESIDENTIAL CANDIDATES |
|---|---|---|---|---|---|
| Ronald Reagan | Republican | 489 | 43,201,220 | 50.80 | George Bush |
| Jimmy Carter | Democratic | 49 | 34,913,332 | 41.05 | Walter Mondale |
| John B. Anderson | Independent | 0 | 5,581,379 | 6.56 | Patrick Lucey |
| Ed Clark | Libertarian | 0 | 881,612 | 1.04 | David Koch |
| Barry Commoner | Citizens | 0 | 221,083 | 0.26 | LaDonna Harris |
| Other candidates | — | 0 | 250,000 | 0.29 | |

QUICK QUIZ: What is the average monthly social security payment for a retiree? See page 735.

# U.S. VICE PRESIDENTS

The Vice President of the United States holds the second most important office in the executive branch of the U.S. government. The Vice President automatically becomes Chief Executive if the President dies, resigns, or is removed from office. If the President cannot perform his duties because of illness or some other reason, the Vice President becomes *acting President* until the President can resume his office.

The only official duty that the U.S. Constitution provides for the Vice President is that of being president of the U.S. Senate. As such he presides over Senate sessions and can vote only to break a tie. The President may assign other responsibilities to the Vice President.

The Vice President receives an annual salary of $75,000, an expense allowance of $10,000, and about $400,000 for administrative and clerical help. The Vice President and his family also are provided with an official residence in Washington, D.C., called Admiral's House.

Thirteen of the 43 Vice Presidents became President—eight because of the death of a President, one because of the resignation of a President, and four by being elected President in their own right. Seven died in office.

| NAME AND POLITICAL PARTY | YEARS IN OFFICE AND AGE AT INAUGURATION | SERVED UNDER PRESIDENT | BIRTHPLACE AND DATE | DEATH DATE | HIGHLIGHTS OF CAREER |
|---|---|---|---|---|---|
| 1. John Adams [1] (Federalist) | 1789–1797 (53) | Washington | Braintree, Mass. Oct. 30, 1735 | July 4, 1826 | Delegate to Continental Congress 1774–77; Commissioner to France 1778–79; wrote Massachusetts constitution 1779; diplomat in Europe 1780–88; 2d President 1797–1801 |
| 2. Thomas Jefferson [1] (Democratic-Republican) | 1797–1801 (53) | J. Adams | Albemarle County, Va. April 13, 1743 | July 4, 1826 | Delegate to Continental Congress 1775–76; wrote Declaration of Independence 1776; Governor of Virginia 1779–81; delegate to Congress 1783–84; Secretary of State 1789–93; 3d President 1801–09 |
| 3. Aaron Burr (Democratic-Republican) | 1801–1805 (45) | Jefferson | Newark, N.J. Feb. 6, 1756 | Sept. 14, 1836 | Attorney general N.Y. 1789–90; U.S. Senator 1791–97; killed Alexander Hamilton in duel 1804; organized expedition against Spanish colonies and Mexico; indicted for treason but acquitted 1807 |
| 4. George Clinton [2] (Democratic-Republican) | 1805–1812 (65) | Jefferson and Madison | Little Britain, N.Y. July 26, 1739 | April 20, 1812 | Delegate to Continental Congress 1775–76; brig. general of militia 1776–77; Governor of New York 1777–95, 1801–04 |
| 5. Elbridge Gerry [2] (Democratic-Republican) | 1813–1814 (68) | Madison | Marblehead, Mass. July 17, 1744 | Nov. 23, 1814 | Delegate to Congress 1776–85; delegate to Constitutional convention 1787; U.S. Representative (R-Mass.) 1789–93; Governor of Massachusetts 1810–12 |
| 6. Daniel D. Tompkins (Democratic-Republican) | 1817–1825 (42) | Monroe | Scarsdale, N.Y. June 21, 1774 | June 11, 1825 | N.Y. State Supreme Court 1804–07; Governor of N.Y. 1807–17; put through state law ending slavery in New York |
| 7. John C. Calhoun [3] (Democratic) | 1825–1832 (42) | J. Q. Adams and Jackson | Abbeville District, S.C. March 18, 1782 | March 31 1850 | First Vice President to resign; U.S. Rep. (D-S.C.) 1811–17; Secretary of War 1817–25; U.S. Senator (D-S.C.) 1832–43, 1845–50; Secretary of State 1844–45 |
| 8. Martin Van Buren [1] (Democratic) | 1833–1837 (50) | Jackson | Kinderhook, N.Y. Dec. 5, 1782 | July 24, 1862 | U.S. Senator (D-N.Y.) 1821–28; Governor of New York 1829; Secretary of State 1829–31; minister to Britain 1831–32; 8th President 1837–41 |
| 9. Richard M. Johnson (Democratic) | 1837–1841 (56) | Van Buren | Beargrass, Ky. Oct. 17, 1780 | Nov. 19, 1850 | Only Vice President ever elected by U.S. Senate; U.S. Rep. (D-Ky.) 1807–19, 1829–37; U.S. Senator (D-Ky.) 1819–29 |
| 10. John Tyler [4] (Whig) | 1841 (50) | W. H. Harrison | Charles City Co., Va. March 29, 1790 | Jan. 18, 1862 | U.S. Rep. (D-R-Va.) 1816–21; Governor of Virginia 1825–27; U.S. Senator (D-Va.) 1827–36; 10th President 1841–45 |
| 11. George M. Dallas (Democratic) | 1845–1849 (52) | Polk | Philadelphia, Pa. July 10, 1792 | Dec. 31, 1864 | Mayor of Philadelphia 1829; U.S. Senator (D-Pa.) 1831–33; minister to Russia 1837–39; minister to Britain 1856–61 |
| 12. Millard Fillmore [4] (Whig) | 1849–1850 (49) | Taylor | Locke, N.Y. Jan. 7, 1800 | March 8, 1874 | U.S. Rep. (W-N.Y.) 1833–35, 1837–43; 13th President 1850–53 |

[1] Elected President.    [2] Died in office.    [3] Resigned as Vice President.    [4] Succeeded to presidency on death of President.

## U.S. VICE PRESIDENTS *(continued)*

| NAME AND POLITICAL PARTY | YEARS IN OFFICE AND AGE AT INAUGURATION | SERVED UNDER PRESIDENT | BIRTHPLACE AND DATE | DEATH DATE | HIGHLIGHTS OF CAREER |
|---|---|---|---|---|---|
| 13. **William R. King** [2] (Democratic) | 1853 (66) | Pierce | Sampson County, N.C. April 7, 1786 | April 18, 1853 | U.S. Rep. (D–R–N.C.) 1811–16; U.S. Senator (D–Ala.) 1819–44, 1848–52; minister to France 1844–46; took vice-presidential oath in Havana, Cuba; died only a month later |
| 14. **John C. Breckinridge** (Democratic) | 1857–1861 (36) | Buchanan | Lexington, Ky. Jan. 15, 1821 | May 17, 1875 | Youngest Vice President; U.S. Rep. (D–Ky.) 1851–55; U.S. Senator (D–Ky.) 1861; Confederate general 1861–64; Confederate secretary of war 1865 |
| 15. **Hannibal Hamlin** (Republican) | 1861–1865 (51) | Lincoln | Paris Hill, Me. Aug. 27, 1809 | July 4, 1891 | U.S. Rep. (D–Me.) 1843–47; U.S. Senator (D–Me.) 1848–57; Governor of Maine 1857; U.S. Senator (R–Me.) 1857–61, 1869–81; minister to Spain 1881–82 |
| 16. **Andrew Johnson** [4] (Democratic) | 1865 (56) | Lincoln | Raleigh, N.C. Dec. 29, 1808 | July 31, 1875 | U.S. Rep. (D.–Tenn.) 1843–53; Governor of Tennessee 1853–57, 1862–64; U.S. Senator (D–Tenn.) 1857–62, 1874–75; 17th President 1865–69 |
| 17. **Schuyler Colfax** (Republican) | 1869–1873 (45) | Grant | New York, N.Y. March 23, 1823 | Jan. 13, 1885 | U.S. Rep. (R–Ind.) 1855–69; Speaker of House 1863–69 |
| 18. **Henry Wilson** [2] (Republican) | 1873–1875 (61) | Grant | Farmington, N.H. Feb. 16, 1812 | Nov. 22, 1875 | Born Jeremiah Jones Colbaith; U.S. Senator (Free Soil–Mass.) 1855–73 |
| 19. **William Wheeler** (Republican) | 1877–1881 (57) | Hayes | Malone, N.Y. June 30, 1819 | June 4, 1887 | U.S. Rep. (R–N.Y.) 1861–63, 1869–77 |
| 20. **Chester Arthur** [4] (Republican) | 1881 (51) | Garfield | Fairfield, Vt. Oct. 5, 1829 | Nov. 18, 1886 | Collector, Port of New York 1871–79; 21st President 1881–85 |
| 21. **Thomas A. Hendricks** [2] (Democratic) | 1885 (65) | Cleveland | Zanesville, Ohio Sept. 7, 1819 | Nov. 25, 1885 | U.S. Rep. (D–Ind.) 1851–55; U.S. Senator (D–Ind.) 1863–69; Governor of Indiana 1872 |
| 22. **Levi P. Morton** (Republican) | 1889–1893 (64) | Harrison | Shoreham, Vt. May 16, 1824 | May 16, 1920 | Wall Street banker; U.S. Rep. (R–N.Y.) 1879–81; minister to France 1881–85; Governor of New York 1889–93 |
| 23. **Adlai E. Stevenson** (Democratic) | 1893–1897 (57) | Cleveland | Christian County, Ky. Oct. 23, 1835 | June 14, 1914 | U.S. Rep. (D–Ill.) 1875–77, 1879–81; Assistant Postmaster General 1885–89 |
| 24. **Garret A. Hobart** [2] (Republican) | 1897–1899 (52) | McKinley | Long Branch, N.J. June 3, 1844 | Nov. 21, 1899 | Member New Jersey legislature 1872–81; member Republican National Committee 1884–96 |
| 25. **Theodore Roosevelt** [4] (Republican) | 1901 (42) | McKinley | New York, N.Y. Oct. 27, 1858 | Jan. 6, 1919 | Police Commissioner, New York City 1895–97; Assistant Secretary of Navy 1897–98; colonel in Spanish–American War 1898; Governor of New York 1899–1900 |
| 26. **Charles W. Fairbanks** (Republican) | 1905–1909 (52) | T. Roosevelt | Unionville Center, Ohio May 11, 1852 | June 4, 1918 | U.S. Senator (R–Ind.) 1897–1905 |
| 27. **James Sherman** [2] (Republican) | 1909–1912 (53) | Taft | Utica, N.Y. Oct. 24, 1855 | Oct. 30, 1912 | Mayor of Utica, N.Y., 1884; U.S. Rep. (R–N.Y.) 1887–91, 1893–1909 |
| 28. **Thomas R. Marshall** (Democratic) | 1913–1921 (58) | Wilson | North Manchester, Ind. March 14, 1854 | June 1, 1925 | Governor of Indiana 1909–13 |
| 29. **Calvin Coolidge** [4] (Republican) | 1921–1923 (48) | Harding | Plymouth, Vt. July 4, 1872 | Jan. 5, 1933 | Massachusetts lieutenant governor 1916–18; Governor of Massachusetts 1919–20; 30th President 1923–29 |
| 30. **Charles G. Dawes** (Republican) | 1925–1929 (59) | Coolidge | Marietta, Ohio Aug. 27, 1865 | April 23, 1951 | U.S. Comptroller of Currency 1898–1901; director Bureau of the Budget 1921–24; won Nobel Peace Prize in 1925 for German reparations plan; ambassador to Britain 1929–32; Chicago banker 1932–51 |
| 31. **Charles Curtis** (Republican) | 1929–1933 (69) | Hoover | N. Topeka, Kan. Jan. 25, 1860 | Feb. 8, 1936 | U.S. Rep. (R.–Kan.) 1893–1907; U.S. Senator (R–Kan.) 1907–13, 1915–29; majority leader U.S. Senate 1924–29 |
| 32. **John N. Garner** (Democratic) | 1933–1941 (64) | F. Roosevelt | Red River Co., Tex. Nov. 22, 1868 | Nov. 7 1967 | U.S. Rep. (D–Tex.) 1903–33; Speaker of House 1931–33 |
| 33. **Henry A. Wallace** (Democratic) | 1941–1945 (52) | F. Roosevelt | Adair County, Iowa Oct. 7, 1888 | Nov. 18, 1965 | Secretary of Agriculture 1933–40; Secretary of Commerce 1945–46 |

[1] Elected President.  [2] Died in office.  [3] Resigned as Vice President.  [4] Succeeded to presidency on death of President.

## U.S. VICE PRESIDENTS (continued)

| NAME AND POLITICAL PARTY | YEARS IN OFFICE AND AGE AT INAUGURATION | SERVED UNDER PRESIDENT | BIRTHPLACE AND DATE | DEATH DATE | HIGHLIGHTS OF CAREER |
|---|---|---|---|---|---|
| 34. Harry S. Truman [4] (Democratic) | 1945 (60) | F.D. Roosevelt | Lamar, Mo. May 8, 1884 | Dec. 26, 1972 | U.S. Senator (D-Mo.) 1935–45; 33d President 1945–53 |
| 35. Alben W. Barkley (Democratic) | 1949–1953 (71) | Truman | Lowes, Graves County, Ky. Nov. 24, 1877 | April 30, 1956 | U.S. Rep. (D-Ky.) 1913–27; U.S. Senator (D-Ky.) 1927–49, 1955–56; majority leader U.S. Senate 1937–47 |
| 36. Richard M. Nixon [1] (Republican) | 1953–1961 (40) | Eisenhower | Yorba Linda, Cal. Jan. 9, 1913 | — | U.S. Rep. (R-Calif.) 1947–50; U.S. Senator (R-Calif.) 1950–53; 37th President 1969–74 |
| 37. Lyndon B. Johnson [4] (Democratic) | 1961–1963 (52) | Kennedy | Stonewall, Tex. Aug. 27, 1908 | Jan. 22, 1973 | U.S. Rep. (D-Tex.) 1937–48; U.S. Senator (D-Tex.) 1949–60; majority leader U.S. Senate 1955–60; 36th President 1963–69 |
| 38. Hubert H. Humphrey Jr. (Democratic) | 1965–1969 (53) | L.B. Johnson | Wallace, S.D. May 27, 1911 | Jan. 13, 1978 | Mayor of Minneapolis 1945–48; U.S. Senator 1949–65, 1971–78; proposed first medical care for aged bill; helped pass civil rights bills |
| 39. Spiro T. Agnew [3] (Republican) | 1969–1973 (50) | Nixon | Baltimore, Md. Nov. 9, 1918 | — | Governor of Maryland 1967–69; forced to resign as Vice President and convicted of income tax evasion 1973 |
| 40. Gerald R. Ford [4] (Republican) | 1973–1974 (60) | Nixon | Omaha, Neb. July 14, 1913 | — | U.S. Rep. (R-Mich.) 1949–73; minority leader U.S. House 1965–73; 38th President 1974–77 |
| 41. Nelson Rockefeller [5] (Republican) | 1974–1977 (66) | Ford | Bar Harbor, Me. July 8, 1908 | Jan. 26, 1979 | Assistant Secretary of State 1944–45; Under Secretary Health, Education, and Welfare 1953–54; Governor N.Y. 1958–73 |
| 42. Walter F. Mondale (Democratic) | 1977–1981 (49) | Carter | Ceylon, Minn. Jan. 5, 1928 | — | Attorney general of Minnesota 1960–64; U.S. Senator (D-Minn.) 1964–77 |
| 43. George Bush (Republican) | 1981– (56) | Reagan | Milton, Mass. June 12, 1924 | — | U.S. Rep. (R-Tex.) 1967–71; ambassador to UN 1971–72; director CIA 1976–77 |

## PRESIDENTS ELECTED WITH MINORITY OF POPULAR VOTE

| ELECTION | PRESIDENT | PARTY | POPULAR VOTE | ELECTION | PRESIDENT | PARTY | POPULAR VOTE |
|---|---|---|---|---|---|---|---|
| 1824 | John Quincy Adams | Independent | 30.60% | 1888 | Benjamin Harrison | Republican | 47.90% |
| 1844 | James K. Polk | Democrat | 49.56% | 1892 | Grover Cleveland | Democrat | 46.04% |
| 1848 | Zachary Taylor | Whig | 47.31% | 1912 | Woodrow Wilson | Democrat | 41.85% |
| 1856 | James Buchanan | Democrat | 45.30% | 1916 | Woodrow Wilson | Democrat | 49.40% |
| 1860 | Abraham Lincoln | Republican | 39.79% | 1948 | Harry S. Truman | Democrat | 49.51% |
| 1876 | Rutherford B. Hayes | Republican | 47.94% | 1960 | John F. Kennedy | Democrat | 49.50% |
| 1880 | James A. Garfield | Republican | 48.50% | 1968 | Richard M. Nixon | Republican | 43.40% |
| 1884 | Grover Cleveland | Democrat | 48.50% | | | | |

## UNCOMPLETED TERMS OF PRESIDENTS

| PRESIDENT | UNCOMPLETED TERM | SUCCESSOR |
|---|---|---|
| William H. Harrison [2] | March 4, 1841–April 4, 1841 | John Tyler |
| Zachary Taylor [2] | March 5, 1849–July 9, 1850 | Millard Fillmore |
| Abraham Lincoln [6] | March 4, 1865–April 15, 1865 (second term) | Andrew Johnson |
| James A. Garfield [6] | March 4, 1881–Sept. 19, 1881 | Chester A. Arthur |
| William McKinley [6] | March 4, 1901–Sept. 14, 1901 (second term) | Theodore Roosevelt |
| Warren G. Harding [2] | March 4, 1921–Aug. 2, 1923 | Calvin Coolidge |
| Franklin D. Roosevelt [2] | Jan. 20, 1945–April 12, 1945 (fourth term) | Harry S. Truman |
| John F. Kennedy [6] | Jan. 20, 1961–Nov. 22, 1963 | Lyndon B. Johnson |
| Richard M. Nixon [3] | Jan. 20, 1973–Aug. 9, 1974 (second term) | Gerald R. Ford |

## VETOES BY THE PRESIDENTS *

| PRESIDENT | Regular | Pocket | PRESIDENT | Regular | Pocket | PRESIDENT | Regular | Pocket | PRESIDENT | Regular | Pocket |
|---|---|---|---|---|---|---|---|---|---|---|---|
| Washington | 2 | – | Polk | 2 | 1 | Arthur | 4 | 8 | Hoover | 21 | 16 |
| Adams | – | – | Taylor | – | – | Cleveland [7] | 304 | 110 | F. Roosevelt | 372 | 263 |
| Jefferson | – | – | Fillmore | – | – | B. Harrison | 19 | 25 | Truman | 180 | 70 |
| Madison | 5 | 2 | Pierce | 9 | – | Cleveland [8] | 42 | 128 | Eisenhower | 73 | 108 |
| Monroe | 1 | – | Buchanan | 4 | 3 | McKinley | 6 | 36 | Kennedy | 12 | 9 |
| J. Q. Adams | – | – | Lincoln | 2 | 4 | T. Roosevelt | 42 | 40 | L. Johnson | 16 | 14 |
| Jackson | 5 | 7 | A. Johnson | 21 | 8 | Taft | 30 | 9 | Nixon | 27 | 16 |
| Van Buren | – | 1 | Grant | 45 | 48 | Wilson | 33 | 11 | Ford | 55 | 11 |
| W. Harrison | – | – | Hayes | 12 | 1 | Harding | 5 | 1 | Carter [9] | 25 | 13 |
| Tyler | 6 | 4 | Garfield | – | – | Coolidge | 20 | 30 | | | |

[1] Elected President.   [2] Died in office.   [3] Resigned.   [4] Succeeded to presidency.   [5] Appointed Vice President.   [6] Assassinated.   [7] 1st term.   [8] 2d term.   [9] To Nov. 1, 1980.   *Source: U.S. Senate Library.

# Home and Family

NUTRITION INFORMATION

PER SERVING
SERVING SIZE = 8 OZ.
SERVINGS PER CONTAINER = 2

Calories .................. 560
Protein ...................... 23g
Carbohydrate ................ 43g
Fat .......................... 33g

PERCENTAGE OF U.S. ... NDED
DAIL... VAN...

Protein ...                    15
...tamin A...

Sixth graders at the Miami Gardens Elementary School in Miami, Fla., learn how the nutrition information on food packages can help in planning a well-balanced diet from an unusual guest lecturer—NUTRO, a 5-foot 2-inch robot. This was just one of many stops made by NUTRO in a national tour sponsored by Hoffmann-La Roche, Inc., to help children and parents become more aware of the importance of good nutrition.

## HIGHLIGHTS: 1980

About 2,000 delegates attended three meetings in 1980 at Baltimore, Minneapolis, and Los Angeles as the central focus of the White House Conference on Families.

The purpose of the meetings was to obtain recommendations for ways the government and other institutions could improve family life in the United States.

Scores of recommendations were approved. Those receiving the most support included:

*Repeal of the Marriage Tax:* Revision of the federal income-tax code to eliminate the marriage penalty by allowing married couples to file income taxes either jointly or separately without penalty.

*Reduce Government Impact on Families:* Laws and regulations of government should be analyzed and revised in terms of their impact on families.

*Health Care for the Aged:* Changes in Medicaid/Medicare policies to encourage home care of the aged instead of institutionalization in old-age centers.

*Increased Efforts to Stem Drug and Alcohol Abuse:* Overwhelming majorities at the three meetings called on government, schools, local communities, and the media to step up efforts against drug and alcohol abuse.

*Improved Job Practices:* Adoption by employers of flextime, job sharing, and other more flexible personnel practices.

*More Aid for the Handicapped:* Development of financial aid programs for families in which a member is handicapped.

# CONSUMERS AND CONSUMERISM: 1980

## DRUG MANUFACTURERS AGREE ON WARNINGS

Manufacturers of such tranquilizers as Valium, Librium, and others agreed in July to issue warnings to doctors that the drugs should not be used to relieve "everyday stress."

Food and Drug Administration Commissioner Jere E. Goyan said that Americans could probably cut in half their intake of an estimated 5 billion tranquilizer pills annually.

According to Goyan, although tranquilizers can be helpful in aiding people through crises or mental illness, millions of Americans "are taking them habitually just to deal with the anxiety of living."

Hoffman-LaRoche, producer of the nation's most prescribed drug, Valium, and four other companies planned to begin their warning literature saying: "Anxiety or tension associated with the stress of everyday life usually does not require treatment with an anxiolytic (anti-anxiety) drug."

## AUTOMATIC GARAGE DOORS POSE HAZARD

Government safety investigators warned that many children are playing a dangerous game with automatic garage doors—a game in which they activate the door's closing mechanism and then try to "beat the door" before it closes. The Consumer Product Safety Commission noted that children under the age of nine are most often involved in automatic garage door injuries and deaths, and may go to great lengths to activate the closing mechanism. A 2-year-old Wisconsin youth is believed to have used a broom handle to trigger the door in a 1980 accident.

The commission advised parents to take steps to minimize the hazards. Suggestions included adjusting to greater sensitivity the automatic reverse mechanism that stops or reverses the door on impact with an object, relocating all operating switches out of easy reach of children, and locking cars that contain radio controls.

## ROLLER SKATES A MAJOR CAUSE OF INJURY

Roller skates have become a significant cause of consumer recreational injuries, surpassing even skateboards in the number of reported accidents, the Consumer Product Safety Commission announced in April.

According to CPSC statistics, nearly one-fourth of the estimated 135,000 roller-skating injuries in 1979 were to people over age 25. At least half of all such injuries were suffered by teenagers, and well over two-thirds of the injuries were to girls and women.

The CPSC believes some injuries might be avoided if skaters wear protective padding

## CONSUMER PRICE INDEX: 1940–1980

Source: U.S. Department of Labor, Bureau of Labor Statistics

The Consumer Price Index of the U.S. Department of Labor is based on the amount of goods and services a consumer could buy for $1 in 1967, so the Index for all items in 1967 is 100. It shows you would have spent 42¢ in 1940 or $2.17 in 1979 for goods and services that cost $2.52 in 1980.

| YEAR | ALL ITEMS | MEDICAL CARE | FOOD | APPAREL AND UPKEEP | HOUSING | TRANS-PORTA-TION | PERSONAL CARE | READING AND ENTERTAINMENT | ALL SERVICES |
|---|---|---|---|---|---|---|---|---|---|
| 1940 | 42.0 | 36.8 | 35.2 | 42.8 | 52.4 | 42.7 | 40.2 | 46.1 | 43.6 |
| 1945 | 53.9 | 42.1 | 50.7 | 61.5 | 59.1 | 47.8 | 55.1 | 62.4 | 48.7 |
| 1950 | 72.1 | 53.7 | 74.5 | 79.0 | 72.8 | 68.2 | 68.3 | 74.4 | 58.9 |
| 1955 | 80.2 | 64.8 | 81.6 | 84.1 | 82.3 | 77.4 | 77.9 | 76.7 | 70.5 |
| 1960 | 88.7 | 79.1 | 88.0 | 89.6 | 90.2 | 89.6 | 90.1 | 87.3 | 83.8 |
| 1962 | 90.6 | 83.5 | 89.9 | 90.9 | 91.7 | 92.5 | 92.2 | 91.3 | 86.2 |
| 1963 | 91.7 | 85.6 | 91.2 | 91.9 | 92.7 | 93.0 | 93.4 | 92.8 | 88.5 |
| 1964 | 92.9 | 87.3 | 92.4 | 92.7 | 93.8 | 94.3 | 94.5 | 95.0 | 90.2 |
| 1965 | 94.5 | 89.5 | 94.4 | 93.7 | 94.9 | 95.9 | 95.2 | 95.9 | 92.2 |
| 1966 | 97.2 | 93.4 | 99.1 | 96.1 | 97.2 | 97.2 | 97.1 | 97.5 | 95.8 |
| 1967 | 100.0 | 100.0 | 100.0 | 100.0 | 100.0 | 100.0 | 100.0 | 100.0 | 100.0 |
| 1968 | 104.2 | 106.1 | 103.6 | 105.4 | 104.2 | 103.2 | 104.2 | 104.7 | 105.2 |
| 1969 | 109.8 | 113.4 | 108.9 | 111.5 | 110.8 | 107.2 | 109.3 | 108.7 | 112.5 |
| 1970 | 116.3 | 120.6 | 114.9 | 116.1 | 118.9 | 112.7 | 113.2 | 113.4 | 121.6 |
| 1971 | 121.3 | 128.4 | 118.4 | 119.8 | 124.3 | 118.6 | 116.8 | 119.3 | 128.4 |
| 1972 | 125.3 | 132.5 | 123.5 | 122.3 | 129.2 | 119.9 | 119.8 | 122.8 | 133.3 |
| 1973 | 133.1 | 137.7 | 141.4 | 126.8 | 135.0 | 123.8 | 125.2 | 125.9 | 139.1 |
| 1974 | 147.7 | 150.5 | 161.7 | 136.2 | 150.6 | 137.7 | 137.3 | 133.8 | 152.1 |
| 1975 | 161.2 | 168.6 | 175.4 | 142.3 | 166.8 | 150.6 | 150.7 | 144.4 | 166.6 |
| 1976 | 170.5 | 197.1 | 180.8 | 147.6 | 177.2 | 165.5 | 160.5 | 151.2 | 180.4 |
| 1977 | 181.5 | 202.4 | 188.0 | 154.2 | 186.5 | 177.2 | 172.1 | 167.7 | 172.2 |
| 1978 | 195.4 | 219.4 | 211.4 | 159.6 | 202.8 | 185.5 | 182.0 | 176.6 | 210.9 |
| 1979 | 217.4 | 239.7 | 234.5 | 166.6 | 227.6 | 212.0 | 195.8 | 188.5 | 234.2 |
| 1980* | 251.7 | 270.6 | 254.2 | 182.2 | 267.7 | 254.7 | 216.7 | 209.8 | 274.8 |

* 1980 data for September.

on elbows and knees, relax their bodies when falling, and watch for stones, twigs, or other surface irregularities while skating.

## NITROSAMINE LEVELS IN BEER REDUCED

The Food and Drug Administration announced in June that brewers have reduced significantly the levels of suspected cancer-causing agents called nitrosamines in beers.

A four-month FDA survey showed that the present nitrosamine level in most beers is well below the level considered dangerous.

## TWO MILLION TIRES RECALLED

Uniroyal Tire Co. announced in March it was recalling 2 million of its steel-belted radial tires because the National Highway Traffic Safety Administration (NHTSA) discovered tread and belt separations.

NHTSA Administrator Joan Claybrook said that most of the recalled tires were original equipment on some full-size General Motors automobiles produced in 1975–77. She estimated that between one-third and one-half of the recalled tires might be in service.

Uniroyal agreed to replace each recalled tire with a new tire, including mounting and balancing at no extra charge, if it had been purchased after Dec. 1, 1976. Tires purchased before that date would be replaced at half-price or on the basis of a prorated share of the treadware, since federal law does not require free replacement of tires more than three years old. Uniroyal estimated the cost of tire replacement at less than $5 million.

## PREGNANT WOMEN WARNED ON CAFFEINE

In September the Food and Drug Administration suggested that pregnant women avoid consumption of caffeine because of a risk of birth defects. However, the agency did not require warning labels on caffeine-containing products because of lack of conclusive evidence.

FDA Commissioner Jere Goyan disclosed that recent tests on rats indicated the possibility that caffeine consumed by the mother could cause her baby to have loss of toes or delays in skeletal development.

Although the FDA believes more studies are needed before requiring a warning label, the agency felt there was enough of a link between caffeine and birth defects to require an informal warning.

Caffeine is found in such widely consumed products as coffee, tea, chocolate, soft drinks, cocoa, and some drugs.

## CRIB MAKER ALERTS PARENTS ON HAZARDS

Bassett Furniture Industries, Inc. signed a consent agreement with the Consumer Product Safety Commission in February, to alert consumers about two styles of cribs that reportedly caused six infant deaths. CPSC staff believed the crib designs were such that infants could trap their heads between a corner post and the headboard (or footboard) and strangle as they stood on the crib mattress.

The main part of the agreement required Bassett to send hazard notifications by direct mail to all parents who had had children within the previous 21 months. It was expected that the mailing would include more than 4 million parents of infants and young children.

In addition, the company agreed to purchase advertising space in popular magazines and mail posters describing the hazards to all obstetricians and gynecologists in the U.S.

Once aware of the potential hazard, consumers were instructed to contact Bassett to obtain a free repair or modification kit.

Bassett further agreed to pay a $175,000 civil penalty to settle the CPSC allegation that the firm failed to promptly report the alleged defect in the cribs.

## PATIENTS TO RECEIVE LEAFLETS ON DRUGS

New Food and Drug Administration rules, to go into effect in mid-1981, require pharmaceutical companies to provide informational leaflets to patients purchasing 10 categories of prescription drugs. The leaflets must include descriptions of each drug's uses and side effects, as well as instructions for taking it effectively.

The 10 drugs include ampicillins, a type of penicillin antibiotic; benzodiazepines, a class of tranquilizer that includes Valium and Librium; cemetidine, used for ulcer treatment; clofibrate, used for treatment of high cholesterol levels in blood; digoxin, used in treating heart problems; methoxsalen, for skin pigmentation problems; thiazides, diuretic drugs used in treatment of high blood pressure; phenytoin, used to control epileptic seizures; propoxyphene, a pain reliever known as Darvon; and warfarin, an anticoagulant.

The new rules were intended to reduce problems caused by inadvertent misuse of drugs by patients.

## CONSUMER HOTLINE PHONE NUMBERS

Here are three toll-free federal hotline numbers you may need to use.

**Product Safety:** To inquire about or report on the safety of products, phone 800-638-8326.

**Solar Energy:** To get information about solar-energy systems for heating and cooling, phone 800-523-2929.

**Auto Recall:** To find out if your car has been recalled by the manufacturer for the repair of defects, phone 800-424-9393.

# CONSUMER DIRECTORY

## U.S. Government Hotlines

The following U.S. government telephone hotlines were in effect at the time the Almanac went to press. Toll-free numbers may be changed, however, and if you have difficulty reaching any of

**ACTION** .......................... 800-424-8580
   Information for potential volunteers.
**Auto Recall Hotline** ................. 800-424-9393
   To find out if your car has been recalled.
**Basic Education Grants Program** ...... 800-638-6700
   In Maryland, 800-492-6602
   General information on education grants.
**Consumer Product Safety Commission** .. 800-638-8326
   In Maryland, 800-492-8363; In Alaska, Hawaii, Puerto Rico, Virgin Islands, 800-638-8333
   To inquire about or report on safety of products.
**Department of Energy Hotline** ........ 800-424-9246
   Receives consumer complaints on gas and heating oil supplies and prices.
**Export-Import Bank** ................. 800-424-5201
   Export information for small businesses.
**Fair Housing and Equal Opportunity** ... 800-424-8590
   For housing and discrimination problems.
**Federal Crime Insurance** ............. 800-638-8780
   Information on insurance in high-risk areas.

the following, we suggest you dial 800-555-1212 to obtain the correct number.
Most of these toll-free numbers are not available in Alaska and Hawaii.

**Federal Election Commission** ......... 800-424-9530
   Regulates campaign financing.
**Interstate Commerce Commission** ...... 800-424-9312
   In Florida, 800-432-4537
   Data on interstate travel and moving companies.
**National Flood Insurance** ............ 800-424-8872
   Information on insurance in flood-exposed areas.
**National Runaway Switchboard** ....... 800-621-4000
   Advice for runaways and parents.
**National Solar Heating and Cooling Information Center** ................. 800-523-2929
   In Pennsylvania, 800-462-4983
   Information on solar installations.
**Tax Hotline** ........................ 800-555-1212
   Phone to find out your state's toll-free IRS number.
**VD Hotline. (Operation Venus)** ........ 800-523-1885
   In Pennsylvania, 800-462-4966
   General information on venereal disease.
**Veterans' Information** ............... 800-555-1212
   Phone to find out your state's toll-free VA number.

# CONSUMER ORGANIZATIONS

The following consumer organizations are among those actively working for and with consumers at national, state and local levels to affect public policy as it relates to inflation.

**Association of Community Organizations for Reform Now (ACORN):** Works for advancement of low-to-moderate-income people.
628 Barrone St., New Orleans, LA 70113 or
523 W. 15th St., Little Rock, AR 72202
**Center for Community Change:** Provides technical assistance to community organizations on housing, manpower, economic development, and other grass-roots concerns.
1000 Wisconsin Ave., NW, Washington, D.C. 20007
**Center for Science in the Public Interest:** Research and education activities focus on nutrition, food programs, and the food industry.
1755 S St., NW, Washington, D.C. 20009
**Common Cause:** Nonpartisan public-affairs lobbying organization concerned mainly with government reform and accountability.
2030 M Street, NW, Washington, D.C. 20036
**Community Nutrition Institute:** Resource center on food and nutrition policy issues; provides technical assistance to community programs.
1146 19th St., NW, Washington, D.C. 20036
**Congress Watch:** Lobbying arm of Public Citizen; active in many areas of national energy and consumer legislation policymaking.
133 C St., SE, Washington, D.C. 20003
**Consumer Coalition for Health:** Coalition of national and local organizations and individuals across the country that develops programs designed to increase public awareness of health-planning issues.
1511 K St., NW, Suite 220, Washington, D.C. 20005
**Consumer Federation of America:** Federation of 225 national, state, and local nonprofit groups that advocates consumer interests on food, energy, credit and banking and health issues.
1012 14th St., NW, Washington, D.C. 20005
**Consumers Union of the U.S., Inc.:** Independent nonprofit product-testing organization that conducts research and prepares education materials on wide variety of consumer concerns.
256 Washington St., Mt. Vernon, NY 10550
**Cooperative League of the U.S.A.:** National organiza-

tion of cooperatives of all types; lobbies, conducts research, publishes educational materials, including "how-to" pamphlets on broad range of subjects such as farm/rural issues, housing, and health.
1828 L St., NW, Washington, D.C. 20036.
**Energy Action Committee:** Nonprofit public-interest organization that monitors government and industry actions in the energy field.
1523 L St., NW, Washington, D.C. 20005
**Environmental Action Foundation:** Education and research organization; publishes information on citizen action in environmental areas including solid waste, electric-utility rate structure and reform, and transportation.
724 Dupont Circle Building, Washington, D.C. 20036
**Environmental Defense Fund:** Nationwide legal-action organization working to protect the public interest in environmental quality, energy, conservation, public health, and consumer welfare.
1525 18th St., NW, Washington, D.C. 20036
**Food Research and Action Center:** Provides legal assistance, organizing aid, training, and information to low-income people and others working to expand and improve federal food programs.
2011 Eye St., NW, Washington, D.C. 20006
**Gray Panthers:** National activist organization that lobbies, advocates in court, and organizes around issues involving health care, nursing homes, age discrimination, and housing.
3700 Chestnut St., Philadelphia, PA 19104
**Health Research Group:** Ralph Nader-affiliated consumer advocacy organization working on consumer-health issues.
2000 P St., NW, Washington, D.C. 20036
**National Consumers League:** Sponsors variety of consumer-education programs and lobbies for consumer rights.
1028 Connecticut Ave., NW, Washington, D.C. 20036
**The National Commission on Neighborhoods:** Presidential advisory group investigates causes of neighborhood decline.
2000 K St., NW, Suite 350, Washington, D.C. 20006

## ADDRESSES OF FEDERAL CONSUMER OFFICES

When corresponding with a federal consumer office, be sure to include photocopies all documents pertinent to your request or complaint.

### ADVERTISING
Director, Bureau of Consumer Protection, Federal Trade Commission, Washington, D.C. 20580.
### AIR TRAVEL
*Routes and Service:* Director, Office of Consumer Protection, Civil Aeronautics Board, Washington, D.C. 20423.
*Safety:* Community and Consumer Liaison Division, Federal Aviation Administration, APA–430, Washington, D.C. 20591.
### ALCOHOLISM, DRUG ABUSE, AND MENTAL ILLNESS
Office of Public Affairs, Alcohol, Drug Abuse, and Mental Health Service, 5600 Fishers Lane, Rockville, MD 20857.
### BANKS
*Federal Credit Unions:* National Credit Union Administration, Washington, D.C. 20456.
*Federally Insured Savings and Loans:* Consumer Division, Office of Community Investment, Federal Home Loan Bank Board, Washington, D.C. 20552.
*Federal Reserve Banks:* Office of Saver and Consumer Affairs, Federal Reserve System, Washington, D.C. 20551.
*National Banks:* Consumer Affairs, Office of the Comptroller of the Currency, Washington, D.C. 20219.
*State Chartered Banks:* Office of Bank Customer Affairs, Federal Deposit Insurance Corporation, Washington, D.C. 20429.
### BOATING
Chief, Information and Administrative Staff, U.S. Coast Guard, Washington, D.C. 20590.
### BUS TRAVEL
Consumer Affairs Office, Interstate Commerce Commission, Washington, D.C. 20423.
### BUSINESS
*General:* Office of the Ombudsman, Department of Commerce, Washington, D.C. 20230.
*Women:* Director, Women-in-Business and Consumer Affairs, Small Business Administration, 1441 L St., NW, Washington, D.C. 20416.
### CHILD ABUSE
National Center on Child Abuse and Neglect, P.O. Box 1182, Washington, D.C. 20013.
### CREDIT
Director, Bureau of Consumer Protection, Federal Trade Commission, Washington, D.C. 20850.
### CUSTOMS
Public Information Division, U.S. Customs, Washington, D.C. 20229.
### DISCRIMINATION
*U.S. Commission on Civil Rights,* 1121 Vermont Ave., Washington, D.C. 20425.
*Equal Employment Opportunity Commission,* 2401 E St., NW, Washington, D.C. 20506.
### DRUGS AND COSMETICS
Consumer Inquiry Section, Food and Drug Administration, 5600 Fishers Lane, Rockville, MD 20852.
### ELDERLY
Administration on Aging, Washington, D.C. 20201.
### ENERGY
*General:* Director, Office of Consumer Affairs, Department of Energy, Washington, D.C. 20585.
*Energy Efficiency:* Information Office, National Bureau of Standards, Washington, D.C. 20234.
### ENVIRONMENT
Office of Public Awareness, Environmental Protection Agency, Washington, D.C. 20460.

### FISH AND WILDLIFE
Fish and Wildlife Service, Office of Public Affairs, Washington, D.C. 20240.
### FOOD
*Assistant Secretary for Food and Consumer Services,* U.S. Department of Agriculture, Washington, D.C. 20250.
*Consumer Inquiry Section,* Food and Drug Administration, 5600 Fishers Lane, Rockville, MD 20852.
### FRAUD
Director, Bureau of Consumer Protection, Federal Trade Commission, Washington, D.C. 20580.
### HANDICAPPED
Director, Division of Public Information, Office of Human Development Services, Department of Health and Human Services, Washington, D.C. 20201.
### IMMIGRATION AND NATURALIZATION
Information Services, Immigration and Naturalization Service, 425 Eye St., NW, Washington, D.C. 20536.
### JOB SAFETY
Office of Information, Occupational Safety and Health Administration, Department of Labor, Washington, D.C. 20210.
### MAIL ORDERS
Federal Trade Commission, Office of the Secretary, Washington, D.C. 20580.
### MAIL SERVICE
Consumer Advocate, U.S. Postal Service, Washington, D.C. 20260.
### MEDICAID AND MEDICARE
Health Care Financing Administration, in the Department of Health and Human Services, Washington, D.C. 20201.
### MEDICAL RESEARCH
*Division of Public Information,* National Institutes of Health, 9000 Rockville Pike, Bethesda, MD 20014.
*Center for Disease Control,* Attention, Public Inquiries, Atlanta, GA 30333.
### MOVING COMPANIES, INTERSTATE
Consumer Assistance Office, Interstate Commerce Commission, Washington, D.C. 20423.
### PARKS AND RECREATION AREAS
*National Forests:* Forest Service, U.S. Department of Agriculture, Washington, D.C. 20250.
*National Parks and Historic Sites:* National Park Service, Washington, D.C. 20240.
### PASSPORTS
Passport Office, Department of State, 1425 K St., NW, Washington, D.C. 20524.
### PATENTS AND TRADEMARKS
*Patents:* Commissioner, Patent Office, Department of Commerce, Washington, D.C. 20231.
*Trademarks:* Commissioner, Trademark Office, Department of Commerce, Washington, D.C. 20231.
### PENSIONS
*Office of Communications,* Pension Benefit Guaranty Corporation, 2020 K St., NW, Washington, D.C. 20006.
*Labor Management Standards Administration,* Department of Labor, Washington, D.C. 20210.
### RADIO AND TELEVISION BROADCASTING AND INTERFERENCE
Consumer Assistance Office, Federal Communications Commission, Washington, D.C. 20554.
### SMOKING
Office on Smoking and Health, 12420 Parklawn Drive, Room 158 Park Building, Rockville, MD 20852.
### WAGES AND WORKING CONDITIONS
Employment Standards Administration, Department of Labor, Washington, D.C. 20210.
### WARRANTIES
Division of Special Statutes, Federal Trade Commission, Washington, D.C. 20580.

# NUTRITION

A basic knowledge of good nutrition is essential for maintaining health. Poor diet in early life may impair both mental and physical development and in later years contribute to heart disease, strokes, and other disorders. Eating wisely also helps to keep desirable body weights.

There are at least 50 known nutrients necessary for health—vitamins, minerals, amino acids (protein), fatty acids, and glucose. No single food can adequately supply all of them. Hence, everyone should eat a varied menu taken from the four basic food groups below:

(1) **The meat group** includes not only beef, pork, lamb, and the like, but also poultry, fish, eggs, dried peas and beans, and nuts. All of these are high in protein.

(2) **The dairy group,** rich in calcium and proteins, includes milk and milk products.

(3) **The cereal group,** which supplies carbohydrates and some protein, consists of breakfast foods and breadstuffs made from oats, barley, wheat, and corn.

(4) **The fruit and vegetable group,** high in vitamins and minerals, includes fruits, berries, leafy and other green vegetables, and the "yellow" vegetables, such as carrots, squash, sweet potatoes, and the like.

A good diet should include two to four servings daily from each of the four groups. Avoid excessive use of sugar and fats.

## RECOMMENDED DAILY DIETARY ALLOWANCES

Source: *Recommended Dietary Allowances,*
  revised 1980, National Academy of Sciences

### WATER-SOLUBLE VITAMINS

| | Age (years) | Weight (kg) | Weight (lbs) | Height (cm) | Height (in) | Energy (calories) | Protein (grams) | Ascorbic Acid * | Folacin † | Niacin * | Riboflavin * | Thiamin * | Vitamin $B_6$ * | Vitamin $B_{12}$ † |
|---|---|---|---|---|---|---|---|---|---|---|---|---|---|---|
| Infants | 0.0-0.5 | 6 | 13 | 60 | 24 | kg x 115 | kg x 2.2 | 35 | 30 | 6 | 0.4 | 0.3 | 0.3 | 0.5 |
| | 0.5-1.0 | 9 | 20 | 71 | 28 | kg x 105 | kg x 2.0 | 35 | 45 | 8 | 0.6 | 0.5 | 0.6 | 1.5 |
| Children | 1-3 | 13 | 29 | 90 | 35 | 1,300 | 23 | 45 | 100 | 9 | 0.8 | 0.7 | 0.9 | 2.0 |
| | 4-6 | 20 | 44 | 112 | 44 | 1,700 | 30 | 45 | 200 | 11 | 1.0 | 0.9 | 1.3 | 2.5 |
| | 7-10 | 28 | 62 | 132 | 52 | 2,400 | 34 | 45 | 300 | 16 | 1.4 | 1.2 | 1.6 | 3.0 |
| Boys | 11-14 | 45 | 99 | 157 | 62 | 2,700 | 45 | 50 | 400 | 18 | 1.6 | 1.4 | 1.8 | 3.0 |
| | 15-18 | 66 | 145 | 176 | 69 | 2,800 | 56 | 60 | 400 | 19 | 1.7 | 1.4 | 2.0 | 3.0 |
| Men | 19-22 | 70 | 154 | 177 | 70 | 2,900 | 56 | 60 | 400 | 18 | 1.7 | 1.5 | 2.2 | 3.0 |
| | 23-50 | 70 | 154 | 178 | 70 | 2,700 | 56 | 60 | 400 | 16 | 1.6 | 1.4 | 2.2 | 3.0 |
| | 51+ | 70 | 154 | 178 | 70 | 2,400 | 56 | 60 | 400 | 15 | 1.4 | 1.2 | 2.2 | 3.0 |
| Girls | 11-14 | 46 | 101 | 157 | 62 | 2,200 | 46 | 50 | 400 | 14 | 1.3 | 1.1 | 1.8 | 3.0 |
| | 15-18 | 55 | 120 | 163 | 64 | 2,100 | 46 | 60 | 400 | 14 | 1.3 | 1.1 | 2.0 | 3.0 |
| Women | 19-22 | 55 | 120 | 163 | 64 | 2,100 | 44 | 60 | 400 | 14 | 1.3 | 1.1 | 2.0 | 3.0 |
| | 23-50 | 55 | 120 | 163 | 64 | 2,000 | 44 | 60 | 400 | 13 | 1.2 | 1.0 | 2.0 | 3.0 |
| | 51+ | 55 | 120 | 163 | 64 | 1,800 | 44 | 60 | 400 | 13 | 1.2 | 1.0 | 2.0 | 3.0 |
| Pregnant mothers ................ | | | | | | +300 | +30 | +20 | +400 | +2 | +0.3 | +0.4 | +0.6 | +1.0 |
| Nursing (lactating) mothers ......... | | | | | | +500 | +20 | +40 | +100 | +5 | +0.5 | +0.5 | +0.5 | +1.0 |

### FAT-SOLUBLE VITAMINS / MINERALS

| | Age (years) | Weight (kg) | Weight (lbs) | Height (cm) | Height (in) | Energy (calories) | Protein (grams) | Vitamin A (RE) [1] | Vitamin D [2] | Vitamin E [2] | Calcium * | Phosphorus * | Iodine † | Iron * | Magnesium * | Zinc * |
|---|---|---|---|---|---|---|---|---|---|---|---|---|---|---|---|---|
| Infants | 0.0-0.5 | 6 | 13 | 60 | 24 | kg x 115 | kg x 2.2 | 420 | 400 | 3 | 360 | 240 | 40 | 10 | 50 | 3 |
| | 0.5-1.0 | 9 | 20 | 71 | 28 | kg x 105 | kg x 2.0 | 400 | 400 | 4 | 540 | 360 | 50 | 15 | 70 | 5 |
| Children | 1-3 | 13 | 29 | 90 | 35 | 1,300 | 23 | 400 | 400 | 5 | 800 | 800 | 70 | 15 | 150 | 10 |
| | 4-6 | 20 | 44 | 112 | 44 | 1,700 | 30 | 500 | 400 | 6 | 800 | 800 | 90 | 10 | 200 | 10 |
| | 7-10 | 28 | 62 | 132 | 52 | 2,400 | 34 | 700 | 400 | 7 | 800 | 800 | 120 | 10 | 250 | 10 |
| Boys | 11-14 | 45 | 99 | 157 | 62 | 2,700 | 45 | 1,000 | 400 | 8 | 1,200 | 1,200 | 150 | 18 | 350 | 15 |
| | 15-18 | 66 | 145 | 176 | 69 | 2,800 | 56 | 1,000 | 400 | 10 | 1,200 | 1,200 | 150 | 18 | 400 | 15 |
| Men | 19-22 | 70 | 154 | 177 | 70 | 2,900 | 56 | 1,000 | 300 | 10 | 800 | 800 | 150 | 10 | 350 | 15 |
| | 23-50 | 70 | 154 | 178 | 70 | 2,700 | 56 | 1,000 | 200 | 10 | 800 | 800 | 150 | 10 | 350 | 15 |
| | 51+ | 70 | 154 | 178 | 70 | 2,400 | 56 | 1,000 | 200 | 10 | 800 | 800 | 150 | 10 | 350 | 15 |
| Girls | 11-14 | 46 | 101 | 157 | 62 | 2,200 | 46 | 800 | 400 | 8 | 1,200 | 1,200 | 150 | 18 | 300 | 15 |
| | 15-18 | 55 | 120 | 163 | 64 | 2,100 | 46 | 800 | 400 | 8 | 1,200 | 1,200 | 150 | 18 | 300 | 15 |
| Women | 19-22 | 55 | 120 | 163 | 64 | 2,100 | 44 | 800 | 300 | 8 | 800 | 800 | 150 | 18 | 300 | 15 |
| | 23-50 | 55 | 120 | 163 | 64 | 2,000 | 44 | 800 | 200 | 8 | 800 | 800 | 150 | 18 | 300 | 15 |
| | 51+ | 55 | 120 | 163 | 64 | 1,800 | 44 | 800 | 200 | 8 | 800 | 800 | 150 | 10 | 300 | 15 |
| Pregnant mothers ................ | | | | | | +300 | +30 | +200 | +200 | +2 | +400 | +400 | +25 | 30+[3] | +150 | +25 |
| Nursing (lactating) mothers ......... | | | | | | +500 | +20 | +400 | +200 | +3 | +400 | +400 | +50 | 30+[3] | +150 | +50 |

\* In milligrams.    † In micrograms.    [1] In retinol equivalents.    [2] In International units.    [3] Supplemental iron recommended.

# CALORIES AND WEIGHT

The weight of an adult man or woman reflects the extent to which he or she balances the intake of energy in food with the expenditure of energy in activity and growth. Weight will stay the same when the number of calories brought into the body by food equals the number of calories used by the body. Similarly, the body loses weight when it receives fewer calories from food than it uses. It gains weight when it receives more calories than are used.

Weight can be controlled by regulating either the amount of food eaten or the extent of physical activity, or both, so that the balance of calories is in the desired direction.

Overweight is a problem shared by more than 60 million Americans of all ages. There are a number of available low-calorie, nutritionally sound diets which, if faithfully followed, will take off excess pounds and help to keep them off. However, it is wise for anyone planning to lose more than a few pounds to consult a doctor.

**DESIRABLE WEIGHTS FOR MEN AGE 25 AND OVER [1]**

Source: National Academy of Sciences

| HEIGHT (WITHOUT SHOES ON) | | | | |
|---|---|---|---|---|
| Feet | Inches | Cm | Pounds | Kilograms |
| 5 | 2 | 158 | 123 (112–141) | 56 (51–64) |
| 5 | 4 | 163 | 130 (118–148) | 59 (54–67) |
| 5 | 6 | 168 | 136 (124–156) | 62 (56–71) |
| 5 | 8 | 173 | 145 (132–166) | 66 (60–75) |
| 5 | 10 | 178 | 154 (140–174) | 70 (64–79) |
| 6 | 0 | 183 | 162 (148–184) | 74 (67–84) |
| 6 | 2 | 188 | 171 (156–194) | 78 (71–88) |
| 6 | 4 | 193 | 181 (164–204) | 82 (74–93) |

**DESIRABLE WEIGHTS FOR WOMEN AGE 25 AND OVER [1]**

Source: National Academy of Sciences

| HEIGHT (WITHOUT SHOES ON) | | | | |
|---|---|---|---|---|
| Feet | Inches | Cm | Pounds | Kilograms |
| 4 | 10 | 147 | 102 (92–119) | 46 (42–54) |
| 5 | 0 | 152 | 107 (96–125) | 49 (44–57) |
| 5 | 2 | 158 | 113 (102–131) | 51 (46–59) |
| 5 | 4 | 163 | 120 (108–138) | 55 (49–63) |
| 5 | 6 | 168 | 128 (114–146) | 58 (52–66) |
| 5 | 8 | 173 | 136 (122–154) | 62 (55–70) |
| 5 | 10 | 178 | 144 (130–163) | 65 (59–74) |
| 6 | 0 | 183 | 152 (138–173) | 69 (63–79) |

[1] Without clothes. Average weight ranges in parentheses.

## AVERAGE HEIGHTS AND WEIGHTS OF BOYS AND GIRLS

Source: National Academy of Sciences

**PHYSICAL GROWTH OF BOYS**
(from age 1 month to 18 years; without clothing)

| AGE (Month or year) | AVERAGE HEIGHT | | AVERAGE WEIGHT | |
|---|---|---|---|---|
| | Centimeters | Inches | Kilograms | Pounds |
| 1 mo. | 54.6 | 21.5 | 4.29 | 9.5 |
| 3 mo. | 61.1 | 24.1 | 5.98 | 13.2 |
| 6 mo. | 67.8 | 26.7 | 7.85 | 17.3 |
| 9 mo. | 72.3 | 28.5 | 9.18 | 20.2 |
| 12 mo. | 76.1 | 30.0 | 10.15 | 22.4 |
| 18 mo. | 82.4 | 32.4 | 11.47 | 25.3 |
| 2 yrs. | 86.8 | 34.2 | 12.34 | 27.2 |
| 3 yrs. | 94.9 | 37.4 | 14.62 | 32.2 |
| 4 yrs. | 102.9 | 40.5 | 16.69 | 36.8 |
| 5 yrs. | 109.9 | 43.3 | 18.67 | 41.2 |
| 6 yrs. | 116.1 | 45.7 | 20.69 | 45.6 |
| 7 yrs. | 121.7 | 47.9 | 22.85 | 50.4 |
| 8 yrs. | 127.0 | 50.0 | 25.30 | 55.8 |
| 9 yrs. | 132.2 | 52.1 | 28.13 | 62.0 |
| 10 yrs. | 137.5 | 54.1 | 31.44 | 69.3 |
| 11 yrs. | 143.3 | 56.4 | 35.30 | 77.8 |
| 12 yrs. | 149.7 | 58.9 | 39.78 | 87.7 |
| 13 yrs. | 156.5 | 61.6 | 44.95 | 99.1 |
| 14 yrs. | 163.1 | 64.2 | 50.77 | 111.9 |
| 15 yrs. | 169.0 | 66.5 | 56.71 | 125.0 |
| 16 yrs. | 173.5 | 68.3 | 62.10 | 136.9 |
| 17 yrs. | 176.2 | 69.4 | 66.31 | 146.2 |
| 18 yrs. | 176.8 | 69.6 | 68.88 | 151.9 |

**PHYSICAL GROWTH OF GIRLS**
(from age 1 month to 18 years; without clothing)

| AGE (Month or year) | AVERAGE HEIGHT | | AVERAGE WEIGHT | |
|---|---|---|---|---|
| | Centimeters | Inches | Kilograms | Pounds |
| 1 mo. | 53.5 | 21.1 | 3.98 | 8.8 |
| 3 mo. | 59.5 | 23.4 | 5.40 | 11.9 |
| 6 mo. | 65.9 | 25.9 | 7.21 | 15.9 |
| 9 mo. | 70.4 | 27.7 | 8.56 | 18.9 |
| 12 mo. | 74.3 | 29.3 | 9.53 | 21.0 |
| 18 mo. | 80.9 | 31.9 | 10.82 | 23.8 |
| 2 yrs. | 86.8 | 34.2 | 11.80 | 26.0 |
| 3 yrs. | 94.1 | 37.0 | 14.10 | 31.0 |
| 4 yrs. | 101.6 | 40.0 | 15.96 | 35.2 |
| 5 yrs. | 108.4 | 42.7 | 17.66 | 38.9 |
| 6 yrs. | 114.6 | 45.1 | 19.52 | 43.0 |
| 7 yrs. | 120.6 | 47.5 | 21.84 | 48.1 |
| 8 yrs. | 126.4 | 49.8 | 24.84 | 54.8 |
| 9 yrs. | 132.2 | 52.0 | 28.46 | 62.7 |
| 10 yrs. | 138.3 | 54.4 | 32.55 | 71.8 |
| 11 yrs. | 144.8 | 57.0 | 36.95 | 81.5 |
| 12 yrs. | 151.5 | 59.6 | 41.53 | 91.6 |
| 13 yrs. | 157.1 | 61.9 | 46.10 | 101.6 |
| 14 yrs. | 160.4 | 63.1 | 50.28 | 110.8 |
| 15 yrs. | 161.8 | 63.7 | 53.68 | 118.3 |
| 16 yrs. | 162.4 | 69.9 | 55.89 | 123.2 |
| 17 yrs. | 163.1 | 64.2 | 56.69 | 125.0 |
| 18 yrs. | 163.7 | 64.4 | 56.62 | 124.8 |

## CALORIE COUNT AND MAIN NUTRIENTS OF BASIC FOODS

Source: U.S. Department of Agriculture.   T = trace.

In nutrition *calorie* expresses the energy-producing value of food. For the average American adult, energy is expended at about the following rates: running, 19.4 calories per minute; swimming, 11.2 calories per minute; bicycle riding, 8.2 calories per minute; walking, 5.2 calories per minute; and repose, 1.3 calories per minute.

Energy values in excess of those used for physical activities are stored in the body in the form of fat.

| KINDS OF FOOD | AMOUNT | FOOD ENERGY (Calories) | PROTEIN (Grams) | FAT (Grams) | CARBOHYDRATES (Grams) |
|---|---|---|---|---|---|
| **BEVERAGES, MILK, FATS** | | | | | |
| Beer | 12 oz. | 150 | 1 | 0 | 14 |
| Butter or margarine (¼ lb.) | ½ cup | 815 | 1 | 92 | T |
| Butter or margarine | 1 pat | 25 | T | 4 | T |
| Buttermilk | 1 cup | 100 | 8 | 2 | 12 |
| Club soda (unsweetened) | 12 oz. | 0 | 0 | 0 | 0 |
| Cocoa | 1 cup | 245 | 10 | 12 | 27 |
| Cola beverages | 12 oz. | 145 | 0 | 0 | 37 |
| Cream, half-and-half | 1 tbsp. | 20 | T | 2 | 1 |
| Cream, sour | 1 tbsp. | 25 | T | 3 | 1 |
| Fats, vegetable | 1 tbsp. | 110 | 0 | 13 | 0 |
| Gin, rum, vodka, whisky | 1½ oz. | 110 | 0 | 0 | T |
| Ginger ale | 12 oz. | 115 | 0 | 0 | 29 |
| Lard | 1 tbsp. | 115 | 0 | 13 | 0 |
| Malted milk | 1 cup | 235 | 11 | 10 | 27 |
| Milk, skim | 1 cup | 85 | 8 | T | 12 |
| Milk, whole | 1 cup | 150 | 8 | 8 | 11 |
| Oils, salad or cooking | 1 tbsp. | 120 | 0 | 14 | 0 |
| Root beer | 12 oz. | 150 | 0 | 0 | 39 |
| Soda, fruit-flavored | 12 oz. | 170 | 0 | 0 | 45 |
| Wine, table | 3½ oz. | 85 | T | 0 | 4 |
| **BREADS, CEREALS, DESSERTS, PASTAS, SNACKS** | | | | | |
| Bagel (egg) | 1 | 165 | 6 | 2 | 28 |
| Biscuit | 1 | 105 | 2 | 5 | 13 |
| Bread: | | | | | |
|   Raisin | 1 slice | 65 | 2 | 1 | 13 |
|   Rye | 1 slice | 60 | 2 | T | 13 |
|   White | 1 slice | 70 | 2 | 1 | 13 |
|   Whole-wheat | 1 slice | 60 | 3 | 1 | 12 |
| Breakfast cereals: | | | | | |
|   Bran flakes | 1 cup | 105 | 4 | 1 | 28 |
|   Corn flakes, plain | 1 cup | 95 | 2 | T | 21 |
|   Oatmeal | 1 cup | 130 | 5 | 2 | 23 |
|   Puffed rice | 1 cup | 60 | 1 | T | 13 |
|   Puffed wheat | 1 cup | 55 | 2 | T | 12 |
|   Shredded wheat | 1 piece | 90 | 2 | 1 | 20 |
| Brownie with nuts | 1 | 95 | 1 | 6 | 10 |
| Cakes (pieces): | | | | | |
|   Angel food | 1 | 135 | 3 | T | 32 |
|   Cupcake (iced) | 1 | 130 | 2 | 5 | 21 |
|   Devil's food (iced) | 1 | 235 | 3 | 8 | 40 |
|   Fruitcake | 1 | 55 | 1 | 2 | 9 |
|   Gingerbread | 1 | 175 | 2 | 4 | 32 |
|   Sponge | 1 | 195 | 5 | 4 | 36 |
|   White (iced) | 1 | 250 | 3 | 8 | 45 |
| Candy: | | | | | |
|   Caramel | 1 oz. | 115 | 1 | 3 | 22 |
|   Chocolate—milk | 1 oz. | 145 | 2 | 9 | 16 |
|   Chocolate—nuts | 1 oz. | 160 | 5 | 12 | 11 |
|   Fudge, plain | 1 oz. | 115 | 1 | 3 | 21 |
|   Gumdrops | 1 oz. | 100 | T | T | 25 |
|   Marshmallows | 1 oz. | 90 | 1 | T | 23 |
|   Mints, uncoated | 1 oz. | 105 | T | 1 | 25 |
| Chocolate, baking | 1 oz. | 145 | 3 | 15 | 8 |
| Chocolate, semisweet | 1 oz. | 145 | 1 | 10 | 16 |
| Chocolate topping | 1 oz. | 125 | 2 | 5 | 20 |
| Corn muffin | 1 | 125 | 3 | 4 | 19 |

| KINDS OF FOOD | AMOUNT | FOOD ENERGY (Calories) | PROTEIN (Grams) | FAT (Grams) | CARBOHYDRATES (Grams) |
|---|---|---|---|---|---|
| Crackers, graham | 4 | 110 | 2 | 2 | 20 |
| Crackers, saltine | 4 | 50 | 1 | 1 | 8 |
| Custard, baked | 1 cup | 305 | 14 | 15 | 29 |
| Danish pastry (4¼" diam.) | 1 | 275 | 5 | 15 | 30 |
| Doughnut | 1 | 205 | 3 | 11 | 16 |
| Fig bar | 1 | 50 | 1 | 1 | 11 |
| Gelatin dessert | 1 cup | 140 | 4 | 0 | 34 |
| Honey | 1 tbsp. | 65 | T | 0 | 17 |
| Ice cream | 1 cup | 270 | 5 | 14 | 32 |
| Ice milk | 1 cup | 185 | 5 | 6 | 29 |
| Jams and preserves | 1 tbsp. | 55 | T | T | 14 |
| Macaroni, plain | 1 cup | 190 | 7 | 1 | 39 |
| Macaroni w/cheese | 1 cup | 430 | 17 | 22 | 40 |
| Muffin | 1 | 120 | 3 | 4 | 17 |
| Noodles | 1 cup | 200 | 7 | 2 | 37 |
| Pancake (4" diam.) | 1 | 50 | 2 | 2 | 9 |
| Pies (⅐ wedges of 9" pie.): | | | | | |
|   Apple | 1 | 345 | 3 | 15 | 51 |
|   Lemon meringue | 1 | 305 | 4 | 12 | 45 |
|   Mince | 1 | 365 | 3 | 16 | 56 |
|   Pecan | 1 | 495 | 6 | 27 | 61 |
| Pizza, cheese (⅛ piece) | 1 | 145 | 6 | 4 | 22 |
| Popcorn, plain | 1 cup | 25 | 1 | T | 5 |
| Popcorn, buttered | 1 cup | 40 | 1 | 2 | 5 |
| Popcorn, caramel | 1 cup | 135 | 2 | 1 | 30 |
| Popsicle | 1 | 70 | 0 | 0 | 18 |
| Pretzel, thin twisted | 1 | 25 | 1 | T | 8 |
| Pudding, chocolate | 1 cup | 385 | 8 | 12 | 67 |
| Pudding, tapioca | 1 cup | 220 | 8 | 8 | 28 |
| Roll, frankfurter | 1 | 120 | 3 | 2 | 21 |
| Sherbet | 1 cup | 260 | 2 | 2 | 59 |
| Spaghetti, plain | 1 cup | 155 | 5 | 1 | 32 |
| Spaghetti, tomato & cheese | 1 cup | 260 | 9 | 9 | 37 |
| Sugar, white granular | 1 tbsp. | 45 | 0 | 0 | 12 |
| Syrup | 1 tbsp. | 60 | 0 | 0 | 15 |
| Waffle (7" diam.) | 1 | 205 | 7 | 8 | 27 |
| Whipped cream | 1 tbsp. | 10 | T | 1 | T |
| **FRUITS AND FRUIT JUICES** | | | | | |
| Apple, raw (2¾ in. dia.) | 1 | 80 | T | 1 | 20 |
| Apple juice | 1 cup | 120 | T | T | 30 |
| Applesauce, sweetened | 1 cup | 230 | T | T | 61 |
| Apricots, raw | 3 | 55 | 1 | T | 14 |
| Apricots, canned in syrup | 1 cup | 220 | 2 | T | 57 |
| Apricots, dried, uncooked | 1 cup | 340 | 7 | 1 | 86 |
| Avocado, raw | 1 | 370 | 5 | 37 | 13 |
| Banana, raw | 1 | 100 | 1 | T | 26 |
| Blackberries, raw | 1 cup | 85 | 2 | 1 | 19 |
| Blueberries, raw | 1 cup | 90 | 1 | 1 | 22 |
| Cantaloupe, raw | ½ | 80 | 2 | T | 20 |
| Cherries, canned | 1 cup | 105 | 2 | T | 26 |
| Cranberry juice, canned | 1 cup | 165 | T | T | 42 |
| Cranberry sauce, sweet | 1 cup | 405 | T | 1 | 104 |
| Dates, pitted | 1 cup | 490 | 4 | 1 | 130 |
| Fruit cocktail, canned | 1 cup | 195 | 1 | T | 50 |
| Grapefruit, raw | ½ | 50 | 1 | T | 13 |
| Grapefruit, canned | 1 cup | 180 | 2 | T | 45 |
| Grapefruit juice | 1 cup | 95 | 1 | T | 23 |

| KINDS OF FOOD | AMOUNT | FOOD ENERGY (Calories) | PROTEIN (Grams) | FAT (Grams) | CARBOHYDRATES (Grams) |
|---|---|---|---|---|---|
| Grape juice, bottled | 1 cup | 165 | T | T | 42 |
| Grapes, raw | 1 cup | 70 | 1 | 1 | 16 |
| Lemon, raw | 1 | 20 | 1 | T | 6 |
| Lemonade | 1 cup | 105 | T | T | 28 |
| Limeade | 1 cup | 100 | T | T | 27 |
| Orange, raw | 1 | 65 | 1 | T | 16 |
| Orange juice | 1 cup | 110 | 2 | T | 26 |
| Peach, raw | 1 | 40 | 1 | T | 10 |
| Peaches, canned in syrup | 1 cup | 200 | T | T | 51 |
| Pear, raw | 1 | 100 | 1 | 1 | 25 |
| Pears, canned in syrup | 1 cup | 195 | T | T | 50 |
| Pineapple, raw, diced | 1 cup | 80 | 1 | T | 21 |
| Pineapple, canned in syrup | 1 cup | 190 | 1 | T | 49 |
| Pineapple juice | 1 cup | 140 | 1 | T | 34 |
| Plum, raw | 1 | 30 | T | T | 8 |
| Prunes, cooked | 1 cup | 255 | 2 | 1 | 67 |
| Prune juice | 1 cup | 195 | 1 | T | 49 |
| Raisins (½ oz. package) | 1 pkg. | 40 | T | T | 11 |
| Raspberries, red, raw | 1 cup | 70 | 1 | 2 | 17 |
| Rhubarb, cooked with sugar | 1 cup | 380 | 1 | T | 97 |
| Strawberries, raw | 1 cup | 55 | 1 | 1 | 13 |
| Watermelon, wedge 4"x8" | 1 | 110 | 2 | 1 | 27 |

**MEAT, CHEESE, EGGS, POULTRY, FISH**

| KINDS OF FOOD | AMOUNT | FOOD ENERGY (Calories) | PROTEIN (Grams) | FAT (Grams) | CARBOHYDRATES (Grams) |
|---|---|---|---|---|---|
| Bacon (slices) | 2 | 85 | 4 | 8 | T |
| Beef, dried or chipped | 2½ oz. | 145 | 24 | 4 | T |
| Beef, hamburger | 3 oz. | 235 | 20 | 17 | 0 |
| Beef, roast (lean only) | 3 oz. | 210 | 25 | 12 | 0 |
| Beef, steak, broiled | 3 oz. | 220 | 24 | 13 | 0 |
| Beef potpie (4¼" diam.) | 1 | 515 | 21 | 30 | 39 |
| Bologna (slices) | 2 | 170 | 6 | 16 | 1 |
| Cheese: | | | | | |
| American | 1 oz. | 105 | 6 | 9 | T |
| American spread | 1 oz. | 82 | 5 | 6 | 2 |
| Blue or Roquefort | 1 oz. | 105 | 6 | 8 | 1 |
| Cheddar | 1 oz. | 115 | 7 | 9 | 1 |
| Cottage | 1 cup | 235 | 28 | 10 | 6 |
| Cream | 1 oz. | 100 | 2 | 10 | 1 |
| Parmesan | 1 oz. | 130 | 12 | 9 | 1 |
| Yogurt | 1 cup | 140 | 8 | 7 | 11 |
| Chicken, broiled | 3 oz. | 115 | 20 | 3 | 0 |
| Chicken, fried | 3 oz. | 215 | 26 | 10 | 2 |
| Chicken potpie (9" diam.) | ⅓ | 545 | 23 | 31 | 42 |
| Chili con carne w/beans | 1 cup | 340 | 19 | 16 | 31 |
| Corned beef (canned) | 3 oz. | 185 | 22 | 10 | 0 |
| Egg, scrambled in fat | 1 | 95 | 6 | 7 | 1 |
| Egg, whole (boiled) | 1 | 80 | 6 | 6 | T |
| Fish and seafood: | | | | | |
| Clams, raw | 3 oz. | 65 | 11 | 1 | 2 |
| Fish sticks | 3 oz. | 150 | 15 | 9 | 6 |
| Haddock, fried | 3 oz. | 140 | 17 | 5 | 5 |
| Lobster, canned | 3 oz. | 80 | 16 | 1 | T |
| Oysters, raw | 1 cup | 160 | 20 | 4 | 8 |
| Salmon, canned | 3 oz. | 120 | 17 | 5 | 0 |
| Sardines, canned | 3 oz. | 175 | 20 | 9 | 0 |
| Tuna, canned | 3 oz. | 170 | 25 | 7 | 0 |
| Ham, baked | 3 oz. | 185 | 25 | 8 | 0 |
| Hot dog (frankfurter) | 2 oz. | 170 | 7 | 16 | 1 |
| Lamb, chop (broiled) | 3.1 oz. | 360 | 18 | 32 | 0 |
| Lamb, leg (roasted) | 3 oz. | 235 | 22 | 16 | 0 |
| Liver, beef (fried) | 3 oz. | 195 | 22 | 9 | 5 |
| Luncheon ham (canned) | slice | 175 | 9 | 15 | 1 |
| Pork, chop | 2.7 oz. | 305 | 19 | 25 | 0 |
| Pork, roast | 3 oz. | 310 | 21 | 24 | 0 |
| Pork, sausage links | 2 | 120 | 4 | 12 | T |
| Salami | 3 oz. | 450 | 20 | 40 | T |
| Veal, cutlet | 3 oz. | 185 | 23 | 9 | 0 |
| Veal, roast | 3 oz. | 230 | 23 | 14 | 0 |

**VEGETABLES AND NUTS**

| KINDS OF FOOD | AMOUNT | FOOD ENERGY (Calories) | PROTEIN (Grams) | FAT (Grams) | CARBOHYDRATES (Grams) |
|---|---|---|---|---|---|
| Almonds, shelled, chopped | 1 cup | 775 | 24 | 70 | 25 |
| Asparagus | 1 cup | 30 | 3 | T | 5 |
| Beans, green | 1 cup | 30 | 2 | T | 7 |
| Beans, lima | 1 cup | 260 | 16 | 1 | 49 |
| Beans, navy | 1 cup | 210 | 14 | 1 | 38 |
| Beans and pork (canned) | 1 cup | 310 | 16 | 7 | 48 |
| Beets | 1 cup | 55 | 2 | T | 12 |
| Broccoli | 1 cup | 40 | 5 | T | 7 |
| Brussels sprouts | 1 cup | 55 | 6 | 1 | 10 |
| Cabbage, cooked | 1 cup | 30 | 2 | T | 6 |
| Cabbage, raw | 1 cup | 15 | 1 | T | 4 |
| Carrot, raw (7" long) | 1 | 30 | 1 | T | 7 |
| Carrots, cooked | 1 cup | 50 | 1 | T | 11 |
| Cashew nuts | 1 cup | 785 | 24 | 64 | 41 |
| Cauliflower, cooked | 1 cup | 31 | 3 | T | 6 |
| Celery, diced, raw | 1 cup | 20 | 1 | T | 5 |
| Coconut, grated | 1 cup | 275 | 3 | 28 | 8 |
| Collards | 1 cup | 65 | 7 | 1 | 10 |
| Corn, canned (whole kernel) | 1 cup | 175 | 5 | 1 | 43 |
| Corn, sweet | 1 ear | 70 | 2 | 1 | 16 |
| Cucumber, peeled | 1 | 20 | 1 | T | 5 |
| Lettuce, iceberg (head) | 1 | 70 | 5 | T | 16 |
| Mushrooms, raw | 1 cup | 20 | 2 | T | 3 |
| Onion, cooked | 1 cup | 60 | 3 | T | 14 |
| Onion, raw (2½" diam.) | 1 | 40 | 2 | T | 10 |
| Parsnips | 1 cup | 100 | 2 | 1 | 23 |
| Peanut butter | 1 tbsp. | 95 | 4 | 8 | 3 |
| Peanuts, roasted | 1 cup | 840 | 38 | 72 | 27 |
| Peas, green, canned | 1 cup | 150 | 8 | 1 | 29 |
| Pecan halves | 1 cup | 810 | 11 | 84 | 17 |
| Pepper, green, raw | 1 pod | 15 | 1 | T | 4 |
| Pickle, sweet | 1 | 20 | T | T | 5 |
| Potato, baked | 1 | 145 | 4 | T | 33 |
| Potato, boiled | 1 | 105 | 3 | T | 23 |
| Potato, french-fry pieces | 10 | 135 | 2 | 7 | 18 |
| Potato, mashed | 1 cup | 135 | 4 | 2 | 27 |
| Potato chips | 10 | 115 | 1 | 8 | 10 |
| Radishes, raw | 10 | 10 | 1 | T | 2 |
| Rice, cooked | 1 cup | 225 | 4 | T | 50 |
| Sauerkraut, canned | 1 cup | 40 | 2 | T | 9 |
| Spinach | 1 cup | 40 | 5 | T | 6 |
| Sweet potato, baked | 1 | 160 | 2 | 1 | 37 |
| Tomato, raw (3" diam.) | 1 | 40 | 2 | T | 9 |
| Tomato catsup | 1 tbsp. | 15 | T | T | 4 |
| Tomato juice | 1 cup | 45 | 2 | T | 10 |
| Tomatoes, canned | 1 cup | 50 | 2 | T | 10 |
| Turnip greens | 1 cup | 30 | 3 | T | 5 |
| Turnips, diced | 1 cup | 35 | 1 | T | 8 |
| Walnuts, black | 1 cup | 785 | 26 | 74 | 19 |

**SALAD DRESSINGS, SAUCES, AND SOUPS**

| KINDS OF FOOD | AMOUNT | FOOD ENERGY (Calories) | PROTEIN (Grams) | FAT (Grams) | CARBOHYDRATES (Grams) |
|---|---|---|---|---|---|
| Barbecue sauce | 1 cup | 230 | 4 | 17 | 20 |
| Bean with pork soup | 1 cup | 170 | 8 | 6 | 22 |
| Beef broth | 1 cup | 30 | 5 | 0 | 3 |
| Bouillon cube | 1 | 5 | 1 | T | T |
| Cream of chicken soup | 1 cup | 180 | 7 | 10 | 15 |
| Cream of mushroom soup | 1 cup | 215 | 7 | 14 | 16 |
| Cream of tomato soup | 1 cup | 175 | 7 | 7 | 23 |
| Salad dressings: | | | | | |
| Blue cheese | 1 tbsp. | 75 | 1 | 8 | 1 |
| French | 1 tbsp. | 65 | T | 6 | 3 |
| Mayonnaise | 1 tbsp. | 100 | T | 11 | T |
| Thousand Island | 1 tbsp. | 80 | T | 8 | 2 |
| Tartar sauce | 1 tbsp. | 75 | T | 8 | 1 |
| Tomato soup | 1 cup | 90 | 2 | 3 | 16 |
| Vegetarian soup | 1 cup | 80 | 2 | 2 | 13 |
| White sauce | 1 cup | 405 | 10 | 31 | 22 |

# FOOD IS THE SOURCE OF HEALTH

Source: U.S. Departments of Agriculture and Health and Human Services; *Food Is More Than Just Something To Eat*

In this land of plenty, millions of Americans aren't eating wisely.

The problem is not that Americans haven't enough to eat, but that they eat too many of the wrong things or too little of the right.

*Food is what you eat; nutrition is how your body uses food.* And if you aren't eating foods to meet your bodily needs, you may be suffering from poor nutrition. Some of the damages caused by severe malnutrition may be irreversible.

## FOOD IS THE BASIS OF LIFE

Food is the source of health and well-being, gives you the energy you need for everyday living, affects your weight and height and even your strength to a great extent.

In other words, everything in life begins with food, and there is much to the saying "You are what you eat."

Food contains protein, carbohydrates, fats, vitamins, minerals, and water. All of these are nutrients; that is, they nourish the body.

The important thing to remember is that no single food does everything and all foods have something to offer. A variety of different types of food will provide all the nutrients most of us need.

## PROTEIN

After water and possibly fat, protein is the most plentiful substance in the body. The substances, called enzymes, which control the processes that keep the body working are made of protein.

Protein is also part of the hemoglobin molecule in red blood cells that carries oxygen into the system.

The antibodies in the bloodstream that fight off disease and infection are also protein.

Another important use of protein in the body is for building the muscle tissue that holds the bone structure together and provides the strength to move and work. *Most Americans get more than enough protein.*

Where is protein found? Meat, poultry, fish, milk, cheese, and eggs provide good quantities of it. Bread and cereal are also important sources.

And such vegetables as soybeans, chickpeas, dry beans, and peanuts are also good sources of protein. You do not have to load up on meat, poultry, or eggs to get enough protein in your diet.

Combining cereal or vegetable foods with a little milk, cheese, or other animal protein can provide good protein in your diet.

For example, eat cereal with milk, rice with fish, spaghetti with meatballs, or simply drink a glass of milk during a meal. All these combinations provide the high-quality protein the body needs.

## FATS

Fats provide energy and add flavor and variety to foods. They make meals more satisfying.

Fats carry vitamins A, D, E, and K and are essential parts of the structure of the cells that make up the body's tissues.

Our body fat protects vital organs by providing a cushion around them.

Fats are plentiful in butter, margarine, shortening, salad oils, cream, most cheeses, mayonnaise, salad dressings, nuts, and bacon.

## CARBOHYDRATES

Carbohydrates are starches and sugars found in cereal grains, fruits, vegetables, and sugar added to foods for sweetening.

Carbohydrates are the major source of energy in the diet. Wheat, oats, corn, and rice—and the foods made from them, such as bread, spaghetti, macaroni, noodles, or grits—provide starch along with other important nutrients. So do potatoes, sweet potatoes, and vegetables such as peas, dry beans, peanuts, and soybeans.

Most of the other vegetables contain smaller amounts of carbohydrates.

Carbohydrates in vegetables are usually in the form of starch; in fruits they occur as sugar. Candies, jams, molasses, and syrups are primarily sugar.

## WATER

Water is a vitally important nutrient. Water stands next to air in importance to life. You can get along for days, even weeks, without food but you can live only a few days without water.

Water is necessary for all the processes of digestion.

Nutrients are dissolved in water so they may pass through the intestinal wall and into the bloodstream for use throughout the body.

Water carries waste out of the body and also helps to regulate body temperature.

The body's most obvious source of water is the water a person drinks, but some is produced by the body's burning of food for energy. Coffee and tea are mostly water, and so are fruit juices and milk.

Soup is a source of water, and so are many fruits and vegetables. Even meat can be up to 80% water.

## MINERALS

The most abundant mineral in the body is calcium and, except for iron, it is the most likely to be inadequate in the diets of many age groups.

From the age of 9, the diets of girls and women may lack as much as 25% to 30% of the calcium they need.

Almost all calcium, and most phosphorus, which works closely with calcium in the body, is in bones and teeth.

The other minerals play a vital role in tissue and body fluids. Soft tissue, or muscle, especially has a high phosphorus content. Calcium is required for blood to clot and for the heart to function normally. The nervous system does not work properly when calcium levels in the blood are below normal.

People who buy from the milk counter are stocking up on calcium supplies.

In the U.S. we rely on milk as a basic source of calcium. Two cups of milk, or an equivalent amount of cheese or other dairy products except butter, go a long way toward supplying all the calcium needed for the day.

But milk is not the only source. Dark-green leafy vegetables like collards, mustard greens, or turnip greens provide some calcium, and salmon and sardines supply useful amounts of it if the very tiny bones are eaten.

## IRON

Iron is another essential mineral. Women of childbearing age require more iron than men do.

The diets of infants and pregnant women may need special attention to see that they contain the iron needed.

Unfortunately, only a few foods provide iron in very useful amounts. However, liver, heart, kidney, and most lean meats are generously supplied with it. So are shellfish, particularly oysters.

Whole-grain and enriched breads and cereals can provide 20% to 25% or more of the daily iron need.

Dark-green leafy vegetables are also sources of iron.

## IODINE

The most important fact about iodine is that a deficiency of it can cause goiter—a swelling of the thyroid gland. The most practical ways to be sure of getting enough iodine are to use iodized salt regularly and to add seafood to the diet whenever possible.

## OTHER ESSENTIAL ELEMENTS

Calcium, iron, and iodine are not the only minerals you need. Most of the others—zinc, copper, sodium, potassium, magnesium, and phosphorus—are widely available in so many foods that a little variety in selecting groceries takes care of them easily. Magnesium, for example, is abundant in nuts, whole-grain products, dry beans, and dark-green vegetables.

Phosphorus shows up in the same foods that supply you with protein and calcium, although leafy vegetables contain little phosphorus.

## FLUORINE

Fluorine—an element that helps protect teeth from decay—is not so readily found in food. Many metropolitan areas add minute amounts of fluorine to local sources of drinking water.

## VITAMINS

Scientists know of a dozen or more vitamins that you must have to enjoy good health. Ordinarily, you can get them from a well-chosen assortment of everyday foods.

A few of these vitamins are of great importance, and you should know what foods provide them.

## VITAMIN A

Vitamin A plays a very important role in eye function, and in keeping the skin and mucous membranes resistant to infection.

Although vitamin A occurs only in foods of animal origin, the deep-yellow and dark-green vegetables and fruits supply a material—carotene—that your body can turn into vitamin A.

Vegetables and fruits can easily supply all the vitamin A you need. Such items as collards, turnip greens, kale, carrots, squash, and sweet potatoes can more than take care of daily needs; yellow peaches, apricots, cantaloupe, and papayas also help.

Many people, however, do not regularly eat these foods.

Liver is an excellent source of vitamin A. A 2-ounce serving of cooked beef liver provides more than 30,000 international units of the vitamin. That amounts to six times more vitamin A than you would need during the day. Kidney is also an excellent source of vitamin A.

There are plenty of other sources of vitamin A. Whole milk is a source, but skim milk doesn't have any vitamin A unless it is fortified—that is, vitamin A has been added to it.

Cheese made from whole milk, and margarine enriched with vitamin A, both supply this vitamin.

## THE B VITAMINS

Three of the best-known vitamins—riboflavin, thiamin, and niacin—release the

**FOOD IS THE SOURCE OF HEALTH** *(continued)*
energy in food. They also have a role in the nervous system, keep the digestive system working calmly, and help maintain healthy skin.

Vitamin $B_2$ (riboflavin) is easy to find and extremely important to your diet. It is plentifully supplied by meats, milk, whole-grain or enriched breads, and cereals.

Organ meats (liver, kidney, etc.) also supply this vitamin.

A lack of thiamin (vitamin $B_1$) causes beriberi. Fortunately, this disease is now almost nonexistent in the U.S., although it is still detected in some alcoholics.

Thiamin is abundant in only a few foods. Lean pork is one. Dry beans and peas, some organ meats, and some nuts supply some thiamin.

Whole-grain and enriched cereals and breads are also dependable sources of the vitamin.

Niacin can be found in whole-grain and enriched cereals, meat and meat products, and peas and beans.

Other B vitamins such as $B_6$, $B_{12}$, and folacin are needed to maintain normal hemoglobin, the substance in blood that carries oxygen to the tissues. The signs of $B_{12}$ deficiency include soreness of the mouth and tongue, numbness and tingling in the hands and legs, anemia, and loss of coordination.

Folacin is available in many foods but in small quantities.

## VITAMIN C

Vitamin C, ascorbic acid, is not completely understood, but it is considered important in helping to maintain the cementing material that holds body cells together.

The citrus-fruit juice you may have for breakfast can give you more than half of the vitamin C needed for the day.

In fact, unless good foods are consciously avoided, the rest of the fruits and vegetables eaten during the day will help to provide the vitamin C required.

Potatoes and sweet potatoes provide helpful amounts of vitamin C, and so do tomatoes and peppers. In addition, green vegetables such as broccoli, turnip greens, raw cabbage, and collards make a contribution of vitamin C.

## VITAMIN D

Although few foods contain vitamin D, it is readily available in milk fortified with it. Sunlight enables the body to produce vitamin D if it shines directly on the skin.

Vitamin D is important in building strong bones and teeth and is needed throughout the growth period.

Without vitamin D the body cannot absorb the calcium supplied by food. For this reason milk is often fortified with vitamin D.

Adults rarely need more vitamin D than they get in food and from the sun. However, infants and young children sometimes do not get enough.

A disease called rickets results from a lack of vitamin D. Children who suffer from this disease have absorbed too little calcium. Their bodies cannot form strong and rigid bones, and consequently they may have enlarged joints, bowed legs, knock-knees, or beaded ribs.

On the other hand, too much vitamin D can be dangerous. This causes a calcium overload in the blood and tissues. Infants given too much vitamin D may develop calcium deposits in the kidneys and end up with permanent kidney damage.

## VITAMIN E

Vitamin E is known to be essential, but its exact role in the body is not fully understood by scientists.

Vitamin E is abundant in vegetable oils and margarine and is contained in such foods as wheat germ and lettuce.

A diet usually does not lack in vitamin E if it regularly includes fruits, vegetables, vegetable oil, milk, meat, and eggs.

## VITAMIN K

Vitamin K is essential for the manufacture of a substance that helps blood to clot. Vitamin K is widely distributed in a variety of foods such as the green and leafy vegetables, tomatoes, cauliflower, egg yolks, soybean oil, and any kind of liver.

## NUTRIENTS AND ENERGY

Almost all foods provide energy—some more than others.

This energy is measured in calories. Foods that are rich in fats, starches, or sugars contain large amounts of calories—or energy.

Fat is the most concentrated source of energy. Ounce for ounce, it provides more than twice as much energy as protein or the carbohydrates.

Foods that contain a lot of water, like watermelon and cucumbers, have few calories because water, which makes up most of their weight, provides no calories and therefore no energy.

When you eat a diet that furnishes more energy—or calories—than you need, the excess supply is stored in the body as fat. And when you continue to overeat you become overweight or fat.

When you eat less calories than the body uses, you lose weight.

# HOW TO STRETCH YOUR FOOD DOLLAR

You can save a great deal of money on food if you shop carefully and cautiously.

Here are some general rules for feeding your family at less cost.

**1. Learn the facts about basic nutrition.** Then you will know how much protein your family needs each day and what foods provide it. You will also understand how to meet the daily minimum requirements of vitamins and minerals. See pages 398-401.

**2. Plan the week's menu ahead of time.** If you shop only once or twice a week instead of every day, you will spend less. Impulse buying of exotic foods will be kept to a minimum.

**3. Shop around for the best prices.** Special sale prices in one store can be attractive enough to make you overlook the fact that the prices of staples, bread, and milk are higher than those in another store.

**4. Watch for specials and sales.** Read supermarket advertisements in the newspapers on Wednesday and Thursday. These advertisements offer bargains from 6% to 34% below regular prices. It often pays to buy in quantity if the items will keep.

**5. Privately labeled foods in supermarket chains usually cost less.** They are often as good as well-known brands.

**6. Learn how to store foods properly.** Waste through spoilage can be a constant drain on your food budget. For example, use frozen foods as quickly as possible, and do not let them thaw before putting them in your freezer. Remove the store wrappings from meat and store it in a covered dish. If you freeze meat, wrap it *tightly* in foil or other material to prevent freezer burn.

**7. Save on meat costs.** Remember that all meat has about the same nutritional value. Lamb chops, T-bone steak, and veal cost more because they are tender and may have superior flavor.

But there are some meats with a high initial cost that, because they have little waste, are good buys—for example, canned ham and round steak. Chicken is one of the best buys in the market.

Most seafood has risen in price. Substitute cheese and egg dishes once or twice a week. Dry beans and peas are also rich in protein.

**8. Stretch food by using leftovers.** Think in terms of double-duty foods, especially meats. Steaks and chops are usually good for one meal only. On the other hand, leftovers from roasts, chicken, turkey, and ham can be made into a wide variety of dishes.

You can grind leftover meats for hash and casseroles, and cut up leftover poultry, meats, and vegetables for pies, stews, salads, or soups. The stripped carcass of a roasted chicken or turkey and the bones from a beef roast or smoked ham can be boiled to make a rich soup stock.

**9. Do not avoid unfamiliar foods, especially meats, that are on sale, just because you don't know how to cook them.** Consult a reputable cookbook that tells you how to prepare such cuts as lamb's breast, beef and lamb kidneys, tripe, and the like.

**10. Be aware of the high cost of convenience foods.** These include TV dinners, frozen pasta and Chinese dishes, and frozen vegetables prepared with butter sauce and other garnishes. A package of frozen green beans with mushrooms may cost from 11 to 15 cents more than one of plain green beans.

**11. Buying staples in large quantities is usually economical if you have sufficient storage space.** Sugar, flour, cereals, rice, potatoes, and canned foods are often better bargains in large quantities. Buying milk in a two-quart container costs less than two separate containers. Do not overlook the various brands of powdered milk, which offer substantial savings.

**12. If you live in or near a large city, discuss the idea of a cooperative food-buying plan with your friends and neighbors.** A dozen or more families can band together to purchase food supplies wholesale from city markets and meat warehouses at savings up to 40%. In order to do this you must have a central place, such as a garage or basement, in which to store the items. The plan also requires some bookkeeping as well as purchasing and distributing work.

## TOO MUCH SALT CAN KILL

The average American eats from 2 to $2\frac{1}{2}$ teaspoons of salt each day—or about $8\frac{1}{2}$ pounds a year, according to the Food and Drug Administration (FDA). Only about one-third comes from sprinkling salt on your food, about one-third occurs naturally in the food you eat, and about one-third comes as flavoring in processed foods in your diet.

However, the National Research Council of the National Academy of Sciences estimates that an "adequate and safe intake" should be only about one-fourth of the amount normally consumed.

Too much salt in the diet can be especially dangerous to the 10% to 30% of persons who have inherited a tendency to develop high blood pressure, according to studies sponsored by the FDA. High blood pressure often leads to stroke, heart disease, and kidney failure.

## PLANTING AND GROWING GARDEN ANNUALS
Source: U.S. Department of Agriculture

Most garden annuals, plants that live only one year, should be planted outdoors only after the last frost of spring.

To find the approximate date of the last frost in your area, see the table *Freeze Dates and Growing Season for Gardeners* on pages 408–411.

| PLANT | WHEN TO PLANT SEEDS | EXPOSURE | GERMINA-TION TIME (days) | PLANT SPACING (inches) | REMARKS |
|---|---|---|---|---|---|
| Ageratum | After last frost | Semishade or full sun | 5 | 10 to 12 | Pinch tips to encourage branching; remove dead flowers. |
| Balsam | After last frost | Sun | 10 | 12 to 14 | |
| Calendula | Early spring or late fall | Shade or sun | 10 | 8 to 10 | |
| Calliopsis | After last frost | Shade or sun | 8 | 10 to 14 | |
| China aster | After last frost | Shade or sun | 8 | 10 to 12 | Start early in cold frame; resow for prolonged blooming. |
| Cockscomb | After last frost | Shade or sun | 10 | 10 to 12 | |
| Coleus | Sow indoors any time; outdoors after last frost | Sun or partial shade | 10 | 10 to 12 | |
| Cornflower | Early spring | Partial shade | 5 | 12 to 14 | |
| Cosmos | After last frost | Sun | 5 | 10 to 12 | |
| Dahlia | After last frost | Sun | 5 | 12 to 14 | For best blooms, sow several weeks before other annuals. |
| Forget-me-not | Spring or summer; shade in summer | Partial shade | 10 | 10 to 12 | |
| Four-o'clock | After last frost | Sun | 5 | 12 to 14 | Store roots; plant next year. |
| Globe amaranth | Early spring | Sun | 15 | 10 to 12 | |
| Impatiens | Indoors any time; outdoors after last frost | Partial or deep shade | 15 | 10 to 12 | |
| Larkspur | South late fall; North early spring | Sun | 20 | 6 to 8 | Hard to transplant; grow in peat pots. |
| Lupine | Early spring or late fall | Sun | 20 | 6 to 8 | |
| Marigold | After last frost | Sun | 5 | 10 to 14 | High fertility delays bloom. |
| Morning glory | After last frost | Sun | 5 | 24 to 36 | Reseeds itself. |
| Nasturtium | After last frost | Sun | 8 | 8 to 12 | For best flowers, grow in soil of low fertility. |
| Pansy | Spring or summer; shade in summer | Sun or shade | 10 | 6 to 8 | Does best in cool season. |
| Petunia | Early spring indoors | Sun | 10 | 12 to 14 | Transplant outdoors early summer; keep cool. |
| Pink | Early spring through summer; shade in summer | Sun or shade | 5 | 8 to 12 | Start early in spring indoors; keep cool; remove dead flowers. |
| Poppy | Early spring through summer; shade in summer | Sun | 10 | 6 to 10 | Difficult to transplant; start in peat pots; make successive plantings. |
| Portulaca | After last frost or in late fall | Sun | 10 | 10 to 12 | |
| Salpiglossis | Early spring | Sun | 15 | 10 to 12 | Needs supports; avoid cold. |
| Scabiosa | Spring or summer; shade in summer | Sun | 10 | 12 to 14 | Remove old flowers. |
| Scarlet sage | Spring or summer; shade in summer | Sun | 15 | 8 to 12 | |
| Snapdragon | Spring or late fall | Sun | 15 | 6 to 10 | Start cool; pinch tips to encourage branching. |
| Spider plant | Early spring, spring, or fall | Sun | 10 | 12 to 14 | Reseeds freely; pinch to keep plant short; water and fertilize freely. |
| Stock | After last frost | Sun | 5 | 6 to 10 | |
| Strawflower | Early spring | Sun | 5 | 10 to 12 | |
| Summer cypress | Early spring | Sun | 15 | 18 to 24 | |
| Sunflower | After last frost | Sun | 5 | 12 to 14 | |
| Sweet alyssum | Early spring | Sun | 5 | 10 to 12 | Damps off easily; sow in hills; do not thin. |
| Sweetpea | Early spring or late summer through late fall | Sun | 15 | 6 to 8 | Select heat-resistant types. |
| Verbena | After last frost | Sun | 20 | 18 to 24 | Pinch to encourage branching. |
| Vinca | After last frost | Sun | 15 | 10 to 12 | Avoid overwatering. |
| Zinnia | After last frost | Sun | 5 | 8 to 12 | Thin after plants begin to bloom; remove poor-flowering plants. |

## PLANTING AND GROWING VEGETABLES
Source: U.S. Department of Agriculture

Home-grown vegetables picked at the peak of their maturity have a tasty quality seldom found in those bought in a store.

Vegetable gardening requires labor and time. But vegetables grown at home can save on grocery bills as well as provide an enjoyable hobby.

Be cautious about how large a garden you plant the first time. A small well-kept garden will give you more enjoyment than a large neglected one.

Even though you live in a one-room apartment, you can have a vegetable garden in containers on a windowsill or balcony.

If you use plastic containers, allow for drainage by boring several small holes in the side of the container near the bottom. Put about half an inch of coarse gravel in the bottom of the

container before filling it with soil.

The inexperienced gardener should choose only a few crops to plant the first year.

When you buy seeds for your garden, check to make sure they are stamped with this year's date. Old seed germinates poorly.

You can get a jump on the growing season by planting your seeds indoors, and then transplanting the plants to your garden when the weather is warmer.

The vegetables suggested in the table below all can be grown in a minigarden. Vegetables such as corn and potatoes take a great deal of space in order to provide a worthwhile harvest.

The approximate date of the last spring frost in your area can be found in the table *Freeze Dates and Growing Season for Gardeners* on pages 408–411.

| VEGETABLE | PLANTING | | | GROWING | COMMENTS |
|---|---|---|---|---|---|
| | Weeks before frost-free date | Depth of seeds | Space between plants | Days from seed to harvest | |
| Beets | 2 to 4 weeks | ½ in. | 2 to 3 in. | 50 to 60 days | Tolerates partial shade; thin plants when 6 to 8 inches high. |
| Cabbage | 4 to 6 weeks | ½ in. | 12 to 18 in. | 65 to 120 days | Tolerates partial shade; can also be set out for a fall crop. |
| Carrots | 2 to 4 weeks | ½ in. | 2 to 3 in. | 65 to 80 days | Tolerates partial shade; for several harvests make plantings at 3-week intervals until 3 months before fall freezing date. |
| Chives | 4 to 6 weeks | ½ in. | 2 to 3 in. between clusters | 60 to 70 days | Grow in partial shade; bulbs should be divided occasionally so they do not get too thick. |
| Cucumbers | 1 week after frost-free date | ½ in. | 18 in. | 70 to 80 days | Need full sunlight and hot weather; start seeds indoors 3 weeks before time to set out. |
| Eggplant | See comments | ½ in. | 18 in. | 100 to 140 days | Start seeds indoors 8 to 9 weeks before planting outdoors; set out on frost-free date in warm soil; needs full sunlight; cover plants during cool weather. |
| Leaf lettuce | 4 to 6 weeks | ¼ in. | 4 to 6 in. | 30 to 35 days | Tolerates partial shade and temperatures as low as 28° F.; make several later plantings for summer lettuce. |
| Mustard greens | 2 to 4 weeks | ¼ in. | 4 to 5 in. | 35 to 40 days | Make plantings at 10-day intervals for successive crops; tolerate partial shade. |
| Onions | 4 to 6 weeks | 1 to 1½ in. | 2 to 3 in. | 100 to 120 days | Green onions grow in partial shade; mature bulbs need full sun; onions need lots of water. |
| Parsley | 4 to 6 weeks | ¼ in. | 6 to 8 in. | 80 to 85 days | Does well in partial shade; start seeds indoors, soaking them overnight before planting; keep soil moist to help seeds germinate. |
| Peppers | 1 week after frost-free date | ½ in. | 14 to 18 in. | 110 to 120 days | Require full sunlight and hot weather; start seeds indoors 5 to 6 weeks before outdoor planting. |
| Radishes | 2 to 4 weeks | ½ in. | 1 in. | 22 to 35 days | Do well in partial shade; cannot withstand heat; make several plantings at 1-week intervals. |
| Summer squash | See comments | 1 to 2 in. | 18 in. | 50 to 60 days | Plant on frost-free date; does best in full sunlight; plant bush types. |
| Tomatoes | See comments | ½ in. | 14 to 18 in. | 55 to 100 days | Start seeds 5 to 7 weeks before transplanting on frost-free date; require full sunlight and warm weather. |
| Turnips | 4 to 6 weeks | ½ in. | 3 to 4 in. | 30 to 80 days | Tolerate partial shade; thin when plants are large enough to use for greens, leaving others to mature as vegetables. |

# FREEZE DATES AND GROWING SEASON FOR GARDENERS

Gardeners and farmers need to know the approximate date they can expect the last freezing day in the spring so they can schedule when to set out plants susceptible to frost. The length of the growing season—the time until the first freezing day in the fall—helps determine what kinds of flowers or vegetables can be grown in a certain climate.

Information in the following table comes from the *Annual Summary of Climatological Data,* National Oceanic and Atmospheric Administration.

| LOCATION | LAST SPRING FREEZE | GROWING SEASON | FIRST FALL FREEZE |
|---|---|---|---|
| **ALABAMA** | | | |
| Athens | March 25 | 27 weeks | Oct. 3 |
| Birmingham | March 22 | 33 weeks | Nov. 13 |
| Gadsden | March 22 | 33 weeks | Nov. 12 |
| Haleyville | April 9 | 25 weeks | Oct. 3 |
| Huntsville | March 22 | 33 weeks | Nov. 13 |
| Jasper | April 10 | 25 weeks | Oct. 3 |
| Mobile | Feb. 27 | 40 weeks | Dec. 1 |
| Montgomery | Feb. 28 | 37 weeks | Nov. 13 |
| Ozark | Feb. 27 | 37 weeks | Nov. 13 |
| Pittsview | April 10 | 25 weeks | Oct. 5 |
| Selma | Feb. 27 | 37 weeks | Nov. 13 |
| Tuscaloosa | April 10 | 25 weeks | Oct. 3 |
| **ALASKA** | | | |
| Adak | May 31 | 20 weeks | Oct. 24 |
| Anchorage | May 18 | 18 weeks | Sept. 28 |
| Fairbanks | May 5 | 20 weeks | Sept. 27 |
| Juneau | May 21 | 18 weeks | Sept. 28 |
| Ketchikan | March 31 | 32 weeks | Nov. 12 |
| Kodiak | May 22 | 19 weeks | Oct. 2 |
| Seward | April 26 | 22 weeks | Sept. 29 |
| Sitka | May 25 | 18 weeks | Oct. 3 |
| Wrangell | April 23 | 23 weeks | Oct. 4 |
| **ARIZONA** | | | |
| Bisbee | April 16 | 24 weeks | Oct. 31 |
| Flagstaff | June 9 | 14 weeks | Sept. 16 |
| Mesa | Feb. 9 | 44 weeks | Dec. 15 |
| Nogales | May 21 | 19 weeks | Oct. 31 |
| Phoenix | Jan. 3 | 49 weeks | Dec. 15 |
| Prescott | May 21 | 19 weeks | Oct. 30 |
| Scottsdale | Feb. 21 | 41 weeks | Dec. 10 |
| Tombstone | March 10 | 37 weeks | Nov. 29 |
| Tucson | April 4 | 33 weeks | Nov. 24 |
| Winslow | May 20 | 24 weeks | Nov. 4 |
| **ARKANSAS** | | | |
| Arkadelphia | April 9 | 31 weeks | Nov. 13 |
| El Dorado | March 24 | 34 weeks | Nov. 14 |
| Fayetteville | April 17 | 26 weeks | Oct. 16 |
| Fort Smith | April 9 | 31 weeks | Nov. 14 |
| Helena | April 6 | 32 weeks | Nov. 15 |
| Hot Springs | March 26 | 33 weeks | Nov. 15 |
| Jonesboro | March 25 | 30 weeks | Oct. 22 |
| Little Rock | April 6 | 32 weeks | Nov. 15 |
| Mammoth Spring | April 17 | 26 weeks | Oct. 16 |
| Pine Bluff | March 24 | 34 weeks | Nov. 15 |
| Stuttgart | March 24 | 34 weeks | Nov. 15 |
| Texarkana | March 24 | 34 weeks | Nov. 15 |
| **CALIFORNIA** | | | |
| Bakersfield | Feb. 7 | 46 weeks | Dec. 23 |
| Barstow | April 10 | 33 weeks | Nov. 24 |
| Death Valley | Jan. 5 | 51 weeks | none |
| El Centro | Feb. 6 | 44 weeks | Dec. 11 |
| Eureka | Feb. 23 | 43 weeks | Dec. 23 |
| Fairmont | April 19 | 31 weeks | Nov. 23 |
| Fresno | Feb. 23 | 40 weeks | Dec. 1 |
| Los Angeles | none | 52 weeks | none |
| Modesto | Feb. 7 | 46 weeks | Dec. 23 |
| Oakland | none | 52 weeks | none |
| Palmdale | May 19 | 24 weeks | Oct. 31 |
| **CALIFORNIA** *(continued)* | | | |
| Paradise | March 3 | 42 weeks | Dec. 22 |
| Red Bluff | Feb. 22 | 40 weeks | Nov. 30 |
| Sacramento | Feb. 8 | 46 weeks | Dec. 24 |
| San Bernardino | Jan. 3 | 51 weeks | Dec. 26 |
| San Diego | none | 52 weeks | none |
| San Francisco | Jan. 8 | 50 weeks | Dec. 25 |
| San Jose | Jan. 9 | 46 weeks | Nov. 28 |
| San Rafael | none | 51 weeks | Nov. 30 |
| Santa Rosa | March 9 | 37 weeks | Nov. 26 |
| Stockton | Feb. 9 | 42 weeks | Nov. 30 |
| Woodland | March 9 | 37 weeks | Nov. 23 |
| **COLORADO** | | | |
| Aspen | June 8 | 12 weeks | Sept. 3 |
| Boulder | April 30 | 19 weeks | Sept. 12 |
| Burlington | April 22 | 28 weeks | Nov. 2 |
| Colorado Springs | May 1 | 21 weeks | Sept. 28 |
| Del Norte | June 3 | 17 weeks | Sept. 28 |
| Denver | April 16 | 29 weeks | Oct. 30 |
| Durango | June 9 | 15 weeks | Sept. 23 |
| Grand Junction | April 15 | 29 weeks | Nov. 5 |
| Greeley | April 16 | 24 weeks | Sept. 28 |
| Lakewood | June 8 | 15 weeks | Sept. 12 |
| Manassa | June 10 | 12 weeks | Sept. 3 |
| Pueblo | April 22 | 27 weeks | Oct. 31 |
| **CONNECTICUT** | | | |
| Bridgeport | April 10 | 24 weeks | Oct. 18 |
| Danbury | May 8 | 20 weeks | Sept. 24 |
| Hartford | May 8 | 20 weeks | Sept. 24 |
| Middletown | May 8 | 20 weeks | Sept. 24 |
| New Haven | April 10 | 24 weeks | Oct. 19 |
| Norfolk | May 8 | 20 weeks | Sept. 24 |
| Stamford | May 8 | 20 weeks | Sept. 24 |
| Storrs | May 2 | 22 weeks | Oct. 4 |
| Westbrook | May 9 | 21 weeks | Oct. 3 |
| **DELAWARE** | | | |
| Bridgeville | April 20 | 24 weeks | Oct. 4 |
| Dover | April 7 | 26 weeks | Oct. 3 |
| Georgetown | May 8 | 26 weeks | Oct. 4 |
| Middletown | April 20 | 24 weeks | Oct. 3 |
| Milford | May 8 | 25 weeks | Oct. 3 |
| Wilmington | April 7 | 26 weeks | Oct. 3 |
| **DIST. OF COLUMBIA** | | | |
| Washington | May 8 | 20 weeks | Sept. 24 |
| **FLORIDA** | | | |
| Fort Lauderdale | none | 52 weeks | none |
| Fort Myers | none | 52 weeks | none |
| Gainesville | Feb. 27 | 40 weeks | Dec. 2 |
| Jacksonville | Feb. 27 | 39 weeks | Nov. 14 |
| Key West | none | 52 weeks | none |
| Miami | none | 52 weeks | none |
| Orlando | Feb. 26 | 51 weeks | none |
| St. Augustine | Feb. 27 | 42 weeks | Dec. 18 |
| St. Petersburg | none | 52 weeks | none |
| Tallahassee | Feb. 28 | 37 weeks | Nov. 13 |
| Tampa | Feb. 27 | 51 weeks | none |
| Tavernier | none | 52 weeks | none |
| Titusville | Feb. 26 | 51 weeks | none |

| LOCATION | LAST SPRING FREEZE | GROWING SEASON | FIRST FALL FREEZE |
|---|---|---|---|
| **GEORGIA** | | | |
| Albany | March 1 | 37 weeks | Nov. 13 |
| Athens | March 22 | 31 weeks | Oct. 22 |
| Atlanta | March 22 | 34 weeks | Nov. 13 |
| Augusta | April 10 | 28 weeks | Oct. 21 |
| Brunswick | Feb. 28 | 40 weeks | Dec. 4 |
| Cartersville | April 25 | 23 weeks | Oct. 3 |
| Columbus | Feb. 28 | 37 weeks | Nov. 15 |
| Gainesville | April 7 | 28 weeks | Oct. 22 |
| Moultrie | Feb. 28 | 37 weeks | Nov. 13 |
| Rome | April 10 | 30 weeks | Oct. 3 |
| Savannah | Feb. 28 | 39 weeks | Nov. 28 |
| Valdosta | Feb. 28 | 37 weeks | Nov. 13 |
| **HAWAII** | | | |
| Honolulu | none | 52 weeks | none |
| Kailua | none | 52 weeks | none |
| **IDAHO** | | | |
| Boise | May 16 | 20 weeks | Oct. 5 |
| Idaho Falls | May 31 | 15 weeks | Sept. 13 |
| Lewiston | April 13 | 25 weeks | Oct. 6 |
| Oakley | June 8 | 18 weeks | Oct. 13 |
| Pocatello | May 16 | 17 weeks | Sept. 13 |
| Potlatch | June 9 | 9 weeks | Aug. 13 |
| Twin Falls | May 16 | 20 weeks | Oct. 5 |
| **ILLINOIS** | | | |
| Chicago | May 7 | 21 weeks | Oct. 1 |
| Decatur | April 24 | 23 weeks | Oct. 2 |
| Joliet | May 7 | 20 weeks | Sept. 23 |
| Marion | April 18 | 24 weeks | Oct. 3 |
| Mount Vernon | April 17 | 24 weeks | Oct. 3 |
| Olney | April 17 | 24 weeks | Oct. 3 |
| Peoria | April 24 | 26 weeks | Sept. 23 |
| Quincy | April 9 | 25 weeks | Oct. 2 |
| Rockford | May 7 | 20 weeks | Sept. 22 |
| Springfield | April 9 | 25 weeks | Oct. 2 |
| Urbana | April 24 | 23 weeks | Oct. 2 |
| **INDIANA** | | | |
| Bloomington | April 10 | 25 weeks | Oct. 3 |
| Columbus | May 8 | 21 weeks | Oct. 2 |
| Crawfordsville | May 8 | 21 weeks | Oct. 2 |
| Evansville | April 9 | 25 weeks | Oct. 3 |
| Fort Wayne | May 7 | 20 weeks | Sept. 23 |
| Greencastle | May 7 | 21 weeks | Oct. 2 |
| Hobart | May 10 | 19 weeks | Sept. 23 |
| Indianapolis | May 7 | 21 weeks | Oct. 2 |
| New Castle | May 8 | 20 weeks | Sept. 23 |
| Scottsburg | May 7 | 21 weeks | Oct. 2 |
| South Bend | May 7 | 21 weeks | Oct. 3 |
| **IOWA** | | | |
| Cedar Rapids | May 6 | 20 weeks | Sept. 22 |
| Davenport | April 24 | 23 weeks | Oct. 2 |
| Des Moines | April 15 | 24 weeks | Oct. 1 |
| Mason City | May 6 | 17 weeks | Sept. 3 |
| Oskaloosa | April 24 | 22 weeks | Sept. 22 |
| Pocahontas | May 6 | 20 weeks | Sept. 22 |
| Sioux City | April 16 | 23 weeks | Sept. 22 |
| Waterloo | May 6 | 20 weeks | Sept. 21 |
| **KANSAS** | | | |
| Atchison | April 8 | 30 weeks | Nov. 6 |
| Dodge City | April 16 | 26 weeks | Oct. 15 |
| Fort Scott | April 5 | 31 weeks | Nov. 6 |
| Healy | April 16 | 20 weeks | Sept. 3 |
| Hill City | April 16 | 26 weeks | Sept. 13 |
| Lawrence | April 5 | 31 weeks | Nov. 6 |
| Lincoln | April 16 | 26 weeks | Oct. 15 |
| Mankato | April 16 | 26 weeks | Oct. 15 |

| LOCATION | LAST SPRING FREEZE | GROWING SEASON | FIRST FALL FREEZE |
|---|---|---|---|
| **KANSAS** *(continued)* | | | |
| Topeka | April 15 | 24 weeks | Oct. 1 |
| Wichita | April 15 | 29 weeks | Nov. 6 |
| **KENTUCKY** | | | |
| Ashland | May 8 | 20 weeks | Sept. 23 |
| Danville | April 10 | 25 weeks | Oct. 3 |
| Frankfort | May 8 | 26 weeks | Oct. 3 |
| Lexington | April 25 | 23 weeks | Oct. 2 |
| Louisville | April 9 | 28 weeks | Oct. 21 |
| Middlesboro | May 7 | 26 weeks | Oct. 3 |
| Owensboro | April 9 | 25 weeks | Oct. 3 |
| Somerset | April 25 | 23 weeks | Oct. 3 |
| **LOUISIANA** | | | |
| Alexandria | Feb. 27 | 40 weeks | Dec. 1 |
| Bastrop | March 24 | 37 weeks | Nov. 15 |
| Baton Rouge | Feb. 27 | 37 weeks | Nov. 15 |
| Lafayette | Feb. 26 | 40 weeks | Dec. 1 |
| Monroe | Feb. 26 | 37 weeks | Nov. 14 |
| Natchitoches | Feb. 26 | 37 weeks | Nov. 15 |
| New Orleans | Feb. 27 | 39 weeks | Nov. 27 |
| Shreveport | Feb. 26 | 37 weeks | Nov. 15 |
| **MAINE** | | | |
| Augusta | May 5 | 20 weeks | Sept. 24 |
| Bangor | May 6 | 20 weeks | Sept. 25 |
| Bar Harbor | May 5 | 24 weeks | Oct. 19 |
| Caribou | May 21 | 18 weeks | Sept. 24 |
| Houlton | May 29 | 16 weeks | Sept. 19 |
| Lewiston | May 2 | 23 weeks | Oct. 14 |
| Portland | May 5 | 22 weeks | Oct. 4 |
| **MARYLAND** | | | |
| Annapolis | March 26 | 28 weeks | Oct. 5 |
| Baltimore | March 26 | 25 weeks | Oct. 21 |
| Bittinger | May 8 | 20 weeks | Sept. 23 |
| Boonsboro | April 20 | 27 weeks | Sept. 24 |
| La Plata | May 8 | 21 weeks | Oct. 3 |
| Salisbury | April 11 | 25 weeks | Oct. 4 |
| **MASSACHUSETTS** | | | |
| Amherst | May 8 | 20 weeks | Sept. 24 |
| Boston | April 10 | 27 weeks | Oct. 19 |
| Chester | May 26 | 15 weeks | Sept. 5 |
| Hyannis | May 2 | 24 weeks | Oct. 19 |
| Provincetown | April 20 | 25 weeks | Oct. 14 |
| Springfield | April 26 | 23 weeks | Oct. 4 |
| Stockbridge | May 21 | 18 weeks | Sept. 24 |
| Woods Hole | April 25 | 30 weeks | Nov. 22 |
| Worcester | May 8 | 21 weeks | Oct. 4 |
| **MICHIGAN** | | | |
| Alpena | May 27 | 16 weeks | Sept. 18 |
| Bad Axe | May 8 | 21 weeks | Oct. 2 |
| Detroit | May 7 | 20 weeks | Sept. 22 |
| Escanaba | May 7 | 20 weeks | Sept. 22 |
| Grand Rapids | May 10 | 19 weeks | Sept. 23 |
| Lansing | May 10 | 19 weeks | Sept. 22 |
| Marquette | May 9 | 21 weeks | Oct. 1 |
| Midland | May 8 | 20 weeks | Sept. 22 |
| Muskegon | May 10 | 21 weeks | Oct. 2 |
| Traverse City | May 10 | 19 weeks | Sept. 23 |
| **MINNESOTA** | | | |
| Albert Lea | May 13 | 19 weeks | Sept. 21 |
| Baudette | May 25 | 17 weeks | Sept. 21 |
| Duluth | May 13 | 16 weeks | Sept. 1 |
| Fergus Falls | May 15 | 16 weeks | Sept. 3 |
| Rochester | May 6 | 20 weeks | Sept. 21 |
| St. Cloud | May 25 | 14 weeks | Sept. 1 |
| St. Paul | May 6 | 20 weeks | Sept. 22 |

## FREEZE DATES AND GROWING SEASON FOR GARDENERS *(continued)*

| LOCATION | LAST SPRING FREEZE | GROWING SEASON | FIRST FALL FREEZE |
|---|---|---|---|
| **MINNESOTA** *(continued)* | | | |
| Stillwater | May 23 | 17 weeks | Sept. 22 |
| Tyler | May 7 | 20 weeks | Sept. 22 |
| **MISSISSIPPI** | | | |
| Aberdeen | March 22 | 34 weeks | Nov. 15 |
| Biloxi | Feb. 27 | 35 weeks | Nov. 28 |
| Greenville | March 24 | 34 weeks | Nov. 15 |
| Grenada | April 7 | 32 weeks | Nov. 15 |
| Hattiesburg | Feb. 28 | 37 weeks | Nov. 13 |
| Jackson | March 22 | 34 weeks | Nov. 14 |
| McComb | March 22 | 34 weeks | Nov. 13 |
| Tupelo | April 10 | 25 weeks | Oct. 3 |
| **MISSOURI** | | | |
| Butler | April 17 | 29 weeks | Nov. 6 |
| Cape Girardeau | April 9 | 25 weeks | Oct. 3 |
| Dexter | April 9 | 31 weeks | Nov. 14 |
| Festus | April 24 | 22 weeks | Sept. 23 |
| Jefferson City | April 24 | 23 weeks | Oct. 2 |
| Joplin | March 25 | 32 weeks | Nov. 6 |
| Kansas City | April 5 | 31 weeks | Nov. 6 |
| Poplar Bluff | April 10 | 28 weeks | Oct. 21 |
| St. Joseph | April 17 | 23 weeks | Sept. 22 |
| St. Louis | April 9 | 25 weeks | Oct. 2 |
| Springfield | April 17 | 29 weeks | Nov. 5 |
| **MONTANA** | | | |
| Bigfork | May 17 | 17 weeks | Sept. 13 |
| Billings | May 16 | 19 weeks | Sept. 27 |
| Butte | June 10 | 12 weeks | Sept. 2 |
| Goldbutte | May 23 | 14 weeks | Sept. 1 |
| Great Falls | May 16 | 19 weeks | Sept. 29 |
| Helena | May 16 | 17 weeks | Sept. 13 |
| Missoula | May 31 | 15 weeks | Sept. 13 |
| Shonkin | June 1 | 14 weeks | Sept. 2 |
| **NEBRASKA** | | | |
| Albion | May 3 | 18 weeks | Sept. 3 |
| Dalton | May 22 | 15 weeks | Sept. 3 |
| Grand Island | April 16 | 24 weeks | Sept. 30 |
| Imperial | April 16 | 24 weeks | Sept. 30 |
| Lincoln | April 23 | 23 weeks | Oct. 1 |
| North Platte | May 12 | 16 weeks | Sept. 3 |
| Omaha | April 16 | 24 weeks | Sept. 29 |
| Scottsbluff | May 12 | 16 weeks | Sept. 3 |
| **NEVADA** | | | |
| Carson City | June 8 | 14 weeks | Sept. 12 |
| Duckwater | May 21 | 19 weeks | Sept. 28 |
| Eureka | June 8 | 10 weeks | Aug. 20 |
| Las Vegas | March 4 | 39 weeks | Nov. 30 |
| **NEW HAMPSHIRE** | | | |
| Benton | May 20 | 18 weeks | Sept. 24 |
| Bethlehem | May 21 | 18 weeks | Sept. 24 |
| Concord | May 21 | 18 weeks | Sept. 24 |
| Hanover | May 5 | 20 weeks | Sept. 24 |
| Lancaster | May 20 | 17 weeks | Sept. 17 |
| Lebanon | May 20 | 18 weeks | Sept. 24 |
| Monroe | May 21 | 18 weeks | Sept. 24 |
| Woodstock | May 20 | 18 weeks | Sept. 24 |
| **NEW JERSEY** | | | |
| Atlantic City | April 10 | 27 weeks | Oct. 19 |
| Jersey City | April 10 | 27 weeks | Oct. 19 |
| Moorestown | May 8 | 21 weeks | Oct. 3 |
| Newark | April 10 | 27 weeks | Oct. 19 |
| Sandy Hook | April 10 | 32 weeks | Nov. 23 |
| Trenton | April 10 | 27 weeks | Oct. 19 |

| LOCATION | LAST SPRING FREEZE | GROWING SEASON | FIRST FALL FREEZE |
|---|---|---|---|
| **NEW MEXICO** | | | |
| Alamogordo | April 5 | 30 weeks | Nov. 4 |
| Albuquerque | April 5 | 30 weeks | Oct. 31 |
| Carlsbad | March 25 | 32 weeks | Nov. 5 |
| Gallup | June 10 | 16 weeks | Sept. 28 |
| Mescalero | May 22 | 21 weeks | Oct. 15 |
| San Mateo | May 21 | 23 weeks | Sept. 27 |
| Santa Fe | April 27 | 27 weeks | Oct. 30 |
| Taos | June 9 | 16 weeks | Sept. 27 |
| Thoreau | May 21 | 21 weeks | Oct. 15 |
| **NEW YORK** | | | |
| Albany | May 5 | 20 weeks | Sept. 24 |
| Angelica | May 28 | 17 weeks | Sept. 23 |
| Buffalo | May 8 | 21 weeks | Oct. 3 |
| Cooperstown | May 20 | 18 weeks | Sept. 23 |
| Glens Falls | May 5 | 20 weeks | Sept. 23 |
| New York City | April 10 | 27 weeks | Oct. 19 |
| Newcomb | May 20 | 18 weeks | Sept. 24 |
| Plattsburgh | May 5 | 20 weeks | Sept. 24 |
| Rochester | May 8 | 21 weeks | Oct. 3 |
| Scarsdale | May 8 | 22 weeks | Oct. 8 |
| Syracuse | May 5 | 24 weeks | Oct. 18 |
| Utica | May 5 | 20 weeks | Sept. 24 |
| **NORTH CAROLINA** | | | |
| Asheville | April 9 | 25 weeks | Oct. 3 |
| Boone | May 7 | 21 weeks | Oct. 3 |
| Charlotte | April 10 | 28 weeks | Oct. 20 |
| Greensboro | April 10 | 25 weeks | Oct. 4 |
| Greenville | March 27 | 27 weeks | Oct. 4 |
| Hatteras | March 15 | 39 weeks | Dec. 10 |
| Lenoir | April 7 | 21 weeks | Oct. 3 |
| Raleigh | April 11 | 25 weeks | Oct. 3 |
| Winston-Salem | April 11 | 25 weeks | Oct. 3 |
| **NORTH DAKOTA** | | | |
| Bismarck | May 24 | 14 weeks | Sept. 1 |
| Fargo | May 15 | 18 weeks | Sept. 21 |
| Grand Forks | May 15 | 16 weeks | Sept. 1 |
| Minot | May 17 | 18 weeks | Sept. 21 |
| Sheyenne | May 15 | 16 weeks | Sept. 1 |
| Washburn | May 24 | 22 weeks | Sept. 28 |
| **OHIO** | | | |
| Cadiz | May 7 | 21 weeks | Oct. 1 |
| Carpenter | May 7 | 20 weeks | Sept. 23 |
| Cincinnati | April 9 | 25 weeks | Oct. 3 |
| Cleveland | May 7 | 21 weeks | Oct. 3 |
| Columbus | May 7 | 21 weeks | Oct. 2 |
| Dayton | April 10 | 28 weeks | Oct. 21 |
| Kenton | May 7 | 20 weeks | Sept. 23 |
| Oberlin | May 10 | 19 weeks | Sept. 23 |
| Toledo | May 7 | 20 weeks | Sept. 22 |
| Youngstown | May 8 | 21 weeks | Oct. 3 |
| Zanesville | May 7 | 20 weeks | Sept. 23 |
| **OKLAHOMA** | | | |
| Ada | April 5 | 32 weeks | Nov. 15 |
| Beaver | April 17 | 26 weeks | Oct. 15 |
| Chattanooga | April 5 | 32 weeks | Nov. 15 |
| Clinton | April 4 | 32 weeks | Nov. 12 |
| McAlester | April 5 | 32 weeks | Nov. 14 |
| Meeker | April 6 | 32 weeks | Nov. 14 |
| Oklahoma City | April 5 | 32 weeks | Nov. 14 |
| Ponca City | April 5 | 31 weeks | Nov. 6 |
| Tulsa | March 25 | 33 weeks | Nov. 14 |
| Tuskahoma | April 9 | 27 weeks | Oct. 16 |
| **OREGON** | | | |
| Astoria | April 13 | 36 weeks | Dec. 22 |

| LOCATION | LAST SPRING FREEZE | GROWING SEASON | FIRST FALL FREEZE |
|---|---|---|---|
| **OREGON** (continued) | | | |
| Baker | June 8 | 14 weeks | Sept. 13 |
| Beulah | May 30 | 17 weeks | Sept. 27 |
| Medford | April 26 | 23 weeks | Oct. 5 |
| Pendleton | April 13 | 25 weeks | Oct. 6 |
| Portland | March 18 | 36 weeks | Nov. 28 |
| Salem | May 13 | 21 weeks | Oct. 5 |
| **PENNSYLVANIA** | | | |
| Allentown | May 8 | 20 weeks | Sept. 24 |
| Altoona | May 11 | 19 weeks | Sept. 23 |
| Butler | May 11 | 19 weeks | Sept. 24 |
| Erie | May 8 | 21 weeks | Oct. 3 |
| Harrisburg | April 7 | 26 weeks | Oct. 4 |
| Lewistown | May 8 | 20 weeks | Sept. 24 |
| Montrose | May 12 | 19 weeks | Sept. 23 |
| Philadelphia | April 11 | 27 weeks | Oct. 19 |
| Pittsburgh | April 10 | 25 weeks | Oct. 4 |
| Scranton | May 5 | 20 weeks | Sept. 23 |
| **RHODE ISLAND** | | | |
| Block Island | April 26 | 25 weeks | Oct. 21 |
| Kingston | May 9 | 21 weeks | Oct. 1 |
| Newport | April 26 | 25 weeks | Oct. 19 |
| Providence | April 11 | 27 weeks | Oct. 14 |
| **SOUTH CAROLINA** | | | |
| Charleston | March 15 | 34 weeks | Nov. 9 |
| Columbia | March 18 | 29 weeks | Oct. 4 |
| Darlington | April 7 | 26 weeks | Oct. 4 |
| Greenville | March 25 | 28 weeks | Oct. 5 |
| Greenwood | April 11 | 25 weeks | Oct. 4 |
| Longcreek | March 26 | 26 weeks | Sept. 25 |
| Ridgeland | April 10 | 25 weeks | Oct. 4 |
| Sumter | March 18 | 29 weeks | Oct. 4 |
| **SOUTH DAKOTA** | | | |
| Aberdeen | May 15 | 16 weeks | Sept. 3 |
| Deadwood | June 1 | 13 weeks | Sept. 2 |
| Dupree | May 24 | 18 weeks | Sept. 28 |
| Huron | May 24 | 15 weeks | Sept. 3 |
| Pierre | May 15 | 19 weeks | Sept. 28 |
| Rapid City | May 23 | 18 weeks | Sept. 28 |
| Sioux Falls | May 6 | 17 weeks | Sept. 3 |
| **TENNESSEE** | | | |
| Chattanooga | April 25 | 26 weeks | Oct. 22 |
| Cleveland | April 25 | 26 weeks | Oct. 21 |
| Jackson | April 9 | 31 weeks | Nov. 14 |
| Knoxville | March 22 | 34 weeks | Nov. 15 |
| Memphis | March 24 | 34 weeks | Nov. 15 |
| Nashville | April 9 | 31 weeks | Nov. 14 |
| Waverly | April 25 | 23 weeks | Oct. 2 |
| **TEXAS** | | | |
| Abilene | April 5 | 33 weeks | Nov. 25 |
| Amarillo | April 16 | 29 weeks | Nov. 4 |
| Austin | Feb. 26 | 40 weeks | Nov. 30 |
| Corpus Christi | None | 52 weeks | None |
| Dallas | March 24 | 36 weeks | Nov. 29 |
| El Paso | March 11 | 35 weeks | Nov. 13 |
| Houston | Feb. 26 | 40 weeks | Nov. 30 |
| San Angelo | April 5 | 33 weeks | Nov. 25 |
| San Antonio | Feb. 26 | 39 weeks | Nov. 26 |
| Texarkana | March 25 | 34 weeks | Nov. 15 |
| Waco | March 24 | 36 weeks | Nov. 29 |
| **UTAH** | | | |
| Bonanza | June 10 | 13 weeks | Sept. 12 |
| Cedar City | June 8 | 16 weeks | Sept. 28 |
| Emery | June 10 | 13 weeks | Sept. 12 |
| Ogden | May 20 | 20 weeks | Oct. 6 |

| LOCATION | LAST SPRING FREEZE | GROWING SEASON | FIRST FALL FREEZE |
|---|---|---|---|
| **UTAH** (continued) | | | |
| Park Valley | June 9 | 14 weeks | Sept. 13 |
| Saint George | March 6 | 38 weeks | Nov. 24 |
| Salt Lake City | April 28 | 27 weeks | Nov. 5 |
| **VERMONT** | | | |
| Bellows Falls | May 6 | 20 weeks | Sept. 24 |
| Burlington | May 20 | 18 weeks | Sept. 24 |
| Chelsea | May 21 | 18 weeks | Sept. 23 |
| Montpelier | May 5 | 20 weeks | Sept. 24 |
| Newport | May 20 | 18 weeks | Sept. 24 |
| Rutland | May 7 | 20 weeks | Sept. 24 |
| Woodstock | May 21 | 18 weeks | Sept. 23 |
| **VIRGINIA** | | | |
| Appomattox | April 11 | 25 weeks | Oct. 3 |
| Boykins | April 11 | 25 weeks | Oct. 4 |
| Elkwood | May 8 | 20 weeks | Sept. 24 |
| Lexington | May 7 | 21 weeks | Oct. 3 |
| Lynchburg | April 11 | 25 weeks | Oct. 3 |
| Norfolk | March 25 | 34 weeks | Nov. 16 |
| Richmond | April 11 | 25 weeks | Oct. 3 |
| Winchester | May 8 | 20 weeks | Sept. 24 |
| Wise | May 7 | 21 weeks | Oct. 3 |
| Wytheville | May 8 | 20 weeks | Sept. 24 |
| **WASHINGTON** | | | |
| Aberdeen | April 13 | 36 weeks | Dec. 22 |
| Cougar | April 8 | 37 weeks | Dec. 23 |
| Goldendale | June 9 | 13 weeks | Sept. 11 |
| Hartline | May 16 | 20 weeks | Oct. 3 |
| Olympia | April 14 | 25 weeks | Oct. 6 |
| Pullman | May 16 | 19 weeks | Sept. 27 |
| Spokane | May 16 | 20 weeks | Oct. 5 |
| Tacoma | March 8 | 38 weeks | Nov. 29 |
| Vancouver | April 13 | 29 weeks | Oct. 5 |
| Walla Walla | March 20 | 33 weeks | Nov. 4 |
| Winthrop | May 20 | 17 weeks | Sept. 13 |
| **WEST VIRGINIA** | | | |
| Beckley | May 7 | 20 weeks | Sept. 24 |
| Bluefield | April 10 | 25 weeks | Oct. 2 |
| Charleston | May 7 | 21 weeks | Oct. 2 |
| Clarksburg | May 8 | 20 weeks | Sept. 24 |
| Franklin | May 8 | 20 weeks | Sept. 23 |
| Lewisburg | May 8 | 20 weeks | Sept. 24 |
| Martinsburg | May 8 | 20 weeks | Sept. 24 |
| Morgantown | May 7 | 20 weeks | Sept. 24 |
| Parkersburg | April 10 | 25 weeks | Oct. 3 |
| **WISCONSIN** | | | |
| Antigo | May 26 | 14 weeks | Sept. 1 |
| Beloit | May 7 | 20 weeks | Sept. 22 |
| Cumberland | May 13 | 19 weeks | Sept. 22 |
| Dodge | May 7 | 17 weeks | Sept. 3 |
| Green Bay | April 10 | 23 weeks | Sept. 21 |
| Madison | May 13 | 19 weeks | Sept. 22 |
| Milwaukee | May 10 | 19 weeks | Sept. 22 |
| Platteville | May 7 | 20 weeks | Sept. 22 |
| Stevens Point | May 13 | 19 weeks | Sept. 22 |
| Superior | May 26 | 17 weeks | Sept. 22 |
| West Bend | May 10 | 19 weeks | Sept. 22 |
| **WYOMING** | | | |
| Buffalo | May 16 | 17 weeks | Sept. 13 |
| Cheyenne | May 3 | 21 weeks | Sept. 28 |
| Clark | June 1 | 13 weeks | Sept. 2 |
| Dillinger | June 11 | 12 weeks | Sept. 4 |
| Grass Creek | June 1 | 11 weeks | Aug. 18 |
| Laramie | June 9 | 12 weeks | Sept. 2 |
| Morrisey | May 14 | 17 weeks | Sept. 13 |
| Wamsutter | June 8 | 12 weeks | Sept. 3 |

## CALENDAR OF TRADITIONAL RETAIL SALES IN STORES

Source: Citibank

| MONTH | ITEMS ON SALE |
|---|---|
| January .... | Storewide clearances; beds; cars; Christmas cards; clothing and accessories; cosmetics; decorating accessories; decorations (Christmas); diamonds; fabrics; floor coverings; furniture; furs; infant needs; linens; lingerie; luggage; major appliances (end of month); notions; radios; stationery; television sets; tires; wrappings. |
| February ... | Storewide sales on Lincoln's and Washington's birthdays; cars; decorating accessories; fabrics; floor coverings; furniture; furs; major appliances; menswear; women's coats; women's stockings. |
| March ...... | China and glassware; housewares. |
| April ....... | Storewide sales after Easter; children's clothing; diamonds; fabrics; fashion clearances; lingerie; sleepwear; women's coats. |
| May ........ | Storewide sales on Memorial Day; clothing for men, women, and children; decorating accessories; diamonds; housewares; infant needs; linens; luggage. |

| MONTH | ITEMS ON SALE |
|---|---|
| June ....... | Floor coverings; furniture and beds; lingerie; men's clothing; sleepwear; stockings; summer sportswear (mid-month). |
| July ........ | Fabrics; furniture and beds; garden equipment and garden furniture (end of month); jewelry; linens; major appliances (end of month); storm windows; summer fashion clearances (men's, women's, and children's); tires. |
| August ..... | Cars; furniture and beds; furs; garden equipment and garden furniture; infant needs; linens; major appliances; rugs; stationery; women's accessories. |
| September . | Labor Day sales on tires and special items; cars (end of model year). |
| October .... | Storewide sales on Columbus Day; cars (old models); children's clothing; infant needs; women's coats. |
| November .. | Storewide sales on Election Day and Veterans Day; furs; women's coats. |
| December .. | After-Christmas sales on cards, decorations, and wrappings; infant needs; women's coats. |

## WEDDING ANNIVERSARY GIFTS

| ANNIVERSARY | GIFTS |
|---|---|
| First | Paper, plastics, clocks |
| Second | Cotton, china |
| Third | Leather, crystal, glass |
| Fourth | Fruit, flowers, silk, appliances |
| Fifth | Wood, silverware |
| Sixth | Iron, candy, sugar, wood |
| Seventh | Wood, copper, brass, desk sets |
| Eighth | Bronze, pottery, appliances, linen |
| Ninth | Leather, willow, pottery, glass |
| Tenth | Tin, aluminum, diamond jewelry |
| Eleventh | Steel, fashion jewelry |
| Twelfth | Silk, linen, pearl, colored gems |
| Thirteenth | Lace, textiles, furs |
| Fourteenth | Gold jewelry, ivory, agate |
| Fifteenth | Crystal, glass, watches |

| ANNIVERSARY | GIFTS |
|---|---|
| Sixteenth | Silver hollowware |
| Seventeenth | Furniture |
| Eighteenth | Porcelain |
| Nineteenth | Bronze |
| Twentieth | China, platinum, furniture |
| Twenty-fifth | Silver |
| Thirtieth | Pearl, diamond |
| Thirty-fifth | Coral, jade |
| Fortieth | Ruby, garnet |
| Forty-fifth | Sapphire, tourmaline |
| Fiftieth | Gold |
| Fifty-fifth | Emerald, turquoise |
| Sixtieth | Diamond |
| Seventy-fifth | Diamond, gold |

## BIRTHSTONES AND FLOWERS

| MONTH | BIRTHSTONE AND MEANING | FLOWER |
|---|---|---|
| January...... | Garnet—constancy, fidelity | Carnation or Snowdrop |
| February..... | Amethyst—sincerity | Violet or Primrose |
| March ....... | Aquamarine or Bloodstone—courage, truthfulness | Jonquil or Violet |
| April ........ | Diamond—innocence | Daisy or Sweet Pea |
| May ........ | Emerald—happiness, success | Hawthorn or Lily of the Valley |
| June ........ | Pearl, Alexandrite, or Moonstone—health | Rose or Honeysuckle |

| MONTH | BIRTHSTONE AND MEANING | FLOWER |
|---|---|---|
| July ......... | Ruby—contentment | Larkspur or Water Lily |
| August ...... | Peridot or Sardonyx—felicity | Gladiolus or Poppy |
| September... | Sapphire—love, wisdom | Morning Glory or Aster |
| October .... | Opal or Tourmaline—hope | Calendula or Cosmos |
| November ... | Topaz—fidelity | Chrysanthemum |
| December ... | Turquoise or Zircon—prosperity, success | Narcissus, Holly, or Poinsettia |

# HOW TO REMOVE COMMON STAINS

Knowing how to remove stains from fabrics can save dollars. Act quickly. Do not permit fresh stains to dry and become set. Because there are so many washable synthetic fibers on the market, it is wise to save the garment tags on which washing or dry-cleaning instructions are given. There are four principal types of stain removers:

**1. Absorbents** include cornstarch, cornmeal, chalk, fuller's earth, and paper towels. Use them to blot grease and liquids from fabrics.

**2. Washing agents** include detergents, soaps, borax, washing soda, and ammonia. Detergents (dry or liquid) remove most nongreasy and some greasy stains. Borax, washing soda, and ammonia loosen dirt and grease from fabrics. Mild soap is often safer than detergents on delicate materials.

**3. Chemical solvents** such as acetone, rubbing alcohol, and turpentine remove many nongreasy stains. Dry-cleaning solutions and "spot lifters" are effective in removing grease stains from both washables and dry-clean-only fabrics, but be certain to follow directions on the label.

**4. Bleaches,** to be used only on washables, include hydrogen peroxide, liquid or dry chlorine bleach, and dry oxygen bleach. Chlorine bleach is safe only for cottons and linens. It will damage other fabrics. Oxygen bleach is less effective than chlorine, but it is safe for most washables.

Many stains can be removed at home by following these simple rules:

**Blood.** While stain is fresh, sponge or soak with cold water (*never* warm or hot) until stain is light brown. Wash in warm suds. Soak stubborn stains in a weak solution of bleach, and then relaunder.

**Candle wax.** Scrape off excess and press stain between white blotters with a hot iron. Rub spot with lard or turpentine and wash.

**Chewing gum.** Rub with a piece of ice until gum hardens and can be lifted off. Then sponge with dry-cleaning fluid.

**Chocolate or cocoa.** Soak in cool water. Rub on detergent. Wash in hot suds with bleach. Treat any remaining stain with a weak solution of bleach or hydrogen peroxide. Then relaunder in hot suds.

**Coffee and tea.** Pour boiling water through fabric. Then wash in hot suds with bleach.

**Egg.** Scrape off excess. Soak fabric in cool water with bleach, then wash in warm suds.

**Fruits and berries.** Sponge peach, pear, cherry, and plum stains at once with cool water and rub with glycerine. After 2 hours apply a few drops of vinegar, then launder.

**Grass and foliage.** Scrub with hot water and suds. If needed, use a mild bleach. Then wash promptly in warm suds.

**Grease, oil, tar, butter.** Apply dry-cleaning fluid. Rub on detergent. Launder. Dry. Soak in weak bleach solution. Relaunder.

**Ice cream.** Sponge with cool water to remove sugar and protein, then with warm suds to remove grease.

**Lipstick.** Soften with glycerine, then wash in hot suds.

**Mildew.** Soak in suds and hang out with stain exposed to sunlight. If spots persist, rub with lemon juice and salt, then bleach in the sun.

**Paint.** If oil-based paint, use lots of hot suds for fresh stains. For stains that have set, apply turpentine, kerosene, or lard, and then wash in hot suds. Water-emulsion paint that is still wet usually comes out in hot suds.

**Pet stains.** When these occur on rugs or upholstery, sponge with cold water. Make a solution of one-fourth cup of white vinegar to a quart of water, and sponge again. Allow the solution to work for 15 minutes. Then wash the stain with cool detergent suds and rinse.

**Rust.** Place the stained portion over a pot of boiling water and pour lemon juice on the fabric. Rinse and then launder.

**Wine.** Once a wine stain has set, it is very hard to remove. Cover wet stains generously with salt, which will absorb the color. Then launder in warm suds.

# BIRTH DATES FOR ASTROLOGY'S SIGNS OF THE ZODIAC

| BIRTH DATES | SIGN NAME | SYMBOL | ASTROLOGICAL PERSONALITY TRAITS |
|---|---|---|---|
| Mar. 21–Apr. 19 | Aries, or Ram | ♈ | Active, dynamic, charming, diplomatic, restless |
| Apr. 20–May 20 | Taurus, or Bull | ♉ | Amusing, honest, affectionate, methodical |
| May 21–June 20 | Gemini, or Twins | ♊ | Intellectual, magnetic, changeable, sensitive |
| June 21–July 22 | Cancer, or Crab | ♋ | Managerial, overly serious, artistic, extroverted |
| July 23–Aug. 22 | Leo, or Lion | ♌ | Generous, sympathetic, imaginative, impulsive |
| Aug. 23–Sept. 22 | Virgo, or Virgin | ♍ | Independent, kind, sincere, reliable, emotional |
| Sept. 23–Oct. 22 | Libra, or Scales | ♎ | Practical, poised, attractive, loyal, quick-tempered |
| Oct. 23–Nov. 21 | Scorpio, or Scorpion | ♏ | Inventive, intuitive, dynamic, obstinate, selfish |
| Nov. 22–Dec. 21 | Sagittarius, or Archer | ♐ | Trustworthy, outgoing, moody, prideful, bright |
| Dec. 22–Jan. 19 | Capricorn, or Goat | ♑ | Calm, pleasant, serious, mild-mannered, reliable |
| Jan. 20–Feb. 18 | Aquarius, or Water Bearer | ♒ | Changeable, indolent, expressive, altruistic |
| Feb. 19–Mar. 20 | Pisces, or Fishes | ♓ | Faithful, perceptive, reserved, imaginative, jealous |

## STATE MARRIAGE LAWS

| STATE | RELATIVES ONE CANNOT MARRY [1] | MINIMUM AGE WITH PARENT CONSENT [2] Male | Female | BLOOD TEST REQUIRED | COMMON-LAW MARRIAGE RECOGNIZED | WAIT BETWEEN APPLICATION AND LICENSE | TIME LICENSE IS VALID |
|---|---|---|---|---|---|---|---|
| Alabama | ABE | 14 | 14 | Yes | Yes | None | 30 days |
| Alaska | — | 16 | 16 | Yes | No | 3 days | 90 days |
| Arizona | F | 16 | 16 | Yes | No [6] | None | NSP [23] |
| Arkansas | F | 17 | 16 | Yes | No [6] | 3 days | NSP [23] |
| California | — | —[3] | —[3] | Yes | No | None | 90 days |
| Colorado | — | 16 | 16 | Yes | Yes | None | 30 days |
| Connecticut | AB | 16 | 16 | Yes | No | 4 days | 65 days |
| Delaware | F | 18 | 16 | Yes | No [6] | None | 30 days |
| Florida | | 16 | 16 | Yes | No [8] | 3 days | 30 days |
| Georgia | ABEILC | —[3] | —[3] | Yes | Yes | 3 days | 30 days |
| Hawaii | — | 16 | 16 | Yes | No | None | 30 days |
| Idaho | F | 16 | 16 | Yes | Yes | None [21] | NSP [23] |
| Illinois | F | 16 | 16 | Yes | No [7] | None | 60 days |
| Indiana | FI | 17 | 17 | Yes | No [9] | 3 days | 60 days |
| Iowa | ABEFIJ | 16 | 16 | Yes | Yes | 3 days | 20 days |
| Kansas | F | 18 [4] | 18 [4] | Yes | Yes [18] | 3 days | NSP [23] |
| Kentucky | FH | 18 [4] | 18 [4] | Yes | No | 3 days | 30 days |
| Louisiana | F | 18 | 16 | Yes | No | None | 30 days |
| Maine | ABEIJKM | 16 | 16 | Yes | No | 5 days | 60 days |
| Maryland | BIJKLM | 16 | 16 | No | No | 2 days | 6 months |
| Massachusetts | ABEIL | 18 [4] | 16 | Yes | No | 3 days | 60 days |
| Michigan | F | 18 | 16 | Yes | No [10] | 3 days | 33 days |
| Minnesota | F | 18 [4] | 16 | No | No [11] | 5 days | 6 months |
| Mississippi | ABEFI | —[3] | —[3] | Yes | No [12] | None [25] | NSP [23] |
| Missouri | F | 15 | 15 | Yes | No [13] | 3 days | NSP [23] |
| Montana | F | 16 | 16 | Yes | Yes | None | 180 days |
| Nebraska | F | 17 | 17 | Yes | No [14] | 2 days | NSP [23] |
| Nevada | F | 16 | 16 | No | No [19] | None | NSP [23] |
| New Hampshire | AEF | 14 | 13 | Yes | No | 5 days | 90 days |
| New Jersey | — | 16 | 16 | Yes | No [15] | 3 days | 30 days |
| New Mexico | — | 16 | 16 | Yes | No | None | NSP [23] |
| New York | — | 16 | 16 | Yes | No [20] | None | 60 days |
| North Carolina | O | 16 | 16 | Yes [5] | No | None | NSP [23] |
| North Dakota | F | 16 | 16 | Yes | No | None | 60 days |
| Ohio | F | 18 | 16 | Yes | Yes | 5 days | 60 days |
| Oklahoma | F | 16 | 16 | Yes | No | None [22] | 30 days |
| Oregon | F | 17 | 17 | Yes | No [6] | 7 days | 30 days |
| Pennsylvania | ABEF | 16 | 16 | Yes | Yes | 3 days | 60 days |
| Rhode Island | BIMQ | 18 | 16 | Yes [5] | Yes | None [26] | 3 months |
| South Carolina | ABEIJKM | 16 | 14 | No | Yes | 24 hours | NSP [23] |
| South Dakota | ABF | 16 | 16 | Yes | No [16] | None | 20 days |
| Tennessee | ABCN | 16 | 16 | Yes | No [6] | None [22] | 30 days |
| Texas | — | 14 | 14 | Yes | Yes | None | 21 days [24] |
| Utah | F | 14 | 14 | Yes | No | None | 30 days |
| Vermont | — | 16 | 16 | Yes | No | None | 60 days |
| Virginia | — | 16 | 16 | Yes | No [6] | None | 60 days |
| Washington | F | 17 | 17 | Yes | No [6] | 3 days | 30 days |
| West Virginia | FO | 18 | 16 | Yes | No | 3 days | 60 days |
| Wisconsin | G | 16 | 16 | Yes | No [17] | 5 days | 30 days |
| Wyoming | ABEIJKM | 16 | 16 | Yes | No | None | NSP [23] |
| Dist. of Columbia | F | 16 | 16 | Yes | Yes | 3 days | NSP [23] |

[1] In every state it is illegal to marry a sister, brother, half sister, half brother, mother, father, daughter, son, granddaughter, grandson, grandmother, grandfather, great-grandmother, great-grandfather, aunt, uncle, niece, or nephew. Many states also prohibit other marriages as indicated by these capital letters: A stepparent; B stepchild; C stepgrandchild; D Half niece or half nephew; E son-in-law or daughter-in-law; F first cousin; G first cousin, except female 55 or older; OH first cousin once removed; I father-in-law or mother-in-law; J spouse of grandchild; K spouse of grandparent; L stepgrandparent; M spouse's grandparent or grandchild; N great-uncle, great-aunt, grandnephew, or grandniece; O double first cousin; P grandnephew or grandniece; Q marriages between Jews permitted by their religion are recognized; R any relative by adoption; S spouse's niece, spouse's grandchild, brother or sister by adoption. [2] Without parental consent, minimum age for marriage is 18, with these exceptions: Arkansas, 21 for men; Georgia, 16; Mississippi, 17 for men, 15 for women; Nebraska, 19. [3] No minimum age with parental consent and court order. [4] Marriage below 18 must have court approval and parental consent. [5] Physical exam also required. [6] However, state recognizes common-law marriage contracted in another state that recognizes its validity. [7] Unless before June 30, 1905. [8] Unless before 1968. [9] Unless before 1958. [10] Unless before 1957. [11] Unless before April 26, 1941. [12] Unless before April 5, 1956. [13] Unless before March 31, 1921. [14] Unless before 1923. [15] Unless before Dec. 1, 1939. [16] Unless before July 1, 1959. [17] Unless before 1917. [18] But both parties guilty of misdemeanor. [19] Unless before March 29, 1943. [20] Unless before April 29, 1933. [21] Except 3-day wait if both parties under 18. [22] Except 3 days if either is under 18. [23] No statutory provision. [24] After medical exam. [25] Except 3 days if either is under 21. [26] Except 5-day waiting period for female nonresident. [27] After blood test.

## MARRIAGES AND DIVORCES

Source: U.S. Public Health Service

The divorce rate in the United States soared to a new high of 5.3 per 1,000 population in 1979, the thirteenth consecutive annual increase. The number of marriages in 1979 jumped to 10.7 per 1,000, higher than it has been since 1974. In spite of the increase in the divorce rate, the total number of marriages in 1979 exceeded the total number of divorces by 1,189,000.

| STATE | MARRIAGES | | MARRIAGE RATE[2] | | DIVORCES | | DIVORCE RATE[2] | |
|---|---|---|---|---|---|---|---|---|
| | 1979[1] | 1970 | 1979[1] | 1970 | 1979[1] | 1970 | 1979[1] | 1970 |
| **UNITED STATES**......... | **2,359,000** | **2,158,802** | **10.7** | **10.6** | **1,170,000** | **708,000** | **5.3** | **3.5** |
| Alabama.............. | 48,807 | 46,959 | 12.9 | 13.6 | 26,900 | 15,109 | 7.1 | 4.4 |
| Alaska............... | 5,071 | 3,390 | 12.5 | 11.2 | 3,513 | 1,695 | 8.7 | 5.6 |
| Arizona............. | 29,549 | 18,508 | 12.1 | 10.4 | 19,917 | 12,714 | 8.1 | 7.2 |
| Arkansas ........... | 24,947 | 23,307 | 11.4 | 12.1 | 19,337 | 9,310 | 8.9 | 4.8 |
| California........... | 201,133 | 172,388 | 8.9 | 8.6 | 133,402 | 112,942 | 6.0 | 5.7 |
| Colorado............ | 31,889 | 24,988 | 11.5 | 11.3 | 16,688 | 10,400 | 6.0 | 4.7 |
| Connecticut ......... | 24,675 | 24,929 | 7.9 | 8.2 | 12,780 | 5,812 | 4.1[3] | 1.9 |
| Delaware............ | 4,418 | 4,254 | 7.6 | 7.8 | 3,166 | 1,732 | 5.4 | 3.2 |
| Florida.............. | 103,406 | 69,249 | 11.7 | 10.2 | 70,155 | 37,208 | 7.9 | 5.5 |
| Georgia............. | 65,898 | 63,896 | 12.9 | 13.9 | 32,842 | 18,649 | 6.4 | 4.1 |
| Hawaii.............. | 11,658 | 10,599 | 12.7 | 13.8 | 5,035 | 2,589 | 5.5 | 3.4 |
| Idaho............... | 13,568 | 10,915 | 15.0 | 15.3 | 6,519 | 3,612 | 7.2[3] | 5.1 |
| Illinois.............. | 108,443 | 115,478 | 9.7 | 10.4 | 53,842 | 36,450 | 4.8 | 3.3 |
| Indiana............. | 59,613 | 55,202 | 11.0 | 10.6 | 40,333[3] | 15,153 | 7.5[3] | N.A. |
| Iowa................ | 27,731 | 24,648 | 9.6[3] | 8.7 | 11,403 | 7,188 | 3.9 | 2.5 |
| Kansas ............. | 24,867 | 22,421 | 10.5 | 10.0 | 13,017 | 8,785 | 5.5 | 3.9 |
| Kentucky ........... | 36,513 | 36,269 | 10.4 | 11.3 | 16,913 | 10,664 | 4.8 | 3.3 |
| Louisiana........... | 41,816 | 35,416 | 10.4 | 9.7 | 13,229[3] | 5,065 | 3.3[3] | N.A. |
| Maine .............. | 11,944 | 10,975 | 10.9 | 11.0 | 6,110 | 3,853 | 5.6 | 3.9 |
| Maryland ........... | 45,903 | 52,237 | 11.1 | 13.3 | 15,541 | 9,252 | 3.7 | 2.4 |
| Massachusetts ...... | 42,652 | 47,403 | 7.4[3] | 8.3 | 17,405 | 10,994 | 3.0 | 1.9 |
| Michigan............ | 86,660 | 89,694 | 9.4 | 10.1 | 45,951 | 29,993 | 5.0 | 3.4 |
| Minnesota........... | 36,298 | 31,280 | 8.9 | 8.2 | 14,705 | 8,290 | 3.6[3] | 2.2 |
| Mississippi.......... | 26,718 | 26,328 | 11.0 | 11.9 | 12,901 | 8,211 | 5.3 | 3.7 |
| Missouri............ | 52,336 | 50,149 | 10.8 | 10.7 | 28,467 | 17,852 | 5.8 | 3.8 |
| Montana............ | 8,246 | 6,919 | 10.5 | 10.0 | 5,159 | 3,047 | 6.6 | 4.4 |
| Nebraska ........... | 14,032 | 15,666 | 8.9 | 10.6 | 6,021 | 3,712 | 3.8 | 2.5 |
| Nevada ............. | 121,874 | 97,605 | 173.6 | 199.7 | 10,465 | 9,138 | 14.9 | 18.7 |
| New Hampshire ..... | 9,175 | 10,006 | 10.3 | 13.6 | 5,051 | 2,433 | 5.7 | 3.3 |
| New Jersey.......... | 54,844 | 56,625 | 7.5 | 7.9 | 23,544 | 10,834 | 3.2 | 1.5 |
| New Mexico......... | 16,785 | 12,422 | 13.5 | 12.2 | 9,329 | 4,375 | 7.5 | 4.3 |
| New York........... | 141,350 | 161,246 | 8.0 | 8.9 | 59,898 | 26,404 | 3.4 | 1.5 |
| North Carolina ...... | 45,233 | 48,291 | 8.1 | 9.5 | 27,523 | 13,702 | 4.9 | 2.7 |
| North Dakota ....... | 5,977 | 5,340 | 9.1 | 8.6 | 2,076 | 985 | 3.2[3] | 1.6 |
| Ohio................ | 102,539 | 90,056 | 9.6 | 8.5 | 60,108 | 39,302 | 5.6 | 3.7 |
| Oklahoma........... | 44,452 | 39,004 | 15.4[3] | 15.2 | 22,823 | 16,842 | 7.9[3] | 6.6 |
| Oregon............. | 21,907 | 17,302 | 8.7 | 8.3 | 17,709 | 9,583 | 7.0 | 4.6 |
| Pennsylvania........ | 89,417 | 94,516 | 7.6 | 8.0 | 39,689 | 22,622 | 3.4 | 1.9 |
| Rhode Island ....... | 7,350 | 7,531 | 7.9 | 7.9 | 3,599 | 1,687 | 3.9 | 1.8 |
| South Carolina ...... | 53,968 | 57,887 | 18.4 | 22.3 | 13,965 | 5,829 | 4.8 | 2.3 |
| South Dakota ....... | 9,098 | 11,034 | 13.2 | 16.6 | 2,635 | 1,357 | 3.8 | 2.0 |
| Tennessee .......... | 59,407 | 45,361 | 13.6 | 11.6 | 32,349 | 16,623 | 7.4 | 4.2 |
| Texas .............. | 174,473 | 139,491 | 13.1 | 12.5 | 91,454 | 51,530 | 6.8 | 4.6 |
| Utah ............... | 16,823 | 11,692 | 12.3 | 11.0 | 7,542 | 3,912 | 5.5 | 3.7 |
| Vermont ............ | 5,228 | 4,524 | 10.6 | 10.2 | 2,296 | 1,028 | 4.7 | 2.3 |
| Virginia............. | 58,739 | 51,964 | 11.3 | 11.2 | 23,648 | 11,879 | 4.6 | 2.6 |
| Washington ......... | 45,809 | 41,313 | 11.7 | 12.1 | 26,802 | 17,887 | 6.8 | 5.2 |
| West Virginia........ | 17,275 | 15,948 | 9.3[3] | 9.1 | 10,066 | 5,584 | 5.4 | 3.2 |
| Wisconsin........... | 39,551 | 34,415 | 8.4 | 7.8 | 16,880 | 8,930 | 3.6 | 2.0 |
| Wyoming ........... | 6,032 | 4,495 | 13.4 | 13.5 | 3,654 | 1,797 | 8.1 | 5.4 |
| District of Columbia ..... | 4,974 | 7,267 | 7.6 | 9.6 | 4,173 | 2,268 | 6.4 | 3.0 |

[1] Provisional 1979 data.   [2] Per 1,000 population.   N.A.=Not available.   [3] Final 1978 data.

# HOW TO RID YOUR HOME OF HOUSEHOLD PESTS

Despite modern building methods and pesticide techniques, certain insects and rodents are still household problems.

There are only two ways in which they can be controlled: systematic and thorough housekeeping and the use of the proper pesticide at the right time.

Housekeepers are concerned chiefly with *insecticides* to control insects and *rodenticides* to kill rats and mice.

Insecticides come in the form of surface sprays, dusts, liquids, and pastes for crawling insects and space sprays or aerosols for flying insects.

Rodenticides are usually small poisoned pellets put out to be eaten by both rats and mice.

Below is a list of 10 insects and rodents that can be eliminated in the home with pesticides. Termite infestation is such a complex problem that it should be referred to an expert exterminator.

**Ants.** If you can find the ant nest by following the insects' line of march, treat it with a liquid or spray insecticide containing diazinon, lindane, or malathion.

Apply the substance to surfaces on which the ants crawl, and treat cracks or openings they may be using to enter the room or house.

**Bedbugs.** Spray the bed slats, springs, and frame. Cover the mattress completely with spray, but do not soak it.

Be sure to use a product on mattresses that does not contain more than 0.1% lindane or 1% malathion.

**Clothes Moths and Carpet Beetles.** Preventive measures should be taken against clothes moths before storing woolens. Have the garments dry-cleaned. Place paradichlorobenzene crystals or naphthalene flakes or balls in the garment bags or other containers before sealing. It is best to store furs at a commercial storage company.

To get rid of carpet beetles, vacuum rugs, upholstered furniture, draperies, and the surrounding floors. Spray rugs and other woolen or mohair fabrics with a stainless insecticide containing methoxychlor, Perthane, or Strobane.

**Cockroaches.** Preparations containing diazinon, malathion, or ronnel will control all types of cockroaches including the shiny brown German variety, which has developed resistance to chlordane and lindane. Apply the insecticide to places where cockroaches hide and breed—under kitchen sinks, in cracks around or beneath cupboards, places where pipes pass along a wall, behind loose baseboards or moldings, and on the undersides of tables and chairs. Powdered insecticide may be applied after spraying. Severe infestations should be handled by an exterminator.

Cockroaches seek warmth, moisture, and food. They hide during the day in sheltered, dark places in the home, and come out at night to forage. They feed on garbage as well as human food. Cockroaches may transmit some diseases caused by food-poisoning organisms, and they may also damage fabrics and books.

**Fleas.** These insects bite humans as well as dogs and cats. The first method for keeping fleas from infesting the home is to treat pets with a powder recommended by a veterinarian or pet shop.

If the fleas are all over the house, thoroughly vacuum carpets, floors, and upholstered furniture.

Apply a nonstaining spray containing methoxychlor, malathion, or ronnel. Treat baseboards, floor cracks, and places where your dog or cat lies or sleeps.

**House Flies.** You can help keep your home free of flies by installing tight-fitting screens in windows and doors. Since flies breed in decaying organic matter, promptly dispose of garbage, pet droppings, and the like. If flies have invaded your home in large numbers, use a household or aerosol spray especially prepared for flying insects.

**Mice and Rats.** The first steps in keeping out these rodents are to seal holes in walls, floors, and foundations and to make certain that food is not left where they can get to it. If you have only a few mice, place snap traps along walls and holes. Bait the traps with peanut butter, bacon, cheese, or soft candy. A pet cat is often a deterrent to mice.

Rats are a more serious problem, as they ruin property, carry disease, and bite when cornered. Poisoned bait is the best weapon against them, although traps will get rid of some of them. If rats are a neighborhood problem, community action must be taken and pest-control operators called in.

**Mosquitoes.** Check for larvae (wigglers) in any potential breeding areas such as filled vases, rain barrels, fish tanks, and the like. Screens will help keep out adult mosquitoes. They may be exterminated with a spray designed to kill flying insects.

**Pantry Pests.** Some types of insect larvae, popularly called "weevils," may infest dry food products such as cornmeal, flour, and cereals. Before buying such foods, examine the packages for tears or cracks. Keep your pantry shelves clean of spilled food particles, and store dry foods in metal or glass containers having tight-fitting lids.

# International Relations

Baring his sole during visit to UN in New York in October 1980, Iran's Prime Minister Mohammed Ali Rajai put his foot on the table to show scars from injuries he said he received while prisoner of the former shah.

## HIGHLIGHTS: 1980

### NEW U.S. MILITARY BASES IN MIDEAST

Because of the Soviet invasion of Afghanistan (see page 9) and the war between Iraq and Iran (see page 25), the United States took action in 1980 to strengthen its military position in the Middle East. President Carter declared that the U.S. would use military force if necessary to protect oil fields of friendly nations, such as Saudi Arabia.

At a cost of more than $300 million in promised military weapons and economic aid, the U.S. obtained the right to use bases in Kenya, Oman, and Somalia.

Ethiopia's dictator, Mengistu Haile Mariam, warned the U.S. that its agreement with Somalia risked involving the U.S. in war with Ethiopia if weapons supplied by the U.S. were used in the continuing war by Somali guerrillas against Ethiopia and its Soviet and Cuban allies.

After the outbreak of the war between Iraq and Iran, the U.S. sent four sophisticated ra-

dar warning planes to Saudi Arabia along with ground radar, communications equipment, and several hundred support personnel.

In July the Organization of African Unity (OAU) in a conference at Freetown, Sierra Leone, denounced the U.S. for its use of a military base on the island of Diego Garcia as a "threat to Africa and the concept of a zone of peace in the Indian Ocean." The OAU called on the U.S. to turn over the island "unconditionally" to the nation of Mauritius.

### NEW RULES OF WAR

Delegates of 72 nations meeting in Geneva, Switzerland, in October approved a treaty laying down additional rules designed to reduce civilian casualties in wars. The treaty is to be presented to the United Nations for approval in 1981 and then will go into force after ratification by 20 countries.

The treaty would ban the use of incendiary

# UNITED STATES AID TO OTHER NATIONS

Source: U.S. Department of Commerce

The United States has supplied other nations with nearly $246 billion in military assistance, economic and technical aid, and loans since the end of World War II.

Over $75 billion of this foreign aid has been in the form of loans, some $62 billion of which has been repaid. The figures in this table are for July 1, 1945, to Jan. 1, 1979.

| NATION | TOTAL AID BY U.S. | LOANS REPAID TO U.S. | LOANS STILL OWED TO U.S.[1] |
|---|---|---|---|
| Afghanistan .. | $ 540,000,000 | $ 51,000,000 | $ 108,000,000 |
| Albania | 20,000,000 | — | — |
| Algeria | 619,000,000 | 57,000,000 | 428,000,000 |
| Angola | 12,000,000 | 7,000,000 | 4,000,000 |
| Argentina | 1,323,000,000 | 843,000,000 | 366,000,000 |
| Australia | 1,073,000,000 | 928,000,000 | 153,000,000 |
| Austria | 1,318,000,000 | 132,000,000 | 35,000,000 |
| Bahamas | 55,000,000 | 49,000,000 | 5,000,000 |
| Bangladesh | 1,136,000,000 | 92,000,000 | 612,000,000 |
| Belgium | 2,187,000,000 | 276,000,000 | 75,000,000 |
| Benin | 38,000,000 | ** | 19,000,000 |
| Bolivia | 857,000,000 | 90,000,000 | 340,000,000 |
| Botswana | 61,000,000 | — | 22,000,000 |
| Brazil | 5,609,000,000 | 2,030,000,000 | 2,465,000,000 |
| Britain | 10,137,000,000 | 3,482,000,000 | 2,252,000,000 |
| Burma | 229,000,000 | 18,000,000 | 42,000,000 |
| Cambodia | 2,207,000,000 | 79,000,000 | 209,000,000 |
| Cameroon | 90,000,000 | 7,000,000 | 39,000,000 |
| Canada | 564,000,000 | 304,000,000 | 251,000,000 |
| Central Africa | 13,000,000 | — | 3,000,000 |
| Chad | 55,000,000 | | |
| Chile | 2,674,000,000 | 1,200,000,000 | 1,022,000,000 |
| Colombia | 1,893,000,000 | 526,000,000 | 903,000,000 |
| Congo | 12,000,000 | ** | ** |
| Costa Rica | 286,000,000 | 65,000,000 | 92,000,000 |
| Cuba | 60,000,000 | 3,000,000 | 36,000,000 |
| Cyprus | 139,000,000 | 8,000,000 | 12,000,000 |
| Czechoslovakia | 199,000,000 | 8,000,000 | 5,000,000 |
| Denmark | 992,000,000 | 69,000,000 | 56,000,000 |
| Dominican Rep. | 696,000,000 | 121,000,000 | 258,000,000 |
| Ecuador | 483,000,000 | 135,000,000 | 132,000,000 |
| Egypt | 3,054,000,000 | 452,000,000 | 1,778,000,000 |
| El Salvador | 226,000,000 | 36,000,000 | 85,000,000 |
| Ethiopia | 641,000,000 | 55,000,000 | 130,000,000 |
| Finland | 225,000,000 | 185,000,000 | 29,000,000 |
| France | 10,988,000,000 | 2,556,000,000 | -151,000,000 |
| Gabon | 32,000,000 | 2,000,000 | 21,000,000 |
| Germany, East | 17,000,000 | — | |
| Germany, West | 5,208,000,000 | 1,460,000,000 | -937,000,000 |
| Ghana | 407,000,000 | 96,000,000 | 195,000,000 |
| Greece | 5,286,000,000 | 492,000,000 | 858,000,000 |
| Guatemala | 572,000,000 | 58,000,000 | 118,000,000 |
| Guinea | 169,000,000 | 15,000,000 | 87,000,000 |
| Guyana | 98,000,000 | 2,000,000 | 67,000,000 |
| Haiti | 239,000,000 | 20,000,000 | 52,000,000 |
| Honduras | 260,000,000 | 32,000,000 | 102,000,000 |
| Hungary | 40,000,000 | 18,000,000 | 5,000,000 |
| Iceland | 95,000,000 | 44,000,000 | 16,000,000 |
| India | 12,944,000,000 | 3,593,000,000 | 3,821,000,000 |
| Indonesia | 3,393,000,000 | 542,000,000 | 1,963,000,000 |
| Iran | 3,260,000,000 | 1,354,000,000 | 551,000,000 |
| Iraq | 97,000,000 | 23,000,000 | 4,000,000 |
| Ireland | 197,000,000 | 148,000,000 | 32,000,000 |
| Israel | 12,063,000,000 | 1,377,000,000 | 4,396,000,000 |
| Italy | 6,612,000,000 | 1,133,000,000 | 194,000,000 |
| Ivory Coast | 101,000,000 | 17,000,000 | 60,000,000 |
| Jamaica | 223,000,000 | 51,000,000 | 115,000,000 |
| Japan | 7,434,000,000 | 3,244,000,000 | -103,000,000 |
| Jordan | 1,696,000,000 | 103,000,000 | 208,000,000 |
| Kenya | 227,000,000 | 18,000,000 | 104,000,000 |
| Korea, South | 14,108,000,000 | 989,000,000 | 2,678,000,000 |

| NATION | TOTAL AID BY U.S. | LOANS REPAID TO U.S. | LOANS STILL OWED TO U.S.[1] |
|---|---|---|---|
| Kuwait | $ 50,000,000 | $ 50,000,000 | $ — |
| Laos | 2,552,000,000 | — | — |
| Lebanon | 303,000,000 | 61,000,000 | 83,000,000 |
| Lesotho | 46,000,000 | — | |
| Liberia | 415,000,000 | 141,000,000 | 102,000,000 |
| Libya | 231,000,000 | 7,000,000 | ** |
| Madagascar | 24,000,000 | — | 6,000,000 |
| Malawi | 50,000,000 | — | 28,000,000 |
| Malaysia | 284,000,000 | 122,000,000 | 94,000,000 |
| Mali | 97,000,000 | ** | 4,000,000 |
| Malta | 85,000,000 | 1,000,000 | 5,000,000 |
| Mauritania | 38,000,000 | ** | 4,000,000 |
| Mauritius | 15,000,000 | — | |
| Mexico | 1,897,000,000 | 1,063,000,000 | 670,000,000 |
| Morocco | 1,367,000,000 | 280,000,000 | 585,000,000 |
| Nepal | 229,000,000 | 1,000,000 | 3,000,000 |
| Netherlands | 2,718,000,000 | 523,000,000 | 77,000,000 |
| New Zealand | 233,000,000 | 116,000,000 | 112,000,000 |
| Nicaragua | 317,000,000 | 50,000,000 | 166,000,000 |
| Niger | 96,000,000 | ** | 3,000,000 |
| Nigeria | 361,000,000 | — | 1,000,000 |
| Norway | 1,657,000,000 | 272,000,000 | 233,000,000 |
| Pakistan | 6,379,000,000 | 667,000,000 | 2,827,000,000 |
| Panama | 491,000,000 | 113,000,000 | 189,000,000 |
| Papua New Guinea | — | 31,000,000 | — |
| Paraguay | 213,000,000 | 41,000,000 | 55,000,000 |
| Peru | 1,437,000,000 | 591,000,000 | 439,000,000 |
| Philippines | 3,399,000,000 | 638,000,000 | 626,000,000 |
| Poland | 2,049,000,000 | 524,000,000 | 852,000,000 |
| Portugal | 2,148,000,000 | 243,000,000 | 836,000,000 |
| Romania | 286,000,000 | 148,000,000 | 128,000,000 |
| Saudi Arabia | 335,000,000 | 283,000,000 | -17,000,000 |
| Senegal | 125,000,000 | 1,000,000 | 14,000,000 |
| Sierra Leone | 99,000,000 | 15,000,000 | 27,000,000 |
| Singapore | 140,000,000 | 10,000,000 | 126,000,000 |
| Somalia | 109,000,000 | 1,000,000 | 23,000,000 |
| Soviet Union | 1,434,000,000 | 721,000,000 | 287,000,000 |
| Spain | 3,079,000,000 | 793,000,000 | 1,019,000,000 |
| Sri Lanka | 387,000,000 | 45,000,000 | 213,000,000 |
| Sudan | 185,000,000 | 30,000,000 | 59,000,000 |
| Suriname | 12,000,000 | 4,000,000 | 3,000,000 |
| Sweden | 162,000,000 | 42,000,000 | 32,000,000 |
| Switzerland | 101,000,000 | 18,000,000 | 83,000,000 |
| Syria | 177,000,000 | 14,000,000 | 104,000,000 |
| Taiwan | 6,316,000,000 | 555,000,000 | 927,000,000 |
| Tanzania | 249,000,000 | 7,000,000 | 86,000,000 |
| Thailand | 2,262,000,000 | 116,000,000 | 167,000,000 |
| Togo | 37,000,000 | 1,000,000 | 1,000,000 |
| Trinidad-Tob. | 74,000,000 | 26,000,000 | 13,000,000 |
| Tunisia | 979,000,000 | 113,000,000 | 355,000,000 |
| Turkey | 7,839,000,000 | 493,000,000 | 1,929,000,000 |
| Uganda | 46,000,000 | 1,000,000 | 11,000,000 |
| Upper Volta | 90,000,000 | — | 1,000,000 |
| Uruguay | 268,000,000 | 51,000,000 | 99,000,000 |
| Venezuela | 707,000,000 | 473,000,000 | 149,000,000 |
| Vietnam | 23,991,000,000 | 459,000,000 | 100,000,000 |
| Yemen | 87,000,000 | — | 1,000,000 |
| Yugoslavia | 3,649,000,000 | 802,000,000 | 927,000,000 |
| Zaire | 873,000,000 | 53,000,000 | 491,000,000 |
| Zambia | 134,000,000 | 24,000,000 | 104,000,000 |

[1] A negative credit indicates an excess of principal payments over new credits utilized.   ** Less than $500,000.

United Press Int'l.

Polish union leader Lech Walesa addresses workers in Gdansk whose strike in August toppled the communist government of Poland and caused tremors in the communist ruling circles of neighboring countries.

**HIGHLIGHTS: 1980** *(continued)*
bombs in attacks on cities and other concentrations of civilians. Records would have to be kept regarding the placement of land mines, so that they could be removed after the war. Weapons could not be used that fragment into pieces of glass, plastic, or other nonmetallic substances, undetectable when X rays are used in an attempt to discover the cause of a wound. The treaty also would ban the use of booby traps that appear to be harmless objects or are attached to objects such as toys that might be triggered by civilians.

The treaty provides for future conferences to discuss additional limitations on the use of specific weapons that cause civilian injuries in war.

### LITTLE PROGRESS TOWARD MIDEAST PEACE

Although Israel and Egypt resumed formal diplomatic relations in February 1980 and Israel returned additional land to Egypt, little progress was made in Israeli-Egyptian negotiations on the issue of providing autonomy to the Arab residents of the West Bank and Gaza areas that are under Israeli military occupation.

The U.S. voted in March in the UN Security Council in favor of a resolution condemning Israel for establishing civilian settlements in its militarily occupied territories. Because

# HISTORY OF THE MIDDLE EAST

The strategic importance of the Middle East, linking the continents of Europe, Asia, and Af- rica, has caused the region to be the scene of bloody wars since the dawn of history.

**3200–2800 B.C.   Egyptians in Africa and Sumerians in Mesopotamia** (Iraq) separately invent writing and begin recorded history.

**3000–539 B.C.   Egypt contends with Sumeria, Babylonia, and Assyria** for control of Middle East.

**539–333 B.C.   Persia (Iran)** conquers Assyria and Egypt, establishing Persian rule of region.

**333–30 B.C.   Alexander the Great** of Macedonia conquers Persia and Egypt; Greek rulers govern region.

**30 B.C.–A.D. 260   Rome** conquers and rules Middle East.

**260–637   Wars between Persia and Roman Empire** (later Byzantine Empire) for control of region.

**637–1055   Arabs conquer and rule Middle East.**

**1055   Turks conquer Middle East;** region ruled as part of Ottoman Empire until World War I.

**1859–69   Suez Canal constructed,** linking Mediterranean Sea with Red Sea and Indian Ocean.

**1878   Britain takes control of Cyprus.**

**1882   British troops occupy Egypt** to protect British interests in Suez Canal.

**1896   Zionist movement** founded by Theodor Herzl, calling for formation of Jewish national state in former Jewish homeland of Palestine.

**1897–1914   About 50,000 Jews migrate to Palestine** to escape persecution in Europe.

**1901   Persian oil fields** discovered.

**1902–25   Ibn Saud conquers most of Arabia;** proclaims himself king of Hejaz and Nejd in 1927; changes country's name to Saudi Arabia in 1932.

**1914   Egypt declared protectorate** by Britain.

**1916–18   Lawrence of Arabia,** British Col. T.E. Lawrence, leads Arabs seeking independence in attacks on Turks.

**1917   Balfour Declaration** issued by Britain to gain Jewish support in World War I; promises Britain's help in establishing "national home" for Jews in Palestine without violating rights of Arab majority (Arabs accounted for about 90% of Palestine's 700,000 population).

**1918   Turkey defeated** by British troops with aid of Arabs in World War I, dismembering Ottoman Empire.

**1920   Britain given mandate over Palestine** by League of Nations.

**1920   France given mandate over Syria and Lebanon** by League of Nations.

**1921   Arab emirate of Transjordan** (later Jordan) founded under British control.

**1921   Arab kingdom of Iraq** established under British control, with Faisal I as king.

**1921   Arabs in Palestine riot,** protesting increased Jewish immigration; Britain issues proposed Palestine constitution, but Arabs refuse to take part in elections.

**1922 (Feb. 28)   Britain formally ends protectorate over Egypt,** but British troops remain.

**1922–23   Turkey's sultanate abolished** and republic proclaimed by Kemal Ataturk; as president (1923–38) Ataturk Westernizes Turkey.

**1926   Lebanon republic founded** under French control.

**1929   Arabs attack and kill Jews in Jerusalem,** Palestine, in dispute over use of Wailing Wall.

**1930   Iraq granted independence** by Britain.

**1933–45   Tens of thousands of Jews migrate to Palestine to escape Nazi persecution** in which 6 million European Jews were killed.

**1935   Saudi Arabia's major oil fields** discovered.

**1935   Persia's name changed to Iran** by Reza Shah Pahlevi, who as army officer had seized control of country in 1921 and deposed shah in 1925.

**1937   British commission recommends partition of Palestine** between Arabs and Jews.

**1939 (May 23)   British parliament approves plan to create independent Palestine state** within 10 years with safeguards to protect rights of Jewish minority; Jewish immigra- tion to Palestine to be banned after 1941.

**1941   Syria and Lebanon granted independence** by Free French leaders after fall of France early in World War II.

**1945   Arab League created** by Egypt, Iraq, Jordan, Lebanon, Saudi Arabia, Syria, and Yemen to coordinate Arab interests.

**1945–48   Thousands of displaced European Jews immi- grate to Palestine** despite efforts of British to stop them.

**1946   British and French troops withdraw from Syria.**

**1946 (April 25)   Kingdom of Transjordan** (later Jordan) becomes independent, but British officers control army.

**1947 (Oct. 26)   British troops withdraw from Iraq.**

**1947 (Nov. 29)   UN General Assembly votes to partition Palestine** into Arab and Jewish states with Jerusalem remaining a UN trusteeship; Arabs reject plan.

**1948 (May 14)   Israel declares its independence** as a Jewish state simultaneously with Britain ending its mandate.

**1948–49   First Arab-Israeli War:** All of Israel's Arab neighbors attack and attempt to destroy new nation, but Israel with help of arms from U.S. is able to drive back Arab forces.

**1949   About 1 million Arab refugees** who had fled from Israel settle in camps in Arab nations, creating major problem in succeeding decades.

**1956 (June 13)   British withdraw troops from Egypt** after 74 years of occupation.

**1956 (July 26)   Egypt nationalizes Suez Canal,** seizing it from British and French owners.

**1956 (Oct. 29–Nov. 6)   Second Arab-Israeli War:** with support of Britain and France, Israel attacks Egypt and drives to Suez Canal.

**1956 (Nov. 15)   UN peace-keeping force sent to Suez Canal.**

**1957 (March 1)   Israel withdraws from Egyptian territory.**

**1958 (July 15)   U.S. Marines land in Lebanon,** carrying out "Eisenhower Doctrine" to prevent communist takeover of government; troops withdrawn in November.

**1958–61   Syria and Egypt unite** to form United Arab Republic, finally dissolved by Syria.

**1960   Britain grants independence to Cyprus.**

**1964   UN sends peace-keeping force to Cyprus** to prevent outbreak of war between Greece and Turkey over island.

**1964   Palestine Liberation Organization** founded by Arab nations to conduct terrorist raids on Israel.

**1967 (May 18)   Egypt demands and obtains immediate withdrawal of UN forces** from its borders with Israel.

**1967 (June 5–10)   Third Arab-Israeli War:** Israel attacks Egypt, Syria, and Jordan; captures all of Jerusalem and Jordanian land west of Jordan River, all of Egypt's Sinai Peninsula, and Syria's Golan Heights; an additional 750,000 Arabs flee from territories, adding to refugee problem.

**1973 (Oct. 6–24)   Fourth Arab-Israeli War:** Egypt and Syria, supported with military supplies from Soviet Union, attack Israel; Israel fights back, aided by arms from U.S., driving across Suez Canal into Egypt and pushing beyond Golan Heights into Syria.

**1974   Truce agreements negotiated** with Egypt and Syria by U.S. Secretary of State Henry Kissinger.

**1974   Turkish troops invade Cyprus** after Greek-led revolt overthrows island's government.

**1975–76   Civil War in Lebanon** with leftist Muslims and Palestinian Arabs fighting against rightist Christians; ends after Syria sends in army to impose peace.

**1977 (Nov. 19–21)   Egypt's President Sadat visits Israel** in effort to achieve lasting peace agreement.

**1979 (Jan. 16)   Muslim revolt overthrows Shah** of Iran, making country Islamic republic.

**1979 (March 26)   Peace treaty signed by Egypt and Israel:** goes into effect April 25; other Arab countries angered, breaking relations with Egypt.

**1979 (Dec. 27)   Soviet troops invade Afghanistan;** set up puppet communist government.

**1980**   For 1980 events, see pages 8–30.

At summit meeting in Venice, Italy, in June, Italy's Prime Minister Francesco Cossiga tries to pull President Carter closer to France's President Valéry Giscard D'Estaing for a group photo. West Germany's Chancellor Helmut Schmidt stands at far left, and Britain's Prime Minister Margaret Thatcher is at far right.

## HIGHLIGHTS: 1980 (continued)

this was the first time the U.S. had not supported Israel on a vote in the UN, American Jews raised a storm of protest. Two days later President Carter repudiated the vote, while members of his administration claimed it had resulted from a "failure in communications."

Israel further defied world opinion in July when its parliament incorporated Arab East Jerusalem as part of the Israeli capital.

### SECRETARY OF STATE VANCE RESIGNS

Secretary of State Cyrus R. Vance resigned on April 28, 1980, because he opposed the U.S. military attempt to rescue the American hostages in Iran (see page 15). He was replaced by Sen. Edmund S. Muskie (D-Maine).

In a commencement address at Harvard University six weeks later, Vance outlined what he believed were the four goals most basic to U.S. foreign policy:

"First, we must preserve the global military balance and achieve, as well, balance in our political relations with the Soviet Union. . . .

"A second and paramount goal for our nation should be to nurture strong alliances among free nations. . . .

"(Third) support for the political independence and economic growth of the poorer nations. . . .

"(Fourth) a strong American economy in a strong international economy."

Vance described the U.S. foreign-aid program as "disgraceful," pointing out that the U.S. ranks 13th among major industrial powers in the percentage of gross national product devoted to economic assistance for developing countries.

### APPEAL FOR WORLD'S POOR

Retiring after 13 years as president of the World Bank, Robert S. McNamara made an impassioned appeal in September for the U.S. and other industrial nations to increase their economic aid to the poor nations of the world. Echoing Vance's term "disgraceful" as a description of the U.S. foreign-aid program, McNamara said the 1.1 billion people of the world's poorest countries have a bleak future. "Their already low per capita income of less than $220 a year," he said, "is likely to grow by no more than 1% a year—an average of only $2 or $3 for each individual."

# HISTORY OF THE UNITED NATIONS

**1941 (June 12) Inter-Allied Declaration** signed in London by all nations then at war with Germany to work for "a world in which, relieved of the menace of aggression, all may enjoy economic and social security."

**1941 (Aug. 14) Atlantic Charter** issued by U.S. President Franklin D. Roosevelt and British Prime Minister Winston Churchill detailing eight points to "base their hopes for a better future for the world."

**1942 (Jan. 1) Declaration by United Nations** signed by 26 nations in Washington approving basic points of Atlantic Charter; first official use of name "United Nations."

**1943 (Oct. 30) Moscow Declaration on General Security** signed by Britain, China, Soviet Union, and United States, recognizing "the necessity of establishing at the earliest practicable date a general international organization, based on the principle of sovereign equality."

**1944 (Aug. 21) Dumbarton Oaks Conference** in Washington, D.C., at which for three months representatives of 39 nations discuss proposals for establishing United Nations organization, agreeing on Security Council as executive branch of UN.

**1945 (June 26) UN Charter** approved by delegates of 50 nations at international conference in San Francisco.

**1945 (Oct. 16) Food and Agriculture Organization of United Nations** established to improve consumption, production, and distribution of food throughout world.

**1945 (Oct. 24) UN Charter goes into effect** upon ratification by majority of nations, including Britain, China, France, Soviet Union, and United States. Day celebrated annually as United Nations Day.

**1946 (Jan. 10) UN General Assembly** begins first meeting in London with delegates of 51 nations as members. Trygve Lie of Norway is elected first secretary-general of UN.

**1946 (June 25) International Bank for Reconstruction and Development** begins operations to assist nations by government loans.

**1946 (Nov. 4) UNESCO,** United Nations Educational, Scientific, and Cultural Organization, formed to promote international cooperation in solving such problems as illiteracy.

**1946 (Dec. 14) Gift of $8,500,000** from U.S. millionaire John D. Rockefeller Jr. accepted by UN to buy 18 acres in New York City as site of permanent headquarters.

**1947 (April 4) International Civil Aviation Organization** established to develop international standards and regulations for civil aviation.

**1948 (April 7) World Health Organization** established to promote world health.

**1948 (Sept. 17) UN peace negotiator Count Folke Bernadotte** of Sweden assassinated in Jerusalem while trying to arrange truce in fighting between Arabs and Israelis.

**1948 (Dec. 10) Universal Declaration of Human Rights** adopted by UN General Assembly.

**1949 (Jan. 1) Cease-fire between India and Pakistan** obtained by UN to end two years of fighting over control of Kashmir.

**1949 (Feb.–July)** Cease-fire agreements arranged between Israel and Arab states by UN negotiator Ralph J. Bunche.

**1949 (Dec. 27) Netherlands grants independence to Indonesia** after conference arranged by UN to settle fighting.

**1950 (March 23) World Meteorological Organization** established to promote international reporting and observation of weather.

**1950 (June 27) UN Security Council calls for member nations to send troops to aid South Korea,** which had been attacked by communist North Korea. Soviet Union was boycotting meetings of Security Council at this time and so could not veto measure. Troops of U.S. and 15 other nations dispatched to aid South Korea.

**1953 (July 27) UN signs truce with North Korea,** ending over three years of fighting.

**1956 (Nov. 7) UN obtains cease-fire in Suez Canal fighting** between Egypt and Israeli-British-French forces; sends UN Emergency Force to supervise truce.

**1957 (July 29) International Atomic Energy Agency** created to promote peaceful uses of atomic energy.

**1961 (Sept. 13) UN troops begin fighting in Congo** (now Zaire) to restore order in civil war.

**1961 (Sept. 18) UN Secretary-General Dag Hammarskjold** killed in air crash in Africa while on Congo peace mission.

**1961 (Nov. 3) U Thant** of Burma elected as UN's third secretary-general to succeed Dag Hammarskjold.

**1964 (March 4) UN peace-keeping force sent to Cyprus** to prevent fighting between Turkish and Greek forces.

**1966 (Dec. 16) UN Security Council asks member nations to stop trading with Rhodesia** because of its policies against blacks.

**1967 (June 10) UN negotiates truce** in Six-Day Israeli-Arab War.

**1971 (Oct. 25) Communist China admitted** to UN and nationalist China expelled by 76–35 vote of General Assembly.

**1971 (Dec. 13) UN General Assembly votes** 79 to 7 with 36 abstentions for Israel to restore to Arab countries territories acquired by force.

**1972 Kurt Waldheim appointed UN secretary-general** on resignation of U Thant.

**1973 (Oct. 22) Cease-fire in 17-day-old Middle East War** ordered by UN Security Council.

**1973 (Oct. 25) UN peace-keeping force sent to Middle East** to prevent further fighting between Arab nations and Israel.

**1974 Special session of UN General Assembly** establishes emergency relief fund for poor nations of world.

**1975 International Women's Year** declared by UN to promote women's equality.

**1977 (Nov. 4) Mandatory embargo on military supply shipments to South Africa** ordered by UN; first such action against UN member.

**1978 UN 6,100-man peace-keeping force** stationed in southern Lebanon: Bring withdrawal of Israeli troops that invaded in March.

**1979 (Sept. 18) UN memberships reaches 152** with admission of Saint Lucia.

**1980** For 1980 events, see pages 7–30.

## THE 154 MEMBERS OF THE UNITED NATIONS

The 154 members of the UN include most of the independent nations in the world.

When the UN charter went into effect on Oct. 24, 1945, there were 51 members. Among them were Belorussia and Ukraine, two of the 15 states or republics of the Soviet Union.

New members of the UN must first be passed on by the UN Security Council, and therefore may be vetoed by any of the five permanent members. Membership then must be approved by a vote of the UN General Assembly.

Some nations are *not* members of the UN, such as: Andorra, Bophuthatswana, North Korea, South Korea, Liechtenstein, Monaco, Namibia, Nauru, San Marino, Switzerland, Taiwan, Tonga, Transkei, Tuvalu, and Vanuatu.

| MEMBER | SINCE | MEMBER | SINCE | MEMBER | SINCE |
|---|---|---|---|---|---|
| Afghanistan | 1946 (Nov. 19) | Germany, West | 1973 (Sept. 18) | Panama | 1945 (Nov. 13) |
| Albania | 1955 (Dec. 14) | Ghana | 1957 (March 8) | Papua New Guinea | 1975 (Oct. 10) |
| Algeria | 1962 (Oct. 8) | Greece | 1945 (Oct. 25) | Paraguay | 1945 (Oct. 24) |
| Angola | 1976 (Dec. 1) | Grenada | 1974 (Sept. 17) | Peru | 1945 (Oct. 31) |
| Argentina | 1945 (Oct. 24) | Guatemala | 1945 (Nov. 21) | Philippines | 1945 (Oct. 24) |
| Australia | 1945 (Nov. 1) | Guinea | 1958 (Dec. 12) | Poland | 1945 (Oct. 24) |
| Austria | 1955 (Dec. 14) | Guinea-Bissau | 1974 (Sept. 17) | Portugal | 1955 (Dec. 14) |
| Bahamas | 1973 (Sept. 18) | Guyana | 1966 (Sept. 20) | Qatar | 1971 (Sept. 21) |
| Bahrain | 1971 (Sept. 21) | Haiti | 1945 (Oct. 24) | Romania | 1955 (Dec. 14) |
| Bangladesh | 1974 (Sept. 17) | Honduras | 1945 (Dec. 17) | Rwanda | 1962 (Sept. 18) |
| Barbados | 1966 (Dec. 9) | Hungary | 1955 (Dec. 14) | Saint Lucia | 1979 (Sept. 18) |
| Belgium | 1945 (Dec. 27) | Iceland | 1946 (Nov. 19) | Saint Vincent | 1980 (Sept. 16) |
| Belorussia | 1945 (Oct. 24) | India | 1945 (Oct. 30) | São Tomé and Príncipe | 1975 (Sept. 16) |
| Benin | 1960 (Sept. 20) | Indonesia | 1950 (Sept. 28) | Saudi Arabia | 1945 (Oct. 24) |
| Bhutan | 1971 (Sept. 21) | Iran | 1945 (Oct. 24) | Senegal | 1960 (Sept. 28) |
| Bolivia | 1945 (Nov. 14) | Iraq | 1945 (Dec. 21) | Seychelles | 1976 (Sept. 28) |
| Botswana | 1966 (Oct. 17) | Ireland | 1955 (Dec. 14) | Sierra Leone | 1961 (Sept. 27) |
| Brazil | 1945 (Oct. 24) | Israel | 1949 (May 11) | Singapore | 1965 (Sept. 21) |
| Britain | 1945 (Oct. 24) | Italy | 1955 (Dec. 14) | Solomons | 1978 (Sept. 19) |
| Bulgaria | 1955 (Dec. 14) | Ivory Coast | 1960 (Sept. 20) | Somalia | 1960 (Sept. 20) |
| Burma | 1948 (April 19) | Jamaica | 1962 (Sept. 18) | South Africa | 1945 (Nov. 7) |
| Burundi | 1962 (Sept. 18) | Japan | 1956 (Dec. 18) | Soviet Union | 1945 (Oct. 24) |
| Cambodia | 1955 (Dec. 14) | Jordan | 1955 (Dec. 14) | Spain | 1955 (Dec. 14) |
| Cameroon | 1960 (Sept. 20) | Kenya | 1963 (Dec. 16) | Sri Lanka | 1955 (Dec. 14) |
| Canada | 1945 (Nov. 9) | Kuwait | 1963 (May 14) | Sudan | 1956 (Nov. 12) |
| Cape Verde | 1975 (Sept. 16) | Laos | 1955 (Dec. 14) | Suriname | 1975 (Dec. 4) |
| Central Africa | 1960 (Sept. 20) | Lebanon | 1945 (Oct. 24) | Swaziland | 1968 (Sept. 24) |
| Chad | 1960 (Sept. 20) | Lesotho | 1966 (Oct. 17) | Sweden | 1946 (Nov. 19) |
| Chile | 1945 (Oct. 24) | Liberia | 1945 (Nov. 2) | Syria | 1945 (Oct. 24) |
| China | 1945 (Oct. 24) | Libya | 1955 (Dec. 14) | Tanzania | 1961 (Dec. 14) |
| Colombia | 1945 (Nov. 5) | Luxembourg | 1945 (Oct. 24) | Thailand | 1946 (Dec. 16) |
| Comoros | 1975 (Nov. 12) | Madagascar | 1960 (Sept. 20) | Togo | 1960 (Sept. 20) |
| Congo | 1960 (Sept. 20) | Malawi | 1964 (Dec. 1) | Trinidad-Tobago | 1962 (Sept. 18) |
| Costa Rica | 1945 (Nov. 2) | Malaysia | 1957 (Sept. 17) | Tunisia | 1956 (Nov. 12) |
| Cuba | 1945 (Oct. 24) | Maldives | 1965 (Sept. 21) | Turkey | 1945 (Oct. 24) |
| Cyprus | 1960 (Sept. 20) | Mali | 1960 (Sept. 28) | Uganda | 1962 (Oct. 25) |
| Czechoslovakia | 1945 (Oct. 24) | Malta | 1964 (Dec. 1) | Ukraine | 1945 (Oct. 24) |
| Denmark | 1945 (Oct. 24) | Mauritania | 1961 (Oct. 27) | United Arab Emirates | 1971 (Dec. 9) |
| Djibouti | 1977 (Sept. 20) | Mauritius | 1968 (April 24) | United States | 1945 (Oct. 24) |
| Dominica | 1978 (Dec. 18) | Mexico | 1945 (Nov. 7) | Upper Volta | 1960 (Sept. 20) |
| Dominican Republic | 1945 (Oct. 24) | Mongolia | 1961 (Oct. 27) | Uruguay | 1945 (Dec. 18) |
| Ecuador | 1945 (Dec. 21) | Morocco | 1956 (Nov. 12) | Venezuela | 1945 (Nov. 15) |
| Egypt | 1945 (Oct. 24) | Mozambique | 1975 (Sept. 16) | Vietnam | 1977 (Sept. 20) |
| El Salvador | 1945 (Oct. 24) | Nepal | 1955 (Dec. 14) | Western Samoa | 1976 (Dec. 15) |
| Equatorial Guinea | 1968 (Nov. 12) | Netherlands | 1945 (Dec. 10) | Yemen, North | 1947 (Sept. 30) |
| Ethiopia | 1945 (Nov. 13) | New Zealand | 1945 (Oct. 24) | Yemen, South | 1967 (Dec. 14) |
| Fiji | 1970 (Oct. 13) | Nicaragua | 1945 (Oct. 24) | Yugoslavia | 1945 (Oct. 24) |
| Finland | 1955 (Dec. 14) | Niger | 1960 (Sept. 20) | Zaire | 1960 (Sept. 20) |
| France | 1945 (Oct. 24) | Nigeria | 1960 (Oct. 7) | Zambia | 1964 (Dec. 1) |
| Gabon | 1960 (Sept. 20) | Norway | 1945 (Nov. 27) | Zimbabwe | 1980 (Aug. 25) |
| Gambia | 1965 (Sept. 21) | Oman | 1971 (Oct. 7) | | |
| Germany, East | 1973 (Sept. 18) | Pakistan | 1947 (Sept. 30) | | |

## UN SECRETARIES-GENERAL

The secretary-general is the UN's chief administrative officer.

Since its beginning in 1945 the United Nations has had four secretaries-general:

**Trygve Lie** (1896–1968) of Norway served from Feb. 1, 1946, until he resigned in September 1952 during his second term in office.

**Dag Hammarskjöld** (1905–61) of Sweden, named in April 1953, was serving a second term when he died in a plane crash while on a UN mission in the Congo on Sept. 18, 1961.

**U Thant** (1909–74) of Burma was appointed in 1962 and resigned in 1972.

**Kurt Waldheim** (1918– ) of Austria was appointed in 1972. He had represented Austria in the UN since 1964.

# UNITED NATIONS ORGANIZATION

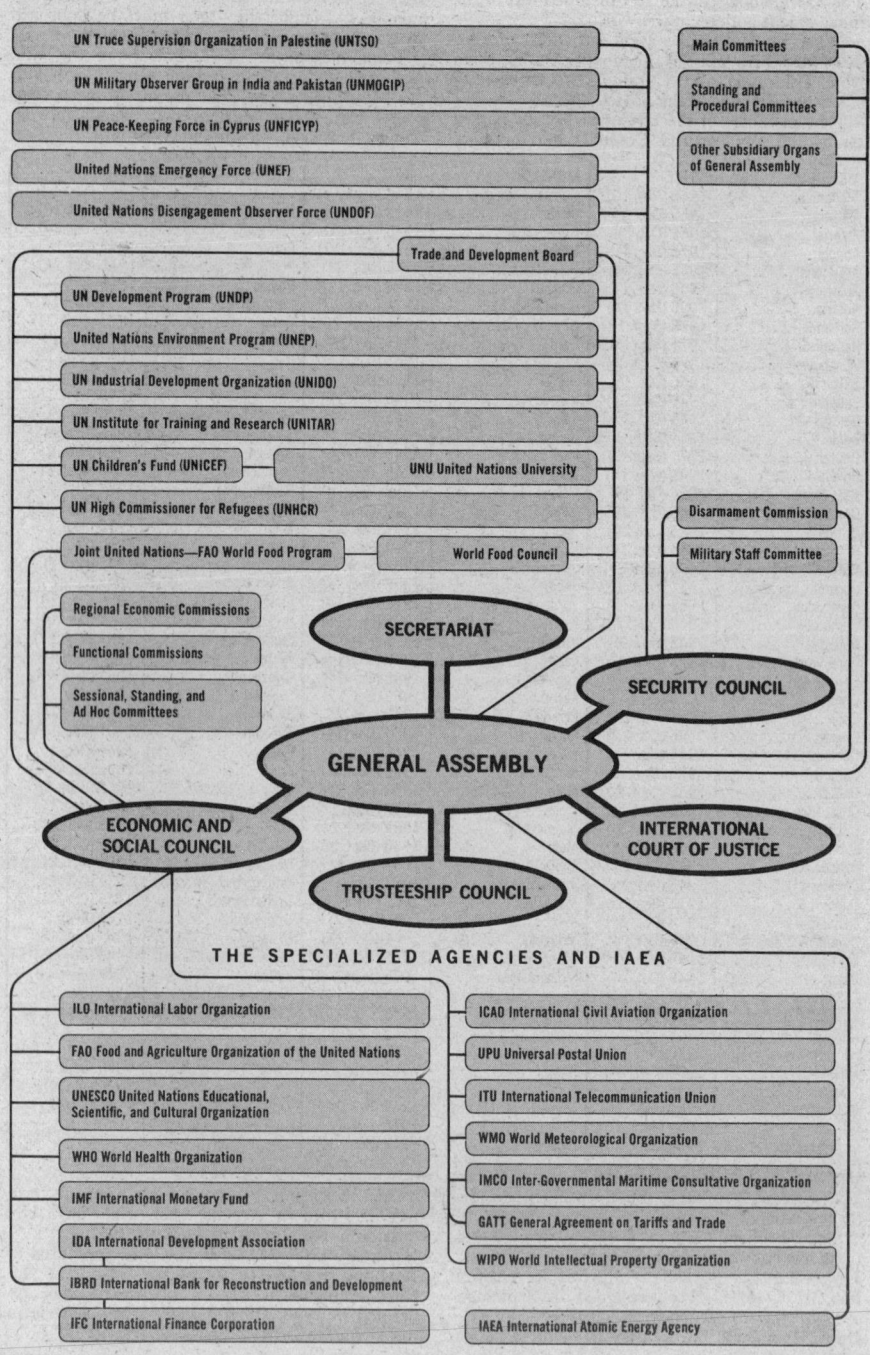

UN Truce Supervision Organization in Palestine (UNTSO)

UN Military Observer Group in India and Pakistan (UNMOGIP)

UN Peace-Keeping Force in Cyprus (UNFICYP)

United Nations Emergency Force (UNEF)

United Nations Disengagement Observer Force (UNDOF)

Main Committees

Standing and Procedural Committees

Other Subsidiary Organs of General Assembly

Trade and Development Board

UN Development Program (UNDP)

United Nations Environment Program (UNEP)

UN Industrial Development Organization (UNIDO)

UN Institute for Training and Research (UNITAR)

UN Children's Fund (UNICEF)

UNU United Nations University

UN High Commissioner for Refugees (UNHCR)

Joint United Nations—FAO World Food Program

World Food Council

Disarmament Commission

Military Staff Committee

Regional Economic Commissions

Functional Commissions

Sessional, Standing, and Ad Hoc Committees

SECRETARIAT

SECURITY COUNCIL

GENERAL ASSEMBLY

ECONOMIC AND SOCIAL COUNCIL

INTERNATIONAL COURT OF JUSTICE

TRUSTEESHIP COUNCIL

## THE SPECIALIZED AGENCIES AND IAEA

ILO International Labor Organization

FAO Food and Agriculture Organization of the United Nations

UNESCO United Nations Educational, Scientific, and Cultural Organization

WHO World Health Organization

IMF International Monetary Fund

IDA International Development Association

IBRD International Bank for Reconstruction and Development

IFC International Finance Corporation

ICAO International Civil Aviation Organization

UPU Universal Postal Union

ITU International Telecommunication Union

WMO World Meteorological Organization

IMCO Inter-Governmental Maritime Consultative Organization

GATT General Agreement on Tariffs and Trade

WIPO World Intellectual Property Organization

IAEA International Atomic Energy Agency

# PRINCIPAL ORGANS OF THE UNITED NATIONS

## GENERAL ASSEMBLY

The General Assembly is the main deliberative organ of the United Nations. Including representatives from all UN member nations, it discusses and makes recommendations on matters within the scope of the organization's Charter. It also approves the UN budget and apportions expenses among the members. A president, elected at the beginning of each session, presides.

The General Assembly convenes annually on the third Tuesday in September. Each member nation has one vote and is permitted to send up to 5 representatives to each session. On ordinary matters, decisions are carried by a simple majority of members present and voting; on more important matters, by a two-thirds majority.

The General Assembly works through 7 main committees: Political and Security; Special Political Committee; Economic and Financial; Social, Humanitarian, and Cultural; Trusteeship; Administrative and Budgetary; and Legal.

## SECURITY COUNCIL

The UN Security Council has primary responsibility for maintaining peace and security. The Council has 5 permanent members—Britain, China, France, the Soviet Union, and the United States—and 10 nonpermanent members elected to 2-year terms by the General Assembly. The Security Council is organized to function continuously. Each member has one vote. Decisions on procedural matters are carried by a majority of 9 members. However, on important matters, the 9 affirmative votes must include concurrence of the 5 permanent members. This is known as the "veto" privilege. Abstention does not constitute a veto.

The Security Council is empowered to investigate any situation that might lead to friction between two or more countries. All UN members are pledged to carry out its decisions, as well as to make available to the Council assistance and facilities—including armed forces—for maintenance of international peace. A country that is a member of the United Nations, but not of the Security Council, may participate in its discussions when that nation's interests are specially affected. Nonmembers can be invited to participate in Security Council discussions of disputes to which they are parties. A member that is a party to a dispute may not vote. The Disarmament Commission includes all UN member nations. It prepares proposals for regulation, limitation, and reduction of armed forces and armaments; for elimination of all weapons adaptable to mass destruction; and for international control of atomic energy to ensure its use for peaceful purposes.

The Military Staff Committee is composed of the chiefs of staff of the 5 permanent members—Britain, China, France, the Soviet Union, and the United States—or their representatives. It advises and assists the Security Council on such questions as the Council's military requirements for the maintenance of peace, the strategic direction of armed forces placed at its disposal, and the regulation of armaments.

## ECONOMIC AND SOCIAL COUNCIL

The UN Economic and Social Council examines and makes recommendations on international economic, social, cultural, educational, and health issues. The Council comprises 54 members, 18 of whom are elected each year to 3-year terms by the General Assembly. It is aided by separate regional commissions for Europe, Asia and the Far East, Latin America, and Africa.

## TRUSTEESHIP COUNCIL

The UN Trusteeship Council is the principal organ assisting the General Assembly in supervision and administration of trust territories. It comprises member nations administering trust territories, permanent members of the Security Council not administering trust territories, and as many other members (elected to 3-year terms by the General Assembly) as are required to provide an equal number of administering and nonadministering members.

Originally, 11 territories were placed under the trusteeship system; 10 have become independent or joined other independent states. The one still under UN trusteeship is the Trust Territory of the Pacific Islands (Micronesia), under U.S. administration.

## INTERNATIONAL COURT OF JUSTICE

The International Court of Justice, or *World Court*, is the judicial organ of the UN. It sits at The Hague, in the Netherlands. Fifteen judges are elected to 9-year terms by the General Assembly and the Security Council, voting independently. Every UN member has automatic access to the Court and is pledged to comply with its decisions. The Court has jurisdiction over all cases specifically referred to it, and over all matters specially provided for in the Charter or in treaties and conventions in force. The Court renders legal opinions on matters referred to it by the General Assembly, Security Council, and specialized agencies authorized by the General Assembly.

## UNITED NATIONS HEADQUARTERS

The present site of the United Nations headquarters is an 18-acre tract along the East River in midtown Manhattan. Purchased with an $8.5 million gift from John D. Rockefeller Jr., the site is now international territory.

In November 1947 the world body unanimously approved a design submitted by an international consulting board under the direction of Wallace K. Harrison, an American architect.

The United States loaned the organization $65 million, and construction began in September 1948. Total cost was $73 million.

The General Assembly met at "United Nations, New York" for the first time in October 1952. (Interim business had been conducted from temporary quarters at Hunter College in New York City and at Lake Success, N.Y.)

The present headquarters comprise three interconnected buildings and a library, surrounded by plazas, gardens, and lawns.

The Secretariat building is a 30-story rectangular column, sheathed in glass and marble. The Secretariat building contains offices and working space for the headquarters staff. It has 5,400 windows.

The General Assembly building faces a landscaped plaza to the north. It is a sloping, doubly concave structure, topped by a shallow dome.

The General Assembly Hall, in which representatives of all the member nations convene in formal session at least once a year, is 165 feet long, 115 feet wide, and three stories high. Seats for delegates and alternates are arranged in curved rows on the floor, facing the officials' podium, and flanked by seats for advisers and observers. In the rear are places for alternate delegates, representatives' guests, and the press. Public galleries overlook the hall.

Translation and press booths line the walls of the General Assembly Hall. All 2,098 seats are equipped with earphones, enabling participants and spectators to listen to proceedings in any of the UN's five official languages: Chinese, English, French, Spanish, and Russian. Translations are simultaneous.

The UN buildings and grounds are decorated by works of art donated by various nations.

Buildings are open to the public from 9 A.M. to 5:30 P.M. daily, except Christmas and New Year's Day. An international staff of guides conducts tours of the headquarters between 9:00 A.M. and 4:45 P.M. daily. About one million persons take the tours each year.

## UNITED STATES MISSION TO THE UNITED NATIONS

Donald F. McHenry, *Ambassador Extraordinary and Plenipotentiary*, Permanent Representative to the United Nations

William J. vanden Heuvel, *Ambassador*, Deputy Permanent Representative to the United Nations

Richard W. Petree, *Ambassador*, Deputy Representative on the Security Council

Joan Edelman Spero, *Ambassador*, Representative, Economic and Social Council

H. Carl McCall, *Ambassador*, Alternate Representative for Special Political Affairs

## MEMBERSHIP IN PRINCIPAL UNITED NATIONS BODIES: 1981

### SECURITY COUNCIL

Fifteen members: Five (indicated by *) are designated in the Charter as permanent. Ten are elected by the General Assembly for 2-year terms, ending December 31 of the year indicated.

| | | | | | |
|---|---|---|---|---|---|
| Britain * | Germany, East (1981) | Mexico (1981) | Philippines (1981) | Spain (1982) | Uganda (1982) |
| China * | Ireland (1982) | Niger (1981) | Soviet Union * | Tunisia (1981) | United States * |
| France * | Japan (1982) | Panama (1982) | | | |

### ECONOMIC AND SOCIAL COUNCIL

Fifty-four members are elected by the General Assembly for 3-year terms, ending December 31 of the year indicated.

| | | | | | |
|---|---|---|---|---|---|
| Algeria (1981) | Britain (1983) | Ecuador (1981) | Iraq (1982) | Nepal (1982) | Spain (1981) |
| Argentina (1983) | Bulgaria (1982) | Ethiopia (1982) | Ireland (1981) | Nicaragua (1983) | Sudan (1983) |
| Australia (1982) | Burundi (1983) | Fiji (1983) | Italy (1982) | Nigeria (1982) | Thailand (1982) |
| Bahamas (1982) | Cameroon (1983) | France (1981) | Jordan (1982) | Norway (1983) | Turkey (1981) |
| Bangladesh (1983) | Canada (1983) | Germany, East (1981) | Kenya (1983) | Pakistan (1981) | United States (1982) |
| Barbados (1981) | Chile (1982) | Germany, West (1981) | Libya (1982) | Peru (1983) | Venezuela (1981) |
| Belgium (1982) | China (1983) | Ghana (1981) | Malawi (1982) | Poland (1983) | Yugoslavia (1981) |
| Belorussia (1983) | Cyprus (1981) | India (1983) | Mexico (1982) | Senegal (1981) | Zaire (1982) |
| Brazil (1981) | Denmark (1983) | Indonesia (1981) | Morocco (1981) | Soviet Union (1983) | Zambia (1981) |

### INTERNATIONAL COURT OF JUSTICE (WORLD COURT)

Fifteen members, elected by the General Assembly and the Security Council to 9-year terms ending February 5 of the year indicated.

President of World Court:

| | |
|---|---|
| Sir Humphrey Waldock, Britain ..........1982 | Hermann Mosler, West Germany ............1985 |
| Taslim O. Elias, Nigeria (Vice President) .....1985 | Shigeru Oda, Japan ......................1985 |
| Isaac Forster, Senegal ....................1982 | Salah El Dine Tarazi, Syria ................1985 |
| André Gros, France .......................1982 | Roberto Ago, Italy ........................1988 |
| José María Ruda, Argentina ...............1982 | Abdullah Ali El-Erian, Egypt ..............1988 |
| Nagendra Singh, India ....................1982 | José Sette Câmara, Brazil .................1988 |
| Manfred Lachs, Poland ....................1985 | Richard R. Baxter, United States ..........1988 |
| | Platon Morozov, Soviet Union ............1988 |

# UN SPECIALIZED AGENCIES AND AUTONOMOUS BODIES

**Food and Agriculture Organization of the United Nations (FAO)**
*Headquarters:* Rome, Italy
Established Oct. 16, 1945, to promote development of agriculture and good nutrition

**General Agreement on Tariffs and Trade (GATT)**
*Headquarters:* Geneva, Switzerland
Established Jan. 1, 1948, to provide international trade and tariff standards

**Intergovernmental Maritime Consultative Organization (IMCO)**
*Headquarters:* London, England
Established March 17, 1958, to promote international cooperation in maritime navigation

**International Atomic Energy Agency (IAEA)**
*Headquarters:* Vienna, Austria
Established July 29, 1957, to promote development of nuclear power for peaceful purposes

**International Bank for Reconstruction and Development (World Bank)**
*Headquarters:* Washington, D.C.
Established Dec. 27, 1945, to assist reconstruction and development of member states

**International Civil Aviation Organization (ICAO)**
*Headquarters:* Montreal, Quebec
Established April 4, 1947, to study international civil aviation problems and set standards

**International Development Association (IDA)**
*Headquarters:* Washington, D.C.
Established Sept. 24, 1960, for the purpose of making loans to less-developed countries

**International Finance Corporation (IFC)**
*Headquarters:* Washington, D.C.
Established July 20, 1956, to further economic development by encouraging private enterprise

**International Fund for Agricultural Development (IFAD)**
*Headquarters:* Rome, Italy.
Established Dec. 29, 1977, to help developing countries obtain investments to aid agricultural production

**International Labor Organization (ILO)**
*Headquarters:* Geneva, Switzerland
Established April 11, 1919, for the purpose of improving labor conditions and living standards through international action

**International Monetary Fund (IMF)**
*Headquarters:* Washington, D.C.
Established Dec. 27, 1945, for the purpose of promoting international monetary cooperation

**International Telecommunication Union (ITU)**
*Headquarters:* Geneva, Switzerland
Founded at Paris May 17, 1865, to establish international regulations for telegraph, telephone, and radio services

**United Nations Capital Development Fund (UNCDF)**
*Headquarters:* New York City.
Established Dec. 13, 1966, to provide grants and loans to developing countries

**United Nations Children's Fund (UNICEF)**
*Headquarters:* United Nations, N.Y.
Established Dec. 11, 1946, to aid the world's children by helping solve problems of health, hunger, and education

**United Nations Conference on Trade and Development (UNCTAD)**
*Headquarters:* Geneva, Switzerland
Established Dec. 30, 1964, to encourage economic growth in countries dependent on international trade

**United Nations Development Program (UNDP)**
*Headquarters:* Geneva, Switzerland
Established Nov. 22, 1966, to assist economic growth of developing nations

**United Nations Disaster Relief Office (UNDRO)**
*Headquarters:* Geneva, Switzerland
Established Dec. 14, 1971, to help coordinate aid in disaster areas

**United Nations Educational, Scientific, and Cultural Organization (UNESCO)**
*Headquarters:* Paris, France
Established Nov. 4, 1946, for the purpose of promoting international collaboration in education, science, and culture

**United Nations Environment Program (UNEP)**
*Headquarters:* Nairobi, Kenya
Established Dec. 15, 1972, as an outgrowth of the Stockholm Conference on the Human Environment, to identify major international environmental problems, monitoring the environment through the "Earthwatch" system

**United Nations Fund for Population Activities (UNFPA)**
*Headquarters:* United Nations, N.Y.
Established Dec. 18, 1972, to study and assist in population and family-planning problems

**United Nations Industrial Development Organization (UNIDO)**
*Headquarters:* Vienna, Austria
Established Nov. 17, 1966, to promote industrial growth in developing countries

**United Nations Institute for Training and Research (UNITAR)**
*Headquarters:* United Nations, N.Y.
Established Dec. 11, 1963, to carry out research and training programs to help developing nations

**United Nations Office of High Commissioner for Refugees (UNHCR)**
*Headquarters:* Geneva, Switzerland
Established Dec. 3, 1949, to protect the rights of refugees in foreign countries

**United Nations Relief and Works Agency for Palestine Refugees in the Near East (UNRWA)**
*Headquarters:* Vienna, Austria, and Amman, Jordan
Established Dec. 8, 1949, to aid refugees from Arab-Israeli War of 1948

**United Nations Research Institute for Social Development (UNRISD)**
*Headquarters:* Geneva, Switzerland
Established July 1, 1964, to research social problems related to economic growth

**United Nations University (UNU)**
*Headquarters:* Tokyo, Japan
Established Dec. 11, 1972, to provide a worldwide network of institutions of higher education

**Universal Postal Union (UPU)**
*Headquarters:* Bern, Switzerland
Established July 1, 1875, to promote cooperation in international postal services

**World Food Council (WFC)**
*Headquarters:* Rome, Italy
Established Dec. 17, 1974, on recommendation of World Food Conference to coordinate international efforts to feed hungry persons and to assist agricultural development of poor nations

**World Health Organization (WHO)**
*Headquarters:* Geneva, Switzerland
Established April 7, 1948, to promote world health through advisory and technical services

**World Intellectual Property Organization (WIPO)**
*Headquarters:* Geneva, Switzerland
Established April 26, 1970; affiliated with UN in 1974; promotes the protection of such intellectual properties as rights to literary, artistic, and scientific works

**World Meteorological Organization (WMO)**
*Headquarters:* Geneva, Switzerland
Established April 4, 1951, to promote international cooperation in weather observation

## INTERNATIONAL ORGANIZATIONS AND ALLIANCES

**Agency for the Prohibition of Nuclear Weapons in Latin America (OPANAL)**
*Headquarters:* Mexico City. Established Sept. 2, 1969, to prevent introduction of nuclear weapons in Latin America. *Members:* Bahamas, Barbados, Bolivia, Brazil, Chile, Colombia, Costa Rica, Dominican Republic, Ecuador, El Salvador, Grenada, Guatemala, Haiti, Honduras, Jamaica, Mexico, Nicaragua, Panama, Paraguay, Peru, Suriname, Trinidad-Tobago, Uruguay, Venezuela.

**Andean Pact**
Established Oct. 16, 1969, to end trade barriers among member nations and create a common market. *Members:* Bolivia, Colombia, Ecuador, Peru, Venezuela.

**ANZUS Pact**
Defense alliance established April 29, 1952. *Members:* Australia, New Zealand, U.S.

**Arab League**
Established March 22, 1945; headquarters in Tunis, Tunisia; fosters cooperation among Arab nations. *Members:* Algeria, Bahrain, Djibouti, Egypt (suspended), Iraq, Jordan, Kuwait, Lebanon, Libya, Mauritania, Morocco, Oman, Palestinians (PLO), Qatar, Saudi Arabia, Somalia, Sudan, Syria, Tunisia, United Arab Emirates, North Yemen, South Yemen.

**Association of Southeast Asian Nations (ASEAN)**
Established Aug. 9, 1967, to stimulate economic growth of region. *Members:* Indonesia, Malaysia, Philippines, Singapore, Thailand.

**Caribbean Community and Common Market (CARICOM)**
Established Aug. 1, 1973, to coordinate economic and foreign policies. *Members:* Antigua, Barbados, Belize, Dominica, Grenada, Guyana, Jamaica, Montserrat, St. Kitts-Nevis, St. Lucia, St. Vincent, Trinidad-Tobago.

**Central African Customs and Economic Union (UDEAC)**
Established Jan. 1, 1966, to aid economic, social, technical, and cultural development of members. *Members:* Cameroon, Central Africa, Congo, Gabon.

**Central American Common Market (CACM)**
Established June 3, 1961, to form a common market. *Headquarters:* Guatemala City. *Members:* Costa Rica, El Salvador, Guatemala, and Nicaragua.

**Colombo Plan**
*Headquarters:* Colombo, Sri Lanka. Established July 1, 1951, to aid development of members: Afghanistan, Australia, Bangladesh, Bhutan, Britain, Burma, Cambodia, Canada, Fiji, India, Indonesia, Iran, Japan, South Korea, Laos, Malaysia, Maldives, Nepal, New Zealand, Pakistan, Papua New Guinea, Philippines, Singapore, Sri Lanka, Thailand, United States, Vietnam.

**Conference on Security and Cooperation in Europe (CSCE—Helsinki Pact)**
Formed in 1975 by signing of Helsinki Agreement to cooperate in economics, peacekeeping, and promotion of human rights. *Members:* Austria, Belgium, Britain, Bulgaria, Canada, Cyprus, Czechoslovakia, Denmark, East Germany, Finland, France, Greece, Hungary, Iceland, Ireland, Italy, Liechtenstein, Luxembourg, Malta, Monaco, Netherlands, Norway, Poland, Portugal, Romania, San Marino, Soviet Union, Spain, Sweden, Switzerland, Turkey, United States, Vatican, West Germany, Yugoslavia.

**Council for Mutual Economic Assistance (COMECON)**
An economic organization of communist-bloc nations, founded Jan. 25, 1949, with headquarters in Moscow. *Members:* Bulgaria, Cuba, Czechoslovakia, East Germany, Hungary, Mongolia, Poland, Romania, Soviet Union, Vietnam. *Associate Member,* Yugoslavia.

**Council of Europe**
*Headquarters:* Strasbourg, France. Established Aug. 3, 1949, to promote unity, economic progress, and social progress among members. *Members:* Austria, Belgium, Britain, Cyprus, Denmark, France, West Germany, Greece, Iceland, Ireland, Italy, Liechtenstein, Luxembourg, Malta, Netherlands, Norway, Portugal, Spain, Sweden, Switzerland, Turkey.

**Economic Community of West African States (ECOWAS)**
Established by treaty signed May 28, 1975, at Lagos, Nigeria, to provide economic cooperation among members: Benin, Cape Verde, Gambia, Ghana, Guinea, Guinea-Bissau, Ivory Coast, Liberia, Mali, Mauritania, Niger, Nigeria, Senegal, Sierra Leone, Togo, Upper Volta.

**European Economic Community (EEC)**
European Common Market, established Jan. 1, 1958; also includes European Coal and Steel Community (ECSC), European Atomic Energy Community (EURATOM), and European Parliament. *Members:* Belgium, Britain, Denmark, France, West Germany, Greece, Italy, Ireland, Luxembourg, Netherlands.

**European Free Trade Association (EFTA)**
Established May 3, 1960, for free trade among members. *Members:* Austria, Iceland, Norway, Portugal, Sweden, Switzerland. *Associate member:* Finland.

**Latin American Free Trade Association (LAFTA)**
Founded June 2, 1961, with headquarters in Montevideo. *Members:* Argentina, Bolivia, Brazil, Chile, Colombia, Ecuador, Mexico, Paraguay, Peru, Uruguay, and Venezuela.

**Nordic Council**
Established Feb. 12, 1953, as an interparliamentary union to promote cooperation of Scandinavian nations in nonmilitary matters. *Members:* Denmark, Finland, Iceland, Norway, Sweden.

**North Atlantic Treaty Organization (NATO)**
Defense alliance, established Sept. 17, 1949. *Headquarters:* Brussels. *Members:* Belgium, Britain, Canada, Denmark, France, West Germany, Greece, Iceland, Italy, Luxembourg, Netherlands, Norway, Portugal, Turkey, United States.

**Organization for Economic Cooperation and Development (OECD)**
Established Sept. 30, 1961, to promote economic cooperation among members: Australia, Austria, Belgium, Britain, Canada, Denmark, Finland, France, West Germany, Greece, Iceland, Ireland, Italy, Japan, Luxembourg, Netherlands, New Zealand, Norway, Portugal, Spain, Sweden, Switzerland, Turkey, United States, Yugoslavia.

**Organization of African Unity (OAU)**
Established May 25, 1963, OAU promotes the unity and development of members: Algeria, Angola, Benin, Botswana, Burundi, Cameroon, Cape Verde, Central Africa, Chad, Comoros, Congo, Djibouti, Egypt, Equatorial Guinea, Ethiopia, Gabon, Gambia, Ghana, Guinea, Guinea-Bissau, Ivory Coast, Kenya, Lesotho, Liberia, Libya, Madagascar, Malawi, Mali, Mauritania, Mauritius, Morocco, Mozambique, Niger, Nigeria, Rwanda, São Tomé and Príncipe, Senegal, Seychelles, Sierra Leone, Somalia, Sudan, Swaziland, Tanzania, Togo, Tunisia, Uganda, Upper Volta, Zaire, Zambia.

**Organization of American States (OAS)**
*Headquarters:* Washington, D.C. Formerly the Pan American Union, the OAS was organized Dec. 31, 1951, for defense and cooperation. *Members:* Argentina, Barbados, Bolivia, Brazil, Chile, Colombia, Costa Rica, Cuba, Dominica, Dominican Republic, Ecuador, El Salvador, Grenada, Guatemala, Haiti, Honduras, Jamaica, Mexico, Nicaragua, Panama, Paraguay, Peru, St. Lucia, Suriname, Trinidad-Tobago, United States, Uruguay, Venezuela.

**Organization of Petroleum Exporting Countries (OPEC)**
Established Nov. 14, 1960, to control production and pricing of crude oil. *Members:* Algeria, Ecuador, Gabon, Indonesia, Iran, Iraq, Kuwait, Libya, Nigeria, Qatar, Saudi Arabia, United Arab Emirates, Venezuela.

**South Pacific Forum**
*Headquarters:* Suva, Fiji. Established August 1971 to promote economic and political cooperation. *Members:* Australia, Cook Islands, Fiji, Kiribati, Nauru, New Zealand, Niue, Papua New Guinea, Solomon Islands, Tonga, Tuvalu, Vanuatu, Western Samoa.

**Warsaw Treaty Organization**
*Headquarters:* Moscow. Military alliance of communist states, established June 5, 1955. *Members:* Bulgaria, Czechoslovakia, East Germany, Hungary, Poland, Romania, Soviet Union.

**Western European Union (WEU)**
Established May 6, 1955, as military alliance. *Members:* Belgium, Britain, France, West Germany, Italy, Luxembourg, Netherlands.

# Language

## NEW WORDS

The American language is growing at a rapid rate as dozens of new words come into use each year. These words come from a wide variety of fields including science, politics, economics, and education. Each specialized group coins new words, and some of these spread quickly, especially when they are picked up by newspapers and the television and radio media. Others may become popular only in one city or geographic region.

Words new in 1980 and in recent years are listed below:

**Abscam**—code name for "Arab scam," in which FBI agents posing as Arab businessmen offered bribes to public officials for promised commercial or political favors

**acid rain**—rainfall containing acids produced by emissions from power plants, smelters, and motor vehicles, considered toxic to wildlife and natural resources

**action grants**—federal funds for distribution to cities that compete for them by submitting urban-development plans; cities must also obtain commitment to projects by private investment sector

**advertorial**—blend of advertisement and editorial; see also *issue ad*

**anticiflation**—increase in prices, wages, and government spending in anticipation of new inflationary pressures

**asset stripping**—practice of buying undervalued companies having solid assets, which are then sold off for funds to make other acquisitions

**bad actor**—waste product from high-level fission in nuclear power plant; including cesium 137, strontium 90, and plutonium

**barn**—in metric system, unit of measurement for atomic nuclei assigned value of 10 to minus 24 square centimeters

**boatlift**—transportation of people by fleet of small boats, especially those fleeing their country for refuge elsewhere

**born-again politics**—conservative political movement based on fundamentalist morality

**bregoil**—waste product of pulp-and-paper industry used for cleaning oil spills by absorbing petroleum, forming hardened mass that later can be used for fuel

**broadbanding**—in industry, broadening of job classification so that each worker in group may do work of others to increase productivity

**bubble concept**—idea that each factory is self-contained within its own bubble and should be allowed to control its total air pollution in its own way unhampered by regulations for each smokestack or other emission site

**bubble memory**—oval-shaped magnetic chip used in microcomputers for data storage and retrieval; single garnet bubble, one-sixteenth diameter of human hair, can store upwards of 250,000 bits of information

**cafeteria plan**—program by which qualified company employees may select fringe benefits to suit long- or short-term needs with respect to insurance coverage, retirement, vacations, and the like

**captive insurer**—subsidiary of company or trade association formed to provide full range of insurance coverage at lower operating costs than if purchased from commercial insurance firm

**cardaholic**—person who habitually uses credit cards for purchases well beyond ability to pay

**channeling radiation**—newly discovered source of X rays, produced when charged subatomic particles moving at speed of light are guided into channels to form perfect single crystal; possibly useful for studying structure of crystalline materials by X-ray diffraction

**chop shop**—auto junk yard that illegally accepts stolen cars for cutting up into parts for resale

**Chunnel**—proposed tunnel under English Channel linking Britain and France

**condomania**—widespread rush to convert rental apartments into condominiums

**creditism**—government control of supply and use of credit to counter inflation

**Cubalift**—airlift for persons fleeing oppression in Cuba

**deadline diplomacy**—diplomacy conducted under pressure of resolving issues before a scheduled date, as in arms-limitation talks

**demand-side economics**—theory that government can regulate nation's economy by controlling total demand for goods and services—stimulating demand to create employment or curbing demand to combat inflation

**diamond anvil**—device by which rock sample placed between pair of diamonds is heated by laser beams and compressed to pressure comparable to that in earth's core, for use in studying formation of earth's interior

**double nickel**—55-mile-per-hour speed limit

**ecological allergy**—allergic reaction from exposure to chemicals in plastics, petroleum-based products or pesticides

**enterprise zone**—blighted area in city in which government controls, restrictions, and taxes are reduced or eliminated to encourage rehabilitation by private enterprise

**equity mortgage**—home-mortgage contract in which lender reduces interest rate by certain percentage in return for same percentage of profit when borrower sells home

**event horizon**—in physics, theoretical region within "black hole" in which object becomes virtually invisible, having lost all physical properties except mass, magnetism, and angular momentum

**fast tracking**—in building, procedure by which elements of construction project, such as excavation and foundation, are begun before

**NEW WORDS** (continued)

design is completed in effort to save time and expense

**favorite daughter**—proposal that each state offer woman candidate for presidential nomination on platform of support for Equal Rights Amendment

**Fourth World**—group of undeveloped nations concentrated in black Africa, Asia, and Caribbean islands whose poverty levels according to UN studies are lowest in world

**Freedom Flotilla**—fleet of boats for carrying people fleeing oppression in their country to sanctuary elsewhere, especially as applied to refugees from Cuba

**friendship price**—reduced price for commodity, such as oil or grain, offered by seller to select group of buyers who belong to same political or trading bloc

**front-end bonus**—payment, in addition to salary and benefits, offered to prospective company executive as inducement to accept position

**fudge factor**—allowance for changing economic conditions built into forecasts of trends determined by statistical formulas or econometric models

**gasohol**—motor-fuel mixture consisting of 90% unleaded gasoline and 10% 200-proof ethyl alcohol

**glutflation**—inflated prices for commodity, such as oil, in spite of its overabundance (glut)

**gnarly**—slang, meaning "good"

**graymail**—threat of disclosing classified information dangerous to national security as means of avoiding prosecution on criminal charges

**grid lock**—complete stoppage of vehicular traffic in city resulting from tie-ups at intersections within given area

**guided missile**—in medicine, drug placed in capsule of fatty material for release only in area of body requiring treatment; application of heat to targeted area causes fatty material to dissolve, releasing drug

**hardship index**—index of economic hardship measured on basis of whether individual's income is below poverty level and person belongs to household with total income less than twice the poverty standard

**hortitherapy**—therapy of growing plants and flowers that aids persons in overcoming physical and emotional problems

**house doctor**—professional expert in determining energy efficiency of residences and commercial buildings and prescribing methods of improvement

**huddling**—informal meeting between two or more persons in large company to solve problems without going through chain of command

**hydrasorter**—device that separates useful solid materials, such as metals and glass, from liquid garbage for recovery and recycling while also producing steam for generating electricity

**inflacession**—economic recession caused by inability to adjust to mounting inflation

**intelligent printer**—copying machine linked electronically to computer, word-processing typewriter, or other automated office equipment to produce printed copy at high speed; machine uses lasers or fiber-optic cathode-ray tubes to convert typed characters to printed form by means of digital signals without physically touching paper

**issue ad**—editorial type of radio or TV commercial presented by corporation on controversial topic; see also *advertorial*

**junk bond**—bond or other debt instrument offering high yield at price that does not reflect underlying value of company's assets

**killer satellite**—space vehicle capable of tracking and destroying other orbiting craft, such as communications or surveillance satellites

**knockout jacket**—jacket made of net fabric treated with pesticide that repels or kills blood-sucking insects

**mastery learning**—educational technique by which students continue study of subject until they demonstrate mastery according to programmed testing

**microprocessor**—miniaturized electronic circuitry usually contained in tiny silicon chip for use in electronic calculators and small computers

**modem**—device that converts data signals into form that can be transmitted over telephone line and be converted back by computers at other end

**narrowcasting**—transmission by cable or subscription TV of programs unrestricted by conventional moral standards of regular commercial or public broadcasting

**necessity stamps**—proposed system of aid, similar to food stamps, to enable needy families to meet rising expenses for housing and energy as well as food

**outplacement**—management-consulting service that handles dismissals of, and procurement of new positions for, executive personnel

**ovenable paperboard**—heat-resistant paperboard material formed into trays for use in heating food in microwave ovens

**palimony**—financial settlement awarded by court decree to woman after termination of living relationship with man to enable her to reestablish independent life style

**passive smoker**—nonsmoker who inhales smoke from other people's cigarettes and is susceptible to deleterious effects, especially of "sidestream smoke" produced by lighted cigarettes not inhaled by smokers

**performance audit**—examination of financial records of public or private agency to determine whether money was well spent or whether goods and services contracted were up to standard

**PET**—acronym for *p*ositron *e*mission *t*omography, technique for scanning brain to study disorders by injecting solution carrying radioactive isotope in bloodstream whose emissions are converted by computer to show areas of greatest activity

**petrocession**—economic recession resulting from inflationary pressures caused by mounting costs of petroleum

**powder metallurgy**—technique for producing metal objects from powdered metal, which is poured into presses or dies, subjected to high pressure, and heated in furnace

**predacide**—chemical agent for killing or warding off predator animals

**psychosocial dwarfism**—arrested growth and development in children resulting from severe emotional disturbances within family

**Qube**—in cable television, device that connects home TV set with computer in transmitting station for polling viewer opinions of programs or topical issues

**rain radar**—radar technique for measuring number and size of falling raindrops

**repo**—agreement by which bank or other financial institution agrees to buy back securities, such as government bonds, from purchaser at specified price higher than that of original purchase

**resegregation**—practice among certain real-estate firms of directing whites and blacks seeking homes or apartments to particular neighborhoods in support of racial separation and denial of desegregation

**satcheleer**—speculator who puts deposit on article offered for sale by auction house in hopes of selling at higher price before balance is due

**shield law**—law designed to protect reporters from being forced by courts to disclose sources of materials developed during investigations or news gathering

**siabon**—hybrid ape, offspring of siamang and gibbon

**sin subsidy**—lower income tax rate for unmarried couple filing as individuals than for married couple filing joint return

**smokeout**—campaign whereby persons voluntarily stop smoking for entire day as step toward permanent abstention

**smoking gun**—incriminating evidence of a crime

**snake box**—electronic display board connected to computer to enable dealers in foreign exchange to keep track of pair of floating currencies (called "snake"); when exchange rate reaches certain level, alarm goes off to alert dealers to buy or sell so as to ensure proper rate

**solar index**—amount of sunshine available for operating solar water heaters on given day, rated on scale of 0 to 100; data compiled by U.S. Energy Department and National Weather Service

**squid**—acronym for *s*uperconductive *q*uantum *i*nterference *d*evice, highly sensitive electronic device capable of detecting slight random interference; used in research for measuring magnetic fields

**stealth aircraft**—military aircraft specially designed and coated to evade detection by enemy radar

**stream walker**—one of group of volunteers who patrol designated stream or creek to monitor water for pollution by illegal discharge of industrial waste

**sunbelt**—region of southern states of U.S.

**sunrise industry**—new industry based on advanced technology, involving risk but offering potential for growth and export

**supply-side economics**—economic theory that government incentives to increase nation's total supply of goods and services will stimulate employment, create greater demand, and lead to prosperity

**supported work**—government-supported program under which welfare recipients train to do jobs while continuing to receive support payments

**survival suit**—flotation suit of neoprene rubber covering entire body, including feet, hands, and forehead, to enable shipwrecked mariners to survive immersion in chilling waters

**sweat equity**—ownership interest in abandoned housing units obtained by persons who furnish their labor to renovate them; type of urban homesteading

**synfuel**—synthetic fuel, such as oil from coal or oil shale

**taggants**—tiny chips of layered paint embedded in batch of dynamite or other explosive for identification by code; useful in tracking source of explosive in police work

**tax creep**—rise in income tax resulting from increased earnings that force taxpayer into higher bracket at greater rate according to system of graduated income tax

**taxflation**—increased government tax revenues caused by inflation as persons move up in tax brackets by inflation raises rather than by adding real income

**teleport**—telecommunication center in metropolitan area for sending and receiving messages worldwide from orbiting satellites

**third kingdom**—newly discovered class of primitive organisms, simpler than bacteria, that use salts and acids as food; called *archaebacteria,* they include methanogens, halophiles, and thermoacidophiles

**tight-sands gas**—natural gas trapped in sandy rock, considered potential source of fuel

**time share**—purchased right to use room or apartment in hotel, motel, or condominium for limited time each year over period stipulated in contract

**tombstone**—financial or securities notice in newspaper or journal that merely presents facts, without further embellishment

**tractorcade**—procession of farmers on tractors in protest against government policy

**transit mall**—system of enclosed shelters within city for convenience of persons waiting for buses, especially in bad weather

**trashformation**—transformation of discarded trash, junk, or other found objects into useful or artistic articles

**trigger pricing**—U.S. government system of pricing steel, designed to protect domestic industry from foreign competition by identifying imports offered for sale at below cost of production

**tunnel vision**—narrowed view of life produced by overspecialization in field of work, learning, or thought that results in ignoring ethical considerations

**urban nomads**—inner-city residents displaced from older, moderate-priced dwellings by developers who renovate them for sale or lease to more affluent persons

**value engineering**—review of proposed engineering projects by independent consultants to evaluate whether plans and specifications are reliable and economically sound

**wind surfing**—water sport using surfboard equipped with hand-held sail

**word processing**—use of automated equipment to type letters or other documents

# HOW TO WRITE A REPORT

Preparing a report is a time-consuming, mentally taxing task. It can also be absorbing and rewarding. Involved are eight essential steps.

**1. Choose and analyze a subject.** Select a subject in which you are interested. It is difficult to write effectively unless you are concerned with your material.

Choose a subject about which sufficient information is available to you in the form of printed materials or from experts who can be reached.

Select a subject about which you can arrive at a conclusion or a set of conclusions. An effective report is a group of facts that *prove* or *disprove* a specific statement, theory, or idea about a particular subject.

**2. Make a careful investigation.** In gathering material for a report, start by reading a good résumé of the subject. Most often you should start with an encyclopedia article. If your topic is not covered in a general or special-subject encyclopedia, you may find the needed summary in a magazine article or in a chapter from a book.

Find the books that can help you. Begin your search in the card catalog of your library for books mentioned in the bibliography following the résumé article you have read.

Search for recently written material. Examine recent issues of the *Reader's Guide to Periodical Literature*. You can then compare what is listed there with entries in the *International Index to Periodicals* and *Bulletin of the Public Affairs Information Service* (P.A.I.S.). In addition, you might consult entries in the *Art Index, Agricultural Index, Education Index, Applied Science and Technology Index,* and *Business Periodical Index.*

If necessary, write or telephone people who can provide information.

**3. Take notes on your findings.** Take notes on 3-by-5-inch cards, which can be easily shuffled into place according to the subject outline. Place no more than one note on a card; *never* use both sides of the card.

Each book or other source used should be entered on a separate card *in full bibliographical detail*, giving full name of the author, title, place of publication, publisher, and date.

You will then have two files of cards: (1) a master file that will include *all* bibliographical details on each book or article used, and (2) a file containing notes taken for the body of your paper.

Notes must be *legible* to avoid misinterpretation later, and must be *full* so that repeated trips to the library to verify them will not be necessary.

Distinguish between fact and opinion in the notes made. They all should be worded so that there will be no confusion later as to what *you* wrote or thought and what the *author* meant.

**4. Prepare an outline.** No one can write an effective report without some sort of outline.

An outline need not be detailed or elaborate. Only a few minutes may be needed to prepare a rough "sketch" outline that may pay big dividends.

You will probably make a number of tentative outlines as your work proceeds. When you are ready to state conclusions and have some idea of the framework of the entire structure, you can rearrange your notes under the outline headings.

**5. Write a first draft.** Prepare a first draft as a working copy. You can then make changes in sequence, strengthen your beginning, eliminate overlapping details, or make your discussion more effective.

Write in a clear, straightforward manner. A research paper need not be stiff, overly formal, or pedantic. It can be enlivened by touches of humor.

You must avoid *plagiarism*. You must *not* copy the words written by someone else unless you put them in quotation marks and name their source. Unless the idea and the phrasing are your own, refer the reader in a footnote to the source for your statement.

**6. Add footnotes or explanatory comments.** The purpose of a footnote is to name the authority for some fact or to develop some point referred to in the body of a paper.

**7. Prepare a bibliography.** In a report a bibliography is an alphabetical, sometimes classified, list containing the names of all works quoted from or generally used in preparation. The bibliography should be placed at the end of the report on a separate page.

Unless instructed otherwise, arrange items in the bibliography alphabetically by last names of the authors. List titles by the same author alphabetically. Citing the publisher's name is optional, but the place and date of publication are usually given.

**8. Revise and proofread with care.** The final version of a report must be carefully prepared. It should be as nearly letter-perfect as possible. To make sure of this, read slowly through the text to correct spelling and punctuation. Larger errors involving revision or addition may necessitate redoing a page.

Check your footnotes and bibliography.

If time permits, lay the paper aside for at least one day. Then reread it with fresh eyes. You may be surprised at how many errors and lapses you discover.

# HOW TO PREPARE A SPEECH

So you were asked to speak at the next club meeting. And you were so flattered that you accepted. But now the time is rapidly approaching when you must make your appearance, and you haven't yet prepared your speech. Worried? Here are some tips that can help you overcome your stage fright.

**1. Choose a topic to interest your audience.** Who are the people you are speaking to? What are their interests? Write out what you believe is a fair profile of your audience. What is their average age? Will there be more men than women, or vice versa? What are their occupations? What common bond or interest brings them together as a group? Once you know your audience you should be ready to make a list of topics that might interest them.

**2. Make sure your topic fits the occasion.** What is the purpose of the meeting? If it is a Little League dinner celebrating the end of the season, you certainly shouldn't give a speech on *How to Pot Geraniums*, even if you happen to be the world's greatest authority on that subject.

**3. Try to make your topic timely.** If the meeting is a week before Christmas, you shouldn't try to speak on the events leading up to the Declaration of Independence. Think ahead to what events are going to take place at the time of the meeting or soon after. What can you talk about that will relate to those events?

**4. Make sure your topic fits the time allowed.** How long is your speech supposed to be? If you have only been allowed five minutes, don't choose such a broad topic that it can't possibly be discussed thoroughly within that period. For example, *The History of Space Exploration* would require much more than five minutes. So reduce your topic to *Man's First Walk on the Moon* to fit the time allowed.

**5. Stimulate your audience to action.** After the audience has heard your speech, what do you want them to do? If you want them to stop littering the streets with waste paper, then you must make them want to use the litter baskets. Even if you are giving a purely informative speech, such as *The History of the Bill of Rights*, you should try to get your audience to go out and read more about the subject because of the interest you have evoked by your speech. So in planning your topic, consider what you are going to ask your audience to do about it.

**6. Be specific with your topic.** Avoid a generalized topic, narrowing it to a specific aspect of the subject. For example, *Baseball* is too broad a subject for a good speech. Instead, talk on a specific aspect of baseball, such as *Four Ways to Hit More Home Runs* or *How One Boy Learned What Team Spirit Means.*

**7. Choose a topic you are interested in.** Avoid choosing a topic that you yourself find uninteresting. Otherwise, how can you possibly excite your audience about it?

**8. Prepare your speech in three parts.** Your speech should be divided into three main parts: (1) the introductory remarks, (2) the main body of the speech, and (3) the conclusion.

As you gather materials for your speech and make notes, arrange them into these three parts.

**9. Wake up the audience at the outset.** The introductory remarks, the first part of your speech, must catch the attention of the audience and make them want to listen to you. You may want to ask a question: "How many of you ever hit a home run?" or "Which one of you threw this gum wrapper on the floor?" Or you may wish to open with a startling statement: "Look down the row you are sitting in. At least one of the people you see will die of a heart attack within the next two years."

**10. Avoid jokes unless you are a practiced storyteller.** If you have tried telling jokes to your family and friends, and have received only weak smiles in return, avoid trying to open your speech with a joke.

If you are determined to use a joke, practice it on strangers. If they don't laugh, discard it.

**11. Limit the main points you want to make.** As you prepare the main body of your speech, limit yourself to making only two, three, or four main points. Organize your speech so that it will be clear to the audience exactly what are the main points you are trying to get across. Many speakers ramble on from one topic to another, and at the end the members of the audience ask each other, "What was he trying to say?"

**12. Use specific examples.** Back up each point with at least one specific example.

**13. Avoid technical vocabulary.** Although you are an authority on your subject, your audience is not. Make sure that the vocabulary you use is simplified so your audience can understand you. If you have to use a technical term, define it for the audience.

**14. Conclude with a climax.** The conclusion should be the best part of the speech and the part the audience remembers longest. You should summarize your main points and make your audience want to act on what you have said.

# PUNCTUATE IT RIGHT!

Too much punctuation may be as confusing as too little. If a sentence is so complicated that no amount of punctuation seems adequate, the writer should reorganize it.

## PERIOD (.)

The period is used at the end of sentences, after an indirect question, and after a polite request resembling a question. It is also the end mark for initials and certain abbreviations.

Here are examples of sentences that end with a period.

Declarative: *Mrs. Morris placed the book on the table.*

Imperative: *Do it today. Sit down.*

Indirect Question: *The members of the committee asked when the meeting would take place.*

Polite Request: *Will you open the door for me, please.*

## QUESTION MARK (?)

The question mark signifies that the sentence asks a question: *What time is it? Am I late?*

Sometimes a sentence consists of several questions, each of which should end with a question mark. However, the separate questions within the sentence do not begin with a capital, since they are part of the sentence: *Who will attend the conference? the president? the vice president? the secretary?*

## EXCLAMATION POINT (!)

The exclamation point at the end of a statement denotes strong emotion or a sense of urgency. Often this may be a phrase or even a single word: *What a show! Hurrah! Please hurry!*

An interjection such as *Oh!* or *Ah!* at the beginning of a sentence is usually followed by a comma, and the sentence is ended with an exclamation point: *Oh, what a day this has been!*

## COMMA (,)

Here are examples of sentence structure that call for the comma:

**Series:** The comma separates various elements in a series—either words, phrases, or clauses—when there are at least three units: *The dog jumped up, barked ferociously, bared his teeth, and took off after the rabbit.*

Style adopted by some newspapers, magazines, and publishing firms does not require the comma before the conjunction in a series, as in: *The flag is red, white and blue.*

When *et cetera,* or its abbreviation *etc.,* ends a series it should be preceded by a comma. A comma should also follow *etc.*

when it is not the last word in a sentence: *She stopped off to get some fruit, vegetables, etc., on the way home.*

**Introductory Elements:** When the main clause of the sentence comes first, there is no need for a comma in the sentence: *Take along a few magazines when you visit him.*

An introductory phrase containing a verb usually should be followed by a comma: *After making the survey, the committee published its report.*

If the introductory phrase is very short or does not contain a verb, it need not be followed by a comma unless the phrase is parenthetical or explanatory: *After much debate the meeting was adjourned.* But: *On the contrary, I believe the President was absolutely right.*

A comma sets off an introductory *yes* or *no*: *No, we shall not be ready on time.*

A parenthetical expression (word, phrase, or clause) that can be omitted without drastically changing the meaning of the sentence should be set off by commas: *The king, who was ill, was not present.*

**Quotations:** Use the comma before direct quotations, unless they are very long—usually a paragraph or more. In such cases a colon should be used: *She asked, "Is the train on time?"*

**Appositives:** A comma or commas should set off an identifying or explanatory word or phrase (called an *appositive*) which helps to make the meaning of the sentence clearer: *Mr. Jones, our grocer, traveled last summer to Canada, his native country.*

**Contrasting Expressions:** Use a comma to separate contrasting expressions—word, phrase, or clause: *We shall leave today, not tomorrow.*

**Parallel Adjectives:** Commas should separate parallel adjectives: *The tall, thin, scowling man made a poor impression.*

**Conjunctions:** The comma should be used before a conjunction (*but, and, or,* etc.) that connects two independent clauses: *John played shortstop, and he filled in a few times when the regular catcher was hurt.*

If the clauses are short and uncomplicated the comma may be omitted: *We were drenched but Mother didn't scold us.*

When two verbs have the same subject, the connecting conjunction is not usually preceded by a comma: *It snowed all morning but stopped at noon.*

**Numbers and Dates:** Use the comma with numbers in the thousands: *1,792 new cars.* Omit the comma in a date using only month and year: *April 1970.* But do use commas with the day of the month: *April 2, 1970.*

## SEMICOLON (;)

The semicolon separates two independent clauses when the conjunction is omitted: *We are enclosing an envelope for your convenience; it requires no postage.*

**Compound Sentences:** The semicolon separates members of a compound sentence when the clauses are connected by such words as *however, nevertheless, consequently, thus: The team was undefeated; however, three games ended in ties.*

When part of a compound sentence contains a comma, the semicolon must be used to separate the members: *If nominated, he will run; but his chances seem rather slim.*

**Series:** Phrases or clauses in a series are separated by the semicolon when one or more contain a comma: *Our profits for the three years were unusually high: 1974, $2,345,000; 1975, $2,070,400; 1976, $2,545,000.*

## COLON (:)

The colon generally indicates that a list, example, or strong assertion will follow: *Johnny had three jobs to do: clean the garage, mow the lawn, and sweep the back porch.*

The colon is also used after the salutation of a formal letter (*Dear Sir:*); between elements of a biblical citation (*Exodus 16:1–4*); after the name of the speaker in a play (*Hamlet: To be, or not to be: that is the question*); and to separate hours and minutes when time is expressed in figures (*We shall be there at 3:30 P.M.*).

## APOSTROPHE (')

The apostrophe commonly forms the possessive of nouns and pronouns. (However, personal pronouns such as *mine, yours, theirs* do not take the apostrophe.) With words ending in an *s,* use *'s* with one-syllable words, but use only an apostrophe with words of two or more syllables unless the *s* is not sounded: *James's, Adams', Arkansas's.*

Be careful not to use an apostrophe in the plurals of proper nouns where no possessive is intended: *We are going to see the Smiths and the Jeffersons* (not *Smith's* or *Smiths', Jefferson's* or *Jeffersons'*).

*Contractions:* An apostrophe is also used to show that one or more letters have been omitted from a word, or that numerals have been omitted from a number: *it's*—it is; *can't*—cannot; *'29*—1929.

## QUOTATION MARKS (" ") (' ')

Double quotation marks (" ") are required at the beginning and end of a word or words spoken in direct discourse: *Roy said, "I'm reading a good book."*

If a direct quotation is interrupted by one or more words, double quotation marks are placed around the quoted matter only, and not around the interrupting words: *"Hurry along," said the coach, "or the game will not start on time."*

Double quotation marks set off words or phrases the writer does not wish to claim as his or her own: *Let my opponent produce his "incontrovertible evidence."*

Single quotation marks (' ') enclose a quotation within a quotation: *Jack remarked, "I believe that Patrick Henry said, 'Give me liberty or give me death.'"*

Enclose in double quotation marks the titles of essays, magazine articles, lectures, term papers, and book chapters.

## HYPHEN (-)

Use the hyphen for end-of-line word divisions and in compound words.

Words may be divided at the end of a line *only* between syllables. (If in doubt as to how to divide a word, check your dictionary.) Never divide one-syllable words.

**Compound Words:** When two or more words precede a noun and form a single idea modifying the noun, they should be hyphenated: *He spoke in a matter-of-fact tone.*

**Prefixes:** Hyphens are sometimes used to separate prefixes from words where the meaning might otherwise be distorted: *The upholsterer re-covered the chair. Mr. Aiken recovered his stolen property.*

The hyphen is generally used when words are compounded with the prefix *self: self-satisfied; self-sufficient.*

The hyphen is also used to separate a prefix from a proper noun: *anti-American.*

**Numbers:** Hyphens are used in all numbers from *twenty-one* to *ninety-nine*, and in fractions: *one-half, three-quarters.*

## DASH (—)

A word of caution against confusing the hyphen (-) and the dash (—). The hyphen connects. The dash often separates. The dash may be used in place of the comma and parentheses in handling appositive and parenthetical expressions. It is also used to mark intentional repetition and interruption: *Exercise every day—I mean every day.*

## PARENTHESES [( )]

Parentheses marks are used to enclose words that give additional information but have little, if any, direct connection with the main thought expressed. They should be used sparingly: *If we win the contest (and I feel certain we shall), we shall compete in the finals.*

Parentheses are widely used to enclose references to statements, authors, and so forth: We are using the book *Effective Business English* (Jones and Smith).

# FORMS OF ADDRESS

Many people either may meet or have the occasion to write letters to persons of importance—high government officials, congressmen, judges, officers of the armed services, clergymen, physicians, and college professors. There are certain proper forms of address that should be used.

## PRESIDENT OF THE UNITED STATES

*Address*    Business: The President
The White House
Washington, D.C. 20500

               Social: The President
and Mrs. . . .
The White House
Washington, D.C. 20500

*Salutation*  Formal: Sir:
          Informal: My Dear Mr. President:

*Closing*    Formal: I have honor to remain,
Most respectfully yours,
          Informal: Very respectfully yours,

In conversation: Mr. President *or* Sir

## CHIEF JUSTICE OF THE UNITED STATES

*Address*    Business: The Chief Justice
The Supreme Court
Washington, D.C. 20543

               Social: The Chief Justice
and Mrs. . . .
Home address

*Salutation*  Formal: Sir:
          Informal: My Dear Mr. Chief Justice:

*Closing*    Formal: Very truly yours,
          Informal: Sincerely yours, *or*
Faithfully yours,

In conversation: Mr. Chief Justice *or* Sir

## ASSOCIATE JUSTICE OF THE SUPREME COURT

*Address*    Business: Mr. Justice . . .
The Supreme Court
Washington, D.C. 20543

               Social: Mr. Justice . . .
and Mrs. . . .
Home address

*Salutation*  Formal: Sir:
          Informal: My Dear Mr. Justice . . . :

*Closing*    Formal: Very truly yours,
          Informal: Sincerely yours,

In conversation: Mr. Justice *or* Mr.
Justice . . . *or* Sir

## CABINET OFFICER

*Address*    Business: The Honorable . . .
The Secretary of the
Treasury *or* The
Attorney General
Washington, D.C.

               Social: The Honorable . . .
The Secretary of the Treas-
ury *or* The Attorney
General and Mrs. . . .
Home address

*Salutation*  Formal: Sir: *or* Dear Sir:
          Informal: My Dear Mr. Secretary:
*or* My Dear Mr. Attorney
General:

*Closing*    Formal: Very truly yours,
          Informal: Sincerely yours,

In conversation: Mr. Secretary *or*
Mr. Attorney General
*or* . . . Sir.

## UNITED STATES SENATOR

*Address*    Business: The Honorable . . .
United States Senate
Washington, D.C. 20510

               Social: The Honorable . . .
and Mrs. . . .
Home address

*Salutation*  Formal: Sir: *or* Madam:
          Informal: My Dear Senator . . . :

*Closing*    Formal: Very truly yours,
          Informal: Sincerely yours,

In conversation: Senator *or* Senator . . .
*or* Sir *or* Madam

## UNITED STATES REPRESENTATIVE

*Address*    Business: The Honorable . . .
United States House of
Representatives
Washington, D.C. 20515

               Social: The Honorable . . .
and Mrs. . . .
Home address
*or* (for a woman member)
Mr. and Mrs. . . .

*Salutation*  Formal: Sir: *or* Madam:
          Informal: My Dear Mr. (or
Mrs.) . . . :

*Closing*    Formal: Very truly yours,
          Informal: Sincerely yours,

In conversation: Mr. . . . *or* Mrs. . . . *or*
Sir *or* Madam

## STATE SENATORS AND REPRESENTATIVES

Address like U.S. senators and representatives.

## AMBASSADOR OF THE UNITED STATES

*Address*    Business: The Honorable . . .
The Ambassador of the
United States
American Embassy
Address

               Social: The Honorable . . .
and Mrs. . . .
Home address
*or* (for a woman ambassador) Mr. and Mrs. . . .

*Salutation*  Formal: Sir: *or* Madam:
          Informal: My Dear Mr. (*or* My Dear
Madam) Ambassador:

*Closing*    Formal: Very truly yours,
          Informal: Sincerely yours,

In conversation: My Dear Mr. (*or* Madam)
Ambassador *or* Sir (*or*
Madam)

## CONSUL OF THE UNITED STATES

*Address*    Business: Mr. . . . .
American Consul
Address

               Social: Mr. and Mrs. . . .
Home Address

*Salutation*  Formal: Sir: *or* My Dear Sir:
          Informal: Dear Mr. . . . .

In conversation: Mr. . . . .

Title of Introduction: Mr. . . . .

## AMBASSADOR OF A FOREIGN COUNTRY

*Address*   Business: His Excellency, . . .
The Ambassador of . . .
Washington, D.C.
Social: His Excellency, . . .
The Ambassador of . . .
Home address
*Salutation*   Formal: Excellency:
Informal: My Dear Mr.
Ambassador:
*Closing*   Formal: Very truly yours,
Informal: Sincerely yours,
In conversation: Mr. Ambassador *or*
Excellency *or* Sir

## GOVERNOR OF A STATE

*Address*   Business: The Honorable . . .
Governor of . . .
(capital city, state)
Social: The Honorable . . .
and Mrs. . . .
Home address
*Salutation*   Formal: Sir:
Informal: Dear Governor . . . :
*Closing*   Formal: Very truly yours,
In conversation: Governor . . . *or* Sir

## MAYOR

*Address*   Business: His (*or* Her) Honor the
Mayor
City Hall
Address
Social: His Honor the Mayor
and Mrs. *or* (*for woman
mayor*) Mr. and Mrs.
Home address
*Salutation*   Formal: Sir: *or* Madam:
Informal: Dear Mayor . . . :
*Closing*   Formal: Very truly yours,
In conversation: Mr. (*or* Madam) Mayor

## JUDGE

*Address*   Business: The Honorable . . .
Justice Appellate
Division
Supreme Court of the
State of . . .
Address
Social: The Honorable . . .
and Mrs. . . .
Home address
*Salutation*   Formal: Sir: *or* Madam:
Informal: Dear Judge . . .
*Closing*   Formal: Very truly yours,
In conversation: Mr. (*or* Madam) Justice

## PROTESTANT CLERGYMAN

*Address*   Business: The Reverend . . . *or* (if
he holds the degree) The
Reverend . . . , D.D.
Social: The Reverend . . . and
Mrs. . . .
Home address
*Salutation*   Formal: Sir: *or* My Dear Sir:
Informal: Dear Mr. (*or* Dr.) . . . :
*Closing*   Formal: Sincerely yours, *or*
Faithfully yours,
In conversation: Mr. (*or* Dr.) . . . (*never*
Reverend . . .)

## RABBI

*Address*   Business: Rabbi . . . *or* (if he
holds the degree)
Dr. . . . , D.D.
Address of his synagogue
Social: Rabbi (*or* Dr.) and
Mrs. . . .
Home address
*Salutation*   Formal: Dear Sir:
Informal: Dear Rabbi (*or* Dr.) . . .
*Closing*   Formal: Sincerely yours,
Informal: Sincerely yours,
In conversation: Rabbi (*or* Dr.)

## CATHOLIC PRIEST

*Address*   Business: The Reverend . . . (and
the initials of his order,
if needed)
Address of his church
*Salutation*   Formal: Reverend Father:
Informal: Dear Father . . . :
*Closing*   Formal: I remain, Reverend
Father, yours faithfully,
Informal: Faithfully yours,
In conversation: Father *or* Father . . .
*or* Your Reverence

## OFFICERS OF THE ARMED SERVICES

(Commander or higher in the Navy; captain or
higher in the Air Force, Army, and Marines)
*Address*   Business: Admiral . . . , USN *or*
Colonel . . . , USMC
*or* General . . . , USA
*or* USAF (plus any title)
Address of base, ship, or
government department
Social: Admiral (*or* Colonel *or*
General) and Mrs. . . .
Home address
*Salutation*   Formal: Sir:
Informal: My Dear Admiral
(*or* Colonel
*or* General) . . . :
*Closing*   Formal: Very truly yours,
Informal: Sincerely yours,

## PHYSICIAN

*Address*   Business: . . . , M.D.
Office address
Social: Dr. and Mrs. . . .
Home address
*Salutation*   Formal: Dear Sir:
Informal: Dear Dr. . . . :
*Closing*   Formal: Very truly yours,
Informal: Sincerely yours,

## COLLEGE (OR UNIVERSITY) PROFESSOR

*Address*   Business: Professor *or* (if he
holds the Ph.D. degree)
Dr. *or* Mr. . . .
Office address
Social: Professor (*or* Dr. *or*
Mr.) and Mrs. . . .
*Salutation*   Formal: Dear Sir:
Informal: Dear Professor (*or* Dr.
*or* Mr.) . . .
*Closing*   Formal: Very truly yours,
Informal: Sincerely yours,
In conversation: Professor (*or* Dr.) . . .
(within the college);
Mr. . . . (elsewhere)

# SPELL IT RIGHT!

Here are five tips to better spelling:

1. Keep a list of your spelling errors and study them.

2. Learn to spell the most commonly misspelled words. (See opposite page.)

3. Use newly acquired words and make them a part of your oral and written vocabulary.

4. When in doubt as to the correct spelling of a word, consult your dictionary.

5. Study the following rules. These will help you overcome many of the most common spelling pitfalls.

**Which is it: -ant or -ent? -ance or -ence?** If you know that a word ends in *-ant*, related words will always end in *-ance* and *-ancy*. And if a word ends in *-ent*, related words will end in *-ence* and *-ency*.

Here are 8 representative *-ant*, *-ance*, *-ancy* words: *acceptance, assistant, attendant, insurance, maintenance, relevancy, resistant, tolerant*. In the *-ent*, *-ence*, *-ency* group the following 12 words are troublesome to many people: *apparent, coincident, conference, confident, consistency, correspondent, dependent, existence, occurrence, persistent, reference, superintendent*.

**Which is it: -cede, -ceed, or sede?** There is only one word that ends in *-sede: supersede.* Only three words end in *-ceed: proceed* (but *procedure*), *exceed, succeed.* All other words with this phonetic sound end in *-cede: precede, recede, secede.*

**Which is it: ie or ei?** After *c*, when the sound is long *e*, the *e* usually precedes the *i* (ei): *ceiling, deceive, receipt, receive.*

After most other letters, the *i* precedes the *e* (ie): *achieve, believe, grief, lien, siege, thief.*

When the sound is not long *e*, and especially if the sound is long *a*, the *e* precedes the *i* (ei): *sleigh, veil, weigh.*

**Which is it: -ary or -ery?** Because the word endings *-ary* and *-ery* sound alike, they can cause spelling problems. However, one fact will solve most of the problems. More than 300 words end in *-ary;* only a few words end in *-ery.* If you learn these few you will conquer the difficulty: *artillery, bakery, brewery, celery, cemetery, confectionery, distillery, dysentery, millinery, monastery, refinery, stationery* (writing paper).

**Which is it: -ar, -er, or -or?** Here are two tips on *-ar, -er,* and *-or* words. First, the ending *-ar* is not common. All you need do is to learn a few common *-ar* words such as *beggar, cedar, collar, dollar, liar, registrar, scholar,* and *similar.*

The more confusing endings are *-er* and *-or.* So here's a second tip: For simple, common words *-er* is usually the right ending.

The Latin *-or* goes with advanced words.

In American English *-re* is not a common ending. Learn the correct spelling of these six *-re* words: *acre, lucre, macabre, massacre, mediocre, ogre.*

**Which is it: -al, -el, or -le?** No good rule has ever been devised to help you decide whether a word ends in *-al, -el,* or *-le.* Pronunciation will not help you either, because all three sound alike when spoken.

You must try to memorize the spelling of words with these endings. When in doubt, consult your dictionary.

**Which is it: -able or -ible?** Two points about *-able* and *-ible* simplify the decision as to which spelling is correct:

1. *-able* is the basic form. Many more words end in *-able* than in *-ible.*

2. An *a* for an *a* and an *i* for an *i:* If the adjective is closely related to a noun that ends in *-ation,* the adjective is almost certain to end in *-able.* If a related noun ends in *-ion* instead of *-ation,* the adjective is pretty sure to end in *-ible.*

**Which is it: c or ck?** If a word ends in a *c,* you must add a *k* before a suffix beginning with *e, i,* or *y* to keep the *c* hard: *frolic* becomes *frolicking; mimic* becomes *mimicking; panic* becomes *panicking; picnic* becomes *picnicking* and *picnicker; traffic* becomes *trafficking* and *trafficker.*

**The final -e rule:** A final silent *e* is usually dropped before a suffix beginning with a vowel (like *-able, -ion, -ing*): *blam(e)able, confus(e)ion, hop(e)ing.* But a final silent *e* is retained before a consonant: *blameworthy, hopeless.*

**Which is it: -efy or -ify?** The ending *-ify* is much more common than *-efy.* In fact, words ending in *-efy* may be considered exceptions. Here are some *-efy* words (the exceptions): *liquefy, putrefy, rarefy, stupefy.*

**Which is it: -ise, -ize, or -yze?** The usual suffix is *-ize,* and *-yze* and *-ise* are rather rare exceptions. Only two common words end in *-yze: analyze* and *paralyze.* Only about 30 common words end in *-ise: advertise, comprise, despise, exercise,* among them.

**Which is it: -ly or -ally?** When the original ends in *-ic,* the adverb-making suffix sometimes is *-ally* instead of *-ly,* as in *artistically* and *fantastically.* One common word ending in *-ic* that is made into an adverb by adding only *-ly* is *public;* the adverb is *publicly.*

**When is a final y changed to i?** If a word ends in *y* preceded by a consonant (any letter other than *a, e, i, o, u*), change the *y* to an *i* when you add a suffix. Here are some examples: *ally* becomes *allies* and *allied; city* becomes *cities; duty* becomes *duties* and *dutiful.*

# SPELLING DEMONS

### SIXTH GRADE SPELLING DEMONS

Here are some of the words most frequently misspelled by sixth-graders. Many adults still misspell some of them. Check yourself to see if you need to relearn any of these words.

| | | | | | |
|---|---|---|---|---|---|
| accommodate | athletics | challenge | February | Halloween | separate |
| across | balloon | coming | forth | minute | similar |
| already | bicycle | deceive | fourth | missile | sincerely |
| arithmetic | business | describe | good night | niece | surprise |
| athlete | ceiling | description | grammar | really | writing |

### HIGH SCHOOL SPELLING DEMONS

Here are some of the words taken from school and job-placement tests most frequently misspelled by high school seniors and graduates. How many of them do you find troublesome?

| | | | | | |
|---|---|---|---|---|---|
| absence | conscious | dispensable | guidance | occasion | receive |
| absurd | convenient | embarrass | humorous | occurred | recommend |
| accidentally | correspondence | environment | immediately | omitted | repetition |
| advertisement | criticize | escape | independent | opportunity | restaurant |
| all right | definite | exaggerate | irresistible | parallel | rhythm |
| amateur | dependent | existence | laboratory | performance | schedule |
| attendance | descend | experience | lightning | permanent | success |
| believe | desperate | fascinate | losing | prejudice | tragedy |
| committee | develop | foreign | necessary | privilege | villain |
| condemn | difference | government | neighbor | professor | weird |

### CIVIL SERVICE WORDS

Since many people who take Civil Service exams are high school graduates, the words most frequently misspelled are much the same as those on high school lists. Civil Service spelling tests also show 24 more demons related to government and office work.

| | | | |
|---|---|---|---|
| accident | enforcement | monetary | simplified |
| auxiliary | expedient | municipal | society |
| career | federal | personnel (*vs.* personal) | supervisor |
| clerical | filing (*vs.* filling) | president | technical |
| county (*vs.* country) | legality | responsibility | tendency |
| comptroller | mechanism | salary | yield |

### COLLEGE WORDS

This list contains words most often misspelled by students who have had two years of college. Demons from the high school list above are not repeated although many of those words continue to be misspelled by college and university students.

| | | | | | |
|---|---|---|---|---|---|
| achieve | competition | desirable | exercise | noticeable | pronunciation |
| aggravate | conscientious | despair | grievance | occurrence | responsibility |
| appearance | convenience | dining | knowledge | permissible | superintendent |
| argument | council | disappear | maintenance | precede | supersede |
| athlete | definitely | enforcement | marriage | procedure | usage |
| cemetery | descend | exceed | mischievous | proceed | wholly |

### ADULT SPELLING DEMONS

Many business executives and professionals with college degrees still have spelling problems. Here are some words they misspell most often, not repeating demons from the above lists.

| | | | | | |
|---|---|---|---|---|---|
| accessible | assistant | coolly | incidentally | irritable | perseverance |
| acquainted | burglar | drunkenness | insistent | license | recognize |
| analyze | campaign | envelope | intercede | mortgage | seize |

### HOW DO THE EXPERTS DO?

Editors, writers, and English teachers are especially good spellers. The following list consists of 60 everyday words most often misspelled by such experts. How many can you spell correctly?

| | | | | | |
|---|---|---|---|---|---|
| abscess | chrysanthemum | fission | inoculate | phlegm | sacrilegious |
| accelerator | connoisseur | fricassee | liquefy | picnicking | sheriff |
| aggressor | demagogue | fuselage | millennium | poliomyelitis | sieve |
| allotted | desiccate | gaiety | millionaire | prairie | subpoena |
| annihilate | dilapidated | gynecologist | miscellaneous | prescription | tariff |
| assassin | discriminate | harebrained | moccasin | propeller | tonsillitis |
| besiege | dissipate | hippopotamus | paraffin | questionnaire | tyranny |
| broccoli | ecstasy | hypocrisy | paralyze | raspberry | vacillate |
| catalyst | effervescent | immaculate | penitentiary | requiem | vengeance |
| category | exhilarate | innocuous | perspiration | rhinoceros | zephyr |

# WAYS TO BUILD YOUR VOCABULARY

Building a large vocabulary—understanding and using a wide variety of words—is important for success in almost any field. To build such a vocabulary sometimes requires bone-hard work.

Each person has three vocabularies.

*First,* there is an *active,* or *speaking,* vocabulary—the words we use every day in speaking.

*Second,* there is our *writing* vocabulary. It contains some words we do not use in speech.

*Third,* each person has a *recognition,* or *reading,* vocabulary, the largest of the three. Through this recognition vocabulary we can understand speakers and read books, magazines, and newspapers.

Consistent effort is needed to move words from our recognition to our active vocabulary.

Here are seven commonsense, time-tested suggestions for building your vocabulary:

**1. Make friends with your dictionary.** The most important element in vocabulary growth is the *will* to learn new words and to learn how to use them.

All reading and listening should lead straight to a good dictionary. You should actually *study* each word you look up. It requires only a moment to learn the spelling, pronunciation, or one meaning of a word. But hasty examination will prevent your mastering the word and adding it to your active vocabulary.

Equip yourself with a large dictionary that contains 100,000 words or more. It is unwise to buy a "cheap" dictionary when an excellent one can be purchased for only a few dollars more.

**2. Learn a few basic word elements.** Numerous word elements rarely appear independently but do form parts of longer words. Such elements, known as "combining forms," may be illustrated by "graph," as in *photograph, lithography, telegraph, phonograph, geography;* and "micro," as in *microphone, microscope, microcosm,* and *microfilm.*

**3. Learn the meanings of common prefixes.** A prefix is a letter of the alphabet (or a group of letters) put before a word to add to or qualify meaning. Understanding the meaning (or meanings) of constantly appearing prefixes, such as *anti-, post-,* and *pre-,* will build your vocabulary by making large numbers of words instantly recognizable and usable

**4. Learn the meaning of common suffixes.** A suffix is an element that is placed after a word or word root to make a term of different meaning or use, such as *-ful, -less, -ly,* or *-some.*

**5. Make a study of synonyms.** A synonym is a word having the same meaning, or nearly the same meaning, as another. A study of synonyms for the word "old" might add these words, among others, to your vocabulary: *aged, immemorial, ancient, aboriginal, hoary, antique, elderly, patriarchal, passé, venerable, antediluvian,* and *antiquated.*

**6. Make a study of antonyms.** An antonym is a word that is opposite in meaning to another word: *small* and *little* are antonyms of "large"; *happy* is an antonym of "sad."

Learning the opposite, or negative, of one or more of the meanings of another word will not be so valuable as studying synonyms, but the effort is worthwhile. Seeking antonyms for the verb *praise* may add these words, among others, to your vocabulary: *abuse, blame, censure, condemn, deprecate, disparage, impugn, inveigh against, lampoon, stigmatize, vilify.* The word *join,* for example, has such opposites as *cleave, disconnect, sever, separate,* and *sunder.*

These opposite meanings are not all-inclusive: A word may be an antonym of another only in a limited meaning. For example, one antonym of *man* (*woman*) concerns sex; another (*child*), age; another (*animal*), biology; another (*God*), religion. Like synonyms, antonyms must be selected carefully and used with exactness.

**7. Use your vocabulary.** How to use words exactly and emphatically is the most important phase of the problem of vocabulary building. It is indeed necessary to increase your vocabulary and not use words incorrectly. But the mere size of your vocabulary is not always a test of speaking or writing ability. Nor does it follow that if you stick to the principles of correct usage you will write effectively. Much dull and feeble speech and writing is correct, but correctness alone is a negative virtue. Using words clearly, exactly, strongly—that is most important and most difficult to do.

Who is the best conversationalist you know? What are the characteristics of his or her language? If you reply honestly, you will probably select a person whose speech seems *forceful* or *vivid* to you, someone who talks clearly, someone whose conversation is *smooth, logical, precise, animated.* Few will select a person whose talk is merely *correct.* Rarely will any comment be made on the niceties of conventional grammar, on violations of established usage, on subject-verb agreement, or on the right case of pronouns. True, the person you choose may use correct English—more often than not he or she will—but your remarks will not be "He uses correct English" nearly so often as "He's interesting to listen to."

and the "father of medicine": first to base medical treatment on scientific observation.

**Chevalier Jackson** (1865–1958), American surgeon: developed lighted esophagoscope.

**Edward Jenner** (1749–1823), British physician: developed vaccination against smallpox (1796).

**Carl Gustav Jung** (1875–1961), Swiss psychiatrist: founded analytical psychology.

**Paul Karrer** (1889–1971), Swiss chemist: did valuable research on vitamins A, E, K, and the carotenes. (N)

**Edward Calvin Kendall** (1886–1972), American biochemist: discovered thyroxine, hormone of thyroid gland (1914); discovered cortisone (1936), used to treat arthritis and other diseases. (N)

**Shibasaburo Kitasato** (1852–1931), Japanese bacteriologist: isolated tetanus germ (1889) and bubonic plague bacillus (1894).

**Edwin Klebs** (1834–1913), German-American bacteriologist: discovered pneumonia bacillus (1875) and, with Friedrich Löffler, diphtheria bacillus (1884).

**Robert Koch** (1843–1910), German physician: established science of bacteriology; discovered microorganisms causing anthrax (1876), tuberculosis (1882), and cholera (1884). (N)

**Emil Theodor Kocher** (1841–1917), Swiss surgeon: performed first goiter operation to remove enlarged thyroid gland (1878). (N)

**Arthur Kornberg** (1918–  ), American biochemist: co-discoverer of synthetic nucleic acids, key substance in heredity; developed nucleic acid that reproduces itself (1967). (N)

**Hans Adolf Krebs** (1900–  ), German biochemist: discovered citric-acid cycle in sugar metabolism (1937), called Krebs cycle. (N)

**Richard Kuhn** (1900–67), German chemist: discovered vitamin $B_2$, riboflavin. (N)

**René Théophile Hyacinthe Laënnec** (1781–1826), French physician: invented stethoscope (1816).

**Karl Landsteiner** (1868–1943), Austrian-American physician: discovered main blood types (1900), polio virus (1908); with A. S. Wiener, discovered Rh blood factor (1940). (N)

**Charles L. A. Laveran** (1845–1922), French physician: discovered parasite causing malaria (1880). (N)

**Anton van Leeuwenhoek** (1632–1723), Dutch biologist: perfected single-lens microscope; first described bacteria, protozoa, and blood cells.

**Sir Joseph Lister** (1827–1912), British surgeon: introduced antisepsis in surgery (1865).

**Friedrich Löffler** (1852–1915), German bacteriologist: with Edwin Klebs, discovered diphtheria bacillus (1884); with Paul Frosch, discovered virus causing hoof-and-mouth disease in cattle (1897).

**Crawford Williamson Long** (1815–78), American physician: first to use ether as anesthetic in surgery (1842).

**Feodor Lynen** (1911–79), German chemist: helped discover how body uses and makes cholesterol and fatty acids. (N)

**John James Rickard Macleod** (1876–1935), British physiologist: co-discoverer of insulin (1921). (N)

**Marcello Malpighi** (1628–94), Italian physician: discovered capillary blood vessels.

**Sir Patrick Manson** (1844–1922), British physi-

cian: discovered parasite causing elephantiasis (1877); called "father of tropical medicine."

**William Worral Mayo** (1819–1911) and sons, **William James Mayo** (1861–1939) and **Charles Horace Mayo** (1865–1939), American surgeons: founded Mayo Clinic in Rochester, Minn. (1889).

**Elmer Verner McCollum** (1879–1967), American biochemist: invented alphabet system of naming vitamins (1915).

**Ephraim McDowell** (1771–1830), American surgeon: performed first successful removal of tumor from ovary (1809).

**Sir Peter Brian Medawar** (1915–  ), British zoologist: proved organs and tissues transplantable between unrelated animals (1953). (N)

**Charles Frederick Menninger** (1862–1953) and sons, **Karl Augustus Menninger** (1893–  ) and **William Claire Menninger** (1899–1966), American psychiatrists: founded Menninger Clinic in Topeka, Kan. (1919).

**Franz Mesmer** (1734–1815), Austrian physician: pioneered hypnotism in medicine (1778).

**Elie Metchnikoff** (1845–1916), Russian biologist: developed theory that white blood cells attack disease germs. (N)

**George Minot** (1885–1950), American physician: discovered liver-extract treatment for pernicious anemia (1926). (N)

**Egas Moniz** (1874–1955), Portuguese neurologist: developed prefrontal lobotomy as surgical treatment of severe mental illness. (N)

**Thomas Hunt Morgan** (1866–1945), American biologist: advanced knowledge of heredity by discovering that genes transmit inherited characteristics (1926). (N)

**Giovanni Battista Morgagni** (1682–1771), Italian physician: pioneered use of autopsies to study causes of diseases.

**William T. G. Morton** (1819–68), American dentist: first to use ether as anesthetic in dentistry (1846).

**Florence Nightingale** (1820–1910), British nurse: founder of nursing as profession.

**Hideyo Noguchi** (1876–1928), Japanese bacteriologist: developed skin test for diagnosis of syphilis; discovered parasite of yellow fever.

**Sir William Osler** (1849–1919), Canadian physician: developed method of teaching new doctors as interns in hospital wards.

**George Nicholas Papanicolaou** (1883–1962), American physician: devised "Pap" smear test for cancer detection.

**Philippus Aureolus Paracelsus** (1493–1541), Swiss physician: introduced use of specific chemicals as treatment for specific illnesses.

**Ambroise Paré** (1510–90), French surgeon: introduced use of artificial limbs.

**Louis Pasteur** (1822–95), French bacteriologist: first proved bacteria cause disease; developed pasteurization to kill bacteria with heat (1864); developed vaccine for rabies (1885).

**Ivan Petrovich Pavlov** (1849–1936), Russian physiologist: proved nerves control flow of digestive juices; pioneered in study of conditioned reflexes. (N)

**Walter Reed** (1851–1902), U.S. Army surgeon: helped discover cause of yellow fever.

**Tadeus Reichstein** (1897–  ), Swiss chemist: discovered how to make ascorbic acid, vitamin C (1933); isolated cortisone (1936). (N)

**PIONEERS IN MEDICINE** (continued)

**Howard Taylor Ricketts** (1871–1910), American pathologist: identified microorganisms (named *rickettsia* after his death) that cause Rocky Mountain spotted fever and typhus.

**Sir Ronald Ross** (1857–1932), British physician: proved *Anopheles* mosquito carries malaria (1898).

**Benjamin Rush** (1745–1813), American physician and signer of Declaration of Independence: established first free U.S. medical clinic at Philadelphia (1786).

**Albert Sabin** (1906–    ), Russian-American bacteriologist: developed oral polio vaccine (1957).

**Jonas Salk** (1914–    ), American physician: developed first successful vaccine for polio (1953).

**Frederick Sanger** (1918–    ), British chemist: helped determine structure of insulin. (N)

**Béla Schick** (1877–1967), Hungarian-American pediatrician: devised test for susceptibility to diphtheria (1913).

**Theodor Schwann** (1810–82), German physiologist and histologist: discovered that cell is fundamental unit of life (1839).

**Ignaz Philipp Semmelweiss** (1818–65), Hungarian physician: pioneered use of antiseptic methods in childbirth (1860).

**Sir James Young Simpson** (1811–70), British physician: first used chloroform as anesthetic in childbirth (1847).

**Lazzaro Spallanzani** (1729–99), Italian biologist: proved bacteria float in the air and heating kills bacteria.

**Wendell M. Stanley** (1904–71), American biochemist: proved viruses are solid particles that contain protein (1935). (N)

**Andrew Taylor Still** (1828–1917), American founder of osteopathic medicine: organized osteopathic college, Kirksville, Mo., in 1892.

**James Batcheller Sumner** (1887–1955), American biochemist: first to isolate pure crystals of an enzyme (1926). (N)

**Albert Szent–Gyorgyi** (1893–    ), Hungarian-American biochemist: discovered actin, a muscle protein. (N)

**Helen Taussig** (1898–    ), American pediatrician: with A. Blalock, developed corrective heart surgery for "blue-babies" (1944).

**Max Theiler** (1899–1972), South African physician: discovered vaccine against yellow fever (1937). (N)

**Andreas Vesalius** (1514–64), Flemish physician: wrote first comprehensive textbook on human anatomy (1543).

**Rudolf Virchow** (1821–1902), German physician: pioneered scientific study of diseases, or *pathology* (1850s).

**Selman A. Waksman** (1888–1973), U.S. microbiologist: discovered streptomycin (1943). (N)

**August von Wassermann** (1866–1925), German physiologist and bacteriologist: developed blood test for diagnosing syphilis (1906).

**James Dewey Watson** (1928–    ), American biochemist: co-discoverer of molecular structure of DNA (1953). (N)

**Maurice H. F. Wilkins** (1916–    ), British biophysicist: first explained structure of deoxyribo-nucleic acid (DNA). (N)

**Daniel Hale Williams** (1856–1931), American black physician: first surgeon to repair pericardium, sac around the heart (1893).

**Alexandre E. J. Yersin** (1863–1943), Swiss-French bacteriologist: independently discovered bubonic plague bacillus (1894).

## MAJOR ADVANCES IN MEDICINE AND DRUGS

| Year | Advance | Year | Advance | Year | Advance |
|---|---|---|---|---|---|
| 1628 | Blood circulation described | 1904 | Chemotherapy first used | 1941 | Fluorides, for prevention of dental caries |
| 1676 | Bacteria and blood cells discovered | 1909 | Salvarsan, for syphilis | 1943 | Streptomycin, a broad-spectrum antibiotic |
| 1707 | Pulse rate measured | 1912 | Phenobarbital, sedative | | |
| 1733 | Blood pressure measured | 1913 | Niacin, antipellagra vitamin | 1943 | ACTH, a pituitary hormone |
| 1794 | Therapeutic oxygen inhalation | 1913 | Vitamin A | 1945 | Methadone, a synthetic narcotic for control of drug addiction |
| 1796 | Smallpox vaccine | 1914 | Blood storage developed | | |
| 1820 | Quinine, for malaria | 1920 | Cod liver oil (vitamin D) | 1946 | Iodine$^{131}$, for exophthalmic goiter and diagnosis of thyroid disorders |
| 1839 | Iodine, as antiseptic | 1921 | Insulin, a pancreatic hormone, to control diabetes mellitus | | |
| 1842 | Ether, as surgical anesthetic | | | 1948 | Aureomycin, antibiotic |
| 1844 | Nitrous oxide, anesthetic | 1921 | BCG tuberculosis vaccine | 1948 | Vitamin B$_{12}$, for pernicious anemia |
| 1847 | Chloroform, anesthetic | 1923 | Scarlet-fever germ isolated | 1950 | First successful human organ transplant operation with kidney |
| 1864 | Pasteurization developed | 1926 | Gene theory of heredity | | |
| 1865 | Phenol (carbolic acid), for surgical asepsis | 1926 | Thiamine, a vitamin | 1952 | Isoniazid, a synthetic chemical effective against tuberculosis |
| | | 1926 | Liver extract, for anemia | | |
| 1869 | Chloral hydrate, sedative | 1927 | Ephedrine, a stimulant and nasal decongestant | 1953 | Salk vaccine, for immunization against poliomyelitis |
| 1876 | Anthrax bacteria discovered | | | | |
| 1878 | First operation to remove goiter | 1928 | Vitamin C (ascorbic acid) isolated | 1953 | DNA structure discovered |
| 1882 | Tuberculosis bacteria discovered | 1929 | Cyclopropane, an anesthetic | 1954 | Reserpine, a tranquilizer obtained from rauwolfia |
| 1884 | Cholera bacteria discovered | 1932 | Curare (arrow poison) alkaloids, for tetanus and spastic disorders | | |
| 1884 | Cocaine, as local anesthetic | | | 1954 | Enovid, first birth-control pill |
| 1885 | Rabies immunization | 1933 | Whooping-cough vaccine | 1957 | Growth (pituitary) hormone, for dwarfism |
| 1890 | Diphtheria antitoxin | 1935 | Sulfa drugs proved effective | | |
| 1890 | Tetanus antitoxin | 1935 | Amphetamine, a stimulant | 1957 | Sabin oral polio vaccine |
| 1894 | Thyroid extract, for goiter | 1935 | Blood bank developed | 1963 | Measles vaccine |
| 1895 | Viruses discovered | 1936 | Cortisone discovered | 1967 | First successful human heart transplant operation |
| 1895 | X rays discovered | 1937 | Yellow-fever vaccine | | |
| 1897 | Blood count developed | 1937 | Antihistamines, to control allergic reactions and motion sickness | 1969 | Rubella vaccine |
| 1898 | Radium discovered | | | 1970 | L-Dopa, for Parkinsonism |
| 1899 | Aspirin, an analgesic | 1937 | Heparin, an anticoagulant | 1977 | Ara-A, first antivirus drug, proved effective |
| 1900 | Blood types discovered | 1940 | Rh blood factor | | |
| 1903 | Barbitol (veronal), barbiturate | 1941 | Penicillin, first antibiotic, proved effective | 1978 | Pneumonia vaccine |

# MEDICAL TERMS AND WHAT THEY MEAN

**abasia**—inability to walk from lack of muscular coordination; caused by damage to brain or nervous system

**abdomen**—region of body below chest and above pelvis; muscular wall of diaphragm separates abdominal cavity from chest; abdomen contains digestive, excretory, and sex organs

**abortion**—induced or natural loss or destruction of fertilized ovum or fetus before birth

**abrasion**—skin scrape with bleeding; can become infected unless cleaned and treated

**abscess**—area of infection in which pus forms, usually caused by bacteria

**acetanilid**—drug used to reduce fever and pain

**Achilles tendon**—thick tendon at back of ankle connecting calf muscles in leg to heel bone

**acid burn**—burn caused by acid or caustic alkali; should be washed for at least 30 minutes with running water; treatment by physician essential

**acidosis**—condition caused by lack of alkali in blood; symptoms include weakness, drowsiness

**acne**—pimples and blackheads caused by skin pores becoming blocked; may come from improper diet or lack of cleanliness; physician should be consulted to prevent disfiguring scars

**acromegaly**—abnormal enlargement of hands, feet, or features of face; results from excess of growth hormones

**acrophobia**—fear of high places

**ACTH**—hormone produced by pituitary gland; has been used to relieve pain in treatment of various diseases

**acute**—having sudden, severe symptoms of comparatively short duration

**addiction**—craving for certain foods or drugs, such as alcohol or habit-forming narcotics

**Addison's disease**—debilitating disease that causes weakness, darkening of skin, low blood pressure; results from insufficient hormone production by cortex of adrenal glands

**adenoids**—glandular tissue at upper part of throat, behind nose; excessive growth or infection of adenoids causes breathing difficulty

**adrenalin**—hormone secreted by adrenal glands; stimulates heart to beat faster, increasing blood pressure, and enabling muscles to work faster and harder

**agraphobia**—fear of large open spaces

**aichmophobia**—fear of sharp instruments

**ailurophobia**—fear of cats

**allergen**—allergy-producing substance

**allergy**—unusual reaction of body to substances normally having no adverse effect on most other persons

**allopathy**—medical treatment to create effects opposed to those of specific disease

**alopecia**—loss of hair or baldness; usually hereditary

**amblyopia**—dimness of vision; may be hereditary or caused by improper diet or excessive use of tobacco or alcohol

**amnesia**—temporary or permanent loss of memory

**analgesic**—medicine that relieves pain; aspirin is one of commonest analgesics

**androgen**—male sex hormone that determines such characteristics as deep voice and beard

**anemia**—blood disorder with reduced hemoglobin or red cells; symptoms: paleness, constant tiredness

**aneurysm**—abnormal weakening of artery wall, forming pulsating blood-filled sac; rupture of weakened artery wall can cause death

**angina pectoris**—pain in chest, shoulder, neck, or left arm, generally caused by *arteriosclerosis*

**anodontia**—failure of teeth to grow in; may be hereditary or glandular malfunction

**anorexia**—loss of appetite for long period

**antacid**—remedy for upset stomach; baking soda is common antacid

**anthrophobia**—fear of human society

**antibiotic**—medicine produced by microorganisms, such as molds; antibiotics prevent growth and reproduction of certain disease germs; common antibiotics include penicillin, streptomycin, Aureomycin, Chloromycetin

**antibody**—natural substance in body that protects against disease or infection

**anticoagulant**—substance that slows clotting of blood; example: heparin

**antidote**—remedy to counteract poison

**antigen**—substance that stimulates production of *antibodies* when it enters body; examples: bacteria, pollen, viruses

**antihistamine**—medicine used to counteract symptoms of hay fever, allergies, and common cold; may cause sleepiness

**antitoxin**—type of *antibody*, acts against poison (toxin) that enters body; antitoxins produced in the blood of animals used to treat such diseases as *tetanus*

**anxiety**—in psychiatry, irrational worry or fear in absence of obvious danger

**aphasia**—loss or impairment of ability to speak, write, or understand others; caused by brain damage, often after *stroke*

**aphonia**—loss of voice or ability to speak louder than whisper; may be caused by excessive use of voice, brain damage, or cancer of larynx (voice box)

**aphrodisiac**—substance supposed to stimulate sexual powers

**apoplexy**—stroke caused by blockage of blood vessel in brain by blood clot

**appendicitis**—inflammation and swelling of appendix; if not surgically removed, it may rupture and cause death; symptom: pain around navel, spreading to lower right of abdomen

**arteriosclerosis**—hardening of arteries; caused by accumulation of calcium and cholesterol on artery walls; brings about clots in blood that may cause stroke in brain or heart attack

**artery**—vessel carrying blood from heart to parts of body

**arthritis**—disease affecting joints and supporting tissues; causes swelling, pain; can cripple hands, arms, and legs

**asepsis**—absence of germs, achieved by use of germ-killing antiseptics and sterilization

**asphyxia**—suffocation from lack of oxygen

**asthma**—chronic disease of bronchial tubes; causes breathing difficulty

**astraphobia**—fear of thunderstorms

**atherosclerosis**—accumulation of fatty deposits on artery walls, causing arteriosclerosis

**MEDICAL TERMS** (*continued*)

**athlete's foot**—contagious infection of foot; caused by fungus in wet, warm places

**autism**—mental disorder in which child or adult ignores others, lives in own dream world

**bacitracin**—antibiotic used as treatment for skin infections

**bedsore**—ulcer of skin caused by lying in bed in same position for long time

**benign tumor**—tissue growth in body not harmful in itself and likely not to recur after being removed

**biopsy**—removal of bit of tissue from living body for microscopic examination; used in diagnosing such diseases as *cancer* and *cirrhosis*

**blood poisoning**—presence in bloodstream of bacteria from infection; symptoms include weakness, chills, fever; fatal if not treated

**blood pressure**—force of blood against artery walls; normal blood pressure for adults aged 18 to 45 is 120/80; first number is *systolic* pressure caused by heart contracting; second number is *diastolic* pressure when heart relaxes; high blood pressure can cause stroke or heart attack

**blood types**—four main types of blood: O, A, B, and AB based on substances found in red blood cells and *plasma*; before *transfusions*, blood types must be determined for correct matching; *Rh factor* also important in classifying blood; only O-type can be given to anyone

**body temperature**—normal heat of body; averages 98.6°F. (37°C.); temperature over 100°F. (37.8°C.) in adult indicates fever

**boil**—pus-filled infection on skin caused by bacteria; never open boil yourself because pus can get into bloodstream, causing *blood poisoning*

**botulism**—dangerous infection caused by bacteria from improperly canned, bottled, or preserved food

**bronchitis**—inflammation of respiratory passages; caused by viral infection, smoking, air pollution

**bubonic plague**—acute contagious disease usually transmitted to people by fleas of rats; in past has caused widespread epidemics, killing millions of persons; symptoms appear suddenly: chills, fever, vomiting, delerium

**bursitis**—painful inflammation at joint caused by irritation of bursa (liquid-filled sac at joint)

**cancer**—group of diseases characterized by abnormal cell growth, crowding out healthy tissue and interfering with vital function of affected organs; malignant tumors develop

**carcinogen**—cancer-causing substance

**carcinoma**—cancer that originates in skin or mucous membranes

**cardiac**—pertaining to heart

**caries**—bacterial decay of tooth or bone

**cataract**—clouded condition in lens of eye, resulting in blurred vision; can be corrected by surgery

**cauterize**—destruction of abnormal or infected tissue by applying hot iron, laser beam, or other means

**cerebral hemorrhage**—bleeding inside brain from ruptured blood vessel; symptoms: headache, nausea, unconsciousness, paralysis

**cerebral palsy**—disorders caused by damage to brain before, during, or after birth

**chemotherapy**—use of chemicals and drugs to treat or to prevent disease

**chicken pox**—contagious disease; symptoms: fever, eruptions on skin; lasts about two weeks

**cholera**—acute epidemic disease; spread by polluted water, contaminated food, insects; symptoms: vomiting, diarrhea

**cholesterol**—substance in fats and oils, main material of *gallstones*; contributes to hardening of arteries; high cholesterol diet may help cause heart disease

**chorea**—involuntary twitching, once called "St. Vitus's dance"; often associated with *rheumatic fever*

**chromosome**—part of every plant or animal cell; carries genes determining physical characteristics of specific plant or animal

**chronic**—lasting long time without rapid change for better or worse

**cirrhosis**—chronic disease of liver; often associated with alcoholism

**claustrophobia**—fear of confined space

**coagulant**—substance that speeds up clotting of blood

**congenital**—existing at birth

**conjunctivitis**—inflammation of conjunctiva (mucous membrane covering eyeball and inner part of eyelids); also called pinkeye

**contraception**—prevention of pregnancy by use of methods of birth control

**coronary thrombosis**—blocking of artery supplying blood to heart muscles; common cause of heart attacks

**cystic fibrosis**—incurable hereditary disease of childhood; sweat glands and mucus-secreting glands do not function properly, involving lungs and pancreas

**cystitis**—bladder infection or inflammation

**cystoscope**—hollow tube with lights and mirrors used to examine interior of bladder

**diabetes**—noncontagious disease in which pancreas does not produce enough insulin or body does not use insulin properly; symptoms: thirst, excessive urination

**electrocardiograph**—instrument that records electrical current produced by action of heart muscle; resulting electrocardiogram (EKG) shows wave pattern traced on paper; used to diagnose heart ailments

**electroencephalograph**—instrument that records electrical impulses in brain (brain waves); resulting electroencephalogram (EEG) used in diagnosing brain disorders

**embolism**—blocking of blood vessel by loose blood clot, air bubble, or other material; can cause *stroke*

**emphysema**—incurable respiratory disorder; air sacs in lungs lose elasticity, causing impaired breathing, heart strain; contributing factors: smoking, air pollution

**encephalitis**—acute inflammation of brain; commonly known as "sleeping sickness" because main symptom is sleepiness; caused by virus carried by mosquitoes and ticks

**endocarditis**—inflammation of heart lining

**enteritis**—inflammation of intestine

**epilepsy**—chronic disorder of nervous system; causes periodic convulsions and unconsciousness; caused by brain injury or brain infection

**erysipelas**—also called "St. Anthony's fire"; skin disease; symptoms: hot red patches on skin,

fever, headache, nausea

**erythrophobia**—fear of blushing

**estrogens**—female hormones responsible for regulating female sex functions

**fluoridation**—addition of fluoride salts to drinking water to reduce tooth decay

**food poisoning**—acute illness caused by eating contaminated food; symptoms: pain in abdomen, vomiting, diarrhea

**frostbite**—injury to skin, ears, nose, toes, or fingers from cold; body tissues freeze without pain when exposed to cold; may cause *gangrene*; any pressure on frozen toes or fingers may cause permanent injury; do not massage frozen parts; professional treatment necessary

**gallstone**—solid rocklike mass that forms in gallbladder; can cause inflammation of gallbladder; symptoms: pain in upper abdomen, fever, vomiting, tiredness; treated by surgery

**gamma globulin**—protein in blood *plasma*; contains numerous kinds of *antibodies*; used as serum to produce immunity for diseases such as measles

**gangrene**—death of body tissues in part of body; may be caused by infection or frostbite; severe cases require surgery

**gastritis**—inflammation of stomach

**gene splicing**—method of combining genetic material from two species in cells to create new life forms

**German measles**—also called rubella; contagious virus infection; symptoms: swollen lymph glands, 3-day rash; if contracted during early pregnancy, can cause miscarriage or birth defects; vaccine available

**gingivitis**—inflammation of gums around teeth; symptom: bleeding gums; can lead to *pyorrhea*

**glaucoma**—disorder of eyes marked by increased pressure within eyeballs; symptoms: pain in eyes, blurred vision, appearance of halos around electric lights

**gonorrhea**—highly contagious bacterial infection; usually transmitted during sexual intercourse; readily cured in early stages by professional treatment

**group therapy**—method of treatment for emotional or mental disorders; several persons under professional supervision analyze own and each other's problems

**hallucination**—vivid perception of something not present in reality

**hallucinogen**—substance that produces *hallucinations*; includes such drugs as marijuana, mescaline, LSD

**hemophilia**—hereditary disorder affecting males; blood clots too slowly to prevent excessive bleeding from minor injuries

**hemorrhoids**—enlarged veins in region of anus, usually painful; also known as "piles"

**hepatic**—pertaining to liver

**hepatitis**—inflammation of liver; usually caused by virus; contagious; symptoms: loss of appetite, fever, pain in upper right abdomen

**hernia**—abnormal protrusion of organ through tissue wall surrounding it; corrected by surgery

**hydrophobia**—fear of water

**hyperglycemia**—condition caused by too much sugar in blood; symptom of diabetes

**hypertension**—high blood pressure

**hypochondria**—excessive concern with one's health; person exaggerates trivial symptoms or suffers imaginary ailments; type of *neurosis*

**hypoglycemia**—condition caused by deficiency of glucose in blood; may be caused by insulin injection

**hysterectomy**—removal by surgery of uterus, and in some cases ovaries, Fallopian tubes, and cervix

**immunization**—procedure for protection against disease; introduces or induces production of antibodies, usually by inoculation; natural immunity may be developed to specific disease after contracting it and recovering

**interferon**—protein substance produced in body cells of humans and other mammals that stops growth of viral infections in uninfected cells; subject of research as possible drug to use in treating or preventing cancer

**intrauterine device (IUD)**—contraceptive device inserted into uterus; common types include spirals or loops of flexible plastic

**L-dopa**—drug used to treat *Parkinsonism*

**leukemia**—type of cancer affecting blood-forming tissues; produces abnormally large number of white blood cells; symptoms: fever, loss of appetite

**lumbago**—pain in lumbar region of lower back; may be due to *arthritis*

**malignant tumor**—tissue growth of *cancer*

**mastectomy**—surgical removal of breast tissue, usually to treat breast cancer

**measles**—also called rubeola; acute virus disease, sometimes followed by complications; vaccine should be given at age 1 year

**meningitis**—contagious disease causing inflammation of membrane covering brain and lung; symptoms: headache, vomiting, fever, spasms pulling head back; in infants, spots on skin

**metabolism**—total of processes by which food, water, and oxygen are converted into living tissue, energy, and waste

**metastasis**—transfer of disease from one part of body to another by germs or by abnormal cells transported in blood or lymph

**microphobia**—fear of germs

**mononucleosis**—contagious disease producing abnormally large number of monocytes (type of white blood cell); sometimes called "kissing disease" because of way it can be transmitted; symptoms: chills, fever, sore throat, tiredness

**multiple sclerosis**—progressive disease forming hardened patches on nerve sheaths in brain and spinal cord, preventing nerves from responding normally; symptoms: unsteady balance, jerky movements of arms and legs, stiff muscles

**mumps**—acute contagious disease, usually of childhood; causes swelling of salivary glands; vaccine available

**muscular dystrophy**—hereditary disease causing muscles to weaken and deteriorate; mostly affects boys

**mysophobia**—fear of dirt

**nephritis**—inflammation of kidneys

**neuralgia**—severe pain along a nerve in the face, mouth, or throat

**neuritis**—inflammation of nerve causing pain in any part of body

**neurosis**—emotional disturbance produced by unresolved and unconscious conflicts; often

**MEDICAL TERMS** *(continued)*

accompanied by *anxiety* and depression

**nyctophobia**—fear of darkness

**oral contraception**—method of birth control by taking pills containing sex hormones

**osteo**—pertaining to bones

**ovulation**—release of egg cell from ovary

**pacemaker**—nerve and muscle cells in heart that establish and regulate heart rhythm; when natural pacemaker does not function properly, artificial pacemaker may be implanted to stimulate heart with small electrical impulses

**palsy**—type of paralysis and disorder marked by constant trembling of parts of body; injury or disorder of nervous system impairs ability to control voluntary muscles

**Pap test**—quick, painless test to detect some types of cancer, especially of cervix; women over 30 should have Pap test annually

**paranoia**—mental disorder characterized by delusions of persecution or power

**Parkinsonism**—chronic, slowly progressive disorder that affects part of brain controlling voluntary movement; also known as Parkinson's disease

**phobia**—extreme fear, usually so overpowering as to prevent person from functioning normally

**phobophobia**—fear of fear

**physical therapy**—treatment of injury, disability, or physical defect by massage, heat, exercise, or other external means

**placebo**—harmless substance given to humor patient; sometimes used in research experiments as control device to check on effectiveness of specific drugs

**plasma**—liquid part of blood; used rather than whole blood for some transfusions; can be used in transfusing persons of any *blood type*

**platelets**—part of blood that causes blood to clot; person with deficiency of platelets may bleed excessively from minor injuries

**pleurisy**—inflammation of pleura (double membrane that covers each lung and lines chest cavity)

**pneumonia**—acute infection of lungs; tiny air sacs become filled with fluid; breathing impaired

**postpartum**—postnatal; occurring after delivery of baby

**prosthesis**—artificial substitute for part of body; prosthetic devices range from dentures to artificial legs

**psychiatrist**—physician specializing in *psychiatry*

**psychiatry**—study, diagnosis, and treatment of mental illness and personality disorders

**psychoanalysis**—technique developed by Sigmund Freud to bring back repressed memories and understand unconscious impulses

**psychology**—science of study of mind, especially concerned with behavior

**psychosis**—severe mental disorder, often involving disintegration of personality

**psychosomatic**—denoting disorders, such as ulcers and migraine headaches, that may be completely or partly due to emotional causes

**psychotherapy**—treatment of emotional and mental disorders largely through discussion of them

**pyorrhea alveolaris**—disease forming pus at roots of teeth; tissue of gums shrinks; teeth become loose, causing loss of teeth

**rabies**—disease usually transmitted by bite of animal; symptoms: muscle spasms, convulsions, periodic rage and calm, spasms of throat when attempting to drink; death follows within 2 to 3 days after appearance of symptoms

**renal**—pertaining to kidneys

**Rh factor**—inherited substance in red blood cells; if present, as in most persons, blood is Rh positive; if absent, blood is Rh negative; person with Rh negative blood never should receive transfusion of Rh positive blood

**rheumatic fever**—bacterial disease of children and young adults; usually follows untreated streptococcus infections; symptoms: fever, swollen joints, nosebleed; may cause heart damage

**ringworm**—fungus infection of skin

**rubella**—German measles

**schizophrenia**—serious mental disorder characterized by delusions, retreat from reality, and possible deterioration of personality

**shock**—signs and symptoms associated with failure or collapse of circulatory system; may follow extensive surgery, severe injury, or heavy bleeding; requires emergency medical treatment

**sphygmomanometer**—instrument used to measure blood pressure

**streptococcus**—type of bacteria that causes scarlet fever and strep throat

**stroke**—damage to brain from blocked or ruptured artery; symptoms: unconsciousness, paralysis of one side of body; high blood pressure and hardening of arteries are underlying causes

**syphilis**—contagious bacterial disease transmitted in sexual intercourse; can cause brain disease, blindness, heart disease; treated with penicillin

**thrombosis**—blocking of blood vessel by blood clot; can cause gangrene, stroke, or heart attack

**toxin**—poisonous substance produced by germs, chemicals, and some plants and animals

**trachoma**—highly contagious virus disease of eyelids; can lead to blindness if untreated; widespread in tropical areas

**transfusion**—injection of blood or blood parts into person's circulatory system

**trauma**—injury caused to organ by blow or wound; in *psychiatry*, grave emotional shock that may have lasting effect on personality

**trichinosis**—disease caused by eating undercooked pork; parasitic roundworms invade blood and body organs; symptoms: fever, nausea, vomiting, diarrhea, abdominal pain

**tuberculosis**—chronic communicable disease; attacks lungs and other body parts

**tumor**—abnormal tissue growth on or in body; may be *benign* or *malignant*

**ulcer**—inflamed open sore on skin or on mucous membrane lining stomach, small intestine, or other body cavity

**uremia**—toxic condition of blood caused by wastes normally removed by kidneys and excreted in urine

**vaccine**—preparation containing bacteria or viruses treated to give immunity against specific diseases

**venereal disease**—infection transmitted mainly by sexual intercourse, such as *syphilis* and *gonorrhea*

**Wassermann test**—method of determining presence of syphilis

**zoophobia**—fear of animals

# National Defense

World's fastest warship: The U.S. Navy's SES-100B, a surface effect ship, broke the world speed record for a warship on Jan. 25, 1980, at the Navy's Chesapeake Bay Test Range with a speed of 91.9 knots (105 mph).

## HIGHLIGHTS: 1980

### QUESTIONING DEFENSE READINESS

Whether or not the U.S. defense forces are ready to fight and win a war became a major issue in the 1980 presidential campaign. Public confidence in the armed forces already had been shaken in April by the failure of a U.S. military task force to rescue American hostages in Iran (see page 15).

During the year newspapers reported the results of several Defense Department confidential reports that showed the forces ready for combat included less than half of the Navy's 13 aircraft carriers, only 12 of the Army's 16 combat divisions, and only 90% of the Air Force's 123 tactical squadrons.

The most comprehensive study of the comparative military strengths of the Soviet Union and the United States in 1980 was a 600-page book by John M. Collins, a defense specialist for the Congressional Research Service. Among Collins' conclusions was that the U.S. ability "to survive a full-scale nuclear assault by the Soviet Union is nearly nil."

Secretary of Defense Harold Brown defended the military capabilities of the armed forces on Oct. 9, declaring that news reports on the lack of readiness were "misleading," and contending that by the same standards two-thirds of the Soviet Union's army divisions would be rated as "not combat ready."

### THE COST OF DEFENSE

A study prepared by former U.S. arms control official Ruth Leger Sivard reported that more than $500 billion was being spent by the world's nations on their military forces in 1980. The report said the U.S. and the Soviet Union had spent 60% of the world's total military expenditures since 1960.

U.S. defense spending in 1981 is expected to be about $161 billion, an increase of some $26 billion over 1980's authorized expenditures.

Among the factors increasing U.S. military spending was an 11.7% pay increase granted by Congress to members of the armed forces

**HIGHLIGHTS: 1980** *(continued)*
on Oct. 1, 1980. Congress also approved the spending of about $53 billion for weapons.

### DRAFT REGISTRATION REVIVED

President Carter asked Congress in February 1980 for funds to revitalize the Selective Service with registration of all men and women born in 1960 or 1961. The proposal touched off antidraft protests on many college campuses, and on March 22 about 30,000 protesters held a rally in Washington, D.C.

The plan met stiff opposition in Congress, where the provision to register women was struck from the measure. Senate opponents of the measure, led by Sen. Mark O. Hatfield (R-Ore.), failed to filibuster it to death. The Senate approved $13.3 million for the registration by a vote of 58 to 34, and the House gave final approval by 234 to 168. President Carter signed it into law on June 27.

On July 18, three days before the registration was to begin, a federal court in Philadelphia ruled that the Selective Service Act was unconstitutional because it excluded women. But the following day Supreme Court Associate Justice William F. Brennan Jr. ruled that the registration could proceed while the Supreme Court pondered how to deal with the lower-court decision.

The registration took place from July 21 to Aug. 2, with the director of Selective Service, Bernard D. Rostker, warning that those who failed to register would face sentences of up to five years in prison.

In September Rostker reported that 3,593,187 men had registered. He said this was 93% of the 3,880,000 that the Census Bureau estimated were eligible.

### FALSE MISSILE ALERTS

Equipment failures in the nation's early warning system on June 3 and June 6, 1980, twice put bomber crews, missile teams, and

## ARMED FORCES MONTHLY BASIC PAY SCALES[1]

| YEARS SERVED | COMMISSIONED OFFICERS' PAY GRADES | | | | | | | | | |
| --- | --- | --- | --- | --- | --- | --- | --- | --- | --- | --- |
| | 0-1[2] | 0-2[2] | 0-3[2] | 0-4 | 0-5 | 0-6 | 0-7 | 0-8 | 0-9 | 0-10[3] |
| Up to 2[2] | $924.30 | $1,064.70 | $1,221.30 | $1,340.30 | $1,559.10 | $1,949.40 | $2,629.60 | $3,165.00 | $3,494.40 | $3,942.90 |
| 2+ .... | 962.10 | 1,163.10 | 1,365.30 | 1,599.90 | 1,830.90 | 2,142.00 | 2,808.90 | 3,259.80 | 3,586.20 | 4,081.50 |
| 3+ .... | 1,163.10 | 1,397.10 | 1,459.50 | 1,707.00 | 1,957.20 | 2,281.80 | 2,808.90 | 3,337.20 | 3,662.40 | 4,081.50 |
| 4+ .... | 1,163.10 | 1,444.20 | 1,614.90 | 1,707.00 | 1,957.20 | 2,281.80 | 2,808.90 | 3,337.20 | 3,662.40 | 4,081.50 |
| 6+ .... | 1,163.10 | 1,474.20 | 1,692.00 | 1,738.20 | 1,957.20 | 2,281.80 | 2,934.60 | 3,337.20 | 3,662.40 | 4,081.50 |
| 8+ .... | 1,163.10 | 1,474.20 | 1,753.20 | 1,815.30 | 1,957.20 | 2,281.80 | 2,934.60 | 3,585.20 | 3,755.70 | 4,238.10[4] |
| 10+ .... | 1,163.10 | 1,474.20 | 1,847.40 | 1,939.20 | 2,016.90 | 2,281.80 | 3,105.00 | 3,585.20 | 3,755.70 | 4,238.10[4] |
| 12+ .... | 1,163.10 | 1,474.20 | 1,939.20 | 2,043.40 | 2,124.90 | 2,281.80 | 3,105.00 | 3,755.70 | 3,911.70 | 4,562.70[4] |
| 14+ .... | 1,163.10 | 1,474.20 | 1,986.90 | 2,142.00 | 2,267.10 | 2,359.20 | 3,259.80 | 3,755.70 | 3,911.70 | 4,562.70[4] |
| 16+ .... | 1,163.10 | 1,474.20 | 1,986.90 | 2,235.60 | 2,436.90 | 2,732.70 | 3,586.20 | 3,911.70 | 4,238.10 | 4,889.10[4] |
| 18+ .... | 1,163.10 | 1,474.20 | 1,986.90 | 2,297.70 | 2,577.00 | 2,872.50 | 3,832.50 | 4,081.50 | 4,238.10 | 4,889.10[4] |
| 20+ .... | 1,163.10 | 1,474.20 | 1,986.90 | 2,297.70 | 2,654.70 | 2,934.60 | 3,832.50 | 4,238.10 | 4,562.70[4] | 5,216.10[4] |
| 22+ .... | 1,163.10 | 1,474.20 | 1,986.90 | 2,297.70 | 2,747.40 | 3,105.00 | 3,832.50 | 4,407.90 | 4,562.70[4] | 5,216.10[4] |
| 26+ .... | 1,163.10 | 1,474.20 | 1,986.90 | 2,297.70 | 2,747.40 | 3,367.50 | 3,832.50 | 4,407.90 | 4,889.10[4] | 5,541.60[4] |

| YEARS SERVED | WARRANT OFFICERS' PAY GRADES | | | | YEARS SERVED | WARRANT OFFICERS' PAY GRADES | | | |
| --- | --- | --- | --- | --- | --- | --- | --- | --- | --- |
| | W-1 | W-2 | W-3 | W-4 | | W-1 | W-2 | W-3 | W-4 |
| Up to 2 | $825.30 | $990.60 | $1,131.00 | $1,244.10 | 12+ ..... | $1,211.10 | $1,319.70 | $1,474.20 | $1,661.40 |
| 2+ .... | 946.20 | 1,071.30 | 1,226.70 | 1,334.70 | 14+ ..... | 1,257.00 | 1,365.30 | 1,521.00 | 1,734.20 |
| 3+ ... | 946.20 | 1,071.30 | 1,226.70 | 1,334.70 | 16+ ..... | 1,303.20 | 1,413.00 | 1,566.60 | 1,799.70 |
| 4+ ... | 1,025.10 | 1,102.50 | 1,242.30 | 1,365.30 | 18+ ..... | 1,348.80 | 1,459.50 | 1,614.90 | 1,847.40 |
| 6+ ... | 1,071.30 | 1,163.10 | 1,257.00 | 1,427.40 | 20+ ..... | 1,397.10 | 1,505.70 | 1,677.30 | 1,907.70 |
| 8+ ... | 1,117.50 | 1,226.70 | 1,348.80 | 1,490.40 | 22+ ..... | 1,397.10 | 1,566.60 | 1,738.20 | 1,971.60 |
| 10+ ... | 1,163.10 | 1,272.90 | 1,427.40 | 1,552.80 | 26+ ..... | 1,397.10 | 1,566.60 | 1,799.70 | 2,124.90 |

| YEARS SERVED | ENLISTED PAY GRADES | | | | | | | | |
| --- | --- | --- | --- | --- | --- | --- | --- | --- | --- |
| | E-1 | E-2 | E-3 | E-4 | E-5 | E-6 | E-7 | E-8 | E-9[5] |
| Up to 2 | $501.30 | $558.60 | $580.50 | $603.60 | $627.90 | $715.20 | $828.00 | — | — |
| 2+ ... | 501.30 | 558.60 | 612.30 | 637.50 | 683.40 | 779.70 | 893.70 | — | — |
| 3+ ... | 501.30 | 558.60 | 636.90 | 674.70 | 716.40 | 812.40 | 927.00 | — | — |
| 4+ ... | 501.30 | 558.60 | 662.10 | 727.20 | 747.60 | 846.60 | 959.10 | — | — |
| 6+ ... | 501.30 | 558.60 | 662.10 | 756.00 | 796.50 | 878.10 | 992.10 | — | — |
| 8+ ... | 501.30 | 558.60 | 662.10 | 756.00 | 828.90 | 910.20 | 1,023.30 | $1,185.90 | — |
| 10+ ... | 501.30 | 558.60 | 662.10 | 756.00 | 862.20 | 943.50 | 1,056.30 | 1,219.20 | $1,413.60 |
| 12+ ... | 501.30 | 558.60 | 662.10 | 756.00 | 893.70 | 992.10 | 1,089.00 | 1,251.60 | 1,445.70 |
| 14+ ... | 501.30 | 558.60 | 662.10 | 756.00 | 910.20 | 1,023.30 | 1,138.20 | 1,284.30 | 1,478.40 |
| 16+ ... | 501.30 | 558.60 | 662.10 | 756.00 | 910.20 | 1,056.30 | 1,170.60 | 1,317.90 | 1,512.60 |
| 18+ ... | 501.30 | 558.60 | 662.10 | 756.00 | 910.20 | 1,072.20 | 1,203.60 | 1,348.50 | 1,546.20 |
| 20+ ... | 501.30 | 558.60 | 662.10 | 756.00 | 910.20 | 1,072.20 | 1,219.20 | 1,381.50 | 1,576.20 |
| 22+ ... | 501.30 | 558.60 | 662.10 | 756.00 | 910.20 | 1,072.20 | 1,301.10 | 1,462.80 | 1,659.30 |
| 26+ ... | 501.30 | 558.60 | 662.10 | 756.00 | 910.20 | 1,072.20 | 1,462.80 | 1,626.00 | 1,820.40 |

[1] Pay scale effective Oct. 1, 1980.   [2] Officers in the first 3 pay grades who have had 4 years of enlisted service receive some additional pay.   [3] Chiefs of staff of each service receive $6,114.30.   [4] Basic pay is limited to $4,176.00 by Level V of the Executive Schedule.   [5] Highest-ranking enlisted person in each service receives $2,212.80.

U.S. Marine Maj. John P. Bland inspects laser-guided air-to-ground Maverick missile, which is mounted under wing of his A-4M attack plane. In his first practice firing of the missile, it accurately destroyed an armored personnel carrier at the test range at Eglin Air Force Base in Florida. The missile was developed primarily for use by the Marine Corps for close air support of ground troops.

United Press Int'l.

submarines on alert for an enemy missile attack. Each time the errors were discovered as such within a few minutes.

The North American Air Defense Command, headquartered near Colorado Springs, Colo., which set off the alerts, later reported that they resulted from the failure of a 46-cent silicon chip in one of the computers. A similar false alert occurred in November 1979.

Secretary of Defense Brown issued assurances that the system contained safeguards that would prevent the automatic launching of retaliatory missiles in the case of such a false alarm.

A congressional report said that in the 18 months from Jan. 1, 1979, to June 30, 1980, the system registered 3,850 false alarms, mostly caused by weather disturbances.

## JOINT CHIEFS OF STAFF

The Joint Chiefs of Staff of the U.S. armed forces was established within the Department of Defense in 1947. The position of Chairman of the Joint Chiefs of Staff was created in 1949.

**CHAIRMAN**
**Gen. David C. Jones, USAF** (June 30, 1978–Current)

Gen. George S. Brown, USAF (July 1974–June 1978)
Adm. Thomas H. Moorer, USN (July 1970–July 1974)
Gen. Earle G. Wheeler, USA (July 1964–July 1970)
Gen. Maxwell D. Taylor, USA (Oct. 1962–July 1964)
Gen. Lyman L. Lemnitzer, USA (Oct. 1960–Sept. 1962)
Gen. Nathan F. Twining, USAF (Aug. 1957–Sept. 1960)
Adm. Arthur W. Radford, USN (Aug. 1953–Aug. 1957)
Gen. of the Army Omar N. Bradley, USA (Aug. 1949–Aug. 1953)

**CHIEF OF STAFF, UNITED STATES ARMY**
**Gen. Edward Charles Meyer** (June 1979–Current)

Gen. Bernard W. Rogers (Sept. 1976–June 1979)
Gen. Frederick C. Weyand (Oct. 1974–Sept. 1976)
Gen. Creighton W. Abrams (Oct. 1972–Sept. 1974)
Gen. William C. Westmoreland (July 1968–June 1972)
Gen. Harold K. Johnson (July 1964–July 1968)
Gen. Earle G. Wheeler (Oct. 1962–July 1964)
Gen. George H. Decker (Sept. 1960–Sept. 1962)
Gen. Lyman L. Lemnitzer (July 1959–Sept. 1960)
Gen. Maxwell D. Taylor (June 1955–June 1959)
Gen. Matthew B. Ridgway (Aug. 1953–June 1955)
Gen. J. Lawton Collins (Aug. 1949–Aug. 1953)
Gen. Omar N. Bradley (Feb. 1948–Aug. 1949)
Gen. of the Army Dwight D. Eisenhower (Nov. 1945–Feb. 1948)

**CHIEF OF NAVAL OPERATIONS**
**Adm. Thomas B. Hayward** (July 1, 1978–Current)

Adm. James J. Holloway III (June 1974–June 1978)
Adm. Elmo R. Zumwalt Jr. (July 1970–June 1974)

Adm. Thomas H. Moorer (Aug. 1967–June 1970)
Adm. David L. McDonald (Aug. 1963–Aug. 1967)
Adm. George W. Anderson (Aug. 1961–July 1963)
Adm. Arleigh A. Burke (Aug. 1955–Aug. 1961)
Adm. Robert B. Carney (Aug. 1953–Aug. 1955)
Adm. William M. Fechteler (Aug. 1951–Aug. 1953)
Adm. Forrest P. Sherman (Nov. 1949–July 1951)
Adm. Louis E. Denfield (Dec. 1947–Nov. 1949)
Fleet Adm. Chester W. Nimitz (Dec. 1945–Dec. 1947)

**CHIEF OF STAFF, UNITED STATES AIR FORCE**
**Gen. Lew Allen Jr.** (July 1, 1978–Current)

Gen. David C. Jones (July 1974–June 1978)
Gen. George S. Brown (July 1973–July 1974)
Gen. John D. Ryan (Aug. 1969–July 1973)
Gen. John P. McConnell (Feb. 1965–Aug. 1969)
Gen. Curtis E. LeMay (June 1961–Jan. 1965)
Gen. Thomas D. White (July 1957–June 1961)
Gen. Nathan F. Twining (June 1953–June 1957)
Gen. Hoyt S. Vandenberg (April 1948–June 1953)
Gen. Carl Spaatz (Sept. 1947–April 1948)

**COMMANDANT OF THE MARINE CORPS**
**Gen. Robert H. Barrow** (July 1979–Current)

Gen. Louis H. Wilson Jr. (July 1975–July 1979)
Gen. R.E. Cushman Jr. (Jan. 1972–July 1975)
Gen. Leonard F. Chapman Jr. (Jan. 1968–Dec. 1971)
Gen. Wallace M. Greene Jr. (Jan. 1964–Dec. 1967)
Gen. David M. Shoup (Jan. 1960–Dec. 1963)
Gen. Randolph McC. Pate (Jan. 1956–Dec. 1959)
Gen. Lemuel C. Shepherd (Jan. 1952–Dec. 1955)

## U.S. MILITARY FORCES ACTIVE STRENGTH

Source: U.S. Department of Defense

| MILITARY PERSONNEL | 1970 | 1975 | 1977 | 1978 | 1979 | 1980 |
|---|---|---|---|---|---|---|
| Army | 1,322,548 | 784,333 | 778,920 | 776,710 | 758,992 | 774,607 |
| Navy | 692,660 | 539,100 | 524,875 | 523,472 | 519,512 | 527,296 |
| Marine Corps | 259,737 | 195,951 | 189,270 | 189,673 | 185,143 | 187,647 |
| Air Force | 791,349 | 612,751 | 580,956 | 573,770 | 559,984 | 559,282 |
| Totals | 3,066,294 | 2,132,136 | 2,074,465 | 2,053,625 | 2,023,631 | 2,048,832 |

## U.S. MILITARY STRENGTH ABROAD

Source: U.S. Department of Defense

| PLACE | NUMBER OF U.S. MILITARY PERSONNEL | | | PLACE | NUMBER OF U.S. MILITARY PERSONNEL | | |
|---|---|---|---|---|---|---|---|
| | 1980 | 1979 | 1975 | | 1980 | 1979 | 1975 |
| West Germany | 250,912 | 239,414 | 220,000 | Netherlands | 2,602 | 2,235 | 2,000 |
| Japan | 46,007 | 46,406 | 48,000 | Iceland | 2,524 | 2,930 | 3,000 |
| South Korea | 42,822 | 38,507 | 42,000 | Cuba (Guantánamo) | 2,392 | 2,203 | 3,000 |
| Afloat, Western Europe | 33,165 | 16,507 | 30,000 | Belgium | 2,122 | 2,079 | 2,000 |
| Britain | 23,802 | 22,828 | 21,000 | Portugal/Azores | 1,401 | 1,429 | 2,000 |
| Afloat in other areas | 20,392 | 3,114 | 10,000 | Bermuda | 1,296 | 1,637 | 1,000 |
| Afloat, Pacific | 20,137 | 28,057 | 28,000 | Diego Garcia | 1,154 | 1,065 | — |
| Philippines | 13,963 | 14,283 | 15,000 | Australia | 838 | 622 | 2,000 |
| Italy | 11,910 | 11,777 | 12,000 | Canada | 699 | 668 | 2,000 |
| Panama | 9,526 | 9,401 | 10,000 | Midway Island | 472 | 505 | — |
| Guam | 9,303 | 8,776 | 10,000 | Saudi Arabia | 460 | 437 | — |
| Spain | 9,057 | 9,141 | 9,000 | Norway | 447 | 194 | — |
| Turkey | 4,871 | 4,755 | 7,000 | Greenland | 298 | 299 | — |
| Greece | 4,497 | 3,377 | 4,000 | Other places | 3,110 | 3,272 | 25,000 |
| Puerto Rico | 3,667 | 3,508 | 5,000 | TOTAL | 523,826 | 478,666 | 517,000 |

## U.S. AIR FORCE ACTIVE AIRCRAFT

| Source: U.S. Department of Defense | 1960 | 1970 | 1975 | 1978 | 1979 | 1980 * | 1981 * |
|---|---|---|---|---|---|---|---|
| U.S. Air Force total | 15,312 | 11,245 | 7,239 | 7,121 | 6,950 | 7,065 | 7,170 |
| Bomber | 2,193 | 570 | 498 | 448 | 417 | 415 | 414 |
| Tanker | 1,230 | 663 | 657 | 525 | 525 | 532 | 532 |
| Fighter/Attack/Interceptor | 3,922 | 3,404 | 2,299 | 2,652 | 2,622 | 2,790 | 2,899 |
| Reconnaissance/Electronic Warfare | 685 | 1,017 | 494 | 419 | 366 | 356 | 356 |
| Cargo/Transport | 2,549 | 1,854 | 927 | 845 | 841 | 834 | 833 |
| Search and Rescue (Fixed Wing) | 129 | 87 | 44 | 37 | 35 | 35 | 35 |
| Helicopter (including Rescue) | 372 | 457 | 269 | 246 | 230 | 231 | 229 |
| Special Research | 2 | — | — | — | — | — | — |
| Trainer | 3,914 | 2,625 | 1,861 | 1,739 | 1,704 | 1,687 | 1,678 |
| Utility/Observation | 316 | 568 | 189 | 210 | 210 | 185 | 189 |
| Support of allied nations | — | 948 | 243 | — | — | — | — |
| Air National Guard | 2,269 | 1,900 | 1,647 | 1,539 | 1,522 | 1,567 | 1,642 |
| Air Force Reserve | 770 | 420 | 448 | 478 | 487 | 467 | 470 |
| Other non-Air Force agencies | 361 | 212 | — | — | — | — | — |
| Total active Air Force aircraft | 18,712 | 14,725 | 9,577 | 9,138 | 8,959 | 9,099 | 9,282 |

## U.S. NAVY AND MARINE CORPS STRENGTH

| Source: U.S. Department of Defense | 1960 | 1968 | 1972 | 1976 | 1978 | 1979 | 1980 | 1981 * |
|---|---|---|---|---|---|---|---|---|
| Warships | 424 | 489 | 381 | 289 | 294 | 302 | 315 | 330 |
| Attack Carriers (CVA/CVAN) | 14 | 15 | 14 | 13 | 13 | 13 | 13 | 12 |
| ASW Carriers (CVS) | 9 | 8 | 3 | — | — | — | — | — |
| Cruisers (CG, CGN, CLG, CA, CC) | 14 | 34 | 28 | 26 | 28 | 28 | 27 | 27 |
| Destroyers (DD, DDR) | 223 | 184 | 93 | 31 | 30 | 36 | 43 | 43 |
| Destroyers (DDG) | 3 | 37 | 38 | 38 | 37 | 37 | 37 | 41 |
| Frigates (FF, FFG) | 41 | 50 | 66 | 64 | 65 | 65 | 71 | 79 |
| Submarines (SS, SSR, SSG, SSN) | 111 | 105 | 94 | 74 | 80 | 80 | 81 | 91 |
| Submarines (SSBN) | 2 | 41 | 41 | 41 | 41 | 41 | 41 | 35 |
| Submarines (AGSS) | 7 | 14 | 4 | 2 | 2 | 2 | 2 | 2 |
| Amphibious ships | 113 | 157 | 77 | 62 | 64 | 65 | 63 | 60 |
| Amphib. Helo/Landing Craft Carr. | 3 | 16 | 22 | 22 | 24 | 25 | 26 | 26 |
| Landing Craft Carriers | 104 | 124 | 51 | 38 | 38 | 38 | 35 | 32 |
| Other Amphibious | 6 | 17 | 74 | 2 | 2 | 2 | 2 | 2 |
| Patrol combatants (PG,PHM,PCER) | 4 | 9 | 16 | 8 | 3 | 3 | 3 | 5 |
| Mine warfare ships | 81 | 84 | 31 | 3 | 3 | 3 | 3 | 3 |
| Auxiliary ships | 190 | 237 | 149 | 114 | 88 | 85 | 78 | 79 |
| TOTAL ACTIVE U.S. FLEET | 812 | 976 | 654 | 476 | 453 | 533 | 540 | 544 |
| U.S. Navy Aircraft, operating | 6,759 | 7,103 | 5,658 | 4,931 | 4,512 | 4,463 | 4,932 | 4,970 |
| Marine Corps Divisions | 3 | 4 | 3 | 3 | 3 | 3 | 3 | 3 |

* Planned strength.

## WORLD MILITARY EXPENDITURES AND SIZE OF ARMED FORCES

Source: U.S. Arms Control and Disarmament Agency, data for 1978.

| NATIONS | MILITARY EXPENDITURES | ARMED FORCES | NATIONS | MILITARY EXPENDITURES | ARMED FORCES |
|---|---|---|---|---|---|
| WORLD TOTAL .... | $477,000,000,000 | 26,639,000 | Laos ............. | $ 42,000,000 | 45,000 |
| Afghanistan ....... | 66,000,000 | 110,000 | Lebanon ......... | 70,000,000 | 9,000 |
| Albania............ | 154,000,000 | 53,000 | Liberia .......... | 9,000,000 | 7,000 |
| Algeria ........... | 431,000,000 | 75,000 | Libya ........... | 469,000,000 | 50,000 |
| Angola ........... | 102,000,000[1] | 47,000 | Luxembourg ...... | 32,000,000 | 1,000 |
| Argentina ........ | 1,567,000,000 | 155,000 | Madagascar ...... | 53,000,000 | 20,000 |
| Australia .......... | 1,658,000,000 | 70,000 | Malawi .......... | 20,000,000 | 5,000 |
| Austria ........... | 649,000,000 | 40,000 | Malaysia ......... | 661,000,000 | 82,000 |
| Bahrain .......... | 80,000,000 | 2,000 | Mali ............ | 24,000,000 | 8,000 |
| Bangladesh ....... | 130,000,000 | 129,000 | Malta ........... | 4,000,000 | 7,000 |
| Barbados.......... | 1,000,000 | 0 | Mauritania........ | 29,000,000 | 12,000 |
| Belgium .......... | 2,847,000,000 | 90,000 | Mauritius ......... | 1,000,000 | 0 |
| Benin ........... | 13,000,000 | 4,000 | Mexico .......... | 403,000,000 | 145,000 |
| Bolivia .......... | 71,000,000 | 20,000 | Mongolia ........ | 73,000,000[1] | 36,000 |
| Brazil ........... | 1,743,000,000 | 450,000 | Morocco ......... | 452,000,000 | 115,000 |
| Britain ........... | 12,951,000,000 | 318,000 | Mozambique ...... | 49,000,000 | 13,000 |
| Bulgaria .......... | 2,346,000,000 | 164,000 | Nepal ........... | 15,000,000 | 32,000 |
| Burma ........... | 167,000,000 | 212,000 | Netherlands ...... | 3,735,000,000 | 100,000 |
| Burundi .......... | 13,000,000 | 8,000 | New Zealand ...... | 281,000,000 | 12,000 |
| Cambodia ........ | 67,000,000[1] | 70,000 | Nicaragua ........ | 43,000,000 | 6,000[3] |
| Cameroon ........ | 55,000,000 | 11,000 | Niger ........... | 8,000,000 | 4,000 |
| Canada .......... | 4,411,000,000 | 80,000 | Nigeria .......... | 1,871,000,000 | 204,000 |
| Cape Verde....... | 1,000,000[2] | 2,000[2] | Norway .......... | 1,281,000,000 | 39,000 |
| Central Africa ..... | 10,000,000 | 4,000 | Oman ........... | 799,000,000 | 12,000 |
| Chad............. | 20,000,000 | 9,000 | Pakistan.......... | 907,000,000 | 518,000 |
| Chile............. | 414,000,000 | 111,000 | Panama .......... | 17,000,000 | 8,000 |
| China ............ | 37,596,000,000 | 4,500,000 | Papua New Guinea . | 26,000,000 | 3,000 |
| Colombia ......... | 159,000,000 | 60,000 | Paraguay ......... | 32,000,000 | 15,000 |
| Congo ........... | 42,000,000 | 11,000 | Peru ............ | 751,000,000 | 125,000 |
| Costa Rica ....... | 0 | 3,000 | Philippines ....... | 655,000,000 | 156,000 |
| Cuba ............ | 987,000,000 | 210,000 | Poland .......... | 6,874,000,000 | 430,000 |
| Cyprus .......... | 22,000,000 | 10,000 | Portugal.......... | 631,000,000 | 58,000 |
| Czechoslovakia .... | 4,053,000,000 | 212,000 | Qatar ........... | 165,000,000[2] | 5,000 |
| Denmark ......... | 1,193,000,000 | 34,000 | Romania ......... | 3,455,000,000 | 218,000 |
| Dominican Republic | 92,000,000 | 19,000 | Rwanda .......... | 14,000,000 | 4,000 |
| Ecuador .......... | 172,000,000 | 35,000 | Saudi Arabia ...... | 10,284,000,000 | 50,000 |
| Egypt ........... | 1,354,000,000 | 350,000 | Senegal ......... | 38,000,000 | 13,000 |
| El Salvador ....... | 45,000,000 | 10,000 | Sierra Leone...... | 6,000,000 | 1,000 |
| Equatorial Guinea .. | 4,000,000[1] | 2,000 | Singapore ........ | 439,000,000 | 64,000 |
| Ethiopia .......... | 100,000,000 | 233,000 | Somalia ......... | 64,000,000 | 54,000 |
| Fiji............... | 3,000,000 | 1,000 | South Africa ...... | 1,738,000,000 | 78,000 |
| Finland........... | 477,000,000 | 39,000 | Soviet Union ...... | 150,700,000,000 | 4,800,000 |
| France ........... | 16,587,000,000 | 502,000 | Spain ........... | 2,265,000,000 | 321,000 |
| Gabon ........... | 8,000,000 | 4,000 | Sri Lanka......... | 23,000,000 | 13,000 |
| Germany, East..... | 5,257,000,000 | 228,000 | Sudan ........... | 233,000,000 | 71,000 |
| Germany, West .... | 19,921,000,000 | 489,000 | Suriname......... | 0 | 1,000 |
| Ghana ........... | 69,000,000 | 19,000 | Swaziland ........ | 4,000,000 | 2,000 |
| Greece ........... | 1,453,000,000 | 184,000 | Sweden .......... | 2,932,000,000 | 68,000 |
| Guatemala........ | 59,000,000 | 14,000 | Switzerland ....... | 1,357,000,000 | 18,000 |
| Guinea .......... | 18,000,000 | 18,000 | Syria............ | 1,176,000,000 | 225,000 |
| Guinea–Bissau ..... | 6,000,000 | 6,000 | Taiwan .......... | 1,967,000,000 | 471,000 |
| Guyana .......... | 13,000,000 | 7,000 | Tanzania ......... | 159,000,000 | 63,000 |
| Haiti ............ | 15,000,000 | 7,000 | Thailand ......... | 720,000,000 | 250,000 |
| Honduras ......... | 31,000,000 | 13,000 | Togo ............ | 21,000,000 | 5,000 |
| Hungary........... | 1,793,000,000 | 110,000 | Trinidad–Tobago ... | 8,000,000 | 1,000 |
| India ............ | 3,645,000,000 | 1,300,000 | Tunisia .......... | 95,000,000 | 20,000 |
| Indonesia.......... | 1,590,000,000 | 250,000 | Turkey .......... | 2,576,000,000 | 566,000 |
| Iran.............. | 10,598,000,000 | 350,000 | Uganda .......... | 134,000,000 | 6,000 |
| Iraq.............. | 2,136,000,000 | 140,000 | United Arab Emirates . | 686,000,000 | 25,000 |
| Ireland ........... | 174,000,000 | 13,000 | UNITED STATES ... | 108,357,000,000 | 2,100,000 |
| Israel ........... | 3,914,000,000 | 165,000 | Upper Volta ...... | 22,000,000 | 6,000 |
| Italy ............ | 5,694,000,000 | 365,000 | Uruguay.......... | 94,000,000 | 28,000 |
| Ivory Coast ....... | 151,000,000 | 8,000 | Venezuela ........ | 652,000,000 | 55,000 |
| Jamaica .......... | 26,000,000 | 1,000 | Vietnam .......... | 459,000,000[1] | 660,000 |
| Japan............ | 7,069,000,000 | 239,000 | Yemen .......... | 122,000,000 | 40,000 |
| Jordan ........... | 280,000,000 | 70,000 | Yemen, Southern... | 79,000,000 | 20,000 |
| Kenya............ | 78,000,000 | 13,000 | Yugoslavia........ | 2,330,000,000 | 260,000 |
| Korea, North ..... | 2,112,000,000 | 632,000 | Zaire ........... | 32,000,000 | 53,000 |
| Korea, South ...... | 2,269,000,000 | 600,000 | Zambia .......... | 76,000,000 | 20,000 |
| Kuwait .......... | 1,028,000,000 | 10,000 | Zimbabwe ........ | 218,000,000 | 24,000 |

[1] 1975 data latest available. [2] 1976 data latest available. [3] 1977 data latest available.

# U.S. ARMED FORCES IN MAJOR CONFLICTS

Source: U.S. Department of Defense

The military services of the U.S. have taken part in nine major wars in which about 650,000 American military personnel were killed in action.

More American men and women served in the armed services in World War II than in any other war—over 16 million. More were killed or wounded in that war than in any other—more than 1 million.

The Continental Army was first formed by order of the Continental Congress on June 15, 1775, with George Washington as commander in chief. A Continental Navy was formed by the Continental Congress on Dec. 22, 1775, with the appointment of Esek Hopkins as its commander. Various congressional committees and boards maintained civilian control over the armed forces during the early part of the Revolutionary War.

The first secretary of war, Maj. Gen. Benjamin Lincoln, was appointed by Congress on Oct. 30, 1781.

The Department of Defense, created by Congress in 1949, provides civilian administration of the armed services. The secretary of defense is a cabinet-level officer.

| WARS | BRANCH OF SERVICE | NUMBER SERVING | MILITARY CASUALTIES Total | Deaths in Action | Other Deaths | Nonfatal Wounds |
|---|---|---|---|---|---|---|
| Revolutionary War 1775–1783 | Total | 184,000 to 250,000 | 10,623 | 4,435 | — | 6,188 |
| | Army | — | 10,048 | 4,044 | — | 6,004 |
| | Navy | — | 456 | 342 | — | 114 |
| | Marines | — | 119 | 49 | — | 70 |
| War of 1812 1812–1815 | Total | 286,730 | 6,765 | 2,260 | — | 4,505 |
| | Army | — | 5,950 | 1,950 | — | 4,000 |
| | Navy | — | 704 | 265 | — | 439 |
| | Marines | — | 111 | 45 | — | 66 |
| Mexican War 1846–1848 | Total | 78,718 | 17,435 | 1,733 | 11,550 | 4,152 |
| | Army | — | 17,373 | 1,721 | 11,550 | 4,102 |
| | Navy | — | 4 | 1 | — | 3 |
| | Marines | — | 58 | 11 | — | 47 |
| Civil War 1861–1865 | Union Forces | 2,213,363 | 646,392 | 140,414 | 224,097 | 281,881 |
| | Army | 2,128,948 | 639,568 | 138,154 | 221,374 | 280,040 |
| | Navy | } 84,415 | 6,233 | 2,112 | 2,411 | 1,710 |
| | Marines | | 591 | 148 | 312 | 131 |
| | Confederate Forces [1] | 600,000 to 1,500,000 | 159,821 to 164,821+ | 74,524 | 85,297 to 90,297 | — |
| Spanish-American War 1898 | Total | 306,760 | 4,108 | 385 | 2,061 | 1,662 |
| | Army | 280,564 | 4,024 | 369 | 2,061 | 1,594 |
| | Navy | 22,875 | 57 | 10 | — | 47 |
| | Marines | 3,321 | 27 | 6 | — | 21 |
| World War I 1917–1918 | Total | 4,734,991 | 320,518 | 53,402 | 63,114 | 204,002 |
| | Army | 4,057,101 | 300,041 | 50,510 | 55,868 | 193,663 |
| | Navy | 599,051 | 8,106 | 431 | 6,856 | 819 |
| | Marines | 78,839 | 12,371 | 2,461 | 390 | 9,520 |
| World War II 1941–1945 | Total | 16,112,566 | 1,076,245 | 291,557 | 113,842 | 670,846 |
| | Army | 11,260,000 | 884,135 | 234,874 | 83,400 | 565,861 |
| | Navy | 4,183,466 | 100,392 | 36,950 | 25,664 | 37,778 |
| | Marines | 669,100 | 91,718 | 19,733 | 4,778 | 67,207 |
| Korean War 1950–1953 | Total | 5,720,000 | 157,530 | 33,629 | 20,617 | 103,284 |
| | Army | 2,834,000 | 114,729 | 27,704 | 9,429 | 77,596 |
| | Navy | 1,177,000 | 6,077 | 458 | 4,043 | 1,576 |
| | Marines | 424,000 | 29,272 | 4,267 | 1,261 | 23,744 |
| | Air Force | 1,285,000 | 7,452 | 1,200 | 5,884 | 368 |
| Vietnam War [2] 1961–1975 | Total | 3,385,000 | 360,851 | 46,752 | 10,395 | 303,704 |
| | Army | — | 239,481 | 30,743 | 7,202 | 201,536 |
| | Navy [3] | — | 12,562 | 1,575 | 909 | 10,078 |
| | Marines | — | 103,345 | 13,031 | 1,681 | 88,633 |
| | Air Force | — | 5,463 | 1,403 | 603 | 3,457 |

[1] Other deaths include 26,000 to 31,000 Confederates who died in Union prisons. [2] Includes *Mayaguez* incident, 1975. [3] Includes small number of Coast Guard casualties.

United Press Int'l.

Urban guerrillas in El Salvador's capital city San Salvador take cover behind a light pole in one of the countless shootouts that kept the Central American nation in turmoil and killed thousands of Salvadorans during the year.

## HIGHLIGHTS: 1980

### FIRST NEW NATION OF 1980s

After 74 years of rule by Britain and France as the condominium New Hebrides, the Pacific island nation of Vanuatu was granted sovereignty on July 30, 1980. A group of 70 islands and islets, Vanuatu has a population larger than only 13 of the smallest independent nations. But its land area is larger than those of 33 other countries.

The birth pangs of the new nation were not easy. Because of the joint British-French administration of the colony, negotiations for independence had dragged on for many years as Britain and France argued about details, each trying to achieve an advantage.

Then, after achieving independence, the new government of Vanuatu immediately had to call in troops from its neighbor Papua New Guinea to put down a rebellion by set-

tlers who wanted to establish a rival nation called Vemerana on Vanuatu's island Espiritu Santo. See page 669.

### RHODESIA BECOMES ZIMBABWE

While Britain was breaking up its worldwide empire in the 1950s–60s, the whites in the African colony of Southern Rhodesia became increasingly fearful that the black majority might be given control of the government. The whites took matters into their own hands in 1965, declaring their independence from British rule.

Shunned by most other nations than neighboring white-ruled South Africa, Rhodesia remained a world trouble spot for over 14 years as black guerrillas battled Rhodesian troops. But British diplomacy finally succeeded in achieving a cease-fire on Dec. 28,

Wide World

Nearly three years after having been ousted from office by voters disenchanted with her increasingly dictatorial rule, Indira Gandhi was restored as India's prime minister by a landslide parliamentary election victory in 1980.

## HIGHLIGHTS: 1980 *(continued)*

1979. Free elections held in February 1980 were won by black guerrilla leader Robert Mugabe, who became prime minister as Rhodesia changed its name to Zimbabwe. See page 680.

### WAR, VIOLENCE, AND REFUGEES

Throughout the world in 1980 millions of persons suffered as refugees from war and violence.

About 1 million Afghans fled from their country, living in hardship in Pakistan to avoid the occupation of Afghanistan by the Soviet Union. Many slipped back and forth across the mountainous border in raids against their communist oppressors. See page 9.

Thousands were driven from their homes and many were killed in the war between Iraq and Iran. See page 25.

Perhaps the largest number of refugees living under the worst conditions were an estimated 2 million in the small poverty-stricken country of Somalia on Africa's east coast. Most were Ethiopians who had fled from the two wars going on in their country—one between Ethiopia and rebelling Eritreans and the other between Ethiopia and Somali guerrillas. See pages 544–545 and 641.

In Southeast Asia about 300,000 Cambodians lived in refugee camps in Thailand, having fled the civil war in their country between Vietnamese-backed and Chinese-backed communists.

### POPULATIONS [1] OF CONTINENTS

| | |
|---|---:|
| Africa | 473,705,000 |
| North America | 251,825,000 |
| South America | 373,121,000 |
| Asia | 2,592,660,000 |
| Europe | 487,250,000 |
| Australia | 14,691,900 |

[1] January 1981 population estimates.

## LARGEST NATIONS IN AREA

| RANK | NATION | AREA (sq. mi.) | LOCATION |
|---|---|---|---|
| 1 | Soviet Union | 8,649,538 | Europe–Asia |
| 2 | Canada | 3,851,809 | North America |
| 3 | China | 3,691,514 | Asia |
| 4 | United States | 3,615,122 | North America |
| 5 | Brazil | 3,286,488 | South America |
| 6 | Australia | 2,967,909 | South Pacific |
| 7 | India | 1,269,346 | Asia |
| 8 | Argentina | 1,068,301 | South America |
| 9 | Sudan | 967,500 | Africa |
| 10 | Algeria | 919,595 | North Africa |

## SMALLEST NATIONS IN AREA

| RANK | NATION | AREA (sq. mi.) | LOCATION |
|---|---|---|---|
| 170 | Vatican City | 0.17 | Europe |
| 169 | Monaco | 0.58 | Europe |
| 168 | Nauru | 8.00 | South Pacific |
| 167 | Tuvalu | 10.00 | South Pacific |
| 166 | San Marino | 23.60 | Europe |
| 165 | Liechtenstein | 61.00 | Europe |
| 164 | Maldives | 115.00 | Indian Ocean |
| 163 | Malta | 122.00 | Mediterranean |
| 162 | Grenada | 133.00 | Caribbean |
| 161 | St. Vincent | 150.00 | Caribbean |

## LARGEST NATIONS IN POPULATION

| RANK | NATION | POPULATION [1] | LOCATION |
|---|---|---|---|
| 1 | China | 1,039,270,000 | Asia |
| 2 | India | 672,541,000 | Asia |
| 3 | Soviet Union | 267,605,000 | Europe–Asia |
| 4 | United States | 223,674,000 | North America |
| 5 | Indonesia | 154,755,255 | Asia |
| 6 | Brazil | 123,675,000 | South America |
| 7 | Japan | 117,800,000 | Asia |
| 8 | Bangladesh | 89,843,300 | Asia |
| 9 | Pakistan | 82,679,500 | Asia |
| 10 | Nigeria | 78,348,000 | Africa |

## SMALLEST NATIONS IN POPULATION

| RANK | NATION | POPULATION [1] | LOCATION |
|---|---|---|---|
| 170 | Vatican City | 1,309 | Europe |
| 168 | Nauru | 7,394 | South Pacific |
| 169 | Tuvalu | 7,759 | South Pacific |
| 167 | San Marino | 21,471 | Europe |
| 166 | Liechtenstein | 25,887 | Europe |
| 165 | Monaco | 27,256 | Europe |
| 164 | Andorra | 30,620 | Europe |
| 163 | Kiribati | 53,146 | South Pacific |
| 162 | Seychelles | 65,478 | Indian Ocean |
| 161 | São Tome-Princ. | 85,519 | South Atlantic |

## 170 NATIONS OF THE WORLD: LOCATION, AREA, POPULATION, CAPITALS

| NATION | LOCATION | AREA In Sq. Mi. | Rank | POPULATION [1] Total | Rank | Per Sq. Mi. | CAPITAL |
|---|---|---|---|---|---|---|---|
| WORLD | — | 57,506,000 | — | 4,463,780,000 | — | 77.6 | New York (UN) |
| Afghanistan | Asia | 250,000 | 40 | 16,235,400 | 42 | 64.9 | Kabul |
| Albania | Europe | 11,100 | 125 | 2,774,630 | 107 | 250.0 | Tiranë |
| Algeria | North Africa | 919,595 | 10 | 20,086,500 | 35 | 21.8 | Algiers |
| Andorra | Europe | 175 | 158 | 30,620 | 164 | 175.0 | Andorra la Vella |
| Angola | Africa | 481,354 | 21 | 7,162,130 | 71 | 14.9 | Luanda |
| Argentina | South America | 1,068,301 | 8 | 27,261,500 | 29 | 25.5 | Buenos Aires |
| Australia | South Pacific | 2,967,909 | 6 | 14,691,900 | 47 | 5.0 | Canberra |
| Austria | Europe | 32,374 | 106 | 7,489,210 | 70 | 231.3 | Vienna |
| Bahamas | Caribbean | 5,380 | 138 | 244,692 | 148 | 45.5 | Nassau |
| Bahrain | Asia | 240 | 154 | 443,597 | 139 | 1,848.3 | Manama |
| Bangladesh | Asia | 55,598 | 87 | 89,843,300 | 8 | 1,615.9 | Dacca |
| Barbados | Caribbean | 166 | 159 | 255,043 | 147 | 1,536.4 | Bridgetown |
| Belgium | Europe | 11,781 | 123 | 9,864,670 | 58 | 837.3 | Brussels |
| Benin | Africa | 43,484 | 95 | 3,619,240 | 98 | 83.2 | Porto Novo |
| Bhutan | Asia | 18,147 | 115 | 1,312,770 | 124 | 72.3 | Thimphu |
| Bolivia | South America | 424,165 | 26 | 5,120,530 | 85 | 12.1 | La Paz; Sucre |
| Bophuthatswana | Africa | 15,610 | 120 | 1,298,500 | 125 | 83.2 | Mmabatho |
| Botswana | Africa | 231,805 | 43 | 800,323 | 132 | 3.5 | Gaborone |
| Brazil | South America | 3,286,488 | 5 | 123,675,000 | 6 | 37.6 | Brasília |
| Britain | Europe | 94,227 | 72 | 55,975,200 | 14 | 594.0 | London |
| Bulgaria | Europe | 42,823 | 98 | 8,902,600 | 61 | 207.9 | Sofia |
| Burma | Asia | 261,218 | 39 | 34,011,400 | 25 | 130.2 | Rangoon |
| Burundi | Africa | 10,747 | 128 | 4,550,150 | 92 | 423.4 | Bujumbura |
| Cambodia | SE Asia | 69,898 | 83 | 5,000,000 | 88 | 71.5 | Phnom Penh |
| Cameroon | Africa | 183,569 | 49 | 8,530,910 | 64 | 46.5 | Yaoundé |
| Canada | North America | 3,851,809 | 2 | 24,152,300 | 31 | 6.3 | Ottawa |
| Cape Verde | South America | 1,557 | 146 | 329,175 | 146 | 211.4 | Praia |
| Central Africa | Africa | 240,535 | 42 | 2,504,830 | 110 | 10.4 | Bangui |
| Chad | Africa | 495,755 | 19 | 4,679,420 | 90 | 9.4 | N'Djaména |
| Chile | South America | 292,258 | 36 | 11,381,700 | 54 | 38.9 | Santiago |
| China | Asia | 3,691,514 | 3 | 1,039,270,000 | 1 | 281.5 | Peking |
| Colombia | South America | 439,737 | 24 | 27,417,400 | 28 | 62.3 | Bogotá |
| Comoros | Indian Ocean | 694 | 150 | 337,949 | 143 | 486.9 | Moroni |
| Congo | Africa | 132,047 | 56 | 1,556,030 | 121 | 11.8 | Brazzaville |
| Costa Rica | Central America | 19,575 | 113 | 2,240,380 | 113 | 114.5 | San José |
| Cuba | Caribbean | 44,218 | 94 | 10,073,000 | 57 | 227.8 | Havana |
| Cyprus | Mediterranean | 3,572 | 143 | 672,045 | 133 | 188.1 | Nicosia |
| Czechoslovakia | Europe | 49,371 | 91 | 15,443,300 | 44 | 312.8 | Prague |
| Denmark | Europe | 16,629 | 116 | 5,142,450 | 84 | 309.2 | Copenhagen |

[1] Jan. 1, 1981, population estimates.

## LOCATION, AREA, POPULATION, CAPITALS *(continued)*

| NATION | LOCATION | AREA In Sq. Mi. | Rank | POPULATION [1] Total | Rank | Per Sq. Mi. | CAPITAL |
|---|---|---|---|---|---|---|---|
| Djibouti | Africa | 8,494 | 132 | 119,338 | 155 | 14.0 | Djibouti |
| Dominica | Caribbean | 290 | 152 | 86,598 | 159 | 298.6 | Roseau |
| Dominican Republic | Caribbean | 18,816 | 114 | 5,518,430 | 82 | 293.3 | Santo Domingo |
| Ecuador | South America | 109,484 | 66 | 8,497,870 | 65 | 77.6 | Quito |
| Egypt | Africa | 386,102 | 28 | 42,583,300 | 20 | 110.3 | Cairo |
| El Salvador | Central America | 8,124 | 133 | 4,666,320 | 91 | 574.4 | San Salvador |
| Equatorial Guinea | Africa | 10,831 | 127 | 366,306 | 141 | 33.8 | Malabo |
| Ethiopia | Africa | 471,778 | 23 | 31,681,500 | 26 | 67.2 | Addis Ababa |
| Fiji | SE Asia | 7,056 | 134 | 627,448 | 134 | 88.9 | Suva |
| Finland | Europe | 130,120 | 57 | 4,787,800 | 89 | 36.8 | Helsinki |
| France | Europe | 211,208 | 46 | 55,175,000 | 15 | 261.2 | Paris |
| Gabon | Africa | 103,347 | 69 | 552,957 | 138 | 5.4 | Libreville |
| Gambia | Africa | 4,361 | 139 | 609,815 | 135 | 139.8 | Banjul |
| Germany, East | Europe | 41,768 | 100 | 16,672,200 | 41 | 399.2 | East Berlin |
| Germany, West | Europe | 95,976 | 71 | 60,850,300 | 12 | 634.0 | Bonn |
| Ghana | Africa | 92,100 | 74 | 11,987,100 | 53 | 130.2 | Accra |
| Greece | Europe | 50,944 | 89 | 9,620,210 | 60 | 188.8 | Athens |
| Grenada | Caribbean | 133 | 162 | 90,348 | 158 | 679.3 | St. George's |
| Guatemala | Central America | 42,042 | 99 | 7,113,280 | 72 | 169.2 | Guatemala City |
| Guinea | Africa | 94,964 | 73 | 5,079,750 | 86 | 53.5 | Conakry |
| Guinea–Bissau | Africa | 13,948 | 121 | 576,873 | 137 | 41.4 | Bissau |
| Guyana | South America | 83,000 | 78 | 855,400 | 131 | 10.3 | Georgetown |
| Haiti | Caribbean | 10,714 | 129 | 5,054,090 | 87 | 471.7 | Port-au-Prince |
| Honduras | Central America | 43,277 | 96 | 3,758,190 | 96 | 86.8 | Tegucigalpa |
| Hungary | Europe | 35,919 | 104 | 10,819,400 | 55 | 301.2 | Budapest |
| Iceland | North Atlantic | 39,768 | 101 | 228,518 | 150 | 5.8 | Rejkjavík |
| India | Asia | 1,269,346 | 7 | 672,541,000 | 2 | 529.8 | New Delhi |
| Indonesia | SE Asia | 788,425 | 13 | 154,755,255 | 5 | 196.3 | Jakarta |
| Iran | Asia | 636,296 | 16 | 37,188,100 | 23 | 58.4 | Teheran |
| Iraq | Asia | 167,925 | 52 | 13,438,400 | 52 | 80.0 | Baghdad |
| Ireland | Europe | 27,136 | 110 | 3,463,450 | 100 | 127.6 | Dublin |
| Israel | Asia | 9,000 | 131 | 3,895,920 | 94 | 432.9 | Jerusalem |
| Italy | Europe | 116,304 | 64 | 57,410,000 | 13 | 493.6 | Rome |
| Ivory Coast | Africa | 124,504 | 62 | 8,461,680 | 67 | 68.0 | Abidjan |
| Jamaica | Caribbean | 4,244 | 141 | 2,214,120 | 114 | 521.7 | Kingston |
| Japan | Asia | 145,809 | 55 | 117,800,000 | 7 | 819.5 | Tokyo |
| Jordan | Asia | 37,738 | 103 | 2,186,738 | 115 | 57.9 | Amman |
| Kenya | Africa | 224,961 | 45 | 16,195,500 | 43 | 72.0 | Nairobi |
| Kiribati | South Pacific | 264 | 155 | 53,146 | 163 | 201.3 | Bairiki, Tarawa |
| Korea, North | Asia | 46,540 | 92 | 19,623,700 | 36 | 421.7 | Pyongyang |
| Korea, South | Asia | 38,025 | 102 | 40,090,600 | 21 | 1,054.3 | Seoul |
| Kuwait | Asia | 6,880 | 135 | 1,391,330 | 122 | 202.2 | Kuwait |
| Laos | SE Asia | 91,429 | 76 | 3,761,340 | 95 | 41.1 | Vientiane |
| Lebanon | Asia | 4,015 | 142 | 3,058,670 | 104 | 761.8 | Beirut |
| Lesotho | Africa | 11,720 | 124 | 1,360,720 | 123 | 116.1 | Maseru |
| Liberia | Africa | 43,000 | 97 | 1,894,460 | 118 | 44.1 | Monrovia |
| Libya | Africa | 679,362 | 15 | 3,046,980 | 105 | 4.5 | Tripoli |
| Liechtenstein | Europe | 61 | 165 | 25,887 | 166 | 424.4 | Vaduz |
| Luxembourg | Europe | 998 | 148 | 359,076 | 142 | 359.8 | Luxembourg-Ville |
| Madagascar | Indian Ocean | 226,658 | 44 | 8,840,230 | 62 | 39.0 | Antananarivo |
| Malawi | Africa | 45,747 | 93 | 6,129,910 | 77 | 134.0 | Lilongwe |
| Malaysia | SE Asia | 127,317 | 60 | 13,923,600 | 50 | 109.4 | Kuala Lumpur |
| Maldives | Indian Ocean | 115 | 164 | 154,951 | 153 | 1,347.4 | Male |
| Mali | Africa | 478,767 | 22 | 6,724,730 | 74 | 14.0 | Bamako |
| Malta | Mediterranean | 122 | 163 | 334,317 | 145 | 2,740.3 | Valletta |
| Mauritania | Africa | 397,955 | 27 | 1,654,750 | 120 | 4.2 | Nouakchott |
| Mauritius | Indian Ocean | 790 | 149 | 960,179 | 128 | 1,215.4 | Port-Louis |
| Mexico | North America | 761,605 | 14 | 73,171,478 | 11 | 96.1 | Mexico City |
| Monaco | Europe | 0.58 | 169 | 27,256 | 165 | 46,993.1 | Monaco-Ville |
| Mongolia | Asia | 604,250 | 17 | 1,697,320 | 119 | 2.8 | Ulaanbaatar |
| Morocco | Africa | 275,117 | 38 | 20,451,638 | 34 | 74.3 | Rabat |
| Mozambique | Africa | 302,330 | 34 | 10,595,700 | 56 | 35.0 | Maputo |
| Namibia | Africa | 318,261 | 32 | 1,035,740 | 127 | 3.3 | Windhoek |
| Nauru | South Pacific | 8 | 168 | 7,394 | 169 | 924.3 | Yaren |
| Nepal | Asia | 54,362 | 88 | 14,173,800 | 49 | 260.7 | Kathmandu |
| Netherlands | Europe | 15,770 | 119 | 14,181,000 | 48 | 899.2 | Amsterdam; The Hague |
| New Zealand | South Pacific | 103,883 | 68 | 3,407,890 | 101 | 32.8 | Wellington |
| Nicaragua | Central America | 50,193 | 90 | 2,617,290 | 108 | 52.1 | Managua |
| Niger | Africa | 489,191 | 20 | 5,582,660 | 81 | 11.4 | Niamey |

[1] Jan. 1, 1981, population estimates.

**LOCATION, AREA, POPULATION, CAPITALS** *(continued)*

| NATION | LOCATION | AREA In Sq. Mi. | Rank | POPULATION [1] Total | Rank | Per Sq. Mi. | CAPITAL |
|---|---|---|---|---|---|---|---|
| Nigeria | Africa | 356,669 | 30 | 78,348,000 | 10 | 219.7 | Lagos |
| Norway | Europe | 125,182 | 61 | 4,099,800 | 93 | 32.8 | Oslo |
| Oman | Asia | 82,030 | 79 | 905,790 | 129 | 11.0 | Muscat |
| Pakistan | Asia | 310,404 | 33 | 82,679,500 | 9 | 266.4 | Islamabad |
| Panama | Central America | 29,762 | 108 | 1,971,360 | 117 | 66.2 | Panama City |
| Papua New Guinea | South Pacific | 178,260 | 50 | 3,223,060 | 103 | 18.1 | Port Moresby |
| Paraguay | South America | 157,048 | 53 | 3,299,170 | 102 | 21.0 | Asunción |
| Peru | South America | 496,225 | 18 | 18,025,400 | 38 | 36.3 | Lima |
| Philippines | SE Asia | 115,830 | 65 | 50,285,100 | 17 | 434.1 | Manila |
| Poland | Europe | 120,725 | 63 | 35,894,100 | 24 | 297.3 | Warsaw |
| Portugal | Europe | 35,553 | 105 | 9,795,264 | 59 | 275.5 | Lisbon |
| Qatar | Asia | 4,247 | 140 | 175,452 | 151 | 41.3 | Doha |
| Romania | Europe | 91,699 | 75 | 22,351,300 | 33 | 243.7 | Bucharest |
| Rwanda | Africa | 10,169 | 130 | 5,291,640 | 83 | 520.4 | Kigali |
| St. Lucia | Caribbean | 238 | 156 | 125,964 | 154 | 529.3 | Castries |
| St. Vincent | Caribbean | 150 | 161 | 116,056 | 156 | 773.7 | Kingstown |
| San Marino | Europe | 23.6 | 166 | 21,471 | 167 | 909.8 | San Marino |
| São Tomé–Príncipe | South Atlantic | 372 | 151 | 85,519 | 161 | 229.9 | São Tomé |
| Saudi Arabia | Asia | 830,000 | 12 | 8,492,180 | 66 | 10.2 | Riyadh |
| Senegal | Africa | 75,750 | 80 | 5,738,840 | 80 | 75.8 | Dakar |
| Seychelles | Indian Ocean | 156 | 160 | 65,478 | 162 | 419.7 | Victoria |
| Sierra Leone | Africa | 27,699 | 109 | 3,510,920 | 99 | 126.8 | Freetown |
| Singapore | SE Asia | 224 | 157 | 2,404,840 | 111 | 10,735.9 | Singapore |
| Solomons | South Pacific | 10,983 | 126 | 237,817 | 149 | 21.7 | Honiara |
| Somalia | Africa | 246,201 | 41 | 3,689,970 | 97 | 15.0 | Mogadiscio |
| South Africa | Africa | 437,538 | 25 | 24,835,400 | 30 | 55.8 | Cape Town; Pretoria |
| Soviet Union | Europe–Asia | 8,649,538 | 1 | 267,605,000 | 3 | 30.9 | Moscow |
| Spain | Europe | 194,897 | 48 | 38,425,200 | 22 | 197.2 | Madrid |
| Sri Lanka | Indian Ocean | 25,332 | 111 | 15,076,400 | 46 | 595.2 | Colombo |
| Sudan | Africa | 967,500 | 9 | 18,896,700 | 37 | 19.5 | Khartoum |
| Suriname | South America | 63,037 | 86 | 413,535 | 140 | 6.6 | Paramaribo |
| Swaziland | Africa | 6,704 | 136 | 590,173 | 136 | 88.0 | Mbabane; Lobamba |
| Sweden | Europe | 173,732 | 51 | 8,340,360 | 68 | 48.0 | Stockholm |
| Switzerland | Europe | 15,941 | 117 | 6,273,700 | 76 | 393.6 | Bern |
| Syria | Asia | 71,498 | 82 | 8,753,150 | 63 | 122.4 | Damascus |
| Taiwan | Asia | 13,892 | 122 | 17,915,600 | 39 | 1,289.6 | Taipei |
| Tanzania | Africa | 364,900 | 29 | 17,653,800 | 40 | 48.4 | Dodoma; Dar es Salaam |
| Thailand | SE Asia | 198,457 | 47 | 46,812,100 | 18 | 235.9 | Bangkok |
| Togo | Africa | 21,622 | 112 | 2,569,200 | 109 | 118.8 | Lomé |
| Tonga | South Pacific | 270 | 153 | 86,178 | 160 | 319.2 | Nukualofa |
| Transkei | Africa | 15,830 | 118 | 2,312,890 | 112 | 146.1 | Umtata |
| Trinidad–Tobago | Caribbean | 1,981 | 145 | 1,179,000 | 126 | 595.5 | Port-of-Spain |
| Tunisia | Africa | 63,170 | 85 | 6,497,010 | 75 | 102.8 | Tunis |
| Turkey | Europe–Asia | 301,382 | 35 | 45,861,400 | 19 | 152.2 | Ankara |
| Tuvalu | South Pacific | 10 | 167 | 7,759 | 168 | 775.9 | Fongafale |
| Uganda | Africa | 91,134 | 77 | 13,898,500 | 51 | 152.5 | Kampala |
| United Arab Emirates | Asia | 32,278 | 107 | 870,915 | 130 | 27.0 | Abu Dhabi |
| UNITED STATES | North America | 3,615,122 | 4 | 223,674,000 | 4 | 61.9 | Washington, D.C. |
| Upper Volta | Africa | 105,869 | 67 | 6,989,850 | 73 | 66.0 | Ouagadougou |
| Uruguay | South America | 68,037 | 84 | 2,907,260 | 106 | 42.7 | Montevideo |
| Vanuatu | South Pacific | 5,700 | 137 | 107,315 | 157 | 18.8 | Port Vila |
| Vatican City | Europe | 0.17 | 170 | 1,309 | 170 | 7,700 | — |
| Venda | Africa | 2,467 | 144 | 336,078 | 144 | 136.2 | Thohoyandou |
| Venezuela | South America | 352,145 | 31 | 15,267,700 | 45 | 43.4 | Caracas |
| Vietnam | SE Asia | 128,402 | 59 | 52,817,900 | 16 | 411.3 | Hanoi |
| Western Samoa | South Pacific | 1,097 | 147 | 156,326 | 152 | 142.5 | Apia |
| Yemen, North | Asia | 75,290 | 81 | 5,979,470 | 78 | 79.4 | Sana |
| Yemen, South | Asia | 128,560 | 58 | 2,000,510 | 116 | 15.6 | Aden |
| Yugoslavia | Europe | 98,766 | 70 | 22,411,700 | 32 | 226.9 | Belgrade |
| Zaire | Africa | 905,568 | 11 | 30,393,800 | 27 | 33.6 | Kinshasa |
| Zambia | Africa | 290,586 | 37 | 5,922,010 | 79 | 20.4 | Lusaka |
| Zimbabwe | Africa | 150,804 | 54 | 7,518,200 | 69 | 49.9 | Harare (Salisbury) |

[1] Jan. 1, 1981, population estimates.

## VITAL STATISTICS, EDUCATION, COMMUNICATIONS

| NATION | VITAL STATISTICS | | | | | COMMUNICATIONS | | | | |
|---|---|---|---|---|---|---|---|---|---|---|
| | Birth Rate [1] | Death Rate [1] | Infant Deaths [2] | Life Expectancy Men/Women | Urban Pop. | Literacy Rate [3] | Phones [1] | Radio Sets [1] | TV Sets [1] | News- papers [4] |
| WORLD .......... | 32.0 | 13.0 | 98.0 | 55.0 | 83.6% | — | 147 | | | |
| Afghanistan ........ | 43.0 | 21.0 | 184.9 | 39.9/40.7 | 15.0% | 10% | 2 | 6 | — | 27 |
| Albania ........... | 33.3 | 8.1 | 86.8 | 64.9/67.0 | 33.8% | 70% | 5 | 71 | 1.8 | 46 |
| Algeria ........... | 48.7 | 15.4 | 86.3 | 51.7/54.8 | 52.0% | 26% | 16 | 173 | 30 | 17 |
| Andorra ........... | 16.5 | 5.0 | — | | 37.0% | 100% | 345 | 228 | 103 | 250 |
| Angola ........... | 47.2 | 24.5 | 24.1 | 37.0/40.1 | 16.6% | 15% | 5 | 17 | — | 2 |
| Argentina ......... | 22.9 | 9.4 | 59.0 | 65.2/71.4 | 80.4% | 90% | 99 | 838 | 180 | 154 |
| Australia ......... | 16.1 | 7.7 | 14.3 | 67.6/74.2 | 86.0% | 98.5% | 415 | 770 | 351 | 394 |
| Austria ........... | 11.3 | 12.2 | 16.9 | 68.1/75.1 | 51.9% | 99% | 320 | 291 | 236 | 320 |
| Bahamas .......... | 24.8 | 4.6 | 24.7 | 64.0/67.3 | 57.9% | 93% | 281 | 475 | | 152 |
| Bahrain ........... | 30.0 | 18.7 | 35.5 | 47.0 | 78.1% | 40% | 142 | 412 | 120 | 21 |
| Bangladesh ........ | 49.5 | 28.1 | 132.0 | 45.8/46.6 | 8.8% | 25% | 1 | | — | 5 |
| Barbados ......... | 18.6 | 9.2 | 28.3 | 62.7/67.4 | 3.7% | 90% | 175 | 526 | 194 | 98 |
| Belgium .......... | 12.4 | 11.4 | 14.0 | 67.8/74.2 | 94.6% | 97% | 315 | 409 | 268 | 239 |
| Benin ............ | 49.9 | 23.0 | 109.6 | 39.4/42.6 | 13.8% | 20% | 3 | 47 | — | 0.3 |
| Bhutan ........... | 43.6 | 20.5 | — | 42.2/45.0 | 4.1% | 5% | 1 | 300 | | |
| Bolivia ........... | 46.6 | 18.0 | 77.3 | 45.7/47.9 | 34.3% | 40% | 21 | 74 | — | 35 |
| Bophuthatswana .... | 43.0 | 14.0 | 100.0 | 55.7/62.7 | 12.1% | — | | | | |
| Botswana ......... | 45.6 | 23.0 | — | 41.9/45.1 | 12.3% | 32% | 11 | 87 | — | 20 |
| Brazil ........... | 37.1 | 8.8 | 97.1 | 57.6/61.0 | 61.2% | 83% | 40 | 58 | 96 | 39 |
| Britain ........... | 11.8 | 11.7 | 14.0 | 67.8/73.8 | 77.7% | 99% | 394 | 706 | 317 | 388 |
| Bulgaria .......... | 16.1 | 10.7 | 23.7 | 68.6/73.9 | 60.5% | 95% | 107 | 314 | 176 | 232 |
| Burma ............ | 39.5 | 15.8 | 247.5 | 48.6/51.5 | 20.0% | 70% | 1 | 22 | — | 10 |
| Burundi .......... | 42.0 | 20.4 | 150.0 | 40.0/43.0 | 2.2% | 15% | 1 | 27 | — | 0.3 |
| Cambodia ......... | 46.7 | 19.0 | 127.0 | 44.2/43.3 | 10.3% | 41% | 1 | 14 | 4.2 | 10 |
| Cameroon ......... | 40.4 | 22.0 | 137.2 | 39.4/42.6 | 20.3% | 50% | 2 | 96 | — | 3.9 |
| Canada ........... | 15.5 | 7.3 | 14.3 | 69.3/76.3 | 75.5% | 99% | 632 | 1,011 | 428 | 235 |
| Cape Verde ....... | 27.6 | 9.4 | 104.9 | 48.3/51.7 | 19.7% | 14% | 6 | 119 | — | — |
| Central Africa ..... | 43.4 | 22.5 | 190.0 | 33.0/36.0 | 26.6% | 18% | 2 | 36 | — | 0.3 |
| Chad ............ | 44.0 | 24.0 | 160.0 | 29.0/35.0 | 18.4% | 10% | 1 | 18 | — | 0.4 |
| Chile ............ | 23.9 | 7.8 | 43.1 | 60.5/66.0 | 79.8% | 90% | 45 | 172 | 68 | 94 |
| China ............ | 17.9 | 10.3 | 55.0 | 59.9/63.3 | 25.5% | 25% | 28 | 16 | 0.6 | 8 |
| Colombia .......... | 40.6 | 8.8 | 88.9 | 59.2/62.7 | 59.5% | 75% | 56 | 117 | 70 | 69 |
| Comoros .......... | 46.6 | 21.7 | 51.7 | 40.9/44.1 | 20.3% | — | 3 | 115 | | |
| Congo ............ | 45.1 | 20.8 | 180.0 | 41.9/45.1 | 29.7% | 20% | 10 | 60 | 2.4 | 1 |
| Costa Rica ........ | 29.7 | 4.6 | 33.6 | 61.8/64.8 | 40.6% | 90% | 69 | 74 | 77 | 88 |
| Cuba ............ | 19.8 | 5.6 | 23.0 | 68.5/71.8 | 60.3% | 96% | 33 | 229 | 69 | 95 |
| Cyprus ........... | 22.2 | 6.8 | 27.2 | 70.0/72.9 | 42.2% | 89% | 111 | 313 | 89 | 124 |
| Czechoslovakia ..... | 18.7 | 11.5 | 19.6 | 66.7/73.6 | 66.7% | 100% | 190 | 263 | 254 | 300 |
| Denmark .......... | 12.2 | 9.9 | 8.9 | 71.1/76.8 | 66.9% | 99% | 529 | 365 | 323 | 341 |
| Djibouti .......... | 42.0 | 7.6 | — | | — | 5% | 12 | 139 | 32 | 307 |
| Dominica .......... | 21.8 | 6.7 | 24.1 | 57.0/59.2 | — | 80% | 54 | — | | 88 |
| Dominican Republic . | 45.8 | 11.0 | 43.5 | 57.2/58.6 | 49.1% | 68% | 28 | 41 | 33 | 42 |
| Ecuador .......... | 41.8 | 9.5 | 65.8 | 54.9/58.1 | 42.8% | 57% | 29 | 279 | 41 | 49 |
| Egypt ............ | 37.7 | 11.8 | 101.3 | 51.6/53.8 | 43.9% | 44% | 14 | 138 | 17 | 21 |
| El Salvador ........ | 41.7 | 7.8 | 59.5 | 56.6/60.4 | 38.8% | 50% | 16 | 340 | 33 | 51 |
| Equatorial Guinea ... | 36.8 | 19.7 | 53.2 | 41.9/45.1 | 35.1% | 20% | 5 | 253 | — | 4 |
| Ethiopia .......... | 49.4 | 25.8 | 84.2 | 36.5/39.6 | 12.9% | 5% | 3 | 7 | 0.7 | 2.5 |
| Fiji ............. | 25.0 | 4.3 | 9.1 | 68.5/71.7 | 37.2% | 80% | 56 | 517 | — | 35 |
| Finland ........... | 13.9 | 9.4 | 12.0 | 67.4/75.4 | 59.0% | 99% | 428 | 461 | 363 | 440 |
| France ........... | 14.0 | 10.1 | 11.4 | 69.0/76.9 | 73.0% | 97% | 329 | 330 | 274 | 214 |
| Gabon ........... | 32.2 | 22.2 | 229.0 | 25.0/45.0 | 32.0% | 12% | 12 | 175 | 16 | — |
| Gambia ........... | 43.3 | 24.1 | 165.0 | 38.5/41.6 | 15.9% | 10% | 6 | 113 | — | 21 |
| Germany, East ..... | 13.3 | 13.4 | 13.1 | 68.9/74.2 | 75.5% | 99% | 171 | 367 | 309 | 472 |
| Germany, West ..... | 9.5 | 11.5 | 15.5 | 68.3/74.8 | 38.4% | 99% | 374 | 329 | 306 | 312 |
| Ghana ........... | 48.8 | 21.9 | 156.0 | 41.9/45.1 | 31.4% | 25% | 7 | 107 | 6 | 51 |
| Greece ........... | 15.4 | 8.9 | 20.3 | 67.5/70.7 | 64.8% | 86% | 251 | 300 | 127 | 107 |
| Grenada .......... | 27.4 | 5.9 | 23.5 | 60.1/65.6 | 14.8% | — | 45 | 229 | — | 31 |
| Guatemala ........ | 42.6 | 9.8 | 76.5 | 48.3/49.7 | 35.6% | 30% | 14 | 42 | 19 | 39 |
| Guinea ........... | 46.6 | 22.9 | 216.0 | 39.4/42.0 | 11.2% | 10% | 2 | 26 | — | 1 |
| Guinea–Bissau ..... | 40.1 | 25.1 | 47.1 | 37.0/40.1 | 18.1% | 5% | 5 | 21 | — | 11 |
| Guyana ........... | 26.6 | 7.1 | 50.5 | 59.0/63.0 | 40.0% | 86% | 33 | 351 | — | 155 |
| Haiti ............ | 35.8 | 16.3 | — | 49.0/51.0 | 24.3% | 12% | 4 | 20 | 3 | 20 |
| Honduras ......... | 49.3 | 14.6 | 31.4 | 52.1/55.0 | 31.4% | 47% | 7 | 57 | 17 | 42 |
| Hungary .......... | 16.7 | 12.4 | 26.2 | 66.5/72.4 | 51.8% | 97% | 103 | 243 | 236 | 233 |
| Iceland ........... | 18.0 | 6.5 | 9.5 | 73.0/79.2 | 87.1% | 99% | 429 | 291 | 241 | 431 |
| India ............ | 35.2 | 15.9 | 122.0 | 41.9/40.6 | 21.2% | 29% | 4 | 24 | 0.5 | 16 |

[1] Per 1,000 population.    [2] Per 1,000 live births.    [3] Percent of population over age 15 who can read and write.
[4] Daily newspaper circulation per 1,000 population.

| NATION | VITAL STATISTICS | | | | | COMMUNICATIONS | | | | |
|---|---|---|---|---|---|---|---|---|---|---|
| | Birth Rate [1] | Death Rate [1] | Infant Deaths [2] | Life Expectancy Men/Women | Urban Pop. | Literacy Rate [3] | Phones [1] | Radio Sets [1] | TV Sets [1] | News-papers [4] |
| Indonesia .......... | 42.9 | 16.9 | 125.0 | 47.5 | 18.2% | 60% | 2 | 37 | 2.3 | 18 |
| Iran................ | 42.5 | 11.5 | 108.1 | 57.6/57.4 | 46.8% | 37% | 25 | 63 | 51 | 15 |
| Iraq .............. | 48.1 | 14.6 | 33.1 | 51.2/54.3 | 65.9% | 40% | 26 | 300 | 207 | 22 |
| Ireland ............ | 21.4 | 10.5 | 15.7 | 68.8/73.5 | 52.2% | 99% | 161 | 287 | 192 | 222 |
| Israel ............. | 26.1 | 6.8 | 20.1 | 71.2/74.8 | 87.2% | 88% | 255 | 189 | 137 | 208 |
| Italy .............. | 13.2 | 9.6 | 17.6 | 69.0/74.9 | 48.0% | 93% | 285 | 232 | 220 | 113 |
| Ivory Coast......... | 45.6 | 20.6 | 138.0 | 41.9/45.1 | 32.4% | 65% | 9 | 120 | 51 | 7.2 |
| Jamaica ........... | 29.8 | 7.1 | 20.4 | 62.7/66.6 | 37.1% | 65% | 56 | 270 | 54 | 90 |
| Japan ............. | 15.5 | 6.1 | 8.9 | 72.1/77.4 | 75.9% | 99% | 442 | 530 | 235 | 526 |
| Jordan ............ | 47.6 | 14.7 | 36.3 | 52.6/52.0 | 42.0% | 55% | 22 | 191 | 45 | 18 |
| Kenya ............. | 48.7 | 16.0 | 51.4 | 46.9/51.2 | 9.9% | 27% | 10 | 37 | 3.6 | 10 |
| Kiribati............ | 22.3 | 6.5 | 48.9 | 56.9/59.0 | 29.7% | 50% | — | 124 | — | — |
| Korea, North ....... | 35.7 | 9.4 | — | 58.8/62.5 | 14.7% | 90% | — | 40 | — | 20 |
| Korea, South ....... | 28.8 | 8.8 | 5.0 | 63.0/67.0 | 48.4% | 90% | 52 | 144 | 48 | 173 |
| Kuwait ............ | 43.3 | 4.4 | 34.3 | 66.1/71.8 | 22.1% | 60% | 131 | 487 | 196 | 86 |
| Laos .............. | 44.6 | 22.8 | 123.0 | 39.1/41.8 | 14.7% | 12% | 2 | 59 | — | 3 |
| Lebanon ........... | 39.8 | 9.9 | 13.6 | 61.4/65.1 | 60.1% | 86% | 77 | 540 | 144 | 92 |
| Lesotho ........... | 36.7 | 14.5 | 114.4 | 44.4/47.6 | 1.0% | 40% | 3 | 19 | — | 1.2 |
| Liberia ............ | 49.8 | 20.9 | 159.2 | 45.8/44.0 | 27.6% | 24% | 6 | 151 | 5.1 | 7.6 |
| Libya ............. | 45.0 | 14.7 | 130.0 | 51.4/54.5 | 29.8% | 35% | 20 | 45 | 4 | 17 |
| Liechtenstein ...... | 12.5 | 6.0 | 16.5 | — | 28.6% | 100% | 715 | 364 | 199 | 277 |
| Luxembourg ....... | 11.4 | 11.5 | 10.6 | 67.0/73.9 | 67.9% | 98% | 523 | 575 | 293 | 463 |
| Madagascar ........ | 46.0 | 25.0 | 102.0 | 37.5/38.3 | 14.1% | 45% | 4 | 74 | 1 | 9 |
| Malawi ............ | 50.5 | 26.5 | 150.9 | 40.9/44.2 | 10.1% | 15% | 4 | 25 | — | 1.8 |
| Malaysia .......... | 30.9 | 6.1 | 30.7 | 66.2/71.4 | 28.8% | 48% | 29 | 118 | 45 | 87 |
| Maldives .......... | 40.5 | 11.8 | 118.8 | — | 11.3% | 40% | 4 | 29 | — | — |
| Mali .............. | 50.1 | 25.9 | 120.0 | 36.5/39.6 | 16.6% | 5% | 1 | 14 | — | 0.5 |
| Malta ............. | 17.9 | 8.6 | 13.5 | 68.3/73.1 | 94.3% | 83% | 218 | 207 | 207 | 195 |
| Mauritania ........ | 44.8 | 24.9 | 187.0 | 37.0/40.1 | 22.8% | 10% | 1 | 64 | — | 0.2 |
| Mauritius ......... | 25.8 | 7.9 | 44.4 | 60.7/65.3 | 43.6% | 60% | 33 | 223 | 46 | 91 |
| Mexico ............ | 42.0 | 8.6 | 54.7 | 62.8/66.6 | 65.2% | 65% | 55 | 301 | 84 | 85 |
| Monaco ........... | 7.5 | 10.6 | 9.3 | — | 100.0% | 99% | 1,231 | 300 | 640 | — |
| Mongolia .......... | 38.8 | 9.3 | — | 59.1/62.3 | 46.4% | 80% | 25 | 77 | 2.4 | 78 |
| Morocco ........... | 46.2 | 15.7 | 149.0 | 51.4/54.5 | 37.9% | 20% | 12 | 92 | 27 | 21 |
| Mozambique........ | 43.1 | 20.1 | 19.1 | 41.9/45.1 | 7.0% | 15% | 6 | 24 | 0.1 | 9 |
| Namibia........... | 45.5 | 23.2 | — | 39.4/42.6 | — | — | 65 | — | — | — |
| Nauru............. | 19.8 | 4.5 | 19.0 | 44.0 | — | 99% | 208 | 450 | — | — |
| Nepal ............. | 42.9 | 20.3 | 169.0 | 42.2/45.0 | 4.0% | 12% | 1 | 12 | — | 3 |
| Netherlands ....... | 12.5 | 7.9 | 9.5 | 71.5/78.0 | 88.4% | 98% | 421 | 290 | 274 | 315 |
| New Zealand ....... | 17.8 | 8.2 | 13.9 | 68.6/74.6 | 83.0% | 98% | 545 | 865 | 259 | 376 |
| Nicaragua ......... | 48.3 | 13.9 | 37.0 | 51.2/54.6 | 48.6% | 52% | 24 | 60 | 40 | 26 |
| Niger ............. | 52.2 | 25.5 | 200.0 | 37.0/40.1 | 8.2% | 6% | 2 | 36 | — | 0.5 |
| Nigeria ............ | 49.3 | 22.7 | 180.0 | 37.2/36.7 | 22.8% | 25% | 2 | 79 | 1.6 | 9 |
| Norway ............ | 12.5 | 9.7 | 10.5 | 71.9/78.1 | 44.2% | 100% | 386 | 320 | 270 | 412 |
| Oman ............. | 50.0 | 19.0 | 138.0 | 46.0 | 5.3% | 10% | 9 | — | — | — |
| Pakistan .......... | 36.0 | 12.0 | 124.0 | 53.7/48.8 | 25.5% | 21% | 3 | 17 | 4.8 | 6 |
| Panama ........... | 36.2 | 7.1 | 28.5 | 64.3/67.5 | 50.8% | 82% | 88 | 157 | 108 | 79 |
| Papua New Guinea.. | 40.6 | 17.1 | 159.0 | 47.7/47.6 | 12.9% | 15% | 13 | — | — | 7 |
| Paraguay .......... | 39.8 | 8.9 | 38.6 | 60.3/63.6 | 39.6% | 74% | 15 | 66 | 20 | 38 |
| Peru .............. | 41.0 | 11.9 | 58.2 | 52.6/55.5 | 62.5% | 50% | 26 | 129 | 37 | 122 |
| Philippines ........ | 43.8 | 10.5 | 58.9 | 56.9/60.0 | 31.8% | 83% | 13 | 43 | 18 | 18 |
| Poland ............ | 19.1 | 9.0 | 24.1 | 66.9/74.6 | 57.0% | 98% | 84 | 239 | 198 | 248 |
| Portugal .......... | 19.2 | 10.5 | 38.9 | 65.3/72.0 | 26.4% | 70% | 120 | 161 | 76 | 70 |
| Qatar ............. | 50.0 | 19.0 | 138.0 | 47.0 | 72.8% | 25% | 154 | 421 | 302 | 149 |
| Romania .......... | 19.6 | 9.6 | 31.2 | 67.4/72.0 | 47.5% | 99% | 51 | 145 | 138 | 129 |
| Rwanda ........... | 51.0 | 22.0 | 127.0 | 39.4/42.6 | 3.5% | 25% | 1 | 16 | — | 0.04 |
| St. Lucia ......... | 35.0 | 7.3 | 36.5 | 55.1/58.5 | — | 80% | 62 | 745 | 16 | — |
| St. Vincent ....... | 32.7 | 10.0 | 99.6 | 58.5/59.7 | — | 80% | 53 | 300 | 7 | — |
| San Marino......... | 14.8 | 6.9 | 24.1 | — | 92.4% | 100% | 305 | 300 | 200 | 350 |
| São Tomé-Príncipe .. | 45.0 | 11.2 | 64.3 | 33.8 | 20.5% | 10% | 9 | 247 | — | — |
| Saudi Arabia ....... | 49.5 | 20.2 | 152.0 | 44.2/46.5 | 14.0% | 15% | 24 | 28 | 14 | 11 |
| Senegal ........... | 47.6 | 23.9 | 92.9 | 38.5/41.6 | 31.7% | 10% | 8 | 57 | 0.4 | 7 |
| Seychelles ........ | 25.9 | 7.7 | 43.2 | 61.9/68.0 | 26.1% | 60% | 74 | 288 | — | 60 |
| Sierra Leone........ | 44.7 | 20.7 | 136.3 | 41.9/45.1 | 13.9% | 10% | 5 | 22 | 2.7 | 10 |
| Singapore ......... | 16.6 | 5.2 | 12.4 | 65.1/70.0 | 100.0% | 70% | 196 | 156 | 129 | 190 |
| Solomons .......... | 36.1 | 13.0 | 52.4 | — | 9.1% | 60% | 10 | 53 | — | — |
| Somalia ........... | 47.2 | 21.7 | 177.0 | 39.4/42.6 | 20.2% | 10% | 2 | 21 | — | 1 |
| South Africa........ | 42.9 | 15.5 | 117.0 | 49.8/53.3 | 47.9% | 85% | 98 | 96 | — | 70 |
| Soviet Union ....... | 18.1 | 9.6 | 27.7 | 64.0/74.0 | 62.2% | 98.5% | 75 | 481 | 217 | 397 |

[1] Per 1,000 population. [2] Per 1,000 live births. [3] Percent of population over age 15 who can read and write. [4] Daily newspaper circulation per 1,000 population.

## VITAL STATISTICS, EDUCATION, COMMUNICATIONS (continued)

| NATION | VITAL STATISTICS | | | | | COMMUNICATIONS | | | | |
|---|---|---|---|---|---|---|---|---|---|---|
| | Birth Rate [1] | Death Rate [1] | Infant Deaths [2] | Life Expectancy Men/Women | Urban Pop. | Literacy Rate [3] | Phones [1] | Radio Sets [1] | TV Sets [1] | News-papers [4] |
| Spain | 18.0 | 7.7 | 15.6 | 69.7/75.0 | 43.0% | 97% | 263 | 259 | 185 | 98 |
| Sri Lanka | 29.9 | 7.7 | 45.1 | 64.8/66.9 | 22.4% | 82% | 5 | 58 | — | 42 |
| Sudan | 47.8 | 17.5 | 93.6 | 47.3/49.9 | 20.4% | 10% | 3 | 77 | 6 | 8 |
| Suriname | 36.9 | 7.2 | 30.4 | 62.5/66.7 | 37.8% | 80% | 55 | 257 | 87 | 57 |
| Swaziland | 49.0 | 21.8 | 149.0 | 41.9/45.1 | 7.9% | 25% | 18 | 121 | — | 17 |
| Sweden | 11.6 | 10.7 | 8.0 | 72.1/77.9 | 82.7% | 99% | 717 | 390 | 363 | 572 |
| Switzerland | 11.5 | 8.7 | 10.7 | 70.3/76.2 | 54.6% | 98% | 659 | 332 | 285 | 402 |
| Syria | 45.4 | 4.8 | 15.3 | 54.5/58.7 | 48.8% | 40% | 25 | 224 | 30 | 9 |
| Taiwan | 26.0 | 5.0 | 25.0 | 70.0 | 77.0% | 90% | 100 | 103 | 79 | 99 |
| Tanzania | 47.0 | 22.0 | 162.5 | 40.0/41.0 | 7.3% | 61% | 5 | 19 | — | 5 |
| Thailand | 43.4 | 10.8 | 25.5 | 53.6/58.7 | 13.2% | 70% | 8 | 131 | 18 | 21 |
| Togo | 50.6 | 23.3 | 127.0 | 31.6/38.5 | 15.2% | 10% | 2 | 23 | — | 32 |
| Tonga | 13.0 | 1.9 | 20.5 | — | 21.8% | 95% | 14 | 108 | — | — |
| Transkei | — | — | — | 55.7/62.7 | 7.1% | — | 5 | — | — | — |
| Trinidad-Tobago | 25.3 | 6.9 | 27.2 | 64.1/68.1 | 49.4% | 95% | 70 | 253 | 103 | 92 |
| Tunisia | 40.0 | 13.8 | 125.0 | 52.5/55.7 | 40.1% | 50% | 25 | 141 | 10 | 36 |
| Turkey | 39.6 | 14.6 | 153.0 | 53.7 | 44.6% | 62% | 33 | 105 | 44 | 41 |
| Tuvalu | 22.3 | 6.5 | 48.9 | 56.9/59.0 | 29.7% | 49% | 0.5 | 0.5 | — | — |
| Uganda | 45.2 | 15.9 | 160.0 | 48.3/51.7 | 7.1% | 40% | 4 | 22 | 6 | 5 |
| United Arab Emirates | 50.0 | 19.0 | 138.0 | 47.0 | 57.0% | 25% | 120 | 240 | — | 25 |
| UNITED STATES | 15.3 | 8.8 | 14.0 | 69.9/77.8 | 73.5% | 99% | 744 | 1,882 | 571 | 287 |
| Upper Volta | 48.5 | 25.8 | 182.0 | 32.1/31.1 | 3.7% | 10% | 1 | 17 | 1 | 0.3 |
| Uruguay | 20.9 | 10.2 | 45.9 | 65.5/71.6 | 83.0% | 91% | 96 | 516 | 114 | 267 |
| Vanuatu | 45.0 | 20.0 | — | — | 23.1% | 20% | 24 | 155 | — | — |
| Vatican City | 0.0 | 11.4 | 0.0 | — | 100.0% | 100% | — | — | — | 250 |
| Venda | — | — | — | — | — | — | — | — | — | — |
| Venezuela | 36.1 | 7.0 | 40.4 | 62.9/66.7 | 75.1% | 74% | 64 | 407 | 116 | 93 |
| Vietnam | 41.5 | 20.5 | 42.8 | 43.2/46.0 | 24.2% | 65% | 1 | 121 | 26 | 29 |
| Western Samoa | 36.9 | 6.7 | 40.0 | 60.8/65.2 | 21.3% | 90% | 25 | 329 | 0.3 | 1 |
| Yemen | 49.6 | 20.6 | 22.7 | 43.7/45.9 | 5.8% | 10% | 1 | 13 | — | 10 |
| Yemen, South | 49.6 | 20.6 | 22.7 | 43.7/45.9 | 33.3% | 15% | 6 | 57 | 18 | 1 |
| Yugoslavia | 17.7 | 8.4 | 35.2 | 65.4/70.2 | 38.6% | 80.3% | 71 | 210 | 161 | 89 |
| Zaire | 45.2 | 20.5 | 104.0 | 41.9/45.1 | 30.3% | 35% | 1 | 101 | 0.3 | 9 |
| Zambia | 51.5 | 20.3 | 259.0 | 42.9/46.1 | 39.3% | 28% | 13 | 21 | 4.9 | 22 |
| Zimbabwe | 47.9 | 14.4 | 122.0 | 49.8/53.3 | 19.6% | 30% | 29 | 39 | 11 | 18 |

[1] Per 1,000 population.  [2] Per 1,000 live births.  [3] Percent of population over age 15 who can read and write.  [4] Daily newspaper circulation per 1,000 population.

## NATIONS OF THE WORLD: MONEY, ECONOMY, TRANSPORTATION

| NATION | MONETARY UNIT | Value [1] | ECONOMY INDICATORS | | Cost of Living | Electric Power [2] | TRANSPORTATION | |
|---|---|---|---|---|---|---|---|---|
| | | | Gross Domestic Product Annual | Per Capita [1] | | | Highways [3] | Rail-roads [4] |
| Afghanistan | afghani | 2⅕¢ | $3,760,000,000 | $ 168 | 142[5] | 50 | 2,960 | 0.6 |
| Albania | lek | 20¢ | 1,200,000,000 | 520 | — | 850 | 1,287 | 277 |
| Algeria | dinar | 24¢ | 24,600,000,000 | 1,374 | 183[5] | 250 | 45,070 | 3,950 |
| Andorra | Fr. franc | 24¢ | — | — | — | 3,448 | 96 | — |
| | Sp. peseta | 1⅓¢ | | | | | | |
| Angola | kwanza | 2¢ | 2,660,000,000 | 440 | — | 210 | 8,577 | 3,189 |
| Argentina | peso | 1/20¢ | 102,500,000,000 | 3,853 | 121,051[5] | 1,090 | 43,900 | 39,738 |
| Australia | dollar | $1.17 | 119,144,000,000 | 8,264 | 244[5] | 6,180 | 207,650 | 40,851 |
| Austria | schilling | 8¢ | 68,579,000,000 | 9,138 | 172[5] | 5,160 | 20,800 | 6,517 |
| Bahamas | dollar | $1.00 | 825,000,000 | 3,650 | 163[8] | 3,150 | 1,350 | — |
| Bahrain | dinar | $2.65 | 1,400,000,000 | 5,130 | — | 13,010 | 93 | — |
| Bangladesh | taka | 6¢ | 9,309,000,000 | 106 | 354[5] | 20 | 4,076 | 2,909 |
| Barbados | dollar | 50¢ | 440,000,000 | 1,840 | 330[5] | 920 | 1,350 | — |
| Belgium | franc | 3½¢ | 107,097,000,000 | 10,861 | 191[5] | 5,190 | 1,051 | 4,219 |
| Benin | CFA franc | ½¢ | 716,300,000 | 220 | 142[5] | 20 | 705 | 579 |
| Bhutan | ngultrum | 11½¢ | 90,000,000 | 70 | — | 6 | 418 | — |
| Bolivia | peso | 4¢ | 4,500,000,000 | 890 | 381[5] | 230 | 1,150 | 3,572 |
| Bophuthatswana | S. Af. rand | $1.33 | 15,168,000 | 110 | — | — | — | — |
| Botswana | pula | $1.20 | 597,000,000 | 779 | 172[6] | 120 | 579 | 726 |
| Brazil | cruzeiro | 2¢ | 187,000,000,000 | 1,620 | 742[5] | 765 | 75,900 | 30,300 |
| Britain | pound | $2.38 | 345,660,000,000 | 6,210 | 305[5] | 5,070 | 343,315 | 18,287 |
| Bulgaria | lev | $1.10 | 48,700,000,000 | 5,285 | — | 3,550 | 6,610 | 4,415 |
| Burma | kyat | 15¢ | 5,000,000,000 | 150 | 257[5] | 30 | 3,200 | 3,285 |

[1] In $U.S.  [2] Kilowatt hours per capita.  [3] Paved kilometers.  [4] Total kilometers.  [5] 100 = 1970 prices.  [6] 100 = 1974 prices.  [7] 100 = 1975 prices.  [8] $100 = 1972 prices.

| NATION | MONETARY UNIT | Value [1] | ECONOMIC INDICATORS Gross Domestic Product Annual [1] | Per Capita [1] | Cost of Living | Electric Power [2] | TRANSPORTATION Highways [3] | Railroads [4] |
|---|---|---|---|---|---|---|---|---|
| Burundi | franc | 1¢ | $ 705,700,000 | $ 140 | 166 [5] | 6 | 300 | — |
| Cambodia | — | — | 500,000,000 | 50 | 1,820 [5] | 30 | 2,622 | 612 |
| Cameroon | CFA franc | ½¢ | 5,800,000,000 | 628 | 234 [5] | 160 | 2,127 | 1,173 |
| Canada | dollar | 85¢ | 249,310,340,000 | 10,390 | 196 [5] | 14,810 | 189,800 | 68,978 |
| Cape Verde | escudo | 2¢ | 66,000,000 | 176 | 437 [5] | 20 | — | — |
| Central Africa | CFA franc | ½¢ | 434,700,000 | 193 | 210 [5] | 60 | 290 | — |
| Chad | CFA franc | ½¢ | 924,600,000 | 220 | 144 [8] | 15 | 242 | — |
| Chile | peso | 2½¢ | 17,087,600,000 | 1,566 | 310,499 [5] | 980 | 9,000 | 6,361 |
| China | yuan | 68¢ | 444,000,000,000 | 440 | — | 260 | 260,000 | 46,000 |
| Colombia | peso | 2¢ | 22,795,000,000 | 881 | 117 [12] | 740 | 8,200 | 3,436 |
| Comoros | CFA franc | ½¢ | 69,500,000 | 200 | — | 10 | 295 | — |
| Congo | CFA franc | ½¢ | 894,700,000 | 500 | 197 [5] | 90 | 555 | 800 |
| Costa Rica | colón | 11⅔¢ | 4,250,000,000 | 1,950 | 236 [5] | 800 | 2,000 | 563 |
| Cuba | peso | $1.32 | 11,800,000,000 | 1,220 | — | 770 | 8,800 | 14,640 |
| Cyprus | pound | $2.68 | 1,990,000,000 | 3,100 | 117 [6] | 1,400 | 4,580 | — |
| Czechoslovakia | koruna | 18¢ | 70,700,000,000 | 4,673 | 108 [5] | 4,560 | 60,157 | 13,186 |
| Denmark | krone | 18¢ | 59,200,000,000 | 11,541 | 277 [5] | 4,070 | 64,551 | 2,591 |
| Djibouti | franc | ½¢ | 336,000,000 | 1,070 | — | 310 | 220 | 97 |
| Dominica | E.C. dollar | 37¢ | 32,000,000 | 410 | 254 [5] | 90 | 500 | — |
| Dominican Rep. | peso | $1.00 | 4,695,000,000 | 868 | 221 [7] | 460 | 5,800 | 1,600 |
| Ecuador | sucre | 3¾¢ | 8,570,000,000 | 1,033 | 289 [5] | 280 | 3,300 | 1,121 |
| Egypt | pound | $1.43 | 16,350,000,000 | 368 | 184 [5] | 365 | 12,300 | 4,857 |
| El Salvador | colón | 40¢ | 3,100,000,000 | 690 | 108 [5] | 280 | 1,500 | 600 |
| Eq. Guinea | ekuele | 1½¢ | 76,000,000 | 264 | — | 50 | 331 | — |
| Ethiopia | birr | 48¢ | 2,899,200,000 | 104 | 203 [5] | 20 | 3,323 | 1,014 |
| Fiji | dollar | $1.21 | 792,250,000 | 1,220 | 227 [5] | 420 | 346 | 644 |
| Finland | markka | 27¢ | 49,950,000,000 | 10,500 | 262 [5] | 7,475 | 31,000 | 6,038 |
| France | franc | 24¢ | 523,600,000,000 | 9,870 | 220 [5] | 4,240 | 840,000 | 36,571 |
| Gabon | CFA franc | ½¢ | 3,000,000,000 | 5,250 | 239 [7] | 670 | 459 | 970 |
| Gambia | dalasi | 48¢ | 168,700,000 | 292 | 250 [5] | 50 | 317 | — |
| Germany, East | mark | 53¢ | 81,000,000,000 | 4,834 | — | 5,730 | 47,530 | 14,215 |
| Germany, West | mark | 55¢ | 775,517,010,000 | 12,630 | 149 [5] | 5,740 | 161,400 | 33,453 |
| Ghana | cedi | 36¢ | 14,327,000,000 | 380 | 276 [5] | 350 | 6,084 | 953 |
| Greece | drachma | 2½¢ | 43,570,000,000 | 4,560 | 355 [5] | 2,450 | 16,090 | 2,476 |
| Grenada | E.C. dollar | 37¢ | 56,000,000 | 520 | — | 230 | 600 | — |
| Guatemala | quetzal | $1.00 | 7,110,000,000 | 1,043 | 149 [8] | 230 | 2,750 | 947 |
| Guinea | syli | 5¢ | 1,209,000,000 | 240 | — | 110 | 4,949 | 805 |
| Guinea-Bissau | peso | 3¢ | 174,000,000 | 280 | — | 30 | 418 | — |
| Guyana | dollar | 39¢ | 472,000,000 | 580 | 196 [5] | 450 | 550 | 109 |
| Haiti | gourde | 20¢ | 1,785,000,000 | 297 | 235 [5] | 42 | 600 | 80 |
| Honduras | lempira | 50¢ | 2,067,000,000 | 500 | 178 [5] | 130 | 1,450 | 574 |
| Hungary | forint | 5¢ | 32,000,000,000 | 2,990 | 142 [5] | 2,380 | 32,583 | 8,523 |
| Iceland | króna | ⅕¢ | 2,133,400,000 | 9,060 | 759 [5] | 10,730 | 166 | — |
| India | rupee | 13¢ | 130,700,000,000 | 200 | 190 [5] | 160 | 415,250 | 62,181 |
| Indonesia | rupiah | ⅙¢ | 45,896,000,000 | 300 | 351 [5] | 80 | 26,583 | 7,843 |
| Iran | rial | 1½¢ | 76,100,000,000 | 2,160 | 247 [5] | 570 | 12,060 | 4,601 |
| Iraq | dinar | $3.38 | 30,000,000,000 | 2,338 | 151 [10] | 570 | 6,490 | 1,700 |
| Ireland | pound | $2.07 | 15,235,200,000 | 4,554 | 304 [5] | 3,060 | 87,422 | 2,190 |
| Israel | shekel | 17¢ | 16,394,022,000 | 4,332 | 1,041 [5] | 3,230 | 4,459 | 767 |
| Italy | lira | 1/10¢ | 323,548,000,000 | 5,685 | 304 [5] | 3,080 | 254,400 | 20,690 |
| Ivory Coast | CFA franc | ½¢ | 10,638,000,000 | 1,293 | 272 [5] | 170 | 2,461 | 657 |
| Jamaica | dollar | 56¢ | 2,426,797,300 | 1,143 | 321 [5] | 1,310 | 7,600 | 330 |
| Japan | yen | ½¢ | 976,411,000,000 | 8,502 | 219 [5] | 5,000 | 338,343 | 28,912 |
| Jordan | dinar | $3.42 | 2,844,000,000 | 1,060 | 156 [8] | 340 | 4,837 | 817 |
| Kenya | shilling | 13⅔¢ | 5,381,000,000 | 341 | 196 [9] | 90 | 4,300 | 2,040 |
| Kiribati | Austr. dollar | $1.17 | — | 740 | — | 870 | 483 | — |
| Korea, North | won | 56¢ | 10,400,000,000 | 570 | — | 1,450 | 304 | 4,750 |
| Korea, South | won | ⅙¢ | 67,821,000,000 | 1,776 | 350 [5] | 720 | — | — |
| Kuwait | dinar | $3.63 | 14,067,000,000 | 11,722 | 175 [9] | 6,645 | 2,255 | — |
| Laos | kip | ¼¢ | 290,000,000 | 90 | 457 [5] | 95 | 1,300 | — |
| Lebanon | pound | 29¢ | 3,624,100,000 | 1,169 | 130 [5] | 470 | 6,270 | 378 |
| Lesotho | S. Af. rand | $1.33 | 203,500,000 | 160 | 193 [10] | — | 218 | 1.6 |
| Liberia | U.S. dollar | $1.00 | 744,000,000 | 433 | 203 [5] | 620 | 603 | 499 |
| Libya | dinar | $3.37 | 19,300,000,000 | 7,280 | 178 [5] | 870 | 7,750 | — |
| Liechtenstein | Swiss franc | 60¢ | 292,000,000 | 16,864 | 147 [5] | 2,590 | 131 | 19 |
| Luxembourg | Belg. franc | 3½¢ | 4,300,000,000 | 11,900 | 178 [5] | 3,910 | 4,912 | 270 |
| Madagascar | franc | ½¢ | 2,400,000,000 | 290 | 205 [5] | 60 | 4,525 | 884 |
| Malawi | kwacha | $1.25 | 1,062,100,000 | 180 | 205 [5] | 60 | 1,870 | 678 |
| Malaysia | ringgit | 47¢ | 19,548,400,000 | 1,467 | 166 [5] | 550 | 16,744 | 1,821 |

[1] In U.S. dollars. [2] Kilowatt hours per capita. [3] Paved km. [4] Total km. [5] 100=1970 prices. [6] 100=1977 prices. [7] 100=1971 prices. [8] 100=1975 prices. [9] 100=1972 prices. [10] 100=1973 prices. [11] 100=1974 prices. [12] 100=1978 prices.

**MONEY, ECONOMY, TRANSPORTATION** (continued)

| NATION | MONETARY UNIT | Value [1] | ECONOMIC INDICATORS Gross Domestic Product Annual [1] | Per Capita [1] | Cost of Living | Electric Power [2] | TRANSPORTATION Highways [3] | Rail-roads [4] |
|---|---|---|---|---|---|---|---|---|
| Maldives ......... | rupee ...... | 13¢ | $ 17,400,000 | $ 135 | — | 40 | — | — |
| Mali ............ | franc ...... | 2¢ | 970,000,000 | 149 | 326 [5] | 20 | 1,669 | 642 |
| Malta .......... | pound ...... | $2.60 | 763,600,000 | 2,463 | 165 [5] | 1,380 | 1,159 | — |
| Mauritania ..... | ouguiya ..... | 2¢ | 518,700,000 | 376 | 135 [8] | 70 | 558 | 650 |
| Mauritius........ | rupee ...... | 13¢ | 695,800,000 | 789 | 273 [5] | 340 | 1,636 | — |
| Mexico.......... | peso ....... | 4 1/3¢ | 120,097,000,000 | 1,757 | 280 [11] | 830 | 63,000 | 19,680 |
| Monaco ........ | French franc | 24¢ | — | — | — | — | — | — |
| Mongolia........ | tugrik ...... | 32¢ | 750,000,000 | 380 | — | 770 | — | 1,516 |
| Morocco ....... | dirham ..... | 22¢ | 16,026,000,000 | 843 | 156 [6] | 210 | 24,700 | 2,625 |
| Mozambique.... | metical ..... | 3¢ | 2,000,000,000 | 112 | 196 [5] | 470 | 4,322 | 3,436 |
| Namibia........ | S. Af. rand ... | $1.33 | — | — | — | 1,110 | 3,800 | 2,340 |
| Nauru.......... | Austr. dollar. | $1.17 | 194,000,000 | 27,000 | — | 3,710 | 21 | — |
| Nepal.......... | rupee ...... | 8¢ | 1,760,000,000 | 111 | 171 [7] | 10 | 1,751 | 63 |
| Netherlands ..... | guilder ..... | 51¢ | 156,712,135,900 | 11,193 | 190 [5] | 4,430 | 86,354 | 9,153 |
| New Zealand .... | pound ...... | 98¢ | 20,215,000,000 | 6,468 | 277 [5] | 8,180 | 46,716 | 4,716 |
| Nicaragua ....... | córdoba .... | 10¢ | 1,319,000,000 | 571 | 127 [6] | 520 | 1,570 | 344 |
| Niger .......... | CFA franc ... | 1/2¢ | 649,300,000 | 297 | 241 [5] | 14 | 1,892 | — |
| Nigeria......... | naira ...... | $1.75 | 46,968,000,000 | 561 | 166 [8] | 60 | 25,180 | 4,257 |
| Norway ........ | krone ...... | 20¢ | 51,020,000,000 | 12,480 | 201 [5] | 19,915 | 17,699 | 4,257 |
| Oman .......... | rial ........ | $2.90 | 2,633,200,000 | 2,992 | — | 1,090 | 5 | — |
| Pakistan ........ | rupee ...... | 10¢ | 22,037,000,000 | 275 | 273 [7] | 200 | 26,855 | 8,816 |
| Panama ........ | balboa ..... | $1.00 | 2,306,000,000 | 1,264 | 122 [8] | 770 | 2,500 | 249 |
| Papua New Guin. | kina ....... | $1.45 | 1,760,000,000 | 480 | 196 [7] | 315 | 640 | — |
| Paraguay........ | guarani ..... | 4/5¢ | 3,087,800,000 | 1,038 | 279 [5] | 200 | 1,100 | 1,043 |
| Peru ........... | sol ........ | 1/3¢ | 13,525,000,000 | 771 | 883 [5] | 510 | 54,000 | 2,148 |
| Phillippines ..... | peso ....... | 13 1/2¢ | 29,234,000,000 | 619 | 250 [11] | 360 | 18,546 | 3,510 |
| Poland ......... | zloty ...... | 3 1/2¢ | 108,300,000,000 | 3,094 | 123 [5] | 3,280 | 65,000 | 26,864 |
| Portugal ........ | escudo ..... | 2¢ | 18,721,000,000 | 2,100 | 127 [12] | 1,410 | 39,938 | 3,593 |
| Qatar .......... | rival ....... | 27¢ | 4,500,000,000 | 20,000 | — | 12,120 | 805 | — |
| Romania ........ | leu ........ | 8¢ | 67,500,000,000 | 3,100 | — | 2,940 | 28,471 | 11,127 |
| Rwanda ........ | franc ...... | 1¢ | 890,000,000 | 185 | 199 [5] | 30 | 320 | — |
| St. Lucia ....... | EC dollar ... | 37¢ | 65,000,000 | 590 | 303 [5] | 360 | 450 | — |
| St. Vincent ..... | EC dollar ... | 37¢ | 33,500,000 | 305 | — | 190 | 300 | — |
| San Marino ..... | It. lira ...... | 1/10¢ | — | — | — | — | 104 | — |
| São Tomé–Prínc. | dobra ...... | 3¢ | 20,000,000 | 250 | — | 70 | — | — |
| Saudi Arabia.... | riyal ........ | 30¢ | 112,000,000,000 | 13,750 | 229 [5] | 1,500 | 16,500 | 575 |
| Senegal ........ | CFA franc ... | 1/2¢ | 2,357,000,000 | 428 | 219 [5] | 120 | 2,960 | 1,033 |
| Seychelles ...... | rupee ...... | 16¢ | 89,400,000 | 1,470 | 359 [5] | 410 | 145 | — |
| Sierra Leone .... | leone ...... | 99¢ | 901,200,000 | 220 | 256 [5] | 90 | 1,148 | 84 |
| Singapore ...... | dollar ...... | 48¢ | 8,964,000,000 | 3,798 | 104 [13] | 2,520 | 1,806 | 38 |
| Solomons ...... | dollar ...... | $1.17 | 70,092,000 | 308 | 114 [10] | 105 | 241 | — |
| Somalia ........ | shilling ..... | 16¢ | 407,000,000 | 110 | 206 [5] | 10 | 1,900 | — |
| South Africa .... | rand ....... | $1.33 | 54,901,000,000 | 1,955 | 243 [5] | 3,240 | 57,435 | 25,560 |
| Soviet Union .... | ruble ....... | $1.47 | 1,253,600,000,000 | 4,800 | — | 4,600 | 322,000 | 140,504 |
| Spain .......... | peseta ...... | 1 1/3¢ | 187,048,000,000 | 4,995 | 100 [5] | 2,650 | 60,747 | 16,087 |
| Sri Lanka........ | rupee ...... | 6¢ | 2,580,000,000 | 179 | 182 [5] | 100 | 24,300 | 1,636 |
| Sudan .......... | pound ...... | $2.00 | 6,066,000,000 | 361 | 294 [5] | 40 | 600 | 5,470 |
| Suriname........ | guilder ..... | 56¢ | 675,000,000 | 1,590 | 223 [5] | 2,350 | 500 | 166 |
| Swaziland ....... | lilangeni .... | $1.33 | 224,000,000 | 470 | 217 [5] | 250 | 390 | 292 |
| Sweden ........ | krona ...... | 24¢ | 101,850,000,000 | 12,203 | 212 [5] | 10,902 | 73,000 | 12,074 |
| Switzerland ..... | franc ...... | 60¢ | 100,302,350,000 | 15,895 | 156 [5] | 6,990 | 62,145 | 5,098 |
| Syria........... | pound ...... | 25¢ | 7,355,800,000 | 864 | 239 [10] | 320 | 12,051 | 1,543 |
| Taiwan ......... | NT dollar ... | 2 3/4¢ | 38,800,000,000 | 2,200 | — | 1,780 | 7,564 | 4,500 |
| Tanzania ........ | shilling ..... | 12 1/2¢ | 3,892,000,000 | 222 | 249 [5] | 80 | 3,588 | 3,555 |
| Thailand ........ | baht ....... | 5¢ | 27,266,000,000 | 591 | 207 [5] | 272 | 16,244 | 3,927 |
| Togo........... | CFA franc | 1/2¢ | 765,500,000 | 319 | 224 [5] | 50 | 1,231 | 442 |
| Tonga ......... | dollar ...... | $1.40 | 39,000,000 | 400 | 228 [5] | 90 | 177 | — |
| Transkei ........ | S. Af. rand ... | $1.33 | 180,000,000 | 90 | — | 140 | 725 | 160 |
| Trinidad–Tobago | dollar ...... | 42¢ | 4,335,000,000 | 3,750 | 289 [5] | 1,913 | 3,600 | — |
| Tunisia ......... | dinar ...... | $2.50 | 7,095,000,000 | 1,133 | 113 [10] | 270 | 7,940 | 2,089 |
| Turkey......... | lira ........ | 1 1/4¢ | 49,932,000,000 | 1,218 | 483 [5] | 510 | 21,000 | 8,468 |
| Tuvalu ......... | Austr. dollar. | $1.17 | — | — | — | 430 | 8 | — |
| Uganda ........ | shilling ..... | 13 1/2¢ | 3,200,000,000 | 267 | 486 [5] | 80 | 1,934 | 1,216 |
| United Arab Emir. | dirham ..... | 27¢ | 15,985,000,000 | 15,800 | 135 [5] | 5,500 | 780 | — |
| UNITED STATES | dollar ...... | $1.00 | 2,523,400,000,000 | 11,282 | 187 [5] | 9,750 | 6,059,200 | 277,686 |
| Upper Volta .... | CFA franc... | 1/2¢ | 847,700,000 | 136 | 127 [5] | 9 | 859 | 1,173 |
| Uruguay ........ | peso ....... | 11 1/2¢ | 7,292,000,000 | 2,553 | 4,769 [5] | 968 | 6,700 | 2,795 |

[1] In U.S. dollars. [2] Kilowatt hours per capita. [3] Paved kilometers. [4] Total kilometers. [5] 100 = 1970 prices. [6] 100 = 1974 prices. [7] 100 = 1971 prices. [8] 100 = 1975 prices. [9] 100 = 1973 prices. [10] 100 = 1977 prices. [11] 100 = 1972 prices. [12] 100 = 1979 prices. [13] 100 = 1978 prices.

## MONEY, ECONOMY, TRANSPORTATION *(continued)*

| NATION | MONETARY UNIT Value [1] | ECONOMIC INDICATORS Gross Domestic Product Annual [1] | Per Capita [1] | Cost of Living | Electric Power [2] | TRANSPORTATION Highways [3] | Rail-roads [4] |
|---|---|---|---|---|---|---|---|
| Vanuatu......... | franc....... 1½¢ | $        — | $   — | | 130 | 240 | — |
| Vatican City ..... | It. lira ...... 1/10¢ | — | — | — | — | — | — |
| Venda .......... | S.Af. rand ... $1.33 | — | — | — | — | — | — |
| Venezuela ....... | bolívar ..... 23¢ | 39,252,000,000 | 2,992 | 184 [5] | 1,990 | 21,800 | 746 |
| Vietnam......... | dong ....... 50¢ | 7,600,000,000 | 150 | — | 75 | 5,471 | — |
| Western Samoa .. | tala ........ $1.10 | 70,000,000 | 451 | 185 [9] | 170 | 375 | — |
| Yemen, North .... | rial........ 22¢ | 2,762,000,000 | 502 | 187 [5] | 20 | 467 | — |
| Yemen, South.... | dinar ....... $2.90 | 550,000,000 | 310 | 171 [5] | 108 | 322 | — |
| Yugoslavia ...... | dinar ....... 3½¢ | 62,910,000,000 | 2,850 | 432 [5] | 2,320 | 44,733 | 9,967 |
| Zaire .......... | zaïre ....... 33¢ | 7,500,000,000 | 271 | 1,132 [5] | 163 | 2,654 | 5,256 |
| Zambia ......... | kwacha ..... $1.29 | 2,707,800,000 | 480 | 231 [5] | 1,390 | 5,403 | 2,014 |
| Zimbabwe ....... | dollar ...... $1.45 | 3,300,000,000 | 480 | 198 [5] | 1,110 | 7,995 | 3,476 |

[1] In U.S. dollars.   [2] Kilowatt hours per capita.   [3] Paved kilometers.   [4] Total kilometers.   [5] 100=1970 prices.   [6] 100=1974 prices.   [7] 100=1971 prices.   [8] 100=1975 prices.   [9] 100=1973 prices.

## SELECTED DEPENDENCIES, TERRITORIES, COLONIES, AND POSSESSIONS

| NAME | CONTROLLED BY | LOCATION | AREA (sq. mi.) | POPULATION [1] Total | Per sq. mi. | CAPITAL |
|---|---|---|---|---|---|---|
| Andamans–Nicobars .. | India | Bay of Bengal | 3,203 | 117,551 | 36.7 | Port Blair |
| Anguilla ............. | British | Caribbean | 35 | 6,832 | 195.2 | The Valley |
| Antigua ............. | Britain | Caribbean | 171 | 77,004 | 450.3 | St. John's |
| Azores .............. | Portugal | Atlantic Ocean | 902 | 254,160 | 281.8 | Ponta Delgada |
| Balearic Islands...... | Spain | Mediterranean | 1,936 | 624,703 | 322.7 | Palma |
| Belize.............. | Britain | Central America | 8,867 | 164,777 | 18.6 | Belmopan |
| Bermuda ............ | Britain | North Atlantic | 20 | 59,909 | 2,995.5 | Hamilton |
| Brunei .............. | Britain | Borneo, SE Asia | 2,226 | 213,003 | 95.7 | Bandar Seri Begawan |
| Canary Islands....... | Spain | Atlantic Ocean | 2,808 | 1,274,280 | 453.8 | Las Palmas; Santa Cruz |
| Cayman Islands...... | Britain | Caribbean | 100 | 10,419 | 104.2 | George Town |
| Channel Islands ...... | Britain | English Channel | 75 | 135,311 | 1,804.1 | St. Peter Port, St. Helier |
| Christmas Island ..... | Australia | South Pacific | 52 | 3,335 | 64.1 | Flying Fish Cove |
| Cook Islands ........ | New Zealand | South Pacific | 90 | 15,693 | 174.4 | Avarua |
| Corsica ............. | France | Mediterranean | 3,352 | 301,486 | 89.9 | Ajaccio; Bastia |
| Faeroe Islands ....... | Denmark | North Atlantic | 540 | 43,502 | 80.6 | Tórshavn |
| Falkland Islands ..... | Britain | South Atlantic | 4,700 | 2,086 | 0.44 | Stanley |
| Galápagos Islands ... | Ecuador | Pacific | 3,028 | 3,800 | 1.3 | Baquerizo Moreno |
| Gibraltar ............ | Britain | Europe | 2.3 | 28,783 | 12,514.3 | Gibraltar |
| Guadeloupe ......... | France | Caribbean | 687 | 332,307 | 483.7 | Basse-Terre |
| Guam ............... | U.S. | Pacific | 212 | 116,644 | 550.2 | Agana |
| Guiana, French ...... | France | South America | 35,135 | 71,428 | 2.0 | Cayenne |
| Hong Kong .......... | Britain | SE Asia | 403 | 4,793,000 | 11,893.3 | Victoria |
| Indian Ocean Terr. .. | Britain | Indian Ocean | 30 | 2,000 | 66.7 | Diego Garcia |
| Lakshadweep ........ | India | Arabian Sea | 12.4 | 35,020 | 2,824.2 | Kavaratti |
| Macao .............. | Portugal | SE Asia | 6.2 | 291,481 | 47,013.1 | Macao |
| Madeira............. | Portugal | Atlantic Ocean | 307 | 270,976 | 882.7 | Funchal |
| Mahore ............. | France | Indian Ocean | 144 | 49,537 | 344.0 | Dzaoudzi |
| Man, Isle of ......... | Britain | Irish Sea | 227 | 68,089 | 300.0 | Douglas |
| Martinique .......... | France | Caribbean | 425 | 328,889 | 773.9 | Fort-de-France |
| Micronesia .......... | U.S. | Pacific Ocean | 533 | 129,282 | 242.6 | Kolonia, Ponape |
| Montserrat .......... | Britain | Caribbean | 38 | 10,272 | 270.3 | Plymouth |
| Netherlands Antilles .. | Netherlands | Caribbean | 371 | 250,338 | 674.8 | Willemstad, Curaçao |
| New Caledonia....... | France | South Pacific | 7,359 | 153,952 | 20.9 | Nouméa |
| Niue ................ | New Zealand | South Pacific | 100 | 3,049 | 30.5 | Tufukla |
| Polynesia, French .... | France | South Pacific | 1,544 | 158,007 | 102.3 | Papeete, Tahiti |
| Puerto Rico ......... | U.S. | Caribbean | 3,435 | 3,615,598 | 1,052.6 | San Juan |
| Réunion............. | France | Indian Ocean | 969 | 512,322 | 528.7 | Saint-Denis |
| Saint Helena ........ | Britain | South Atlantic | 47 | 5,200 | 110.6 | Jamestown |
| Saint Kitts–Nevis..... | Britain | Caribbean | 104 | 49,947 | 480.3 | Basseterre, St. Kitts |
| Saint Pierre–Miquelon . | France | North Atlantic | 93 | 5,904 | 63.5 | St. Pierre |
| Samoa, American .... | U.S. | South Pacific | 76 | 35,490 | 467 | Pago Pago |
| Sardinia.........•.... | Italy | Mediterranean | 9,194 | 1,522,770 | 165.6 | Cagliari |
| Sicily .............. | Italy | Mediterranean | 9,817 | 4,795,750 | 488.5 | Palermo |
| Turks and Caicos .... | Britain | Caribbean | 166 | 6,228 | 37.5 | Cockburn Town |
| Virgin Islands, British | Britain | Caribbean | 59 | 14,024 | 237.7 | Road Town |
| Virgin Islands, U.S... | U.S. | Caribbean | 133 | 71,236 | 535.6 | Charlotte Amalie |
| Wallis and Futuna.... | France | South Pacific | 77 | 9,400 | 22.1 | Matu Utu |

[1] Jan. 1, 1981, population estimates.

NORTH AMERICA

CUBA

JAMAICA

HAITI

DOM.
REP.

*WEST INDIES*

PUERTO
RICO

GRENADA
ST. GEORGE'S

BARBADOS

TRINIDAD-
TOBAGO

NETHERLANDS
ANTILLES

*CARIBBEAN*

*SEA*

PANAMA
CANAL

Barranquilla

Maracaibo

CARACAS

PORT OF
SPAIN

Orinoco R.

Medellín

GUYANA

SURINAM

GEORGETOWN

PARAMARIBO

FRENCH GUIANA

CAYENNE

VENEZUELA

Cali

BOGOTÁ

COLOMBIA

Quito

ECUADOR

*AMAZON*

Amazon R.

Belém

Guayaquil

Fortaleza

PERU

Manaus

*BASIN*

Natal

Trujillo

Recife

*ANDES*

Callao

LIMA

Cuzco

BRAZIL

LAKE
TITICACA

LA PAZ

Arequipa

BOLIVIA

Cochabamba

MATO GROSSO

Salvador

BRASÍLIA

Oruro

SUCRE

Belo Horizonte

Antofagasta

PARAGUAY

*MOUNTAINS*

*CHACO*

São Paulo

Rio de Janeiro

CHILE

Tucumán

ASUNCIÓN

Santos

*DESERT OF ATACAMA*

*Paraná*

Porto Alegre

Santa Fe

Córdoba

URUGUAY

Valparaíso

SANTIAGO

Rosario

JUAN
FERNÁNDEZ

BUENOS
AIRES

MONTEVIDEO

*PAMPAS*

Concepción

ARGENTINA

Mar del Plata

*ANDES*

*PATAGONIA*

Puerto
Montt

STRAIT
OF
MAGELLAN

FALKLAND
ISLANDS
(Brit.)

Punta Arenas

TIERRA DEL FUEGO

CAPE HORN

*PACIFIC*

*OCEAN*

*ATLANTIC*

*OCEAN*

*ATLANTIC OCEAN*

SOUTH AMERICA

0    200    400    600    800    1000

MILES

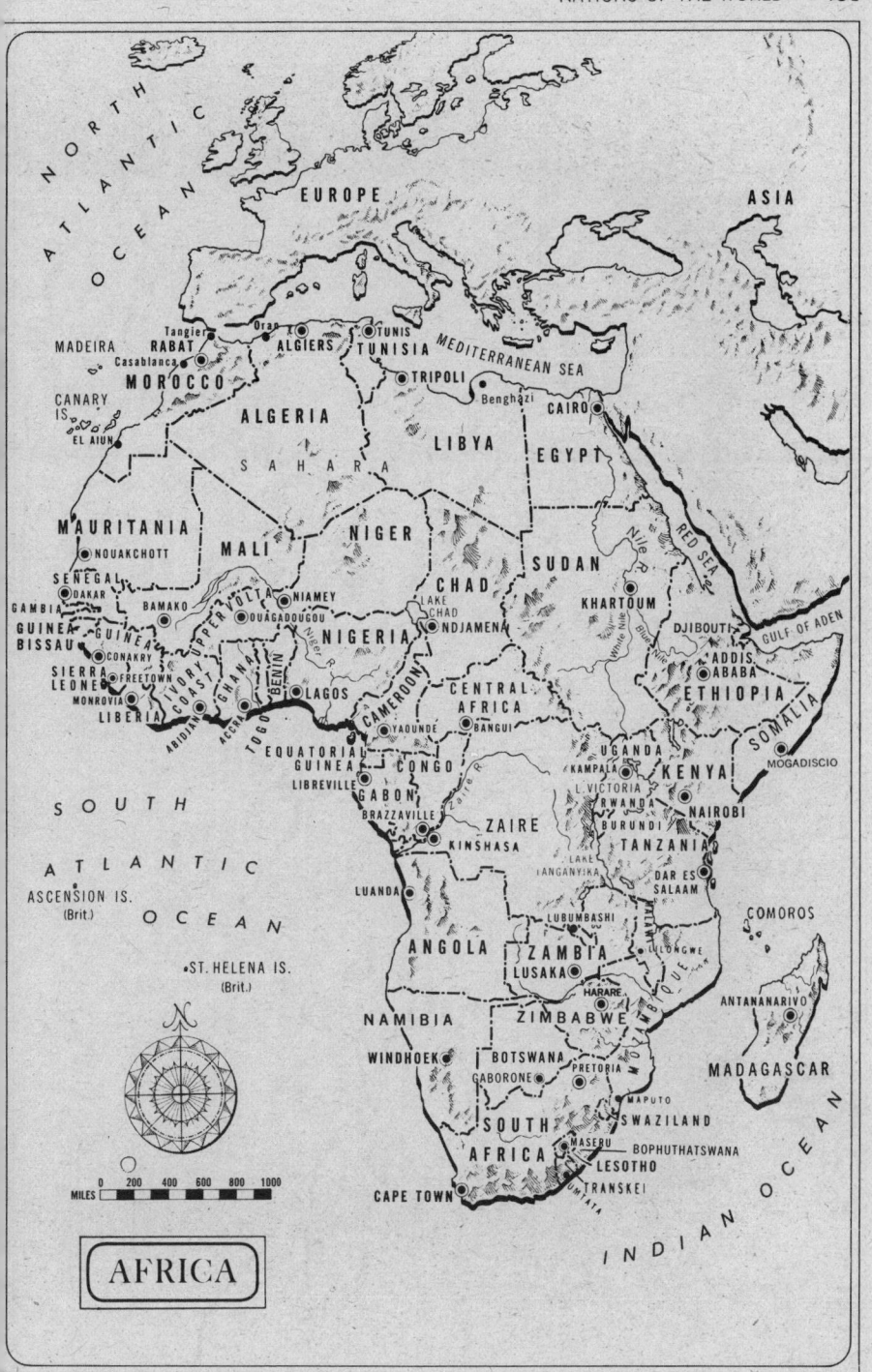

NORTH ATLANTIC OCEAN

EUROPE

ASIA

MADEIRA
CANARY IS.
EL AIUN

Tangier
RABAT
Casablanca
MOROCCO

Oran
ALGIERS

TUNIS
TUNISIA
TRIPOLI

MEDITERRANEAN SEA

Benghazi
CAIRO

ALGERIA

SAHARA

LIBYA

EGYPT

RED SEA

MAURITANIA
NOUAKCHOTT
SENEGAL
DAKAR
GAMBIA
GUINEA
BISSAU
CONAKRY
SIERRA
LEONE
FREETOWN
MONROVIA
LIBERIA
ABIDJAN

MALI
BAMAKO
UPPER VOLTA
OUAGADOUGOU
GUINEA
IVORY
COAST
GHANA
ACCRA
TOGO
BENIN
LAGOS

NIGER
NIAMEY

Niger R.

NIGERIA

LAKE CHAD

CHAD
NDJAMENA

SUDAN
KHARTOUM

Nile R.
White Nile
Blue Nile

DJIBOUTI
ADDIS
ABABA

GULF OF ADEN

ETHIOPIA

SOMALIA
MOGADISCIO

CAMEROON
YAOUNDE

CENTRAL
AFRICA
BANGUI

EQUATORIAL
GUINEA
LIBREVILLE
GABON
BRAZZAVILLE

CONGO

Zaire R.

ZAIRE
KINSHASA

UGANDA
KAMPALA
L. VICTORIA
RWANDA
BURUNDI

KENYA
NAIROBI

TANZANIA
DAR ES
SALAAM

Lake TANGANYIKA

SOUTH
ATLANTIC
OCEAN

ASCENSION IS.
(Brit.)

•ST. HELENA IS.
(Brit.)

N

MILES
0  200  400  600  800  1000

LUANDA

ANGOLA

LUBUMBASHI

ZAMBIA
LUSAKA

MOZAMBIQUE

COMOROS

LILONGWE

ANTANANARIVO

NAMIBIA
WINDHOEK

ZIMBABWE
HARARE

BOTSWANA
GABORONE
PRETORIA

MADAGASCAR

SOUTH
AFRICA

CAPE TOWN

MAPUTO
SWAZILAND
MASERU
LESOTHO
BOPHUTHATSWANA
TRANSKEI
UMTATA

INDIAN OCEAN

AFRICA

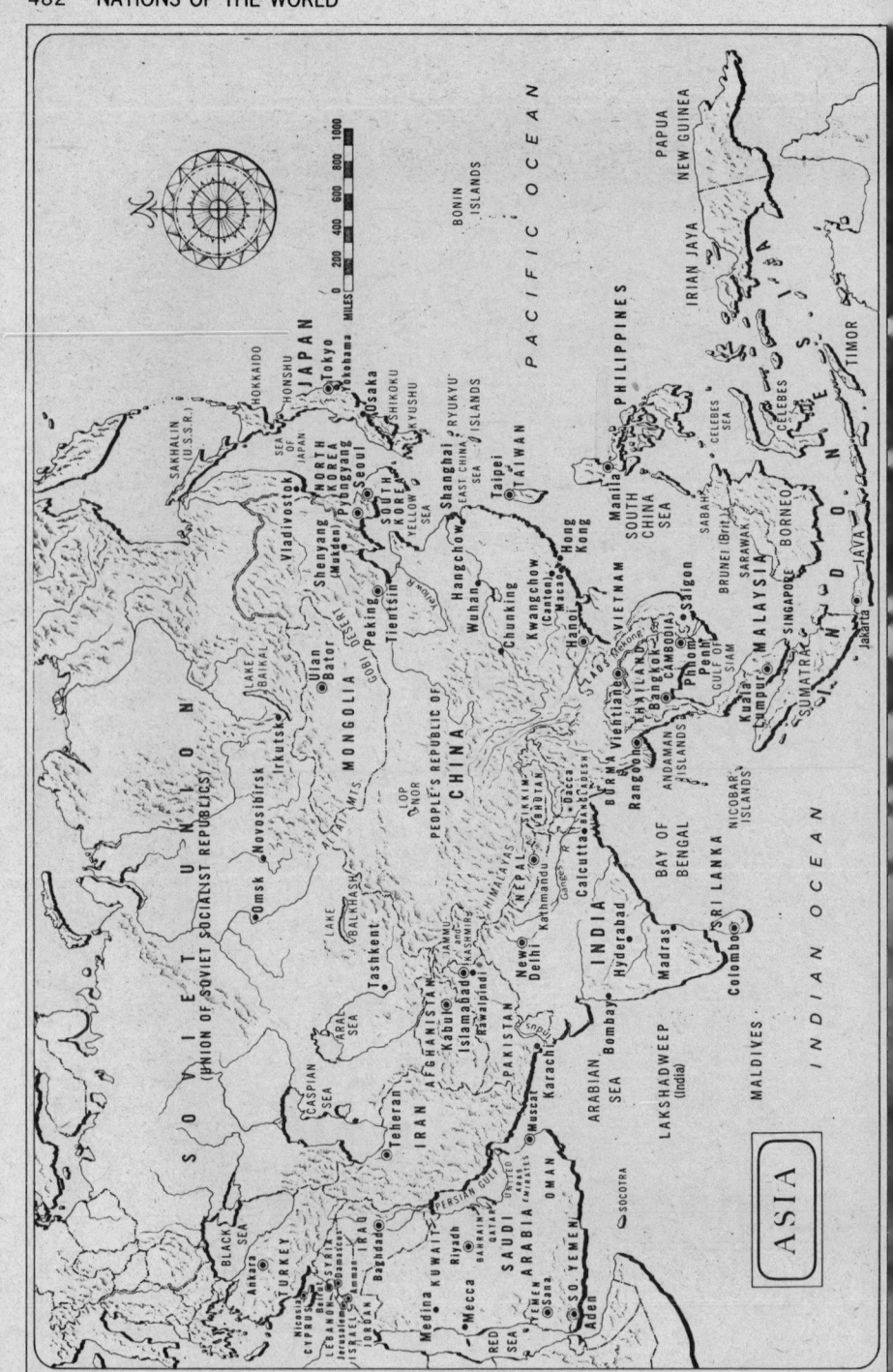

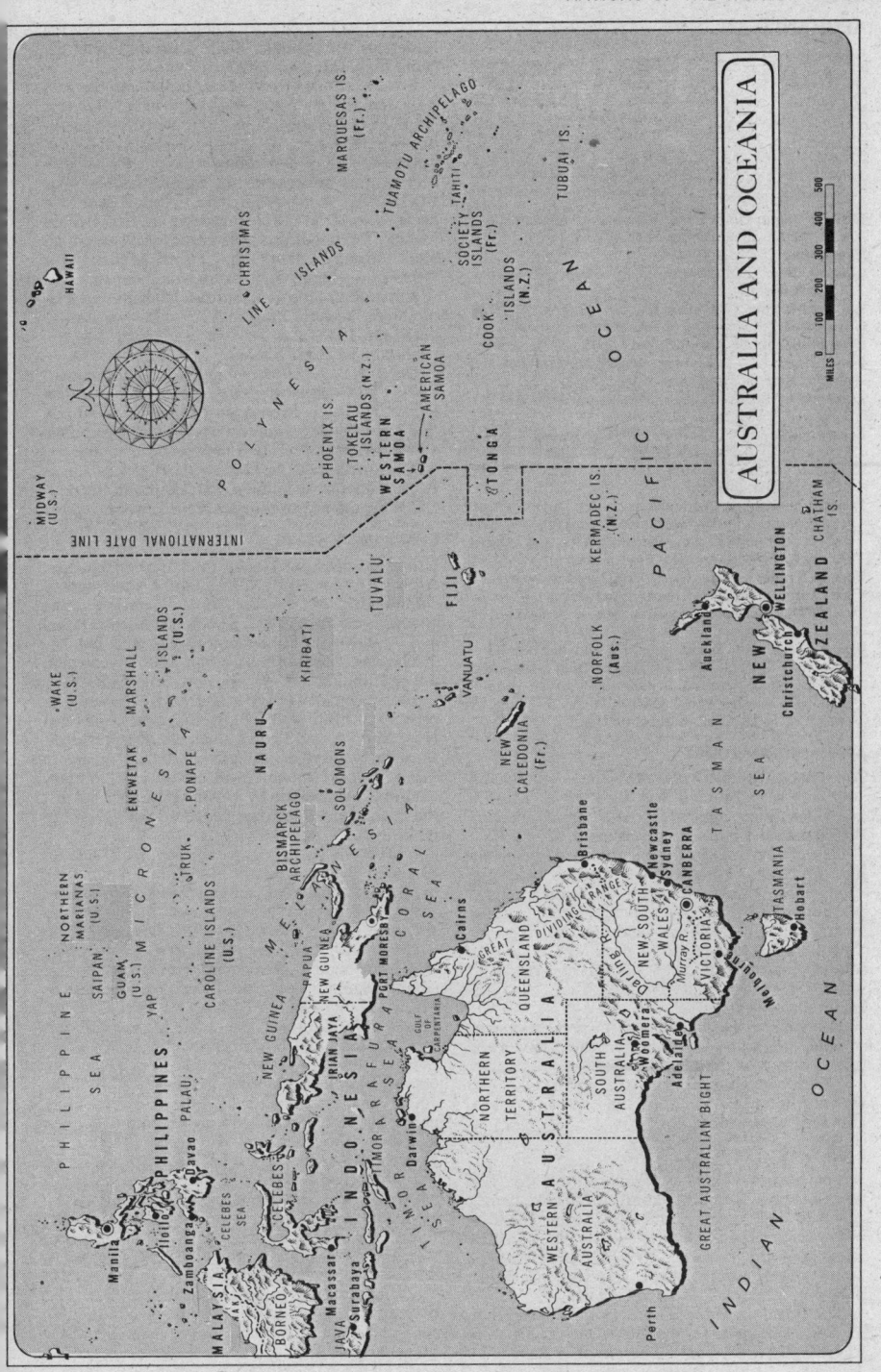

AUSTRALIA AND OCEANIA

# AFGHANISTAN

**Official Name:** Democratic Republic of Afghanistan.
**Area:** 250,000 square miles (647,497 sq. km.).
**Population:** 16,235,400.
**Chief Cities:** Kabul, capital, 318,094; Kandahar, 209,000; Herat, 157,000.
**Largest Metropolitan Area:** Kabul, 749,000.
**Government:** Soviet-controlled communist state.
**President:** Babrak Karmal (since 1979).
**Flag:** Black, red, and green stripes; emblem has star above rising sun and open book.
**Languages:** Pushtu (50%), Persian or Dari (35%), Turkic (11%).
**Ethnic Groups:** Pushtuns (50%), Tajiks (25%), Uzbeks (9%), Hazaras (9%).
**Religion:** Sunni Muslim (87%), Shia Muslim (12%), other (1%).
**Leading Industries:** Agriculture (sheep, goats, fruits, wheat, cotton, nuts, vegetables); mining (natural gas, copper, iron); manufacturing (fur and leather products, carpets, textiles, food processing).
**Foreign Trade:** *major exports*—fruits and nuts, natural gas, karakul skins, raw cotton, carpets, wool; *major imports*—petroleum products, sugar, tea, machinery, textiles.
**Places of Interest:** Kabul museum and bazaar; Khyber Pass; ancient ruins of Balkh; Blue Mosque at Mazar-i-Sharif; Paghman summer resort; largest Buddha statue in world (180 ft. high) in Valley of the Gods at Bamian; temples of Herat.

## AFGHANISTAN TODAY

A landlocked country of southwest Asia, Afghanistan was torn by civil war in 1980 as Muslim guerrillas fought against Soviet troops supporting the communist national government.

One of the world's poor nations, Afghanistan has difficulty raising enough food to meet the needs of its population. The mountainous terrain prevents most land from being farmed. Most farmers have just enough land to raise crops for their families. Only about 1 person in 27 goes to school, and no more than 1 in 10 can read and write. Most live and dress as they have for hundreds of years.

The country has substantial mineral resources of coal, gas, and petroleum, but these have been mined only to a limited degree.

The Soviet Union lies to the north, China to the northeast, Pakistan to the east and south, and Iran to the west.

## EARLY HISTORY

In ancient times the region was called *Bactria.* It was the home of the two-humped Bactrian camel, still used as a beast of burden in Afghanistan.

Persian rulers of Bactria were overthrown by Alexander the Great in the 300s B.C. Then the country was overrun by a series of overlords, including Greeks, Turks, and Arabs.

The invading Mongol hordes of Genghis Khan in the 1200s and Tamerlane in the 1300s were followed by the Mogul emperors of India.

Afghanistan achieved independence under the leadership of Ahmad Shah Durrani, who became shah (king) in 1747.

British efforts to control India and central Asia led to the First Afghan War (1832–42). Afghan resistance caused the British to withdraw temporarily.

British fear of expanding Russian influence in central Asia brought on the Second Afghan War (1878–79), won by Britain. Abdur Rahman became king in 1881, agreeing to let Britain manage foreign affairs. His grandson, Amanullah Shah, brought about the Third Afghan War (1919), in which Afghanistan won independence.

Amanullah's cousin, Sardar Mohammad Nadir Shah, became king in 1929. He was assassinated in 1933 and was succeeded by his son Mohammad Zahir Shah.

On July 17, 1973, while King Mohammad Zahir was visiting Italy, his brother-in-law Prime Minister Mohammad Daoud overthrew the government. Daoud proclaimed a republic with himself as president and prime minister.

The opening of the Trans-Asia Highway across Afghanistan from Istanbul to Calcutta in the mid-1970s brought auto tourists from Europe.

## COMMUNIST STATE

Using Soviet-built tanks and fighter planes, Afghan troops led by Col. Abdul Qader, deputy commander of the air force, overthrew the government on April 27, 1978. President Daoud and 30 members of his family were executed.

The rebels established a communist government under domination of the pro-Soviet People's Democratic Party (PDP). The rebels released from prison the head of the PDP, 61-year-old novelist Noor Mohammad Taraki, and made him president. Moscow poured in millions of dollars of aid to Taraki's government and sent in "military advisers." A rebellion by Muslim tribesmen against the communist central government grew in intensity.

In a bloody palace coup on Sept. 14, 1979, U.S.-educated Prime Minister Hafizullah Amin took over the government, making himself president. Former President Taraki and many of his supporters were killed during the takeover.

Dissatisfied with Amin's leadership, the Soviet Union invaded Afghanistan with about 85,000 troops beginning on Christmas 1979. Amin was executed on Dec. 27 and was replaced as president by Babrak Karmal, an Afghan communist in exile under Soviet protection.

U.S. President Carter led Western powers in denouncing the Soviet action. On Jan. 4, 1980, he embargoed U.S. grain sales to the Soviet Union, called for a boycott of Moscow's Olympic Games, and took other steps aimed at forcing the Soviets to withdraw their troops. See page 9.

Fighting spread throughout the country as Muslims opposed the Soviet occupation. An estimated 1 million Afghans fled to neighboring Pakistan and Iran during 1980. Most of Afghanistan's 143,000-man army joined the guerrillas. Although Soviet troops managed to control the main cities and highways, Muslim guerrillas dominated the countryside. Thousands died in the fighting and in executions of opponents of the Soviet regime.

# ALBANIA

**Official Name:** People's Socialist Republic of Albania.
**Area:** 11,100 square miles (28,748 sq. km.).
**Population:** 2,774,630.
**Capital:** Tirana (Tiranë), 169,300.
**Government:** One-party communist state.
**Heads of Government:** First Secretary of Albanian Workers Party (AWP), Enver Hoxha (took office in 1946); Premier Mehmet Shehu (took office in 1954); President of the Presidium, Haxhi Lleshi (took office in 1953).
**Legislature:** *National Assembly,* 250 members.
**Flag:** Red field with centered black two-headed eagle topped by gold-edged red star.
**Language:** Albanian (Gheg and Tosk dialects).
**Main Ethnic Group:** Albanians (96%).
**Religions:** Abolished in 1967, but Albanians are believed to be about 70% Muslims and 30% Christians.
**Leading Industries:** Agriculture (corn, wheat, goats, sheep, cattle, cotton, sugar beets, tobacco, vegetables); mining (chrome, copper, nickel, petroleum, bitumen); manufacturing (food processing, textiles, chemicals, metalwork).
**Foreign Trade:** *major exports*—metal ores, petroleum, bitumen, tobacco; *major imports*—machinery, iron and steel, coke, sugar, wheat, processed food.
**Places of Interest:** 15th century Mesi Bridge near Shkodër; various mosques; old quarter and Venetian clock tower in Tirana.

## ALBANIA TODAY

About the size of Maryland, Albania is the poorest nation of Europe. Fearful of foreign domination, Albania's communist dictatorship has largely isolated the country. The U. S. has had no diplomatic relations with Albania since 1939.

Two-thirds of the Albanian people live on state-owned farms or in small villages, making their living by raising crops or livestock. Few Albanians had any education before World War II, but the government reports that today 3 out of 4 Albanians can read and write. The government closed 2,169 churches and mosques in 1967, proclaiming Albania "the first atheist state in the world." Since then the government has carried on an active campaign against all religions.

The Adriatic Sea lies to the west, Yugoslavia to the northeast, and Greece to the southeast.

## EARLY HISTORY

Once part of the kingdom of Illyria and then of the Roman and Byzantine empires, Albania was later invaded by Slavic tribes and was absorbed in the 800s by Bulgaria.

The country became a target of Ottoman Turkish expansion in the late 1300s. The Turks controlled Albania from 1478 (when they completed its conquest) until 1912 (when the Albanians won independence).

Italian, Greek, French, and Serbo-Monteneg-

rin forces occupied the land during World War I. The Albanians eventually expelled all foreign troops and also successfully resisted Yugoslav and Greek encroachments.

Ahmed Zogu emerged from Albania's internal political struggle to seize power in 1925. At first he proclaimed a republic with himself as president, but in 1928 he established a monarchy and became King Zog I. He ruled as a dictator until the spring of 1939, when Italy invaded and annexed the country.

## A COMMUNIST NATION

Following Italy's World War II surrender in 1943, German troops replaced the Italians. The Nazis withdrew at the end of 1944, leaving Albania to the communist-led National Liberation Front headed by Enver Hoxha. He set up a communist state in 1946.

With over 750,000 Albanians living in neighboring Yugoslavia, fear of that country has been a constant factor in Albania.

When Stalin expelled Yugoslavia from the Cominform in 1948, Albania sided with Moscow. After Stalin's death in 1953, Hoxha continued to follow a hard "Stalinist" line.

## SPLIT WITH MOSCOW

When communist China split with the Soviet Union over ideology in 1960, Albania sided with China. The Soviets broke diplomatic relations with Albania in 1961 and then cut off all military and economic aid. The vacuum was filled by China, which provided hundreds of industrial and military experts and financed industrial projects.

Albania played a conspicuous role in the expulsion of nationalist China (Taiwan) from the United Nations in 1971.

Albania isolated itself from its neighbors from 1946 to 1971, when diplomatic relations were finally resumed with Greece and Yugoslavia.

An attempted coup in 1973, said by Hoxha to have been led by Defense Minister Beqir Balluka, brought a purge of hundreds of officials.

In October 1974 Hoxha again denounced the Soviet Union, declaring: "We will never reconcile with them, will never make friends with them, we will always be their enemies."

A new constitution in 1976 made it illegal to accept loans or aid from capitalist nations.

Albania improved its relations with Greece in 1977, signing a $23 million trade agreement in March, and an air-travel pact in July.

Albania lost its last powerful friend when China on July 13, 1978, cut off aid to the Balkan nation after having supplied about $5 billion over the past 24 years. Chinese technicians withdrew from Albania, and Albanian students left China. The break came after Albania sided with Vietnam in that country's dispute with China.

In August 1978 Albania launched a propaganda barrage, declaring China had tried to force Albania to join Yugoslavia and Romania in a military alliance. The government said 15 senior army officers were executed in 1975 for plotting with China to end Albania's sovereignty.

Albania signed a trade agreement with Yugoslavia in October 1979.

QUICK QUIZ: What general won the Nobel Peace Prize in 1953? See page 73.

# ALGERIA

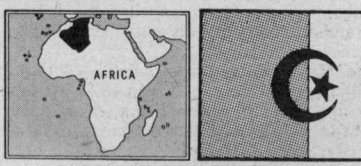

**Official Name:** Democratic and Popular Republic of Algeria.
**Area:** 919,595 square miles (2,381,741 sq. km.).
**Population:** 20,086,500.
**Chief Cities:** Alger (Algiers), capital, 903,530; Ouahran (Oran), 327,493; Constantine, 243,558; Annaba (Bône), 152,006.
**Largest Metropolitan Area:** Algiers, 2,000,000.
**Government:** Socialist military junta.
**President:** Chadli Benjedid (since 1979).
**Prime Minister:** Mohammed Benahmed Abdelghani (since 1979).
**Legislature:** *National Assembly,* 261 members.
**U.S. Ambassador to Algeria:** Ulric St. Clair Haynes Jr.
**Algerian Ambassador to U.S.:** Redha Malek.
**Languages:** Arabic (80%), Berber (18%), French (1%), other (1%).
**Flag:** Green and white bar, with centered red crescent enclosing red star.
**Principal Ethnic Group:** Arabic-Berber (98%).
**State Religion:** Islam (99%).
**Leading Industries:** Mining (petroleum, gas, iron ore, phosphates, lead, zinc, mercury); agriculture (wheat, barley, oats, wine grapes, citrus fruits, olives, vegetables, figs, dates, tobacco, livestock); manufacturing (oil refining, chemicals, iron and steel, fertilizers, textiles, transportation equipment); tourism.
**Foreign Trade:** *major exports*—crude petroleum, wine, citrus fruits; *major imports*—grain, food, manufactured goods, machinery.
**Places of Interest:** Sahara Desert; Atlas Mountains. *In Algiers:* Court of the Great Mosque; the Casbah; government buildings. *In Constantine:* Perregaux Bridge; Muslim College.

## ALGERIA TODAY

Although Algeria ranks as the world's 10th-largest country in area, 34 other nations have larger populations. This disparity between population and area exists because the sandy wastelands of the Sahara Desert cover seven-eighths of Algeria.

Most Algerians live on the narrow strip of fertile land along the Mediterranean coast between Morocco to the west and Tunisia to the east. The majority farm crops or raise livestock. Only about 1 in 4 can read and write. Over half of the people are under the age of 20 with a life expectancy of 53 years.

Few Algerians live in the Sahara, but large petroleum and natural-gas deposits found there have made Algeria one of the world's important producers of oil and natural gas. The country has 6% to 7% of the world's reserves of oil and gas. Revenues from oil and gas pay for much of Algeria's industrial development.

## EARLY HISTORY

The Phoenician colony of Carthage in nearby Tunisia controlled the Algerian coast from about 800 to 146 B.C.

After crushing Carthage, Rome governed the coastal areas and parts of the interior.

Islam was introduced by Arab invaders in the 600s A.D. Berber Muslim rulers united Algeria with Morocco and Spain.

A Turkish pirate, Barbarossa, helped Algeria expel Spanish invaders in the 1500s. He then declared himself sultan. Thus Algeria came under the rule of the Ottoman Empire.

In the 1700s and 1800s Algeria fought wars with the U.S. as a Barbary Coast pirate state.

## FRENCH RULE

France invaded Algeria in 1830. Northern Algeria was made an integral part of France in 1848.

Fierce Berber resistance delayed French control of the Sahara region for many years.

On Nov. 1, 1954, the National Liberation Front (FLN) began a war for independence that lasted over seven years. Thousands died as a 500,000-man French army tried to put down the revolt. The war ended with a cease-fire on March 18, 1962.

## INDEPENDENCE

France granted independence to Algeria on July 3, 1962.

A power struggle among FLN leaders was resolved when Ahmed Ben Bella gained control in August 1962. A new constitution was approved in 1963, and Ben Bella was elected Algeria's first president.

On June 19, 1965, a military coup led by Col. Houari Boumediene overthrew Ben Bella, and he was imprisoned until 1979. All political parties except the FLN were outlawed. Boumediene implemented a socialist program.

Algeria joined with other Arab nations in halting oil shipments to the United States and other nations in the energy crisis of 1973–74.

Diplomatic relations with the United States, broken in 1967 as a result of the third Arab-Israeli war, were resumed on Nov. 12, 1974.

Algeria broke relations with Morocco and Mauretania in 1976 when those countries took possession of Spain's former colony, the Spanish Sahara. Algerian troops aided guerrillas seeking independence for the region in 1976–80.

Algerians voted on Nov. 19, 1976, ratifying a new constitution. All persons 18 or over could vote, with women allowed to cast ballots for the first time.

The nation's economy soared in the 1970s with per capita national income nearly tripling from 1973 to 1979. The United States replaced France as Algeria's main trading partner with the purchase of over $3 billion a year in petroleum and natural gas.

Algerians took a major step toward democracy on Feb. 24, 1977, when for the first time in 14 years they elected a 261-member parliament. Although all 783 candidates were members of the FLN, voters were urged to choose the most competent.

The 46-year-old Boumediene died on Dec. 27, 1978. The FLN chose as his successor 49-year-old Col. Chadli Benjedid, who was formally elected president on Feb. 7, 1979, in a national election in which he was the only candidate.

A severe earthquake destroyed the town of Al Asnam on Oct. 10, 1980, killing about 2,950 persons and leaving 300,000 homeless.

# ANDORRA

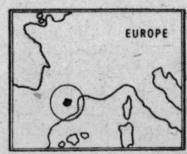 

**Official Name:** Principality of Andorra.
**Area:** 175 square miles (453 sq. km.).
**Population:** 30,620.
**Capital:** Andorra la Vella, 19,764.
**Government:** Parliamentary principality.
**Chiefs of State:** President of France and bishop of Urgel (Spain).
**Flag:** Blue, yellow, and red bars, with coat of arms in yellow bar.
**Legislature:** *General Council of the Valleys,* 24 members.
**Languages:** Catalan (official), Spanish, French.
**Principal Ethnic Group:** Catalan.
**Official Religion:** Roman Catholicism (99%).
**Leading Industries:** Tourism; agriculture (sheep, cattle, oats, barley, tobacco); manufacturing (electricity, cigarettes, handicrafts, matches, postage stamps, anisette, footwear); mining (iron ore, lead).
**Places of Interest:** Pyrenees Mountains; Engolasters Lake; Valira River; Les Escaldes thermal springs; Our Lady of Meritxell shrine and government building at Andorra la Vella.

## ANDORRA TODAY

Located high in the Pyrenees Mountains between Spain and France, Andorra is a 700-year-old nation with a land area smaller than the city of Chicago. Isolated from the wars and political turmoil of Europe, the people of Andorra lead peaceful lives. Winters in Andorra are cold with much snow, while summer weather is usually mild.

Over 7 million tourists visit Andorra each year to buy products cheaply and to enjoy winter skiing. Andorra has over 250 hotels and restaurants. Smuggling of goods between Spain and France is a thriving industry because Andorra is a free port. Thus, manufactured goods cost less there than in Spain or France.

The land is rugged and mountainous. Little of it can be farmed for crops. Most of the farmers, therefore, raise sheep or cattle.

## HISTORY

Tradition says that Charlemagne granted the Andorrans a charter for their support after driving the Muslim Moors from Andorra in the 800s. The bishop of Urgel and the count of Foix were established as co-princes of Andorra in 1278. The rights of the latter passed to the kings, and later the presidents, of France.

Women first won the right to vote in 1970.

An influx of foreign residents in the 1960s and 1970s gave foreigners about a 2 to 1 majority over native-born Andorrans.

With prosperity brought by the booming tourist industry in the 1970s and 1980s, Andorrans debate whether they should change their constitution, which limits the vote to heads of families who are third-generation residents. This gives the right to vote to only about 10% of the population.

# ANGOLA

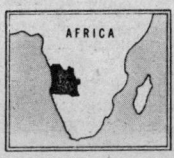 

**Official Name:** People's Republic of Angola.
**Area:** 481,354 square miles (1,246,700 sq. km.).
**Population:** 7,162,130.
**Capital:** Luanda, 475,328.
**Government:** Communist state.
**President:** José Eduardo dos Santos (since 1979).
**Flag:** Red stripe over black stripe; yellow symbol represents socialism, industry, and agriculture.
**Languages:** Portuguese, Bantu.
**Ethnic Groups:** Ovimbundu (33%), Bakongo (25%), Kimbundu (25%), Chokwe (8%), Portuguese and Cunhama (9%).
**Religions:** Animism, Roman Catholicism, Protestant.
**Leading Industries:** Mining (diamonds, iron ore, petroleum); agriculture (coffee, cotton, sisal, corn, livestock); manufacturing (chemicals, tobacco products, food processing).
**Foreign Trade:** *major exports*—coffee, petroleum, diamonds, iron ore; *major imports*—raw materials, consumer goods.
**Places of Interest:** Government buildings in Luanda; Matala Dam on the Cunene River.

## ANGOLA TODAY

Almost twice as large as Texas, Angola was the last major European colony in Africa to gain independence, after nearly five centuries of Portuguese domination. Aided by the Soviet Union and Cuba, communists won control of the country in a civil war in 1975–76. However, some 30,000 Cuban troops based in Angola continue to battle anticommunist guerrillas in border areas.

A small part of Angola, called Cabinda, lies north of the Congo (Zaire) River, separated from Angola proper by a strip of land that is Zaire's only outlet to the Atlantic Ocean. Cabinda has major oil reserves.

Like most other developing countries, Angola has many severe problems. Although the country has rich mineral resources of diamonds, iron ore, and petroleum, most of the people are uneducated Bantu tribesmen. Few Angolans can read and write, much less perform the skilled work needed for modern industry. Many Angolans work on huge coffee plantations that provide the country's second major export after minerals.

Northern Angola is forested and has hot tropical temperatures from November to April. Southern Angola is a dry semidesert.

## HISTORY

Portuguese explorer Diogo Cão landed at the mouth of the Congo River in 1483, establishing Portugal's control of Angola. The Dutch occupied Angola's ports briefly from 1641 to 1648. From the 1500s to the 1800s Portugal shipped an estimated 3 million slaves from Angola to Brazil.

Guerrilla warfare began in Angola in 1961 as the black majority sought independence. For

QUICK QUIZ: If it is 12 noon EST in New York, what time is it in Angola? See page 108.

**ANGOLA** *(continued)*

more than 13 years 50,000 Portuguese soldiers fought the guerrillas. After Portugal's government was ousted by a military revolt in 1974, Angola was promised independence.

Civil war raged throughout 1975 as rival political groups battled for control of Angola. With independence on Nov. 11, 1975, Portuguese troops withdrew from Angola. The U.S. Congress in January 1976 forbade sending military aid to the anticommunists.

By mid-February 1976, the Marxist Popular Movement for the Liberation of Angola (MPLA) led by Agostinho Neto won control, aided by Soviet weapons and Cuban troops. South Africa, which had intervened on the side of the anticommunists, withdrew its troops on March 27, 1976.

South African paratroops raided Angola on May 5, 1978, killing between 400 and 500 Namibian guerrillas at Cassinga. South Africa continued similar raids on Angola in 1979-80.

President Neto died of cancer in Moscow on Sept. 10, 1979. The ruling Marxist party chose as his successor as president Soviet-educated José Eduardo dos Santos, 37, who had served as first deputy prime minister.

The government executed by firing squad in August 1980 more than 20 persons accused as anticommunist guerrillas. In retaliation the guerrillas bombed government petroleum facilities at the port of Lobito.

# ARGENTINA

**Official Name:** Republic of Argentina.
**Area:** 1,068,301 square miles (2,766,889 sq. km.).
**Population:** 27,261,500.
**Chief Cities:** Buenos Aires, capital, 2,982,000; Córdoba, 781,565; Rosario, 750,455; La Plata, 391,247; Tucumán, 321,567.
**Largest Metropolitan Area:** Buenos Aires, 9,749,000.
**Government:** Military junta.
**President:** Jorge Rafael Videla (since 1976).
**U.S. Ambassador to Argentina:** Harry Schlaudeman.
**Argentinian Ambassador to U.S.:** Jorge A. Aja Espil.
**Flag:** Blue, white, and blue stripes; golden sun in white stripe has 32 rays.
**Official Language:** Spanish.
**Main Ethnic Group:** Spanish ancestry.
**Official Religion:** Roman Catholicism (94%).
**Leading Industries:** Manufacturing (steel, food processing, textiles, chemicals, vehicles, machinery, petroleum refining); agriculture (cattle, sheep, hogs, corn, wheat, cotton, citrus fruits, rye, alfalfa); mining (petroleum, gas, coal, iron ore, salt, uranium).
**Foreign Trade:** *major exports*—meat, corn, wheat, hides and skins, wool, Quebracho extract, linseed; *major imports*—nonelectric machinery, iron, steel, motor vehicles, paper and paperboard.
**Places of Interest:** Iguassú Falls; Nahuel Huapi National Park; Lake Traful; Mar del Plata beach resort; colonial buildings in La Plata; Mendoza; Córdoba; Salta. *In Buenos Aires:* Paleimo Park; Casa Rosada (Government House); National Historical Museum; cathedral.

## ARGENTINA TODAY

The world's eighth-largest country in area, Argentina has many natural resources. Its people enjoy high standards of living and education. But freedom is limited by the ruling military junta.

Argentina shares with Chile the majestic mountain peaks of the Andes range. In the east are the fertile plains of the Pampa, home of the Argentine cowboy, the gaucho. To the northeast lie subtropical deltas, dense forests, and grassy savannas. In the north are dry lowlands. South of the Pampa lies uninhabited Patagonia.

## EARLY HISTORY

The Spanish navigator Juan Díaz de Solís discovered Argentina in 1516.

In 1810 revolutionists seeking independence from Spain overthrew the viceroyalty and set up a governing junta in Buenos Aires. Other Argentine provinces joined, led by Gen. José de San Martín, and in 1816 declared independence.

## PERONISM

An army colonel, Juan Perón, became Argentina's president in 1946 and ruled dictatorially for a decade. In 1955 anti-Peronists overthrew Perón. He fled and later settled in Spain.

A series of provisional, military-dominated governments then succeeded each other.

The 77-year-old Perón returned from exile in 1973 and was elected president. His third wife, Isabel Martínez de Perón, became vice president.

Upon Perón's death on July 1, 1974, his 43-year-old widow succeeded him as president, becoming the first woman to head a national government in the Western Hemisphere.

## MILITARY RULE

Commanders of the armed forces overthrew and imprisoned Mrs. Perón in a bloodless coup on March 24, 1976. Martial law was proclaimed and the nation's congress was dismissed.

The commander in chief of the army, Lt. Gen. Rafael Videla, was sworn in as Argentina's 39th president on March 29, 1976.

The military junta arrested some 6,000 to 15,000 persons in 1976–79 in an effort to end terrorist activities. Thousands disappeared and were presumed to have been executed.

The United States reduced military aid to Argentina in 1977 because of the military regime's violation of human rights in suppressing political opposition.

Videla's regime began a program to revive the economy, emphasizing free enterprise, encouraging foreign investments, and selling off to private investors hundreds of companies taken over by previous governments. Inflation declined from an annual rate of 350% in 1976 to 160% in 1979, but consumer prices in 1980 were nearly 300 times those of 1974. Interest rates on bank loans reached a level of 130% a year in 1980.

To reinstitute "civilian" government, President Videla on Aug. 1, 1978, resigned from the army. However, he remained responsible to the military junta of heads of the armed forces. He promised to restore political parties in the 1980s.

The junta chose Gen. Roberto Eduardo Viola, 56, retired commander of the armed forces, to replace Videla as president in March 1981.

# AUSTRALIA

**Official Name:** Commonwealth of Australia.
**Area:** 2,967,909 square miles (7,686,848 sq. km.).
**Population:** 14,691,900.
**Chief Metropolitan Areas:** Canberra, capital, 196,539; Sydney, 3,021,983; Melbourne, 2,604,035; Brisbane, 957,743; Adelaide, 900,431; Perth, 805,747; Newcastle, 363,011; Wollongong, 211,068; Hobart, 162,062; Geelong, 131,636; Gold Coast, 116,195.
**Government:** Federal parliamentary state.
**Prime Minister:** Malcolm Fraser (took office in 1975).
**Chief of State:** Queen Elizabeth II, represented by Governor-General Sir Zelman Cowen (since 1977).
**Parliament:** *Senate,* 64 members; *House of Representatives,* 124 members.
**U.S. Ambassador to Australia:** Philip H. Alston Jr.
**Australian Ambassador to U.S.:** Sir Nicholas F. Parkinson
**Flag:** Blue field with red, white, and blue Union Jack in upper left and large white seven-pointed star below; five smaller white stars on right represent Southern Cross.
**Official Language:** English.
**Principal Ethnic Group:** British descent.
**Main Religions:** Anglicanism (38%), Roman Catholicism (23%), Methodism (11%), Presbyterianism (10%).
**Leading Industries:** Manufacturing (steel, aluminum, vehicles, textiles, machines); agriculture (cattle, sheep, hogs, wheat, oats, fruits, vegetables); mining (bauxite, iron ore, coal, tin, copper, zinc, lead, gold, uranium); fishing.
**Foreign Trade:** *major exports*—wheat, meat, sugar, metal ores; *major imports*—machinery, transport equipment, electrical machinery, textiles, drugs and chemicals.
**Places of Interest:** Great Barrier Reef off Queensland coast; Botany Bay; Blue Mountains, with Jenolan Caves; Mount Kosciusko National Park; Parliament House and St. Paul's Cathedral in Melbourne; St. James' Church, Opera House, and Australian Museum in Sydney; Canberra; Shepparton resort in Victoria; Ballarat, reconstructed village of 1850s; 12,000-year-old rock paintings in Queensland.

## AUSTRALIA TODAY

The only nation to cover an entire continent, Australia is the world's sixth-largest country. It is a federation of six states.

### STATES AND MAINLAND TERRITORIES

|                       | Area [1] | Population [2] | Capital   |
| --------------------- | -------- | -------------- | --------- |
| New South Wales ...   | 309,433  | 4,776,200      | Sydney    |
| Queensland.........   | 667,000  | 2,037,000      | Brisbane  |
| South Australia.....  | 380,070  | 1,244,600      | Adelaide  |
| Tasmania..........    | 26,383   | 402,800        | Hobart    |
| Victoria ...........  | 87,884   | 3,646,300      | Melbourne |
| Western Australia ..  | 975,920  | 1,144,400      | Perth     |
| Capital Territory.... | 939      | 197,578        | Canberra  |
| Northern Territory .. | 520,280  | 97,100         | Darwin    |

[1] In square miles.    [2] 1976 census.

The land is rich in natural resources, and the people, mostly of British descent, enjoy one of the highest standards of living in the world. Most Australians live along the east coast.

However, Australia is sparsely settled in relation to its size. Nearly as large as the United States, it has only about one-fifteenth as many people. Government encouragement of immigration has helped double the population in the past four decades.

Transportation is a major problem because there are few highways or railroads. Air travel is the only way to reach many parts of the interior.

Bordering the narrow eastern coastal plain is the Great Dividing Range, which extends from Queensland to the south of New South Wales. The highest peak, Mt. Kosciusko in New South Wales, is only 7,310 feet. Much of the interior is barren desert. Major rivers include the Murray and its tributary, the Darling. Northern Australia has a tropical climate.

## DISCOVERY AND COLONIZATION

Aborigines were the continent's only inhabitants when Capt. James Cook took formal possession of the east coast for Britain in 1770.

The first European settlement was a British penal colony established in 1788 at Port Jackson (the port of Sydney). Many of the early settlers were convicts or soldiers. As the number of free settlers increased, the practice of transporting convicts from Britain was curtailed and finally was discontinued altogether in 1868.

Gold strikes in the colonies of Victoria and New South Wales in 1851 brought thousands of new settlers. By 1859 six colonies, including the island of Tasmania, had been organized.

## FORMATION OF THE COMMONWEALTH

A constitution[9] drafted in 1897–98 was approved by the colonists and the British parliament. The Commonwealth of Australia came into being in 1901. The parliament of the federal government met in Melbourne until moved to Canberra in 1927. Australian soldiers fought with distinction on the side of the Allies in both world wars.

## EXPANDING INDUSTRIAL NATION

Australia began the century as an agricultural country but by the end of World War II had become an industrial one.

A surprise victory by the Labor Party in a national election in December 1972 ended 23 years of coalition rule. The head of the Labor Party, Edward Gough Whitlam, became prime minister and immediately launched a series of liberal reforms in domestic and foreign policies.

In a general election on May 18, 1974, Prime Minister Whitlam's Labor Party won a 5-vote majority in the House of Representatives. In the Senate, Labor tied with the Liberal-Country coalition, each receiving 29 seats.

In October-November 1975 a coalition of the Liberal and National Country parties forced a governmental crisis by blocking appropriations in the Senate because Whitlam refused to call new national elections. On Nov. 11 Governor-General Sir John Kerr removed Prime Minister

QUICK QUIZ: What entertainer won the Spingarn Medal in 1968? See page 86.

## AUSTRALIA (continued)

Whitlam from office and appointed opposition leader Malcolm Fraser to succeed him as head of a coalition cabinet. In national elections on Dec. 13, 1975, Fraser's coalition parties won majorities in both houses of parliament.

Parliament in August 1977 passed legislation outlawing strikes by public employees and giving the government the right to dismiss strikers.

In August 1977 Prime Minister Fraser lifted a ban on mining and exporting uranium imposed by the Labor government in 1972.

Australian uranium deposits, valued at about $150 billion, account for 20% of the known reserves of noncommunist nations. The first uranium ore was scheduled for shipment in 1981 under the new policy.

The government announced plans in 1977 for a $2.5 to $3 billion development of natural-gas fields off the northwest coast.

Fraser called early parliamentary elections on Dec. 10, 1977, in which his conservative coalition surprised political forecasters by winning a larger majority than in the 1975 election.

The nation's inflation rate rose from 7.8% in 1978 to 10% in 1979. The unemployment rate declined slightly from 7.7% in 1978 to 7.2% in 1979.

A large-scale diamond rush developed in northwestern Australia after the discovery in July 1978 of major deposits of the valuable gems. Some 20 mining companies quickly staked claims.

Labor unrest grew in Australia in 1979 as a result of government efforts to prevent unauthorized strikes. When the government arrested 10 union leaders for failing to obtain police permits before addressing meetings, 200 unions called a 24-hour general strike on June 21, 1979, that shut down most industry. Prime Minister Fraser declared on July 22: "Industrial disputes are tearing this nation apart when we should be building and working together with a sense of purpose."

Prime Minister Fraser's government reacted strongly in 1980 against the Soviet Union's invasion of Afghanistan, substantially increasing spending on national defense and offering the U.S. a naval base at Cockburn Sound near Perth. The government also restricted the amount of grain that could be sold to the Soviet Union in order not to make up for the grain lost to that country by the U.S. embargo on grain sales.

Fraser's conservative coalition won parliamentary elections on Oct. 18, 1980, but with a sharply reduced majority.

## AUSTRALIAN DEPENDENCIES

### AUSTRALIAN CAPITAL TERRITORY

Area: 939 square miles (2,432 sq. km.).
Capital: Canberra, 196,539.

The Capital Territory is bordered on all sides by New South Wales. The land was transferred to the commonwealth for the seat of government in 1911. Residents are represented in parliament by one elected member. The federal minister for the interior supervises general administration.

### NORTHERN TERRITORY

Area: 520,280 square miles (1,347,519 sq. km.).
Population: 98,170.
Capital: Darwin, 43,000.

## PRIME MINISTERS OF AUSTRALIA

| | | |
|---|---|---|
| 1901–03 | Edmund Barton.......... | Protectionist |
| 1903–04 | Alfred Deakin ........... | Protectionist |
| 1904 | John C. Watson.......... | Labor |
| 1904–05 | George H. Reid .......... | Free trade |
| 1905–08 | Alfred Deakin ........... | Protectionist |
| 1908–09 | Andrew Fisher........... | Labor |
| 1909–10 | Alfred Deakin ........... | Fusion |
| 1910–13 | Andrew Fisher........... | Labor |
| 1913–14 | Joseph Cook ............ | Liberal |
| 1914–15 | Andrew Fisher........... | Labor |
| 1915–17 | William M. Hughes ....... | Labor |
| 1917–23 | William M. Hughes ....... | Nationalist |
| 1923–29 | Stanley M. Bruce......... | Nationalist |
| 1929–32 | James Scullin ........... | Labor |
| 1932–39 | Joseph A. Lyons ......... | United |
| 1939 | Earle Page .............. | Country |
| 1939–41 | Robert G. Menzies ....... | United |
| 1941 | Arthur Fadden........... | Country |
| 1941–45 | John Curtin ............. | Labor |
| 1945 | Francis M. Forde ......... | Labor |
| 1945–49 | Ben Chifley ............. | Labor |
| 1949–66 | Robert G. Menzies ....... | Liberal |
| 1966–67 | Harold E. Holt .......... | Liberal |
| 1967–68 | John McEwen ........... | Country |
| 1968–71 | John G. Gorton ......... | Liberal |
| 1971–72 | William McMahon ........ | Liberal |
| 1972–75 | Edward Gough Whitlam... | Labor |
| 1975– | Malcolm Fraser .......... | Liberal |

The Northern Territory is largely a tableland that rises to a maximum elevation of 1,200 feet from the 1,040-mile-long coastline. There are large areas of fine pasturelands, especially in the north and northeast, but much of the interior is desert, especially in the west.

Products include manganese, gold, sorghum, beef, and pearl shell.

South Australia formally transferred the territory to the federal government in 1911.

In an election on Aug. 13, 1977, voters gave a majority of seats in the new 19-member legislative assembly to the Liberal-Country Party, which had promised to win statehood for the territory.

### AUSTRALIAN ANTARCTIC TERRITORY

Area: 2,360,000 square miles (6,112,372 sq. km.).
Australia claimed the area in 1936.

### CHRISTMAS ISLAND

Area: 52 square miles (135 sq. km.).
Population: 3,335.

Christmas Island is in the Indian Ocean, 220 miles south of Java Head. Sovereignty was transferred to Australia from Singapore in 1958. About 60% of its people are Chinese. The island's only economic activity is phosphate extraction and export.

### COCOS (KEELING) ISLANDS

Area: 5.4 square miles (14 sq. km.).
Population: 1,237.
Capital: Bantam.

The territory, two atolls comprising 27 small coral islands, lies in the Indian Ocean, about 1,400 miles south of Sri Lanka. The Cocos Islands were discovered in 1609 by Capt. William Keeling. The islands were given to the Clunies-Ross family by Queen Victoria in 1886. Australia reached agreement in 1978 to purchase the islands for $7.2 million from the Clunies-Ross family.

## HEARD AND McDONALD ISLANDS
**Area:** 142 square miles (368 sq. km.).
The islands, in the Indian Ocean about 2,500 miles southwest of Perth, were transferred to Australia by Britain in 1947. The territory is governed under the laws of the Australian Capital Territory and is uninhabited.

## LORD HOWE ISLAND
**Area:** 5 square miles (13 sq. km.).
**Population:** 23.
Lord Howe Island, the most southerly island known to have coral reefs, is situated in the Tasman Sea, 436 miles northeast of Sydney. It was discovered in 1788. It is a dependency of New South Wales.

## MACQUARIE ISLAND
Macquarie, about 1,000 miles southeast of Hobart, has been a dependency of Tasmania since the 1800s. It is uninhabited except for a federal government weather and research base.

## NORFOLK ISLAND
**Area:** 14 square miles (36 sq. km.).
**Population:** 2,117.
**Capital:** Kingston.
Norfolk Island, situated in the Tasman Sea, 1,035 miles northeast of Sydney, was discovered by Capt. James Cook in 1774. It has been a distinct settlement since 1856, when 194 descendants of the *Bounty* mutineers were taken from Pitcairn to Norfolk Island as a result of an offer made to them by Queen Victoria of Britain. The descendants of these people make up about one-fourth of the population.

Among the crops produced are bean seeds, maize, pineapples, citrus fruits, potatoes, onions, and other vegetables.

The scenic beauty and climate attract many visitors, making tourism a major industry.

## AUSTRIA

**Official Name:** Republic of Austria.
**Area:** 32,374 square miles (83,849 sq. km.).
**Population:** 7,489,210.
**Largest Cities:** Wien (Vienna), capital, 1,592,800; Graz, 250,893; Linz, 208,000; Salzburg, 139,000; Innsbruck, 120,355.
**Government:** Federal republic.
**Chancellor:** Bruno Kreisky (took office in 1970).
**President:** Rudolf Kirchschläger (since 1974).
**Legislature:** *Bundesrat,* 58 members; *Nationalrat,* 183 members.
**U.S. Ambassador to Austria:** Philip M. Kaiser.
**Austrian Ambassador to U.S.:** Karl Herbert Schober.
**Flag:** Red, white, and red stripes, with coat of arms in center.
**Official Language:** German.
**Main Ethnic Group:** German descent (98%).

**Religions:** Roman Catholic (90%), Protestant (6%).
**Leading Industries:** Manufacturing (steel, chemicals, machinery, consumer products); agriculture (livestock, dairy products, barley, oats, corn, sugar beets, potatoes); tourism; mining (magnesite, graphite, iron ore, lignite).
**Foreign Trade:** *major exports*—iron and steel, machinery, yarn and fabrics, lumber;. *major imports*—automobiles, coal, petroleum products.
**Places of Interest:** Danube River; Vienna Woods; Mozart's birthplace ·at Salzburg and the Salzburg Music Festival; Tyrol; Innsbruck old quarters; Graz. *In Vienna:* Schönbrunn Palace; St. Stephen's Cathedral; State Opera House; Spanish Riding School; UN City.

## AUSTRIA TODAY
Austria's major problem is its location between the communist powers of eastern Europe and the West. Defeated as an ally of Germany in World Wars I and II, Austria today is about the size of the state of Maine—only a remnant of an empire that once dominated central Europe. Austria endeavors to maintain its neutrality by constitutional law. It takes part in no military alliances and has no foreign military bases.

Other than fearing the consequences of a war between East and West, the Austrians are contented and prosperous. Most live in cities, working in business and industry.

Thousands of tourists visit Austria each year for winter sports in the snow-covered Alps, to attend music festivals, to go to art museums, or to view the scenic attractions along the beautiful Danube River.

## EARLY HISTORY
From prehistoric times Austria has been a crossroads of Europe. Rome conquered the territory between 16 and 9 B.C. From the end of the Roman Empire until 803, when it became part of Charlemagne's empire, it was overrun by Germanic tribes. In the 900s Austria was added to the Holy Roman Empire.

By 1273 the Austrian lands had come under the control of the House of Hapsburg, which ruled until 1918. With one brief interruption, the Hapsburgs were rulers of the Holy Roman Empire from 1438 until 1806, when it was dissolved by Napoleon.

By the end of the 1400s the Hapsburg territories ranged from the plains north of the Danube to the Adriatic. They formed a multinational empire with the German-speaking lands (in substance, the future Austrian republic) in the center. To the north, east, and south were Czech, Hungarian, Italian, Polish, Ruthenian, Romanian, Slovak, and southern Slav territories.

The cultural development of present-day Austria was strongly influenced both by its German ethnic, social, and political composition and by ties to Slavic and Romance peoples and to the Magyars (Hungarians).

An Austrian empire was officially established in 1804. By 1815 Austria became the leading power in the German confederation and in the Holy Alliance. Austria's skillful foreign minister, Prince Klemens von Metternich, acted as chief arbiter of Europe. Revolutions in Hungary,

QUICK QUIZ: What is the average annual rainfall in Vienna, Austria? See page 148.

**AUSTRIA** *(continued)*

Bohemia, and Vienna brought an end to the Age of Metternich in 1848.

Hungary forced Emperor Franz Josef I to accord it equal rights in a dual monarchy, forming the Austro-Hungarian Empire in 1867.

The assassination on June 28, 1914, of Archduke Franz Ferdinand, the emperor's nephew and heir, triggered World War I. Defeat of Austria and Germany by the Allies ended the Austro-Hungarian Empire in 1918. Austria became a republic.

## FEDERAL REPUBLIC OF AUSTRIA

In the 1920s Austria suffered economic collapse and social and political unrest. Austrian Nazis assassinated Chancellor Engelbert Dollfuss in 1934 but failed in an attempted coup. In March 1938 Adolf Hitler annexed Austria to Germany.

After World War II Austria was divided into four occupation zones. The Soviet Union refused to end the occupation until Oct. 25, 1955, when Austria was finally reestablished as an independent republic obligated to remain neutral. The country was then permitted to join the UN.

After parliamentary elections in March 1970, Bruno Kreisky, the new chancellor, formed Austria's first socialist government since World War II. Upon the death in 1974 of Franz Jonas, who had been president since 1965, Rudolf Kirchschläger, a socialist, was elected president. He was reelected in 1980. Kreisky's Socialist Party won a parliamentary majority in national elections on Oct. 5, 1975.

In a national referendum on Nov. 5, 1978, voters turned down by $\frac{1}{2}\%$ the nation's first atomic power plant. Chancellor Kreisky had supported use of the $530 million facility, which had been ready to start operation.

The 68-year-old Kreisky led his Socialist Party to victory in national parliamentary elections on May 6, 1979, increasing its majority to 96 seats in the lower house.

The nation's strong economy grew at a rate of more than 5% in 1979 with inflation held to only 3.7%. Unemployment remained at 2%.

Kreisky's Socialist Party was shaken in 1980 by a major scandal involving bribes and kickbacks in the construction of a 2,100-bed hospital in Vienna at a cost of about $3.25 billion.

# BAHAMAS

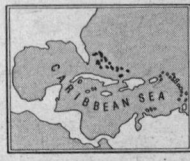 

**Official Name:** Commonwealth of The Bahamas.
**Area:** 5,380 square miles (13,935 sq. km.).
**Population:** 244,692.
**Capital:** Nassau, 3,233 (metropolitan area, 101,503).
**Government:** Parliamentary state.
**Prime Minister:** Lynden O. Pindling (since 1968).
**Chief of State:** Queen Elizabeth II, represented by Governor-General Gerald C. Cash (since 1976).
**Legislature:** *House of Assembly,* 38 members; *Senate,* 16 members.

**U.S. Ambassador to Bahamas:** William B. Schwartz Jr.
**Bahamian Ambassador to U.S.:** Reginald L. Wood.
**Flag:** Black triangle and three stripes, with aquamarine stripes at top and bottom and gold band in middle.
**Language:** English.
**Main Ethnic Group:** Black (85%).
**Chief Religions:** Anglicanism, Roman Catholicism, Methodism, Baptist.
**Leading Industries:** Tourism; banking; fishing; petroleum refining; agriculture (fruits, vegetables); cement; salt; chemicals.
**Foreign Trade:** *major exports*—petroleum products, tomatoes, salt, rum, seafood, cement, pulpwood; *major imports*—food, manufactured products.
**Places of Interest:** San Salvador (Watling) Island, believed to have been Christopher Columbus' first landing place in New World; Exuma Cays National Land and Sea Park, 176-square-mile preserve for sea life; gambling casinos at Freeport on Grand Bahama Island; resort hotels; swimming beaches. *In Nassau:* Fort Fincastle, the Bahamian Museum, Fort Charlotte, Seafloor Aquarium.

## BAHAMAS TODAY

An island country off the east coast of Florida, the Bahamas attract about 2 million American tourists each year. Money spent by the tourists represents over three-fourths of the Bahamas' income.

Since 1955 gambling has been legalized in the Freeport area of Grand Bahama Island, only a few minutes flight from Florida. Many gambling casinos and resort hotels have been built.

The islands' second major industry is banking. Because of the nation's low taxation, many foreign corporations had established headquarters there. But in 1976 the government imposed taxes on corporations that were not 60% Bahamian owned. As a result many corporations moved to other tax havens.

The government seeks to diversify the islands' economy by encouraging new industries and better utilization of the natural resources.

A large oil refinery completed in the late 1960s at Freeport caused a 70% increase in the value of the nation's exports and made petroleum products the Bahamas' leading export commodity. In addition, the Freeport area has seen the development of cement, pharmaceutical, and light manufacturing plants.

Before the development of the tourist industry and oil refining, the islands depended largely on fishing and agriculture.

The more than 700 islands that make up the Bahamas extend over about 90,000 square miles. They lie in a band 500 miles long and 200 miles wide, starting about 50 miles east of Florida.

Only about 40 of the largest islands are inhabited. Most of the rest are little more than small sandy or rocky beaches.

The largest, Andros Island, lies about midway between Florida and Cuba. The capital, Nassau, is on New Providence Island. The closest large island to the United States is Grand Bahama Island whose largest city is Freeport. Other major islands include Acklins, Cat, Eleuthera, Great Abaco, Great Exuma, Great Inagua, Little Abaco, and San Salvador.

## DISCOVERY AND COLONIZATION

The Bahamas were the first land discovered by

Christopher Columbus in the New World in 1492 when he landed on San Salvador (or Watling) Island. Although Columbus claimed the islands for Spain, the Spaniards made no effort to colonize them.

British colonists began developing the islands after Charles I granted the Bahamas to Sir Robert Heath in 1626.

The Bahamas became a crown colony of Britain in 1717.

The first royal governor, Capt. Woodes Rogers, devoted his efforts to rooting out the pirates. The motto of the islands, part of the Great Seal of the Bahamas, became *Expulsis Piratis Restituta Commercia*, or "Pirates Expelled, Commerce Restored."

During the American Revolution, the islands were the scene of one of the first operations of the new U.S. Continental Navy, when its first commander, Esek Hopkins, led a raid in 1776. U.S. Marines landed and carried off cannon and gunpowder. Many British Loyalists fled from the United States to settle in the Bahamas.

During the American Civil War, the Bahamas were a center for blockade runners carrying goods to the Southern states.

In the 1920s American bootleggers used the Bahamas as a smuggling base as did drug smugglers in the 1960s-1980s.

The Bahamas were granted complete internal self-government in 1964.

The islands were ruled until 1967 by the white-dominated United Bahamian Party. But widespread government scandals involving payoffs for gambling licenses in the late 1960s led to victory in the national election of 1967 by the black-led Progressive Liberal Party (PLP) and the appointment of Lynden O. Pindling as prime minister. Pindling's PLP strengthened its position by again winning an election in September 1972.

## INDEPENDENCE

The Bahamas received full independence from Britain on July 10, 1973, retaining their status as a member of the Commonwealth of Nations. Pindling continued in office as the sovereign nation's first prime minister. On Aug. 1, 1973, the first Bahamian took office as governor-general—Sir Milo Butler.

In August 1975 the government banned fishing for lobsters in the Bahama Banks to the south and east of the islands. The action severely hurt the Florida fishing industry.

In the first national election since independence, on July 19, 1977, Pindling's PLP party won a landslide victory, taking 30 of the seats in the 38-member assembly. The main opposition, the new Bahamian Democratic Party (BDP), won only five seats.

In the 1970s–80s the islands became the main transshipment point for illegal drugs being smuggled into the United States. Smugglers hide their boats by day among the islands' thousands of cays and then run their cargoes overnight to the coast of Florida. With only a handful of police boats to search among the hundreds of islands, the government has expressed helplessness in trying to halt the smuggling.

# BAHRAIN

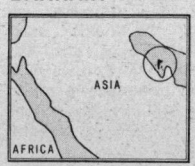 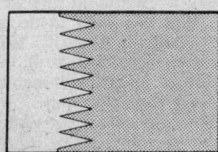

**Official Name:** State of Bahrain.
**Area:** 240 square miles (622 sq. km.).
**Population:** 443,597.
**Capital:** Manama, 88,785.
**Government:** Arab emirate.
**Chief of State:** Emir Isa bin Salman Al Khalifa (reigned since 1961).
**Premier:** Khalifa bin Salman Al Khalifa (appointed in 1970).
**U.S. Ambassador to Bahrain:** Peter A. Sutherland.
**Bahrainian Ambassador to U.S.:** Abdulaziz Abdulrahman Buali.
**Flag:** Red flag with broad white serrated band in hoist.
**Languages:** Arabic (official), Persian, English.
**Main Ethnic Group:** Arab (80%).
**Religion:** Islam.
**Leading Industries:** Petroleum mining and refining; aluminum refining; construction; ship repairs; fishing; agriculture (dates, vegetables, livestock).
**Foreign Trade:** *major export*—crude petroleum; *major imports*—consumer goods, automobiles, machinery, food, oil-industry equipment.
**Places of Interest:** Ancient burial mounds in uplands; oil refineries; royal residences.

## BAHRAIN TODAY

Bahrain is an island nation in the Persian Gulf, important as an oil-refining and trading center. Its 33 islets halfway down the gulf, off Saudi Arabia, form an archipelago 30 miles long and 10 miles wide. Bahrain enjoys a temperate climate and splendid offshore fishing.

About 70% of Bahrain's annual government budget of over $700 million derives from oil income. The government uses the revenues to provide free education and health services, to subsidize housing, and to develop industries.

Bahrain collects no customs duties on goods passing through the country, promoting use of port facilities by export-import companies.

## HISTORY

From the mid-1500s Bahrain was occupied successively by the Portuguese, Persians, and Omanese. In 1783 it was taken over by the Atabi Arabs from the mainland, founders of the present ruling dynasty. In 1820 the sheik signed a general treaty of peace with Britain. Bahrain became a British protectorate in 1861.

Oil deposits were discovered in 1932, the first in the Arabian peninsula. One of the largest oil refineries in the Middle East, with a capacity of 200,000 barrels a day, was built at Sitrah. More than half the oil refined comes by pipeline from Saudi Arabia.

Iran abandoned its long-standing claim to Bahrain in 1970, paving the way for the termination of the British protectorate.

To help diversify the nation's economy, an international consortium in 1971 completed the

## BAHRAIN *(continued)*

largest aluminum smelter in the Middle East.

Emir Al Khalifa declared the country independent on Aug. 15, 1971, and proclaimed the nation's first constitution in 1973. Leftists won control of the 30-member national assembly. Then the emir ended the nation's experiment with democracy on Aug. 26, 1975, dissolving the assembly.

Since 1974 Bahrain has enjoyed a construction boom, especially in housing and new hotels. To hold inflation down to a rate of 14% in 1977, the government subsidized the cost of food.

Bahrain's banking industry flourished in the 1970s–80s as some 40 international banks transferred operations from Lebanon after that country was devastated by civil war. Bahrain levies no taxes on the banks, satisfied with the additional employment brought by their presence.

A major new industry was launched in 1977 as South Korean workers completed a new $150 million supertanker repair drydock.

Bahrain did not renew the U.S. Navy's lease on port facilities when it expired in June 1977, ending the stigma of being an Arab country with a U.S. military base. However, arrangements were made to continue to service the U.S. Middle Eastern fleet.

Plans were put out for bid in 1980 for a $1 billion 15-mile overseas highway bridge to link Bahrain to the Saudi Arabian mainland for the first time. It is scheduled for completion by 1986.

# BANGLADESH

**Official Name:** People's Republic of Bangladesh.
**Area:** 55,598 square miles (143,998 sq. km.).
**Population:** 89,843,300.
**Chief Metropolitan Areas:** Dacca, capital, 1,730,253; Chittagong, 889,760; Khulna, 437,304; Narayanganj, 186,769.
**Government:** Republic.
**President:** Maj. Gen. Ziaur (Zia) Rahman (since 1977).
**Prime Minister:** Shah Azizur Rahman (since 1979).
**Parliament:** 330 seats (300 elected, 30 appointed).
**U.S. Ambassador to Bangladesh:** David T. Schneider.
**Bangladesh Ambassador to U.S.:** Tabarak Husain.
**Flag:** Off-centered brilliant orange circle on field of brilliant bottle green.
**Languages:** Bengali (official), English.
**Main Ethnic Group:** Bengali (98%).
**Chief Religions:** Islam (85%), Hinduism (14%).
**Leading Industries:** Agriculture (rice, jute, cattle, sugarcane, tobacco, cotton, tea); food processing; jute processing; manufacturing (rope, textiles, chemicals, paper); fishing.
**Foreign Trade:** *major exports*—jute, animal hides, fish, tea; *major imports*—food, coal, machines, vehicles, textiles.
**Places of Interest:** Bay of Bengal; Chittagong; Cox's Bazaar beach resort. *In Dacca:* Lal Bagh fort; tomb of Bibi Peri; Bara Katra caravansary; Husaini Dalan monument; Tejgaon Church; Shrine of Ba Yazid.

## BANGLADESH TODAY

The eighth-largest country in the world in population, Bangladesh also is one of the most poverty-stricken. Although Bangladesh covers an area only about the size of Wisconsin, it has about as many people as live in all the states west of the Mississippi River. And four or more babies are born every minute—about 6,000 a day. With so many people to feed and so little land on which to grow food, the Bangladeshis constantly verge on starvation even when the rice harvest is good. Most of the people cannot read and write.

Food shortages and poor sanitation contribute to continual epidemics of cholera and other diseases. Cyclones and tidal waves from the Bay of Bengal have repeatedly flooded low-lying areas, killing tens of thousands of persons.

Jute, a fiber used in making burlap bags, is Bangladesh's most important export.

### EARLY HISTORY

Located in the northeastern corner of India at the mouth of the Ganges River, Bangladesh was known for many years as East Bengal. In the 1200s Turkish Muslims conquered the area, converting the population to Islam. In the 1500s it became part of the Mogul empire. In the 1700s and 1800s the region became part of Britain's colonial empire in India.

When the British gave up colonial rule of India in 1947, the subcontinent was divided into Muslim Pakistan and Hindu India. East Bengal became East Pakistan, although separated from West Pakistan by 1,000 miles of Indian territory.

In November 1970 about 300,000 Bengalis drowned in a massive tidal wave during a cyclone.

Sheik Mujibur (Mujib) Rahman led his Awami Party to victory in the East Pakistan parliamentary elections of December 1970, giving strong support to a Bengali separatist movement. When the Pakistan government refused to let the new parliament meet in March, the Bengalis began a civil disobedience demonstration.

Gen. Agha Yahya Khan, president of Pakistan, led his army in a bloody repression of East Bengal on March 25, 1971. Mujib was arrested and tried for treason. The Bengalis fought back in a civil war that produced thousands of casualties plus nearly 9 million refugees who fled to India. In support of Bangladesh independence, India entered the war on Dec. 3, 1971, and in 13 days defeated Pakistan.

### INDEPENDENCE

Bangladesh became an independent nation on Dec. 16, 1971. Released from prison in January 1972, Mujib returned to become Bangladesh's first prime minister under a constitution proclaimed on Jan. 11, 1972. Indian troops withdrew in March 1972.

In March 1973, in the first national election, Mujib's Awami League party won all but a handful of the 315 seats in the national parliament.

Mujib became president with dictatorial powers on Jan. 26, 1975, a day after parliament had amended the constitution to enable him to do so. A month later, on Feb. 24, Mujib decreed Bangladesh a one-party state.

On Aug. 15, 1975, Mujib and members of his family were slain by rebelling army officers.

Khandaker Moshtaque Ahmed, the commerce minister, seized power, becoming the nation's president. However, on Nov. 5, 1975, he was overthrown in another coup and imprisoned.

Maj. Gen. Ziaur (Zia) Rahman, commander of the army, took control of the government in November 1975, invoking martial law. The former chief justice of the supreme court, Abu Sadat Mohammed Sayem, was named president.

On April 21, 1977, Zia took over the position of president in addition to his posts as chief martial-law administrator and head of the army.

The United States provided Bangladesh with 200,000 metric tons of wheat in 1977.

Over 230 persons were killed on Oct. 2, 1977, in an unsuccessful coup by lower-echelon army and air force officers. Subsequently, the government convicted more than 400 persons of taking part in the rebellion, and 92 were sentenced to death. On Oct. 14 President Zia banned the three main political parties for inciting violence.

The government ended restrictions on political activities in April 1978 in preparation for the nation's first presidential election on June 3. In the short campaign that followed, opposition parties rallied behind the candidacy of Gen. M. A. G. Osmani, who led the Bangladesh army in the 1971 war of independence. But President Zia won the election by a majority of nearly 4 to 1 of the more than 19 million votes cast.

The economy suffered a new blow in 1978 when neighboring Burma expelled more than 200,000 Muslims, driving them across the border into Bangladesh. The government, with the aid of the U.S. and international aid organizations, established refugee camps. Burma agreed to accept repatriation of the refugees in September 1978, but few chose to return.

In the first parliamentary election in six years, on Feb. 18, 1979, President Zia's Nationalist Party won two-thirds of the elective seats. Seven weeks later, on April 7, Zia ended martial law, restoring civilian rule.

The government reported in 1979 that the country had cut its import food needs by 50% in the 5-year period 1974–79.

A new 5-year plan for 1980–85 calls for doubling food production to achieve self-sufficiency.

# BARBADOS

**Official Name:** Barbados.
**Area:** 166 square miles (431 sq. km.).
**Population:** 255,043.
**Capital:** Bridgetown, 100,000 (metropolitan area).
**Government:** Parliamentary democracy.
**Prime Minister:** J.M.G. Adams (since 1976).
**Chief of State:** Queen Elizabeth II.
**Legislature:** *Senate,* 21 members; *House of Assembly,* 24 members.

**U.S. Ambassador to Barbados:** Sally Shelton.
**Barbadian Ambassador to U.S.:** Oliver H. Jackman.
**Flag:** Blue, gold, and blue bars, with black trident in gold bar.
**Official Language:** English.
**Main Ethnic Groups:** Blacks (80%), mixed (15%).
**Principal Religion:** Anglicanism (70%).
**Leading Industries:** Tourism; agriculture (sugarcane, corn, yams, fruits); sugar refining; manufacturing (rum, molasses, soap); fishing.
**Foreign Trade:** *major exports*—raw sugar, seafood, molasses, rum; *major imports*—petroleum, meat, dairy products, automobiles, steel.
**Places of Interest:** Deep-sea fishing ports and marinas; beach resorts; Andromeda Gardens at Bathsheba; Welchman Hall Gully gardens; sugar farms; old plantation homes. *In Bridgetown:* St. Michael's Anglican Cathedral; Sam Lord's Castle.

## BARBADOS TODAY

A prosperous Caribbean island nation with a stable democratic government, Barbados has an economy based on tourism and sugar.

Barbados is the most densely populated island in the West Indies. But a determined family-planning program has succeeded in reducing the population growth rate to less than 1%.

The island has many resort hotels for tourists attracted to Barbados by the year-round warm weather and the hundreds of miles of swimming beaches.

All Barbadians 18 or older can vote. The island's educational system is so well developed that almost everyone is literate.

Barbados lies on the eastern edge of the Lesser Antilles, with its eastern coast facing the Atlantic Ocean and its western coast on the Caribbean Sea. The generally flat land rises to a central high point of 1,104 feet at Mt. Hillaby.

## HISTORY

Barbados was claimed for England by Capt. John Powell in 1625 and was settled in 1627. Its parliament, founded in 1639, is the third oldest in the Americas (after Bermuda's and Virginia's).

The slaves who were imported to work the extensive sugar plantations were freed in 1834. However, the plantation owners retained political control of the island. Their power was broken only after universal suffrage was achieved in 1951, largely as a result of the efforts of a black attorney, Sir Grantley Adams.

The country has two major political parties. Adams' Barbados Labour Party (BLP) headed the government from 1954 to 1961. The Democratic Labour Party (DLP) led by Errol Barrow won majority control of parliament in 1961.

Barbados received independence from Britain on Nov. 30, 1966.

Barrow became the nation's first prime minister. His DLP party won national elections in 1966 and 1971.

In an election upset, the BLP party won 17 of the 24 seats in the national assembly on Sept. 2, 1976. BLP leader J.M.G. (Tom) Adams, son of Sir Grantley Adams, became prime minister.

Adams promised to cut taxes, establish free national health insurance, end corruption, and reduce unemployment.

QUICK QUIZ: What is a pocket veto? See page 157.

# BELGIUM

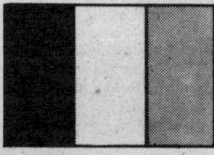

**Official Name:** Kingdom of Belgium.
**Area:** 11,781 square miles (30,513 sq. km.).
**Population:** 9,864,670.
**Chief Cities:** Bruxelles (Brussels), capital, 103,712; Antwerp, 222,775; Ghent, 148,166; Liège, 144,875; Schaerbeek, 118,950; Bruges, 118,023.
**Largest Metropolitan Area:** Brussels, 1,028,972.
**Government:** Constitutional monarchy.
**Prime Minister:** Wilfried Martens (since 1979).
**King:** Baudouin (since 1951).
**Parliament:** *Senate,* 181 members; *Chamber of Representatives,* 212 members.
**U.S. Ambassador to Belgium:** Anne Cox Chambers.
**Belgian Ambassador to U.S.:** Raoul Shoumaker.
**Flag:** Bars of black, yellow, and red.
**Official Languages:** Flemish (Dutch) and French.
**Chief Ethnic Groups:** Flemish (Dutch-speaking; 56%), Walloon (French-speaking; 32%).
**Main Religion:** Roman Catholicism (75%).
**Leading Industries:** Manufacturing (steel, textiles, machinery, chemicals); agriculture (wheat, oats, rye, barley, cattle, poultry, horses, sugar beets, vegetables); mining (coal, zinc, lead, copper).
**Foreign Trade:** *major exports*—iron and steel, transport equipment, textile yarn and fabrics, cut diamonds, glassware, chemical products, nonferrous metals; *major imports*—motor vehicles, copper, wool, machinery, iron ore, cotton, wheat, petroleum products.
**Places of Interest:** Ardennes Forest; Meuse Valley; cathedrals, palaces, and museums in Brussels; cathedral and Rubens' house in Antwerp; Bruges city canals; Mons churches; Ypres war memorials; Ghent; Liège; Ostend seaside resort; Industrial Exhibition Halls and Palace of Fine Arts at Charleroi; Grottoes of Han at Han-sur-Lesse; Namur resort.

## BELGIUM TODAY

A small industrial nation in western Europe, Belgium is a little larger than the state of Maryland. Because of its location between France and Germany, Belgium historically has been a battleground for its more powerful neighbors. In Belgium's best interests, therefore, its leaders have worked hard since World War II to achieve economic unity and peace in western Europe. As a consequence Belgium's capital, Brussels, has become the headquarters of western Europe's two most powerful organizations, the Common Market and NATO.

Belgium's highly industrialized economy has prospered since the establishment of the European Common Market in 1958. Because the country has few natural resources, Belgium imports raw materials from other countries and processes them them into products for export. West Germany supplies Belgium with most of its needed raw materials, while the Netherlands is the best customer for Belgium's manufactured products.

Farming plays a minor role in Belgium's economy. Only 6 of every 100 Belgians earn their living from agriculture.

A parliamentary democracy whose king is a figurehead, Belgium has been less successful in achieving internal political harmony. The root of the nation's domestic problems lies in the country's division into three language regions, each having its own goals. The Dutch-speaking Flemish people live in Flanders, the northern part of the country along the border with the Netherlands. French-speaking Walloons live in the southern Ardennes region along the border with France. Brussels, in the central plain between the two, is a bilingual political battleground.

Because of the conflicting regional and language-group interests, the people of Belgium divide their votes among six or more political parties none of which is able to win a majority of seats in the parliament. As a result, coalition governments representing two or more parties join forces to run Belgium's government. When the parties to the coalition disagree, the government falls.

## EARLY HISTORY

The country was part of the Roman province of *Belgica* and later part of Charlemagne's empire. Under Burgundian rule since the mid-1300s, Belgium became a hereditary possession of the Germanic Hapsburg dynasty by marriage in 1477.

Hapsburg King Felipe II of Spain gained control of Belgium in 1555 when his father, Karl V, divided his kingdom. In 1568 the Low Countries (modern Belgium, the Netherlands, and Luxembourg) revolted against King Felipe. The northern provinces won their independence, but Belgium was reconquered by Spain.

France took Belgium in 1797 and held it until Napoleon's final defeat at the Battle of Waterloo, fought in Belgium in 1815.

The victorious powers of the Napoleonic wars again united Belgium with the Netherlands and Luxembourg under Dutch King Willem I to form a buffer state against France.

## INDEPENDENCE

When the Belgians revolted in 1830, England and France imposed an armistice, dissolved the unitary kingdom, and guaranteed Belgium's independence and neutrality.

The new state chose Leopold of Saxe-Coburg as its king in 1831. Upon his death in 1865 he was succeeded by his son Leopold II, whose encouragement of rapid industrialization and colonial acquisition brought prosperity. He established the African Congo as a private colony, but it was transferred to the state in 1908.

## BELGIUM IN WORLD WARS I AND II

Albert I, nephew of Leopold II, succeeded to the throne in 1909.

Disregarding Belgium's neutrality, Germany invaded Belgium in 1914, crossing it to attack France. In protest Britain immediately declared war on Germany. King Albert's small army was quickly overpowered by the Germans.

After World War I Belgium ended its status of guaranteed neutrality and entered into a defensive alliance with France. King Albert died in 1934 and was succeeded by Leopold III.

With the resurgence of Germany under Hitler, Belgium withdrew from alliance with France in 1936 and declared a policy of independent neutral-

ity. When the Germans invaded Belgium in 1940, King Leopold, as chief of his country's army, resisted for 18 days. He then surrendered and refused to accompany his government to London. The cabinet declared the surrender illegal.

## POSTWAR BELGIUM

Leopold's unpopularity caused a long political crisis after the liberation of Belgium in 1944. Leopold finally gave up the throne to his son Baudouin, who became king on July 17, 1951.

Belgium gave up its colonial empire, granting independence to the Congo (now Zaire) in 1960.

A government crisis was brought about by the resignation of Prime Minister Gaston Eyskens in November 1972. It ended in January 1973 with the formation of a coalition government under Prime Minister Edmond Leburton, the first socialist to head the government since 1958. The new coalition included the country's three major political parties: the Socialist, the Social Christian (Roman Catholic), and the Party of Liberty and Progress (Liberal).

Leburton's coalition government collapsed early in 1974. In elections in March the moderate Social Christians won the largest bloc, 72 seats, in the Chamber of Deputies. Their leader, Dutch-speaking Leo Tindemans, became premier.

In a national election on April 17, 1977, the Social Christians won the largest number of seats, 80, in the 212-member chamber of deputies.

Tindemans began a new term as prime minister in June 1977, forming a coalition government of four parties that agreed to constitutional revisions to solve Belgium's regional and language-group problems. The plan called for three autonomous regions for the Flemish, the Walloons, and bilingual Brussels. Each region would have its own executive and legislative assembly.

Paul vanden Boeynants, leader of the French-speaking members of the Social Christian Party, became prime minister on Oct. 20, 1978, after Tindemans resigned when parliament turned down his regionalization plan to settle the country's language conflict. Boeynants previously served as prime minister in 1966–68.

A new parliamentary election was held on Dec. 17, 1978. Boeyants resigned the following day, declaring the election had decided nothing, although his Social Christian Party had gained 2 seats, increasing its plurality to 82.

After four months of negotiations among the political parties, Wilfried Martens, leader of the Flemish Social Christians, became prime minister on April 3, 1979.

Belgium sent a contingent of 250 paratroops to Zaire in 1979 to assist in training Zairian troops. The Belgian force also was expected to provide protection for the nearly 30,000 Belgians working in Zaire.

The parliament approved legislation on Aug. 5, 1980, granting partial autonomy to Dutch-speaking Flanders and French-speaking Wallonia. Each region was given the power to elect its own assembly to control such matters as public health and highways. The legislation was achieved by a compromise that delayed until 1982 consideration of similar autonomy for Brussels.

# BENIN

Official Name: People's Republic of Benin.
Area: 43,484 square miles (112,622 sq. km.).
Population: 3,619,240.
Chief Cities: Porto Novo, official capital, 104,000; Cotonou, political capital, 178,000.
Government: One-party communist state.
President and Premier: Mathieu Kerekou (seized power in 1972).
U.S. Ambassador to Benin: James B. Engle.
Benin Ambassador to U.S.: Thomas Setondji Boya.
Parliament: Revolutionary National Assembly, 350 members.
Flag: Green field with red star in upper hoist corner.
Official Language: French.
Ethnic Groups: Fons or Dahomey (50%), Samba, Baroba, Chabe.
Religions: Animism (65%), Roman Catholicism (15%), Islam (13%).
Leading Industries: Agriculture (corn, rice, manioc, beans, palm products, peanuts, yams, cotton, kapok, tobacco, cashew nuts); manufacturing and processing (cotton ginning, palm-kernel oil, textiles, beer, soap, cement).
Foreign Trade: major exports—palm products, raw cotton, peanuts; major imports—fabrics, motor vehicles, petroleum products, iron and steel.
Places of Interest: Pendjari Game Preserve; national park of the "W"; Cotonou floating fishing village; Porto Novo Ethnographic Museum; Abomey historical museum; Temple of the Serpents in Ouidah.

## BENIN TODAY

A small, densely populated West African nation, Benin (formerly called Dahomey) is a poverty-stricken communist one-party state.

About the size of Tennessee, Benin is entirely dependent on agriculture for its economy. Cotton and palm-kernel oil account for about three-fourths of the country's exports. What little manufacturing and processing industry Benin has is concerned mostly with the ginning of cotton and the production of palm products. The government opened the nation's largest single industrial plant in 1975, a textile mill employing 2,000.

About 9 out of every 10 Beninese farm for their living. Few can read and write.

Most of the country's foreign trade passes through the port of Cotonou, Benin's largest city, which lies on the 75-mile-long coastline. Most government operations are located in Cotonou, the unofficial political capital.

Long beaches, a tradition of hospitality to visitors, and unspoiled wildlife reserves provide the potential for a tourist industry.

Togo lies to the west, with Upper Volta and Niger to the north, and Nigeria to the east.

## EARLY HISTORY AND FRENCH RULE

Benin's earliest known settlers, the Adja, established a kingdom near the coast before the

QUICK QUIZ: Who is chairman of the Senate Foreign Relations Committee? See page 162.

**BENIN** *(continued)*

1100s. The kingdom of Benin grew to control the interior region in the 1300s to 1400s. Both Benin and the adjacent kingdom of Dahomey were subject to the larger empire of Oyo. At annual festivals the kings sacrificed hundreds of their subjects to tribal gods.

In 1485 Portuguese traders reached the area. Dahomey and Benin soon became centers of the African slave trade.

In 1822 King Gezo of Dahomey, leading an army of female warriors, ended Oyo supremacy.

French influence began in 1851. After several attacks by tribesmen on French coastal trading posts between 1889 and 1891, France established a protectorate. In 1904 Dahomey became a territory of French West Africa.

The people of Dahomey were given French citizenship in 1946 and the opportunity to take part in local assemblies. In 1958 Dahomey received a large measure of self-government.

## INDEPENDENCE

The country was granted independence on Aug. 1, 1960. Hubert Maga (from the north), the first president, was deposed in October 1963 by Col. Christophe Soglo, a southerner. In December 1967 Soglo was deposed in a bloodless coup led by Lt. Col. Alphonse Alley.

Alley's regime was overthrown by the army in December 1969.

Maga again became president in May 1970 and was peacefully succeeded in May 1972 by Justin Ahomadegbé Tometin. On Oct. 26, 1972, an army coup overthrew the government, and Mathieu Kerekou was installed as president and premier.

Kerekou announced on Feb. 28, 1973, that a plot to overthrow him had been discovered and that 15 persons had been arrested, including Col. Alphonse Alley, who had led the 1967 coup.

A severe drought in 1972–74 set back the nation's already poor economy.

In November 1974 Kerekou proclaimed that the country would thenceforth be a Marxist-Leninist state. The government then nationalized banks, insurance companies, and manufacturing and processing plants.

On Jan. 23, 1975, the government announced the arrest and imprisonment of Minister of Labor Capt. Janvier Assogba, who was accused of leading an attempted coup. In June 1975 President Kerekou ordered the execution of Interior Minister Michel Aikpe, whom he had surprised in bed with Mrs. Kerekou.

Kerekou renamed the country the *People's Republic of Benin* on Nov. 30, 1975.

An armed force landed by transport plane at Cotonou on Jan. 16, 1977, and then escaped after an unsuccessful attempt to overthrow Kerekou. The Beninese leader blamed "French imperialists" aided by Morocco, Gabon, Togo, Ivory Coast, and Senegal.

The UN Security Council, after an investigation and lengthy debate, condemned the raid on April 14, 1977, but avoided naming those responsible.

To provide a broader base for his Marxist-Leninist government, Kerekou established a one-party Revolutionary National Assembly of 350 members that began meeting in February 1980.

## BHUTAN

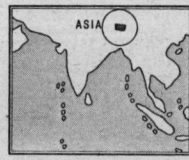 

**Official Name:** Kingdom of Bhutan.
**Area:** 18,147 square miles (47,000 sq. km.).
**Population:** 1,312,770.
**Capital:** Thimphu, 8,922.
**Government:** Constitutional monarchy.
**King:** Jigme Singye Wangchuk (reigned since 1972).
**Legislature:** *National Assembly (Tsongdu),* not more than 150 members.
**Flag:** Yellow triangle above orange one, divided diagonally; white dragon in center.
**Official Language:** Druk-ke.
**Religions:** Buddhism (75%), Hinduism (25%).
**Ethnic Groups:** Bhotia (60%), Nepalese (25%), Lepcha and Santal (15%).
**Leading Industries:** Agriculture (rice, corn, wheat, barley, yaks, fruits); forestry; handicrafts; mining (dolomite, coal).
**Foreign Trade:** *major exports*—postage stamps, rice, dolomite, handicrafts, fruits; *major imports*—kerosene, sugar, textiles.
**Places of Interest:** Royal residences in Punakka and Thimphu; fortified town of Wangdu Phodrang; 16th century bridge over Sankosh River; Buddhist monasteries.

### BHUTAN TODAY

Bhutan, a small country in the eastern Himalayan hill area, is bordered on the north by the Tibet region of China and on the south by India.

The terrain varies from the icy 24,000-foot peaks of the Himalaya to the steamy jungles of the southern lowland. Between these extremes lie eight fertile valleys.

Most Bhutanese farm or raise yaks. Few know how to read and write. They produce enough food to support themselves without importing food products. The country's major source of revenue for foreign trade is money received from about 1,500 tourists yearly. India provides about $10 million a year in aid.

### HISTORY

Bhutan's early history is obscure. About 1630 a refugee Dukpa Lama from Tibet became the first Dharma Raja, with both spiritual and temporal powers. In the following centuries Bhutan was beset by internal rivalry among powerful penlops (governors). After a war in 1865 the British annexed part of southern Bhutan and in 1910 assumed control of Bhutan's foreign relations.

A hereditary monarchy was established in 1907. A government council selected Sir Ugyen Wangchuk as the country's first maharaja. He was succeeded in 1927 by his son, and in 1952 by his grandson Jigme Dorji Wangchuk. India in 1949 returned part of the lands previously annexed by Britain.

Jigme Singye Wangchuck, 16, succeeded to the throne upon the death of his father in 1972. The new king, the fourth of his line, was crowned at Thimphu on June 2, 1974.

# BOLIVIA

**Official Name:** Republic of Bolivia.
**Area:** 424,165 square miles (1,098,581 sq. km.).
**Population:** 5,120,530.
**Chief Cities:** La Paz, administrative capital, 654,713; Sucre, legal capital, 106,590; Santa Cruz, 237,128; Cochabamba, 194,156; Oruro, 124,091.
**Government:** Military dictatorship.
**President:** Gen. Luis García Meza Tejada (since 1980).
**National Congress:** *Senate,* 27 members; *Chamber of Deputies,* 117 members.
**Flag:** Stripes of red, gold, and green, with coat of arms on center stripe.
**Official Languages:** Spanish, Quechua, Aymará.
**Ethnic Groups:** Indian (65%), Cholo (mixed Indian-European descent; 25%), Spanish descent (10%).
**Official Religion:** Roman Catholicism (95%).
**Leading Industries:** Agriculture (potatoes, corn, sugarcane, cassava, cotton, barley, rice, wheat, coffee, bananas, llamas, alpacas); mining (tin, petroleum, natural gas, lead, zinc, copper, tungsten, bismuth, antimony, gold, sulfur, silver, iron ore); manufacturing (textiles, handicrafts, food processing).
**Foreign Trade:** *major exports*—tin, antimony, tungsten, zinc, silver, lead, oil, natural gas; *major imports*—flour, motor vehicles.
**Places of Interest:** Lake Titicaca; Chacaltaya ski resort; San Francisco Church and Tiwanaci ancient ruins in La Paz.

## BOLIVIA TODAY

A landlocked South American country, Bolivia has extensive natural resources. However, Bolivians have benefited little from them because of two disastrous wars and many revolutions.

Over half the people are Indians, who live in thatched mud huts and raise just enough food to feed their families. Corn and potatoes are the staples. Few Indians have gone to school, and most cannot read and write. Many work in the country's tin mines and oil fields.

Bolivia is divided into three regions. Two bleak Andean ranges that flank a high plateau (Altiplano) stretch along the Chilean border in the west. The valleys (Yungas) scar the eastern slopes of the Andes. The tropical plains (Llanos and Chaco) are in the east.

## SPANISH CONQUEST

Pre-Inca ruins, such as those at Tiahuanaco, indicate the existence of an early Indian civilization in Bolivia. About 1200 the country came under the rule of the Incas.

The Spanish conquest of the Inca empire, which began in 1532, brought the subjugation of the Bolivian region by 1538.

## INDEPENDENCE

Called Upper Peru under Spanish rule, Bolivia was one of the first colonies to rebel. Its War of Independence lasted from 1809 to 1825.

Bolivia became an independent republic on Aug. 6, 1825. It was named for its liberator, Gen. Simón Bolívar.

For most of its independent history, Bolivia has endured factional strife and dictators. It lost much of its territory in wars.

In 1879 Chile seized Bolivia's only exit to the ocean, the mineral-rich Atacama Desert.

In 1903 Brazil took a huge rubber-tree area.

From 1932 to 1935 Bolivia fought the bloody Chaco War with Paraguay. Paraguay was frustrated in trying to occupy the petroleum fields of the southeast, but Bolivia lost much land and suffered a humiliating defeat.

The Movement of the National Revolution (MNR), which seized power in 1952, gave equality to the Indian masses, began land reforms, and nationalized big foreign mining companies.

## MILITARY RULE

In 1964 Vice President René Barrientos Ortuño overthrew the government. He died in a plane crash in April 1969, and Vice President Luis Siles Salinas was named president.

Siles was ousted by a military coup on Sept. 26, 1969. Gen. Alfredo Ovando Candia assumed the presidency. Ovando was forced to resign on Oct. 6, 1970. Gen. Juan José Torres, a leftist, became president.

Col. Hugo Banzer Suárez overthrew Torres in August 1971, becoming president. All strikes and union activities were outlawed.

Bolivia conducted extensive negotiations with Chile and Peru in 1975–77 in an effort to obtain a land corridor to the Pacific Ocean. On July 6, 1976, Argentina granted Bolivia a free-port zone at Rosario on the Paraná River. When negotiations with Chile bogged down, Bolivia broke diplomatic relations with Chile on March 17, 1978, and both increased troops on their joint border.

Bolivia held its first presidential election in a dozen years on July 9, 1978, but fraud was so prevalent that a court annulled the results.

Air Force Gen. Juan Pereda Asbún, the military junta's presidential candidate in the disputed election, seized power on July 21, 1978, deposing Banzer and making himself president. Four months later, on Nov. 24, 1978, Army Gen. David Padilla Arancibia ousted Pereda.

Under Gen. Padilla's guidance, Bolivia made a new effort to return to democracy in 1979. A national election was held on July 1, 1979, for a new congress and a civilian president. Because none of the eight presidential candidates received a majority of the popular vote, choice of a new president was left to congress. Unable to agree on any of the presidential candidates, congress decided on Aug. 6, 1979, to give the presidency on an interim basis to Walter Guevara Arze, 68, a former foreign minister.

Conservative Col. Alberto Natusch Busch overthrew Guevara on Nov. 1, 1979. When the people of La Paz demonstrated against his attempt to return the country to military rule, Natusch's troops and planes fired into the crowds, killing about 60 persons.

The Bolivian Congress, supported by former

**BOLIVIA** *(continued)*

president Padilla, refused to accept Natusch as the country's leader. Natusch agreed to step down on Nov. 16, and the president of Congress, Lydia Gueiler Tejada, 51, was chosen by that body as the nation's interim president.

In a national election on June 29, 1980, 67-year-old Hernan Siles Suazo, a leftist former president, won a plurality in the race for president against 13 other candidates, including four other former presidents.

With support from the militiary dictatorship of neighboring Argentina, army commander Gen. Luis García Meza Tejada overthrew the government on July 17, 1980, to prevent the new president from taking office. He launched a campaign of terror against opponents, arresting and killing hundreds. The U.S. cut off all military and economic aid to the new regime.

Siles Suazo announced from hiding on Aug. 6, 1980, the day he was supposed to take office as president, that he was forming an underground government to fight the military dictatorship. The nation's 50,000 miners refused to work for the new government, but Gen. Garcia Meza sent troops to attack mining villages and cut off food supplies to the mining areas.

## BOPHUTHATSWANA

**Official Name:** Republic of Bophuthatswana.
**Area:** 15,610 square miles (40,430 sq. km.).
**Population:** 1,298,500.
**Leading Cities:** Mmabatho, capital, 5,000; GaRanku-wa, 72,518; Mabopane, 64,854; Mafikeng, 10,000.
**Government:** Republic.
**President:** Chief L.M, Mangope (since 1977).
**National Assembly:** 96 members (48 elected).
**Flag:** Dark blue background divided by diagonal orange bar; leopard's head in white circle in upper hoist corner.
**Official Languages:** Tswana, English, Afrikaans.
**Chief Ethnic Group:** Tswana (Western Sotho of Bantus).
**Main Religion:** Animism.
**Leading Industries:** Agriculture (wheat, corn, peanuts, vegetables, alfalfa, cotton, cattle, sheep, goats); manufacturing (food processing, pottery, furniture, textiles, plastics); mining (platinum, asbestos, iron ore, manganese, chrome, vanadium, diamonds).
**Foreign Trade:** *major exports*—asbestos, chrome, diamonds, iron ore, manganese, platinum; *major imports*—consumer goods, food.
**Places of Interest:** *In Mmabatho:* government buildings; Babeligi industrial area, north of Pretoria.

### BOPHUTHATSWANA TODAY

Although declared an independent nation by South Africa, Bophuthatswana has failed to gain recognition as sovereign by any other country.

Given its freedom as part of South Africa's apartheid policy of separating the races, Bophuthatswana is made up of six areas separated by land that remains part of South Africa. Two regions lie along the boundary of Botswana.

Bophuthatswana is the main source of platinum for Western industrial countries.

Several large South African cities lie adjacent to parts of Bophuthatswana, including Pretoria, South Africa's administrative capital.

### HISTORY

The Bantu-speaking Sotho tribes, from which the Tswana are descended, migrated to southern Africa in the 900s to 1600s. About 75 Tswana tribes developed, often warring with each other.

By the 1700s the Tswana were living in large villages with houses made of stone.

In the 1820s and 1830s life in the region was disrupted by invasions of tribes driven from the coastal areas by European colonists.

By the late 1800s white colonists had brought an end to the tribal wars. The remaining Tswana tribes moved back to their original homelands.

In 1961 a Tswana territorial authority was established. Eleven years later, on June 1, 1972, the territory was given self-government.

In the first national election, on Oct. 4, 1972, the Bophuthatswana National Party (BNP) won 20 of the 24 elective seats. BNP leader Chief L.M. Mangope became chief minister of the Bophuthatswana government.

Bophuthatswana was granted independence on Dec. 6, 1977, by South Africa, which at the same time deprived the 1 million Tswana who live and work in South Africa of South African citizenship.

Chief Mangope became Bophuthatswana's first president, his party having won control of the national assembly in an election held on Aug. 24, 1977. During the election campaign, Chief H.T.R. Masseloane's National Party opposed independence for Bophuthatswana.

A new capital, Mmabatho, was built in 1977, just outside the South African city of Mafeking.

South Africa on Sept. 19, 1980, transferred the city of Mafeking to Bophuthatswana, which changed the name to Mafikeng.

## BOTSWANA

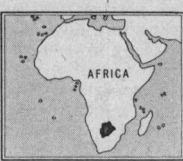
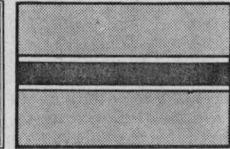

**Official Name:** Republic of Botswana.
**Area:** 231,805 square miles (600,372 sq. km.).
**Population:** 800,323.
**Capital:** Gaborone, 18,799.
**Government:** Parliamentary democracy.
**President:** Quett Masire (since 1980).
**Legislature:** *National Assembly,* 36 members.
**U.S. Ambassador to Botswana:** Horace G. Dawson Jr.
**Botswana Ambassador to U.S. :** Bias Mookodi.
**Flag:** Wide light-blue bands separated from a central black band by narrow white stripes.
**Languages:** English (official), Bantu (Tswana).
**Main Ethnic Group:** Tswana (98%).
**Religion:** Animism (85%).
**Leading Industries:** Agriculture (cattle, corn, sorghum); mining (diamonds, copper, nickel, manganese, coal); tourism; food processing.

Foreign Trade: *major exports*—meat, hides, diamonds, manganese; *major imports*—grains, fuels, motor vehicles, textiles, clothing.

Places of Interest: Kalahari Desert; Okavango swamps; Makarikari salt pans; game and bird sanctuaries; Gaborone gambling casino; Stone Age rock paintings on cliffs of Tsodilo Hills.

## BOTSWANA TODAY

The southern African country of Botswana is one of the few nations on the continent that has maintained a multiparty democracy since attaining independence. However, Botswana remains economically dependent on South Africa.

With about the same area and climate as Texas, Botswana has specialized for many years in cattle raising. Most of the people follow a tribal way of life that has changed little in hundreds of years.

Tourists from Rhodesia and South Africa visit Botswana to gamble at the casino in Gaborone and to hunt, fish, bird-watch, and photograph at the parks in the Okavango delta region, the Chobe game park, and the Khutse game reserve.

Most of Botswana's exports and imports pass through South Africa and parts of Bophuthatswana, which lie to the south. Zambia and Zimbabwe border Botswana on the northeast. Namibia is to the west and north.

The Kalahari Desert covers much of the south. The Okavango River forms an extensive swamp in the northwest.

## HISTORY

Under Khama the Great and other chiefs, the Bechuana (Tswana) people sought British protection against the Transvaal Boers in the 1880s. Britain established the Bechuanaland Protectorate in 1885. In 1909–55 it was threatened by incorporation into South Africa.

In 1948 the country was thrown into turmoil when Oxford-educated Seretse Khama, heir to the throne of the leading Bamandwato tribe, married a white English girl, Ruth Williams. He was forced by the British to live in exile. When he renounced his claim to the chieftainship, he was allowed to return to Bechuanaland in 1956.

Organizing the Bechuanaland Democratic Party, Khama helped lead his people to self-government. In the first general election, in 1965, his party won an overwhelming majority, and he became chief minister.

The nation achieved full independence on Sept. 30, 1966, and was renamed Botswana. Sir Seretse Khama was elected by the national assembly as the first president of the new republic. He was reelected in 1969, 1974, and 1979 when his Botswana Democratic Party (BDP) again won parliamentary elections.

The discovery of substantial mineral deposits in Botswana in the 1970s stimulated its impoverished economy. British and American interests developed a diamond mine at Orapa. A large copper-nickel mine began production at Selbi-Pikwe in 1975. The country's GNP grew at an annual rate of about 20%.

Upon the death of Sir Seretse Khama in 1980, he was succeeded as president by Dr. Quett Masire, who had served as vice president.

# BRAZIL

 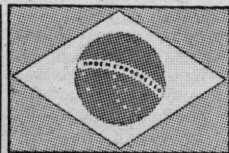

Official Name: Federative Republic of Brazil.
Area: 3,286,488 square miles (8,511,965 sq. km.).
Population: 123,675,000.
Largest Metropolitan Areas: Brasília, capital, 763,254; São Paulo, 7,198,608; Rio de Janeiro, 4,857,716; Belo Horizonte, 1,557,464; Recife, 1,249,821; Salvador, 1,237,393; Fortaleza, 1,109,839; Pôrto Alegre, 1,043,964.
Government: Republic under military rule.
President: Gen. João Figueiredo (since 1979).
National Congress: *Senate,* 67 members; *Chamber of Deputies,* 420 members.
U.S. Ambassador to Brazil: Robert M. Sayre.
Brazilian Ambassador to U.S.: Antonio da Silveira.
Flag: Green field with centered yellow diamond enclosing blue globe with 22 stars (five of which form Southern Cross) and motto "Ordem e Progresso."
Main Ethnic Groups: European descent (62%), mixed European-Indian-black (26%).
Official Language: Portuguese.
Main Religion: Roman Catholicism (93%).
Leading Industries: Agriculture (cattle, coffee, corn, rice, sugarcane, rubber, cocoa, soybeans); manufacturing (steel, automobiles, plastics, paper, alcohol, chemicals, machinery, consumer goods); mining (iron ore, manganese, coal, petroleum, bauxite, nickel); construction.
Foreign Trade: *major exports*—industrial products, cocoa, coffee, soybeans, sugar, iron ore; *major imports*—petroleum, wheat, machinery.
Places of Interest: Brasília; Rio de Janeiro; Christ of Corcovado statue; Amazon River; Iguassú Falls; Portuguese colonial sites at Salvador; Ouro Preto, Congonhas, Sabara—the "Cities of Gold"; Ipiranga Museum and Monument at São Paulo; St. John del Rey gold mine; Copacabana and Santos beach resorts; scenic highway between São Paulo and Santos.

## BRAZIL TODAY

The world's fifth-largest country in area, Brazil also is the seventh largest in population. As such, it faces many major problems.

Brazil's government is dominated by military leaders who prevent constitutional democracy from functioning and restrict freedom in the name of national security and stability. A high percentage of Brazilians live in poverty in the cities and in rural areas.

Brazil has made tremendous strides in industrializing its economy. By the 1980's exports of industrial products exceeded those of agricultural products. However, this was accomplished at the expense of political and civil liberties.

Almost as large as the United States, but with half as many people, Brazil has huge undeveloped areas in the interior along the Amazon River. The Amazon basin accounts for 60% of Brazil's area but contains only 8% of its population. The government has made a concerted effort to open up and settle the western region. One of the keys to this program has been

QUICK QUIZ: What is the geographic center of the United States? See page 180.

**BRAZIL** *(continued)*

the construction of a $100 million 3,500-mile Trans-Amazon Highway, begun in 1970. The highway has created boom towns along its route, just as the coming of the railroads once brought boom towns in the western U.S. Settlers are given interest-free loans to start farms.

The same spirit of lawlessness and treatment of Indians that marked the American West is prevalent on the new Brazilian frontier. Indians wearing war paint have attacked settlers and highway construction crews invading their territory. In turn the Indians often have been mistreated and killed with little provocation. Only about 100,000 Indians survive of the 1 to 5 million who once lived in Brazil.

The country has vast natural resources, but must import about 80% of the petroleum it uses.

## GEOGRAPHY

Occupying almost half the South American continent, Brazil is bordered on the north by French Guiana, Surinam, Guyana, Venezuela, and Colombia. Peru and Bolivia lie to the west. Paraguay and Argentina are to the southwest and Uruguay to the south.

A tropical climate prevails in the Amazon River basin in the north. Over half the country's area consists of highlands between 650 and 3,000 feet above sea level, where the climate is temperate. Brazil's major waterways are the Amazon, the second-longest river in the world, the Paraná, and the São Francisco.

## PORTUGUESE DISCOVERY AND COLONIZATION

In 1500 Pedro Álvares Cabral, a Portuguese admiral, claimed the region for his country. In 1532 Martim Afonso de Sousa founded the first colony at São Vicente and introduced sugarcane cultivation. When Brazil became the major source of sugar in the 17th century, many Negro slaves were imported.

Between 1693 and 1700 mineral wealth was discovered in central Brazil, and the region flourished for a century as a major world supplier of gold and diamonds. By 1763 Rio de Janeiro had replaced Salvador as the colony's capital. In 1808, after Napoleon's capture of Lisbon, Portugal's royal family fled to Brazil. Rio became the seat of the Portuguese empire.

## BRAZILIAN EMPIRE

King João VI returned to Portugal in 1821, leaving his son, Dom Pedro, as regent. In 1822, acceding to widespread demands for liberty, Dom Pedro became Pedro I, emperor of an independent Brazil. His popularity diminished, and in 1831 he abdicated in favor of his son Pedro de Alcântara (Pedro II), who governed until 1889. The progressive rule of Pedro II laid the foundation of modern Brazil.

Foreign demand for rubber stimulated the growth of such cities as Belém and Manaus.

The abolition of slavery in 1888 fanned rebellion as the owners of plantations supported the republican movement.

## REPUBLIC OF BRAZIL

In 1889 a bloodless revolt established the United States of Brazil, with Manuel Deodoro da Fonseca as first president.

By 1914 Brazil had gained political stability and international recognition. The country's rubber monopoly ended, however, with the development of plantations in Southeast Asia.

In 1930 a revolution brought Getúlio Vargas to the presidency. His regime degenerated into a dictatorship and was overthrown in 1945. Vargas became president again in 1950, this time by popular vote, but a serious political crisis led to his suicide in 1954.

Juscelino Kubitschek, elected president in 1955, initiated heavy construction programs and industrial expansion. He created a new capital, Brasília, in the country's wilderness to encourage development of the interior.

Jânio Quadros, elected president in 1960 by the largest plurality vote in Brazil's history, failed to stem the economic crisis. He resigned after seven months. João Goulart, the vice president, took over in 1961. His 30-month regime was marked by economic slowdowns, strikes, riots, and inflation. Goulart turned increasingly leftward.

## MILITARY RULE

A military uprising forced Goulart into exile in 1964. Congress elected Marshal Humberto de Alencar Castello Branco interim president. In 1966 the same congress elected Marshal Artur da Costa e Silva to a 4-year presidential term.

Faced with growing opposition from members of the national assembly, President Costa e Silva yielded to right-wing military pressure and arrested opposition political leaders. He dissolved the national assembly, suspended constitutional rights, imposed strict censorship, and seized total power on Dec. 13, 1968. He suffered a stroke and died in December 1969.

A triumvirate of Brazil's military leaders named Gen. Emilio Garrastazú Médici to the presidency on Oct. 7, 1969. He set up ambitious economic and social goals, including redistribution of wealth. Prosperity made him popular.

Gen. Ernesto Geisel was sworn in as president on March 15, 1974, having been chosen to succeed Médici by the military leadership.

Work got under way in 1976 on the world's biggest hydroelectric project—the Itaipu Dam on the Paraná River, which will cost about $9 billion by the time it is completed in the 1980s.

High coffee prices in 1977 helped turn Brazil's economy around, overcoming part of the imbalance in foreign trade that had been caused by soaring oil prices since 1973.

The military government's emphasis on industrialization caused the nation's gross national product to increase five-fold during the decade of the 1970's—from about $40 billion to $200 billion annually.

Despite objections by U.S. President Carter, Brazil went ahead in 1977 with plans to purchase from West Germany nuclear reactors and plants to enrich and process uranium. Carter had pointed out that the plants could lead to the proliferation of nuclear weapons, giving Brazil the capability of making its own atomic bombs.

Because the U.S. State Department criticized human-rights practices in Brazil, the government in March 1977 canceled its 25-year-old military

assistance treaty with the U.S. and rejected $50 million in American military aid for 1978.

The military regime also took action in April 1977 to strengthen its hold on the government. President Geisel decreed that future presidents would continue to be chosen indirectly rather than by public election, as would state governors and one-third of the senate.

President Geisel extended his own term of office by an additional year to six years and made it possible for a simple majority in congress to approve a constitutional amendment instead of the previous two-thirds majority.

Despite the opposition of Roman Catholic leaders, the Brazilian congress passed legislation in 1977 legalizing divorce in what is the world's largest Roman Catholic country.

President Carter visited Brazil on March 29–30, 1978, receiving a rather cool reception from the nation's military leaders who still resented criticisms by the U.S. government about their restrictions on human rights for Brazilians.

However, during the next several months the government relaxed several of its limitations on human rights. For the first time in a decade, unions were allowed to strike against private employers. In June the government ended its pre-publication censorship of newspapers, but continued controls on radio and TV broadcasting.

Gen. João Baptista de Figueiredo, chief of the national intelligence service, was elected president by a special 592-member electoral college in 1978. He took office on March 15, 1979, pledging to return his country to full civilian control at the end of his 6-year term.

The government announced plans in 1979 to reduce dependency on imported petroleum by investing $5 billion through 1985 to produce alcohol fuel from sugarcane and other farm crops. Plans called for auto manufacturers to produce nearly 2 million cars to use 100% alcohol as fuel, while other automobiles would use a gasohol mixture including 20% alcohol.

President Figueiredo signed an amnesty on Aug. 28, 1979, that permitted an estimated 5,000 political exiles to return to Brazil in the following months. The amnesty excluded about 200 persons accused of acts of political violence. The government announced it had freed its last political prisoner on Oct. 8, 1980.

In an effort to stem inflation, the government devalued the cruzeiro by 30% in December 1979. However, in 1980 inflation rose to an annual rate of 109%.

Rightist terrorists opposed to the government's liberalization policies and especially to the lack of censorship of leftist publications stepped up bombing attacks in 1980, killing scores of liberal leaders and known criminals.

Despite efforts by the government to increase agricultural production to make the nation self-sufficient in growing food, recurrent droughts in 1978–80 seriously damaged crops.

The Roman Catholic Church again called on the government in 1980 to break up landed estates and end the country's feudal system of sharecropping, pointing out that only 1% of rural families own half of the agricultural land.

# BRITAIN

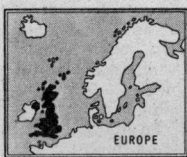

**Official Name:** United Kingdom of Great Britain and Northern Ireland.
**Area:** 94,227 square miles (244,046 sq. km.).
**Population:** 55,975,200.
**Largest Metropolitan Areas:** London, capital, 7,167,600; Manchester, 2,389,260; Birmingham, 2,358,980; Leeds, 1,735,700; Glasgow, 1,727,625; Liverpool, 1,226,310.
**Government:** Constitutional monarchy.
**Prime Minister:** Margaret Thatcher (since 1979).
**Queen:** Elizabeth II (since 1952).
**Parliament:** *House of Lords,* 1,075 members; *House of Commons,* 635 members.
**U.S. Ambassador to Britain:** Kingman Brewster Jr.
**British Ambassador to U.S.:** Sir Nicholas Henderson.
**Flag:** The Union Jack, combination of red-on-white crosses of England's St. George and Ireland's St. Patrick, with white-on-blue cross of Scotland's St. Andrew.
**Main Religions:** Anglicanism (66%), Roman Catholicism (9%), Presbyterianism (2%).
**Languages:** English (official), Gaelic, Irish, Welsh.
**Leading Industries:** Manufacturing (steel, machinery, cement, paper, electricity, motor vehicles, chemicals, aluminum, textiles, consumer goods); agriculture (sheep, cattle, dairy products, poultry, barley, potatoes, sugar beets, wheat, oats, fruits, vegetables); mining (coal, iron ore, natural gas, tin, petroleum); tourism; fishing.
**Foreign Trade:** *major exports*—machinery, motor vehicles, metals and metal products, chemicals and drugs, textiles; *major imports*—food products, raw materials and fuels, machinery, motor vehicles, petroleum.
**Places of Interest:** *England*—Windsor Castle; Hampton Court; Shakespeare country around Stratford; Brighton; Lake District; Stonehenge; Devon and Cornwall; Oxford and Cambridge university towns; cathedral towns; Bath. *In London*—Westminster Abbey; Tower of London; Buckingham Palace; British Museum; Museum of London. *Wales*—Tintern Abbey; Caernarvon Castle. *Scotland*—Edinburgh; Scottish Highlands; the Trossachs. *Northern Ireland*—Giant's Causeway; County Fermanagh.

## BRITAIN TODAY

An island kingdom that once was the most powerful nation in the world, Britain faces many serious economic problems. With the loss of the bulk of its worldwide empire in the past three decades, Britain today is a nation only half as large as its ancient rival France.

Britain is a union of England, Scotland, Wales, and Northern Ireland. A scattering of islands and small territories around the world still are British colonies and dependencies. But most of Britain's former colonies have been granted complete independence. Many, such as Australia and Canada, retain membership in the British Commonwealth of Nations.

Britain was the birthplace of the Industrial

**BRITAIN** *(continued)*

Revolution in the mid-1700s and became the world's first industrial nation. But with the loss of the captive markets of its major colonies, Britain has been unable to compete successfully in today's free-for-all foreign trade. As recently as 1958 Britain ranked second only to the United States in world trade, but today it stands fifth in the value of its exports behind the U.S., West Germany, Japan, and France.

The British people also have seen a decline in their standard of living. The per capita gross domestic product has fallen to about half that of the United States. Because Britain must import much of the food its people eat and many of the raw materials its factories process, the nation has been hard hit by worldwide inflation. The average Briton has to pay taxes equal to about a third of his income.

The idea that many problems might be solved by membership in the European Common Market, accomplished in 1973, has proved illusory. However, a bright hope for Britain's future developed in the 1970s–1980s as offshore oil discoveries promised petroleum self-sufficiency.

### EARLY HISTORY

A people called the Iberians are thought to have inhabited Britain during the Stone Age. Sometime before the 500s B.C. Celtic tribes from northern Europe began a centuries-long series of invasions. Troops under Julius Caesar landed in Britain in 55 B.C. By A.D. 142 Rome held all the land to the River Clyde, where Hadrian's Wall was put up to keep out the Picts of Scotland. The Romans introduced Christianity.

As their empire declined, the Romans withdrew their legions, and Germanic invaders from northern Europe—Angles, Saxons, and Jutes—took their place in Britain. Driving the Britons west to Wales and Cornwall, they formed the kingdoms of Kent, Essex, Wessex, Sussex, East Anglia, Mercia, and Northumbria in the south and east between 500 and 800.

Late in the 700s Danish Vikings began to harass the Anglo-Saxon kingdoms. In the 860s the Danes invaded the island. By 1016 Canute, a Dane, was king of England, and Anglo-Saxon rule was over, except for a brief period under Edward the Confessor.

### MIDDLE AGES

In 1066 a Norman duke, William the Conqueror, led the last successful invasion of Britain. He became William I (1066–87) of England when his Norman troops beat a force of Anglo-Saxons under Harold at Hastings. William imposed a feudal system.

The first Plantagenet ruler, Henry II (1154–89), began the conquest of Ireland.

Feudal nobles forced King John (1199–1216) to approve the Magna Carta in 1215, the first step toward the parliamentary system.

Edward I (1272–1307), who completed the conquest of Wales in 1282, enlarged parliament, increasing its powers. In 1296 he conquered Scotland, but the defeat of his son Edward II (1307–27) at Bannockburn by Robert the Bruce in 1314 restored Scottish independence, which England recognized by treaty in 1328. Long-

standing English claims to French territory and commercial rivalry with France precipitated the Hundred Years War (1338–1453). In 1346 Edward III (1327–77) invaded Normandy. He crushed the French at Crécy in 1346. Ten years later his son Edward, the Black Prince, won a second victory for England at Poitiers.

The war continued under Henry IV (1399–1413), Britain's first ruler of the Lancastrian line. Henry V (1413–22) routed the French at Agincourt (1415) and was acknowledged heir to the throne of France. After Henry's death the French rallied under Joan of Arc. The French victory at Orléans was the first of a series which, in time, left England only the port of Calais.

At the end of the Hundred Years War the rival families of York and Lancaster began a bloody struggle for the English throne: the Wars of the Roses (1455–85). Henry Tudor, a Lancastrian, ended the wars by defeating Richard III (1483–85) of York at Bosworth Field in 1485, and founded the Tudor dynasty as Henry VII (1485–1509).

### REFORMATION

Henry VIII (1509–47) broke with the pope when denied the right to divorce the first of his six wives. He then claimed supreme authority over the Catholic Church in England. Under Henry, the Church of England emerged as Anglican Protestant. His eldest daughter, Mary (1553–58), restored Catholicism as the state religion, but supremacy of the Protestant Church of England was permanently reestablished by another of Henry's daughters, Elizabeth I (1558–1603).

### BUILDING A COLONIAL EMPIRE

Elizabeth's reign was one of the glories of English history. The defeat of the Spanish Armada in 1588 made England a major naval power. The previous year Mary Stuart, Queen of Scots, a Catholic rival for the throne, had been executed. Men of daring such as Sir Walter Raleigh and Sir Francis Drake staked out an overseas empire. Men of genius such as William Shakespeare and Francis Bacon brought a flowering of English arts and science.

Elizabeth was succeeded by James VI of Scotland, the Protestant son of Mary Stuart. Ruling over Scotland and England as James I (1603–25), he established the first English colonies in North America at Jamestown and Plymouth.

### COMMONWEALTH AND RESTORATION

Conflict with parliament arose from James' belief in the divine right of kings. His son Charles I (1625–49) aggravated the conflict. Civil war broke out in 1642 between his supporters and the Puritan partisans of parliament. Oliver Cromwell led the Puritans to victory, and King Charles was captured and beheaded in 1649.

England, now a commonwealth, was governed by parliamentary committee until 1653, when Cromwell dismissed parliament and ruled as Lord Protector, or dictator.

In 1660, two years after Cromwell's death, the monarchy was restored with the popular reign of Charles II (1660–85), a Stuart. The austere Puritan social code was replaced by a renewed sense of freedom. Political and religious strife re-

turned when Charles was succeeded by his brother
James II (1685–88), who reasserted the discredited divine right of kings and plotted to restore
Roman Catholicism. James was deposed in 1688,
without bloodshed, in the "Glorious Revolution."
His Protestant daughter Mary and her husband,
William of Orange, the ruler of Holland, were
invited to govern England. The rule of William III
(1689–1702) and Mary II (1689–94) ushered in a
period of political stability. The Bill of Rights was
passed, parliament became supreme, and political
parties were established.

## CREATING THE UNITED KINGDOM

Under Queen Anne (1702–14), last of the
Protestant Stuarts, the Act of Union (1707)
created the United Kingdom of Great Britain by
uniting Scotland with England and Wales.

Anne's death brought her German cousin
George I (1714–27), the first of the Hanover line,
to the throne. Like him, his son and successor
George II (1727–60) spoke little English. The
parliament became more powerful than the king.
Under George II Britain added to its empire,
chiefly at the expense of Bourbon France,
emerging from the Seven Years War (1756–63) in
possession of India and of North America from
the Atlantic coastline to the Mississippi River.

King George III (1760–1820) dismissed Wil-
liam Pitt the Elder, the prime minister responsible
for Britain's colonial successes. He then attempted
to impose his own views on parliament. In the
American Revolution (1775–83) all the North
American colonies except Canada were lost.
Following the defeat of Napoleon (1815) by an
army under the command of the Duke of
Wellington, Britain acquired new colonies in the
Mediterranean, the Caribbean, Africa, and Asia.

## INDUSTRIAL REVOLUTION

The Industrial Revolution, which began in the
mid-1700s, gave Britain the world's first industrial economy. But the factory system brought
many abuses to workers.

The first of a series of reforms, in 1832,
extended the right to vote to the middle classes
and made parliament more truly representative.
In the following year child-labor and factory-
inspection laws were passed, and slavery was
abolished in the colonies. Repeal of the Corn
Laws in 1846 was intended to lower the price of
grain for ordinary consumers. Prime Minister
Benjamin Disraeli's Reform Bill of 1867 extended voting privileges to many factory laborers.
Prime Minister William Gladstone's Reform Bill
of 1884 established universal male suffrage.

Many of these reforms occurred during the
long reign of Queen Victoria (1837–1901),
which also witnessed the transfer of India from
rule by the British East India Company to the
British crown (1859) and the annexation of
South Africa after the Boer War (1899–1902).
The globe-girdling British Empire, rich, stable,
and prosperous, was at the peak of its power.

## WORLD WARS I AND II

Britain allied itself with its traditional enemy,
France, in 1904. Ten years later Britain and
France fought World War I against the empires
of Germany and Austria-Hungary. Under Prime
Minister David Lloyd George, Britain emerged
victorious. To its empire were added former
German colonies in Africa and former Turkish
provinces in the Middle East.

World War I marked the end of British
expansion. Ireland's rebellion (1916–21) ended
with the division of the island into the Irish Free
State and Northern Ireland. Britain was racked by
economic upheaval and severe unemployment in
the worldwide depression beginning in 1929.

Britain granted independence in 1931 to
Australia, Canada, Ireland, New Zealand, and
South Africa, which became the first members
of the British Commonwealth of Nations.

In 1936 Edward VIII abdicated to marry an
American divorcée, a marriage disapproved of
by the Church of England and the cabinet. His
brother became king as George VI.

Hoping to avoid another war, Neville Chamberlain's government adopted a policy of ap-
peasement toward Nazi Germany. But when
Hitler's troops invaded Poland in 1939, Britain
immediately declared war on Germany.

During World War II the British people
rallied under the inspired leadership of Prime
Minister Winston Churchill and held out against
intensive air attacks by Nazi bombers.

## SOCIALIST BRITAIN

The return to peace was marked by popular
demand for radical change. In July 1945 the
Labour Party, led by Clement Attlee, won an
overwhelming electoral victory. In the next six
years the Labour Party made Britain a socialist
nation, nationalizing such basic industries as
coal mines, steel mills, the railways, and the
Bank of England. An extensive social-welfare
program included socialized medicine.

The Labour government in 1947 granted independence within the Commonwealth to India
and Pakistan, heralding the end of Britain's empire. In the following decades most of Britain's

## PRIME MINISTERS OF BRITAIN

| 1902-05 | Arthur J. Balfour | Conservative |
|---|---|---|
| 1905-08 | Henry Campbell-Bannerman | Liberal |
| 1908-16 | Herbert H. Asquith | Liberal |
| 1916-22 | David Lloyd George | Liberal |
| 1922-23 | Andrew Bonar Law | Conservative |
| 1923-24 | Stanley Baldwin | Conservative |
| 1924 | J. Ramsay MacDonald | Labour |
| 1924-29 | Stanley Baldwin | Conservative |
| 1929-35 | J. Ramsay MacDonald | Labour |
| 1935-37 | Stanley Baldwin | Conservative |
| 1937-40 | Neville Chamberlain | Conservative |
| 1940-45 | Winston Churchill | Conservative |
| 1945-51 | Clement R. Attlee | Labour |
| 1951-55 | Winston Churchill | Conservative |
| 1955-57 | Anthony Eden | Conservative |
| 1957-63 | Harold Macmillan | Conservative |
| 1963-64 | Alexander Douglas-Home | Conservative |
| 1964-70 | Harold Wilson | Labour |
| 1970-74 | Edward Heath | Conservative |
| 1974-76 | Harold Wilson | Labour |
| 1976-79 | James Callaghan | Labour |
| 1979- | Margaret Thatcher | Conservative |

QUICK QUIZ: What is the highest mountain in Europe? See page 183.

**BRITAIN** *(continued)*

remaining colonies received independence.

Churchill returned to power in 1951–55. King George VI died in 1952, and his daughter became Queen Elizabeth II.

The Labour Party won elections in 1964, making Harold Wilson prime minister. Conservatives led by Edward Heath won control in June 1970.

Britain joined the European Economic Community (the Common Market) on Jan. 1, 1973. The action marked the end of a 10-year effort by Britain to enter the Common Market. Entry had been delayed by the opposition of President Charles de Gaulle of France.

Britain was hard hit by the Arab oil embargo that began in October 1973. The crisis worsened with a nationwide strike by coal miners in February 1974. A parliamentary election called for Feb. 28, 1974, resulted in neither the Conservative nor Labour Party receiving a majority, although Labour won the largest number of seats. Wilson again became prime minister, met the coal miners' wage demands, and ended the crisis.

Prime Minister Wilson called new parliamentary elections on Oct. 10, 1974, in which his Labour Party won a firm majority in the House of Commons for the next five years.

Because many Britons blamed the nation's slumping economy on its membership in the European Common Market, the Labour government set an unprecedented national referendum on the issue for June 5, 1975. In the voting 67.2% of the people supported continued British participation. The 2 to 1 majority was viewed as a major triumph for Labour.

On March 16, 1976, Prime Minister Wilson announced his retirement from public life. The Labour Party chose as his successor Foreign Minister James Callaghan, who was sworn in as prime minister on April 5.

The worst drought in 250 years struck Britain in the spring and summer of 1976, damaging crops and reducing water supplies.

Reflecting Britain's declining prestige, the value of the pound dropped as low as $1.57 late in October 1976—35% lower than its value of $2.40 in 1975.

The House of Lords in November 1976 prevented the socialist Labour government from adding the aircraft and shipbuilding industries to those nationalized.

Racial tensions caused by an influx of some 2 million black and Asian immigrants in the 1960s and 1970s brought race riots in 1977.

**FIRST WOMAN PRIME MINISTER**

The nation's continuing inflation and a wave of strikes as labor unions sought large wage increases brought increasing disenchantment with Callaghan's government. On March 28, 1979, he became the first prime minister in 55 years to be forced out of office by a parliamentary no-confidence vote.

In a national election on May 3, 1979, the Conservative Party won a landslide victory with a 43-seat majority in the House of Commons. Conservative leader Margaret Thatcher, 53, became Britain's first woman prime minister, promising to move the nation away from socialism.

During their first few months in office in 1979,

the Conservatives cut government spending by about $9 billion, reduced government controls on business, and announced plans for income tax cuts and restrictions on labor unions. The sales tax was raised to 15%. The government also began selling to private investors $2 billion of shares in nationalized industries. But by mid-1979 Britain's inflation rate was more than 16%, higher than that of any other industrialized nation.

Increasing production of petroleum from the North Sea enabled Britain to reduce its imports of foreign oil in 1979 and 1980.

As Britain slid deeper into recession in 1980, Prime Minister Thatcher in a TV address said:

"Change cannot be painless, particularly at a time of world recession and rapidly rising oil prices. But much of what we are going through today is the result of past folly and neglect. After any major operation you feel worse before you convalesce. But you don't refuse the operation when you know that without it you won't survive."

In an effort to control inflation, the Conservative government cut government expenditures in 1980 and raised gasoline taxes. Unemployment soared to more than 2 million persons by August—the largest number of jobless Britons since the Great Depression in 1935. And it continued to climb, reaching a rate of 8.5% of the whole force in October 1980. Inflation also continued to rise, reaching an annual rate of 21.9%.

However, there were a few good signs in the 1980 economy as reduced imports shrank Britain's trade deficit and the value of the pound sterling reached the 1973 level of $2.46.

The Conservatives took further steps to get the government out of private business, ending the Post Office monopoly on delivering mail and telephone services. Plans also were announced to sell to their tenants some 6 million government-owned houses and apartments.

# THE FOUR COUNTRIES OF THE UNITED KINGDOM

## ENGLAND

**Area:** 50,333 square miles (130,362 sq. km.).
**Population:** 46,831,500.
**Capital:** London, 7,167,600 (metropolitan area).
**Members in House of Commons:** 516.

England is the largest of the four countries of the United Kingdom. It covers the southeastern three-fifths of the island of Great Britain. Its explorers and colonists spread the English language to all parts of the world and made London the capital of a worldwide empire. The history of England is detailed on preceding pages.

## WALES

**Area:** 8,017 square miles (20,764 sq. km.).
**Population:** 2,779,460.
**Capital:** Cardiff, 284,700.
**Members in House of Commons:** 36.

Wales is the third largest of the four countries of the United Kingdom.

Wales has huge reserves of coal that helped make Britain a leading industrial power.

When the Germanic Angles and Saxons conquered England in the 400s, the original Britons escaped to Wales, the mountainous western part of

the island of Great Britain. They preserved the independence of Wales until William the Conqueror proclaimed himself Lord of Wales in 1071.

English King Edward I claimed control of Wales in 1284. He started naming the heir to the English throne the Prince of Wales in 1301.

In 1536 Henry VIII of England united the two countries, giving the Welsh seats in the English parliament and making English the country's official language. In 1976 the Welsh language was returned to equal status with English in the schools. Bilingual road signs replaced English-only signs.

Nationalist demands for home rule suffered a setback on March 1, 1979, when voters rejected a plan for limited self-government.

## SCOTLAND

**Area:** 30,414 square miles (78,772 sq. km.).
**Population:** 5,153,090.
**Capital:** Edinburgh, 470,085.
**Largest Metropolitan Area:** Glasgow, 1,727,625.
**Members in House of Commons:** 71.

Scotland is the second largest of the four countries of the United Kingdom. A mountainous country, Scotland covers the northern third of the island of Great Britain.

When the Roman general Agricola conquered Scotland in A.D. 80, he called the country *Caledonia* and the people *Picts*, meaning painted, because they painted their bodies. In the 500s a Celtic tribe from Ireland, called the *Scots*, invaded and conquered Scotland.

In succeeding centuries English kings endeavored to make Scotland part of England, but the Scots resisted. In 1603 the Scottish king James VI inherited the English throne upon the death of Queen Elizabeth I. He became James I of England but ruled Scotland as a separate country.

During the reign of Queen Anne, the Scottish parliament voted in 1707 to unite with England and Wales to form the United Kingdom.

The discovery of oil and gas fields offshore from eastern Scotland in 1973–74 brought an economic boom. It also stimulated demands by Scottish nationalists for home rule and for Scotland to be given a major share of the oil revenues.

But a plan for home rule was defeated in a referendum on March 1, 1979, when fewer than 40% of Scotland's registered voters cast ballots in favor of the measure.

## NORTHERN IRELAND

**Area:** 5,463 square miles (14,148 sq. km.).
**Population:** 1,570,710.
**Capital:** Belfast, 362,400.
**Members in House of Commons:** 12.

The smallest of the four countries of the United Kingdom, Northern Ireland is the northeastern tip of the island of Ireland. About two-thirds of the people are Protestants and one-third Roman Catholics.

Because of Irish revolts against attempted English domination, England's King James I in 1603 forced Irish Roman Catholics in Northern Ireland to give up their land to English and Scottish Protestants whose descendants still constitute a majority in Northern Ireland.

# BRITISH COMMONWEALTH OF NATIONS

The Commonwealth of Nations is an association of countries and dependencies that formerly were part of the British Empire. Independent members voluntarily maintain trade and military ties.

## INDEPENDENT MEMBERS

| | | | |
|---|---|---|---|
| Australia | Grenada | New Zealand | Tanzania |
| Bahamas | Guyana | Nigeria | Tonga |
| Bangladesh | India | Papua | Trinidad- |
| Barbados | Jamaica | New Guinea | Tobago |
| Botswana | Kenya | Saint Lucia | Tuvalu |
| Britain | Kiribati | Saint Vincent | Uganda |
| Canada | Lesotho | Seychelles | Vanuatu |
| Cyprus | Malawi | Sierra Leone | Western Samoa |
| Dominica | Malaysia | Singapore | Zambia |
| Fiji | Malta | Solomons | Zimbabwe |
| Gambia | Mauritius | Sri Lanka | |
| Ghana | Nauru | Swaziland | |

## BRITISH COLONIES AND DEPENDENCIES

| | | |
|---|---|---|
| Anguilla | British Virgin | Montserrat |
| Antigua | Islands | Pitcairn |
| Belize | Cayman Islands | Islands |
| Bermuda | Channel Islands | Saint Helena |
| British Antarctic | Falkland Islands | St. Kitts-Nevis |
| Territory | Gibraltar | Turks and |
| British Indian Ocean | Hong Kong | Caicos Islands |
| Territory | Isle of Man | |

**PROTECTORATE:** Brunei

In 1801 the British parliament united all of Ireland with the United Kingdom. After a revolt in Ireland during World War I, Britain separated Northern Ireland from the rest of Ireland in 1920. The Protestant majority of Northern Ireland chose to remain part of the United Kingdom.

Seeking to unite all of Ireland, the outlawed Irish Republican Army (IRA) has carried on a campaign of assassinations and bombings against the Northern Ireland Protestants and British soldiers stationed in the country since 1969. Protestant extremists have retaliated.

On May 1, 1975, voters elected 78 members to a convention given the task of devising a government acceptable to both Protestants and Catholics. But the convention disbanded on March 3, 1976, after 10 months of futile efforts to write a new constitution. Britain announced it would continue direct rule of Northern Ireland.

In the 10-year period 1969–79 over 1,900 persons were killed and nearly 21,000 injured in shootings and bombings. On Aug. 27, 1979, the IRA shocked the world by assassinating the senior statesman of the British royal family, Earl Mountbatten of Burma, 79, near his vacation home in Ireland. In September 1979, Pope John Paul II begged the IRA to end its terrorism.

Britain made new efforts in 1980 to get Protestant and Catholic leaders of Northern Ireland to agree on a home-rule plan.

# BRITISH DEPENDENCIES

## ANGUILLA

**Area:** 35 square miles (91 sq. km.).
**Population:** 6,832.
**Capital:** The Valley.

One of the northernmost Caribbean islands, Anguilla lies about 160 miles east of Puerto Rico and

**BRITISH DEPENDENCIES** *(continued)*
about 60 miles north of St. Kitts. Fishing is the main industry.

The island first became a British colony about 1650. After being ruled from St. Kitts for two centuries, Anguillans revolted on May 30, 1967, demanding self-government. Two years later the islanders declared independence and announced the severing of all ties with Britain. British paratroops and London police invaded the island on March 19, 1969, and put down the revolt.

On Feb. 10, 1976, Britain granted Anguilla a constitution as a separate self-governing dependency. The People's Progressive Party led by Ronald Webster won 6 of the 7 seats in the national assembly elected on March 15, 1976.

When Webster lost a confidence vote in the assembly in 1977, the British governor-general named Emile Gumbs as chief minister.

Webster regained power as chief minister in 1980 when his Anguilla United Movement won 6 of the 7 elective seats in the legislative assembly.

## ANTIGUA

**Area:** 171 square miles (442 sq. km.).
**Population:** 77,004.
**Capital:** St. John's, 21,814.

The associated state of Antigua includes three eastern Caribbean islands: Antigua (108 sq. mi.), Barbuda (62 sq. mi.), and Redonda (0.5 sq. mi.).

Discovered by Christopher Columbus in 1493, Antigua was first colonized in 1632 by the British led by Sir Thomas Warner. Most of the people are descendants of African slaves. Tourism and agriculture are the main industries.

On Feb. 18, 1976, an election threw out of office the ruling Progressive Labour Movement (PLM), which had called for the island's independence. Vere Bird of the Antigua Labour Party (ALP) became prime minister.

Antigua and the United States signed an 11-year agreement in 1977 providing continued U.S. military installations on the island.

## BELIZE

**Area:** 8,867 square miles (22,965 sq. km.).
**Population:** 164,777.
**Cities:** Belmopan, capital, 3,000; Belize, 39,050.

Belize, formerly British Honduras, is bordered on the north by Mexico, on the west and south by Guatemala, and on the east by the Caribbean Sea. The land is generally low and jungle-covered. Rainfall ranges from 69 to 156 inches a year.

The first European settlers were shipwrecked British seamen, who founded Belize City in 1638. In 1798 Britain defeated a Spanish attack on the colony. British Honduras became a colony in 1862 and was made self-governing in 1964.

The new city of Belmopan became the capital in 1970. The government announced in June 1973 the country's change of name to Belize. In 1975 and in 1977 Britain sent troops to protect Belize from threatened Guatemalan attacks.

Britain has promised Belize independence when Guatemala gives up its claims to the area.

## BERMUDA

**Area:** 20 square miles (53 sq. km.).
**Population:** 59,909.
**Capital:** Hamilton, 2,060.

Situated in the Atlantic Ocean some 580 miles east of Cape Hatteras, N.C., Bermuda consists of 150 coral islands, 20 inhabited.

Discovered in 1503 by the Spaniard Juan de Bermúdez, the islands were settled in 1612 by a group of Englishmen who had been shipwrecked while on their way to Virginia. The crown acquired the islands from a chartered company in 1684. Bermuda has the oldest British colonial legislature in the world. The crown-appointed governor is assisted by a 9-member executive council, an appointed legislative council of 11 members, and a 40-member house of assembly.

In 1968 Bermuda was granted internal autonomy. The governing, mainly white, United Bermuda Party (UNP) won reelection on May 19, 1976, over the black Progressive Labour Party.

Rioting broke out in December 1977, and British troops were flown in to help put down the disorders. The unrest was touched off by the island's first execution in 30 years on Dec. 2, 1977, of two convicted murderers, one of whom confessed killing the British governor of Bermuda in 1973. A British royal commission that investigated the rioting recommended in 1978 that Bermudans be given an opportunity to vote on becoming independent in the near future.

## BRITISH ANTARCTIC TERRITORY

**Area:** 2,025 square miles (5,245 sq. km.), excluding Graham Land.

The British Antarctic Territory was formed in 1962 to include the South Shetland Islands (1,785 square miles), the South Orkney Islands (240 square miles), and Graham Land (the British territory on Palmer Peninsula, Antarctica, 473,000 square miles).

## BRITISH INDIAN OCEAN TERRITORY

**Area:** 30 square miles (78 sq. km.).
**Population:** 2,000.

Situated in the Indian Ocean about 700 miles south of India, the territory consists only of the Chagos Archipelago, or Oil Islands. The three main inhabited islands are Diego Garcia, Peros Banhos, and Salomon. The people fish and raise coconuts for a living.

The U.S. Navy built a major base on Diego Garcia in the 1970s.

From 1965 to 1976 the territory included the Aldabra Islands, Desroches Island, and the Farquhar Group, all of which were transferred to the administration of Seychelles in 1976.

## BRITISH VIRGIN ISLANDS

**Area:** 59 square miles (153 sq. km.).
**Population:** 14,024.
**Capital:** Road Town, 2,260.

The British Virgin Islands consist of 36 islands and islets in the Caribbean east of Puerto Rico. Almost all the people are of African descent. Britain obtained the islands in 1666. The crown-appointed administrator is assisted by an executive council and a partly elected legislative council. Livestock raising, farming, fishing, and tourism all contribute to the economy.

## BRUNEI

**Area:** 2,226 square miles (5,765 sq. km.).
**Population:** 213,003.
**Capital:** Bandar Seri Begawan, 36,987.

The sultanate of Brunei, lying on the northwest coast of Borneo, is split into two noncontiguous parts. It is bordered by the Malaysian state of Sarawak and the South China Sea. The climate is tropical. Some 55% of the people are Malaysian. More than 25% are Chinese.

Petroleum is the base of the economy. Natural gas, timber, and rubber also are exported.

Once a powerful state controlling Borneo, Sulu, and some of the Philippine Islands, Brunei lost much of its territory to European colonists in the mid-1800s. Britain established a protectorate in 1888. Brunei's first constitution was promulgated in 1959. Sultan Omar Ali Saifuddin abdicated in October 1967. He was succeeded on Aug. 1, 1968, by his son Sultan Hassanal Bolkiah Waddaulah. All political parties were banned.

The UN General Assembly called upon Britain in 1975 to hold free elections in Brunei. In 1979 Britain and Brunei signed an agreement that Brunei would receive full independence on Jan. 1, 1984.

## CAYMAN ISLANDS

**Area:** 100 square miles (259 sq. km.).
**Population:** 10,419.
**Capital:** Georgetown, 3,975.

The Cayman Islands consist of Grand Cayman, the principal island, Little Cayman, and Cayman Brac. They lie in the Caribbean Sea some 200 miles northwest of Jamaica. About a third of the people are European, a fifth black, and the rest of mixed races. Tourism is the chief industry.

Although discovered by Columbus in 1503, the islands were never settled by the Spanish. They were colonized by British from Jamaica and were its dependency until 1959. In 1962 they became a separate colony. A crown-appointed administrator rules with the advice and consent of an elected legislative assembly and executive council.

## CHANNEL ISLANDS

**Area:** 75 square miles (195 sq. km.).
**Population:** 135,311.
**Capitals:** St. Helier, Jersey, 26,351; St. Peter Port, Guernsey, 16,800.

Lying in the English Channel near the French coast, the main Channel Islands are Jersey, Guernsey, Alderney, and Sark.

The islands were acquired by the Duke of Normandy in the 900s and became part of Britain after the Norman Conquest (1066). Despite French efforts to regain the islands in the 1300s and later, they have remained loyal to Britain. In World War II they were occupied by Germany.

The islands ship large quantities of vegetables, fruits, and flowers to the English market. Jersey and Guernsey cattle are raised.

## FALKLAND ISLANDS

**Area:** 4,700 square miles (12,173 sq. km.).
**Population:** 2,086.
**Capital:** Stanley, 1,098.

Situated in the South Atlantic some 480 miles northeast of Cape Horn, the Falklands crown colony has two principal islands, East Falkland and West Falkland. They are mostly hilly moorlands with a cool, rainy, and windy climate. The people

are Christians of British stock.

An English navigator, John Davis, sighted the islands in 1592, but the first settlement was made by the French in 1764 on East Falkland. The British settled West Falkland in 1765, but both colonies were later abandoned. In 1820 Argentina colonized East Falkland. The British recaptured it in 1832–33. South Georgia, a whaling settlement 800 miles to the east, and the South Sandwich Islands are part of the colony. The main industry is sheep farming. Argentina claims the islands, calling them the *Malvinas*.

## GIBRALTAR

**Area:** 2.3 square miles (6 sq. km.).
**Population:** 28,783.
**Capital:** Gibraltar, 31,117.

The Rock of Gibraltar, towering 1,400 feet high, is a peninsula jutting into the Mediterranean from Spain's southwest coast.

The Moors settled Gibraltar in 711, naming it Jebel-al-Tarik (Mount of Tarik). The Spanish took it in 1309, lost it again to the Moors, and regained it in 1462. The English won possession in 1704 and have maintained it since, although besieged many times by the Spanish and French. Spain renewed its claim after World War II.

Britain's proposal that the Gibraltar issue be placed before the International Court of Justice was rejected by Spain. In a referendum on Sept. 10, 1967, the people of Gibraltar voted overwhelmingly to keep their special ties with Britain. In 1969 the border was sealed by the Spanish government. Britain and Spain reached agreement on April 10, 1980, to reopen the border.

## HONG KONG

**Area:** 403 square miles (1,045 sq. km.).
**Population:** 4,793,000.
**Chief Cities:** Victoria, capital, 633,138; New Kowloon, 1,478,581; Kowloon, 716,272.

Hong Kong lies on the China coast, 91 miles southeast of Canton, and has access to the Pacific.

The British crown colony comprises Hong Kong Island (29 square miles), the mainland peninsula of Kowloon (3.5 square miles), the New Territories (369.5 square miles) that includes the area between Kowloon and China, and over 230 offshore islands. The climate is subtropical.

Hong Kong harbor is one of the world's busiest. Victoria, the administrative capital, rises sharply from the waterfront and extends halfway up Victoria Peak. Kowloon and New Kowloon are crowded commercial and industrial centers. The New Territories are partially under cultivation. However, there are steep hillsides and swamps that have never been developed.

More than 98% of the people are of Chinese descent. English and Chinese are both official languages.

China ceded Hong Kong Island to Britain in 1842 following British occupation during the Opium War. Kowloon became part of the colony in 1860. China leased the New Territories to Britain in 1898 for 99 years.

The colony's location, its deep, sheltered harbor, abundant labor supply, and free-port economy have made it an important center of trade, com-

**BRITISH DEPENDENCIES** (continued)

merce, and industry. The largest industry is textile manufacturing. Much food, raw material, and water come from communist China. The colony is also an international banking center.

In May 1975 Elizabeth II became the first reigning British monarch to visit Hong Kong.

Work began in 1975 on a $1.2 billion subway transit system to be completed in the 1980s.

Hong Kong was inundated in 1979 by a flood of "boat people" refugees from Indochina.

In the 1970s and 1980s Hong Kong had one of the most rapidly growing economies in the world, expanding at an average annual rate of 10% or more.

## ISLE OF MAN

**Area:** 227 square miles (588 sq. km.).
**Population:** 68,089.
**Capital:** Douglas, 19,897.

The Isle of Man lies in the north Irish Sea midway between Britain and Northern Ireland.

Inhabited since Neolithic times, Man was ruled by the Vikings until about 800, by the Norwegians until 1266, and by the Scots until the 1300s, when it passed to the earls of Salisbury and Derby. It came under the direct administration of the British crown in 1765.

Tourism, dairying, fishing, quarrying, and agriculture support the economy.

## MONTSERRAT

**Area:** 38 square miles (98 sq. km.).
**Population:** 10,272.
**Capital:** Plymouth, 1,267.

Montserrat was discovered by Christopher Columbus in 1493 and named after a monastery in Spain. First settlers were English and Irish colonists from the nearby island of St. Kitts in 1632. The French disputed British control of the island, holding it briefly for the last time in 1782–83.

Montserrat became a self-governing British colony in 1960.

Tourism, construction, and agriculture are the main industries. Cotton is the main export.

## PITCAIRN ISLANDS

**Area:** 18.5 square miles (48 sq. km.).
**Population:** 124.
**Capital:** Adamstown.

Pitcairn is a volcanic, mountainous Pacific island about 1,200 miles southeast of Tahiti. Its area is 1.75 sq. mi., but the colony also includes three uninhabited islands: Henderson (12 sq. mi.), Ducie (2.5 sq. mi.), and Oeno (2 sq. mi.).

Pitcairn was discovered by the British in 1767 and settled in 1790 by mutineers off H.M.S. *Bounty* and some Tahitian women. Most of the islanders are their descendants. The island came under British jurisdiction in 1898 and was transferred to the control of Fiji. When Fiji became independent in 1970 the British high commissioner in New Zealand became governor of Pitcairn.

## SAINT HELENA

**Area:** 47 square miles (122 sq. km.).
**Population:** 5,365.
**Capital:** Jamestown, 1,475.

A mountainous island in the South Atlantic Ocean about 1,200 miles west of Africa, St. Helena was discovered by the Portuguese in 1502 and claimed by the Dutch in 1633. The British East India Company took the island in 1659 and established a colony two years later. The Dutch attempted to regain it in 1673 but held it less than a year.

Napoleon I was exiled on the island after his defeat at Waterloo in 1815 until his death in 1821. In 1834 St. Helena became a crown colony. The colony is administered by a crown-appointed governor and a legislative council.

**Ascension Island** (34 sq. mi. [88 sq. km.]; population: 1,146), about 700 miles northwest of St. Helena, was annexed in 1922.

**Tristan da Cunha** (40 sq. mi. [104 sq. km.]; population: 292) and the uninhabited islands of Gough, Nightingale, and Inaccessible became dependencies of St. Helena in 1938. The four islands lie about 1,500 miles southwest of St. Helena. Tristan da Cunha was evacuated after a volcanic eruption in 1961, but its people returned in 1963.

## SAINT KITTS–NEVIS

**Area:** 104 square miles (269 sq. km.).
**Population:** 49,947.
**Capital:** Basseterre, St. Kitts, 15,930.

The eastern Caribbean islands of St. Kitts (or St. Christopher) and Nevis are volcanic islands separated by a 2-mile-wide channel. St. Kitts has an area of 68 sq. mi. and Nevis of 36 sq. mi.

St. Kitts and Nevis were discovered by Christopher Columbus in 1493. St. Kitts became the first West Indies island settled by the British when Sir Thomas Warner led colonists there in 1623. French colonists settled on the island in 1625. In the following year the European colonists massacred about 2,000 Carib Indians. For the next 150 years Britain and France battled for possession of the islands until France gave up its claims in 1783.

The islands became a self-governing associated state with Britain on Feb. 27, 1967. At that time the island of Anguilla, 60 miles to the north, was included as part of the associated state. But Anguilla rebelled against rule by St. Kitts and since 1967 has been administered as a separate colony.

Tourism and agriculture are the main industries of the island. Sugarcane is the major export crop. In 1974 legislation was approved to nationalize the large sugar plantations. The first casino-hotel opened on St. Kitts in 1977.

## TURKS AND CAICOS ISLANDS

**Area:** 166 square miles (430 sq. km.).
**Population:** 2,287.
**Capital:** Cockburn Town, Grand Turk, 2,287.

The Turks and Caicos lie east of Cuba. The only regularly inhabited of the eight Turk Islands are Grand Turk and Salt Cay. South and North Caicos are the most important of the Caicos group. The population is mostly black.

Though discovered by Juan Ponce de León in 1512, the islands were uninhabited until Bermudians arrived to gather salt in 1678. Administered as part of Jamaica until 1962, the islands are administered by a crown-appointed governor and a partly elected state council. Salt, crayfish, and sisal are exported.

Britain promised to grant the islands independence in 1982.

# BULGARIA

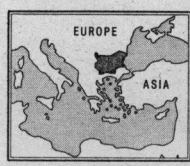

**Official Name:** People's Republic of Bulgaria.
**Area:** 42,823 square miles (110,912 sq. km.).
**Population:** 8,902,600.
**Chief Cities:** Sofia, capital, 976,015; Plovdiv, 307,414; Varna, 257,731; Ruse, 161,605; Bourgas, 146,709.
**Government:** Communist state.
**Head of Government:** First Secretary of the Communist Party, Todor Zhivkov (since 1954).
**Premier:** Stanko Todorov (took office in 1971).
**Legislature:** *National Assembly,* 400 members.
**U.S. Ambassador to Bulgaria:** Jack Richard Perry.
**Bulgarian Ambassador to U.S.:** Konstantin Nicolou Grigorov.
**Flag:** Stripes of white, green, and red, with national coat of arms in top left-hand corner.
**Main Language:** Bulgarian.
**Ethnic Groups:** Bulgarian (85%), Turk (9%).
**Principal Religion:** Eastern Orthodox.
**Leading Industries:** Manufacturing (machinery, food and tobacco processing, metals, leather goods, lumber, textiles, chemicals, fertilizers); agriculture (livestock, wheat, grapes, roses, tobacco, barley, tomatoes, mushrooms, sugar beets).
**Foreign Trade:** *major exports*—food, tobacco, metals, textiles, machinery, rose oil, wine, leather; *major imports*—oil, gas, steel, wood.
**Places of Interest:** Shipka Pass; Kazanluk, in Valley of Roses; Varna Black Sea resort; Old Plovdiv; Rila Monastery; Veliko Turnovo. *In Sofia:* Alexander Nevsky Memorial Church; Boyana Church; Georgi Dimitrov mausoleum; Park of Liberty; museums.

## BULGARIA TODAY

Bulgaria is a communist nation on the Black Sea northeast of Greece. A mountainous country about the size of Tennessee, Bulgaria has changed from an agricultural to an industrial nation in the decades since World War II. The major industries are food processing and the production of chemicals and machinery.

However, about a third of the Bulgarians still depend on farming for their living. A leading tobacco-grower, Bulgaria makes many of the cigarettes smoked in the Soviet Union.

The Balkan Mountains cross Bulgaria from east to west between the Danubian tableland in the north and the Thracian Plain in the south. The Danube flows along Bulgaria's northern boundary, and the Maritsa River drains the Thracian Plain region.

## EARLY HISTORY

Bulgaria, part of ancient Thrace and Moesia, was settled by Slavic tribes in the 500s A.D. The Bulgars, a Turkic-speaking people, crossed the Danube, conquered the Slavs, and founded the first Bulgarian empire in 681.

Under the leadership of Krum (802?–814), the Bulgars expanded and consolidated their empire. Krum's forces captured Sofia and killed the Byz-

antine emperor Nicephorus I. Under Boris I the Bulgars adopted Christianity (865). The first Bulgarian empire fell in 1018, when it was annexed by the Byzantine empire. The second empire, founded in 1186, lasted until the Ottoman Turks subdued the Bulgars in 1396.

## TURKISH RULE

For nearly 500 years the Turks held Bulgaria. A revolt in 1876 was savagely put down by the Turks in the "Bulgarian Massacres." Russia intervened, defeated the Turks, and created an expanded, pro-Russian Bulgaria.

Other European powers, particularly Britain and Austria-Hungary, feared Russian penetration into the Balkans. At their insistence Russia was forced to accept a treaty revision at the Congress of Berlin (1878). Northern Bulgaria was made a principality under Ottoman control. Alexander of Battenberg was its first prince.

Eastern Rumelia, south of the Balkan Mountains, was annexed by Bulgaria in 1885. His successor, Prince Ferdinand of Saxe-Coburg-Gotha, came to power in 1887.

## INDEPENDENT KINGDOM

In 1908 Ferdinand proclaimed full independence and assumed the title of czar.

Bulgaria sided with Germany in World War I. In 1918 Ferdinand abdicated in favor of his son Boris III. Bulgaria lost much territory as the result of the peace treaty.

Bulgaria backed the Axis powers in World War II. Boris died in 1943. His 6-year-old son was named King Simeon II.

## COMMUNIST RULE

Soviet troops seized the country in 1944. A Soviet-supervised election overthrew the monarchy, and Simeon II went into exile. A communist state was organized in 1945 under the leadership of Prime Minister Georgi Dimitrov.

After Dimitrov's death in 1949, his brother-in-law Vulko Chervenkov became dictator.

The United States suspended diplomatic relations with Bulgaria from 1950 to 1959 because of charges of espionage that Bulgaria made against the American ambassador.

Following Stalin's death in 1953, Chervenkov lost influence in Moscow. In 1954 he gave up his position as head of the Communist Party to Todor Zhivkov but remained premier.

In 1961 Zhivkov ousted Chervenkov, consolidating power in his own hands. In 1971 Zhivkov took the title of chairman of the state council, making Stanko Todorov premier.

Direct railroad ferry service between Bulgaria and the Soviet Union was initiated in 1978.

Trying to encourage foreign investment and trade, the government established new rules in 1980 permitting foreign companies to own up to 90% of joint ventures.

The success of Bulgaria's industrialization was emphasized with figures released in 1980 that showed Bulgaria's per capita gross national product was $5,285—nearly 25% higher than that of Spain and almost as high as that of Britain.

QUICK QUIZ: What is the largest lake in Louisiana? See page 189.

# BURMA

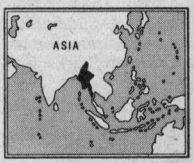
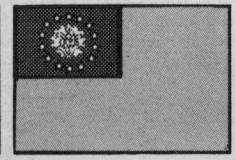

**Official Name:** Socialist Republic of the Union of Burma.
**Area:** 261,218 square miles (676,552 sq. km.).
**Population:** 34,011,400.
**Chief Cities:** Rangoon, capital, 2,276,000; Mandalay, 458,000; Karbe, 253,600; Moulmein, 188,000.
**Government:** One-party republic.
**President:** U Ne Win (since 1962).
**Prime Minister:** U Maung Maung Kha (since 1977).
**Legislature:** *National Assembly,* 451 members.
**U.S. Ambassador to Burma:** Patricia M. Byrne.
**Burmese Ambassador to U.S.:** U Hla Shwe.
**Flag:** Red field with blue rectangle in upper hoist corner containing gear wheel and rice encircled by 14 white stars representing Burma's states.
**Languages:** Burmese (official), English.
**Main Ethnic Groups:** Burman (65%), Shan (11%), Karen (7%), Kachin (6%), Chin (2%).
**Religion:** Buddhism (85%).
**Leading Industries:** Agriculture (rice, tobacco, sugarcane, rubber, jute, peanuts); forestry and lumber; mining (petroleum, natural gas, lead, zinc, tungsten, nickel); manufacturing (food processing, textiles, construction materials).
**Foreign Trade:** *major exports*—rice, teak, jute, rubber; *major imports*—textile yarn and fabrics, nonelectric machinery, vehicles, chemicals.
**Places of Interest:** Inle Lake; Sagaing Hills. *In Rangoon:* Shwedagon and Sule pagodas; national museum. *In Pegu:* Shwemaudaw Pagoda and 181-foot-long Shwethalyaung (Reclining Buddha). *In Pagan:* Over 2,500 monuments in ancient royal capital.

## BURMA TODAY

About the size of Texas, Burma is a Southeast Asian nation that for nearly two decades rejected most contact with the outside world. An isolationist socialist-military regime allowed the country's once prosperous economy to stagnate.

Nearly all of its people are poor with an average income of less than $150 per year. Only about 7 in 10 can read and write.

Burma was relatively unaffected by the soaring oil prices of the 1970s because it is nearly self-sufficient in petroleum. However, inflation was fueled by a thriving black market in consumer goods smuggled in from Thailand to avoid the government's ban on luxury imports.

The country has fertile plains and delta in the south and central area. Uplands form a protective arc of hills across the northern frontiers with Bangladesh, India, China, Laos, and Thailand.

## BRITISH RULE

Conflict between the British and the Burmese for influence over states bordering Burma brought about an Anglo-Burmese war (1824–26), as a result of which the British gained control of part of lower Burma. A second Anglo-Burmese war in 1852 and a third in 1885 ended Burma's independence. Grafted onto India as a province, Burma was governed from New Delhi.

Under British rule Burma became the world's largest exporter of rice—"the rice bowl of Asia."

In 1937 Burma was separated from India. A new constitution was drawn up that gave Burma an elected parliament.

In 1942 the Japanese, aided by Burmese nationalists, expelled the British from most of Burma. British rule was restored in 1946.

## INDEPENDENCE

The independent Union of Burma was formed on Jan. 4, 1948. U Nu was named premier. His party repeatedly won parliamentary elections, and U Nu led the country for most of its first 10 years.

In the late 1950s U Nu's party split into rival groups. Fearing the outbreak of civil war, he asked the head of the armed forces, Gen. U Ne Win, to take charge of the government temporarily in 1958. When U Nu's party won the parliamentary election in 1960, Ne Win stepped aside and U Nu again became premier.

When civil war once more threatened in 1962, Ne Win again took over the government and established a socialist military dictatorship. U Nu was imprisoned, and then exiled from 1966 to 1980.

Under Ne Win's socialist leadership the government took over ownership of most businesses and industries. Foreign private investment and aid were rejected.

A new constitution was adopted on Jan. 4, 1974, making the country a one-party state under Ne Win's Burmese Socialist Program Party.

Sporadic fighting has gone on along Burma's borders for more than three decades. In northeast Burma communist rebels hold an estimated 7,000 square miles along the Chinese border. Altogether some 13 different ethnic groups carry on warfare against the government.

The government on Sept. 1, 1976, ended martial law that had been imposed in 1974 when students rioted at funeral ceremonies for former UN Secretary-General U Thant. About 1,600 persons were ordered released from prison, and sentences were reduced for 3,300 others.

In March 1977 the ruling Socialist Party reported that goals in the 1973–77 economic plan had not been met.

Prime Minister U Sein Win resigned on March 29, 1977, after he and other cabinet members were criticized for failure to follow the nation's economic plan. He was replaced as prime minister by 57-year-old U Maung Maung Kha, who had been minister of mines and labor.

Ne Win's regime became disenchanted with communist domination of the third-world movement and announced its official withdrawal in 1979. Subsequently a more friendly relationship developed with Western nations. U.S. economic aid to Burma resumed in 1980 with the signing of an agreement for $5 million assistance to the nation's rural health-care program.

A bumper rice crop in 1978–79 stimulated a spurt in growth in Burma's economy, permitting the export of about 700,000 tons of rice.

An ambitious 4-year development plan for 1978–82 calls for loans from international organizations to finance improvements in agriculture and transportation. The government also hopes to exploit potential offshore petroleum deposits.

# BURUNDI

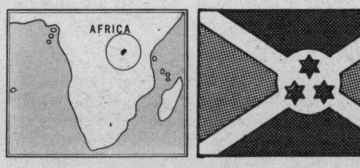

**Official Name:** Republic of Burundi.
**Area:** 10,747 square miles (27,834 sq. km.).
**Population:** 4,550,150.
**Capital:** Bujumbura, 78,810.
**Government:** One-party dictatorship.
**President:** Jean-Baptiste Bagaza (since 1976).
**U.S. Ambassador to Burundi:** Frances D. Cook.
**Burundi Ambassador to U.S.:** Simon Sabimbona.
**Flag:** White diagonal cross, with red quarters on top and bottom and green quarters to left and right; centered white circle bears three red stars edged in green.
**Official Languages:** Kirundi, French.
**Ethnic Groups:** Hutu (85%), Tutsi (14%), Twa (1%).
**Religions:** Roman Catholicism (50%), animism (40%), Protestantism (10%).
**Leading Industries:** Agriculture (coffee, cotton, tea, peanuts, cattle); food processing; fishing.
**Foreign Trade:** *major exports*—coffee, cotton, hides; *major imports*—textiles, motor vehicles, flour, petroleum products.
**Places of Interest:** Lake Tanganyika; Ruvuvu River, source of Nile; Bujumbura.

## BURUNDI TODAY

About the size of Maryland in area and population, Burundi is one of the poorest countries of Africa. It has few natural resources. Even its soil is mostly eroded and unfertile. The country's main export is coffee.

Most people lead primitive tribal lives, raising beans, corn, and yams, or fishing in Lake Tanganyika. Few can read or write.

The country has few villages or towns. Most Burundians live with members of their own extended families in rural compounds called *rugos.*

A land of grassy plains, forests, and rocky hills, Burundi has a hot equatorial climate in its lowlands. But its upland regions have cool nights with an occasional frost. The White Nile River has its southernmost source in Burundi.

Landlocked Burundi has no railroads and less than 200 miles of paved roads. Rwanda lies to the north, Tanzania to the east and south, and Zaire to the west. Burundi's border with Zaire runs down the middle of Lake Tanganyika.

## HISTORY

Tall Watutsi (Tutsi) warriors dominated the shorter Bahutu (Hutu) for centuries under an absolute monarch call the *mwami.*

Burundi was absorbed by German East Africa in 1898. Then it was mandated to Belgium after World War I as part of Ruanda-Urundi.

On July 1, 1962, Urundi was granted independence as a monarchy, renamed Burundi.

Mwami (king) Mwambutsa IV was deposed on July 8, 1966, by his son, who became Ntare V.

Prime Minister Michel Micombero overthrew Ntare V on Nov. 28, 1966, and proclaimed Burundi a republic. Micombero, a Tutsi, named himself president. He ruled as dictator by decree.

The Hutu majority revolted in April 1972 and May 1973. An estimated 150,000 Hutu and tens of thousands of Tutsi died in the fighting.

The Minority Rights Group (MRG), a British organization, accused Micombero's government in 1976 of having systematically killed all Hutus who had more than a high school education.

Lt. Col. Jean-Baptiste Bagaza led a military coup on Nov. 1, 1976, that overthrew Micombero. A Belgian-educated political scientist, Bagaza said he would try to end tribal strife.

President Bagaza established "civilian government" in 1980, making the Central Committee of Burundi's sole political party the main legislative body to approve his decrees and dissolving the military junta of army officers, the Supreme Revolutionary Council.

# CAMBODIA

**Official Name:** Democratic Kampuchea.
**Area:** 69,898 square miles (181,035 sq. km.).
**Population:** 5,000,000.
**Capital:** Phnom Penh, 150,000.
**Government:** One-party communist state.
**President:** Heng Samrin (since 1979).
**Flag:** Red field with Angkor Wat pagoda in yellow.
**Official Language:** Khmer.
**Main Ethnic Groups:** Khmer (85%), Chinese (6%).
**Religion:** Buddhism (85%).
**Leading Industries:** Agriculture (rubber, rice, corn); fishing; forest products.
**Foreign Trade:** *major export*—rubber; *major imports*—food, fuel, machinery.
**Places of Interest:** Angkor Wat ruins and other ornamental monuments, temples, and palaces covering over 60 square miles, located at Siemreap. *In Phnom Penh:* national museum; royal palace; Silver Pagoda; floating villages on Mekong River.

## CAMBODIA TODAY

A devastated country of Southeast Asia, Cambodia was ruined in the 1970s by wars and by the repressive measures of its communist leaders. Millions of Cambodians—half the population—died or fled to neighboring countries.

Throughout 1979–80 civil war raged between two rival communist governments, one supported by China and the other by Vietnam and the Soviet Union.

Most Cambodians are farmers. Before the disasters of the 1970s, the country exported large amounts of rice, corn, and rubber.

Mountains along the border with Thailand rise sharply from the Gulf of Thailand coast, drop to a plains region, and ascend again in the north. Much of the best land for rice farming lies in the central basin along the Mekong River and around

QUICK QUIZ: The world's population is expected to increase how much by 2000? See page 193.

**CAMBODIA** *(continued)*
Tonle Sap (Great Lake).

About the size of Oklahoma, Cambodia lies south of Thailand. Laos is to the northeast. Vietnam lies to the east and south.

## EARLY HISTORY

About A.D. 100 the Kingdom of Funan was established in southern Cambodia. Three centuries later an Indian Brahman took control of Funan. Indian influences shaped the country's customs, alphabet, and legal code.

The Khmer Empire was established in northern Cambodia in 802. It conquered Funan and most of Southeast Asia. A vast complex of shrines and temples was built at its capital, Angkor.

After disintegration of the Khmer Empire in the 1400s, Cambodia was dominated alternately by the Thais and the Vietnamese. In the 1700s Thailand annexed three of Cambodia's provinces.

France established a protectorate over Cambodia in 1863. It later became part of French Indochina.

Anti-French sentiment spread during World War II, when Vichy France bowed to Japan's demands for Cambodian bases. King Norodom Sihanouk, who had become monarch in 1941 at the age of 18, cooperated with Japan.

France granted Cambodia independence under King Sihanouk within the French Union on Nov. 9, 1953. Sihanouk abdicated in favor of his parents in 1955. He then became premier. Cambodia left the French Union in 1955, declaring its complete independence. In 1960 Prince Sihanouk was installed as chief of state.

Beginning in 1963, Sihanouk permitted North Vietnamese and Vietcong troops to build up military bases along Cambodia's border. The communists armed the Khmer Rouge, Cambodia's Communist Party, and staged border raids into South Vietnam. The U.S. Air Force at President Nixon's direction secretly began bombing communist forces in Cambodia in 1969.

In March 1970 Cambodian Premier Lon Nol overthrew Sihanouk, who fled to communist China. Relations with Hanoi were severed in May. On April 30 the U.S. and South Vietnam sent 20,000 troops into Cambodia to destroy communist bases. American troops were withdrawn on June 29, but South Vietnamese forces remained and the U.S. continued bombing communist forces in Cambodia.

On Oct. 9, 1970, Lon Nol proclaimed the nation a republic named the *Khmer Republic.* In elections on June 4, 1972, Lon Nol became the nation's first elected president.

President Nixon announced on March 27, 1973, that U.S. planes would continue to bomb communist troops in Cambodia until the communists agreed to a cease-fire. But the U.S. Congress, angered because Nixon had not consulted it, passed legislation that ended all U.S. military action in Indochina on Aug. 15, 1973.

The communists closed Phnom Penh's major supply route, the Mekong River, in February 1975. The U.S. then initiated an airlift to supply government forces fighting around the capital. Communist troops pressed their offensive on Phnom Penh, and on April 1 President Lon Nol fled from Cambodia, leaving the government in the hands of Premier Long Boret. On April 12 the U.S. ambassador and his staff flew out of Phnom Penh, and the U.S. airlift ended.

## COMMUNIST RULE

Refusing attempts by Premier Long Boret to negotiate a cease-fire, Khmer Rouge troops captured Phnom Penh on April 16, 1975, ending the war. Communist firing squads executed Long Boret and other officials and generals of the former government.

Hundreds of thousands died when communists forced city dwellers to march into the countryside and work as farm laborers.

The Khmer Rouge announced on April 25, 1975, that Prince Norodom Sihanouk would be chief of state for life. But Sihanouk resigned on April 2, 1976, and went into seclusion. Khieu Samphan then took the title of president, but the government was controlled by Pol Pot as secretary-general of the Cambodian Communist Party.

The communists changed the country's official name to *Democratic Kampuchea.* However, the government was the reverse of "democratic," creating a repressive police state that took over all private property, paid workers with scanty food rations instead of wages, and closed all schools. Thousands of opponents were tortured and executed, some for nothing more than criticizing the quantity or quality of their food rations. Few foreigners were allowed to remain in the country.

In April 1978 President Carter denounced Cambodia as "the worst violator of human rights in the world today." Officials estimated that about 2.5 million Cambodians had been killed by the Pol Pot government.

Vietnam launched a full-scale invasion of Cambodia on Dec. 25, 1978, and two weeks later captured Phnom Penh on Jan. 7, 1979.

Pol Pot and members of his government fled to the jungles, where they carried on guerrilla warfare with supplies provided by China.

Soviet-supported Vietnam set up a new government with Heng Samrin as president.

Prince Shihanouk escaped from Cambodia in January 1979, appearing at a special meeting of the UN Security Council, where he denounced the Vietnamese invasion. Later Sihanouk quit his role as a representative of the Pol Pot government, condemning it for the atrocities committed against Cambodians.

International agencies mounted a huge relief effort in 1979–80 to prevent Cambodians from starving because continued fighting prevented the growing of rice. The U.S. provided over $200 million in food and aid for relief.

An additional 150,000 Cambodians were estimated to have fled to Thailand during 1979.

Khieu Samphan, prime minister of the Pol Pot government, called Western news correspondents to his jungle headquarters in August 1980 to announce that the Khmer Rouge had decided to reject communism as a philosophy and would restore democracy and private enterprise if successful in its civil war against the Vietnamese-controlled government of Heng Samrin. Khieu Samphan indicated he would welcome military aid from the United States.

The Pol Pot regime was aided by the U.S. in retaining Cambodia's seat in the UN in 1979–80.

# CAMEROON

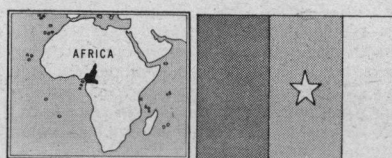

**Official Name:** United Republic of Cameroon.
**Area:** 183,569 square miles (475,442 sq. km.).
**Population:** 8,530,910.
**Chief Cities:** Yaoundé, capital, 250,000; Douala, 350,000; Nkongsamba, 100,000.
**Government:** One-party republic.
**President:** El Hadj Ahmadou Ahidjo (since 1961).
**National Assembly:** 120 members.
**U.S. Ambassador to Cameroon:** Hume A. Horan.
**Cameroonian Ambassador to U.S.:** Benoit Bindzi.
**Flag:** Tricolor of green, red, and yellow bars, with yellow star centered on red bar.
**Official Languages:** French and English.
**Main Ethnic Group:** Over 200 Bantu tribes.
**Religions:** Animism (40%), Islam (25%), Roman Catholicism (20%).
**Leading Industries:** Agriculture (cocoa, coffee, cotton, bananas, cattle, rice, sugarcane, palm oil); mining (petroleum); forestry; manufacturing (food processing, aluminum, textiles, jute bags, soap).
**Foreign Trade:** *major exports*—cocoa, coffee, cotton, wood, prawns, aluminum; *major imports*—machinery, textiles, transport equipment, petroleum products, alumina, chemicals.
**Places of Interest:** Bamiléké Plateau; Waza Forest and wildlife preserve; Bamoun country; beaches.

## CAMEROON TODAY

Cameroon is a West African country that is making progress in its efforts to leap from primitive to modern times in a few decades.

Somewhat larger than California, Cameroon has not experienced the political unrest that has set back many of its neighbors.

While establishing extensive preserves to protect its wildlife, Cameroon has moved ahead to improve agricultural production.

About four-fifths of the Cameroonians live in the French-speaking eastern part of the country. Altogether there are over 200 tribes that speak 24 different African languages.

Poor nutrition and lack of health facilities give Cameroonians a life expectancy of only 41 years.

The people are poor, and the majority still follow a primitive tribal culture. But Cameroon boasts that a higher proportion of its children are in school or have graduated from school than in any other African nation.

By encouraging foreign investment, Cameroon has been able to build hydroelectric power plants and railroads to develop its large deposits of bauxite, thus becoming the largest aluminum-producing nation in Africa. Cameroon also is one of the world's important producers of cocoa.

Southern Cameroon rises eastward from the coastal plains to a densely wooded plateau about 1,000 feet high. In the central interior region is the Adamaoua Plateau, 2,500 to 4,500 feet above sea level. The principal rivers are the Benoué and the Sanaga.

Mount Cameroon, the highest point in the country, rises to 13,350 feet on the Atlantic coastline northeast of Douala.

Nigeria lies to the north. Chad and Central Africa are to the east. Congo, Gabon, and Equatorial Guinea are to the south.

### EARLY HISTORY

The Portuguese visited the area in the 1400s but made no permanent settlements. From the 1500s to the 1800s the Cameroon coast was a regular source of supply for the slave trade of Spain, Britain, and the Netherlands.

Germany established a protectorate in 1884. British and French armies invaded the German protectorate in 1914. After World War I the western part of Cameroon was turned over to Britain. The remainder, about four-fifths of the total territory, was ceded to France.

During World War II French Cameroon was seized by the Free French, who made it a training base for troops that later saw action in North Africa and Syria.

The French and British Cameroons became United Nations trusteeships in 1946. The Cameroonians were granted limited self-government by the administering European powers.

### INDEPENDENCE

The French Cameroon assembly voted for full independence in 1957. France and the UN concurred, and the Republic of Cameroon became independent on Jan. 1, 1960.

Plebiscites were held in British Cameroons in 1961. The northern region chose to unite with Nigeria. The southern region elected to join with Cameroon.

The northern region of British Cameroons became part of Nigeria on June 1, 1961.

The southern region, newly named West Cameroon, joined East Cameroon, formerly French Cameroon, on Oct. 1, 1961, forming the new Federal Republic of Cameroon. West Cameroon and East Cameroon each had its own parliament and ministries.

Ahmadou Ahidjo was chosen as first president of the federal republic in 1961. He was reelected without opposition to new 5-year terms in 1965, 1970, 1975, and 1980. All political parties in the country were consolidated into one party, the National Cameroonian Union (UNC), in 1966.

After Cameroon had functioned for 11 years as a federal government, President Ahidjo proposed that the separate state governments be abolished. In a referendum on May 20, 1972, the people approved Ahidjo's proposal, changing from a federal to a unitary state.

In the 1970s Cameroon had a low rate of growth because of bad weather and a decline in the price of cocoa, the leading export.

The Trans-Cameroon Railway was completed in 1974, linking Douala and Ngaoundere.

Offshore wells began producing petroleum in 1977, and construction began in 1978 on the nation's first oil refinery, to be completed in 1981.

A 5-year economic plan for 1976–81 emphasizes tourism, timber exploitation, cattle raising, and the development of processing industries.

QUICK QUIZ: What was the U.S. unemployment rate in 1933? See page 196.

# CANADA

**Official Name:** Canada.
**Area:** 3,851,807 square miles (9,976,139 sq. km.).
**Population:** 24,152,300.
**Chief Cities:** Ottawa, capital, 304,462; Montreal, 1,080,546; Toronto, 633,318; Winnipeg, 560,874; Calgary, 469,917; Edmonton, 461,361; Vancouver, 410,188.
**Largest Metropolitan Areas:** Toronto, 2,856,500; Montreal, 2,823,000; Vancouver, 1,173,300; Ottawa, 726,400; Winnipeg, 589,100; Edmonton, 581,400.
**Government:** Federal parliamentary state.
**Prime Minister:** Pierre Trudeau (since 1980).
**Chief of State:** Queen Elizabeth II, represented by Governor-General Edward Schreyer (since 1979).
**Parliament:** *Senate,* 102 members (appointed); *House of Commons,* 282 members (elected to 5-year terms).
**U.S. Ambassador to Canada:** Kenneth Curtis.
**Canadian Ambassador to U.S.:** Peter M. Towe.
**Flag:** Red maple leaf on white field, with red bars at each side.
**Official Languages:** English and French.
**Ethnic Backgrounds:** British (44%); French (30%); native Indian and Eskimo (1%); other (25%).
**Main Religions:** Roman Catholicism (46%), United Church of Canada (18%), Anglicanism (12%).
**Leading Industries:** Manufacturing (steel, paper, electricity, aluminum, food processing, vehicles); mining (petroleum, copper, zinc, iron, lead, natural gas, asbestos, nickel, salt); agriculture (cattle, hogs, poultry, dairy products, wheat, barley, potatoes, corn, rapeseed, tobacco); forestry; fishing; tourism.
**Foreign Trade:** *major exports*—manufactured goods, newsprint, wood, wood pulp, wheat, natural gas; *major imports*—motor vehicles and parts, chemical products, tools, machinery, aircraft, petroleum, communications equipment.
**Places of Interest:** Banff National Park, Alta.; Barkerville (gold-rush town), B.C.; Bell Homestead, Brantford, Ont.; Calgary Stampede, Alta.; Citadel, Quebec City, Que.; CN Tower, Toronto, Ont.; Fort Macleod Mounted Police Museum, Alta.; Fortress of Louisbourg, N.S.; Gaspé Peninsula, Que.; Man and His World exhibition, Montreal, Que.; L'Anse aux Meadows (Viking site), Nfld.; Niagara Falls, Ont.; parliament buildings, Ottawa, Ont.; parks, Vancouver, B.C.; Royal Botanical Gardens, Hamilton, Ont.; Thunderbird Park totem pole collection, Victoria, B.C.; white sand beaches, P.E.I.

## CANADA TODAY

The second-largest nation in the world in land area, Canada is rich in natural resources. But Canada, like Australia, is underpopulated. Only 7% of the land is under cultivation, and only about 27% of its area is used for production of lumber or paper. The difficulties in transporting oil to the east coast from its large but dwindling western reserves explain Canada's unique position as both a leading oil exporter and an increasingly dependent oil importer.

One of Canada's major problems has been in maintaining its identity as a nation in relation to the more powerful United States, which lies to the south and is Canada's best foreign-trade customer. U.S. investments are important to Canada's economy. Investment proposals by foreign companies are subject to screening under the Foreign Investment Review Act (1973) to assure that they benefit Canada.

Another major problem is the division of the nation into two language groups: French-speaking, mainly in Quebec, and English-speaking, throughout most of the rest of Canada.

## GEOGRAPHY

Canada is a federation of 10 provinces and two territories.

Most of the country's population is concentrated in the southeastern region in Ontario and Quebec near the Great Lakes and the St. Lawrence River.

To the east of this region is the Atlantic coastal area of New Brunswick, Newfoundland, Nova Scotia, and Prince Edward Island.

The Canadian Shield, a vast, U-shaped, rocky expanse, surrounds Hudson Bay. Thousands of lakes are scattered over this area. To the north are the Hudson Bay lowlands. Farther north is Canada's Arctic Archipelago, which includes Baffin, Victoria, and Ellesmere islands.

Canada's interior plains stretch to the west of the Shield.

The far west is mountainous. Major mountain systems are the Canadian Rockies, the Cascades, and the Coast Mountains.

Vancouver Island and the Queen Charlotte Islands lie in the Pacific Ocean near the west coast.

Canada has more lakes than any other country in the world. Among the largest are Great Bear Lake, Great Slave Lake, and Lake Winnipeg. Major rivers include the St. Lawrence, Yukon, Fraser, Columbia, Mackenzie, Peace, and Slave.

The southeast and far west have generally temperate climates with mild winters and warm summers. Seasonal variations are more extreme in the

## CANADA'S PROVINCES AND TERRITORIES

| NAME | AREA Sq. Mi. | Sq. Km. | Rank | POPULATION Number | Rank | ADMISSION Date | Rank | CAPITAL |
|---|---|---|---|---|---|---|---|---|
| Alberta | 255,285 | 661,185 | 5 | 2,036,300 | 4 | 1905 (Sept. 1) | 8 | Edmonton |
| British Columbia | 366,255 | 948,596 | 4 | 2,598,730 | 3 | 1871 (July 20) | 6 | Victoria |
| Manitoba | 251,000 | 650,087 | 7 | 1,041,660 | 5 | 1870 (July 15) | 5 | Winnipeg |
| New Brunswick | 28,354 | 73,437 | 10 | 709,035 | 8 | 1867 (July 1) | 1 | Fredericton |
| Newfoundland | 156,185 | 404,517 | 9 | 581,136 | 9 | 1949 (Mar. 31) | 10 | St. John's |
| Nova Scotia | 21,425 | 55,490 | 11 | 856,336 | 7 | 1867 (July 1) | 1 | Halifax |
| Ontario | 412,582 | 1,068,582 | 3 | 8,598,950 | 1 | 1867 (July 1) | 1 | Toronto |
| Prince Edward Island | 2,184 | 5,657 | 12 | 124,356 | 10 | 1873 (July 1) | 7 | Charlottetown |
| Quebec | 594,860 | 1,540,680 | 2 | 6,370,660 | 2 | 1867 (July 1) | 1 | Quebec |
| Saskatchewan | 251,700 | 651,900 | 6 | 968,459 | 6 | 1905 (Sept. 1) | 8 | Regina |
| Northwest Territories | 1,304,903 | 3,379,683 | 1 | 43,676 | 11 | — | — | Yellowknife |
| Yukon Territory | 207,076 | 536,324 | 8 | 21,939 | 12 | — | — | Whitehorse |

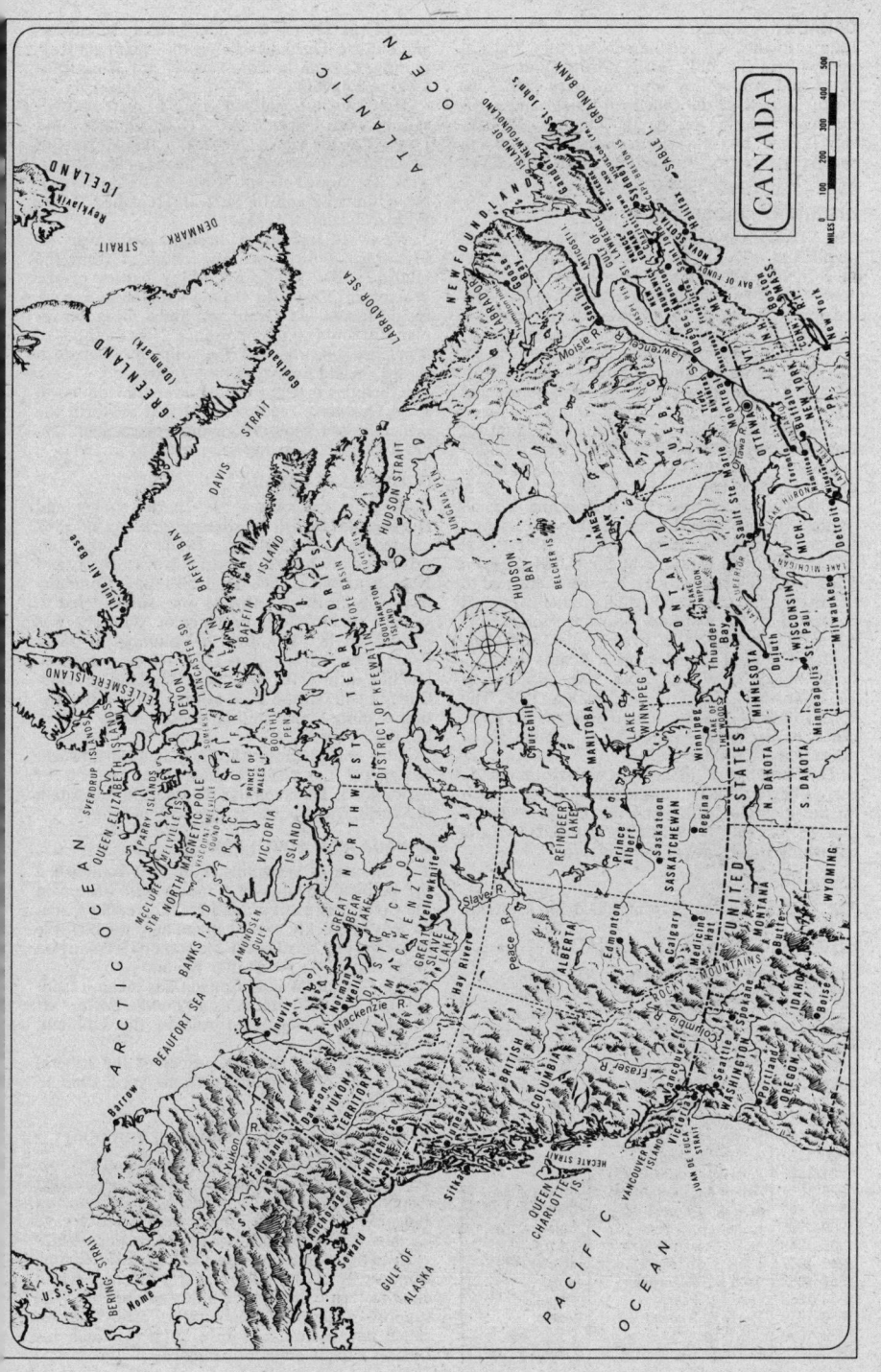

**CANADA** *(continued)*

interior plains, where summers are dry and hot and winters are cold. To the north, summers are short and winters are long and very cold. The northern part of the Canadian Shield and areas northward have an Arctic climate. Rainfall ranges from 2.40 in. (6.1 cm.) a year at Eureka in the Arctic to 115.39 in. (293.1 cm.) at Estevan Point, British Columbia.

## DISCOVERY AND COLONIZATION

The Vikings explored the coast of Newfoundland about A.D. 1000, but their colonies did not survive. In 1497 Canada was claimed for England by John Cabot, an Italian-born explorer in the service of Henry VII. In 1524 Giovanni da Verrazano explored the coast, and in 1534 Jacques Cartier erected a cross at Gaspé and claimed the land for the king of France. There followed visits by British and French explorers, but the first permanent settlement was established by the Frenchmen Samuel de Champlain and the Sieur de Monts at Port Royal in Nova Scotia (1605). They founded Quebec in 1608. In 1610–11 Henry Hudson explored Hudson Bay and James Bay.

The struggle between the British and French became intense after Britain established its first settlement in Nova Scotia in 1623. Port Royal and Quebec were captured by Sir David Kirke in 1628 and 1629, respectively, but were returned to the French in 1632. The French gradually pushed westward in search of furs, following such explorers as Nicolet, La Salle, Brulé, Joliet, and Marquette. The French settlement in Acadia was captured by an expedition from New England in 1654 but was restored to the French in 1655. The colony of New France, centered on the St. Lawrence River, grew steadily to a population of more than 12,400 by 1692.

The French and Indian Wars with Britain in the early 1700s culminated in the defeat of the French on the Plains of Abraham and the surrender of Quebec in 1759. New France was ceded to the British by the Treaty of Paris in 1763.

## BRITISH RULE

The Quebec Act of 1774 provided for preserva-

tion of the French-Canadian language, religion, and culture. During and after the American Revolution, Canada became a haven for Americans loyal to England.

The Constitutional Act of 1791 created a division between Upper Canada (later Ontario) and Lower Canada (later Quebec), making a total of six colonial units with Nova Scotia, New Brunswick (separated from Nova Scotia in 1784), Newfoundland and Ile St. Jean (renamed Prince Edward Island in 1798).

Westward expansion brought settlement of Manitoba in 1812 on land obtained from the Hudson's Bay Company. Many battles of the War of 1812 between Britain and the U.S. were fought in Canada. Grain and timber began to replace fur and fish in importance. New methods of transport appeared with the building of canals in the 1820s and railways in the 1840s.

Rebellions in Upper and Lower Canada led to Lord Durham's report (1839) that set forth the principles of responsible cabinet government. Upper and Lower Canada were reunited in 1841.

## DOMINION OF CANADA

Following conferences at Charlottetown and Quebec, the British North America Act of 1867 created the Dominion of Canada with the four provinces of Quebec, Ontario, Nova Scotia, and New Brunswick. The Hudson's Bay Company territories in the Northwest were surrendered to Canada in 1869. The province of Manitoba was established in 1870, British Columbia in 1871, Prince Edward Island in 1873, Alberta and Saskatchewan in 1905, and Newfoundland in 1949. Canada entered the 20th century with a population of more than 5 million and a railway system linking its coasts.

After confederation the Canadian government recognized the need to develop all aspects of nationhood. Participation on the side of Britain in World War I led to strong nationalism.

## CANADA AS A WORLD POWER

The Statute of Westminster in 1931 established the political equality of Canada with Britain in the Commonwealth of Nations. Thereafter Canada moved quickly to develop an autonomous role in the world. Canada declared war on Germany on Sept. 10, 1939, a week after Britain.

Since World War II Canada has taken a leading part in world affairs as a "middle power." It has played a significant role in the UN and NATO.

Lester Bowles Pearson, leader of the Liberal Party, was prime minister from April 1963 to April 1968.

## CANADA UNDER PRIME MINISTER TRUDEAU

Pierre Elliott Trudeau, a French-Canadian lawyer who had been minister of justice, succeeded Pearson in 1968. Trudeau called for elections on June 25, 1968. The decisive Liberal victory gave Canada its first majority government since 1962.

In national elections on Oct. 30, 1972, Prime Minister Trudeau's Liberal Party failed to win a clear majority, but formed a new cabinet with the support of the New Democratic Party. Trudeau called new elections in July 1974, in which his Liberal Party won a clear majority.

## PRIME MINISTERS OF CANADA

| 1867–1873 | Sir John A. Macdonald | Conservative |
|---|---|---|
| 1873–1878 | Alexander Mackenzie | Liberal |
| 1878–1891 | Sir John A. Macdonald | Conservative |
| 1891–1892 | Sir John J. C. Abbott | Conservative |
| 1892–1894 | Sir John S. D. Thompson | Conservative |
| 1894–1896 | Sir Mackenzie Bowell | Conservative |
| 1896 | Sir Charles Tupper | Conservative |
| 1896–1911 | Sir Wilfrid Laurier | Liberal |
| 1911–1917 | Sir Robert L. Borden | Conservative |
| 1917–1920 | Sir Robert L. Borden | Unionist |
| 1920–1921 | Arthur Meighen | Unionist |
| 1921–1926 | W. L. Mackenzie King | Liberal |
| 1926 | Arthur Meighen | Conservative |
| 1926–1930 | W. L. Mackenzie King | Liberal |
| 1930–1935 | Richard B. Bennett | Conservative |
| 1935–1948 | W. L. Mackenzie King | Liberal |
| 1948–1957 | Louis S. St. Laurent | Liberal |
| 1957–1963 | John G. Diefenbaker | Prog. Cons. |
| 1963–1968 | Lester B. Pearson | Liberal |
| 1968–1979 | Pierre E. Trudeau | Liberal |
| 1979–1980 | Joe Clark | Prog. Cons. |
| 1980– | Pierre E. Trudeau | Liberal |

Canada began a 6-year conversion to the metric system on April 1, 1975.

The 1970s recession was slower in hitting Canada than other industrial nations partly because of its oil export income. However, in October 1975 Prime Minister Trudeau established Canada's first peacetime controls on wages and prices to combat inflation.

On Jan. 1, 1977, Canada declared a 200-mile fishing limit off its east and west coasts. The new limit was recognized in bilateral treaties signed with most major offshore fishing powers.

Prime Minister Trudeau and President Carter announced agreement on Sept. 8, 1977, on plans to build a $10 billion, 2,700-mile trans-Canada pipeline to carry Alaskan natural gas south through Canada to the U.S. by 1983.

Complete regular live TV coverage of the Canadian parliament began on Oct. 17, 1977.

Following the lead of Britain earlier in the month, Canadians turned conservative at parliamentary elections held on May 22, 1979. The Progressive Conservative Party won a plurality of 137 members in the 282-seat House of Commons, enabling Conservative 39-year-old Joe Clark to become prime minister on June 4.

The first electricity from the $13.8 billion James Bay hydroelectric project in northern Quebec began to be generated in 1979, producing about 5,000 megawatts. Started in 1971, the project will supply about half the province's energy needs when it is completed in the late 1980s.

Canada's economy continued to falter in 1979. Inflation rose to an annual rate of 9%, while unemployment dropped only slightly to 7.5%.

Less than six months after attaining office, Clark was defeated in a vote of confidence in the House of Commons on Dec. 13, 1979, for failing to make good on campaign promises to cut taxes and instead proposing an excise tax of 18 cents per gallon on gasoline.

Trudeau led his Liberal Party to victory in a national election on Feb. 18, 1980, winning a clear majority of 146 seats to the Conservatives' 103 in the House of Commons and regaining the office of prime minister.

Efforts by Quebec's premier René Lévesque to win sovereignty for his French-speaking province were defeated in a referendum on May 20, 1980, when Quebecers voted 58.2% to 41.8% against a proposal that would have initiated negotiations for Quebec's independence.

Parliament adopted the song "O Canada" as the official national anthem in June 1980.

Seeking to develop a Canadian constitution to replace the British North America Act of 1867, Prime Minister Trudeau convened a conference of provincial premiers in Ottawa on Sept. 8–13, 1980. However, the meeting ended in failure because the provincial leaders feared that a new constitution would increase the powers of the federal government at their expense.

Determined that Canada should have its own constitution containing a bill of rights, Trudeau convened a special session of parliament. The lower house approved a resolution to reform the constitution 156–83 on Oct. 26, 1980, sending the measure on to the senate for debate.

QUICK QUIZ: Which nation is the leader in exports? See page 198.

# CAPE VERDE

**Official Name:** Republic of Cape Verde.
**Area:** 1,557 square miles (4,033 sq. km.).
**Population:** 329,175.
**Capital:** Praia, 20,000.
**Government:** One-party state.
**President:** Aristedes Pereira (since 1975).
**Prime Minister:** Pedro Pires (since 1975).
**National Assembly:** 56 members.
**U.S. Ambassador to Cape Verde:** Peter Jon de Vos.
**Ambassador to U.S.:** Jose Luis Fernandes Lopes.
**Flag:** Red vertical bar at hoist with black star flanked by two green cornstalks and yellow seashell; two horizontal stripes, yellow over green.
**Languages:** Portuguese (official), Crioulo.
**Main Ethnic Groups:** Creole (mulatto—71%), black (28%).
**Principal Religions:** Roman Catholicism (65%), animism (30%).
**Leading Industries:** Agriculture (coffee, bananas, corn, vegetables, sugarcane, beans, potatoes, peanuts, fruits); fishing; shipping; tourism; food processing.
**Foreign trade:** *major exports*—fish, bananas, coffee, salt, peanuts; *major imports*—petroleum, consumer goods, corn, rice, sugar.
**Places of Interest:** White sand beaches; 9,281-foot Pico volcano and Chã das Caldeiras, black sand lake on Fogo; ruins of first European settlement on São Tiago; 15th century capital city of Ribeira Grande on Santo Antão, ancient fortress, tiled cathedral, Gothic tombs.

## CAPE VERDE TODAY

Ranking among the smallest of the world's nations in area and population, Cape Verde faces a bleak future because of its lack of resources.

Lying about 400 miles off the coast of West Africa, the nation's main islands are São Tiago (383 sq. mi.), Santa Antão (301), Boa Vista (239), Fogo (184), São Nicolau (132), Maio (104), and Sal (83).

Most Cape Verdeans make their living by herding livestock or farming. But years of drought from 1968 to 1980 severely hurt agriculture. As a result about 40,000 Cape Verdeans migrated to Portugal to find work. Money they send home to their families helps pay for imports.

Tourism promises to become an important industry because of the white sand beaches, year-round mild climate, and absence of cloudy or rainy weather. Some islands have recorded no rainfall in more than 11 years.

## HISTORY

Portuguese explorer Diogo Gomes discovered the uninhabited islands in 1460. The islands soon became an important provisioning stop for ships sailing around Africa and to Brazil. Portuguese trade in slaves from Guinea was controlled from the islands for hundreds of years. The wealthy capital city of Ribeira Grande on Santo Antão was often attacked by pirates.

**CAPE VERDE** *(continued)*

Severe droughts repeatedly caused many deaths: 20,000 in 1900–03, 25,000 in 1920–22, 20,000 in 1940–43, and 3,000 in 1946–48.

After more than five centuries of Portuguese rule the islands were granted independence on July 5, 1975.

Aristedes Pereira, leader of the nation's only political party, the African Party for the Independence of Guinea-Bissau and Cape Verde (PIAGC), became Cape Verde's first president.

# CENTRAL AFRICA

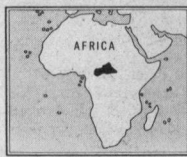 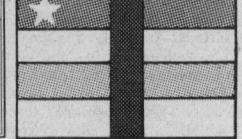

**Official Name:** Central African Republic.
**Area:** 240,535 square miles (622,984 sq. km.).
**Population:** 2,504,830.
**Chief Cities:** Bangui, capital, 187,000.
**Government:** One-party republic.
**President:** David Dacko (since 1979).
**U.S. Ambassador to Central Africa:** A. H. Woodruff.
**Ambassador to U.S.:** Jacques Topanda Makombo.
**Flag:** Blue, white, green, and yellow stripes crossed by vertical red bar; gold star in upper hoist corner.
**Languages:** French (official), Sangho.
**Ethnic Groups:** Banda (29%), Baya (28%), Mandia (24%), Ubangi (14%), Sara (5%).
**Religions:** Protestantism (40%), Roman Catholicism (28%), animism (24%), Islam (8%).
**Leading Industries:** Agriculture (cattle, cotton, coffee, bananas, rubber, mangoes, manioc); mining (diamonds, uranium); manufacturing (textiles, food processing); forestry and lumbering.
**Foreign Trade:** *major exports*—diamonds, cotton, coffee, wood; *major imports*—textile and leather machinery, textiles.
**Places of Interest:** Game reserves in north; Bangui.

## CENTRAL AFRICA TODAY

A little larger than New Mexico and Arizona combined, Central Africa is a poor, landlocked country that has few resources. Nine out of ten of the people raise crops and livestock, mostly to feed their families. The country's only two important cash crops are coffee and cotton.

Large tropical forests provide the potential for a substantial lumber industry, but the lack of good transportation facilities makes the export of large amounts of lumber difficult.

The country's best hope for improving its economic situation seems to lie in the development of its mining industry. Gem and industrial diamonds account for over half the value of the country's exports. In the 1970s the French Atomic Energy Commission cooperated in the development of mining and refining facilities to work a large deposit of uranium found in the eastern part of the country. France is the nation's main trading partner.

The nation stretches north to Chad, east to the Sudan, south to Congo and Zaire, and west to Cameroon. The terrain is chiefly rolling plateau, becoming tropical forest in the south and hilly savanna in the north.

From October to June the weather is dry and hot; temperatures exceed 110° F. in the daytime and range from 55° to 70° F. at night. From June through September temperatures range from 75° to 110° F. Tornadoes and floods are frequent.

## HISTORY

In 1889 the French established an outpost at Bangui. In 1894 the area between the Ubangi and Shari rivers was made a French territory. It was united with Chad in 1905 to form the Ubangi-Shari-Chad Colony. In 1910 the colony became part of French Equatorial Africa. Chad was detached from Ubangi-Shari in 1920.

The first representative assembly was created in 1945. A year later Ubangi-Shari received representation in the French parliament.

As the Central African Republic, the country was proclaimed autonomous within the French Community in 1958. Its first president, Barthelemy Boganda, was killed in a plane crash in 1959.

The nation won full independence on Aug. 13, 1960. David Dacko, Boganda's nephew and leader of the African Social Evolution Party (MESAN), was elected president in 1960 and 1964. He outlawed opposition parties.

Col. Jean-Bédel Bokassa ousted Dacko by a military coup on Jan. 1, 1966. He dissolved the national assembly and abolished the constitution. Suspected political opponents were jailed without trial, tortured, and often beaten to death.

In 1975 President Bokassa appointed Elisabeth Domitien as prime minister, the first woman to achieve that office in any African nation. But she was dismissed the following year.

Bokassa escaped an attempted assassination on Feb. 3, 1976. His son-in-law, Maj. Fidel Odrou, and seven others were executed 11 days later.

In 1976 Bokassa converted to Islam, changing his name to Salah Eddine Ahmed Bokassa.

Bokassa renamed the country the *Central African Empire* on Dec. 4, 1976, and crowned himself as Emperor Bokassa I in a ceremony at the Bangui sports stadium. A year later he staged a more elaborate official coronation on Dec. 4, 1977, at a cost of $50 million.

The emperor arrested his eldest son, Prince George, and expelled him on Oct. 5, 1978, fearing the crown prince might seize the throne.

When schoolboys demonstrated against a government decree ordering them to buy uniforms from a shop partly owned by one of Bokassa's three wives, Bokassa ordered them arrested and about 100 were killed on April 18–19, 1979. Despite Bokassa's denials of involvement, an international investigative team of lawyers from five African countries reported in August 1979 that Bokassa was responsible, quoting witnesses that the emperor personally killed 39 of the students. In reaction to the incident, the U.S. cut off $2.5 million annual foreign aid and France reduced its economic assistance to Bokassa's government.

Former President Dacko, 49, who had acted as an adviser to Bokassa, overthrew the emperor on Sept. 20, 1979, reestablishing a republic with himself as president. The coup was accomplished with the aid of French troops. Bokassa was in Libya at the time of the coup and was granted asylum by Ivory Coast. Dacko retained many of Bokassa's leading officials in his government.

# CHAD

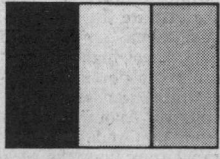

**Official Name:** Republic of Chad.
**Area:** 495,755 square miles (1,284,000 sq. km.).
**Population:** 4,679,420.
**Capital:** N'Djaména, 179,000.
**Government:** Transitional.
**President:** Goukouni Oueddei (since 1979).
**Flag:** Blue, yellow, red bars.
**Languages:** French (official), Arabic, Sara.
**Ethnic Groups:** Arab, Bantu, Sudanese.
**Religions:** Animism (50%), Islam (45%), Roman Catholicism (5%).
**Leading Industries:** Agriculture (cotton, cattle, millet, sorghum, rice, sweet potatoes); mining (natron); manufacturing (textiles, food processing).
**Foreign Trade:** *major exports*—cotton, cattle; *major imports*—petroleum products, machinery, motor vehicles.
**Places of Interest:** Lake Chad; Sahara Desert.

## CHAD TODAY

Chad is almost as large as the combined area of California, Arizona, New Mexico, and Nevada, but about half the country is covered by the wasteland of the Sahara Desert. It is one of the world's poorest countries, made even poorer by many years of civil war.

The nation's economy is almost entirely dependent upon agriculture and foreign aid. Most of the people of the northern part of the country are Muslim nomads who tend flocks of sheep, goats, and cattle, and live mostly on milk and dates. The people of southern Chad are mostly black farmers who grow grain crops, especially millet and sorghum. Their diet is largely gruel and beer.

Animosity between the Arabs of northern Chad and the blacks of southern Chad has existed for hundreds of years. The Arabs call southern Chad *Dar al-Abib*, meaning "Territory of Slaves," because it was the region where the Arabs frequently captured blacks for slaves.

The northern Sahara region of Chad is a dry barren land relieved only by occasional oases. Chad's central area is semidesert with some tropical trees and grazing land.

Lake Chad, on the western border, is a broad body of water surrounded by huge marshes.

Landlocked Chad is bordered by Libya on the north, Sudan to the east, Central Africa to the south, Cameroon and Nigeria to the southwest, and Niger to the west.

## EARLY HISTORY OF CHAD

In the 700s A.D. peoples from the upper Nile built walled city-states on the eastern shores of Lake Chad. Saharan Berbers forged these states into a centralized kingdom called *Kanem*, which later was absorbed into the empire of Bornu in what is now Nigeria.

British explorers first entered the area in 1822.

The French pushed northward into Chad in the 1890s, killing Rabeh, a military adventurer who had devastated the Muslim states (1892–98). The French created the Military Territory of Chad in 1900. Chad was united in 1906 with Ubangi-Shari (now Central Africa). In 1910 it became a part of French Equatorial Africa. Chad was detached from Ubangi-Shari in 1920. In 1958 it became an autonomous state.

## INDEPENDENCE

Chad won independence on Aug. 11, 1960, remaining within the French Community. François Tombalbaye, head of the Parti Progressiste Tchadien (PPT), became president. He outlawed all other political parties in 1962.

A civil war began in 1965 between the Muslim northerners and the Christian-led but largely animist blacks of the south.

A severe drought that lasted for six years, from 1969 to 1974, killed thousands of persons.

In June 1973 Tombalbaye arrested and imprisoned Gen. Félix Malloum, commander of the army, on charges of plotting his overthrow.

The army attacked the presidential palace on April 13, 1975, killing Tombalbaye and ending his 15-year dictatorship. Malloum was released from prison and became president of the military junta that took charge of the government.

Malloum dismissed the national assembly, banned Tombalbaye's PPT political party, freed the former president's political opponents from prison, and restored religious freedom. He appealed to Muslim rebels to lay down their arms.

The government agreed to a cease-fire on Jan. 22, 1978, with Arab rebel leader Hissene Habre. On Aug. 29, 1978, the ruling military junta was dissolved. Malloum became president and Habre became prime minister.

Civil war broke out anew in February 1979 between troops of Malloum and Habre. French paratroops flew into N'Djaména to rescue about 4,000 westerners from the fighting in which thousands were killed and most of the capital city's population fled to the countryside. Missionaries reported that thousands of Muslims were massacred throughout southern Chad as blacks sought revenge for reported atrocities by Muslim troops.

After a cease-fire was negotiated with the assistance of Nigeria, President Malloum resigned on March 23, 1979, and flew into exile in Nigeria.

A new government was agreed to on Aug. 21, 1979, with Muslim guerrilla leader Goukouni Oueddei as president and the head of black Christian forces, Col. Wadal Abdelkadar Kamougue, as vice president.

New fighting began on March 22, 1980, between troops of President Goukouni and those of former Prime Minister Habre. Because of the intensity of the new civil war, most Westerners, including the U.S. embassy staff, were evacuated. In May 1980 France withdrew its last 1,100 troops from the country.

Despite efforts of the Organization of African Unity (OAU) to obtain a truce, fighting continued to rage in 1980 with thousands of new casualties.

QUICK QUIZ: How many U.S. students graduated from high school in 1869-70? See page 202.

# CHILE

**Official Name:** Republic of Chile.
**Area:** 292,258 square miles (756,945 sq. km.).
**Population:** 11,381,700.
**Chief Cities:** Santiago, capital, 3,448,700; Viña del Mar, 262,100; Valparaíso, 248,200; Talcahuano, 204,200; Concepción, 172,800; Antofagasta, 157,000.
**Largest Metropolitan Area:** Santiago, 3,691,548.
**Government:** Military dictatorship.
**President:** Gen. Augusto Pinochet Ugarte (seized power in 1973).
**U.S. Ambassador to Chile:** John A. Bushnell.
**Chilean Ambassador to U.S.:** José Miguel Barros.
**Flag:** Stripes of white and red; union is blue square with five-pointed white star.
**Language:** Spanish.
**Principal Ethnic Group:** Mestizo (mixed Spanish-Indian ancestry).
**Main Religions:** Roman Catholicism (official, 67%), Protestantism (9%).
**Leading Industries:** Mining (copper, iron ore, sodium nitrate, coal); manufacturing (steel, textiles, food processing, consumer goods); agriculture (wheat, sugar beets, livestock, potatoes, corn, beans).
**Foreign Trade:** *major exports*—copper, iron ore, nitrates, coal; *major imports*—electrical machinery, chemical products, cereals, crude petroleum.
**Places of Interest:** Chilean lake country; Valparaíso; Indian ruins of Antofagasta province; Villarrica mountain area; Viña del Mar beach resort. *In Santiago:* Santa Lucia and San Cristóbal hills; presidential palace, cathedral; historical museum and national library; Forestal and President Balmaceda parks.

## CHILE TODAY

A long narrow country, Chile stretches 2,650 miles along the western coast of South America. It averages only 110 miles in width and is 221 miles across at its widest point.

For many years Chile was one of the few Latin American countries where the government was regularly chosen by constitutional free elections and human rights were respected. But today Chile is ruled by a military dictatorship that has suspended all civil liberties. The change came in September 1973 when the armed forces overthrew the country's elected Marxist president because they feared he was leading Chile to become a satellite of the Soviet Union.

Although rich in natural resources and one of the world's leading producers of copper, Chile has lagged in developing improved farming methods and manufacturing industries. As a result it must import much of its food and consumer products.

Chile's people are better educated and have a higher standard of living than those of many other Latin American countries. About three-fourths of the people live in cities.

A land of dramatic contrasts, Chile is hemmed by natural frontiers of desert, mountains, and ocean. Its white deserts in the north, especially the Atacama Desert, are among the driest regions in the world. They are rich in nitrate, copper, and other mineral deposits. In the east are the immense Andes Mountains. Mt. Aconcagua, on the border with Argentina, is 22,834 feet high—the loftiest peak in the Western Hemisphere. The Andes decrease in height as they run south to Chile's beautiful lake country. About 30 rivers drain into the Pacific from the Andes. To the west, a lower coastal range runs along the ocean.

A fertile central valley, about 600 miles long and 45 miles wide, is the center of Chile's agriculture and industry and the home of 90% of the population. Chile has many earthquakes.

## EARLY HISTORY

Led by Pedro de Valdivia, the Spanish conquistadores founded Santiago in 1541 and later established other settlements in the central region. During Chile's colonial period, which was marked by savage Indian wars and internal dissension, the country was essentially a neglected land of pioneers.

On Sept. 18, 1810, Chile declared its independence from Spain. A 7-year war followed in which Chilean patriots led by Bernardo O'Higgins won the country's freedom. The constitution of 1833, chiefly the work of Diego Portales, paved the way for parliamentary government. It lasted until 1925 with few amendments. The years 1841 to 1861 were marked by political reform and material progress. Chile won the "War of the Pacific" against Bolivia and Peru in 1884, acquiring the northern desert regions with their mineral wealth.

In 1891 a split in the Chilean aristocracy precipitated a civil war, culminating in the defeat and suicide of President José Manuel Balmaceda. For nearly 35 years thereafter, the congress was virtually omnipotent.

In 1920, when employment and political unrest had brought Chile to the verge of revolution, Arturo Alessandri was elected president with the support of the working and middle classes. He was ousted by a military coup in 1924, but was recalled in 1925. Alessandri introduced labor reforms and a new constitution. Conservative opposition led to his second ouster in 1925 and to the 6-year military dictatorship of Col. Carlos Ibáñez, which in turn collapsed in 1931.

Constitutional government was restored with Alessandri again elected to the presidency in 1932. In 1938 a "Popular Front" of Democrats, Radicals, Socialists, and Communists carried Pedro Aguirre Cerda into the presidency. Various coalitions of the center and left parties held power to the end of the decade.

Chile established traditions of constitutional democracy with the successive elections to the presidency of Juan Antonio Ríos in 1942, of Gabriel Gonzáles Videla in 1946, of former dictator Carlos Ibáñez in 1952, and of Jorge Alessandri in 1958.

The presidential election of 1964 was won by Eduardo Frei of the Christian Democratic Party. He emphasized a "revolution in freedom" by democratic rather than totalitarian means. Frei's policies were moderately socialistic and nationalistic, aiming at greater independence in foreign affairs.

## MARXIST REGIME

In a presidential election in September 1970, Salvador Allende Gossens, head of Chile's Socialist Party, was the candidate of a leftist Popular Unity (UP) coalition that included the Communists. He won by a narrow plurality, with 36.3% of the vote in a three-way race. Congress confirmed his election after amending the constitution to guarantee continued democratic government. Allende was the first avowed Marxist to become the freely elected president of a nation.

Former U.S. President Richard Nixon revealed in 1976 that he had ordered the CIA to try to prevent Allende from becoming Chile's president. The CIA was unsuccessful in attempts to foment a military coup.

President Allende established diplomatic relations with communist states. He expropriated many banks, vital industries, and farm estates. His government nationalized foreign-owned businesses, among them properties of four U.S. corporations—Anaconda, Kennecott, Cerro, and ITT.

Chile's economic situation worsened as wage increases led to increased demands for consumer goods, while curbs on profits and declining productivity reduced total output.

In national congressional elections on March 4, 1973, Allende's opposition, the Democratic Confederation (CODE), retained control of both the senate and the chamber of deputies. CODE candidates received 54.7% of the vote.

## MILITARY DICTATORSHIP

On Sept. 11, 1973, military forces led by the commander of the army, Gen. Augusto Pinochet Ugarte, surrounded and bombarded the presidential palace. Allende died during the coup.

The country was placed under strict military rule at all levels of government.

In the weeks following the coup 2,500 or more of Allende's followers were summarily executed. Many were imprisoned in military camps without trial—estimates of those jailed ranged from 10,000 to more than 80,000. The UN and the World Council of Churches helped more than 6,000 foreign refugees leave the country.

In 1975 the U.S. Congress cut off military aid to Chile because of human-rights violations.

The U.S. State Department further blocked $9.6 million in economic loans to Chile in June 1977 because of the military regime's continued disregard for human rights.

The military government was buoyed in January 1978 when a national referendum was held in which 75% of the voters expressed approval for Pinochet's administration.

Relations between the U.S. and Chile worsened in 1978–79 when the U.S. formally demanded the extradition of Gen. Juan Manuel Contreras Sepulveda, former head of the secret police, and two of his associates on charges of plotting and carrying out the assassination in Washington D.C., in 1976 of Chilean diplomat Orlando Letelier, a critic of the Pinochet government. But after Chile's supreme court refused U.S. requests for extradition of the three officers on Oct. 1, 1979, the U.S. backed down on carrying through retaliation it previously had threatened.

Although strikes had been outlawed since 1973, the government announced new decrees in July 1979 banning labor-union from any activity that affected national security, public services, or the public interest.

Pinochet received a stinging international rebuff in March 1980 when he was forced to cancel a tour of Asia. After already starting the trip, he received word that the president of the Philippines would not meet with him.

The military government launched new crackdowns on opponents in 1980, arresting and imprisoning them without trial. Hundreds of university teachers suspected of opposing the government were dismissed from their posts.

A national referendum on Sept. 12, 1980, approved a new constitution to continue Pinochet's military government in power until 1989. Although opponents were not able to campaign freely against the measure, almost a third of the voters cast "no" ballots. However, Pinochet hailed his winning margin of 67% as a great victory.

## CHILE'S DEPENDENCIES

### EASTER ISLAND

**Area:** 63 square miles (163 sq. km.).
**Population:** 1,600.
**Capital:** Hanga Roa.
Easter Island (or Rapa Nui) is a volcanic island in the South Pacific about 2,350 miles west of Chile. It is famed for its hieroglyphics and large stone heads carved from soft volcanic stone. The people are of Polynesian origin and raise yams, taro roots, bananas, potatoes, and sugarcane. The island is governed by Valparaíso province.

### JUAN FERNÁNDEZ

**Area:** 57 square miles (148 sq. km.).
**Population:** 615.
The Juan Fernández group includes two major islands: Robinson Crusoe (36 sq. mi.) and Alexander Selkirk (21 sq. mi.). They are the largest of several volcanic islands in the group, which is located about 400 miles west of Valparaíso. Lobster fishing is the main industry.

The islands are believed to have been discovered by a Spanish explorer, possibly before 1572. The English author Daniel Defoe is believed to have based his story *Robinson Crusoe* on the four-year confinement of the Scottish sailor Alexander Selkirk on Más Atierra (the original name of Robinson Crusoe Island).

### CHILEAN ANTARCTIC TERRITORY

**Area:** 482,625 square miles (1,249,993 sq. km.).
**Population:** 200.
Chile claimed the Palmer Peninsula section of Antarctica in 1940 and has established four bases there. Parts of the territory also are claimed by Britain and Argentina.

### DIEGO RAMÍREZ ISLANDS

This group of uninhabited islands is situated 60 miles southwest of Cape Horn.

### SALAY GOMEZ IŞLAND, SAN AMBROSIO ISLAND, AND SAN FÉLIX ISLAND

These islands are small, uninhabited Pacific Ocean possessions of Chile.

QUICK QUIZ: How many students are enrolled in U.S. colleges and universities? See page 243.

# CHINA

**Official Name:** People's Republic of China.
**Area:** 3,691,514 square miles (9,560,951 sq. km.).
**Population:** 1,039,270,000.
**Chief Metropolitan Areas:** Peking (Beijing), capital, 8,626,050; Shanghai, 10,820,000; Tientsin (Tianjin), 4,280,000; Shenyang, 2,411,000; Wuhan, 2,146,000; Chungking (Chongqing), 2,121,000; Canton (Guangzhou), 1,840,000; Harbin, 1,552,000; Dairen-Port Arthur (Dalian-Lushun), 1,508,000; Nanking (Nanjing), 1,419,000; Sian (Xian), 1,310,000; Tsingtao (Qingdao), 1,121,000; Chengtu (Chengdu), 1,107,000; Taiyuan, 1,020,000.
**Government:** One-party communist state.
**Heads of Government:** Hua Guofeng, chairman of the Communist Party (since 1976); Deng Xiaoping, vice-chairman of the Communist Party (since 1977); Zhao Ziyang, prime minister (since 1980); Ye Jianying, chief of state (since 1976).
**Legislature:** *National People's Congress,* 3,221 members.
**U.S. Ambassador to China:** Leonard Woodcock.
**Chinese Ambassador to U.S.:** Chai Zemin.
**Flag:** Red field, with gold star in upper hoist corner; four smaller gold stars form arc on right.
**Official Language:** Chinese
**Main Ethnic Group:** Han Chinese (94%).
**Religions:** Confucianism, Buddhism, and Taoism.
**Leading Industries:** Agriculture (rice, cotton, sugarcane, sugar beets, jute and hemp, livestock, tobacco, vegetables, corn, tea, wheat, potatoes, soybeans); fishing; manufacturing (steel, machinery, fertilizer, vehicles, chemicals, textiles); mining (coal, petroleum, natural gas, iron ore, other minerals).
**Foreign Trade:** *major exports*—petroleum, agricultural products, iron and steel, textiles, tin, consumer products; *major imports*—machinery, grain.
**Places of Interest:** Great Wall of China; waterfalls in the Kweichow Mountains; Gobi Desert; Shanghai; Hangchow. *In Peking:* former Imperial Palace; Temple of Heaven complex; Summer Palace; city gate.

## CHINA TODAY

China has the largest population of any country in the world—about five times that of the United States. Even so, it is not as crowded as other large countries of Asia, such as Bangladesh and India, because it has the third-largest area after the Soviet Union and Canada. It is rich in resources.

Many of China's problems stem from trying to change in only a few decades from a largely agricultural country into a modern industrial nation. Its problems have been similar to those of the Soviet Union in the 1920s and 1930s.

The success of China's industrialization is not accurately known because the communist government's economic statistics have often been issued for their propaganda effect. However, the nation's science and technology have enabled it to build and test atomic and hydrogen bombs and launch space satellites without assistance from the Soviet Union or the United States.

About one-fifth of China, principally in the east, is a region of lowlands. The rest consists of great plateaus, plains, and massive mountains. The diverse regions range from areas of tropical abundance to barren deserts, and from dense evergreen forests to depleted woodlands.

The principal mountain systems are the Altai in the northwest, the Himalaya in the southwest, the Tien Shan range in the far west, and the Kunlun range in the east.

The country's main waterways include the mighty Yangtze River, over 3,600 miles long, in central China; the Yellow River, the chief waterway of northern China; the Amur, on the northeastern border; and the Min, Si, and headwaters of the Mekong and Red rivers in the south.

## EARLY HISTORY

The story of the Hsia, traditionally China's first dynasty, is largely legendary. The recording of history began only during the subsequent Shang dynasty (about 1766–1123 B.C.).

The Chou dynasty (about 1122–256 B.C.), ruled during a classical era that produced the philosophers Confucius and Lao-tzu.

The Ch'in dynasty (221–207 B.C.) gave China its name and its first emperor, ended feudalism, and centralized the government. Roads, canals, and much of the Great Wall were constructed.

The Han dynasty (202 B.C.–A.D. 220) was noted for its artistry and territorial expansion.

## CHINA'S PROVINCES AND REGIONS

| NAME [1] | AREA | | POPULATION [3] |
|---|---|---|---|
| | Sq.Mi. | Sq. Km. | |
| Anhwei (Anhui) .... | 54,016 | 139,900 | 30,633,407 |
| Chekiang (Zhejiang) | 39,305 | 101,800 | 22,865,747 |
| Fukien (Fujian) .... | 47,529 | 123,100 | 13,142,721 |
| Heilungkiang (Heilongjiang) ... | 178,997 | 463,600 | 11,897,309 |
| Honan (Henan) .... | 64,479 | 167,000 | 44,214,594 |
| Hopei (Hebei) ...... | 78,263 | 202,700 | 37,886,020 |
| Hunan (Hunan) .... | 81,275 | 210,500 | 33,226,954 |
| Hupeh (Hubei) .... | 72,394 | 187,500 | 27,789,693 |
| Inner Mongolia [2] (Nei Monggol) ... | 454,635 | 1,177,500 | 7,338,000 |
| Kansu (Gansu) .... | 141,506 | 366,500 | 11,000,000 |
| Kiangsi (Jiangxi) .. | 63,630 | 164,800 | 16,772,865 |
| Kiangsu (Jiangsu).. | 39,460 | 102,200 | 40,963,000 |
| Kirin (Jilin)........ | 72,200 | 187,000 | 11,290,073 |
| Kwangsi-Chuang [2] (Guangxi Zhuang) | 85,097 | 220,400 | 17,591,000 |
| Kwangtung (Guangdong) .... | 89,344 | 231,400 | 36,740,000 |
| Kweichow (Guizhou)....... | 67,182 | 174,000 | 15,037,310 |
| Liaoning (Liaoning) | 57,915 | 150,000 | 20,566,000 |
| Ningsia Hui [2] (Ningxia Hui).... | 25,637 | 66,400 | 1,800,000 |
| Shansi (Shanxi).... | 60,657 | 157,100 | 14,314,485 |
| Shantung (Shandong) .... | 59,189 | 153,300 | 48,876,548 |
| Shensi (Shaanxi) ... | 75,600 | 195,800 | 15,881,281 |
| Sinkiang-Uighur [2] (Xinjiang Uygur) . | 635,833 | 1,646,800 | 4,873,608 |
| Szechwan (Sichuan) | 219,692 | 569,000 | 65,685,063 |
| Tibet [2] (Xizang) ... | 471,662 | 1,221,600 | 1,273,969 |
| Tsinghai (Qinghai) . | 278,380 | 721,000 | 1,676,534 |
| Yunnan (Yunnan) .. | 168,418 | 436,200 | 17,472,737 |

[1] New Pinyin spellings in parentheses. [2] Autonomous region. [3] 1953 census.

## RULING DYNASTIES OF CHINA

**c.2200–1766 B.C. Legendary Hsia dynasty:** Stone Age civilization; used painted, then black, pottery.

**c.1766–1123 B.C. Shang (or Yin) dynasty:** Bronze Age civilization; writing developed.

**c.1122–256 B.C. Chou dynasty:** Advanced feudal society.

**221–207 B.C. Ch'in dynasty:** First emperors with centralized government; Great Wall built.

**202 B.C.–A.D. 220 Han dynasty:** Science and arts flourished; paper invented.

**220–589 Six dynasties:** China divided among local feudal rulers; invasions by Huns and Turks.

**589–618 Sui dynasty:** Empire reunited; Buddhism flourished; poetry and sculpture outstanding.

**618–907 T'ang dynasty:** Printing on paper and mechanical clocks invented.

**907–959 Five dynasties:** Anarchy prevailed.

**960–1279 Sung dynasty:** Advanced civilization; magnetic compass invented; gunpowder used in warfare.

**1260–1368 Yuan dynasty** of Mongol rulers, founded by Kublai Khan; extensive public works; advancements in science and arts; novel developed in literature.

**1368–1644 Ming dynasty:** Mongols driven out of China; many cultural achievements.

**1644–1912 Manchu (or Ch'ing) dynasty:** European colonial incursions, ended with establishment of republic.

Under the Sung dynasty (960–1279) many innovations occurred, including gunpowder for military use, printing, the magnetic compass, and a new literary form, the novel.

The Mongols, under Genghis Khan, invaded and by 1215 had taken northern China. Genghis' grandson Kublai Khan founded the Yuan dynasty and completed the conquest of the Sung.

The Mongols were ousted in 1368 by the founders of the Ming dynasty.

European penetration began in 1557 when the Portuguese established a colony at Macao.

## MANCHU DYNASTY

The Manchus, meanwhile, were advancing from the north. They took Peking in 1644. Their dynasty, the Ch'ing, ruled until 1911.

China's vast riches increasingly lured European and American traders. China forbade the import of opium, but foreign traders smuggled in huge quantities of the narcotic. This precipitated the first Opium War (1839–42). China was forced to open five ports to British trade and to cede Hong Kong.

In the second Opium War (1856–60), the British and French joined forces. Ports were opened from the Yangtze north to Manchuria.

The U.S. sought equal trading rights, calling in 1900 for an Open Door policy to give all nations the right to trade in Chinese ports. The Boxer Rebellion of 1900 marked a desperate popular attempt to eliminate foreign domination.

## NATIONALIST CHINA

A revolution in 1911 led by Dr. Sun Yat-sen forced the abdication of the boy emperor Hsüant'ung (P'u-i) on Feb. 12, 1912. Sun was named provisional president of the new Republic of China, but soon resigned. His successor's dictatorial rule brought another revolt led by Sun in 1913. It failed and Sun was exiled.

Sun created the Kuomintang (Nationalist) Party, returning to China in 1917. Civil war began. Sun died in 1925, but the Kuomintang army went on under Chiang Kai-shek to defeat the central and northern warlords. In 1928 his government received foreign recognition. Chiang continued to fight the communists, forcing them into the 6,000-mile Long March to the northwest, where they settled in Shensi province in 1935.

Japan invaded Manchuria in 1931, setting up a puppet state called *Manchukuo* with China's former emperor P'u-i as the figurehead ruler.

Japan launched full-scale war on China in 1937. World War II brought Allied aid to China.

## COMMUNIST TAKEOVER OF CHINA

After World War II Chiang received U.S. support and supplies, but by 1949 communists had won control of the mainland. Chiang and his supporters fled to the island of Taiwan.

The *People's Republic of China* was declared by the communists on Oct. 1, 1949, under leadership of Mao Tse-tung (Mao Zedong) as chairman of the Communist Party and Chou En-lai (Zhou Enlai) as prime minister. Agriculture was collectivized and industry was nationalized.

In 1950 China intervened in the Korean War on the side of the North Koreans. Also in 1950 China conquered Tibet. In 1962 an undeclared border war was waged with India.

In 1960 China split with the Soviet Union in a continuing controversy over ideology.

China became a nuclear power with its first explosion of an atomic bomb in 1964. It exploded its first hydrogen bomb in 1967.

Mao launched the Great Proletarian Cultural Revolution in 1966 in an attempt to purge his enemies from power. The chief target of the revolution was the Communist Party establishment and its leader, Liu Shao-chi, who was chairman of the party in 1959–66. China veered toward anarchy as millions of zealous Red Guard students battled for power in provincial capitals. By the end of 1968 the Cultural Revolution appeared to be over, with the expulsion of Liu Shao-chi from the party in October.

In the summer of 1971, Defense Minister Lin Biao, who had been believed to be Mao's handpicked successor, was accused of plotting to assassinate Mao. He fled in a plane that crashed in Mongolia in September, killing all occupants.

## COMMUNIST CHINA IN THE EARLY 1970s

China's seat in the United Nations from 1949 to 1971 was held by Taiwan (Chiang's Republic of China). Admission of mainland China was repeatedly voted down, because of U.S. opposition. But in 1971 the U.S. reversed its position. Then the UN General Assembly voted to admit the Peking government and expelled Taiwan.

A weeklong visit by President Nixon to China in February 1972 demonstrated easing relations.

Climaxing a 6-day visit to Peking on Sept. 29, 1972, Japan's Premier Kakuei Tanaka agreed to establish diplomatic relations.

In mid-February 1973, U.S. Secretary of State Henry Kissinger visited Peking where he had cordial talks with Chairman Mao and Premier Chou that resulted in the establishment

QUICK QUIZ: U.S. petroleum reserves are what percentage of the world total? See page 258.

**CHINA** *(continued)*

of "liaison offices"—one step below formal diplomatic recognition.

China launched a New Cultural Revolution under the leadership of Chairman Mao in February 1974. The new campaign was directed at "reactionaries" who clung to the beliefs of the ancient philosopher Confucius.

A new constitution was adopted in 1975 which made the chairman of the Communist Party, Mao Tse-tung, commander of the armed forces.

Communists supported by China conquered Cambodia, South Vietnam, and Laos in 1975, turning those Southeast Asian countries into communist states.

In September 1975 China established diplomatic relations with the European Common Market.

U.S. President Gerald Ford and First Lady Betty Ford visited China on Dec. 2–5, 1975, meeting with Chairman Mao and other leaders.

The 77-year-old Chou En-lai, who had served as prime minister of China since it was taken over by the communists, died on Jan. 8, 1976. He was succeeded as prime minister by Hua Guofeng.

Chou's chosen successor, Deputy Prime Minister Deng Xiaoping, was stripped of all offices and branded a reactionary. In April 1976 riots broke out in Peking and other cities when the people believed Chou's memory was being degraded.

Major earthquakes in July 1976 caused severe damage to the industrial region of Tientsin and Tangshan. An estimated 242,000 persons were killed.

## CHINA UNDER HUA AND DENG

After ruling China for nearly 27 years, 82-year-old Mao died on Sept. 9, 1976. More than 750,000 Chinese attended a memorial for Mao on Sept. 18, which was presided over by his successor, Hua Guofeng, who became chairman of the Communist Party as well as prime minister.

Mao's widow, Chiang Ching, and three other members of the Communist Party's politburo were arrested in October 1976. They were branded as a radical "Gang of Four" who were trying to take over China. In following months there were reports that over a million of their followers were arrested and over 7,000 killed.

The 74-year-old Deng was restored as deputy prime minister in July 1977, and it soon became clear he had been placed in charge of running the government. His previous downfall was officially blamed on the discredited "Gang of Four."

Well known as a pragmatist, Deng told the Chinese Communist Party's 11th congress in August 1977: "The minimum requirement for a communist is to be an honest person. There must be less empty talk and more hard work."

The new leaders of China turned the country's foreign and domestic policies in new directions. A concerted campaign was launched to discredit the supposed infallibility of Chairman Mao. Chinese officials openly spoke of the last years of his reign as "10 lost years." Hundreds of persons who had been purged during Mao's "cultural revolutions" were restored to official positions.

Obviously envious of the economic prosperity of neighboring Japan, China signed a $20 billion trade pact with Japan on Feb. 16, 1978. This was followed on Aug. 12 with the signing of a treaty of peace and friendship with Japan. Ratification documents were exchanged on Oct. 23, 1978, bringing a formal end to four decades of war between China and Japan. The pact was denounced by the Soviet Union as an alliance that threatened to bring war in Asia.

China actively began encouraging Western tourists to visit the country in 1978, ending the reclusiveness that had barred most visitors for three decades.

Chairman Hua declared in July 1978 that the new leadership had restored the economy from the "brink of collapse."

A new constitution was approved on March 5, 1978, by the national legislature, restoring rights to citizens and to ethnic groups.

China and the U.S. established formal diplomatic relations on Jan. 1, 1979, as the U.S. ended diplomatic ties with the Taiwan government. In late January and early February 1979, Deng made a 9-day visit to the U.S., the first by a Chinese communist leader. He and President Carter signed a series of agreements to strengthen relations. Later in the year, on July 7, China and the U.S. signed a comprehensive trade agreement giving China most-favored-nation trade status. The pact was approved by the U.S. Congress on Jan. 24, 1980. Within a year the U.S. became China's second most important trading partner, next to Japan.

Angered by what it regarded as the mistreatment of ethnic Chinese by the Vietnamese government and by Vietnam's overthrow of the pro-Chinese government of Cambodia, China "punished" its pro-Soviet Union neighbor to the south with a large-scale four-week border war from Feb. 17 to March 15, 1979.

For the first time in 20 years, China announced its government budget for 1979–80, a surprisingly low figure of $70.7 billion based on deficit spending of about $11 billion.

Avowedly to prepare for younger leadership of the nation, Hua and Deng resigned their government posts in September 1980, but retained control of the government through their Communist Party positions.

Zhao Ziyang, 61, was appointed prime minister on Sept. 7, 1980, to manage the day-to-day affairs of the government. Zhao promised to carry on the economic reforms initiated by Deng and make China a "modernized, highly democratic and civilized socialist state" within two decades.

A meeting of the National People's Congress in September 1980 ratified the changes in leadership. It approved an amendment to the constitution abolishing the right of people to air dissenting views in critical wall posters. The congress also ratified a law designed to reduce the birthrate by raising the minimum age for marriage to 22 for men and 20 for women. The Communist Party called on its 38 million members to have no more than one child per family.

The U.S. and China signed new agreements on Sept. 17, 1980, paving the way for scheduled airline service and mutual use of each other's ports by merchant ships.

Drought and floods cut China's food production in 1980, causing it to sign a 4-year agreement with the U.S. on Oct. 22, 1980, to buy 6 to 8 million tons of grain annually.

# COLOMBIA

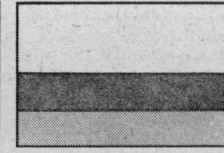

**Official Name:** Republic of Colombia.
**Area:** 439,737 square miles (1,138,914 sq. km.).
**Population:** 27,417,400.
**Largest Cities:** Bogotá, capital, 3,522,000; Medellín, 1,748,000; Cali, 1,189,000; Barranquilla, 868,000; Buvaramanga, 443,000; Cartagena, 355,000.
**Government:** Republic.
**President:** Julio César Turbay Ayala (since 1978).
**Parliament:** *Senate,* 118 members; *House of Representatives,* 210 members.
**U.S. Ambassador to Colombia:** Thomas D. Boyatt.
**Colombian Ambassador to U.S.:** Virgilio Barco.
**Flag:** Tricolor with wide yellow stripe atop narrower blue and red stripes.
**Official Language:** Spanish.
**Main Ethnic Groups:** Mestizo (mixed Indian-Spanish, 58%), European descent (20%), mulatto (14%).
**Principal Religion:** Roman Catholicism (95%).
**Leading Industries:** Agriculture (coffee, cattle, bananas, sugar, tobacco, cotton, rice, wheat, potatoes); mining (petroleum, gold, silver, platinum, emeralds, coal, iron, nickel); food processing; manufacturing (textiles, steel, chemicals).
**Foreign Trade:** *major exports*—coffee, petroleum, coal, bananas, cotton, beef, sugar; *major imports*—machinery, motor vehicles, consumer goods.
**Places of Interest:** Island of San Andrés; Zipaquira underground Salt Mine Cathedral; Guatavita Lake; San Agustín Archaeological Park. *In Bogotá:* Plaza Bolívar; Gold Museum; national museum; Museum of July 20th, 1810; colonial buildings; planetarium; museum of modern art.

## COLOMBIA TODAY

Colombia is a South American nation larger than Texas and California combined. With a wealth of natural resources, Colombia is an important petroleum producer and contains 60% of South America's coal reserves. It is second only to Brazil in coffee production. Colombia also has prospered as one of the main sources of marijuana and cocaine smuggled into the U.S.

Colombia is one of the few South American nations governed by freely elected civilians.

Most Colombians are poor. Many farm workers, eke out a subsistence for their families by growing corn and beans.

An intensive family-planning program reduced the population growth rate from 3.2% in 1965 to 2.9% by the mid-1970s.

Government-owned oil refineries and hydroelectric plants have been developed to speed industrialization. The government welcomes foreign investors and protects their interests.

Since 1970 leftist guerrillas have ambushed government troops, carried out political kidnappings, and conducted other acts of terrorism. The government carries on an unceasing war against guerrillas and drug smugglers.

Colombia has coastlines on the Caribbean to the north and the Pacific to the west. Called the "Gateway to South America," the country is bordered on the northwest by Panama, on the northeast by Venezuela, on the southeast by Brazil, and on the south by Peru and Ecuador.

Three ranges of the Andes Mountains cross Colombia, roughly paralleling the Pacific coast. The Magdalena and Cauca rivers converge in the north and empty into the Caribbean.

## SPANISH COLONIZATION

Spanish explorers who came to Colombia in 1499 found some gold and jewels. The Colimas Indians of the Cauca Valley were especially noted for their works of gold. Over 15,000 gold objects of pre-Spanish art are preserved today in Bogotá's Gold Museum.

Permanent colonization on the isthmus began after 1514. The region—including portions of present-day Panama, Venezuela, Ecuador, and most of Colombia—was called New Granada, a Spanish colony for three centuries.

## INDEPENDENCE

The colonists began their struggle for independence from Spain on July 20, 1810. In 1819 Simón Bolívar became president of the republic of Gran Colombia. By 1830 Venezuela and Ecuador had declared themselves separate states. The remaining territory became the republic of New Granada, which assumed its present name, Colombia, in 1866.

Two political parties developed: Conservatives, favoring centralized government and close ties with the church, and Liberals, advocating a loose federal government and separation of church and state. Their rivalry caused nearly a hundred civil wars by 1899, when the War of a Thousand Days took 100,000 lives.

In 1903 Colombia refused to ratify the leasing of territory to the U.S. to build a canal, and Panama declared itself independent.

An undeclared civil war, called *La Violencia,* between Conservatives and Liberals in 1948–57 resulted in over 200,000 deaths.

Constitutional amendments adopted in 1957 established a unique system that required the presidency to alternate between the Liberal and Conservative parties until 1974.

## RETURN TO TWO-PARTY DEMOCRACY

In the first major two-party national election in more than two decades, on April 21, 1974, Alfonso López Michelsen, the Liberal Party candidate, was elected president.

On June 26, 1975, the government suspended civil rights, imposing a state of siege in efforts to halt a wave of terrorist kidnappings and killings by leftist guerrillas.

The tripling of coffee prices in the late 1970s brought a "coffee bonanza" of $2 to $3 billion to Colombia, but caused inflation to soar.

In a closely contested election on June 4, 1978, Liberal candidate Julio César Turbay Ayala defeated Conservative Belisario Betancur, 2,506,228 to 2,358,644, to win a 4-year term as president. He was inaugurated on Aug. 7.

One of the world's 50 largest hydroelectric

QUICK QUIZ: What is the largest hydroelectric generating plant in the U.S.? See page 262.

## COLOMBIA *(continued)*

projects is under construction on the Patia River in southwest Colombia. Planned for completion in 1983, it will have a capacity of 1,540 megawatts.

To make up for the 30% inflation rate experienced in 1979, the government granted a 30% increase in minimum wages in 1980.

Guerrillas of the Movement of April 19 (M–19) took the embassy of the Dominican Republic on Feb. 27, holding hostage 58 persons, including ambassadors of the U.S. and 13 other countries. Colombian troops besieged the embassy for two months until April 27 when the guerrillas were allowed to fly to Cuba with 12 remaining hostages who were let go there.

Amnesty International condemned the Colombian government in April 1980 for permitting the military to torture political prisoners. It urged the government to stop its practice of allowing the army to hunt down and imprison suspected guerrillas under military law.

With illegal marijuana and cocaine exports at an estimated rate of $1.5 billion a year—about 50% of the country's legal exports—influential voices were raised in 1980 calling for legalization of the drug traffic so that the government could obtain tax revenues from it.

## COMOROS

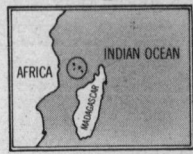 

**Official Name:** Federal and Islamic Republic of the Comoros.
**Area:** 694 square miles (1,797 sq. km.).
**Population:** 337,949.
**Capital:** Moroni, Grande Comore, 12,000.
**Government:** Political-military directorate.
**President:** Ahmed Abdallah (since 1978).
**Prime Minister:** Salim Ben Ali (since 1978).
**Parliament:** Federal Assembly, 39 elected members.
**Flag:** Green field with white crescent and four white stars in center.
**Languages:** Arabic and Swahili.
**Main Ethnic Group:** Antalaotra (mixed Arab-Malay-African ancestry).
**Principal Religion:** Islam.
**Leading Industries:** Agriculture (coconuts, coffee, sisal, vanilla, cocoa, sugarcane, cassava, sweet potatoes, vegetables, mangoes, bananas, goats, cattle); fishing; manufacturing (food processing, soap, lumber).
**Foreign Trade:** *major exports*—copra, vanilla, spices, cocoa; *major imports*—food, consumer goods.
**Places of Interest:** Kartala volcano (7,746 feet) on Grande Comore; swimming beaches; fishing villages; plantations.

## COMOROS TODAY

Lying between the east coast of Africa and the island of Madagascar, Comoros is one of the smallest and poorest nations in the world.

The main islands of Comoros are: Grande Comore, 443 sq. mi.; Anjouan, 164 sq. mi.; and Moheli, 81 sq. mi. The Comoros island Mahore (Mayotte) remains a French dependency.

The Comoro islanders make their living mainly by farming and fishing. Many work on the large plantations that produce vanilla, coffee, coconuts, sisal, cocoa, spices, and plants from which are made essential oils used in perfumes. Families grow their own food on small farms that provide sweet potatoes, cassava, fruits, and vegetables. However, much food has to be imported.

Few people can read and write, and only 3 of every 10 children attend school.

The islands have a hot climate the year round. The dry season, from May to October, has temperatures that fall to about 70° F. in the evening. In the wet season, from November to April, the temperature rarely falls below 80° F.

There are many tropical storms. Reservoirs catch water during the rainy season, but deep wells must be sunk to supplement the supply of drinking water in the dry season.

The mountainous islands are of volcanic origin. The highest volcano is 7,746-foot Kartala on Grande Comore.

## HISTORY

The islands became part of the East African empire of the sultan of Oman in the 800s. They appeared on Portuguese sailing charts by 1527.

France acquired rights to Mahore from the local chiefs, making it a colony in 1843. A protectorate was extended over all the Comoros in 1886. On July 25, 1912, France made all the Comoros a colony. From 1914 they were administered from Madagascar.

France gave the Comoros the status of an overseas territory on Jan. 1, 1947. Local self-government developed with a 30-member assembly.

The islands were granted complete internal self-government in 1960. In a referendum on Dec. 22, 1974, 95% of the people voted for immediate independence.

## INDEPENDENCE

The Comoros national assembly declared independence from France on July 6, 1975, and elected Ahmed Abdallah as president.

The residents of Mahore appealed to France to preserve their colonial status. When French troops withdrew from most of the Comoros in July, some remained on Mahore as a sign of continued French protection.

On Aug. 3, 1975, President Abdallah was overthrown in a bloodless coup led by Ali Soilih, head of the National United Front. A revolutionary council took charge of the government, nationalizing all French-owned property. Soilih tried to create a Chinese Maoist state. His youthful followers persecuted conservatives and attempted to stamp out the Islamic religion.

France terminated its annual $18.5 million aid, causing great economic hardship.

The people of Mahore voted almost unanimously on Feb. 8, 1976, to remain a dependency of France. See page 551.

A military coup on May 13, 1978, overthrew Soilih. He was killed while trying to escape.

Former president Abdallah was restored to power, winning election as president without opposition on Oct. 22, 1978. He proclaimed that people were again free to practice religions of their choice.

# CONGO

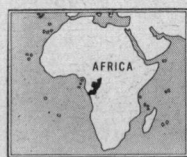

**Official Name:** People's Republic of the Congo.
**Area:** 132,047 square miles (342,000 sq. km.).
**Population:** 1,556,030.
**Largest Metropolitan Areas:** Brazzaville, capital, 136,200; Pointe-Noire, 115,000.
**Government:** Marxist communist military junta.
**President:** Denis Sassou-Nguessou (since 1979).
**Prime Minister:** Col. Louis-Sylvain Goma (since 1975).
**U.S. Ambassador to Congo:** William Lacy Swing.
**Congo Ambassador to U.S.:** Nicolas Mondjo.
**Flag:** Red field with green wreath, yellow star, hammer, and hoe in upper corner.
**Languages:** French (official), Lingala, Kikongo.
**Main Ethnic Groups:** Bakongo (45%), Bateke (20%), M'Bochi (10%).
**Religions:** Animism (48%); Roman Catholicism (47%); Islam (5%).
**Leading Industries:** Agriculture (corn, bananas, cassava, rice, peanuts, goats, poultry, palm nuts, sugarcane, tobacco, coffee, cocoa); forestry and lumbering; manufacturing (cement, textiles, food processing, tobacco products, soap, sugar, palm oil); mining (petroleum, potash).
**Foreign Trade:** *major exports*—wood, sugar, palm nuts, coffee, cocoa, peanuts, tobacco; *major imports*—machinery, vehicles.
**Places of Interest:** Mayombé Mountains; rain forest; Bateke Plateau; Brazzaville.

## CONGO TODAY

Ruled by a Marxist communist military junta, Congo is a hot African country that straddles the equator. It is about the size of New Mexico both in area and population. Thick tropical forests cover much of the country. These have long been Congo's most important resource, with lumber the major export. Congo's Atlantic coast port of Pointe-Noire is a major shipping center.

The majority of Congolese make their living by subsistence agriculture. But about 4 out of 10 people live in cities and towns, employed in businesses and services. As a result a higher percentage of the people can read and write and have a somewhat better standard of living than those in many other black countries of Africa.

A narrow, treeless coastal plain is bordered by the Mayombé Mountains, which run parallel to the coastline. To the north is a grassy plateau region, and to the east the Niari River valley.

The Congo (Zaire) and Ubangi rivers form the eastern border with Zaire. Gabon and Cameroon lie to the east and Central Africa to the north.

## EARLY HISTORY

A large Congo empire reached the peak of its power during the 1500s. In the preceding century the Portuguese were the first European explorers of the coastal areas of the Congo, discovering the mouth of the Congo River in 1484.

Beginning in the 1600s French traders, interested in slaves and ivory, began to establish trading centers. By 1785 at least a hundred French ships a year visited the region.

Exploration of the interior was undertaken by the French beginning in the 1870s. The Congress of Berlin in 1885 recognized French claims to the area.

The colony was first called *French Congo* and was later renamed *Middle Congo*. In 1910 Middle Congo, Gabon, and Ubangi-Shari were combined as French Equatorial Africa. By 1956 Middle Congo had gained local autonomy, and in 1958 the colony's voters approved making it the autonomous *Congo Republic*.

## INDEPENDENCE

On Aug. 15, 1960, the Congo Republic became fully independent. Fulbert Youlou was elected first president, with the support of all parties. On Aug. 13–15, 1963, Youlou was toppled by a revolt. In December 1963 a new constitution was approved. Alphonse Massamba-Débat was elected to a 5-year term as president.

On Aug. 3, 1968, four days after President Massamba-Débat had dissolved the national assembly, the army seized power. Massamba-Débat was forced to resign on Sept. 5.

Maj. Marien Ngouabi, head of the army, declared himself president on Jan. 1, 1969.

Ngouabi proclaimed a new constitution on Jan. 3, 1970, establishing a one-party Marxist communist state. The official name of the Congo was changed to the *People's Republic of the Congo*. A Marxist Congolese Labor Party (CLP) was created with Ngouabi as its leader.

An offshore oil field began production in 1972, contributing to an improvement in the economy. However, the fields were expected to be depleted by the mid-1980s.

Ngouabi was slain on March 18, 1977, by assassins who escaped. Four days later the Roman Catholic archbishop of Brazzaville, Emile Cardinal Biayenda, was murdered in reprisal by members of Ngouabi's family.

The ruling military junta executed former President Massamba-Débat on March 25, 1977, after announcing that he had confessed to plotting Ngouabi's assassination. Sixteen other persons also were executed for complicity.

Col. Joachim Yhombi Opango, 38, was made president on April 13, 1977, by the military junta. Two days later he abolished the national assembly and made the military junta supreme.

Diplomatic relations between Congo and the United States were restored on June 7, 1977, after a 12-year break that had begun in 1965.

The economy stagnated from 1975 to 1979 with reduced oil production. Inadequate transportation facilities hampered shipment of goods.

The Marxist military junta announced on Feb. 8, 1979, that Col. Denis Sassou-Nguessou had become head of state, replacing President Opango, who was imprisoned on charges of treason. The new leader previously had been minister of defense.

The president appealed in 1980 for foreign investors to aid the country's economy, promising the government would not interfere with private enterprise.

QUICK QUIZ: Which is the world's leading commercial fishing country? See page 264.

# COSTA RICA

 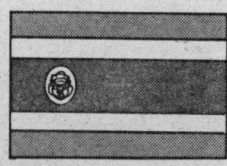

**Official Name:** Republic of Costa Rica.
**Area:** 19,575 square miles (50,700 sq. km.).
**Population:** 2,240,380.
**Chief Cities:** San José, capital, 236,707.
**Largest Metropolitan Area:** San José, 395,401.
**Government:** Democratic republic.
**President:** Rodrigo Carazo Odio (since 1978).
**Parliament:** *Legislative Assembly,* 57 members.
**U.S. Ambassador to Costa Rica:** Francis J. McNeil.
**Costa Rican Ambassador to U.S.:** José Rafael Echeverría.
**Flag:** Stripes top to bottom of blue, white, red, white, blue; national crest in white oval on red stripe.
**Official Language:** Spanish.
**Ethnic Groups:** Spanish descent and mestizo (97%), black (2%), Indian (1%).
**Official Religion:** Roman Catholicism (97%).
**Leading Industries:** Agriculture (coffee, bananas, cattle, cocoa, maize, pineapples, sugarcane, tobacco, rice, potatoes); food processing; manufacturing (textiles, clothing, footwear, cigarettes, furniture, construction materials); mining (gold, salt).
**Foreign Trade:** *major exports*—coffee, bananas, beef, sugar, cocoa; *major imports*—paper products, machinery, iron and steel, pharmaceuticals, petroleum, chemicals, food, manufactured goods.
**Places of Interest:** Irazú Volcano; Arenal and Poas volcanoes; Osa Peninsula, national biological preserve; basalt balls near Palmar Monte; Valley of Orosi; Puntarenas. *In San José:* Canvillo Park; national museum; national palace; national theater.

## COSTA RICA TODAY

About the size of West Virginia in area and population, Costa Rica has a more prosperous economy as well as a more stable democratic government than other Central American countries.

In the 1970s the gross national product grew at an annual rate of 3% to 6%. Bananas and coffee remained the most important products, but other agricultural and manufacturing products now account for more than 40% of the exports.

The development of bauxite mining and the manufacture of aluminum as well as an expanding tourist industry provide the best opportunities for continued economic growth.

Many Americans retire to Costa Rica because the government collects no tax on the income of retirees and allows them to import automobiles and household goods duty free.

Costa Rica lies entirely within the tropical zone, but its climate, flora, and living conditions are tempered by the altitude.

The capital, San José, is located in a fertile central valley.

Most Costa Ricans live at altitudes of 3,000 to 4,000 feet. At these heights the climate is springlike throughout the year.

Costa Rica has several active volcanoes, two of which, Irazú, 11,260 ft., and Arenal, 5,092 ft., erupted in the 1960s.

Nicaragua lies to the north; Panama to the east.

## HISTORY

The country was discovered and probably named by Columbus during his voyage of 1502. Spain ignored its small colony because of the scarcity of minerals, and the province grew slowly.

Costa Rica, along with the rest of Central America, declared independence from Spain without violence on Sept. 15, 1821. In 1824 it became a state in the Federal Republic of Central America. When that government failed in 1838, Costa Rica resumed independence.

An invasion led by the American military adventurer William Walker was put down in 1856 by a united Costa Rican people.

The 1890s saw the arrival of the great fruit companies and the construction of a railroad from the Caribbean to the city of San José.

Since independence Costa Rica's political life has been characterized by a series of smooth, democratic changes of government. Only for three periods (1870–82, 1917–19, and 1948) was the country ruled by dictatorship. Gen. Tomás Guardia seized power in 1870 and ruled by dictatorial means for a dozen years until his death in 1882.

A second military rule, established by Gen. Federico Tinoco in 1917, was overthrown by a popular revolt in 1919. After the restoration of democratic government in 1919, Costa Rica enjoyed a long period of political stability.

In 1948 the national assembly declared invalid the presidential election of Otilio Ulate. Col. José Figuéres Ferrer, a supporter of Ulate, led a revolt and temporarily seized power. He then turned over the presidency to Ulate in 1949.

Figuéres himself was chosen president in the 1953 election, serving until 1958. Since that time elections have been orderly. Figuéres staged an impressive political comeback in the February 1970 presidential election.

Daniel Oduber Quirós, candidate of the ruling National Liberation Party (PLN), was elected president on Feb. 3, 1974, with 42.5% of the popular vote.

Costa Rica's traditional foreign policy has been one of nonintervention in the affairs of neighboring Central American countries. The country has been an active participant in the Organization of American States (OAS).

The government announced on July 6, 1976, the discovery of a plot by right-wing extremists to overthrow President Oduber and eliminate other leading government officials. A spokesman accused Guatemalan rightists of aiding the plot.

Rodrigo Carazo Odio, leader of the opposition Unity Party, won a 4-year term as president in a national election on Feb. 5, 1978. He defeated the governing-PLN candidate Luis Alberto Monge with 51% to 43% of the vote. Carazo, a businessman and economist, had campaigned on charges of corruption in the government.

Costa Rica broke diplomatic relations with Nicaragua in November 1978 after Nicaraguan troops killed two Costa Rican border guards.

In 1979 the government permitted Nicaragua's Sandinista rebels to use Costa Rican border areas as bases in their successful civil war that overthrew Nicaragua's Somoza dictatorship. In addition Costa Rica provided camps for many of the estimated 100,000 Nicaraguan refugees who fled their homeland before and during the civil war.

# CUBA

**Official Name:** Republic of Cuba.
**Area:** 44,218 square miles (114,524 sq. km.).
**Population:** 10,073,000.
**Chief Cities:** Havana (La Habana), capital, 1,008,500; Santiago de Cuba, 315,801; Camagüey, 221,826; Holguín, 151,938; Guantánamo, 148,833; Santa Clara, 146,651.
**Largest Metropolitan Area:** Havana, 1,861,442.
**Government:** One-party communist state.
**President:** Fidel Castro Ruz (since 1959).
**Legislature:** *Council of Ministers,* 23 members.
**U.S. Diplomatic Representative to Cuba:** Lyle Franklin Lane.
**Cuban Diplomatic Representative to U.S.:** Ramón Sánchez Parodi.
**Flag:** Alternate blue and white stripes; red triangle at hoist bears five-pointed white star.
**Official Language:** Spanish.
**Ethnic Groups:** Spanish descent (75%), mixed (13%), black (12%).
**Main Religion:** Roman Catholicism (85%).
**Leading Industries:** Agriculture (sugarcane, tobacco, bananas, pineapples, citrus fruits, cattle, rice, cotton, coffee, cocoa, vegetables); fishing; manufacturing (sugar refining, textiles, rum, tobacco products, oil refining, cement, machine parts); mining (nickel, iron, chromite, copper, manganese, clay, petroleum).
**Foreign Trade:** *major exports*—sugar, inorganic chemicals, tobacco, nickel; *major imports*—crude petroleum, wheat, tractors, cotton fabrics, nonelectrical machinery.
**Places of Interest:** Morro Castle fortress in Havana Harbor; Guantánamo U.S. Naval Base; Bay of Pigs; Isle of Pines (Isle of Youth); Santa Maria Beach; Hanabanilla Mountain and Lake Resort.

## CUBA TODAY

Cuba is the only communist country in the Western Hemisphere. The communist government of the Caribbean island has survived since 1959 largely because of aid estimated at about $3 billion a year from the Soviet Union.

As the world's third-ranking sugarcane-producing nation, Cuba's economy relies heavily on the export of sugar. Soaring sugar prices in 1975 brought Cuba a surge of prosperity, but the fall of sugar prices to a few cents a pound in the late 1970s forced the government to tighten rationing of food and consumer products for its people.

All power rests with President Fidel Castro. Radio and television speeches and mass meetings have replaced parliamentary deliberations. Political opponents are subject to summary trial by a revolutionary tribunal.

The Castro regime has made sweeping economic changes aimed at increasing Cuba's production and replacing capitalism with a controlled communist economy. All land, industries, and businesses have been placed under state control. Socialized medicine provides health services for families, and elementary education is almost universal.

The largest island in the Caribbean Sea, Cuba lies 90 miles south of Key West, Fla. Jamaica is about 100 miles to the southeast. Windward Passage separates Cuba's eastern tip from Haiti.

The island is about 745 miles long and 60 miles wide. Its nearly 2,500-mile-long coast has many bays, inlets, coral reefs, and marshes.

There are three mountainous regions. The rugged Sierra Maestra in the easternmost province, Orjente, rise to 6,542 feet. The lower Sierra de los Organos are in the west. The Sierra de Trinidad stand in central Cuba. Tropical forests cover the mountains.

Several small islands lie off the coast. The largest is the Isle of Pines, renamed the Isle of Youth by Castro in 1978. The island is said to be the setting of Robert Louis Stevenson's *Treasure Island.*

Cuba's largest river, the Cauto, winds across the southeastern corner of the island.

The climate of Cuba remains hot throughout the year with an average of 70° F. in the winter and 81° F. in the summer. About 54 inches of rain fall annually.

## SPANISH RULE

Discovered by Columbus on his first voyage to America in 1492, Cuba remained under Spanish rule until 1898. During the early colonial period Havana served as the last port visited by ships carrying treasure back to Spain.

In 1762 the British captured Havana. Their occupation lasted only a year.

In 1868 Carlos Manuel de Céspedes and other patriots issued a proclamation calling for revolt against Spain. The civil conflict lasted 10 years before being crushed.

Patriot and writer José Marti formed the Cuban Revolutionary Party while in exile in the United States. His call to arms in 1895 sparked a new civil war. He was killed in battle the same year, but the revolt continued.

## INDEPENDENCE

After the U.S. battleship *Maine* was blown up in Havana harbor in 1898, the United States declared war on Spain. Spain was defeated by U.S. forces in the Spanish-American War, and Cuba became independent. Cuba's constitution was adopted in 1901. The island remained under U.S. occupation until 1902, when Tomás Estrada Palma became the republic's first president.

Cuba was ostensibly free, but the U.S. government had insisted that it ratify the Platt Amendment, giving the United States the right to intervene in Cuban affairs. In addition, U.S. companies owned or controlled about half of Cuba's economic resources.

In a 1903 treaty, Cuba gave the U.S. perpetual rights to a naval base at Guantánamo Bay.

In 1906 President Estrada Palma, unable to suppress a revolt by the opposition Liberal Party, called in U.S. troops. A U.S. military governor took over for the next two years and four months. U.S. Marines also intervened briefly in 1912 and 1917. Beginning in 1920 a U.S. supervisor was imposed on the Cuban government for several years.

QUICK QUIZ: In what year did *Gone with the Wind* win an Oscar for best picture? See page 268.

**CUBA** *(continued)*

The Platt Amendment was abrogated by President Franklin D. Roosevelt in 1934.

With the post-World War I economic decline, Cuba fell victim to increasing unemployment and poverty. President Gerardo Machado y Morales, inaugurated in 1925, established dictatorial rule. He was ousted in 1933 by the democratic opposition, which in turn fell victim in 1934 to a coup led by Fulgencio Batista y Zaldívar, then an army sergeant. Batista ruled through puppet presidents until 1940, when he proclaimed a new constitution and was elected president. He was supported by the communists, to whom he gave control of the trade-union movement. His candidate lost the 1944 election. In 1952 Batista again seized power through an army coup. In 1953 a raid on an army barracks by rebels led by Fidel Castro resulted in about 100 deaths. Castro was captured, but he was released from prison in 1955 under a general amnesty and left Cuba.

## COMMUNIST TAKEOVER OF CUBA

In December 1956 Castro launched an uprising. The rebellion spread. On Jan. 1, 1959, Batista fled the country.

Once in power, Castro failed to implement his promise to restore the democratic constitution. U.S.-owned property, valued at about $1.8 billion, was seized and nationalized in 1960.

The United States retaliated by halting purchases of Cuban sugar and beginning a trade boycott. On Jan. 3, 1961, the United States broke off diplomatic relations.

On April 17, 1961, an invasion force of Cuban exiles, trained and equipped by the American CIA, landed at the Bay of Pigs with the intention of launching a rebellion against the Castro government. The invaders were quickly overwhelmed, and many were captured.

Castro announced on May 1, 1961, that Cuba would become a one-party communist state.

At the urging of the United States, the Organization of American States (OAS) voted in January 1962 by a slim majority to exclude Cuba from further participation in OAS activities.

The U.S. and the Soviet Union came close to war in 1962 when the Soviets secretly began to install atomic missiles on Cuban soil. Faced with a naval blockade of Cuba ordered by President Kennedy in October 1962, the Soviets removed their missiles.

Because of Cuba's support of a communist guerrilla movement in Venezuela, the OAS voted on July 26, 1964, to brand Cuba an aggressor, to break all diplomatic ties, and to suspend all trade except for food and medical supplies.

## CUBA IN THE 1970s-80s

The United States and Cuba on Feb. 15, 1973, signed an agreement to prevent the hijacking of planes and boats between the two countries. Between 1961 and 1973 some 85 airplanes had been hijacked in the U. S. and flown to Cuba.

The U.S. joined 15 Latin American nations on July 29, 1975, in voting to end the OAS sanctions against Cuba.

U.S.-Cuban relations took a turn for the worse in 1976. President Ford called Castro "an international outlaw" for sending Cuban troops to intervene in Angola's civil war.

In the first nationwide vote since the revolution, 5.5 million Cubans went to the polls on Feb. 15, 1976, to give 97.7% approval to a new constitution formalizing Communist Party rule.

Castro said in 1977 that he had released all but 2,000 to 3,000 of the more than 15,000 political prisoners arrested in the early years of his regime.

The United States took several major steps toward restoration of normal relations with Cuba in 1977. In March restrictions were lifted on the spending of U.S. dollars by Americans in Cuba, and American tourists again began visiting the island on Caribbean cruises. On Sept. 1, 1977, Cuba and the United States exchanged diplomatic representatives, calling them "counselors" rather than ambassadors. Restoration of full diplomatic relations hinged on settlement of the U.S. claim of $1.8 billion for American property confiscated by Castro's government and of Cuba's demand that the U.S. withdraw from its naval base at Guantánamo Bay.

The U.S. State Department warned Cuba on Nov. 17, 1977, that its buildup of 27,000 troops in Angola, Ethiopia, and 14 other African countries "will have an impact on the pace and even the possibility of normalizing relations."

There were repeated angry exchanges between Castro and U.S. President Carter in 1978 over the use of Cuban troops in Africa. On May 13 Carter said U.S.-Cuban relations could not improve so long as Cuba disregarded human rights by holding thousands of political prisoners.

In August 1978 Cuba agreed to release 480 Cuban-Americans who had been prevented for 17 years from emigrating to the U.S. The first planeload of Cuban-Americans arrived in Miami, Fla., on Sept. 14.

Meanwhile, the Cuban government also offered on Aug. 31, 1978, to free up to 1,000 political prisoners if the U.S. would accept them. The first planeload reached the U.S. on Oct. 21, 1978.

Revelation in August 1979 that a brigade of 3,000 Soviet troops had been stationed in Cuba caused a temporary crisis. Cuba and the Soviet Union said the troops had been there since 1962 for training purposes, and not as a threat to the U.S. In response, President Carter ordered strengthening of U.S. defenses in the Caribbean area and a major combat training exercise at the U.S. military base at Guantánamo, Cuba.

Castro sought to enhance his leadership among developing nations by hosting a meeting of heads of state of about 60 of those countries in Cuba in 1979. Later, in a speech to the UN General Assembly on Oct. 12, 1979, he called on the U.S. and other industrial nations to contribute $300 billion over the next 10 years to aid the poor countries of the world.

Disease struck Cuba's two most important export crops, sugar and tobacco, in 1980, causing an economic slump that increased unemployment and caused shortages in consumer goods.

In the first wage increase in 15 years, agricultural workers had their monthly pay raised to $115 on July 1, 1980.

To help relieve the bad economic conditions, Castro allowed about 126,000 persons to leave the country in 1980, most of whom made their way to the U.S. See page 17.

# CYPRUS

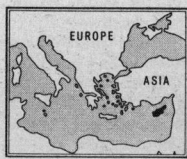

**Official Name:** Republic of Cyprus.
**Area:** 3,572 square miles (9,251 sq. km.).
**Population:** 672,045.
**Capital:** Nicosia, 115,700.
**Government:** Republic.
**President:** Spyros Achilles Kyprianou (since 1977).
**Legislature:** *House of Representatives,* 50 members.
**U.S. Ambassador to Cyprus:** Galen L. Stone.
**Cyprus Ambassador to U.S.:** Andreas J. Jacovides.
**Flag:** White field with outline map of Cyprus in gold above crossed green olive branches.
**Languages:** Greek, Turkish.
**Chief Ethnic Groups:** Greeks (78%), Turks (22%).
**Main Religions:** Greek Orthodox (78%), Islam (22%).
**Leading Industries:** Agriculture (grapes, wheat, barley, citrus fruits, potatoes, vegetables); mining (asbestos, copper, iron); tourism; food processing (wine, olive oil); manufacturing (textiles, shoes, furniture).
**Foreign Trade:** *major exports*—citrus fruits, copper, potatoes, iron; *major imports*—machinery, textiles, motor vehicles, petroleum products, medicines, meat and prepared foods, agricultural machinery.
**Places of Interest:** Troodos Mountains; Mt. Olympus; Selimiye Mosque and national museum in Nicosia; Kyrenia Castle; Kolossi Castle; St. Barnabas Monastery in Famagusta; Tomb of St. Lazarus in Larnaca; ruins of Curium near Paphos; beach resorts.

## CYPRUS TODAY

Cyprus is a war-torn island in the Mediterranean about 44 miles south of Turkey and 60 miles west of Syria. Although Cyprus is about the size of Puerto Rico, it has only one-fifth as many people.

The island has been divided into two separate states since 1974. Greek Cypriots rule two-thirds of the island as the government officially recognized by the U.S. and Britain. The northern third of the island is governed by Turkish Cypriots.

More than half the people make their living as farmers, with grapes, olives, oranges, lemons, and grapefruit among the important products.

The island has a warm climate and pleasant swimming beaches.

## EARLY HISTORY

Cyprus was inhabited as long ago as 6000 B.C. By 2200 B.C. it was the major source of the ancient world's copper. After 1500 B.C. Greeks began to colonize the island. For centuries Cyprus was ruled variously by the Egyptian, Persian, Greek, and Byzantine empires. Christianity was brought by the Apostles Paul and Mark. King Richard I of England took the island from its Byzantine rulers in 1191. It was annexed by Venice in 1489 and fell under Ottoman rule by 1571.

The Congress of Berlin in 1878 placed Cyprus under the administration of Britain, which annexed the island in 1914 and made it a crown colony in 1925.

The Greek Cypriot movement for *enosis* (union with Greece) was resisted by the Turkish Cypriots and the British. It flared in violence in 1931 and again in 1954. In 1955 a Greek ex-army officer, Col. George Grivas, launched a terrorist campaign for enosis. The campaign intensified in 1956, when the British deported Greek Orthodox Archbishop Makarios III.

## INDEPENDENCE AND CIVIL WAR

Britain granted independence to Cyprus on Aug. 16, 1960, with Archbishop Makarios as president.

In 1963 an attempt by Makarios to give the Greek Cypriots control of the government precipitated civil war. A UN peacekeeping force arrived in 1964 to keep Greeks and Turks apart.

Renewed violence in 1966–67 brought a Turkish threat of invasion. The UN, NATO, and the United States succeeded in averting a Greco-Turkish war.

Makarios began a third 5-year term as president on Feb. 8, 1973, after elections were canceled because no opposition candidate had registered. Grivas, leader of the forces calling for union with Greece, had ordered his followers to boycott the elections, as had the Turkish Cypriots.

The Cyprus national guard led by Greek army officers on July 15, 1974, overthrew Makarios, who escaped capture and fled to Malta. Five days later some 40,000 Turkish troops invaded Cyprus to protect Turkish Cypriots.

Amid fears of war between Greece and Turkey, the UN ordered a cease-fire on July 22, 1974. Fighting continued sporadically on the island throughout the year. About 180,000 Greeks driven from their homes in northern Cyprus were settled in refugee camps.

On Dec. 7, 1974, President Makarios returned from his temporary exile and resumed control.

Antagonism between Greece and Turkey over Cyprus continued in 1975–76 to threaten disruption of the NATO military alliance. Greek Cypriots blamed the U.S. for the Turkish invasion.

Turkey proclaimed the Turkish-held northern part of Cyprus an autonomous state on Feb. 13, 1975. It includes about 40% of the island. Rauf Denktash became its acting president. Denktash won the first presidential election held by the Turkish state on June 20, 1976.

Archbishop Makarios in 1976 rejected Turkish proposals for a federal republic with separate Greek and Turkish states.

Makarios died of a heart attack on Aug. 3, 1977. He was succeeded as president by Spyros Kyprianou, leader of the largest Greek Cypriot political party, the conservative Democratic Party. He had served as foreign minister in 1960–72.

Turkey refused to recognize Kyprianou as president of all of Cyprus. Turkish Cypriots threatened to declare complete independence of their state.

After about 1,500 Turkish troops were withdrawn from the island in May 1979, UN Secretary-General Kurt Waldheim succeeded in getting the nation's Greek and Turkish leaders to meet for discussions about settlement of their differences. Talks continued in 1980.

QUICK QUIZ: How many Founding Fathers signed the U.S. Constitution? See page 321.

# CZECHOSLOVAKIA

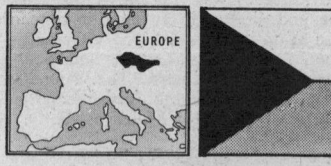

**Official Name:** Czechoslovak Socialist Republic.
**Area:** 49,371 square miles (127,869 sq. km.).
**Population:** 15,443,300.
**Chief Cities:** Praha (Prague), capital, 1,173,031; Brno, 361,561; Bratislava, 345,515; Ostrava, 302,111.
**Government:** Communist state.
**Heads of Government:** Gustav Husák, president (since 1975) and first secretary of the Czechoslovak Communist Party (since 1969); premier, Lubomír Štrougal (since 1970).
**Federal Assembly:** *Chamber of the Nations,* 75 Czechs and 75 Slovaks; *Chamber of the People,* 200 members.
**U.S. Ambassador to Czechoslovakia:** Thomas R. Byrne.
**Czechoslovakian Ambassador to U.S.:** Jaromir Johanes.
**Flag:** White over red stripe with blue triangle at hoist.
**Official Languages:** Czech and Slovak.
**Chief Ethnic Groups:** Czech (65%), Slovak (30%).
**Main Religions:** Roman Catholicism (77%), Protestantism (20%).
**Leading Industries:** Manufacturing (steel, coke, iron, cement, fertilizers, textiles, chemicals, vehicles, weapons); agriculture (potatoes, sugar beets, wheat, barley, oats, rye, corn, cattle, dairy products, hogs, sheep); mining (coal, iron ore, uranium, mercury, antimony, magnesium).
**Foreign Trade:** *major exports*—motor vehicles, iron and steel, footwear, metalworking machinery, railway vehicles, coal; *major imports*—metal scrap, crude petroleum, agricultural machinery, cotton, motor vehicles.
**Places of Interest:** High Tatras Mountains; Carlsbad and Marienbad resorts; Primate's Castle in Bratislava; Spílberk Castle in Brno; Capuchin Monastery; Košice; Olomouc. *In Prague:* Hradčany Castle; Charles Bridge; St. Vitus Cathedral; Old Town Square.

## CZECHOSLOVAKIA TODAY

Czechoslovakia is a communist industrial nation about the size of the state of New York. Many of its problems stem from rivalry by its two major ethnic groups: a Czech majority and a Slovak minority.

Struggles between the Czechs and Slovaks contributed to political instability that enabled communists to take over after World War II.

Efforts by Czech leaders to liberalize the communist state in 1968 were smashed by an invasion of tanks and troops of the Soviet Union and its eastern European satellites.

One of the world's 10 leading steelmaking nations, Czechoslovakia supplies the Soviet Union and other communist nations with such products as machinery, chemicals, and textiles. However, about half the people are farmers.

## GEOGRAPHY

Landlocked in central Europe, Czechoslovakia is bordered on the north by Poland, on the east by the Soviet Union, and on the south by Hungary and Austria. West Germany lies to the southwest, and East Germany to the northwest.

The Carpathian Mountains and the Sudeten range form a natural boundary in the north, as do the Erzgebirge (Ore Mountains) in the northwest and the Bohemian Forest in the west. From these northern heights the country slopes to an area of hills, lowlands, and plains.

The country's three main regions are Bohemia in the west, central Moravia, and eastern Slovakia. The Moravian Gate cuts across the country from north to south, a natural line of travel along the Oder and Morava rivers. Other principal rivers are the Danube, the Elbe, and the Moldau (Vltava).

## EARLY HISTORY

The first known settlers of the Czech lands of Bohemia and Moravia were Celts, followed by Germanic tribes about 100 B.C. Slovak settlers from the east displaced both the Celtic and Germanic peoples by the 400s A.D., and Slavs spread into Slovakia by the 500s. Christianity was introduced by the 800s.

The kingdom of Bohemia emerged under "Good King Wenceslas" in the 900s, but was soon absorbed into the Holy Roman Empire. The Thirty Years War (1618–48) began between the Catholic Hapsburg emperor and the Protestant Czech nobility.

As part of the Austrian Empire for 300 years until 1918, the country was superficially Germanized, with Czech used only as the language of the peasants. Between 1848 and 1914 the refusal of the Germans, particularly in Bohemia, to grant the Czechs equality contributed to the collapse of the Austro-Hungarian Empire in World War I.

## FIRST CZECHOSLOVAK REPUBLIC

On Oct. 28, 1918, the first Czechoslovak Republic came into being. It included formerly Austrian Bohemia and Moravia, which were mainly Czech, and formerly Hungarian Slovakia. Ruthenia, which was mainly Ukrainian, was added in 1919. Tomáš G. Masaryk became the first president. Eduard Beneš succeeded him in 1935.

The first Czechoslovak Republic enjoyed the benefits of a liberal, democratic constitution, internationally respected leadership, and economic advantages because most of Austria-Hungary's industries were in territory incorporated into Czechoslovakia. However, ethnic-group differences resulted in serious problems.

The large German minority living in the Sudeten border districts of Bohemia demanded union with Hitler's Germany. In September 1938 the Munich Pact, signed by Czechoslovakia's allies Britain and France, awarded the Sudetenland to Germany. Czechoslovakia was not consulted. In March 1939 Hitler occupied the rest of Bohemia as well as Moravia.

Beneš established a Czech government-in-exile in London during World War II.

## COMMUNIST TAKEOVER

After Germany's defeat in 1945, Beneš returned to Prague and resumed the presidency of Czechoslovakia. In the 1946 elections the communists emerged as the strongest among many minority

parties. Klement Gottwald, the communist leader, headed a coalition cabinet.

A Moscow-directed coup in February 1948 and the threat of Soviet invasion forced the democratic Prague government to surrender all power to the communist minority. Beneš resigned in June 1948. Gottwald became president.

The Soviet subjection of Czechoslovakia shocked the free world and is often regarded as the start of the Cold War. The event led to the formation of the Western NATO military alliance, which was soon matched by the Warsaw Pact of communist countries.

For the next two decades Czech life was marked by political purges, rigid censorship, concentration camps, and suppression of freedoms. In the late 1950s purge trials took the lives of many Czech leaders. Czechoslovakia's economy and living standards declined steadily.

Gottwald was succeeded as president in 1953 by Antonín Zapotocký. In 1957 Communist Party head Antonín Novotny took over the presidency.

## PERIOD OF LIBERALIZATION

During the first half of 1968 old-guard Stalinists were replaced in the Czech government by younger, more moderate men. Antonín Novotny was deposed as secretary of the Communist Party and replaced by Alexander Dubček. Ludvík Svoboda became president. A new cabinet pledged liberal political and economic reforms.

The press, radio, theater, and all other media became increasingly outspoken, subjecting the past history of the regime to criticism.

In mid-July 1968 Dubček refused demands by Moscow and the Warsaw Pact nations that the new leaders of Czechoslovakia slow the pace of liberalization.

## SOVIET INVASION

On Aug. 21, 1968, Soviet, East German, Polish, Hungarian, and Bulgarian troops, led by Soviet tanks and planes, suddenly invaded and occupied Czechoslovakia.

In mid-April 1969 Dubček was ousted as party secretary and succeeded by Gustav Husák.

As a warning to other communist states, the Kremlin announced the "Brezhnev doctrine," asserting the right of the Soviet Union to intervene forcibly in any "socialist" country it considered menaced from within or without.

Political purge trials continued to 1973. Supporters of the liberal Dubček were charged with antigovernment activities. The trials all ended with convictions and prison terms.

The first direct word from Dubček on the results of his ouster came in a letter smuggled into Italy in 1974 in which he described himself as "dishonored and defenseless."

When Dubček wrote a letter of complaint about being harassed by the secret police in 1975, he was denounced as a traitor by Husák, who said Dubček could leave Czechoslovakia if he did not like living there.

## COMMUNIST CONSOLIDATION

Soviet communist leader Leonid I. Brezhnev visited Prague in February 1973 during the country's celebration of the 25th anniversary of communist rule. He declared that the situation in Czechoslovakia had "returned to normal" and that the role of the Communist Party had been "consolidated." As part of the celebration, President Svoboda declared an amnesty for the 50,000 persons who fled the country after the 1968 invasion. But few took the opportunity to return.

Through agreement with the Vatican, the first Roman Catholic bishops in 25 years were appointed in Czechoslovakia in 1973.

The Czechoslovakian federal assembly ratified a treaty with West Germany in July 1974, normalizing relations between the two nations for the first time since World War II.

When Svoboda became too ill to continue in office, Husák took over the title of president in 1975 while retaining his position as head of the Communist Party.

Early in January 1977 a group of Czech intellectuals calling themselves "Charter 77" issued a manifesto declaring that their nation's government was violating the human-rights covenants of the 1975 Helsinki agreement by depriving the people of freedom of speech, freedom of religion, and many other civil rights. The statement was signed by 242 prominent writers, artists, scientists, and others.

On Jan. 26, 1977, the U.S. State Department officially charged Czechoslovakia with violating the Helsinki pact by arresting and harassing human-rights activists.

The government in October 1977 tried and convicted three of the signers of Charter 77 and a fourth dissident for "antistate activities." Two were sent to jail for terms of 3 and 3½ years. The other two received suspended sentences.

The communist government moved to collectivize in 1978 the remaining privately owned farms, which had continued to provide about half the fruits and vegetables produced in the country. As a result, food production fell, and by June potatoes, the staple of the Czech diet, no longer could be bought in shops in Prague.

An American reporter, Robert H. Reid of the Associated Press, was expelled from Czechoslovakia on May 1, 1978, for having interviewed a member of the Charter 77 movement.

When Brezhnev visited Czechoslovakia on May 30, 1978, police arrested many persons suspected of being human-rights activists to prevent any embarrassing demonstrations.

On Aug. 21, 1978, on the 10th anniversary of Soviet occupation, a few students gathered at the statue of St. Wenceslas in Prague. Riot police in armored trucks stood ready, but no large-scale demonstrations developed.

Reflecting worldwide inflation, the government raised prices in July 1979 by 50% to 100% on a wide range of products and services from gasoline to children's clothes.

Six Czech human-rights activists, including the playwright Vaclav Havel, were tried and convicted of subversion on Oct. 22–23, 1979. The six were given jail terms up to 5 years. Many others were arrested in 1980.

The country's 5-year plan for 1976–80 called for a one-third increase in production.

QUICK QUIZ: In what year was Princeton, N.J., capital of the United States? See page 324.

# DENMARK

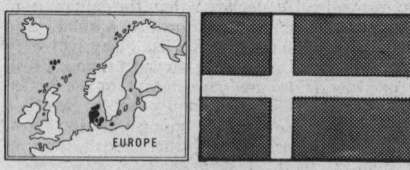

**Official Name:** Kingdom of Denmark.
**Area:** 16,629 square miles (43,069 sq. km.).
**Population:** 5,142,450.
**Chief Cities:** Kobenhaven (Copenhagen), capital, 699,300; Arhus, 246,111; Odense, 167,911; Alborg, 154,605; Frederiksberg, 101,899.
**Largest Metropolitan Area:** Copenhagen, 1,327,940.
**Government:** Constitutional monarchy.
**Prime Minister:** Anker Jorgensen (since 1975).
**Queen:** Margrethe II (since 1972).
**Legislature:** *Folketing*, 179 members.
**U.S. Ambassador to Denmark:** Warren Manshel.
**Danish Ambassador to U.S.:** Otto Rose Borch.
**Flag:** White Latin cross on red field.
**Official Language:** Danish.
**Principal Ethnic Group:** Danes (98%).
**Official Religion:** Evangelical Lutheranism (97%).
**Leading Industries:** Manufacturing (electronic equipment, machinery, furniture, engines, chemicals, food processing, ships); tourism; agriculture (dairy products, hogs, poultry, cattle, barley, rye, potatoes, oats, wheat); fishing; mining (iron ore).
**Foreign Trade:** *major exports*—manufactured goods, bacon, butter; *major imports*—machinery, motor vehicles, steel, petroleum.
**Places of Interest:** Silkeborg lakes; Kronborg (Hamlet's) Castle at Elsinore; Hans Christian Andersen's House at Odense; Egeskov Castle at Funen; Old Town Museum at Arhus; ancient town of Ribe; Ebeltoft. *In Copenhagen:* Little Mermaid statue; Christiansborg Palace; zoo; Tivoli amusement park.

## DENMARK TODAY

Once the homeland of a Viking empire that stretched from England to Russia, Denmark today is a small industrial country in Europe. It ranks as one of the 10 leading fishing nations.

The Danes enjoy a high standard of living and have strong democratic traditions. More than half the people make their living from service industries, many in the booming tourist industry.

The government provides free medical care and extensive social-welfare benefits, supporting the programs with high taxation.

Denmark has many political parties reflecting a variety of political views. Usually no one party can command majority support.

The homeland of Denmark is slightly smaller than the combined areas of Vermont and New Hampshire, but the island of Greenland, an integral part of Denmark since 1953, is bigger than Alaska and Texas combined.

The country's only land connection with the European continent is its 42-mile southern boundary with West Germany.

On the north Denmark faces the Skagerrak. On the east are the Kattegat, the Sound, and the Baltic Sea. The North Sea lies to the west.

Denmark consists of the peninsula of Jutland and 483 neighboring islands, of which 97 are inhabited. The five largest islands are Fyn (Funen), Lolland, Bornholm, Falster, and Zealand (Sjaelland), where Copenhagen is located.

The countryside is predominantly rolling flatlands. The climate is moderate.

## EARLY HISTORY

In the Viking Age (about A.D. 790–1030) Danish Vikings raided France and invaded England. Harold Bluetooth became a Christian in 960. He fell in battle (985) against his son Sweyn Forkbeard. Sweyn held parts of Norway and all of England. His son Canute the Great ruled over a huge northern empire that included England.

In 1397 Norway and Sweden joined Denmark in the Union of Kalmar under Danish Queen Margrethe I, who reigned from 1387 to 1412. A Swedish revolt in 1523 ended the union, but Norway remained united with Denmark until 1814. The Lutheran creed was adopted in 1536. In 1660 Frederik III established royal absolutism.

In the Napoleonic wars, Frederik VI allied with the French. By the Treaty of Kiel (1814) Denmark had to give up Norway to Sweden.

## CONSTITUTIONAL MONARCHY

Under Frederik VII (1848–63) liberal trends brought domestic reforms. Absolutism was abolished. A liberal constitution was adopted in 1849.

An uprising in the duchies of Schleswig and Holstein led to two wars with Prussia in 1848–49 and 1864. At the conclusion of the last war, Denmark had to cede the duchies.

Denmark was neutral during World War I, but the nation's economy was disrupted by the Allied blockade. A plebiscite was held in 1920 in the northern parts of Schleswig, and the mainly Danish-speaking areas were returned to Denmark.

Nazi Germany invaded Denmark and occupied the country in 1940–45.

## POSTWAR DENMARK

After World War II Denmark joined the United Nations, NATO, and the inter-Scandinavian Nordic Council.

The Social Democrats were ousted from the government by a centrist coalition in January 1968, but they returned to power in October 1971 with Jens Otto Krag as prime minister.

King Frederik IX died on Jan. 14, 1972. His eldest daughter was crowned the next day as Queen Margrethe II, the first woman to sit on the throne of Denmark in over five centuries.

Social Democrat Anker Jorgensen succeeded Krag as prime minister in October 1972.

Denmark's entry into the European Common Market on Jan 1, 1973, opened new opportunities for the expansion of the economy.

After parliamentary elections in December 1973, Poul Hartling, leader of the Liberal Party, formed a new minority government.

In an election on Jan. 9, 1975, the Social Democrats won and Jorgensen again became prime minister.

Prime Minister Jorgensen called a new parliamentary election on Feb. 15, 1977, to win support for wage controls. His Social Democrats gained 11 seats for a total of 65.

In a national referendum on Sept. 19, 1978, Danes approved a constitutional amendment lowering the voting age and the age to stand for parliament to 18.

Jorgensen's cabinet resigned on Sept. 28, 1979, when his coalition partner, the Liberal Party, refused to support demands by the Social Democratic Party for compulsory profit-sharing by industries with their workers.

In a new election on Oct. 23, 1979, Jorgensen's Social Democratic Party gained 4 seats to increase its plurality to 69. Conservatives and Liberals tied for second with 22 seats each.

Prime Minister Jorgensen formed a new minority cabinet on Oct. 26, 1979.

Hit by recession and inflation in 1980, Denmark experienced a growing deficit in its foreign-trade balance. Unemployment rose to nearly 7% with about 170,000 workers losing their jobs. To avoid raising taxes, the government announced plans to cut back the country's extensive welfare programs.

## DENMARK'S OVERSEAS AREAS

### GREENLAND (Kâlatdlit-Numât)

**Area:** 840,000 square miles (2,175,600 sq. km.).
**Population:** 52,158.
**Capital:** Godthaab (Nuuk), 3,585.
**Languages:** Greenlandic (official) and Danish.

Greenland, the world's largest island (1,660 miles long, with a maximum width of 650 miles), is considered part of North America.

The ice cap that covers 84% of the island's surface has an average thickness of nearly 5,000 feet, but may be over 14,000 feet thick in some areas. Most of the inhabitants are of mixed Eskimo and European ancestry. The main industry is fishing.

Greenland was first colonized about A.D. 981 by Eric the Red. The early colonists died out in the 1400s when the climate turned colder. Modern colonization by Europeans was begun in 1721 by Hans Egede, a Norwegian missionary. Greenland became a possession of Denmark in 1380.

An offer to purchase Greenland by U.S. Secretary of State James F. Byrnes in 1946 was rejected by Denmark.

Denmark formally turned over local rule of the island to the Greenlanders on May 1, 1979. Greenlandic (Eskimo) replaced Danish as the official language. Denmark retained control of foreign relations and continued to provide about $250 million annual aid.

The U.S. maintains two air bases and several early-warning radar stations in Greenland.

### FAEROE ISLANDS

**Area:** 540 square miles (1,399 sq. km.).
**Population:** 43,502.
**Capital:** Tórshavn, 10,726.

The Faeroe Islands lie in the Atlantic between Scotland's Shetland Islands and Iceland.

Seventeen of the 19 islands are inhabited. The capital, Tórshavn, is located on Streymoy, the largest island. The main industry of the Faeroes is fishing. The principal language is Faeroese.

Celts were the earliest known inhabitants, but in the 700s Norsemen settled the islands.

With Norway the Faeroes came under the Danish crown in 1380. The islands obtained home rule in 1948. The popularly elected parliament (the Lagting) meets in Tórshavn. Two Faeroese representatives sit in the Danish parliament.

## DJIBOUTI

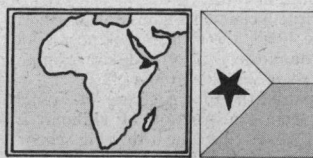

**Official Name:** Republic of Djibouti.
**Area:** 8,494 square miles (22,000 sq. km.).
**Population:** 119,338.
**Capital:** Djibouti, 62,000.
**Government:** Republic.
**President:** Hassan Gouled Aptidon (since 1977).
**Legislature:** Assembly, 65 deputies.
**U.S. Ambassador to Djibouti:** Jerrold M. North.
**Flag:** Light green stripe over light blue with red star on white triangle.
**Languages:** Arabic (official), Somali, Afar, French.
**Main Ethnic Groups:** Issa (Somali; 45%), Afar (45%).
**Religion:** Islam.
**Leading Industries:** Service (port facilities, transportation, ship repairs); commerce; agriculture (cattle, sheep, goats, donkeys, dates); mining (salt); processing (hides, skins); handicrafts.
**Foreign Trade** (excluding transit shipments to and from Ethiopia): major exports—hides, skins, cattle; major imports—food, textiles, consumer goods.
**Places of Interest:** Free-port shops in Djibouti; beach resorts; Lake Assal (512 feet below sea level).

### DJIBOUTI TODAY

A little larger than Massachusetts, Djibouti is an East African country that was known as French Somaliland and later as Afars and Issas. It owes its existence as a nation largely to its location at the southern entrance to the Red Sea, making it an important stopping place for vessels traveling through the Suez Canal.

The majority of people live in and around Djibouti, the port city and capital. Most make their living in service industries connected with the extensive shipping trade. The bulk of Ethiopia's exports and imports flow through the port, linked by rail to Ethiopia's capital, Addis Ababa.

Most of the country's land away from the coast is barren and desolate with little or no vegetation other than thorn bushes. Only about 10% of the land can provide pasture for livestock. Nomadic tribesmen lead poverty-stricken lives tending herds of goats, sheep, camels, and cattle.

Mountains near the northern coast of the Gulf of Tadjoura rise to a height of 5,426 feet.

The country has a hot climate with little rainfall. Temperatures average above 90° F. from May to October, often soaring above 110° F.

### EARLY HISTORY

In early times Muslim Arabs and Persians established trading posts on the Gulf of Tadjoura. Camel caravans from Ethiopia brought gems, ostrich feathers, coffee, and slaves that were carried by ship to the Arab and Persian empires. The local people converted to Islam and were ruled by Muslim sultans.

The French purchased from the local sultan an anchorage at Obock on the north coast of the

QUICK QUIZ: When did the 50-star United States flag become official? See page 328.

**DJIBOUTI** *(continued)*
Gulf of Tadjoura in 1862.

When the British claimed what is now northern Somalia in the 1880s, the French took possession of the area around the Gulf of Tadjoura, naming the colony French Somaliland in 1888.

Leonce Lagarde, the first governor of French Somaliland, began construction of Djibouti in 1888. The city quickly became a thriving seaport and was made the capital in 1892.

Completion of a 486-mile railroad between Djibouti and Addis Ababa on June 7, 1917, brought the area increased prosperity.

In World War II the colony was administered by the pro-Nazi Vichy government of France from 1940 to 1942. But an allied blockade of Djibouti forced the colony to come over to the side of the Free French.

**STEPS TOWARD INDEPENDENCE**

In a referendum in September 1958 the people voted by a narrow margin to accept the status of an overseas territory with representation in France's parliament.

Members of the Afar tribes supported retaining ties with France, while Issa or Somali tribes called for independence.

When Somalia (former British and Italian Somalilands) became independent in 1960, agitation for joining French Somaliland to the new nation was begun by the Somalis. Subsequently, the French expelled thousands of Somalis from the territory of French Somaliland.

In a new referendum in March 1967 on the issue of independence, 60% of the voters chose to maintain dependency with France. The name of the territory was changed on July 5, 1967, to the *French Territory of Afars and Issas.*

The pro-French political party of the Afars won control of the territory's government in elections in 1963, 1968, and 1973 with their leader, Ali Aref Bourhan, chosen as president of the executive council.

The French government announced on Dec. 31, 1975, that it planned to grant Afars and Issas independence but would maintain troops in the country to protect French interests.

Tensions remained high in Afars and Issas throughout 1976. In May and July outbreaks of fighting between Afars and Issas tribesmen resulted in at least 24 killed and 300 wounded.

The people of the territory voted on May 8, 1977, in favor of independence. At the same time they elected a national assembly from a single list of 65 candidates that had previously been agreed to by the four main political parties.

**INDEPENDENCE**

Djibouti was granted its independence by France on June 27, 1977. Hassan Gouled Aptidon, leader of the Issas majority in the legislature, was chosen by his fellow representatives as the nation's first president.

Gouled declared the new nation would remain neutral in the undeclared war between its larger neighbors, Somalia and Ethiopia, both of which promised to respect Djibouti's independence.

About 30,000 refugees from the Somali-Ethiopian war and drought in 1979–80 increased hardship in poverty-stricken Djibouti.

**DOMINICA**

**Official Name:** Commonwealth of Dominica.
**Area:** 290 square miles (751 sq. km.).
**Population:** 86,598.
**Capital:** Roseau, 16,000.
**Government:** Parliamentary republic.
**Prime Minister:** Eugenia Charles (since 1980).
**President:** Jenner Armour (since 1979).
**Legislature:** *House of Assembly,* 21 members.
**U.S. Ambassador to Dominica:** Sally Shelton.
**Flag:** Dark green field with parrot on red disk in center; tricolor cross of yellow, white, and black bars.
**Languages:** English (official), French patois.
**Chief Ethnic Group:** Black
**Principal Religion:** Roman Catholicism.
**Leading Industries:** Agriculture (bananas, citrus fruits, coconuts, cocoa); manufacturing (food processing, floor mats); mining (pumice); tourism.
**Foreign Trade:** *major exports*—bananas, citrus fruits, copra, cocoa; *major imports*—food, tobacco, clothing, machinery, petroleum.
**Places of Interest:** Black volcanic sand beach; scenic mountain rivers; tropical forests; hot mineral springs; Carib Indian reserve.

The Caribbean island of Dominica lies between the French islands of Guadeloupe to the north and Martinique to the south. Tourism and raising bananas and citrus fruits are the main industries.

Sparsely populated compared with most other Caribbean islands, mountainous Dominica has preserved much of its natural tropical beauty. The island is about 20 miles long and 16 miles wide. The highest point is Morne Diablotins (4,747 ft.).

The island was discovered on Nov. 3, 1493, by Christopher Columbus. Settlement began with French colonists in 1632.

Dominica was taken by Britain in 1759, recaptured by the French in 1778, and finally restored to Britain in 1783. It became self-governing on March 1, 1967.

Edward Leblanc, head of the dominant Labor Party, served as chief minister from 1962 to 1974, when he was succeeded by Patrick R. John.

Britain granted Dominica independence on Nov. 3, 1978, with John as the first prime minister of the sovereign nation.

One person was killed and eight wounded on May 29, 1979, when soldiers fired into a crowd demonstrating against restrictive labor legislation proposed by Prime Minister John. Labor unions then began a strike against the government that lasted four weeks until the national legislature replaced John as prime minister on June 21, 1979, with Oliver J. Seraphin.

In the first national election since independence, on July 21, 1980, the Dominica Freedom Party won 17 of the 21 seats in parliament. Its leader, Eugenia Charles, 61, became prime minister—the first woman head of government in the Caribbean.

# DOMINICAN REPUBLIC

**Official Name:** Dominican Republic.
**Area:** 18,816 square miles (48,734 sq. km.).
**Population:** 5,518,430.
**Chief Cities:** Santo Domingo, the capital, 673,470; Santiago de los Caballeros, 155,000.
**Largest Metropolitan Area:** Santo Domingo, 817,645.
**Government:** Republic.
**President:** Antonio Guzmán Fernandez (since 1978).
**National Congress:** *Senate,* 27 members; *Chamber of Deputies,* 91 members.
**U.S. Ambassador to Dom. Rep.:** Robert L. Yost.
**Dominican Republic Ambassador to U.S.:** Antonio del Rosario Ceballos.
**Flag:** White cross bearing national coat of arms; two red and two blue quarters.
**Languages:** Spanish (official), French, English.
**Ethnic Groups:** Mulatto (73%), Spanish descent (16%), black (11%).
**Official Religion:** Roman Catholicism (97%).
**Leading Industries:** Agriculture (sugarcane, tobacco, vegetables, coffee, cocoa, bananas, rice, corn, cattle, poultry); food processing (sugar, molasses, rum); tourism; manufacturing (textiles, cement, bottles, paper, matches, tobacco products); mining (bauxite, gold, silver, iron ore, salt, gypsum).
**Foreign Trade:** *major exports*—sugar, gold, silver, nickel, coffee, cacao, bauxite, tobacco, *major imports*—iron and steel, machinery, chemical and pharmaceutical products, foodstuffs.
**Places of Interest:** *In Santo Domingo:* Basilica Santa Maria la Menor, with the Columbus Tomb and Cross; Alcázar de Colón, built by Columbus' son; viceregal museum; Tower of Homage; national capitol; Plaza de la Cultura.

## DOMINICAN REPUBLIC TODAY

The Dominican Republic is a Caribbean island nation about twice the size of New Hampshire.

About 200,000 American visitors a year come to enjoy the nation's beaches and resorts.

Dominicans have a much lower standard of living than the people of nearby Puerto Rico. Most are farm workers. About a third of the people cannot read and write. Many Dominicans live close to starvation the year round.

The Dominican Republic covers the eastern two-thirds of the island of Hispaniola. It has a 193-mile border on the west with Haiti. The Mona Passage separates it from Puerto Rico.

The climate is mildly tropical and humid. Temperatures range from 72° to 83° F., but the winters are colder in the mountain areas.

## HISTORY

Columbus discovered the island in 1492, claimed it for Spain, and named it Las Española (Hispaniola). Santo Domingo, founded in 1496, was the first permanent European settlement in the Western Hemisphere.

In 1697 Spain was forced by the Treaty of Ryswick to cede to France the western third of the island now known as Haiti. France acquired the rest of Hispaniola in 1795.

With British aid the Dominicans revolted against French rule in 1809, proclaiming the first Dominican Republic. The 1814 Treaty of Paris returned the country to Spanish rule. In 1821 a republic was again proclaimed, but it was overrun and annexed by Haiti the following year.

Led by Juan Pablo Duarte, the Dominicans rebelled, drove out the Haitians, and once again proclaimed a republic on Feb. 27, 1844.

In 1870 the Dominicans approved a treaty that would have annexed the republic to the United States, but the U.S. Senate refused to ratify it.

In 1904 several foreign powers threatened to intervene to collect their debts. To forestall such a move, the U.S. in 1905 took over the administration of Dominican customs. In 1916 the U.S. occupied the republic and established a military government that ruled until 1924. The U.S. retained customs control until 1941.

From 1930 to 1961 the Dominican Republic was governed by Gen. Rafael Leonidas Trujillo Molina, a ruthless dictator. Trujillo was assassinated on May 30, 1961.

Joaquín Balaguer, a conservative, who had been appointed president by Trujillo in 1960, continued to rule after the dictator's death until forced to resign on Jan. 17, 1962.

At the nation's first free elections in four decades, on Dec. 20, 1962, leftist Juan Bosch of the Dominican Revolutionary Party (PR) won the presidency. He took office in February 1963 but was overthrown seven months later by a military coup. A junta took control.

Early in 1965 civil war broke out between leftwing forces trying to restore Bosch to power, and right-wing military elements. Fearing a communist takeover of the nation, President Lyndon B. Johnson sent in 28,000 U.S. Marines in April, intervening against the pro-Bosch forces. After the revolt was put down, the last U.S. troops were withdrawn in September 1966.

Balaguer defeated Bosch in a presidential election in 1966. He was reelected in 1970 and 1974.

Antonio Guzmán Fernandez of the leftist Dominican Revolutionary Party defeated Balaguer in a presidential election on May 16, 1978. When it became apparent Guzmán was going to win, conservative military leaders seized election headquarters and stopped the vote count on May 17. However, when the U.S. sent word that aid would be cut off unless the interference ended, the military allowed the count to resume. Guzmán finally was declared the winner on May 26 with 55% of the more than 1.5 million votes cast.

The 67-year-old Guzmán, a cattle farmer, took office for a 4-year term as the nation's 77th president on Aug. 16, 1978.

The country was devastated on Aug. 31, 1979, by hurricane David that killed 1,380 persons, injured 4,000, and left 200,000 without homes. Property damage was estimated at $837 million.

Inflation soared in 1979–80, increasing by 26% because of accelerated government spending and shortages of consumer goods.

QUICK QUIZ: What lake did James Bridger discover? See page 332.

# ECUADOR

**Official Name:** Republic of Ecuador.
**Area:** 109,484 square miles (283,561 sq. km.).
**Population:** 8,497,870.
**Chief Cities:** Quito, capital, 742,858; Guayaquil, 1,022,010.
**Government:** Democratic republic.
**President:** Jaime Roldós Aquilera (since 1979).
**Congress:** 69 members.
**Ambassador to U.S.:** Ricardo Crespo Zaldumbide.
**U.S. Ambassador to Ecuador:** Raymond E. Gonzáles.
**Flag:** Yellow, blue, and red stripes, with national coat of arms at center.
**Languages:** Spanish (official), Quechua, Jivaro.
**Ethnic Groups:** Mestizo (40%), Indian (40%), black (10%), Spanish descent (10%).
**Official Religion:** Roman Catholicism (95%).
**Leading Industries:** Agriculture (bananas, cocoa, coffee, sugarcane, cattle, dairying); mining (petroleum, gold, copper, sulfur, natural gas); manufacturing (textiles, cement, lumber, tobacco products, sugar); fishing.
**Foreign Trade:** *major exports*—petroleum, bananas, coffee, cocoa, sugar, seafood; *major imports*—machinery, vehicles, paper, textiles, consumer goods.
**Places of Interest:** Andes Mountains; Panecillo; Cotopaxi Volcano; Equatorial Monument; Valley of Chillos; Guayas River; Galápagos Islands; Playas beach resort; Guayaquil; Quito.

## ECUADOR TODAY

About the size of Nevada, Ecuador for many years was one of the poor "banana republics" of Latin America. But in the 1970s its economy boomed as it became an important oil-producing nation. However, most Ecuadoreans remain poor.

Ecuador is so named because the equator passes through the country. Colombia lies to the north and Peru to the south.

The Pacific coast region is a rich agricultural belt in which most of Ecuador's export crops are grown. Two parallel ranges of the Andes run north-south in mid-country.

About three-fourths of Ecuador is covered by forests. Climate varies with the region. Most of the northern coast is a wet, tropical forest. The southern coastal area, including Guayaquil, is cooled by the Peru Current.

## HISTORY

The small tribes of Indians who first inhabited Ecuador were conquered near the end of the 1400s by Incas from the south. The Incas ruled until the Spanish conquest in 1534.

Ecuador won independence from Spain on May 24, 1822. It then became part of Simón Bolívar's Gran Colombia. When that confederation was dissolved in 1830, Ecuador became a separate, independent nation. The country's first and second presidents were conservative Juan José Flores and liberal Vicente Rocafuerte.

From 1830 to 1948 Ecuador had 62 presidents, dictators, and juntas.

More stable government began in 1948 with the election of Galo Plaza Lasso, the first freely elected president to serve his full term. He was followed in 1952 by liberal José María Velasco Ibarra. A conservative, Camilo Ponce Enríquez, was elected in 1956. In 1960 Velasco, running as an independent, was reelected, but he was forced into exile in 1961 by a leftist coup. Vice President Carlos Julio Arosemena Monroy held the presidency until ousted by a military junta in July 1963.

A constitutional assembly elected in 1966 chose a provisional president, Otto Arosemena Gómez. In June 1968 Velasco was again elected. He assumed dictatorial powers in June 1970. On Feb. 15, 1972, he was overthrown by a military junta, and Gen. Guillermo Rodríguez Lara assumed the presidency. The coup aimed to forestall scheduled elections.

Ecuador became an oil-exporting nation with completion in August 1972 of a pipeline from oil fields in the Amazon basin across the Andes mountains to the Pacific coast.

The government took over 25% of the production of U.S.-owned oil companies in 1974.

A military junta headed by Vice Adm. Alfredo Poveda Burbano deposed Rodríguez in 1976.

Under pressure from the U.S. to restore political democracy, the military junta took steps in 1978 to establish civilian rule.

On Jan. 15, 1978, voters approved a new constitution that would give illiterates the vote.

The first presidential election in 10 years was held on July 16, 1978. The most popular politician, Assad Bucaram, a populist former mayor of Guayaquil, was not allowed to run by the military junta because he was born in Lebanon. Bucaram's 38-year-old nephew-in-law, Jaime Roldós Aquilera, the leftist candidate of Bucaram's Coalition of Popular Forces, won a plurality over other candidates, receiving 31% of the vote.

In a runoff presidential election on April 29, 1979, Roldós won with 68% of the popular vote. At the same election his party captured a 45-seat majority in the new unicameral national congress.

Democratic civilian rule was restored on Aug. 10, 1979, when the military junta turned the government over to Roldós and the congress.

A stalemate in government developed as Bucaram, a leader of Congress, blocked Roldós, legislative plans in an effort to assert his control of the government. The popular Roldós threatened to call a referendum to change the constitution to give himself power to dissolve Congress. When congressmen agreed in May 1980 to remove Bucaram as leader and support Roldós' program, the president canceled plans for the referendum.

## GALÁPAGOS ISLANDS

**Area:** 3,028 square miles (7,842 sq. km.).
**Population:** 3,100.
**Capital:** Baquerizo Moreno.

This Ecuadorian territory—60 volcanic islands in the Pacific about 650 miles west of Ecuador—was declared a national park in 1936 to protect its unique wildlife. The British scientist Charles Darwin studied the animal life of the islands in 1835 as he was developing his theory of evolution. The Galápagos tortoises, with a life span of over 200 years, are said to be the world's longest-living animals.

# EGYPT

**Official Name:** Arab Republic of Egypt.
**Area:** 386,102 square miles (1,000,000 sq. km.).
**Population:** 42,583,300.
**Chief Cities:** Cairo, capital, 5,084,463; Alexandria, 2,318,655; Giza, 1,246,713; Shubra El-Khema, 393,700; El-Mahalla El-Kubra, 292,853; Tanta, 284,636; Port Said, 262,620; Mansura, 257,866.
**Government:** Strong-president parliamentary republic.
**President:** Anwar al-Sadat (since 1970).
**Legislature:** *National Assembly,* 392 members.
**U.S. Ambassador to Egypt:** Alfred L. Atherton Jr.
**Egyptian Ambassador to U.S.:** Ashraf A. Ghorbal.
**Flag:** Red, white, and black stripes, with gold hawk emblem in white stripe.
**Languages:** Arabic (official), English.
**Ethnic Groups:** Egyptian, Copt, Bedouin, Nubian.
**Main Religions:** Islam (85%), Coptic Christian (15%).
**Leading Industries:** Agriculture (cotton, rice, corn, wheat, barley, beans, sugarcane, poultry, cattle); manufacturing (textiles, chemicals, steel, machinery, electrical equipment, food processing); tourism; mining (iron ore, petroleum, uranium, phosphate).
**Foreign Trade:** *major exports*—petroleum, cotton, textiles; *major imports*—machinery, wheat, transport equipment, iron and steel, tea.
**Places of Interest:** Pyramids and Sphinx at Giza; Nile River; Abu Simbel temples; Aswan Dam; Alexandria; Luxor and Karnak temples, Valley of the Kings, Queen Hatshepsut Temple, and Memmon Colossi at Luxor. *In Cairo:* Citadel; Mohammed Ali Mosque; Coptic churches.

## EGYPT TODAY

Egypt is the largest and most powerful of the Arab countries of the Middle East. Petroleum is its major export, but it has limited oil reserves. With few other natural resources than its soil and electric power generated by the Nile River, Egypt must rely on other nations for aid in developing its industries. The U.S. provides over $1 billion in aid annually.

Most Egyptians live a hand-to-mouth existence as farmers and livestock herdsmen. Only 4 of 10 Egyptians can read and write.

Antiquated farming methods prevent Egypt from growing enough food to feed its people.

Four wars with Israel in 1948–73 cost Egypt the lives of 100,000 soldiers and left it with huge foreign debts.

The northward-flowing Nile River divides eastern and western Egypt. The vast, rainless Sahara covers most of Egypt.

Lower Egypt in the north includes the Nile Delta, 8,500 square miles of rich cropland.

The productive portion of Upper Egypt in the south consists of a narrow strip of irrigated land about 20 miles wide that follows the course of the Nile River from Cairo to the Sudan.

Libya lies to the west, Sudan to the south, and Israel to the east.

## EARLY HISTORY

The earliest Egyptian dynasty united the kingdoms of Upper and Lower Egypt about 3200 B.C. The great pyramids were built as tombs for kings about 2650–2500 B.C.

Egypt fell under Persian control in 525 B.C. Greek rule by the Macedonians under Alexander the Great and the Ptolemy dynasty followed. Then came Roman rule. The present culture of Egypt was basically set by the Muslim conquest of A.D. 640 that brought the Islamic religion.

After the breakup of the Abbasid empire in the 800s, Egypt was ruled by local caliphs and sultans.

The Ottoman Turks conquered Egypt in 1517 and held it for nearly 300 years.

Napoleon invaded Egypt in 1798. After French withdrawal, a soldier named Mohammed Ali seized power. Under his rule Egypt remained part of the Ottoman Empire.

France and Britain exerted increasing influence on Egyptian affairs after completion of the Suez Canal in 1869.

In 1882 a nationalist revolt caused Britain to send troops to protect British interests. Britain remained in political control, formally making Egypt a British protectorate in 1914.

## INDEPENDENT MONARCHY

In 1922 Britain granted Egypt its independence under the former sultan as King Fuad I. However, Britain kept troops in Egypt to protect the Suez Canal. Upon Fuad's death in 1936, his son Farouk succeeded him.

In World War II Egypt was a crucial base for the Allies in North Africa.

Egypt took the major part in the Arab-Israeli war of 1948. The defeat of Egyptian forces and corruption brought decline in royal prestige. In 1952 Farouk was exiled after a bloodless military coup.

## ARAB REPUBLIC OF EGYPT

Egypt became a republic on June 18, 1953. Gen. Mohammed Naguib was the first president.

Col. Gamal Abdel Nasser ousted Naguib in November 1954, making himself dictator.

Nasser had his most successful moment during the Suez crisis of 1956 when he turned a military defeat at the hands of Britain, France, and Israel into a political victory—retaining control of the Suez Canal, which he had seized. During the crisis he had the support of the Soviet Union, and he benefited from the neutrality of the U.S.

In 1958 Nasser established a federation with Syria called the United Arab Republic (U.A.R.). The federation collapsed in 1961.

Israel attacked Egypt on June 5, 1967, and won a six-day war, capturing the Sinai Peninsula.

During the next three years, Egypt rebuilt its armed forces with Soviet assistance.

## EGYPT UNDER SADAT

Nasser died of a heart attack on Sept. 28, 1970. He was succeeded by Anwar al-Sadat.

Relations with the Soviet Union became strained. In mid-1972 President Sadat ordered the withdrawal of Soviet military personnel.

Egypt and Syria attacked Israel in October

QUICK QUIZ: Who was George Clinton? See page 334.

**EGYPT** *(continued)*

1973 in a fourth war, which lasted 18 days. Israel counterattacked, making new territorial gains.

U.S.-Egyptian diplomatic relations, broken in 1967, resumed in 1974.

In March 1976 Sadat abrogated the 1971 treaty of friendship and cooperation with the Soviet Union. The following month he canceled the Soviet navy's right to use Egyptian ports.

Sadat was reelected to a 6-year term as president on Sept. 16, 1976. He was unopposed.

In a referendum on May 21, 1978, Sadat won 98.3% voter approval for power to silence newspaper critics and political opponents.

Sadat announced on July 22, 1978, the formation of a new political party, the National Democratic Party (NDP), as part of a plan to restore what he called "ethical democracy." It replaced Nasser's Arab Socialist Union. Three other parties also exist: the Socialist Labor Party, the Liberal Socialist Party, and the leftist National Progressive Unionist Party.

In a dramatic reversal of policy, Sadat initiated a drive to achieve peace in the Mideast by visiting Israel in November 1977.

After months of negotiation, Sadat and Israeli Prime Minister Menachem Begin signed a peace treaty on March 26, 1979. Eighteen Arab League countries denounced the treaty, ordering an economic boycott of Egypt and breaking diplomatic relations with Sadat's government. However, the treaty was popular with Egyptians, over 99% of whom voted their approval in a referendum on April 19, 1979.

As part of negotiating the peace agreement, the U.S. granted Egypt $1.5 billion in military sales credits. The first arms under the arrangement were delivered in September 1979.

The first multiparty parliamentary elections since 1952 were held on June 7 and 14, 1979, with Sadat's party winning a landslide victory by capturing 330 of the 372 contested seats.

Sadat won an overwhelming vote of confidence in a national referendum on May 22, 1980, when 98.96% of Egyptian voters approved constitutional amendments he had proposed. Among the amendments, Sadat was given an unlimited term as president, Islamic law was made the basis for legislation, and a multiparty political system was institutionalized.

The government announced in 1980 the discovery of the largest uranium deposit in the Middle East. Plans were made to develop three mines to exploit the deposits.

In February 1980 Egypt ended its boycott of Israel and established formal diplomatic relations for the first time.

Egypt's 5-year plan for 1978–82 provided huge capital expenditures to improve transportation and communication. Work was undertaken to widen and deepen the Suez Canal so that it could be used by supertankers, increasing revenues to about $1 billion a year.

A $140 million tunnel under the canal was completed in 1980, connecting Cairo by highway to Israel and Jordan.

The development of new oil fields enabled Egypt to become an oil-exporting nation in 1977. Government plans called for increased oil production in the 1980s.

# EL SALVADOR

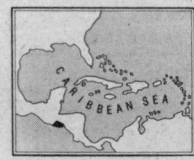 

**Official Name:** Republic of El Salvador.
**Area:** 8,124 square miles (21,041 sq. km.).
**Population:** 4,666,320.
**Capital:** San Salvador, 335,930.
**Government:** Military-civilian junta.
**U.S. Ambassador to El Salvador:** Robert E. White.
**El Salvador Ambassador to U.S.:** Francisco Aquino Herrera.
**Flag:** Blue, white, and blue stripes, with nation's coat of arms in center.
**Official Language:** Spanish.
**Main Ethnic Groups:** Mestizo (89%), Indian (10%).
**Religion:** Roman Catholicism (98%).
**Leading Industries:** Agriculture (coffee, cotton, corn, millet, sugarcane, henequen, beans, cattle, sheep, goats); mining (gold, silver); food processing; manufacturing (textiles, steel, cement, consumer goods); fishing (shrimp).
**Foreign Trade:** *major exports*—coffee, cotton, sugar, shrimp, textiles; *major imports*—crude petroleum, iron and steel, fertilizers, medicines, paper.
**Places of Interest:** San Salvador; Izalco Volcano; El Tazumal ruins at Chalchuapa; Santa Ana Cathedral; Ilopango and Coatepeque lakes.

## EL SALVADOR TODAY

About the size of Massachusetts, El Salvador is the most densely populated country in Central America. Ruled by military dictators and juntas for nearly half a century, it is economically dependent on the world price of coffee, which accounts for over half of the country's exports.

The majority of people work as farm laborers, barely earning food and shelter. Only about half of all Salvadorans can read and write.

Most of the people live in the central plateau between volcanic mountain ranges.

## EARLY HISTORY

Before the Spanish conquest, El Salvador, called *Cuscatlán* (Land of Jewels), was the home of the Aztec-related Pipil Indians and probably an Aztec colony. Spanish conquistador Pedro de Alvarado conquered El Salvador in 1525.

Subsequently, Spain neglected the area in favor of wealthier territories.

San Salvador declared independence from Spain on Sept. 22, 1821, becoming part of the United Provinces of Central America.

## INDEPENDENCE

The country became independent in 1838. Much of El Salvador's history has been beset by internal strife and military dictatorship.

One of the longest stable periods was from 1931 to 1944, when Gen. Maximiliano Hernández Martínez ran the government.

In the 1950s and 1960s some 300,000 Salvadorans migrated to sparsely populated neighboring Honduras in search of jobs and land. On July 14, 1969, El Salvador's army invaded Honduras. A cease-fire was arranged after five days, but the

war took at least 1,000 lives and left bitter feelings on both sides.

Troops of El Salvador and Honduras clashed along their jungle frontier in July 1976, but a cease-fire was achieved on July 22.

The National Conciliation Party (PCN), controlled by the armed forces, governed from 1961.

Col. José Julio Rivera was president in 1962–67, Col. Fidel Sánchez Hernández in 1967–72, and Col. Arturo Armando Molina in 1972–77.

Gen. Carlos Humberto Romero became president in 1977. Romero's inauguration was boycotted by Roman Catholic Archbishop Oscar Arnulfo Romero, protesting the government's treatment of the church and of the peasants.

Military officers overthrew President Romero in a bloodless coup on Oct. 15, 1979, permitting the dictator to flee to exile. A junta that included three civilians and two military officers was appointed.

Although the junta promised amnesty for political prisoners and eventual free elections, leftist groups denounced the new government as a sham to preserve military rule.

The U.S. openly supported the junta, promising some $90 million in aid in 1980. Under U.S. pressure to end dominance of the nation by wealthy families, the junta in 1980 announced nationalization of banks and financial institutions, seized about two-thirds of the best farmland from landowners, and abolished share-cropping, promising to sell small farms to rural families.

As the nation's leading spokesman for human rights and a return to democracy, Roman Catholic Archbishop Romero wrote to U.S. President Carter on Feb. 18, 1980, warning that continued U.S. aid would "sharpen the repression" by the ruling junta. A few weeks later, on March 14, 1980, Romero was slain by rightist terrorists while conducting mass. About 30 persons were killed when battling broke out at his funeral.

Violence escalated throughout 1980 as more than 7,000 civilians and 1,000 troops were killed in assassinations, atrocities, and fighting among rightist terrorists, leftist guerrillas, and soldiers.

The Red Cross reported on Oct. 20, 1980, that heavy fighting between troops and guerrillas had driven 15,000 peasants from their homes in northeastern El Salvador.

# EQUATORIAL GUINEA

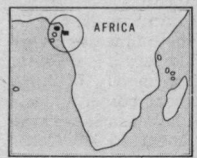

Official Name: Republic of Equatorial Guinea.
Area: 10,831 square miles (28,051 sq. km.).
Population: 336,306.
Capital: Malabo, 37,237.
Government: Military dictatorship.
President: Col. Teodoro Obiang Nguema (since 1979).
National Assembly: 60 members.
U.S. Ambassador: Hume Alexander Horan.

Equatorial Guinean Ambassador to U.S.: Don Carmelo Nvono-Nca Memene Oluy.
Flag: Green, white, and red stripes, with blue triangle at hoist; coat of arms centered in white stripe.
Languages: Spanish (official), tribal dialects.
Chief Ethnic Group: Fang (75%).
Main Religion: Roman Catholicism (60%).
Leading Industries: Agriculture (cocoa, coffee, bananas, oil palms, sisal, cattle, vegetables, fruits); forestry and lumbering; food processing.
Foreign Trade: major exports—cocoa, coffee, wood; major imports—food, tobacco, textiles.
Places of Interest: Swimming beaches; tropical islets.

A small African country, Equatorial Guinea is seeking to recover from a decade of terror and mass killings by its former dictator.

Equatorial Guinea has few mineral resources. A former colony of Spain, it still relies on Spanish aid and trade to support its economy. Only about 1 person in 5 can read and write.

Somewhat smaller than Maryland, Equatorial Guinea has two widely separated provinces:

(1) The mainland area of Río Muni (10,046 sq. mi.) is a forested region with about three-fourths of the population.

(2) The island of Bioko (formerly Fernando Po) (785 sq. mi.) lies about 20 miles off the coast of Cameroon. It also controls the smaller island of Pagalu (formerly Annobíon), over 200 miles to the southwest, and many islets.

The farms and plantations of the offshore island of Bioko grow cocoa. Exports of coffee and okume wood, used in the production of plywood, come from Río Muni.

Bioko was discovered by the Portuguese in 1471 and was ceded to Spain in 1778.

Río Muni was awarded to Spain by the Treaty of Berlin (1885). The two areas were joined as the colony of Spanish Guinea.

On Oct. 12, 1968, Spanish Guinea became independent and took the name Republic of Equatorial Guinea. Francisco Macias Nguema was elected the nation's first president.

On March 9, 1969, President Macias assumed dictatorial powers and began a purge of all opponents. He established his United National Party (PUN) as the only political party in 1970.

In 1975–76 Nigeria evacuated about 45,000 contract laborers from Bioko, charging they had been mistreated.

The U.S. broke diplomatic relations on March 15, 1976, after Equatorial Guinea charged the U.S. with engaging in subversive activities.

In 1976 the president Africanized his name by changing it to Masie and dropped "Francisco."

During Masie's 11-year reign about one-third of the population, some 100,000, fled to exile, and an estimated 40,000 were tortured and killed.

Col. Teodoro Obiang Nguema, 33, a nephew of the dictator, overthrew President Masie on Aug. 3, 1979. The former ruler was captured, tried for genocide, and executed with 6 aides on Sept. 29, 1979. The four-day trial of the former dictator was held in a movie theater with loudspeakers broadcasting testimony to crowds outside.

The U.S. restored diplomatic relations with Equatorial Guinea in 1980.

QUICK QUIZ: Who did Horace Greeley run against for President? See page 336.

# ETHIOPIA

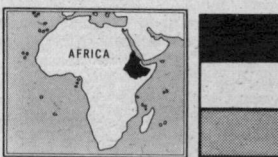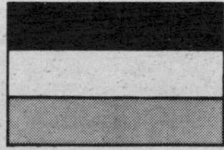

**Official Name:** Ethiopia.
**Area:** 471,778 square miles (1,221,900 sq. km.).
**Population:** 31,681,500.
**Chief Cities:** Addis Ababa, capital, 1,196,300; Asmara, 393,800.
**Government:** Communist military junta.
**Dictator:** Mengistu Haile Mariam (since 1977).
**Flag:** Green, yellow, and red stripes.
**Languages:** Amharic (official), Gallinya, Tigrinya, Arabic.
**Main Ethnic Groups:** Galla (40%), Amhara (25%), Tigre (12%), Sidama (9%), Somali (2%).
**Leading Religions:** Islam (40%), Ethiopian Orthodox Christian (35%), animism (20%).
**Leading Industries:** Agriculture (coffee, cotton, cattle, grains, fruits, vegetables, sugarcane); manufacturing (processing farm products, textiles, cement); mining (gold, platinum).
**Foreign Trade:** *major exports*—coffee, cereal, oilseeds, hides and skins; *major imports*—petroleum products, vehicles, machinery, steel, textiles.
**Places of Interest:** Addis Ababa; Gondar fortress city; Lake Tana; Blue Nile Falls; Lalibela churches carved out of solid rock; ruins at Axum; Asmara; Harar; Awash Game Reserve; beach resorts.

## ETHIOPIA TODAY

Ethiopia is a large but poor African country wracked by war, revolution, and famine.

The people of Ethiopia are divided among more than 40 different tribes. Most are farmers or cattle-raising herdsmen who lead primitive lives unaffected by modern technology. Only about 1 in 10 can read and write.

The third most heavily populated country in Africa after Nigeria and Egypt, Ethiopia covers an area about the size of Texas, Oklahoma, and New Mexico combined. Coffee is the most important cash product.

Ethiopia is a land of geographical contrasts. Snow-capped Ras Dashan, the highest mountain, rises to 15,158 feet. The Great Rift Valley slices through the plateau region that makes up about two-thirds of the land. Lake Tana is the headwater of the Blue Nile River.

The Red Sea lies to the north, Djibouti and Somalia to the east, Kenya to the south, and Sudan to the west.

## EARLY HISTORY

Menelik, the legendary first son of Solomon and the Queen of Sheba, is said to have founded the Ethiopian empire about 1000 B.C. Semitic tribes from Arabia arrived in the 900s to 600s B.C. Christianity was introduced in the 300s A.D.

About A.D. 1260 a new Ethiopian dynasty came to power that allegedly returned the throne to the line of Solomon. By 1855 authority was centralized under Emperor Theodore II.

Menelik II became emperor of Ethiopia in 1889. Italy's army invaded the country in 1895 but was defeated the next year at Aduwa.

Ras Tafari Makonnen, a favorite grandnephew of Menelik II, had Menelik's daughter Judith crowned empress in 1916 with himself as regent.

On the death of the empress in 1930, Ras Tafari became emperor as Haile Selassie I.

In 1935 the Italians invaded and conquered the country, forcing the emperor to flee to Britain in 1936. With British help in World War II, Haile Selassie regained his throne in 1941.

Ethiopia obtained its Red Sea coastline in 1952 when Eritrea, with UN approval, federated with Ethiopia. Eritrea became a province in 1962, but at the same time Eritrean nationalists began a civil war for independence.

A drought in the Tigre and Wallo regions caused 100,000 to 500,000 Ethiopians to die of starvation in 1973–74.

## REVOLUTIONARY ETHIOPIA

On June 29, 1974, Ethiopian troops seized control of the government, declaring a "war on feudalism." They arrested 200 former cabinet members and advisers to the emperor.

The army deposed Haile Selassie on Sept. 12, 1974, ending his 58 years of rule. He died a prisoner in 1975. The junta officially abolished the Ethiopian monarchy on March 21, 1975.

A 120-man military committee known as the *Dergue* took power, headed by Lt. Gen. Aman Michael Andom. General Aman, an Eritrean, was himself arrested and killed by the junta on Nov. 24, 1974. On the same day 59 nobles and former officials were executed, including two former premiers. Leadership of the junta was taken over by Gen. Teferi Bante as chairman.

The communist military rulers announced on April 21, 1976, the establishment of a commission to prepare the way for formation of a Soviet-style "People's Democratic Republic."

Chief of state Gen. Teferi Bante was too slow on the draw on Feb. 3, 1977, when a shoot-out developed at a meeting of the military junta. When the smoke cleared, Teferi and 10 other junta members were dead. Lt. Col. Mengistu Haile Mariam emerged as dictator.

A reign of terror inspired by Mengistu swept Ethiopia in 1977. An estimated 100 to 150 assassinations and executions took place each day.

Ethiopia expelled 300 U.S. officials in April 1977 and closed U.S. aid agencies. Western news correspondents also were expelled.

Full-scale war developed with Somalia in 1977 as Somalis sought to take the southeastern Ogaden region from Ethiopia. On Sept. 14, 1977, the Somalis captured the Ethiopian city of Jijiga, about 100 miles from the Somali border.

But in 1978, with some $1 billion in Soviet arms flown in by airlift, with about 16,000 Cuban troops, and with a Soviet general and 1,500 Soviet "military advisers," the Ethiopians succeeded in driving the Somalis back and recapturing Jijiga on March 5. Fighting continued with Somali guerrillas in the Ogaden throughout 1978–80.

In the northeast, an estimated 100,000 Ethiopian troops launched a counteroffensive in May 1978 against Eritrean rebels supplied by Arab nations. On July 27 Ethiopia broke the 10-month siege by the rebels of the major city of Asmara. In August the Ethiopian government

announced that 33,000 of its troops had been killed or wounded fighting the Eritreans. By the end of November 1978, Ethiopians reported they had recaptured all cities from the Eritreans and that the rebellion had been "smashed."

Meanwhile, Mengistu's campaign of "red terror" against his opponents continued through February 1978 with thousands of persons imprisoned or summarily executed. The government announced in June 1978 that nine assassination attempts had been made on the life of Mengistu. Many members of the ruling military junta were among those killed in reprisal.

Mengistu flew to Moscow in 1978, where on Nov. 20 he signed a 20-year treaty of friendship with the Soviet Union.

An army of about 50,000 Ethiopian, Cuban, and Soviet troops launched a new offensive on Eritrean rebels in mid-July 1979. But by July, Eritreans claimed to have broken the back of the offensive, killing some 15,000 Ethiopian soldiers. Fighting continued throughout 1980.

The U.S. ended economic aid to Ethiopia in 1979, and recalled its ambassador in 1980 at the request of the Mengistu government.

# FIJI

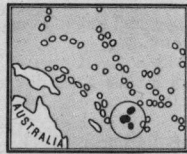 

**Official Name:** Dominion of Fiji.
**Area:** 7,056 square miles (18,274 sq. km.).
**Population:** 627,448.
**Capital:** Suva, 63,628.
**Government:** Parliamentary state.
**Prime Minister:** Sir Kamisese K.T. Mara (since 1970).
**Chief of State:** Queen Elizabeth II, represented by Governor-General Ratu Sir George Cakobau.
**Parliament:** *Senate*, 22 members; *House of Representatives*, 52 members.
**U.S. Ambassador to Fiji:** William Bodde Jr.
**Fijian Ambassador to U.S.:** Filipe Nagera Bole.
**Flag:** Azure blue with Fiji shield centered on right; Union Jack in upper hoist quarter.
**Languages:** English (official), Fijian, Hindustani.
**Main Ethnic Groups:** Indian (50%), Fijian (42%).
**Religions:** Christianity (41%), Hinduism (35%), Islam (12%).
**Leading Industries:** Agriculture (sugarcane, coconuts, rice, bananas, cocoa, tobacco, fruits, vegetables, poultry); mining (gold); tourism; food processing; forestry and lumbering; fishing; manufacturing (cement, consumer goods).
**Foreign Trade:** *major exports*—sugar, coconut products, gold; *major imports*—machinery, manufactured goods, foodstuffs.
**Places of Interest:** Beach resorts; native villages; volcanic islands. *In Suva:* Fiji Museum, Botanical Gardens; University of the South Pacific.

## FIJI TODAY

The South Pacific nation of Fiji has many economic problems that stem from poor roads, lack of cheap electric power, the difficulties of farmers obtaining land, and the lack of technicians and managers for industry. Asian Indians make up a majority of the population.

Fiji's economy depends on four principal industries—sugar, copra, gold mining, and tourism.

Sugarcane, the main crop, is almost entirely raised by Asian Indian farmers, descendants of plantation laborers imported in the 1870s.

Industrial development and tourism are becoming increasingly important. Many new hotels have been built. Fiji is an important port of call for cruise ships. More than 130,000 tourists visit each year.

The native Fijians, a mixture of Melanesians and Polynesians, own about 83% of the land, which is held in trust for them by a government agency. The protective land-tenure system has limited development. Asian Indians can lease the land only for periods of 10 years at a time.

About 100 of Fiji's 844 islands are inhabited. The two main islands are Viti Levu (4,011 sq. mi.) and Vanua Levu (2,137 sq. mi.). Suva, the capital, is located on Viti Levu.

Most of Fiji's larger islands are mountainous and volcanic, with rugged, craggy interiors. Mount Victoria, on Viti Levu, is the highest mountain (about 4,300 feet). Fertile river deltas thick with mangroves intersect the coastal plains. Most of the smaller islands are of limestone and coral, their cliffs rising steeply to flat tops with little vegetation. The climate is warm and humid. A 300-mile arc of coral, the Great Sea Reef, protects the western archipelago.

## EARLY HISTORY

Discovered by the Dutch explorer Abel Tasman in 1643, the Fiji islands were visited by British Capt. James Cook in 1774. Later, trading vessels came for sandalwood.

For many years the region was known as the "Cannibal Islands" because of the reputation of the Fijians as fearsome man-eaters.

Tribal wars for island supremacy were climaxed in 1855 by the victory of the chief of Bau, with the help of neighboring Tonga. Fiji remained under Tonga's domination for the next 20 years. Attempts at confederation failed, and tribal chiefs asked the British to intervene. In 1874 Britain accepted Fiji's offer, and thereafter British governors administered the islands. Local government was set up in 1876.

## INDEPENDENCE

Britain granted Fiji independence on Oct. 10, 1970—the 96th anniversary of the cession of the islands to Queen Victoria. Sir Kamisese K.T. Mara became the newly independent nation's first prime minister.

The country's two main political parties are the Alliance Party, which has governed since 1967, and the opposition National Federation Party (NFP), made up largely of Asian Indians.

In a general election on Sept. 25, 1977, Mara's Alliance Party won a majority of 36 seats in the 52-member lower house of parliament, soundly defeating the NFP.

Fiji sent half of its army, 500 men, to Lebanon in 1978 as part of the UN peace-keeping force in that country.

QUICK QUIZ: Why did Carry Nation carry a hatchet? See page 339.

# FINLAND

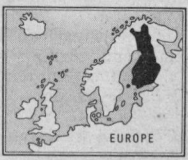
EUROPE

**Official Name:** Republic of Finland.
**Area:** 130,120 square miles (337,009 sq. km.).
**Population:** 4,787,800.
**Chief Cities:** Helsinki, capital, 496,263; Tampere, 166,177; Turku, 164,344; Espoo, 122,010.
**Largest Metropolitan Area:** Helsinki, 871,294.
**Government:** Multiparty parliamentary democracy.
**Prime Minister:** Mauno Koivisto (since 1979).
**President:** Urho K. Kekkonen (took office in 1956).
**Parliament:** 200 members.
**U.S. Ambassador to Finland:** James Eugene Goodbody.
**Finnish Ambassador to U.S.:** Jaakko Olavi Iloniemi.
**Flag:** Light blue cross on a white field.
**Official Languages:** Finnish, Swedish.
**Ethnic Groups:** Finnish (94%), Swedish (6%).
**Main Religions:** Lutheran (92%), Russian Orthodox (1%).
**Leading Industries:** Manufacturing (paper, furniture, machinery, electrical products, vehicles, chemicals, textiles, ships, ceramics, furs); forestry and lumbering; agriculture (dairy products, poultry, cattle, wheat, rye, potatoes); mining (copper).
**Foreign Trade:** *major exports*—paper, wood, machinery, furs; *major imports*—petroleum, machinery, electronics, food, aircraft.
**Places of Interest:** *In Helsinki,* Temple Square underground church, Mannerheim's house, cathedral, Finlandia Hall, Suomenlinna island fortress; *in Järvenpää,* Jean Sibelius' house; *in Vuokatti,* Kainuu Nature and Play Park; Savonlinna Opera Festival in July; inland waterway cruises; Lapland.

## FINLAND TODAY

Somewhat smaller than Montana, Finland lies northwest of the Soviet Union. After having fought three wars with its huge neighbor in this century, Finland today walks a tightrope of neutrality to preserve its democratic freedom.

Finland is one of the world's leading producers of newsprint. Like most industrialized nations of the West, Finland has struggled in the 1970s to cope with the problems of inflation.

About one-third its hardworking people live in cities, making their living from manufacturing and service industries. The others live in small towns or on farms. The people enjoy a much higher standard of living than that of the neighboring Soviet Union. Finland has no illiteracy.

The U.S. maintains an exchange program with Finland financed in part from a trust fund established in 1976 from Finland's final repayment of its post-World War I debt to the U.S.

## GEOGRAPHY AND CLIMATE

More than 60,000 lakes dot Finland's forested landscape. Northern Finland above the Arctic Circle forms part of Lapland. It has many low mountains. In the central and southern regions the land is mainly low-lying and undulating.

July temperatures in Helsinki rarely go above 75°F. In February, winter temperatures range from 12°F. to –30°F.

Norway lies to the north, Sweden and the Gulf of Bothnia to the west, the Gulf of Finland and the Baltic Sea to the south, and the Soviet Union to the east.

## EARLY HISTORY

The Finns' ancestors came into the land from the south through Estonia and Russia about 2,000 years ago. By the 700s the Finns had taken the country from the Lapps.

From the 1100s Sweden controlled the region. In 1809 Czar Alexander I joined Finland to the Russian Empire as an autonomous grand duchy. In 1863 the Finnish legislature met for the first time since the Russian annexation.

## INDEPENDENCE

During Russia's communist revolution the Finns declared their independence on Dec. 6, 1917. After a war of independence Finland adopted a republican constitution on July 17, 1919.

The Soviet Union invaded Finland in 1939–40. The Finns put up stiff resistance, but were forced to cede one-tenth of their land.

Finland began a second war with the Soviet Union in June 1941. The Soviets mounted a fierce offensive in 1944 that made Finland accept an armistice in September. The boundaries and peace terms of 1940 were reestablished, and Finland was forced to pay huge war reparations.

A friendship treaty with the Soviet Union in 1948 accepted the principle of Finnish neutrality, but provided for Soviet military assistance if Finland is attacked.

Under the leadership of Presidents J. K. Paasikivi (1944–56) and Urho Kekkonen (first elected in 1956), Finland has pursued a policy of cooperation with the Soviet Union as well as friendship with the West.

Parliament in 1973 approved an agreement for free trade in industrial products with the Common Market nations. In 1974 free-trade agreements also were made with Bulgaria and Hungary—the first free-trade pacts between capitalist and communist nations.

In an election on Jan. 15–16, 1978, 77-year-old President Kekkonen was reelected to another 6-year term, receiving 82% of the vote.

In parliamentary elections on March 18–19, 1979, voters shifted to the right as the largest party, the Social Democrats, lost 2 seats for a total of 52. The Conservative Party gained 12 seats for a total of 47, making it the second strongest. The remaining 101 seats were split among smaller parties. Women candidates won 26% of the seats.

Social Democrat Mauno Koivisto, 55, president of the Bank of Finland, became prime minister on May 26, 1979, heading a left-center cabinet.

The nation experienced an economic boom in 1979–80 with foreign trade expanding by 73% during the two-year period. Full employment was achieved and average per capita gross domestic product rose to $10,500, about equal to that of the United States.

Although Finnish newspapers in 1980 denounced the Soviet Union's invasion of Afghanistan, the government tried to maintain neutrality, abstaining from voting on the issue in the UN.

# FRANCE

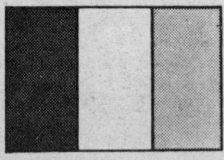

**Official Name:** French Republic.
**Area:** 211,208 square miles (547,026 sq. km.).
**Population:** 55,175,000.
**Chief Cities:** Paris, capital, 2,296,945; Marseille, 912,130; Lyon, 457,410; Toulouse, 371,835; Nice, 344,040; Bordeaux, 223,845; Nantes, 255,700; Strasbourg, 253,355; Saint-Étienne, 220,810.
**Largest Metropolitan Area:** Paris, 8,547,625.
**Government:** Presidential-parliamentary democracy.
**President:** Valéry Giscard d'Estaing (since 1974).
**Prime Minister:** Raymond Barre (appointed in 1976).
**Parliament:** *Senate,* 283 members; *National Assembly,* 491 members.
**U.S. Ambassador to France:** Arthur A. Hartman.
**French Ambassador to U.S.:** François Lefebvre de Laboulaye.
**Flag:** Tricolor of blue, white, and red bars.
**Official Language:** French.
**Main Religions:** Roman Catholicism (90%), Islam (4%), Protestantism (2%), Judaism (1%).
**Leading Industries:** Manufacturing (steel, paper, electricity, aluminum, cement, automobiles, aircraft, chemicals, textiles, perfume, furniture); food processing; tourism; construction; agriculture (cattle, sheep, dairy products, poultry, hogs, sugar beets, corn, wheat, oats, barley, potatoes, grapes, fruits, vegetables); mining (iron ore, bauxite, uranium, salt, coal, natural gas, petroleum); fishing.
**Foreign Trade:** *major exports*—automobiles, iron and steel, alcoholic beverages, petroleum products, clothing; *major imports*—crude petroleum, fruits, office machines, chemicals, copper.
**Places of Interest:** Angoulême; Avignon; Bourges; Brittany peninsula; Carcassonne; Chartres; the château country (Loire Valley); Clermont-Ferrand; Colmar; Dijon; Grasse; Grenoble; Nîmes; Pau; Rheims; the Riviera; Rouen; Strasbourg; Vienne. *In Paris:* Nôtre-Dame, Ste. Chapelle, the Madeleine, Tuileries gardens, the Louvre, Arc de Triomphe, Montmartre, Sorbonne, Luxembourg Palace and Gardens, Hôtel des Invalides, Opéra, Panthéon, Eiffel Tower. *Near Paris:* Fontainebleau, Versailles.

## FRANCE TODAY

About a third larger than California, France has more land than any other nation in western Europe. However, France ranks fourth in population after West Germany, Italy, and Britain.

France is a leading producer of bauxite, cement, electric power, steel, and uranium.

For hundreds of years France fought wars with Germany, Britain, Austria, and Italy to establish itself as a world power. With the rise of the United States and the Soviet Union as superpowers, France has had difficulty reconciling itself to a secondary role in world politics.

To enhance its status and military independence, France developed its own atomic weapons. Like China, France test-explodes them in the atmosphere in defiance of world opinion.

Although France granted independence in the past quarter of a century to most of its former colonies, many of these new nations continued as members of the French Community. This organization preserves use of the French franc as its money and establishes economic and military links. France also maintains control over a scattering of its former colonial possessions as overseas departments and territories, described at the end of this article.

France is a highly industrialized nation. But about half its people continue to live on farms or in rural villages. With a long tradition of democracy and freedom, the people take a vigorous part in their government.

## GEOGRAPHY AND CLIMATE

France is bordered on the north by Belgium, Luxembourg, and West Germany; on the east by Switzerland and Italy; and on the south by Monaco, Spain, and Andorra.

The land is varied and rich. In the southwest the Pyrenees rise along the Spanish border. In the east are the rugged peaks of the Alps and the Jura Mountains, and the wooded mountains of the Vosges range and the Ardennes plateau.

Four major river systems water the country. The Seine rises in the Plateau de Langres and flows northwest through the Paris Basin to the English Channel. The Loire, flowing from the Massif Central, courses westward to the Atlantic. The Garonne runs northwest from the Pyrenees to the Atlantic estuary of the Gironde. The Rhone-Saône system flows from the Alps into the Mediterranean. The Rhine River runs along the Franco-German frontier.

The country has four distinct climatic regions. The dry Mediterranean south has hot summers and mild winters. The central and eastern uplands are moist and seasonally varied. The oceanic west and northwest have cool temperatures and considerable rainfall. The mountainous regions in the southwest and southeast have cold winters, often with heavy snowstorms.

## EARLY HISTORY

France was a crossroads of migrant agricultural peoples for hundreds of years. Conquering Celtic invaders brought a degree of order among the quarreling inhabitants, imposed their language to some extent, and gave the area the name *Gaul.*

Greek settlers began colonizing southern France about 600 B.C.

Roman armies in the 100s B.C. conquered part of Gaul. Julius Caesar subjugated the rest of the region in 58–44 B.C. A Latin tongue took root, and a network of military roads brought some degree of unity. Christianity was introduced.

When the Roman Empire weakened after the 200s A.D., a northern tribe, the Salian Franks, subdued much of the country. After making an alliance with the Roman Catholic Church, Clovis, a leader of the Franks, extended Frankish rule and Christianity by force of arms in the 400s. Clovis founded the Merovingian dynasty.

## MIDDLE AGES

Beset by Muslim invaders moving up from Spain,

QUICK QUIZ: Who was George Washington's Vice President? See page 344.

**FRANCE** *(continued)*

the Frank leader Charles Martel defeated the Arab cavalry at the Battle of Tours in 732, preventing a Muslim conquest of France.

Charlemagne was Charles Martel's grandson. A militant imperialist and ally of the church, he was crowned emperor of the Western Roman Empire on Christmas Day in the year 800. Under Charlemagne, France was only part of a vast Frankish domain.

Following Charlemagne's death the empire fell apart from Viking invasions and regional revolts.

In 987 a fresh beginning was made with the election to the throne of Hugh Capet, duke of Francia. The Capetians, as the new ruling group was known, allied themselves with the church and the growing urban classes to extend their rule slowly over all of France.

For more than 300 years the Capetians wore down the feudal forces in France. They disciplined the bishops, created the beginnings of a central administrative system, crusaded against infidels and heretics, and warded off the English. Their line ended in 1328.

In the Hundred Years War (1337–1453) with England, France was devastated. At the Battle of Orléans on May 7, 1429, Joan of Arc inspired the French army to rout the English, leading to ultimate French victory.

## KINGDOM OF FRANCE

In the late 1550s the Reformation swept through France, pitting Catholic against Protestant. Civil war followed.

A strong central government with a high degree of religious tolerance was now considered necessary to save the nation. A Protestant, the Bourbon Prince Henri of Navarre, took the throne. Embracing Catholicism himself and granting religious freedom to the Protestants (Huguenots) in the Edict of Nantes (1598), he became the most popular king France ever had. Although the wealthy urban classes enjoyed power, France was still a feudal monarchy.

The assassination of Henri in 1610 left the royal government open to challenges from both nobles and bourgeoisie. In this struggle Henri's successors were supported by two great statesmen, Cardinals Richelieu and Mazarin, who were enemies of the nobles, of Protestantism, and of urban democratic tendencies. Guiding France through the perils of the Thirty Years War (1618–48), the cardinals put down internal revolt (the Fronde of 1648–53), continued the colonial expansion begun in the previous century, and helped project the Bourbon house in the person of Louis XIV (1643–1715) to the peak of France's power.

Louis XIV and his lieutenants held the nobility in check, helped industry expand, and systematically eliminated old provincial, municipal, and religious liberties. Royal control was absolute.

Warlike and authoritarian, Louis made France the greatest of Europe's powers, but he also brought the country to economic ruin.

The reign of Louis XV was marked by opposition at home, the loss of empire abroad (Canada fell to England in 1763), and a dazzling display of art and literature. This was the great age of the Enlightenment, and France was the intellectual capital of Europe.

## FRENCH REVOLUTION

The French state, however, was insolvent, and the farmers suffered from landlords seeking higher revenues in an expanding economy. The monarchy was finally bankrupted, in part through involvement in the American Revolution.

The bourgeois creditors of the state refused to advance more credit unless they got social and political concessions from the crown.

The aristocracy was determined to reverse the trend toward absolute monarchy and to regain its former authority.

The common people of rural France waited for some royal action that would ease their lot.

Nobles and bourgeois joined forces to compel Louis XVI to summon the States-General, which had not met since 1614. Then the struggle for power became more complex.

The middle-class representatives of the common people challenged the aristocracy in 1789. They rallied the king temporarily to their side. Within months, following riots against crown and nobility, they seized control of the state.

The revolutionary government overturned the social and political structure of France, launched the egalitarian creed throughout Europe, and reduced the church to a department of state. Finally the revolutionaries executed the king, who had turned against them and had hoped to be rescued by other European monarchs.

The strains of war and resultant unrest at home precipitated a bloody reign of terror that set the stage for the rise of Napoleon.

## NAPOLEONIC ERA

By 1799, after a decade of domestic turmoil, the epochal French Revolution ended in military dictatorship. Young, brilliant, ambitious Gen. Napoleon Bonaparte seized total power.

Napoleon crowned himself emperor of the French in 1804. At home he squashed political conflict and restricted the powers of the church.

France reached its height of power as Napoleon won victory after victory until he controlled most of Europe.

After Napoleon's disastrous defeat in Russia in 1812, his conquests were stripped away by the victory of an allied coalition in 1814.

Napoleon returned from exile in 1815 to rally France again, but was routed at Waterloo.

The former emperor was imprisoned on St. Helena, where he died in 1821.

## RESTORATION OF MONARCHY

The unpopular Bourbons were restored under Louis XVIII in 1814 by allied arms, but the old order never returned.

In 1830 Charles X was driven out by the revolt of the middle and lower classes in the cities.

His successor, Louis Philippe, was ousted in the 1848 revolution.

## SECOND REPUBLIC AND NAPOLEON III

The Second Republic, founded in 1848, was undermined by clashes between the new French factions. The republic then was eliminated by its elected president, Louis Napoleon Bonaparte.

Like his uncle, France's new ruler established a dictatorship to end political quarrels and to preserve the social order. Proclaimed Emperor

Napoleon III in 1852, he presided until 1870.

The regime enriched the industrial and commercial classes but won no loyalty from them.

Napoleon III expanded the empire in Southeast Asia but was unsuccessful in Mexico. He helped bring about the unification of Italy but was defeated in a war with Germany (Prussia).

## THIRD REPUBLIC AND WORLD WARS I AND II

Out of defeat by Germany (1870–71) another republic was born. It accepted severe peace terms, mastered the revolt of the Paris commune, and by 1875 had all but banished the ghost of monarchy.

The Third Republic had a conservative parliamentary government. It expanded the school system and extended its empire in Africa and Asia. It made an ally of Russia in 1894 and of Britain in 1904.

Like much of armed and divided Europe, France took up arms in 1914 hoping to win security. It also hoped to recover Alsace-Lorraine, surrendered to Germany in 1871.

France emerged victorious but exhausted from World War I.

France reacted to Hitler's invasion of Poland by declaring war on Germany in 1939. It suffered swift and total defeat in 1940. World War I hero Marshal Henri Philippe Pétain established a government in southern France at Vichy that collaborated with the Nazis.

A Free French movement led by Gen. Charles de Gaulle from abroad condemned the government at Vichy, won over the loyalty of much of the empire, and fought on the side of the Allies. After liberation, France was ruled by de Gaulle until he resigned in 1946.

## FOURTH REPUBLIC

For 12 years the unstable Fourth Republic struggled to modernize the economy and cope with nationalist movements in the crumbling empire, while French prestige sank in the world.

The regime collapsed in 1958 when faced with a French army rebellion in Algeria.

To avoid civil war, Paris called de Gaulle from retirement. The nation gave him a mandate to rule and to prepare a new constitution.

## FIFTH REPUBLIC

General de Gaulle in September 1958 established a Fifth Republic with himself as a strong president. He governed by decree when necessary.

Driving forcefully toward the leadership of western Europe, de Gaulle granted independence to Algeria. He prevented Britain from joining the European Common Market. And in 1968 he withdrew French military forces from NATO as a protest against U.S. foreign policy.

The regime concentrated on foreign affairs and building atomic weapons while social and economic problems continued to await solution.

In May 1968 a student revolt and a nationwide general strike brought the republic close to anarchy. De Gaulle, however, appealed for law and order, promising reforms. His government received an overwhelming endorsement in general elections on June 23, 1968.

In April 1969, however, de Gaulle resigned after a proposed constitutional reform was defeated in a nationwide referendum.

Georges Pompidou was elected president in 1969 to succeed de Gaulle. Pompidou reversed de Gaulle's policy of opposing Britain's entry into the European Common Market. On July 5, 1972, he named Pierre Messmer, an orthodox Gaullist, as prime minister.

In March 1973, in the first parliamentary elections since the death of de Gaulle, the Gaullist coalition of parties won a reduced majority.

On April 12, 1973, Messmer, who had been reappointed by President Pompidou, completed the formation of a new cabinet. He received a 254–206 vote of confidence on a reform program pushing up the minimum wage, lowering the retirement age to 60, increasing old-age pensions, and raising taxes.

The French government caused a storm of world criticism by test-exploding atomic weapons at Mururoa Atoll in the South Pacific Ocean in the summers of 1973 and 1974. The International Court of Justice, acting on complaints by Australia and New Zealand, ordered France to cancel the tests. The French government, however, proceeded with the explosions.

The death of President Pompidou on April 2, 1974, brought new national elections.

## FRANCE UNDER GISCARD d'ESTAING

Valéry Giscard d'Estaing, a conservative who had served as minister of finance, won the presidency in the runoff election on May 19, 1974.

President Giscard d'Estaing appointed Jacques Chirac, Pompidou's former minister of the interior, as premier on May 27, 1974. Giscard d'Estaing quickly established himself as more liberal than his Gaullist predecessors. He added a woman to the cabinet, lowered to 18 the age for voting and attaining full legal rights of an adult, and increased the minimum wage for workers. French workers were guaranteed a year's pay if thrown out of work.

Chirac resigned as prime minister in August 1976, declaring he had not been given enough power by President Giscard d'Estaing.

An economist, Raymond Barre, was appointed prime minister on Aug. 25, 1976.

Despite protests from many Western nations, a French court on Jan. 11, 1977, freed Abu Daoud, a Palestinian terrorist said to have organized the massacre of Israeli athletes at the 1972 Olympics in Munich. He was allowed to fly to safety in Algeria.

Early in 1977 a socialist-communist coalition looked forward to parliamentary elections, confident of winning control because public-opinion polls showed about 60% of the French favor the leftists. But on Sept. 23, 1977, the alliance of Communist, Socialist, and Left Radical parties suddenly collapsed as leaders disagreed on renewing a platform of objectives adopted in 1972. The leftists resolved their differences in March 1978, agreeing to campaign for nationalization of major private industries.

President Giscard D'Estaing's center-right coalition won a resounding victory in the elections on March 19, 1978, capturing 290 of the 491 seats

QUICK QUIZ: Who was U.S. minister to Russia during Napoleon's invasion? See page 350.

**FRANCE** *(continued)*

in the national assembly. The number of seats won by each of the four main parties were: Gaullists, 153 (a decline of 20); Giscardians, 137 (a gain of 10), Socialists, 104 (a gain of 9), and Communists, 86 (a gain of 12). Barre was reappointed prime minister.

The government took an increasingly stiff stand against the spread of communist influence in Africa in 1978. French troops intervened both in Zaire and Chad to help those African governments fight communist-supported guerrillas.

Because France imports about three-fourths of the energy it uses, the country was particularly hard hit by soaring fuel prices in the 1970s. To help reduce dependency on imported fuel, the government ordered a speed-up in the construction and planning of nuclear power plants. Eighteen already were functioning in 1979 with a capacity of almost 10,000 megawatts. Altogether 38 more would be completed or under construction in 1981. Nuclear power will supply 55% of France's electricity needs by 1985. By constructing breeder reactors that produce more atomic fuel than they use, France hopes to reach energy self-sufficiency.

Although plagued by an unemployment rate that rose to 5.9%, France continued its economic growth in 1979–80, giving its people a living standard one-third higher than that of Britain.

France took a major step to improve its status as a military power when the government announced on June 26, 1980, the successful test of a neutron bomb, a type of atomic bomb designed to kill enemy soldiers while limiting damage to surrounding structures. President Giscard d'Estaing said the government was undecided whether to produce large quantities of the neutron bomb.

During 1980 France was plagued by a growing anti-Semitic movement. The worst terrorist incident took place on Oct. 3 when a bomb was exploded at a Jewish synagogue in Paris, killing 4 persons and injuring 20.

The government announced plans for the next presidential election to be held on April 26, 1981, with a run-off two weeks later on May 10.

## FRANCE'S DEPENDENCIES

### CORSICA

**Area:** 3,352 square miles (8,681 sq. km.).
**Population:** 301,486.
**Cities:** Ajaccio, capital, 40,834; Bastia, 49,375.

Called *Corse* in French, the mountainous Mediterranean island of Corsica is nearly three times as large as the state of Rhode Island. It lies about 100 miles southeast of France. Corsica is separated from the Italian island of Sardinia by an 8-mile-wide strait. It is best known as the birthplace of Napoleon I.

Most of the people make their living farming and raising livestock. Great herds of sheep graze on the mountain slopes, providing the island's two most profitable products, wool and cheese.

Prehistoric people lived on the island at least as early as 2000 B.C., leaving large stone monuments. Greeks from Phocaea, in what is now Turkey, established a colony on Corsica about 560 B.C. These invaders were followed by Carthaginians, Romans, Vandals, and Arabs. The Italian cities of

## THE FRENCH COMMUNITY

Independent nations that once were part of the French colonial empire and present dependencies of France are bound together by economic and military agreements similar to those of the British Commonwealth of Nations.

### INDEPENDENT MEMBERS

| | | |
|---|---|---|
| Central Africa | Djibouti | Gabon |
| Chad | France | Senegal |

### OVERSEAS DEPARTMENTS OF FRANCE

| | | |
|---|---|---|
| French Guiana | Martinique | Réunion  St. Pierre and |
| Guadeloupe | Mahore | Miquelon |

### OVERSEAS TERRITORIES OF FRANCE

| | |
|---|---|
| French Polynesia | New Caledonia |
| French Southern and | Wallis and Futuna |
| Antarctic Territories | Islands |

### ASSOCIATES BY SPECIAL AGREEMENTS

| | | |
|---|---|---|
| Algeria | Ivory Coast | Niger |
| Benin | Mali | Togo |
| Cameroon | Mauritania | Upper Volta |

Pisa and Genoa drove out the Arabs in the 1000s A.D. and then fought each other for control of the island for several centuries.

France invaded and conquered Corsica in 1768, and the following year Napoleon was born there. British forces landed on the island in the 1790s and during the Napoleonic wars. But Corsica was restored to France in 1815.

In the 1970s–80s Corsican nationalists committed a series of demonstrations and terrorist bombings, demanding independence from France, which administers the island as one of the nation's departments with an appointed prefect.

### FRENCH GUIANA (GUYANE)

**Area:** 35,135 square miles (91,000 sq. km.).
**Population:** 71,428.
**Capital:** Cayenne, 34,000.

Located on the northern coast of South America, French Guiana is bordered on the north by the Atlantic Ocean, on the east and south by Brazil, and on the west by Surinam

Most French Guianese are blacks. About 7 in 10 are literate in the French language.

Guiana's farmers raise cattle, bananas, pineapples, sugarcane, fruits, and vegetables. Gold is mined, but large deposits of bauxite have not been developed.

France began to colonize Guiana in 1635 but did not establish firm control until 1677. For nearly a century (1852–1947) French convicts were sent to Guiana's penal colony, Devil's Island. The territory's borders were settled in 1854. It became an overseas department of France in 1946 with representation in France's parliament.

In the 1960s France built its main space-research center at the former prison camp at Kourou. In 1975 the French government began investing $160 million to develop paper manufacturing to utilize the area's forests.

### FRENCH POLYNESIA

**Area:** 1,544 square miles (4,000 sq. km.).
**Population:** 158,007.
**Capital:** Papeete, Tahiti, 25,342.

The nearly 130 islands of French Polynesia are scattered over a vast area of the South Pacific.

For administrative purposes, the islands have been divided into five groups: the *Windward Islands,* including Tahiti and Moorea; the *Leeward Islands,* including Raiatea and Bora-Bora (the Windward and Leeward islands make up the Society Islands); the *Tuamotu and Gambier islands;* the *Austral Islands;* and the *Marquesas Islands.*

Most of the people are French-speaking Christian Polynesians.

Exports include copra, vanilla, coffee, and phosphates.

Tourism is an important revenue source.

The Society Islands were discovered and claimed for England in 1767, but French claims were established a year later. In 1842 France declared a protectorate, and in 1880 the islands became a French colony.

The Tuamotu Islands were discovered by Spain in 1606. They became a French protectorate in 1844 and were annexed in 1881.

The Gambier Islands, discovered by the British in 1797, were annexed by France in 1881.

The Austral Islands came under French control in 1880.

The southern Marquesas were discovered by Spain in 1595, and the northern Marquesas were sighted by an American in 1791. In 1842 French sovereignty over the Marquesas was recognized by local chieftains.

The islands of French Polynesia were grouped into a single colony in 1903. They became an overseas territory of France in 1946.

France's nuclear-testing center, on Mururoa (720 miles southeast of Tahiti), began operating in 1966, when France exploded its first atomic bomb. In 1968 France's first hydrogen bomb was detonated near Mururoa.

## GUADELOUPE AND DEPENDENCIES

**Area:** 687 square miles (1,779 sq. km.).
**Population:** 332,307.
**Capital:** Basse-Terre, 20,000.
**Largest City:** Point-à-Pitre, 29,522.

Guadeloupe is located in the Leeward Islands of the Lesser Antilles in the eastern Caribbean Sea. It consists of two islands, Basse-Terre and Grande-Terre, separated by a narrow channel, the Rivière Salée. Volcanic Basse-Terre lies to the west, while the flat island of Grande-Terre is to the east.

Most of the French-speaking inhabitants of Guadeloupe are of black or mixed descent.

The economy is based on tourism and farming. The main crops are sugarcane, bananas, and pineapples.

Guadeloupe's dependencies include the islands of Marie Galante, Les Saintes, Désirade, and St. Barthélemy. About two-thirds of the island of St. Martin, located about 110 miles northeast of Guadeloupe, is administered by Guadeloupe. The other third is the Dutch St. Maarten.

Columbus discovered Guadeloupe in 1493, and France founded the first permanent colony in 1635. Except for British occupation in the 1700s and during the Napoleonic wars, Guadeloupe remained French. It became an overseas department of France in 1946.

The people enjoy the same social-welfare benefits as the people of France, including family allowances and medical aid.

Guadeloupe has become a popular winter resort for Americans and Canadians. Its climate is warm the year round with mean temperatures of 74° F. in January and 87° F. in August.

More than 72,000 persons evacuated the southern half of the island of Basse-Terre before the 4,813-foot La Soufrière volcano exploded on Aug. 30, 1976, throwing out lava and rocks.

## MARTINIQUE

**Area:** 425 square miles (1,102 sq. km.).
**Population:** 328,889.
**Capital:** Fort-de-France, 96,943.

Martinique is situated in the Windward Islands of the Lesser Antilles in the eastern Caribbean Sea. The island's terrain is generally mountainous, and the highest peak is volcanic Mt. Pelée (4,583 feet).

The people are French-speaking and mostly of black or mixed descent. Sugar, pineapples, bananas, and rum are the main products.

Famed for the beauty of its forested mountains and sandy beaches, Martinique has been called the *Pearl of the Antilles.* The island has a thriving tourist industry, as many visitors come to enjoy the warm climate that averages from 76° to 81° F. the year round.

Columbus discovered Martinique in 1502. France settled the island in 1635. Britain occupied the island in 1762–63 and 1794–1815.

An eruption of Mt. Pelée on May 8, 1902, destroyed the city of St. Pierre, killing about 40,000 persons.

Martinique became an overseas department of France in 1946. It is represented in the French parliament by two senators and three deputies.

## MAHORE

**Area:** 144 square miles (373 sq. km.).
**Population:** 49,537.
**Capital:** Dzaoudzi.

The island of Mahore (formerly Mayotte) lies in the Mozambique Channel off the coast of Africa about midway between Madagascar and Mozambique. It is the southernmost of the Comoro Islands and the only one whose people chose to remain a French dependency when the Comoros declared their independence.

The majority of the people earn their living by farming or fishing. Their most important export products are essential oils, used in perfume making, and spices. The economy depends on subsidies from France to import food and necessities.

France obtained the right from the local chiefs to use Mahore as a military base in 1840–41. Mahore was made a French colony in 1843. French settlers began cultivating sugarcane plantations on the island. By 1912 France had taken over all the Comoros as a colony administered from Madagascar. The islands became an overseas territory of France in 1958 and were granted internal self-government in 1960.

When the other Comoros declared their independence in July 1975, the people of Mahore refused to go along and repelled an attempted inva-

QUICK QUIZ: Who was the first President never before to have held elective office? See page 356.

**FRENCH DEPENDENCIES** *(continued)*

sion by the new Comoros government. On Feb. 8, 1976, Mahore voted 99% in favor of remaining a French dependency. In a vote on April 11, 1976, the islanders chose by an 80% majority to become an overseas department of France.

## NEW CALEDONIA

**Area:** 7,358 square miles (19,058 sq. km.).
**Population:** 153,952.
**Capital:** Nouméa, 56,078.

New Caledonia is a territory of France that includes several island groups in the South Pacific. The island of New Caledonia itself has an area of 6,530 square miles.

Main dependencies of New Caledonia include: the *Loyalty Islands* (area 756 sq. mi.), a chain of islands that lie about 78 miles to the east; the *Chesterfield Islands*, uninhabited coral islets about 400 miles to the northwest; the *Isle of Pines*, about 30 miles to the southeast.

Located about 750 miles east of Australia, the island is mountainous and covered with lush vegetation. Nearly half the people are Melanesian. About 40% are European, mostly French.

Mining is the most important industry. New Caledonia has large reserves of nickel, iron, manganese, and chrome.

The French explorer Louis Antoine de Bougainville sailed near New Caledonia in 1768. Capt. James Cook gave the island its name, landing there on Sept. 4, 1774. The island was annexed by France in 1853 and was used as a penal colony from 1864 to 1894. Following occupation by U.S. forces in World War II, the island became an overseas territory of France in 1946.

A French-appointed governor heads the island's administration. He is assisted by a council of government chosen by the popularly elected territorial assembly. In 1979 France sent 100 riot police to cope with increased violence by nationalists demanding independence.

## RÉUNION

**Area:** 969 square miles (2,510 sq. km.).
**Population:** 512,322.
**Capital:** Saint-Denis, 103,512.

Réunion is located in the Indian Ocean about 450 miles east of the island of Madagascar. The island has one active and nine inactive volcanoes. The people are descendants of French settlers, blacks, Malays, Indochinese, and Malabar Indians.

The island has a prosperous economy based largely on growing sugarcane. All children attend school, and most people read and write French. About 25% of the people are of French descent. Portuguese explorers visited Réunion in the 1500s. The island was claimed for France in 1638 and settled in 1665. Until 1793 Réunion was called Bourbon Island. In 1946 it became an overseas department of France.

## SAINT PIERRE AND MIQUELON

**Area:** 93 square miles (242 sq. km.).
**Population:** 5,904.
**Capital:** Saint Pierre, 4,287.

Saint Pierre and Miquelon lie in the Atlantic Ocean about 15 miles southwest of Newfoundland. There are two main islands—Saint Pierre (10 sq. mi.) and Miquelon (83 sq. mi.). The southern part of Miquelon sometimes is considered to be a separate island called Lauglade.

Most of the people are descendants of early Basque and French settlers and are Roman Catholics. Fishing is the main industry. The soil is so rocky and the climate so cold that no food crops can be grown.

The Portuguese explorer Faguendez visited Saint Pierre and Miquelon in 1520. The islands were claimed for France in 1535 by Jacques Cartier. The first French settlement was founded in 1604. The islands were ceded to Britain in 1713, restored to France in 1763, retaken by Britain from 1778 to 1783 and during the Napoleonic wars, and finally returned to the French in 1816. In 1935 the islands were granted local autonomy. They were made a department of France in 1976.

## SOUTHERN AND ANTARCTIC TERRITORIES

**Area:** 2,918 square miles (7,557 sq. km.).
**Population:** 183.
**Capital:** Port aux Français, Kerguélen.

The French Southern and Antarctic Territories consists of two archipelagos, two islands, and an area on the Antarctic continent.

*Kerguélen Archipelago,* a large subantarctic island and 300 smaller islands in the South Indian Ocean, was discovered by Yves Joseph de Kerguélen-Trémarec in 1772. Research stations, a hospital, and a military camp are located there.

*Crozet Archipelago,* 5 large and 15 small islands in the South Indian Ocean about 800 miles west of Kerguélen, was also discovered in 1772. A meteorological station was built there in 1964.

*Saint Paul* is a tiny, uninhabited island in the Indian Ocean northeast of Kerguélen.

*New Amsterdam Island,* located about 50 miles north of Saint Paul, has research stations and a hospital.

*Terre Adélie,* situated on the Antarctic continent, was discovered on Jan. 19, 1840, by Dumont d'Urville. Nearby Commonwealth Bay is said to be the windiest place in the world, with wind speeds reaching 200 mph.

## WALLIS AND FUTUNA

**Area:** 77 square miles (200 sq. km.).
**Population:** 9,400.
**Capital:** Mata Utu, Uvéa, 6,000.

Wallis and Futuna are two small groups of Pacific islands located about 250 miles west of Samoa. The Wallis Islands consist of Uvéa and about 20 smaller islands. The islands of Futuna and Alofi make up the Hoorn (or Horne) Islands, located about 125 miles west of the Wallis Islands. Most of the population is Polynesian, and the main economic activities are copra production and fishing.

Dutch navigators discovered the Hoorn Islands in 1617. The Wallis Islands were sighted in 1767 by the English explorer Samuel Wallis. France established a protectorate over the islands in 1887–88.

In 1961 Wallis and Futuna became an overseas territory of France. The islands are governed by a French administrator with the assistance of a territorial council consisting of the kings of each of the three main islands and three appointed members.

# GABON

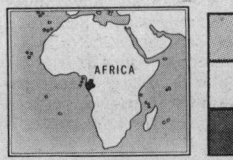 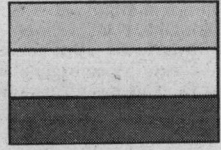

**Official Name:** Gabonese Republic.
**Area:** 103,347 square miles (267,667 sq. km.).
**Population:** 552,957.
**Capital:** Libreville, 57,000.
**Government:** One-party state.
**President:** Omar Bongo (since 1967).
**Premier:** Léon Mebiame (since 1975).
**National Assembly:** 47 members.
**U.S. Ambassador to Gabon:** Arthur T. Tienken.
**Ambassador to U.S.:** Aboubakar C. Bokoko.
**Flag:** Stripes of green (top), yellow (middle), and blue (bottom).
**Official Language:** French.
**Chief Ethnic Groups:** Fang (32%), Eshira (19%), Adouma (12%), Okande (5%).
**Religions:** Christianity (46%), animism, Islam.
**Leading Industries:** Mining (petroleum, manganese, uranium, iron ore, lead, zinc, copper, diamonds); forestry and lumbering; agriculture (cocoa, coffee, vegetables, fruits); construction; fishing.
**Foreign Trade:** *major exports*—petroleum, wood, manganese, uranium; *major imports*—petroleum products, iron and steel, trucks, agricultural machinery, clothing.
**Places of Interest:** Dense hardwood forests; Crystal Mountains; Mt. Iboundji; Libreville; Lambaréné, site of Dr. Albert Schweitzer's hospital; national parks.

## GABON TODAY

Gabon, about the size of Colorado, is one of the most prosperous of the countries of Africa.

Rich in natural resources, Gabon is one of the world's leading producers of uranium, with about 1,000 tons exported to France each year.

Gabon also has large deposits of petroleum, manganese, and iron ore. Oil accounts for about three-fourths of its export income.

Its forests support a thriving lumber industry, and its rivers provide substantial hydroelectric potential.

The government has offered encouragement to foreign investors to develop the natural resources, and has worked hard to improve port and transportation facilities.

Most of the people are poor. The nation's economic boom has eliminated unemployment. But most of the people do not have enough education to handle high-paying jobs in industry. Only about 1 person in 5 can read and write.

Disease and malnutrition give the Gabonese one of the lowest life expectancies in the world, with the average man dying by the age of 25.

An equatorial country in western Africa, Gabon has a hot and humid climate. Much of the land is covered by dense tropical rain forests. The country's major waterway is the Ougooé River.

During the rainy season, from February to June, more than 100 inches of rain fall in Libreville. The heavy rains make jungle roads impassable, so the country relies on aircraft for interior travel. As a result Gabon has some 120 airports.

The coastal lowlands extend 20 to 125 miles into the interior and adjoin a 60-mile-wide belt of rocky cliffs.

Equatorial Guinea and Cameroon lie to the north, and Congo to the east and south.

## EARLY HISTORY

Portuguese exploration began about 1470, followed by the British, Dutch, Spanish, and French during the centuries of slave trading.

In 1839 French explorer Édouard Bouet-Willaumez signed a treaty of peace with "King" Denis of Gabon. Denis, a notorious African slave trader, turned over part of northern Gabon to France in return for protection.

The capital, Libreville (place of liberation), was founded in 1849 when the French captured a slave ship and released its captives at the mouth of the Como River.

Control by France gradually expanded, and the colony of Gabon was established in 1885. Gabon became one of the four territories of French Equatorial Africa in 1910.

Dr. Albert Schweitzer established the first hospital in the region in 1913 at Lambaréné.

Gabon was granted internal self-government in 1957. Leon M'ba became chief minister.

## INDEPENDENCE

Gabon was proclaimed fully independent on Aug. 17, 1960. Leon M'ba was elected president.

M'ba was reelected in March 1967, but died in office that November. Vice President Albert-Bernard Bongo became president.

Bongo declared Gabon a one-party state in March 1968, dissolving the powerful Gabonese Democratic bloc and creating a new party, the Gabonese Democratic Party (PDG). He was reelected president in 1973 without opposition.

Gabon became a full member of the Organization of Petroleum Exporting Countries (OPEC) in 1975. Symbolizing his nation's closer relations with the Arab oil producers, President Bongo changed his French given name of Albert-Bernard to the Arabic name *Omar*.

Work began in 1975 on the 600-mile Trans-Gabon Railway from Libreville to the interior cities of Mékambo and Franceville. The first 115-mile section of the railroad opened to regular traffic in 1979. The line, planned for completion in 1985, will permit expansion of uranium and iron mining.

Bongo expelled 10,000 Benin workers from Gabon by airlift in July 1978. The action came after Benin's ruler Mathieu Kerekou accused Gabon of attempting to overthrow him.

As host to a 1977 conference of the Organization of African Unity (OAU), Gabon borrowed more than $2 billion to prepare for the meeting. As a result, the government had to use nearly half its revenues in 1979–80 in paying off interest and part of the debt. An austerity program caused a decline of about 20% in the gross national product.

However, new oil finds in 1979 indicated petroleum production could be increased in the 1980s with consequent growth in the economy.

QUICK QUIZ: Adlai E. Stevenson was Vice President under which President? See page 391.

# GAMBIA

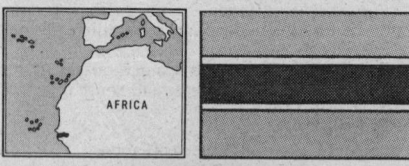

**Official Name:** Republic of The Gambia.
**Area:** 4,361 square miles (11,295 sq. km.).
**Population:** 609,815.
**Capital:** Banjul, 45,604.
**Government:** Presidential-parliamentary democracy.
**President:** Sir Dawda Kairaba Jawara (since 1970).
**House of Representatives:** 37 members.
**U.S. Ambassador to Gambia:** Larry Gordon Piper.
**Gambia Ambassador to U.S.:** Ousman Ahmadou Sallah.
**Flag:** Red, blue, and green stripes from top to bottom, separated by narrow white stripes.
**Official Language:** English.
**Chief Ethnic Groups:** Mandingo (40%), Fula (13%), Wolof (12%), Serahuli (7%), Jola (7%).
**Leading Religions:** Islam (85%), animism, Christianity.
**Leading Industries:** Agriculture (peanuts, cattle, rice, palm kernels, bees, vegetables, fruits); fishing; tourism; food processing; handicrafts.
**Foreign Trade:** *major exports*—peanuts, palm kernels, hides, fish, beeswax; *major imports*—textiles, food, machinery, hardware, consumer goods.
**Places of Interest:** Flora and fauna along the Gambia River; Banjul; beaches.

## GAMBIA TODAY

Africa's smallest independent country, Gambia is a shining example of two-party democracy amid the many dictatorships of the continent.

With less area than the state of Connecticut, Gambia averages only about 20 miles in width but is about 200 miles long from east to west. It is surrounded by Senegal, except for an Atlantic shoreline of about 50 miles.

Unlike most of the small nations of Africa that quickly eradicated signs of colonialism upon attaining independence, Gambia remains proud of its British colonial heritage. Many Britons continue to work in the government offices. And the capital, Banjul, retains the appearance of a British city of the Victorian age.

The Gambia River, which extends the length of the country, provides excellent transportation. However, Gambia has few natural resources.

Most of the people are poor tribesmen. Some are nomads who raise cattle. Many of the others are farmers who raise just enough food to feed their families. Only about 12 persons in 100 can read and write, and only about 20,000 children go to school.

Peanuts, the only sizable cash crop, provide 95% of Gambia's exports.

The government uses much of its limited resources to promote tourism. About 50,000 visitors each year, mostly from Europe.

The village of Juffure attracts an unusual number of foreign visitors as the ancestral home of Kunta Kinte of the book *Roots* written by American author Alex Haley. President Jawara declared Juffure a national monument. The village has changed little since Kunta Kinte was stolen by slave traders in 1767.

Because Gambia has relatively low import duties and low prices compared with Senegal, a substantial amount of smuggling takes place between the two countries. Senegal tries to prevent the smuggling with roving border patrols. This has often resulted in friction between the two governments because the long border is largely unmarked.

The country is generally low-lying and flat, with elevations ranging from sea level to 120 feet. Temperatures vary from a low of 60° F. in winter to a high of 110° F. in summer. The country averages 11 hours of sunshine every day from November to May. Rainfall averages 30 to 55 inches a year, largely in June to September.

## EARLY HISTORY

The Gambia River was discovered in 1456 by Portuguese explorers. It was then part of the kingdom of Mali. Portugal controlled the region until the late 1500s.

Britain and France fought for the territory and the moderately profitable slave trade until the 1800s.

After 1815 France regained Saint-Louis and Gorée islands, and British dominance was maintained by the merchants who traded on the Gambia River.

The British established the first permanent settlement at Bathurst (now Banjul) in 1816. Gambia was administered through a governor-general in Sierra Leone in 1821–43 and 1866–88. It was a separate colony between 1843 and 1866 and returned to crown-colony status in 1888. The country's present boundaries were established by agreement with France in 1889.

Sir Dawda K. Jawara was elected prime minister in 1962. Under his leadership Gambia was granted full internal self-government in 1963.

## INDEPENDENCE

Gambia received independence from Britain on Feb. 18, 1965.

The nation became a republic within the British Commonwealth of Nations with a new constitution promulgated on April 24, 1970. It took the official name *Republic of the Gambia.* Jawara became the nation's first president.

One of the few African countries with a multiparty political system, Gambia held its first national elections in March 1972. Jawara was elected to a 5-year term as president. His People's Progressive Party (PPP) won 28 seats in the house of representatives, and the opposition United Party won 3 seats. Four representatives are appointed by the tribal chiefs.

The 53-year-old Jawara was elected to another 5-year term as president on April 5, 1977, when his PPP party won a national election with a majority of 27 seats in the national house of representatives.

Jawara's chief opponent in the election was Sherrif Dibba, head of the National Convention Party, which won five seats in the national legislature.

A drought during 1977–78 caused a devastating loss of about 40% of the nation's grain crops. Then too much rain in 1978–79 again damaged the peanut crops.

# GERMANY, EAST

**Official Name:** German Democratic Republic.
**Area:** 41,768 square miles (108,178 sq. km.).
**Population:** 16,672,200.
**Chief Cities:** East Berlin, capital, 1,111,398; Leipzig, 565,178; Dresden, 511,223; Karl-Marx-Stadt, 309,457; Magdeburg, 280,570; Halle, 233,049.
**Government:** One-party communist state.
**Heads of Government:** First Secretary of Communist Party, Erich Honecker (since 1971); President, Willi Stoph (appointed in 1973); Premier, Horst Sindermann (since 1973).
**Legislature:** *Volkskammer,* 500 members.
**U.S. Ambassador to East Germany:** Herbert Stuart Okun.
**East German Ambassador to U.S.:** Horst Grunert.
**Flag:** Black, red, and gold stripes, with centered coat of arms.
**Official Language:** German.
**Principal Ethnic Group:** German (99.8%).
**Main Religions:** Protestantism (59%), Roman Catholicism (8%).
**Leading Industries:** Manufacturing (steel, chemicals, textiles, cement, machinery, electronic computers, consumer products); agriculture (dairy products, cattle, poultry, potatoes, sugar beets, wheat, rye, barley, oats); construction; mining (lignite, potash, coal, iron ore, copper, uranium, cobalt).
**Foreign Trade:** *major exports*—machinery, coal briquettes, chemicals; *major imports*—coal, crude petroleum, coke, machinery, wheat, iron ore.
**Places of Interest:** East Berlin's Brandenburg Gate; Dresden's Frauenkirche; Jena's Goethe monument; Leipzig. *In Potsdam:* state buildings; Karl-Marx-Stadt.

## EAST GERMANY TODAY

The communist leaders of East Germany look enviously at the booming industrial production of neighboring West Germany, while the people look equally enviously at the freedom and higher standard of living across the border. Although forbidden to watch TV broadcasts from West Germany, most East Germans do so in the privacy of their homes.

A repressive communist police state, East Germany guards its borders with barbed wire and machine guns to prevent its people from escaping to the West. Even so several hundred each year do escape, although dozens are killed by guards and land mines. About 5,000 people who unsuccessfully try to escape are imprisoned. Some 1,000 to 1,500 are permitted to leave each year for ransom payments of about $20,000 apiece by the West German government.

The government owns and controls all industrial and agricultural facilities. It emphasizes heavy industry at the expense of consumer goods.

## GEOGRAPHY AND CLIMATE

The sandy Baltic coast in the north has hills and lakes. The central region has fertile plains as well as the Harz Mountains. The Thuringian Forest range dominates the southern region. In the southeast the Erzgebirge range forms a natural frontier with Czechoslovakia. The principal rivers are the Elbe, Saale, Havel, and Spree.

Winter temperatures average at freezing or below, while summer temperatures rise to an average of about 64° F.

West Germany lies to the west and south, Poland and Czechoslovakia are to the east, and the Baltic Sea is to the north.

## COMMUNIST STATE

East Germany and East Berlin came under Soviet occupation at the end of World War II. For the earlier history of Germany see article *Germany, West,* on the following pages.

The Soviet Union turned its occupied zone into the *German Democratic Republic (GDR)* on Oct. 7, 1949. This followed the creation of the Federal Republic of Germany (West Germany) three weeks earlier by the Allies.

The Western powers refused to recognize the new government of East Germany, but all Soviet-bloc countries extended recognition immediately.

Soviet troops effectively crushed an anticommunist revolt in East Germany in June 1953.

Between 1949 and 1961 some 3.5 million East Germans escaped to West Germany.

In August 1961 the East German government constructed a wall of barbed wire and concrete around the western sector of Berlin to stop the flow of East Germans into West Berlin.

## DEVELOPMENTS IN 1970s

As head of the Communist Party, Walter Ulbricht dominated the GDR from its formation until 1971, when he resigned party leadership.

After long negotiations, East and West Germany began to relax relations in 1972. A treaty establishing diplomatic relations between the two states was signed on Dec. 21, 1972. Ratification by the parliaments of both states was completed in six months, and the pact went into effect on June 21, 1973.

The new understanding opened the door to UN membership for both Germanys in September 1973, and brought about diplomatic recognition by the U.S. and other Western nations.

Amnesty International reported in October 1977 that from 100,000 to 200,000 East Germans had asked permission to emigrate but had been refused. The report said thousands of them had been jailed as political prisoners.

New restrictive laws went into effect Aug. 1, 1979, providing long jail terms for anyone taking part in an antigovernment demonstration or for passing on any information damaging to the government to "foreign organizations."

East Germany's 5-year plan for 1976–1980 called for a 34% to 36% increase in industrial production by promoting a 30% improvement in the productivity of workers.

Reacting to strikes in neighboring Poland, the government ordered new restrictions in 1980 to prevent western visitors from entering East Germany.

QUICK QUIZ: How many calories are in a 7-inch carrot? See page 401.

# GERMANY, WEST

**Official Name:** Federal Republic of Germany.
**Area:** 95,976 square miles (248,577 sq. km.).
**Population:** 60,850,300.
**Chief Cities:** Bonn, capital, 284,003; West Berlin, 1,926,826; Hamburg, 1,680,340; Munich, 1,313,939; Cologne (Köln), 976,761; Essen, 664,408; Frankfurt am Main, 632,565; Dortmund, 617,590; Düsseldorf, 607,560; Stuttgart, 584,554.
**Government:** Parliamentary democracy.
**Chancellor:** Helmut Schmidt (since 1974).
**President:** Karl Carstens (since 1979).
**Legislature:** *Bundesrat,* 41 members; *Bundestag,* 496 members.
**U.S. Ambassador to W. Germany:** Walter J. Stoessel Jr.
**West German Ambassador to U.S.:** Peter Hermes.
**Flag:** Black, red, and gold stripes.
**Language:** German.
**Principal Ethnic Group:** German (99%).
**Leading Religions:** Protestantism (47%), Roman Catholicism (45%).
**Leading Industries:** Manufacturing (steel, cement, paper, aluminum, electricity, machinery, motor vehicles, chemicals, textiles); agriculture (dairy products, cattle, hogs, poultry, potatoes, sugar beets, rye, wheat, oats, barley, vegetables, fruits); mining (coal, lignite, zinc, natural gas, gold, salt, petroleum); construction.
**Foreign Trade:** *major exports*—automobiles, organic chemicals, plastics, scientific instruments; *major imports*—crude petroleum, fresh fruits, foodstuffs, copper, petroleum products, clothing, automobiles.
**Places of Interest:** The Alps; Black Forest; Harz Mountains; Weser Hills; Rhine and Danube rivers; Heidelberg; Bremen; Bayreuth; Berchtesgaden; Goethe's house and museum in Frankfurt; Germanic National Museum in Nuremberg; Hamburg botanical gardens and flower park; Cologne Cathedral; Charlemagne's throne in Aachen; Passau medieval town. *In Berlin:* Wall between West and East Berlin; Grünewald Hunting Lodge; Kaiser Wilhelm Memorial Church; Hansa Quarter; Dahlem Museum.

## WEST GERMANY TODAY

West Germany is smaller than Oregon, but it has risen from destruction and defeat in World War II to become the leading industrial nation of western Europe. The main competitor of the U.S. and Japan in world trade, West Germany ranks among the world's leading producers of steel, cement, aluminum, electricity, coal-lignite, gold, paper, natural gas, and zinc.

West Germany has the largest population of any country of western Europe. It is also the most crowded of the major European nations because of land lost by World War II. As a result West Germany depends heavily on imports to feed its population.

Although ruled for hundreds of years by kings, emperors, and dictators, the West German people in the generations since World War II have developed a stable, democratic government that has become a beacon of freedom for refugees from communist eastern Europe, Ancient enmities with

France and Britain have been healed.

West Germany today plays an important role in cooperative international organizations, such as NATO, the European Common Market, and the United Nations.

## GEOGRAPHY AND CLIMATE

Wide lowlands extend from the Netherlands to East Germany in the north.

The upland regions of the central German mountains stretch from the Rhine to the East German border.

The wide valley and gorge of the Rhine cross the southeastern part of West Germany.

Mountains and plateaus range across southern Germany, with the Black Forest in the west, the Bavarian Forest in the east, and the Bavarian Alps in the far south.

The Rhine River, whose two main tributaries are the Mosel and the Main, empties into the North Sea. To the east are the Ems, Weser, and Elbe rivers, all with important ports on their estuaries. To the south the Danube flows eastward for about 400 miles.

Lake Constance, lying on the Swiss and Austrian borders, is the largest lake.

The average temperature ranges from below 21° F. in the mountains during the winter to about 68° F. in the valleys during the summer. Rain, falling throughout the year, varies from 20 to 78 inches, depending on the region and altitude. Snow may reach a depth of 6 feet in some areas during January and February.

West Germany is bordered on the north by Denmark; on the east by East Germany and Czechoslovakia; on the south by Austria and Switzerland; and on the west by France, Luxembourg, Belgium, and the Netherlands.

## EARLY HISTORY

The Teutons and the Cimbri are thought to be among the earliest Germanic tribes. Roman records report their defeat by the general Marius in 102–101 B.C. Germanic tribes that included the Alemanni, Burgundians, Franks, Lombards, Ostrogoths, and Visigoths advanced south as the Roman Empire weakened and collapsed.

Charlemagne, the Germanic leader of the Franks who was crowned Roman emperor in A.D. 800, extended his sovereignty over most of Germany.

## MIDDLE AGES

Powerful feudal princes divided Germany at a time when it was being invaded by Slavs, Norsemen, and Magyars.

Otto I, Saxon king of the Germans, created the Holy Roman Empire. He was crowned its first emperor in Rome in 962. However, rivalry among the feudal states in Germany and the struggle for supremacy between the emperors and the popes rendered the empire a loose and ineffective federation with little central authority.

The empire was strengthened under the Hohenstaufens, who subdued many of the large duchies. In 1180 Friedrich I Barbarossa dismembered Saxony, the last remaining great duchy.

His grandson Friedrich II was king of Sicily. He also became king of the Germans (1212) and emperor of the Holy Roman Empire (1220–

1250). Friedrich II ruled from Sicily, paying little attention to German problems. By the end of his reign the French monarchy and Italian city-states had begun their ascendancy.

## REFORMATION

The weakness of the Holy Roman Empire became particularly evident when Germany found itself the center of the Reformation, the religious schism initiated by Martin Luther in 1517.

The Roman Catholic German emperor could not enforce his own religious policies or halt the conversion to Protestantism of many nobles.

The empire was torn by the Thirty Years War (1618–48). The Treaty of Westphalia in 1648 elevated the territorial sovereignty of the states above that of the empire.

## PRUSSIA AND AUSTRIA COMPETE

Prussia grew into the only German state that could challenge Austria. When Friedrich the Great defeated Austria in 1740, Prussia joined the ranks of the great European powers.

Napoleon's rise to power in Europe brought an end to the Holy Roman Empire.

At the Congress of Vienna (1814–15) the German states were reduced in number, and a national structure was formed through the German Confederation, with Prussia and Austria as the dominant states. Austria, however, gained control of the confederation.

In 1848 liberal revolutions in Germany failed to unify the nation. The Prussian monarchy tried its own scheme of unification, but in 1850 Austria checked Prussian ambitions by threatening war.

## GERMAN EMPIRE

In 1862 Prime Minister Otto von Bismarck of Prussia resolved to eliminate Austrian influence over Germany.

Bismarck achieved his goal with victory over Austria in the Austro-Prussian War (1866). Prussia went on to win the Franco-Prussian War of 1870–71 and was able to unify Germany under Emperor Wilhelm I in 1871. Bismarck became Germany's first chancellor.

From 1871 to 1914 the German Empire expanded rapidly. Its economy flourished. The acquisition of colonies and construction of a navy enhanced its power and prestige.

In 1888 Wilhelm II became emperor and two years later dismissed Bismarck as chancellor.

The rulers of Germany and Austria seized upon the assassination of the heir to the Austrian throne in 1914 as an opportune occasion to defeat or at least to divide their enemies.

Europe was thus plunged into World War I, which ended with Germany's defeat.

## WEIMAR REPUBLIC

With the German defeat the Weimar Republic replaced the empire. At its inception the republic was saddled with the humiliating Treaty of Versailles (1919). Germany lost its overseas possessions and had to pay heavy reparations.

In the late 1920s the worldwide depression hit the German economy particularly hard, causing massive unemployment and social chaos.

## HITLER'S NAZI GERMANY

By 1932 Adolf Hitler's National Socialist (Nazi) Party was the largest in the Reichstag. He became chancellor in January 1933. Within the year Hitler assumed dictatorial powers.

Hitler launched a campaign to eliminate all Jews from Germany. The official policy of anti-Semitism culminated during World War II in the "final solution" to the "Jewish problem"— the extermination of an estimated 6 million Jews in death camps.

In violation of the Versailles Treaty, Hitler remilitarized the Rhineland in 1936, annexed Austria in March 1938, and seized the Sudetenland of Czechoslovakia in September 1938.

In March 1939 Germany took over the rest of Czechoslovakia and demanded Danzig and the Polish Corridor that separated most of Germany from East Prussia.

World War II began when Germany invaded Poland on Sept. 1, 1939. The Nazis enjoyed spectacular successes up to 1941, but beginning with the invasion of Russia in that year, the tide gradually turned.

The war ended in May 1945 with Germany's unconditional surrender after Hitler's suicide.

## ALLIED OCCUPATION

At conferences in Yalta and Potsdam the U.S., Britain, and the Soviet Union decided to divide Germany into four occupation zones, with Berlin under four-power control.

The Soviet Union, however, embarked on its own policy, and efforts to govern Germany through the Allied Control Commission collapsed.

In 1948–49 East Germany cut off land access to Berlin from West Germany. The U.S., Britain, and France organized an airlift to supply Berlin. As a result, the East Germans restored land access.

On Sept. 21, 1949, the democratic *Federal Republic of Germany* was granted self-government. It was created out of the U.S., British, and French zones of Germany. Theodor Heuss was elected president, and the Bundestag chose Konrad Adenauer as chancellor.

## INDEPENDENCE FOR WEST GERMANY

West Germany was granted full independence on May 5, 1955, by the U.S., Britain, and France. The United States gave West Germany over $5 billion in aid to rebuild its industries and become a bulwark against the Soviet Union.

Under Adenauer the country achieved economic recovery and political stability.

Adenauer's foreign policy was built on cooperation with the United States, support of NATO, and reconciliation with France. In 1955 West Germany was allowed to rearm under supervision of NATO members. It established diplomatic relations with the Soviet Union. Efforts to reunite East and West Germany were defeated by Cold War tensions.

In 1961 East Germany built the Berlin Wall between the east and west sectors of Berlin to try to prevent East Germans from escaping.

Adenauer retired in 1963. Ludwig Erhard, who as economics minister had been largely responsible for Germany's "economic miracle," became

QUICK QUIZ: What is the most abundant mineral in the human body? See page 403.

## GERMANY, WEST *(continued)*

chancellor. Erhard continued the foreign and domestic policies of Adenauer.

Erhard was succeeded in 1966 by Kurt Georg Kiesinger, who governed until 1969 with a coalition of Christian Democrats and Social Democrats. The Allies gave up their last occupation rights in May 1968.

## OSTPOLITIK OF CHANCELLOR BRANDT

Following the parliamentary elections on Sept. 28, 1969, a coalition of Social Democrats and Free Democrats was formed under Chancellor Willy Brandt, who had been foreign minister in the Kiesinger cabinet.

The German political scene under Brandt was dominated by his *Ostpolitik,* a drive to normalize relations with the communist bloc, including East Germany. *Ostpolitik* led to treaties with the Soviet Union and Poland in 1970 that recognized the inviolability of postwar borders. The Bundestag ratified the treaties on May 17–19, 1972.

The first formal treaty between West and East Germany was ratified and went into effect Oct. 17, 1972. The treaty relaxed some border traffic regulations, enabling more West Germans to visit East Germany. Brandt then went on to win a November election with his coalition parties receiving over 54% of the popular vote.

A week after Brandt's reelection, his government signed a new and more important treaty with East Germany on Dec. 21, 1972, establishing diplomatic relations between the two. The treaty was ratified and went into effect on June 21, 1973. The two Germanys then were admitted to the UN in September 1973.

## REGIME OF CHANCELLOR SCHMIDT

New leaders were chosen in 1974 for both of Germany's top political posts. Chancellor Brandt resigned suddenly on May 6, accepting complete responsibility for "negligence" in having employed a communist East German spy as his assistant for party affairs. Brandt designated 55-year-old Helmut Schmidt, his finance minister, as his successor. Schmidt's elevation as West Germany's fifth chancellor was ratified on May 16 by a 267 to 225 vote of the Bundestag. A day before, 54-year-old Walter Scheel, vice chancellor and foreign minister since 1969, was elected to the ceremonial office of president.

Schmidt turned the foreign policy of West Germany from one of reconciliation with communist eastern Europe toward one of strengthening unity with Western allies.

On June 20, 1974, when the Bundestag gave final approval to a treaty establishing normal relations with communist Czechoslovakia, Schmidt described it as "the final stone" in the building of Brandt's *Ostpolitik.*

Chancellor Schmidt's coalition of the Social Democratic Party (SPD) and Free Democratic Party (FDP) won a close election over the Christian Democratic Party (CDU) on Oct. 3, 1976.

Terrorists of the left, attempting to bring anarchy to West Germany, stepped up their attacks in 1977. On April 7 they assassinated by machine gun West Germany's chief prosecutor of the anarchist Baader-Meinhof gang, Siegfried Buback. On July 30 they killed international banker

## CHANCELLORS OF WEST GERMANY

| 1949–63 | Konrad Adenauer .... | Christian Democrat |
|---------|----------------------|--------------------|
| 1963–66 | Ludwig Erhard ....... | Christian Democrat |
| 1966–69 | Kurt Georg Kiesinger . | Christian Democrat |
| 1969–74 | Willy Brandt ......... | Social Democrat |
| 1974– | Helmut Schmidt...... | Social Democrat |

Jürgen Ponto. On Sept. 5 the terrorists kidnapped and later killed one of the nation's leading industrialists, Hanns-Martin Schleyer.

The terrorism reached a crescendo when four of the gang hijacked a Lufthansa Boeing 737 airliner at Majorca on Oct. 13, 1977. The terrorists took the airliner on a 6,000-mile four-day flight to Somalia, killed the pilot en route, and threatened to kill the remaining passengers and crew by blowing up the plane.

Chancellor Schmidt's government won widespread acclaim when a 60-man West German commando unit made a daring raid on the hijacked airliner at Mogadishu, Somalia, on Oct. 18, 1977, freeing the 86 hostages while killing three of the hijackers and wounding the fourth. Within hours after the raid, three of the convicted members of the gang, including its leader Andreas Baader, were reported to have killed themselves in their prison cells.

Schmidt and Soviet Leader Leonid I. Brezhnev signed on May 6, 1978, a 25-year economic cooperation agreement. As the Soviet Union's largest trading partner among Western nations, West Germany sells more than $5 billion in exports to the Soviet Union annually.

Karl Carstens, 64, speaker of the Bundestag and a former member of the Nazi Party, was elected president to succeed Scheel by an electoral assembly on May 23, 1979. As the Christian Democratic candidate, Carstens won by a vote of 528 to 431 over the candidate of the governing Social Democrats.

Parliament in 1979 lifted the statute of limitations that would have prevented the continued prosecution in the 1980s of former Nazis.

West Germany and East Germany continued to strengthen ties in 1980 with agreement on a $282 million pact to improve road, rail, and waterway links between the two nations. However, labor unrest in Poland caused postponement in August of a planned trip to East Germany by Chancellor Schmidt that would have been the first such visit by a West German leader.

Although West Germany was weathering the 1980 recession better than most other Western industrial countries, it experienced its first trade deficit in 15 years in August as imports exceeded exports by about $100 million. The nation's gross national product also fell by about 1% in the second quarter of 1980. However, unemployment remained low at 3.7%.

West Germany was shocked when a neo-Nazi terrorist group set off a bomb at Munich's Oktoberfest celebration on Sept. 26, 1980, killing 13 persons and injured 215. The bomb thrower was among those killed.

In a national election on Oct. 5, 1980, Chancellor Schmidt's coalition strengthened its majority control of the lower house of parliament, winning 53.5% of the vote and gaining 16 seats. He had been opposed by the conservative governor of Bavaria, Franz Josef Strauss.

# GHANA

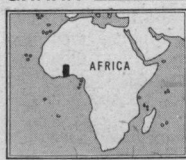

**Official Name:** Republic of Ghana.
**Area:** 92,100 square miles (238,537 sq. km.).
**Population:** 11,987,100.
**Chief Cities:** Accra, capital, 564,194; Kumasi, 260,286; Sekondi-Takoradi, 91,874.
**Largest Metropolitan Area:** Accra, 738,498.
**Government:** Multiparty republic.
**President:** Hilla Limann (since 1979).
**National Assembly:** 140 members.
**U.S. Ambassador to Ghana:** Thomas W.M. Smith.
**Ghana Ambassador to U.S.:** J.K. Baffour-Senkyire.
**Flag:** Red, gold, and green stripes, with black star in gold stripe.
**Languages:** English (official), Akan, Ewe, Ga, Hausa.
**Main Ethnic Group:** Black.
**Religions:** Animism (45%), Christianity (43%), Islam (12%).
**Leading Industries:** Agriculture (cocoa, coffee, palm kernels, corn, rice, peanuts, rabbits, tobacco, rubber, cassava, sweet potatoes, tomatoes, cotton, vegetables, fruits); forestry and lumbering; mining (gold, diamonds, manganese, bauxite); manufacturing (electricity, aluminum, steel, tires, vehicle assembly, oil refining).
**Foreign Trade:** *major exports*—cocoa, wood, gold, diamonds, manganese; *major imports*—auto parts, crude petroleum, automobiles, medicines, textile machinery.
**Places of Interest:** Cape Coast Castle; Boti Waterfall; Elmina resort; national museum, Accra; Kumasi Cultural Center; Bolgatanga market; Mole Game Reserve at Damongo; Aburi Botanical Garden; Paga crocodile pond; Dawhenya irrigation project.

## GHANA TODAY

About the size of Illinois and Indiana combined, Ghana is the world's leading grower of cacao beans, from which cocoa and chocolate are made.

Most of the people are poor. Only about 1 in 4 can read and write.

The country's tropical forests produce lumber, Ghana's second-leading export.

Petroleum was discovered in commercial amounts in 1978. Completion of a large hydroelectric project on the Volta River and the building of smelters for bauxite promise to make Ghana a leading aluminum producer.

Irrigation projects were undertaken in the 1970s to turn the barren Accra plain into farmland.

In the west a forested belt extends north from the coast into the hilly Ashanti region.

The climate is hot and humid in the south, and warm and humid in the north. A rainy season lasts from May to September.

Upper Volta lies to the north, Togo to the east, and Ivory Coast to the west.

## EARLY HISTORY

The ancient Ghana empire flourished from the 300s to the 1000s.

The Portuguese came in 1470, developing gold mining and slave trading. The first British trading visit to the area was by Thomas Windham in 1553.

After Britain declared the slave trade illegal in 1807, all Europeans except the British withdrew.

From 1826 to 1900 the British fought a long series of campaigns against the Ashantis of the interior. The coastal region was annexed by Britain as the Gold Coast Colony in 1874.

The Gold Coast became one of the most politically advanced African colonies. Blacks were admitted into the government in 1942.

The Convention People's Party (CPP), founded by Kwame Nkrumah, won legislative elections in 1951, and for the first time the black majority had power.

## INDEPENDENCE

On March 6, 1957, Ghana (as the Gold Coast was renamed) became the first black African colony granted independence by Britain.

In 1960 Ghana became a republic. Nkrumah, a communist, was elected president. He then established a one-party dictatorship.

In 1966 while in Peking, Nkrumah was deposed by a military coup, reportedly with the aid of the American CIA.

A military junta headed by Gen. A.A. Afrifa ruled until 1969.

Ghana's first·free general elections since 1956 were held Aug. 29, 1969. The Progress Party of Kofi Busia, leader of the opposition to Nkrumah, won a majority of seats in the national assembly.

On Jan. 13, 1972, a military coup, led by Col. Ignatius Kutu Acheampong, dismissed Prime Minister Busia, who was abroad.

Lt. Gen. Fred W.K. Akuffo, Acheampong's No. 2 deputy in the military junta, seized power in a bloodless coup on July 5, 1978. Akuffo said civilian government would be restored in 1979.

Flight Lt. Jerry J. Rawlings, 31, led a coup that overthrew the government on June 4, 1979, with the aid of junior officers and enlisted men.

Declaring that his was a "moral revolution," Rawlings arrested dozens of government officials and senior military officers on charges of corruption. After summary military trials in June 1979, eight were executed, including three former heads of state, Akuffo, Acheampong, and Afrifa.

After a new constitution similar to that of the U.S. was drawn up, Rawlings ordered the first free multiparty elections since 1969. They were held on June 18 and July 10, 1979.

Ghanaians elected the 140 members of a new national assembly and chose as president Dr. Hilla Limann, 52, an economist and head of the center-left People's National Party.

Less than four months after he had seized power, Rawlings turned over the government to President Limann and the new national assembly in a ceremony on Sept. 24, 1979.

During his first year in office, Limann worked to strengthen the economy. By imposing an austerity program on government spending in 1980, he managed to resume payments on foreign debts that had gone unpaid for five years. However, he was repeatedly denounced by Rawlings as moving too slowly to improve the way of life for the average Ghanian.

QUICK QUIZ: Should cucumbers be grown in partial shade or full sunlight? See page 407.

# GREECE

**Official Name:** Hellenic Republic.
**Area:** 50,944 square miles (131,944 sq. km.).
**Population:** 9,620,210.
**Chief Cities:** Athinai (Athens), capital, 867,023; Thessaloniki (Salonika), 345,799; Piraiéus (Piraeus), 187,362; Péristéri, 118,413.
**Largest Metropolitan Area:** Athens, 2,101,103.
**Government:** Parliamentary democracy.
**Prime Minister:** George John Rallis (since 1980).
**President:** Constantine Karamanlis (since 1980).
**Parliament:** 300 members.
**Greek Ambassador to U.S.:** John Tzounis.
**U.S. Ambassador to Greece:** Robert J. McCloskey.
**Flag:** White cross on blue field in upper hoist corner; blue and white stripes.
**Language:** Greek.
**Chief Ethnic Group:** Greek (97%).
**Main Religion:** Greek Orthodox (98%).
**Leading Industries:** Manufacturing (textiles, chemicals, steel, tobacco products, aluminum, consumer products); agriculture (tobacco, cotton, wheat, raisins, currants, olives, grapes, fruits, vegetables); shipping; tourism; mining (petroleum, bauxite, iron, zinc, lead, lignite, chrome, nickel).
**Foreign Trade:** *major exports*—tobacco, currants, raisins, grapes; *major imports*—machinery, transport equipment, iron and steel, crude petroleum.
**Places of Interest:** Mount Olympus; Pindus Mountains; islands of Corfu, Rhodes, Cyclades, Mykonos, and Crete—Minoan ruins; Temple of Apollo in Corinth; Delphi ruins; Temple of Poseidon in Sounion. *In Athens:* Parthenon, Acropolis, and Acropolis Museum; temples of Nike, Theseus, Zeus.

## GREECE TODAY

Although ancient Greece was the birthplace of democracy, modern Greece has experienced only a few brief periods of democratic government. Civilian government, civil rights, and political democracy were restored only as recently as 1974.

The people of Greece have one of the lowest standards of living in western Europe. About 4 out of 10 are farmers, barely making a living for their families. But most people are educated. Only about 1 in 10 cannot read and write.

Greece has lacked basic mineral and energy resources to become a leading industrial nation. Manufacturing provides only about one-fifth of the national income. As a result, Greece has a huge annual trade deficit with the cost of imports three times that of exports. Petroleum from deposits discovered in the Aegean Sea in 1973 fills only about one-fifth of Greece's requirements.

The tourism and shipping industries provide a major share of the money Greece uses to import needed petroleum, consumer goods, raw materials, and machinery.

Hundreds of thousands of visitors each year are attracted by the Acropolis, the Parthenon, and other ruins of ancient Greece. Others come to Greece to enjoy the blue skies and warm beaches of the Greek isles.

Greece is a mountainous and heavily wooded country. The Pindus range, running north and south, is the most important. Mount Olympus, home of the gods in Greek mythology, is the highest peak (9,551 feet). Valleys and plains lie between the mountains.

The main rivers are in the north and have their origins in other countries. None is navigable. Southern Greece includes the Peloponnesian peninsula and some 437 offshore islands, the largest of which is Crete.

Greece, the southernmost country of the Balkan peninsula, is bordered on the north by Albania, Yugoslavia, and Bulgaria; on the east by Turkey and the Aegean Sea; on the south by the Mediterranean Sea; and on the west by the Ionian Sea.

## EARLY HISTORY

Neolithic man lived in Greece at least as early as 4000 B.C. Beginning about 2000 B.C., successive waves of Greek-speaking Achaeans, an Indo-European people, migrated into the area, supplanting the existing cultures.

By 1100 B.C. two major civilizations had flourished and vanished. The Minoan civilization was centered on the island of Crete and later influenced the mainland from the south. The Mycenaean civilization, generally less advanced than the Minoan, was on the mainland.

## ANCIENT GREEK EMPIRE

Greek city-states began to develop about 1000 B.C. They were sufficiently well established by 800 B.C. to become the source of democracy and of colonization efforts. By 600 B.C. colonies founded from the city-states were located on islands in the Ionian, Aegean, and Mediterranean seas, in Asia Minor, on the African coast, and as far west as France and Spain.

Ancient Greek civilization reached its zenith in the 400s B.C., when Athens was the center of a vast overseas empire.

After the death of Alexander the Great in 323 B.C., Greek power disintegrated. By 146 B.C. Greece had become a province of the new Mediterranean power, the Roman Empire.

## BYZANTINE AND TURKISH RULE

After Roman Emperor Constantine moved the capital of the empire in A.D. 330 to Constantinople (now Istanbul, Turkey), the Grecian influence was strongly felt.

While Rome languished under barbarian control, Constantinople and Greece were the centers of a thriving Byzantine Greek civilization.

In the Fourth Crusade, Constantinople was sacked by crusaders en route to the Holy Land (1204). The Greeks won it back in 1261.

Constantinople fell to the Turks in 1453. Greece then became a Turkish province in 1460.

## INDEPENDENT MONARCHY

After almost four centuries of subjugation by the Turks, a war of independence was begun by the Greeks on March 25, 1821. Supported by Britain, France, and Russia, the revolt was ultimately successful, and in July 1832 the sultan recognized the independence of Greece.

Prince Otto of Bavaria was made king of

Greece in 1833. He was overthrown in 1862 and was succeeded by Prince William George of Denmark, who became George I.

Greece unsuccessfully attempted to enlarge its territory in the Greco-Turkish war of 1897.

In the early 1900s the Greeks fought with neighboring Slavs and Turks in an effort to reclaim national territory. In the two Balkan wars (1912 and 1913), Greece obtained Epirus, parts of Thrace and Macedonia, and Crete.

Greece fought on the side of the Allies in World War I and was rewarded with territory from Bulgaria and Turkey.

The people voted for a monarchy in 1920 and for a republic in 1924. King George II, who was dethroned in 1924, returned in 1935 following a plebiscite. On Aug. 4, 1936, the crown accepted Gen. Ioannis Metaxas as dictator.

Metaxas headed the resistance when Italian fascists invaded Greece in 1940. King George II fled the country. Greece was occupied by Italy and Germany in 1941–44.

Following World War II, five years of civil war ensued between the government and communist guerrillas. U.S. aid under the Truman Doctrine helped bring final defeat of the communists in 1949, after about 120,000 Greeks were killed in the fighting. King George II had returned to Greece in September 1946, following a plebiscite.

King George II died in 1947 and was succeeded by his brother Paul I, who reigned until 1964. Upon Paul's death his son Constantine II came to the throne.

A political crisis developed in 1965 between the king and Prime Minister George Papandreou over the issue of an investigation of a secret organization within the army (ASPIDA). In June 1965 Papandreou resigned, and a period of unstable governments ensued.

## MILITARY RULE

A military coup took place on April 21, 1967. A military junta took control, naming Col. George Papadopoulos as premier and defense minister.

On Dec. 13, 1967, King Constantine unsuccessfully attempted a countercoup. In its aftermath, he and the royal family fled to Rome.

Papadopoulos deposed the exiled king on June 1, 1973. He decreed Greece a republic and took the title of president.

On Nov. 25, 1973, military leaders overthrew Papadopoulos. Brig. Gen. Dimitrios Ioannides seized control of the government. Lt. Gen. Phaidon Gizikis was named president.

The Greek military junta supported the overthrow of the government of Archbishop Makarios on Cyprus in July 1974. When Turkey invaded Cyprus and threatened war if Greece intervened, the military junta collapsed.

## DEMOCRATIC REPUBLIC

Constantine Karamanlis, a conservative former premier in 1955–63 who had been living in France, was called home and sworn in as premier on July 24, 1974. He appointed George Mavros as foreign minister with the immediate task of representing Greece in Cyprus peace talks.

Premier Karamanlis ordered a general amnesty for political prisoners. He restored freedom of the press and freedom of speech.

Anti-American demonstrations broke out in August 1974 as Greeks blamed the U.S. for failing to prevent Turkey's invasion of Cyprus. Karamanlis withdrew Greek military forces from the NATO military alliance, but later applied for readmission in 1976.

The first free parliamentary elections in 10 years were held on Nov. 17, 1974. Karamanlis' New Democracy Party won a sweeping victory, capturing more than two-thirds of the 300 seats.

In a referendum held on Dec. 8, 1974, voters overwhelmingly rejected a return to monarchy.

A new constitution was adopted in June 1975, establishing a parliamentary republic. The constitution provided extensive guarantees of civil liberties. Parliament elected Constantine Tsatsos, 76, as president.

After a month-long trial former President Papadopoulos and two other leaders of the 1967 coup were sentenced to death for treason on Aug. 23, 1975. But the Greek cabinet commuted the sentences to life imprisonment.

A dispute between Greece and Turkey over claims to oil deposits in the Aegean Sea caused Greece to place its military forces on a war footing in August 1976. Tensions decreased when both sides agreed to a UN Security Council resolution that called for peaceful negotiation of the issue. However, the issue remained unresolved as discussions continued into the 1980s.

Because of opposition claims that Karamanlis' huge majority in parliament no longer reflected public opinion, the prime minister agreed to a new national election on Nov. 20, 1977. His New Democracy Party won a reduced majority with 174 seats, 41 fewer than before the election. The main opposition, the Panhellenic Socialist Movement, won 91 seats.

To overcome dependence on imported oil, the government announced plans in 1978 to build 18 new hydroelectric generating plants, 10 new lignite-fired generators, and one 600-megawatt nuclear power plant, all to be completed by 1987. The program would more than double the nation's present output of electric power.

The government signed a treaty on May 28, 1979, with the European Economic Community that will make Greece a full partner in the European Common Market on Jan. 1, 1981.

Having led Greece back to democracy, the 73-year-old Karamanlis decided in 1980 to turn leadership of his party over to younger men and accepted parliamentary election to the less demanding post as the nation's president. Foreign minister George John Rallis, 62, was chosen on May 8 to succeed Karamanlis as prime minister.

Angry because Greece's application for readmission to the NATO military alliance had been blocked by Turkey, the Greek government notified the U.S. in 1980 that, unless it acted quickly to settle the problem, Greece would take over the four military bases the U.S. has maintained in Greece since the 1950s.

After a military coup overthrew its government, Turkey agreed to Greece's readmission to NATO, which was achieved on Oct. 20, 1980.

QUICK QUIZ: What is the birthstone for May? See page 412.

# GRENADA

**Official Name:** State of Grenada.
**Area:** 133 square miles (344 sq. km.).
**Population:** 90,348.
**Capital:** St. George's, 7,303.
**Government:** Socialist revolutionary.
**Prime Minister:** Maurice Bishop (since 1979).
**U.S. Ambassador to Grenada:** Sally Shelton.
**Grenada Ambassador to U.S.:** Bernard K. Radix.
**Flag:** Red border with yellow stars above and below green and yellow triangles; red circle with yellow star in center; nutmeg on green triangle.
**Official Language:** English.
**Main Ethnic Group:** Black.
**Principal Religions:** Roman Catholic, Anglican.
**Leading Industries:** Tourism; agriculture (nutmegs, cocoa, bananas, fruits, vegetables, sugarcane, cotton, spices); fishing; food processing.
**Foreign Trade:** *major exports*—nutmegs, cocoa beans, mace, bananas; *major imports*—petroleum, food, consumer goods.
**Places of Interest:** *In St. George's:* Fort George, government buildings, shops; Sauteurs; Grenville; island of Carricou; beaches.

## GRENADA TODAY

A Caribbean island nation with close Soviet and Cuban relations, Grenada is one of the smallest nations in the world. Part of the Windward Islands chain, the mountainous island of Grenada lies less than 100 miles off the coast of Venezuela. The country also includes part of the small Grenadines islands to the north.

The source of much of the world's nutmeg, the island displays a nutmeg on its national flag.

## HISTORY

Settled by French colonists in the 1600s, Grenada became a British possession in 1763.

Grenada was granted self-government in 1967. Prime Minister Eric M. Gairy's United Labor Party won elections in 1967 and 1972.

The nation achieved full independence within the British Commonwealth of Nations on Feb. 7, 1974, with Gairy continuing as prime minister.

A coup in which two persons were killed overthrew Gairy's dictatorial rule on March 13, 1979, while Gairy was visiting the U.S. The head of the leftist New Jewel Movement, Maurice Bishop, 33, whose father was killed by Gairy's secret police in 1974, became prime minister. Bishop suspended the constitution and set up a governing 14-member socialist revolutionary council.

Despite pressure from the U.S., Bishop's government in 1979 formed close ties with communist Cuba, signing a 2-year technical aid pact.

On Oct. 15, 1979, Bishop's government shut down the only opposition newspaper. About 100 political opponents were jailed.

Construction moved forward in 1980 on an international airport, largely financed by Cuba, which is expected to use it for planes supplying Cuban troops in Africa.

# GUATEMALA

**Official Name:** Republic of Guatemala.
**Area:** 42,042 square miles (108,889 sq. km.).
**Population:** 7,113,280.
**Capital:** Guatemala City, 700,504.
**Government:** Military-controlled republic.
**President:** Romeo Lucas García (since 1978).
**National Congress:** 61 members.
**U.S. Ambassador to Guatemala:** George W. Landau.
**Guatemalan Ambassador to U.S.:** Felipe Doroteo Monterroso Miranda.
**Flag:** Blue, white, and blue bars, with national coat of arms in center.
**Languages:** Spanish (official), Maya.
**Main Ethnic Groups:** Maya-Quiché Indians (55%), mestizo (42%).
**Religion:** Roman Catholicism (92%).
**Leading Industries:** Agriculture (coffee, cotton, bananas, sugarcane, cattle, corn, rice, beans, wheat, tobacco); manufacturing (tobacco products, chemicals, textiles, plastics, consumer goods); food processing; construction; mining (nickel, petroleum).
**Foreign Trade:** *major exports*—coffee, cotton, bananas, sugar, beef, wood, chicle; *major imports*—iron and steel, textiles, pharmaceuticals, vehicles, petroleum, food, consumer goods.
**Places of Interest:** National palace at Guatemala City; Mayan ruins at Tikal, Uaxactum, Piedras Negras, Zaculeu; Spanish ruins at Antigua Guatemala.

## GUATEMALA TODAY

About the size of Tennessee, Guatemala is a poor Central American nation dominated by its generals. Although elections are held, they are rigged to come out as the military rulers desire. About 2,000 to 3,000 persons are killed or disappear each year in conflicts between the military regime and its opponents.

The U.S. is Guatemala's main trading partner, buying about one-third of its exports.

Guatemala's economy depends largely on agriculture. Coffee makes up about a third of the country's exports, followed in importance by cotton, bananas, and sugar. Most Guatemalans are poor farmers.

The country has a 50-mile coastline on the Caribbean and a 200-mile coast on the Pacific. The land ranges from a coastal plain to mountainous areas. There are 30 volcanoes, 8 of which are active.

Mexico lies to the west and north. Belize is to the northeast. Honduras lies to the east and El Salvador to the southeast.

## EARLY HISTORY

Guatemala was part of the territory occupied originally by the Mayas, whose influence and power began to decline in the 1100s.

From 1524 to 1821 Central America from Yucatán to Panama was ruled by the Spanish.

By the mid-1700s Antigua, the capital, was one of the great cities of the New World, comparable to Mexico City and Lima. Severe earthquakes in

1773 destroyed the city, and the capital was moved to Guatemala City.

## INDEPENDENCE

Guatemala declared its independence from Spain on Sept. 15, 1821. It was briefly annexed by Mexico, and then was a member of the Central American Federation until 1838.

Guatemala suffered a major disaster on Feb. 4, 1976, when a devastating earthquake destroyed much of the capital city and scores of other towns and villages. Some 22,934 persons were killed.

Petroleum in commercial quantities was discovered in 1976, but supplies only part of the nation's needs.

On March 13, 1978, the nation's congress chose Gen. Romeo Lucas García as president, although 26 of the 61 members refused to take part. Lucas was sworn in on July 1.

Amnesty International on Sept. 12, 1979, charged the military regime of President Lucas with complicity in a wave of political murders.

About 30 Indian peasants occupied the Spanish embassy in Guatemala City in January to protest army repression and occupation of their land. Although the Spanish government asked that authorities not intervene, police attacked on Jan. 31. In the skirmish the embassy burned, killing 39 persons. Spain broke diplomatic relations in protest against the police action.

Guatemala's Vice President Francisco Villagran Kramer, a lawyer and moderate politician, fled to voluntary exile in the United States in September 1980, charging that the military government was protecting assassins of moderate political leaders. Villagren said the continued violence and repression of Indian workers by the government inevitably would lead to full-scale civil war.

## GUINEA

 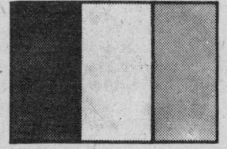

**Official Name:** Republic of Guinea.
**Area:** 94,964 square miles (245,957 sq. km.).
**Population:** 5,079,750.
**Capital:** Conakry, 197,267.
**Government:** One-party communist state.
**President:** Ahmed Sékou Touré (since 1958).
**Premier:** Lansana Beavogui (took office in 1972).
**National Assembly:** 75 members.
**U.S. Ambassador to Guinea:** Allen Clayton Davis.
**Guinean Ambassador to U.S.:** Mamady L. Conde.
**Flag:** Red, yellow, and green bars.
**Languages:** French (official), Fulani, Malinké, Susu.
**Principal Religion:** Islam.
**Main Ethnic Groups:** Fulani (Hamitic; 28%), Malinké (17%), Susu (9%).
**Leading Industries:** Agriculture (rice, palm kernels, tea, bananas, coffee, yams, pineapples, peanuts, manioc, millet, corn, vegetables, fruits, livestock); mining (bauxite, diamonds, gold, iron): manufac-

turing (bauxite refining); fishing.
**Foreign Trade:** *major exports*—alumina, pineapples, bananas, palm kernels, coffee; *major imports*—machinery, metals, food, transport equipment.
**Places of Interest:** Mount Nimba National Reserve; national museum in Conakry.

## GUINEA TODAY

About the size of Oregon, Guinea is a communist police state and one of Africa's poorest countries. Most of the people live in thatched mud huts in tribal villages, growing enough food to feed their families and little else. Few adults can read or write, and few children go to school.

However, Guinea has large deposits of bauxite, iron, gold, and diamonds, as well as the potential for hydroelectric development

The coastal plain ascends to a mountainous region called Futa Jallon. Interior Guinea is a rolling plain, partly woodland and partly grassy savanna, averaging about 1,000 feet in height. In the forested highlands Mt. Nimba rises to 5,748 feet. The Niger, the Senegal, and the Gambia rivers flow from the Futa Jallon.

The climate is humid and tropical. Temperatures range from 60° to 100° F. Annual rainfall has measured 168 inches at Conakry.

Guinea is bordered on the north by Guinea-Bissau, Senegal, and Mali; on the east by Mali and Ivory Coast; and on the south by Liberia and Sierra Leone.

## HISTORY

The empires of Ghana and the Malinkés dominated Guinea in medieval times.

Portuguese explorers and slave traders came to the Guinea coast in the 1400s. The Treaty of Paris of 1814 secured French rights in Guinea. In 1849 a French protectorate was declared.

Guinea declared itself independent on Oct. 2, 1958, with Ahmed Sékou Touré as its first president.

Touré—an avowed Marxist—turned to the Soviet Union and communist China for help. Guinea remained nonaligned, however, and has since received assistance from Western nations.

In November 1970 Guinea defeated an antiregime invasion by land and sea, allegedly backed by Portugal. Some 92 persons were sentenced to death for treason (34 in absentia).

Guinea's export revenues rose nearly 800% from 1972 to 1976 as two large bauxite mining developments got into production.

The International League for Human Rights appealed to the UN in 1977 to intervene in Guinea to halt what it called a "reign of terror" by Touré in which thousands of Guineans were imprisoned and tortured and from which more than 2 million fled to other countries.

Touré released several hundred political prisoners in 1978–79 to improve his human rights image.

In August 1979 Touré visited President Carter in Washington, D.C., seeking an increase in U.S. economic aid.

Touré escaped an assassination attempt on May 14, 1980, but 1 person was killed and 30 injured in the bomb attack.

QUICK QUIZ: Did the marriage rate increase or decrease in the U.S. in 1979? See page 415.

## GUINEA–BISSAU

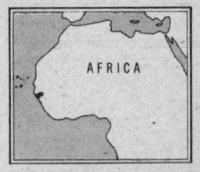
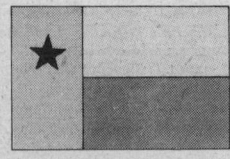

**Official Name:** Republic of Guinea-Bissau.
**Area:** 13,948 square miles (36,125 sq. km.).
**Population:** 576,873.
**Capital:** Bissau, 60,000.
**Government:** One-party socialist state.
**Head of Government:** João Bernardo Veira (since 1980).
**National People's Assembly:** 150 members.
**U.S. Ambassador to Guinea-Bissau:** Peter Jon de Vos.
**Guinea-Bissau Ambassador to U.S.:** Gil Vincente Vaz Fernandes.
**Flag:** Red vertical bar at hoist with black star; two horizontal stripes, yellow above green.
**Languages:** Portuguese, Fulani, Malinké, Felup, Papel, Balanta, Mandyako.
**Main Ethnic Group:** Bantu (97%).
**Principal Religions:** Animism (66%), Islam (30%).
**Leading Industries:** Agriculture (rice, millet, palm kernels, peanuts, cattle); fishing; forestry.
**Foreign Trade:** *major exports*—peanuts, palm kernels; *major imports*—food, consumer goods.
**Places of Interest:** Bissau; islands of the Bijagos archipelago; Boloma, capital until 1948.

About the size of Massachusetts and Connecticut combined, Guinea-Bissau was the first of Portugal's African colonies to win independence.

One of the poorest countries of Africa, Guinea-Bissau has an economy that depends on farming, fishing, livestock raising, and lumbering. It spends four time more for imports than it receives from exports. Most of the people live in tribes whose way of life has changed little in thousands of years.

A tropical country with a hot humid climate the year round, Guinea-Bissau has an Atlantic coastline indented by many rivers. Much of the coast is low and swampy. Inland hills rise to about 800 feet. Many people live in the offshore islands of the Bijagos archipelago.

Senegal is to the north and Guinea to the south.

The Portuguese explorer Nuno Tristão first visited the area in 1446. The region became a center for the Portuguese slave trade.

Called Portuguese Guinea for over 500 years of Portuguese rule, the area was made an overseas province in 1951. An independence movement began in 1959 with guerrilla warfare that raged for the next 15 years.

The African Independence Party (PAIGC) declared independence on Sept. 24, 1973, with Luis Cabral as president. The new country swiftly won recognition from about 90 nations. Portugal recognized Guinea-Bissau's independence on Sept. 10, 1974.

In the 1970s and 1980s the government sought assistance from wealthier countries to develop rice farming to become self-sufficient in food production. Mineral exploration was begun seeking bauxite and petroleum deposits.

Prime Minister João Bernardo Veira overthrew and imprisoned President Cabral on Nov. 15, 1980.

## GUYANA

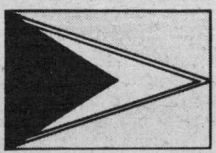

**Official Name:** Cooperative Republic of Guyana.
**Area:** 83,000 square miles (214,969 sq. km.).
**Population:** 855,400.
**Capital:** Georgetown, 72,049.
**Government:** Marxist socialist republic.
**President:** Forbes Burnham (since 1980).
**National Assembly:** 53 members.
**U.S. Ambassador to Guyana:** George B. Roberts Jr.
**Guyanese Ambassador to U.S.:** Laurence Everil Mann.
**Flag:** Green field with black-edged red triangle superimposed on white-edged yellow triangle.
**Languages:** English (official), East Indian dialects.
**Main Ethnic Groups:** East Indian (55%), black (35%).
**Principal Religions:** Christianity (57%), Hinduism (33%), Islam (9%).
**Leading Industries:** Mining (bauxite, gold, diamonds); agriculture (rice, sugarcane, palm kernels, coffee, fruits, vegetables); processing bauxite into alumina; food processing; fishing; forestry and lumbering.
**Foreign Trade:** *major exports*—sugar, bauxite, alumina, rice, gold, diamonds, shrimp; *major imports*—machinery, petroleum, textiles, motor vehicles, wheat.
**Places of Interest:** Kaieteur Waterfall; St. George's Cathedral and Guyana Museum in Georgetown; Bartica area; Rupununi savanna country.

Guyana is the only South American country with a British cultural background. It is also the only communist country on the continent.

The government owns and operates most industry, including the profitable bauxite mines.

About the size of Idaho, the country is largely covered by a thick, uninhabited tropical forest. The people mostly live in the narrow plain along the Atlantic coast.

By 1620 the Dutch had partially settled the country. The three colonies of Berbice, Demerara, and Essequibo were ceded to Britain in 1814 and united as British Guiana in 1831.

Competition between the People's Progressive Party (PPP), generally supported by East Indians, and the People's National Congress (PNC), representing blacks, led to outbreaks of violence in 1962 and 1963. This delayed granting of independence by Britain until May 26, 1966.

In 1964 elections Forbes Burnham of the PNC became prime minister. He was reelected in 1968 and 1973.

Guyana became a republic on Feb. 23, 1970.

A national referendum on July 10, 1978, gave the government the right to change the constitution without holding national votes.

World attention focused on Guyana in 1978 when members of an American religious cult murdered a visiting U.S. congressman on Nov. 18 and then committed mass suicide. The cult's founder, the Rev. Jim Jones, and over 900 of his followers died.

Burnham became president on Oct. 6, 1980, under a new constitution that gave the office strengthened powers as chief executive and commander of the armed forces.

# HAITI

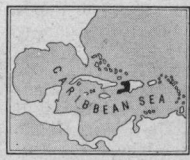

**Official Name:** Republic of Haiti.
**Area:** 10,714 square miles (27,750 sq. km.).
**Population:** 5,054,090.
**Capital:** Port-au-Prince, 745,700.
**Government:** Dictatorship.
**President:** Jean-Claude Duvalier (since 1971).
**National Assembly:** 58 members.
**U.S. Ambassador to Haiti:** Henry L. Kimelman.
**Haitian Ambassador to U.S.:** Serge Elie Charles.
**Flag:** Black and red bars; centered white rectangle contains emblems of war around palm tree.
**Languages:** French (official), Creole.
**Ethnic Groups:** Black (95%), Mulatto (5%).
**Religions:** Roman Catholicism (official; 80%), voodooism.
**Leading Industries:** Agriculture (coffee, sisal, sugar cane, rice, cocoa, poultry, vegetables, fruits); food processing; mining (copper, bauxite); tourism; manufacturing (textiles, soap, cement, assembly plants); fishing.
**Foreign Trade:** *major exports*—coffee, bauxite, sugar, sisal; *major imports*—cotton textiles. foodstuffs, petroleum, machinery.
**Places of Interest:** Sans Souci Palace ruins and King Henri Christophe fortress La Citadelle; Toussaint L'Ouverture Monument in Cap-Haïtien; national museum in Port-au-Prince; vacation resorts at Pétionville and Kenscoff.

## HAITI TODAY

About the size of Maryland, Haiti is a poor, overpopulated Caribbean nation. It has been ruled as a police state by the Duvalier family for over two decades.

Only about 1 in 10 Haitians can read and write. Some farm only to raise their own food. Others work on coffee or sugar plantations, or in the mining of bauxite, Haiti's major mineral.

Because of the availability of low-cost labor, some new assembly plants opened in Haiti in the 1970s to make clothing, sporting goods, and electronic equipment.

About two-thirds of the government's national budget comes from foreign loans and aid by the U.S. and other nations. The U.S. has provided over $200 million in aid in the past three decades.

Development of the island's resources has been hampered by corruption and by the lack of highways. About two-thirds of the country is too mountainous to be farmed.

Haiti occupies the western third of the island of Hispaniola, which it shares with the Dominican Republic to the east.

## EARLY HISTORY

The island of Hispaniola was discovered for Spain by Christopher Columbus in 1492.

Having killed most of the Arawak natives by 1533, the Spanish settled mainly on the eastern side of the island in the vicinity of Santo Domingo. The western area became a base for French and English pirates.

By the Treaty of Ryswick (1697) Spain ceded the western region, now Haiti, to France. French settlers imported many slaves.

The French Revolution, which began in 1789, sparked black slave rebellions in which most of the white colonists were killed or fled.

In 1792 French troops were sent to crush the revolt but were defeated by a self-educated, freed slave, Pierre-Dominique Toussaint L'Ouverture. Agreeing in 1799 to govern for France, Toussaint occupied Santo Domingo in the eastern part of the island, abolished slavery, and gave the island a constitution. In 1802, however, France's new ruler, Napoleon Bonaparte, sent troops to restore French authority. Toussaint, captured by treachery, died in a French prison.

## INDEPENDENT KINGDOM

The French troops were decimated by disease and by clashes with blacks led by Jean-Jacques Dessalines. The army withdrew in 1803, and in 1804 Dessalines declared Haiti's independence. Dessalines ruled as a despot under the title of Emperor Jacques I until his assassination in 1806.

The country then divided, with the north ruled autocratically by Henri Christophe, a black who proclaimed himself King Henri I. A republic in the south and west was governed by a mulatto, Alexandre Pétion, until his death in 1818. His successor, was Jean Pierre Boyer. Following the suicide of King Henri in 1820, the entire island was united in 1822 when Boyer's forces conquered Santo Domingo. A year after Boyer's ouster in 1843, Santo Domingo gained independence as the Dominican Republic. From 1843 to 1915, Haiti was ruled by 22 dictators.

## HAITI IN THE 1900s

In 1905 the U.S. took Haiti's customs into receivership, and 10 years later the U.S. seized full control. The U.S. withdrew its troops in 1934, but retained financial control until 1947.

François "Papa Doc" Duvalier became dictator after being elected president in 1957. His regime, faced by economic decline and political unrest, became repressive, with all opposition held in check by secret-police terror. The economy of Haiti stagnated.

Duvalier died on April 21, 1971, and was succeeded by his 19-year-old son, Jean-Claude "Baby Doc" Duvalier, as president for life.

The Duvalier fortune, acquired during more than two decades of rule, is unofficially estimated at over $400 million.

As a gesture to the U.S., Duvalier released 104 political prisoners in September 1977. Many others remained in prison.

Faced by increasing demands for freedom of human rights, Duvalier cracked down on opponents in 1979, launching a new wave of arrests by his secret police.

About 30,000 Haitians fled to the United States in 1980 and were granted political asylum. During the Duvalier regimes an estimated 300,000 to 400,000 Haitians have made their way to new homes in the U.S.

QUICK QUIZ: How much U.S. aid was given to Afghanistan in the years since World War II? See page 418.

# HONDURAS

**Official Name:** Republic of Honduras.
**Area:** 43,277 square miles (112,088 sq. km.).
**Population:** 3,758,190.
**Chief Cities:** Tegucigalpa, capital, 273,894; San Pedro Sula, 150,991.
**Government:** Transitional.
**Provisional President:** Gen. Policarpo Paz Garcia (since 1980).
**U.S. Ambassador to Honduras:** Jack R. Binns.
**Honduran Ambassador to U.S.:** Ricardo A. Midence.
**Flag:** Stripes of blue, white, and blue, with five blue stars in center.
**Official Language:** Spanish.
**Main Ethnic Groups:** Mestizo (90%), African (5%), Indian (4%).
**Main Religion:** Roman Catholicism (90%).
**Leading Industries:** Agriculture (bananas, coffee, cattle, corn, beans, rice, sugarcane, tobacco, vegetables, fruits); forestry and lumbering; manufacturing (textiles, detergents, cement, paper, chemicals, food products, clothing); mining (gold, silver, copper, lead, zinc).
**Foreign Trade:** *major exports*—bananas, coffee, wood, silver, tobacco; *major imports*—paper and paperboard, textile yarn and fabrics, electrical machinery, petroleum products.
**Places of Interest:** Tegucigalpa; Mayan ruins at Copán; Comayagua and Trujillo ancient cities; Bay Islands; Yojoa Lake; San Fernando Castle at Omoa; La Ceiba, Puerto Cortés, Tela beaches.

## HONDURAS TODAY

About the size of Tennessee, Honduras is a poor Central American country. Banana-growing is its most important industry. About two-thirds of the people are impoverished farm workers. Over half cannot read or write.

Development of the country has been hampered because there are few roads and highways. Much of the eastern part of Honduras can only be reached by airplanes or coastal boats.

Narrow lowlands along the Gulf of Fonseca and the Caribbean coast fringe this mountainous land, whose northern peaks exceed 7,500 feet.

The climate varies from wet and tropical on the coastal plains to dry and cool in the highlands. The capital, Tegucigalpa (elevation 3,500 feet), has a continual springlike climate. The wet season is May to November.

Rainfall averages 100 inches annually on the northern coast and 30 inches in the south.

Nicaragua lies to the south, El Salvador to the southwest, and Guatemala to the west.

## EARLY HISTORY

A center of Mayan civilization before A.D. 900, Honduras was discovered by Columbus in 1502 on his fourth voyage to the New World.

Attracted by exaggerated tales of gold and silver in Honduras, adventurers made the country's early days a chronicle of revolution and intrigue. Rival Spanish factions from Mexico, Guatemala, and Panama struggled for control. Invaders included Hernán Cortés, who in 1524 made a historic march from Mexico to impose his rule on the region. In 1538 Honduras became a part of Guatemala.

On Sept. 15, 1821, Honduras and the other Central American provinces declared their independence from Spain. They were annexed by Mexico, but broke away within a year. Honduras joined its neighbors in the United Provinces of Central America from 1823 to 1838.

Honduras declared its independence as a republic on Nov. 5, 1838.

U.S. Marines were sent to the country several times between 1912 and 1925 to preserve order.

## HONDURAS IN THE 1970s

On Dec. 4, 1972, Gen. Oswaldo López Arellano, who had ruled as dictator in 1963–71, overthrew the government and made himself president.

In 1972 the U.S. gave up to Honduras its claim to the Swan Islands, about 100 miles off the Caribbean coast.

Hurricane Fifi devastated Honduras with 110-mph winds and tidal waves on Sept. 18–19, 1974, killing 2,000 persons and destroying property and banana crops worth $500 million.

In March 1975 army officers forced President López to give up command of the armed forces to Col. Juan Melgar Castro.

Early in April 1975 the U.S. Securities and Exchange Commission (SEC) accused a U.S. firm, United Brands, of concealing from its stockholders the payment of a $1.25 million bribe to an unnamed "high" Honduran official to reduce banana export taxes. When López refused to cooperate with investigators, the junta deposed him, making Colonel Melgar president on April 22. Melgar ruled as dictator by decree.

The new government promised to expropriate 1.5 million acres of land and distribute it to 120,000 landless farm families.

In 1975 tens of thousands of peasants demonstrated, urging a speed-up in land reforms. Soldiers killed about 15 peasants to halt a mass march on the capital. Gunfights broke out between landowners and peasants who occupied uncultivated estates.

Border clashes between troops of Honduras and El Salvador broke out in July 1976. The two nations agreed in August to pull back their troops and allow an observer force of the Organization of American States to patrol the region.

Gen. Policarpo Paz Garcia, commander of the armed forces, and two other generals overthrew President Melgar in a bloodless coup on Aug. 7, 1978. They formed a military junta that ruled the country.

As a step toward restoring civilian government, an election was held on April 20, 1980, for a 71-member constituent assembly to write a new constitution and prepare for national elections in 1981. The Liberal Party, which had opposed the military government, won the largest number of seats.

Gen. Paz Garcia formally turned over the government to the assembly on July 20, 1980, and accepted the title of provisional president to head a transitional government until the 1981 elections.

# HUNGARY

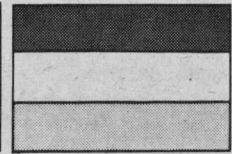

**Official Name:** Hungarian People's Republic.
**Area:** 35,929 square miles (93,030 sq. km.).
**Population:** 10,819,400.
**Chief Cities:** Budapest, capital, 2,085,615; Miskolc, 205,610; Debrecen, 193,958; Szeged, 174,607.
**Government:** One-party communist state.
**Heads of Government:** Janós Kádár, first secretary, Hungarian Socialist Workers Party (since 1956); Gyorgy Lazar, prime minister (since 1975); president of the presidential council, Pál Losonczi (took office in 1967).
**National Assembly:** 352 members.
**U.S. Ambassador to Hungary:** Harry E. Bergold Jr.
**Hungarian Ambassador to U.S.:** Ferenc Esztergalyos.
**Flag:** Red, white, and green tricolor.
**Official Language:** Hungarian.
**Main Ethnic Group:** Magyar (96%).
**Religions:** Roman Catholicism (67%), Protestantism (25%), Unitarianism, Judaism (8%).
**Leading Industries:** Manufacturing (steel, cement, textiles, chemicals, machinery, transportation equipment); agriculture (corn, wheat, sugar beets, potatoes, fruits, vegetables, livestock); mining (bauxite, coal, natural gas).
**Foreign Trade:** *major exports*—transport equipment, machinery, fruits and vegetables, meat, steel; *major imports*—petroleum, coke, textile fibers.
**Places of Interest:** Visegrad fortress on the Danube Bend; Lake Balaton; Eger fortress; Esztergom Palace and Cathedral; Tihanyi and Pannonhalma abbeys; Heviz thermal spa; Hortebagy Horse Show. *In Budapest:* The Citadel; Matthias Church; opera house.

## HUNGARY TODAY

About the size of Indiana, Hungary is a communist country in eastern Europe.

Hungarians enjoy a higher standard of living than the people of neighboring communist nations because of an innovative economic system that enables managers and workers to make profits. The government encourages U.S. corporations to invest in joint ventures and share in profits on goods made and sold in Hungary.

The Danube River forms over one-third the length of the northern border with Czechoslovakia, and then veers south through Budapest and into Yugoslavia. Plains lie to the east and west of the Danube. The Tisza is Hungary's second most important river.

The uplands in the northeast occupy about one-third of the land area. The highest mountain is Kekes (3,300 feet). Lake Balaton, in west central Hungary, is the country's largest lake.

Hungary has hot summers (average July temperature 71° F.) and cold winters (average January temperature 31° F.). Rainfall averages 25 inches a year. Summer droughts are frequent.

Austria lies to the west, Czechoslovakia to the north, the Soviet Union to the northeast, Romania to the east, and Yugoslavia to the south.

## EARLY HISTORY

Hungary was founded by Árpád, a semilegendary chief of the Magyars, who brought his people from beyond the Urals in the 800s A.D.

In 1001 Hungary was unified as a kingdom under István (Stephen) I. He carried on his father's Christianization efforts and was canonized as St. István in 1087. Nobles forced András II to sign in 1222 the Golden Bull, the "Magna Carta of Hungary." The country fell into anarchy after András III died in 1301.

Mátáyas Hollos (Matthias Corvinus), elected king in 1458, restored Hungary to an era of glory. After his death in 1490 the country weakened.

By 1526 Hungary fell under Turkish domination. Hungary was divided into three regions: the west was controlled by the Austrian Hapsburgs, the central plains by the Turks, and the east (Transylvania) by nobles in vassalage to the Turks.

At the end of the 1600s the Austrian Hapsburg armies expelled the Turks and took control of Hungary. Resistance against Austria was led by Francis II Rákoczy, one of Hungary's national heroes, but by 1711 he had been defeated.

A rebellion exploded in 1848 led by Louis Kossuth, who declared Hungary an independent republic in 1849. With Russian assistance, Austria put down the revolt. Following Austria's defeat by the Prussians in 1866, Hungarian nationalism was recognized by creation of the Austro-Hungarian dual empire.

## INDEPENDENCE

Hungary declared itself an independent republic on Nov. 16, 1918. In March 1919 the communist dictator Béla Kun took over the government. Romanian troops intervened, and Kun fled. In November a new government was established with Adm. Nicholas Horthy as regent and head of state. His authoritarian regime lasted 25 years.

During World War II German troops occupied the country and in 1944 arrested Horthy. Soviet troops took Hungary in February 1945.

Hungary's last free election, held in November 1945, gave anticommunists a majority. A Hungarian republic was proclaimed in 1946 with Zoltan Tildy as president.

## COMMUNIST RULE

Tildy was ousted in 1948 by a Soviet-assisted communist coup. A Soviet-style *Hungarian People's Republic* came into being on Aug. 20, 1949.

After Stalin's death in 1953 Premier Imre Nagy relaxed controls, but two years later he and his cabinet were ousted for "anti-Marxism."

In October 1956 a revolt erupted in Budapest. Imre Nagy again became premier. He announced that free multiparty elections would be held. Two days later Soviet troops intervened. Communist rule was forcibly restored under János Kádár. Thousands of Hungarians fled as refugees to other countries. Nagy was executed.

For a dozen years Hungary remained one of the most repressive communist police states.

In 1968 Hungary and the United States formally resumed full diplomatic relations. Kádár's government introduced the New Eco-

QUICK QUIZ: How many Arab-Israeli wars have been fought since World War II? See page 420.

**HUNGARY** *(continued)*

nomic Mechanism (NEM) in 1968, which allows profits at various levels.

On Jan. 6, 1978, U.S. Secretary of State Cyrus R. Vance returned to Hungary the country's most treasured symbol, the 10-century-old crown of St. István (Stephen). The crown had been turned over to the U.S. for safekeeping in World War II. Many Hungarian-Americans protested giving the crown to communists.

Hungary received most-favored nation trade status with the U.S. in a pact approved by the U.S. Congress in 1978.

A national election was held on June 8, 1980, for the 352 members of a new parliament. The voters had few choices among the candidates, all of whom were nominated by the communist-controlled People's Patriotic Front.

# ICELAND

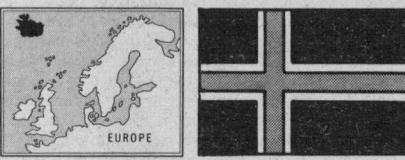

**Official Name:** Republic of Iceland.
**Area:** 39,768 square miles (103,000 sq. km.).
**Population:** 228,518.
**Capital:** Reykjavík, 83,887.
**Government:** Parliamentary republic.
**Prime Minister:** Gunnar Thoroddsen (since 1980).
**President:** Vigdis Finnbogadottir (since 1980).
**Parliament** *(Althing):* Upper House, 20 members; Lower House, 40 members.
**U.S. Ambassador to Iceland:** Richard A. Ericson Jr.
**Icelandic Ambassador to U.S.:** Hans G. Andersen.
**Flag:** White-bordered red cross on blue field.
**Official Language:** Icelandic.
**Principal Ethnic Group:** Norwegian descent (99%).
**Official Religion:** Evangelical Lutheranism.
**Leading Industries:** Fishing and fish processing; manufacturing (electricity, metal products, clothing, furniture, fertilizer, cement); construction; agriculture (cattle, sheep, hay, vegetables); mining (diatomite).
**Foreign Trade:** *major exports*—frozen fish, salted fish, herring meal fodder, herring oil, aluminum; *major imports*—ships and boats, petroleum products, aircraft, cord nets and netting.
**Places of Interest:** Surtsey Island; Golden Fall; Great Geyser; Myvatn; Mt. Hekla. *In Reykjavík:* hot spring reservoirs that heat city; Lutheran Cathedral.

## ICELAND TODAY

About the size of Kentucky, Iceland is an island in the North Atlantic. It lies just south of the Arctic Circle, 200 miles southeast of Greenland.

The sparsely settled island has few mineral resources. Fishing has been developed as Iceland's most profitable industry. The island's hydroelectric potential has been tapped to create an aluminum manufacturing industry. The geothermal energy of hot springs and volcanoes is used to heat homes as well as greenhouses where vegetables are raised. The people have achieved a high standard of living, but depend on imports of oil and manufactured goods.

Iceland has many active volcanoes. The high-est peak, Hvannadalshnúkur, rises 6,952 feet. Huge glaciers cover much of the interior. But the Gulf Stream provides a relatively mild coastal climate.

## EARLY HISTORY

Norse settlers colonized the island about A.D. 870. The *Althing,* established in 930, is the oldest active parliament in the world.

Iceland came under Norwegian control in 1262 and became part of the Danish-Norwegian state in 1381.

Jón Sigurdsson, an Icelandic statesman, helped win a constitution and limited home rule in 1874. With the 1918 Act of Union, the country obtained full self-government under the Danish crown.

## INDEPENDENCE

On June 17, 1944, while Denmark was occupied by Germany, Iceland declared its independence. Under the terms of a 1951 agreement, the U.S. is responsible for the island's defense.

Asgeir Asgeirsson was elected president in 1952 and regularly reelected until his retirement in 1968. He was succeeded by Kristján Eldjárn, who was elected in 1968 and reelected without opposition in 1972 and 1976.

A major issue in national elections on June 30, 1974, was continued U.S. operation of the NATO air base at Keflavík, which was opposed by leftists and supported by conservatives. The leftist parties lost their majority in parliament, and Geir Hallgrimsson became prime minister in July as head of a conservative coalition. The new government rescinded leftist plans to close the U.S. base.

Iceland on Oct. 15, 1975, banned foreign fishing within 200 miles of its coastline. The resulting "cod war" with Britain was settled in 1977 when all British fishing trawlers were excluded from Iceland's 200-mile zone pending an agreement between Iceland and the European Common Market nations.

A strike for higher pay by 12,000 government employees in October 1977 isolated Iceland for about two weeks. The walkout cut off flights in and out of the country.

In a national election on June 25, 1978, socialists and communists made substantial gains at the expense of the governing conservative-center coalition, causing Prime Minister Hallgrimsson to resign.

Olafur Johannesson, of the centrist Progressive Party, became prime minister after forming a coalition cabinet on Aug. 31, 1978.

Unable to reduce the nation's 55% inflation rate, Johannesson's coalition government collapsed and new elections were held on Dec. 2–3, 1979. Results were inconclusive as none of the four main parties won a majority.

After two months of wrangling, Gunnar Thoroddsen, 69, of the Independence Party formed a coalition cabinet. He became prime minister on Feb. 8, 1980, with Johannesson as foreign minister.

Iceland became the first European country to elect a woman as ceremonial head of state on June 29, 1980, when voters chose Vigdis Finnbogadottir, 50, as the nation's president by a narrow margin over three other candidates.

# INDIA

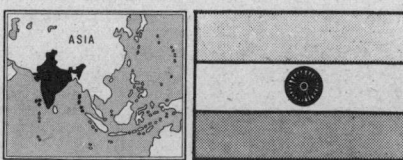

**Official name:** Republic of India.
**Area:** 1,269,346 square miles (3,287,590 sq. km.).
**Population:** 672,541,000.
**Chief Cities:** New Delhi, capital, 301,801; Bombay, 5,970,575; Delhi, 3,287,883; Calcutta, 3,148,746; Madras, 2,469,449; Hyderabad, 1,607,396; Ahmedabad, 1,585,544; Bangalore, 1,540,741; Kanpur, 1,154,388.
**Largest Metropolitan Areas:** Calcutta, 8,297,000; Bombay, 7,605,000; Delhi, 4,891,000; Madras, 3,169,930.
**Government:** Parliamentary republic.
**Prime Minister:** Indira Gandhi (since 1980).
**President:** Neelam Sanjiva Reddy (since 1977).
**U.S. Ambassador to India:** Robert F. Goheen.
**Indian Ambassador to U.S.:** K. R. Narayanan.
**Parliament:** *Rajya Sabha* (Council of States), 240 members; *Lok Sabha* (House of the People), 545 members.
**Flag:** Deep saffron, white, and green stripes, with centered 24-spoke Wheel of Asoka in blue.
**Official Languages:** Hindi, English, Assamese, Bengali, Gujarati, Kannada, Kashmiri, Malayallam, Marathi, Oriya, Punjabi, Sanskrit, Tamil, Telegu, Urdu.
**Main Ethnic Groups:** Aryan in the north (72%), Dravidian in the south (25%).
**Chief Religions:** Hinduism (84%), Islam (10%).
**Leading Industries:** Agriculture (sugarcane, pepper, tea, peanuts, rice, jute, bananas, tobacco, cotton, wheat, vegetables, cattle); manufacturing (steel, machinery, cement, motor vehicles, sugar refining, textiles, jute products, handicrafts); construction; tourism; mining (iron ore, coal, chrome, thorium, nickel, copper, lead, zinc, bauxite, petroleum, natural gas, manganese).
**Foreign Trade:** *major exports*—jute, tea, iron ore, leather, cotton; *major imports*—wheat, fertilizer, chemicals, machinery, steel, petroleum.
**Places of Interest:** Taj Mahal in Agra; Ganges River; Khajuraho temples; Ajanta and Ellora temple caves; Red Fort and Qutb Minar tombs and mosques in Delhi; Amber Palace in Jaipur; ancient temples in Madras; Srinagar in the Vale of Kashmir; Dal Lake.

## INDIA TODAY

India is the second most heavily populated country in the world, next to China. Although India has less than one-third the area of the U.S., it has nearly three times as many people. And the population increases at the rate of 25 babies born each minute—over 13 million a year.

India's people are among the poorest in the world. Many nearly starve year after year. Almost half the people earn less than $7.50 a month. Only 1 person in 4 can read and write.

Rich in natural resources, India ranks among the world's leading nations in production of coal, electricity, forestry products, iron, and natural rubber.

In the north the Himalaya mountains—rising to the highest elevations in the world—serve as

a barrier between India and China. The area's three great rivers—Indus, Ganges, and Brahmaputra—start in the Himalaya.

The lowlands of India stretch eastward for 2,000 miles from the Indus River delta to the delta of the Ganges and the Brahmaputra. Centered in the peninsula, the Deccan Plateau is surrounded by hills and mountains. Beyond the Eastern Ghat mountain range are the plains of the Coromandel Coast on the Bay of Bengal.

The coasts and the Ganges delta are hot and humid. In the far west are the semiarid steppes and the barren Thar Desert, while in the north the climate changes from near tropical to arctic as the land rises in the Himalaya.

## EARLY HISTORY

About 3000 B.C. civilization developed in the Indus Valley. About 1500 B.C. Aryans invaded the country and absorbed this civilization. The following 2,000 years saw Hinduism and the caste system come into being. The first important Aryan kingdom, Magadha, during the reign of Bimbisara (542–490 B.C.), heard the teachings of Jainism and Buddhism from the mouths of their founders.

Alexander the Great in 327–325 B.C. invaded, but his armies were overcome by Chandragupta, who founded the Maurya empire.

Asoka (273–236 B.C.) unified northern India and established Buddhism as the state religion.

The Gupta dynasty reached its height under Samudragupta (about A.D. 340–380).

In the 1000s the Muslim Mahmud of Ghanzi invaded India and extended his empire to the Ganges and the deserts of Rajputana.

The greatest Mogul emperor, Akbar (reigned 1556–1605) extended his rule from northern India well into the Deccan. His policy of religious toleration was not continued by his successors.

European colonization of India began with the arrival of Vasco da Gama in 1498.

By the mid-1800s Britain had won control of most of India. British domination and rising internal strife led to the Sepoy Mutiny of 1857, a rebellion by native troops. In 1877 Queen Victoria was crowned empress of India.

After World War I the nationalist movement came under the sway of Mohandas K. (Mahatma) Gandhi. He organized a series of passive-resistance campaigns.

## INDEPENDENCE

Britain partitioned the peninsula in 1947 into Hindu India and Muslim Pakistan. On Aug. 15, India was granted independence. Jawaharlal Nehru became India's first prime minister.

Partition led to religious riots, killings, and a crisscrossing migration of millions of people. Gandhi attempted to stop the religious violence, but on Jan. 30, 1948, he was assassinated.

India fought Pakistan for control of Kashmir in 1948–49 and again in 1965.

On Jan. 26, 1950, India became a parliamentary republic in the British Commonwealth.

Chinese troops invaded Kashmir and northeastern India on Oct. 20, 1962. After stiff Indian resistance, the Chinese withdrew a month later.

QUICK QUIZ: The United Nations has how many members? See page 423.

**INDIA** *(continued)*

Nehru died in 1964, and Lal Bahadur Shastri succeeded him as prime minister.

When Shastri died suddenly, Mrs. Indira Gandhi, Nehru's daughter, was chosen prime minister on Jan. 19, 1966, and won general elections in 1967 and 1971.

## DEVELOPMENTS IN THE 1970s

A flood of 9 million Bengali refugees poured into India after the outbreak of civil war in east Pakistan (now Bangladesh) in March 1971. In support of the rebels, India invaded the province on Dec. 3. Pakistan surrendered 13 days later.

India, on May 18, 1974, became the first of the world's underdeveloped nations to explode an atomic device.

In 1975 India annexed the independent nation of Sikkim, making it India's 22d state.

When a court ruled that Mrs. Gandhi was guilty of violating election laws, she declared a state of emergency on June 26, 1975, suspended civil liberties, and imposed censorship. Mrs. Gandhi had 28,836 political opponents arrested and jailed "to save India from anarchy."

In 1976 India resumed full diplomatic relations with China for the first time since 1961, and with Pakistan for the first time since 1971.

In an effort to reduce the population growth rate, the government in 1976 raised the minimum age for marriage to 21 for men and 18 for women and launched a vigorous sterilization program.

Mrs. Gandhi put through constitutional amendments, in December 1976, that gave her dictatorial powers. But a month later she surprised the nation by relaxing her 19-month-old arbitrary rule, announcing parliamentary elections to be held in March.

The world was amazed when Mrs. Gandhi and her Congress Party were overwhelmingly defeated in the election held on March 16–20, 1977. The opposition Janata Party captured a majority of 298 seats in the 542-member Lok Sabha, while the Congress Party that had ruled for three decades won only 153 seats.

Morarji Ranchhodji Desai, 81, leader of the Janata Party became prime minister. A follower of Mohandas Gandhi, he had been imprisoned for seven years by the British during the crusade for independence and for 18 months by Mrs. Gandhi during her emergency rule. He had served as her deputy prime minister in 1967–69, before breaking with her to join the opposition.

The new government of Prime Minister Desai moved swiftly to release the remaining 17,000 political prisoners still in jail and to restore all human rights curbed during Mrs. Gandhi's rule.

Desai, who had criticized Mrs. Gandhi as being pro-Soviet, declared India would observe "true nonalignment" in international affairs.

By agreement between the Janata and Congress parties, Neelam Sanjiva Reddy, 64, was

## INDIA'S 22 STATES

| STATE | AREA (sq. mi.) | CAPITAL |
|---|---|---|
| Andhra Pradesh | 106,855 | Hyderabad |
| Assam | 30,318 | Shillong |
| Bihar | 67,134 | Patna |
| Gujarat | 75,670 | Ahmadabad |
| Haryana | 17,074 | Chandigarh |
| Himachal Pradesh | 21,495 | Simla |
| Jammu and Kashmir * | 85,806 | Srinagar |
| Karnataka | 74,044 | Bangalore |
| Kerala | 15,005 | Trivandrum |
| Madhya Pradesh | 170,982 | Bhopal |
| Maharashtra | 118,828 | Bombay |
| Manipur | 8,632 | Imphal |
| Meghalaya | 8,683 | Shillong |
| Nagaland | 6,381 | Kohima |
| Orissa | 60,171 | Bhubaneswar |
| Punjab | 19,445 | Chandigarh |
| Rajasthan | 132,130 | Jaipur |
| Sikkim | 2,744 | Gangtok |
| Tamil Nadu | 50,220 | Madras |
| Tripura | 4,045 | Agartala |
| Uttar Pradesh | 133,674 | Lucknow |
| West Bengal | 33,920 | Calcutta |

* Disputed by Pakistan.

chosen unanimously as president of India in July 1977.

Desai's government, pledged to total prohibition of alcoholic beverages by 1981, increased the number of days on which liquor cannot be sold to 158 in 1978. The number of dry days will be increased each year.

Relations between the U.S. and India improved in 1978 with a visit to India by President Carter on Jan. 1–3, and a return visit by Desai to the White House in June. In April Carter overruled objections by the Nuclear Regulatory Commission to let 8 tons of enriched uranium be sold to India for use in generating electric power.

The grain harvest for 1977–78 set a new record of about 125 million tons, but because of the rapidly expanding population only a marginal increase in food was available to each person.

Although the caste system was officially abolished when India attained independence, persecution of the lowest caste, the untouchables, has continued. Riots occurred in many villages in 1978–80 as untouchable activists sought to end discrimination.

Mrs. Gandhi began efforts to make a political comeback after being ousted from the Congress Party on Jan. 3, 1978. She set up her own political party and won election to parliament in November 1978. But in December 1978 she was ousted from parliament and jailed for one week for having harassed officials in 1975.

Development of the Bombay High oil field, 100 miles offshore in the Arabian Sea, reached 80,000 barrels a day in 1978. Officials believed the field would make India self-sufficient in petroleum by the early 1980s.

The worst floods of the century struck West Bengal in September 1978. Over 1,200 persons drowned, and 40 million persons suffered losses as rivers overflowed because of heavy rains.

Because of a split in his Janata Party, the 83-year-old Desai resigned as prime minister on July 15, 1979. He was succeeded by his deputy prime

## PRIME MINISTERS OF INDIA

| | | |
|---|---|---|
| 1947–64 | Jawaharlal Nehru | Congress |
| 1964–66 | Lal Bahadur Shastri | Congress |
| 1966–77 | Indira Gandhi | Congress |
| 1977–79 | Morarji Desai | Janata |
| 1979–80 | Charan Singh | Janata-Secular |
| 1980– | Indira Gandhi | Congress (I) |

minister, Charan Singh, 77, whose defection to form the Janata-Secular Party had helped cause the fall of Desai's cabinet.

When Singh was unable to put together a coalition majority government, President Reddy dissolved parliament on Aug. 22, 1979, and ordered new elections.

## MRS. GANDHI RESTORED TO POWER

Indira Gandhi's new Congress(I) Party won a landslide victory in elections in January 1980, capturing four-fifths of the seats in parliament. The 62-year-old Mrs. Gandhi resumed office as prime minister on Jan. 14, 1980, after being out of power for 33 months.

Strengthening her socialist government's control over business, Mrs. Gandhi nationalized six of India's largest banks by decree in April 1980, giving the government ownership of 90% of the country's banking system.

India put a space satellite into orbit on July 18, 1980, the sixth nation to do so. The achievement demonstrated India's ability to develop long-range ballistic missiles for use in war. In another move to strengthen the nation's military might, the government contracted with the Soviet Union in May 1980 for purchase of $1.6 billion in weapons.

Throughout 1980 new riots and fighting took place between Hindus and Muslims in northern provinces with 2,000 or more persons killed. Drought in the northern provinces brought thousands to the verge of starvation.

To bolster U.S. relations with India, President Carter overruled the U.S. Nuclear Regulatory Commission in 1980 to permit the export of 38 tons of enriched uranium for use in generating electric power. The action was taken despite India's refusal to guarantee that the atomic fuel would not be used for weapons.

Mrs. Gandhi had promised during her election campaign that she would not reinstate dictatorial rule, but on Sept. 23, 1980, she decreed a law giving the government power to imprison anyone for a year without trial. Several hundred persons were arrested under the new law in the next several weeks.

# INDIA'S TERRITORIES

In addition to those below, India also administers the cities of Chandigarth and Delhi as territories.

## ANDAMAN AND NICOBAR ISLANDS

With an area of 3,203 sq. mi., the islands lie in the Bay of Bengal. Port Blair, the capital is 780 miles southeast of Calcutta. The Andamans include 5 large islands designated the Great Andamans, an island to the south called Little Andaman, and more than 200 islets. The Nicobars, 75 miles to the south, consist of 19 islands, 12 inhabited.

The Negrito people of the Andamans lead a tribal life in the interior—hunting, fishing, and avoiding contact with modern civilization. Most of the Andaman islanders are Indians, with some Burmese Karennis. The Nicobarese are of Mongoloid stock.

The Andamans were first settled as a penal colony by the British in 1858. In World War II the Japanese occupied them in 1942. Britain settled the Nicobars in 1869.

## ARUNACHAL PRADESH

The mountainous 32,270 sq. mi. region on the border with China and Burma formerly was known as the North East Frontier Agency.

Most of the people are Mongol tribesmen.

The northern boundary with the Tibet region of China, called the McMahon Line, was established by Britain in 1914. China invaded the North East Frontier Agency briefly in 1962.

The region was renamed and made a union territory of India on Jan. 21, 1972.

## DADRA AND NAGAR HAVELI

These 190 sq. mi. former colonies of Portugal lie north of Bombay, India. More than a third of the region is covered with teak forests.

Portugal obtained the region in 1780. In 1954 Indian nationalists invaded. It was made a union territory of India on Aug. 11, 1961.

## GOA, DAMAN, AND DIU

The 1,472 sq. mi. territory encompasses what once was Portuguese India. It includes three widely separated former Portuguese colonies on India's west coast: Goa, Daman, and Diu.

Goa was captured for Portugal in March 1510 by Afonso de Albuquerque and became the capital of Portugal's empire in Asia. The Portuguese acquired Damão (now Daman) in 1531 and Diu in 1534.

On Dec. 18, 1961, Indian troops invaded and captured all three colonies. The colonies were made a union territory of India in March 1962.

In 1974–75 many Roman Catholics traveled to Goa for an exposition in which the body of missionary St. Francis Xavier was displayed in a glass coffin in the Se Cathedral. The fact that his body has not decomposed since his death in 1522 is regarded as a miracle by Catholics.

## LAKSHADWEEP

With an area of 12.4 sq. mi., the 27 islands in the territory lie in the Arabian Sea 200 miles west of Kerala. They include the Laccadives and Amindivis. The largest is Minicoy.

## MIZORAM

The 8,142 sq. mi. Mizoram territory borders on Bangladesh and Burma. During British rule of India efforts were made to stamp out headhunting among the Lushai tribes that live in the evergreen forests covering Mizoram's hills.

Until it was made a union territory on Jan. 21, 1972, Mizoram was known as the Mizo Hills district of Assam.

## PONDICHERRY

The 185 sq. mi. Pondicherry administers four widely separated former French colonies in India. *Pondicherry* itself lies on India's east coast, south of the city of Madras. The district of *Karikal* is a coastal enclave 90 miles south of Pondicherry. The district of *Yanam* lies about 400 miles to the north of Pondicherry. *Mahé*, the fourth district, stands on India's west coast, a few miles north of the city of Calicut.

Settled by the French in 1674. Pondicherry was ceded to India on May 28, 1956. It was made a union territory on Aug. 16, 1962.

QUICK QUIZ: Where does the International Court of Justice meet? See page 425.

# INDONESIA

**Official Name:** Republic of Indonesia.
**Area:** 788,425 square miles (2,042,005 sq. km.)
**Population:** 154,755,255.
**Chief Cities:** Jakarta, capital, 4,576,009; Surabaja, 1,556,255; Bandung, 1,201,730; Semarang, 646,590; Medan, 635,562; Palembang, 582,961.
**Government:** Military-controlled republic.
**President:** General Suharto (took office in 1967).
**Parliament:** *People's Representation Council,* 460 members.
**U.S. Ambassador to Indonesia:** Edward E. Masters.
**Indonesian Ambassador to U.S.:** Ashari Danudirdjo.
**Flag:** Red stripe above white stripe.
**Languages:** Indonesian (official), English.
**Ethnic Groups:** Malay (95%), Chinese, Papuan, Arab.
**Leading Religions:** Islam (90%), Christianity (4%), Hinduism (3%), Buddhism (1%).
**Leading Industries:** Agriculture (rice, corn, sugarcane, tea, coffee, rubber, tobacco, cassava, coconuts, peanuts, spices, vegetables, fruits); manufacturing (textiles, assembly of motor vehicles, food processing, cement, consumer goods); mining (petroleum, tin, bauxite, coal, natural gas, copper, diamonds, gold, silver, sulfur, nickel, manganese); fishing; forestry and lumbering.
**Foreign Trade:** *major exports*—crude petroleum and products, rubber, coffee, tin, spices, timber; *major imports*—rice, cotton, machinery, flour, consumer goods.
**Places of Interest:** Botanical gardens of Bogor; Puntjak resort area; Tangkuban Prahu Volcano; Borobudur Temple on Java; Bali; Sumatra; Beautiful Indonesia in Miniature, near Jakarta.

## INDONESIA TODAY

Indonesia includes 13,677 islands between the mainland of Southeast Asia and Australia. The islands stretch 3,300 miles from east to west—nearly as far as from New York to Paris.

Once known as the *East Indies,* Indonesia has the fifth-largest population in the world, after China, India, the Soviet Union, and the United States. Indonesia's islands cover an area about five times larger than that of California. However, its people cannot raise enough farm products to feed themselves. So Indonesia is one of the largest importers of rice.

The government imposes strict censorship on news and holds thousands of political prisoners.

Transportation is one of the country's major problems. Boats and planes must be used for travel between islands. The larger islands are mountainous and heavily forested with relatively few paved roads.

Indonesia has many natural resources. It is one of the world's leading nations in the production of natural rubber, petroleum, and tin. However, Indonesia's industrial production remains underdeveloped. Its gross national product is only about one-twentieth that of Japan.

Indonesians are among the poorest people in the world. Less than half can read and write. About two-thirds do not get enough to eat daily. About one-fourth of the workers are unemployed.

With aid from the United States and other nations, Indonesia has pressed forward to make greater use of the islands' natural resources. New highways have been built, port facilities have been improved, and many electric-power projects have been constructed.

The islands of Indonesia have many mountains and volcanoes. The highest, Jaya in Irian Jaya (western New Guinea), rises to 16,500 feet. Mt. Kerintji on Sumatra is 12,467 feet high.

Indonesia straddles the equator, so the coastal lowland areas have a hot, tropical climate the year round. The interior upland regions of the larger islands enjoy a cooler climate.

## EARLY HISTORY

Migrants from the Asian mainland populated Indonesia between 2500 and 1000 B.C.

In the precolonial period Indian cultural influence was dominant. The great Shrivijaya maritime empire, with its capital in southern Sumatra, was a renowned center of Buddhist learning. About A.D. 800 the Sailendra dynasty built the great Buddhist temple Borobudur in central Java.

From the 1100s, Arab traders spread the Islamic religion. In the 1300s Hinduism was ascendant in the powerful, Java-based Majapahit empire.

Western dominance began in 1511 when the Portuguese landed at Malacca, on the Malayan peninsula, "in search of Christians and spices."

## NETHERLANDS EAST INDIES

By 1623 the Netherlands East India Company was able to establish a monopoly. The Dutch government revoked the company's charter in 1790 and assumed full administration of the islands 10 years later.

Independence movements began in the early 1900s. The first successful mass organization was Sarakat Islam (Islamic Association). Immediately after World War I the organization's Marxist faction founded the Indonesian Communist Party. Tension mounted between the communist and noncommunist branches. In 1921 the communists were expelled from the Islamic Association.

The Indonesian Nationalist Party was formed in 1927 by Sukarno and Mohamad Hatta. The Dutch exiled Sukarno and other nationalist leaders to remote island outposts.

Japanese occupation of the islands during World War II further stimulated the nationalist movement.

## INDEPENDENCE

With Japan's defeat, Sukarno and Hatta declared the independence of the Republic of Indonesia on Aug. 17, 1945. For the next four years the Indonesians battled to keep the Dutch from resuming colonial rule.

The UN succeeded in getting both sides to end the conflict. Sukarno was elected president on Dec. 16, 1949. Eleven days later, on Dec. 27, the Netherlands formally recognized Indonesia's independence.

The first elections to the nation's parliament, held in 1955, sharpened party cleavages and indicated strength for the Communist Party.

Tensions developed between President Sukarno and Vice President Hatta, due partly to Sukarno's tolerance of the communists and his antagonism to the Muslim Masjumi Party, favored by Hatta. In 1956 the vice president resigned.

Sukarno became dictator, declaring martial law in 1957.

New agitation against the Netherlands increased as Indonesia sought control of Netherlands New Guinea (Irian Jaya). Indonesia expelled Dutch nationals and started to expropriate their properties. In 1960 diplomatic relations with the Netherlands were severed, and Indonesian troops began infiltration of Irian Jaya. The Netherlands turned the region over to the United Nations in 1962. The UN placed the territory under Indonesia's jurisdiction in May 1963.

Sukarno strongly opposed the formation of Malaysia in 1963, and openly waged war against that nation.

After the failure of an attempted communist coup on Oct. 1, 1965, a power struggle erupted. Anticommunist rioting that swept the country in 1965 turned into a bloodbath in which 100,000 to 400,000 persons were killed.

Lt. Gen. Suharto emerged as the strong man of a new regime. He ordered the army to eliminate all traces of the Communist Party. An estimated 500,000 persons were jailed.

In March 1967 the national assembly formally revoked Sukarno's governing authority and appointed Suharto as acting president. In March 1968 Suharto was elected to a 5-year term as president by the assembly. Sukarno was arrested in 1969 and died in June 1970.

## DEVELOPMENTS IN THE 1970s

Elections were held in July 1971, and Suharto's Golkar political coalition won 73% of the total seats in parliament.

The People's Consultative Assembly, a 960-member presidential electoral body, unanimously reelected President Suharto to a second 5-year term on March 22, 1973.

In August 1975 a civil war broke out in the Portuguese colony on the island of Timor, the western half of which already was part of Indonesia. Indonesian troops intervened in the fighting. Indonesia formally incorporated the former Portuguese colony on July 17, 1976, making it the nation's 27th province, Loro Sae.

Indonesia in 1976 became the fourth nation to own its own space satellite communications system. The satellites link 40 earth stations.

The U.S. Securities and Exchange Commission (SEC) charged in February 1977 that dozens of U.S. corporations had been shaken down for $1.11 million by the former head of Indonesia's government-owned oil company. In April 1977 the official, Gen. Ibnu Sutowo, was placed under house arrest along with other close associates. The government reported it also was investigating bribery and corruption in the development of its satellite communications system.

The first national election in six years was held on May 2, 1977. However, the government censored the topics that could be discussed, preventing corruption from becoming an issue. Opposi-

### INDONESIA'S 27 PROVINCES (by island groups)

| | AREA (sq. mi.) | CAPITAL |
|---|---|---|
| Borneo (Kalimantan) ... | 208,286 | |
| Central Kalimantan ... | — | Palangkaraya |
| East Kalimantan ..... | — | Samarinda |
| South Kalimantan .... | — | Bandjarmasin |
| West Kalimantan ..... | — | Pontianak |
| Celebes (Sulawesi) .... | 69,255 | |
| Central Sulawesi ..... | — | Palu |
| North Sulawesi ...... | — | Manado |
| South Sulawesi ...... | — | Ujung Pandang |
| Southeast Sulawesi ... | — | Kendari |
| Java (Djawa) .......... | 48,763 | |
| Central Djawa ....... | — | Semarang |
| East Djawa .......... | — | Surabaja |
| Djakarta ............. | — | Jakarta |
| Jogjakarta ........... | — | Jogjakarta |
| West Djawa.......... | — | Bandung |
| Lesser Sunda Islands (Nusatenggara) ... | 36,179 | |
| Bali ................. | — | Denpasar |
| East Nusatenggara ... | — | Kupang, Timor |
| West Nusatenggara .. | — | Mataram, Lombok |
| Loro Sae (East Timor) | — | Dili |
| Moluccas (Maluku) .... | 28,766 | Ambon |
| Sumatra (Sumatera) ... | 165,000 | |
| Atjeh ............... | — | Banda Atjeh |
| Bengkulu ............ | — | Bengkulu |
| Djambi .............. | — | Djambi |
| Lampung ............ | — | Tandjungkarang-Telukbetung |
| North Sumatera...... | — | Medan |
| Riau ................ | — | Pakanbaru |
| South Sumatera ..... | — | Palembang |
| West Sumatera ...... | — | Padang |
| West New Guinea (Irian Jaya).......... | 151,789 | Kotabaru |

tion candidates were screened. The ruling Golkar movement won 62% of the vote. President Suharto's party took control of 332 seats in the 460-member parliament.

A national assembly reelected Suharto to a third 5-year term as president on March 22, 1978.

In October 1977 Amnesty International reported that Indonesia still was holding about 100,000 political prisoners, disputing a claim by the Indonesian government that only 30,000 remained in prison. From December 1977 through 1979 the government released a total of 31,226 political prisoners.

To combat inflation, which rose to an annual rate of about 12% in 1978, the government devalued its currency by 33.6% on Nov. 15, 1978.

Indonesia's economy was stimulated in 1979–80 by rising oil prices that contributed to a 50% increase in export income.

Opposition to President Suharto's military government was aired in 1980 with publication of charges that he and other high officials enriched themselves with multimillion dollar kickbacks from government projects.

The government's third 5-year plan for 1979–84 called for an annual economic growth rate of 6.5%, down from the 7.5% rate of the 1974–79 plan because of the leveling off of petroleum production.

# IRAN

**Official Name:** Islamic Republic of Iran.
**Area:** 636,296 square miles (1,648,000 sq. km.).
**Population:** 37,188,100.
**Chief Cities:** Teheran, capital, 4,496,159; Esfahan, 671,825; Mashdad, 670,180; Tabriz, 598,576.
**Government:** Islamic dictatorship.
**Head of State:** Ayatollah Ruhollah Khomeini (since 1979).
**President:** Abol Hasan Bani-Sadr (since 1980).
**Prime Minister:** Mohammed Ali Rajai (since 1980).
**Parliament:** *Majlis,* 270 members.
**Flag:** Stripes of green (*top*), white, and red; word "Allah" in red on white center stripe.
**Main Languages:** Iranian, Kurdish, Arabic, Turkic, English, French.
**Chief Ethnic Groups:** Iranian, Turk, Kurd, Arab, Armenian.
**Main Religion:** Islam (98%).
**Leading Industries:** Mining (petroleum, natural gas, coal, salt, chromite, lead, copper, iron ore); agriculture (sheep, cattle, goats, wheat, sugar beets, barley, rice, cotton, tea, tobacco); manufacturing (oil refining, steel, electrical equipment, cement, textiles, sugar, flour, furniture, building materials); fishing.
**Foreign Trade:** *major exports*—petroleum, carpets and rugs, cotton textiles; *major imports*—machinery, iron and steel, pharmaceuticals and medicinal products, wheat.
**Places of Interest:** Elburz Mountains; Caspian shore resorts; gold-domed mosque in shrine city of Meshed; Mt. Damavaud; ruins of Persepolis and royal tombs; Sepah Mosque and Golestan Palace Museum in Teheran; Shiraz; Esfahan.

## IRAN TODAY

About five times the size of California, Iran is an oil-rich nation in the Middle East wracked by revolution and war. It is ruled by radical-conservative Islamic religious leaders.

The majority of people are very poor. Only about 1 in 4 can read and write.

Most of Iran is a plateau averaging 4,000 feet above sea level. The Elburz and Zagros mountains cover extensive areas. Large sections of the interior are desert. Rainfall is generally meager.

Iran is bordered on the north by the Soviet Union. Afghanistan and Pakistan lie to the east, and Iraq and Turkey to the west.

## EARLY HISTORY

The early inhabitants of present-day Iran, the Elamites, developed a high degree of civilization by about 3100 B.C. Two Aryan tribes, the Medes and the Persians, settled in the area about 900 B.C. The Medes established their domain over a region of what is now western Iran. The Persians controlled an area extending northeast from the Persian Gulf.

The powerful Persian ruler Cyrus (559–530 B.C.) brought the Medes under his control. He then conquered Babylonia, founding the Persian Empire that eventually encompassed Egypt and eastern Greece. Persian power was crushed in 331 B.C. by Alexander the Great. Alexander's empire crumbled after his death, and his successors battled for supremacy. Most of Persia went to Seleucus I, the Greek ruler of Syria who had been one of Alexander's generals. The Seleucid dynasty tried to follow the Persian pattern of government, but its hold was weak. Parthian rule succeeded the Seleucids. A stronger, more energetic dynasty, the Sassanian, overthrew the Parthians in A.D. 224 and built a flourishing empire that successfully opposed Rome.

Arabs invaded Persia and crushed the Sassanian dynasty about 651. Islam became the dominant religion. Turkish invasions and settlement followed in the 900s. The land later fell to the Mongol invaders, Genghis Khan in the 1200s and Tamerlane in the 1300s.

Native Iranian rule was restored by the Safavid rulers (1502–1736). The dynasty reached its peak during the regime of Shah Abbas I (1587–1629).

A Turkish general, Nadir Shah, ruled in 1736–47, raiding and looting India.

The Zand dynasty (1750–94) restored order before being overthrown by Aga Mohammed Khan, whose Kajar dynasty lasted until 1925. Persia's borders shrank steadily. Land was lost to the Afghans, and in 1813 and 1828 Caucasian territories were taken over by Russia, which exploited the oil deposits.

In 1906 the shah approved formation of a parliament, or Majlis, and the constitution it enacted. In 1907 an Anglo-Russian pact divided Persia into spheres of influence, but the treaty was annulled after World War I.

## MODERN EMPIRE OF IRAN

In 1921 a coup directed by army officer Reza Khan resulted in a military dictatorship. Four years later Reza Khan deposed the shah and adopted the title Reza Shah Pahlevi.

He undertook reforms in all aspects of Persian life, and in 1935 officially changed the country's name to Iran. In 1935 Teheran University was opened. In 1937 women were unveiled. In 1938 the first railroad was built.

The shah's friendly relations with Germany, however, led to the occupation of Iran by British and Russian troops in 1941. The shah abdicated in favor of his son, Mohammed Reza Pahlevi.

In 1945 the Soviets, who had occupied northern Iran, refused to evacuate their troops. But promised U.S. aid under the Truman Doctrine led to the withdrawal of the Soviet troops.

When militant nationalist Mohammed Mossadegh, leader of the extremist National Front, became premier in 1951, he promptly seized control of the Anglo-Iranian Oil Company. The British retaliated with a blockade.

With aid by the U.S., royalists overthrew Mossadegh in 1953, and the shah regained absolute power.

The shah announced on March 16, 1973, the nationalization of the oil industry.

The shah decreed Iran a one-party state on March 2, 1975, establishing the National Resurrection Party. The shah's secret police imprisoned, tortured, and killed his opponents.

When the shah visited the U.S. for the 12th

time in November 1977, a riot by Iranian students occurred outside the White House. More than 100 persons were injured. President Carter returned the shah's visit in January 1978, traveling to Iran during a tour of the Middle East.

Riots in Iran grew in intensity throughout 1978, with hundreds of persons killed as police and troops battled the demonstrators. The demonstrations were organized by Muslim extremists who object to the shah's efforts to modernize Iran.

Failure to control the riots resulted in the shah appointing a military government.

As riots and demonstrations continued, the shah restored civilian government with the appointment as prime minister of Shahpur Bakhtiar, an opposition political leader, who took office on Jan. 6, 1979. But turmoil continued.

Convinced that he no longer could maintain order, the shah flew to exile on Jan. 16, 1979, and died in Egypt in 1980.

## ISLAMIC STATE

The uprising against the shah had been directed from abroad by Ayatollah Ruhollah Khomeini, a Muslim religious leader who had been exiled by the shah 15 years earlier. Khomeini returned to Iran on Feb. 1, 1979. The shah's prime minister, Bakhtiar, resigned on Feb. 11 and fled to exile. Terror swept Iran as Khomeini's militia arrested and executed hundreds of former officials and military officers. On March 30–31, 1979, a national referendum overwhelmingly approved establishment of an Islamic republic.

Khomeini's government nationalized banks, insurance companies, and most remaining heavy industry in June and July 1979. The government imposed strict censorship, forced opposition newspapers to close, and ejected most foreign journalists.

Khomeini called on Iranian women to give up modern dress and smoking and return to the wearing of the Muslim veil.

An uprising by Kurds seeking independence for their region in western Iran brought heavy fighting in 1979–80.

Relations between the U.S. and Iran reached a crisis after Iranian terrorists seized the U.S. embassy in Teheran on Nov. 4, 1979, holding over 50 Americans hostage. The Iranian government refused to negotiate release of the hostages, and a U.S. attempt to free them by military force failed in 1980 (see page 15).

In a national referendum on Dec. 2–3, 1979, Iranians approved a new constitution that made Khomeini leader of Iran for life.

Abol Hasan Bani-Sadr, who had served as finance minister, was elected as Iran's first president on Jan. 25, 1980, winning 75% of the votes against six other candidates. An elected 270-member parliament controlled by conservative Muslims began meeting on May 28, 1980. In August parliament approved the appointment of Mohammed Ali Rajai, formerly education minister, as prime minister.

Border clashes between Iran and Iraq escalated into a full-scale war on Sept. 22, 1980, with each side inflicting severe damage to the other's oil facilities (see page 25).

# IRAQ

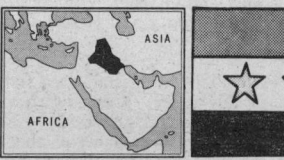 

**Official Name:** Republic of Iraq.
**Area:** 167,925 square miles (434,924 sq. km.).
**Population:** 13,438,400.
**Chief Cities:** Baghdad, capital, 1,490,759; Basra, 310,950; Mosul, 264,146; Kirkuk, 175,303; Najaf, 134,027; Hilla, 84,704.
**Largest Metropolitan Area:** Baghdad, 1,657,424.
**Government:** One-party socialist-military state.
**President:** Saddam Hussein (since 1979).
**Legislature:** *National Assembly,* 250 members.
**Flag:** Red, white, and black stripes, with three green stars in center stripe.
**Languages:** Arabic (official), Kurdish.
**Main Ethnic Groups:** Arab (75%), Kurd (20%).
**Chief Religion:** Islam (95%).
**Leading Industries:** Mining (petroleum); agriculture (sheep, dates, wheat, barley, rice, cotton, cattle, goats, camels); food processing; manufacturing (textiles, cement, leather products).
**Foreign Trade:** *major exports*—petroleum, dates, cement, wool; *major imports*—motor vehicles, sugar, textiles.
**Places of Interest:** Ruins of Babylon, Hanging Gardens, throne room of "writing on the wall," Lion of Babylon; Agarguf ruins; Arch of Ctesiphon. *In Baghdad:* Iraq Museum; mosques; tomb of Sitt Zubaidah.

## IRAQ TODAY

A little larger than California, Iraq ranks among the leading oil-producing nations of the world, but its petroleum facilities were damaged in a war with Iran in 1980.

Most of the people are poor, and only about 4 out of 10 can read and write. The majority are farmers or nomadic herdsmen. The most important cash crop of the farmers is dates, of which Iraq is the world's leading exporter.

The leftist military government runs the country as a police state with human rights severely restricted. As an implacable foe of Israel, Iraq has supported and trained Palestinian terrorists.

Iraq broke diplomatic relations with the United States in 1967 because of U.S. aid to Israel in the Arab-Israeli war in June of that year. But the U.S. maintains a diplomatic mission at the Belgian embassy, and U.S. companies carry on foreign trade with Iraq.

Rising oil prices in the 1970s brought a rapid expansion of the economy.

The Mesopotamian plain, between the great Tigris and Euphrates rivers, was the site of the ancient civilizations of Sumer and Babylonia.

The desert and semidesert uplands in the west correspond roughly to ancient Assyria.

The mountains in the northeast are the home of the Kurds.

The northern climate is temperate, but the plains suffer heat and strong northeasterly winds during the summer. Temperatures may reach

QUICK QUIZ: When was the Organization of Oil Exporting Countries (OPEC) founded? See page 428.

**IRAQ** *(continued)*

120° F. between May and October. Winters are damp, with average temperatures of 50° F.

## ANCIENT MESOPOTAMIA

Archaeological excavations have established that cultures existed in this region, once known as Mesopotamia, for more than 10,000 years.

The written history of the area began about 4000 B.C. when the Sumerians established city-states in southern Mesopotamia. In the 2300s B.C. Sumer was absorbed into a huge empire ruled by Sargon, king of Akkad. The area later became part of the Assyrian and Babylonian empires.

Arabs overran Mesopotamia in the 600s A.D. Baghdad was made the capital of the Abbasid caliphate in 762. The fifth caliph, Harun-al-Rashid, figured in the stories of *the Thousand and One Nights.*

Mongol conquerors devastated the country in 1258 and again in 1401. Baghdad was captured in 1534 by the Ottoman Turks, and Mesopotamia stayed under Turkish control until World War I.

## KINGDOM OF IRAQ

During World War I, Britain, with the help of Hussein, the sharif of Mecca, gained control of the country, known since 1918 as Iraq.

The League of Nations in 1920 made Iraq a mandated territory under British administration. Britain arranged for Faisal I, the son of Hussein, to become king of Iraq. In 1932 the League of Nations mandate was ended, and Iraq joined the League as an independent nation.

Upon Faisal's death in 1933, he was succeeded by his son Ghazi, who was killed in an auto accident in 1939. The throne was inherited by Ghazi's three-year-old son Faisal II.

A pro-Axis government, briefly in power in 1941, collapsed under British military pressure.

Led by pro-Western statesman Nuri es-Said, Iraq in 1955 joined Turkey, Iran, Pakistan, and Britain in a defense treaty known as the Baghdad Pact.

## REPUBLIC OF IRAQ

On July 14, 1958, Gen. Abdul Karim Kassem overthrew the regime. He killed Nuri es-Said and young King Faisal II, establishing the Republic of Iraq. Kassem withdrew Iraq from the Baghdad Pact in 1959.

A military coup on Feb. 8, 1963, overthrew Kassem. He and many Iraqi communists were executed. The Arab Socialist Baath Party took control with Abdul Salam Arif as president. Iraq became a one-party military-socialist state. Most private businesses were nationalized.

In April 1966 Abdul Salam Arif died in a helicopter crash. He was succeeded as president by his elder brother, Abdul Rahman Arif.

President Arif, who was held responsible for Iraq's defeat in the 1967 war with Israel, was ousted by a bloodless military coup on July 17, 1968. The leader of the coup, former premier Ahmed Hassan al-Bakr, took over as president and formed a new government.

## DEVELOPMENTS IN THE 1970s–1980s

A lengthy rebellion of the Kurdish minority in the Zagros Mountains against the Iraqi government temporarily ended in March 1970 when the Baathist regime agreed to grant autonomy to the Kurds within four years.

Iraq joined in the October 1973 Middle East War between the Arab nations and Israel and cut off oil shipments to the U.S. for several months.

Angered at not being given independence, the Kurds took up arms in March 1974, receiving military support from Iran.

In an agreement with Iraq on March 5, 1975, Iran stopped providing supplies to the Kurdish rebels, after which the revolt collapsed.

Iraq completed nationalizing its entire oil industry in December 1975.

The International League for Human Rights reported to the UN in 1977 that the Iraqi government was systematically destroying the Kurdish minority. Refugees said in July 1977 that scores of Kurdish villages had been destroyed and thousands of Kurds pressed into forced labor. Iraq was reported clearing a strip 20 kilometers (12.4 miles) wide along the border facing Iran and Turkey.

The government executed 21 communists in May 1978 and imprisoned 10 others after discovery of a plot to overthrow the government by infiltrating the military forces.

Iraq's relations with the Soviet Union noticeably cooled after exposure of the plot. The government, which has been dependent on Soviet weapons for two decades, began negotiating with France and other Western nations for acquisition of arms.

The government also cracked down on the extremist Palestine Liberation Organization (PLO) in 1978, seizing arms and supplies valued by the PLO at $80 million. The PLO retaliated with an attack on the Iraqi embassy in Paris in August 1978 and an unsuccessful attempt to kill the Iraqi ambassador in London.

The government began a $36 million project in 1978 to excavate and restore the ancient city of Babylon, which stands about 55 miles south of Baghdad. Archaeologists estimated the project would not be completed before the 1990s.

After 11 years as president, the 68-year-old Bakr resigned on July 16, 1979, because of illness. He was succeeded by Gen. Saddam Hussein, 42, who had been vice chairman of the Revolutionary Command Council.

Within two weeks of taking over as president, Hussein arrested scores of officials, charging them with plotting to overthrow him. A firing squad executed 21 of the plotters on Aug. 8, 1979, including five members of the Revolutionary Command Council. A special court had condemned them to death and sentenced 33 others to prison terms for the coup attempt.

In the first national election in 20 years, on June 20, 1980, voters chose the 250 members of a new parliament from among 800 candidates approved by the country's only political party, the Arab Baath Socialist Party.

Ayatollah Khomeini, ruler of neighboring Iran, called in 1980 for the overthrow of Hussein by the Shiite Muslims, who make up the majority of Iraq's population.

In retaliation, Hussein launched attacks on Iran that escalated into a full-scale war beginning on Sept. 22, 1980 (see page 25).

# IRELAND

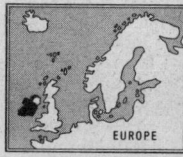
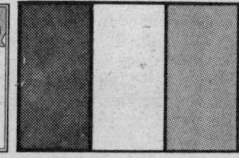

EUROPE

**Official Name:** Ireland (*Eire* in Gaelic).
**Area:** 27,136 square miles (70,283 sq. km.).
**Population:** 3,463,450.
**Chief Cities:** Dublin, capital, 566,034; Cork, 128,235.
**Largest Metropolitan Area:** Dublin, 650,153.
**Government:** Parliamentary republic.
**Prime Minister:** Charles J. Haughey (since 1979).
**President:** Patrick Hillery (since 1976).
**Parliament:** *Seanad Eireann* (Senate), 60 members; *Dáil Eireann* (House), 148 members.
**U.S. Ambassador to Ireland:** William V. Shannon.
**Irish Ambassador to U.S.:** Sean Donlon.
**Flag:** Green, white, and orange bars.
**Official Languages:** Irish (Gaelic) and English.
**Leading Ethnic Group:** Irish.
**Main Religions:** Roman Catholicism (94%), Anglicanism (4%).
**Leading Industries:** Manufacturing (electronics, brewing, distilling, food processing, textiles, paper, machinery, chemicals, vehicle assembly); agriculture (sheep, cattle, horses, hay, potatoes, turnips, sugar beets, barley, wheat, oats, rye); fishing; tourism.
**Foreign Trade:** *major exports*—machinery, textiles, chemicals, meat, dairy products; *major imports*—machinery, iron and steel, textiles, petroleum.
**Places of Interest:** Blarney Castle near Cork; Great Rock of Cashel; Killarney lakes; River Shannon; Galway castles; Limerick; Waterford; Kennedy family home and memorial park at Dunganstown. *In Dublin:* Castle; St. Patrick's Cathedral; Daniel O'Connell Monument; Phoenix Park; Abbey Theatre.

## IRELAND TODAY

Somewhat larger than the state of West Virginia, the Republic of Ireland covers five-sixths of the island of Ireland. It shares the island with Northern Ireland, which is part of Britain's United Kingdom. Ireland is separated from the island of Great Britain by the narrow Irish Sea.

Although industrialization proceeded rapidly in the 1960s–80s, about half the people live on farms or in small villages. Because it must import more than it can export, Ireland depends on income from tourism to make up the difference.

Coastal highlands and a central plain give a saucer shape to the island.

Mild winds from Europe and warm, damp air from the Gulf Stream combine to give the country a temperate climate. Temperatures average 40°F. in the winter and 60°F. in the summer.

## EARLY HISTORY

Prehistoric people lived in Ireland as early as 6000 B.C. They were conquered by Celtic tribes from Britain and Europe about 400 B.C.

St. Patrick brought Christianity in A.D. 432.

In the 700s to 1000s Norse Vikings established seaports in Ireland.

King Henry II of England forced Irish nobles

to recognize his overlordship in 1171.

To stem rising rebellion after the Reformation in the 1500s, Britain gave confiscated Irish lands to pro-British Irish and English Protestants. In the 1700s Irish Catholics lost all legal rights.

In 1801 the Act of Union created the United Kingdom of Great Britain and Ireland.

In the 1840s the country was devastated by a great potato famine. A million Irish died in five years, and 1.6 million emigrated.

Sinn Fein, the political arm of the secret Irish Republican Army (IRA), instigated the 1916 Easter Rebellion in Dublin. In the 1919 general elections Sinn Fein won enough seats to set up its own parliament (Dáil Eireann) in Dublin, and the IRA waged guerrilla warfare against Britain.

The Irish Free State was established in 1922 as a British dominion, with six northern (Protestant) counties remaining in the United Kingdom as Northern Ireland. Sinn Fein extremists under Eamon De Valera continued to fight for full independence. In 1937 a new constitution changed the country's name to *Eire*. De Valera was named prime minister.

## INDEPENDENT REPUBLIC OF IRELAND

John A. Costello, head of the Fine Gael Party, became prime minister in 1948. On April 18, 1949, he declared Ireland an independent republic.

De Valera, of the Fianna Fáil Party, returned to power as prime minister in 1951–54 and 1957–59. He then served as president in 1959–73.

In parliamentary elections on Feb. 28, 1973, a coalition of the Fine Gael and smaller Labor Party won a narrow victory. Liam Cosgrave of the Fine Gael became prime minister.

Cosgrave acknowledged officially for the first time in March 1974 that Northern Ireland was part of Britain's United Kingdom.

To combat the terrorists of the outlawed Irish Republican Army (IRA), the Irish parliament voted on Sept. 1, 1976, to approve a state of emergency and antiterrorist measures.

The Fianna Fail Party won a surprise victory in a national election on June 16, 1977, winning 84 seats in the 148-member Dáil Eireann. John Lynch, head of the Fianna Fail, became prime minister in July. He had promised tax cuts and called for the British to leave Northern Ireland.

Over 700 new manufacturing plants, many owned by U.S. corporations, opened in the 1960s–1970s. Ireland's economy expanded faster than those of other European countries.

In the first visit of a Roman Catholic pope to Ireland, John Paul II in September 1979 drew the largest crowds in the nation's history as millions turned out to receive his blessing.

Charles J. Haughey, 54, a nationalist who believes in the unification of Northern Ireland with Ireland, succeeded Lynch as prime minister and head of Fianna Fail on Dec. 11, 1979, after Lynch resigned because of criticism of his policy of conciliation with Britain.

Prime Minister Haughey called on Britain in 1980 to end the violence in Northern Ireland by giving up its control of that state and by permitting Ireland to unify.

See also *Northern Ireland,* pages 512–513.

QUICK QUIZ: What is Ireland's rank in size among the world's nations? See page 470.

# ISRAEL

**Official Name:** State of Israel.
**Area:** 9,000 sq. mi. (23,309 sq. km.).
**Population:** 3,895,920.
**Chief Cities:** Jerusalem, capital, 376,000; Tel Aviv–Yafo (Jaffa), 343,300; Haifa, 227,800; Ramat Gan, 120,900; Bat Yam, 124,100; Holon, 121,200.
**Largest Metropolitan Area:** Tel Aviv–Yafo, 1,219,900.
**Government:** Parliamentary republic.
**Prime Minister:** Menachem Begin (since 1977).
**President:** Yitzhak Navon (since 1978).
**Parliament:** *Knesset*, 120 members.
**U.S. Ambassador to Israel:** Samuel W. Lewis.
**Israeli Ambassador to U.S.:** Ephraim Evron.
**Flag:** White field bearing blue Star of David between two blue stripes.
**Languages:** Hebrew, Arabic, English.
**Main Ethnic Groups:** Jewish (85%), Arab (15%).
**Leading Religions:** Judaism (official–85%), Islam, Christianity.
**Leading Industries:** Manufacturing (food processing, textiles, clothing, aircraft, chemicals, metal products, vehicle assembly, machinery, cut diamonds, cement); agriculture (poultry, dairy products, citrus fruits, grapes, wheat, sugar beets, cotton, olives, figs, vegetables); mining (potash, petroleum, phosphates, bromine, natural gas); construction.
**Foreign Trade:** *major exports*—diamonds, citrus fruits, textile yarn and thread, potassic fertilizers; *major imports*—diamonds, crude petroleum, ships and boats, meat, corn.
**Places of Interest:** Many Old and New Testament sites; ruins of Masada on Dead Sea; Mt. Carmel in Haifa; Nazareth; Bethlehem; Capernaum; Sodom; King Solomon's copper mines. *In Jerusalem:* Wailing Wall; Dome of the Rock; Church of the Holy Sepulchre.

## ISRAEL TODAY

About the size of New Jersey, Israel is a small Middle Eastern nation on the east coast of the Mediterranean Sea. It is the only nation in the world in which Judaism is the official religion. Most of the people are or descend from Jewish immigrants to their biblical homeland.

Surrounded by Arab nations that wanted to destroy the Jewish state, Israel fought four wars for its existence since declaring its independence in 1948. Its troops occupied over 25,000 sq. mi. claimed by Palestinian Arabs. The nation remained continually on the alert against attack from its neighbors, spending two-thirds of its national budget for military preparedness.

The nation has few natural resources, and much of the land is desert. However, with hard work and $1.8 billion annual aid from the U.S., Israel has developed a booming industrial economy.

Israeli pioneers have reclaimed large desert areas for farming and citrus-fruit orchards.

Israel's people enjoy a much higher standard of living than Arabs in neighboring countries. Most Israelis live in cities and make their living from manufacturing or service industries.

The northern part of the country is hilly, with valleys and plains. South of this region is a narrow coastal plain. In the south is the Negev Desert.

The climate ranges from moderate in the northern part of the country to very hot in the desert. Rain falls from September to May.

Arab nations surround Israel. Lebanon lies to the north, Syria to the northeast and east, Jordan to the east, and Egypt to the southwest.

## EARLY HISTORY

About 1000 B.C. scattered Hebrew tribes in Israel (then called Canaan) banded together under King Saul to fight invading Philistines.

Political unity was achieved under King David, who established the capital at Jerusalem. His son and successor, Solomon, built the Temple and made Jerusalem the cultural and religious capital of Israel about 961–922 B.C.

After Solomon's death the kingdom split into two quarrelsome parts, Judah and Israel. Both soon fell to Assyrian conquerors, who enslaved about 27,000 Israelites in 722 B.C.

In Judah the Assyrians were followed by Egyptians and Babylonians, who exiled the ruling class of Judah in 587–582 B.C. Although the exiles were soon allowed to return, the area was repeatedly overrun by conquerors—Persians, Greeks, Seleucids, Romans, Byzantines, Arabs, Crusaders, and Turks. In 1516 the region became part of the Ottoman Empire.

In the 1890s Zionism, an international movement, was founded by Theodor Herzl to restore Palestine to the Jews. Many European Jews left their homes to settle in Palestine.

In World War I the region fell into British hands. Anxious for Jewish help, England in 1917 issued the Balfour Declaration, promising a national home for the Jews.

As Jews fled to Israel in the 1930s and 1940s to escape Nazi German persecution, an Arab rebellion caused Britain to limit Zionist immigration during and after World War II.

## INDEPENDENT ISRAEL

In 1947 the United Nations agreed to divide Palestine into two independent states, one Jewish and one Arab, with Jerusalem serving as an international or neutral zone.

The plan was accepted by the Jews. On May 14, 1948, they proclaimed Israel's independence when the British withdrew.

On the same day Egypt, Iraq, Jordan, Lebanon, Syria, and Saudi Arabia attacked Israel. Armistices were concluded in 1949.

## SECOND ARAB–ISRAELI WAR

In 1956 an Egyptian-Syrian-Jordanian military alliance threatened Israel with hostile encirclement. At the same time Egypt's expropriation of the Suez Canal Company alienated Britain and France. While an Anglo-French attack knocked out the Egyptian air force, Israeli forces quickly overran Egypt's Sinai region.

Combined pressure from the U.S. and the Soviet Union in the UN caused Israel's eventual withdrawal. A UN emergency force was stationed along the Egyptian-Israeli border.

For the first two decades of independence, the Mapai Workers' Party governed.

## THIRD ARAB–ISRAELI WAR

Israeli armed forces launched air and land strikes on Egypt, Jordan, and Syria on June 5, 1967.

In six days Israeli forces captured Jerusalem, the Sinai peninsula, the West Bank of the Jordan, the Gaza strip, and Golan Heights of Syria. A cease-fire was negotiated on June 11, 1967.

About 2 million Arabs displaced from their homes by the Arab-Israeli wars lived in refugee camps in Arab countries. In 1964 the militant Palestine Liberation Organization (PLO) was formed by the refugees to create an armed force that would compel Israel to give up land for an independent Arab Palestine. In the years that followed, the PLO carried out terrorist attacks on Israel, and Israelis retaliated with raids on PLO installations in Lebanon and elsewhere.

## FOURTH ARAB–ISRAELI WAR

Egypt and Syria launched a new war on Israel on two fronts on Oct. 6, 1973, during Yom Kippur. Other Arab nations soon joined the war.

After heavy fighting, Israeli troops were advancing in Syria and Egypt when the UN Security Council ordered a cease-fire on October 22. Three days later the UN sent a peace-keeping force to the Middle East to prevent further fighting.

The war resulted in a worldwide fuel crisis when Arab oil-producing nations cut off oil shipments for six months to the United States, Japan, and other nations that had aided Israel.

## AN UNEASY PEACE

Domestically Israel was torn by dissension as to who was responsible for being caught off guard in October 1973. Prime Minister Golda Meir resigned on April 10, 1974, and was succeeded by Yitzhak Rabin.

In September 1975 Israel and Egypt reached agreement on a further pullback of Israeli troops in the Sinai. U.S. technicians were sent to maintain electronic early warning stations between Israel and Egypt.

The UN Commission on Human Rights adopted a resolution on Feb. 13, 1976, accusing Israel of "war crimes" in its occupied Arab territories. Violent demonstrations by Arabs and Israeli nationalists took place 1976 in the Israeli-occupied area on the west bank of the Jordan River.

Israel denied news reports in 1976 that it had assembled 13 atomic bombs and further reports in 1980 that it had tested one in cooperation with South Africa.

Prime Minister Rabin resigned on April 8, 1977, after disclosures he had violated currency regulations.

He was succeeded by Shimon Peres, who had been defense minister.

In a national election on May 17, 1977, the right-wing Likud Party won an upset victory, capturing a plurality of 41 seats to Labor's 34 in the Knesset. Remaining seats in the 120-member parliament were split among 10 other parties.

Menachem Begin, 63, leader of the Likud Party, became prime minister on June 21, 1977. Considered one of Israel's founding fathers, Begin had headed the guerrilla army called Irgun Zvai

## ISRAEL'S PRIME MINISTERS

| 1948–63 | David Ben-Gurion . . . . . | Mapai Workers' Party |
| 1963–69 | Levi Eshkol . . . . . . . . . . . | Mapai Workers' Party |
| 1969–74 | Golda Meir . . . . . . . . . . . | Labor Party |
| 1974–77 | Yitzhak Rabin . . . . . . . . . | Labor Party |
| 1977 | Shimon Peres . . . . . . . . . | Labor Party |
| 1977– | Menachem Begin . . . . . . | Likud Party |

Leumi in the 1940s that was responsible for killing many British soldiers in an effort to drive Britain out of Palestine.

Begin appointed as his foreign minister Moshe Dayan, 62, who had commanded the Israeli army in the 1956 Arab-Israeli war and directed the 1967 victory as defense minister. Dayan resigned the post in October 1979.

Events took a dramatic turn on Nov. 19–21, 1977, when Egyptian President Sadat flew to Israel to address the Israeli parliament at the invitation of Prime Minister Begin, breaking the 30-year deadlock in which Arab leaders had refused to meet face to face with Israeli officials.

Begin returned Sadat's visit in December 1977, becoming the first Israeli prime minister to travel to Egypt. Formal peace negotiations began in January 1978.

Fears of a new Mideast war rose in March 1978 when Israel invaded southern Lebanon to destroy Palestinian terrorists. After the UN sent a 4,000-man peacekeeping force to the area, Israeli troops withdrew from Lebanon by June. However, Israel continued to raid PLO bases in southern Lebanon in 1978–80.

Culminating more than a year of negotiations spearheaded by U.S. President Carter, Israel and Egypt signed a peace treaty in Washington, D.C., on March 26, 1979. Upon ratification, the treaty became effective on April 25, 1979.

Israel began withdrawing from Egypt's Sinai peninsula on May 25, 1979, turning over the town of El Arish to Egyptian control. The first Israeli ships were allowed to sail through Egypt's Suez Canal on May 29. The U.S. began construction of two air bases at a cost of $800 million to be turned over to Israel as compensation for two bases it must give up when it completes withdrawal from the Sinai in 1982.

Meanwhile, Israel continued steps toward absorbing former Jordanian territories on the West Bank of the Jordan River, establishing new settlements there in 1979–80 in disregard of protests from Arab nations, the UN, and the U.S.

Israel and Egypt restored formal diplomatic relations with the exchange of ambassadors on Feb. 26, 1980. However, negotiations with Egypt broke down in 1980 on providing Arab autonomy in the West Bank and Gaza areas that are under Israeli military rule.

A storm of world criticism was unleashed when the Israeli parliament on July 30, 1980, formally made the Arab eastern part of Jerusalem part of the nation's capital.

Inflation continued unabated in 1980 at a rate of 134% despite government efforts to bring it under control. The monetary unit of the nation was changed to the shekel in October 1980 with each shekel worth 10 of the former Israeli pounds.

QUICK QUIZ: Is Israel's birthrate higher or lower than that of Japan? See page 473.

# ITALY

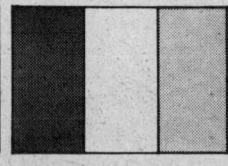

**Official Name:** Italian Republic.
**Area:** 116,304 square miles (301,225 sq. km).
**Population:** 57,410,000.
**Chief Cities:** Roma (Rome), capital, 2,897,505; Milano (Milan), 1,706,268; Napoli (Naples), 1,225,227; Torino (Turin), 1,181,567.
**Government:** Parliamentary republic.
**Prime Minister:** Arnaldo Forlani (since 1980).
**President:** Alessandro Pertini (since 1978).
**Parliament:** *Senate,* 322 members; *Chamber of Deputies,* 630 members.
**U.S. Ambassador to Italy:** Richard Gardner.
**Italian Ambassador to U.S.:** Paolo Pansa Cedronio.
**Flag:** Green, white, and red bars.
**Official Language:** Italian.
**Main Ethnic Group:** Italian.
**Official Religion:** Roman Catholicism (99%).
**Leading Industries:** Manufacturing (steel, automobiles, chemicals, electricity, office machines, electronic equipment, appliances, machinery, clothing, shoes, publishing); food processing; tourism; agriculture (sheep, goats, cattle, wheat, potatoes, corn, rice, grapes, olives, barley, oats, tobacco, fruits, vegetables); mining (natural gas, petroleum, mercury, sulfur, marble, asbestos, bauxite).
**Foreign Trade:** *major exports*—automobiles, petroleum products, clothing, shoes, office machines, citrus fruits, vegetables; *major imports*—petroleum, machinery, food, scrap iron and steel, coal, cotton.
**Places of Interest:** Renaissance art galleries in Florence; Isle of Capri; St. Mark's Square in Venice; La Scala opera house in Milan; Adriatic coast resorts; Dolomite winter-sports at Trentino; Naples; Genoa; Sicily; Sardinia. *In Rome:* St. Peter's Basilica; Vatican; Sistine Chapel; Colosseum; Pantheon.

## ITALY TODAY

About the size of Florida and Georgia combined, Italy has few natural resources. Lack of such mineral resources as iron ore, coal, and petroleum has handicapped Italy's industrial growth. However, it is among the world's leading producers of cement, electricity, natural gas, and steel.

Almost a third of Italy is mountainous and unable to be farmed. This along with backward farming methods combine to limit food production, making Italy dependent on imports to feed its people.

Italy's government lacks stability because no party has a majority of seats in the parliament. The conservative Christian Democrats control only a few more seats than the Communist Party.

In the 1970s–80s leftist and rightist terrorist groups defied government authority with thousands of kidnappings, bombings, and killings.

Only the Po River valley, the coastal plains, and lowland relieve the mountainous landscape of Italy. Alpine ranges in the north include the Maritime, Graian, Pennine, Bergamasque, Dolomites, and Carnic mountains. Below them lies the great fertile basin of the Po Valley, Italy's agricultural and industrial core.

From the valley's lower limits rise the rugged Apennine chain. It runs down the length of the peninsula and leaps the Strait of Messina to cover much of northern Sicily.

Southern Italy and Sicily are in the midst of an earthquake belt that has given rise to Europe's three best-known active volcanoes; Vesuvius (4,190 feet), Etna (10,958 feet), and Stromboli (3,308 feet).

Italy's largest and most famous lakes—Maggiore, Como, and Garda—are all located in the Alps. The country's most important rivers are the Po and the Adige in the north, and the Arno and the Tiber in the central region.

## EARLY HISTORY

The earliest known settlers—Latins, Sabines, Umbrians, and Ligurians—took over large areas in the northern part of the peninsula. They were displaced in the 800s B.C. by the Etruscans. Greeks and Phoenicians began their expansion into Sicily and the southern part of the peninsula about the 700s B.C..

Rome, the home of the Latins, lay between the Etruscan and Greek settlements. The Roman republic annexed the Etruscan kingdom in the 400s B.C. and united most of Italy by 270 B.C.

The Punic Wars (264–146 B.C.) between Rome and Carthage ended with Carthage destroyed and Rome the dominant power in the Mediterranean region. During the next century the Romans expanded into Gaul (France) and Britain.

## ROMAN EMPIRE

In 27 B.C. Rome became an empire with Augustus as its first emperor. Early in the 300s A.D. Emperor Constantine accepted Christianity, and churches spread throughout Italy and all of the Roman Empire. At the same time, Constantine moved the imperial capital to Constantinople (now Istanbul).

Rome subsequently declined, and fell in 476 to German tribes.

The Ostrogoths and Lombards occupied the peninsula in the 500s, but in 774 their kingdom was absorbed by the Frankish empire headed by Charlemagne. During the 900s the powerful German king Otto I extended his rule into the Italian peninsula. In 962 he was crowned emperor of the Holy Roman Empire by the pope.

## ITALIAN CITY-STATES

From the 900s to the 1300s the Italian city-states, the popes, and the Holy Roman emperors vied for power. Towns were divided and most noble families backed one of the two opposition parties: the papal Guelphs and the imperial Ghibellines. After the 1200s the Italian cities of Venice, Bologna, and Florence emerged as autonomous centers of political power and of learning. By the 1500s the Italian Renaissance had breathed new life into European art and learning.

Invasions by France, Spain, and Austria during the 1500s and 1600s divided the Italian states and brought most of them under foreign rule. In the early 1800s Austria became the dominant power in the Italian peninsula. Sporadic attempts to drive out the Austrians were effectively checked. Failing to achieve their goals in the revolutions of 1848 and 1849, nationalist leaders such as Giuseppe

Garibaldi and Giuseppe Mazzini turned for help to Piedmont, the only Italian state to gain a liberal constitution, and to its able prime minister, Count Camillo Cavour. With the aid of France, Piedmont drove out the Austrians in 1859.

## INDEPENDENT KINGDOM AND FASCIST RULE

Cavour succeeded in uniting most of the Italian states in the Kingdom of Italy, proclaimed on March 17, 1861, under the rule of Victor Emmanuel II of Savoy. The entire Italian peninsula was unified by 1870 with Rome as the capital.

Although at first neutral in World War I, promises of territories and concessions induced Italy to enter the war on the Allied side.

Fascist leader Benito Mussolini seized control in 1923. His dictatorship soon controlled all aspects of Italian life. Mussolini set out to assert Italy's power by the conquest of Ethiopia in 1935–36 and by annexing Albania in 1939.

Italy entered World War II on the side of Germany on June 11, 1940. Italian defeats aroused popular discontent with the fascist regime. In July 1943 King Victor Emmanuel III ordered Mussolini's arrest. The new government concluded an armistice with the Allies, who had already begun to invade Sicily. But German forces took control of northern and central Italy. The Allies entered Rome on June 4, 1944. Mussolini was executed by Italian partisans in April 1945. A peace treaty was signed between Italy and the Allies on Feb. 10, 1947.

## ITALIAN REPUBLIC

A popular referendum on June 2, 1946, ended Italy's monarchy. The Italian Republic officially came into being with promulgation of its constitution on Jan. 1, 1948.

Alcide de Gasperi, leader of the Christian Democratic Party, had headed Italy's first postwar cabinet in December 1945. After the formation of the republic, de Gasperi continued as prime minister until 1953.

A quarrel with Austria over the South Tyrol (Alto Adige), a part of Austria ceded to Italy after World War I, was settled in 1969.

The declining influence of the Roman Catholic Church in Italy was demonstrated when Italians voted 3 to 2 on May 12, 1974, in favor of the nation's 1970 divorce law.

Italy and Yugoslavia agreed on a draft treaty on Oct. 1, 1975, bringing final settlement of their 30-year Trieste dispute. The treaty formally gave the area south of Trieste to Yugoslavia.

In national elections on June 20–21, 1976, the Christian Democrats won the largest share of the votes with 39%, but the Communist Party was a close second with 36%.

The United States, Britain, France and West Germany warned in 1976 they would make no more loans to Italy if any cabinet posts were given to communists.

The U.S. and other Western nations agreed in April 1977 to bolster Italy's economy with a $1 billion loan upon promises by the Italian government to try to reduce the rate of inflation.

Communist demands for seats in the cabinet forced Prime Minister Andreotti to resign in mid-

### ITALY'S PRIME MINISTERS* SINCE 1945

| | | | |
|---|---|---|---|
| 1945-53 | Alcide de Gasperi | 1968 | Giovanni Leone |
| 1953-54 | Giuseppe Pella | 1968-70 | Mariano Rumor |
| 1954-55 | Mario Scelba | 1970-72 | Emilio Colombo |
| 1955-57 | Antonio Segni | 1972-73 | Giulio Andreotti |
| 1957-58 | Adone Zoli | 1973-74 | Mariano Rumor |
| 1958-59 | Amintri Fanfani | 1974-76 | Aldo Moro |
| 1959-60 | Antonio Segni | 1976-79 | Giulio Andreotti |
| 1960-63 | Amintri Fanfani | 1979-80 | Francesco Cossiga |
| 1963-64 | Giovanni Leone | 1980- | Arnaldo Forlani |
| 1964-68 | Aldo Moro | | |

*All members of Christian Democratic Party.

January 1978. After two months of crisis, the communists agreed to support a new Christian Democratic government without participating at the cabinet level. Andreotti again became prime minister in mid-March.

The wave of terror by which the anarchist Red Brigades sought to disrupt Italy reached a peak in 1978 with the kidnapping and murder of former Prime Minister Aldo Moro. The terrorists killed Moro's five body guards to capture him on March 16. The government refused ransom demands to free Red Brigade leaders then being tried in Turin. Nearly two months later Moro was slain and his body left in Rome on May 9. In June, 29 Red Brigade members, including several of the founders of the group, were sentenced to prison terms of up to 15 years by the court in Turin.

Despite opposition by the Roman Catholic church, parliament legalized abortion on May 18, 1978, for the first time in the nation's history.

Giovanni Leone, who had served as Italy's president since 1971, resigned on June 15, 1978, after newspaper charges of tax fraud in relation to $1.6 million in bribes allegedly paid by the U.S. Lockheed corporation to Italian officials.

Socialist Alessandro Pertini was chosen as Italy's new president by a special electoral assembly on July 8, 1978.

Italy experienced its longest government crisis in 1979 after the communists withdrew their support from the Christian Democratic government. Prime Minister Andreotti resigned on Jan. 31, and for more than six months neither he nor other politicians could form a new cabinet that could win the majority support of parliament.

New parliamentary elections were held June 3–4, 1979. Christian Democrats retained their plurality in the 630-seat lower house, losing only 1 seat and holding 262. The communists lost 27 seats, ending with 201 as the second-largest party.

The government crisis ended on Aug. 5, 1979, with the swearing-in as prime minister of Christian Democrat Francesco Cossiga, 51, a former minister of interior.

In one of the worst terrorist incidents neofascists killed 84 persons in the bombing of the railway station in Bologna on Aug. 2, 1980.

After 13 years of work and an expenditure of about $375 million, a 9-mile subway line was opened in Rome in Feb. 16, 1980, designed to serve commuters from southeastern suburbs.

Prime Minister Cossiga survived a vote of confidence in July 1980 after he had been accused of aiding the son of a fellow legislator to escape from arrest as a terrorist. But on Sept. 27

QUICK QUIZ: Is Italy's per capita GNP higher or lower than that of Israel? See page 475.

## ITALY (continued)

he was defeated and forced to resign when he lost by one vote on an austerity program that had sought to overcome the rising inflation rate by increasing taxes that raised the price of gasoline to $3.37 per gallon.

Arnaldo Forlani, president of the Christian Democratic Party, was invited by President Pertini on Oct. 2, 1980, to become prime minister.

A major earthquake struck southern Italy on Nov. 23–24, 1980, destroying 133 towns and villages, killing more than 3,000 persons, and leaving over 300,000 homeless.

## ITALY'S SEMIAUTONOMOUS ISLANDS

### SARDINIA

**Area:** 9,194 square miles (23,812 sq. km.)
**Population:** 1,522,770.
**Capital:** Cagliari, 236,931.

About the size of New Hampshire, Sardinia is the second-largest island in the Mediterranean after Sicily. It lies about 100 miles west of Italy. It is separated only by a narrow strait from the French island of Corsica to the north.

Thousands of stone monuments built by prehistoric Stone Age people dot the countryside.

In about the 800s B.C. Phoenicians established trading colonies on the coast. They were followed by Carthaginians, Romans, Vandals, and the Greek Byzantine Empire.

In the 1000s A.D. Arab rulers of Spain took control of the island. The Italian city-states of Pisa and Genoa contended for mastery of the island in the 1100s and 1200s. In the 1300s it passed to rule by Spain. In 1718 it was awarded to the rulers of Savoy in northern Italy, who became kings of Sardinia until 1861, when they became rulers of Italy. In 1948 Sardinia was granted semiautonomous status.

### SICILY

**Area:** 9,817 square miles (25,426 sq. km.).
**Population:** 4,795,750.
**Chief Cities:** Palermo, capital, 662,567; Catania, 398,642; Messina, 261,332; Siracusa (Syracuse), 118,025.

The largest island in the Mediterranean Sea, Sicily has been a stepping-stone between Italy and Africa throughout its history. It lies southwest of the toe of Italy's boot, separated from the mainland by the 2- to 10-mile-wide Strait of Messina.

Because of its year-round warm climate, the island attracts many tourists during the winter.

Peoples called the Sicani and Siculi lived on the island in prehistoric times. Greeks began colonies in the 700s B.C., making Syracuse a major center. Carthage won control in the 300s B.C.

The Romans took Sicily in 211 B.C., making it their first overseas province. It fell to the Byzantine Empire in A.D. 535. Arabs from Africa conquered Sicily in the 800s. Normans under Roger I captured Sicily in the 1000s. It came under the rule of German kings in the 1100s and was the seat of the Holy Roman Empire under Frederick II in 1215–1250. French, Spanish, Austrian, and Italian rulers contended for Sicily for the next 600 years.

In 1861 Sicily became part of the new Kingdom of Italy. The island was granted semiautonomous status on May 15, 1946.

## IVORY COAST

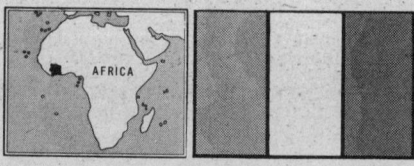

**Official Name:** Republic of the Ivory Coast.
**Area:** 124,504 square miles (322,463 sq. km.).
**Population:** 8,461,680.
**Capital:** Abidjan, 282,000.
**Government:** One-party republic.
**President:** Félix Houphouët-Boigny (since 1960).
**National Assembly:** 120 members.
**U.S. Ambassador to Ivory Coast:** Nancy Y. Rawls.
**Ivory Coast Ambassador to U.S.:** Timothée N' Guetta Ahoua.
**Flag:** Tricolor of orange, white, and green bars.
**Languages:** French (official), Baoulé, Dioula, Mandingo, Mande.
**Main Ethnic Group:** Black.
**Religions:** Animism (54%), Islam (24%), Christianity (12%).
**Leading Industries:** Agriculture (coffee, cocoa, cotton, bananas, pineapples, coconuts, rubber, sugar); forestry and lumbering; food processing; tourism; manufacturing (textiles, shoes, consumer products); mining (petroleum, diamonds, iron ore).
**Foreign Trade:** *major exports*—coffee, cocoa, wood, palm oil, cotton, pineapples, sugar; *major imports*—cotton fabrics, petroleum, automobiles, tractors.
**Places of Interest:** Abidjan plateau; Ebrié lagoon; Banco National Park; Grand Bassam; Dabou; Bingerville; Bouaké; beach resorts.

### IVORY COAST TODAY

A little larger than New Mexico, the Ivory Coast is the most prosperous of the small countries of West Africa. Its people enjoy a standard of living much higher than among their neighbors.

Benefiting from a stable government since becoming independent in 1960, Ivory Coast has maintained a steady pace of economic growth. It has used foreign aid and loans to diversify its agriculture so that coffee, cocoa, and wood each provide a major share of export income.

The country's valuable resources include petroleum, iron ore, and timber.

From the coast the land slopes gradually to a height of about 1,400 feet in the north. The narrow 340-mile coastline—flat and sandy in the east—becomes more indented and rocky in the west. Beyond the coast is a vast forest region occupying nearly one-third of the country. In the northwest mountain ranges reach 5,000 feet.

The coastal region has a tropical climate with year-round temperatures of 73° to 80° F. Annual rainfall of 80 to 120 inches falls mostly from mid-May to mid-July.

Liberia and Guinea lie to the west, Mali and Upper Volta to the north, and Ghana to the east.

### EARLY HISTORY

Before its organization as a French colony, the area that is now the Ivory Coast had no political or cultural unity. Several traditional kingdoms existed in parts of the country, while in others political organization rarely exceeded the village level.

French explorers reached the region in 1483, beginning the lucrative ivory trade from which the area later derived its name.

French missionaries, landing at Assinie in 1687, were the first white settlers. The settlement was soon abandoned, however, and the Ivory Coast remained relatively free of European influence until the 1800s, thus avoiding being drawn into the slave trade.

French interest was reasserted in 1842 with the establishment of a protectorate over the coastal area. Thereafter, mostly as a result of private initiative, French influence was carried to the interior. In 1893 the territory was declared a colony. Treaties with local chieftains strengthened France's hold, but major military action was necessary to establish effective control. Complete French control of the Ivory Coast was finally achieved in 1917.

The French began to develop the country in the 1920s. Yet the colonial administration, based on government by decree, was little changed until the creation of the French Union in 1946. At that time some political rights were extended to native Africans.

Over the next 10 years the Parti Démocratique de Côte d'Ivoire (PDCI), under the leadership of Félix Houphouët-Boigny, emerged as the dominant political force. Most of its opposition had been eliminated by 1956, the year internal autonomy was granted.

## INDEPENDENCE

The Ivory Coast became an autonomous state within the French Community in 1958. Two years later, on Aug. 7, 1960, it proclaimed its independence as a republic. Houphouët-Boigny became president after winning 98% of the votes in an election in November 1960. He was reelected in 1965, 1970, 1975, and 1980.

Since independence the economic development of the nation has proceeded rapidly, spurred in large part by the unusually liberal terms offered to foreign investors. The government has maintained strong ties with France, the United States, and West Germany.

In April 1972 at a meeting of the African-Malagasy Common Organization (OCAM) in Togo, President Houphouët-Boigny was formally reconciled with Gen. Yakubu Gowon, president of Nigeria. They had been estranged since Ivory Coast opposed the Nigerian government's attack on Biafra. But the exiled Biafran leader, Gen. Odumegwo Ojukwu, continued to reside in Ivory Coast. In 1972 Ivory Coast was among seven French-speaking states that set up a West African Economic Community (CEAO) to promote trade among its members.

France's President Giscard d'Estaing visited in 1978, praising the country for having "proved it is possible to escape from the curse of underdevelopment in the framework of a free economy."

Production of petroleum began in 1980 from fields discovered in 1978–80. Predictions that the size of the reserves would enable the country to become an oil exporting nation by the mid-1980s brought optimism that the economy would soar to new heights of prosperity.

# JAMAICA

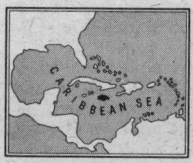 

**Official Name:** Jamaica.
**Area:** 4,244 square miles (10,991 sq. km.).
**Populaton:** 2,214,120.
**Capital:** Kingston, 111,879.
**Government:** Parliamentary democracy.
**Prime Minister:** Edward P. G. Seaga (since 1980).
**Chief of State:** Governor-general Florizel Glasspole (appointed in 1973).
**Parliament:** *Senate,* 21 members; *House of Representatives,* 60 members.
**U.S. Ambassador to Jamaica:** Loren E. Lawrence.
**Jamaican Ambassador to U.S.:** Alfred Adolphus Rattray.
**Flag:** Gold cross with green field in top and bottom quarters; black to left and right.
**Official Language:** English.
**Main Ethnic Groups:** Black (76%), mulatto (15%).
**Leading Religions:** Anglicanism (20%), Baptist (19%), Church of God (12%), Roman Catholicism (7%).
**Leading Industries:** Agriculture (sugarcane, bananas, cattle, hogs, poultry, cocoa, coconuts, fruits, vegetables); mining (bauxite, gypsum); tourism; manufacturing and processing (alumina, rum, molasses, cement, chemicals, petroleum products, consumer products); fishing.
**Foreign Trade:** *major exports*—alumina, bauxite, sugar, bananas; *major imports*—crude petroleum, automobiles.
**Places of Interest:** Kingston; Port Royal; Montego Bay; Ocho Rios resort; Negril Beach; Port Antonio; Royal Botanical Gardens at Hope.

## JAMAICA TODAY

About the size of Connecticut, Jamaica is the world's second-largest producer of bauxite (aluminum ore). The mining of bauxite, the processing of alumina, sugar, and tourism support the economy of the British Commonwealth nation.

Sugar and other agricultural products for many years provided the bulk of the island's income, but today farm products account for less than a fifth of Jamaica's exports. The decreasing importance of agriculture brought many families to the cities, causing serious unemployment.

The island of Jamaica lies in the Caribbean, about 90 miles south of Cuba. A limestone-based plateau, its average elevation is about 1,500 feet. Alluvial coastal deposits surround a mountainous interior dominated in the east by the Blue Mountains, which rise to 7,402 feet.

## EARLY HISTORY

Jamaica was discovered by Columbus in 1494. It was settled 15 years later by Spaniards, who introduced the cultivation of sugarcane. The native Arawaks, unaccustomed to hard labor, soon died out. Then the Spaniards imported Africans to work the plantations.

At war with Spain, England captured Jamaica in 1655. The Spaniards left after freeing their

QUICK QUIZ: Does Jamaica have more or fewer paved highways than Ivory Coast? See page 475.

## JAMAICA (continued)

slaves, who took to the hills and harassed the settlers. The former slaves, called Maroons, were finally granted land and freedom in 1739.

The island became a base for pirates, who grew rich plundering Spanish galleons. Port Royal, the capital, acquired a reputation for wickedness.

The English imported large numbers of African slaves to raise sugarcane. Slavery was abolished in 1838.

Jamaica became a crown colony in 1866. It was granted full internal autonomy in 1953.

In 1958 Jamaica joined with several other British Caribbean possessions in a West Indian Federation. Three years later Jamaica withdrew.

### INDEPENDENCE

On Aug. 6, 1962, Jamaica was granted full independence, with Sir Alexander Bustamante, a labor leader, as the first prime minister. Hugh Shearer became prime minister in 1967.

The ruling Jamaica Labour Party lost in general elections on Feb. 29, 1972, to the People's National Party. The PNP leader, Michael Manley, became the prime minister. Manley, a socialist, led the government in acquiring majority control of the island's sugar industry in 1974 and its bauxite mines in 1975.

The government requires all high school graduates except those going on to college to devote a year to public service.

Manley, who has expressed admiration of Cuba's Fidel Castro, said he hoped to preside over "the most peaceful and constitutional revolution in history."

The government began a land-reform program that from 1973 to 1975 allocated land to 11,000 small farmers and farm cooperatives in an effort to increase food production. Thousands of unemployed persons were hired by the government at $26 a week to clean streets and improve the island's appearance in what was called the Crash Work Program. A minimum wage of $20 for a 40-hour week was adopted in 1975.

Despite claims by the opposition that Prime Minister Manley would soon turn Jamaica into "another Cuba," his PLP party won a landslide victory in an election on Dec. 15, 1976, taking 48 of the 60 seats in the house of representatives.

The island's economy declined year after year during the late 1970s with 1 worker in 3 unemployed by the 1980s while prices rose at an annual rate of more than 30%.

The U.S. and other Western nations reduced economic aid as Manley's government leaned closer to communism.

In a bitter 9-month election campaign in 1980 some 450 persons were killed in battles between opposing political parties.

The pro-Western Jamaica Labor Party (JLP) won a surprise landslide victory on Oct. 30, 1980, capturing 51 of the 60 seats in parliament's lower house. Its leader, Edward P. G. Seaga, 50, was sworn in as prime minister on Nov. 1.

As one of his first acts as prime minister, Seaga asked Cuba to withdraw its ambassador. He promised to restore Jamaica's economy in the 1980s by revitalizing the tourist industry while turning the government from socialism to encouragement of free enterprise.

## JAPAN

 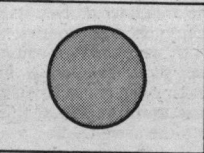

**Official Name:** Japan.
**Area:** 145,809 square miles (377,644 sq. km.).
**Population:** 117,800,000.
**Chief Cities:** Tokyo, capital, 8,543,775; Osaka, 2,723,752; Yokohama, 2,694,569; Nagoya, 2,083,616; Kyoto, 1,464,964; Kobe, 1,366,397; Sapporo, 1,306,686; Kitakyushu, 1,067,915; Fukuoka, 1,039,286; Kawasaki, 1,032,852.
**Largest Metropolitan Area:** Tokyo, 11,683,613.
**Government:** Constitutional monarchy.
**Prime Minister:** Zenko Suzuki (since 1980).
**Emperor:** Hirohito (since 1926).
**Diet:** *House of Councillors,* 252 members; *House of Representatives,* 511 members.
**U.S. Ambassador to Japan:** Michael J. Mansfield.
**Japanese Ambassador to U.S.:** Yoshio Okawara.
**Flag:** Red sun on white field.
**Official Language:** Japanese.
**Principal Ethnic Group:** Japanese.
**Main Religions:** Shintoism and Buddhism.
**Leading Industries:** Manufacturing (shipbuilding, textiles, aluminum, electricity, electrical and electronic equipment, steel, cement, paper, consumer goods); shipping; agriculture (rice, barley, tea, poultry, wheat, soybeans, sweet potatoes, sugar beets, vegetables, fruits); fishing; forestry; mining (coal, manganese, zinc, copper, lead, sulfur); tourism.
**Foreign Trade:** *major exports*—ships and boats, electrical and electronic products, steel, synthetic fabrics, automobiles; *major imports*—crude petroleum, wood, iron ore, cotton.
**Places of Interest:** Mt. Fuji; Fuji-Hakone-Izu National Park; Nikko National Park and resort; Lake Chuzenji; Island of Hokkaido; Kyoto; Osaka; Kobe; Nagoya; Hiroshima; Nagasaki; Tanegashima Island space center. *In Tokyo:* Tokyo Tower atop Kasumigaseki Building; Imperial Palace; Hibiya and Meiji parks; Shiba Zojo-ji Temple; Great Buddha at Kamakura.

### JAPAN TODAY

Although smaller than Montana, Japan is the third most important industrial nation in the world after the United States and the Soviet Union. It is the major competitor of the United States in world trade. Because Japan lacks the three most important minerals needed for industrialization—iron, petroleum, and coking coal, it must import raw materials from other countries.

Japan also lacks sufficient hydroelectric potential to power its industries and light its cities, so it has become a leading developer of atomic electric generating plants. It plans to decrease dependence on foreign oil imports to 50% of energy needs by the 1990s.

Japan is so mountainous that only 19% of its

### AREA OF JAPAN'S MAIN ISLANDS

| | SQ. MI. | SQ. KM. | LARGEST CITY |
|---|---|---|---|
| Honshu | 87,805 | 227,414 | Tokyo |
| Hokkaido | 30,144 | 78,073 | Sapporo |
| Kyushu | 14,114 | 36,555 | Kitakyushu |
| Shikoku | 7,049 | 18,257 | Matsuyama |

land is suitable for farming. By use of up-to-date scientific methods Japanese farmers attain the world's highest crop yields per acre, but even so the country must import about 35% of its food.

About three-fourths of the Japanese people live in and around the cities. Consequently Japan has many problems of urban pollution and urban transit. Most Japanese are well educated. Their standard of living is at about the same level as that of Americans.

Stretching in a 1,500-mile arc from north to south are four main islands: Hokkaido, Honshu, Shikoku, and Kyushu; and nearly 3,000 smaller islands, mostly tiny islets. Japan has 192 volcanoes, 40 of them still active. Dormant Mt. Fuji (12,388 feet) is the tallest.

## EARLY HISTORY

Japanese myths say Jimmu Tenno, descendant of the sun goddess and ancestor of the present emperor, founded the empire about 660 B.C.

Anthropologists believe Chinese colonists about 200 B.C. brought China's ideographic script as well as its philosophy, literature, arts, and sciences to Japan. Buddhism was officially introduced in the 500s A.D.

Under the empress Suiko (593–628) a constitution and an official calendar were adopted.

In the 1100s power fell into the hands of the Minamoto, whose leader, Yoritomo, set up a military government in 1192 at Kamakura. For 700 years military governors, called *shoguns,* ruled Japan in the emperor's name.

China's Mongol ruler Kublai Khan twice launched invasions of Japan in 1274 and 1281, but each time the Mongols were driven off.

Portuguese navigators, arriving in 1542, were the first Europeans seen in Japan. They brought with them the first firearms. In 1549 St. Francis Xavier introduced Christianity.

By 1601 Ieyasu Tokugawa, a warrior, had unified Japan. He was appointed shogun in 1603 and established the Tokugawa shogunate that ruled until 1868. Ieyasu's center of government was Edo, the present Tokyo. After Ieyasu's death in 1616 a policy of national isolation was adopted. Christians were executed. Society became ossified under the ruling lords into four classes: *samurai* (warriors), merchants, artisans, and peasants. For the next two centuries Japan remained isolated from the world, permitting only the Dutch to conduct foreign trade.

## JAPAN'S GROWTH AS A MILITARY POWER

U.S. Commodore Matthew C. Perry forced Japan to open its ports to trade with a treaty concluded on March 3, 1854. The first Japanese ambassador arrived in Washington in 1860.

Ruling power was restored to the emperor in 1868, and the capital was moved from Kyoto to Tokyo. This development was known as the Meiji Restoration. Feudalism was abolished. In 1889 the emperor granted a new constitution, establishing a bicameral parliament.

Japan took Formosa (now Taiwan) and the Pescadores from China in the Sino-Japanese War of 1894–95. After forming an alliance with Britain in 1902, Japan defeated Russia in the Russo-

### JAPAN'S PRIME MINISTERS SINCE 1945

| 1945–46 | Kijuro Shidehara . . . . . . | Nonpartisan |
|---|---|---|
| 1946–47 | Shigeru Yoshida . . . . . . | Coalition |
| 1947–48 | Tetsu Katayama . . . . . . | Socialist |
| 1948 | Hitoshi Ashida . . . . . . . . | Democratic |
| 1948–54 | Shigeru Yoshida . . . . . . | Democratic-Liberal |
| 1954–56 | Ichiro Hatoyama . . . . . . | Democratic |
| 1956–57 | Tanzan Ishibashi . . . . . . | Liberal Democratic |
| 1957–60 | Nobusuke Kishi . . . . . . . | Liberal Democratic |
| 1960–64 | Hayato Ikeda . . . . . . . . . | Liberal Democratic |
| 1964–72 | Eisaku Sato . . . . . . . . . . | Liberal Democratic |
| 1972–74 | Kakuei Tanaka . . . . . . . . | Liberal Democratic |
| 1974–76 | Takeo Miki . . . . . . . . . . . | Liberal Democratic |
| 1976–78 | Takeo Fukuda . . . . . . . . | Liberal Democratic |
| 1978–80 | Masayoshi Ohira . . . . . . | Liberal Democratic |
| 1980– | Zenko Suzuki . . . . . . . . . | Liberal Democratic |

Japanese War of 1904–05. It gained the Liaotung peninsula in Manchuria and half of Sakhalin Island. Korea was annexed in 1910.

As a reward for supporting the Allies in World War I, Japan received a mandate over the northern Pacific islands formerly held by Germany. At the Washington Naval Conference of 1922, Japan was recognized as the third-leading naval power.

Universal manhood suffrage was introduced in 1925. Hirohito became emperor in 1926.

Japan's military leaders invaded and occupied China's province of Manchuria in 1931, and they ended Japan's parliamentary government in 1932.

Beginning in 1937 Japan waged an undeclared war with China. Japan signed a military alliance in 1939 with Nazi Germany and Fascist Italy. The defeat of France by Germany in 1940 enabled Japan to gain a foothold in Indochina.

## JAPAN'S DEFEAT IN WORLD WAR II

In an attempt to halt Japanese aggression in Asia, the U.S. began to reduce its shipments of oil and steel to Japan. On Dec. 7, 1941, Japan launched a surprise attack on Pearl Harbor, Hawaii, nearly wiping out the entire U.S. fleet. The U.S. immediately declared war.

After 1944 Japan's losses grew swiftly and steadily, culminating in the atomic bombing of Hiroshima and Nagasaki by the U.S. on Aug. 6 and 9, 1945.

Japan capitulated on Aug. 14, 1945, and the formal surrender was signed on September 2. The country was demilitarized and occupied by U.S. forces. A new constitution, adopted in 1946, established a parliamentary government.

A Japanese peace treaty was signed in San Francisco on Sept. 8, 1951, by Japan and 48 other nations, including the U.S. Japan signed a bilateral security treaty with the U.S. the same day.

## JAPAN'S RECOVERY AS A WORLD POWER

Japan regained full independence on April 28, 1952, when the peace treaty became effective.

The United States returned the Bonin Islands and Iwo Jima to Japan in 1968 and the Ryukyu Islands in May 1972, while retaining military installations on Okinawa.

Ending an era of conflict that had begun in 1937, Japan and China in 1972 reestablished diplomatic relations.

In a national election for the house of representa-

QUICK QUIZ: Montserrat is a dependency of what country? See page 477.

## JAPAN *(continued)*

tives on Dec. 5, 1976, the ruling Liberal Democratic Party lost its majority, winning only 249 of the 511 seats. However, 9 conservative independent members joined the party to keep it in power.

The U.S. and Japan reached agreement in September 1977 enabling Japan to open the Tokai Mura atomic fuel reprocessing plant north of Tokyo to produce fuel for its increasing number of atomic power stations.

A dispute within the ruling party over economic policies resulted in Masayoshi Ohira, 68, replacing Takeo Fukuda as prime minister on Dec. 7, 1978.

Prime Minister Ohira traveled to Washington, D.C., in May 1979 for meetings with President Carter to discuss steps Japan might take to make it easier for American businessmen to sell products in Japan and thus reduce the growing trade gap between the two nations.

President Carter returned Ohira's visit in June 1979 when he attended a two-day economic conference in Tokyo that included the leaders of Britain, Canada, France, Italy, and West Germany.

In a parliamentary election on Oct. 7, 1979, the governing Liberal Democratic Party lost ground after Prime Minister Ohira called for higher taxes during the campaign. The party won 249 seats, 1 less than in 1976. It retained its governing majority in the lower house by a slim 2 votes with the assistance of 10 independent conservatives.

After achieving a record balance-of-trade surplus of $16.53 in 1978, Japan's economy slowed in 1979–80, registering a trade deficit of more than $9 billion in 1979, largely because of rising prices of oil imports.

The nation was rocked in 1980 by a spy scandal. Maj. Gen. Yukihisa Miyanaga, chief of army intelligence until his retirement in 1974, was arrested on Jan. 18, along with two junior officers still on active duty, on charges of passing military secrets to the Soviet Union. The civilian head of the defense forces and the army's chief of staff were dismissed from their posts a few days later, blamed for lack of discipline in allowing the situation to develop.

On May 16, 1980, Ohira's government was defeated by a no-confidence vote, 243–187, the first such loss by a Japanese prime minister in 27 years.

After scheduling national elections, the 70-year-old Ohira died of a heart attack on June 12, 1980, at the height of the political campaign.

The governing Liberal Democratic Party in the election on June 22, 1980, strengthened its leadership with clear majorities in both the lower and upper houses of parliament. It made its largest gain in winning a majority of 284 in the 511-member lower house.

Zenko Suzuki, 69, a former cabinet minister, became prime minister on July 17, 1980. He reaffirmed close ties with the U.S., but said Japan should build its armed forces without relying entirely on the U.S.-Japanese military alliance for Japan's defense.

Treasure hunters discovered in September 1980 the wreck of the Russian cruiser *Admiral Nakhimov,* which sank in 1905 off Tushima island. The ship's cargo of gold and platinum ingots was estimated to be worth as much as $3.7 billion.

## JORDAN

**Official Name:** Hashemite Kingdom of Jordan.
**Area:** 37,738 square miles (97,740 sq. km.).
**Population:** 2,186,738.
**Chief Cities:** Amman, capital, 711,850; Zarka, 263,400; Irbid, 136,770.
**Government:** Absolute monarchy.
**King:** Hussein (reigned since 1952).
**Prime Minister:** Mudar Badran (since 1980).
**Parliament:** *Senate,* 30 members; *House of Representatives,* 60 members.
**U.S. Ambassador to Jordan:** Nicholas A. Veliotes.
**Jordanian Ambassador to U.S.:** Al-Sharif Fawaz Sharaf.
**Flag:** Black, white, and green stripes, with seven-pointed white star in red triangle on left.
**Languages:** Arabic (official), Circassian.
**Main Ethnic Group:** Arab (95%).
**Religions:** Islam (95%), Christianity (5%).
**Leading Industries:** Agriculture (wheat, barley, figs, olives, grapes, tobacco, sheep, goats, poultry, fruits, vegetables); mining (phosphate); manufacturing (cement, textiles, chemicals, petroleum refining, food processing); tourism.
**Foreign Trade:** *major exports*—phosphates, tomatoes; *major imports*—motor vehicles, crude petroleum, sugar, rice, textiles, machinery, weapons, consumer goods.
**Places of Interest:** Citadel Hill and Roman theater in Amman; Petra, city of red rock; Greco-Roman ruins at Jerash; Crusader architecture at Kerak; Aqaba seaport; Azraq National Park; Wadi Rum Valley; forts and palaces.

## JORDAN TODAY

A little larger than Indiana, Jordan lacks the petroleum resources that have vitalized the economies of other formerly poor Arab nations. However, Jordan has received about $1.7 billion in economic aid from the U.S. since World War II. It has used this aid wisely in developing its agriculture and the mining of its phosphate deposits. Irrigation projects have opened new farmland.

About half of the people are Arab refugees made homeless by the Arab-Israeli wars.

## EARLY HISTORY

Jordan includes the biblical lands of Gilead, Ammon, Bashan, Edom, and Moab. The later Nabataean kingdom was annexed to the Roman Empire in A.D. 106. Arabs conquered the land in the 600s. After the Crusades it fell to the Mamelukes of Egypt, then in the 1500s to the Ottoman Turks. It remained part of their empire until British armies took the area in 1917–18.

Called Transjordan, the region became a British mandate in 1920. The British placed Abdullah ibn Hussein on the throne as emir in 1921.

## INDEPENDENCE

Britain ended its mandate and on May 25, 1946, recognized Abdullah as king of independent Transjordan (renamed Jordan in 1950).

In 1948 Jordan joined the Arab states in attacking the newly independent state of Israel. Jordan's British-led troops captured Jerusalem on May 15, 1948. After concluding an armistice with Israel in 1949, Abdullah annexed the Palestine area west of the Jordan River.

Abdullah was assassinated in 1951 and was succeeded by his son Talal, who was in turn deposed by parliament in 1952 because of mental illness. Talal's son Hussein became king in 1952 and was formally crowned on May 2, 1953.

Because Britain sided with Israel in the second Arab-Israeli war, in 1956, Jordan ordered Britain to remove its troops that had remained stationed in the country since 1946.

In the third Arab-Israeli war, in 1967, Israel defeated Jordan, capturing Arab Jerusalem and all of Jordan's territory west of the Jordan River.

After that war Palestine Arab guerrillas in Jordan continued attacks on Israel until King Hussein agreed to a new Arab-Israeli cease-fire on Aug. 7, 1970. This prompted the guerrillas to focus attention on their cause with a series of dramatic skyjackings. The Jordanian army persuaded Hussein to attack the Palestinians. A brief civil war erupted.

Although Jordan did not directly attack Israel in the fourth Arab-Israeli war, in October 1973, it sent troops to assist Syria.

In 1975 King Hussein, bowing to a decision by other Arab nations, gave up his claims to the west bank of the Jordan to the Palestine Liberation Organization (PLO), which hopes to establish an Arab Palestine state. Hussein's action brought him improved status with other Arab leaders and an influx of financial aid from oil-rich Arab nations.

King Hussein in February 1976 convened the nation's parliament that had been elected in 1967. It adopted a constitutional amendment enabling the king to postpone indefinitely any new parliamentary election.

In May 1976 the king revealed a $2 billion development plan designed to increase the nation's economic growth at a rate of 12% a year.

King Hussein denied reports published in American newspapers in February 1977 that he had received millions of dollars in payments from the CIA over the past 20 years.

Hussein met with PLO leader Yasir Arafat in March 1977 for the first time since the Jordanian army fought the Palestinians in 1970. The two discussed plans for a future Palestinian state on the west bank of the Jordan River.

The 41-year-old Hussein celebrated his silver jubilee as monarch in 1977, having ruled longer than any other contemporary Arab leader.

On June 15, 1978, Hussein married Elizabeth Halaby, 26, daughter of an American businessman. As queen she adopted the Arabic name Noor al-Hussein, meaning "Light of Hussein."

Hussein refused invitations to join peace negotiations in 1978–80 between Israel and Egypt.

In the Iraq-Iran war that broke out in 1980 Jordan supported Iraq. Jordan's port of Aqaba on the Red Sea became the main base for ships of the Soviet Union and other nations that brought war supplies to Iraq.

# KENYA

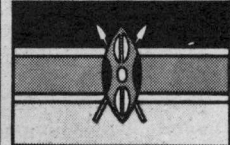

**Official Name:** Republic of Kenya.
**Area:** 224,961 square miles (582,646 sq. km.).
**Population:** 16,195,500.
**Chief Metropolitan Areas:** Nairobi, capital, 818,000; Mombasa, 391,000.
**Government:** One-party republic.
**President:** Daniel arap Moi (since 1978).
**National Assembly:** 170 members.
**U.S. Ambassador to Kenya:** William Harrop.
**Kenyan Ambassador to U.S.:** Peter Mbogua.
**Flag:** Black, red, and green bands separated by white stripes; red, black, and white shield over crossed white spears in center.
**Languages:** English and Swahili (official), Arabic.
**Main Ethnic Groups:** Kikuyu (20%), Luo (15%), Baluhya (13%), Kamba (11%), Kisii (6%), Meru (5%).
**Religions:** Animism (38%), Protestantism (37%), Roman Catholicism (22%), Islam (3%).
**Leading Industries:** Agriculture (coffee, tea, cattle, sugar cane, dairy products, poultry, pyrethrum [flower used in insecticides], sisal, corn, fruits, vegetables); tourism; manufacturing (processing farm products, oil refining, consumer goods); forestry and lumbering; mining (copper).
**Foreign Trade:** *major exports*—coffee, tea, sugar, sisal; *major imports*—crude petroleum, motor vehicles, agricultural machinery.
**Places of Interest:** Rift Valley; Treetops Hotel, west of Mt. Kenya; national museum in Nairobi; Nairobi, Tsavo, Aberdare, Lake Nakuru national parks; Masai Mara, Amboseli, and Samburu game reserves.

## KENYA TODAY

About as large as Arizona and New Mexico combined, Kenya has few important natural resources. Although the country's economy depends largely on agriculture, only about 12% of the land can be farmed and about 6% used for grazing livestock. Kenya's major exports are coffee and tea.

About three-fourths of the people depend on agriculture for a living. Only about 1 Kenyan in 5 can read and write, and many children never attend school.

Because Kenya must import all the petroleum it needs for energy, the nation was hard hit by soaring oil prices of the 1970s–80s. About one-third of its income from foreign trade goes to the purchase of petroleum, severely limiting the amount of money that can be used in development projects to broaden the base of the economy.

The single most important contribution to cash income is tourism, which brings more than 300,000 visitors each year. The nation's leading tourist attractions are the national park sanctuaries for lions, elephants, leopards, cheetahs, giraffes, zebras, gazelles, and other wild animals.

The country is noted for its topographic variety. The low-lying coast rises gently to a dry coast-

QUICK QUIZ: What is the postage to send a 2-ounce air-mail letter to Kenya? See page 695.

**KENYA** *(continued)*

al plain that gives way to a high plateau in the southwest (10,000 feet above sea level at some points). Most of the people and economic activity are located in the plateau area. Mt. Kenya, a perpetually snow-clad 17,058-foot peak, stands in the semidesert northern region.

The Great Rift Valley includes Lake Turkana (formerly Rudolf), the country's largest lake.

## EARLY HISTORY

Throughout the Middle Ages Kenya attracted Indian Ocean trade. In 1498 Portuguese explorers arrived and established trading posts, but they were driven out by the Arabs in 1729. From 1740 Arabs ruled the Kenyan coast from Zanzibar.

In 1887 the British East Africa Company leased the Kenyan coast from the sultan of Zanzibar. Kenya became a British protectorate in 1895. It was organized as a crown colony in 1920.

Jomo Kenyatta, as secretary of an association of the Kikuyu tribe, began campaigning in 1928 for land reform and political rights for Africans. When his campaign was ignored, Kenyatta organized a group called the Mau Mau that began a rebellion in 1952. During the next eight years over 12,000 persons died in the fighting. The British jailed Kenyatta from 1954 to 1961.

Britain agreed in 1960 to grant self-government to the black majority. Although Kenyatta's party, the Kenyan African National Union (KANU), won an election in February 1961, its members refused to take office until Kenyatta was released from confinement in August. KANU won another election in May 1963.

## INDEPENDENCE

Kenya was granted independence by Britain on Dec. 12, 1963, with Kenyatta as prime minister. Exactly one year later Kenya became a republic in the British Commonwealth of Nations with Kenyatta taking office as president.

In the spring of 1966 Ogingo Odinga, the nation's vice president, broke with Kenyatta and formed an opposition party, the Kenya People's Union (KPU).

Odinga was put under house arrest on Oct. 27, 1969, following an antigovernment demonstration by the KPU. Three days later the KPU was banned, leaving KANU the only legal political party in Kenya. On Nov. 11, 1969, Kenyatta was reelected to a second term.

The Kenyan government began a campaign to Africanize the country in March 1968. In the next six years thousands of Asian shopkeepers and businessmen were forced to leave Kenya.

The nation was hard hit by drought in 1974. Some 250,000 cattle—90% of the herds of the Masai tribes—were reported to have died.

Although Kenya is a one-party state, voters chose between rival KANU candidates in the 1974 parliamentary election. The voters defeated four of Kenyatta's cabinet ministers.

In July 1976 President Idi Amin of neighboring Uganda threatened to bomb Kenya. His threats came because Kenya had allowed Israel's planes to land for refueling after the daring July 4 raid on Uganda to rescue hostages held by Arab hijackers. Kenya called on its nationals to leave Uganda as war threatened. However, friendly relations were reestablished in August.

Because Kenyatta was in his eighties, concern rose in the 1970s as to what would happen to the nation when he died. When politicians attempted to hold public meetings on the subject they were warned by the attorney general in October 1976 that it was a crime punishable by death even to imagine the death of the president. No more meetings were held.

Tanzania closed its border with Kenya on Feb. 3, 1977, in a dispute over the shutting down of an airline that had been jointly operated by Kenya, Tanzania, and Uganda. Kenyan officials said it was an effort to prevent the people of socialist Tanzania from coming to Kenya to see the economic growth possible under free enterprise.

The first national election in 10 years for offices in KANU had been scheduled for April 3, 1977, but on April 2 they were postponed indefinitely "due to unavoidable circumstances."

In an effort to preserve Kenya's wildlife, which attracts thousands of tourists each year, the government announced on May 19, 1977, a ban on the killing of elephants, rhinoceroses, leopards, zebras, and other wild animals. The move was applauded by conservationists but was deplored by Kenya's 300 or more professional hunters, who were told to convert hunting trips for tourists into photographic safaris.

Kenya complained in June 1977 that its border was being violated by Somali troops and guerrillas crossing through Kenya to fight in Ethiopia. On July 20 Kenya and Somalia reached agreement on setting up a border commission to resolve the problem.

Kenyatta died in his sleep on Aug. 22, 1978. He was believed to be about 89, but had no record of his birth. Hundreds of thousands of Kenyans lined the route of his funeral procession that included representatives of 82 nations.

Daniel arap Moi, 54, who had served as vice president under Kenyatta, succeeded to the presidency without opposition. He was formally inaugurated as president on Oct. 14, 1978.

A former school headmaster, President Moi made one of his first decrees the abolition of school fees. He also ordered free milk served at schools and promised to increase the number of teachers and other school personnel by 10%.

To emphasize his belief in human rights, President Moi on Dec. 12, 1978, released all 16 prisoners who had been jailed by the Kenyatta regime for political reasons.

Kenya's fourth 5-year plan, for 1979–83, was initiated by President Moi in March 1979. It calls for major investments to be directed to increase the income levels of the poor by aiding small farmers and by providing greater employment opportunities in the cities. One of the major projects planned was to resettle farmers on unused or mismanaged land to increase the country's agricultural output.

In a national election on Nov. 8, 1979, President Moi was elected to a 5-year term. He was the only candidate for the office.

Kenya and the U.S. reached agreement on June 27, 1980, for American ships, planes and troops to use Kenya's ports and military bases. In return, the U.S. promised increased economic and military aid.

# KIRIBATI

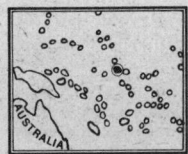

**Official Name:** Republic of Kiribati.
**Area:** 332 square miles (860 sq. km.).
**Population:** 53,146.
**Capital:** Bairiki, Tarawa, 10,616.
**Government:** Democratic republic.
**President:** Ieremia Tabai (since 1979).
**National Assembly:** 35 members.
**U.S. Ambassador to Kiribati:** William Bodde Jr.
**Flag:** Bird flying over rising gold sun in red sky; white and blue wavy stripes.
**Languages:** English and Gilbertese.
**Main Ethnic Group:** Micronesians.
**Major Religion:** Christianity.
**Leading Industries:** Agriculture (coconuts, breadfruit, pandanus, bananas, pawpaws); fishing (tuna, shrimp); handicrafts.
**Foreign Trade:** *major exports*—copra from coconuts, shrimp, handicrafts, postage stamps; *major imports*—food, fuel, clothing, lumber, consumer goods.
**Places of Interest:** Island villages, beaches.

Formerly known as the British colony of the Gilbert Islands, Kiribati includes 33 islands scattered across about 2 million square miles of the central and south Pacific Ocean.

The islands stretch about 3,000 miles from Ocean Island (Banaba) in the west to the southern Line Islands in the east.

The islands have almost no natural resources. Even the sandy soil is of poor quality for growing crops. The national economy is largely dependent on aid from Britain.

The first Europeans to sight the islands were Spanish navigators in the 1500s and 1600s.

The first European settlers in 1837 were deserters from whaling ships. From the 1850s to the 1870s trading ships visited the islands, kidnapping islanders to work as laborers on plantations elsewhere in the South Pacific.

Christianity was brought to the islands with the arrival in 1857 of the American protestant missionary Hiram Bingham.

In 1892 a British protectorate was declared for the Gilberts and the neighboring Ellice Islands (now Tuvalu). In 1916 Britain made the Gilbert and Ellice Islands a colony.

The islands were occupied by Japan in World War II, but they were recovered by the Allies in a fierce battle on Tarawa on Nov. 20–23, 1943, in which 4,690 Japanese troops and 1,087 U.S. Marines were killed.

Britain granted independence to Kiribati on July 12, 1979.

Ieremia (Jeremiah) Tabai, 29, was chosen in 1979 as Kiribati's first president.

In a treaty with the U.S. signed in September 1979, Kiribati received sovereignty over 14 islands in the Phoenix and Line groups, including Canton and Enderbury islands.

# KOREA, NORTH

**Official Name:** Democratic People's Republic of Korea.
**Area:** 46,540 square miles (120,538, sq. km.).
**Population:** 19,623,700.
**Chief Cities:** Pyongyang, the capital, 653,100; Chongjin, 184,300; Hungnam, 143,600; Kaesong, 139,900.
**Government:** One-party communist state.
**President:** Kim Il Sung (ruler since 1948).
**Prime Minister:** Li Jong Ok (since 1977).
**Supreme People's Assembly:** 541 members.
**Flag:** Large red center stripe bordered by thin white stripes and wider blue stripes; white circle enclosing red 5-pointed star on center stripe near hoist.
**Language:** Korean.
**Main Ethnic Group:** Korean.
**Major Religions:** Confucianism, Buddhism.
**Leading Industries:** Manufacturing (machines, electricity, chemicals, steel, textiles, cement, petroleum refining, aluminum); agriculture (rice, corn, vegetables); mining (coal, iron ore, graphite, petroleum, lead, nickel, tungsten, zinc).
**Foreign Trade:** *major exports*—food products, minerals; *major imports*—oil, wheat, machines.
**Places of Interest:** Diamond Mountains; Buddhist monasteries; Mt. Kwanmo; Pyongyang.

## NORTH KOREA TODAY

About the size of Mississippi, North Korea is a communist police state.

With economic and technical assistance from the Soviet Union and China, the country has developed heavy industry to produce machinery. It is among the world's leading nations in mining coal, lead, and zinc.

About half the people work and live on collective farms. The most important crop is rice.

The Korean peninsula is mountainous. The highest peak is Mt. Paektu (9,003 feet).

## COMMUNIST RULE

Korea's history (see Korea, South) is regionally inseparable until 1945. With the Japanese defeat at the end of World War II, the 38th parallel was established as an administrative convenience, not as a political dividing line. Americans accepted the surrender of Japanese forces in the south, and Soviet forces did the same in the north.

The Soviet Union set up the communist government of North Korea on Sept. 9, 1948. Kim Il Sung, a guerrilla in Manchuria before he fled to the Soviet Union in 1941, was made head of the government.

On June 25, 1950, the North Korean army invaded South Korea. The U.S. and 15 other United Nations members sent military forces to aid South Korea. Communist China entered the conflict in support of North Korea. A cease-fire agreement was reached in July 1953, and Korea was again divided at the 38th parallel.

On Jan. 23, 1968, the North Koreans cap-

QUICK QUIZ: What is the rate to send an air parcel-post package of 4 ounces to Kiribati? See page 698.

**KOREA, NORTH** *(continued)*
tured the USS *Pueblo* and imprisoned the crew for nearly a year before releasing them.

A new constitution was adopted in December 1972, establishing the office of president. Kim Il Sung, who had ruled for 24 years as premier, became president.

In 1974–75 South Koreans discovered that North Korea had made extensive new preparations for war, digging highway-wide tunnels under defenses at the 38th parallel.

North Korea established a 200-mile economic sea limit on Aug. 1, 1977, banning Japanese fishermen from an area extending all the way to Japan itself. At the same time it forbade all foreign military craft from coming closer than 50 miles of its coast without permission.

A recession and failure to meet economic goals by its heavy industry forced North Korea to default in 1977 on its estimated $2 billion in foreign debts, causing Japan, Switzerland, Sweden and other creditors to cut off further loans.

North Korea rejected in July 1979 a proposal by U.S. President Carter for three-way talks among the two Koreas and the U.S. to reduce tension and lead to eventual unification of North and South Korea.

In September 1979 the U.S. disclosed discovery of a new North Korean tunnel, the fourth found since 1974, that had been dug under the demilitarized zone to prepare for a sneak attack on South Korea.

To ensure that his 39-year-old son Kim Jong Il would succeed him as ruler, 68-year-old President Kim Il Sung in 1980 named his son to the influential post of secretary of the country's Communist Party.

## KOREA, SOUTH

**Official Name:** Republic of Korea.
**Area:** 38,025 square miles (98,484 sq. km.).
**Population:** 40,090,600.
**Chief Cities:** Seoul, capital, 6,879,464; Pusan, 2,450,125; Taegu, 1,309,131; Inchon, 797,143.
**Largest Metropolitan Area:** Seoul, 7,500,000.
**Government:** Martial law.
**President:** Chun Doo Hwan (since 1980).
**Prime Minister:** Nam Duck Woo (since 1980).
**National Assembly:** 231 members.
**U.S. Ambassador to South Korea:** William H. Gleysteen Jr.
**South Korean Ambassador to U.S.:** Yong Shik Kim.
**Flag:** White field with circular emblem divided in half by curved line (red top and blue bottom); black bar design in each corner.
**Language:** Korean.
**Principal Ethnic Group:** Korean.
**Religions:** Confucianism, Shamanism, Christianity, Buddhism, Chodokyo.
**Leading Industries:** Agriculture (rice, wheat, barley, beans, cotton, livestock, poultry); manufacturing (steel, textiles, cement, electricity, plastics, clothing, plywood, electronics, chemicals); fishing; forestry

and lumbering; mining (coal, iron ore, tungsten, graphite).
**Foreign Trade:** *major exports*—plywood, raw silk, cotton fabrics, electronics, iron and steel; *major imports*—transport equipment, rice, raw cotton, wheat, crude petroleum, textile machinery.
**Places of Interest:** Restored ancient capital, Kyongju; Cheju Island. *In Seoul:* National museum in Duksoo Palace; Changduk Palace and Secret Garden; Kyungbok Palace; Pagoda Park; Kings' Tomb.

## SOUTH KOREA TODAY

About the size of Indiana, South Korea is a small Asian country that won its independence from Japan after World War II. In the 1950s the U.S. and the United Nations helped South Korea preserve its independence during the Korean War, in which communist North Korea and China attempted to overrun the country.

South Korea had one of the most rapidly expanding economies in the world in the 1960s–70s. Its gross national product grew from $2.27 billion in 1962 to $58.6 billion in 1979. However, most of the people are poor.

Although South Korea is a constitutional republic, the country has been ruled since it was created by dictators with little regard for human rights.

The U.S. maintains armed forces in South Korea to protect it from attack by North Korea.

The mountainous peninsula has many harbors along the west coast. Summers are hot and humid. Winters are cold and dry.

## EARLY HISTORY

According to Korean legend, Tangun founded Korean civilization about 4,300 years ago. Korea's recorded history began in the 1100s B.C. when a Chinese prince, Ki-tze, founded a colony at Pyongyang. Chinese influence remained until about 100 B.C., when three warring tribes (Silla, Koguryo, and Paekche) came to power.

Silla kings with their capital at Kyongju united the country in A.D. 668. A new kingdom, Koryo, ruled the Korean peninsula in 935–1392. In the 1200s the Mongols conquered the land. In 1637 Korea fell to the Manchu rulers of China. Because of its isolation, Korea became known as the Hermit Kingdom.

In 1876 Korea was forced by Japan to open its ports to outside trade. Six years later Korea signed a commercial treaty with the U.S. In 1895 Japan won a war against the Chinese in Korea. Russia tried to acquire Korea but was defeated by Japan in 1905.

In 1910 Japan formally annexed Korea as a colony. The Koreans opposed Japanese rule. In 1919 a government-in-exile was formed in Shanghai under Syngman Rhee.

In 1945, near the end of World War II, Soviet troops entered the northern part of Korea. A month later, American forces landed in the south. The U.S. and Soviet Union agreed on a purely administrative dividing line across Korea—the 38th parallel.

## INDEPENDENT SOUTH KOREA

On Aug. 15, 1948, a separate pro-western government was established for South Korea. Syngman Rhee became president.

U.S. troops were withdrawn by June 1949.

On June 25, 1950, the North Korean army invaded South Korea. The U.S. and UN came to the support of South Korea, and 16 member nations sent troops. Communist China entered the war on the side of North Korea in 1951. A cease-fire was achieved in July 1953. Korea remained divided at the 38th parallel.

President Rhee served from 1948 to 1960, when charges of election-rigging led to his resignation and subsequent exile. New elections were held, but on May 16, 1961, the government was ousted by a military junta headed by Gen. Park Chung Hee. In 1963 he was elected president.

In the fall of 1972 President Park imposed martial law on South Korea, closed the schools, established press censorship, and changed the constitution to permit his reelection.

In 1975 President Park made it a crime for anyone to criticize the constitution or to criticize the government to foreigners.

President Park in February 1977 announced that a new capital would be built by 1981 about 60 miles south of Seoul.

U.S. President Jimmy Carter announced plans in 1977 for a gradual withdrawal by 1982 of American troops from South Korea, leaving about 12,000 noncombat personnel as the only U.S. military forces based on Asia's mainland.

President Park was reelected to a fourth term on July 6, 1978, by a special 2,583-member electoral assembly.

In a parliamentary election on Dec. 12, 1978, the opposition New Democratic Party (NDP) won 34% of the vote to 32% by President Park's Democratic Republican Party (DRP). However, 15 independent members joined with the governing party to give it a majority of 86 to the NDP's 68 among the elected members. Park's control of parliament was augmented by the appointment of 77 additional members to give the DRP a total of 163 seats.

For the first time in almost six years, South Korean and North Korean officials met in 1979 at Panmunjom in a series of sessions to discuss possible reunification of Korea.

U.S. President Carter visited South Korea from June 29 to July 1, 1979. After returning to the United States, he announced on July 20 that the withdrawal of the remaining 32,000 U.S. combat troops in South Korea would be postponed at least until 1981.

President Park was assassinated on Oct. 26, 1979, by Kim Jae Kyu, head of the Korean central intelligence agency, who was arrested and executed. Martial law was imposed throughout the nation with army chief of staff Gen. Chung Seung Hwa in charge. Prime Minister Choi Kyu Han became president.

Younger military officers overthrew Gen. Chung on Dec. 12, 1979. Maj. Gen. Chun Doo Hwan emerged as the new military strongman.

When thousands of students rioted in May 1980, protesting continued military rule, the government closed the universities. A rebellion in Kwangju was put down with troops and tanks on May 27.

In the following months tens of thousands of opponents to the regime were imprisoned without trial. Former presidential candidate Kim Dae Jung, the most prominent spokesman for democracy, was arrested, tried by a military court, and on Sept. 17, 1980, was sentenced to death.

After forcing President Choi to resign, Chun had himself made president. In his inaugural address on Sept. 1, 1980, he promised elections in 1981 under a new constitution that opponents said was designed to keep him in power.

# KUWAIT

 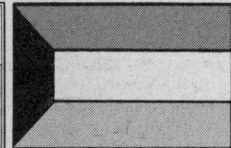

**Official Name:** State of Kuwait.
**Area:** 6,880 square miles (17,818 sq. km.).
**Population:** 1,391,330.
**Chief Cities:** Kuwait, capital, 700,000; Hawalli, 106,542; Salmiyyah, 38,791.
**Government:** Monarchy (emirate).
**Emir:** Sheik Jabir al-Ahmad al-Sabah (since 1977).
**Prime Minister and Crown Prince:** Sheik Saad al-Abdullah Al-Sabah (since 1977).
**National Assembly:** 50 members.
**U.S. Ambassador to Kuwait:** Francois M. Dickman.
**Kuwaiti Ambassador to U.S.:** Khalid M. Jaffar.
**Flag:** Green, white, and red stripes, with black trapezoid at flagstaff.
**Languages:** Arabic (official), Persian, English.
**Main Ethnic Group:** Arab (85%).
**Religion:** Islam (99%).
**Leading Industries:** Mining (petroleum, natural gas); construction; manufacturing and processing (electricity, desalination of seawater, oil refining, ammonia, fertilizer, cement, consumer products); shipping; fishing; agriculture (sheep, goats, wheat, dates, vegetables).
**Foreign Trade:** *major export*—petroleum; *major imports*—food, oil refinery equipment, automobiles, trucks, machinery, consumer goods.
**Places of Interest:** Oil wells; modern city of Kuwait; royal residences; seaport of Mina al-Ahmad.

## KUWAIT TODAY

About the size of New Jersey, Kuwait is one of the most prosperous countries in the world. The Middle East's third-largest producer of oil, Kuwait has about one-quarter of the world's oil reserves. Its people pay no taxes.

Kuwait has given and loaned billions of dollars to poorer Arab states, has invested billions in the United States and other industrial countries, and has purchased planes and other equipment for Arab states opposing Israel.

The government also has used its oil wealth to give free medical services, education, a 124-acre amusement park, and other benefits to everyone in Kuwait. Local telephone service is also free, and almost every family owns at least one car and one TV set.

The government holds down food costs by

QUICK QUIZ: How many seconds are there in one day? See page 719.

## KUWAIT *(continued)*

subsidizing food imports.

Abundant natural gas provides energy for Kuwait's expanding industries. The nation's capital is a thriving modern city on Kuwait Bay.

### EARLY HISTORY

Kuwait was founded about 1740 by Arab nomads who migrated from northern Arabia to the Persian Gulf coast. Sabah Abu Abdullah founded an emirate there in 1756. Under his successors, Kuwait's population grew to several thousand.

The British came to Kuwait's aid when it was threatened in the first half of the 1800s by the Wahabi of Arabia, a puritanical Muslim sect that waged holy war against all other forms of Islam. Following a struggle for supremacy by the two great tribal families of the area, the al-Rashids and the Saudis, the latter fled to Kuwait. Emir al-Sabah helped Abdul-Aziz ibn Saud regain his territories, the nucleus of modern Saudi Arabia.

In 1897 the emir of Kuwait, fearful that the Turks would extend more than nominal control over his territory, asked the British for protection. An agreement in 1899 made Kuwait a quasi-protectorate of Britain.

In 1919 Saudi Arabia invaded Kuwait but was repelled with the help of the British. The Saudis placed a land blockade on Kuwait that lasted 20 years, although in 1922 the two governments established the Neutral Zone in which they shared sovereignty until 1966, when the zone was partitioned between them.

With the discovery of oil in Kuwait in 1938, and its development after 1945, Iraq decided in 1952 to renew an ancient claim to Kuwait. This was promptly rejected by the British.

### INDEPENDENCE

By mutual consent the British protectorate was revoked on June 19, 1961, and Kuwait became a fully independent nation.

Several hundred thousand Arab refugees from the Arab-Israeli wars (1948–73) were allowed to settle in Kuwait.

Kuwait and Saudi Arabia signed an agreement on Dec. 18, 1969, dividing a previous 2,000-square-mile Neutral Zone between them and establishing a new boundary.

Iraqi troops invaded Kuwait on March 20, 1973, near the Persian Gulf, claiming the boundary between the countries had never been settled. After Saudi Arabia sent more than 15,000 troops to assist Kuwait, Iraq withdrew.

In 1975 the government bought complete control of the oil and gas industry from the U.S. and other foreign owners. Its gross national product doubled from 1974 to 1975, reaching more than $10.6 billion a year.

Sheik Sabah, who had ruled since 1965, dissolved the elected parliament and ended freedom of the press on Aug. 29, 1976, in a dispute with Palestinian radicals.

Sheik Jabir al-Ahmad al-Sabah became emir on Dec. 31, 1977, after Sheik Sabah died of a heart attack. He announced plans in 1980 to hold an election in 1981 for a new parliament.

The nation's 1976–81 development plan calls for spending $16.6 billion with emphasis placed on new housing and manufacturing enterprises.

# LAOS

**Official Name:** Lao People's Democratic Republic.
**Area:** 91,429 square miles (236,800 sq. km.).
**Population:** 3,761,340.
**Chief Cities:** Vientiane, capital, 132,253; Luang Prabang, 42,000.
**Government:** Communist one-party state.
**President:** Prince Souphanouvong (since 1975).
**Prime Minister:** Kaysone Phomvihan (since 1975).
**Flag:** Narrow red stripes top and bottom; wide blue stripe in middle with large white circle.
**Languages:** Lao (official), French.
**Main Ethnic Group:** Lao.
**Religions:** Buddhism and animism.
**Leading Industries:** Agriculture (rice, coffee, tea, cattle, fruits, vegetables, corn, cotton, tobacco); mining (tin, iron ore); fishing; manufacturing (textiles, handicrafts); forestry and lumbering.
**Foreign Trade:** *major exports*—tin, teak, coffee; *major imports*—rice and other foods, petroleum, transport equipment, consumer goods.
**Places of Interest:** Annamite Cordillera; former royal palace, wats (temples) and pagodas. *In Vientiane:* Shrine of That Luang; Luang Prabang.

### LAOS TODAY

Somewhat smaller than Oregon, Laos is a mountainous Southeast Asian country ruled by communists. It is the only communist-ruled nation of former French Indochina with which the U.S. has not broken diplomatic relations.

One of the poorest and most underdeveloped nations of the world, Laos depends on aid from other countries to import the food and other goods its people need to survive. Most of the people are poverty-stricken rice farmers. Few can read or write.

Over 80% of the country is rugged jungle terrain. The flatlands are mostly in the valleys of the Mekong River and its tributaries.

### EARLY HISTORY

First settled in the 1100s by refugee Thai tribes from China, Laotian territory was the seat of the Buddhist kingdom of Lan Xang, founded in 1353 by King Fa Ngum. In 1707 the kingdom split into two regions: Luang Prabang in the north and Vientiane in the south.

France made Laos a protectorate in 1893.

Japanese forces invaded Laos in 1941. Just before Japan's World War II surrender in September 1945, King Sisavang Vong of Luang Prabang proclaimed himself king of all Laos. On Oct. 12, 1945, nationalists of the Free Laos movement declared the country independent. French troops reoccupied Laos in May 1946.

### INDEPENDENT KINGDOM

Laos became an associated state in the French Union on July 19, 1949. France granted Laos full independence on Oct. 22, 1953.

A communist movement, the Pathet Lao, was

created by Prince Souphanouvong in 1950. Three years later Vietnamese communists invaded Laos to assist the Pathet Lao. The conference at Geneva in 1954 that ended the Indochina War brought a cease-fire to Laos.

In 1957 Laos' premier, Prince Souvanna Phouma, and his half-brother, Prince Souphanouvong, formed a coalition government. Sri Savang Vatthanna became king on Nov. 4, 1959, after the death of his father, King Sisavang Vong.

Civil war with the communist Pathet Lao again broke out in 1960. The U.S. supported government forces.

On Feb. 8, 1971, South Vietnam forces, with U.S. air support, drove into Laos to cut the Ho Chi Minh Trail, a road used by North Vietnam.

Following the Vietnam War cease-fire in early 1973, the Laotian government signed a cease-fire agreement with the Pathet Lao, ending 10 years of war at noon on Feb. 22, 1973.

## COMMUNIST TAKE-OVER OF LAOS

After communists conquered South Vietnam in the spring of 1975, the Pathet Lao moved to occupy strategic positions held by government forces. On Dec. 3, 1975, the communists forced King Sri Savang Vatthanna to abdicate, ending the 622-year-old monarchy. The communists proclaimed a new government called the *Lao People's Democratic Republic.* Prince Souphanouvong became the first president of Laos. The new premier was Kaysone Phomvihan, secretary-general of the Laotian Communist Party.

The government arrested hundreds of former political leaders in April 1976 in what was called a "cultural revolution." About 500 of the prisoners broke out of jail in Vientiane on April 25, 1976, and some escaped to Thailand.

With financial support from the Asian Development Bank in 1976, Laos planned to complete the Nam Ngum River hydroelectric project.

In an effort to build a larger population, the government in 1976 banned all birth control.

In March 1977 the government reported that it had arrested 69-year-old former King Sri Savang Vatthanna, his wife, and children, sending them to a "reeducation center" to be taught to grow vegetables and learn Marxist-Leninist principles.

A severe drought in 1977 caused an estimated 60% loss in the rice crop. The government appealed to other countries to send rice to save the Laotian people from starvation.

France broke diplomatic relations with Laos on Aug. 22, 1978, after the Laotian government expelled French diplomats on charges they were aiding guerrillas in attacks on the communists.

An American congressional delegation that visited Laos in August 1978 received the bodies of four U.S. pilots, the first information on 230 servicemen missing in action in Laos.

As an ally of Vietnam and the Soviet Union, Laos sent troops to aid Vietnam in its 1979 conquest of Cambodia.

Thousands of Lao people fled from the country to neighboring Thailand in 1979, adding to the estimated 200,000 Laotian refugees who had left the country in 1975–78 to escape the repression of the communist regime.

# LEBANON

**Official Name:** Republic of Lebanon.
**Area:** 4,015 square miles (10,400 sq. km.).
**Population:** 3,058,670.
**Chief Cities:** Beirut, capital, 474,870; Tripoli, 127,611.
**Largest Metropolitan Area:** Beirut, 938,940.
**Government:** Parliamentary republic.
**Prime Minister:** Shafiq al-Wazan (since 1980).
**President:** Elias Sarkis (since 1976).
**Chamber of Deputies:** 99 members.
**U.S. Ambassador to Lebanon:** John Gunther Dean.
**Lebanese Ambassador to U.S.:** Khalil Itani.
**Flag:** Red, white, and red stripes, with green cedar tree in white stripe.
**Languages:** Arabic (official), French, English, Armenian.
**Principal Ethnic Groups:** Arab (94%), Armenian (6%).
**Religions:** Christianity (50%), Islam (50%).
**Leading Industries:** Trade and banking; manufacturing (oil refining, textiles, food processing, cement, tobacco products); agriculture (sheep, poultry, fruits, vegetables, grapes, figs, wheat, cotton); tourism.
**Foreign Trade:** *major exports*—apples, pears, quinces, eggs, dried beans, wool; *major imports*—animals, automobiles, wheat, beans, gasoline.
**Places of Interest:** Baalbeck temple; ruins at Anjar and Byblos; Tyre excavations; Beit-Eddine Palace; Castle of the Sea at Saida (Sidon); Jeita Grotto; Beirut Museum; Tripoli citadel.

## LEBANON TODAY

Smaller than Connecticut, Lebanon is a Middle Eastern Arab nation torn by civil war, fought among Christian rightists, Muslim leftists, and troops of Syria, Israel, and the UN. The fighting wrecked the nation's cities and destroyed Lebanon's previously prosperous economy. Hundreds of people continued to be killed each year in the 1980s as opposing militants battled each other.

Prior to the civil war, Lebanon had been the trading and banking center of the Arab world, being known as the "Zurich of the Middle East." As the most industrialized of the Arab nations, Lebanon supplied many trained technicians and managers to assist other Arab countries.

With a population almost evenly divided between Christians and Muslims, Lebanon had endeavored to achieve political stability by traditionally choosing a Christian as president and a Muslim as prime minister. Unlike the people in other Arab countries, most Lebanese could read and write and took an active part in elective politics.

A major factor leading to political dissension was the presence of refugee camps for about 400,000 Palestinian Arabs made homeless by the Arab-Israeli wars. The Palestine Liberation Organization (PLO) used these camps as a training ground for Arab guerrillas to make frequent terrorist attacks on Israel. In turn Israeli armed

**LEBANON** (continued)

forces have made retaliatory strikes into Lebanon. Syrian and UN troops became involved in the fighting in an effort to impose peace.

The Lebanon Mountains dominate the country's landscape. To the west is a narrow coastal plain where the largest cities are located.

The Mediterranean coast has a mild climate the year round. But the mountain regions have heavy snows that attract skiing enthusiasts.

## EARLY HISTORY

In ancient times the Phoenicians, who lived in what is now Lebanon, spread civilization throughout the Mediterranean as seafaring traders and colonizers. The Phoenician city-state of Tyre reached its peak of prosperity about 1000 B.C. Persians, Assyrians, Babylonians, Egyptians, and the Greeks under Alexander the Great fought in turn for the area. In time it came under Roman rule along with Syria. A Christian sect, the Maronites, settled there, and while Syria became Muslim, Lebanon remained mainly Christian.

After centuries of warfare and invasion, the Middle East was unified under the Ottoman Empire in the 1500s. Egyptian occupation in 1832 increased tension between the Christian Maronites and the Islamic Druses. Fearing annihilation, the Maronites appealed for help.

European powers in 1864 forced the Turks to agree to a pro-Christian government for the province of Mount Lebanon that was created.

After World War I France received a mandate over Lebanon. It became a republic in 1926.

## INDEPENDENCE

Lebanon declared its independence on Nov. 26, 1941, but France refused to recognize Lebanon's sovereignty until Nov. 27, 1943. French troops withdrew in December 1946.

Although a member of the Arab League, Lebanon had a minor role in the Arab-Israeli wars of 1948 and 1956. It did not participate in the 1967 and 1973 wars.

A civil war began in 1975 among rightist Christians, leftist Muslims, and Palestinian guerrillas. With the acquiescence of the U.S. and Israel, 30,000 Syrian troops intervened in April 1976 on the side of the rightists.

The Syrian army took control of Beirut on Nov. 15, 1976, putting an end to the heaviest fighting that had killed about 60,000.

Israeli troops invaded southern Lebanon on March 14, 1978, destroying Palestinian strongholds, but withdrew in June after a UN peacekeeping force arrived in the area.

Lebanon's parliament elected a Christian banker, Elias Sarkis, as president in 1976.

Despite the presence of 6,000 UN peace-keeping troops, fighting continued between Christian militia and Palestinians in southern Lebanon. Israeli artillery repeatedly bombarded the region in support of the Christian militia, and Israeli forces raided in retaliation for Palestinian terrorist attacks in Israel.

The leader of the Christian militia in southern Lebanon, Maj. Saad Haddad, 45, on April 19, 1979, declared independence for the region, which he called *Free Lebanon*. Lebanon's government in Beirut charged Haddad with treason.

# LESOTHO

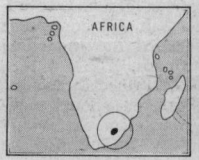 

**Official Name:** Kingdom of Lesotho.
**Area:** 11,720 square miles (30,355 sq. km.).
**Population:** 1,360,720.
**Capital:** Maseru, 13,312.
**Government:** Dictatorship.
**Prime Minister:** Leabua Jonathan (since 1965).
**King:** Motlotlehi Moshoeshoe II (since 1966).
**Parliament:** *National Assembly,* 60; *Senate,* 33.
**U.S. Ambassador to Lesotho:** John R. Clingerman.
**Lesotho Ambassador to U.S.:** 'M'alineo N. Tau.
**Flag:** Parallel bars of green and red at hoist, with white conical Basuto hat on blue field.
**Official Languages:** English and Sesotho.
**Ethnic Groups:** Sotho (85%), Ngun (15%).
**Religions:** Christianity (70%), animism (30%).
**Leading Industries:** Agriculture (corn, wheat, sorghum, peas, beans, sheep, cattle); mining (diamonds); manufacturing (carpets, candles, fertilizer, pottery, jewelry).
**Foreign Trade:** *major exports*—wool, cattle, mohair, diamonds; *major imports*—food, machinery, vehicles, consumer goods.
**Places of Interest:** Drakensberg Mountains; bushmen cave and cliff paintings in Cave Sandstone area; Sehlabathebe National Park.

A little larger than the state of Maryland, Lesotho has few known natural resources. About a fourth of the country's men travel to South Africa for several months each year to earn cash by working in the mines. Otherwise most of the people live in tribal villages, farming for a living. About 4 of 10 persons can read and write. Heavily dependent on foreign aid, Lesotho imports food and other goods worth 12 times its exports.

Lesotho is a rugged, mile-high plateau country nestled amid the 11,000-foot peaks of the Drakensberg Mountains. Only about 10% of the land can be farmed. Temperatures average 45° F. in July and 70° F. in January.

Formerly called *Basutoland,* Lesotho is landlocked by South Africa on three sides and by Transkei to the south.

The Basotho nation came into being in 1818 under the leadership of Moshesh I. In 1867 the Basotho requested British protection against Boer advances from South Africa, and in 1868 Britain annexed Basutoland. Internal self-government was introduced in 1959.

Independence was granted on Oct. 4, 1966, with Leabua Jonathan as prime minister.

The country's first election since independence was held on Jan. 31, 1970. Jonathan declared the results invalid, suspended the constitution, and arrested members of the opposition.

Jonathan ruled as dictator by decree. In April 1973 he established an appointed national assembly. Opponents tried to overthrow Jonathan's rule in January 1975. A court found 18 persons guilty of treason in the coup attempt.

Guerrilla warfare against Chief Jonathan's dictatorship intensified in 1979–80.

# LIBERIA

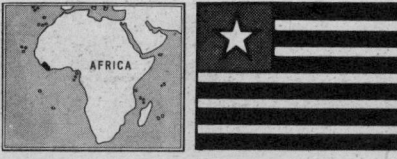

**Official Name:** Republic of Liberia.
**Area:** 43,000 square miles (111,369 sq. km.).
**Population:** 1,894,460.
**Capital:** Monrovia, 96,226.
**Government:** Military dictatorship.
**President:** Samuel K. Doe (since 1980).
**Military Junta:** People's Redemption Council (PRC), 17 members.
**U.S. Ambassador to Liberia:** Robert P. Smith.
**Flag:** Alternating stripes of red and white, with blue square containing white star in upper hoist corner.
**Religions:** Animism (75%), Islam (15%), Christianity (10%).
**Main Ethnic Group:** Black.
**Languages:** English (official), many tribal languages.
**Leading Industries:** Agriculture (rice, cassava, coffee, sugarcane, tobacco, cocoa, rubber, palm kernels, citrus fruits, vegetables); mining (iron ore, diamonds, gold); shipping; manufacturing (soap, plastics, paint, paper products, textiles, building materials, fertilizer, tobacco products); forestry and lumbering; tourism.
**Foreign Trade:** *major exports*—iron ore, rubber, diamonds, coffee, cacao; *major imports*—machinery, transport equipment, manufactured goods.
**Places of Interest:** Atlantic coast beaches and resorts; Providence Island; Monrovia; Lake Piso; Bong mine; Totota Zoo; LAMCO mining site.

## LIBERIA TODAY

About the size of Ohio, Liberia is one of the world's 10 leading producers of iron ore and natural rubber. Most of the people lead a tribal life in the country's tropical forests.

One of Liberia's most pressing problems as it seeks to become an industrial nation is to improve and expand its educational system to provide skilled workers and technicians and managers. Only about 2 in 10 Liberians can read and write. The majority of the people speak tribal dialects.

The world's largest merchant fleet sails under the Liberian flag—over 2,600 ships. Most are owned by Americans, Greeks, and other foreigners who register the ships in Liberia to avoid strict control. Ship registration fees make up about 8% of Liberia's gross national product.

Liberia lies on the west coast of Africa. Guinea is to the north, Ivory Coast to the east, and Sierra Leone to the northwest.

## LIBERIA'S HISTORY

The colony of Liberia was founded for liberated American slaves in 1822 by the National Colonization Society, a white abolitionist group whose agents governed the area until 1847.

The Republic of Liberia was established on July 26, 1847, becoming the first black African colony to gain independence.

Beginning in 1926, in exchange for a U.S. loan, it allowed American companies to develop rubber plantations.

Huge iron-ore deposits were discovered in 1955 at Mt. Nimba on the border with Guinea. Shipments from the mines began in 1963. Iron ore accounts for over half of the nation's exports.

From 1877 to 1980 the True Whigs governed as the country's only political party. William V. S. Tubman, president of Liberia from 1943 until his death on July 23, 1971, was responsible for many social and economic reforms. Tubman was succeeded by William R. Tolbert Jr.

U.S. President Carter visited Liberia on April 3, 1978, in the first trip by an American chief executive to black nations of Africa.

When the government proposed an increase in the consumer price of rice in 1979, protesters marched on the presidential mansion. Soldiers killed 41 demonstrators.

Master Sgt. Samuel K. Doe, 28, led a coup on April 12, 1980, in which President Tolbert and 27 others were killed. Doe made himself president, forming a 17-member military junta called the People's Redemption Council (PRC) to run the government under martial law. On April 22 the new rulers publicly executed 13 of the leading officials of Tolbert's government.

# LIBYA

**Official Name:** Socialist People's Libyan Arab Jamahiriya.
**Area:** 679,362 square miles (1,759,540 sq. km.).
**Population:** 3,046,980.
**Chief Cities:** Tripoli, capital, 213,506; Benghazi, 137,295.
**Government:** Socialist military dictatorship.
**Head of State:** Col. Mu'ammar al-Qadhafi (since 1969).
**Flag:** Green field.
**Languages:** Arabic (official), Berber.
**Main Ethnic Groups:** Arab and Berber.
**Official Religion:** Islam (97%).
**Leading Industries:** Mining (petroleum); agriculture (cattle, sheep, goats, peanuts, olives, grapes, dates, barley, wheat); construction; manufacturing (petroleum products, textiles, tobacco products).
**Foreign Trade:** *major exports*—petroleum, hides and skins, peanuts; *major imports*—machinery, clothing, automobiles, wheat flour.
**Places of Interest:** Marble arch of Marcus Aurelius in Tripoli; 2d century amphitheater at Sabratha; ancient city of Leptis; Cyrene archaeological site.

## LIBYA TODAY

Over twice as large as Texas, Libya is largely covered by the hot, nearly uninhabited Sahara Desert. Most Libyans live along the 1,100-mile Mediterranean coast. Yet oil fields in the Sahara make Libya a leading oil-producing nation.

The socialist military dictator who rules Libya gives the people little voice in their government.

The government uses much of its oil riches to

QUICK QUIZ: The fraction ¹⁸/₂₅ is the equivalent of what percent? See page 721.

## LIBYA *(continued)*

purchase jet fighter planes and other military equipment, and to finance Palestine Arab terrorists. But substantial sums also are spent to provide social services, public works, agriculture, and industrial development.

Most of the people are very poor, and only about 3 in 10 can read and write. Three-fourths of the Libyans are farmers or livestock herders. The orthodox Islamic religion is the official faith, placing women in a secondary role to men.

Egypt and Sudan lie to the east, Tunisia and Algeria to the west, and Niger and Chad to the south.

### EARLY HISTORY

Beginning about 630 B.C. Greeks colonized northeastern Libya, called Cyrenaica. About the same time Phoenicians colonized northwestern Libya, or Tripolitania, which became part of the state of Carthage. In the 1st century B.C. both became part of the Roman Empire.

In A.D. 642–643 Libya was conquered by Arabs, who converted the local Berber peoples to Islam.

Libya became part of the Ottoman Turkish Empire in 1551. Ottoman rule ended when Italy invaded Libya in 1911, making it a colony.

The Muslim leader Mohammed Idris fought Italian rule from 1916 until British troops captured Libya during World War II in October 1942. The country remained under British administration as a UN trust until 1951.

### INDEPENDENCE

Libya became independent on Dec. 24, 1951, with Idris as king. The discovery of oil in 1959 brought wealth.

The 79-year-old King Idris was overthrown on Sept. 1, 1969, in a bloodless military coup led by Col. Mu'ammar al-Qadhafi. He proclaimed the country a republic with himself as head of state. Qadhafi then ruled as a socialist dictator.

Libya nationalized foreign-owned oil companies in 1973–74 and joined the Arab oil embargo of countries that had befriended Israel in the Arab-Israeli war in 1973.

The Libyan leader completed publication of his 2-volume *Green Book* in 1978 in which he described a utopian "new socialist society" that he hopes to create in Libya.

Qadhafi helped lead Arab opposition to Egypt's peace treaty with Israel in 1979.

A Libyan mob attacked and burned the U.S. embassy in Tripoli on Dec. 2, 1979. Four months later, in May 1980, the U.S. withdrew all diplomats but did not break diplomatic relations.

The Libyan government paid $220,000 to the U.S. President Carter's brother Billy in 1980 in an effort to influence U.S. government policies.

Syria and Libya signed an agreement on Sept. 10, 1980, to merge their governments into a single state. However, most observers believed the arrangement was little more than a military alliance.

After war broke out between Iran and Iraq in 1980, both Libya and Syria supported Iran with military supplies.

Agents of Qadhafi carried out a wave of assassinations in Europe in 1980, killing opposition Libyans living in exile.

## LIECHTENSTEIN

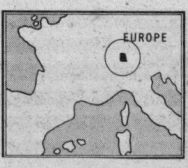 

**Official Name:** Principality of Liechtenstein.
**Area:** 61 square miles (157 sq. km.).
**Population:** 25,887.
**Capital:** Vaduz, 4,000.
**Government:** Constitutional principality.
**Prime Minister:** Hans Brunhart (since 1978).
**Chief of State:** Prince Franz Josef II (since 1938).
**Legislature:** *Diet,* 15 members.
**Flag:** Blue and red; gold crown in blue stripe.
**Language:** German.
**Principal Ethnic Group:** German.
**Religion:** Roman Catholicism (92%).
**Leading Industries:** Manufacturing (precision instruments, textiles, ceramics, pharmaceuticals, false teeth, food processing); banking; tourism; agriculture (cattle, dairy products, grapes, corn, potatoes, wheat, vegetables).
**Foreign Trade:** *major exports*—textiles, pottery, instruments, pharmaceuticals, postage stamps; *major imports*—food, manufactured goods.
**Place of Interest:** Mt. Naafkopf; medieval village of Vaduz and the prince's 700-year-old castle; ski resort at Malbun.

Liechtenstein is the most highly industrialized country in the world, with only 7% of the people dependent on farming for their living. Its prosperous people enjoy a high standard of living.

Because of low taxes, about 25,000 foreign businesses have headquarters in Liechtenstein.

Thousands of tourists visit each year. There are many hotels and ski resorts.

The sale of postage stamps provides a large share of the government's annual budget.

Covering an area smaller than Cleveland, Ohio, Liechtenstein is bordered by Austria on the east and Switzerland on the north, south, and west. Warm winds protect the country from temperature extremes. Summers are cool and winters are cold with much snow.

The barony of Schellenberg and the county of Vaduz, founded in 814, were bought by Johann Adam von Liechtenstein in 1699 and 1712. The Holy Roman emperor joined the two areas to create the principality of Liechtenstein in 1719.

Following French and Russian invasions during the Napoleonic wars, Liechtenstein joined the German Confederation in 1815. Ties with Austria developed, leading to withdrawal from the confederation in 1866. It remained neutral in both World War I and World War II.

Since 1924 Switzerland has administered the principality's defense, foreign affairs, and customs.

In 1973 a national referendum was held in which the men voted 2,128 to 1,675 against giving women the right to vote.

In a national election, Feb. 3, 1978, the Patriotic Union Party won control of parliament, making its leader, 32-year-old Hans Brunhart, the youngest prime minister in Europe.

The nation in 1978 celebrated the 40th anniversary of rule by 72-year-old Franz Josef II.

# LUXEMBOURG

# MADAGASCAR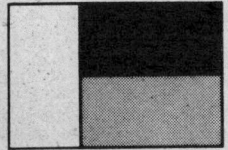

**Official Name:** Grand Duchy of Luxembourg.
**Area:** 998 square miles (2,586 sq. km.).
**Population:** 359,076.
**Capital:** Luxembourg-Ville, 78,400.
**Government:** Constitutional grand duchy.
**Prime Minister:** Pierre Werner (since 1979).
**Chief of State:** Grand Duke Jean (since 1964).
**Legislature:** *Council of State,* 21 members; *Chamber of Deputies,* 59 members.
**U.S. Ambassador to Luxembourg:** James Lowenstein.
**Luxembourgian Ambassador to U.S.:** Adrien Meisch.
**Flag:** Red, white, and light blue stripes.
**Languages:** French, German, Luxembourgish.
**Principal Ethnic Group:** Gallo-Germanic.
**Religion:** Roman Catholicism (97%).
**Leading Industries:** Manufacturing (steel, machinery, rubber, chemicals, wine, fertilizer); mining (iron ore); trade and banking; agriculture (grapes, poultry, hogs, cattle, dairy products, sheep, oats, potatoes, wheat, vegetables).
**Foreign Trade:** *major exports*—iron and steel; *major imports*—coal, petroleum.
**Places of Interest:** Grand ducal palace; national museum; Cathedral of Notre Dame; Citadel of St. Espirit; Quirinus rock chapel; Chervaux and Vianden castles.

Somewhat smaller than Rhode Island, Luxembourg is one of the world's 20 most important steel-producing nations.

Luxembourg has the highest per capita usage of electricity among industrialized nations—50% greater than that of the United States.

Lowlands rise gradually from the Luxembourg-Lorraine iron-mining basin in the southwest to the Ardennes Plateau in the north.

Belgium lies to the west, France to the south, and West Germany to the east.

Luxembourg began as a feudal domain in A.D. 963. In 1308 the count of Luxembourg became Holy Roman Emperor Henry VII, and in 1354 Luxembourg was raised to a duchy.

After 1443 it was governed by the rulers of the Netherlands. Luxembourg was granted autonomy in 1839, but Dutch kings continued to rule.

In 1867 the Treaty of London declared Luxembourg an independent, neutral state. It became a parliamentary democracy under a constitution adopted in 1868. At the death of Dutch King Willem III in 1890, the grand duchy went to Duke Adolf of Nassau.

Luxembourg was occupied by German troops in both world wars.

Grand Duke Jean became the country's ruler on Nov. 12, 1964, when his mother, Grand Duchess Charlotte, abdicated.

In a national election on June 10, 1979, the opposition Christian Social Party won a plurality of 24 seats. Christian Social leader Pierre Werner became prime minister, forming a coalition cabinet with the Liberal Party.

**Official Name:** Democratic Republic of Madagascar.
**Area:** 226,658 square miles (587,041 sq. km.).
**Population:** 8,840,230.
**Capital:** Antananarivo (Tananarive), 347,466.
**Government:** One-party Marxist socialist state.
**President:** Didier Ratsiraka (since 1975).
**Prime Minister:** Desire Rakotoarijaona (since 1977).
**Ambassador to U.S.:** Fernando E. Rondon.
**Parliament:** *National People's Assembly,* 137 members.
**Flag:** White bar; stripes of red over green.
**Official Languages:** Malagasy and French.
**Main Ethnic Group:** Merina (Malayo-Polynesian descent).
**Religions:** Christianity (40%), animism, Islam.
**Leading Industries:** Agriculture (coffee, cotton, cloves, vanilla, tobacco, rice, sugar, sisal, cattle); mining (chromite, graphite, mica); food processing; manufacturing (leather products, textiles, paper, consumer goods, tobacco products); fishing.
**Foreign Trade:** *major exports*—chromite, graphite, coffee, vanilla, cloves, meat, sugar, sisal; *major imports*—machinery, electrical equipment, chemicals, rice, textiles, trucks, petroleum.
**Places of Interest:** Antananarivo marketplaces.

## MADAGASCAR TODAY

Although larger than Texas, Madagascar is an underdeveloped island nation with few known natural resources.

The country's revolutionary socialist government rules through a one-party parliamentary system. Banks, insurance companies, mines, and shipping have been nationalized.

The former French colony depends heavily on economic aid from communist nations.

Most of the people are poor farmers. Only 4 in 10 persons can read and write.

Madagascar, the world's fourth-largest island, lies in the Indian Ocean about 250 miles east of the African coast of Mozambique. Its west coast is deeply indented and bordered by a gradually rising plain leading to a central plateau. The highest mountain, 9,450-foot Mt. Tsaratanana, stands in the north.

### EARLY HISTORY

Immigration to Madagascar from the southwest Pacific began before the Christian era and continued until the 1400s. These immigrants, later known as Merinas, settled mainly in the central highlands. The coastal regions were colonized by immigrants from Africa and Arabia. In the 1500s and 1600s the Merina kingdom became the strongest on the island and later imposed its rule over most of Madagascar.

In the 1800s King Radama I (reigned 1810–28) allowed English and French missionaries to open churches and schools, and they devised a written form of the Malagasy language.

QUICK QUIZ: What would $1 grow to if saved 30 years at 15% compound interest? See page 722.

## MADAGASCAR *(continued)*

French efforts to take Madagascar were opposed by the Merina rulers in the wars of 1883–85 and 1895–96. Madagascar became a French colony in 1896. The monarchy was abolished and the last queen was exiled.

In 1947 an armed uprising broke out. Between 60,000 and 90,000 people were killed before it was crushed by French troops in 1947.

Madagascar was granted self-government as the autonomous Malagasy Republic within the French Community on Oct. 14, 1958.

### INDEPENDENCE

Madagascar attained full independence on June 26, 1960. Philibert Tsiranana, head of the dominant Social Democratic Party, became president. He was reelected president in 1965 and 1972. During his administration French settlers continued to dominate the economy.

After a week of student riots and a general strike, President Tsiranana turned over his powers to the army chief, Maj. Gen. Gabriel Ramanantsoa, on May 18, 1972.

At a national referendum in October 1972 the voters approved extending military rule for five years, ousting Tsiranana from the government and closing the legislature.

Riots that caused great destruction broke out in 1972–73, caused by anger at the Merina tribesmen who control the military government. The rioters belonged to other tribes.

On Feb. 5, 1975, Lt. Col. Richard Ratsimandrava became the new military government leader. Six days later, on Feb. 11, Ratsimandrava was assassinated in an ambush in Antananarivo.

On Feb. 13–14, 1975, government troops stormed military police barracks and socialist headquarters, killing 21 persons and arresting 297, including former President Tsiranana.

About two-thirds of the 140,000 French settlers fled from Madagascar in 1975, leaving the nation short of managers and technicians.

The new government forced the United States and France to close military bases and a space tracking station on the island.

Didier Ratsiraka, a former naval officer, who had served as foreign minister since 1972, was chosen president and head of the 19-member military junta on June 15, 1975, to succeed Ratsimandrava.

At a referendum on Dec. 21, 1975, the people approved a new constitution written by Ratsiraka and elected him without opposition to a 7-year term as president. The constitution promised severe punishment for anyone opposing "the objectives of the revolution."

In an election on June 30, 1977, the 137 members of the national assembly were elected to 5-year terms. All were selected by the single political party, the National Front for the Defense of the Malagasy Socialist Revolution.

After riots in which up to 1,000 Comoros immigrants were killed in northwestern Madagascar, the Comoros government in 1977 undertook to repatriate the remaining 25,000 or more Comorians living in Madagascar.

Three persons were killed and 150 were arrested in two days of riots on May 29–30, 1978, by students protesting lowered educational standards.

## MALAWI

**Official Name:** Republic of Malawi.
**Area:** 45,747 square miles (118,484 sq. km.).
**Population:** 6,129,910.
**Chief Cities:** Lilongwe, capital, 75,000; Balantyre-Limbe, 219,000.
**Government:** One-party republic.
**President:** Hastings Kamuzu Banda (since 1966).
**National Assembly:** 87 members.
**U.S. Ambassador to Malawi:** John A. Burroughs Jr.
**Malawi Ambassador to U.S.:** Jacob T.X. Muwamba.
**Flag:** Black, red, and green stripes, with red rising sun on black stripe.
**Official Languages:** Chichewa and English.
**Main Ethnic Groups:** Chewa, Nyanja.
**Religions:** Animism (67%), Christianity, Islam.
**Leading Industries:** Agriculture (cotton, peanuts, coffee, tea, tobacco, maize, cattle, sorghum, sugar, millet); fishing; food processing; construction.
**Foreign Trade:** *major exports*—sugar, tobacco, tea, peanuts, cotton; *major imports*—machinery, consumer products, motor vehicles, petroleum.
**Places of Interest:** Lake Malawi; Mlanje Mountains; Great Rift Valley; public gardens at Lilongwe; Blantyre-Limbe tea estates.

### MALAWI TODAY

About the size of Pennsylvania, Malawi has few resources other than farm and grazing land. Lake Malawi (formerly Lake Nyasa) covers about 20% of the country's area, and much of the rest is too mountainous to be farmed.

Most of the people live in tribal villages, seldom seeing any money from one year to the next. They live by fishing and farming. Only about 1 in 7 persons can read and write.

Long and narrow, Malawi is a landlocked country in southeast Africa. Lake Malawi extends along the eastern border with Tanzania and Mozambique. Zambia is to the west.

Lake Malawi drains south into the Shire River. The steep cliffs of the Rift Valley rise to the west.

### EARLY HISTORY

For several centuries Lake Malawi attracted Bantu tribes from the northwest. The Malawi kingdom was established in the region in the 1300s. By the 1600s the Malawi people had fallen under dominance of the Yao tribes, who sold the Malawi as slaves to Arab traders.

The Scottish missionary-explorer David Livingstone became the first European to reach Lake Malawi, on Sept. 16, 1859. He and Scottish missionaries who followed him fought the Arab slave trade.

Britain established a protectorate in 1891, calling the area *Nyasaland.*

Resentful of mistreatment by British plantation owners, Malawi tribesmen led by John Chilembwe staged an unsuccessful uprising in 1915.

In 1953 Nyasaland was forced by the British into federation with North and South Rhodesia.

The Nyasaland African Congress (NAC), founded in 1944, opposed the federation. The NAC gained strength in 1958 when its leaders recalled Dr. Hastings Kamuzu Banda from 40 years of study abroad.

The British, faced with rising protests, outlawed the NAC in 1959 and imprisoned Banda and 1,200 of his followers. Other followers, however, built up the Malawi Congress Party (MCP). They persuaded the British to release Banda in 1960.

In elections in August 1961 Banda won control of the territorial government. The federation was dissolved on Dec. 31, 1963.

## INDEPENDENCE

Under Banda's leadership, Nyasaland became the independent state of Malawi within the British Commonwealth of Nations on July 6, 1964. A coup in 1964 proved unsuccessful, and Banda was able to resolve dissension within his party.

Malawi became a republic on July 6, 1966, with Banda as its first president.

Since 1967 a program of persecution has been carried on against the Jehovah's Witnesses sect, whose members refuse to salute the Malawi flag. The government banned the group and placed about 30,000 in prison camps. In December 1975 officials of the sect protested their members were being beaten, tortured, and raped.

In 1970 Banda was acclaimed president for life by a convention of the Malawi Congress Party, the only authorized political party in the country.

In ruling his country Banda brooks no opposition. When one of his cabinet ministers, Aleke Banda, mentioned himself as a possible successor to the president in an article published in Zambia, he was dismissed in March 1973 from both the cabinet and the party.

Malawi passed a law in 1974 banning miniskirts, with a penalty of six months in prison for any woman baring her knees.

The government moved its capital in 1975 to the new centrally located city of Lilongwe to encourage opening up the interior of the country. The capital was developed at a cost of more than $250 million by a profit-making corporation. Lilongwe's extensive public gardens employ 2,000 workers.

Some $68 million was budgeted by the government in 1976 for expenditure on agricultural development and hydroelectric power projects. Wages and prices were controlled by the government in an effort to reduce inflation.

The former head of the secret police, Martin Gwede, and the former head of the MCP party, Albert Andrew Muwalo Nqumayo, were convicted of treason on Feb. 14, 1977, and sentenced to death for plotting to overthrow President Banda.

On July 4, 1977, Banda released most of the remaining 2,000 political prisoners he had jailed.

The first general election in 17 years was held on June 29, 1978. Although all candidates were members of the MCP party, several contested for 47 of the 87 seats in the national assembly. As a result, two cabinet members and 29 other members lost their seats. Banda praised the results as a democratic expression of the people's will.

# MALAYSIA

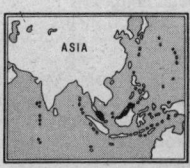

**Official Name:** Malaysia.
**Area:** 127,317 square miles (329,749 sq. km.).
**Population:** 13,923,600.
**Chief Cities:** Kuala Lumpur, capital, 451,977; George Town, 269,603; Ipoh, 247,953; Johore Bahru, 136,234; Klang, 113,611.
**Government:** Constitutional monarchy.
**Prime Minister:** Datuk Hussein Onn (since 1976).
**King:** Sultan Ahmad Shah of Pahang (since 1979).
**Parliament:** *Senate* (Dewan Negara), 58 members; *House of Representatives* (Dewan Ra'ayat), 154.
**U.S. Ambassador to Malaysia:** Barbara M. Watson.
**Malaysian Ambassador to U.S.:** Zain Azraai.
**Flag:** Red and white stripes with blue field containing gold crescent and 14-pointed gold star.
**Languages:** Malay and English (both official), Chinese, Tamil.
**Main Ethnic Groups:** Malay (44%), Chinese (36%), Indian and Pakistani (10%).
**Religions:** Islam, Buddhism, Christianity, Hinduism.
**Leading Industries:** Agriculture (rubber, rice, palm kernels, tea, peppers, coconuts, vegetables, fruits); mining (tin, petroleum, iron ore, natural gas, bauxite); forestry and lumbering; manufacturing (steel, automobiles, electronics, petroleum products, rubber products, palm oil, chemicals, textiles); fishing; tourism.
**Foreign Trade:** *major exports*—rubber, tin, timber, palm oil, iron ore, petroleum; *major imports*—machinery, rice, textiles.
**Places of Interest:** Batu Cave; Cameron Highlands; Malaysia National Park. *In Kuala Lumpur:* National museum; national mosque; houses on stilts.

## MALAYSIA TODAY

About the size of New Mexico, Malaysia has more than 10 times as many people.

The nation has two parts separated by 400 miles of the South China Sea. West Malaysia lies on a peninsula in Southeast Asia just south of Thailand. East Malaysia covers the northern coast of the island of Borneo.

Malaysia is the world's leading producer of tin and natural rubber and is an oil-exporting nation.

Because Malaysia has abundant natural resources, it has a stronger economy and more industry than most other nations of Southeast Asia. But the majority of Malaysians are poor farm workers who cannot read and write.

Malaysia's king is elected for a 5-year term by the sultans of the nine states of West Malaysia from among their own members.

About 80% of West Malaysia is covered by mountains and tropical forests. Most of the people live along the more than 1,200 miles of coast.

The East Malaysian states of Sarawak and Sabah lie on the island of Borneo. The nation's highest mountain, Mt. Kinabalu (13,455 feet), stands in Sabah.

The climate along the coasts is hot, but it

QUICK QUIZ: What is the square root of 88? See page 723.

## MALAYSIA *(continued)*

becomes cool in the hills and mountains of the interior. Annual rainfall averages 100 inches.

### EARLY HISTORY

Portuguese traders first arrived on the Malay peninsula in 1511. In 1786 the British East India Company leased the island of Penang. By the early 1900s Britain controlled all the Malay states as colonies or protectorates.

In 1946 the Union of Malaya was formed, uniting Penang and Malacca with the nine Malay states. The union became the Federation of Malaya in 1948.

Communist insurrections erupted in 1948. The guerrilla terrorism in the countryside finally was brought under control in 1959.

### INDEPENDENT MALAYSIA

The Federation of Malaya was granted independence by Britain on Aug. 31, 1957.

In 1961 Malaya's Prime Minister Tunku Abdul Rahman, fearing the creation of an independent Singapore controlled by procommunist forces, proposed uniting Malaya, Sarawak, North Borneo, and Brunei as Malaysia.

Malaysia became an independent constitutional monarchy on Sept. 16, 1963. It incorporated the former Federation of Malaya and the former British colonies of Singapore, Sarawak, and North Borneo (Sabah). The sultans of the Malaya states elect one of their number every five years as paramount ruler (king).

Tensions developed between Rahman's Malay-dominated Alliance government and the predominantly Chinese government of Singapore. In August 1965 Rahman decided that only Singapore's expulsion could prevent racial outbreaks. Singapore reluctantly accepted independence.

The worst racial rioting in Malaysia's history broke out May 13, 1969, in Kuala Lumpur. Violent strife between Malays and Chinese brought the assumption of emergency powers by a National Operations Council under Deputy Prime Minister Tun Abdul Razak.

### DEVELOPMENTS IN THE 1970s

On Jan. 12, 1970, the government announced the formation of a 65-member national consultative council to avert a recurrence of racial strife.

Rahman retired in September 1970, and Razak succeeded him as prime minister. Parliamentary rule was resumed in February 1971.

Razak's national front won a huge majority in parliamentary elections on Aug. 24, 1974.

Offshore oil strikes made in 1973 went into production in 1975, boosting the economy.

Razak died of leukemia on Jan. 14, 1976. He was succeeded as prime minister on the following day by his brother-in-law Datuk Hussein Onn.

Prime Minister Datuk Hussein's National Front coalition won a comfortable two-thirds majority in parliamentary elections held in 1978.

Malaysia took a strong stand in 1979 against admitting more refugee "boat people" from Vietnam. Its forces compelled many refugee boats to put back out to sea. The government called on other nations to find homes for the more than 75,000 refugees already being cared for in Malaysian camps.

## MALDIVES

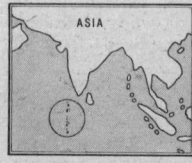 

**Official Name:** Republic of Maldives.
**Area:** 115 square miles (298 sq. km.).
**Population:** 154,951.
**Capital:** Malé, 29,555.
**Government:** Republic ruled by decree.
**President:** Maumoon Abdul Gayoom (since 1978).
**Legislature:** *Majlis,* 48 members.
**U.S. Ambassador to Maldives:** W. Howard Wriggins.
**Maldivian Ambassador to U.S.:** Abdul Sattar.
**Flag:** Red field with green panel containing white crescent.
**Languages:** Divehi (official), Arabic.
**Ethnic Groups:** Sinhalese, Arab, Dravidian.
**Official Religion:** Sunni Islam.
**Leading Industries:** Fishing; agriculture (coconuts, corn, millet, pumpkins, sweet potatoes, fruits); tourism; shipping; handicrafts, rope making.
**Foreign Trade:** *major exports*—dried fish, rope, copra, ambergris, lace, shells, handicrafts; *major imports*—grain, drugs, textiles, consumer goods.
**Places of Interest:** Plants and animals of the various islands; Malé; beach resorts.

One of the 10 smallest and poorest nations in the world, the Maldives have a land area smaller than the city of Philadelphia. Only a few Maldivians can read and write.

The 2,000 or more Maldive islands string out over 550 miles of the Indian Ocean. The largest has an area of about 5 square miles. About 215 are inhabited. The climate is hot and humid.

Almost all the men of the Maldives fish for a living. Dried fish is the country's main export, with Sri Lanka the main customer. Rice, the main staple of the islanders, must be imported.

About 30,000 tourists visit the islands each year. A tourist who breaks the law is subject to punishment by banishment to an uninhabited isle with no food other than what he can catch from the sea or pick from coconut palms.

The islands were ruled as a sultanate by members of the Didi clan from about 1100 until 1968. Arab traders visited in 1153, converting the people to Islam. In the 1600s the Maldives came under the protection of Sri Lanka (Ceylon), then under Dutch rule.

The Maldives became a protectorate of Britain in December 1887. Britain established an air base in 1939 on Gan, an island in Addu, the southernmost atoll, but closed it in 1976.

The Maldives were granted full independence on July 26, 1965. The nation was a constitutional monarchy until Nov. 11, 1968, when Sultan Mohammed Farid Didi I was deposed. A republic was proclaimed under President Amir Ibrahim Nasir, the sultan's prime minister in 1956–68.

President Nasir suspended the constitution and imposed rule by decree on March 6, 1975. Nasir resigned because of illness in 1978. He was succeeded by Maumoon Abdul Gayoom, who was elected without opposition by the national legislature.

# MALI

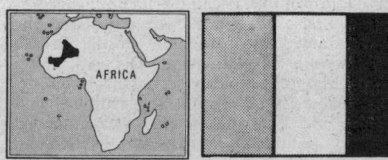

**Official Name:** Republic of Mali.
**Area:** 478,767 square miles (1,240,000 sq. km.).
**Population:** 6,724,730.
**Capital:** Bamako, 404,022.
**Government:** Military dictatorship.
**President:** Col. Moussa Traoré (since 1968).
**U.S. Ambassador to Mali:** Anne F. Holloway.
**Mali Ambassador to U.S.:** Maki Koreissi Aguibou Tall.
**Flag:** Bars of green, yellow, and red.
**Languages:** French (official), Bambra.
**Ethnic Groups:** Mande (50%), Peul (17%), Voltaic (12%), Songhai (6%), Tuareg and Moors (5%).
**Main Religion:** Islam (90%).
**Leading Industries:** Agriculture (cattle, cotton, rice, peanuts, sorghum, millet, goats, sheep); fishing; mining (gold); manufacturing (textiles, cigarettes, matches, baskets, food processing).
**Foreign Trade:** *major exports*—cotton, peanuts, fish, livestock; *major imports*—textiles, food, machinery, motor vehicles, petroleum products.
**Places of Interest:** Cliff-dwelling Dogon tribes near Sangha; Bamako; Timbuktu; Lake Débo.

## MALI TODAY

A little larger than the combined areas of Texas and California, Mali is one of the most poverty-stricken nations in the world. Ironically, the country counts among its mineral resources bauxite, uranium, iron ore, copper, manganese, phosphate, and gold. Currently only gold is mined, and that in small quantities, because the primitive transportation system of the landlocked country cannot handle large ore shipments. The military government hopes to find foreign investors willing to develop the minerals and the necessary transportation and communications facilities.

Meanwhile, most of the people farm crops or herd livestock, barely raising enough food to feed their families.

Mali is bordered by Senegal, Mauritania, Algeria, Niger, Upper Volta, Ivory Coast, and Guinea. The greater part of the country spreads north, east, and west of the great bend of the Niger River, while a rather small area lies south of the Niger.

The northern half of Mali is covered by the Sahara Desert. To the south is semidesert, and in the far southwest are savanna lands. The country generally has a hot climate with little rainfall.

## EARLY HISTORY

For many years Mali was part of the empire of Ghana. As Islam expanded in the western Sahara, Almoravid Berbers from Mauritania launched a *jihad,* or holy war, against peoples to the south. In 1076 Abu Bakr overthrew Ghana. Although in 1087 the Soninke leaders of Ghana recovered their independence for a century, their great empire had been disrupted.

In the 1000s the small Malinke state of Kangaba, south of Ghana, also embraced Islam and began to annex nearby kingdoms. The emperor Sundiata Keita conquered Ghana in 1235 and established the Muslim empire of Mali, which became the richest and most powerful of the western Sudanese empires.

Under the leadership of Mansa Musa (1307–32), Mali reached its peak as a center of Muslim trade and learning. The empire disintegrated after his death.

The Songhai controlled the next great Islamic empire, with its center at Gao, until 1591, when the Moroccans defeated the Songhai at Tondibi and became the new rulers.

French troops conquered the region in 1881 to 1898. It became known as the territory of *French Soudan* in the colony of French West Africa, which was established in 1904.

## INDEPENDENT REPUBLIC OF MALI

The French Soudan was granted self-government in 1958 as a member state in the French Community. In 1959 the colony, renamed the *Sudanese Republic,* joined Senegal in the Mali Federation, which became independent on June 20, 1960. The federation dissolved on Aug. 20, 1960.

The former French Soudan proclaimed itself the *Republic of Mali* on Sept. 22, 1960, and withdrew from the French Community.

Modibo Keita, head of the Sudanese Union Party, became Mali's first president. Keita socialized Mali's economy, and formed close ties with the Soviet Union and communist China. These moves had a disastrous effect on Mali's economy and caused a split in the Sudanese Union Party among pro-Soviet, pro-Chinese, and pro-French factions. In 1967 Keita tried to appease the pro-French faction by reestablishing economic ties with France.

Keita took steps to strengthen his power in late 1967 and 1968. He dissolved the national assembly and began ruling by decree.

Mali's army, fearing the growing role of Keita's Chinese-trained militia, overthrew and imprisoned Keita on Nov. 19, 1968.

Lt. Moussa Traoré became president, and Capt. Yoro Diakité was named premier. Following an attempt to reinstate Keita on Aug. 13, 1969, Traoré assumed the premiership. For attempting a coup in 1971, Diakité was sentenced to life imprisonment in 1972.

Six years of drought from 1969 to 1974 killed up to 100,000 people and about three-fourths of the cattle in the nation. Many of the 700,000 Tuareg nomads of northern Mali migrated to other countries.

President Traoré invoked emergency powers in 1977 after demonstrations in May at the funeral of former President Keita, who died after being imprisoned since the 1968 coup.

Traoré arrested several cabinet members in February 1978, charging them with treason and fraud of more than $1.2 million in distribution of grain to drought victims.

New drought in 1980 brought an appeal from President Traoré for aid to save his people from famine.

QUICK QUIZ: The symbol Au stands for what chemical element? See page 725.

## MALTA

 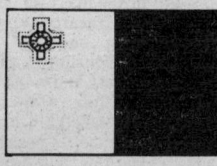

**Official Name:** Republic of Malta.
**Area:** 122 square miles (316 sq. km.).
**Population:** 334,317.
**Cities:** Valletta, capital, 14,096; Sliema, 22,000.
**Government:** Parliamentary republic.
**Prime Minister:** Dom Mintoff (appointed in 1971).
**President:** Anton Buttigieg (since 1976).
**House of Representatives:** 65 members.
**U.S. Ambassador to Malta:** Joan Margaret Clark.
**Flag:** White and red bars, with George Cross in silver on white bar.
**Languages:** Maltese, English.
**Official Religion:** Roman Catholicism (99%).
**Ethnic Groups:** Arab, Italian, English.
**Leading Industries:** Shipbuilding and ship repairs; tourism; agriculture (poultry, dairy products, flowers, vegetables, fruits); manufacturing (textiles, yarn, clothing, electronic equipment, food processing).
**Foreign Trade:** *major exports*—cotton yarn, textiles, cut flowers, ships and boats, wine; *major imports*—food, petroleum, automobiles, consumer products.
**Places of Interest:** Valletta; Hypogeum underground Neolithic temple at Paola; cave of Ghar Dalam; Blue Grotto at Zurrieq; cathedral museum at Mdina.

### MALTA TODAY

With a land area about as large as Kansas City, Mo., the island nation of Malta has only one major resource—its strategic location. It lies at the geographic center of the Mediterranean Sea, about 60 miles south of Sicily.

The socialist government depends on foreign aid to develop industries in an effort to become a "nonaligned" neutral nation.

The government also seeks to expand tourism to exploit Malta's year-round sunny climate and many historic monuments and buildings.

Malta includes two main islands, Malta and Gozo, and the small island of Comino.

### HISTORY

Malta's strategic position has attracted successive waves of invaders. Phoenicians, Greeks, Carthaginians, Romans, Byzantines, and Arabs occupied the islands. In 1090 Malta was seized by the Normans.

In 1530 the Holy Roman emperor Charles V awarded Malta to the Knights of St. John of Jerusalem, who beat off repeated Turkish attacks.

Napoleon seized control in 1798. The Maltese rose against the French and, with the help of Britain, threw them two years later.

In 1814 Malta became a British colony.

Maltese courage while under siege during World War II was rewarded in 1942, when the George Cross was bestowed on Malta itself—the first time an entire people had been so honored.

Malta became independent on Sept. 21, 1964. The country was governed from 1964 to 1971 by the Nationalist Party, led by Prime Minister Giorgio Borg Olivier.

In a national election held in June 1971, the Malta Labor Party won by a narrow margin. Its leader, Dom Mintoff, became prime minister.

Malta's house of representatives declared the nation an independent republic in the British Commonwealth of Nations on Dec. 13, 1974. Anthony Mamo, who had served as governor-general since 1971, became the nation's first president. The constitution also was amended to restrict political activities of the Roman Catholic Church.

Mintoff's socialist policies narrowly received voter approval in an election on Sept. 18, 1976, when the Labor Party won a majority of 34 seats in the 65-member House of Representatives.

For nearly two centuries Malta's economy had been dependent on jobs and money provided by British military bases located there. But the socialist government refused to renew leases on the bases. On April 1, 1979, the British military presence in Malta ended after 179 years with the departure of the warship HMS *Hood.*

Libya promised aid to Malta to make up for the loss of income from Britain.

After receiving aid from Libya for several years, Malta expelled Libyan advisers in August 1980 in a dispute over rights to offshore oil.

In September 1980 Malta and Italy signed an agreement under which Italy would provide military assistance to protect Malta's neutrality.

## MAURITANIA

**Official Name:** Islamic Republic of Mauritania.
**Area:** 397,955 square miles (1,030,700 sq. km.).
**Population:** 1,654,750.
**Capital:** Nouakchott, 134,986.
**Government:** Military junta.
**President:** Lt. Col. Mohammed Khouno Haidala (since 1980).
**U.S. Ambassador to Mauritania:** Henry Precht.
**Mauritanian Ambassador to U.S.:** Sidi Bouna Ould Sidi.
**Flag:** Gold star and crescent on green field.
**Languages:** French (official), Arabic.
**Ethnic Groups:** Arab-Berber (80%), black (20%).
**Religion:** Islam.
**Leading Industries:** Agriculture (cattle, sheep, goats, horses, millet, dates, gum arabic, vegetables, fruits); mining (iron ore, copper, gold, salt); fishing.
**Foreign Trade:** *major exports*—iron ore, copper, livestock, gum arabic, fish, salt, dates; *major imports*—food, vehicles, petroleum, machinery, textiles.
**Places of Interest:** Kédia d'Idjit Mountains; iron mines; Nouakchott; Port-Étienne.

### MAURITANIA TODAY

Larger than Texas and California combined, Mauritania depends on the export of iron ore and copper for most of the cash income that has enabled it to obtain a few benefits of modern civilization. European companies share profits from the mining operations with the government.

Most Mauritanians live as they have for

hundreds of years—the Arabs and Berbers as nomadic herdsmen and the black tribesmen as subsistence farmers and livestock raisers. Few can read and write, and only about 10% of the children attend school.

Although the government officially forbids slavery, many of the blacks are held as slaves by Arab masters.

Most of the country is desert. The Senegal River on the southern border is the only waterway. Mauritania's climate is mostly hot and dry.

## MAURITANIA'S HISTORY

In Roman times *Mauretania* was the name of a vast kingdom that included western Algeria, Morocco, and part of what is now Mauritania.

In the 1000s A.D. Berber invasions into the present-day Mauritania area pushed the black African inhabitants southward. The area became the base for holy wars in which the Muslims conquered Morocco, Algeria, Spain, and Ghana.

The French began invading Mauritania in 1904. Mauritania became part of French West Africa in 1920 and was administered from Saint-Louis along with Senegal. In 1958 it became the self-governing Islamic Republic of Mauritania within the French Community.

Mauritania was granted full independence on Nov. 28, 1960, under President Mokhtar Ould Daddah, who previously had been prime minister. He was reelected to 5-year terms as president in 1966, 1971, and 1976.

In 1966 Mauritania withdrew from the French Community.

Mauritania's 1961 constitution was amended in 1964 to establish a single-party system.

Six years of drought and famine brought the nation to the verge of disaster in 1974. Over 80% of the country's livestock died.

In November 1974 the government nationalized the iron-mining industry.

Mauritania joined with Morocco in 1976 in partitioning the former Spanish Sahara. In an agreement signed on April 14, 1976, Mauritania annexed the southern third of the former Spanish colony, an area about the size of South Carolina. Mauritanian troops clashed with those of the Algerian-backed Polisario guerrillas who sought independence for the Western Sahara.

Army Chief of Staff Lt. Col. Mustapha Ould Salek overthrew and imprisoned President Daddah and his cabinet on July 9, 1978.

The Polisaro guerrillas declared a unilateral cease-fire with Mauritania in July 1978.

Prime Minister Ahmed Ould Bousseif and 11 other persons were killed in a plane crash in the Atlantic Ocean off Senegal on May 27, 1979. A week later on June 3, President Salek resigned and was replaced by Lt. Col. Mohammed Mahmoud Ould Luly. Lt. Col. Mohammed Khouno Haidala was appointed prime minister.

A peace agreement was signed with the Polisario guerrillas on Aug. 8, 1979, in which Mauritania gave up its claims to the Western Sahara region. Mauritania also ended its military alliance with Morocco.

Haidala overthrew Luly on Jan. 4, 1980, making himself president.

# MAURITIUS

**Official Name:** Mauritus.
**Area:** 790 square miles (2,045 sq. km.).
**Population:** 960,179.
**Capital:** Port-Louis, 141,022.
**Government:** Parliamentary state.
**Prime Minister:** Sir Seewoosagur Ramgoolam (appointed in 1964).
**Chief of State:** Governor-General Sir Abdul Raman Osman (since 1973).
**Legislative Assembly:** 70 members.
**U.S. Ambassador to Mauritius:** Robert C. F. Gordon.
**Flag:** Red, blue, yellow, and green stripes.
**Languages:** English (official), Creole, Hindi, Urdu, French.
**Main Ethnic Groups:** Asian Indian descent (67%), Creole (28%), Chinese descent (3%).
**Chief Religions:** Hinduism (47%), Christianity (34%), Islam (16%).
**Leading Industries:** Agriculture (sugarcane, rice, tea, tobacco, aloe, potatoes, onions, vegetables, fruits, cattle, sheep, goats, poultry); food processing; fishing.
**Foreign Trade:** *major exports*—sugar, molasses, tea; *major imports*—rice, wheat, cotton fabrics, petroleum products, fertilizers, machinery, consumer goods.
**Places of Interest:** Pamplemousses Garden; Nicolière Reservoir; Plaine Champagne; Black River gorges; Grand Bassin Lake; Morne Brabant; Mahebourg Naval Museum; Blue Bay Beach; Belle Mare.

## MAURITIUS TODAY

About two-thirds the size of Rhode Island, Mauritius has no important mineral deposits. The economy depends almost entirely on sugar, which accounts for more than 90% of its exports. Tea and molasses are also exported. Tourism is being developed as a source of foreign exchange.

Mauritius was the home of the flightless dodo bird until it became extinct in the 1600s.

An island of volcanic origin, Mauritius lies in the Indian Ocean about 500 miles east of Madagascar. The island of Mauritius itself has an area of 720 square miles. The nation also includes several smaller islands, including Rodriguez (42 sq. mi.), Agalega, and Cargados Carajos. On Mauritius a plain rises toward a central plateau of about 2,200 feet before dropping to the southern and western coasts.

## HISTORY OF MAURITIUS

Although Mauritius was probably visited by Arabs, Malays, and Portuguese, the first colonists were the Dutch in 1589. They named the island after their ruler, Prince Maurice of Nassau. A Dutch settlement, established in 1638, was abandoned in 1710.

The French claimed the island in 1713, but it was taken by the British in 1810. It was formally ceded to Britain by the Treaty of Paris

QUICK QUIZ: Who invented the microwave oven? See page 727.

**MAURITIUS** *(continued)*
in 1814. The island was administered jointly with Seychelles until 1903.

Mauritius was granted full independence as a parliamentary state within the British Commonwealth of Nations on March 12, 1968. It was admitted to UN membership in April 1968.

Parliamentary elections in 1967 were won by a coalition that included the island's Labor Party and parties representing Muslims and Hindus.

Sir Seewoosagur Ramgoolam, who had headed the colonial government since 1947 as leader of the Labor Party, became prime minister upon independence in 1968.

The Marxist Militant Mauritian Movement (MMM) won a parliamentary by-election in 1970. Although parliamentary elections are required every five years, the government decided to postpone the 1972 elections to 1976 in order to avert political strife.

The government moved in 1976 to resettle on the Agalega Islands the 1,200 to 1,400 persons removed in 1972 from the Indian Ocean island of Diego Garcia, which was sold to Britain and made into a U.S. naval base.

As president of the Organization of African Unity (OAU), Prime Minister Ramgoolam helped lead the drive for black majority rule in South Africa, even though South Africa is one of Mauritius' main trading partners.

In a national election on Dec. 20, 1976, the Marxist MMM party won 34 seats in the 70-member national assembly, but the other parties joined in a coalition that kept Ramgoolam as prime minister.

## STATES OF MEXICO

| NAME | AREA (sq. mi.) | CAPITAL |
|---|---|---|
| Aguascalientes | 2,158 | Aguascalientes |
| Baja California Norte | 27,071 | Mexicali |
| Baja California Sur | 28,447 | La Paz |
| Campeche | 21,666 | Campeche |
| Chiapas | 28,528 | Tuxtla |
| Chihuahua | 95,401 | Chihuahua |
| Coahuila | 58,522 | Saltillo |
| Colima | 2,106 | Colima |
| Durango | 46,196 | Durango |
| Federal District | 579 | Mexico City |
| Guanajuato | 11,810 | Guanajuato |
| Guerrero | 24,631 | Chilpancingo |
| Hidalgo | 8,103 | Pachuca |
| Jalisco | 30,941 | Guadalajara |
| México | 8,286 | Toluca |
| Michoacán | 23,114 | Morelia |
| Morelos | 1,908 | Cuernavaca |
| Nayarit | 10,665 | Tepic |
| Nuevo León | 24,925 | Monterrey |
| Oaxaca | 36,820 | Oaxaca |
| Puebla | 13,096 | Puebla |
| Querétaro | 4,544 | Querétaro |
| Quintana Roo | 16,228 | Chetumal |
| San Luis Potosí | 24,266 | San Luis Potosí |
| Sinaloa | 22,429 | Culiacán |
| Sonora | 71,403 | Hermosillo |
| Tabasco | 9,522 | Villahermosa |
| Tamaulipas | 30,822 | Ciudad Victoria |
| Tlaxcala | 1,511 | Tlaxcala |
| Veracruz | 28,114 | Jalapa |
| Yucatán | 16,749 | Mérida |
| Zacatecas | 28,973 | Zacatecas |

# MEXICO

**Official Name:** United Mexican States.
**Area:** 761,605 square miles (1,972,547 sq. km.).
**Population:** 73,171,478.
**Chief Cities:** Mexico City, capital, 8,988,230; Netzahualcoyotl, 2,067,992; Guadalajara, 1,813,131; Monterrey, 1,054,029; Puebla de Zaragoza, 677,959; Juárez, 597,096; León, 589,950; Tijuana, 534,993; Acapulco, 421,088; Chihuahua, 369,545; Mexicali, 338,423.
**Largest Metropolitan Area:** Mexico City, 13,993,866.
**Government:** Federal republic.
**President:** José Lopez Portillo (since 1976).
**National Congress:** *Senate,* 64 members; *Chamber of Deputies,* 400 members.
**U.S. Ambassador to Mexico:** Julian Nava.
**Mexican Ambassador to U.S.:** Hugo B. Margain.
**Flag:** Green, white, and red bars; coat of arms in white bar—brown eagle on cactus devouring green serpent (representing Aztec legend), encircled by laurel wreath.
**Official Language:** Spanish.
**Main Ethnic Groups:** Mestizo (mixed Spanish-Indian descent), (60%), American Indian (30%).
**Religion:** Roman Catholicism (97%).
**Leading Industries:** Trade and services; manufacturing (steel, petroleum products, cement, automobiles, fertilizers, textiles, paper, aluminum, electricity); tourism; agriculture (sugarcane, coffee, cattle, cotton, wheat, rice, maize, fruits, vegetables); mining (petroleum, natural gas, coal, iron ore, copper, manganese, zinc, lead); fishing; construction.
**Foreign Trade:** *major exports*—petroleum, cotton, sugar, coffee, shrimp, zinc, lead, copper; *major imports*—food, machinery, consumer goods.
**Places of Interest:** Mayan archaeological ruins on Yucatán peninsula; Aztec ruins and pyramids near Mexico City; Popocatépetl, Parícutin, Ixtaccíhuatl and Citlaltépetl volcanoes; Sierra Madre mountains; Acapulco; Guadalajara; Oaxaca. *In and near Mexico City:* Cathedral of Zócalo; University of Mexico; national palace; Chapultepec Park; Xochimilco floating gardens; National Museum of Anthropology.

## MEXICO TODAY

With huge oil reserves and one of the most stable governments in Latin America, Mexico has hopes of becoming a major industrial nation.

Because one-third of the people still depend on agriculture for their living, Mexico has been a leader in the "green revolution" that encourages farmers to use more productive seed, hybrids, and fertilizers. The government has spent millions of dollars on irrigation projects to reclaim unproductive land. However, many Mexicans still live at a subsistence level. About 1 in 3 cannot read and write.

In an effort to encourage decentralization of manufacturing, the government gives tax reductions to industries locating in rural areas.

Mexico has about one-fourth the area of the U.S., which lies to the north. Guatemala and Belize lie to the south.

The land is dominated by a high central pla-

teau running north and south, enclosed by the mountain ranges of the Sierra Madre. The longest river is the Rio Grande.

Climate ranges from subtropical in the coastal zones to extreme cold in the mountains.

## EARLY HISTORY

Indian civilizations developed in Mexico more than 2,000 years ago.

The Maya Indians in the Yucatán peninsula mastered the arts of construction and stone-carving, built cities, developed a calendar, and studied astronomy. The Nahuatl culture, established much later in the central plains, included the Toltecs and the Aztecs.

Mexico came under Spanish rule after conquistador Hernán Cortés landed at Veracruz in 1519 and conquered the highly civilized Aztec nation.

## INDEPENDENCE

A drive for independence began on Sept. 16, 1810, led by Miguel Hidalgo, a Mexican priest. Independence from Spain was finally achieved in 1821 under the leadership of Agustín de Iturbide and Vicente Guerrero. Iturbide became emperor in 1822, but was deposed when a republic was formed in 1823.

Gen. Antonio López de Santa Anna ruled in the 1830s and 1840s. The territory of Texas seceded in 1836 and joined the U.S. in 1844.

After the Mexican War (1846–48), Mexico was forced to cede half its territory to the U.S.

In 1861, during a period of internal disorder, French troops captured the capital and crowned Austrian Archduke Maximilian as emperor. After the French withdrew, the forces of Benito Juárez regained control, and in 1867 Maximilian was executed. Mexico again became a republic.

Gen. Porfirio Díaz seized power in 1876 and ruled as dictator. He was overthrown in 1911 by a liberal revolt led by Francisco Madero.

Liberal factions disputed, and leaders such as Francisco Villa and Emiliano Zapata rose and fell. A violent anticlerical movement persecuted the Roman Catholic Church.

A reform constitution was adopted in 1917. A succession of leaders attempted to bring stability to the political and governmental structure. Most notable of the leaders were Álvaro Obregón and Plutarco Elías Calles.

From 1934 to 1940 the liberal regime of Lázaro Cárdenas instituted widespread reforms.

In 1938 Mexico became the first noncommunist country to nationalize its petroleum industry, taking over all foreign-owned oil companies. Pemex, a government corporation, was established to manage the petroleum holdings.

## POLITICAL STABILITY

Mexican affairs since 1940 have been marked by political stability with the dominance of the Institutional Revolutionary Party (PRI) during the presidency of Gen. Manuel Ávila Camacho (1940–46) and his successors.

Mexico became an oil exporter after major oil finds in the 1970s–80s.

José López Portillo, 55, who had served as minister of finance, was elected president on July

## PRESIDENTS AND RULERS OF MEXICO

| YEARS | NAME | PARTY |
|---|---|---|
| 1821–22 | Agustín de Iturbide, president | |
| 1822–23 | Agustín de Iturbide, emperor | |
| 1824–28 | Gen. Guadalupe Victoria | |
| 1828–29 | Vicente Guerrero | C |
| 1829–32 | Gen. Anastasio Bustamante | C |
| 1833–36 | Gen. Antonio López de Santa Anna | C |
| 1837–41 | Gen. Anastasio Bustamante | C |
| 1841–44 | Gen. Antonio López de Santa Anna | C |
| 1844–46 | José Joaquín Herrera | M |
| 1846 | Mariano Paredes | C |
| 1846–47 | Gen. Antonio López de Santa Anna | C |
| 1848–51 | José Joaquín Herrera | M |
| 1851–53 | Mariano Arista | M |
| 1853–55 | Gen. Antonio López de Santa Anna | C |
| 1855 | Juan Álvarez | L |
| 1855–58 | Ignacio Comonfort | L |
| 1858–72 | Benito Juárez | L |
| 1864–67 | Maximilian, emperor | |
| 1872–76 | Sebastián Lerdo de Tejada | L |
| 1876–80 | Gen. Porfirio Díaz | L |
| 1880–84 | Manuel González | L |
| 1884–1911 | Gen. Porfirio Díaz, dictator | |
| 1911–13 | Francisco Madero | L |
| 1913–14 | Gen. Victoriano Huerta, dictator | |
| 1914–20 | Venustiano Carranza | L |
| 1920–24 | Álvaro Obregón | L |
| 1924–28 | Plutarco Elías Calles | L |
| 1929 | Emilio Portes Gil | PNR |
| 1929–32 | Pascual Ortíz Rubio | PNR |
| 1932–34 | Abelardo Rodríguez | PNR |
| 1934–40 | Lázaro Cárdenas | PNR |
| 1940–46 | Gen. Manuel Ávila Camacho | PRM |
| 1946–52 | Miquel Alemán Valdéz | PRI |
| 1952–58 | Adolfo Ruiz Corines | PRI |
| 1958–64 | Adolfo López Mateos | PRI |
| 1964–70 | Gustavo Díaz Ordaz | PRI |
| 1970–76 | Luis Echeverría Álvarez | PRI |
| 1976– | José López Portillo | PRI |

C = Conservative;  M = Moderate;  L = Liberal; PNR = National Revolutionary Party; PRM = Party of the Mexican Revolution; PRI = Institutional Revolutionary Party.

4, 1976, as the PRI candidate.

Portillo instituted tough austerity measures, including wage controls. Inflation was brought under control, and the country's balance of trade deficit was reduced. Portillo announced plans to expand oil production to 2.7 million barrels a day by 1982, with half designated for export.

The U.S. and Mexico sought to improve relations in 1979 as President Portillo and U.S. President Carter exchanged visits. Carter traveled to Mexico in February. Portillo reciprocated with a visit to Washington, D.C., in September.

In a national election on July 1, 1979, the governing PRI won 296 of 300 contested seats in the National Congress. The Communist Party was permitted to run candidates for the first time in 33 years, winning more than 5% of the vote.

President Portillo declared on Sept. 1, 1979, that Mexico's energy needs were secure for the next 60 years with proven reserves of oil and natural gas at the equivalent of nearly 46 billion barrels and potential reserves of 200 billion barrels.

Despite the growth in Mexico's economy in 1980 caused by expanded production of oil, the nation spends about 50% more on imports than it receives for exports.

QUICK QUIZ: What did Edwin Armstrong invent? See page 729.

## MONACO

**Official Name:** Principality of Monaco.
**Area:** 0.58 square miles (1.49 sq. km.).
**Population:** 27,256.
**Capital:** Monaco-Ville, 25,000.
**Government:** Constitutional principality.
**Chief of State:** Prince Rainier III (since 1949).
**Head of Government:** Minister of State André Saint-Mleux (since 1972).
**National Council:** 18 members.
**Flag:** Red stripe over white stripe.
**Main Ethnic Groups:** French (58%), Italian (17%), Monegasque (15%).
**Languages:** French (official), English, Italian, Monegasque.
**Official Religion:** Roman Catholicism (95%).
**Leading Industriés:** Tourism and gambling, chemicals, food products, plastics, instruments.
**Places of Interest:** Royal palace; oceanographic museum; garden; Monte Carlo Casino.

Less than half as large as New York City's Central Park, Monaco is the second-smallest nation in the world after Vatican City. It is surrounded by France except for its coast on the Mediterranean Sea. Tourists provide more than half of Monaco's income.

Because Monaco has no income tax and no direct corporation tax, many wealthy persons and foreign corporations locate there.

Rocky cliffs overhang sandy beaches of the Riviera coast. Two peninsulas enclose an excellent harbor. Winters are mild, and summer temperatures are moderated by sea breezes.

Monaco was probably settled by Phoenicians. In 1215 the Genoese built a fortified castle on the site of present-day Monaco. In 1297 control passed to the Grimaldi family of Genoa. Monaco was a Spanish protectorate from 1524 to 1641, a French protectorate from 1641 to 1793, and part of France from 1793 to 1814. Following Napoleon's defeat, the Treaty of Vienna (1815) established Monaco as a protectorate of Sardinia.

In 1861 France assumed the protectorate. The casino at Monte Carlo opened in 1863.

The last absolute monarch, Prince Albert, reigned from 1889 to 1922. He provided the first constitution in 1911 and signed a treaty in 1918 establishing French protection of Monaco.

Louis II ruled from 1922 until 1949, when he was followed by his grandson Prince Rainier III. In 1956 Prince Rainier married American movie actress Grace Kelly.

Prince Rainier in 1962 announced a new constitution giving women the right to vote and abolishing the death penalty.

The government revitalized the resort in the 1970s after buying from private owners the Monte Carlo gambling casino and the main hotels.

In a national election on Jan. 15, 1978, the National and Democratic Union (UND) won all 18 seats in the National Council.

## MONGOLIA

 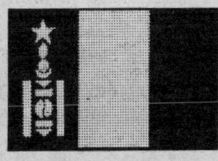

**Official Name:** Mongolian People's Republic.
**Area:** 604,250 square miles (1,565,000 sq. km.).
**Population:** 1,697,320.
**Capital:** Ulaanbaatar, 300,000.
**Government:** One-party communist state.
**Chief of State:** Yumjaagiyn Tsedenbal, chairman, Presidium of Great People's Khural, and first secretary of Communist Party (since 1952).
**Premier:** Jambyn Batmonh (since 1974).
**Legislature:** *People's Great Khural,* 354 members.
**Flag:** Red, blue, and red bars, with national "soyombo" emblem in gold below five-pointed gold star.
**Official Language:** Mongolian.
**Main Ethnic Groups:** Mongolian (90%), Turk (7%).
**Religion:** Buddhism.
**Leading Industries:** Agriculture (cattle, horses, sheep, goats, camels, dairy products, wheat, hay, potatoes, vegetables); manufacturing (processing agricultural products); mining (coal, petroleum, copper, molybdenum, gold, fluorspar).
**Foreign Trade:** *major exports*—livestock, butter, wool and hair, hides, furs; *major imports*—machinery, petroleum, cloth, building materials.
**Places of Interest:** Khangai Mountains; Erdeni-Dzuu monastery, ruins of ancient Mongol capital. *In Ulaanbaatar:* government buildings, opera house.

### MONGOLIA TODAY

Over twice as large as Texas but with fewer people than live in the Houston metropolitan area, Mongolia is a sparsely populated communist country.

Landlocked between the Soviet Union to the north and China to the east, west, and south, Mongolia allies itself with the Soviet Union. Its 1,500-mile border with China's Inner Mongolia is heavily fortified.

Mongolia is a large plateau, with an average elevation of 3,000 to 4,000 feet. In the southeast is the vast Gobi Desert. The climate is generally dry, with cold winters and hot summers.

Forests in the northern mountains, hills, and highland steppes give way gradually to lower steppe grasslands, semidesert country, and barren desert. The principal rivers are the Selenga, Orkhon, and Kerulen.

The most densely populated part of the country follows the valley of the Selenga River northward from Ulaanbaatar.

### HISTORY OF MONGOLIA

In the 1200s Genghis Khan established the Mongolian Empire, with its capital at Karakorum. After 1368 Mongolia fell under the rule of China.

The revolution in China in 1911 led to Mongolia's autonomy.

Russian-supported Mongolian communists took over the government in July 1921. The Jebtsun Damba Khutukhtu remained as titular leader until his death in 1924, when the *Mongolian People's Republic* was established. Khorloin

# NEW ZEALAND

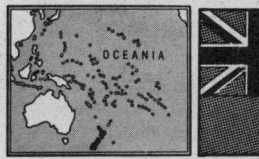 

**Official Name:** Dominion of New Zealand.
**Area:** 103,883 square miles (269,056 sq. km.).
**Population:** 3,407,890.
**Chief Cities:** Wellington, capital, 139,200; Christ-church, 172,400; Auckland, 149,000; Manukau, 142,200.
**Largest Metropolitan Areas:** Auckland, 746,300; Manukau, 746,300.
**Government:** Parliamentary democracy.
**Prime Minister:** Robert D. Muldoon (since 1975).
**Chief of State:** Queen Elizabeth II, represented by Governor-General Sir Denis Blundell (since 1976).
**House of Representatives:** 92 members.
**U.S. Ambassador to New Zealand:** Ann Clark Martindell.
**New Zealand Ambassador to U.S.:** Thomas Francis Gill.
**Flag:** Blue field with British Union Jack at upper hoist corner; four red stars outlined in white represent Southern Cross constellation.
**Languages:** English (official), Maori.
**Ethnic Groups:** European (92%), Maori (8%).
**Main Religions:** Anglicanism (34%), Presbyterianism (22%), Roman Catholicism (15%), Methodism (7%).
**Leading Industries:** Trade and services; manufacturing (food processing, machinery, clothing, furniture, cement, fertilizers); agriculture (sheep, cattle, dairy products, wheat, barley, oats, corn, fruits, vegetables); forestry and lumbering; fishing; mining (gold, coal, petroleum, natural gas); tourism.
**Foreign Trade:** *major exports*—wool, lamb and mutton, butter; *major imports*—automobiles, petroleum and petroleum products, cotton fabrics, agricultural machinery.
**Places of Interest:** Tongariro and Egmont national parks; Franz Josef and Fox glaciers; Milford Sound fjords; Hanmer (thermal) Springs resort; Glow-worm Grotto at Waitomo; Mt. Cook ski resort.

## NEW ZEALAND TODAY

About the size of Colorado, New Zealand is a mountainous island nation some 1,200 miles southeast of Australia. Most of its people are of British descent, and they preserve British traditions. New Zealand also administers several island dependencies (see next page).

Despite expansion of the nation's manufacturing industry, agricultural products account for 95% of New Zealand's exports.

New Zealand has one of the most comprehensive social-welfare programs of any nation, including old-age pensions, free hospital care for everyone, and compensation for all accidents, no matter what their cause.

Most New Zealanders take a summer vacation from mid-December to mid-January.

The nation includes two principal islands, North Island (44,190 sq. mi.) and South Island (58,192 sq. mi.), separated by Cook Strait. Other islands are Steward Island, off the south-

ern tip of South Island, and the Chatham Islands, about 500 miles east of South Island.

The Southern Alps run the length of South Island and contain several glaciers. The highest of these mountains is 12,349-foot Mt. Cook.

The majority of people live in the narrow coastlands in the eastern part of North Island. This island has many active volcanoes, including 9,175-foot Mt. Ruapehu.

The climate ranges from year-round warm temperatures at the northern tip of North Island to cold winters in August on South Island.

## EARLY HISTORY

The race of Polynesians called Maoris came to New Zealand from Southeast Asia at least as early as 1350. When the Dutch explorer Abel J. Tasman discovered the islands in 1642, the unfriendly Maoris prevented him from landing. In 1769 Capt. James Cook of England visited the islands, and in the 1790s several small English whaling settlements were established. In the early 1800s whaling, sealing, and a little primitive agriculture were the only activities carried on by the few settlers, some of whom were navy deserters and escaped convicts from Australia.

In 1840 the New Zealand Company organized the first large migration to the islands and established a settlement at Wellington. In that year the Maoris granted sovereignty over New Zealand to the British crown. In 1845–48 and 1860–70 Maori uprisings were suppressed by military force.

The first real stimulus to New Zealand's settlement was the discovery of gold on South Island in 1861. Development of an export trade in butter and meat, primarily to Britain, was accelerated by refrigerated ships after 1882.

Parliamentary democracy was well established by 1890. New Zealand became a self-governing dominion on Sept. 26, 1907.

## INDEPENDENT NEW ZEALAND

In 1947 New Zealand was the last dominion to ratify the Statute of Westminster, passed in 1931 to grant independence to members of the British Commonwealth. In recent years New Zealand has broadened its international contacts through Commonwealth programs such as the Colombo Plan and through UN activities.

The conservative National Party headed the government for 12 years from 1960 to 1972, winning elections in 1960, 1963, 1966, and 1969. Sir Keith J. Holyoake was prime minister until he retired in February 1972 and was succeeded by John Ross Marshall.

In national elections held on Nov. 25, 1972, the Labour Party won a surprise victory, and its leader, Norman Eric Kirk, became prime minister. Previously, the Labour Party had governed New Zealand in 1935–49 and 1957–60. Kirk died of a heart attack in August 1974, and Wallace Rowling, 46, who had been finance minister, became prime minister.

New Zealand placed new restrictions on immigration in 1974 to limit newcomers to 12,000 to 15,000 persons a year.

Discovery of a large offshore gas field in 1975 promised to reduce New Zealand's dependency

**NEW ZEALAND** *(continued)*

on imported oil in the 1980s.

In elections on Nov. 29, 1975, the National Party defeated Labour. Its leader, Robert D. Muldoon, became prime minister.

New Zealand established a 200-mile fishing and economic zone off its coast on Oct. 1, 1977.

Muldoon's party won a national election on Nov. 25, 1978, but with a reduced majority of 49 seats to the opposition's 43.

The government expelled the Soviet Union's ambassador on Jan. 25, 1980, on charges of contributing a large sum of money to the New Zealand Communist Party.

## NEW ZEALAND DEPENDENCIES

### COOK ISLANDS

**Area:** 90 square miles (234 sq. km.).
**Population:** 15,693.
**Capital:** Avarua, on Rarotonga.

The Cook Islands in the South Pacific divide into two groups.

The seven Northern Group islands are low-lying, sparsely populated, scattered coral atolls.

The fertile islands in the Lower Group are more heavily populated. Rarotonga, the largest Cook island, is volcanic.

Citrus fruits and juices, copra, and tomatoes are the leading exports.

Some of the islands were discovered in 1773 by Capt. James Cook, others by John Williams 50 years later. They became a British protectorate in 1888 and were annexed to New Zealand in 1901. The islands' constitution, adopted in 1965, provides for full internal self-government in association with New Zealand.

A monthly ship and a weekly airplane carry passengers, freight, and mail between New Zealand and Rarotonga. A $22 million jet airport was completed at Rarotonga in 1974 to encourage increased tourism.

### NIUE

**Area:** 100 square miles (259 sq. km.).
**Population:** 3,049.
**Capital:** Tufukla.

Niue, part of the Cook group but separately administered since 1903, lies in the Pacific 580 miles northwest of Rarotonga. The people are Polynesian and speak Samoan. Niue became self-governing in 1974 with a prime minister and a 14-member elected assembly. The soil is fertile.

### ROSS DEPENDENCY

**Area:** 160,000 square miles (414,398 sq. km.).

This region includes the Antarctic continent between longitude 160° E. and 150° W. and the islands south of latitude 60° S. New Zealand took jurisdiction in 1923. The region includes a whaling center and a research station.

### TOKELAU

**Area:** 4 square miles (10 sq. km.).
**Population:** 1,700.

The islands, consisting of three atolls, lie about 300 miles north of Western Samoa and are administered from there. Once part of the Gilbert and Ellice Islands colony, they became a New Zealand territory in 1925. The people are Polynesian. Copra is the islands' principal export.

## NICARAGUA

**Area:** 50,193 square miles (130,000 sq. km.).
**Population:** 2,513,910.
**Capital:** Managua, 398,514.
**Government:** Revolutionary military junta.
**U.S. Ambassador to Nicaragua:** Lawrence A. Pezzullo.
**Nicaraguan Ambassador to U.S.:** Rafael Solis.
**Flag:** Blue, white, and blue stripes, with coat of arms on white stripe.
**Languages:** Spanish (official), English, Indian dialects.
**Ethnic Groups:** Mestizo (70%), European descent (17%), black (9%), Indian (4%).
**Religion:** Roman Catholicism (95%).
**Leading Industries:** Trade and services; agriculture (coffee, cotton, sugarcane, cattle, bananas, corn, tobacco, rice, beans, fruits, vegetables); mining (gold, silver, gypsum); fishing; manufacturing (food processing, textiles, clothing, footwear, tobacco products).
**Foreign Trade:** *major exports*—cotton, meat, coffee, sugar, sesame, cottonseed; *major imports*—insecticides, motor vehicles, pharmaceuticals, iron and steel, petroleum, machinery.
**Places of Interest:** Lake Nicaragua; Mt. Momotombo and other volcanoes; earthquake ruins and rebuilding in Managua; Granada; León Cathedral; Pacific beach resorts; Great Corn Island in the Caribbean.

### NICARAGUA TODAY

About the size of Iowa, Nicaragua is a poverty-stricken Central American country torn by civil war and natural disasters. Although the nation has substantial natural resources and hydroelectric potential, these have remained largely undeveloped. More than half of its fertile land remains covered by tropical forests.

Most of the people are poor. Only about half can read and write.

The nation's population, principal cities, and major industries are largely concentrated in a narrow, fertile, volcanic belt between Lakes Nicaragua and Managua and the Pacific Ocean.

Tropical rain forests grow in the sultry lowland plains of the Mosquito Coast, near the Caribbean.

Farther inland large stands of pines extend to a central plateau that is broken by mountains.

The climate is warm and humid, with an average annual temperature of 81° F.

Honduras lies to the north and Costa Rica to the south.

### HISTORY

Discovered by Christopher Columbus in 1502, Nicaragua was explored in 1522 and 1523 by the Spanish conquistadores Gil González Dávila and Francisco Hernández de Córdoba. The latter founded Granada and León.

Nicaragua was ruled by the captaincy-general of Guatemala until it declared independence from Spain on Sept. 15, 1821. Nicaragua belonged to the United Provinces of Central America from 1823 until it became an independent republic in 1838.

William Walker, an American military adventurer, led an expeditionary army to Nicaragua in 1855. He became president of the country the following year, but was expelled in 1857. He was executed in 1860 in Honduras.

Internal chaos led to the stationing of U.S. Marines in Nicaragua in 1912–25 and 1927–33. In the 1920s and early 1930s the U.S. occupation was fought by guerrillas led by Augusto Cesar Sandino, who was assassinated in 1934.

Gen. Anastasio Somoza seized the presidency in 1936. He ruled as dictator until his assassination in 1956. His son Luis Somoza then served as president in 1956–63. René Schick, controlled by the Somozas, was president in 1963–66.

Anastasio Somoza Debayle, another son of the former dictator, ruled the country as president from 1967.

A revolutionary movement called the Sandinistas (after the guerrilla martyr Sandino) was formed in 1962 with the object of overthrowing the Somozas.

For the next 15 years the Sandinistas carried out sporadic terrorist attacks on the Somozas' U.S.-armed National Guard. But the Somozas merely became more powerful, amassing a fortune estimated at $900 million. When an earthquake devastated Managua in 1972, much of the aid that poured in was believed to have been diverted to the Somozas' personal fortune.

The Sandinista guerrillas launched a major offensive on Oct. 13, 1977, but were soon crushed by Somoza's National Guard.

Popular support for the Sandinistas grew after the government arranged the assassination on Jan. 10, 1978, of Pedro Joaquin Chamorro, owner-editor of *La Prensa,* a newspaper that criticized Somoza.

On Aug. 22, 1978, guerrillas led by Eden Pastora stormed the national palace in Managua. They captured most members of the nation's congress, holding them hostage for two days until Somoza paid $500,000 ransom and freed 83 political prisoners.

Full-scale civil war raged throughout September 1978 as Somoza's troops attacked guerrilla strongholds, destroying the business centers in the country's larger cities.

The Sandinistas began a major offensive from Costa Rica on May 29, 1979, that carried them to victory. Somoza fled into exile on July 17. A 5-member Sandinista military junta took control of the government on July 20.

The civil war was estimated to have cost 40,000 lives and an estimated $1.3 billion in property damage.

The revolutionary junta expropriated the property of Somoza and his associates, which included about 30% of Nicaragua's farmland, and distributed it to landless peasants directly or as cooperatives. About 5,000 of Somoza's supporters were jailed, but the junta restored freedom of the press and other civil liberties. Elections were promised within three to five years.

The revolutionary junta appealed to the U.S., the Soviet Union, and other countries for additional aid in 1980 to rebuild the country's war-torn economy.

# NIGER

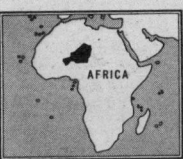 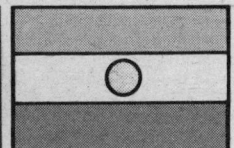

**Official Name:** Republic of Niger.
**Area:** 489,191 square miles (1,267,000 sq. km.).
**Population:** 5,582,660.
**Capital:** Niamey, 130,299.
**Government:** Military junta.
**Chief of State and Head of Government:** Lt. Col. Seyni Kountché (seized power in 1974).
**Supreme Military Council:** 12 members.
**U.S. Ambassador to Niger:** James Keough Bishop.
**Niger Ambassador to U.S.:** André Joseph Wright.
**Flag:** Orange, white, and green stripes, with centered orange disk—the sun.
**Languages:** French (official), Hausa, Djerma.
**Main Ethnic Groups:** Hausa (50%), Djerma (23%), Fulani (15%), Tuareg (10%).
**Leading Religion:** Islam (85%).
**Foreign Trade:** *major exports*—uranium, peanuts, cotton, meat, hides; *major imports*—fuels, machinery, transport equipment, food, consumer goods.
**Chief Agricultural Products:** Peanuts, cattle, millet, beans, manioc, cotton, sorghum.
**Places of Interest:** Lake Chad; native villages.

## NIGER TODAY

Although larger than Texas and California combined, Niger is a poor, landlocked African nation. The northern four-fifths of Niger is covered by the wasteland of the Sahara Desert. The climate is hot, dry, and dusty.

Most of the people are desert nomads or farmers who raise only enough food to support their families. Only about 1 in 20 can read and write. Children under 15 make up almost half the population.

Niger's main political problems result from internal antagonisms—between Arab-Berber nomads and black farmers, between Djerma-Songhai and Hausa ethnic groups, and between traditional conservatives and Western-educated young radicals.

Deposits of high-grade uranium ore that began to be mined and exported in 1971 provide the country's main source of foreign exchange. Large deposits of iron ore have been discovered but cannot be mined until transportation is improved.

The nation has no railroad to the nearest port, about 1,000 miles away on the Atlantic coast.

The most fertile cropland is in the southwestern part of Niger in the 300-mile-long valley of the Niger River.

Algeria and Libya lie to the north, Chad to the east, Nigeria and Benin to the south, and Mali and Upper Volta to the west.

## EARLY HISTORY OF NIGER

From the 600s until the late 1800s, portions of Niger successively belonged to the Songhai, Hausa, and Fulani empires. In the 1600s Tuareg

QUICK QUIZ: In what months can Venus be viewed as an evening star? See Page 749.

## NIGER *(continued)*

tribes formed confederations in the north.

European explorers who first reached Niger in the 1800s found a state of chronic warfare and anarchy. French penetration began in the 1890s with the establishment of military posts along the Niger River. Through conquest and treaties with local sultans and Britain, most of the country's present boundaries were set by 1914.

In 1922 Niger became a French colony under civil administration in the French West Africa federation. Niger became autonomous in 1958.

### INDEPENDENCE

France granted Niger full independence on Aug. 3, 1960. Hamani Diori was elected president in 1960 and was reelected in 1965 and 1970. He banned political parties other than his own Parti Progressiste Nigérien (PPN).

On April 15, 1974, Lt. Col. Seyni Kountché, chief of staff of Niger's 2,500-man army, overthrew Diori. He charged that Diori had failed to deal with the "catastrophic situation" of Niger's many years of drought.

In August 1975 Kountché arrested his chief aide, Vice President Sani Souna Sido, on charges of plotting against him.

Oil and phosphate deposits were discovered in 1975, but their extent remained to be determined.

In February 1976 the government made an emergency appeal to other nations for 200,000 tons of food to save 1.2 million of its people from starving. The problem was caused by the continuing drought that caused crop failures in 1974–75 and 1975–76. The government also asked for $2.7 million in economic aid to fight rats that attacked the nation's scanty remaining food supplies.

Loyal troops put down an attempt to overthrow Kountché's government on March 15, 1976. The leader of the revolt, Capt. Sidi Mohamed, and nine others were sentenced to death.

The government's development plan for 1979–83 emphasizes agricultural development and improvement of education and health services.

## NIGERIA

 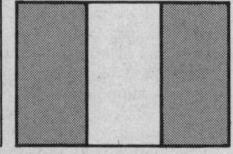

**Official Name:** Federal Republic of Nigeria.
**Area:** 356,669 square miles (923,768 sq. km.).
**Population:** 78,348,000.
**Chief Cities:** Lagos, capital, 1,060,848; Ibadan, 847,000; Ogbomosho, 432,000; Kano, 399,000.
**Largest Metropolitan Area:** Lagos, 1,476,837.
**Government:** Multiparty democratic republic.
**President:** Alhaji Shehu Shagari (since 1979).
**Congress:** *Senate,* 95 members; *House of Representatives,* 449.
**U.S. Ambassador to Nigeria:** Stephen Low.
**Nigerian Ambassador to U.S.:** Olujimi Jolaoso.
**Flag:** Bars of green, white, and green.
**Main Ethnic Groups:** Hausa (21%), Yoruba (20%), Ibo (17%), Fulani (8%).
**Languages:** English (official), tribal dialects.

**Leading Religions:** Islam (47%), Christianity (34%), animism (19%).
**Leading Industries:** Mining (petroleum, natural gas, tin, coal, iron ore); agriculture (peanuts, cattle, cotton, palm kernels, cocoa, rubber, bananas, corn, yams, rice, fruits, vegetables); manufacturing (food processing, cement, petroleum products, textiles, tobacco products, consumer goods).
**Foreign Trade:** *major exports*—crude petroleum, cacao, peanuts and oil, tin, palm nuts and oil, rubber, cotton; *major imports*—food, iron and steel, textiles, automobiles.
**Places of Interest:** Museum of Nigerian antiquities in Lagos; Muslim city of Kano; Ibadan; Benin.

### NIGERIA TODAY

Nigeria is the world's richest, most heavily populated, black nation. A federation of 19 states, it is somewhat larger than Texas and Oklahoma combined.

Nigeria is one of the world's 10 leading producers of petroleum, forestry products, natural rubber, and tin.

Using its oil wealth to build needed facilities of all kinds, the government has placed emphasis on improving the educational system to reduce illiteracy and enable more Nigerians to find jobs as skilled workers and managers. Additional money was spent in building and improving roads to open up interior regions.

The government also has invested large sums to create a "green revolution" to improve the country's agriculture. Most Nigerians continue to live as subsistence farmers.

Nigeria has about 250 tribes, each with its own language. Three groups are dominant: Hausa-Fulani in the north, Yoruba in the west, and Ibo in the east.

Benin lies to the west, Niger to the north, Lake Chad to the northeast, and Cameroon to the east.

### EARLY HISTORY OF NIGERIA

Nigeria's earliest known culture, Nok, flourished in 500 B.C. Later, migrants from the northeast founded the Yoruba and Edo kingdoms of Oyo and Benin and the spiritual center of Ife.

Sub-Saharan states were founded in the 600s to 700s A.D. by the Zaghawa nomads, thought to be of Berber origin. These states were the forerunners of the Kanem empire established in the 700s. Islamic traditions of the Kanem empire were diffused through the seven Hausa city-states on the savanna fringes of the Sahara.

In the 1400s and 1500s the Portuguese and then the British engaged in slave trading on the Atlantic coast.

The Hausa city-states were conquered in the early 1800s in the Islamic crusade of the Fulani warrior Usman dan Fodio.

Slavery ended after 1861 when Britain annexed Lagos as a colony.

In 1883 the Niger Coast Protectorate was declared, and in 1885 the Berlin Conference recognized Britain's claim to southern Nigeria. British troops captured the Muslim stronghold at Kano in 1903. The British created the unified colony and protectorate of Nigeria in 1914.

A nationalist movement after World War I received strong support from Ibo leaders. In 1954 Nigeria became a federation of three autonomous regions, later increased to four.

## INDEPENDENCE

Nigeria was granted full independence on Oct. 1, 1960, with a constitution providing for a federal parliamentary democracy.

Through 1965 an uneasy political balance was maintained by a coalition in the federal government between the northern Hausa-Fulani and the eastern Ibo. The Yoruba of the west formed the opposition.

On Jan. 15, 1966, the Nigerian national government was ousted by a military coup attributed to young Ibo officers. The federal prime minister, Sir Abubakr Tafawa Balewa, and the premiers of the western and northern regions were among those murdered. Army Chief of Staff Maj. Gen. Johnson Aguiyi-Ironsi, an Ibo, became chief of state.

Ironsi dissolved the federation and established a unitary republic in May 1966, triggering anti-Ibo riots in the north.

A new military coup on July 29, 1966, killed Ironsi and brought to power Lt. Col. Yakubu Gowon, a northern Christian from a non-Hausa minority group. Some 30,000 Ibo were massacred, and over one million were driven from the north.

## THE BIAFRA CIVIL WAR

On May 30, 1967, the young Ibo leader Col. Odumegwu Ojukwu proclaimed the independence of the Republic of Biafra (the 29,484-square-mile former Eastern Region). Biafra's secession was resisted on three grounds: (1) much of the oil wealth lay in Biafra; (2) its 12 million inhabitants included 5 million non-Ibo; (3) its secession would fragment Nigeria. Federal troops invaded Biafra on July 6, 1967.

The civil war lasted over 30 months. France and Portugal aided the Biafrans, while Britain and the Soviet Union helped the Nigerian central government. In Biafra starvation brought a high death toll, despite international relief.

The Biafrans, convinced that surrender meant annihilation, managed to hold out against overwhelming odds during 1968. In 1969 Biafra forces reclaimed some territory lost to federal troops. In January 1970, however, federal troops stepped up their offensive. On Jan. 15, 1970, Biafran leaders surrendered.

## MILITARY RULE IN THE 1970s

Except for a few incidents the reconstruction of Nigeria proceeded smoothly. Biafran fears of annihilation proved unfounded. On April 20 Biafra was reinstated as the Central Eastern State on an equal standing with the other federal Nigerian states. In May 1972 Gowon announced that the postwar rehabilitation had been completed.

Hostility between Nigeria and Ivory Coast, growing out of Ivory Coast's opposition to the attack on Biafra, ended in April 1972.

President Gowon announced agreement with Togo on May 1, 1972, to form the Nigerian-Togolese Economic Community.

Nigeria took over thousands of foreign-owned businesses in March 1974, as the government forbade foreign ownership of 55 kinds ranging from dry-cleaning shops to publishing houses.

The six years of drought that ended in 1974

hurt Nigeria's economy despite increased revenue from petroleum and gas.

Brig. Gen. Murtala Muhammed ousted Gowon in a bloodless coup on July 29, 1975.

Muhammed made himself chief of state and head of the ruling 22-member Supreme Military Council while Gowon was in Uganda at an international conference. The new regime accused Gowon's government of widespread corruption. Muhammed's council purged hundreds of public officials from their posts.

On Feb. 13, 1976, Gen. Muhammed was killed in an unsuccessful coup.

Lt. Gen. Olusegun Obasanjo, commander of the army, was chosen by the military council to succeed Muhammed as head of state.

Thirty persons were executed on March 11, 1976, for implication in Muhammed's assassination, including Maj. Gen. Ilyasu Bisalla, who had been promoted to minister of defense after the unsuccessful coup. Seven more were executed on May 15, including Lt. Col. Bukar Dimka, who was said to have confessed heading the plot.

The Nigerian government in 1976 denounced Britain for refusing to extradite former President Gowon to stand trial. In London, Gowon denied any connection with the coup attempt.

## MULTIPARTY DEMOCRACY

The first nationwide elections in over 11 years were held on Aug. 31, 1977, to choose members for an assembly to write a new constitution. The 231-member body began meeting on Oct. 6, 1977.

The growing importance of Nigeria in international affairs was emphasized in 1978 when U.S. President Carter visited Nigeria on March 31–April 3—the first tour by an American chief executive to a black African nation.

The constituent assembly completed work on the nation's new constitution, presenting it to Obasanjo on Aug. 29, 1978. It provided for a government modeled on that of the U.S. with a strong president elected for a 4-year term and a bicameral national congress.

Obasanjo ended the 12-year state of emergency on Sept. 21, 1978, lifting a ban on political activities in preparation for national elections.

The military government nationalized British petroleum interests in Nigeria on July 31, 1979, as a protest against Britain's policies regarding racial problems in Zimbabwe-Rhodesia.

In a series of elections in July and August 1979, Nigerians elected a president, members of a national congress, 19 state governors, and state legislators.

As the nation's first civilian president since 1966, Alhaji Shehu Shagari, 54, winner of the presidential election, took office on Oct. 1, 1979, as Obasanjo followed through on his promise to end military control of the government.

President Shagari's National Party held pluralities of 36 seats in the 95-member senate and 168 in the 449-member house of representatives. The second-leading party, the Unity Party, took 111 seats in the house and 28 in the senate.

In 1980 President Shagari visited the United States to appeal for aid in improving Nigeria's farm production.

QUICK QUIZ: About what time does the sun rise in New Orleans during January? See page 750.

# NORWAY

**Official Name:** Kingdom of Norway.
**Area:** 125,182 square miles (324,219 sq. km.).
**Population:** 4,099,800.
**Chief Cities:** Oslo, capital, 461,437; Bergen, 212,308; Trondheim, 135,322.
**Largest Metropolitan Area:** Oslo, 645,413.
**Government:** Constitutional monarchy.
**Prime Minister:** Odvar Nordli (since 1976).
**King:** Olav V (reigned since 1957).
**Legislature:** *Storting,* 155 members.
**U.S. Ambassador to Norway:** Sidney Anders Rand.
**Norwegian Ambassador to U.S.:** Knut Hedemann.
**Flag:** Blue Latin cross bordered in white on red field.
**Language:** Norwegian (Bokmal and Nynorsk dialects).
**Principal Ethnic Group:** Norwegian.
**State Religion:** Lutheranism (96%).
**Leading Industries:** Manufacturing (aluminum, paper, chemicals, ships, furniture); trade and shipping; services; construction; mining (petroleum, natural gas, iron ore, lead, zinc, copper, molybdenum); agriculture (cattle, sheep, goats, dairy products, barley, potatoes, fruits, vegetables); fishing; forestry and lumbering.
**Foreign Trade:** *major exports*—petroleum, gas, manufactured goods, shipping services, aluminum, fish, paper, pulp; *major imports*—machinery, ships, food.
**Places of Interest:** North Cape and "land of the midnight sun"; fjord country; old Bergen; Nidaros Cathedral at Trondheim; Stavanger Cathedral; Maihaugen museum at Lillehammer. *In Oslo:* Akershus Castle; Vigeland sculptures, Frogner Park; museums.

## NORWAY TODAY

Somewhat larger than New Mexico, Norway is an important industrial and trading nation of northern Europe. Production from huge offshore deposits of oil and gas has brought Norway increased prosperity.

Since the time of the Vikings, Norwegians have been seafarers. Norway has the world's third-largest merchant fleet, and, until surpassed by oil exports, income from shipping was Norway's largest source of foreign exchange.

Norway has experienced tremendous economic expansion, especially in mining, shipbuilding, and manufacturing industries. Growth has enabled mining and manufacturing to surpass in importance the country's traditional industries of agriculture, forestry, and fishing, bringing the Norwegian people a high standard of living.

Wealth from its offshore oil and gas fields has enabled Norway to cut income taxes, while at the same time increasing social benefits. The government placed restrictions on the production of petroleum and gas to ensure a steady income for many years into the future.

To protect its well-paid labor force from an influx of cheap labor, Norway severely limits most immigration.

Norway occupies the western and northernmost part of the Scandinavian peninsula. Sweden lies to the east and south. Finland and the

Soviet Union are to the northeast.

About one-third of the country lies within the Arctic Circle. The terrain is mountainous, and the 1,700-mile coastline is deeply marked with fjords, bays, and inlets. Numerous offshore island chains dot the coastline.

, The warming waters of the Gulf Stream keep Norway's climate comparatively mild. The far north is the land of the midnight sun with continuous daylight from mid-May to the last of July. From late November to the end of January the sun does not rise above the horizon.

## EARLY HISTORY

Hunters and fishermen lived in Norway at least 8,000 years ago. Fortified settlements began to be built about A.D. 400.

The Viking Age in which Norwegian seafarers raided and plundered along the coasts of Europe began about 900. Much of Norway was united for the first time in 900–940 by King Harold Fairhair (Harold I). Christianity was introduced by Olav I (995–1000). Olav II was killed by a peasant army in 1030, and Norway then passed under the rule of Canute the Great of England and Denmark.

The latter half of the 1100s was a period of warfare among contenders for the Norwegian throne. In the 1200's Haakon IV acquired Iceland, Greenland, the Faeroe Islands, the Shetlands, and the Orkneys.

The royal male line died out with Haakon V in 1319, so Norway entered into union with Sweden under Magnus V. Queen Margrethe I of Denmark united the three Scandinavian kingdoms in the Union of Kalmar (1397), which lasted until Sweden broke away in 1523. Union between Norway and Denmark continued until 1814, when Denmark ceded Norway to Sweden.

## INDEPENDENT KINGDOM OF NORWAY

On June 7, 1905, the Norwegian parliament declared the union with Sweden dissolved. Norway became an independent kingdom under Haakon VII, a Danish prince.

Norway was neutral in World War I and sought neutrality in World War II. However, Germany invaded in April 1940, occupying the country until 1945. A puppet government was established under Vidkun Quisling, whose name became a synonym for traitor.

The postwar period saw rapid economic and industrial development. Haakon VII died in 1957 and was succeeded by Olav V.

In January 1972 the Norwegian government agreed to enter the European Common Market, but in September the voters rejected entry.

In September 1973 the socialist parties won a one-seat majority in parliamentary elections. Trygve Bratteli of the Labor Party became premier.

Odvar Nordli, head of the Labor Party, became prime minister on Jan. 12, 1976, upon the retirement of the 66-year-old Bratteli.

Norway established a 200-mile fishing and economic zone along its coast on Jan. 1, 1977, closing the Norwegian part of the North Sea to foreign fishermen. In June 1977 Norway also claimed a fishing protection zone around Svalbard in the Arctic Ocean. Negotiations were undertaken to determine a dividing line between claims of Norway and the Soviet Union.

Prime Minister Nordli's government won another four years in office in a national election on Sept. 11–12, 1977. His Labor Party gained 14 seats for a total of 76 in the 155-member Storting. However, his coalition partner, the Left Socialist Party, lost 14 seats, retaining only two.

The government agreed in September 1980 to stockpile large amounts of military equipment and arms for use by U.S. Marines who would be flown in by airlift in the event of a war with the Soviet Union, but continued its policy of not permitting troops of NATO allies to be stationed in Norway.

## NORWEGIAN OVERSEAS AREAS

### SVALBARD

**Area:** 23,957 square miles (62,004 sq. km.).
**Population:** 3,700.
Svalbard, some 400 miles north of Norway, is a barren archipelago with an Arctic climate. West Spitsbergen is the largest island.

The islands first were found by Norwegians in the 1100s. The Dutch rediscovered them in 1596, and in the 1600s rival claims were made by the Dutch, British, and Norwegians. Sovereignty disappeared as an issue until the 1900s, when rich coal deposits were discovered. In 1920 Norway's sovereignty was recognized. Svalbard officially became part of Norway in 1925.

**JAN MAYEN:** Island (144 sq. mi.) 300 miles north of Iceland; annexed in 1929.

**BOUVET ISLAND:** Uninhabited South Atlantic island (23 sq. mi.); became a dependency in 1930.

**PETER I ISLAND:** Uninhabited Antarctic island (96 sq. mi.); became a dependency in 1933.

**QUEEN MAUD LAND:** Part of Antarctic continent; claimed by Norway in 1939.

## OMAN

**Official Name:** Sultanate of Oman.
**Area:** 82,030 square miles (212,457 sq. km.).
**Population:** 905,790.
**Cities:** Muscat, capital, 10,000; Matrah, 70,000.
**Government:** Absolute monarchy.
**Sultan:** Qaboos Bin Said (reigned since 1970).
**U.S. Ambassador to Oman:** Marshall W. Wiley.
**Omani Ambassador to U.S.:** Sadek Jawad Sulaiman.
**Flag:** Red bar with crossed white swords next to staff; white, red, and green stripes.
**Official Language:** Arabic.
**Chief Ethnic Groups:** Arab, Iranian, Baluchi.
**Main Religion:** Islam.
**Leading Industries:** Mining (petroleum, copper); construction; agriculture (dates, livestock, pomegranates, coconuts, grains, fruits, vegetables); oil refining; fishing; food processing.
**Foreign Trade:** *major exports*—petroleum, dates, pomegranates, limes, fish, hides; *major imports*—food, cotton goods, rice, coffee, tea, motor vehicles, construction materials.
**Places of Interest:** Royal palace; ancient forts.

### OMAN TODAY

About the size of Kansas, Oman is an oil-rich Arab sultanate on the Arabian Sea.

Oman has used much of its oil wealth to educate its children, to provide free outdoor color television sets for each community, to build a lavish new palace for the sultan, and to equip its army. Airports, highways, and sewerage systems have been constructed.

Because about three-fourths of the people depend on farming for their living, the government stimulated agriculture by importing new breeds of livestock and constructing model farms.

The country generally has a hot desert climate, averaging between 69° and 90°F. Average annual rainfall is less than 4 inches in Muscat.

### HISTORY

Oman was an important farming and trading area with many towns and villages and an elaborate irrigation system in the 2000s B.C.

In the 600s A.D. Saudi Arabian traders spread Muslim influence to the Persian Gulf. In the 1500s the Portuguese conquered the land, using Muscat as a base to control Persian Gulf trade. Arabs ejected the Portuguese in 1650.

In 1696–98 Oman drove the Portuguese out of bases in East Africa, captured Mombassa in Kenya, and won control of Zanzibar.

The present Said dynasty came to power in Muscat and Oman in 1741. British influence was established with a treaty of friendship in 1798.

In the early 1800s Oman was the most powerful state in Arabia, controlling much of East Africa. But when the ruler died in 1856, his sons quarreled and then divided the empire in 1861. Zanzibar continued to pay tribute to the sultans until its independence in 1964.

Before oil began to be produced in 1967, Oman had become a poor country.

In July 1970 the sultan's son, Qaboos Bin Said, overthrew his father. The new sultan changed the name of the country from Muscat and Oman to Oman. He began using the oil income for progressive economic and social reforms.

The sultan took majority control of the oil industry on Jan. 1, 1974.

After a dozen years of fighting in southern Oman, the government announced in January 1976 that rebel leaders had surrendered. The civil war had begun in 1964 as rebels sought independence for the Dhofar area. The rebels were supplied with Chinese and Soviet arms from Southern Yemen.

Britain closed its military base at Masira, Oman, on March 31, 1977, its last military outpost in the Middle East.

The U.S. on June 5, 1980, announced an agreement with Oman for use of ports and air bases by American military forces.

The country's 5-year plan for 1981–85 placed emphasis on the development of companies to oversee expansion of production from agriculture and fisheries.

QUICK QUIZ: How long does it take the Sun to make one orbit around the Milky Way? See page 752.

# PAKISTAN

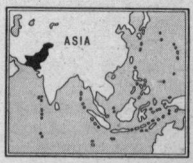 

**Official Name:** Islamic Republic of Pakistan.
**Area:** 310,404 square miles (803,943 sq. km.).
**Population:** 82,679,500.
**Chief Cities:** Islamabad, capital, 77,318; Karachi, 3,498,634; Lahore, 2,165,372; Shah Faisalabad (formerly Lyallpur), 822,263; Hyderabad, 628,310; Rawalpindi, 615,392.
**Government:** Military dictatorship.
**President:** Gen. Mohammad Zia al-Haq (since 1978).
**U.S. Ambassador to Pakistan:** Arthur W. Hummel Jr.
**Pakistani Ambassador to U.S.:** Muhammad Khan.
**Flag:** Green field with white crescent and star; white bar along hoist.
**Chief Ethnic Groups:** Punjabi (65%), Sindhi (11%), Urdu (9%), Pathan (8%).
**Principal Languages:** Urdu (official), English, Punjabi.
**Main Religion:** Islam (97%).
**Leading Industries:** Agriculture (wheat, cattle, sugarcane, rice, cotton, barley, corn, tobacco); manufacturing (textiles, chemicals, steel, electricity); mining (natural gas, petroleum, coal); fishing.
**Foreign Trade:** *major exports*—cotton, rice, textiles; *major imports*—grains, machinery, raw materials.
**Places of Interest:** Modern capital of Islamabad; Karachi museum; Shalimar Gardens, fort and Badshahi Mosque in Lahore; Peshawar museum and bazaars; Mohenjo-Daro excavations; Taxila ruins near Rawalpindi; Khyber Pass near Peshawar; Kaghan Valley; Tarbela Dam.

## PAKISTAN TODAY

About as large as Texas and Louisiana combined, Pakistan has the ninth-largest population among the nations of the world.

Most of Pakistan's people are poor farm workers who live at the subsistence level, earning less than $300 per year. Less than 1 in 5 can read and write.

The government owns most large basic manufacturing industries, as well as transportation, banking, and insurance.

However, the country's major export is its workers for construction projects in other Muslim countries. They send home nearly $2 billion in annual earnings.

Because Pakistan is an Islamic state, the oil-rich Arab nations of the Middle East have invested hundreds of millions of dollars to help develop its industrialization program. In addition, large amounts of aid have been provided by the United States, China, and other nations.

Pakistan rises from the deserts of Sind in the south and Baluchistan in the west to the forested hills in the north, and then to the soaring Himalayas. The Indus River waters much of the eastern and central region.

The climate is hot and dry near the coast of the Arabian Sea, but is cool and temperate in the northeastern uplands.

Iran lies to the west, Afghanistan to the north, China to the northeast, and India to the east.

## EARLY HISTORY

In the 700s the Islamic faith was introduced by Arab traders. In the 900s Muslim warriors swept into the subcontinent and conquered most of Pakistan. Muslim rule lasted 1,000 years, reaching its peak under the Mogul empire in the 1500s.

Portuguese traders arrived in the 1400s. By the 1800s the British East India Company had become the dominant power, with the last Mogul emperor deposed in 1859.

Under the leadership of Mohammed Ali Jinnah and Liaquat Ali Khan, the Muslim League began demanding in 1940 a separate state composed of areas where Muslims were in the majority.

## INDEPENDENCE

In 1947 Britain agreed to the formation of separate Hindu and Islamic states. Pakistan came into being as an independent dominion within the British Commonwealth of Nations on Aug. 15, 1947, with Liaquat Ali Khan as prime minister and with Mohammed Ali Jinnah as governor-general. Islamic Pakistan consisted of two provinces, East and West Pakistan, separated from each other by 1,000 miles of Indian territory.

Muslim-Hindu disputes intensified after independence. States with Hindu majorities but Muslim rulers were forcibly joined to India. Kashmir, a state with a majority of Muslim residents but ruled by a Hindu minority, became the chief point of contention, and fighting over control of Kashmir broke out between Pakistan and India in 1948. The UN negotiated a cease-fire the following year, but tension remained high. Pakistani-Indian fighting resumed in September 1965. A peace accord was signed early in 1966.

Elsewhere, Pakistan faced economic and political difficulties. Following the death of Mohammed Ali Jinnah in 1948 and the assassination of Liaquat Ali Khan in 1951, the precarious control of the new government gradually disintegrated.

A new constitution went into effect on March 23, 1956, making the nation the *Islamic Republic of Pakistan*. Maj. Gen. Iskander Mirza became the first president.

By 1958 the East Pakistan provincial legislature was in turmoil. In West Pakistan the khan of Kalat moved toward secession. On Oct. 7, 1958, the commander in chief of the army, Gen. Mohammed Ayub Khan, took over the government. Violent antigovernment riots erupted in late 1968 and early 1969.

On March 25, 1969, President Ayub resigned and turned the government over to Gen. Agha Mohammed Yahya Khan, commander in chief of the armed forces.

## WAR WITH INDIA AND BANGLADESH

In general elections in March 1971 the nationalist Awami League, led by Sheik Mujibur (Mujib) Rahman, won nearly all of East Pakistan's seats, giving it a majority in the national assembly.

When President Yahya postponed convocation of the assembly, a massive uprising swept East Pakistan.

The league proclaimed the province an independent nation called *Bangladesh*. Pakistan outlawed the league and imprisoned Mujib.

The Pakistani army attempted to crush the rebellion in East Pakistan. About 9 million

Bengali refugees flooded into India.

India, which sided with the rebels, began an armed invasion of Pakistan on Dec. 3, 1971. Pakistani forces surrendered on Dec. 16.

Some 90,000 Pakistani soldiers and former officials in Bangladesh were interned as prisoners of war. During the war hostilities had also broken out with India on the West Pakistan border in Kashmir, producing a million more refugees.

## RULE BY BHUTTO IN THE 1970s

Under the impact of the defeat, the military junta in Pakistan collapsed. Zulfikar Ali Bhutto, head of the National Party, was sworn in as provisional president in late December 1971.

Bhutto released Mujib, who returned to Bangladesh. Soon thereafter the displaced Pakistani president, General Yahya, and his top military associates were arrested.

In January 1972 Pakistan withdrew from the Commonwealth of Nations because Britain had established diplomatic relations with Bangladesh.

An interim constitution approved by the national assembly in April gave Bhutto almost dictatorial powers. Martial law was lifted on April 21, 1972.

On April 12, 1973, President Bhutto signed into law a new constitution that provided for a president and a prime minister elected by the national assembly. In August 1973 Bhutto gave up the presidency to become prime minister.

On April 9, 1974, Pakistan, India, and Bangladesh signed an agreement disposing of outstanding problems remaining from the 1971 war.

The socialist government of Prime Minister Bhutto completed the nationalization of basic industries in 1974 by taking over private banks and shipping companies. Previously the government had nationalized airlines, railways, iron and steel, automobile manufacturing, and other heavy manufacturing industries.

The government also began a program in 1974 of giving 1,350 square feet of free land to each homeless rural family.

Bhutto in August 1974 announced restoration of basic civil rights that had been suspended since 1970. But six months later, on Feb. 10, 1975, he banned the main opposition political party, the National Awami Party (NAP).

The United States ended a 10-year arms embargo against Pakistan on Feb. 23, 1975, enabling the country to purchase modern arms for its military forces.

After six years of construction the world's second-largest dam, the $1.3 billion Tarbela Dam on the Indus River, was completed in 1976, providing needed irrigation for thousands of acres of farmland. The dam is 9,000 feet long and 480 feet high. Work continued on the development of the dam's 12 hydroelectric generating units that will produce 2,100 megawatts.

The government announced plans in 1976 to construct 24 nuclear power plants by 1996.

Some 40,000 Chinese engineers and workers spent six years, in 1972–78, constructing a 468-mile highway through Pakistan's Karakoram Range, providing China with its first modern land route to the Middle East.

After a parliamentary election on March 7, 1977, Bhutto announced that his Pakistan People's Party had won a landslide victory, taking 133 of the 200 elective seats.

Opponents declared the election had been stolen by fraud. In the next four months Pakistan was thrown into turmoil with strikes, riots, and demonstrations in which at least 350 persons were killed. Bhutto declared martial law, imposed censorship, and jailed opponents.

## MILITARY RULE

Gen. Mohammad Zia al-Haq, 53, chief of staff of the army, seized control of the government on July 5, 1977, jailing Bhutto and his closest aides. Zia imposed martial law but freed the press, radio, and TV of censorship. He established severe Islamic punishments, including amputations of hands and public whipping, for such crimes as theft and annoying women.

Bhutto was convicted of murder in 1978. He was hanged on April 4, 1979.

When President Fazal Elahi Chaudry completed his elected 5-year term, Zia took the title of president for himself on Sept. 16, 1978, while retaining his titles as chief martial-law administrator and armed forces commander.

After the CIA confirmed in 1979 that Pakistan was building a secret plant to manufacture enriched uranium that could be used to make atomic weapons, the U.S. cut off economic and military aid of about $40 million a year. Zia denied Pakistan planned to build atomic weapons and appealed for restoration of U.S. aid, but he said Pakistan might explode a nuclear device for research purposes.

Relations between Pakistan and Afghanistan worsened in 1979–80 when Zia permitted about 1 million Afghan tribesmen to take refuge and use Pakistan as a base for guerrilla raids against Afghanistan's communist government and troops of its Soviet ally. The influx of Afghan refugees added to Pakistan's difficult economic and social problems.

After scheduling a national election for November 1979, Zia canceled it on Oct. 16, 1979, banned political activities, and arrested hundreds of politicians, including the widow and daughter of executed former prime minister Bhutto. He also tightened martial law, putting most civilian crimes under military courts.

Mobs of Pakistani Muslims, inflamed by anti-American statements by Iran's Ayatollah Khomeini, attacked and burned the U.S. embassy in Islamabad on Nov. 21, 1979, killing two Americans and two Pakistani employees. U.S. installations in other Pakistani cities also were attacked. Although the Pakistani government apologized, the U.S. evacuated hundreds of personnel and dependents.

After Soviet troops invaded Afghanistan to control its communist government, the U.S. in January 1980 offered $400 million in military aid to bolster Pakistan's defenses. However, President Zia rejected the offer as "peanuts," explaining that substantially more aid was necessary. He also indicated he feared the U.S. would attach strings to the aid to try to halt Pakistan's effort to develop an atomic bomb.

QUICK QUIZ: How many moons does Saturn have? See page 753.

# PANAMA

 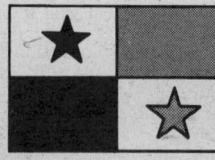

**Official Name:** Republic of Panama.
**Area:** 29,762 square miles (77,083 sq. km.).
**Population:** 1,971,360.
**Capital:** Panama City, 439,870.
**Government:** Republic.
**President:** Aristedes Royo (since 1978).
**Parliament:** *Legislative Council,* 57 members; *National Assembly,* 505 members.
**U.S. Ambassador to Panama:** Ambler H. Moss Jr.
**Ambassador to U.S.:** Juan Jose Amado.
**Flag:** Quarters of blue, red, and white, with blue and red stars on the two white portions.
**Official Language:** Spanish.
**Main Ethnic Groups:** Mestizo (70%), black (13%), European descent (10%), Indian (6%).
**Official Religion:** Roman Catholicism (93%).
**Leading Industries:** Agriculture (rice, bananas, corn, cocoa, abaca, tobacco, coffee, palm kernels, livestock); fishing; trade and services; manufacturing (food processing, oil refining, tobacco products, textiles, soap, cement); forestry and lumbering; mining (gold).
**Foreign Trade:** *major exports*—bananas, refined petroleum, shrimp, cocoa; *major imports*—crude petroleum, motor vehicles, foodstuffs.
**Places of Interest:** Panama Canal; Panama City; El Valle; Darién; Contadora, Taboga, San Blas islands; Pacific coast beaches; Piñas Bay; Portobelo ruins near Colón.

## PANAMA TODAY

Almost as large as South Carolina, Panama numbers among its resources large copper deposits, rich farmland, and the Panama Canal. About half the people are farmers. Most of the rest make a living directly or indirectly from the canal.

For many years U.S. control of the Panama Canal had been a major point of contention between the U.S. and Panama. Panamanians felt that their country did not receive a fair share of the profits from operation of the canal and that Panama should have sovereignty over the Panama Canal Zone. In 1979 the U.S. gave up sovereignty over the canal zone.

Panama lies between the Caribbean and the Pacific on the isthmus linking North and South America.

There are lowlands on both coasts of Panama. The eastern portion of the country is covered by rain forest. Colombia is to the east and Costa Rica to the west.

## EARLY HISTORY

Panama's history has been shaped by its strategic location between two oceans. The Spanish explorer Rodrigo de Bastidas visited eastern Panama in 1501, and Columbus claimed the area for Spain in the following year. In 1513 Vasco Núñez de Balboa became the first European to cross the narrow isthmus to reach the Pacific. Occupied by Spaniards, Panama served as the route for shipping Inca treasures to Spain in the 1500s and 1600s. Spanish rule was overthrown in 1821, and Panama became a province of Colombia.

The California gold rush in 1849 revived interest in Panama's geographical importance as a route from the Atlantic to the Pacific. The Panama Railroad (completed in 1855) carried gold-rush traffic across the isthmus.

French attempts during the 1880s to build a canal were unsuccessful because 20,000 workers died of yellow fever.

The U.S. bought the canal rights from France, but Colombia demanded more money.

## INDEPENDENCE AND THE PANAMA CANAL

On Nov. 3, 1903, Panamanians revolted and declared independence from Colombia. President Theodore Roosevelt immediately sent U.S. Marines to protect the new government. On Nov. 18, 1903, the U.S. and Panama signed the Hay–Bunau-Varilla Treaty giving the U.S. control of the 10-mile-wide Panama Canal Zone for a payment of $10 million plus $250,000 a year.

U.S. Col. William C. Gorgas in 1904–13 wiped out the mosquitoes in Panama that caused yellow fever and malaria.

Construction of the canal began in 1907 under Col. George W. Goethals. On Aug. 15, 1914, the first ship went through the canal from the Atlantic to the Pacific. Officially opened on July 12, 1920, the canal cost about $350 million.

Brig. Gen. Omar Torrijos Herrera, commander of the national guard, seized control of the government on Oct. 11, 1968. Torrijos abolished all political parties in 1969.

A new constitution was proclaimed in 1972 establishing a 505-member assembly to meet for one 30-day session each year.

After 13 years of negotiations, the U.S. and Panama agreed in 1977 to new Panama Canal treaties returning control of the waterway to Panama. Ratification by the U.S. Senate was completed on April 18, 1978.

President Carter visited on June 16, 1978, for formal ceremonies concluding the new treaties.

In October 1978 Torrijos stepped down as chief of state after the national assembly elected his choice as president, former education minister Aristedes Royo. Torrijos remained head of the armed forces and the power behind the Panamanian government.

The U.S. on Oct. 1, 1979, formally returned to Panama sovereignty over the 553-square-mile Panama Canal Zone that had been governed by the U.S. since 1904. After Panama's flag was raised over the former U.S. Canal Zone, President Royo declared: "A state within a state no longer exists."

All U.S. control over the canal will end at noon on Dec. 31, 1999.

The self-exiled shah of Iran sought refuge in Panama in 1979, but left for Egypt in March 1980 to escape Iranian efforts to extradite him for trial.

Panamanians were given a taste of democracy for the first time in 12 years on Sept. 28, 1980, when a multiparty election was held for 19 of the 57 seats in the national Legislative Council. A majority of the seats were won by the government party while many opponents boycotted the election.

# PAPUA NEW GUINEA

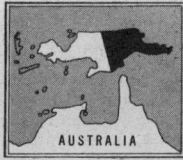 

AUSTRALIA

**Official Name:** Papua New Guinea.
**Area:** 178,260 square miles (461,691 sq. km.).
**Population:** 3,223,060.
**Capital:** Port Moresby, 113,449.
**Government:** Parliamentary state.
**Prime Minister:** Sir Julius Chan (since 1980).
**Chief of State:** Queen Elizabeth II, represented by Governor-General Tore Lokoloko (since 1977).
**Parliament:** *House of Assembly*, 109 members.
**U.S. Ambassador:** Harvey Feldman.
**Papua New Guinean Ambassador to U.S.:** Paulias Nguna Matane.
**Flag:** Five-star constellation on black triangle on lower left; gold bird of paradise on red triangle on upper right.
**Languages:** English, Pidgin English, Motu, more than 700 tribal dialects.
**Ethnic Groups:** Melanesians, Asians, Australians, Europeans.
**Religions:** Christianity, tribal religions.
**Leading Industries:** Mining (copper, gold); agriculture (cocoa, copra, rubber, tea, fruits, vegetables); forestry and lumbering; fishing; food processing.
**Foreign Trade:** *major exports*—copper, gold, plywood, lumber, seafood, cocoa, rubber, tea; *major imports*—machinery, vehicles, food.
**Places of Interest:** Port Moresby government buildings; thatched-roof tribal villages; copper mines on island of Bougainville; Rabaul on island of New Britain; towns of Mt. Hagan, Lae, Goroka, Aitape, Wewak, Popondetta, Madang, Kerema, and Daru on mainland New Guinea.

## PAPUA NEW GUINEA TODAY

Larger than California, Papua New Guinea faces a multitude of problems. Most of the mountainous country is covered by tropical rain forests with few roads. The extent of the country's mineral resources is unknown, but copper and gold are mined for export. Only a small portion of the nation's land is farmed.

Communication among the people is a major difficulty. More than 700 tribal dialects are spoken, with one tribe being unable to understand another. Many of the people speak Pidgin English. Few can read and write. Most people live in tribal villages leading the same primitive life as their ancestors.

Wars between tribes are frequent.

The country depends heavily on over $200 million annual aid from Australia.

Papua New Guinea covers the eastern half of the island of New Guinea, just north of Australia. The country also includes many offshore islands, the largest of which are New Britain (14,600 sq. mi.), Bougainville (3,880 sq. mi.), and New Ireland (3,340 sq. mi.). The western half of New Guinea is the Indonesian province of Irian Jaya.

The coastal plain of New Guinea is 50 to 150 miles wide. Inland mountains tower to a height of 14,500 feet.

The climate is hot along the coasts, with cooler temperatures in the uplands. There is much rain.

## EARLY HISTORY

The people of Papua New Guinea are believed to have come to the islands from the Asian mainland thousands of years ago.

The first European known to have visited New Guinea was the Portuguese governor of the Molucca Islands, Jorge de Meneses, in 1526.

In 1884 Britain made southeastern New Guinea a protectorate, and Germany claimed northeastern New Guinea and the offshore islands.

Southeastern New Guinea became Australia's Territory of Papua on Sept. 1, 1906. With the defeat of Germany in World War I, the League of Nations transferred administration of northeastern New Guinea and the offshore islands to Australia in 1920.

During World War II the Japanese captured northern New Guinea, but Port Moresby became an important Allied military base. The U.S. and Australia recaptured all New Guinea by 1944.

In 1949 Australia united northeastern and southeastern New Guinea under a single administration called *Papua New Guinea.*

Papua New Guinea's first house of assembly convened in 1964 with debates conducted in pidgin English. In 1968 new elections were held for the house of assembly, and an executive council, or cabinet, was formed.

After national elections in 1972 a coalition government was formed with Michael Somare of the Pangu Party as chief minister.

Australia granted complete self-government on Dec. 1, 1973.

The government in September 1974 reached an agreement with copper-mining companies to turn over about half their profits in taxes.

Nationalists on the copper-rich island of Bougainville declared their independence from Papua New Guinea on Sept. 1, 1975, naming their government the Republic of the Northern Solomons.

The Papua New Guinea government responded by suspending Bougainville's provincial government and taking over administration.

## INDEPENDENCE

Australia gave Papua New Guinea complete independence on Sept. 16 1975, with Somare as the nation's first prime minister.

Papua New Guinea reached agreement with the European Economic Community (EEC) in March 1977, allowing it to export most of its products to the EEC without having to pay tariffs.

The first national election since independence was held June 18 to July 9, 1977. Prime Minister Somare's coalition parties won a majority of 60 seats in the 109-member parliament.

Increasing unemployment and a soaring crime rate brought criticism of Somare's administration. On March 11, 1980, he lost a vote of confidence 57 to 49. He was succeeded as prime minister by Sir Julius Chan, 43, head of the opposition People's Progress Party.

QUICK QUIZ: When is the first U.S. spacecraft scheduled to fly past Uranus? See page 755.

# PARAGUAY

**Official Name:** Republic of Paraguay.
**Area:** 157,048 square miles (406,752 sq. km.).
**Population:** 3,299,170.
**Capital:** Asunción, 434,928 (met. area, 565,363).
**Government:** Republic under dictatorship.
**President:** Gen. Alfredo Stroessner (since 1954).
**Legislature:** *Senate,* 30 members; *Chamber of Deputies,* 60 members.
**U.S. Ambassador to Paraguay:** Lyle F. Lane.
**Paraguayan Ambassador to U.S.:** Mario Lopez Escobar.
**Flag:** Red, white, and blue stripes; national coat of arms in center.
**Official Languages:** Spanish, Guaraní.
**Principal Ethnic Group:** Mestizo (95%).
**Official Religion:** Roman Catholicism (97%).
**Leading Industries:** Agriculture (wheat, corn, manioc, sweet potatoes, beans, rice, sugarcane, livestock, fruits, vegetables); lumbering and forestry; food processing; manufacturing (electricity, oil refining, cement, consumer goods).
**Foreign Trade:** *major exports*—meat, timber, oilseed, tobacco, cotton, quebracho extract, hides; *major imports*—machinery, food, steel, consumer goods.
**Places of Interest:** Guairá Falls; Port President Stroessner; San Bernardino and El Tirol tourist resorts; Jesuit missions in south. *In Asunción:* Cathedral; Pantheon of the Heroes; botanical garden.

## PARAGUAY TODAY

About the size of California, Paraguay is one of the poorest nations of South America. The majority of the people are farmers and ranch workers. Most raise only enough food to support their own families. The nation has no mineral resources to aid in building a modern economy. Hopes for industrialization are pinned on completion in the 1980s of $10 billion in hydroelectric projects financed by Brazil and Argentina.

In the past two decades about a million Paraguayans have migrated to Argentina to escape poverty and political repression.

Throughout most of its history the nation has been ruled by a succession of dictators, so that the people have grown used to lack of political freedom. Two major wars with its neighbors in the 1870s and 1930s contributed to the nation's poverty. The country's only paved highway links the capital, Asunción, with Brazil. Most villages and towns have dirt streets and no sidewalks.

The Paraguay and Alto Paraná rivers are important waterways. To the west of the Paraguay River lies the arid, sparsely settled region of the Chaco Boreal.

Argentina lies to the south and west, Brazil to the northeast, and Bolivia to the northwest.

## HISTORY OF PARAGUAY

Spanish conquistadores came to Paraguay in 1524, establishing Asunción in 1537 and intermarrying with the docile Guaraní Indians. In the 1500s and 1600s Jesuit missionaries instituted a written form of the Guaraní language, still used by most Paraguayans today.

In 1721 a successful revolt led by José de Antequera enabled him to rule an independent Paraguay for about 10 years.

Paraguay declared independence from Spain on May 14, 1811. The first of three strong dictators who shaped the nation took power in 1814—José Gaspar Rodríguez Francia, who ruled until his death in 1840. Then came Carlos Antonio López (1842–62) and López's son, Francisco Solano López (1862–70).

In 1865 López plunged his country into the War of the Triple Alliance against Brazil, Argentina, and Uruguay. At the war's end in 1870 Paraguay had lost 55,000 square miles of territory and over 500,000 people.

Economic problems and political instability plagued the country thereafter.

In 1932 a territorial dispute led to a 3-year Chaco War with Bolivia. Paraguay won, although at a cost of some 40,000 men.

Higinio Morínigo established a dictatorship in 1940, but resigned in 1948 after a revolt by leftists. From 1949 to 1954 the country was ruled by Federico Chavez.

In 1954 Gen. Alfredo Stroessner, commander of the army, made himself dictator.

In March 1973 the British Anti-Slavery Society urged the UN Human Rights Commission to take action to prevent the extermination of the Ache Indians in Paraguay, charging that most men of the tribe had been slain and the women and children sold into slavery.

Paraguay and Brazil signed an agreement on April 26, 1973, to build a $3 billion dam and hydroelectric project at Itaipu on the Paraná River between the two countries. The Itaipu Dam would be 720 feet high and create a reservoir of 555 square miles of water. Two other major hydroelectric projects were undertaken jointly with Argentina, the Yacyreta Dam and the Corpus Project, costing about $7 billion. Construction of the huge hydroelectric projects brought an economic boom in the late 1970s and early 1980s.

In apparent response to U.S. President Jimmy Carter's call for human rights, the government in January 1977 freed three communists who had been jailed for 19 years. In February the government also released 11 women political prisoners and their 17 children. However, human-rights organizations said that about 350 political prisoners remain in Paraguay's jails.

Opposition political parties boycotted an election on Feb. 6, 1977, for a constituent assembly, so supporters of Stroessner won all 120 seats. The assembly met on March 7–11 to amend the constitution to enable the president to be elected to office more than twice.

Stroessner won his sixth 5-year term as president in an election on Feb. 12, 1978, receiving 86% of the vote against candidates of the Liberal and Liberal-Radical parties.

President Stroessner in 1979 provided a haven in Paraguay for deposed Nicaraguan dictator Anastasio Somoza Debayle, who had been refused admission by other nations. Somoza was assassinated in Asunción on Sept. 17, 1980. Stroessner's government broke diplomatic relations with Nicaragua a few days later, charging its government with complicity in the slaying.

# PERU

**Official Name:** Republic of Peru.
**Area:** 496,225 square miles (1,285,216 sq. km.).
**Population:** 18,025,200.
**Chief Cities:** Lima, capital, 2,833,069; Arequipa, 302,316; Callao, 296,721; Trujillo, 240,322.
**Largest Metropolitan Area:** Lima, 3,302,523.
**Government:** Multiparty democracy.
**President:** Fernando Belaúnde Terry (since 1980).
**Prime Minister:** Manuel Ulloa (since 1980).
**Congress:** *Chamber of Deputies*, 180 members; *Senate*, 60 members.
**U.S. Ambassador to Peru:** Edwin G. Corr.
**Peruvian Ambassador to U.S.:** Alfonso Arias-Schreiber.
**Flag:** Red, white, and red bars, with coat of arms centered on white bar.
**Official Languages:** Spanish, Quechua.
**Ethnic Groups:** Indian (46%), mestizo (43%), European descent (11%).
**Official Religion:** Roman Catholicism.
**Leading Industries:** Agriculture (sugarcane, cotton, rice, wheat, coffee, potatoes, livestock, fruits, vegetables); mining (petroleum, iron ore, copper, gold, silver, lead, zinc, tungsten, manganese, coal); fishing; food processing; manufacturing (textiles, cement, leather products, plastics, chemicals).
**Foreign Trade:** *major exports*—fish meal, copper, sugar, iron ore, silver, cotton, zinc, coffee, lead; *major imports*—machinery, food, trucks, chemicals.
**Places of Interest:** Inca ruins Machu Picchu and Cuzco; prehistoric ruins of Chavín de Huantar near Huarás; Lake Titicaca; El Misti Volcano. *In Lima:* Cathedral and tomb of Pizarro; Court of the Inquisition; Plaza de Armas; Torre Tagle Palace. *In Arequipa:* Cathedral; Lucioni Gardens.

## PERU TODAY

Almost twice as large as Texas, Peru is a South American country enjoying the restoration of democracy after years of military rule. Richer in natural resources than most other nations of its size, it is among the world's leading nations in fishing and the mining of lead and zinc. But its people have remained poor. About a third have no education.

The Andes Mountains split the country into three areas. A narrow coastal desert, from 10 to 100 miles wide, extends about 1,400 miles along the Pacific coast. The temperate slopes of the Andes make up Peru's most populous region. About half of Peru lies east of the Andes—a sparsely populated lowland area of rain forests.

Ecuador and Colombia lie on the north, Brazil and Bolivia on the east, and Chile on the south.

## HISTORY OF PERU

As early as 300 B.C. the Nazca people of Peru drew on the ground hundreds of huge pictures, such as a hummingbird with a 900-foot wing-span.

The Nazca and other early cultures were absorbed by the Inca Empire in the 1400s A.D. The Incas, with their capital at Cuzco, controlled territory from Ecuador to Chile.

Drawn by the Inca treasure, Francisco Pizarro conquered the empire in 1533. Lima, established in 1535, was for three centuries the seat of Spanish control over all Hispanic South America except Venezuela. In the 1780s Inca leader Túpac Amaru led an unsuccessful revolt against Spain.

Peru's independence was declared on July 28, 1821, by Gen. José de San Martín. Venezuela's liberator Simón Bolívar led Peru's armies in battling Spain's troops to final victory in 1826.

Peru suffered a costly defeat by Chile in the War of the Pacific in 1879–83, losing its southern provinces of Tacna, Arica, and Tarapacá. Later, in 1929, Tacna was restored to Peru.

Although military leaders and dictators have dominated Peru's government throughout most of its history, Fernando Belaúnde Terry of the Popular Action Party was elected president in a free multiparty election in 1963.

A military coup on Oct. 3, 1968, overthrew Belaúnde, who was exiled to Argentina. Gen. Juan Velasco Alvarado, army chief of staff, became president, heading a socialist military junta that began nationalizing privately owned property. About 17 million acres of land were distributed to 300,000 peasants. During the next several years, the socialist economic policies drove the nation to the verge of bankruptcy.

Gen. Francisco Morales Bermúdez, a moderate, was named premier by Velasco on Feb. 1, 1975. Seven months later, on Aug. 29, 1975, Morales led a bloodless coup, overthrowing Velasco and making himself president. The new president dropped Marxists from the government and began turning a number of nationalized industries back to private ownership.

In September 1975 Morales decreed amnesty for exiled politicians, permitting former President Belaúnde to return to Peru.

Completion of several investment projects that cost about $2 billion began helping Peru's ailing economy in 1977. The trans-Andean pipeline began delivering oil to the coast at a rate of 35,000 barrels per day. The large Cerro Verde copper mine also began production.

The nation's state of emergency was ended by President Morales on Aug. 29, 1977, restoring most civil rights.

In the first free election in 15 years, Peruvians elected a 100-member constituent assembly on June 18, 1978. The assembly drafted a new constitution that took effect in 1980.

A national election was held on May 18, 1980, to choose a president and members of a new Congress. It was a triumph for 68-year-old former President Belaúnde, who regained the office with a 5-year term, receiving 45% of the popular vote against 14 other candidates. His Popular Action Party also won control of the Congress.

The military turned the government over to Belaúnde and the new Congress on Peru's Independence Day, July 28, 1980.

Belaúnde's government appealed to international loan agencies for $2 billion to finance a 5-year development plan for 1981-85 to develop agriculture, transportation, and public services.

QUICK QUIZ: When was the U.S. weather satellite system inaugurated? See page 757.

# 626 NATIONS OF THE WORLD

## PHILIPPINES

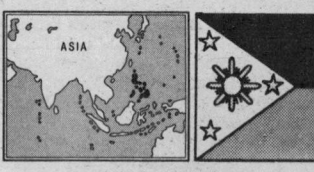

**Official name:** Republic of the Philippines.
**Area:** 115,830 square miles (300,000 sq. km.).
**Population:** 50,285,100.
**Chief Cities:** Manila, capital, 7,800,000; Davao, 515,520; Cebu, 418,517; Iloilo, 247,956; Zamboanga, 240,066.
**Government:** Republic under martial law.
**President and Prime Minister:** Ferdinand Edralin Marcos (took office in 1965).
**National Assembly:** 192 members.
**U.S. Ambassador to Philippines:** Richard W. Murphy.
**Philippine Ambassador to U.S.:** Eduardo Z. Romualdez.
**Flag:** Blue and red stripes bordered by white triangle containing yellow stars and sun.
**Official Languages:** Filipino, English, Spanish.
**Main Ethnic Group:** Malayo-Polynesian (90%).
**Religions:** Roman Catholicism (83%), Protestantism (9%); Islam (5%), animism (3%).
**Leading Industries:** Agriculture (rice, abaca, coconuts, sugarcane, corn, tobacco, livestock, fruits, vegetables); food processing; manufacturing (tobacco products, textiles, clothing, automobiles, oil refining); forestry and lumbering; fishing; mining (gold, silver, copper, iron, chromite, nickel).
**Foreign Trade:** *major exports*—coconut products, sugar, wood, abaca; *major imports*—food, petroleum, consumer goods.
**Places of Interest:** Nayong Filipino (Philippine village) and Malacanang Palace in Manila; Tagaytay Ridge overlooking Lake Taal; Pagsanjan Falls; Corregidor Island; Banawe rice terraces at Ifugao; Mayon Volcano at Legaspi; Baguio; Cebu City.

## PHILIPPINES TODAY

Once called "the show window of democracy in Asia," the Philippines today is ruled as a dictatorship under martial law by Ferdinand Marcos.

The Philippines is among the world's leading producers of copper, gold, and natural rubber. Agriculture employs over half of the nation's workers and provides about a third of the national income.

The Philippines include 7,107 islands, stretching some 1,100 miles from within 150 miles of Taiwan to less than 15 miles of Borneo.

From May to November, typhoons are a seasonal hazard. Temperatures range from the hot steaming jungles and rain forests to the cool pine-clad highlands.

## EARLY HISTORY

In prehistoric times the Philippines were settled by peoples who came from the islands of Indonesia and the Malay peninsula. In the 1200s the islands became part of the Indo-Malay empires. The missionary zeal of Islam swept the region in the 1300s.

Ferdinand Magellan claimed the islands for Spain in 1521. He was slain during his stay, but one of his vessels went on to become the first to circle the earth. The islands were named the Phil-

## MAIN ISLANDS OF THE PHILIPPINES

| NAME | AREA (sq. mi.) | LARGEST CITY |
|---|---|---|
| Luzon | 47,765 | Manila |
| Mindanao | 38,344 | Davao |
| Palawan | 5,751 | Puerto Princesa |
| Negros | 5,278 | Bacolod |
| Samar | 5,185 | Calbayog |
| Panay | 4,748 | Iloilo |
| Mindoro | 3,955 | Pinamalayan |
| Leyte | 3,090 | Tacloban |
| Cebu | 1,965 | Cebu |
| Bohol | 1,590 | Tagbilaran |
| Masbate | 1,563 | Masbate |
| Catanduanes | 583 | Virac |

ippines in honor of Philip (Felipe) II of Spain. In 1564 Miguel López de Legaspi arrived with soldiers instructed to Christianize the islands. In 20 years he was able to establish control over the major inhabited areas except for Muslim Mindanao and Sulu. The colony was placed under the administration of the viceroy of Mexico.

Growing Filipino nationalism, inspired by the writings of José Rizal, found expression in an unsuccessful revolt in 1896. Although Rizal was executed by the Spanish authorities, the rebellion continued under the leadership of Emilio Aguinaldo. Taking advantage of the weakening power of the Spanish empire, the Filipino rebels declared their independence in 1898.

## AMERICAN RULE

After Adm. George Dewey destroyed the Spanish fleet in Manila Bay on May 1, 1898, U.S. troops landed to force the surrender of Spanish authorities. When the U.S. paid Spain $20 million to acquire the Philippines and then established U.S. rule, Aguinaldo angrily began fighting the U.S. troops. The battles went on for two years until Aguinaldo was captured. William Howard Taft, later President, became the first U.S. governor of the Philippines in 1901.

Beginning in 1907 representatives to the national legislature were elected. In 1935 the Tydings-McDuffie Act gave the islands commonwealth status with complete self-government.

On Dec. 8, 1941, Japan launched a surprise attack and within a month occupied Manila. Gen. Douglas MacArthur, commanding some 90,000 American and Filipino troops, was forced to retreat to Luzon. He withdrew to Australia, but U.S. troops, commanded by Gen. Jonathan Wainwright, held out on Bataan and then on the island of Corregidor, until May 6, 1942.

On Oct. 20, 1944, a U.S. invasion force, under MacArthur's command, landed on the central Philippine island of Leyte. On July 5, 1945, MacArthur announced that all of the Philippines had been recaptured.

## INDEPENDENCE

The United States granted the Philippines independence on July 4, 1946. The republic crushed a communist insurrection in 1946-50. The U.S. supplied $2.3 billion in economic and military assistance to help rebuild the nation.

The presidents of the new republic in succession were Manuel Roxas (1946-48), Elpidio Quirino (1948-53), Ramón Magsaysay (1953-57), Carlos P. Garcia (1957-61), and Diosado

Macapagal (1961–65). Ferdinand Marcos was elected president in 1965 and reelected in 1969.

Claiming that communist subversion threatened the Philippines, President Marcos declared martial law on Sept. 21, 1972, arresting opposition leaders and newsmen.

A 317-man convention completed a draft of a new constitution, which Marcos proclaimed on Jan. 17, 1973. He took titles of both president and prime minister.

President Marcos enlarged Manila on Nov. 6, 1975, merging it with the former official capital Quezon City and 15 other cities and towns. Marcos appointed his wife, Imelda Marcos, as governor of Manila, succeeding the mayors of the communities who had been elected in 1971.

A national referendum held in October 1976 ratified constitutional amendments that in effect permit President Marcos to remain in office for life with dictatorial powers.

A cease-fire agreement was reached on Dec. 23, 1976, with Muslim leaders of the four-year revolt in the southern Philippines, bringing a temporary end to fighting.

The eight-month truce in the southern Philippines broke down on Sept. 20, 1977, when government planes attacked Muslim rebels on Basilan Island. Fighting continued in 1978–80.

President Marcos temporarily relaxed his ban on political activity for 45 days in 1978 to hold an election for a new interim national assembly on April 7. Not surprisingly, the candidates of Marcos' New Society Movement won most of the seats.

Although he denounced U.S. President Carter's international campaign for human rights as "moral imperialism," Marcos freed more than 1,000 political prisoners during 1978.

The government signed an agreement with the U.S. on Jan. 7, 1979, that assured continued U.S. use of air and naval bases in the islands until 1983. The U.S. agreed to pay $500 million during the 5-year period. The U.S. also gave up its sovereignty over the bases, agreeing to the appointment of Filipino commanders and the stationing of Filipino troops at the bases.

As Marcos entered his eighth year as dictator of the Philippines in September 1979, he granted amnesty to 2,307 persons arrested for subversion and other acts.

After 7½ years in solitary confinement under sentence of death, the man who had been expected to become president if national elections had been held in 1973, Benigno S. Aquino Jr., was permitted to leave prison to fly to the U.S. on May 8, 1980, to undergo a heart operation to save his life. Aquino, regarded as Marcos' best-known opponent, said he would not seek political asylum in the U.S. but would return to the Philippines upon recovery from the operation.

As opposition to Marcos mounted in the Philippines, scores of persons were killed and injured in 1980 in a series of bombings by a guerrilla group calling itself the April 6 Liberation Movement. More moderate opponents issued a Covenant for Freedom pledging peaceful efforts to get Marcos to restore democratic freedom and human rights.

# POLAND

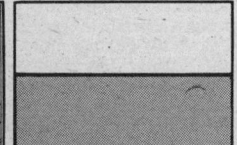

**Official Name:** Polish People's Republic.
**Area:** 120,725 square miles (312,677 sq. km.).
**Population:** 35,894,100.
**Chief Cities:** Warszawa (Warsaw), capital, 1,474,200; Lódz, 814,800; Kraków, 707,000; Wroclaw, 588,700; Poznań, 531,600; Gdansk, 439,200; Szcezecin, 380,100; Katowice, 349,800; Bydgoszcz, 333,200.
**Government:** Communist state.
**Head of Government:** First Secretary, Central Committee of the PZPR, Stanislaw Kania (since 1980).
**Prime Minister:** Josef Pinkowski (since 1980).
**Chief of State:** President, Council of State, Henryk Jablonski (took office in 1972).
**Legislature:** *Sejm,* 460 members.
**U.S. Ambassador to Poland:** Francis J. Meehan.
**Polish Ambassador to U.S.:** Romuald Spasowski.
**Flag:** White stripe over red stripe.
**Official Language:** Polish.
**Principal Ethnic Group:** Polish (98%).
**Religion:** Roman Catholicism (95%).
**Leading Industries:** Manufacturing (steel, electricity, cement, chemicals, ships, vehicles, machinery, textiles, paper); mining (coal, lignite, zinc, lead, natural gas, copper, sulfur); agriculture (wheat, sugar beets, potatoes, oats, barley, corn, livestock, fruits, vegetables); construction; trade and services.
**Foreign Trade:** *major exports*—coal, lignite, coke, railway rolling stock, ships, cement; *major imports*—iron ore, petroleum and petroleum products, fertilizers, wheat.
**Places of Interest:** Masurian and Augustow Lake district; Baltic Sea resorts; Sudetan and Tatra Mountains; Malbork Castle near Gdansk; Kraków. *In Warsaw:* Palace of Culture and Science; Kampinos Forest National Park; Old Town; Wilanow Palace; birthplace of Chopin.

## POLAND TODAY

About the size of New Mexico, Poland has ample mineral resources as well as rich farmland. It is one of the world's 10 leading producers of cement, coal, copper, electricity, steel, and zinc. But more Poles make their living from farming than from any other industry.

As with other communist nations, the standard of living of the people is substantially below that of the industrial nations of western Europe.

However, the people are allowed greater religious freedom than in most other communist states, with the official policy that a person can be both a member of the Communist Party and a member of the Roman Catholic Church.

Poland also is the only communist country in Europe where farmers still own as much as 85% of the land.

The communist government used huge subsidies to hold down prices in the face of worldwide inflation in the 1970s–80s.

The Soviet Union maintains large armed forces in Poland.

QUICK QUIZ: What is the temperature when it is midnight on the Moon? See page 761.

**POLAND** (continued)

The land is generally low and flat, about nine-tenths of it lying below 1,000 feet. Temperatures range from an average of 60° F. in summer to below 30° F. in winter. The principal rivers are the Vistula, Oder, Bug, and Warta.

The Soviet Union lies to the east, Czechoslovakia to the south, East Germany to the west, and the Baltic Sea to the north.

**EARLY HISTORY AND PARTITION**

Slavic tribes in Poland were united during the 800s A.D. by the Piast dynasty. In 966 Duke Mieszko I adopted Christianity. His son, Boleslaw the Brave, became king in 1025.

A new dynasty was established in 1386 by a Lithuanian grand duke, Jagiello, who became King Wladyslaw II of Poland. The Polish-Lithuanian union encompassed an empire extending from the Baltic to the Black Sea.

The Jagiellonian dynasty ended without heir in 1572. The throne became elective.

In 1772 Russia, Prussia, and Austria seized about one-third of Poland's territory in the *first partition*. In the *second partition* in 1793 Russia acquired Lithuania and the Ukraine from Poland while Prussia took about 22,000 square miles of western Poland.

The Polish patriot Thaddeus Kosciusko, who had served in the Continental Army during the American Revolution, led an unsuccessful Polish uprising in 1794. His defeat by the Russians led to the *third partition* in 1795–96, in which the remainder of Poland was divided among Russia, Prussia, and Austria.

**INDEPENDENCE AND WORLD WAR II**

Poland remained under foreign rule until after World War I when a Polish republic was formed in 1918. Józef Pilsudski became the first president. The noted pianist Jan Paderewski served as prime minister. Pilsudski ruled as dictator from 1926 until his death in 1935. Turmoil then ensued as various leaders contended for power.

In 1939 a Soviet-German pact opened the way for a new invasion and partition of Poland. The Nazi march into the country on Sept. 1, 1939, began World War II. Less than three weeks later the Soviets invaded from the east. The Germans murdered 6 million Poles, half of them Jews. The Russians executed 15,000 Polish army officers and deported 1.7 million Poles.

After World War II the Soviet Union annexed 70,000 square miles of Poland, but gave the new Poland 40,000 square miles of former German East Prussia, Pomerania, and Silesia.

**COMMUNISTS TAKE OVER**

The 1945 Yalta agreement by the Allies pledged free and unrestricted elections in Poland at the end of the war. But the Soviets installed 20,000 Polish communists to rule the country. After a two-year campaign of internal terrorism, national elections were held in 1947. The communists, led by Wladyslaw Gomulka, formed a coalition that claimed 80% of the vote. A communist puppet government was established under Gomulka.

When Soviet dictator Joseph Stalin feared Gomulka was becoming too independent, he had him removed in 1948.

Stalin's death in 1953 initiated relaxation of communist tyranny in Poland. After a violent strike and riots at Poznań in 1956 cost many lives, Gomulka was restored to power.

**DEVELOPMENTS IN THE 1970s–80s**

On December 12, 1970, strikes and riots erupted at Gdansk (formerly Danzig), Szczecin (Stettin), and other cities, in protest against food price increases. Police and troops crushed the disorders, with heavy casualties. Gomulka resigned as head of the Communist Party on Dec. 20, 1970, and was replaced by Edward Gierek.

In May 1972 Poland and West Germany ratified a treaty recognizing the western Oder-Neisse frontier with Germany that gave Poland territory that was part of Germany before World War II.

Fearing a repetition of the 1970 riots, the communist government kept food prices frozen for five years by paying $1 billion or more in subsidies. But on June 24, 1976, the government announced it was increasing retail food prices by as much as 100%. The next day, riots broke out in Warsaw, Radom, and Plock. That night the government backed down, canceling the price rise.

On Oct. 16, 1978, Karol Cardinal Wojtyla was elevated to pope as John Paul II—the first Polish pope. He visited Poland in June 1979, drawing huge crowds as he denounced the communist government for regarding man "merely as a means of production" and called on communist leaders to grant the people greater freedom.

Widespread labor unrest flared in the weeks that followed a government order on July 1, 1980, raising meat prices 40% to 60%. The climax came during 17 days, Aug. 13–31, when 17,000 workers seized a Gdansk shipyard and were supported by hundreds of thousands of strikers in other cities.

Under leadership of 37-year-old Lech Walesa, the strikers won written agreement from the government to permit the organization of independent labor unions instead of those controlled by the government, to free dissidents arrested during the crisis, and to regularly broadcast Roman Catholic church services.

Although the Soviet Union refrained from crushing the labor revolt with tanks, Gierek and other leaders of the communist government were purged. Stanislaw Kania, 53, a former head of the secret police, replaced Gierek on Sept. 6, 1980, as leader of the Polish Communist Party and of the government. He promised to fulfill the pledges to the workers.

When Walesa's independent Solidarity union was granted its registration by a district court in Warsaw on Oct. 24, 1980, the court changed the union's charter by inserting a clause recognizing the supremacy of the Communist Party. The union immediately announced plans for a nationwide strike to begin on Nov. 12 unless the clause was removed from the charter.

As the Soviet Union conducted military maneuvers with the implication of armed intervention in the dispute, the Polish government capitulated to the union with the Polish Supreme Court ruling on Nov. 9, 1980, that the Solidarity movement's charter could stand without the offensive clause—making it the first free labor union to be officially recognized in a communist nation.

# PORTUGAL

**Official Name:** Republic of Portugal.
**Area:** 35,553 square miles (92,082 sq. km.).
**Population:** 9,795,624.
**Chief Cities:** Lisboa (Lisbon), capital, 829,900; Pôrto, 335,700.
**Largest Metropolitan Area:** Lisbon, 1,611,887.
**Government:** Multiparty democratic republic.
**President:** Gen. António Ramalho Eanes (since 1976).
**Prime Minister:** Francisco Pinto Balsemão (since 1980).
**National Assembly:** 250 members.
**U.S. Ambassador to Portugal:** Richard J. Bloomfield.
**Portuguese Ambassador to U.S.:** João Hall Themido.
**Flag:** Green and red bars with national coat of arms.
**Official Language:** Portuguese.
**Principal Ethnic Group:** Portuguese.
**Religion:** Roman Catholicism (97%).
**Leading Industries:** Trade and services; manufacturing (textiles, cork products, cement, petroleum refining, steel, wine, food processing; agriculture (wheat, potatoes, maize, rye, oats, olives, livestock, fruits, vegetables); forestry and lumbering; mining (coal, pyrites, copper, tungsten); fishing.
**Foreign Trade:** *major exports*—wine, cork, fish, tomato paste, textiles; *major imports*—diamonds, automobiles, petroleum products, peanuts, plastics, textile machinery, sugar.
**Places of Interest:** Bucaco mountain and forest; Praja de Rocha beach resort; Nazaré fishing village; Azores and Madeira islands; Fatima sanctuary; Queluz; Coimbra; Pôrto. *In Lisbon:* Moorish fortress and palace; Jerónimos monastery; Monument to Christ.

## PORTUGAL TODAY

Somewhat smaller than Indiana, Portugal is a poor European nation struggling to achieve a stable political democracy after half a century of fascist dictatorship.

Lying between the Atlantic on the west and Spain on the east, Portugal occupies about one-sixth of the Iberian peninsula.

Extensive plains extend from the Tagus River south to Cape Saint Vincent, Europe's southwestern tip.

Portugal's highest point is the 6,532-foot Serra da Estréla, northeast of Lisbon.

Important rivers include the Douro, Tagus, Minho, and Guadiana, all originating in Spain.

The weather varies with cool summers and cold winters in the north, and a warm Mediterranean climate in the south.

## EARLY HISTORY

Ancient Phoenicians, Carthaginians, and Greeks all established colonies on the coast. In 27 B.C. the Romans made the region a province called *Lusitania.* After the Romans, Visigoths controlled the region until they were defeated in 711 by the Moors.

In 1143 Portugal became an independent nation under King Afonso Henriques.

QUICK QUIZ: What are *novae*? See page 764.

Portugal's era of glory began with the reign of João I (1385–1433). His son, Henry the Navigator, encouraged exploration that gave Portugal a huge overseas empire.

From 1580 to 1640 Spain ruled Portugal. Independence was reestablished in 1640 when the Portuguese revolted and installed João VI as king.

Napoleon's forces invaded Portugal in 1807, and the royal family fled to Brazil. King João VI returned to Portugal in 1820.

## THE PORTUGUESE REPUBLIC

The monarchy was overthrown in 1910, and a republic was established.

From 1928 Portugal was ruled as a fascist dictatorship, first by António de Oliveira Salazar and then from 1968 by Marcello Caetano.

On April 25, 1974, Gen. António de Spinola, a leftist, led army troops in overthrowing Caetano.

The military junta replaced Spinola on Sept. 30, 1974, with Gen. Francisco da Costa Gomes as president. On March 11, 1975, Spinola unsuccessfully attempted to overthrow Gomes' government.

The junta let voters go to the polls on April 25, 1975, in the first free election since 1926, choosing an assembly to draw up a constitution.

The revolutionary government in 1975 nationalized most industries and expropriated large landholdings. It also ended Portugal's 500-year-old African colonial empire.

Under a new democratic constitution, a national assembly was elected on April 25, 1976, with socialists led by Mário Soares winning a plurality of 106 of the 263 seats.

Army Chief of Staff Gen. António Ramalho Eanes, 41, was elected president on June 27, 1976, with the support of the socialists. Soares became prime minister.

The U.S. and 10 other industrial nations agreed on June 22, 1977, to lend $750 million to Portugal to help its shaky economy, in which about 40% of the work force was unemployed.

Many persons were injured in riots in farming areas after parliament adopted a law on Aug. 11, 1977, that small farms seized in the 1975 revolution should be returned to their owners.

When Soares' coalition cabinet disintegrated in 1978, President Eanes dismissed him and appointed a politically independent industrialist, Alfredo Nobre da Costa, as prime minister. Seventeen days later, on Sept. 14, the national assembly rejected Nobre da Costa's program.

President Eanes then appointed as prime minister a law professor, Carlos da Mota Pinto, 42, who took office on Nov. 22, 1978, with a nonpartisan cabinet.

After socialists and communists introduced motions to censure Mota Pinto's government, the prime minister resigned on June 6, 1979.

Weary of the bickering between the political parties that created instability, President Eanes ordered new parliamentary elections and appointed as caretaker prime minister the nation's first woman head of state, Maria de Lurdes Pintassilgo, 49, a moderate leftist.

Portuguese voters moved toward the right in

**PORTUGAL** *(continued)*

parliamentary elections held on Dec. 2, 1979, and on Oct. 5, 1980. The conservative Democratic Alliance of Francisco Sá Carneiro, who became prime minister on Jan. 3, 1980, won majorities in both elections, with 128 seats and then with 134.

Sá Carneiro was killed in a plane crash on Dec. 4, 1980. Deputy Prime Minister Diogo Freitas do Amaral briefly succeeded him. Then Minister of State Francisco Pinto Balsemão was named as prime minister.

In a presidential election on Dec. 7, 1980, President Eanes, supported by independents, socialists, and communists, won reelection to another 4-year term, receiving about 57% of the vote.

## PORTUGUESE OVERSEAS AREAS

### AZORES

**Area:** 902 square miles (2,336 sq. km.).
**Population:** 254,160.
**Capital:** Ponta Delgada, 69,930.

Lying in the Atlantic Ocean about 750 miles west of Europe, the Azores include nine main islands and several small ones. Most people make their living as fishermen and farmers. Main exports include canned fish, pineapples, butter, and cheese.

The Azores were discovered in 1427–31 by the Portuguese explorer Diogo de Sevilla. Settled by Portuguese and Flemish colonists, the Azores became an important stop for ships during the exploration of the Americas.

The U.S. maintains an air base on Terceira Island. Portugal and the U.S. signed a treaty on June 18, 1979, providing for continued U.S. use of the air base until 1983.

On April 30, 1976, Portugal granted the Azores internal self-government with an elected assembly. Nationalists continued to demonstrate in 1977–80, calling for complete independence.

### MACAO

**Area:** 6.2 square miles (16 sq. km.).
**Population:** 291,481.
**Capital:** Macao City, 241,413.

Macao, at the mouth of mainland China's Pearl River, is about 40 miles from Hong Kong.

The colony consists of Macao City on Macao peninsula, and two smaller islands—Taipa and Coloane. About 99% of the people are Chinese.

Portugal colonized Macao in 1557 and paid rent to China until 1949. When Portugal began freeing its colonies in 1975, China indicated it preferred Macao's status to remain unchanged.

### MADEIRA

**Area:** 307 square miles (795 sq. km.).
**Population:** 270,976.
**Capital:** Funchal, 105,791.

Situated in the Atlantic Ocean about 600 miles southwest of Portugal, the group includes two main islands, Madeira and Pôrto Santo, and several uninhabited smaller islands.

Thousands of tourists go to Madeira each year to enjoy the beaches and tropical scenery.

The Portuguese explorer João Goncalves Zarco first sighted the islands in 1418. Portuguese settlers colonized Madeira, importing slaves to work the plantations. On April 30, 1976, Portugal granted Madeira autonomy with an elected assembly for internal self-government.

# QATAR

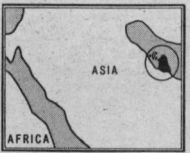 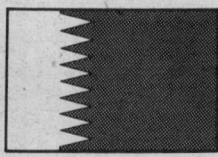

**Official Name:** State of Qatar.
**Area:** 4,247 square miles (11,000 sq. km.).
**Population:** 175,452.
**Capital:** Doha, 100,000.
**Government:** Absolute monarchy.
**Emir:** Khalifa bin Hamad al-Thani (since 1972).
**U.S. Ambassador to Qatar:** Charles E. Marthinsen.
**Ambassador to U.S.:** Abdelkader Braik al-Ameri.
**Flag:** Maroon field; white serrated band at hoist.
**Official Language:** Arabic.
**Main Ethnic Groups:** Qatari (45%), Pakistani (35%).
**Religion:** Islam (98%).
**Leading Industries:** Mining (petroleum, natural gas); construction; manufacturing (electricity, cement, oil refining, steel); agriculture (livestock, vegetables, fruits); fishing.
**Foreign Trade:** *major exports*—petroleum, steel, chemicals, tomatoes; *major imports*—consumer goods.
**Places of Interest:** Royal residence; oil refineries.

## QATAR TODAY

About the size of Massachusetts, Qatar is an oil-rich Arab country that is largely a hot, sandy desert. Most of the people live in and around the capital city of Doha.

New industries have been developed with oil revenues, including an electric power plant, a desalting plant to supply drinking water from the sea, and improved harbor facilities.

Qatar's population more than doubled in the 1970s as thousands of Pakistanis and other foreigners came to work on development projects.

The desert land has sparse vegetation, although vegetables, grain, and fruits are grown.

Qatar is a peninsula jutting into the Persian Gulf. Saudi Arabia and the United Arab Emirates border it on the south.

## HISTORY

For many years Qatar was dominated by the rulers of Bahrain. In 1868 Britain undertook negotiations to end Bahrain's rule. But in 1872 the Ottoman Turks absorbed Qatar.

With the collapse of the Turkish empire in World War I, Britain in 1916 made Qatar a protectorate.

Oil was discovered in Qatar in 1940. Commercial production began in 1949.

Qatar declared its independence on Sept. 1, 1971. A treaty of friendship replaced the "special treaty" relationship with Britain.

Emir Ahmed bin Ali al-Thani ruled from 1960 to 1972. He was deposed in a bloodless coup on Feb. 22, 1972, by his cousin Sheik Khalifa bin Hamad al-Thani.

The ruler uses a substantial part of the nation's oil and gas income to develop social services, free housing for Qataris, and heavy industry, including a $300 million steel plant completed in 1978 and a $500 million petrochemical industry that began production in 1980.

# ROMANIA

**Official Name:** Socialist Republic of Romania.
**Area:** 91,699 square miles (237,500 sq. km.).
**Population:** 22,351,300.
**Chief Cities:** Bucureşti (Bucharest), capital, 1,807,044; Timişoara, 268,785; Iaşi, 264,947; Cluj, 262,421.
**Government:** Communist state.
**President:** Nicolae Ceausescu (since 1967).
**Prime Minister:** Ilie Verdet (since 1979).
**Grand National Assembly:** 465 members.
**U.S. Ambassador to Romania:** O. Rudolph Aggrey.
**Romanian Ambassador to U.S.:** Nicolae Ionescu.
**Flag:** Blue, yellow, and red bars, with national coat of arms in center.
**Languages:** Romanian (official), Hungarian, German.
**Main Ethnic Groups:** Romanian (88%), Magyar (9%), German (2%).
**Leading Religions:** Eastern Orthodox (80%), Roman Catholic (9%).
**Leading Industries:** Agriculture (wheat, corn, sheep, cattle, hogs, poultry, fruits, potatoes, vegetables, sunflower seeds); manufacturing (steel, chemicals, cement, textiles, machinery); trade and services; mining (natural gas, petroleum, coal, iron, copper, bauxite, chromium, manganese, salt); forestry and lumbering.
**Foreign Trade:** *major exports*—food, lumber, chemicals, natural gas, machinery; *major imports*—steel, metals, iron ore, petroleum.
**Places of Interest:** Danube delta; Black Sea beach resorts; mountain resorts; Bukovina monasteries at Suceava; Brukenthal Museum at Sibiu; Felix and Herculane spas. *In Bucharest:* Cismigiu Park; Stavropoleos church.

## ROMANIA TODAY

One of the least industrialized communist countries of eastern Europe, Romania depends heavily on agriculture, which long has made it one of the leading wheat- and corn-growing nations.

Under leadership of President Nicolae Ceausescu since 1965, Romania has become increasingly politically independent of the Soviet Union. However, it is economically dependent on the Soviet Union as its main trading partner.

Government economic planning has placed emphasis on the development of heavy industry, especially in the areas of machine building, metal processing, chemicals, electric power, mining, manufacture of construction materials, petroleum production, and forestry.

About the size of Oregon, Romania is a land of great geographical contrasts. The Carpathian Mountains surround the central plateau of Transylvania. Beyond are three major plateaus: Moldavia to the east, Wallachia to the south, and Dobruja on the Black Sea coast between Bulgaria and the Soviet Union.

The Soviet Union lies to the north and northeast, Bulgaria to the south, and Hungary and Yugoslavia to the west.

## EARLY HISTORY

The Roman province of Dacia included most of present-day Romania in the 100s A.D. After Rome withdrew, the area was overrun successively by Goths, Huns, Avars, Slavs, and Mongols.

In the 1000s Hungary took control of Transylvania, ruling it until the early 1900s.

Prince Vlad Tepes of Wallachia, said to be the original for the fictional vampire Count Dracula, fought off Turkish invaders until he was killed when they finally conquered Wallachia in 1476. The Turks then took Moldavia in 1504.

For the next three centuries Moldavia and Wallachia were part of the Ottoman Turkish Empire.

## KINGDOM OF ROMANIA

In 1861 Moldavia and Wallachia united under Prince Alexander John Cuza, with the principality taking the name *Romania.* Cuza was cast aside in 1866 in favor of Prince Karl of the house of Hohenzollern-Sigmaringen.

Romania became independent in 1877. Prince Karl became King Carol I in 1881.

After fighting on the side of the Allies in World War I, Romania acquired Transylvania and the Banat from Hungary, Bukovina from Austria, and Bessarabia from Russia.

In June 1940 Hungary seized Transylvania, the Soviet Union annexed the northern part of Romania called Bessarabia, and Bulgaria took Dobruja in the southeast.

In September 1940 Marshal Ion Antonescu ousted King Carol II, placing his young son Michael on the throne with the help of the Iron Guard—a fascist military organization. Romania joined the Axis Powers.

In August 1944 Antonescu was overthrown by King Michael, and Romania switched to the Allied side.

## COMMUNIST RULE

After the Soviet advance into the country in 1944–45, a communist-led coalition headed by Petri Groza came to power. In 1947 Michael was forced to abdicate, and Romania was declared a communist republic.

A peace treaty in 1947 restored Transylvania to Romania, but gave Bessarabia to the Soviet Union and part of Dobruja to Bulgaria.

Romania remained an obedient Soviet satellite until 1962, when the Soviet Union attempted unsuccessfully to persuade it to abandon its plan for industrialization and become an agricultural reserve for the Soviet bloc. Since then Romanian leaders Gheorghe Gheorgiu-Dej (1961–65) and Nicolae Ceausescu (since 1965) have pursued an independent course.

While the Soviet bloc supported the Arab countries during the June 1967 Arab-Israeli war, Romania refused to condemn Israel as the aggressor and did not break relations with it.

The Ceausescu regime supported the liberalization program in Czechoslovakia, refusing to join in Warsaw Pact military action against the Dubček government in Czechoslovakia in 1968.

In 1974 Romania modified its press laws to end censorship prior to publication, putting the

QUICK QUIZ: What is the distance in light-years to the star Altair? See page 766.

**ROMANIA** *(continued)*
burden on editors to delete anticommunist ideas from articles before printing them.

Although the Soviet Union broke off trade agreements with the U.S. in a dispute over freedom of immigration, Romania negotiated a new trade agreement with the U.S. on April 2, 1975, and eased immigration restrictions.

An earthquake on March 4, 1977, destroyed many buildings in Bucharest and nearby cities, killing 1,570 persons and injuring 11,300.

The government on May 8, 1977, freed about 30,000 prisoners who were granted amnesty as part of Romania's celebration of its 100th anniversary of independence.

In an effort to strengthen relations with the U.S., President Ceausescu in April 1978 made his fourth trip in eight years to visit a U.S. President in Washington, D.C.

A visit to Romania in August 1978 by China's Chairman Hua Kuo-feng emphasized Romania's growing independence from the Soviet Union.

In September 1978 the government fired several cabinet ministers and other high officials, including its UN ambassador, as a result of secret disclosures to the U.S. CIA by Romanian Lt. Gen. Ion Pacepa, No. 2 man in Romania's spy organization, who defected to the U.S. on July 29, 1978.

Ceausescu took a major step toward independence from the Soviet Union on Nov. 26, 1978, when he announced his refusal to sign an agreement imposed by Moscow to increase military spending.

Subsequently in public speeches the Romanian president called for recognition of "the sacred right of each nation to decide its own destiny without outside interference."

Ceausescu appointed his brother-in-law, Ilie Verdet, 54, as prime minister on March 30, 1979.

Increased energy usage caused Romania to become a net importer of petroleum in 1979. The government announced plans to build six nuclear power plants and turn to other energy sources to achieve energy self-sufficiency by 1990.

# RWANDA

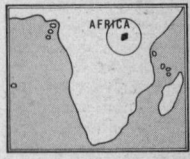 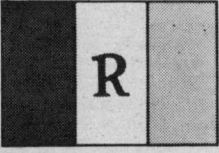

**Official Name:** Republic of Rwanda.
**Area:** 10,169 square miles (26,338 sq. km.).
**Population:** 5,291,640.
**Capital:** Kigali, 54,403.
**Government:** One-party dictatorship.
**President:** Juvenal Habyarimana (since 1973).
**U.S. Ambassador to Rwanda:** Harry R. Melone.
**Rwandan Ambassador to U.S.:** Bonaventure Ubalijoro.
**Flag:** Bars of red, yellow, and green, with black *R* in center.
**Official Languages:** French and Kinyarwanda.
**Main Ethnic Groups:** Hutu (89%), Tutsi (10%).
**Religions:** Christianity (60%), Islam, animism.
**Leading Industries:** Agriculture (coffee, cattle, pyrethrum, tea, beans, corn); manufacturing (light consumer goods); mining (tin, wolfram).

**Foreign Trade:** *major exports*—coffee, tin, tea; *major imports*—textiles, oil and gasoline, food, machinery.
**Places of Interest:** Kigali; Gisenyi; Butare Museum; Kagera and Volcanoes national parks; Rusumo Falls; Gabiro guesthouse at Kibungo.

## RWANDA TODAY

About the size of Vermont, Rwanda is one of the poorest countries in the world.

Most of the people live as they have for centuries, growing enough food and raising enough cattle to subsist, but not enough to afford more than a primitive existence. Only about 10% can read and write. The average Rwandan lives only to age 44.

Only a few Europeans live in Rwanda, and most of those who do supervise the tin and wolfram mines—the country's only substantial industry other than agriculture.

Violence between the Hutu and the Tutsi has continued sporadically since independence. The Tutsi government of neighboring Burundi has accused the Hutu government of Rwanda of massacring Tutsi tribesmen. In turn the Rwanda government has accused Burundi of harboring Tutsi guerrillas.

Rwanda's exports and imports travel by truck along a 1,000-mile road through Uganda to the port of Mombasa, Kenya.

The land is mountainous, with elevations ranging from 4,800 feet at Lake Kivu in the west to 14,787-foot Mt. Karisimbi in the northwest. In the east are a hilly plateau and lakes. The climate is tropical.

Uganda lies to the north, Tanzania to the east, Burundi to the south, and Zaire to the west.

## EARLY HISTORY

The kingdom of Rwanda can be traced back to the 1500s. Under leadership of a royal clan from Ethiopia, successive waves of Tutsi conquered the local Hutu tribes.

In 1899 Rwanda was incorporated as a colony into German East Africa. After World War I the League of Nations mandated Rwanda and its neighbor Burundi to Belgium as the territory of Rwanda-Urundi.

After World War II, Rwanda-Urundi became a UN trust territory administered by Belgium.

In November 1959 an uprising by the Hutu against the Tutsi brought the massacre of thousands of Tutsi and the flight of thousands of others to neighboring Burundi.

The Tutsi king was overthrown and a republic was proclaimed in 1961.

## INDEPENDENCE

Belgium granted self-government to Rwanda on Jan. 1, 1962, with Gregoire Kayibanda, head of the Parmehutu Party, as president.

Rwanda received independence on July 1, 1962. Kayibanda was reelected in 1965 and 1969.

In a bloodless coup on July 5, 1973, Defense Minister Maj. Gen. Juvenal Habyarimana overthrew Kayibanda. He dissolved the national assembly and ruled by decree. He made his National Revolutionary Movement for Development (MRND) the only political party in 1975. Habyarimana was elected without opposition to a 5-year term as president on Dec. 17, 1978.

# SAINT LUCIA

**Official Name:** State of St. Lucia.
**Area:** 238 square miles (616 sq. km.).
**Population:** 125,964.
**Capital:** Castries, 45,000.
**Government:** Multiparty parliamentary democracy.
**Prime Minister:** Allan Louisy (since 1979).
**House of Assembly:** 17 members.
**U.S. Ambassador to St. Lucia:** Sally A. Shelton.
**Saint Lucian Ambassador to U.S.:** Barry Bertrand Lucas Auguste.
**Flag:** Blue field with white, black, and yellow triangle in center.
**Main Languages:** English (official); French patois widely spoken.
**Ethnic Groups:** Black (97%), white (3%).
**Principal Religion:** Roman Catholicism.
**Leading Industries:** Agriculture (bananas, coconuts, cocoa, citrus fruits, spices); fishing; forestry; manufacturing (rum, food processing, clothing, electricity, fertilizer, batteries); tourism.
**Foreign Trade:** *major exports*—bananas, coconut products, coconuts, fruits and vegetables, spices; *major imports*—flour, meat, fish, sugar, milk, alcoholic beverages, metals, lumber, fuel oil, clothing, shoes, machinery, automobiles.
**Places of Interest:** Fort Rodney on Pigeon Island; Morne Fortune (Lucky Hill) battlefield; beach resorts; Piton volcanoes near Soufrière.

## ST. LUCIA TODAY

A volcanic Caribbean island about one-twelfth the size of Puerto Rico, St. Lucia lies closer to South America than to the United States. Its nearest neighbors are the French island of Martinique to the north, St. Vincent to the south, and Barbados to the east.

Most of the people are descendants of African slaves. Although English is generally understood, most of the people speak a French patois. Most of the islanders make their living from tourism or from agriculture. About one-third of the population live in the capital city of Castries.

The agricultural land largely is divided into small family farms of less than 5 acres. More than 10,000 families raise bananas, which account for about 80% of the island's exports. Coconuts provide the second most important export crop.

Income from tourism amounts to almost as much as receipts from exports. Over 100,000 tourists visit St. Lucia each year, about half of whom are passengers on cruise ships.

Tropical rain forests cover the steep slopes of the island's volcanoes. The highest peak is 3,117-foot Mt. Gimie. Twin volcanoes called the Pitons rise sharply from the sea near Soufrière on the southwest coast.

The island has a year-round tropical climate with an average temperature of 80°F. (26°C.).

Annual rainfall of 60 to 138 inches comes mainly from May to August.

### EARLY HISTORY

The earliest inhabitants of St. Lucia were the Arawak Indians from South America. They later were driven out by the fierce Carib Indians.

The first attempts to settle the island were made by English colonists in 1605 and 1638. Both times the English were killed or driven off by the Carib Indians.

French colonists forced the Carib Indians to give up their claim to the island in 1660.

During the next 150 years the French and English battled for possession of the island.

In 1778 some 1,300 British troops repulsed an attack by 5,000 French soldiers.

In May 1781 French Adm. Comte de Grasse attacked the island with a fleet of 25 warships but was beaten off by bombardment from Fort Rodney on Pigeon Island, a few miles north of Castries. However, St. Lucia was given to France in the 1783 peace treaty.

Britain took the island again in April 1796 with an assault by 12,000 troops under command of Lt. Gen. Sir Ralph Abercrombie with most of the fighting taking place on Morne Fortune (Lucky Hill) near Castries. But France again won possession in a peace treaty.

The final battle for St. Lucia took place in June 1803, during the Napoleonic wars, when British troops again stormed ashore and defeated French defenders. In the 1814 Treaty of Paris, France ceded the island to Britain.

Britain ended slavery on St. Lucia in 1834, compensating owners for freeing 13,291 slaves, who made up the bulk of the island's population of 16,000 at the time.

St. Lucia was administered as a separate British colony until 1838, when it was annexed to the British Windward Islands Colony.

With the abolition of the governorship of the Windward Islands in 1959, St. Lucia received its own British governor. It then was part of the short-lived Federation of the West Indies until its dissolution in 1962.

Britain granted St. Lucia complete self-government on May 3, 1967, as an associated state of the Commonwealth of Nations.

The government was controlled for 15 years by the conservative United Workers Party (UWP), which won national elections in 1964, 1968, and 1974. UWP leader John Compton served as prime minister.

### INDEPENDENT NATION

Prime Minister Compton conducted lengthy negotiations with Britain that culminated in gaining independence for Saint Lucia on Feb. 22, 1979. The new nation remained part of the British Commonwealth of Nations, recognizing Britain's Queen Elizabeth II as chief of state.

The leftist Labor Party, which had campaigned for closer relations with communist nations, won a national election on July 2, 1979, capturing 12 of the 17 seats in the House of Assembly. Allan Louisy, 62, head of the Labor Party, replaced Compton as prime minister.

QUICK QUIZ: When did A.J. Foyt first win the Indianapolis 500? See page 772.

# SAINT VINCENT

**Official Name:** St. Vincent and the Grenadines.
**Area:** 150 square miles (388 sq. km.)
**Population:** 116,056.
**Capital:** Kingstown, 23,645.
**Government:** Multiparty parliamentary democracy.
**Prime Minister:** Robert Milton Cato (since 1974).
**House of Assembly:** 13 members.
**Flag:** Vertical stripes of blue, yellow, and green; green coat of arms on yellow stripe.
**Language:** English.
**Main Ethnic Group:** Black.
**Chief Religions:** Methodism, Anglicanism, Roman Catholicism.
**Leading Industries:** Agriculture (bananas, sweet potatoes, arrowroot, coconuts, nutmegs, peanuts, mace, cocoa, food crops); tourism; manufacturing and processing (starch, coconut oil, cigarettes, rum distilling, furniture, flour, clothing); fishing; forestry.
**Foreign Trade:** *major exports*—bananas, sweet potatoes, arrowroot, coconut oil, nutmegs, peanuts; *main imports*—food, textiles, cement, lumber, petroleum products, fertilizer, automobiles.
**Places of Interest:** Soufrière volcano; beach resorts; in Layou, prehistoric Carib Indian altar; in Kingstown, botanic garden.

## ST. VINCENT TODAY

One of the chain of Windward Islands in the eastern Caribbean Sea, St. Vincent has an area about the size of Carson City, Nev. But its population is over four times that of Carson City.

The nation also includes hundreds of islets called the Grenadines that stretch to the south.

Most Vincentians earn their living from agriculture or from industries that process farm products. About half the farmland is divided among huge plantations and the rest among small farms of 10 acres or less.

The island's fastest-growing industry is tourism. About 20,000 visitors come to St. Vincent annually to enjoy the black sand beaches, the tropical scenery, and the climate.

Although many of the people are poor, most can read and write because of the excellent school system in which primary education is free. About one-fourth of the population is made up of children who are enrolled in schools.

The island's tallest volcano, 4,048-foot Soufrière, erupts periodically. Its eruption in 1902 killed about 2,000 persons. The volcano came to life in April 1979, sending smoke thousands of feet into the air. Some 20,000 persons were evacuated from the northern part of the island around the volcano, but later returned to their homes after the volcano quieted.

St. Vincent often experiences water shortages during the dry season from January to May. In the rest of the year, annual rainfall varies from 60 inches on the coast to 150 inches in the mountains of the interior.

Temperatures seldom rise to more than 90° F.

in daytime and may fall to 64° F. at night.

St. Vincent lies 21 miles south of St. Lucia and about 100 miles west of Barbados.

## HISTORY

The earliest known inhabitants were the Arawak Indians, who later were killed or driven out by the warlike Carib Indians.

Christopher Columbus landed on St. Vincent on Jan. 22, 1498.

The Carib Indians remained in control of the island throughout most of the 1700s, although a few European colonists, mostly French, established some settlements.

British forces captured the island from the French in 1762. It was retaken by the French in 1779 during the American Revolution, but was restored to Britain by treaty in 1783.

In 1795–96 the British deported most of the Carib Indians to the island of Rattan in the Bay of Honduras.

From 1958 to 1962 St. Vincent was part of the Federation of the West Indies. During this period the island received internal self-government, beginning in 1960.

The island received the status of an associated state in the British Commonwealth of Nations on Oct. 27, 1969, with complete control of its own domestic affairs.

In a general election on Dec. 9, 1974, the conservative St. Vincent Labor Party (SVLP) won control of the House of Assembly with SLVP leader Robert Milton Cato as prime minister.

Responding to the rising tide of nationalism among its neighbors in the Carribean, St. Vincent was granted independence by Britain, on Oct. 27, 1979, with Cato as prime minister. Britain promised to provide the new nation with $23 million in aid.

In the first national election since independence, held on Dec. 5, 1979, Cato's party won a landslide victory, taking 11 of parliament's 13 seats.

Leftist rebels on Union Island tried to secede from St. Vincent, but were subdued in a battle with police on Dec. 8, 1979, in which one was killed and 19 arrested.

# SAN MARINO

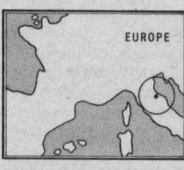 

**Official Name:** Most Serene Republic of San Marino.
**Area:** 23.6 square miles (61 sq. km.).
**Population:** 21,471.
**Capital:** San Marino, 4,628.
**Government:** Communist-governed republic.
**Chiefs of State:** Co-regents chosen for 6-month terms; 11-man Congress of State (cabinet).
**Legislature:** *Grand and General Council*, 60 members.
**Flag:** White stripe over blue stripe with national coat of arms in center.
**Language:** Italian.
**Main Ethnic Group:** Sanmarinese.
**Principal Religion:** Roman Catholicism.

NATIONS OF THE WORLD    635

**Leading Industries:** Tourism; agriculture (wheat, grapes, vegetables, livestock); manufacturing (wine, textiles, leather products, ceramics).

**Foreign Trade:** *major exports*—wine, textiles, ceramics, postage stamps; *major imports*—manufactured goods.

**Places of Interest:** Mt. Titano; Rocca medieval fortress; San Marino Cathedral; Pinacoteca di Stato Museum; Palazzo dei Valloni.

## SAN MARINO TODAY

With an area only as large as Newark, N.J. San Marino is surrounded by the mountains of northeast Italy. It has two main industries—farming and tourism.

The government has two main sources of income: (1) the sale of postage stamps and (2) an annual subsidy paid by Italy.

More tourists usually visit each day in the summer than the country's entire population.

The capital city, also called San Marino, lies on the slopes of 2,425-foot Mt. Titano, about 65 miles east of Florence, Italy.

## HISTORY

According to legend, San Marino was founded in the 300s by Marinus, a Christian stonecutter from Dalmatia fleeing religious persecution. The independence of San Marino was recognized in 1631 by Pope Urban VIII.

Since 1862 San Marino and Italy have had treaties regulating customs and common interests. San Marino declared war on Germany in World War I but tried to remain neutral in World War II.

A coalition of communists and socialists governed from 1945 to 1957. Women received the right to vote in 1960.

The neutrality of San Marino was confirmed in a new agreement with Italy in 1971.

In parliamentary elections on May 28, 1978, leftist parties gained seats. Although the conservative Christian Democrats retained their plurality with 26 seats, they were unable to form a coalition cabinet with the socialists after the election.

A communist-led coalition government with the socialists was approved by parliament by a vote of 31 to 29 on July 17, 1978.

The leftists won 56% of the votes in a new election on May 25, 1980.

## SÃO TOMÉ AND PRÍNCIPE

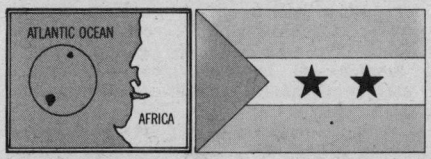

**Official Name:** Democratic Republic of São Tomé and Príncipe.
**Area:** 372 square miles (964 sq. km.).
**Population:** 85,519.
**Capital:** São Tomé, 5,714.
**Government:** One-party socialist state.
**President:** Manuel Pinto da Costa (since 1975).
**Prime Minister:** Miguel Trovoada (since 1975).

**U.S. Ambassador to:** Arthur T. Tienken.
**Flag:** Stripes of green, yellow, and green with red triangle at hoist; two black stars on center yellow stripe.
**Language:** Portuguese.
**Main Ethnic Groups:** Black (90%), mixed Portuguese black ancestry (7%).
**Religions:** Roman Catholicism, animism.
**Leading Industries:** Agriculture (coffee, cocoa, coconuts, palm kernels, vegetables, fruits); fishing; turtle shell products; food processing; tourism.
**Foreign Trade:** *major exports*—coffee, cocoa; *major imports*—food, consumer goods.
**Places of Interest:** Swimming beaches; medieval plays and festivals on religious feast days; saltwater fishing; coffee plantations; volcanic craters.

## SÃO TOMÉ AND PRÍNCIPE TODAY

Only one-third the size of Rhode Island, the island country of São Tomé and Príncipe lies in the Gulf of Guinea, about 125 miles off the west coast of Africa. The largest island is São Tomé (330 sq. mi.). Príncipe (42 sq. mi.) lies about 93 miles to the northeast.

Most of the people are descendants of African slaves. They make their living by farming or fishing. The main exports are coffee and cocoa.

São Tomé has 10 volcanic peaks. The highest, Pico de São Tomé, rises to 6,640 feet. Rain forests cover the mountain slopes, harboring 60 types of tropical birds.

Beaches, saltwater fishing, and a mild climate that averages 62.6° F. attract tourists.

## HISTORY

São Tomé was discovered by Portuguese explorers João de Santarém and Pedro Escobar on Dec. 21, 1470. Príncipe was sighted almost a month later, on Jan. 17, 1471. Neither island was inhabited.

In the late 1400s Portugal sent convicts and exiled Jews to the islands. Sugar plantations were founded, worked by slaves from Africa. São Tomé became a major slave trading port for transshipment of African slaves to the Americas. Coffee was introduced in 1800 and cocoa in 1822.

Prosperity declined after 1909 when Britain and Germany boycotted cocoa from the islands because plantation laborers continued to be treated as slaves by their Portuguese masters.

The islands were made an overseas province of Portugal in 1951.

Full independence was granted by Portugal on July 12, 1975, with Manuel Pinto da Costa as the first president. Most of the islands' 4,000 Portuguese residents returned to Portugal.

Under a constitution that became effective on Dec. 12, 1975, the socialist Movement for the Liberation of São Tomé and Príncipe (MLSTP) was designated as the only political party. The president was given absolute power to choose or dismiss a prime minister and cabinet officers.

The country depends on foreign aid and loans to make up annual trade deficits as the import costs outweigh revenues from exports. The main trading partners are Portugal and Netherlands.

The government's economic plans for the 1980s call for diversification of agriculture to end the country's dependence on food imports.

QUICK QUIZ: What team won baseball's World Series in 1972, 1973, and 1974? See page 776.

# SAUDI ARABIA

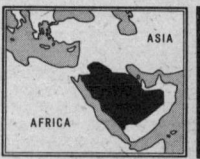

**Official Name:** Kingdom of Saudi Arabia.
**Area:** 830,000 square miles (2,149,690 sq. km.).
**Population:** 8,492,180.
**Chief Cities:** Riyadh, capital, 666,840; Jidda, 561,104; Mecca, 366,801; Taif, 204,857; Medina, 198,186.
**Government:** Absolute monarchy.
**King and Prime Minister:** Khalid Abdul-Aziz (since 1975).
**First Deputy Prime Minister:** Crown Prince Fahd Abdul-Aziz (since 1975).
**U.S. Ambassador to Saudi Arabia:** John C. West.
**Saudi Arabian Ambassador to U.S.:** Faisal Alhegelan.
**Flag:** Green, with inscription "There is no god but Allah and Mohammed is His messenger" in white Arabic characters above white sword.
**Official Language:** Arabic.
**Principal Ethnic Group:** Arab (99%).
**State Religion:** Islam (99%).
**Leading Industries:** Mining (petroleum); construction; agriculture (livestock, dates, wheat, corn, alfalfa, grapes, rice, coffee, fruits, vegetables); manufacturing (oil refining, cement, steel).
**Foreign Trade:** *major export*—petroleum; *major imports*—vehicles, machinery, iron and steel.
**Places of Interest:** Kaaba, Islam's most sacred shrine, in Mecca; mosques and palaces; Asir Kingdom National Park.

## SAUDI ARABIA TODAY

About one-fourth the size of the United States, Saudi Arabia is a desert kingdom populated by nomadic Arab tribes. But huge deposits of petroleum have changed Saudi Arabia in a few decades from a poor underdeveloped nation to one of the world's richest with an annual oil income of about $100 billion.

The king has used part of the wealth to build highways and other public works. Thousands of new schools have been opened. Skyscrapers rise in the cities. Much money also has been given to poor Arab countries.

Occupying most of the Arabian peninsula, Saudi Arabia stretches from the Persian Gulf in the east to the Red Sea and the Gulf of Aqaba in the west. Qatar and the United Arab Emirates lie to the east. To the north are Jordan, Iraq, and Kuwait. To the south are Oman, Southern Yemen, and Yemen.

Most of Saudi Arabia is desert. In the west is a fertile coastal plain 10 to 40 miles wide, giving way to steep mountains that rise to over 8,000 feet in the southwest. The Nejd plateau slopes eastward and is bordered by the desert areas of Nefud in the north, Dahna and Nefud Dahi in the east, and Rab al Khali in the south.

Coastal regions have a high, tropical humidity. In the deserts, temperatures range from 70° to 130° F.

## EARLY HISTORY

Historians believe Arabia was the original home of the Semitic peoples of the Middle East.

Mohammed founded the religion of Islam at Mecca and Medina about A.D. 622–632. The Muslim armies of the caliph Omar conquered most of the Middle East by 644. The Arab empire extended from Spain and North Africa to the subcontinent of India from the 700s to 1000s. Baghdad, the capital of the Arab empire, fell to the Seljuk Turks in 1055.

From the 1500s Arabia was part of the Ottoman Turkish empire.

In the 1700s Mohammed ibn Saud, the Arab ruler of Nejd, gathered a Bedouin army to gain control of Arabia. His son and successor Abdullah I was defeated by Egypt's Mohammed Ali in 1815–16.

In 1902 young Abdul Aziz ibn Saud regained control of Nejd. By 1925 he had annexed the Kingdom of Hejaz. Britain endorsed independence of his dominions in 1927.

## KINGDOM OF SAUDI ARABIA

Saudi Arabia was proclaimed a unified kingdom in 1932 under King Abdul Aziz ibn Saud. Huge oil deposits were discovered in 1935.

In 1945 Saudi Arabia joined the United Nations and the Arab League, ending its isolation.

Ibn Saud was succeeded by his son Saud in 1953. But King Saud was deposed in 1964 to be followed by his younger brother Faisal.

Saudi Arabia did not join directly in the Arab-Israeli war of October 1973, but led in the 1973–74 oil embargo of nations friendly to Israel.

In June 1974 the government took 60% control of foreign-owned oil companies.

King Faisal was assassinated by a nephew on March 25, 1975, and was succeeded by his half-brother Khalid Abdul-Aziz.

The discovery of new offshore oil fields in the Persian Gulf in 1975 pushed the nation's known oil reserves to about 180 billion barrels, enough to last 60 years at the present rate of production.

Saudi Arabia's 5-year development program for 1976–81 spent $142 billion for housing, highways, electrification of towns and cities, education, and industry. Two new cities, each planned for a population of 250,000, were built—Yanbu on the Red Sea and Jubail on the Persian Gulf.

Saudi Arabia's royal family was shaken when several hundred rebels seized Islam's holiest shrine, the Grand Mosque, in Mecca on Nov. 20, 1979, and their leader proclaimed himself the savior of Islam. Saudi troops besieged the mosque for two weeks before forcing the rebels to surrender. About 220 persons died in the fighting, including 120 soldiers. On Jan. 9, 1980, 63 of the captured rebels were beheaded in public executions in eight Saudi cities.

With the outbreak of war between Iraq and Iran in 1980, Saudi Arabia announced it would step up oil production to stabilize the world supply available to oil-importing nations. As a gesture of friendship, the U.S. sent sophisticated radar search planes to the nation to provide early warning for any attack that might be launched on the kingdom.

The government announced plans for a 5-year development plan for 1981–86 that would invest $250 billion, largely to develop manufacturing industries to broaden the nation's economy.

# SENEGAL

**Official Name:** Republic of Senegal.
**Area:** 75,750 square miles (196,192 sq. km.).
**Population:** 5,738,840.
**Capital:** Dakar, 798,792.
**Government:** Multiparty socialist republic.
**President:** Léopold Sédar Senghor (took office in 1960).
**Premier:** Abdou Diouf (appointed in 1970).
**National Assembly:** 100 members.
**U.S. Ambassador to Senegal:** Walter C. Carrington.
**Senegalese Ambassador to U.S.:** André Coulbary.
**Flag:** Bars of green, gold, and red, with centered green star.
**Languages:** French (official), English, tribal dialects.
**Main Ethnic Groups:** Wolof (36%), Peuhl (18%), Serere (17%), Toucouleur (9%), Diola (9%), Mandingo (7%).
**Religions:** Islam (80%), animism, Christianity.
**Leading Industries:** Agriculture (peanuts, millet, sorghum, cotton, sugarcane, rice, livestock, vegetables, fruits); fishing; mining (phosphates); food processing; tourism.
**Foreign Trade:** *major exports*—peanuts and peanut oil, phosphates, fish; *major imports*—food, consumer goods, machinery, transport equipment.
**Places of Interest:** Gorée Island; Niokolo-Koba national park. *In Dakar:* Native markets; French Institute of Black Africa.

## SENEGAL TODAY

About the size of South Dakota, Senegal has few natural resources. Its people are poor, and few can read or write.

Because Dakar was for half a century the capital of French colonies in west Africa, Senegal is more industrially developed than most other West African countries. However, its economy depends heavily on aid from France.

Peanuts account for about two-thirds of Senegal's exports and most of the cash income for farmers.

Most of Senegal consists of hot, dry savanna with light, low-fertility soil. Some parts of the north are semidesert. The south is forested and rises to a height of 1,315 feet. Chief rivers include the Gambia and the Senegal.

Located on the west coast of Africa's bulge into the Atlantic Ocean, Senegal lies south of Mauritania. Mali is to the east. Guinea and Guinea-Bissau are to the south. Senegal surrounds the small country of Gambia, except for that nation's outlet to the Atlantic.

The capital, Dakar, lies on Cape Verde, the westernmost port of the African continent.

## EARLY HISTORY

Stone Age artifacts indicate that Senegal has been populated for thousands of years.

The name *Senegal* came from the Zenaga Berbers of Mauritania who invaded the region in the 100s, converting the Toucouleur people of the region to Islam.

By the mid-1400s Portuguese explorers reached the area. They were followed by Dutch, French, and British traders.

## FRENCH RULE

After the Napoleonic wars Britain recognized French claims to the area north of the Gambia River.

The French first built a fort at Dakar in 1857. French designs on the interior were long blocked by the Toucouleur empire of El Hadj Omar, which did not fall to French conquest until 1893, although by 1861 the French had absorbed western Senegal.

France agreed to give Britain control of the Gambia River in a treaty in 1889, resulting in the present-day nation of Gambia.

In 1902 Dakar became the administrative center for French West Africa.

Remaining loyal to the Vichy regime in World War II, Senegal repulsed an attempt by the Free French to take Dakar in 1940.

After the war, Senegalese leaders worked for a viable French Union, but when Guinea defected from the union in 1958, Senegal became an autonomous member of the French Community.

In 1959 the country joined with the Sudanese Republic to form the Mali Federation.

## INDEPENDENCE

On Aug. 20, 1960, Senegal declared itself independent, with Léopold Sédar Senghor as the first president. It was admitted to the UN that year.

An attempt to overthrow Senghor in 1962 resulted in the imprisonment of Premier Mamadou Dia until 1974 and in a new constitution vesting greater power in the presidency.

Throughout the 1960s and early 1970s Senghor and his ruling party forbade political opposition while winning reelection to 5-year terms in 1963, 1968, and 1973.

Senghor's one-party government followed a moderate form of socialism. Its development plan for 1973–77 emphasized agricultural projects and industrial expansion.

Senegal's economy suffered from drought in 1966–73 and in 1977–78.

In February 1976 Senegal extended its territorial limits 150 miles to sea and forbade foreign fishing within 200 miles of its coast.

The constitution was amended in 1976 to allow two opposition parties to exist in addition to Senghor's ruling Socialist Party.

In the nation's first multiparty election on Feb. 26, 1978, Senghor won 82% of the vote and his Socialist Party took 83 of the 100 seats in the national assembly. The opposition Democratic Party won the other 17 seats.

A $500 million dam building project on the Senegal River got under way in 1979. Sponsored by Senegal, Mali, and Mauritania, the project will provide irrigation for 100,000 acres of new farmland when completed in the mid-1980s.

Senegal sent troops into Gambia in November 1980 to prevent what it said was a threatened invasion by Libya.

QUICK QUIZ: What baseball player scored the most runs in his career? See page 779.

## SEYCHELLES

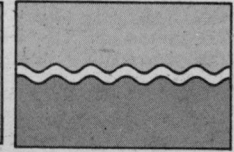

**Official Name:** Republic of Seychelles.
**Area:** 156 square miles (404 sq. km.).
**Population:** 65,478.
**Capital:** Victoria, 13,736.
**Government:** One-party socialist state.
**President:** Albert René (since 1977).
**Legislative Assembly:** 19 members.
**U.S. Ambassador to Seychelles:** William Harrop.
**Flag:** Red stripe at top, wavy white band in middle, and green stripe at bottom.
**Languages:** English and French (official), Creole.
**Main Ethnic Group:** Creole (mixed French and black descent; 94%).
**Principal Religion:** Roman Catholicism.
**Leading Industries:** Agriculture (coconuts, cinnamon, vanilla, fruits, vegetables); tourism; fishing.
**Foreign Trade:** *major exports*—cinnamon, coconuts; *major imports*—machinery, vehicles, food.
**Places of Interest:** Vallée de Mai on Praslin Island; tourist resorts; swimming beaches; Bird Island bird sanctuary.

An island nation off the east coast of Africa, Seychelles is one of the 10 smallest countries in the world. The Seychelles include 86 islands and islets. The largest islands are Mahé (57 sq. mi.) and Praslin (17 sq. mi.).

The luxuriant tropical beauty of the islands has made them increasingly popular to tourists.

The people make their living providing services for the tourists, farming, and fishing. About 2 out of 3 Seychellois can read and write.

The climate seldom varies from a temperature of 75° to 85° F. on the coast. Mountains rise to a height of 2,993 feet on Mahé. Rainfall ranges from 70 to 135 inches a year.

Arabs are believed to have visited in the 1100s. But the islands remained uninhabited until French settlers brought African slaves in the 1770s.

The British captured the islands in 1810, and the French formally gave them up in the Treaty of Paris of 1814. The islands were administered as part of the British colony of Mauritius until 1903, when they were made a separate crown colony. Islanders were first given the opportunity to vote in 1948.

A U.S. space-tracking station was established on Mahé in 1963.

The conservative Seychelles Democratic Party (SDP) won elections in 1970 and 1974 with SDP leader James R. Mancham as chief minister.

Britain granted Seychelles independence on June 29, 1976, with Mancham as president.

Sixty armed rebels overthrew Mancham's government on June 5, 1977. For president they chose Albert René, head of the Seychelles People's United Party (SPUP). René said his new socialist government was pro-Western.

René announced he had thwarted an attempted coup on Nov. 16, 1979, arresting about 100 persons. The prisoners were freed in 1980 after agreeing to leave the country.

## SIERRA LEONE

**Official Name:** Republic of Sierra Leone.
**Area:** 27,699 square miles (71,740 sq. km.).
**Population:** 3,510,920.
**Capital:** Freetown 214,443.
**Government:** One-party republic.
**President:** Siaka Stevens (since 1971).
**House of Representatives:** 97 members.
**U.S. Ambassador to Sierra Leone:** Theresa Ann Healy.
**Sierra Leone Ambassador to U.S.:** Mohamed Morlai Turay.
**Flag:** Stripes of green (top), white, and blue.
**Languages:** English (official), Krio (Pidgin English), tribal dialects.
**Ethnic Groups:** Mende (30%), Temne (30%), others (40%).
**Religions:** Animism (66%), Islam (28%), Christianity (6%).
**Leading Industries:** Mining (diamonds, iron, bauxite, rutile); agriculture (rice, peanuts, coffee, palm kernels, cocoa, cassava, ginger, livestock); fishing; forestry and lumbering; food processing; tourism.
**Foreign Trade:** *major exports*—diamonds, iron ore, palm kernels; *major imports*—cotton fabrics, petroleum products, mining machinery, rice.
**Places of Interest:** Mountainous area of the Sierra Leone peninsula; Freetown; swimming beaches.

### SIERRA LEONE TODAY

Although Sierra Leone has large deposits of diamonds, bauxite, and other minerals, it is a poor country. Most people are farmers, but they do not raise even enough of their basic crop, rice, to feed everyone.

Britain is Sierra Leone's largest customer, purchasing more than half the nation's exports.

About the size of South Carolina, Sierra Leone is bordered by Guinea in the north and by Liberia in the southeast.

The peninsula in the extreme west is a hilly area. The remainder of western Sierra Leone consists of a coastal plain. Farther inland the land rises abruptly to a low plateau. Freetown, the capital, has one of the world's largest harbors.

### HISTORY

The area was named *Serra Lyoa* (later corrupted to Sierra Leone)—meaning "Lion Mountains"—in the 1400s by Portuguese seamen.

In 1787 British abolitionists, in a plan to return former English and American slaves to Africa, sent a small expedition to Sierra Leone. They were driven away by the local tribal chief, but other expeditions followed. By 1792 nearly all of England's destitute blacks had been transported to Sierra Leone. They were joined by captured Maroons from Jamaica and by former slaves from other British colonies.

In 1808 the British took over the colony for use as a naval base.

During the next 60 years Sierra Leone received thousands of liberated slaves.

The British expanded inland from Freetown, and in 1896 the interior was declared a protectorate. The two areas later were merged.

Sierra Leone was granted independence on April 21, 1961, remaining in the British Commonwealth of Nations.

The results of the March 17, 1967, elections gave a slight edge to the All People's Congress, led by Siaka Stevens, over the ruling Sierra Leone People's Party, led by Prime Minister Albert Margai. The results were contested, and army officers staged a coup, installing a military government.

A group of noncommissioned army officers ousted the military regime in 1968. Siaka Stevens was sworn in as prime minister.

In March 1971 Stevens survived a military coup and two attempted assassinations. A month later he declared Sierra Leone a republic, becoming its president.

Stevens' APC party won general elections in 1973, after the opposition party boycotted the election because of police intimidation.

Sierra Leone and its neighbor Liberia formed the Mano River Union in 1973 for mutual economic cooperation. The first major undertaking of the new organization was the construction of a bridge over the Mano River begun in 1974 to link the two countries.

On May 6, 1977, President Stevens' APC again won a general election as opposition parties charged murder and police brutality had prevented them from fully participating.

Stevens hosted the organization of African Unity (OAU) conference in June 1980.

# SINGAPORE

**Official Name:** Republic of Singapore.
**Area:** 224 square miles (581 sq. km.).
**Population:** 2,404,840.
**Capital:** Singapore, 2,334,400.
**Government:** Parliamentary republic.
**Prime Minister:** Lee Kuan Yew (appointed in 1959).
**President:** Benjamin H. Sheares (since 1971).
**Legislative Assembly:** 69 members.
**U.S. Ambassador to Singapore:** Harry E.T. Thayer.
**Singapore Ambassador to U.S.:** Punch Coomaraswamy.
**Flag:** Red and white stripes, with white crescent and five white stars on red stripe.
**Languages:** Malay, Chinese, English, and Tamil.
**Main Ethnic Groups:** Chinese (74%), Malay (14%), Indian and Pakistani (8%).
**Religions:** Buddhism, Islam, Hinduism, Christianity.
**Foreign Trade:** *major exports*—petroleum products, rubber; *major imports*—petroleum products, rubber, crude petroleum.
**Places of Interest:** St. Andrew's Cathedral; Muslim Holy Sultan Mosque; Fort Canning Hill garrison; national museum; botanical gardens; various Chinese temples; Van Cleef Aquarium; House of Jade.

## SINGAPORE TODAY

Singapore is a prosperous island nation with an area about the same as that of Chicago but with only about three-fourths as large a population. Its people have the highest standard of living in east Asia after Japan.

Most of the main island of Singapore is a sprawling city. Little land is available for farming, so most food is imported, as are fuel and raw materials. To reduce population growth, extra taxes are levied on couples who have more than two children. Stiff license fees on automobiles and taxicabs entering the downtown area have reduced traffic congestion.

Public opposition to the government's suppressive measures against political opponents has been blunted by Singapore's remarkable prosperity and low unemployment rate. As a regional center for banking, finance, and technology, the island nation attracts ever-larger foreign investment.

The nation's economy depends on processing, packing, and transshipping to world markets the basic products of Southeast Asia. It also distributes within the region manufactured goods from the world's industrial nations.

Singapore's oil-refinery complex, the third largest in the world, provides about one-fourth of the nation's manufacturing income. Oil-rig construction became a growth industry.

Malaysia and the United States are Singapore's major trading partners.

Singapore lies between the southern tip of Southeast Asia's Malay peninsula and Indonesia's island of Sumatra. The weather is usually hot and humid with much rain.

## EARLY HISTORY

The earliest known colonizers of Singapore were Sumatrans in the 1000s.

In the 1700s Singapore became part of the Dutch colony of Johore.

In 1819 Sir Thomas Stamford Raffles, an agent of the British East India Company, set up a trading station at Singapore. Five years later the British bought the island from the Dutch. Singapore was made a part of the Straits Settlements, with Malacca and Penang in 1826. The island became a British crown colony in 1867.

Singapore was an important British naval base before World War II. In 1941 Japanese forces seized the city after a fierce battle. It was retaken, without fighting, in 1945. In 1946 Singapore was made a separate crown colony. It became a self-governing state in 1959.

In 1963 Singapore joined the Federation of Malaysia, but tensions grew between Singapore's local Chinese leaders and the Malaysians.

## INDEPENDENCE

On Aug. 9, 1965, it withdrew from Malaysia and became the independent *Republic of Singapore.*

In 1971 Prime Minister Lee Kuan Yew, charging that communists were fomenting racial rioting, restricted freedom of the press.

In general elections in 1972 the People's Action Party, which has dominated Singapore since 1959, won all the parliamentary seats, assuring Lee's continuance as prime minister.

QUICK QUIZ: Who led the National League in batting six times in 1943–52? See page 783.

In a war on crime, the government requires mandatory death sentences for criminals convicted of armed robbery and other crimes of violence. In 1976 the death penalty was extended to anyone found in possession of 15 grams of heroin or 30 grams of morphine.

Prime Minister Lee's party won its fifth general election in 17 years on Dec. 23, 1976, taking all 69 seats in parliament.

In 1977 the government launched a new drive against its critics, imprisoning and fining newsmen and others who spoke out against Lee.

The government announced plans in 1980 for a "second industrial revolution" to spur its expanding economy.

# SOLOMONS

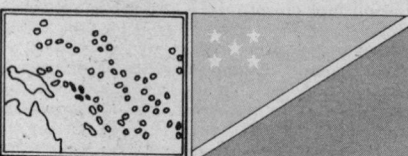

**Official Name:** Solomon Islands.
**Area:** 10,983 square miles (28,446 sq. km.).
**Population:** 237,817.
**Capital:** Honiara, 14,942.
**Government:** Parliamentary democracy.
**Prime Minister:** Peter Kenilorea (since 1978).
**Legislative Assembly:** 24 elected members.
**U.S. Ambassador to Solomons:** Harvey Feldman.
**Solomons Ambassador to U.S.:** Francis Bugotu.
**Flag:** Blue and green triangles divided by diagonal yellow stripe; five white stars in upper hoist corner.
**Languages:** English (official), Pidgin English, tribal dialects.
**Main Ethnic Groups:** Melanesians (93%), Polynesians (4%), Micronesians (2%), others (1%).
**Leading Industries:** Agriculture (coconuts and oil palms, rice, cocoa, yams, taro, cassava, vegetables, peanuts, cattle), processing (copra and palm oil), forestry (lumber), fishing, mining (gold, bauxite, copper, nickel).
**Foreign Trade:** *major exports*—fish, timber, copra, cocoa, seashells, gold; *major imports*—petroleum, manufactured goods.
**Places of Interest:** Swimming beaches, tropical forests, shell-money manufacturing on Malaita, palm plantations, Mt. Popomanaseu on Guadalcanal.

## SOLOMONS TODAY

A South Pacific nation of six large islands and many smaller ones, the Solomons lie about 1,800 miles southwest of Hawaii and some 1,100 miles northeast of Australia. The island chain extends about 900 miles in a southeasterly direction from Papua New Guinea's island of Bougainville.

Although the thatch-roofed shops of the small capital city of Honiara on Guadalcanal boast air conditioning and a plentiful supply of Japanese-made products, most of the dark-skinned Melanesian people of the Solomons follow much the same way of life their ancestors did hundreds of years ago. However, all have given up the practice of cannibalism that persisted into the early 1900s.

Most people live by raising their own fruits and vegetables and by fishing. About half the children attend church-sponsored elementary schools. The islands have only limited secondary education

facilities, a teacher-training school, and a technology institute. Several hundred students go abroad each year to continue their education.

Dense tropical rain forests cover the mountainous islands, erasing the scars of the furious World War II battles fought between Americans and Japanese. The highest mountain, Mt. Popomanaseu, rises 7,647 feet on Guadalcanal. That 2,500-square-mile island also has extensive palm plantations and beef cattle ranches.

Altogether the Solomons have a land area somewhat larger than the state of Maryland, but stretch out over an ocean area larger than Texas. The main islands include Guadalcanal, Malaita, San Cristóbal, New Georgia, Santa Isabel, and Choiseul.

The nation's Shortland Islands lie just east of Bougainville, about 340 miles northwest of Honiara. The northernmost island is the coral atoll of Ontong Java, about 290 miles north of Honiara. The most southeasterly islet is Fataka in the Santa Cruz group, about 650 miles southeast of Honiara.

Airlines provide service among the islands and to Australia and Fiji.

Lying south of the equator, the Solomons have a year-round average temperature of about 80°F. (about 27°C.). Annual rainfall of 63 to 95 inches falls mostly from November through April.

## HISTORY OF THE SOLOMONS

Melanesians settled the islands centuries ago, possibly from Malaysia in Southeast Asia.

The first European to find the islands was the Spaniard Álvaro de Mendaña in 1568. He gave them their name because he believed they contained the lost gold mines of King Solomon. His beliefs were not completely without foundation, because in this century gold mining has become the islands' fifth-ranking export.

In the 1800s British sea captains began enslaving the islanders, taking them to Fiji and to Australia as plantation workers.

Britain established a protectorate over the main islands in 1893. In 1898–99 the Santa Cruz Islands to the southeast were added to the protectorate. In 1900 the Shortland Islands to the northwest, Ontong Java to the north, and other islands were transferred to British control by Germany in exchange for British recognition of German rights in what is now Western Samoa.

The Solomons were the scene of heavy fighting in World War II. The Japanese captured the islands in May–July 1942. The U.S. began its counteroffensive in the South Pacific with the landing of Marines on Guadalcanal on Aug. 8, 1942. Fighting in the Solomons continued until late 1943 when the Japanese finally were driven out after about 20,000 had been killed.

Britain began preparing the islands for independence in 1953 when local councils began to be set up on each of the islands. Central legislative and executive councils were established in 1960. Elections were introduced in 1964.

A new constitution was adopted in 1975, giving the islanders policy-making powers.

Britain granted the Solomons independence on July 7, 1978. Highly dependent on aid from Britain, the Solomons remained part of the British Commonwealth of Nations. Peter Kenilorea became the first prime minister.

# SOMALIA

**Official Name:** Somali Democratic Republic.
**Area:** 246,201 square miles (637,657 sq. km.).
**Population:** 3,689,970.
**Capital:** Mogadiscio, 230,000.
**Government:** One-party socialist state.
**President:** Maj. Gen. Mohammed Siad Barre (since 1969).
**Parliament:** People's Assembly, 171 members.
**U.S. Ambassador to Somalia:** Donald K. Petterson.
**Somali Ambassador to U.S.:** Mohamed Warsama Ali.
**Flag:** Light blue field with centered white star.
**Languages:** Somali, Arabic.
**Main Ethnic Group:** Somali (mixture of Arab, Persian, and Cushitic descent).
**State Religion:** Islam.
**Leading Industries:** Agriculture (cattle, sheep, goats, camels, bananas, sorghum, corn, beans, peanuts, sugarcane, cotton); fishing; food processing; manufacturing (leather products, textiles); mining (tin).
**Foreign Trade:** *major exports*—livestock, bananas, hides and skins; *major imports*—rice, cotton, fabrics, petroleum products, machinery, transport equipment, paper products, tea.
**Places of Interest:** Lac Badana National Park; Gedka-Dabley, Benadir, and Lower Juba wildlife reserves; Dallo forests; Indian Ocean resorts; Bajuni Islands.

## SOMALIA TODAY

Although almost as large as Texas, Somalia is one of the world's 25 poorest countries. Most Somalis live as nomadic herdsmen, raising camels, cattle, goats, and sheep.

The country has some deposits of iron and other minerals, but there is little mining and almost no manufacturing.

Somalia's economy worsened with the influx in 1978–80 of an estimated 2 million refugees from revolution and war in Ethiopia. The UN and other international organizations sent food and economic aid while searching for some long-range solution to the massive refugee problem.

The greater part of the country is covered by the vast Ogaden plateau, mountain-bordered in the north but sloping in the south to a lowland area crossed by the Webi Shebeli and Juba rivers.

Kenya and Ethiopia lie to the west, and Djibouti to the northwest.

## EARLY HISTORY

Somali tribes have occupied the region for more than 2,000 years. From the 900s to 1400s it was part of the Zenj empire, which was overthrown by the Portuguese in the 1500s.

In the 1600s Muscat and Oman gained control of the coastal towns. In the 1800s their authority passed to the sultan of Zanzibar.

## BRITISH AND ITALIAN RULE

A British protectorate was established in the north between 1884 and 1886, and an Italian protectorate in the south in 1889. British rule was constantly threatened by Somali resistance, led by Mohammed Ibn Abdullah Hassan, who was finally defeated in 1920 by British forces.

From 1934 to 1936 Italian Somalia was a staging area for the Italian conquest of Ethiopia. During World War II Italian troops briefly occupied British Somaliland. Italian Somalia was returned to Italian control in 1950 under a 10-year UN trusteeship. In 1954 part of British Somaliland was transferred to Ethiopia.

## INDEPENDENCE

British Somaliland and Italian Somalia joined on July 1, 1960, to form independent Somalia.

Large numbers of Somalis live in Ethiopia, Kenya, and adjacent areas. Pressures for a Greater Somalia have been, and remain, a source of conflict with neighbors. In 1963 Somalia broke off relations with Britain to protest against its grant of substantial autonomy to northern Kenya.

Aden Abdulla Osman was president of Somalia from 1960 to 1967, when he was defeated by Abdirashid Ali Shermarke. President Shermarke was assassinated on Oct. 15, 1969. Sheik Mukhtar Mohammed Mussein became interim president.

On Oct. 21, 1969, a leftist military junta led by Maj. Gen. Mohammed Siad Barre seized power, dissolved the legislature, and outlawed political parties.

In 1970 the country was renamed the *Somali Democratic Republic.* All foreign banks and oil companies were nationalized. The army was equipped and trained by Soviet advisers.

The first Somali written language was introduced by the government in 1972.

The U.S. government reported in 1975 that the Soviet Union had installed atomic guided-missile facilities in Somalia. The Soviet activities were cited as a major reason for the building of a U.S. Navy base on the island of Diego Garcia in the Indian Ocean.

In June 1976 the Socialist Revolutionary Party was organized as the nation's only political party. The following month the party's 7-man central committee was made Somalia's ruling body under President Mohammed Siad Barre.

In mid-1977 Somali guerrillas began a major drive to capture the Ogaden region of Ethiopia. When the Soviet Union and Cuba aided Ethiopia, Somalia on Nov. 13, 1977, canceled its treaty of friendship with the Soviet Union and broke relations with Cuba. An Ethiopian offensive in March 1978 forced Somali troops to withdraw from Ethiopia's northern Ogaden region. But fighting continued into the 1980s.

The first election since Barre seized power was held on Dec. 30, 1979, with members of the national People's Assembly and local district assemblies approved from a single slate of candidates.

The U.S. and Somalia signed an agreement on Aug. 22, 1980, permitting the U.S. to use military bases in Somalia in return for $45 million in economic and military aid over a two-year period. Ethiopia warned the U.S. that its action could involve the U.S. "in an endless war in Africa."

Quick Quiz: What metropolitan area has the largest population in the world? See page 110.

# SOUTH AFRICA

 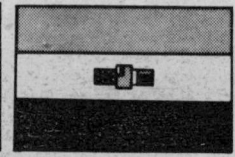

**Official Name:** Republic of South Africa.
**Area:** 437,538 square miles (1,133,218 sq. km.).
**Population:** 24,835,400.
**Chief Metropolitan Areas:** Cape Town, legislative capital, 1,096,597; Pretoria, administrative capital, 561,703; Bloemfontein, judicial capital, 180,179; Johannesburg, 1,432,643; Soweto, 1,200,000; Durban, 843,327; Port Elizabeth, 468,577.
**Government:** Parliamentary republic.
**President:** Marais Viljoen (since 1979).
**Prime Minister:** Pieter Willem Botha (since 1978).
**Parliament:** Senate, 51 members; House of Assembly, 165 members.
**U.S. Ambassador to South Africa:** William B. Edmondson.
**South African Ambassador to U.S.:** Donald Bell Sole.
**Flag:** Orange, white, and blue stripes; in center, replicas of Union Jack, old flag of Orange Free State, and old Transvaal Vierkleur (four-color).
**Languages:** Afrikaans, English (both official), many black languages.
**Ethnic Groups:** Black (67%), European descent (19%), mulatto (11%), Asian descent (3%).
**Main Religions:** Christianity (73%), animism (13%), Hinduism (2%), Islam (1%).
**Leading Industries:** Trade and services; manufacturing (steel, chemicals, automobiles, textiles, metal products, machinery, consumer products); mining (diamonds, gold, coal, iron, copper, uranium, many others); agriculture (corn, sheep, dairy products, cattle, wheat, sugarcane, tobacco, fruits, vegetables); fishing.
**Foreign Trade:** *major exports*—gold, metal products, food, diamonds, wool; *major imports*—automobiles, petroleum, machinery, manufactured goods.
**Places of Interest:** Kruger National Park; Cape Point; Kirstenbosch National Botanical Gardens; garden route tour from Cape Town to Durban; Oudtshoorn caves; Johannesburg gold mines; Kimberley diamond mine; Indian market and beaches at Durban; Zululand game reserves; Sudwala caves and adjoining Dinosaur Park.

## SOUTH AFRICA TODAY

Rich in natural resources, white-ruled South Africa leads the world in gold mining and produces about a third of the world's diamonds. It also has large amounts of iron, coal, copper, tin, and uranium. It lacks only natural petroleum, but has undertaken large scale production of petroleum from coal. South Africa's farmlands produce ample amounts of wheat and other food crops to have some left over for export.

Most of the world opposes South Africa's racial segregation policies, which include barring blacks from voting in national elections.

About three times the size of California, South Africa is bordered on the northwest by Namibia (South West Africa), on the north by Botswana and Zimbabwe Rhodesia, and on the northeast by Mozambique and Swaziland. The eastern part of South Africa surrounds Lesotho, Transkei, Bophuthatswana, and Venda.

Most of South Africa is a plateau, with an average height of 4,000 feet. In the east the land rises steeply from fertile coastal lowlands to the Drakensberg Mountains. In the east central and northern regions are the prairie-like veld. Cape Agulhas is the continent's southern tip.

The Orange River rises in the Drakensberg Mountains and with its tributary, the Vaal, flows westward into the Atlantic. The Limpopo River rises in the Witwatersrand in the Transvaal.

## APARTHEID (SEPARATE RACIAL DEVELOPMENT)

Less than 1 person in 5 in South Africa is white. Yet whites control the government and all aspects of life by the policy of racial segregation called *apartheid*. To enforce the policy, parliament passed restrictive racial laws in the 1950s and 1960s. Some restrictions in sports and other areas were lifted in the 1970s, including removal in 1979 of the ban on black labor unions.

Police can arrest and imprison people without a court order and hold them indefinitely without letting them communicate with lawyers, families, or friends. Or they can be "banned" to their homes and denied rights of free speech. The security police are protected from court restraints, but may be prosecuted for excesses.

About two-thirds of the blacks live on tribal reserves that cover about 13% of the country's land area. Millions of blacks have been forcibly moved from white areas to nine *homelands*: Bophuthatswana, Ciskei, Gazankulu, KwaZulu, Lebowa, Qwaqwa, Swazi, Transkei, and Venda. South Africa granted sovereignty to Transkei in 1976, to Bophuthatswana in 1977, and to Venda in 1979. It planned to give independence to the others later.

Other nations have refused to recognize the sovereignty of the South Africa homelands because they view the homelands program as part of the nation's apartheid policy of racial segregation. The program requires blacks who are members of tribes that have independent homelands to give up their South African citizenship, even though they live in South Africa. Thus, by the time all the homelands are "independent" most blacks would no longer be citizens of South Africa, so the whites then would be the majority of South African citizens and could validly control the government.

Wholly dependent on South Africa for their economic existence, the homelands are "landlocked islands" surrounded by South Africa.

Migrant blacks who take jobs in the cities of South Africa are forbidden to bring their wives and children with them. They and permanent black resident families live in "locations" set aside on the outskirts of cities or towns. Asians and those of mixed ancestry are similarly restricted to specific living areas. Education is segregated, except in some private schools.

Most professional and supervisory jobs are held by whites. Blacks do most unskilled and semiskilled labor on farms, in mines, in manufacturing plants, and in public service.

## EARLY HISTORY

Hottentots, Bushmen, and other Africans lived in southern Africa for thousands of years, but little is known of their history other than the cave paintings they drew.

Portuguese explorer Bartolomeu Dias in 1488 became the first European to reach the Cape of Good Hope. The first permanent European settlement was made at Cape Town in 1652 by the Dutch East India Company. The Dutch were soon joined by French and German settlers. These early arrivals came to be known as *Boers*.

## BRITISH RULE

Through the Napoleonic wars, Britain gained formal possession of the Cape Colony in 1814.

Because of dissatisfaction with British rule and the abolition of slavery in 1833, many Boers migrated to the interior in the Great Trek of 1835–48. There they founded the Transvaal, Natal, and the Orange Free State territories. Their migration led to war with the Zulus and other Bantu tribesmen. The Boers defeated the Zulus in 1838 at the Battle of Blood River.

Britain annexed Natal in 1843. After discovery of gold and diamonds, it annexed part of the Orange Free State in 1871 and the South Africa Republic (Transvaal) in 1877.

Boer resentment of British encroachment erupted in 1899 into the Boer War, or South African War, which the British won in 1902.

Britain formed the Union of South Africa on May 31, 1910, joining Cape Colony, Natal, the Orange River Colony (Orange Free State), and the Transvaal. The Union of South Africa gained sovereignty in 1934.

Apartheid became official policy under Prime Minister Dr. Daniel Malan, whose party won the 1948 elections.

## REPUBLIC OF SOUTH AFRICA

On May 31, 1961, the country became the independent *Republic of South Africa*. Six months later it withdrew from the British Commonwealth of Nations, reacting to criticism of its racial policies.

With the growing number of independent black African nations, pressures mounted in the U.S. and UN against South African apartheid. The U.S. ended the sale of all military equipment to South Africa on Dec. 31, 1963.

The most prominent black leader, Nelson R. Mandela, head of the African National Congress, was convicted of treason in 1964 and sentenced to life imprisonment.

South Africa continued its rigid policy of apartheid under Prime Minister Hendrik F. Verwoerd, who was assassinated in 1966, and under his successor, Balthazar Johannes Vorster.

In November 1974 the UN General Assembly suspended South Africa's voting privileges in the international organization.

The government announced in May 1976 that it would build its first atomic power plant, planned for completion in 1982.

A wave of protest riots and strikes by black students began on June 16, 1976, in Soweto, a black suburb of Johannesburg. Over 500 were killed and nearly 4,000 injured.

The government on Oct. 19, 1977, banned 18 black activist groups and jailed over 50 black leaders in an effort to stop black demonstrations. The UN Security Council on Nov. 4, 1977,

unanimously ordered a worldwide mandatory embargo on the shipment of military supplies to South Africa—the first such action ever taken by the UN against a member nation.

Vorster's National Party easily won national elections on Nov. 30, 1977, capturing 134 of the 165 seats in the House of Assembly.

In December 1977 the UN General Assembly adopted by huge majorities resolutions calling on the UN Security Council to embargo oil shipments to South Africa and to cut off foreign investment in South African enterprises.

President Nicolaas Diederichs, 75, died on Aug. 21, 1978. A month later Vorster resigned as prime minister and was elected president by the electoral college of parliament.

Pieter Willem Botha, 62, formerly defense minister under Vorster, was chosen as prime minister on Sept. 28, 1978, by the ruling National Party.

Vorster resigned as president in June 1979 and was succeeded by Marais Viljoen, 63, who previously had been president of the senate.

The resignation of Vorster came after a government investigation commission disputed his denials that he had tried to cover up a secret expenditure of more than $70 million to influence public opinion in favor of apartheid.

As the price of gasoline rose to $2.43 a gallon in 1979, the government rushed construction of several plants to convert coal into oil. The plants are expected to provide from one-third to one-half of the country's oil needs by the mid-1980s.

In April 1979 relations between South Africa and the U.S. were shaken when the government expelled three members of the U.S. embassy staff on charges of spying on South Africa with an aerial camera concealed in the plane of the U.S. ambassador. The U.S. retaliated by expelling two South African diplomats from Washington, D.C.

A flash of light detected by a U.S. satellite off the southern coast of South Africa on Sept. 22, 1979, was interpreted by some nuclear scientists as evidence South Africa had tested an atomic bomb. However, the government denied doing so.

The soaring price of gold in 1979–80 brought South Africa unexpected bonanzas of about $3.5 billion in 1979 and more in 1980. The surplus enabled the government to drastically cut income taxes in 1980, eliminating all income taxes for workers receiving $2,500 a year or less in wages.

In 1980 South Africa experienced the worst wave of racial violence since 1976. In June guerrillas bombed two of the country's new coal-to-oil conversion plants and an oil refinery. Later in the same month police fired on black demonstrators in Cape Town, killing about 30. A strike for higher pay by about 3,000 black city workers in Johannesburg in July was broken by forcibly deporting about half of them to their tribal homelands.

The severest drought in the nation's history hit South Africa's tribal homelands in 1980, damaging food crops and causing starvation.

More than three decades of wrangling between the UN and South Africa over the status of Namibia (South West Africa) continued into the 1980s as South Africa refused to give up control of the former German colony. See page 609.

QUICK QUIZ: Who was the first speaker of the U.S. House of Representatives? See page 166.

# SOVIET UNION

**Official Name:** Union of Soviet Socialist Republics.
**Area:** 8,649,538 square miles (22,402,200 sq. km.).
**Population:** 267,605,000.
**Chief Cities:** Moskva (Moscow), capital, 6,941,961; Leningrad, 3,512,974; Kiev, 2,131,000; Tashkent, 1,732,000; Kharkov, 1,428,000; Gorki, 1,332,000; Novosibirsk, 1,324,000; Kuibyshev, 1,221,000; Sverdlovsk, 1,204,000.
**Largest Metropolitan Areas:** Moscow, 7,909,000; Leningrad, 4,480,000.
**Government:** Communist one-party state.
**Chief of State:** Leonid I. Brezhnev, president (since 1977) and general secretary of the Communist Party (since 1964).
**Prime Minister:** Nilolai A. Tikhonov (since 1980).
**Supreme Soviet:** *Soviet of the Union,* 750 members; *Soviet of Nationalities,* 750 members.
**U.S. Ambassador to Soviet Union:** Thomas J. Watson Jr.
**Soviet Ambassador to U.S.:** Anatoliy F. Dobrynin.
**Flag:** Red field with gold hammer and sickle below gold-bordered star in upper hoist corner.
**Major Languages:** Russian (official), Slavic (76%), Altaic (8%), other (16%).
**Main Ethnic Groups:** Russian (52%), Ukrainian (16%), Uzbek (5%), Belorussian (4%).
**Religions:** Atheism (official), Russian Orthodoxy (18%).
**Leading Industries:** Manufacturing (steel, cement, paper, electricity, vehicles, electronics, armaments); agriculture (wheat, livestock, corn, rye, oats, potatoes, fruits, vegetables); mining (petroleum, natural gas, coal, lignite, iron ore, diamonds, bauxite, copper, lead, zinc, salt); forestry and lumbering; fishing.
**Foreign Trade:** *major exports*—equipment for industrial plants, petroleum; *major imports*—machinery, clothing, ships, raw sugar, metal ores, wheat.
**Places of Interest:** Lake Baikal; Black Sea resorts; Caucasus area; the Crimea; Baltic Sea area; Kiev. *In Moscow:* The Kremlin, containing Nikolai Palace (now home of Supreme Soviet), Kremlin Theater, belfry of Ivan the Terrible, Cathedral of the Archangel Michael, Patriarch's Palace; Lenin Mausoleum; St. Basil's Cathedral. *In Leningrad:* Hermitage Museum (former Winter Palace).

## SOVIET UNION TODAY

As one of the world's two great superpowers, the Soviet Union competes with the United States for world leadership.

Stretching from eastern Europe across the continent of Asia, the Soviet Union has nearly two-and-a-half times the area of the U.S. and a population about 20% larger.

The Soviet Union has a communist form of government with one-party domination of political activities and state ownership of economic activities. It suppresses such civil rights as freedom of speech and freedom of the press. Refusing to work is a crime punishable by imprisonment.

Since World War II the Soviet Union and the U.S. have engaged in a costly arms race in which each nation has built atomic interconti-

nental missiles capable of destroying the other.

As a by-product of the armament buildup, the two superpowers competed in a space race. The Soviet Union became the first to fire a satellite into orbit around the earth in 1957 and the first to launch a cosmonaut into earth orbit in 1961. However, the United States came back to win the space race by being the first to place men on the moon in 1969.

## SOVIET GOVERNMENT

Though the constitution of the Soviet government is patterned somewhat after those of Western democracies, there are no checks and balances and little real separation of powers.

The country is ruled by the Communist Party's Politburo, whose 14 members are also the chief officials of the government and of the party.

In theory, the highest legislative body is the bicameral Supreme Soviet, elected by universal suffrage from single lists of Communist Party-approved candidates. It meets twice yearly but functions as a rubber stamp. It elects a 38-member Presidium empowered to act for it when it is not in session.

The Communist Party controls all levels of government and practically every phase of Soviet life. It is the only political party in the country—its power guaranteed by the constitution. Membership in the party is about 14.5 million, or 9% of the adult population.

The party's highest organ, theoretically, is its congress, which normally meets every four years to formalize broad policies of the Politburo. The congress elects a central committee to act for it between sessions.

## GEOGRAPHY

The world's largest country, the Soviet Union covers nearly one-sixth of the earth's land area.

The Soviet Union extends through 11 time zones, varying widely in terrain and climate.

Its Ural Mountains are considered the dividing line between Europe and Asia. The Carpathian Mountains fringe the Soviet Union in the west. The Caucasus Mountains lie between the Black and Caspian seas. The Pamir, Tien Shan, Altai, and other ranges rise along the southern border.

The Soviet Union includes 15 Soviet states. The largest is Russia (Russian Soviet Federated Socialist Republic), with 70% of the total land area and more than half the people. Second

## STATES OF THE SOVIET UNION

| NAME | AREA (sq. mi.) | CAPITAL |
|---|---|---|
| Armenia | 11,506 | Yerevan |
| Azerbaijan | 33,436 | Baku |
| Belorussia | 80,155 | Minsk |
| Estonia | 17,413 | Tallinn |
| Georgia | 26,911 | Tbilisi |
| Kazakhstan | 1,048,306 | Alma-Ata |
| Kirghizstan | 76,641 | Frunze |
| Latvia | 24,595 | Riga |
| Lithuania | 25,174 | Vilnius |
| Moldavia | 13,012 | Kishinev |
| Russia | 6,592,850 | Moscow |
| Tadzhikistan | 55,251 | Dushanbe |
| Turkmenistan | 188,456 | Ashkhabad |
| Ukraine | 233,090 | Kiev |
| Uzbekistan | 173,592 | Tashkent |

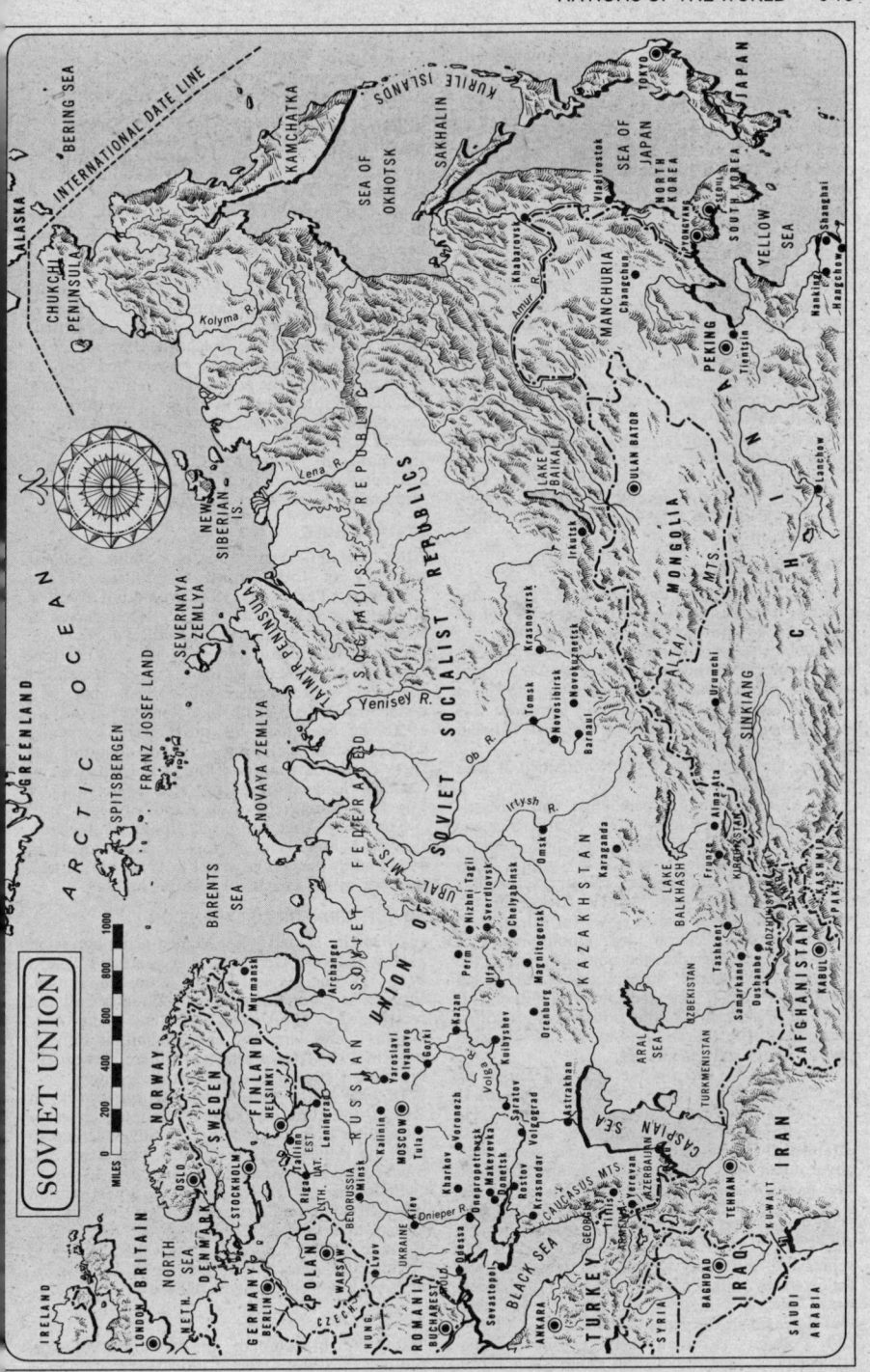

**SOVIET UNION** *(continued)*

most populous is the Ukraine (Ukrainian Soviet Socialist Republic), with 20% of the people.

## EARLY HISTORY OF RUSSIA

Rurik, the almost legendary Swede, is generally credited with founding the Russian state when he led his Varangian tribe into Novgorod in the year 862. Rurik's dynasty later ruled the duchy of Moscow and eventually all of Russia.

Saint Vladimir (Vladimir I, reigned 980–1015), initially a pagan, became the first Christian ruler of Kiev. Through his victories over Lithuanians, Bulgars, and the Greeks in the Crimea, he is considered the founder of the powerful Kievan state. Under Yaroslav the Wise in the 1000s, Kiev reached a peak of prosperity and culture. In 1240 Kiev fell to the Mongols, who, under Batu Khan, created an empire called the Golden Horde that ruled most of what is now the eastern and southern Soviet Union.

Northern Russia fell under domination of Moscow. Its power was solidified by Dmitri Donskoi. Under Ivan III (1462–1505), who drove out the Mongols, and Vasily III (1505–33), many principalities were brought under Russian control.

## CZARIST RUSSIA

Ivan IV, better known as "Ivan the Terrible" and the first ruler to be crowned czar (caesar) of all Russia (1547), further enlarged the country.

After the reign of Boris Godunov (1598–1605) came dynastic upheavals, civil war, and territorial losses to Sweden and Poland. Following the defeat of the Poles, the nobleman Mikhail Romanov was elected czar (1613), founding the last Russian dynasty.

Peter the Great (1689–1725) opened Russia to Westernization.

Continuing Peter's expansionist and authoritarian policies, Ekaterina II (Catherine the Great; 1762–96) made Russia a leading power.

Under Aleksandr I (1801–25) more lands were added to the empire. With Napoleon's defeat on Russian soil (1812), Aleksandr became one of Europe's most powerful rulers.

The spread of liberal ideas among many of the aristocrats and educated bourgeois led to the abortive Decembrist Conspiracy (1825), an attempt to block the accession of Nikolai I. Though unsuccessful, the conspiracy is often viewed as the initial phase of the Russian revolutionary movement.

After Britain and France defeated Russia in the Crimean War (1854–56), Czar Aleksandr II (1855–81) inaugurated a series of reforms. He freed the serfs, modernized the courts, and established provincial, county, and town self-government on a modest scale. He also extended the Russian empire in the Far East. He was assassinated in 1881 by a terrorist group.

Aleksandr III (1881–94) repudiated his father's policies and instituted a period of severe repression, especially against the Jews. He was followed by Nikolai II (1894–1917), the last czar. During Nikolai's administration, Russia was defeated in the Russo-Japanese War (1904–05). Popular discontent in 1905 forced Nikolai to accept a constitution and establish a representative parliament, the Duma.

In World War I a poorly prepared Russia joined the battle against the Central Powers. Russian armies suffered massive setbacks.

## RUSSIAN REVOLUTION

Revolution erupted in February 1917, when troops refused to fire upon crowds milling in the streets of St. Petersburg (Leningrad) as part of a general strike. The czar abdicated, and a moderate provisional government took over, headed successively by Prince Georgi Lvov and Aleksandr Kerensky.

In November 1917 the Bolsheviks (communists), led by Vladimir Lenin and Leon Trotsky, seized power. The royal family was executed. Lenin had founded the Bolshevik Party in 1903. Although the communists represented only a small minority of the population, Lenin ruled as a dictator until his death in 1924. His government successfully fought off attempts to overthrow it during a civil war (1918–20). The Communist International (Comintern), founded in 1919, attempted through local communist parties to undermine western European governments.

## STALIN'S RULE

After Lenin's death, Joseph Stalin, general secretary of the Central Committee of the Communist Party since 1922, won a bitter power struggle against Leon Trotsky (murdered in Mexico, 1940). Stalin created a brutal police state. He pushed the nation into rapid industrialization, forcibly collectivized agriculture, and expanded the secret police, censorship, forced labor, and concentration camps. In "blood purges" in the late 1930s he executed tens of thousands, mostly without trials, including surviving founding fathers of the Soviet state and a majority of the military leadership. Stalin also systematically imprisoned hundreds of thousands of people.

The Soviet Union received diplomatic recognition by a number of European governments in 1924 and by the United States in 1933. It became a member of the League of Nations in 1934.

## SOVIET TERRITORIAL EXPANSION

In 1939 the Soviet Union signed a nonagression pact with Nazi Germany that preceded World War II. The Soviet Union absorbed Latvia, Lithuania, Estonia (political conquests still not recognized by the United States and many other nations), and later the eastern half of Poland. Also in 1939 Russia attacked Finland, eventually taking a large part of its eastern territory.

In 1941 Hitler launched a surprise attack on Russia, inflicting civilian and military losses of 20 million lives and driving the Soviet Union to join the Allied side. With U.S. lend-lease aid, Soviet armies drove back the Germans.

Following Allied victory, the Soviet Union imposed communist governments in eastern European countries occupied by the Red Army. By mid-1948 Poland, Czechoslovakia, Hungary, Romania, Bulgaria, East Germany, Yugoslavia, and Albania were Soviet satellites.

## COLD WAR

With the breakup of the wartime alliance, mutual hostility (the Cold War) came to

characterize Soviet relations with the West.

The Soviet Union's test explosion of its first atomic bomb in 1949, using secrets stolen from Britain and the U.S., brought fears that an attack on noncommunist countries might be launched without warning.

The formation of the NATO military alliance by the U.S., Canada, and western European nations in 1950 was countered by Moscow with the Warsaw Pact alliance of its satellites.

After Stalin's death in 1953, Georgi M. Malenkov became chairman of the Council of Ministers, but in 1955 he was replaced by Nikolai Bulganin. In October 1956 Soviet troops crushed a popular revolt in Hungary.

By 1956 Nikita S. Khrushchev, Communist Party first secretary, emerged as the most powerful figure in the Soviet Union. In 1963 he agreed to a limited nuclear test-ban treaty with the U.S.

The Chinese communists rejected destalinization and the "peaceful coexistence" formula. Sino-Soviet differences produced a schism that divided the communist movement throughout the world.

The Soviet Union and the United States came close to war in 1962 when Khrushchev installed atomic missiles in Cuba that could be used to attack the U.S. However, war was averted after President Kennedy imposed a naval blockade on Cuba, forcing Khrushchev to withdraw the missiles.

## RULE BY LEONID BREZHNEV

In 1964 Khrushchev was abruptly removed from office, to be succeeded by Leonid Brezhnev as Communist Party first secretary and Alexei Kosygin as premier.

In August 1968 the Soviet Union and its Warsaw Pact allies (except Romania) invaded Czechoslovakia and crushed a more liberal communist government under Alexander Dubček. Moscow announced the "Brezhnev Doctrine," proclaiming the Soviet Union's right to intervene in any "socialist" country.

As part of his "détente" policies to ease tensions with communist regimes, President Nixon held a summit meeting with Brezhnev in Moscow on May 22–30, 1972, where they signed two agreements limiting production of nuclear weapons, as formulated during four years of SALT (Strategic Arms Limitation Talks) negotiations.

In June 1973 Brezhnev made a 9-day visit to the U.S. for a meeting with President Nixon hailed as the official end to the Cold War.

When Nobel Prize-winner Aleksandr I. Solzhenitsyn published a book, *The Gulag Archipelago, 1918–1956*, exposing the horrors of Soviet secret labor-prisons, he was arrested and exiled in 1974.

President Ford met with Brezhnev in Vladivostok in November 1974. They agreed to continue efforts to limit atomic weapons.

The Soviet Union began construction of a second Trans-Siberian railroad in 1974. A work force of 100,000 was employed in building the 2,000-mile line to be completed in 1985.

The Soviet government on Jan. 10, 1975, canceled its 1972 trade agreement with the U.S. because of requirements by the U.S. Congress that the Soviet Union relax its restrictive emigration policies.

In May 1977 the 70-year-old Brezhnev ousted 74-year-old Nikolai V. Podgorny from the presidency. He then took the title of president, becoming the first Soviet ruler to hold titles as both head of the party and chief of state.

The Supreme Soviet adopted a new constitution on Oct. 7, 1977, that emphasized the Communist Party's dominant role.

A new "hot line" communication system using space satellites to carry messages between the White House and the Kremlin went into service on Jan. 16, 1978. It replaced a land cable "hot line" that had been installed in 1963 in an effort to prevent misunderstandings between the two leading nuclear powers.

Soviet-U.S. relations deteriorated in 1977–78 as President Carter repeatedly denounced Soviet violations of human rights of its citizens. The Soviet government responded with trials and harsh sentences for several human-rights activists. But in 1979 five of the Soviet dissidents were given their freedom in exchange with the United States for two convicted Soviet spies. The Soviet government also eased restrictions on the emigration of Jews in 1979, permitting a record 51,000 to leave the country and bringing to about 240,000 the number allowed to leave during the 1970s.

Seven years of negotiations between the U.S. and the Soviet Union for a new pact limiting strategic arms resulted in a SALT II treaty signed by Brezhnev and President Carter on June 18, 1979. But deteriorating relations with the U.S. prevented U.S. ratification of the treaty.

Sagging industrial production and poor crop harvests caused the Soviet government to issue a decree in 1979 calling for greater efficiency and production, especially in consumer goods. During 1979 the country had a 3.4% rate of industrial growth, the lowest since World War II, and considerably short of the planned rate of 5.7%.

The Soviet Union invaded Afghanistan in December 1979, setting up a puppet communist government loyal to Moscow. Soviet troops battled Afghan guerrillas opposed to the communist takeover of their country (see page 9).

On Jan. 4, 1980, U.S. President Carter denounced the Soviet actions in Afghanistan, cut grain sales to the Soviet Union, and suspended the sale of high-technology equipment such as computers. He also took the lead in organizing a partial boycott of the summer Olympic Games held in Moscow (see pages 836–837).

As relations with the U.S. worsened, the Soviet government became harsher with its treatment of human-rights dissidents. On Jan. 22, 1980, Andrei D. Sakharov, Nobel Prize-winning father of the Soviet hydrogen bomb, was arrested and exiled without trial to the city of Gorki for having criticized the Soviet invasion of Afghanistan. Many less prominent Soviet dissidents were arrested or were given passports and escorted out of the country.

Nikolai A. Tikhonov, 75, was appointed prime minister on Oct. 23, 1980, succeeding the 76-year-old Kosygin, who resigned because of illness. Tikhonov had served as Kosygin's deputy for four years.

QUICK QUIZ: What is the world's highest waterfall? See page 188.

# SPAIN

**Official Name:** Spanish State.
**Area:** 194,897 square miles (504,782 sq. km.).
**Population:** 38,425,200.
**Chief Cities:** Madrid, capital, 3,520,320; Barcelona, 1,809,722; Valencia, 713,026; Seville, 588,784; Zaragoza, 547,317; Bilbao, 457,655; Málaga, 402,978.
**Government:** Parliamentary monarchy.
**King:** Juan Carlos I (since 1975).
**Prime Minister:** Adolfo Suárez Gonzáles (since 1976).
**Legislature:** *Upper House,* 248 members; *Lower House,* 350 members.
**U.S. Ambassador to Spain:** Terence A. Todman.
**Spanish Ambassador to U.S.:** José Llado y Fernandez-Urrutia.
**Flag:** Wide yellow stripe in center with narrow red stripes at top and bottom.
**Official Language:** Castilian Spanish.
**Ethnic Groups:** Spanish-Castilian, Basque, Catalan, Galician, Andalusian.
**Main Religion:** Roman Catholicism.
**Leading Industries:** Trade and services; manufacturing (steel, ships, automobiles, textiles, cement, paper, cork products, consumer goods); agriculture (livestock, wheat, sugar beets, potatoes, barley, olives, grapes, fruits, vegetables); tourism; mining (lead, coal, iron, petroleum, uranium); forestry and lumbering; fishing.
**Foreign Trade:** *major exports*—citrus fruits, olive oil, wine; *major imports*—crude petroleum, corn, soybeans, meat.
**Places of Interest:** *In Madrid,* Prado Museum, royal palace, nearby El Escorial palace and monastery; *in Toledo,* cathedral, Sto. Tomé Church; *in Barcelona,* Sagrada Familia Church, Gothic Quarter, cathedral; *in Seville,* Giralda tower and cathedral, Alcázar palaces; *in Granada,* Alhambra Moorish palace-citadel; *in Cordoba,* Great Mosque; Costa del Sol resort area; *in Segovia,* Roman aqueduct.

## SPAIN TODAY

Larger than California both in area and population, Spain is the fifth most important industrial nation of western Europe. It is among the leading producers of cement, fish, and uranium.

Although Spain has experienced substantial economic growth with the aid of large loans from the United States, it has a per capita income about half that of West Germany.

Over 30 million tourists visit Spain each year because of its mild climate and many historical and cultural attractions.

Spain is bounded on the north by the rugged Pyrenees that separate it from France and the independent republic of Andorra. Portugal lies to the west. The British colony of Gibraltar stands at the southern tip of Spain.

Spain has six mountain ranges, grazing lands, a vast central plateau, plains, and rocky coastlines. The most important rivers are the Ebro, Douro, Tagus, Guadalquivir, and Guadiana.

## EARLY HISTORY

In the 800s B.C. Phoenician traders settled on the southwest coast. Carthaginians colonized the east coast and the Balearic Islands, where Greeks also planted colonies.

In the 200s B.C. the Carthaginians conquered most of Iberia but subsequently were defeated by the Romans.

Christianity was established in the 200s and 300s A.D. Then hordes of Germanic tribes began sweeping into the peninsula in 409.

In the 700s Spain was conquered by Muslim Berbers (Moors). Under Abd-ar-Rahman III (891–961) Muslim Spain reached its apex.

## KINGDOM OF SPAIN

The Moors lost their last stronghold (Granada) in 1492, when it fell to the forces of Fernando V and Isabel I, rulers of Castile and Aragon. In that same year Columbus made his first voyage of discovery to America.

Spain's "golden century" was the 1500s, coinciding with the Hapsburg dynasty's accession to the throne. The country acquired a huge overseas empire that included nearly all of South America, the southern part of North America, and the Philippines.

Vast wealth came from the Americas. Spain ruled the seas and had the strongest military force in Europe. But incessant wars with England, the Netherlands, and France brought a decline in Spanish power.

Spain's deepest humiliation came in 1808, when Napoleon forced King Carlos IV to abdicate and installed Joseph Bonaparte as king of Spain. By 1814 British forces under the Duke of Wellington succeeded in driving out the French. Colonial rebellions and the Spanish-American War (1898) brought an end to most of Spain's overseas empire.

A military dictatorship led by Primo de Rivera took power in 1923 under the Bourbon king Alfonso XIII. De Rivera was ousted in 1930.

## REPUBLIC OF SPAIN AND CIVIL WAR

A republican victory at the polls in 1931 brought an end to the monarchy. A Popular Front (republicans, socialists, communists, and syndicalists) won elections in February 1936.

Gen. Francisco Franco began a revolt on July 18, 1936, taking command of the Spanish army in Morocco. He led an invasion of Spain and began three years of devastating civil war.

Franco was supported by conservatives, including the Fascist Falange Party, founded in 1933 by the son of ex-dictator de Rivera. The defending Loyalists (republicans) were backed by the Popular Front and the Basques and Catalans. Franco received substantial aid from Nazi Germany and Fascist Italy. The Loyalists received help from the Soviet Union. By 1939 Franco defeated the republican forces, made himself dictator, and suppressed all opposition.

## RULE BY FRANCISCO FRANCO

Spain was ruled as a dictatorship by Franco for 36 years in 1939–75. He headed the only legal political party, the National Movement.

During World War II Spain favored the Axis Powers but remained technically neutral.

Speculation about the probable successor to General Franco ended in 1969 with his an-

nouncement in July that he had chosen Prince Juan Carlos de Borbón y Borbón to be his legal successor and heir to the Spanish throne.

Because Spain must import most petroleum, it was hard hit by the Arab oil embargo of 1973–74 and soaring oil prices that slowed economic growth and brought high inflation.

## CONSTITUTIONAL MONARCHY

Juan Carlos was proclaimed king on Nov. 22, 1975, two days after Franco's death. He promised to restore political liberties.

Spain gave up its last large overseas colony on Feb. 26, 1976, turning over the 102,703-square-mile Spanish Sahara on the west coast of Africa to Morocco and Mauritania.

The U.S. and Spain signed a 5-year pact in 1976 that extended American use of military bases in Spain in return for $1.2 billion in aid.

The parliament lifted the long-standing ban on political parties in June 1976.

King Juan Carlos I dismissed Franco's last prime minister, Carlos Arias Navarro, on July 2, 1976, replacing him with Adolfo Suárez González, head of the National Movement Party.

In 1977 Spain removed its ban on the Communist Party and restored diplomatic relations with the Soviet Union for the first time since 1939.

The first free national election since the Spanish civil war was held on June 15, 1977, to elect a new two-house parliament to replace the unicameral *Cortes* of the Franco years. A coalition of center-right parties led by Prime Minister Suárez won a majority in the senate and the largest number of seats in the lower house. The socialists were a close second.

The government restored some self-rule to the northeastern region of Catalonia in September 1977 with revival of its governing body, called the *Generalitat*, which had been abolished by Franco in 1939.

A national referendum on Dec. 6, 1978, approved by a vote of 87.7% a new democratic constitution to replace the dictatorial "Fundamental Laws" of Generalissimo Franco under which Spain had been governed since the 1930s. King Juan Carlos signed the constitution on Dec. 27, 1978, making Spain a parliamentary democracy with guarantees of human rights and free enterprise. It also removed the official status of Roman Catholicism, which previously had been the state religion.

In the first election under the new constitution on March 1, 1979, Prime Minister Suárez's centrist party, the Union of the Democratic Center (UCD), won control of parliament with 168 seats in the lower house and a majority of the elective seats in the senate. The second-largest party, the Marxist Spanish Socialist Workers' Party (PSOE), won 121 seats in the lower house.

During the worldwide economic slowdown in 1979, Spain's rate of unemployment climbed to more than 9% while inflation dropped only slightly to about 15%. The nation's overall growth rate fell to less than 2%.

The Basque and Catalonia regions in northern Spain won autonomous status on Jan. 11, 1980, with the right to control local governmental affairs with their own elected parliaments. Both regions had been deprived of home rule by the Franco regime.

However, the Basque terrorist organization ETA continued its campaign to seek full Basque independence with murders, kidnappings, and bombings especially directed at resort areas in an effort to hurt the Spanish tourist industry. More people were slain in terrorist assassinations in 1980 than in any other European country, including Italy and Northern Ireland.

# SPANISH OVERSEAS AREAS

## BALEARIC ISLANDS

**Area:** 1,936 square miles (5,014 sq. km.).
**Population:** 624,703.
**Capital:** Palma, 267,081.

The Balearic Islands *(Islas Baleares)* lie in the Mediterranean Sea off the east coast of Spain. The largest islands are Majorca *(Mallorca),* 1,400 sq. mi.; Minorca *(Menorca),* 266 sq. mi.; Ibiza *(Iviza),* 209 sq. mi.; and Formentera, 32 sq. mi. The year-round warm climate makes the islands a popular tourist resort area.

Many Stone Age monuments built by prehistoric people dot the countryside of Majorca and Minorca. The islands were colonized by Phoenicians and Carthaginians. Fought over for centuries by contending powers, the islands came under the rule of Spanish kings in the 1200s. Limited local autonomy was granted on June 30, 1978.

## CANARY ISLANDS

**Area:** 2,808 square miles (7,273 sq. km.).
**Population:** 1,274,280.
**Capitals:** Las Palmas de Gran Canaria, 328,187; Santa Cruz de Tenerife, 157,791.

The 13 Canary Islands lie off the northwest coast of Morocco in the Atlantic Ocean. The largest islands are Tenerife, 795 sq. mi.; Fuerteventura, 668 sq. mi.; and Grand Canary, 592 sq. mi. The islands have many mountains and volcanoes, the highest of which is snow-capped 12,198-foot Pico de Teide on Tenerife.

The warm subtropical climate of the Canaries attracts over a million tourists each year.

The islands received their name from the Latin word for dog, *canis,* because of the fierce dogs found there. Songbirds called canaries were first discovered in these islands by ancient Phoenician traders. The French explorer Jean de Béthencourt conquered the islands in 1402–04, making himself king. Spain gained sovereignty over the Canaries in 1479. The islands were divided into two provinces by Spain on Sept. 21, 1927.

## CEUTA AND MELILLA

**Area:** 12 square miles (31 sq. km.).
**Population:** 167,879.

These two city enclaves stand on the Mediterranean coast of Morocco. Both are governed as parts of Spain. Ceuta was built on the site of a Phoenician colony and may have been the location of one of the ancient Pillars of Hercules. It was seized from the Arabs by Portugal in 1415 and passed into Spanish hands in 1580. Melilla has been Spanish since 1496. Morocco pressed claims for the cities in the 1970s–80s.

QUICK QUIZ: The U.S. leads in producing which 7 major resources? See page 264.

# SRI LANKA

**Official Name:** Democratic Socialist Republic of Sri Lanka.
**Area:** 25,332 square miles (65,610 sq. km.).
**Population:** 15,076,400.
**Chief Cities:** Colombo, capital, 592,000; Dahiwala–Mt. Lavinia, 162,000; Jaffna, 114,000.
**Government:** Presidential-parliamentary republic.
**President:** Junius Richard Jayewardene (since 1978).
**Prime Minister:** Ranasinghe Premadasa (since 1978).
**Legislature:** *National State Assembly,* 168 members.
**U.S. Ambassador to Sri Lanka:** Donald R. Toussaint.
**Sri Lanka Ambassador to U.S.:** W.S. Karunaratne.
**Flag:** Yellow border around maroon rectangle with bo leaves in each corner; yellow sword-carrying lion in center; green and orange bars at hoist.
**Languages:** Sinhala (official), English, Tamil.
**Main Ethnic Groups:** Sinhalese (72%), Tamil (20%).
**Principal Religions:** Buddhism (67%), Hinduism (17%), Christianity (8%), Islam (7%).
**Leading Industries:** Agriculture (tea, rubber, coconuts, rice, cocoa, corn, spices, fruits, vegetables); forestry and lumbering; fishing; manufacturing (cement, textiles); mining (gems, salt, graphite).
**Foreign Trade:** *major exports*—tea, rubber, coconut products; *major imports*—wheat, rice, food, fertilizer, machinery, textiles, petroleum products, sugar, flour, transportation equipment.
**Places of Interest:** Gal Oya Valley, Wilpattu, Ruhunu national parks; ruins at Anuradhapura and Polonnaruwa; Fortress in the Sky at Sigiriya; Buddhist Temple of the Tooth at Kandy; Bentota, Ambalangoda, Mt. Lavinia beach resorts. *In Colombo:* Pettah (Old Town); Colombo Museum; Victoria Park.

## SRI LANKA TODAY

An island-nation about the size of West Virginia, Sri Lanka lies in the Indian Ocean only 18 miles off India's southern coast. Unlike many other developing nations, Sri Lanka has maintained a democratic government since gaining independence in 1948. Although the people are poor, 9 out of 10 can read and write.

Sri Lanka has few natural resources. Because much of the land is used to raise tea, rubber, and coconuts for export, Sri Lanka does not grow enough food to feed its people.

Plains sweep in a broad band from northern Sri Lanka around the island's coast, bordering the mountains and rugged plateaus in central and southern Sri Lanka. The island's highest point is Pidurutalagala (8,281 feet), but most of Sri Lanka has altitudes of 1,000 feet or less.

## EARLY HISTORY

Formerly called *Ceylon,* Sri Lanka was settled in the 500s B.C. by Sinhalese from northern India, conquering the ancient Veddas. In 483 B.C. Vijaya, an Indian prince, established the first Sinhalese kingdom, with the capital at Anuradhapura. Buddhism was introduced in the 200s B.C.

Rajaraja I, ruler of the Tamil kingdom of Chola in southern India, extended his domain to Ceylon in the 1000s A.D. Polonnaruwa became the capital of Chola.

During the "Golden Age of Lanka" in the mid-1100s, the Sinhalese under King Prakrama Bahu I ruled the whole island.

The first Western conquerors were Portuguese, who began to introduce Christianity in 1505. They were followed by the Dutch in the 1600s. In 1796 the British took over. Britain conquered the last free Ceylonese kingdom, Kandy, in 1815.

## INDEPENDENCE

On Feb. 4, 1948, Ceylon became independent as a British dominion. Don Stephen Senanayake, the first prime minister, was succeeded in 1952 by his son Dudley. In elections that year his United National Party (UNP) retained power.

The Sri Lanka Freedom Party (SLEP) won the 1956 elections. S.W.R.D. Bandaranaike, who became prime minister, was assassinated in 1959.

New elections held in 1960 made Bandaranaike's widow, Sirimavo Bandaranaike, the world's first woman prime minister.

From 1965 to 1970 Senanayake returned as prime minister of a pro-Western government.

Mrs. Bandaranaike again became prime minister in 1970, forming a leftist coalition government.

On May 22, 1972, the nation became a republic. It remained within the British Commonwealth of Nations.

J.R. Jayewardene, a 70-year-old Buddhist nicknamed "Yankee Dick" because of his pro-Western views, became prime minister in 1977. His UNP party had overwhelmingly defeated Mrs. Bandaranaike's leftist SLEP party in parliamentary elections on July 21, capturing 140 of the 168 seats. SLEP won only 8 seats.

Parliament amended the constitution in October 1977 to establish a strong presidential-parliamentary system similar to that of France, with a presidential election to be held every six years. Jayewardene became president on Feb. 3, 1978.

A new constitution was proclaimed on Sept. 7, 1978, strengthening the powers of the presidency. Parliamentary elections will be held by a system of proportional representation to prevent control by a minority party.

The country's economy had stagnated for many years as the government emphasized consumer subsidies at the expense of capital expenditures. Jayewardene's government reversed these priorities, seeking to stimulate private industry. This shift in policy brought an economic growth rate of 7.3% in 1979, while inflation was held below an annual rate of 6%. The government ended the long-standing policy of free rice distribution to all persons in September 1979, substituting a food stamp program embracing the low-income half of the population.

The government began construction in March 1980 of the huge Victoria Reservoir on the Mahaweli River in the north-central part of the island. The 5-year hydroelectric project, which will help relieve the nation's dependence on imported petroleum, was financed in large part by about $250 million in aid from Britain.

Parliament expelled Mrs. Bandaranaike on Oct. 16, 1980, on charges she had abused her powers as prime minister. She was barred from running for public office in the future.

# SUDAN

**Official Name:** Democratic Republic of the Sudan.
**Area:** 967,500 square miles (2,505,813 sq. km.).
**Population:** 18,896,700.
**Chief Cities:** Khartoum, capital, 261,840; Omdurman, 258,532; Khartoum North, 127,672; Port Sudan, 110,091.
**Government:** One-party republic.
**President:** Maj. Gen. Gaafar Muhammed Nimeiri (seized power in 1969).
**Legislature:** *National Assembly*, 304 members.
**U.S. Ambassador to Sudan:** C. William Kontos.
**Sudanese Ambassador to U.S.:** Omer Salih Eissa.
**Flag:** Green triangle; red, white, and black stripes.
**Official Language:** Arabic.
**Main Ethnic Groups:** Arab (70%), black (23%).
**Principal Religions:** Islam (70%), animism (25%), Christianity (5%).
**Leading Industries:** Agriculture (livestock, cotton, sorghum, wheat, sesame, peanuts, castor beans, fruits, vegetables); food processing; mining (petroleum); manufacturing (textiles, handicrafts).
**Foreign Trade:** *major exports*—cotton, sesame, peanuts; *major imports*—fertilizers, sugar, machinery, petroleum, chemicals.
**Places of Interest:** Archaeological ruins along Nile; Nubian Desert; Dindar National Park.

## SUDAN TODAY

About one-fourth the size of the United States, Sudan is the largest country in Africa. But it also is one of the 25 poorest countries in the world. Its major resource is soil.

New strains were put on the economy in 1978–80 as half a million refugees came to Sudan from wars and revolutions in Chad, Ethiopia, Uganda, and Zaire. The Sudanese government sought aid from the UN and international agencies to ease the burden of caring for the homeless refugees.

Despite government development of huge irrigation projects, agricultural production declined in the late 1970s.

Most people live by subsistence farming or by herding livestock. Only about 1 person in 10 can read and write.

The Nile River flows north through the Sudan plain. A rain forest in the south gives way to savanna grasslands in the central region and to a desert in the north.

Egypt lies to the north; the Red Sea and Ethiopia to the east; Kenya, Uganda, and Zaire to the south; and Central Africa, Chad, and Libya to the west.

## EARLY HISTORY

Ancient Egypt established outposts in the Sudan from which developed the kingdom of Kush. In A.D. 350 Kush was destroyed by the Aksumites from Ethiopia.

In the 500s Christian missionaries established states that coexisted with Muslim-Arab Egypt for over 600 years. By the end of the 1200s Arabs had taken over Christian Nubia and settled in the Sudan, where they introduced Islam.

In 1820–21 troops of the Ottoman viceroy of Egypt, Mohammed Ali, imposed Turko-Egyptian rule over northern Sudan. Southern Sudan was conquered by Egypt in 1863–79.

The Sudanese revolted, under the leadership of Mohammed Ahmed, the Mahdi. His forces massacred a British army led by Gen. Charles Gordon at Khartoum on Jan. 26, 1885, drove out the Egyptians, and established an independent, theocratic Mahdist state. British Gen. Herbert Kitchener invaded the Sudan in 1898, ending Mahdist rule. From 1899 to 1956 Britain and Egypt controlled Sudan.

## INDEPENDENCE

On Jan. 1, 1956, Sudan gained independence from Britain and Egypt as a republic. Two years later army officers seized control.

A popular revolution in 1964 reestablished civilian rule. The assembly elected in 1965 was controlled by Mohammed Ahmed Mahgoub, a conservative. Sayyid Saddiq-al-Mahdi, a grandson of the original Mahdi, unseated Mahgoub in July 1966, but was replaced by Mahgoub in February 1968.

In May 1969 the Mahgoub regime was ousted in a military coup. Maj. Gen. Gaafar Muhammed Nimeiri became president.

On July 19, 1971, a group of communist-oriented officers, allegedly with Soviet support, overthrew President Nimeiri. But within three days, helped by Egypt, his government regained control, and rebel leaders were executed.

In October 1971 Nimeiri was elected president in a national referendum. He then dissolved the military revolutionary council and announced creation of a new political party, the Sudanese Socialist Union (SSU).

An uprising by blacks in the south against the government's Arabization policies raged from 1955 to 1972. The 17-year civil war cost perhaps 500,000 lives. In March 1972, however, the southern rebel leader, Gen. Joseph Lagu, agreed to a cease-fire.

The nation's first constitution was approved on April 12, 1973, making the SSU the only legal political party.

President Nimeiri was reelected to a 6-year term in an unopposed election on April 3, 1977.

In May 1977 Sudan expelled Soviet military advisers, asked the Soviet Union to cut in half the size of its embassy staff, and then appealed to the United States for military aid.

Nimeiri granted amnesty to political prisoners in 1977–78 and encouraged opponents to return to Sudan from exile. In elections for the national assembly in February 1978, more than half the seats were won by dissidents, but Nimeiri's government retained control.

The first major oil find in Sudan was made in July 1979 at Abu Jabra by the American Chevron company, bringing in a 500-barrel-a-day well. Estimates that Sudan might export 20,000 barrels of oil per day by the mid-1980s gave hope for improvement in the economy.

QUICK QUIZ: What is Woody Allen's real name? See page 275.

# SURINAME

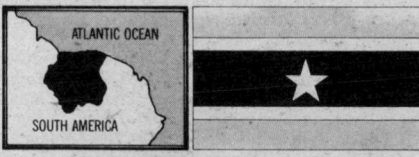

**Official Name:** Republic of Suriname.
**Area:** 63,037 square miles (163,265 sq. km.).
**Population:** 413,535.
**Capital:** Paramaribo, 150,000.
**Government:** Military-civilian junta.
**President:** Henk Chin A Sen (since 1980).
**U.S. Ambassador to Suriname:** John J. Crowley Jr.
**Suriname's Ambassador to U.S.:** Roel F. Karamat.
**Flag:** Stripes of green, white, red, white, and green with yellow star centered on red stripe.
**Languages:** Dutch (official), English, Sranang Tongo.
**Main Ethnic Groups:** Asian Indian descent (37%), Creole (mixed black-European descent) (31%), Javanese descent (13%), Bush Negro (8%).
**Principal Religions:** Hinduism (26%), Islam (26%), Roman Catholicism (21%), Protestantism (18%).
**Leading Industries:** Mining (bauxite); agriculture (rice, bananas, coconuts, fruits, vegetables); manufacturing (aluminum, electricity, food processing, clothing); forestry and lumbering; fishing.
**Foreign Trade:** *major exports*—bauxite, aluminum, alumina; *major imports*—food, machinery, petroleum, steel, cotton, grain, consumer goods.
**Places of Interest:** *In Paramaribo:* colonial buildings, oriental bazaars; swimming beaches; jungle villages; sport fishing and hunting; river canoeing.

## SURINAME TODAY

Somewhat larger than the state of Georgia, Suriname is the smallest and newest of South America's independent nations.

The former Dutch Colony's most important resource is bauxite, the ore from which aluminum is made. Suriname ranks as the world's fourth-leading producer of the ore. In addition, the country's rivers have been harnessed to produce electricity to power aluminum-making plants.

Farms produce ample quantities of rice, the people's major food staple.

Most of Suriname's farms are along the northern coast at the mouths of the Suriname, Saramacca, Coppername, and Nickerie rivers. The center of the country is heavily forested. The southern three-fourths of the land is a hilly, largely uninhabited area that rises to 4,120 feet in the Wilhelmina Mountains.

The country has a hot tropical climate that averages 79 ° F. the year round. There are two rainy seasons—from November to February and from March through July.

Suriname lies on the northeast coast of South America. Guyana is to the west, Brazil to the south, and French Guiana to the east.

## HISTORY

The first European settlement was established in 1651 by Lord Willoughby of England. He encouraged experienced colonists to emigrate from other settlements in the Americas. Among them were Portuguese Jews from Brazil, who built the first synagogue in the Western Hemisphere in 1665.

After the English captured New York from the Dutch, the Treaty of Breda was signed in 1667 by which the Dutch received Suriname in exchange for giving up their claims to New York.

During the 1700s and early 1800s the colony, known as *Dutch Guiana,* changed hands several times but ended in possession of the Dutch by the Vienna treaty of 1815.

Some 300,000 slaves were imported from Africa before slavery was abolished on July 1, 1863. Then indentured plantation workers were brought from India and Indonesia.

Suriname became an autonomous territory of the Netherlands on Dec. 15, 1954.

After elections in December 1973, the head of the Creole political party, Henck Arron, became prime minister. The new government began negotiations for independence despite opposition by Asian Indians.

About 100,000 Surinamese migrated to the Netherlands in 1974–75, fearing that such movement would be restricted after independence.

The Netherlands granted Suriname independence on Nov. 25, 1975, and promised $1.5 billion in aid for 1976–86.

On Nov. 1, 1977, Arron's National Party Combination (NPK) won the first parliamentary election since independence.

A group of army sergeants, angered at not being allowed to form a union to seek better pay, overthrew Prime Minister Arron on Feb. 25, 1980. They formed a 9-member junta called the National Military Council to supervise the government and made Henk Chin A Sen, a civilian, prime minister.

In a second coup, on Aug. 13, 1980, led by army commander Desi Bouterse, the sergeants who had headed the junta were arrested and charged with plotting a communist Cuban-type government. The army also ousted President Johan Ferrier and jailed former Prime Minister Arron. The junta then named Chin A Sen as president at the head of a civilian cabinet.

# SWAZILAND

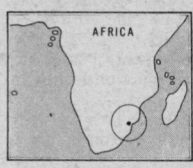

**Official Name:** Kingdom of Swaziland.
**Area:** 6,704 square miles (17,363 sq. km.).
**Population:** 590,173.
**Capital:** (administrative) Mbabane, 20,800; (traditional) Lobamba.
**Government:** Absolute monarchy.
**King:** Sobhuza II (since 1921).
**Prime Minister:** Prince Mandabala Fred Dlamini (since 1979).
**U.S. Ambassador to Swaziland:** Richard C. Matheron.
**Swaziland Ambassador to U.S.:** Musa Simon Kunene.
**Flag:** Stripes of blue, yellow, red, yellow, and blue, with black and white Swazi shield of Emasotsha regiment.
**Languages:** siSwati and English (both official), Zulu.
**Main Ethnic Groups:** Swazi, Zulu.
**Religions:** Christianity (60%), animism (40%).
**Leading Industries:** Agriculture (cattle, goats, poultry, sugarcane, rice, citrus fruits, cotton, maize, sorghum,

tobacco, pineapples); forestry and lumbering; mining (iron, coal, asbestos); manufacturing (food processing, chemicals, machinery, consumer goods); tourism.

**Foreign Trade:** *major exports*—iron ore, sugar, wood products, asbestos, coal, canned fruits; *major imports*—food, clothing, vehicles, machinery, petroleum.

**Places of Interest:** Mountain scenery in the west; hot springs at Mbabane; game preserves.

## SWAZILAND TODAY

Once dependent on subsistence farming for its economy, Swaziland became one of the most prosperous small nations of Africa during the 1970s. British and South African investors helped develop iron mines, sugar refineries, a pulp paper mill, and sugar, pineapple, and orange plantations. An east-west railroad also was built across the country to carry exports to the port of Maputo, Mozambique.

Called "the Switzerland of Africa," Swaziland attracts over 100,000 tourists each year to its gambling casinos, fine hotels, golf courses, and game preserves.

Despite efforts to develop a diversified economy, about three-fourths of Swaziland's people live by raising cattle and corn. Only about 1 Swazi in 3 can read and write.

Somewhat larger than Connecticut, Swaziland is bordered on the north, west, and south by South Africa and on the east by Mozambique. Three topographical regions extend from north to south: a mountainous region in the west averages between 3,500 and 4,500 feet above sea level; a middle plateau; and a low plain in the east, averaging about 1,000 feet.

## HISTORY

The Swazi settled in northern Zululand about 1750. They had their first formal relations with Britain in the 1840s when they sought help against the Zulus. Mineral rights were granted to the Europeans by the Swazi, and in 1894 South Africa assumed responsibility for the protection and administration of the country.

After the Boer War, Swaziland was administered by the British governor of the Transvaal. In 1907 a British resident commissioner was appointed. Sobhuza II became king in 1921.

Political parties were formed in the 1960s that demanded independence from British rule. In 1964 the first election was held in which the Swazi could vote. The king's political party, Imbokodvo, won all 24 seats in the national assembly.

Swaziland became independent on Sept. 6, 1968. The country is a member of the British Commonwealth of Nations.

In 1973 King Sobhuza II scrapped the constitution that had been prepared with the help of the British and took over absolute power. He outlawed political parties and political meetings.

King Sobhuza II celebrated his 80th birthday on July 22, 1979. His people speculated which of his more than 100 sons by his scores of wives might succeed him.

The king's main political opponent, Dr. Ambrose Zwane, was jailed without trial in February 1978 after being arrested at his medical clinic. Dr. Zwane later escaped to Mozambique, directing guerrilla activities from there.

# SWEDEN

 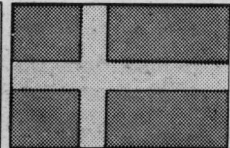

**Official Name:** Kingdom of Sweden.
**Area:** 173,732 square miles (449,964 sq. km.).
**Population:** 8,340,360.
**Chief Cities:** Stockholm, capital, 661,258; Göteborg, 442,410; Malmö, 240,220; Uppsala, 139,893; Norrköping, 119,967; Västerås, 118,055; Örebro, 117,383; Linköping, 110,053; Jönköping, 108,171.
**Largest Metropolitan Area:** Stockholm, 1,364,175.
**Government:** Constitutional monarchy.
**Prime Minister:** Thorbjorn Falldin (since 1979).
**King:** Karl XVI Gustaf (since 1973).
**Legislature:** *Riksdag,* 349 members.
**U.S. Ambassador to Sweden:** Rodney Kennedy-Minott.
**Swedish Ambassador to U.S.:** Count Wilhelm Wachtmeister.
**Flag:** Light blue field with yellow cross.
**Official Language:** Swedish.
**Main Ethnic Group:** Swedes.
**State Religion:** Evangelical Lutheranism (95%).
**Leading Industries:** Trade and services; manufacturing (paper, electricity, steel, metal products, machinery, automobiles, aircraft, consumer goods); mining (iron, coal, copper, lead, zinc, manganese); agriculture (dairy products, cattle, hay, sugar beets, barley, oats, wheat, potatoes, fruits, vegetables); forestry; lumbering; fishing.
**Foreign Trade:** *major exports*—machinery and transport equipment, manufactured goods, paper, wood pulp, wood, iron ore; *major imports*—machinery and transport equipment, manufactured goods, fuels.
**Places of Interest:** "Land of the Midnight Sun"—Lapland; Gotland Island; Lake Siljan; "The Crystal Land"—glassworks near Kalmar; Göta Canal; New Älvsborg Fortress in Göteborg. *In Stockholm:* Drottningholm Palace; Royal Warship Wasa Museum.

## SWEDEN TODAY

About twice as large as Minnesota, Sweden has a higher standard of living than the United States and the world's longest life expectancy.

Although governed by socialists for over four decades until 1976, only a few basic industries are owned by the government. But the country has one of the most extensive social-welfare programs in the world, paid for with taxes that absorb more than half of the national income.

The south has a temperate climate with about a two-month winter and four-month summer. The long, cold winter in the north lasts more than seven months.

Norway lies to the west and Finland to the northeast. Sweden's largest islands are Gotland and Oland in the Baltic Sea.

## EARLY HISTORY

Tacitus, the Roman historian, first mentioned the Swedes (Suiones) about A.D. 100. In the 800s their semilegendary chieftain Rurik is said to have founded Russia. By the 900s Swedish influence extended south to the Black Sea. Warfare against

QUICK QUIZ: Which U.S. state has the highest crime rate? See page 170.

## SWEDEN (continued)

Norsemen and Danes went on for centuries. In 1397 all the Scandinavian crowns were united under Queen Margrethe I of Denmark.

### INDEPENDENT MONARCHY

Sweden became an independent kingdom in 1523, when the Swedes elected Gustaf I as ruler. By the time of its involvement in the Thirty Years War (1618–48), Sweden, under Gustaf II Adolf (1611–32), was the foremost Protestant power.

Sweden became a constitutional monarchy under Queen Ulrika Eleonora (1718–20).

Sweden warred with Napoleon I and lost Finland to Russia (1809).

Napoleon's brilliant marshal Jean Baptiste Jules Bernadotte was elected by the *Riksdag* to succeed the childless Karl XIII. Bernadotte ascended the throne in 1818 as Karl XIV, founding the present Swedish dynasty.

The last war in Swedish history was fought in 1814, when Bernadotte enforced the Treaty of Kiel's award of Norway to Sweden. Norway remained in union with Sweden until 1905.

With neutrality as its foreign policy, Sweden remained uninvolved in both world wars.

The Social Democratic Party was dominant in 1932–76, except for a short period in 1936.

A coalition of opposition parties defeated the socialists after 44 years of rule in national elections on Sept. 19, 1976. Thorbjorn Falldin, head of the Center Party, became prime minister.

Liberal leader Ola Ullsten became prime minister on Oct. 13, 1978, after Falldin's coalition collapsed over the issue of whether to build more nuclear power plants.

In a national election on Sept. 16, 1979, the governing nonsocialist parties won a one-seat majority in parliament with 175 members to 174 for the socialists and communists. Falldin again became prime minister in October.

Less affected than most other countries by the worldwide economic recession of the 1970s, Sweden's economy boomed in 1978–80. Average income per person topped $12,000 in 1979 for the first time. The economic improvement was achieved largely by government deficit spending.

In Sweden's first nationwide strike-lockout in 70 years, about 1 million workers were idled for 10 days on May 2–11, 1980, shutting down most of the nation's public transportation, communication, and manufacturing industries. The dispute was settled when management negotiators accepted government urging to grant a 7% wage increase.

A nationwide referendum on March 23, 1980, decided 3 to 2 favor of an ambitious program to double the number of Sweden's nuclear electric generating plants to reduce dependency on oil imports.

When one member of the Swedish parliament was late arriving for a session on May 21, 1980, because of a delay in taking a child to school, a tie vote resulted in a proposal to cut $475 million from the defense budget. To settle the issue, lots were drawn and the budget cut won.

By a 1-vote margin parliament adopted on Sept. 6, 1980, the highest value-added tax (sales tax) in Europe—a record 23.46%. The measure was an effort to overcome the nation's $5 billion annual trade deficit.

## SWITZERLAND

**Official Name:** Swiss Confederation.
**Area:** 15,941 square miles (41,288 sq. km.).
**Population:** 6,273,700.
**Chief Cities:** Bern, capital, 145,500; Zurich, 379,600; Basel, 185,300; Geneva, 150,100; Lausanne, 132,400.
**Largest Metropolitan Area:** Zurich, 707,500.
**Government:** Federal republic of 23 cantons.
**Executive:** *Federal Council,* 7 members elected by Federal Assembly. President chosen annually.
**Federal Assembly:** *Council of States,* 46 members; *National Council,* 200 members.
**U.S. Ambassador to Switzerland:** Richard D. Vine.
**Swiss Ambassador to U.S.:** Anton Hegner.
**Flag:** White cross on red field.
**Languages:** German (65%), French (18%), Italian (12%), Romansch (1%), other (4%).
**Main Religions:** Roman Catholicism (49.4%), Protestantism (47.8%).
**Leading Industries:** Manufacturing (machinery, electrical equipment, watches, precision instruments, chocolate, cheese, chemicals, textiles, electricity, consumer products); tourism; banking, trade, and services; agriculture (dairy products, cattle, goats, hogs, sheep, sugar beets, grains, potatoes, grapes, fruits, vegetables); forestry and lumbering; mining (salt, building stone).
**Foreign Trade:** *major exports*—watches, instruments, cheese, chocolate, textile machinery, organic chemicals, medical supplies, metalworking machine tools; *major imports*—iron and steel, automobiles, petroleum, clothing.
**Places of Interest:** Swiss National Park; Alps; Lake Lucerne; Interlaken, Gstaad, St. Moritz resorts; Rhone Valley. *In Zurich:* Grossmünster Cathedral; churches. *In Geneva:* Ariana Park, UN headquarters in Europe. *In Basel:* Art museum; 11th century cathedral. *In Bern:* Clock tower; the Bear Pit; town hall, Gothic cathedral and rose gardens. *In Lucerne:* Lion Monument; Wagner's home, Tribschen.

### SWITZERLAND TODAY

About twice the size of New Jersey, Switzerland has enjoyed peace and neutrality for more than a century and a half. It has become an international banking and finance center and a favorite meeting place for diplomats. Its people enjoy one of the highest standards of living in the world.

About half the country's income comes from manufacturing. Most of the rest comes from service industries, particularly those accommodating the many tourists who visit Switzerland each year to enjoy the mountain scenery or take part in winter sports.

Lacking coal and oil to develop an industrialized economy, the Swiss use their mountain rivers to provide electric power for factories.

Only about a fourth of the land can be used for crops, so much food must be imported.

In a $3 billion civil-defense program begun in 1962, underground nuclear shelters will be provided for the entire population by the year 2000.

Swiss citizens have more of a voice in their

laws than those of other countries, voting in national referendums up to four times each year to approve or reject proposed laws. A petition with only 50,000 signatures can force a referendum.

Switzerland is bordered on the north by West Germany, on the east by Austria and Liechtenstein, on the south by Italy, and on the west by France.

Two mountain systems cover most of the country—the Alps in the south and the Jura in the west and northwest. In the central Alps rise the Rhine, the Rhone, and the Ticino rivers. The highest peak is 15,203-foot Monte Rosa.

## HISTORY

The Helvetians, who lived in the northern foothills of the Alps, were conquered by the Romans in 58 B.C. After A.D. 401, the area was dominated by a succession of rival neighbors.

In the 800s the area was part of the Empire of Charlemagne. As the Carolingian Empire fell into decay, the Hapsburg, Zähringer, and Savoy dynasties made encroachments.

In 1291 a defensive league against the Hapsburgs was formed by the cantons of Unterwalden, Uri, and Schwyz (from which the country takes its name). This marks the beginning of the *Swiss Confederation,* the nation's present official name.

By 1513 the confederation had grown to 13 largely autonomous cantons. The Treaty of Westphalia, which in 1648 ended the Thirty Years War, recognized Swiss independence.

In 1798 French revolutionary forces invaded Switzerland and formed the Helvetic Republic. Napoleon's Act of Mediation in 1803 restored the old confederation, but under French dominance.

## NEUTRAL SWITZERLAND

In 1815 the Treaty of Paris and the Congress of Vienna guaranteed Switzerland's perpetual neutrality.

Switzerland is governed today under a constitution adopted in 1874.

In February 1971, Swiss women for the first time won the right to vote in federal elections.

Parliamentary elections on Oct. 26, 1975, left unchanged the moderate four-party coalition that had governed since 1971.

A national referendum on Sept. 24, 1978, approved establishing Jura as the 23d canton of Switzerland—its first new state since 1815.

Swiss voters, in a referendum on Dec. 3, 1978, turned down a plan to create a national police force to combat terrorism.

In national elections on Oct. 21, 1979, conservative parties increased their majority in parliament. Women more than doubled the number of seats they had previously held, increasing their parliamentary representatives from 11 to 24.

In a national referendum on March 1, 1980, Swiss voters rejected by about 4 to 1 a proposal to sever ties between government and religion. The proposal would have ended the practice of supporting religious sects with government taxes.

Unemployment in Switzerland fell to a new low in mid-1980 with fewer than 6,000 persons out of work, while employers sought to fill more than 12,000 vacant jobs. Wage and price controls held inflation to an annual rate of less than 2%.

# SYRIA

**Official Name:** Syrian Arab Republic.
**Area:** 71,498 square miles (185,180 sq. km.).
**Population:** 8,753,150.
**Chief Cities:** Damascus, capital, 1,142,000; Aleppo, 878,000; Homs, 306,000; Lattakia, 204,000; Hana, 180,000.
**Government:** Republic.
**President:** Hafez al-Assad (since 1971).
**Prime Minister:** Abdul Rauf al-Kasm (since 1980).
**Legislature:** *People's Council,* 195 members.
**U.S. Ambassador to Syria:** Talcott W. Seelye.
**Syrian Ambassador to U.S.:** Sabah Kabbani.
**Flag:** Red, white, and black stripes, with hawk in center stripe.
**Languages:** Arabic (official), Armenian, Kurdish, French, English.
**Ethnic Groups:** Arab (90%), Kurd, Armenian, Turkmen, Circassian.
**Main Religions:** Islam (86%), Christianity (13%).
**Leading Industries:** Agriculture (livestock, cotton, wheat, barley, sugar beets, fruits, vegetables); mining (petroleum, phosphates); construction; manufacturing (textiles, cement, ceramics, food processing, oil refining, electricity); trade and services; tourism.
**Foreign Trade:** *major exports*—cotton, barley, wool, wheat; *major imports*—iron and steel, machinery, petroleum products, weapons.
**Places of Interest:** Palmyra monuments; Krak des Chevaliers (Crusaders Castle) in Homs district; Aleppo; waterwheels at Hama. *In Damascus:* Omayyad Mosque; Azem Palace; Hamidieh Bazaar; biblical street called Straight.

## SYRIA TODAY

A militant Arab state, Syria has joined in four wars in three decades against its neighbor Israel. Its leaders refuse to negotiate peace until Israel gives back all territory it won in those wars.

Syria's socialist government has nationalized most industry and expropriated and redistributed most large landholdings. New varieties of wheat and fertilizers enable Syrian farmers to raise enough grain so that some could be exported. Syria's economy suffered in 1980 from a high rate of inflation and the cost of its armed forces, which absorb half the national budget.

Western Syria consists of a narrow Mediterranean coastal plain and the Alawite and Anti-Lebanon mountains and plateau. A fertile region in the north gives way to a central steppe area and a desert region in the south. The main rivers are the Euphrates, Khabur, and Barada.

Somewhat larger than North Dakota, Syria lies at the eastern end of the Mediterranean Sea. Turkey is on the north, Iraq on the east and southeast, Jordan on the south, Israel on the southwest, and Lebanon on the west.

## EARLY HISTORY

Ancient Syria was the home of the Amorites,

QUICK QUIZ: Who won the Orange Bowl on Jan. 1, 1981? See page 30.

**SYRIA** *(continued)*

Canaanites, Phoenicians, and Hebrews. It was conquered by several waves of foreign invaders—Aramaeans, Assyrians, Babylonians, and Persians. Syria was unified after its conquest by Alexander the Great in 332 B.C. It passed to the Romans in 63 B.C. and to the Byzantines in A.D. 395.

In the 600s Syria fell to the Arabs, who introduced the Arabic language and culture. From 661 to 750, under the Damascus caliphate of the Omayyads, Syria controlled a vast Islamic domain.

From 1516 to World War I Syria was part of the Ottoman Turkish Empire.

From 1920 to 1946 France controlled Syria as a League of Nations mandate.

### INDEPENDENCE

Syria gained independence as a republic on April 17, 1946.

From 1958 to 1961 Syria was part of the United Arab Republic (Egypt and Syria) under the presidency of Egypt's President Nasser.

Syrian troops participated in four Arab-Israeli wars (1948, 1956, 1967, 1973).

A military coup in February 1968 installed Nureddin al-Attassi as head of state. His regime received substantial military equipment from the Soviet Union. In November 1970, however, he was ousted by rightist military officers, who made Hafez al-Assad president in 1971.

In 1972 Syria nationalized all properties of the Western-owned Iraq Petroleum Company.

A new constitution in 1973 provided for freedom of religion and did not declare Islam the official state religion.

Syria joined Egypt in attacking Israel in October 1973. After the UN-ordered cease-fire on October 24, artillery duels and border clashes between Syria and Israel continued into 1974. Finally, on May 31, 1974, Syria signed a U.S.-negotiated pact with Israel for mutual withdrawal of their armed forces.

In 1974 the U.S. and Syria resumed diplomatic relations, broken since 1967.

Syria sent troops and tanks into Lebanon on May 31, 1976, and within six months ended the civil war in that country. Syrian troops remained in Lebanon to preserve the peace.

In May 1977 U.S. President Carter met with Assad in Geneva but failed to obtain Syria's cooperation in establishing a Mideast peace.

On Feb. 8, 1978, Assad was elected without opposition to a second 7-year term as president.

Muslim fanatics seeking Islamic control of the government waged a campaign of terrorism in 1978–80. Troops were called out to put down antigovernment riots in March 1980 in Aleppo, Hama, and other cities.

Syria and Iraq broke diplomatic relations in August 1980 after Iraq expelled Syrian diplomats for stocking their Baghdad embassy with arms and ammunition.

Syria and Libya announced on Sept. 10, 1980, that the two nations would merge. However, details remained to be worked out. When war broke out between Iraq and Iran later in the month, Libya and Syria aided Iran.

On Oct. 8, 1980, Syria and the Soviet Union signed a 20-year military and economic treaty similar to one signed in 1972 by Iraq and the Soviet Union.

## TAIWAN

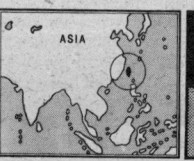

**Official Name:** Republic of China.
**Area:** 13,892 square miles (35,981 sq. km.).
**Population:** 17,915,600.
**Chief Cities:** Taipei, capital, 1,769,568; Kaohsiung, 1,000,000; Taichung, 575,000; Tainan, 550,000.
**Government:** One-party parliamentary republic.
**President:** Chiang Ching-kuo (took office in 1978).
**Prime Minister:** Sun Yun-suan (since 1978).
**Legislature:** *Legislative Yüan,* about 430 members.
**Flag:** Red field bearing blue rectangle, upper left, that contains 12-pointed white sun.
**Languages:** Chinese (Peking dialect; official), English, Japanese, Hokkien, Hakka.
**Ethnic Groups:** Taiwanese (87%), Chinese (13%).
**Religions:** Confucianism, Taoism, Buddhism, Christianity.
**Leading Industries:** Manufacturing (electronics, textiles, chemicals, fertilizer, cement, glass, plastics, aircraft); agriculture (poultry, hogs, rice, sugarcane, tea, fruits, vegetables); forestry and lumbering; tourism; fishing; mining (coal, natural gas, sulfur).
**Foreign Trade:** *major exports*—textiles, electronic equipment, plywood, canned food; *major imports*—machinery, iron and steel, raw cotton, soybeans, motor vehicles, wheat, petroleum.
**Places of Interest:** Sun-Moon Lake; Fo Kuang Mountain temple; Taroko Gorge. *In Taipei:* national palace museum; botanical gardens; temples; Grass Mountain resort area; 75th Buddha, near Changhua. *In Tainan:* forts and temples.

### TAIWAN TODAY

About twice the size of Hawaii, Taiwan has achieved a strong and prosperous economy in the nearly three decades since the government of nationalist China retreated to the island. Its people enjoy one of the highest standards of living in the Far East.

With a variety of major public works and industrial projects under way, the government hopes to move from the status of a developing nation to that of a developed nation. Projects include improved port facilities, railroad and highway construction, airport development, and the building of a steel mill, shipyards, and petrochemical plants.

Tourism is a major industry with about 1.5 million visitors each year.

While Taiwan's economy has grown, its influence in world politics has diminished because of the insistence of its leaders that it represents the legal government of mainland China. As a result many nations, including the U.S., have broken diplomatic relations with Taiwan, and it has lost its seat in the UN. But many of the nations who refuse diplomatic recognition continue to trade with Taiwan.

The authoritarian government controls communication with strict censorship and prevents expression of political opposition.

Taiwan (formerly called *Formosa*) is an island about 100 miles from the China main-

land. It measures some 240 miles north to south, and 85 miles at its greatest width.

The Pescadores (Penghu Islands), an island group belonging to Taiwan, lie about 25 miles from the southwest coast. Matsu and Quemoy (Kinmen), two small island groups controlled by Taiwan, are just off the mainland coast.

Mountains cover about two-thirds of Taiwan. Their eastern slope is rugged and sparsely settled, while the western slope is fertile and has one of the world's greatest population densities. The highest mountain, Yü Shan, rises to 13,110 feet.

The U.S. government has emphasized that it does not intend to build up Taiwan's armies for an invasion of communist-governed mainland China, and has advised Peking that it would not support any nationalist attempt to land forces on the mainland.

## HISTORY OF TAIWAN

Chinese immigration to Taiwan began as early as the T'ang dynasty (618–907). In 1628 Dutch forces defeated Spaniards for control of Taiwan. After the Manchu conquest of the island in 1683, Taiwan was administered as part of China. In 1895 it was ceded to Japan following the Sino-Japanese War. Uprisings continued for decades.

After World War II, Japan surrendered Taiwan to China in 1945. Japan renounced all claims to Taiwan in 1951.

In 1949 the advancing communist forces of Mao Tse-tung forced President Chiang Kai-shek's nationalist government and his remaining armies to flee from the mainland to Taiwan. Communist China's plans to invade the island were blocked in 1950 when President Harry S. Truman sent the U.S. Seventh Fleet to patrol Taiwan Strait.

The U.S. signed an agreement in 1955 to defend Taiwan and the Pescadores from any attack by Communist China.

In October 1971 the UN General Assembly with U.S. support voted for Red China's admission but, despite U.S. objections, expelled Taiwan. President Nixon declared that U.S.-Taiwan alliances would be maintained.

In 1972, at the age of 85, Chiang Kai-shek turned over the running of the government to his eldest son, Chiang Ching-kuo, as premier.

After Chiang Kai-shek died in 1975, Premier Chiang became head of the ruling Nationalist Party (Kuomintang).

The 65-year-old Chiang Ching-kuo was elected president without opposition by the national assembly on March 21, 1978. Two months later he was sworn into the office that had been held by his father for three decades. He apppointed Sun Yun-suan as prime minister.

To extend diplomatic recognition to China, the U.S. ended formal relations with Taiwan on Jan. 1, 1979. President Carter also abrogated the 1955 mutual defense pact with Taiwan, effective Dec. 31, 1979. However, the U.S. continued to maintain unofficial diplomatic relations with Taiwan through an organization called the American Institute.

Taiwan's foreign trade expanded 30% in 1979 with a favorable balance of $1.3 billion.

# TANZANIA

**Official Name:** United Republic of Tanzania.
**Area:** 364,900 square miles (945,087 sq. km.).
**Population:** 17,653,800.
**Capital:** Official capital, Dodoma, 60,000; actual capital, Dar es Salaam, 517,000.
**Government:** One-party socialist republic.
**President:** Julius Kambarage Nyerere (since 1961).
**Prime Minister:** Edward Sokoine (since 1977).
**Legislature:** *National Assembly* (mainland), 219 members; House of Representatives (Zanzibar), 40 members.
**U.S. Ambassador to Tanzania:** Richard N. Viets.
**Tanzanian Ambassador to U.S.:** Paul Bomani.
**Flag:** Green triangle (upper left) and blue triangle (lower right) separated by diagonal gold-bordered black stripe.
**Languages:** Swahili (official), English.
**Main Ethnic Group:** Black.
**Principal Religions:** Islam (35%), Christianity (35%); animism (30%).
**Leading Industries:** Agriculture (livestock, cotton, coffee, sisal, cloves, coconuts, tea, tobacco, cashews, sugarcane); mining (diamonds, gold, tin, gemstones); manufacturing (food processing, oil refining, textiles, cement, consumer goods); tourism.
**Foreign Trade:** *major exports*—cotton, coffee, sisal, diamonds, cloves; *major imports*—machinery, transport equipment, iron and steel, crude petroleum.
**Places of Interest:** Mt. Kilimanjaro; Ngorongoro Crater; nine national parks; five game preserves; Olduvai Gorge; Amboni Caves; Zanzibar and Mafia islands; Dar es Salaam.

## TANZANIA TODAY

Although more than twice as large as California, Tanzania is one of the poorest African nations. It is a federation of a mainland area formerly called Tanganyika and the island of Zanzibar.

Tanzania is one of the world's leading diamond-mining nations. But its economy is largely based on agriculture.

Most Tanzanians scratch out a bare living, raising corn, beans, and cassava. Few can read and write.

Most of mainland Tanzania is an infertile plateau, 1,000 to 4,000 feet high, bisected from north to south by the Great Rift Valley. On the more fertile margins of the plateau are Lakes Victoria, Tanganyika, and Malawi. Mt. Kilimanjaro (19,340 feet), the highest mountain in Africa, is in the northeast.

Tanzania is bordered on the south by Zambia, Malawi, and Mozambique; on the west by Rwanda, Burundi, and Zaire; and on the north by Kenya and Uganda.

## EARLY HISTORY OF TANZANIA

Archaeological discoveries at Olduvai Gorge indicate that manlike creatures lived in the area 3 million years ago. Ancient Greek mariners

QUICK QUIZ: What is the name of the era when dinosaurs lived? See page 179.

## TANZANIA *(continued)*

called the coast *Azania.*

Zanzibar and various coastal cities, especially Kilwa, were colonized from the Persian Gulf area, probably in the 700s. A series of autonomous Muslim city-states flourished with a Swahili language and culture.

In the 1500s the Portuguese destroyed the Muslim city-states and then controlled the coast until ousted by Arabs from Oman in the 1700s.

European colonization led to establishment in 1890 of a British protectorate in Zanzibar and to German colonization of Tanganyika, as the mainland area was called. German control ended after World War I when Britain took over Tanganyika under a League of Nations mandate.

### INDEPENDENCE

The Tanganyika African National Union (TANU), headed by Julius Nyerere, led Tanganyika to independence on Dec. 9, 1961. Zanzibar became independent in December 1963.

On April 26, 1964, Tanganyika and Zanzibar united with Nyerere as president. The new country was named the *United Republic of Tanzania* in October 1964.

The socialist government nationalized clove plantations in Zanzibar in 1964 and took over many major companies in 1967 and 1968.

Nyerere was unopposed in reelections in 1970, 1975, and 1980.

With massive economic and technical aid from China, a 1,162-mile railroad was built in 1970–76 from Dar es Salaam to Kapiri Mposhi, Zambia.

Centrally located Dodoma has been named the official capital, but few government offices have been transferred there from Dar es Salaam pending completion of a $550 million construction program by 1985.

President Nyerere reported that by mid-1975 over 9 million Tanzanians had been moved into more than 6,900 socialist collective villages. The government in 1976 moved thousands of unemployed from Dar es Salaam to the countryside.

President Nyerere uses the Swahili word *ujamaa,* meaning "familyhood," to describe the village socialism he fosters. He explains that familyhood calls for sharing. But when Nyerere points out each person must work hard, many seem to lose interest.

Full-scale war began in 1978 after Ugandan President Idi Amin announced on Nov. 1 that his troops had annexed 710 square miles of Tanzanian territory. Tanzania fought back, invaded Uganda, and drove Amin into exile, capturing Uganda's capital on April 11, 1979. Victorious Tanzanian troops began withdrawing from Uganda in July 1979. Tanzania's economy suffered because of the estimated $500 million cost of the war.

Zanzibar was granted autonomy in 1979 with a separate constitution. In the first Zanzibar election since 1964, its people chose a 40-member House of Representatives on Jan. 7, 1980, from among 80 candidates nominated by the only political party, Chama Cha Mapinduzi (CCM). Aboud Jumbe was elected president of Zanzibar on Oct. 26, 1980.

Hard hit by drought in 1980, Tanzania appealed for aid to prevent starvation.

# THAILAND

**Official Name:** Kingdom of Thailand.
**Area:** 198,457 square miles (514,000 sq. km.).
**Population:** 46,812,100.
**Chief Cities:** Bangkok, capital, 4,178,000; Thonburi, 627,989.
**Government:** Monarchy controlled by military.
**King:** Phumiphon Adunyadet (reigned since 1950).
**Prime Minister:** Prem Tinsulanonde (since 1980).
**Parliament:** *House of Representatives,* 301 elected members; *Senate,* 225 appointed members.
**U.S. Ambassador to Thailand:** Morton I. Abramowitz.
**Thailand Ambassador to U.S.:** Prok Amaranand.
**Flag:** From top to bottom, five stripes: red, white, blue (double width), white, and red.
**Official Language:** Thai.
**Main Ethnic Groups:** Thai (75%), Chinese (14%).
**Principal Religions:** Buddhism (96%), Islam (4%).
**Leading Industries:** Agriculture (rice, corn, sugarcane, rubber, cotton, livestock, poultry); mining (tin, gems, tungsten); forestry and lumbering; fishing; manufacturing (food processing, cement, paper).
**Foreign Trade:** *major exports*—rice, corn, rubber, tin, tapioca products, kenaf; *major imports*—machinery, textiles, petroleum.
**Places of Interest:** Chiangmai; Ayutthaya palaces and temples; Lop Buri ruins; old city of Nakhon Pathom. *In Bangkok:* Grand Palace; Emerald Buddha Temple; Temple of Dawn; rose garden; floating market.

### THAILAND TODAY

Larger than California, Thailand is a noncommunist country in Southeast Asia. The word *Thai* means "free," and the Thais, unlike their neighbors, have maintained independence from both European colonialism and communist expansion.

Thailand is one of the world's leading producers of natural rubber and tin. The Thai government has done little to foster the development of industry or manufacturing. The economy depends on rice farming and U.S. aid.

The country has four main regions. The north is a forest highland area. A series of mountain ranges in the northwest rise to more than 8,500 feet in Inthanon Peak. The central plains are a fertile lowland with silt accumulations from the Chao Phraya River, which flows into the Gulf of Siam. The most fertile region is the Bangkok Delta, known as the rice basket or heartland of the country. To the northeast rises a dry upland area, ending at the Mekong River on the border with Laos. Peninsular Thailand, reaching to Malaysia, is a mountainous ridge.

Laos lies to the east, Cambodia and Malaysia to the south, and Burma to the west.

### EARLY HISTORY OF THAILAND

Archaeological discoveries indicate that an early civilization developed in the 4000s B.C. in Thailand. By 3600 B.C. it had become the first culture in history to use bronze.

But the ancestors of the present-day Thai people, who lived in what is now China's

Yunnan province, only began migrating to the region about 1,000 years ago. They established a kingdom at Sukhothai in the 1200s.

The Thai capital was moved in the 1300s to Ayutthaya on the Chao Phraya River north of present-day Bangkok.

In 1782 the Chakkri dynasty was established with its capital at Bangkok. That dynasty has continued to reign to the present time.

Modernization began under the enlightened rule of King Mongkut (Rama IV, 1851–68) and his son Chulalongkorn (Rama V, 1868–1910), who abolished slavery. The Western powers acquired extensive extraterritorial privileges, which they retained until 1937.

## CONSTITUTIONAL MONARCHY

In 1932 a coup by young radicals forced King Prajadipok (Rama VII, 1925–35), to give up his absolute powers and accept a constitution.

During World War II Japan occupied Thailand. After the war King Phumiphon Adunyadet (Rama IX) became ruler in 1946 while still a student in Switzerland. He returned to Thailand in 1950.

A military coup brought Field Marshal Sarit Thanarat to power in 1957, and the constitution was suspended. Upon Sarit's death in 1963, Lt. Gen. Thanom Kittikachorn became premier.

During the Vietnam War, the U.S. built some 93 military installations including a dozen air bases from which B-52s bombed communist forces in Cambodia, Laos, and Vietnam. Some 48,000 U.S. servicemen were stationed in Thailand. Subsidized with $50 million a year by the U.S., Thailand sent 11,000 troops to fight in Vietnam from 1968 to 1972.

In October 1973, college students demanding a new constitution led mobs that overthrew Thanom. A democratic constitution was adopted on Oct. 7, 1974. Free national elections were held on Jan. 26, 1975, and 22 parties divided the 269 seats in the house of representatives.

Kukrit Pramoj became premier on March 13, 1975. He immediately called on the U.S. to withdraw its remaining 350 planes and 25,000 military personnel from Thailand within a year.

U.S. relations with Thailand became strained in May 1975 when the U.S. used Thai bases without permission to rescue the crew of the U.S. freighter *Mayaguez* who had been taken prisoner by Cambodian communists.

When communists took over neighboring Cambodia and Laos in 1975, thousands of refugees fled to Thailand.

In elections on April 4, 1976, Kukrit Pramoj lost his seat in parliament. His 71-year-old brother Seni Pramoj became prime minister.

American military forces completed their withdrawal on July 20, 1976, leaving behind only about 250 military advisers.

The U.S. pullout brought a depression to Thailand's economy. The U.S. promised to provide $94 million in economic aid over a 6-year period in 1976–82.

A right-wing military junta led by Defense Minister Adm. Sa-ngad Chaloryu seized power on Oct. 6, 1976. The constitution and civil rights were suspended. Over 5,000 students and suspected leftists were arrested.

The junta chose a civilian judge, Thanin Kraivichien, as prime minister on Oct. 8, 1976.

Gen. Kriangsak Chamanand, supreme commander of the military forces, led a bloodless coup on Oct. 20, 1977, that overthrew Prime Minister Thanin. Kriangsak, secretary-general of the military revolutionary party, also became prime minister on Nov. 11, 1977.

A new constitution adopted in December 1978 ensured continued control of the government by the military, but provided for election of the lower house of parliament. The prime minister and members of the cabinet do not have to be elected.

In the first national election under the new constitution on April 22, 1979, the Social Action Party of former prime minister Kukrit Pramoj won the largest number of elected seats in parliament, but Prime Minister Kriangsak remained in power with the support of members he had appointed.

Vietnam's conquest of neighboring Cambodia in 1979 brought an influx of additional tens of thousands of refugees, bringing to about 300,000 the number living in camps in Thailand.

Soaring oil prices brought antigovernment demonstrations in Bangkok in 1980, causing Kriangsak to resign as prime minister on Feb. 29. He was succeeded by Gen. Prem Tinsulanonde, 59, head of the armed forces. Seeking widespread support, Prem appointed many civilian political leaders to his new cabinet.

Vietnamese troops invaded Thailand on June 23, 1980, in pursuit of Cambodian guerrillas, but withdrew within 10 hours in the face of Thai military resistance. The U.S. airlifted arms and supplies to bolster Thailand's defenses.

# TOGO

**Official Name:** Republic of Togo.
**Area:** 21,622 square miles (56,000 sq. km.).
**Population:** 2,569,200.
**Capital:** Lomé, 148,156.
**Government:** One-party dictatorship.
**President:** Gen. Gnassingbe Eyadema (since 1967).
**U.S. Ambassador to Togo:** Marilyn Priscilla Johnson.
**Togo Ambassador to U.S.:** Yao Grunitzky.
**Parliament:** General Assembly.
**Flag:** Green and yellow stripes, with white star centered in red square at upper hoist corner.
**Languages:** French (official), tribal dialects.
**Main Ethnic Groups:** Hamitic and Bantu tribes.
**Religions:** Animism (75%), Christianity (20%), Islam (5%).
**Leading Industries:** Agriculture (cocoa, coffee, palm kernels, corn, peanuts, cotton, manioc, millet, sorghum, livestock, fruits, vegetables); mining (phosphates); manufacturing (textiles, food processing, construction materials); fishing.

## TOGO *(continued)*

**Foreign Trade:** *major exports*—phosphates, cocoa, coffee, palm nuts, cotton, peanuts, fish, manioc flour and starch: *major imports*—manufactured goods, machinery, transport equipment, food, cotton fabrics, tobacco.

**Places of Interest:** Togo Mountains; native villages; Lomé.

## TOGO TODAY

Togo is a hot tropical country of West Africa, about the size of West Virginia. Its most important resource, other than its farmland, is a huge deposit of phosphates. Otherwise the country's economy depends mostly on agriculture and fishing.

To balance the annual budget, the government counts on foreign aid each year.

The people are poor. Most struggle for their existence by raising food on plots of land owned in common by several families. Some work on large plantations that grow coffee for export. Few children go to school. The hard life of the people of Togo results in one of the lowest life-expectancy rates in the world, with the average Togolese living only to the age of 40.

The government has endeavored to diversify the economy with the construction of roads, hotels, and industrial plants financed by foreign loans. It encourages foreign investors with relief from taxation.

Togo is a narrow country about 75 miles wide and 360 long. Upper Volta lies on the north, Dahomey on the east, and Ghana on the west.

Because of coastal sandbars and lagoons, there is no good harbor. Inland the terrain is hilly and mountainous.

## HISTORY OF TOGO

As a nation Togo has little precolonial history. The colony of Togoland, created by Germany in 1885, consisted of today's Togo in the east and part of present-day Ghana in the west.

In 1922 the League of Nations divided Togoland into French and British mandates, with Togo going to the French.

The United Nations assumed trusteeship of the territory in 1946. In a 1956 plebiscite the Togolese voted 3 to 1 for autonomy, and in April 1960 Togo became an independent state.

Sylvanus Olympio, a man of great ability, was president of Togo until his assassination in the military coup of 1963. His successor was Nicolas Grunitzky, appointed by the military.

In January 1967 Grunitzky was peacefully ousted by Gen. Gnassingbe Eyadema, who became president on April 14. Eyadema rules Togo with the help of a 12-man council.

In an effort to get a larger share of the profits from the mining of phosphate, the government nationalized the phosphate industry on Feb. 4, 1975.

The government began an active campaign in 1976–77 to obtain the 11,200-square-mile area of the former colony of British Togoland, which was absorbed by Ghana in 1957.

Running unopposed, Eyadema was reelected to a 7-year term on Dec. 30, 1979. A general assembly also was elected from among candidates submitted by the only political party, the Togolese People's Rally.

## TONGA

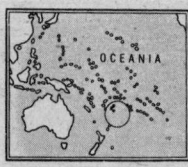

**Official Name:** Kingdom of Tonga.
**Area:** 270 square miles (699 sq. km.).
**Population:** 86,178.
**Capital:** Nuku'alofa, 22,000.
**Government:** Constitutional monarchy.
**King:** Taufa'ahau Tupou IV (reigned since 1965).
**Prime Minister:** Prince Tu'ipelehake (since 1965).
**Legislative Assembly:** 23 members.
**Tonga Ambassador to U.S.:** 'Inoke Faletau
**U.S. Ambassador to Tonga:** William Bodde Jr.
**Flag:** Red field with red cross on white square in upper hoist corner.
**Language:** Tongan (official), English.
**Main Ethnic Group:** Tongan (98%).
**Religions:** Methodism (60%), Mormonism (20%), other Christian denominations (20%).
**Leading Industries:** Agriculture (bananas, coconuts, fruits, vegetables); fishing; food processing.
**Foreign Trade:** *major exports*—bananas, coconut products; *major imports*— textiles, food, timber, steel.
**Places of Interest:** Royal palace and chapel; terraced tombs; blow holes; sacred flying foxes; Nuku'alofa.

## TONGA TODAY

The South Pacific island kingdom of Tonga has a land area about equal to the city of Dallas, Texas, but only about one-eighth as many people. Two-thirds of Tonga's people live on the largest island, Tongatapu, which covers about 99 square miles.

The government owns all the land. But each man, upon reaching the age of 16, is entitled to rent an *api* of 8.25 acres for farming and a village plot of 0.375 acre on which to build a house. Most Tongans live by raising tropical fruits and vegetables and catching fish to feed their families.

An archipelago of 150 islands and islets, Tonga lies east of Fiji and south of Western Samoa. The islands stretch across about 500 miles of ocean from north to south.

## HISTORY OF TONGA

Tonga's hereditary monarchs date at least from the 1000s A.D. In the 1200s the power of the Tonga monarchy extended as far as Hawaii.

One of the islands was discovered by the Dutch in 1616, and others by Capt. James Cook in 1773 and 1777. Cook called them the Friendly Islands because of their good-natured inhabitants.

The famous mutiny aboard the British ship *Bounty* took place in 1789 in waters off Tonga.

British missionaries arrived in 1797.

The present dynasty was founded by the Christian king George Tupou I in 1845.

A British protectorate was proclaimed in 1900. On June 4, 1970, Tonga was granted independence with membership in the British Commonwealth of Nations.

The nation's third 5-year development program for 1975–80 encouraged diversification of agriculture and development of light industry.

# TRANSKEI

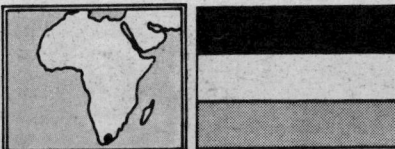

# TRINIDAD-TOBAGO

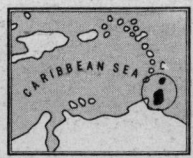

**Official Name:** Republic of Transkei.
**Area:** 15,830 square miles (41,000 sq. km).
**Population:** 2,312,890.
**Capital:** Umtata, 30,000.
**Government:** Parliamentary republic.
**Prime Minister:** Chief George Matanzima (since 1979).
**President:** Chief Kaiser Matanzima (since 1979).
**Flag:** Stripes of red (top), white, and green (bottom).
**National Assembly:** *The Bunga,* 150 members (75 tribal chiefs and 75 elected members).
**Chief Languages:** Xhosa (official), English, Afrikaans, Sesotho.
**Principal Ethnic Group:** Xhosa-speaking Bantus.
**Main Religions:** Methodist (60%), animism (40%).
**Leading Industries:** Agriculture (cattle, sheep, corn, tea, coffee, nuts); manufacturing (electricity, food processing, textiles); fishing; forestry; tourism.
**Foreign Trade:** *major exports*—livestock, meat products, wool, hides; *major imports*—petroleum products, consumer goods, vehicles, machinery.
**Places of Interest:** Wild Coast nature area between Kei and Umtamvuna rivers; Magwa Falls; beaches.

A poor south African nation about twice the size of New Jersey, Transkei is completely dependent on South Africa. It has a 168-mile coastline on the Indian Ocean, with a harbor at Port St. Johns.

The small capital city of Umtata boasts a twin-tower 14-story government building. But most of the people live in tribal villages.

Cattle and corn are the main products. When in need of cash money, the men go to South Africa to work in the mines. Polygamy is legal.

The climate is mild. Winters are cool and dry with an occasional frost. Summers are warm to hot with about 25 inches of rain.

South Africa borders Transkei on the west and the northeast. Lesotho lies to the north.

Britain annexed the region in 1872–94.

South Africa gave Transkei independence as a republic on Oct. 26, 1976. Chief Kaiser Matanzima, head of the Transkei National Independence Party, became the first prime minister.

With Transkei's independence, 1.5 million Xhosa tribesmen living outside Transkei automatically lost their South African citizenship and became citizens of Transkei. Other nations refused to grant Transkei diplomatic recognition, claiming it was a puppet of South Africa.

In an effort to demonstrate Transkei's sovereignty, Chief Matanzima broke diplomatic relations with South Africa on April 10, 1978. Relations were restored on Feb. 7, 1980.

Chief Botha Sigcau, the country's president since 1976, died on Dec. 1, 1978. Chief Kaiser Matanzima gave up the office of prime minister in February 1979 to accept election as president. He appointed his brother, George Matanzima, as prime minister.

**Official Name:** Republic of Trinidad and Tobago.
**Area:** 1,981 square miles (5,130 sq. km.).
**Population:** 1,179,100.
**Capital:** Port of Spain, 11,032.
**Government:** Parliamentary republic.
**Prime Minister:** Eric Eustace Williams (since 1962).
**President:** Sir Ellis Clarke (since 1976).
**Parliament:** *Senate,* 31 appointed members; *House of Representatives,* 36 elected members.
**U.S. Ambassador to Trinidad-Tobago:** Irving Cheslaw.
**Trinidad-Tobago Ambassador to U.S.:** Victor C. McIntyre.
**Flag:** Red field crossed diagonally by white-bordered black stripe.
**Languages:** English (official), Spanish.
**Main Ethnic Groups:** Black (43%), Asian Indian (40%).
**Principal Religions:** Roman Catholicism (32%), Protestantism (29%), Hinduism (20%), Islam (6%).
**Leading Industries:** Mining (petroleum, natural gas); manufacturing (oil refining, chemicals, textiles, cement, food processing); agriculture (sugarcane, cocoa, coconuts, fruits, vegetables); tourism; fishing.
**Foreign Trade:** major exports—petroleum, sugar, cocoa, natural asphalt, chemicals; major imports—steel, food, chemicals, machinery, vehicles.
**Places of Interest:** *On Trinidad:* The Saddle; Caroni Bird Sanctuary; Maracas Bay; Pitch Lake; Port of Spain. *On Tobago:* Bird of Paradise Sanctuary; Man O'War Bay; Pigeon Point; Coral Sea Gardens; Turtle Beach.

## TRINIDAD-TOBAGO TODAY

The mining and refining of petroleum are the largest industries of Trinidad-Tobago. Oil products make up about 85% of the country's exports. Huge natural gas reserves promise a source of power for developing industry.

Other important industries are the raising of sugarcane and the refining of sugar. Many islanders work in the cane fields.

The revenues from oil and sugar provide the islanders with one of the highest per capita incomes in the Caribbean. However, unemployment stands between 17% and 30%.

The warm climate, ocean beaches, and mountain scenery of Trinidad and Tobago make the islands a popular winter vacation spot for tourists from the United States. Calypso, the steel band, and limbo all originated in Trinidad. These are featured in the colorful celebrations and carnival leading up to Ash Wednesday each year. Tourists enjoy seeing the bird of paradise and scarlet ibis in bird sanctuaries.

The islands of Trinidad and Tobago lie about 20 miles apart in the Caribbean Sea off Venezuela's northeast coast.

Trinidad, the largest island, has an area of 1,864 square miles. It has three mountain ranges, which run roughly east to west. Moun-

QUICK QUIZ: Which U.S. state capital city was established in 1610? See page 306.

tains in the northern range rise to 3,085 feet. Small streams flow to the sea through gently rolling flatlands between the mountains.

Tobago (116 sq. mi.) is generally more rugged than Trinidad. It has a central volcanic core that ascends to 1,890 feet.

Daily high temperatures average 92°F. throughout the year.

## EARLY HISTORY

The islands were discovered by Columbus in 1498, bringing them under Spanish rule.

During the 1600s and 1700s cocoa and sugar plantations were established with slave labor imported from Africa. In 1783 the Spanish government offered free land grants that attracted many non-Spanish settlers, especially French.

Trinidad was captured by the British in 1797 during a war with France. It was officially ceded to Britain in 1802, when it became a crown colony. Tobago was acquired by Britain in 1814 and was made a crown colony in 1877. Trinidad and Tobago were joined as a single colony in 1889.

Slaves on Trinidad were emancipated in 1833. To replace these plantation workers, the British brought in 150,000 Hindus and Muslims from India between 1845 and 1917.

## INDEPENDENCE

A drive for self-government, under the leadership of Dr. Eric Williams, culminated in independence on Aug. 31, 1962. Williams became the nation's first prime minister.

In 1970 the government acquired a 51% interest in the nation's main sugar-processing industry, Caroni Limited.

Black-power demonstrations marked by arson and looting shook the country in the first months of 1970. They reached a climax in a mutiny staged by half of the 800-man army. The government suppressed the rebellion in three days.

Offshore oil fields discovered in 1972–75 brought Trinidad-Tobago sudden wealth as it joined the rolls of the oil-exporting nations. The oil revenues made it possible for the government to cut personal income taxes, to increase social-welfare benefits, and at the same time to subsidize food prices to prevent inflation from soaring.

To stabilize its currency the government in May 1976 tied its money to that of the United States at a rate of $1 U.S. to $1.20 of Trinidad-Tobago currency.

Trinidad-Tobago became a republic within the British Commonwealth on Aug. 1, 1976. Sir Ellis Clarke, who had served as governor-general, was chosen as the first president.

Prime Minister Williams' PNM party won its fifth 5-year term in national elections on Sept. 13, 1976, taking 24 of the 36 seats in the house of representatives. The main political party, the People's Nationalist Movement (PNM), draws its strength primarily from the blacks, who make up 43% of the population. The chief opposition is the leftist United Labor Front (ULF).

The government encourages foreign investment in new manufacturing plants in order to reduce the country's dependence on the petroleum and sugar industries.

# TUNISIA

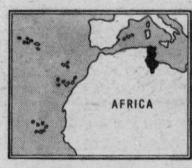 

**Official Name:** Republic of Tunisia.
**Area:** 63,170 square miles (163,610 sq. km.).
**Population:** 6,497,010.
**Chief Cities:** Tunis, capital, 468,997; Bizerte, 95,023; Sousse, 82,666; Sfax, 79,595.
**Government:** One-party republic.
**President:** Habib Bourguiba (since 1957).
**Prime Minister:** Mohammed Mzali (since 1980).
**Legislature:** *National Assembly,* 112 members.
**U.S. Ambassador to Tunisia:** Stephen W. Bosworth.
**Tunisian Ambassador to U.S.:** Ali Hedda.
**Flag:** Red field with white circle containing red crescent and star.
**Languages:** Arabic (official), French.
**Main Ethnic Group:** Arab-Berber (98%).
**Official Religion:** Islam.
**Leading Industries:** Agriculture (olives, grapes, wheat, fruits, vegetables); manufacturing (oil refining), chemicals, textiles, wine, electricity, cement, consumer products); mining (petroleum, natural gas, phosphates, iron, zinc, lead); tourism; fishing.
**Foreign Trade:** *major exports*—crude oil, olive oil, phosphates, citrus fruits, iron, wine, lead; *major imports*—wheat, motor vehicles, textile yarn and thread, vegetable oils, sulfur, wood.
**Places of Interest:** Roman ruins; beach resorts; Djerba Island; ancient city of Kairouan; fortified city of Monastir; Bardo Museum and Belvédère Park in Tunis; site of ancient Carthage; Sousse; Sfax.

## TUNISIA TODAY

Helped by nearly $1 billion in aid from the United States since World War II, Tunisia has developed a diversified economy that is no longer solely dependent on agriculture.

While its richer North African neighbors Algeria and Libya have turned to state-controlled socialism, Tunisia has relied on private enterprise to develop its economy. Tourism has become the main industry.

However, not enough new industries have been developed to provide jobs for the many Tunisians who leave their farms each year to seek a better life in the cities. Many young people educated in Tunisia's colleges and universities must go to Europe to obtain well-paying jobs.

Most of the people are poor. About half earn a living as farmers. Only about 4 of 10 Tunisians can read and write.

Somewhat larger than the state of Georgia, Tunisia lies on the Mediterranean coast of Africa between Algeria in the west and Libya in the southeast.

The east-west Atlas mountain range divides Tunisia into two main regions. North of the mountains is the relatively well-watered, fertile Tell zone with groves of olive trees and pastures for livestock. To the south are a semiarid plain and plateau that extend into the Sahara Desert.

The majority of people live in the coastal plain bordering the Mediterranean Sea. Nomadic tribes live in the southern region.

## EARLY HISTORY OF TUNISIA

Tunisia was the center of ancient Carthage and later, from the 100s B.C., of a Roman province.

Tunisia was occupied by the Vandals in the 400s A.D. and recovered by the Byzantine Empire in the 500s. The country was finally conquered by the Arabs in the 600s.

During the Middle Ages it was the center from which Arab power and Islam spread south and west and also north across the Mediterranean. In 1535 Carthage was captured by the Holy Roman Emperor Karl V. The ruling dynasty turned for help to the Turks, who expelled the Spaniards in 1574 and made Tunisia a Turkish province.

Britain, France, and Italy assumed financial control of Tunisia in 1869. Tunisia became a French protectorate in 1883.

Opposition to French rule was stirred by formation of the Young Tunisian Party in 1907 and by the Destour (Constitutional) Party after World War I.

After the fall of France in World War II, Tunisia remained loyal to the Vichy government. The country became a central theater of the war in North Africa.

Habib Bourguiba, leader of the Neo-Destour Party, led the struggle for independence from France in the 1940s and 1950s.

## INDEPENDENCE

On March 20, 1956, France granted Tunisia independence as a monarchy.

Tunisia's constituent assembly abolished the monarchy on July 25, 1957, establishing a republic with Habib Bourguiba as president. He won election without opposition in 1959, 1964, and 1969. The national assembly elected Bourguiba president for life in 1974.

Devastating floods struck Tunisia late in March 1973, leaving 53,000 homeless and 119 dead or missing.

To clarify the line of succession, Bourguiba changed the constitution in 1973. It provides that on his death he will be succeeded as head of the government by the prime minister. Then a presidential election will be held within 45 days.

Plans for uniting Tunisia and Libya as one nation were aborted by President Bourguiba in January 1974.

Soaring oil and phosphate prices in the mid-1970s brought Tunisia added revenues, which enabled it to expand its manufacturing and processing industries.

Guerrillas crossed into Tunisia from Algeria on Jan. 27, 1980, attacking the mining city of Gafsa. Forty-five persons were killed and over 100 injured before most of the guerrillas were captured. The Tunisian government claimed Libya had trained the guerrillas and had planned to invade Tunisia to support the attackers. Thirteen of the captured guerrillas were hanged on April 17, 1980, and others were sentenced to prison. Tunisia expelled Libya's ambassador and recalled its own ambassador.

Bourguiba named former education minister Mohammed Mzali, 54, as prime minister on April 23, 1980, replacing ailing 69-year-old Hedi Nouira, who had held the office since 1970.

# TURKEY

**Official Name:** Republic of Turkey.
**Area:** 301,382 square miles (780,576 sq. km.).
**Population:** 45,861,400.
**Chief Cities:** Ankara, capital, 1,698,542; Istanbul, 2,534,839; Izmir, 636,078; Adana, 467,122; Bursa, 346,084; Gaziantep, 300,801; Eskisehir, 258,266.
**Largest Metropolitan Area:** Istanbul, 3,864,493.
**Government:** Military junta.
**Chief of State:** Gen. Kenan Evren (since 1980).
**Prime Minister:** Bulent Ulusu (since 1980).
**Military Junta:** *National Security Council,* 5 members.
**U.S. Ambassador to Turkey:** James W. Spain.
**Turkish Ambassador to U.S.:** Sukru Elekdag.
**Flag:** White star and crescent on red field.
**Languages:** Turkish (official), Kurdish.
**Main Ethnic Groups:** Turk (90%), Kurd (7%).
**Religion:** Islam (98%).
**Leading Industries:** Manufacturing (steel, textiles, electricity, tobacco products, food processing, consumer products); agriculture (wheat, barley, corn, cotton, sugar beets, livestock, tobacco, fruits, vegetables); mining (coal, lignite, iron, petroleum); services; fishing.
**Foreign Trade:** *major exports*—cotton, tobacco; *major imports*—petroleum, motor vehicles, machinery.
**Places of Interest:** Bosporus bridge; Black Sea and Mediterranean resorts; Göreme Valley; ruins of Troy; ancient city of Sardis; Temple of Diana at Ephesus; tomb of Antiochus I on Mt. Nimrud; Ankara; Izmir. *In Istanbul:* Topkapi Palace; Grand Bazaar; St. Sofia; the Blue Sofia; the Blue Mosque.

## TURKEY TODAY

Larger than Texas, Turkey was for 1,600 years the seat of empires that dominated southeastern Europe and the Middle East. Today Turkey's largest city, Istanbul (once called Constantinople), stands on the southeastern tip of Europe, but 97% of Turkey lies in Asia.

The country's strategic position on the Soviet Union's southwestern frontier makes Turkey a key member of the NATO military alliance. The U.S. uses 12 military bases in Turkey.

Turkey is a developing country striving to become an industrial nation. The people of Turkey are poorer than those of neighboring countries. About half cannot read or write. Hundreds of thousands of Turkish workers have gone to West Germany and other European nations to find work. The money they send home to their families has been an important part of the foreign exchange used in developing new industries in Turkey. In addition the U.S. has given and loaned Turkey over $7.8 billion in economic and military assistance in the past three decades.

Lacking most important industrial natural resources, Turkey pins its hopes for the future on developing oil wells in the adjacent Aegean Sea in areas disputed with Greece.

Turkey controls the only outlet for Soviet

QUICK QUIZ: Where is the world's largest atomic electric-power generator? See page 263.

**TURKEY** (continued)

ships from the Black Sea to the Mediterranean Sea, including the Bosporus, the Sea of Marmara, and the Dardanelles. Completion of the huge Bosporus bridge across the strait in 1973 linked European and Asian Turkey by highway.

Greece lies to the west, Bulgaria to the north, the Soviet Union to the northeast, Syria and Iraq to the south, and Iran to the east.

### EARLY HISTORY

In about 600 B.C. Greeks founded the city of Byzantium (now Istanbul) on hills strategically commanding the Bosporus. Roman legions captured Byzantium in A.D. 196.

In A.D. 330 the Christian emperor Constantine moved his capital from Rome to Byzantium, renamed Constantinople. The Byzantine Empire ruled eastern Europe and the Middle East for more than 1,000 years.

In 1453 the Turks, led by Ottoman Sultan Mohammed II, ended the Byzantine Empire with the capture of Constantinople. Islam supplanted Christianity. The Ottoman Empire dominated the Middle East until the early 1900s.

Turkey entered World War I on the German side. After Turkey's surrender in 1918, Sultan Mohammed VI, last of the Ottoman rulers, accepted the Treaty of Sèvres (1920), which reduced the empire to a minor state.

### REPUBLIC OF TURKEY

A Turkish national resistance movement, led by Mustafa Kemal (later called Kemal Ataturk), rejected the Sèvres settlement. Ataturk declared the sultan deposed in 1922 and repulsed a Greek offensive in the west.

A republic, with Kemal Ataturk as president, was proclaimed in 1923. The Treaty of Lausanne (1923) established the present Turkish boundaries. The next year Ataturk introduced a new constitution that set up a national legislative assembly. Ataturk abolished Islam as the state religion, replaced Islamic law with European law. He moved the capital to Ankara.

Former Premier Ismet Inonu became president after Ataturk's death in 1938. Turkey did not declare war on Germany and Japan until 1945. Ataturk's successors remained in power until 1950, when Celal Bayar, leader of the Democratic Party, won the presidency. He appointed Adnan Menderes as premier.

In May 1960 an army revolt overthrew the elected government. Menderes was sentenced to death and hanged in 1961. In the same year a new constitution was adopted restoring parliamentary democracy.

Gen. Cemal Gursel, head of a faction favoring strict adherence to the principles of Ataturk, won the presidency in 1961. Gursel died in 1966. Gen. Cevdet Sunay succeeded him.

### TURBULENT 1970s–80s

In 1973 parliament elected Adm. Fahri Koruturk to a 7-year term as president. He retired in April 1980 when the politically divided parliament was unable to agree on a successor.

Throughout the 1970s neither of the country's leading political parties was able to hold a clear majority in parliament. Conservative Suleyman Demirel, head of the Justice Party, and Bulent Ecevit, leader of the socialist Republican People's Party (RPU), alternated in serving as prime minister.

The Greek-led overthrow of the Cyprus government in July 1974 caused Turkey to invade the island with 40,000 troops.

The U.S. cut off arms shipments to Turkey on Feb. 5, 1975, because Turkey had used NATO arms in its invasion of Cyprus. In retaliation, Turkey took over U.S. military bases.

In a national parliamentary election on June 5, 1977, the socialist RPU won the largest number of seats, 213, but not a clear majority. RPU leader Ecevit again became prime minister, but after 10 days in office he was defeated in a confidence vote, 229 to 217. He regained the office in January 1978.

Threatening to change the East-West balance of power in the Middle East unless the U.S. ended its arms ban on Turkey, Ecevit visited Moscow and signed pacts on June 23, 1978, that pledged nonaggression and expanded trade with the Soviet Union. The U.S. Congress repealed its ban on arms sales to Turkey in September 1978. The Turkish government agreed in October to let the U.S. reopen four military bases.

Martial law was declared in 13 Turkish provinces on Dec. 26, 1978, after riots caused by Muslim fanatics resulted in the deaths of more than 100 persons and injuries to more than 1,000. The martial law was repeatedly extended.

Lacking petroleum resources of its own, Turkey was especially hard hit by soaring oil prices in the 1970s–80s. The country's economy reached a state of crisis in 1979 with inflation at a rate of 70% and an estimated 25% of its workers unemployed. In an effort to temporarily ease the crisis, the government obtained agreement from the International Monetary Fund in 1980 for loans of $1.16 billion.

The U.S. and Turkey signed a 5-year agreement on March 29, 1980, providing continued use by the U.S. of 12 military bases. In return, the U.S. promised $2.5 billion in economic and military aid to Turkey over the period of the agreement.

After his conservative party won all five seats at stake in parliamentary by-elections, Demirel became prime minister on Nov. 12, 1979.

Violence between terrorists of the left and right increased during the first 9 months of 1980 with some 2,000 persons killed.

Promising to end the violence, Gen. Kenan Evren, chief of the armed forces, led a bloodless coup on Sept. 12, 1980. Demirel, Ecevit, and other political leaders were arrested, but later were released after agreeing to take no part in political activities. Evren became chief of state as head of a military junta called the National Security Council. The junta appointed a retired admiral, Bulent Ulusu, as prime minister. In all, some 11,500 persons were arrested within six weeks after the junta seized power.

Gen. Evren assured the U.S. and other NATO allies of continued cooperation. He said democratic government would be restored once violence had been ended and a new constitution for a more stable government had been adopted.

Inflation reached an annual rate of 40% in October 1980.

# TUVALU

**Official Name:** Tuvalu.
**Area:** 10 square miles (26 sq. km.).
**Population:** 7,759.
**Capital:** Fongafale on Funafuti, 826.
**Government:** Parliamentary state.
**Prime Minister:** Toalipi Lauti (since 1978).
**Chief of State:** Queen Elizabeth II of Britain.
**Tuvalu Ambassador to U.S.:** Ionatana Ionatana.
**U.S. Ambassador to Tuvalu:** William Bodde Jr.
**Parliament:** 12 members.
**Flag:** British blue ensign with nine yellow stars representing the nation's islands.
**Languages:** Tuvaluan, English.
**Main Ethnic Group:** Tuvaluans of Polynesian descent.
**Principal Religion:** Christianity, largely Protestant.
**Leading Industries:** Agriculture (coconuts, pulaka or taro, pandanus fruit, bananas, pawpaws); fishing.
**Foreign Trade:** *major export*—copra from coconuts; *major imports*—food, fuel.
**Places of Interest:** villages; beaches.

One of the smallest of the world's nations, Tuvalu encompasses nine tropical islands in the South Pacific, about 600 miles north of Fiji. The group formerly was the Ellice Islands.

The Tuvaluans lead a simple existence, living in thatched huts on a diet of tropical fruits, vegetables, and fish. The only export is copra from coconuts, which provides money to import additional food, fuel, and manufactured goods. Islanders receive an elementary education.

The islands are scattered over an area of about half a million square miles of ocean. Stretching about 450 miles from northwest to southeast, the nine islands are: Nanumea, Nanumanga, Niutao, Nui, Vaitupu, Nukufetau, Funafuti, Nukulaelae, and Niulakita.

All the islands are coral atolls, rising no more than 15 feet above sea level. Only Funafuti and Nukufetau have sheltered lagoons that can accommodate ships for anchorage.

In prehistoric times, Polynesians from Samoa settled the islands.

The first European explorer to visit was the Spanish navigator Álvaro de Mendaña, who discovered Nui in 1568 and Niulakita in 1595.

In the mid-1800's "blackbirders" raided the islands, carrying off as slaves all but about 3,000 of an estimated population of 20,000.

In 1892 Britain established a protectorate over Tuvalu, then called the Ellice Islands, governing them from the Gilbert Islands, which lie to the northwest. Britain created the Gilbert and Ellice Islands colony in 1916. During World War II the islands were occupied by Japanese troops in 1942–43, until driven out by U.S. forces.

The islanders voted in 1974 to separate from the Gilberts, becoming the separate territory of Tuvalu on Jan. 1, 1976. Britain granted Tuvalu complete independence on Oct. 1, 1978.

# UGANDA

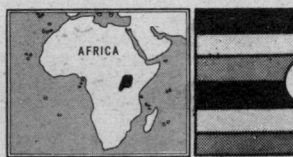

**Official Name:** Republic of Uganda.
**Area:** 91,134 square miles (236,036 sq. km.).
**Population:** 13,898,500.
**Capital:** Kampala, 330,700.
**Government:** Transitional.
**Ambassador to U.S.:** Joshua Luyimbaze Zake.
**U.S. Ambassador to Uganda:** Gordon R. Beyer.
**Flag:** Black, yellow, and red stripes, with crested crane on white circle in center.
**Languages:** English (official), Luganda, Swahili.
**Main Ethnic Group:** Black.
**Religions:** Christianity (50%), animism (35%), Islam (15%).
**Leading Industries:** Agriculture (coffee, cotton, tea, tobacco, peanuts, livestock, fruits, vegetables); manufacturing (food, copper smelting, textiles, cement, shoes, fertilizer); mining (copper, tin).
**Foreign Trade:** *major exports*—coffee, cotton, copper, tea; *major imports*—petroleum products, machinery, cotton fabrics, vehicles.
**Places of Interest:** Lake Victoria; "Mountains of the Moon" in the Ruwenzori Range; Queen Elizabeth and Kidepo Valley national parks; Kabalega Falls; wildlife preserves; Kampala.

## UGANDA TODAY

Somewhat smaller than Oregon, Uganda was a nation under military junta rule in 1980.

Dependent largely on agriculture, forestry, and fishing to support its economy, Uganda has few mineral resources other than copper and tin. Only about 1 out of 5 Ugandans can read and write.

Although the equator runs through the southern part of the country, the high altitude gives Uganda a moderate climate. The Ruwenzori Mountains are in the west with Mt. Margherita rising to 16,763 feet on the Zaire border. Lake Victoria is in the southeast.

Kenya lies to the east, Sudan to the north, Zaire to the west, and Tanzania and Rwanda to the south.

## EARLY HISTORY

Powerful kingdoms began to develop in the lakes area south of the Nile during the 1400s or early 1500s. Bunyoro was the most powerful of the southern kingdoms until the 1800s. Then a succession of able rulers made Buganda the leading kingdom. The first visitors were Arab and Swahili ivory and slave traders.

Britain and Germany agreed in 1890 that Britain should control the region. In 1894 Britain established a protectorate over Buganda that was later extended to the rest of Uganda.

## INDEPENDENCE

Uganda gained its independence on Oct. 9, 1962, remaining a member of the British Commonwealth of Nations. In 1963 King Mutesa of

QUICK QUIZ: Which musical was judged best in 1980 by the Tony Awards? See page 271.

**UGANDA** *(continued)*

Buganda became Uganda's first president with Milton Obote as prime minister.

In February 1966 Obote suspended the constitution, and the king fled to Britain. Obote then made himself president.

On Jan. 25, 1971, while Obote was abroad, Gen. Idi Amin seized power.

In 1972 Amin expelled about 60,000 British Asians, seizing their businesses and property.

The United States, Britain, Canada, and other countries cut off financial aid and technical assistance in 1973. The U.S. closed its embassy in Uganda in November 1973.

Israeli commandos attacked Uganda's Entebbe airport on July 3–4, 1976, freeing over 100 hostages held by Palestinian airplane hijackers.

Britain broke diplomatic relations with Uganda on July 28, 1976, the first such action against a British Commonwealth nation.

The human-rights organization Amnesty International reported that during Amin's first six years in office he had been responsible for killing as many as 300,000 persons.

Amin began a war with neighboring Tanzania in 1978, announcing on Nov. 1 that his troops had annexed 710 square miles of Tanzania.

Determined to destroy the Ugandan dictator, Tanzania resisted the invasion and then counterattacked, routing Amin's forces and capturing Uganda's capital, Kampala, on April 11, 1979. Amin escaped into exile, keeping his whereabouts unknown because of a huge reward offered for his capture. Fighting continued until July 1979 when the last of Amin's forces surrendered or fled into exile. The liberation army captured secret documents and uncovered mass graves that revealed horrors inflicted by the dictator.

About 10,000 of Tanzania's troops remained in Uganda to preserve order.

A provisional government approved by Tanzania was sworn in on April 13, 1979, with a former college teacher, Yusufu Kironde Lule, as president. A 30-man legislature called the National Consultative Council was formed by Amin's opponents who returned from exile. On June 20, 1979, the legislature ousted Lule as president, giving the office to Godfrey L. Binaisa, a former attorney general under President Milton Obote who had practiced law in the U.S. in 1977–79. The U.S. and Britain restored diplomatic relations with the new government.

Drought and armed cattle rustlers brought starvation in northeast Uganda in 1980, causing thousands of deaths despite UN relief efforts.

When President Binaisa tried to dismiss his army chief of staff, Brig. Gen. David Oyite Ojok, he was overthrown and arrested on May 12, 1980. A 6-man military junta, called the Military Commission of the National Liberation Front, took over the government with the consent of Tanzania. Although controlled by Ojok, the junta was headed by Paulo Muwanga, who had served as a cabinet minister under Binaisa.

The junta permitted former president Milton Obote to return to Uganda later in May 1980 to campaign for president as candidate of the Uganda People's Congress. He was opposed by Paul Semogerere of the Democratic Party. The election was set for Dec. 10, 1980 (see page 30).

# UNITED ARAB EMIRATES

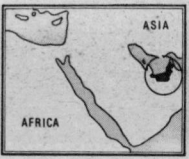 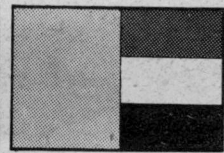

**Official Name:** United Arab Emirates.
**Area:** 32,278 square miles (83,600 sq. km.).
**Population:** 870,915.
**Largest Cities:** Abu Dhabi, capital, 85,000; Dubai, 60,000.
**Government:** Confederation of monarchies.
**President:** Sheik Zayid bin Sultan al Nuhayan, ruler of Abu Dhabi (since 1971).
**Prime Minister and Vice President:** Sheik Rashid bin Said al Maktum, ruler of Dubai (since 1979).
**Legislature:** *National Assembly,* 40 members.
**U.S. Ambassador to United Arab Emirates:** William D. Wolle.
**United Arab Emirates Ambassador to U.S.:** Hamad Abdel Rahman al Madfa.
**Flag:** Red bar at hoist; stripes of green, white, and black.
**Languages:** Arabic (official), Persian, English.
**Main Ethnic Group:** Arab (72%).
**Principal Religion:** Islam (96%).
**Leading Industries:** Mining (petroleum, natural gas); manufacturing (petroleum refining, gas liquefaction, aluminum, chemicals, fertilizer, cement, plastics); agriculture (dates, sheep, goats, tobacco, vegetables, fruits).
**Foreign Trade:** *major exports*—petroleum, natural gas; *major imports*—manufactured goods, machinery, vehicles, construction materials.
**Places of Interest:** Oil refineries; royal residences; national zoo at Al Ain; beaches.

## UNITED ARAB EMIRATES TODAY

About the size of the state of Maine, the country is mostly a desert with temperatures of 120 ° F. in the shade. Until oil began to be produced in 1962, the sheikdoms were very poor. But in the 1980s oil income soared over $15 billion a year.

The government receives 60% of all oil produced. Much of the income is spent for welfare projects, port improvements, water desalinization, oil refineries, and industrial plants. Free education, health care, and phone service are provided by the government. There are no income taxes.

The United Arab Emirates (UAE) is a confederation of seven Arab sheikdoms on the Persian Gulf. The sheikdoms are: Abu Dhabi, Dubai, Sharjah, Ajman, Ras al-Khaimah, Umm al-Qaiwain, and Fujairah.

Saudi Arabia and Qatar lie to the west. Oman is to the east.

## EARLY HISTORY

The coastal area was ruled by Portugal in the 1500s to 1600s and then by Iran. The Iranians were expelled in 1783 by an Arab tribe.

Known as the *Trucial States,* the Persian Gulf sheikdoms subsequently were called the Pirate Coast, a base of operation for over 800 Arab pirate ships as well as European marauders.

From 1806 onward, the Persian Gulf states gradually came under British protection. Piracy was brought to an end in 1853 when sheiks

signed the Perpetual Maritime Truce, which was arranged and supervised by Britain.

Between 1880 and 1916 the sheiks of the Persian Gulf states concluded protective treaties with Britain. Economic development began after oil was discovered in Abu Dhabi in 1958.

After Britain announced in 1967 that it would withdraw its military forces from the Persian Gulf area by the end of 1971, the sheikdoms set up a provisional government.

## INDEPENDENCE

On Dec. 2, 1971, six of the sheikdoms proclaimed themselves the independent United Arab Emirates with Sheik Zayid of Abu Dhabi as president. A seventh sheikdom joined the union on Feb. 1, 1972.

The country also has large natural-gas deposits, and in 1974–75 huge plants were built on Das Island to liquefy 3 million tons of gas a year for shipment to Japan.

In December 1976 Sheik Zayid was elected to a second 5-year term as president by the rulers of the other emirates. They also agreed to turn over to his control the military forces.

In the 1970s and 1980s the government spent huge sums to build industries to support the country when its oil reserves are exhausted. A port with berths for 66 large ships was built at Jebel Ali, an island of Dubai about 19 miles off the main coast. A $1.4 billion aluminum smelter and freshwater plant also was constructed on the island.

## UPPER VOLTA

**Official Name:** Republic of Upper Volta.
**Area:** 105,869 square miles (274,200 sq. km.).
**Population:** 6,989,850.
**Capital:** Ouagadougou, 200,000.
**Government:** Military junta.
**President:** Col. Saye Zerbo (since 1980).
**U.S. Ambassador to Upper Volta:** Thomas D. Boyatt.
**Ambassador to U.S.:** Telesphore Yaguibou.
**Flag:** Black, white, and red stripes.
**Official Language:** French.
**Main Ethnic Groups:** Mossi (67%), Bobo (15%).
**Principal Religion:** Animism.
**Leading Industries:** Agriculture (cattle, poultry, millet, sorghum, corn, cotton, peanuts, fruits, vegetables); fishing; forestry and lumbering; manufacturing (electricity, bicycles, food processing, textiles, soap); mining (manganese).
**Foreign Trade:** *major exports*—livestock, meat, peanuts, cotton; *major imports*—petroleum products, textiles, clothing, machinery.
**Places of Interest:** Spiked mosque at Bobo Dioulasso; Ouagadougou.

## UPPER VOLTA TODAY

About the size of Colorado, Upper Volta is a poor nation that depends on aid from wealthier countries. It is one of the few African countries with multiparty democratic elections.

Most of the people consider themselves lucky if they can get enough food to keep from starving. Only about 1 person in 10 can read and write. Most live by farming or herding cattle.

A landlocked country, Upper Volta covers a plateau 650 to 1,000 feet high. The main rivers are the Black, White, and Red Volta rivers.

Much of the fertile land in the valleys remains fallow because people fear the river-blindness disease carried by black flies along the rivers.

Mali lies to the northwest, Niger to the northeast, and Ivory Coast, Ghana, Togo, and Dahomey to the south.

## HISTORY OF UPPER VOLTA

By the 1300s the Mossi people of the area were raiding the wealthy trading cities on the Niger River and beyond. They organized the state of Ouagadougou, Yatenga, and Fada-n-Gurma. They later established the Dagomba state.

The French claimed the region in 1896. At first Upper Volta was included in the Ivory Coast colony. In 1919 it was detached. In 1933 the territory was divided among the Ivory Coast, Niger, and French Sudan colonies.

France granted independence to the Republic of Upper Volta on Aug. 5, 1960. Maurice Yaméogo, the only candidate for the presidency, was elected.

In January 1966, following antigovernment riots, Lt. Col. Aboubakar Sangoulé Lamizana seized power. President Yaméogo, who had been reelected several days earlier, was imprisoned.

Lamizana suspended the constitution and assumed all legislative and executive powers. New elections held in 1970 were won by the Democratic Union. Its leader, Gerard Kango Ouedraogo, was named premier in February 1971.

On Feb. 8, 1974, Lamizana, with the help of the army, threw out the elected government of Premier Ouedraogo and again took control.

Like other African nations bordering the Sahara Desert, Upper Volta suffered six years of drought in 1969–74 that destroyed cattle and crops, bringing widespread famine.

Lack of rain continued to plague Upper Volta in the late 1970s, causing reduced production of grains. As a result, emergency food aid continued to be supplied by other nations.

Lamizana restored multiparty democracy in 1978. In parliamentary elections on April 30, Ouedraogo's Democratic Union won a majority of 28 seats in the national assembly. In a presidential election in May Lamizana defeated Macaire Ouedraogo, a banker, by a margin of 56% to 44% for a 5-year term.

Pope John Paul II visited Upper Volta on May 10, 1980, as part of a 6-nation African tour. He appealed to the world for more aid to help the poor country.

Col. Saye Zerbo, a former foreign minister, led a coup that overthrew the government on Nov. 25, 1980. He headed a military junta called the Military Committee of Recovery for National Progress. The new government banned all political activity.

QUICK QUIZ: What was the name of the first constitution of the U.S.? See page 317.

# URUGUAY

**Official Name:** Oriental Republic of Uruguay.
**Area:** 68,536 square miles (177,508 sq. km.).
**Population:** 2,907,260.
**Capital:** Montevideo, 1,173,254.
**Government:** Military junta.
**President:** Aparicio Méndez (since 1976).
**U.S. Ambassador to Uruguay:** Robert S. Gershenson.
**Uruguayan Ambassador to U.S.:** Jorge Pacheco Areco.
**Flag:** Blue stripes on white field, with golden sun in upper hoist corner.
**Language:** Spanish.
**Ethnic Groups:** European descent (85%), mestizo (10%), mulatto and black (5%).
**Principal Religions:** Roman Catholicism (66%), Protestantism (2%), Judaism (2%).
**Leading Industries:** Agriculture (cattle, sheep, hogs, rice, wheat, corn, fruits, vegetables); manufacturing (food processing, electricity, leather products, glass, ceramics, furniture, clothing); forestry and lumbering; tourism; fishing; construction.
**Foreign Trade:** *major exports*—meat, wool, leather, fish, rice, shoes, glass, ceramics, cement; *major imports*—petroleum, machinery, motor vehicles and aircraft, chemicals, iron and steel.
**Places of Interest:** Santa Teresa National Park; beach resorts; Pan de Azúcar (Sugar Loaf peak); Castle of Piria; Lobos Island. *In Montevideo:* Plaza Independencia; town hall (*cabildo*); legislative palace.

## URUGUAY TODAY

About the size of Missouri, Uruguay is a small South American country with few natural resources. Uruguay's economy depends primarily upon tourism, banking, and livestock raising.

Because Uruguay is poor in natural mineral resources, it has lagged in the development of manufacturing. The government owns and operates basic industries.

Austerity in government spending and reduced taxes on imports have stimulated the economy, while holding inflation to a lower rate than in neighboring countries.

With a highly educated population, Uruguay for many years was considered the most outstanding example of political democracy in South America. However, a stagnating economy, inflation, government spending, and a leftist guerrilla movement caused the military in 1973 to force the nation to abandon democracy and civil rights.

Brazil lies to the northeast and Argentina to the west.

## EARLY HISTORY OF URUGUAY

Spaniards explored the Río de la Plata as early as 1515, but permanent settlement did not occur until 1624. Uruguay's native Charrúa Indians, who strenuously resisted Spanish occupation, were killed off or absorbed by the 1830s. Portuguese from Brazil fortified the present site of Montevideo in 1717, but the Spaniards later drove them off, and Uruguay became part of the Spanish vice-royalty centered in Argentina.

Montevideo was permanently settled in 1726.

A war of independence, led by José Gervasio Artigas, began in 1810. Portuguese forces captured Montevideo in 1820, and for five years Uruguay was part of Brazil.

## INDEPENDENCE

In 1825 the "Thirty-three Immortals," led by Juan Antonio Lavalleja, declared Uruguay's independence. On Aug. 25, 1828, Uruguay was established as an independent buffer state between Brazil and Argentina. A constitution was adopted in 1830. Fructuoso Rivera became president.

The following decades were marked by internal strife, disputes with Brazil and Argentina, and violent changes of government.

José Batlle y Ordóñez, a liberal, served two terms as president (1903–07, 1911–15). He launched social, economic, and political reforms.

From 1952 to 1966 Uruguay was governed by a council. In November 1966 the people elected as president Oscar Daniel Gestido of the liberal Colorado Party.

President Gestido died in 1967 and was succeeded by Vice President Jorge Pacheco Areco.

Strikes and unrest brought periods of limited martial law in 1968 and 1969. Terrorist activities included abductions of foreign diplomats by leftist urban guerrillas called *Tupamaros*.

## URUGUAY IN THE 1970s

In 1971 conservative Juan M. Bordaberry was elected president after a 79-day recount.

The army, air force, and navy rebelled in February 1973, demanding an important voice in running the country. In June 1973 Bordaberry ended 40 years of democratic government in Uruguay by dissolving the legislature and elected municipal councils. Many opposition political leaders fled to asylum in Argentina. The government used troops and tanks to break a general protest strike by labor unions, imprisoned union leaders, and imposed censorship on the press. All political activities were banned. The last of the *Tupamaros* terrorists were eliminated by 1974.

Military leaders ousted Bordaberry on June 12, 1976. He was temporarily replaced as president by Vice President Alberto Demicheli, 79.

A 45-member council in July 1976 elected 72-year-old Aparicio Méndez, a conservative lawyer, to a 5-year term as president.

When President Méndez took office on Sept. 1, 1976, he immediately banned the political rights of all Uruguayans who had held office in the past 10 years. Only officeholders in the existing government were exempted.

The U.S. Congress on Sept. 15, 1976, cut off military aid to Uruguay because of accusations that the Uruguayan government was using torture and other violations of human rights in a crackdown on leftist subversives.

In March 1977 the government said it would reject all U.S. aid because of American criticism.

The government announced plans for a gradual return to democracy. A referendum was scheduled for 1980 to approve a new constitution drafted by the military. A presidential election was set for Nov. 29, 1981, with a single candidate to be agreed upon by the country's political parties.

# VANUATU

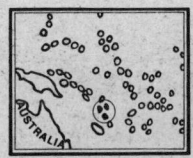

**Official Name:** Republic of Vanuatu.
**Area:** 5,700 square miles (14,763 sq. km.).
**Population:** 107,315.
**Capital:** Vila, Efate, 3,072.
**Government:** Democratic parliamentary republic.
**President:** George Sokomanu (since 1980).
**Prime Minister:** Rev. Walter Lini (since 1980).
**Representative Assembly:** 42 members.
**Flag:** Emblem of crossed mele leaves surrounded by yellow hog tusk on black triangle at hoist; red upper panel and green lower panel separated by thin black and yellow stripes.
**Languages:** English and French (official), Bislama (New Hebrides pidgin), Melanesian languages.
**Chief Ethnic Group:** Melanesian (92%).
**Main Religions:** Christianity, animism.
**Leading Industries:** Agriculture (coconuts, cocoa, coffee, cattle, taros, yams); fishing; food processing; mining (manganese); tourism; handicrafts.
**Foreign Trade:** *major exports*—copra, fish, manganese, meat; *major imports*—food, petroleum, machinery; consumer goods.
**Places of Interest:** Swimming beaches; tropical rain forests; villages; volcanoes.

## VANUATU TODAY

The first nation to win independence in the 1980s, Vanuatu had been jointly ruled by Britain and France for 74 years as the condominium of New Hebrides.

A group of more than 70 islands and islets in the southwest Pacific Ocean, Vanuatu has an area nearly as large as Hawaii. The main islands are Espiritu Santo, Malekula, Efate, Erromango, Tanna, Ambrym, Pentecost, Maevo, Aoba, and Aneityum. The island chain stretches about 500 miles from the Torres Islands in the north to Aneityum in the south.

Vanuatu lies about 1,000 miles northeast of Australia, 600 miles west of Fiji, and 250 miles northeast of New Caledonia.

The larger islands are covered by thick rain forests. Active volcanoes stand on several islands, including Ambrym and Tanna. The highest peak, Tabwemasana, on Espiritu Santo Island, is 6,160 feet high.

Most Vanuatuans are dark-skinned Melanesians, whose ancestors were cannibals less than a century ago. Most make their living from agriculture or fishing. Only about 1 person in 10 can read and write.

Because the value of imports are three times that of exports, Vanuatu depends heavily on economic aid from Britain and France.

Tourism is a growing industry. Some 40,000 cruise-ship passengers visit each year. Several hotels are located at Vila on Efate Island and at Luganville on Espiritu Santo. Commercial airlines provide two flights a week to and from Australia.

The climate is generally hot, humid, and rainy. Annual rainfall averages 91 inches.

## EARLY HISTORY

The Portuguese explorer Pedro Fernándes de Queirós discovered the islands in 1606, naming the main one Australia del Espiritu Santo. British explorer Capt. James Cook gave the islands the name New Hebrides in 1774.

During the early 1800s French and British missionaries, planters, and traders settled in the islands. The native Melanesians suffered depredations by "blackbirder" ships that shanghaied them to work as laborers on plantations in Fiji.

To protect the lives and property of French and British settlers, Britain and France agreed in 1887 to place the islands under the administration of a joint naval commission.

## ANGLO-FRENCH CONDOMINIUM

The government of the New Hebrides was established as an Anglo-French condominium by the London Convention of Oct. 20, 1906. This agreement was replaced by the Anglo-French Protocol of Aug. 6, 1914, which was ratified in 1922.

The islands were placed under joint administration of British and French commissioners.

During World War II the U.S. constructed a huge air and naval base at Esperitu Santo that was used as a staging facility for the invasions of Japanese-held Guadalcanal, Tarawa, and other islands in the south Pacific. The U.S. built 17 airstrips and many miles of roads on the islands.

From 1957 to 1975 an appointed advisory council, including the French and British resident commissioners, controlled local government.

The advisory council was replaced in 1976 with a 42-member representative assembly, including 29 elected members.

The first general election, in November 1975, was won by the Vanu aku Party (VAP), which captured 21 seats. However, disagreements among the political parties, which represent French, British, and local interests, delayed formation of a unified government until Dec. 22, 1978.

Parliamentary elections in November 1979 were won by the VAP, whose leader, Rev. Walter Lini, an Anglican priest, became chief minister.

## INDEPENDENCE

France and Britain granted Vanuatu independence as a republic on July 30, 1980, with Lini as the sovereign nation's first prime minister. George Sokomanu, who had served as Lini's deputy chief minister, was chosen as Vanuatu's first president by vote of a special electoral college.

One of the first acts of the new government was to ask a force of 200 British and French troops to temporarily remain in occupation of the island of Espiritu Santo, where rebels armed with bows and arrows threatened to secede from Vanuatu as the separate nation of Vemarana.

The French and British troops were replaced in mid-August by 150 soldiers loaned by Papua New Guinea. On Aug. 31, 1980, they captured the rebel leader, Jimmy Stevens, and about 70 of his followers, breaking the back of the rebellion.

QUICK QUIZ: When did the U.S. annex Hawaii? See page 883.

## VATICAN CITY

## VENDA

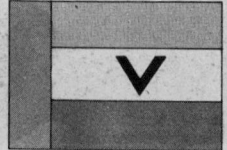

**Official Name:** State of the Vatican City.
**Area:** 0.17 sq. mi. (109 acres) (0.44 sq. km.).
**Population:** 1,309.
**Government:** Ecclesiastical state.
**Pope:** John Paul II (since 1978).
**Flag:** Yellow and white bars; crossed keys of St. Peter under papal tiara on white bar.
**Languages:** Latin (official), Italian.
**Official Religion:** Roman Catholicism (100%).
**Places of Interest:** St. Peter's Basilica; Vatican museums, including the Sistine Chapel.

### VATICAN CITY TODAY

The world's smallest sovereign nation, Vatican City lies entirely within the Italian city of Rome. It occupies a small triangle on the west bank of the Tiber River. Vatican City also has jurisdiction over several churches and palaces in Rome and nearby Castel Gandolfo.

The government is an absolute monarchy with all powers vested in the pope of the Roman Catholic Church. He in turn delegates most of these powers, including diplomatic relations with other nations, to a secretary of state that he appoints. The government is often called merely the *Vatican.* The pope's court is known as the *Holy See.*

The government's security force consists of 75 Swiss guards. The official radio station is Radio Vatican. The official newspaper is *l'Osservatore Romano.* The state has its own postal and telephone systems.

The nation's citizens are largely the several hundred employees who reside in Vatican City and can buy tax-free food and goods.

Through the pope, the Vatican affects the lives of more than half a billion Roman Catholics throughout the world. In addition, the state has large real estate holdings in many countries.

### HISTORY

For many centuries after the fall of the Roman Empire, popes ruled Rome and central Italy, which were called the *Papal States.* With the unification of Italy in 1861, most of the Papal States except Rome were added to the new kingdom of Italy. In 1870 the Italian king took Rome from the pope, annexing it to Italy and making it his capital. Then, for more than half a century, Pope Pius IX and his successors refused to acknowledge Italy's sovereignty and regarded themselves as prisoners in Vatican City.

Treaties called the Lateran Accords signed on Feb. 11, 1929, by Italy and the Vatican established the independence and sovereignty of Vatican City. The accords were brought up to date with revisions in 1976–77, ending Roman Catholicism's status as the official religion of Italy and reducing the pope's authority over education and marriage in Italy.

See also the list of popes on page 709.

**Official Name:** Republic of Venda.
**Area:** 2,467 square miles (6,390 sq. km.).
**Population:** 336,078.
**Capital:** Thohoyandou.
**Government:** Parliamentary republic.
**Prime Minister:** Chief Patrick Mphephu (since 1973).
**Flag:** Blue stripe at hoist; green, yellow and brown horizontal stripes; brown Von yellow stripe.
**Parliament:** Legislative Assembly, 84 members (42 elected and 42 tribal chiefs).
**Chief Languages:** Venda (official), English, Afrikaans.
**Principal Ethnic Group:** Venda-speaking Bantus.
**Main Religions:** Christianity, animism.
**Leading Industries:** Agriculture (cattle, sheep, corn); personal services; forestry; mining (graphite).
**Foreign Trade:** *main exports*—agricultural products; *main imports*—petroleum products, consumer goods, vehicles, machinery.

One of the black homelands established by South Africa as part of its apartheid policy of separation of the races, Venda is a small country about the size of Delaware.

Granted independence by South Africa, Venda has been unable to gain recognition for its sovereignty from other nations.

Most of the people live on the food they raise, seldom seeing any money except what they receive from relatives working in South Africa.

The country is divided into two parts, both surrounded by South Africa. Although Venda lies close to the southern border of Zimbabwe, a South African defense zone separates Venda from Zimbabwe. South Africa's Kruger Game Park lies between Venda and Mozambique to the east.

The Venda people, a division of the Bantus, are believed to have come to their present homeland from Zimbabwe. Stone structures made by the Venda resemble ancient ruins in Zimbabwe.

Chief Patrick Mphephu became chief minister of Venda when it was granted internal self-government in 1973. In elections that year his Venda National Party won only 5 of the 18 elective seats in the legislative assembly, but he was made chief minister by the vote of tribal chiefs who were automatically assembly members.

In a new election in 1978, Mphephu retained power, again with the vote of the nonelected chiefs, even though his party won only 11 of the 42 elective seats in the new legislature.

When the Venda Independence Party of Baldwin Mudau challenged his leadership in 1978, Mphephu ordered the arrest of about 50 of its members. The Independence Party had won 31 of the elective seats in the legislature.

South Africa granted Venda independence on Sept. 13, 1979, while continuing to provide about $35 million annual aid to support its economy. The UN Security Council denounced Venda's independence as a "totally invalid" effort "to perpetuate" South African apartheid.

# VENEZUELA

**Official Name:** Republic of Venezuela.
**Area:** 352,145 square miles (912,050 sq. km.).
**Population:** 15,267,700.
**Chief Cities:** Caracas, capital, 1,662,627; Maracaibo, 792,000; Valencia, 439,000; Barquisimeto, 430,000; Maracay, 301,000; Barcelona–Puerto La Cruz, 242,000; San Cristóbal, 241,000; Ciudad Guayana, 180,000.
**Largest Metropolitan Area:** Caracas, 2,576,000.
**Government:** Republic.
**President:** Luis Herrera Campins (since 1979).
**Congress:** *Senate,* 49 members; *Chamber of Deputies,* 200 members.
**U.S. Ambassador to Venezuela:** William H. Luers.
**Venezuelan Ambassador to U.S.:** Marcial Perez Chiriboga.
**Flag:** Yellow, blue, and red stripes, with seven white stars in semicircle in center; national coat of arms in upper hoist corner.
**Official Language:** Spanish.
**Ethnic Groups:** Mestizo (70%), mulatto (13%), European descent (10%), black (5%), Indian (2%).
**Religions:** Roman Catholicism (96%), Protestantism (2%), Judaism (0.1%).
**Leading Industries:** Manufacturing (steel, motor vehicles, ships, oil refining, chemicals, food processing, textiles, cement); mining (petroleum, iron, diamonds, manganese); services; agriculture (livestock, coffee, cocoa, corn, rice, sugar, tobacco, cotton, fruits, vegetables); tourism; forestry and lumbering.
**Foreign Trade:** *major exports*—petroleum and petroleum products, iron ore, coffee, cocoa; *major imports*—machinery, steel, automobiles, wheat.
**Places of Interest:** Angel Falls; Mt. Avila; Margarita Island; Lake Maracaibo; Bavarian village of Colonía Tovar; beach resorts; home of Simón Bolívar in Caracas; Spanish colonial buildings in Merida.

## VENEZUELA TODAY

Larger than California, Oregon, and Washington combined, Venezuela is the most prosperous country in South America.

Venezuela is a leading oil-exporting nation. It also is one of the world's 10 most important producers of iron ore. Oil and iron ore account for about 98% of the value of the country's annual exports, although these industries employ only about 2% of Venezuela's workers. A fifth of the people are farmers.

Caracas, the capital, resembles Los Angeles or Miami with many skyscrapers and freeways.

The government's vigorous support of education has nearly wiped out illiteracy.

Venezuela has a 1,750-mile coastline on the Caribbean Sea. Its beaches and resorts attract many tourists. Colombia lies to the west, Brazil to the south, and Guyana to the east.

## EARLY HISTORY

Columbus discovered the Orinoco River in 1498.

German adventurers followed, but organization of the country was undertaken by Spain. Caracas was founded in 1567.

In 1811 Francisco de Miranda led a revolt against Spanish leaders. Independence was declared on July 5, 1811. Simón Bolívar completed the struggle for independence in 1821. Bolívar's dream of a Greater Colombia to include Venezuela was realized briefly, but after his death in 1830 Venezuela became independent. Dictator followed dictator in succeeding decades.

A revolution in 1945 brought to power a liberal democratic government headed by Rómulo Betancourt. In 1947 Rómulo Gallegos won a free presidential election but was ousted by a military coup in 1948. Gen. Carlos Delgado Chalbaud became president but was assassinated in 1950. Marcos Pérez Jiménez became president and dictator in 1953.

## DECADES OF DEMOCRACY

After the overthrow of Pérez Jiménez in 1958, Rómulo Betancourt of the Democratic Action Party was elected president. During his administration a new constitution was adopted limiting the presidency to one 5-year term. Betancourt began a land-reform program that redistributed millions of acres of land to more than 100,000 small farmers.

After Venezuela broke relations with Cuba in 1961, Cuban-supported communist guerrillas tried to overthrow Betancourt.

Raúl Leoni of Betancourt's Democratic Action Party was elected president in 1963.

Rafael Caldera of the Christian Social Party won the 1968 presidential election. At his inauguration in March 1969 a milestone was achieved as Leoni became the first president in Venezuelan history to peacefully turn over the government to an opposition party. Caldera instituted a policy of "pacification" with the leftists, legalizing the Communist Party and granting amnesty to the terrorists of the 1960s.

Carlos Andrés Pérez of the Democratic Action Party won the presidential election of December 1973. His party also received a majority in both houses of congress.

On Jan. 1, 1975, the government nationalized U.S.-owned iron mines, and on Jan. 1, 1976, nationalized the petroleum industry, paying the foreign owners with government bonds.

Work began in 1977 on a new $1.5 billion subway system for Caracas. It is scheduled for completion in 1983.

Luis Herrera Campins became president on March 12, 1979. As candidate of the Social Christian Party, he had won an upset victory in a national election on Dec. 3, 1978, that ousted the governing Democratic Action Party from office. President Herrera criticized the outgoing regime for having run up a national debt of more than $11 billion despite Venezuela's huge income from petroleum exports.

To stimulate production, the government ended price controls on most goods in August 1979.

Cuts in government spending brought a minor recession in 1980 as the nation's growth rate slowed.

QUICK QUIZ: How many U.S. servicemen were killed in action in World War I? See page 466.

# VIETNAM

**Official Name:** Socialist Republic of Vietnam.
**Area:** 128,402 square miles (332,561 sq. km.).
**Population:** 52,817,900.
**Chief Cities:** Hanoi, capital, 414,620; Ho Chi Minh City (Saigon), 1,825,297; Danang, 492,194; Nhatrang, 216,227; Quinhon, 213,757; Hué, 209,043; Haiphong, 182,490.
**Government:** One-party communist state.
**Government Leaders:** Le Duan, secretary-general of the Communist Party (since 1960); prime minister, Pham Van Dong (since 1955).
**Legislature:** *National Assembly,* 492 members.
**Flag:** Gold star centered on red field.
**Languages:** Vietnamese (official), French, Chinese.
**Main Ethnic Groups:** Kinh (87%), Chinese (6%).
**Principal Religions:** Buddhism (70%), Roman Catholicism (10%).
**Leading Industries:** Agriculture (rice, poultry, rubber, tea, livestock, coffee, tobacco, sugarcane, corn, manioc, fruits, vegetables); manufacturing (food processing, textiles, cement, fertilizer, consumer products); fishing; forestry and lumbering; mining (coal, phosphates, iron, bauxite, gold, petroleum, chrome, zinc, tungsten).
**Foreign Trade:** *major exports*—coal, rubber; *major imports*—food, petroleum, machinery, vehicles.
**Places of Interest:** Hanoi, government buildings; Ho Chi Minh City (Saigon), gardens, zoos, museums.

## VIETNAM TODAY

Although somewhat smaller than Montana, Vietnam has the third-largest population of any communist nation after China and the Soviet Union. The country was united by the communists in 1976.

Wars from the 1940s to 1970s devastated many of Vietnam's cities, towns, and villages, leaving behind countless political, social, health, and economic problems to be solved. About half of Vietnamese adults cannot read and write. In the area of health, diseases that have been eliminated in more developed countries kill from one-third to one-half of Vietnamese babies before they reach the age of six.

The nation's economy depends largely on agriculture. Most Vietnamese earn their living as rice farmers. However, Vietnam has the potential for substantial industrial development with ample mineral resources that include coal and iron ore.

Vietnam is a long, narrow country that extends for about 1,000 miles from north to south. Northern Vietnam is hilly and mountainous while southern Vietnam is the low, flat delta of the Mekong River. Tropical forests cover much of the country.

Vietnam has a year-round warm and wet tropical climate. Mountain regions are cool from about October to March. Heavy rains fall from May to September.

China lies to the north. Laos and Cambodia are to the west. The Gulf of Tonkin and the South China Sea are to the east.

## EARLY HISTORY

Vietnamese legend attributes the founding of the nation more than 4,000 years ago to King Hung.

China's Han dynasty conquered Vietnam in 111 B.C. For more than 1,000 years China ruled northern Vietnam. A revolt by the Vietnamese threw off Chinese rule in A.D. 939.

Meanwhile, in southern Vietnam a kingdom called Champa had been founded by an Indonesian people. Champa carried on trade with India for many centuries and was influenced by Hindu art and religion.

Vietnam's emperor Le Thanh-Ton conquered Champa in 1471, unifying the region. But by the early 1600s Vietnam again had become divided with the kingdoms of Tonkin in the north and Cochin China in the south.

European traders began visiting the region in the 1500s.

## FRENCH CONTROL

In the late 1700s French military officers helped Prince Nguyen Anh of Cochin China win control of the entire country. In 1802 he established himself as Emperor Gia-Long with his capital at Hué. His descendants continued to rule for the next century and a half.

By the mid-1800s French missionaries had converted about 2 million Vietnamese to Roman Catholicism. Fearing the foreign influence of the Christians, the government began a campaign of persecution, killing many of them.

France's Emperor Napoleon III demanded in 1858 that Vietnamese Emperor Tu-Duc stop the persecution of Christians. Then France, in 1859, began its conquest of the country, first capturing Saigon with the aid of Spain.

France made southern Vietnam (Cochin China) a colony in 1867. After much fighting, France established a protectorate over all of Vietnam on June 6, 1884.

By 1893 France also had won control of Cambodia and Laos. It then incorporated these countries with Vietnam into the Indochinese Union, headed by a French governor-general. Vietnam was divided into three parts: Tonkin in the north, Annam in the center, and Cochin China in the south.

During the next half century Indochina became France's most prosperous colony. Hanoi became the capital of French Indochina.

In the 1930s Vietnamese aspirations for independence were spurred by the Indochinese Communist Party founded by Ho Chi Minh, who had been educated in France.

After the defeat of France by Germany in World War II, the Vichy French colonial administration gave Japan complete control of Indochina. Ho Chi Minh organized Vietnamese patriots into the Vietminh movement, which carried out guerrilla attacks on the Japanese.

## INDOCHINA WAR

When Japan surrendered to the U.S. in World War II in August 1945, the Vietminh seized control of Hanoi and forced Emperor Bao Dai to abdicate. Ho Chi Minh declared Vietnam an independent republic on Sept. 2, 1945.

France tried to reassert its control of Vietnam, establishing a separate regime in Cochin

China (southern Vietnam) in June 1946. Fighting soon began between the French troops and the Vietminh. The Indochina War dragged on for eight years, ending with French defeat in 1954 and a peace settlement at Geneva.

The nation was divided at the 17th parallel into North Vietnam (capital at Hanoi) and South Vietnam (capital at Saigon). The settlement provided that elections should be held in 1956 to vote on reuniting the country. However, the U.S. and South Vietnam refused to sign the Geneva agreement and repudiated a unification referendum. The U.S. signed a defense treaty with South Vietnam in 1954.

## VIETNAM WAR

In South Vietnam, Emperor Bao Dai was ousted in October 1955 by his prime minister, Ngo Dinh Diem, who declared the nation a republic with himself as its first president. Communists began guerrilla warfare against South Vietnam.

The U.S. sent constantly increasing supplies and military advisers to South Vietnam.

In the belief Diem was incapable of winning the war, the U.S. government encouraged a coup in 1963 in which Diem was assassinated.

After attacks by North Vietnamese patrol craft on U.S. destroyers in the Gulf of Tonkin in 1964, the U.S. Congress gave President Lyndon Johnson authority to use any means to prevent further aggression by North Vietnam.

U.S. troops began combat operations in Vietnam in 1965. Within four years more than 500,000 U.S. servicemen were fighting against North Vietnamese troops and guerrillas.

Meanwhile, Nguyen Van Thieu had been elected president of South Vietnam in 1967.

Ho Chi Minh, the leader of North Vietnam, died in September 1969. He was succeeded as president by Ton Duc Thang, who died in 1980.

Antiwar sentiment in the U.S. caused President Richard Nixon to begin withdrawing U.S. forces from Vietnam in 1969. A cease-fire agreement became effective on Jan. 28, 1973. All U.S. forces left by March 29, 1973. Over 56,000 Americans had died in the war.

North Vietnam launched a new offensive in March 1975. South Vietnam's defenses quickly collapsed. The war ended on April 30, 1975, with South Vietnam's unconditional surrender.

## REUNIFIED COMMUNIST VIETNAM

The communists quickly moved to reunify Vietnam. Hanoi became the capital for the entire country. Saigon was renamed Ho Chi Minh City.

On July 2, 1976, the national assembly approved reunification and elected North Vietnam leaders as heads of the new state.

American and Vietnamese diplomats met in Paris on Nov. 12, 1976, for the first talks since the end of the Vietnam War. The meetings, which continued intermittently into 1977, sought to settle problem issues and lead to the establishment of regular diplomatic relations.

Letters made public in 1977 showed that President Nixon secretly had promised North Vietnam

## HIGHLIGHTS OF THE INDOCHINA AND VIETNAM WARS: 1945-1975

**1945 (Sept. 2) Independence** of Democratic Republic of Vietnam proclaimed by communist Ho Chi Minh.

**1946 (March 6) France recognizes** Ho's government, granting internal self-rule to Vietnam.

**1946 (June 1) After disputes with Ho,** France declares southern Vietnam independent, calling it Cochin China.

**1946 (Dec. 19) War begins with surprise attack** by troops of Ho Chi Minh launched on French military bases.

**1954 (May 7) French army surrenders fortress** of Dien Bien Phu after 55-day siege by North Vietnamese.

**1954 (July 21) Truce signed,** ending 8-year Indochina War; nation divided into North and South Vietnam.

**1954 (Aug. 11) Peace agreement signed** in Geneva, Switzerland, providing referendum in 1956 to decide government of unified Vietnam. United States and South Vietnam refuse to sign agreement.

**1954 (Sept. 8) Southeast Asia Collective Defense Treaty** signed by U.S. and seven other nations pledging joint action to protect South Vietnam and other nations in area.

**1964 (Aug. 2–4) U.S. destroyers** in Gulf of Tonkin attacked by North Vietnamese torpedo boat.

**1964 (Aug. 5) Retaliatory bombing of North Vietnam** by U.S. planes ordered by President Johnson.

**1964 (Aug. 7) Congress votes Gulf of Tonkin Resolution,** giving President authority "to prevent further aggression."

**1965 (June 28) First U.S. combat operations** on ground authorized by President Johnson.

**1968 (Jan. 30) Tet offensive,** biggest communist attack of war begun, directed at Saigon.

**1968 (March 16) My Lai massacre** of 100 to 400 Vietnamese civilians by U.S. troops led by Lt. William L. Calley Jr.

**1968 (May 13) Peace talks begin** in Paris between U.S. and North Vietnam as war rages.

**1969 (March) U.S. troops fighting in Vietnam** reach peak level of 541,500.

**1969 (June 8) President Nixon** announces U.S. will

**1969 (Nov. 15) About 300,000 antiwar demonstrators** march on Washington.

**1970 (April 30–June 30) U.S. troops enter Cambodia** to destroy North Vietnamese supply bases.

**1972 (April 2) North Vietnamese troops** invade South Vietnam in major new offensive.

**1972 (May 8) Mining of North Vietnam's ports** and bombing of supply routes to China ordered by Nixon.

**1972 (August) Last U.S. combat troops leave** Vietnam.

**1972 (Oct. 26) Peace Negotiator Henry Kissinger** reports U.S. and North Vietnam are in substantial agreement on 9-point plan; expresses belief "peace is at hand."

**1972 (Dec. 13) U.S. suspends Kissinger-Tho talks,** claiming North Vietnamese have changed their position on previously agreed-upon points.

**1972 (Dec. 18) President Nixon** orders heaviest bombing of war on North Vietnam; 28 U.S. planes lost in 13 days.

**1973 (Jan. 27) Truce agreements** formally signed in Paris by U.S., North Vietnam, South Vietnam, and Vietcong.

**1973 (Jan. 28) Cease-fire begins** in Vietnam at 8 A.M.

**1973 (March 29) Last U.S. military personnel** leave.

**1973 (April 1) Last of 590 U.S. prisoners** of war released.

**1975 (March 10) North Vietnamese troops begin offensive** on provincial capital of Ban Me Thuot.

**1975 (March 16) South Vietnam orders withdrawal of troops** from northern and central provinces; withdrawal quickly turns into headlong retreat.

**1975 (April 21) South Vietnam's President Nguyen Van Thieu** resigns and flees to safety in Taiwan a few days later.

**1975 (April 29) U.S. ambassador and 1,000 Americans** evacuate Saigon by helicopter as communist troops attack city's outskirts.

**1975 (April 30) Unconditional surrender of South Vietnam** announced by President Duong Van Minh.

QUICK QUIZ: Did the U.S. birthrate increase or decrease in 1978? See page 449.

**VIETNAM** *(continued)*

$4.75 billion in postwar aid when the communists agreed to a Vietnam War cease-fire in 1973.

The U.S. Congress passed legislation in July 1977 forbidding the expenditure of funds for aid to Vietnam.

In September 1977 Vietnam was admitted to membership in the United Nations after the U.S. withdrew its objections.

Relations worsened between the U.S. and Vietnam in February 1978 when the U.S. government expelled Vietnam's UN representative Dinh Ba Thi for participation in espionage in the U.S. with an American and a Vietnamese refugee.

The Vietnamese government announced in March 1978 that it was banning all private business and confiscating the property of capitalists.

Because many of the merchants whose property and fortunes were confiscated were of Chinese descent, China accused Vietnam of persecution and reduced its financial aid to Vietnam. Some 160,000 Chinese were reported to have been forced to flee to China in 1978.

The government announced in May 1978 that it had resettled some 1.3 million persons from cities into previously uninhabited forest areas. In all, the government's plan calls for more than 10 million persons to be moved to sparsely settled regions during a 20-year period.

Vietnam signed an alliance with the Soviet Union on Nov. 3, 1978, which the Chinese denounced as directed against them.

Soviet-equipped Vietnamese troops launched an offensive on Dec. 25, 1978, against the Chinese-supported regime of Pol Pot in Cambodia. In a lightning drive the Vietnamese army captured the Cambodian capital Phnom Penh on Jan. 7, 1979, and set up a new government allied with Vietnam. However, Pol Pot's forces took to the jungles and fought a guerrilla war in 1979–80 against the 200,000 Vietnamese troops in Cambodia. Vietnamese troops invaded Thailand in June 1980, claiming the Thais were aiding Pol Pot's troops, but withdrew after a day's fighting.

Vowing that Vietnam needed to be "punished," China invaded northern Vietnam on Feb. 17, 1979, with about 200,000 troops. In a hard-fought four-week war, the Chinese destroyed Vietnamese cities and towns within about 40 miles of the Chinese border. After withdrawing its troops on March 15, China announced that it had inflicted about 50,000 casualties on the Vietnamese while claiming Chinese forces suffered 20,000.

In 1978–79 hundreds of thousands of refugees left Vietnam, becoming known as "boat people" because of the leaky boats in which they escaped. Evidence mounted that Vietnam was extorting millions of dollars from the refugees to allow them to leave. After protests by neighboring countries about the burden of caring for them, an international conference of 65 nations was called in Geneva, Switzerland, in July 1979. At the conference, the Vietnamese government promised to try to stem the flow of refugees. However, an estimated 4,000 refugees per month continued to escape from Vietnam in 1980.

Because of poor harvests, Vietnam was forced to import an estimated 2 million tons of rice in 1980.

# WESTERN SAMOA

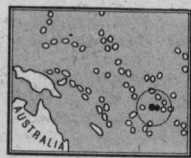

**Official Name:** Western Samoa.
**Area:** 1,097 square miles (2,842 sq. km.).
**Population:** 156,326.
**Capital:** Apia, 32,616.
**Government:** Parliamentary democracy.
**Chief of State:** Malietoa Tanumafili II (since 1963).
**Prime Minister:** Tupuola Efi (since 1976).
**Legislature:** *Legislative Assembly,* 47 members.
**U.S. Ambassador to Western Samoa:** Anne Clark Martindell.
**Samoan Ambassador to U.S.:** Iulia Toma.
**Flag:** Red field with blue rectangle in upper hoist corner; five white stars represent Southern Cross.
**Official Languages:** Samoan and English.
**Main Ethnic Group:** Samoan (89%).
**Religions:** Congregationalism (50%), Methodism (20%), Roman Catholicism (20%).
**Leading Industries:** Agriculture (bananas, coconuts, cocoa, poultry, fruits, vegetables); fishing; forestry and lumbering; manufacturing (food processing, handicrafts); tourism.
**Foreign Trade:** *major exports*—copra, cocoa, bananas; *major imports*—food, manufactured goods.
**Places of Interest:** Home of Robert Louis Stevenson; Mt. Vaea on Upolu Island.

About the size of Rhode Island, Western Samoa has an economy that depends mostly on agriculture and fishing.

The nation's major exports are bananas, copra, and cocoa. Tourism also brings cash.

The Samoans live in tribal villages, following social customs that have survived for many centuries. There are no political parties. Most Samoans are Christians.

Situated in the Pacific Ocean, halfway between Honolulu and Sydney, Western Samoa has two principal islands (Savai'i and Upolu) and seven small islands.

Average annual rainfall is about 113 inches, mostly from October to March.

The first Europeans to sight the islands were the Dutch in 1772.

English missionaries arrived in 1830, in the midst of a long struggle among the native chiefs that ended in 1889 when Samoa was declared neutral and independent. Malietoa Laupepa was recognized as king.

In 1900 Eastern Samoa was annexed by the U.S. and Western Samoa by Germany.

From 1919 to 1962 New Zealand administered Western Samoa.

The country was granted independence by New Zealand on Jan. 1, 1962. Malietoa Tanumafili II became chief of state in 1963. Western Samoa became a member of the British Commonwealth of Nations in 1970 and the UN in 1976.

A modern airport and a highway were completed in the mid-1970s.

Government development plans call for improvements in electric power and communications facilities as well as diversification of industry.

# YEMEN, NORTH

**Official Name:** Yemen Arab Republic.
**Area:** 75,290 square miles (195,000 sq. km.).
**Population:** 5,979,470.
**Chief Cities:** Sana, capital, 134,588; Taiz, 40,000; Hodeida, 40,000.
**Government:** Military-controlled republic.
**President:** Lt. Col. Ali Abdullah Saleh (since 1978).
**Prime Minister:** Abd al-Aziz Abd al-Ghani (since 1978).
**Constituent People's Assembly:** 99 members.
**U.S. Ambassador to Yemen:** George M. Lane.
**Yemen Ambassador to U.S.:** Yahya M. al-Mutawakel.
**Flag:** Red, white, and black stripes, green star.
**Language:** Arabic.
**Main Ethnic Group:** Arab.
**Official Religion:** Islam.
**Leading Industries:** Agriculture (wheat, sorghum, coffee, cattle, sheep, qat, cotton, fruits); manufacturing (handicrafts, textiles, cement, cigarettes, nails, shoes).
**Foreign Trade:** *major exports*—qat, coffee, cotton; *major imports*—food, machinery, vehicles.
**Places of Interest:** Dhafar antiquities; Throne of Belgis and ruins of Marib Dam at Marib; Al-Janad Mosque; Salah Palace in Taiz.

North Yemen is about the size of South Dakota. Its government, which fosters private enterprise, remains in a state of cold war with its Marxist neighbor South Yemen.

The country has a cooler climate, more rain, and greater possibilities for agriculture development than other areas of the Arabian peninsula.

In North Yemen's interior, mountains rise to a height of more than 12,000 feet. Hills and mountainsides have been terraced by the farmers.

Most of the people are poor. Only 1 in 10 can read and write. Over a million Yemeni men work in Saudi Arabia, sending home about $2 billion to their families each year

Saudi Arabia lies to the north, South Yemen to the south, and the Red Sea to the west.

North Yemen contained the biblical kingdom of Sheba. The area was ruled by the Himyarites from 115 B.C. to A.D. 525. Yemenis claim to have built the first skyscraper 2,000 years ago, the 20-story Palace of Ghamdan at Sana.

About 885 the Zaidi founded the Rassid dynasty of imams (rulers). Two successive periods of Egyptian control began in the 1200s. In 1517 the Turks occupied the region. After Turkey's defeat in World War I, Yemen was ruled by the Hamid al-Din dynasty of imams.

In 1962 Imam Ahmed's death and the succession of his son Muhammad Badr were followed by a republican revolution led by Col. Abdullah al-Sallal and supported by Egyptian troops. The Yemen Arab Republic was established on Sept. 26, 1962. Republican control soon was established in the coastal Tihama area, while royalist Imani forces held the highlands.

Egypt, the Soviet Union, and communist China supported the republicans in the ensuing civil war, while Saudi Arabia backed the royalists.

Republican forces broke a siege of Sana by royalist troops in 1968. The 8-year civil war came to an end in 1970 with agreement to include royalist leaders in future cabinets.

Col. Ibrahim al-Hamdi, deputy commander of the army, overthrew the government in a bloodless coup on June 13, 1974. A 5-man military command council took control.

President Hamdi and his brother Lt. Col. Abdullah al-Hamdi were assassinated on Oct. 11, 1977. Lt. Col. Ahmed Hussein al-Ghashmi, Hamdi's second in command, took control of the military government.

President Ghashmi was assassinated on June 24, 1978, by a bomb carried by a South Yemen envoy, who also was killed. He was succeeded by 36-year-old Lt. Col. Ali Abdullah Saleh.

Nine high-ranking army officers were reported killed in another unsuccessful coup on Oct. 15, 1978. Twenty-one persons, including a former cabinet minister, were executed for the plot.

Soviet-supplied South Yemen troops invaded North Yemen on Feb. 23, 1979. Reacting to this attempted communist expansion in the Middle East, the U.S. announced on March 9 it was rushing $390 million in arms to North Yemen to aid its army. On March 16 the two nations agreed to a truce, and South Yemen withdrew its troops.

# YEMEN, SOUTH

**Official Name:** People's Democratic Republic of Yemen.
**Area:** 128,560 square miles (332,968 sq. km.).
**Population:** 2,000,510.
**Capital:** Aden, 271,590.
**Government:** One-party Marxist state.
**Chief of State and Prime Minister:** Ali Nasser Mohammed (since 1980).
**People's Supreme Assembly:** 111 members.
**Flag:** Red, white, and black stripes with light blue triangle containing red star at hoist.
**Languages:** Arabic (official), English.
**Main Ethnic Group:** Arab (90%).
**Religion:** Islam.
**Leading Industries:** Agriculture (cotton, livestock, coffee, sorghum, sesame, millet, tobacco, fruits); oil refining; manufacturing (soap, cigarettes, handicrafts); fishing; mining (salt).
**Foreign Trade:** *major exports*—petroleum products, cotton, cottonseed, salt, hides and skins, coffee; *major imports*—food, building materials, automobiles, machinery, manufactured goods, crude oil.
**Places of Interest:** Ancient ruined cities; Socotra Island; biblical valley of Hadhramant at Shibam.

## SOUTH YEMEN TODAY

South Yemen is the only Arab Marxist nation. About the size of Nevada, it is a desert country at

## YEMEN, SOUTH *(continued)*

the southern end of the Arabian peninsula. The main industry is the refining of petroleum at the port city and capital of Aden.

Most of the people are poor farmers or nomadic livestock herders. Only about 1 person in 10 can read and write. With few natural resources, the country depends on foreign aid largely from communist nations.

South Yemen has a hot dry climate. Summer temperatures soar above 130°F.

Extending the length of the Arabian Sea coast is a low, rugged plain. The interior contains a series of increasingly higher ridges that merge into a rugged highland plateau fragmented by a series of deep, dry valleys (wadis).

### EARLY HISTORY

South Yemen was included in the Minaean, Sabaean, and Himyarite kingdoms of Arabia that flourished from about 1200 to 50 B.C.

The spread of Judaism and Christianity to southern Yemen in the 500s A.D. brought about religious rivalry. Abyssinian and Persian occupation followed.

By 885 the highland areas of southern Yemen belonged to the Islamic rulers of Yemen. The coastal area recognized the Baghdad caliphate, and was later ruled by Egyptians and Turks.

The British captured Aden in 1839, making it part of the British Empire for more than a century. Aden increased in importance after the opening of the Suez Canal in 1869.

In 1962 Aden joined the British-sponsored Federation of South Arabia to protect itself from Yemeni republicans who had deposed the imam. A United Nations investigation in 1963 indicated that most southern Yemenis wanted union with Yemen and British withdrawal.

### INDEPENDENCE

In September 1967, as British troops withdrew from all parts of the country except Aden, the National Liberation Front (NLF) took charge. In November fierce street battles broke out in Aden, and Britain decided to withdraw its military forces.

South Yemen became independent on Nov. 30, 1967. The moderate government of President Qahtan al-Shaabi resigned on June 22, 1969, and was replaced by a Marxist regime.

South Yemen broke diplomatic relations with the United States on Oct. 24, 1969.

On June 26, 1978, President Salim Rubayya Ali of South Yemen was overthrown and executed by his Marxist colleagues. Ali Nasser Mohammed, who had been prime minister since 1972, succeeded to the presidency.

Six months later, on Dec. 28, 1978, Abd al-Fattah Ismail, secretary-general of the Marxist National Front, took over the presidency.

An invasion of North Yemen in a 3-week war from Feb. 23 to March 16, 1979, ended with a truce negotiated by other Arab countries.

South Yemen signed a 20-year friendship pact with the Soviet Union in October 1979.

On April 21, 1980, Prime Minister Mohammed overthrew Ismail, taking over as chief of state. Seeking better international relations, he went to Saudi Arabia in June 1980 for the first official visit since South Yemen's independence.

## YUGOSLAVIA

**Official Name:** Socialist Federal Republic of Yugoslavia.
**Area:** 98,766 square miles (255,804 sq. km.).
**Population:** 22,411,700.
**Chief Cities:** Beograd (Belgrade), capital, 746,105; Zagreb, 566,224; Skoplje, 312,980; Sarajevo, 243,980; Ljubljana, 173,853.
**Largest Metropolitan Area:** Belgrade, 774,744.
**Government:** One-party communist republic.
**President:** Chosen annually from among 8-member presidency committee.
**Prime Minister:** Veselin Djuranovic (since 1977).
**Legislature:** *Assembly—Federal Council,* 220 delegates; *Council of the Republics and Provinces,* 58 delegates.
**U.S. Ambassador to Yugoslavia:** Lawrence S. Eagleburger.
**Yugoslavian Ambassador to U.S.:** Budomir Loncar.
**Flag:** Red star outlined in gold, centered on stripes of blue, white, and red.
**Languages:** Serbo-Croatian, Slovenian, Macedonian, Hungarian, Albanian.
**Main Ethnic Groups:** Serb (40%), Croat (22%), Slovene and Bosnian (8%), Macedonian (6%), Albanian (6%), Montenegrin and Hungarian (2%), Turk (1%).
**Principal Religions:** Eastern Orthodox (41%), Roman Catholicism (32%), Islam (12%).
**Leading Industries:** Agriculture (wheat, potatoes, corn, barley, tobacco, sugar beets, fruits, vegetables, livestock); manufacturing (steel, cement, chemicals, food processing, fertilizer, textiles); mining (bauxite, lignite, zinc, lead, petroleum, natural gas, iron, coal, copper, gold); forestry and lumbering; tourism.
**Foreign Trade:** *major exports*—timber, nonferrous metals, livestock and meat, machinery, metal products; *major imports*—machinery, metal products, chemicals, textiles, petroleum.
**Places of Interest:** Mountain and coastal resorts; Roman, Byzantine, Serbian, and Turkish antiquities at Skoplje; Plitvice lakes; Postoina caves; Dubrovnik; Split; Opatija; Ljubljana; Zagreb. *In Belgrade:* national museum; Museum of Modern Art; Kalemegdan citadel (now a museum).

### YUGOSLAVIA TODAY

About the size of Wyoming, Yugoslavia is a communist nation in southeastern Europe. It is among the world's leading producers of bauxite, lead, and lignite.

The country's main problem in international relations has been to maintain independence from the Soviet Union and play a leading role among the nonaligned nations of the world.

About two-thirds of the people speak the Serbo-Croatian language. This majority is divided into two ethnic groups, the Serbs and Croatians, who have feuded with each other for hundreds of years. The remaining third of the population includes large minority groups of Slovenes, Macedonians, Albanians, Bosnian Muslims, Montenegrins, Hungarians, and Turks.

In an effort to give these various ethnic groups local self-government, Yugoslavia is divided into

six republics and two autonomous provinces within Serbia (Kosovo and Vojvodina).

Croatian nationalists, many living in exile, continue to work for independence of a Croatian state, sometimes carrying out bombings and airplane hijackings to call attention to their cause.

Although Yugoslavia has made progress toward industrialization through use of its wealth of natural resources, almost three-fourths of the people still live on farms and in villages. However, Yugoslavs enjoy more consumer goods then most other communist nations of Europe.

The nation's official name is the *Socialist Federal Republic of Yugoslavia.*

The Danube River and its tributaries drain Yugoslavia's fertile lowland area in the north and northeast. Yugoslavia's coastline along the Adriatic Sea is about 1,000 miles long. About two-thirds of the country is covered by mountain ranges that run northwest to southeast a few miles inland from the Adriatic coast. The climate is similar to that of the U.S. east coast.

Yugoslavia is bounded on the north by Italy, Austria, and Hungary; on the east by Romania and Bulgaria; and on the south by Greece and Albania.

## EARLY HISTORY

The various parts of Yugoslavia had never been united under one government before 1918:

*Serbia* was under Turkish domination from 1371 to 1878. After the Balkan Wars of 1912–13, Serbia became independent and acquired Macedonia, an ancient kingdom that had been under Turkish control.

*Montenegro,* under Turkish rule for centuries, became independent in 1878.

*Slovenia,* passing to Austrian Hapsburg rule in 1335, was under their domination until 1918.

*Croatia* was part of Hungary from the 1000s to 1500s, under the Turks until the 1800s, and later regained by Hungary.

*Bosnia and Herzegovina* became Turkish possessions in the 1500s and were annexed by Austria in 1908.

The 1914 assassination by Serbian nationalists in Sarajevo, Bosnia, of Austria's Archduke Franz Ferdinand led to World War I. The collapse of the Austro-Hungarian and Turkish empires opened the way for unification of the Balkan Slavs.

King Peter I of Serbia became the ruler of the new Kingdom of the Serbs, Croats, and Slovenes in 1918, but his son Alexander ruled as regent until Peter's death in 1921.

King Alexander declared himself absolute ruler in 1929 and changed the kingdom's name to Yugoslavia. In 1934 Alexander was assassinated. His heir, Peter II, succeeded under the regency of Prince Paul.

Yugoslavia attempted to remain neutral in World War II, but Germany invaded the country on April 6, 1941, and defeated its army in two weeks. King Peter II fled to London.

Several resistance movements emerged. The most important were the royalist Chetniks, led by a Serb general, Draja Mikhailovich, and the pro-Soviet partisans led by the Croat communist Josip Broz Tito. Both guerrilla armies fought

## REPUBLICS OF YUGOSLAVIA

| REPUBLIC | CAPITAL | AREA |
|---|---|---|
| Bosnia and Herzegovina | Sarajevo | 19,741 sq. mi. |
| Croatia | Zagreb | 21,829 sq. mi. |
| Macedonia | Skoplje | 9,928 sq. mi. |
| Montenegro | Titograd | 5,333 sq. mi. |
| Serbia | Belgrade | 34,116 sq. mi. |
| Slovenia | Ljubljana | 7,819 sq. mi. |

against the Germans and each other.

By 1944 Britain and the U.S. switched support to Tito, who also received military aid from the Soviet Union.

## COMMUNIST RULE

A leftist coalition headed by Tito declared a republic on Nov. 29, 1945. Tito became president. Mikhailovich was captured, tried as a war criminal, and executed on July 17, 1946.

Although the Communist Party ruled the country, it resisted Soviet efforts to penetrate and control Yugoslavia. Matters came to a head in January 1948 when the recently created Communist Information Bureau (Cominform), dominated by Moscow, expelled Yugoslavia, charging it with "revisionism." This break forced Tito to draw closer to the West.

After the death of Stalin in 1953, however, diplomatic and trade relations with the Soviet Union were resumed. A dramatic visit to Yugoslavia by Soviet leader Nikita Khrushchev in 1955 restored cooperative relations.

A meeting between President Tito and Chancellor Willy Brandt of West Germany in 1973 worked out differences between the two nations regarding reparations Yugoslavia claimed for damages during World War II.

Yugoslavia signed a joint-venture agreement with the U.S. in 1973, providing tax benefits for American investors.

In 1974 Yugoslavia proclaimed its fourth constitution under communist rule. The new government structure provides for a bicameral national assembly similar to the U.S. Congress.

To combat low productivity, the government for the first time in 1975 gave the managers of communist businesses the right to fire workers who fail to meet production goals.

In January 1976 the U.S. resumed selling arms to Yugoslavia. American military aid had been suspended since 1961.

At a meeting between Soviet leader Leonid Brezhnev and Tito in Yugoslavia in November 1976, the Yugoslav president turned down Soviet requests for closer military cooperation.

After a protracted illness, Tito died on May 4, 1980, three days short of his 88th birthday.

Upon Tito's death, under terms of the country's 1974 constitution, the executive powers of the federal government were transferred to an 8-member presidency committee that will annually choose one to hold the title of president.

After being criticized for not attending Tito's funeral, U.S. President Jimmy Carter made amends by visiting Yugoslavia's new leaders on June 24, 1980, urging them to continue to pursue an independent course in international affairs.

QUICK QUIZ: How large are Yugoslavia's armed forces? See page 465.

# ZAIRE

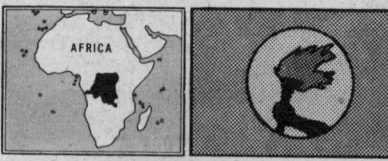

**Official Name:** Republic of Zaire.
**Area:** 905,568 square miles (2,345,409 sq. km.).
**Population:** 30,393,800.
**Chief Cities:** Kinshasa, capital, 2,008,352; Kananga, 601,239; Luluabourg, 506,033; Lubumbashi, 403,623; Mbuji-Mayi, 336,654; Kisangani, 310,705.
**Government:** One-party dictatorship.
**President:** Mobutu Sese Seko (seized power in 1965).
**Prime Minister:** Nguza Karl-i-Bond (since 1980).
**Legislature:** *National Assembly,* 420 members.
**U.S. Ambassador to Zaire:** Robert B. Oakley.
**Zaire's Ambassador to U.S.:** Kasongo Mutuale.
**Flag:** Green field with yellow circle in center showing arm carrying torch.
**Languages:** French (official), tribal dialects.
**Main Ethnic Group:** Bantu (80%).
**Religions:** Animism (50%), Christianity (50%).
**Leading Industries:** Agriculture (coffee, cocoa, tea, rubber, palm kernels, cotton, sugarcane, livestock, fruits, vegetables); mining (copper, petroleum, zinc, tin, cobalt, diamonds, gold); forestry and lumbering; manufacturing (food processing, textiles, clothing, cement, consumer goods).
**Foreign Trade:** *major exports*—copper, diamonds, coffee, tin, palm oil; *major imports*—motor vehicles, cotton fabrics, petroleum products.
**Places of Interest:** Boyoma Falls, Point Kalina, Cristal Mountains—all on Zaire River. *In Kinshasa:* Botanical and zoological gardens; Museum of Native Life; St. Anne's Cathedral; Pioneers and Stanley monuments.

## ZAIRE TODAY

About one-fourth the size of the United States, Zaire is rich in natural resources. But the country has suffered an economic recession and high inflation since 1975, caused by a sharp drop in government revenues that resulted from low copper prices and by disruption from two invasions of rebel exiles from Angola.

Zaire is the world's largest producer of cobalt and industrial diamonds and the sixth most important copper-mining country. It ranks eighth in tin-ore mining and ninth in natural rubber. Offshore oil wells began production in 1975. In addition its rivers provide potential for hydroelectric power. Hopeful of becoming the leading industrial nation of Africa; the government has sought loans and investments from both communist and noncommunist nations.

As with most other African countries, a problem equal to the lack of capital is the scarcity of educated skilled workers. Most of the people belong to the more than 200 Bantu tribes that live in the tropical forests or on the upland plains. Few can read and write. The tribesmen support themselves with primitive subsistence farming that has changed little in hundreds of years.

The third-largest nation in Africa, Zaire derives its name from the Zaire (Congo) River, whose course lies within the country's borders. Except for a narrow corridor on the northern bank of the Zaire River, the country is landlocked.

Much of the central Zaire River basin area, comprising nearly half the country, is densely forested. The land in the higher regions to the north and south is savanna or bush country. Southeast of the central plateau the elevation gradually rises to 6,000 feet, and to the east mountain ranges reach a height of 16,763 feet at the crest of Margherita Peak.

In the lower western and central regions the climate is tropically hot and humid. The climate in the higher eastern elevations is more temperate. South of the equator rains are heavy and frequent from fall to late spring. North of the equator the season of heaviest rainfall is from April to November.

Congo lies to the west; Central Africa and Sudan to the north; Uganda, Rwanda, Burundi, and Tanzania to the east; and Zambia and Angola to the south.

## EARLY HISTORY

Pygmies or Bushmen probably first occupied the Zaire basin. They were later displaced by migrants (mostly Bantu), who settled the area in the 600s and 700s and established kingdoms. The kingdom of Kongo (Congo) gave its name to the river and to the French and Belgian colonial territories carved from the basin.

Henry Stanley of Britain explored the Congo River in 1877. His reports sparked the interest of King Leopold II of Belgium, who in 1878 formed a company to exploit the region.

The Congress of Berlin in 1885 recognized Leopold's claims, and he became absolute monarch of the Congo Free State.

International protests over reported abuse of the Congolese population forced Leopold to cede his private state to Belgium. It became the colony of Belgian Congo in 1908.

## INDEPENDENCE

Belgium granted the country independence on June 30, 1960. Parliament chose Joseph Kasavubu as president and Patrice Lumumba as premier. Almost immediately the country was swept by disorders. Belgian troops intervened to protect Belgian nationals. The gravest challenge was the secession of the richest province, Katanga, led by Moïse Tshombe.

When rivalry between Kasavubu and Lumumba crippled the government, Col. Joseph-Désiré Mobutu (now Mobutu Sese Seko), head of the army, supported Kasavubu. Lumumba was jailed but escaped, and then was murdered.

In January 1963 the central government, with UN military aid, took over Katanga province.

Tshombe was invited in 1964 to return from exile and become premier. Fighting intensified in Katanga.

In October 1965 Kasavubu replaced Tshombe as premier with Evariste Kimba.

Mobutu, now a general, proclaimed himself president and assumed total power on Nov. 24, 1965. Kimba and other opponents were hanged. Mobutu changed European geographical names in Zaire to African names. He changed his own name to Mobutu Sese Seko.

In 1967 white mercenaries formerly used by Tshombe staged an unsuccessful revolt in the

eastern province. Meanwhile, Tshombe, suspected of planning to return from exile, was kidnapped by Algerians and died in 1969.

In 1973–74 Zaire confiscated stores and plantations owned by foreigners, and in January 1975 nationalized all industries, building trades, and distribution services.

On March 8, 1977, Katangan rebels invaded Zaire's eastern province of Shaba from Angola. They were defeated in May after Morocco sent 1,500 troops to aid Zaire.

In May 1978 Katangan rebels again invaded Zaire from Angola. Capturing the copper-mining town of Kolwezi, they massacred about 200 whites. French and Belgian paratroops drove out the invaders. Zaire and Angola agreed in July 1978 to end their border differences.

The U.S. released $26 million in aid to Zaire in August 1978. The funds had been frozen until President Mobutu agreed to undertake political and economic reforms.

With inflation running at an annual rate of about 100% and the production of copper and cobalt at a low level because of the havoc caused by the rebel invasions, Zaire faced an economic crisis in 1979–80, unable to meet the payments on its foreign debt of about $6 billion. In an effort to prevent economic collapse, the International Monetary Fund agreed to advance a loan of $150 million.

The human rights organization Amnesty International issued a report on May 20, 1980, accusing Mobutu's regime of executing and starving to death hundreds of political prisoners in jungle detention camps.

## ZAMBIA

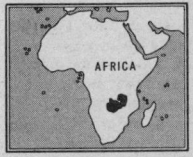
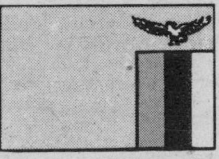

**Official Name:** Republic of Zambia.
**Area:** 290,586 square miles (752,614 sq. km.).
**Population:** 5,922,010.
**Chief Cities:** Lusaka, capital, 559,000; Kitwe, 310,000; Ndola, 291,000; Chingola, 173,000.
**Government:** One-party republic.
**President:** Kenneth D. Kaunda (took office in 1964).
**Prime Minister:** Daniel Lisulo (since 1978).
**Legislature:** *National Assembly,* 136 members.
**U.S. Ambassador to Zambia:** Frank George Wisner II.
**Zambian Ambassador to U.S.:** Putteho Muketoi Ngonda.
**Flag:** Green field with red, black, and orange bars on right surmounted by eagle.
**Languages:** English (official), tribal languages, including Bemba, Tnga, Nyanja.
**Main Ethnic Group:** Black (99%).
**Religions:** Animism (70%), Christianity (30%).
**Leading Industries:** Agriculture (corn, tobacco, peanuts, cotton, livestock, fruits, vegetables); mining (copper, cobalt, zinc, lead, coal); manufacturing (textiles, food processing, tobacco products).
**Foreign Trade:** *major exports*—copper, lead, zinc, cobalt; *major imports*—machinery, vehicles.

**Places of Interest:** Victoria Falls; Lake Tanganyika; Zambezi River; Luangwa Valley and Kafue national parks; Lusaka; Maramba Cultural Center and national museum in Livingstone.

## ZAMBIA TODAY

Somewhat larger than Texas, Zambia has an abundance of natural resources. It is one of the world's largest producers of copper. It is also an important source of cobalt, zinc, and lead.

The Zambian government obtained a majority interest in previously foreign-owned mining industries in 1970, agreeing to compensate the owners out of future earnings. Since then, the government has financed large-scale agricultural and industrial development projects.

Although Zambia's per capita national income is three to four times that of most of Africa's black nations, most Zambians still are poor farmers who barely raise enough food to live. Only about half the people can read and write.

Most of the country is a plateau of flat, wooded grassland broken by scrub-covered hills and by valleys of the Zambezi and Luangwa rivers.

Landlocked Zambia is surrounded by Zaire, Tanzania, Malawi, Mozambique, Zimbabwe (Rhodesia), Botswana, Namibia, and Angola.

## HISTORY

In the 1400s Bantu tribesmen moved into the area from the north.

In the early 1800s Nguni-speaking Africans and Swahili-speaking slave traders arrived.

Explorer David Livingstone first saw Victoria Falls in 1855. British developer Cecil Rhodes in 1888 obtained mineral rights. The region became known as *Northern Rhodesia.* The British South African Company, developing the copper resources, governed the territory.

In 1924 Northern Rhodesia became a British protectorate. In 1953 Britain founded the Federation of Rhodesia and Nyasaland, transferring control to white-ruled Southern Rhodesia (now Zimbabwe). The federation was dissolved in 1963. Northern Rhodesia then proceeded toward independence under African majority rule.

Zambia, as the new republic was named, became independent within the British Commonwealth of Nations on Oct. 24, 1964. Kenneth Kaunda was elected as Zambia's first president.

A new constitution adopted in 1973 made Kaunda's United National Independence Party (UNIP) the nation's only political party.

On July 1, 1975, President Kaunda decreed the nationalization of privately owned land, movie theaters, private hospitals, and newspapers.

Completion of the 1,162-mile TanZam Railway in 1976, linking Zambia's copper mines with the Tanzanian port of Dar es Salaam, promised increased economic growth.

Faced with a worsening economy, Zambia lifted its trade embargo on neighboring Zimbabwe on Oct. 6, 1978, in order to use its rail lines for trade with Mozambique and South Africa.

Running as the only candidate, Kaunda was easily reelected to another 5-year term as president in a national election on Dec. 12, 1978.

QUICK QUIZ: Which country leads the world in producing newsprint paper? See page 264.

## ZIMBABWE

**Official Name:** Republic of Zimbabwe.
**Area:** 150,804 square miles (390,580 sq. km.).
**Population:** 7,518,200.
**Chief Cities:** Harare (Salisbury), capital, 568,000; Bulawayo, 340,000.
**Government:** Parliamentary democracy.
**Prime Minister:** Robert Mugabe (since 1980).
**President:** Rev. Canaan Banana (since 1980).
**U.S. Ambassador to Zimbabwe:** Robert V. Keeley.
**Zimbabwe Ambassador to U.S.:** Elleck K. Mashingaidze.
**Parliament:** *House of Assembly,* 100 members (80 black, 20 white); *Senate,* 40 members.
**Flag:** Zimbabwe bird on red star in white triangle at hoist; stripes, top to bottom, of green, gold, red, black, red, gold, and green.
**Languages:** English (official), Shona, Ndebele.
**Main Ethnic Groups:** Blacks (96%), European descent (4%).
**Religions:** Animism, Anglicanism, Presbyterianism, Roman Catholicism.
**Leading Industries:** Agriculture (corn, tobacco, sugarcane, cotton, wheat, tea, millet, sorghum, livestock, vegetables, fruits); mining (coal, chrome, asbestos, gold, copper); manufacturing (electricity, clothing, chemicals, steel, vehicles, petroleum products).
**Foreign Trade:** *major exports*—tobacco, asbestos, copper, clothing, meat; *major imports*—textiles, fertilizers, automobiles, petroleum, tobacco.
**Places of Interest:** Victoria Falls; Wankie National Park; Inyanga and Vumba mountains; Mana pools; Harare (Salisbury); Bulawayo; Zimbabwe ruins.

## ZIMBABWE TODAY

Formerly called Rhodesia, Zimbabwe won international recognition as an independent nation in 1980. After 15 years in which a white minority resisted world pressure and guerrilla warfare to retain control, a peaceful transition to black majority rule was achieved.

The new black government pledged itself to protect the rights of whites, who have enjoyed a standard of living comparable to that of Americans. At the same time it sought massive international aid to improve the lot of blacks, most of whom live as tribal subsistence farmers. Fewer than 1 black in 3 can read and write.

One of the leading gold-mining countries, Zimbabwe lies between the Limpopo and Zambezi rivers. Mt. Inyangani, on the eastern border, rises to 8,514 feet. Zambia is on the north, Mozambique on the east, South Africa on the south, and Botswana on the west.

## EARLY HISTORY

The name Zimbabwe comes from the stone ruins of a city built by a black civilization in the 1000s to 1400s.

In the 1890s the British South Africa Company of Cecil Rhodes acquired the area.

In 1923 the British government took over the region, calling the colony Southern Rhodesia.

Britain refused independence to Southern Rhodesia in 1964 unless representative government was assured for the black majority.

In the 1965 elections the Rhodesia Front, representing white nationalism, won an overwhelming victory, retaining in office Ian Smith, who had been prime minister since 1964.

## INDEPENDENCE

On Nov. 11, 1965, Southern Rhodesia declared independence from Britain.

Britain and other nations refused to grant diplomatic recognition because the all-white government restricted the rights of blacks. The United Nations in 1966 called for a trade embargo on Rhodesia. The U.S. joined in the trade boycott.

All ties between Britain and Rhodesia were severed on March 2, 1970, when the government proclaimed itself the *Republic of Rhodesia.*

Black guerrillas based in neighboring black-ruled countries fought against government troops and civilians from 1965 to 1979.

On March 3, 1978, the Rhodesian government signed an agreement with leaders of the United African National Council (UANC) providing for a transitional government leading to black majority rule. On March 21 the head of the UANC, American-educated Methodist Bishop Abel Muzorewa, and two other black leaders were sworn in to an executive council to share leadership with Prime Minister Smith.

In a national election on April 17–21, 1979, some 1.7 million blacks voted for the first time, giving 51 seats in the new parliament to Muzorewa's UANC party. On May 29, 1979, Muzorewa became the nation's first black prime minister. Parliament also elected a black, Josiah Gumede, as president. However, Muzorewa was unable to convince the U.S. or Britain that his new government was fully representative.

Under the leadership of Lord Carrington, Britain's foreign minister, Muzorewa and guerrilla leaders signed a peace agreement on Dec. 21, 1979, after a conference in London that had begun on Sept. 10. A cease-fire went into effect on Dec. 28, 1979, supervised by a Commonwealth peace-keeping force.

In an election on Feb. 27–29, the Zanu-Patriotic Front party of former guerrilla leader Robert Mugabe won control of parliament with 57 of the 80 seats reserved for blacks.

Britain formally recognized independence for the Republic of Zimbabwe on April 18, 1980, with Mugabe as prime minister. Parliament elected a Methodist minister, Rev. Canaan Banana, to the largely ceremonial post of president of Zimbabwe.

Mugabe, formerly known as a Marxist socialist, pledged to seek economic revitalization of the nation through private enterprise rather than government nationalization of industries. Britain, the U.S., and other industrial nations agreed to provide millions of dollars in aid. Despite Mugabe's assurances of protection, whites continued to leave the country in 1980 at the rate of about 1,200 a month.

To display opposition to South Africa's apartheid policy, Zimbabwe broke diplomatic relations on Sept. 3, 1980. But because of economic dependence on South Africa, trade relations remained unchanged.

# Newspapers and Magazines

CBS news commentator Walter Cronkite, 63, *right*, with Dan Rather, 48, who will succeed Cronkite as anchorman for the *CBS Evening News* in 1981. Cronkite asked CBS to relieve him of the daily grind of live news broadcasting. Considered the dean of news analysts by many Americans, Cronkite plans to work on special assignments and a new science TV series. Rather has been one of the principal editors and anchormen of the award-winning *60 Minutes* TV newsmagazine.

United Press Int'l.

## HIGHLIGHTS: 1980

### NEWSPAPERS SHOW GAINS

Daily newspaper circulation in the United States rose to 62,223,040 in 1979, a gain of more than 200,000 over 1978. There were 1,763 daily newspapers at the end of 1979, an increase of seven.

Other figures compiled by the *Editor & Publishers International Yearbook* showed a total of 382 morning newspapers with a circulation of 28,574,879.

Sunday newspapers also continued to show gains in 1979. A record circulation of 54,379,923 was reported for the 720 Sunday editions.

### ELECTRONIC NEWSPAPERS

The inauguration of electronic newspapers, which transmit editorial content to private homes via personal computer systems, was begun in Columbus, Ohio, and Coral Gables, Fla., in July 1980.

The *Columbus Dispatch* began transmitting its entire editorial content, through a computer system called CompuServe, to 3,000 home terminals. Subscribers pay $5 per hour to call up an index of the day's stories and select any article for viewing. The viewer also has access to Associated Press articles. Plans were under way for 13 other newspapers to be added to the CompuServe system by the summer of 1981. These include the *New York Times, Chicago Sun-Times, St. Louis Post-Dispatch,* and *San Francisco Chronicle.*

In Coral Gables, Knight-Ridder Newspapers, Inc., began a test of its Viewdata system in 200 homes. The families receive news, advertising, and consumer services free of charge, on computers provided by the corporation. Thirty-one advertisers are participating in the Coral Gables experiment. Viewers can order products advertised by typing messages into their computer terminals, indicating which credit card should be used for billing, and when the products should be delivered.

In both experiments, telephone lines are used to link the home viewers to a central computer. Similar forms of these two-way communications systems are in use in Eu-

**HIGHLIGHTS: 1980** *(continued)*
rope, Japan, and Canada.

## HARPER'S MAGAZINE SAVED FROM EXTINCTION

*Harper's,* the nation's oldest monthly magazine, announced in June that the August
1980 issue would be its last. The 130-year-old
literary and political monthly was facing losses of a reported $1.5 million per year.

Just as the last issue came off the presses,
two foundations announced they would purchase the magazine and operate it as a nonprofit enterprise.

The John D. and Catherine T. MacArthur
Foundation purchased the assets and assumed the liabilities of the magazine from the
Minneapolis Star and Tribune Company for
an undisclosed amount. The asking price had
been $250,000. The Atlantic Richfield Foun-
dation agreed to help pay the operating costs.
Together, the two foundations committed $3
million toward future operations.

Over its 130-year history, the prestigious
journal has published work by almost every
famous short-story writer, including Mark

Chicago news vendor John Haupt looks over a copy of
an early edition of the July 17 *Chicago Sun-Times* that
declared Gerald Ford the GOP vice-presidential candidate. Printed before George Bush was announced as
Ronald Reagan's running mate, copies of the paper
were scooped up by collectors. Later editions changed
the headline.

Twain, Sherwood Anderson, Rudyard Kipling, Joseph Conrad, Willa Cather, Aldous
Huxley, and John Fowles.

The foundations hoped that the nonprofit
status would reduce postage rates and the operating deficit. Editor Lewis H. Lapham and
his staff were asked to remain.

## NEWSPAPER OFFERS TAX HELP

*Las Vegas Sun* publisher and editor Hank
Greenspun, facing his own battle against the
Internal Revenue Service, offers free tax
counseling to any home-delivery subscriber
who faces an IRS audit. Available is free telephone advice from a qualified tax counsel,
two hours of free consultation, and a tax lawyer to appear with the subscriber at the tax
audit. The paper received more than 300 requests for tax help during the first six months
of 1980.

## SYNDICATED COLUMNS CREATE CONTROVERSY

Columns by political writer Jack Anderson
caused controversy in the journalistic community when some newspapers, including the
*Washington Post,* refused to print them and
other papers printed them with editors' notes.

The columns, released in August, alleged
that the Carter administration had planned
an invasion of Iran for October, in order to
boost Carter's reelection chances.

In omitting the columns, the *Post* carried a
news story including Anderson's charges, but
added that it could not confirm any of the
details and that sources in Washington vehe-
mently denied the assertions. The *Miami
Herald* did not run the first column, but then
ran the first and second columns together after numerous calls from readers.

Many papers that carried the first column
put it next to stories containing denials by the
Pentagon and other officials. Other papers
put an editor's disclaimer with the column.
The *Montrose Daily Press,* in Montrose,
Colo., noted that the allegations "... are the
most serious ever made against any president
of the United States ...."

In a speech on Aug. 19, Anderson called
his decision to print the details of the alleged
invasion "anguishing" and said he chose to
disclose them because he felt that the invasion could never succeed.

## SPIRIT OF COOPERATION SEEN IN DETROIT

In a generous gesture of goodwill the *Detroit
News* agreed to print its rival daily, the *Detroit Free Press,* after the latter was shut down
by a strike two days before the opening of the
Republican National Convention. The two
papers were printed under a joint masthead
from July 15 through July 24, with profits
from advertising revenue shared.

# NEWSPAPER AND MAGAZINE AWARDS: 1980

In addition to awards listed below, see the Pulitzer Prizes on pages 78–85.

## NEWSPAPER GUILD HEYWOOD BROUN AWARD

The annual Heywood Broun Award of the Newspaper Guild is named after the guild's founder and first president.

**Gene Miller, Carl Hiaasen, Patrick Malone,** and **William Montalbano** of the *Miami Herald* received a check and citation for a series of articles spotlighting "dangerous doctors" practicing medicine in Florida.

**Honorable mention** was given to: Walter Bogdanich and Walter Johns Jr., *Cleveland Press,* for a series on a Cleveland area hospital's victimization of poor and elderly patients; Peter Almond, *Cleveland Press,* for series on a chemical plant's poisoning of its employees and neighbors and steps taken to correct the situation; Larry Eichel, *Philadelphia Inquirer,* for series on the Asian boat people's exodus.

## GEORGE POLK AWARDS

The George Polk Awards, sponsored by Long Island University (New York) to honor the memory of a CBS correspondent killed in Greece in 1948, included:

**Foreign Reporting:** John Kifner, *New York Times,* for his reporting from Iran.

**National Reporting:** Brian Donovan, Bob Wyrick, Stuart Diamond, *Newsday,* for their probes of the 1979 summer gasoline shortage.

**Regional Reporting:** Jim Adams, Jim Detjen, *Louisville Courier-Journal,* for exposing illegal dumping of chemical wastes in Brooks, Kentucky.

**Local Reporting:** Ed Petykiewicz, *Saginaw News,* for a series on the quality of justice in Saginaw County, Michigan.

**Metropolitan Reporting:** Walt Bogdanich, Walter Johns Jr., *Cleveland Press,* for exposing corruption and profiteering at a suburban Cleveland hospital.

**Political Reporting:** Jack Newfield, *Village Voice,* for investigative articles on the integrity of public officials.

**Commentary:** 'Notes and Comment,' "Talk of the Town," *The New Yorker,* for originality and trenchancy of its observations on important events of the day.

**Special Interest Reporting:** Wilbert Rideau and Billy Sinclair, editors of *The Angolite,* news-magazine published by and for inmates of Angola (La.) State Prison.

## U.S. DAILY NEWSPAPERS

Source: *Editor & Publisher*

| YEAR | NO. | CIRCULATION | YEAR | NO. | CIRCULATION |
|------|------|-------------|------|------|-------------|
| 1945 | 1,749 | 48,384,188 | 1971 | 1,749 | 61,743,141 |
| 1950 | 1,772 | 53,829,000 | 1972 | 1,761 | 62,510,242 |
| 1955 | 1,760 | 56,147,000 | 1973 | 1,774 | 63,147,280 |
| 1960 | 1,763 | 58,882,000 | 1974 | 1,768 | 61,877,197 |
| 1962 | 1,760 | 59,848,688 | 1975 | 1,756 | 60,655,431 |
| 1965 | 1,751 | 60,358,000 | 1976 | 1,762 | 60,977,011 |
| 1968 | 1,752 | 62,535,000 | 1977 | 1,753 | 61,495,140 |
| 1969 | 1,758 | 62,060,000 | 1978 | 1,756 | 61,989,997 |
| 1970 | 1,748 | 62,108,000 | 1979 | 1,763 | 62,223,040 |

**News Photography:** *United Press International* for "Firing Squad" photo showing executioners mowing down row of prisoners in Iran.

**Special Award:** Alden Whitman, obituary writer, *New York Times,* for establishing new standards of excellence.

## OVERSEAS PRESS CLUB AWARDS

The annual awards presented by the Overseas Press Club for distinguished reporting and interpretation of foreign affairs included:

**Daily Newspaper or Wire Service Reporting from Abroad:** Sajid Rizvi, *United Press International,* for coverage from Iran.

**Daily Newspaper or Wire Service Interpretation of Foreign Affairs (Bob Considine Memorial Award):** Ray Vicker, *Wall Street Journal,* for coverage of the Middle East.

**Robert Capa Gold Medal for Photography:** Kaveh Golestan, *Time* magazine, for photos from Iran.

**Photographic Reporting from Abroad:** David Burnett, *Contact Press Images,* for coverage of refugees in Southeast Asia and the Iran revolution.

**Magazine Reporting from Abroad:** Walter Isaacson and Donald Neff, *Time* magazine, for "The Colombian Connection: Billions in Pot and Coke."

**Magazine Interpretation of Foreign Affairs:** Sidney Zion and Uri Dan, *New York Times Magazine,* for "The Untold Story of the Middle East Talks."

**Cartoon on Foreign Affairs:** Don Wright, *Miami News* and *New York Times Syndicate,* for commentary on Iran.

**Business News Reporting from Abroad:** William J. Holstein, *United Press International,* for reporting from China.

## NATIONAL MAGAZINE AWARDS

Sponsored by the American Society of Magazine Editors and administered by the Columbia University Graduate School of Journalism:

**Reporting Excellence:** "To *Mother Jones* for 'The Corporate Crime of the Century,' by Mark Dowie, a . . . cleanly written exposé of large-scale dumping in Third World countries . . . of hazardous products declared illegal within the U.S."

**Fiction:** "To *Antaeus* and Joy Williams for 'The Farm,' a story of a woman . . . who kills a boy in a car accident and is increasingly haunted by the mishap."

**Essays and Criticism:** "To *Natural History* for Stephen Jay Gould's consistently excellent column on evolutionary biology. . . ."

**Specialized Journalism:** "To *IEEE Spectrum* for its diligent and intensive analysis of the Three Mile Island nuclear accident."

**Public Service:** "To *Texas Monthly* for 'Why Teachers Can't Teach,' by Gene Lyons."

**Service to the Individual:** "To *Saturday Review* and Susan Schiefelbein for 'Children and Cancer,' . . . of great potential service to families facing the tragedy of a child afflicted with the disease."

**Design:** "To *GEO,* an outstanding new entry in the magazine field, for its unparalleled achievement in the art of photographic essay."

## U.S. DAILY NEWSPAPER CIRCULATION LEADERS: 1979

| NEWSPAPER (M) Morning (E) Evening | CIRCULATION Daily | Weekend or Sunday | NEWSPAPER (M) Morning (E) Evening | CIRCULATION Daily | Weekend or Sunday |
|---|---|---|---|---|---|
| New York Daily News (M) | 1,606,365 | 2,237,494 | Philadelphia Bulletin (E) | 462,137 | 542,924 |
| Wall Street Journal (M) | 1,599,559 | — | Milwaukee Journal (E) | 324,167 | 530,683 |
| New York Times (M) | 841,890 | 1,403,077 | Atlanta Journal (E) | 219,455 | 505,829 [2] |
| Los Angeles Times (M) | 1,013,565 | 1,273,536 | Cleveland Plain Dealer (M) | 386,194 | 447,816 |
| Chicago Tribune (M) | 780,626 | 1,147,699 | St. Louis Post-Dispatch (E) | 253,948 | 430,711 |
| Philadelphia Inquirer (M) | 418,148 | 844,472 | Houston Chronicle (E) | 339,573 | 428,494 |
| Detroit News (E) | 628,574 | 818,741 | Portland Oregonian (M) | 242,621 | 409,780 |
| Washington (D.C.) Post (M) | 578,831 | 809,403 | Kansas City Star (E) | 317,370 | 406,194 |
| Detroit Free Press (M) | 607,647 | 712,190 | Des Moines Register (M) | 208,856 | 392,500 |
| Chicago Sun-Times (M) | 675,995 | 710,633 | Houston Post (M) | 325,085 | 386,640 |
| Boston Globe (M & E) | 482,578 | 694,211 | Baltimore Sun (M) | 178,987 | 369,139 |
| San Francisco Chronicle (M) | 504,644 | 667,335 [1] | Arizona Republic (M) | 232,152 | 357,971 |
| Pittsburgh Press (E) | 262,778 | 656,734 | Denver Post (E) | 266,571 | 351,839 |
| New York Post (E) | 631,104 | 412,106 | Dallas News (M) | 286,781 | 350,820 |
| Minneapolis Tribune (M) | 229,754 | 600,287 | Washington (D.C.) Star (E) | 342,760 | 313,860 |
| Newark (N.J.) Star Ledger (M) | 408,038 | 563,120 | Dallas Times Herald (E) | 247,629 | 341,126 |
| Miami Herald (M) | 420,400 | 552,426 | Louisville Courier-Journal (M) | 191,738 | 333,694 [3] |
| Newsday, Garden City, N.Y. (E) | 497,759 | 543,825 | Boston Herald-American (M) | 263,584 | 329,891 |

[1] Sunday Examiner & Chronicle    [2] Atlanta Journal Constitution    [3] Courier Journal & Times

## CANADIAN DAILY NEWSPAPER CIRCULATION LEADERS: 1979

| Newspaper | Daily | Weekend | Newspaper | Daily | Weekend |
|---|---|---|---|---|---|
| Toronto Star (E) | 481,667 | 760,666 | Edmonton Journal (E) | 169,502 | — |
| Toronto Sun (M) | 213,050 | 355,717 | Ottawa Citizen (E) | 121,170 | 155,318 |
| Toronto Globe and Mail (M) | 314,695 | — | Hamilton Spectator (E) | 142,933 | — |
| Le Journal de Montreal (M) | 306,693 | 270,083 | Winnipeg Free Press (E) | 141,547 | — |
| Montreal, La Presse (E) | 155,874 | 228,360 | Quebec, La Soleil (E) | 122,842 | 129,700 |
| Vancouver Sun (E) | 219,503 | — | Calgary Herald (E) | 128,178 | — |
| Montreal, The Gazette (M) | 165,820 | 202,197 | Vancouver Province (M) | 121,000 | — |

## NEW U.S. DAILY NEWSPAPERS: 1979

Abbeville (LA) Meridional
Amherst (MA) Record
Auburn (CA) Journal
Auburn (WA) Globe News
Broken Arrow (OK) Ledger

Duncan (OK) Eagle
Kent (WA) News Journal
Nogales (AZ) International
Oakland (CA) Eastbay
Today

Renton (WA) Record Chronicle
Sequin (TX) Gazette
Sylacauga (AL) Advance
Vero Beach (FL)
Press-Journal

## MERGED AND SUSPENDED U.S. DAILY NEWSPAPERS: 1979

Champaign-Urbana (IL) Courier (suspended)
Beaver Falls (PA) New Tribune merged with Beaver County (PA) Times
East St. Louis (IL) Metro East Journal (suspended)
Homestead (PA) Messenger (suspended)
Huntington (WV) Advertiser merged with Huntington (WV) Herald-Dispatch

Midland (MI) Times (suspended)
Redwood City (CA) Times merged with Palo Alto (CA) Times
Rockford (IL) Star merged with Rockford (IL) Register Republic
St. Charles (MO) News (suspended)
Tucumcari (NM) News (suspended)
Yuba City (CA) Herald (suspended)

## U.S. MAGAZINE CIRCULATION LEADERS*: 1979
Source: Magazine Publishers Association

| MAGAZINE | CIRCULATION | MAGAZINE | CIRCULATION | MAGAZINE | CIRCULATION |
|---|---|---|---|---|---|
| TV Guide | 19,043,358 | American Legion | 2,592,065 | Workbasket | 1,569,788 |
| Reader's Digest | 17,888,680 | Sports Illustrated | 2,274,819 | Midnight Globe | 1,552,579 |
| National Geographic | 10,413,639 | People Weekly | 2,264,087 | Boys' Life | 1,516,405 |
| Better Homes & Gardens | 8,097,651 | U.S. News & World Rept. | 2,042,910 | Parents Magazine | 1,456,311 |
| Family Circle | 7,753,604 | Field & Stream | 2,021,381 | Seventeen | 1,450,625 |
| Woman's Day | 7,560,329 | Glamour | 1,879,402 | Sunset | 1,403,481 |
| McCall's | 6,526,745 | Southern Living | 1,862,667 | Farm Journal | 1,337,873 |
| Ladies' Home Journal | 5,502,149 | V.F.W. Magazine | 1,829,180 | Life | 1,332,074 |
| Good Housekeeping | 5,271,172 | Smithsonian | 1,812,084 | Ebony | 1,262,619 |
| Playboy | 5,249,010 | Popular Science | 1,800,319 | Nation's Business | 1,256,270 |
| National Enquirer | 5,024,180 | Outdoor Life | 1,709,872 | Changing Times | 1,233,718 |
| Penthouse | 4,711,849 | Hustler | 1,700,873 | Sport | 1,207,633 |
| Redbook | 4,303,951 | Today's Education | 1,694,024 | New Woman | 1,195,756 |
| Time | 4,272,888 | Mechanix Illustrated | 1,680,245 | Psychology Today | 1,177,988 |
| The Star | 3,292,106 | Elks Magazine | 1,644,618 | Bon Appetit | 1,144,718 |
| Newsweek | 2,934,530 | Popular Mechanics | 1,642,570 | House & Garden | 1,084,277 |
| Cosmopolitan | 2,747,042 | True Story | 1,604,178 | 'Teen | 1,059,325 |

* Circulation of national newspaper supplements: Parade, 21,623,793; Family Weekly, 12,300,000.

# People in the News

Edwin E. Robinson, 62, of Falmouth, Me., hugs granddaughters, Christine, 8, *left*, and Kimberly Robinson, 9, as he sees them for the first time on June 9. He had regained his sight a week before when struck by lightning, having been blind since a 1971 truck accident. The lightning also enabled him to converse without a hearing aid.

## WOMEN IN THE NEWS

**Pauline Frederick** became the first woman to receive the Paul White Award, the highest honor of the Television News Directors' Association. Ms. Frederick was United Nations correspondent for NBC News in 1954–74. . . . Pulitzer Prize-winning poet **Maxine Kumin** was named consultant in poetry by the Library of Congress.

**Beverly J. Bimes,** who teaches English at Hazelwood High School in St. Louis, Mo., was named Teacher of the Year. . . . **Betty Lieder,** 56, of Spencer, Iowa, was named Mother of the Year.

San Francisco **Mayor Dianne Feinstein** invited all residents of the city to her January wedding to businessman **Richard Blum** at City Hall, where cake and champagne were served. The mayor paid a memorable visit to Washington, D.C., in July, were she tripped and broke her arm leaving the White House after visiting with old friend **Vice President Walter Mondale.**

**Barbara Shelton,** a Campbell, Cal., bookkeeper, won $67,261 in a Reno, Nev., slot machine. It was the largest jackpot ever paid on a quarter. . . . Actress **Bo Derek** was named worst-dressed woman of 1979 by designer Mr. Blackwell. Others on his worst-dressed list included actresses **Jill Clayburgh, Loni Anderson, Valerie Perrine,** and **Margaux Hemingway,** singers **Deborah "Blondie" Harry** and **Dolly Parton,** San Francisco **Mayor Dianne Feinstein, Christina Onassis,** and Britain's **Princess Margaret.**

**Rosanna Giannini,** 28, gave birth to sextuplets in Florence, Italy, on Jan. 11. The four boys and two girls became the world's second set of surviving sextuplets. . . . **Julie Martinez,** 42, gave birth in January to her 21st child in 25 years. Mrs. Martinez had no multiple births and 18 children have survived.

Former Swedish diplomat **Alva Myrdal,** 78, received the $50,000 Albert Einstein Peace Prize for her service as Sweden's Minister for Disarmament and delegate to the Geneva disarmament talks. . . . **Rosa Parks,** 67, received the Martin Luther King Jr. Nonviolent Peace Prize in recognition of her refusal, in 1955, to give her bus seat to a white

man in Montgomery, Ala., starting the bus boycott that brought King fame.

Poet, novelist, translator **Marguerite Yourcenar**, 76, was the first woman elected to the French Academy.... **Mother Theresa**, winner of the 1979 Nobel Peace Prize, was awarded Haiti's Legion of Honor for her work with the poor.... A nun, **Sister Sophia**, of the Sisters of the Holy Family of Nazareth, became the first female fire fighter in Sea Cliff, N.Y.

**Katharine Graham**, chairman of the Washington Post Company, became president of the American Newspaper Publishers Association.... Actress **Jean Marsh**, who dropped out of school as a teenager, received an honorary doctorate of humane letters from Marymount College in Tarrytown, N.Y.

Pulitzer Prize-winning historian **Barbara Tuchman** was selected as the 1980 Jefferson Lecturer by the National Endowment for the Humanities. The $10,000 grant is the federal government's highest award for distinguished achievement outside of science.

**Debra R. Hachen** was ordained as a rabbi at the Hebrew Union College-Jewish Institute of Religion in New York in June as her proud father, **Rabbi David S. Hachen**, watched. It was the first time in history the daughter of a rabbi became a rabbi.... During the April visit to the U.S. of Egyptian **President Anwar al-Sadat**, his wife, **Jihan**, received a pyramid-shaped telephone from the wives of Washington officials.

## LIFE AMONG THE ENTERTAINERS

Harvard's Hasty Pudding Club, the oldest dramatic organization in the U.S., chose actress **Meryl Streep** and actor **Alan Alda** for its Woman and Man of the Year awards.... **Ray Stevens**, **Kris Kristofferson**, and **Roy Orbison** were among 200 friends helping country singer **Johnny Cash** celebrate 25 years in show business at a party at Cash's Nashville home.

Veteran TV commentator **Hugh Downs** had his first science-fiction story published in *Omni* magazine.... Actor **Larry Hagman**, who plays the villainous J.R. Ewing in the *Dallas* TV series, escorted his wife, Maj, to the races at Ascot, England, wearing top hat and morning suit. His reception exceeded that for **Queen Elizabeth II**.

Comedian **Richard Pryor** won widespread admiration for his courage and will to live following a household accident in June in

Jerry Rubin, anti-establishment Yippie leader of the 1960s wears shirt and tie, *left,* in Wall Street office where he began work in July as a research analyst for investment firm John Muir and Co. Rubin is shown, *right,* as he appeared in 1968, carrying toy M16 rifle on arrival to appear before the House Un-American Activities Committee.

United Press Int'l.

Special Congressional Gold Medal honoring actor John Wayne, who died in 1979, was presented to members of Wayne's family in Washington, D.C., in March. A bronze replica of the medal was sold by the U.S. Mint in a 3-inch size costing $8 and a 1$\frac{5}{16}$-inch size costing $1. The first such medal went to George Washington. Only 85 other people or groups have been similarly honored since 1776.

Wide World

which he suffered third-degree burns over the upper half of his body. Although his chances of survival were considered poor, his strong will and thousands of letters from fans helped him recover.

Choreographer **Jerome Robbins** was honored at the White House with a program entitled *Salute to the American Musical—West Side Story*. A 44-member cast performed dances and songs from the show.... Opera star **Marilyn Horne** received the Handel Medallion, New York City's highest cultural award.

Lyricist **Hal David** was elected president of the American Society of Composers, Authors, and Publishers (Ascap).... **Frank Sinatra** received the Humanitarian Award of Variety Clubs International. **Princess Grace** of Monaco presented the award, with **Gregory Peck, Cary Grant, Gene Kelly, Henry Winkler, Red Buttons,** and **Jack Klugman** also on hand.

Actor **Burt Reynolds** became the first actor to receive more than $5 million for a film, with his role in *Cannonball*.... Dancer **Juliet Prowse** became a U.S. citizen 20 years after moving to this country from her native South Africa to appear in the film *Can Can*.

**Henry Winkler,** known for his role as "The Fonze" in the *Happy Days* TV series, donated the brown leather jacket worn by the character to the Smithsonian Institution's History of Entertainment Collection.

With opera tenor **Jan Peerce** acting as cantor, comedian **Henny Youngman,** 73, realized a lifelong dream to have a bar mitzvah in a ceremony in Atlantic City, N.J.... **Claudette Colbert** was named Best Actress of the Year by the Sarah Siddons Society of Chicago.

After 25 years as host of the Miss America Pageant in Atlantic City, **Bert Parks** was fired because pageant officials wanted a new image. **Ron Ely,** television game-show host who once played Tarzan, was chosen to replace Parks.... **Homer Shockley,** president of the Elvis Presley Fan Hall of Fame, announced that a 74-acre park will be developed in Asheville, N.C., as a memorial to the late singer. A central A-frame building will house a theater that will show Presley movies continuously and a restaurant featuring the singer's favorite dishes.

Choreographer **George Balanchine** received the Gold Medal of Merit for dance from the National Society of Arts and Letters.... Dance critic **Walter Terry** won the Capezio Dance Award for his contributions in promoting the public's awareness of dance.

Talk-show host **Phil Donahue** married actress **Marlo Thomas,** culminating a three-year courtship.... Dancer **Fred Astaire,** 80, married jockey **Robyn Smith,** 36.

Former Beatle **Paul McCartney** was arrested in January at Tokyo International Air-

port on charges of smuggling marijuana into the country in his luggage. After spending nine days in jail, he was deported. He was not prosecuted because the marijuana was for his own use and because he sustained heavy financial losses due to the cancellation of 11 scheduled concerts in Japan.

Writer and director **John Huston** was guest of honor at a tribute by the Film Society of Lincoln Center. Among those at the gala who introduced clips from his famous films were **Richard Burton, Lauren Bacall,** and **Paul Newman.**

After receiving an honorary degree from Harvard University, TV newsman **Walter Cronkite** was cheered by students shouting "Walter, Walter." Earlier in the year he received the Servant of Justice award from the Legal Aid Society because "the public has profound trust in him as a newsman. . . ."

Actor **James Stewart** received the Life Achievement Award from the American Film Institute. . . . **Ellen Stewart,** founder of the La Mama Experimental Theater, won the Margo Jones award "for the encouragement of new playwrights through a policy of regularly introducing new works."

Jacques Bailly, 14, holds his trophy aloft after winning the 1980 National Spelling Bee in Washington, D.C., on May 29. The Denver, Colo., 8th grader won by successfully spelling the word "elucubrate."

Deaf since birth, **Phyllis Frelich** triumphed over her handicap to become a founding member of the National Theater for the Deaf. Married to a nondeaf person, she was the inspiration for author **Mark Medoff** to write his play *Children of a Lesser God* about a deaf woman who marries a man with normal hearing. Miss Frelich was chosen to play the role on Broadway, and her success culminated in her Tony award as best actress in a play.

## STATESMEN, POLITICIANS, OTHERS

Former Secretary of State **Cyrus R. Vance** had the pleasure of sponsoring his daughter, **Amy Vance,** when she was admitted to practice law in the federal courts in July. . . . **John Robinette** smashed two bottles of Russian vodka to dedicate a new bridge in Vulcan, W. Va., in recognition of the worldwide publicity received in 1976 when he asked the Soviet Union for foreign aid to build the bridge when local officials refused funds for the project. After the Russians sent an official to investigate, the states of West Virginia and Kentucky agreed to construct the bridge, which links the isolated community with Pike County, Ky.

**President Carter** presented the Medal of Freedom, in June, to Adm. **Hyman G. Rickover,** photographer **Ansel Adams,** ballerina **Lucia Chase,** Greek Orthodox **Archbishop Iakovos,** ornithologist **Roger Tory Peterson,** opera singer **Beverly Sills,** writers **Eudora Welty** and **Robert Penn Warren,** and playwright **Tennessee Williams.** Posthumous medals were presented to the scientist and author **Rachel Carson,** Sen. **Hubert H. Humphrey,** and actor **John Wayne.**

**Elmer Vincent,** 49, of Muldrow, Okla., and **Arthur Vincent Scamardo,** 40, of Fort Smith, Ark., who had been friends and business associates for 15 years, were astonished to discover that they are brothers. Elmer Vincent was nine when his mother died after giving birth to Arthur, who was adopted before his four other siblings were put in a Fort Smith orphanage. Organizers of an orphanage reunion discovered the relationship, to the delight and amazement of both men.

**Richard W. Lyman,** 57, resigned as president of Stanford University to become president of the Rockefeller Foundation. . . . **Gilbert M. Grosvenor** was named president of the National Geographic Society. . . . Nobel laureate in medicine, **Dr. Frederick C. Robbins,** was appointed president of the National Academy of Sciences Institute of Medicine.

The Westinghouse Science Talent Search ended in a tie for the first time in its 39-year history. The winners, **Lisa J. Randall,** 17, of New York City, and **John M. Andersland,**

Actor Henry Fonda, *left*, celebrated his 75th birthday and 55th year in show business with his son Peter, *center*, and daughter Jane in Beverly Hills, Calif., on May 16. He took a break from work to enjoy some birthday cake.

United Press Int'l.

17, of East Lansing, Mich., each received $12,000.... **Dr. Joseph Pursch** received a Distinguished Service Medal on his retirement from the military and as head of the Alcohol and Drug Abuse Center at the Long Beach (Calif.) Naval Hospital.

**George H. Brown Jr.** became the first black appointed to the Tennessee Supreme Court.... **William Reece Smith Jr.** became president of the American Bar Association.... **Henry Ford II** received the American Heritage Award from the Anti-Defamation League of B'nai B'rith.

Three volunteers at Duke University in Durham, N.C., emerged from a pressure tank after a 28-day test in which they set a world record of 2,132 feet in a simulated dive. A mixture of helium and oxygen with 10% nitrogen allowed **Stephen Porter, Delmar Shelton,** and **William Bell** to successfully complete the experiment. Some scientists believe the results will allow wider exploration of the ocean depths.

**Dr. Thomas C. MacAvoy,** former president of the Corning Glass Works, became president of the Boy Scouts of America.... **John G. Gelinas Jr.,** of Scarsdale, N.Y., succeeded in earning the last of all 118 merit badges offered by the Boy Scouts.

A survey by the International Platform Association showed the speakers most in demand on the lecture circuit in 1980 were **Jack Anderson, Isaac Asimov, Joyce Brothers, Art Buchwald, Milton Friedman, Paul Harvey, James J. Kilpatrick, Henry Kissinger, Ralph Nader, Dan Rather, Jessica Savitch, Beverly Sills, Abigail Van Buren, Mike Wallace,** and **Barbara Walters.**

Assistant Treasury Secretary **Curtis Hessler** was sworn in at Sibley Memorial Hospital in Washington, D.C., so his wife, Christine, who had just given birth to a baby could be present. Also present was their 18-hour-old son, **Alexander William Hessler.** ... **Michael S. Ainslie,** 36-year-old businessman of Cincinnati, was named president of the National Trust for Historic Preservation.... **Curtis Brewer,** 55, who has been paralyzed from the neck down for 25 years, was named Handicapped American of the Year by the President's Committee on Employment of the Handicapped. He founded an organization, in 1964, called Untapped Resources to help disabled individuals cut through red tape to obtain jobs.

**Fred A. Grewe III,** originally from West Virginia, won the Maxi the Taxi award as the funniest of all 23,000 New York City cabdrivers after a "joke-off" held at a New York City restaurant.... **Mrs. Jerry Randolph,** 43, of Houston, Tex., was named Secretary of the Year at a convention of the National Secretaries Association.

When **Lillian Carter** was asked to provide

her personal list of the best Presidents of the United States, she put her son, **Jimmy Carter**, sixth. In order, she listed **Abraham Lincoln, Woodrow Wilson, Harry S. Truman, Theodore Roosevelt, John F. Kennedy,** her son, and then, **George Washington.**

**Sir Edmund Hillary,** first man to climb Mt. Everest, presented the community of Solukhumbi, in northeast Nepal, with the keys to a 15-bed hospital built with money from the Himalayan Trust of New Zealand, of which he is the president.... **Howard Earle Skipper** received a $25,000 Bristol-Myers award for distinguished achievement in cancer research for his work in chemotherapy.

Chief U.S. delegate to the United Nations, **Donald F. McHenry,** accepted an honorary doctor of laws degree at his alma mater, Illinois State University at Normal, Ill.... Speaker of the House of Representatives **Thomas (Tip) O'Neill Jr.** received the University of Notre Dame's Laetare Medal, the oldest honor accorded to American Roman Catholic laymen.

Kentucky **Gov. John Y. Brown** had the honor of swearing in fellow Kentuckian **Drew Von Bergen,** reporter for United Press International's Washington bureau, as presi-

Adopted grandfather Jim Donovan, 78, of Miami, Fla., poses with his new family, Mrs. Debbie Wilkinson, her son John, 10, and daughter Michelle, 9. The retired electrician, poet, and musician had offered himself for adoption in a newspaper advertisement.

dent of the National Press Club.... **Herbert Klein,** President Nixon's former director of communications, became editor-in-chief of Copley Newspapers.... The Overseas Press Club gave its President's Award to **Kenneth D. Taylor,** the Canadian Ambassador in Iran who protected six Americans in Teheran and helped them to escape.

The nation's highest award for bravery, the Medal of Honor, was awarded, 12 years after his death in a Vietcong prison, to **Col. Donald Gilbert Cook.** His widow, **Laurette,** accepted the award at the Pentagon. Cook heroically refused to provide information to the Vietcong during three years of interrogation.

In what may be the largest "palimony" settlement in the U.S., **Philip Schwartz,** 47, of Miami, agreed to pay former roommate, **June Schwartz,** 53, of Elizabeth, N.J., $245,000 after she filed suit when he left her to move to Texas.... To pay off a $17,500 divorce settlement, **Bob Taylor,** of Tulsa, Okla., hired a security company to pay his former wife in quarters, nickels, and dimes. Annoyed at receiving a call from a collection agency, Taylor made sure the 30-odd bags of coins were delivered to his ex-wife's lawyer's office after regular banking hours.

Eager to expand the membership of their Parent-Teacher Association, students at Whitney Junior High School in Tulsa, Okla., wrote to celebrities giving honorary membership cards. Among those who wrote acknowledgments were **Erma Bombeck, Amy Carter, Art Linkletter, Jane Fonda, Carol Burnett, George Burns, Miss Piggy,** and **Snoopy....** **Caroline Kennedy,** 22, daughter of late **President John F. Kennedy,** and her cousin **Michael L. Kennedy,** 22, son of late **Sen. Robert F. Kennedy,** both received degrees at Harvard University in June.

Soviet **President Leonid Brezhnev** accepted the Lenin Prize for Literature during a ceremony at the Kremlin for his three volumes of memoirs.... **Pope John Paul II** was voted best-dressed statesman of 1979 by the Fashion Foundation of America. Others on the list included New York **Mayor Edward I. Koch, President Carter, Gen. Alexander Haig,** and Saudi Arabian oil minister **Sheik Ahmed Zaki Yamani.**

The Brandeis University Creative Arts Awards went to playwright **Lanford Wilson,** poet **Edgar Bowers,** painter **Philip Guston,** sculptor **Betty Parsons,** and ballerina **Suzanne Farrell.**

The National Association for the Advancement of Colored People (NAACP) presented a posthumous award to late President **Lyndon B. Johnson** for his role in encouraging passage of the 1964 Civil Rights Act and 1975 Voting Rights Act.

Edward W. Scheffler, 73, of Pipersville, Pa., graduated from Central Bucks West High School in Doylestown, Pa. He had returned to high school after having quit more than half a century earlier.

A 12-year-old Ukrainian immigrant, **Walter Polovchak,** of Chicago, refused to accompany his parents back to the Soviet Union when they became disenchanted with the U.S. He and his 17-year-old sister, **Natalie,** both were granted political asylum by the U.S. and were placed in a foster home where they could consider their decision more thoroughly.

**THE GOLDEN YEARS**

Thirty-five years late, retired Army **Lt. Col. Matt Urban,** 62, received the Congressional Medal of Honor from **President Carter** in July. Although a recommendation for the medal was made in 1945, for heroism in World War II in France, it had been lost and only turned up in the files in 1978. The Holland, Mich., resident was reunited with members of his old infantry division at the ceremony.

**Dr. Eugene Fanta,** 70, of Brooklyn, N.Y., was named Family Doctor of the Year.... Photographer **P. H. Polk,** 81, received an award from the International Black Photographers for 50 years of work in portraying the lives of blacks in America.

Stalled in a New York City traffic jam in April, 80-year-old artist **Louise Nevelson** was over an hour late for the dedication of the Louise Nevelson Laboratory for Cancer Immunobiology at Memorial Sloan-Kettering Cancer Center. She later viewed the ceremony on videotape.... Nobel laureate **Isaac Bashevis Singer** received the 1980 award for literature from the National Arts Club.

Londoners helped celebrate the 80th birthday of Britain's **Queen Mother Elizabeth.** The popular "Queen Mum," mother of **Queen Elizabeth II,** was honored with a thanksgiving service at St. Paul's Cathedral in July.

More than 70,000 persons cheered Japanese **Emperor Hirohito** on his 79th birthday. He is the world's longest-reigning monarch, having held the throne for 55 years.

The Woodland Nursing Home in New Rochelle, N.Y., threw a champagne party for three of its residents, **Helen Hatch, Christina Morrison,** and **Emilie Sommerville,** who all turned 100 in February.... **Mary Bobo,** owner of a boarding house in Lynchburg, Tenn., received 5,000 greeting cards for her 99th birthday. A nearby distillery had advertised in national publications for readers to send birthday greetings to the popular Lynchburg resident.

New York City's Second Avenue Deli dedicated the **Molly Picon** Dining Room and decorated it with posters of the 82-year-old actress' plays in the Yiddish theater.... Ragtime pianist **Eubie Blake** had his 97th

birthday party at the Songwriter's Hall of Fame, where more than 100 persons turned out to honor him.

**Isaac Corkland**, 83, married **Martha Munzer**, 80, in Pompano Beach, Fla., after a romance that spanned 62 years. After meeting in 1918, Corkland was shipped off to Europe to fight in World War I and they lost touch. Each married another and became widowed. They met accidentally in 1978 and decided to take up where they had left off.

Chicago theologian **Ralph Wendell Burhoe**, 68, became the first American to win the Templeton Prize for Progress in Religion. The former chairman of the theology department at Meadville Theological School in Chicago received $206,000, the most lucrative award in the field of religion.

Composer **William Schuman**, winner of the first Pulitzer Prize for Music in 1943, was presented with an 8-by-4-foot cake on stage at the Aspen Music Festival in Colorado to celebrate his 70th birthday. . . . **William J. Moore**, 108, of Harrison, Ark., was declared the oldest living U.S. war veteran by the Veterans Administration. . . . **Col. William Kelly**, of Buffalo, N.Y., the oldest living graduate of the U.S. Military Academy at West Point, celebrated his 103d birthday.

Physical fitness expert **Jack LaLanne**, who runs a chain of health spas, turned 65 and registered for Medicare. . . . **Davis Johnson Jr.**, 74, received his bachelor's degree at Bucknell University, 50 years late. He had dropped out of college four credits short of the degree requirements during the Great Depression, but finally wrote a paper fulfilling the credit requirement in time to graduate with the class of 1980. The following weekend he returned to the campus to attend the 50th reunion of his original class of 1930.

Acting coach **Lee Strasberg**, 79, found a surprise waiting for him one day as he arrived at the former Greek Orthodox Church in New York City that houses his famous Actors Studio. One of his former students, **Shelley Winters**, greeted him and showed him a wall plaque proclaiming the 103-seat theater the Lee Strasberg Theater.

**Harold Taylor**, 83, became one of the oldest persons to complete the 3-week training course given by Guide Dog Foundation for the Blind in New York City. The rigorous training course included walking with the dog on subways, buses, and trains, and in all types of city conditions. . . . Pioneer cancer researcher **Dr. Alton Ochsner**, 83, received the George Washington Award, highest honor given by the Freedoms Foundation at Valley Forge, Pa.

Mrs. Mary Marvich, 107, is congratulated by federal Judge Robert A. Maxwell, *left*, after she received her citizenship papers in Fairmont, W. Va., in June. Born in Yugoslavia in 1873, she came to the U.S. in 1894 and recently applied for citizenship, which at first was denied because she could not prove her birth date or remember the ship she arrived on. Flanking her are her daughter and son-in-law, Frank and Betty Nicoletti.

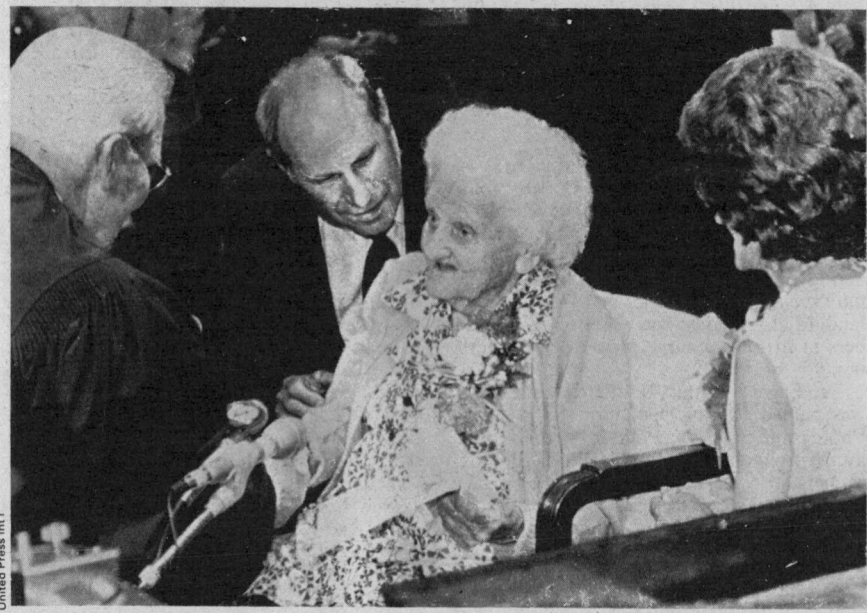

United Press Int'l

## Postal Service

# HIGHLIGHTS: 1980

Postmaster General William F. Bolger proposed a record rate increase for the U.S. Postal Service in April. Stating that "this is the leanest, trimmest rate package we could devise," Mr. Bolger requested an increase of first-class postage rates to 20 cents for the first ounce and 17 cents for each additional ounce. The price of a postcard would go from 10 cents to 13 cents. Rates for second-class mail, mainly mass-circulation newspapers and magazines, would rise by 1.9%. However, the proposal included reductions in rates for rural newspapers and nonprofit organizations.

Postage rates, which have not been increased since May 1978, are subject to approval by the Postal Rate Commission, which has 10 months to consider them.

The overall rate increase of 28% was requested because of an estimated deficit of $593 million for fiscal year 1980.

In other developments, Congress assured continuation of Saturday mail deliveries when the House Post Office and Civil Service Committee approved a $947 million expense-cutting bill required by the 1981 budget. Under the proposed budget, the committee was required to cut $1 billion from programs it funds. An estimated $500 million could have been saved by eliminating mail deliveries on Saturdays.

The committee agreed to cut only $250 million from the subsidy going to the Postal Service, and the committee added specific wording requiring the continuation of six-day-a-week mail delivery.

The 9-number zip code will come into use on Feb. 1, 1981, increasing the number of zip codes in use to 19.8 million from 1.2 million. Primarily for use by businesses, the new digits should enable mail to be sorted into smaller geographic areas, such as one building or city block.

The present Zip Code was implemented in 1963, and its usage has grown to the extent that approximately 97% of all mail now contains a 5-digit Zip Code. The first five digits of the expanded Zip Code will be identical to the present ones, and the added digits will more specifically identify the section of the block or building.

The governing board of the U.S. Postal Service announced on Aug. 15 that a proposed electronic mail system for business will go into effect on Jan. 4, 1982. The Electronic

Neither rain, nor snow, nor volcanic ash keeps Mary DeShazer from her appointed rounds in Kelso, Wash., in June. Mary, like others in the town, wears a mask to filter out from the air volcanic ash blown out from the nearby Mount St. Helens volcano eruption.

Computer-Originated Mail service, known as E-COM, will allow business to transmit messages electronically to certain post offices, where the messages would be printed, placed in envelopes, and delivered by hand. Messages supposedly would be received anywhere in the continental U.S. within two days.

The board of governors said it would ask a federal appeals court in Washington to rule on an April decision by the Postal Rate Commission that the electronic mail plan be considered temporary, with an expiration date of Oct. 1, 1984, at which time renewal would be necessary.

The Postal Service reported the results of a national survey on direct-mail advertising conducted by Robert Hansen, marketing professor at the University of Minnesota. Contrary to popular belief, Hansen found that only about 7% of the people in the U.S. feel that direct mail advertising is "junk." The most popular direct-mail items were free samples and catalogs.

# TIPS ON USING THE POSTAL SERVICE

The U.S. Postal Service tries to meet your needs as a sender and receiver of mail by providing a variety of services. Some services and regulations that may be unfamiliar to you are described below.

## MINIMUM AND MAXIMUM SIZES

The Postal Service will not handle cards or letters less than 3½ inches high and 5 inches long unless they are more than ¼ inch thick. Cards less than seven-thousandths of an inch thick also are prohibited.

Cards or letters more than 6⅛ inches high or 11½ inches wide are subject to a surcharge, as is letter mail of odd shapes in which the length is more than 1.3 times the height or less than 2.5 times the height.

## EXPRESS MAIL

If you send a letter or package up to 70 pounds by Express Mail, the U.S. Postal Service *guarantees* to return your money if it is not delivered within the time stated.

The Express Mail customer can choose one of four delivery options: (1) custom designed service, (2) next-day service, (3) same-day airport service, and (4) international service.

Express Mail became a permanent class of mail on Oct. 8, 1977. In 1979 the Postal Service inaugurated Express Mail Metro Service, with same-day delivery for urgent matter. It is available in the 25 largest metropolitan areas of the country.

## FORWARDING MAIL TO A NEW ADDRESS

If you move to a new address, you can obtain a "Change of Address Kit" from your local post office.

The kit contains change of address cards for you to send to magazines, charge accounts, and friends. There is also a change of address form with which to notify your local post office as to when you plan to move and your new address.

After you have given the post office this information, postal workers will forward to your new address for one year mail that comes to your former address.

## ADDRESS CORRECTION SERVICE

If one of your friends or correspondents moves and neglects to notify you of the new address, the Postal Service may be able to help you obtain the new address.

Mail a letter to your friend at the old address, and mark on the envelope "Address Correction Requested."

If your friend has notified the post office of his new address, the post office will then forward your letter to the new address, and return to you a form containing your friend's new address with a charge of 25 cents.

If the post office cannot determine the new address of your friend, it will merely return your letter at no charge.

## PACKAGING FOR SECURE DELIVERY

The way you package a parcel sent by mail can affect the condition in which the contents arrive at their destination.

Packages containing breakable items should be marked "Fragile" above the address and below the postage. Those containing food that can spoil should be marked "Perishable."

Before sealing the carton, place a list of the contents, your address, and the address of the person to whom it is being sent *inside* the package.

Wrap your package in paper at least as strong as that used for large grocery bags.

Use tape to seal all openings in the wrapping, including those at each end of the parcel.

Reinforce the package by tying strong twine around it several times in both directions. Knot the twine at each intersection. You can use nylon filament tape instead of twine to reinforce the package, running it completely around the length and the width of the parcel.

## ZIP CODES

If you put the correct ZIP Code on the address of all mail that you send, the post office can deliver it more quickly. The ZIP Codes for many cities and towns are listed on pages 114–137.

Here is how ZIP Code works. The first digit of every five-digit ZIP Code designates a national area, from "0" in the Northeast states to "9" in the Western states. The first three digits together stand for one of 552 large cities or sectional centers. The last two digits designate a delivery area or post office within the sectional center.

The *National Zip Code and Post Office Directory* lists the names of all the post offices and the five-digit codes for every postal delivery zone in the United States.

You can use the directory at your local post office, or buy it there for $7.50. You also can obtain a copy by sending $7.50 to:

Superintendent of Documents
Government Printing Office
Washington, D.C. 20420

If you own an out-of-date *National Zip Code Directory*, you no longer can exchange it free for a new one at your local post office.

# U.S. POSTAL RATES AND FEES *

| DOMESTIC MAIL | RATE |
|---|---|
| **First Class:** | |
| 1st ounce | 15¢ |
| 2d to 12th ounces | 13¢ per ounce |
| Over 12 ounces | See Priority Mail table on page 696 |
| Postal and postcards | 10¢ |
| Double postcards | 10¢ each half |
| Business reply letters: | |
| with advance deposit | 3.5¢ |
| without advance deposit | 12¢ |
| **Second Class** (newspapers, periodicals): | |
| Mailed singly by public | 10¢ for 2 oz.; 6¢ for each extra ounce, or the parcel post rate, whichever is lower |
| **Bulk rates:** | |
| In county per pound | 3.1¢ |
| In county per piece | 1.6¢ |
| Outside county | Consult postmaster |
| **Third Class:** | |
| Mailed singly | 20¢ up to 2 ounces |
| (circulars, books, catalogs, | 40¢ up to 4 ounces |
| merchandise, etc., weighing | 53¢ up to 6 ounces |
| less than one lb. each) | 66¢ up to 8 ounces |
| | 79¢ up to 10 ounces |
| | 92¢ up to 12 ounces |
| | $1.05 up to 14 ounces |
| | $1.18 up to 15.9 ounces |
| Keys and identification devices | 32¢ up to 2 ounces |
| Bulk rates | Consult postmaster |
| **Fourth Class:** | |
| Parcel Post | See table on page 696 |
| Books and records rate: | |
| 1st pound | 59¢ |
| 2d to 7th pounds | 22¢ per pound |
| Over 7 pounds | 13¢ for each additional pound |
| Library rate: | |
| 1st pound | 19¢ |
| 2d to 7th pounds | 7¢ |
| Over 7 pounds | 5¢ |
| **Special Delivery** (fee in addition to postage): | |
| 1st class | $2 to $2.85 |
| 2d, 3d, and 4th class | $2.25 to $3.25 |
| **Certified Mail:** | |
| Regular delivery | 80¢ plus postage |
| **Money Orders** (for safe transmission of money): | |
| Amount $0.01 to $400 | 55¢ to $1.10 |
| **Special Handling** (fee in addition to postage; 3d and 4th class only): | 70¢ for first 10 lbs. $1.25 over 10 lbs. |
| **Restricted delivery** (not available for mail insured for $15 or less): | Additional 80¢ fee |
| **Special Services:** | |
| Address Correction | 25¢ |
| Certificate of mailing | 15¢ |
| **Insurance** (in addition to postage): | |
| Liability up to $15 | 50¢ |
| Liability up to $50 | 85¢ |
| Liability up to $100 | $1.10 |
| Liability up to $150 | $1.40 |
| Liability up to $200 | $1.75 |
| Liability up to $300 | $2.25 |
| Liability up to $400 | $2.75 |

| DOMESTIC MAIL (continued) | RATE |
|---|---|
| **Registered Mail** (in addition to postage): | |
| Value $0.00 to $25,000 | $3 to $14.50 |
| **Return Receipts** for certified, registered, or insured (not available for mail insured for $15 or less): | |
| Requested at time of mailing: | |
| Showing to whom and date delivered | Additional 45¢ fee |
| Also showing address where delivered | Additional 55¢ fee |
| Requested after mailing to show to whom and date delivered | Additional $2.10 fee |
| **C.O.D. Mail:** | |
| Up to limit of $400 | $1.10 to $3.25 |

| INTERNATIONAL MAIL | RATE |
|---|---|
| **Mail to Canada or Mexico:** | |
| Surface Mail—1 ounce | 15¢ |
| Surface Mail—2d to 12th ounce | 13¢ per ounce |
| Surface Mail—over 12 ounces (Max. weights: Canada, 60 lbs.; Mexico, 4 lbs.) | Use 8th zone Priority Mail rates (see page 696) |
| Postal and postcards (surface) | 10¢ |
| Small packets of merchandise or samples, or printed matter: | |
| up to 2 ounces | 20¢ |
| over 2 oz. to 4 oz. | 40¢ |
| over 4 oz. to 6 oz. | 53¢ |
| over 6 oz. to 8 oz. | 66¢ |
| over 8 oz. to 10 oz. | 79¢ |
| over 10 oz. to 12 oz. | 92¢ |
| over 12 oz. to 14 oz. | $1.05 |
| over 14 oz. to 1 lb. | $1.18 |
| Mexico only, up to 2 lbs. | $1.26 |
| **Mail to Other Countries:** | |
| Surface rates—1 ounce | 30¢ |
| over 1 oz. to 2 oz. | 47¢ |
| over 2 oz. to 4 oz. | 81¢ |
| over 4 oz. to 8 oz. | $1.49 |
| over 8 oz. to 1 lb. | $2.76 |
| over 1 lb. to 2 lbs. | $4.80 |
| over 2 lbs. to 4 lbs. | $7.80 |
| Air letters: (To Central America, Colombia, Venezuela, Caribbean islands, Bahamas, Bermuda, and St. Pierre and Miquelon) | 35¢ per ½ oz. up to 2 oz.; 30¢ for each additional ½ oz. |
| Air letters: (To all other countries) | 40¢ per ½ oz. up to 2 oz.; 35¢ each additional ½ oz. |
| Aerogrammes (folded as envelope and sent by air) | 30¢ each |
| Postal and postcards—surface | 19¢ |
| Postal and postcards—airmail | 28¢ |
| Small packets of merchandise or samples, 1 or 2 lbs. maximum—surface: | |
| up to 2 oz. | 20¢ |
| over 2 oz. to 4 oz. | 40¢ |
| over 4 oz. to 8 oz. | 66¢ |
| over 8 oz. to 1 lb. | $1.05 |
| over 1 lb. to 2 lbs. | $1.26 |

* Effective Jan. 1, 1981; does not include rate changes planned to be effective later in 1981.

## U.S. FOURTH CLASS (PARCEL POST)

| Weight in pounds up to: | Zone: Local | Up to 150 miles 1-2 | 150-300 miles 3 | 300-600 miles 4 | 600-1,000 miles 5 | 1,000-1,400 miles 6 | 1,400-1,800 miles 7 | Over 1,800 miles 8 |
|---|---|---|---|---|---|---|---|---|
| 2 | $1.15 | $1.35 | $1.39 | $1.56 | $1.72 | $1.84 | $1.98 | $2.22 |
| 3 | 1.23 | 1.45 | 1.53 | 1.73 | 1.86 | 2.04 | 2.24 | 2.61 |
| 4 | 1.29 | 1.56 | 1.65 | 1.82 | 2.00 | 2.23 | 2.50 | 3.00 |
| 5 | 1.36 | 1.66 | 1.77 | 1.92 | 2.14 | 2.43 | 2.77 | 3.39 |
| 6 | 1.42 | 1.71 | 1.84 | 2.01 | 2.28 | 2.62 | 3.03 | 3.78 |
| 7 | 1.47 | 1.76 | 1.90 | 2.11 | 2.41 | 2.82 | 3.29 | 4.17 |
| 8 | 1.51 | 1.80 | 1.97 | 2.20 | 2.55 | 3.02 | 3.56 | 4.56 |
| 9 | 1.54 | 1.85 | 2.03 | 2.29 | 2.69 | 3.21 | 3.82 | 4.95 |
| 10 | 1.57 | 1.89 | 2.10 | 2.39 | 2.83 | 3.41 | 4.08 | 5.34 |
| 11 | 1.60 | 1.94 | 2.17 | 2.50 | 3.00 | 3.65 | 4.42 | 5.73 |
| 12 | 1.64 | 1.98 | 2.22 | 2.56 | 3.09 | 3.77 | 4.57 | 6.12 |
| 13 | 1.67 | 2.02 | 2.27 | 2.63 | 3.17 | 3.89 | 4.72 | 6.41 |
| 14 | 1.70 | 2.05 | 2.32 | 2.69 | 3.25 | 3.99 | 4.86 | 6.62 |
| 15 | 1.73 | 2.09 | 2.36 | 2.74 | 3.33 | 4.09 | 4.99 | 6.80 |
| 16 | 1.76 | 2.13 | 2.41 | 2.80 | 3.40 | 4.19 | 5.11 | 6.98 |
| 17 | 1.79 | 2.16 | 2.45 | 2.85 | 3.47 | 4.28 | 5.23 | 7.15 |
| 18 | 1.82 | 2.20 | 2.49 | 2.91 | 3.54 | 4.37 | 5.34 | 7.31 |
| 19 | 1.86 | 2.23 | 2.53 | 2.96 | 3.61 | 4.46 | 5.45 | 7.47 |
| 20 | 1.89 | 2.27 | 2.58 | 3.01 | 3.67 | 4.54 | 5.55 | 7.62 |
| 21 | 1.92 | 2.30 | 2.62 | 3.06 | 3.74 | 4.62 | 5.66 | 7.76 |
| 22 | 1.95 | 2.34 | 2.66 | 3.14 | 3.85 | 4.78 | 5.80 | 7.90 |
| 23 | 1.98 | 2.37 | 2.72 | 3.25 | 3.99 | 4.96 | 6.02 | 8.03 |
| 24 | 2.01 | 2.44 | 2.80 | 3.35 | 4.12 | 5.13 | 6.24 | 8.16 |
| 25 | 2.04 | 2.51 | 2.89 | 3.46 | 4.26 | 5.31 | 6.46 | 8.28 |
| 26 | 2.07 | 2.58 | 2.97 | 3.56 | 4.39 | 5.48 | 6.68 | 8.40 |
| 27 | 2.11 | 2.65 | 3.06 | 3.67 | 4.53 | 5.66 | 6.90 | 8.52 |
| 28 | 2.14 | 2.72 | 3.14 | 3.77 | 4.66 | 5.83 | 7.12 | 8.63 |
| 29 | 2.17 | 2.79 | 3.23 | 3.88 | 4.80 | 6.01 | 7.34 | 8.75 |
| 30 | 2.20 | 2.86 | 3.31 | 3.98 | 4.93 | 6.18 | 7.56 | 8.85 |
| 31 | 2.68 | 3.09 | 3.46 | 4.09 | 5.07 | 6.36 | 7.78 | 9.41 |
| 32 | 2.71 | 3.12 | 3.49 | 4.19 | 5.20 | 6.53 | 8.00 | 9.51 |
| 33 | 2.74 | 3.16 | 3.57 | 4.30 | 5.34 | 6.71 | 8.22 | 9.61 |
| 34 | 2.77 | 3.19 | 3.65 | 4.40 | 5.47 | 6.88 | 8.44 | 9.80 |
| 35 | 2.80 | 3.22 | 3.74 | 4.51 | 5.61 | 7.06 | 8.66 | 10.06 |
| 36 | 2.83 | 3.28 | 3.82 | 4.61 | 5.74 | 7.23 | 8.89 | 10.32 |
| 37 | 2.86 | 3.35 | 3.91 | 4.72 | 5.88 | 7.41 | 9.10 | 10.58 |
| 38 | 2.89 | 3.42 | 3.99 | 4.82 | 6.01 | 7.58 | 9.32 | 10.84 |
| 39 | 2.93 | 3.49 | 4.08 | 4.93 | 6.15 | 7.76 | 9.54 | 11.10 |
| 40 | 2.96 | 3.56 | 4.16 | 5.03 | 6.28 | 7.93 | 9.76 | 11.36 |
| 41 | 2.99 | 3.63 | 4.25 | 5.14 | 6.42 | 8.11 | 9.98 | 11.62 |
| 42 | 3.02 | 3.70 | 4.33 | 5.24 | 6.55 | 8.28 | 10.20 | 11.88 |
| 43 | 3.05 | 3.77 | 4.42 | 5.35 | 6.69 | 8.46 | 10.42 | 12.14 |
| 44 | 3.08 | 3.84 | 4.50 | 5.45 | 6.82 | 8.63 | 10.64 | 12.40 |
| 45 | 3.11 | 3.91 | 4.59 | 5.56 | 6.96 | 8.81 | 10.86 | 12.66 |
| 46 | 3.14 | 3.98 | 4.67 | 5.66 | 7.09 | 8.98 | 11.08 | 12.92 |
| 47 | 3.17 | 4.05 | 4.76 | 5.77 | 7.23 | 9.16 | 11.30 | 13.18 |
| 48 | 3.20 | 4.12 | 4.84 | 5.87 | 7.36 | 9.33 | 11.52 | 13.44 |
| 49 | 3.23 | 4.19 | 4.93 | 5.98 | 7.50 | 9.51 | 11.74 | 13.70 |
| 50 | 3.27 | 4.26 | 5.01 | 6.08 | 7.63 | 9.68 | 11.96 | 13.96 |
| 51 | 3.30 | 4.33 | 5.10 | 6.19 | 7.77 | 9.86 | 12.18 | 14.22 |
| 52 | 3.33 | 4.40 | 5.18 | 6.29 | 7.90 | 10.03 | 12.40 | 14.48 |
| 53 | 3.36 | 4.47 | 5.27 | 6.40 | 8.04 | 10.21 | 12.62 | 14.74 |
| 54 | 3.39 | 4.54 | 5.35 | 6.50 | 8.17 | 10.38 | 12.84 | 15.00 |
| 55 | 3.42 | 4.61 | 5.44 | 6.61 | 8.31 | 10.56 | 13.06 | 15.26 |
| 56 | 3.45 | 4.68 | 5.52 | 6.71 | 8.44 | 10.73 | 13.28 | 15.52 |
| 57 | 3.48 | 4.75 | 5.61 | 6.82 | 8.58 | 10.91 | 13.50 | 15.78 |
| 58 | 3.51 | 4.82 | 5.69 | 6.92 | 8.71 | 11.08 | 13.72 | 16.04 |
| 59 | 3.54 | 4.89 | 5.78 | 7.03 | 8.85 | 11.26 | 13.94 | 16.30 |
| 60 | 3.57 | 4.96 | 5.86 | 7.13 | 8.98 | 11.43 | 14.16 | 16.56 |
| 61 | 3.60 | 5.03 | 5.95 | 7.24 | 9.12 | 11.61 | 14.38 | 16.82 |
| 62 | 3.64 | 5.10 | 6.03 | 7.34 | 9.25 | 11.78 | 14.60 | 17.08 |
| 63 | 3.67 | 5.17 | 6.12 | 7.45 | 9.39 | 11.96 | 14.82 | 17.34 |
| 64 | 3.70 | 5.24 | 6.20 | 7.55 | 9.52 | 12.13 | 15.04 | 17.60 |
| 65 | 3.73 | 5.31 | 6.29 | 7.66 | 9.66 | 12.31 | 15.26 | 17.86 |
| 66 | 3.76 | 5.38 | 6.37 | 7.76 | 9.79 | 12.48 | 15.48 | 18.12 |
| 68 | 3.82 | 5.52 | 6.54 | 7.97 | 10.06 | 12.83 | 15.92 | 18.64 |
| 70 | 3.88 | 5.66 | 6.71 | 8.18 | 10.33 | 13.18 | 16.36 | 19.16 |

## U.S. PRIORITY MAIL (over 12 oz.)

| Weight in pounds up to: | Zone: Local 1-2-3 | 300-600 miles 4 | 600-1,000 miles 5 | 1,000-1,400 miles 6 | 1,400-1,800 miles 7 | Over 1,800 miles 8 |
|---|---|---|---|---|---|---|
| 1 | $1.71 | $1.81 | $1.88 | $1.97 | $2.06 | $2.25 |
| 1.5 | 1.86 | 1.96 | 2.07 | 2.21 | 2.34 | 2.50 |
| 2 | 1.99 | 2.12 | 2.27 | 2.44 | 2.61 | 2.83 |
| 2.5 | 2.11 | 2.27 | 2.46 | 2.68 | 2.89 | 3.16 |
| 3 | 2.23 | 2.42 | 2.65 | 2.91 | 3.17 | 3.50 |
| 3.5 | 2.35 | 2.58 | 2.84 | 3.15 | 3.45 | 3.83 |
| 4 | 2.47 | 2.73 | 3.03 | 3.38 | 3.73 | 4.16 |
| 4.5 | 2.59 | 2.89 | 3.22 | 3.62 | 4.01 | 4.50 |
| 5 | 2.72 | 3.04 | 3.42 | 3.85 | 4.29 | 4.83 |
| 6 | 2.96 | 3.35 | 3.80 | 4.32 | 4.84 | 5.50 |
| 7 | 3.20 | 3.66 | 4.18 | 4.79 | 5.40 | 6.16 |
| 8 | 3.44 | 3.96 | 4.56 | 5.26 | 5.96 | 6.83 |
| 9 | 3.69 | 4.27 | 4.95 | 5.73 | 6.51 | 7.49 |
| 10 | 3.93 | 4.58 | 5.33 | 6.20 | 7.07 | 8.16 |
| 11 | 4.17 | 4.89 | 5.71 | 6.67 | 7.63 | 8.83 |
| 12 | 4.42 | 5.20 | 6.10 | 7.14 | 8.18 | 9.49 |
| 13 | 4.66 | 5.50 | 6.48 | 7.61 | 8.74 | 10.16 |
| 14 | 4.90 | 5.81 | 6.86 | 8.08 | 9.30 | 10.82 |
| 15 | 5.15 | 6.12 | 7.25 | 8.55 | 9.86 | 11.49 |
| 16 | 5.39 | 6.43 | 7.63 | 9.02 | 10.41 | 12.16 |
| 17 | 5.63 | 6.74 | 8.01 | 9.49 | 10.97 | 12.82 |
| 18 | 5.87 | 7.04 | 8.39 | 9.96 | 11.53 | 13.49 |
| 19 | 6.12 | 7.35 | 8.78 | 10.43 | 12.08 | 14.15 |
| 20 | 6.36 | 7.66 | 9.16 | 10.90 | 12.64 | 14.82 |
| 21 | 6.60 | 7.97 | 9.54 | 11.37 | 13.20 | 15.49 |
| 22 | 6.85 | 8.28 | 9.93 | 11.84 | 13.75 | 16.15 |
| 23 | 7.09 | 8.58 | 10.31 | 12.31 | 14.31 | 16.82 |
| 24 | 7.33 | 8.89 | 10.69 | 12.78 | 14.87 | 17.48 |
| 25 | 7.58 | 9.20 | 11.08 | 13.25 | 15.43 | 18.15 |
| 26 | 7.82 | 9.51 | 11.46 | 13.72 | 15.98 | 18.82 |
| 27 | 8.06 | 9.82 | 11.84 | 14.19 | 16.54 | 19.48 |
| 28 | 8.30 | 10.12 | 12.22 | 14.66 | 17.10 | 20.15 |
| 29 | 8.55 | 10.43 | 12.61 | 15.13 | 17.65 | 20.81 |
| 30 | 8.79 | 10.74 | 12.99 | 15.60 | 18.21 | 21.48 |
| 31 | 9.03 | 11.05 | 13.37 | 16.07 | 18.77 | 22.15 |
| 32 | 9.28 | 11.36 | 13.76 | 16.54 | 19.32 | 22.81 |
| 33 | 9.52 | 11.66 | 14.14 | 17.01 | 19.88 | 23.48 |
| 34 | 9.76 | 11.97 | 14.52 | 17.48 | 20.44 | 24.14 |
| 35 | 10.01 | 12.28 | 14.91 | 17.95 | 21.00 | 24.81 |
| 36 | 10.25 | 12.59 | 15.29 | 18.42 | 21.55 | 25.48 |
| 37 | 10.49 | 12.90 | 15.67 | 18.89 | 22.11 | 26.14 |
| 38 | 10.73 | 13.20 | 16.05 | 19.36 | 22.67 | 26.81 |
| 39 | 10.98 | 13.51 | 16.44 | 19.83 | 23.22 | 27.47 |
| 40 | 11.22 | 13.82 | 16.82 | 20.30 | 23.78 | 28.14 |
| 41 | 11.46 | 14.13 | 17.20 | 20.77 | 24.34 | 28.81 |
| 42 | 11.71 | 14.44 | 17.59 | 21.24 | 24.89 | 29.47 |
| 43 | 11.95 | 14.74 | 17.97 | 21.71 | 25.45 | 30.14 |
| 44 | 12.19 | 15.05 | 18.35 | 22.18 | 26.01 | 20.80 |
| 45 | 12.44 | 15.36 | 18.74 | 22.65 | 26.57 | 31.47 |
| 46 | 12.68 | 15.67 | 19.12 | 23.12 | 27.12 | 32.14 |
| 47 | 12.92 | 15.98 | 19.50 | 23.59 | 27.68 | 32.80 |
| 48 | 13.16 | 16.28 | 19.88 | 24.06 | 28.24 | 33.47 |
| 49 | 13.41 | 16.59 | 20.27 | 24.53 | 28.79 | 34.13 |
| 50 | 13.65 | 16.90 | 20.65 | 25.00 | 29.35 | 34.80 |
| 51 | 13.89 | 17.21 | 21.03 | 25.47 | 29.91 | 35.47 |
| 52 | 14.14 | 17.52 | 21.42 | 25.94 | 30.46 | 36.13 |
| 53 | 14.38 | 17.82 | 21.80 | 26.41 | 31.02 | 36.80 |
| 54 | 14.62 | 18.13 | 22.18 | 26.88 | 31.58 | 37.46 |
| 55 | 14.87 | 18.44 | 22.57 | 27.35 | 32.14 | 38.13 |
| 56 | 15.11 | 18.75 | 22.95 | 27.82 | 32.69 | 38.80 |
| 58 | 15.59 | 19.36 | 23.71 | 28.76 | 33.81 | 40.14 |
| 60 | 16.08 | 19.98 | 24.48 | 29.70 | 34.92 | 41.46 |
| 62 | 16.57 | 20.60 | 25.25 | 30.64 | 36.03 | 42.79 |
| 64 | 17.03 | 21.21 | 26.01 | 31.58 | 37.15 | 44.12 |
| 66 | 17.54 | 21.83 | 26.78 | 32.52 | 38.26 | 45.46 |
| 68 | 18.02 | 22.44 | 27.54 | 33.46 | 39.38 | 46.79 |
| 70 | 18.51 | 23.06 | 28.31 | 34.40 | 40.49 | 48.12 |

# POSTAL SERVICE ADDRESS ABBREVIATIONS

## STATES AND TERRITORIES

| | | | | |
|---|---|---|---|---|
| Alabama ..............AL | Georgia ...GA | Maryland .........MD | New Mexico .....NM | South Dakota ....SD |
| Alaska ...............AK | Guam ....GU | Massachusetts ....MA | New York .........NY | Tennessee ......TN |
| Arizona .............AZ | Hawaii......HI | Michigan .........MI | North Carolina ...NC | Texas ...........TX |
| Arkansas............AR | Idaho......ID | Minnesota ......MN | North Dakota .....ND | Utah............UT |
| California ...........CA | Illinois ......IL | Mississippi ....MS | Ohio.............OH | Vermont.........VT |
| Canal Zone ..........CZ | Indiana ....IN | Missouri .......MO | Oklahoma ......OK | Virginia .........VA |
| Colorado ............CO | Iowa........IA | Montana ........MT | Oregon ..........OR | Virgin Islands ....VI |
| Connecticut .........CT | Kansas....KS | Nebraska ........NE | Pennsylvania .....PA | Washington .....WA |
| Delaware ............DE | Kentucky...KY | Nevada .........NV | Puerto Rico......PR | West Virginia ....WV |
| District of Columbia ..DC | Louisiana ..LA | New Hampshire....NH | Rhode Island .....RI | Wisconsin ......WI |
| Florida ..............FL | Maine .....ME | New Jersey .......NJ | South Carolina ...SC | Wyoming .......WY |

## OTHER POSTAL SERVICE ADDRESS ABBREVIATIONS

| | | | | |
|---|---|---|---|---|
| Academy..ACAD | Central ....CTL | Fort..........FT | Junction ....JCT | Parkway ....PKY | Spring.....SPG |
| Airport....ARPRT | Church ....CHR | Fountain ....FTN | Lake .........LK | Place ........PL | Square......SQ |
| Alley........ALY | Circle ....CIR | Freeway ....FWY | Lane.........LN | Plaza .......PLZ | State ........ST |
| Annex......ANX | City .........CY | Gateway ..GTWY | Light ......LGT | Point ........PT | Station ....STA |
| Avenue....AVE | College ..CLG | Great .......GR | Little........LTL | Prairie ......PR | Street........ST |
| Bayou......BYU | Court ......CT | Grove ....GRV | Lower ....LWR | Ridge ......RDG | Terrace .....TER |
| Beach ......BCH | Creek ......CRK | Harbor ....HBR | Manor .....MNR | River.......RIV | Tower......TWR |
| Boulevard .BLVD | Crossing ...XING | Heights ....HTS | Meadows .MDWS | Road ......RD | Trail........TRL |
| Bluff........BLF | Drive .......DR | High ..........HI | Memorial ..MEM | Rural ........R | Trailer....TRLR |
| Branch......BR | East .........E | Highway ....HWY | Middle ....MDL | Saint........ST | Turnpike..TPKE |
| Bridge......BRG | Estates ....EST | Hill ..........HL | Mission ..MSN | Sainte ......ST | Upper ....UPR |
| Brook ......BRK | Expressway EXPY | Hospital ...HOSP | Mount ....MT | San.........SN | Union .....UN |
| Camp........CP | Extension ...EXT | House .....HSE | Mountain ..MTN | Santa .......SN | University .UNIV |
| Cape ......CPE | Ferry ......FRY | Institute ..INST | National ..NAT | School ....SCH | Valley ......VLY |
| Causeway .CWSY | Field........FLD | Island .......IS | North ........N | Seminary SMNRY | Village ......VLG |
| Center......CTR | Forest .....FRST | Isle ..........IS | Park .........PK | South .........S | West ........W |

# AIR PARCEL POST RATES* FROM THE U.S. TO OTHER COUNTRIES

Air parcel post service is available to most countries of the world. Registered or insured parcels must be sealed. To most countries the greatest length of a package allowed is 3½ feet, and the greatest length and girth combined is 6 feet. To some countries, parcels may measure 4 feet in length if not more than 16 inches in girth. Consult your local post office.

| Country | First 4 oz. | Each added 4 oz. or fraction | Max. insurance available | Max. weight in lbs. | Country | First 4 oz. | Each added 4 oz. or fraction | Max. insurance available | Max. weight in lbs. |
|---|---|---|---|---|---|---|---|---|---|
| Afghanistan .......... | $5.40 | $1.10 | No | 22 | Canada ............. | — | — | $ 400 | 35 |
| Albania ............. | 4.60 | .90 | No | 22 | Canary Islands........ | $4.60 | $0.90 | $ 200 | 44 |
| Algeria ............. | 5.40 | 1.10 | No | 44 | Cape Verde ......... | 5.40 | 1.10 | $ 20 | 22 |
| Andorra............. | 3.80 | .70 | $ 395 | 44 | Central Africa ........ | 6.20 | 1.30 | No | 44 |
| Angola............. | 6.20 | 1.30 | $ 20 | 22 | Chad ............. | 5.40 | 1.10 | No | 44 |
| Antigua ............. | 3.00 | .50 | $ 100 | 22 | Chile ............. | 5.40 | 1.10 | No | 22 |
| Argentina ........... | 5.40 | 1.10 | $ 200 | 44 | China[1] ............ | 6.20 | 1.30 | No | 44 |
| Aruba ............. | 3.00 | .50 | $ 200 | 44 | Colombia .......... | 3.80 | .70 | $ 200 | 44 |
| Australia ........... | 5.40 | 1.10 | $ 225 | 44 | Comoros ........... | 6.20 | 1.30 | No | 44 |
| Austria ............. | 3.80 | .70 | $ 395 | 44 | Congo ............. | 5.40 | 1.10 | No | 44 |
| Azores ............. | 4.60 | .90 | $ 395 | 44 | Corsica ............ | 6.20 | 1.30 | $ 395 | 44 |
| Bahamas............ | 3.00 | .50 | $ 120 | 22 | Costa Rica .......... | 3.00 | .50 | No | 44 |
| Bahrain ............ | 5.40 | 1.10 | $ 100 | 22 | Curacao ........... | 3.00 | .50 | $ 200 | 44 |
| Balearic Islands ....... | 4.60 | .90 | $ 200 | 44 | Cyprus ............ | 5.40 | 1.10 | $ 200 | 44 |
| Bangladesh .......... | 6.20 | 1.30 | $ 200 | 22 | Czechoslovakia ...... | 4.60 | .90 | $ 200 | 44 |
| Barbados ........... | 3.80 | .70 | $ 100 | 22 | Denmark............ | 3.80 | .70 | $ 395 | 44 |
| Belgium ............ | 6.20 | 1.30 | $ 200 | 44 | Djibouti ............ | 6.20 | 1.30 | $ 395 | 44 |
| Belize ............. | 3.00 | .50 | No | 22 | Dominica .......... | 3.00 | .50 | $ 100 | 22 |
| Benin ............. | 5.40 | 1.10 | No | 44 | Dominican Republic ... | 3.00 | .50 | No | 44 |
| Bermuda ........... | 3.00 | .50 | No | 33 | Ecuador ............ | 3.80 | .70 | $ 50 | 44 |
| Bolivia ............. | 3.80 | .70 | No | 44 | Egypt ............. | 4.60 | .90 | $ 200 | 44 |
| Botswana ........... | 6.20 | 1.30 | No | 22 | El Salvador ......... | 3.00 | .50 | No | 44 |
| Brazil............. | 6.20 | 1.30 | No | 44 | Equatorial Guinea .... | 5.40 | 1.10 | No | 44 |
| Britain ............. | 4.60 | .90 | $1,200 | 44 | Ethiopia ........... | 5.40 | 1.10 | $ 200 | 44 |
| Brunei ............. | 5.40 | 1.10 | No | 22 | Faeroe Islands ....... | 4.60 | .90 | $ 395 | 44 |
| Bulgaria ............ | 5.40 | 1.10 | No | 22 | Falkland Islands...... | 5.40 | 1.10 | No | 22 |
| Burma ............. | 5.40 | 1.10 | No | 22 | Fiji ............. | 3.80 | .70 | $ 120 | 22 |
| Burundi ............ | 6.20 | 1.30 | No | 22 | Finland ............ | 5.40 | 1.10 | $ 395 | 44 |
| Cameroon .......... | 4.60 | .90 | No | 22 | France ............ | 6.20 | 1.30 | $ 395 | 44 |

* Effective Jan. 1, 1981. [1] Mail must be addressed to the "People's Republic of China."

## AIR PARCEL POST RATES TO OTHER COUNTRIES (continued)

| Country | First 4 oz. | Each added 4 oz. or fraction | Max. insurance available | Max. weight in lbs. | Country | First 4 oz. | Each added 4 oz. or fraction | Max. insurance available | Max. weight in lbs. |
|---|---|---|---|---|---|---|---|---|---|
| French Guiana | $4.60 | $ .90 | No | 44 | Niger | $5.40 | $1.10 | No | 44 |
| French Polynesia | 5.40 | 1.10 | $ 395 | 44 | Nigeria | 4.60 | .90 | No | 22 |
| Gabon | 5.40 | 1.10 | No | 44 | Norway | 5.40 | 1.10 | $395 | 44 |
| Gambia | 3.80 | .70 | No | 22 | Oman | 5.40 | 1.10 | $100 | 22 |
| Germany, East | 4.60 | .90 | $ 200 | 22 | Pakistan | 5.40 | 1.10 | $200 | 22 |
| Germany, West | 4.60 | .90 | $ 395 | 44 | Panama | 3.00 | .50 | No | 70 |
| Ghana | 5.40 | 1.10 | $ 80 | 22 | Papua New Guinea | 5.40 | 1.10 | $100 | 22 |
| Gibraltar | 5.40 | 1.10 | $ 50 | 22 | Paraguay | 4.60 | .90 | No | 44 |
| Greece | 4.60 | .90 | $ 200 | 44 | Peru | 3.80 | .70 | No | 44 |
| Greenland | 5.40 | 1.10 | $ 395 | 44 | Philippines | 5.40 | 1.10 | $200 | 44 |
| Grenada | 3.80 | .70 | $ 100 | 22 | Pitcairn Islands | 3.80 | .70 | No | 22 |
| Guadeloupe | 3.00 | .50 | No | 44 | Poland | 4.60 | .90 | No | 44 |
| Guatemala | 3.00 | .50 | $ 100 | 44 | Portugal | 3.80 | .70 | $395 | 22 |
| Guinea | 3.80 | .70 | No | 44 | Qatar | 4.60 | .90 | $100 | 22 |
| Guinea–Bissau | 3.80 | .70 | $ 20 | 22 | Réunion | 6.20 | 1.30 | No | 44 |
| Guyana | 3.80 | .70 | $ 200 | 22 | Romania | 4.60 | .90 | No | 22 |
| Haiti | 3.00 | .50 | No | 44 | Rwanda | 5.40 | 1.10 | No | 22 |
| Honduras | 3.80 | .70 | No | 44 | Saba | 3.00 | .50 | $200 | 44 |
| Hong Kong | 4.60 | .90 | $ 395 | 22 | St. Helena | 3.80 | .70 | No | 22 |
| Hungary | 4.60 | .90 | $ 400 | 44 | St. Kitts | 3.00 | .50 | $100 | 22 |
| Iceland | 5.40 | 1.10 | $ 395 | 44 | St. Lucia | 3.00 | .50 | $100 | 22 |
| India | 5.40 | 1.10 | $ 200 | 44 | St. Pierre & Miquelon | 3.00 | .50 | No | 44 |
| Indonesia | 6.20 | 1.30 | No | 22 | St. Vincent | 3.00 | .50 | $100 | 22 |
| Iran | 5.40 | 1.10 | $ 200 | 44 | San Marino | 4.60 | .90 | $120 | 44 |
| Iraq | 5.40 | 1.10 | No | 44 | Santa Cruz Islands | 3.80 | .70 | No | 22 |
| Ireland | 4.60 | .90 | $1,000 | 22 | Saudi Arabia | 4.60 | .90 | No | 22 |
| Israel | 4.60 | .90 | No | 33 | Senegal | 5.40 | 1.10 | No | 44 |
| Italy | 4.60 | .90 | $ 120 | 44 | Seychelles | 5.40 | 1.10 | No | 22 |
| Ivory Coast | 5.40 | 1.10 | No | 44 | Sierra Leone | 4.60 | .90 | No | 22 |
| Jamaica | 3.00 | .50 | No | 22 | Singapore | 5.40 | 1.10 | $100 | 22 |
| Japan | 6.20 | 1.30 | $ 395 | 22 | Solomons | 4.60 | .90 | No | 22 |
| Jordan | 4.60 | .90 | No | 22 | Somalia | 5.40 | 1.10 | No | 22 |
| Kenya | 5.40 | 1.10 | No | 22 | South Africa | 6.20 | 1.30 | No | 22 |
| Kiribati | 3.80 | .70 | No | 44 | Soviet Union | 6.20 | 1.30 | $200 | 44 |
| Korea, South | 5.40 | 1.10 | $ 200 | 22 | Spain | 4.60 | .90 | $200 | 44 |
| Kuwait | 4.60 | .90 | $ 200 | 44 | Sri Lanka | 5.40 | 1.10 | $200 | 22 |
| Laos | 6.20 | 1.30 | No | 22 | Sudan | 5.40 | 1.10 | No | 22 |
| Lebanon | 4.60 | .90 | No | 44 | Suriname | 3.80 | .70 | $100 | 44 |
| Lesotho | 6.20 | 1.30 | No | 22 | Swaziland | 5.40 | 1.10 | No | 22 |
| Liberia | 3.80 | .70 | $ 100 | 22 | Sweden | 5.40 | 1.10 | $395 | 44 |
| Libya | 4.60 | .90 | No | 44 | Switzerland | 3.80 | .70 | $395 | 44 |
| Liechtenstein | 3.80 | .70 | $ 395 | 44 | Syria | 4.60 | .90 | $200 | 44 |
| Luxembourg | 3.80 | .70 | $ 200 | 44 | Taiwan | 4.60 | .90 | $200 | 44 |
| Macao | 4.60 | .90 | $ 120 | 22 | Tanzania | 6.20 | 1.30 | No | 22 |
| Madagascar | 4.60 | .90 | No | 44 | Thailand | 5.40 | 1.10 | $120 | 22 |
| Madeira Islands | 3.80 | .70 | $ 395 | 22 | Togo | 5.40 | 1.10 | No | 44 |
| Malawi | 5.40 | 1.10 | No | 22 | Tonga | 3.80 | .70 | No | 22 |
| Malaysia | 5.40 | 1.10 | $ 100 | 22 | Trinidad–Tobago | 3.80 | .70 | $145 | 22 |
| Maldives | 5.40 | 1.10 | No | 22 | Tristan da Cunha | 3.80 | .70 | No | 22 |
| Mali | 4.60 | .90 | No | 44 | Tunisia | 4.60 | .90 | No | 44 |
| Malta | 4.60 | .90 | No | 22 | Turkey | 4.60 | .90 | $200 | 44 |
| Martinique | 3.00 | .50 | No | 44 | Turks and Caicos Is. | 3.00 | .50 | No | 22 |
| Mauritania | 5.40 | 1.10 | No | 44 | Tuvalu | 3.80 | .70 | No | 22 |
| Mauritius | 6.20 | 1.30 | No | 22 | Uganda | 5.40 | 1.10 | No | 22 |
| Mexico | 3.00 | .50 | No | 44 | United Arab Emirates | 5.40 | 1.10 | $100 | 22 |
| Monaco | 6.20 | 1.30 | $ 395 | 44 | Upper Volta | 4.60 | .90 | No | 44 |
| Montserrat | 3.00 | .50 | $ 100 | 22 | Uruguay | 3.80 | .70 | No | 44 |
| Morocco | 4.60 | .90 | No | 44 | Vanuatu | 3.80 | .70 | No | 44 |
| Mozambique | 6.20 | 1.30 | $ 100 | 22 | Vatican City | 4.60 | .90 | No | 44 |
| Namibia | 6.20 | 1.30 | No | 22 | Venezuela | 3.80 | .70 | No | 44 |
| Nauru | 4.60 | .90 | $ 200 | 22 | Wallis and Futuna | 2.81 | .93 | $395 | 44 |
| Nepal | 5.40 | 1.10 | No | 22 | Western Samoa | 3.80 | .70 | $200 | 22 |
| Netherlands | 4.60 | .90 | $ 395 | 44 | Yemen, North | 5.40 | 1.10 | No | 44 |
| Netherlands Antilles | 3.00 | .50 | $ 200 | 44 | Yemen, South | 5.40 | 1.10 | No | 44 |
| Nevis | 3.00 | .50 | $ 100 | 22 | Yugoslavia | 4.60 | .90 | $200 | 44 |
| New Calendonia | 5.40 | 1.10 | $ 395 | 44 | Zaire | 5.40 | 1.10 | No | 44 |
| New Zealand | 5.40 | 1.10 | $ 200 | 22 | Zambia | 6.20 | 1.30 | No | 22 |
| Nicaragua | 3.80 | 0.70 | $ 200 | 44 | Zimbabwe | 6.20 | 1.30 | No | 22 |

# Religion

An estimated 200,000 Christians gathered on the Mall in Washington, D.C., April 29, 1980, for a day of prayer, intended to bring the nation back to God. Called "Washington for Jesus," the rally was sponsored by One Nation Under God, a coalition of independent church leaders. The evangelical and fundamentalist participants heard Rev. Bill Bright, of San Bernardino, Calif., founder of the Campus Crusade for Christ, say that deterioration of morals had led to "a world aflame in sin." Earlier, a statement by 20 religious organizations, including the National Council of Churches, denounced the rally, accusing its sponsors of "trying to Christianize the government."

## HIGHLIGHTS: 1980

### TRAVELS OF POPE JOHN PAUL II

Pope John Paul II traveled thousands of miles in 1980, visiting three continents. He began with a six-nation, 11,000-mile tour of black Africa on May 2.

Terming it a "journey of friendship and brotherly love," the pope stopped first in Zaire, where more than a million people cheered him during a motorcade from the airport into the heart of Kinshasa. Tragedy marred his visit to Kinshasa when nine people were trampled to death by a crowd heading for a papal mass on May 4.

In Kenya, the pope urged the continent's 200 million Christians to participate more in the politics of their countries.

In Ghana, the pope met with Dr. Robert Runcie, archbishop of Canterbury, who was also visiting Africa. The two men, who together spiritually lead the largest number of

Christians in Africa, termed their meeting a "joyful and moving occasion," and a step toward closer relations between their churches.

In Upper Volta, the pope called for efforts to battle the problems of the advancing Sahara Desert and assailed the industrialized nations for not coming to the aid of the drought-stricken nation.

The pope's last stop in Africa was the Ivory Coast, where he chided officials on the great differences between the rich and poor.

Late in May, the pope made a historic 4-day visit to France, the first by a Roman Catholic pontiff since 1814. At Notre Dame Cathedral John Paul II urged the French clergy to remain constant against the turbulence of the outside world. He later assailed the French for decline in the church's influence. It was reported that although 85% of France's

population are baptized as Catholics, only about 15% actively practice and adhere to the tenets of the religion.

In the longest papal trip outside Italy in modern times, John Paul II visited 13 cities in Brazil during June 30–July 11. He spoke out strongly for social justice for the poor and oppressed. At one point, he was so touched by the conditions in a Rio de Janeiro slum, that he slid his gold ring of office from his finger and gave it to a local priest for his parish. In his talks he also gave special emphasis to the plight of Brazil's Indian tribes, faced with extinction as the nation tries to industrialize the Amazon jungles. Tragedy again marred the pope's journeys, when three people were trampled to death as crowds stormed a soccer stadium in Fortaleza, where he was to speak.

### ANGLICAN PRIESTS JOIN CATHOLIC CLERGY

In a break with tradition, the Vatican announced in August that it will admit dissident Anglican priests to the Roman Catholic priesthood. The priests, many of whom are married, are among thousands of persons who split with the Episcopal Church when it decided, in 1976, to ordain women.

Acting on an appeal by one dissident group, the California-based Pro-Diocese of St. Augustine of Canterbury, the Vatican stated that those Anglican priests wishing to become Roman Catholic priests would be reviewed individually and would have to accept the tenets of the Roman Catholic Church, though they could keep some of the traditions of their former church. Married priests could not become bishops, nor remarry if widowed.

The Episcopal Church is part of the Anglican Communion, founded in Britain after King Henry VIII broke with the Roman Catholic Church in 1533 when refused permission to divorce Catherine of Aragon to marry Anne Boleyn.

### MORMON CHURCH MARKS 150th ANNIVERSARY

Thousands of Mormons flocked to Salt Lake City, Utah, the first weekend in April to mark the 150th anniversary of the founding of the Mormon Church, or Church of Jesus Christ of Latter-day Saints. In marking the occasion, church officials reported that there are 4.3 million Mormons in more than 60 countries, growing by over 30% in the past five years. Much of the growth, however, has taken place in foreign countries, where some 30,000 church missionaries have successfully presented Mormonism's gospel.

In the United States the church has been increasingly concerned about the erosion of the family and other secular influences. The 1979 excommunication of Virginia housewife Sonia Johnson for her support of the Equal Rights Amendment caused controversy and divided church members.

Church authorities, while confident that its family-centered gospel will continue to hold and attract followers, note greater attention to increasing the role of women in the main worship service.

### WOMEN MAKE GAINS IN RELIGION

Women did make inroads toward full participation in religious practice during 1980. Rev. Marjorie S. Matthews, of Traverse City, Mich., was elected a bishop of the United Methodist Church in July by delegates to the North Central regional conference in Dayton, Ohio. Rev. Matthews, 64, became the first woman to be named to the ruling hierarchy of an American church body.

In May, delegates to the Rabbinical Assembly, representing Conservative Judaism, passed a resolution favoring the ordination of women as rabbis. At present, only Reform Jews have female rabbis. Although the vote did not in itself order the ordination of women, it will present the opinion of the rabbinate to the Jewish Theological Seminary of America, which trains and ordains most Conservative rabbis.

### GLASS CATHEDRAL OPENS IN CALIFORNIA

A recital by opera star Beverly Sills helped mark the opening of the Garden Grove (Calif.) Community Church in May. Known also as the Crystal Cathedral, the new building was designed by architect Philip Johnson and built at a cost of $18 million.

Rev. Robert H. Schuller established the church in 1955 when he began his ministry in the Reformed Church in America, using a drive-in movie theater snack bar as a pulpit for four years. In 1959 a chapel was built, but soon proved too small, and he began piping his sermons by loudspeakers to cars parked outside.

The cathedral, shaped like a four-point star, is 415 feet long, 207 feet wide, and rises to a peak of 128 feet. It seats 2,862 people and has a choir loft for 120. The walls and roof are made of more than 10,000 plates of tinted glass, and there is a 185-foot-long altar of red marble.

Rev. Schuller encouraged the use of all glass construction, claiming, "It's the first time you have a religious building you can see the sky through."

Known for his weekly TV evangelical program, *The Hour of Power*, Rev. Schuller held the first worship services inside the suburban Los Angeles cathedral in September.

# MAJOR WORLD RELIGIONS

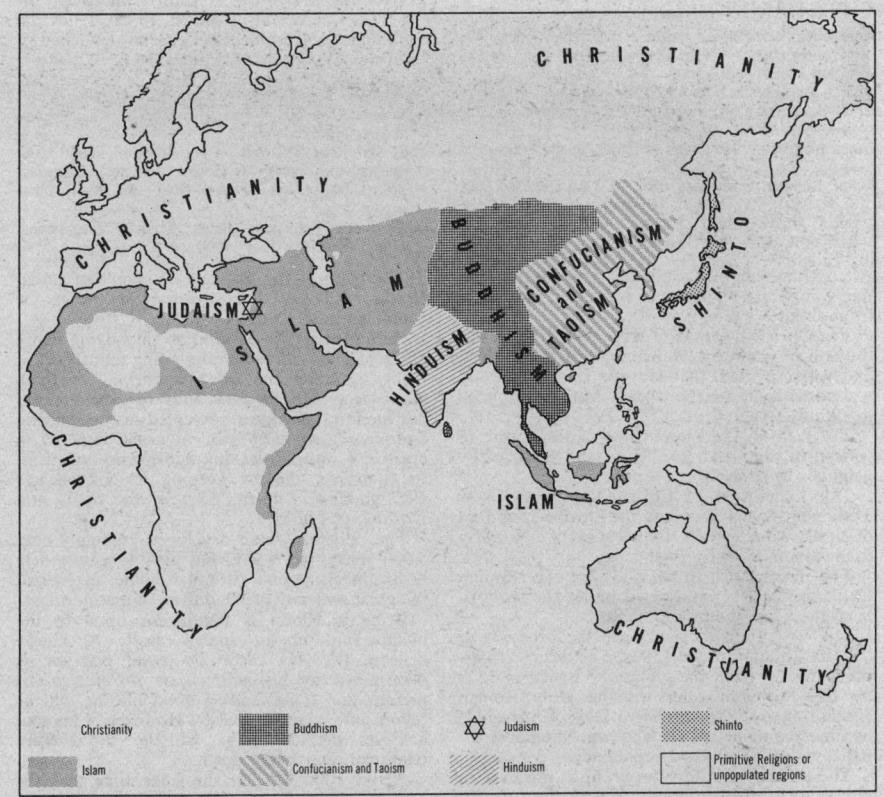

| | | | |
|---|---|---|---|
| Christianity | Buddhism | ✡ Judaism | Shinto |
| Islam | Confucianism and Taoism | Hinduism | Primitive Religions or unpopulated regions |

This map gives a general idea of the areas where the world's major religions have exerted their strongest direct influence. Not shown are North and South America, where the Christian religion has been predominant.

Throughout history man has turned to religion to find meaning for life and to explain the unknown.

Man's awareness of God, or of some supernatural power or powers, has impelled belief in a sacred, transcendent order that deals with human experience in the world or beyond it.

The nine largest world religions are: Buddhism, Christianity, Confucianism, Hinduism, Islam, Judaism, Shinto, Sikhism, and Taoism.

## BUDDHISM

**Adherents Worldwide:** About 245 million, chiefly in Southeast Asia, Sri Lanka, Korea, China, Japan, and Tibet.
**Adherents in U.S.:** About 60,000.
**Chief Scripture:** The Pali Canon.
**Dates from:** The time of Prince Siddhartha Gautama, the Buddha (about 2,500 years ago).

Buddhism teaches that the way beyond sorrow and suffering is a middle path between striving and spiritual contemplation. Its ethical system is based upon compassion and elimination of self-interest. Its theology accepts the rebirth of persons through the transmigration of souls.

An object of Buddhist life is to achieve nirvana, blissful detachment from the world, through which the cycle of rebirth stops.

Early Buddhism was close to Hinduism, but eventually split into several branches. The main branches include: Mahayana Buddhism, which stresses salvation and contemplation; and Hinayana, which preserves the monastic tradition of the early believers. Zen Buddhism is a Japanese type of Mahayana. The Lamaism of Tibet is a combination of Buddhism and the primitive beliefs of the region.

Buddhism has long ceased to be an important influence on the Indian subcontinent, the area where it originated. About A.D. 1000 many areas in southern Asia that were formerly Buddhist fell to the influence of Islam.

Buddhist precepts have influenced some Western philosophers, most notably Arthur Schopenhauer (1788–1860).

The Buddhist Churches of America were incorporated under that name in 1942.

**MAJOR WORLD RELIGIONS** *(continued)*

# CHRISTIANITY

**Adherents Worldwide:** About 1 billion (including 565 million Roman Catholics, 324 million Protestants, and 92 million Eastern Orthodox).

**Church Members in U.S.:** About 134 million.

**Chief Scripture:** The Bible (the Old Testament and the New Testament).

**Dates from:** The time of Jesus Christ (about 2,000 years ago).

**Major Holidays:** Christmas (Dec. 25), the Epiphany (Jan. 6), All Saints' Day (Nov. 1); Ash Wednesday, Palm Sunday, Good Friday, Easter Sunday, Ascension Day, and Pentecost; dates vary annually.

A continuation of the Judaic tradition, Christianity began with Jesus of Nazareth, who lived from about 5 B.C. to A.D. 30.

The Christian article of faith is that Jesus was the Son of God, that He came to save the world and was crucified, that He was resurrected and will come again on the world's last day to judge mankind.

The primary commandments of Jesus were to believe in God and love Him, and to love thy neighbor as thyself.

The foundation of Christianity is the New Testament, which recounts the life and teachings of Jesus Christ, and the works of his early followers, notably St. Paul.

The largest Christian body is the Roman Catholic Church, centralized under the authority of the pope, the bishop of Rome.

The Protestant churches are the products of the Reformation of the 1500s. The term "Protestant" derives from the *protestatio* issued in 1529 by the Lutheran rulers in the Holy Roman Empire against the repressive Diet of Speyer. It became the name for all who argued against the papal claim of universal supremacy.

The third great Christian group is the Eastern Orthodox, arising mainly from the ancient political split of the Roman Empire into East and West. The patriarch of Constantinople (in Istanbul) is first in honor among all the Orthodox leaders, and most of the churches consider him the spiritual leader of Eastern Orthodoxy. Over 4 million Americans belong to various branches of Eastern Orthodoxy.

# CONFUCIANISM

**Adherents Worldwide:** About 275 million, mainly in China and Taiwan.

**Chief Scripture:** The Analects.

**Dates from:** The time of Confucius (about 2,500 years ago).

Confucianism is primarily a body of ethics, and can be considered an institutional religion only in that it requires sacrifices to the gods and ancestors. However, Confucianism does not restrict itself to any formalized theology.

Confucians generally conduct their lives according to five cardinal virtues: kindness, righteousness, decorous behavior, wisdom, and uprightness. Confucius taught that the chief ethic was benevolence, and one of his prime precepts was "Treat inferiors with propriety."

The basis of Confucianism derives from the Analects of Confucius and the writings of Mencius, a sage of the 4th century B.C. Confucius was the foremost philosopher of China.

With the overthrow of China's monarchy in 1911-12, Confucianism waned. In the 1970s the communist government of China launched a campaign to wipe out Confucianism.

# HINDUISM

**Adherents:** Over 500 million live in India or in Indian communities in other lands.

**Chief Scriptures:** The Veda, a huge body of sacred texts, including the Upanishads (Secret Doctrines), Bhagavad-Gita (Song of the Blessed One), and many other writings.

**Dates from:** Prehistoric times, although the earliest writings date from about 1000 B.C.

The religion of the majority of people of India, Hinduism holds that divinity, or *ātman*, is contained in all beings.

Hinduism interprets God as embodying many different personalities, representing all aspects of reality. Among the most important of these deities are: *Siva*, a god both of creation and destruction, usually represented as a dancing figure with an extra pair of arms; *Brahma*, a creator; *Vishnu*, a sleeping figure who dreams of the universe, thereby keeping it in existence; *Kali*, goddess of death, sickness, and chaos; and *Krishna*, god of love.

The religion, which developed gradually over 5,000 years, has not given birth to any widely held ethical system. Although some sects exist, the great majority of Hindus are not sectarians.

Being a Hindu is contingent upon having membership in an Indian caste. A Hindu believes that his caste, or social position, is determined by his actions, or *Karma*, in his present life. If he leads a good life, he will be reborn into a superior caste. However, if his soul achieves perfection, he will be saved from continual rebirth and death.

About 1000 B.C., at the same time that the earliest of the Vedas were being recorded, the caste system began to become important in the Hindu social structure. The Brahman caste became the high priests of Hinduism about 800 B.C., a position that they hold to the present time.

Since India won independence in 1947, the government has tried to end the caste system. Most of today's Hindus worship according to the Puranic creed, a theological school that stabilized about A.D. 1500.

# ISLAM

**Adherents Worldwide:** About 700 million.

**Adherents in U.S.:** About 1 million.

**Chief Scripture:** The Koran.

**Dates from:** The time of Mohammed (about 1,400 years ago).

**Major Holidays:** Eid-al-Fitr (after fasting month of Ramadan) and Eid-al-Azha (feast of sacrifice on last day of Hajj).

Islam, an Arabic word meaning "submission to Allah (God)," is based on the revelations of Allah to Mohammed, who was born in Mecca (now in Saudi Arabia) and who lived from about A.D. 570 to 632. Among Muslims, Mohammed is believed to have been a descendant of Abraham, the founder of Judaism.

Mohammed received the revelations of Allah

compiled in the Koran, and provided explanations of Koranic teachings in the Sunna.

The main Islamic article of faith is a simple one: "There is no god but God (Allah), and Mohammed is His messenger." In addition, the followers of Islam have other major articles of faith: recitation of five daily prayers; observance of Ramadan (a monthlong period of fasting and self-examination); giving of alms (zakat); and, if possible, a pilgrimage to Mecca, the birthplace of Mohammed. The most important religious service is held at midday each Friday.

Islam divides into four interpretations: Hanafi, Shafai, Hanbali, and Maliki.

In the century after the death of Mohammed, Arab Muslim armies conquered the Middle East, North Africa, Spain, and southern France.

Although Muslim influence was prevented from spreading farther into Europe after Charles Martel's Christian military victory at Tours in 732, Islam continued its eastern growth. It served as a unifying force among the many Arab tribes.

Islam's missionary organization, the Ahmadiyya movement, was founded in 1889 by Hazrat Ahmad (1815–1908). It brought Islam to the U.S. in 1920. Today a majority of persons in 57 nations are Muslims.

## JUDAISM

**Adherents Worldwide:** About 15 million.
**Adherents in U.S.:** About 5.9 million.
**Chief Scriptures:** The Torah (Old Testament) and the Talmud.
**Dates from:** The time of Abraham (about 1800 B.C.).
**Major Holidays:** Pesach (Passover), Shavuot (Pentecost), Sukkot (Tabernacles), Rosh Hashanah (New Year), Yom Kippur (Day of Atonement), Hanukkah (Festival of Lights); dates vary annually.

Judaism recognizes one God, sometimes called *Elohim* or *Jehovah*.

The basic prayer of Judaism, called the Shema, begins: "Hear, O Israel, the Lord our God, the Lord is one."

The Jewish Sabbath is from sunset Friday to sunset Saturday.

Beginning with the patriarch Abraham, the Jews have had many great leaders and prophets, including Moses, who freed his people from Egyptian bondage in the 1200s B.C. and received the Ten Commandments and the Torah as a constitution for a new nation.

The ancient city of Jerusalem once was, and again is, central to Judaism. However, in ancient times Jerusalem was repeatedly destroyed and rebuilt. About A.D. 135 the Romans put down a Jewish revolt and forced the Jews to leave the Holy Land in what is called the *Diaspora*.

For many centuries Jews were persecuted by Christians in the belief they were responsible for the death of Jesus Christ. About 6 million Jews were slaughtered by Germans and others during World War II.

The Zionist movement for a Jewish homeland, which began in the 1800s, bore fruit in 1948, when the Jewish state of Israel was created in Palestine.

In the United States and in much of Europe, Jewish congregations are classified as Orthodox, Conservative, or Reform, depending on their degree of adherence to ancient religious customs and dietary laws.

## SHINTO

**Adherents Worldwide:** About 63 million, all of whom are Japanese.
**Chief Scripture:** None.
**Dates from:** Antiquity; originated with the beginnings of the Japanese culture.

Shinto is a set of rituals and customs involving pilgrimages, festivals, and worship of a great host of gods. It is a folk religion, limited strictly to the Japanese people, and thus without any universal prophetic message. The word *shin-to* means "way of the gods."

The highest deity is the sun goddess, known as the Ruler of Heaven.

Gods are worshiped through the sacrifice of rice and rice wine (sake).

Shinto did not evolve an ethical system of its own, but gradually borrowed ethical principles from Buddhism and Confucianism.

From about the 500s A.D., the emperor of Japan was considered the chief Shinto priest and had the immortal status of a deity. In the 1800s a state form of Shinto was organized in coordination with Japan's newly awakened imperialism. This militaristic form of Shinto disappeared after World War II, when Emperor Hirohito disavowed his divinity. Many of today's Shinto sects stress world peace and brotherhood.

## SIKHISM

**Adherents Worldwide:** About 8 million.
**Chief Scripture:** Granth Sahib.
**Dates from:** About A.D. 1500.

Most of the people who follow the religion of Sikhism live in the state of Punjab in northwestern India. The religion combines the beliefs of Islam and Hinduism.

Sikhism was founded by Guru Nanak (1469–1539). He taught that there was a single God, rejecting the many deities of Hinduism and the worship of idols. He attempted to eliminate the caste system of Hinduism, uniting his followers into one class.

The sacred writings of Sikhism began to be compiled by Guru Arjan (1563–1606), who also built the Sikhs' sacred city of Amritsar.

## TAOISM

**Adherents Worldwide:** About 30 million.
**Chief Scripture:** Tao-te ching.
**Dates from:** About 2,600 years ago, founded by Lao-tzu.

*Tao* in Chinese means "path," and the basis of early Taoism is the allowance of the affairs of men to take the path of nature. The religion stresses quietism, contemplation, and the elimination of all striving and strong passions.

After the 500s A.D., Taoism took on aspects of Confucianism and Buddhism. Taoist monasteries were established throughout China.

Taoism developed beliefs concerning an afterlife, which included a heaven and hell, as well as a cosmology that divided all reality into male and female principles, or *yang* and *yin*. In its later development, Taoism became concerned with magic and also provided the basis for many secret societies.

## PATRON SAINTS

Since the early days of Christianity certain saints and angels have been regarded as patrons of specific occupations, groups, localities, and nations.

| SUPPLIANTS | SAINTS | SUPPLIANTS | SAINTS | SUPPLIANTS | SAINTS |
|---|---|---|---|---|---|
| Accountants | St. Matthew | France | St. Joan of Arc; St. Thérèse; Our Lady of Assumption | Pilgrims | St. Alexius; St. James |
| Actors | St. Genesius | | | Plasterers | St. Bartholomew |
| Advertisers | St. Bernardine of Siena | Funeral dirs. | St. Dismas; St. Joseph of Arimathea | Poets | St. David; St. Cecilia |
| Altar boys | St. John Berchmans | | | Poison sufferers | St. Benedict |
| Anesthetists | St. René Goupil | Gardeners | St. Dorothy; St. Adelard; St. Tryphon; St. Fiacre; St. Phocas | Poland | St. Casimir; St. Stanislaus of Kracow; Our Lady of Czestochowa |
| Archers | St. Sebastian | | | | |
| Architects | St. Thomas, apostle; St. Barbara | Germany | St. Boniface; St. Michael | Policemen | St. Michael |
| Art | St. Catherine of Bologna | Glassworkers | St. Luke | Poor | St. Lawrence; St. Anthony of Padua |
| Artists | St. Luke | Gravediggers | St. Anthony, abbot | Possessed | St. Bruno; St. Denis |
| Astronomers | St. Dominic | Greece | St. Nicholas; St. Andrew | Postal workers | St. Gabriel |
| Athletes | St. Sebastian | | | Preg. mothers | St. Margaret; St. Raymund Nonnatus; St. Gerard Majella |
| Authors | St. Francis de Sales | Grocers | St. Michael | | |
| Aviators | Our Lady of Loreto; St. Thérèse of Lisieux; St. Joseph of Cupertino | Headaches | St. Teresa of Avila | Priests | St. Jean-Baptiste Vianney |
| | | Heart Patients | St. John of God | | |
| | | Housewives | St. Anne | Printers | St. John of God; St. Augustine of Hippo; St. Genesius |
| Bakers | St. Elizabeth of Hungary; St. Nicholas | Hunters | St. Hubert; St. Eustachius | | |
| Bankers | St. Matthew | India | Our Lady of Ass'pt'n | Prisoners | St. Dismas; St. Barbara; St. Joseph Cafasso |
| Barbers | Sts. Cosmas and Damian; St. Louis | Infantrymen | St. Maurice | | |
| | | Innkeepers | St. Amand | Public relations | St. Bernardino, Siena |
| Barren women | St. Anthony of Padua; St. Felicitas | Invalids | St. Roch | Radio workers | St. Gabriel |
| | | Ireland | St. Patrick; St. Brigid; St. Columba | Rheumatics | St. James the Greater |
| Beggars | St. Alexius | | | Sailors | St. Cuthbert; St. Brendan; St. Eulalia; St. Christopher; St. Peter Gonzales; St. Erasmus |
| Blacksmiths | St. Dunstan | Italy | St. Francis of Assisi; St. Catherine of Siena | | |
| Blind | St. Odilia; St. Raphael | | | | |
| Bookkeepers | St. Matthew | Japan | St. Peter Baptist | Scholars | St. Brigid |
| Booksellers | St. John of God | Jewelers | St. Eligius | Scientists | St. Albert |
| Boy Scouts | St. George | Journalists | St. Francis de Sales | Scotland | St. Andrew; St. Columba |
| Brewers | St. Augustine of Hippo; St. Luke; St. Nicholas of Myra | Jurists | St. Catherine of Alexandria; St. John Capistrano | Sculptors | St. Claude |
| | | Laborers | St. Isidore; St. James; St. John Bosco | Searchers for lost articles | St. Anthony of Padua |
| Bricklayers | St. Stephen | | | | |
| Brides | St. Nicholas of Myra | Lawyers | St. Ivo; St. Genesius; St. Thomas More | Secretaries | St. Genesius |
| Builders | St. Vincent Ferrer | | | Servants | St. Martha; St. Zita |
| Butchers | St. Anthony of Egypt; St. Hadrian; St. Luke | Librarians | St. Jerome | Shoemakers | Sts. Crispin and Crispinian |
| | | Maids | St. Zita | | |
| Cabinetmakers | St. Anne | Mentally ill | St. Dympna | Sick | St. Michael; St. John of God; St. Camillus de Lellis |
| Canada | St. Joseph; St. Anne | Merchants | St. Francis of Assisi; St. Nicholas of Myra | | |
| Cancer patients | St. Peregrine | | | Singers | St. Gregory; St. Cecilia |
| Carpenters | St. Joseph | Messengers | St. Gabriel | | |
| Children | St. Nicholas of Myra | Metal workers | St. Eligius | Skaters | St. Lidwina |
| China | St. Joseph | Mexico | Our Lady of Guad'l'pe | Skiers | St. Bernard |
| Choir boys | St. Dominic Savio | Miners | St. Barbara | Social workers | St. Louise de Marillac |
| Comedians | St. Vitus | Mothers | St. Monica | Soldiers | St. Hadrian; St. George; St. Ignatius; St. Sebastian; St. Martin of Tours; St. Joan of Arc |
| Confessors | St. Alphonsus Liguori; St. John Nepomucene | Motorcyclists | Our Lady of Grace | | |
| | | Motorists | St. Christopher; St. Frances of Rome | Spain | St. James; St. Teresa |
| Cooks | St. Lawrence; St. Martha | | | Stenographers | St. Genesius; St. Cassian |
| | | Mountaineers | St. Bernard, Menthon | | |
| Dairy workers | St. Brigid | Musicians | St. Gregory the Great; St. Cecilia; St. Dunstan | Students | St. Thomas Aquinas; St. Catherine of Alexandria |
| Deaf | St. Francis de Sales | | | | |
| Denmark | St. Ansgar; St. Canute | Norway | St. Olaf | Sweden | St. Bridget; St. Eric |
| Dentists | St. Apollonia | Nurses | St. Camillus de Lellis; St. John of God; St. Agatha; St. Alexius; St. Raphael | Tailors | St. Homobonus |
| Dying | St. Joseph; St. Barbara | | | Tax collectors | St. Matthew |
| Ecology | St. Francis of Assisi | | | Taxi drivers | St. Fiacre |
| Editors | St. John Bosco | Orators | St. John Chrysostom | Teachers | St. Gregory the Great; St. Catherine of Alexandria; St. John Baptist de la Salle |
| Emigrants | St. Frances Xavier Cabrini | Orphans | St. Jerome Aemilian | | |
| | | Painters | St. Luke | | |
| Engineers | St. Ferdinand III | Paratroopers | St. Michael | | |
| England | St. George | Pawnbrokers | St. Nicholas | TV workers | St. Gabriel |
| Ethiopia | St. Frumentius | Pharmacists | Sts. Cosmas and Damian; St. James the Greater | Throat sufferers | St. Blaise |
| Eye Sufferers | St. Lucy | | | Travelers | St. Christopher; St. Anthony of Padua; St. Nicholas of Myra; St. Raphael |
| Falsely accused | St. Raymund Nonnatus | | | | |
| Farmers | St. George; St. Isidore | Philosophers | St. Justin; St. Catherine of Alexandria | | |
| Firemen | St. Florian | | | United States | Immaculate Concept. |
| Fishermen | St. Andrew | Physicians | St. Pantaleon; Sts. Cosmas and Damian; St. Luke, St. Raphael | Wales | St. David |
| Florists | St. Dorothy; St. Thérèse of Lisieux | | | Women in labor | St. Anne |
| | | | | Young girls | St. Agnes |

# U.S. RELIGIOUS DENOMINATIONS

Church membership in the United States increased in 1979 to 133,748,776 from a total of 132,812,470, according to the National Council of Churches of Christ.

Some 60.7% of the U.S. population belonged to an organized religion in 1979, and there were 332,970 churches.

**Adventist: Advent Christian Church:** Organized, 1860; address, P.O. Box 23152, Charlotte, NC 28212; churches, 372; membership, 31,000.

**Adventist: Seventh-day Adventists:** Organized, 1863; address, 6840 Eastern Ave. N.W., Washington, DC 20012; churches, 3,591; membership, 535,735.

**Apostolic Christian Churches of America:** Founded, 1847; address, 3528 N. Linden Lane, Peoria, IL 61604; churches, 80; membership; 18,000.

**Baha'i Faith:** Founded in Iraq, 1863; address, National Spiritual Assembly, 536 Sheridan Rd., Wilmette, IL 60091; assemblies, 900.

**Baptist: American Baptist Association:** Organized, 1905; address, 4605 N. State Line Ave., Texarkana, TX 75501; churches, 5,000; membership, 1,500,000.

**Baptist: American Baptist Churches in the U.S.A.:** Organized, 1907; address, Valley Forge, PA 19481; churches, 5,815; membership, 1,316,760.

**Baptist: Baptist General Conference:** Organized, 1879; address, 1233 Central St., Evanston, IL 60201; churches, 772; membership, 131,000.

**Baptist: Baptist Missionary Association of America:** Organized, 1950; address, 720 Main St., Little Rock, AR 72201; churches, 1,487; membership, 219,697.

**Baptist: Conservative Baptist Association of America:** Organized, 1947; address, Geneva Rd., Box 66, Wheaton, IL 60187; churches, 1,114; membership, 300,000.

**Baptist: Free Will Baptists:** Organized, 1727; address, 1134 Murfreesboro Road, Nashville,

Roman Catholicism remained the largest single religion in the U.S. Its 49,602,035 members in 1979 represented a decrease of 134,141 since 1978.

Because of space limitations, only U.S. religious denominations reporting 16,000 or more members are listed in the following table.

TN 37217; churches, 2,436; membership, 216,831.

**Baptist: General Association of Regular Baptist Churches:** Organized, 1932; address, 1300 N. Meacham Rd., Schaumberg, IL 60195; churches, 1,544; membership, 240,000.

**Baptist: General Baptists, General Association of:** Founded in England, 1607; address, Box 537, Poplar Bluff, MO 63901; churches, 867; membership, 72,000.

**Baptist: National Baptist Convention of America:** Organized, 1880; address, 2823 N. Houston, Fort Worth, TX 76106; churches, 11,398; membership, 2,668,799.

**Baptist: National Baptist Convention, United States of America, Inc.:** Organized, 1880; address, 405 E. 31st St., Chicago, IL 60616; churches, 26,000; membership, 6,300,000.

**Baptist: National Primitive Baptist Convention, Inc.:** Organized, 1907; address, P.O. Box 2355, Tallahassee, FL 32301; churches, 606; membership, 250,000.

**Baptist: North American Baptist Conference:** 1 S. 210 Summit Ave., Oakbrook Terrace, IL 60181; churches, 253; membership, 42,499.

**Baptist: Primitive Baptists:** Address, S. Second St., Thornton, AR 71766; churches, 1,000; membership, 72,000.

**Baptist: Progressive National Baptist Convention, Inc.:** Organized, 1961; address, 601 50th St., N.E., Washington, DC 20019; churches, 655; membership, 521,692.

**Baptist: Southern Baptist Convention:** Formed,

## 50 LARGEST U.S. RELIGIOUS DENOMINATIONS

| DENOMINATION | MEMBERSHIP | DENOMINATION | MEMBERSHIP |
|---|---|---|---|
| Roman Catholic Church | 49,602,035 | Progressive National Baptist Convention, Inc. | 521,692 |
| Southern Baptist Convention | 13,191,394 | Jehovah's Witnesses | 519,218 |
| United Methodist Church | 9,731,779 | (Pentecostal) Church of God in Christ, Intl. | 501,000 |
| National Baptist Convention, U.S.A., Inc. | 6,300,000 | Christian Methodist Episcopal Church | 466,718 |
| Judaism | 5,860,900 | Church of the Nazarene | 462,724 |
| Church of Jesus Christ of Latter-day Saints | 3,300,000 | United Pentecostal Church, Intl. | 450,000 |
| Churches of Christ | 3,000,000 | (Pentecostal) Church of God in Christ | 425,000 |
| Lutheran Church in America | 2,942,002 | Salvation Army | 414,035 |
| Episcopal Church | 2,815,359 | Wisconsin Evangelical Lutheran Synod | 402,972 |
| National Baptist Convention of America | 2,668,799 | Church of God (Cleveland, Tenn.) | 392,551 |
| Lutheran Church—Missouri Synod | 2,631,374 | Reformed Church in America | 348,080 |
| United Presbyterian Church in the U.S.A. | 2,520,367 | Armenian Church of America (Eastern | |
| American Lutheran Church | 2,377,235 | Orthodox) | 326,500 |
| African Methodist Episcopal Church | 1,970,000 | Conservative Baptist Association of America | 300,000 |
| Greek Orthodox Archdiocese | 1,950,000 | Polish National Catholic Church of America | 282,411 |
| United Church of Christ | 1,769,104 | National Primitive Baptist Convention | 250,000 |
| American Baptist Association | 1,500,000 | General Assn. of Regular Baptist Churches | 240,000 |
| American Baptist Churches in the U.S.A. | 1,316,760 | Baptist Missionary Association of America | 219,697 |
| (Pentecostal) Assemblies of God | 1,293,394 | Free Will Baptists | 216,831 |
| Christian Church (Disciples of Christ) | 1,231,807 | Christian Reformed Church | 211,302 |
| African Methodist Episcopal Zion Church | 1,093,001 | National Council of Community Churches | 190,000 |
| Christian Church and Churches of Christ | 1,054,266 | Reorganized Church of Jesus Christ of | |
| Islam | 1,000,000 | Latter Day Saints | 185,636 |
| Orthodox Church in America (Russian) | 1,000,000 | Church of the Brethren | 177,335 |
| Presbyterian Church in the U.S. | 862,416 | Church of God (Anderson, Ind.) | 173,753 |
| Seventh-day Adventists | 535,705 | Christian and Missionary Alliance | 158,218 |

**U.S. RELIGIOUS DENOMINATIONS** *(continued)*
1845; address, 460 James Robertson Pkwy., Nashville, TN 37219; churches, 35,357; membership, 13,191,394.

**Baptist: United Free Will Baptist Church:** Organized, 1870; address, Kinston College, 1000 University St., Kinston, NC 28501; churches, 836; membership, 100,000.

**Bible Way Church of Our Lord Jesus Christ World Wide, Inc.:** Established, 1957; address, 1100 New Jersey Ave., N.W., Washington, DC 20001; churches, 350; membership, 30,000.

**Brethren: Brethren Church:** Separated from Church of the Brethren in 1882; address, 524 College Ave., Ashland, OH 44805; churches, 120; membership, 16,000.

**Brethren: Church of the Brethren:** Founded in Germany, 1708; address, 1451 Dundee Ave., Elgin, IL 60120; churches, 1,061; membership, 175,335.

**Brethren: Fellowship of Grace Brethren Churches:** Separated from Church of the Brethren in 1882; address, Box 587, Winona Lake, IN 46590; churches, 262; membership, 39,605.

**Buddhist Churches of America:** Founded, 1899; 1710 Octavia St., San Francisco, CA 94109; churches, 60; membership, 60,000.

**Christadelphians:** Organized, 1844; address, 1002 Webster Lane, Des Plaines, IL 60012; churches, 850; membership, 16,000.

**Christian and Missionary Alliance:** Organized, 1887; address, 350 N. Highland Ave., Nyack, NY 10960; churches, 1,300; membership, 158,218.

**Christian Church (Disciples of Christ):** Organized, 1832; address, Box 1986, 222 S. Downey Ave., Indianapolis, IN 46206; churches, 4,347; membership, 1,231,817.

**Christian Churches and Churches of Christ:** Founded, early 1800s; address, Box 39456, Cincinnati, OH 45231; churches, 5,535; membership, 1,054,266.

**Christian Science: Church of Christ, Scientist:** Founded, 1879; address, Christian Science Center, Boston, MA 02115; branches, 3,000 throughout world.

**Church of God:** Organized, about 1880; address, Box 2420, Anderson, IN 46011; churches, 2,264; membership, 173,753.

**Church of God: General Conference of Churches of God:** Organized, 1825; address, 2200 Jennifer Lane, Findlay, OH 45840; churches, 347; membership, 36,016.

**Church of the Living God:** Organized, 1889; address, 801 N.E. 17th St., Oklahoma City, OK 73105; temples, 276; membership, 45,320.

**Church of the Nazarene:** Organized, 1908; address, 6401 The Paseo, Kansas City, MO 64131; churches, 4,719; membership, 462,724.

**Churches of Christ:** No general organization higher than local congregation; churches, 17,550; membership, 3,000,000.

**Community Churches, National Council of:** Organized, 1946; address, 89 E. Wilson Bridge Rd., Worthington, OH 43085; churches, 200; membership, 190,000.

**Congregational Christian Churches, National Association of:** Organized, 1955; address, P.O. Box 1620, Oak Creek, WI 53154; churches, 382; membership, 95,000.

**Congregational Christian Conference, Conser-** vative: Founded, 1948; address, 25 W. 626 St. Charles Rd., Wheaton, IL 60187; churches, 130; membership, 22,750.

**Eastern Orthodox: Albanian Orthodox Archdiocese in America:** Established, 1908; address, 523 E. Broadway, S. Boston, MA 02127; churches, 16; membership, 40,000.

**Eastern Orthodox: American Carpatho-Russian Orthodox Greek Catholic Church:** Organized, 1938; address, Johnstown, PA 15906; churches, 70; membership, 100,000.

**Eastern Orthodox: Antiochian Orthodox Christian Archdiocese of All North America:** Established, 1975; address, 358 Mountain Rd., Englewood, NJ 07631; churches, 110; membership, 152,000.

**Eastern Orthodox: Armenian Apostolic Church of America:** Established, 1887; address, 138 E. 39th St., New York, NY 10016; churches, 30; membership, 125,000.

**Eastern Orthodox: Armenian Church of America, Diocese of the:** Established, 1889; address, 630 Second Ave., New York, NY 10016; churches, 58; membership, 326,500.

**Eastern Orthodox: Bulgarian Eastern Orthodox Church:** Founded, 1907; address, 312 W. 101st St., New York, NY 10025; churches, 13; membership, 86,000.

**Eastern Orthodox: Greek Orthodox Archdiocese of North and South America:** Founded, 1864; address, 8–10 East 79th St., New York, NY 10021; churches, 535; membership, 1,950,000.

**Eastern Orthodox: Orthodox Church in America** (formerly Russian Orthodox Greek Catholic Church of America): Established, 1792; address, P.O. Box 675, Syosset, NY 11791; churches, 440; membership, 1,000,000.

**Eastern Orthodox: Romanian Orthodox Episcopate of America:** Organized, 1929; address, 2522 Grey Tower Rd., Jackson, MI 49201; churches, 34; membership, 40,000.

**Eastern Orthodox: Russian Orthodox Church in the U.S.A., Patriarchal Parishes of the:** Address, 15 E. 97th St., New York, NY 10029; churches, 41; membership, 51,500.

**Eastern Orthodox: Russian Orthodox Church Outside Russia:** Organized, 1920; address, 75 E. 93d St., New York, NY 10028; churches, 81; membership, 55,000.

**Eastern Orthodox: Serbian Eastern Orthodox Church for the U.S.A. and Canada:** Address, P.O. Box 519, Libertyville, IL 60048; churches, 52; membership, 65,000.

**Eastern Orthodox: Syrian Orthodox Church of Antioch:** 293 Hamilton Pl., Hackensack, NJ 07601; churches, 13; membership, 30,000.

**Eastern Orthodox: Ukrainian Orthodox Church in the U.S.A.:** Organized, 1919; address, South Bound Brook, NJ 08880; churches, 107; membership, 87,745.

**Eastern Orthodox: Ukrainian Orthodox Church in America (Ecumenical Patriarchate):** Organized, 1928; address, 90–34 139th St., Jamaica, NY 11435; churches, 28; membership, 25,000.

**Episcopal Church:** Became autonomous from the Anglican Church of England in 1789; address, 815 Second Avenue, New York City, NY 10017; churches, 7,009; membership, 2,815,359.

**Evangelical Congregational Church:** Formed, 1928; 100 W. Park Ave., Myerstown, PA 17067; churches, 161; membership, 28,459.

**Evangelical Covenant Church of America:** Organized, 1885; address, 5101 N. Francisco Ave., Chicago, IL 60625; churches, 520; membership, 74,678.

**Evangelical Free Church of America:** Organized, 1880s; address, 1515 E. 66th St., Minneapolis, MN 55423; churches, 621; membership, 100,000.

**Evangelistic: Christian Congregation, Inc.:** Incorporated, 1887; address, 804 W. Hemlock St., La Follette, TN 37766; churches, 1,133; membership, 81,604.

**Evangelistic: Missionary Church:** Formed by merger of United Missionary Church and Missionary Church Association, 1969; address, 3901 S. Wayne Ave., Fort Wayne, IN 46807; churches, 273; membership, 20,078.

**Free Christian Zion Church of Christ:** Organized, 1905; address, 1315 Hutchinson St., Nashville, AR 71852; churches, 742; membership, 22,260.

**Independent Fundamental Churches of America:** Organized, 1930; address, 1860 Mannheim Rd., Box 250, Westchester, IL 60153; churches, 614; membership, 87,582.

**Islam:** Address, Islamic Center, 2551 Massachusetts Ave., N.W., Washington, DC 20008.

**Jehovah's Witnesses:** Organized, 1870s; 124 Columbia Heights, Brooklyn, NY 11201; congregations, 7,526; membership, 519,218.

**Judaism:** First congregation in America, 1654; total membership, 5,860,900.

**Judaism (Conservative):** United Synagogue of America: Address, 155 Fifth Ave., New York, NY 10010; congregations, 800.

**Judaism (Orthodox):** Union of Orthodox Jewish Congregations of America: Address, 116 E. 27th St., New York, NY 10016; congregations, 3,000.

**Judaism (Reform):** Union of American Hebrew Congregations: Address, 838 Fifth Ave., New York, NY 10021; congregations, 700.

**Lutheran: American Lutheran Church:** Organized, 1960; address, 422 S. 5th St., Minneapolis, MN 55415; churches, 4,837; membership, 2,377,235.

**Lutheran: Evangelical Lutheran Churches, Association of:** Organized, 1976; address, 12015 Manchester Rd., Ste. 80LL, St. Louis, MO 63131; churches, 250; membership, 106,684.

**Lutheran: Evangelical Lutheran Synod:** Organized, 1853; address, Bethany Lutheran College, Mankato, MN 56001; churches, 108; membership, 19,705.

**Lutheran Church in America:** Organized, 1962; address, 231 Madison Ave., New York, NY 10016; churches, 5,800; membership, 2,942,002.

**Lutheran Church—Missouri Synod:** Organized, 1847; address, 500 N. Broadway, St. Louis, MO 63102; churches, 5,700; membership, 2,631,374.

**Lutheran: Wisconsin Evangelical Lutheran Synod:** Organized, 1850; address, 3512 W. North Ave., Milwaukee, WI 53208; churches, 1,116; membership, 402,972.

**Mennonite: General Conference of Mennonite Brethren Churches:** Established in America, 1874; address, Hillsboro, KS 67063; churches, 120; membership, 16,042.

**Mennonite Church:** Established in America, 1683; address, 528 E. Madison St., Lombard, IL 60148; churches, 1,081; membership, 97,142.

**Mennonite Church, The General Conference:** Organized, 1860; address, 722 Main St., Newton, KS 67114; churches, 187; membership, 36,397.

**Methodist: African Methodist Episcopal Church:** Founded, 1787; address, 1002 Kirkwood Ave., Nashville, TN 37203; churches, 3,050; membership, 1,970,000.

**Methodist: African Methodist Episcopal Zion Church:** Founded, 1796; address, P.O. Box 31005, Charlotte, NC 28230; churches, 6,020; membership, 1,093,001.

**Methodist: Christian Methodist Episcopal Church:** Organized, 1870; address, P.O. Box 74, Memphis, TN 38126; churches, 2,598; membership, 466,718.

**Methodist: Free Methodist Church of North America:** Organized, 1860; address, 901 College Ave., Winona Lake, IN 46590; churches, 1,148; membership, 73,294.

**Methodist: Reformed Zion Union Apostolic Church:** Organized, 1869; address, 416 South Hill Ave., South Hill, VA 23970; churches, 50; membership, 16,000.

**Methodist: United Methodist Church:** Formed, 1968; address, 1100 W. 42nd St., Indianapolis, IN 46208; churches, 36,682; membership, 9,731,779.

**Metropolitan Community Churches, Universal Fellowship of:** Founded, 1968; address, 5300 Santa Monica Blvd., #304, Los Angeles, CA 90029; churches, 118; membership, 25,520.

**Moravian Church in America:** Established, 1735; address, P.O. Box 1245, 69 W. Church St., Bethlehem, PA 18018; churches, 147; membership, 53,521.

**Mormon: Church of Jesus Christ of Latter-day Saints:** Organized, 1830; address, 50 East North Temple St., Salt Lake City, UT 84111; churches, 7,500; membership, 3,300,000.

**New Apostolic Church of North America:** Established, 1863; address, 3753 N. Troy St., Chicago, IL 60618; churches, 362; membership, 26,384.

**Old Roman Catholic Church (English Rite):** Established in America, 1916; address, 4200 N. Kedvale Ave., Chicago, IL 60641; churches, 121; membership, 67,314.

**Pentecostal: Apostolic Overcoming Holy Church of God:** Organized, 1916; address, 514 10th Ave. W., Birmingham, AL 35204; churches, 300; membership, 75,000.

**Pentecostal: Assemblies of God:** Founded, 1914; address, 1445 Boonville Ave., Springfield, MO 65802; churches, 9,410; membership, 1,293,394.

**Pentecostal: Church of God:** Organized, 1903; 2504 Arrow Wood Dr., S.E., Huntsville, AL 35803; churches, 2,035; membership, 75,890.

**Pentecostal: Church of God (Cleveland, Tenn.):** Organized, 1886; address, Keith St. at 25th N.W., Cleveland, TN 37311; churches, 4,847; membership, 392,551.

**Pentecostal: Church of God in Christ:** Organized, 1895; address, 938 Mason St., Memphis, TN 38126; churches, 4,500; membership, 425,000.

## 708 RELIGION

**U.S. RELIGIOUS DENOMINATIONS** *(continued)*

**Pentecostal: Church of God in Christ, International:** Organized, 1969; address, 170 Adelphi St., Brooklyn, NY 11025; churches, 1,041; membership, 501,000.

**Pentecostal: Church of God of Prophecy:** Organized, 1903; Bible Pl., Cleveland, TN 37311; churches, 1,791; membership, 65,801.

**Pentecostal: Church of Our Lord Jesus Christ of the Apostolic Faith, Inc.:** Organized, 1919; address, 2081 Seventh Ave., New York, NY 10027; churches, 160; membership, 45,000.

**Pentecostal: International Church of the Foursquare Gospel:** Organized, 1927; address, Angelus Temple, 1100 Glendale Blvd., Los Angeles, CA 90026; churches, 714; membership, 89,215.

**Pentecostal: Open Bible Standard Churches, Inc.:** Formed, 1935; address, Bell Ave. at Fleur Dr., P.O. Box 1737, Des Moines, IA 50306; churches, 280; membership, 60,000.

**Pentecostal: The (Original) Church of God, Inc.:** Organized, 1886; address, P.O. Box 3086, Chattanooga, TN 37404; churches, 70; membership, 20,000.

**Pentecostal Church of God of America, Inc.:** Organized, 1919; address, Messenger Plaza, 221 Main St., Joplin, MO 64801; churches, 1,189; membership, 110,870.

**Pentecostal Holiness Church, Inc.:** Organized, about 1895; address, P.O. Box 12609, Oklahoma City, OK 73112; churches, 2,340; membership, 86,103.

**Pentecostal: United Holy Church of America, Inc.:** Organized, 1886; address, 159 W. Coulter St., Philadelphia, PA 19144; churches, 470; membership, 28,980.

**Pentecostal: United Pentecostal Church International:** Formed, 1945; address, 8855 Dunn Rd., Hazelwood, MO 63042; churches, 2,830; membership, 450,000.

**Plymouth Brethren:** Organized, 1820s; address, P.O. Box 294, 218 W. Willow, Wheaton, IL 60187; churches, 800; membership, 74,000.

**Polish National Catholic Church of America:** Organized, 1897; address, 529 E. Locust St., Scranton, PA 18505; churches, 162; membership, 282,411.

**Presbyterian: Associate Reformed Presbyterian Church (General Synod):** Reorganized, 1935; address, 1 Cleveland St., Greenville, SC 29601; churches, 158; membership, 32,139.

**Presbyterian Church in America:** Established, 1973; address, Box 256, Clinton, MS 39056; churches, 440; membership, 82,095.

**Presbyterian Church in the U.S.:** Established, 1861; address, 341 Ponce de Leon Ave. N.E., Atlanta, GA 30308; churches, 4,007; membership, 862,416.

**Presbyterian: Cumberland Presbyterian Church:** Organized, 1810; address, Box 4149, 1978 Union Ave., Memphis, TN 38104; churches, 850; membership, 93,268.

**Presbyterian: Orthodox Presbyterian Church:** Organized, 1936; address, 7401 Old York Rd., Philadelphia, PA 19126; churches, 136; membership, 15,806.

**Presbyterian: Reformed Presbyterian Church, Evangelical Synod:** Formed, 1965; address, 107 Hardy Rd., Lookout Mountain, TN 37350; churches, 145; membership, 25,448.

**Presbyterian: Second Cumberland Presbyterian Church in U.S.:** Organized, 1869; address, 545 Vanderhorst Dr., Nashville, TN 37209; churches, 120; membership, 30,000.

**Presbyterian: United Presbyterian Church in U.S.A.:** Established, 1706; merger, 1958; address, 475 Riverside Dr., New York, N.Y. 10027; churches, 8,567; membership, 2,520,367.

**Quaker: Evangelical Friends Alliance:** Formed, 1965; address, 3343 E. 114 Dr., Thornton, CO 80233; churches, 257; membership, 25,531.

**Quaker: Friends General Conference:** Organized, 1900; address, 1520-B Race St., Philadelphia, PA 19102; churches, 233; membership, 26,184.

**Quaker: Friends United Meeting:** Organized, 1965; address, 101 Quaker Hill Dr., Richmond, IN 47374; churches, 522; membership, 62,080.

**Reformed Church in America:** Established 1628 as the Reformed Protestant Dutch Church; address, 475 Riverside Dr., New York, NY 10027; churches, 900; membership, 348,080.

**Reformed Churches: Christian Reformed Church:** Founded, 1857; address, 2850 Kalamazoo Ave., S.E., Grand Rapids, MI 49508; churches, 623; membership, 211,302.

**Reorganized Church of Jesus Christ of Latter Day Saints:** Reorganized, 1860; address, The Auditorium, Independence, MO 64051; churches, 1,048; membership, 185,636.

**Roman Catholic Church:** Established in Maryland, 1634; address, 1312 Massachusetts Ave. N.W., Washington, DC 20005; parishes, churches, and missions, 25,542; membership, 49,602,035.

**Salvation Army:** Established, 1880; address, 120–130 W. 14th St., New York, NY 10011; churches, 1,100; membership, 414,435.

**Scientology, Church of:** Founded, 1950; address, 5930 Franklin Ave., Los Angeles, CA 90028; churches, 47.

**Triumph the Church and Kingdom of God in Christ (International):** Founded, 1902; address, 213 Farrington Ave., Atlanta, GA 30318; churches, 475; membership, 54,307.

**Unitarian Universalist Association:** Universalists organized, 1793; Unitarians organized, 1825; merger, 1961; address, 25 Beacon St., Boston, MA 02108; churches, 936; membership, 136,207.

**United Brethren in Christ:** Founded, 1800; address, 302 Lake St., P.O. Box 650, Huntington, IN 46750; churches, 285; membership, 28,035.

**United Church of Christ:** Union, 1957, of the Evangelical and Reformed Church and the Congregational Christian Churches; 105 Madison Ave., New York, NY 10016; churches, 6,500; membership, 1,769,104.

**Volunteers of America:** Founded, 1896; address, 340 W. 85th St., New York, NY 10024; churches, 607; membership, 36,634.

**Wesleyan Church:** Union, 1968, of the Pilgrim Holiness Church and Wesleyan Methodist Church; address, P.O. Box 2000, Marion, IN 46952; churches, 1,714; membership, 99,016.

**Worldwide Church of God:** Founded, 1934; address, 300 West Green St., Pasadena, CA 91123; churches, 530; membership, 50,710.

# ROMAN CATHOLIC POPES

| POPE | REIGN | POPE | REIGN | POPE | REIGN | POPE | REIGN |
|---|---|---|---|---|---|---|---|
| St. Peter | d.67 | St. Boniface IV | 608–15 | Benedict V[2] | 964–66 | Innocent VI | 1352–62 |
| St. Linus | 67–76 | St. Deusdedit or | | John XIII | 965–72 | Urban V | 1362–70 |
| St. Cletus or | | Adeodatus I | 615–18 | Benedict VI | 973–74 | Gregory XI | 1370–78 |
| Anacletus | 76–88 | Boniface V | 619–25 | Benedict VII | 974–83 | Urban VI | 1378–89 |
| St. Clement I | 88–97 | Honorius I | 625–38 | John XIV | 983–84 | Boniface IX | 1389–1404 |
| St. Evaristus | 97–105 | Severinus | 640 | John XV | 985–96 | Innocent VII | 1404–06 |
| St. Alexander I | 105–15 | John IV | 640–42 | Gregory V | 996–99 | Gregory XII | 1406–15 |
| St. Sixtus I | 115–25 | Theodore I | 642–49 | Sylvester II | 999–1003 | Martin V | 1417–31 |
| St. Telesphorus | 125–36 | St. Martin I | 649–55 | John XVII | 1003 | Benedict XIV | 1425–30 |
| St. Hyginus | 136–40 | St. Eugene I | 654–57 | John XVIII | 1004–09 | Eugene IV | 1431–47 |
| St. Pius I | 140–55 | St. Vitalian | 657–72 | Sergius IV | 1009–12 | Nicholas V | 1447–55 |
| St. Anicetus | 155–66 | Adeodatus II | 672–76 | Benedict VIII | 1012–24 | Callistus III | 1455–58 |
| St. Soter | 166–75 | Donus | 676–78 | John XIX | 1024–32 | Pius II | 1458–64 |
| St. Eleutherius | 175–89 | St. Agatho | 678–81 | Benedict IX[3] | 1032–44 | Paul II | 1464–71 |
| St. Victor I | 189–99 | St. Leo II | 682–83 | | 1045, 1047–48 | Sixtus IV | 1471–84 |
| St. Zephyrinus | 199(?)–217 | St. Benedict II | 684–85 | Sylvester III[3] | 1045 | Innocent VIII | 1484–92 |
| St. Callistus I | 217–22 | John V | 685–86 | Gregory VI[3] | 1045–46 | Alexander VI | 1492–1503 |
| St. Urban I | 222–30 | Conon | 686–87 | Clement II[3] | 1046–47 | Pius III | 1503 |
| St. Pontian | 230–35 | St. Sergius I | 687–701 | Damasus II | 1048 | Julius II | 1503–13 |
| St. Anterus | 235–36 | John VI | 701–05 | St. Leo IX | 1049–54 | Leo X | 1513–21 |
| St. Fabian | 236–50 | John VII | 705–07 | Victor II | 1055–57 | Adrian VI | 1522–23 |
| St. Cornelius | 251–53 | Sisinnius | 708 | Stephen IX (X) | 1057–58 | Clement VII | 1523–34 |
| St. Lucius I | 253–54 | Constantine | 708–15 | Nicholas II | 1059–61 | Paul III | 1534–49 |
| St. Stephen I | 254–57 | St. Gregory II | 715–31 | Alexander II | 1061–73 | Julius III | 1550–55 |
| St. Sixtus II | 257–58 | St. Gregory III | 731–41 | St. Gregory VII | 1073–85 | Marcellus II | 1555 |
| St. Dionysius | 259–68 | St. Zacharias | 741–52 | Victor III | 1086–87 | Paul IV | 1555–59 |
| St. Felix I | 269–74 | Stephen II | 752 | Urban II | 1088–99 | Pius IV | 1559–65 |
| St. Eutychian | 275–83 | Stephen II (III) | 752–57 | Paschal II | 1099–1118 | St. Pius V | 1566–72 |
| St. Caius | 283–96 | St. Paul I | 757–67 | Gelasius II | 1118–19 | Gregory XIII | 1572–85 |
| St. Marcellinus | 296–304 | Stephen III (IV) | 768–72 | Callistus II | 1119–24 | Sixtus V | 1585–90 |
| St. Marcellus I | 308–09 | Adrian I | 772–95 | Honorius II | 1124–30 | Urban VII | 1590 |
| St. Eusebius | 309 or 310 | St. Leo III | 795–816 | Innocent II | 1130–43 | Gregory XIV | 1590–91 |
| St. Miltiades | 311–14 | Stephen IV (V) | 816–17 | Victor IV | 1138 | Innocent IX | 1591 |
| St. Sylvester I | 314–35 | St. Paschal | 817–24 | Celestine II | 143–44 | Clement VIII | 1592–1605 |
| St. Marcus | 336 | Eugene II | 824–27 | Lucius II | 1144–45 | Leo XI | 1605 |
| St. Julius I | 337–52 | Valentine | 827 | Eugene III | 1145–53 | Paul V | 1605–21 |
| Liberius | 352–66 | Gregory IV | 827–44 | Anastasius IV | 1153–54 | Gregory XV | 1621–23 |
| St. Damasus I | 366–84 | Sergius II | 844–47 | Adrian IV | 1154–59 | Urban VIII | 1623–44 |
| St. Siricius | 384–99 | St. Leo IV | 847–55 | Alexander III | 1159–81 | Innocent X | 1644–55 |
| St. Anastasius I | 399–401 | Benedict III | 855–58 | Lucius III | 1181–85 | Alexander VII | 1655–67 |
| St. Innocent I | 401–17 | St. Nicholas I | 858–67 | Urban III | 1185–87 | Clement IX | 1667–69 |
| St. Zosimus | 417–18 | Adrian II | 867–72 | Gregory VIII | 1187 | Clement X | 1670–76 |
| St. Boniface I | 418–22 | John VIII | 872–82 | Clement III | 1187–91 | Innocent XI | 1676–89 |
| St. Celestine I | 422–32 | Marinus I | 882–84 | Celestine III | 1191–98 | Alexander VIII | 1689–91 |
| St. Sixtus III | 432–40 | St. Adrian III | 884–85 | Innocent III | 1198–1216 | Innocent XII | 1691–1700 |
| St. Leo I | 440–61 | Stephen V (VI) | 885–91 | Honorius III | 1216–27 | Clement XI | 1700–21 |
| St. Hilarius | 461–68 | Formosus | 891–96 | Gregory IX | 1227–41 | Innocent XIII | 1721–24 |
| St. Simplicius | 468–83 | Boniface VI | 896 | Celestine IV | 1241 | Benedict XIII | 1724–30 |
| St. Felix III (II)[1] | 483–92 | Stephen VI (VII) | 896–97 | Innocent IV | 1243–54 | Clement XII | 1730–40 |
| St. Gelasius I | 492–96 | Romanus | 897 | Alexander IV | 1254–61 | Benedict XIV | 1740–58 |
| Anastasius II | 496–98 | Theodore II | 897 | Urban IV | 1261–64 | Clement XIII | 1758–69 |
| St. Symmachus | 498–514 | John IX | 898–900 | Clement IV | 1265–68 | Clement XIV | 1769–74 |
| St. Hormisdas | 514–23 | Benedict IV | 900–03 | Gregory X | 1271–76 | Pius VI | 1775–99 |
| St. John I | 523–26 | Leo V | 903 | Innocent V | 1276 | Pius VII | 1800–23 |
| St. Felix IV (III) | 526–30 | Sergius III | 904–11 | Adrian V | 1276 | Leo XII | 1823–29 |
| Boniface II | 530–32 | Anastasius III | 911–13 | John XXI | 1276–77 | Pius VIII | 1829–30 |
| John II | 533–35 | Lando | 913–14 | Nicholas III | 1277–80 | Gregory XVI | 1831–46 |
| St. Agapetus I | 535–36 | John X | 914–28 | Martin IV | 1281–85 | Pius IX | 1846–78 |
| St. Silverius | 536–37 | Leo VI | 928 | Honorius IV | 1285–87 | Leo XIII | 1878–1903 |
| Vigilius | 537(?)–55 | Stephen VII (VIII) | 928–31 | Nicholas IV | 1288–92 | St. Pius X | 1903–14 |
| Pelagius I | 556–61 | John XI | 931–35 | St. Celestine V | 1294 | Benedict XV | 1914–22 |
| John III | 561–74 | Leo VII | 936–39 | Boniface VIII | 1294–1303 | Pius XI | 1922–39 |
| Benedict I | 575–79 | Stephen VIII (IX) | 939–42 | Benedict XI | 1303–04 | Pius XII | 1939–58 |
| Pelagius II | 579–90 | Marinus II | 942–46 | Clement V | 1305–14 | John XXIII | 1958–63 |
| St. Gregory I | 590–604 | Agapetus II | 946–55 | John XXII | 1316–34 | Paul VI | 1963–78 |
| Sabinianus | 604–06 | John XII[2] | 955–64 | Benedict XII | 1334–42 | John Paul I | 1978 |
| Boniface III | 607 | Leo VIII[2] | 963–65 | Clement VI | 1342–52 | John Paul II | 1978– |

[1] The presence of antipopes (not listed here) sometimes places question on a pope's number. In all such cases, the alternate number is cited on this list in parentheses. [2] John XII was deposed in 963 by a church council. If this deposition was invalid, Leo was an antipope. If the deposition was valid, Leo was the legitimate pope and Benedict was an antipope. [3] Benedict IX was deposed on three different occasions (in 1044, 1046, and 1048). If the depositions were illegitimate, Sylvester III, Gregory VI, and Clement II were antipopes.

# THEOLOGIANS AND PHILOSOPHERS

**Peter Abelard** (1079–1142), French philosopher and theologian who used a dialectic method in an effort to support Christian dogma. He is best known for his tragic romance with Héloïse, an abbess, and their exchange of love letters.

**Aristotle** (384–322 B.C.), Greek philosopher whose writings have greatly influenced Western thought. His philosophy became dominant in the 13th century when it was largely adopted by the Christian scholastic philosophers.

**Asoka** (died 232 B.C.), Indian emperor who galvanized growth of Buddhism in Asia by making it India's state religion and by sending Buddhist missionaries to distant countries. Asoka thus transformed Buddhism from a local religion to a faith of world importance.

**Averroës** (1126–98), Islamic Spanish philosopher whose studies and interpretations of Aristotle's thought exerted considerable influence on European philosophy and Christian theology, including that of Thomas Aquinas.

**Karl Barth** (1886–1968), Swiss Protestant theologian whose views stress the importance of Christian revelation and tend to favor the theology of the prescientific age.

**Henri Bergson** (1859–1941), French philosopher of Jewish origin but inclined toward Christian mysticism, who stressed the importance of intuition in the perception of reality.

**George Berkeley** (1685–1753), Anglo-Irish clergyman and philosopher who saw an ordered coherence in the world as proof of God's existence. He spent three years in America attempting to establish a college to train missionaries to convert the Indians.

**Bernard of Clairvaux** (1090–1153), French abbot whose mystical teachings exerted a powerful influence on Christianity throughout western Europe.

**John Biddle** (1615–62), English theologian who founded Unitarianism, a Christian denomination that affirms the existence of God but denies the Holy Trinity.

**Jakob Böhme** or **Boehme** (1575–1624), German theosophist and mystic whose writings were concerned with the necessity of evil because of the dualism of the divine nature of God. One of his works was declared heretical.

**Dietrich Bonhoeffer** (1906–45), German theologian and Lutheran pastor who advocated a secularized reinterpretation of Christianity. His anti-Hitler sentiments resulted in his execution by the Nazis.

**Martin Buber** (1878–1965), Jewish mystical philosopher who was influenced by the Christian existentialism of Kierkegaard. In turn, Buber exerted influence on modern Christian thought in the form of a highly personalized ("I-Thou") approach to God and the world.

**Buddha (Siddhartha Gautama;** c. 563–483 B.C.), Indian nobleman who founded Buddhism, one of the major Asian religions. He renounced sensual pleasures and advocated total spiritual detachment from the world.

**Rudolf Karl Bultmann** (1884–1976), German Protestant existentialist theologian and scholar who attempted to distinguish between what he interpreted as the mythical and the historical elements in the New Testament.

**John Calvin** (1509–64), French theologian who was one of the most important figures of the Reformation. His doctrines are central to the Presbyterian and Reformed churches.

**Chuang-tse** (369?–275? B.C.), Chinese Taoist philosopher whose writings are among the most important in Taoist literature.

**Clement of Alexandria** (150?–215?), Greek Christian theologian who was possibly the first to attempt to reconcile Platonistic and Stoic thought with Christian belief and ethics.

**Confucius** (c. 551–479? B.C.), Chinese philosopher whose ethical precepts, the *Analects,* set forth standards of personal behavior with a view toward social harmony in an ideal state.

**Thomas Cranmer** (1489–1556), English churchman who was archbishop of Canterbury and a supporter of Henry VIII against Rome. He contributed to the preparation of the Book of Common Prayer.

**René Descartes** (1596–1650), French philosopher and scientist whose method of achieving certitude began with the assertion of self (*cogito ergo sum*) and proceeded to attempt a rational proof of God's existence.

**Jonathan Edwards** (1703–58), American theologian whose preaching, based largely on the thought of Calvin, Berkeley, and Locke, exerted a powerful influence on colonial America.

**Ralph Waldo Emerson** (1803–82), American essayist, poet, and philosopher whose belief in a mystical unity of nature (transcendentalism) has been an important influence in American thought.

**Gamaliel II** (1st century A.D.), Jewish teacher and an innovator of Jewish prayers and rituals in the wake of the upheaval following the Roman destruction of Jerusalem. He was a grandson of Gamaliel, cited in the New Testament (Acts 5:33–39).

**Georg Wilhelm Friedrich Hegel** (1770–1831), German idealist philosopher whose dialectical interpretation of history influenced such diverse thinkers as Marx, Kierkegaard, and Dewey.

**Martin Heidegger** (1889–1976), German philosopher whose writing, an extension of the phenomenological school of Edmund Husserl, interprets "being" as the continual, elusive process of "becoming." His major work, *Being and Time* (1927), has influenced existentialism.

**Theodor Herzl** (1860–1904), Hungarian Jewish religious leader, considered the father of modern Zionism. Primarily a writer, his best-known work is the pamphlet *Der Judenstaat* (The Jewish State). He convened the first Zionist Congress at Basel, Switzerland, in 1897.

**Hillel** (1st century B.C.), Jewish scholar and one of the leading figures in the compilation of Talmudic law. He laid the foundation of a systematic legal interpretation of Hebrew writings. Although born in Babylonia, he went to Palestine, the center of Judaism, at age 40 and was elected leader of the Sanhedrin.

**Richard Hooker** (1554?–1600), English theologian whose writings constitute a major influence on Anglican theological concepts and ecclesiastical organization.

**John Huss or Jan Hus** (1369?–1415), Bohemian religious reformer whose denunciation of abuses of the Catholic hierarchy ultimately led to his martyrdom. He is considered a forerunner of the Protestant Reformation and is regarded as a Czech national hero.

**William Ralph Inge** (1860–1954), English theologian who was influential as a teacher at Cambridge and Oxford universities. His writings explore the mystical aspects of Christianity.

**Jesus Christ** (c. 5 B.C.–A.D. 30), founder of Christianity. The books of the New Testament tell about his life on earth, his teachings, the miracles that he performed, and his trial, crucifixion, and resurrection. His disciples and followers spread Christianity throughout the Roman Empire.

**Immanuel Kant** (1724–1804), German philosopher who ranks among the greatest figures in the history of Western thought. His *Critique of Pure Reason* (1781) denies that God's existence can be verified by rational proofs.

**Sören Kierkegaard** (1813–55), Danish philosopher whose belief in the superiority of subjective over objective truth led him to conclude that adherence to Christian belief is of less value than the acting out of a Christian life. He is considered the father of existentialism.

**John Knox** (1513?–72), Scottish religious leader who founded Scottish Presbyterianism. He was closely associated with John Calvin.

**Lao-tzu** (604–531 B.C.), Chinese philosopher who is considered the founder of the Taoist religion. His only known writing is a treatise on the origins of the universe, entitled *Tao Teh King.*

**Hugh Latimer** (1485?–1555), English bishop whose staunch faithfulness to Protestantism led to his martyrdom by Queen Mary I.

**John Locke** (1632–1704), English philosopher who believed that all ideas originate from sensory perception. This set the foundation for the empirical school of philosophy. His belief in man's tendency toward social good influenced modern democratic thought.

**Martin Luther** (1483–1546), German leader of the Protestant Reformation whose rebellion against abuses of the Roman Catholic Church marked a major turning point in Europe's social and religious history. Founder of the Lutheran Church, his teachings have been a major influence on all of Protestantism.

**Maimonides (Moses ben Maimon;** 1135–1204), Jewish philosopher and physician who organized Jewish oral law into concepts that were understandable to the layman. His most important work is *Moreh Nevukhim* (Guide for the Perplexed).

**Jacques Maritain** (1882–1973), French Catholic philosopher who attempted to reconcile Aquinas' teachings with contemporary thought.

**Cotton Mather** (1663–1728), American Puritan clergyman who exercised great influence through his preaching and writings in colonial New England. He was among the chief investigators of suspected witchcraft in Salem, Mass.

**Increase Mather** (1639–1723), American clergyman and a leading advocate of Puritan theocracy. He was the father of Cotton Mather.

**Philipp Melanchthon** (1497–1560), German theologian and humanist who was an associate of Martin Luther and an important voice in the Reformation.

**Mencius or Meng-tse** (372–289 B.C.), Chinese religious reformer and sage who influenced a resurgence of Confucian thought during his lifetime, and who was later venerated in Confucian temples.

**Moses Mendelssohn** (1729–86), German Jewish philosopher who espoused reforms of Jewish ritual law, thus pioneering a faith adaptable to modern needs.

**Mohammed** (570?–632), Arab prophet of the religion of Islam. Incorporating Jewish and Christian beliefs with his own distinctive theology, he is believed by his Muslim followers to be the last great prophet of the Jewish and Christian traditions and successor to Jesus. He wrote the Koran as the revelations of Allah (God).

**John Courtney Murray** (1904–67), American Catholic theologian and scholar who was a leader in the liberal Catholic movement.

**Nestorius** (died after 451), Middle Eastern theologian who founded the Nestorian Church, an early Christian heretical sect.

**John Henry Newman** (1801–90), English Roman Catholic cardinal and a leader of the Oxford Movement, a major reorganizational effort within the Anglican Church. His decision to become a Roman Catholic stirred controversy within England's church circles; he justified his action in *Apologia pro Vita Sua.*

**Helmut Richard Niebuhr** (1894–1962), American Protestant theologian who attempted to reconcile Christian doctrine with the dominant ideas of the 20th century.

**Reinhold Niebuhr** (1892–1971), American Protestant theologian who wrote extensively on the social aspects of modern Christian life.

**Friedrich Wilhelm Nietzsche** (1844–1900), German moral philosopher who viewed his contemporary Christian civilization as decadent and looked forward to an era when a new breed of men would revivify the civilization.

**Matthew Parker** (1504–75), English religious leader who, as archbishop of Canterbury, led the Anglican Church in a middle course between Roman Catholicism and Protestantism.

**Blaise Pascal** (1623–62), French religious thinker and scientist who stressed that faith was the ultimate bridge between man and God.

**Philo Judaeus** (20? B.C.–A.D. 50?), Jewish Alexandrian philosopher whose teachings regarding God's perfection and total transcendence over man had a marked influence on early Christian writings. His thought amounts to a fusion of Platonic philosophy with the doctrines of Hebrew scriptures.

**Plato** (427?–347? B.C.), Greek philosopher and disciple of Socrates. Plato's writings have had immense influence on the religious and secular thought of Western civilization.

**Plotinus** (205–270), Alexandrian philosopher of the Neoplatonist school whose thought influenced early Christian doctrine.

**Nicholas Ridley** (1500?–55), English church reformer who took part in compiling the Book of Common Prayer. A staunch adherent of Anglicanism, he was martyred, along with Hugh Latimer, by Queen Mary I.

**THEOLOGIANS AND PHILOSOPHERS** *(continued)*

**Saint Thomas Aquinas** (1225–74), Italian theologian and philosopher who ranks as the most influential figure in medieval philosophy. He formulated the official Roman Catholic philosophy, most explicitly in *Summa Theologica.*

**Saint Augustine** (354–430), Latin bishop and doctor of the Christian church, considered by many to be the founder of a formalized Christian theology. His books include the *Confessions*, a spiritual autobiography; and *City of God*, a defense of Christian beliefs.

**Saint Thomas à Becket** (1118?–70), archbishop of Canterbury. A defender of church rights against lay power, he quarreled with Henry II and was murdered in Canterbury Cathedral by the king's knights.

**Saint Francis of Assisi** (1182–1226), Italian friar and preacher who founded the Franciscan order in 1209. His monastic rule demanded poverty, and the members of his order lived by begging. According to legend he experienced the miracle of the stigmata in 1224.

**Saint John of the Cross** (San Juan de la Cruz; 1542–91), Spanish mystic and poet. With St. Theresa of Ávila he founded the Discalced Carmelites. His works include three great mystical poems: *The Dark Night of the Soul, The Flame of Divine Love*, and *The Spiritual Canticle.*

**Saint Ignatius Loyola** (1491–1556), Spanish Catholic founder of the Jesuit order.

**Saint John Nepomucene Neuman** (1811–60), first American man canonized by Roman Catholic Church (1977). Born in Bohemia (now Czechoslovakia), he came to U.S. in 1836. He was vicar of the Redemptionists order, 1847–52, and then served as bishop of Philadelphia, 1852–60, expanding parochial school enrollment from 500 to 9,000.

**Saint Patrick** (389?–461?), patron saint of Ireland who converted the Irish people to Christianity and established churches.

**Saint Paul** (died A.D. 67?), an organizer of the Christian church. Jewish by birth, he tried to stamp out the Christian movement in Jerusalem, but he was converted on the way to Damascus. He made several missionary journeys and founded churches to which he sent letters (the Pauline epistles of the New Testament).

**Saint Peter** (died A.D. 67?), one of Jesus' disciples, helped organize the early Christian church. He is regarded as the first pope by the Roman Catholic Church.

**Saint Elizabeth Ann Seton** (1774–1821), first person born in U.S. canonized a saint by Roman Catholic Church (1975). Founded Sisters of Charity in 1809. Pioneered parochial education and charitable institutions in U.S.

**Saint Theresa of Ávila** (1515–82), Spanish Roman Catholic nun of the Carmelite order. Both a vigorous administrator and author of religious tracts, she exerted great influence on the 16th century Catholic Reformation.

**Girolamo Savonarola** (1452–98), Italian Catholic reformer and religious leader of Florence whose attacks against the papacy ultimately led to his execution.

**Friedrich Daniel Ernst Schleiermacher** (1768–1834), German theologian who claimed that religion and philosophy do not contradict each other, but that religion should be purged of metaphysical overtones.

**Arthur Schopenhauer** (1788–1860), German philosopher whose writings utilized the philosophy of Kant and showed influences of Buddhism in negation of the individual will. His major work is *The World as Will and Representation* (1818).

**Albert Schweitzer** (1875–1965), Alsatian theologian and medical missionary who established a hospital for African natives in Lambaréné, Gabon. His ethical principle, Reverence for Life, requires a respect for all living creatures.

**Joseph Smith** (1805–44), American religious leader who founded the Church of Jesus Christ of the Latter–day Saints (Mormons), published the *Book of Mormon* in 1830.

**Baruch Spinoza** (1632–77), Dutch Jewish rationalist philosopher. He believed God to be identical with nature and thus conceived of man as an extension, or attribute, of divinity.

**Emanuel Swedenborg** (1688–1772), Swedish theologian and scientist who wrote extensively on physiology before writing religious tracts. His religious thinking became most widely known after his death.

**Jeremy Taylor** (1613–67), Anglican bishop and religious writer whose finely styled prose was widely popular in the 1600s.

**William Temple** (1881–1944), archbishop of Canterbury considered the leading influence in forming the British Council of Churches and the World Council of Churches.

**Thomas à Kempis** (1379?–1471), German monk and devotional writer. He probably wrote *The Imitation of Christ*, still widely read.

**Paul Johannes Tillich** (1886–1965), German-American existentialist theologian who incorporated psychology into his theological system.

**William Tyndale** (1494?–1536), English Protestant martyr whose scriptural translations later formed the basis of the King James Bible.

**Vardhamana** (called **Mahavira;** 500s B.C.), Indian prophet. He founded Jainist religion in reaction against certain Hindu beliefs and practices. Jainism emphasizes man's need to transcend all of his passions.

**John Wesley** (1703–91), English Anglican minister who founded the Methodist Church. In 1784 he ordained the first American Methodist bishops.

**William of Ockham** (1285?–1347), English scholastic philosopher who drew a sharp distinction between the realms of philosophy and theology to avoid purported contradictions.

**John Wyclif** or **Wycliffe** (1330?–84), English ecclesiastical reformer and forerunner of the Reformation. He insisted on the supremacy of scripture over the authority of the church.

**Brigham Young** (1801–77), American Mormon preacher who led his sect in its migration west.

**Zoroaster** or **Zarathustra** (628?–551? B.C.), ancient Persian religious teacher and prophet. He founded Zoroastrianism, which disappeared only with rise of Islam in 600s A.D. Zoroastrianism introduced the idea of an ultimate resurrection of the dead.

**Huldreich Zwingli** (1484–1531), Swiss religious leader who was major figure behind Protestant Reformation in Switzerland.

# Science and Invention

United Press Int'l.

Heavy smoking machine in the Federal Trade Commission laboratory in Washington, D.C., tests amount of carbon monoxide found in smoke. Recent studies indicate carbon monoxide may be a "possible critical factor" in certain diseases, making its content in cigarette smoke as important as measurements of tar and nicotine.

## HIGHLIGHTS: 1980

In addition to the 1980 developments in science and invention included in this section, see also the sections on *Awards, Climate and Weather, Earth, Ecology and Environment, Energy and Resources, Medicine and Health,* and *Space and Astronomy.*

### INVENTORS HONORED

The National Inventors Hall of Fame added four more persons in a ceremony on Feb. 10, 1980. They were: Lewis H. Sarett, who invented synthetic cortisone in 1944; James Hillier, who developed the first practical electron microscope in 1937; the late Charles F. Kettering, who invented the automobile self-starter in 1911; and the late Edwin H. Armstrong, who invented FM radio in 1933.

At the same ceremony at the Patent and Trademark offices in Arlington, Va., William

A. Thornton Jr. was named Inventor of the Year for 1979 for his invention of a fluorescent lamp that gives off light of the same color as that of an incandescent lamp.

### BUDGET CUTS DELAY PATENTS

Budget reductions by the federal government were blamed in 1980 for increasing delays in the issuance of patents and trademarks. A total of 51,686 patents were granted in 1979, some 14,000 fewer than in 1978. The average time to obtain a patent has grown from 18 months to 21 months. However, the rate of applications received continues at about 100,000 per year.

The average time a company must wait for obtaining approval of a trademark has increased from 3 months in 1976 to 26 months in 1980. In the same period the staff of the

**HIGHLIGHTS: 1980** *(continued)*

trademark office was increased by about 12% while the number of applications for trademarks rose from 37,074 in 1976 to 53,100 in 1979.

### EDISON LAB DECLARED A HAZARD

The laboratory of inventor Thomas A. Edison in West Orange, N.J., ordinarily draws more than 50,000 visitors a year as a National Historic site. However, in 1980 the federal Environmental Protection Agency temporarily closed the lab to visitors until plans could be made to dispose of chemicals left in the laboratory after Edison's death in 1931.

Michael Polito, the federal EPA official who recommended the closing, said many of the 10,000 items in the chemistry laboratory were considered potentially hazardous.

Other buildings at the site were allowed to remain open to the public.

### SUPERSPEEDY COMPUTER USING SQUIDS

International Business Machines (IBM) scientists announced a breakthrough in 1980 in experiments to develop a computer 20 times faster than those currently used that depend on transistor circuits in silicon chips.

A patent was granted to IBM for a process to make the world's thinnest metal wires—as small in diameter as only 20 atoms. The wires are for use in making *squids,* or superconductive quantum interference devices. Signals as small as 120 microvolts have been measured by squids developed by the IBM research staff.

IBM hopes to have a computer using such devices by 1984.

### STEREOPHONIC AM RADIOS

The Federal Communications Commission (FCC) approved in 1980 a plan that is expected to antiquate most existing AM radios during the 1980s. Radio broadcasters and radio manufacturers began gearing up to use the new system that enables stereophonic sound to be broadcast on AM frequencies.

The FCC chose among several systems proposed by various manufacturers in selecting one submitted by Magnavox. The corporation will license others to use its system, which combines amplitude and phase modulation to achieve stereo sound.

### LIFETIME ELECTRIC WATCH BATTERIES

The Bulova Watch Company announced plans for the production of electric wristwatches that wearers will not have to periodically open to replace batteries. The new watches will have built into them a device called a *thermatron,* which will use the body heat of the wearer to generate electricity to recharge the watch battery. The company hopes that the new watch will enable it to increase its share in the annual market of about 27 million electrically powered watches.

### NEW CALIFORNIA ATOM SMASHER

The largest U.S. atom smasher built to date went into operation in May 1980 at the Stanford Linear Accelerator Center in California. Called a colliding beam particle accelerator, the new machine fires beams of electrons and positrons at each other so that their collision generates tinier subatomic particles. In the first tests of the machine the collisions produced 16 billion electron volts.

### PATENTING NEW FORMS OF LIFE

A U.S. Supreme Court ruling in June that man-made life forms could be patented was

Sony Corporation's chief executive officer, Akio Morita, demonstrates new combination video camera-recorder.

Hundreds of thousands of personal microcomputers were sold to homes, schools, and small businesses in 1980. Providing as much "brain power" as did room-sized computers of the 1950s, the microcomputers have an infinite number of uses, limited only by the imagination of the user. Accessories enable the microcomputers to "speak," to print out letters, to play games, or even to compose music.

United Press Int'l.

expected to further stimulate the growing science of gene splicing. The court decision gave the General Electric Company protection for a bacteria developed by its scientists that eats oil in cleaning up oil spills.

Hundreds of applications already are on file for newly developed life forms. Many of these are for new kinds of bacteria used in producing drugs, such as insulin.

Organisms also have been developed that can eat specific kinds of chemicals or minerals. These are being tested by mining and metallurgical industries to determine whether it is possible to have these bacteria eat away the impurities in various ores, leaving behind only the valuable minerals and thus eliminate the need to smelt the ore.

The use of gene splicing in laboratory experiments was further stimulated in 1980 when the National Institutes of Health eased safety rules to make such research less expensive in research centers that use federal funds. No restrictions are placed on industries or private researchers using their own funds.

## CLONING A PREHISTORIC MAMMOTH
Soviet research scientist V. Mikhelson reported that efforts were under way to create a living mammoth. Using cells taken from the body of a prehistoric mammoth found preserved in a glacier, the Soviet scientist hopes to clone mammoth cells that can then be implanted in a female elephant, which would give birth to the cloned mammoth.

## DELAYED MILITARY PATENTS
Delayed to preserve national-defense secrecy, several patents were granted in 1980 on inventions whose applications had been pending for more than three decades. One was for a 1944 invention by Joseph C. Tellier of a proximity fuse that enables bombs from aircraft to be exploded at a predetermined height. Another was for the 1945 invention by Frank P. Wipff of a voice scrambler to protect phone conversations from eavesdroppers. The third was for the 1947 invention by William B. McLean of the Sidewinder missile used to home in on the exhaust pipe of an aircraft and destroy it.

## SYNTHETIC SKUNK SCENT
One of the most unusual inventions to receive a patent in 1980 was a synthetic skunk smell invented by Arthur F. Isbell of College Station, Texas. Because the skunk scent prevents wildlife from smelling the odor of humans, the synthetic will be sold to animal-watchers, hunters, and trappers to enable them to mask their presence.

The scent would be released downwind from the animals being hunted.

## LENGTH AND DISTANCE: U.S. MEASURES (AND METRIC EQUIVALENTS)

1 **mil** = 0.001 inch = 0.0254 millimeter
1 **inch** (in.) = 25.4 millimeters = 2.54 centimeters
1 **foot** (ft.) = 12 inches = $\frac{1}{3}$ yard = 0.00018939 mile
  = 30.48 centimeters = 0.3048 meter
1 **yard** (yd.) = 3 feet = 36 inches = 0.9144 meter
1 **rod** (rd.) = $16\frac{1}{2}$ feet = $5\frac{1}{2}$ yards = 5.0292 meters

1 **furlong** (fur.) = $\frac{1}{8}$ mile = 40 rods = 220 yards
  = 660 feet = 201.168 meters
1 **statute mile** (mi.) = 8 furlongs = 320 rods
  = 1,760 yards = 5,280 feet = 1.609344 kilometers
  = 0.86897624 nautical mile
1 **league** (land) = 3 statute miles = 4.8280 kilometers

### NAUTICAL MEASURES OF LENGTH AND DISTANCE

1 **span** = 9 inches = 22.86 centimeters
1 **fathom** (fm.) = 8 spans = 72 inches = 6 feet
  = 1.8288 meters
1 **cable** = 120 fathoms = 240 yards = 720 feet
  = 219.4560 meters
1 **league** (nautical) = 3 nautical miles
  = 5,556 meters = 3.452338 statute miles

1 **nautical mile** (or international mile) (mi.)
  = 2,025.37182852 yards = 6,076.11548556 feet
  = 1,852 meters = 1.852 kilometers
  = 1.150779448 statute miles
  = 1' (minute) latitude
1 ° (degree) **latitude**
  = 60 nautical miles

### SURVEYOR'S (or GUNTER'S) CHAIN MEASURES

1 **link** (li.) = 7.92 inches = 0.201168 meter
1 **chain** (ch.) = 100 links = 66 feet = 20.1168 meters
1 **furlong** (fur.) = 10 chains = 40 rods = 660 feet
  = 201.168 meters
1 **statute mile** = 80 chains = 8 furlongs = 5,280 feet
  = 1.609344 kilometers

### ENGINEER'S CHAIN MEASURES

1 **link** (li.) = 1 foot
  = 0.3048 meter
1 **chain** (ch.) = 100 links
  = 100 feet = 30.48 meters
1 **statute mile** = 52.8 chains = 5,280 feet
  = 1.609344 kilometers

## AREA: U.S. MEASURES (AND METRIC EQUIVALENTS)

1 **square inch** (sq. in.) = 6.45160 square centimeters
  = 0.00694444 square foot
1 **square foot** (sq. ft.) = 144 square inches
  = 929.0304 square centimeters
1 **square yard** (sq. yd.) = 1,296 square inches
  = 9 square feet = 0.83612736 square meter

1 **square rod** (sq. rd.) = $30\frac{1}{4}$ square yards
  = $272\frac{1}{4}$ square feet = 25.29285264 square meters
1 **acre** (A.) = 160 square rods = 4,840 square yards
  = 43,560 square feet = 0.40468564224 hectare
1 **square mile** (sq. mi.) = 640 acres = 27,878,400 sq. ft.
  = 2.589988110336 square kilometers

### SURVEYOR'S MEASURES OF LAND AREA

1 **square link** (sq. li.) = 62.7264 square inches
  = 404.68564 square centimeters
1 **square pole** (sq. p.) = 625 square links
  = $30\frac{1}{4}$ square yards = 25.29285264 square meters
1 **square chain** (sq. ch.) = 16 square poles
  = 484 square yards = 404.68564224 square meters

1 **acre** (A.) = 10 square chains = 4,840 square yards
  = 43,560 square feet = 0.40468564324 hectare
1 **section** (sec.) = 640 acres = 1 square mile
  = 2.589988110336 square kilometers
1 **township** (tp.) = 36 sections = 36 square miles
  = 93.23957 square kilometers

## WEIGHT OR MASS: U.S. MEASURES (AND METRIC EQUIVALENTS)

### AVOIRDUPOIS UNITS OF WEIGHT

Everyday weights are measured in avoirdupois units in the United States. When necessary to distinguish these units from other measuring units, such as fluid ounces or troy ounces, use the abbreviation **avdp.**

1 **grain** (gr.) = 0.00228571 ounce = 0.00208333 troy ounce
  = 64.79891 milligrams = 0.00017361 troy pound
1 **dram** (dr.) = $27\frac{11}{32}$ grains = 27.34375 grains
  = 1.7718449 grams
1 **ounce** (oz.) = 16 drams = $437\frac{1}{2}$ grains
  = 0.9114583 troy ounce = 0.9114583 apothecaries' ounce
  = 0.0625 pound = 0.07595486 troy pound
  = 28.349523125 grams

1 **pound** (lb.) = 16 ounces = 256 drams = 7,000 grains
  = 1.215278 troy pound = 1.215278 apothecaries' lbs.
  = 453.59237 grams = 0.45359237 kilogram
1 **hundredweight** (cwt.) = 100 pounds = 0.05 ton
  = 45.359237 kilograms
1 **ton** (designated as **short** ton or **net** ton)
  = 2,000 pounds = 0.8928571 long ton (or gross ton)
  = 907.18474 kilograms = 0.90718474 metric ton

### BRITISH UNITS OF AVOIRDUPOIS WEIGHT

1 **stone** = 14 pounds = 6.35029318 kilograms
1 **hundredweight** = 112 pounds = 50.80234544 kilograms

1 **ton** (designated as **long** ton or **gross** ton)
  = 2,240 pounds = 1.12 short tons = 1,016.0469088 kilograms

### TROY UNITS OF WEIGHT

Gems and precious metals are measured using troy weight.

1 **grain** = 0.0022857 avdp. ounce = 64.79891 milligrams
1 **carat** = 3.086 grains = 0.00705 avdp. ounce
  = 200 milligrams = 0.2 gram
1 **assay ton** (AT) = $29,166\frac{2}{3}$ milligrams (same as number
  of troy ounces in short ton)
1 **pennyweight** (dwt.) = 24 grains = T0.05485715 avdp. ounce
  = 1.55517384 grams

1 **ounce** = 480 grains = 20 pennyweights
  = 1.097143 avdp. ounces = 31.1034768 grams
1 **pound** = 5,760 grains = 240 pennyweights
  = 12 troy ounces = 0.8228571 avdp. pound
  = 13.16571 avdp. ounces = 373.2417216 grams
  = 0.3732417216 kilogram
1 **short ton** = 2,000 avdp. pounds = $29,166\frac{2}{3}$ troy ounces

### APOTHECARIES' UNITS OF WEIGHT

1 **grain** = 0.0022857 avdp. ounce = 64.79891 milligrams
1 **scruple** = 20 grains = 0.04571429167 avdp. ounce
  = 1.29584782 grams
1 **dram** = 60 grains = 3 scruples = 0.137142875 avdp. ounce
  = 3.8879346 grams

1 **ounce** = 480 grains = 24 scruples = 8 drams
  = 1.097143 avdp. ounces = 31.1034768 grams
1 **pound** = 5,760 grains = 288 scruples = 96 drams
  = 12 apothecaries' ounces = 13.16571 avdp. ounces
  = 373.2417216 grams = 0.3732417216 kilogram

## VOLUME AND CAPACITY: U.S. MEASURES (AND METRIC EQUIVALENTS)

1 **cubic inch** (cu. in.) = 16.387064 cubic centimeters
= 0.5541126 fluid ounce = 0.016387064 liter

1 **cubic foot** = 1,728 cubic inches = 957.5065 fluid ounces
= 0.028316846592 cubic meter = 29.92208 fluid quarts
= 7.480519 U.S. gallons = 28.316846592 liters
= 6.228822724 British imperial gallons

1 **cubic yard** (cu. yd.) = 46,656 cubic inches
= 27 cubic feet
= 0.764554857984 cubic meter
= 201.9740 U.S. gallons
= 168.1782135 British imperial gallons
= 764.554857984 liters

### MEASURES OF VOLUME-MASS

1 **cubic foot of seawater** = 64 pounds

1 **cubic foot of fresh water** = 62.428 pounds at 39.2° F.

1 **cubic foot of ice** = 56 pounds

1 **measurement ton** = 40 cubic feet = 1 freight ton

1 **displacement ton** = 35 cubic feet of seawater
= 1 long ton

1 **register ton** = 100 cubic feet
= 2.8316846592 cubic meters

### HOUSEHOLD MEASURES OF LIQUID CAPACITY

1 **teaspoon** = $\frac{1}{3}$ tablespoon = $\frac{1}{6}$ fluid ounce = 80 drops
= 4.928921667 milliliters

1 **tablespoon** = 3 teaspoons = $\frac{1}{2}$ fluid ounce = 240 drops
= 14.786765 milliliters

1 **fluid ounce** (fl. oz.) = 2 tablespoons = 6 teaspoons
= 29.57353 milliliters = 1.8046875 cubic inches

1 **gill** (gi.) = $\frac{1}{2}$ cup = 4 fluid ounces = 7.21875 cubic inches
= 118.29411825 milliliters = 1,920 minims

1 **cup** = 16 tablespoons = 8 fluid ounces
= 14.4375 cubic inches = 236.58824 milliliters

1 **pint** (pt.) = 2 cups = 4 gills = 16 fluid ounces
= 28.875 cubic inches = 0.473176473 liter

1 **quart** (qt.) = 2 pints = 4 cups = 32 fluid ounces
= 57.75 cubic inches = 0.832672482 British quart
= 0.946352946 liter = 0.03342014 cubic foot

1 **British imperial quart** = 1.20095 U.S. quarts
= 69.355 cubic inches = 1.1365248824 liters

1 **gallon** (gal.) = 4 quarts = 8 pints = 16 cups
= 128 fluid ounces = 231 cubic inches
= 3,785.411784 milliliters
= 0.832672482 British imperial gallon
= 3.785411784 liters

1 **British imperial gallon** = 1.20095 U.S. gallons
= 160 British fluid ounces = 277.42 cubic inches
= 4.546099295 liters

1 **barrel (liquids)** = 31.5 U.S. gallons = 4.21 cubic feet
= 119.2404712 liters

1 **barrel (petroleum)** = 42 U.S. gallons
= 0.1589872949 cubic meter = 5.6145852 cubic feet
= 158.9872949 liters

### APOTHECARIES' MEASURES OF LIQUID CAPACITY

1 **minim** (or **drop**) (min.) = $\frac{1}{60}$ fluid dram
= $\frac{1}{480}$ fluid ounce = 0.0020833 fluid ounce
= 0.0037597656 cubic inch = 0.06161152 milliliter

1 **British fluid drachm** = 0.961 U.S. fluid dram
= 0.216734 cubic inch = 3.55164 milliliters

1 **fluid dram** (fl. dr.) = 60 minims = $\frac{1}{8}$ fluid ounce
= 0.125 fluid ounce = 0.225585937 cubic inch
= 3.69669125 cubic centimeters = 3.69669125 milliliters

1 **British fluid ounce** = 0.961 U.S. fluid ounce
= 1.733875 cubic inches = 28.41312 milliliters

1 **fluid ounce** (fl. oz.) = 8 fluid drams = $\frac{1}{16}$ fluid pint
= 1.8046875 cubic inches = 29.57353 cubic centimeters
= 29.57353 milliliters = 1.041 British fluid ounces

1 **pint** = 128 fluid drams = 16 fluid ounces = 7,680 minims
= 28.875 cubic inches = 473.176473 cubic centimeters
= 473.176473 milliliters
= 0.473176473 liter

1 **quart** = 2 pints = 32 fluid ounces = 256 fluid drams
= 57.75 cubic inches = 946.352946 cubic centimeters
= 0.946352946 liter
= 0.832672482 British quart

1 **gallon** = 4 quarts = 8 pints = 128 fluid ounces
= 231 cubic inches
= 3,785.411784 cubic centimeters
= 3.785411784 liters
= 0.832672482 British gallon

### CUSTOMARY DRY MEASURES OF CAPACITY

1 **pint** = 33.6003125 cubic inches
= 550.61047 cubic centimeters = 0.55061047 liters

1 **quart** = 2 pints = 67.200625 cubic inches
= 1,101.22094 cubic centimeters
= 1.10122094 liters = 0.969 British dry quart

1 **British imperial dry quart** = 1.032 U.S. dry quarts
= 69.355 cubic inches = 1.1365 liters

1 **peck** (pk.) = 8 quarts = 16 pints = 0.25 bushel
= 537.605 cubic inches = 8,809.7675 cubic centimeters
= 8.8097675 liters

1 **bushel** (bu.), **U.S. struck measure** = 4 pecks = 32 dry quarts
= 64 dry pints = 2,150.42 cubic inches = 35.23907 liters

1 **British imperial bushel** = 1.032 U.S. struck measure bushels
= 2,219.36 cubic inches = 36.368735 liters

1 **bushel, U.S. heaped measure** = $1\frac{1}{4}$ struck measure bushels = 1.278 struck measure bushels
= 2,747.715 cubic inches = 45.035527 liters

1 **barrel** (bbl.), **cranberries** = 5,286 cubic inches
= $86\frac{45}{64}$ dry quarts = 2.709 struck measure bushels

1 **barrel** (bbl.), **standard** (other fruits and vegetables and dry commodities) = 7,056 cubic inches = 105 dry quarts
= 3.281 struck measure bushels
= 0.115627 cubic meter

## LENGTH: METRIC MEASURES AND EQUIVALENTS

1 **nanometer** (nm.) = 0.00000003937008 inch

1 **micron** (m.) = 1,000 nanometers = 0.00003937008 inch

1 **millimeter** (mm.) = 0.03937008 inch

1 **centimeter** (cm.) = 10 millimeters = 0.3937008 inch

1 **decimeter** (dm.) = 100 millimeters = 10 centimeters
= 3.937008 inches

1 **meter** (m.) = 1,000 millimeters = 100 centimeters
= 10 decimeters = 39.37008 inches = 3.280840 feet
= 1.093613 yards = 0.54680665 fathom
= 0.00062137 statute mile = 0.00053996 nautical mile

1 **decameter** (dam.) = 10 meters
= 32.80840 feet = 10.93613 yards
= 393.7008 inches = 0.0062137 mile

1 **hectometer** (hm.) = 10 decameters = 100 meters
= 328.0840 feet
= 109.3613 yards

1 **kilometer** (km.) = 1,000 meters = 100 decameters
= 10 hectometers = 3,280.83990 feet = 1,093.61330 yards
= 0.621371192 statute mile
= 0.53995680 nautical mile

## AREA: METRIC MEASURES AND EQUIVALENTS

1 **square millimeter** (mm.$^2$) = 0.0015500031 square inch
1 **square centimeter** (cm.$^2$) = 100 square millimeters
  = 0.15500031 square inch = 0.001076391 square foot
1 **square decimeter** (dm.$^2$) = 100 square centimeters
  = 15.500031 square inches = 0.1076391 square foot
1 **square meter** (m.$^2$) = 1,000,000 square millimeters
  = 10,000 square centimeters = 100 square decimeters
  = 10.76391045 square feet = 1.19599005 square yards

1 **are** (a.) = 100 square meters = 119.599005 square yards
  = 0.02471053815 acre
1 **hectare** (ha.) = 10,000 square meters = 100 ares
  = 2.471053815 acres
1 **square kilometer** (km.$^2$) = 1,000,000 square meters
  = 100 hectares = 247.1053815 acres
  = 0.38610216 square statute mile
  = 0.29155335 square nautical mile

## VOLUME: METRIC MEASURES AND EQUIVALENTS

1 **cubic millimeter** (mm.$^3$) = 0.001 cubic centimeter
  = 0.00006102374 cubic inch
1 **cubic centimeter** (cm.$^3$) = 1,000 cubic millimeters
  = 0.06102374 cubic inch = 0.00026417205 U.S. gallon
1 **cubic decimeter** (dm.$^3$) = 1,000 cubic centimeters = 1 liter
  = 61.02374 cubic inches = 0.03531467 cubic foot
1 **stere** (s) = 1 cubic meter

1 **cubic meter** (m.$^3$) = 1,000,000 cubic centimeters
  = 1,000 cubic decimeters = 35.31467 cubic feet
  = 1.30795059 cubic yards = 264.17205 U.S. gallons
1 **cubic decameter** (dam.$^3$) = 1,000 cubic meters
  = 1,307.9506 cubic yards
1 **cubic hectometer** (hm.$^3$) = 1,000 cubic decameters
  = 1,307,950.6 cubic yards

## CAPACITY: METRIC MEASURES AND EQUIVALENTS

1 **milliliter** (ml.) = 0.001 liter = 0.03381402 fluid ounce
  = 16.23073 minims = 0.06102374 cubic inch
1 **centiliter** (cl.) = 10 milliliters = 0.01 liter
  = 0.3381402 fluid ounce = 0.6102374 cubic inch
1 **deciliter** (dl.) = 100 milliliters = 10 centiliters
  = 3.381402 fluid ounces = 6.102374 cubic inches
1 **liter** (l.) = 1,000 milliliters = 10 deciliters
  = 33.81402 fluid ounces = 1 cubic decimeter
  = 61.02374 cubic inches = 1.056688 fluid quarts
  = 0.26417205 U.S. gallon = 0.90808298 dry quart

1 **decaliter** (dal.) = 10 liters
  = 2.6417205 U.S. gallons
1 **hectoliter** (hl.) = 100 liters
  = 10 decaliters
  = 26.417205 U.S. gallons
  = 2.837759 U.S. bushels
  = 3.531467 cubic feet
1 **kiloliter** (kl.) = 1,000 liters = 10 hectoliters
  = 35.31467 cubic feet
  = 264.17205 U.S. gallons

## WEIGHT: METRIC MEASURES AND EQUIVALENTS

1 **microgram** (μg.) = 0.000001 gram
  = 0.00001543236 grain
1 **milligram** (mg.) = 1,000 micrograms = 0.001 gram
  = 0.01543236 grain
1 **centigram** (cg.) = 10 milligrams = 0.01 gram
  = 0.1543236 grain = 0.003527396 avdp. ounce
1 **decigram** (dg.) = 10 centigrams = 0.1 gram
  = 1.543236 grains = 0.03527396 avdp. ounce
1 **gram** (g.) = 1,000 milligrams = 10 decigrams
  = 15.43236 grains = 0.03527396 avdp. ounce
1 **decagram** (dag.) = 10 grams = 0.3527396 avdp. ounce

1 **hectogram** (hg.) = 100 grams = 10 decagrams
  = 3.527396 avdp. ounces
1 **kilogram** (kg.) = 1,000 grams = 10 hectograms
  = 35.27396 avdp. ounces = 32.15075 troy ounces
  = 2.204623 avdp. pounds
  = 2.679229 troy pounds
1 **quintal** (q.) = 100 kilograms = 220.4623 avdp. pounds
1 **metric ton** (M.T.) = 1,000 kilograms
  = 2,204.623 avdp. pounds
  = 1.1023113 short tons
  = 0.9842065 long ton

## HOW TO CONVERT UNITS OF MEASURE BY MULTIPLICATION

| U.S. MEASURE | MULTIPLY BY | TO GET METRIC | METRIC MEASURE | MULTIPLY BY | TO GET U.S. |
|---|---|---|---|---|---|
| **LENGTH AND DISTANCE** | | | | | |
| inches | × 25.4 | = millimeters | millimeters | × 0.03937008 | = inches |
| inches | × 2.54 | = centimeters | centimeters | × 0.3937008 | = inches |
| feet | × 0.3048 | = meters | meters | × 3.280840 | = feet |
| yards | × 0.9144 | = meters | meters | × 1.093613 | = yards |
| miles | × 1.609344 | = kilometers | kilometers | × 0.62137 | = miles |
| **AREA OR SURFACE** | | | | | |
| square inches | × 6.4516 | = square centimeters | square centimeters | × 0.1550003 | = square inches |
| square feet | × 0.09290304 | = square meters | square meters | × 10.76391 | = square feet |
| square yards | × 0.83612736 | = square meters | square meters | × 1.195990 | = square yards |
| acres | × 0.40468564224 | = hectares | hectares | × 2.47105 | = acres |
| square miles | × 2.58998811 | = square kilometers | square kilometers | × 0.386102 | = square miles |
| **VOLUME** | | | | | |
| cubic inches | × 16.387064 | = cubic centimeters | cubic centimeters | × 0.06102374 | = cubic inches |
| cubic feet | × 0.028316846592 | = cubic meters | cubic meters | × 35.31467 | = cubic feet |
| cubic yards | × 0.764554857984 | = cubic meters | cubic meters | × 1.3079506 | = cubic yards |
| **CAPACITY** | | | | | |
| fluid ounces | × 29.57353 | = milliliters | milliliters | × 0.03381402 | = fluid ounces |
| liquid pint | × 0.473176473 | = liters | liters | × 2.113376 | = liquid pints |
| liquid quart | × 0.946352946 | = liters | liters | × 1.056688 | = liquid quarts |
| gallons | × 3.785411784 | = liters | liters | × 0.26417205 | = gallons |
| bushels | × 35.23907 | = liters | liters | × 0.02837759 | = bushels |
| **WEIGHT** | | | | | |
| grains | × 0.06479891 | = grams | grams | × 15.43236 | = grains |
| ounces avdp. | × 28.349523125 | = grams | grams | × 0.03527396 | = ounces avdp. |
| pounds avdp. | × 0.45359237 | = kilograms | kilograms | × 2.204623 | = pounds avdp. |
| tons | × 0.90718474 | = metric tons | metric tons | × 1.1023113 | = tons |

## TIME MEASUREMENTS

1 **microsecond** = 0.000001 second
1 **second** = 1,000,000 microseconds = 0.016667 minute
= 0.00027778 hour = 0.00069444 day = 15″ longitude
1 **minute** = 60 seconds = 0.0166667 hour
= 0.00069444 day = 15′ longitude
1 **hour** = 3,600 seconds = 60 minutes = 15° longitude
= 0.04166667 day
1 **day** = 24 hours = 1,440 minutes = 86,400 seconds
= 360° longitude
1 **mean solar day** (1 rotation of Earth with respect to Sun)
= 24 hours, 3 minutes, 56.55536 seconds
= 1.00273791 rotations with respect to vernal equinox
= 1.0027378118868 rotations of Earth with respect to stars

1 **sidereal month** = 27.321661 days
= 27 days, 7 hours, 43 minutes, 11.5 seconds
1 **synodical month** = 29.530588 days
= 29 days, 12 hours, 44 minutes, 2.8 seconds
1 **calendar year** = 31,536,000 seconds
= 525,600 minutes = 8,760 hours = 365 days
1 **solar year** = 31,556,925.975 seconds
= 525,948.766 minutes = 8,765.8128 hours
= 365 days, 5 hours, 48 minutes, 46 seconds
1 **light-year** = 5,880,000,000,000 statute miles
= 9,460,000,000,000 kilometers
= 5,110,000,000,000 nautical miles

## SPEED: U.S. AND METRIC MEASURES

1 **foot per minute** = 0.01666667 foot per second
= 0.00508 meter per second
1 **yard per minute** = 3 feet per minute
= 0.05 foot per second
= 0.03409091 statute mile per hour
= 0.02962419 knot = 0.01524 meter per second
1 **statute mile per hour** = 88 feet per minute
= 29.333 yards per minute = 1.466667 feet per second
= 1.609344 kilometers per hour = 0.86897624 knot
= 0.44704 meter per second
1 **knot** = 101.26859143 feet per minute
= 6,076.11548556 feet per hour
= 33.75619714 yards per minute
= 1.852 kilometers per hour
= 1.68780986 feet per second
= 1.15077945 statute miles per hour
= 0.51444444 meter per second
1 **meter per second** = 196.85039340 feet per minute
= 65.6167978 yards per minute
= 3.6 kilometers per hour
= 3.28083990 feet per second
= 2.23693632 statute miles per hour
= 1.94384449 knots

1 **kilometer per hour**
= 0.53995680 knot
= 0.62137119 statute mile per hour
**Speed of light** (in vacuum)
= 186,282 statute miles per second
= 161,875 nautical miles per second
= 299,792 kilometers per second
= 983.570 feet per microsecond
**Speed of light** (in air)
= 186,230 statute miles per second
= 299,708 kilometers per second
= 161,829 nautical miles per second
= 983.294 feet per microsecond
**Speed of sound** (in air at 60° F. at sea level)
= 1,116.99 feet per second
= 761.59 statute miles per hour
= 661.80 knots
= 340.46 meters per second
**Speed of sound** (in salt water at 60° F.)
= 4,945.37 feet per second
= 3,371.85 statute miles per hour
= 2,930.05 knots
= 1,507.35 meters per second

## SPECIAL UNITS OF MEASUREMENT

**Ampere:** Unit of electric current. A potential difference of 1 volt across a resistance of 1 ohm produces a current of 1 ampere.
**Bale:** Bale of cotton weighs 500 pounds gross or 480 pounds net.
**Board Foot:** Volume of 1-inch-thick, 1-foot-square board, rough sawn.
**BTU:** British thermal unit, equal to 252 calories; amount of heat needed to increase temperature of 1 pound of pure water by 1° F.
**Calorie:** Amount of heat needed to increase the temperature of 1 gram of pure water by 1° C.
**Carat:** Used to indicate purity of gold alloys, on a scale of 24: 14 carats means 14 parts gold to 10 parts alloy.
**Cord:** Equals 128 cubic feet of firewood (4 ft. × 4 ft. × 8 ft.).
**Decibel:** Unit of relative loudness in acoustics.
**Hand:** Unit used in measuring height of horses; equals 4 inches.
**Hertz:** Modern unit in electronics, equivalent to and replacing the former "cycles per second"; abbreviated as *hz.*
**Horsepower:** Standard theoretical unit of the time rate of work or power. It is equal to the work done in lifting 550 pounds 1 foot in 1 second; equals 745.7 watts.
**Joule:** Unit of energy measurement equal to 0.24 calorie or 10 million ergs.

**Kilowatt-hour:** Equal to consumption of 1,000 watts of power over a period of 1 hour.
**Ohm:** Unit of electrical resistance. A circuit in which a potential difference of 1 volt produces a current of 1 ampere has a resistance of 1 ohm.
**Pi** ($\pi$): Ratio (3.14159 . . . ) of the circumference of circle to its total diameter.
**Pica:** In typography, equals 12 points; about 1/6 inch; 0.166044 inch; 4.2175176 millimeters.
**Point:** In typography, about 1/72 inch; 0.013837 inch; 0.3514598 millimeter.
**Quire:** Either 24 or 25 sheets of paper of uniform size and quality; equal to 1/20 of a ream.
**Ream:** Twenty quires or 480 uniform sheets of paper, except newsprint or book paper (equal to 500 sheets), or a "perfect ream" of 516.
**Roentgen:** Dosage unit of radiation exposure produced by X rays and gamma rays, alpha, beta, and neutron; it applies to biological effects only.
**Talent:** Ancient unit of coin and weight equal to about 3,600 shekels as a weight, and about 3,000 shekels as silver or gold revenue. Hebrew gold *shekel* probably weighed about 252 grains troy, or slightly over 1/2 ounce.
**Volt:** Unit of electromotive force, or potential difference; potential difference of 1 volt across a resistance of 1 ohm produces a current of 1 ampere.
**Watt:** Power expended by current of 1 ampere across potential difference of 1 volt equals 1 watt.

## TEMPERATURE CONVERSION TABLE *
Source: Ever Ready Thermometer Company

The numbers in boldface type in the center columns—the key to the table—refer to the temperature in either Celsius (formerly centigrade) or Fahrenheit degrees. Thus, for example, +30 in the center column, if chosen to represent 30° Fahrenheit, will convert to -1.1° Celsius, the figure found to the left of the column. If, on the other hand, it is made to represent 30° Celsius, it will convert to 86.0° Fahrenheit, the figure to the right of the column.

For degrees of temperature not included in this table, the following formulas provide the necessary conversion:

$$F° = (C° \times 1.8) + 32 \quad \text{or} \quad C° = (F° - 32) \times 5 \div 9$$

| DEGREES C. | DEGREES | DEGREES F. | DEGREES C. | DEGREES | DEGREES F. | DEGREES C. | DEGREES | DEGREES F. |
|---|---|---|---|---|---|---|---|---|
| -34.4 | -30 | -22.0 | -9.4 | +15 | +59.0 | +15.6 | +60 | +140.0 |
| -33.9 | -29 | -20.2 | -8.9 | +16 | +60.8 | +16.1 | +61 | +141.8 |
| -33.3 | -28 | -18.4 | -8.3 | +17 | +62.6 | +16.7 | +62 | +143.6 |
| -32.8 | -27 | -16.6 | -7.8 | +18 | +64.4 | +17.2 | +63 | +145.4 |
| -32.2 | -26 | -14.8 | -7.2 | +19 | +66.2 | +17.8 | +64 | +147.2 |
| -31.7 | -25 | -13.0 | -6.7 | +20 | +68.0 | +18.3 | +65 | +149.0 |
| -31.1 | -24 | -11.2 | -6.1 | +21 | +69.8 | +18.9 | +66 | +150.8 |
| -30.6 | -23 | -9.4 | -5.5 | +22 | +71.6 | +19.4 | +67 | +152.6 |
| -30.0 | -22 | -7.6 | -5.0 | +23 | +73.4 | +20.0 | +68 | +154.4 |
| -29.4 | -21 | -5.8 | -4.4 | +24 | +75.2 | +20.6 | +69 | +156.2 |
| -28.9 | -20 | -4.0 | -3.9 | +25 | +77.0 | +21.1 | +70 | +158.0 |
| -28.3 | -19 | -2.2 | -3.3 | +26 | +78.8 | +21.7 | +71 | +159.8 |
| -27.8 | -18 | -0.4 | -2.8 | +27 | +80.6 | +22.2 | +72 | +161.6 |
| -27.2 | -17 | +1.4 | -2.2 | +28 | +82.4 | +22.8 | +73 | +163.4 |
| -26.7 | -16 | +3.2 | -1.7 | +29 | +84.2 | +23.3 | +74 | +165.2 |
| -26.1 | -15 | +5.0 | -1.1 | +30 | +86.0 | +23.9 | +75 | +167.0 |
| -25.6 | -14 | +6.8 | -0.6 | +31 | +87.8 | +24.4 | +76 | +168.8 |
| -25.0 | -13 | +8.6 | 0.0 | +32 | +89.6 | +25.0 | +77 | +170.6 |
| -24.4 | -12 | +10.4 | +0.6 | +33 | +91.4 | +25.6 | +78 | +172.4 |
| -23.9 | -11 | +12.2 | +1.1 | +34 | +93.2 | +26.1 | +79 | +174.2 |
| -23.3 | -10 | +14.0 | +1.7 | +35 | +95.0 | +26.7 | +80 | +176.0 |
| -22.8 | -9 | +15.8 | +2.2 | +36 | +96.8 | +27.2 | +81 | +177.8 |
| -22.2 | -8 | +17.6 | +2.8 | +37 | +98.6 | +27.8 | +82 | +179.6 |
| -21.7 | -7 | +19.4 | +3.3 | +38 | +100.4 | +28.3 | +83 | +181.4 |
| -21.1 | -6 | +21.2 | +3.9 | +39 | +102.2 | +28.9 | +84 | +183.2 |
| -20.6 | -5 | +23.0 | +4.4 | +40 | +104.0 | +29.4 | +85 | +185.0 |
| -20.0 | -4 | +24.8 | +5.0 | +41 | +105.8 | +30.0 | +86 | +186.8 |
| -19.4 | -3 | +26.6 | +5.5 | +42 | +107.6 | +30.6 | +87 | +188.6 |
| -18.9 | -2 | +28.4 | +6.1 | +43 | +109.4 | +31.1 | +88 | +190.4 |
| -18.3 | -1 | +30.2 | +6.7 | +44 | +111.2 | +31.7 | +89 | +192.2 |
| -17.8 | 0 | +32.0 | +7.2 | +45 | +113.0 | +32.2 | +90 | +194.0 |
| -17.2 | +1 | +33.8 | +7.8 | +46 | +114.8 | +32.8 | +91 | +195.8 |
| -16.7 | +2 | +35.6 | +8.3 | +47 | +116.6 | +33.3 | +92 | +197.6 |
| -16.1 | +3 | +37.4 | +8.9 | +48 | +118.4 | +33.9 | +93 | +199.4 |
| -15.6 | +4 | +39.2 | +9.4 | +49 | +120.2 | +34.4 | +94 | +201.2 |
| -15.0 | +5 | +41.0 | +10.0 | +50 | +122.0 | +35.0 | +95 | +203.0 |
| -14.4 | +6 | +42.8 | +10.6 | +51 | +123.8 | +35.6 | +96 | +204.8 |
| -13.9 | +7 | +44.6 | +11.1 | +52 | +125.6 | +36.1 | +97 | +206.6 |
| -13.3 | +8 | +46.4 | +11.7 | +53 | +127.4 | +36.7 | +98 | +208.4 |
| -12.8 | +9 | +48.2 | +12.2 | +54 | +129.2 | +37.2 | +99 | +210.2 |
| -12.2 | +10 | +50.0 | +12.8 | +55 | +131.0 | +37.8 | +100 | +212.0 |
| -11.7 | +11 | +51.8 | +13.3 | +56 | +132.8 | +38.3 | +101 | +213.8 |
| -11.1 | +12 | +53.6 | +13.9 | +57 | +134.6 | +38.9 | +102 | +215.6 |
| -10.6 | +13 | +55.4 | +14.4 | +58 | +136.4 | +39.4 | +103 | +217.4 |
| -10.0 | +14 | +57.2 | +15.0 | +59 | +138.2 | +40.0 | +104 | +219.2 |

* Absolute zero is -273.15° C.  or  -459.67° F.

## KELVIN SCALE

The British physicist Lord Kelvin (1824–1907) devised a temperature scale based on thermodynamic laws. Known also as the absolute scale, Kelvin's system became a fundamental temperature scale used in scientific measurement. Absolute temperatures are used in formulas derived from the laws governing the behavior of gases, which expand and contract in volume at high and low temperatures. According to the kinetic molecular theory, absolute zero is the point at which the molecules of substances have no heat energy. Absolute zero, -273.15° on the Celsius scale, is 0° Kelvin. Thus degrees Kelvin are equivalent to degrees of Celsius plus 273.15. The freezing point of water (0° Celsius and 32° Fahrenheit) is 273.15° Kelvin. The conversion formulas are: $K° = C° + 273.15$ or $K° = (F° - 32) \times (5 \div 9) + 273.15$

# MATHEMATICAL TABLES

## NAMES OF LARGE NUMBERS

| NAME | EQUIVALENT | Number of Zeros | Power of 10 | NAME | EQUIVALENT | Number of Zeros | Power of 10 |
|---|---|---|---|---|---|---|---|
| million | 1,000 thousands | 6 | $10^6$ | duodecillion | 1,000 undecillions | 39 | $10^{39}$ |
| billion | 1,000 millions | 9 | $10^9$ | tredecillion | 1,000 duodecillions | 42 | $10^{42}$ |
| trillion | 1,000 billions | 12 | $10^{12}$ | quattuordecillion | 1,000 tredecillions | 45 | $10^{45}$ |
| quadrillion | 1,000 trillions | 15 | $10^{15}$ | quindecillion | 1,000 quattuordecillions | 48 | $10^{48}$ |
| quintillion | 1,000 quadrillions | 18 | $10^{18}$ | sexdecillion | 1,000 quindecillions | 51 | $10^{51}$ |
| sextillion | 1,000 quintillions | 21 | $10^{21}$ | septendecillion | 1,000 sexdecillions | 54 | $10^{54}$ |
| septillion | 1,000 sextillions | 24 | $10^{24}$ | octodecillion | 1,000 septendecillions | 57 | $10^{57}$ |
| octillion | 1,000 septillions | 27 | $10^{27}$ | novemdecillion | 1,000 octodecillions | 60 | $10^{60}$ |
| nonillion | 1,000 octillions | 30 | $10^{30}$ | vigintillion | 1,000 novemdecillions | 63 | $10^{63}$ |
| decillion | 1,000 nonillions | 33 | $10^{33}$ | googol | —— | 100 | $10^{100}$ |
| undecillion | 1,000 decillions | 36 | $10^{36}$ | | | | |

## ROMAN NUMERALS

| | | | | | | | | | | | | | | |
|---|---|---|---|---|---|---|---|---|---|---|---|---|---|---|
| I | 1 | V | 5 | IX | 9 | XIII | 13 | XVII | 17 | XXX | 30 | LXX | 70 | D ... 500 |
| II | 2 | VI | 6 | X | 10 | XIV | 14 | XVIII | 18 | XL | 40 | LXXX | 80 | M ... 1,000 |
| III | 3 | VII | 7 | XI | 11 | XV | 15 | XIX | 19 | L | 50 | XC | 90 | V̄ ... 5,000 |
| IV | 4 | VIII | 8 | XII | 12 | XVI | 16 | XX | 20 | LX | 60 | C | 100 | X̄ ... 10,000 |

## DECIMAL EQUIVALENTS OF FRACTIONS

| | | | | | | |
|---|---|---|---|---|---|---|
| .015625 = 1/64 | .171875 = 11/64 | .350000 = 7/20 | .531250 = 17/32 | .687500 = 11/16 | .857143 = 6/7 |
| .031250 = 1/32 | .187500 = 3/16 | .359375 = 23/64 | .546875 = 35/64 | .700000 = 7/10 | .859375 = 55/64 |
| .046875 = 3/64 | .200000 = 1/5 | .375000 = 3/8 | .550000 = 11/20 | .707125 = 45/64 | .875000 = 7/8 |
| .050000 = 1/20 | .203125 = 13/64 | .390625 = 25/64 | .555555 = 5/9 | .714286 = 5/7 | .888889 = 8/9 |
| .062500 = 1/16 | .218750 = 7/32 | .400000 = 2/5 | .562500 = 9/16 | .718750 = 23/32 | .890625 = 57/64 |
| .078125 = 5/64 | .222222 = 2/9 | .406250 = 13/32 | .571429 = 4/7 | .734375 = 47/64 | .900000 = 9/10 |
| .083333 = 1/12 | .234375 = 15/64 | .416667 = 5/12 | .578125 = 37/64 | .750000 = 3/4 | .906250 = 29/32 |
| .093750 = 3/32 | .250000 = 1/4 | .421875 = 27/64 | .583333 = 7/12 | .765625 = 49/64 | .916667 = 11/12 |
| .100000 = 1/10 | .265625 = 17/64 | .428571 = 3/7 | .593750 = 19/32 | .777778 = 7/9 | .921875 = 59/64 |
| .109375 = 7/64 | .281250 = 9/32 | .437500 = 7/16 | .600000 = 3/5 | .781250 = 25/32 | .950000 = 19/20 |
| .111111 = 1/9 | .285714 = 2/7 | .444444 = 4/9 | .609375 = 39/64 | .796875 = 51/64 | .953125 = 61/64 |
| .125000 = 1/8 | .296875 = 19/64 | .450000 = 9/20 | .625000 = 5/8 | .800000 = 4/5 | .968750 = 31/32 |
| .140625 = 9/64 | .300000 = 3/10 | .453125 = 29/64 | .640625 = 41/64 | .812500 = 13/16 | .984375 = 63/64 |
| .142857 = 1/7 | .312500 = 5/16 | .468750 = 15/32 | .650000 = 13/20 | .828125 = 53/64 | |
| .150000 = 3/20 | .328125 = 21/64 | .484375 = 31/64 | .656250 = 21/32 | .833333 = 5/6 | |
| .156250 = 5/32 | .333333 = 1/3 | .500000 = 1/2 | .666667 = 2/3 | .843750 = 27/32 | |
| .166667 = 1/6 | .343750 = 11/32 | .515625 = 33/64 | .671875 = 43/64 | .850000 = 17/20 | |

## PERCENTS AS FRACTIONS

| | | | | | | | | | |
|---|---|---|---|---|---|---|---|---|---|
| 1% | = 0.01 | = 1/100 | 29% | = 0.29 | = 29/100 | 57% | = 0.57 | = 57/100 | 84% = 0.84 = 21/25 |
| 2% | = 0.02 | = 1/50 | 30% | = 0.30 | = 3/10 | 58% | = 0.58 | = 29/50 | 85% = 0.85 = 17/20 |
| 3% | = 0.03 | = 3/100 | 31% | = 0.31 | = 31/100 | $58\frac{1}{3}$% | = $0.58\frac{1}{3}$ | = 7/12 | 86% = 0.86 = 43/50 |
| 4% | = 0.04 | = 1/25 | 32% | = 0.32 | = 8/25 | 59% | = 0.59 | = 59/100 | 87% = 0.87 = 87/100 |
| 5% | = 0.05 | = 1/20 | 33% | = 0.33 | = 33/100 | 60% | = 0.60 | = 3/5 | $87\frac{1}{2}$% = $0.87\frac{1}{2}$ = 7/8 |
| 6% | = 0.06 | = 3/50 | $33\frac{1}{3}$% | = $0.33\frac{1}{3}$ | = 1/3 | 61% | = 0.61 | = 61/100 | 88% = 0.88 = 22/25 |
| 7% | = 0.07 | = 7/100 | 34% | = 0.34 | = 17/50 | 62% | = 0.62 | = 31/50 | 89% = 0.89 = 89/100 |
| 8% | = 0.08 | = 2/25 | 35% | = 0.35 | = 7/20 | $62\frac{1}{2}$% | = 0.625 | = 5/8 | 90% = 0.90 = 9/10 |
| $8\frac{1}{3}$% | = $0.08\frac{1}{3}$ | = 1/12 | 36% | = 0.36 | = 9/25 | 63% | = 0.63 | = 63/100 | 91% = 0.91 = 91/100 |
| 9% | = 0.09 | = 9/100 | 37% | = 0.37 | = 37/100 | 64% | = 0.64 | = 16/25 | $91\frac{2}{3}$% = $0.91\frac{2}{3}$ = 11/12 |
| 10% | = 0.10 | = 1/10 | $37\frac{1}{2}$% | = 0.375 | = 3/8 | 65% | = 0.65 | = 13/20 | 92% = 0.92 = 23/25 |
| 11% | = 0.11 | = 11/100 | 38% | = 0.38 | = 19/50 | 66% | = 0.66 | = 33/50 | 93% = 0.93 = 93/100 |
| 12% | = 0.12 | = 3/25 | 39% | = 0.39 | = 39/100 | $66\frac{2}{3}$% | = $0.66\frac{2}{3}$ | = 2/3 | 94% = 0.94 = 47/50 |
| $12\frac{1}{2}$% | = 0.125 | = 1/8 | 40% | = 0.40 | = 2/5 | 67% | = 0.67 | = 67/100 | 95% = 0.95 = 19/20 |
| 13% | = 0.13 | = 13/100 | 41% | = 0.41 | = 41/100 | 68% | = 0.68 | = 17/25 | 96% = 0.96 = 24/25 |
| 14% | = 0.14 | = 7/50 | $41\frac{2}{3}$% | = $0.41\frac{2}{3}$ | = 5/12 | 69% | = 0.69 | = 69/100 | 97% = 0.97 = 97/100 |
| 15% | = 0.15 | = 3/20 | 42% | = 0.42 | = 21/50 | 70% | = 0.70 | = 7/10 | 98% = 0.98 = 49/50 |
| 16% | = 0.16 | = 4/25 | 43% | = 0.43 | = 43/100 | 71% | = 0.71 | = 71/100 | 99% = 0.99 = 99/100 |
| $16\frac{2}{3}$% | = $0.16\frac{2}{3}$ | = 1/6 | 44% | = 0.44 | = 11/25 | 72% | = 0.72 | = 18/25 | 100% = 1.00 = 1 |
| 17% | = 0.17 | = 17/100 | 45% | = 0.45 | = 9/20 | 73% | = 0.73 | = 73/100 | 110% = 1.10 = 1 1/10 |
| 18% | = 0.18 | = 9/50 | 46% | = 0.46 | = 23/50 | 74% | = 0.74 | = 37/50 | $112\frac{1}{2}$% = 1.125 = 1 1/8 |
| 19% | = 0.19 | = 19/100 | 47% | = 0.47 | = 47/100 | 75% | = 0.75 | = 3/4 | $116\frac{2}{3}$% = $1.16\frac{2}{3}$ = 1 1/6 |
| 20% | = 0.20 | = 1/5 | 48% | = 0.48 | = 12/25 | 76% | = 0.76 | = 19/25 | 120% = 1.20 = 1 1/5 |
| 21% | = 0.21 | = 21/100 | 49% | = 0.49 | = 49/100 | 77% | = 0.77 | = 77/100 | 125% = 1.25 = 1 1/4 |
| 22% | = 0.22 | = 11/50 | 50% | = 0.50 | = 1/2 | 78% | = 0.78 | = 39/50 | $133\frac{1}{3}$% = $1.33\frac{1}{3}$ = 1 1/3 |
| 23% | = 0.23 | = 23/100 | 51% | = 0.51 | = 51/100 | 79% | = 0.79 | = 79/100 | $137\frac{1}{2}$% = 1.375 = 1 3/8 |
| 24% | = 0.24 | = 6/25 | 52% | = 0.52 | = 13/25 | 80% | = 0.80 | = 4/5 | 150% = 1.50 = 1 1/2 |
| 25% | = 0.25 | = 1/4 | 53% | = 0.53 | = 53/100 | 81% | = 0.81 | = 81/100 | $166\frac{2}{3}$% = $1.66\frac{2}{3}$ = 1 2/3 |
| 26% | = 0.26 | = 13/50 | 54% | = 0.54 | = 27/50 | 82% | = 0.82 | = 41/50 | 175% = 1.75 = 1 3/4 |
| 27% | = 0.27 | = 27/100 | 55% | = 0.55 | = 11/20 | 83% | = 0.83 | = 83/100 | 180% = 1.80 = 1 4/5 |
| 28% | = 0.28 | = 7/25 | 56% | = 0.56 | = 14/25 | $83\frac{1}{3}$% | = $0.83\frac{1}{3}$ | = 5/6 | 200% = 2.00 = 2 |

## COMMON AREA FORMULAS

| FIGURE | FORMULA | MEANING OF LETTERS |
|---|---|---|
| Rectangle | $A = ab$ | a = base, b = height |
| Square | $A = a^2$ | a = one side |
| Triangle | $A = \dfrac{ab}{2}$ | a = base, b = height |
| Parallelogram | $A = ab$ | a = base, b = height |
| Regular pentagon | $A = 1.720a^2$ | a = one side |
| Regular hexagon | $A = 2.598a^2$ | a = one side |
| Regular octagon | $A = 4.828a^2$ | a = one side |
| Circle | $A = \pi r^2$ | $\pi$ = 3.1416, r = radius |

## COMMON VOLUME FORMULAS

| FIGURE | FORMULA | MEANING OF LETTERS |
|---|---|---|
| Cube | $V = a^3$ | a = one side |
| Pyramid | $V = \dfrac{ah}{3}$ | a = area of base<br>h = height |
| Cylinder | $V = \pi r^2 h$ | $\pi$ = 3.1416<br>h = height<br>r = radius of base |
| Cone | $V = \dfrac{\pi r^2 h}{3}$ | $\pi$ = 3.1416<br>r = radius of base<br>h = height |
| Sphere | $V = \dfrac{4\pi r^3}{3}$ | $\pi$ = 3.1416<br>r = radius |

## MULTIPLES OF PI

| No. | Value | No. | Value |
|---|---|---|---|
| $1\pi$ | 3.1416 | $\dfrac{1}{\pi}$ | 0.3183 |
| $2\pi$ | 6.2832 | $1/2\pi$ | 1.5708 |
| $3\pi$ | 9.4248 | $1/3\pi$ | 1.0472 |
| $4\pi$ | 12.5664 | $1/4\pi$ | 0.7854 |
| $5\pi$ | 15.7080 | $1/5\pi$ | 0.6283 |
| $6\pi$ | 18.8496 | $1/6\pi$ | 0.5236 |
| $7\pi$ | 21.9912 | $1/7\pi$ | 0.4488 |
| $8\pi$ | 25.1328 | $1/8\pi$ | 0.3927 |
| $9\pi$ | 28.2744 | $1/9\pi$ | 0.3491 |
| $\pi^2$ | 9.8696 | $\sqrt{\pi}$ | 1.7725 |

## GEOMETRY OF REGULAR POLYGONS

| No. of Sides | Name of Polygon | If length of side = 1, then: Area = | Radius of Circumscribed Circle = | Radius of Inscribed Circle = | If Radius of Circumscribed Circle = 1, then Side = |
|---|---|---|---|---|---|
| 3 | triangle | 0.433013 | 0.5773 | 0.2887 | 1.7321 |
| 4 | square | 1.000000 | 0.7071 | 0.5000 | 1.4142 |
| 5 | pentagon | 1.720477 | 0.8056 | 0.6882 | 1.1756 |
| 6 | hexagon | 2.598076 | 1.0000 | 0.8660 | 1.0000 |
| 7 | heptagon | 3.633912 | 1.1524 | 1.0383 | 0.8677 |
| 8 | octagon | 4.828427 | 1.3066 | 1.2071 | 0.7653 |
| 9 | nonagon | 6.181824 | 1.4619 | 1.3737 | 0.6840 |
| 10 | decagon | 7.694209 | 1.6180 | 1.5388 | 0.6180 |

## POWERS OF 10

| | |
|---|---|
| $10^1$ | = 10 |
| $10^2$ | = 100 |
| $10^3$ | = 1,000 |
| $10^4$ | = 10,000 |
| $10^5$ | = 100,000 |
| $10^6$ | = 1,000,000 |
| $10^7$ | = 10,000,000 |
| $10^{-1}$ | = 0.1 |
| $10^{-2}$ | = 0.01 |
| $10^{-3}$ | = 0.001 |
| $10^{-4}$ | = 0.0001 |
| $10^{-5}$ | = 0.00001 |
| $10^{-6}$ | = 0.000001 |
| $10^{-7}$ | = 0.0000001 |

## HOW $1 GROWS AT COMPOUND INTEREST

| YEARS | 2% | 4% | 5% | 6% | 7% | 10% | 12% | 15% | 20% |
|---|---|---|---|---|---|---|---|---|---|
| 1 | $1.0200 | $1.0400 | $1.0500 | $1.0600 | $1.0700 | $1.1000 | $1.1200 | $1.1500 | $1.2000 |
| 2 | 1.0404 | 1.0816 | 1.1025 | 1.1236 | 1.1449 | 1.2100 | 1.2544 | 1.3225 | 1.4400 |
| 3 | 1.0612 | 1.1249 | 1.1576 | 1.1910 | 1.2250 | 1.3310 | 1.4049 | 1.5209 | 1.7280 |
| 4 | 1.0824 | 1.1699 | 1.2155 | 1.2625 | 1.3108 | 1.4641 | 1.5735 | 1.7490 | 2.0736 |
| 5 | 1.1041 | 1.2167 | 1.2763 | 1.3382 | 1.4026 | 1.6105 | 1.7623 | 2.0114 | 2.4883 |
| 6 | 1.1262 | 1.2653 | 1.3401 | 1.4185 | 1.5007 | 1.7716 | 1.9738 | 2.3131 | 2.9860 |
| 7 | 1.1487 | 1.3159 | 1.4071 | 1.5036 | 1.6058 | 1.9487 | 2.2107 | 2.6600 | 3.5832 |
| 8 | 1.1717 | 1.3686 | 1.4775 | 1.5938 | 1.7182 | 2.1436 | 2.4760 | 3.0590 | 4.2998 |
| 9 | 1.1951 | 1.4233 | 1.5513 | 1.6895 | 1.8385 | 2.3579 | 2.7731 | 3.5179 | 5.1598 |
| 10 | 1.2190 | 1.4802 | 1.6289 | 1.7908 | 1.9672 | 2.5937 | 3.1058 | 4.0456 | 6.1917 |
| 11 | 1.2434 | 1.5395 | 1.7103 | 1.8983 | 2.1049 | 2.8531 | 3.4785 | 4.6524 | 7.4301 |
| 12 | 1.2682 | 1.6010 | 1.7959 | 2.0122 | 2.2522 | 3.1384 | 3.8960 | 5.3503 | 8.9161 |
| 13 | 1.2936 | 1.6651 | 1.8856 | 2.1329 | 2.4098 | 3.4523 | 4.3635 | 6.1528 | 10.6993 |
| 14 | 1.3195 | 1.7317 | 1.9799 | 2.2609 | 2.5785 | 3.7975 | 4.8871 | 7.0757 | 12.8392 |
| 15 | 1.3459 | 1.8009 | 2.0789 | 2.3966 | 2.7590 | 4.1772 | 5.4736 | 8.1371 | 15.4070 |
| 16 | 1.3728 | 1.8730 | 2.1829 | 2.5404 | 2.9522 | 4.5950 | 6.1304 | 9.3576 | 18.4884 |
| 17 | 1.4002 | 1.9479 | 2.2920 | 2.6928 | 3.1588 | 5.0545 | 6.8660 | 10.7613 | 22.1861 |
| 18 | 1.4282 | 2.0258 | 2.4066 | 2.8543 | 3.3799 | 5.5599 | 7.6900 | 12.3755 | 26.6234 |
| 19 | 1.4568 | 2.1068 | 2.5270 | 3.0256 | 3.6165 | 6.1159 | 8.6128 | 14.2318 | 31.9480 |
| 20 | 1.4859 | 2.1911 | 2.6533 | 3.2071 | 3.8697 | 6.7275 | 9.6463 | 16.3665 | 38.3376 |
| 21 | 1.5157 | 2.2788 | 2.7860 | 3.3996 | 4.1406 | 7.4002 | 10.8038 | 18.8215 | 46.0052 |
| 22 | 1.5460 | 2.3699 | 2.9253 | 3.6035 | 4.4304 | 8.1403 | 12.1003 | 21.6447 | 55.2062 |
| 23 | 1.5769 | 2.4647 | 3.0715 | 3.8197 | 4.7405 | 8.9543 | 13.5524 | 24.8915 | 66.2474 |
| 24 | 1.6084 | 2.5633 | 3.2251 | 4.0489 | 5.0724 | 9.8497 | 15.1786 | 28.6252 | 79.4969 |
| 25 | 1.6406 | 2.6658 | 3.3864 | 4.2919 | 5.4274 | 10.8347 | 17.0001 | 32.9189 | 95.3963 |
| 26 | 1.6734 | 2.7725 | 3.5557 | 4.5494 | 5.8074 | 11.9182 | 19.0401 | 37.8568 | 114.4760 |
| 27 | 1.7069 | 2.8834 | 3.7335 | 4.8223 | 6.2139 | 13.1100 | 21.3249 | 43.5353 | 137.3710 |
| 28 | 1.7410 | 2.9987 | 3.9201 | 5.1117 | 6.6488 | 14.4210 | 23.8839 | 50.0656 | 164.8450 |
| 29 | 1.7758 | 3.1187 | 4.1161 | 5.4184 | 7.1143 | 15.8631 | 26.7499 | 57.5754 | 197.8140 |
| 30 | 1.8114 | 3.2434 | 4.3219 | 5.7435 | 7.6123 | 17.4494 | 29.9599 | 66.2117 | 237.3770 |

# SQUARES, CUBES, SQUARE ROOTS, AND CUBE ROOTS

| NO. | SQUARE | CUBE | SQUARE ROOT | CUBE ROOT | NO. | SQUARE | CUBE | SQUARE ROOT | CUBE ROOT |
|---|---|---|---|---|---|---|---|---|---|
| 1 | 1 | 1 | 1.000 | 1.000 | 51 | 2,601 | 132,651 | 7.141 | 3.708 |
| 2 | 4 | 8 | 1.414 | 1.260 | 52 | 2,704 | 140,608 | 7.211 | 3.733 |
| 3 | 9 | 27 | 1.732 | 1.442 | 53 | 2,809 | 148,877 | 7.280 | 3.756 |
| 4 | 16 | 64 | 2.000 | 1.587 | 54 | 2,916 | 157,464 | 7.348 | 3.780 |
| 5 | 25 | 125 | 2.236 | 1.710 | 55 | 3,025 | 166,375 | 7.416 | 3.803 |
| 6 | 36 | 216 | 2.449 | 1.817 | 56 | 3,136 | 175,616 | 7.483 | 3.826 |
| 7 | 49 | 343 | 2.646 | 1.913 | 57 | 3,249 | 185,193 | 7.550 | 3.849 |
| 8 | 64 | 512 | 2.828 | 2.000 | 58 | 3,364 | 195,112 | 7.616 | 3.871 |
| 9 | 81 | 729 | 3.000 | 2.080 | 59 | 3,481 | 205,379 | 7.681 | 3.893 |
| 10 | 100 | 1,000 | 3.162 | 2.154 | 60 | 3,600 | 216,000 | 7.746 | 3.915 |
| 11 | 121 | 1,331 | 3.317 | 2.224 | 61 | 3,721 | 226,981 | 7.810 | 3.936 |
| 12 | 144 | 1,728 | 3.464 | 2.289 | 62 | 3,844 | 238,328 | 7.874 | 3.958 |
| 13 | 169 | 2,197 | 3.606 | 2.351 | 63 | 3,969 | 250,047 | 7.937 | 3.979 |
| 14 | 196 | 2,744 | 3.742 | 2.410 | 64 | 4,096 | 262,144 | 8.000 | 4.000 |
| 15 | 225 | 3,375 | 3.873 | 2.466 | 65 | 4,225 | 274,625 | 8.062 | 4.021 |
| 16 | 256 | 4,096 | 4.000 | 2.520 | 66 | 4,356 | 287,496 | 8.124 | 4.041 |
| 17 | 289 | 4,913 | 4.123 | 2.571 | 67 | 4,489 | 300,763 | 8.185 | 4.062 |
| 18 | 324 | 5,832 | 4.243 | 2.621 | 68 | 4,624 | 314,432 | 8.246 | 4.082 |
| 19 | 361 | 6,859 | 4.359 | 2.668 | 69 | 4,761 | 328,509 | 8.307 | 4.102 |
| 20 | 400 | 8,000 | 4.472 | 2.714 | 70 | 4,900 | 343,000 | 8.367 | 4.121 |
| 21 | 441 | 9,261 | 4.583 | 2.759 | 71 | 5,041 | 357,911 | 8.426 | 4.141 |
| 22 | 484 | 10,648 | 4.690 | 2.802 | 72 | 5,184 | 373,248 | 8.485 | 4.160 |
| 23 | 529 | 12,167 | 4.796 | 2.844 | 73 | 5,329 | 389,017 | 8.544 | 4.179 |
| 24 | 576 | 13,824 | 4.899 | 2.884 | 74 | 5,476 | 405,224 | 8.602 | 4.198 |
| 25 | 625 | 15,625 | 5.000 | 2.924 | 75 | 5,625 | 421,875 | 8.660 | 4.217 |
| 26 | 676 | 17,576 | 5.099 | 2.962 | 76 | 5,776 | 438,976 | 8.718 | 4.236 |
| 27 | 729 | 19,683 | 5.196 | 3.000 | 77 | 5,929 | 456,533 | 8.775 | 4.254 |
| 28 | 784 | 21,952 | 5.292 | 3.037 | 78 | 6,084 | 474,552 | 8.832 | 4.273 |
| 29 | 841 | 24,389 | 5.385 | 3.072 | 79 | 6,241 | 493,039 | 8.888 | 4.291 |
| 30 | 900 | 27,000 | 5.477 | 3.107 | 80 | 6,400 | 512,000 | 8.944 | 4.309 |
| 31 | 961 | 29,791 | 5.568 | 3.141 | 81 | 6,561 | 531,441 | 9.000 | 4.327 |
| 32 | 1,024 | 32,768 | 5.657 | 3.175 | 82 | 6,724 | 551,368 | 9.055 | 4.344 |
| 33 | 1,089 | 35,937 | 5.745 | 3.208 | 83 | 6,889 | 571,787 | 9.110 | 4.362 |
| 34 | 1,156 | 39,304 | 5.831 | 3.240 | 84 | 7,056 | 592,704 | 9.165 | 4.380 |
| 35 | 1,225 | 42,875 | 5.916 | 3.271 | 85 | 7,225 | 614,125 | 9.220 | 4.397 |
| 36 | 1,296 | 46,656 | 6.000 | 3.302 | 86 | 7,396 | 636,056 | 9.274 | 4.414 |
| 37 | 1,369 | 50,653 | 6.083 | 3.332 | 87 | 7,569 | 658,503 | 9.327 | 4.431 |
| 38 | 1,444 | 54,872 | 6.164 | 3.362 | 88 | 7,744 | 681,472 | 9.381 | 4.448 |
| 39 | 1,521 | 59,319 | 6.245 | 3.391 | 89 | 7,921 | 704,969 | 9.434 | 4.465 |
| 40 | 1,600 | 64,000 | 6.325 | 3.420 | 90 | 8,100 | 729,000 | 9.487 | 4.481 |
| 41 | 1,681 | 68,921 | 6.403 | 3.448 | 91 | 8,281 | 753,571 | 9.539 | 4.498 |
| 42 | 1,764 | 74,088 | 6.481 | 3.476 | 92 | 8,464 | 778,688 | 9.592 | 4.514 |
| 43 | 1,849 | 79,507 | 6.557 | 3.503 | 93 | 8,649 | 804,357 | 9.644 | 4.531 |
| 44 | 1,936 | 85,184 | 6.633 | 3.530 | 94 | 8,836 | 830,584 | 9.695 | 4.547 |
| 45 | 2,025 | 91,125 | 6.708 | 3.557 | 95 | 9,025 | 857,375 | 9.747 | 4.563 |
| 46 | 2,116 | 97,336 | 6.782 | 3.583 | 96 | 9,216 | 884,736 | 9.798 | 4.579 |
| 47 | 2,209 | 103,823 | 6.856 | 3.609 | 97 | 9,409 | 912,673 | 9.849 | 4.595 |
| 48 | 2,304 | 110,592 | 6.928 | 3.634 | 98 | 9,604 | 941,192 | 9.899 | 4.610 |
| 49 | 2,401 | 117,649 | 7.000 | 3.659 | 99 | 9,801 | 970,299 | 9.950 | 4.626 |
| 50 | 2,500 | 125,000 | 7.071 | 3.684 | 100 | 10,000 | 1,000,000 | 10.000 | 4.642 |

# MULTIPLICATION TABLE

| | 2 | 3 | 4 | 5 | 6 | 7 | 8 | 9 | 10 | 11 | 12 | 13 | 14 | 15 | 16 | 17 | 18 | 19 | 20 |
|---|---|---|---|---|---|---|---|---|---|---|---|---|---|---|---|---|---|---|---|
| 2 | 4 | 6 | 8 | 10 | 12 | 14 | 16 | 18 | 20 | 22 | 24 | 26 | 28 | 30 | 32 | 34 | 36 | 38 | 40 |
| 3 | 6 | 9 | 12 | 15 | 18 | 21 | 24 | 27 | 30 | 33 | 36 | 39 | 42 | 45 | 48 | 51 | 54 | 57 | 60 |
| 4 | 8 | 12 | 16 | 20 | 24 | 28 | 32 | 36 | 40 | 44 | 48 | 52 | 56 | 60 | 64 | 68 | 72 | 76 | 80 |
| 5 | 10 | 15 | 20 | 25 | 30 | 35 | 40 | 45 | 50 | 55 | 60 | 65 | 70 | 75 | 80 | 85 | 90 | 95 | 100 |
| 6 | 12 | 18 | 24 | 30 | 36 | 42 | 48 | 54 | 60 | 66 | 72 | 78 | 84 | 90 | 96 | 102 | 108 | 114 | 120 |
| 7 | 14 | 21 | 28 | 35 | 42 | 49 | 56 | 63 | 70 | 77 | 84 | 91 | 98 | 105 | 112 | 119 | 126 | 133 | 140 |
| 8 | 16 | 24 | 32 | 40 | 48 | 56 | 64 | 72 | 80 | 88 | 96 | 104 | 112 | 120 | 128 | 136 | 144 | 152 | 160 |
| 9 | 18 | 27 | 36 | 45 | 54 | 63 | 72 | 81 | 90 | 99 | 108 | 117 | 126 | 135 | 144 | 153 | 162 | 171 | 180 |
| 10 | 20 | 30 | 40 | 50 | 60 | 70 | 80 | 90 | 100 | 110 | 120 | 130 | 140 | 150 | 160 | 170 | 180 | 190 | 200 |
| 11 | 22 | 33 | 44 | 55 | 66 | 77 | 88 | 99 | 110 | 121 | 132 | 143 | 154 | 165 | 176 | 187 | 198 | 209 | 220 |
| 12 | 24 | 36 | 48 | 60 | 72 | 84 | 96 | 108 | 120 | 132 | 144 | 156 | 168 | 180 | 192 | 204 | 216 | 228 | 240 |
| 13 | 26 | 39 | 52 | 65 | 78 | 91 | 104 | 117 | 130 | 143 | 156 | 169 | 182 | 195 | 208 | 221 | 234 | 247 | 260 |
| 14 | 28 | 42 | 56 | 70 | 84 | 98 | 112 | 126 | 140 | 154 | 168 | 182 | 196 | 210 | 224 | 238 | 252 | 266 | 280 |
| 15 | 30 | 45 | 60 | 75 | 90 | 105 | 120 | 135 | 150 | 165 | 180 | 195 | 210 | 225 | 240 | 255 | 270 | 285 | 300 |
| 16 | 32 | 48 | 64 | 80 | 96 | 112 | 128 | 144 | 160 | 176 | 192 | 208 | 224 | 240 | 256 | 272 | 288 | 304 | 320 |
| 17 | 34 | 51 | 68 | 85 | 102 | 119 | 136 | 153 | 170 | 187 | 204 | 221 | 238 | 255 | 272 | 289 | 306 | 323 | 340 |
| 18 | 36 | 54 | 72 | 90 | 108 | 126 | 144 | 162 | 180 | 198 | 216 | 234 | 252 | 270 | 288 | 306 | 324 | 342 | 360 |
| 19 | 38 | 57 | 76 | 95 | 114 | 133 | 152 | 171 | 190 | 209 | 228 | 247 | 266 | 285 | 304 | 323 | 342 | 361 | 380 |
| 20 | 40 | 60 | 80 | 100 | 120 | 140 | 160 | 180 | 200 | 220 | 240 | 260 | 280 | 300 | 320 | 340 | 360 | 380 | 400 |

# THE CHEMICAL ELEMENTS

At one time a chemical element could be defined as a substance that could not be broken down into two or more different kinds of matter. But in the late 1930s and early 1940s, scientists found that atoms of elements could be broken apart into subatomic particles. Ever since, scientists have had to qualify their definition of an element as a substance that cannot be broken down into anything else *by ordinary chemical means*.

The ancients and medieval alchemists are usually credited with the discovery of 12 elements, including gold, silver, tin, carbon, sulfur, iron, copper, zinc, arsenic, mercury, lead, and bismuth.

The concept of an "element" was not really developed until about 200 years ago. In 1789 the French scientist Antoine Lavoisier proposed a definition of an "element" and listed 23 of what scientists now regard as true chemical elements.

Alessandro Volta's discoveries concerning electric current (about 1800) led to Sir Humphry Davy's discovery of 6 new elements in the early 1800s.

In the 1860s and 1870s almost 30 new elements were discovered because of the new technique of spectroscopy and the arrangement of known elements into a periodic table with elements grouped according to their atomic numbers and atomic weights. Finally, the advent of atom smashers led to the discovery of more than a dozen elements with atomic numbers above uranium.

American physicists announced the discovery of element 126 in the mineral monazite in June 1976, but attempts to duplicate the experiment later in the year were unsuccessful. They concluded that there are no unknown elements in monazite.

The atomic number of an element tells the number of protons (positively charged particles) it contains in its nucleus.

| SYMBOL, NAME, AND ATOMIC NUMBER | | | ATOMIC WEIGHT [1] | DATE OF DISCOVERY AND DISCOVERER |
|---|---|---|---|---|
| H | Hydrogen | 1 | 1.00797 | 1766  H. Cavendish, Britain |
| He | Helium | 2 | 4.0026 | 1868  In the sun: P. Janssen, France |
| | | | | 1895  On the earth: W. Ramsay, Britain; N. Langlet and P. T. Cleve, Sweden |
| Li | Lithium | 3 | 6.939 | 1817  J. A. Arfvedson, Sweden |
| Be | Beryllium | 4 | 9.01218 | 1798  L. N. Vauquelin, France |
| B | Boron | 5 | 10.811 | 1808  H. Davy, Britain; J. L. Gay–Lussac and L. J. Thénard, France |
| C | Carbon | 6 | 12.01115 | —  Ancient |
| N | Nitrogen | 7 | 14.0067 | 1772  D. Rutherford, Britain |
| O | Oxygen | 8 | 15.9994 | 1774  J. Priestley, Britain |
| F | Fluorine | 9 | 18.9984 | 1886  H. Moissan, France |
| Ne | Neon | 10 | 20.179 | 1898  W. Ramsay and M. W. Travers, Britain |
| Na | Sodium | 11 | 22.98977 | 1807  H. Davy, Britain |
| Mg | Magnesium | 12 | 24.312 | 1808  H. Davy, Britain |
| Al | Aluminum | 13 | 26.98154 | 1825  H. C. Oersted, Denmark |
| Si | Silicon | 14 | 28.86 | 1823  J. J. Berzelius, Sweden |
| P | Phosphorus | 15 | 30.97376 | 1669  H. Brand, Germany |
| S | Sulfur | 16 | 32.064 | —  Ancient |
| Cl | Chlorine | 17 | 35.453 | 1774  K. W. Scheele, Sweden |
| A | Argon | 18 | 39.948 | 1894  W. Ramsay and J. Rayleigh, Britain |
| K | Potassium | 19 | 39.102 | 1807  H. Davy, Britain |
| Ca | Calcium | 20 | 40.08 | 1808  H. Davy, Britain |
| Sc | Scandium | 21 | 44.9559 | 1879  L. F. Nilson, Sweden |
| Ti | Titanium | 22 | 47.90 | 1791  W. Gregor, Britain |
| V | Vanadium | 23 | 50.9414 | 1830  N. G. Sefström, Sweden |
| Cr | Chromium | 24 | 51.996 | 1797  L. N. Vauquelin, France |
| Mn | Manganese | 25 | 54.938 | 1774  K. W. Scheele and J. G. Gahn, Sweden |
| Fe | Iron | 26 | 55.847 | —  Ancient |
| Co | Cobalt | 27 | 58.9332 | 1735  G. Brandt, Sweden |
| Ni | Nickel | 28 | 58.70 | 1751  A. F. Cronstedt, Sweden |
| Cu | Copper | 29 | 63.546 | —  Ancient |
| Zn | Zinc | 30 | 65.37 | 1746  A. Marggraf, Germany |
| Ga | Gallium | 31 | 69.72 | 1875  L. de Boisbaudran, France |
| Ge | Germanium | 32 | 72.59 | 1886  C. A. Winkler, Germany |
| As | Arsenic | 33 | 74.9216 | —  Medieval |
| Se | Selenium | 34 | 78.96 | 1817  J. J. Berzelius, Sweden |
| Br | Bromine | 35 | 79.904 | 1826  A. J. Balard, France |
| Kr | Krypton | 36 | 83.80 | 1898  W. Ramsay and M. W. Travers, Britain |
| Rb | Rubidium | 37 | 85.4678 | 1861  R. W. Bunsen and G. R. Kirchhoff, Germany |
| Sr | Strontium | 38 | 87.62 | 1790  A. Crawford, Scotland |
| Y | Yttrium | 39 | 88.905 | 1794  J. Gadolin, Finland |
| Zr | Zirconium | 40 | 91.22 | 1789  M. H. Klaproth, Germany |
| Nb | Niobium | 41 | 92.9064 | 1801  C. Hatchett, Britain |

| SYMBOL, NAME, AND ATOMIC NUMBER | | | ATOMIC WEIGHT [1] | DATE OF DISCOVERY AND DISCOVERER |
|---|---|---|---|---|
| Mo | Molybdenum | 42 | 95.94 | 1778  K. W. Scheele, Sweden |
| Tc | Technetium | 43 | 97 [2] | 1937  E. Segre and C. Perrier, Italy |
| Ru | Ruthenium | 44 | 101.07 | 1844  K. Klaus, Estonia |
| Rh | Rhodium | 45 | 102.9055 | 1803  W. H. Wollaston, Britain |
| Pd | Palladium | 46 | 106.4 | 1803  W. H. Wollaston, Britain |
| Ag | Silver | 47 | 107.868 | —    Ancient |
| Cd | Cadmium | 48 | 112.40 | 1817  F. Stromeyer, Germany |
| In | Indium | 49 | 114.82 | 1863  F. Reich and H. T. Richter, Germany |
| Sn | Tin | 50 | 118.69 | —    Ancient |
| Sb | Antimony | 51 | 121.75 | —    Ancient |
| Te | Tellurium | 52 | 127.60 | 1782  M. von Reichenstein, Austria |
| I | Iodine | 53 | 126.9044 | 1811  B. Courtois, France |
| Xe | Xenon | 54 | 131.30 | 1898  W. Ramsay and M. W. Travers, Britain |
| Cs | Cesium | 55 | 132.9054 | 1860  R. Bunsen and G. R. Kirchhoff, Germany |
| Ba | Barium | 56 | 137.34 | 1808  H. Davy, Britain |
| La | Lanthanum | 57 | 138.9055 | 1839  C. G. Mosander, Sweden |
| Ce | Cerium | 58 | 140.12 | 1803  J. J. Berzelius and W. von Hisinger, Sweden; M. H. Klaproth, Germany |
| Pr | Praseodymium | 59 | 140.9077 | 1885  C. A. von Welsbach, Austria |
| Nd | Neodymium | 60 | 144.24 | 1885  C. A. von Welsbach, Austria |
| Pm | Promethium | 61 | 145 [2] | 1945  J. A. Marinsky, L. E. Glendenin, and C. D. Coryell, U.S. |
| Sm | Samarium | 62 | 150.35 | 1879  L. de Boisbaudran, France |
| Eu | Europium | 63 | 151.96 | 1896  E. A. Demarçay, France |
| Gd | Gadolinium | 64 | 157.25 | 1880  J. C. de Marignac, Switzerland |
| Tb | Terbium | 65 | 158.9254 | 1843  C. G. Mosander, Sweden |
| Dy | Dysprosium | 66 | 162.50 | 1886  L. de Boisbaudran, France |
| Ho | Holmium | 67 | 164.9304 | 1878  J. L. Soret, Switzerland |
| Er | Erbium | 68 | 167.26 | 1843  C. G. Mosander, Sweden |
| Tm | Thulium | 69 | 168.9342 | 1879  P. T. Cleve, Sweden |
| Yb | Ytterbium | 70 | 173.04 | 1878  J. de Marignac, Switzerland |
| Lu | Lutetium | 71 | 174.97 | 1907  G. Urbain, France |
| Hf | Hafnium | 72 | 178.49 | 1923  G. von Hevesy, Sweden; D. Coster, Netherlands |
| Ta | Tantalum | 73 | 180.9479 | 1802  A. G. Ekeberg, Sweden |
| W | Tungsten | 74 | 183.85 | 1783  J. J. d'Elhuyar and D. F. d'Elhuyar, Spain |
| Re | Rhenium | 75 | 186.207 | 1925  W. Noddack and I. E. Tacke, Germany |
| Os | Osmium | 76 | 190.2 | 1804  S. Tennant, Britain |
| Ir | Iridium | 77 | 192.22 | 1804  S. Tennant, Britain |
| Pt | Platinum | 78 | 195.09 | 1735  A. De Ulloa, Spain |
| Au | Gold | 79 | 196.9665 | —    Ancient |
| Hg | Mercury | 80 | 200.59 | —    Ancient |
| Tl | Thallium | 81 | 204.37 | 1861  W. Crookes, Britain |
| Pb | Lead | 82 | 207.19 | —    Ancient |
| Bi | Bismuth | 83 | 208.9804 | —    Medieval |
| Po | Polonium | 84 | 210 [2] | 1898  M. Curie and P. Curie, France |
| At | Astatine | 85 | 210 [2] | 1940  E. G. Segre, D. R. Corson, and K. R. MacKenzie, U.S. |
| Rn | Radon | 86 | 222 [2] | 1900  F. E. Dorn, Germany |
| Fr | Francium | 87 | 223 [2] | 1939  M. Perey, France |
| Ra | Radium | 88 | 226 [2] | 1898  M. Curie and P. Curie, France |
| Ac | Actinium | 89 | 227 [2] | 1899  A. L. Debierne, France |
| Th | Thorium | 90 | 232.0381 | 1828  J. J. Berzelius, Sweden |
| Pa | Protactinium | 91 | 231.0359 | 1917  O. Hahn and L. Meitner, Germany; J. Cranston and F. Soddy, Britain |
| U | Uranium | 92 | 238.029 | 1789  M. H. Klaproth, Germany |
| Np | Neptunium | 93 | 237 [2] | 1940  E. McMillan and P. Abelson, U.S. |
| Pu | Plutonium | 94 | 244 [2] | 1940  G. T. Seaborg, E. M. McMillan, A. C. Wahl, and J. W. Kennedy, U.S. |
| Am | Americium | 95 | 243 [2] | 1945  G. T. Seaborg, R. A. James, S. G. Thompson, and A. Ghiorso, U.S. |
| Cm | Curium | 96 | 247 [2] | 1944  G. T. Seaborg, R. A. James and A. Ghiorso, U.S. |
| Bk | Berkelium | 97 | 247 [2] | 1949  S. G. Thompson, A. Ghiorso and G. T. Seaborg, U.S. |
| Cf | Californium | 98 | 251 [2] | 1950  S. G. Thompson, K. Street Jr., A. Ghiorso, and G. T. Seaborg, U.S. |
| E | Einsteinium | 99 | 254 [2] | 1952  A. Ghiorso et al., U.S. |
| Fm | Fermium | 100 | 257 [2] | 1953  A. Ghiorso et al., U.S. |
| Mv | Mendelevium | 101 | 258 [2] | 1955  A. Ghiorso, B. Harvey, G. Choppin, S. G. Thompson, G. T. Seaborg, U.S. |
| No | Nobelium | 102 | 255 [2] | 1958  A. Ghiorso, T. Sikkeland, J. Walton, and G. T. Seaborg, U.S. |
| Lr | Lawrencium | 103 | 260 [2] | 1961  A. Ghiorso, A. E. Larsh, R. M. Latimer, and T. Sikkeland, U.S. |
| Rf | Kurchatovium } Rutherfordium } | 104 | 257 [2] | 1964  G. N. Flerov et al., U.S.S.R.} 1969  A. Ghiorso et al., U.S. } Soviet claim disputed by U.S. |
| Ha | Bohrium } Hahnium { | 105 | 261 [2] | 1968  G. N. Flerov et al., U.S.S.R.} 1970  A. Ghiorso et al., U.S. } Soviet claim disputed by U.S. |
| | Unnamed | 106 | 263 [2] | 1974  G. N. Flerov et al., U.S.S.R. } 1974  G. T. Seaborg, A. Ghiorso, et al., U.S.} Soviet claim disputed by U.S. |

[1] The standard for chemical atomic weights (adopted in 1961) is that of carbon—12.011.    [2] Most stable known isotope.

# GREAT INVENTIONS

The origins of many great inventions are shrouded in the distant past. The inventors of writing, the wheel, and fire making will forever remain anonymous. And subsequent development of innovations such as the abacus, the windmill, gunpowder, the cannon, and the concrete arch must be attributed to countries or civilizations rather than to any particular individual or group of individuals.

**Abacus:** Uncertain; possibly by Babylonians as long ago as 3,500 years. In various forms it was known and used by ancient Chinese, Hindus, Egyptians, and Greeks

**Adding machine (first commercially successful):** William Burroughs, United States (1888)

**Adding machine (simple):** Blaise Pascal, France (1642)

**Addressograph:** J. S. Duncan, United States (1893)

**Air brake, Westinghouse:** George Westinghouse, U.S. (1868)

**Air conditioning:** Willis H. Carrier, United States (1902)

**Air pump:** Otto von Guericke, Germany (1654)

**Airplane (first successful heavier-than-air):** Orville and Wilbur Wright, United States (1903)

**Airship (nonrigid):** Henri Giffard, France (1852)

**Aluminum (processing):** Charles M. Hall, United States (1886); Paul Héroult, France (1886)

**Atomic bomb:** International team of scientists, U.S. (1945)

**Atomic pile (self-sustaining nuclear chain reaction):** Enrico Fermi and staff, United States (1942)

**Automatic pilot (airplane):** William Green, U.S. (1929)

**Automobile:** Karl Benz, Germany (1885)

**Bakelite (plastic):** Leo H. Baekeland, United States (1909)

**Balloon (hot air):** Jacques and Joseph Montgolfier, France (1783)

**Barbed wire:** Joseph F. Glidden, United States (1873)

**Barometer:** Evangelista Torricelli, Italy (1643)

**Bessemer steel process:** Henry Bessemer, England (1856)

**Bicycle:** Baron Karl Drais von Sauerbronn, Germany (1816–18)

**Bifocal lens:** Benjamin Franklin, United States (1780)

**Bottle-making machine (automatic):** M. J. Owens, U.S. (1898)

**Braille printing:** Louis Braille, France (1829)

**Bridge, suspension (chain):** James Finley, U.S. (1800)

**Bridge, suspension (wire cable):** John A. Roebling, United States (1845)

**Bunsen burner:** Robert Wilhelm von Bunsen, Germany (1855)

**Camera (camera obscura):** Europe (early 1500s)

**Camera (photographic):** Joseph Niepce, France (1826)

**Camera (Kodak):** George Eastman, United States (1888)

**Canning (food):** Nicolas Appert, France (1809)

**Cannon (iron):** Germans, Germany (c.1320)

**Car (steam-driven):** Nicolas Cugnot, France (c.1769)

**Carburetor:** Gottlieb Daimler, Germany (1892)

**Carpet sweeper:** M. R. Bissell, United States (1876)

**Cash register:** James Ritty, United States (1879)

**Cathode-ray tube:** Sir William Crookes, Britain (1878)

**Cellophane:** Jacques E. Brandenberger, Switzerland (1908)

**Celluloid:** Alexander Parkes, Britain (1855)

**Cement:** Joseph Aspdin, England (1824)

**Chronometer:** John Harrison, England (1759)

**Clock (mechanical):** I-Hsing and Liang Ling-Tsan, China (725)

**Clock (pendulum):** Christiaan Huygens, Netherlands (1656)

**Compass (mariner's):** Arabs (800s)

**Computer (analog):** Vannevar Bush, United States (1930)

**Computer (digital):** Howard Aiken, United States (1944)

**Cotton gin:** Eli Whitney, United States (1793)

**Cream separator:** Carl Gustaf de Laval, Sweden (1876)

**Cyclotron:** Ernest O. Lawrence, United States (1930)

**Cylinder lock:** Linus Yale, United States (1860)

**Daguerreotype:** Louis J. M. Daguerre, France (1839)

**Diesel engine:** Rudolf Diesel, Germany (1892)

**Disc brake:** Frederick W. Lanchester, Britain (1902)

**Dynamite:** Alfred B. Nobel, Sweden (1867)

**Electric fan:** Schuyler S. Wheeler, United States (1886)

**Electric flat iron:** H. W. Seeley, United States (1882)

**Electric generator (disk):** Michael Faraday, England (1831)

**Electric generator (coil):** Hippolyte Pixii, France (1832)

**Electric motor (A.C.):** Nikola Tesla, United States (1888)

**Electric motor (D.C.):** Zenobe Gramme, Belgium (1873)

**Electric power generating plant (commercial):** Thomas A. Edison, United States (1882)

**Electrocardiograph:** Willem Einthoven, Netherlands (1903)

**Electroencephalograph:** Hans Berger, Germany (1929)

**Electromagnet:** Joseph Henry, United States; William Sturgeon, England (1824)

**Electroplating:** George and Henry Elkington, Britain (1840)

**Elevator (safety):** Elisha G. Otis, United States (1852)

**Engraving (half-tone process):** Frederick E. Ives, U.S. (1878)

**Flush toilet:** Joseph Brahmah, Britain (1778)

**Frequency modulation (FM):** Edwin H. Armstrong, U.S. (1933)

**Frozen food (retail):** Clarence Birdseye, U.S. (1917–29)

**Gas lighting:** William Murdock, Scotland (1792)

**Gasoline (antiknock tetraethyl lead):** Thomas Midgley, United States (1921)

**Geiger counter:** Hans Geiger, Germany (1908)

**Glider:** Sir George Cayley, England (1804)

**Gunpowder:** Chinese, China (800s)

**Gyrocompass:** Elmer A. Sperry, United States (1911)

**Gyroscope:** G. C. Bohnenberger, Germany (1810)

**Helicopter:** Igor Sikorsky, United States (1939)

**Holography:** Dennis Gabor, England (1948)

**Hydroplane:** Glenn H. Curtiss, United States (1911)

**Ice-making machine:** John Gorrie, United States (1851)

**Internal-combustion engine (first workable):** Jean Joseph E. Lenoir, France (1860)

**Internal-combustion engine (high-speed):** Gottlieb Daimler, Germany (1885); Karl Benz, Germany (1885)

**Jet engine:** Sir Frank Whittle, England (1930)

**Kaleidoscope:** Sir David Brewster, Britain (1817)

**Kerosene (coal oil):** Abraham Gesner, Canada (1852)

**Knitting machine:** William Lee, England (1589)

**Lamp (arc):** Humphry Davy, England (1809)

**Lamp (arc, commercial):** Paul Jablochkov, Russia (1876)

**Lamp (carbon-filament electric):** Joseph W. Swan, England (1850)

**Lamp (incandescent carbon-filament electric):** Thomas A. Edison, United States (1879)

**Lamp (incandescent drawn tungsten-filament electric):** William D. Coolidge, United States (1910)

**Lamp (miner's safety):** Humphry Davy, England (1815)

**Lamp (neon):** Georges Claude, France (1915)

**Lamp (oil with glass chimney):** Aimé Argand, Switzerland (1784)

**Laser:** Gordon Gould, United States (1957)

**Lathe:** Greeks, Greece (c.1500 B.C.)

**Lever:** Archimedes, Greece (200s B.C.)

**Lightning rod:** Benjamin Franklin, Pennsylvania (1752)

**Linoleum:** Frederick Walton, England (1860)

**Lithography:** Aloys Senefelder, Bohemia (1798)

**Lock (cylinder):** Linus Yale Jr., United States (1861)

**Locomotive (steam):** Richard Trevithick, Wales (1804)

**Locomotive (electric):** Werner von Siemens, Germany (1879)

**Loom (power):** Edmund Cartwright, England (1786)

**Machine gun:** Richard J. Gatling, United States (1862)

**Mass spectrograph:** F. Aston, Britain (1919)

**Match (book):** Joshua Pusey, United States (1892)

**Match (friction):** John Walker, England (1827)

**Match (safety):** Gustave E. Pasch, Sweden (1844)

**Microcomputer (silicon chip):** Michael J. Cochrane, Gary W. Boone, U.S. (1971)

**Micrometer:** William Gascoigne, Britain (1636)

**Microphone:** Alexander Graham Bell, United States (1876)

**Microscope (compound):** Hans and Zacharias Janssen, Netherlands (1590)

Microscope (electron): Ernst Ruska, Germany (1933)
Microscope (field ion): Erwin W. Mueller, U.S. (1936)
Microwave oven: Percy L. Spencer, United States (1945)
Milking machine: Anna Baldwin, U.S. (1878)
Motion pictures (camera): Thomas A. Edison, United States (1891)
Motion picture (peep show): Thomas A. Edison, U.S. (1894)
Motion picture (projected): Auguste Marie Louis Nicolas Lumière and Louis Jean Lumière, France (1895)
Motor scooter: Greville Bradshaw, England (1919)
Motorcycle: Gottlieb Daimler, Germany (1885)
Nylon: Wallace H. Carothers, United States (1935)
Oil well (modern): Edwin Drake, United States (1859)
Outboard engine: Ole Evinrude, United States (1909)
Parachute: André-Jacques Garnerin, France (1797)
Parking meter: Carlton C. Magee, United States (1935)
Patent leather: Seth Boyden, United States (1819)
Pen (ball-point): John Loud, United States (1888)
Pen (fountain): Lewis Waterman, United States (1884)
Pen (lever-fill): W. A. Sheaffer, United States (1913)
Phonograph (cylinder): Thomas A. Edison, U.S. (1877)
Phonograph (disk): Emile Berliner, United States (1890–94)
Photoelectric cell: G. R. Carey, United States (1875)
Photoengraving: William Fox Talbot, United States (1852)
Photography (color): Gabriel Lippmann, France (1891)
Photography (on celluloid film): Rev. Hannibal W. Goodwin, United States (1887)
Photography (on transparent paper strip film): George Eastman, United States (1884)
Photography (on metal): Joseph Niepce, France (1826)
Photography (on paper): William Fox Talbot, England (1839)
Pipeline (oil): Samuel van Syckel, United States (1865)
Plastic (celluloid): John W. Hyatt, United States (1869)
Plow (steel): John Deere, United States (1837)
Polaroid Land camera: Edwin Land, United States (1947)
Porcelain: Chinese, China (700s A.D.)
Potter's wheel: Asia Minor (c.6500 B.C.)
Printing (movable type): Pi Sheng, China (c. 1045); Johann Gutenberg, Germany (c. 1454)
Printing (offset): Ira Rubel, United States (1905)
Printing (rotary): Richard Hoe, United States (1846)
Radar: Albert H. Taylor and Leo C. Young, United States (1922)
Radio (wireless): Guglielmo Marconi, Italy (1895)
Radio (transatlantic): Guglielmo Marconi, Italy (1901)
Radio (voice): Valdemar Poulsen, Denmark (1904)
Radio (automobile): William P. Lear, U.S. (1926)
Radio tube diode: John A. Fleming, England (1904)
Radio tube triode: Lee De Forest, United States (1906)
Railroad (steam): George Stephenson, England (1825)
Railway car coupling: Eli H. Jannery, United States (1868)
Railway sleeping coach: George M. Pullman, U.S. (1859)
Raincoat (waterproof): Charles Macintosh, Scotland (1819)
Rayon: Hilaire Chardonnet, France (1884)
Razor (electric): Col. Jacob Schick, United States (1931)
Razor (safety): King C. Gillette, United States (1895)
Reaping machine: Cyrus H. McCormick, United States (1831)
Record (long playing): Peter Goldmark, United States (1948)
Recording (magnetic tape): J. A. O'Neill, United States (1927)
Recording (magnetic wire): Valdemar Poulsen, Denmark (1898)
Revolver: Samuel Colt, United States (1835)
Rifle (automatic): John Moses Browning, United States (1917)
Rifle (repeating): O. F. Winchester, United States (1860)
Rocket (liquid-fuel): Robert H. Goddard, U.S.; Hermann Oberth, Germany; Konstantin E. Tsiolkovsky, Soviet Union (1920s)
Rocket (military): Sir William Congreve, Britain (1808)
Rubber (latex foam): Dunlop Rubber Co., England (1928)
Rubber (vulcanized): Charles Goodyear, United States (1839)
Rubber tire (pneumatic): John B. Dunlop, Britain (1888)
Rubber tire (solid): Thomas Hancock, England (1846)
Rudder (ship): Vikings (1100s)
Safety pin: Walter Hunt, United States (1849)
Screw propeller: John Ericsson, United States (1837)
Self-starter (internal-combustion engine): Charles F. Kettering, United States (1911)

Sewing machine: Elias Howe, United States (1846)
Sewing machine (foot-operated): Isaac Singer, United States (1851)
Sewing machine (electric): Singer Sewing Machine Co., United States (1889)
Sextant: John Hadley, England; Thomas Godfrey, U.S. (1730)
Ship (seagoing): Egyptians or Phoenicians (2500 B.C.)
Ship (steam): J. C. Périer, France (1775)
Ship (steam, commercial): Robert Fulton, U.S. (1807)
Ship (turbine): Sir Charles Parsons, Britain (1894)
Slot machine: Charles Fey, U.S. (1895)
Spectacles (curved glass): Salvino D'Armato, Italy (1285)
Spectroscope: Joseph von Fraunhofer, Germany (1814)
Spinning frame: Sir Richard Arkwright, England (1769)
Spinning jenny: James Hargreaves, England (1770)
Spinning mule: Samuel Crompton, England (1779)
Stainless steel: Harry Brearley, England (1913)
Steam engine (no moving parts): Thomas Savery, England (1698)
Steam engine (piston): Thomas Newcomen, England (c.1712)
Steam engine (condenser): James Watt, Scotland (1769)
Steam shovel: William S. Otis, U.S. (1838)
Steel production: Henry Bessemer, England (1856)
Stethoscope: René Laënnec, France (1816)
Stirrups (metal): China (500s A.D.)
Stove (coal): Jordan L. Mott, United States (1833)
Stove (Franklin): Benjamin Franklin, United States (1740)
Stove (gas): Robert W. Bunsen, Germany (1855)
Stove (electric): W. S. Hadaway, United States (1896)
Submarine: David Bushnell, United States (1776)
Submarine (nuclear-powered, *Nautilus*): Government scientists, United States (1955)
Tank (armored): Sir Ernest Swinton, England (1914)
Telegraph (electric): Samuel F. B. Morse, U.S. (1832–37)
Telegraph (visual semaphore): Claude Chappe, France (1793)
Telephone: Alexander Graham Bell, United States (1875–76)
Telescope (simple): Hans Lippershey, Netherlands (1608)
Telescope (refracting): Galileo Galilei, Italy (1609)
Telescope (reflecting): Isaac Newton, England (1668)
Telescope (radio): Karl Jansky, United States (1931)
Television (electronic): Vladimir K. Zworykin, United States (1923)
Television (mechanical): John L. Baird, Scotland (1926)
Thermometer: Galileo Galilei, Italy (1593)
Thermometer (improved): Gabriel D. Fahrenheit, Germany (1714)
Thermos bottle: Sir James Dewar, Britain (1892)
Torpedo (self-propelled): Robert Whitehead, Scotland (1866)
Tractor (steam): Nicolas Cugnot, France (1769)
Tractor (track-type): Benjamin Holt, United States (1906)
Tram (railed): Mine rail tracks, Alsace (1550)
Transformer: Otto Bláthy, Hungary (1884)
Transistor: John Bardeen, William Shockley, and Walter Brattain, United States (1947)
Tungsten filament: Irving Langmuir, United States (1915)
Typesetting machine (Linotype): Ottmar Mergenthaler, United States (1884)
Typesetting machine (Monotype): Tolbert Lanston, United States (1885)
Typewriter: Christopher L. Sholes, Carlos Glidden, U.S. (1867)
Vacuum cleaner: I. W. McGaffey, United States (1869)
Vacuum tube (triode): Lee De Forest, United States (1906)
Washing machine (manual): Hamilton E. Smith, U.S. (1858)
Washing machine (electric): Alva J. Fisher, U.S. (1907)
Watch (mainspring): Peter Henlein, Germany (c.1500)
Watch (self-winding): Louis Recordon, Britain (1780)
Welder (electric): Elihu Thomson, United States (1877)
Wheel (solid): Sumerians (c.3300 B.C.)
Wheel (spoked): Egypt (c.1900 B.C.)
Windmill: Iran (corn-grinding mills; c.600 A.D.)
Xerography: Chester Carlson, United States (1937–48)
X ray: Wilhelm Roentgen, Germany (1895)
Zipper: Whitcomb L. Judson, United States (1891)
Zipper (meshed-tooth): Gideon Sundback, United States (1913)

## HOW TO PROTECT YOUR INVENTION

**What Can Be Patented?** If you have invented something that you wish to patent, it would have to meet the statutory standard that "whoever invents or discovers any new and useful process, machine, manufacture, or composition of matter, or any new and useful improvements thereof may obtain a patent." These classes of subject matter taken together include practically everything made by man and the processes for making them.

Patents may also be granted on any distinct and new variety of plant, other than a tuber-propagated plant, which is asexually reproduced, or any new, original, and ornamental design for an article of manufacture.

**What Cannot Be Patented?** A patent may *not* be granted on a useless invention, on a method of doing business, on mere printed matter, or on a device or machine that will not operate. Furthermore, even if your invention is novel or new, a patent may not be obtained if your invention would have been obvious to a person having ordinary skill in the same area at the time of your invention.

And a patent may not be obtained if the invention was in public use or on sale in the U.S. for more than one year prior to the filing of your patent application, or the invention has been patented or described in a printed publication anywhere in the world more than a year before your U.S. patent application is filed. Finally, you may not receive a patent for an invention useful only in applying nuclear material for military purposes.

**Applying for a Patent.** If your invention appears worthy of a patent, how can you know for certain that it is?

The law gives you the privilege of preparing your own application, but since the law is complicated, you would be wise to consult an expert—a registered patent attorney or agent.

Your application will include a claim or claims describing the scope of your invention.

Patentability (novelty and unobviousness) is judged by the claims.

After a patent is granted, questions of patent validity and infringement are determined by a court on the basis of the claims.

Obviously you cannot know that your invention is unique unless you have done some research. The Patent and Trademark Office has a Public Search Room at its offices (2021 Jefferson Davis Highway, Arlington, Va.). Here you can conduct your own search, or employ a patent attorney to do so.

Once the search is done and it appears that your invention may be unique and patentable, your attorney will prepare a final draft of your application. The original should be signed by you and sent to the Commissioner of Patents and Trademarks, Washington, D.C. 20231. There is a basic filing fee of $65. Small additional amounts are charged if claims exceed a certain number.

**Patent Rights.** If you are to receive a patent, there is a basic $100 issuance fee plus printing charges.

After payment, you will receive your patent, which gives you "the right to exclude others from making, using, or selling" the invention for a period of 17 years from the date of the patent. Information from your patent will also be published in the Patent and Trademark Office's *Official Gazette.*

The entire process, from application to grant, currently averages 21 months.

**Patent Laws.** Your right to be granted a patent—the exclusive privilege to control something that you have invented and to share in any compensation that your invention brings—is derived from Article I, Section 8, of the United States Constitution. The first U.S. patent law was passed by Congress in 1790. In 1836 the patent laws were revised, the office of Commissioner of Patents was established, and Patent No. 1, the first numbered patent, was issued to Sen. John Ruggles of Maine on July 13, 1836. The Patent and Trademark Office was transferred to the Interior Department in 1849 and to the Commerce Department in 1925.

**Trademarks and Service Marks.** A trademark is a word, name, symbol, or device used to indicate the source of goods being sold. It distinguishes these goods from other similar goods.

Trademark rights may be used to prevent others from using a confusingly similar mark. But trademark rights do NOT prevent others from making the same kind of goods or selling similar goods using a nonconfusing mark.

A *service mark* is similar to a trademark but is used in the sale or advertising of services rather than goods.

Trademarks or service marks used in interstate or foreign commerce may be registered in the Patent and Trademark Office.

You can obtain more information about trademarks by writing to Commissioner of Patents and Trademarks, Washington, D.C. 20231.

## WHAT IS A COPYRIGHT?

A copyright protects an author or artist from having others make copies of his work without permission. Plays, articles, books, musical compositions, pictures, and other forms of art can be protected by copyright.

A copyright protects the *form* of the expression, rather than the subject matter. For example, you might copyright your written description of how an automobile works. This copyright would prevent others from copying *your* description without your permission. But it

would NOT prevent others from writing their own descriptions of how an automobile works.

Under a revised copyright law effective on Jan. 1, 1978, works copyrighted on or after that date are protected for the life of the author and for 50 years after the author's death.

Copyrights are registered in the Copyright Office in the Library of Congress. You can obtain more information about copyrights by writing to Register of Copyrights, Library of Congress, Washington, D.C. 20559.

# SCIENTISTS AND INVENTORS

Scientists who have won Nobel Prizes are indicated below by (N). Their prize-winning achievements are listed on pages 70–77. For deaths of scientists and inventors in 1980, see pages 981–986.

**Jean Louis Agassiz** (1807–73), Swiss-American biologist and geologist: proved glaciers once covered much of the Earth.

**Howard Hathaway Aiken** (1900–73), American mathematician: designed world's first large-scale digital computer, the Mark I, for International Business Machines Corp. (1944).

**André Marie Ampère** (1775–1836), French physicist and mathematician: developed laws of electromagnetism, using electric currents; *ampere*, unit to measure flow of electric current, named after him.

**Carl D. Anderson** (1905–    ), American physicist: discovered *positron*, or anti-electron, a unit of matter (1932). (N)

**Sir Edward Victor Appleton** (1892–1965), British physicist: discovered Appleton layer of free electrons in ionosphere that bounces radio waves back to Earth, leading to development of radar. (N)

**Archimedes** (287–212 B.C.), Greek mathematician and engineer: father of experimental science; discovered laws of lever, pulley, displacement, and buoyancy; invented catapult and Archimedean screw, a kind of pump.

**Aristarchus** (200s B.C.) Greek astronomer: first to say Earth revolves around Sun, but theory disregarded for hundreds of years.

**Aristotle** (384–322 B.C.) Greek philosopher: father of objective science; developed syllogism in logic; made first scientific study of biology.

**Sir Richard Arkwright** (1732–92), British inventor: developed water-powered spinning machine (1769), starting Industrial Revolution.

**Edwin Howard Armstrong** (1890–1954), American electrical engineer: invented FM (frequency modulation) radio, eliminating static (1933).

**Francis W. Aston** (1877–1945), British physicist: invented mass spectrograph (1919). (N)

**Amedeo Avogadro** (1776–1856), Italian physicist: developed Avogadro's law of gases (1811); differentiated molecules and atoms; provided basis for determining correct atomic weights.

**Roger Bacon** (1214?–94), English philosopher and scientist: pioneered in controlled experiments and observation of phenomena; introduced gunpowder formula to Europe (1242).

**Leo Hendrik Baekeland** (1863–1944), Belgian-American chemist: invented Bakelite, first artificial resin plastic (1909).

**Adolf von Baeyer** (1835–1917), German chemist: developed synthetic dyes. (N)

**John Bardeen** (1908–    ), American physicist: co-inventor of transistor (1947). (N)

**Nikolai G. Basov** (1922–    ), Russian physicist: developed masers (1955), using molecular energy to amplify radio waves. (N)

**Antoine Henri Becquerel** (1852–1908), French physicist: co-discoverer with Curies of natural radioactivity. (N)

**Alexander Graham Bell** (1847–1922), American scientist: invented telephone (1875–76).

**Karl Benz** (1844–1929), German engineer: invented first gasoline-powered automobile (1885).

**Friedrich Bergius** (1884–1949), German chemist: converted coal dust to oil. (N)

**Jöns Jakob Berzelius** (1779–1848), Swedish chemist: developed system still used to write chemical symbols and formulas; discovered elements selenium (1817), silicon (1823), thorium (1828); co-discovered cerium (1803).

**Sir Henry Bessemer** (1813–98), British inventor: developed Bessemer process for converting pig iron into steel (1856).

**Clarence Birdseye** (1886–1956), American inventor: invented fast-frozen food processing (1925) and dehydrated food processing (1949).

**Max Bodenstein** (1871–1942), German chemist: first described chain reactions (1916) in chemical processes.

**Niels Bohr** (1885–1962), Danish physicist: described atom as miniature solar system with electrons in orbits around nucleus (1913). (N)

**William Cranch Bond** (1789–1859) and his son **George Phillips Bond** (1825–65), American astronomers: took first photograph of star (1850); discovered dark ring of Saturn and Saturn's eighth moon.

**Max Born** (1882–1970), German physicist: pioneered research in quantum mechanics. (N)

**Carl Bosch** (1874–1940), German chemist: developed commercial process using Friedrich Bergius' discovery to convert coal into oil. (N)

**Johann Friedrich Böttger** (1682–1719), German chemist: first European to discover how to make porcelain (1708).

**Nathaniel Bowditch** (1773–1838), American astronomer and mathematician: wrote *The American Practical Navigator* (1799).

**Seth Boyden** (1788–1870), American inventor: developed patent-leather process (1819).

**Robert Boyle** (1627–91), Irish alchemist and chemist: proved air, earth, fire, and water were not elements as alchemists had believed; developed Boyle's law of gases.

**James Bradley** (1693–1762), English astronomer: discovered aberration of light.

**Sir William Henry Bragg** (1862–1942) and his son **Sir William Lawrence Bragg** (1890–1971), British physicists: developed X-ray spectrometer to explore atomic structures. (N)

**Tycho Brahe** (1546–1601), Danish astronomer: proved changes occur in stars with discovery of new star (1572); proved comets originate in outer space (1577).

**Jacques Edwin Brandenberger** (1872–1954), Swiss chemist: invented cellophane (1908).

**Walter Houser Brattain** (1902–    ), American physicist: co-inventor of transistor (1947). (N)

**John Moses Browning** (1855–1926), American inventor: designed Browning machine gun (1890) and Browning automatic rifle (1917).

**Robert Wilhelm Bunsen** (1811–99), German chemist: developed electrolytic cell to produce magnesium (1852), Bunsen burner (1855).

**William Burroughs** (1855–98), American inventor: first reliable adding machine (1889).

**Vannevar Bush** (1890–1974), American electrical engineer: invented first analog computer, called differential analyzer, in 1930, used in World War II to aim antiaircraft guns.

**Melvin Calvin** (1911–    ), American chemist:

**SCIENTISTS AND INVENTORS** *(continued)*
discovered how plants make food by photosynthesis. (N)

**Georg Cantor** (1845–1918), German mathematician: developed theory of sets (1870s).

**Chester F. Carlson** (1906–68), American physicist: invented xerography method of electrostatic printing in 1937–48.

**Wallace H. Carothers** (1896–1937), American chemist: developed nylon (1935).

**Rachel Carson** (1907–64), American biologist: her book *Silent Spring* warned of dangers to wildlife by misuse of insecticides.

**Edmund Cartwright** (1743–1823), English clergyman and inventor: invented first successful steam-powered loom to weave cloth (1786).

**George Washington Carver** (1859?–1943), American botanist and chemist: invented hundreds of products made from peanuts, sweet potatoes, pecans, and other farm crops.

**Henry Cavendish** (1731–1810), English physicist and chemist: discovered hydrogen (1766); demonstrated water is compound of oxygen and hydrogen.

**Sir James Chadwick** (1891–1974), British physicist: discovered neutron (1932). (N)

**Owen Chamberlain** (1920–   ), American physicist: co-discoverer of antiproton (1955). (N)

**Hilaire Chardonnet** (1839–1924), French chemist: invented rayon (1884).

**Rudolf J. E. Clausius** (1822–88), German physicist: discovered thermodynamics laws (1850).

**Sir John Douglas Cockcroft** (1897–1967), British physicist: with Ernest T. S. Walton, first to split atoms by bombardment with protons. (N)

**Samuel Colt** (1814–62), American inventor: developed first successful revolver (1835).

**Arthur Holly Compton** (1892–1962), American physicist: helped prove quantum theory with discovery of Compton effect in which X rays act as atomic particles; helped develop atomic bomb. (N)

**Sir William Congreve** (1772–1828), British inventor: developed military rockets (1808), used by British Army against Napoleon and against Americans in War of 1812.

**Peter Cooper** (1791–1883), American inventor: built *Tom Thumb*, first U.S. steam locomotive used on commercial railroad (1830).

**Nicolaus Copernicus** (1473–1543), Polish astronomer: revolutionized astronomy by demonstrating that Earth moves around Sun instead of being the stationary center of universe.

**Frederick Gardener Cottrell** (1877–1948), American chemist: invented first electrical precipitator to reduce pollution from industrial smokestacks (1910).

**Bernard Courtois** (1777–1838), French chemist: discovered element iodine (1811).

**Jacques-Yves Cousteau** (1910–   ), French inventor: developed Aqua-Lung (1943) for skin divers to breathe underwater.

**Sir William Crookes** (1832–1919), British chemist: discovered element thallium (1861); invented a cathode-ray tube, the radiometer, and the spinthariscope.

**Pierre Curie** (1859–1906) and his wife **Marie Sklodowska Curie** (1867–1934), French chemists and physicists: discovered radioactive elements radium and polonium (1898). (N)

**John Dalton** (1766–1844), English chemist: developed atomic theory (1803); made first table of atomic weights.

**Charles Robert Darwin** (1809–82), British naturalist: wrote *On the Origin of Species* (1859), his theory of evolution.

**Leonardo da Vinci** (1452–1519), Italian artist and scientist: drew sketches and plans for many devices invented hundreds of years later, including helicopter, machine gun, parachute.

**Sir Humphry Davy** (1778–1829), English chemist: discovered elements potassium and sodium (1807); invented electric arc (1808); discovered elements barium, calcium, and magnesium (1808); invented miner's safety lamp (1815).

**Louis Victor de Broglie** (1892–   ), French physicist: developed wave mechanics (1923).

**Lee De Forest** (1873–1961), American inventor: developed triode vacuum tube (1906), making possible long-distance radio and TV.

**Willem de Sitter** (1872–1934), Dutch astronomer: first proposed theory of expanding universe (1917).

**John Deere** (1804–86), American inventor: invented first steel plow (1837).

**Arthur Jeffrey Dempster** (1886–1950), American physicist: discovered uranium 235 (in 1935), basic material used in atomic bombs.

**René Descartes** (1596–1650), French philosopher and mathematician: developed analytical geometry (1637).

**Joseph Dixon** (1799–1869), American inventor: made lead pencils from graphite (1827).

**Amos E. Dolbear** (1837–1910), American physicist and inventor: invented "talking machine" (1864), 12 years before Bell patented telephone; produced first radio waves (1882).

**Charles E. Duryea** (1861–1938) and **J. Frank Duryea** (1869–1967), brothers, American inventors: built first successful gasoline-powered automobile in U.S. (1893).

**James Buchanan Eads** (1820–87), American engineer: developed armored warships (1862).

**George Eastman** (1854–1932), American inventor: developed first Kodak camera using roll film (1888); began mass-producing cameras at $1 each (1900).

**Sir Arthur Stanley Eddington** (1882–1944), British astronomer: discovered relationship between mass and brightness in stars; discovered deflection of light by Sun's gravitational field (1919).

**Harold Eugene Edgerton** (1903–   ). American electrical engineer: invented photographic electronic flash equipment (1931).

**Thomas Alva Edison** (1847–1931), American inventor: among his more than 1,100 inventions were phonograph (1877), electric light (1879), stencil duplicating process for mimeograph machines (1887), and motion-picture projector (1889).

**Albert Einstein** (1879–1955), German-American physicist: developed theory of relativity (1905) and unified field theory (1929); his theories made possible development of atomic bombs and atomic energy.

**John Ericsson** (1803–89), Swedish-American engineer: invented first successful propeller with blades for use on ships (1837).

**Euclid** (c.300 B.C.), Greek mathematician: com-

piled first geometry textbook.

**Oliver Evans** (1755–1819), American inventor: built first steam-powered land vehicle in U.S. (1805).

**Gabriel Daniel Fahrenheit** (1686–1736), German physicist: developed Fahrenheit scale of temperatures.

**Thaddeus Fairbanks** (1796–1886), American inventor: platform weighing scale (1831).

**Michael Faraday** (1791–1867), English chemist and physicist: discovered electromagnetic induction (1831), leading to development of electric generators and motors; formulated laws of electrolysis.

**Philo Taylor Farnsworth** (1906–71), American inventor: patented image dissector (1928), electronic device basic to television.

**Pierre de Fermat** (1601–65), French mathematician: introduced theory of mathematical probability and modern theory of numbers.

**Enrico Fermi** (1901–54), Italian-American physicist: split the atom in nuclear fission (1934); produced first atomic chain reaction (1942); helped develop atomic bomb. (N)

**Cyrus West Field** (1819–92), American businessman: laid first successful telegraph cable across Atlantic (1858); laid new cable in 1866.

**John Fitch** (1743–98), American inventor: built first successful steamboat (1787).

**Henry Ford** (1863–1947), American inventor and businessman: introduced moving assembly line to produce "Model T" Fords (1913).

**Jean B. L. Foucault** (1819–68), French physicist: proved light travels more slowly in water (1850); used pendulum to prove rotation of Earth (1851); built first gyroscope (1852).

**Benjamin Franklin** (1706–90), American statesman and scientist: proved lightning is electricity (1752); invented lightning rod (1752) and bifocal glasses (1780).

**R. Buckminster Fuller** (1895–    ), American inventor: designed Dymaxion prefabricated metal home in 1927; invented geodesic dome of triangular elements in 1960s.

**Robert Fulton** (1765–1815), American artist and inventor: built *Clermont*, first commercially successful steamboat in U.S. (1807).

**Galileo Galilei** (1564–1642), Italian physicist and astronomer: discovered law of pendulum (1584), law of falling bodies (1589), four moons of Jupiter (1610); proved Copernican theory of astronomy.

**Richard Jordan Gatling** (1818–1903), American inventor: developed first practical machine gun in U.S. (1862).

**Karl Friedrich Gauss** (1777–1855), German mathematician: helped develop modern number theory and laws of electromagnetism.

**Joseph Louis Gay-Lussac** (1778–1850), French chemist and physicist: made discoveries about gases; co-discovered element boron (1808),

**Hans Geiger** (1882–1947), German physicist: invented Geiger counter (1908).

**Josiah Willard Gibbs** (1839–1903), American mathematician and physicist: founder of physical chemistry and thermodynamics; member American Hall of Fame.

**Donald Arthur Glaser** (1926–    ), American physicist: invented bubble chamber (1953), device used to study subatomic particles. (N)

**Carlos Glidden** (1834–77), American co-inventor of typewriter (1867).

**Robert Hutchings Goddard** (1882–1945), American physicist: built first successful liquid-fueled rocket (1926), making space travel possible.

**Charles Goodyear** (1800–60), American inventor: discovery of vulcanization process (1839) initiated rubber industry.

**John Gorrie** (1803–55), American physician: invented first ice-making machine (1851).

**Thomas Graham** (1805–69), Scottish chemist: pioneer in physical chemistry; stated how gases mix in Graham's law of diffusion (1833).

**Otto von Guericke** (1602–86), German scientist: invented 34-foot-high water barometer; invented air pump (1650).

**Johann Gutenberg** (1395?–1468?), German inventor: invented metal type molding of letters, making mass printing possible (c. 1455).

**Fritz Haber** (1868–1934), German chemist: developed process for making synthetic ammonia (1913) for fertilizers and explosives. (N)

**Otto Hahn** (1879–1968), German chemist: co-discoverer of element protactinium (1917); with Fritz Strassman, split nucleus of uranium atom (1938). (N)

**George Ellery Hale** (1868–1938), American astronomer: invented spectroheliograph (1889) for photographing Sun; founded three major observatories, Yerkes (1895), Mt. Wilson (1904), and Mt. Palomar (1928).

**Charles Martin Hall** (1863–1914), American chemist: discovered how to make aluminum from bauxite (1886), working independently of **Paul Héroult** (1863–1914), French chemist who discovered same process in same year.

**Edmund Halley** (1656–1742), English astronomer: developed star catalog for Southern Hemisphere; correctly forecast return of Halley's comet in 1910.

**James Hargreaves** (1722?–78), English inventor: developed first spinning jenny to spin many threads at same time (1770).

**Werner Heisenberg** (1901–76), German physicist: founded study of subatomic particles (1927). (N)

**Hermann L. F. von Helmholtz** (1821–94), German physicist: developed law of conservation of energy; invented ophthalmoscope (1851).

**Sir William Herschel** (1738–1822), British astronomer: first person to discover a planet since prehistoric times when he sighted Uranus in 1781; discovered infrared radiation (1800).

**Heinrich Rudolf Hertz** (1857–94), German physicist: discovered electromagnetic waves (1887), making possible radio and TV.

**Georg von Hevesy** (1885–1966), Hungarian chemist: co-discoverer of element hafnium (1923). (N)

**Hipparchus** (100s B.C.), Greek astronomer: made first catalog of stars; discovered changes of equinoxes.

**John Philip Holland** (1840–1914), Irish-American inventor: built first practical submarine for U.S. Navy (1898).

**Elias Howe** (1819–67), American inventor: built first practical sewing machine (1846).

**James Hutton** (1726–97), Scottish geologist: founded modern geology with theory that rocks were formed by lava from volcanoes (1785).

**SCIENTISTS AND INVENTORS** (*continued*)

**Christian Huygens** (1629–95), Dutch scientist: developed telescope lens (1655) with which he discovered Saturn's ring and one of Saturn's moons; discovered wave theory of light; invented micrometer to measure small objects; invented pendulum clock (1673).

**Joseph M. Jacquard** (1752–1834), French inventor: invented automatic pattern loom (1801–04).

**Karl Guthe Jansky** (1905–50), American engineer: discovered radio waves from outer space (1932), leading to radio astronomy.

**Thomas Jefferson** (1743–1826), American President and inventor: among his many inventions were swivel chair and dumbwaiter.

**Charles Francis Jenkins** (1867–1934), American inventor: developed phantascope (1891–94), first successful motion-picture projector.

**J. Hans Jensen** (1906– ), German physicist: discovered nuclear shell structure of 'atomic nuclei. (N)

**Frédéric Joliot** (1900–58) and his wife **Irène Joliot-Curie** (1897–1956), French physicists: produced isotopes by high-energy bombardment of elements (1934). (N)

**James Prescott Joule** (1818–89), English physicist: determined relationship between heat and mechanical energy (conservation of energy).

**Lord Kelvin** (William Thomson; 1824–1907), British physicist: invented Kelvin temperature scale for use with gas thermometers, with absolute zero equal to –273 ° C.

**Johannes Kepler** (1571–1630), German astronomer and mathematician: wrote laws of motion of the planets.

**Donald William Kerst** (1911– ), American physicist: developed betatron (1940), an atomic accelerator.

**Charles Franklin Kettering** (1876–1958), American inventor: invented automobile self-starter (1911) and other auto improvements.

**Chevalier de Lamarck** (1744–1829), French naturalist: founder of invertebrate paleontology; concluded plants and animals change to adapt to their environments; made first efforts to scientifically forecast weather.

**Edwin Herbert Land** (1909– ), American inventor: invented polarized plastic sheets (1928); developed polaroid camera that takes and prints pictures in a few seconds (1947); invented self-developing color film (1963).

**Marquis de Laplace** (1749–1827), French astronomer and mathematician: described origin of solar system from a nebula (1796).

**Antoine Laurent Lavoisier** (1743–94), French chemist: gave first scientific explanation of fire as union of material with oxygen (1777); proved law of conservation of matter; wrote first modern textbook of chemistry (1789).

**Ernest Orlando Lawrence** (1901–58), American physicist: invented cyclotron (1930) and bevatron (1954), atomic particle accelerators; produced first man-made mesons (1948). (N)

**Nicolas Leblanc** (1742–1806), French physician: discovered process for making soda from common salt (1790).

**Gottfried Wilhelm von Leibniz** (1646–1716), German mathematician: developed theories of differential and integral calculus; invented an early type of calculating or adding machine.

**Jean Joseph Étienne Lenoir** (1822–1900), French inventor: invented first internal-combustion engine, using illuminating gas as fuel (1860); built vehicle using his engine (1863).

**Willard Frank Libby** (1908–80), American chemist: discovered carbon 14 (radiocarbon) in 1947; developed method of using it to date prehistoric plant and animal fossils. (N)

**Carolus Linnaeus** (1707–78), Swedish botanist: established present-day scientific method of naming and classifying plants and animals.

**Hendrick Antoon Lorentz** (1853–1928), Dutch physicist: developed electron theory. (N)

**Sir Bernard Lovell** (1913– ), British astronomer: built first completely directional radio telescope, at Jodrell Bank, England.

**Archibald M. Low** (1888–1956), British physicist: demonstrated principles of television (1914); invented radio control systems for torpedoes and rockets.

**Percival Lowell** (1855–1916), American astronomer: predicted discovery of Pluto (1905).

**Guglielmo Marconi** (1874–1937), Italian electrical engineer: invented first practical radio system (1895); sent first transatlantic radio signal (1901). (N)

**Sir Hiram Stevens Maxim** (1840–1916), British-American inventor: invented first completely automatic machine gun (1889).

**James Clerk Maxwell** (1831–79), British mathematician and physicist: developed mathematical descriptions of electricity and magnetism; predicted (1864) electromagnetic waves.

**Julius Robert von Mayer** (1814–78), German physician and physicist: independently discovered law of conservation of energy (1842).

**Maria Goeppert Mayer** (1906–72), German-American physicist: independently developed theory of structure of atomic nuclei. (N)

**Cyrus Hall McCormick** (1809–84), American inventor: invented reaping machine to harvest wheat (1831).

**Lise Meitner** (1878–1968), Austrian physicist: co-discoverer of element protactinium (1917); mathematically determined energy released by nuclear fission, helping lead to atomic bomb.

**Gregor Johann Mendel** (1822–84), Austrian monk and botanist: developed theory of heredity and founded science of genetics.

**Dmitri Ivanovich Mendeleev** (1834–1907), Russian chemist: developed periodic table of elements, predicting elements not yet discovered.

**Ottmar Mergenthaler** (1854–99), German-American inventor: invented Linotype typesetting machine (1883).

**Charles Messier** (1730–1817), French astronomer: made first star catalog of northern sky (1784).

**Julius Lothar Meyer** (1830–95), German chemist: demonstrated relationship of atomic weights to properties of elements (1869).

**Albert Abraham Michelson** (1852–1931), German-American physicist: with Edward W. Morley, disproved that substance called ether fills vacuums (1887); invented interferometer (1880); made first accurate measurements of diameter of a star (1920) and speed of light (1926). (N)

**Robert Andrews Millikan** (1868–1953), American physicist: measured electric charge of elec-

tron and intensity of cosmic rays. (N)

**Samuel Finley Breese Morse** (1791–1872), American artist and inventor: invented electric telegraph (1832–37).

**Paul Mueller** (1899–1965), Swiss chemist: discovered power of DDT insecticide (1939). (N)

**Walther Hermann Nernst** (1864–1941), German chemist: developed third law of thermodynamics. (N)

**Simon Newcomb** (1835–1909), American astronomer: computed new, more accurate, tables of orbits of Moon and planets.

**Thomas Newcomen** (1663–1729), English inventor: with Thomas Savery, built first piston steam engine (c.1712).

**Sir Isaac Newton** (1642–1727), English scientist and mathematician: described basic laws of gravity and motion (1687); invented calculus, new branch of mathematics (independently of Leibniz); invented reflecting telescope.

**Joseph Nicéphore Niepce** (1765–1833), French scientist: made first crude photograph (1826), using process called *heliography.*

**Alfred Otto Carl Nier** (1911– ), American physicist: separated from uranium the isotope U-235, basic atomic material (1940).

**Alfred Bernhard Nobel** (1833–96), Swedish chemist: invented dynamite (1867); established Nobel prizes to encourage peace and progress.

**Robert N. Noyce** (1927– ), American physicist: developed electronic integrated circuit on silicon chip, making possible development of microcomputers and hand-held calculators.

**Hans Christian Oersted** (1777–1851), Danish physicist: discovered magnetic field surrounds any wire carrying electricity (1819); made first aluminum (1825).

**Ransom Eli Olds** (1864–1950), American inventor: first to use assembly line to mass-produce automobiles (1901).

**J. Robert Oppenheimer** (1904–67), American physicist: directed construction of first atomic bombs (1943–45).

**Elisha Graves Otis** (1811–61), American inventor: invented safety elevator (1852), steam plow (1857), bake oven (1858).

**Blaise Pascal** (1623–62), French mathematician and scientist: formulated Pascal's law, explaining pressures of liquid; invented theory of probability; invented adding machine (1642).

**Linus Carl Pauling** (1901– ), American chemist: built accurate models of molecules; led scientists in trying to ban atomic testing. (N)

**Karl Pearson** (1857–1936), British mathematician: founded science of statistics.

**Sir William Henry Perkin** (1838–1907), British chemist: made synthetic aniline dye (1856).

**Auguste Piccard** (1884–1962), Swiss physicist: invented stratosphere balloon to ascend to high altitudes (1931); invented bathyscaph to descend to depths of ocean (1953).

**Max Planck** (1858–1947), German physicist: revolutionized physics with quantum theory of energy (1901). (N)

**Joseph Priestley** (1733–1804), British clergyman and chemist: discovered hydrochloric acid (1772), laughing gas (1772), sulfur dioxide (1774), oxygen (1774).

**Alexander M. Prokhorov** (1916– ), Russian physicist: with Nikolai Basov, discovered masers

(1955), a means of amplifying radio waves with molecular energy.

**Ptolemy** (100s A.D.), Greek astronomer and geographer: his theory of Earth being motionless at center of universe was accepted for 1,500 years; his miscalculation of size of Earth led Columbus to believe he had reached Asia when he discovered Americas.

**Michael Idvorsky Pupin** (1858–1935), Hungarian-American physicist: invented 34 devices to improve telephone, telegraph, and radio.

**Pythagoras** (500s B.C.), Greek philosopher and mathematician: believed Earth was round and had motions, but his ideas were discounted for hundreds of years.

**Isidor Isaac Rabi** (1898– ), Austrian-American physicist: supervised U.S. development of radar (1940–45); developed data on magnetic properties of atomic nuclei. (N)

**Sir William Ramsay** (1852–1916), British chemist: co-discoverer of elements argon (1894), helium (1895), and krypton, neon, xenon (all 1898). (N)

**Ira Remsen** (1846–1927), American physician and chemist: founded *American Chemical Journal* (1879), first scientific journal in U.S.

**David Rittenhouse** (1732–96), American astronomer: accurately measured Earth's distance from Sun (1769); built accurate model of solar system (1770).

**James Ritty** (1836–1918), American inventor: invented first practical cash register (1879).

**Wilhelm Conrad Roentgen** (1845–1923), German physicist: discovered X rays (1895). (N)

**Henry Augustus Rowland** (1848–1901), American physicist: determined value of *ohm*, unit for measuring resistance to electric current.

**Bertrand Arthur William Russell** (1872–1970), English mathematician and philosopher: coauthor of *Principia Mathematica*, landmark in symbolic logic.

**Ernest Rutherford** (1871–1937), British physicist: called father of nuclear physics; stated theory of atomic transmutation (1902); described nuclear structure of atom (1911); produced protons by bombarding nitrogen atoms with alpha particles (1919). (N)

**Andrei Dmitriyevich Sakharov** (1921– ): Soviet physicist: developed first hydrogen bomb for Soviet Union in 1950s; became outspoken critic of communist restrictions on human rights. (N)

**Carl Wilhelm Scheele** (1742–86), German-Swedish chemist: discovered oxygen (1774), chlorine (1774), and molybdenum (1778).

**Erwin Schrödinger** (1887–1961), Austrian physicist: provided mathematical basis for quantum theory with Schrödinger equation. (N)

**Glenn Theodore Seaborg** (1912– ), American physicist: co-discoverer of six elements—plutonium (1940), curium (1944), americium (1945), berkelium (1949), californium (1950), mendelevium (1955); chairman, U.S. Atomic Energy Commission (1961–71).

**Alois Senefelder** (1771–1834), German inventor: invented lithography (1798).

**Harlow Shapley** (1885–1972), American astronomer: developed new information about Milky Way.

**William Shockley** (1910– ), American physicist: co-discoverer of transistor (1947). (N)

**SCIENTISTS AND INVENTORS** *(continued)*

**Christopher Latham Sholes** (1819–90), American inventor: co-invented typewriter (1867–68).

**Sir Charles William Siemens** (1823–83), German-British inventor: invented furnace (1856) that led to open-hearth steelmaking process.

**Igor I. Sikorsky** (1889–1972), Russian-American aircraft designer: designed and built first four-engine plane (1913) and first successful single-rotor helicopter (1939).

**Isaac Merrit Singer** (1811–75), American inventor: invented improvements on early sewing machines to make them practical (1851).

**Frederick Soddy** (1877–1956), British chemist: coined term *isotopes* for atoms of same element that have different weights. (N)

**Elmer Ambrose Sperry** (1860–1930), American inventor: invented gyrocompass (1911), leading to automatic pilots for aircraft.

**Hermann Staudinger** (1881–1965), German chemist: his exploration of giant molecules led to development of many plastics. (N)

**Charles Proteus Steinmetz** (1865–1923), German-American mathematician and engineer: solved problems of using alternating current in generating and transmitting electricity.

**George Stephenson** (1781–1848), British inventor: built one of first practical locomotives, *Puffing Billy* (1814); his locomotive *The Rocket* (1829) reached speed of 30 mph.

**Fritz Strassmann** (1902– ), German chemist: co-discoverer of method of splitting uranium atom (1938).

**Theodor Svedberg** (1884–1971), Swedish chemist: invented ultracentrifuge. (N)

**Richard L. M. Synge** (1914– ), British biochemist: invented partition chromatography, method of analyzing tiny samples. (N)

**Leo Szilard** (1898–1964), Hungarian-American physicist: helped develop nuclear reactor (1942).

**Edward Teller** (1908– ), American physicist: developed hydrogen bomb (1952).

**Nikola Tesla** (1856–1943), Slavic-American electrical engineer: invented alternating-current electric motor (1888).

**Thales** (c.640–c.546 B.C.), Greek philosopher: pioneered scientific method of observation; used geometry to predict eclipse of Sun.

**Sir Joseph John Thomson** (1856–1940), British physicist: discovered electron (1897). (N)

**Clyde William Tombaugh** (1906– ), American astronomer: discovered planet Pluto (1930).

**Evangelista Torricelli** (1608–47), Italian mathematician and physicist: invented mercury barometer (1643).

**Charles Hard Townes** (1915– ), American physicist: pioneered in development of laser-maser principle (1953–58). (N)

**John Tyndall** (1820–93), British scientist: discovered Tyndall effect in scattering of light passing through small particles; described effects of *Penicillium* mold slowing growth of bacteria (1876) half a century before its value in medicine was recognized.

**Harold Clayton Urey** (1893– ), American chemist: discovered heavy hydrogen (1932), used in development of atomic energy. (N)

**Jacobus Henricus Van't Hoff** (1852–1911), Dutch chemist: pioneered in stereochemistry, study of internal molecular structure. (N)

**Alessandro Volta** (1745–1827), Italian physicist: invented electric battery (1800); electromagnetic unit, *volt*, named after him.

**Wernher Von Braun** (1912–77), German-American rocket engineer: developed V-2 guided missile rocket for Germany in World War II; developed Jupiter and Saturn rockets for U.S. space program.

**John Von Neumann** (1903–57), Hungarian-American mathematician: wrote *The Mathematical Foundations of Quantum Mechanics* (1944); helped develop high-speed electronic computers.

**Ernest T. S. Walton** (1903– ), British physicist: co-developer of first nuclear accelerators (1932). (N)

**Sir Robert Alexander Watson-Watt** (1892–1973), British electronics engineer and inventor: invented practical radar (1935).

**James Watt** (1736–1819), Scottish engineer: made steam engines practical with invention of separate condenser (1769); invented steam radiators for heating (1784).

**Carl Auer Welsbach** (1858–1929), Austrian chemist: discovered elements neodymium and praseodymium (1885); invented mantle used in gas lighting before invention of electric lights.

**George Westinghouse** (1846–1914), American inventor: invented railroad air brake (1868).

**Sir Charles Wheatstone** (1802–75), British physicist and inventor: independently invented electric telegraph (1837).

**Alfred North Whitehead** (1861–1947), British mathematician and philosopher: coauthor of *Principia Mathematica.*

**Eli Whitney** (1765–1825), American inventor: invented cotton gin to remove seeds from cotton (1793); introduced use of interchangeable parts, enabling mass production of guns (1798).

**Sir Frank Whittle** (1907– ), British inventor: invented turbojet engine for airplanes (1930).

**Norbert Wiener** (1894–1964), American mathematician: devised mathematical theory of cybernetics (1948); helped develop high-speed electronic computers.

**Eugene Paul Wigner** (1902– ), Hungarian-American physicist: made many contributions to development of atomic energy. (N)

**Charles T. R. Wilson** (1869–1959), British physicist: invented Wilson cloud chamber (1912), device to make visible tracks of high-speed atomic particles. (N)

**Friedrich Wöhler** (1800–82), German chemist: first to synthesize organic compounds from inorganic material (1828).

**Jethro Wood** (1774–1834), American inventor: invented cast-iron plow (1819).

**Wilbur Wright** (1867–1912) and his brother **Orville Wright** (1871–1948), American inventors: invented first successful airplane (1903).

**Hideki Yukawa** (1907– ), Japanese physicist: developed theory showing existence of meson (1935), discovered next year. (N)

**Richard Zsigmondy** (1865–1929), Austrian chemist: invented ultramicroscope, aiding in research in colloid chemistry. (N)

**Vladimir Kosma Zworykin** (1889– ), Russian-American physicist and electronics engineer: invented iconoscope TV camera tube (1923) and kinescope TV picture tube (1929); perfected electron microscope (1939).

## Social Welfare

# HIGHLIGHTS: 1980

To allay concerns by older Americans that Congress might decide to impose a federal income tax on social security benefits, the U.S. House of Representatives on July 21, 1980, approved by 384 to 1 a resolution that the benefits remain tax exempt.

A congressional study group, the National Commission on Social Security, reported the results of a survey showing that 77% of the people think so well of social security that they voluntarily would join the system and pay the required tax if given the option. Some 60% said they were counting on social security as the major source of retirement income. However, the survey also showed that 73% of the persons interviewed between the ages of 25 and 44 believed the system would have no money left with which to pay them benefits when they reach retirement age.

The number of persons receiving government payments under social security, supplemental security income, and welfare totaled about 49.6 million in 1980.

The nation's social security and supplemental security income recipients received a 14.3% automatic increase in their benefits in July 1980. This was the sixth such increase for inflation as measured by the Consumer Price Index.

The increase brought the average monthly payments for a retired worker without dependents to $330 and for a retired couple both receiving benefits to $563.

The maximum benefit for a worker retiring in 1980 at age 65 was increased to $653.80.

The maximum federal monthly payment for an aged couple on supplemental income rose to $357.

Welfare rolls for Aid to Families with Dependent Children (AFDC) averaged about 10.3 million recipients in 1979, with annual benefits of about $10 billion.

## SOCIAL WELFARE EXPENDITURES: 1950–1978

Source: Social Security Bulletin, data for fiscal years

From 1977 to 1978 social welfare expenditures rose by 9%, and in 1978 equaled 18.5% of the total U.S. gross national product of $2.1 trillion.

Combined federal, state, and local government expenditures for social welfare programs are shown in millions of dollars (add 000,000).

| | 1950 | 1960 | 1965 | 1970 | 1975 | 1977 | 1978 |
|---|---|---|---|---|---|---|---|
| TOTAL | $23,508.4 | $52,293.3 | $77,175.3 | $145,761.1 | $290,064.0 | $361,552.9 | $394,462.4 |
| Social insurance | 4,946.6 | 19,306.7 | 28,122.8 | 54,691.2 | 123,013.1 | 160,866.9 | 175,101.1 |
| Social security and Medicare | 784.1 | 11,032.3 | 16,997.5 | 36,835.4 | 78,429.9 | 105,410.1 | 117,432.9 |
| Railroad retirement | 306.4 | 934.7 | 1,128.1 | 1,609.9 | 3,085.1 | 3,818.6 | 4,019.8 |
| Public employee retirement | 817.9 | 2,569.9 | 4,528.5 | 8,658.7 | 20,118.6 | 26,495.9 | 29,929.1 |
| Unemployment benefits | 2,190.1 | 2,829.6 | 3,002.6 | 3,819.5 | 13,877.5 | 15,448.8 | 12,599.8 |
| State temporary disability | 72.1 | 347.9 | 483.5 | 717.7 | 990.0 | 1,042.2 | 1,102.9 |
| Workers' compensation | 625.1 | 1,308.5 | 1,859.4 | 2,950.4 | 6,479.2 | 8,462.2 | 9,809.1 |
| Public aid | 2,496.2 | 4,101.1 | 6,283.4 | 16,487.7 | 40,706.1 | 52,894.7 | 59,620.2 |
| Public assistance | 2,490.2 | 4,041.7 | 5,874.9 | 14,433.5 | 26,758.2 | 34,714.2 | 36,983.8 |
| Supplemental security income | — | — | — | — | 6,091.6 | 6,818.9 | 7,193.7 |
| Food stamps | — | — | — | 576.9 | 4,693.9 | 5,472.0 | 5,590.0 |
| Health and medical programs | 2,063.5 | 4,463.8 | 6,246.4 | 9,906.8 | 17,787.7 | 20,438.1 | 23,003.7 |
| Hospital and medical care | 1,222.3 | 2,853.3 | 3,452.3 | 5,313.4 | 9,490.4 | 10,033.4 | 10,950.6 |
| Maternal and child health | 29.8 | 141.3 | 227.3 | 431.4 | 545.5 | 632.0 | 663.5 |
| Medical research | 69.2 | 448.9 | 1,165.2 | 1,635.4 | 2,599.0 | 3,313.0 | 3,903.0 |
| School health | 30.6 | 101.0 | 142.2 | 246.6 | 350.8 | 414.0 | 467.0 |
| Other public health | 350.8 | 401.2 | 671.0 | 1,348.0 | 2,953.0 | 4,050.0 | 4,868.0 |
| Veterans' programs | 6,865.7 | 5,479.2 | 6,031.0 | 9,078.0 | 17,018.8 | 19,015.3 | 19,742.4 |
| Pensions and compensation | 2,092.1 | 3,402.7 | 4,141.4 | 5,393.8 | 7,578.5 | 9,081.9 | 9,676.5 |
| Health and medical | 748.0 | 954.0 | 1,228.7 | 1,784.0 | 3,516.7 | 4,670.6 | 5,235.9 |
| Education | 2,691.6 | 490.6 | 40.9 | 1,018.5 | 4,433.8 | 3,925.5 | 3,405.6 |
| Life insurance | 475.7 | 494.1 | 434.3 | 502.3 | 556.1 | 607.2 | 614.3 |
| Education | 6,674.1 | 17,626.2 | 28,107.9 | 50,845.5 | 80,833.4 | 94,420.8 | 101,187.9 |
| Elementary and secondary | 5,596.2 | 15,109.0 | 22,357.7 | 38,632.3 | 59,744.9 | 68,682.6 | 73,694.4 |
| Higher | 914.7 | 2,190.7 | 4,826.4 | 9,907.1 | 16,384.1 | 20,055.2 | 21,014.4 |
| Vocational and adult | 160.8 | 298.0 | 853.9 | 2,144.4 | 4,441.3 | 5,338.0 | 6,050.4 |
| Housing | 14.6 | 176.8 | 318.1 | 701.2 | 3,172.3 | 4,358.1 | 5,224.6 |
| Other social welfare | 447.7 | 1,139.4 | 2,065.7 | 4,145.2 | 7,532.6 | 9,559.0 | 10,582.5 |
| Vocational rehabilitation | 30.0 | 96.3 | 210.5 | 703.8 | 1,036.4 | 1,251.9 | 1,295.9 |
| Institutional care | 145.5 | 420.5 | 789.5 | 201.7 | 296.1 | 359.7 | 421.9 |
| Child nutrition | 160.2 | 398.7 | 617.4 | 896.0 | 2,517.6 | 3,263.9 | 3,507.9 |
| Child welfare | 104.9 | 211.5 | 354.3 | 585.3 | 597.0 | 810.0 | 800.0 |

# YOUR SOCIAL SECURITY BENEFITS

Source: Social Security Administration

For most Americans, social security provides a partial replacement of income when family earnings drop or stop because of retirement, disability, or death.

In addition, social security's Medicare program helps pay hospital and medical bills for most persons 65 and over and for some younger disabled persons.

Almost every American is covered by social security. Today about 1 of every 7 Americans receives a monthly social security benefit check.

## SOCIAL SECURITY NUMBER AND RECORD

You should have a social security card that contains your number, your name, and your signature. *You keep this same social security identification number all your life.*

If you do not have a social security number, you should apply for one at once at any local social security office. You will be advised to provide proof of your age, identity, and citizenship.

You must have a social security number when you obtain a job. Even if you do not work, you need a social security number of your own for such purposes as identification on tax forms or in case you ever have to apply for public assistance.

Make sure your employer has your correct social security number. If your employer does not use your correct number, you may not receive credit for your work under social security. This could reduce the amount of social security benefits you or your family eventually can receive.

Once you have a social security number, the Social Security Administration will maintain a separate earnings record in your name for the rest of your life. This record keeps track of the credits you accumulate toward social security benefits. Information in your social security record is confidential and cannot be disclosed without authorization.

If the Social Security Administration does not have an accurate record of your earnings, the amount of your benefits can be jeopardized at the time you need them. Therefore, officials recommend that each wage earner and person who is self-employed check on their social securities earning record *every three years.*

To do so, you should obtain a "Request for Statement of Earnings" form from any local social security office.

After you fill out the form and mail it in, the Social Security Administration will send back a report that shows what earnings have been accumulated each year for the past three years, the total for which you have been credited since 1950, and the total of earnings reported since 1936. If these figures disagree with your records, ask for a correction.

At the end of each year your employer provides you with a Form W-2 that gives you a record of gross wages paid to you and social security contributions deducted from your pay. Keep copies to check the accuracy of your social security record.

Before you or your family can get monthly cash social security benefits, you or your spouse (or one of your parents, if you are a

## GROWTH OF SOCIAL SECURITY: 1940–1979

Source: Social Security Administration, data for fiscal years

| YEAR | PENSION PAYMENT EXPENDITURES | | | BENEFICIARIES | | AVERAGE MONTHLY BENEFITS | | | |
|---|---|---|---|---|---|---|---|---|---|
| | Total | Retirement & Survivors | Disability | Retirement & Survivors | Disability | Retired Worker | Retired Couple | Widow or Widower | Disabled Worker |
| 1940 | $   23,500,000 | $   15,805,000 | — | 222,488 | — | $ 22.60 | $ 34.73 | $ 20.28 | — |
| 1945 | 247,800,000 | 239,834,000 | — | 1,288,107 | — | 24.19 | 37.01 | 20.19 | — |
| 1950 | 928,400,000 | 727,266,000 | — | 3,477,243 | — | 43.86 | 67.46 | 36.54 | — |
| 1955 | 4,855,300,000 | 4,333,147,000 | — | 7,960,616 | — | 61.90 | 94.97 | 48.69 | — |
| 1960 | 11,080,500,000 | 10,269,709,000 | $ 528,304,000 | 14,157,138 | 687,451 | 74.04 | 112.76 | 57.68 | $ 89.31 |
| 1963 | 15,220,800,000 | 13,844,584,000 | 1,170,678,000 | 17,583,017 | 1,452,472 | 76.88 | 116.82 | 66.84 | 90.59 |
| 1964 | 16,006,700,000 | 14,579,166,000 | 1,251,207,000 | 18,236,173 | 1,563,366 | 77.57 | 117.80 | 67.85 | 91.12 |
| 1965 | 18,093,700,000 | 15,225,894,000 | 1,392,190,000 | 19,127,716 | 1,739,051 | 83.92 | 127.55 | 73.75 | 97.76 |
| 1966 | 19,811,300,000 | 18,071,453,000 | 1,721,133,000 | 20,796,930 | 1,970,322 | 84.35 | 128.16 | 74.10 | 98.09 |
| 1967 | 21,154,300,000 | 18,885,714,000 | 1,860,789,000 | 21,564,773 | 2,140,214 | 85.37 | 129.61 | 74.99 | 98.43 |
| 1968 | 24,667,300,000 | 20,737,093,000 | 2,088,352,000 | 22,225,263 | 2,335,134 | 98.86 | 150.07 | 86.43 | 111.86 |
| 1969 | 26,459,600,000 | 23,732,010,000 | 2,443,437,000 | 22,826,514 | 2,487,548 | 100.40 | 152.28 | 87.27 | 112.74 |
| 1970 | 31,569,600,000 | 26,266,928,000 | 2,778,118,000 | 23,563,634 | 2,664,995 | 118.10 | 179.29 | 101.71 | 131.29 |
| 1971 | 36,865,100,000 | 31,101,018,000 | 3,381,448,000 | 24,361,500 | 2,930,008 | 132.17 | 200.52 | 113.17 | 146.52 |
| 1972 | 41,275,200,000 | 34,540,813,000 | 4,045,895,000 | 25,204,542 | 3,271,486 | 162.35 | 246.44 | 137.66 | 179.32 |
| 1973 | 51,130,500,000 | 42,169,744,000 | 5,161,840,000 | 26,309,163 | 3,558,982 | 166.40 | 251.18 | 156.35 | 183.00 |
| 1974 | 58,194,100,000 | 47,848,838,000 | 6,158,569,000 | 26,941,483 | 3,911,334 | 188.20 | 283.96 | 176.03 | 205.70 |
| 1975 | 66,585,700,000 | 54,838,818,000 | 7,629,796,000 | 25,732,311 | 4,352,200 | 207.18 | 312.37 | 192.33 | 225.89 |
| 1976 | 75,332,100,000 | 62,140,449,000 | 9,222,211,000 | 28,399,725 | 4,623,827 | 224.86 | 338.99 | 207.13 | 245.17 |
| 1977 | 84,263,800,000 | 71,270,519,000 | 11,135,237,000 | 29,228,350 | 4,854,206 | 242.98 | 366.05 | 221.95 | 265.19 |
| 1978 | 92,530,700,000 | 78,524,090,000 | 12,213,895,000 | 29,718,195 | 4,868,576 | 263.19 | 439.00 | 238.84 | 288.25 |
| 1979 | 103,967,300,000 | 87,591,968,000 | 13,428,454,000 | 30,347,848 | 4,777,218 | 294.27 | 442.63 | 266.87 | 322.03 |

child) must have credit for a certain amount of work under social security. The exact amount of work credit required depends on your age and the type of benefit.

## SOCIAL SECURITY CONTRIBUTIONS

If you are employed, your employer deducts social security contributions from your paycheck and matches them with an equal contribution. If you are self-employed you pay contributions at a somewhat lower rate than the combined rate for an employee and his employer.

The money collected in social security taxes is maintained in separate trust funds by the U.S. Treasury. The funds can be used only for payment of social security benefits and expenses.

## RETIREMENT BENEFITS

If you have enough work credits you can retire with benefits as early as the age of 62, but if you do you will receive for the rest of your life only 80% of the monthly benefits to which you would be entitled if you waited until you were 65 to retire.

The size of the monthly benefits you will collect when you retire at age 65 depends on your average earnings under social security over a period of years.

You do not have to pay federal income tax on social security benefits. And the government will deposit your benefits directly in your bank account if you wish.

A retired worker 65 or older can earn up to $5,500 without losing any social security benefits. For every $2 earned above that amount the retiree loses $1 of benefits. There are no earnings restrictions on anyone who is 72 or older.

There is a special rule that generally applies only in the first year of retirement: Even though earnings may exceed the annual exempt amount, a benefit can be paid for any *month* a person performs little or no work. More information on this can be obtained at any social security office.

A worker who does not receive benefits before 65 and delays retirement past 65 will have his benefits increased by 1/12 of 1% for each month in which he does not collect benefits from 65 to 72.

For persons who reach 65 in 1982 or later, the credit will be 3% for each year (1/4% for each month).

Your social security retirement benefits will be automatically increased whenever the Consumer Price Index rises by 3% or more over a comparable measuring period of the previous year.

If you plan to retire in the next few years and wish to estimate your retirement income, consult officials at your local social security office and they will assist you.

## DISABILITY BENEFITS

If you become disabled by accident or illness so that your physical or mental condition prevents you from working before you reach 65, social security provides income protection. The disability must have lasted or be expected to last at least a year.

Your checks can start for the sixth full month of your disability. You will receive checks monthly as long as you are disabled.

The amount of the monthly benefit for disability depends on the worker's age and average earnings under social security.

An insured worker's unmarried child 18 or older who becomes severely disabled before reaching 22 can receive monthly checks as long as the disability continues.

## SOCIAL SECURITY TAXES

Source: Social Security Administration

In the more than four decades that the Social Security System has existed, payroll taxes to support it have increased dramatically from the maximum of $30 paid yearly by an employee in 1937.

| YEARS | MAXIMUM TAXABLE WAGE | EMPLOYEE TAXES[1] Rate | EMPLOYEE TAXES[1] Maximum Tax | SELF-EMPLOYED TAX Rate | SELF-EMPLOYED TAX Maximum Tax | YEARS | MAXIMUM TAXABLE WAGE | EMPLOYEE TAXES[1] Rate | EMPLOYEE TAXES[1] Maximum Tax | SELF-EMPLOYED TAX Rate | SELF-EMPLOYED TAX Maximum Tax |
|---|---|---|---|---|---|---|---|---|---|---|---|
| 1937-49 | $3,000 | 1.00% | $ 30.00 | — | — | 1969-70 | $ 7,800 | 4.80% | $ 374.40 | 6.90% | $ 538.20 |
| 1950 | 3,000 | 1.50% | 45.00 | — | — | 1971 | 7,800 | 5.20% | 405.60 | 7.50% | 585.00 |
| 1951-53 | 3,600 | 1.50% | 54.00 | 2.25% | $ 81.00 | 1972 | 9,000 | 5.20% | 468.00 | 7.50% | 675.00 |
| 1954 | 3,600 | 2.00% | 72.00 | 3.00% | 108.00 | 1973 | 10,800 | 5.85% | 631.80 | 8.00% | 864.00 |
| 1955-56 | 4,200 | 2.00% | 84.00 | 3.00% | 126.00 | 1974 | 13,200 | 5.85% | 772.20 | 7.90% | 1,042.80 |
| 1957-58 | 4,200 | 2.25% | 94.50 | 3.375% | 141.75 | 1975 | 14,100 | 5.85% | 824.85 | 7.90% | 1,113.90 |
| 1959 | 4,800 | 2.50% | 120.00 | 3.75% | 180.00 | 1976 | 15,300 | 5.85% | 895.05 | 7.90% | 1,208.70 |
| 1960-61 | 4,800 | 3.00% | 144.00 | 4.50% | 216.00 | 1977 | 16,500 | 5.85% | 965.25 | 7.90% | 1,303.50 |
| 1962 | 4,800 | 3.125% | 150.00 | 4.70% | 225.60 | 1978 | 17,700 | 6.05% | 1,070.85 | 8.10% | 1,433.70 |
| 1963-65 | 4,800 | 3.625% | 174.00 | 5.40% | 259.20 | 1979 | 22,900 | 6.13% | 1,403.77 | 8.10% | 1,854.90 |
| 1966 | 6,600 | 4.20% | 277.20 | 6.15% | 405.90 | 1980 | 25,900 | 6.13% | 1,587.67 | 8.10% | 2,097.90 |
| 1967 | 6,600 | 4.40% | 290.40 | 6.40% | 422.40 | 1981 | 29,700 | 6.65% | 1,975.05 | 9.30% | 2,762.10 |
| 1968 | 7,800 | 4.40% | 343.20 | 6.40% | 499.20 | | | | | | |

[1] Payroll taxes deducted from wages are equally matched by employers.

And the disabled worker's spouse can receive checks if 62 or older or if caring for children who are under 18 or disabled.

Total monthly benefits to the family of a disabled worker who first becomes entitled to disability benefits after June 1980 are limited to the *lower* of 85% of the worker's average earnings before becoming disabled or 150% of the worker's disability benefit.

## SURVIVORS' BENEFITS

Like life insurance, social security provides monthly benefits for the family of a worker who dies.

A lump-sum payment of $255 also is usually made for burial expenses.

The dependents of a deceased worker who are eligible for monthly cash benefits include:

1. Unmarried children under 18 (or 22 if full-time students).
2. Unmarried son or daughter 18 or over who was severely disabled before 22 and continues to be disabled.
3. Widow or widower 60 or older.
4. Widow or widower under 60, or surviving divorced spouse, if caring for worker's child under 18 (or disabled) who is getting a benefit based on the deceased worker's earnings.
5. Widow or widower 50 or older who becomes disabled not later than seven years after worker's death, or within seven years after ceasing to receive checks for care of deceased worker's children.
6. Dependent parents 62 or older.
7. Unmarried divorced wife 60 or older (50 if disabled), if marriage to insured worker lasted 10 years before divorce.
8. Grandchildren, under certain conditions.

The monthly payments to these survivors may range from 50% to 100% of the amount the worker would receive at 65 as retirement benefits.

## APPLYING FOR SOCIAL SECURITY BENEFITS

Before you or your family can get any social security checks, you must apply for them at a social security office. When you apply, you should have with you:

1. **Social security number:** Your own social security card or a record of your number. If your claim is on another person's record, you will need that person's social security number.
2. **Proof of your age:** A birth certificate or a baptismal certificate that records birth date.
3. **Your marriage certificate,** if applying for spouse's benefits, or widow's or widower's benefits.
4. **Your children's birth certificates,** if applying for children's benefits.
5. **Your Form W-2 for the previous year,** or a copy of your last federal income tax return if you are self-employed.
6. **Proof of your dependence for support** on the insured worker, if you are applying for benefits as a dependent parent.

If you do not have these proofs, do not delay applying. When you apply, a social security official will tell you about alternate means of proof that you can obtain.

## RIGHT OF APPEAL

If you believe that a decision made on your claim is not correct, you may ask the Social Security Administration to reconsider it. Employees of any social security office will explain how you may appeal and will help you get your claim reconsidered or request a hearing.

---

# FOOD STAMPS

The Food Stamp Program helps low-income people buy more food.

Food stamps are available to all low-income persons who qualify, *not* just those receiving public assistance or social security benefits.

Unemployed families and working families with low incomes also may qualify.

The number of food stamp recipients rose in 1980 to about 22 million.

The amount of benefits in food stamps is adjusted yearly to compensate for inflation in food prices.

To find out whether or not you are eligible for food stamps, inquire at your local food stamp or welfare office. Eligibility depends on your household's income and assets.

Food stamps can be used at any approved supermarket or grocery store for the purchase of any food item.

### FOOD STAMP PROGRAM
Source: U.S. Department of Agriculture

| YEAR | NUMBER OF PARTICIPANTS | TOTAL BENEFITS | AV. MONTHLY BENEFITS PER PERSON |
|---|---|---|---|
| 1962 | 143,000 | $ 13,153,000 | $ 7.67 |
| 1963 | 226,000 | 18,639,000 | 6.89 |
| 1964 | 367,000 | 28,643,000 | 6.51 |
| 1965 | 424,000 | 32,494,000 | 6.38 |
| 1966 | 864,000 | 64,781,000 | 6.25 |
| 1967 | 1,447,000 | 105,455,000 | 6.08 |
| 1968 | 2,211,000 | 172,985,000 | 6.52 |
| 1969 | 2,878,000 | 228,587,000 | 6.63 |
| 1970 | 4,340,000 | 550,806,000 | 10.55 |
| 1971 | 9,368,000 | 1,522,904,000 | 13.55 |
| 1972 | 11,103,000 | 1,794,875,000 | 13.48 |
| 1973 | 12,190,000 | 2,102,133,000 | 14.60 |
| 1974 | 12,896,000 | 2,725,988,000 | 17.62 |
| 1975 | 17,063,000 | 4,386,144,000 | 21.43 |
| 1976 | 18,557,008 | 5,310,133,000 | 23.85 |
| 1977 | 17,085,000 | 5,077,357,000 | 24.77 |
| 1978 | 16,044,000 | 5,165,209,000 | 26.83 |
| 1979 | 17,770,000 | 6,478,066,000 | 30.55 |
| 1980 | 22,000,000 | 8,717,000,000 | 34.40 |

# MEDICARE AND MEDICAID

Medicare includes separate social security hospital and medical insurance programs administered by the Health Care Financing Administration of the Department of Health, Education, and Welfare.

Medicaid, on the other hand, is a health assistance program for about 23 million low-income people, especially for those receiving welfare or Supplementary Security Income.

## MEDICARE HOSPITAL INSURANCE

Persons 65 and older eligible for social security or rail retirement benefits automatically receive free Medicare hospital insurance. Others 65 and older can purchase hospital insurance by paying a monthly premium of $78.

Younger persons can receive Medicare if they have been entitled for 24 consecutive months to disability benefits under social security, somewhat longer under railroad retirement, or, under certain conditions, if they need continuing hemodialysis treatment for kidney disease or a kidney transplant.

Anyone 65 or over, or anyone under 65 entitled to Medicare hospital insurance, may enroll for medical insurance.

A person who is not already receiving social security benefits should check with the local social security office about Medicare 3 months before the 65th birthday.

The Medicare hospital insurance provides:
**Hospitalization:** Coverage of up to 90 days of hospital benefits in a period of time called a "benefit period." A benefit period begins when you enter the hospital and ends when you have been out of a hospital or skilled nursing or rehabilitation home for 60 days in a row.

The patient pays the first $204 of costs during the first 60 days of inpatient hospital care, and then pays $51 for each day of hospitalization from 61 to 90 days.

If all 90 days are used up, a "lifetime reserve" can be drawn on for up to 60 more days of benefits. During these additional days, the Medicare beneficiary pays $102 a day of the hospital expenses.

After each "benefit period," the 90 days of hospital benefits are renewed but "lifetime reserve" days are not renewable.

Subject to those limitations, hospital insurance covers (1) the cost of a semiprivate room (two to four patients to a room), a private room only if medically necessary (if the patient elects a private room, he pays the difference); (2) board; (3) hospital services except private-duty nursing; (4) the services of interns or residents in approved teaching programs; and (5) drugs and medical supplies used by the patient in the hospital.

The same coverage extends to hospitalization in tuberculosis or psychiatric institutions. There is a lifetime limit of 190 days of coverage for treatment in a psychiatric hospital.
**Skilled Nursing Facility:** Up to 100 days in a skilled nursing facility after at least 3 days of hospitalization.

The patient pays $25.50 for each day in excess of 20 days, up to the limit of 100 days. Subject to that limitation, insurance covers cost of a semiprivate room, board, general nursing (but not private-duty nursing), prescribed drugs, and therapy by employees of the skilled nursing facility.
**Home Health Services:** Up to 100 home visits by nurses or therapists of an approved home health agency during a one-year period following the patient's discharge from a hospital or skilled nursing facility, when recommended by an attending physician.

## MEDICARE MEDICAL INSURANCE

A person who enrolls when first eligible pays $9.60 a month for coverage by Medicare medical insurance. The person also pays the first $60 of covered medical expenses each year. Medicare then pays 80% of reasonable charges for covered services received for the rest of the year.

The medical insurance covers physicians' and surgeons' services and medical and health services such as diagnostic tests, surgical dressings, certain ambulance services, hospital outpatient charges, and home health services. Payments for home health services are 100% of reasonable costs after the $60 deductible.

## MEDICARE AND MEDICAID: 1970-1979

Source: Health Care Financing Administration

| YEAR | MEDICARE PAYMENTS | | | NUMBER OF MEDICARE BILLS PAID | | MEDICAID |
|------|-------|----------|---------|----------|---------|-------------|
| | Total | Hospital | Medical | Hospital | Medical | Expenditures |
| 1970 | $ 7,099,000,000 | $ 5,124,000,000 | $1,975,000,000 | 7,512,000 | 39,695,000 | $ 4,516,000,000 |
| 1971 | 7,868,000,000 | 5,751,000,000 | 2,117,000,000 | 7,415,000 | 44,947,000 | 5,895,000,000 |
| 1972 | 8,643,000,000 | 6,318,000,000 | 2,325,000,000 | 7,677,000 | 51,754,000 | 7,346,000,000 |
| 1973 | 9,583,000,000 | 7,057,000,000 | 2,526,000,000 | 8,295,000 | 43,508,000 | 8,714,000,000 |
| 1974 | 12,418,000,000 | 9,099,000,000 | 3,318,000,000 | 9,562,000 | 67,995,000 | 9,737,000,000 |
| 1975 | 15,588,000,000 | 11,315,000,000 | 4,273,000,000 | 10,318,000 | 83,106,000 | 12,086,000,000 |
| 1976 | 18,420,000,000 | 13,340,000,000 | 5,080,000,000 | 11,169,000 | 87,116,000 | 13,977,000,000 |
| 1977 | 21,774,000,000 | 15,737,000,000 | 6,038,000,000 | 11,743,000 | 111,723,000 | 16,355,000,000 |
| 1978 | 24,934,000,000 | 17,682,000,000 | 7,252,000,000 | 12,233,000 | 112,660,000 | 18,168,000,000 |
| 1979 | 29,331,000,000 | 20,623,000,000 | 8,708,000,000 | 12,689,000 | 142,725,000 | 20,582,000,000 |

# VETERANS' BENEFITS

Source: Veterans Administration

Almost 100 million Americans are potentially eligible for veterans' benefits and services, including 30 million living veterans, their 66 million family members, and 4 million survivors of deceased veterans.

In 1980 the federal government will spend more than $20 billion for veterans' benefits.

To find out about your own eligibility for specific veterans' benefits, contact your local Veterans Administration (VA) office. Consult your telephone directory for the number to call. Toll-free special telephone service is available for calls to the VA.

Veterans with dishonorable discharges are *not* eligible for most benefits described here.

### FREE HOSPITALIZATION

Veterans with service-connected disabilities have priority for free treatment at Veterans Administration hospitals.

However, if beds are available, free hospitalization is provided for (1) any war veteran who is 65 or older, or (2) any younger veteran who cannot pay the cost of hospitalization.

### AUTOMOBILES FOR THE DISABLED

The VA will pay up to $3,800 toward the purchase of a car plus the cost of adaptive equipment for a veteran whose service-connected disability resulted in loss of use of one

or both hands or feet or permanent impairment of vision in both eyes.

### CLOTHING ALLOWANCE

An annual clothing allowance of $240 can be paid to any veteran entitled to receive compensation for a service-connected disability for which he or she wears or uses a prosthetic or orthopedic appliance that tends to wear out clothing.

### PENSIONS AND DISABILITY COMPENSATION

The VA has two basic programs providing monthly cash benefits to veterans and their survivors.

**Disability Compensation.** Veterans with service-connected disabilities receive monthly payments ranging from $48 to $2,536, depending on the extent of their disability. Additional allowances are paid for dependents if the veteran's disability is rated at 30% or more.

**Veterans' Pensions.** Needy war veterans 65 or older (or younger war veterans totally disabled by nonservice injury or illness) are eligible for monthly pension payments.

The size of the pension depends on the amount of the veteran's additional yearly income. Eligible veterans are guaranteed an annual income level of $4,460 if they are single. Those with one dependent receive a pension to bring their income level to $5,844, and this is increased by $755 for each additional dependent.

**Death Pensions.** Dependents of a veteran who dies of service-connected injuries or illness are eligible for substantial pensions. Lesser amounts are payable to needy widows or widowers of veterans who die of a nonservice related cause.

### DRUG TREATMENT

All veterans who have not been dishonorably discharged can receive free hospitalization and treatment for drug dependency.

### MEDICAL AND DENTAL TREATMENT

Veterans can receive free medical and dental treatment for service-connected disabilities.

Medical aid also covers the purchase of needed prosthetic appliances and aids for the blind, including a trained guide dog.

### EDUCATIONAL BENEFITS

Veterans with service between Feb. 1, 1955, and Dec. 31, 1976, can receive up to 45 months of GI Bill payments for attending school or on-the-job training. Eligibility expires 10 years after discharge.

## VETERANS' BENEFITS: 1940–1980

Source: U.S. Veterans Administration

| YEAR | RETIREMENT, DISABILITY, AND SURVIVORS' BENEFITS | | | ANNUAL MEDICAL OUTLAYS |
|---|---|---|---|---|
| | Benefits | Veteran Beneficiaries | Survivor Beneficiaries | |
| 1940 | $ 423,500,000 | 610,000 | 323,000 | $ 70,000,000 |
| 1945 | 952,100,000 | 1,534,000 | 698,000 | 97,000,000 |
| 1950 | 2,223,800,000 | 2,366,000 | 1,010,000 | 573,000,000 |
| 1955 | 2,745,900,000 | 2,707,000 | 1,156,000 | 688,000,000 |
| 1960 | 3,436,900,000 | 3,064,000 | 1,393,000 | 848,000,000 |
| 1961 | 3,640,700,000 | 3,137,000 | 1,547,000 | 899,000,000 |
| 1962 | 2,732,700,000 | 3,177,000 | 1,653,000 | 940,000,000 |
| 1963 | 3,864,300,000 | 3,195,000 | 1,750,000 | 971,000,000 |
| 1964 | 3,942,500,000 | 3,204,000 | 1,848,000 | 1,019,000,000 |
| 1965 | 4,196,000,000 | 3,216,000 | 1,924,000 | 1,072,000,000 |
| 1966 | 4,373,500,000 | 3,194,000 | 1,995,000 | 1,137,000,000 |
| 1967 | 4,456,400,000 | 3,175,000 | 2,077,000 | 1,328,000,000 |
| 1968 | 4,616,000,000 | 3,171,000 | 2,151,000 | 1,429,000,000 |
| 1969 | 5,154,200,000 | 3,179,000 | 2,208,000 | 1,573,000,000 |
| 1970 | 5,480,100,000 | 3,210,000 | 2,301,000 | 1,793,000,000 |
| 1971 | 5,934,500,000 | 3,251,000 | 2,365,000 | 2,087,000,000 |
| 1972 | 6,340,100,000 | 3,288,000 | 2,393,000 | 2,409,000,000 |
| 1973 | 6,438,600,000 | 3,267,000 | 2,360,000 | 2,681,000,000 |
| 1974 | 7,069,300,000 | 3,250,000 | 2,282,000 | 3,076,000,000 |
| 1975 | 7,429,400,000 | 3,227,000 | 2,256,000 | 3,475,000,000 |
| 1976 | 8,072,971,000 | 3,236,000 | 2,221,000 | 3,730,700,000 |
| 1977 | 8,999,600,000 | 3,258,267 | 1,635,736 | 4,483,900,000 |
| 1978 | 9,636,400,000 | 3,274,804 | 1,631,897 | 5,169,100,000 |
| 1979 | 10,426,194,000 | 3,281,278 | 1,629,856 | 5,600,087,000 |
| 1980 | 11,204,421,000 | 3,195,221 | 1,779,058 | 6,428,959,000 |

A single veteran with a full-time course of study at an approved institution receives $311 per month.

On-the-job payments for a single trainee start at $226 for the first 6 months.

A separate voluntary contributory program is available for veterans who initially entered active duty on or after Jan. 1, 1977.

Another separate program is available for disabled veterans.

The children and spouse of a veteran who died or was totally service-disabled also are eligible for educational benefits. Eligibility for children extends until they are 26 years old. Eligibility for a spouse extends for 10 years from the time the veteran became totally disabled or died.

About 7.6 million Vietnam-era veterans—almost 65%—have participated.

Only 50.5% of World War II veterans took advantage of the GI Bill.

## LOANS FOR HOMES, FARMS, AND BUSINESSES

Veterans, service personnel on active duty, and certain unmarried surviving spouses of veterans may apply for home loans guaranteed or insured by the VA. The VA guarantee may be 60% or $25,000, whichever is less, for conventionally built homes. The maximum guarantee for mobile homes is 50% or $17,500, whichever is less.

There is no time limit on using this loan privilege. Such loans often can be arranged with no down payment by the borrower. Veterans also have preferences for FHA insured loans.

Since 1944 the VA has guaranteed or insured over 11.2 million loans with a value of more than $187 billion.

## GRANTS FOR "SPECIALLY ADAPTED" HOMES

Certain disabled veterans may be entitled to a grant for as much as $30,000 to acquire, build, or remodel a home specially adapted for use by the disabled. For example, such a grant might be used to adapt a home for use by a veteran confined to a wheelchair.

In addition the VA provides up to $40,000 mortgage life insurance on such a home.

## GI INSURANCE

Up to $10,000 of Service-Disabled Veterans Insurance (S-DVI) can be issued to veterans separated on or after April 25, 1951, with a service-connected disability. Application must be made within one year of notice granting such a disability.

Dividends are paid on government life insurance policies prefixed with the letters K, V, RS, W, J, JR, and JS. On all but K, dividends may purchase paid-up insurance additions.

Most VA policies waive premiums if the insured becomes totally disabled for 6 or more months with total disability prior to the 65th birthday. Some policies have riders providing income in cases of total disability.

VA programs include Servicemen's Group Life Insurance (SGLI), Veterans Group Life Insurance (VGLI), and Veterans Mortgage Life Insurance (VMLI).

SGLI provides $20,000 group life insurance to active-duty service personnel, ready reservists, and retired reservists. Upon separation from active duty veterans may convert their SGLI to VGLI.

VGLI provides up to $20,000 group life insurance for a 5-year term. At the end of the term, VGLI may be converted to an individual policy with a participating commercial insurance company.

VMLI provides up to $40,000 of mortgage life insurance protection to disabled veterans with specially adapted housing.

## BURIAL BENEFITS

The VA will pay up to $300 of the burial expenses and up to $150 for a burial plot for a war veteran or service-disabled peacetime veteran. Additional benefits are payable if the veteran died of a service-connected disability. When a veteran dies, his or her family usually is also eligible for a $255 lump-sum death payment from Social Security.

An American flag to drape the casket of a veteran can be obtained from a local VA office or from most local post offices. After the funeral, the flag is given to the next of kin or a close friend.

A headstone or a small allowance for its purchase will be supplied for the burial place of a deceased veteran.

Burial space will be provided for a deceased veteran in a national cemetery as well as for the veteran's spouse, minor children, and, under special conditions, adult unmarried children. Special restrictions apply to burial in Arlington National Cemetery.

When a member of the armed forces dies on active duty and the body is not recovered, the family may obtain a headstone or marker for placement in a private cemetery or in the memorial section of a national cemetery.

## REEMPLOYMENT AND UNEMPLOYMENT

Veterans with 5 years or less of military service have their job rights protected in their previous employment and acquire seniority for the time in military service. The veteran must apply for reemployment within 90 days after discharge. Veterans seeking a job can apply for unemployment benefits from the state immediately upon discharge.

# UNEMPLOYMENT INSURANCE

If you have lost your job through no fault of your own, you may be eligible to receive weekly unemployment insurance payments while looking for new employment.

You should apply for the benefits at your local state employment office.

## FEDERAL–STATE UNEMPLOYMENT INSURANCE

About 86 million workers in the United States are covered by federal-state unemployment insurance.

The federal and state governments collect payroll taxes from employers at a rate of 3.4% of up to the first $6,000 of each worker's wages to pay the benefits.

In a few states employees also pay a small tax to the unemployment fund.

Because each state has its own laws regarding unemployment insurance, the benefits vary from state to state. Depending on how much you previously were earning, your benefits may range from a low of $5 weekly in some states to a high of $160 a week in another. The average amount received is about $90 a week.

Regular benefits end after 26 to 39 weeks of unemployment.

## INELIGIBILITY

You cannot collect unemployment insurance if you voluntarily quit your last job or if you were fired because of misconduct. Most states also will not pay unemployment benefits to workers who are unemployed because of a labor dispute.

While collecting unemployment benefits, you lose your eligibility if you refuse to take a suitable job that is offered you.

If you believe you are being unfairly denied unemployment benefits, each state has a procedure by which you can appeal the decision to a review tribunal.

## OTHER UNEMPLOYMENT COMPENSATION

The federal government funds separate unemployment compensation plans for federal civilian employees and for military personnel who cannot find jobs after they have been discharged. And the federal government also administers a separate unemployment insurance program for railroad workers.

Some corporations and labor unions also have programs that pay an unemployed worker extra benefits over those received from the regular state plan.

## HISTORY

The first state unemployment insurance law was adopted by Wisconsin in 1932.

When the federal government enacted the Social Security Act of 1935, it instituted the present system of unemployment insurance in which the federal government collects payroll taxes and makes money available to states whose unemployment compensation laws meet federal standards.

## FEDERAL–STATE UNEMPLOYMENT INSURANCE: 1940–1979

Source: U.S. Department of Labor

| Year | Average Weekly Benefit | Average Weekly Beneficiaries | Total Benefits Paid | Number of First Payments | Weeks Compensated | Claimants Exhausting Benefits | Funds Available for Benefits at End of Year |
|---|---|---|---|---|---|---|---|
| 1940 | $10.56 | 982,392 | $ 518,700,000 | 5,220,073 | 51,084,375 | 2,596,128 | $ 1,817,108,000 |
| 1945 | 18.77 | 464,996 | 445,866,000 | 2,861,190 | 24,179,769 | 254,271 | 6,914,009,000 |
| 1950 | 20.76 | 1,304,991 | 1,373,114,000 | 5,211,883 | 67,859,529 | 1,853,336 | 6,972,295,000 |
| 1955 | 25.04 | 1,099,466 | 1,350,268,000 | 4,507,894 | 56,099,729 | 1,272,232 | 8,263,850,000 |
| 1960 | 32.87 | 1,640,429 | 2,726,656,000 | 6,753,387 | 85,630,399 | 1,603,372 | 6,643,257,000 |
| 1961 | 33.80 | 2,004,177 | 3,422,698,000 | 7,066,467 | 104,217,226 | 2,370,833 | 5,802,038,000 |
| 1962 | 34.56 | 1,525,481 | 2,675,447,000 | 6,073,668 | 79,324,955 | 1,638,359 | 6,272,863,000 |
| 1963 | 35.28 | 1,541,092 | 2,774,668,000 | 6,040,335 | 80,137,101 | 1,568,558 | 6,648,314,000 |
| 1964 | 35.96 | 1,372,695 | 2,522,100,000 | 5,497,903 | 71,380,122 | 1,370,857 | 7,296,220,000 |
| 1965 | 37.19 | 1,131,025 | 2,166,004,000 | 4,813,229 | 58,813,298 | 1,085,977 | 8,357,350,000 |
| 1966 | 39.76 | 895,133 | 1,771,298,000 | 4,140,026 | 46,546,925 | 780,700 | 9,828,244,000 |
| 1967 | 41.25 | 1,017,356 | 2,092,338,000 | 4,628,083 | 52,902,523 | 867,403 | 10,778,138,000 |
| 1968 | 43.43 | 935,930 | 2,031,617,000 | 4,197,699 | 48,668,357 | 848,179 | 11,717,246,000 |
| 1969 | 46.17 | 922,503 | 2,127,877,000 | 4,213,803 | 47,948,702 | 811,532 | 12,637,508,000 |
| 1970 | 50.34 | 1,516,500 | 3,848,467,000 | 6,401,782 | 78,857,992 | 1,295,319 | 11,895,901,000 |
| 1971 | 54.02 | 1,813,700 | 4,957,026,000 | 6,540,358 | 94,312,380 | 2,006,700 | 9,703,424,000 |
| 1972 | 56.76 | 1,562,706 | 4,470,969,000 | 5,703,866 | 81,260,712 | 1,809,450 | 9,422,799,000 |
| 1973 | 59.00 | 1,369,669 | 4,007,562,000 | 5,328,998 | 71,222,809 | 1,495,092 | 10,933,767,000 |
| 1974 | 64.25 | 1,880,833 | 5,974,922,000 | 7,729,590 | 97,803,299 | 1,926,147 | 10,593,936,000 |
| 1975 | 70.23 | 3,371,246 | 11,754,684,646 | 11,160,042 | 175,304,812 | 4,195,023 | 4,522,933,588 |
| 1976 | 75.16 | 2,450,476 | 8,974,546,269 | 8,560,107 | 127,424,765 | 3,270,042 | 3,361,647,042 |
| 1977 | 78.79 | 2,188,672 | 8,357,160,144 | 7,985,099 | 113,244,354 | 2,850,136 | 4,387,301,806 |
| 1978 | 83.67 | 1,946,073 | 8,214,290,495 | 7,580,045 | 101,195,817 | 2,032,776 | 9,307,267,000 |
| 1979 | 89.67 | 2,036,552 | 9,263,468,406 | 8,077,727 | 106,307,994 | 2,044,131 | 9,380,457,000 |

## WORKERS' COMPENSATION

State workers' compensation laws cover about 88 of every 100 civilian workers, providing cash benefits and medical payments to workers and their survivors for work-related deaths, injuries, and illnesses.

Each state has its own workers' compensation laws, so benefits vary considerably from state to state. Employers are held responsible for work-related injuries and occupational diseases regardless of fault. Employers are required to purchase insurance with private insurance companies, pay premiums into a state insurance fund, or qualify as self-insurers.

Cash benefits to the worker and his or her family may be paid in weekly payments or a lump-sum settlement. In addition, hospital and other medical expenses are paid. Generally the weekly benefits amount to two-thirds of the worker's average weekly wages, but most states set a maximum payment of about $210 a week.

A disabled worker or survivor can collect workers' compensation payments in addition to those provided by federal social security, although a social security offset exists that is based on the worker's average weekly wage.

You can find out more about your coverage by talking to your employer or writing to your state compensation agency.

You or your family will not automatically receive these benefits if you are injured or are killed at work. You or your family must file a claim for the benefits with your employer or the appropriate state agency.

### WORKERS' COMPENSATION: 1940–1979
Source: Social Security Administration

| YEAR | TOTAL BENEFITS | CASH BENEFITS | MEDICAL |
|------|----------------|---------------|---------|
| 1940 | $ 256,000,000 | $ 161,000,000 | $ 95,000,000 |
| 1945 | 408,000,000 | 283,000,000 | 125,000,000 |
| 1950 | 615,000,000 | 415,000,000 | 200,000,000 |
| 1955 | 916,000,000 | 591,000,000 | 325,000,000 |
| 1960 | 1,295,000,000 | 860,000,000 | 435,000,000 |
| 1962 | 1,489,000,000 | 994,000,000 | 495,000,000 |
| 1963 | 1,582,000,000 | 1,057,000,000 | 525,000,000 |
| 1964 | 1,707,000,000 | 1,142,000,000 | 565,000,000 |
| 1965 | 1,814,000,000 | 1,214,000,000 | 600,000,000 |
| 1966 | 2,000,000,000 | 1,320,000,000 | 680,000,000 |
| 1967 | 2,189,000,000 | 1,439,000,000 | 750,000,000 |
| 1968 | 2,376,000,000 | 1,546,000,000 | 830,000,000 |
| 1969 | 2,634,000,000 | 1,714,000,000 | 920,000,000 |
| 1970 | 3,031,000,000 | 1,981,000,000 | 1,050,000,000 |
| 1971 | 3,563,000,000 | 2,433,000,000 | 1,130,000,000 |
| 1972 | 4,039,000,000 | 2,799,000,000 | 1,240,000,000 |
| 1973 | 5,092,000,000 | 3,622,000,000 | 1,470,000,000 |
| 1974 | 5,765,000,000 | 4,015,000,000 | 1,750,000,000 |
| 1975 | 6,522,000,000 | 4,492,000,000 | 2,030,000,000 |
| 1976 | 7,671,000,000 | 5,231,000,000 | 2,380,000,000 |
| 1977 | 8,660,000,000 | 5,890,000,000 | 2,740,000,000 |
| 1978 | 9,729,000,000 | 6,769,000,000 | 2,960,000,000 |
| 1979 | 10,690,000,000 | 7,480,000,000 | 3,210,000,000 |

## PENSION AND RETIREMENT BENEFIT PLANS

Because social security payments amount to only a fraction of the annual amount earned before retirement, most retired persons must supplement their social security benefits with additional income if they are to maintain their accustomed standard of living.

Most commonly such supplemental income, often with benefits larger than those of social security, comes from pension and retirement benefit plans.

Pension plans may be provided to their employees by federal, state, or local governments, by private businesses, or by the individuals themselves.

The first pensions by the U.S. government were established for disabled veterans of the American Revolution in legislation by Congress in 1792. The first local government pensions were established by New York City in 1859 for its police. The first pension plan by a U.S. business came in 1875 by the American Express Company. Columbia University adopted the first American college pension plan for professors in 1892. The following year Chicago established the first pension plan for public school teachers. Pensions for federal Civil Service employees were first adopted by Congress in 1920.

Private pension and retirement plans are regulated by the federal government under the Employee Retirement Income Security Act (ERISA) of 1974. The plans are supervised by the office of Pension and Welfare Benefit Programs of the U.S. Department of Labor and by the Internal Revenue Service. Under ERISA, the Pension Benefit Guaranty Corporation of the federal government insures certain private pension plans to make sure that employees will not be deprived of their benefits if their companies go out of business.

Private companies can establish a variety of pension or profit-sharing plans in which the company does not have to pay income taxes on the money contributed. The individuals receiving benefits under such plans only have to pay income taxes on amounts they receive after retirement.

The federal pension laws also permit a self-employed person or an individual who is not protected by an employer-sponsored pension or retirement plan to start his or her own individual tax-free retirement plan.

About 50 million Americans are participants in more than a half-million private pension and retirement plans.

# PUBLIC ASSISTANCE—SSI AND AFDC

The federal government pays monthly checks to people in financial need who are 65 or older or who are blind or disabled.

The Supplemental Security Income (SSI) program began in 1974, replacing earlier federal-state public assistance programs for the aged, blind, and disabled.

The federal government also pays a major share of the welfare benefits to needy families with children under the state-administered program called Aid to Families with Dependent Children (AFDC).

## MONTHLY INCOME FLOOR

The SSI program, administered by the Social Security Administration, establishes a basic nationwide monthly payment for persons in financial need who are 65 or over, or blind, or disabled.

This basic monthly payment automatically rises to keep pace with the cost of living. Such an automatic increase of 14.3% went into effect on July 1, 1980, raising the SSI monthly payment to $238.00 for individuals and $357.00 for couples.

Monthly checks sent by the federal government make up the difference between a person's low income and the basic payment amount.

Benefits for eligible recipients are higher in some states because those states add to the federal payments.

## INELIGIBILITY

Supplemental Security Income payments may be suspended, reduced, or terminated in

any of the following circumstances:
1. An increase in income or resources.
2. Confinement in a public institution.
3. Refusal to accept or undergo treatment for drug addiction or alcoholism.
4. Absence from the U.S. for 30 or more consecutive days.
5. Refusal to accept vocational rehabilitation services without good cause.
6. Loss of U.S. citizenship or of permission to live in the U.S.
7. Failure to apply for or obtain benefits under other programs that may be payable to the recipient.
8. Termination of blindness or disability.
9. Death of a person getting SSI payments.

A recipient must be given written notice of any proposed change in his payments and has 60 days to appeal the action.

## WELFARE—AFDC

The nation's largest cash-assistance welfare program—Aid to Families with Dependent Children (AFDC)—was not included in the SSI program. It is operated by the states with federal help. In this program about 10.3 million needy parents and children received about $11.5 billion in support payments in 1979.

Because most of the persons receiving this assistance are mothers and children who have been deserted by fathers, the government has made an effort to find the missing fathers, getting them to provide $1.3 billion in support for their children in 1979.

AFDC grants average $259.37 a month per family.

## PUBLIC ASSISTANCE, AFDC, AND SSI: 1940–1979

Source: Social Security Administration

| YEAR | FEDERAL PAYMENTS | | | | | RECIPIENTS OF BENEFITS | | | |
|------|------------------|--|--|--|--|------------------------|--|--|--|
| | Total [1] | Old-age | Blind | Disabled | AFDC [2] | Old-age | Blind | Disabled | AFDC [2] |
| 1940 | $1,020,115,000 | $ 472,778,000 | $21,735,000 | — | $ 133,393,000 | 2,070,000 | 73,400 | — | 1,222,000 |
| 1945 | 987,934,000 | 725,683,000 | 26,515,000 | — | 149,475,000 | 2,056,000 | 71,500 | — | 943,000 |
| 1950 | 2,354,485,000 | 1,453,917,000 | 52,567,000 | $ 8,042,000 | 547,174,000 | 2,786,000 | 97,500 | 69,000 | 2,233,000 |
| 1955 | 2,516,590,000 | 1,487,991,000 | 67,804,000 | 134,630,000 | 612,209,000 | 2,538,000 | 104,100 | 241,000 | 2,192,000 |
| 1960 | 3,262,769,000 | 1,626,021,000 | 86,080,000 | 236,402,000 | 994,425,000 | 2,305,000 | 106,900 | 369,000 | 3,073,000 |
| 1963 | 3,647,906,000 | 1,610,310,000 | 85,122,000 | 317,656,000 | 1,355,538,000 | 2,152,000 | 96,900 | 464,000 | 3,930,000 |
| 1964 | 3,817,446,000 | 1,606,561,000 | 86,189,000 | 355,643,000 | 1,496,525,000 | 2,120,000 | 95,500 | 509,000 | 4,219,000 |
| 1965 | 3,995,907,000 | 1,594,183,000 | 77,308,000 | 416,765,000 | 1,644,096,000 | 2,087,000 | 85,100 | 557,000 | 4,396,000 |
| 1966 | 4,305,507,000 | 1,630,131,000 | 84,708,000 | 487,212,000 | 1,849,886,000 | 2,073,000 | 83,700 | 588,000 | 4,666,000 |
| 1967 | 4,931,681,000 | 1,698,145,000 | 86,950,000 | 573,575,000 | 2,249,673,000 | 2,073,000 | 82,700 | 646,000 | 5,309,000 |
| 1968 | 5,672,143,000 | 1,673,191,000 | 87,828,000 | 655,792,000 | 2,823,841,000 | 2,027,000 | 80,700 | 702,000 | 6,086,000 |
| 1969 | 6,866,956,000 | 1,746,714,000 | 91,300,000 | 786,757,000 | 3,533,281,000 | 2,074,000 | 80,600 | 803,000 | 7,313,000 |
| 1970 | 8,860,998,000 | 1,866,087,000 | 97,496,000 | 975,504,000 | 4,857,178,000 | 2,082,000 | 81,000 | 935,000 | 9,659,000 |
| 1971 | 10,863,635,000 | 1,919,693,000 | 100,691,000 | 1,185,314,000 | 6,230,447,000 | 2,024,000 | 80,300 | 1,068,000 | 10,653,000 |
| 1972 | 11,199,944,000 | 1,893,982,000 | 104,736,000 | 1,392,896,000 | 7,019,621,000 | 1,934,000 | 79,800 | 1,168,000 | 11,065,000 |
| 1973 | 11,438,246,000 | 1,749,324,000 | 102,978,000 | 1,566,140,000 | 7,291,925,000 | 1,820,000 | 77,900 | 1,275,000 | 10,815,000 |
| 1974 | 14,125,100,000 | 2,414,034,000 | 125,791,000 | 2,556,988,000 | 7,990,787,000 | 2,285,909 | 74,616 | 1,635,539 | 11,006,000 |
| 1975 | 16,446,200,000 | 2,516,515,000 | 132,155,000 | 3,335,028,000 | 9,348,869,000 | 2,307,105 | 74,489 | 1,932,681 | 11,383,000 |
| 1976 | 17,265,300,000 | 2,472,571,000 | 134,060,000 | 3,345,778,000 | 10,140,420,000 | 2,147,697 | 76,366 | 2,011,876 | 11,184,000 |
| 1977 | 16,327,252,000 | 2,363,887,000 | 142,138,000 | 3,628,060,000 | 10,602,611,000 | 2,050,921 | 77,362 | 2,109,409 | 10,761,000 |
| 1978 | 17,111,300,000 | 2,342,080,000 | 148,027,000 | 3,881,531,000 | 10,739,662,000 | 1,967,900 | 77,135 | 2,171,890 | 10,325,000 |
| 1979[3] | 18,435,875,000 | 2,420,720,000 | 162,444,000 | 4,285,559,000 | 11,567,150,000 | 1,871,716 | 77,250 | 2,200,609 | 10,314,985 |

[1] Total includes general assistance federal payments. The total also includes state payments under the Supplemental Security Income program after 1973.  [2] Aid to Families with Dependent Children.  [3] Estimates.

# Space and Astronomy

United Press Int'l.

Astronaut Dr. Anna Fisher takes the controls to practice Space Shuttle launches and landings in the Orbiter Aeroflight Simulator (OAS). Dr. Fisher had been in training for Space Shuttle flights since being accepted as an astronaut candidate in 1978. In May 1980 her husband, Dr. William F. Fisher, was named by NASA as one of 19 new astronaut candidates, making the two the first married couple to become astronauts.

# HIGHLIGHTS: 1980

## SPACE SHUTTLE READY TO FLY

Two years behind schedule, the United States manned space program was ready to resume in 1981 after a $5\frac{1}{2}$-year hiatus. Astronauts were set to explore space once again, this time using the Space Shuttle, a reusable space ship designed to land like an ordinary airplane upon its return to Earth from space journeys.

With the first launch of the Space Shuttle planned for March 1981, officials of the National Aeronautics and Space Administration (NASA) were keeping their fingers crossed in hopes that no new problems would arise that might cause new delays.

The *Columbia*, the ship to be used for the first test flight, will be flown by astronauts John W. Young and Robert L. Crippen. The ship, about the size of a DC-9 jetliner, is covered with more than 30,000 ceramic tiles to protect it from burning up upon reentry from space into the Earth's atmosphere.

In cooperation with the European Space Agency, the Space Shuttle will be used beginning in 1982 to carry a European-made Spacelab in its cargo bay. Scientists will be able to conduct a wide range of experiments in space in such fields as physics, astronomy, and the life sciences.

## PLANS LAID FOR ORBITING TELESCOPE

Scores of universities and other organizations competed in 1980 to be the site of the new Space Telescope Science Institute to be estab-

**HIGHLIGHTS: 1980** *(continued)*

lished by NASA. The institute seems likely to become the source of most new astronomical discoveries during the next decade or so as the agency in charge of the planned Large Space Telescope, which is to be put into orbit in 1983 or 1984 at a cost of about $1.1 billion.

Orbiting 310 miles above the Earth, the 10-ton telescope is expected to enable astronomers to see 350 times as much of the universe as they can presently see from the largest Earth-based telescope. Although the telescope itself will be a comparatively small 95 inches in diameter, it will be able to see much farther than larger telescopes on Earth because of lack of interference by dust and gases in the atmosphere.

The Space Telescope Science Institute will be staffed by 25 astronomers and about 125 other personnel. The institute will decide

what astronomical features will be studied and which visiting astronomers may use the telescope for their own projects.

### NEW MOONS OF SATURN AND JUPITER

The U.S. spacecraft *Voyager 1*, which passed within 77,000 miles of Saturn on Nov. 12, 1980, sent back thousands of photographs. The photos revealed the planet has 15 moons, instead of 11 as earlier believed. Two of the moons seem to be in the same orbit, chasing each other around the planet. The close-up photos also revealed that what previously was thought to be six rings around Saturn actually divide into scores of separate rings, some of which seem to be unexplainably braided. Scientists expect to learn even more about Saturn when the *Voyager 2* spaceship flies by the planet on Aug. 27, 1981.

The 15th and 16th satellites of Jupiter were

"Project Private Enterprise," as Robert Truax calls the 25-foot rocket he built from spare parts, is planned for launch late in 1981. Truax says the rocket will carry a volunteer astronaut into a 10-minute suborbital flight. The rocket engine completed a successful ground test in June 1980. If the launch takes place, it will be the first such spaceflight in a vehicle built entirely with private funds.

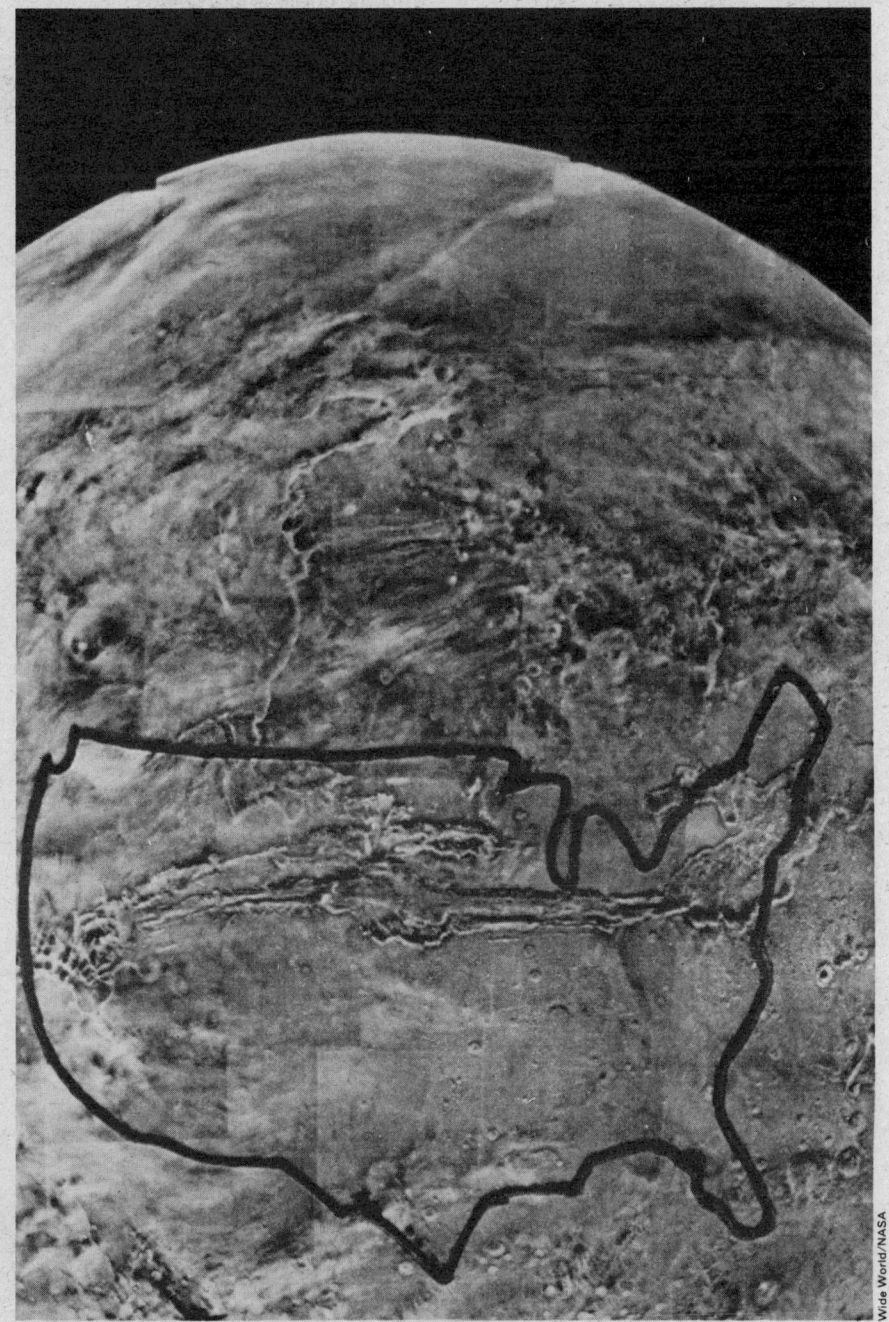

A "Super Grand Canyon" as long as the United States is wide is shown in this mosaic of photos of Mars taken by *Viking Orbiter 1*. The canyon is called Valles Marineris. The photos also revealed that the planet has thin clouds at an altitude of about 18 miles that slowly drift across the Martian sky.

**HIGHLIGHTS: 1980** *(continued)*

discovered in 1980 by Dr. Stephen P. Synnott of the Jet Propulsion Laboratory in Pasadena, Calif. He spotted them while studying photographs taken in March 1979 by the spacecraft *Voyager 1* and *2* during their closest approaches to Jupiter. Synnott made the discoveries while confirming the existence of the 14th moon of the planet, which also was first seen in *Voyager 1* photographs by other researchers in 1979.

## SUPERHOT, SUPERLARGE SUPERBUBBLE

A strange new phenomenon about 6,000 light-years from Earth was discovered in 1980 by scientists studying data received from the X-ray telescope of NASA's High Energy Astronomy Observatory-1 (HEAO-1). What they found was a huge glowing ring of gas about 1,200 light-years in diameter.

Invisible to visual telescopes, the gas bubble is located in the summer constellation Cygnus, the Swan. The discovery was made by Dr. Webster Cash of the University of Colorado and Dr. Philip Charles of the University of California.

Dr. Cash said the sphere contains gas that is superheated to a temperature of 3.5 million degrees Fahrenheit and is filled with enough material to create 10,000 stars the size of the Sun.

## STRANGE COMINGS AND GOINGS

For two decades astronomers have been puzzling over the peculiar motions of a star called SS433.

Part of the time the star seems to be zooming toward the Earth at a speed of nearly 50,000 miles per second. And then suddenly the star begins to move away from the Earth at a similar speed.

Astronomers believe that the object may be emitting two strong jets of gas in opposite directions and that, as the star turns, its gas jets merely give it the appearance of coming and going.

A similar phenomenon on a much grander scale was recently discovered by the National Radio Astronomy Observatory at Socorro, N.M. Found in the distant galaxy 3C449 were jet beams of energy flowing from the core in opposite directions at a speed of about 600 miles per second with each jet extending into space for more than 1 million light-years.

## SHRINKING SUN

Astronomers reported in 1980 that measurements of the Sun compared with similar data recorded in 1715 by the British astronomer Edmund Halley show that it has become smaller and seems to continue to be shrinking. They said the Sun is now one-twentieth of 1% smaller than 265 years ago.

Visitor from outer space looks like a monster alien but actually is a dust particle believed to have been shed from a passing comet. In this photo the dust particle has been magnified about 15,000 times by an electron microscope. Such dust particles collected by NASA aircraft are studied by scientists seeking information on the chemical composition of the materials that formed the solar system about 4.6 billion years ago.

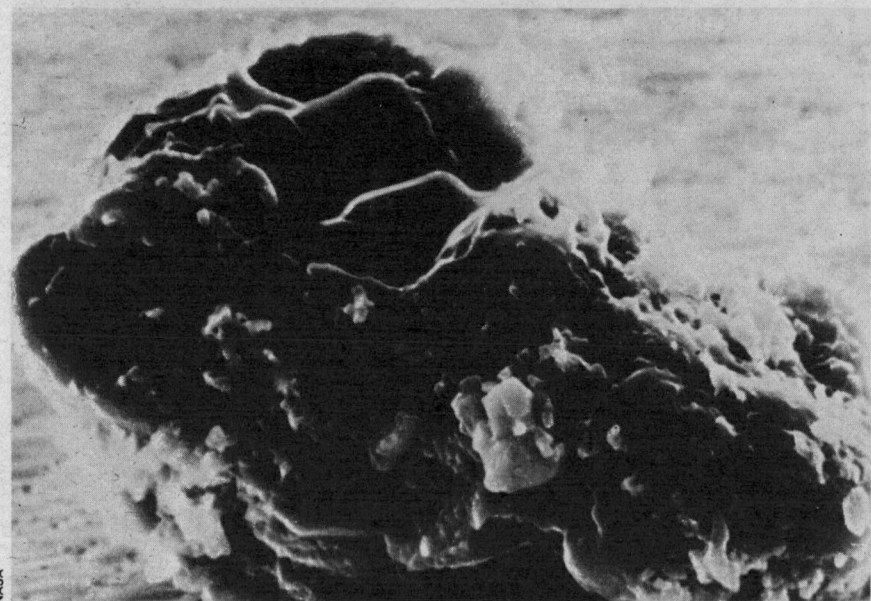

NASA

# SKY-WATCHER'S CALENDAR: 1981

Source: *Astronomical Phenomena*, U.S. Naval Observatory

The calendar below lists various astronomical phenomena that will occur in 1981.

**Evening and Morning Stars.** The planets in the western sky shortly after sunset are *evening stars*, and those seen in the eastern sky shortly before sunrise are *morning stars*.

**Occultation.** When the Moon passes between the Earth and one of the planets or bright stars, this phenomenon is called *occultation*. The occultation of Venus by a crescent moon is depicted on the flags of many Islamic countries.

**Meteor Showers.** Meteors, or shooting stars, are visible on almost any night of the year, but at certain times the Earth encounters large numbers of meteors all moving together along the same orbit. These groups of meteors are named for the constellations from which they seem to radiate.

Meteors are pieces of rock or metal traveling in orbit around the Sun. Scientists estimate that about 1,000 tons of meteorites fall on the Earth every day.

**Comets** are bodies traveling around the Sun in greatly elongated orbits. Most comets can only be seen with telescopes, but from time to time a comet develops a tail of gas or dust that reflects the light from the Sun.

**Conjunction of Planets.** The orbits of the planets work out so that from time to time the planets appear to pass quite close to each other or to the sun.

**Jan. 1–Jan. 26 Mars** seen as evening star.
**Jan. 1–Feb. 25 Venus** seen as morning star.
**Jan. 1–March 26 Jupiter** seen as morning star.
**Jan. 1–March 27 Saturn** seen as morning star.
**Jan. 4 Quadrantid meteor shower** at maximum: About 110 meteors per hour visible, seeming to radiate from handle of Big Dipper.
**Jan. 14 Conjunction of Jupiter and Saturn.**
**Jan. 15–Feb. 12 Mercury** seen as evening star.
**Jan. 20 (2:39 A.M. EST) Full Moon.**
**Jan. 23 Conjunction of Mars and Mercury.**
**Jan. 28 Penumbral eclipse of Moon:** Visible in U.S. and many parts of world; begins at 12:36 A.M. EST and ends at 5:04 A.M. EST.
**Feb. 4–5 Annular eclipse of Sun:** Not visible in U.S.; seen only in Southern Hemisphere.
**Feb. 10 Conjunction of Mars and Mercury.**
**Feb. 18 (5:58 P.M. EST) Full Moon.**
**Feb. 19 Conjunction of Jupiter and Saturn.**
**Feb. 23–April 20 Mercury** seen as morning star.
**March 20 (10:22 A.M. EST) Full Moon.**
**March 20 Spring begins** in Northern Hemisphere with spring equinox at 12:03 P.M. EST when Sun crosses celestial equator on its journey north.
**March 26–Oct. 1 Jupiter** seen as evening star.
**March 27–Sept. 19 Saturn** seen as evening star.
**April 19 (2:59 A.M. EST) Full Moon.**
**April 26 (2 A.M. EST) Daylight-saving time begins.** Set clocks ahead 1 hour.
**May 5 Aquarids meteor shower** at maximum: About 20 per hour visible, seeming to radiate from constellation Aquarius.
**May 5–June 14 Mercury** seen as evening star.
**May 16–Dec. 31 Venus** seen as evening star.
**May 18 (8:04 P.M. EDT) Full Moon.**
**June 8–Dec. 31 Mars** seen as morning star.
**June 9 Conjunction of Venus and Mercury.**
**June 17 (11:04 A.M. EDT) Full Moon.**
**June 21 Summer begins** in Northern Hemisphere as Sun reaches solstice at 7:45 A.M. EDT, with Sun at greatest altitude as seen from north of Tropic of Cancer.
**June 30–Aug. 2 Mercury** seen as morning star.
**July 16–17 Partial eclipse of Moon:** Visible in most of U.S. except northwest; begins on July 16 at 10:05 P.M. EDT and ends on July 17 at 3:28 A.M. EDT.

**July 17 (12:39 A.M. EDT) Full Moon.**
**July 27–28 Aquarids meteor shower** at maximum: About 35 per hour visible, seeming to radiate from constellation Aquarius.
**July 30 Conjunction of Jupiter and Saturn.**
**July 30–31 Total eclipse of Sun:** Only visible in northwestern North America and Asia; begins on July 30 at 9:11 P.M. EDT and ends on July 31 at 2:20 A.M. EDT.
**Aug. 12 Perseid meteor shower** at maximum: About 70 per hour visible, seeming to radiate from constellation Perseus.
**Aug. 15 (12:37 A.M. EDT) Full Moon.**
**Aug. 19–Oct. 13 Mercury** seen as evening star.
**Aug. 25 Conjunction of Venus and Saturn.**
**Aug. 28 Conjunction of Venus and Jupiter.**
**Sept. 10 Conjunction of Saturn and Mercury.**
**Sept. 13 Conjunction of Jupiter and Mercury.**
**Sept. 13 (11:09 P.M. EDT) Full Moon.**
**Sept. 22 Autumn begins** in Northern Hemisphere as Sun reaches equinox at 11:05 P.M. EDT, crossing celestial equator on journey south.
**Oct. 13 (8:49 A.M. EDT) Full Moon.**
**Oct. 21 Orionid meteor shower** at maximum: About 30 per hour visible, seeming to radiate from constellation Orion.
**Oct. 23–Dec. 31 Saturn** seen as morning star.
**Oct. 25 (2 A.M. EDT) Daylight-saving time ends.** Set clocks back 1 hour.
**Oct. 25–Nov. 24 Mercury** seen as morning star.
**Oct. 27–Dec. 31 Jupiter** seen as morning star.
**Nov. 6 Conjunction of Jupiter and Mercury.**
**Nov. 11 (5:26 P.M. EST) Full Moon.**
**Nov. 17 Leonid meteor shower** at maximum: About 10 per hour visible, seeming to radiate from the constellation Leo. Next major shower is due in 1999 with thousands visible.
**Dec. 11 (3:41 A.M. EST) Full Moon.**
**Dec. 14 Geminid meteor shower** at maximum: Over 55 per hour visible, seeming to radiate from constellation Gemini.
**Dec. 16 Venus** at greatest brilliance.
**Dec. 21 Winter begins** in Northern Hemisphere as Sun reaches its solstice at 5:51 P.M. EST, its lowest altitude seen from Northern Hemisphere.
**Dec. 26–Dec. 31 Mercury** seen as evening star.

# SUNRISE AND SUNSET CALENDAR: 1981

Tables on this and the opposite page enable you to find the times for sunrise and sunset. Suggestions for using the tables follow.

## CONVERTING TIME TO A.M. AND P.M.

The times used in the table are based on a 24-hour clock. The time 0 00 is midnight and 12 00 is noon. The times from 0 01 to 11 59 are morning or A.M., and the times from 12 01 to 23 59 are afternoon and evening or P.M.

To convert the times shown to those commonly used with a 12-hour clock, subtract 12 hours from all times from 13 00 to 23 59. Thus 14 12 would be the same as 2:12 P.M., or 20 23 would be 8:23 P.M.

## LATITUDE AND LONGITUDE

To use the table below to find the time of sunrise or sunset, you need to know the latitude and longitude of the place where you live. The latitude and longitude of more than 300 cities are listed on pages 138–140. Use the latitude and longitude of your nearest city listed.

The table below shows the time of events in northern latitudes—those north of the equator. For your convenience a state or city is named in each of the latitude columns. Thus 20 ° N. latitude passes through the state of Hawaii, New Orleans is close to the line of 30 ° N. latitude, and so on.

## CONVERT MEAN TIME TO REAL TIME

The times given in the table are for local *mean* time. This is the time on the standard time meridian that passes through your time zone. The standard time meridians (longitude) are Atlantic 60 °, Eastern 75 °, Central 90 °, Mountain 105 °, Pacific 120 °, and Alaska-Hawaii 150 °.

To convert mean time to real local time, find out the longitude of the place where you live. For each degree of longitude that your home is east of the standard time meridian, subtract 4 minutes from the mean time shown in the table. For each degree of longitude west, add 4 minutes. For example, if you live at 78 ° longitude, you are 3 ° west of the Eastern Standard Time meridian

(78 ° – 75 ° = 3 ° west). Therefore, add 12 minutes to the times shown (3 ° × 4 min. = 12 min.). Thus, for the place where you live a mean time 4 42 shown in the table actually should be changed to 4 54 (4 42 + 0 12 = 4 54).

## INTERPOLATING TIME FOR YOUR LATITUDE

Because the times in the table are given for specific degrees of latitude and it is unlikely that your home lies exactly on one of these parallels, it is necessary also to correct the times by interpolating for your own latitude.

Suppose, for example, that your home has a latitude of 38 °. This falls between the 35 ° and 40 ° columns shown in the table. The difference between 35 ° and 40 ° is 5 ° (40 °– 35 = 5 °), and the difference between 35 ° and 38 ° is 3 ° (38 ° – 35 °= 3 °). To correct the times for your latitude, you would have to subtract 3/5 of the difference between the times shown for 35 ° and 40 °. For example, in the sunrise table for May 6, the difference in time between 35 ° and 40 ° is 10 minutes (5 04 – 4 54 = 10 min.). Three-fifths of 10 minutes is 6 minutes (10 × 3/5= 6). So you would subtract 6 minutes from the time shown for 35 ° to obtain the local mean time for the place where you live (5 04 – 6 min.= 4 58). Note: If the time at the higher latitude is *later* (instead of earlier), you would *add* the difference (rather than subtract).

## STANDARD AND DAYLIGHT TIMES

The times given in the sunrise and sunset table are for the local standard time zone where you live. During those periods of the year in which you use daylight time, add 1 hour to the time shown in a table to change it to daylight time.

## CALCULATING SUNRISE AND SUNSET

Using the suggestions above, correct the times shown in the sunrise and sunset table:
(1) Interpolate them for your latitude.
(2) Convert them from mean time to real time (based on your longitude).
(3) If you are using daylight time, add 1 hour.

## SUNRISE AND SUNSET: 1981
Source: U.S. Naval Observatory.

| | TIME OF SUNRISE | | | | | | TIME OF SUNSET | | | | | |
| DATE | 20 ° N. Latitude (Hawaii) | 30 ° N. Latitude (New Orleans) | 35 ° N. Latitude (Albuquerque) | 40 ° N. Latitude (Philadelphia) | 48 ° N. Latitude (Seattle) | 60 ° N. Latitude (Alaska) | 20 ° N. Latitude (Hawaii) | 30 ° N. Latitude (New Orleans) | 35 ° N. Latitude (Albuquerque) | 40 ° N. Latitude (Philadelphia) | 48 ° N. Latitude (Seattle) | 60 ° N. Latitude (Alaska) |
|---|---|---|---|---|---|---|---|---|---|---|---|---|
| | h m | h m | h m | h m | h m | h m | h m | h m | h m | h m | h m | h m |
| Jan. 10 | 6 37 | 6 57 | 7 09 | 7 22 | 7 48 | 8 55 | 17 38 | 17 18 | 17 07 | 16 54 | 16 28 | 15 21 |
| Jan. 14 | 6 38 | 6 57 | 7 08 | 7 21 | 7 46 | 8 49 | 17 41 | 17 22 | 17 11 | 16 58 | 16 33 | 15 29 |
| Jan. 18 | 6 38 | 6 56 | 7 07 | 7 19 | 7 43 | 8 43 | 17 43 | 17 25 | 17 14 | 17 02 | 16 38 | 15 39 |
| Jan. 22 | 6 38 | 6 55 | 7 05 | 7 17 | 7 39 | 8 36 | 17 46 | 17 28 | 17 18 | 17 07 | 16 44 | 15 48 |
| Jan. 26 | 6 37 | 6 54 | 7 03 | 7 14 | 7 35 | 8 28 | 17 48 | 17 32 | 17 23 | 17 12 | 16 50 | 15 58 |
| Feb. 3 | 6 35 | 6 49 | 6 57 | 7 07 | 7 25 | 8 09 | 17 53 | 17 39 | 17 31 | 17 21 | 17 03 | 16 19 |
| Feb. 7 | 6 33 | 6 47 | 6 54 | 7 03 | 7 20 | 7 59 | 17 55 | 17 42 | 17 35 | 17 26 | 17 09 | 16 30 |
| Feb. 11 | 6 31 | 6 43 | 6 50 | 6 58 | 7 13 | 7 49 | 17 57 | 17 45 | 17 39 | 17 31 | 17 16 | 16 40 |
| Feb. 15 | 6 29 | 6 40 | 6 46 | 6 53 | 7 07 | 7 38 | 17 59 | 17 49 | 17 43 | 17 36 | 17 22 | 16 51 |
| Feb. 19 | 6 27 | 6 36 | 6 42 | 6 48 | 7 00 | 7 27 | 18 01 | 17 52 | 17 46 | 17 40 | 17 29 | 17 01 |
| Feb. 23 | 6 24 | 6 32 | 6 37 | 6 42 | 6 53 | 7 16 | 18 03 | 17 55 | 17 50 | 17 45 | 17 35 | 17 12 |
| Mar. 3 | 6 18 | 6 24 | 6 27 | 6 31 | 6 38 | 6 53 | 18 06 | 18 00 | 17 57 | 17 54 | 17 47 | 17 32 |
| Mar. 7 | 6 15 | 6 20 | 6 22 | 6 25 | 6 30 | 6 41 | 18 07 | 18 03 | 18 01 | 17 58 | 17 53 | 17 42 |

| DATE | TIME OF SUNRISE | | | | | | TIME OF SUNSET | | | | | |
|---|---|---|---|---|---|---|---|---|---|---|---|---|
| | 20° N. Latitude (Hawaii) | 30° N. Latitude (New Orleans) | 35° N. Latitude (Albuquerque) | 40° N. Latitude (Philadelphia) | 48° N. Latitude (Seattle) | 60° N. Latitude (Alaska) | 20° N. Latitude (Hawaii) | 30° N. Latitude (New Orleans) | 35° N. Latitude (Albuquerque) | 40° N. Latitude (Philadelphia) | 48° N. Latitude (Seattle) | 60° N. Latitude (Alaska) |
| | h m | h m | h m | h m | h m | h m | h m | h m | h m | h m | h m | h m |
| Mar. 11.. | 6 12 | 6 15 | 6 17 | 6 18 | 6 22 | 6 29 | 18 08 | 18 06 | 18 04 | 18 02 | 17 59 | 17 52 |
| Mar. 15.. | 6 09 | 6 10 | 6 11 | 6 12 | 6 14 | 6 17 | 18 10 | 18 08 | 18 07 | 18 07 | 18 05 | 18 02 |
| Mar. 19.. | 6 05 | 6 05 | 6 05 | 6 05 | 6 05 | 6 05 | 18 11 | 18 11 | 18 11 | 18 11 | 18 11 | 18 12 |
| Mar. 23.. | 6 02 | 6 01 | 6 00 | 5 59 | 5 57 | 5 53 | 18 12 | 18 13 | 18 14 | 18 15 | 18 17 | 18 22 |
| Mar. 27.. | 5 58 | 5 56 | 5 54 | 5 52 | 5 49 | 5 41 | 18 13 | 18 16 | 18 17 | 18 19 | 18 23 | 18 31 |
| Apr. 4.. | 5 51 | 5 46 | 5 43 | 5 40 | 5 33 | 5 17 | 18 15 | 18 20 | 18 24 | 18 27 | 18 34 | 18 51 |
| Apr. 8.. | 5 48 | 5 41 | 5 38 | 5 33 | 5 25 | 5 05 | 18 16 | 18 23 | 18 27 | 18 31 | 18 40 | 19 01 |
| Apr. 12.. | 5 45 | 5 37 | 5 32 | 5 27 | 5 17 | 4 53 | 18 17 | 18 25 | 18 30 | 18 35 | 18 46 | 19 10 |
| Apr. 16.. | 5 41 | 5 32 | 5 27 | 5 21 | 5 09 | 4 41 | 18 18 | 18 28 | 18 33 | 18 39 | 18 51 | 19 20 |
| Apr. 20.. | 5 38 | 5 28 | 5 22 | 5 15 | 5 02 | 4 29 | 18 20 | 18 30 | 18 36 | 18 43 | 18 57 | 19 30 |
| Apr. 24.. | 5 35 | 5 24 | 5 17 | 5 10 | 4 54 | 4 18 | 18 21 | 18 33 | 18 40 | 18 47 | 19 03 | 19 40 |
| May 2.. | 5 30 | 5 16 | 5 08 | 4 59 | 4 41 | 3 56 | 18 24 | 18 38 | 18 46 | 18 55 | 19 14 | 20 00 |
| May 6.. | 5 28 | 5 13 | 5 04 | 4 54 | 4 34 | 3 45 | 18 25 | 18 40 | 18 49 | 18 59 | 19 20 | 20 10 |
| May 10.. | 5 26 | 5 10 | 5 01 | 4 50 | 4 28 | 3 35 | 18 27 | 18 43 | 18 53 | 19 03 | 19 25 | 20 20 |
| May 14.. | 5 24 | 5 07 | 4 57 | 4 46 | 4 23 | 3 25 | 18 28 | 18 46 | 18 56 | 19 07 | 19 31 | 20 29 |
| May 18.. | 5 23 | 5 05 | 4 54 | 4 42 | 4 18 | 3 16 | 18 30 | 18 48 | 18 59 | 19 11 | 19 36 | 20 39 |
| May 22.. | 5 22 | 5 03 | 4 52 | 4 39 | 4 13 | 3 07 | 18 32 | 18 51 | 19 02 | 19 15 | 19 41 | 20 47 |
| May 26.. | 5 21 | 5 01 | 4 50 | 4 36 | 4 09 | 2 59 | 18 33 | 18 53 | 19 05 | 19 18 | 19 45 | 20 56 |
| June 3.. | 5 20 | 4 59 | 4 47 | 4 32 | 4 04 | 2 47 | 18 36 | 18 57 | 19 10 | 19 24 | 19 53 | 21 11 |
| June 7.. | 5 20 | 4 58 | 4 46 | 4 31 | 4 02 | 2 42 | 18 38 | 18 59 | 19 12 | 19 26 | 19 56 | 21 17 |
| June 11.. | 5 20 | 4 58 | 4 45 | 4 31 | 4 00 | 2 38 | 18 39 | 19 01 | 19 14 | 19 29 | 19 59 | 21 21 |
| June 15.. | 5 20 | 4 58 | 4 45 | 4 30 | 4 00 | 2 36 | 18 40 | 19 02 | 19 15 | 19 30 | 20 01 | 21 25 |
| June 19.. | 5 21 | 4 59 | 4 46 | 4 31 | 4 00 | 2 35 | 18 42 | 19 04 | 19 17 | 19 32 | 20 03 | 21 27 |
| June 23.. | 5 22 | 5 00 | 4 47 | 4 32 | 4 01 | 2 36 | 18 42 | 19 04 | 19 17 | 19 33 | 20 03 | 21 28 |
| July 1.. | 5 24 | 5 02 | 4 49 | 4 35 | 4 04 | 2 42 | 18 43 | 19 05 | 19 18 | 19 33 | 20 03 | 21 25 |
| July 5.. | 5 25 | 5 04 | 4 51 | 4 37 | 4 07 | 2 47 | 18 44 | 19 05 | 19 17 | 19 32 | 20 02 | 21 21 |
| July 9.. | 5 27 | 5 06 | 4 53 | 4 39 | 4 10 | 2 53 | 18 43 | 19 04 | 19 17 | 19 31 | 20 00 | 21 17 |
| July 13.. | 5 28 | 5 08 | 4 56 | 4 42 | 4 14 | 2 59 | 18 43 | 19 03 | 19 15 | 19 29 | 19 57 | 21 11 |
| July 17.. | 5 30 | 5 10 | 4 58 | 4 45 | 4 18 | 3 07 | 18 42 | 19 02 | 19 13 | 19 27 | 19 54 | 21 04 |
| July 21.. | 5 31 | 5 12 | 5 01 | 4 48 | 4 22 | 3 15 | 18 41 | 19 00 | 19 11 | 19 24 | 19 50 | 20 56 |
| July 25.. | 5 33 | 5 15 | 5 04 | 4 52 | 4 27 | 3 24 | 18 40 | 18 58 | 19 08 | 19 21 | 19 45 | 20 47 |
| Aug. 2.. | 5 36 | 5 19 | 5 10 | 4 59 | 4 37 | 3 42 | 18 37 | 18 53 | 19 02 | 19 13 | 19 34 | 20 28 |
| Aug. 6.. | 5 37 | 5 22 | 5 13 | 5 03 | 4 42 | 3 52 | 18 34 | 18 49 | 18 58 | 19 08 | 19 28 | 20 18 |
| Aug. 10.. | 5 38 | 5 24 | 5 16 | 5 06 | 4 48 | 4 02 | 18 32 | 18 46 | 18 54 | 19 03 | 19 22 | 20 07 |
| Aug. 14.. | 5 40 | 5 27 | 5 19 | 5 10 | 4 53 | 4 11 | 18 29 | 18 42 | 18 50 | 18 58 | 19 15 | 19 56 |
| Aug. 18.. | 5 41 | 5 29 | 5 22 | 5 14 | 4 58 | 4 21 | 18 27 | 18 38 | 18 45 | 18 53 | 19 08 | 19 45 |
| Aug. 22.. | 5 42 | 5 31 | 5 25 | 5 18 | 5 04 | 4 31 | 18 24 | 18 34 | 18 40 | 18 47 | 19 01 | 19 33 |
| Aug. 26.. | 5 43 | 5 33 | 5 28 | 5 22 | 5 09 | 4 40 | 18 20 | 18 30 | 18 35 | 18 41 | 18 53 | 19 22 |
| Sept. 3.. | 5 45 | 5 38 | 5 34 | 5 29 | 5 20 | 4 59 | 18 14 | 18 20 | 18 24 | 18 29 | 18 37 | 18 58 |
| Sept. 7.. | 5 46 | 5 40 | 5 37 | 5 33 | 5 26 | 5 09 | 18 10 | 18 15 | 18 19 | 18 22 | 18 29 | 18 46 |
| Sept. 11.. | 5 46 | 5 42 | 5 40 | 5 37 | 5 31 | 5 18 | 18 06 | 18 11 | 18 13 | 18 16 | 18 21 | 18 34 |
| Sept. 15.. | 5 47 | 5 44 | 5 43 | 5 41 | 5 37 | 5 27 | 18 03 | 18 06 | 18 07 | 18 09 | 18 13 | 18 22 |
| Sept. 19.. | 5 48 | 5 47 | 5 46 | 5 44 | 5 42 | 5 37 | 17 59 | 18 01 | 18 01 | 18 02 | 18 04 | 18 09 |
| Sept. 23.. | 5 49 | 5 49 | 5 48 | 5 48 | 5 48 | 5 46 | 17 55 | 17 56 | 17 56 | 17 56 | 17 56 | 17 57 |
| Oct. 1.. | 5 51 | 5 53 | 5 55 | 5 56 | 5 59 | 6 05 | 17 48 | 17 46 | 17 44 | 17 43 | 17 40 | 17 33 |
| Oct. 5.. | 5 52 | 5 56 | 5 58 | 6 00 | 6 04 | 6 15 | 17 45 | 17 41 | 17 39 | 17 36 | 17 32 | 17 21 |
| Oct. 9.. | 5 53 | 5 58 | 6 01 | 6 04 | 6 10 | 6 24 | 17 41 | 17 36 | 17 33 | 17 30 | 17 24 | 17 09 |
| Oct. 13.. | 5 54 | 6 00 | 6 04 | 6 08 | 6 16 | 6 34 | 17 38 | 17 32 | 17 28 | 17 24 | 17 16 | 16 57 |
| Oct. 17.. | 5 55 | 6 03 | 6 07 | 6 12 | 6 22 | 6 44 | 17 35 | 17 27 | 17 23 | 17 18 | 17 08 | 16 46 |
| Oct. 21.. | 5 57 | 6 06 | 6 11 | 6 17 | 6 28 | 6 54 | 17 32 | 17 23 | 17 18 | 17 12 | 17 01 | 16 34 |
| Oct. 25.. | 5 58 | 6 09 | 6 14 | 6 21 | 6 34 | 7 04 | 17 30 | 17 19 | 17 13 | 17 07 | 16 54 | 16 23 |
| Nov. 2.. | 6 02 | 6 15 | 6 22 | 6 30 | 6 46 | 7 24 | 17 25 | 17 12 | 17 05 | 16 57 | 16 40 | 16 02 |
| Nov. 6.. | 6 04 | 6 18 | 6 26 | 6 35 | 6 52 | 7 35 | 17 23 | 17 09 | 17 01 | 16 52 | 16 34 | 15 52 |
| Nov. 10.. | 6 06 | 6 21 | 6 29 | 6 39 | 6 59 | 7 45 | 17 22 | 17 07 | 16 58 | 16 48 | 16 29 | 15 42 |
| Nov. 14.. | 6 08 | 6 24 | 6 33 | 6 44 | 7 05 | 7 55 | 17 21 | 17 05 | 16 55 | 16 45 | 16 24 | 15 33 |
| Nov. 18.. | 6 11 | 6 27 | 6 37 | 6 48 | 7 11 | 8 05 | 17 20 | 17 03 | 16 53 | 16 42 | 16 19 | 15 25 |
| Nov. 22.. | 6 13 | 6 31 | 6 41 | 6 53 | 7 16 | 8 15 | 17 19 | 17 01 | 16 51 | 16 39 | 16 15 | 15 17 |
| Nov. 26.. | 6 15 | 6 34 | 6 45 | 6 57 | 7 22 | 8 24 | 17 19 | 17 00 | 16 49 | 16 37 | 16 12 | 15 10 |
| Dec. 4.. | 6 21 | 6 40 | 6 52 | 7 05 | 7 32 | 8 41 | 17 20 | 17 00 | 16 48 | 16 35 | 16 08 | 14 59 |
| Dec. 8.. | 6 23 | 6 43 | 6 55 | 7 09 | 7 37 | 8 48 | 17 21 | 17 00 | 16 48 | 16 35 | 16 07 | 14 56 |
| Dec. 12.. | 6 25 | 6 46 | 6 58 | 7 12 | 7 41 | 8 54 | 17 22 | 17 01 | 16 49 | 16 35 | 16 07 | 14 54 |
| Dec. 16.. | 6 28 | 6 49 | 7 01 | 7 15 | 7 44 | 8 58 | 17 24 | 17 02 | 16 50 | 16 36 | 16 07 | 14 53 |
| Dec. 20.. | 6 30 | 6 51 | 7 04 | 7 18 | 7 46 | 9 01 | 17 25 | 17 04 | 16 52 | 16 37 | 16 09 | 14 54 |
| Dec. 24.. | 6 32 | 6 53 | 7 05 | 7 20 | 7 48 | 9 03 | 17 27 | 17 06 | 16 54 | 16 40 | 16 11 | 14 56 |
| Jan. 1(82) | 6 35 | 6 56 | 7 08 | 7 22 | 7 50 | 9 03 | 17 32 | 17 11 | 16 59 | 16 45 | 16 17 | 15 05 |
| Jan. 5(82) | 6 36 | 6 57 | 7 09 | 7 22 | 7 50 | 9 00 | 17 35 | 17 14 | 17 02 | 16 49 | 16 21 | 15 11 |

NASA

Although the surface of the planet Venus cannot be seen because of its continuous cloud cover, radar measurements of the planet by NASA's *Pioneer Venus Orbiter* reveal that there are three mountainous landmasses. In this artist's conception, Ishtar Terra, *right*, is about the size of Australia. Aphrodite Terra, *bottom center*, is about half as large as Africa. Beta Regio, *top*, is a huge chain of volcanoes about 1,300 miles in length.

# EXPLORING THE SOLAR SYSTEM

The solar system includes the Sun and all the celestial objects that orbit it—planets, asteroids, meteors, comets, dust, gas, and man-made satellites. The nine planets in order of distance from the Sun are Mercury, Venus, Earth, Mars, Jupiter, Saturn, Uranus, Neptune, and Pluto.

Since the advent of the Space Age, space probes have been sent to the Sun and the planets, greatly expanding knowledge about man's neighbors in space.

## FACTS ABOUT THE SUN

**Distance from Earth:** Closest, 91.4 million miles; farthest, 94.5 million miles; average, 92.9 million miles.

**Diameter:** About 864,000 miles, or more than 109 times the width of Earth.

**Source of life on Earth:** All life on Earth depends on heat and light from the Sun. Sunlight travels at the speed of light, reaching Earth about 8 minutes and 20 seconds after being radiated from the Sun.

**Speed:** The Sun travels around the center of the Milky Way at about 150 miles per second, taking 225 million years to make one orbit around the galaxy.

**Rotation:** The Sun revolves on its axis from west to east, like Earth. It makes a complete revolution in about 30 days. Because the Sun is a ball of gases, its equator rotates faster than its polar regions.

**Age:** About 4.6 billion years. This means that in the lifetime of the Sun, it has only revolved around the center of the Milky Way galaxy 20 times. Thus, if we consider that one revolution is the equivalent of one year in the Sun's life, the Sun would be only 20 years old.

## THE SUN

One of the many stars in the Milky Way galaxy, the Sun has a surface temperature of about 11,000 ° F. The main form of energy radiating from this sphere of seething gas is light. Other radiations include gamma rays, X rays, infrared rays, cosmic rays, and radio waves. The Sun also sprays out what is known as the *solar wind,* a continuous flow of charged particles, protons and electrons.

The Sun is essentially a huge ball of hydrogen. In its interior, where temperatures approach 25,000,000 ° F., this element is converted into helium, releasing immense quantities of energy.

The Sun has polar caps, as have Earth and Mars. However, with a temperature of about 1,800,000 ° F., the caps are not frozen ice.

The atmosphere of the Sun consists of several layers of gases. The layer next to the surface, about 10,000 miles thick, is called the *chromosphere.* Enveloping this layer are the inner and outer *coronas.* You can see the corona during a total solar eclipse.

Sunspots are dark, turbulent regions often seen within larger, brighter areas known as *flocculi* on the surface of the Sun. The presence of a sunspot is frequently accompanied by a surge of energy called a *solar flare.* They often disrupt radio communications.

## MERCURY

Mercury is the planet nearest the Sun. It is also the smallest, fastest, and hottest.

Because Mercury orbits between Earth and the Sun, it is seen in phases like those of the Moon. Its eccentric orbit makes it appear largest when in the crescent phases and much smaller when it is full. It has many craters, like those of the Moon and Mars.

Mercury's atmosphere is made up largely of the gas helium.

## VENUS

Venus is the planet closest to Earth. After the Sun and Moon, it is the brightest object in our view.

The diameter of Venus is only about 400 miles less than that of the Earth.

Venus revolves about the Sun in a nearly circular orbit at a distance of 67,200,000 miles. When Venus is closest to Earth, it is about 26,000,000 miles away.

The U.S. and the Soviet Union have sent

## NATURAL SATELLITES OF THE PLANETS

An (R) following the satellite's name indicates that it revolves in a retrograde manner, opposite to the direction of its planet's rotation. The numbers given the satellites are noted, but the satellites are listed in the order of their distance from their primary planet.

| PLANETS AND SATELLITES | AVERAGE DISTANCE FROM PLANET (in miles) | DIAMETER (in miles) | PERIOD OF REVOLUTION AROUND PLANET | | | APPARENT MAGNITUDE | DISCOVERER AND DATE |
|---|---|---|---|---|---|---|---|
| | | | days | hrs. | mins. | | |
| **EARTH** | | | | | | | |
| Moon .......... | 238,866 | 2,057.6 | 27 | 7 | 43 | –12.7 | — |
| **MARS** | | | | | | | |
| Phobos.......... | 5,825 | 5 | 0 | 57 | 39 | 11.5 | Asaph Hall, 1877 |
| Deimos.......... | 14,580 | 3 | 1 | 6 | 18 | 12.5 | Asaph Hall, 1877 |
| **JUPITER** | | | | | | | |
| XVI 1979 J-3 ... | 35,000 | 25 | 0 | 7 | 4 | — | Stephen P. Synnott, 1980 |
| XIV 1979 J-1 ... | 36,000 | 19–25 | 0 | 7 | 8 | — | Voyager 1, 1979 |
| XV 1979 J-2 .... | 93,900 | 43–50 | 0 | 16 | 16 | — | Stephen P. Synnott, 1980 |
| V Amalthea ..... | 112,779 | 149 | 0 | 11 | 57 | 13.0 | Edward Barnard, 1892 |
| I Io ............ | 262,219 | 2,256 | 1 | 18 | 28 | 5.5 | Galileo, 1610 |
| II Europa........ | 417,189 | 1,942 | 3 | 13 | 14 | 5.8 | Galileo, 1610 |
| III Ganymede .... | 665,489 | 3,278 | 7 | 3 | 43 | 5.1 | Galileo, 1610 |
| IV Callisto ...... | 1,170,663 | 2,994 | 16 | 16 | 32 | 6.3 | Galileo. 1610 |
| XIII Leda ........ | 6,893,492 | 4 | 239 | — | — | 20.0 | Charles Kowal, 1974 |
| VI Himalia....... | 7,137,691 | 106 | 251 | — | — | 14.0 | Charles Perrine, 1904 |
| VII Elara ........ | 7,299,247 | 50 | 260 | — | — | 18.0 | Charles Perrine, 1905 |
| X Lysithea....... | 7,370,084 | 9 | 264 | — | — | 19.0 | Seth Nicholson, 1938 |
| XII Ananke (R) ... | 13,204,137 | 3.7–17 | 631 | — | — | 19.0 | Seth Nicholson, 1951 |
| XI Carme (R) .... | 14,005,706 | 5–25 | 692 | — | — | 19.0 | Seth Nicholson, 1938 |
| VIII Pasiphae (R) . | 14,608,436 | 5–28.5 | 739 | — | — | 18.5 | P.J. Melotte, 1908 |
| IX Sinope (R) .... | 14,707,856 | 3.7–22 | 758 | — | — | 19.0 | Seth Nicholson, 1914 |
| **SATURN** | | | | | | | |
| XV ............. | 83,500 | 100 | 0 | 14 | 20 | — | Voyager 1, 1980 |
| XIV ............. | 86,000 | 310 | 0 | 14 | 43 | — | Voyager 1, 1980 |
| XIII ............. | 87,600 | 370 | 0 | 15 | 5 | — | Voyager 1, 1980 |
| X ............. | 93,000 | 440 | 0 | 16 | 40 | — | Voyager 1, 1980 |
| XI ............. | 93,000 | 440 | 0 | 16 | 40 | — | Pioneer 11, 1980 |
| I Mimas ........ | 115,624 | 218 | 0 | 22 | 37 | 12.1 | Sir William Herschel, 1789 |
| II Enceladus ..... | 147,886 | 324 | 1 | 8 | 53 | 11.8 | Sir William Herschel, 1789 |
| III Tethys........ | 183,118 | 634 | 1 | 21 | 18 | 10.3 | Giovanni Cassini, 1684 |
| IV Dione ........ | 234,506 | 684 | 2 | 17 | 41 | 10.4 | Giovanni Cassini, 1684 |
| XII ............. | 234,506 | 50 | 2 | 17 | 44 | — | Voyager 1, 1980 |
| V Rhea ......... | 327,463 | 932 | 4 | 12 | 25 | 9.8 | Giovanni Cassini, 1672 |
| VI Titan ........ | 759,316 | 3,624 | 15 | 23 | 20 | 8.4 | Christian Huygens, 1655 |
| VII Hyperion ..... | 922,115 | 187 | 21 | 7 | 40 | 14.2 | G.P. & W.C. Bond, 1848 |
| VIII Iapetus....... | 2,213,324 | 994 | 79 | 22 | 6 | 11.0 | Giovanni Cassini, 1671 |
| IX Phoebe (R) ... | 8,052,971 | 50 | 550 | 10 | 50 | 16.5 | William Pickering, 1898 |
| **URANUS** | | | | | | | |
| V Miranda........ | 80,700 | 124 | 1 | 9 | 56 | 16.9 | Gerard Kuiper, 1948 |
| I Ariel .......... | 119,100 | 370 | 2 | 12 | 29 | 14.0 | William Lassell, 1851 |
| II Umbriel ....... | 165,900 | 250 | 4 | 3 | 28 | 15.0 | William Lassell, 1851 |
| III Titania ....... | 272,100 | 620 | 8 | 16 | 56 | 13.8 | Sir William Herschel, 1787 |
| IV Oberon ....... | 363,900 | 500 | 13 | 11 | 7 | 14.0 | Sir William Herschel, 1787 |
| **NEPTUNE** | | | | | | | |
| Triton (R) ....... | 219,500 | 2,300 | 5 | 21 | 3 | 13.6 | William Lassell, 1846 |
| Nereid .......... | 3,461,000 | 200? | 359 | 10 | — | 19.7 | Gerard Kuiper, 1949 |
| **PLUTO** | | | | | | | |
| Charon.......... | 12,000 | 735 | 6 | 9 | 17 | 17.0 | James W. Christy, 1978 |

**EXPLORING THE SOLAR SYSTEM** *(continued)*

many unmanned spaceships to explore the planet, whose surface is obscured from view by a heavy cloud layer. Using radar to penetrate the clouds, the spaceships have discovered that the surface is much more rugged than that of Earth, with higher mountains and deeper canyons.

Incapable of supporting life as known on Earth, Venus has a surface temperature of 854 ° F. that seems to be evenly distributed in all regions. Huge thunderstorms apparently rage continually.

Although the clouds have winds of 100 to 200 mph, winds at the surface of the planet were measured at only 10 mph.

Sulfur gases in the planet's atmosphere seem to burn and glow continuously from the intense heat.

### MARS

Mars is half again as far from the Sun as is Earth, and thus is colder. Its summer noon temperature reaches only about 80 ° F. at its equator.

The planet takes 1.88 years to orbit the Sun, so its seasons are about twice as long as those on Earth. It is inclined 24 ° to its orbit, nearly the same as is Earth.

A day on Mars is just slightly longer than Earth's—24 hours and 37 minutes. The planet, which is 4,218 miles in diameter, has about 11% of Earth's mass and is of lower density—an object of 100 pounds on Earth would weigh a mere 38 pounds on Mars.

Circling Mars are two small satellites, Phobos *(fear)* and Deimos *(panic)*. Deimos orbits Mars once a day, but Phobos makes almost three daily revolutions.

Two U.S. *Viking* spacecraft landed on Mars in 1976, sending back the first photos and data from the surface of the planet.

The *Viking I* lander reported in July 1976 that the Martian atmosphere is composed of 95% carbon dioxide, 2% to 3% nitrogen, 1% to 2% argon-40, and 0.3% oxygen.

The planet's low atmospheric pressure prevents water from remaining on the surface, except as ice in the northern polar region.

There are regions of quite different geological character on Mars: vast valleys and "stream" channels, towering mountains, and some densely cratered Moon-like areas. The 1972 photo map of Mars, produced from *Mariner 9* data, revealed such remarkable features as Nix Olympica, a volcanic mountain 300 miles wide and 10½ miles high. The photos also showed channels apparently once cut by rivers of water on the planet's surface.

Mars is best seen when opposite the Sun in the sky. Because of the motion of Mars and Earth about the Sun, this point at "opposition" occurs every two years and two months—next in June 1982.

### ASTEROIDS

About 20,000 to 30,000 asteroids, or minor planets, circle the Sun, mostly in orbits that lie between those of Mars and Jupiter. The first and largest asteroid, Ceres, was discovered on Jan. 1, 1801, by Italian astronomer Giuseppe Piazzi.

All the asteroids are smaller than the Moon. Diameters of the larger asteroids include: Ceres, 600 miles; Pallas, 350 miles; Vesta, 310 miles; Hygeia, 240 miles; Interamnia, 200 miles; and Davida, 170 miles.

Some scientists believe that asteroids and comets are pieces of a large planet that exploded about 6 million years ago.

### JUPITER

The largest planet, Jupiter has a volume that would engulf 1,347 Earths. Its mass is twice that of the rest of the planets combined.

Scientists believe there is a possibility that some forms of life exist in Jupiter's atmosphere, which has zones of water vapor at temperatures comparable to those on Earth.

Jupiter rotates once in somewhat less than 10 hours. Because of this rapid rotation—fastest of all the planets—Jupiter is oblate, its poles are flattened, and its equator bulges. Jupiter has 16 moons. Ganymede, the larg-

## PLANETS OF OUR SOLAR SYSTEM

| PLANET | DIAMETER | MASS | DENSITY | GRAVITY | ESCAPE VELOCITY | INCLI- NATION OF AXIS | ALBEDO OR REFLEC- TIVITY | SPEED IN SOLAR ORBIT |
|---|---|---|---|---|---|---|---|---|
| | (in miles) | (Earth=1) | (water=1) | (Earth=1) | (in miles) per sec.) | | | (in miles per sec.) |
| MERCURY | 3,100 | 0.056 | 5.13 | 0.36 | 2.6 | unknown | 0.056 | 29.8 |
| VENUS | 7,519 | 0.815 | 5.26 | 0.87 | 6.4 | 6° | 0.76 | 21.8 |
| EARTH | 7,926 | 1.00 | 5.52 | 1.00 | 7.0 | 23°27' | 0.36 | 18.5 |
| MARS | 4,218 | 0.108 | 3.94 | 0.38 | 3.1 | 24° | 0.16 | 15.0 |
| JUPITER | 88,732 | 317.9 | 1.33 | 2.61 | 37.9 | 3°1' | 0.73 | 8.1 |
| SATURN | 74,316 | 95.2 | 0.69 | 0.90 | 23.0 | 26°7' | 0.76 | 6.0 |
| URANUS | 29,200 | 14.6 | 1.56 | 1.07 | 13.7 | 97°9' | 0.93 | 4.2 |
| NEPTUNE | 27,700 | 17.3 | 2.27 | 1.41 | 15.5 | 28°8' | 0.84 | 3.4 |
| PLUTO | 2,160-1,750 | 0.06? | 4.00? | 0.3? | unknown | unknown | 0.14? | 3.0 |

## PLANETARY EXPLORATION BY U.S. SPACECRAFT

| PLANET | DISTANCE[1] | SPACECRAFT | ENCOUNTER |
|---|---|---|---|
| Venus | 26,000,000 | Mariner 2 | Flyby: Dec. 14, 1962; returns surface temperature measurements |
| | | Mariner 5 | Flyby: Oct. 19, 1967; closes within 2,480 miles of planet |
| | | Mariner 10 | Flybys: March 29, 1974; Sept. 21, 1974; March 16, 1975 |
| | | Pioneer Venus 1 | Eight-month orbiting of planet, beginning Dec. 5, 1978 |
| | | Pioneer Venus 2 | Five probes sent into Venus' atmosphere on Dec. 9, 1978 |
| Mars | 35,000,000 | Mariner 4 | Flyby: July 14, 1965; sends first close photos from 6,118 miles |
| | | Mariner 6 | Flyby: July 31, 1969 |
| | | Mariner 7 | Flyby: Aug. 5, 1969 |
| | | Mariner 9 | Orbited Mars from Nov. 13, 1971, to Oct. 27, 1972 |
| | | Viking 1 | Lander 1 touched down on planet's surface on July 20, 1976; sends first photos from surface of Mars |
| | | Viking 2 | Lander 2 touched down on Sept. 3, 1976; analysis of soil samples failed to prove or disprove existence of microbial life |
| Mercury | 48,000,000 | Mariner 10 | Flybys: March 29, 1974; Sept. 21, 1974; March 16, 1975 |
| Jupiter | 366,000,000 | Pioneer 10 | Flyby: Dec. 4, 1973 |
| | | Pioneer 11 | Flyby: Dec. 5, 1974 |
| | | Voyager 1 | Flyby: March 5, 1979; discovered ring around planet and 3 new moons |
| | | Voyager 2 | Flyby: July 9, 1979 |
| Saturn | 743,000,000 | Pioneer 11 | Flyby: Sept. 1, 1979; discovered new 11th moon and new rings |
| | | Voyager 1 | Flyby: Nov. 12, 1980; discovered 4 new moons and many rings |
| | | Voyager 2 | Flyby: scheduled Aug. 27, 1981 |
| Uranus | 1,606,000,000 | Voyager 2 | Flyby: scheduled Jan. 30, 1986 |

[1] Minimum distance from Earth in miles.

est, is bigger than Mercury.

Approaching Jupiter from space, an observer would see a huge yellowish globe striped with multicolored dark and light bands—all in a kind of mottled motion that reveals a turbulent cloud layer.

The planet also is surrounded by a thin ring of rock and dust particles.

The smooth surface of the planet is a gigantic sea of compressed hydrogen and helium. Jupiter has a central rocky core surrounded by liquid metallic hydrogen at a temperature of 54,000 ° F., about six times the heat of the surface of the Sun. Because of its internal heat, Jupiter gives off more heat than it receives from the Sun.

Clouds of methane, ammonia, water, and other compounds float in bands around the planet, whipped along by winds of 200 mph.

Hydrogen makes up more than 76% of Jupiter's mass. Helium is about 22%.

Photos sent back by space probes indicate Jupiter's Great Red Spot—an oval about 30,000 miles long and 7,000 miles wide—is a huge hurricane-like storm.

### SATURN

Some 700,000,000 miles from Earth, Saturn is yellowish overall and has atmospheric bands across its face. It is girdled by many glittering rings in the plane of its equator. These rings extend about 600,000 miles from the planet.

Most experts think the rings are probably bits of ice-covered rock, between dust and gravel in size—or perhaps chunks of water ice itself. The rings are incredibly thin for their span and are so tenuous that stars can be seen through them. Their thickness is at most a few thousand feet.

Saturn, second-largest planet in the solar system, is so gaseous that it is also the least dense. If there were a celestial sea of water to dunk it in, it would float.

| PERIOD OF ROTATION | | | | PERIOD OF REVOLUTION (in Earth days) | UNIT SOLAR RADIATION AVAILABLE (Earth=1) | AVERAGE DISTANCE FROM SUN (in million miles) | MINIMUM DISTANCE FROM EARTH (in million miles) | AVERAGE TRAVEL TIME FROM EARTH | PLANET |
|---|---|---|---|---|---|---|---|---|---|
| days | hrs. | min. | sec. | | | | | | |
| 58.65 | — | — | — | 88 days | 6.7 | 36.0 | 48 | 115 days | MERCURY |
| 243.10 | — | — | — | 116.8 days | 1.9 | 67.2 | 26 | 146 days | VENUS |
| — | 23 | 56 | 4 | 365.26 days | 1.00 | 92.9 | — | 146 days | EARTH |
| — | 24 | 37 | 23 | 687 days | 0.43 | 141.5 | 35 | 237 days | MARS |
| — | 9 | 55 | 33 | 11.86 years | 0.04 | 483.4 | 366 | 2.6 years | JUPITER |
| — | 10 | 39.4 | — | 29.46 years | 0.01 | 886.0 | 743 | 5.6 years | SATURN |
| — | 12 | 18 | — | 84.01 years | 0.0031 | 1,782.0 | 1,606 | 15 years | URANUS |
| — | 14? | — | — | 164.8 years | 0.001 | 2,792.0 | 2,678 | 30 years | NEPTUNE |
| 6.387 | — | — | — | 247.7 years | 0.0006 | 3,675.0 | 2,650 | 30 years | PLUTO |

**EXPLORING THE SOLAR SYSTEM** (continued)

The planet has 15 moons. The largest of these moons—Titan, with a diameter of 3,624 miles—has an atmosphere, the only satellite in the solar system so endowed. Some scientists believe Titan may be sufficiently warm to support some primitive forms of life.

**URANUS**

The pale green planet Uranus orbits 1.79 billion miles from the Sun. About 29,200 miles in diameter, Uranus has its axis inclined 8° from the orbital plane. An observer living at one of the poles would see a "midnight Sun" for about 42 years and live in darkness the next 42 years.

Uranus has eight rings encircling it, like those of Saturn but smaller.

Uranus has 5 moons. Like the other giant planets, it is rich in light elements, especially hydrogen and helium. But it is denser than Jupiter and Saturn.

**NEPTUNE**

The bluish green hue of Neptune, a near twin of Uranus, stems from the methane in its atmosphere. It has two moons. One, Triton, is remarkably similar to Earth's moon. At 2.8 billion miles from the Sun, a spacecraft orbiting Neptune would chill to –370° F. if it were not heated.

Since Neptune's discovery in 1846, it has made less than three-quarters of one revolution of the Sun.

**PLUTO**

At 3.7 billion miles from the Sun, Pluto is so cold and dark as to numb the imagination. It is believed to be smaller than Earth and made up of frozen methane and water.

Its orbit about the Sun departs by 17° from the plane of the other planets' orbits.

A moon circling around Pluto was discovered on June 22, 1978, by U.S. astronomer James W. Christy.

# HIGHLIGHTS OF THE U.S. SPACE PROGRAM

The first U.S. satellite program, Project Vanguard, was initiated as part of the 1957–58 International Geophysical Year (IGY). The project launched America's first satellite, *Explorer 1*, on Jan. 31, 1958, four months after *Sputnik 1*, the first man-made satellite was orbited by the Soviet Union on Oct. 4, 1957.

*Vanguard 1*, the project's second satellite, launched on March 17, 1958, was the first with solar-powered batteries.

On Nov. 7, 1957, President Eisenhower created a Scientific Advisory Committee, headed by Massachusetts Institute of Technology's president, Dr. James R. Killian. In March 1958 the Killian Committee recommended the creation of a civilian space agency. Congress passed the National Aeronautics and Space Act of 1958, and on July 29 it was signed into law by President Eisenhower.

Two months later, on October 1, the National Aeronautics and Space Administration (NASA) was born. Its nucleus was the National Advisory Committee for Aeronautics (NACA), which for 43 years had been active in U.S. aeronautical research.

President John F. Kennedy said in a historic address to Congress on May 25, 1961:

"I believe that this Nation should commit itself to achieving the goal, before this decade is out, of landing a man on the Moon and returning him safely to Earth."

This goal was achieved with man's first walk on the Moon in July 1969.

The NASA program has been marred by only one major tragedy. On Jan. 27, 1967, a fire erupted inside an *Apollo* spacecraft during ground testing, resulting in the death of three astronauts—Lt. Col. Virgil I. Grissom, USAF; Lt. Col. Edward H. White II, USAF; and Lt. Comdr. Roger B. Chaffee, USN.

**1958 (Oct. 11) First NASA launch:** *Pioneer I* reached altitude of 70,717 miles. The 84-pound spacecraft had a life of only 43 hours.

**1958 (Jan. 31) First U.S. satellite successfully launched:** *Explorer 1* remains in orbit until March 31, 1970, circling the Earth 58,408 times and traveling 2.67 billion miles.

**1959 (Aug. 7) First TV photo of Earth from space:** Transmitted by *Explorer 6* as it orbits Earth.

**1960 (April 1) First meteorological satellite launched:** *Tiros 1* led off series of 10 consecutive successful research missions, providing 22,952 cloud-cover photos.

**1960 (Aug. 12) First passive communications satellite:** 100-foot balloon, *Echo 1*, inflated in orbit.

**1961 (May 5) First U.S. manned suborbital space flight:** Astronaut Alan B. Shepard Jr. flew in *Freedom 7* spacecraft.

**1961 (July 21) Second U.S. suborbital flight:** Astronaut Virgil I. (Gus) Grissom piloted *Liberty Bell 7* over the Atlantic Ocean, achieving altitude of 118 miles and covering distance of 305 miles.

**1962 (Feb. 20) First U.S. manned orbital spaceflight:** Astronaut John H. Glenn Jr. in *Friendship 7* (Mercury-Atlas 6) flew 81,000 miles in 4 hours and 55 minutes.

**1962 (March 7) First scientific observatory spacecraft:** OSO 1 placed in orbit with 13 experiments to study Sun.

**1962 (May 24) Second U.S. manned orbital flight:** Astronaut M. Scott Carpenter piloted *Aurora 7* in 3 orbits of the Earth.

**1962 (July 10) First privately-financed satellite:** *Telstar 1* carries out series of communication transmission tests, including TV, telephone, data, and photo facsimile.

**1962 (Aug. 27) First U.S. planetary exploration spacecraft:** *Mariner 2* launched on flight to Venus; passed within 21,648 miles of planet on Dec. 14, returning surface temperature measurements to Earth by radio.

**1962 (Oct. 3) Third U.S. manned orbital space flight:** Astronaut Walter M. Schirra Jr. made nearly 6 orbits, traveling 160,000 miles in 9 hours and 13 minutes in *Sigma 7*.

**1963 (May 15-16) Final flight of Mercury Project:** Astronaut Gordon Cooper in *Faith 7* made 22 orbits of Earth in 34 hours and 20 minutes.

**1963 (July 26) First satellite communication between U.S. and Africa:** *Syncom 2* communications satellite placed in stationary orbit over Brazil.

**1964 (Jan. 25) First joint U.S.-Soviet Union space experiment:** *Echo 2* passive communications satellite placed in polar orbit.

**1964 (July 20) First successful electric rocket engine tested in space:** Used aboard *Sert 1* spacecraft.

**1964 (July 28-31) Spacecraft photographs Moon:** *Ranger 7* sends back 4,316 clear photos before crashing onto lunar surface.

**1964 (Sept. 5) Orbiting Geophysical Observatory program:** *OGO 1* placed in orbit to carry on 20 space experiments.

**1965 (March 23) First maneuvering of manned spacecraft in orbit:** Second phase of U.S. manned space program begun with 3-orbit flight of *Gemini 3* by Astronauts Virgil I. (Gus) Grissom and John W. Young.

**1965 (April 6) First commercial communications satellite:** *Early Bird (Intelsat 1)* placed in synchronous equatorial orbit over Atlantic Ocean.

**1965 (June 3-7) First U.S. space walk:** *Gemini 4* orbits earth 62 times with Astronauts James A. McDivitt and Edward H. White; White leaves spaceship for first U.S. walk in space.

**1965 (Aug. 21-29) Third Gemini flight:** Astronauts L. Gordon Cooper and Charles Conrad Jr. make 120 orbits around Earth during 8-day mission.

**1965 (Dec. 4-18) Fourth Gemini flight:** 14-day endurance mission flown by Astronauts Frank Borman and James A. Lovell Jr. in *Gemini 7.*

**1965 (Dec. 15) First rendezvous by spacecraft:** *Gemini 6,* piloted by Astronauts Walter Schirra Jr. and Thomas P. Stafford, rendezvousing within 6 feet of *Gemini 7* in orbit.

**1966 (Feb. 3) Weather satellite system inaugurated:** Weather Bureau's satellite information system becomes operational with launch of 305-pound *ESSA 1.*

**1966 (March 16-17) First space docking experiment:** Performed by Astronauts Neil Armstrong and David R. Scott in *Gemini 8* with a Gemini unmanned target vehicle.

**1966 (May 30-June 2) First U.S. unmanned space landing on Moon:** Spacecraft *Surveyor 1* makes soft landing on Moon's Ocean of Storms; sends back total of 11,237 photos.

**1966 (July 18-21) First successful docking of spacecraft:** *Gemini 10,* piloted by Astronauts John W. Young and Michael Collins, overtakes and docks with Gemini target vehicle.

**1966 (Aug. 10) First U.S. spacecraft orbits Moon:** Unmanned *Lunar Orbiter 1* takes first photos of Earth as seen from vicinity of Moon.

**1966 (Nov. 11-15) Final Gemini mission:** Astronauts James A. Lovell Jr. and Edwin A. Aldrin Jr. in *Gemini 12* successfully docked with a target vehicle in Earth orbit; Aldrin performed two walks in space.

**1967 (Jan. 27) Disaster in Apollo flight experiment:** Three astronauts training as crew for first Apollo mission killed when fire sweeps through vehicle while it was being tested on the ground.

**1967 (Aug. 1) Mapping of Moon completed by spacecraft:** *Lunar Orbiter 5* launched, completing mapping mission preparatory to manned Apollo flights to Moon.

**1967 (Sept. 7-9) First successful U.S. biological research spacecraft:** *Biosatellite 2* carries radiation and general biology experiments into orbit around Earth.

**1967 (Sept. 8-11) Spacecraft explores possible landing sites for Apollo mission:** *Surveyor 5* lands on Moon, takes photos of potential landing areas and begins chemical analysis of Moon's surface.

**1967 (Nov. 9) First Apollo unmanned flight test:** *Saturn V* three-stage launch vehicle sent aloft and brought back to Earth at lunar-return velocity.

**1968 (Jan. 7-10) Laser beam from Earth received on Moon:** Unmanned *Surveyor 7* received light signal from Earth while returning TV pictures of Moon's surface and per-

forming digging experiments.

**1968 (July 4) Astronomy research craft launched:** *Radio Astronomy Explorer Satellite* provides data on new elements and distant regions of the universe.

**1968 (Oct. 11-22) First manned Apollo flight:** Mission lasts 10 days and 20 hours orbiting Earth with *Apollo 7* manned by Astronauts Walter M. Schirra Jr., Donn F. Eisele, and R. Walter Cunningham; crew seen by home TV viewers in first telecast from space.

**1968 (Dec. 21-27) First manned Moon-orbiting mission:** Astronauts Frank Borman, James A. Lovell, and William Anders in *Apollo 8* orbit Moon 10 times.

**1969 (May 18-26) Second manned Moon-orbiting mission:** *Apollo 10,* manned by Astronauts Eugene A. Cernan, John W. Young, and Thomas P. Stafford, circles Moon 31 times; *Lunar Module* (LM) flown to within 47,000 feet of Moon's surface; first live color TV pictures sent from space.

**1969 (July 20) First astronauts land on Moon:** Launched on July 16, *Apollo 11* was manned by Astronauts Neil A. Armstrong, Edwin E. Aldrin Jr., and Michael Collins; Armstrong and Aldrin became first man to walk on Moon; President Nixon congratulates astronauts in first telephone call to Moon; astronauts remain on Moon for more than 21 hours; return to Earth on July 24.

**1969 (Nov. 14-24) Second Moon landing flight:** *Apollo 12* flown by Astronauts Charles Conrad Jr., Richard E. Godron Jr., and Alan L. Bean; Conrad and Bean stay on Moon for 32 hours.

**1970 (April 13) Accident in space aborts Moon flight:** *Apollo 13* was launched on April 11, manned by Astronauts James A. Lovell, John L. Swigert Jr., and Fred W. Haise Jr. Rupture of oxygen tank aboard spacecraft forces crew to take emergency action and return to Earth on April 17.

**1971 (Jan. 31-Feb. 9) Third successful lunar landing mission:** *Apollo 14* manned by Astronauts Alan B. Shepard Jr., Stuart A. Roosa, and Edgar D. Mitchell; Shepard and Mitchell stay on Moon over 33 hours.

**1971 (July 26-Aug. 7) Fourth lunar landing mission:** *Apollo 15* flown by Astronauts David R. Scott, James B. Irwin, and Alfred M. Worden; Scott and Irwin became first to use *Lunar Roving Vehicle* (LRV) to travel over 17 miles exploring Moon's surface.

**1972 (March 3) *Pioneer 10* launched to explore distant planets:** Unmanned spacecraft is first powered completely by nuclear energy; after photographing Jupiter and Saturn, will escape from solar system in 1987.

**1972 (April 16-27) *Apollo 16* mission to Moon:** Fifth lunar landing flight manned by Astronauts John W. Young, Thomas K. Mattingly II, and Charles M. Duke Jr.; Young and Duke remain on Moon 71 hours.

**1972 (Dec. 7-19) Final Apollo flight to Moon:** *Apollo 17* flown by Astronauts Eugene A. Cernan, Ronald B. Evans, and Harrison H. Schmitt; Cernan and Schmitt stay on Moon over 3 days.

**1973 (April 6) *Pioneer 11* sent to explore planets:** Unmanned craft to explore Jupiter, Saturn, and Uranus.

**1973 (May 14) *Skylab* becomes first U.S. space station:** Orbits 268.7 miles above Earth.

**1973 (May 25-June 22) First manned *Skylab* expedition:** Astronauts Charles Conrad Jr., Joseph P. Kerwin, and Paul J. Weitz repair *Skylab* and conduct experiments during 28-day mission aboard space station.

**1973 (July 28-Sept. 25) Second manned *Skylab* mission:** Astronauts Alan L. Bean, Jack R. Lousma, and Owen K. Garriott spend over 59 days in space.

**1973 (Nov. 16) to 1974 (Feb. 8) Final *Skylab* mission:** Astronauts Gerald Carr, Edward Gibson, and William Pogue remain in space more than 84 days.

**1975 (July 15-24) Final manned spaceflight of Apollo Project:** U.S. Apollo spaceship manned by Thomas P. Stafford, Vance D. Brand, and Donald K. Slayton; docked on July 17 with Soviet *Soyuz 19* spaceship for a "handshake in space."

**1980 For space events of year,** see pages 745–748 and 8–30.

## OUTSTANDING MANNED SPACEFLIGHTS

Sources: National Aeronautics and Space Administration; Library of Congress

The Soviet Union and the United States use different methods of measuring Earth orbital flights. The Soviets measure in "orbits," the Americans in revolutions. Because of the Earth's rotation, there is one less revolution than orbit in a 24-hour period.

| ASTRONAUT COUNTRY AND DATE | ORBITS | ALTITUDE [1] | FLIGHT TIME | WEIGHT OF CRAFT [2] | CRAFT NAME | ROCKET THRUST [2] |
|---|---|---|---|---|---|---|
| Yuri A. Gagarin (U.S.S.R.) April 12, 1961 . . . . . . . . . . . . | 1 | 112.5 to 203.2 | 1 hr. 48 min. | 10,418 | Vostok I | 1,124,550 |
| Gherman S. Titov (U.S.S.R.) Aug. 6, 1961 . . . . . . . . . . . . . | 17.5 | 111 to 160 | 25 hrs. 18 min. | 10,430 | Vostok II | 1,124,550 |
| John Glenn (U.S.) Feb. 20, 1962 . . . . . . . . . . . . | 3 | 100.3 to 162.7 | 4 hrs. 55 min. | 2,900 | Friendship 7 | 360,000 |
| M. Scott Carpenter (U.S.) May 24, 1962 . . . . . . | 3 | 100 to 166.8 | 4 hrs. 56 min. | 2,975 | Aurora 7 | 360,000 |
| Andrian G. Nikolayev (U.S.S.R.) Aug. 11, 1962 . . . . . . . . . . . . | 64 | 114 to 156 | 94 hrs. 35 min. | 10,400 | Vostok III | 1,124,550 |
| Pavel R. Popovich (U.S.S.R.) Aug. 12, 1962 . . . . . . . . . . . . | 48 | 112 to 158 | 70 hrs. 57 min. | 10,400 | Vostok IV | 1,124,550 |
| Walter M. Schirra Jr. (U.S.) Oct. 3, 1962 . . . . . . . . | 6 | 100 to 176 | 9 hrs. 13 min. | 2,900 | Sigma 7 | 360,000 |
| L. Gordon Cooper (U.S.) May 15, 1963 . . . . . . | 22 | 100.2 to 166.1 | 34 hrs. 20 min. | 2,900 | Faith 7 | 360,000 |
| Valery F. Bykovsky (U.S.S.R.) June 14, 1963 . . . . . . . . . . . | 81 | 109 to 138 | 119 hrs. 6 min. | 10,360 | Vostok V | 1,124,550 |
| Valentina V. Tereshkova (U.S.S.R.) June 16, 1963 . . . . . . . . . . . | 48 | 114 to 145 | 79 hrs. 50 min. | 10,360 | Vostok VI | 1,124,550 |
| Konstantin Feoktistov Vladimir Komarov Boris Yegorov (U.S.S.R.) Oct. 12, 1964 . . . . . . . . . . . . | 16 | 111 to 254 | 24 hrs. 17 min. | 16,000 | Voskhod I | 1,124,550 |
| Pavel I. Belyayev Alexei Leonov (U.S.S.R.) March 18, 1965 . . . . . . . . . . | 17 | 107 to 308 | 26 hrs. 2 min. | 13,200 | Voskhod II | 1,124,550 |
| Virgil I. Grissom John W. Young (U.S.) March 23, 1965 . . . . | 3 | 100 to 139 | 4 hrs. 53 min. | 7,111 | Gemini 3 | 530,000 |
| James A. McDivitt Edward H. White (U.S.) June 3, 1965 . . . . . . . | 62 | 100 to 175 | 97 hrs. 56 min. | 7,879 | Gemini 4 | 530,000 |
| L. Gordon Cooper Charles Conrad Jr. (U.S.) Aug. 21, 1965 . . . . . . | 120 | 101 to 217 | 190 hrs. 56 min. | 7,947 | Gemini 5 | 530,000 |
| Frank Borman James A. Lovell Jr. (U.S.) Dec. 4, 1965 . . . . . . . | 206 | 100 to 204 | 330 hrs. 35 min. | 8,076 | Gemini 7 | 530,000 |
| Walter M. Schirra Jr. Thomas P. Stafford (U.S.) Dec. 15, 1965 . . . . . . | 15 | 100 to 161 | 25 hrs. 51 min. | 7,817 | Gemini 6 | 530,000 |
| Neil A. Armstrong David R. Scott (U.S.) March 16, 1966 . . . . | 6.6 | 99 to 164 | 10 hrs. 42 min. | 7,116 | Gemini 8 | 530,000 |
| Thomas P. Stafford Eugene A. Cernan (U.S.) June 3, 1966 . . . . . . . | 44 | 167 to 169 | 72 hrs. 20 min. | 8,100 | Gemini 9 | 530,000 |
| John W. Young Michael Collins (U.S.) July 18, 1966 . . . . . . . | 43 | 185 to 468 | 70 hrs. 46 min. | 8,250 | Gemini 10 | 530,000 |
| Charles Conrad Jr. Richard F. Gordon Jr. (U.S.) Sept. 12, 1966 . . . . . | 44 | 180 to 850 | 71 hrs. 17 min. | 8,260 | Gemini 11 | 530,000 |
| James A. Lovell Jr. Edwin E. Aldrin Jr. (U.S.) Nov. 11, 1966 . . . . . . | 59 | 158 to 179 | 94 hrs. 34 min. | 8,290 | Gemini 12 | 530,000 |

[1] In miles.    [2] In pounds.

| ASTRONAUT COUNTRY AND DATE | ORBITS | ALTITUDE[1] | FLIGHT TIME | WEIGHT OF CRAFT[2] | CRAFT NAME | ROCKET THRUST[2] |
|---|---|---|---|---|---|---|
| Walter M. Schirra Jr.<br>Donn F. Eisele<br>Walter Cunningham<br>(U.S.) Oct. 11, 1968....... | 163 | 140 to 183 | 260 hrs. | 12,500 | Apollo 7 | 1,600,000 |
| Georgi T. Beregovoi<br>(U.S.S.R.) Oct. 26, 1968 ... | 64 | 127 to 140 | 94 hrs. 51 min. | 14,495 | Soyuz 3 | 1,124,550 |
| Frank Borman<br>James A. Lovell Jr.<br>William A. Anders<br>(U.S.) Dec. 21, 1968 ...... | 10[1] | — | 147 hrs. | 87,297 | Apollo 8 | 7,500,000 |
| Vladimir A. Shatalov<br>(U.S.S.R.) Jan. 15, 1969 ... | 45 | 107 to 140 | 771 hrs. 14 min. | 14,605 | Soyuz 4 | 1,124,550 |
| Boris V. Volynov<br>Aleksei S. Yeliseyev<br>Yevgeny V. Khrunov<br>(U.S.S.R.) Jan. 15, 1969 ... | 46 | 124 to 143 | 72 hrs. 46 min. | 14,517 | Soyuz 5 | 1,124,550 |
| James A. McDivitt<br>David R. Scott<br>Russell L. Schweickart<br>(U.S.) March 3, 1969 ...... | 151 | 118 to 120 | 241 hrs. 1 min. | 95,022 | Apollo 9 | 7,700,000 |
| Thomas R. Stafford<br>Eugene A. Cernan<br>John W. Young<br>(U.S.) May 18, 1969........ | 31[3] | — | 192 hrs. 3 min. | 98,267 | Apollo 10 | 7,681,000 |
| Neil A. Armstrong<br>Edwin E. Aldrin Jr.<br>Michael Collins<br>(U.S.) July 16, 1969 ....... | 31[4] | — | 195 hrs. 18 min. | 100,602 | Apollo 11 | 7,654,000 |
| Georgy S. Shonin<br>Valery N. Kubasov<br>(U.S.S.R.) Oct. 11, 1969 ... | 79 | 124 to 140 | 118 hrs. 42 min. | 14,500 | Soyuz 6 | 1,124,550 |
| Anatoly V. Filipchenko<br>Vladislav N. Volkov<br>Viktor V. Gorbatko<br>(U.S.S.R.) Oct. 12, 1969 ... | 79 | 124 to 140 | 118 hrs. 41 min. | 14,484 | Soyuz 7 | 1,124,550 |
| Vladimir A. Shatalov<br>Aleksei S. Yeliseyev<br>(U.S.S.R.) Oct. 13, 1969 ... | 79 | 124 to 140 | 118 hrs. 50 min. | 14,652 | Soyuz 8 | 1,124,550 |
| Charles Conrad Jr.<br>Richard F. Gordon<br>Alan L. Bean<br>(U.S.) Nov. 14, 1969 ...... | 45[4] | — | 244 hrs. 36 min. | 101,131 | Apollo 12 | 7,620,000 |
| James A. Lovell Jr.<br>Fred W. Haise Jr.<br>John L. Swigert Jr.<br>(U.S.) April 11, 1970 ...... | — | — | 142 hrs. 54 min. | 110,210 | Apollo 13 | 7,620,000 |
| Andrian G. Nikolayev<br>Vitali I. Sevastyanov<br>(U.S.S.R.) June 1, 1970 ... | 286 | 166 | 424 hrs. 59 min. | 14,331 | Soyuz 9 | 1,124,550 |
| Alan B. Shepard Jr.<br>Stuart A. Roosa<br>Edgar D. Mitchell<br>(U.S.) Jan. 31, 1971........ | 34[4] | 60 | 216 hrs. 42 min. | 102,177 | Apollo 14 | 7,500,000[5] |
| Vladimir A. Shatalov<br>Aleksei S. Yeliseyev<br>Nikolai Rukavishmikov<br>(U.S.S.R.) April 22, 1971 .. | 32 | 153 | 47 hrs. 46 min. | 14,500 | Soyuz 10 | 1,124,500 |
| Georgi T. Dobrovolsky<br>Vladislav N. Volkov<br>Viktor I. Patsayev<br>(U.S.S.R.) June 6, 1971 ... | 385 | 175 | 570 hrs. 22 min.[6] | 14,500 | Soyuz 11 | 1,124,500 |
| David R. Scott<br>James B. Irwin<br>Alfred M. Worden<br>(U.S.) July 26, 1971....... | 74[4] | 60 | 295 hrs. 12 min. | 107,185 | Apollo 15 | 7,500,000[5] |
| John W. Young<br>Charles M. Duke Jr.<br>Thomas K. Mattingly II<br>(U.S.) April 16, 1972 ...... | 64[4] | 60 | 265 hrs. 51 min. | 116,363 | Apollo 16 | 7,723,726 |

[1] In miles.  [2] In pounds.  [3] Moon orbits.  [4] Moon orbits in command module.  [5] Approximate.  [6] Plus or minus 10 minutes.

## OUTSTANDING MANNED SPACEFLIGHTS *(continued)*

| ASTRONAUT COUNTRY AND DATE | ORBITS | ALTITUDE [1] | FLIGHT TIME | WEIGHT OF CRAFT | CRAFT NAME | ROCKET THRUST [2] |
|---|---|---|---|---|---|---|
| Eugene A. Cernan<br>Ronald E. Evans<br>Harrison H. Schmitt<br>(U.S.) Dec. 7-19, 1972..... | 75 [3] | 60 | 301 hrs. 52 min. | 116,269 [2] | Apollo 17 | 7,665,111 |
| Charles Conrad Jr.<br>Joseph P. Kerwin<br>Paul J. Weitz<br>(U.S.) May 25 to<br>June 22, 1973 ........... | 434 [4] | 268.7 | 28 days 50 min. | 100 tons | Skylab 1 | — |
| Alan L. Bean<br>Jack R. Lousma<br>Owen K. Garriott<br>(U.S.) July 28 to<br>Sept. 25, 1973........... | 914 [4] | 268.7 | 59 days 11 hrs.<br>9 min. | 100 tons | Skylab 2 | — |
| Gerald P. Carr<br>Edward G. Gibson<br>William Pogue<br>(U.S.) Nov. 16, 1973, to<br>Feb. 8, 1974 ............. | 1,295 [4] | 268.7 | 84 days 1 hr.<br>16.5 min. | 100 tons | Skylab 3 | — |
| Thomas P. Stafford<br>Donald K. Slayton<br>Vance Brand<br>Alexei Leonov<br>Valeri Kubasov<br>(U.S.–Soviet Union)<br>July 15-24, 1975......... | — | 140 | 9 days | — | Apollo–<br>Soyuz | — |
| Pyotr I. Klimuk<br>Vitaly I. Sevastyanov<br>(Soviet Union) May 24 to<br>July 26, 1975 ............ | — | 217 | 62 days 23 hrs.<br>20 min. | 25 tons | Soyuz 18–<br>Salyut 4 | — |
| Boris Volynov<br>Vitaly Zhobolov<br>(Soviet Union) July 26 to<br>Aug. 24, 1976 ............ | — | 168–152 | 50 days | 25 tons | Soyuz 21–<br>Salyut 5 | — |
| Viktor V. Garbatko<br>Yuri Glazkov<br>(Soviet Union) Feb. 7 to<br>Feb. 25, 1977 ............ | — | 168–152 | 18 days | 25 tons | Soyuz 24–<br>Salyut 5 | — |
| Yuri Romanenko<br>Georgi Grechko<br>(Soviet Union) Dec. 1, 1977,<br>to March 16, 1978 ........ | — | 168–152 | 96 days 10 hrs. | 25 tons | Soyuz 26–<br>Salyut 6–<br>Soyuz 27 | — |
| Vladimir Kovalyonok<br>Aleksandr Ivanchenokov<br>(Soviet Union) June 5,<br>1978, to Nov. 2, 1978....... | — | 168–152 | 139 days 15 hrs. | 25 tons | Soyuz 29–<br>Salyut 6–<br>Soyuz 31 | — |
| Vladimir Lyakhov<br>Valery Ryumin<br>(Soviet Union) Feb. 25,<br>1979, to Aug. 19, 1979 ..... | — | 168–152 | 175 days | 25 tons | Soyuz 32–<br>Salyut 6–<br>Soyuz 34 | — |
| Leonid Popov<br>Valery Ryumin<br>(Soviet Union) April 9,<br>1980, to Oct. 11, 1980 ...... | — | 168–152 | 185 days | 25 tons | Soyuz 35–<br>Salyut 6–<br>Soyuz 37 | — |

[1] In miles.   [2] In pounds.   [3] Moon orbits in command module.   [4] Approximate.

## SPACE CAPSULES

**Perfect NASA launch record in 1979.** NASA achieved a perfect score in 1979 when it was successful in all its nine launch attempts. This was its fourth perfect score in 21 years.

**A total of 43 U.S. astronauts** took part in 31 manned spaceflights from May 1961 through July 1975. Thirty of the 73 persons named as U.S. astronauts did not make spaceflights.

## FACTS ABOUT THE MOON

More has been learned about the Moon than any other of the Earth's neighbors in space because of the Apollo program that enabled men to walk on the Moon and bring back hundreds of pounds of rocks. Following are some of the important facts we now know about the Moon.

**Age of the Moon:** Over 4.6 billion years. Moon rocks brought back by the astronauts have been dated as old as 4.6 billion years.

**Composition of the Moon:** The content of rocks on the Moon is much different from that of the Earth. The Moon has only an estimated 8.5% iron, while the Earth is about 36% iron. The Moon has proportionately three times as much uranium as the Earth, but only about one-third the Earth's percentage of gold and only about half the proportion of potassium.

**Diameter of the Moon:** 2,160 miles, about the distance from San Francisco to Chicago.

**Circumference of the Moon:** 6,785 miles, about the distance from Chicago to Athens, Greece.

**Surface area:** 14,650,000 square miles, about four times the area of the United States.

**Mass:** 81,000 trillion tons.

**Gravity:** One-sixth that of the Earth. A man who weighs 180 pounds on Earth weighs only 30 pounds when on the surface of the Moon.

**Sidereal month** (period of Moon's revolution around Earth in relation to the stars): 27 days, 7 hours, 43 minutes, 11.5 seconds.

**Synodic month** (period of Moon's revolution around Earth in relation to Sun): 29 days, 12 hours, and 44 minutes.

**Average speed traveling around the Earth:** 2,287 miles an hour.

**Distance from the Earth:** *Closest,* 221,456 miles; *farthest,* 252,711 miles, *mean distance,* 238,875 miles.

**Length of a day on the Moon:** 14 Earth days.

**Distance traveled in orbit each year:** 1,500,000 miles.

**Temperature at noon on the Moon:** 243 ° F., hot enough to boil water.

**Temperature at midnight on the Moon:** -297 ° F., cold enough to freeze carbon dioxide into dry ice.

**Escape velocity from the Moon:** 1.5 miles per second, or about 5,400 miles an hour.

## CALENDAR OF PHASES OF THE MOON: 1981

Source: *Astronomical Phenomena,* U.S. Naval Observatory; all times are Eastern Standard Time (EST)

| NEW MOON | | FIRST QUARTER | | FULL MOON | | LAST QUARTER | |
|---|---|---|---|---|---|---|---|
| Day | Time | Day | Time | Day | Time | Day | Time |
| Jan. 6 | 2:24 A.M. | Jan. 13 | 5:10 A.M. | Jan. 20 | 2:39 A.M. | Jan. 27 | 11:19 P.M. |
| Feb. 4 | 6:14 P.M. | Feb. 11 | 12:49 P.M. | Feb. 18 | 5:58 P.M. | Feb. 26 | 8:14 P.M. |
| Mar. 6 | 5:31 A.M. | Mar. 12 | 8:50 P.M. | Mar. 20 | 10:22 A.M. | Mar. 28 | 2:34 P.M. |
| Apr. 4 | 3:19 P.M. | Apr. 11 | 6:11 A.M. | Apr. 19 | 2:59 A.M. | Apr. 27 | 5:14 A.M. |
| May 3 | 11:19 P.M. | May 10 | 5:22 P.M. | May 18 | 12:04 A.M. | May 26 | 4:00 P.M. |
| June 2 | 6:32 A.M. | June 9 | 6:33 A.M. | June 17 | 10:04 A.M. | June 24 | 11:25 P.M. |
| July 1 | 2:03 P.M. | July 8 | 9:39 P.M. | July 16 | 11:39 P.M. | July 24 | 4:40 A.M. |
| July 30 | 10:52 P.M. | Aug. 7 | 2:26 P.M. | Aug. 15 | 11:37 A.M. | Aug. 22 | 9:16 A.M. |
| Aug. 29 | 9:43 A.M. | Sep. 6 | 8:26 A.M. | Sep. 13 | 10:09 P.M. | Sep. 20 | 2:47 P.M. |
| Sep. 27 | 11:07 P.M. | Oct. 6 | 2:45 A.M. | Oct. 13 | 7:49 A.M. | Oct. 19 | 10:40 P.M. |
| Oct. 27 | 3:13 P.M. | Nov. 4 | 8:09 P.M. | Nov. 11 | 5:26 P.M. | Nov. 18 | 9:54 A.M. |
| Nov. 26 | 9:38 A.M. | Dec. 4 | 11:22 A.M. | Dec. 11 | 3:41 A.M. | Dec. 18 | 12:47 A.M. |
| Dec. 26 | 5:10 A.M. | | | | | | |

## PHASES OF THE MOON

The Moon shines only by reflected light. Its phases, or apparent changes in shape, result from the varying part of the sunlit hemisphere of the Moon visible to observers on Earth. Its lighted portion varies in shape because of the relative positions of the Moon, the Sun, and the Earth.

At New Moon, when the Moon is on the line between the Sun and the Earth, eclipses of the Sun by the Moon may occur if the Moon is properly positioned.

The Moon moves on in its orbit of the Earth from west to east. It passes through its waxing Crescent phase into First Quarter when it is at Half Moon.

Through the waxing Gibbous phase, it comes then to Full Moon, on the opposite side of the Earth from the Sun, when the Earth's shadow may be cast across the Moon in lunar eclipses.

The Moon moves on through waning Gibbous into Last Quarter. It then passes through the waning Crescent phase into New Moon again.

Occasionally the unlit portion of the Moon facing the Earth glows in "earthshine" (sunlight reflected from the Earth to the Moon and back again). Certain parts of the Moon, such as the bright crater Aristarchus, are especially reflective.

The worst storms have been found to be significantly related to lunar phases. Such storms are more likely to occur, in the long run, from 1 to 3 days after New Moon and from 3 to 5 days after Full Moon. Similar relationships between storms and the phases of the Moon have been reported in many parts of the world.

The magnetic disturbances that sometimes disrupt radio communications, and the beginning of hurricanes in the Caribbean, have been found to be similarly related to lunar positions. The way in which these effects are produced is still a mystery.

# THE CONSTELLATIONS

When you look up on a clear night at the stars, many of them appear to be clustered in groups called constellations.

Ancient observers gave 48 constellations names suggested by the patterns of their stars.

Usually the stars forming these apparent groups are entirely unrelated and are located at greatly varying distances, although all the stars visible to the naked eye are in our own Milky Way galaxy.

Modern astronomers recognize 88 constellations, including most of the ancient ones.

Strict boundaries for the constellations were established by the International Astronomical Union in 1928.

The constellation boundaries are used as reference areas for locating, naming, and classifying the stars, and for roughly fixing the positions of comets, meteors, and other celestial bodies viewed in the sky.

The table names the constellations. Those marked with an asterisk (*) are not visible from midnorthern latitudes.

| LATIN NAME | ENGLISH | LATIN NAME | ENGLISH | LATIN NAME | ENGLISH |
|---|---|---|---|---|---|
| Andromeda | Chained Maiden | Boötes | Herdsman | Carina * | Keel |
| Antila | Air Pump | Caelum | Chisel | Cassiopeia | Lady in Chair |
| Apus * | Bird of Paradise | Camelopardalis | Giraffe | Centaurus * | Centaur |
| Aquarius | Water Bearer | Cancer | Crab | Cepheus | King |
| Aquila | Eagle | Canes Venatici | Hunting Dogs | Cetus | Whale |
| Ara * | Altar | Canis Major | Great Dog | Chamaeleon * | Chameleon |
| Aries | Ram | Canis Minor | Small Dog | Circinus * | Compasses |
| Auriga | Charioteer | Capricornus | Sea Goat | Columba | Dove |

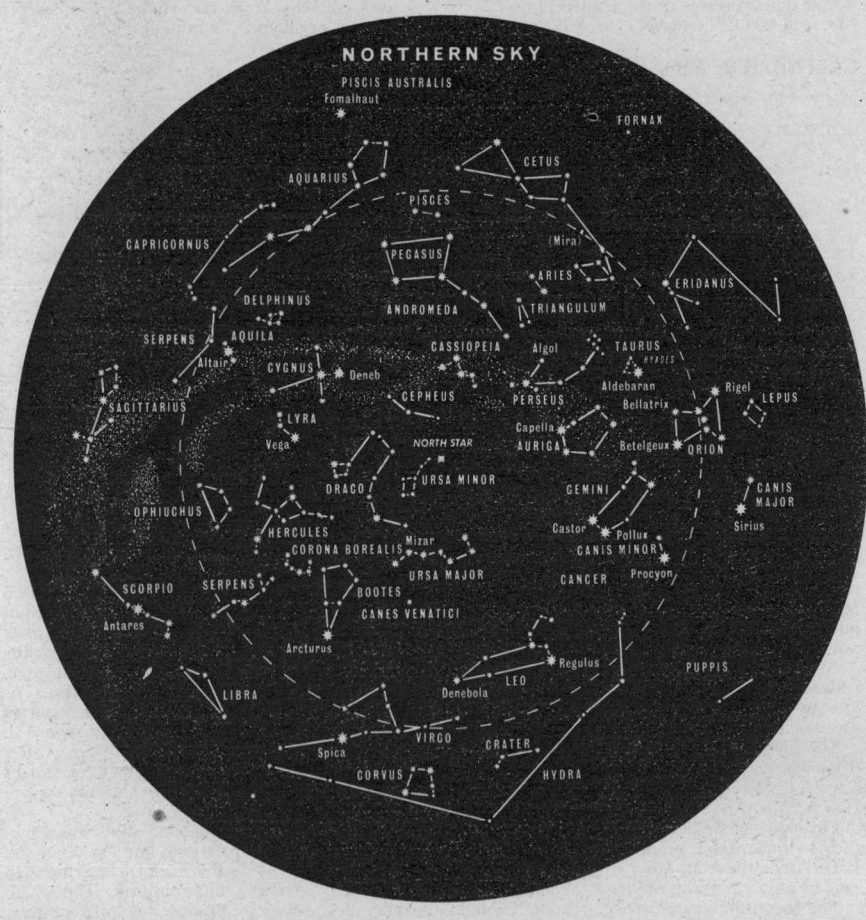

| LATIN NAME | ENGLISH | LATIN NAME | ENGLISH | LATIN NAME | ENGLISH |
|---|---|---|---|---|---|
| Coma Berenices .. | Berenice's Hair | Leo Minor........ | Small Lion | Pyxis .............. | Compass |
| Corona Australis.. | Southern Crown | Lepus ........... | Hare | Reticulum * ........ | Net |
| Corona Borealis .. | Northern Crown | Libra ............ | Scales | Sagitta ........... | Arrow |
| Corvus............ | Crow | Lupus * .......... | Wolf | Sagittarius ......... | Archer |
| Crater ............ | Cup | Lynx ............. | Lynx | Scorpius ........... | Scorpion |
| Crux * ........... | (Southern) Cross | Lyra ............. | Lyre | Sculptor ........... | Sculptor |
| Cygnus .......... | Swan | Mensa *.......... | Table (Mountain) | Scutum............ | Shield |
| Delphinus ........ | Dolphin | Microscopium .... | Microscope | Serpens ........... | Serpent |
| Dorado * ......... | Swordfish | Monoceros ...... | Unicorn | Sextans........... | Sextant |
| Draco............. | Dragon | Musca *.......... | Fly | Taurus ........... | Bull |
| Equuleus ......... | Little Horse | Norma * ......... | Square | Telescopium *..... | Telescope |
| Eridanus ......... | River Eridanus | Octans * ......... | Octant | Trianguium ........ | Triangle |
| Fornax ........... | Furnace | Ophiuchus ....... | Serpent Bearer | Triangulum Australe* | Southern Triangle |
| Gemini ........... | Twins | Orion ............ | Hunter | Tucana * .......... | Toucan |
| Grus * ........... | Crane | Pavo * ........... | Peacock | Ursa Major ........ | Great Bear |
| Hercules ......... | Hercules | Pegasus ......... | Pegasus | Ursa Minor ........ | Small Bear |
| Horologium * ..... | Clock | Perseus ......... | Champion | Vela * ............ | Sails |
| Hydra ............ | Sea Serpent | Phoenix * ........ | Phoenix | Virgo ............. | Virgin |
| Hydrus * ......... | Water Snake | Pictor * .......... | Painter's (Easel) | Volans * .......... | Flying Fish |
| Indus * .......... | Indian | Pisces ........... | Fishes | Vulpecula ......... | Fox |
| Lacerta .......... | Lizard | Piscis Austrinus .. | Southern Fish | | |
| Leo.............. | Lion | Puppis ........... | Poop (Stern) | | |

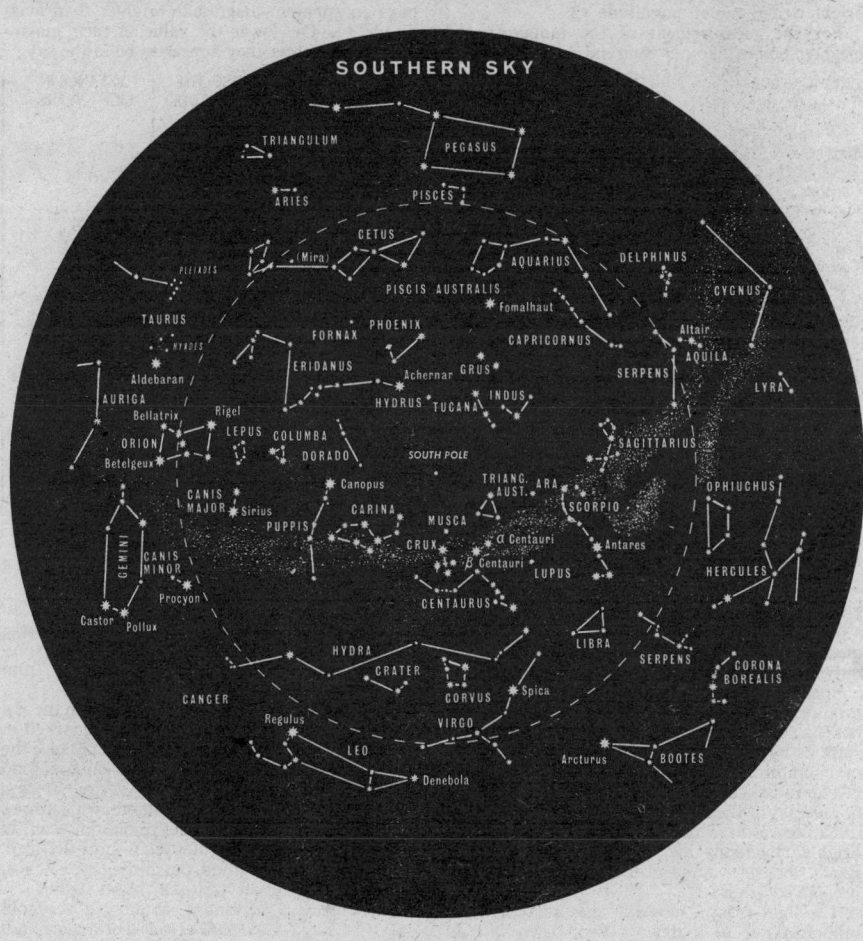

SOUTHERN SKY

# BRIGHTEST STARS

Ptolemy, the Greek astronomer, made the first significant attempt to classify the stars by their brightness in the 100s A.D. According to his system, all the stars that can be seen with the naked eye fall into six groups of brightness, called apparent magnitudes.

The first positive (+) magnitude stars are the very brightest, and the sixth positive magnitude stars are the faintest. The planet Uranus is near the limit of naked-eye visibility with a magnitude of +5.7.

With the use of the telescope, photographic plates, and other equipment, fainter stars of much higher apparent magnitude can be seen. Ptolemy's scale of decreasing visible brightness has been extended to over +20. Stars of magnitude +23 have recorded their dim images on photographic plates made with large telescopes. On the present magnitude scale, a difference of one magnitude represents a difference in brightness of 2.512 times. Therefore, a celestial body of magnitude +1 appears to be about +2.5 times brighter than one of magnitude +2.

For the measurement of the luminosity of brighter bodies like our Sun and nearby planets, the magnitude scale has been extended into negative (−) magnitudes.

The higher negative magnitudes represent greater brightness. Thus the Sun has an apparent magnitude of −26.73 as shown in the table, the full Moon −12.7, Venus at its brightest −4.2, and Jupiter −2.5.

The brightest star, other than the Sun, is Sirius, with a magnitude of −1.42.

The estimated magnitude of the supernova explosion that created the Crab Nebula in A.D. 1054 was −6 at its height.

Since a small but bright star at a great distance appears approximately as bright as a nearby but cooler one, an absolute magnitude scale has also been devised. The absolute brightness of a star is the numerical value it would have if it were seen at a set distance from the Earth. The distance that has been chosen is 10 parsecs. One parsec is equal to 3.262 light-years, or about 19 trillion miles.

The following table lists all those stars that have an apparent magnitude brighter than magnitude +1. The lower the value of their magnitude, the brighter they appear to be in the sky.

| BRIGHT STARS | GREEK LETTER AND CONSTELLATION | APPARENT MAGNITUDE *Variable star | ABSOLUTE MAGNITUDE | DISTANCE IN LIGHT-YEARS |
|---|---|---|---|---|
| Sun | Sun | −26.73 | 4.84 | — |
| Sirius | Alpha Canis Majoris | − 1.42 | 1.45 | 8.7 |
| Canopus | Alpha Carinae | − 0.72 | −3.10 | 98 |
| Rigil Kentaurus | Alpha Centauri A | − 0.01 | 4.39 | 4.3 |
| Arcturus | Alpha Boötis | − 0.06 | −0.3 | 36 |
| Vega | Alpha Lyrae | 0.04 | 0.5 | 26.5 |
| Capella | Alpha Aurigae | 0.05 | −0.6 | 45 |
| Rigel | Beta Orionis | 0.14* | −7.1 | 900 |
| Procyon | Alpha Canis Minoris | 0.37 | 2.7 | 11.3 |
| Betelgeuse | Alpha Orionis | 0.41* | −5.6 | 520 |
| Achernar | Alpha Eridani | 0.51 | −2.3 | 118 |
| Hadar | Beta Centauri AB | 0.63 | −5.2 | 490 |
| Altair | Alpha Aquilae | 0.77 | 2.2 | 16.5 |
| Aldebaran | Alpha Tauri | 0.86* | −0.7 | 68 |
| Antares | Alpha Scorpii | 0.92* | −5.1 | 520 |
| Spica | Alpha Virginis | 0.91* | −3.3 | 220 |
| Acrux | Alpha Crucis | 1.10 | −3.03 | 245 |
| Pollux | Beta Geminorum | 1.16 | 1.0 | 35 |
| Fomalhaut | Alpha Piscis Austrinus | 1.19 | 2.0 | 22.6 |
| Deneb | Alpha Cygni | 1.25 | −6.2 | 1,630 |

# VARIABLE AND EXPLODING STARS

Changes in the brightness of the many different kinds of variable stars have taught astronomers a great deal about the nature, evolution, and distances of stars, and even about events going on within them.

Some pulsating variable stars, whose light brightens and dims regularly, are caused by the passage of companions in front of the brighter stars or by the relations of several stars orbiting in a complex system.

The radiation of other stars may vary because of changes in their outer layers.

Explosive variables are stars that suddenly brighten by many magnitudes. They are called novae, or new stars, because they suddenly become so bright.

The light from a new star may increase by a million times in a day or two. Then it may decrease slowly to about its original magnitude.

Novae may be stars that have reached an unbalanced state in which they blow off large portions of their substance in cataclysmic explosions. Novae have been known to recur from one to three times.

The 400th anniversary of the sighting in the sky of "a new star" never seen before was marked in 1972. It is best known as Tycho's star because the Danish astronomer Tycho Brahe gave a good published account of his observations. It was actually first noticed by the little-known astronomer Schuler at Wittenberg, Prussia, on Aug. 6, 1572. Tycho himself did not see it until the 11th, when it was at its brightest, outshining even Venus, and visible in daytime. Called a "Nova Stella," it is today termed a supernova, actually a very old

(continued at bottom of opposite page)

# ASTRONOMICAL TELESCOPES

A *refractor* telescope uses a lens to collect light from a distant object and bring it to a focus. A *reflector* telescope uses a concave mirror for the same purpose.

Because lenses fail to bring all colors to the same focus, most large astronomical telescopes built in the past 50 years are reflectors.

Today, visual observations are rarely made with astronomical telescopes, for photographs can record objects much fainter than the eye can see. Large telescopes thus are used as cameras or to collect light for analysis in other ways.

Radio telescopes are used to study radio waves coming from celestial objects.

## LARGE REFRACTING TELESCOPES

Source: U. S. Naval Observatory

| DIAMETER OF LENS | OBSERVATORY AND LOCATION | YEAR |
| --- | --- | --- |
| 40.0 in. (1.02 m.) | Yerkes Observatory, Williams Bay, Wisconsin . . . . . . . . . . | 1897 |
| 36.0 in. (0.91 m.) | Lick Observatory, Mt. Hamilton, California . . . . . . . | 1888 |
| 32.7 in. (0.83 m.) | Paris Observatory, Meudon, France . . . . . . . . . . . . . . . . . . | 1889 |
| 32.0 in. (0.81 m.) | Astrophysical Observatory, Potsdam, East Germany . . . | 1899 |
| 30.0 in. (0.76 m.) | Allegheny Observatory, Pittsburgh, Pennsylvania . . | 1914 |
| 29.1 in. (0.74 m.) | Nice Observatory at Mont Gros, Nice, France . . . . . . . . | 1886 |

## LARGE RADIO AND RADAR TELESCOPES

Source: U.S. National Radio Astronomy Observatory

| SIZE | OBSERVATORY | YEAR |
| --- | --- | --- |
| 27 x 82 ft., 38 mi. (61 km.) [1] . . . . . . | National Radio Astronomy Observatory, Socorro, N.M. . | 1980 |
| 16,000 ft. (4.9 km.) [1] . . . . . . . . . | Mullard Observatory, Cambridge, England . . . . . . . . . . | 1972 |
| 2.05 mi. (3.3 km.) [1] interferometer . . | Clark Lake Radio Obs., Borrego Springs, Calif. . . . . | 1975 |
| 1.86 mi. (3 km.) [2] . . | CSIRO, Culgoora, Australia . . | 1967 |
| 1.86 mi. (3 km.) [1] . . | Netherlands Foundation for Radio Astronomy, Westerbork, Neth. . . . . . . . | 1973 |
| 1.44 mi. (2.3 km.) [1] interferometer . . | U. of Tokyo Observatory, Nobeyama, Japan . . . . . . . . | 1970 |
| 1,890 ft. (576 m.) [3] | Special Astrophysical Obs., Zelenschukskaya, USSR . . . | 1976 |
| 1,000 ft. (305 m.) [3] | Arecibo Observatory, Puerto Rico . . . . . . . . . . . . . . . . . . | 1974 [5] |
| 984 ft. (300 m.) [3] . | Radio Astronomy Station, Nancy, France . . . . . . . . . . . | 1964 |
| 328 ft. (100 m.) [3] . | Max Planck Institute, Effelsberg, West Germany . . . . . | 1970 |
| 300 ft. (91.4 m.) [3] . | National Radio Astronomy Obs., Green Bank, W. Va. | 1963 |
| 250 ft. (76.2 m.) [3] . | Nuffield Laboratories, Jodrell Bank, England . . . . | 1971 [5] |
| 45 ft. (13.7 m.) [4] . . | Five College Observatory, New Salem, Mass. . . . . . . . | 1977 |

## LARGE REFLECTING TELESCOPES

Source: U.S. Naval Observatory

| DIAMETER OF MIRROR | OBSERVATORY AND LOCATION | YEAR |
| --- | --- | --- |
| 236 in. (6 m.) . . . . | Special Astrophysical Obs., Zelenschukskaya, USSR . . | 1976 |
| 200 in. (5.08 m.) . . | Hale Obs., Palomar Mountain, California . . . . . . . | 1948 |
| 175 in. (4.5 m.) . . . (6 x 72 in. mirrors) | Smithsonian Astrophysical Observatory and U. of Arizona, Mt. Hopkins, Ariz. | 1979 |
| 158 in. (4 m.) . . . . | Kitt Peak National Observatory, Tucson, Arizona . . . | 1973 |
| 158 in. (4 m.) . . . . | Cerro Tololo Inter-American Observatory, Chile . . . . . . . | 1974 |
| 153 in. (3.9 m.) . . . | Anglo-Australian Telescope, Siding Spring, Australia . . . | 1975 |
| 150 in. (3.8 m.) [6] . . | British Infrared Telescope, Mauna Kea, Hawaii . . . . . . . | 1978 |
| 144 in. (3.66 m.) . . | Canada-France-Hawaii Telescope, Mauna Kea, Hawaii | 1979 |
| 142 in. (3.6 m.) . . . | European Southern Observatory, La Silla, Chile . . . . . | 1976 |
| 138 in. (3.5 m.) . . . | Max Planck Institute of Astrophysics, W. Germany . . . | UC |
| 126 in. (3.2) m.) [6] . . | NASA-U. of Hawaii, Mauna Kea, Hawaii . . . . . . . . . . . . | 1979 |
| 120 in. (3.05 m.) . . | Lick Observatory, Mt. Hamilton, California . . . . . . | 1959 |
| 107 in. (2.72 m.) . . | McDonald Observatory, Fort Davis, Texas . . . . . . . . . . | 1968 |
| 102 in. (2.59 m.) . . | Crimean Astrophysical Obs., Simferopol, USSR . . . . . . . . | 1960 |
| 100 in. (2.54 m.) . . | Hale Obs., Mt. Wilson, California . . . . . | 1917 |
| 100 in. (2.54 m.) . . | Carnegie Institution, Las Campanas, Chile . . . . . . . . | 1976 |
| 98 in. (2.49 m.) . . . | Royal Greenwich Observatory, Herstmonceux Castle, Sussex, England . . . . . . | 1966 |

[1] Baseline interferometer.  [2] Diameter, radioheliograph.  [3] Diameter, single antenna for centimeter wavelengths and longer.  [4] Diameter, single antennas for millimeter wavelengths.  [5] Upgraded.  [6] Infrared telescope.  UC=under construction.

## VARIABLE AND EXPLODING STARS *(continued)*

star that became unstable and exploded, increasing greatly in brightness and appearing where no star had been visible before to the unaided eye. By the end of 1572 the new star had faded until it was at the limit of visibility, and it disappeared entirely by March 1574.

The importance of Tycho's star was that it helped show that the heavens are not immutable. This was important at a time when the beginnings of astronomy were throwing off the dogma of Aristotelian cosmology. At the time of its appearance, some religious fanatics considered it to be a reappearance of the Star of Bethlehem, and thought the Second Coming was imminent. And astrologers of the time had a field day interpreting this unique portent.

Supernovae are rare, and only a few have been seen in our galaxy, the Milky Way. Many have been found, however, in other galaxies, and a supernova seen in 1885 in the Andromeda galaxy even provided astronomers with a clue to the nature of the galaxies.

Based on rather scanty information, astronomers estimate that we should see one supernova in our galaxy every several hundred years—and there has not been a sighting since Kepler observed one in 1604.

## DISTANCES OF THE STARS

We live some 93 million miles from the nearest star, our Sun.

Light from the Sun takes over 8 minutes to reach Earth, even though it travels at some 186,282 miles a second.

Other distances in our solar system are so immense that the Astronomical Unit (AU) is used to measure them—one AU is the average Earth-Sun distance.

The AU is too small, however, to measure the distances to stars other than our Sun. Instead, the light-year unit is used. A light-year is the distance light travels in a year—about 6 *trillion* miles.

Thus the next nearest star to Earth—a double

one named Rigil Centaurus (Alpha Centauri A) and a companion—is 4.3 light-years distant, as shown below.

The table shows some other stars known to be located within a distance of 17 light-years. Also indicated are the spectral types of these stars and their luminosity, or brightness.

Beyond these "nearby" stars lie other stars in our galaxy, the Milky Way. Containing billions of stars, the Milky Way is a great disk about 100,000 light-years in diameter.

The nearest galaxies to the Earth are the Magellanic Clouds, at a distance of about 170,000 light-years.

| STAR | SPEC-TRAL TYPE | DISTANCE IN LIGHT-YEARS | BRIGHT-NESS (Sun=1.0) | STAR | SPEC-TRAL TYPE | DISTANCE IN LIGHT-YEARS | BRIGHT-NESS (Sun=1.0) |
|---|---|---|---|---|---|---|---|
| Sun ............ | G2 | — | 1.0 | BD-12°4523 ... | M5 | 13.1 | 0.0013 |
| Alpha Cen A* .... | G2 | 4.3 | 1.3 | van Maanen's... | white | | |
| Barnard's* ...... | M5 | 5.9 | 0.00044 | | dwarf F | 13.9 | 0.00017 |
| Wolf 359 ...... | M6 | 7.6 | 0.00002 | Wolf 424 A* .... | M6 | 14.1 | 0.0014 |
| Lalande 21185*. | M2 | 8.1 | 0.0052 | CD-37°15492.. | M3 | 14.5 | 0.0058 |
| Sirius A* ........ | A1 | 8.6 | 23.0 | Groombridge | | | |
| Luyten 726-8A* . | M6 | 8.9 | 0.00006 | 1618 ........ | M0 | 15.0 | 0.040 |
| Ross 154 ...... | M5 | 9.4 | 0.0004 | CD-46°11540.. | M4 | 15.1 | 0.0030 |
| Ross 248 ...... | M6 | 10.3 | 0.00011 | CD-49°13515.. | M3 | 15.2 | 0.0058 |
| Epsilon Eri ...... | K2 | 10.7 | 0.30 | CD-44°11909.. | M5 | 15.3 | 0.00063 |
| Luyten 789-6 ... | M6 | 10.8 | 0.00012 | Luyten 1159-16. | M7 | 15.4 | 0.00023 |
| Ross 128 ...... | M5 | 10.8 | 0.00033 | Lalande 25372.. | M3.5 | 15.7 | 0.0076 |
| 61 Cygni A* ..... | K5 | 11.2 | 0.083 | AOe 17415-6* .. | M3.5 | 15.7 | 0.0044 |
| Epsilon Ind ...... | K5 | 11.2 | 0.13 | CC 658........ | white | | |
| Procyon A* ..... | F5 | 11.4 | 7.6 | | dwarf | 15.8 | 0.0008 |
| Sigma 2398 A*.. | M3.5 | 11.5 | 0.0028 | Ross 780 ...... | M5 | 15.8 | 0.0016 |
| Groombridge 34A* | M1 | 11.6 | 0.0058 | Omicron² Eri A* . | K0 | 15.9 | 0.33 |
| Lacaille 9352 ... | M2 | 11.7 | 0.012 | BD+20°2465*.. | M4.5 | 16.1 | 0.0036 |
| Tau Ceti ...... | G8 | 11.9 | 0.44 | Altair ........ | A7 | 16.6 | 10.0 |
| BD+5°1668 ... | M4 | 12.2 | 0.0014 | 70 Oph. A* .... | K1 | 16.7 | 0.44 |
| Lacaille 8760 ... | M1 | 12.5 | 0.025 | AC+79°3888.. | M4 | 16.8 | 0.0009 |
| Kapteyn's...... | M0 | 12.7 | 0.0040 | BD+43°4305*.. | M5 | 16.9 | 0.0021 |
| Kruger 60 A*.... | M4 | 12.8 | 0.0017 | Stein 2051A* ... | M5 | 17.0 | 0.0008 |
| Ross 614 A* .... | M5 | 13.1 | 0.0004 | | | | |

* These stars are binary or larger multiples—that is, they have one or more smaller stars associated with them.

## STAR COLORS AND TEMPERATURES

The floods of radiation given off by stars range the whole electromagnetic spectrum from gamma rays and X rays through light and heat to radio waves.

These radiations come from nuclear-fusion reactions maintained by the great pressures and temperatures deep within the stars. The calculated temperature of the center of the Sun is about 25,000,000°F. At such extremes, hydrogen atoms will fuse into helium atoms with a loss in total mass and the release of tremendous quantities of energy.

Stars vary greatly in color and temperature as well as in size. Astronomers analyze the radiations from stars with many instruments, including the spectroscope, which divides light into a color spectrum. The spectra of stars indicate their temperatures. The standard spectral classification of stars is given in the capital letters in the following table, with the color and approximate surface temperatures of stars in these classes.

The stars that fall into intermediate positions are indicated by a range of numbers from 0 to 9 with each letter. Our Sun, for example, has the spectral classification of G2 and a surface temperature of about 10,440°F.

| SPECTRAL CLASSIFICATION | COLOR SCALE | STAR SURFACE TEMPERATURE (°Fahrenheit) |
|---|---|---|
| O ............. | Blue.......... | 63,000 |
| B ............. | Bluish ........ | 45,000 |
| A .............. | White ........ | 19,800 |
| F .............. | Yellowish ..... | 13,500 |
| G Dwarf ....... | Yellow ....... | 10,440 |
| G Giant ....... | Yellow ....... | 9,540 |
| K Dwarf ........ | Orange ....... | 8,820 |
| K Giant ......... | Orange ....... | 7,200 |
| M Dwarf ....... | Orange-red ... | 6,120 |
| M Giant ........ | Orange-red ... | 5,400 |
| S ............. | Red .......... | 4,680 |
| N ............. | Red .......... | 4,680 |
| R ............. | Red .......... | 4,140 |

# Sports and Games

U.S. speed skater Eric Heiden became the first athlete ever to win five gold medals for single events during one Olympic competition in the Winter Olympics at Lake Placid, N.Y., in February 1980. Heiden, of Madison, Wis., set new Olympic records in each of the five events. He skated the 500 meters in 38.03 seconds, the 1,000 meters in 1:15.18, the 1,500 meters in 1:55.44, the 5,000 meters in 7:02.09, and the 10,000 meters in 14:28.33.

United Press Intl.

## SPORTS AND GAMES: CONTENTS

# MAJOR U.S. SPORTS AWARDS

## ATHLETE OF THE YEAR (Associated Press)

| YEAR | MALE ATHLETE | SPORT | YEAR | FEMALE ATHLETE | SPORT |
|---|---|---|---|---|---|
| 1937 | Don Budge | Tennis | 1937 | Katherine Rawls | Swimming |
| 1938 | Don Budge | Tennis | 1938 | Patty Berg | Golf |
| 1939 | Nile Kinnick | Football | 1939 | Alice Marble | Tennis |
| 1940 | Tommy Harmon | Football | 1940 | Alice Marble | Tennis |
| 1941 | Joe DiMaggio | Baseball | 1941 | Betty Hicks Newell | Golf |
| 1942 | Frank Sinkwich | Football | 1942 | Gloria Callen | Swimming |
| 1943 | Gunder Haegg | Track | 1943 | Patty Berg | Golf |
| 1944 | Byron Nelson | Golf | 1944 | Ann Curtis | Swimming |
| 1945 | Byron Nelson | Golf | 1945 | Babe Didrikson Zaharias | Golf |
| 1946 | Glenn Davis | Football | 1946 | Babe Didrikson Zaharias | Golf |
| 1947 | Johnny Lujack | Football | 1947 | Babe Didrikson Zaharias | Golf |
| 1948 | Lou Boudreau | Baseball | 1948 | Fanny Blankers—Koen | Track |
| 1949 | Leon Hart | Football | 1949 | Marlene Bauer | Golf |
| 1950 | Jim Konstanty | Baseball | 1950 | Babe Didrikson Zaharias | Golf |
| 1951 | Dick Kazmaier | Football | 1951 | Maureen Connolly | Tennis |
| 1952 | Bob Mathias | Track and Football | 1952 | Maureen Connolly | Tennis |
| 1953 | Ben Hogan | Golf | 1953 | Maureen Connolly | Tennis |
| 1954 | Willie Mays | Baseball | 1954 | Babe Didrikson Zaharias | Golf |
| 1955 | Hopalong Cassady | Football | 1955 | Patty Berg | Golf |
| 1956 | Mickey Mantle | Baseball | 1956 | Pat McCormick | Diving |
| 1957 | Ted Williams | Baseball | 1957 | Althea Gibson | Tennis |
| 1958 | Herb Elliott | Track | 1958 | Althea Gibson | Tennis |
| 1959 | Ingemar Johansson | Boxing | 1959 | Maria Bueno | Tennis |
| 1960 | Rafer Johnson | Decathlon | 1960 | Wilma Rudolph | Track |
| 1961 | Roger Maris | Baseball | 1961 | Wilma Rudolph | Track |
| 1962 | Maury Wills | Baseball | 1962 | Dawn Fraser | Swimming |
| 1963 | Sandy Koufax | Baseball | 1963 | Mickey Wright | Golf |
| 1964 | Don Schollander | Swimming | 1964 | Mickey Wright | Golf |
| 1965 | Sandy Koufax | Baseball | 1965 | Kathy Whitworth | Golf |
| 1966 | Frank Robinson | Baseball | 1966 | Kathy Whitworth | Golf |
| 1967 | Carl Yastrzemski | Baseball | 1967 | Billie Jean King | Tennis |
| 1968 | Denny McLain | Baseball | 1968 | Peggy Fleming | Ice Skating |
| 1969 | Tom Seaver | Baseball | 1969 | Debbie Meyer | Swimming |
| 1970 | George Blanda | Football | 1970 | Chi Cheng | Track |
| 1971 | Lee Trevino | Golf | 1971 | Evonne Goolagong | Tennis |
| 1972 | Mark Spitz | Swimming | 1972 | Olga Korbut | Gymnastics |
| 1973 | O.J. Simpson | Football | 1973 | Billie Jean King | Tennis |
| 1974 | Muhammad Ali | Boxing | 1974 | Chris Evert | Tennis |
| 1975 | Fred Lynn | Baseball | 1975 | Chris Evert | Tennis |
| 1976 | Bruce Jenner | Track | 1976 | Nadia Comaneci | Gymnastics |
| 1977 | Steve Cauthen | Horse Racing | 1977 | Chris Evert | Tennis |
| 1978 | Ron Guidry | Baseball | 1978 | Nancy Lopez | Golf |
| 1979 | Willie Stargell | Baseball | 1979 | Tracy Austin | Tennis |

## JAMES E. SULLIVAN MEMORIAL TROPHY (Amateur Athletic Union)

| | | | | | |
|---|---|---|---|---|---|
| 1930 | Bobby Jones | Golf | 1955 | Harrison Dillard | Track (Sprinter) |
| 1931 | Bernard E. Berlinger | All-Around Athlete | 1956 | Pat McCormick | Diving |
| 1932 | James A. Bausch | All-Around Athlete | 1957 | Bobby Joe Morrow | Track (Sprinter) |
| 1933 | Glenn Cunningham | Track | 1958 | Glenn Davis | Track (Sprinter) |
| 1934 | Bill Bonthron | Track | 1959 | Parry O'Brien | Track (Shot Put) |
| 1935 | Lawson Little | Golf | 1960 | Rafer Johnson | Track (Decathlon) |
| 1936 | Glenn Morris | Track (Decathlon) | 1961 | Wilma Rudolph | Track (Sprinter) |
| 1937 | Don Budge | Tennis | 1962 | Jim Beatty | Track |
| 1938 | Don Lash | Track | 1963 | John Pennel | Track (Pole Vaulter) |
| 1939 | Joe Burk | Rowing | 1964 | Don Schollander | Swimming |
| 1940 | Greg Rice | Track | 1965 | Bill Bradley | Basketball |
| 1941 | Les MacMitchell | Track | 1966 | Jim Ryun | Track (Mile Runner) |
| 1942 | Cornelius Warmerdam | Track (Pole Vaulter) | 1967 | Randy Matson | Track (Shot Put) |
| 1943 | Gil Dodds | Track | 1968 | Debbie Meyer | Swimming |
| 1944 | Ann Curtis | Swimming | 1969 | Bill Toomey | Track (Decathlon) |
| 1945 | Doc Blanchard | Football | 1970 | John Kinsella | Swimming |
| 1946 | Arnold Tucker | Football | 1971 | Mark Spitz | Swimming |
| 1947 | Jack Kelly Jr. | Rowing | 1972 | Frank Shorter | Track (Distance Runner) |
| 1948 | Bob Mathias | Track (Decathlon) | 1973 | Bill Walton | Basketball |
| 1949 | Dick Button | Figure Skating | 1974 | Rick Wohlhuter | Track |
| 1950 | Fred Wilt | Track | 1975 | Tim Shaw | Swimming |
| 1951 | Bob Richards | Track (Pole Vaulter) | 1976 | Bruce Jenner | Track |
| 1952 | Horace Ashenfelter | Track (Distance Runner) | 1977 | John Naber | Swimming |
| 1953 | Sammy Lee | Diving | 1978 | Tracy Caulkins | Swimming |
| 1954 | Mal Whitfield | Track (Runner) | 1979 | Kurt Thomas | Gymnastics |

# PEOPLE IN SPORTS

Father Bill Magill, *right*, 61, leads his "Over the Hill Gang" down Copper Mountain, Colo. The Episcopal minister from Denver founded the club for skiers over 45 in 1977. The club has a waiting list.

**Bill Rodgers** won the Boston Marathon on April 22, but the question of who really won the women's race will go down in history as doubtful. Veteran marathoner Rodgers crossed the finish line in 2 hours, 12 minutes, 11 seconds to take his fourth Boston title. The first woman to cross the finish line was New Yorker **Rosie Ruiz**, in a purported 2:31:56, the third-fastest time recorded in any marathon by a woman.

Race officials and runners immediately questioned whether the 26-year-old administrative assistant had run the entire race, and officials launched an investigation. Other runners denied ever seeing her. She did not appear in any of the videotapes of the race. Some Harvard students reported seeing her jump into the race less than a mile from the finish. Consequently, Ruiz was stripped of her crown by marathon officials on April 29. **Jacqueline Gareau**, of Montreal, was declared the official winner, with Ms. Ruiz still insisting she was the true winner.

During the investigation, a woman claimed that she had ridden the subway with Ms. Ruiz during the 1979 New York Marathon, and that Ruiz did not really run the race in 2:56:29, which time enabled her to enter the Boston race. New York officials disqualified her as a finisher in the 1979 competition on April 25.

**Curt Brinkman**, 26, of Orem, Utah, won the wheelchair division of the Boston Marathon in 1 hour, 55 minutes, 17 minutes faster than Bill Rodgers. The wheelchair entrants pushed off 15 minutes ahead of the regular runners, completely separate from them.

**Alberto Salazar**, 22, won the New York City Marathon Oct. 26, in a course record 2 hours, 9 minutes, 41 seconds. The University of Oregon senior, running his first marathon, beat 12,622 other finishers to the tape.

**Grete Waitz**, won the race for the third consecutive time, in 2:25:42, her third world record for the New York Marathon.

Among the finishers in the New York City race was **Mort Schlein**, 47, of New York City. Though blind, he attached a four-foot string to his little finger and to the finger of a friend running ahead of him for the first 16 miles. Another friend took over for the last 10 miles, and Schlein finished 10,896th in 4:28:32. The oldest finisher was **Chick Mostow**, 77, of Chicago, who placed 11,674th.

Yachtsman **David Scott-Cowper**, 38, set a new round-the-world sailing record of 249

**PEOPLE IN SPORTS** (continued)

days. Traveling in a 40-foot aluminum hull sailboat, *Ocean Bound*, Scott-Cowper landed in Plymouth, England, on April 24. Only 225 days were actually spent at sea; the others in port. The sailing time of 225 days bettered by one day the record set by the late **Sir Francis Chichester** in 1967, and shattered by 23 days the solo record of 272 days set by **Naomi James** in 1978.

**Juan Antonio Samaranch,** Spanish ambassador to the Soviet Union, was elected as the new president of the International Olympic Committee, succeeding **Lord Killanin** of Ireland. . . . **Will F. Nicholson, Jr.** assumed the presidency of the United States Golf Association.

**Lynn Swann,** wide receiver of the Pittsburgh Steelers, became a trustee of the Pittsburgh Ballet Theater. . . . Steeler quarterback **Terry Bradshaw** reigned as king of the Mardi Gras in New Orleans in February.

**Cheryl Hanchar,** 10, of Congers, N.Y., retrieved the 400th home-run ball hit by New York Yankee **Reggie Jackson.** . . . **Nigel Short,** 14, became the world's youngest international chessmaster at an International Chess League tournament at Hastings, England, in January. Nigel was the third 14-year-old in chess history to qualify as an international master.

U.S. Olympic hockey team goalie **Jim Craig** played his first professional game in a NHL game with the Atlanta Flames in March. For his debut, he deflected 24 shots, resulting in a 4–1 Atlanta victory over the Colorado Rockies. He later was traded to the Boston Bruins, his hometown team.

Tennis ace **Arthur Ashe** ended his playing career in April, citing health as a major factor in his decision. He underwent bypass surgery after a heart attack in 1979. In September he was named captain of the U.S. Davis Cup team. . . . Dallas quarterback **Roger Staubach** retired from professional football in March at age 38, after 11 seasons with the Cowboys that included four Super Bowl games.

**Joe May,** of Trapper Creek, Alaska, won the Iditarod Trail Race in record time in March. The fur trapper drove his team of eight sled dogs from Anchorage to Nome in 14 days, 7 hours, 11 minutes.

**Ed (Too Tall) Jones,** who quit professional football in 1979 to pursue a boxing career, returned to the Dallas Cowboys for the 1980–81 football season.

Teammates of Pittsburgh Pirates first baseman **Willie Stargell** presented the veteran baseball player with a cake for his 39th birthday. Then they shoved the entire whipped-cream-filled pastry in his face.

World champion ice skaters **Linda Fratianne,** of the U.S., and **Robin Cousins,** of Britain, both turned professional in 1980. Ms. Fratianne, who won a silver medal at the Olympics, signed a contract with producer Burt Sugarman, reportedly guaranteeing her $1 million. Cousins joined the Holiday on Ice company.

**Tracee Talavera,** 13, won the women's title at the two-day American Cup gymnastics competition at New York City's Madison Square Garden in March. The Walnut Creek, Calif., teenager beat the world's eighth-ranked all-around gymnast, Emilia Eberle, of Romania, for the title. Kurt Thomas took the men's title, scoring a perfect 10.0 in the high bar during the competition.

Several climbing teams successfully conquered Mt. Everest in 1980. In February, **Leszek Cichy,** 29, of Warsaw, and **Krzysztof Wielicki,** 30, of Wroclaw. Poland, reached the summit for the first successful assault in the winter. In May, two Japanese climbers became the first to scale the 29,028-foot peak by the previously unconquered North Wall. **Tsuneo Shigehiro** and **Takashi Ozaki** reached the summit after two failed attempts. In early September, **Reinhold Messner,** of Italy, claimed the highest honor in mountaineering with a solo ascent without oxygen equipment. Messner, 35, reportedly reached the peak on Aug. 20 from the Chinese side.

**Rohn Roskelly,** 32, of Spokane, Wash., a photojournalist, became the first American to climb Mt. Makalu, in Nepal, the fifth-highest mountain in the world. . . . **Marco Broggi,** 40, of Switzerland, became the first person to cross the 6,910-foot St. Gotthard pass in a hang glider. The trip took 2 hours, 15 minutes.

**Bettye McClendon,** of Atlanta, became the first woman referee to officiate at a men's college basketball game when Clark College played at Morris Brown in January. . . . Apprentice jockey **Karen Rogers,** 17, became the first female to win both races in a daily double at Aqueduct race track in Queens, New York. The double paid $362.80.

Swedish tennis ace **Bjorn Borg** married **Mariana Simionescu,** in Bucharest, Romania, in July. . . . Welterweight boxing champion **Sugar Ray Leonard** married his sweetheart of nine years, **Juanita Wilkinson,** in Landover, Md., in January.

**AWARDS AND HONORS**

Associated Press named **Muhammad Ali** as its Athlete of the Decade for the 1970s. . . . Soccer star **Pelé** was chosen Champion of the Century by a group of 20 sports newspapers from all over the world.

**Jean-Marc Boivin** of Dijon, France, re-

ceived the International Award for Valor in Sport for scaling the 24,930-foot Himalayan peak, K2, second highest in the world, then jumping off the top in a hang glider. The 29-year-old, from Chamonix, France, took 4½ months to reach the top, and became partially blinded in the ascent. He received a $220,000 gold wreath, which he must relinquish in 1981, but was later given an $11,000 facsimile to keep.

Boston College basketball captain **Jim Sweeney** received the Naismith Hall of Fame Award, given annually to the nation's outstanding college basketball player under 6 feet tall.

*The Sporting News* named Louisville's **Darrell Griffith** college basketball player of the year. Both AP and UPI named DePaul's **Mark Aguirre** college basketball player of the year, and his coach, **Ray Meyer**, as coach of the year.

Inductees to the newly created Women's Sports Hall of Fame included racing-car driver **Janet Guthrie**, runner **Wilma Rudolph**, tennis ace **Billie Jean King**, swimmer **Eleanor Holm Whalen**, golfer **Patty Berg**. Posthumous inductees were track star **Babe Didrikson Zaharias**, aviator **Amelia Earhart**, swimmer **Gertrude Ederle**, and tennis star and golfer **Althea Gibson**.

**Jack Tuthill**, tournament director of the PGA tour, received the William C. Richardson award from the Golf Writers Association of America, given annually to the individual who "consistently has made an outstanding contribution to golf." ... Former Champion **Jim Stefanich** and Professional Bowlers Assn. business secretary **Lorraine Stitzlein** were inducted into the Professional Bowlers Assn. Hall of Fame.

Baseball great **Willie Mays** received the A. Philip Randolph Humanitarian Award from the Harlem-Downing Children's Service for "unselfish contributions to children's causes." ... A plaque dedicated to the late New York Yankee catcher **Thurman Munson** was dedicated at Yankee Stadium in September. The memorial incorporates a likeness of the former team captain, who died in a 1979 plane crash.

Gymnast Bart Conner displays his form on the rings during the American Cup gymnastic championships at New York's Madison Square Garden on March 9. In the two-day competition Conner scored a 9.9 of a possible 10.0 on the high bar, and totaled 58.4 points to win the silver medal. The first-place gold was won by teammate Kurt Thomas, who scored 58.85 points, including a perfect 10.0 on the high bar.

Wide World

# AUTOMOBILE RACING

Wide World

After winning the Indianapolis 500 for the third time, Johnny Rutherford receives congratulations from rookie driver Tim Richmond. During Rutherford's victory lap, Richmond hitched a ride after his car had stalled.

## WINNERS OF THE INDIANAPOLIS 500

| YEAR | WINNER | CAR | AVG. SPEED | YEAR | WINNER | CAR | AVG. SPEED |
|------|--------|-----|-----------|------|--------|-----|-----------|
| 1911 | Ray Harroun... | Marmon............ | 74.590 | 1947 | Mauri Rose.... | Blue Crown Special | 116.338 |
| 1912 | Joe Dawson ... | National........... | 78.720 | 1948 | Mauri Rose.... | Blue Crown Special | 119.814 |
| 1913 | Jules Goux.... | Peugeot........... | 75.930 | 1949 | Bill Holland.... | Blue Crown Special | 121.327 |
| 1914 | Rene Thomas | Delage............ | 82.470 | 1950 | Johnny Parsons | Wynn's Special...... | 124.002 [3] |
| 1915 | Ralph De Palma | Mercedes.......... | 89.840 | 1951 | Lee Wallard.... | Balanger Special | 126.244 |
| 1916 | Dario Resta.... | Peugeot........... | 84.000 [1] | 1952 | Troy Ruttman | Agajanian Special ... | 128.922 |
| 1919 | Howard Wilcox. | Peugeot........... | 88.050 | 1953 | Bill Vukovich... | Fuel Injection Special | 128.740 |
| 1920 | Gaston Chevrolet | Monroe.......... | 88.620 | 1954 | Bill Vukovich... | Fuel Injection Special | 130.840 |
| 1921 | Tommy Milton | Frontenac......... | 89.620 | 1955 | Bob Sweikert.. | John Zink Special.... | 128.209 |
| 1922 | Jim Murphy ... | Murphy Special ... | 94.480 | 1956 | Pat Flaherty ... | John Zink Special.... | 128.490 |
| 1923 | Tommy Milton | H.C.S. Special....... | 90.950 | 1957 | Sam Hanks.... | Belond Exhaust Spcl.. | 135.601 |
| 1924 | L. L. Corum, | | | 1958 | Jimmy Bryan .. | Belond AP Special ... | 133.791 |
|  | Joe Boyer... | Duesenberg Special | 98.230 | 1959 | Rodger Ward .. | Leader Card 500.... | 135.857 |
| 1925 | Peter De Paolo . | Duesenberg Special | 101.130 | 1960 | Jim Rathman .. | Ken-Paul Special ... | 138.767 |
| 1926 | Frank Lockhart | Miller Special ....... | 95.904 [2] | 1961 | A. J. Foyt...... | Bowes Seal Special .. | 139.130 |
| 1927 | George | | | 1962 | Rodger Ward .. | Leader Card 500 .... | 140.293 |
|  | Souders..... | Duesenberg......... | 97.545 | 1963 | Parnelli Jones | Agajanian-Willard Spcl. | 143.137 |
| 1928 | Louis Meyer ... | Miller Special...... | 99.482 | 1964 | A. J. Foyt...... | S.T.W. Offenhauser .. | 147.350 |
| 1929 | Ray Keech... | Simplex Special ... | 97.585 | 1965 | Jim Clark .... | Lotus-Ford......... | 150.686 |
| 1930 | Billy Arnold.... | Hartz-Miller....... | 100.448 | 1966 | Graham Hill ... | Lotus-Ford.......... | 144.317 |
| 1931 | Louis | | | 1967 | A. J. Foyt...... | Coyote Ford ........ | 151.207 |
|  | Schneider ... | Bowes Special..... | 96.629 | 1968 | Bobby Unser ... | Eagle-Offenhauser ... | 152.882 |
| 1932 | Fred Frame.... | Miller Special...... | 104.144 | 1969 | Mario Andretti | Hawk-Ford.......... | 156.867 |
| 1933 | Louis Meyer ... | Miller Special...... | 104.162 | 1970 | Al Unser ...... | Lola-Ford........... | 155.749 |
| 1934 | Bill Cummings | Miller Special...... | 104.863 | 1971 | Al Unser ...... | P.J. Colt-Ford ...... | 157.735 |
| 1935 | Kelly Petillo... | Gilmore Special ..... | 106.240 | 1972 | Mark Donohue | McLaren-Offenhauser | 162.962 [4] |
| 1936 | Louis Meyer ... | Ring Free Special .... | 109.069 | 1973 | Gordon Johncock | McLaren-Offenhauser | 158.589 [5] |
| 1937 | Wilbur Shaw... | Shaw-Gilmore Spcl. | 113.580 | 1974 | Johnny | | |
| 1938 | Floyd Roberts | Burd Piston Reg. | | | Rutherford .. | McLaren-Offenhauser | 158.589 |
|  |  | Special........... | 117.200 | 1975 | Bobby Unser .. | Eagle-Offenhauser ... | 149.213 [6] |
| 1939 | Wilbur Shaw... | Boyle Special....... | 115.035 | 1976 | J. Rutherford... | McLaren-Offenhauser | 148.725 [7] |
| 1940 | Wilbur Shaw... | Boyle Special....... | 114.277 | 1977 | A. J. Foyt...... | Coyote Foyt......... | 161.331 |
| 1941 | Mauri Rose, | Noc-Out Hose Clamp. | | 1978 | Al Unser ...... | Lola-Cosworth ...... | 161.363 |
|  | Floyd Davis | Special........... | 115.117 | 1979 | Rick Mears .... | Penske-Cosworth .... | 158.899 |
| 1946 | George Robson | Thorne Eng. Special | 114.820 | 1980 | J. Rutherford .. | Chaparral-Cosworth . | 142.862 |

[1] 300 miles.   [2] 400 miles.   [3] 345 miles.   [4] Track record.   [5] 332.5 miles.   [6] 435 miles.   [7] 255 miles.

## U.S. AUTO CLUB NATIONAL CHAMPIONS (Indy-type cars)

| | | | |
|---|---|---|---|
| 1910 Ray Harroun | 1925 Peter De Paolo | 1946–48 Ted Horn | 1967 A. J. Foyt |
| 1911 Ralph Mulford | 1926 Harry Hartz | 1949 Johnnie Parsons | 1968 Bobby Unser |
| 1912 Ralph De Palma | 1927 Peter De Paolo | 1950 Henry Banks | 1969 Mario Andretti |
| 1913 Earl Cooper | 1928–29 Louis Meyer | 1951 Tony Bettenhausen | 1970 Al Unser |
| 1914 Ralph De Palma | 1930 Billy Arnold | 1952 Chuck Stevenson | 1971–72 Joe Leonard |
| 1915 Earl Cooper | 1931 Louis Schneider | 1953 Sam Hanks | 1973 Roger McCluskey |
| 1916 Dario Resta | 1932 Bob Carey | 1954 Jimmy Bryan | 1974 Bobby Unser |
| 1917 Earl Cooper | 1933 Louis Meyer | 1955 Bob Sweikert | 1975 A. J. Foyt |
| 1918 Ralph Mulford | 1934 Bill Cummings | 1956–57 Jimmy Bryan | 1976 Gordon Johncock |
| 1919 Howard Wilcox | 1935 Kelly Petillo | 1958 Tony Bettenhausen | 1977–78 Tom Sneva |
| 1920 Gaston Chevrolet | 1936 Mauri Rose | 1959 Rodger Ward | 1979 A. J. Foyt |
| 1921 Tommy Milton | 1937 Wilbur Shaw | 1960–61 A. J. Foyt | 1980 Johnny Rutherford |
| 1922 James Murphy | 1938 Floyd Roberts | 1962 Rodger Ward | |
| 1923 Eddie Hearne | 1939 Wilbur Shaw | 1963–64 A. J. Foyt | |
| 1924 James Murphy | 1940–41 Rex Mays | 1965–66 Mario Andretti | |

## GRAND PRIX WORLD CHAMPIONS (Formula 1 cars)

| | | |
|---|---|---|
| 1959–60 Jack Brabham, Australia | 1967 Denis Hulme, New Zealand | 1974 Emerson Fittipaldi, Brazil |
| 1961 Phil Hill, United States | 1968 Graham Hill, Britain | 1975 Niki Lauda, Austria |
| 1962 Graham Hill, Britain | 1969 Jackie Stewart, Britain | 1976 James Hunt, Britain |
| 1963 Jim Clark, Britain | 1970 Jochen Rindt, Austria | 1977 Niki Lauda, Austria |
| 1964 John Surtees, Britain | 1971 Jackie Stewart, Britain | 1978 Mario Andretti, United States |
| 1965 Jim Clark, Britain | 1972 Emerson Fittipaldi, Brazil | 1979 Jody Scheckter, South Africa |
| 1966 Jack Brabham, Australia | 1973 Jackie Stewart, Britain | 1980 Alan Jones, Australia |

## SPORTS CAR CLUB OF AMERICA (SCCA) CAN-AM CHALLENGE

| YEAR | SERIES WINNER | CAR | YEAR | SERIES WINNER | CAR |
|---|---|---|---|---|---|
| 1968 | Denis Hulme | McLaren M8A-Chevy | 1974 | Jackie Oliver | Shadow DN4-Dodge |
| 1969 | Bruce McLaren .... | McLaren M8B-Chevy | 1975–76 | Not Held | |
| 1970 | Denis Hulme....... | McLaren M8D-Chevy | 1977 | Patrick Tambay .... | Lola T-333CS-Chevy |
| 1971 | Peter Revson .... | McLaren M8F-Chevy | 1978 | Alan Jones ........ | Lola T-333CS-Chevy |
| 1972 | George Follmer .... | Porsche 917/10-Porsche (T) | 1979 | Jacky Ickx ........ | Lola T-333CS-Chevy |
| 1973 | Mark Donohue ..... | Porsche 917/30-Porsche (T) | 1980 | Patrick Tambay .... | Lola T-530-Chevy |

## WINSTON CUP GRAND NATIONAL CHAMPIONS OF NASCAR (National Association for Stock Car Auto Racing)

| YEAR | CHAMPION | CAR | YEAR | CHAMPION | CAR | YEAR | CHAMPION | CAR |
|---|---|---|---|---|---|---|---|---|
| 1949 | Red Byron | Oldsmobile | 1958–59 | Lee Petty | Olds./Plym. | 1968–69 | David Pearson | Ford |
| 1950 | Bill Rexford | Oldsmobile | 1960 | Rex White | Chevrolet | 1970 | Bobby Isaac | Dodge |
| 1951 | Herb Thomas | Plymouth-Hudson | 1961 | Ned Jarrett | Chevrolet | 1971–72 | Richard Petty | Plym./Dodge |
| 1952 | Tim Flock | Hudson | 1962 | Joe Weatherly | Pontiac | 1973 | Benny Parsons | Chevrolet |
| 1953 | Herb Thomas | Hudson | 1963 | Joe Weatherly | Pontiac-Merc. | 1974–75 | Richard Petty | Dodge |
| 1954 | Lee Petty | Chrysler | 1964 | Richard Petty | Plymouth | 1976–77 | Cale Yarborough | Chevrolet |
| 1955 | Tim Flock | Chrysler | 1965 | Ned Jarrett | Ford | 1978 | Cale Yarborough | Oldsmobile |
| 1956 | Buck Baker | Chrysler-Dodge | 1966 | David Pearson | Dodge | 1979 | Richard Petty | Olds./Chev. |
| 1957 | Buck Baker | Chevrolet | 1967 | Richard Petty | Plymouth | 1980 | Dale Earnhardt | Chevrolet |

## WINNERS OF THE DAYTONA 500 (Stock Cars)

| YEAR | WINNER | CAR | SPEED (mph) | YEAR | WINNER | CAR | SPEED (mph) |
|---|---|---|---|---|---|---|---|
| 1961 | Marvin Panch .... | Pontiac ... | 149.601 | 1971 | Richard Petty .... | Plymouth | 144.462 |
| 1962 | Fireball Roberts .. | Pontiac ... | 152.529 | 1972 | A. J. Foyt ........ | Mercury .. | 161.550 |
| 1963 | Tiny Lund ........ | Ford ...... | 151.566 | 1973 | Richard Petty .... | Dodge ..... | 157.205 |
| 1964 | Richard Petty .... | Plymouth | 154.334 | 1974 | Richard Petty .... | Dodge ..... | 140.894 |
| 1965 [1] | Fred Lorenzen .... | Ford ...... | 141.539 | 1975 | Benny Parsons ... | Chevrolet | 153.649 |
| 1966 [2] | Richard Petty .... | Plymouth | 160.627 | 1976 | David Pearson ... | Mercury .. | 152.181 |
| 1967 | Mario Andretti .... | Ford ...... | 146.926 | 1977 | Cale Yarborough | Chevrolet | 153.218 |
| 1968 | Cale Yarborough | Mercury .. | 143.251 | 1978 | Bobby Allison .... | Ford ...... | 159.730 |
| 1969 | Lee Roy Yarborough | Ford ...... | 157.950 | 1979 | Richard Petty .... | Oldsmobile | 143.997 |
| 1970 | Pete Hamilton .... | Plymouth | 149.601 | 1980 | Buddy Baker ..... | Oldsmobile | 177.602 |

[1] 332.5 miles (rain). [2] 495 miles (rain).

## WORLD SPEED RECORDS (One Mile)

| YEAR | DRIVER | CAR | SPEED (mph) | YEAR | DRIVER | CAR | SPEED (mph) |
|---|---|---|---|---|---|---|---|
| **Gasoline-engine cars** | | | | **Gasoline-engine cars** | | | |
| 1898 | Chasseloup Laubat .. | Jeantaud ....... | 39.24 | 1935 | Sir Malcolm Campbell | Bluebird Special | 301.13 |
| 1904 | Henry Ford ........ | Ford .......... | 91.37 | 1939 | John R. Cobb ...... | Railton ........ | 368.90 |
| 1910 | Barney Oldfield ..... | Benz ......... | 131.72 | 1947 | John R. Cobb ...... | Railton-Mobil ... | 394.19 |
| 1919 | Ralph De Palma ..... | Packard ...... | 149.88 | 1964 | Donald Campbell .... | Bluebird ....... | 403.10 |
| 1920 | Tommy Milton ...... | Duesenberg .... | 155.05 | 1965 | Bob Summers ....... | Goldenrod ..... | 409.23 |
| 1927 | H. O. D. Seagrave .... | Sunbeam ...... | 203.79 | | | | |
| 1928 | Ray Keech .......... | White Triplex ... | 207.55 | **Jet- or rocket-powered cars** | | | |
| 1929 | H. O. D. Seagrave .... | Irving Napier ... | 231.45 | 1963 | Craig Breedlove .... | Spirit of America | 407.45 |
| 1931 | Sir Malcolm Campbell | Napier-Campbell | 246.09 | 1964 | Art Arfons ........ | Green Monster | 536.71 |
| 1932 | Sir Malcolm Campbell | Napier-Campbell | 253.96 | 1965 | Craig Breedlove .... | Spirit of America | 600.60 |
| 1933 | Sir Malcolm Campbell | Napier-Campbell | 272.11 | 1970 | Gary Gabelich ....... | Blue Flame ..... | 622.41 |

# BASEBALL

George Brett, of the Kansas City Royals, hits a double at Royals Stadium on Aug. 18, against Toronto's Mike Barlow, bringing his batting average to .401. He pushed his average up to .407 by the end of the month, but ended the regular season with a league-leading .390. Brett was voted the American League's Most Valuable Player.

United Press Int'l.

Defying the odds makers, the Philadelphia Phillies won the National League pennant in a thrilling playoff series with Houston 3 games to 2, and then went on to defeat the Kansas City Royals, 4 games to 2, for their first World Series championship. In their last World Series appearance, in 1950, the Phillies folded before the New York Yankees, 4 games to 0.

The Royals were believed to have the advantage going into the World Series, having clobbered the Yankees 3 games to 0 in the playoffs for the American League title.

In the first game of the World Series at Philadelphia, the Royals took the lead with two-run homers by Amos Otis and Willie Aikens, but the Phillies fought back to win 7–6 despite a second two-run homer by Aikens.

After trailing 4–2 at the end of the seventh inning, Philadelphia won the second game with four runs in the eighth that made the final score 6–4.

Performing before their home fans, the Royals regained winning form in the third game. The Phillies tied the game in the second, fifth, and eighth innings, but Kansas City finally took it 4–3 with a game-winning hit by Aikens in the tenth.

The Royals evened the series by taking the fourth game 5–3, helped by the big bat of Willie Aikens, who again hit two home runs—the first player ever to hit two homers in two separate games of a World Series.

The Phillies' ace reliever Tug McGraw was a hero in the fifth game when, with the bases loaded by the Royals in the bottom half of the ninth, he struck out Jose Cardenal to win the game 4–3.

Trailing 4–1, Kansas City again had the bases loaded in the ninth inning of the sixth game in Philadelphia. And the Phillies' McGraw again became a hero with a strike-out fastball pitch to Willie Wilson that ended the series.

Japan's star home-run hitter Sadaharu Oh, 40, retired in November after 21 seasons in which he compiled a lifetime record of 868 homers and a batting average of .301.

In Little League baseball, Taiwan won its fourth consecutive title, beating Tampa, Fla., at Williamsport, Pa., on Aug. 30, in a closely contested game, 4–3.

Philadelphia Phillies' Mike Schmidt, *above,* who hit safely in all six games of the World Series, was named its Most Valuable Player. He later was named the National League's Most Valuable Player.

Phillie relief pitcher Tug McGraw, *right,* throws hard during sixth and final game of World Series. Relieving winning pitcher Steve Carlton in the eighth inning, he held on to strike out Kansas City's Willie Wilson for the last out and the championship title. McGraw pitched in three of the six World Series games after taking part in all five of the National League playoff games against Houston.

United Press Int'l.

United Press Int'l.

## WORLD SERIES BOX SCORES: 1980

### 1st GAME: PHILADELPHIA 7, KANSAS CITY 6

| | | | | | | | | | | R | H | E |
|---|---|---|---|---|---|---|---|---|---|---|---|---|
| Kansas City | 0 | 2 | 2 | 0 | 0 | 0 | 0 | 2 | 0 | 6 | 9 | 1 |
| Philadelphia | 0 | 0 | 5 | 1 | 1 | 0 | 0 | 0 | x | 7 | 11 | 0 |

Pitchers: Philadelphia—Walk (winner, 7), McGraw (2); Kansas City—Leonard (loser, 3⅔), Martin (4), Quisenberry (⅓).
Home runs: Otis, Aikens (2), McBride.
Attendance at Philadelphia Oct. 14: 65,791.

### 2nd GAME: PHILADELPHIA 6, KANSAS CITY 4

| | | | | | | | | | | R | H | E |
|---|---|---|---|---|---|---|---|---|---|---|---|---|
| Kansas City | 0 | 0 | 0 | 0 | 0 | 1 | 3 | 0 | 0 | 4 | 11 | 0 |
| Philadelphia | 0 | 0 | 0 | 0 | 0 | 2 | 0 | 4 | x | 6 | 8 | 1 |

Pitchers: Philadelphia—Carlton (winner, 8), Reed (1); Kansas City—Gura (6), Quisenberry (loser, 2).
Home runs: None.
Attendance at Philadelphia Oct. 15: 65,775.

### 3rd GAME: KANSAS CITY 4, PHILADELPHIA 3

| | | | | | | | | | | R | H | E |
|---|---|---|---|---|---|---|---|---|---|---|---|---|
| Philadelphia | 0 | 1 | 0 | 0 | 1 | 0 | 0 | 1 | 0 | 3 | 14 | 0 |
| Kansas City | 1 | 0 | 0 | 1 | 0 | 0 | 1 | 0 | 1 | 4 | 11 | 0 |

Pitchers: Kansas City—Gale (4⅓), Martin (3⅓), Quisenberry (winner, 2⅓); Philadelphia—Ruthven (9), McGraw (loser, ⅔).
Home runs: G. Brett, Schmidt, Otis.
Attendance at Kansas City Oct. 17: 42,380.

### 4th GAME: KANSAS CITY 5, PHILADELPHIA 3

| | | | | | | | | | | R | H | E |
|---|---|---|---|---|---|---|---|---|---|---|---|---|
| Philadelphia | 0 | 1 | 0 | 0 | 0 | 0 | 1 | 1 | 0 | 3 | 10 | 1 |
| Kansas City | 4 | 1 | 0 | 0 | 0 | 0 | 0 | 0 | x | 5 | 10 | 2 |

Pitchers: Kansas City—Leonard (winner, 7), Quisenberry (2); Philadelphia—Christenson (loser, ⅓), Noles (4⅔), Saucier (⅔), Brusstar (2⅓).
Home runs: Aikens (2).
Attendance at Kansas City Oct. 18: 42,363.

### 5th GAME: PHILADELPHIA 4, KANSAS CITY 3

| | | | | | | | | | | R | H | E |
|---|---|---|---|---|---|---|---|---|---|---|---|---|
| Philadelphia | 0 | 0 | 0 | 2 | 0 | 0 | 0 | 0 | 2 | 4 | 7 | 0 |
| Kansas City | 0 | 0 | 0 | 0 | 1 | 2 | 0 | 0 | x | 3 | 12 | 2 |

Pitchers: Philadelphia—Bystrom (5), Reed (1), McGraw (winner, 3); Kansas City—Gura (6⅓), Quisenberry (loser 2⅔).
Home runs: Schmidt, Otis.
Attendance at Kansas City Oct. 19: 42,369.

### 6th GAME: PHILADELPHIA 4, KANSAS CITY 1

| | | | | | | | | | | R | H | E |
|---|---|---|---|---|---|---|---|---|---|---|---|---|
| Kansas City | 0 | 0 | 0 | 0 | 0 | 0 | 0 | 1 | 0 | 1 | 7 | 2 |
| Philadelphia | 0 | 0 | 2 | 0 | 1 | 1 | 0 | 0 | x | 4 | 9 | 0 |

Pitchers: Philadelphia—Carlton (winner, 7), McGraw (2); Kansas City—Gale (loser, 2), Martin (2⅓), Splittorff (1⅔), Pattin (1), Quisenberry (1).
Home runs: None.
Attendance at Philadelphia Oct. 20: 65,838.

## WORLD SERIES RESULTS: 1903–1980

| YEAR | WINNERS | LOSERS | GAMES | YEAR | WINNERS | LOSERS | GAMES |
|---|---|---|---|---|---|---|---|
| 1903 [1] | Boston (A) | Pittsburgh | 5–3 | 1942 | St. Louis (N) | New York (A) | 4–1 |
| 1904 | Not played | | – | 1943 | New York (A) | St. Louis (N) | 4–1 |
| 1905 | New York (N) | Philadelphia (A) | 4–1 | 1944 | St. Louis (N) | St. Louis (A) | 4–2 |
| 1906 | Chicago (A) | Chicago (N) | 4–2 | 1945 | Detroit (A) | Chicago (N) | 4–3 |
| 1907 [2] | Chicago (N) | Detroit (A) | 4–0 | 1946 | St. Louis (N) | Boston (A) | 4–3 |
| 1908 | Chicago (N) | Detroit (A) | 4–1 | 1947 | New York (A) | Brooklyn (N) | 4–3 |
| 1909 | Pittsburgh (N) | Detroit (A) | 4–3 | 1948 | Cleveland (A) | Boston (N) | 4–2 |
| 1910 | Philadelphia (A) | Chicago (N) | 4–1 | 1949 | New York (A) | Brooklyn (N) | 4–1 |
| 1911 | Philadelphia (A) | New York (N) | 4–2 | 1950 | New York (A) | Philadelphia (N) | 4–0 |
| 1912 [2] | Boston (A) | New York (N) | 4–3 | 1951 | New York (A) | New York (N) | 4–2 |
| 1913 | Philadelphia (A) | New York (N) | 4–1 | 1952 | New York (A) | Brooklyn (N) | 4–3 |
| 1914 | Boston (N) | Philadelphia (A) | 4–0 | 1953 | New York (A) | Brooklyn (N) | 4–2 |
| 1915 | Boston (A) | Philadelphia (N) | 4–1 | 1954 | New York (N) | Cleveland (A) | 4–0 |
| 1916 | Boston (A) | Brooklyn (N) | 4–1 | 1955 | Brooklyn (N) | New York (A) | 4–3 |
| 1917 | Chicago (A) | New York (N) | 4–2 | 1956 | New York (A) | Brooklyn (N) | 4–3 |
| 1918 | Boston (A) | Chicago (N) | 4–2 | 1957 | Milwaukee (N) | New York (A) | 4–3 |
| 1919 [1] | Cincinnati (N) | Chicago (A) | 5–3 | 1958 | New York (A) | Milwaukee (N) | 4–3 |
| 1920 [1] | Cleveland (A) | Brooklyn (N) | 5–2 | 1959 | Los Angeles (N) | Chicago (A) | 4–2 |
| 1921 [1] | New York (N) | New York (A) | 5–3 | 1960 | Pittsburgh (N) | New York (A) | 4–3 |
| 1922 [2] | New York (N) | New York (A) | 4–0 | 1961 | New York (A) | Cincinnati (N) | 4–1 |
| 1923 | New York (A) | New York (N) | 4–2 | 1962 | New York (A) | San Francisco (N) | 4–3 |
| 1924 | Washington (A) | New York (N) | 4–3 | 1963 | Los Angeles (N) | New York (A) | 4–0 |
| 1925 | Pittsburgh (N) | Washington (A) | 4–3 | 1964 | St. Louis (N) | New York (A) | 4–3 |
| 1926 | St. Louis (N) | New York (A) | 4–3 | 1965 | Los Angeles (N) | Minnesota (A) | 4–3 |
| 1927 | New York (A) | Pittsburgh (N) | 4–0 | 1966 | Baltimore (A) | Los Angeles (N) | 4–0 |
| 1928 | New York (A) | St. Louis (N) | 4–0 | 1967 | St. Louis (N) | Boston (A) | 4–3 |
| 1929 | Philadelphia (A) | Chicago (N) | 4–1 | 1968 | Detroit (A) | St. Louis (N) | 4–3 |
| 1930 | Philadelphia (A) | St. Louis (N) | 4–2 | 1969 | N.Y. Mets (N) | Baltimore (A) | 4–1 |
| 1931 | St. Louis (N) | Philadelphia (A) | 4–3 | 1970 | Baltimore (A) | Cincinnati (N) | 4–1 |
| 1932 | New York (A) | Chicago (N) | 4–0 | 1971 | Pittsburgh (N) | Baltimore (A) | 4–3 |
| 1933 | New York (N) | Washington (A) | 4–1 | 1972 | Oakland (A) | Cincinnati (N) | 4–3 |
| 1934 | St. Louis (N) | Detroit (A) | 4–3 | 1973 | Oakland (A) | N.Y. Mets (N) | 4–3 |
| 1935 | Detroit (A) | Chicago (N) | 4–2 | 1974 | Oakland (A) | Los Angeles (N) | 4–1 |
| 1936 | New York (A) | New York (N) | 4–2 | 1975 | Cincinnati (N) | Boston (A) | 4–3 |
| 1937 | New York (A) | New York (N) | 4–1 | 1976 | Cincinnati (N) | New York (A) | 4–0 |
| 1938 | New York (A) | Chicago (N) | 4–0 | 1977 | New York (A) | Los Angeles (N) | 4–2 |
| 1939 | New York (A) | Cincinnati (N) | 4–0 | 1978 | New York (A) | Los Angeles (N) | 4–2 |
| 1940 | Cincinnati (N) | Detroit (A) | 4–3 | 1979 | Pittsburgh (N) | Baltimore (A) | 4–3 |
| 1941 | New York (A) | Brooklyn (N) | 4–1 | 1980 | Philadelphia (N) | Kansas City (A) | 4–2 |

[1] A nine-game World Series was scheduled.   [2] One tie game played.

# PENNANT WINNERS—MAJOR LEAGUE BASEBALL

| NATIONAL LEAGUE | | | | | | AMERICAN LEAGUE | | | | | |
|---|---|---|---|---|---|---|---|---|---|---|---|
| YEAR | CLUB | W | L | PCT. | MANAGER | YEAR | CLUB | W | L | PCT. | MANAGER |
| 1910 | Chicago | 104 | 50 | .675 | Frank Chance | 1910 | Philadelphia | 102 | 48 | .680 | Connie Mack |
| 1911 | New York | 99 | 54 | .647 | John McGraw | 1911 | Philadelphia | 101 | 50 | .669 | Connie Mack |
| 1912 | New York | 103 | 48 | .682 | John McGraw | 1912 | Boston | 105 | 47 | .691 | J. Stahl |
| 1913 | New York | 101 | 51 | .664 | John McGraw | 1913 | Philadelphia | 96 | 57 | .627 | Connie Mack |
| 1914 | Boston | 94 | 59 | .614 | G. Stallings | 1914 | Philadelphia | 99 | 53 | .651 | Connie Mack |
| 1915 | Philadelphia | 90 | 62 | .592 | P. Moran | 1915 | Boston | 101 | 50 | .669 | W. Carrigan |
| 1916 | Brooklyn | 94 | 60 | .610 | W. Robinson | 1916 | Boston | 91 | 63 | .591 | W. Carrigan |
| 1917 | New York | 98 | 56 | .636 | John McGraw | 1917 | Chicago | 100 | 54 | .649 | C. Rowland |
| 1918 | Chicago | 84 | 45 | .651 | F. Mitchell | 1918 | Boston | 75 | 51 | .595 | E. Barrow |
| 1919 | Cincinnati | 96 | 44 | .686 | P. Moran | 1919 | Chicago | 88 | 52 | .629 | W. Gleason |
| 1920 | Brooklyn | 93 | 61 | .604 | W. Robinson | 1920 | Cleveland | 98 | 56 | .636 | Tris Speaker |
| 1921 | New York | 94 | 59 | .614 | John McGraw | 1921 | New York | 98 | 55 | .641 | M. Huggins |
| 1922 | New York | 93 | 61 | .604 | John McGraw | 1922 | New York | 94 | 60 | .610 | M. Huggins |
| 1923 | New York | 95 | 58 | .621 | John McGraw | 1923 | New York | 98 | 54 | .645 | M. Huggins |
| 1924 | New York | 93 | 60 | .608 | John McGraw | 1924 | Washington | 92 | 62 | .597 | S. Harris |
| 1925 | Pittsburgh | 95 | 58 | .621 | W. McKechnie | 1925 | Washington | 96 | 55 | .636 | S. Harris |
| 1926 | St. Louis | 89 | 65 | .578 | R. Hornsby | 1926 | New York | 91 | 63 | .591 | M. Huggins |
| 1927 | Pittsburgh | 94 | 60 | .610 | O. Bush | 1927 | New York | 110 | 44 | .714 | M. Huggins |
| 1928 | St. Louis | 95 | 59 | .617 | W. McKechnie | 1928 | New York | 101 | 53 | .656 | M. Huggins |
| 1929 | Chicago | 98 | 54 | .645 | Joe McCarthy | 1929 | Philadelphia | 104 | 46 | .693 | Connie Mack |
| 1930 | St. Louis | 92 | 62 | .597 | C. Street | 1930 | Philadelphia | 102 | 52 | .662 | Connie Mack |
| 1931 | St. Louis | 101 | 53 | .656 | C. Street | 1931 | Philadelphia | 107 | 45 | .704 | Connie Mack |
| 1932 | Chicago | 90 | 64 | .584 | C. Grimm | 1932 | New York | 107 | 47 | .695 | Joe McCarthy |
| 1933 | New York | 91 | 61 | .599 | Bill Terry | 1933 | Washington | 99 | 53 | .651 | Joe Cronin |
| 1934 | St. Louis | 95 | 58 | .621 | Frank Frisch | 1934 | Detroit | 101 | 53 | .656 | G. Cochrane |
| 1935 | Chicago | 100 | 54 | .649 | C. Grimm | 1935 | Detroit | 93 | 58 | .616 | G. Cochrane |
| 1936 | New York | 92 | 62 | .597 | Bill Terry | 1936 | New York | 102 | 51 | .667 | Joe McCarthy |
| 1937 | New York | 95 | 57 | .625 | Bill Terry | 1937 | New York | 102 | 52 | .662 | Joe McCarthy |
| 1938 | Chicago | 89 | 63 | .586 | C. Hartnett | 1938 | New York | 99 | 53 | .651 | Joe McCarthy |
| 1939 | Cincinnati | 97 | 57 | .630 | W. McKechnie | 1939 | New York | 106 | 45 | .702 | Joe McCarthy |
| 1940 | Cincinnati | 100 | 53 | .654 | W. McKechnie | 1940 | Detroit | 90 | 64 | .584 | D. Baker |
| 1941 | Brooklyn | 100 | 54 | .649 | Leo Durocher | 1941 | New York | 101 | 53 | .656 | Joe McCarthy |
| 1942 | St. Louis | 106 | 48 | .688 | W. Southworth | 1942 | New York | 103 | 51 | .669 | Joe McCarthy |
| 1943 | St. Louis | 105 | 49 | .682 | W. Southworth | 1943 | New York | 98 | 56 | .636 | Joe McCarthy |
| 1944 | St. Louis | 105 | 49 | .682 | W. Southworth | 1944 | St. Louis | 89 | 65 | .578 | J. Sewell |
| 1945 | Chicago | 98 | 56 | .636 | C. Grimm | 1945 | Detroit | 88 | 65 | .575 | S. O'Neill |
| 1946 | St. Louis | 98 | 58 | .628 | E. Dyer | 1946 | Boston | 104 | 50 | .675 | Joe Cronin |
| 1947 | Brooklyn | 94 | 60 | .610 | B. Shotton | 1947 | New York | 97 | 57 | .630 | S. Harris |
| 1948 | Boston | 91 | 62 | .595 | W. Southworth | 1948 | Cleveland | 97 | 58 | .626 | Lou Boudreau |
| 1949 | Brooklyn | 97 | 57 | .630 | B. Shotton | 1949 | New York | 97 | 57 | .630 | Casey Stengel |
| 1950 | Philadelphia | 91 | 63 | .591 | E. Sawyer | 1950 | New York | 98 | 56 | .636 | Casey Stengel |
| 1951 | New York | 98 | 59 | .624 | Leo Durocher | 1951 | New York | 98 | 56 | .636 | Casey Stengel |
| 1952 | Brooklyn | 96 | 57 | .627 | C. Dressen | 1952 | New York | 95 | 59 | .617 | Casey Stengel |
| 1953 | Brooklyn | 105 | 49 | .682 | C. Dressen | 1953 | New York | 99 | 52 | .656 | Casey Stengel |
| 1954 | New York | 97 | 57 | .630 | Leo Durocher | 1954 | Cleveland | 111 | 43 | .721 | Al Lopez |
| 1955 | Brooklyn | 98 | 55 | .641 | Walt Alston | 1955 | New York | 96 | 58 | .623 | Casey Stengel |
| 1956 | Brooklyn | 93 | 61 | .604 | Walt Alston | 1956 | New York | 97 | 57 | .630 | Casey Stengel |
| 1957 | Milwaukee | 95 | 59 | .617 | F. Haney | 1957 | New York | 98 | 56 | .636 | Casey Stengel |
| 1958 | Milwaukee | 92 | 62 | .597 | F. Haney | 1958 | New York | 92 | 62 | .597 | Casey Stengel |
| 1959 | Los Angeles | 88 | 68 | .564 | Walt Alston | 1959 | Chicago | 94 | 60 | .610 | Al Lopez |
| 1960 | Pittsburgh | 95 | 59 | .617 | D. Murtaugh | 1960 | New York | 97 | 57 | .630 | Casey Stengel |
| 1961 | Cincinnati | 93 | 61 | .604 | F. Hutchinson | 1961 | New York | 109 | 53 | .673 | Ralph Houk |
| 1962 | San Fran. | 103 | 62 | .624 | A. Dark | 1962 | New York | 96 | 66 | .593 | Ralph Houk |
| 1963 | Los Angeles | 99 | 63 | .611 | Walt Alston | 1963 | New York | 104 | 57 | .646 | Ralph Houk |
| 1964 | St. Louis | 93 | 69 | .574 | J. Keane | 1964 | New York | 99 | 63 | .611 | Yogi Berra |
| 1965 | Los Angeles | 97 | 65 | .599 | Walt Alston | 1965 | Minnesota | 102 | 60 | .630 | Sam Mele |
| 1966 | Los Angeles | 95 | 67 | .586 | Walt Alston | 1966 | Baltimore | 97 | 63 | .606 | H. Bauer |
| 1967 | St. Louis | 101 | 60 | .627 | A. Schoendienst | 1967 | Boston | 92 | 70 | .568 | R. Williams |
| 1968 | St. Louis | 97 | 65 | .599 | A. Schoendienst | 1968 | Detroit | 103 | 59 | .636 | M. Smith |
| 1969 | N.Y. Mets | 100 | 62 | .617 | Gil Hodges | 1969 | Baltimore | 109 | 53 | .673 | Earl Weaver |
| 1970 | Cincinnati | 102 | 60 | .630 | S. Anderson | 1970 | Baltimore | 108 | 54 | .667 | Earl Weaver |
| 1971 | Pittsburgh | 97 | 65 | .599 | D. Murtaugh | 1971 | Baltimore | 101 | 57 | .639 | Earl Weaver |
| 1972 | Cincinnati | 95 | 59 | .617 | S. Anderson | 1972 | Oakland | 93 | 62 | .600 | Dick Williams |
| 1973 | N.Y. Mets | 82 | 79 | .509 | Yogi Berra | 1973 | Oakland | 94 | 68 | .580 | Dick Williams |
| 1974 | Los Angeles | 102 | 60 | .630 | Walt Alston | 1974 | Oakland | 90 | 72 | .556 | Alvin Dark |
| 1975 | Cincinnati | 108 | 54 | .667 | S. Anderson | 1975 | Boston | 95 | 65 | .594 | Darrell Johnson |
| 1976 | Cincinnati | 102 | 60 | .630 | S. Anderson | 1976 | New York | 97 | 62 | .610 | Billy Martin |
| 1977 | Los Angeles | 98 | 64 | .605 | T. Lasorda | 1977 | New York | 100 | 62 | .617 | Billy Martin |
| 1978 | Los Angeles | 95 | 67 | .586 | T. Lasorda | 1978 | New York | 100 | 63 | .613 | Bob Lemon |
| 1979 | Pittsburgh | 98 | 64 | .605 | Chuck Tanner | 1979 | Baltimore | 102 | 57 | .642 | Earl Weaver |
| 1980 | Philadelphia | 91 | 71 | .562 | Dallas Green | 1980 | Kansas City | 97 | 65 | .599 | Jim Frey |

## SELECTED WORLD SERIES BASEBALL RECORDS: 1903–1980

### TEAM RECORDS:

| | |
|---|---|
| World championships won | New York Yankees (AL)—22; St. Louis Cardinals (NL)—8 |
| Played in most World Series | New York Yankees (AL)—32 times from 1921 through 1978 |
| Games won | New York Yankees (AL)—107 |
| Played in most World Series, National League | Giants, New York/San Francisco (NL)—15 times from 1905 through 1962 (14 times representing New York and once San Francisco) |
| Hits by one team, one game | New York Giants (NL) and St. Louis Cardinals (NL), tie—20. The Giants made 20 hits against the Yankees in the Oct. 7, 1921, World Series game; the Cardinals did the same against the Boston Red Sox in the Oct. 10, 1946, series game |
| Batting average, highest | New York Yankees (AL)—.338 in the seven-game series against the Pittsburgh Pirates in 1960 |
| Batting average, lowest, one series | Los Angeles Dodgers (NL)—.142 against Baltimore pitchers in 1966 |
| Runs batted in, one series | New York Yankees (AL)—54 runs in seven games in 1960 |
| Home runs, one series | New York Yankee batters (AL)—12 home runs in seven games against the Brooklyn Dodgers in 1956 |
| Home runs, one game | New York Yankee batters (AL)—5 home runs against St. Louis Cardinal pitching in a game played Oct. 9, 1928 |
| Doubles, one series | St. Louis Cardinals (NL)—19 doubles against the Boston Red Sox in 1946; the Philadelphia Athletics (AL) also scored 19 series doubles against the Chicago Cubs in 1910 |
| Bases on balls received, one series | New York Yankee batters (AL)—38 times against Brooklyn Dodger pitching in seven games in 1947 |
| Strike outs, one series | Oakland A's batters (AL)—62 times against New York Mets pitching in seven games in 1973 |
| Double plays, one series | Brooklyn Dodgers (NL)—12, in a seven-game series against the New York Yankees in 1955 |
| Triple plays, one series | Cleveland Indians (AL)—1. The only World Series triple play was an unassisted one made by Cleveland 2d baseman Billy Wambsganss in the 1920 series against Brooklyn |
| Fielding record, one series | New York Yankees (AL)—1.000 (no errors) in the 1937 World Series against the New York Giants; Baltimore Orioles (AL)—1.000 (no errors) in the 1966 World Series against Los Angeles |

### INDIVIDUAL RECORDS:

| | |
|---|---|
| Home runs, one game | Babe Ruth, New York Yankees (AL)—3 home runs on Oct. 6, 1926, and again on Oct. 9, 1928; Reggie Jackson, New York Yankees (AL)—3 consecutive home runs on Oct. 18, 1977 |
| Home runs in single World Series | Reggie Jackson, New York Yankees (AL)—5 against Los Angeles Dodgers (NL) in 1977 |
| Home runs in World Series, lifetime | Mickey Mantle, New York Yankees (AL)—18 |
| Batting average, lifetime, 20 or more games | Lou Brock, St. Louis (NL)—.391, in three World Series: 1964, 1967, 1968 (21 games, 87 at-bats, 34 hits) |
| Hits, lifetime | Yogi Berra, New York Yankees (AL)—71, between 1947 and 1963 |
| Batting average in single World Series by regular starting player | Babe Ruth, New York Yankees (AL)—.625, in the 1928 series against the St. Louis Cardinals (four games) |
| Game-winning home runs, one series | Casey Stengel, New York Giants (NL)—won two games with home runs in 1923 series; Rudy York of Boston Red Sox (AL) also won two games with home runs in 1946 series |
| Game-winning home runs, lifetime | Hank Greenberg, Detroit Tigers (AL)—won three series games with home runs: in 1935 against Chicago Cubs; in 1940 against Cincinnati Reds; and in 1945 against Chicago Cubs |
| Runs batted in, one game | Bobby Richardson, New York Yankees (AL)—6 on Oct. 8, 1960, against the Pittsburgh Pirates (NL) |
| Runs, in one series | Reggie Jackson, N.Y. Yankees (AL)—10 in 1977 |
| Runs, lifetime | Mickey Mantle, N.Y. Yankees (AL)—42 in 12 series, 65 games (1951–64) |
| Errors, one game | Willie Davis, Los Angeles Dodgers (NL)—three errors, all in the same inning against the Baltimore Orioles on Oct. 6, 1966 |
| Played in most World Series | Yogi Berra, New York Yankees (AL)—14 times from 1947 to 1963 |
| Played on most championship teams | Yogi Berra, New York Yankees (AL)—10 times |
| Pitching no-hitter, one game | Don Larsen, New York Yankees (AL)—won a perfect no-hitter against the Brooklyn Dodgers, Oct. 8, 1956. He faced the minimum 27 batters, threw 97 pitches, and allowed no base runners |
| Pitcher with most World Series wins, lifetime | Whitey Ford, New York Yankees (AL)—10, between 1950 and 1964 |
| Pitcher with most strikeouts, one game | Bob Gibson, St. Louis Cardinals (NL)—17, against the Detroit Tigers in the first game of the 1968 World Series |
| Pitching consecutive scoreless innings | Whitey Ford, New York Yankees (AL)—33 ²/₃ innings, during the 1960, 1961, and 1962 series |

# INDIVIDUAL MAJOR LEAGUE BASEBALL RECORDS: 1900–1980

| BATTING | AMERICAN LEAGUE | NATIONAL LEAGUE |
|---|---|---|
| Games, career | 3,033 — Ty Cobb (1905–28) | 3,298 — Hank Aaron (1954–76) * |
| Years leading league | 12 — Ty Cobb, Detroit (1907–15, 1917–19) | 8 — Honus Wagner, Pittsburgh (1900, 1903–04, 1906–09, 1911) |
| Batting average, career | .367 — Ty Cobb, Detroit (1905–26), Philadelphia (1927–28) | .359 — Rogers Hornsby, St. Louis, New York, Boston, Chicago (1915–32) |
| Batting average, season | .422 — Napoleon Lajoie, Phila. (1901) | .424 — Rogers Hornsby, St. Louis (1924) |
| Games, consecutive | 2,130 — Lou Gehrig, New York (1925–39) | 1,117 — Billy Williams, Chicago (1963–70) |
| Runs scored, career | 2,244 — Ty Cobb, Detroit, Phil. (1905–28) | 2,174 — Hank Aaron (1954–76) * |
| Runs scored, season | 177 — Babe Ruth, New York (1921) | 158 — Chuck Klein, Philadelphia (1930) |
| Runs scored, game | 6 — John Pesky, Boston (1946) | 6 — Mel Ott, New York (1934, 1944); Frank Torre, Milwaukee (1957) |
| Runs batted in, career | 2,209 — Babe Ruth, Boston (1914–19), New York (1920–34), Boston (NL) (1935) * | 2,297 — Hank Aaron, Milwaukee (NL), Atlanta (NL), Milwaukee (AL) (1954–76) * |
| Runs batted in, season | 184 — Lou Gehrig, New York (1931) | 190 — Hack Wilson, Chicago (1930) |
| Runs batted in, game | 11 — Tony Lazzeri, New York (1936) | 12 — Jim Bottomley, St. Louis (1924) |
| Hits, career | 4,191 — Ty Cobb, Detroit, Philadelphia | 3,771 — Hank Aaron (1954–76) * |
| Hits, season | 257 — George Sisler, St. Louis (1920) | 254 — Frank O'Doul, Philadelphia (1929); Bill Terry, New York (1930) |
| Games batted safely, consecutive | 56 — Joe DiMaggio, New York (1941) | 44 — Pete Rose, Cincinnati (1978) |
| Long hits (doubles, triples, home runs) career | 1,356 — Babe Ruth, Boston, New York, Boston (NL) (1914–35) * | 1,477 — Hank Aaron, Milwaukee (NL), Atlanta (NL), Milwaukee (AL) (1954–76) * |
| Long hits, season | 119 — Babe Ruth (1921) | 107 — Chuck Klein, Philadelphia (1930) |
| Slugging average, career | .690 — Babe Ruth (1914–35) * | .578 — Rogers Hornsby (1915–32) |
| Home runs, career | 714 — Babe Ruth (1914–35) * | 755 — Hank Aaron, Milwaukee (NL), Atlanta (NL), Milwaukee (AL) (1954–76) * |
| Home runs, season | 61 (162 games) — Roger Maris, N.Y. (1961) 60 (154 games) — Babe Ruth, N.Y. (1927) | 56 — Hack Wilson, Chicago (1930) 54 — Ralph Kiner, Pittsburgh (1949) |
| Home runs, game | 4 — Lou Gehrig, New York (1932) | 4 — Chuck Klein, Philadelphia (1936) |
| Home runs with bases filled, career | 23 — Lou Gehrig, New York (1925–39) | 18 — Willie McCovey, San Fran., San Diego, Oakland, San Fran. (1959–80) |
| Home runs with bases filled, season | 5 — Jim Gentile, Baltimore (1961) | 5 — Ernie Banks, Chicago (1955) |
| Strikeouts, career | 1,728 — Reggie Jackson, K.C., Oakland, Baltimore, New York (1967–80) | 1,903 — Willie Stargell, Pittsburgh (1962–80) |
| Games, no strikeouts, consecutive | 98 — Nelson Fox, Chicago (1958) | 77 — Lloyd Waner, Pittsburgh, Boston, Cincinnati (1941) |
| Stolen bases, career | 892 — Ty Cobb, Detroit, Philadelphia (1905–28) | 938 — Lou Brock, Chicago, St. Louis, (1961–79) |
| Stolen bases, season | 100 — Rickey Henderson, Oakland (1980) | 118 — Lou Brock, St. Louis (1974) |
| Stolen bases, game | 6 — Eddie Collins, Philadelphia (1912) | 5 — Dennis McGann, New York (1904) |
| Stealing home, career | 35 — Ty Cobb, Detroit, Philadelphia | 27 — George Burns, N.Y., Cincinnati, Philadelphia (1911–25) |
| Stealing home, season | 7 — Rod Carew, Minnesota (1969) | 7 — Pete Reiser, Brooklyn (1946) |

| PITCHING | AMERICAN LEAGUE | NATIONAL LEAGUE |
|---|---|---|
| Games pitched, career | 802 — Walter Johnson, Washington (1907–27) | 846 — ElRoy Face, Pittsburgh (1953, 1955–68), Montreal (1969) |
| Games pitched, season | 88 — Wilbur Wood, Chicago (1968) | 106 — Mike Marshall, Los Angeles (1974) |
| Games started, career | 666 — Walter Johnson, Wash. (1907–27) | 665 — Warren Spahn (1942–65) |
| Games started, season | 51 — Jack Chesbro, N.Y. Yankees (1904) | 48 — Joe McGinnity, N.Y. Giants (1903) |
| Games completed, career | 531 — Walter Johnson, Wash. (1907–27) | 437 — Grover Alexander (1911–29) |
| Games completed, season | 48 — Jack Chesbro, N.Y. Yankees (1904) | 45 — Victor Willis, Boston Braves (1902) |
| Earned run average, career (2,000 or more innings) | 2.37 — Walter Johnson, Wash. (1907–1927) | 2.33 — James L. Vaughn, Chicago (1913–21) |
| Earned run average, season | 1.01 — Hubert Leonard, Boston (1914) | 1.12 — Bob Gibson, St. Louis (1968) |
| Games won, career | 416 — Walter Johnson, Wash. (1907–27) | 373 — Grover Alexander, Christy Mathewson, N.Y., Cin. (1900–16) |
| Games won, season | 41 — Jack Chesbro, N.Y. Yankees (1904) | 37 — Christy Mathewson (1908) |
| Games won, consecutive | 17 — Johnny Allen, Cleveland (1936–37); Dave McNally, Baltimore (1968–69) | 24 — Carl Hubbell, New York (1936–37) |
| Shutout games, career | 113 — Walter Johnson, Wash. (1907–27) | 90 — Grover Alexander (1911–29) |
| Shutout games, season | 13 — John Coombs, Philadelphia (1910) | 16 — Grover Alexander (1916) |
| Shutout innings, consecutive | 56 — Walter Johnson, Wash. (1913) | 58 — Don Drysdale, Los Angeles (1968) |
| No-hit games, career | 4 — Nolan Ryan, California Angels, 1973 (2), 1974 (1), 1975 (1) | 4 — Sandy Koufax, Los Angeles (1962–65) |
| Strikeouts, 9-inning game | 19 — Nolan Ryan, Calif. (1974) | 19 — Steve Carlton, St. Louis (1969); Tom Seaver, New York (1970) |
| Strikeouts, season | 383 — Nolan Ryan, Calif. (1973) | 382 — Sandy Koufax, Los Angeles (1965) |
| Strikeouts, career | 3,508 — Walter Johnson, Wash. (1907–27) | 3,117 — Bob Gibson, St. Louis (1959–75) |
| Won-lost percentage, season, 16 or more decisions | .938 — John Allen, Cleveland (1937), won 15, lost 1 | .947 — ElRoy Face, Pittsburgh (1959), won 18, lost 1 |

* Career total includes play in both leagues.

## POSTSEASON BASEBALL PLAYOFFS: 1969–1980

### NATIONAL LEAGUE

| | |
|---|---|
| 1969 | New York defeated Atlanta, 3 games to 0 |
| 1970 | Cincinnati defeated Pittsburgh, 3 games to 0 |
| 1971 | Pittsburgh defeated San Francisco, 3 games to 1 |
| 1972 | Cincinnati defeated Pittsburgh, 3 games to 2 |
| 1973 | New York defeated Cincinnati, 3 games to 2 |
| 1974 | Los Angeles defeated Pittsburgh, 3 games to 1 |
| 1975 | Cincinnati defeated Pittsburgh, 3 games to 0 |
| 1976 | Cincinnati defeated Philadelphia, 3 games to 0 |
| 1977 | Los Angeles defeated Philadelphia, 3 games to 1 |
| 1978 | Los Angeles defeated Philadelphia, 3 games to 1 |
| 1979 | Pittsburgh defeated Cincinnati, 3 games to 0 |
| 1980 | Philadelphia defeated Houston, 3 games to 2 |

### AMERICAN LEAGUE

| | |
|---|---|
| 1969 | Baltimore defeated Minnesota, 3 games to 0 |
| 1970 | Baltimore defeated Minnesota, 3 games to 0 |
| 1971 | Baltimore defeated Oakland, 3 games to 0 |
| 1972 | Oakland defeated Detroit, 3 games to 2 |
| 1973 | Oakland defeated Baltimore, 3 games to 2 |
| 1974 | Oakland defeated Baltimore, 3 games to 1 |
| 1975 | Boston defeated Oakland, 3 games to 0 |
| 1976 | New York defeated Kansas City, 3 games to 2 |
| 1977 | New York defeated Kansas City, 3 games to 2 |
| 1978 | New York defeated Kansas City, 3 games to 1 |
| 1979 | Baltimore defeated California, 3 games to 1 |
| 1980 | Kansas City defeated New York, 3 games to 0 |

## POSTSEASON PLAYOFF GAMES: 1980

**NATIONAL LEAGUE:** Philadelphia won National League Pennant, 3 games to 2.

**AMERICAN LEAGUE:** Kansas City won American League Pennant, 3 games to 0.

**1st GAME: PHILADELPHIA 3, HOUSTON, 1**

| | | R | H | E |
|---|---|---|---|---|
| Houston | 0 0 0 1 0 0 0 0 0 | 1 | 7 | 0 |
| Philadelphia | 0 0 0 0 0 2 1 0 x | 3 | 8 | 1 |

Pitchers: Philadelphia—Carlton (winner, 7), McGraw (2); Houston—Forsch (loser, 8).
Home runs: Luzinski.
Attendance at Philadelphia Oct. 7: 65,277.

**2d GAME: HOUSTON 7, PHILADELPHIA 4**

| | | R | H | E |
|---|---|---|---|---|
| Houston | 0 0 1 0 0 0 1 1 0 4 | 7 | 8 | 1 |
| Philadelphia | 0 0 0 2 0 0 0 1 1 | 4 | 14 | 2 |

Pitchers: Houston—Ryan (6⅓), Sambito (⅓), D. Smith (1⅓), LaCorte (winner, 1), Andujar (1); Philadelphia—Ruthven (7), McGraw (1), Reed (loser, 1 ⅓), Saucier (⅔).
Home runs: None.
Attendance at Philadelphia Oct. 8: 65,476.

**3d GAME: HOUSTON 1, PHILADELPHIA 0**

| | | R | H | E |
|---|---|---|---|---|
| Philadelphia | 0 0 0 0 0 0 0 0 0 0 0 | 0 | 7 | 1 |
| Houston | 0 0 0 0 0 0 0 0 0 0 1 | 1 | 6 | 1 |

Pitchers: Houston—Niekro (10); Smith, (winner, 1); Philadelphia—Christenson (6), Noles (1⅓), McGraw (loser, 3).
Home runs: None.
Attendance at Houston Oct. 10: 44,443.

**4th GAME: PHILADELPHIA 5, HOUSTON 3**

| | | R | H | E |
|---|---|---|---|---|
| Philadelphia | 0 0 0 0 1 0 0 3 0 2 | 5 | 13 | 0 |
| Houston | 0 0 0 1 1 0 0 0 1 0 | 3 | 5 | 1 |

Pitchers: Philadelphia—Carlton (5⅓), Noles (1⅓), Saucier (0), Reed (⅓), Brusstar (winner, 2), McGraw (1). Houston—Ruhle (7), Smith (0), Sambito (loser, 3).
Home runs: None.
Attendance at Houston Oct. 11: 44,952.

**1st GAME: KANSAS CITY 7, NEW YORK 2**

| | | R | H | E |
|---|---|---|---|---|
| New York | 0 2 0 0 0 0 0 0 0 | 2 | 10 | 1 |
| Kansas City | 0 2 2 0 0 0 1 2 x | 7 | 10 | 0 |

Pitchers: Kansas City—Gura (winner, 9); New York—Guidry (loser, 3), Davis (4), Underwood (1).
Home runs: Cerone, Piniella, G. Brett.
Attendance at Kansas City Oct. 8: 42,598.

**2d GAME: KANSAS CITY 3, NEW YORK 2**

| | | R | H | E |
|---|---|---|---|---|
| New York | 0 0 0 0 2 0 0 0 0 | 2 | 8 | 0 |
| Kansas City | 0 0 3 0 0 0 0 0 x | 3 | 6 | 0 |

Pitchers: Kansas City—Leonard (winner, 8), Quisenberry (1); New York—May (loser, 8).
Home runs: Nettles.
Attendance at Kansas City Oct. 9: 42,633.

**3d GAME: KANSAS CITY 4, NEW YORK 2**

| | | R | H | E |
|---|---|---|---|---|
| Kansas City | 0 0 0 0 1 0 3 0 0 | 4 | 12 | 1 |
| New York | 0 0 0 0 0 2 0 0 0 | 2 | 8 | 0 |

Pitchers: Kansas City—Splittorff (5⅓), Quisenberry (winner, 3⅔); New York—John (6⅔), Gossage (loser, ⅓), Underwood (2).
Home runs: White, G. Brett (2).
Attendance at New York Oct. 10: 56,588.

**5th GAME: PHILADELPHIA 8, HOUSTON 7**

| | | R | H | E |
|---|---|---|---|---|
| Philadelphia | 0 2 0 0 0 0 0 5 1 | 8 | 13 | 2 |
| Houston | 1 0 0 0 0 1 3 2 0 | 7 | 14 | 0 |

Pitchers: Philadelphia—Bystrom (5⅓), Brusstar (⅔), Christenson (⅔), Reed (⅓), McGraw (1), Ruthven (winner, 2); Houston—Ryan (7), Sambito (⅓), Forsch (⅔), LaCorte (loser, 2).
Home runs: None.
Attendance at Houston Oct. 12: 44,802.

## TEAM BATTING—MAJOR LEAGUE BASEBALL REGULAR SEASON: 1980

### NATIONAL LEAGUE

| Club | PCT. | G | AB | R | H | HR |
|---|---|---|---|---|---|---|
| St. Louis | .275 | 162 | 5608 | 738 | 1541 | 101 |
| Philadelphia | .270 | 162 | 5625 | 728 | 1517 | 117 |
| Pittsburgh | .266 | 162 | 5517 | 666 | 1469 | 116 |
| Los Angeles | .263 | 163 | 5568 | 663 | 1462 | 148 |
| Cincinnati | .262 | 163 | 5516 | 707 | 1445 | 113 |
| Houston | .261 | 163 | 5566 | 637 | 1455 | 75 |
| Montreal | .257 | 162 | 5465 | 694 | 1407 | 114 |
| New York | .257 | 162 | 5478 | 611 | 1407 | 61 |
| San Diego | .255 | 163 | 5540 | 591 | 1410 | 67 |
| Chicago | .251 | 162 | 5619 | 614 | 1411 | 107 |
| Atlanta | .250 | 161 | 5402 | 630 | 1352 | 144 |
| San Francisco | .244 | 161 | 5368 | 573 | 1310 | 80 |

### AMERICAN LEAGUE

| Club | PCT. | G | AB | R | H | HR |
|---|---|---|---|---|---|---|
| Kansas City | .286 | 162 | 5714 | 809 | 1633 | 115 |
| Texas | .284 | 163 | 5690 | 756 | 1616 | 124 |
| Boston | .283 | 160 | 5603 | 757 | 1588 | 162 |
| Cleveland | .277 | 160 | 5470 | 738 | 1517 | 89 |
| Milwaukee | .275 | 162 | 5653 | 811 | 1555 | 203 |
| Detroit | .273 | 163 | 5648 | 830 | 1543 | 143 |
| Baltimore | .273 | 162 | 5589 | 805 | 1523 | 156 |
| New York | .267 | 162 | 5553 | 820 | 1484 | 189 |
| Minnesota | .265 | 161 | 5530 | 670 | 1468 | 99 |
| California | .265 | 160 | 5443 | 698 | 1442 | 106 |
| Oakland | .259 | 162 | 5495 | 686 | 1424 | 137 |
| Chicago | .259 | 162 | 5444 | 587 | 1408 | 91 |
| Toronto | .251 | 162 | 5571 | 624 | 1398 | 126 |
| Seattle | .248 | 163 | 5489 | 610 | 1359 | 104 |

# 1980 FINAL STANDINGS—MAJOR LEAGUE BASEBALL

## NATIONAL LEAGUE

| EASTERN DIVISION | WON | LOST | PCT. | G.B. [1] | WESTERN DIVISION | WON | LOST | PCT. | G.B. [1] |
|---|---|---|---|---|---|---|---|---|---|
| Philadelphia [2] | 91 | 71 | .562 | — | Houston | 93 | 70 | .571 | — |
| Montreal | 90 | 72 | .556 | 1 | Los Angeles | 92 | 71 | .564 | 1 |
| Pittsburgh | 83 | 79 | .512 | 8 | Cincinnati | 89 | 73 | .549 | 3 ½ |
| St. Louis | 74 | 88 | .457 | 17 | Atlanta | 81 | 80 | .503 | 11 |
| New York | 67 | 95 | .414 | 24 | San Francisco | 75 | 86 | .466 | 17 |
| Chicago | 64 | 98 | .395 | 27 | San Diego | 73 | 89 | .451 | 19 ½ |

## AMERICAN LEAGUE

| EASTERN DIVISION | WON | LOST | PCT. | G.B.[1] | WESTERN DIVISION | WON | LOST | PCT. | G.B.[1] |
|---|---|---|---|---|---|---|---|---|---|
| New York | 103 | 59 | .636 | — | Kansas City [2] | 97 | 65 | .599 | — |
| Baltimore | 100 | 62 | .617 | 3 | Oakland | 83 | 79 | .512 | 14 |
| Milwaukee | 86 | 76 | .531 | 17 | Minnesota | 77 | 84 | .478 | 19 ½ |
| Boston | 83 | 77 | .519 | 19 | Texas | 76 | 85 | .472 | 20 ½ |
| Detroit | 84 | 78 | .519 | 19 | Chicago | 70 | 90 | .438 | 26 |
| Cleveland | 79 | 81 | .494 | 23 | California | 65 | 95 | .406 | 31 |
| Toronto | 67 | 95 | .414 | 36 | Seattle | 59 | 103 | .364 | 38 |

[1] Games behind.   [2] League pennant winner.

# 1980 TEAM-BY-TEAM VICTORIES—MAJOR LEAGUE BASEBALL

To determine a team's regular-season wins read horizontally. To determine a team's regular-season losses read down the proper column. For postseason playoff results, see page 780.

## NATIONAL LEAGUE

| EASTERN DIVISION | Phil. | Mon. | Pitt. | St. L. | N.Y. | Chi. | Atl. | Cin. | Hou. | L.A. | S.D. | S.F. | TOTAL WINS |
|---|---|---|---|---|---|---|---|---|---|---|---|---|---|
| Philadelphia | – | 9 | 7 | 9 | 12 | 13 | 7 | 5 | 9 | 6 | 8 | 6 | 91 |
| Montreal | 9 | – | 6 | 12 | 10 | 12 | 7 | 9 | 7 | 1 | 10 | 7 | 90 |
| Pittsburgh | 11 | 12 | – | 10 | 8 | 10 | 1 | 6 | 5 | 6 | 6 | 8 | 83 |
| St. Louis | 9 | 6 | 8 | – | 9 | 9 | 6 | 7 | 5 | 5 | 5 | 5 | 74 |
| New York | 6 | 8 | 10 | 9 | – | 8 | 9 | 4 | 4 | 5 | 1 | 3 | 67 |
| Chicago | 5 | 6 | 8 | 9 | 10 | – | 4 | 7 | 1 | 5 | 4 | 5 | 64 |

| WESTERN DIVISION | Hou. | L.A. | Cin. | Atl. | S.F. | S.D. | Chi. | Mon. | N.Y. | Phil. | Pitt. | St. L. | TOTAL WINS |
|---|---|---|---|---|---|---|---|---|---|---|---|---|---|
| Houston | – | 9 | 10 | 11 | 11 | 11 | 11 | 5 | 8 | 3 | 7 | 7 | 93 |
| Los Angeles | 10 | – | 9 | 7 | 13 | 9 | 7 | 11 | 7 | 6 | 6 | 7 | 92 |
| Cincinnati | 8 | 9 | – | 16 | 7 | 15 | 5 | 3 | 8 | 7 | 6 | 5 | 89 |
| Atlanta | 7 | 11 | 2 | – | 11 | 12 | 8 | 5 | 3 | 5 | 11 | 6 | 81 |
| San Francisco | 7 | 5 | 11 | 6 | – | 8 | 7 | 5 | 9 | 6 | 4 | 7 | 75 |
| San Diego | 7 | 9 | 3 | 6 | 10 | – | 8 | 2 | 11 | 4 | 6 | 7 | 73 |

## AMERICAN LEAGUE

| EASTERN DIVISION | N.Y. | Balt. | Mil. | Bos. | Det. | Clev. | Tor. | Cal. | Chi. | K.C. | Min. | Oak. | Sea. | Tex. | TOTAL WINS |
|---|---|---|---|---|---|---|---|---|---|---|---|---|---|---|---|
| New York | – | 6 | 8 | 10 | 8 | 8 | 10 | 10 | 7 | 4 | 8 | 8 | 9 | 7 | 103 |
| Baltimore | 7 | – | 7 | 8 | 10 | 6 | 11 | 10 | 6 | 6 | 10 | 7 | 6 | 6 | 100 |
| Milwaukee | 5 | 6 | – | 7 | 6 | 10 | 5 | 6 | 7 | 6 | 6 | 7 | 9 | 5 | 86 |
| Boston | 3 | 5 | 6 | – | 8 | 7 | 7 | 9 | 6 | 5 | 6 | 9 | 7 | 5 | 83 |
| Detroit | 5 | 3 | 7 | 5 | – | 10 | 9 | 7 | 10 | 2 | 6 | 6 | 10 | 4 | 84 |
| Cleveland | 5 | 7 | 3 | 6 | 3 | – | 8 | 6 | 7 | 5 | 9 | 6 | 8 | 6 | 79 |
| Toronto | 3 | 2 | 8 | 6 | 4 | 5 | – | 9 | 7 | 3 | 5 | 4 | 6 | 5 | 67 |

| WESTERN DIVISION | K.C. | Oak. | Min. | Tex. | Chi. | Cal. | Sea. | Balt. | Bos. | Clev. | Det. | Mil. | N.Y. | Tor. | TOTAL WINS |
|---|---|---|---|---|---|---|---|---|---|---|---|---|---|---|---|
| Kansas City | – | 6 | 5 | 10 | 8 | 8 | 7 | 6 | 7 | 7 | 10 | 6 | 8 | 9 | 97 |
| Oakland | 7 | – | 7 | 7 | 7 | 10 | 8 | 5 | 3 | 6 | 6 | 5 | 4 | 8 | 83 |
| Minnesota | 8 | 6 | – | 9 | 8 | 6 | 7 | 2 | 6 | 3 | 6 | 8 | 7 | 7 | 77 |
| Texas | 3 | 6 | 3 | – | 7 | 2 | 9 | 6 | 4 | 7 | 8 | 7 | 5 | 5 | 76 |
| Chicago | 5 | 6 | 5 | 6 | – | 10 | 6 | 6 | 4 | 5 | 2 | 5 | 5 | 5 | 70 |
| California | 5 | 3 | 7 | 11 | 3 | – | 11 | 2 | 3 | 4 | 5 | 6 | 2 | 3 | 65 |
| Seattle | 6 | 5 | 6 | 4 | 7 | 2 | – | 6 | 5 | 4 | 2 | 3 | 3 | 6 | 59 |

## 1980 LEADING BASEBALL BATTERS[1]

### AMERICAN LEAGUE
(Close of regular season)

| PLAYER—CLUB | PCT. | AB | R | H | HR | RBI |
|---|---|---|---|---|---|---|
| Brett, Kansas City | .390 | 449 | 87 | 175 | 24 | 118 |
| Cooper, Milwaukee | .352 | 622 | 96 | 219 | 25 | 122 |
| Dilone, Cleveland | .341 | 528 | 82 | 180 | 0 | 40 |
| Rivers, Texas | .333 | 630 | 96 | 210 | 7 | 60 |
| Carew, California | .331 | 540 | 74 | 179 | 3 | 59 |
| Bell, B., Texas | .329 | 489 | 76 | 161 | 17 | 83 |
| Wilson, Kansas City | .326 | 705 | 133 | 230 | 3 | 49 |
| Oliver, Texas | .319 | 656 | 96 | 209 | 19 | 117 |
| Bumbry, Baltimore | .318 | 645 | 118 | 205 | 9 | 53 |
| Watson, B., New York | .307 | 469 | 62 | 144 | 13 | 68 |

### NATIONAL LEAGUE
(Close of regular season)

| PLAYER—CLUB | PCT. | AB | R | H | HR | RBI |
|---|---|---|---|---|---|---|
| Buckner, Chicago | .324 | 578 | 69 | 187 | 10 | 68 |
| Hernandez, K., St. Louis | .321 | 595 | 111 | 191 | 16 | 99 |
| Templeton, St. Louis | .319 | 504 | 83 | 161 | 4 | 43 |
| McBride, Philadelphia | .309 | 554 | 68 | 171 | 9 | 87 |
| Cedeno, Houston | .309 | 499 | 71 | 154 | 10 | 73 |
| Dawson, A., Montreal | .308 | 577 | 96 | 178 | 17 | 87 |
| Garvey, S., Los Angeles | .304 | 658 | 78 | 200 | 26 | 106 |
| Collins, D., Cincinnati | .303 | 551 | 94 | 167 | 3 | 35 |
| Simmons, T., St. Louis | .303 | 495 | 84 | 150 | 21 | 98 |
| Hendrick, G., St. Louis | .302 | 572 | 73 | 173 | 25 | 109 |

[1] Based on 502 or more plate appearances.

## 1980 LEADING BASEBALL PITCHERS[1]

### AMERICAN LEAGUE

| PITCHER—CLUB | ERA | W | L | IP | H | BB | SO |
|---|---|---|---|---|---|---|---|
| May, New York | 2.47 | 15 | 5 | 175 | 144 | 39 | 133 |
| Norris, Oakland | 2.54 | 22 | 9 | 284 | 215 | 83 | 180 |
| Burns, Chicago | 2.84 | 15 | 13 | 238 | 213 | 63 | 133 |
| Keough, Oakland | 2.92 | 16 | 13 | 250 | 218 | 94 | 121 |
| Gura, Kansas City | 2.96 | 18 | 10 | 283 | 272 | 76 | 113 |
| Haas, Milwaukee | 3.11 | 16 | 15 | 252 | 246 | 56 | 146 |
| Stone, Baltimore | 3.23 | 25 | 7 | 251 | 224 | 101 | 149 |
| Erickson, Minnesota | 3.25 | 7 | 13 | 191 | 198 | 56 | 97 |
| Langford, Oakland | 3.26 | 19 | 12 | 290 | 276 | 64 | 102 |
| Clancy, Toronto | 3.30 | 13 | 16 | 251 | 217 | 128 | 152 |

### NATIONAL LEAGUE

| PITCHER—CLUB | ERA | W | L | IP | H | BB | SO |
|---|---|---|---|---|---|---|---|
| Sutton, Los Angeles | 2.21 | 13 | 5 | 212 | 163 | 47 | 128 |
| Carlton, Philadelphia | 2.34 | 24 | 9 | 304 | 243 | 90 | 286 |
| Reuss, Los Angeles | 2.52 | 18 | 6 | 229 | 193 | 40 | 111 |
| Blue, San Francisco | 2.97 | 14 | 10 | 224 | 202 | 61 | 129 |
| Rogers, Montreal | 2.98 | 16 | 11 | 281 | 247 | 85 | 147 |
| Zachry, New York | 3.00 | 6 | 10 | 165 | 145 | 58 | 88 |
| Soto, Cincinnati | 3.08 | 10 | 8 | 190 | 126 | 84 | 182 |
| Whitson, San Fran. | 3.10 | 11 | 13 | 212 | 222 | 56 | 90 |
| Sanderson, Montreal | 3.11 | 16 | 11 | 211 | 206 | 56 | 125 |
| Forsch, Houston | 3.20 | 12 | 13 | 222 | 230 | 41 | 84 |

[1] 162 or more innings pitched.

## STAR BASEBALL PITCHERS OF THE PAST

| PITCHERS | CAREER | YEARS | G | IP | W | L | PCT | H | R | ER | SO | BB | ERA |
|---|---|---|---|---|---|---|---|---|---|---|---|---|---|
| Grover Cleveland Alexander | 1911–1930 | 20 | 696 | 5,189 | 373 | 208 | .642 | 4,868 | 1,851 | — | 2,198 | 951 | 2.56 |
| Charles (Chief) Bender | 1903–1925 | 15 | 433 | 2,847 | 208 | 112 | .650 | 2,455 | 987 | — | 1,630 | 667 | — |
| Mordecai (Three-finger) Brown | 1903–1916 | 12 | 411 | 2,697 | 208 | 111 | .652 | 2,284 | 863 | — | 1,166 | 548 | — |
| Jack Chesbro | 1899–1909 | 11 | 392 | 2,886 | 198 | 127 | .609 | 2,602 | 1,292 | — | 1,276 | 674 | — |
| John Clarkson | 1882–1894 | 12 | 517 | 4,514 | 327 | 176 | .650 | 4,384 | — | — | 2,013 | 1,192 | — |
| Stan Coveleski | 1912–1925 | 14 | 450 | 3,092 | 214 | 141 | .603 | 3,055 | 1,237 | 982 | 981 | 802 | 2.88 |
| Jerome (Dizzy) Dean | 1930–1947 | 12 | 317 | 1,966 | 150 | 83 | .644 | 1,921 | 776 | 663 | 1,155 | 458 | 3.04 |
| Urban (Red) Faber | 1914–1933 | 20 | 669 | 4,087 | 254 | 212 | .545 | 4,104 | 1,813 | 1,430 | 1,471 | 1,213 | 3.15 |
| Bob Feller | 1936–1956 | 18 | 570 | 3,828 | 266 | 162 | .621 | 3,271 | 1,557 | 1,384 | 2,581 | 1,764 | 3.25 |
| Whitey Ford | 1950–1967 | 16 | 498 | 3,171 | 236 | 106 | .690 | 2,766 | 1,107 | 967 | 1,956 | 1,086 | 2.74 |
| James (Pud) Galvin | 1876–1892 | 14 | 685 | 5,959 | 361 | 309 | .539 | 6,334 | — | — | 1,786 | 744 | — |
| Vernon (Lefty) Gomez | 1930–1942 | 14 | 368 | 2,503 | 189 | 102 | .649 | 2,290 | 1,091 | 929 | 1,468 | 1,095 | 3.34 |
| Clark Griffith | 1891–1914 | 21 | 416 | 3,370 | 240 | 140 | .632 | 3,372 | — | — | 962 | 800 | — |
| Burleigh Grimes | 1916–1934 | 19 | 615 | 4,178 | 270 | 212 | .560 | 4,406 | 2,048 | 1,638 | 1,512 | 1,295 | 3.52 |
| Robert (Lefty) Grove | 1925–1941 | 17 | 616 | 3,940 | 300 | 140 | .682 | 3,849 | 1,594 | 1,339 | 2,266 | 1,187 | 3.06 |
| Jesse J. (Pop) Haines | 1920–1937 | 19 | 555 | 3,207 | 210 | 158 | .571 | 3,460 | 1,556 | 1,298 | 981 | 871 | 3.64 |
| Waite Hoyte | 1919–1938 | 21 | 675 | 3,762 | 237 | 182 | .566 | 4,037 | 1,780 | 1,500 | 1,206 | 1,003 | 3.59 |
| Carl Hubbell | 1928–1943 | 16 | 535 | 3,591 | 253 | 154 | .622 | 3,461 | 1,380 | 1,188 | 1,677 | 725 | 2.98 |
| Walter Johnson | 1907–1927 | 21 | 802 | 5,924 | 416 | 279 | .599 | 4,920 | 1,902 | 1,103 | 3,508 | 1,353 | — |
| Tim Keefe | 1880–1893 | 14 | 599 | 5,050 | 344 | 225 | .605 | — | — | — | 2,542 | 1,225 | — |
| Sandy Koufax | 1955–1966 | 12 | 397 | 2,325 | 165 | 87 | .655 | 1,754 | 806 | 713 | 2,396 | 817 | 2.76 |
| Ted Lyons | 1923–1946 | 21 | 594 | 4,162 | 260 | 230 | .531 | 4,489 | 2,056 | 1,696 | 1,073 | 1,121 | 3.67 |
| Richard (Rube) Marquard | 1908–1925 | 18 | 536 | 3,307 | 201 | 177 | .532 | 3,233 | 1,443 | — | 1,593 | 858 | — |
| Christy Mathewson | 1900–1916 | 17 | 635 | 4,781 | 373 | 188 | .655 | 4,203 | 1,613 | — | 2,505 | 837 | — |
| Joe McGinnity | 1899–1908 | 10 | 467 | 3,455 | 247 | 145 | .630 | 3,236 | 1,442 | — | 1,064 | 803 | — |
| Charles (Kid) Nichols | 1890–1906 | 15 | 582 | 5,067 | 360 | 202 | .641 | 4,854 | — | — | 1,866 | 1,245 | — |
| Herb Pennock | 1912–1934 | 22 | 617 | 3,558 | 240 | 162 | .597 | 3,900 | 1,699 | 1,403 | 1,227 | 916 | 3.60 |
| Eddie Plank | 1901–1917 | 16 | 581 | 4,234 | 305 | 181 | .628 | 3,688 | 1,470 | — | 2,112 | 984 | — |
| Charles (Hoss) Radbourne | 1880–1891 | 12 | 517 | 4,543 | 308 | 191 | .617 | 4,500 | 2,300 | — | 1,746 | 856 | — |
| Eppa Rixey | 1912–1933 | 21 | 692 | 4,494 | 266 | 251 | .515 | 4,633 | 1,986 | 1,572 | 1,350 | 1,082 | 3.15 |
| Charles (Red) Ruffing | 1924–1947 | 22 | 624 | 4,342 | 273 | 225 | .548 | 4,294 | 2,117 | 1,833 | 1,987 | 1,541 | 3.80 |
| Warren Spahn | 1940–1967 | 21 | 750 | 5,246 | 363 | 245 | .597 | 4,830 | 2,016 | 1,798 | 2,583 | 1,434 | 3.08 |
| Arthur (Dazzy) Vance | 1915–1935 | 16 | 442 | 2,967 | 197 | 140 | .585 | 2,809 | 1,246 | 1,068 | 2,045 | 840 | 3.24 |
| George (Rube) Waddell | 1897–1910 | 13 | 407 | 2,958 | 191 | 142 | .574 | 2,480 | 1,079 | — | 2,310 | 771 | — |
| Ed Walsh | 1904–1917 | 14 | 431 | 2,968 | 195 | 126 | .607 | 2,335 | 882 | — | 1,731 | 620 | — |
| Mickey Welch | 1880–1892 | 13 | 564 | 4,775 | 311 | 207 | .600 | 4,637 | 2,548 | — | 1,837 | 1,305 | — |
| Early Wynn | 1939–1963 | 23 | 691 | 4,566 | 300 | 244 | .551 | 4,291 | 2,037 | 1,796 | 2,334 | 1,775 | 3.54 |
| Denton T. (Cy) Young | 1890–1911 | 22 | 906 | 7,377 | 511 | 313 | .620 | 7,078 | 3,168 | — | 2,819 | 1,209 | — |

## BATTING CHAMPIONS—MAJOR LEAGUE BASEBALL

### NATIONAL LEAGUE

| Year | Player | Avg |
|---|---|---|
| 1912 | Heinie Zimmerman, Chicago | .372 |
| 1913 | Jake Daubert, Brooklyn | .350 |
| 1914 | Jake Daubert, Brooklyn | .329 |
| 1915 | Larry Doyle, New York | .320 |
| 1916 | Hal Chase, Cincinnati | .339 |
| 1917 | Edd Roush, Cincinnati | .341 |
| 1918 | Zack Wheat, Brooklyn | .335 |
| 1919 | Edd Roush, Cincinnati | .321 |
| 1920 | Rogers Hornsby, St. Louis | .370 |
| 1921 | Rogers Hornsby, St. Louis | .397 |
| 1922 | Rogers Hornsby, St. Louis | .401 |
| 1923 | Rogers Hornsby, St. Louis | .384 |
| 1924 | Rogers Hornsby, St. Louis | .424 |
| 1925 | Rogers Hornsby, St. Louis | .403 |
| 1926 | Gene Hargrave, Cincinnati | .353 |
| 1927 | Paul Waner, Pittsburgh | .380 |
| 1928 | Rogers Hornsby, Boston | .387 |
| 1929 | Lefty O'Doul, Philadelphia | .398 |
| 1930 | Bill Terry, New York | .401 |
| 1931 | Chick Hafey, St. Louis | .349 [1] |
| 1932 | Lefty O'Doul, Brooklyn | .368 |
| 1933 | Chuck Klein, Philadelphia | .368 |
| 1934 | Paul Waner, Pittsburgh | .362 |
| 1935 | Arky Vaughan, Pittsburgh | .385 |
| 1936 | Paul Waner, Pittsburgh | .373 |
| 1937 | Joe Medwick, St. Louis | .374 |
| 1938 | Ernie Lombardi, Cincinnati | .342 |
| 1939 | Johnny Mize, St. Louis | .349 |
| 1940 | Debs Garms, Pittsburgh | .355 |
| 1941 | Pete Reiser, Brooklyn | .343 |
| 1942 | Ernie Lombardi, Boston | .330 |
| 1943 | Stan Musial, St. Louis | .357 |
| 1944 | Dixie Walker, Brooklyn | .357 |
| 1945 | Phil Cavarretta, Chicago | .355 |
| 1946 | Stan Musial, St. Louis | .365 |
| 1947 | Harry Walker, St. Louis–Philadelphia | .363 |
| 1948 | Stan Musial, St. Louis | .376 |
| 1949 | Jackie Robinson, Brooklyn | .342 |
| 1950 | Stan Musial, St. Louis | .346 |
| 1951 | Stan Musial, St. Louis | .355 |
| 1952 | Stan Musial, St. Louis | .336 |
| 1953 | Carl Furillo, Brooklyn | .344 |
| 1954 | Willie Mays, New York | .345 |
| 1955 | Richie Ashburn, Philadelphia | .338 |
| 1956 | Hank Aaron, Milwaukee | .328 |
| 1957 | Stan Musial, St. Louis | .351 |
| 1958 | Richie Ashburn, Philadelphia | .350 |
| 1959 | Hank Aaron, Milwaukee | .355 |
| 1960 | Dick Groat, Pittsburgh | .325 |
| 1961 | Roberto Clemente, Pittsburgh | .351 |
| 1962 | Tommy Davis, Los Angeles | .346 |
| 1963 | Tommy Davis, Los Angeles | .326 |
| 1964 | Roberto Clemente, Pittsburgh | .339 |
| 1965 | Roberto Clemente, Pittsburgh | .329 |
| 1966 | Matty Alou, Pittsburgh | .342 |
| 1967 | Roberto Clemente, Pittsburgh | .357 |
| 1968 | Pete Rose, Cincinnati | .335 |
| 1969 | Pete Rose, Cincinnati | .348 |
| 1970 | Rico Carty, Atlanta | .366 |
| 1971 | Joe Torre, St. Louis | .363 |
| 1972 | Billy Williams, Chicago | .333 |
| 1973 | Pete Rose, Cincinnati | .338 |
| 1974 | Ralph Garr, Atlanta | .353 |
| 1975 | Bill Madlock, Chicago | .354 |
| 1976 | Bill Madlock, Chicago | .339 |
| 1977 | Dave Parker, Pittsburgh | .338 |
| 1978 | Dave Parker, Pittsburgh | .334 |
| 1979 | Keith Hernandez, St Louis | .344 |
| 1980 | Bill Buckner, Chicago | .324 |

### AMERICAN LEAGUE

| Year | Player | Avg |
|---|---|---|
| 1912 | Ty Cobb, Detroit | .410 |
| 1913 | Ty Cobb, Detroit | .390 |
| 1914 | Ty Cobb, Detroit | .368 |
| 1915 | Ty Cobb, Detroit | .369 |
| 1916 | Tris Speaker, Cleveland | .386 |
| 1917 | Ty Cobb, Detroit | .383 |
| 1918 | Ty Cobb, Detroit | .382 |
| 1919 | Ty Cobb, Detroit | .384 |
| 1920 | George Sisler, St. Louis | .407 |
| 1921 | Harry Heilmann, Detroit | .394 |
| 1922 | George Sisler, St. Louis | .420 |
| 1923 | Harry Heilmann, Detroit | .403 |
| 1924 | Babe Ruth, New York | .378 |
| 1925 | Harry Heilmann, Detroit | .393 |
| 1926 | Heinie Manush, Detroit | .378 |
| 1927 | Harry Heilmann, Detroit | .398 |
| 1928 | Goose Goslin, Washington | .379 |
| 1929 | Lew Fonseca, Cleveland | .369 |
| 1930 | Al Simmons, Philadelphia | .381 |
| 1931 | Al Simmons, Philadelphia | .390 |
| 1932 | Dale Alexander, Detroit–Boston | .367 |
| 1933 | Jimmy Foxx, Philadelphia | .356 |
| 1934 | Lou Gehrig, New York | .363 |
| 1935 | Buddy Myer, Washington | .349 |
| 1936 | Luke Appling, Chicago | .388 |
| 1937 | Charley Gehringer, Detroit | .371 |
| 1938 | Jimmy Foxx, Boston | .349 |
| 1939 | Joe DiMaggio, New York | .381 |
| 1940 | Joe DiMaggio, New York | .352 |
| 1941 | Ted Williams, Boston | .406 |
| 1942 | Ted Williams, Boston | .356 |
| 1943 | Luke Appling, Chicago | .328 |
| 1944 | Lou Boudreau, Cleveland | .327 |
| 1945 | George Sternweiss, New York | .309 |
| 1946 | Mickey Vernon, Washington | .353 |
| 1947 | Ted Williams, Boston | .343 |
| 1948 | Ted Williams, Boston | .369 |
| 1949 | George Kell, Detroit | .343 [2] |
| 1950 | Billy Goodman, Boston | .354 |
| 1951 | Ferris Fain, Philadelphia | .344 |
| 1952 | Ferris Fain, Philadelphia | .327 |
| 1953 | Mickey Vernon, Washington | .337 |
| 1954 | Bobby Avila, Cleveland | .341 |
| 1955 | Al Kaline, Detroit | .340 |
| 1956 | Mickey Mantle, New York | .353 |
| 1957 | Ted Williams, Boston | .388 |
| 1958 | Ted Williams, Boston | .328 |
| 1959 | Harvey Kuenn, Detroit | .353 |
| 1960 | Pete Runnels, Boston | .320 |
| 1961 | Norm Cash, Detroit | .361 |
| 1962 | Pete Runnels, Boston | .326 |
| 1963 | Carl Yastrzemski, Boston | .321 |
| 1964 | Tony Oliva, Minnesota | .323 |
| 1965 | Tony Oliva, Minnesota | .321 |
| 1966 | Frank Robinson, Baltimore | .316 |
| 1967 | Carl Yastrzemski, Boston | .326 |
| 1968 | Carl Yastrzemski, Boston | .301 |
| 1969 | Rod Carew, Minnesota | .332 |
| 1970 | Alex Johnson, California | .329 |
| 1971 | Tony Oliva, Minnesota | .337 |
| 1972 | Rod Carew, Minnesota | .318 |
| 1973 | Rod Carew, Minnesota | .350 |
| 1974 | Rod Carew, Minnesota | .364 |
| 1975 | Rod Carew, Minnesota | .359 |
| 1976 | George Brett, Kansas City | .333 |
| 1977 | Rod Carew, Minnesota | .388 |
| 1978 | Rod Carew, Minnesota | .333 |
| 1979 | Fred Lynn, Boston | .333 |
| 1980 | George Brett, Kansas City | .390 |

[1] In 1931 Hafey compiled an average of .3489. Bill Terry of New York was second with .3486, and Jim Bottomley of St. Louis was third with .3482. [2] In 1949 Kell compiled .3429. Ted Williams of Boston was second with .3427.

# HOME RUN CHAMPIONS—MAJOR LEAGUE BASEBALL

| NATIONAL LEAGUE | | | AMERICAN LEAGUE | | |
|---|---|---|---|---|---|
| YEAR | PLAYER AND CLUB | HOME RUNS | YEAR | PLAYER AND CLUB | HOME RUNS |
| 1918 | Cliff Cravath, Philadelphia | 8 | 1918 | Babe Ruth, Boston | 11 |
| | | | | Clarence Walker, Philadelphia | 11 |
| 1919 | Cliff Cravath, Philadelphia | 12 | 1919 | Babe Ruth, Boston | 29 |
| 1920 | Fred Williams, Philadelphia | 15 | 1920 | Babe Ruth, New York | 54 |
| 1921 | George Kelly, New York | 23 | 1921 | Babe Ruth, New York | 59 |
| 1922 | Rogers Hornsby, St. Louis | 42 | 1922 | Kenneth R. Williams, St. Louis | 39 |
| 1923 | Fred Williams, Philadelphia | 41 | 1923 | Babe Ruth, New York | 41 |
| 1924 | Jacques Fournier, Brooklyn | 27 | 1924 | Babe Ruth, New York | 46 |
| 1925 | Rogers Hornsby, St. Louis | 39 | 1925 | Bob Meusel, New York | 33 |
| 1926 | Hack Wilson, Chicago | 21 | 1926 | Babe Ruth, New York | 47 |
| 1927 | H. Wilson, Chi.; F. Williams, Phil. | 30 | 1927 | Babe Ruth, New York | 60 |
| 1928 | Hack Wilson, Chicago | 31 | 1928 | Babe Ruth, New York | 54 |
| | Jim Bottomley, St. Louis | 31 | | | |
| 1929 | Chuck Klein, Philadelphia | 43 | 1929 | Babe Ruth, New York | 46 |
| 1930 | Hack Wilson, Chicago | 56 | 1930 | Babe Ruth, New York | 49 |
| 1931 | Chuck Klein, Philadelphia | 31 | 1931 | B. Ruth and L. Gehrig, N.Y. | 46 |
| 1932 | C. Klein, Phil.; M. Ott, N.Y. (tie) | 38 | 1932 | Jimmy Foxx, Philadelphia | 58 |
| 1933 | Chuck Klein, Philadelphia | 28 | 1933 | Jimmy Foxx, Philadelphia | 48 |
| 1934 | M. Ott, N.Y.; R. Collins, St. L. (tie) | 35 | 1934 | Lou Gehrig, New York | 49 |
| 1935 | Wally Berger, Boston | 34 | 1935 | J. Foxx, Phil.; H. Greenberg, Det. | 36 |
| 1936 | Mel Ott, New York | 33 | 1936 | Lou Gehrig, New York | 49 |
| 1937 | M. Ott, N.Y.; J. Medwick, St. L. | 31 | 1937 | Joe DiMaggio, New York | 46 |
| 1938 | Mel Ott, New York | 36 | 1938 | Hank Greenberg, Detroit | 58 |
| 1939 | Johnny Mize, St. Louis | 28 | 1939 | Jimmy Foxx, Boston | 35 |
| 1940 | Johnny Mize, St. Louis | 43 | 1940 | Hank Greenberg, Detroit | 41 |
| 1941 | Dolph Camilli, Brooklyn | 34 | 1941 | Ted Williams, Boston | 37 |
| 1942 | Mel Ott, New York | 30 | 1942 | Ted Williams, Boston | 36 |
| 1943 | Bill Nicholson, Chicago | 29 | 1943 | Rudy York, Detroit | 34 |
| 1944 | Bill Nicholson, Chicago | 33 | 1944 | Nick Etten, New York | 22 |
| 1945 | Tommy Holmes, Boston | 28 | 1945 | Vern Stephens, St. Louis | 24 |
| 1946 | Ralph Kiner, Pittsburgh | 23 | 1946 | Hank Greenberg, Detroit | 44 |
| 1947 | R. Kiner, Pitt.; J. Mize, N.Y. | 51 | 1947 | Ted Williams, Boston | 32 |
| 1948 | Ralph Kiner, Pittsburgh | 40 | 1948 | Joe DiMaggio, New York | 39 |
| | Johnny Mize, New York | 40 | | | |
| 1949 | Ralph Kiner, Pittsburgh | 54 | 1949 | Ted Williams, Boston | 43 |
| 1950 | Ralph Kiner, Pittsburgh | 47 | 1950 | Al Rosen, Cleveland | 37 |
| 1951 | Ralph Kiner, Pittsburgh | 42 | 1951 | Gus Zernial, Chicago–Phil. | 33 |
| 1952 | R. Kiner, Pitt.; H. Sauer, Chi. | 37 | 1952 | Larry Doby, Cleveland | 32 |
| 1953 | Eddie Mathews, Milwaukee | 47 | 1953 | Al Rosen, Cleveland | 43 |
| 1954 | Ted Kluszewski, Cincinnati | 49 | 1954 | Larry Doby, Cleveland | 32 |
| 1955 | Willie Mays, New York | 51 | 1955 | Mickey Mantle, New York | 37 |
| 1956 | Duke Snider, Brooklyn | 43 | 1956 | Mickey Mantle, New York | 52 |
| 1957 | Hank Aaron, Milwaukee | 44 | 1957 | Roy Sievers, Washington | 42 |
| 1958 | Ernie Banks, Chicago | 47 | 1958 | Mickey Mantle, New York | 42 |
| 1959 | Eddie Mathews, Milwaukee | 46 | 1959 | Rocky Colavito, Cleveland | 42 |
| | | | | Harmon Killebrew, Washington | 42 |
| 1960 | Ernie Banks, Chicago | 41 | 1960 | Mickey Mantle, New York | 40 |
| 1961 | Orlando Cepeda, San Francisco | 46 | 1961 | Roger Maris, New York | 61 |
| 1962 | Willie Mays, San Francisco | 49 | 1962 | Harmon Killebrew, Minnesota | 48 |
| 1963 | Hank Aaron, Milwaukee | 44 | 1963 | Harmon Killebrew, Minnesota | 45 |
| | Willie McCovey, San Francisco | 44 | | | |
| 1964 | Willie Mays, San Francisco | 47 | 1964 | Harmon Killebrew, Minnesota | 49 |
| 1965 | Willie Mays, San Francisco | 52 | 1965 | Tony Conigliaro, Boston | 32 |
| 1966 | Hank Aaron, Atlanta | 44 | 1966 | Frank Robinson, Baltimore | 49 |
| 1967 | Hank Aaron, Atlanta | 39 | 1967 | Carl Yastrzemski, Boston | 44 |
| | | | | Harmon Killebrew, Minnesota | 44 |
| 1968 | Willie McCovey, San Francisco | 36 | 1968 | Frank Howard, Washington | 44 |
| 1969 | Willie McCovey, San Francisco | 45 | 1969 | Harmon Killebrew, Minnesota | 49 |
| 1970 | Johnny Bench, Cincinnati | 45 | 1970 | Frank Howard, Washington | 44 |
| 1971 | Willie Stargell, Pittsburgh | 48 | 1971 | Bill Melton, Chicago | 33 |
| 1972 | Johnny Bench, Cincinnati | 40 | 1972 | Dick Allen, Chicago | 37 |
| 1973 | Willie Stargell, Pittsburgh | 44 | 1973 | Reggie Jackson, Oakland | 32 |
| 1974 | Mike Schmidt, Philadelphia | 36 | 1974 | Dick Allen, Chicago | 32 |
| 1975 | Mike Schmidt, Philadelphia | 38 | 1975 | Reggie Jackson, Oakland | 36 |
| | | | | George Scott, Milwaukee | 36 |
| 1976 | Mike Schmidt, Philadelphia | 38 | 1976 | Graig Nettles, New York | 32 |
| 1977 | George Foster, Cincinnati | 52 | 1977 | Jim Rice, Boston | 39 |
| 1978 | George Foster, Cincinnati | 40 | 1978 | Jim Rice, Boston | 46 |
| 1979 | Dave Kingman, Chicago | 48 | 1979 | Gorman Thomas, Milwaukee | 45 |
| 1980 | Mike Schmidt, Philadelphia | 48 | 1980 | Ben Oglivie, Milwaukee | 41 |
| | | | | Reggie Jackson, New York | 41 |

# RUNS-BATTED-IN LEADERS — MAJOR LEAGUE BASEBALL

Hack Wilson of the Chicago Cubs set the National League record of 190 in 1930. Lou Gehrig of the New York Yankees established the American League mark of 184 in 1931.

| NATIONAL LEAGUE | | | AMERICAN LEAGUE | | |
|---|---|---|---|---|---|
| 1914 | Sherwood Magee, Philadelphia | 101 | 1914 | Sam Crawford, Detroit | 112 |
| 1915 | Cliff Cravath, Philadelphia | 118 | 1915 | Sam Crawford, Detroit | 116 |
| 1916 | Hal Chase, Cincinnati | 84 | 1916 | Wally Pipp, New York | 99 |
| 1917 | Heinie Zimmerman, New York | 100 | 1917 | Robert Veach, Detroit | 115 |
| 1918 | Fred Merkle, Chicago | 71 | 1918 | G. Burns, Phil.; R. Veach, Det. | 74 |
| 1919 | Henry (Hi) Myers, Brooklyn | 72 | 1919 | Babe Ruth, Boston | 112 |
| 1920 | George Kelly, New York | 94 | 1920 | Babe Ruth, New York | 137 |
|  | Rogers Hornsby, St. Louis | 94 |  |  |  |
| 1921 | Rogers Hornsby, St. Louis | 126 | 1921 | Babe Ruth, New York | 170 |
| 1922 | Rogers Hornsby, St. Louis | 152 | 1922 | Ken Williams, St. Louis | 155 |
| 1923 | Irish Meusel, New York | 125 | 1923 | Tris Speaker, Cleveland; Babe Ruth, N.Y. | 130 |
| 1924 | George Kelly, New York | 136 | 1924 | Goose Goslin, Washington | 129 |
| 1925 | Rogers Hornsby, St. Louis | 143 | 1925 | Bob Meusel, New York | 138 |
| 1926 | Jim Bottomley, St. Louis | 120 | 1926 | Babe Ruth, New York | 145 |
| 1927 | Paul Waner, Pittsburgh | 131 | 1927 | Lou Gehrig, New York | 175 |
| 1928 | Jim Bottomley, St. Louis | 136 | 1928 | Babe Ruth and Lou Gehrig, N.Y. | 142 |
| 1929 | Hack Wilson, Chicago | 159 | 1929 | Al Simmons, Philadelphia | 157 |
| 1930 | Hack Wilson, Chicago | 190 | 1930 | Lou Gehrig, New York | 174 |
| 1931 | Chuck Klein, Philadelphia | 121 | 1931 | Lou Gehrig, New York | 184 |
| 1932 | Frank Hurst, Philadelphia | 143 | 1932 | Jimmy Foxx, Philadelphia | 169 |
| 1933 | Chuck Klein, Philadelphia | 120 | 1933 | Jimmy Foxx, Philadelphia | 163 |
| 1934 | Mel Ott, New York | 135 | 1934 | Lou Gehrig, New York | 165 |
| 1935 | Wally Berger, Boston | 130 | 1935 | Hank Greenberg, Detroit | 170 |
| 1936 | Joe Medwick, St. Louis | 138 | 1936 | Hal Trosky, Cleveland | 162 |
| 1937 | Joe Medwick, St. Louis | 154 | 1937 | Hank Greenberg, Detroit | 183 |
| 1938 | Joe Medwick, St. Louis | 122 | 1938 | Jimmy Foxx, Boston | 175 |
| 1939 | Frank McCormick, Cincinnati | 128 | 1939 | Ted Williams, Boston | 145 |
| 1940 | Johnny Mize, St. Louis | 137 | 1940 | Hank Greenberg, Detroit | 150 |
| 1941 | Dolph Camilli, Brooklyn | 120 | 1941 | Joe DiMaggio, New York | 125 |
| 1942 | Johnny Mize, New York | 110 | 1942 | Ted Williams, Boston | 137 |
| 1943 | Bill Nicholson, Chicago | 128 | 1943 | Rudy York, Detroit | 118 |
| 1944 | Bill Nicholson, Chicago | 122 | 1944 | Vern Stephens, St. Louis | 109 |
| 1945 | Dixie Walker, Brooklyn | 124 | 1945 | Nick Etten, New York | 111 |
| 1946 | Enos Slaughter, St. Louis | 130 | 1946 | Hank Greenberg, Detroit | 127 |
| 1947 | Johnny Mize, New York | 138 | 1947 | Ted Williams, Boston | 114 |
| 1948 | Stan Musial, St. Louis | 131 | 1948 | Joe DiMaggio, New York | 155 |
| 1949 | Ralph Kiner, Pittsburgh | 127 | 1949 | Ted Williams, Vern Stephens, Boston | 159 |
| 1950 | Del Ennis, Philadelphia | 126 | 1950 | Vern Stephens, Boston | 144 |
|  |  |  |  | Walt Dropo, Boston | 144 |
| 1951 | Monte Irvin, New York | 121 | 1951 | Gus Zernial, Chicago-Philadelphia | 129 |
| 1952 | Hank Sauer, Chicago | 121 | 1952 | Al Rosen, Cleveland | 105 |
| 1953 | Roy Campanella, Brooklyn | 142 | 1953 | Al Rosen, Cleveland | 145 |
| 1954 | Ted Kluszewski, Cincinnati | 141 | 1954 | Larry Doby, Cleveland | 126 |
| 1955 | Duke Snider, Brooklyn | 136 | 1955 | R. Boone, Det.; J. Jensen, Bost. | 116 |
| 1956 | Stan Musial, St. Louis | 109 | 1956 | Mickey Mantle, New York | 130 |
| 1957 | Hank Aaron, Milwaukee | 132 | 1957 | Roy Sievers, Washington | 114 |
| 1958 | Ernie Banks, Chicago | 129 | 1958 | Jackie Jensen, Boston | 122 |
| 1959 | Ernie Banks, Chicago | 143 | 1959 | Jackie Jensen, Boston | 112 |
| 1960 | Hank Aaron, Milwaukee | 126 | 1960 | Roger Maris, New York | 112 |
| 1961 | Orlando Cepeda, San Francisco | 142 | 1961 | Roger Maris, New York | 142 |
| 1962 | Tommy Davis, Los Angeles | 153 | 1962 | Harmon Killebrew, Minnesota | 126 |
| 1963 | Hank Aaron, Milwaukee | 130 | 1963 | Dick Stuart, Boston | 118 |
| 1964 | Ken Boyer, St. Louis | 119 | 1964 | Brooks Robinson, Baltimore | 118 |
| 1965 | Deron Johnson, Cincinnati | 130 | 1965 | Rocky Colavito, Cleveland | 108 |
| 1966 | Hank Aaron, Atlanta | 121 | 1966 | Frank Robinson, Baltimore | 122 |
| 1967 | Orlando Cepeda, St. Louis | 111 | 1967 | Carl Yastrzemski, Boston | 121 |
| 1968 | Willie McCovey, San Francisco | 105 | 1968 | Ken Harrelson, Boston | 109 |
| 1969 | Willie McCovey, San Francisco | 126 | 1969 | Harmon Killebrew, Minnesota | 140 |
| 1970 | Johnny Bench, Cincinnati | 148 | 1970 | Frank Howard, Washington | 126 |
| 1971 | Joe Torre, St. Louis | 137 | 1971 | Harmon Killebrew, Minnesota | 119 |
| 1972 | Johnny Bench, Cincinnati | 125 | 1972 | Dick Allen, Chicago | 113 |
| 1973 | Willie Stargell, Pittsburgh | 119 | 1973 | Reggie Jackson, Oakland | 117 |
| 1974 | Johnny Bench, Cincinnati | 129 | 1974 | Jeff Burroughs, Texas | 118 |
| 1975 | Greg Luzinski, Philadelphia | 120 | 1975 | George Scott, Milwaukee | 109 |
| 1976 | George Foster, Cincinnati | 121 | 1976 | Lee May, Baltimore | 109 |
| 1977 | George Foster, Cincinnati | 149 | 1977 | Larry Hisle, Minnesota | 119 |
| 1978 | George Foster, Cincinnati | 120 | 1978 | Jim Rice, Boston | 139 |
| 1979 | Dave Winfield, San Diego | 118 | 1979 | Don Baylor, California | 139 |
| 1980 | Mike Schmidt, Philadelphia | 121 | 1980 | Cecil Cooper, Milwaukee | 122 |

## PITCHERS WITH LOWEST EARNED RUN AVERAGE (ERA) [1]

| | NATIONAL LEAGUE | | | AMERICAN LEAGUE | | |
|---|---|---|---|---|---|---|
| YEAR | PITCHER AND CLUB | INNINGS | ERA | PITCHER AND CLUB | INNINGS | ERA |
| 1951 | Chet Nichols, Boston | 156 | 2.88 | Saul Rogovin, Detroit–Chicago | 217 | 2.78 |
| 1952 | Hoyt Wilhelm, New York | 159 | 2.43 | Allie Reynolds, New York | 244 | 2.07 |
| 1953 | Warren Spahn, Milwaukee | 266 | 2.10 | Eddie Lopat, New York | 178 | 2.43 |
| 1954 | John Antonelli, New York | 259 | 2.29 | Mike Garcia, Cleveland | 259 | 2.64 |
| 1955 | Bob Friend, Pittsburgh | 200 | 2.84 | Billy Pierce, Chicago | 206 | 1.97 |
| 1956 | Lew Burdette, Milwaukee | 256 | 2.71 | Whitey Ford, New York | 226 | 2.47 |
| 1957 | John Podres, Brooklyn | 196 | 2.66 | Bobby Shantz, New York | 173 | 2.45 |
| 1958 | Stu Miller, San Francisco | 182 | 2.47 | Whitey Ford, New York | 219 | 2.01 |
| 1959 | Sam Jones, San Francisco | 271 | 2.82 | Hoyt Wilhelm, Baltimore | 226 | 2.19 |
| 1960 | Mike McCormick, San Francisco | 253 | 2.70 | Frank Baumann, Chicago | 185 | 2.68 |
| 1961 | Warren Spahn, Milwaukee | 263 | 3.01 | Dick Donovan, Washington | 169 | 2.40 |
| 1962 | Sandy Koufax, Los Angeles | 184 | 2.54 | Hank Aguirre, Detroit | 216 | 2.21 |
| 1963 | Sandy Koufax, Los Angeles | 311 | 1.88 | Gary Peters, Chicago | 243 | 2.33 |
| 1964 | Sandy Koufax, Los Angeles | 223 | 1.74 | Dean Chance, Los Angeles | 278 | 1.65 |
| 1965 | Sandy Koufax, Los Angeles | 336 | 2.04 | Sam McDowell, Cleveland | 274 | 2.17 |
| 1966 | Sandy Koufax, Los Angeles | 323 | 1.73 | Gary Peters, Chicago | 204 | 2.03 |
| 1967 | Phil Niekro, Atlanta | 207 | 1.96 | Joe Horlen, Chicago | 258 | 2.06 |
| 1968 | Bob Gibson, St. Louis | 304 | 1.12 | Luis Tiant, Cleveland | 258 | 1.60 |
| 1969 | Juan Marichal, San Francisco | 299 | 2.10 | Dick Bosman, Washington | 193 | 2.19 |
| 1970 | Tom Seaver, New York | 291 | 2.81 | Diego Segui, Oakland | 162 | 2.56 |
| 1971 | Tom Seaver, New York | 286 | 1.76 | Vida Blue, Oakland | 312 | 1.82 |
| 1972 | Steve Carlton, Philadelphia | 346 | 1.98 | Luis Tiant, Boston | 179 | 1.91 |
| 1973 | Tom Seaver, New York | 290 | 2.07 | Jim Palmer, Baltimore | 296 | 2.40 |
| 1974 | Buzz Capra, Atlanta | 217 | 2.28 | Jim (Catfish) Hunter, Oakland | 318 | 2.49 |
| 1975 | Randy Jones, San Diego | 285 | 2.24 | Jim Palmer, Baltimore | 323 | 2.09 |
| 1976 | John Denny, St. Louis | 207 | 2.52 | Mark Fidrych, Detroit | 250 1/3 | 2.34 |
| 1977 | John Candelaria, Pittsburgh | 231 | 2.34 | Frank Tanana, California | 241 | 2.54 |
| 1978 | Craig Swan, New York | 207 | 2.43 | Ron Guidry, New York | 274 | 1.74 |
| 1979 | James Richard, Houston | 292 | 2.71 | Ron Guidry, New York | 236 | 2.78 |
| 1980 | Don Sutton, Los Angeles | 212 | 2.21 | Rudy May, New York | 175 | 2.47 |

## PITCHERS WITH HIGHEST WON-LOST PERCENTAGES [2]

| | NATIONAL LEAGUE | GAMES | | PCT. | AMERICAN LEAGUE | GAMES | | PCT. |
|---|---|---|---|---|---|---|---|---|
| YEAR | PITCHER AND CLUB | Won | Lost | | PITCHER AND CLUB | Won | Lost | |
| 1950 | Sal Maglie, New York | 18 | 4 | .818 | Vic Raschi, New York | 21 | 8 | .724 |
| 1951 | Preacher Roe, Brooklyn | 22 | 3 | .880 | Bob Feller, Cleveland | 22 | 8 | .733 |
| | | | | | Morrie Martin, Philadelphia | 11 | 4 | .733 |
| 1952 | Hoyt Wilhelm, New York | 15 | 3 | .833 | Bobby Shantz, Philadelphia | 24 | 7 | .774 |
| 1953 | Carl Erskine, Brooklyn | 20 | 6 | .769 | Eddie Lopat, New York | 16 | 4 | .800 |
| 1954 | John Antonelli, New York | 21 | 7 | .750 | Sandy Consuegra, Chicago | 16 | 3 | .842 |
| | Hoyt Wilhelm, New York | 12 | 4 | .750 | | | | |
| 1955 | Don Newcombe, Brooklyn | 20 | 5 | .800 | Tommy Byrne, New York | 16 | 5 | .762 |
| 1956 | Don Newcombe, Brooklyn | 27 | 7 | .794 | Whitey Ford, New York | 19 | 6 | .760 |
| 1957 | Bob Buhl, Milwaukee | 18 | 7 | .720 | Dick Donovan, Chicago | 16 | 6 | .727 |
| 1958 | Warren Spahn, Milwaukee | 22 | 11 | .667 | Tom Sturdivant, New York | 16 | 6 | .727 |
| | Lew Burdette, Milwaukee | 20 | 10 | .667 | Bob Turley, New York | 21 | 7 | .750 |
| 1959 | Elroy Face, Pittsburgh | 18 | 1 | .947 | Bob Shaw, Chicago | 18 | 6 | .750 |
| 1960 | Lindy McDaniel, St. Louis | 12 | 4 | .750 | Jim Coates, New York | 13 | 3 | .813 |
| 1961 | Johnny Podres, Los Angeles | 18 | 5 | .783 | Whitey Ford, New York | 25 | 4 | .862 |
| 1962 | Bob Purkey, Cincinnati | 23 | 5 | .821 | Ray Herbert, Chicago | 20 | 9 | .690 |
| 1963 | Ron Perranoski, Los Angeles | 16 | 3 | .842 | Whitey Ford, New York | 24 | 7 | .774 |
| 1964 | Sandy Koufax, Los Angeles | 19 | 5 | .792 | Wally Bunker, Baltimore | 19 | 5 | .792 |
| 1965 | Sandy Koufax, Los Angeles | 26 | 8 | .765 | Jim Grant, Minnesota | 21 | 7 | .750 |
| 1966 | Juan Marichal, San Francisco | 25 | 6 | .806 | Dave Boswell, Minnesota | 12 | 5 | .706 |
| 1967 | Nelson Briles, St. Louis | 14 | 5 | .736 | Joel Horlen, Chicago | 19 | 7 | .730 |
| 1968 | Steve Blass, Pittsburgh | 18 | 6 | .750 | Dennis McLain, Detroit | 31 | 6 | .843 |
| 1969 | Bob Moose, Pittsburgh | 14 | 3 | .824 | Jim Palmer, Baltimore | 16 | 4 | .800 |
| 1970 | Wayne Simpson, Cincinnati | 14 | 3 | .824 | Dave McNally, Baltimore | 24 | 9 | .727 |
| 1971 | Tug McGraw, New York | 11 | 4 | .733 | Dave McNally, Baltimore | 21 | 5 | .807 |
| 1972 | Gary Nolan, Cincinnati | 15 | 5 | .750 | Jim Hunter, Oakland | 21 | 7 | .750 |
| 1973 | George Stone, New York | 12 | 3 | .800 | Roger Moret, Boston | 13 | 2 | .866 |
| 1974 | Tommy John, Los Angeles | 13 | 3 | .813 | Bill Champion, Milwaukee | 11 | 4 | .733 |
| 1975 | Al Hrabosky, St. Louis | 13 | 3 | .813 | Roger Moret, Boston | 14 | 3 | .824 |
| 1976 | Richard Rhoden, Los Angeles | 12 | 3 | .800 | Bill Campbell, Minnesota | 17 | 5 | .773 |
| 1977 | John Candelaria, Pittsburgh | 20 | 5 | .800 | Don Gullett, New York | 14 | 4 | .778 |
| 1978 | Gaylord Perry, San Diego | 21 | 6 | .778 | Ron Guidry, New York | 25 | 3 | .893 |
| 1979 | James Bibby, Pittsburgh | 12 | 4 | .750 | Ron Davis, New York | 14 | 2 | .875 |
| 1980 | Jerry Reuss, Los Angeles | 18 | 6 | .750 | Steve Stone, Baltimore | 25 | 7 | .781 |

[1] Must have pitched 162 innings.    [2] Must have been involved in 15 won-lost decisions.

## MAJOR LEAGUE BASEBALL PARKS

| TEAM | STADIUM | SEATING CAPACITY | DISTANCE FROM HOME PLATE (in feet) | | |
|------|---------|------------------|-------------|---------------|------------|
| | | | Right Field | Center Field | Left Field |
| **NATIONAL LEAGUE** | | | | | |
| Atlanta Braves ..... | Atlanta Stadium ............... | 52,194 | 330 | 402 | 330 |
| Chicago Cubs ...... | Wrigley Field ................. | 37,741 | 353 | 400 | 355 |
| Cincinnati Reds .... | Riverfront Stadium............. | 52,392 | 330 | 404 | 330 |
| Houston Astros .... | The Astrodome ................ | 45,000 | 340 | 406 | 340 |
| Los Angeles Dodgers | Dodger Stadium ............... | 56,000 | 330 | 395 | 330 |
| Montreal Expos .. | Olympic Stadium .............. | 59,984 | 325 | 404 | 325 |
| New York Mets ..... | Shea Stadium ................. | 55,300 | 338 | 410 | 338 |
| Philadelphia Phillies | Veterans Stadium ............. | 64,976 | 330 | 408 | 330 |
| Pittsburgh Pirates .. | Three Rivers Stadium ......... | 50,230 | 335 | 400 | 335 |
| St. Louis Cardinals.. | Busch Memorial Stadium ........ | 50,222 | 330 | 414 | 330 |
| San Diego Padres... | San Diego Stadium ............ | 51,362 | 330 | 420 | 330 |
| San Francisco Giants | Candlestick Park ............. | 58,000 | 335 | 410 | 335 |
| **AMERICAN LEAGUE** | | | | | |
| Baltimore Orioles... | Memorial Stadium ............. | 52,862 | 309 | 405 | 309 |
| Boston Red Sox .... | Fenway Park ................. | 33,536 | 302 | 390 | 315 |
| California Angels ... | Anaheim Stadium.............. | 43,250 | 370 | 404 | 370 |
| Chicago White Sox .. | White Sox Park............... | 44,492 | 352 | 445 | 352 |
| Cleveland Indians... | Cleveland Stadium ............ | 76,713 | 320 | 400 | 320 |
| Detroit Tigers ...... | Tiger Stadium ................ | 52,067 | 325 | 440 | 340 |
| Kansas City Royals . | Royals Stadium ............... | 40,628 | 330 | 410 | 330 |
| Milwaukee Brewers . | County Stadium ............... | 53,192 | 362 | 402 | 362 |
| Minnesota Twins ... | Metropolitan Stadium ......... | 45,919 | 370 | 402 | 360 |
| New York Yankees .. | Yankee Stadium .............. | 57,545 | 353 | 417 | 387 |
| Oakland A's........ | Oakland Coliseum ............ | 50,000 | 330 | 400 | 330 |
| Seattle Mariners.... | The Kingdome ................ | 59,438 | 316 | 410 | 316 |
| Texas Rangers .... | Arlington Stadium ............ | 41,097 | 370 | 400 | 370 |
| Toronto Blue Jays .. | Exhibition Stadium ........... | 43,737 | 330 | 400 | 330 |

## MAJOR LEAGUE BASEBALL ATTENDANCE FIGURES AT HOME PARKS

| NATIONAL LEAGUE CLUB | TOTAL 1980 ATTENDANCE | RECORD SEASON Attendance | Year | NATIONAL LEAGUE CLUB | TOTAL 1980 ATTENDANCE | RECORD SEASON Attendance | Year |
|------|------|------|------|------|------|------|------|
| Atlanta .......... | 1,048,411 | 1,539,801 | 1966 | New York......... | 1,192,073 | 2,697,479 | 1970 |
| Chicago .......... | 1,206,776 | 1,674,993 | 1969 | Philadelphia....... | 2,651,650 | 2,775,011 | 1979 |
| Cincinnati ........ | 2,022,450 | 2,629,708 | 1976 | Pittsburgh ........ | 1,646,757 | 1,705,828 | 1960 |
| Houston .......... | 2,278,217 | 2,278,217 | 1980 | St. Louis ......... | 1,385,147 | 2,090,145 | 1967 |
| Los Angeles ...... | 3,249,287 | 3,347,845 | 1978 | San Diego ........ | 1,139,026 | 1,670,107 | 1978 |
| Montreal ......... | 2,208,175 | 2,208,175 | 1980 | San Francisco..... | 1,096,115 | 1,795,356 | 1960 |

| AMERICAN LEAGUE CLUB | TOTAL 1980 ATTENDANCE | RECORD SEASON Attendance | Year | AMERICAN LEAGUE CLUB | TOTAL 1980 ATTENDANCE | RECORD SEASON Attendance | Year |
|------|------|------|------|------|------|------|------|
| Baltimore ......... | 1,797,438 | 1,797,438 | 1980 | Milwaukee ........ | 1,857,408 | 1,918,343 | 1979 |
| Boston ........... | 1,956,092 | 2,353,114 | 1979 | Minnesota ........ | 769,206 | 1,483,547 | 1967 |
| California ......... | 2,297,327 | 2,523,575 | 1979 | New York......... | 2,627,417 | 2,627,417 | 1980 |
| Chicago .......... | 1,200,365 | 1,657,135 | 1977 | Oakland .......... | 842,259 | 1,077,684 | 1975 |
| Cleveland ......... | 1,033,827 | 2,620,627 | 1948 | Seattle ........... | 836,204 | 1,338,523 | 1977 |
| Detroit ........... | 1,785,293 | 2,031,847 | 1968 | Texas ............ | 1,198,275 | 1,519,671 | 1979 |
| Kansas City....... | 2,288,714 | 2,288,714 | 1980 | Toronto .......... | 1,400,327 | 1,701,052 | 1977 |

## ALL-STAR BASEBALL GAME RESULTS

| YEAR | WINNING LEAGUE | SCORE | YEAR | WINNING LEAGUE | SCORE | YEAR | WINNING LEAGUE | SCORE | YEAR | WINNING LEAGUE | SCORE |
|------|------|------|------|------|------|------|------|------|------|------|------|
| 1933 | American | 4–2 | 1946 | American | 12–0 | 1959 | National | 5–4 | 1968 | National | 1–0 |
| 1934 | American | 9–7 | 1947 | American | 2–1 | | American | 5–3 | 1969 | National | 9–3 |
| 1935 | American | 4–1 | 1948 | American | 5–2 | 1960 | National | 5–3 | 1970 | National | 5–4 |
| 1936 | National | 4–3 | 1949 | American | 11–7 | | National | 6–0 | 1971 | American | 6–4 |
| 1937 | American | 8–3 | 1950 | National | 4–3 | 1961 | National | 5–4 | 1972 | National | 4–3 |
| 1938 | National | 4–1 | 1951 | National | 8–3 | | Tie game | 1–1 | 1973 | National | 7–1 |
| 1939 | American | 3–1 | 1952 | National | 3–2 | 1962 | National | 3–1 | 1974 | National | 7–2 |
| 1940 | National | 4–0 | 1953 | National | 5–1 | | American | 9–4 | 1975 | National | 6–3 |
| 1941 | American | 7–5 | 1954 | American | 11–9 | 1963 | National | 5–3 | 1976 | National | 7–1 |
| 1942 | American | 3–1 | 1955 | National | 6–5 | 1964 | National | 7–4 | 1977 | National | 7–5 |
| 1943 | American | 5–3 | 1956 | National | 7–3 | 1965 | National | 6–5 | 1978 | National | 7–3 |
| 1944 | National | 7–1 | 1957 | American | 6–5 | 1966 | National | 2–1 | 1979 | National | 7–6 |
| 1945 | No game | | 1958 | American | 4–3 | 1967 | National | 2–1 | 1980 | National | 4–2 |

# BASEBALL HALL OF FAME

| PITCHERS | CAREER | Won | Lost |
|---|---|---|---|
| Grover Alexander | 1911–1930 | 373 | 208 |
| Charles (Chief) Bender | 1903–1925 | 212 | 128 |
| Mordecai (Three-finger) Brown | 1903–1916 | 239 | 130 |
| Jack Chesbro | 1899–1909 | 199 | 128 |
| John Clarkson | 1882–1894 | 328 | 175 |
| Stan Coveleski | 1912–1925 | 216 | 142 |
| W. A. Cummings * | 1872–1877 | 146 | 92 |
| Jerome (Dizzy) Dean | 1930–1947 | 150 | 83 |
| Urban (Red) Faber | 1914–1933 | 253 | 211 |
| Bob Feller | 1936–1956 | 266 | 162 |
| Edward (Whitey) Ford | 1950–1967 | 236 | 106 |
| James (Pud) Galvin | 1876–1892 | 365 | 309 |
| Vernon (Lefty) Gomez | 1930–1942 | 189 | 95 |
| Clark Griffith | 1891–1914 | 237 | 140 |
| Burleigh Grimes | 1916–1934 | 270 | 212 |
| Robert (Lefty) Grove | 1925–1941 | 300 | 141 |
| Jesse J. (Pop) Haines | 1920–1937 | 210 | 158 |
| Waite Hoyte | 1919–1938 | 237 | 182 |
| Carl Hubbell | 1928–1943 | 253 | 154 |
| Walter Johnson | 1907–1927 | 416 | 279 |
| Addie Joss | 1902–1910 | 159 | 96 |
| Tim Keefe | 1880–1893 | 346 | 225 |
| Sandy Koufax | 1955–1966 | 165 | 87 |
| Bob Lemon | 1946–1958 | 207 | 128 |
| Ted Lyons | 1923–1946 | 260 | 230 |
| Joe McGinnity | 1899–1908 | 247 | 142 |
| Richard (Rube) Marquard | 1908–1925 | 201 | 177 |
| Christy Mathewson | 1900–1916 | 373 | 188 |
| Charles (Kid) Nichols | 1890–1906 | 360 | 202 |
| Leroy (Satchel) Paige | 1948–1952 | 28 | 31 |
| Herb Pennock | 1912–1934 | 241 | 163 |
| Eddie Plank | 1901–1917 | 325 | 190 |
| Charles (Hoss) Radbourne | 1880–1891 | 308 | 191 |
| Eppa Rixey | 1912–1933 | 266 | 251 |
| Robin Roberts | 1948–1966 | 286 | 245 |
| Charles (Red) Ruffing | 1924–1947 | 273 | 225 |
| Amos Rusie | 1889–1901 | 243 | 160 |
| Warren Spahn | 1940–1967 | 363 | 245 |
| A. G. Spalding * | 1871–1877 | 252 | 68 |
| Arthur (Dazzy) Vance | 1915–1935 | 197 | 140 |
| George (Rube) Waddell | 1897–1910 | 193 | 140 |
| Ed Walsh | 1904–1917 | 195 | 126 |
| John Ward | 1878–1894 | 158 | 102 |
| Mickey Welch | 1880–1892 | 309 | 211 |
| Early Wynn | 1939–1963 | 300 | 244 |
| Denton T. (Cy) Young | 1890–1911 | 511 | 315 |

| CATCHERS | CAREER | AVERAGE |
|---|---|---|
| Lawrence (Yogi) Berra | 1946–1965 | .285 |
| Roger Bresnahan | 1897–1915 | .279 |
| Roy Campanella | 1948–1957 | .276 |
| Gordon (Mickey) Cochrane | 1925–1937 | .320 |
| Bill Dickey | 1928–1946 | .313 |
| William (Buck) Ewing | 1880–1897 | .311 |
| Charles (Gabby) Hartnett | 1922–1941 | .297 |
| Mike Kelly | 1878–1893 | .315 |
| Connie Mack | 1886–1896 | .249 |
| Wilbert Robinson | 1886–1902 | .280 |
| Ray Schalk | 1912–1929 | .253 |

| FIRST BASEMEN | CAREER | AVERAGE |
|---|---|---|
| Adrian (Cap) Anson | 1876–1897 | .339 |
| Jake Beckley | 1888–1907 | .309 |
| Sunny Jim Bottomley | 1922–1935 | .310 |
| Dennis (Dan) Brouthers | 1879–1896 | .348 |
| Frank Chance | 1898–1914 | .297 |
| Charles Comiskey | 1882–1894 | .269 |
| Roger Connor | 1880–1897 | .317 |
| Jimmy Foxx | 1925–1945 | .325 |
| Henry (Lou) Gehrig | 1923–1939 | .340 |
| Henry (Hank) Greenberg | 1933–1947 | .313 |
| George Kelly | 1915–1932 | .297 |
| Buck Leonard | 1930–1944 | (Negro leag.) |
| George Sisler | 1915–1930 | .340 |
| Bill Terry | 1923–1936 | .341 |

| SECOND BASEMEN | CAREER | AVERAGE |
|---|---|---|
| Eddie Collins | 1906–1930 | .333 |
| Johnny Evers | 1902–1919 | .270 |
| Frank Frisch | 1919–1937 | .316 |
| Charley Gehringer | 1924–1942 | .321 |
| Billy Herman | 1931–1947 | .304 |
| Rogers Hornsby | 1915–1937 | .359 |
| Napoleon Lajoie | 1896–1916 | .339 |
| Jackie Robinson | 1947–1956 | .311 |

| THIRD BASEMEN | CAREER | AVERAGE |
|---|---|---|
| Frank (Home Run) Baker | 1908–1922 | .307 |
| Jimmy Collins | 1895–1908 | .294 |
| William (Judy) Johnson | 1918–1938 | .340 |
| Eddie Mathews | 1952–1968 | .271 |
| John McGraw | 1891–1906 | .334 |
| Harold (Pie) Traynor | 1920–1937 | .320 |

| SHORTSTOPS | CAREER | AVERAGE |
|---|---|---|
| Luke Appling | 1930–1950 | .310 |
| Dave Bancroft | 1915–1929 | .279 |
| Ernie Banks | 1953–1971 | .274 |
| Lou Boudreau | 1938–1952 | .295 |
| Joe Cronin | 1926–1945 | .302 |
| Hugh Jennings | 1891–1918 | .314 |
| Walter (Rabbit) Maranville | 1912–1935 | .258 |
| Joe Sewell | 1920–1933 | .312 |
| Joe Tinker | 1902–1916 | .264 |
| John (Honus) Wagner | 1897–1917 | .329 |
| Roderick (Bobby) Wallace | 1894–1918 | .267 |
| George Wright * | 1876–1882 | .251 |

| OUTFIELDERS | CAREER | AVERAGE |
|---|---|---|
| Earl Averill | 1929–1941 | .318 |
| James (Cool Papa) Bell | 1921–1950 | (Negro leag.) |
| Jesse Burkett | 1890–1905 | .342 |
| Max Carey | 1910–1929 | .285 |
| Oscar Charleston | 1915–1944 | (Negro leag.) |
| Fred Clarke | 1894–1915 | .315 |
| Roberto Clemente | 1955–1972 | .317 |
| Ty Cobb | 1905–1928 | .367 |
| Earl B. Combs | 1924–1935 | .325 |
| Sam Crawford | 1899–1917 | .309 |
| Hazen (Kiki) Cuyler | 1921–1938 | .321 |
| Ed Delahanty | 1888–1903 | .346 |
| Martin Dihigo | 1923–1950 | .320 |
| Joe DiMaggio | 1936–1951 | .325 |
| Hugh Duffy | 1888–1906 | .330 |
| Elmer Flick | 1898–1910 | .315 |
| Josh Gibson | 1929–1946 | (Negro leag.) |
| Leon (Goose) Goslin | 1921–1938 | .316 |
| Billy Hamilton | 1888–1901 | .344 |
| Harry Heilmann | 1914–1932 | .342 |
| Harry Hooper | 1909–1925 | .281 |
| Monte Irvin | 1930s–40s | (Negro leag.) |
| Al Kaline | 1953–1974 | .297 |
| Willie Keeler | 1892–1910 | .345 |
| Joe Kelley | 1892–1910 | .321 |
| Ralph Kiner | 1946–1955 | .279 |
| Chuck Klein | 1928–1944 | .320 |
| Fred Lindstrom | 1924–1936 | .311 |
| John Henry Lloyd | 1905–1931 | .362 |
| Mickey Mantle | 1951–1968 | .298 |
| Henry (Heinie) Manush | 1923–1939 | .330 |
| Willie Mays | 1951–1973 | .302 |
| Thomas McCarthy | 1884–1896 | .294 |
| Joe Medwick | 1932–1948 | .324 |
| Stan Musial | 1941–1963 | .331 |
| James O'Rourke | 1876–1894 | .315 |
| Mel Ott | 1926–1947 | .304 |

* Elected for meritorious service.

## BASEBALL HALL OF FAME (continued)

### OUTFIELDERS (continued)

| | | |
|---|---|---|
| Edgar (Sam) Rice | 1915–1934 | .322 |
| Edd Roush | 1913–1931 | .323 |
| George (Babe) Ruth | 1914–1935 | .342 |
| Al Simmons | 1924–1944 | .334 |
| Duke Snider | 1947–1964 | .295 |
| Tris Speaker | 1907–1928 | .344 |
| Sam Thompson | 1885–1898 | .336 |
| Lloyd Waner | 1927–1945 | .316 |
| Paul Waner | 1926–1945 | .333 |
| Zack Wheat | 1909–1927 | .317 |
| Ted Williams | 1939–1960 | .344 |
| Lewis R. (Hack) Wilson | 1923–1934 | .319 |
| Ross Youngs | 1917–1926 | .322 |

### OTHERS ELECTED FOR MERITORIOUS SERVICE

Edward G. Barrow, American League executive
Morgan G. Bulkeley, first National League president
Alexander J. Cartwright, organized first baseball club
Henry Chadwick, wrote first baseball rule book
Charles A. Comiskey, player, manager, and executive
John (Jocko) Conlan, National League umpire (1941–65)
Tom Connolly, American League umpire for 52 years
Billy Evans, umpire and later general manager of
Cleveland Indians and Boston Red Sox
Ford C. Frick, National League president (1934–51) and baseball commissioner (1951–65)
Warren Giles, president of the National League (1951–69)
Will Harridge, president of the American League (1931–58)
Bucky Harris, player and manager (1919–47)
Cal Hubbard, American League umpire (1936–52)
Miller Huggins, managed N.Y. Yankees to six pennants
Ban Johnson, first American League president
Bill Klem, National League umpire for 46 years
Kenesaw M. Landis, baseball's first commissioner
Al Lopez, catcher 1928–47; manager, Cleveland Indians 1951–57, Chicago White Sox 1957–65, 1968–69
Leland MacPhail, manager, Cincinnati, Brooklyn, N.Y. Yankees (1933–47); introduced night games (1935)
Joe McCarthy, managed N.Y. Yankees to nine pennants and won seven World Series
Bill McKechnie, managed three different clubs to pennants
Branch Rickey, executive of three National League clubs
Casey Stengel, manager N.Y. Yankees and N.Y. Mets
George Weiss, general manager of N.Y. Yankees and Mets
Harry Wright, National League manager for 30 years
Tom Yawkey, owner of Boston Red Sox (1933–76)

## CY YOUNG AWARD (Top Major League Pitchers)

| National League | | American League | |
|---|---|---|---|
| 1970 | Bob Gibson, St. Louis | 1970 | Jim Perry, Minnesota |
| 1971 | Ferguson Jenkins, Chicago | 1971 | Vida Blue, Oakland |
| 1972 | Steve Carlton, Philadelphia | 1972 | Gaylord Perry, Cleveland |
| 1973 | Tom Seaver, New York | 1973 | Jim Palmer, Baltimore |
| 1974 | Mike Marshall, Los Angeles | 1974 | Jim (Catfish) Hunter, Oakland |
| 1975 | Tom Seaver, New York | 1975 | Jim Palmer, Baltimore |
| 1976 | Randy Jones, San Diego | 1976 | Jim Palmer, Baltimore |
| 1977 | Steve Carlton, Philadelphia | 1977 | Sparky Lyle, New York |
| 1978 | Gaylord Perry, San Diego | 1978 | Ron Guidry, New York |
| 1979 | Bruce Sutter, Chicago | 1979 | Mike Flanagan, Baltimore |
| 1980 | Steve Carlton, Philadelphia | 1980 | Steve Stone, Baltimore |

## LEADING HOME RUN HITTERS—LIFETIME TOTALS

| PLAYER | HR | PLAYER | HR | PLAYER | HR | PLAYER | HR |
|---|---|---|---|---|---|---|---|
| Hank Aaron | 755 | Eddie Mathews | 512 | Duke Snider | 407 | Johnny Mize | 359 |
| Babe Ruth | 714 | Ernie Banks | 512 | Al Kaline | 399 | Yogi Berra | 358 |
| Willie Mays | 660 | Mel Ott | 511 | Frank Howard | 382 | Johnny Bench * | 356 |
| Frank Robinson | 586 | Lou Gehrig | 493 | Orlando Cepeda | 379 | Lee May * | 351 |
| Harmon Killebrew | 573 | Stan Musial | 475 | Norm Cash | 377 | Dick Allen | 351 |
| Mickey Mantle | 536 | Willie Stargell * | 472 | Rocky Colavito | 374 | Ron Santo | 342 |
| Jimmy Foxx | 534 | Billy Williams | 426 | Gil Hodges | 370 | John (Boog) Powell | 339 |
| Ted Williams | 521 | Carl Yastrzemski * | 419 | Ralph Kiner | 369 | Joe Adcock | 336 |
| Willie McCovey * | 521 | Reggie Jackson * | 410 | Joe DiMaggio | 361 | Hank Greenberg | 331 |

* Active player as of 1980 season.

## STAR BASEBALL HITTERS OF THE PAST

| PLAYER AND TEAM(S) | YEARS | GAMES | AT BAT | RUNS | HITS | BAT. AV. |
|---|---|---|---|---|---|---|
| Ty Cobb, Detroit, Philadelphia (AL) | 1905–28 | 3,033 | 11,429 | 2,244 | 4,191 | .367 |
| Rogers Hornsby, St. Louis, N.Y., Boston, Chicago (NL) | 1915–32 | 2,259 | 8,173 | 1,579 | 2,930 | .359 |
| Tris Speaker, Bost., Clev., Wash., Phil. (AL) | 1907–28 | 2,789 | 10,208 | 1,881 | 3,515 | .344 |
| Ted Williams, Boston (AL) | 1939–60 | 2,292 | 7,706 | 1,798 | 2,654 | .344 |
| Babe Ruth, Boston, New York (AL), Boston (NL) | 1914–35 | 2,503 | 8,399 | 2,174 | 2,873 | .342 |
| Harry Heilmann, Detroit (AL), Cincinnati (NL) | 1914–32 | 2,146 | 7,787 | 1,291 | 2,660 | .342 |
| Bill Terry, New York (NL) | 1923–36 | 1,721 | 6,428 | 1,120 | 2,193 | .341 |
| Lou Gehrig, New York (AL) | 1923–39 | 2,164 | 8,001 | 1,888 | 2,721 | .340 |
| George Sisler, mainly with St. Louis (AL) | 1915–30 | 2,055 | 8,267 | 1,284 | 2,812 | .340 |
| Napoleon Lajoie, mainly with Philadelphia (AL) | 1896–1916 | 2,475 | 9,589 | 1,503 | 3,251 | .339 |
| Eddie Collins, Philadelphia, Chicago (AL) | 1906–30 | 2,826 | 9,952 | 1,818 | 3,313 | .333 |
| Paul Waner, Pitt., Brooklyn, Boston (NL), N.Y. (AL) | 1926–45 | 2,549 | 9,459 | 1,626 | 3,152 | .333 |
| Stan Musial, St. Louis (NL) | 1941–63 | 3,026 | 10,972 | 1,949 | 3,630 | .331 |
| Jimmy Foxx, Phil., Boston (AL), Chicago, Phil. (NL) | 1925–45 | 2,317 | 8,134 | 1,751 | 2,646 | .325 |
| Joe DiMaggio, New York (AL) | 1936–51 | 1,736 | 6,821 | 1,390 | 2,214 | .325 |
| Joe Medwick, St. Louis, Brooklyn, N.Y., Boston (NL) | 1932–48 | 1,984 | 7,635 | 1,198 | 2,471 | .324 |
| Charley Gehringer, Detroit (AL) | 1924–42 | 2,323 | 8,858 | 1,773 | 2,838 | .321 |
| Chuck Klein, Philadelphia, Chicago, Pittsburgh (NL) | 1928–44 | 1,753 | 6,486 | 1,168 | 2,076 | .320 |
| Frank Frisch, New York, St. Louis (NL) | 1919–37 | 2,311 | 9,112 | 1,532 | 2,880 | .316 |
| Hank Aaron, Milw., Atlanta (NL), Milw. (AL) | 1954–76 | 3,298 | 12,364 | 2,174 | 3,771 | .305 |
| Willie Mays, N.Y. (NL), San. Fran. (NL), N.Y. (NL) | 1951–73 | 2,992 | 10,881 | 2,062 | 3,283 | .302 |
| Mickey Mantle, New York (AL) | 1951–68 | 2,401 | 8,102 | 1,677 | 2,415 | .298 |

## BASEBALL MOST VALUABLE PLAYER AWARDS

| NATIONAL LEAGUE | | | AMERICAN LEAGUE | | |
|---|---|---|---|---|---|
| YEAR | PLAYER | CLUB | YEAR | PLAYER | CLUB |
| 1942 | Mort Cooper | St. Louis | 1942 | Joe Gordon | New York |
| 1943 | Stan Musial | St. Louis | 1943 | Spud Chandler | New York |
| 1944 | Marty Marion | St. Louis | 1944 | Hal Newhouser | Detroit |
| 1945 | Phil Cavarretta | Chicago | 1945 | Hal Newhouser | Detroit |
| 1946 | Stan Musial | St. Louis | 1946 | Ted Williams | Boston |
| 1947 | Bob Elliott | Boston | 1947 | Joe DiMaggio | New York |
| 1948 | Stan Musial | St. Louis | 1948 | Lou Boudreau | Cleveland |
| 1949 | Jackie Robinson | Brooklyn | 1949 | Ted Williams | Boston |
| 1950 | Jim Konstanty | Philadelphia | 1950 | Phil Rizzuto | New York |
| 1951 | Roy Campanella | Brooklyn | 1951 | Yogi Berra | New York |
| 1952 | Hank Sauer | Chicago | 1952 | Bobby Shantz | Philadelphia |
| 1953 | Roy Campanella | Brooklyn | 1953 | Al Rosen | Cleveland |
| 1954 | Willie Mays | New York | 1954 | Yogi Berra | New York |
| 1955 | Roy Campanella | Brooklyn | 1955 | Yogi Berra | New York |
| 1956 | Don Newcombe | Brooklyn | 1956 | Mickey Mantle | New York |
| 1957 | Hank Aaron | Milwaukee | 1957 | Mickey Mantle | New York |
| 1958 | Ernie Banks | Chicago | 1958 | Jackie Jensen | Boston |
| 1959 | Ernie Banks | Chicago | 1959 | Nellie Fox | Chicago |
| 1960 | Dick Groat | Pittsburgh | 1960 | Roger Maris | New York |
| 1961 | Frank Robinson | Cincinnati | 1961 | Roger Maris | New York |
| 1962 | Maury Wills | Los Angeles | 1962 | Mickey Mantle | New York |
| 1963 | Sandy Koufax | Los Angeles | 1963 | Elston Howard | New York |
| 1964 | Ken Boyer | St. Louis | 1964 | Brooks Robinson | Baltimore |
| 1965 | Willie Mays | San Francisco | 1965 | Zoilo Versalles | Minnesota |
| 1966 | Roberto Clemente | Pittsburgh | 1966 | Frank Robinson | Baltimore |
| 1967 | Orlando Cepeda | St. Louis | 1967 | Carl Yastrzemski | Boston |
| 1968 | Bob Gibson | St. Louis | 1968 | Dennis McLain | Detroit |
| 1969 | Willie McCovey | San Francisco | 1969 | Harmon Killebrew | Minnesota |
| 1970 | Johnny Bench | Cincinnati | 1970 | Boog Powell | Baltimore |
| 1971 | Joe Torre | St. Louis | 1971 | Vida Blue | Oakland |
| 1972 | Johnny Bench | Cincinnati | 1972 | Dick Allen | Chicago |
| 1973 | Pete Rose | Cincinnati | 1973 | Reggie Jackson | Oakland |
| 1974 | Steve Garvey | Los Angeles | 1974 | Jeff Burroughs | Texas |
| 1975 | Joe Morgan | Cincinnati | 1975 | Fred Lynn | Boston |
| 1976 | Joe Morgan | Cincinnati | 1976 | Thurman Munson | New York |
| 1977 | George Foster | Cincinnati | 1977 | Rod Carew | Minnesota |
| 1978 | Dave Parker | Pittsburgh | 1978 | Jim Rice | Boston |
| 1979 | Willie Stargell | Pittsburgh | 1979 | Don Baylor | California |
|  | Keith Hernandez | St. Louis |  |  |  |
| 1980 | Mike Schmidt | Philadelphia | 1980 | George Brett | Kansas City |

## BASEBALL ROOKIE OF THE YEAR AWARDS

| NATIONAL LEAGUE | | | AMERICAN LEAGUE | | |
|---|---|---|---|---|---|
| YEAR | PLAYER AND POSITION | CLUB | YEAR | PLAYER AND POSITION | CLUB |
| 1955 | Bill Virdon, outfielder | St. Louis | 1955 | Herb Score, pitcher | Cleveland |
| 1956 | Frank Robinson, outfielder | Cincinnati | 1956 | Luis Aparicio, shortstop | Chicago |
| 1957 | John Sanford, pitcher | Philadelphia | 1957 | Tony Kubek, infielder | New York |
| 1958 | Orlando Cepeda, first baseman | San Francisco | 1958 | Albie Pearson, outfielder | Washington |
| 1959 | Willie McCovey, first baseman | San Francisco | 1959 | Bob Allison, outfielder | Washington |
| 1960 | Frank Howard, outfielder | Los Angeles | 1960 | Ron Hansen, shortstop | Baltimore |
| 1961 | Billy Williams, outfielder | Chicago | 1961 | Don Schwall, pitcher | Boston |
| 1962 | Ken Hubbs, second baseman | Chicago | 1962 | Tom Tresh, outfielder-shortstop | New York |
| 1963 | Pete Rose, second baseman | Cincinnati | 1963 | Gary Peters, pitcher | Chicago |
| 1964 | Dick Allen, third baseman | Philadelphia | 1964 | Tony Oliva, outfielder | Minnesota |
| 1965 | Jim Lefebvre, second baseman | Los Angeles | 1965 | Curt Blefary, outfielder | Baltimore |
| 1966 | Tommy Helms, third baseman | Cincinnati | 1966 | Tommie Agee, outfielder | Chicago |
| 1967 | Tom Seaver, pitcher | New York | 1967 | Rod Carew, second baseman | Minnesota |
| 1968 | Johnny Bench, catcher | Cincinnati | 1968 | Stan Bahnsen, pitcher | New York |
| 1969 | Ted Sizemore, second baseman | Los Angeles | 1969 | Lou Piniella, outfielder | Kansas City |
| 1970 | Carl Morton, pitcher | Montreal | 1970 | Thurman Munson, catcher | New York |
| 1971 | Earl Williams, catcher | Atlanta | 1971 | Chris Chambliss, first baseman | Cleveland |
| 1972 | Jon Matlack, pitcher | New York | 1972 | Carlton Fisk, catcher | Boston |
| 1973 | Gary Matthews, outfielder | San Francisco | 1973 | Al Bumbry, outfielder | Baltimore |
| 1974 | Bake McBride, outfielder | St. Louis | 1974 | Mike Hargrove, first baseman | Texas |
| 1975 | John Montefusco, pitcher | San Francisco | 1975 | Fred Lynn, outfielder | Boston |
| 1976 | Pat Zachry, pitcher | Cincinnati | 1976 | Mark Fidrych, pitcher | Detroit |
|  | Butch Metzger, pitcher | San Diego |  |  |  |
| 1977 | Andre Dawson, outfielder | Montreal | 1977 | Eddie Murray, DH, outfielder | Baltimore |
| 1978 | Bob Horner, third baseman | Atlanta | 1978 | Lou Whitaker, second baseman | Detroit |
| 1979 | Rick Sutcliffe, pitcher | Los Angeles | 1979 | Alfredo Griffin, shortstop | Toronto |
|  |  |  |  | John Castino, third baseman | Minnesota |
| 1980 | Steve Howe, pitcher | Los Angeles | 1980 | Joe Charboneau, outfielder | Cleveland |

# BASKETBALL
## COLLEGE BASKETBALL: 1979–1980

The University of Louisville defeated 10-time winner UCLA, 59–54, to capture the 42d NCAA basketball tournament at Indianapolis, Ind., on March 24.

All-America guard Darrell Griffith, who scored 23 points, led the Cardinals to their first NCAA title, after being down 4 points with 4½ minutes to play. He was voted most valuable player of the tournament.

The victory was especially sweet for coach Denny Crum, who played college basketball at UCLA and was once an assistant coach there. On their way to the championship his Cardinals trounced LSU, 86–66, in the Midwest regional final, and beat Iowa, 80–72, in the semifinals. The team finished the season with a record of 33 wins, 3 losses.

Purdue soundly defeated Iowa, 75–58, in the consolation game.

Virginia, a fifth-place finisher in the Atlantic Coast Conference defeated Minnesota, 58–55, to win the National Invitation Tournament (NIT) at Madison Square Garden in New York City on March 19. Virginia center Ralph Sampson was selected the tournament's most valuable player. He tallied 15 points and 15 rebounds in the final game.

Before reaching the NIT final, Virginia beat Lafayette, 67–56, in the first round, edged Boston College, 57–55, in the second round; defeated Michigan, 79–68, in the third round; and whipped Nevada-Las Vegas, 90–71, in the semifinals.

Illinois beat Nevada-Las Vegas, 84–74, in the NIT consolation game.

At the end of the regular season, United Press International sportswriters ranked the top teams: (1) DePaul, (2) Louisville, (3) Louisiana State, (4) Kentucky, (5) Oregon State, (6) Syracuse, (7) Indiana, (8) Maryland, (9) Notre Dame, (10) Ohio State.

Top-ranked DePaul was beaten by UCLA early in the second round of the Western regional playoffs.

Also in March, Cameron University, of Lawton, Okla., defeated Alabama State, 84–77, to win the National Association of Intercollegiate Athletics (NAIA) championship.

In women's basketball, Old Dominion won its second consecutive Association for Intercollegiate Athletics for Women (AIAW) championship at Mount Pleasant, Mich., by defeating Tennessee, 68–53. Led by their two All-Americans, Nancy Lieberman and Inge Nissen, the Lady Monarchs led 32–24 at the half and never gave up the lead. Tennessee shot a poor 33% from the floor, and made only 13 of 23 free throws. Old Dominion finished the season with a 37–1 record.

In the AIAW consolation game, South Carolina defeated Louisiana Tech, 77–69.

University of Louisville's All-America guard Darrell Griffith (35) is fouled by Iowa guard Kenny Arnold during NCAA semifinal game at Indianapolis on March 22. Griffith scored 34 points leading his team to an 80–72 victory. Louisville went on to beat UCLA, 59–54, on March 24, for its first NCAA basketball title.

## ALL-AMERICA COLLEGE
## BASKETBALL TEAMS: 1979–1980
Source: Associated Press

FIRST TEAM: Joe Barry Carroll, Purdue; Albert King, Maryland; Mark Aguirre, De Paul; Darrell Griffith, Louisville; Kyle Macy, Kentucky.

SECOND TEAM: Mike Gminski, Duke; Don Collins, Washington State; Michael Brooks, La Salle; Reggie Carter, St. John's; Ray Blume, Oregon State.

THIRD TEAM: Herb Williams, Ohio State; John Stroud, Mississippi; Lewis Lloyd, Drake; Rolando Blackman, Kansas State; Sam Worthen, Marquette.

## NATIONAL COLLEGIATE ATHLETIC ASSOCIATION TOURNAMENT

| YEAR | CHAMPION | COACH | YEAR | CHAMPION | COACH |
|---|---|---|---|---|---|
| 1941 | Wisconsin | Harold Foster | 1963 | Loyola (Chicago) | George Ireland |
| 1942 | Stanford | Everett Dean | 1964 | UCLA | John Wooden |
| 1943 | Wyoming | Everett Shelton | 1965 | UCLA | John Wooden |
| 1944 | Utah | Vadal Peterson | 1966 | Texas Western | Donald Haskins |
| 1945–46 | Oklahoma A & M | Henry Iba | 1967 | UCLA | John Wooden |
| 1947 | Holy Cross | Alvin Julian | 1968 | UCLA | John Wooden |
| 1948–49 | Kentucky | Adolph Rupp | 1969 | UCLA | John Wooden |
| 1950 | City College, N.Y. | Nat Holman | 1970 | UCLA | John Wooden |
| 1951 | Kentucky | Adolph Rupp | 1971 | UCLA | John Wooden |
| 1952 | Kansas | Forest C. Allen | 1972 | UCLA | John Wooden |
| 1953 | Indiana | Branch McCracken | 1973 | UCLA | John Wooden |
| 1954 | La Salle | Kenneth Loeffler | 1974 | North Carolina State | Norm Sloan |
| 1955–56 | San Francisco | Phil Woolpert | 1975 | UCLA | John Wooden |
| 1957 | North Carolina | Frank McGuire | 1976 | Indiana | Bobby Knight |
| 1958 | Kentucky | Adolph Rupp | 1977 | Marquette | Al McGuire |
| 1959 | California | Pete Newell | 1978 | Kentucky | Joe B. Hall |
| 1960 | Ohio State | Fred Taylor | 1979 | Michigan State | Jud Heathcote |
| 1961–62 | Cincinnati | Edward Jucker | 1980 | Louisville | Denny Crum |

### NCAA 42d ANNUAL BASKETBALL CHAMPIONSHIP TOURNAMENT: 1980

| NATIONAL FINALS | REGIONAL FINALS | REGIONAL SEMIFINALS |
|---|---|---|
| **Championship:** | **East:** | Iowa 88, Syracuse 77 |
| Louisville 59, UCLA 54 | Iowa 88, Georgetown 80 | Georgetown 74, Maryland 68 |
| **Consolation** | **Mideast:** | Purdue 76, Indiana 69 |
| Purdue 75, Iowa 58 | Purdue 68, Duke 60 | Duke 55, Kentucky 54 |
| | **Midwest:** | LSU 68, Missouri 63 |
| NATIONAL SEMIFINALS | Louisville 86, LSU 66 | Louisville 66, Texas A&M 55 |
| Louisville 80, Iowa 72 | **West:** | UCLA 72, Ohio State 68 |
| UCLA 67, Purdue 62 | UCLA 85, Clemson 74 | Clemson 74, Lamar 66 |

### NCAA OUTSTANDING PLAYER AWARD

| | | | |
|---|---|---|---|
| **1955** Bill Russell, San Francisco | **1961** Jerry Lucas, Ohio St. | **1967–69** Lew Alcindor, UCLA | **1976** Kent Benson, Indiana |
| **1956** Hal Lear, Temple | **1962** Paul Hogue, Cincinnati | **1970** Sidney Wicks, UCLA | **1977** Butch Lee, Marquette |
| **1957** Wilt Chamberlain, Kansas | **1963** Art Heyman, Duke | **1971** vacated | **1978** Jack Givens, Kentucky |
| **1958** Elgin Baylor, Seattle | **1964** Walt Hazzard, UCLA | **1972–73** Bill Walton, UCLA | **1979** Earvin Johnson, Mich. St. |
| **1959** Jerry West, W. Va. | **1965** Bill Bradley, Princeton | **1974** David Thompson, NCS | **1980** Darrell Griffith, Louisville |
| **1960** Jerry Lucas, Ohio St. | **1966** Jerry Chambers, Utah | **1975** Rick Washington, UCLA | |

## NATIONAL INVITATION TOURNAMENT

| YEAR | CHAMPION | COACH | YEAR | CHAMPION | COACH |
|---|---|---|---|---|---|
| 1946 | Kentucky | Adolph Rupp | 1964 | Bradley | Chuck Orsborn |
| 1947 | Utah | Vadal Peterson | 1965 | St. John's (N.Y.) | Joe Lapchick |
| 1948 | St. Louis | Edward Hickey | 1966 | Brigham Young | Stanley Watts |
| 1949 | San Francisco | Pete Newell | 1967 | Southern Illinois | Jack Hartman |
| 1950 | City College, N.Y. | Nat Holman | 1968 | Dayton | Don Donoker |
| 1951 | Brigham Young | Stanley Watts | 1969 | Temple | Harry Litwack |
| 1952 | La Salle | Kenneth Loeffler | 1970 | Marquette | Al McGuire |
| 1953 | Seton Hall | John Russell | 1971 | North Carolina | Dean Smith |
| 1954 | Holy Cross | Lester Sheary | 1972 | Maryland | Lefty Driesell |
| 1955 | Duquesne | Donald Moore | 1973 | Virginia Tech | Don DeVoe |
| 1956 | Louisville | Bernard Hickman | 1974 | Purdue | Fred Schaus |
| 1957 | Bradley | Chuck Orsborn | 1975 | Princeton | Pete Carril |
| 1958 | Xavier of Ohio | James McCafferty | 1976 | Kentucky | Joe Hall |
| 1959 | St. John's (N.Y.) | Joe Lapchick | 1977 | St. Bonaventure (N.Y.) | Jim Satalin |
| 1960 | Bradley | Chuck Orsborn | 1978 | Texas | Abe Lemons |
| 1961 | Providence College | Joe Mullaney | 1979 | Indiana | Bobby Knight |
| 1962 | Dayton | Tom Blackburn | 1980 | Virginia | Terry Holland |
| 1963 | Providence College | Joe Mullaney | | | |

### NATIONAL INVITATION TOURNAMENT WINNERS: 1980

| FINALS | | | |
|---|---|---|---|
| **Championship:** | Minnesota 94, SW La. 73 | St. Peter's 34, Duquesne 33 | Boston Col. 95, Boston U. 74 |
| Virginia 58, Minnesota 55 | Nev.-Las Vg. 67, St. Peter's 62 | Mich. 74, Texas-El Paso 65 | Duquesne 65, Pittsburgh 63 |
| **Consolation:** | Illinois 65, Murray State 63 | Murray St. 70, Oklahoma 62 | Michigan 76, Nebraska 69 |
| Illinois 84, Nev.-Las Vegas 74 | SECOND ROUND | FIRST ROUND | Mississippi 76, Grambling 74 |
| NATIONAL SEMIFINALS | Virginia 57, Boston College 55 | Virginia 67, Lafayette 56 | St. Peter's 71, Conn. 61 |
| Virginia 90, Nev.-Las Vegas 71 | Illinois 75, Illinois St. 65 | Minnesota 64, Bowling Gr. 50 | Murray St. 53, Jacksonville 49 |
| Minnesota 65, Illinois 63 | Nevada-Las Vegas 90, Long | Illinois 105, Loyola 87 | Ill. St. 80, W. Texas St. 63 |
| THIRD ROUND | Beach State 81 | Nev.-Las Vegas 93, Wash. 73 | Alabama 53, Penn St. 49 |
| Virginia 79, Michigan 68 | SW Louisiana 77, Texas 76 | SW La. 74, Ala.-Birm. 72 | Texas 70, St. Joseph's 61 |
| | | Tex.-El Paso 58, Wichita St. 56 | Lg. Bch. St. 104, Pepperdine 87 |

## BEST WON-LOST BASKETBALL RECORDS:[1] 1979–1980

| TEAM | TOTAL WON | TOTAL LOST | PCT. | TEAM | TOTAL WON | TOTAL LOST | PCT. |
|---|---|---|---|---|---|---|---|
| Alcorn State | 28 | 2 | .933 | St. John's | 24 | 5 | .828 |
| DePaul | 26 | 2 | .929 | Georgetown | 26 | 6 | .813 |
| Louisville | 33 | 3 | .917 | Louisiana State | 26 | 6 | .813 |
| Weber State | 26 | 3 | .897 | Missouri | 25 | 6 | .806 |
| Oregon State | 26 | 4 | .867 | South Alabama | 23 | 6 | .793 |
| Syracuse | 26 | 4 | .867 | Toledo | 23 | 6 | .793 |
| Iona | 29 | 5 | .853 | Notre Dame | 22 | 6 | .786 |
| Old Dominion | 25 | 5 | .833 | Washington State | 22 | 6 | .786 |
| Kentucky | 29 | 6 | .829 | Maryland | 24 | 7 | .774 |
| Brigham Young | 24 | 5 | .828 | Furman | 23 | 7 | .767 |

## TEAM SCORING LEADERS:[1] 1979–1980

| TOP OFFENSIVE TEAMS | GAMES | POINTS FOR | AVERAGE | TOP DEFENSIVE TEAMS | GAMES | POINTS AGAINST | AVERAGE |
|---|---|---|---|---|---|---|---|
| Alcorn State | 30 | 2,729 | 91.0 | St. Peter's | 31 | 1,563 | 50.4 |
| Drake | 27 | 2,398 | 88.8 | Princeton | 30 | 1,654 | 55.1 |
| Oral Roberts | 28 | 2,447 | 87.4 | Penn State | 28 | 1,600 | 57.1 |
| Utah State | 27 | 2,329 | 86.3 | Wyoming | 28 | 1,644 | 58.7 |
| Syracuse | 30 | 2,575 | 85.8 | Fresno State | 24 | 1,412 | 58.8 |
| West Texas State | 30 | 2,565 | 85.5 | Texas A & M | 34 | 2,032 | 59.8 |
| Southern University | 29 | 2,457 | 84.7 | Jacksonville | 29 | 1,736 | 59.9 |
| Loyola (III.) | 29 | 2,453 | 84.6 | Georgia Tech. | 26 | 1,558 | 59.9 |
| DePaul | 28 | 2,346 | 83.8 | Arkansas | 29 | 1,745 | 60.2 |
| Brigham Young | 29 | 2,421 | 83.5 | Brown | 26 | 1,571 | 60.4 |
| Southwestern Louisiana | 30 | 2,499 | 83.3 | St. Joseph's (Pa.) | 30 | 1,821 | 60.7 |

## INDIVIDUAL SCORING LEADERS[1]

| PLAYER AND SCHOOL | GAMES | POINTS | AVG. |
|---|---|---|---|
| T. Murphy, Southern | 29 | 932 | 32.1 |
| L. Lloyd, Drake | 27 | 815 | 30.2 |
| H. Kelly, Texas Southern | 26 | 753 | 29.0 |
| K. Page, New Mexico | 28 | 784 | 28.0 |
| J. Tillman, E. Kentucky | 27 | 734 | 27.2 |
| E. Belcher, St. Bonaventure | 24 | 646 | 26.9 |
| R. Bowers, American | 27 | 726 | 26.9 |
| C. Nicks, Indiana State | 27 | 723 | 26.8 |
| M. Aguirre, DePaul | 28 | 749 | 26.8 |
| A. Toney, SW Louisiana | 24 | 627 | 26.1 |

## INDIVIDUAL REBOUND LEADERS[1]

| PLAYER AND SCHOOL | GAMES | REBOUNDS | AVG. |
|---|---|---|---|
| L. Smith, Alcorn State | 26 | 392 | 15.1 |
| L. Lloyd, Drake | 27 | 406 | 15.0 |
| R. Brown, Mississippi State | 27 | 389 | 14.4 |
| M. Davis, Tennessee State | 26 | 347 | 13.3 |
| G. Hooker, Murray State | 29 | 356 | 12.3 |
| T. Grooms, Kent State | 26 | 319 | 12.3 |
| J. Schoen, St. Francis (Pa.) | 25 | 303 | 12.1 |
| K. Green, Pan American | 28 | 337 | 12.0 |
| J. Ruland, Iona | 34 | 407 | 12.0 |
| A. Martin, Oral Roberts | 28 | 334 | 11.9 |

## INDIVIDUAL SINGLE GAME HIGHS[1]

| PLAYER AND SCHOOL (AGAINST OPPONENT) | POINTS | PLAYER AND SCHOOL (AGAINST OPPONENT) | REBOUNDS |
|---|---|---|---|
| M. Brooks, La Salle (Brigham Young) | 51 | G. Charles, NW Louisiana (Nicholls St.) | 25 |
| T. Murphy, Southern (Miss. Valley) | 50 | M. Davis, Tennessee St. (N.C. Central) | 24 |
| M. Olliver, Lamar (Portland St.) | 50 | S. Green, Nevada-Las Vegas (Nevada-Reno) | 24 |
| J. McCloskey, Loyola, Cal. (St. Mary's, Cal.) | 49 | R. Brown, Mississippi State (Vanderbilt) | 23 |
| H. Kelly, Texas Southern (Paul Quinn) | 48 | M. Davis, Tennessee St. (Towson St.) | 23 |
| M. Ferrara, Colgate (Cornell) | 47 | B. Johnson, Miss. Valley (Jackson St.) | 23 |
| L. Lloyd, Drake (Wisconsin-Superior) | 47 | J. Lombardo, St. Francis, N.Y. (Canisius) | 23 |
| T. Murphy, Southern (Jackson St.) | 47 | L. Smith, Alcorn St. (Miss. Valley) | 23 |
| K. Page, New Mexico (Illinois Tech.) | 47 | A. Taylor, Brigham Young (San Diego St.) | 23 |

## COLLEGE BASKETBALL CONFERENCE CHAMPIONS:[2] 1979–1980

| CONFERENCE | CHAMPION | WON | LOST | CONFERENCE | CHAMPION | WON | LOST |
|---|---|---|---|---|---|---|---|
| Atlantic Coast | Maryland | 24 | 7 | Mid-Eastern | Howard | 21 | 7 |
| Big East | Georgetown | 26 | 6 | Midwestern City | Loyola (Illinois) | 19 | 10 |
| | Syracuse | 26 | 4 | Missouri Valley | Bradley | 23 | 10 |
| | St. John's | 24 | 5 | Ohio Valley | Murray State | 23 | 8 |
| Big Eight | Missouri | 25 | 6 | | Western Kentucky | 21 | 8 |
| Big Sky | Weber State | 26 | 3 | Pacific Ten | Oregon State | 26 | 4 |
| Big Ten | Indiana | 21 | 8 | Pacific Coast | Utah State | 19 | 8 |
| East Coast (Eastern) | St. Joseph's | 21 | 9 | Southeastern | Kentucky | 29 | 6 |
| East Coast (Western) | Bucknell | 20 | 7 | Southern | Furman | 23 | 7 |
| | Lafayette | 21 | 8 | Southland | Lamar | 22 | 11 |
| Eastern Eight | Villanova | 23 | 8 | Southwest | Texas A&M | 26 | 8 |
| | Duquesne | 18 | 10 | Southwestern | Alcorn State | 28 | 2 |
| | Rutgers | 14 | 14 | Sun Belt | South Alabama | 23 | 6 |
| Ivy | Penn | 17 | 12 | Trans-America | NE Louisiana | 18 | 10 |
| | Princeton | 15 | 15 | West Coast | San Francisco | 22 | 7 |
| Metro | Louisville | 33 | 3 | Western Athletic | Brigham Young | 24 | 5 |
| Mid-American | Toledo | 23 | 6 | | | | |

[1] Source: NCAA Statistics Service; Statistics include playoff games. [2] Playoff games not included.

# PROFESSIONAL BASKETBALL: 1979–80

Los Angeles Lakers' Earvin "Magic" Johnson shoots over the head of Philadelphia 76ers' Julius Erving during sixth and final game of NBA championship May 16. The Lakers won the series, 4 games to 2, with Johnson named most valuable player of the tournament.

The Los Angeles Lakers, without the aid of star center Kareem Abdul-Jabbar, won the National Basketball Association (NBA) championship on May 16, 1980, by defeating the Philadelphia 76ers, 123–107. The Lakers took the series, 4 games to 2.

During the final game at the Spectrum in Philadelphia, rookie guard Earvin (Magic) Johnson substituted for the injured Abdul-Jabbar, and contributed 42 points. Johnson was later voted most valuable player of the tournament. With the score tied 60–60 at the half, Los Angeles opened the third quarter with 14 straight points, and the 76ers were never able to catch up.

On their way to the championship, the Lakers trounced the 1979 champions, the Seattle SuperSonics, 4 games to 1, after defeating Phoenix, 4 games to 1, in the conference semifinals.

George Gervin of San Antonio was the NBA leading scorer during the regular season for the third consecutive year. He had a 33.1 season average, and scored 40 or more points in 18 games. Runner-up Lloyd Free, of San Diego, had a 30.2 average.

The Lakers' Kareem Abdul-Jabbar was voted by NBA players as the season's most valuable player. He finished the regular season with a .604 field goal percentage and averaged 24.8 points per game. Abdul-Jabbar led the league in blocked shots, averaging 3.41 per game.

Larry Bird of the Boston Celtics was named Rookie of the Year. During his first professional season he averaged 21.3 points per game. Earvin (Magic) Johnson, also a rookie, averaged 18.0 points per game during the regular season.

Houston's Rick Barry won his sixth crown for free-throw percentage, by making 143 of 153 attempts for .935 and a lifetime average of .900.

Boston's Cedric Maxwell won the field goal percentage title for the second consecutive year. The Celtics' forward shot .609.

Seattle's Fred Brown became the first winner in the NBA's new category—three-point field goal percentage. Brown shot a .443, against the league average of .280.

The 1979–80 All-Star team, chosen in balloting following the conclusion of the regular season consisted of: forwards Julius Erving, Philadelphia, and Larry Bird, Boston; center Kareem Abdul-Jabbar, Los Angeles; and guards George Gervin, San Antonio, and Paul Westphal, Phoenix.

East defeated West 144-136 in the 30th annual NBA All-Star game.

## NATIONAL BASKETBALL ASSOCIATION FINAL STANDINGS: 1979–80

| TEAM | WON | LOST | PCT. | TEAM | WON | LOST | PCT. |
|---|---|---|---|---|---|---|---|
| **Atlantic Division** | | | | **Midwest Division** | | | |
| Boston | 61 | 21 | .744 | Milwaukee | 49 | 33 | .598 |
| Philadelphia | 59 | 23 | .720 | Kansas City | 47 | 35 | .573 |
| Washington | 39 | 43 | .476 | Denver | 30 | 52 | .366 |
| New York | 39 | 43 | .476 | Chicago | 30 | 52 | .366 |
| New Jersey | 34 | 48 | .415 | Utah | 24 | 58 | .293 |
| **Central Division** | | | | **Pacific Division** | | | |
| Atlanta | 50 | 32 | .610 | Los Angeles | 60 | 22 | .732 |
| Houston | 41 | 41 | .500 | Seattle | 56 | 26 | .683 |
| San Antonio | 41 | 41 | .500 | Phoenix | 55 | 27 | .671 |
| Indiana | 37 | 45 | .451 | Portland | 38 | 44 | .463 |
| Cleveland | 37 | 45 | .451 | San Diego | 35 | 47 | .527 |
| Detroit | 16 | 66 | .195 | Golden State | 24 | 58 | .293 |

United Press Int'l.

## NBA INDIVIDUAL SCORING LEADERS: 1979–80

| PLAYER AND TEAM | G [1] | FG [2] | FT [3] | PTS [4] | AVG [5] | PLAYER AND TEAM | G [1] | FG [2] | FT [3] | PTS [4] | AVG [5] |
|---|---|---|---|---|---|---|---|---|---|---|---|
| Gervin, San Antonio | 78 | 1,024 | 505 | 2,585 | 33.1 | Williams, G. Seattle | 82 | 739 | 331 | 1,816 | 22.1 |
| Free, San Diego | 68 | 737 | 572 | 2,055 | 30.2 | Westphal, Phoenix | 82 | 692 | 382 | 1,792 | 21.9 |
| Dantley, Utah | 68 | 730 | 443 | 1,903 | 28.0 | Cartwright, N.Y. | 82 | 665 | 451 | 1,781 | 21.7 |
| Erving, Philadelphia | 78 | 838 | 420 | 2,100 | 26.9 | Johnson, Milwaukee | 77 | 689 | 291 | 1,671 | 21.7 |
| Malone, Houston | 82 | 778 | 563 | 2,119 | 25.8 | Davis, Phoenix | 75 | 657 | 299 | 1,613 | 21.5 |
| Abdul-Jabbar, L.A. | 82 | 835 | 364 | 2,034 | 24.8 | Bird, Boston | 82 | 693 | 301 | 1,745 | 21.3 |
| Issel, Denver | 82 | 715 | 517 | 1,951 | 23.8 | Newlin, N.J. | 78 | 611 | 367 | 1,634 | 20.9 |
| Hayes, Washington | 81 | 761 | 334 | 1,859 | 23.0 | Williams, R., N.Y. | 82 | 687 | 333 | 1,714 | 20.9 |
| Birdsong, Kan. City | 82 | 781 | 286 | 1,858 | 22.7 | Theus, Chicago | 82 | 566 | 500 | 1,660 | 20.2 |
| Mitchell, Cleveland | 82 | 775 | 270 | 1,820 | 22.2 | Kenon, San Antonio | 78 | 647 | 270 | 1,565 | 20.1 |

[1] Games. [2] Field Goals. [3] Free Throws. [4] Total Points. [5] Average per Game.

## NATIONAL BASKETBALL ASSOCIATION TEAM STATISTICS: 1979–80

| TEAM | GAMES | SCORING AVERAGE | | | FIELD GOALS | | | FREE THROWS | | |
|---|---|---|---|---|---|---|---|---|---|---|
| | | For | Against | Difference | Made | Attempts | Pct. | Made | Attempts | Pct. |
| San Antonio | 82 | 119.4 | 119.7 | −0.3 | 4,000 | 7,997 | .500 | 2,024 | 2,528 | .801 |
| Los Angeles | 82 | 115.1 | 109.2 | +5.9 | 3,723 | 7,921 | .470 | 1,622 | 2,092 | .775 |
| Cleveland | 82 | 114.1 | 113.8 | +0.3 | 3,811 | 7,610 | .501 | 1,702 | 2,205 | .772 |
| New York | 82 | 114.0 | 115.1 | −1.1 | 3,707 | 7,492 | .495 | 1,698 | 2,274 | .747 |
| Boston | 82 | 113.5 | 105.7 | +7.8 | 3,439 | 7,313 | .470 | 1,907 | 2,449 | .779 |
| Indiana | 82 | 111.2 | 111.9 | −0.7 | 3,693 | 7,545 | .489 | 1,753 | 2,333 | .751 |
| Phoenix | 82 | 111.1 | 107.5 | +3.6 | 3,563 | 7,480 | .476 | 1,906 | 2,466 | .773 |
| Houston | 82 | 110.8 | 110.6 | +0.2 | 3,658 | 7,382 | .496 | 1,782 | 2,326 | .766 |
| Milwaukee | 82 | 110.1 | 106.1 | +4.0 | 3,456 | 7,487 | .462 | 1,605 | 2,102 | .764 |
| Philadelphia | 82 | 109.1 | 104.9 | +4.2 | 3,444 | 7,561 | .455 | 1,876 | 2,431 | .772 |
| Detroit | 82 | 108.9 | 117.2 | −8.3 | 3,847 | 7,761 | .496 | 1,590 | 2,149 | .740 |
| Seattle | 82 | 108.5 | 103.8 | +4.7 | 3,408 | 7,424 | .459 | 1,730 | 2,253 | .768 |
| New Jersey | 82 | 108.3 | 109.5 | −1.2 | 3,480 | 7,427 | .469 | 1,882 | 2,406 | .782 |
| Denver | 82 | 108.3 | 112.7 | −4.4 | 3,736 | 7,591 | .492 | 1,871 | 2,539 | .737 |
| Kansas City | 82 | 108.0 | 104.9 | +3.1 | 3,328 | 6,992 | .476 | 1,671 | 2,205 | .743 |
| San Diego | 82 | 107.6 | 111.7 | −4.1 | 3,752 | 7,508 | .500 | 1,595 | 2,167 | .736 |
| Chicago | 82 | 107.5 | 110.2 | −2.7 | 3,585 | 7,222 | .496 | 2,019 | 2,592 | .779 |
| Washington | 82 | 107.0 | 109.5 | −2.5 | 3,615 | 7,771 | .465 | 1,552 | 2,048 | .758 |
| Atlanta | 82 | 104.5 | 101.6 | +2.9 | 3,144 | 6,872 | .458 | 2,038 | 2,645 | .771 |
| Golden State | 82 | 103.6 | 108.0 | −4.4 | 3,438 | 6,975 | .493 | 1,412 | 1,914 | .738 |
| Portland | 82 | 102.5 | 103.3 | −0.8 | 3,349 | 7,008 | .478 | 1,560 | 2,100 | .743 |
| Utah | 82 | 102.4 | 108.4 | −6.0 | 3,559 | 7,182 | .496 | 1,571 | 1,943 | .809 |

## NATIONAL BASKETBALL ASSOCIATION CHAMPIONS: 1960–80

REGULAR SEASON        PLAYOFF CHAMPIONSHIP

| Year | Eastern Conference | Won | Lost | Pct. | Western Conference | Won | Lost | Pct. | Winner |
|---|---|---|---|---|---|---|---|---|---|---|
| 1960 | Boston | 59 | 16 | .787 | St. Louis | 46 | 29 | .613 | Boston over St. Louis (4–3) |
| 1961 | Boston | 57 | 22 | .722 | St. Louis | 51 | 28 | .646 | Boston over St. Louis (4–1) |
| 1962 | Boston | 60 | 20 | .750 | Los Angeles | 54 | 26 | .675 | Boston over Los Angeles (4–3) |
| 1963 | Boston | 58 | 22 | .725 | Los Angeles | 53 | 27 | .663 | Boston over Los Angeles (4–2) |
| 1964 | Boston | 59 | 21 | .737 | San Francisco | 48 | 32 | .600 | Boston over San Francisco (4–1) |
| 1965 | Boston | 62 | 18 | .775 | Los Angeles | 49 | 31 | .612 | Boston over Los Angeles (4–1) |
| 1966 | Philadelphia | 55 | 25 | .687 | Los Angeles | 45 | 35 | .562 | Boston over Los Angeles (4–3) |
| 1967 | Philadelphia | 68 | 13 | .840 | St. Louis | 56 | 26 | .683 | Philadelphia over San Fran. (4–2) |
| 1968 | Philadelphia | 62 | 20 | .756 | San Francisco | 44 | 37 | .643 | Boston over Los Angeles (4–2) |
| 1969 | Baltimore | 57 | 25 | .695 | Los Angeles | 55 | 27 | .671 | Boston over Los Angeles (4–3) |
| 1970 | New York | 60 | 22 | .732 | Atlanta | 48 | 34 | .585 | New York over Los Angeles (4–3) |
| 1971* | New York (Atlantic) | 52 | 30 | .634 | Milwaukee (Midwest) | 66 | 16 | .805 | Milwaukee over Baltimore (4–0) |
| | Baltimore (Central) | 42 | 40 | .512 | Los Angeles (Pacific) | 48 | 34 | .585 | |
| 1972 | Boston (Atlantic) | 56 | 26 | .683 | Los Angeles (Pacific) | 69 | 13 | .841 | Los Angeles over New York (4–1) |
| | Baltimore (Central) | 38 | 44 | .463 | Milwaukee (Midwest) | 63 | 19 | .768 | |
| 1973 | Boston (Atlantic) | 68 | 14 | .829 | Milwaukee (Midwest) | 60 | 22 | .732 | New York over Los Angeles (4–1) |
| | Baltimore (Central) | 52 | 30 | .634 | Los Angeles (Pacific) | 60 | 22 | .732 | |
| 1974 | Boston (Atlantic) | 56 | 26 | .683 | Milwaukee (Midwest) | 59 | 23 | .720 | Boston over Milwaukee (4–3) |
| | Washington (Central) | 47 | 35 | .573 | Los Angeles (Pacific) | 47 | 35 | .573 | |
| 1975 | Boston (Atlantic) | 60 | 22 | .732 | Chicago (Midwest) | 47 | 35 | .573 | Golden St. over Washington (4–0) |
| | Washington (Central) | 60 | 22 | .732 | Golden State (Pacific) | 48 | 34 | .585 | |
| 1976 | Boston (Atlantic) | 54 | 28 | .659 | Milwaukee (Midwest) | 38 | 44 | .463 | Boston over Phoenix (4–2) |
| | Cleveland (Central) | 49 | 33 | .598 | Golden State (Pacific) | 59 | 23 | .720 | |
| 1977 | Philadelphia (Atlantic) | 50 | 32 | .610 | Denver (Midwest) | 50 | 32 | .610 | Portland over Philadelphia (4–2) |
| | Houston (Central) | 49 | 33 | .598 | Los Angeles (Pacific) | 53 | 29 | .646 | |
| 1978 | Philadelphia (Atlantic) | 55 | 27 | .671 | Denver (Midwest) | 48 | 34 | .585 | Washington over Seattle (4–3) |
| | San Antonio (Central) | 52 | 30 | .634 | Portland (Pacific) | 58 | 24 | .707 | |
| 1979 | Washington (Atlantic) | 54 | 28 | .659 | Kansas City (Midwest) | 48 | 34 | .585 | Seattle over Washington (4–1) |
| | San Antonio (Central) | 48 | 34 | .585 | Seattle (Pacific) | 52 | 30 | .634 | |
| 1980 | Boston (Atlantic) | 61 | 21 | .744 | Milwaukee (Midwest) | 49 | 33 | .598 | Los Angeles over Philadelphia (4–2) |
| | Atlanta (Central) | 50 | 32 | .610 | Los Angeles (Pacific) | 60 | 22 | .732 | |

* In 1970–71 the NBA reorganized into four conferences: Atlantic, Central, Midwest, and Pacific.

# NATIONAL BASKETBALL ASSOCIATION INDIVIDUAL AWARDS

## MOST VALUABLE PLAYER (PODOLOFF CUP) AND ROOKIE OF THE YEAR

| YEAR | MVP | ROOKIE OF THE YEAR | YEAR | MVP | ROOKIE OF THE YEAR |
|------|-----|--------------------|------|-----|--------------------|
| 1958 | Bill Russell, Boston | Woody Sauldsberry, Phil. | 1970 | Willis Reed, N.Y. | Abdul-Jabbar, Milw. |
| 1959 | Bob Pettit, St. Louis | Elgin Baylor, Minn. | 1971 | Abdul-Jabbar, Milw. | Dave Cowens, Boston |
| 1960 | Wilt Chamberlain, Phil. | Wilt Chamberlain, Phil. | | | Geoff Petrie, Portland (tie) |
| 1961 | Bill Russell, Boston | Oscar Robertson, Cinn. | 1972 | Abdul-Jabbar, Milw. | Sidney Wicks, Portland |
| 1962 | Bill Russell, Boston | Walt Bellamy, Chicago | 1973 | Dave Cowens, Boston | Bob McAdoo, Buffalo |
| 1963 | Bill Russell, Boston | Terry Dischinger, Chicago | 1974 | Abdul-Jabbar, Milw. | Ernie DiGregorio, Buffalo |
| 1964 | Oscar Robertson, Cinn. | Jerry Lucas, Cinn. | 1975 | Bob McAdoo, Buffalo | Keith Wilkes, Golden State |
| 1965 | Bill Russell, Boston | Willis Reed, New York | 1976 | Abdul-Jabbar, L.A. | Alvan Adams, Phoenix |
| 1966 | Wilt Chamberlain, Phil. | Rick Barry, San Francisco | 1977 | Abdul-Jabbar, L.A. | Adrian Dantley, Buffalo |
| 1967 | Wilt Chamberlain, Phil. | Dave Bing, Detroit | 1978 | Bill Walton, Portland | Walter Davis, Phoenix |
| 1968 | Wilt Chamberlain, Phil. | Earl Monroe, Baltimore | 1979 | Moses Malone, Houston | Phil Ford, Kansas City |
| 1969 | Wes Unseld, Baltimore | Wes Unseld, Baltimore | 1980 | Abdul-Jabbar, L.A. | Larry Bird, Boston |

## NBA LEADERS IN REBOUNDS: 1979–80

| PLAYER AND TEAM | GAMES | NUMBER | AVG. |
|-----------------|-------|--------|------|
| Nater, San Diego | 81 | 1,216 | 15.0 |
| Malone, Houston | 82 | 1,190 | 14.5 |
| Unseld, Washington | 82 | 1,094 | 13.3 |
| Jones, Philadelphia | 80 | 950 | 11.9 |
| Sikma, Seattle | 82 | 908 | 11.1 |
| Hayes, Washington | 81 | 896 | 11.1 |
| Parish, Golden State | 72 | 783 | 10.9 |
| Abdul-Jabbar, L.A. | 82 | 886 | 10.8 |
| Washington, Portland | 80 | 842 | 10.5 |
| Bird, Boston | 82 | 852 | 10.4 |

## NBA LEADERS IN ASSISTS: 1979–80

| PLAYER AND TEAM | GAMES | NUMBER | AVG. |
|-----------------|-------|--------|------|
| Richardson, N.Y. | 82 | 832 | 10.1 |
| Archibald, Boston | 80 | 671 | 8.4 |
| Walker, Cleveland | 76 | 607 | 8.0 |
| Nixon, Los Angeles | 82 | 642 | 7.8 |
| Lucas, Golden State | 80 | 602 | 7.5 |
| Ford, Kansas City | 82 | 610 | 7.4 |
| Johnson, Los Angeles | 77 | 563 | 7.3 |
| Cheeks, Philadelphia | 79 | 556 | 7.0 |
| Jordan, New Jersey | 82 | 557 | 6.8 |
| Porter, Washington | 70 | 457 | 6.5 |

# NATIONAL BASKETBALL ASSOCIATION PLAYOFFS: 1980

**Championship Series:**
Los Angeles defeated Philadelphia, 4 games to 2.
**Conference Finals:**
Los Angeles defeated Seattle, 4 games to 1.
Philadelphia defeated Boston, 4 games to 1.

**Conference Semifinals:**
Los Angeles defeated Phoenix, 4 games to 1.
Seattle defeated Milwaukee, 4 games to 3.
Boston defeated Houston, 4 games to 0.
Philadelphia defeated Atlanta, 4 games to 1.

# NATIONAL BASKETBALL ASSOCIATION SCORING LEADERS

| SEASON | PLAYER AND TEAM | G [1] | FG [2] | FT [3] | TP [4] | AVG [5] |
|--------|-----------------|-------|--------|--------|--------|---------|
| 1948–49 | George Mikan, Minneapolis Lakers | 60 | 583 | 532 | 1,698 | 28.3 |
| 1949–50 | George Mikan, Minneapolis Lakers | 68 | 649 | 567 | 1,865 | 27.4 |
| 1950–51 | George Mikan, Minneapolis Lakers | 68 | 678 | 576 | 1,932 | 28.4 |
| 1951–52 | Paul Arizin, Philadelphia Warriors | 66 | 548 | 578 | 1,674 | 25.4 |
| 1952–53 | Neil Johnston, Philadelphia Warriors | 70 | 504 | 556 | 1,564 | 22.3 |
| 1953–54 | Neil Johnston, Philadelphia Warriors | 72 | 591 | 577 | 1,759 | 24.4 |
| 1954–55 | Neil Johnston, Philadelphia Warriors | 72 | 521 | 589 | 1,631 | 22.7 |
| 1955–56 | Bob Pettit, St. Louis Hawks | 72 | 646 | 557 | 1,849 | 25.7 |
| 1956–57 | Paul Arizin, Philadelphia Warriors | 71 | 613 | 591 | 1,817 | 25.6 |
| 1957–58 | George Yardley, Detroit Pistons | 72 | 673 | 655 | 2,001 | 27.8 |
| 1958–59 | Bob Pettit, St. Louis Hawks | 72 | 719 | 667 | 2,105 | 29.2 |
| 1959–60 | Wilt Chamberlain, Philadelphia Warriors | 72 | 1,065 | 577 | 2,707 | 37.6 |
| 1960–61 | Wilt Chamberlain, Philadelphia Warriors | 79 | 1,251 | 531 | 3,033 | 38.4 |
| 1961–62 | Wilt Chamberlain, Philadelphia Warriors | 80 | 1,597 | 835 | 4,029 | 50.4 |
| 1962–63 | Wilt Chamberlain, San Francisco Warriors | 80 | 1,463 | 660 | 3,586 | 44.8 |
| 1963–64 | Wilt Chamberlain, San Francisco Warriors | 80 | 1,204 | 540 | 2,948 | 36.5 |
| 1964–65 | Wilt Chamberlain, Philadelphia 76ers | 73 | 1,063 | 408 | 2,534 | 34.7 |
| 1965–66 | Wilt Chamberlain, Philadelphia 76ers | 79 | 1,074 | 501 | 2,649 | 33.5 |
| 1966–67 | Rick Barry, San Francisco Warriors | 78 | 1,011 | 753 | 2,775 | 35.6 |
| 1967–68 | Dave Bing, Detroit Pistons | 79 | 835 | 472 | 2,142 | 27.1 |
| 1968–69 | Elvin Hayes, San Diego Rockets | 82 | 930 | 467 | 2,327 | 28.4 |
| 1969–70 | Jerry West, Los Angeles Lakers | 74 | 831 | 647 | 2,309 | 31.2 |
| 1970–71 | Lew Alcindor (Kareem Abdul-Jabbar), Milwaukee Bucks | 82 | 1,063 | 470 | 2,596 | 31.7 |
| 1971–72 | Kareem Abdul-Jabbar, Milwaukee Bucks | 81 | 1,159 | 504 | 2,822 | 34.8 |
| 1972–73 | Nate Archibald, Kansas City–Omaha Kings | 82 | 1,028 | 603 | 2,719 | 34.0 |
| 1973–74 | Bob McAdoo, Buffalo Braves | 74 | 901 | 459 | 2,261 | 30.6 |
| 1974–75 | Bob McAdoo, Buffalo Braves | 82 | 1,095 | 641 | 2,831 | 34.5 |
| 1975–76 | Bob McAdoo, Buffalo Braves | 78 | 934 | 559 | 2,427 | 31.1 |
| 1976–77 | Pete Maravich, New Orleans Jazz | 73 | 886 | 501 | 2,273 | 31.1 |
| 1977–78 | George Gervin, San Antonio Spurs | 82 | 864 | 504 | 2,232 | 27.2 |
| 1978–79 | George Gervin, San Antonio Spurs | 80 | 947 | 471 | 2,365 | 29.6 |
| 1979–80 | George Gervin, San Antonio Spurs | 78 | 1,024 | 505 | 2,585 | 33.1 |

[1] Games.   [2] Field Goals.   [3] Free Throws.   [4] Total Points.   [5] Average per Game.

# BICYCLING

## UNITED STATES BICYCLING CHAMPIONS

Source: U.S. Cycling Federation and *Velo-news*

### SENIOR MEN BICYCLING CHAMPIONS

| | ROAD | SPRINT | 4,000–METER PURSUIT | POINTS RACE | 1,000 METERS |
|---|---|---|---|---|---|
| 1973 | John Howard | Roger Young | Mike Neel | — | Steve Woznick |
| 1974 | John Allis | Steve Woznick | Ralph Therrio | — | Steve Woznick |
| 1975 | John Howard | Steve Woznick | Ron Skarin* | — | Steve Woznick |
| 1976 | Wayne Stetina | L. Barczewski | Leonard Nitz | — | Bob Vehe |
| 1977 | Wayne Stetina | L. Barczewski | Paul Deem | Nelson Saldana | Jerry Ash |
| 1978 | Dale Stetina | L. Barczewski | Dave Grylls | Ron Skarin | Jerry Ash |
| 1979 | Steve Wood | L. Barczewski | Dave Grylls | Gus Pipenhagen | Jerry Ash |
| 1980 | Dale Stetina | Mark Gorski | Leonard Nitz | Scott Hembree | Brent Emery |

### SENIOR WOMEN BICYCLING CHAMPIONS / JUNIOR MEN BICYCLING CHAMPIONS

| | ROAD | SPRINT | 3,000–METER PURSUIT | ROAD | TRACK |
|---|---|---|---|---|---|
| 1971 | Mary Jane Reoch | Sheila Young | Kathy Ecroth | Ralph Therrio | Ralph Therrio |
| 1972 | Debbie Bradley | Sue Novara | Clara Teyssier | Ted Waterbury | Nelson Saldana |
| 1973 | Eileen Brennan | Sheila Young | Mary Jane Reoch | Pat Nielson | Gilbert Hatton |
| 1974 | Jane Robinson | Sue Novara | Mary Jane Reoch | David Mayer-Oakes | Gilbert Hatton |
| 1975 | Linda Stein | Sue Novara | Mary Jane Reoch | Larry Shields | Kurtis Miller |
| 1976 | Connie Carpenter | Sheila Young | Connie Carpenter | Larry Shields | Chris Springer |
| 1977 | Connie Carpenter | Sue Novara | Connie Carpenter | Greg LeMond | Chris Springer |
| 1978 | Barbara Hintzen | Sue Novara | Mary Jane Reoch | Jeff Bradley | Eric Baltes |
| 1979 | Connie Carpenter | Sue Novara | Connie Carpenter | Greg LeMond | Mark Whitehead |
| 1980 | Beth Heiden | Sue Novara | Elizabeth Davis | Sterling McBride | John Butler |

# BOWLING

## U.S. MEN'S OPEN CHAMPIONSHIP (Bowling Proprietors Association of America)

| | | | | | |
|---|---|---|---|---|---|
| 1946 Joe Wilman | 1953–54 Don Carter | 1961 Bill Tucker | 1969 Billy Hardwick | 1975 Steve Neff | |
| 1947–48 Andy Varipapa | 1955 Steve Nagy | 1962–63 Dick Weber | 1970 Bobby Cooper | 1976 Paul Moser | |
| 1949 Connie Schwoegler | 1956 Bill Lillard | 1964 Bob Strampe | 1971 Mike Lemongello | 1977 Johnny Petraglia | |
| 1950 Junie McMahon | 1957–58 Don Carter | 1965–66 Dick Weber | 1972 Don Johnson | 1978 Nelson Burton Jr. | |
| 1951 Dick Hoover | 1959 Billy Welu | 1967 Les Schissler | 1973 Mike McGrath | 1979 Joe Berardi | |
| 1952 Junie McMahon | 1960 Harry Smith | 1968 Jim Stefanich | 1974 Larry Laub | 1980 Steve Martin | |

## U.S. WOMEN'S OPEN CHAMPIONSHIP (Bowling Proprietors Association of America)

| | | | | |
|---|---|---|---|---|
| 1962 Shirley Garms | 1966 Joy Abel | 1971 Paula Sperber | 1975 Paula Sperber | 1979 Diana Silva |
| 1963 Marion Ladewig | 1967 Gloria Bouvia | 1972 Lorrie Koch | 1976 Patty Costello | 1980 Pat Costello |
| 1964 La Verne Carter | 1968–69 D. Fothergill | 1973 Millie Martorella | 1977 Betty Morris | |
| 1965 Ann Slattery | 1970 Mary Baker | 1974 Pat Costello | 1978 Donna Adamek | |

## AMERICAN BOWLING CONGRESS ALL–EVENTS CHAMPIONSHIP

| | | | | |
|---|---|---|---|---|
| 1946 Joe Wilman | 1953 Frank Santore | 1960 Vince Lucci | 1967 Gary Lewis | 1974 Bob Hart |
| 1947 Junie McMahon | 1954 Brad Lewis | 1961 Luke Karan | 1968 Vince Mazzanti | 1975 Bobby Meadows |
| 1948 Ned Day | 1955 Fred Bujack | 1962 Billy Young | 1969 Edward Jackson | 1976 Jim Lindquist |
| 1949 John Small | 1956 Bill Lillard | 1963 Bus Oswalt | 1970 Mike Berlin | 1977 Bud Debenham |
| 1950 Frank Santore | 1957 Jim Spalding | 1964 Les Zikes | 1971 Al Cohn | 1978 Chris Cobus |
| 1951 Tony Lindemann | 1958 Al Faragalli | 1965 Tom Hathaway | 1972 Mac Lowry | 1979 Bob Busacchi |
| 1952 Steve Nagy | 1959 Ed Lubanski | 1966 John Wilcox | 1973 Ron Woolet | 1980 Steve Fehr |

## WOMEN'S INTERNATIONAL BOWLING CONGRESS ALL–EVENTS CHAMPIONSHIP

| | | | | |
|---|---|---|---|---|
| 1951 LaVerne Haverley | 1957 Anita Cantaline | 1963 Helen Shablis | 1969 Helen Duval | 1975 Virginia Park |
| 1952 Virginia Turner | 1958 Mae Ploegman | 1964 Jean Havlish | 1970 D. Fothergill | 1976 Betty Morris |
| 1953 Doris Knechtges | 1959 Pat McBride | 1965 D. Zimmerman | 1971 Lorrie Koch | 1977 Akiko Yamaga |
| 1954 Anne Johnson | 1960 Judy Roberts | 1966 Kate Helbig | 1972 Millie Martorella | 1978 Annese Kelly |
| 1955 Marion Ladewig | 1961 Evelyn Teal | 1967 Carol Miller | 1973 Toni Calvary | 1979 Betty Morris |
| 1956 Doris Knechtges | 1962 Flossie Argent | 1968 Susie Reichley | 1974 Judy Soutar | 1980 Cheryl Robinson |

## AMERICAN BOWLING CONGRESS MASTERS CHAMPIONSHIP

| | | | | |
|---|---|---|---|---|
| 1954 Eugene Elkins | 1960 Bill Golembiewski | 1966 Bob Strampe | 1971 Jim Godman | 1976 Nelson Burton Jr. |
| 1955 Buzz Fazio | 1961 Don Carter | 1967 Lou Scalia | 1972 Bill Beach | 1977 Earl Anthony |
| 1956–57 Dick Hoover | 1962 Bill Golembiewski | 1968 Pete Tountas | 1973 Dave Soutar | 1978 Frank Ellenburg |
| 1958 Tom Hennessey | 1963 Harry Smith | 1969 Jim Chestney | 1974 Paul Colwell | 1979 Doug Myers |
| 1959 Ray Bluth | 1964–65 Billy Welu | 1970 Don Glover | 1975 Ed Ressler | 1980 Neil Burton |

## AMERICAN BOWLING CONGRESS CLASSIC SINGLES CHAMPIONSHIP

| | | | | |
|---|---|---|---|---|
| 1963 Fred Delello | 1967 Frank Perry | 1971 Al Cohn | 1975 Jim Setser | 1978 Rick Peters |
| 1964 Jim Stefanich | 1968 Wayne Kowalski | 1972 Bill Pointer | 1976 Mike Putzer | 1980 Mike Eaton |
| 1965 Ken Roeth | 1969 Greg Campbell | 1973 Ed Thompson | 1977 Frank Gadaleto | |
| 1966 Don Chapman | 1970 Jake Yoder | 1974 Gene Krause | 1978 Rich Mersek | |

## PROFESSIONAL BOWLERS ASSOCIATION FIRESTONE TOURNAMENT OF CHAMPIONS

| | | | | |
|---|---|---|---|---|
| 1966 Wayne Zahn | 1969 Jim Godman | 1972 Mike Durbin | 1975 Dave Davis | 1978 Earl Anthony |
| 1967 Jim Stefanich | 1970 Don Johnson | 1973 Jim Godman | 1976 Marshall Holman | 1979 George Pappas |
| 1968 Dave Davis | 1971 John Petraglia | 1974 Earl Anthony | 1977 Mike Berlin | 1980 Wayne Webb |

# BOXING

Wide World

Sixteen years after he first won the world's heavyweight championship, Muhammad Ali at the age of 38 failed in his effort to regain the title from Larry Holmes, *left*, the champion recognized by the World Boxing Council (WBC). Displaying few remnants of the speed and power that enabled him to become the only boxer in history to win and then twice regain the heavyweight title, Ali was unable to answer the bell for the 11th round in the fight held in Las Vegas, Nev., on Oct. 2.

As a result of the Leonard-Duran rematch title fight (see opposite page), the World Boxing Council (WBC) ruled on Dec. 6 that in the future "direct rematches" would not be sanctioned, forcing the loser of a championship boxing match to earn the right to a rematch by defeating other challengers.

Johnny Owen, 24, a Welsh bantamweight fighter, died on Nov. 3 in Los Angeles, having remained in a coma for six weeks after being knocked out in a title fight with WBC champion Lupe Pintor of Mexico.

In one of the worst accidents in sports history, 14 American Amateur Athletic Union

## NATIONAL AAU BOXING CHAMPIONS: 1980

Source: AAU, National AAU Boxing Championships, Las Vegas, Nev., May 5–11, 1980

| CLASS | CHAMPION | CLASS | CHAMPION |
|---|---|---|---|
| 106 pounds ...... | Robert Shannon, Edmonds, Wash. | 147 pounds ...... | Gene Hatcher, Fort Worth, Texas |
| 112 pounds ...... | Richard Sandoval, Pomona, Calif. | 156 pounds ...... | Donald Bowers, Jackson, Tenn. |
| 119 pounds ...... | Jackie Beard, Jackson, Tenn. | 165 pounds ...... | Martin Pierce, Flint, Mich. |
| 125 pounds ...... | Clifford Gray, Boynton Beach, Fla. | 178 pounds ...... | Jeff Lampkin, Youngstown, Ohio |
| 132 pounds ...... | Melvin Paul, New Orleans, La. | Heavyweight ...... | Marvis Frazier, Philadelphia, Pa. |
| 139 pounds ...... | Johnny Bumphus, Nashville, Tenn. | Outstanding Boxer | Jackie Beard (119 pounds) |

In the most controversial title match of the year, Sugar Ray Leonard, *right*, regained his WBC welterweight title on Nov. 25 from Roberto Duran, to whom he had lost his crown five months earlier. Duran, formerly the lightweight champion for seven years, suddenly quit in the middle of the 8th round at New Orleans, telling the referee, "No more box." Later, he said he was suffering stomach cramps. The following day the state boxing commission fined Duran $7,500 for an "unsatisfactory performance." However, Duran received about $8 million for his share of the fight receipts.

(AAU) boxers, their coach, and seven team aides were killed on March 14 in the crash of a Polish airliner at Warsaw Poland. All 87 persons aboard the plane died.

Because the two rival professional boxing associations, the WBA and the WBC, have generally managed to prevent the fighters they separately recognize as champions from meeting each other in decisive title bouts, the table below has been prepared by the editors of *The Ring Magazine* to reflect their choice of the fighter in each division who most nearly deserves the title of "world champion" at the end of 1980.

## PROFESSIONAL BOXING CHAMPIONS BY CLASSES: 1980

Source: *The Ring Magazine*

| CLASS AND WEIGHT | WORLD BOXING ASSOCIATION (WBA) | WORLD BOXING COUNCIL (WBC) |
|---|---|---|
| Heavyweight (over 190 pounds) | Mike Weaver [1], United States | *Larry Holmes [2], United States |
| Cruiserweight (175–190 pounds) | Vacant | Carlos DeLeon [1], Puerto Rico |
| Light Heavyweight (161–175 pounds) | Eddie Mustafa Muhammad [1], U.S. | *Matthew Saad Muhammad [2], U.S. |
| Middleweight (155–160 pounds) | *Marvin Hagler [1], United States | *Marvin Hagler [1], United States |
| Junior Middleweight (148–154 pounds) | *Ayub Kaluie [2], Denmark | Maurice Hope [2], England |
| Welterweight (141–147 pounds) | Thomas Hearns [1], United States | *Sugar Ray Leonard [2], United States |
| Junior Welterweight (136–140 pounds) | *Aaron Pryor [1], United States | Saoul Mamby [1], United States |
| Lightweight (131–135 pounds) | Hilmer Kenty [1], United States | Jim Watt [2], Scotland |
| Junior Lightweight (127–130 pounds) | *Yasutsune Uehara [1], Japan | Vacant |
| Featherweight (123–126 pounds) | Eusebio Pedroza [2], Panama | *Salvador Sanchez [1], Mexico |
| Junior Featherweight (119–122 pounds) | Sergio Palma [1], Argentina | *Wilfredo Gomez [2], Puerto Rico |
| Bantamweight (113–118 pounds) | *Jeff Chandler [1], United States | Lupe Pintor [2], Mexico |
| Flyweight (109–112 pounds) | Tae-Shik Kim [1], South Korea | *Shoji Oguma [1], Japan |
| Junior Flyweight (under 109 pounds) | Yoko Gushiken [2], Japan | Vacant |

* Rated as World Champion by *The Ring Magazine*. [1] Won title in 1980. [2] Successfully defended title in 1980.

## HEAVYWEIGHT BOXING CHAMPIONS (over 175 pounds)

Source: *The Ring Magazine*; World Boxing Association (WBA) champions in 1970s-1980s

| CHAMPION | REIGN | CHAMPION | REIGN | CHAMPION | REIGN |
|---|---|---|---|---|---|
| John L. Sullivan | 1889–92 | Primo Carnera | 1933–34 | Cassius Clay [6] | 1964–67 |
| James J. Corbett | 1892–97 | Max Baer | 1934–35 | Jimmy Ellis | 1968–70 |
| Bob Fitzsimmons | 1897–99 | Jim Braddock | 1935–37 | Joe Frazier | 1970–73 |
| James J. Jeffries [1] | 1899–1905 | Joe Louis [4] | 1937–49 | George Foreman | 1973–74 |
| Tommy Burns | 1906–08 | Ezzard Charles | 1949–51 | Muhammad Ali | 1974–78 |
| Jack Johnson | 1908–15 | Jersey Joe Walcott | 1951–52 | Leon Spinks Jr. | 1978 |
| Jess Willard | 1915–19 | Rocky Marciano [5] | 1952–56 | Muhammad Ali | 1978–79 |
| Jack Dempsey | 1919–26 | Floyd Patterson | 1956–59 | John Tate | 1979–80 |
| Gene Tunney [2] | 1926–28 | Ingemar Johannson | 1959–60 | Mike Weaver | 1980– |
| Max Schmeling [3] | 1930–32 | Floyd Patterson | 1960–62 | | |
| Jack Sharkey | 1932–33 | Sonny Liston | 1962–64 | | |

[1] Jeffries retired in 1905. [2] Tunney retired undefeated in 1928. [3] In 1931 the New York Boxing Commission reversed its decision in favor of Schmeling's opponent, Jack Sharkey. [4] Louis retired in 1949. [5] Marciano retired undefeated in 1956. [6] In 1967 Clay's title was declared vacant by the World Boxing Association (WBA) and the New York Athletic Commission after Clay failed to answer a draft call for military service. Earlier that year Clay changed his name to Muhammad Ali.

## LIGHT HEAVYWEIGHT BOXING CHAMPIONS (Up to 175 pounds)

Source: *The Ring Magazine:* World Boxing Association (WBA) champions in 1970s–1980s

| CHAMPION | REIGN | CHAMPION | REIGN | CHAMPION | REIGN |
|---|---|---|---|---|---|
| Jack Root | 1903 | Tommy Loughran | 1927–29 | Willie Pastrano | 1963–65 |
| George Gardner | 1903 | Maxie Rosenbloom [2] | 1930–34 | Jose Torres | 1965–66 |
| Bob Fitzsimmons | 1903–05 | Bob Olin | 1934–35 | Dick Tiger | 1966–68 |
| "Philadelphia" Jack O'Brien | 1905–12 | John Henry Lewis | 1935–38 | Bob Foster [5] | 1968–70 |
| Jack Dillon | 1912–16 | Melio Bettina [3] | 1939 | Vincente Paul Rondon | 1971–72 |
| Battling Levinsky | 1916–20 | Billy Conn | 1939–40 | Bob Foster | 1972–74 |
| Georges Carpentier | 1920–22 | Anton Christoforidis | 1941 | Victor Galindez | 1974–78 |
| Battling Siki | 1922–23 | Gus Lesnevich | 1941–48 | Mike Rossman | 1978–79 |
| Mike McTigue | 1923–25 | Freddie Mills | 1948–50 | Victor Galindez | 1979 |
| Paul Berlenbach | 1925–26 | Joey Maxim | 1950–52 | Marvin Johnson | 1979–80 |
| Jack Delaney | 1926–27 | Archie Moore | 1952–61 | Eddie Mustafa Muhammad | 1980– |
| Mike McTigue [1] | 1927 | Harold Johnson [4] | 1961–63 | | |

[1] Delaney resigned the crown and McTigue reclaimed it in 1927.  [2] Loughran resigned the title and Rosenbloom became champion.  [3] Bettina was the victor in an elimination tournament after Lewis resigned as titleholder.  [4] Moore was stripped of his title by the NBA. Johnson won the title by defeating Jesse Bowdry.  [5] Foster's title declared vacant in 1970.

## MIDDLEWEIGHT BOXING CHAMPIONS (Up to 160 pounds)

Source: *The Ring Magazine:* World Boxing Association (WBA) champions in 1970s–1980s

| CHAMPION | REIGN | CHAMPION | REIGN | CHAMPION | REIGN |
|---|---|---|---|---|---|
| Jack Dempsey ("The Nonpareil") | 1884–91 | Tony Zale | 1941–47 | Paul Pender | 1960–62 |
| Bob Fitzsimmons | 1891–97 | Rocky Graziano | 1947–48 | Dick Tiger | 1962–63 |
| Tommy Ryan | 1897–1907 | Tony Zale | 1948 | Joey Giardello | 1963–65 |
| Stanley Ketchel | 1908 | Marcel Cerdan | 1948–49 | Dick Tiger | 1965–66 |
| Billy Papke | 1908 | Jake LaMotta | 1949–51 | Emile Griffith | 1966–67 |
| Stanley Ketchel | 1908–10 | Sugar Ray Robinson | 1951 | Nino Benvenuti | 1967 |
| Frank Klaus [1] | 1913 | Randy Turpin | 1951 | Emile Griffith | 1967–68 |
| George Chip | 1913–14 | Sugar Ray Robinson | 1951–52 | Nino Benvenuti | 1968–70 |
| Al McCoy | 1914–17 | Bobo Olson [3] | 1953–55 | Carlos Monzon | 1970–77 |
| Mike O'Dowd | 1917–20 | Sugar Ray Robinson [3] | 1955–57 | Rodrigo Valdes | 1977–78 |
| Johnny Wilson | 1920–23 | Gene Fullmer | 1957 | Hugo Corro | 1978–79 |
| Harry Greb | 1923–26 | Sugar Ray Robinson | 1957 | Vito Antuofermo | 1979–80 |
| Tiger Flowers | 1926 | Carmen Basilio | 1957–58 | Alan Minter | 1980 |
| Mickey Walker [2] | 1926–31 | Sugar Ray Robinson | 1958–60 | Marvin Hagler | 1980– |
| | | Gene Fullmer [4] | 1959–62 | | |

[1] Ketchel was shot and killed in 1910. Papke reclaimed the title and Klaus defeated him in 1913 to gain the middleweight crown.  [2] Walker relinquished the title in 1931. The NBA and New York State Athletic Commission each sponsored separate tournaments to determine a new champion. During the next ten years Gorilla Jones, Ben Jeby, Marcel Thil, Lou Brouillard, Vince Dundee, Teddy Yarosz, Babe Risko, Freddy Steele, Al Hostak, Solly Krieger, Fred Apostoli, Ceferino Garcia, Ken Overlin, and Billy Soose were all recognized as champions.  [3] Robinson retired from the ring in 1952. Olson outpointed Randy Turpin to become world champion in 1953. Robinson returned to the ring in 1955.  [4] The NBA vacated Robinson's title in 1959 and Fullmer fought Basilio for the title. When, in 1962, he defeated Pender, who outpointed Robinson in 1960, he was universally recognized as champion.

## WELTERWEIGHT BOXING CHAMPIONS (Up to 147 pounds)

Source: *The Ring Magazine:* World Boxing Association (WBA) champions in 1970s–1980s

| CHAMPION | REIGN | CHAMPION | REIGN | CHAMPION | REIGN |
|---|---|---|---|---|---|
| Mysterious Billy Smith | 1892–94 | Tommy Freeman | 1930–31 | Carmen Basilio | 1955–56 |
| Tommy Ryan | 1894–96 | Young Jack Thompson | 1931 | Johnny Saxton | 1956 |
| Kid McCoy | 1896 | Lou Brouillard | 1931–32 | Carmen Basilio | 1956–57 |
| Mysterious Billy Smith | 1896–1900 | Jackie Fields | 1932–33 | Virgil Akins | 1958 |
| Matty Matthews | 1900–01 | Young Corbett 3d | 1933 | Don Jordan | 1958–60 |
| Rube Ferns | 1901 | Jimmy McLarnin | 1933–34 | Benny (Kid) Paret | 1960–61 |
| Joe Walcott | 1901–04 | Barney Ross | 1934 | Emile Griffith | 1961 |
| Dixie Kid | 1904 | Jimmy McLarnin | 1934–35 | Benny (Kid) Paret | 1961–62 |
| Joe Walcott | 1904–06 | Barney Ross | 1935–38 | Emile Griffith | 1962–63 |
| Honey Mellody | 1906–07 | Henry Armstrong | 1938–40 | Luis Rodriguez | 1963 |
| Mike (Twin) Sullivan [1] | 1907–10 | Fritzie Zivic | 1940–41 | Emile Griffith | 1963–66 |
| Ted Lewis | 1915–19 | Freddie Cochrane | 1941–46 | Curtis Cokes [4] | 1966–69 |
| Jack Britton | 1919–22 | Marty Servo | 1946 | Jose Napoles | 1969–70 |
| Mickey Walker | 1922–26 | Sugar Ray Robinson [2] | 1946–51 | Billy Backus | 1970–71 |
| Peter Latzo | 1926–27 | Johnny Bratton | 1951 | Jose Napoles | 1971–75 |
| Joe Dundee | 1927–29 | Kid Gavilan [3] | 1951–54 | Angel Espada | 1975–76 |
| Jackie Fields | 1929–30 | Johnny Saxton | 1954–55 | Pipino Cuevas | 1976–80 |
| Young Jack Thompson | 1930 | Tony DeMarco | 1955 | Thomas Hearns | 1980– |

[1] Sullivan vacated his title in 1910 by becoming a middleweight.  [2] Because Servo refused to fight Robinson, the New York State Commission declared his title vacant.  [3] Robinson gave up the crown in 1951 after winning the middleweight title.  [4] Cokes was accepted as titleholder when Griffith became middleweight champion.

## LIGHTWEIGHT BOXING CHAMPIONS (Up to 135 pounds)

Source: *The Ring Magazine:* World Boxing Association (WBA) champions in 1970s–1980s

| CHAMPION | REIGN | CHAMPION | REIGN | CHAMPION | REIGN |
|---|---|---|---|---|---|
| Joe Gans | 1901–08 | Tony Canzoneri [2] | 1935–36 | Wallace (Bud) Smith | 1955–56 |
| Battling Nelson | 1908–10 | Lou Ambers | 1936–38 | Joe Brown | 1956–62 |
| Ad Wolgast | 1910–12 | Henry Armstrong | 1938–39 | Carlos Ortiz | 1962–65 |
| Willie Ritchie | 1912–14 | Lou Ambers | 1939–40 | Ismael Laguna | 1965 |
| Freddie Welsh | 1914–17 | Lew Jenkins | 1940–41 | Carlos Ortiz | 1965–68 |
| Benny Leonard [1] | 1917–24 | Sammy Angott [3] | 1941–42 | Teo Cruz | 1968–69 |
| Jimmy Goodrich | 1925 | Ike Williams | 1947–51 | Mando Ramos | 1969–70 |
| Rocky Kansas | 1925–26 | Jimmy Carter | 1951–52 | Ismael Laguna | 1970 |
| Sammy Mandell | 1926–30 | Lauro Salas | 1952 | Ken Buchanan | 1970–72 |
| Al Singer | 1930 | Jimmy Carter | 1952–54 | Roberto Duran | 1972–79 |
| Tony Canzoneri | 1930–33 | Paddy DeMarco | 1954 | Ernesto Espana | 1979–80 |
| Barney Ross | 1933–35 | Jimmy Carter | 1954–55 | Hilmer Kenty | 1980– |

[1] Leonard retired undefeated.  [2] Ross relinquished his title.  [3] Angott resigned his title in 1942. From 1943 to 1947, the NBA and the New York State Athletic Commission recognized different champions. The dispute was settled in 1947.

## FEATHERWEIGHT BOXING CHAMPIONS (Up to 126 pounds)

Source: *The Ring Magazine:* World Boxing Association (WBA) champions in 1970s–1980s

| CHAMPION | REIGN | CHAMPION | REIGN | CHAMPION | REIGN |
|---|---|---|---|---|---|
| Abe Attell | 1904 | Freddie Miller | 1933–36 | Davey Moore | 1959–63 |
| Tommy Sullivan | 1904–08 | Petey Sarron | 1936–37 | Sugar Ramos | 1963–64 |
| Abe Atell | 1908–12 | Henry Armstrong | 1937–38 | Vicente Saldivar | 1964–67 |
| Johnny Kilbane | 1912–23 | Joey Archibald | 1938–40 | Raul Rojas | 1968 |
| Eugene Criqui | 1923 | Harry Jeffra | 1940–41 | Sho Saijo | 1968–71 |
| Johnny Dundee | 1923–25 | Joey Archibald | 1941 | Alfredo Marcano | 1971–72 |
| Louis (Kid) Kaplan | 1926–27 | Chalky Wright | 1941–42 | Ernesto Marcel | 1972–74 |
| Benny Bass | 1927–28 | Willie Pep | 1942–48 | Ruben Olivares | 1974 |
| Tony Canzoneri | 1928 | Sandy Saddler | 1948–49 | Alexis Arguello | 1974–77 |
| Andre Routis | 1928–29 | Willie Pep | 1949–50 | Cecilio Lastra | 1977–78 |
| Battling Battalino | 1929–32 | Sandy Saddler | 1950–57 | Eusebio Pedroza | 1978– |
| Tommy Paul | 1932 | Kid Bassey | 1957–59 | | |

## BANTAMWEIGHT BOXING CHAMPIONS (Up to 118 pounds)

Source: *The Ring Magazine:* World Boxing Association (WBA) champions in 1970s–1980s

| CHAMPION | REIGN | CHAMPION | REIGN | CHAMPION | REIGN |
|---|---|---|---|---|---|
| George Dixon | 1890–92 | Eddie Martin | 1924–25 | Alphonse Halimi | 1957–59 |
| Vacant | 1893 | Charley Rosenberg | 1925–27 | Jose Becerra | 1959–60 |
| Jimmy Barry | 1894–99 | Bud Taylor | 1927–28 | Eder Jofre | 1961–65 |
| Terry McGovern | 1899–1900 | Al Brown | 1929–35 | Masahiko Harada | 1965–68 |
| Harry Harris | 1901–02 | Baltazar Sangchili | 1935–36 | Lionel Rose | 1968–69 |
| Harry Forbes | 1902–03 | Tony Marino | 1936 | Ruben Olivares | 1969–70 |
| Frankie Neil | 1903–04 | Sixto Escobar | 1936–37 | Jesus Castillo | 1970–71 |
| Joe Bowker | 1904 | Harry Jeffra | 1937–38 | Ruben Olivares | 1971–72 |
| Jimmy Walsh | 1905–07 | Sixto Escobar | 1938–40 | Rafael Herrera | 1972 |
| Vacant | 1908–09 | Georgie Pace | 1940 | Enrique Pinder | 1972–73 |
| Johnny Coulon | 1910–14 | Lou Salica | 1940–42 | Romero Anaya | 1973 |
| Kid Williams | 1914–17 | Manuel Ortiz | 1942–47 | Arnold Taylor | 1973–74 |
| Pete Herman | 1917–20 | Harold Dade | 1947 | Soo Hwan Hong | 1974–75 |
| Joe Lynch | 1920–21 | Manuel Ortiz | 1947–50 | Alfonso Zamora | 1975–77 |
| Pete Herman | 1921 | Vic Toweel | 1950–52 | Jorge Lujan | 1977–80 |
| Johnny Buff | 1921–22 | Jimmy Carruthers | 1952–54 | Jeff Chandler | 1980– |
| Joe Lynch | 1922–24 | Robert Cohen | 1954–56 | | |
| Abe Goldstein | 1924 | Mario D'Agata | 1956–57 | | |

## FLYWEIGHT BOXING CHAMPIONS (Up to 112 pounds)

Source: *The Ring Magazine:* World Boxing Association (WBA) champions in 1970s–1980s

| CHAMPION | REIGN | CHAMPION | REIGN | CHAMPION | REIGN |
|---|---|---|---|---|---|
| Jimmy Wilde | 1916–23 | Dado Marino | 1950–52 | Bernabe Villacampo | 1969–70 |
| Pancho Villa | 1923–25 | Yoshio Shirai | 1952–54 | Berkrerk Chartvachai | 1970 |
| Fidel La Barba | 1925–27 | Pascual Perez | 1954–60 | Masao Ohba | 1970–73 |
| Frankie Genaro | 1928–31 | Pone Kingpetch | 1960–62 | Chartchai Chionoi | 1973–74 |
| Victor Perez | 1931–32 | Masahiko Harado | 1962–63 | Erbito Salavarria | 1975 |
| Jackie Brown | 1932–35 | Pone Kingpetch | 1963 | Alfonso Lopez | 1976 |
| Benny Lynch | 1935–38 | Hiroyuki Ebihara | 1963–64 | Guty Espades | 1976–78 |
| Peter Kane | 1938–41 | Pone Kingpetch | 1964–65 | Bertulio Gonzalez | 1978–80 |
| Vacant | 1941–42 | Salvatore Burruni | 1965–66 | Tae-Shik Kim | 1980– |
| Jackie Paterson | 1943–47 | Horacio Accavallo | 1966–68 | | |
| Rinty Monaghan | 1948–50 | Hiroyuki Ebihara | 1969 | | |

# CHESS

By the end of 1980, two chess masters had emerged as the prime candidates to challenge Anatoly Karpov for the world championship title in 1981. After victories throughout the year, West Germany's Robert Hübner and Viktor Korchnoi, now residing in Switzerland, were scheduled to meet in a final candidates' match in Italy in December 1980–January 1981. The winner will meet Karpov lat-er in 1981.

The United States chess championship tournament, held in Greenville, Pa., in June, resulted in a three-way tie. The winners were Larry Christiansen of Modesto, Calif., Larry Evans of Reno, Nev., and Walter Browne of Berkeley, Calif.

Gari Kasparov, 17, of the Soviet Union, won the World Junior championship tournament in Dortmund, West Germany, in October.

## WORLD CHESS CHAMPIONS

| YEARS | CHAMPION | COUNTRY | YEARS | CHAMPION | COUNTRY |
|-------|----------|---------|-------|----------|---------|
| 1851–58 | Adolph Anderssen | Germany | 1948–57 | Mikhail Botvinnik | Soviet Union |
| 1858–62 | Paul C. Morphy | United States | 1957–58 | Vassily Smyslov | Soviet Union |
| 1862–66 | Adolph Anderssen | Germany | 1958–60 | Mikhail Botvinnik | Soviet Union |
| 1866–94 | Wilhelm Steinitz | Austria, U.S. | 1960–61 | Mikhail Tal | Soviet Union |
| 1894–1921 | Emanuel Lasker | Germany | 1961–63 | Mikhail Botvinnik | Soviet Union |
| 1921–27 | José R. Capablanca | Cuba | 1963–69 | Tigran Petrosian | Soviet Union |
| 1927–35 | Alexander A. Alekhine | France | 1969–72 | Boris Spassky | Soviet Union |
| 1935–37 | Max Euwe | Netherlands | 1972–75 | Bobby Fischer | United States |
| 1937–46 | Alexander A. Alekhine | France | 1975– | Anatoly Karpov | Soviet Union |

# FENCING

## NATIONAL COLLEGIATE ATHLETIC ASSOCIATION FENCING CHAMPIONSHIPS

### TEAM CHAMPIONSHIPS

| | | | | | |
|---|---|---|---|---|---|
| 1947 New York U. | 1954 Columbia; | 1959 Navy | 1966–67 New York U. | 1972 Detroit |
| 1948 City College, N.Y. | New York U. | 1960–61 New York U. | 1968 Columbia | 1973–74 New York U. |
| 1949 Army; Rutgers | 1955 Columbia | 1962 Navy | 1969 Pennsylvania | 1975 Wayne State |
| 1950 Navy | 1956 Illinois | 1963 Columbia | 1970 New York U. | 1976 New York U. |
| 1951–52 Columbia | 1957 New York U. | 1964 Princeton | 1971 New York U.; | 1977–78 Notre Dame |
| 1953 Pennsylvania | 1958 Illinois | 1965 Columbia | Columbia | 1979–80 Wayne State |

### FOIL CHAMPIONS

| | | |
|---|---|---|
| 1941 Edward McNamara, Northwestern | 1956 Ralph DeMarco, Columbia | 1967 Mike Gaylor, New York U. |
| 1942 Byron Kreiger, Wayne State | 1957 Bruce Davis, Wayne State | 1968 Gerard Esponda, San Francisco |
| 1947 Abraham Balk, New York U. | 1958 Bruce Davis, Wayne State | 1969 Norman Braslow, Pennsylvania |
| 1948 Albert Axelrod, City College, N.Y. | 1959 Joe Paletta, Navy | 1970 Walter Krause, New York U. |
| 1949 Ralph Tedeschi, Rutgers | 1960 Gene Glazer, New York U. | 1971–72 Tyrone Simmons, Detroit |
| 1950 Robert Nielsen, Columbia | 1961 Herbert Cohen, New York U. | 1973 Brooke Makler, Pennsylvania |
| 1951 Robert Nielsen, Columbia | 1962 Herbert Cohen, New York U. | 1974–76 Greg Benko, Wayne State |
| 1952 Harold Goldsmith, City College, N.Y. | 1963 Jay Lustig, Columbia | 1977 Pat Gerard, Notre Dame |
| 1953 Ed Nober, Brooklyn College | 1964 Bill Hicks, Princeton | 1978 Ernest Simon, Wayne State |
| 1954 Robert Goldman, Pennsylvania | 1965 Joe Nalven, Columbia | 1979 Andy Bonk, Wayne State |
| 1955 Herman Velasco, Illinois | 1966 Al Davis, New York U. | 1980 Ernie Simon, Wayne State |

### SABER CHAMPIONS

| | | |
|---|---|---|
| 1942 Andre Deladrier, St. John's | 1957 Bernie Balaban, New York U. | 1967–68 Todd Makler, Pennsylvania |
| 1947 Oscar Parsons, Temple | 1958 Art Schankin, Illinois | 1969 Antony Kestler, Columbia |
| 1948 James Day, Navy | 1959 Al Morales, Navy | 1970–72 Bruce Soriano, Columbia |
| 1949–50 Alex Treves, Rutgers | 1960 Mike Desaro, New York U. | 1973 Peter Westbrook, New York U. |
| 1951 Chambless Johnston, Princeton | 1961 Israel Colon, New York U. | 1974 Steve Danosi, Wayne State |
| 1952 Frank Zimolzak, Navy | 1962 Barton Nisonson, Columbia | 1975 Yuri Rabinovich, Wayne State |
| 1953 Robert Parmacek, Pennsylvania | 1963 Bela Szentivanyi, Wayne State | 1976 Brian Smith, Columbia |
| 1954 Steve Sobel, Columbia | 1964 Craig Bell, Illinois | 1977–78 Mike Sullivan, Notre Dame |
| 1955 Barry Pariser, Columbia | 1965 Howard Goodman, New York U. | 1979 Yuri Rabinovich, Wayne State |
| 1956 Gerald Kaufman, Columbia | 1966 Paul Apostol, New York U. | 1980 Paul Friedberg, Pennsylvania |

### ÉPÉE CHAMPIONS

| | | |
|---|---|---|
| 1941 G. H. Boland, Illinois | 1956 Kinmont Hoitsma, Princeton | 1968 Don Sieja, Cornell |
| 1942 Ben Burtt, Ohio State | 1957 James Margolis, Columbia | 1969 James Wetzler, Pennsylvania |
| 1947 Abraham Balk, New York U. | 1958 Roland Wommack, Navy | 1970 John Nadas, Case Western Reserve |
| 1948 William Bryan, Navy | 1959 Roland Wommack, Navy | 1971 George Szunyogh, New York U. |
| 1949 Richard C. Bowman, Army | 1960 Gil Eisner, New York U. | 1972 Ernesto Fernandez, Pennsylvania |
| 1950 Thomas Stuart, Navy | 1961 Jerry Halpern, New York U. | 1973–75 Risto Hurme, New York U. |
| 1951 Daniel Chafetz, Columbia | 1962 Thane Hawkins, Navy | 1976 Randy Eggleton, Pennsylvania |
| 1952 James Wallner, New York U. | 1963 Larry Crum, Navy | 1977 Hans Wieselgren, New York U. |
| 1953 Jack Tori, Pennsylvania | 1964–65 Paul Pesthy, Rutgers | 1978 Bjorne Vaggo, Notre Dame |
| 1954 Henry Kolowrat, Princeton | 1966 Bernhardt Hermann, Iowa | 1979 Carlo Songini, Cleveland State |
| 1955 Donald Tadrawski, Notre Dame | 1967 George Masin, New York U. | 1980 Gil Pezza, Wayne State |

# FISHING

## WORLD FRESHWATER FISHING RECORDS

Source: *Field & Stream*

| SPECIES | WEIGHT [1] | LENGTH [2] | GIRTH [2] | PLACE CAUGHT | DATE | ANGLER |
|---|---|---|---|---|---|---|
| Bass (largemouth) .. | 22– 4 | 32 ½" | 28 ½" | Montgomery Lake, Ga. | June 2, 1932 | George W. Perry |
| Bass (redeye)....... | 8– 3 | 23" | 16 ½" | Flint River, Ga. .... | Oct. 23, 1977 | David A. Hubbard |
| Bass (rock)......... | 3– 0 | 13 ½" | 10 ¾" | York River, Ont. ..... | Aug. 1, 1974 | Peter Gulgin |
| Bass (smallmouth) .. | 11–15 | 27" | 21 ⅔" | Dale Hollow Lake, Ky. | July 9, 1955 | David L. Hayes |
| Bass (spotted) ..... | 8–15 | — | — | Smith Lake, Ala. ..... | Mar. 18, 1978 | Philip C. Terry, Jr. |
| Bass (white) ....... | 5– 6 | — | — | Grenada, Miss. .... | April 21, 1979 | William C. Mulvihill |
| Bass (yellow) ...... | 2– 4 | 16 ¼" | 12 ¾" | Lake Monroe, Ind. ... | Mar. 27, 1977 | Donald L. Stalker |
| Bluegill ............ | 4–12 | 15" | 18 ¼" | Ketona Lake, Ala. ... | Apr. 9, 1950 | T. S. Hudson |
| Bowfin ............. | 21–8 | — | — | Florence, N.C. ..... | Jan. 29, 1980 | Robert L. Harmon |
| Buffalo (bigmouth) .. | 70–5 | — | — | Bastrop, La. ....... | Apr. 21, 1980 | Delbert Sisk |
| Buffalo (smallmouth) | 32– 8 | 34 ½" | 29" | Sardis Reservoir, Miss. | Oct. 22, 1977 | Eddie O'Daniel |
| Bullhead (black) .... | 8 | 24" | 17 ¾" | Lake Waccabuc, N.Y. | Aug. 1, 1951 | Kani Evans |
| Carp............... | 55– 5 | 42" | 31" | Clearwater Lake, Minn. | July 10, 1952 | Frank J. Ledwein |
| Catfish (blue)....... | 97 | 57" | 37" | Missouri River, S.D. . | Sept. 16, 1959 | Edward B. Elliott |
| Catfish (channel).... | 58 | 47 ¼" | 29 ⅛" | Santee-Cooper Res., S.C. | July 7, 1964 | W. B. Whaley |
| Catfish (flathead) ... | 79– 8 | 44" | 27" | White River, Ind. .... | Aug. 13, 1966 | Glenn T. Simpson |
| Catfish (white)...... | 10– 5 | 25" | 17 ½" | Raritan River, N.J. .. | June 23, 1976 | Lewis M. Lomerson |
| Char (Arctic) ....... | 29–11 | 39 ¾" | 26" | Arctic River, N.W.T. . | Aug. 21, 1968 | Jeanne P. Branson |
| Crappie (black) ..... | 5 | 19 ¼" | 18 ⅝" | Santee-Cooper Res., S.C. | Mar. 15, 1957 | Paul E. Foust |
| Crappie (white) ..... | 5– 3 | 21" | 19" | Enid Dam, Miss. ... | July 31, 1957 | Fred L. Bright |
| Dolly Varden........ | 32 | 40 ½" | 29 ¾" | L. Pend Oreille, Idaho | Oct. 27, 1949 | N. L. Higgins |
| Drum (freshwater) .. | 54– 8 | 31 ½" | 29" | Nickajack Dam, Tenn. | Apr. 20, 1972 | Benny E. Hull |
| Gar (alligator) ...... | 279 | 93" | — | Rio Grande, Texas ... | Dec. 2, 1951 | Bill Valverde |
| Gar (longnose)...... | 50– 5 | 72 ¼" | 22 ¼" | Trinity River, Texas .. | July 30, 1954 | Townsend Miller |
| Grayling (Arctic) .... | 5–15 | 29 ⅞" | 15 ⅛" | Katseyedie R., N.W.T. | Aug. 16, 1967 | Jeanne P. Branson |
| Kokanee ........... | 6– 9 ¾ | 24 ½" | 14 ½" | Priest Lake, Idaho ... | June 9, 1975 | Jerry Verge |
| Muskellunge........ | 69–15 | 64 ½" | 31 ¾" | St. Lawrence R., N.Y. | Sept. 22, 1957 | Arthur Lawton |
| Perch (white) ....... | 4–12 | 19 ½" | 13" | Messalonskee Lake, Me. | June 4, 1949 | Mrs. Earl Small |
| Perch (yellow) ...... | 4– 3 ½ | — | — | Bordentown, N.J. .... | May 1865 | Dr. C. C. Abbot |
| Pickerel (chain) ..... | 9– 6 | 31" | 14" | Homerville, Ga. ..... | Feb. 17, 1961 | Baxley McQuaig Jr. |
| Pike (northern) ..... | 46– 2 | 52 ½" | 25" | Sacandaga Res., N.Y. | Sept. 15, 1940 | Peter Dubuc |
| Redhorse (silver).... | 4– 2 | 20 ½" | 14" | Gasconade R., Mo. .. | Oct. 5, 1974 | C. Larry McKinney |
| Salmon (Atlantic) ... | 79– 2 | — | — | Tana River, Norway .. | 1928 | Henrik Henriksen |
| Salmon (chinook) ... | 93 | 50" | 39" | Alaska Kelp Bay, Alas. | June 24, 1977 | Howard Rider |
| Salmon (chum) ..... | 27– 3 | 39 ⅜" | 24 ½" | Raymond Cove, Alas. | June 11, 1977 | Robert A. Jahnke |
| Salmon (coho or silver) | 31 | — | — | Cowichan Bay, B.C. .. | Oct. 11, 1947 | Mrs. Lee Hallberg |
| Salmon (landlocked). | 22– 8 | 36" | — | Sebago Lake, Maine . | Aug. 1, 1907 | Edward Blakely |
| Sauger............. | 8–12 | 28" | 15" | Lake Sakakawea, N.D. | Oct. 6, 1971 | Mike Fischer |
| Shad (American) .... | 9– 4 | — | — | Delaware River, Pa... | Apr. 26, 1979 | J. Edward Whitman |
| Sturgeon (white) .... | 360 | 111" | 86" | Snake River, Idaho ... | Apr. 24, 1956 | Willard Cravens |
| Sunfish (green) ..... | 2– 2 | 14 ¾" | 14" | Stockton Lake, Mo. .. | June 18, 1971 | Paul M. Dilley |
| Sunfish (redbreast) . | 1– 8 ½ | 11" | 12 ⅝" | Suwannee River, Fla. | Apr. 30, 1977 | Tommy D. Cason Jr. |
| Sunfish (red ear) .... | 4– 8 | 16 ¼" | 17 ¾" | Chase City, Va. ..... | June 19, 1970 | Maurice E. Ball |
| Trout (brook) ....... | 14– 8 | 31 ½" | — | Nipigon River, Ontario | July 1916 | Dr. W. J. Cook |
| Trout (brown) ....... | 35–15 | — | — | Nahuel Huapi, Argentina | Dec. 16, 1952 | Eugenio Cavaglia |
| Trout (cutthroat).... | 41 | 39" | — | Pyramid Lake, Nev. . | Dec. 1925 | John Skimmerhorn |
| Trout (golden) ...... | 11 | 28" | 16" | Cook's Lake, Wyo. .. | Aug. 5, 1948 | Charles S. Reed |
| Trout (lake) ........ | 65 | 52" | 38" | Great Bear Lake, N.W.T. | Aug. 8, 1970 | Lary Daunis |
| Trout (rainbow) [3] ... | 42– 2 | 43" | 23 ½" | Bell Island, Alaska .. | June 22, 1970 | David R. White |
| Trout (sunapee)..... | 11– 8 | 33" | 17 ¼" | Lake Sunapee, N.H. . | Aug. 1, 1954 | Ernest Theoharis |
| Trout (tiger) ........ | 17 | 31" | 21" | Lake Michigan, Wis. . | Aug. 2, 1977 | Edward Rudnicki |
| Walleye ............ | 25 | 41" | 29" | Old Hickory Lake, Tenn. | Aug. 1, 1960 | Mabry Harper |
| Warmouth.......... | 2 | 12" | 12 ½" | Sylvania, Ga. ....... | May 4, 1974 | Carlton Robbins |
| Whitefish (lake) ..... | 13 | 32 ¼" | 19" | Great Bear L., N.W.T. | July 14, 1974 | Robert L. Stintsman |
| Whitefish (mountain) | 5 | 19" | 14" | Athabasca R., Alberta | June 3, 1963 | Orville Welch |

[1] In pounds and ounces.  [2] In inches.  [3] Also known as Steelhead or Kamloops.

## AMERICAN CASTING ASSOCIATION RECORDS

| | | | | | | | | |
|---|---|---|---|---|---|---|---|---|
| Men: All Distance [1] ... | Steve Rajeff .. | 1980 | 5,594 ft. | Women: All Accuracy [2] | Mollie Light... | 1973 | 544 pts. |
| Men: All Accuracy [2] .. | Steve Rajeff .. | 1977 | 593 pts. | Women: Accuracy Plugs [4] | Mollie Light... | 1973 | 277 pts. |
| Men: Distance Plugs [3] . | Chris Korich .. | 1980 | 3,785 ft. | Women: Accuracy Flies [4] | Pauline Cathcart | 1973 | 277 pts. |
| Men: Distance Flies [3] .. | Steve Rajeff .. | 1980 | 1,860 ft. | Intm.: All Accuracy [2] .. | Steve Willson . | 1970 | 564 pts. |
| Men: Accuracy Plugs [4] . | Steve Rajeff .. | 1977 | 297 pts. | Intm.: Accuracy Plugs [4] | Don Lanser ... | 1970 | 284 pts. |
| Men: Accuracy Flies [4] .. | Steve Rajeff .. | 1978 | 298 pts. | Intm.: Accuracy Flies [4] | Luke Brugnara | 1978 | 298 pts. |

[1] Total of 12 casts.  [2] Of possible 600 points.  [3] Total of 6 casts.  [4] Of possible 300 points.

## SALTWATER FISHING ALL–TACKLE RECORDS

Source: International Game Fish Association

| SPECIES | WEIGHT (in lbs. and oz.) | LENGTH (in ft. and in.) | GIRTH (in inches) | WHERE CAUGHT | DATE | ANGLER |
|---|---|---|---|---|---|---|
| Albacore | 88–2 | 4' 2" | 37" | Canary Islands | Nov. 19, 1977 | Siegfried Dickemann |
| Amberjack (greater) | 149 | 5' 11" | 41¾" | Bermuda | June 21, 1964 | Peter Simons |
| Barracuda (great) | 83 | 6' ¼" | 29" | Lagos, Nigeria | Jan. 13, 1952 | K. J. W. Hackett |
| Bass (black sea) | 8-12 | — | — | Oregon Inlet, N.C. | Apr. 21, 1979 | Joe W. Mizelle Sr. |
| Bass (giant sea) | 563–8 | 7' 5" | 72" | Anacapa Island, Calif. | Aug. 20, 1968 | James D. McAdam Jr. |
| Bass (striped) | 72 | 4' 6½" | 31" | Cuttyhunk, Mass. | Oct. 10, 1969 | Edward J. Kirker |
| Bluefish | 31–12 | 3' 11" | 23" | Hatteras Inlet, N.C. | Jan. 30, 1972 | James M. Hussey |
| Bonefish | 19 | 3' 3⅝" | 17" | Zululand, South Africa | May 26, 1962 | Brian W. Batchelor |
| Bonito (Pacific) | 23–8 | 2' 11¼" | 23¼" | Seychelles | Feb. 19, 1975 | Mrs. Ann Cochain |
| Cobia | 110–5 | 5' 3" | 34" | Mombasa, Kenya | Sept. 8, 1964 | Eric Tinworth |
| Cod | 98–12 | 5' 3" | 41" | Isle of Shoals, Mass. | June 8, 1969 | Alphonse J. Bielevich |
| Dolphin | 87 | 6' 9⅔" | 28" | Costa Rica | Sept. 25, 1976 | Manual Salazar |
| Drum (black) | 113–1 | 4' 5⅛" | 43½" | Lewes, Del. | Sept. 15, 1975 | Gerald M. Townsend |
| Drum (red) | 90 | 4' 7½" | 38¼" | Rodanthe, N.C. | Nov. 7, 1973 | Elvin Hooper |
| Flounder | 30–12 | 3' 2½" | 30½" | Viña del Mar, Chile | Nov. 1, 1971 | Augusto Núñez Moreno |
| Jack (crevalle) | 51 | 4' 5½" | 29½" | Lake Worth, Fla. | June 30, 1978 | Stephen V. Schwenk |
| Jewfish | 680 | 7' 1½" | 66" | Fernandina Beach, Fla. | May 20, 1961 | Lynn Joyner |
| Kawakawa | 26 | — | — | New South Wales, Australia | Jan. 26, 1980 | Wally Elfring |
| Mackerel (king) | 90 | 5' 11" | 30" | Key West, Fla. | Feb. 16, 1976 | Norton I. Thomton |
| Marlin (Atlantic blue) | 1,282 | 14' 8" | 76½" | St. Thomas, Virgin Is. | Aug. 6, 1977 | Larry Martin |
| Marlin (black) | 1,560 | 14' 6" | 81" | Cabo Blanco, Peru | Aug. 4, 1953 | Alfred C. Glassell Jr. |
| Marlin (Pacific blue) | 1,153 | 14' 8" | 73" | Ritidian Point, Guam | Aug. 21, 1969 | Greg D. Perez |
| Marlin (striped) | 417–8 | 11' 7½" | 52½" | Cavalli Island New Zealand | Jan. 14, 1977 | Phillip Bryers |
| Marlin (white) | 181–14 | — | — | Vitoria, Brazil | Dec. 8, 1979 | Evandro Luiz Caser |
| Permit | 51–8 | 3' 8¼" | 35" | Lake Worth, Fla. | April 28, 1978 | William M. Kenney |
| Pollock | 46–7 | 4' 2½" | 30" | Brielle, N.J. | May 6, 1975 | James T. Holton |
| Pompano (African) | 41–8 | — | — | Fort Lauderdale, Fla. | Feb. 15, 1979 | Wayne Sommers |
| Roosterfish | 114 | 5' 4" | 33" | LaPaz, Mexico | June 1, 1960 | Abe Sackheim |
| Runner (rainbow) | 33–10 | 4' 7¼" | 22½" | Clarion Is., Mexico | Mar. 14, 1976 | Ralph Mikkelsen |
| Sailfish (Atlantic) | 128–1 | 8' 10" | 34" | Luanda, Angola | Mar. 27, 1974 | Harm Steyn |
| Sailfish (Pacific) | 221 | 10' 9" | — | Galápagos Islands | Feb. 12, 1947 | C. W. Stewart |
| Seabass (white) | 83–12 | 5' 5½" | 34" | San Felipe, Mexico | Mar. 31, 1953 | L. C. Baumgardner |
| Seatrout (spotted) | 16 | 2' 8½" | 21¾" | Mason's Beach, Va. | May 28, 1977 | William G. Katko |
| Shark (blue) | 437 | — | — | Catherine Bay, Australia | Oct. 2, 1976 | Peter Hyde |
| Shark (hammerhead) | 703 | 14' 4" | 63" | Jacksonville Beach, Fla. | July 5, 1975 | H. B. Reasor |
| Shark (porbeagle) | 465 | 9' 3" | 56" | Padstow, England | July 23, 1976 | Jorge Potier |
| Shark (shortfin mako) | 1,061 | 12' 2" | 79½" | Mayor Island, New Zealand | Feb. 17, 1970 | James B. Penwarden |
| Shark (thresher) | 739 | 8' 10" | 68" | Tutukaka, New Zealand | Feb. 17, 1975 | Brian Galvin |
| Shark (tiger) | 1,780 | 13' 10½" | 103" | Cherry Grove, S.C. | June 14, 1964 | Walter Maxwell |
| Shark (white) | 2,664 | 16' 10" | 114" | Ceduna, Australia | Apr. 21, 1959 | Alfred Dean |
| Snook | 53–10 | — | — | Rio de Parasmina, Costa Rica | Oct. 18, 1978 | Gilbert Ponzi |
| Swordfish | 1,182 | 14' 11¼" | 78" | Iquique, Chile | May 7, 1953 | L. Marron |
| Tanguigue | 85–6 | 5' 8¾" | 30½" | Rottnest Is., W. Australia | May 5, 1978 | Barry Wrightson |
| Tarpon | 283 | 7' 2⅗" | — | L. Maracaibo, Venezuela | Mar. 19, 1956 | M. Salazar |
| Tautog (blackfish) | 21–6 | 2' 7½" | 23½" | Cape May, N.J. | June 12, 1954 | R. N. Sheafer |
| Trevally | 116 | 5' 3¼" | 39¾" | Pago Pago, Am. Samoa | Feb. 20, 1978 | William G. Foster |
| Tuna (Atlantic bigeye) | 375–8 | — | — | Ocean City, Md. | Aug. 26, 1977 | Cecil Browne |
| Tuna (blackfin) | 42 | 3' 6½" | 29½" | Bermuda | June 2, 1978 | Alan J. Card |
| Tuna (bluefin) | 1,235 | — | — | North Lake, Canada | Oct. 17, 1978 | Michael MacDonald |
| Tuna (dogtooth) | 189–2 | — | — | Dar es Salaam, Tanzania | Nov. 12, 1978 | Luke John Samaras |
| Tuna (longtail) | 65 | 4' 5¾" | 31" | Port Stevens, Australia | Apr. 20, 1978 | Michael James |
| Tuna (Pacific bigeye) | 435 | 7' 9" | 63½" | Cabo Blanco, Peru | Apr. 17, 1957 | Dr. Russel V. A. Lee |
| Tuna (skipjack) * | 39–15 | 3' 3" | 28" | Walker Cay, Bahamas | Jan. 21, 1952 | F. Drowley |
| | 40 | 3' 2¾" | 27½" | Mauritius | Apr. 19, 1971 | Joseph R. P. Caboche Jr. |
| Tuna (southern bluefin) | 220–7 | 6' 5½" | 50¾" | Tasman Is., Australia | June 10, 1978 | Stanley Gibbon |
| Tuna (yellowfin) | 388–12 | 7' 7¼" | 62¼" | San Benedicto Is., Mexico | Apr. 1, 1977 | Curt Wiesenhutter |
| Tunny (little) | 27 | 3' 3" | 22" | Key Largo, Fla. | Apr. 20, 1976 | William E. Allison |
| Wahoo | 149 | 6' 7¾" | 37½" | Cat Cay, Bahamas | June 5, 1962 | John Pirovano |
| Weakfish | 19–8 | 3' 1" | 25¾" | Trinidad | Apr. 13, 1962 | Dennis B. Hall |
| Yellowtail | 111 | 5' 2" | 38" | New Zealand | June 11, 1961 | A.F. Plim |
| Yellowtail (California) | 71–15 | — | — | Alijos Rocks, Mexico | June 24, 1979 | Michael Carpenter |

* = Tie.

# FOOTBALL—PROFESSIONAL FOOTBALL HIGHLIGHTS

## NATIONAL FOOTBALL LEAGUE FINAL STANDINGS: 1980

### AMERICAN FOOTBALL CONFERENCE (AFC)

| Eastern Division | W | L | T | PCT. | PTS. | OP |
|---|---|---|---|---|---|---|
| Buffalo † | 11 | 5 | 0 | .688 | 320 | 260 |
| New England | 10 | 6 | 0 | .625 | 441 | 325 |
| Miami | 8 | 8 | 0 | .500 | 266 | 305 |
| Baltimore | 7 | 9 | 0 | .438 | 355 | 387 |
| Jets | 4 | 12 | 0 | .250 | 302 | 395 |
| **Central Division** | | | | | | |
| Cleveland † | 11 | 5 | 0 | .688 | 357 | 310 |
| Houston * | 11 | 5 | 0 | .688 | 295 | 251 |
| Pittsburgh | 9 | 7 | 0 | .563 | 352 | 313 |
| Cincinnati | 6 | 10 | 0 | .375 | 244 | 312 |
| **Western Division** | | | | | | |
| San Diego † | 11 | 5 | 0 | .688 | 418 | 327 |
| Oakland * | 11 | 5 | 0 | .688 | 364 | 306 |
| Denver | 8 | 8 | 0 | .500 | 310 | 323 |
| Kansas City | 8 | 8 | 0 | .500 | 319 | 336 |
| Seattle | 4 | 12 | 0 | .250 | 291 | 408 |

### NATIONAL FOOTBALL CONFERENCE (NFC)

| Eastern Division | W | L | T | PCT. | PTS. | OP |
|---|---|---|---|---|---|---|
| Philadelphia † | 12 | 4 | 0 | .750 | 384 | 222 |
| Dallas * | 12 | 4 | 0 | .750 | 454 | 311 |
| Washington | 6 | 10 | 0 | .375 | 251 | 293 |
| St. Louis | 5 | 11 | 0 | .313 | 299 | 350 |
| Giants | 4 | 12 | 0 | .250 | 249 | 427 |
| **Central Division** | | | | | | |
| Minnesota † | 9 | 7 | 0 | .563 | 317 | 308 |
| Detroit | 9 | 7 | 0 | .563 | 334 | 272 |
| Chicago | 7 | 9 | 0 | .438 | 304 | 264 |
| Green Bay | 5 | 10 | 1 | .344 | 231 | 371 |
| Tampa Bay | 5 | 10 | 1 | .344 | 271 | 341 |
| **Western Division** | | | | | | |
| Atlanta † | 12 | 4 | 0 | .750 | 405 | 272 |
| Los Angeles * | 11 | 5 | 0 | .688 | 424 | 289 |
| San Francisco | 6 | 10 | 0 | .375 | 320 | 415 |
| New Orleans | 1 | 15 | 0 | .063 | 289 | 487 |

† Division Champion.   * Qualified for postseason playoffs.

## SUPER BOWL GAMES: 1967–1980

**1967** — Super Bowl I
The Coliseum, Los Angeles, California

| | | | | | |
|---|---|---|---|---|---|
| **Green Bay (NFL)** | 7 | 7 | 14 | 7 | **35** |
| Kansas City (AFL) | 0 | 10 | 0 | 0 | **10** |

**1968** — Super Bowl II
Orange Bowl Stadium, Miami, Florida

| | | | | | |
|---|---|---|---|---|---|
| **Green Bay (NFL)** | 3 | 13 | 10 | 7 | **33** |
| Oakland (AFL) | 0 | 7 | 0 | 7 | **14** |

**1969** — Super Bowl III
Orange Bowl Stadium, Miami, Florida

| | | | | | |
|---|---|---|---|---|---|
| **New York (AFL)** | 0 | 7 | 6 | 3 | **16** |
| Baltimore (NFL) | 0 | 0 | 0 | 7 | **7** |

**1970** — Super Bowl IV
Tulane Stadium, New Orleans, Louisiana

| | | | | | |
|---|---|---|---|---|---|
| **Kansas City (AFL)** | 3 | 13 | 7 | 0 | **23** |
| Minnesota (NFL) | 0 | 0 | 7 | 0 | **7** |

**1971** — Super Bowl V
Orange Bowl Stadium, Miami, Florida

| | | | | | |
|---|---|---|---|---|---|
| **Baltimore (AFC)** | 0 | 6 | 0 | 10 | **16** |
| Dallas (NFC) | 3 | 10 | 0 | 0 | **13** |

**1972** — Super Bowl VI
Tulane Stadium, New Orleans, Louisiana

| | | | | | |
|---|---|---|---|---|---|
| **Dallas (NFC)** | 3 | 7 | 7 | 7 | **24** |
| Miami (AFC) | 0 | 3 | 0 | 0 | **3** |

**1973** — Super Bowl VII
The Coliseum, Los Angeles, California

| | | | | | |
|---|---|---|---|---|---|
| **Miami (AFC)** | 7 | 7 | 0 | 0 | **14** |
| Washington (NFC) | 0 | 0 | 0 | 7 | **7** |

**1974** — Super Bowl VIII
Rice Stadium, Houston, Texas

| | | | | | |
|---|---|---|---|---|---|
| **Miami (AFC)** | 14 | 3 | 7 | 0 | **24** |
| Minnesota (NFC) | 0 | 0 | 0 | 7 | **7** |

**1975** — Super Bowl IX
Tulane Stadium, New Orleans, Louisiana

| | | | | | |
|---|---|---|---|---|---|
| **Pittsburgh (AFC)** | 0 | 2 | 7 | 7 | **16** |
| Minnesota (NFC) | 0 | 0 | 0 | 6 | **6** |

**1976** — Super Bowl X
Orange Bowl Stadium, Miami, Florida

| | | | | | |
|---|---|---|---|---|---|
| **Pittsburgh (AFC)** | 7 | 0 | 0 | 14 | **21** |
| Dallas (NFC) | 7 | 3 | 0 | 7 | **17** |

**1977** — Super Bowl XI
Rose Bowl, Pasadena, California

| | | | | | |
|---|---|---|---|---|---|
| **Oakland (AFC)** | 0 | 16 | 3 | 13 | **32** |
| Minnesota (NFC) | 0 | 0 | 7 | 7 | **14** |

**1978** — Super Bowl XII
Louisiana Superdome, New Orleans, Louisiana

| | | | | | |
|---|---|---|---|---|---|
| **Dallas (NFC)** | 10 | 3 | 7 | 7 | **27** |
| Denver (AFC) | 0 | 0 | 10 | 0 | **10** |

**1979** — Super Bowl XIII
Orange Bowl, Miami, Florida

| | | | | | |
|---|---|---|---|---|---|
| **Pittsburgh (AFC)** | 7 | 14 | 0 | 14 | **35** |
| Dallas (NFC) | 7 | 7 | 3 | 14 | **31** |

**1980** — Super Bowl XIV
Rose Bowl, Pasadena, California

| | | | | | |
|---|---|---|---|---|---|
| **Pittsburgh (AFC)** | 3 | 7 | 7 | 14 | **31** |
| Los Angeles (NFC) | 7 | 6 | 6 | 0 | **19** |

## CONFERENCE CHAMPIONSHIP GAME COMPOSITE STANDINGS

| AFC 1960–1979 | W | L | Pct. | Pts. | OP |
|---|---|---|---|---|---|
| Kansas City Chiefs[1] | 3 | 0 | 1.000 | 68 | 31 |
| Miami Dolphins | 3 | 0 | 1.000 | 69 | 27 |
| Pittsburgh Steelers | 4 | 2 | .667 | 125 | 86 |
| New York Jets | 1 | 0 | 1.000 | 27 | 23 |
| Denver Broncos | 1 | 0 | 1.000 | 20 | 17 |
| Buffalo Bills | 2 | 1 | .667 | 50 | 38 |
| Baltimore Colts | 1 | 1 | .500 | 27 | 38 |
| Houston Oilers | 2 | 4 | .333 | 76 | 140 |
| Oakland Raiders[2] | 2 | 7 | .222 | 161 | 172 |
| San Diego Chargers[2] | 1 | 4 | .200 | 77 | 87 |
| New England Patriots[3] | 0 | 1 | .000 | 10 | 51 |

| NFC 1933–1979 | W | L | Pct. | Pts. | OP |
|---|---|---|---|---|---|
| Green Bay Packers | 8 | 2 | .800 | 223 | 116 |
| Detroit Lions | 4 | 1 | .800 | 129 | 100 |
| Minnesota Vikings | 4 | 1 | .800 | 98 | 63 |
| Baltimore Colts | 3 | 1 | .750 | 88 | 60 |
| Philadelphia Eagles | 3 | 1 | .750 | 59 | 41 |
| Chicago Bears | 6 | 4 | .600 | 259 | 194 |
| Dallas Cowboys | 5 | 4 | .556 | 176 | 134 |
| St. Louis Cardinals[4] | 1 | 1 | .500 | 28 | 28 |
| Washington Redskins[5] | 3 | 4 | .429 | 109 | 180 |
| Cleveland Browns | 4 | 7 | .364 | 224 | 253 |
| Los Angeles Rams[6] | 3 | 7 | .300 | 120 | 216 |
| New York Giants | 3 | 11 | .214 | 208 | 309 |
| Tampa Bay Buccaneers | 0 | 1 | .000 | 0 | 9 |
| San Francisco 49ers | 0 | 2 | .000 | 13 | 31 |

[1] One game played when franchise in Dallas (Texans) (Won 20–17).   [2] One game played when franchise in Los Angeles (Lost 24–16).   [3] Game played when franchise in Boston (Lost 51–10).   [4] Both games played when franchise in Chicago (Won 28–21, lost 7–0).   [5] One game played when franchise in Boston (Lost 21–6).   [6] One game played when franchise in Cleveland (Won 15–14).

# NFL TEAM-BY-TEAM SCORES IN REGULAR SEASON: 1980

## NATIONAL CONFERENCE

### EASTERN DIV.

**DALLAS**
17—Washington 3
20—Denver 41
28—Tampa Bay 17
28—Green Bay 7
24—N.Y. Giants 3
59—San Fran. 14
10—Phila. 17
42—San Diego 31
27—St. Louis 24
35—N.Y. Giants 38
31—St. Louis 17
14—Washington 10
51—Seattle 7
19—Oakland 13
14—Los Angeles 38
35—Phila. 27

**N.Y. GIANTS**
41—St. Louis 35
21—Washington 23
3—Phila. 35
7—Los Angeles 28
3—Dallas 24
16—Phila. 31
7—San Diego 44
9—Denver 14
13—Tampa Bay 30
38—Dallas 35
27—Green Bay 12
0—San Fran. 12
6—St. Louis 23
27—Seattle 14
13—Washington 16
17—Oakland 33

**PHILA.**
27—Denver 6
42—Minnesota 7
35—N.Y. Giants 3
14—St. Louis 24
24—Washington 14
31—N.Y. Giants 16
17—Dallas 10
17—Chicago 14
27—Seattle 20
34—N. Orleans 21
24—Washington 0
10—Oakland 7
21—San Diego 22
17—Atlanta 20
17—St Louis 21
27—Dallas 35

**ST. LOUIS**
35—N.Y. Giants 41
21—San Fran. 24
7—Detroit 24
24—Phila. 14
40—New Orleans 7
13—Los Angeles 21
0—Washington 23
17—Baltimore 10
24—Dallas 27
27—Atlanta 33
21—Dallas 31
13—Kansas City 21
23—N.Y. Giants 6
24—Detroit 23
3—Phila. 17
7—Washington 31

**WASHINGTON**
3—Dallas 17
23—N.Y. Giants 21
21—Oakland 24
0—Seattle 14
14—Phila. 24
17—Denver 20
23—St. Louis 0
22—N. Orleans 14
14—Minnesota 39
21—Chicago 35
0—Phila. 24
10—Dallas 14
6—Atlanta 10
30—N.Y. Giants 13
40—San Diego 17
16—N.Y. Giants 13
31—St. Louis 17

### CENTRAL DIV.

**CHICAGO**
6—Green Bay 12
22—New Orleans 3
34—Minnesota 14
3—Pittsburgh 38
13—Tampa Bay 0
7—Minnesota 13
24—Detroit 7
14—Phila. 17
21—Cleveland 27
35—Washington 21
6—Houston 10
17—Atlanta 28
23—Detroit 17
61—Green Bay 7
14—Cincinnati 17
14—Tampa Bay 13

**DETROIT**
41—Los Angeles 20
29—Green Bay 7
20—St. Louis 10
27—Minnesota 7
28—Atlanta 43
24—N. Orleans 13
7—Chicago 24
17—Kansas City 20
17—San Fran. 13
0—Minnesota 34
24—Tampa Bay 10
17—Chicago 23
3—St. Louis 24
27—Tampa Bay 24
24—Green Bay 3

**GREEN BAY**
12—Chicago 6
7—Detroit 29
21—Los Angeles 51
7—Dallas 28
14—Cincinnati 17
14—Tampa Bay 14
21—Cleveland 26
16—Minnesota 3
20—Pittsburgh 22
23—San Fran. 16
21—N.Y. Giants 27
25—Minnesota 13
17—Tampa Bay 20
7—Chicago 61
3—Houston 22
3—Detroit 24

**MINNESOTA**
24—Atlanta 23
7—Phila. 42
34—Chicago 14
7—Detroit 27
17—Pittsburgh 23
13—Chicago 7
0—Cincinnati 14
3—Green Bay 16
39—Washington 14
34—Detroit 0
38—Tampa Bay 30
13—Green Bay 25
23—N. Orleans 20
21—Tampa Bay 10
28—Cleveland 23
16—Houston 20

**TAMPA BAY**
17—Cincinnati 12
10—Los Angeles 9
17—Dallas 28
27—Cleveland 34
0—Chicago 23
14—Green Bay 7
14—Houston 20
24—San Fran. 23
30—N.Y. Giants 13
21—Pittsburgh 24
10—Minnesota 38
10—Detroit 24
20—Green Bay 17
10—Minnesota 21
14—Detroit 27
13—Chicago 14

### WESTERN DIV.

**ATLANTA**
23—Minnesota 24
37—N. England 21
17—Miami 20
43—Detroit 28
35—N.Y. Jets 14
41—N. Orleans 14
13—Los Angeles 10
30—Buffalo 14
33—St. Louis 27
31—N. Orleans 13
17—Chicago 28
20—Washington 6
35—San Fran. 10
17—Los Angeles 31

**LOS ANGELES**
20—Detroit 41
9—Tampa Bay 10
51—Green Bay 21
28—N.Y. Giants 7
48—San Fran. 26
21—St. Louis 13
10—Atlanta 13
45—N. Orleans 31
14—Miami 35
17—N. England 14
27—New Orleans 7
38—N.Y. Jets 13
7—Buffalo 10
38—Dallas 14
20—Atlanta 17

**NEW ORLEANS**
23—San Fran. 26
3—Chicago 22
24—Buffalo 35
16—Miami 21
27—St. Louis 40
13—Detroit 24
14—Atlanta 41
14—Washington 22
31—Los Angeles 45
21—Phila. 34
13—Atlanta 31
7—Los Angeles 27
20—Minnesota 23
35—San Fran. 38
21—N.Y. Jets 24
27—N. England 38

**SAN FRAN.**
26—N. Orleans 23
24—St. Louis 21
37—N.Y. Jets 27
17—Atlanta 20
26—Los Angeles 48
14—Dallas 59
17—Los Angeles 31
23—Tampa Bay 24
13—Detroit 17
16—Green Bay 23
13—Miami 17
12—N.Y. Giants 0
10—Pittsburgh 23
24—Baltimore 14
17—N.Y. Jets 24

## AMERICAN CONFERENCE

### EASTERN DIV.

**BALTIMORE**
17—N.Y. Jets 14
17—Pittsburgh 20
16—Houston 21
35—N.Y. Jets 21
30—Miami 17
10—Buffalo 12
21—N. England 37
10—St. Louis 17
31—Kansas City 24
27—Cleveland 28
10—Detroit 9
21—N. England 47
28—Buffalo 24
33—Cincinnati 34
14—Miami 24
28—Kansas City 38

**BUFFALO**
17—Miami 7
20—N.Y. Jets 10
35—N. Orleans 24
24—Oakland 7
26—San Diego 24
12—Baltimore 17
14—Miami 17
31—N. England 13
14—Atlanta 30
31—N.Y. Jets 24
14—Cincinnati 0
28—Pittsburgh 13
26—Los Angeles 7
2—N. England 24
18—San Fran. 13

**N.Y. JETS**
14—Baltimore 17
10—Buffalo 20
27—San Fran. 37
21—Baltimore 35
11—N. England 21
14—Atlanta 7
17—Seattle 27
17—Miami 14
21—N. England 34
24—Buffalo 31
24—Denver 31
31—Houston 28
13—Los Angeles 38
17—Cleveland 17
24—Miami 17

**MIAMI**
7—Buffalo 17
17—Cincinnati 16
20—Atlanta 17
21—N. Orleans 16
17—Baltimore 30
0—N. England 34
17—Buffalo 14
14—N.Y. Jets 17
10—Oakland 16
35—Los Angeles 14
17—San Fran. 13
24—San Diego 27
10—Pittsburgh 23
16—N. England 13
24—Baltimore 14
17—N.Y. Jets 24

**N. ENGLAND**
34—Cleveland 17
21—Atlanta 37
37—Seattle 31
23—Denver 14
21—N.Y. Jets 11
34—Miami 0
37—Baltimore 21
13—Buffalo 31
34—N.Y. Jets 21
34—Houston 38
14—Los Angeles 17
47—Baltimore 21
17—San Fran. 21
13—Miami 16
24—Buffalo 2
38—N. Orleans 27

### CENTRAL DIV.

**CINCINNATI**
12—Tampa Bay 17
16—Miami 17
30—Pittsburgh 28
0—Houston 13
9—Green Bay 14
17—Pittsburgh 16
14—Minnesota 0
3—Houston 23
14—San Diego 31
17—Oakland 28
0—Buffalo 14
7—Cleveland 31
34—Baltimore 33
17—Chicago 14
24—Cleveland 27

**CLEVELAND**
17—N. England 34
7—Houston 16
34—Kansas City 13
34—Tampa Bay 27
16—Denver 19
27—Seattle 3
26—Green Bay 21
27—Pittsburgh 26
27—Chicago 21
28—Baltimore 27
13—Pittsburgh 16
31—Cincinnati 7
16—Houston 14
17—N.Y. Jets 17
17—Kansas City 13
27—Cincinnati 24

**HOUSTON**
17—Pittsburgh 31
16—Cleveland 7
21—Baltimore 16
13—Cincinnati 10
7—Seattle 26
20—Kansas City 21
20—Tampa Bay 14
23—Cincinnati 3
20—Denver 16
38—N. England 34
10—Chicago 6
28—N.Y. Jets 31
14—Cleveland 17

**PITTSBURGH**
31—Houston 17
20—Baltimore 17
28—Cincinnati 30
38—Chicago 3
23—Minnesota 17
16—Cincinnati 17
45—Oakland 34
26—Cleveland 27
22—Green Bay 20
24—Tampa Bay 21
16—Cleveland 13
13—Buffalo 28
23—Miami 10
0—Houston 6
21—Kansas City 16
17—San Diego 26

### WESTERN DIV.

**DENVER**
6—Phila. 27
41—Dallas 20
13—San Diego 30
14—N. England 23
19—Cleveland 16
20—Washington 17
17—Kansas City 23
14—N.Y. Giants 9
16—Houston 20
20—San Diego 13
31—N.Y. Jets 30
36—Seattle 20
3—Oakland 9
14—Kansas City 31
21—Oakland 24
25—Seattle 17

**KANSAS CITY**
14—Oakland 27
16—Seattle 17
13—Cleveland 20
7—San Diego 24
31—Oakland 14
21—Houston 20
23—Denver 17
20—Detroit 17
24—Baltimore 31
31—Seattle 30
20—St. Louis 13
6—Cincinnati 20
31—Denver 14
16—Pittsburgh 21
38—Baltimore 28

**OAKLAND**
27—Kansas City 14
24—San Diego 30
24—Washington 21
7—Buffalo 24
17—Kansas City 31
38—San Diego 24
45—Pittsburgh 34
33—Seattle 14
16—Miami 14
28—Cincinnati 17
19—Seattle 17
9—Phila. 10
9—Denver 3
13—Dallas 19
24—Denver 21
33—N.Y. Giants 17

**SAN DIEGO**
34—Seattle 13
30—Oakland 24
30—Denver 16
24—Kansas City 7
24—Buffalo 26
44—N.Y. Giants 7
31—Dallas 42
31—Cincinnati 14
13—Denver 20
20—Kansas City 7
27—Miami 24
21—Phila. 22
17—Washington 40
14—Seattle 0
26—Pittsburgh 17

**SEATTLE**
13—San Diego 34
17—Kansas City 16
31—N. England 37
14—Washington 0
26—Houston 7
3—Cleveland 27
27—N.Y. Jets 17
14—Oakland 33
20—Phila. 27
30—Kansas City 31
4—Oakland 19
20—Denver 36
7—Dallas 51
21—N.Y. Giants 27
14—San Diego 0
25—Denver 17

# NATIONAL FOOTBALL LEAGUE TOP PLAYERS: 1979

## TOP PASSERS (168 or more attempts)

### AMERICAN CONFERENCE

| | ATTEMPTS | COMPLETIONS | | AVERAGE GAIN | TOUCHDOWNS | | INTERCEPTIONS | | RATING [1] |
|---|---|---|---|---|---|---|---|---|---|
| | | Total | Pct. | Yards | | Total | Pct. | Total | Pct. | |
| Dan Fouts, San Diego .. | 530 | 332 | 62.6 | 4,082 | 7.70 | 24 | 4.5 | 24 | 4.5 | 82.6 |
| Ken Stabler, Oakland ... | 498 | 304 | 61.0 | 3,615 | 7.26 | 26 | 5.2 | 22 | 4.4 | 82.2 |
| Ken Anderson, Cincinnati | 339 | 189 | 55.8 | 2,340 | 6.90 | 16 | 4.7 | 10 | 2.9 | 80.9 |
| Jim Zorn, Seattle....... | 505 | 285 | 56.4 | 3,661 | 7.25 | 20 | 4.0 | 18 | 3.6 | 77.6 |
| Steve Grogan, New Eng. . | 423 | 206 | 48.7 | 3,286 | 7.77 | 28 | 6.6 | 20 | 4.7 | 77.5 |
| Terry Bradshaw, Pitt. ... | 472 | 259 | 54.9 | 3,724 | 7.89 | 26 | 5.5 | 25 | 5.3 | 77.0 |
| Greg Landry, Baltimore . | 457 | 270 | 59.1 | 2,932 | 6.42 | 15 | 3.3 | 15 | 3.3 | 75.3 |
| Joe Ferguson, Buffalo .. | 458 | 238 | 52.0 | 3,572 | 7.80 | 14 | 3.1 | 15 | 3.3 | 74.5 |

### NATIONAL CONFERENCE

| | ATTEMPTS | COMPLETIONS | | AVERAGE GAIN | TOUCHDOWNS | | INTERCEPTIONS | | RATING [1] |
|---|---|---|---|---|---|---|---|---|---|
| | | Total | Pct. | Yards | | Total | Pct. | Total | Pct. | |
| Roger Staubach, Dallas .. | 461 | 267 | 57.9 | 3,586 | 7.78 | 27 | 5.9 | 11 | 2.4 | 92.4 |
| Joe Theismann, Wash. .. | 395 | 233 | 59.0 | 2,797 | 7.08 | 20 | 5.1 | 13 | 3.3 | 84.0 |
| Ron Jaworski, Phil. ...... | 374 | 190 | 50.8 | 2,669 | 7.14 | 18 | 4.8 | 12 | 3.2 | 76.8 |
| Archie Manning, N.O. .... | 420 | 252 | 60.0 | 3,169 | 7.55 | 15 | 3.6 | 20 | 4.8 | 75.6 |
| Steve DeBerg, San. Fran. . | 578 | 347 | 60.0 | 3,652 | 6.32 | 17 | 2.9 | 21 | 3.6 | 73.1 |
| Tommy Kramer, Minn... | 566 | 315 | 55.7 | 3,397 | 6.00 | 23 | 4.1 | 24 | 4.2 | 69.7 |
| Mike Phipps, Chicago... | 255 | 134 | 52.5 | 1,535 | 6.02 | 9 | 3.5 | 8 | 3.1 | 69.7 |
| Pat Haden, Los Angeles .. | 290 | 163 | 56.2 | 1,854 | 6.39 | 11 | 3.8 | 14 | 4.8 | 68.2 |

[1] NFL combined rating points awarded for percent of completions, TDs, interceptions, and average gain.

## AMERICAN CONFERENCE

### TOP RECEIVERS

| | COMPLETIONS | | | TDs |
|---|---|---|---|---|
| | No. | Yards | Avg. | |
| Joe Washington, Balt. .... | 82 | 750 | 9.1 | 3 |
| Charlie Joiner, S.D. ..... | 72 | 1,008 | 14.0 | 4 |
| John Stallworth, Pitt. .... | 70 | 1,183 | 16.9 | 8 |
| Steve Largent, Seattle ... | 66 | 1,237 | 18.7 | 9 |
| Rick Upchurch, Denver .. | 64 | 937 | 14.6 | 7 |
| John Jefferson, S.D. .... | 61 | 1,090 | 17.9 | 10 |
| Dave Logan, Cleveland .. | 59 | 982 | 16.6 | 7 |
| Cliff Branch, Oakland ... | 59 | 844 | 14.3 | 6 |

### TOP SCORERS

| | TDs | X PTs | FGs | TOTAL |
|---|---|---|---|---|
| John Smith, New. Eng. .. | 0 | 46 | 23 | 115 |
| Earl Campbell, Houston . | 19 | 0 | 0 | 114 |
| Matt Bahr, Pittsburgh ... | 0 | 50 | 18 | 104 |
| Toni Fritsch, Houston ... | 0 | 41 | 21 | 104 |
| Efren Herrera, Seattle... | 0 | 43 | 19 | 100 |
| Uwe von Schamann, Mia. . | 0 | 36 | 21 | 99 |
| Jim Breech, Oakland.... | 0 | 41 | 18 | 95 |
| Pete Johnson, Cin. ..... | 15 | 0 | 0 | 90 |
| Sherman Smith, Seattle . | 15 | 0 | 0 | 90 |

### TOP RUSHERS

| | YARDS | AVG. | TDs |
|---|---|---|---|
| Earl Campbell, Houston .. | 1,697 | 4.6 | 19 |
| Mike Pruitt, Cleveland ...... | 1,294 | 4.9 | 9 |
| Franco Harris, Pittsburgh ... | 1,186 | 4.4 | 11 |
| Clark Gaines, N.Y. Jets ... | 905 | 4.9 | 0 |
| Joe Washington, Baltimore.. | 884 | 3.7 | 4 |
| Pete Johnson, Cinn. ....... | 865 | 3.6 | 14 |
| Larry Csonka, Miami ...... | 837 | 3.8 | 12 |
| Mark van Eeghen, Oakland . | 818 | 3.7 | 7 |

### TOP PUNTERS

| | NO. | YARDS | AVG. |
|---|---|---|---|
| Bob Grupp, Kansas City .... | 90 | 3,883 | 43.6 |
| Ray Guy, Oakland.......... | 70 | 2,939 | 42.6 |
| Pat McInally, Cincinnati..... | 91 | 3,678 | 41.3 |
| Johnny Evans, Cleveland ... | 71 | 2,844 | 41.2 |
| Chuck Ramsey, N.Y. Jets ... | 73 | 2,979 | 40.8 |
| Cliff Parsley, Houston ...... | 93 | 3,777 | 40.6 |
| Craig Colquitt, Pittsburgh... | 68 | 2,733 | 40.2 |
| George Roberts, Miami .... | 70 | 2,772 | 40.2 |

### PASS INTERCEPTORS

| | TOTAL | YARDS | AVG. |
|---|---|---|---|
| Mike Reinfeldt, Houston .... | 12 | 205 | 17.1 |
| Gary Barbaro, Kan. City .... | 7 | 142 | 20.3 |
| Lester Hayes, Oakland ..... | 7 | 100 | 14.3 |
| J.C. Wilson, Houston ....... | 6 | 135 | 22.5 |
| Jeff Nixon, Buffalo.......... | 6 | 81 | 13.5 |
| Dick Jauron, Cincinnati..... | 6 | 41 | 6.8 |
| Burgess Owens, N.Y. Jets .. | 6 | 41 | 6.8 |
| Jack Lambert, Pittsburgh ... | 6 | 29 | 4.8 |

## NATIONAL CONFERENCE

### TOP RECEIVERS

| | COMPLETIONS | | | TDs |
|---|---|---|---|---|
| | No. | Yards | Avg. | |
| Ahmad Rashad, Minn... | 80 | 1,156 | 14.5 | 9 |
| Wallace Francis, Atlanta . | 74 | 1,013 | 13.7 | 8 |
| Rickey Young, Minn. .... | 72 | 519 | 7.2 | 4 |
| Wes Chandler, N.O. ..... | 65 | 1,069 | 16.4 | 6 |
| Freddie Scott, Detroit ... | 62 | 929 | 15.0 | 5 |
| Tony Hill, Dallas ....... | 60 | 1,062 | 17.7 | 10 |
| Paul Hofer, San. Fran. .. | 58 | 662 | 11.4 | 2 |
| Tony Galbreath, N.O..... | 58 | 484 | 8.3 | 1 |

### TOP SCORERS

| | TDs | X PTs | FGs | TOTAL |
|---|---|---|---|---|
| Mark Moseley, Washington | 0 | 39 | 25 | 114 |
| Tony Franklin, Philadelphia | 0 | 36 | 23 | 105 |
| Rafael Septien, Dallas ... | 0 | 40 | 19 | 97 |
| Walter Payton, Chicago ... | 16 | 0 | 0 | 96 |
| Ray Wersching, San. Fran.. | 0 | 32 | 20 | 92 |
| Wilbert Montgomery, Phil. | 14 | 0 | 0 | 84 |
| Bob Thomas, Chicago.... | 0 | 34 | 16 | 82 |
| Frank Corral, L.A. ...... | 0 | 36 | 13 | 75 |
| Garo Yepremian, N.O. .... | 0 | 39 | 12 | 75 |

### TOP RUSHERS

| | YARDS | AVG. | TDs |
|---|---|---|---|
| Walter Payton, Chicago........ | 1,610 | 4.4 | 14 |
| Ottis Anderson, St. Louis ... | 1,605 | 4.8 | 8 |
| Wilbert Montgomery, Phil. .. | 1,512 | 4.5 | 9 |
| Ricky Bell, Tampa Bay ..... | 1,263 | 4.5 | 7 |
| Chuck Muncie, New Orleans . | 1,198 | 5.0 | 11 |
| John Riggin, Washington ... | 1,153 | 4.4 | 9 |
| Wendell Tyler, Los Angeles . | 1,109 | 5.1 | 9 |
| Tony Dorsett, Dallas ........ | 1,107 | 4.4 | 6 |

### TOP PUNTERS

| | NO. | YARDS | AVG. |
|---|---|---|---|
| Dave Jennings, N.Y. Giants . | 104 | 4,445 | 42.7 |
| Danny White, Dallas ....... | 76 | 3,168 | 41.7 |
| Rick Partridge, New Orleans | 57 | 2,330 | 40.9 |
| David Beverly, Green Bay... | 69 | 2,785 | 40.4 |
| Ken Clark, Los Angeles .... | 95 | 3,731 | 40.1 |
| Larry Swider, Detroit ....... | 88 | 3,523 | 40.0 |
| John James, Atlanta ....... | 84 | 3,296 | 39.7 |
| Tom Blanchard, Tampa Bay . | 95 | 3,679 | 39.6 |

### PASS INTERCEPTORS

| | TOTAL | YARDS | AVG. |
|---|---|---|---|
| Lemar Parrish, Washington . | 9 | 65 | 7.2 |
| Tom Myers, New Orleans . | 7 | 127 | 18.1 |
| Rolland Lawrence, Atlanta . | 6 | 120 | 20.0 |
| Joe Lavender, Washington .. | 6 | 77 | 12.8 |
| Ken Stone, St. Louis ....... | 6 | 70 | 11.7 |
| Terry Schmidt, Chicago .... | 6 | 44 | 7.3 |
| Gary Fencik, Chicago....... | 6 | 31 | 5.2 |
| Carl Allen, St. Louis........ | 5 | 126 | 25.2 |

## STARS OF THE NATIONAL FOOTBALL LEAGUE

### LEADING PASSERS

| Year | Player | A[1] | C[2] | YG[3] | Year | Player | A[1] | C[2] | YG[3] |
|---|---|---|---|---|---|---|---|---|---|
| 1944 | Frank Filchock, Washington | 147 | 84 | 1,139 | 1962 | Bart Starr, Green Bay ..... | 285 | 178 | 2,438 |
| 1945 | Sammy Baugh, Washington | 182 | 128 | 1,669 | 1963 | Y.A. Tittle, New York ...... | 367 | 221 | 3,145 |
| 1946 | Bob Waterfield, Los Angeles | 251 | 127 | 1,747 | 1964 | Bart Starr, Green Bay ..... | 272 | 163 | 2,144 |
| 1947 | Sammy Baugh, Washington. | 354 | 121 | 2,938 | 1965 | Rudy Bukich, Chicago Bears | 312 | 176 | 2,641 |
| 1948 | Tom Thompson, Philadelphia | 246 | 141 | 1,965 | 1966 | Bart Starr, Green Bay ..... | 251 | 156 | 2,257 |
| 1949 | Sammy Baugh, Washington. | 255 | 145 | 1,903 | 1967 | Sonny Jurgensen, Washington | 508 | 288 | 3,747 |
| 1950 | Norm Van Brocklin, L.A. ... | 233 | 127 | 2,061 | 1968 | Earl Morrall, Baltimore..... | 317 | 182 | 2,909 |
| 1951 | Bob Waterfield, L.A. ....... | 176 | 88 | 1,556 | 1969 | Sonny Jurgensen, Washington | 442 | 274 | 3,102 |
| 1952 | Norm Van Brocklin, L.A. ... | 205 | 113 | 1,736 | 1970 | John Brodie, San Francisco | 378 | 223 | 2,941 |
| 1953 | Otto Graham, Cleveland.... | 258 | 167 | 2,722 | 1971 | Bob Griese, Miami......... | 263 | 145 | 2,089 |
| 1954 | Norm Van Brocklin, L.A. ... | 260 | 139 | 2,637 | 1972 | Norm Snead, N.Y. Giants ... | 325 | 196 | 2,307 |
| 1955 | Otto Graham, Cleveland.... | 185 | 98 | 1,721 | 1973 | Roger Staubach, Dallas ... | 286 | 179 | 2,428 |
| 1956 | Ed Brown, Chicago Bears .. | 168 | 96 | 1,667 | 1974 | Ken Anderson, Cincinnati .. | 328 | 213 | 2,667 |
| 1957 | Tom O'Connell, Cleveland .. | 110 | 63 | 1,229 | 1975 | Ken Anderson, Cincinnati .. | 377 | 228 | 3,169 |
| 1958 | Eddie LeBaron, Washington | 145 | 79 | 1,365 | 1976 | Ken Stabler, Oakland ..... | 291 | 194 | 2,737 |
| 1959 | Charley Conerly, New York . | 194 | 113 | 1,706 | 1977 | Bob Griese, Miami......... | 307 | 180 | 2,252 |
| 1960 | Milt Plum, Cleveland....... | 250 | 151 | 2,297 | 1978 | Roger Staubach, Dallas .... | 413 | 231 | 3,190 |
| 1961 | Milt Plum, Cleveland....... | 302 | 177 | 2,416 | 1979 | Roger Staubach, Dallas .... | 461 | 267 | 3,586 |

### LEADING PASS RECEIVERS

| Year | Player | PASSES RECEIVED | Year | Player | PASSES RECEIVED |
|---|---|---|---|---|---|
| 1944 | Don Hutson, Green Bay .......... | 58 | 1961 | Jim Phillips, Los Angeles .......... | 78 |
| 1945 | Don Hutson, Green Bay .......... | 47 | 1962 | Bobby Mitchell, Washington ...... | 72 |
| 1946 | Jim Benton, Los Angeles ........ | 63 | 1963 | Bobby Joe Conrad, St. Louis....... | 73 |
| 1947 | Jim Keane, Chicago Bears ........ | 64 | 1964 | Johnny Morris, Chicago Bears ..... | 93 |
| 1948 | Tom Fears, Los Angeles .......... | 51 | 1965 | Dave Parks, San Francisco ....... | 80 |
| 1949 | Tom Fears, Los Angeles .......... | 77 | 1966 | Charles Taylor, Washington ....... | 72 |
| 1950 | Tom Fears, Los Angeles .......... | 84 | 1967 | Charles Taylor, Washington ....... | 70 |
| 1951 | Elroy Hirsch, Los Angeles ....... | 66 | 1968 | Clifton Mcneil, San Francisco ...... | 71 |
| 1952 | Mac Speedie, Cleveland ......... | 62 | 1969 | Dan Abramowicz, New Orleans .... | 73 |
| 1953 | Pete Pihos, Philadelphia ........ | 63 | 1970 | Dick Gordon, Chicago ........... | 71 |
| 1954 | Pete Pihos, Philadelphia (tie) .... | 60 | 1971 | Fred Biletnikoff, Oakland ........ | 61 |
|  | Billy Wilson, San Francisco (tie).... | 60 | 1972 | Harold Jackson, Philadelphia ...... | 62 |
| 1955 | Pete Pihos, Philadelphia ........ | 62 | 1973 | Harold Carmichael, Philadelphia.... | 67 |
| 1956 | Billy Wilson, San Francisco ...... | 60 | 1974 | Lydell Mitchell, Baltimore ........ | 72 |
| 1957 | Billy Wilson, San Francisco ...... | 52 | 1975 | Chuck Foreman, Minnesota ...... | 73 |
| 1958 | Ray Berry, Baltimore (tie) ........ | 56 | 1976 | MacArthur Lane, Kansas City ...... | 66 |
|  | Pete Retzlaff, Philadelphia (tie) .... | 56 | 1977 | Lydell Mitchell, Baltimore ........ | 71 |
| 1959 | Ray Berry, Baltimore ........... | 66 | 1978 | Rickey Young, Minnesota ......... | 88 |
| 1960 | Ray Berry, Baltimore........... | 74 | 1979 | Joe Washington, Baltimore ....... | 82 |

### RUSHING LEADERS

| Year | Player | YARDS GAINED | Year | Player | YARDS GAINED |
|---|---|---|---|---|---|
| 1944 | Bill Paschal, New York ........... | 737 | 1962 | Jim Taylor, Green Bay ........... | 1,474 |
| 1945 | Steve Van Buren, Philadelphia ..... | 832 | 1963 | Jim Brown, Cleveland ........... | 1,863 |
| 1946 | Bill Dudley, Pittsburgh .......... | 604 | 1964 | Jim Brown, Cleveland ........... | 1,446 |
| 1947 | Steve Van Buren, Philadelphia ..... | 1,008 | 1965 | Jim Brown, Cleveland ........... | 1,544 |
| 1948 | Steve Van Buren, Philadelphia ..... | 845 | 1966 | Gale Sayers, Chicago Bears........ | 1,231 |
| 1949 | Steve Van Buren, Philadelphia ..... | 1,146 | 1967 | Leroy Kelly, Cleveland .......... | 1,205 |
| 1950 | Marion Motley, Cleveland ........ | 810 | 1968 | Leroy Kelly, Cleveland .......... | 1,239 |
| 1951 | Eddie Price, New York ........... | 971 | 1969 | Gale Sayers, Chicago............ | 1,032 |
| 1952 | Dan Towler, Los Angeles ........ | 894 | 1970 | Larry Brown, Washington ........ | 1,125 |
| 1953 | Joe Perry, San Francisco ........ | 1,018 | 1971 | Floyd Little, Denver ............ | 1,133 |
| 1954 | Joe Perry, San Francisco ........ | 1,049 | 1972 | O.J. Simpson, Buffalo .......... | 1,251 |
| 1955 | Alan Ameche, Baltimore ......... | 961 | 1973 | O.J. Simpson, Buffalo .......... | 2,003[4] |
| 1956 | Rick Casares, Chicago Bears....... | 1,126 | 1974 | Otis Armstrong, Denver .......... | 1,407 |
| 1957 | Jim Brown, Cleveland .......... | 942 | 1975 | O.J. Simpson, Buffalo .......... | 1,817 |
| 1958 | Jim Brown, Cleveland ........... | 1,527 | 1976 | O.J. Simpson, Buffalo .......... | 1,503 |
| 1959 | Jim Brown, Cleveland ........... | 1,329 | 1977 | Walter Payton, Chicago.......... | 1,852 |
| 1960 | Jim Brown, Cleveland ........... | 1,257 | 1978 | Earl Campbell, Houston ......... | 1,450 |
| 1961 | Jim Brown, Cleveland ........... | 1,408 | 1979 | Earl Campbell, Houston ......... | 1,697 |

### SCORING LEADERS

| Year | Player | POINTS | Year | Player | POINTS |
|---|---|---|---|---|---|
| 1943 | Don Hutson, Green Bay .......... | 117 | 1953 | Gordon Soltau, San Francisco...... | 114 |
| 1944 | Don Hutson, Green Bay .......... | 85 | 1954 | Bob Walston, Philadelphia ........ | 114 |
| 1945 | Steve Van Buren, Philadelphia ..... | 110 | 1955 | Doak Walker, Detroit............. | 96 |
| 1946 | Ted Fritsch, Green Bay........... | 100 | 1956 | Bobby Layne, Detroit............ | 99 |
| 1947 | Pat Harder, Chicago Cardinals ..... | 102 | 1957 | Sam Baker, Washington .......... | 77 |
| 1948 | Pat Harder, Chicago Cardinals ..... | 110 |  | Lou Groza, Cleveland ........... | 77 |
| 1949 | Pat Harder, Chi., Gene Roberts, N.Y... | 102 | 1958 | Jimmy Brown, Cleveland ......... | 108 |
| 1950 | Doak Walker, Detroit............. | 128 | 1959 | Paul Hornung, Green Bay ........ | 94 |
| 1951 | Elroy Hirsch, Los Angeles ........ | 102 | 1960 | Paul Hornung, Green Bay ........ | 176[4] |
| 1952 | Gordon Soltau, San Francisco...... | 94 | 1961 | Paul Hornung, Green Bay ........ | 146 |

[1] Attempts.    [2] Completions.    [3] Yards gained.    [4] Record.

## SCORING LEADERS *(continued)*

| YEAR | PLAYER | POINTS |
|------|--------|--------|
| 1962 | Jim Taylor, Green Bay | 114 |
| 1963 | Don Chandler, New York | 106 |
| 1964 | Lenny Moore, Baltimore | 128 |
| 1965 | Gale Sayers, Chicago | 132 |
| 1966 | Bruce Gossett, Los Angeles | 120 |
| 1967 | Jim Bakken, St. Louis | 132 |
| 1968 | Leroy Kelly, Cleveland | 113 |
| 1969 | Fred Cox, Minnesota | 117 |
| 1970 | Fred Cox, Minnesota | 120 |

| YEAR | PLAYER | POINTS |
|------|--------|--------|
| 1971 | Garo Yepremian, Miami | 121 |
| 1972 | Chester Marcol, Green Bay | 125 |
| 1973 | David Ray, Los Angeles | 130 |
| 1974 | Chester Marcol, Green Bay | 94 |
| 1975 | O.J. Simpson, Buffalo | 138 |
| 1976 | Toni Linhart, Baltimore | 109 |
| 1977 | Errol Mann, Oakland | 99 |
| 1978 | Frank Corral, Los Angeles | 118 |
| 1979 | John Smith, New England | 115 |

## TOP NFL COLLEGE DRAFT CHOICES: 1979

| NUMBER | PLAYER | POSITION | FROM SCHOOL | TO PRO TEAM |
|--------|--------|----------|-------------|-------------|
| 1 | Billy Sims | Running Back | Oklahoma | Detroit |
| 2 | Johnny (Lam) Jones | Wide Receiver | Texas | New York Jets |
| 3 | Anthony Munoz | Offensive Tackle | Southern California | Cincinnati |
| 4 | Bruce Clark | Defensive Tackle | Penn State | Green Bay |
| 5 | Curtis Dickey | Running Back | Texas A & M | Baltimore |
| 6 | Curtis Greer | Defensive Tackle | Michigan | St. Louis |
| 7 | Junior Miller | Tight End | Nebraska | Atlanta |
| 8 | Mark Haynes | Defensive Back | Colorado | New York Giants |
| 9 | Doug Martin | Defensive Tackle | Washington | Minnesota |
| 10 | Jacob Green | Defensive End | Texas A & M | Seattle |
| 11 | Brad Budde | Guard | Southern California | Kansas City |
| 12 | Stan Brock | Offensive Tackle | Colorado | New Orleans |

## NO. 1 NFL DRAFT CHOICES: 1963–1979

| YEAR | CLUB | PLAYER | POSITION | SCHOOL |
|------|------|--------|----------|--------|
| 1963 | Kansas City Chiefs (AFL) | Buck Buchanan | Tackle | Grambling |
| 1963 | Los Angeles Rams (NFL) | Terry Baker | Quarterback | Oregon State |
| 1964 | Denver Broncos (AFL) | Bob Brown | Tackle | Nebraska |
| 1964 | San Francisco 49ers (NFL) | Dave Parks | End | Texas Tech |
| 1965 | New York Jets (AFL) | Joe Namath | Quarterback | Alabama |
| 1965 | New York Giants (NFL) | Tucker Frederickson | Running Back | Auburn |
| 1966 | Miami Dolphins (AFL) | Jim Grabowski | Running Back | Illinois |
| 1966 | Atlanta Falcons (NFL) | Tommy Nobis | Line Backer | Texas |
| 1967 | Baltimore Colts | Bubba Smith | Tackle | Michigan State |
| 1968 | Minnesota Vikings | Ron Yary | Tackle | Southern California |
| 1969 | Buffalo Bills | O.J. Simpson | Running Back | Southern California |
| 1970 | Pittsburgh Steelers | Terry Bradshaw | Quarterback | Louisiana Tech |
| 1971 | New England Patriots | Jim Plunkett | Quarterback | Stanford |
| 1972 | Buffalo Bills | Walt Patulski | Defensive End | Notre Dame |
| 1973 | Houston Oilers | John Matuszak | Defensive End | Tampa |
| 1974 | Dallas Cowboys | Ed Jones | Defensive End | Tennessee State |
| 1975 | Atlanta Falcons | Steve Bartkowski | Quarterback | California |
| 1976 | Tampa Bay Buccaneers | Leroy Selmon | Defensive End | Oklahoma |
| 1977 | Tampa Bay Buccaneers | Ricky Bell | Running Back | Southern California |
| 1978 | Houston Oilers | Earl Campbell | Running Back | Texas |
| 1979 | Buffalo Bills | Tom Cousineau | Line Backer | Ohio State |
| 1980 | Detroit Lions | Billy Sims | Running Back | Oklahoma |

## NATIONAL FOOTBALL LEAGUE STADIUMS

### NATIONAL CONFERENCE

| TEAM | STADIUM | SEATING |
|------|---------|---------|
| Atlanta Falcons | Atlanta Stadium | 60,498 |
| Chicago Bears | Soldier Field | 58,064 |
| Dallas Cowboys | Texas Stadium | 65,101 |
| Detroit Lions | Pontiac Silverdome | 80,638 |
| Green Bay Packers | Lambeau Field & | 56,194 |
|  | Milwaukee Co. Stadium | 55,958 |
| Los Angeles Rams | Anaheim Stadium | 69,000 |
| Minnesota Vikings | Metropolitan Stadium | 48,446 |
| New Orleans Saints | Louisiana Superdome | 71,330 |
| New York Giants | Giants Stadium, N.J. | 76,500 |
| Philadelphia Eagles | Veterans Stadium | 71,434 |
| St. Louis Cardinals | Civic Center Busch | |
|  | Memorial Stadium | 51,392 |
| San Francisco 49ers | Candlestick Park | 61,185 |
| Tampa Bay Buccaneers | Tampa Stadium | 72,112 |
| Washington Redskins | Robert F. Kennedy | |
|  | Stadium | 55,045 |

### AMERICAN CONFERENCE

| TEAM | STADIUM | SEATING |
|------|---------|---------|
| Baltimore Colts | Memorial Stadium | 60,020 |
| Buffalo Bills | Rich Stadium | 80,020 |
| Cincinnati Bengals | Riverfront Stadium | 59,754 |
| Cleveland Browns | Cleveland Stadium | 80,385 |
| Denver Broncos | Denver Mile High | |
|  | Stadium | 75,103 |
| Houston Oilers | Astrodome | 50,000 |
| Kansas City Chiefs | Arrowhead Stadium | 78,094 |
| Miami Dolphins | Orange Bowl | 75,250 |
| New England Patriots | Schaefer Stadium, | |
|  | Foxboro, Mass. | 61,297 |
| New York Jets | Shea Stadium | 60,372 |
| Oakland Raiders | Oakland-Alameda | |
|  | County Coliseum | 54,615 |
| Pittsburgh Steelers | Three Rivers Stadium | 54,000 |
| San Diego Chargers | San Diego Stadium | 52,660 |
| Seattle Seahawks | Kingdome | 64,757 |

## NATIONAL FOOTBALL LEAGUE CONFERENCE CHAMPIONS

| YEAR | EASTERN CONFERENCE | W | L | T | YEAR | WESTERN CONFERENCE | W | L | T |
|------|--------------------|---|---|---|------|--------------------|---|---|---|
| 1936 | Boston Redskins | 7 | 5 | 0 | 1936 | Green Bay Packers | 10 | 1 | 1 |
| 1937 | Washington Redskins | 8 | 3 | 0 | 1937 | Chicago Bears | 9 | 1 | 1 |
| 1938 | New York Giants | 8 | 2 | 1 | 1938 | Green Bay Packers | 8 | 3 | 0 |
| 1939 | New York Giants | 9 | 1 | 1 | 1939 | Green Bay Packers | 9 | 2 | 0 |
| 1940 | Washington Redskins | 9 | 2 | 0 | 1940 | Chicago Bears | 8 | 3 | 0 |
| 1941 | New York Giants | 8 | 3 | 0 | 1941 | Chicago Bears | 10 | 1 | 1 |
| 1942 | Washington Redskins | 10 | 1 | 1 | 1942 | Chicago Bears | 11 | 0 | 0 |
| 1943 | Washington Redskins | 6 | 3 | 1 | 1943 | Chicago Bears | 8 | 1 | 1 |
| 1944 | New York Giants | 8 | 1 | 1 | 1944 | Green Bay Packers | 8 | 2 | 0 |
| 1945 | Washington Redskins | 8 | 2 | 0 | 1945 | Cleveland Rams | 9 | 1 | 0 |
| 1946 | New York Giants | 7 | 3 | 1 | 1946 | Chicago Bears | 8 | 2 | 1 |
| 1947 | Philadelphia Eagles | 8 | 4 | 0 | 1947 | Chicago Cardinals | 9 | 3 | 0 |
| 1948 | Philadelphia Eagles | 9 | 2 | 1 | 1948 | Chicago Cardinals | 11 | 1 | 0 |
| 1949 | Philadelphia Eagles | 11 | 1 | 0 | 1949 | Los Angeles Rams | 8 | 2 | 2 |
| 1950 | Cleveland Browns | 10 | 2 | 0 | 1950 | Los Angeles Rams | 9 | 3 | 0 |
| 1951 | Cleveland Browns | 11 | 1 | 0 | 1951 | Los Angeles Rams | 8 | 4 | 0 |
| 1952 | Cleveland Browns | 8 | 4 | 0 | 1952 | Detroit Lions | 9 | 3 | 0 |
| 1953 | Cleveland Browns | 11 | 1 | 0 | 1953 | Detroit Lions | 10 | 2 | 0 |
| 1954 | Cleveland Browns | 9 | 3 | 0 | 1954 | Detroit Lions | 9 | 2 | 1 |
| 1955 | Cleveland Browns | 9 | 2 | 1 | 1955 | Los Angeles Rams | 8 | 3 | 1 |
| 1956 | New York Giants | 8 | 3 | 1 | 1956 | Chicago Bears | 9 | 2 | 1 |
| 1957 | Cleveland Browns | 9 | 2 | 1 | 1957 | Detroit Lions | 8 | 4 | 0 |
| 1958 | New York Giants | 9 | 3 | 0 | 1958 | Baltimore Colts | 9 | 3 | 0 |
| 1959 | New York Giants | 10 | 2 | 0 | 1959 | Baltimore Colts | 9 | 3 | 0 |
| 1960 | Philadelphia Eagles | 10 | 2 | 0 | 1960 | Green Bay Packers | 8 | 4 | 0 |
| 1961 | New York Giants | 10 | 3 | 1 | 1961 | Green Bay Packers | 11 | 3 | 0 |
| 1962 | New York Giants | 12 | 2 | 0 | 1962 | Green Bay Packers | 13 | 1 | 0 |
| 1963 | New York Giants | 11 | 3 | 0 | 1963 | Chicago Bears | 11 | 1 | 2 |
| 1964 | Cleveland Browns | 10 | 3 | 1 | 1964 | Baltimore Colts | 12 | 2 | 0 |
| 1965 | Cleveland Browns | 11 | 3 | 0 | 1965 | Green Bay Packers | 10 | 3 | 1 |
| 1966 | Dallas Cowboys | 10 | 3 | 1 | 1966 | Green Bay Packers | 12 | 2 | 0 |
| 1967 | Dallas Cowboys | 9 | 5 | 0 | 1967 | Green Bay Packers | 9 | 4 | 1 |
| 1968 | Cleveland Browns | 10 | 4 | 0 | 1968 | Baltimore Colts | 13 | 1 | 0 |
| 1969 | Cleveland Browns | 10 | 3 | 1 | 1969 | Minnesota Vikings | 12 | 2 | 0 |
| | AMERICAN CONFERENCE [1] | | | | | NATIONAL CONFERENCE [1] | | | |
| 1970 | Baltimore Colts | 11 | 2 | 1 | 1970 | Dallas Cowboys | 10 | 4 | 0 |
| 1971 | Miami Dolphins | 10 | 3 | 1 | 1971 | Dallas Cowboys | 11 | 3 | 0 |
| 1972 | Miami Dolphins | 14 | 0 | 0 | 1972 | Washington Redskins | 11 | 3 | 0 |
| 1973 | Miami Dolphins | 12 | 2 | 0 | 1973 | Minnesota Vikings | 12 | 2 | 0 |
| 1974 | Pittsburgh Steelers | 10 | 3 | 1 | 1974 | Minnesota Vikings | 10 | 4 | 0 |
| 1975 | Pittsburgh Steelers | 12 | 2 | 0 | 1975 | Dallas Cowboys | 10 | 4 | 0 |
| 1976 | Oakland Raiders | 13 | 1 | 0 | 1976 | Minnesota Vikings | 11 | 2 | 1 |
| 1977 | Denver Broncos | 12 | 2 | 0 | 1977 | Dallas Cowboys | 12 | 2 | 0 |
| 1978 | Pittsburgh Steelers | 14 | 2 | 0 | 1978 | Dallas Cowboys | 12 | 4 | 0 |
| 1979 | Pittsburgh Steelers | 12 | 4 | 0 | 1979 | Los Angeles Rams | 9 | 7 | 0 |

[1] NFL reorganization in 1970 (records exclude playoff games).

## DIVISIONAL CHAMPIONSHIP PLAYOFF GAMES

**AMERICAN FOOTBALL CONFERENCE**        **NATIONAL FOOTBALL CONFERENCE**

| Season | Winner | Loser | Score | Site | Winner | Loser | Score | Site |
|--------|--------|-------|-------|------|--------|-------|-------|------|
| 1960 | Houston | San Diego | 24–16 | Houston | Philadelphia | Green Bay | 17–13 | Philadelphia |
| 1961 | Houston | San Diego | 10–3 | San Diego | Green Bay | N.Y. Giants | 37–0 | Green Bay |
| 1962 | Dallas | Houston | 20–17 | Houston | Green Bay | N.Y. Giants | 16–7 | New York |
| 1963 | San Diego | New England | 51–10 | San Diego | Chicago | N.Y. Giants | 14–10 | Chicago |
| 1964 | Buffalo | San Diego | 20–7 | Buffalo | Cleveland | Baltimore | 27–10 | Cleveland |
| 1965 | Buffalo | San Diego | 23–0 | San Diego | Green Bay | Cleveland | 23–12 | Green Bay |
| 1966 | Kansas City | Buffalo | 31–7 | Buffalo | Green Bay | Dallas | 34–27 | Dallas |
| 1967 | Oakland | Houston | 40–7 | Oakland | Green Bay | Dallas | 21–17 | Green Bay |
| 1968 | N.Y. Jets | Oakland | 27–23 | New York | Baltimore | Cleveland | 34–0 | Cleveland |
| 1969 | Kansas City | Oakland | 17–7 | Oakland | Minnesota | Cleveland | 27–7 | Minnesota |
| 1970 | Baltimore | Oakland | 21–17 | Baltimore | Dallas | San Francisco | 17–10 | San Francisco |
| 1971 | Miami | Baltimore | 21–0 | Miami | Dallas | San Francisco | 14–3 | Dallas |
| 1972 | Miami | Pittsburgh | 21–17 | Pittsburgh | Washington | Dallas | 25–3 | Washington |
| 1973 | Miami | Oakland | 27–10 | Miami | Minnesota | Dallas | 27–10 | Dallas |
| 1974 | Pittsburgh | Oakland | 24–13 | Oakland | Minnesota | Los Angeles | 14–10 | Minnesota |
| 1975 | Pittsburgh | Oakland | 16–10 | Pittsburgh | Dallas | Los Angeles | 37–7 | Los Angeles |
| 1976 | Oakland | Pittsburgh | 24–7 | Oakland | Minnesota | Los Angeles | 24–13 | Minnesota |
| 1977 | Denver | Oakland | 20–17 | Denver | Dallas | Minnesota | 23–6 | Dallas |
| 1978 | Pittsburgh | Houston | 34–5 | Pittsburgh | Dallas | Los Angeles | 28–0 | Los Angeles |
| 1979 | Pittsburgh | Houston | 27–13 | Pittsburgh | Los Angeles | Tampa Bay | 9–0 | Tampa Bay |

## PRO FOOTBALL INDIVIDUAL ALL-TIME RECORDS

The records listed on this page do not include statistics from the 1980 season unless indicated, because those figures were incomplete when the *Reader's Digest Almanac* went to press.

### INDIVIDUAL RECORDS

**Seasons, active player:** 26, George Blanda (1949–75)
**Points, lifetime:** 2,002, George Blanda (1949–75), Chicago Bears, Baltimore, Houston, Oakland
**Points, season:** 176, Paul Hornung, Green Bay, (1960)—15 touchdowns, 41 points after touchdown, 15 field goals
**Points, one game:** 40, Ernie Nevers for Chicago Cardinals against Chicago Bears, Nov. 28, 1929—6 touchdowns and 4 points after touchdown
**Touchdowns, lifetime:** 126, Jim Brown, Cleveland (1957–65), 106 running, 20 on passes
**Touchdowns, season:** 23, O. J. Simpson, Buffalo Bills (1975), 16 running, 7 on passes
**Touchdowns, game:** 6, Ernie Nevers, Chicago Cardinals against Chicago Bears, Nov. 28, 1929
**Field goals, lifetime:** 335, George Blanda (1949–75), Chicago Bears, Baltimore, Houston, Oakland
**Field goals, season:** 34, Jim Turner, N.Y. Jets (1968)
**Field goals, one game:** 7, Jim Bakken for St. Louis against Pittsburgh, Sept. 24, 1967
**Field goal, longest:** 63 yards, Tom Dempsey for New Orleans against Detroit, Nov. 8, 1970
**Field goals, highest completion percentage, season:** 88.46, Lou Groza, Cleveland (1953)
**Rushing—most seasons leading league:** 8, Jim Brown, Cleveland (1957–61) and (1963–65)
**Rushing—most yards gained lifetime:** 12,312, Jim Brown, Cleveland (1957–65)
**Rushing—most yards gained, season:** 2,003, O. J. Simpson, Buffalo (1973)
**Rushing—most yards gained, game:** 275, Walter Payton for Chicago against Minnesota, Nov. 20, 1977
**Run, longest from scrimmage:** 97 yards for touchdown, by Andy Uram for Green Bay against Chicago Cardinals, Oct. 8, 1939.
**Touchdowns rushing, lifetime:** 106, Jim Brown, Cleveland (1957–65)
**Touchdowns rushing, season:** 19, Jim Taylor, Green Bay (1962)
**Touchdowns rushing, game:** 6, Ernie Nevers, Chicago Cardinals against Chicago Bears, Nov. 28, 1929
**Passing—most seasons leading league:** 6, Sammy Baugh, Washington (1937, '40, '43, '45, '47, '49)
**Passes completed, lifetime:** 3,686, Fran Tarkenton,
N.Y. Giants (1967–71), Minnesota (1961–66; 1972–78), 6,467 attempts
**Passes completed, season:** 347, Steve DeBerg, San Francisco (1979), 578 attempts
**Passes completed, game:** 42, Richard Todd for New York Jets against San Francisco 49ers, Sept. 21, 1980, 59 attempts
**Passes, most consecutive completed:** 17, Bert Jones for Baltimore against N.Y. Jets, Dec. 15, 1974
**Passing, most yards gained, career:** 47,003, Fran Tarkenton, N.Y. Giants (1967–71), Minnesota (1961–66; 1972–78)
**Passing, most yards gained, season:** 4,082, Dan Fouts, San Diego Chargers (1979).
**Touchdown passes, lifetime:** 342, Fran Tarkenton, N.Y. (1967–71), Minnesota (1961–66; 1972–78)
**Touchdown passes, season:** 36, George Blanda, Houston (1961).
**Touchdown passes, game:** 7, Sid Luckman for Chicago Bears against New York, Nov. 14, 1943.
**Pass receptions, lifetime:** 649, Charley Taylor, Washington (1964–75, 1977)
**Pass receptions, season:** 101, Charlie Hennigan, Houston (1964)
**Pass receptions, game:** 18, Tom Fears for Los Angeles against Green Bay, Dec. 3, 1950
**Pass interception return, longest:** 102 yards for touchdown, Bob Smith, Detroit against Chicago Bears, Nov. 24, 1949
**Punt, longest:** 98 yards by Steve O'Neal for New York Jets against Denver, Sept. 21, 1969
**Punting, highest average, lifetime:** 45.1 yards, Sammy Baugh, Washington (1937–52)
**Punting, highest average, season:** 51.4 yards, Sammy Baugh, Washington (1940)
**Punting, highest average, game (at least 4 punts):** 61.75, Bob Cifers, Detroit against Chicago Bears, Nov. 24, 1946
**Kickoff return, longest:** 106 yards for a touchdown, by Al Carmichael for Green Bay against Chicago, Oct. 7, 1956.
**Yards gained, lifetime:** 15,459 yards, Jim Brown, Cleveland (1957–65)
**Yards gained, season:** 2,462, Terry Metcalf, St. Louis (1975)

## NFL TOP PASSERS—LIFETIME [1]

| PLAYER | YEARS | ATTEMPTS | COMPLETIONS Total | COMPLETIONS Pct. | YARDS | TOUCHDOWNS Total | TOUCHDOWNS Pct. | INTERCEPTIONS Total | INTERCEPTIONS Pct. | AVERAGE GAIN | RATING |
|---|---|---|---|---|---|---|---|---|---|---|---|
| Roger Staubach... | 11 | 2,958 | 1,685 | 57.0 | 22,700 | 153 | 5.2 | 109 | 3.7 | 7.67 | 83.5 |
| Sonny Jurgenson . | 18 | 4,262 | 2,433 | 57.1 | 32,224 | 255 | 6.0 | 189 | 4.4 | 7.56 | 82.8 |
| Len Dawson ...... | 19 | 3,741 | 2,136 | 57.1 | 28,711 | 239 | 6.4 | 183 | 4.9 | 7.67 | 82.6 |
| Fran Tarkenton ... | 18 | 6,467 | 3,686 | 57.0 | 47,003 | 342 | 5.3 | 266 | 4.1 | 7.27 | 80.5 |
| Bert Jones ....... | 7 | 1,592 | 890 | 55.9 | 11,435 | 78 | 4.9 | 56 | 3.5 | 7.18 | 80.3 |
| Bart Starr ........ | 16 | 3,149 | 1,808 | 57.4 | 24,718 | 152 | 4.8 | 138 | 4.4 | 7.85 | 80.3 |
| Ken Stabler ...... | 10 | 2,481 | 1,486 | 59.9 | 19,978 | 150 | 6.0 | 143 | 5.8 | 7.69 | 79.9 |
| Ken Anderson .... | 9 | 2,785 | 1,570 | 56.4 | 20,030 | 125 | 4.5 | 101 | 3.6 | 7.19 | 79.1 |
| Johnny Unitas .... | 18 | 5,186 | 2,830 | 54.6 | 40,239 | 290 | 5.6 | 253 | 4.9 | 7.76 | 78.2 |
| Otto Graham .... | 6 | 1,565 | 872 | 55.7 | 13,499 | 88 | 5.6 | 94 | 6.0 | 8.63 | 78.1 |
| Frank Ryan ....... | 13 | 2,133 | 1,090 | 51.1 | 16,042 | 149 | 7.0 | 111 | 5.2 | 7.52 | 77.7 |
| Bob Griese ...... | 12 | 3,019 | 1,689 | 55.9 | 22,142 | 172 | 5.7 | 152 | 5.0 | 7.33 | 77.4 |
| Norm Van Brocklin | 12 | 2,895 | 1,553 | 53.6 | 23,611 | 173 | 6.0 | 178 | 6.1 | 8.16 | 75.3 |
| Sid Luckman ..... | 12 | 1,744 | 904 | 51.8 | 14,686 | 137 | 7.9 | 132 | 7.6 | 8.42 | 75.0 |
| Don Meredith ..... | 9 | 2,308 | 1,170 | 50.7 | 17,199 | 135 | 5.8 | 111 | 4.8 | 7.45 | 74.7 |
| Roman Gabriel ... | 16 | 4,498 | 2,366 | 52.6 | 29,444 | 201 | 4.5 | 149 | 3.3 | 6.55 | 74.5 |
| Earl Morrall ...... | 21 | 2,689 | 1,379 | 51.3 | 20,809 | 161 | 6.0 | 148 | 5.5 | 7.74 | 74.2 |
| Y. A. Tittle ....... | 15 | 3,817 | 2,118 | 55.5 | 28,339 | 212 | 5.6 | 221 | 5.8 | 7.42 | 73.8 |
| Greg Landry ...... | 11 | 1,747 | 957 | 54.8 | 12,451 | 80 | 4.6 | 81 | 4.6 | 7.13 | 73.6 |
| Daryle Lamonica .. | 12 | 2,601 | 1,288 | 49.5 | 19,154 | 164 | 6.3 | 138 | 5.3 | 7.36 | 72.9 |

[1] Does not include 1980. Rating points awarded for percent of completions, TDs, interceptions, and average gain.

## NATIONAL PROFESSIONAL FOOTBALL HALL OF FAME

Herb Adderley, defensive back: Green Bay (1961–69), Dallas (1970–72)

Lance Alworth, wide receiver: San Diego (1962–70)

Cliff Battles, halfback: Boston, Washington (1932–37)

Sammy Baugh *, quarterback: Washington (1937–52)

Chuck Bednarik, center: Philadelphia (1949–62)

Bert Bell *, NFL commissioner (1949–59)

Raymond Berry, end: Baltimore (1955–67)

Charles W. Bidwill, owner: Chicago Cardinals (1933–47)

Jim Brown, fullback: Cleveland (1957–65)

Paul Brown, coach: Cleveland (1946–52), Cincinnati (1968–69)

Roosevelt Brown, tackle: New York Giants (1953–65)

Dick Butkus, linebacker: Chicago (1965–73)

Tony Canadeo, halfback: Green Bay (1940–52)

Joe Carr *, NFL president (1921–38)

Guy Chamberlin, end, coach: Canton, Cleveland, Frankford, Chicago (1919–28)

Jack Christiansen, defensive back: Detroit (1951–58)

Dutch Clark *, quarterback: Portsmouth, Detroit (1931–38)

George Connor, tackle, linebacker: Chicago Bears (1948–55)

Jimmy Conzelman, quarterback, coach, executive: Decatur, Rock Island, Milwaukee, Detroit, Providence, Chicago (1920–48)

Art Donovan, defensive tackle: Baltimore, New York, Dallas (1950–61)

Paddy Driscoll, quarterback, coach: Decatur, Chicago Cardinals, Chicago Bears (1920–57)

Bill Dudley, halfback: Pittsburgh, Detroit, Washington (1942–53)

Turk Edwards, tackle, Boston, Washington (1932–53)

Weeb Ewbank, coach: Baltimore Colts (1954–62), N.Y. Jets (1963–73)

Tom Fears, end: Los Angeles (1948–56)

Ray Flaherty, coach: (1926–49)

Len Ford, end: Los Angeles, Cleveland (1948–58)

Danny Fortmann, M.D., guard: Chicago Bears, New York Yankees (1936–43)

Bill George, linebacker: Chicago Bears, Los Angeles (1952–66)

Frank Gifford, halfback: New York Giants (1952–60, 1962–64)

Otto Graham, quarterback: Cleveland (1946–55)

Red Grange *, halfback: Chicago Bears, New York Yankees (1925–34)

Forrest Gregg, tackle: Green Bay, Dallas (1956, 1958–71)

Lou Groza, tackle, kicker: Cleveland (1946–59, 1961–67)

Joe Guyon, halfback: Canton, Cleveland, Oorang Indians, Rock Island, Kansas City, New York (1918–27)

George Halas *, end, coach, owner: Chicago Bears (1920–67)

Ed Healey, tackle: Rock Island, Chicago Bears (1920–27)

Mel Hein *, center: New York (1931–45)

Pete (Fats) Henry *, tackle: Canton, Akron, New York, Pottsville, Pittsburgh (1920–30)

Arnie Herber, quarterback: Green Bay, New York (1930–45)

Bill Hewitt, end: Chicago Bears, Philadelphia, Pittsburgh (1932–39, 1943)

Clarke Hinkle, fullback: Green Bay (1932–41)

Elroy (Crazylegs) Hirsch, end, halfback: Chicago Rockets, Los Angeles (1946–57)

Cal Hubbard *, tackle, end: N.Y., Green Bay, Pittsburgh (1927–36)

Lamar Hunt, first president of the AFL (1960)

Don Hutson *, end: Green Bay (1935–45)

David (Deacon) Jones, defensive end: Los Angeles (1961–71), San Diego (1972–73), Washington (1974)

Walter Kiesling, guard, coach: Duluth, Pottsville, Boston, Chicago Bears, Green Bay, Pittsburgh (1926–56)

Frank (Bruiser) Kinard, tackle: Brooklyn, N.Y. (1938–47)

Curly Lambeau *, coach: Green Bay Packers (1919–49), Chicago Cardinals (1950–51), Washington Redskins (1952–53)

Dick (Night Train) Lane, defensive back: Los Angeles, Chicago Cardinals, Detroit (1952–65)

Yale Lary, defensive back punter: Detroit (1952–53, 1956–64)

Dante Lavelli, end: Cleveland (1946–56)

Bobby Layne, quarterback: Chicago Bears, New York, Detroit, Pittsburgh (1948–62)

Alphonse (Tuffy) Leemans, fullback: N.Y. Giants (1937–43)

Bob Lilly, defensive tackle: Dallas (1961–74)

Vince Lombardi, coach: Green Bay, Washington (1958–69)

Sid Luckman, quarterback: Chicago Bears (1939–50)

Roy (Link) Lyman, tackle: Canton, Cleveland, Frankford, Chicago Bears (1922–34)

Tim Mara *, owner: New York Giants (1925–59)

Gino Marchetti, defensive end: Dallas, Baltimore (1953–66)

George Preston Marshall *, owner: Boston Braves (1932), Boston Redskins (1933–36), Washington Redskins (1937–69)

Ollie Matson, halfback: Chicago Cardinals, Los Angeles, Detroit, Philadelphia (1952–66)

George McAfee, halfback: Chicago Bears (1940–41, 1945–50)

Hugh McElhenny, halfback: San Francisco (1952–60)

John Blood McNally *, halfback: Milwaukee, Duluth, Pottsville, Green Bay, Pittsburgh (1925–39)

Mike Michalske, guard: New York, Green Bay (1927–37)

Wayne Millner, end: Boston, Washington (1936–41, 1945)

Ron Mix, tackle: San Diego (1960–69), Oakland (1971)

Lenny Moore, running back: Baltimore (1956–67)

Marion Motley, fullback: Cleveland, Pittsburgh (1946–55)

Bronko Nagurski *, fullback: Chicago Bears (1930–37, 1943)

Earle (Greasy) Neale, coach: Philadelphia (1941–50)

Ernie Nevers *, fullback: Duluth, Chicago Cardinals (1926–37)

Ray Nitschke, linebacker: Green Bay Packers (1958–72)

Leo Nomellini, defensive tackle: San Francisco (1953–63)

Jim Otto, center: Oakland (1960–74)

Steve Owen, tackle: Kansas City Cowboys (1924–25), New York Giants (1926–30); coach, New York Giants (1931–53)

Ace Parker, quarterback: Brooklyn Dodgers, Boston Yanks, New York Yankees (1937–46)

Jim Parker, guard: tackle: Baltimore (1957–67)

Joe Perry, fullback: San Francisco, Baltimore (1948–62)

Pete Pihos, end: Philadelphia (1947–55)

Hugh (Shorty) Ray, NFL official (1938–56)

Daniel F. Reeves, owner: Los Angeles Rams (1941–71)

Andy Robustelli, end: Los Angeles, New York Giants (1951–64)

Art Rooney, owner: Pittsburgh Pirates (1933–40), Pittsburgh Steelers (1941–42, 1949–77)

Gale Sayers, running back: Chicago Bears (1965–71)

Joe Schmidt, linebacker: Detroit (1953–65)

Bart Starr, quarterback: Green Bay (1956–71)

Ernie Stautner, defensive tackle: Pittsburgh (1950–63)

Ken Strong, halfback, place-kicker: Staten Island, New York (1929–39, 1944–47)

Joe Stydahar, tackle: Chicago Bears (1936–42, 1945–46)

Jim Taylor, fullback: Green Bay, New Orleans (1958–67)

Jim Thorpe *, halfback: Canton, Oorang Indians, Cleveland, Toledo, Rock Island, New York (1915–26, 1929)

Y. A. Tittle, quarterback: Baltimore, San Francisco, New York Giants (1948–64)

George Trafton, center: Decatur, Chicago Staleys, Chicago Bears (1920–32)

Charley Trippi, halfback: Chicago Cardinals (1947–55)

Emlen Tunnell, safety: New York, Green Bay (1948–61)

Clyde (Bulldog) Turner, center: Chicago Bears (1940–52)

Johnny Unitas, quarterback: Baltimore (1956–72), San Diego (1973)

Norm Van Brocklin, quarterback: Los Angeles, Phila. (1949–60)

Steve Van Buren, halfback: Philadelphia (1944–52)

Bob Waterfield, quarterback: Cleveland, Los Angeles (1945–52)

Bill Willis, guard: Cleveland (1946–53)

Larry Wilson, defensive back: St. Louis Cardinals (1960–72)

Alex Wojciechowicz, center: Detroit, Philadelphia (1938–50)

* Charter member.

# COLLEGE FOOTBALL HIGHLIGHTS: 1980

Herschel Walker, of the University of Georgia, bounds over the goal line in run for a touchdown against Vanderbilt University on Oct. 18. He gained over 200 yards rushing in the game, which Georgia won, 41–0. By the end of the regular season, Walker had shattered the NCAA record for a first-year runner, carrying 1,616 yards, breaking the record of 1,586 set by Pittsburgh's Tony Dorsett in 1973.

United Press Int'l.

The University of Georgia was the only undefeated major college football team at the end of the 1980 regular season, finishing with 11–0–0. Georgia took the Southeastern Conference title, and was ranked number one in the nation by both United Press International and Associated Press.

The prestigious Heisman Trophy, for the outstanding college football player, was awarded to George Washington Rogers Jr., University of South Carolina running back. He led the nation in rushing with 1,781 yards. The Duluth, Ga., senior completed his college career with 4,598 yards rushing, fourth on the NCAA career rushing charts.

Brigham Young, which won the Western Athletic Conference title, was first in the nation in total offense, averaging 535 yards per game. Brigham Young's Jim McMahon led the nation in passing, with 4,571 yards and 47 touchdown passes.

For the results of postseason college football bowl games in December 1980 and on Jan. 1–2, 1981, see page 30.

## ALL-AMERICA COLLEGE FOOTBALL TEAMS: 1980

### ASSOCIATED PRESS

| OFFENSIVE TEAM | POSITIONS | DEFENSIVE TEAM | POSITIONS |
|---|---|---|---|
| Ken Margerum, Stanford | Wide Receiver | Hugh Green, Pittsburgh | End |
| Anthony Carter, Michigan | Wide Receiver | Scott Zettek, Nortre Dame | End |
| Dave Young, Purdue | Tight End | Leonard Mitchell, Texas | Tackle |
| Mark May, Pittsburgh | Tackle | Kenneth Sims, Texas | Tackle |
| Keith Van Horne, Southern California | Tackle | E.J. Junior, Alabama | Linebacker |
| Frank Ditta, Baylor | Guard | David Little, Florida | Linebacker |
| Randy Schleusener, Nebraska | Guard | Mike Singletary, Baylor | Linebacker |
| John Scully, Notre Dame | Center | Lawrence Taylor, North Carolina | Linebacker |
| Mark Herrmann, Purdue | Quarterback | Ronnie Lott, Southern California | Back |
| George Rogers, South Carolina | Running Back | John Simmons, SMU | Back |
| Herschel Walker, Georgia | Running Back | Ken Easley, UCLA | Back |

### UNITED PRESS INTERNATIONAL

| OFFENSIVE TEAM | POSITIONS | DEFENSIVE TEAM | POSITIONS |
|---|---|---|---|
| Ken Margerum, Stanford | Wide Receiver | Hugh Green, Pittsburgh | End |
| Dave Young, Purdue | Tight End | E. J. Junior, Alabama | End |
| Mark May, Pittsburgh | Tackle | Kenneth Sims, Texas | Tackle |
| Keith Van Horne, Southern California | Tackle | Leonard Mitchell, Houston | Tackle |
| Randy Schleusener, Nebraska | Guard | Ron Simmons, Florida State | Middle Guard |
| Roy Foster, Southern California | Guard | Mike Singletary, Baylor | Linebacker |
| John Scully, Notre Dame | Center | Bob Crable, Notre Dame | Linebacker |
| Mark Herrmann, Purdue | Quarterback | Lawrence Taylor, North Carolina | Linebacker |
| George Rogers, South Carolina | Running Back | Scott Woerner, Georgia | Back |
| Herschel Walker, Georgia | Running Back | Ronnie Lott, Southern California | Back |
| Jarvis Redwine, Nebraska | Running Back | Ken Easley, UCLA | Back |
| Rex Robinson, Georgia | Place Kicker | Rohn Stark, Florida State | Punter |

## TOP-RATED COLLEGE FOOTBALL TEAMS: 1980 (end of regular season)

| COACHES' POLL (UPI) | | | | | WRITERS' RATINGS (AP) | | | | |
|---|---|---|---|---|---|---|---|---|---|
| RANK | TEAM | W | L | T | POINTS | RANK | TEAM | W | L | T | POINTS |
| 1 | Georgia | 11 | 0 | 0 | 582 | 1 | Georgia | 11 | 0 | 0 | 1,274 |
| 2 | Florida State | 10 | 1 | 0 | 540 | 2 | Florida State | 10 | 1 | 0 | 1,208 |
| 3 | Pittsburgh | 10 | 1 | 0 | 489 | 3 | Pittsburgh | 10 | 1 | 0 | 1,127 |
| 4 | Oklahoma | 9 | 2 | 0 | 417 | 4 | Oklahoma | 9 | 2 | 0 | 1,027 |
| 5 | Michigan | 9 | 2 | 0 | 386 | 5 | Michigan | 9 | 2 | 0 | 947 |
| 6 | Alabama | 9 | 2 | 0 | 332 | 6 | Baylor | 10 | 1 | 0 | 914 |
| 7 | Baylor | 10 | 1 | 0 | 313 | 7 | Notre Dame | 9 | 1 | 1 | 860 |
| 8 | Notre Dame | 9 | 1 | 1 | 271 | 8 | Nebraska | 9 | 2 | 0 | 801 |
| 9 | Nebraska | 9 | 2 | 0 | 269 | 9 | Alabama | 9 | 2 | 0 | 800 |
| 10 | Penn State | 9 | 2 | 0 | 237 | 10 | Penn State | 9 | 2 | 0 | 644 |

## WON-LOST SEASON RECORDS OF MAJOR COLLEGE FOOTBALL TEAMS: 1980

| TEAM | W | L | T | TEAM | W | L | T | TEAM | W | L | T |
|---|---|---|---|---|---|---|---|---|---|---|---|
| Air Force | 2 | 9 | 1 | Iowa | 4 | 7 | 0 | Princeton | 6 | 4 | 0 |
| Alabama | 9 | 2 | 0 | Iowa State | 6 | 5 | 0 | Purdue | 8 | 3 | 0 |
| Alcorn St. | 6 | 4 | 0 | Jackson State | 8 | 3 | 0 | Rice | 5 | 6 | 0 |
| Arizona | 5 | 6 | 0 | Kansas | 4 | 5 | 2 | Rutgers | 7 | 4 | 0 |
| Arizona State | 7 | 4 | 1 | Kansas State | 3 | 8 | 0 | San Diego State | 4 | 8 | 0 |
| Arkansas | 6 | 5 | 0 | Kentucky | 3 | 8 | 0 | South Carolina | 8 | 3 | 0 |
| Auburn | 5 | 6 | 0 | Long Beach State | 8 | 3 | 0 | South Carolina State | 10 | 1 | 0 |
| Army | 3 | 7 | 1 | Louisiana State | 7 | 4 | 0 | SMU | 8 | 3 | 0 |
| Baylor | 10 | 1 | 0 | Maryland | 8 | 3 | 0 | Southern California | 8 | 2 | 1 |
| Boise State | 8 | 3 | 0 | Massachusetts | 7 | 3 | 0 | Syracuse | 5 | 6 | 0 |
| Boston College | 7 | 4 | 0 | Memphis State | 2 | 9 | 0 | Temple | 4 | 7 | 0 |
| Boston University | 9 | 2 | 0 | Michigan | 9 | 2 | 0 | Tennessee State | 9 | 1 | 0 |
| Brigham Young | 11 | 1 | 0 | Michigan State | 3 | 8 | 0 | Texas | 7 | 4 | 0 |
| Brown | 7 | 5 | 0 | Minnesota | 5 | 6 | 0 | Texas A & M | 4 | 7 | 0 |
| Central Mich. | 9 | 2 | 0 | Mississippi | 3 | 8 | 0 | Texas Tech | 5 | 6 | 0 |
| Clemson | 6 | 5 | 0 | Mississippi State | 9 | 2 | 0 | Tulane | 7 | 4 | 0 |
| Colgate | 5 | 4 | 1 | Missouri | 8 | 3 | 0 | Tulsa | 8 | 3 | 0 |
| Colorado State | 6 | 4 | 1 | Navy | 8 | 3 | 0 | UCLA | 9 | 2 | 0 |
| Dartmouth | 4 | 6 | 0 | Nebraska | 9 | 2 | 0 | Utah State | 6 | 5 | 0 |
| Florida State | 10 | 1 | 0 | North Carolina | 10 | 1 | 0 | Villanova | 6 | 5 | 0 |
| Grambling | 9 | 1 | 0 | North Carolina State | 6 | 5 | 0 | VMI | 3 | 7 | 1 |
| Fresno State | 5 | 6 | 0 | North Texas State | 6 | 5 | 0 | Wake Forest | 5 | 6 | 0 |
| Furman | 9 | 1 | 1 | Notre Dame | 9 | 1 | 1 | Washington | 9 | 2 | 0 |
| Georgia | 11 | 0 | 0 | Ohio State | 9 | 2 | 0 | Washington State | 4 | 7 | 0 |
| Harvard | 7 | 3 | 0 | Oklahoma | 9 | 2 | 0 | West Texas State | 5 | 6 | 0 |
| Hawaii | 8 | 3 | 0 | Oklahoma State | 3 | 7 | 1 | West Virginia | 6 | 6 | 0 |
| Houston | 6 | 5 | 0 | Oregon | 6 | 3 | 2 | Wisconsin | 4 | 7 | 0 |
| Illinois | 3 | 7 | 1 | Penn State | 9 | 2 | 0 | Wyoming | 6 | 5 | 0 |
| Indiana | 6 | 5 | 0 | Pittsburgh | 10 | 1 | 0 | Yale | 8 | 2 | 0 |

## HEISMAN MEMORIAL TROPHY WINNERS

The John W. Heisman Memorial Trophy is awarded annually to the nation's leading college football player. It was originated in 1935 by the Downtown Athletic Club of New York.

| YEAR | PLAYER | POSITION | TEAM | YEAR | PLAYER | POSITION | TEAM |
|---|---|---|---|---|---|---|---|
| 1935 | Jay Berwanger | Back | Chicago | 1958 | Pete Dawkins | Back | Army |
| 1936 | Larry Kelley | End | Yale | 1959 | Billy Cannon | Back | Louisiana State |
| 1937 | Clint Frank | Quarterback | Yale | 1960 | Joe Bellino | Back | Navy |
| 1938 | Davey O'Brien | Quarterback | TCU | 1961 | Ernie Davis | Back | Syracuse |
| 1939 | Nile Kinnick | Back | Iowa | 1962 | Terry Baker | Back | Oregon State |
| 1940 | Tom Harmon | Back | Michigan | 1963 | Roger Staubach | Quarterback | Navy |
| 1941 | Bruce Smith | Back | Minnesota | 1964 | John Huarte | Quarterback | Notre Dame |
| 1942 | Frank Sinkwich | Back | Georgia | 1965 | Mike Garrett | Back | So. California |
| 1943 | Angelo Bertelli | Quarterback | Notre Dame | 1966 | Steve Spurrier | Quarterback | Florida |
| 1944 | Les Horvath | Quarterback | Ohio State | 1967 | Gary Beban | Quarterback | UCLA |
| 1945 | Felix Blanchard | Back | Army | 1968 | O. J. Simpson | Tailback | So. California |
| 1946 | Glenn Davis | Back | Army | 1969 | Steve Owens | Back | Oklahoma |
| 1947 | Johnny Lujack | Quarterback | Notre Dame | 1970 | Jim Plunkett | Quarterback | Stanford |
| 1948 | Doak Walker | Back | So. Methodist | 1971 | Pat Sullivan | Quarterback | Auburn |
| 1949 | Leon Hart | End | Notre Dame | 1972 | Johnny Rodgers | Back | Nebraska |
| 1950 | Vic Janowicz | Back | Ohio State | 1973 | John Cappelletti | Tailback | Penn State |
| 1951 | Dick Kazmaier | Back | Princeton | 1974 | Archie Griffin | Tailback | Ohio State |
| 1952 | Billy Vessels | Back | Oklahoma | 1975 | Archie Griffin | Tailback | Ohio State |
| 1953 | Johnny Lattner | Back | Notre Dame | 1976 | Tony Dorsett | Tailback | Pittsburgh |
| 1954 | Alan Ameche | Back | Wisconsin | 1977 | Earl Campbell | Back | Texas |
| 1955 | Howard Cassady | Back | Ohio State | 1978 | Billy Sims | Tailback | Oklahoma |
| 1956 | Paul Hornung | Quarterback | Notre Dame | 1979 | Charles White | Running Back | So. California |
| 1957 | John Crow | Back | Texas A&M | 1980 | George Rogers | Running Back | So. Carolina |

## UNDEFEATED, UNTIED MAJOR TEAMS: 1968–80

| YEAR | COLLEGE | WINS [1] | YEAR | COLLEGE | WINS [1] | YEAR | COLLEGE | WINS [1] |
|---|---|---|---|---|---|---|---|---|
| 1968 | Ohio State | 9 ‡ | 1971 | Alabama | 11 ‡ | 1975 | Arizona State | 11 † |
| | Ohio University | 10 † | | Michigan | 11 ‡ | | Ohio State | 11 ‡ |
| | Penn State | 10 ‡ | | Nebraska | 12 † | 1976 | Pittsburgh | 11 † |
| 1969 | Penn State | 10 † | | Toledo | 11 † | | Rutgers | 11 |
| | San Diego State | 10 ‡ | 1972 | Southern California | 11 † * | | Maryland | 11 ‡ |
| | Texas | 10 ‡ | 1973 | Alabama | 11 ‡ | 1977 | Texas | 11 ‡ |
| | Toledo | 10 ‡ | | Miami (Ohio) | 10 † | 1978 | Penn State | 11 ‡ |
| 1970 | Arizona State | 10 † | | Notre Dame | 10 † | 1979 | Alabama | 11 † |
| | Dartmouth | 9 | | Penn State | 11 † | | Ohio State | 11 ‡ |
| | Ohio State | 9 ‡ | 1974 | Alabama | 11 ‡ | | Florida State | 11 ‡ |
| | Texas | 10 ‡ | | Oklahoma | 11 ‡ | | Brigham Young | 11 ‡ |
| | Toledo | 11 ‡ | | | | 1980 | Georgia | 11 † |

[1] Regular season games only.  Subsequent bowl win is indicated by (†), loss (‡), and tie (§).

## COLLEGE RUSHING CHAMPIONS

| YEAR | PLAYER, TEAM | GAMES | PLAYS | YARDS [1] |
|---|---|---|---|---|
| 1951 | Ollie Matson, San Francisco | 9 | 245 | 1,566 |
| 1952 | Howie Waugh, Tulsa | 10 | 164 | 1,372 |
| 1953 | J. C. Caroline, Illinois | 9 | 194 | 1,256 |
| 1954 | Art Luppino, Arizona | 10 | 179 | 1,359 |
| 1955 | Art Luppino, Arizona | 10 | 209 | 1,313 |
| 1956 | Jim Crawford, Wyoming | 10 | 200 | 1,104 |
| 1957 | Leon Burton, Arizona State | 10 | 117 | 1,126 |
| 1958 | Dick Bass, Pacific | 10 | 205 | 1,361 |
| 1959 | Pervis Atkins, New Mexico St. | 10 | 130 | 971 |
| 1960 | Bob Gaiters, New Mexico State | 10 | 197 | 1,338 |
| 1961 | Jim Pilot, New Mexico State | 10 | 191 | 1,278 |
| 1962 | Jim Pilot, New Mexico State | 10 | 208 | 1,247 |
| 1963 | Dave Casinelli, Memph. State | 10 | 219 | 1,016 |
| 1964 | Brian Piccolo, Wake Forest | 10 | 252 | 1,044 |
| 1965 | Mike Garrett, Southern Calif. | 10 | 267 | 1,440 |
| 1966 | Ray McDonald, Idaho | 10 | 259 | 1,329 |
| 1967 | O. J. Simpson, Southern Calif. | 9 | 266 | 1,415 |
| 1968 | O. J. Simpson, Southern Calif. | 10 | 355 | 1,709 |
| 1969 | Steve Owens, Oklahoma | 10 | 358* | 1,523 |
| 1970 | Ed Marinaro, Cornell | 9 | 285 | 158.3 |
| 1971 | Ed Marinaro, Cornell | 9 | 356 | 209.0* |
| 1972 | Pete VanValkenburg, Brig. Young | 10 | 232 | 138.6 |
| 1973 | Mark Kellar, Northern Illinois | 11 | 291 | 156.3 |
| 1974 | Louie Giammona, Utah State | 10 | 329 | 153.4 |
| 1975 | Ricky Bell, Southern Calif. | 11 | 357 | 170.5 |
| 1976 | Tony Dorsett, Pittsburgh | 11 | 338 | 177.1 |
| 1977 | Earl Campbell, Texas | 11 | 267 | 158.5 |
| 1978 | Billy Sims, Oklahoma | 11 | 231 | 160.2 |
| 1979 | Charles White, Southern Calif. | 10 | 293 | 180.3 |
| 1980 | George Rogers, So. Carolina | 11 | 297 | 161.9 |

## COLLEGE SCORING CHAMPIONS

| YEAR | PLAYER, TEAM | GAMES | TD | XPT. | FG | PTS. [2] |
|---|---|---|---|---|---|---|
| 1951 | Ollie Matson, San Francisco | 9 | 21 | 0 | 0 | 126 |
| 1952 | Jackie Parker, Miss. State | 9 | 16 | 24 | 0 | 120 |
| 1953 | Earl Lindley, Utah State | 11 | 13 | 3 | 0 | 81 |
| 1954 | Art Luppino, Arizona | 10 | 24 | 22 | 0 | 166 |
| 1955 | Jim Swink, TCU | 10 | 20 | 5 | 0 | 125 |
| 1956 | Clendon Thomas, Okla. | 10 | 18 | 0 | 0 | 108 |
| 1957 | Leon Burton, Arizona State | 10 | 16 | 0 | 0 | 96 |
| 1958 | Dick Bass, Pacific | 10 | 18 | 8 | 0 | 116 |
| 1959 | Pervis Atkins, N.M. State | 10 | 17 | 5 | 0 | 107 |
| 1960 | Bob Gaiters, N.M. State | 10 | 23 | 7 | 0 | 145 |
| 1961 | Jim Pilot, New Mexico State | 10 | 21 | 12 | 0 | 138 |
| 1962 | Jerry Logan, W. Texas State | 10 | 13 | 32 | 0 | 110 |
| 1963 | Cosmo Iacavazzi, Princeton | 9 | 14 | 0 | 0 | 84 |
| | Dave Casinelli, Memph. State | 10 | 14 | 0 | 0 | 84 |
| 1964 | Brian Piccolo, Wake Forest | 10 | 17 | 9 | 0 | 111 |
| 1965 | Howard Twilley, Tulsa | 10 | 16 | 31 | 0 | 127 |
| 1966 | Ken Hebert, Houston | 10 | 11 | 41 | 2 | 113 |
| 1967 | Leroy Keyes, Purdue | 10 | 19 | 0 | 0 | 114 |
| 1968 | Jim O'Brien, Cincinnati | 10 | 12 | 31 | 13 | 142 |
| 1969 | Steve Owens, Oklahoma | 10 | 23 | 0 | 0 | 138 |
| 1970 | Brian Bream, Air Force | 10 | 20 | 0 | 0 | 12.0 |
| | Gary Kosins, Dayton | 9 | 18 | 0 | 0 | 12.0 |
| 1971 | Ed Marinaro, Cornell | 9 | 24 | 4 | 0 | 16.4 |
| 1972 | Harold Henson, Ohio State | 10 | 20 | 0 | 0 | 12.0 |
| 1973 | Jim Jennings, Rutgers | 11 | 21 | 2 | 0 | 11.6 |
| 1974 | Bill Marek, Wisconsin | 9 | 19 | 0 | 0 | 12.7 |
| 1975 | Pete Johnson, Ohio State | 11 | 25 | 0 | 0 | 13.6 |
| 1976 | Tony Dorsett, Pittsburgh | 11 | 22 | 2 | 0 | 12.2 |
| 1977 | Earl Campbell, Texas | 11 | 19 | 0 | 0 | 10.4 |
| 1978 | Billy Sims, Oklahoma | 11 | 20 | 0 | 0 | 10.9 |
| 1979 | Billy Sims, Oklahoma | 11 | 22 | 0 | 0 | 12.0 |
| 1980 | Sammy Windner, So. Miss. | 11 | 20 | 0 | 0 | 10.9 |

\* Record.  [1] Beginning in 1970, ranked on per-game (instead of total) yards.  [2] Beginning in 1970, ranked on per-game (instead of total) points.  Source: National Collegiate Sports Services.

## COLLEGE FOOTBALL PASSING CHAMPIONS[1]: 1980

Source: NCAA Statistics Service.

| | GAMES | ATT. | CMP. | CMP. PCT. | INT. | INT. PCT. | YDS. | YDS./ ATT. | TD | TD PCT. | RATING POINTS |
|---|---|---|---|---|---|---|---|---|---|---|---|
| Jim McMahon, Brigham Young | 12 | 445 | 284 | 63.82 | 18 | 4.04 | 4,571 | 10.27 | 47 | 10.56 | 176.9 |
| Joe Adams, Tennessee State | 10 | 333 | 200 | 60.06 | 21 | 6.31 | 2,848 | 8.55 | 30 | 9.01 | 149.0 |
| John Elway, Stanford | 11 | 379 | 248 | 65.44 | 11 | 2.90 | 2,889 | 7.62 | 27 | 7.12 | 147.2 |
| Steve Woods, Tenn.—Chattanooga | 10 | 194 | 100 | 51.55 | 13 | 6.70 | 1,827 | 9.42 | 17 | 8.76 | 146.2 |
| Mark Herrmann, Purdue | 10 | 340 | 220 | 64.71 | 17 | 5.00 | 2,923 | 8.60 | 19 | 5.59 | 145.4 |
| Larry Gentry, Nevada—Las Vegas | 11 | 209 | 113 | 54.07 | 16 | 7.66 | 1,691 | 8.09 | 22 | 10.53 | 141.5 |
| Art Schlichter, Ohio State | 11 | 191 | 102 | 53.40 | 8 | 4.19 | 1,628 | 8.52 | 12 | 6.28 | 137.4 |
| Ricky Hardin, Utah | 11 | 290 | 179 | 61.72 | 19 | 6.55 | 2,459 | 8.48 | 15 | 5.17 | 136.9 |
| Tom Flick, Washington | 11 | 280 | 168 | 60.00 | 11 | 3.93 | 2,178 | 7.78 | 15 | 5.36 | 135.2 |
| Rick Stockstill, Florida State | 11 | 201 | 121 | 60.20 | 8 | 3.98 | 1,377 | 6.85 | 15 | 7.46 | 134.4 |
| Kevin Starkey, Long Beach State | 11 | 248 | 138 | 55.65 | 16 | 6.45 | 1,995 | 7.88 | 19 | 7.66 | 134.2 |
| Mark Lockenmeyer, Princeton | 9 | 185 | 110 | 59.46 | 5 | 2.70 | 1,284 | 6.94 | 12 | 6.49 | 133.8 |
| John Wangler, Michigan | 11 | 192 | 105 | 54.69 | 9 | 4.69 | 1,377 | 7.17 | 15 | 7.81 | 131.3 |
| Oliver Luck, West Virginia | 12 | 254 | 135 | 53.15 | 12 | 4.72 | 1,874 | 7.38 | 19 | 7.48 | 130.4 |

[1] Minimum of 15 attempts per game.

## COLLEGE FOOTBALL NATIONAL CHAMPIONSHIP TEAMS

Various groups have picked the annual college football team champion since 1924. The Associated Press started polling sportswriters in 1936 to determine the team winner. In 1950 United Press International began to poll football coaches. The NCAA recognizes both polls.

| | | | | | |
|---|---|---|---|---|---|
| 1925 | Dartmouth | 1941 | Minnesota | 1956 | Oklahoma |
| 1926 | Stanford | 1942 | Ohio State | 1957 | Auburn (AP) |
| 1927 | Illinois | 1943 | Notre Dame | | Ohio State (UPI) |
| 1928 | So. California | 1944 | Army | 1958 | Louisiana State |
| 1929 | Notre Dame | 1945 | Army | 1959 | Syracuse |
| 1930 | Notre Dame | 1946 | Notre Dame | 1960 | Minnesota |
| 1931 | So. California | 1947 | Notre Dame | 1961 | Alabama |
| 1932 | Michigan | 1948 | Michigan | 1962 | So. California |
| 1933 | Michigan | 1949 | Notre Dame | 1963 | Texas |
| 1934 | Minnesota | 1950 | Oklahoma | 1964 | Alabama |
| 1935 | Southern Methodist | 1951 | Tennessee | 1965 | Alabama |
| 1936 | Minnesota | 1952 | Michigan State | 1966 | Notre Dame |
| 1937 | Pittsburgh | 1953 | Maryland | 1967 | So. California |
| 1938 | Texas Christian | 1954 | Ohio State (AP); | 1968 | So. Calif. (UPI) |
| 1939 | Texas A & M | | UCLA (UPI) | | Ohio State (AP) |
| 1940 | Minnesota | 1955 | Oklahoma | 1969 | Texas |

| | |
|---|---|
| 1970 | Nebraska (AP) |
| | Texas (UPI) |
| 1971 | Nebraska |
| 1972 | So. California |
| 1973 | Notre Dame |
| 1974 | Oklahoma (AP) |
| | So. Calif. (UPI) |
| 1975 | Oklahoma |
| 1976 | Pittsburgh |
| 1977 | Notre Dame |
| 1978 | Alabama (AP) |
| | So. Calif. (UPI) |
| 1979 | Alabama |
| 1980 | Georgia |

## COLLEGE FOOTBALL CONFERENCE CHAMPIONS

### ATLANTIC COAST CONFERENCE CHAMPIONS

| | | | | | | | |
|---|---|---|---|---|---|---|---|
| 1955* | Maryland—Duke | 1962 | Duke | 1969 | South Carolina | 1976 | Maryland |
| 1956 | Clemson | 1963 | North Carolina State | 1970 | Wake Forest | 1977 | North Carolina |
| 1957 | North Carolina State | 1964 | North Carolina State | 1971 | North Carolina | 1978 | Clemson |
| 1958 | Clemson | 1965 | Duke | 1972 | North Carolina | 1979 | North Carolina State |
| 1959 | Clemson | 1966 | Clemson | 1973 | North Carolina State | 1980 | North Carolina |
| 1960 | Duke | 1967 | Clemson | 1974 | Maryland | | |
| 1961 | Duke | 1968 | North Carolina State | 1975 | Maryland | | |

### BIG EIGHT CONFERENCE CHAMPIONS

| | | | | | | | |
|---|---|---|---|---|---|---|---|
| 1936 | Nebraska | 1948 | Oklahoma | 1960 | Missouri | 1972 | Oklahoma |
| 1937 | Nebraska | 1949 | Oklahoma | 1961 | Colorado | 1973 | Oklahoma |
| 1938 | Oklahoma | 1950 | Oklahoma | 1962 | Oklahoma | 1974 | Oklahoma |
| 1939 | Missouri | 1951 | Oklahoma | 1963 | Nebraska | 1975* | Oklahoma—Nebraska |
| 1940 | Nebraska | 1952 | Oklahoma | 1964 | Nebraska | 1976* | Oklahoma—Colorado |
| 1941 | Missouri | 1953 | Oklahoma | 1965 | Nebraska | | —Oklahoma State |
| 1942 | Missouri | 1954 | Oklahoma | 1966 | Nebraska | 1977 | Oklahoma |
| 1943 | Oklahoma | 1955 | Oklahoma | 1967 | Oklahoma | 1978* | Oklahoma—Nebraska |
| 1944 | Oklahoma | 1956 | Oklahoma | 1968 | Kansas | 1979 | Oklahoma |
| 1945 | Missouri | 1957 | Oklahoma | 1969* | Missouri—Nebraska | 1980 | Oklahoma |
| 1946* | Oklahoma—Kansas | 1958 | Oklahoma | 1970 | Nebraska | | |
| 1947* | Oklahoma—Kansas | 1959 | Oklahoma | 1971 | Nebraska | | |

### BIG TEN CHAMPIONS

| | | | | | | | |
|---|---|---|---|---|---|---|---|
| 1937 | Minnesota | 1949* | Ohio State—Michigan | 1961 | Ohio State | 1972* | Ohio State—Michigan |
| 1938 | Minnesota | 1950 | Michigan | 1962 | Wisconsin | 1973* | Ohio State—Michigan |
| 1939 | Ohio State | 1951 | Illinois | 1963 | Illinois | 1974* | Ohio State—Michigan |
| 1940 | Minnesota | 1952* | Wisconsin—Purdue | 1964 | Michigan | 1975 | Ohio State |
| 1941 | Minnesota | 1953* | Illinois—Mich. State | 1965 | Michigan State | 1976* | Michigan—Ohio State |
| 1942 | Ohio State | 1954 | Ohio State | 1966 | Michigan State | 1977* | Michigan—Ohio State |
| 1943* | Michigan—Purdue | 1955 | Ohio State | 1967* | Indiana—Purdue— | 1978* | Michigan— |
| 1944 | Ohio State | 1956 | Iowa | | Minnesota | | Michigan State |
| 1945 | Indiana | 1957 | Ohio State | 1968 | Ohio State | 1979 | Ohio State |
| 1946 | Illinois | 1958 | Iowa | 1969* | Michigan—Ohio State | 1980 | Michigan |
| 1947 | Michigan | 1959 | Wisconsin | 1970 | Ohio State | | |
| 1948 | Michigan | 1960* | Minnesota—Iowa | 1971 | Michigan | | |

### IVY LEAGUE CHAMPIONS

| | | | | | | | |
|---|---|---|---|---|---|---|---|
| 1957 | Princeton | 1965 | Dartmouth | 1970 | Dartmouth | 1977 | Yale |
| 1958 | Dartmouth | 1966* | Dartmouth—Harvard | 1971* | Cornell—Dartmouth | 1978 | Dartmouth |
| 1959 | Pennsylvania | | —Princeton | 1972 | Dartmouth | 1979 | Yale |
| 1960 | Yale | 1967 | Yale | 1973 | Dartmouth | 1980 | Yale |
| 1961* | Columbia—Harvard | 1968* | Harvard—Yale | 1974* | Harvard—Yale | | |
| 1962 | Dartmouth | 1969* | Dartmouth— | 1975 | Harvard | | |
| 1963* | Dartmouth—Princeton | | Princeton—Yale | 1976* | Yale—Brown | | |
| 1964 | Princeton | | | | | | |

### PACIFIC COAST ATHLETIC CONFERENCE CHAMPIONS

| | | | | | | | |
|---|---|---|---|---|---|---|---|
| 1969 | San Diego State | 1972-74 | San Diego State | 1977 | Fresno State | 1979 | San Jose State |
| 1970 | Long Beach State | 1975 | San Jose State | 1978* | Utah State— | 1980 | Long Beach State |
| 1971 | Long Beach State | 1976 | San Diego State | | San Jose State | | |

* Tie.

## PACIFIC TEN CHAMPIONS

| | | | |
|---|---|---|---|
| 1936* Washington—So. Cal. | 1949–50 California | 1960 Washington | 1970 Stanford |
| 1937 California | 1951 Stanford | 1961 UCLA | 1971 Stanford |
| 1938* California—So. Cal. | 1952 Southern California | 1962 Southern California | 1972 Southern California |
| 1939 Southern California | 1953 UCLA | 1963 Washington | 1973 Southern California |
| 1940 Stanford | 1954 UCLA | 1964* Oregon State— | 1974 Southern California |
| 1941 Oregon State | 1955 UCLA | Southern California | 1975* California—UCLA |
| 1942 UCLA | 1956 Oregon State | 1965 UCLA | 1976 Southern California |
| 1943–45 Southern California | 1957* Oregon State—Oregon | 1966 Southern California | 1977 Washington |
| 1946 UCLA | 1958 California | 1967 Southern California | 1978 Southern California |
| 1947 Southern California | 1959* Washington— Southern | 1968 Southern California | 1979 Southern California |
| 1948* Oregon—California | California—UCLA | 1969 Southern California | 1980 Washington |

## SOUTHEASTERN CONFERENCE CHAMPIONS

| | | | |
|---|---|---|---|
| 1935–36 LSU | 1948 Georgia | 1959 Georgia | 1970 LSU |
| 1937 Alabama | 1949 Tulane | 1960 Mississippi | 1971 Alabama |
| 1938 Tennessee | 1950 Kentucky | 1961* Alabama—LSU | 1972 Alabama |
| 1939* Tennessee—Ga. Tech. | 1951* Georgia Tech—Tenn. | 1962 Mississippi | 1973 Alabama |
| 1940 Tennessee | 1952 Georgia tech | 1963 Mississippi | 1974 Alabama |
| 1941 Mississippi State | 1953 Alabama | 1964 Alabama | 1975 Alabama |
| 1942 Georgia | 1954 Mississippi | 1965 Alabama | 1976 Georgia |
| 1943–44 Georgia Tech | 1955 Mississippi | 1966* Georgia—Alabama | 1977* Alabama—Kentucky |
| 1945 Alabama | 1956 Tennessee | 1967 Tennessee | 1978 Alabama |
| 1946* Georgia—Tennessee | 1957 Auburn | 1968 Georgia | 1979 Alabama |
| 1947 Mississippi | 1958 LSU | 1969 Tennessee | 1980 Georgia |

## SOUTHERN CONFERENCE CHAMPIONS

| | | | |
|---|---|---|---|
| 1935 Duke | 1947 William & Mary | 1959–60 VMI | 1970 William & Mary |
| 1936 Duke | 1948 Clemson | 1961 Citadel | 1971 Richmond |
| 1937 Maryland | 1949 North Carolina | 1962 VMI | 1972 East Carolina |
| 1938 Duke | 1950 Washington & Lee | 1963 Virginia Tech | 1972 East Carolina |
| 1939 Duke | 1951* Maryland—VMI | 1964 West Virginia | 1973 East Carolina |
| 1940 Clemson | 1952 Duke | 1965 West Virginia | 1974 VMI |
| 1941 Duke | 1953 West Virginia | 1966* William & Mary— | 1975 Richmond |
| 1942 William & Mary | 1954 West Virginia | East Carolina | 1976 East Carolina |
| 1943 Duke | 1955 West Virginia | 1967 West Virginia | 1977* Tenn.-Chat.—VMI |
| 1944 Duke | 1956 West Virginia | 1968 Richmond | 1978* Tenn.-Chat.—Furman |
| 1945 Duke | 1957 VMI | 1969* Davidson— | 1979 Tennessee-Chat. |
| 1946 North Carolina | 1958 West Virginia | Richmond | 1980 Furman |

## SOUTHWEST CONFERENCE CHAMPIONS

| | | | |
|---|---|---|---|
| 1937 Rice | 1949 Rice | 1960 Arkansas | 1972 Texas |
| 1938 TCU | 1950 Texas | 1961* Texas—Arkansas | 1973 Texas |
| 1939 Texas A & M | 1951 TCU | 1962 Texas | 1974 Baylor |
| 1940 Texas A & M—SMU | 1952 Texas | 1963 Texas | 1975* Texas A & M— |
| 1941 Texas A & M | 1953* Rice—Texas | 1964–65 Arkansas | Arkansas—Texas |
| 1942–43 Texas | 1954 Arkansas | 1966 SMU | 1976* Houston—Texas Tech |
| 1944 TCU | 1955 Texas | 1967 Texas A & M | 1977 Texas |
| 1945 Texas | 1956 Texas A & M | 1968 Texas | 1978 Houston |
| 1946* Arkansas—Rice | 1957 Rice | 1969 Texas | 1979* Arkansas—Houston |
| 1947 SMU | 1958 TCU | 1970 Texas | 1980 Baylor |
| 1948 SMU | 1959* Texas—TCU—Ark. | 1971 Texas | |

## MISSOURI VALLEY CONFERENCE CHAMPIONS

| | | | |
|---|---|---|---|
| 1938 Tulsa | 1949 Detroit | 1960 Wichita | 1971 North Texas |
| 1939 Washington | 1950 Tulsa | 1961 Wichita | 1972* Louisville—West |
| 1940 Tulsa | 1951 Tulsa | 1962 Tulsa | Texas—Drake |
| 1941 Tulsa | 1952 Houston | 1963* Cincinnati—Wichita | 1973 North Texas |
| 1942 Tulsa | 1953* Okla. A&M—Detroit | 1964 Cincinnati | 1974–75 Tulsa |
| 1943 Tulsa | 1954 Wichita | 1965 Tulsa | 1976* Tulsa— |
| 1944 Oklahoma A & M | 1955* Detroit—Wichita | 1966* North Texas—Tulsa | New Mexico State |
| 1945 Oklahoma A & M | 1956 Houston | 1967 North Texas | 1977 West Texas State |
| 1946 Tulsa | 1957 Houston | 1968 Memphis State | 1978 New Mexico State |
| 1947 Tulsa | 1958 North Texas | 1969 Memphis State | 1979 West Texas State |
| 1948 Oklahoma A & M | 1959* North Texas—Houston | 1970 Louisville | 1980 Tulsa |

## WESTERN ATHLETIC CONFERENCE CHAMPIONS

| | | | |
|---|---|---|---|
| 1962–63 New Mexico | 1969 Arizona State | 1974 Brigham Young | 1978 Brigham Young |
| 1964* New Mexico— | 1970 Arizona State | 1975 Arizona State | 1979 Brigham Young |
| Utah—Arizona | 1971 Arizona State | 1976* Brigham Young—Wyo. | 1980 Brigham Young |
| 1965 Brigham Young | 1972 Arizona State | 1977* Brigham Young— | |
| 1966–68 Wyoming | 1973* Arizona—Arizona State | Arizona State | |

* Tie.

# COLLEGE FOOTBALL'S MAJOR BOWL GAMES

## ROSE BOWL (at Pasadena, Calif.) (played in January)

| | | |
|---|---|---|
| 1902 Michigan 49, Stanford 0 | 1936 Stanford 7, SMU 0 | 1958 Ohio State 10, Oregon 7 |
| 1916 Washington State 14, Brown 0 | 1937 Pittsburgh 21, Washington 0 | 1959 Iowa 38, California 12 |
| 1917 Oregon 14, Pennsylvania 0 | 1938 California 13, Alabama 0 | 1960 Washington 44, Wisconsin 8 |
| 1918 Mare Island Marines 19, Camp Lewis (Army) 7 | 1939 Southern California 7, Duke 3 | 1961 Washington 17, Minnesota 7 |
| | 1940 So. Calif. 14, Tennessee 0 | 1962 Minnesota 21, UCLA 3 |
| 1919 Great Lakes (Navy) 17, Mare Island Marines 0 | 1941 Stanford 21, Nebraska 13 | 1963 So. Calif. 42, Wisconsin 37 |
| | 1942 Oregon State 20, Duke 16 [1] | 1964 Illinois 17, Washington 7 |
| 1920 Harvard 7, Oregon 6 | 1943 Georgia 9, UCLA 0 | 1965 Michigan 34, Oregon State 7 |
| 1921 California 28, Ohio State 0 | 1944 So. Calif. 29, Wash. 0 [2] | 1966 UCLA 14, Michigan State 12 |
| 1922 Washington and Jefferson 0, California 0 | 1945 Southern California 25, Tennessee 0 | 1967 Purdue 14, So. Calif. 13 |
| | | 1968 So. Calif. 14, Indiana 3 |
| 1923 So. Calif. 14, Penn State 3 | 1946 Alabama 34, Southern California 14 | 1969 Ohio State 27, So. Calif. 16 |
| 1924 Navy 14, Washington 14 | | 1970 So. Calif. 10, Michigan 3 |
| 1925 Notre Dame 27, Stanford 10 | 1947 Illinois 45, UCLA 14 | 1971 Stanford 27, Ohio State 17 |
| 1926 Alabama 20, Washington 19 | 1948 Michigan 49, So. Calif. 0 | 1972 Stanford 13, Michigan 12 |
| 1927 Alabama 7, Stanford 7 | 1949 Northwestern 20, California 14 | 1973 So. Calif. 42, Ohio State 17 |
| 1928 Stanford 7, Pittsburgh 6 | 1950 Ohio State 17, California 14 | 1974 Ohio State 42, So. Calif. 21 |
| 1929 Georgia Tech. 8, California 7 | 1951 Michigan 14, California 6 | 1975 So. Calif. 18, Ohio State 17 |
| 1930 So. Calif. 47, Pittsburgh 14 | 1952 Illinois 40, Stanford 7 | 1976 UCLA 23, Ohio State 10 |
| 1931 Alabama 24, Washington State 0 | 1953 So. Calif. 7, Wisconsin 0 | 1977 So. Calif. 14, Michigan 6 |
| 1932 So. Calif. 21, Tulane 12 | 1954 Michigan State 28, UCLA 20 | 1978 Washington 27, Michigan 20 |
| 1933 So. Calif. 35, Pittsburgh 0 | 1955 Ohio State 20, So. Calif. 7 | 1979 So. Calif. 17, Michigan 10 |
| 1934 Columbia 7, Stanford 0 | 1956 Michigan State 17, UCLA 14 | 1980 So. Calif. 17, Ohio State 16 |
| 1935 Alabama 29, Stanford 13 | 1957 Iowa 35, Oregon State 19 | 1981 See page 30. |

[1] Because of World War II restrictions, the 1942 Rose Bowl game was played at Duke Stadium, Durham, North Carolina.
[2] The only Rose Bowl game between two Pacific Coast Conference teams.

## ORANGE BOWL (at Miami, Fla.) (played in January)

| | | |
|---|---|---|
| 1934 Duquesne 33, Miami (Fla.) 7 | 1950 Santa Clara 21, Kentucky 13 | 1967 Florida 27, Georgia Tech 12 |
| 1935 Bucknell 26, Miami (Fla.) 0 | 1951 Clemson 15, Miami 14 | 1968 Oklahoma 26, Tennessee 24 |
| 1936 Catholic University 20, Mississippi 19 | 1952 Georgia Tech 17, Baylor 14 | 1969 Penn State 15, Kansas 14 |
| | 1953 Alabama 61, Syracuse 6 | 1970 Penn State 10, Missouri 3 |
| 1937 Duquesne 13, Miss. State 12 | 1954 Oklahoma 7, Maryland 0 | 1971 Nebraska 17, LSU 12 |
| 1938 Alabama Poly 6, Michigan State 0 | 1955 Duke 36, Nebraska 7 | 1972 Nebraska 38, Alabama 6 |
| 1939 Tennessee 17, Oklahoma 0 | 1956 Oklahoma 20, Maryland 6 | 1973 Nebraska 40, Notre Dame 6 |
| 1940 Georgia Tech 21, Missouri 7 | 1957 Colorado 27, Clemson 21 | 1974 Penn State 16, LSU 9 |
| 1941 Miss. State 14, Georgetown 7 | 1958 Oklahoma 48, Duke 21 | 1975 Notre Dame 13, Alabama 11 |
| 1942 Georgia 40, Texas Christian 26 | 1959 Oklahoma 21, Syracuse 6 | 1976 Oklahoma 14, Michigan 6 |
| 1943 Alabama 37, Boston College 21 | 1960 Georgia 14, Missouri 0 | 1977 Ohio State 27, Colorado 10 |
| 1944 LSU 19, Texas A & M 14 | 1961 Missouri 21, Navy 14 | 1978 Arkansas 31, Oklahoma 6 |
| 1945 Tulsa 26, Georgia Tech 12 | 1962 LSU 25, Colorado 7 | 1979 Oklahoma 31, Nebraska 24 |
| 1946 Miami (Fla.) 13, Holy Cross 6 | 1963 Alabama 17, Oklahoma 0 | 1980 Oklahoma 24, Fla. State 7 |
| 1947 Rice 8, Tennessee 0 | 1964 Nebraska 13, Auburn 7 | 1981 See page 30. |
| 1948 Georgia Tech 20, Kansas 14 | 1965 Texas 21, Alabama 17 | |
| 1949 Texas 41, Georgia 28 | 1966 Alabama 39, Nebraska 28 | |

## SUGAR BOWL (at New Orleans, La.) (played in January)

| | | |
|---|---|---|
| 1935 Tulane 20, Temple 14 | 1950 Oklahoma 35, Louisiana State 0 | 1967 Alabama 34, Nebraska 7 |
| 1936 Texas Christian 3, La. State 2 | 1951 Kentucky 13, Oklahoma 7 | 1968 LSU 20, Wyoming 13 |
| 1937 Santa Clara 21, La. State 14 | 1952 Maryland 28, Tennessee 13 | 1969 Arkansas 16, Georgia Tech 2 |
| 1938 Santa Clara 6, Louisiana State 0 | 1953 Georgia Tech 24, Mississippi 7 | 1970 Mississippi 27, Arkansas 22 |
| 1939 Texas Christian 15, Carnegie Tech 7 | 1954 Georgia Tech 42, West Virginia 19 | 1971 Tennessee 34, Air Force 13 |
| | 1955 Navy 21, Mississippi 0 | 1972 Oklahoma 40, Auburn 22 |
| 1940 Texas A&M 14, Tulane 13 | 1956 Georgia Tech 7, Pittsburgh 0 | 1973 Oklahoma 14, Penn State 0 |
| 1941 Boston College 19, Tennessee 13 | 1957 Baylor 13, Tennessee 7 | 1974 Notre Dame 24, Alabama 23 |
| 1942 Fordham 2, Missouri 0 | 1958 Mississippi 39, Texas 7 | 1975 Nebraska 13, Florida 10 |
| 1943 Tennessee 14, Tulsa 7 | 1959 Louisiana State 7, Clemson 0 | 1976 Alabama 13, Penn State 6 |
| 1944 Georgia Tech 20, Tulsa 18 | 1960 Mississippi 21, LSU 0 | 1977 Pittsburgh 27, Georgia 3 |
| 1945 Duke 29, Alabama 26 | 1961 Mississippi 14, Rice 6 | 1978 Alabama 35, Ohio State 6 |
| 1946 Oklahoma A & M 33, St. Mary's (Calif.) 13 | 1962 Alabama 10, Arkansas 3 | 1979 Alabama 14, Penn State 7 |
| | 1963 Mississippi 17, Arkansas 13 | 1980 Alabama 24, Arkansas 9 |
| 1947 Georgia 20, North Carolina 10 | 1964 Alabama 12, Mississippi 7 | 1981 See page 30. |
| 1948 Texas 27, Alabama 7 | 1965 La. State 13, Syracuse 10 | |
| 1949 Oklahoma 14, North Carolina 6 | 1966 Missouri 20, Florida 18 | |

## COTTON BOWL (at Dallas) (played in January)

| | | |
|---|---|---|
| 1937 Texas Christian 16, Marquette 6 | 1942 Alabama 29, Texas A & M 21 | 1947 Louisiana State 0, Arkansas 0 |
| 1938 Rice 28, Colorado 14 | 1943 Texas 14, Georgia Tech 7 | 1948 So. Methodist 13, Penn State 13 |
| 1939 St. Mary's 20, Texas Tech 13 | 1944 Randolph Field 7, Texas 7 | 1949 So. Methodist 21, Oregon 13 |
| 1940 Clemson 6, Boston College 3 | 1945 Oklahoma A & M 34, TCU 0 | 1950 Rice 27, North Carolina 13 |
| 1941 Texas A & M 13, Fordham 12 | 1946 Texas 40, Missouri 27 | 1951 Tennessee 20, Texas 14 |

## COTTON BOWL *(continued)*

| | | |
|---|---|---|
| 1952 Kentucky 20, Texas Christian 7 | 1962 Texas 12, Mississippi 7 | 1972 Penn State 30, Texas 6 |
| 1953 Texas 16, Tennessee 0 | 1963 Louisiana State 13, Texas 0 | 1973 Texas 17, Alabama 13 |
| 1954 Rice 28, Alabama 6 | 1964 Texas 28, Navy 6 | 1974 Nebraska 19, Texas 3 |
| 1955 Georgia Tech 14, Arkansas 6 | 1965 Arkansas 10, Nebraska 7 | 1975 Penn State 41, Baylor 20 |
| 1956 Miss. 14, Texas Christian 13 | 1966 Louisiana State 14, Arkansas 7 | 1976 Arkansas 31, Georgia 10 |
| 1957 Texas Christian 28, Syracuse 27 | 1967 Georgia 24, So. Methodist 9 | 1977 Houston 30, Maryland 21 |
| 1958 Navy 20, Rice 7 | 1968 Texas A & M 20, Alabama 16 | 1978 Notre Dame 38, Texas 10 |
| 1959 Air Force 0, Texas Christian 0 | 1969 Texas 36, Tennessee 13 | 1979 Notre Dame 35, Houston 34 |
| 1960 Syracuse 23, Texas 14 | 1970 Texas 21, Notre Dame 17 | 1980 Houston 17, Nebraska 14 |
| 1961 Duke 7, Arkansas 6 | 1971 Notre Dame 24, Texas 11 | 1981 See page 30. |

## SUN BOWL (at El Paso, Texas)*

| | | |
|---|---|---|
| 1936 Hardin Simmons 14, N. Mex. St. 14 | 1952 Texas Tech 25, Col. Pacific 14 | 1968 U. Texas El Paso 14, Mississippi 7 |
| 1937 Hardin Simmons 34, Texas Mines 6 | 1953 Col. Pacific 26, Miss. Southern 7 | 1969 Auburn 34, Arizona 10 |
| 1938 West Virginia 7, Texas Tech 6 | 1954 U. Tex. El Paso 37, Miss. South. 14 | 1970 Nebraska 45, Georgia 6 |
| 1939 Utah 26, New Mexico 0 | 1955 U. Texas El Paso 47, Florida St. 20 | 1971 Georgia Tech 17, Texas Tech 9 |
| 1940 Catholic U. 0, Arizona St. 0 | 1956 Wyoming 21, Texas Tech 14 | 1972 LSU 33, Iowa State 15 |
| 1941 Western Reserve 26, Arizona St. 13 | 1957 Geo. Wash. 13, U. Texas El Paso 0 | 1973 North Carolina 32, Texas Tech 28 |
| 1942 Tulsa 6, Texas Tech 0 | 1958 Louisville 34, Drake 20 | 1974 Missouri 34, Auburn 17 |
| 1943 2d Air Force 13, Hardin-Simmons 7 | 1959 Wyoming 14, Hardin-Simmons 6 | 1975 Mississippi St. 26, N. Carolina 24 |
| 1944 Southwest. (Tex.) 7, N. Mexico 0 | 1960 New Mexico St. 28, No. Texas St. 8 | 1976 Pittsburgh 33, Kansas 19 |
| 1945 Southwest. (Tex.) 35, U. of Mex. 0 | 1961 New Mexico St. 20, Utah State 13 | 1977 Oklahoma 44, Wyoming 7 |
| 1946 New Mexico 34, Denver 24 | 1962 Villanova 17, Wichita 9 | 1978 Stanford 24, Louisiana State 14 |
| 1947 Cincinnati 38, Virginia Tech 6 | 1963 West Texas St. 15, Ohio U. 14 | 1979 Texas 42, Maryland 0 |
| 1948 Miami (O.) 13, Texas Tech 12 | 1964 Oregon 21, So. Methodist 14 | 1980 Washington 14, Texas 7 |
| 1949 West Virginia 21, Texas Mines 12 | 1965 Georgia 7, Texas Tech 0 | 1981 See page 30. |
| 1950 U. Tex. El Paso 33, Georgetown 20 | 1966 U. Texas El Paso 13, TCU 12 | |
| 1951 West Texas St. 14, Cincinnati 13 | 1967 Wyoming 28, Florida St. 20 | |

\* Games for 1970–80 played in December of previous year.

## GATOR BOWL (at Jacksonville, Fla.) (played in December)

| | | |
|---|---|---|
| 1945 Wake Forest 26, S.C. 14 | 1957 Tennessee 3, Texas A & M 0 | 1969 Florida 14, Tennessee 13 |
| 1946 Oklahoma 34, N.C. State 13 | 1958 Mississippi 7, Florida 3 | 1970 Auburn 35, Mississippi 28 |
| 1947 Maryland 20, Georgia 20 | 1959 Arkansas 14, Georgia Tech 7 | 1971 Georgia 7, North Carolina 3 |
| 1948 Clemson 24, Missouri 23 | 1960 Florida 13, Baylor 12 | 1972 Auburn 24, Colorado 3 |
| 1949 Maryland 20, Missouri 7 | 1961 Penn State 30, Georgia Tech 15 | 1973 Texas Tech 28, Tennessee 19 |
| 1950 Wyoming 20, Washington & Lee 7 | 1962 Florida 17, Penn State 7 | 1974 Auburn 27, Texas 3 |
| 1951 Miami (Fla.) 14, Clemson 0 | 1963 North Carolina 35, Air Force 0 | 1975 Maryland 13, Florida 0 |
| 1952 Florida 14, Tulsa 13 | 1964 Florida State 36, Oklahoma 19 | 1976 Notre Dame 20, Penn State 9 |
| 1953 Texas Tech 35, Auburn 13 | 1965 Georgia Tech 31, Texas Tech 21 | 1977 Pittsburgh 34, Clemson 3 |
| 1954 Auburn 33, Baylor 13 | 1966 Tennessee 18, Syracuse 12 | 1978 Clemson 17, Ohio State 15 |
| 1955 Vanderbilt 25, Auburn 13 | 1967 Penn State 17, Fla. State 17 | 1979 No. Carolina 17, Michigan 15 |
| 1956 Georgia Tech 21, Pittsburgh 14 | 1968 Missouri 35, Alabama 10 | 1980 See page 30. |

## ASTRO-BLUEBONNET BOWL (at Houston, Texas) (played in December)

| | | |
|---|---|---|
| 1959 Clemson 23, TCU 7 | 1967 Colorado 31, Miami (Fla.) 21 | 1975 Texas 38, Colorado 21 |
| 1960 Texas 3, Alabama 3 | 1968 SMU 28, Oklahoma 27 | 1976 Nebraska 27, Texas Tech 24 |
| 1961 Kansas 33, Rice 7 | 1969 Houston 36, Auburn 7 | 1977 So. Calif. 47, Texas A & M 28 |
| 1962 Missouri 14, Georgia Tech 10 | 1970 Oklahoma 24, Alabama 24 | 1978 Stanford 25, Georgia 22 |
| 1963 Baylor 14, LSU 7 | 1971 Colorado 29, Houston 17 | 1979 Purdue 27, Tennessee 22 |
| 1964 Tulsa 14, Mississippi 7 | 1972 Tennessee 24, Louisiana St. 17 | 1980 See page 30. |
| 1965 Tennessee 27, Tulsa 6 | 1973 Houston 47, Tulane 7 | |
| 1966 Texas 19, Mississippi 0 | 1974 Houston 31, N. Carolina State 31 | |

## LIBERTY BOWL (at Memphis, Tenn.) (played in December)

| | | |
|---|---|---|
| 1959 Penn State 7, Alabama 0 | 1967 N.C. State 14, Georgia 7 | 1975 So. Calif. 20, Texas A & M 0 |
| 1960 Penn State 41, Oregon 12 | 1968 Mississippi 34, Va. Tech 17 | 1976 Alabama 36, UCLA 6 |
| 1961 Syracuse 15, Miami 14 | 1969 Colorado 47, Alabama 33 | 1977 Nebraska 21, North Carolina 17 |
| 1962 Oregon 6, Villanova 0 | 1970 Tulane 17, Colorado 3 | 1978 Missouri 20, LSU 15 |
| 1963 Miss. State 16, N.C. State 12 | 1971 Tennessee 14, Arkansas 13 | 1979 Penn State 9, Tulane 6 |
| 1964 Utah 32, West Virginia 6 | 1972 Georgia Tech 31, Iowa State 30 | 1980 See page 30. |
| 1965 Mississippi 13, Auburn 7 | 1973 No. Carolina St. 31, Kansas 18 | |
| 1966 Miami (Fla.) 14, Va. Tech 7 | 1974 Tennessee 7, Maryland 3 | |

## PEACH BOWL (at Atlanta, Georgia) (played in December)

| | | |
|---|---|---|
| 1968 LSU 31, Florida State 27 | 1973 Georgia 17, Maryland 16 | 1978 Purdue 41, Georgia Tech 21 |
| 1969 West Virginia 14, South Carolina 3 | 1974 Texas Tech 6, Vanderbilt 6 | 1979 Baylor 24, Clemson 18 |
| 1970 Arizona State 48, N. Carolina 26 | 1975 West Virginia 13, N.C. State 10 | 1980 See page 30. |
| 1971 Mississippi 41, Georgia Tech 18 | 1976 Kentucky 21, N. Carolina 0 | |
| 1972 North Carolina St. 49, West Va. 13 | 1977 N.C. State 24, Iowa State 14 | |

## FIESTA BOWL (at Tempe, Arizona) (played in December)

| | | |
|---|---|---|
| 1971 Arizona State 45, Florida State 38 | 1975 Arizona State 17, Nebraska 14 | 1979 Pittsburgh 16, Arizona 10 |
| 1972 Arizona State 49, Missouri 35 | 1976 Oklahoma 41, Wyoming 7 | 1980 See page 30. |
| 1973 Arizona State 28, Pittsburgh 7 | 1977 Penn State 42, Arizona State 30 | |
| 1974 Okla. State 16, Brigham Young 6 | 1978 UCLA 10, Arkansas 10 | |

# MAJOR COLLEGE FOOTBALL RECORDS

## INDIVIDUAL RECORDS

**Touchdowns scored in one game:** 7 by Arnold Boykin, Mississippi versus Mississippi State, Dec. 1, 1951; 11* by Philip King, Princeton versus Columbia, Nov. 4, 1890; 11 by Jefferson Fletcher, Harvard versus Exeter, Nov. 3, 1886; 11 by Henry Beecher, Yale versus Wesleyan, Oct. 30, 1886.

**Touchdowns scored in one season:** 29 by Lydell Mitchell, Penn State, in 1971; 38* by Mayes McLain, Haskell, in 1926.

**Touchdowns scored in a career:** 59 by Glenn Davis, Army, 1943–46; 72* by Willie Heston, Michigan, 1901–04; 66 by Henry Beecher, Yale, 1885–87.

**Points scored in one game:** 43 by Jim Brown, Syracuse versus Colgate, Nov. 17, 1956 (6 TDs, 7 PATs); 64* by Bernard Trafford, Harvard versus Wesleyan, Nov. 3, 1891 (7 TDs, 4 points each; 18 PATs, 2 points each).

**Points scored in a season:** 174 by Lydell Mitchell, Penn State, 1971 (29 TDs); 270* by Bernard Trafford, Harvard, 1891 (24 TDs, 4 points each; 77 PATs, 2 points each; 4 FGs, 5 points each).

**Points scored in a career:** 356 by Tony Dorsett, Pittsburgh, 1973–76; 730* by Knowlton Ames, Princeton, 1886–89 (62 TDs, 4 points each; 176 PATs, 2 points each; 6 FGs, 5 points each).

**Yards gained in one game:** 599 by Virgil Carter, Brigham Young versus U. Texas–El Paso, Nov. 5, 1966 (86 rushing, 513 passing).

**Yards gained in a season:** 4,627 by Jim McMahon, Brigham Young, 1979 (56 rushing, 4,571 passing).

**Yards gained in a career:** 8,444 by Mark Herrmann, Purdue (1977–80).

**Yards gained by rushing in one game:** 356 by Eddie Lee Ivery, Georgia State versus Air Force, Nov. 11, 1978; 362* by Jim Thorpe, Carlisle versus Pennsylvania, Nov. 16, 1912 (29 rushes).

**Yards gained by rushing in one season:** 1,948 by Tony Dorsett, Pittsburgh, 1976 (338 rushes); 1,881 by Ed Marinaro, Cornell, 1971 (356 rushes); 1,869* by Jim Thorpe, Carlisle, 1912 (191 rushes).

**Yards gained by rushing in a career:** 6,082 by Tony Dorsett, Pittsburgh, 1973–76; 4,854 by Charles White, Southern California, 1977–79.

**Passes completed in one game:** 43 by Rich Campbell, California, against Florida, Sept. 13, 1980; 43 by Dave Wilson, Illinois, versus Ohio State, Nov. 8, 1980.

**Passes completed in one season:** 296 by Bill Anderson, Tulsa, 1965 (attempted 509).

**Passes completed in a career:** 717 by Mark Herrmann, Purdue, 1977–80 (attempted 1,218).

**Passes, consecutive completed:** 21 by Rich Campbell, California, (last 15 versus Michigan, Oct. 4, 1980, first 6 versus Oregon, Oct. 11, 1980).

**Passes, highest percentage completed in one game** (minimum 15 completed): 94.1% by Tom Flick, Washington versus Arizona, Nov. 8, 1980 (16 of 17).

**Passes, highest percentage completed in a season** (minimum 150 attempts): 69.3% by Chris Kupec, North Carolina, 1974 (104 of 150).

**Passes, highest percentage completed in a career** (minimum 300 attempts): 64.4% by Rich Campbell, California, 1977–80 (574 of 891).

**Passing yards gained in one game:** 621 by Dave Wilson, Illinois, against Ohio State, Nov. 8, 1980.

**Passing yards gained in one season:** 4,571 by Jim McMahon, Brigham Young, 1980.

**Touchdown passes in one game:** 9 by Dennis Shaw, San Diego State versus New Mexico State, Nov. 15, 1969.

**Touchdown passes in a season:** 47 by Jim McMahon, Brigham Young, 1980.

**Touchdown passes in a career:** 81 by Joe Adams, Tennessee State, 1977–80.

**Passes caught in one game:** 22 by Jay Miller, Brigham Young versus New Mexico, Nov. 3, 1973 (263 yards).

**Touchdown passes caught in one game:** 6 by Tim Delaney, San Diego State versus New Mexico State, Nov. 15, 1969.

**Field goals in one game:** 6 by Charley Gogolak, Princeton versus Rutgers, Sept. 25, 1965 (attempted 6); 7* by Edward Robertson, Purdue versus Rose Poly, Oct. 27, 1900 (attempted 12).

**Field goals, season:** 23, Obed Ariri, Clemson, 1980.

**Points by kicker, game:** 20 by Charley Gogolak, Princeton versus Rutgers, Sept. 25, 1965.

**Points by kicker, season:** 104, Bill Capec, Florida State, 1980.

**Field goal, longest made:** 67 yards by Russell Erxleben, Texas versus Rice, Oct. 1, 1977.

**Points kicked after touchdown in one game:** 13 by Terry Leiweke, Houston versus Tulsa, Nov. 23, 1968 (attempted 14). 23* by Arlo Davis, Oklahoma versus Kingfisher, Sept. 29, 1917 (attempted 26).

## TEAM RECORDS

**Touchdowns in one game:** 15 by Wyoming versus Colorado State College, Nov. 5, 1949 (9 rushing, 6 passing). 32* by Georgia Tech versus Cumberland, Oct. 7, 1916.

**Touchdowns in one season:** 74 by Army in 1944. 144* by Harvard in 1886 (4 points each).

**Points scored in one game:** 103 by Wyoming versus Colorado State (0), Nov. 5, 1949. 222* by Georgia Tech versus Cumberland (0), Oct. 7, 1916.

**Points scored in one season:** 560 by Brigham Young, 1980.

**Yards gained in one game:** 875 by Oklahoma versus Colorado, Oct. 4, 1980. 1,261* by Michigan versus Buffalo, Oct. 26, 1901.

**Yards gained rushing in one game:** 758 by Oklahoma versus Colorado, Oct. 4, 1980. 1,261* by Michigan versus Buffalo, Oct. 16, 1901 (76 rushes).

**Passes completed in one game:** 43 by California versus Florida, Sept. 13, 1980.

**Touchdown passes in one game:** 10 by San Diego State versus New Mexico State, Nov. 15, 1969.

**First downs in one game:** 40 by Vanderbilt versus Davidson, Nov. 22, 1969 (27 by rushing, 13 passing).

**Points kicked after touchdown in one game:** 13 by Wyoming versus Northern Colo., Nov. 5, 1949.

**Yards gained by passes in one game:** 698 by Tulsa versus Idaho State, Oct. 7, 1967 (completed 39 of 62).

**Yards on punt returns in one game:** 319 by Texas A & M versus North Texas State, Sept. 21, 1946 (10 returns).

**Yards on kickoff returns in one game:** 295 by Cincinnati versus Memphis State, Oct. 30, 1971.

**Average points per game in a season:** 56.0 by Army in 1949 (504 points in 9 games).

**Fumbles lost in a game:** 10 by Wichita State versus Florida State, Sept. 20, 1969.

* Pre-1937 records: There was no general clearinghouse for national records until the NCAA took over the task in 1937. Touchdowns — TDs; points after touchdown — PATs; field goals — FGs.

# GOLF

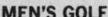

Jack Nicklaus studiously concentrates on his putt as he gets a birdie on the ninth hole in the third round of the Professional Golfers' Association championship tournament at Rochester, N.Y. Nicklaus went on to win his fifth PGA championship title on Aug. 10, with a total of 274. Earlier in the year he captured his fourth U.S. Open crown when he carded an 8-under-par 272 at the Baltusrol Golf Club in Springfield, N.J., on June 15, breaking his own U.S. Open scoring record of 275, set in 1967.

## MEN'S GOLF

For the fourth straight year, Tom Watson was the leading money winner on the 1980 PGA tour, with a total of $530,808. He became the first golfer to win over a half-million dollars in one season.

Watson won seven championships during the 1980 PGA Tour, including the World Series of Golf, which boasts the biggest prize in golf—$100,000. Watson totaled a 10-under-par 270 on the Firestone Country Club course at Akron, Ohio, on Aug. 24.

Earlier in the year Watson won the Tournament of Champions at Carlsbad, Calif., by three strokes, even after he was penalized two strokes for giving advice to partner Lee Trevino during the tournament.

He captured his third British Open at Muirfield, Scotland, on July 20 with a 13-under-par 271. Trevino was second with 275.

The Masters Tournament was won by Spanish golfer Severiano Ballesteros on April 13. At 23, he was the youngest ever to win this competition. He carded a 13-under-par 272 on the difficult Augusta, Ga., course.

Trevino captured the Tournament Players Championship March 23, at Ponte Vedra, Fla., shooting a 72-hole score of 278, one stroke better than Ben Crenshaw.

## WOMEN'S GOLF

Beth Daniel was the leading money winner on the LPGA tour, totaling $231,000. She captured four major tournaments in 1980, including the World Series of Women's Golf. In the tournament, held on Sept. 4–8, at Pepper Pike, Ohio, she carded a 6-under-par 282, one stroke ahead of Nancy Lopez-Melton.

Amy Alcott broke the U.S. Women's Open championship record with a 4-under-par 280 at the Richland Country Club in Nashville, Tenn., on July 13. Two-time Open champion Hollis Stacy was runner-up with 289.

South African Sally Little scored a 3-under-par 285 to win the 26th Ladies Professional Golf Association Championship at Kings Island, Ohio, on June 9.

The U.S. Women's Amateur, held in Hutchinson, Kan., in August, was won by Julie Simpson Inkster, of Santa Cruz, Calif.

## U.S. PROFESSIONAL GOLF ASSOCIATION CHAMPIONS

| Year | Champion | Year | Champion | Year | Champion | Year | Champion |
|---|---|---|---|---|---|---|---|
| 1916 | Jim Barnes | 1934 | Paul Runyan | 1947 | Jim Ferrier | 1959 | Bob Rosburg | 
| 1917–18 | No play | 1935 | Johnny Revolta | 1948 | Ben Hogan | 1960 | Jay Hebert |
| 1919 | Jim Barnes | 1936–37 | Denny Shute | 1949 | Sam Snead | 1961 | Jerry Barber |
| 1920 | Jock Hutchison | 1938 | Paul Runyan | 1950 | Chandler Harper | 1962 | Gary Player |
| 1921 | Walter Hagen | 1939 | Henry Picard | 1951 | Sam Snead | 1963 | Jack Nicklaus |
| 1922–23 | Gene Sarazen | 1940 | Byron Nelson | 1952 | Jim Turnesa | 1964 | Bobby Nichols |
| 1924–27 | Walter Hagen | 1941 | Victor Ghezzi | 1953 | Walter Burkemo | 1965 | Dave Marr |
| 1928–29 | Leo Diegel | 1942 | Sam Snead | 1954 | Chick Harbert | 1966 | Al Geiberger |
| 1930 | Tommy Armour | 1943 | No play | 1955 | Doug Ford | 1967 | Don January |
| 1931 | Tom Creavy | 1944 | Bob Hamilton | 1956 | Jack Burke | 1968 | Julius Boros |
| 1932 | Olin Dutra | 1945 | Byron Nelson | 1957 | Lionel Hebert | 1969 | Ray Floyd |
| 1933 | Gene Sarazen | 1946 | Ben Hogan | 1958 | Dow Finsterwald | 1970 | Dave Stockton |

1971 Jack Nicklaus; 1972 Gary Player; 1973 Jack Nicklaus; 1974 Lee Trevino; 1975 Jack Nicklaus; 1976 Dave Stockton; 1977 Lanny Wadkins; 1978 John Mahaffey; 1979 David Graham; 1980 Jack Nicklaus

## U.S. WOMEN'S OPEN GOLF CHAMPIONS

| Year | Champion | Score | Year | Champion | Score | Year | Champion | Score |
|---|---|---|---|---|---|---|---|---|
| 1948 | Babe Didrikson Zaharias | 300 | 1959 | Mickey Wright | 287 | 1970 | Donna Caponi | 287 |
| 1949 | Louise Suggs | 291 | 1960 | Betsy Rawls | 292 | 1971 | JoAnne Carner | 288 |
| 1950 | Babe Didrikson Zaharias | 291 | 1961 | Mickey Wright | 293 | 1972 | Susie Maxwell Berning | 299 |
| 1951 | Betsy Rawls | 293 | 1962 | Murie Lindstrom | 301 | 1973 | Susie Maxwell Berning | 290 |
| 1952 | Louise Suggs | 284 | 1963 | Mary Mills | 289 | 1974 | Sandra Haynie | 295 |
| 1953 | Betsy Rawls [1] | 302 | 1964 | Mickey Wright [1] | 290 | 1975 | Sandra Palmer | 295 |
| 1954 | Babe Didrikson Zaharias | 291 | 1965 | Carol Mann | 290 | 1976 | JoAnne Carner [1] | 292 |
| 1955 | Fay Crocker | 299 | 1966 | Sandra Spuzich | 297 | 1977 | Hollis Stacy | 292 |
| 1956 | Kathy Cornelius [1] | 302 | 1967 | Catherine Lacoste [2] | 294 | 1978 | Hollis Stacy | 289 |
| 1957 | Betsy Rawls | 299 | 1968 | Susie Maxwell Berning | 289 | 1979 | Jerilyn Britz | 284 |
| 1958 | Mickey Wright | 290 | 1969 | Donna Caponi | 294 | 1980 | Amy Alcott | 280 |

## MASTERS GOLF CHAMPIONS

| Year | Champion | Score | Year | Champion | Score | Year | Champion | Score |
|---|---|---|---|---|---|---|---|---|
| 1936 | Horton Smith | 285 | 1953 | Ben Hogan | 274 | 1967 | Gay Brewer | 280 |
| 1937 | Byron Nelson | 283 | 1954 | Sam Snead | 289 | 1968 | Bob Goalby | 277 |
| 1938 | Henry Picard | 285 | 1955 | Cary Middlecoff | 279 | 1969 | George Archer | 281 |
| 1939 | Ralph Guldahl | 279 | 1956 | Jack Burke | 289 | 1970 | Billy Casper | 279 |
| 1940 | Jimmy Demaret | 280 | 1957 | Doug Ford | 283 | 1971 | Charles Coody | 279 |
| 1941 | Craig Wood | 280 | 1958 | Arnold Palmer | 284 | 1972 | Jack Nicklaus | 286 |
| 1942 | Byron Nelson | 280 | 1959 | Art Wall Jr. | 284 | 1973 | Tommy Aaron | 283 |
| 1946 | Herman Keiser | 282 | 1960 | Arnold Palmer | 282 | 1974 | Gary Player | 278 |
| 1947 | Jimmy Demaret | 281 | 1961 | Gary Player | 280 | 1975 | Jack Nicklaus | 276 |
| 1948 | Claude Harmon | 279 | 1962 | Arnold Palmer | 280 | 1976 | Ray Floyd | 271 |
| 1949 | Sam Snead | 282 | 1963 | Jack Nicklaus | 286 | 1977 | Tom Watson | 276 |
| 1950 | Jimmy Demaret | 283 | 1964 | Arnold Palmer | 276 | 1978 | Gary Player | 277 |
| 1951 | Ben Hogan | 280 | 1965 | Jack Nicklaus | 271 | 1979 | Fuzzy Zoeller [1] | 280 |
| 1952 | Sam Snead | 286 | 1966 | Jack Nicklaus | 288 | 1980 | S. Ballesteros | 275 |

## PGA TOUR LEADING MONEY WINNERS

| Year | Winner | Amount | Year | Winner | Amount | Year | Winner | Amount |
|---|---|---|---|---|---|---|---|---|
| 1938 | Sam Snead | $19,534 | 1953 | Lew Worsham | $34,002 | 1967 | Jack Nicklaus | $188,988 |
| 1939 | Henry Picard | 10,303 | 1954 | Bob Toski | 65,820 | 1968 | Billy Casper | 205,169 |
| 1940 | Ben Hogan | 10,655 | 1955 | Julius Boros | 65,122 | 1969 | Frank Beard | 175,224 |
| 1941 | Ben Hogan | 18,358 | 1956 | Ted Kroll | 72,836 | 1970 | Lee Trevino | 150,037 |
| 1942 | Ben Hogan | 13,143 | 1957 | Dick Mayer | 65,835 | 1971 | Jack Nicklaus | 244,491 |
| 1944 | Byron Nelson | 37,968 | 1958 | Arnold Palmer | 42,407 | 1972 | Jack Nicklaus | 320,542 |
| 1945 | Byron Nelson | 63,336 | 1959 | Art Wall Jr. | 53,168 | 1973 | Jack Nicklaus | 308,362 |
| 1946 | Ben Hogan | 42,556 | 1960 | Arnold Palmer | 75,263 | 1974 | Johnny Miller | 353,201 |
| 1947 | Jimmy Demaret | 27,937 | 1961 | Gary Player | 64,540 | 1975 | Jack Nicklaus | 323,149 |
| 1948 | Ben Hogan | 32,112 | 1962 | Arnold Palmer | 81,448 | 1976 | Jack Nicklaus | 266,438 |
| 1949 | Sam Snead | 31,594 | 1963 | Arnold Palmer | 128,230 | 1977 | Tom Watson | 310,653 |
| 1950 | Sam Snead | 35,759 | 1964 | Jack Nicklaus | 113,285 | 1978 | Tom Watson | 362,429 |
| 1951 | Lloyd Mangrum | 26,089 | 1965 | Jack Nicklaus | 140,752 | 1979 | Tom Watson | 462,636 |
| 1952 | Julius Boros | 37,033 | 1966 | Billy Casper | 121,945 | 1980 | Tom Watson | 530,808 |

## LPGA TOUR LEADING MONEY WINNERS

| Year | Winner | Amount | Year | Winner | Amount | Year | Winner | Amount |
|---|---|---|---|---|---|---|---|---|
| 1951 | Babe Zaharias | $15,087 | 1961 | Mickey Wright | $22,236 | 1971 | Kathy Whitworth | $41,182 |
| 1952 | Betsy Rawls | 14,505 | 1962 | Mickey Wright | 21,641 | 1972 | Kathy Whitworth | 65,064 |
| 1953 | Louise Suggs | 19,816 | 1963 | Mickey Wright | 31,270 | 1973 | Kathy Whitworth | 82,864 |
| 1954 | Patty Berg | 16,011 | 1964 | Mickey Wright | 29,800 | 1974 | JoAnne Carner | 87,094 |
| 1955 | Patty Berg | 16,492 | 1965 | Kathy Whitworth | 28,658 | 1975 | Sandra Palmer | 94,805 |
| 1956 | Marlene Hagge | 20,235 | 1966 | Kathy Whitworth | 33,518 | 1976 | Judy Rankin | 150,734 |
| 1957 | Patty Berg | 16,272 | 1967 | Kathy Whitworth | 32,938 | 1977 | Judy Rankin | 122,890 |
| 1958 | Beverly Hanson | 12,640 | 1968 | Kathy Whitworth | 48,380 | 1978 | Nancy Lopez | 189,813 |
| 1959 | Betsy Rawls | 26,774 | 1969 | Carol Mann | 49,153 | 1979 | Nancy Lopez | 215,987 |
| 1960 | Louise Suggs | 16,892 | 1970 | Kathy Whitworth | 30,235 | 1980 | Beth Daniel | 231,000 |

[1] Won in playoff.  [2] Amateur golfer.

## U.S. OPEN GOLF CHAMPIONS

| YEAR | CHAMPION | SCORE[1] | YEAR | CHAMPION | SCORE[1] | YEAR | CHAMPION | SCORE[1] |
|---|---|---|---|---|---|---|---|---|
| 1895 | Horace Rawlins | 173 | 1924 | Cyril Walker | 297 | 1955 | Jack Fleck | 287* |
| 1896 | James Foulis | 152 | 1925 | Willie Macfarlane | 291* | 1956 | Cary Middlecoff | 281 |
| 1897 | Joe Lloyd | 162 | 1926 | Bobby Jones[2] | 293 | 1957 | Dick Mayer | 282* |
| 1898 | Fred Herd | 328 | 1927 | Tommy Armour | 301* | 1958 | Tommy Bolt | 283 |
| 1899 | Willie Smith | 315 | 1928 | Johnny Farrell | 294* | 1959 | Billy Casper | 282 |
| 1900 | Harry Vardon | 313 | 1929 | Bobby Jones[2] | 294* | 1960 | Arnold Palmer | 280 |
| 1901 | Willie Anderson | 331* | 1930 | Bobby Jones[2] | 287 | 1961 | Gene Littler | 281 |
| 1902 | L. Auchterlonie | 307 | 1931 | Billie Burke | 292* | 1962 | Jack Nicklaus | 283* |
| 1903 | Willie Anderson | 307* | 1932 | Gene Sarazen | 286 | 1963 | Julius Boros | 293* |
| 1904 | Willie Anderson | 303 | 1933 | Johnny Goodman[2] | 287 | 1964 | Ken Venturi | 278 |
| 1905 | Willie Anderson | 314 | 1934 | Olin Dutra | 293 | 1965 | Gary Player | 282* |
| 1906 | Alex Smith | 295 | 1935 | Sam Parks Jr. | 299 | 1966 | Billy Casper | 278* |
| 1907 | Alex Ross | 302 | 1936 | Tony Manero | 282 | 1967 | Jack Nicklaus | 275 |
| 1908 | Fred McLeod | 322* | 1937 | Ralph Guldahl | 281 | 1968 | Lee Trevino | 275 |
| 1909 | George Sargent | 290 | 1938 | Ralph Guldahl | 284 | 1969 | Orville Moody | 281 |
| 1910 | Alex Smith | 298* | 1939 | Byron Nelson | 284* | 1970 | Tony Jacklin | 281 |
| 1911 | John McDermott | 307* | 1940 | Lawson Little | 287* | 1971 | Lee Trevino | 280* |
| 1912 | John McDermott | 294 | 1941 | Craig Wood | 284 | 1972 | Jack Nicklaus | 290 |
| 1913 | Francis Ouimet[2] | 304 | 1942–45 | No match | | 1973 | Johnny Miller | 279 |
| 1914 | Walter Hagen | 290 | 1946 | Lloyd Mangrum | 284* | 1974 | Hale Irwin | 287 |
| 1915 | J. D. Travers[2] | 297 | 1947 | Lew Worsham | 282* | 1975 | Lou Graham | 287* |
| 1916 | Chick Evans Jr.[2] | 286 | 1948 | Ben Hogan | 276 | 1976 | Jerry Pate | 277 |
| 1917–18 | No match | | 1949 | Cary Middlecoff | 286 | 1977 | Hubert Green | 278 |
| 1919 | Walter Hagen | 301* | 1950 | Ben Hogan | 287* | 1978 | Andrew North | 285 |
| 1920 | Edward Ray | 295 | 1951 | Ben Hogan | 287 | 1979 | Hale Irwin | 284 |
| 1921 | Jim Barnes | 289 | 1952 | Julius Boros | 281 | 1980 | Jack Nicklaus | 272 |
| 1922 | Gene Sarazen | 288 | 1953 | Ben Hogan | 283 | | | |
| 1923 | Bobby Jones[2] | 296* | 1954 | Ed Furgol | 284 | | | |

* Tie for first place, playoff determined champion.  [1] For 72 holes except for 1895-97 when 36 holes were played.  [2] Amateur.

## BRITISH OPEN GOLF CHAMPIONS

The oldest prestigious golf tournament, the British Open, initiated formal competition in golf in 1860. The first American champion was Jock Hutchison in 1921. American golfers who have won the British open are indicated by an asterisk (*).

| | | | | | | | | | |
|---|---|---|---|---|---|---|---|---|---|
| 1860 | Willie Park Sr. | 1883 | W. L. Fernie | 1905 | James Braid | 1931 | Tommy Armour * | 1958 | Peter Thomson * |
| 1861-62 | Tom Morris Sr. | 1884 | Jack Simpson | 1906 | James Braid | 1932 | Gene Sarazen * | 1959 | Gary Player |
| 1863 | Willie Park Sr. | 1885 | Bob Martin | 1907 | Arnaud Massy | 1933 | Denny Shute * | 1960 | Kel Nagle |
| 1864 | Tom Morris Sr. | 1886 | D. L. Brown | 1908 | James Braid | 1934 | Henry Cotton | 1961-62 | Arnold Palmer * |
| 1865 | A. L. Strath | 1887 | Willie Park Jr. | 1909 | J. H. Taylor | 1935 | Alf Perry | 1963 | Bob Charles |
| 1866 | Willie Park Sr. | 1888 | Jack Burns | 1910 | James Braid | 1936 | Alf Padgham | 1964 | Tony Lema * |
| 1867 | Tom Morris Sr. | 1889 | Willie Park Jr. | 1911 | Harry Vardon | 1937 | Henry Cotton | 1965 | Peter Thomson |
| 1868 | Tom Morris Jr. | 1890 | John Ball | 1912 | Ted Ray | 1938 | R.A.Whitecombe | 1966 | Jack Nicklaus * |
| 1869 | Tom Morris Jr. | 1891 | Hugh Kirkaldy | 1913 | J. H. Taylor | 1939 | Richard Burton | 1967 | R. de Vicenzo |
| 1870 | Tom Morris Jr. | 1892 | H. H. Hilton | 1914 | Harry Vardon | 1940-45 | No play | 1968 | Gary Player |
| 1871 | No play | 1893 | W. Auchterlonie | 1915-19 | No play | 1946 | Sam Snead * | 1969 | Tony Jacklin |
| 1872 | Tom Morris Jr. | 1894 | J. H. Taylor | 1920 | George Duncan | 1947 | Fred Daly | 1970 | Jack Nicklaus * |
| 1873 | Tom Kidd | 1895 | J. H. Taylor | 1921 | Jock Hutchison * | 1948 | Henry Cotton | 1971 | Lee Trevino * |
| 1874 | Mungo Park | 1896 | Harry Vardon | 1922 | Walter Hagen * | 1949 | Bobby Locke * | 1972 | Lee Trevino * |
| 1875 | Willie Park Sr. | 1897 | H. H. Hilton | 1923 | Arthur Havers | 1950 | Bobby Locke * | 1973 | Tom Weiskopf * |
| 1876 | Bob Martin | 1898 | Harry Vardon | 1924 | Walter Hagen * | 1951 | Max Faulkner | 1974 | Gary Player |
| 1877 | Jamie Anderson | 1899 | Harry Vardon | 1925 | Jim Barnes * | 1952 | Bobby Locke * | 1975 | Tom Watson * |
| 1878 | Jamie Anderson | 1900 | J. H. Taylor | 1926 | Bobby Jones * | 1953 | Ben Hogan * | 1976 | Johnny Miller * |
| 1879 | Jamie Anderson | 1901 | James Braid | 1927 | Bobby Jones * | 1954 | Peter Thomson | 1977 | Tom Watson * |
| 1880 | Bob Ferguson | 1902 | Alex Herd | 1928 | Walter Hagen * | 1955 | Peter Thomson | 1978 | Jack Nicklaus * |
| 1881 | Bob Ferguson | 1903 | Harry Vardon | 1929 | Walter Hagen * | 1956 | Peter Thomson | 1979 | Severiano Ballesteros |
| 1882 | Bob Ferguson | 1904 | Jack White | 1930 | Bobby Jones * | 1957 | Bobby Locke | 1980 | Tom Watson * |

## RYDER CUP INTERNATIONAL PROFESSIONAL GOLF MATCH

| | | | |
|---|---|---|---|
| 1927 | United States 9½, Britain 2½ | 1957 | Britain 7½, United States 4½ |
| 1929 | Britain 7, United States 5 | 1959 | United States 8½, Britain 3½ |
| 1931 | United States 9, Britain 3 | 1961 | United States 14½, Britain 9½ |
| 1933 | Britain 6½, United States 5½ | 1963 | United States 23, Britain 9 |
| 1935 | United States 9, Britain 3 | 1965 | United States 19½, Britain 12½ |
| 1937 | United States 8, Britain 4 | 1967 | United States 23½, Britain 8½ |
| 1939–45 | No matches | 1969 | United States 16, Britain 16 (tie) |
| 1947 | United States 11, Britain 1 | 1971 | United States 18½, Britain 13½ |
| 1949 | United States 7, Britain 5 | 1973 | United States 18, Britain 13 |
| 1951 | United States 9½, Britain 2½ | 1975 | United States 21, Britain 11 |
| 1953 | United States 6½, Britain 5½ | 1977 | United States 12½, Britain 7½ |
| 1955 | United States 8, Britain 4 | 1979 | United States, 17, Britain 11 |

## UNITED STATES AMATEUR GOLF CHAMPIONS: MEN

The United States Golf Association (USGA) held its first amateur men's championship in 1895. Robert T. "Bobby" Jones Jr., generally regarded as America's greatest amateur golfer, won the championship a record five times in 1924, 1925, 1927, 1928, and 1930.

| | | | |
|---|---|---|---|
| 1895 C. MacDonald | 1913 Jerry Travers | 1931 Francis Ouimet | 1950 Sam Urzetta | 1966 Gary Cowan |
| 1896–98 H. Whigham | 1914 Francis Ouimet | 1932 Ross Somerville | 1951 Billy Maxwell | 1967 Bob Dickson |
| 1899 H. Harriman | 1915 Robert Gardner | 1933 George Dunlap, Jr. | 1952 Jack Westland | 1968 Bruce Fleisher |
| 1900-01 Walter Travis | 1916 Chick Evans, Jr. | 1934–35 Lawson Little | 1953 Gene Littler | 1969 Steve Melnyk |
| 1902 Louis James | 1917–18 No play | 1936 John Fischer | 1954 Arnold Palmer | 1970 Lanny Wadkins |
| 1903 Walter Travis | 1919 Davidson Herron | 1937 John Goodman | 1955–56 Harvie Ward | 1971 Gary Cowan |
| 1904 Chandler Egan | 1920 Chick Evans, Jr. | 1938 Willie Turnesa | 1957 Hillman Robbins | 1972 Vinny Giles |
| 1905 Chandler Egan | 1921 Jesse Guilford | 1939 Bud Ward | 1958 Charles Coe | 1973 Craig Stadler |
| 1906 Eben Byers | 1922 Jess Sweetser | 1940 Dick Chapman | 1959 Jack Nicklaus | 1974 Jerry Pate |
| 1907 Jerry Travers | 1923 Max Marston | 1941 Bud Ward | 1960 Deane Beman | 1975 Fred Ridley |
| 1908 Jerry Travers | 1924–25 Bobby Jones | 1942–45 No play | 1961 Jack Nicklaus | 1976 Bill Sander |
| 1909 Robert Gardner | 1926 George Von Elm | 1946 Ted Bishop | 1962 Labron Harris Jr. | 1977 John Faught |
| 1910 William Fownes Jr. | 1927–28 Bobby Jones | 1947 Skee Riegel | 1963 Deane Beman | 1978 John Cook |
| 1911 Harold Hilton | 1929 Harrison Johnston | 1948 Willie Turnesa | 1964 Bill Campbell | 1979 Mark O'Meara |
| 1912 Jerry Travers | 1930 Bobby Jones | 1949 Charles Coe | 1965 Robert Murphy Jr. | 1980 Hal Sutton |

## NATIONAL COLLEGIATE ATHLETIC ASSOCIATION GOLF CHAMPIONS

| | | |
|---|---|---|
| 1897 Louis Bayard Jr., Princeton | 1927 Watts Gunn, Georgia Tech | 1955 Joe Campbell, Purdue |
| 1898 James Reid Jr., Yale | 1928 Maurice McCarthy, Georgetown | 1956 Rick Jones, Ohio State |
| James Curtis, Harvard | 1929 Tom Aycock, Yale | 1957 Rex Baxter Jr., Houston |
| 1899 Percy Pyne, Princeton | 1930–31 George Dunlap Jr., Princeton | 1958 Phil Rodgers, Houston |
| 1901 H. Lindsley, Harvard | 1932 J. W. Fischer, Michigan | 1959–60 Dick Crawford, Houston |
| 1902 Charles Hitchcock Jr., Yale | 1933 Walter Emery, Oklahoma | 1961 Jack Nicklaus, Ohio State |
| 1903 F. O. Reinhart, Princeton | 1934 Charles Yates, Georgia Tech | 1962 Kermit Zarley, Houston |
| 1904 A. L. White, Harvard | 1935 Ed White, Texas | 1963 R. H. Sikes, Arkansas |
| 1905 Robert Abbott, Yale | 1936 Charles Kocsis, Michigan | 1964 Terry Small, San Jose State |
| 1906 W. E. Clow Jr., Yale | 1937 Fred Haas Jr., Louisiana State | 1965 Marty Fleckman, Houston |
| 1907 Ellis Knowles, Yale | 1938 John Burke, Georgetown | 1966 Bob Murphy, Florida |
| 1908 H. H. Wilder, Harvard | 1939 Vincent D'Antoni, Tulane | 1967 Hale Irwin, Colorado |
| 1909 Albert Seckel, Princeton | 1940 Dixon Brooke, Virginia | 1968 Grier Jones, Oklahoma State |
| 1910 Robert Hunter, Yale | 1941 Earl Stewart, Louisiana State | 1969 Bob Clark, Los Angeles State |
| 1911 George Stanley, Yale | 1942 Frank Tatum Jr., Stanford | 1970 John Mahaffey, Houston |
| 1912 F. C. Davison, Harvard | 1943 Wallace Ulrich, Carleton | 1971 Ben Crenshaw, Texas |
| 1913 Nathaniel Wheeler, Yale | 1944 Louis Lick, Minnesota | 1972 Ben Crenshaw, Texas |
| 1914 Edward Allis, Harvard | 1945 John Lorms, Ohio State | Tom Kite, Texas |
| 1915 Francis Blossom, Yale | 1946 George Hamer, Georgia | 1973 Ben Crenshaw, Texas |
| 1916 J. W. Hubbell, Harvard | 1947 Dave Barclay, Michigan | 1974 Curtis Strange, Wake Forest |
| 1917–18 No play | 1948 Bob Harris, San Jose State | 1975 Jay Haas, Wake Forest |
| 1919 A. L. Walker Jr., Columbia | 1949 Harvie Ward, North Carolina | 1976–77 Scott Simpson, USC |
| 1920 Jess Sweetser, Yale | 1950 Fred Wampler, Purdue | 1978 David Edwards, Oklahoma State |
| 1921 Simpson Dean, Princeton | 1951 Tom Nieporte, Ohio State | 1979 Gary Hallberg, Wake Forest |
| 1922 Pollack Boyd, Dartmouth | 1952 Jim Vickers, Oklahoma | 1980 Jay Don Blake, Utah State |
| 1923–24 Dexter Cummings, Yale | 1953 Earl Moeller, Oklahoma State | |
| 1925–26 Fred Lamprecht, Yale | 1954 Hillman Robbins, Memphis State | |

## BRITISH AMATEUR GOLF CHAMPIONS

The oldest golf tournament for amateurs is the British Amateur Tournament, played since 1885. It has been won 18 times by American amateur golfers, most recently in 1979.

| | | | | |
|---|---|---|---|---|
| 1885 A. F. MacFie | 1904 W. J. Travis | 1925 Robert Harris | 1948 Frank Stranahan* | 1965 Mike Bonallack |
| 1886–87 H. G. Hutchinson | 1905 A. G. Barry | 1926 Jess Sweetser* | 1949 Sam McCready | 1966 Bobby Cole |
| 1888 John Ball | 1906 James Robb | 1927 W. Tweddell | 1950 Frank Stranahan* | 1967 Bob Dickson* |
| 1889 J. E. Laidlay | 1907 John Ball | 1928 T. P. Perkins | 1951 Dick Chapman* | 1968–70 Mike Bonallack |
| 1890 John Ball | 1908 E. A. Lassen | 1929 Cyril Tolley | 1952 Harvie Ward* | 1971 Steve Melnyk* |
| 1891 J. E. Laidlay | 1909 R. Maxwell | 1930 Bobby Jones* | 1953 Joseph Carr | 1972 Trevor Homer |
| 1892 John Ball | 1910 John Ball | 1931 E. Martin Smith | 1954 Doug Bachli | 1973 Dick Siderowf* |
| 1893 P. L. Anderson | 1911 H. H. Hilton | 1932 J. De Forest | 1955 Joseph Conrad* | 1974 Trevor Homer |
| 1894 John Ball | 1912 John Ball | 1933 Michael Scott | 1956 John Beharrell | 1975 Marvin M. Giles |
| 1895 L. M. B. Melville | 1913 H. H. Hilton | 1934–35 Lawson Little* | 1957 Reid Jack | 1976 Dick Siderowf* |
| 1896 F. G. Tait | 1914 J. L. C. Jenkins | 1936 H. Thompson | 1958 Joseph Carr | 1977–78 Peter McEvoy |
| 1897 A. J. T. Allan | 1915–19 No play | 1937 Robert Sweeny Jr. | 1959 Deane Beman* | 1979 Jay Sigel* |
| 1898 F. G. Tait | 1920 Cyril J. Tolley | 1938 C. R. Yates* | 1961 Mike Bonallack | 1980 David Evans |
| 1899 John Ball | 1921 W. I. Hunter | 1939 Alex Kyle | 1960 Joseph Carr | |
| 1900-01 H. H. Hilton | 1922 E. W. Holderness | 1940–45 No play | 1962 Richard Davies* | |
| 1902 C. Hutchings | 1923 R. Wethered | 1946 James Bruen | 1963 Michael Lunt | |
| 1903 R. Maxwell | 1924 E. W. Holderness | 1947 Willie Turnesa* | 1964 Gordon Clark | |

*United States golfer.

## U.S. AMATEUR GOLF CHAMPIONS: WOMEN

The United States Golf Association (USGA) held its first amateur women's championship in 1895. Glenna Collett Vare won the championship six times between 1922 and 1935.

| | | | |
|---|---|---|---|
| 1895  Mrs. C. S. Brown | 1916  Alexa Stirling | 1941  Mrs. Frank Newell | 1963  Anne Quast Welts |
| 1896–98  Beatrix Hoyt | 1917–18  No play | 1942–45  No play | 1964  Barbara McIntire |
| 1899  Ruth Underhill | 1919  Alexa Stirling | 1946  Babe Zaharias | 1965  Jean Ashley |
| 1900  Frances Griscom | 1920  Alexa Stirling | 1947  Louise Suggs | 1966  JoAnne Carner |
| 1901  Genevieve Hecker | 1921  Marion Hollins | 1948  Grace Lenczyk | 1967  Lou Dill |
| 1902  Genevieve Hecker | 1922  Glenna Collett | 1949  Dorothy Porter | 1968  JoAnne Carner |
| 1903  Bessie Anthony | 1923  Edith Cummings | 1950  Beverly Hanson | 1969  Catherine Lacoste |
| 1904  Georgiana Bishop | 1924  Dorothy Campbell Hurd | 1951  Dorothy Kirby | 1970  Martha Wilkinson |
| 1905  Pauline Mackay | 1925  Glenna Collett | 1952  Jacqueline Pung | 1971  Laura Baugh |
| 1906  Harriot Curtis | 1926  Helen Stetson | 1953  Mary Lena Faulk | 1972  Mary Budke |
| 1907  Margaret Curtis | 1927  Miriam Burns Horn | 1954  Barbara Romack | 1973  Carol Semple |
| 1908  Kate Harley | 1928–30  Glenna Collett | 1955  Patricia Lesser | 1974  Cynthia Rill |
| 1909  Dorothy Campbell | 1931  Helen Hicks | 1956  Marlene Stewart | 1975  Beth Daniel |
| 1910  Dorothy Campbell | 1932–34  Virginia Van Wie | 1957  JoAnne Gunderson | 1976  Donna Horton |
| 1911  Margaret Curtis | 1935  Glenna Collett Vare | 1958  Anne Quast | 1977  Beth Daniel |
| 1912  Margaret Curtis | 1936  Pamela Barton | 1959  Barbara McIntire | 1978  Cathy Sherk |
| 1913  Gladys Ravenscroft | 1937  Mrs. J. A. Page Jr. | 1960  JoAnne Gunderson | 1979  Carolyn Hill |
| 1914  Mrs. H. A. Jackson | 1938  Patty Berg | 1961  Anne Quast Decker | 1980  Julie Simpson Inkster |
| 1915  Mrs. C. H. Vanderbeck | 1939–40  Betty Jameson | 1962  JoAnne Gunderson | |

## CURTIS CUP INTERNATIONAL WOMEN'S GOLF TEAM MATCH

The United States has dominated this series of matches between women amateur golf teams representing the U.S. and Britain. The matches are played every two years in even years.

| | | |
|---|---|---|
| 1932  United States 5½, Britain 3½ | 1954  United States 6, Britain 3 | 1968  United States 10½, Britain 7½ |
| 1934  United States 6½, Britain 2½ | 1956  Britain 5, United States 4 | 1970  United States 11½, Britain 6½ |
| 1936*  United States 4½, Britain 4½ | 1958*  Britain 4½, United States 4½ | 1972  United States 10, Britain 8 |
| 1938  United States 5½, Britain 3½ | 1960  United States 6½, Britain 2½ | 1974  United States 13, Britain 5 |
| 1948  United States 6½, Britain 2½ | 1962  United States 8, Britain 1 | 1976  United States 11½, Britain 8½ |
| 1950  United States 7½, Britain 1½ | 1964  United States 10½, Britain 7½ | 1978  United States 12, Britain 6 |
| 1952  Britain 5, United States 4 | 1966  United States 13, Britain 5 | 1980  United States 13, Britain 5 |

* Tie.

## WALKER CUP INTERNATIONAL MEN'S GOLF TEAM MATCH

The oldest international amateur golf team match, the Walker Cup competition is played between teams representing the United States and Britain. The cup was presented by G. Herbert Walker, former president of the United States Golf Association, and the first competition was held in 1922. Since 1924 the match has taken place every two years.

| YEAR | RESULTS | COURSE AND LOCATION |
|---|---|---|
| 1922 | United States 8; Britain 4 . . . . . . . . . . . . . . . . . . . . . | National Golf Links of America, Southampton, N.Y. |
| 1923 | United States 6; Britain 5; one match halved . . . . . . | St. Andrews, Scotland |
| 1924 | United States 9; Britain 3 . . . . . . . . . . . . . . . . . . . . . | Garden City Golf Club, Garden City, N.Y. |
| 1926 | United States 6; Britain 5; one match halved . . . . . . | St. Andrews, Scotland |
| 1928 | United States 11; Britain 1 . . . . . . . . . . . . . . . . . . . | Chicago Golf Club, Wheaton, Ill. |
| 1930 | United States 10; Britain 2 . . . . . . . . . . . . . . . . . . . | Royal St. George's Golf Club, Sandwich, England |
| 1932 | United States 8; Britain 1; three matches halved . . . | The Country Club, Brookline, Mass. |
| 1934 | United States 9; Britain 2; one match halved . . . . . . | St. Andrews, Scotland |
| 1936 | United States 9; Britain 0; three matches halved . . . | Pine Valley Golf Club, Clementon, N.J. |
| 1938 | Britain 7; United States 4; one match halved . . . . . . | St. Andrews, Scotland |
| 1940–45 | No competition because of World War II . . . . . . . . . | |
| 1947 | United States 8; Britain 4 . . . . . . . . . . . . . . . . . . . . . | St. Andrews, Scotland |
| 1949 | United States 10; Britain 2 . . . . . . . . . . . . . . . . . . . | Winged Foot Golf Club, Mamaroneck, N.Y. |
| 1951 | United States 6; Britain 3; three matches halved . . . | Birkdale Golf Club, Southport, England |
| 1953 | United States 9; Britain 3 . . . . . . . . . . . . . . . . . . . . . | Kittansett Club, Marion, Mass. |
| 1955 | United States 10; Britain 2 . . . . . . . . . . . . . . . . . . . | St. Andrews, Scotland |
| 1957 | United States 8; Britain 3; one match halved . . . . . . | Minikahda Club, Minneapolis, Minn. |
| 1959 | United States 9; Britain 3 . . . . . . . . . . . . . . . . . . . . . | Muirfield, Scotland |
| 1961 | United States 11; Britain 1 . . . . . . . . . . . . . . . . . . . | Seattle Golf Club, Seattle, Wash. |
| 1963 | United States 12; Britain 8; four matches halved . . . | Turnberry, Scotland |
| 1965 | United States 11; Britain 11 . . . . . . . . . . . . . . . . . . . | Baltimore Country Club, Baltimore, Md. |
| 1967 | United States 13; Britain 7 . . . . . . . . . . . . . . . . . . . . | Royal St. George's Golf Club, Sandwich, England |
| 1969 | United States 10; Britain 8 . . . . . . . . . . . . . . . . . . . . | Milwaukee Country Club, Milwaukee, Wis. |
| 1971 | Britain 13; United States 11 . . . . . . . . . . . . . . . . . . . | St. Andrews, Scotland |
| 1973 | United States 14; Britain 10 . . . . . . . . . . . . . . . . . . . | The Country Club, Brookline, Mass. |
| 1975 | United States 15½; Britain 8½ . . . . . . . . . . . . . . . . . | St. Andrews, Scotland |
| 1977 | United States 16; Britain 8 . . . . . . . . . . . . . . . . . . . . | Shinnecock Hills Golf Club, Southampton, N.Y. |
| 1979 | United States 15½; Britain 8½ . . . . . . . . . . . . . . . . . | Muirfield, Scotland |

# HOCKEY

United Press Int'l.

New York Islanders' Bob Nystrom shoots puck past Philadelphia Flyers' goalie Pete Peeters to score winning goal in overtime during final game of NHL playoffs May 24. The Islanders captured their first Stanley Cup by defeating the Flyers, 5–4, taking the series, 4 games to 2. The winning goal occurred 7 minutes, 11 seconds into the overtime period at the Nassau Coliseum in Uniondale, N.Y.

An overtime goal by right wing Bob Nystrom clinched the first NHL Stanley Cup for the New York Islanders on their home ice in Uniondale, N.Y., on May 24, 1980. They defeated the Philadelphia Flyers, 5–4, taking the playoff final series, 4 games to 2.

In the sixth and final game, each team scored two goals in the first period, though the New York goals were mired in controversy caused by questionable officiating. The Islanders scored two more goals in the second period, leading Philadelphia, 4–2. The hard-playing Flyers fought back with two of their own goals in the third period, tying the score at 4–4 and forcing a sudden-death overtime. It took New York 7 minutes and 11 seconds to score the winning goal.

The Islanders' center Bryan Trottier was voted the Conn Smythe Trophy as most valuable player in the playoffs. His two assists in the final game brought his playoff points to 29, a new NHL record for most points in the playoffs in one season.

During the regular season, the Islanders won 39 games, lost 28, and tied 13, leaving them in fifth place in the 21-team league. The Philadelphia Flyers finished first in the league with 48 wins, 12 losses, and 20 ties.

On their way to the Stanley Cup, the Islanders defeated the Boston Bruins, 4 games to 1, in the quarterfinals, and beat the Buffalo Sabres, 4 games to 2, in the semifinals.

Hockey superstar Gordie Howe announced his retirement at age 52 in June, after 32 active seasons. Holder of several NHL records, Howe played with the Detroit Red Wings from the 1946–47 season through the 1970–71 season, then joined the now-defunct World Hockey Association, playing for the Houston Aeros from 1973 to 1977. He completed the 1979–80 season with the Hartford Whalers.

In college action, North Dakota outskated Northern Michigan, 5–2, to win the National Collegiate Hockey Championship at Providence, R. I., on March 29. North Dakota's Doug Smail was voted outstanding player.

## NATIONAL COLLEGIATE ATHLETIC ASSOCIATION HOCKEY CHAMPIONSHIPS

| | | | |
|---|---|---|---|
| 1959 | North Dakota over Michigan State, 4–3 | 1970 | Cornell over Clarkson, 6–4 |
| 1960 | Denver over Michigan Tech, 5–3 | 1971 | Boston U. over Minnesota, 4–2 |
| 1961 | Denver over Saint Lawrence, 12–2 | 1972 | Boston U. over Cornell, 4–0 |
| 1962 | Michigan Tech over Clarkson, 7–1 | 1973 | Wisconsin over Denver, 4–2 |
| 1963 | North Dakota over Denver, 6–5 | 1974 | Minnesota over Michigan Tech, 4–2 |
| 1964 | Michigan over Denver, 6–3 | 1975 | Michigan Tech over Minnesota, 6–1 |
| 1965 | Michigan Tech over Boston College, 8–2 | 1976 | Minnesota over Michigan Tech, 6–4 |
| 1966 | Michigan State over Clarkson, 6–1 | 1977 | Wisconsin over Michigan, 6–5 |
| 1967 | Cornell over Boston U., 4–1 | 1978 | Boston U. over Boston College, 5–3 |
| 1968 | Denver over North Dakota, 4–0 | 1979 | Minnesota over North Dakota, 4–3 |
| 1969 | Denver over Cornell, 4–3 | 1980 | North Dakota over Northern Michigan, 5–2 |

## NATIONAL HOCKEY LEAGUE FINAL STANDINGS: 1979–80

### PRINCE OF WALES CONFERENCE

#### James Norris Division

| TEAM | WON | LOST | TIED | GOALS | POINTS |
|------|-----|------|------|-------|--------|
| Montreal | 47 | 20 | 13 | 328 | 107 |
| Los Angeles | 30 | 36 | 14 | 290 | 74 |
| Pittsburgh | 30 | 37 | 13 | 251 | 73 |
| Hartford | 27 | 34 | 19 | 303 | 73 |
| Detroit | 26 | 43 | 11 | 268 | 63 |

#### Charles F. Adams Division

| TEAM | WON | LOST | TIED | GOALS | POINTS |
|------|-----|------|------|-------|--------|
| Buffalo | 47 | 17 | 16 | 318 | 110 |
| Boston | 46 | 21 | 13 | 310 | 105 |
| Minnesota | 36 | 28 | 16 | 311 | 88 |
| Toronto | 35 | 40 | 5 | 304 | 75 |
| Quebec | 25 | 44 | 11 | 248 | 61 |

### CLARENCE CAMPBELL CONFERENCE

#### Lester Patrick Division

| TEAM | WON | LOST | TIED | GOALS | POINTS |
|------|-----|------|------|-------|--------|
| Philadelphia | 48 | 12 | 20 | 327 | 116 |
| N.Y. Islanders | 39 | 28 | 13 | 281 | 91 |
| N.Y. Rangers | 38 | 32 | 10 | 308 | 86 |
| Atlanta | 35 | 32 | 13 | 282 | 83 |
| Washington | 27 | 40 | 13 | 261 | 67 |

#### Conn Smythe Division

| TEAM | WON | LOST | TIED | GOALS | POINTS |
|------|-----|------|------|-------|--------|
| Chicago | 34 | 27 | 19 | 241 | 87 |
| St. Louis | 34 | 34 | 12 | 266 | 80 |
| Vancouver | 27 | 37 | 16 | 256 | 70 |
| Edmonton | 28 | 39 | 13 | 301 | 69 |
| Winnipeg | 20 | 49 | 11 | 214 | 51 |
| Colorado | 19 | 48 | 13 | 234 | 51 |

## NHL STANLEY CUP PLAYOFFS: 1980

**Finals:**
New York Islanders won finals and Stanley Cup, defeating Philadelphia Flyers, 4 games to 2.

**Semifinals:**
New York Islanders defeated Buffalo Sabres,
    4 games to 2.
Philadelphia Flyers defeated Minnesota North Stars,
    4 games to 1.

**Quarterfinals:**
New York Islanders defeated Boston Bruins,
    4 games to 1.
Philadelphia Flyers defeated N.Y. Rangers,
    4 games to 1.
Buffalo Sabres defeated Chicago Black Hawks,
    4 games to 0.
Minnesota North Stars defeated Montreal Canadiens,
    4 games to 3.

## STANLEY CUP NHL CHAMPIONS

| | | | | | | | |
|------|----|------|----|------|----|------|----|
| 1893–94 | Montreal A.A.A. | 1914 | Toronto Blueshirts | 1934 | Ch. Black Hawks | 1955 | Detroit Red Wings |
| 1895 | Montreal Victorias | 1915 | Vancouver Mil. | 1935 | Montreal Maroons | 1956 | Montreal Canadiens |
| 1896 | Winnipeg Victorias, | 1916 | Montreal Canadiens | 1936–37 | Detroit Red Wings | 1957–60 | Montreal Canadiens |
| | Montreal Victorias | 1917 | Seattle Met. | 1938 | Chi. Black Hawks | 1961 | Chi. Black Hawks |
| 1897–98 | Montreal Victorias | 1918 | Toronto Arenas | 1939 | Boston Bruins | 1962 | Toronto Maple Leafs |
| 1899 | Montreal Shamrocks | 1919 | No decision | 1940 | New York Rangers | 1963 | Toronto Maple Leafs |
| 1900 | Montreal Shamrocks | 1920–21 | Ottawa Senators | 1941 | Boston Bruins | 1964 | Toronto Maple Leafs |
| 1901 | Winnipeg Victorias | 1922 | Toronto St. Pats | 1942 | Toronto Maple Leafs | 1965 | Montreal Canadiens |
| 1902 | Montreal A.A.A. | 1923 | Ottawa Senators | 1943 | Detroit Red Wings | 1966 | Montreal Canadiens |
| 1903–05 | Ottawa Silver Seven | 1924 | Montreal Canadiens | 1944 | Montreal Canadiens | 1967 | Toronto Maple Leafs |
| 1906 | Montreal Wanderers | 1925 | Victoria Cougars | 1945 | Toronto Maple Leafs | 1968–69 | Montreal Canadiens |
| 1907 | Kenora Thistles, | 1926 | Montreal Maroons | 1946 | Montreal Canadiens | 1970 | Boston Bruins |
| | Mont. Wanderers | 1927 | Ottawa Senators | 1947–49 | Toronto Maple Leafs | 1971 | Montreal Canadiens |
| 1908 | Montreal Wanderers | 1928 | New York Rangers | 1950 | Detroit Red Wings | 1972 | Boston Bruins |
| 1909 | Ottawa Senators | 1929 | Boston Bruins | 1951 | Toronto Maple Leafs | 1973 | Montreal Canadiens |
| 1910 | Montreal Wanderers | 1930–31 | Montreal Canadiens | 1952 | Detroit Red Wings | 1974–75 | Philadelphia Flyers |
| 1911 | Ottawa Senators | 1932 | Toronto Maple Leafs | 1953 | Montreal Canadiens | 1976–79 | Montreal Canadiens |
| 1912–13 | Quebec Bulldogs | 1933 | New York Rangers | 1954 | Detroit Red Wings | 1980 | New York Islanders |

## NATIONAL HOCKEY LEAGUE LEADING SCORERS: 1979–80

| PLAYER | TEAM | GAMES | GOALS | ASSISTS | POINTS |
|--------|------|-------|-------|---------|--------|
| Marcel Dionne | Los Angeles | 80 | 53 | 84 | 137 |
| Wayne Gretzky | Edmonton | 79 | 51 | 86 | 137 |
| Guy Lafleur | Montreal | 74 | 50 | 75 | 125 |
| Gil Perreault | Buffalo | 80 | 40 | 66 | 106 |
| Mike Rogers | Hartford | 80 | 44 | 61 | 105 |
| Bryan Trottier | N.Y. Islanders | 78 | 42 | 62 | 104 |
| Charlie Simmer | Los Angeles | 64 | 56 | 45 | 101 |
| Blaine Stoughton | Hartford | 80 | 56 | 44 | 100 |
| Darryl Sittler | Toronto | 73 | 40 | 57 | 97 |
| Blair MacDonald | Edmonton | 80 | 46 | 48 | 94 |
| Bernie Federko | St. Louis | 79 | 38 | 56 | 94 |
| Al Macadam | Minnesota | 80 | 42 | 51 | 93 |
| Kent Nilsson | Atlanta | 80 | 40 | 53 | 93 |
| Mike Bossy | N.Y. Islanders | 75 | 51 | 41 | 92 |
| Rick Middleton | Boston | 80 | 40 | 52 | 92 |
| Pierre Larouche | Montreal | 73 | 50 | 41 | 91 |
| Dave Taylor | Los Angeles | 61 | 37 | 53 | 90 |
| Danny Gare | Buffalo | 76 | 56 | 33 | 89 |
| Steve Shutt | Montreal | 77 | 47 | 42 | 89 |
| Real Cloutier | Quebec | 67 | 42 | 46 | 88 |
| Steve Payne | Minnesota | 80 | 42 | 43 | 85 |
| Bobby Smith | Minnesota | 61 | 27 | 56 | 83 |

# NATIONAL HOCKEY LEAGUE TROPHY WINNERS

## ART ROSS TROPHY
(Leading scorer in regular season)

| YEAR | PLAYER | GAMES PLAYED | GOALS | ASSISTS | POINTS |
|------|--------|-------------|-------|---------|--------|
| 1950–51 | Gordie Howe, Detroit | 70 | 43 | 43 | 86 |
| 1951–52 | Gordie Howe, Detroit | 70 | 47 | 39 | 86 |
| 1952–53 | Gordie Howe, Detroit | 70 | 49 | 46 | 95 |
| 1953–54 | Gordie Howe, Detroit | 70 | 33 | 48 | 81 |
| 1954–55 | Bernie Geoffrion, Montreal | 70 | 38 | 37 | 75 |
| 1955–56 | Jean Beliveau, Montreal | 70 | 47 | 41 | 88 |
| 1956–57 | Gordie Howe, Detroit | 70 | 44 | 45 | 89 |
| 1957–58 | Dickie Moore, Montreal | 70 | 36 | 48 | 84 |
| 1958–59 | Dickie Moore, Montreal | 70 | 41 | 55 | 96 |
| 1959–60 | Bobby Hull, Chicago | 70 | 39 | 42 | 81 |
| 1960–61 | Bernie Geoffrion, Montreal | 64 | 50 | 45 | 95 |
| 1961–62 | Bobby Hull, Chicago | 70 | 50 | 34 | 84 |
| 1962–63 | Gordie Howe, Detroit | 70 | 38 | 48 | 86 |
| 1963–64 | Stan Mikita, Chicago | 70 | 39 | 50 | 89 |
| 1964–65 | Stan Mikita, Chicago | 70 | 28 | 59 | 87 |
| 1965–66 | Bobby Hull, Chicago | 65 | 54 | 43 | 97 |
| 1966–67 | Stan Mikita, Chicago | 70 | 35 | 62 | 97 |
| 1967–68 | Stan Mikita, Chicago | 72 | 40 | 47 | 87 |
| 1968–69 | Phil Esposito, Boston | 74 | 49 | 77 | 126 |
| 1969–70 | Bobby Orr, Boston | 76 | 33 | 87 | 120 |
| 1970–71 | Phil Esposito, Boston | 78 | 76 | 76 | 152 |
| 1971–72 | Phil Esposito, Boston | 76 | 66 | 67 | 133 |
| 1972–73 | Phil Esposito, Boston | 78 | 55 | 75 | 130 |
| 1973–74 | Phil Esposito, Boston | 78 | 68 | 77 | 145 |
| 1974–75 | Bobby Orr, Boston | 80 | 46 | 89 | 135 |
| 1975–76 | Guy Lafleur, Montreal | 80 | 56 | 69 | 125 |
| 1976–77 | Guy Lafleur, Montreal | 80 | 56 | 80 | 136 |
| 1977–78 | Guy Lafleur, Montreal | 78 | 60 | 72 | 132 |
| 1978–79 | Bryan Trottier, N.Y. Islanders | 76 | 47 | 87 | 134 |
| 1979–80 | Marcel Dionne, L.A. Kings | 80 | 53 | 84 | 137 |

## HART MEMORIAL TROPHY (Most valuable player)

| YEAR | PLAYER | YEAR | PLAYER | YEAR | PLAYER |
|------|--------|------|--------|------|--------|
| 1945–46 | Max Bentley, Chicago | 1955–56 | Jean Beliveau, Montreal | 1966–68 | Stan Mikita, Chicago |
| 1946–47 | Maurice Richard, Montreal | 1956–58 | Gordie Howe, Detroit | 1968–69 | Phil Esposito, Boston |
| 1947–48 | Herbert O'Connor, New York | 1958–59 | Andy Bathgate, New York | 1969–72 | Bobby Orr, Boston |
| 1948–49 | Sid Abel, Detroit | 1959–60 | Gordie Howe, Detroit | 1972–73 | Bobby Clarke, Philadelphia |
| 1949–50 | Chuck Rayner, New York | 1960–61 | Bernie Geoffrion, Montreal | 1973–74 | Phil Esposito, Boston |
| 1950–51 | Milt Schmidt, Boston | 1961–62 | Jacques Plante, Montreal | 1974–76 | Bobby Clarke, Philadelphia |
| 1951–53 | Gordie Howe, Detroit | 1962–63 | Gordie Howe, Detroit | 1976–78 | Guy Lafleur, Montreal |
| 1953–54 | Al Rollins, Chicago | 1963–64 | Jean Beliveau, Montreal | 1978–79 | Bryan Trottier, N.Y. Islanders |
| 1954–55 | Ted Kennedy, Detroit | 1964–66 | Bobby Hull, Chicago | 1979–80 | Wayne Gretzky, Edmonton |

## VEZINA TROPHY (Best goalkeeper record)

| YEAR | PLAYER | YEAR | PLAYER | YEAR | PLAYER |
|------|--------|------|--------|------|--------|
| 1961–62 | Jacques Plante, Montreal | 1967–68 | Lorne Worsley and Rogatien Vachon, Montreal | 1972–73 | Ken Dryden, Montreal |
| 1962–63 | Glenn Hall, Chicago | | | 1973–74 | Tony Esposito, Chicago, and Bernie Parent, Philadelphia |
| 1963–64 | Charlie Hodge, Montreal | 1968–69 | Jacques Plante and Glenn Hall, St. Louis | | |
| 1964–65 | Terry Sawchuk and Johnny Bower, Toronto | 1969–70 | Tony Esposito, Chicago | 1974–75 | Bernie Parent, Philadelphia |
| | | 1970–71 | Ed Giacomin and | 1975–76 | Ken Dryden, Montreal |
| 1965–66 | Lorne Worsley and Charlie Hodge, Montreal | 1970–71 | Gilles Villemure, New York | 1976–79 | Ken Dryden, Montreal, and Michel Larocque, Montreal |
| 1966–67 | Denis De Jordy and Glenn Hall, Chicago | 1971–72 | Tony Esposito and Gary Smith, Chicago | 1979–80 | Bob Suave and Don Edwards, Buffalo |

## CALDER MEMORIAL TROPHY (Rookie of the year)

| YEAR | PLAYER | YEAR | PLAYER | YEAR | PLAYER |
|------|--------|------|--------|------|--------|
| 1950–51 | Terry Sawchuk, Detroit | 1960–61 | Dave Keon, Toronto | 1970–71 | Gil Perreault, Buffalo |
| 1951–52 | Bernie Geoffrion, Montreal | 1961–62 | Bobby Rousseau, Montreal | 1971–72 | Ken Dryden, Montreal |
| 1952–53 | Lorne Worsley, New York | 1962–63 | Kent Douglas, Toronto | 1972–73 | Steve Vickers, New York |
| 1953–54 | Camille Henry, New York | 1963–64 | Jacques Laperriere, Montreal | 1973–74 | Denis Potvin, N.Y. Islanders |
| 1954–55 | Ed Litzenberger, Chicago | 1964–65 | Roger Crozier, Detroit | 1974–75 | Eric Vail, Atlanta |
| 1955–56 | Glenn Hall, Detroit | 1965–66 | Brit Selby, Toronto | 1975–76 | Bryan Trottier, N.Y. Islanders |
| 1956–57 | Larry Regan, Boston | 1966–67 | Bobby Orr, Boston | 1976–77 | Willi Plett, Atlanta |
| 1957–58 | Frank Mahovlich, Toronto | 1967–68 | Derek Sanderson, Boston | 1977–78 | Mike Bossy, N.Y. Islanders |
| 1958–59 | Ralph Backstrom, Montreal | 1968–69 | Danny Grant, Minnesota | 1978–79 | Bobby Smith, Minnesota |
| 1959–60 | Bill Hay, Chicago | 1969–70 | Tony Esposito, Chicago | 1979–80 | Ray Bourque, Boston |

## LADY BYNG MEMORIAL TROPHY (For skillful and sportsmanlike play)

| YEAR | PLAYER | YEAR | PLAYER | YEAR | PLAYER |
|------|--------|------|--------|------|--------|
| 1950–51 | Leonard Kelly, Detroit | 1960–61 | Leonard Kelly, Toronto | 1971–72 | Jean Ratelle, New York |
| 1951–52 | Sid Smith, Toronto | 1961–63 | Dave Keon, Toronto | 1972–73 | Gil Perreault, Buffalo |
| 1952–54 | Leonard Kelly, Detroit | 1963–64 | Ken Wharram, Chicago | 1973–74 | Johnny Bucyk, Boston |
| 1954–55 | Sid Smith, Toronto | 1964–65 | Bobby Hull, Chicago | 1974–75 | Marcel Dionne, Detroit |
| 1955–56 | Earl Reibel, Detroit | 1965–66 | Alex Delvecchio, Detroit | 1975–76 | Jean Ratelle, Boston |
| 1956–57 | Andy Hebenton, New York | 1966–68 | Stan Mikita, Chicago | 1976–77 | Marcel Dionne, Los Angeles |
| 1957–58 | Camille Henry, New York | 1968–69 | Alex Delvecchio, Detroit | 1977–78 | Butch Goring, Los Angeles |
| 1958–59 | Alex Delvecchio, Detroit | 1969–70 | Phil Goyette, St. Louis | 1978–79 | Bob MacMillan, Atlanta |
| 1959–60 | Don McKenney, Boston | 1970–71 | Johnny Bucyk, Boston | 1979–80 | Wayne Gretzky, Edmonton |

## JAMES NORRIS MEMORIAL TROPHY (Outstanding defenseman)

| YEAR | PLAYER | YEAR | PLAYER | YEAR | PLAYER |
|------|--------|------|--------|------|--------|
| 1958–59 | Tom Johnson, Montreal | 1965–66 | J. Laperriere, Montreal | 1975–76 | Denis Potvin, N.Y. Islanders |
| 1959–61 | Doug Harvey, Montreal | 1966–67 | Harry Howell, New York | 1976–77 | Larry Robinson, Montreal |
| 1961–62 | Doug Harvey, New York | 1967–75 | Bobby Orr, Boston | 1977–79 | Denis Potvin, N.Y. Islanders |
| 1962–65 | Pierre Pilote, Chicago | 1974–75 | Bobby Orr, Boston | 1979–80 | Larry Robinson, Montreal |

## CONN SMYTHE TROPHY (Most valuable player in the Stanley Cup playoffs)

| YEAR | PLAYER | YEAR | PLAYER | YEAR | PLAYER |
|------|--------|------|--------|------|--------|
| 1968–69 | Serge Savarad, Montreal | 1972–73 | Yvan Cournoyer, Montreal | 1976–77 | Guy Lafleur, Montreal |
| 1969–70 | Bobby Orr, Boston | 1973–74 | Bernie Parent, Philadelphia | 1977–78 | Larry Robinson, Montreal |
| 1970–71 | Ken Dryden, Montreal | 1974–75 | Bernie Parent, Philadelphia | 1978–79 | Bob Gainey, Montreal |
| 1971–72 | Bobby Orr, Boston | 1975–76 | Reggie Leach, Philadelphia | 1979–80 | Bryan Trottier, N.Y. Islanders |

## NATIONAL HOCKEY LEAGUE PRINCE OF WALES TROPHY WINNERS

| | | | | | | | |
|---|---|---|---|---|---|---|---|
| 1925 | Montreal Canadiens | 1941 | Boston Bruins | 1954 | Detroit Red Wings | 1967 | Chicago Black Hawks |
| 1926 | Montreal Maroons | 1942 | New York Rangers | 1955 | Detroit Red Wings | 1968 | Montreal Canadiens |
| 1927 | Ottawa Senators | 1943 | Detroit Red Wings | 1956 | Montreal Canadiens | 1969 | Montreal Canadiens |
| 1928–31 | Boston Bruins | 1944 | Montreal Canadiens | 1957 | Detroit Red Wings | 1970 | Chicago Black Hawks |
| 1932 | New York Rangers | 1945 | Montreal Canadiens | 1958 | Montreal Canadiens | 1971–72 | Boston Bruins |
| 1933 | Boston Bruins | 1946 | Montreal Canadiens | 1959 | Montreal Canadiens | 1973 | Montreal Canadiens |
| 1934 | Detroit Red Wings | 1947 | Montreal Canadiens | 1960 | Montreal Canadiens | 1974 | Boston Bruins |
| 1935 | Boston Bruins | 1948 | Toronto Maple Leafs | 1961 | Montreal Canadiens | 1975 | Buffalo Sabres |
| 1936 | Detroit Red Wings | 1949 | Detroit Red Wings | 1962 | Montreal Canadiens | 1976 | Montreal Canadiens |
| 1937 | Detroit Red Wings | 1950 | Detroit Red Wings | 1963 | Toronto Maple Leafs | 1977 | Montreal Canadiens |
| 1938 | Boston Bruins | 1951 | Detroit Red Wings | 1964 | Montreal Canadiens | 1978 | Montreal Canadiens |
| 1939 | Boston Bruins | 1952 | Detroit Red Wings | 1965 | Detroit Red Wings | 1979 | Montreal Canadiens |
| 1940 | Boston Bruins | 1953 | Detroit Red Wings | 1966 | Montreal Canadiens | 1980 | Buffalo Sabres |

## NATIONAL HOCKEY LEAGUE CLARENCE S. CAMPBELL BOWL WINNERS

| | | | | | |
|---|---|---|---|---|---|
| 1968 | Philadelphia Flyers | 1972 | Chicago Black Hawks | 1978 | New York Islanders |
| 1969–70 | St. Louis Blues | 1973 | Chicago Black Hawks | 1979 | New York Rangers |
| 1971 | Chicago Black Hawks | 1974–77 | Philadelphia Flyers | 1980 | Philadelphia Flyers |

## NATIONAL HOCKEY LEAGUE ALL-STAR GAMES

When All-Star games began to be played in 1947, the All-Star team played the defending champion team of the previous season. Later, East Division All-Stars played West Division All-Stars in mid-season. In the 1978–79 season, a team of All-Stars from the NHL opposed the best players of the Soviet Union in a three-game series. The first six players of the NHL team were selected in continent-wide voting among fans. The coach and manager chose the other players on the squad.

| | | | | | |
|---|---|---|---|---|---|
| 1947 | All-Stars 4, Toronto 3 | 1960 | All-Stars 2, Montreal 1 | 1974 | West 6, East 4 |
| 1948 | All-Stars 3, Toronto 1 | 1961 | All-Stars 3, Chicago 1 | 1975 | Prince of Wales Conf. 7, |
| 1949 | All-Stars 3, Toronto 1 | 1962 | Toronto 4, All-Stars 1 | | C.F. Campbell Conf. 1 |
| 1950 | Detroit 7, All-Stars 1 | 1963 | All-Stars 3, Toronto 3 | 1976 | Prince of Wales Conf. 7, |
| 1951 | 1st Team 2, 2d Team 2 | 1964 | All-Stars 3, Toronto 2 | | C.F. Campbell Conf. 5 |
| 1952 | 1st Team 1, 2d Team 1 | 1965 | All-Stars 5, Montreal 2 | 1977 | Prince of Wales Conf. 4, |
| 1953 | All-Stars 3, Montreal 1 | *1967 | Montreal 3, All-Stars 0 | | C.F. Campbell Conf. 3 |
| 1954 | All-Stars 2, Detroit 2 | 1968 | Toronto 4, All-Stars 3 | 1978 | Prince of Wales Conf. 3, |
| 1955 | Detroit 3, All-Stars 1 | 1969 | East 3, West 3 | | C.F. Campbell Conf. 2 |
| 1956 | All-Stars 1, Montreal 1 | 1970 | East 4, West 1 | 1979 | Soviet National Stars 2, |
| 1957 | All-Stars 5, Montreal 1 | 1971 | West 2, East 1 | | NHL All-Stars 1 |
| 1958 | Montreal 6, All-Stars 3 | 1972 | East 3, West 2 | 1980 | Prince of Wales Conf. 6, |
| 1959 | Montreal 6, All-Stars 1 | 1973 | East 5, West 4 | | C.F. Campbell Conf. 3 |

*Game shifted to midseason.

## SELECTED NATIONAL HOCKEY LEAGUE RECORDS

### TEAM RECORDS

| | |
|---|---|
| Most points, one season | 132—Montreal Canadiens, 1976–77, won 60, lost 8, tied 12 |
| Most wins, one season | 60—Montreal Canadiens, 1976–77 |
| Longest winning record | 14 games—Boston Bruins, Dec. 3, 1929–Jan. 9, 1930 |
| Most goals, one season | 399—Boston Bruins, 1970–71 |
| Most goals, both teams, one game | 21—Jan. 10, 1920: Montreal Canadiens defeated Toronto St. Patricks, 14-7 |
| Most penalties, one team, one game | 30—Philadelphia Flyers, Oct. 25, 1974, at California |
| Most penalty minutes, one team, one game | 194—Philadelphia Flyers, March 11, 1979, against Los Angeles Kings |

### INDIVIDUAL RECORDS

| | |
|---|---|
| Most seasons | 26—Gordie Howe, Detroit Red Wings, 1946–47 through 1970–71; Hartford Whalers, 1979–80 |
| Most games | 1,767—Gordie Howe, Detroit Red Wings, Hartford Whalers, 1946–71, 1979–80 |
| Most goals | 801—Gordie Howe, Detroit Red Wings, Hartford Whalers, 1946–71, 1979–80 |
| Most assists | 1,049—Gordie Howe, Detroit Red Wings, Hartford Whalers, 1946–71, 1979–80 |
| Highest goals-per-game average, career (among players with 200 or more goals) | .767—Cy Denneny, Ottawa Senators, Boston Bruins, 1917–18 through 1928–29 |
| Most 50-or-more goal seasons | 5—Bobby Hull, Chicago Black Hawks in 15 seasons |
| Most goals, one season | 76—Phil Esposito, Boston Bruins, 1970–71 |
| Most penalty minutes, one season | 472—Dave Schultz, Philadelphia Flyers, 1974–75 |
| Longest consecutive goal-scoring streak | 16 games—Harry (Punch) Broadbent, Ottawa Senators, 1921–22 |
| Most goals, one game | 7—Joe Malone, Quebec Bulldogs, Jan. 31, 1920, against Toronto St. Patricks |
| Most points, one game | 10—Darryl Sittler, Toronto Maple Leafs, Feb. 7, 1976, against Boston; 6 goals, 4 assists |

# HORSE RACING

Jacinto Vasquez guides Genuine Risk to victory in 106th Kentucky Derby at Churchill Downs May 3, 1980.

Genuine Risk became the second filly in history to win the Kentucky Derby when she outdistanced Rumbo and Jaklin Klugman in the 106th run for the roses on May 3. The last filly to win the race was Regret, in 1915.

The three-year-old ran the 1¼-mile track in 2:02, as a 13–1 shot. Rockhill Native, the favorite, was fifth.

Genuine Risk was beaten in the Preakness, the second leg of the Triple Crown, by Codex, a horse known mainly on the West Coast, by 4¾ lengths. The filly's jockey, Jacinto Vasquez, protested the outcome because he claimed Codex had "brushed" his horse. Although millions of TV viewers watched the alleged foul replayed several times, stewards at the track declared no foul was committed. Codex covered the track at Pimlico, in Baltimore, Md., in 1:54⅕.

The Belmont Stakes, third leg of the Triple Crown, was won by a 53–1 shot, Temperence Hill. The colt edged Genuine Risk by two lengths. Codex finished seventh.

In harness racing, 3-year-old pacer Niatross became the first winner of pacing's Triple Crown since 1970. During the Little Brown Jug, second leg of the crown, Niatross shattered six world pacing records in the two-heat race at Delaware, Ohio, on Sept. 18. Driven by Clint Galbraith, Niatross earned $104,717 in the Jug, bringing his 1980 winnings to more than $1,133,000. He was Harness Horse of the Year in 1979 and 1980.

Harness racing's prestigious Hambletonian race was won by Burgomeister, at the Du-Quoin, Ill., track on Aug. 30. Jockey Bill Haughton guided Burgomeister to victory in the third and deciding heat in 1:56⅗.

## THOROUGHBRED HORSE OF THE YEAR (ECLIPSE AWARD)

| YEAR | HORSE | YEAR | HORSE | YEAR | HORSE | YEAR | HORSE |
|------|-------|------|-------|------|-------|------|-------|
| 1936 | Granville | 1948 | Citation | 1959 | Sword Dancer | 1970 | Personality |
| 1937 | War Admiral | 1949 | Capot | 1960 | Kelso | 1971 | Ack Ack |
| 1938 | Seabiscuit | 1950 | Hill Prince | 1961 | Kelso | 1972 | Secretariat |
| 1939–40 | Challedon | 1951 | Counterpoint | 1962 | Kelso | 1973 | Secretariat |
| 1941 | Whirlaway | 1952 | Native Dancer | 1963 | Kelso | 1974 | Forego |
| 1942 | Whirlaway | 1953 | Tom Fool | 1964 | Kelso | 1975 | Forego |
| 1943 | Count Fleet | 1954 | Native Dancer | 1965 | Moccasin | 1976 | Forego |
| 1944 | Twilight Tear | 1955 | Nashua | 1966 | Buckpasser | 1977 | Seattle Slew |
| 1945 | Busher | 1956 | Swaps | 1967 | Damascus | 1978 | Affirmed |
| 1946 | Assault | 1957 | Dedicate | 1968 | Dr. Fager | 1979 | Affirmed |
| 1947 | Armed | 1958 | Round Table | 1969 | Arts and Letters | 1980 | Spectacular Bid |

## LEADING MONEY-WINNING RACEHORSES

Source: Thoroughbred Racing Association of North America

| YEAR | HORSE | AGE (in years) | STARTS | WINS | SECONDS | THIRDS | AMOUNT WON | YEAR | HORSE | AGE (in years) | STARTS | WINS | SECONDS | THIRDS | AMOUNT WON |
|---|---|---|---|---|---|---|---|---|---|---|---|---|---|---|---|
| 1945 | Busher | 3 | 13 | 10 | 2 | 1 | $273,735 | 1963 | Candy Spots | 3 | 12 | 7 | 2 | 1 | $604,481 |
| 1946 | Assault | 3 | 15 | 8 | 2 | 3 | 424,195 | 1964 | Gun Bow | 4 | 16 | 8 | 4 | 2 | 580,100 |
| 1947 | Armed | 6 | 17 | 11 | 4 | 1 | 376,325 | 1965 | Buckpasser | 2 | 11 | 9 | 1 | 0 | 568,096 |
| 1948 | Citation | 3 | 20 | 19 | 1 | 0 | 709,470 | 1966 | Buckpasser | 3 | 14 | 13 | 1 | 0 | 669,078 |
| 1949 | Ponder | 3 | 21 | 9 | 5 | 2 | 321,825 | 1967 | Damascus | 3 | 16 | 12 | 3 | 1 | 817,944 |
| 1950 | Noor | 5 | 12 | 7 | 4 | 1 | 346,940 | 1968 | Forward Pass | 3 | 13 | 7 | 2 | 0 | 546,674 |
| 1951 | Counterpoint | 3 | 15 | 7 | 2 | 1 | 250,525 | 1969 | Arts and Letters | 3 | 14 | 8 | 5 | 1 | 555,604 |
| 1952 | Crafty Admiral | 4 | 16 | 9 | 4 | 1 | 277,225 | 1970 | Personality | 3 | 18 | 8 | 2 | 1 | 444,049 |
| 1953 | Native Dancer | 3 | 10 | 9 | 1 | 0 | 513,425 | 1971 | Riva Ridge | 2 | 9 | 7 | 0 | 0 | 503,263 |
| 1954 | Determine | 3 | 15 | 10 | 3 | 2 | 328,700 | 1972 | Droll Roll | 4 | 8 | 4 | 1 | 2 | 471,633 |
| 1955 | Nashua | 3 | 12 | 10 | 1 | 1 | 752,550 | 1973 | Secretariat | 3 | 21 | 16 | 3 | 1 | 860,404 |
| 1956 | Needles | 3 | 8 | 4 | 2 | 0 | 440,850 | 1974 | Chris Evert | 3 | 7 | 4 | 1 | 2 | 551,063 |
| 1957 | Round Table | 3 | 22 | 15 | 1 | 3 | 600,383 | 1975 | Foolish Pleasure | 3 | 11 | 5 | 4 | 1 | 716,278 |
| 1958 | Round Table | 4 | 20 | 14 | 4 | 0 | 662,780 | 1976 | Forego | 6 | 8 | 6 | 1 | 1 | 491,701 |
| 1959 | Sword Dancer | 3 | 13 | 8 | 4 | 0 | 537,004 | 1977 | Seattle Slew | 3 | 7 | 6 | 0 | 0 | 641,370 |
| 1960 | Bally Ache | 3 | 15 | 10 | 3 | 1 | 455,045 | 1978 | Affirmed | 3 | 11 | 8 | 2 | 0 | 901,541 |
| 1961 | Carry Back | 3 | 16 | 9 | 1 | 3 | 565,349 | 1979 | Spectacular Bid | 3 | 12 | 10 | 1 | 1 | 1,279,333 |
| 1962 | Never Bend | 2 | 10 | 7 | 1 | 2 | 402,969 | 1980 | Temperence Hill | 3 | 17 | 8 | 3 | 1 | 1,130,452 |

## THOROUGHBRED HORSE RACING'S TRIPLE CROWN

The Triple Crown of thoroughbred horse racing in the United States consists of winning three races for 3-year-olds: the Kentucky Derby, the Preakness Stakes, and the Belmont Stakes.

Only 11 horses have won the Triple Crown: Sir Barton in 1919, Gallant Fox in 1930, Omaha in 1935, War Admiral in 1937, Whirlaway in 1941, Count Fleet in 1943, Assault in 1946, Citation in 1948, Secretariat in 1973, Seattle Slew in 1977, and Affirmed in 1978.

### KENTUCKY DERBY

The Kentucky Derby is the oldest continually run horse race in the U.S. The 1¼-mile race for 3-year-old horses is run annually at Churchill Downs in Louisville, Ky., on the first Saturday in May. From 1875 through 1895 the race was 1½ miles. Two jockeys have won five times: Eddie Arcaro in 1938, 1941, 1945, 1948, and 1952; and Bill Hartack in 1957, 1960, 1962, 1964, and 1969.

| YEAR | WINNER | PURSE | JOCKEY | TIME | YEAR | WINNER | PURSE | JOCKEY | TIME |
|---|---|---|---|---|---|---|---|---|---|
| 1875 | Aristides | $2,850 | Oliver Lewis | 2:37 ¾ | 1910 | Donau | $4,850 | Robert Herbert | 2:06 ⅖ |
| 1876 | Vagrant | 2,950 | Bobby Swim | 2:38 ¼ | 1911 | Meridian | 4,850 | George Archibald | 2:05 |
| 1877 | Baden Baden | 3,300 | Billy Walker | 2:38 | 1912 | Worth | 4,850 | Carroll Shilling | 2:09 ⅖ |
| 1878 | Day Star | 4,050 | J. Carter | 2:37 ¼ | 1913 | Donerail | 5,475 | Roscoe Goose | 2:04 ⅘ |
| 1879 | Lord Murphy | 3,550 | C. Shaver | 2:37 | 1914 | Old Rosebud | 9,125 | John McCabe | 2:03 ⅖ |
| 1880 | Fonso | 3,800 | George Lewis | 2:37 ½ | 1915 | Regret | 11,450 | Joe Notter | 2:05 ⅖ |
| 1881 | Hindoo | 4,410 | Jimmy McLaughlin | 2:40 | 1916 | George Smith | 9,750 | Johnny Loftus | 2:04 |
| 1882 | Apollo | 4,560 | Babe Hurd | 2:40 ¼ | 1917 | Omar Khayyam | 16,600 | Charles Borel | 2:04 ⅗ |
| 1883 | Leonatus | 3,760 | Billy Donohue | 2:43 | 1918 | Exterminator | 14,700 | Willie Knap | 2:10 ⅘ |
| 1884 | Buchanan | 3,990 | Isaac Murphy | 2:40 ¼ | 1919 | Sir Barton | 20,825 | Johnny Loftus | 2:09 ⅘ |
| 1885 | Joe Cotton | 4,630 | Erskine Henderson | 2:37 ⅕ | 1920 | Paul Jones | 30,375 | Ted Rice | 2:09 |
| 1886 | Ben Ali | 4,890 | P. Duffy | 2:36 ½ | 1921 | Behave Yourself | 38,450 | Charles Thompson | 2:04 ⅕ |
| 1887 | Montrose | 4,200 | Isaac Lewis | 2:39 ¼ | 1922 | Morvich | 46,775 | Albert Johnson | 2:04 ⅗ |
| 1888 | Macbeth II | 4,740 | G. Covington | 2:38 ¼ | 1923 | Zev | 53,600 | Earl Sande | 2:05 ⅖ |
| 1889 | Spokane | 4,970 | Thomas Kiley | 2:34 ½ | 1924 | Black Gold | 52,775 | John D. Mooney | 2:05 ⅕ |
| 1890 | Riley | 5,460 | Isaac Murphy | 2:45 | 1925 | Flying Ebony | 52,950 | Earl Sande | 2:07 ⅗ |
| 1891 | Kingman | 4,680 | Isaac Murphy | 2:52 ½ | 1926 | Bubbling Over | 50,075 | Albert Johnson | 2:03 ⅘ |
| 1892 | Azra | 4,230 | Alonzo Clayton | 2:41 ½ | 1927 | Whiskey | 51,000 | Linus McAtee | 2:06 |
| 1893 | Lookout | 4,090 | E. Kunze | 2:39 ¼ | 1928 | Reigh Count | 55,375 | Chick Lang | 2:10 ⅖ |
| 1894 | Chant | 4,020 | Frank Goodale | 2:41 | 1929 | Clyde Van Dusen | 53,950 | Linus McAtee | 2:10 ⅘ |
| 1895 | Halma | 2,970 | James Perkins | 2:37 ½ | 1930 | Gallant Fox | 50,725 | Earl Sande | 2:07 ⅗ |
| 1896 | Ben Brush | 4,850 | Willie Simms | 2:07 ¾ | 1931 | Twenty Grand | 48,725 | Charles Kurtsinger | 2:01 ⅘ |
| 1897 | Typhoon II | 4,850 | Buttons Garner | 2:12 ½ | 1932 | Burgoo King | 52,350 | Eugene James | 2:05 ⅕ |
| 1898 | Plaudit | 4,850 | Willie Simms | 2:09 | 1933 | Brokers Tip | 48,925 | Don Meade | 2:06 ⅘ |
| 1899 | Manuel | 4,850 | Fred Taral | 2:12 | 1934 | Cavalcade | 28,175 | Mack Garner | 2:04 |
| 1900 | Lt. Gibson | 4,850 | Jimmy Boland | 2:06 ¼ | 1935 | Omaha | 39,525 | Willie Saunders | 2:05 |
| 1901 | His Eminence | 4,850 | Jimmy Winkfield | 2:07 ¾ | 1936 | Bold Venture | 37,725 | Ira Hanford | 2:03 ⅗ |
| 1902 | Alan-a-Dale | 4,850 | Jimmy Winkfield | 2:08 ¾ | 1937 | War Admiral | 52,050 | Charles Kurtsinger | 2:03 ⅕ |
| 1903 | Judge Himes | 4,850 | Hal Booker | 2:09 | 1938 | Lawrin | 47,050 | Eddie Arcaro | 2:04 ⅘ |
| 1904 | Elwood | 4,850 | Frankie Prior | 2:08 ½ | 1939 | Johnstown | 46,350 | James Stout | 2:03 ⅖ |
| 1905 | Agile | 4,850 | Jack Martin | 2:10 ¾ | 1940 | Gallahadion | 60,150 | Carroll Bierman | 2:05 |
| 1906 | Sir Huron | 4,850 | Roscoe Troxler | 2:08 ⅘ | 1941 | Whirlaway | 61,275 | Eddie Arcaro | 2:01⅖ |
| 1907 | Pink Star | 4,850 | Andy Minder | 2:12 ⅗ | 1942 | Shut Out | 64,225 | Wayne D. Wright | 2:04⅖ |
| 1908 | Stone Street | 4,850 | Arthur Pickens | 2:15 ⅕ | 1943 | Count Fleet | 60,725 | Johnny Longden | 2:04 |
| 1909 | Wintergreen | 4,850 | Vince Powers | 2:08 ⅕ | 1944 | Pensive | 64,675 | Con McCreary | 2:04⅕ |

## KENTUCKY DERBY (continued)

| YEAR | WINNER | PURSE | JOCKEY | TIME | YEAR | WINNER | PURSE | JOCKEY | TIME |
|---|---|---|---|---|---|---|---|---|---|
| 1945 | Hoop Jr. | $64,850 | Eddie Arcaro | 2:07 | 1963 | Chateaugay | $108,900 | Braulio Baeza | 2:01 4/5 |
| 1946 | Assault | 96,400 | Warren Mehrtens | 2:06 3/5 | 1964 | Northern Dancer | 114,300 | Bill Hartack | 2:00 |
| 1947 | Jet Pilot | 92,160 | Eric Guerin | 2:06 4/5 | 1965 | Lucky Debonair | 112,000 | Willie Shoemaker | 2:01 1/5 |
| 1948 | Citation | 83,400 | Eddie Arcaro | 2:05 2/5 | 1966 | Kauai King | 120,500 | Don Brumfield | 2:02 |
| 1949 | Ponder | 91,600 | Steve Brooks | 2:04 1/5 | 1967 | Proud Clarion | 119,700 | Bobby Ussery | 2:00 3/5 |
| 1950 | Middleground | 92,650 | Willie Boland | 2:01 3/4 | 1968 | Dancer's Image | 122,600 | Ismael Valenzuela | 2:02 1/5 |
| 1951 | Count Turf | 98,050 | Conn McCreary | 2:02 3/5 | 1969 | Majestic Prince | 155,700 | Bill Hartack | 2:01 4/5 |
| 1952 | Hill Gail | 96,300 | Eddie Arcaro | 2:01 3/5 | 1970 | Dust Commander | 128,000 | Mike Manganello | 2:03 2/5 |
| 1953 | Dark Star | 90,050 | Henry Moreno | 2:02 | 1971 | Canonero II | 125,000 | Gustavo Avila | 2:03 1/5 |
| 1954 | Determine | 102,050 | Ray York | 2:03 | 1972 | Riva Ridge | 140,300 | Ron Turcotte | 2:01 4/5 |
| 1955 | Swaps | 108,400 | Willie Shoemaker | 2:01 4/5 | 1973 | Secretariat | 155,050 | Ron Turcotte | 1:59 2/5 |
| 1956 | Needles | 123,450 | Dave Erb | 2:03 2/5 | 1974 | Cannonade | 274,000 | Angel Cordero Jr. | 2:04 |
| 1957 | Iron Liege | 109,550 | Bill Hartack | 2:02 1/5 | 1975 | Foolish Pleasure | 209,600 | Jacinto Vasquez | 2:02 |
| 1958 | Tim Tam | 116,400 | Ismael Valenzuela | 2:05 | 1976 | Bold Forbes | 165,200 | Angel Cordero Jr. | 2:01 3/5 |
| 1959 | Tomy Lee | 119,650 | Willie Shoemaker | 2:02 1/5 | 1977 | Seattle Slew | 214,700 | Jean Cruguet | 2:02 1/5 |
| 1960 | Venetian Way | 114,850 | Bill Hartack | 2:02 2/5 | 1978 | Affirmed | 186,900 | Steve Cauthen | 2:01 1/5 |
| 1961 | Carry Back | 120,500 | John Sellers | 2:04 | 1979 | Spectacular Bid | 324,900 | Ron Franklin | 2:02 2/5 |
| 1962 | Decidedly | 119,650 | Bill Hartack | 2:00 2/5 | 1980 | Genuine Risk | 339,300 | Jacinto Vasquez | 2:02 |

## PREAKNESS STAKES (at Pimlico, Baltimore, Md., 1 3/16 miles for 3-year-olds)

| YEAR | WINNER | PURSE | JOCKEY | TIME | YEAR | WINNER | PURSE | JOCKEY | TIME |
|---|---|---|---|---|---|---|---|---|---|
| 1931 | Mate | $48,225 | G. Ellis | 1:59 | 1956 | Fabius | $84,250 | Bill Hartack | 1:58 2/5 |
| 1932 | Burgoo King | 50,375 | Eugene James | 1:59 4/5 | 1957 | Bold Ruler | 62,250 | Eddie Arcaro | 1:56 1/5 |
| 1933 | Head Play | 26,850 | Charles Kurtsinger | 2:02 | 1958 | Tim Tam | 97,900 | Ismael Valenzuela | 1:57 1/5 |
| 1934 | High Quest | 25,175 | R. Jones | 1:58 1/5 | 1959 | Royal Orbit | 136,200 | W. Harmatz | 1:57 |
| 1935 | Omaha | 25,325 | Willie Saunders | 1:58 2/5 | 1960 | Bally Ache | 121,000 | Bobby Ussery | 1:57 3/5 |
| 1936 | Bold Venture | 27,325 | G. Woolf | 1:59 | 1961 | Carry Back | 126,200 | John Sellers | 1:57 3/5 |
| 1937 | War Admiral | 45,600 | Charles Kurtsinger | 1:58 2/5 | 1962 | Greek Money | 135,800 | J. L. Rotz | 1:56 1/5 |
| 1938 | Dauber | 51,875 | M. Peters | 1:59 4/5 | 1963 | Candy Spots | 127,500 | Willie Shoemaker | 1:56 1/5 |
| 1939 | Challedon | 53,710 | G. Seabo | 1:59 4/5 | 1964 | Northern Dancer | 124,200 | Bill Hartack | 1:56 4/5 |
| 1940 | Bimelech | 53,230 | F.A. Smith | 1:58 3/5 | 1965 | Tom Rolfe | 128,100 | Ron Turcotte | 1:56 1/5 |
| 1941 | Whirlaway | 49,365 | Eddie Arcaro | 1:58 4/5 | 1966 | Kauai King | 129,000 | Don Brumfield | 1:55 2/5 |
| 1942 | Alsab | 58,175 | B. James | 1:57 | 1967 | Damascus | 141,500 | Willie Shoemaker | 1:55 1/5 |
| 1943 | Count Fleet | 43,190 | Johnny Longden | 1:57 2/5 | 1968 | Forward Pass | 142,700 | Ismael Valenzuela | 1:56 4/5 |
| 1944 | Pensive | 60,075 | Conn McCreary | 1:59 1/5 | 1969 | Majestic Prince | 129,500 | Bill Hartack | 1:55 3/5 |
| 1945 | Polynesian | 66,170 | Wayne D. Wright | 1:58 4/5 | 1970 | Personality | 150,000 | E. Belmonte | 1:56 1/5 |
| 1946 | Assault | 96,620 | Warren Mehrtens | 2:01 2/5 | 1971 | Canonero II | 137,400 | Gustavo Avila | 1:54 |
| 1947 | Faultless | 96,005 | D. Dodson | 1:59 | 1972 | Bee Bee Bee | 135,300 | E. Nelson | 1:55 3/5 |
| 1948 | Citation | 91,870 | Eddie Arcaro | 2:02 2/5 | 1973 | Secretariat | 129,900 | Ron Turcotte | 1:54 2/5 |
| 1949 | Capot | 79,985 | T. Atkinson | 1:56 | 1974 | Little Current | 156,500 | Miguel Rivera | 1:54 3/5 |
| 1950 | Hill Prince | 56,115 | Eddie Arcaro | 1:59 1/5 | 1975 | Master Derby | 158,100 | Darrel McHargue | 1:56 2/5 |
| 1951 | Bold | 83,110 | Eddie Arcaro | 1:56 2/5 | 1976 | Elocutionist | 129,700 | John Lively | 1:55 |
| 1952 | Blue Man | 86,135 | Conn McCreary | 1:57 2/5 | 1977 | Seattle Slew | 138,600 | Jean Cruguet | 1:54 2/5 |
| 1953 | Native Dancer | 65,200 | Eric Guerin | 1:57 4/5 | 1978 | Affirmed | 136,200 | Steve Cauthen | 1:54 2/5 |
| 1954 | Hasty Road | 91,600 | J. Adams | 1:57 2/5 | 1979 | Spectacular Bid | 295,300 | Ron Franklin | 1:54 1/5 |
| 1955 | Nashua | 67,550 | Eddie Arcaro | 1:54 1/5 | 1980 | Codex | 250,600 | Angel Cordero Jr. | 1:54 1/5 |

## BELMONT STAKES (at Belmont Park, L.I., N.Y., 1 1/2 miles for 3-year-olds)

| YEAR | WINNER | PURSE | JOCKEY | TIME | YEAR | WINNER | PURSE | JOCKEY | TIME |
|---|---|---|---|---|---|---|---|---|---|
| 1931 | Twenty Grand | $58,770 | Charles Kurtsinger | 2:29 4/5 | 1956 | Needles | $83,600 | Dave Erb | 2:29 4/5 |
| 1932 | Fairena | 55,120 | T. Malley | 2:32 4/5 | 1957 | Gallant Man | 77,300 | Willie Shoemaker | 2:26 3/5 |
| 1933 | Hurryoff | 49,490 | M. Garner | 2:32 3/5 | 1958 | Cavan | 73,430 | P. Anderson | 2:30 1/5 |
| 1934 | Peace Chance | 43,140 | Wayne D. Wright | 2:29 1/5 | 1959 | Sword Dancer | 93,525 | Willie Shoemaker | 2:28 2/5 |
| 1935 | Omaha | 35,480 | Willie Saunders | 2:30 3/5 | 1960 | Celtic Ash | 96,785 | Bill Hartack | 2:29 3/5 |
| 1936 | Granville | 29,800 | Willie Saunders | 2:30 3/5 | 1961 | Sherluck | 104,900 | Braulio Baeza | 2:29 1/5 |
| 1937 | War Admiral | 38,020 | Charles Kurtsinger | 2:28 3/5 | 1962 | Jaipur | 109,500 | Willie Shoemaker | 2:28 4/5 |
| 1938 | Pasteurized | 34,530 | James Stout | 2:29 3/5 | 1963 | Chateaugay | 101,700 | Braulio Baeza | 2:30 1/5 |
| 1939 | Johnstown | 37,020 | James Stout | 2:29 3/5 | 1964 | Quadrangle | 110,850 | Manuel Ycaza | 2:28 1/5 |
| 1940 | Bimelech | 35,030 | F.A. Smith | 2:29 3/5 | 1965 | Hail to All | 104,150 | John Sellers | 2:28 1/5 |
| 1941 | Whirlaway | 39,770 | Eddie Arcaro | 2:31 | 1966 | Amberoid | 117,700 | Willie Boland | 2:29 3/5 |
| 1942 | Shut Out | 44,520 | Eddie Arcaro | 2:29 1/5 | 1967 | Damascus | 104,950 | Willie Shoemaker | 2:28 4/5 |
| 1943 | Count Fleet | 35,340 | Johnny Longden | 2:28 1/5 | 1968 | Stage Door Johnny | 117,700 | H. Gustines | 2:27 1/5 |
| 1944 | Bounding Home | 55,000 | G.L. Smith | 2:32 1/5 | 1969 | Arts and Letters | 104,050 | Braulio Baeza | 2:28 4/5 |
| 1945 | Pavot | 52,675 | Eddie Arcaro | 2:30 1/5 | 1970 | High Echelon | 125,000 | J. L. Rotz | 2:34 |
| 1946 | Assault | 75,400 | Warren Mehrtens | 2:30 4/5 | 1971 | Pass Catcher | 125,000 | W. Blum | 2:30 3/5 |
| 1947 | Phalanx | 78,900 | R.Donoso | 2:29 3/5 | 1972 | Riva Ridge | 93,540 | Ron Turcotte | 2:28 |
| 1948 | Citation | 77,700 | Eddie Arcaro | 2:28 1/5 | 1973 | Secretariat | 90,120 | Ron Turcotte | 2:24 |
| 1949 | Capot | 60,900 | T. Atkinson | 2:30 1/5 | 1974 | Little Current | 52,564 | Miguel Rivera | 2:29 1/5 |
| 1950 | Middleground | 61,350 | Willie Boland | 2:28 3/5 | 1975 | Avatar | 116,160 | Willie Shoemaker | 2:28 1/5 |
| 1951 | Counterpoint | 82,000 | D. Gorman | 2:29 | 1976 | Bold Forbes | 117,000 | Angel Cordero Jr. | 2:29 |
| 1952 | One Count | 82,400 | Eddie Arcaro | 2:30 1/5 | 1977 | Seattle Slew | 109,080 | Jean Cruguet | 2:29 3/5 |
| 1953 | Native Dancer | 82,500 | Eric Guerin | 2:28 3/5 | 1978 | Affirmed | 110,580 | Steve Cauthen | 2:26 4/5 |
| 1954 | High Gun | 89,000 | Eric Guerin | 2:30 4/5 | 1979 | Coastal | 269,000 | Ruben Hernandez | 2:28 3/5 |
| 1955 | Nashua | 83,700 | Eddie Arcaro | 2:29 | 1980 | Temperence Hill | 293,700 | Eddie Maple | 2:29 4/5 |

# THOROUGHBRED RACING WORLD RECORDS

Source: The American Racing Manual (Daily Racing Form)

| DISTANCE | TIME | HORSE | AGE | WEIGHT | TRACK OR PLACE | DATE |
|---|---|---|---|---|---|---|
| 1/4 mile | 0:20 4/5 | Big Racket | 4 | 114 | Hipodromo, Mexico City | 1945 (Feb. 5) |
| 2 1/2 furlongs | 0:26 4/5 | Tie Score | 5 | 115 | Hipodromo, Mexico City | 1946 (Feb. 5) |
| 3/8 mile | 0:33 1/5 | Atoka | 6 | 105 | Butte, Mont. | 1906 (Sept. 7) |
| 3 1/2 furlongs | 0:38 4/5 | Tango King | 6 | 116 | Northlands Park, Alta., Canada | 1978 (Apr. 22) |
| 1/2 mile | 0:44 3/5 | Norgor | 9 | 118 | Ruidoso Downs, N.M. | 1976 (Aug. 14) |
| 4 1/2 furlongs | 0:50 2/5 | Kathryn's Doll | 2 | 111 | Turf Paradise, Phoenix, Ariz. | 1967 (April 9) |
| | 0:50 2/5 | Dear Ethel | 2 | 114 | Miles Park, Louisville, Ky. | 1967 (July 4) |
| | 0:50 2/5 | Bold Liz | 2 | 118 | Sunland Park, N.M. | 1972 (March 19) |
| | 0:50 2/5 | Scott's Poppy | 2 | 118 | Turf Paradise, Phoenix, Ariz. | 1975 (Feb. 22) |
| 5/8 mile | 0:55 2/5 | Zip Pocket | 3 | 122 | Turf Paradise, Phoenix, Ariz. | 1967 (April 22) |
| 5 1/2 furlongs | 1:01 3/5 | Zip Pocket | 3 | 129 | Turf Paradise, Phoenix, Ariz. | 1967 (Nov. 19) |
| 5 3/4 furlongs | 1:07 1/5 | Last Freeby | 4 | 116 | Timonium, Md. | 1974 (July 20) |
| 3/4 mile [1] | 1:06 1/5 | Gelding [2] | 3 | 123 | Brighton, England [3] | 1929 (Aug. 6) |
| | 1:07 1/5 | Grey Papa | 6 | 116 | Longacres, Seattle, Wash. | 1972 (Sept. 4) |
| 6 1/2 furlongs | 1:13 4/5 | Best Hitter | 4 | 114 | Longacres, Seattle, Wash. | 1973 (Aug. 4) |
| 7/8 mile | 1:19 2/5 | Rich Cream | 5 | 115 | Hollywood Park, Inglewood, Calif. | 1980 (May 16) |
| 1 mile | 1:32 1/5 | Dr. Fager | 4 | 134 | Arlington Heights, Ill. | 1968 (Aug. 24) |
| 1 mile, 40 yards | 1:38 4/5 | Impecunious | 3 | 126 | Salem Depot, N.H. | 1973 (Sept. 3) |
| 1 mile, 70 yards [1] | 1:37 1/5 | Aborigine | 6 | 119 | Penn National, Pa. | 1978 (Aug. 20) |
| 1 1/16 miles | 1:38 | Told | 4 | 123 | Penn National, Pa. | 1980 (Sept. 14) |
| 1 1/8 miles [1] | 1:45 2/5 | Tentam | 4 | 118 | Saratoga Springs, N.Y. | 1973 (Aug. 10) |
| 1 1/8 miles | 1:45 2/5 | Secretariat | 3 | 124 | Belmont Park, Elmont, N.Y. | 1973 (Sept. 15) |
| 1 3/16 miles | 1:51 2/5 | Toonerville | N.A. | N.A. | Hialeah, Hialeah, Fla. | 1976 (Feb. 7) |
| 1 1/4 miles | 1:57 3/5 | King Pellinore | 4 | 124 | Santa Anita Park, Arcadia, Calif. | 1976 (Oct. 10) |
| | 1:57 3/5 | Double Discount | 4 | 116 | Santa Anita, Arcadia, Calif. | 1977 (Oct. 6) |
| 1 5/16 miles | 2:07 | Roberto | 3 | 122 | York, England | 1972 (Aug. 15) |
| 1 3/8 miles [1] | 2:11 | Cougar II | 6 | 126 | Hollywood Park, Inglewood, Calif. | 1972 (April 29) |
| 1 1/2 miles | 2:23 | John Henry | 5 | 126 | Santa Anita, Arcadia, Calif. | 1980 (March 16) |
| 1 9/16 miles | 2:37 3/5 | Lone Wolf | 5 | 115 | Keeneland, Lexington, Ky. | 1961 (Oct. 31) |
| 1 5/8 miles | 2:37 4/5 | Red Reality | 6 | 113 | Saratoga Springs, N.Y. | 1972 (Aug. 23) |
| 1 5/8 miles | 2:37 4/5 | Malwak | 5 | 110 | Saratoga Springs, N.Y. | 1973 (Aug. 22) |
| 1 mi., 5 1/2 furlongs | 2:51 3/5 | Distribute | 9 | 109 | River Downs, Cincinnati, Ohio | 1940 (Sept. 7) |
| 1 3/4 miles | 2:50 4/5 | Swartz Pete | 6 | N.A. | Auckland, New Zealand | 1966 (Jan. 1) |
| 1 7/8 miles [1] | 3:11 4/5 | El Moro | 8 | 116 | Delaware Park, Wilmington, Del. | 1963 (July 22) |
| 2 miles [1] | 3:15 | Polazel | 3 | N.A. | Salisbury, England | 1924 (July 8) |
| 2 miles, 40 yards | 3:29 1/5 | Winning Mark | 4 | 107 | Thistledown, Cleveland, Ohio | 1940 (July 20) |
| 2 miles, 70 yards | 3:30 2/5 | Sun n Shine | 4 | 113 | Hawthorne, Cicero, Ill. | 1974 (Oct. 19) |
| 2 1/16 miles | 3:29 3/5 | Midafternoon | 4 | 126 | Jamaica, L.I., N.Y. | 1956 (Nov. 15) |
| 2 1/8 miles | 3:35 | Centuron | 5 | 119 | Newbury, England | 1923 (Sept. 29) |
| 2 3/16 miles | 3:51 1/8 | Santiago | 5 | 112 | Narragansett Park, Pawtucket, R.I. | 1941 (Sept. 27) |
| 2 1/4 miles [1] | 3:37 2/5 | Dakota | 4 | 116 | Lingfield, England | 1927 (May 27) |
| 2 3/8 miles | 4:15 | Wiki Jack | 4 | 97 | Tijuana, Mexico | 1925 (Feb. 8) |
| 2 1/2 miles | 4:14 3/5 | Miss Grillo | 6 | 118 | Pimlico, Baltimore, Md. | 1948 (Nov. 12) |
| 2 5/8 miles [4] | 4:51 2/5 | Worthman | 5 | 101 | Tijuana, Mexico | 1925 (Feb. 22) |
| 2 3/4 miles | 4:48 4/5 | Shot Put | 4 | 126 | Washington Park, Homewood, Ill. | 1940 (Aug. 14) |
| 2 7/8 miles [5] | 5:23 | Bosh | 5 | 100 | Tijuana, Mexico | 1925 (March 8) |
| 3 miles | 5:15 | Farragut | 5 | 113 | Agua Caliente, Mexico | 1941 (March 9) |
| 3 3/8 miles | 6:13 | Winning Mark | 4 | 104 | Washington Park, Homewood, Ill. | 1940 (Aug. 21) |
| 4 miles | 7:10 4/5 | Sotemia | 5 | 119 | Churchill Downs, Louisville, Ky. | 1912 (Oct. 7) |

[1] Turf.  [2] By Blink-Broken Tendril.  [3] Downhill course.  [4] Track heavy.  [5] Track sloppy.  [6] N.A.=Not available.

# HARNESS RACING'S TRIPLE CROWN FOR 3-YEAR-OLDS

Source: The United States Trotting Association

## HAMBLETONIAN (at Du Quoin, Ill.—1 mile)

| YEAR | PURSE | WINNER | DRIVER | TIME | YEAR | PURSE | WINNER | DRIVER | TIME |
|---|---|---|---|---|---|---|---|---|---|
| 1952 | $ 87,638 | Sharp Note | Bion Shively | 2:02 3/5 | 1967 | 122,650 | Speedy Streak | Del Cameron | 2:00 |
| 1953 | 117,118 | Helicopter | Harry Harvey | 2:01 3/5 | 1968 | 116,190 | Nevele Pride | Stanley Dancer | 1:59 3/5 |
| 1954 | 106,831 | Newport Dream | Del Cameron | 2:02 4/5 | 1969 | 124,910 | Lindy's Pride | Howard Beissinger | 1:57 3/5 |
| 1955 | 86,863 | Scott Frost | Joe O'Brien | 2:00 3/5 | 1970 | 143,620 | Timothy T | John Simpson, Jr. | 1:58 2/5 |
| 1956 | 100,604 | The Intruder | Ned Bower | 2:01 2/5 | 1971 | 129,770 | Speedy Crown | Howard Beissinger | 1:57 2/5 |
| 1957 | 111,126 | Hickory Smoke | John Simpson | 2:00 1/5 | 1972 | 119,090 | Super Bowl | Stanley Dancer | 1:56 3/5 |
| 1958 | 106,719 | Emily's Pride | Flave Nipe | 1:59 4/5 | 1973 | 144,710 | Flirth | Ralph Baldwin | 1:57 1/5 |
| 1959 | 125,283 | Diller Hanover | Frank Ervin | 2:01 1/5 | 1974 | 160,150 | Christopher T | Billy Haughton | 1:58 3/5 |
| 1960 | 147,481 | Blaze Hanover | Joe O'Brien | 1:59 3/5 | 1975 | 232,192 | Bonefish | Stanley Dancer | 1:59 |
| 1961 | 131,573 | Harlan Dean | James Arthur | 1:58 2/5 | 1976 | 263,524 | Steve Lobell | Billy Haughton | 1:56 3/5 |
| 1962 | 116,612 | A. C.'s Viking | Sanders Russell | 1:59 3/5 | 1977 | 284,131 | Green Speed | Billy Haughton | 1:55 3/5 |
| 1963 | 115,549 | Speedy Scot | Ralph Baldwin | 1:57 3/5 | 1978 | 241,280 | Speedy Somolli | Howard Beissinger | 1:55 |
| 1964 | 115,281 | Ayers | John Simpson | 1:56 4/5 | 1979 | 300,000 | Legend Hanover | George Sholty | 1:56 1/5 |
| 1965 | 122,245 | Egyptian Candor | Del Cameron | 2:03 4/5 | 1980 | 300,000 | Burgomeister | Wm. Haughton | 1:56 3/5 |
| 1966 | $122,540 | Kerry Way | Frank Ervin | 1:58 4/5 | | | | | |

## KENTUCKY FUTURITY (at Lexington, Ky.)

| YEAR | PURSE | WINNER | DRIVER | TIME | YEAR | PURSE | WINNER | DRIVER | TIME |
|---|---|---|---|---|---|---|---|---|---|
| 1953 | $ 67,485 | Kimberly Kid .... | Thomas Berry ... | 2:00 3/5 | 1967 | $ 58,642 | Speed Model .... | Art Hult ......... | 1:59 1/5 |
| 1954 | 63,121 | Harlan ......... | Del Miller ...... | 2:01 | 1968* | 57,000 | Nevele Pride .... | Stanley Dancer .. | 1:57 |
| 1955 | 62,702 | Scott Frost...... | Joe O'Brien .... | 2:00 3/5 | 1969 | 64,757 | Lindy's Pride ... | Howard Beissinger | 1:59 |
| 1956 | 53,731 | Nimble Colby ... | Ralph Baldwin .. | 2:02 | 1970 | 76,351 | Timothy T ...... | Joe Simpson Jr.. | 1:59 4/5 |
| 1957 | 50,460 | Cassin Hanover . | Fred Egan ...... | 2:02 1/5 | 1971 | 63,415 | Savoir ......... | James Arthur ... | 1:58 1/5 |
| 1958 | 53,330 | Emily's Pride ... | Flave Nipe ..... | 1:59 1/5 | 1972 | 56,210 | Super Bowl ..... | Stanley Dancer .. | 1:59 |
| 1959 | 53,810 | Diller Hanover... | Ralph Baldwin .. | 2:01 1/5 | 1973 | 64,174 | Arnie Almahurst.. | Joe O'Brien .... | 1:59 1/5 |
| 1960 | 64,040 | Elaine Rodney .. | Clint Hodgins .. | 1:58 3/5 | 1974 | 100,000 | Waymaker ...... | John Simpson Jr. | 1:58 1/5 |
| 1961 | 59,330 | Duke Rodney ... | Eddie Wheeler .. | 1:58 1/5 | 1975 | 100,000 | Noble Rouge ... | William Herman .. | 1:59 3/5 |
| 1962 | 55,230 | Safe Mission ... | Joe O'Brien .... | 1:59 1/5 | 1976 | 100,000 | Quick Pay ...... | Peter Haughton.. | 1:59 |
| 1963 | 61,128 | Speedy Scot ... | Ralph Baldwin .. | 1:57 1/5 | 1977 | 100,000 | Texas ......... | Billy Herman ... | 1:57 3/5 |
| 1964 | 57,096 | Ayres ......... | John Simpson .. | 1:58 1/5 | 1978 | 100,000 | Doublemint .... | Peter Haughton . | 1:58 3/5 |
| 1965 | 65,133 | Armbro Flight ... | Joe O'Brien .... | 1:59 3/5 | 1979 | 100,000 | Classical Way ... | John Simpson Jr. | 1:57 4/5 |
| 1966 | $ 61,602 | Governor Armbro | Joe O'Brien .... | 2:00 3/5 | 1980 | 100,000 | Final Score ..... | Tom Haughton .. | 1:58 |

## YONKERS TROT (at Yonkers, N.Y.—1 1/16-mile race before 1963, now 1 mile)

| YEAR | PURSE | WINNER | DRIVER | TIME | YEAR | PURSE | WINNER | DRIVER | TIME |
|---|---|---|---|---|---|---|---|---|---|
| 1959 | $ 56,397 | John A. Hanover . | Stanley Dancer .. | 2:11 | 1970 | $106,770 | Victory Star ..... | Vernon Dancer .. | 2:03 |
| 1960 | 74,265 | Duke of Decatur . | Del Miller ...... | 2:13 3/5 | 1971 | 110,795 | Quick Pride ..... | Stanley Dancer .. | 2:02 4/5 |
| 1961 | 100,330 | Duke Rodney .... | Eddie Wheeler ... | 2:10 3/5 | 1972 | 94,097 | Super Bowl ..... | Stanley Dancer .. | 2:02 |
| 1962 | 105,422 | A. C.'s Viking ... | Sanders Russell .. | 2:10 4/5 | 1973 | 93,242 | Tamerlane ...... | Charles Clark ... | 2:04 4/5 |
| 1963 | 135,127 | Speedy Scot ... | Ralph Baldwin ... | 2:03 3/5 | 1974 | 125,822 | Spitfire Hanover . | Del Miller ...... | 2:05 2/5 |
| 1964 | 116,691 | Ayres ......... | John Simpson ... | 2:01 3/5 | 1975 | 200,000 | Surefire Hanover . | Stanley Dancer .. | 2:03 |
| 1965 | 122,236 | Noble Victory ... | Stanley Dancer .. | 2:02 | 1976 | 202,004 | Steve Lobell..... | Billy Haughton .. | 2:01 4/5 |
| 1966 | 123,375 | Polaris ......... | George Sholty ... | 2:06 | 1977 | 239,000 | Green Speed .... | Billy Haughton .. | 1:59 |
| 1967 | 150,000 | Pomp ......... | Harry Pownall ... | 2:04 4/5 | 1978 | 233,594 | Speedy Somolli .. | Howard Beissinger | 1:59 3/5 |
| 1968 | 150,000 | Nevele Pride .... | Stanley Dancer .. | 2:03 3/5 | 1979 | 237,765 | Chiola Hanover .. | James Allen ..... | 2:04 2/5 |
| 1969 | 100,000 | Lindy's Pride ... | Howard Beissinger | 2:03 4/5 | 1980 | 263,540 | Nevele Impulse .. | Dick Macomber .. | 2:03 2/5 |

# PACING'S TRIPLE CROWN

## LITTLE BROWN JUG (at Delaware, Ohio—1 mile)

Source: United States Trotting Association.

| YEAR | PURSE | WINNER | DRIVER | TIME | YEAR | PURSE | WINNER | DRIVER | TIME |
|---|---|---|---|---|---|---|---|---|---|
| 1953 | $ 54,972 | Keystoner ...... | Frank Ervin ..... | 2:02 3/5 | 1967 | $ 84,778 | Best of All ...... | Jim Hackett ..... | 1:59 1/5 |
| 1954 | 69,332 | Adios Harry .... | Morris MacDonald | 2:02 3/5 | 1968 | 104,226 | Rum Customer ... | William Haughton | 1:59 3/5 |
| 1955 | 66,608 | Quick Chief .... | William Haughton | 2:00 | 1969 | 109,731 | Laverne Hanover . | William Haughton | 2:00 2/5 |
| 1956 | 52,666 | Noble Adios .... | John Simpson ... | 2:00 4/5 | 1970 | 100,110 | Most Happy Fella | Stanley Dancer .. | 1:57 1/5 |
| 1957 | 73,528 | Torpid ......... | John Simpson ... | 2:00 3/5 | 1971 | 102,964 | Nansemond ..... | Herve Filion ... | 1:57 3/5 |
| 1958 | 65,252 | Shadow Wave ... | Joe O'Brien .... | 2:01 | 1972 | 104,916 | Strike Out ...... | Keith Waples ... | 1:56 3/5 |
| 1959 | 76,582 | Adios Butler ... | Clint Hodgins ... | 1:59 2/5 | 1973 | 120,000 | Melvin's Woe .... | Joe O'Brien .... | 1:57 3/5 |
| 1960 | 66,510 | Bullet Hanover .. | John Simpson ... | 1:58 3/5 | 1974 | 132,630 | Armbro Omaha... | William Haughton | 1:57 3/5 |
| 1961 | 70,069 | Henry T. Adios .. | Stanley Dancer .. | 1:58 3/5 | 1975 | 147,813 | Seatrain ....... | Ben Webster ... | 1:56 4/5 |
| 1962 | 75,038 | Lehigh Hanover .. | Stanley Dancer .. | 1:58 4/5 | 1976 | 153,799 | Keystone Ore ... | Stanley Dancer .. | 1:56 4/5 |
| 1963 | 68,294 | Overtrick ...... | John Patterson .. | 1:57 1/5 | 1977 | 150,000 | Governor Skipper | John Chapman .. | 1:56 1/5 |
| 1964 | 66,590 | Vicar Hanover ... | William Haughton | 2:00 4/5 | 1978 | 186,760 | Happy Escort ... | Bill Popfinger ... | 1:57 2/5 |
| 1965 | 70,000 | Bret Hanover ... | Frank Ervin .... | 1:57 | 1979 | 226,455 | Hot Hitter ...... | Herve Filion .... | 1:55 3/5 |
| 1966 | 74,616 | Romeo Hanover . | George Sholty ... | 1:59 3/5 | 1980 | 207,361 | Niatross ........ | Clint Galbraith .. | 1:54 4/5 |

## CANE PACE (at Yonkers, N.Y.—1 mile)

| YEAR | PURSE | WINNER | DRIVER | TIME | YEAR | PURSE | WINNER | DRIVER | TIME |
|---|---|---|---|---|---|---|---|---|---|
| 1961 | $110,950 | Cold Front ..... | Clint Hodgins ... | 2:08 3/5 | 1971 | $106,795 | Albatross ...... | Stanley Dancer .. | 2:00 |
| 1962 | 117,542 | Ranger Knight .. | Clint Hodgins ... | 2:13 1/5 | 1972 | 107,097 | Hilarious Way ... | John Simpson Jr. | 2:02 2/5 |
| 1963 | 163,187 | Meadow Skipper | Earle Avery .... | 1:58 4/5 | 1973 | 101,242 | Smog ......... | Vernon Dancer .. | 1:58 4/5 |
| 1964 | 123,191 | Race Time ..... | George Sholty ... | 2:01 4/5 | 1974 | 121,822 | Boyden Hanover . | William Herman . | 1:59 4/5 |
| 1965 | 125,236 | Bret Hanover ... | Frank Ervin .... | 2:01 | 1975 | 200,000 | Nero .......... | Joe O'Brien .... | 1:58 4/5 |
| 1966 | 126,915 | Romeo Hanover . | William Myer ... | 1:59 4/5 | 1976 | 200,000 | Keystone Ore ... | Stanley Dancer .. | 1:57 1/5 |
| 1967 | 150,000 | Meadow Paige... | William Haughton | 2:03 | 1977 | 286,500 | Jade Princess ... | Jack Kopas ..... | 1:59 |
| 1968 | 150,000 | Rum Customer .. | William Haughton | 1:59 4/5 | 1978 | 307,594 | Armbro Tiger ... | Herve Filion .... | 1:59 1/5 |
| 1969 | 100,000 | Kat Byrd ...... | Eldon Harner ... | 2:02 3/5 | 1979 | 336,420 | Happy Motoring .. | Wm. Popfinger .. | 1:57 3/5 |
| 1970 | 102,770 | Most Happy Fella | Stanley Dancer .. | 1:58 3/5 | 1980 | 321,365 | Niatross ........ | Clint Galbraith .. | 1:57 3/5 |

## MESSENGER STAKE (at Westbury, L.I., N.Y.—1 mile)

| YEAR | PURSE | WINNER | DRIVER | TIME | YEAR | PURSE | WINNER | DRIVER | TIME |
|---|---|---|---|---|---|---|---|---|---|
| 1961 | $145,377 | Adios Don ..... | Howard Camper . | 2:02 4/5 | 1971 | $114,977 | Albatross ...... | Stanley Dancer .. | 2:00 2/5 |
| 1962 | 169,430 | Thor Hanover .. | John Simpson .. | 2:01 1/5 | 1972 | 154,733 | Silent Majority .. | William Haughton | 2:01 4/5 |
| 1963 | 146,324 | Overtrick ...... | John Patterson .. | 2:00 4/5 | 1973 | 122,732 | Valiant Bret ..... | Lucien Fontaine . | 2:00 3/5 |
| 1964 | 150,960 | Race Time ..... | Ralph Baldwin .. | 2:01 2/5 | 1974 | 151,044 | Armbro Omaha.. | William Haughton | 1:59 3/5 |
| 1965 | 151,252 | Bret Hanover ... | Frank Ervin .... | 2:02 | 1975 | 154,223 | Bret's Champ ... | William Haughton | 1:59 1/5 |
| 1966 | 169,885 | Romeo Hanover . | George Sholty ... | 2:01 | 1976 | 161,290 | Windshield Wiper | William Haughton | 1:59 |
| 1967 | 178,064 | Romulus Hanover | William Haughton | 1:59 1/10 | 1977 | 159,155 | Governor Skipper | John Chapman .. | 1:59 1/5 |
| 1968 | 189,018 | Rum Customer .. | William Haughton | 2:01 4/5 | 1978 | 167,862 | Abercrombie .... | Glen Garnsey ... | 1:58 2/5 |
| 1969 | 182,976 | Bye Bye Sam ... | Stanley Dancer .. | 2:02 3/5 | 1979 | 180,225 | Hot Hitter ...... | Henri Filion .... | 1:59 4/5 |
| 1970 | 123,450 | Most Happy Fella | Stanley Dancer .. | 2:00 3/5 | 1980 | 173,522 | Niatross ........ | Clint Galbraith .. | 1:59 3/5 |

# HARNESS HORSE RACING RECORDS AND CHAMPIONS

Source: United States Trotting Association

## WORLD HARNESS RACE ONE-MILE RECORDS

| HORSE | SEX | DRIVER | YEAR | TRACK | TIME |
|---|---|---|---|---|---|
| **Trotting—Mile Track** | | | | | |
| Lindy's Crown . . . . . . . . . . . . . . . . . . | Horse | Howard Beissinger | 1980 | Du Quoin, Ill. | 1:54 4/5 |
| Colonial Charm . . . . . . . . . . . . . . . . | Mare | Glen Garnsey | 1974 | Lexington, Ky. | 1:56 1/5 |
| Pride of Carlisle (tie) . . . . . . . . . . . . | Gelding | Ben Webster | 1977 | East Rutherford, N.J. | 1:56 3/5 |
| Crown's Star (tie) . . . . . . . . . . . . . . | Gelding | Wm. Herman | 1980 | East Rutherford, N.J. | 1:56 3/5 |
| **Pacing—Mile Track** | | | | | |
| Niatross . . . . . . . . . . . . . . . . . . . . . . . | Horse | Clint Galbraith | 1980 | Inglewood, Calif. | 1:52 1/5 |
| Guiding Beam (tie) . . . . . . . . . . . . . | Mare | Steve Waller | 1980 | Du Quoin, Ill. | 1:53 4/5 |
| Toy Poodle (tie) . . . . . . . . . . . . . . . | Mare | Wm. Herman | 1980 | Lexington, Ky. | 1:53 4/5 |
| New Lew . . . . . . . . . . . . . . . . . . . . . . | Gelding | Lew Williams | 1979 | East Rutherford, N.J. | 1:54 |
| **Trotting—Five-eighths-mile Track** | | | | | |
| Lindy's Crown . . . . . . . . . . . . . . . . . . | Horse | Howard Beissinger | 1980 | Wilmington, Dela. | 1:57 1/5 |
| Keystone Pioneer . . . . . . . . . . . . . . | Mare | Richard DeSantis | 1976 | Philadelphia, Pa. | 1:58 1/5 |
| Dudate Windswept . . . . . . . . . . . . . | Gelding | Stephen Guy | 1978 | Laurel, Md. | 1:58 |
| **Pacing—Five-eighths-mile Track** | | | | | |
| Storm Damage . . . . . . . . . . . . . . . . . | Horse | Joe O'Brien | 1980 | Meadow Lands, Pa. | 1:53 2/5 |
| Meadow Blue Chip . . . . . . . . . . . . . | Mare | Ross Hayter | 1976 | Wilmington, Dela. | 1:55 1/5 |
| Rambling Willie . . . . . . . . . . . . . . . . | Gelding | Robert Farrington | 1977 | Wilmington, Dela. | 1:54 3/5 |
| **Trotting—Half-mile Track** | | | | | |
| Nevele Pride . . . . . . . . . . . . . . . . . . . | Horse | Stanley Dancer | 1969 | Saratoga Springs, N.Y. | 1:56 4/5 |
| Armbro Flight . . . . . . . . . . . . . . . . . . | Mare | Joe O'Brien | 1965 | Delaware, Ohio | 1:59 1/5 |
| Darn Safe . . . . . . . . . . . . . . . . . . . . . | Gelding | James Arthur | 1957 | Saratoga Springs, N.Y. | 1:59 4/5 |
| **Pacing—Half-mile Track** | | | | | |
| Niatross . . . . . . . . . . . . . . . . . . . . . . . | Horse | Clint Galbraith | 1980 | Delaware, Ohio | 1:54 4/5 |
| Roses Are Red . . . . . . . . . . . . . . . . . | Mare | Jack Kopas | 1979 | Delaware, Ohio | 1:56 3/5 |
| Try Scotch . . . . . . . . . . . . . . . . . . . . | Gelding | Shelly Goudreau | 1979 | Westbury, N.Y. | 1:56 3/5 |

## HARNESS HORSE OF THE YEAR

| YEAR | HORSE | GAIT | YEAR | HORSE | GAIT | YEAR | HORSE | GAIT |
|---|---|---|---|---|---|---|---|---|
| 1949 | Good Time . . . . . . | pacer | 1959 | Bye Bye Byrd . . . . | pacer | 1971–72 | Albatross . . . . . . . . | pacer |
| 1950 | Proximity . . . . . . . . | trotter | 1960-61 | Adios Butler . . . . . | pacer | 1973 | Sir Dalrae . . . . . . . | pacer |
| 1951 | Pronto Don . . . . . | trotter | 1962 | Su Mac Lad . . . . . | trotter | 1974 | Delmonica Hanover | trotter |
| 1952 | Good Time . . . . . . | pacer | 1963 | Speedy Scot . . . . . | trotter | 1975 | Savoir . . . . . . . . . . | trotter |
| 1953 | Hi-Lo's Forbes . . . | pacer | 1964 | Bret Hanover . . . . | pacer | 1976 | Keystone Ore . . . . | pacer |
| 1954 | Stenographer . . . . | trotter | 1965 | Bret Hanover . . . . | pacer | 1977 | Green Speed . . . . | trotter |
| 1955–56 | Scott Frost . . . . . . | trotter | 1966 | Bret Hanover . . . . | pacer | 1978 | Abercrombie . . . . | pacer |
| 1957 | Torpid . . . . . . . . . . | pacer | 1967–69 | Nevele Pride . . . . | trotter | 1979 | Niatross . . . . . . . . | pacer |
| 1958 | Emily's Pride . . . . | trotter | 1970 | Fresh Yankee . . . . | trotter | 1980 | Niatross . . . . . . . . | pacer |

# QUARTER HORSE RACING

Source: American Quarter Horse Association

## WORLD RECORDS

| DIST. | HORSE | AGE | WT. | DATE | TIME | DIST. | HORSE | AGE | WT. | DATE | TIME |
|---|---|---|---|---|---|---|---|---|---|---|---|
| 440 yds. | Truckle Feature . . . | 3 | 120 | 8/26/73 | 0:21.02 | 300 yds. | Jolly Jet Deck . . . . | 5 | 125 | 9/07/70 | 0:15.24 |
| 400 yds. | Truckle Feature . . . | 3 | 120 | 5/06/73 | 0:19.38 | 250 yds. | Junior Meyers . . . | 6 | 121 | 5/16/71 | 0:13.00 |
| 350 yds. | Van Too Too . . . . . | 5 | 118 | 9/03/73 | 0:17.24 | 220 yds. | Junior Meyers . . . | 4 | 120 | 8/10/69 | 0:11.62 |
| 330 yds. | Good N Tension . . | 2 | 120 | 4/06/74 | 0:16.47 | | | | | | |

## ALL AMERICAN FUTURITY, RUIDOSO DOWNS, N.M., 2-YEAR-OLD QUARTER HORSES [s]

| YEAR | WINNER | TIME | PURSE | OWNER | TRAINER | JOCKEY |
|---|---|---|---|---|---|---|
| 1963 | Goetta . . . . . . . . . . . | 0:20.30 | $ 285,000.00 | Hugh Huntley | Newton Keck | Charles Smith |
| 1964 | Decketta . . . . . . . . . | 0:20.30 | $ 302,060.00 | W. W. Wilson | W. W. Wilson | Boyd Morris |
| 1965 | Savannah Jr. . . . . . . | 0:20.30 | $ 419,460.00 | J. R. & R. E. Cates | Ted W. Wells Jr. | Jack Wallace |
| 1966 | Go Dick Go . . . . . . . | 0:20.27 | $ 430,600.00 | Joseph Leitner | Clarence V. Jay | Buddy Nesmith |
| 1967 | Laico Bird . . . . . . . . | 0:20.11 | $ 486,600.00 | Floyd H. Jones Jr. | Jimmie Jones | Bobby Harmon |
| 1968 | Three Oh's . . . . . . . | 0:20.07 | $ 602,000.00 | Dr. D. G. Strole | C. W. Cascio | Jerry Nicodemus |
| 1969 | Easy Jet . . . . . . . . . | 0:20.49 | $ 600,000.00 | Walter Merrick | Walter Merrick | Willie Lovell |
| 1970 | Rocket Wrangler . . | 0:20.09 | $ 670,000.00 | J. R. Adams | Charles Cascio | Jerry Nicodemus |
| 1971 | Mr. Kid Charge . . . | 0:19.65 | $ 753,910.00 | Will F. Whitehead | James Chapman | Johnny Cox |
| 1972 | Possumjet . . . . . . . | 0:20.04 | $1,035,900.00 | Jack M. Byers | Jack Byers | Pete Herrera |
| 1973 | Timeto Thinkrich . . | 0:21.58 | $1,030,000.00 | Frank Vessels | Jerry Fisher | John Watson |
| 1974 | Easy Date . . . . . . . | 0:21.60 | $1,030,000.00 | Walter Merrick | James McArthur | Don Knight |
| 1975 | Bugs Alive in 75 . . | 0:21.98 | $1,030,000.00 | Ralph W. Shebester | J. B. Montgomery | Jerry Burgess |
| 1976 | Real Wind . . . . . . . | 0:21.70 | $1,030,000.00 | J.D. & E. Kitchens | T. A. Walker | Gary Sumpter |
| 1977 | Hot Idea . . . . . . . . | 0:21.76 | $ 766,000.00 | Jackson/Bruce | G. Tefertiller | Terry Lipham |
| 1978 | Moon Lark . . . . . . . | 0:21.85 | $1,000,000.00 | Jas/Paul/Sam Howard | Jack Brooks | Jackie Martin |
| 1979 | Pie in the Sky . . . . | 0:21.76 | $1,000,000.00 | Dan & Jolene Urschel | Leo Wood | Danny Cardoza |
| 1980 | Higheasterjet . . . . | 0:22.15 | $1,000,000.00 | Jerry Highsmith | Johnie Goodman | Billy Hunt |

[s] Previously 400 yards, the All American Futurity was changed to 440 yards in 1973.

# OLYMPIC GAMES

United Press Int'l.

Shot by John Harrington, *left,* of the U.S., bounces off pads of Soviet goalie Vladislav Tretjak in first period of semifinal game during Winter Olympics hockey competition on Feb. 22. The U.S. went on to surprise the powerful Soviet team with a 4–3 upset, and then won the gold medal by defeating Finland, 4–2, in the final game on Feb. 24.

Although the U.S. came in third after East Germany and the Soviet Union in the XIII Winter Olympic Games, held at Lake Placid, N.Y., in February, American speed skater Eric Heiden was the outstanding single performer, winning five individual gold medals (see page 767).

The U.S. hockey team, made up of amateur minor league players and college players, stunned the sports world when they beat the reigning Olympic and world champion Soviet team in the semifinal round, and then trounced Finland, 4–2, for the gold medal. Goalie Jim Craig allowed only 15 goals in seven games and stopped 91% of his opponents' goal attempts.

In other action, hopes for a U.S. medal in pairs figure skating were dimmed when world champions Tai Babilonia and Randy Gardner had to withdraw from competition at the last minute because of an injury to Gardner. The gold medal was captured by the Soviet Union's Rodnina and Zaitsev.

The U.S. took third in the Winter Games, winning 12 medals. East Germany was first with 23 and the USSR second with 22.

The XXII Summer Olympic Games were held in Moscow July 19–Aug. 3, with only 81 nations participating. The United States and about 57 other countries boycotted the games as a protest to the Soviet Union's invasion of Afghanistan. The U.S.-led boycott diminished the quality of competition in many events, such as track and field and swimming, because of the absence of prominent athletes from such boycotting countries as the U.S., West Germany, Japan, and Kenya.

The USSR captured a total of 197 medals, and took first place. East Germany was second with 126, and Bulgaria third with 40. Soviet gymnast Aleksandr Dityatin collected eight medals, more than any other athlete had ever won at any of the modern Olympic Games.

One dramatic confrontation involved two British track rivals, Sebastian Coe and Steve Ovett. The two met in the 800-meter final July 26, when Ovett won the gold in 1:45.4. Coe got his revenge Aug. 1, when he beat Ovett in the 1,000-meters for the gold.

## SUMMER OLYMPIC GAMES: 1896–1984

| | YEAR | PLACE | NATIONS | EVENTS | LEADING WINNERS OF GOLD MEDAL CHAMPIONSHIPS | | |
|---|---|---|---|---|---|---|---|
| | | | | | First | Second | Third |
| I | 1896 | Athens, Greece | 10 | 42 | United States (11) | Greece (8) | Germany (3½) |
| II | 1900 | Paris, France | 20 | 60 | France (28) | United States (22) | Britain (14) |
| III | 1904 | St. Louis, Mo. | 10 | 67 | United States (78) | Cuba (5) [2] Germany (5) [2] | |
| —[1] | 1906 | Athens, Greece | 21 | 75 | France (14) | United States (12) | Greece (8) [2] Britain (8) [2] |
| IV | 1908 | London, England | 22 | 104 | Britain (56) | United States (22) | Sweden (8) |
| V | 1912 | Stockholm, Sweden | 28 | 106 | Sweden (24½) | United States (23) | Britain (10) |
| VI | 1916 | Berlin, Germany | —— | —— | Canceled because of World War I | | |
| VII | 1920 | Antwerp, Belgium | 29 | 154 | United States (41) | Sweden (19) | Finland (15) |
| VIII | 1924 | Paris, France | 44 | 137 | United States (45) | Finland (14) | France (13) |
| IX | 1928 | Amsterdam, Neth. | 46 | 120 | United States (22) | Germany (9½) | Italy (7) [2] Switzerland (7) [2] |
| X | 1932 | Los Angeles, Calif. | 37 | 124 | United States (41) | Italy (12) | France (10) |
| XI | 1936 | Berlin, Germany | 49 | 142 | Germany (33) | United States (24) | Hungary (10) |
| XII | 1940 | Helsinki, Finland | —— | —— | Canceled because of World War II | | |
| XIII | 1944 | Unawarded | —— | —— | Canceled because of World War II | | |
| XIV | 1948 | London, England | 59 | 138 | United States (38) | Sweden (17) | Hungary (10) |
| XV | 1952 | Helsinki, Finland | 69 | 149 | United States (40) | Soviet Union (22) | Hungary (16) |
| XVI | 1956 | Melbourne, Australia | 67 | 145 | Soviet Union (37) [4] | United States (32) | Australia (13) |
| XVII | 1960 | Rome, Italy | 84 | 150 | Soviet Union (43) | United States (34) | Italy (13) |
| XVIII | 1964 | Tokyo, Japan | 94 | 162 | United States (36) | Soviet Union (30) | Japan (16) |
| XIX | 1968 | Mexico City, Mexico | 109 | 172 | United States (45) | Soviet Union (28) | France (10) [2] Japan (10) [2] |
| XX | 1972 | Munich, W. Germany | 112 | 195 | Soviet Union (50) | United States (33) | East Germany (20) |
| XXI | 1976 | Montreal, Canada | 89 | 198 | Soviet Union (47) | East Germany (40) | United States (34) |
| XXII | 1980 | Moscow, Soviet Union | 81 | 203 | Soviet Union (80) | East Germany (47) | Bulgaria (8) |
| XXIII | 1984 | Los Angeles, Calif. | —— | —— | —— | —— | —— |

## WINTER OLYMPICS: 1924–1984

| | YEAR | PLACE | NATIONS | EVENTS | LEADING WINNERS OF GOLD MEDAL CHAMPIONSHIPS | | |
|---|---|---|---|---|---|---|---|
| | | | | | First | Second | Third |
| I | 1924 | Chamonix, France | 16 | 16 | Norway (4) | Finland (3) | Austria (2) |
| II | 1928 | St. Moritz, Switzerland | 25 | 15 | Norway (5½) | United States (2) [2] Sweden (2) [2] | —— |
| III | 1932 | Lake Placid, N.Y. | 17 | 19 | United States (6) | Norway (3) | France (1) [2] Sweden (1) [2] Finland (1) [2] Canada (1) [2] Austria (1) [2] |
| IV | 1936 | Garmisch-Partenkirchen, Germany | 28 | 21 | Norway (7) | United States (3) | Sweden (2) |
| V | 1948 | St. Moritz, Switzerland | 28 | 24 | Sweden (4) [2] Norway (4) [2] | —— | United States (3) [2] Switzerland (3) [2] |
| VI | 1952 | Olso, Norway | 30 | 23 | Norway (7) | United States (4) | Finland (3) [2] Germany (3) [2] |
| VII | 1956 | Cortina, Italy | 32 | 24 | Soviet Union (6) | Austria (4) | Finland (3) |
| VIII | 1960 | Squaw Valley, Calif. | 30 | 27 | Soviet Union (6) | Germany (4) | United States (3) [2] Sweden (3) [2] Norway (3) [2] |
| IX | 1964 | Innsbruck, Austria | 36 | 34 | Soviet Union (11) | Austria (4) [2] | Germany (3) [2] France (3) [2] Finland (3) [2] Sweden (3) [2] Norway (3) [2] |
| X | 1968 | Grenoble, France | 37 | 35 | Norway (6) | Soviet Union (5) | France (4) [2] Italy (4) [2] |
| XI | 1972 | Sapporo, Japan | 35 | 35 | Soviet Union (8) | Switzerland (4) [2] Netherlands (4) [2] East Germany (4) [2] | |
| XII | 1976 | Innsbruck, Austria | 37 | 35 | Soviet Union (13) | East Germany (7) | United States (3) [2] Norway (3) [2] |
| XIII | 1980 | Lake Placid, N.Y. | 38 | 39 | Soviet Union (10) | East Germany (9) | United States (6) |
| XIV | 1984 | Sarajevo, Yugoslavia | —— | —— | —— | | |

[1] Unofficial Olympics.  [2] Tie.  [3] Equestrian events held in Stockholm, Sweden.  [4] Includes full credit for ties.

## WINTER OLYMPIC GAMES FINAL MEDAL STANDINGS: 1980

| NATION | GOLD | SILVER | BRONZE | TOTAL | NATION | GOLD | SILVER | BRONZE | TOTAL |
|---|---|---|---|---|---|---|---|---|---|
| East Germany.. | 9 | 7 | 7 | 23 | Sweden......... | 3 | 0 | 1 | 4 |
| Soviet Union ... | 10 | 6 | 6 | 22 | Italy........... | 0 | 2 | 0 | 2 |
| United States .. | 6 | 4 | 2 | 12 | Canada........ | 0 | 1 | 1 | 2 |
| Norway......... | 1 | 3 | 6 | 10 | Britain ........ | 1 | 0 | 0 | 1 |
| Finland ........ | 1 | 5 | 3 | 9 | Hungary ....... | 0 | 1 | 0 | 1 |
| Austria ........ | 3 | 2 | 2 | 7 | Japan ......... | 0 | 1 | 0 | 1 |
| West Germany . | 0 | 2 | 3 | 5 | Bulgaria ....... | 0 | 0 | 1 | 1 |
| Switzerland .... | 1 | 1 | 3 | 5 | Czechoslovakia . | 0 | 0 | 1 | 1 |
| Liechtenstein... | 2 | 2 | 1 | 5 | France ......... | 0 | 0 | 1 | 1 |
| Netherlands.... | 1 | 2 | 1 | 4 | | | | | |

## SUMMER OLYMPIC GAMES FINAL MEDAL STANDINGS: 1980

| NATION | GOLD | SILVER | BRONZE | TOTAL | NATION | GOLD | SILVER | BRONZE | TOTAL |
|---|---|---|---|---|---|---|---|---|---|
| Soviet Union ... | 80 | 70 | 47 | 197 | North Korea ... | 0 | 3 | 2 | 5 |
| East Germany.. | 47 | 36 | 43 | 126 | Brazil ......... | 2 | 0 | 2 | 4 |
| Bulgaria ....... | 8 | 16 | 16 | 40 | Ethiopia ........ | 2 | 0 | 2 | 4 |
| Hungary ....... | 7 | 10 | 15 | 32 | Mongolia ...... | 0 | 2 | 2 | 4 |
| Poland ......... | 3 | 14 | 14 | 31 | Netherlands..... | 0 | 1 | 3 | 4 |
| Romania ....... | 6 | 6 | 13 | 25 | Mexico ........ | 0 | 1 | 3 | 4 |
| Britain ........ | 5 | 7 | 9 | 21 | Greece ......... | 1 | 0 | 2 | 3 |
| Cuba .......... | 8 | 7 | 5 | 20 | Jamaica ....... | 0 | 0 | 3 | 3 |
| Italy........... | 8 | 3 | 4 | 15 | Switzerland .... | 2 | 0 | 0 | 2 |
| France ......... | 6 | 5 | 3 | 14 | Tanzania ...... | 0 | 2 | 0 | 2 |
| Czechoslovakia . | 2 | 2 | 9 | 13 | Ireland ........ | 0 | 1 | 1 | 2 |
| Sweden........ | 3 | 3 | 6 | 12 | Belgium ....... | 1 | 0 | 0 | 1 |
| Australia ...... | 2 | 2 | 5 | 9 | India .......... | 1 | 0 | 0 | 1 |
| Yugoslavia ..... | 2 | 3 | 4 | 9 | Zimbabwe ..... | 1 | 0 | 0 | 1 |
| Finland ........ | 3 | 1 | 4 | 8 | Venezuela ..... | 0 | 1 | 0 | 1 |
| Spain ......... | 1 | 3 | 2 | 6 | Uganda ....... | 0 | 1 | 0 | 1 |
| Denmark ...... | 2 | 1 | 2 | 5 | Lebanon ....... | 0 | 0 | 1 | 1 |
| Austria ....... | 1 | 3 | 1 | 5 | Guyana ........ | 0 | 0 | 1 | 1 |

# SUMMER OLYMPIC WINNERS AND RECORDS

## ARCHERY: MEN

| | | POINTS |
|---|---|---|
| 1972 | John Williams, United States ........... | 2,528 |
| 1976* | Darrell Pace, United States............. | 2,571 |
| 1980 | T. Poikolainen, Finland................. | 2,455 |

## ARCHERY: WOMEN

| | | POINTS |
|---|---|---|
| 1972 | Doreen Wilber, United States ........... | 2,424 |
| 1976* | Luann Ryon, United States ............. | 2,499 |
| 1980 | K. Losabexidze, USSR.................. | 2,491 |

## BASKETBALL: MEN

| 1936 | United States | 1952 | United States | 1960 | United States | 1968 | United States | 1976 | United States |
|---|---|---|---|---|---|---|---|---|---|
| 1948 | United States | 1956 | United States | 1964 | United States | 1972 | Soviet Union | 1980 | Yugoslavia |

## BASKETBALL: WOMEN

| 1976 | Soviet Union | 1980 | Soviet Union |
|---|---|---|---|

## BOXING: LIGHT FLYWEIGHT

| 1968 | Francisco Rodriguez, Venezuela | 1976 | Jorge Hernandez, Cuba | 1980 | Shamil Sabyrov, USSR |
|---|---|---|---|---|---|
| 1972 | Gyoergy Gedeo, Hungary | | | | |

## BOXING: FLYWEIGHT

| 1904 | G. Finnegan, U.S.A. | 1932 | I. Enekes, Hungary | 1956 | T. Spinks, Britain | 1972 | G. Kostadinov, Bulgaria |
|---|---|---|---|---|---|---|---|
| 1920 | F. De Genaro, U.S.A. | 1936 | W. Kaiser, Germany | 1960 | G. Torck, Hungary | 1976 | Leo Randolph, U.S.A. |
| 1924 | F. La Barba, U.S.A. | 1948 | P. Perez, Argentina | 1964 | F. Atzori, Italy | 1980 | Petar Lessov, Bulgaria |
| 1928 | A. Kocsis, Hungary | 1952 | N. Brooks, U.S.A. | 1968 | R. Delgado, Mexico | | |

## BOXING: BANTAMWEIGHT

| 1904 | O. L. Kirk, U.S.A. | 1928 | V. Tamagnini, Italy | 1952 | P. Hamalainen, Finland | 1968 | V. Sokolov, USSR |
|---|---|---|---|---|---|---|---|
| 1908 | A. Thomas, Britain | 1932 | H. Gwynne, Canada | 1956 | W. Behrendt, W. Ger. | 1972 | O. Martinez, Cuba |
| 1920 | C. Walker, S. Africa | 1936 | U. Sergo, Italy | 1960 | O. Grigoryev, USSR | 1976 | Gu Yong Jo, N. Korea |
| 1924 | W. Smith, S. Africa | 1948 | T. Csik, Hungary | 1964 | T. Sakurai, Japan | 1980 | Juan Hernandez, Cuba |

## BOXING: FEATHERWEIGHT

| 1904 | O. L. Kirk, U.S.A. | 1928 | L. Van Klaveren, Neth. | 1952 | J. Zachara, Czech. | 1968 | A. Roldan, Mexico |
|---|---|---|---|---|---|---|---|
| 1908 | R. K. Gunn, Britain | 1932 | C. Robledo, Argentina | 1956 | V. Sefronov, USSR | 1972 | B. Kousnetsov, USSR |
| 1920 | P. Fritsch, France | 1936 | O. Casanovas, Argentina | 1960 | F. Musso, Italy | 1976 | A. Herrara, Cuba |
| 1924 | J. Fields, U.S.A. | 1948 | E. Formenti, Italy | 1964 | S. Stepashkin, USSR | 1980 | Rudi Fink, E. Germany |

## BOXING: LIGHTWEIGHT

| 1904 | H. J. Spanger, U.S.A. | 1928 | C. Orlandi, Italy | 1952 | Bolognesi, Italy | 1968 | R. Harris, U.S.A. |
|---|---|---|---|---|---|---|---|
| 1908 | F. Grace, Britain | 1932 | L. Stevens, S. Africa | 1956 | R. McTaggart, Britain | 1972 | J. Szczepanski, Poland |
| 1920 | S. Mosberg, U.S.A. | 1936 | I. Harangi, Hungary | 1960 | K. Pazdzier, Poland | 1976 | Howard Davis, U.S.A. |
| 1924 | H. Nielsen, Denmark | 1948 | G. Dreyer, S. Africa | 1964 | J. Grudzien, Poland | 1980 | Angel Herrera, Cuba |

\* Olympic record.

## BOXING: LIGHT WELTERWEIGHT

| | | | |
|---|---|---|---|
| 1952 C. Adkins, U.S.A. | 1960 B. Nemecek, Czech. | 1968 J. Kulei, Poland | 1976 Ray Leonard, U.S.A. |
| 1956 V. Engoibarian, USSR | 1964 J. Kulei, Poland | 1972 R. Seales, U.S.A. | 1980 Patrizio Oliva, Italy |

## BOXING: WELTERWEIGHT

| | | | |
|---|---|---|---|
| 1904 A. Yong, U.S.A. | 1932 E. Flynn, U.S.A. | 1956 N. Linca, Romania | 1972 E. Correa, Cuba |
| 1920 T. Schneider, Canada | 1936 S. Súvio, Finland | 1960 G. Benvenuti, Italy | 1976 J. Bachfeld, E. Germany |
| 1924 J. Delarge, Belgium | 1948 J. Torma, Czech. | 1964 M. Kasprzyk, Poland | 1980 A. Aldama, Cuba |
| 1928 E. Morgan, N. Zealand | 1952 Z. Chychia, Poland | 1968 M. Wolke, E. Germany | |

## BOXING: LIGHT MIDDLEWEIGHT

| | | | |
|---|---|---|---|
| 1952 L. Papp, Hungary | 1960 W. McClure, U.S.A. | 1968 B. Lagutin, USSR | 1976 J. Rybicki, Poland |
| 1956 L. Papp, Hungary | 1964 M. Kasprzyk, Poland | 1972 D. Kottysch, W. Ger. | 1980 A. Martinez, Cuba |

## BOXING: MIDDLEWEIGHT

| | | | |
|---|---|---|---|
| 1904 C. Mayer, U.S.A. | 1928 P. Toscani, Italy | 1952 Floyd Patterson, U.S.A. | 1968 C. Finnegan, Britain |
| 1908 J. Douglas, Britain | 1932 C. Barth, U.S.A. | 1956 G. Chatkov, USSR | 1972 V. Lemechev, USSR |
| 1920 H. Mallin, Britain | 1936 J. Despeaux, France | 1960 E. Crook, U.S.A. | 1976 Mike Spinks, U.S.A. |
| 1924 H. Mallin, Britain | 1948 L. Papp, Hungary | 1964 V. Popenchenko, USSR | 1980 Jose Gomez, Cuba |

## BOXING: LIGHT HEAVYWEIGHT

| | | | |
|---|---|---|---|
| 1920 E. Eagan, U.S.A. | 1936 R. Michelot, France | 1960 Cassius Clay, U.S.A. | 1976 Leon Spinks, U.S.A. |
| 1924 H. Mitchell, Britain | 1948 G. Hunter, S. Africa | 1964 C. Pinto, Italy | 1980 Slobodan Kacar, |
| 1928 V. Avendano, Argentina | 1952 Norvel Lee, U.S.A. | 1968 D. Pozdniak, USSR | Yugoslavia |
| 1932 D. Carstens, S. Africa | 1956 James Boyd, U.S.A. | 1972 M. Parlov, Yugoslavia | |

## BOXING: HEAVYWEIGHT

| | | | |
|---|---|---|---|
| 1904 S. Berger, U.S.A. | 1928 R. Jurado, Argentina | 1952 E. Sanders, U.S.A. | 1968 George Foreman, U.S.A. |
| 1908 A. Oldham, Britain | 1932 S. Lovell, Argentina | 1956 P. Rademacher, U.S.A. | 1972 T. Stevenson, Cuba |
| 1920 R. Rawson, Britain | 1936 H. Runge, Germany | 1960 F. De Piccoli, Italy | 1976 T. Stevenson, Cuba |
| 1924 O. von Porat, Norway | 1948 R. Iglesias, Argentina | 1964 Joe Frazier, U.S.A. | 1980 T. Stevenson, Cuba |

## CANOEING: KAYAK SINGLES—WOMEN: 500 METERS

| | | | | | |
|---|---|---|---|---|---|
| 1948 K. Hoff, Denmark | 2:31.9 | 1960 A. Seredina, USSR | 2:08.08 | 1972 Y. Ryabchinskaya, USSR 2:03.17 | |
| 1952 S. Saimo, Finland | 2:18.4 | 1964 L. Khvedosiuk, USSR | 2:12.87 | 1976 C. Zirzow, E. Germany 2:01.05 | |
| 1956 E. Dementieva, USSR | 2:18.9 | 1968 L. Pinaeva, USSR | 2:11.09 | 1980 B. Fischer, E. Germany 1:57.96* | |

## CANOEING: KAYAK PAIRS—WOMEN: 500 METERS

| | | | |
|---|---|---|---|
| 1960 USSR: M. Shubina, A. Seredina | 1:54.76 | 1972 USSR: L. Pinaeva, E. Kuryshko | 1:53.50 |
| 1964 W. Germany: R. Esser, A. Zimmerman | 1:56.95 | 1976 USSR: Popova, Kreft | 1:51.15 |
| 1968 W. Germany: A. Zimmermann, R. Esser | 1:56.44 | 1980 E. Germany, Bischoff, Genauss | 1:43.88 |

## CANOEING: KAYAK PAIRS—MEN: 500 METERS

| | | | |
|---|---|---|---|
| 1976 E. Germany: Mattern, Olbricht | 1:35.87 | 1980 Soviet Union: Parfenovich, Chukrai | 1:32.38 |

## CANOEING: KAYAK SINGLES—MEN: 1,000 METERS

| | | | | | |
|---|---|---|---|---|---|
| 1936 G. Hradetzky, Austria | 4:22.9 | 1960 E. Hansen, Denmark | 3:53.0 | 1976 R. Helm, E. Germany | 3:48.20 |
| 1948 G. Fredriksson, Sweden | 4:33.2 | 1964 R. Peterson, Sweden | 3:57.13 | 1980 R. Helm, E. Germany | 3:48.77 |
| 1952 G. Fredriksson, Sweden | 4:07.9 | 1968 M. Hesz, Hungary | 4:02.63 | | |
| 1956 G. Fredriksson, Sweden | 4:12.8 | 1972* A. Shaparenko, USSR | 3:48.06 | | |

## CANOEING: CANADIAN SINGLES—MEN: 1,000 METERS

| | | | | | |
|---|---|---|---|---|---|
| 1936 F. Amyot, Canada | 5:32.1 | 1960 J. Parti, Hungary | 4:33.9 | 1976 M. Ljubek, Yugoslavia | 4:09.51 |
| 1948 J. Holocek, Czech | 5:42.0 | 1964 J. Eschert, W. Germany | 4:35.14 | 1980 L. Lubenkov, Romania | 4:12.38 |
| 1952 J. Holocek, Czech | 4:56.3 | 1968 T. Tatai, Hungary | 4:36.14 | | |
| 1956 L. Rottman, Romania | 5:05.3 | 1972* I. Patzaichin, Romania | 4:08.94 | | |

## CANOEING: KAYAK PAIRS—MEN: 1,000 METERS

| | | | | |
|---|---|---|---|---|
| 1936 Austria: A. Kainz, A. Dorfner | 4:03.8 | 1964 Sweden: S. Sjodelius, G. Utterberg | 3:28.54 |
| 1948 Sweden: H. Berglund, L. Klingstroem | 4:07.3 | 1968 USSR: A. Shaparenko, V. Morozov | 3:37.54 |
| 1952 Finland: K. Wires, Y. Hietanen | 3:51.1 | 1972 USSR: N. Gorbachev, V. Kratassyuk | 3:31.23 |
| 1956 W. Germany: M. Scheuer, M. Miltenberger | 3:49.6 | 1976 USSR: Nagorny, Romanovsky | 3:29.01 |
| 1960 Sweden: G. Fredriksson, S. Sjodelius | 3:34.73 | 1980 USSR: V. Parfenovich, S Chukh | 3:26.72* |

## CANOEING: CANADIAN PAIRS—MEN: 1,000 METERS

| | | | | |
|---|---|---|---|---|
| 1936 Czechoslovakia: V. Syrovatka, J. Brzak | 4.50.1 | 1964 USSR: A. Khimich, S. Oschepkov | 4:04.65 |
| 1948 Czechoslovakia: J. Brzak, B. Kudrna | 5:07.1 | 1968 Romania: I. Patzaichin, S. Covaliov | 4:07.18 |
| 1952 Denmark: B. Rasch, F. Haunstoft | 4:38.3 | 1972 USSR: V. Chessyunas, Y. Lobanov | 3:52.60 |
| 1956 Romania: A. Dumitru, S. Ismailciuc | 4:47.4 | 1976 USSR: Petrenko, Vinogradov | 3:52.76 |
| 1960 USSR: L. Geyshter, S. Makarenko | 4:17.9 | 1980 Romania: Potzaichin, Simionov | 3:47.65* |

## CANOEING: KAYAK RELAY—MEN: 1,000 METERS

| | | | | | |
|---|---|---|---|---|---|
| 1960 W. Germany | 7:39.43 | 1968 Norway | 3:14.38 | 1976* USSR | 3:06.69 |
| 1964 USSR | 3:14.67 | 1972 USSR | 3:14.02 | 1980 E. Germany | 3:13.76 |

## CANOEING: SLALOM—MEN: 500 METERS

| KAYAK SLALOM: SINGLES | CANADIAN SLALOM: SINGLES | CANADIAN SLALOM: PAIRS |
|---|---|---|
| 1972 Siegbert Horn, E. Germany | 1972 Reinhard Eiben, E. Germany | 1972 E. Germany: W. Hofmann, R. Amend |
| 1976 V. Diba, Romania | 1976 A. Rogov, USSR | 1976 USSR: Petrenko, Vinogradov |
| 1980 V. Parfenovich, USSR | 1980 S. Postrekhin, USSR | 1980 Hungary: Foltan, Vaskuti |

## CYCLING: ROAD RACE—INDIVIDUAL: 200 KILOMETERS

| | | | |
|---|---|---|---|
| 1896 A. Konstantinidis, Greece | 1928 H. Hansen, Denmark | 1956 E. Baldini, Italy | 1976 B. Johansson, Sweden |
| 1906 Vast, Bardonneau (tie), France | 1932 A. Pavesi, Italy | 1960 V. Kapitonov, USSR | 1980 S. Sukharuchenkov, |
| 1912 R. Lewis, S. Africa | 1936 R. Charpentier, France | 1964 M. Zanin, Italy | USSR |
| 1920 H. Stenquist, Sweden | 1948 J. Bayaert, France | 1968 P. Vianelli, Italy | |
| 1924 A. Blanchonnet, France | 1952 A. Noyelle, Belgium | 1972 H. Kuiper, Neth. | |

*Olympic record.

## SUMMER OLYMPIC WINNERS AND RECORDS (continued)

### CYCLING: ROAD RACE—TEAM: 100 KILOMETERS

| | | | | | | | | | |
|---|---|---|---|---|---|---|---|---|---|
| 1912 | Sweden | 1928 | Denmark | 1948 | Belgium | 1960 | Italy | 1972 | USSR |
| 1920 | France | 1932 | Italy | 1952 | Belgium | 1964 | Netherlands | 1976 | USSR |
| 1924 | France | 1936 | France | 1956 | France | 1968 | Netherlands | 1980 | USSR |

### CYCLING: INDIVIDUAL TIME TRIAL—1,000 METERS

| | | | | | | | | |
|---|---|---|---|---|---|---|---|---|
| 1928 | W. Falck-Hansen, Denmark | 1:14.2 | 1952 | Mockridge, Australia | 1:11.1 | 1968 | P. Trentin, France | 1:03.91 |
| 1932 | E. Gray, Australia | 1:13.0 | 1956 | L. Faggin, Italy | 1:09.8 | 1972 | N. Fredborg, Denmark | 1:06.44 |
| 1936 | A. van Vliet, Netherlands | 1:12.0 | 1960 | S. Gaiardoni, Italy | 1:07.27 | 1976 | K.J. Gruenke, E. Germany | 1:05.927 |
| 1948 | J. Dupont, France | 1:13.5 | 1964 | P. Sercu, Belgium | 1:09.59 | 1980* | L. Thoms | 1:02.955 |

### CYCLING: INDIVIDUAL PURSUIT—4,000 METERS

| | | | | | |
|---|---|---|---|---|---|
| 1964 | J. Daller, Czechoslovakia | 5:04.7 | 1976 | G. Braun, W. Germany | 4:47.61 |
| 1968 | D. Rebillard, France | 4:41.71 | 1980* | R. Dill-Bundi, Switzerland | 4:35.66 |
| 1972 | K. Knudsen, Norway | 4:45.74 | | | |

### CYCLING: TEAM PURSUIT—4,000 METERS

| | | | | | | | | | | | |
|---|---|---|---|---|---|---|---|---|---|---|---|
| 1920 | Italy | 5:20.0 | 1932 | Italy | 4:53.0 | 1952 | Italy | 4:46.1 | 1964 | W. Germany 4:35.6 | 1976 | W. Germany | 4:21.06 |
| 1924 | Italy | 5:15.0 | 1936 | France | 4:45.0 | 1956 | Italy | 4:37.4 | 1968 | Denmark | 4:22.44 | 1980* | USSR | 4:15.70 |
| 1928 | Italy | 5:01.8 | 1948 | France | 4:57.8 | 1960 | Italy | 4:30.9 | 1972 | W. Germany 4:22.14 | | |

### CYCLING: SCRATCH SPRINT (Time for final 200 meters in seconds)

| | | | | | | | | |
|---|---|---|---|---|---|---|---|---|
| 1924 | L. Michard, France | 12.8 | 1948 | M. Ghella, Italy | 12.0 | 1968* | D. Morelon, France | 10.68 |
| 1928 | R. Beaufrand, France | 13.2 | 1952 | E. Sacchi, Italy | 12.0 | 1972 | D. Morelon, France | —[1] |
| 1932 | J. van Edmond, Netherlands | 12.2 | 1956 | M. Rousseau, France | 11.4 | 1976 | A. Tkac, Czechoslovakia | —[1] |
| 1936 | T. Merkens, Germany | 11.8 | 1964 | G. Pettenella, Italy | 13.6 | 1980 | L. Hesslich, E. Germany | —[1] |

### CYCLING: TANDEM—2,000 METERS

| | | | | | | | | | |
|---|---|---|---|---|---|---|---|---|---|
| 1908 | France | 1928 | Netherlands | 1948 | Italy | 1960 | Italy | 1972 | USSR |
| 1920 | Britain | 1932 | France | 1952 | Australia | 1964 | Italy | | |
| 1924 | France | 1936 | Germany | 1956 | Australia | 1968 | France | | |

### EQUESTRIAN: INDIVIDUAL—THREE-DAY EVENT

| | | | | | |
|---|---|---|---|---|---|
| 1912 | A. Nordlander, Sweden | 1936 | L. Stubbendorff, Germany | 1964 | M. Checcoli, Italy |
| 1920 | Helmer Morner, Sweden | 1948 | B. Chevallier, France | 1968 | J. Guyon, France |
| 1924 | A. van der Voort van Zijp, Neth. | 1952 | H. von Blixen-Finecke, Sweden | 1972 | R. Meade, Britian |
| 1928 | F.P. de Mortanges, Netherlands | 1956 | P. Kastenman, Sweden | 1976 | E. Coffin, U.S.A. |
| 1932 | F. P. de Mortanges, Netherlands | 1960 | L. Morgan, Australia | 1980 | F.E. Roman, Italy |

### EQUESTRIAN: INDIVIDUAL—DRESSAGE

| | | | | | |
|---|---|---|---|---|---|
| 1912 | C. Bonde, Sweden | 1936 | H. Pollary, Germany | 1964 | H. Chammartin, Switzerland |
| 1920 | J. Lundblad, Sweden | 1948 | H. Moser, Switzerland | 1968 | I. Kizimov, USSR |
| 1924 | E. Linder, Sweden | 1952 | H. St. Cyr, Sweden | 1972 | L. Linsenhoff, W. Germany |
| 1928 | C. von Langen, Germany | 1956 | H. St. Cyr, Sweden | 1976 | C. Stueckelberger, Switzerland |
| 1932 | R. Lesage, France | 1960 | S. Filatov, USSR | 1980 | E. Theurer, Austria |

### EQUESTRIAN: INDIVIDUAL—GRAND PRIX JUMPING

| | | | | | |
|---|---|---|---|---|---|
| 1912 | J. Cariou, France | 1936 | K. Hasse, Germany | 1964 | P. d'Oriola, France |
| 1920 | T. Lequio, Italy | 1948 | H. Mariles Cortes, Mexico | 1968 | W.C. Steinkraus, U.S.A. |
| 1924 | A. Gemuseus, Switzerland | 1952 | P. d'Oriola, France | 1972 | G. Mancinelli, Italy |
| 1928 | F. Ventura, Czechoslovakia | 1956 | H. Winkler, W. Germany | 1976 | A. Schockemoehle, W. Germany |
| 1932 | T. Nishi, Japan | 1960 | R. d'Inzeo, Italy | 1980 | J. Kowalczyk, Poland |

### EQUESTRIAN: TEAM—THREE-DAY EVENT

| | | | | | | | | | |
|---|---|---|---|---|---|---|---|---|---|
| 1912 | Sweden | 1928 | Netherlands | 1948 | U.S.A. | 1960 | Australia | 1972 | Britain |
| 1920 | Sweden | 1932 | U.S.A. | 1952 | Sweden | 1964 | Italy | 1976 | U.S.A. |
| 1924 | Netherlands | 1936 | Germany | 1956 | Britain | 1968 | Britain | 1980 | USSR |

### EQUESTRIAN: TEAM—DRESSAGE

| | | | | | | | | |
|---|---|---|---|---|---|---|---|---|
| 1928 | Germany | 1948 | France | 1964 | W. Germany | 1976 | W. Germany |
| 1932 | France | 1952 | Sweden | 1968 | W. Germany | 1980 | USSR |
| 1936 | Germany | 1956 | Sweden | 1972 | USSR | | |

### EQUESTRIAN: TEAM—GRAND PRIX JUMPING

| | | | | | | | | | |
|---|---|---|---|---|---|---|---|---|---|
| 1912 | Sweden | 1928 | Spain | 1952 | Britain | 1964 | W. Germany | 1976 | France |
| 1920 | Sweden | 1936 | Germany | 1956 | W. Germany | 1968 | Canada | 1980 | USSR |
| 1924 | Sweden | 1948 | Mexico | 1960 | W. Germany | 1972 | W. Germany | | |

### FENCING: FOILS—MEN: INDIVIDUAL

| | | | | | |
|---|---|---|---|---|---|
| 1896 | E. Gravelotte, France | 1928 | L. Gauldin, France | 1960 | V. Zhdanovich, USSR |
| 1900 | C. Coste, France | 1932 | G. Marzi, Italy | 1964 | E. Franke, Poland |
| 1904 | R. Fonst, Cuba | 1936 | G. Gaudini, Italy | 1968 | I. Drima, Romania |
| 1912 | N. Nadi, Italy | 1948 | J. Buhan, France | 1972 | W. Woyda, Poland |
| 1920 | N. Nadi, Italy | 1952 | C. d'Oriola, France | 1976 | F. dal Zotto, Italy |
| 1924 | R. Ducret, France | 1956 | C. d'Oriola, France | 1980 | V. Smirnov, USSR |

\* Olympic record.    [1] Time not available.

## FENCING: FOILS—WOMEN: INDIVIDUAL

| Year | Winner | Year | Winner | Year | Winner |
|---|---|---|---|---|---|
| 1924 | E. Osiier, Denmark | 1952 | I. Camber, Italy | 1972 | Ragno Lonzi, Italy |
| 1928 | H. Mayer, Germany | 1956 | G. Sheen, Britain | 1976 | I. Schwarczenberger, Hungary |
| 1932 | E. Preis, Austria | 1960 | A. Schmid, W. Germany | 1980 | P. Trinquet, France |
| 1936 | I. Elek, Hungary | 1964 | I. Rejto, Hungary | | |
| 1948 | I. Elek, Hungary | 1968 | E. Novikova, USSR | | |

## FENCING: FOILS—MEN: TEAM

| Year | Winner | Year | Winner | Year | Winner | Year | Winner | Year | Winner |
|---|---|---|---|---|---|---|---|---|---|
| 1904 | Cuba | 1928 | Italy | 1948 | France | 1960 | USSR | 1972 | Poland |
| 1920 | Italy | 1932 | France | 1952 | France | 1964 | USSR | 1976 | W. Germany |
| 1924 | France | 1936 | Italy | 1956 | Italy | 1968 | France | 1980 | France |

## FENCING: FOILS—WOMEN: TEAM

| Year | Winner | Year | Winner | Year | Winner | Year | Winner | Year | Winner | Year | Winner |
|---|---|---|---|---|---|---|---|---|---|---|---|
| 1960 | USSR | 1964 | Hungary | 1968 | USSR | 1972 | USSR | 1976 | USSR | 1980 | France |

## FENCING: ÉPÉE—MEN: INDIVIDUAL

| Year | Winner | Year | Winner | Year | Winner |
|---|---|---|---|---|---|
| 1900 | R. Fonst, Cuba | 1928 | L. Gaudin, France | 1960 | G. Delfino, Italy |
| 1904 | R. Fonst, Cuba | 1928 | C. Cornaggia-Medici, Italy | 1964 | G. Kriss, USSR |
| 1908 | G. Alibert, France | 1936 | F. Riccardi, Italy | 1968 | G. Kulcsar, Hungary |
| 1912 | P. Anspach, Belgium | 1948 | L. Cantone, Italy | 1972 | C. Fenyvesi, Hungary |
| 1920 | A. Massard, France | 1952 | E. Mangiarotti, Italy | 1976 | A. Pusch, W. Germany |
| 1924 | C. Delporte, Belgium | 1956 | C. Pavesi, Italy | 1980 | J. Harmenberg, Sweden |

## FENCING: ÉPÉE—MEN: TEAM

| Year | Winner | Year | Winner | Year | Winner | Year | Winner | Year | Winner | Year | Winner |
|---|---|---|---|---|---|---|---|---|---|---|---|
| 1908 | France | 1924 | France | 1936 | Italy | 1956 | Italy | 1968 | Hungary | 1980 | France |
| 1912 | Belgium | 1928 | Italy | 1948 | France | 1960 | Italy | 1972 | Hungary | | |
| 1920 | Italy | 1932 | Italy | 1952 | Italy | 1964 | Hungary | 1976 | Sweden | | |

## FENCING: SABRE—MEN: INDIVIDUAL

| Year | Winner | Year | Winner | Year | Winner |
|---|---|---|---|---|---|
| 1896 | J. Georgiadis, Greece | 1928 | O. Tersztyanszky, Hungary | 1964 | T. Pezsa, Hungary |
| 1900 | G. de la Falaise, France | 1932 | G. Piller, Hungary | 1968 | J. Pawlowski, Poland |
| 1904 | M. Diaz, Cuba | 1936 | E. Kabos, Hungary | 1972 | V. Sidiak, USSR |
| 1908 | J. Fuchs, Hungary | 1948 | A. Gerevich, Hungary | 1976 | V. Krovopuskov, USSR |
| 1912 | J. Fuchs, Hungary | 1952 | P. Kovacs, Hungary | 1980 | V. Krovopuskov, USSR |
| 1920 | N. Nadi, Italy | 1956 | R. Karpati, Hungary | | |
| 1924 | S. Posta, Hungary | 1960 | R. Karpati, Hungary | | |

## FENCING: SABRE—MEN: TEAM

| Year | Winner | Year | Winner | Year | Winner | Year | Winner | Year | Winner | Year | Winner |
|---|---|---|---|---|---|---|---|---|---|---|---|
| 1904 | Cuba | 1920 | Italy | 1932 | Hungary | 1952 | Hungary | 1964 | USSR | 1976 | USSR |
| 1908 | Hungary | 1924 | Italy | 1936 | Hungary | 1956 | Hungary | 1968 | USSR | 1980 | USSR |
| 1912 | Hungary | 1928 | Hungary | 1948 | Hungary | 1960 | Hungary | 1972 | Italy | | |

## FIELD HOCKEY—MEN

| Year | Winner | Year | Winner | Year | Winner | Year | Winner | Year | Winner | Year | Winner | Year | Winner |
|---|---|---|---|---|---|---|---|---|---|---|---|---|---|
| 1908 | Britain | 1928 | India | 1948 | India | 1956 | India | 1964 | India | 1972 | W. Germany | 1980 | India |
| 1920 | Britain | 1936 | India | 1952 | India | 1960 | Pakistan | 1968 | Pakistan | 1976 | New Zealand | | |

## FIELD HOCKEY—WOMEN

| Year | Winner |
|---|---|
| 1980 | Zimbabwe |

## GYMNASTICS: ALL-AROUND—MEN: TEAM

| Year | Winner | Year | Winner | Year | Winner | Year | Winner | Year | Winner | Year | Winner |
|---|---|---|---|---|---|---|---|---|---|---|---|
| 1896 | Germany | 1912 | Italy | 1928 | Switzerland | 1948 | Finland | 1960 | Japan | 1972 | Japan |
| 1904 | U.S.A. | 1920 | Italy | 1932 | Italy | 1952 | USSR | 1964 | Japan | 1976 | Japan |
| 1908 | Sweden | 1924 | Italy | 1936 | Germany | 1956 | USSR | 1968 | Japan | 1980 | USSR |

## GYMNASTICS: ALL-AROUND—WOMEN: TEAM

| Year | Winner | Year | Winner | Year | Winner | Year | Winner | Year | Winner | Year | Winner |
|---|---|---|---|---|---|---|---|---|---|---|---|
| 1928 | Netherlands | 1948 | Czechoslovakia | 1956 | USSR | 1964 | USSR | 1972 | USSR | 1980 | USSR |
| 1936 | Germany | 1952 | USSR | 1960 | USSR | 1968 | USSR | 1976 | USSR | | |

## GYMNASTICS: ALL-AROUND—MEN: INDIVIDUAL

| Year | Winner | Year | Winner | Year | Winner |
|---|---|---|---|---|---|
| 1900 | S. Sandras, France | 1928 | G. Miez, Switzerland | 1960 | B. Shakhlin, USSR |
| 1904 | A. Heida, U.S.A. | 1932 | R. Neri, Italy | 1964 | Y. Endo, Japan |
| 1908 | A. Braglia, Italy | 1936 | A. Schwarzmann, Germany | 1968 | S. Kato, Japan |
| 1912 | A. Braglia, Italy | 1948 | V. Huhtanen, Finland | 1972 | S. Kato, Japan |
| 1920 | G. Zampori, Italy | 1952 | V. Chukarin, USSR | 1976 | N. Andrianov, USSR |
| 1924 | L. Stukelj, Yugoslavia | 1956 | V. Chukarin, USSR | 1980 | A. Dityatin, USSR |

## GYMNASTICS: ALL-AROUND—WOMEN: INDIVIDUAL

| Year | Winner | Year | Winner | Year | Winner | Year | Winner |
|---|---|---|---|---|---|---|---|
| 1952 | M. Gorokhovskaja, USSR | 1960 | L. Latynina, USSR | 1968 | V. Caslavska, Czech. | 1976 | N. Comaneci, Romania |
| 1956 | L. Latynina, USSR | 1964 | V. Caslavska, Czech. | 1972 | L. Turischeva, USSR | 1980 | Y. Davydova, USSR |

## GYMNASTICS: LONG HORSE—MEN

| Year | Winner | Year | Winner | Year | Winner |
|---|---|---|---|---|---|
| 1896 | K. Schumann, Germany | 1948 | P. Aaltonen, Finland | 1964 | H. Yamashita, Japan |
| 1904 | (tie) A. Heida, G. Eyser, U.S.A. | 1952 | V. Chukarin, USSR | 1968 | M. Voronin, USSR |
| 1924 | F. Kriz, U.S.A. | 1956 | (tie) H. Bantz, W. Germany; V. Mouratov, USSR | 1972 | K. Koeste, E. Germany |
| 1928 | E. Mack, Switzerland | | | 1976 | N. Andrianov, USSR |
| 1932 | S. Guglielmetti, Italy | 1960 | (tie) B. Shakhlin, USSR; T. Ono, Japan | 1980 | N. Andrianov, USSR |
| 1936 | K. Schwarzmann, Germany | | | | |

## GYMNASTICS: LONG HORSE—WOMEN

| Year | Winner | Year | Winner | Year | Winner | Year | Winner |
|---|---|---|---|---|---|---|---|
| 1952 | Y. Kalinthouk, USSR | 1960 | M. Nikolaeva, USSR | 1968 | V. Caslavska, Czech. | 1976 | N. Kim, USSR |
| 1956 | L. Latynina, USSR | 1964 | V. Caslavska, Czech. | 1972 | K. Janz, E. Germany | 1980 | N. Shaposhnikova, USSR |

## GYMNASTICS: PARALLEL BARS—MEN

| Year | Winner | Year | Winner | Year | Winner | Year | Winner |
|---|---|---|---|---|---|---|---|
| 1896 | A. Flatow, Germany | 1932 | R. Neri, Italy | 1956 | V. Chukarin, USSR | 1972 | S. Kato, Japan |
| 1904 | G. Eyser, U.S.A. | 1936 | K. Frey, Germany | 1960 | B. Shakhlin, USSR | 1976 | S. Kato, Japan |
| 1924 | A. Guttinger, Switz. | 1948 | M. Reusch, Switz. | 1964 | Y. Endo, Japan | 1980 | A. Tkachyov, USSR |
| 1928 | L. Vacha, Czech. | 1952 | H. Eugster, Switz. | 1968 | A. Nakayama, Japan | | |

## SUMMER OLYMPIC WINNERS AND RECORDS *(continued)*

### GYMNASTICS: PARALLEL BARS—WOMEN

| | | | |
|---|---|---|---|
| 1952 M. Korondi, Hungary | 1960 P. Astakhova, USSR | 1968 V. Caslavska, Czech. | 1976 N. Comaneci, Romania |
| 1956 A. Keleti, Hungary | 1964 P. Astakhova, USSR | 1972 K. Janz, E. Germany | 1980 M. Gnauck, E. Germany |

### GYMNASTICS: FLOOR EXERCISES—MEN

| | | | |
|---|---|---|---|
| 1956 V. Mouratov, USSR | 1964 F. Menichelli, Italy | 1972 N. Andrianov, USSR | 1980 R. Bruckner, E. Germany |
| 1960 N. Aihara, Japan | 1968 S. Kato, Japan | 1976 N. Andrianov, USSR | |

### GYMNASTICS: FLOOR EXERCISES—WOMEN

| | | |
|---|---|---|
| 1952 A. Keleti, Hungary | 1964 L. Latynina, USSR | 1976 N. Kim, USSR |
| 1956 (tie) A. Keleti, Hungary; L. Latynina, USSR | 1968 (tie) V. Caslavska, Czech.; L. Petrik, USSR | 1980 N. Kim, USSR; N. Comaneci, Romania |
| 1960 L. Latynina, USSR | 1972 Olga Korbut, USSR | |

### GYMNASTICS: BALANCE BEAM—WOMEN

| | | | |
|---|---|---|---|
| 1952 N. Botcharova, USSR | 1960 E. Bosakova, Czech. | 1968 N. Kutchinskava, USSR | 1976 N. Comaneci, Romania |
| 1956 A. Keleti, Hungary | 1964 V. Caslavska, Czech. | 1972 Olga Korbut, USSR | 1980 N. Comaneci, Romania |

### GYMNASTICS: POMMELED HORSE—MEN

| | | | |
|---|---|---|---|
| 1896 L. Zutter, Switzerland | 1948 (tie) P. Aaltonen, V. Houtanen, I. Savolainen, Finland | 1964 M. Cerar, Yugoslavia | |
| 1904 A. Heida, U.S.A. | | 1968 M. Voronin, USSR | |
| 1924 J. Wilhelm, Switzerland | 1952 V. Chukarin, USSR | 1972 V. Klimenko, USSR | |
| 1928 H. Hanggi, Switzerland | 1956 B. Shakhlin, USSR | 1976 Z. Magyar, Hungary | |
| 1932 I. Pelle, Hungary | 1960 (tie) E. Ekman, Finland; B. Shakhlin, USSR | 1980 Z. Magyar, Hungary | |
| 1936 K. Frey, Germany | | | |

### GYMNASTICS: FLYING RINGS—MEN

| | | | |
|---|---|---|---|
| 1986 J. Mitropoulos, Greece | 1932 G. Gulack, U.S.A. | 1956 A. Azarian, USSR | 1972 A. Nakayama, Japan |
| 1904 H. Glass, U.S.A. | 1936 A. Hudec, Czech. | 1960 A. Azarian, USSR | 1976 N. Andrainov, USSR |
| 1924 F. Martino, Italy | 1948 K. Frei, Switz. | 1964 T. Hayata, Japan | 1980 A. Dityatin, USSR |
| 1928 L. Stukelj, Yugoslavia | 1952 G. Chaguinian, USSR | 1968 A. Nakayama, Japan | |

### GYMNASTICS: HORIZONTAL BAR—MEN

| | | | |
|---|---|---|---|
| 1896 H. Weingaertner, Ger. | 1932 D. Bixler, U.S.A. | 1960 T. Ono, Japan | 1976 M. Tsukahara, Japan |
| 1904 (tie) A. Heida, E. Hennig, U.S.A. | 1936 A. Saarvala, Finland | 1964 B. Shakhlin, USSR | 1980 S. Deltchev, Bulgaria |
| | 1948 J. Stalder, Switz. | 1968 (tie) M. Voronin, USSR; A. Nakayama, Japan | |
| 1924 L. Stukelj, Yugoslavia | 1952 J. Gunthard, Switz. | | |
| 1928 G. Miez, Switzerland | 1956 T. Ono, Japan | 1972 M. Tsukahara, Japan | |

### HANDBALL: TEAM (MEN)  /  HANDBALL: TEAM (WOMEN)

| | | | |
|---|---|---|---|
| 1972 Yugoslavia | 1976 USSR | 1980 E. Germany | 1980 USSR |

### JUDO

| LIGHTWEIGHT | MIDDLEWEIGHT | HEAVYWEIGHT | OPEN CLASS |
|---|---|---|---|
| 1964 T. Nakatani, Japan | 1964 I. Okano, Japan | 1964 I. Inokuma, Japan | 1964 A. Geesink, Neth. |
| 1972 T. Kawaguchi, Japan | 1972 S. Sekine, Japan | 1972 W. Ruska, Neth. | 1972 W. Ruska, Neth. |
| 1976 N. Rodriguez, Cuba | 1976 I. Sonada, Japan | 1976 S. Novikov, USSR | 1976 H. Uemura, Japan |
| 1980 E. Gamba, Italy; T. Rey, France [1] N. Soludkhin, USSR [2] | 1980 J. Roethlisberger, Switzerland; S. Khabareli, USSR [3] | 1980 A. Parisi, France; R. Van DeWalle, Belgium [4] | 1980 D. Lorenzo, E. Germany |
| WELTERWEIGHT | | LIGHT HEAVYWEIGHT | |
| 1972 T. Nomura, Japan | 1976 V. Nevzorov, USSR | 1972 S. Chochoshvily, USSR | 1976 K. Ninomiya, Japan |

### PENTATHLON: WOMEN—INDIVIDUAL

| | | |
|---|---|---|
| 1964 I. Press, USSR | 1972 Mary Peters, Britain | 1980* O. Tkachenko, USSR |
| 1968 I. Becker, W. Germany | 1976 Sigurn Siegl, E. Germany | |

### MODERN PENTATHLON: MEN—INDIVIDUAL

| | | | |
|---|---|---|---|
| 1912 Jim Thorpe, U.S.A. | 1928 S. Thofelt, Sweden | 1952 L. Hall, Sweden | 1968 B. Ferm, Sweden |
| G. Lilliehood, Sweden | 1932 J. Oxenstierna, Sweden | 1956 L. Hall, Sweden | 1972 A. Balczo, Hungary |
| 1920 J. Dyrssen, Sweden | 1936 G. Handrick, Germany | 1960 F. Nemeth, Hungary | 1976 J. Pyciak-Peciak, Poland |
| 1924 Bo Lindman, Sweden | 1948 W. Grut, Sweden | 1964 F. Torok, Hungary | 1980 A. Starostin, USSR |

### MODERN PENTATHLON: MEN—TEAM

| | | | |
|---|---|---|---|
| 1952 Hungary | 1960 Hungary | 1968 Hungary | 1976 Britain |
| 1956 USSR | 1964 USSR | 1972 USSR | 1980 USSR |

### ROWING SINGLE SCULLS—MEN

| | | | |
|---|---|---|---|
| 1900 H. Barrelet, France | 1928 H. Pearce, Australia | 1956 V. Ivanov, USSR | 1976 P. Karppinen, Finland |
| 1908 H. Blackstaffe, Britain | 1932 H. Pearce, Australia | 1960 V. Ivanov, USSR | 1980 P. Karppinen, Finland |
| 1912 W. Kinnear, Britain | 1936 G. Schafer, Germany | 1964 V. Ivanov, USSR | |
| 1920 John Kelly, U.S.A. | 1948 M. Wood, Australia | 1968 J. Wienese, Neth. | |
| 1924 J. Beresford, Britain | 1952 Y. Chukalov, USSR | 1972 Y. Malishev, USSR | |

### ROWING: DOUBLE SCULLS—MEN

| | | | | |
|---|---|---|---|---|
| 1920 U.S.A. | 1932 Britain | 1952 Argentina | 1964 USSR | 1976 Norway |
| 1924 U.S.A. | 1936 Germany | 1956 USSR | 1968 USSR | 1980 E. Germany |
| 1928 U.S.A. | 1948 Britain | 1960 Czechoslovakia | 1972 USSR | |

### ROWING: PAIRS WITHOUT COXSWAIN—MEN

| | | | | |
|---|---|---|---|---|
| 1908 Britain | 1928 Germany | 1948 Britain | 1960 USSR | 1972 E. Germany |
| 1920 Italy | 1932 Britain | 1952 U.S.A. | 1964 Canada | 1976 E. Germany |
| 1924 Netherlands | 1936 Germany | 1956 U.S.A. | 1968 E. Germany | 1980 E. Germany |

### ROWING: PAIRS WITH COXSWAIN—MEN

| | | | | | | |
|---|---|---|---|---|---|---|
| 1900 Netherlands | 1928 Switzerland | 1936 Germany | 1952 France | 1960 W. Germany | 1968 Italy | 1976 E. Germany |
| 1924 Switzerland | 1932 U.S.A. | 1948 Denmark | 1956 U.S.A. | 1964 U.S.A. | 1972 E. Germany | 1980 E. Germany |

* Olympic record. [1] Extra Lightweight. [2] Half Lightweight. [3] Half middleweight. [4] Half Heavyweight.

## ROWING: FOURS WITHOUT COXSWAIN—MEN

| | | | | | | |
|---|---|---|---|---|---|---|
| 1908 Britain | 1928 Britain | 1936 Germany | 1952 Yugoslavia | 1960 U.S.A | 1968 E. Germany | 1976 E. Germany |
| 1924 Britain | 1932 Britain | 1948 Italy | 1956 Canada | 1964 Denmark | 1972 W. Germany | 1980 E. Germany |

## ROWING: FOURS WITH COXSWAIN—MEN

| | | | | |
|---|---|---|---|---|
| 1912 Germany | 1928 Italy | 1948 U.S.A. | 1960 W. Germany | 1972 W. Germany |
| 1920 Switzerland | 1932 Germany | 1952 Czechoslovakia | 1964 W. Germany | 1976 USSR |
| 1924 Switzerland | 1936 Germany | 1956 Italy | 1968 New Zealand | 1980 E. Germany |

## ROWING: EIGHTS WITH COXSWAIN—MEN

| | | | | | |
|---|---|---|---|---|---|
| 1900 U.S.A. | 1920 U.S.A. | 1932 U.S.A. | 1952 U.S.A. | 1964 U.S.A. | 1976 E. Germany |
| 1908 Britain | 1924 U.S.A. | 1936 U.S.A. | 1956 U.S.A. | 1968 W. Germany | 1980 E. Germany |
| 1912 Britain | 1928 U.S.A. | 1948 U.S.A. | 1960 W. Germany | 1972 New Zealand | |

## ROWING: WOMEN

| SINGLE SCULLS | DOUBLE SCULLS | PAIRS WITHOUT COXSWAIN |
|---|---|---|
| 1976 E. Germany | 1976 Bulgaria | 1976 Bulgaria |
| 1980 Romania | 1980 USSR | 1980 E. Germany |
| FOURS WITH COXSWAIN | EIGHTS WITH COXSWAIN | QUADRUPLE SCULLS WITH COXSWAIN |
| 1976 E. Germany | 1976 E. Germany | 1976 E. Germany |
| 1980 E. Germany | 1980 E. Germany | 1980 E. Germany |

## SHOOTING: TRAPSHOOTING

| | | |
|---|---|---|
| 1908 W.H. Ewing, Canada ........72 | 1952 G. Genereux, Canada ..192 | 1968 J. Brathwaite, Britain ....198 |
| 1912 James Graham, U.S.A. ......96 | 1956 G. Rossini, Italy ........195 | 1972 *A. Scalzone, Italy ........199 |
| 1920 Mark Arie, U.S.A. ..........95 | 1960 I. Dumitrescu, Romania 192 | 1976 D. Haldeman, U.S.A. ......190 |
| 1924 G. Halasy, Hungary ........98 | 1964 E. Mattarelli, Italy......198 | 1980 L. Giovannetti, Italy ....198 |

## SHOOTING: PISTOL—RAPID FIRE: 25 METERS

| | | |
|---|---|---|
| 1936 C. van Oyen, Germany .....36 | 1960 W. McMillan, U.S.A. ....587 | 1976 *N. Klaar, E. Germany ....597 |
| 1948 K. Takacs, Hungary .......580 | 1964 P. Linnosvuop, Finland .592 | 1980 C. Ion .................596 |
| 1952 K. Takacs, Hungary .......579 | 1968 J. Zapedski, Poland ....593 | |
| 1956 S. Petrescu, Romania ....587 | 1972 J. Zapedzki, Poland ....595 | |

## SHOOTING: PISTOL—FREE: 50 METERS

| | | |
|---|---|---|
| 1936 T. Ullmann, Sweden......539 | 1960 A. Gustchin, USSR .....560 | 1976 V. Potteck, E. Germany ..573 |
| 1948 C.E. Vasquez, Peru .....545 | 1964 V. Markkanen, Finland ..560 | 1980 *A. Melentev, USSR ....581 |
| 1952 Huelet Benner, U.S.A. ....553 | 1968 G. Kosykh, USSR ......562 | |
| 1956 P. Linnosvuoo, Finland ....556 | 1972 R. Skanaker, Sweden ...567 | |

## SHOOTING: SMALL-BORE RIFLE—PRONE: 50 METERS

| | | |
|---|---|---|
| 1960 P. Kohnke, W. Germany ...590 | 1968 Jan Kurka, Czech. ....598 | 1976 * K. Smiezek, W. Germany .599 |
| 1964 L. Hammerl, Hungary ....597 | 1972 * Ho Jun Li, North Korea ....599 | 1980 K. Varga, Hungary, H. Heilfort, E. Germany ..............599 |

## SHOOTING: SMALL-BORE RIFLE—3-POSITION

| | | |
|---|---|---|
| 1960 V. Shamburkin, USSR ..1,149 | 1968 B. Klingner, W. Ger. ..1,157 | 1976 L. Bassham, U.S.A. ....1,162 |
| 1964 Lones Wigger, U.S.A. .....1,164 | 1972 John Writer, U.S.A...1,166 | 1980 * V. Vlasov, USSR ....1,173 |

## SHOOTING: SKEET SHOOTING

| | |
|---|---|
| 1968 *Evgeny Petrov, USSR .......198 | 1976 * J. Panacek, Czech......198 |
| 1972 Konrad Wirnhier, W. Germany ..195 | 1980 H. Rasmussen, Den. ...196 |

## SHOOTING: MOVING TARGET

| |
|---|
| 1972 Lakov Zhelezniak, USSR .569 |
| 1976 A. Gazov, USSR ........579 |
| 1980 * I. Sokolav, USSR ........589 |

## SOCCER

| | | | | | |
|---|---|---|---|---|---|
| 1900 Britain | 1912 Britain | 1928 Uruguay | 1952 Hungary | 1964 Hungary | 1976 E. Germany |
| 1904 Canada | 1920 Belgium | 1936 Italy | 1956 USSR | 1968 Hungary | 1980 Czech. |
| 1908 Britain | 1924 Uruguay | 1948 Sweden | 1958 Yugoslavia | 1972 Poland | |

## SWIMMING: 100-METER FREESTYLE—MEN

| | | |
|---|---|---|
| 1896 A. Hajos, Hungary ....... 1:22.2 | 1928 John Weissmuller, U.S.A. 0:58.6 | 1964 D. Schollander, U.S.A. 0:53.40 |
| 1900 Jarvis, Britain ....... 1:16.0 | 1932 Y. Miyazaki, Japan .... 0:58.2 | 1968 M. Wenden, Australia 0:52.20 |
| 1904 de Halmay, Hungary (100 yds.) 1:02.8 | 1936 Ferenc Csik, Hungary . 0:57.6 | 1972 Mark Spitz, U.S.A.... 0:51.22 |
| 1908 Charles Daniels, U.S.A. 1:05.6 | 1948 Walter Ris, U.S.A. ..... 0:57.3 | 1976 *J. Montgomery, U.S.A. 0:49.99 |
| 1912 Duke Kahanamoku, U.S.A. 1:03.4 | 1952 Clarke Scholes, U.S.A..0:57.4 | 1980 J. Woithe, E. Germany 0:50.40 |
| 1920 Duke Kahanamoku, U.S.A. 1:01.4 | 1956 Jon Henricks, Australia 0:55.4 | |
| 1924 John Weissmuller, U.S.A. ..0:59.0 | 1960 J. Devitt, Australia .... 0:55.2 | |

## SWIMMING: 100-METER FREESTYLE—WOMEN

| | | |
|---|---|---|
| 1912 F. Durack, Australia .. 1:22.2 | 1936 H. Mastenbroek, Neth. 1:05.9 | 1964 Dawn Fraser, Australia .. 0:59.50 |
| 1920 Ethelda Bleibtrey, U.S.A. .. 1:13.6 | 1948 Greta Andersen, Denmark 1:06.3 | 1968 Margo Jan Henne, U.S.A. 1:00.00 |
| 1924 Ethel Lackie, U.S.A. .... 1:12.4 | 1952 Katalin Szoke, Hungary 1:06.8 | 1972 Sandra Neilson, U.S.A. 0:58.59 |
| 1928 Albina Osipowich, U.S.A. . 1:11.0 | 1956 Dawn Fraser, Australia 1:02.0 | 1976 K. Ender, E. Germany 0:55.65 |
| 1932 Helene Madison, U.S.A. . 1:06.8 | 1960 Dawn Fraser, Australia .1:01.2 | 1980 * B. Krause, E. Germany 0:54.79 |

## SWIMMING: 400-METER FREESTYLE—MEN

| | | |
|---|---|---|
| 1908 Henry Taylor, Britain . 5:35.8 | 1936 Jack Medica, U.S.A. ..4:44.5 | 1968 Michael Burton, U.S.A. 4:09.00 |
| 1912 G. Hodgson, Canada . 5:24.4 | 1948 William Smith, U.S.A. ..4:41.0 | 1972 B. Cooper, Australia 4:00.27 |
| 1920 Norman Ross, U.S.A. .. 5:26.8 | 1952 Jean Boiteux, France .. 4:30.7 | 1976 B. Goodell, U.S.A. ... 3:51.93 |
| 1924 John Weissmuller, U.S.A. 5:04.2 | 1956 Murray Rose, Australia 4:27.3 | 1980 * V. Salnikov.......... 3:51.31 |
| 1928 A. Zorilla, Argentina .. 5:01.6 | 1960 Murray Rose, Australia 4:18.3 | |
| 1932 Clarence Crabbe, U.S.A. 4:48.4 | 1964 Don Schollander, U.S.A. . 4:12.2 | |

\* Olympic record.

## SUMMER OLYMPIC WINNERS AND RECORDS (continued)

### SWIMMING: 400-METER FREESTYLE—WOMEN

| | | | | | | |
|---|---|---|---|---|---|---|
| 1924 | Martha Norelius, U.S.A. | 6:02.2 | 1952 | V. Gyenge, Hungary | 5:12.1 | 1972 Shane Gould, Australia 4:19.04 |
| 1928 | Martha Norelius, U.S.A. | 5:26.4 | 1956 | L. Crapp, Australia | 4:54.6 | 1976 Petra Thuemer, E. Ger. 4:09.89 |
| 1932 | Helene Madison, U.S.A. | 5:28.5 | 1960 | C. von Saltza, U.S.A. | 4:50.6 | 1980* Ines Diers, E. Germany . 4:08.76 |
| 1936 | H. Mastenbroek, Neth | 5:26.4 | 1964 | Ginny Duenkel, U.S.A. | 4:43.3 | |
| 1948 | Ann Curtis, U.S.A. | 5:17.8 | 1968 | Deborah Meyer, U.S.A. | 4:31.8 | |

### SWIMMING: 100-METER BACKSTROKE—MEN

| | | | | | | |
|---|---|---|---|---|---|---|
| 1908 | Arno Bieberstein, Germany | 1:24.6 | 1936 | Adolf Kiefer, U.S.A. | 1:05.9 | 1968 R. Matthes, E. Germany 0:58.7 |
| 1912 | Harry Hebner, U.S.A. | 1:21.2 | 1948 | Allen Stack, U.S.A. | 1:06.4 | 1972 R. Matthes, E. Germany 0:56.58 |
| 1920 | Warren Kealoha, U.S.A. | 1:15.2 | 1952 | Y. Oyakawa, U.S.A. | 1:05.4 | 1976* J. Naber, U.S.A. 0:55.49 |
| 1924 | Warren Kealoha, U.S.A. | 1:13.2 | 1956 | D. Thiele, Australia | 1:02.2 | 1980 B. Baron, Sweden 0:56.53 |
| 1928 | George Kojac, U.S.A. | 1:08.2 | 1960 | D. Thiele, Australia | 1:01.9 | |
| 1932 | M. Kiyokawa, Japan | 1:08.6 | 1964 | Event not held | | |

### SWIMMING: 100-METER BACKSTROKE—WOMEN

| | | | | | | |
|---|---|---|---|---|---|---|
| 1924 | Sybil Bauer, U.S.A. | 1:23.2 | 1952 | J. Harrison, S. Africa | 1:14.3 | 1972 Melissa Belote, U.S.A. 1:05.78 |
| 1928 | Marie Braun, Netherlands | 1:22.0 | 1956 | J. Grinham, Britain | 1:12.9 | 1976 U. Richter, E. Germany 1:01.83 |
| 1932 | Eleanor Holm, U.S.A. | 1:19.4 | 1960 | Lynn Burke, U.S.A. | 1:09.3 | 1980* R. Reinisch, E. Germany . 1:00.86 |
| 1936 | Dina Senff, Netherlands | 1:18.9 | 1964 | Cathy Ferguson, U.S.A. | 1:07.7 | |
| 1948 | Karen Harup, Denmark | 1:14.4 | 1968 | Kaye Hall, U.S.A. | 1:06.2 | |

### SWIMMING: 200-METER BREASTSTROKE—MEN

| | | | | | | |
|---|---|---|---|---|---|---|
| 1908 | F. Holman, Britain | 3:09.2 | 1936 | T. Hamuro, Japan | 2:41.5 | 1968 F. Munoz, Mexico 2:28.7 |
| 1912 | W. Bathe, Germany | 3:01.8 | 1948 | Joseph Verduer, U.S.A. | 2:39.3 | 1972 John Hencken, U.S.A. 2:21.55 |
| 1920 | H. Malmroth, Sweden | 3:04.4 | 1952 | J. Davis, Australia | 2:34.4 | 1976 D. Wilkie, Britain 2:15.11 |
| 1924 | Robert Skelton, U.S.A. | 2:56.6 | 1956 | M. Furukawa, Japan | 2:34.7 | 1980* R. Zulpa, USSR 2:15.85 |
| 1928 | Y. Tsuruta, Japan | 2:48.8 | 1960 | W. Mulliken, U.S.A. | 2:37.4 | |
| 1932 | Y. Tsuruta, Japan | 2:45.4 | 1964 | Ian O'Brian, Australia | 2:27.8 | |

### SWIMMING: 200-METER BREASTSTROKE—WOMEN

| | | | | | | |
|---|---|---|---|---|---|---|
| 1924 | Lucy Morton, Britain | 3:33.2 | 1952 | Eva Szekely, Hungary | 2:51.7 | 1968 Sharon Wichman, U.S.A. 2:44.4 |
| 1928 | Hilde Schrader, Germany | 3:12.6 | 1956 | U. Happe, W. Germany | 2:53.1 | 1972 B. Whitfield, Australia 2:41.71 |
| 1932 | C. Dennis, Australia | 3:06.3 | 1960 | A. Lonsbrough, Britain | 2:49.5 | 1976 M. Koshevaia, USSR 2:33.35 |
| 1936 | H. Maehata, Japan | 3:03.6 | 1964 | G. Prozumenschikova, | | 1980 L. Kachushite, USSR 2:29.54 |
| 1948 | Nel Vliet, Netherlands | 2:57.2 | | USSR | 2:46.4 | |

### SWIMMING: 100-METER BUTTERFLY STROKE—MEN

| | | | | | |
|---|---|---|---|---|---|
| 1968 | Douglas Russell, U.S.A. | 0:55.9 | 1976 | M. Vogel, U.S.A. | 54.35 |
| 1972* | Mark Spitz, U.S.A. | 0:54.27 | 1980 | P. Arvidsson, Sweden | 54.92 |

### SWIMMING: 100-METER BUTTERFLY STROKE—WOMEN

| | | | | | | |
|---|---|---|---|---|---|---|
| 1956 | Shelley Mann, U.S.A. | 1:11.0 | 1968 | L. McClements, Australia | 1:05.5 | 1976* K. Ender, E. Germany 1:00.13 |
| 1960 | Carolyn Schuler, U.S.A. | 1:09.5 | 1972 | M. Aoki, Japan | 1:03.34 | 1980 C. Metschuck 1:00.42 |
| 1964 | Sharon Stouder, U.S.A. | 1:04.7 | | | | |

### SWIMMING: 400-METER INDIVIDUAL MEDLEY—MEN

| | | | | | | |
|---|---|---|---|---|---|---|
| 1964 | Dick Roth, U.S.A. | 4:45.4 | 1972 | G. Larsson, Sweden | 4:31.98 | 1980* A. Sidorenko, USSR 4:22.89 |
| 1968 | Charles Hickcox, U.S.A. | 4:48.4 | 1976 | R. Strachan, U.S.A. | 4:23.68 | |

### SWIMMING: 400-METER INDIVIDUAL MEDLEY—WOMEN

| | | | | | | |
|---|---|---|---|---|---|---|
| 1964 | Donna de Varona, U.S.A. | 5:18.7 | 1972 | G. Neall, Australia | 5:02.97 | 1980* P. Schneider, E. Germany 4:36.29 |
| 1968 | Claudia Kolb, U.S.A. | 5:08.5 | 1976 | U. Tauber, E. Germany | 4:42.77 | |

### SWIMMING: 400-METER FREESTYLE RELAY—WOMEN

| | | | | | | | | |
|---|---|---|---|---|---|---|---|---|
| 1912 | Britain | 5:52.8 | 1932 | U.S.A. 4:38.0 | 1956 | Australia 4:17.1 | 1972 | U.S.A. 3:55.19 |
| 1920 | U.S.A. | 5:11.6 | 1936 | Netherlands 4:36.0 | 1960 | U.S.A. 4:08.9 | 1976 | U.S.A. 3:44.82 |
| 1924 | U.S.A. | 4:58.8 | 1948 | U.S.A. 4:29.2 | 1964 | U.S.A. 4:03.8 | 1980* | E. Germany 3:42.71 |
| 1928 | U.S.A. | 4:47.6 | 1952 | Hungary 4:24.4 | 1968 | U.S.A. 4:02.5 | | |

### SWIMMING: 400-METER MEDLEY RELAY—MEN

| | | | | | | |
|---|---|---|---|---|---|---|
| 1960 | U.S.A. | 4:05.4 | 1968 | U.S.A. 3:54.9 | 1976* U.S.A. 3:42.22 | |
| 1964 | U.S.A. | 3:58.4 | 1972 | U.S.A. 3:48.16 | 1980 Australia 3:45.70 | |

### SWIMMING: 400-METER MEDLEY RELAY—WOMEN

| | | | | | | |
|---|---|---|---|---|---|---|
| 1960 | U.S.A. | 4:41.1 | 1968 | U.S.A. 4:28.3 | 1976 E. Germany 4:07.95 | |
| 1964 | U.S.A. | 4:33.9 | 1972 | U.S.A. 4:20.75 | 1980* E. Germany 4:06.67 | |

### SWIMMING: 200-METER BACKSTROKE—MEN

| | | | | | | |
|---|---|---|---|---|---|---|
| 1964 | Jed Graef, Australia | 2:10.3 | 1972 | R. Matthes, E. Germany | 2:02.82 | 1980 S. Wladar, Hungary 2:01.93 |
| 1968 | R. Matthes, E. Germany | 2:09.6 | 1976* | J. Naber, U.S.A. | 1:59.19 | |

### SWIMMING: 200-METER BACKSTROKE—WOMEN

| | | | | | | |
|---|---|---|---|---|---|---|
| 1968 | Lillian Watson, U.S.A. | 2:24.8 | 1976 | U. Richter, E. Germany | 2:13.43 | |
| 1972 | Melissa Belote, U.S.A. | 2:19.19 | 1980* | R. Reinisch, E. Germany | 2:11.77 | |

### SWIMMING: 200-METER BUTTERFLY STROKE—MEN

| | | | | | | |
|---|---|---|---|---|---|---|
| 1956 | William Yorzyk, U.S.A. | 2:19.3 | 1968 | Carl Robie, U.S.A. | 2:08.7 | 1980 S. Fesenko, USSR 1:59.76 |
| 1960 | Michael Troy, U.S.A. | 2:12.8 | 1972 | Mark Spitz, U.S.A. | 2:00.70 | |
| 1964 | Kevin Berry, Australia | 2:06.6 | 1976* | M. Bruner, U.S.A. | 1:59.23 | |

### SWIMMING: 200-METER BUTTERFLY STROKE—WOMEN

| | | | | | | |
|---|---|---|---|---|---|---|
| 1968 | Ada Kok, Netherlands | 2:24.7 | 1976 | A. Pollack, E. Germany | 2:11.43 | |
| 1972 | Karen Moe, U.S.A. | 2:15.57 | 1980* | I. Geissler, E. Germany | 2:10.44 | |

\* Olympic record.

## SWIMMING: 100-METER BREASTSTROKE—MEN

| | | | |
|---|---|---|---|
| 1968 Donald McKenzie, U.S.A. | 1:07.7 | 1976* J. Hencken, U.S.A. | 1:03.11 |
| 1972 Nobutaka Taguchi, Japan | 1:04.94 | 1980 D. Goodhew, Britain | 1:03.34 |

## SWIMMING: 100-METER BREASTSTROKE—WOMEN

| | | | |
|---|---|---|---|
| 1968 D. Bjedov, Yugoslavia | 1:15.8 | 1976* H. Anke, E. Germany | 1:11.16 |
| 1972 Catherine Carr, U.S.A. | 1:13.58 | 1980 U. Geweniger, E. Germany | 1:10.22 |

## SWIMMING: 200-METER FREESTYLE—MEN

| | | | |
|---|---|---|---|
| 1968 Mike Wenden, Australia | 1:55.2 | 1976 B. Furniss, U.S.A. | 1:50.29 |
| 1972 Mark Spitz, U.S.A. | 1:52.78 | 1980* S. Kopliakov, USSR | 1:49.81 |

## SWIMMING: 200-METER FREESTYLE—WOMEN

| | | | |
|---|---|---|---|
| 1968 Deborah Meyer, U.S.A. | 2:10.5 | 1976 K. Ender, E. Germany | 1:59.26 |
| 1972 Shane Gould, Australia | 2:03.56 | 1980* B. Krause, E. Germany | 1:58.33 |

## SWIMMING: 200-METER INDIVIDUAL MEDLEY—MEN

| | | | |
|---|---|---|---|
| 1968 Charles Hickcox, U.S.A. | 2:12.0 | 1972* Gunnar Larsson, Sweden | 2:07.17 |

## SWIMMING: 200-METER INDIVIDUAL MEDLEY—WOMEN

| | | | |
|---|---|---|---|
| 1968 Claudia Kolb, U.S.A. | 2:24.7 | 1972* Shane Gould, Australia | 2:23.07 |

## SWIMMING: 800-METER FREESTYLE—WOMEN

| | | | |
|---|---|---|---|
| 1968 Deborah Meyer, U.S.A. | 9:24.0 | 1976 P. Thuemer, E. Germany | 8:37.14 |
| 1972 Keena Rothhammer, U.S.A. | 8:53.68 | 1980* M. Ford, Australia | 8:28.90 |

## SWIMMING: 800-METER FREESTYLE RELAY—MEN

| | | | | | | | |
|---|---|---|---|---|---|---|---|
| 1908 Britain | 10:55.6 | 1928 U.S.A. | 9:36.2 | 1952 U.S.A. | 8:31.1 | 1968 U.S.A. | 7:52.3 |
| 1912 Australia | 10:11.6 | 1932 Japan | 8:58.2 | 1956 Australia | 8:23.6 | 1972 U.S.A. | 7:35.78 |
| 1920 U.S.A. | 10:04.4 | 1936 Japan | 8:51.5 | 1960 U.S.A. | 8:10.2 | 1976* U.S.A. | 7:23.22 |
| 1924 U.S.A. | 9:53.4 | 1948 U.S.A. | 8:46.0 | 1964 U.S.A. | 7:52.1 | 1980 USSR | 7:23.50 |

## SWIMMING: 1,500—METER FREESTYLE—MEN

| | | | | | |
|---|---|---|---|---|---|
| 1908 H. Taylor, Britain | 22:48.4 | 1936 N. Terada, Japan | 19:13.7 | 1968 Michael Burton, U.S.A. | 16:38.9 |
| 1912 G. Hodgson, Canada | 22:00.0 | 1948 James McLane, U.S.A. | 19:18.5 | 1972 Michael Burton, U.S.A. | 15:52.58 |
| 1920 Norman Ross, U.S.A. | 22:23.2 | 1952 Ford Konno, U.S.A. | 18:30.0 | 1976 B. Goodell, U.S.A. | 15:02.40 |
| 1924 A. Charlton, Australia | 20:06.6 | 1956 M. Rose, Australia | 17:58.9 | 1980* V. Salnikov, USSR | 14:58.27 |
| 1928 Arne Borg, Sweden | 19:51.8 | 1960 J. Konrads, Australia | 17:19.6 | | |
| 1932 K. Kitamura, Japan | 19:12.4 | 1964 R. Windle, Australia | 17:01.7 | | |

## SWIMMING: 3-METER SPRINGBOARD DIVING—MEN

| | | |
|---|---|---|
| 1908 A. Zurner, Germany | 1936 Richard Degener, U.S.A. | 1968 Bernard Wrightson, U.S.A. |
| 1912 P. Gunther, Germany | 1948 Bruce Harlan, U.S.A. | 1972 Vladimir Vasin, USSR |
| 1920 Louis Keuhn, U.S.A. | 1952 David Browning, U.S.A. | 1976 Phil Boggs, U.S.A. |
| 1924 Albert White, U.S.A. | 1956 Robert Clotworthy, U.S.A. | 1980 Aleksandr Portnov, USSR |
| 1928 Pete Desjardins, U.S.A. | 1960 Gary Tobian, U.S.A. | |
| 1932 Michael Galitzen, U.S.A. | 1964 Ken Sitzberger, U.S.A. | |

## SWIMMING: 3-METER SPRINGBOARD DIVING—WOMEN

| | | |
|---|---|---|
| 1920 Aileen Riggin, U.S.A. | 1948 Victoria Draves, U.S.A. | 1968 Sue Gossick, U.S.A. |
| 1924 Elizabeth Becker, U.S.A. | 1952 Patricia McCormick, U.S.A. | 1972 Micki King, U.S.A. |
| 1928 Helen Meany, U.S.A. | 1956 Patricia McCormick, U.S.A. | 1976 Jennifer Chandler, U.S.A. |
| 1932 Georgia Coleman, U.S.A. | 1960 Ingrid Kramer, W. Germany | 1980 Irina Kalinina, USSR |
| 1936 Marjorie Gestring, U.S.A. | 1964 Ingrid Engel—Kramer, W. Germany | |

## SWIMMING: 10-METER PLATFORM DIVING—MEN

| | | | |
|---|---|---|---|
| 1904 G.E. Sheldon, U.S.A. | 1928 P. Desjardins, U.S.A. | 1956 J. Capilla, Mexico | 1976 K. Di Biasi, Italy |
| 1908 H. Johansson, Sweden | 1932 Harold Smith, U.S.A. | 1960 R. Webster, U.S.A. | 1980 F. Hoffmann, E. Germany |
| 1912 E. Adlerz, Sweden | 1936 M. Wayne, U.S.A. | 1964 R. Webster, U.S.A. | |
| 1920 Clarence Pinkston, U.S.A. | 1948 Samuel Lee, U.S.A. | 1968 K. Di Biasi, Italy | |
| 1924 Albert White, U.S.A | 1952 Samuel Lee, U.S.A. | 1972 K. Di Biasi, Italy | |

## SWIMMING: 10-METER PLATFORM DIVING—WOMEN

| | | |
|---|---|---|
| 1912 G. Johansson, Sweden | 1936 D. Poynton-Hill, U.S.A. | 1964 Lesley Bush, U.S.A. |
| 1920 S. Fryland-Clausen, Denmark | 1948 Victoria Draves, U.S.A. | 1968 M. Duchkova, Czechoslovakia |
| 1924 Caroline Smith, U.S.A. | 1952 Patricia McCormick, U.S.A. | 1972 Ulrika Knape, Sweden |
| 1928 Elizabeth Pinkston, U.S.A. | 1956 Patricia McCormick, U.S.A. | 1976 E. Vaytsekhovskaia, USSR |
| 1932 Dorothy Poynton, U.S.A. | 1960 Ingrid Kramer, W. Germany | 1980 M. Jaschke, E. Germany |

## TRACK AND FIELD: 100-METER DASH—MEN

| | | | | | |
|---|---|---|---|---|---|
| 1896 Thomas Burke, U.S.A. | 0:12.0 | 1928 P. Williams, Canada | 0:10.8 | 1964 Bob Hayes, U.S.A. | 0:10.0 |
| 1900 Francis Jarvis, U.S.A. | 0:10.8 | 1932 Eddie Tolan, U.S.A. | 0:10.3 | 1968* James Hines, U.S.A. | 0:09.9 |
| 1904 Archie Hahn, U.S.A. | 0:11.0 | 1936 Jesse Owens, U.S.A. | 0:10.3 | 1972 Valery Borzov, USSR | 0:10.14 |
| 1908 R. Walker, S. Africa | 0:10.8 | 1948 J. Dillard, U.S.A. | 0:10.3 | 1976 Hasley Crawford, | |
| 1912 Ralph Craig, U.S.A. | 0:10.8 | 1952 L. Remigino, U.S.A. | 0:10.4 | Trinidad-Tobago | 0:10.06 |
| 1920 C. Paddock, U.S.A. | 0:10.8 | 1956 Bobby Morrow, U.S.A. | 0:10.5 | 1980 Allan Wells, Britain | 0:10.25 |
| 1924 H. Abrahams, Britain | 0:10.6 | 1960 Armin Hary, W. Germany | 0:10.2 | | |

\* Olympic record.

## SUMMER OLYMPIC WINNERS AND RECORDS *(continued)*

### TRACK AND FIELD: 100-METER DASH—WOMEN

| | | | | | |
|---|---|---|---|---|---|
| 1928 | Elizabeth Robinson, U.S.A. | 0:12.2 | 1952 | M. Jackson, Australia | 0.11.5 |
| 1932 | S. Walasiewicz, Poland | 0:11.9 | 1956 | B. Cuthbert, Australia | 0:11.5 |
| 1936 | Helen Stephens, U.S.A. | 0:11.5 | 1960 | Wilma Rudolph, U.S.A. | 0:11.0 |
| 1948 | F. Blankers-Koen, Neth. | 0:11.9 | 1964 | Wyomia Tyus, U.S.A. | 0:11.4 |

| 1968* | Wyomia Tyus, U.S.A. | 0:11.0 |
| 1972 | R. Stecher, E. Germany | 0:11.07 |
| 1976 | A. Richter, W. Germany | 0:11.08 |
| 1980 | L. Kondratyeva, USSR | 0:11.06 |

### TRACK AND FIELD: 200-METER DASH—MEN

| | | | | | |
|---|---|---|---|---|---|
| 1900 | John Tewksbury, U.S.A. | 0:22.2 | 1928 | P. Williams, Canada | 0:21.8 |
| 1904 | Archie Hahn, U.S.A. | 0:21.6 | 1932 | Eddie Tolan, U.S.A. | 0:21.2 |
| 1908 | R. Kerr, Canada | 0:22.6 | 1936 | Jesse Owens, U.S.A. | 0:20.7 |
| 1912 | Ralph Craig, U.S.A. | 0:21.7 | 1948 | Mel Patton, U.S.A. | 0:21.1 |
| 1920 | Allan Woodring, U.S.A. | 0:22.0 | 1952 | A. Stanfield, U.S.A. | 0:20.7 |
| 1924 | Jackson Scholz, U.S.A. | 0:21.6 | 1956 | Bobby Morrow, U.S.A. | 0:20.6 |

| 1960 | Livio Berruti, Italy | 0:20.5 |
| 1964 | Henry Carr, U.S.A. | 0:20.3 |
| 1968* | Tommie Smith, U.S.A. | 0:19.0 |
| 1972 | Valery Borzov, USSR | 0:20.0 |
| 1976 | D. Quarrie, Jamaica | 0:20.23 |
| 1980 | Pietro Mennea, Italy | 0:20.19 |

### TRACK AND FIELD: 200-METER DASH—WOMEN

| 1948 | F. Blankers-Koen, Netherlands | 0:24.4 |
| 1952 | M. Jackson, Australia | 0:23.7 |
| 1956 | Betty Cuthbert, Australia | 0:23.4 |

| 1960 | Wilma Rudolph, U.S.A. | 0:24.0 |
| 1964 | Edith McGuire, U.S.A. | 0:23.0 |
| 1968 | I. Kirszenstein, Poland | 0:22.5 |
| 1972 | R. Stecher, E. Germany | 0:22.40 |

| 1976* | B. Eckert, E. Germany | 0:22.37 |
| 1980 | B. Wockel, E. Germany | 0.22.03 |

### TRACK AND FIELD: 400-METER RACE—MEN

| | | | | | |
|---|---|---|---|---|---|
| 1896 | Thomas Burke, U.S.A. | 0:54.2 | 1928 | Ray Barbuti, U.S.A. | 0:47.8 |
| 1900 | Maxey Long, U.S.A. | 0:49.4 | 1932 | William Carr, U.S.A. | 0:46.2 |
| 1904 | Harry Hillman, U.S.A. | 0:49.2 | 1936 | Archie Williams, U.S.A. | 0:46.5 |
| 1908 | W. Halswelle, Britain | 0:50.0 | 1948 | Arthur Wint, Jamaica | 0:46.2 |
| 1912 | Charles Reidpath, U.S.A. | 0:48.2 | 1952 | G. Rhoden, Jamaica | 0:45.9 |
| 1920 | Bevil Rudd, S. Africa | 0:49.6 | 1956 | Charles Jenkins, U.S.A. | 0:46.7 |
| 1924 | Eric Liddell, Britain | 0:47.6 | 1960 | Otis Davis, U.S.A. | 0:44.9 |

| 1964 | Mike Larrabee, U.S.A. | 0:45.1 |
| 1968* | Lee Evans, U.S.A. | 0:43.8 |
| 1972 | Vincent Mattews, U.S.A. | 0:44.66 |
| 1976 | A. Juantorena, Cuba | 0:44.26 |
| 1980 | V. Markin, USSR | 0:44.60 |

### TRACK AND FIELD: 400-METER RACE—WOMEN

| 1964 | Betty Cuthbert, Australia | 0:52.0 |
| 1968 | C. Besson, France | 0:52.0 |

| 1972 | M. Zehrt, E. Germany | 0:51.08 |
| 1976 | Irena Szcwinska, Poland | 0:49.29 |

| 1980* | Marita Koch, E. Germany | 0:48.88 |

### TRACK AND FIELD: 800-METER RACE—MEN

| | | | | | |
|---|---|---|---|---|---|
| 1896 | E. Flack, Australia | 2:11.0 | 1928 | Douglas Lowe, Britain | 1:51.8 |
| 1900 | A. Tysoe, Britain | 2:01.4 | 1932 | T. Hampson, Britain | 1:49.8 |
| 1904 | James Lightbody, U.S.A. | 1:56.0 | 1936 | John Woodruff, U.S.A. | 1:52.9 |
| 1908 | Melvin Sheppard, U.S.A. | 1:52.8 | 1948 | Mal Whitfield, U.S.A. | 1:49.2 |
| 1912 | James Meredith, U.S.A. | 1:51.9 | 1952 | Mal Whitfield, U.S.A. | 1:49.2 |
| 1920 | Albert Hill, Britain | 1:53.4 | 1956 | Thomas Courtney, U.S.A. | 1:47.7 |
| 1924 | Douglas Lowe, Britain | 1:52.4 | 1960 | P. Snell, New Zealand | 1:46.3 |

| 1964 | P. Snell, New Zealand | 1:45.1 |
| 1968 | R. Doubell, Australia | 1:44.3 |
| 1972 | David Wottle, U.S.A. | 1:45.9 |
| 1976* | A. Juatorena, Cuba | 1:43.50 |
| 1980 | Steve Ovett, Britain | 1:45.40 |

### TRACK AND FIELD: 800-METER RACE—WOMEN

| 1928 | L. Radke-Batschauer, Germany | 2:16.8 |
| 1960 | L. Shevcova, USSR | 2:04.3 |

| 1964 | Ann Packer, Britain | 2:01.1 |
| 1968 | Madeline Manning, U.S.A. | 2:00.9 |

| 1972 | H. Falck, W. Germany | 1:58.6 |
| 1976 | Tatiana Kazankina, USSR | 1:54.94 |
| 1980* | N. Olizaryenko, USSR | 1:53.50 |

### TRACK AND FIELD: 1,500-METER RACE—MEN

| | | | | | |
|---|---|---|---|---|---|
| 1896 | E. Flack, Australia | 4:33.2 | 1928 | Harri Larva, Finland | 3:53.2 |
| 1900 | E. Bennett, Britain | 4:06.2 | 1932 | Luigi Beccali, Italy | 3:51.2 |
| 1904 | James Lightbody, U.S.A. | 4:05.4 | 1936 | Jack Lovelock, N. Zealand | 3:47.8 |
| 1908 | Melvin Sheppard, U.S.A. | 4:03.4 | 1948 | H. Ericksson, Sweden | 3:49.8 |
| 1912 | A. Jackson, Britain | 3:56.8 | 1952 | J. Barthel, Luxembourg | 3:45.2 |
| 1920 | Albert Hill, Britain | 4:01.8 | 1956 | Ron Delany, Ireland | 3:41.2 |
| 1924 | Paavo Nurmi, Finland | 3:53.6 | 1960 | H. Elliott, Australia | 3:35.6 |

| 1964 | P. Snell, N. Zealand | 3:38.1 |
| 1968* | K. Keino, Kenya | 3:34.9 |
| 1972 | P. Vasala, Finland | 3:36.3 |
| 1976 | John Walker, N. Zealand | 3:39.17 |
| 1980* | Sebastian Coe, Britain | 3:38.4 |

### TRACK AND FIELD: 1,500-METER RACE—WOMEN

| 1972 | Ludmila Bragina, USSR | 4:01.4 |
| 1976 | Tatiana Kazankina, USSR | 4:05.48 |

| 1980* | Tatiana Kazankina, USSR | 3:56.6 |

### TRACK AND FIELD: 5,000-METER RACE—MEN

| | | | | | |
|---|---|---|---|---|---|
| 1912 | H. Kolehmainen, Finland | 14:36.6 | 1936 | G. Hockert, Finland | 14:22.2 |
| 1920 | J. Guillemot, France | 14:55.6 | 1948 | G. Reiff, Belgium | 14:17.6 |
| 1924 | Paavo Nurmi, Finland | 14:31.2 | 1952 | E. Zatopek, Czech. | 14:06.6 |
| 1928 | Villie Ritola, Finland | 14:38.0 | 1956 | Vladimir Kuts, USSR | 13:39.6 |
| 1932 | L. Lehtinen, Finland | 14:30.0 | 1960 | M. Halberg, N. Zealand | 13:43.4 |

| 1964 | Bob Schul, U.S.A. | 13:48.8 |
| 1968 | M. Gammoudi, Tunisia | 14:05.0 |
| 1972 | L. Viren, Finalnd | 13:26.4 |
| 1976 | L. Viren, Finland | 13:24.76 |
| 1980 | M. Yifter, Ethiopia | 13:21.0 |

### TRACK AND FIELD: 10,000-METER RACE—MEN

| | | | | | |
|---|---|---|---|---|---|
| 1912 | H. Kolehmainen, Finland | 31:20.8 | 1936 | I. Salminen, Finland | 30:15.4 |
| 1920 | Paavo Nurmi, Finland | 31:45.8 | 1948 | Emil Zatopek, Czech | 29:59.6 |
| 1924 | Villie Ritola, Finland | 30:23.2 | 1952 | Emil Zatopek, Czech | 29:17.0 |
| 1928 | Paavo Nurmi, Finland | 30:18.8 | 1956 | Vladimir Kuts, USSR | 28:45.6 |
| 1932 | J. Kusocinski, Poland | 30:11.4 | 1960 | P. Bolotnikov, USSR | 28:32.2 |

| 1964 | Billy Mills, U.S.A. | 28:24.4 |
| 1968 | N. Temu, Kenya | 29:27.4 |
| 1972* | L. Viren, Finland | 27:38.4 |
| 1976 | L. Viren, Finland | 27:40.38 |
| 1980 | M. Yifter | 27:42.7 |

* Olympic record.

## TRACK AND FIELD: MARATHON—MEN

| | | | | | |
|---|---|---|---|---|---|
| 1896 | S. Loues, Greece .....2:58:50.0 | 1928 | A.B. El Ouafi, France .2:32:57.0 | 1964 | A. Bikila, Ethiopia ...2:12:11.2 |
| 1900 | M. Theato, France ....2:59:45.0 | 1932 | J. Zabala, Argentina ..2:31:36.0 | 1968 | M. Wolde, Ethiopia ...2:20:26.4 |
| 1904 | Thomas Hicks, U.S.A. .3:28:53.0 | 1936 | K. Son, Japan .......2:29:19.2 | 1972 | Frank Shorter, U.S.A. 2:12:19.8 |
| 1908 | John Hayes, U.S.A.....2:55:18.4 | 1948 | D. Cabrera, Argentina 2:34:51.6 | 1976* | W. Cierpinski, E. Ger. 2:09:55.0 |
| 1912 | K. McArthur, S. Africa .2:36:54.8 | 1952 | E. Zatopek, Czech. ...2:23:03.2 | 1980 | W. Cierpinski, E. Ger. 2:11:03.0 |
| 1920 | H. Kolehmainen, Finland 2:32:35.8 | 1956 | A. Mimoun, France....2:25:00.0 | | |
| 1924 | A. Stenroos, Finland ..2:41:22.6 | 1960 | A. Bikila, Ethiopia ....2:15:16.2 | | |

## TRACK AND FIELD: 110-METER HURDLES—MEN

| | | | | | |
|---|---|---|---|---|---|
| 1896 | Thomas Curtis, U.S.A...0:17.6 | 1928 | S. Atkinson, S. Africa ...0:14.8 | 1964 | Hayes Jones, U.S.A....0:13.6 |
| 1900 | Alvin Kraenzlein, U.S.A. ..0:15.4 | 1932 | George Saling, U.S.A. ...0:14.6 | 1968 | W. Davenport, U.S.A. ..0:13.3 |
| 1904 | Frederick Schule, U.S.A. .0:16.0 | 1936 | Forrest Towns, U.S.A. ...0:14.2 | 1972* | Rodney Milburn, U.S.A. 0:13.24 |
| 1908 | Forrest Smithson, U.S.A. .0:15.0 | 1948 | William Porter, U.S.A. ...0:13.9 | 1976 | Guy Drut, France .....0:13.30 |
| 1912 | Frederick Kelly, U.S.A. ..0:15.1 | 1952 | H. Dillard, U.S.A. ......0:13.7 | 1980 | Thomas Munkelt, |
| 1920 | E. Thomson, Canada .....0:14.8 | 1956 | Lee Calhoun, U.S.A. ....0:13.5 | | E. Germany ........0:13.39 |
| 1924 | Daniel Kinsey, U.S.A.....0:15.0 | 1960 | Lee Calhoun, U.S.A. ....0:13.8 | | |

## TRACK AND FIELD: 100-METER HURDLES—WOMEN

| | | | |
|---|---|---|---|
| 1972 | Annelie Ehrhardt, E. Germany ..........0:12.59 | 1980* | V. Komisova, USSR....................0:12.56 |
| 1976 | J. Schaller, E. Germany .................0:12.77 | | |

## TRACK AND FIELD: 400-METER HURDLES—MEN

| | | | | | |
|---|---|---|---|---|---|
| 1900 | John Tewksbury, U.S.A. ..0:57.6 | 1932 | Robert Tisdall, Ireland ..0:51.8 | 1964 | Rex Cawley, U.S.A. ....0:49.6 |
| 1904 | Harry Hilman, U.S.A. ....0:53.0 | 1936 | Glenn Hardin, U.S.A. ...0:52.4 | 1968 | David Hemery, Britain .0:48.1 |
| 1908 | Charles Bacon, U.S.A....0:55.0 | 1948 | Roy Cochran, U.S.A. ....0:51.1 | 1972 | J. Akii-bua, Uganda ...0:47.82 |
| 1920 | Frank Loomis, U.S.A. ....0:54.0 | 1952 | Charles Moore, U.S.A....0:50.8 | 1976* | Edwin Moses, U.S.A....0:47.64 |
| 1924 | Morgan Taylor, U.S.A. ...0:52.6 | 1956 | Glenn Davis, U.S.A. ....0:50.1 | 1980 | Volker Beck, E. Ger. ...0:48.70 |
| 1928 | Lord David Burgley, Britain ..0:53.4 | 1960 | Glenn Davis, U.S.A. ....0:49.3 | | |

## TRACK AND FIELD: 3,000-METER STEEPLECHASE—MEN

| | | | | | |
|---|---|---|---|---|---|
| 1920 | P. Hodges, Britain ......10:00.4 | 1948 | T. Sjostrand, Sweden ...9:04.6 | 1968 | Amos Biwott, Kenya ....8:51.0 |
| 1924 | V. Ritola, Finland .......9:33.6 | 1952 | H. Ashenfelter, U.S.A. ..8:45.4 | 1972 | K. Keino, Kenya .......8:23.6 |
| 1928 | T. Loukola, Finland .....9:21.8 | 1956 | Chris Brasher, Britain ...8:41.2 | 1976* | A. Garderud, Sweden ..8:08.02 |
| 1932 | V. Iso-Hollo, Finland ....10:33.4 | 1960 | Z. Krzyszkowiak, Poland .8:34.2 | 1980 | B. Malinowski, Poland .8:09.70 |
| 1936 | V. Iso-Hollo, Finland ....9:03.8 | 1964 | Gaston Roelants, Belgium ..8:30.8 | | |

## TRACK AND FIELD: 400-METER RELAY—MEN

| | | | | | | | |
|---|---|---|---|---|---|---|---|
| 1912 | Britain ........0:42.4 | 1932 | U.S.A. .....0:40.0 | 1956 | U.S.A.......0:39.5 | 1972* | U.S.A.....0:38.19 |
| 1920 | U.S.A.........0:42.2 | 1936 | U.S.A. .....0:40.0 | 1960 | W. Germany 0:39.5 | 1976 | U.S.A.....0:38.33 |
| 1924 | U.S.A.........0:41.0 | 1948 | U.S.A. .....0:40.3 | 1964 | U.S.A.......0:39.0 | 1980 | USSR ....0:38.26 |
| 1928 | U.S.A.........0:41.0 | 1952 | U.S.A. .....0:40.1 | 1968 | U.S.A.......0:38.2 | | |

## TRACK AND FIELD: 400-METER RELAY—WOMEN

| | | | | | | | |
|---|---|---|---|---|---|---|---|
| 1928 | Canada........0:48.4 | 1948 | Netherlands 0:47.5 | 1960 | U.S.A.......0:44.5 | 1972 | W. Germany .0:42.81 |
| 1932 | U.S.A.........0:47.0 | 1952 | U.S.A. .....0:45.9 | 1964 | Poland......0:43.6 | 1976 | E. Germany .0:42.55 |
| 1936 | U.S.A.........0:46.9 | 1956 | Australia ...0:44.5 | 1968 | U.S.A.......0:42.8 | 1980* | E. Germany .0:41.60 |

## TRACK AND FIELD: 1,600-METER RELAY—MEN

| | | | | | | | |
|---|---|---|---|---|---|---|---|
| 1908 | U.S.A.........3:29.4 | 1928 | U.S.A. .....3:14.2 | 1952 | Jamaica ...3:03.9 | 1968* | U.S.A. ....2:56.1 |
| 1912 | U.S.A.........3:16.6 | 1932 | U.S.A. .....3:08.2 | 1956 | U.S.A.......3:04.8 | 1972 | Kenya ....2:59.8 |
| 1920 | Britain ........3:22.2 | 1936 | Britain .....3:09.0 | 1960 | U.S.A.......3:02.2 | 1976 | U.S.A.....2:59.52 |
| 1924 | U.S.A.........3:16.0 | 1948 | U.S.A. .....3:10.4 | 1964 | U.S.A.......3:00.7 | 1980 | USSR.....3:01.1 |

## TRACK AND FIELD: 1,600-METER RELAY—WOMEN

| | | | | | |
|---|---|---|---|---|---|
| 1972 | E. Germany.............3:23.0 | 1976* | E. Germany...........3:19.23 | 1980 | USSR................3:20.2 |

## TRACK AND FIELD: 20-KILOMETER WALK—MEN

| | | | | |
|---|---|---|---|---|
| 1956 | L. Spirine, USSR ....................1:31:27.0 | 1972 | P. Frenkel, E. Germany .............1:26:42.4 |
| 1960 | V. Golubnichy, USSR ................1:34:07.2 | 1976 | D. Bautista, Mexico.................1:24:40.6 |
| 1964 | Ken Matthews, U.S.A.................1:29:34.0 | 1980 | M. Damilano, Italy ..................1:23:35.5 |
| 1968 | L. Golubnichy, USSR .................1:33:58.4 | | |

## TRACK AND FIELD: 50-KILOMETER WALK—MEN

| | | | | |
|---|---|---|---|---|
| 1932 | T. Green, Britain ..........4:50:10.0 | 1956 | N. Read, N. Zealand .... 4:30:42.8 | 1972 | B. Kannenberg, W. Ger.  3:56:11.6 |
| 1936 | H. Whitlock, Britain .......4:30:41.4 | 1960 | D. Thompson, Britain.... 4:25:30.0 | 1980 | H. Gauder, E. Germany 3:49:24 |
| 1948 | J. Ljunggren, Sweden........4:41:52.0 | 1964 | A. Pamich, Italy ........ 4:1.1:12.4 | | |
| 1952 | G. Dordoni, Italy ..........4:28:07.8 | 1968 | C. Hohne, E. Germany .. 4:20:13.6 | | |

## TRACK AND FIELD: HIGH JUMP—MEN

| | | | | | |
|---|---|---|---|---|---|
| 1896 | Ellery Clark, U.S.A. ...... 5' 11¼" | 1928 | R.W. King, U.S.A......6' 4⅜" | 1964 | V. Brumel, USSR ..... 7' 1⅝" |
| 1900 | Irving Baxter, U.S.A. ..... 6' 2⅘" | 1932 | D. McNaughton, Can. ...6' 5⅝" | 1968 | Dick Fosbury, U.S.A. .. 7' 4¼" |
| 1904 | Samuel Jones, U.S.A. .... 5' 11" | 1936 | C. Johnson, U.S.A. ...6' 7¹⁵⁄₁₆" | 1972 | Yuri Tarmak, USSR .. 7' 3¾" |
| 1908 | Harry Porter, U.S.A. ..... 6' 2¾" | 1948 | J. Winter, Australia ....6' 6" | 1976 | J. Wszola, Poland .... 7' 4½" |
| 1912 | Almer Richards, U.S.A. ... 6' 4" | 1952 | Walter Davis, U.S.A. ...6' 8¼" | 1980* | G. Wessig, E. Germany 7' 9" |
| 1920 | R. Landon, U.S.A. ....... 6' 4¼" | 1956 | Charles Dumas, U.S.A. ..6' 11¼" | | |
| 1924 | Harold Osborn, U.S.A. ... 6' 5¹⁵⁄₁₆" | 1960 | R. Shavlakadze, USSR...7' 1" | | |

\* Olympic record.

## SUMMER OLYMPIC WINNERS AND RECORDS *(continued)*

### TRACK AND FIELD: HIGH JUMP—WOMEN

| | | |
|---|---|---|
| 1928 E. Catherwood, Canada 5'3" | 1952 E. Brand, S. Africa 5'5¾" | 1968 M. Rezkova, Czech. ............ 5'11¾" |
| 1932 Jean Shiley, U.S.A. .... 5'5¼" | 1956 M. McDaniel, U.S.A. 5'9¼" | 1972 U. Meyfarth. W. Germany ... 6'3¼" |
| 1936 I. Csak, Hungary ...... 5'3" | 1960 I. Balas, Romania . 6'¼" | 1976 R. Ackermann, W. Germany ...... 6'3¾" |
| 1948 Alice Coachman, U.S.A. 5'6⅛" | 1964 I. Balas, Romania . 6'2⅖" | 1980* S. Simeoni, Italy ............... 6'5½" |

### TRACK AND FIELD: LONG JUMP—MEN

| | | |
|---|---|---|
| 1896 Ellery Clark, U.S.A. ..... 20'10" | 1924 DeHart Hubbard, U.S.A. . 24'5⅛" | 1960 Ralph Boston, U.S.A. . 26'7¾" |
| 1900 A. Kraenzlein, U.S.A. ... 23'6⅞" | 1928 Edward Hamm, U.S.A.... 25'4¾" | 1964 L. Davies, Britain.... 26'5⁷⁄₁₀" |
| 1904 Myer Prinstein, U.S.A.... 24'1⅜" | 1932 Edward Gordon, U.S.A. .. 25'¾" | 1968* Bob Beamon, U.S.A. . 29'2½" |
| 1908 Frank Irons, U.S.A......... 24'6½" | 1936 Jesse Owens, U.S.A..... 26'5⅜" | 1972 Randy Williams, U.S.A. 27'½" |
| 1912 A. Gutterson, U.S.A. ... 24'11¼" | 1948 Willie Steele, U.S.A. .... 25'8" | 1976 Arnie Robinson, U.S.A. 27'4½" |
| 1920 W. Pettersson, | 1952 Jerome Biffle, U.S.A. .. 24'10" | 1980 L. Dombroski, |
| Sweden ............. 23'5½" | 1956 Gregory Bell, U.S.A..... 25'8¼" | E. Germany .... 28'¼" |

### TRACK AND FIELD: LONG JUMP—WOMEN

| | | |
|---|---|---|
| 1948 O. Gyarmati, Hungary ... 18'8¼" | 1960 V. Krepkina, USSR ... 20'10¾" | 1972 Rosendahl, W. Germany ... 22'3" |
| 1952 Y. Williams, New Zealand . 20'5¾" | 1964 Mary Rand, Britain ... 22'2⅛" | 1976 A. Voigt, E. Germany . 22'2½" |
| 1956 E. Krzesinska, Poland .... 20'9¾" | 1968 V. Viscopoleanu, Rom. 22'4½" | 1980* T. Kolpakova, USSR .. 23'2" |

### TRACK AND FIELD: DISCUS THROW—MEN

| | | |
|---|---|---|
| 1896 R. Garrett, U.S.A..... 95'7½" | 1928 C. Houser, U.S.A..... 155'2⅖" | 1964 A. Oerter, U.S.A. .... 200'1½" |
| 1900 R. Bauer, Hungary .... 118'2⅞" | 1932 J. Anderson, U.S.A. .. 162'4⅞" | 1968 A. Oerter, U.S.A. .... 212'6½" |
| 1904 M. Sheridan, U.S.A. .... 128'10½" | 1936 K. Carpenter, U.S.A. . 165'7½" | 1972 L. Danek, Czech..... 211'3" |
| 1908 M. Sheridan, U.S.A. ... 134'2" | 1948 A. Consolini, Italy .... 173'2" | 1976* Mac Wilkens, U.S.A. . 221'5.4" |
| 1912 A. Taipale, Finland .... 145'⁹⁄₁₆" | 1952 Sim Iness, U.S.A. .... 180'6½" | 1980 V. Rasshchupkin, USSR 218'7" |
| 1920 E. Niklander, Finland .. 146'7" | 1956 A. Oerter, U.S.A. .... 184'10½" | |
| 1924 C. Houser, U.S.A. ...... 151'5¼" | 1960 A. Oerter, U.S.A. .... 194'2" | |

### TRACK AND FIELD: DISCUS THROW—WOMEN

| | | |
|---|---|---|
| 1928 Konopacka, Poland . 129'11⅞" | 1952 N. Romaschkova, | 1968 L. Manoliu, Romania . 191'2½" |
| 1932 L. Copeland, U.S.A. . 132'2" | USSR............ 168'8½" | 1972 Faina Melnik, USSR ........ 218'7" |
| 1936 Mauermayer, Germany 156'3³⁄₁₆" | 1956 O. Fikotova, Czech.. 176'11½" | 1976 E. Schlaak, E. Germany .. 226'4½" |
| 1948 M. Ostermeyer, | 1960 N. Ponomareva, USSR 180'8¼" | 1980* E. Jahl, E. Germany ....... 229'6½" |
| France ......... 137'6½" | 1964 Tamara Press, USSR ... 187'10¾" | |

### TRACK AND FIELD: SHOT PUT—MEN

| | | |
|---|---|---|
| 1896 R. Garrett, U.S.A....... 36'9¾" | 1928 John Kuck, U.S.A..... 52'11⁄₁₆" | 1964 Dallas Long, U.S.A. ... 66'8⅔" |
| 1900 R. Sheldon, U.S.A. .... 46'3⅛" | 1932 Leo Sexton, U.S.A. ... 52'6³⁄₁₆" | 1968 R. Matson, U.S.A. .... 67'4¾" |
| 1904 Ralph Rose, U.S.A. .... 48'7" | 1936 H. Woellke, Germany . 53'1¾" | 1972 W. Komar, Poland .... 69'6" |
| 1908 Ralph Rose, U.S.A. .... 46'7½" | 1948 W. Thompson, U.S.A. . 56'2" | 1976 U. Beyer, E. Germany . 69'¾" |
| 1912 P. McDonald, U.S.A. .... 50'4" | 1952 P. O'Brien Jr., U.S.A. . 57'1½" | 1980* V. Kiselyov, USSR .... 70'½" |
| 1920 V. Porhola, Finland .... 48'7⅛" | 1956 P. O'Brien Jr., U.S.A. . 60'11" | |
| 1924 C. Houser, U.S.A. ........ 49'2½" | 1960 W. Nieder, U.S.A. .... 64'6¾" | |

### TRACK AND FIELD: SHOT PUT—WOMEN

| | | |
|---|---|---|
| 1948 M. Ostermeyer, France ... 45'1½" | 1960 Tamara Press, USSR . 56'9⅝" | 1972 N. Chizova, USSR .... 69'0" |
| 1952 G. Zybina, USSR ....... 50'1½" | 1964 Tamara Press, USSR . 59'6⅛" | 1976 I. Christova, Bulgaria . 69'5" |
| 1956 T. Tishkyevich, USSR..... 54'5" | 1968 M. Gummel, E. Ger. .. 64'4" | 1980* I. Slupianek, E. Germany 73'6¼" |

### TRACK AND FIELD: JAVELIN THROW—MEN

| | | |
|---|---|---|
| 1908 E. Lemming, Sweden ... 179'10½" | 1936 G. Stock, Germany .. 235'8⁵⁄₁₆" | 1964 P. Nevala, Finland ... 271'2⅓" |
| 1912 E. Lemming, Sweden ... 198'11¼" | 1948 T. Rautavaara, | 1968 Jan Lusis, USSR ..... 295'7¼" |
| 1920 Jonni Myrra, Finland ... 215'9¾" | Finland ............ 228'10½" | 1972 W. Wolfermann, |
| 1924 Jonni Myrra, Finland ... 206'6¾" | 1952 Cy Young, U.S.A. .... 242'¾" | W. Germany........ 296'10" |
| 1928 E. Lundquist, Sweden ... 218'6⅛" | 1956 E. Danielson, Norway . 281'2¼" | 1976* M. Nemeth, Hungary . 310'4" |
| 1932 M. Jarvinen, Finland .... 238'7" | 1960 V. Tsibulenko, USSR . 277'8⅜" | 1980 D. Kula, USSR ....... 299'2" |

### TRACK AND FIELD: JAVELIN THROW—WOMEN

| | | |
|---|---|---|
| 1932 Mildred Didrikson, U.S.A. 143'4" | 1956 I. Janzeme, USSR ... 176'8" | 1972 R. Fuchs, E. Germany . 209'7" |
| 1936 T. Fleischer, Germany . 148'2¾" | 1960 E. Ozolina, USSR..... 183'8" | 1976 R. Fuchs, E. Germany . 216'4" |
| 1948 H. Baume, Austria ...... 149'6" | 1964 M. Penes, Romania .... 198'7½" | 1980* M. Colon, Cuba ..... 224'5" |
| 1952 D. Zatopkova, Czech. ... 165'7" | 1968 A. Nemeth, Hungary... 198'½" | |

### TRACK AND FIELD: POLE VAULT—MEN

| | | |
|---|---|---|
| 1896 William Hoyt, U.S.A. ................ 10'9¾" | 1936 Earle Meadows, U.S.A. .............. 14'3¼" |
| 1900 Irving Baxter, U.S.A. .............. 10'9⅞" | 1948 Guinn Smith, U.S.A................. 14'1¼" |
| 1904 Charles Dvorak, U.S.A. .............. 11'6" | 1952 Bob Richards, U.S.A. .............. 14'11¼" |
| 1908 (tie) A. Gilbert; E. Cook Jr., U.S.A. ...... 12'2" | 1956 Bob Richards, U.S.A. .............. 14'11½" |
| 1912 Harry Babcock, U.S.A. ............ 12'11½" | 1960 Don Bragg, U.S.A. ................ 15'5⅛" |
| 1920 Frank Foss, U.S.A. .............. 12'5⁵⁄₁₆" | 1964 Fred Hansen, U.S.A. ............... 16'8¾" |
| 1924 Lee Barnes, U.S.A.................. 12'11½" | 1968 Bob Seagren, U.S.A. ............... 17'8½" |
| 1928 . Sabin Carr, U.S.A................. 13'9⅜" | 1972 W. Nordwig, E. Germany ............ 18'½" |
| 1932 W. Miller, U.S.A.................. 14'1⅞" | 1976 T. Slusarski, Poland................ 18'½" |
| | 1980* W. Kozakiewicz, Poland ............ 18'11½" |

* Olympic record.

### TRACK AND FIELD: TRIPLE JUMP—MEN

| | | | | | |
|---|---|---|---|---|---|
| 1896 | James Connolly, U.S.A. | 45′ | 1948 | A. Ahman, Sweden | 50′ 6¼″ |
| 1900 | Myer Prinstein, U.S.A. | 47′ 4¼″ | 1952 | A. Ferreira da Silva, Brazil | 53′ 2½″ |
| 1904 | Myer Prinstein, U.S.A. | 47′ | 1956 | A. Ferreira da Silva, Brazil | 53′ 7½″ |
| 1908 | T. Ahearne, Britain | 48′ 11¼″ | 1960 | J. Schmidt, Poland | 55′ 1⅜″ |
| 1912 | G. Lindblom, Sweden | 48′ 5⅛″ | 1964 | J. Schmidt, Poland | 55′ 3⅖″ |
| 1920 | V. Tuulos, Finland | 47′ 7 7/16″ | 1968* | V. Saneev, USSR | 57′ ¾″ |
| 1924 | A. Winter, Australia | 50′ 11⅛″ | 1972 | V. Saneev, USSR | 56′ 11″ |
| 1928 | M. Oda, Japan | 49′ 10 13/16″ | 1976 | V. Saneev, USSR | 56′ 8¾″ |
| 1932 | C. Nambu, Japan | 51′ 7″ | 1980 | J. Uudmae, USSR | 56′ 11⅛″ |
| 1936 | N. Tajima, Japan | 52′ 5⅞″ | | | |

### TRACK AND FIELD: HAMMER THROW—MEN

| | | | | | |
|---|---|---|---|---|---|
| 1900 | John Flanagan, U.S.A. | 167′ 4″ | 1948 | I. Nemeth, Hungary | 183′ 11½″ |
| 1904 | John Flanagan, U.S.A. | 168′ 1″ | 1952 | J. Csermak, Hungary | 197′ 11¾″ |
| 1908 | John Flanagan, U.S.A. | 170′ 4¼″ | 1956 | H. Connolly, U.S.A. | 207′ 3½″ |
| 1912 | M. McGrath, U.S.A. | 179′ 7⅛″ | 1960 | V. Rudenkov, USSR | 220′ 1⅝″ |
| 1920 | Patrick Ryan, U.S.A. | 173′ 5⅝″ | 1964 | R. Klim, USSR | 228′ 9⅔″ |
| 1924 | F. Tootell, U.S.A. | 174′ 10¼″ | 1968 | G. Zsivotzky, Hungary | 240′ 8″ |
| 1928 | P. O'Callaghan, Ireland | 168′ 7½″ | 1972 | A. Bondarchuk, USSR | 248′ 8″ |
| 1932 | P. O'Callaghan, Ireland | 176′ 11⅛″ | 1976 | J. Sedych, USSR | 254′ 4″ |
| 1936 | Karl Hein, Germany | 185′ 4¼″ | 1980* | Y. Sedykh, USSR | 268′ 4½″ |

### TRACK AND FIELD: DECATHLON—MEN

| | | | | | |
|---|---|---|---|---|---|
| 1912 | Jim Thorpe, U.S.A. | 1936 | Glenn Morris, U.S.A. | 1964 | W. Holdorf, W. Germany |
| 1920 | H. Lovland, Norway | 1948 | Bob Mathias, U.S.A. | 1968 | Bill Toomey, U.S.A. |
| 1924 | Harold Osborn, U.S.A. | 1952 | Bob Mathias, U.S.A. | 1972 | Nikolai Avilov, USSR |
| 1928 | P. Yrjola, Finland | 1956 | Milt Campbell, U.S.A. | 1976 | Bruce Jenner, U.S.A. |
| 1932 | James Bausch, U.S.A. | 1960 | Rafer Johnson, U.S.A. | 1980 | Daley Thompson, Britain |

### VOLLEYBALL—MEN

| | | | | | |
|---|---|---|---|---|---|
| 1964 | USSR | 1972 | Japan | 1980 | USSR |
| 1968 | USSR | 1976 | Poland | | |

### VOLLEYBALL—WOMEN

| | | | | | |
|---|---|---|---|---|---|
| 1964 | Japan | 1972 | USSR | 1980 | USSR |
| 1968 | USSR | 1976 | Japan | | |

### WATER POLO—MEN

| | | | | | | | | | | | |
|---|---|---|---|---|---|---|---|---|---|---|---|
| 1900 | Britain | 1912 | Britain | 1928 | Germany | 1948 | Italy | 1960 | Italy | 1972 | USSR |
| 1904 | U.S.A. | 1920 | Britain | 1932 | Hungary | 1952 | Hungary | 1964 | Hungary | 1976 | Hungary |
| 1908 | Britain | 1924 | France | 1936 | Hungary | 1956 | Hungary | 1968 | Yugoslavia | 1980 | USSR |

### WEIGHTLIFTING: FLYWEIGHT (114.5 lbs.)

| | | | | | |
|---|---|---|---|---|---|
| 1972 | Z. Smalcerz, Poland | 745 lbs. | 1980* | K. Osmonalieu, USSR | 540 lbs. |
| 1976 | A. Voronin, USSR | 534.5 lbs. | | | |

### WEIGHTLIFTING: BANTAMWEIGHT (123 lbs.)

| | | POUNDS | | | POUNDS | | | POUNDS |
|---|---|---|---|---|---|---|---|---|
| 1948 | Joe DePietro, U.S.A. | 677 | 1960 | Charles Vinci, U.S.A. | 760 | 1972 | Imre Foldi, Hungary | 833 |
| 1952 | Ivan Udovov, USSR | 694 | 1964 | A. Vakhonin, USSR | 788.1 | 1976 | N. Nourikian, Bulgaria | 578.5 |
| 1956 | Charles Vinci, U.S.A. | 754.5 | 1968 | M.N. Seresht, Iran | 808.5 | 1980 | D. Nunez, Cuba | 606.2 |

### WEIGHTLIFTING: FEATHERWEIGHT (132 lbs.)

| | | | | | | | | |
|---|---|---|---|---|---|---|---|---|
| 1920 | L. de Haes, Belgium | 485 | 1948 | M. Fayad, Egypt | 733 | 1968 | Y. Miyake, Japan | 863.5 |
| 1924 | P. Gabetti, Italy | 887 | 1952 | R. Chimishyan, USSR | 743.5 | 1972 | N. Nourikian, Bulgaria | 888 |
| 1928 | F. Andrysek, Austria | 633 | 1956 | Isaac Berger, U.S.A. | 776.75 | 1976 | N. Kolenisnikov, USSR | 628 |
| 1932 | R. Suvigny, France | 633 | 1960 | Y. Minaev, USSR | 821 | 1980 | V. Mazin, USSR | 639 |
| 1936 | A. Teriazzo, U.S.A. | 688 | 1964 | Y. Miyake, Japan | 876.3 | | | |

### WEIGHTLIFTING: LIGHTWEIGHT (149 lbs.)

| | | | | | | | | |
|---|---|---|---|---|---|---|---|---|
| 1920 | A. Neyland, Estonia | 567 | 1936 | M. Mesbah, Egypt | 755 | 1964 | W. Baszanowski, Poland | 953.5 |
| 1924 | E. Decottignies, France | 970 | 1948 | I. Shams, Egypt | 793 | 1968 | W. Baszanowski, Poland | 962.5 |
| 1928 | (tie) D. Helbig, Germany; | | 1952 | Tommy Kono, U.S.A. | 798.75 | 1972 | M. Kirzhinov, USSR | 1,014 |
| | H. Haas, Austria | 710 | 1956 | Igor Rybak, USSR | 837 | 1976 | Z. Kaczmarek, Poland | 677.5 |
| 1932 | R. Duverger, France | 716 | 1960 | V. Bushuev, USSR | 876 | 1980 | Y. Roussev, Bulgaria | 755 |

### WEIGHTLIFTING: MIDDLEWEIGHT (165 lbs.)

| | | | | | | | | |
|---|---|---|---|---|---|---|---|---|
| 1920 | B. Gance, France | 540 | 1948 | Frank Spellman, U.S.A. | 859 | 1968 | V. Kurentsov, USSR | 1,045 |
| 1924 | C. Galimberti, Italy | 1,085 | 1952 | Peter George, U.S.A. | 881.5 | 1972 | Y. Bikov, Bulgaria | 1,069.23 |
| 1928 | F. Roger, France | 738 | 1956 | F. Bogdanovskii, USSR | 925.5 | 1976 | Y. Mitkov, Bulgaria | 738.5 |
| 1932 | R. Ismayr, Germany | 760 | 1960 | A. Kurynov, USSR | 964.25 | 1980 | A. Zlatev, Bulgaria | 792 |
| 1936 | K. El Touni, Egypt | 854 | 1964 | H. Zdrazila, Czech | 981 | | | |

### WEIGHTLIFTING: LIGHT HEAVYWEIGHT (181.5 lbs.)

| | | | | | | | | |
|---|---|---|---|---|---|---|---|---|
| 1920 | E. Cadine, France | 639 | 1948 | S. Stanczyk, U.S.A. | 920.00 | 1968 | B. Selitsky, USSR | 1,067.00 |
| 1924 | C. Rigoulot, France | 1,107 | 1952 | T. Lomakin, USSR | 920.25 | 1972 | L. Jenssen, Norway | 1,118.00 |
| 1928 | S. Nosseir, Egypt | 782 | 1956 | Tommy Kono, U.S.A. | 986.25 | 1976 | V. Shary, USSR | 803.00 |
| 1932 | L. Hostin, France | 804 | 1960 | I. Palinski, Poland | 975.25 | 1980 | Y. Vardanyan, USSR | 882 |
| 1936 | L. Hostin, France | 821 | 1964 | R. Plyukfeider, USSR | 1,047.20 | | | |

* Olympic record.

**SUMMER OLYMPIC WINNERS AND RECORDS** (*continued*)

### WEIGHTLIFTING: MIDDLE HEAVYWEIGHT (198 lbs.)

| | | |
|---|---|---|
| 1952  N. Schemansky, U.S.A. 980.75 | 1964  V. Golovanov, USSR . 1,074.70 | 1976  D. Rigert, USSR ..... 841.50 |
| 1956  A. Vorobiev, USSR .. 1,019.25 | 1968  K. Kangasniemi, Finland 1,138.50 | 1980  P. Baczako, Hungary 832.2 |
| 1960  A. Vorobiev, USSR ,. 1,041.25 | 1972  A. Nikolov, Bulgaria . 1,157.00 | |

### WEIGHTLIFTING: 1st HEAVYWEIGHT (220 lbs.)

1980  O. Zaremba, Czechoslovakia .........870.8

### WEIGHTLIFTING: 2d HEAVYWEIGHT (Up to 242 lbs.)

| | | |
|---|---|---|
| 1920  F. Bottini, Italy ......... 595 | 1948  John Davis, U.S.A. .... 997.00 | 1968  L. Zhabotinsky, USSR 1,259.50 |
| 1924  G. Tonani, Italy ....... 1,140 | 1952  John Davis, U.S.A. .. 1,013.75 | 1972  Yan Talts, USSR ... 1,278.00 |
| 1928  J. Strassberger, Germany 821 | 1956  Paul Anderson, U.S.A. . 1,102.00 | 1976  V. Khristov, Bulgaria ... 880 |
| 1932  J. Skobia, Czechoslovakia 837 | 1960  Y. Vlasov, USSR..... 1,184.25 | 1980  L. Taranenko, USSR .. 931.4 |
| 1936  J. Manger, Germany ..... 903 | 1964  L. Zhabotinsky, USSR· 1,262.10 | |

### WEIGHTLIFTING: SUPER HEAVYWEIGHT (Over 242 lbs.)

| | | |
|---|---|---|
| 1972  Vasily Alexeev, USSR .... 1,411 | 1976  Vasily Alexeev, USSR....... 968 | 1980  S. Rakhmanov, USSR..... 970 |

### WRESTLING: FREESTYLE—PAPERWEIGHT (105.5 lbs.)

| | | |
|---|---|---|
| 1972  Roman Dmitriev, USSR | 1976  K. Issaev, Bulgaria | 1980  C. Pollio, Italy |

### WRESTLING: FREESTYLE—FLYWEIGHT (114.5 lbs.)

| | | | |
|---|---|---|---|
| 1948 L.Viitala, Finland | 1960  A. Bilek, Turkey | 1968  S. Nakata, Japan | 1976  Y. Takada, Japan |
| 1952 H. Gemici, Turkey | 1964  Y. Yoshida, Japan | 1972  K. Kato, Japan | 1980  A. Beloglazov, USSR |
| 1956 M. Tzalkalmanidze, USSR | | | |

### WRESTLING: FREESTYLE—BANTAMWEIGHT (125.5 lbs.)

| | | | |
|---|---|---|---|
| 1904  G. Mehnert, U.S.A. | 1932  Robert Pearce, U.S.A. | 1956  M. Dagistanli, Turkey | 1972  H. Yanagida, Japan |
| 1908  G. Mehnert, U.S.A. | 1936  O. Zombori, Hungary | 1960  Terrence McCann, U.S.A. | 1976  V. Umin, USSR |
| 1924  K. Pihlajamaki, Finland | 1948  N. Akar, Turkey | 1964  Y. Uetake, Japan | 1980  S. Beloglazov, USSR |
| 1928  K. Makinen, Finland | 1952  S. Ishii, Japan | 1968  Y. Uetake, Japan | |

### WRESTLING: FREESTYLE—FEATHERWEIGHT (136.5 lbs.)

| | | | |
|---|---|---|---|
| 1908  George Dole, U.S.A. | 1932  H. Pihlajamaki, Finland | 1956  S. Sasahara, Japan | 1972  Z. Abdulbekov, USSR |
| 1920  Charles Ackerly, U.S.A. | 1936  K. Pihlajamaki, Finland | 1960  M. Dagistanli, Turkey | 1976  Yang Jung Mo, S. Korea |
| 1924  Robin Reed, U.S.A. | 1948  G. Bilge, Turkey | 1964  O. Watanabe, Japan | 1980  M. Abushev, USSR |
| 1928  Allie Morrison, U.S.A. | 1952  B. Sit, Turkey | 1968  M. Kaneko, Japan | |

### WRESTLING: FREESTYLE—LIGHTWEIGHT (149.5)

| | | | |
|---|---|---|---|
| 1908  G. de Relwyskow, Britain | 1928  O. Kapp, Estonia | 1952  O. Anderberg, Sweden | 1968  A. Movahed, Iran |
| 1920  K. Antilla, Finland | 1932  C. Pacome, France | 1956  E. Habibi, Iran | 1972  Dan Gable, U.S.A. |
| 1924  Russell Vis, U.S.A. | 1936  K. Karpati, Hungary | 1960  Shelby Wilson, U.S.A. | 1976  P. Pinegin, USSR |
| | 1948  C. Atik, Turkey | 1964  E. Dimov, Bulgaria | 1980  S. Absaidov, USSR |

### WRESTLING: FREESTYLE—WELTERWEIGHT (163 lbs.)

| | | | |
|---|---|---|---|
| 1924  H. Gehri, Switzerland | 1948  Y. Dogu, Turkey | 1964  I. Ogan, Turkey | 1980  V. Raitchev, Bulgaria |
| 1928  A. Haavisto, Finland | 1952  William Smith, U.S.A. | 1968  M. Atalay, Turkey | |
| 1932  Jack Van Bebber, U.S.A. | 1956  M. Ikeda, Japan | 1972  Wayne Wells, U.S.A. | |
| 1936  Frank Lewis, U.S.A. | 1960  D. Blubaugh, U.S.A. | 1976  I. Date, Japan | |

### WRESTLING: FREESTYLE—MIDDLEWEIGHT (180 lbs.)

| | | | |
|---|---|---|---|
| 1908  S. Bacon, Britain | 1928  E. Kyburz, Switzerland | 1952  D. Cimakuridze, USSR | 1968  B. Gurevitch, USSR |
| 1920  E. Leino, Finland | 1932  I. Johansson, Sweden | 1956  N. Nikolov, Bulgaria | 1972  L. Tediashvili, USSR |
| 1924  F. Haggmann, Switzerland. | 1936  E. Poilve, France | 1960  H. Gungor, Turkey | 1976  J. Peterson, U.S.A. |
| | 1948  Glen Brand, U.S.A. | 1964  P. Gardjev, Bulgaria | 1980  I. Abilov, Bulgaria |

### WRESTLING: FREESTYLE—LIGHT HEAVYWEIGHT (198 lbs.)

| | | | |
|---|---|---|---|
| 1920  A. Larsson, Sweden | 1936  K. Fridell, Sweden | 1960  I. Atli, Turkey | 1976  L. Tediashvili, USSR |
| 1924  John Spellman, U.S.A. | 1948  Henry Wittenberg, U.S.A. | 1964  A. Medved, USSR | 1980  S. Oganesyan, USSR |
| 1928  T. Sjostedt, Sweden | 1952  W. Palm, Sweden | 1968  A. Ayuk, Turkey | |
| 1932  Peter Mehringer, U.S.A. | 1956  G. Takhti, Iran | 1972  Ben Peterson, U.S.A. | |

### WRESTLING: FREESTYLE—HEAVYWEIGHT (220 lbs.)

| | | | |
|---|---|---|---|
| 1908  G.C. O'Kelly, Britain | 1932  J. Richthoff, Sweden | 1956  H. Kaplan, Turkey | 1968  A. Medved, USSR |
| 1920  R. Roth, Switzerland | 1936  K. Palusalu, Estonia | 1960  W. Dietrich, W. Germany | 1972  Ivan Yarygin, USSR |
| 1924  Harry Steele, U.S.A. | 1948  G. Bobis, Hungary | | 1976  Ivan Yarygin, USSR |
| 1928  J. Richthoff, Sweden | 1952  A. Mekokishvili, USSR | 1964  A. Ivanitsky, USSR | 1980  Ilya Mate, USSR |

### WRESTLING: FREESTYLE—SUPER HEAVYWEIGHT (Over 220 lbs.)

| | | |
|---|---|---|
| 1972  Aleksandr Medved, USSR | 1976  Soslan Andiev, USSR | 1980  S. Andiev, USSR |

### WRESTLING: GRECO-ROMAN—PAPERWEIGHT (105.5 lbs.)

| | | |
|---|---|---|
| 1972  Gheorghe Berceanu, Romania | 1976  A. Shumakov, USSR | 1980  Z. Ushkempirov, USSR |

## WRESTLING: GRECO-ROMAN—FLYWEIGHT (114.5 lbs.)

| | | |
|---|---|---|
| 1948 P. Lombardi, Italy | 1960 D. Pirvulescu, Romania | 1972 P. Kirov, Bulgaria |
| 1952 B. Gourevitch, USSR | 1964 T. Hanahara, Japan | 1976 V. Konstantinov, USSR |
| 1956 N. Soloviev, USSR | 1968 P. Kirov, Bulgaria | 1980 V. Blagidze, USSR |

## WRESTLING: GRECO-ROMAN—BANTAMWEIGHT (125.5 lbs.)

| | | | |
|---|---|---|---|
| 1924 E. Putsep, Estonia | 1948 K. Pettersen, Sweden | 1960 O. Karavaev, USSR | 1972 R. Kazakov, USSR |
| 1928 K. Leucht, Germany | 1952 I. Hodos, Hungary | 1964 M. Ichiguchi, Japan | 1976 P. Ukkola, Finland |
| 1932 J. Brendel, Germany | 1956 K. Vyropaev, USSR | 1968 J. Varga, Hungary | 1980 S. Serikov, USSR |
| 1936 M. Lorinc, Hungary | | | |

## WRESTLING: GRECO—ROMAN—FEATHERWEIGHT (136.5 lbs.)

| | | | |
|---|---|---|---|
| 1912 K. Koskelo, Finland | 1932 G. Gozzo, Italy | 1956 R. Makinen, Finland | 1972 G. Markov, Bulgaria |
| 1920 O. Friman, Finland | 1936 Y. Erkan, Turkey | 1960 M. Sille, Turkey | 1976 K. Lipien, Poland |
| 1924 K. Anttila, Finland | 1948 M. Oktav, Turkey | 1964 I. Polyak, Hungary | 1980 S. Migiakis, Greece |
| 1928 V. Vali, Estonia | 1952 Y. Punkin, USSR | 1968 R. Rurua, USSR | |

## WRESTLING: GRECO-ROMAN—LIGHTWEIGHT (149.5 lbs.)

| | | | |
|---|---|---|---|
| 1908 E. Porro, Italy | 1928 L. Keresztes, Hungary | 1952 C. Safin, USSR | 1968 M. Mumemura, Japan |
| 1912 E. Vare, Finland | 1932 E. Malmberg, Sweden | 1956 K. Lehtonen, Finland | 1972 S. Khisamutdinov, USSR |
| 1920 E. Vare, Finland | 1936 I. Koskela, Finland | 1960 A. Kordidze, USSR | 1976 S. Nalbandian, USSR |
| 1924 O. Friman, Finland | 1948 K. Freij, Sweden | 1964 K. Ayvaz, Turkey | 1980 S. Rusu, Romania |

## WRESTLING: GRECO-ROMAN—WELTERWEIGHT (163 lbs.)

| | | | |
|---|---|---|---|
| 1932 I. Johansson, Sweden | 1952 M. Szilvasi, Hungary | 1964 A. Kolesov, USSR | 1976 A. Bykov, USSR |
| 1936 R. Svedberg, Sweden | 1956 M. Bayrak, Turkey | 1968 R. Vesper, E. Germany | 1980 F. Kocsis, Hungary |
| 1948 G. Andersson, Sweden | 1960 M. Bayrak, Turkey | 1972 V. Macha, Czechoslovakia | |

## WRESTLING: GRECO-ROMAN—MIDDLEWEIGHT (180 lbs.)

| | | |
|---|---|---|
| 1908 F. Martenson, Sweden | 1936 I. Johansson, Sweden | 1968 L. Metz, E. Germany |
| 1912 C. Johansson, Sweden | 1948 A. Gronberg, Sweden | 1972 C. Hegedus, Hungary |
| 1920 C. Westergren, Sweden | 1952 A. Gronberg, Sweden | 1976 M. Petkovic, Yugoslavia |
| 1924 E. Vesterland, Finland | 1956 G. Kartosa, USSR | 1980 G. Korban, USSR |
| 1928 V. Kokkinen, Finland | 1960 D. Dobrev, Bulgaria | |
| 1932 V. Kokkinen, Finland | 1964 B. Simic, Yugoslavia | |

## WRESTLING: GRECO-ROMAN—LIGHT HEAVYWEIGHT (198 lbs.)

| | | |
|---|---|---|
| 1908 V. Weckmann, Finland | 1932 R. Svensson, Sweden | 1964 B. Alexandrov, Bulgaria |
| 1912 (tie) A. Ahlgren, Sweden | 1936 A. Cadier, Sweden | 1968 B. Radev, Bulgaria |
| I. Boling, Finland | 1948 N. Nilsson, Sweden | 1972 V. Rezantsev, USSR |
| 1920 C. Johansson, Sweden | 1952 K. Grondhal, Finland | 1976 V. Rezantsev, USSR |
| 1924 C. Westergren, Sweden | 1956 V. Nikolaev, USSR | 1980 N. Nottny, Hungary |
| 1928 I. Moustafa, Egypt | 1960 Tevik Kis, Turkey | |

## WRESTLING: GRECO-ROMAN—HEAVYWEIGHT (220 lbs.)

| | | | |
|---|---|---|---|
| 1896 K. Schumann, Germany | 1928 R. Svensson, Sweden | 1956 A. Parfenov, USSR | 1976 N. Bolboshin, USSR |
| 1908 R. Weisz, Hungary | 1932 C. Westergren, Sweden | 1960 I. Bogdan, USSR | 1980 G. Raikov, Bulgaria |
| 1912 Y. Saarela, Finland | 1936 K. Palusalu, Estonia | 1964 I. Kozma, Hungary | |
| 1920 A. Lindfors, Finland | 1948 A. Kirecci, Turkey | 1968 I. Kozma, Hungary | |
| 1924 H. Degiane, France | 1952 J. Kotkas, USSR | 1972 N. Martinescu, Romania | |

## WRESTLING: GRECO-ROMAN—SUPER HEAVYWEIGHT (Over 220 lbs.)

| | | |
|---|---|---|
| 1972 Anatoly Roshin, USSR | 1976 A. Kolchinsky, USSR | 1980 A. Kolchinsky, USSR |

## YACHTING: FINN CLASS

| | | | |
|---|---|---|---|
| 1952 Denmark | 1960 Denmark | 1968 USSR | 1976 East Germany |
| 1956 Denmark | 1964 West Germany | 1972 France | 1980 Finland |

## YACHTING: FLYING DUTCHMAN CLASS

| | | | | | |
|---|---|---|---|---|---|
| 1960 Norway | 1964 New Zealand | 1968 Britain | 1972 Britain | 1976 West Germany | 1980 Spain |

## YACHTING: TEMPEST CLASS / YACHTING: SOLING CLASS / YACHTING: TORNADO CLASS / YACHTING: 470 CLASS

| YACHTING: TEMPEST CLASS | YACHTING: SOLING CLASS | YACHTING: TORNADO CLASS | YACHTING: 470 CLASS |
|---|---|---|---|
| 1972 USSR | 1972 U.S.A. | 1976 Britain | 1976 West Germany |
| 1976 Sweden | 1976 Denmark | 1980 Brazil | 1980 Brazil |
| | 1980 Denmark | | |

## YACHTING: STAR CLASS

| | | | | |
|---|---|---|---|---|
| 1932 U.S.A. | 1948 U.S.A. | 1956 U.S.A. | 1964 Bahamas | 1972 Australia |
| 1936 Germany | 1952 Italy | 1960 USSR | 1968 U.S.A. | 1980 USSR |

## YACHTING: DRAGON CLASS

| | | | | |
|---|---|---|---|---|
| 1948 Norway | 1956 Sweden | 1964 Denmark | 1968 U.S.A. | 1972 Australia |
| 1952 Norway | 1960 Greece | | | |

# WINTER OLYMPIC WINNERS AND RECORDS

### BIATHLON—10 km
1980  Frank Ullrich, E. Germany . . . . . . . . . . . . .  0:32:10.69

### BIATHLON—20 km
| | |
|---|---|
| 1960  Klas Lestander, Sweden . . . . . . . . . 1:33:21.6 | 1972  Magnar Solberg, Norway . . . . . . . . . . . . . . .1:15:55.50 |
| 1964  Vladimir Melanin, USSR . . . . . . . . . 1:20:26.8 | 1976  Nikolai Kruglov, USSR . . . . . . . . . . . . . . . .1:14:12.26 |
| 1968  Magnar Solberg, Norway . . . . . . . . . . . . 1:13:45.9 | 1980* Anatoli Aljabiev, USSR . . . . . . . . . . . . . . . .1:08:16.31 |

### BIATHLON RELAY
1968  USSR . . .   2:13.02 | 1972  USSR . . .  1:51.44 | 1976  USSR . . .   1:57:55.67 | 1980*  USSR . . 1:34:03.27

### BOBSLED: 2-MAN BOB (winning driver)
| | |
|---|---|
| 1932  U.S.A., Hubert Stevens . . . . . . . . . . . . . . . . 8:14.74 | 1964  Britain, Antony Nash . . . . . . . . . . . . . . . . . . 4:21.90 |
| 1936  U.S.A., Ivan Brown . . . . . . . . . . . . . . . . . . . 5:29.29 | 1968  Italy, Eugenio Monti . . . . . . . . . . . . . . . . . 4:41.54 |
| 1948  Switzerland, F. Endrich . . . . . . . . . . . . . . . 5:29.2 | 1972  W. Germany, Wolfgang Zimmerer . . . . . . . 4:47.07 |
| 1952  W. Germany, Andreas Ostler . . . . . . . . . . 5:24.54 | 1976* E. Germany, Meinhard Nehmer . . . . . . . . 3:40.43 |
| 1956  Italy, Dalla Costa . . . . . . . . . . . . . . . . . . . . 5:30.14 | 1980  Switzerland, Erich Schaerer . . . . . . . . . . . . 4:09.36 |

### BOBSLED: 4-MAN BOB (winning driver)
| | |
|---|---|
| 1924  Switzerland, Edward Scherrer . . . . . . . . . 5:45.54 | 1956  Switzerland, Franz Kapus . . . . . . . . . . . . . 5:10.44 |
| 1928  U.S.A., William Fiske . . . . . . . . . . . . . . . . . 3:20.5 | 1964  Canada, Victor Emery . . . . . . . . . . . . . . . . 4:14.46 |
| 1932  U.S.A., William Fiske . . . . . . . . . . . . . . . . . 7:53.68 | 1968* Italy, Eugenio Monti . . . . . . . . . . . . . . . . . 2:17.39 |
| 1936  Switzerland, Perre Musy . . . . . . . . . . . . . . 5:19.85 | 1972  Switzerland, Jean Wicki . . . . . . . . . . . . . . . 4:43.07 |
| 1948  U.S.A., Edward Rimkus . . . . . . . . . . . . . . . . 5:20.1 | 1976  E. Germany, Meinhard Nehmer . . . . . . . . 3:44.42 |
| 1952  W. Germany, Andreas Ostler . . . . . . . . . . 5:07.84 | 1980  E. Germany, Meinhard Nehmer . . . . . . . . 3:59.92 |

### ICE HOCKEY
| | | | | | | | |
|---|---|---|---|---|---|---|---|
| 1920  Canada | 1928   Canada | 1936   Britain | 1952   Canada | 1960   U.S.A. | 1968   USSR | 1976   USSR |
| 1924  Canada | 1932   Canada | 1948   Canada | 1956   USSR | 1964   USSR | 1972   USSR | 1980   U.S.A. |

### SKATING: FIGURE SKATING—MEN
| | | |
|---|---|---|
| 1908  Ulrich Salchow, Sweden | 1936  Karl Schafer, Austria | 1964  Manfred Schnelldorfer, W. Germ. |
| 1920  Gillis Grafstrom, Sweden | 1948  Richard Button, U.S.A. | 1968  Wolfgang Schwarz, Austria |
| 1924  Gillis Grafstrom, Sweden | 1952  Richard Button, U.S.A. | 1972  Ondrej Nepela, Czechoslovakia |
| 1928  Gillis Grafstrom, Sweden | 1956  H.A. Jenkins, U.S.A. | 1976  John Curry, Britain |
| 1932  Karl Schafer, Austria | 1960  David Jenkins, U.S.A. | 1980  Robin Cousins, Britain |

### SKATING: FIGURE SKATING—WOMEN
| | | |
|---|---|---|
| 1908  Madge Syers, Britain | 1936  Sonja Henie, Norway | 1964  Sjoukje Dijkstra, Netherlands |
| 1920  Magda Julin-Mauroy, Sweden | 1948  Barbara Ann Scott, Canada | 1968  Peggy Fleming, U.S.A. |
| 1924  Heima von Szabo-Planck, Austria | 1952  Jeanette Altwegg, Britain | 1972  Beatrix Schuba, Austria |
| 1928  Sonja Henie, Norway | 1956  Tenley Albright, U.S.A. | 1976  Dorothy Hamill, U.S.A. |
| 1932  Sonja Henie, Norway | 1960  Carol Heiss, U.S.A. | 1980  Anett Poetzsch, E. Germany |

### SKATING: FIGURE SKATING—PAIRS
| | |
|---|---|
| 1908  Germany: Anna Hubler, Heinrich Burger | 1956  Austria: Elizabeth Schwarz, Kurt Oppelt |
| 1920  Finland: Ludovika and Walter Jakobsson | 1960  Canada: Barbara Wagner, Robert Paul |
| 1924  Austria: Helene Engelmann, Alfred Berger | 1964  USSR: Ludmila Beloussova, Oleg Protopopov |
| 1928  France: Andrée Joly, Pierre Brunet | 1968  USSR: Ludmila Beloussova, Oleg Protopopov |
| 1932  France: Andrée and Pierre Brunet | 1972  USSR: Irina Rodnina, Alexel Ulanov |
| 1936  Germany: Maxie Heber, Ernest Baier | 1976  USSR: Irina Rodnina, Aleksandr Zaitsev |
| 1952  W. Germany: Ria and Paul Falk | 1980  USSR: Irina Rodnina, Aleksandr Zaitsev |

### SKATING: ICE DANCING
1976  USSR: Ludmila Pakhoma, Aleksandr Gorshkov | 1980  USSR: Natalia Linichuk, Gennadi Karponosov

### SKATING: SPEED SKATING—MEN: 500 METERS
| | |
|---|---|
| 1924  Charles Jewtraw, U.S.A. . . . . . . . . . . . . . . . 0:44.0 | 1956  Evgeniy Grishin, USSR . . . . . . . . . . . . . . . . 0:40.20 |
| 1928  Clas Thunberg, Finland, and | 1960  Evgeniy Grishin, USSR . . . . . . . . . . . . . . . . 0:40.20 |
| Bernt Evensen, Norway (tie) . . . . . . . . . . 0:43.4 | 1964  Richard McDermott, U.S.A. . . . . . . . . . . . . 0:40.10 |
| 1932  John A. Shea, U.S.A. . . . . . . . . . . . . . . . . . 0:43.4 | 1968  Erhard Keller, W. Germany . . . . . . . . . . . . 0:40.30 |
| 1936  Ivar Ballangrud, Norway . . . . . . . . . . . . . . 0:43.4 | 1972  Erhard Keller, W. Germany . . . . . . . . . . . . 0:39.40 |
| 1948  Finn Helgesen, Norway . . . . . . . . . . . . . . . 0:43.1 | 1976  Evgeny Kulikov, USSR . . . . . . . . . . . . . . . . 0:39.17 |
| 1952  Kenneth Henry, U.S.A. . . . . . . . . . . . . . . . 0:43.2 | 1980* Eric Heiden, U.S.A. . . . . . . . . . . . . . . . . . . . 0:38.03 |

### SKATING: SPEED SKATING—WOMEN: 500 METERS
| | |
|---|---|
| 1932  Jean Wilson, Canada . . . . . . . . . . . . . . . . . . 0:58.0 | 1972  Anne Henning, U.S.A. . . . . . . . . . . . . . . . . . 0:43.3 |
| 1960  Helga Haase, W. Germany . . . . . . . . . . . . 0:45.9 | 1976  Sheila Young, U.S.A. . . . . . . . . . . . . . . . . . 0:42.76 |
| 1964  Lydia Skoblikova, USSR . . . . . . . . . . . . . . . 0:45.0 | 1980* Karin Enke, E. Germany . . . . . . . . . . . . . . . 0:41.78 |
| 1968  Ludmila Titova, USSR . . . . . . . . . . . . . . . . 0:46.1 | |

### SKATING: SPEED SKATING—MEN: 1,000 METERS
1976  Peter Mueller, U.S.A. . . . . . . . . . . . . . . 1:19.32 | 1980* Eric Heiden, U.S.A. . . . . . . . . . . . . . . . 1:15.18

### SKATING: SPEED SKATING—WOMEN: 1,000 METERS
| | |
|---|---|
| 1932  Elizabeth Du Bois, U.S.A. . . . . . . . . . . . . . 2:04.0 | 1972  Monika Pflug, W. Germany . . . . . . . . . . . . 1:31.40 |
| 1960  Kara Guseva, USSR . . . . . . . . . . . . . . . . . . 1:34.1 | 1976  Tatiana Averina, USSR . . . . . . . . . . . . . . . . 1:28.43 |
| 1964  Lidia Skoblikova, USSR . . . . . . . . . . . . . . . 1:33.2 | 1980* Natalia Petruseva, USSR . . . . . . . . . . . . . . 1:24.10 |
| 1968  Carolina Geijssen, Netherlands . . . . . . . . . . 1:32.60 | |

*Olympic record.

## SKATING: SPEED SKATING—MEN: 1,500 METERS

| 1924 | Clas Thunberg, Finland | 2:20.8 |
| 1928 | Clas Thunberg, Finland | 2:21.1 |
| 1932 | John A. Shea, U.S.A. | 2:57.5 |
| 1936 | Charles Mathisen, Norway | 2:19.2 |
| 1948 | Sverre Farstad, Norway | 2:17.6 |
| 1952 | Hjalmar Anderson, Norway | 2:20.4 |
| 1956 | Evgeniy Grishin and Y. Mikhailov, USSR (tie) | 2:08.6 |
| 1960 | Edgar Roadaas, Norway, and Evgeniy Grishin, USSR (tie) | 2:10.4 |
| 1964 | Ants Antson, USSR | 2:10.3 |
| 1968 | Cornelis Verkerk, Netherlands | 2:03.4 |
| 1972 | Ard Schenk, Netherlands | 2:02.96 |
| 1976 | Jan-Egil Storholt, Norway | 1:59.38 |
| 1980 | * Eric Heiden, U.S.A. | 1:55.44 |

## SKATING: SPEED SKATING—WOMEN: 1,500 METERS

| 1932 | Kit Klein, U.S.A. | 3:06.0 |
| 1960 | Lidia Skoblikova, USSR | 2:52.2 |
| 1964 | Lidia Skoblikova, USSR | 2:22.6 |
| 1968 | Kaija Mustonen, Finland | 2:22.40 |
| 1972 | Dianne Holum, U.S.A. | 2:20.80 |
| 1976 | Galina Stepanskaya, USSR | 2:16.58 |
| 1980 | * Annie Borckink, Netherlands | 2:10.95 |

## SKATING: SPEED SKATING—MEN: 5,000 METERS

| 1924 | Clas Thunberg, Finland | 8:39.0 |
| 1928 | Ivar Ballangrud, Norway | 8:50.5 |
| 1932 | Irving Jaffee, U.S.A. | 9:40.8 |
| 1936 | Ivar Ballangrud, Norway | 8:19.6 |
| 1948 | Reidar Liaklev, Norway | 8:29.4 |
| 1952 | Hjalmar Anderson, Norway | 8:10.6 |
| 1956 | Boris Shilkov, USSR | 7:48.70 |
| 1960 | Victor Kosichkin, USSR | 7:51.30 |
| 1964 | Knut Johannesen, Norway | 7:38.40 |
| 1968 | Fred Anton Maier, Norway | 7:22.40 |
| 1972 | Ard Schenk, Netherlands | 7:23.60 |
| 1976 | Sten Stenson, Norway | 7:24.48 |
| 1980 | * Eric Heiden, U.S.A. | 7:02.29 |

## SKATING: SPEED SKATING—WOMEN: 3,000 METERS

| 1960 | Lidia Skoblikova, USSR | 5:14.3 |
| 1964 | Lidia Skoblikova, USSR | 5:14.9 |
| 1968 | Johanna Schut, Netherlands | 4:56.2 |
| 1972 | Stien Kaiser-Baas, Netherlands | 4:52.14 |
| 1976 | Tatiana Averina, USSR | 4:45.19 |
| 1980 | * Bjoerg Eva Jensen, Norway | 4:32.13 |

## SKATING: SPEED SKATING—MEN: 10,000 METERS

| 1924 | Julien Skutnabb Finland | 18:04.8 |
| 1928 | No decision because of thawing ice | |
| 1932 | Irving Jaffee, U.S.A. | 19:13.6 |
| 1936 | Ivar Ballangrud, Norway | 17:24.3 |
| 1948 | Ake Seyffarth, Norway | 17:26.3 |
| 1952 | Hjalmar Anderson, Norway | 16:45.8 |
| 1956 | Sigvard Ericsson, Sweden | 16:35.9 |
| 1960 | Knut Johannesen, Norway | 15:46.6 |
| 1964 | Jonny Nilsson, Sweden | 15:50.1 |
| 1968 | Johnny Hoëglin, Sweden | 15:23.6 |
| 1972 | Ard Schenk, Netherlands | 15:01.35 |
| 1976 | Piet Kleine, Netherlands | 14:50.59 |
| 1980 | * Eric Heiden, U.S.A. | 14:28.13 |

## SKIING: ALPINE—MEN: DOWNHILL

| 1948 | Henry Oreiller, France | 2:55.0 |
| 1952 | Zeno Colo, Italy | 2:30.8 |
| 1956 | Anton Sailer, Austria | 2:52.2 |
| 1960 | Jean Vuarnet, France | 2:06.0 |
| 1964 | Egon Zimmermann, Austria | 2:18.16 |
| 1968 | Jean-Claude Killy, France | 1:59.85 |
| 1972 | Bernhard Russi, Switzerland | 1:51.43 |
| 1976 | Franz Klammer, Austria | 1:45.73 |
| 1980 | * Leonhard Stock, Austria | 1:45.50 |

## SKIING: ALPINE—WOMEN: DOWNHILL

| 1948 | Hedi Schlunegger, Switzerland | 2:28.3 |
| 1952 | Trude Jochum-Beiser, Austria | 1:47.1 |
| 1956 | Madeleine Berthod, Switzerland | 1:40.7 |
| 1960 | Heidi Biebl, W. Germany | 1:37.6 |
| 1964 | Christi Haas, Austria | 1:55.3 |
| 1968 | Olga Pall, Austria | 1:40.8 |
| 1972 | * Marie Therese Nadig, Switzerland | 1:36.68 |
| 1976 | Rosi Mittermaier, W. Germany | 1:46.16 |
| 1980 | Annemarie Moser, Austria | 1:37.52 |

## SKIING: ALPINE—MEN: GIANT SLALOM

| 1952 | Stein Eriksen, Norway | 2:25.0 |
| 1956 | Anton Sailer, Austria | 3:00.1 |
| 1960 | Roger Staub, Switzerland | 1:48.3 |
| 1964 | * Francois Bonlieu, France | 1:46.7 |
| 1968 | Jean-Claude Killy, France | 3:29.28 |
| 1972 | Gustavo Thoeni, Italy | 3:09.62 |
| 1976 | Heini Hemmii, Switzerland | 3:26.97 |
| 1980 | Ingemar Stenmark, Sweden | 2:40.74 |

## SKIING: ALPINE—WOMEN: GIANT SLALOM

| 1952 | Andrea Mead Lawrence, U.S.A. | 2:06.8 |
| 1956 | Ossi Reichert, W. Germany | 1:56.5 |
| 1960 | Yvonne Ruegg, Switzerland | 1:39.9 |
| 1964 | Marielle Goitschel, France | 1:52.2 |
| 1968 | Nancy Greene, Canada | 1:51.97 |
| 1972 | Marle Therese Nadig, Switzerland | 1:29.90 |
| 1976 | * Kathy Kreiner, Canada | 1:29.13 |
| 1980 | Hanni Wenzel, Liechtenstein | 2:41.66 |

## SKIING: ALPINE—MEN: SLALOM

| 1948 | Edi Reinalter, Switzerland | 2:10.3 |
| 1952 | Othmar Schneider, Austria | 2:00.0 |
| 1956 [1] | Anton Sailer, Austria | — |
| 1960 | Ernst Hinterseer, Austria | 2:08.9 |
| 1964 | Josef Stiegler, Austria | 2:11.13 |
| 1968 | Jean-Claude Killy, France | 1:39.73 |
| 1972 | * Francisco Fernandez Ochoa, Spain | 1:09.27 |
| 1976 | Piero Gros, Italy | 2:03.29 |
| 1980 | Ingemar Stenmark, Sweden | 1:44.26 |

## SKIING: ALPINE—WOMEN: SLALOM

| 1948 | Gretchen Fraser, U.S.A. | 1:57.2 |
| 1952 | Andrea Mead Lawrence, U.S.A. | 2:10.6 |
| 1956 [1] | Renee Colliard, Switzerland | — |
| 1960 | Anne Heggtveigt, Canada | 1:49.6 |
| 1964 | Christine Goitschel, France | 1:29.8 |
| 1968 | Marielle Goitschel, France | 1:25.86 |
| 1972 | Barbara Cochran, U.S.A. | 1:31.24 |
| 1976 | Rosi Mittermaier, W. Germany | 1:30.54 |
| 1980 | * Hanni Wenzel, Liechtenstein | 1:25.09 |

* Olympic record.  [1] Scored in points instead of time.

## WINTER OLYMPIC WINNERS AND RECORDS (continued)

### SKIING: NORDIC—WOMEN: 5 KILOMETERS

| | | | | | |
|---|---|---|---|---|---|
| 1964 | Claudia Boyarskikh, USSR | 17:50.5 | 1976 | Helena Takalo, Finland | 15:48.69 |
| 1968 | Toini Gustafsson, Sweden | 16:45.2 | 1980 *Raisa Smetanina, USSR | | 15:06.92 |
| 1972 | Galina Koulacova, USSR | 17:00.50 | | | |

### SKIING: NORDIC—WOMEN: 10 KILOMETERS

| | | | | | |
|---|---|---|---|---|---|
| 1952 | Lydia Wideman, Finland | 41:40.0 | 1968 | Toini Gustafsson, Sweden | 36:46.50 |
| 1956 | Ljubavi Kazyreva, USSR | 38:11.0 | 1972 | Galina Koulacova, USSR | 34:17.80 |
| 1960 | Marija Gusakova, USSR | 39:46.6 | 1976 *Raisa Smetanina, USSR | | 30:13.41 |
| 1964 | Claudia Boyarskikh, USSR | 40:24.3 | 1980 | Barbara Petzold, E. Germany | 30:31.54 |

### SKIING: NORDIC—WOMEN: 20–KILOMETER RELAY

| | | | | | | | | | |
|---|---|---|---|---|---|---|---|---|---|
| 1956 | Finland 1:09:01.0 | 1964 | USSR | 59:20.2 | 1972 * | USSR | 48:46.10 | 1980 | E. Ger. 1:02:11.10 |
| 1960 | Sweden 1:04:21.4 | 1968 | Norway | 57:30.00 | 1976 | USSR | 1:07:49.75 | | |

### SKIING: NORDIC—MEN: 15 KILOMETERS

| | | | | | |
|---|---|---|---|---|---|
| 1956 | Hallgier Brenden, Norway | 49:39.0 | 1972 | Sven-Ake Lundback, Sweden | 45:28.20 |
| 1960 | Hakon Brusveen, Norway | 51:55.5 | 1976 | N. Bashukov, USSR | 43:58.47 |
| 1964 | Eero Maentyranta, Finland | 50:54.1 | 1980 *Thomas Wassberg, Sweden | | 41:57.63 |
| 1968 | Harald Groenningen, Norway | 47:54.20 | | | |

### SKIING: NORDIC—MEN: 30 KILOMETERS

| | | | | | |
|---|---|---|---|---|---|
| 1956 | Veikko Hakulinen, Finland | 1:44:06.0 | 1972 | Vyacheslav Vedenin, USSR | 1:36:31.10 |
| 1960 | Sixten Jernberg, Sweden | 1:51:03.9 | 1976 | Sergei Saveliev, USSR | 1:30:29.38 |
| 1964 | Eero Maentyranta, Finland | 1:30:50.7 | 1980 *Nikolai Zimjatov, USSR | | 1:27:02.80 |
| 1968 | Franco Nones, Italy | 1:35:39.20 | | | |

### SKIING: NORDIC—MEN: 50 KILOMETERS

| | | | | | |
|---|---|---|---|---|---|
| 1924 | Thorlief Haug, Norway | 3:44:32.0 | 1960 | Kalevi Hamalainen, Finland | 2:59:06.30 |
| 1928 | Per E. Hedlund, Sweden | 4:52:03.0 | 1964 | Sixten Jernberg, Sweden | 2:43:52.60 |
| 1932 | Veli Saarinen, Finland | 4:28:00.0 | 1968 | Ole Ellefsaeter, Norway | 2:28:45.80 |
| 1936 | Elis Viklund, Sweden | 3:30:11.0 | 1972 | Paal Tyldum, Norway | 2:43:14.75 |
| 1948 | Nils Karlsson, Sweden | 3:47:48.0 | 1976 | Ivar Formo, Norway | 2:37:30.05 |
| 1952 | Veikko Hakulinen, Finland | 3:33:33.0 | 1980 *Nikolai Zimjatov, USSR | | 2:27:24.50 |
| 1956 | Sixten Jernberg, Sweden | 2:50:27.00 | | | |

### SKIING: NORDIC—MEN: 40–KILOMETER RELAY

| | | | | | | | | | |
|---|---|---|---|---|---|---|---|---|---|
| 1936 | Finland 2:41:33.0 | 1956 | USSR | 2:15:30.0 | 1968 | Norway | 2:08:33.50 | 1980 * | USSR 1:57:03.46 |
| 1948 | Sweden 2:32:08.0 | 1960 | Finland | 2:18:45.6 | 1972 | USSR | 2:04:47.90 | | |
| 1952 | Finland 2:20:16.0 | 1964 | Sweden | 2:18:34.6 | 1976 | Finland | 2:07:59.72 | | |

### SKIING: NORDIC—MEN: COMBINED CROSS COUNTRY AND JUMPING

| | | | | | |
|---|---|---|---|---|---|
| 1924 | Thorlief Haug, Norway | 453.800 | 1960 | Georg Thoma, W. Germany | 457.952 |
| 1928 | Johan Grottumsbraaten, Norway | 427.800 | 1964 | Tormod Knutsen, Norway | 469.280 |
| 1932 | Johan Grottumsbraaten, Norway | 446.200 | 1968 | Franz Keller, W. Germany | 449.040 |
| 1936 | Oddbjorn Hagen, Norway | 430.300 | 1972 | Ulrich Wehling, E. Germany | 413.340 |
| 1948 | Heikki Hasu, Finland | 448.800 | 1976 | Ulrich Wehling, E. Germany | 423.390 |
| 1952 | Simon Slattvik, Norway | 451.621 | 1980 | Ulrich Wehling, E. Germany | 432.200 |
| 1956 | Sverre Stenersen, Norway | 455.000 | | | |

### SKIING: NORDIC—MEN: 90–METER SKI JUMPING

| | | | | | |
|---|---|---|---|---|---|
| 1924 | Jacob Thams, Norway | 227.5 | 1960 | Helmut Recknagel, W. Germany | 227.2 |
| 1928 | Alfred Andersen, Norway | 330.5 | 1964 | Toralf Engan, Norway | 230.7 |
| 1932 | Birger Ruud, Norway | 228.0 | 1968 | Vladimir Beloussov, USSR | 231.3 |
| 1936 | Birger Ruud, Norway | 232.0 | 1972 | Wojiech Fortuna, Poland | 219.9 |
| 1948 | Petter Hugsted, Norway | 228.1 | 1976 | Karl Schnabl, Austria | 234.8 |
| 1952 | Arnfinn Bergmann, Norway | 226.0 | 1980 | Jouko Tormanen, Finland | 271.0 |
| 1956 | Antti Hyvarinen, Finland | 227.0 | | | |

### SKIING: NORDIC—MEN: 70–METER SKI JUMPING

| | | | | | |
|---|---|---|---|---|---|
| 1964 | Veikko Kankkonen, Finland | 229.9 | 1976 | Hans-Georg Aschenbach, E. Germany | 252.0 |
| 1968 | Jiri Raska, Czechoslovakia | 216.5 | 1980 | Anton Innauer, Austria | 266.3 |
| 1972 | Yukio Kasaya, Japan | 244.2 | | | |

### TOBOGGAN (LUGE)—MEN: SINGLES

| | | | | | |
|---|---|---|---|---|---|
| 1964 | Thomas Koehler, W. Germany | 3:26.77 | 1976 | Detlef Guenther, E. Germany | 3:27.688 |
| 1968 *Manfred Schmid, Austria | | 2:52.48 | 1980 | Bernhard Glass, E. Germany | 2:54.796 |
| 1972 | Wolfgang Scheidel, E. Germany | 3:27.580 | | | |

### TOBOGGAN (LUGE)—WOMEN: SINGLES

| | | | | | |
|---|---|---|---|---|---|
| 1964 | Ortrun Enderlein, W. Germany | 3:24.67 | 1976 | Margit Schumann, E. Germany | 2:50.621 |
| 1968 *Erica Lechner, Italy | | 2:28.66 | 1980 | Vera Zozulia, USSR | 2:36.537 |
| 1972 | Anna Muller, E. Germany | 2:59.180 | | | |

### TOBOGGAN (LUGE)—MEN: DOUBLES

| | | | | | |
|---|---|---|---|---|---|
| 1964 | Austria: Josef Feistmantl, Manfred Stengl | 1:41.62 | 1976 | E. Germany: Hans Rinn, Norbert Hahn | 1:25.604 |
| 1968 | E. Germany: Klaus Bonsack, Thomas Koehler | 1:35.85 | 1980 *E. Germany: Hans Rinn, Norbert Hahn | | 1:19.331 |
| 1972 | tie: Italy and E. Germany | 1:28.35 | | | |

* Olympic record.

# PETS

## BEST-IN-SHOW CHAMPION DOGS AT THE WESTMINSTER KENNEL CLUB SHOW

| YEAR | BREED | BEST-IN-SHOW CHAMPION | OWNER |
|---|---|---|---|
| 1967 | Scottish Terrier | Ch. Bardene Bingo | E.H. Stuart |
| 1968 | Lakeland Terrier | Ch. Stingray of Derryabah | Mr. and Mrs. James A. Farrell Jr. |
| 1969 | Skye Terrier | Ch. Glamoor Good News | Walter and Mrs. Adele F. Goodman |
| 1970 | Boxer | Ch. Arriba's Prima Donna | Dr. and Mrs. P.J. Pagano and Dr. T.S. Fickles |
| 1971–72 | English Springer Spaniel | Ch. Chinoe's Adamant James | Dr. Milton Prickett |
| 1973 | Standard Poodle | Ch. Acadia Command Performance | Mrs. Jo Ann Sering and Edward B. Jenner |
| 1974 | German Shorthaired Pointer | Ch. Gretchenhof Columbia River | Dr. Richard P. Smith |
| 1975 | Old English Sheepdog | Ch. Sir Lancelot of Barvan | Mr. and Mrs. Ronald Vanword |
| 1976 | Lakeland Terrier | Ch. Jo-Ni's Red Baron of Crofton | Virginia Dickson |
| 1977 | Sealyham Terrier | Ch. Dersade Bobby's Girl | Dorothy Wimer |
| 1978 | Yorkshire Terrier | Ch. Cede Higgens | Barbara and Charles Switzer |
| 1979 | Irish Water Spaniel | Ch. Oak Tree's Aristocrat | Mrs. Ann Snelling |
| 1980 | Siberian Husky | Ch. Innisfree's Sierra Cinnar | Mrs. Trish Kanzler |

## BREEDS OF DOGS

The following chart compiled by the American Kennel Club (AKC) lists the 105 largest breeds of the 965,250 purebred dogs registered by the AKC for the year 1979.

| Breed | Count | Breed | Count | Breed | Count |
|---|---|---|---|---|---|
| Poodles | 94,950 | Scottish Terriers | 6,343 | Soft-Coated Wheaten Terriers | 797 |
| Doberman Pinschers | 80,363 | Cairn Terriers | 6,262 | Australian Terriers | 784 |
| Cocker Spaniels | 65,685 | West Highland White Terriers | 6,210 | Welsh Terriers | 691 |
| German Shepherd Dogs | 57,683 | Keeshonden | 5,850 | Standard Schnauzers | 687 |
| Labrador Retrievers | 46,077 | Norwegian Elkhounds | 5,794 | Salukis | 619 |
| Golden Retrievers | 38,060 | Dalmatians | 5,558 | Bearded Collies | 588 |
| Beagles | 35,374 | Pugs | 5,497 | Belgian Sheepdogs | 584 |
| Dachshunds | 32,777 | Weimaraners | 4,605 | Papillons | 576 |
| Miniature Schnauzers | 32,666 | Fox Terriers | 3,762 | Manchester Terriers | 534 |
| Shetland Sheepdogs | 25,943 | Chesapeake Bay Retrievers | 3,460 | Italian Greyhounds | 515 |
| Lhasa Apsos | 22,714 | Rottweilers | 3,286 | Kerry Blue Terriers | 499 |
| Yorkshire Terriers | 22,458 | Silky Terriers | 2,565 | Giant Schnauzers | 496 |
| Collies | 21,210 | Newfoundlands | 2,345 | Belgian Tervuren | 452 |
| Irish Setters | 20,912 | Welsh Corgis (Pembroke) | 2,216 | Japanese Chin | 411 |
| English Springer Spaniels | 20,071 | Bichons Frises | 2,146 | Pointers | 398 |
| Siberian Huskies | 19,876 | Akitas | 1,878 | Tibetan Terriers | 343 |
| Pekingese | 17,992 | Vizslas | 1,737 | Pulik | 341 |
| Brittany Spaniels | 17,038 | Bloodhounds | 1,671 | Welsh Corgis (Cardigan) | 341 |
| Pomeranians | 16,184 | Miniature Pinschers | 1,428 | Bernese Mountain Dogs | 318 |
| Shih Tzu | 16,042 | Basenjis | 1,393 | Irish Terriers | 316 |
| Chihuahuas | 15,512 | Schipperkes | 1,353 | Bedlington Terriers | 311 |
| Great Danes | 15,322 | Bouviers des Flandres | 1,345 | Black And Tan Coonhounds | 302 |
| Basset Hounds | 14,930 | Great Pyrenees | 1,345 | American Water Spaniels | 282 |
| Boxers | 13,250 | Whippets | 1,296 | Staffordshire Bull Terriers | 257 |
| Old English Sheepdogs | 12,018 | Borzois | 1,283 | Briards | 246 |
| Chow Chows | 11,739 | English Setters | 1,263 | Welsh Springer Spaniels | 224 |
| Boston Terriers | 11,125 | Iris Wolfhounds | 1,189 | Norwich Terriers | 205 |
| German Shorthaired Pointers | 10,579 | English Cocker Spaniels | 1,156 | Flat Coated Retrievers | 200 |
| Samoyeds | 8,653 | Gordon Setters | 1,140 | Dandie Dinmont Terriers | 192 |
| St. Bernards | 7,444 | Mastiffs | 1,097 | Lakeland Terriers | 192 |
| Alaskan Malamutes | 7,377 | American Staffordshire Terriers | 1,072 | Skye Terriers | 190 |
| Afghan Hounds | 6,833 | Bull Terriers | 1,042 | Kuvaszok | 180 |
| Maltese | 6,806 | Rhodesian Ridgebacks | 1,029 | Scottish Deerhounds | 174 |
| Airedale Terriers | 6,594 | German Wirehaired Pointers | 978 | Border Terriers | 163 |
| Bulldogs | 6,566 | Bullmastiffs | 804 | Greyhounds | 157 |

## BREEDS OF CATS

**Abyssinian:** *Coat:* ruddy (brown) or red, banded or ticked with darker brown, black, or red: *Eyes:* gold, green hazel.

**American Short Hair:** *Body:* heavily built; *Coat:* short and lustrous, same colors as Persian.

**Angora,** or **Turkish Angora:** *Body and Head:* more elongated than Persian; *Coat:* long-haired, silky; *Eyes:* blue, copper, odd (one blue, one copper).

**Balinese,** or **Long-haired Siamese:** *Body and Coat:* like Siamese except coat is long.

**Himalayan:** *Body:* like Persian; *Coat:* like Balinese.

**Maine Coon:** *Coat:* long-haired in all colors; *Body:* long and powerful; *Head:* medium to broad.

**Manx:** *Body:* tailless and often hops like rabbit; *Coat:* thick, double coat in variety of colors.

**Persian:** *Body:* Short and cobby, wide across shoulders; *Head:* wide with small ears; *Nose:* short; *Coat:* long, flowing, glossy; *Color:* there are five color divisions—Solid, Tabby and Tortie, Smoke, Silver, and Cameo.

**Rex:** *Coat:* curly, like lamb fleece; *Color:* all colors.

**Russian Blue:** *Body:* fine-boned, slender; *Coat:* double-coated, short, thick; *Eyes:* deep green; *Color:* blue with silver tipping.

**Siamese:** *Body:* long, slender with long tail; *Head:* triangular; *Eyes:* deep blue, almond-shaped; *Coat:* short-haired, sandy brown with points (darker colors on face, ears, paws, tail), which from darkest to lightest are called seal, chocolate, blue, lilac, and red. Points may be tortoise or striped.

# RODEOS

Source: The Rodeo Cowboys Association

## ALL-AROUND RODEO COWBOY CHAMPIONS

| Year | Name | Amount | Year | Name | Amount | Year | Name | Amount |
|------|------|--------|------|------|--------|------|------|--------|
| 1951 | Casey Tibbs | $29,104 | 1961 | Benny Reynolds | $31,309 | 1971 | Phil Lyne | $49,245 |
| 1952 | Harry Tompkins | $30,934 | 1962 | Tom Nesmith | $32,611 | 1972 | Phil Lyne | $60,852 |
| 1953 | Bill Linderman | $33,674 | 1963 | Dean Oliver | $31,329 | 1973 | Larry Mahan | $64,447 |
| 1954 | Buck Rutherford | $40,404 | 1964 | Dean Oliver | $31,150 | 1974 | Tom Ferguson | $66,929 |
| 1955 | Casey Tibbs | $42,065 | 1965 | Dean Oliver | $33,163 | 1975 | Leo Camarillo | $50,300 |
| 1956 | Jim Shoulders | $43,381 | 1966 | Larry Mahan | $40,358 | | Tom Ferguson | $50,300 |
| 1957 | Jim Shoulders | $33,299 | 1967 | Larry Mahan | $51,996 | 1976 | Tom Ferguson | $96,913 |
| 1958 | Jim Shoulders | $32,212 | 1968 | Larry Mahan | $49,129 | 1977 | Tom Ferguson | $76,730 |
| 1959 | Jim Shoulders | $32,905 | 1969 | Larry Mahan | $57,726 | 1978 | Tom Ferguson | $131,233 |
| 1960 | Harry Tompkins | $32,522 | 1970 | Larry Mahan | $41,493 | 1979 | Tom Ferguson | $117,222 |

# SHOOTING

## NATIONAL OUTDOOR RIFLE AND PISTOL CHAMPIONSHIPS: 1980

Source: National Rifle Association of America

| EVENT AND WINNER | SCORE | EVENT AND WINNER | SCORE |
|------------------|-------|------------------|-------|
| **High Power Rifle (Perfect Score: 2400-240X)** | | **Pistol (Perfect score: 2700-270X)** | |
| National: C. Bernosky, Gordon, PA | 2374-120X | National: SFC J. Pascarella, NGUS, Las Cruces, NM | 2657-139X |
| Civilian: C. Bernosky, Gordon, PA | 2374-120X | Civilian: Guigno D. Carapellottti, Darby, PA | 2633-111X |
| Service: CW4 Robert L. Goller, USMC, Quantico, VA | 2363-095X | Regular Service: MSG Bonnie Harmon, USA, Ft. Benning, GA | 2635-133X |
| Woman: SSG Anne Joseph, USMCR, Blue Ridge, GA | 2312-066X | Woman: SP4 Ruby E. Fox, USAR, Parker, AZ | 2597-082X |
| Junior: Mark Liebetrau, Black Earth, WI | 2346-077X | Senior: Gil Hebard, Knoxville, IL | 2571-080X |
| Senior: Gerritt Stekeur, Latham, NY | 2319-069X | Police: John L. Farley, Americus, GA | 2604-085X |
| Collegiate: Lt. D. Erickson, USAR, Bellevue, WA | 2353-070X | Collegiate: Russell L. May, Sarasota, FL | 2539-073X |
| **Smallbore Rifle—Prone (Perfect Score: 6400-640X)** | | Junior: Kenneth O. Swanson, Birmingham, AL | 2539-072X |
| National: CPT E. Vande Zande, USA, Ft. Benning, GA | 6396-057X | **National Police Revolver (Perfect Score: 1500-150X)** | |
| Civilian: Carl Jooss, New Albany, OH | 6396-530X | National: Richard M. Collins, Stockton Police Dept., CA | 1495-099X |
| Woman: SP5 M. Stidworthy, Prescott, AZ | 6394-571X | Woman: C. Compton, Dallas–Ft. Worth Air. Police, TX | 1486-090X |
| Junior: R. Wigger, Ft. Benning, GA | 6390-495X | Federal: Larry L. Hausman, U.S. Border Patrol, TX | 1489-103X |
| Sub-Junior: J. Fell, Wallingford, CT | 6345-356X | State: Frank Glenn, Dept. of Public Safety, AZ | 1492-102X |
| Senior: Ransford Triggs, Madison, NJ | 6390-510X | County: A. W. Arrington, Guilford Cty. Sheriff's Dept., NC | 1488-097X |
| Collegiate: SP5 M. Stidworthy, Prescott, AZ | 6394-571X | Municipal: Richard L. Jarvis, Medley Police Dept., FL | 1492-103X |
| **Smallbore Rifle—Position (Perfect Score: 2400)** | | Industrial: Carl S. Kates, McDonnell-Douglas Corp., MO | 1478-079X |
| National: LTC Lones W. Wigger Jr., USA, Ft. Benning, GA | 1745 | Sheriff: A. W. Arrington, Guilford Cty. Sheriff's Dept., NC | 1488-097X |
| Civilian: John Foster, Bozeman, MT | 1693 | Retired: Angelo D. Torrise, San Mateo, CA | 1488-088X |
| Woman: Lt. D. Cannella, Ft. Benning, GA | 1974 | Conservation: Cliff Miller, Alabama Game Game & Fish | 1481-089X |
| Junior: K. Fitz-Randolph, Palm Bay, FL | 1691 | | |
| Sub-Junior: T.M. Leone, Arlington, VA | 1581 | Distinguished: James E. Collins, Alabama State Troopers, AL | 595-034X |
| Senior: D. W. Burtis, Levittown, PA | 1509 | President's: James E. Collins, Ala. State Troopers, AL | 1193-081X |
| College: K. Fitz-Randolph, Palm Bay, FL | 1691 | Shotgun: T.E. Wright, El Paso Police Dept., TX | 749-003X |

## NATIONAL SKEET SHOOTING ASSOCIATION CHAMPIONS: 1980

Source: *Skeet Shooting Review*

**Champion of Champions:**
Champion: T. Bender, San Antonio, TX
Woman: C. Confer, Warren, MI
Senior: J. Vint, Tulsa, OK
Junior: J.C. Martin IV, Laredo, TX

**High Overall Championships:**
Champion: A. Magyar, Allen Pk., MI
Woman: C. Brundage, San Antonio, TX
Senior: E. Farley Jr., Mattapoisett, MA
Junior: B. Wren, Punta Gorda, FL

**28-Gauge Championships:**
Champion: G. Desatoff, Hacienda Hts., Canada
Woman: I. Hill, Brimingham, MI
Senior: L. McAlister, Huntsville, AL
Junior: D. Park, Clemmons, NC

**20-Gauge Championships:**
Champion: B. Evans, Burnet, TX
Woman: S. McCurley, Mobile, AL
Senior: A. Beard, Fairfax, VA
Junior: B. Wren, Punta Gorda, FL

**12-Gauge Championships:**
Champion: T. Killian, San Antonio, TX
Woman: B. Thomas, Brooklyn, NY
Senior: E. Farley Jr., Mattapoisett, MA
Junior: B. Wren, Punta Gorda, FL

**.410-Gauge Championships:**
Champion: W. Mayes, Hixon, TN
Woman: C. Confer, Warren, MI
Senior: J. Vint, Tulsa, OK
Junior: J.C. Martin IV, Laredo, TX

# SHUFFLEBOARD

Source: National Shuffleboard Assn., Inc.

**National Shuffleboard Association Tournament: 1980**

**MEN**
Men's Open: Robert Douthit, Upper Arlington, Ohio
Men's Closed: Charles McGee, Jackson, Michigan
Men's Doubles: Larry Faris, Cincinnati, Ohio
Jay Snoddy, Florida

**WOMEN**
Women's Open: Virginia Worden, Coldwater, Michigan
Women's Closed: Katherine McGreery, Ontario, Canada
Women's Doubles: Mildred Davis, Newcastle, Indiana
Virginia Worden, Coldwater, Michigan

# SKATING

## WORLD SPEED SKATING RECORDS

Source: International Skating Union

**500 METERS: MEN**
Evgeny Kulikov, USSR, March 29, 1975 ..........0:37.00

**1,000 METERS: MEN**
Eric Heiden, U.S., Jan. 13, 1980 ................1:13.60

**1,500 METERS: MEN**
Eric Heiden, U.S., Jan. 19, 1980 ................1:54.79

**3,000 METERS: MEN**
Eric Heiden, U.S., March 2, 1978 ..............4:07.01

**5,000 METERS: MEN**
Kay Arne Stenshjemmet, Norway, March 19, 1977 ......6:56.90

**10,000 METERS: MEN**
Eric Heiden, U.S., Feb. 23, 1980 ...............14:28.13

**500, 1,500, 5,000, AND 10,000 METERS: MEN**
Jan Egil Storholt, Norway, March 19–20, 1977......163.221 pts.

**500, 500, 1,000, AND 1,000 METERS: MEN**
Evgeny Kulikov, USSR, March 20–21, 1976...151.190 pts.

**500 METERS: WOMEN**
Sheila Young, U.S., March 13, 1976 ..............0:40.68

**1,000 METERS: WOMEN**
Natalya Petruseva, USSR, March 27, 1980 . .......1:23.01

**1,500 METERS: WOMEN**
Khalida Vorobyova, USSR, April 10, 1978 .........2:07.18

**3,000 METERS: WOMEN**
Galina Stepanskaya, USSR, March 23, 1976 ......4:31.00

**5,000 METERS: WOMEN**
Bjoerg Eva Jensen, Norway, Nov. 30, 1980........8:05.00

**500, 1,000, 1,500, AND 3,000 METERS: WOMEN**
Galina Stepanskaya, USSR, March 22–23, 1976 ....173.811 pts.

**500, 500, 1,000, AND 1,000 METERS: WOMEN**
Sheila Young, U.S., March 12–13, 1976 ......166.210 pts.

## AMATEUR SKATING UNION OF THE U.S. SPEED SKATING CHAMPIONS: 1980

### NATIONAL OUTDOOR (St. Paul, Minn., Jan. 26–27, 1980)

| | | | |
|---|---|---|---|
| Senior Men | Greg Oly, Minneapolis, Minn. | Senior Women | Shari Miller, Butte, Montana |
| Intermediate Boys | Tom Grannes, Minneapolis, Minn. | Intermediate Girls | Sandra Chobot, West Allis, Wis. |
| Junior Boys | Mike Jansen, West Allis, Wis. | Junior Girls | Angela Zuckerman, Whitefish Bay, Wis. |
| Juvenile Boys | Brian Tetzlaff, St. Paul, Minn. | Juvenile Girls | Anne Hills, St. Paul, Minn. |
| Midget Boys | Frank Filardi, Park Ridge, Ill. | Midget Girls | Maura D'Andrea, Saratoga Spgs., N.Y. |

### NORTH AMERICAN OUTDOOR (Saratoga Springs, N.Y., Feb. 2–3, 1980)

| | | | |
|---|---|---|---|
| Senior Men | Barth Levy, Lakewood, Ohio | Senior Women | Shari Miller, Butte, Montana |
| Intermediate Boys | Tom Grannes, Minneapolis, Minn. | Intermediate Girls | Katie Class, St. Paul, Minn. |
| Junior Boys | Paul Grannes, Minneapolis, Minn. | Junior Girls | Angela Zuckerman, Whitefish Bay, Wis. |
| Juvenile Boys | Brian Tetzlaff, St. Paul, Minn. | Juvenile Girls | Anne Hills, St. Paul, Minn. |
| Midget Boys | Derrick Auch, Manitoba, Canada | Midget Girls | Maura D'Andrea, Saratoga Spgs., N.Y. |

### NATIONAL INDOOR (Wyandotte, Mich., Mar. 21–23, 1980)

| | | | |
|---|---|---|---|
| Senior Men | Barth Levy, Lakewood, Ohio | Senior Women (tie) | Pam Mercer, Wyandotte, Mich. |
| Intermediate Boys | Charles Riddle, Wyandotte, Mich. | | Debbie Carlstrom, Des Plaines, Ill. |
| Junior Boys | Tom Carter, Park Ridge, Ill. | Intermediate Girls | Ann Klopp, St. Paul, Minn. |
| Juvenile Boys | Tony Meibock, Fairview Park, Ohio | Junior Girls | Lisa Parfitt, Alpena, Mich. |
| Midget Boys | Jeff Frank, Ossineke, Mich. | Juvenile Girls | Megan McConville, Lakewood, Ohio |
| | | Midget Girls | Maura D'Andrea, Saratoga Spgs., N.Y. |

### NORTH AMERICAN INDOOR (Esquimalt B.C., Canada, Mar. 28–30, 1980)

| | | | |
|---|---|---|---|
| Senior Men | Gaetan Boucher, Quebec, Canada | Senior Women | Cathy Turnbull, Saskat., Canada |
| Intermediate Boys | Michel Desisle, Quebec, Canada | Intermediate Girls | Louise Begin, Quebec, Canada |
| Junior Boys | Randy Ljuden, B.C., Canada | Junior Girls | Maryse Perreault, Quebec, Canada |
| Juvenile Boys | Benoit Lamarche, Quebec, Canada | Juvenile Girls | Loi Ljuden, B.C., Canada |
| Midget Boys | Derrick Auch, Manitoba, Canada | Midget Girls | Maura D'Andrea, Saratoga Spgs., N.Y. |

## FIGURE SKATING CHAMPIONS

### UNITED STATES FIGURE SKATING CHAMPIONS: MEN

| | | | | | | | |
|---|---|---|---|---|---|---|---|
| 1951–52 | Dick Button | 1962 | Monty Hoyt | 1966 | Scott Allen | 1972 | Ken Shelley |
| 1953–56 | Hayes Jenkins | 1963 | Tommy Litz | 1967 | Gary Visconti | 1973–75 | Gordon McKellen Jr. |
| 1957–60 | Dave Jenkins | 1964 | Scott Allen | 1968–70 | Tim Wood | 1976 | Terry Kubicka |
| 1961 | Bradley Lord | 1965 | Gary Visconti | 1971 | John Petkvich | 1977–80 | Charles Tickner |

### UNITED STATES FIGURE SKATING CHAMPIONS: WOMEN

| | | | | | | | |
|---|---|---|---|---|---|---|---|
| 1957–60 | Carol Heiss | 1962 | Barbara Pursley | 1964–68 | Peggy Fleming | 1974–76 | Dorothy Hamill |
| 1961 | Laurence Owen | 1963 | Lorraine Hanlon | 1968–73 | Janet Lynn | 1977–80 | Linda Fratianne |

### WORLD FIGURE SKATING CHAMPIONS: MEN

| | | | | | |
|---|---|---|---|---|---|
| 1951–52 | Dick Button, U.S. | 1964 | M. Schnelldorfer, W. Germany | 1975 | Sergei Volkov, USSR |
| 1953–56 | Hayes Jenkins, U.S. | 1965 | Alain Calmat, France | 1976 | John Curry, Britain |
| 1957–59 | Dave Jenkins, U.S. | 1966–68 | Emmerich Danzer, Austria | 1977 | Vladimir Kovalev, USSR |
| 1960 | Alain Giletti, France | 1969–70 | Tim Wood, U.S. | 1978 | Charles Tickner, U.S. |
| 1962 | Don Jackson, Canada | 1971–73 | Ondrej Nepela, Czech. | 1979 | Vladimir Kovalev, USSR |
| 1963 | Don McPherson, Canada | 1974 | Jan Hoffman, E. Germany | 1980 | Jan Hoffman, E. Germany |

### WORLD FIGURE SKATING CHAMPIONS: WOMEN

| | | | | | |
|---|---|---|---|---|---|
| 1952 | Jacqueline du Bief, France | 1965 | Petra Burka, Canada | 1975 | Dianne deLeeuw, Netherlands |
| 1953 | Tenley Albright, U.S. | 1966–68 | Peggy Fleming, U.S. | 1976 | Dorothy Hamill, U.S. |
| 1954 | Gundi Busch, W. Germany | 1969–70 | Gabriele Seyfert, E. Germany | 1977 | Linda Fratianne, U.S. |
| 1955 | Tenley Albright, U.S. | 1971–72 | Beatrix Schuba, Austria | 1978 | Anett Poetzsch, E. Germany |
| 1956–60 | Carol Heiss, U.S. | 1973 | Karen Magnussen, Canada | 1979 | Linda Fratianne, U.S. |
| 1962–64 | Sjoukje Dijkstra, Netherlands | 1974 | Christine Errath, E. Germany | 1980 | Anett Poetzsch, E. Germany |

# SKIING

A brother and sister from Liechtenstein captured World Cups in Alpine skiing in March 1980. Hanni Wenzel, 23, captured the women's overall title, and her brother, Andreas Wenzel, 22, won the men's crown.

Three-time World Cup winner Ingemar Stenmark won every other honor in international skiing during the season, including two gold medals at the Olympic Games.

American skiers Steve Mahre and Christin Cooper swept to victory in the slalom competition at the U.S. Alpine skiing championships in Squaw Valley, Calif., in March. Miss Cooper also won the giant slalom race.

Stan Dunklee and Alison Owen-Spencer won the first United States cross-country skiing championships ever held in Canada when they swept to victory at Mont Ste. Anne, Quebec, in the 30-kilometer and 10-kilometer races, respectively, on Jan. 28.

## WORLD CUP CHAMPIONS—MEN

| | | | | | |
|---|---|---|---|---|---|
| 1967–68 | Jean-Claude Killy, France | 1973 | Gustavo Thoeni, Italy | 1977 | Ingemar Stenmark, Sweden |
| 1969–70 | Karl Schranz, Austria | 1974 | Piero Gros, Italy | 1978 | Ingemar Stenmark, Sweden |
| 1971 | Gustavo Thoeni, Italy | 1975 | Gustavo Thoeni, Italy | 1979 | Peter Luescher, Switzerland |
| 1972 | Gustavo Thoeni, Italy | 1976 | Ingemar Stenmark, Sweden | 1980 | Andreas Wenzel, Liechtenstein |

## WORLD CUP CHAMPIONS—WOMEN

| | | | | | |
|---|---|---|---|---|---|
| 1967–68 | Nancy Greene, Canada | 1971–75 | Annemarie Proell, Austria | 1978 | Hanni Wenzel, Liechtenstein |
| 1969 | Gertrud Gabl, Austria | 1976 | Rosi Mittermaier, W. Germany | 1979 | Annemarie Proell Moser, Austria |
| 1970 | Michele Jacot, France | 1977 | Lisa-Marie Morerod, Switzerland | 1980 | Hanni Wenzel, Liechtenstein |

## NCAA SKIING CHAMPIONSHIPS

The University of Vermont won its first NCAA skiing championship at Stowe, Vt., in March 1980. Vermont finished with 171 points, while second-place Utah collected 151. Colorado ended its eight-year reign by finishing third, with 98 points.

### NCAA TEAM CHAMPIONS

| | | | | | | | | | | | |
|---|---|---|---|---|---|---|---|---|---|---|---|
| 1954–57 | Denver | 1961 | Denver | 1965 | Denver | 1969–71 | Denver | 1975 | Colorado | 1978 | Colorado |
| 1958 | Dartmouth | 1962 | Denver | 1966 | Denver | 1972 | Colorado | 1976 | Colorado | 1979 | Colorado |
| 1959 | Colorado | 1963 | Denver | 1967 | Denver | 1973 | Colorado | | Dartmouth | 1980 | Vermont |
| 1960 | Colorado | 1964 | Denver | 1968 | Wyoming | 1974 | Colorado | 1977 | Colorado | | |

### NCAA DOWNHILL CHAMPIONS

| | | | | | |
|---|---|---|---|---|---|
| 1954 | Pat Myers, Nevada | 1963 | Dave Gorusch, Western Colorado | 1970–72 | Otto Tschudi, Denver |
| 1955 | Chiharu Igaya, Dartmouth | | Bill Marolt, Colorado | 1973 | Bob Cochran, Vermont |
| 1956 | Walt Taulvee, Washington | | Buddy Werner, Colorado | 1974 | Larry Kennison, Wyoming |
| 1957 | Ralph Miller, Dartmouth | 1964 | John Clough, Middlebury | 1975 | Mark Ford, Colorado |
| 1958 | Gary Vaughn, Norwich | 1965 | Bill Marolt, Colorado | 1976 | Dave Cleveland, Dartmouth * |
| 1959 | Marvin Melville, Utah | 1966 | Terje Overland, Denver | 1977 | Stephen Hienzsch, Colorado |
| 1960 | Dave Butts, Colorado | 1967 | Dennis McCoy, Denver | 1978 | Dale Merrill, Wyoming * |
| 1961 | Gordon Eaton, Middlebury | 1968 | Barney Peet, Fort Lewis | 1979 | Chris Mikell, Vermont * |
| 1962 | Mike Baar, Denver | 1969 | Mike Lafferty, Colorado | 1980 | John Teague, Vermont * |

\* Giant Slalom

### NCAA SLALOM CHAMPIONS

| | | | | | |
|---|---|---|---|---|---|
| 1955–57 | Chiharu Igaya, Dartmouth | 1965 | Rick Chaffee, Denver | 1973 | Peik Christensen, Denver |
| 1958 | Robert Gebhardt, Dartmouth | 1966 | Bill Marolt, Colorado | 1974 | Bill Shaw, Boise State |
| 1959 | Marvin Melville, Utah | 1967 | Rick Chaffee, Denver | 1975 | Peik Christensen, Denver |
| 1960 | Rudy Ruana, Montana | 1968 | Dennis McCoy, Denver | 1976 | Mike Meleski, Wyoming |
| 1961 | Buddy Werner, Colorado | 1969 | Paul Rachetto, Denver | 1977 | Stephen Hienzsch, Colorado |
| 1962 | Jim Gaddis, Utah | 1970 | Mike Porcarelli, Colorado | 1978 | Dan Brelsford, Montana |
| 1963 | James Heuga, Colorado | 1971 | Otto Tschudi, Denver | 1979 | Per Nicholaysen, Utah |
| 1964 | John Clough, Middlebury | 1972 | Mike Porcarelli, Colorado | 1980 | Bret Williams, No. Michigan |

### NCAA JUMPING CHAMPIONS

| | | | | | |
|---|---|---|---|---|---|
| 1958 | Oddvar Ronnestead, Denver | 1965 | Erik Jansen, Denver | 1973 | Vidar Nilsgard, Colorado |
| 1959 | Dave Butts, Colorado | 1966 | Frithjof Prydz, Utah | 1974–75 | Didrik Ellefsen, Colorado |
| 1960 | Dag Helgestad, Washington State | 1967 | Bjorn Loken, Utah | 1976 | Kip Sundgaard, Utah |
| 1961 | Cris Selback, Denver | 1968 | Peter Robes, Wyoming | 1977 | Ron Steele, Utah |
| 1962 | Oyvind Floystad, Denver | 1969 | Odd Hammernes, Denver | 1978 | Tom Jensen, Colorado |
| 1963 | Tom Nord, Washington | 1970 | Jay Rand, Colorado | | Kare Herje, Vermont |
| 1964 | Frithjof Prydz, Utah | 1971 | Vidar Nilsgard, Colorado | 1979 | Roger Holden, Vermont |
| | Erik Jansen, Denver | 1972 | Odd Hammernes, Denver | 1980 | Jorn Stromberg, Wyoming |

### NCAA CROSS COUNTRY CHAMPIONS

| | | | | | |
|---|---|---|---|---|---|
| 1955 | Larry Damon, Vermont | 1963 | Eddie Demers, Western Colorado | 1973–75 | Steinar Hypertsen, Wyoming |
| 1956 | Erik Berggren, Idaho | 1964 | Eddie Demers, Western Colorado | 1976 | Stan Dunklee, Vermont |
| 1957 | Mack Miller, Western Colorado | 1965–66 | Mike Elliot, Fort Lewis | 1977 | Helge Aamodt, Colorado |
| 1958–59 | Clarence Servold, Denver | 1967 | Ned Gillette, Dartmouth | 1978 | Sigurd Kjerpeseth, Colarado |
| 1960 | John Denhahl, Colorado | 1968–69 | Clark Matis, Colorado | 1979 | Svein Arne Olsen, Utah |
| 1961 | Charles Akers, Maine | 1970–71 | Ole Hansen, Denver | 1980 | Pal Sjulstad, Vermont |
| 1962 | James Page, Dartmouth | 1972 | Stale Engen, Wyoming | | |

# SOCCER

The New York Cosmos won Soccer Bowl-80, the North American Soccer League championship, on Sept. 21, at RFK Stadium in Washington, D.C. New York captured its third league title by defeating the Fort Lauderdale Strikers, 3–0. Giorgio Chinaglia scored two goals in the second half after Julio Cesar Romero got the first at 2 minutes 55 seconds after the halftime intermission.

Chinaglia won the NASL scoring championship for the third time in five years. He scored 32 goals in 32 games during the regular season, along with 13 assists. The Cosmos' Jeff Durgan was voted NASL Rookie of the Year.

On their way to the championship, the Cosmos defeated the Los Angeles Aztecs, 3–1, to gain the National Conference title. The Fort Lauderdale Strikers downed San Diego, 2–0, for the American Conference championship.

## NORTH AMERICAN SOCCER LEAGUE

### 1980 FINAL STANDINGS

| | Games Played | Won | Lost | Goals For | Goals Against | Bonus Points | Points |
|---|---|---|---|---|---|---|---|
| **NATIONAL CONFERENCE** | | | | | | | |
| **Eastern Division** | | | | | | | |
| New York Cosmos | 32 | 24 | 8 | 87 | 41 | 69 | 213 |
| Washington Diplomats | 32 | 17 | 15 | 72 | 61 | 57 | 159 |
| Toronto Blizzard | 32 | 14 | 18 | 49 | 65 | 44 | 128 |
| Rochester Lancers | 32 | 12 | 20 | 42 | 67 | 37 | 109 |
| **Central Division** | | | | | | | |
| Dallas Tornado | 32 | 18 | 14 | 57 | 58 | 49 | 157 |
| Minnesota Kicks | 32 | 16 | 16 | 66 | 56 | 51 | 147 |
| Tulsa Roughnecks | 32 | 15 | 17 | 56 | 62 | 49 | 139 |
| Atlanta Chiefs | 32 | 7 | 25 | 34 | 84 | 32 | 74 |
| **Western Division** | | | | | | | |
| Seattle Sounders | 32 | 25 | 7 | 74 | 31 | 57 | 207 |
| Los Angeles Aztecs | 32 | 20 | 12 | 61 | 52 | 54 | 174 |
| Vancouver Whitecaps | 32 | 16 | 16 | 52 | 47 | 43 | 139 |
| Portland Timbers | 32 | 15 | 17 | 50 | 53 | 43 | 133 |
| **AMERICAN CONFERENCE** | | | | | | | |
| **Eastern Division** | | | | | | | |
| Tampa Bay Rowdies | 32 | 19 | 13 | 61 | 50 | 54 | 168 |
| Fort Lauderdale Strikers | 32 | 18 | 14 | 61 | 55 | 55 | 163 |
| New England Tea Men | 32 | 18 | 14 | 54 | 56 | 46 | 154 |
| Philadelphia Fury | 32 | 10 | 22 | 42 | 68 | 38 | 98 |
| **Central Division** | | | | | | | |
| Chicago Sting | 32 | 21 | 11 | 80 | 50 | 61 | 187 |
| Houston Hurricane | 32 | 14 | 18 | 56 | 69 | 46 | 130 |
| Detroit Express | 32 | 14 | 18 | 51 | 52 | 45 | 129 |
| Memphis Rogues | 32 | 14 | 18 | 49 | 57 | 42 | 126 |
| **Western Division** | | | | | | | |
| Edmonton Drillers | 32 | 17 | 15 | 58 | 51 | 47 | 149 |
| California Surf | 32 | 15 | 17 | 61 | 67 | 54 | 144 |
| San Diego Sockers | 32 | 16 | 16 | 53 | 51 | 44 | 140 |
| San Jose Earthquakes | 32 | 9 | 23 | 45 | 68 | 41 | 95 |

### NASL CHAMPIONS: 1968–1980

| | | | | | | | |
|---|---|---|---|---|---|---|---|
| 1968 | Atlanta Chiefs | 1971 | Dallas Tornado | 1974 | Los Angeles Aztecs | 1977–78 | New York Cosmos |
| 1969 | Kansas City Spurs | 1972 | New York Cosmos | 1975 | Tampa Bay Rowdies | 1979 | Vancouver Whitecaps |
| 1970 | Rochester Lancers | 1973 | Philadelphia Atoms | 1976 | Toronto Metros | 1980 | New York Cosmos |

## WORLD CUP

The World Cup soccer championship is played every four years, although the cycle was broken between 1938 and 1950 because of World War II. The 1982 games are to be in Spain.

| YEAR | CHAMPIONSHIP FINAL | HOST | YEAR | CHAMPIONSHIP FINAL | HOST |
|---|---|---|---|---|---|
| 1934 | Italy 2, Czechoslovakia 1 | Italy | 1962 | Brazil 3, Czechoslovakia 1 | Chile |
| 1938 | Italy 4, Hungary 2 | France | 1966 | England 4, West Germany 2 | England |
| 1950 | Uruguay 2, Brazil 1 | Brazil | 1970 | Brazil 4, Italy 1 | Mexico |
| 1954 | West Germany 3, Hungary 2 | Switzerland | 1974 | West Germany 2, Netherlands 1 | West Germany |
| 1958 | Brazil 5, Sweden 2 | Sweden | 1978 | Argentina 3, Netherlands 1 | Argentina |

## NCAA SOCCER

| YEAR | CHAMPION | RUNNER-UP | SCORE | HOST |
|---|---|---|---|---|
| 1973–74 | St. Louis University | UCLA | 2–1 | Orange Bowl, Miami, Fla. |
| 1974–75 | Howard University | St. Louis University | 2–1 | St. Louis University |
| 1975–76 | San Francisco University | Southern Illinois University | 4–0 | Southern Illinois University |
| 1976–77 | San Francisco University | Indiana | 1–0 | University of Pennsylvania |
| 1977–78 | Hartwick College | San Francisco University | 2–1 | San Francisco University |
| 1978–79 | San Francisco University | Indiana | 2–0 | Tampa Stadium |
| 1979–80 | Southern Illinois, Edwardsville | Clemson | 3–2 | Tampa Stadium |
| 1980–81 | San Francisco University | Indiana | 4–3 | Tampa Stadium |

# SWIMMING

## U.S. INDOOR SWIMMING AND DIVING NATIONAL CHAMPIONSHIPS: 1980

Held at Austin, Texas, April 9–12, 1980.

### MEN'S EVENTS

**Freestyle:**
50-Meter: Gary Schatz, 0:22.86
100-Meter: Rowdy Gaines, 0:49.61*
200-Meter: Rowdy Gaines, 1:49.16*
400-Meter: Mike Bruner, 3:52.24
800-Meter: Djan Madruga, 7:59.85*
1,500-Meter: Mike Bruner, 15:19.76
**Breaststroke:**
100-Meter: Steve Lundquist, 1:03.08*
200-Meter: Glenn Mills, 2:18.03
**Backstroke:**
100-Meter: Peter Rocca, 56.66
200-Meter: Peter Rocca, 2:00.73

**Butterfly:**
100-Meter: Par Arvidsson, 54.20*
200-Meter: Mike Bruner, 1:59.48
**Individual Medley:**
200-Meter: Chris Cavanaugh, 2:04.77
400-Meter: Djan Madruga, 4:25.30
**Relay Events:**
400-Meter Medley: Concord Pleasant Hill 'A' team, 3:46.06
400-Meter Freestyle: Florida Aquatics, 3:21.93
800-Meter Freestyle: Concord Pleasant Hill 'A' team, 7:29.29

**Diving Events:**
One-Meter Springboard: Greg Louganis, 857.43 pts.
Three-Meter Springboard: Greg Louganis, 963.30 pts.
Ten-Meter Platform: Bruce Kimball, 816.97 pts.

**Swimming Team Champion:**
Mission Viejo Nadadores
**Individual High Point Award (Kiputh Award):**
Mike Bruner, Mesa Aquatics

### WOMEN'S EVENTS

**Freestyle:**
50-Meter: Jill Sterkel, 25.96*
100-Meter: Jill Sterkel, 56.12
200-Meter: Marybeth Linzmeier, 2:00.21
400-Meter: Kim Linehan, 4:09.58
800-Meter: Kim Linehan, 8:27.82
1,500-Meter: Kim Linehan, 16:15.56
**Breaststroke:**
100-Meter: Tracy Caulkins, 1:11.34
200-Meter: Tracy Caulkins, 2:33.06*
**Backstroke:**
100-Meter: Sue Walsh, 1:03.34
200-Meter: Libby Kinkead, 2:14.59

**Butterfly:**
100-Meter: Mary T. Meagher, 59.26*
200-Meter: Mary T. Meagher, 2:08.69
**Individual Medley:**
200-Meter: Tracy Caulkins, 2:14.73
400-Meter: Anne Tweedy, 4:49.69
**Relay Events:**
400-Meter Medley: Cincinnati Pepsi Marlins 'A', 4:11.59
400-Meter Freestyle: Longhorn Aquatics 'A', 3:48.23
800-Meter Freestyle: Longhorn Aquatics 'A', 8:14.76*

**Diving Events:**
One-Meter Springboard: Karen Gorham, 647.77 pts.
Three-Meter Springboard: Carrie Finneran, 685.65 pts.
Ten-Meter Platform: Christine Loock, 585.87 pts.

**Swimming Team Champions:**
Cincinnati Pepsi Marlins
**Individual High Point Award (Kiputh Award):**
Tracy Caulkins, Nashville AC

\* New American Record

## WORLD SWIMMING RECORDS

Source: United States Swimming

### MEN'S RECORDS

| EVENTS | TIME | SWIMMER AND NATION | DATE | SITE |
|---|---|---|---|---|
| 100-Meter Freestyle | 0:49.44 | Jonty Skinner, South Africa | 8-14-76 | Philadelphia, Pa. |
| 200-Meter Freestyle | 1:49.16 | Rowdy Gaines, U.S. | 4-11-80 | Austin, Texas |
| 400-Meter Freestyle | 3:50.49 | Peter Szmidt, Canada | 7-16-80 | Ontario, Canada |
| 800-Meter Freestyle | 7:56.49 | Vladimir Salnikov, Soviet Union | 3-23-79 | Moscow, Soviet Union |
| 1,500-Meter Freestyle | 14:58.27 | Vladimir Salnikov, Soviet Union | 7-22-80 | Moscow, Soviet Union |
| 100-Meter Breaststroke | *1:02.86 | Gerald Moerken, E. Germany | 8-17-77 | Jönköping, Sweden |
| 200-Meter Breaststroke | 2:15.11 | David Wilkie, U.S. | 7-24-76 | Montreal, Canada |
| 100-Meter Butterfly | 0:54.15 | Par Arvidsson, Sweden | 4-11-80 | Austin, Texas |
| 200-Meter Butterfly | 1:58.21 | Craig Beardsley, U.S. | 7-30-80 | Irvine, California |
| 100-Meter Backstroke | 0:55.49 | John Naber, U.S. | 7-19-76 | Montreal, Canada |
| 200-Meter Backstroke | 1:59.19 | John Naber, U.S. | 7-24-76 | Montreal, Canada |
| 200-Meter Individual Medley | 2:03.24 | Bill Barrett, U.S. | 8-1-80 | Irvine, California |
| 400-Meter Individual Medley | 4:20.05 | Jesse Vassallo, U.S. | 8-22-78 | Berlin, W. Germany |
| 400-Meter Freestyle Relay | 3:19.74 | United States team | 8-22-78 | Berlin, W. Germany |
| 800-Meter Freestyle Relay | 7:20.82 | United States team | 8-24-78 | Berlin, W. Germany |
| 400-Meter Medley Relay | 3:42.22 | United States team | 7-22-76 | Montreal, Canada |

### WOMEN'S RECORDS

| 100-Meter Freestyle | 0:54.79 | Barbara Krause, East Germany | 7-21-80 | Moscow, Soviet Union |
|---|---|---|---|---|
| 200-Meter Freestyle | 1:58.23 | Cynthia Woodhead, U.S. | 9-3-79 | Tokyo, Japan |
| 400-Meter Freestyle | 4:06.28 | Tracey Wickham, Australia | 8-24-78 | Berlin, W. Germany |
| 800-Meter Freestyle | *8:18.77 | Cynthia Woodhead, U.S. | 2-8-80 | Paris, France |
| 1,500-Meter Freestyle | 16:04.49 | Kim Linehan, U.S. | 8-19-79 | Fort Lauderdale, Fla. |
| 100-Meter Breaststroke | 1:10.11 | Ute Geweniger, East Germany | 7-24-80 | Moscow, Soviet Union |
| 200-Meter Breaststroke | 2:28.36 | Lina Kachushite, Soviet Union | 4-6-79 | Potsdam, E. Germany |
| 100-Meter Butterfly | *0:59.26 | Mary Meagher, U.S. | 4-11-80 | Austin, Texas |
| 200-Meter Butterfly | 2:06.37 | Mary Meagher, U.S. | 7-30-80 | Irvine, California |
| 100-Meter Backstroke | 1:00.86 | Rica Reinisch, East Germany | 7-23-80 | Moscow, Soviet Union |
| 200-Meter Backstroke | 2:11.77 | Rica Reinisch, East Germany | 7-27-80 | Moscow, Soviet Union |
| 200-Meter Individual Medley | *2:13.00 | Petra Schneider, East Germany | 5-24-80 | Magdeburg, E. Germany |
| 400-Meter Individual Medley | 4:36.29 | Petra Schneider, East Germany | 7-26-80 | Moscow, Soviet Union |
| 400-Meter Freestyle Relay | 3:42.71 | East German team | 7-27-80 | Moscow, Soviet Union |
| 400-Meter Medley Relay | 4:07.95 | East German team | 7-18-76 | Montreal, Canada |

\* Pending official recognition.

# 1980 UNITED STATES OUTDOOR SWIMMING NATIONAL CHAMPIONSHIPS

Held at Irvine, Calif., July 29-Aug. 2, 1980.

## MEN'S EVENTS

| EVENT | SWIMMER AND CLUB | TIME |
|---|---|---|
| 50 meter Freestyle | Joe Bottom, Walnut Creek | 23.07 |
| 100 meter Freestyle | Rowdy Gaines, Florida Aquatic | 50.19 |
| 200 meter Freestyle | Rowdy Gaines, Florida Aquatic | 1:50.02 |
| 400 meter Freestyle | Mike Bruner, Mesa Aquatics | 3:52.19 |
| 800 meter Freestyle | Brian Goodell, Mission Viejo Nadadores | 7:59.66 |
| 1500 meter Freestyle | Mike Bruner, Mesa Aquatics | 15:19.80 |
| 100 meter Backstroke | Peter Rocca, Concord Pleasant Hill | 56.64 |
| 200 meter Backstroke | Steve Barnicoat, Mission Viejo Nadadores | 2:01.06 |
| 100 meter Breaststroke | Steve Lundquist, Dr. Pepper | 1:02.88 |
| 200 meter Breaststroke | Glenn Mills, Cincinnati Pepsi Marlins | 2:18.78 |
| 100 meter Butterfly | William Paulus, Longhorn Aquatic | 54.34 |
| 200 meter Butterfly | Craig Beardsley, Florida Aquatic | 1:58.21 |
| 200 meter Individual Medley | Bill Barrett, Cincinnati Pepsi Marlins | 2:03.62 |
| 400 meter Individual Medley | Jesse Vassallo, Mission Viejo Nadadores | 4:21.51 |
| 400 meter Medley Relay | Dr. Pepper Swim Team | 3:47.13 |
| 400 meter Freestyle Relay | Florida Aquatic Swim Team | 3:22.24 |
| 800 meter Freestyle Relay | Florida Aquatic Swim Team | 7:26.67 |

## WOMEN'S EVENTS

| EVENT | SWIMMER AND CLUB | TIME |
|---|---|---|
| 50 meter Freestyle | Jill Sterkel, Longhorn Aquatic | 26.21 |
| 100 meter Freestyle | Cynthia Woodhead, Unattached | 56.57 |
| 200 meter Freestyle | Cynthia Woodhead, Unattached | 1:59.44 |
| 400 meter Freestyle | Kim Linehan, Longhorn Aquatic | 4:07.77 |
| 800 meter Freestyle | Kim Linehan, Longhorn Aquatic | 8:27.86 |
| 1500 meter Freestyle | Kim Linehan, Longhorn Aquatic | 16:21.74 |
| 100 meter Backstroke | Linda Jezek, Cardinal | 1:03.16 |
| 200 meter Backstroke | Linda Jezek, Cardinal | 2:14.52 |
| 100 meter Breaststroke | Tracy Caulkins, Nashville Aquatic | 1:10.40 |
| 200 meter Breaststroke | TIE—Tracy Caulkins, Nashville Aquatic, and Terri Baxter, Ladera Oaks | 2:34.66 |
| 100 meter Butterfly | Mary T. Meagher, Cincinnati Pepsi Marlins | 59.41 |
| 200 meter Butterfly | Mary T. Meagher, Cincinnati Pepsi Marlins | 2:06.37 |
| 200 meter Individual Medley | Tracy Caulkins, Nashville Aquatic | 2:14.64 |
| 400 meter Individual Medley | Tracy Caulkins, Nashville Aquatic | 4:40.61 |
| 400 meter Medley Relay | Cincinnati Pepsi Marlins | 4:17.81 |
| 400 meter Freestyle Relay | Cincinnati Pepsi Marlins | 3:48.83 |
| 800 meter Freestyle Relay | Cincinnati Pepsi Marlins | 8:13.07 |

## TEAM CHAMPIONS
MEN: TIE—Florida Aquatic Swim Team and Mission Viejo Nadadores; WOMEN: Cincinnati Pepsi Marlins; COMBINED: Cincinnati Pepsi Marlins

## INDIVIDUAL HIGH POINT WINNERS
MEN: Mike Bruner, Mesa Aquatics; WOMEN: Tracy Caulkins, Nashville Aquatic

# NATIONAL COLLEGIATE ATHLETIC ASSOCIATION SWIMMING CHAMPIONS

## NCAA TEAM CHAMPIONS

| | | | | |
|---|---|---|---|---|
| 1949–50 Ohio State | 1953 Yale | 1960 USC | 1963–66 USC | 1974–77 USC |
| 1951 Yale | 1954–56 Ohio State | 1961 Michigan | 1967 Stanford | 1978 Tenn. |
| 1952 Ohio State | 1957–59 Michigan | 1962 Ohio State | 1968–73 Indiana | 1979–80 California |

## 50-YARD FREESTYLE

| | | |
|---|---|---|
| 1969 Dan Frawley, USC 0:21.040 | 1973 John Trembley, Tenn. 0:20.377 | 1977 Joe Bottom, USC 0:19.750 |
| 1970 David Edgar, Tennessee 0:20.930 | 1974 John Trembley, Tenn. 0:20.230 | 1978 Andy Coan, Tennessee 0:20.290 |
| 1971 David Edgar, Tennessee 0:20.300 | 1975 Joe Bottom, USC 0:20.118 | 1979 Ambrose Gaines, Auburn 0:19.990 |
| 1972 David Edgar, Tennessee 0:20.442 | 1976 Joe Bottom, USC 0:20.081 | 1980 Andy Coan, Tennessee 0:19.920 |

## 100-YARD FREESTYLE

| | | |
|---|---|---|
| 1969 Fran Heath, UCLA 0:46.240 | 1973 John Trembley, Tenn. 0:45.090 | 1977 David Fairbank, Stanford 0:43.680 |
| 1970 David Edgar, Tennessee 0:46.060 | 1974 Joe Bottom, USC 0:45.067 | 1978 Andy Coan, Tennessee 0:44.100 |
| 1971 David Edgar, Tennessee 0:44.690 | 1975 Jonty Skinner, Alabama 0:43.927 | 1979 Andy Coan, Tennessee 0:43.420 |
| 1972 David Edgar, Tennessee 0:45.003 | 1976 James Montgomery, Ind. 0:44.400 | 1980 Ambrose Gaines, Auburn 0:43.360 |

## 200-YARD FREESTYLE

| | | |
|---|---|---|
| 1969 Mark Spitz, Indiana 1:39.530 | 1973 James McConica, USC 1:39.600 | 1977 Bruce Furniss, USC 1:36.160 |
| 1970 Juan Bello, Michigan 1:42.700 | 1974 James Montgomery, Ind. 1:39.188 | 1978 Bruce Furniss, USC 1:37.020 |
| 1971 James McConica, USC 1:39.750 | 1975 G. McDonnell, UCLA 1:38.042 | 1979 Andy Coan, Tennessee 1:35.620 |
| 1972 J. Heidenreich, So. Meth. 1:38.357 | 1976 James Montgomery, Ind. 1:36.530 | 1980 Ambrose Gaines, Auburn 1:34.570 |

## 500-YARD FREESTYLE

| | | |
|---|---|---|
| 1969 Mark Spitz, Indiana 4:33.480 | 1973 John Kinsella, Indiana 4:27.593 | 1977 Tim Shaw, Long Beach St. 4:17.390 |
| 1970 Mike Burton, UCLA 4:37.290 | 1974 John Naber, USC 4:26.855 | 1978 Brian Goodell, UCLA 4:18.050 |
| 1971 John Kinsella, Indiana 4:27.390 | 1975 John Naber, USC 4:20.450 | 1979 Brian Goodell, UCLA 4:16.430 |
| 1972 John Kinsella, Indiana 4:24.496 | 1976 Tim Shaw, Long Beach St. 4:19.053 | 1980 Brian Goodell, UCLA 4:17.810 |

## NCAA SWIMMING AND DIVING CHAMPIONS (continued)

### 1,650–YARD FREESTYLE

| | | | |
|---|---|---|---|
| 1969 H. Fassnacht, Long B. .. 15:54.210 | 1973 John Kinsella, Indiana .. 15:29.200 | 1977 Keith Converse, Alabama . 14:57.300 |
| 1970 Mike Burton, UCLA...... 16:10.590 | 1974 Jack Tingley, USC ..... 15:29.287 | 1978 Brian Goodell, UCLA .... 14:55.530 |
| 1971 John Kinsella, Indiana ... 15:26.510 | 1975 M. Bruner, Stanford ... 15:16.540 | 1979 Brian Goodell, UCLA ..... 14:54.130 |
| 1972 John Kinsella, Indiana ... 15:33.582 | 1976 Tim Shaw, Long Beach St. 15:06.760 | 1980 Brian Goodell, UCLA ..... 14:54.070 |

### 100–YARD BACKSTROKE

| | | |
|---|---|---|
| 1969 Fred Haywood, Stanford . 0:52.440 | 1973 Mike Stamm, Indiana.... 0:50.910 | 1977 John Naber, USC ........ 0:49.360 |
| 1970 Larry Barbiere, Indiana .. 0:51.910 | 1974 John Naber, USC ....... 0:50.516 | 1978 Robert Jackson, Long Bch. . 0:49.880 |
| 1971 S. Esteva, Indiana ........ 0:51.710 | 1975 John Naber, USC ....... 0:49.947 | 1979 Carlos Berrocal, Alabama .. 0:49.710 |
| 1972 Paul Gilbert, Yale ........ 0:51.293 | 1976 John Naber, USC ....... 0:49.940 | 1980 Clay Britt, Texas .......... 0:49.520 |

### 200–YARD BACKSTROKE

| | | |
|---|---|---|
| 1969 Charlie Hickcox, Indiana . 1:53.670 | 1973 Mike Stamm, Indiana .... 1:50.560 | 1977 John Naber, USC ........ 1:46.090 |
| 1970 Mitch Ivey, Long Bch. ... 1:52.770 | 1974 John Naber, USC ....... 1:48.950 | 1978 Pete Rocca, California ... 1:47.480 |
| 1971 Gary Hall, Indiana ....... 1:50.600 | 1975 John Naber, USC ....... 1:46.827 | 1979 Pete Rocca, California ... 1:45.530 |
| 1972 C. Campbell, Princeton .. 1:50.557 | 1976 John Naber, USC ....... 1:46.960 | 1980 James Fowler, USC ....... 1:47.760 |

### 100–YARD BREASTSTROKE

| | | |
|---|---|---|
| 1969 Don McKenzie, Indiana... 0:58.360 | 1973 John Hencken, Stanford . 0:57.110 | 1977 Graham Smith, California . 0:55.100 |
| 1970 Brian Job, Stanford ..... 0:57.570 | 1974 David Wilkie, Miami ..... 0:56.720 | 1978 Scott Spann, Auburn ..... 0:56.620 |
| 1971 Brian Job, Stanford ..... 0:57.240 | 1975 John Hencken, Stanford . 0:55.596 | 1979 Graham Smith, California . 0:54.910 |
| 1972 Thomas Bruce, UCLA..... 0:56.998 | 1976 John Hencken, Stanford . 0:56.040 | 1980 Steve Lundquist, SMU ... 0:53.590 |

### 200–YARD BREASTSTROKE

| | | |
|---|---|---|
| 1969 Mike Dirksen, Oregon.... 2:08.620 | 1973 David Wilkie, Miami ..... 2:03.400 | 1977 Graham Smith, California . 2:00.050 |
| 1970 Brian Job, Stanford ..... 2:05.990 | 1974 John Hencken, Stanford . 2:01.748 | 1978 Graham Smith, California . 2:02.240 |
| 1971 Brian Job, Stanford ..... 2:03.390 | 1975 John Hencken, Stanford . 2:00.839 | 1979 Graham Smith, California . 2:00.370 |
| 1972 Brian Job, Stanford ..... 2:02.592 | 1976 David Wilkie, Miami ..... 2:00.740 | 1980 William Barrett, UCLA ... 1:58.430 |

### 100–YARD BUTTERFLY

| | | |
|---|---|---|
| 1969 Mark Spitz, Indiana....... 0:49.690 | 1973 John Trembley, Tenn. ... 0:48.680 | 1977 Joe Bottom, USC ........ 0:47.770 |
| 1970 Mark Spitz, Indiana....... 0:49.820 | 1974 John Trembley, Tenn. ... 0:48.718 | 1978 Greg Jagenburg, Calif. St. . 0:48.770 |
| 1971 Mark Spitz, Indiana....... 0:49.420 | 1975 Jeff Rolan, Utah ........ 0:48.953 | 1979 Par Arvidsson, California . 0:47.760 |
| 1972 Mark Spitz, Indiana....... 0:47.988 | 1976 Matt Vogel, Tennessee . 0:48.950 | 1980 Par Arvidsson, California . 0:47.360 |

### 200–YARD BUTTERFLY

| | | |
|---|---|---|
| 1969 John Ferris, Stanford ..... 1:49.610 | 1973 Gary Hall, Indiana ..... 1:48.480 | 1977 Mike Bruner, Stanford ... 1:45.270 |
| 1970 Mike Burton, UCLA ..... 1:51.600 | 1974 Robin Backhaus, Wash.. 1:47.040 | 1978 Greg Jagenburg .......... 1:46.010 |
| 1971 Mark Spitz, Indiana ..... 1:50.100 | 1975 Robin Backhaus, Wash.. 1:47.168 | 1979 Par Arvidsson, California . 1:45.530 |
| 1972 Mark Spitz, Indiana ..... 1:46.898 | 1976 Steve Gregg, N.C. St.... 1:47.000 | 1980 Par Arvidsson, California . 1:44.430 |

### 200–YARD INDIVIDUAL MEDLEY

| | | |
|---|---|---|
| 1969 Charlie Hickcox, Indiana . 1:54.430 | 1973 Steve Furniss, USC ..... 1:51.385 | 1977 Scott Spann, Auburn ..... 1:48.260 |
| 1970 Frank Heckl, USC ...... 1:55.210 | 1974 Steve Furniss, USC ..... 1:51.522 | 1978 Scott Spann, Auburn ..... 1:49.300 |
| 1971 Gary Hall, Indiana ...... 1:52.200 | 1975 Fredrick Tyler, USC ..... 1:50.628 | 1979 Graham Smith, California . 1:48.440 |
| 1972 Gary Hall, Indiana ........ 1:51.507 | 1976 Leroy Engstrand, Tenn... 1:50.129 | 1980 William Barrett, UCLA ... 1:46.250 |

### 400–YARD INDIVIDUAL MEDLEY

| | | |
|---|---|---|
| 1969 Hans Fassnacht, Long Bch. 4:07.660 | 1973 Steve Furniss, USC ..... 3:56.160 | 1977 Rodney Strachan, USC .. 3:54.760 |
| 1970 Gary Hall, Indiana ....... 4:07.310 | 1974 Steve Furniss, USC ..... 3:57.800 | 1978 Brian Goodell, UCLA .... 3:53.610 |
| 1971 Gary Hall, Indiana ........ 3:58.250 | 1975 Leroy Engstrand, Tenn... 3:57.801 | 1979 Brian Goodell, UCLA ..... 3:50.800 |
| 1972 Gary Hall, Indiana ........ 3:58.717 | 1976 Rodney Strachan, USC .. 3:55.640 | 1980 Brian Goodell, UCLA ..... 3:31.380 |

### 400–YARD FREESTYLE RELAY

| | | | | |
|---|---|---|---|---|
| 1965 Yale.......... 3:07.200 | 1969 USC ......... 3:02.770 | 1973 Tennessee .... 3:00.363 | 1977 USC .......... 2:55.280 |
| 1966 USC ......... 3:08.050 | 1970 USC ......... 3:03.910 | 1974 Indiana ...... 3:00.359 | 1978 Tennessee .... 2:55.280 |
| 1967 Stanford ... 3:05.000 | 1971 USC ......... 3:02.380 | 1975 Indiana ...... 2:58.421 | 1979 Tennessee .... 2:54.740 |
| 1968 Yale.......... 3:04.090 | 1972 Tennessee ... 3:01.118 | 1976 USC ......... 2:57.540 | 1980 Auburn ....... 2:55.160 |

### 800–YARD FREESTYLE RELAY

| | | | |
|---|---|---|---|
| 1969 USC ......... 6:49.480 | 1972 USC ......... 6:38.635 | 1975 Indiana ...... 6:36.293 | 1978 Auburn ....... 6:31.930 |
| 1970 USC ......... 6:51.770 | 1973 Indiana ...... 6:36.490 | 1976 USC ......... 6:33.130 | 1979 Florida ...... 6:28.010 |
| 1971 USC ......... 6:39.040 | 1974 Indiana ...... 6:40.321 | 1977 USC ......... 6:28.010 | 1980 Auburn ....... 6:28.070 |

### 400–YARD MEDLEY RELAY

| | | | | |
|---|---|---|---|---|
| 1965 Indiana ...... 3:30.700 | 1969 Indiana ...... 3:25.890 | 1973 Tennessee .... 3:22.988 | 1977 Indiana ...... 3:17.140 |
| 1966 Michigan .... 3:33.360 | 1970 Stanford .... 3:24.990 | 1974 Tennessee .... 3:22.788 | 1978 California .... 3:18.260 |
| 1967 UCLA ....... 3:29.450 | 1971 Stanford..... 3:22.510 | 1975 USC ......... 3:19.221 | 1979 California .... 3:15.220 |
| 1968 Texas Arl. ... 3:31.530 | 1972 USC ......... 3:23.116 | 1976 USC ......... 3:20.020 | 1980 Texas ....... 3:14.590 |

### ONE–METER DIVING

| | | |
|---|---|---|
| 1969 Jim Henry, Indiana ......... 531.06 | 1973 Tim Moore, Ohio St. ..... 487.90 | 1977 Matthew Chelich, Mich. ... 503.13 |
| 1970 Jim Henry, Indiana ......... 487.56 | 1974 Tim Moore, Ohio St. ..... 494.25 | 1978 Wayne Chester, Alabama .. 485.10 |
| 1971 M. Finneron, Ohio St. ...... 520.98 | 1975 Tim Moore, Ohio St. ..... 502.71 | 1979 Greg Louganis, Miami (Fla.) 513.75 |
| 1972 Todd Smith, Ohio St. ...... 503.25 | 1976 James Kennedy, Tenn. ... 514.29 | 1980 Greg Louganis, Miami (Fla.) 557.20 |

### THREE–METER DIVING

| | | |
|---|---|---|
| 1969 Jim Henry, Indiana ......... 574.68 | 1973 Tim Moore, Ohio St. ..... 539.61 | 1977 Brian Bungum, Indiana ... 542.40 |
| 1970 Jim Henry, Indiana ......... 550.59 | 1974 Rick McAllister, Air Force .. 526.41 | 1978 Christopher Snode, Florida 543.18 |
| 1971 Phil Boggs, Florida St. ...... 552.93 | 1975 Tim Moore, Ohio St. ..... 590.61 | 1979 Matthew Chelich, Michigan 527.85 |
| 1972 Craig Lincoln, Minnesota .... 545.94 | 1976 Brian Bungum, Indiana .. 542.19 | 1980 Greg Louganis, Miami (Fla.) 608.10 |

# TENNIS

Wide World

John McEnroe serves to Jimmy Connors in their semifinal match at the U.S. Open Tennis Championships in Queens, N.Y., on Sept. 6. McEnroe defeated Connors in the five-set match, which lasted 4 hours and 16 minutes and ended in a tie breaker. McEnroe went on to defeat Bjorn Borg for the U.S. Open men's singles title.

Sweden's Bjorn Borg became the first man to win five consecutive Wimbledon singles titles in modern history when he defeated John McEnroe of the U.S. in a grueling five-set match, lasting 3 hours and 53 minutes. British player H. Doherty won five titles in 1902–06, but the requirements for defending a title were less stringent in those days.

The highlight of the game was the dramatic fourth set, in which McEnroe saved seven match points, including five in an electrifying 34-point tie breaker. Borg captured the fifth set, to win the match and the title 1–6, 7–5, 6–3, 3–7, 8–6.

On his way to the championship, Borg crushed Gene Mayer, 7–5, 6–3, 7–5, in the quarterfinals, and downed Brian Gottfried, 6–2, 4–6, 6–2, 6–0, in the semifinals.

In the women's singles, Australia's Evonne Goolagong whipped Chris Evert Lloyd, 6–1, 7–6, in only 1 hour and 33 minutes. The second set was decided on a 7–4 tie breaker, the first Wimbledon championship that was ever decided in this way.

To reach the finals, Goolagong downed Australia's Wendy Turnbull, 6–3, 6–2, in the quarterfinals, and beat Tracy Austin, 6–3, 0–6, 6–4, in the semifinals.

**TENNIS** *(continued)*

American Andrea Jaeger, 15, was the youngest player ever to be seeded at Wimbledon. Early in the tournament she beat 1977 Wimbledon winner Virginia Wade, 6–2, 7–6, and won the hearts of the fans. But the 14th seeded teenager from Illinois lost to Chris Evert Lloyd, 6–1, 6–1, in the quarterfinals.

At the U.S. Open championships in Queens, N.Y., in September, John McEnroe avenged his Wimbledon loss to Bjorn Borg by defeating Borg, 7–6, 6–1, 6–7, 5–7, 6–4, to win the men's singles title, Sept. 7, for the second straight year. The match lasted over four hours, with McEnroe winning in the 55th game. The same total number of games were played in the Wimbledon final.

McEnroe reached the final after a five-set, four-hour-plus semifinal victory over Jimmy Connors, 6–4, 5–7, 0–6, 6–3, 7–6, which ended in a tiebreaker.

In women's competition, Chris Evert Lloyd defeated Czechoslovakian teenager Hana Mandlikova, 5–7, 6–1, 6–1. It was her fifth U.S. Open crown in six years. To reach the final, she defeated Yugoslavia's Mima Jausovec, 7–6, 6–2, in the quarterfinals, and beat Tracy Austin, 4–6, 6–1, 6–1, in the semifinals. Earlier in 1980 she had taken a four-month leave of absence from the tennis tour.

At the U.S. Open, Stan Smith and Bob Lutz won the men's doubles, and Billie Jean King and Martina Navratilova captured the women's doubles title. Wendy Turnbull and Marty Reissen won the mixed doubles.

By early December, Martina Navratilova was the top money-winner on the women's circuit, with $611,900. John McEnroe topped the men's earnings list with $523,383 in 1980.

The United States was eliminated from Davis Cup competition on March 9, when Argentina beat the U.S. team, 4–1, in Buenos Aires, to win the American Zone Davis Cup title. The U.S. had been hoping for a third consecutive Davis Cup title.

In college tennis, Stanford University won the NCAA team title at the championship matches held at the University of Georgia, at Athens, Ga., in May. The Stanford team beat the University of California, 5–3. The University of Southern California was third. It was Stanford's fifth team championship since 1973.

Fifth-seeded Robert Van't Hof, of USC, upset top-seeded Peter Rennert, of Stanford, 6–3, 7–5, to win the NCAA singles title.

Tennessee's Mel Purcell and Rodney Harmon won the NCAA doubles championship by defeating Gony Gimmalva and John Benson of Trinity (Texas), 7–6, 7–6. They were the first Tennessee players to win a national championship doubles title.

## U.S. OPEN TENNIS CHAMPIONS

### U.S. MEN'S SINGLES CHAMPIONS

| | | | |
|---|---|---|---|
| 1915 | William M. Johnston (U.S.) | 1942 | Ted Schroeder (U.S.) |
| 1916 | R. Norris Williams II (U.S.) | 1943 | Joe Hunt (U.S.) |
| 1917–18 | R. Lindley Murray (U.S.) | 1944 | Frank Parker (U.S.) |
| 1919 | William M. Johnston (U.S.) | 1945 | Frank Parker (U.S.) |
| 1920–25 | Bill Tilden (U.S.) | 1946 | Jack Kramer (U.S.) |
| 1926–27 | Rene Lacoste (France) | 1947 | Jack Kramer (U.S.) |
| 1928 | Henri Cochet (France) | 1948 | Pancho Gonzales (U.S.) |
| 1929 | Bill Tilden (U.S.) | 1949 | Pancho Gonzales (U.S.) |
| 1930 | John Doeg (U.S.) | 1950 | Art Larsen (U.S.) |
| 1931–32 | Ellsworth Vines (U.S.) | 1951–52 | Frank Sedgman (Australia) |
| 1933–34 | Fred Perry (England) | 1953 | Tony Trabert (U.S.) |
| 1935 | Wilmer Allison (U.S.) | 1954 | Vic Seixas (U.S.) |
| 1936 | Fred Perry (England) | 1955 | Tony Trabert (U.S.) |
| 1937 | Don Budge (U.S.) | 1956 | Ken Rosewall (Australia) |
| 1938 | Don Budge (U.S.) | 1957 | Mal Anderson (Australia) |
| 1939 | Bobby Riggs (U.S.) | 1958 | Ashley Cooper (Australia) |
| 1940 | Don McNeill (U.S.) | 1959–60 | Neale Fraser (Australia) |
| 1941 | Bobby Riggs (U.S.) | 1961 | Roy Emerson (Australia) |

| | |
|---|---|
| 1962 | Rod Laver (Australia) |
| 1963 | Rafael Osuna (Mexico) |
| 1964 | Roy Emerson (Australia) |
| 1965 | Manuel Santana (Spain) |
| 1966 | Fred Stolle (Australia) |
| 1967 | John Newcombe (Australia) |
| 1968 | Arthur Ashe (U.S.) |
| 1969 | Rod Laver (Australia) |
| 1970 | Ken Rosewall (Australia) |
| 1971 | Stan Smith (U.S.) |
| 1972 | Ilie Nastase (Romania) |
| 1973 | John Newcombe (Australia) |
| 1974 | Jimmy Connors (U.S.) |
| 1975 | Manuel Orantes (Spain) |
| 1976 | Jimmy Connors (U.S.) |
| 1977 | Guillermo Vilas (Argentina) |
| 1978 | Jimmy Connors (U.S.) |
| 1979–80 | John McEnroe (U.S.) |

### U.S. WOMEN'S SINGLES CHAMPIONS

| | | | | | |
|---|---|---|---|---|---|
| 1920–22 | Molla Bjurstedt Mallory (U.S.) | 1947 | Louise Brough (U.S.) | 1969 | Margaret S. Court (Australia) |
| 1923–25 | Helen Wills (U.S.) | 1948–50 | Margaret O. du Pont (U.S.) | 1970 | Margaret S. Court (Australia) |
| 1926 | Molla Bjurstedt Mallory (U.S.) | 1951–53 | Maureen Connolly (U.S.) | 1971 | Billie Jean King (U.S.) |
| 1927–29 | Helen Wills (U.S.) | 1954–55 | Doris Hart (U.S.) | 1972 | Billie Jean King (U.S.) |
| 1930 | Betty Nuthall (England) | 1956 | Shirley Fry (U.S.) | 1973 | Margaret S. Court (Australia) |
| 1931 | Helen Wills Moody (U.S.) | 1957–58 | Althea Gibson (U.S.) | 1974 | Billie Jean King (U.S.) |
| 1932–35 | Helen Hull Jacobs (U.S.) | 1959 | Maria Bueno (Brazil) | 1975 | Chris Evert (U.S.) |
| 1936 | Alice Marble (U.S.) | 1960–61 | Darlene Hard (U.S.) | 1976 | Chris Evert (U.S.) |
| 1937 | Anita Lizana (Chile) | 1962 | Margaret Smith (Australia) | 1977 | Chris Evert (U.S.) |
| 1938–40 | Alice Marble (U.S.) | 1963–64 | Maria Bueno (Brazil) | 1978 | Chris Evert (U.S.) |
| 1941 | Sarah Palfrey Cooke (U.S.) | 1965 | Margaret Smith (Australia) | 1979 | Tracy Austin (U.S.) |
| 1942–44 | Pauline Betz (U.S.) | 1966 | Maria Bueno (Brazil) | 1980 | Chris Evert Lloyd (U.S.) |
| 1945 | Sarah Palfrey Cooke (U.S.) | 1967 | Billie Jean King (U.S.) | | |
| 1946 | Pauline Betz (U.S.) | 1968 | Virginia Wade (England) | | |

## DAVIS CUP—MEN'S TEAM TENNIS

The most highly prized trophy of international men's team tennis, the Davis Cup, was put up in 1900 by Dwight F. Davis, an outstanding sportsman and U.S. public official.

In the early years of play, the United States, England, and Australasia (Australia and New Zealand) held a monopoly on the Davis Cup trophy.

By 1927, however, France, and then other nations, developed high-caliber teams.

The annual Davis Cup Challenge Round is played in the country of the defending champion.

### DAVIS CUP CHALLENGE ROUND

| YEAR | WINNER | LOSER | SCORE | YEAR | WINNER | LOSER | SCORE |
|------|--------|-------|-------|------|--------|-------|-------|
| 1900 | United States | England | 5–0 | 1940–45 | Not held | — | — |
| 1902 | United States | England | 3–2 | 1946 | United States | Australia | 5–0 |
| 1903 | England | United States | 4–1 | 1947 | United States | Australia | 4–1 |
| 1904 | England | Belgium | 5–0 | 1948 | United States | Australia | 5–0 |
| 1905 | England | United States | 5–0 | 1949 | United States | Australia | 4–1 |
| 1906 | England | United States | 5–0 | 1950 | Australia | United States | 4–1 |
| 1907 | Australia | England | 3–2 | 1951 | Australia | United States | 3–2 |
| 1908 | Australia | United States | 3–2 | 1952 | Australia | United States | 4–1 |
| 1909 | Australasia | United States | 5–0 | 1953 | Australia | United States | 3–2 |
| 1910 | Not held | — | — | 1954 | United States | Australia | 3–2 |
| 1911 | Australasia | United States | 5–0 | 1955 | Australia | United States | 5–0 |
| 1912 | England | Australasia | 3–2 | 1956 | Australia | United States | 5–0 |
| 1913 | United States | England | 3–2 | 1957 | Australia | United States | 3–2 |
| 1914 | Australasia | United States | 3–2 | 1958 | United States | Australia | 3–2 |
| 1915–18 | Not held | — | — | 1959 | Australia | United States | 3–2 |
| 1919 | Australasia | England | 4–1 | 1960 | Australia | Italy | 4–1 |
| 1920 | United States | Australasia | 5–0 | 1961 | Australia | Italy | 5–0 |
| 1921 | United States | Japan | 5–0 | 1962 | Australia | Mexico | 5–0 |
| 1922 | United States | Australasia | 4–1 | 1963 | United States | Australia | 3–2 |
| 1923 | United States | Australasia | 4–1 | 1964 | Australia | United States | 3–2 |
| 1924 | United States | Australasia | 5–0 | 1965 | Australia | Spain | 4–1 |
| 1925 | United States | France | 5–0 | 1966 | Australia | India | 4–1 |
| 1926 | United States | France | 4–1 | 1967 | Australia | Spain | 4–1 |
| 1927 | France | United States | 3–2 | 1968 | United States | Australia | 4–1 |
| 1928 | France | United States | 4–1 | 1969 | United States | Romania | 5–0 |
| 1929 | France | United States | 3–2 | 1970 | United States | West Germany | 5–0 |
| 1930 | France | United States | 4–1 | 1971 | United States | Romania | 3–2 |
| 1931 | France | England | 3–2 | 1972 | United States | Romania | 3–2 |
| 1932 | France | United States | 3–2 | 1973 | Australia | United States | 5–0 |
| 1933 | England | France | 3–2 | 1974 | South Africa | India [1] | — |
| 1934 | England | United States | 4–1 | 1975 | Sweden | Czechoslovakia | 3–2 |
| 1935 | England | United States | 5–0 | 1976 | Italy | Chile | 4–1 |
| 1936 | England | Australia | 3–2 | 1977 | Australia | Italy | 4–1 |
| 1937 | United States | England | 4–1 | 1978 | United States | Britain | 4–1 |
| 1938 | United States | Australia | 3–2 | 1979 | United States | Italy | 5–0 |
| 1939 | Australia | United States | 3–2 | 1980 | Czechoslovakia | Italy | 4–1 |

## WIGHTMAN CUP—WOMEN'S TEAM TENNIS

Donated in 1923 by Mrs. Hazel Wightman, an American tennis champion and socialite, the Wightman Cup is the premier prize in women's international competition. Teams from the U.S. and Britain compete for the trophy. The site alternates between the two countries.

| YEAR | WINNER | SCORE | YEAR | WINNER | SCORE | YEAR | WINNER | SCORE |
|------|--------|-------|------|--------|-------|------|--------|-------|
| 1923 | United States | 7–0 | 1946 | United States | 7–0 | 1964 | United States | 5–2 |
| 1924 | Britain | 6–1 | 1947 | United States | 7–0 | 1965 | United States | 5–2 |
| 1925 | Britain | 4–3 | 1948 | United States | 6–1 | 1966 | United States | 4–3 |
| 1926 | United States | 4–3 | 1949 | United States | 7–0 | 1967 | United States | 6–1 |
| 1927 | United States | 5–2 | 1950 | United States | 7–0 | 1968 | Britain | 4–3 |
| 1928 | Britain | 4–3 | 1951 | United States | 6–1 | 1969 | United States | 5–2 |
| 1929 | United States | 4–3 | 1952 | United States | 7–0 | 1970 | United States | 4–3 |
| 1930 | Britain | 4–3 | 1953 | United States | 7–0 | 1971 | United States | 4–3 |
| 1931 | United States | 5–2 | 1954 | United States | 6–0 [2] | 1972 | United States | 5–2 |
| 1932 | United States | 4–3 | 1955 | United States | 6–1 | 1973 | United States | 5–2 |
| 1933 | United States | 4–3 | 1956 | United States | 5–2 | 1974 | Britain | 6–1 |
| 1934 | United States | 5–2 | 1957 | United States | 6–1 | 1975 | Britain | 5–2 |
| 1935 | United States | 4–3 | 1958 | Britain | 4–3 | 1976 | United States | 5–2 |
| 1936 | United States | 4–3 | 1959 | United States | 4–3 | 1977 | United States | 7–0 |
| 1937 | United States | 6–1 | 1960 | Britain | 4–3 | 1978 | Britain | 4–3 |
| 1938 | United States | 5–2 | 1961 | United States | 6–1 | 1979 | United States | 7–0 |
| 1939 | United States | 5–2 | 1962 | United States | 4–3 | 1980 | United States | 5–2 |
| 1940–45 | Not held | — | 1963 | United States | 6–1 | | | |

[1] India defaulted in protest against South Africa's racial policies.   [2] One doubles match was not played because of rain.

# WIMBLEDON TENNIS CHAMPIONS

## WIMBLEDON MEN'S SINGLES CHAMPIONS

| | | |
|---|---|---|
| 1920–21 Bill Tilden (U.S.) | 1939 Bobby Riggs (U.S.) | 1960 Neale Fraser (Australia) |
| 1922 Gerald Patterson (Australia) | 1940–45 No matches | 1961–62 Rod Laver (Australia) |
| 1923 Bill Johnston (U.S.) | 1946 Yvon Petra (France) | 1963 Chuck McKinley (U.S.) |
| 1924 Jean Borotra (France) | 1947 Jack Kramer (U.S.) | 1964–65 Roy Emerson (Australia) |
| 1925 René Lacoste (France) | 1948 Bob Falkenburg (U.S.) | 1966 Manuel Santana (Spain) |
| 1926 Jean Borotra (France) | 1949 Ted Schroeder (U.S.) | 1967 John Newcombe (Australia) |
| 1927 Henri Cochet (France) | 1950 Budge Patty (U.S.) | 1968–69 Rod Laver (Australia) |
| 1928 René Lacoste (France) | 1951 Dick Savitt (U.S.) | 1970–71 John Newcombe (Australia) |
| 1929 Henri Cochet (France) | 1952 Frank Sedgman (Australia) | 1972 Stan Smith (U.S.) |
| 1930 Bill Tilden (U.S.) | 1953 Vic Seixas (U.S.) | 1973 Jan Kodes (Czech.) |
| 1931 Sid Wood (U.S.) | 1954 Jaroslav Drobny (Egypt) | 1974 Jimmy Connors (U.S.) |
| 1932 Ellsworth Vines (U.S.) | 1955 Tony Trabert (U.S.) | 1975 Arthur Ashe (U.S.) |
| 1933 Jack Crawford (Australia) | 1956–57 Lew Hoad (Australia) | 1976–80 Bjorn Borg (Sweden) |
| 1934–36 Fred Perry (Britain) | 1958 Ashley Cooper (Australia) | |
| 1937–38 Don Budge (U.S.) | 1959 Alex Olmedo (U.S.) | |

## WIMBLEDON WOMEN'S SINGLES CHAMPIONS

| | | |
|---|---|---|
| 1924 Kitty McKane (Britain) | 1940–45 No matches | 1964 Maria Bueno (Brazil) |
| 1925 Suzanne Lenglen (France) | 1946 Pauline Betz (U.S.) | 1965 Margaret Smith (Australia) |
| 1926 Kitty McK. Godfree (Britain) | 1947 Margaret Osborne (U.S.) | 1966–68 Billie Jean King (U.S.) |
| 1927–29 Helen Wills (U.S.) | 1948–50 Louise Brough (U.S.) | 1969 Ann Jones (Britain) |
| 1930 Helen Wills Moody (U.S.) | 1951 Doris Hart (U.S.) | 1970 Margaret Smith Court (Australia) |
| 1931 Cilly Aussen (Germany) | 1952–54 Maureen Connolly (U.S.) | 1971 Evonne Goolagong (Australia) |
| 1932–33 Helen Wills Moody (U.S.) | 1955 Louise Brough (U.S.) | 1972–73 Billie Jean King (U.S.) |
| 1934 Dorothy Round (Britain) | 1956 Shirley Fry (U.S.) | 1974 Chris Evert (U.S.) |
| 1935 Helen Wills Moody (U.S.) | 1957–58 Althea Gibson (U.S.) | 1975 Billie Jean King (U.S.) |
| 1936 Helen Hull Jacobs (U.S.) | 1959–60 Maria Bueno (Brazil) | 1976 Chris Evert (U.S.) |
| 1937 Dorothy Round (Britain) | 1961 Angela Mortimer (Britain) | 1977 Virginia Wade (Britain) |
| 1938 Helen Wills Moody (U.S.) | 1962 Karen Hantze Susman (U.S.) | 1978–79 Martina Navratilova (U.S.) |
| 1939 Alice Marble (U.S.) | 1963 Margaret Smith (Australia) | 1980 Yvonne Goolagong (Australia) |

## WIMBLEDON MEN'S DOUBLES CHAMPIONS

| | |
|---|---|
| 1954–55 Rex Hartwig and Mervyn Rose (Australia) | 1967 Bob Hewitt (Australia) and Frew McMillan (South Africa) |
| 1956 Lew Hoad and Ken Rosewall (Australia) | 1968–70 John Newcombe and Tony Roche (Australia) |
| 1957 Gardnar Mulloy and Budge Patty (U.S.) | 1971 Roy Emerson and Rod Laver (Australia) |
| 1958 Sven Davidson and Ulf Schmidt (Sweden) | 1972 Bob Hewitt (Australia) and Frew McMillan (South Africa) |
| 1959 Neale Fraser and Roy Emerson (Australia) | 1973 Ilie Nastase (Romania) and Jimmy Connors (U.S.) |
| 1960 Rafael Osuna (Mexico) and Dennis Ralston (U.S.) | 1974 John Newcombe and Tony Roche (Australia) |
| 1961 Neale Fraser and Roy Emerson (Australia) | 1975 Sandy Mayer and Vitas Gerulaitis (U.S.) |
| 1962 Fred Stolle and Bob Hewitt (Australia) | 1976 Brian Gottfried (U.S.) and Raul Ramirez (Mexico) |
| 1963 Rafael Osuna and Antonio Palafox (Mexico) | 1977 Ross Case and Geobb Masters (Australia) |
| 1964 Fred Stolle and Bob Hewitt (Australia) | 1978 Bob Hewitt and Frew McMillan (South Africa) |
| 1965 John Newcombe and Tony Roche (Australia) | 1979 Peter Fleming and John McEnroe (U.S.) |
| 1966 Ken Fletcher and John Newcombe (Australia) | 1980 Paul McNamee and Peter McNamara (Australia) |

## WIMBLEDON WOMEN'S DOUBLES CHAMPIONS

| | |
|---|---|
| 1956 Angela Buxton (Britain) and Althea Gibson (U.S.) | 1969 Margaret Smith Court and Judy Tegart (Australia) |
| 1957 Althea Gibson and Darlene Hard (U.S.) | 1970–71 Rosemary Casals and Billie Jean King (U.S.) |
| 1958 Althea Gibson (U.S.) and Maria Bueno (Brazil) | 1972 Billie Jean King (U.S.) and Betty Stove (Netherlands) |
| 1959 Jeanne Arth and Darlene Hard (U.S.) | 1973 Billie Jean King and Rosemary Casals (U.S.) |
| 1960 Maria Bueno (Brazil) and Darlene Hard (U.S.) | 1974 Peggy Michel (U.S.) and Evonne Goolagong (Australia) |
| 1961–62 Karen Hantze and Billie Jean Moffitt (U.S.) | 1975 Ann Kiyomura (U.S.) and Kazuko Sawamatsu (Japan) |
| 1963 Darlene Hard (U.S.) and Maria Bueno (Brazil) | 1976 Martina Navratilova (Czech.) and Chris Evert (U.S.) |
| 1964 Margaret Smith and Lesley Turner (Australia) | 1977 Helen Cawley (Australia) and Joanne Russell (U.S.) |
| 1965 Billie Jean Moffitt (U.S.) and Maria Bueno (Brazil) | 1978 Wendy Turnbull and Kerry Reid (Australia) |
| 1966 Maria Bueno (Brazil) and Nancy Richey (U.S.) | 1979 Martina Navratilova and Billie Jean King (U.S.) |
| 1967–68 Billie Jean King and Rosemary Casals (U.S.) | 1980 Kathy Jordan and Anne Smith (U.S.) |

## WIMBLEDON MIXED DOUBLES CHAMPIONS

| | |
|---|---|
| 1956 Shirley Fry and Vic Seixas (U.S.) | 1969 Ann Jones (U.K.) and Fred Stolle (Australia) |
| 1957 Darlene Hard (U.S.) and Mervyn Rose (Australia) | 1970 Rosemary Casals (U.S.) and Ilie Nastase (Romania) |
| 1958 Lorraine Coughlan and Robert Howe (Australia) | 1971 Billie Jean King (U.S.) and Owen Davidson (Aust.) |
| 1959–60 Darlene Hard (U.S.) and Rod Laver (Australia) | 1972 Rosemary Casals (U.S.) and Ilie Nastase (Romania) |
| 1961 Lesley Turner and Fred Stolle (Australia) | 1973–74 Billie Jean King (U.S.) and Owen Davidson (Aust.) |
| 1962 Margaret O. du Pont (U.S.) and Neale Fraser (Aust.) | 1975 Margaret Court (Australia) and Marty Riessen (U.S.) |
| 1963 Margaret Smith and Ken Fletcher (Australia) | 1976 Francoise Durr (France) and Tony Roche (Australia) |
| 1964 Lesley Turner and Fred Stolle (Australia) | 1977 Bob Hewitt and Greer Stevens (S. Africa) |
| 1965–66 Margaret Smith and Ken Fletcher (Australia) | 1978 Frew McMillan (Australia) and Betty Stove (Neth.) |
| 1967 Billie Jean King (U.S.) and Owen Davidson (Aust.) | 1979 Bob Hewitt and Greer Stevens (S. Africa) |
| 1968 Margaret Court (Aust.) and K. Fletcher (Hong Kong) | 1980 John and Tracy Austin (U.S.) |

# TRACK AND FIELD

Sebastian Coe of Britain crosses finish line Aug. 1 to win the gold medal in the 1,500-meter race at the 1980 Olympic Games in Moscow. Perennial rival Steve Ovett, *left*, was third. East Germany's Jurgen Straub, *right*, was second. Coe's time of 3:38.40 later was surpassed on Aug. 21 by Ovett, who ran the 1,500 meters in a record 3:31.36 at Koblenz, West Germany.

The 1980 season in track and field saw the setting of new world records in many events.

Although the U.S. boycott prevented American athletes from competing at the Summer Olympic Games held in Moscow July 19–Aug. 3, the games produced several outstanding performances and new records, particularly in field events (see pages 836–851).

Poland's Wladyslaw Kozakiewicz broke the world record in the pole vault with a new mark of 18′ 11″ on July 30. The next day Yuriy Sedykh, of the Soviet Union, tossed a hammer a world record distance of 266′ 4″.

Gerd Wessig, of West Germany, scored a world record 7′ 8¾″ in the high jump on Aug. 1.

The Soviet Union's Nadyezhda Tkachenko broke her own world record in the pentathlon, with a new high of 5,038 points on July 24. Three days later, Nadyezhda Olizaryenko, of the Soviet Union set a new world mark of 1:53.5 in the 800 meters. On Aug. 1, the East German team ran the 400-meter relay in world record time of 41.60.

Among the most eagerly awaited competitions at the Olympics were between two Britons, Sebastian Coe and Steve Ovett, considered the two fastest runners of all time. Ovett won the gold medal in the 800 meters on July 26 with a time of 1:45.4, although Coe holds the world record in that event—1:42.4, set in 1979. Six days later, Coe won the gold in the 1,500 meters with 3:38.4, below his 1979 world-record performance of 3:32.1. Ovett went on to set a new world record of 3:31.36 in the 1,500 meters on August 27, at Koblenz, West Germany.

Other world records set in 1980 included American Mary Decker's 4:21.7 in the mile, at Auckland, New Zealand, on Jan. 26; West German Guido Kratschmer's 8,649 points in the decathlon, at Filderstadt, West Germany on June 14; and American Edwin Moses' 47.13 in the 400-meter hurdles, at Milan, Italy, on July 3.

Mary Decker is all alone at the finish line during the 1,500-meter race at the U.S. Olympic Trials in Eugene, Ore., June 30. She completed the race in 4:04.91. In August, she set a new American record for the 1,500 meters of 3:59.43. Earlier in 1980, she had broken the world's record for the mile race, completing it in 4:21.7 at Auckland, New Zealand on Jan. 26.

**TRACK AND FIELD** (continued)

## AAU INDOOR TRACK AND FIELD CHAMPIONSHIPS: 1980

### MEN'S EVENTS

| | | | |
|---|---|---|---|
| 60-Yard Dash: Curtis Dickey (Texas A & M) | 0:06.09 | 35-lb. Weight Throw: Ed Kania (Unat.) | 72' 8" |
| 600-Yard Dash: Mark Enyeart (Unat., Logan, Utah) | 1:09.20 | Long Jump: Larry Myricks (Athletic Attic) | 26' 11½" |
| 1,000-Yard Run: Billy Martin (Iona College) | 2:07.70 | Triple Jump: Ron Livers (Phila. Pioneer Club) | 55' 1½" |
| One-Mile Run: Craig Masback (N.Y. Pioneer Club) | 4:02.20 | High Jump: Franklin Jacobs (Fairleigh Dickinson) | 7' 4½" |
| 3-Mile Run: Eamonn Coghlan (New York AC/Ireland) | 13:02.80 | Pole Vault: Earl Bell (Unat.) | 18' 2½" |
| 2-Mile Walk: Todd Scully (Shore AC) | 12:35.10 | Sprint Medley Relay: (Philadelphia Pioneer Club 'A') | 2:01.0 |
| 60-Yard Hurdles: Ron Milburn (Houston TC) | 0:07.09 | One-Mile Relay: (Philadelphia Pioneer Club) | 3:10.9 |
| Shot Put: Jesse Stuart (Univ. of Chicago TC) | 66' 5" | Two-Mile Relay: (Virginia Tech.) | 7:29.2 |

### WOMEN'S EVENTS

| | | | |
|---|---|---|---|
| 60-Yard Dash: Evelyn Ashford (Amer. Council of Athletics) | 0:06.76 | Shot Put: Maren Seidler (San Jose Stars) | 57' ¾" |
| 220-Yard Dash: Wanda Hooker (Memphis State Univ.) | 0:24.00 | Long Jump: Pat Johnson (Univ. of Wisconsin) | 20' 11½" |
| 440-Yard Dash: Rosalyn Bryant (Ali TC) | 0:53.92 | High Jump: Louise Ritter (Texas Women's Univ.) | 6' 3" |
| 880-Yard Run: Madeline Manning (Oral Roberts TC) | 2:04.50 | 640-Yard Relay: D.C. International | 1:09.5 |
| One-Mile Run: Maggie Keyes (Maccabi Union TC) | 4:39.30 | One-Mile Relay: Ali TC | 3:41.0 |
| Two-Mile Run: Cindy Bremser (Wisconsin United TC) | 9:45.00 | One-Mile Walk: Susan Brodock (So. Calif. Roadrunners) | 7:06.9 |
| 60-Yard Hurdles: Stephanie Hightower (Ohio State Univ.) | 0:07.40 | Sprint Medley Relay: Los Angeles Mercurettes | 1.45.0 |

## AAU OUTDOOR TRACK AND FIELD CHAMPIONSHIPS: 1980

### MEN'S EVENTS

| | | | |
|---|---|---|---|
| 100-Meter Dash: Stanley Floyd (Auburn TC) | 0:10.19 | 10,000-Meter Run: Rodolfo Gomez (Mexico) | 28:44.00 |
| 200-Meter Dash: LaMonte King (Stars & Stripes TC) | 0:20.08 | High Jump: Franklin Jacobs (Athletic Attic) | 7' 4¼" |
| 400-Meter Dash: Willie Smith (Auburn TC) | 0:45.36 | Pole Vault: Tom Hintnaus (So. Calif. Striders) | 18' 2½" |
| 800-Meter Run: James Robinson (Inner City AC) | 1:46.20 | Long Jump: Larry Myricks (Athletic Attic) | 27' 1¼" |
| 1,500-Meter Run: Steve Lacy (So. Calif. Striders) | 3:40.86 | Triple Jump: Willie Banks (Amer. Council of Athletics) | 56' 11½" |
| 5,000-Meter Run: Matt Centrowitz (Oregon TC) | 13:33.61 | Shot Put: Brian Oldfield (Univ. of Chicago TC) | 71' 7" |
| 110-Meter High Hurdles: Renaldo Nehemiah (DC Internatl.) | 13:49.00 | Discus Throw: Mac Wilkins (Athletics West) | 224' 3" |
| 400-Meter Hurdles: David Lee (Southern Illinois) | 0:49.38 | Hammer Throw: Gian Paolo Urlando (Italy) | 251' 3" |
| 3,000-Meter Steeplechase: Doug Brown (Athletics West) | 8:26.20 | Javelin Throw: Duncan Atwood (Athletics West) | 273' 10" |
| 5-Kilometer Walk: Ray Sharp (unattached) | 20:27.80 | Outstanding Performer: LaMonte King | Stars & Stripes TC |

### WOMEN'S EVENTS

| | | | |
|---|---|---|---|
| 100-Meter Dash: Alice Brown (Los Angeles Nat. TC) | 0:11.21 | 400-Meter Relay: Los Angeles Naturite TC | 0:43.81 |
| 200-Meter Dash: Karen Hawkins (Texas Southern) | 0:22.80 | 1,600-Meter Relay: Ali TC | 3:34.16 |
| 400-Meter Dash: Sherri Howard (Ali TC) | 0:51.51 | 3,200-Meter Relay: Los Angeles Naturite TC | 8:32.30 |
| 800-Meter Run: Madeline Manning (Oral Roberts TC) | 1:58.75 | 5,000-Meter Walk: Sue Brodock (So. Calif. Roadrunners) | 23:19.10 |
| 1,500-Meter Run: Francie Larrieu (Pacific Coast Club) | 4:12.72 | High Jump: Coleen Rienstra (Sun Devil Sports) | 6' 4" |
| 3,000-Meter Run: Julie Brown (Los Angeles Nat. TC) | 9:07.90 | Long Jump: Jodi Anderson (Los Angeles Naturite TC) | 21' 9¾" |
| 10,000-Meter Run: Judi St. Hilaire (Liberty AC) | 33:31.02 | Shot Put: Maren Seidler (San Jose Stars) | 59' 1" |
| 100-Meter Hurdles: Stephanie Hightower (Ohio State) | 0:13.14 | Discus Throw: Lorna Griffin (Amer. Council of Athletics) | 191' 9" |
| 400-Meter Hurdles: Esther Mahr (KCBQ TC) | 0:56.30 | Javelin Throw: Karin Smith (Amer. Council of Athletics) | 199' 1" |
| Sprint Medley Relay: Ali TC | 1:37.40 | Outstanding Performer: Madeline Manning | Oral Roberts TC |

## NCAA OUTDOOR TRACK AND FIELD CHAMPIONSHIPS: 1980

| | | |
|---|---|---|
| **100-Meter Dash** | **110-Meter Hurdles** | **Hammer Throw** |
| Stanley Floyd, Auburn ... 0:10.10 | Greg Foster, UCLA ... 0:13.42 | Thommie Sjoholm, Texas-El Paso  225' 0" |
| **200-Meter Dash** | **400-Meter Hurdles** | **Long Jump** |
| Michael Roberson, Florida State ... 0:19.96 | David Lee, Southern Illinois ... 0:48.87 | Carl Lewis, Houston ... 27' 4¾" |
| **400-Meter Dash** | **3,000-Meter Steeplechase** | **Triple Jump** |
| Bert Cameron, Texas-El Paso ... 0:45.23 | Randy Jackson, Wisconsin ... 8:22.81 | Steve Hanna, Texas-El Paso ... 55' 1" |
| **800-Meter Run** | **400-Meter Relay** | **Javelin Throw** |
| Don Paige, Villanova ... 1:45.81 | Southern California ... 0:39.16 | Curt Ransford, San Jose State ... 269' 3" |
| **1,500-Meter Run** | **1,600-Meter Relay** | **Shot Put** |
| Sydney Maree, Villanova ... 3:38.64 | Tennessee ... 3:03.94 | Michael Carter, So. Methodist ... 66' 11¼" |
| **5,000-Meter Run** | **High Jump** | **Discus** |
| Suleiman Nyambui, Texas-El Paso .. 13:44.43 | Jeff Woodard, Alabama ... 7' 7¼" | Goran Svensson, Brigham Young . 202' 6" |
| **10,000-Meter Run** | **Pole Vault** | **Decathlon** |
| Suleiman Nyambui, Texas-El Paso .. 29:21.85 | Randy Hall, Texas A&M ... 18' 2¼" | Mark Anderson, UCLA ... 7,893 pts. |

## NCAA TEAM CHAMPIONSHIPS: 1922–1980

| | | | | |
|---|---|---|---|---|
| 1922 California | 1932 Indiana | 1949–55 USC | 1964 Oregon | 1973 UCLA |
| 1923 Michigan | 1933 Louisiana State | 1956 UCLA | 1965 Oregon, USC | 1974 Tennessee |
| 1924 No meet | 1934 Stanford | 1957 Villanova | 1966 UCLA | 1975 Texas-El Paso |
| 1925 Stanford [1] | 1935–43 USC | 1958 USC | 1967–68 USC | 1976 USC |
| 1926 USC | 1944 Illinois | 1959 Kansas | 1969 San Jose State | 1977 Arizona State |
| 1927 Illinois [1] | 1945 Navy | 1960 Kansas | 1970 Brigham Young, | 1978 USC |
| 1928 Stanford | 1946 Illinois | 1961 USC | Kansas, Oregon | 1979 Texas-El Paso |
| 1929 Ohio State | 1947 Illinois | 1962 Oregon | 1971 UCLA | 1980 Texas-El Paso |
| 1930–31 USC | 1948 Minnesota | 1963 USC | 1972 UCLA | |

[1] Unofficial.

# WORLD TRACK AND FIELD RECORDS: MEN

| EVENT | RECORD | RECORD HOLDER | NATION | DATE | SITE |
|---|---|---|---|---|---|
| **Running** | | | | | |
| 100 Yards ...... | 0:09.0 | Ivory Crockett ... | United States ... | 5-11-74 | Knoxville, Tennessee |
| | | Houston McTear ... | United States ... | 5-9-75 | Winter Park, Florida |
| 220 Yards ...... | 0:19.5 | Tommie Smith ... | United States ... | 5-7-66 | San Jose, California |
| 220 Yards (turn) | 0:19.9 | Don Quarrie ..... | Jamaica ..... | 6-7-75 | Eugene, Oregon |
| 440 Yards ..... | 0:44.5 | J. Smith ......... | United States ... | 6-26-71 | Eugene, Oregon |
| 880 Yards ..... | 1:44.1 | Rich Wohlhuter .. | United States ... | 6-8-74 | Eugene, Oregon |
| 1 Mile ........ | * 3:48.80 | Steve Ovett ...... | Britain ......... | 7-1-80 | Oslo, Norway |
| 2 Miles ...... | 8:13.5 | Steve Ovett ...... | Britain ......... | 9-15-78 | London, England |
| 3 Miles ...... | 12:47.8 | Emiel Puttemans . | Belgium ...... | 9-20-72 | Brussels, Belgium |
| 6 Miles ...... | 26:47.0 | R. Clarke ...... | Australia ...... | 7-14-65 | Oslo, Norway |
| 10 Miles ...... | 45:57.2 | Jos Hermens .... | Netherlands ..... | 9-14-75 | Papendal, Netherlands |
| 15 Miles ...... | 1:11:52.6 | Pekka Paivarinta . | Finland .......... | 5-15-75 | Oulu, Finland |
| 1 Hour ........ | 20,944 meters [1] | Jos Hermens .... | Netherlands ..... | 5-1-76 | Arnhem, Netherlands |
| 100 Meters .... | 0:09.9 | J. Hines ........ | United States ... | 10-14-68 | Mexico City, Mexico |
| 200 Meters .... | 0:19.72 | Pietro Mennea ... | Italy ........... | 9-12-79 | Mexico City, Mexico |
| 200 Meters (turn) | 0:19.8 | Donald Quarrie... | Jamaica ....... | 8-3-71 | Cali, Colombia |
| 400 Meters .... | 0:43.9 | Lee Evans ...... | United States ... | 10-18-68 | Mexico City, Mexico |
| 600 Meters .... | 1:14.3 | Lee Evans ...... | United States ... | 8-31-68 | Lake Tahoe, California |
| 800 Meters .... | 1:42.4 | Sebastian Coe ... | Britain ......... | 7-5-79 | Oslo, Norway |
| 1,000 Meters .... | * 2:13.4 | Sebastian Coe ... | Britain ......... | 7-1-80 | Oslo, Norway |
| 1,500 Meters .... | * 3:31.36 | Steve Ovett ...... | Britain ......... | 8-27-80 | Koblenz, W. Germany |
| 2,000 Meters .... | 4:51.4 | John Walker ..... | New Zealand ... | 6-30-76 | Oslo, Norway |
| 3,000 Meters .... | 7:32.1 | Henry Rono...... | Kenya ......... | 6-27-78 | Oslo, Norway |
| 5,000 Meters .... | 13:08.4 | Henry Rono...... | Kenya ......... | 4-8-78 | Berkeley, California |
| 10,000 Meters .... | 27:22.5 | Henry Rono...... | Kenya ......... | 6-11-78 | Vienna, Austria |
| 20,000 Meters .... | 57:24.2 | Jos Hermens .... | Netherlands ..... | 5-1-76 | Arnhem, Netherlands |
| | 57:31.6 | Jos Hermens .... | Netherlands ..... | 9-28-75 | Papendal, Netherlands |
| 25,000 Meters .... | 1:14.12 | Bill Rodgers .... | United States ... | 2-21-79 | Saratoga, Calif. |
| 30,000 Meters .... | 1:31:30.4 | Jim Adler........ | Britain.......... | 9-5-70 | London, England |
| **Relays** | | | | | |
| 400 Meters ..... | 0:38.0 | U.S. Team ...... | United States ... | 9-3-77 | Düsseldorf, Germany |
| 440 Yards ..... | 0:38.6 | So. California .... | United States ... | 6-17-67 | Provo, Utah |
| 800 Meters ..... | 1:20.3 | So. California .... | United States ... | 5-27-78 | Tempe, Arizona |
| 880 Yards ..... | 1:21.7 | Texas A & M .... | United States ... | 4-24-70 | Des Moines, Iowa |
| 1,600 Meters .... | 2:56.1 | U.S. National team | United States ... | 10-20-68 | Mexico City, Mexico |
| 1 Mile ........ | 3:02.42 | U.S. team ...... | United States ... | 7-19-75 | Durham, North Carolina |
| 3,200 Meters ..... | 7:08.1 | Soviet team...... | Soviet Union .... | 8-13-78 | Podolsk, Soviet Union |
| 2 Miles ...... | 7:10.4 | Chicago TC ...... | United States ... | 5-12-73 | Durham, North Carolina |
| 6,000 Meters .... | 14:49.0 | French team ..... | France .......... | 6-25-65 | St. Maur, France |
| 4 Miles ...... | 10:02.8 | N.Z. team ...... | New Zealand ... | 2-3-72 | Auckland, New Zealand |
| **Hurdles** | | | | | |
| 120 Yards ..... | 0:13.0 | Rod Milburn ..... | United States ... | 6-25-71 | Eugene, Oregon |
| 220 Yards ..... | 0:21.9 | Don Styron ...... | United States ... | 4-2-60 | Baton Rouge, Louisiana |
| 440 Yards ..... | 0:48.7 | Jim Bolding...... | United States ... | 7-27-74 | Turin, Italy |
| 110 Meters ..... | 0:13.00 | Renaldo Nehemiah | United States ... | 5-6-79 | Westwood, California |
| 200 Meters ..... | 0:21.9 | Don Styron ...... | United States ... | 4-2-60 | Baton Rouge, Louisiana |
| 200 Meters (turn) | 0:22.5 | Martin Lauer ..... | West Germany .. | 7-7-59 | Zurich, Switzerland |
| 400 Meters ..... | * 0:47.13 | Edwin Moses .... | United States ... | 7-3-80 | Milan, Italy |
| 3,000 Meters † .... | * 8:05.4 | Henry Rono...... | Kenya ......... | 5-13-78 | Seattle, Washington |
| **Walking** | | | | | |
| 20 Miles.......... | 2:30:38.6 | Gerhard Weidner | West Germany ... | 5-25-74 | Hamburg, West Germany |
| 30 Miles.......... | 3:51:48.6 | Gerhard Weidner | West Germany ... | 4-8-73 | Hamburg, West Germany |
| 20 Kilometers..... | 1:20:06.8 | Daniel Bautista | Mexico .......... | 10-17-79 | Montreal, Canada |
| 30 Kilometers..... | 2:08:00 | Jose Marin ...... | Spain........... | 4-8-79 | Barcelona, Spain |
| 50 Kilometers..... | 3:41.39 | Raul Gonzalez ... | Mexico ........ | 5-25-79 | Fana, Norway |
| 2 Hours .......... | 28,165 meters [2] | Jose Marin ...... | Spain........... | 4-8-79 | Barcelona, Spain |
| **Jumping** | | | | | |
| High Jump ...... | * 7 ' 8 ¾ " | Gerd Wessig ..... | East Germany ... | 8-1-80 | Moscow, Soviet Union |
| Long Jump ....... | 29 ' 2 ½ " | Bob Beamon ..... | United States ... | 10-18-68 | Mexico City, Mexico |
| Triple Jump ..... | 58 ' 8 ½ " | João Oliveira ... | Brazil ......... | 10-15-75 | Mexico City, Mexico |
| Pole Vault ...... | * 18 ' 11 ½ " | W. Kozakiewicz .. | Poland ......... | 7-30-80 | Moscow, Soviet Union |
| **Throwing** | | | | | |
| Shot ............. | 72 ' 8" | Udo Beyer....... | East Germany ... | 7-6-78 | Göteborg, Sweden |
| Discus ........... | 233 ' 5 ½ " | Wolfgang Schmidt | East Germany ... | 8-9-78 | Berlin, East Germany |
| Hammer .......... | * 268 ' 4 " | Yuriy Sedykh .... | Soviet Union ... | 7-31-80 | Moscow, Soviet Union |
| Javelin .......... | 317 ' 4 " | Ferenc Paragi ... | Hungary ....... | 4-23-80 | Tata, Hungary |
| **Decathlon**........ | 8,649 pts | Guido Kratschmer | West Germany .. | 6-14-80 | Filderstadt, W. Germany |

* Pending official recognition.   † Steeplechase.   [1] 13 miles, 25 yards.   [2] 17 miles, 881 yards.

## WORLD TRACK AND FIELD RECORDS: WOMEN

| EVENT | RECORD | RECORD HOLDER | NATION | DATE | SITE |
|---|---|---|---|---|---|
| **Running** | | | | | |
| 60  Meters | 0:07.2 | Betty Cuthbert | Australia | 2-27-60 | Sydney, Australia |
| 100  Yards | 0:10.0 | Chi Cheng | Taiwan | 6-13-70 | Portland, Oregon |
| 100  Meters | *0:10.87 | Lyudmila Kondratyeva | Soviet Union | 6-3-80 | Leningrad, Soviet Union |
| 200  Meters | 0:21.71 | Marita Koch | East Germany | 6-10-79 | Berlin, East Germany |
| 220  Yards | 0:22.6 | Chi Cheng | Taiwan | 7-3-70 | Los Angeles, California |
| 400  Meters | 0:48.60 | Marita Koch | East Germany | 8-4-79 | Turin, Italy |
| 440  Yards | 0:51.71 | Irena Szewinska | Poland | 8-6-76 | Edinburgh, Scotland |
|  | 0:52.2 | Kathy Hammond | United States | 8-12-72 | Urbana, Illinois |
| 800  Meters | *1:53.5 | Nadyezhda Olizaryenko | Soviet Union | 7-27-80 | Moscow, Soviet Union |
| 880  Yards | 2:02.0 | Dixie Willis | Australia | 3-3-62 | Perth, Australia |
| 1,500  Meters | *3:52.5 | Tatiana Kazankina | Soviet Union | 8-13-80 | Zurich, Switzerland |
| 1  Mile | *4:21.7 | Mary Decker | United States | 1-26-80 | Auckland, New Zealand |
| 3,000  Meters | 8:27.2 | Ludmilla Bragina | Soviet Union | 8-7-76 | College Park, Maryland |
|  | 8:45.4 | Grete Waitz | Norway | 6-21-76 | Oslo, Norway |
| **Hurdles** | | | | | |
| 100  Meters | *0:12.36 | Grazyna Rabsztyn | Poland | 6-13-80 | Warsaw, Poland |
| 200  Meters | 0:25.7 | Pamela Ryan | Australia | 11-25-71 | Melbourne, Australia |
| 400  Meters | *0:54.29 | Karin Rossley | East Germany | 5-18-80 | Jena, East Germany |
| **Jumping** | | | | | |
| High Jump | 6 ′ 7 ″ | Sara Simeoni | Italy | 8-4-78 | Brescia, Italy |
| Long Jump | 23 ′ 3 ¼ ″ | Vilma Bardauskiene | Soviet Union | 8-29-78 | Prague, Czechoslovakia |
| **Throwing** | | | | | |
| Shot | *73 ′ 8 ″ | Ileana Slupianek | East Germany | 5-11-80 | Celje, Yugoslavia |
| Discus | *235 ′ 7 ″ | Maria Vergova | Bulgaria | 7-13-80 | Sofia, Bulgaria |
| Javelin | *229 ′ 11 ″ | Tatyana Birylina | Soviet Union | 7-12-80 | Moscow, Soviet Union |
| Pentathlon | *5,083 pts. | Nadyezhda Tkachenko | Soviet Union | 7-24-80 | Moscow, Soviet Union |
| **Running Relays** | | | | | |
| 400  Meters | *0:41.60 | East German team | East Germany | 6-10-79 | Berlin, East Germany |
| 440  Yards | 0:44.1 | West German team | West Germany | 7-19-75 | Durham, North Carolina |
| 800  Meters | *1:28.15 | East German Team | East Germany | 8-9-80 | Jena, East Germany |
| 880  Yards | 1:35.8 | Australian team | Australia | 11-9-69 | Brisbane, Australia |
| 1,600  Meters | 3:19.23 | East German team | East Germany | 7-31-76 | Montreal, Canada |
| 1  Mile | 3:29.1 | Soviet team | Soviet Union | 8-7-76 | College Park, Maryland |
|  | 3:30.3 | West German team | West Germany | 7-19-75 | Durham, North Carolina |
| 3,200  Meters | *7:52.3 | Soviet team | Soviet Union | 8-16-76 | Podolsk, Soviet Union |
|  | 8:05.2 | Bulgarian team | Bulgaria | 8-30-75 | Sofia, Bulgaria |

## OTHER WOMEN'S OUTDOOR AMERICAN RECORDS

| | | | | | |
|---|---|---|---|---|---|
| **Running** | | | | | |
| 60  Meters | 0:07.3 | Barbara Ferrell | United States | 8-25-68 | Walnut, California |
| 100  Yards | 0:10.0 | Chi Cheng | United States | 6-13-70 | Portland, Oregon |
| 100  Meters | 0:10.97 | Evelyn Ashford | United States | 6-16-79 | Walnut, California |
| 200  Meters | 0:21.83 | Evelyn Ashford | United States | 8-25-79 | Montreal, Canada |
| 220  Yards | 0:22.6 | Chi Cheng | United States | 7-3-70 | Los Angeles, California |
| 400  Meters | 0:50.6 | Rosalyn Bryant | United States | 7-28-76 | Montreal, Canada |
| 440  Yards | 0:52.2 | Kathy Hammond | United States | 8-12-72 | Urbana, Illinois |
| 800  Meters | 1:57.9 | Madeline Jackson | United States | 8-7-76 | College Park, Maryland |
| 880  Yards | 2:04.6 | Charlotte Cooke | United States | 7-23-66 | Los Angeles, California |
| 1,500  Meters | *3:59.43 | Mary Decker | United States | 8-13-80 | Zurich, Switzerland |
| 1  Mile | 4:21.7 | Mary Decker | United States | 1-26-80 | Auckland, New Zealand |
| 3  Mile | 15:04.1 | Kathy Mills | United States | 5-26-78 | Knoxville, Tennessee |
| 3,000  Meters | *8:38.73 | Mary Decker | United States | 7-15-80 | Oslo, Norway |
| 5,000  Meters | *15:30.6 | Jan Merrill | United States | 3-22-80 | Stanford, California |
| 10,000  Meters | *32:52.5 | Mary Shea | United States | 6-15-79 | Walnut, California |
| **Hurdles** | | | | | |
| 100  Meters | 0:12.86 | Deby LaPlante | United States | 6-16-79 | Walnut, California |
| 200  Meters | 0:26.1 | Pat Hawkins | United States | 7-10-71 | Bakersfield, California |
| 400  Meters | *0:56.16 | Esther Mahr | United States | 8-15-80 | Sittard, Netherlands |
| **Race Walking** | | | | | |
| 1,500  Meters | 6:46.6 | Lisa Metheny | United States | 6-28-75 | White Plains, New York |
| 1  Mile | 7:20.1 | Sue Brodock | United States | 2-2-74 | Los Angeles, California |
| 5,000  Meters | *23:19.1 | Sue Brodock | United States | 6-13-80 | Walnut, California |
| 10,000  Meters | *50:32.8 | Sue Brodock | United States | 6-17-79 | Walnut, California |
| **Jumping** | | | | | |
| High Jump | *6 ′ 4 ¾ ″ | Louise Ritter | United States | 5-30-80 | Wichita, Kansas |
| Long Jump | *22 ′ 11 ¾ ″ | Jodi Anderson | United States | 6-28-80 | Eugene, Oregon |
| **Throwing** | | | | | |
| Shot | *62 ′ 7 ¾ ″ | Maren Seidler | United States | 6-16-79 | Walnut, California |
| Discus | *207 ′ 5 ″ | Lorna Griffin | United States | 5-24-80 | Long Beach, California |
| Javelin | *227 ′ 5 ″ | Kathy Schmidt | United States | 9-11-77 | Pacific Palisades, California |

* Pending official recognition.

# WEIGHTLIFTING

## 1980 NATIONAL AAU SENIOR WEIGHTLIFTING CHAMPIONSHIPS

### 52 KILOGRAMS (114.5 POUNDS)
1. Leslie Sewall (unattached), 182.5 kg. (402.3 lbs.)
2. Brian Miyamoto (Hawaiian Lifters), 177.5 kg. (391.3 lbs.)
3. Mark Kappes (unattached), 167.5 kg. (369.3 lbs.)
4. John Jones (N.W. Co. YMCA), 155.0 kg. (341.7 lbs.)
5. Adrian Johnson (Crushers), 152.5 kg. (336.2 lbs.)

### 56 KILOGRAMS (123 POUNDS)
1. Joe Widdel (unattached), 210.0 kg. (463.0 lbs.)
2. Richard Palmer (unattached), 205.0 kg. (451.9 lbs.)
3. Ronald Crawley (Crushers), 200.0 kg. (440.9 lbs.)
4. Stefan Swett (unattached), 190.0 kg. (418.8 lbs.)

### 60 KILOGRAMS (132 POUNDS)
1. Philip Sanderson (York Barbell), 242.5 kg. (534.6 lbs.)
2. Gerald Fukuoka (Hawaii), 230.0 kg. (507.1 lbs.)
3. Bill Leblanc (Metairie YMCA), 225.0 kg. (490.5 lbs.)
4. Steven Kenjitazum (Bellmar Rec.), 222.5 kg. (490.5 lbs.)
5. Ron Johnson (Oregon Wt. Club), 217.5 kg. (479.5 lbs.)

### 67.5 KILOGRAMS (148¾ POUNDS)
1. Cal Schake (Butler YMCA), 290.0 kg. (639.3 lbs.)
2. James Benjamin (Columbus Y), 270.0 kg. (595.2 lbs.)
3. Donnie Warner (York Barbell), 265.0 kg. (584.2 lbs.)
4. Don Abrahamson (Catharsis), 255.0 kg. (562.2 lbs.)
5. Mark Levell (Sayre Park), 255.0 kg. (562.2 lbs.)
6. David Toguchi (Hawaii A.C.), 235.0 kg. (518.1 lbs.)

### 75 KILOGRAMS (165¼ POUNDS)
1. Myron Davis (N.W. Co. YMCA), 297.5 kg. (655.9 lbs.)
2. Fred Lowe (MSU Wt. Club), 290.0 kg. (639.3 lbs.)
3. Curt White (unattached), 285.0 kg. (628.3 lbs.)
4. Leo Temoshenko (York Barbell), 275.0 kg. (606.3 lbs.)
5. Toney Sims (Crushers), 265.0 kg. (584.2 lbs.)

### 82.5 KILOGRAMS (181¾ POUNDS)
1. Michael Karchut (Sayre Park), 327.5 kg. (722.0 lbs.)
2. Michael Cohen (Savannah BBC), 325.0 kg. (716.5 lbs.)
3. Tom Hirtz (Sports Palace), 322.5 kg. (711.0 lbs.)
4. John Julius (Olympic H.C.), 322.4 kg. (711.0 lbs.)
5. Pete Cline (Sports Palace), 305.0 kg. (672.4 lbs.)
6. Val Balison (unattached), 305.0 kg. (672.4 lbs.)

### 90 KILOGRAMS (198¼ POUNDS)
1. James Curry Jr. (Sports Palace), 337.5 kg. (744.1 lbs.)
2. Joseph Puleo (York Barbell), 330.0 kg. (727.5 lbs.)
3. Luke Klaja (Sports Palace), 327.5 kg. (722.0 lbs.)
4. Lou Macardo (Woodbridge Rec.), 322.5 kg. (711.0 lbs.)

### 100 KILOGRAMS (220 POUNDS)
1. Brian Derwin (Belleville), 362.5 kg. (799.2 lbs.)
2. Guy Carlton (York Barbell), 360.0 kg. (793.7 lbs.)
3. Kurt Setterberg (unattached), 350.0 kg. (771.6 lbs.)
4. Ken Clark (Sports Palace), 345.0 kg. (760.6 lbs.)
5. Phil Grippaldi (Giordano's Gym), 325.0 kg. (716.5 lbs.)

### 110 KILOGRAMS (242 POUNDS)
1. Mark Cameron (York Barbell), 372.5 kg. (821.2 lbs.)
2. Robert Giordano (Giordano's Gym), 365.0 kg. (804.7 lbs.)
3. Mario Martinez (Sport Palace), 347.5 kg. (766.1 lbs.)
4. Phillip Hall (Dallas Spoon), 347.5 kg. (766.1 lbs.)
5. Raymond Blaha (La Naturite), 345.0 kg. (760.6 lbs.)

### SUPERHEAVYWEIGHT
1. Tom Stock (York Barbell), 392.5 kg. (865.3 lbs.)
2. Jerome Hannan (Giordano's Gym), 385.0 kg. (848.8 lbs.)
3. Joseph Dube Sr. (York Barbell), 352.5 kg. (777.1 lbs.)
4. Richard Johnson (Sayre Park), 337.5 kg. (744.1 lbs.)
5. Donald Lingerfelt (Michigan H.A.), 322.5 kg. (711.0 lbs.)

# WRESTLING

## NATIONAL COLLEGIATE ATHLETIC ASSOCIATION WRESTLING CHAMPIONSHIPS

### NCAA TEAM CHAMPIONSHIPS

| | | | | | | | | | |
|---|---|---|---|---|---|---|---|---|---|
| 1928–31 | Oklahoma St. | 1937–46 | Oklahoma St. | 1954–56 | Oklahoma St. | 1964 | Oklahoma St. | 1971 | Oklahoma St. |
| 1932 | Indiana | 1947 | Cornell Col. | 1957 | Oklahoma | 1965 | Iowa State | 1972–73 | Iowa State |
| 1933 (tie) | Iowa State; Oklahoma St. | 1948–49 | Oklahoma St. | 1958–59 | Oklahoma St. | 1966 | Oklahoma St. | 1974 | Oklahoma |
| | | 1950 | No. Iowa | 1960 | Oklahoma | 1967 | Michigan St. | 1975–76 | Iowa |
| 1934–35 | Oklahoma St. | 1951–52 | Oklahoma St. | 1961–62 | Oklahoma St. | 1968 | Oklahoma St. | 1977 | Iowa State |
| 1936 | Oklahoma | 1953 | Penn State | 1963 | Oklahoma | 1969–70 | Iowa State | 1978–80 | Iowa |

### NCAA OUTSTANDING WRESTLER AWARDS

| | | | | | |
|---|---|---|---|---|---|
| 1947–48 | William Koll, No. Iowa | 1959 | Ron Gray, Iowa St. | 1971 | Darrell Keller, Oklahoma St. |
| 1949 | Charles Hetrick, Oklahoma St. | 1960 | Dave Auble, Cornell U. | 1972 | Wade Schalles, Clarion St. |
| 1950 | A. Gizoni, Waynesburg | 1961–62 | E. Simons, Lock Haven St. | 1973 | Greg Strobel, Oregon St. |
| 1951 | W. Romanowski, Cornell Col. | 1963 | Mickey Martin, Oklahoma | 1974 | Floyd Hitchcock, Bloomsburg St. |
| 1952 | Tommy Evans, Oklahoma | 1964 | Dean Lahr, Colorado | 1975 | Mike Frick, Lehigh |
| 1953 | Frank Bettucci, Cornell U. | 1965–66 | Yojiro Uetake, Oklahoma St. | 1976 | Chuck Yagla, Iowa |
| 1954 | Tommy Evans, Oklahoma | 1967 | Richard Sanders, Portland St. | 1977 | Nick Gallo, Hofstra |
| 1955 | Ed Eichelberger, Lehigh | 1968 | Dwayne Keller, Oklahoma St. | 1978 | Mark Churella, Michigan |
| 1956–57 | Dan Hodge, Oklahoma | 1969 | Dan Gable, Iowa St. | 1979 | Bruce Kinseth, Iowa |
| 1958 | Dick Delgado, Oklahoma | 1970 | Larry Owings, Washington | 1980 | Howard Harris, Oregon St. |

### NCAA INDIVIDUAL WRESTLING CHAMPIONS: 1980

| | | | | | |
|---|---|---|---|---|---|
| Heavyweight | Howard Harris, Oregon St. | 158 Pounds | Rickey Stewart, Oklahoma St. | 126 Pounds | John Azevedo, Bakersfield St. |
| 190 Pounds | Noel Loban, Clemson | 150 Pounds | Andy Rein, Wisconsin | 118 Pounds | Joe Gonzales, Bakersfield St. |
| 177 Pounds | Ed Banach, Iowa | 142 Pounds | Lee Roy Smith, Oklahoma St. | | |
| 167 Pounds | Matt Reiss, N. Carolina St. | 134 Pounds | Randy Lewis, Iowa | | |

## NATIONAL AAU SENIOR SOMBO WRESTLING CHAMPIONSHIPS: 1980

### DIVISION CHAMPIONS

| | | | |
|---|---|---|---|
| 105.5 Pounds: | Lewis Dorrance, USMA | 180.5 Pounds: | Jim Martin, Washington Judo |
| 114.5 Pounds: | James Howard, USMC | 198.5 Pounds: | Jerry Shedd, Washington |
| 125.5 Pounds: | Wilfredo Leiva, USMC | 220 Pounds: | Greg Gibson, USMC |
| 136.5 Pounds: | Katsuji Nerio, Southland | Open (Over 220 Pounds): | Carl Dambman, AIA |
| 149.5 Pounds: | Josh Henson, Potomac | Team Championship: | U.S. Marine Corps |
| 163 Pounds: | Ross Papke, NCIJA | Outstanding Wrestler: | Greg Gibson, USMC |

# YACHTING

## THE AMERICA'S CUP RACES

The 24th challenge for the America's Cup was made in 1980 by the Australian contender *Australia*. The U.S. entry, *Freedom*, skippered by Dennis Connor, won the cup, taking four races and losing one off Newport, R.I.

The most prestigious series of international yacht races began in the mid-1800s.

A feature of the London Exhibition of 1851 was a 58-mile yacht race around the Isle of Wight. Among the entries was a 100-foot schooner from the United States, named the *America* and sponsored by members of the New York Yacht Club. The *America* took the race, defeating 14 English cutters and schooners, and winning a trophy called the Hundred-Guineas Cup.

The *America* was sold and left in England, but the cup was brought back to the U.S. and presented to the New York Yacht Club. Used as a trophy for international yacht racing, it became known as the America's Cup.

The first international challenge race took place in 1870 and set a pattern that is still followed. In the first contest the America's Cup was successfully defended, as were successive challenges over the years.

Specifications for yachts in America's Cup races have undergone several changes since the first race in 1851. The race in 1881 was restricted to sloop-rigged craft. Since 1956 only 12-meter (39.4-foot) sloops have been eligible to compete.

| YEAR | WINNING YACHT | OWNER | RESULTS | LOSING YACHT | OWNER |
|---|---|---|---|---|---|
| 1851 | America, U.S. .... | John C. Stevens | 1 race to 0 | Aurora .......... | T. Le Marchant, England |
| 1870 | Magic, U.S. ...... | Franklin Osgood | 1 race to 0 | Cambria [1] ....... | James Ashbury, England |
| 1871 | Columbia [2], U.S. .. | Franklin Osgood | 2 races to 0 | Livonia .......... | James Ashbury, England |
|  | Sappho [2], U.S.... | William P. Douglass | 2 races to 0 |  |  |
| 1876 | Madeleine, U.S... | John S. Dickerson | 2 races to 0 | Countess of |  |
|  |  |  |  | Dufferin ........ | Charles Gifford, Canada |
| 1881 | Mischief, U.S. .... | J.R. Busk | 2 races to 0 | Atlanta .......... | Alexander Cuthbert, Canada |
| 1885 | Puritan, U.S. ..... | J.M. Forbes, | 2 races to 0 | Genesta ......... | Sir Richard Sutton, England |
|  |  | Charles Paine |  |  |  |
| 1886 | Mayflower, U.S. .. | Charles Paine | 2 races to 0 | Galatea .......... | William Henn, England |
| 1887 | Volunteer, U.S. ... | Charles Paine | 2 races to 0 | Thistle .......... | James Bell, England |
| 1893 | Vigilant, U.S. ..... | Oliver Iselin | 3 races to 0 | Valkyrie II ....... | Lord Dunraven, England |
| 1895 | Defender, U.S. ... | Oliver Iselin, | 3 races to 0 | Valkyrie III ...... | Lord Dunraven |
|  |  | E.D. Morgan, |  |  | Lord Lonsdale, |
|  |  | W.K. Vanderbilt |  |  | Lord Wolverton, England |
| 1899 | Columbia, U.S. ... | Oliver Iselin, J.P. Morgan | 3 races to 0 | Shamrock I....... | Sir Thomas Lipton, Ireland |
| 1901 | Columbia, U.S. ... | E.D. Morgan | 3 races to 0 | Shamrock II ..... | Sir Thomas Lipton, Ireland |
| 1903 | Reliance, U.S. .... | Cornelius Vanderbilt | 3 races to 0 | Shamrock III..... | Sir Thomas Lipton, Ireland |
| 1920 | Resolute, U.S. .... | Harry Walters | 3 races to 2 | Shamrock IV ..... | Sir Thomas Lipton, Ireland |
| 1930 | Enterprise, U.S. .. | Harold S. Vanderbilt | 4 races to 0 | Shamrock V ..... | Sir Thomas Lipton, Ireland |
| 1934 | Rainbow, U.S. .... | Harold S. Vanderbilt | 4 races to 0 | Endeavour ...... | T.O.M. Sopwith, England |
| 1937 | Ranger, U.S. ..... | Harold S. Vanderbilt | 4 races to 0 | Endeavour II ..... | T.O.M. Sopwith, England |
| 1958 | Columbia, U.S. ... | Henry Sears | 4 races to 0 | Sceptre ......... | Hugh Goodson, England |
| 1962 | Weatherly, U.S.... | Henry Mercer | 4 races to 1 | Gretel .......... | Sir Frank Packer, Australia |
| 1964 | Constellation, U.S. | Walter Gubelmann | 4 races to 0 | Sovereign ........ | Anthony Boyden, England |
| 1967 | Intrepid, U.S..... | N.Y. Yacht Club's | 4 races to 0 | Dame Pattie .... | Royal Sydney Yacht Squadron's |
|  |  | Intrepid Syndicate |  |  | Syndicate, Australia |
| 1970 | Intrepid, U.S...... | N.Y. Yacht Club's | 4 races to 1 | Gretel II......... | Sir Frank Packer, Australia |
|  |  | Intrepid Syndicate |  |  |  |
| 1974 | Courageous, U.S. . | N.Y. Yacht Club's | 4 races to 0 | Southern Cross ... | Royal Perth Y.C. Challenger |
|  |  | Courageous Syndicate |  |  | Syndicate, Australia |
| 1977 | Courageous, U.S.. | Kings Point | 4 races to 0 | Australia ......... | Sun City Yacht Club, |
|  |  | Maritime Acad. Synd. |  |  | Australia |
| 1980 | Freedom, U.S...... | N.Y. State | 4 races to 1 | Australia ........ | Sun City Yacht Club, |
|  |  | Maritime College, |  |  | Australia |
|  |  | Fort Schuyler Found. |  |  |  |

[1] *Cambria*, the only English schooner in the race, finished tenth in a field of 24.
[2] After winning the first two races, the *Columbia* was disabled. *Sappho* substituted and won the fourth and fifth races.

## NORTH AMERICAN YACHT RACING UNION CHAMPIONSHIPS

| MALLORY CUP—MEN | | ADAMS CUP—WOMEN | |
|---|---|---|---|
| 1970 | John Jennings, St. Petersburg, Florida | 1970 | Jan O'Malley, Mantoloking, New Jersey |
| 1971 | John Kolius, Corinthian Yacht Club, Texas | 1971 | Mrs. Romeyn Everdell, Duxbury, Massachusetts |
| 1972 | Edwin H. Sherman Jr., St. Petersburg, Florida | 1972 | Sally Lindsay, Swampscott, Massachusetts |
| 1973 | John Jennings, St. Petersburg, Florida | 1973 | Mrs. David Larr, Oyster Bay, New York |
| 1974 | Vann Wilson, San Anselmo, California | 1974 | Deborah Freeman, Beachwood, New Jersey |
| 1975 | Christopher Pollak, Westport, Connecticut | 1975 | Cindy S. Batchelor, Essex, Connecticut |
| 1976 | David J. Crockett, Los Alamitos, California | 1976 | Ellen Gerloff, Galveston, Texas |
| 1977 | Marvin Beckman, Houston, Texas | 1977 | Cindy Stieffel, Bay Waveland, Missouri |
| 1978 | Glenn Darden, Fort Worth, Texas | 1978 | Bonnie Shore, Newport, Rhode Island |
| 1979 | Glenn Darden, Fort Worth, Texas | 1979 | Allison Jolly, St. Petersburg, Florida |
| 1980 | Dave Ullman, Corona del Mar, California | 1980 | Judy McKinney, Bay St. Louis, Mississippi |

# States of the United States

Louisiana's first Republican governor in 103 years, David Treen, happily waves to the crowd while seated next to his wife in an inauguration day parade on March 10, 1980. The state's skyscraper capitol at Baton Rouge, La., looms in the background.

Wide World

## HIGHLIGHTS: 1980

One of the most important tasks facing state governments in 1981 will be the redrawing of congressional district boundaries based on the 1980 census. The party in power has an advantage for the next 10 years in the way these districts are designed. Therefore, the Democrats were happy that they had managed to hold control of a majority of state legislatures and governorships despite the Republican victory in 1980.

Democrats retained 27 governorships, although they lost four to Republicans in the 1980 elections—Arkansas, Missouri, North Dakota, and Washington (see page 248).

The Democrats also held control of both houses of the legislature in 28 states, while the Republicans have both in only 14. Seven states are divided, with each party controlling one house. The 50th state, Nebraska, has a one-house nonpartisan legislature.

Rolling in money because of its 12.5% royalty on oil production, Alaska's government repealed the state's income tax on Sept. 24, 1980, and began refunding about $185.5 mil-

**HIGHLIGHTS: 1980** *(continued)*

lion in taxes already collected for 1979 and 1980. The state's oil income amounts to about $5 billion a year, almost four times the normal budget of state government.

Faced with a projected surplus of funds of nearly $100 million in 1981, Nebraska's government reduced the state's individual income tax rate to 15% from 17%, making the reduction retroactive to Jan. 1, 1980. The state also reduced its corporate tax rates.

In a major tax rebellion, voters in Massachusetts approved a measure called Proposition 2½ because it requires local govern-

ments to reduce property taxes to no more than 2½% of assessed valuations. Local governments were faced with having to curtail services or restructure their system of tax revenues. The city of Boston faced a particularly large problem because its property tax has been 20% of assessed valuation.

Voters in Washington, D.C., approved preliminary measures aimed at making the District of Columbia the nation's 51st state.

The only woman governor in the U.S., Ella T. Grasso of Connecticut, developed cancer in 1980, resigning at the end of the year to turn the office over to Lt. Gov. William O'Neill.

## 25 LARGEST STATES IN AREA

| RANK | STATE | SQUARE MILES |
|---|---|---|
| 1 | Alaska | 586,412 |
| 2 | Texas | 267,338 |
| 3 | California | 158,693 |
| 4 | Montana | 147,138 |
| 5 | New Mexico | 121,666 |
| 6 | Arizona | 113,909 |
| 7 | Nevada | 110,540 |
| 8 | Colorado | 104,247 |
| 9 | Wyoming | 97,914 |
| 10 | Oregon | 96,981 |
| 11 | Utah | 84,916 |
| 12 | Minnesota | 84,068 |
| 13 | Idaho | 83,557 |
| 14 | Kansas | 82,264 |
| 15 | Nebraska | 77,227 |
| 16 | South Dakota | 77,047 |
| 17 | North Dakota | 70,665 |
| 18 | Oklahoma | 69,919 |
| 19 | Missouri | 69,686 |
| 20 | Washington | 68,192 |
| 21 | Georgia | 58,876 |
| 22 | Florida | 58,560 |
| 23 | Michigan | 58,216 |
| 24 | Illinois | 56,400 |
| 25 | Iowa | 56,290 |

## 25 SMALLEST STATES IN AREA

| RANK | STATE | SQUARE MILES |
|---|---|---|
| 50 | Rhode Island | 1,214 |
| 49 | Delaware | 2,057 |
| 48 | Connecticut | 5,009 |
| 47 | Hawaii | 6,450 |
| 46 | New Jersey | 7,836 |
| 45 | Massachusetts | 8,257 |
| 44 | New Hampshire | 9,304 |
| 43 | Vermont | 9,609 |
| 42 | Maryland | 10,577 |
| 41 | West Virginia | 24,181 |
| 40 | South Carolina | 31,055 |
| 39 | Maine | 33,215 |
| 38 | Indiana | 36,291 |
| 37 | Kentucky | 40,395 |
| 36 | Virginia | 40,817 |
| 35 | Ohio | 41,222 |
| 34 | Tennessee | 42,244 |
| 33 | Pennsylvania | 45,333 |
| 32 | Mississippi | 47,716 |
| 31 | Louisiana | 48,523 |
| 30 | New York | 49,576 |
| 29 | Alabama | 51,609 |
| 28 | North Carolina | 52,586 |
| 27 | Arkansas | 53,104 |
| 26 | Wisconsin | 56,154 |

## 25 LARGEST STATES IN POPULATION [1]

| RANK | STATE | POPULATION |
|---|---|---|
| 1 | California | 23,510,372 |
| 2 | New York | 17,476,798 |
| 3 | Texas | 14,152,339 |
| 4 | Pennsylvania | 11,824,561 |
| 5 | Illinois | 11,321,350 |
| 6 | Ohio | 10,578,421 |
| 7 | Florida | 9,579,495 |
| 8 | Michigan | 9,236,891 |
| 9 | New Jersey | 7,335,808 |
| 10 | Massachusetts | 5,728,288 |
| 11 | North Carolina | 5,846,159 |
| 12 | Indiana | 5,454,154 |
| 13 | Georgia | 5,396,425 |
| 14 | Virginia | 5,321,521 |
| 15 | Missouri | 4,901,678 |
| 16 | Wisconsin | 4,688,055 |
| 17 | Tennessee | 4,539,834 |
| 18 | Louisiana | 4,194,299 |
| 19 | Maryland | 4,193,378 |
| 20 | Washington | 4,109,634 |
| 21 | Minnesota | 4,068,856 |
| 22 | Alabama | 3,863,698 |
| 23 | Kentucky | 3,642,143 |
| 24 | Connecticut | 3,096,951 |
| 25 | South Carolina | 3,067,061 |

## 25 SMALLEST STATES IN POPULATION [1]

| RANK | STATE | POPULATION |
|---|---|---|
| 50 | Alaska | 400,331 |
| 49 | Wyoming | 468,909 |
| 48 | Vermont | 511,299 |
| 47 | Delaware | 594,779 |
| 46 | North Dakota | 652,437 |
| 45 | South Dakota | 687,643 |
| 44 | Montana | 783,674 |
| 43 | Nevada | 800,312 |
| 42 | New Hampshire | 919,114 |
| 41 | Idaho | 943,629 |
| 40 | Rhode Island | 945,761 |
| 39 | Hawaii | 964,624 |
| 38 | Maine | 1,123,560 |
| 37 | New Mexico | 1,290,551 |
| 36 | Utah | 1,454,630 |
| 35 | Nebraska | 1,564,727 |
| 34 | West Virginia | 1,928,524 |
| 33 | Arkansas | 2,280,687 |
| 32 | Kansas | 2,355,536 |
| 31 | Mississippi | 2,503,250 |
| 30 | Oregon | 2,617,444 |
| 29 | Arizona | 2,714,013 |
| 28 | Colorado | 2,877,726 |
| 27 | Iowa | 2,908,797 |
| 26 | Oklahoma | 2,998,124 |

[1] Bureau of Census preliminary data for April 1, 1980, Census.

## U.S. STATES AND TERRITORIES—Important Facts: 1981

| | AREA Sq. Mi. | POPULATION[1] Total | Density | GOVERNOR Name | Party | Term Years | Term Expires | LEGISLATURE Senate Majority Party | House Majority Party |
|---|---|---|---|---|---|---|---|---|---|
| Alabama | 51,609 | 3,863,698 | 74.9 | Forest James Jr. | D | 4 | Jan. '83 | Democratic | Democratic |
| Alaska | 586,412 | 400,331 | 0.7 | Jay S. Hammond | R | 4 | Dec. '82 | Tie | Democratic |
| Arizona | 113,909 | 2,714,013 | 23.8 | Bruce Babbitt | D | 4 | Jan. '83 | Republican | Republican |
| Arkansas | 53,104 | 2,280,687 | 42.9 | Frank D. White | R | 2 | Jan. '83 | Democratic | Democratic |
| California | 158,693 | 23,510,372 | 148.2 | Edmund G. Brown Jr. | D | 4 | Jan. '83 | Democratic | Democratic |
| Colorado | 104,247 | 2,877,726 | 27.6 | Richard D. Lamm | D | 4 | Jan. '83 | Republican | Republican |
| Connecticut | 5,009 | 3,096,951 | 618.3 | William A. O'Neill | D | 4 | Jan. '83 | Democratic | Democratic |
| Delaware | 2,057 | 594,779 | 289.1 | Pierre S. duPont IV | R | 4 | Jan. '85 | Democratic | Republican |
| Florida | 58,560 | 9,579,495 | 163.6 | Robert Grahm | D | 4 | Jan. '83 | Democratic | Democratic |
| Georgia | 58,876 | 5,396,425 | 91.7 | George Busbee | D | 4 | Jan. '83 | Democratic | Democratic |
| Hawaii | 6,450 | 964,624 | 149.6 | George R. Ariyoshi | D | 4 | Dec. '82 | Democratic | Democratic |
| Idaho | 83,557 | 943,629 | 11.3 | John V. Evans | D | 4 | Jan. '83 | Republican | Republican |
| Illinois | 56,400 | 11,321,350 | 200.7 | James R. Thompson | R | 4 | Jan. '83 | Republican | Republican |
| Indiana | 36,291 | 5,454,154 | 150.3 | Robert D. Orr | R | 4 | Jan. '85 | Republican | Republican |
| Iowa | 56,290 | 2,908,797 | 51.7 | Robert D. Ray | R | 4 | Jan. '83 | Republican | Republican |
| Kansas | 82,264 | 2,355,536 | 28.6 | John W. Carlin | D | 4 | Jan. '83 | Republican | Republican |
| Kentucky | 40,395 | 3,642,143 | 90.2 | John Y. Brown Jr. | D | 4 | Dec. '83 | Democratic | Democratic |
| Louisiana | 48,523 | 4,194,299 | 86.4 | David C. Treen | R | 4 | Mar. '84 | Democratic | Democratic |
| Maine | 33,215 | 1,123,560 | 33.8 | Joseph E. Brennan | D | 4 | Jan. '83 | Republican | Democratic |
| Maryland | 10,577 | 4,193,378 | 396.5 | Harry R. Hughes | D | 4 | Jan. '83 | Democratic | Democratic |
| Massachusetts | 8,257 | 5,728,288 | 693.7 | Edward J. King | D | 4 | Jan. '83 | Democratic | Democratic |
| Michigan | 58,216 | 9,236,891 | 158.7 | William G. Milliken | R | 4 | Jan. '83 | Democratic | Democratic |
| Minnesota | 84,068 | 4,068,856 | 48.4 | Albert H. Quie | R | 4 | Jan. '83 | Democratic | Democratic |
| Mississippi | 47,716 | 2,503,250 | 52.5 | William Winter | D | 4 | Jan. '84 | Democratic | Democratic |
| Missouri | 69,686 | 4,901,678 | 70.3 | Christopher S. Bond | R | 4 | Jan. '85 | Democratic | Democratic |
| Montana | 147,138 | 783,674 | 5.3 | Ted Schwinden | D | 4 | Jan. '85 | Republican | Democratic |
| Nebraska | 77,227 | 1,564,727 | 20.3 | Charles Thone | R | 4 | Jan. '83 | Nonpartisan | — |
| Nevada | 110,540 | 800,312 | 7.2 | Robert F. List | R | 4 | Jan. '83 | Democratic | Democratic |
| New Hampshire | 9,304 | 919,114 | 98.8 | Hugh Gallen | D | 2 | Jan. '85 | Republican | Republican |
| New Jersey | 7,836 | 7,335,808 | 936.2 | Brendan T. Byrne | D | 4 | Jan. '82 | Democratic | Democratic |
| New Mexico | 121,666 | 1,290,551 | 10.6 | Bruce King | D | 4 | Jan. '83 | Democratic | Democratic |
| New York | 49,576 | 17,476,798 | 352.6 | Hugh L. Carey | D | 4 | Jan. '83 | Republican | Democratic |
| North Carolina | 52,586 | 5,846,159 | 111.2 | James B. Hunt Jr. | D | 4 | Jan. '85 | Democratic | Democratic |
| North Dakota | 70,665 | 652,437 | 9.2 | Allen I. Olson | R | 4 | Jan. '85 | Republican | Republican |
| Ohio | 41,222 | 10,758,421 | 261.0 | James A. Rhodes | R | 4 | Jan. '83 | Republican | Democratic |
| Oklahoma | 69,919 | 2,998,124 | 42.9 | George Nigh | D | 4 | Jan. '83 | Democratic | Democratic |
| Oregon | 96,981 | 2,617,444 | 27.0 | Victor Atiyeh | R | 4 | Jan. '83 | Republican | Republican |
| Pennsylvania | 45,333 | 11,824,561 | 260.8 | Richard L. Thornburgh | R | 4 | Jan. '83 | Republican | Republican |
| Rhode Island | 1,214 | 945,761 | 779.0 | J. Joseph Garrahy | D | 2 | Jan. '83 | Democratic | Democratic |
| South Carolina | 31,055 | 3,067,061 | 98.8 | Richard W. Riley | D | 4 | Jan. '83 | Democratic | Democratic |
| South Dakota | 77,047 | 687,643 | 8.9 | William J. Janklow | R | 4 | Jan. '83 | Republican | Republican |
| Tennessee | 42,244 | 4,539,834 | 107.5 | Lamar Alexander | R | 4 | Jan. '83 | Democratic | Democratic |
| Texas | 267,338 | 14,152,339 | 52.9 | William Clements | R | 4 | Jan. '83 | Democratic | Democratic |
| Utah | 84,916 | 1,454,630 | 17.1 | Scott M. Matheson | D | 4 | Jan. '85 | Republican | Republican |
| Vermont | 9,609 | 511,299 | 53.2 | Richard A. Snelling | R | 2 | Jan. '83 | Republican | Republican |
| Virginia | 40,817 | 5,321,521 | 130.4 | John N. Dalton | R | 4 | Jan. '82 | Democratic | Democratic |
| Washington | 68,192 | 4,109,634 | 60.3 | John Spellman | R | 4 | Jan. '85 | Democratic | Republican |
| West Virginia | 24,181 | 1,928,524 | 79.8 | John D. Rockfeller IV | D | 4 | Jan. '85 | Democratic | Democratic |
| Wisconsin | 56,154 | 4,689,055 | 83.6 | Lee Sherman Dreyfus | R | 4 | Jan. '83 | Democratic | Democratic |
| Wyoming | 97,914 | 468,909 | 4.8 | Ed Herschler | D | 4 | Jan. '83 | Democratic | Republican |
| Dist. of Columbia | 67 | 635,233 | 7,301.5 | Marion Barry[3] | D | 4 | Jan. '83 | Democratic | — |
| Am. Samoa | 76 | 35,490[2] | 467.0 | Peter T. Coleman | — | 4 | Jan. '85 | Nonpartisan | Nonpartisan |
| Guam | 212 | 116,644[2] | 550.2 | Paul M. Calvo | R | 4 | Jan. '83 | Republican | — |
| Micronesia | 533 | 129,282[2] | 242.6 | Adrian Paul Winkel | — | — | — | — | — |
| Northern Marianas | 184 | 15,000[2] | 81.5 | Carlos S. Camacho | — | — | — | — | — |
| Puerto Rico | 3,435 | 3,187,550[1] | 928.0 | Carlos Romero-Barcelo[4] | — | 4 | Jan. '85 | Pop. Dem.[5] | New Prog.[4] |
| Virgin Islands | 133 | 71,236[2] | 535.6 | Juan Luis | I | 4 | Jan. '83 | — | — |

[1] Bureau of Census preliminary data for April 1, 1980, Census. [2] Jan. 1, 1981, estimate. [3] Mayor. [4] New Progressive Party. [5] Popular Democratic Party.

UNITED STATES

## PERSONAL INCOME IN STATES BY BASIC INDUSTRIES: 1979

Source: U.S. Department of Commerce, Bureau of Economic Analysis

Total personal income increased 12.1% in 1979, with average personal income rising to $8,706 per capita.

Alaska had the highest personal income per capita with $11,252. The District of Columbia, with $10,911 per capita, was higher than any state except Alaska. Mississippi's $6,167 per capita was the lowest in the country.  •

| REGION AND STATE | PER CAPITA | TOTAL [1] | MANU- FACTUR- ING [1] | GOVERN- MENT [1] | SERVICES | RETAIL TRADE [1] | CON- STRUC- TION [1] | FARM- ING [1] | MIN- ING [1] |
|---|---|---|---|---|---|---|---|---|---|
| United States ...... | $8,706 | $1,915,999 | $387,627 | $237,189 | $253,466 | $147,280 | $90,706 | $41,763 | $24,579 |
| New England....... | 8,816 | 108,351 | 25,765 | 11,390 | 16,281 | 7,958 | 3,811 | 443 | 101 |
| Connecticut ...... | 9,959 | 31,021 | 8,416 | 2,614 | 4,170 | 2,089 | 1,105 | 90 | 54 |
| Maine .......... | 7,057 | 7,741 | 1,614 | 1,077 | 957 | 622 | 339 | 99 | 3 |
| Massachusetts ... | 8,844 | 51,019 | 11,319 | 5,658 | 8,688 | 3,808 | 1,549 | 101 | 20 |
| New Hampshire .. | 8,231 | 7,301 | 1,743 | 696 | 882 | 596 | 384 | 20 | 8 |
| Rhode Island ..... | 8,266 | 7,679 | 1,864 | 951 | 1,080 | 556 | 262 | 9 | 4 |
| Vermont ......... | 7,280 | 3,589 | 810 | 394 | 503 | 286 | 172 | 125 | 13 |
| Mideast .......... | 9,092 | 382,753 | 76,254 | 50,230 | 58,293 | 26,046 | 13,321 | 2,018 | 1,682 |
| Delaware ........ | 9,537 | 5,550 | 1,680 | 615 | 630 | 407 | 267 | 121 | 4 |
| District of Columbia | 10,911 | 7,157 | 345 | 6,432 | 3,182 | 527 | 261 | — | 3 |
| Maryland ........ | 9,150 | 37,955 | 4,556 | 6,845 | 5,369 | 3,075 | 1,751 | 264 | 35 |
| New Jersey ...... | 9,702 | 71,135 | 14,990 | 7,465 | 9,249 | 4,797 | 2,515 | 144 | 59 |
| New York ........ | 9,098 | 160,555 | 28,520 | 19,028 | 26,811 | 10,110 | 4,286 | 628 | 212 |
| Pennsylvania ..... | 8,559 | 100,400 | 26,161 | 9,845 | 13,050 | 7,128 | 4,242 | 862 | 1,369 |
| Great Lakes ....... | 9,118 | 376,445 | 109,680 | 36,687 | 43,654 | 27,512 | 16,262 | 6,988 | 2,384 |
| Illinois ......... | 9,823 | 110,302 | 25,199 | 10,718 | 13,996 | 7,909 | 4,844 | 2,168 | 883 |
| Indiana .......... | 8,686 | 46,903 | 15,035 | 4,128 | 4,493 | 3,478 | 2,229 | 1,133 | 279 |
| Michigan ......... | 9,269 | 85,341 | 29,503 | 9,123 | 9,789 | 6,094 | 3,377 | 999 | 358 |
| Ohio ............ | 8,775 | 94,162 | 28,856 | 8,793 | 11,022 | 7,037 | 4,039 | 1,000 | 809 |
| Wisconsin........ | 8,419 | 39,738 | 11,088 | 3,924 | 4,354 | 2,993 | 1,774 | 1,689 | 55 |
| Plains ............ | 8,460 | 144,813 | 26,080 | 16,085 | 16,849 | 11,419 | 7,321 | 10,337 | 1,276 |
| Iowa ........... | 8,589 | 24,925 | 4,987 | 2,415 | 2,529 | 1,879 | 1,245 | 2,107 | 51 |
| Kansas ......... | 9,055 | 21,451 | 3,488 | 2,377 | 2,157 | 1,495 | 988 | 1,616 | 337 |
| Minnesota ....... | 8,760 | 35,567 | 7,077 | 3,799 | 4,471 | 2,916 | 1,891 | 1,994 | 465 |
| Missouri ......... | 8,132 | 39,581 | 8,257 | 4,353 | 5,137 | 3,262 | 1,944 | 1,531 | 191 |
| Nebraska ........ | 8,341 | 13,129 | 1,619 | 1,672 | 1,466 | 1,043 | 650 | 1,622 | 39 |
| North Dakota .... | 7,774 | 5,108 | 252 | 765 | 549 | 408 | 366 | 704 | 133 |
| South Dakota .... | 7,334 | 5,053 | 399 | 703 | 540 | 414 | 238 | 766 | 60 |
| Southeast ........ | 7,589 | 378,639 | 68,525 | 51,861 | 44,313 | 29,925 | 19,375 | 8,853 | 7,120 |
| Alabama......... | 6,976 | 26,294 | 5,831 | 3,952 | 2,684 | 1,881 | 1,234 | 567 | 416 |
| Arkansas ........ | 6,785 | 14,792 | 2,982 | 1,624 | 1,458 | 1,137 | 723 | 1,024 | 114 |
| Florida .......... | 8,532 | 75,597 | 6,895 | 8,777 | 10,578 | 6,630 | 3,844 | 1,688 | 195 |
| Georgia.......... | 7,515 | 38,456 | 7,490 | 5,742 | 4,586 | 3,229 | 1,657 | 899 | 132 |
| Kentucky ........ | 7,342 | 25,896 | 5,198 | 3,133 | 2,659 | 1,924 | 1,338 | 784 | 1,476 |
| Louisiana ........ | 7,477 | 30,042 | 4,080 | 3,459 | 3,741 | 2,469 | 2,440 | 436 | 1,862 |
| Mississippi....... | 6,167 | 14,979 | 3,095 | 2,109 | 1,502 | 1,149 | 753 | 801 | 205 |
| North Carolina ... | 7,359 | 41,257 | 10,780 | 5,504 | 4,412 | 3,263 | 1,807 | 1,291 | 85 |
| South Carolina ... | 7,027 | 20,605 | 5,467 | 3,211 | 1,967 | 1,534 | 1,066 | 365 | 28 |
| Tennessee ...... | 7,299 | 31,972 | 7,735 | 4,292 | 3,957 | 2,594 | 1,471 | 532 | 204 |
| Virginia.......... | 8,605 | 44,719 | 6,456 | 8,588 | 5,498 | 3,182 | 2,278 | 418 | 616 |
| West Virginia .... | 7,470 | 14,029 | 2,515 | 1,470 | 1,271 | 933 | 764 | 48 | 1,787 |
| Southwest ........ | 8,461 | 168,911 | 24,638 | 21,431 | 20,419 | 14,371 | 11,090 | 4,346 | 8,013 |
| Arizona.......... | 8,305 | 20,347 | 2,585 | 3,077 | 2,589 | 1,819 | 1,602 | 393 | 556 |
| New Mexico...... | 7,294 | 9,052 | 507 | 1,812 | 1,190 | 779 | 565 | 366 | 667 |
| Oklahoma ....... | 8,226 | 23,791 | 3,129 | 3,060 | 2,451 | 1,832 | 1,113 | 1,166 | 1,557 |
| Texas .......... | 8,649 | 115,721 | 18,417 | 13,482 | 14,189 | 9,942 | 7,809 | 2,421 | 5,234 |
| Rocky Mountain .... | 8,205 | 51,527 | 6,386 | 7,728 | 6,557 | 4,507 | 3,478 | 1,613 | 2,414 |
| Colorado ........ | 8,945 | 24,795 | 3,342 | 3,727 | 3,457 | 2,214 | 1,566 | 541 | 832 |
| Idaho............ | 7,446 | 6,739 | 971 | 887 | 819 | 574 | 437 | 475 | 92 |
| Montana......... | 7,412 | 5,826 | 489 | 922 | 705 | 533 | 356 | 229 | 200 |
| Utah ............ | 7,185 | 9,822 | 1,407 | 1,631 | 1,194 | 840 | 683 | 110 | 443 |
| Wyoming ........ | 9,657 | 4,346 | 177 | 560 | 391 | 345 | 435 | 259 | 846 |
| Far West ......... | 9,766 | 291,518 | 49,614 | 38,469 | 45,149 | 24,376 | 15,101 | 6,955 | 1,325 |
| California ........ | 9,913 | 224,969 | 38,237 | 29,565 | 35,586 | 18,562 | 10,633 | 5,176 | 1,108 |
| Nevada .......... | 10,204 | 7,163 | 331 | 929 | 2,237 | 701 | 613 | 75 | 90 |
| Oregon .......... | 8,842 | 22,345 | 4,510 | 2,667 | 2,722 | 2,035 | 1,314 | 593 | 52 |
| Washington ...... | 9,435 | 37,041 | 6,536 | 5,308 | 4,603 | 3,078 | 2,541 | 1,111 | 76 |
| Alaska........... | 11,252 | 4,568 | 320 | 1,388 | 626 | 382 | 442 | 6 | 261 |
| Hawaii........... | 9,353 | 8,474 | 364 | 1,922 | 1,316 | 785 | 505 | 204 | 1 |

[1] In millions of dollars (add 000,000 to each amount shown).

## ALABAMA

**Area:** 51,609 square miles; 133,667 sq. km.
**Population:** 3,769,000 (1979); 3,444,165 (1970).
**Capital:** Montgomery.
**Flower:** Camellia; **Tree:** Southern (longleaf) pine.
**Bird:** Yellowhammer.
**Stone:** Marble; **Mineral:** Hematite; **Fish:** Tarpon.
**Song:** *Alabama.*
**Nickname:** The Heart of Dixie.
**Motto:** We Dare Defend Our Rights.
**Flag:** Diagonal red cross on white field.
**Leading Industries:** Manufacturing (iron, steel, aluminum, chemicals, paper), agriculture (poultry, dairy products, beef cattle, cotton, peanuts, pecans), mining (coal, iron ore, petroleum).
**Climate** (Montgomery): *Normal temperatures:* Jan. high 58 ° F., low 37 ° F.; July high 89 ° F., low 69 ° F. *Normal yearly precipitation:* 50" (water). *Record snowstorm:* 11" in December 1886.
**Recreation Areas:** National forests, 4; state parks and recreation areas, 20; Gulf Coast beaches.
**Points of Interest:** George C. Marshall Space Flight Center (Huntsville); Horseshoe Bend National Memorial Park; Russell Cave National Monument; White House of Confederacy in Montgomery; battleship USS *Alabama* in Mobile Bay.

### KEY EVENTS IN ALABAMA

**1519   Mobile Bay believed to have been discovered** by Spanish explorer Alonso Ívarez de Piñeda.
**1702   French settlement** at Fort Louis founded; colony moves in 1711 to present site of Mobile, Ala.
**1763   Britain wins** region from France.
**1783   Spain acquires southern Alabama** from Britain, while U.S. receives northern Alabama.
**1795   U.S. obtains rest of Alabama except Mobile** from Spain in Treaty of San Lorenzo.
**1813   (April 15)   U.S. captures Mobile** from Spain.
**1814   (March 27)   Battle of Horseshoe Bend:** Gen. Andrew Jackson defeats Creek Indians.
**1817   (March 3)   Territory of Alabama** organized.
**1819   (Dec. 14)   Alabama becomes 22d U.S. state.**
**1861   First capital of Confederacy** at Montgomery.
**1861   (Jan. 11)   Alabama secedes** from Union.
**1864   (Aug. 5–23)   Battle of Mobile Bay:** Union Adm. David Farragut conquers Mobile's forts.
**1868   (June 25)   Alabama readmitted** to Union.
**1880   Iron and steel industry** begins growth at Birmingham with opening of first blast furnace.
**1944   State's first oil well** produces at Gilbertown.
**1949   Space research center** established at Huntsville.
**1955   Black civil-rights crusade** by Rev. Martin Luther King Jr. begins bus boycott in Montgomery.
**1961–76   Confederate flag** flown above U.S. flag on state capitol.
**1975   George C. Wallace** becomes state's first three-term governor.
**1979   Low population growth** of 9.4% since 1970 drops Alabama to 22d among states in population.

## ALASKA

**Area:** 586,412 square miles; 1,518,800 sq. km.
**Population:** 406,000 (1979); 302,173 (1970).
**Capital:** Juneau.
**Flower:** Forget-me-not; **Tree:** Sitka spruce; **Bird:** Willow ptarmigan; **Gem:** Jade; **Fish:** King salmon.
**Song:** *Alaska's Flag.*
**Nickname:** The Last Frontier.
**Motto:** North to the Future.
**Flag:** Blue field with 7 gold stars on left representing Big Dipper and one on right representing Polaris.
**Leading Industries:** Government, mining (petroleum, gold, coal), food processing, forestry, agriculture (dairy products, poultry, cattle, hogs, sheep, potatoes,

barley, oats, vegetables), tourism.
**Climate** (Fairbanks): *Normal temperatures:* Jan. high –2.2 ° F., low –22 ° F.; July high 72 ° F., low 50 ° F. *Normal yearly precipitation:* 11" (water). *Record snowstorm:* 20.1" in February 1966.
**Recreation Areas:** National park, 1; national forests, 2; state parks and recreation areas, 64.
**Points of Interest:** Mt. McKinley National Park; Mendenhall Glacier (in North Tongass National Forest); Glacier Bay and Katmai national monuments; Sitka National Historical Park; Klondike Gold Rush National Historical Park; Russian-era relics in Ketchikan and Sitka; Eskimo villages.

### KEY EVENTS IN ALASKA

**1741   Alaska discovered** by Danish sea captain Vitus Bering, exploring for Russia.
**1784   (Aug. 14)   First Russian settlement** established on Kodiak Island by fur trader Grigori Shelekhov.
**1867   (Oct. 18)   U.S. acquires Alaska** from Russia for $7.2 million.
**1896–99   Discoveries of gold** bring rush of prospectors to Klondike and Alaska.
**1912   (Aug. 24)   Territory of Alaska** organized.
**1942   (June 12)   Japan invades and occupies** Attu Island in Aleutians; later takes Kiska and Agattu.
**1943   (May 11–30)   U.S. troops recapture Attu;** reoccupy Kiska on Aug. 15.
**1959   (Jan. 3)   Alaska becomes 49th U.S. state.**
**1964   (March 27)   Severe earthquake** in south central Alaska kills 131 persons, causes widespread damage.
**1968   Discovery of oil at Prudhoe Bay,** believed largest oil reserve in world.
**1975   (May 27)   Alaska becomes first state to legalize use of marijuana** in ruling by state court.
**1976   Voters approve moving state capital** from Juneau to Willow, 70 miles from Anchorage.
**1977   Trans-Alaska pipeline completed** at cost of $7.7 billion; oil flows south 799 miles from Prudhoe Bay to Valdez at rate of 1.2 million barrels a day.
**1978   (Dec. 1)   About 56 million acres of land** made into 17 national monuments by President Carter.
**1979   State population** grows 34.3% since 1970.
**1980   (April 27)   Time zone shift** moves Juneau and area to north into Yukon Time Zone, two hours later than Nome.
**1980   State income tax abolished;** $185 million already collected is refunded to taxpayers; state government grows rich with 12.5% royalty on oil production.

## ARIZONA

**Area:** 113,909 square miles; 295,023 sq. km.
**Population:** 2,450,000 (1979); 1,772,482 (1970).
**Capital:** Phoenix.
**Flower:** Saguaro cactus blossom.
**Tree:** Palo verde; **Bird:** Cactus wren.
**Gemstone:** Turquoise; **Song:** *Arizona.*
**Nickname:** The Grand Canyon State.
**Motto:** *Ditat Deus* (God Enriches).
**Flag:** Copper-colored star centered on radiating red and yellow stripes above horizontal blue stripe.
**Leading Industries:** Manufacturing (machinery, smelting, metal products), mining (copper, molybdenum, gold, silver, zinc), agriculture (beef cattle, cotton, lettuce, dairy products, sheep, vegetables, fruits), tourism.
**Climate** (Phoenix): *Normal temperatures:* Jan. high 65 ° F., low 38 ° F.; July high 102 ° F., low 78 ° F. *Normal yearly precipitation:* 7" (water). *Record snowstorm:* 1" in January 1937.
**Recreation Areas:** National parks, 2; national forests, 7; national recreation area, 1; state parks and recreation areas, 11.
**Points of Interest:** Grand Canyon and Petrified Forest national parks; Monument Valley; Painted Desert;

**ARIZONA** (continued)

Indian reservations; Tombstone; Fort Apache: numerous national monuments (including Chiricahua, Saguaro, Organ Pipe Cactus, Pipe Spring, Canyon de Chelly, Navajo, Casa Grande Ruins, Hohokam Pima, Montezuma Castle, Tonto, Tumacacori, Tuzigoot, Walnut Canyon, Wupatki, Sunset Crater, and Marble Canyon); Oak Creek Canyon (in Coconino National Forest); Fort Bowie and Hubbell Trading Post national historical parks; Kitt Peak National Observatory.

## KEY EVENTS IN ARIZONA

**1539–40   Arizona explored for Spain:** Marcos de Niza (1539); Francisco de Coronado (1540).
**1690s   Roman Catholic missions** founded in Arizona by Spanish Jesuit priest Eusebio Kino.
**1776   Fort Tucson established** by Spaniards.
**1848   U.S. acquires Arizona** in Mexican War.
**1853   Southern Arizona obtained from Mexico** in Gadsden Purchase.
**1863   Navajo Indians subdued** by Kit Carson leading 400 troops against stronghold in Canyon de Chelly.
**1863   (Feb. 24)   Arizona Territory created.**
**1871–86   Apache War:** Chief Geronimo captured.
**1912   (Feb. 14)   Arizona becomes 48th U.S. state.**
**1948   Indians win right to vote** in Arizona.
**1973   Biggest dam in world** completed: New Cornelia Tailings Dam, near Ajo, containing 274,026,000 cubic yards of material, 98 feet high, 6.7 miles long.
**1978   Arizona moves ahead of Kansas** to rank 31st in population among the states.
**1979   Second-fastest growth** of any state increases population 38.0% since 1970.

## ARKANSAS

**Area:** 53,104 square miles; 137,539 sq. km.
**Population:** 2,180,000 (1979); 1,923,295 (1970).
**Capital:** Little Rock.
**Flower:** Apple blossom; **Tree:** Pine; **Bird:** Mockingbird; **Stone:** Diamond; **Song:** Arkansas.
**Nickname:** The Land of Opportunity.
**Motto:** Regnat Populus (The People Rule).
**Flag:** Star-studded white diamond on red field.
**Leading Industries:** Food processing, manufacturing (machinery, appliances, paper), agriculture (soybeans, cotton, rice, poultry, beef cattle, dairy products), mining (petroleum, bauxite, bromine).
**Climate** (Little Rock): Normal temperatures: Jan. high 50° F., low 29° F.; July high 93° F., low 70° F. Normal yearly precipitation: 49" (water). Record snowstorm: 13" in January 1893.
**Recreation Areas:** National park, 1; national forests, 3; state parks and recreation areas, 34.
**Points of Interest:** Hot Springs National Park; Pea Ridge National Military Park; Arkansas Territorial Capitol Restoration (Little Rock); Fort Smith National Historic Site; Arkansas Post National Memorial; Buffalo National River; Crater of Diamonds mine near Murfreesboro; Dogpatch U.S.A., amusement park near Harrison.

## KEY EVENTS IN ARKANSAS

**1541   Arkansas region explored** by Hernando de Soto of Spain, discoverer of Mississippi River.
**1686   Arkansas Post established** as fort by French explorer Henri de Tonti.
**1803   U.S. acquires area** in Louisiana Purchase.
**1819   (March 2)   Territory of Arkansas** organized.
**1836   (June 15)   Arkansas becomes 25th U.S. state.**
**1861   (May 6)   Arkansas secedes** from Union.
**1862   (March 7–8)   Battle of Pea Ridge:** Union troops defeat Confederate army.
**1868   (June 22)   Arkansas readmitted** to Union.
**1887   Bauxite discovered** near Little Rock.

**1906   Only diamond deposit** in North America found near Murfreesboro.
**1921   Oil production begins** in El Dorado field.
**1957   (Sept. 24–Nov. 27)   President Eisenhower sends federal troops into Little Rock** to enforce school racial desegregation barred by Gov. Orval Faubus.
**1970   Arkansas River made navigable waterway.**
**1979   Population grows 13.4%** since 1970.

## CALIFORNIA

**Area:** 158,693 square miles; 411,013 sq. km.
**Population:** 22,694,000 (1979); 19,953,134 (1970).
**Capital:** Sacramento.
**Flower:** Golden poppy; **Tree:** California redwood; **Bird:** California valley quail; **Stone:** Serpentine; **Mineral:** Native gold; **Animal:** California grizzly bear; **Fish:** California golden trout; **Reptile:** California desert tortoise; **Insect:** California dog-face butterfly; **Marine mammal:** California gray whale; **Fossil:** Saber-toothed cat.
**Song:** I Love You, California.
**Nickname:** The Golden State.
**Motto:** Eureka (I Have Found It).
**Flag:** Bear and red star on white field above "California Republic" with red stripe at bottom.
**Leading Industries:** Manufacturing (aircraft, automobiles, electronic equipment, appliances, weapons, steel, chemicals), food processing, agriculture (beef cattle, dairying, sheep, grain, fruits, vegetables, nuts), mining (petroleum, natural gas, boron, gold), tourism.
**Climate** (Sacramento): Normal temperatures: Jan. high 53° F., low 37° F.; July high 93° F., low 58° F. Normal yearly precipitation: 17" (water). Record snowstorm: 7.24" in April 1880.
**Recreation Areas:** National parks, 5; national forests, 22; national seashore, 1; national recreation areas, 2; state parks and recreation areas, 186; many beaches.
**Points of Interest:** Yosemite, Kings Canyon, Sequoia, Lassen Volcanic, and Redwood national parks; Cabrillo, Channel Islands, Death Valley, Devils Postpile, Joshua Tree, Pinnacles, Lava Beds, and Muir Woods national monuments; Mt. Wilson Observatory, Disneyland, and Hollywood in Los Angeles area; Civic Center and Golden Gate Bridge and Park in San Francisco; San Simeon State Park; Point Reyes National Seashore.

## KEY EVENTS IN CALIFORNIA

**1542   California coast explored** for Spain by Juan Rodríguez Cabrillo.
**1769   First Spanish fort and mission** in California established at San Diego.
**1826   First American explorer reaches California** by land: Jedediah Strong Smith.
**1846–48   U.S. troops capture California.**
**1848   (Jan. 24)   Gold discovered** at Sutter's Mill by James W. Marshall, starting gold rush to California.
**1850   (Sept. 9)   California becomes 31st U.S. state.**
**1906   (April 18)   Severe earthquake** destroys most of San Francisco, killing 700 persons.
**1911   First movie studio** built in Hollywood.
**1963   California tops New York** to become largest state in population.
**1968   Highest dam in U.S.** built on Feather River near Oroville, 770 feet high.
**1971   (Feb. 9)   Earthquake in southern California** kills 64 persons, causes $500 million damage.
**1976   Nation's first right-to-die law** approved.
**1976–77   Drought** causes $3 billion in farm losses.
**1977   First woman** appointed as state chief justice: Rose Elizabeth Bird.
**1978   Voters approve Proposition 13,** cutting property taxes about 60%, limiting growth of local government.
**1979   Population grows 13.6%** since 1970.

# COLORADO

**Area:** 104,247 square miles; 269,998 sq. km.
**Population:** 2,772,000 (1979); 2,207,259 (1970).
**Capital:** Denver.
**Flower:** Rocky Mountain columbine.
**Tree:** Colorado blue spruce.
**Bird:** Lark bunting; **Stone:** Aquamarine.
**Animal:** Rocky Mountain bighorn sheep.
**Song:** *Where the Columbines Grow.*
**Nickname:** The Centennial State.
**Motto:** *Nil Sine Numine* (Nothing Without Providence).
**Flag:** Red "C" enclosing gold bell against blue, white, and blue stripes.
**Leading Industries:** Food processing, manufacturing (metal products, machinery), agriculture (beef cattle, sheep, dairy products, wheat, corn, sugar beets), tourism, mining (petroleum, molybdenum, coal, lead).
**Climate** (Denver): *Normal temperatures:* Jan. high 44° F., low 16° F.; July high 87° F., low 59° F. *Normal yearly precipitation:* 16″ (water). *Record snowstorm:* 23″ in April 1885.
**Recreation Areas:** National parks, 2; national forests, 12; national recreation areas, 2; state parks and recreation areas, 26.
**Points of Interest:** Rocky Mountain and Mesa Verde national parks; Dinosaur, Colorado, Black Canyon of Gunnison, Florissant Fossil Beds, Hovenweep, Yucca House, and Great Sand Dunes national monuments; Pikes Peak; Garden of the Gods; U.S. Air Force Academy; Durango-Silverton narrow-gauge railway; Central City; Aspen resort area; Bent's Old Fort National Historic Site.

## KEY EVENTS IN COLORADO

**1706** Colorado claimed for Spain by Juan de Ulibarri.
**1803** U.S. acquires eastern Colorado in Louisiana Purchase.
**1806** Colorado explored by Lt. Zebulon M. Pike, who discovers Pikes Peak.
**1833** First permanent American settlement established at Bent's Fort, near present-day La Junta.
**1845** Central Colorado acquired by U.S. with admission of Texas as state.
**1848** Western Colorado obtained in Mexican War.
**1858** Discovery of gold by Green Russell on Cherry Creek near present-day Denver begins gold rush.
**1861** (Feb. 28) Territory of Colorado organized.
**1864** Sand Creek Massacre: Settlers attack and kill hundreds of Cheyenne Indians.
**1870** Railroads link Colorado with eastern states.
**1875** Rich silver deposits discovered.
**1876** (Aug. 1) Colorado becomes 38th U.S. state.
**1891** Gold discovered at Cripple Creek.
**1934–35** Drought develops "dust bowl" in eastern Colorado, causing abandonment of farms.
**1974** Dwight D. Eisenhower 1.7-mile automobile tunnel completed through Rocky Mountains west of Denver, longest auto tunnel in U.S.
**1976** Nation's first sunset law approved to disband agencies that do not serve public.
**1977** Gem-quality diamonds discovered in northeastern Colorado.
**1979** Population grows 25.5% since 1970.

# CONNECTICUT

**Area:** 5,009 square miles; 12,973 sq. km.
**Population:** 3,115,000 (1979); 3,032,217 (1970).
**Capital:** Hartford.
**Flower:** Mountain laurel; **Tree:** White oak; **Mineral:** Garnet; **Insect:** Praying mantis; **Animal:** Sperm whale; **Bird:** American robin; **Nickname:** The Constitution State; **Song:** *Yankee Doodle.*

**Motto:** *Qui Transtulit Sustinet* (He Who Transplanted Still Sustains).
**Flag:** State seal centered on blue field.
**Leading Industries:** Manufacturing (aircraft, machinery, metal products), tourism, agriculture (dairy products, poultry, tobacco).
**Climate** (Hartford): *Normal temperatures:* Jan. high 33° F., low 16° F.; July high 84° F., low 61° F. *Normal yearly precipitation:* 43″ (water). *Record snowstorm:* 19″ in February 1949.
**Recreation Areas:** State parks and recreation areas, 9; Long Island Sound beaches.
**Points of Interest:** Mystic Seaport Museum of Maritime America; Yale University (New Haven); Nathan Hale Homestead (South Coventry); Wadsworth Atheneaum, Harriet Beecher Stowe House, State Capitol, and Mark Twain Memorial (Hartford); U.S. Coast Guard Academy (New London); U.S. Navy submarine base (Groton); American Shakespeare Festival Theater (Stratford).

## KEY EVENTS IN CONNECTICUT

**1614** Connecticut region claimed for Netherlands by Adriaen Block.
**1633** Dutch build fort at site of Hartford.
**1633** English colonists from Massachusetts settle Windsor.
**1636–37** Pequot War: Colonists slaughter Pequot Indians near Mystic and Fairfield.
**1639** (Jan. 24) Connecticut colony organized under Fundamental Orders, unifying early settlements.
**1662** (May 3) Royal charter granted Connecticut: serves as constitution until 1818.
**1665** Connecticut expanded, unifying with New Haven colony.
**1687** Colonists save charter by hiding it in Charter Oak at Hartford to prevent being ruled by British governor of New England Sir Edmund Andros.
**1776** (June 14) Independence from Britain approved in resolution by Connecticut assembly.
**1788** (Jan. 9) Connecticut becomes 5th U.S. state, ratifying U.S. Constitution.
**1794** Eli Whitney begins manufacture of cotton gins at New Haven; starts mass production of firearms with interchangeable parts in 1798.
**1960** (Oct. 1) County governments abolished.
**1974** (Nov. 5) Connecticut elects first woman governor: Ella T. Grasso; first woman governor in U.S. who was not wife or widow of preceding governor.
**1977** Reorganization plan adopted by legislature reduces 256 state agencies and commissions to 23.
**1979** Population increases only 2.7% since 1970.

# DELAWARE

**Area:** 2,057 square miles; 5,328 sq. km.
**Population:** 582,000 (1979); 548,104 (1970).
**Capital:** Dover.
**Flower:** Peach blossom.
**Tree:** American holly.
**Bird:** Blue hen chicken.
**Song:** *Our Delaware.*
**Nickname:** The First State.
**Motto:** Liberty and Independence.
**Flag:** Blue field with centered state seal in yellow diamond above date Delaware ratified U.S. Constitution (Dec. 7, 1787).
**Leading Industries:** Manufacturing (chemicals, plastics, leather products), food processing, agriculture (poultry, dairy products, corn, hogs, beef cattle, soybeans).
**Climate** (Wilmington): *Normal temperatures:* Jan. high 40° F., low 23° F.; July high 86° F., low 66° F. *Normal yearly precipitation:* 40″ (water). *Record rainfall in 24 hours:* 6.5″ in August 1945.

**DELAWARE** *(continued)*

**Recreation Areas:** State parks with recreation areas, 9; Rehoboth, Bethany, Dewey, and Fenwick Island beaches.

**Points of Interest:** Henry Francis du Pont Winterthur Museum (near Wilmington); several historic towns, including New Castle, Dover, Odessa.

## KEY EVENTS IN DELAWARE

**1609    Delaware Bay** discovered for Dutch by Henry Hudson.

**1631    First Dutch colonists** settle at Zwaanendael (near Lewes).

**1638    Swedish colonists** found New Sweden; establish Fort Christina at Wilmington; led by Peter Minuit.

**1655    New Sweden captured by Dutch** led by Peter Stuyvesant.

**1664    England makes Delaware** part of colony of New York.

**1682    Delaware region made part of Pennsylvania colony.**

**1704    Separate Delaware legislature** granted by Pennsylvania.

**1776    (Sept. 20)    First state constitution** adopted.

**1777    (Sept. 3)    Battle of Coochs Bridge:** British defeat Americans in Revolutionary War battle.

**1787    (Dec. 7)    Delaware becomes first U.S. state,** ratifying U.S. Constitution.

**1802    Gunpowder manufacturing plant** established by Éleuthère Irénée du Pont near Wilmington.

**1861–65    In Civil War,** although slave state, Delaware fights on side of Union.

**1951    Delaware Memorial Bridge** completed across Delaware River at Wilmington; second span opened in 1968.

**1963    Delaware Turnpike opens,** completing superhighway from Boston to Washington, D.C.

**1979    Delaware's population** increases 6.2% since 1970, while state drops in rank to 47th in population size.

## FLORIDA

**Area:** 58,560 square miles; 151,670 sq. km.
**Population:** 8,860,000 (1979); 6,789,443 (1970).
**Capital:** Tallahassee.
**Flower:** Orange blossom.
**Tree:** Sabal palmetto palm.
**Bird:** Mockingbird.
**Saltwater fish:** Atlantic sailfish.
**Saltwater mammal:** Dolphin.
**Gem:** Moonstone.
**Shell:** Horse conch.
**Beverage:** Orange juice.
**Song:** *Swanee River.*
**Nickname:** The Sunshine State.
**Motto:** In God We Trust.
**Flag:** Centered state seal and diagonal red bars on white field.
**Leading Industries:** Tourism, manufacturing (chemicals, metal products, transportation equipment, missiles), food processing, agriculture (fruits, nuts, vegetables, tobacco, beef cattle, dairy products), mining (phosphates).
**Climate** (Miami): *Normal temperatures:* Jan. high 76° F., low 59° F.; July high 89° F., low 76° F. *Normal yearly precipitation:* 60″ (water). *Record snowstorm (Jacksonville):* 1.9″ in February 1899.
**Recreation Areas:** National park, 1; national forests, 3; national seashore, 1; state parks and recreation areas, 103; numerous beaches.
**Points of Interest:** Everglades National Park; Biscayne, Castillo de San Marcos, Fort Jefferson, and Fort Matanzas national monuments; Fort Caroline National Memorial near St. Augustine; Marineland;

Silver Springs; Ringling museums (Sarasota); Cypress Gardens (near Winter Haven); Kennedy Space Center, Cape Canaveral; Walt Disney World; Miami Beach; Gulf Islands National Seashore.

## KEY EVENTS IN FLORIDA

**1513    (April 2)    Florida discovered,** named, and claimed for Spain by Juan Ponce de Léon.

**1564    French Huguenot colonists** establish Fort Caroline on St. Johns River near Jacksonville.

**1565    (Sept. 8)    Spaniards** found St. Augustine.

**1565    (Sept. 20)    Spaniards** under Pedro Menéndez de Avilés capture Fort Caroline, massacring French.

**1763–83    Britain wins Florida** in Seven Years War, but loses it back to Spain in Revolutionary War.

**1810    (Oct. 27)    U.S. annexes West Florida** from Spain.

**1814    (Nov. 7)    Pensacola captured** by Gen. Andrew Jackson.

**1818    (April–May)    East Florida captured** from Spain by Gen. Jackson during First Seminole War.

**1821    (Feb. 22)    East Florida acquired** by U.S. from Spain for $5 million in Adams-Onís Treaty (signed on Feb. 22, 1819).

**1822    (March 30)    Territory of Florida** organized.

**1835–43    Second Seminole War** fought by settlers, ending with removal of Indians west of Mississippi.

**1845    (March 3)    Florida becomes 27th U.S. state.**

**1861    (Jan. 10)    Florida secedes** from Union.

**1868    (June 25)    Florida readmitted** to Union.

**1906    State drains Everglades** near Fort Lauderdale.

**1912–15    Miami Beach created** as resort by Carl Fisher.

**1938    Overseas highway** links Key West to mainland.

**1969    First men to land on Moon** launched in *Apollo 11* from Cape Canaveral.

**1977    (January)    Cold wave** causes $385 million in agricultural losses; throws 50,000 out of work.

**1979    Population grows** 30.5% since 1970.

## GEORGIA

**Area:** 58,876 square miles; 152,488 sq. km.
**Population:** 5,117,000 (1979); 4,589,575 (1970).
**Capital:** Atlanta.
**Flower:** Cherokee rose.
**Tree:** Live oak.
**Bird:** Brown thrasher.
**Fish:** Largemouth bass.
**Song:** *Georgia on My Mind.*
**Nickname:** The Empire State of the South.
**Motto:** Wisdom, Justice, and Moderation.
**Flag:** State seal on blue bar, with Confederate flag on right.
**Leading Industries:** Manufacturing (textiles, aircraft, automobiles), food processing, forestry, agriculture (poultry, beef cattle, hogs, peanuts, tobacco, corn, cotton), mining (kaolin, barite, bauxite).
**Climate** (Atlanta): *Normal temperatures:* Jan. high 51° F., low 33° F.; July high 87° F., low 69° F. *Normal yearly precipitation:* 48″ (water). *Record snowstorm:* 5.67″ in February 1961.
**Recreation Areas:** National forests, 2; state parks and recreation areas, 70.
**Points of Interest:** Okefenokee National Wildlife Refuge; Andersonville National Historic Site; Chickamauga and Chattanooga National Military Park; Little White House (Warm Springs); Sea Island; Stone Mountain; Fort Frederica, Fort Pulaski, and Ocmulgee national monuments; Kennesaw Mountain National Battlefield Park; Cumberland Island National Seashore.

## KEY EVENTS IN GEORGIA

**1732    (June 9)    Royal charter for Georgia** granted to

Gen. James Edward Oglethorpe by King George II.

**1733 (Feb. 12) First permanent settlement** established by Oglethorpe at site of Savannah.

**1742 (July) Battle of Bloody Marsh:** Oglethorpe defeats Spanish invasion at Fort Frederica on St. Simons Island.

**1753 Georgia becomes royal colony.**

**1776 (Jan. 18) Patriots** imprison last royal governor.

**1777 (Feb. 5) First state constitution** adopted.

**1778 (Dec. 29) British capture and hold Savannah** until July 11, 1782.

**1788 (Jan. 2) Georgia becomes 4th U.S. state,** ratifying U.S. Constitution.

**1793 Eli Whitney invents cotton gin** near Savannah.

**1795 Yazoo Fraud:** Speculators bribe legislature to sell about 50,000 square miles of western land.

**1838 Cherokees forced to move** to Oklahoma.

**1861 (Jan. 19) Georgia secedes,** joins Confederacy.

**1864 (Nov. 14–Dec. 22) March to the Sea:** Union Gen. William T. Sherman burns Atlanta, destroys 60-mile-wide path to coast, captures Savannah.

**1870 (July 15) Georgia readmitted** to Union.

**1943 First state to give vote to 18-year-olds.**

**1961 (Aug. 30) Atlanta begins to end segregation** of public schools under court order.

**1972 State government reorganized** by Gov. Jimmy Carter, reducing agencies from 300 to 22 departments.

**1973 First black mayor of Atlanta elected:** Maynard H. Jackson Jr.

**1979 Population increases 11.5%** since 1970.

## HAWAII

**Area:** 6,450 square miles; 16,705 sq. km.
**Population:** 915,000 (1979); 769,913 (1970).
**Capital:** Honolulu.
**Flower:** Hibiscus.
**Tree:** Candlenut.
**Bird:** Hawaiian goose.
**Song:** *Hawaii Ponoi.*
**Nickname:** The Aloha State.
**Motto:** *Ua Mau Ke Ea O Ka Aina I Ka Pono* (The Life of the Land Is Perpetuated in Righteousness).
**Flag:** Alternating white, red, and blue stripes, with Union Jack in upper left.
**Leading Industries:** Tourism, military installations, food processing, agriculture (sugarcane, pineapples, beef cattle, coffee).
**Climate** (Honolulu): *Normal temperatures:* Jan. high 79° F., low 65° F.; July high 87° F., low 73° F. *Normal yearly rain:* 23". *Record rainfall in 24 hours:* 17.07" in March 1958.
**Recreation Areas:** National parks, 2; state parks and recreation areas, 46; many fine beaches.
**Points of Interest:** Hawaii Volcanoes National Park (Hawaii) and Haleakala National Park (Maui); City of Refuge National Historical Park (Hawaii); Polynesian Cultural Center (Oahu, near Laie); Waimea Canyon (Kauai); USS *Arizona* Memorial (Pearl Harbor); Iolani Palace, Bishop Museum, and the Waikiki area (all in Honolulu); Nuuanu Pali (near Honolulu); Puukohola Heiau National Historic Site (Hawaii).

### KEY EVENTS IN HAWAII

**1778 (Jan. 18) British Capt. James Cook** discovers Hawaiian Islands, naming them Sandwich Islands.

**1795 Hawaii unified** by King Kamehameha I.

**1820 Protestant missionaries** from New England led by Hiram Bingham begin converting Hawaiians.

**1893 (Jan. 17) Queen Liliuokalani** deposed.

**1894 (July 4) Republic of Hawaii** established with Sanford B. Dole as president.

**1898 (Aug. 12) U.S. annexes Hawaii.**

**1900 (June 14) Territory of Hawaii** organized.

**1941 (Dec. 7) Japanese attack** Pearl Harbor.

**1959 (Aug. 21) Hawaii becomes 50th U.S. state.**

**1979 Population grows** 18.8% since 1970.

## IDAHO

**Area:** 83,557 square miles; 216,412 sq. km.
**Population:** 905,000 (1979); 713,008 (1970).
**Capital:** Boise.
**Flower:** Syringa.
**Tree:** White pine.
**Bird:** Mountain bluebird.
**Horse:** Appaloosa.
**Gemstone:** Star garnet.
**Song:** *Here We Have Idaho.*
**Nickname:** The Gem State.
**Motto:** *Esto Perpetua* (It Is Perpetual).
**Flag:** State seal and inscription "State of Idaho" centered on blue field.
**Leading Industries:** Agriculture (potatoes, wheat, barley, beans, hay, sugar beets, beef cattle, sheep, dairy products), food processing, forestry, mining (silver, lead, zinc, copper).
**Climate** (Boise): *Normal temperatures:* Jan. high 37° F., low 21° F.; July high 91° F., low 59° F. *Normal yearly precipitation:* 11.5" (water). *Record snowstorm:* 17" in December 1884.
**Recreation Areas:** National park, 1; national forests, 15; state parks and recreation areas, 19.
**Points of Interest:** Yellowstone National Park; Hells Canyon–Seven Devils scenic area; Sun Valley resort area; Shoshone Falls (near Twin Falls); Craters of the Moon National Monument; Nez Percé National Historical Park.

### KEY EVENTS IN IDAHO

**1805 Idaho explored** by Lewis and Clark.

**1846 (Aug. 5) Idaho acquired by U.S.** as Oregon Treaty with Britain becomes effective.

**1860 First permanent settlement** established by Mormons at Franklin.

**1860 (Sept. 30) Gold discovered** on Orofino Creek.

**1863 (March 4) Territory of Idaho** established.

**1877–79 Battles** between U.S. troops and Nez Percé, Bannock, and Sheepeater Indians.

**1880 Railroad completed** to southeastern Idaho.

**1890 (July 3) Idaho becomes 43d U.S. state.**

**1951 (Dec. 20) First electricity generated with atomic power** near Idaho Falls.

**1959–68 Three hydroelectric plants** built on Snake River, providing over 1 million kilowatts.

**1975 Snake River project** opens 469-mile navigable waterway from Lewiston, Idaho, to Astoria, Oregon.

**1976 (June 5) 300-foot-high Teton Dam collapses,** causing 11 deaths and $1 billion in damage.

**1979 Population grows** 26.9% since 1970.

## ILLINOIS

**Area:** 56,400 square miles; 146,075 sq. km.
**Population:** 11,229,000 (1979); 11,113,976 (1970).
**Capital:** Springfield.
**Flower:** Native violet.
**Tree:** White oak.
**Bird:** Cardinal.
**Mineral:** Fluorite.
**Insect:** Monarch butterfly.
**Song:** *Illinois.*
**Nickname:** The Prairie State.
**Motto:** State Sovereignty–National Union.
**Flag:** State seal and "Illinois" centered on white field.
**Leading Industries:** Manufacturing (machinery, appliances, iron and steel, construction materials), food processing, agriculture (corn, hogs, oats, beef cattle, poultry, dairy products, soybeans, fruits), mining (coal, petroleum).

**ILLINOIS** *(continued)*
**Climate** (Chicago): *Normal temperatures:* Jan. high
32° F., low 17° F.; July high 84° F., low 65° F.
*Normal yearly precipitation:* 34″ (water). *Record
snowstorm:* 19.8″ in January 1967.
**Recreation Areas:** National forest, 1; state parks and
recreation areas, 144; Lake Michigan beach and
boating areas.
**Points of Interest:** Dickson Mounds Indian burial
ground (near Lewistown); New Salem restoration;
homestead and mansion of Joseph Smith (Nauvoo);
Lincoln's home and burial place (Springfield). *In
Chicago:* Art Institute; Field Museum; Museum of
Science and Industry; Shedd Aquarium; Adler Planetarium; Merchandise Mart; Chicago Portage National
Historic Site.

### KEY EVENTS IN ILLINOIS

**1673**  Illinois explored by Louis Joliet and Jesuit
priest Jacques Marquette for France.
**1675**  Roman Catholic mission founded at Kaskaskia,
near present-day Utica, by Father Marquette.
**1699**  French settlers establish first permanent town
at Cahokia, near present-day East St. Louis.
**1763**  Britain obtains region in settlement of French
and Indian War.
**1778**  George Rogers Clark captures Kaskaskia and
Cahokia during American Revolutionary War.
**1787**  Region becomes part of Northwest Territory.
**1809**  (Feb. 3)  Territory of Illinois organized.
**1812**  (Aug. 15–16)  In War of 1812 Britain's Indian
allies massacre U.S. troops and settlers at Fort
Dearborn, at site of present-day Chicago.
**1818**  (Dec. 3)  Illinois becomes 21st U.S. state.
**1832**  (April 6–Aug. 2)  Black Hawk War fought by
settlers and Indians along Mississippi River.
**1844**  (June 27)  Carthage mob kills Joseph Smith,
founder of Mormon church, and his brother Hyrum.
**1848**  Illinois and Michigan Canal completed, linking
Great Lakes to Mississippi River.
**1855**  Railroad links Chicago to East Coast.
**1871**  (Oct. 8–9)  Fire destroys most of Chicago, killing 300 persons.
**1942**  (Dec. 2)  Atomic Age begins with first successful nuclear chain reaction achieved in Chicago.
**1973**  World's tallest building completed in Chicago:
1,454-foot Sears Tower.
**1977**  State legislature tied up 6 weeks as record 186
roll calls are taken in choosing senate president.
**1979**  Population grows only 1.1% since 1970.

# INDIANA

**Area:** 36,291 square miles; 93,993 sq. km.
**Population:** 5,400,000 (1979); 5,193,669 (1970).
**Capital:** Indianapolis.
**Flower:** Peony.
**Tree:** Tulip poplar.
**Bird:** Cardinal.
**Stone:** Limestone.
**Song:** *On the Banks of the Wabash, Far Away.*
**Nickname:** The Hoosier State.
**Motto:** Crossroads of America.
**Flag:** Gold torch with 18 gold stars on blue field.
**Leading Industries:** Manufacturing (machinery, appli-
ances, steel, transportation equipment), agriculture
(corn, hogs, soybeans, tomatoes, wheat, sheep,
poultry, dairy products), mining (coal, natural gas,
petroleum).
**Climate** (Indianapolis): *Normal temperatures:* Jan.
high 36° F., low 20° F.; July high 85° F., low 65° F.
*Normal yearly precipitation:* 39″ (water). *Record
snowstorm:* 6.4″ on Feb. 24, 1974.
**Recreation Areas:** National forest, 1; national lakeshore, 1; state park and recreation areas, 22.

**Points of Interest:** Prehistoric Indian mounds; Indiana
Dunes National Lakeshore; mineral springs at French
Lick; Motor Speedway (Indianapolis); Lincoln Boy-
hood National Memorial (near Lincoln City);
George Rogers Clark National Historical Park.

### KEY EVENTS IN INDIANA

**1679–80**  Indiana explored for France by Robert
Cavelier, Sieur de La Salle.
**1731–33**  French settlers establish Vincennes.
**1763**  Britain wins region in French and Indian War.
**1779**  (Feb. 24)  George Rogers Clark captures
Vincennes from British in Revolutionary War.
**1787**  Becomes part of Northwest Territory.
**1800**  (May 7)  Indiana Territory organized.
**1811**  (Nov. 7)  Battle of Tippecanoe: Shawnees defeated near present-day Lafayette by Gen. William H.
Harrison, then governor of Indiana Territory and
later President of the United States.
**1816**  (Dec. 11)  Indiana becomes 19th U.S. state.
**1861–65**  In Civil War Indiana supports Union with
about 200,000 soldiers.
**1906**  Gary established as steelmaking center.
**1911**  First Memorial Day 500-mile auto race held at
Indianapolis.
**1913**  (March 25–27)  Floods in Indiana and Ohio
kill 732 persons, cause over $180 million in damage.
**1956**  Indiana Turnpike opened.
**1963**  Studebaker Corporation ends auto production
at South Bend; began as wagonmaker in 1852.
**1979**  Low population growth of 3.9% since 1970
causes Indiana to drop from 11th to 12th most
heavily populated state.

# IOWA

**Area:** 56,290 square miles; 145,790 sq. km.
**Population:** 2,902,000 (1979); 2,825,041 (1970).
**Capital:** Des Moines.
**Flower:** Wild rose.
**Tree:** Oak.
**Bird:** Eastern goldfinch.
**Stone:** Geode.
**Song:** *The Song of Iowa.*
**Nickname:** The Hawkeye State.
**Motto:** Our Liberties We Prize and Our Rights We
Will Maintain.
**Flag:** Blue, white, and red bars, with eagle and
"Iowa" in larger white bar.
**Leading Industries:** Agriculture (beef cattle, hogs,
corn, dairy products, poultry, soybeans, oats, hay),
manufacturing (machinery, chemicals), food process-
ing.
**Climate** (Des Moines): *Normal temperatures:* Jan.
high 28° F., low 11° F.; July high 85° F., low 65° F.
*Normal yearly precipitation:* 31″ (water). *Record
snowstorm:* 19.8″ in January 1942.
**Recreation Areas and State Parks:** 92.
**Points of Interest:** Herbert Hoover National Historic
Site (West Branch); Amana Colonies; Fort Dodge
Historical Museum, Fort, and Stockade; Effigy
Mounds National Monument.

### KEY EVENTS IN IOWA

**1682**  Iowa region claimed for France.
**1762**  Region ceded to Spain by France.
**1788**  First settler, French-Canadian Julien Dubuque, begins mining lead near present-day Dubuque.
**1803**  U.S. acquires region in Louisiana Purchase.
**1808**  Fort Madison established by U.S. Army.
**1838**  (June 12)  Territory of Iowa organized.
**1846**  (Dec. 28)  Iowa becomes 29th U.S. state.
**1857**  Des Moines becomes state capital.
**1867**  Railroad completed west to Council Bluffs.
**1929–35**  During Great Depression more than half of

Iowa's farmers lose land by mortgage foreclosures.

**1960  Majority of state's people live in cities and towns** for first time.

**1979  Low population growth** of 2.7% since 1970, drops state to 26th in rank behind South Carolina.

# KANSAS

**Area:** 82,264 square miles; 213,063 sq. km.
**Population:** 2,369,000 (1979); 2,249,071 (1970).
**Capital:** Topeka.
**Flower:** Native sunflower.
**Tree:** Cottonwood.
**Bird:** Western meadowlark.
**Animal:** American buffalo.
**Insect:** Honeybee.
**Song:** *Home on the Range.*
**Nickname:** The Sunflower State.
**Motto:** *Ad Astra per Aspera* (To the Stars Through Difficulties).
**Flag:** Sunflower atop state seal on blue field.
**Leading Industries:** Manufacturing (aircraft, railroad equipment, chemicals, machinery), food processing, agriculture (beef cattle, wheat, hogs, sorghum grains, corn), mining (petroleum, natural gas, helium).
**Climate** (Topeka): *Normal temperatures:* Jan. high 38°F., low 18°F.; July high 89°F., low 67°F. *Normal yearly precipitation:* 35" (water). *Record snowstorm:* 18.7" on Feb. 27–28, 1900.
**Recreation Areas:** State parks and recreation areas, 29.
**Points of Interest:** Fort Larned and Fort Scott national historic sites; Hollenberg Pony Express Station; Fort Leavenworth; Eisenhower Library and boyhood home (Abilene); 1870s restoration of Dodge City; Kansas State Historical Society and Museum (Topeka); Museum of Art (Lawrence); John Brown Memorial State Park (Osawatomie).

## KEY EVENTS IN KANSAS

**1541  Region explored for Spain** by Francisco de Coronado.
**1682  Kansas region claimed** for France.
**1803  U.S. acquires Kansas** in Louisiana Purchase.
**1806  Kansas explored** by U.S. Lt. Zebulon Pike.
**1821  Santa Fe Trail route** across Kansas pioneered by William Becknell.
**1827  First permanent settlement:** Fort Leavenworth.
**1854  (May 30)  Territory of Kansas created,** setting off guerrilla warfare between proslavery and antislavery factions seeking to control government.
**1860  (July 19)  First railroad** reaches Kansas.
**1861  (Jan. 29)  Kansas becomes 34th U.S. state.**
**1863  (Aug. 21)  Lawrence burned** and 150 settlers killed by Confederate guerrillas led by William C. Quantrill.
**1865–80  Over 3,000 miles of railroad** open across Kansas, making such towns as Abilene cattle-shipping centers for trail drives from Texas.
**1870s  Mennonite settlers introduce winter wheat,** making Kansas leading wheat producer.
**1892  Petroleum discovered** near Neodesha.
**1919  First airplane factory** opens in Wichita; city becomes leading plane manufacturer in nation.
**1934–35  Drought develops "dust bowl"** in southwestern Kansas, driving many farmers from homes.
**1979  Slow growth** of 5.3% since 1970 drops Kansas to 32d rank in population.

# KENTUCKY

**Area:** 40,395 square miles; 104,623 sq. km.
**Population:** 3,527,000 (1979); 3,219,311 (1970).
**Capital:** Frankfort.
**Flower:** Goldenrod.
**Tree:** Coffee tree.
**Bird:** Cardinal.
**Song:** *My Old Kentucky Home.*
**Nickname:** The Bluegrass State.
**Motto:** United We Stand, Divided We Fall.
**Flag:** State seal on blue field.
**Leading Industries:** Manufacturing and processing (machinery, food, tobacco products, chemicals), distilling (bourbon whisky), agriculture (beef cattle, dairy products, tobacco, corn, hay, hogs, poultry, horses), mining (coal, petroleum, gas).
**Climate** (Louisville): *Normal temperatures:* Jan. high 42°F., low 25°F.; July high 87°F., low 66°F. *Normal yearly precipitation:* 43" (water). *Record snowstorm:* 15" in December 1917.
**Recreation Areas:** National park, 1; national forests, 2; state parks and recreation areas, 48.
**Points of Interest:** Mammoth Cave National Park; Kentucky Woodlands National Wildlife Refuge; Abraham Lincoln Birthplace National Historical Site (near Hodgenville); Cumberland Gap National Historical Park; Bluegrass region (around Lexington); Churchill Downs (Louisville); My Old Kentucky Home (Bardstown); Constitution Square restoration (Danville).

## KEY EVENTS IN KENTUCKY

**1750  Cumberland Gap** pass in Appalachian Mountains discovered by Thomas Walker.
**1774  First permanent settlement** established at Harrodsburg by James Harrod.
**1775  Daniel Boone** blazes Wilderness Road through Cumberland Gap; established Boonesborough on Kentucky River.
**1792  (June 1)  Kentucky becomes 15th U.S. state.**
**1798  (Nov. 16)  Kentucky Resolution** written by Thomas Jefferson adopted by state legislature declaring federal Alien and Sedition Acts unconstitutional.
**1800  (July)  "Great revival" of religion** begins with huge camp meeting at Gaspar River.
**1815  First steamboat** reaches Louisville from New Orleans.
**1861–65  In Civil War** Kentucky remains in Union despite opposition by state's slave owners; battles fought in Kentucky at Mill Springs on Jan. 19, 1862, at Richmond on Aug. 30, 1862, and at Perryville on Oct. 8, 1862.
**1875  First Kentucky Derby** horse race run at Louisville.
**1979  State population** grows 9.5% since 1970.

# LOUISIANA

**Area:** 48,523 square miles; 125,674 sq. km.
**Population:** 4,018,000 (1979); 3,643,180 (1970).
**Capital:** Baton Rouge.
**Flower:** Magnolia.
**Tree:** Cypress.
**Bird:** Eastern brown pelican.
**Songs:** *Give Me Louisiana,* and *You Are My Sunshine.*
**Nickname:** The Pelican State.
**Motto:** Union, Justice and Confidence.
**Flag:** Pelican atop state motto on blue field.
**Leading Industries:** Mining (petroleum, natural gas, salt, sulfur), manufacturing (chemicals, metal products), food processing, forestry, agriculture (beef cattle, poultry, cotton, rice, sugarcane, soybeans), services, fishing.
**Climate** (New Orleans): *Normal temperatures:* Jan. high 62°F., low 44°F.; July high 90°F., low 73°F. *Normal yearly precipitation:* 57" (water). *Record snowstorm:* 8.2" February 1895.
**Recreation Areas:** National forest, 1; state park and recreation areas, 31.
**Points of Interest:** New Orleans, including French Quarter, Superdome; plantation homes near Natchitoches and New Iberia; Cajun country (in Mississippi

**LOUISIANA** *(continued)*
River delta region); Chalmette National Historical Park; Evangeline Oak in St. Martinville.

## KEY EVENTS IN LOUISIANA

**1541** **Hernando de Soto** explores part of region, discovering Mississippi River for Spain.
**1682** **(April 9)** **Region claimed for France** by Robert Cavelier, Sieur de La Salle.
**1714 First permanent French settlement:** Natchitoches.
**1718** **New Orleans founded** by Jean Baptiste le Moyne, Sieur de Bienville.
**1762** **(Nov. 3)** **Spain acquires Louisiana.**
**1800** **France regains Louisiana** from Spain.
**1803** **(Dec. 20)** **U.S. takes formal possession of most of Louisiana** after purchase from France.
**1804** **(March 26)** **Region organized by U.S. as Territory of Orleans.**
**1810** **(Oct. 27)** **U.S. annexes West Feliciana District (Baton Rouge)** from Spain after uprising by Americans captures area.
**1812** **(April 30)** **Louisiana becomes 18th U.S. state.**
**1815** **(Jan. 8)** **Battle of New Orleans:** Gen. Andrew Jackson defeats larger British army; neither side aware treaty already signed ending War of 1812.
**1840** **New Orleans** becomes second-largest U.S. port as result of steamboat traffic on Mississippi River.
**1861** **(Jan. 26)** **Louisiana secedes from Union,** joins Confederacy.
**1862** **(May 1)** **New Orleans surrenders** to Union forces after Adm. David Farragut bombards its forts.
**1868** **(June 25)** **Louisiana readmitted to Union.**
**1877** **(April 20)** **Reconstruction ends** with withdrawal of federal troops.
**1879** **New Orleans becomes ocean port** with dredging of Mississippi River channel by U.S. Army.
**1901** **Petroleum discovered** near Jennings and White Castle.
**1927** **Mississippi River flood** drives 300,000 persons from homes, causes huge property losses.
**1935** **(Sept. 8)** **Assassination** in Baton Rouge of U.S. Sen. Huey P. Long, political boss of state.
**1975** **(Jan. 1)** **New constitution** becomes effective, ending property taxes for homes of $30,000 or less.
**1979** **Population grows** 10.5% since 1970.
**1980** **(March 10)** **First Republican governor in 103 years,** David C. Treen, sworn in.

## MAINE

**Area:** 33,215 square miles; 86,026 sq. km.
**Population:** 1,097,000 (1979); 993,663 (1970).
**Capital:** Augusta.
**Flower:** White pine cone and tassel.
**Tree:** Eastern white pine.
**Bird:** Chickadee. **Insect:** Honeybee.
**Mineral:** Tourmaline. **Fish:** Landlocked salmon.
**Song:** *State of Maine Song.*
**Nickname:** The Pine Tree State.
**Motto:** *Dirigo* (I Direct).
**Flag:** State seal centered on blue field.
**Leading Industries:** Manufacturing (paper, leather products, lumber), food processing, agriculture (poultry, dairy products, potatoes, oats, corn, vegetables, fruits), fishing.
**Climate** (Portland): *Normal temperatures:* Jan. high 31° F., low 12° F.; July high 79° F., low 57° F. *Normal yearly precipitation:* 41" (water). *Record snowstorm:* 23.3" in January 1935.
**Recreation Areas:** National park, 1; national forest, 1; state parks and recreation areas, 39.
**Points of Interest:** Bar Harbor; Acadia National Park; Allagash National Wilderness Waterway; Baxter State Park; Wadsworth-Longfellow House (Portland); Roosevelt Campobello International Park; Saint Croix

Island National Monument; Old Gaol Museum (York).

## KEY EVENTS IN MAINE

**1498** **John Cabot explores Maine coast.**
**1604** **First French colony** established at Saint Croix Island by Pierre du Guast, Sieur de Monts.
**1607** **First English colony** founded on Kennebec River by George Popham and Raleigh Gilbert (abandoned 1608).
**1622** **(Aug. 10)** **Maine and New Hampshire granted** to Sir Ferdinando Gorges and John Mason.
**1623** **First English settlements** established.
**1629** **Region divided** by Gorges and Mason with Gorges keeping Maine.
**1677** **(March 13)** **Massachusetts gains title to Maine** by purchase for about $6,000.
**1775** **(June 12)** **First naval action of Revolutionary War:** Patriots capture British sloop *Margaretta* off Machias, Me.
**1775** **(Oct. 18)** **British burn Falmouth** (now Portland).
**1814** **In War of 1812,** Eastport and eastern Maine captured and occupied by British.
**1820** **(March 15)** **Maine becomes 23d U.S. state** as part of Missouri Compromise.
**1838–39** **Aroostook War:** Militia of Maine and New Brunswick prepare to fight in boundary dispute.
**1842** **(Aug. 9)** **Webster-Ashburton Treaty** signed, settling Maine's boundary with Canada.
**1851** **First state prohibition law enacted.**
**1948** **First woman elected by Maine to U.S. Senate:** Margaret Chase Smith.
**1958** **First Democrat elected to U.S. Senate by popular vote in Maine:** Edmund S. Muskie.
**1972** **Penobscot and Passamaquoddy Indians** file suit asking $300 million in damages because over 12 million acres of their land were seized illegally.
**1974** **First Maine governor independent of both major political parties** elected: James B. Longley.
**1977** **Legal age raised to 20 from 18** for drinking alcoholic beverages.
**1979** **Population grows** 10.4% since 1970.

## MARYLAND

**Area:** 10,577 square miles; 27,394 sq. km.
**Population:** 4,148,000 (1979); 3,922,399 (1970).
**Capital:** Annapolis.
**Flower:** Black-eyed Susan.
**Tree:** White oak.
**Bird:** Baltimore oriole.
**Animal:** Chesapeake Bay retriever.
**Fish:** Striped bass.
**Song:** *Maryland, My Maryland.*
**Nickname:** The Old Line State.
**Motto:** *Fatti Maschii, Parole Femine* (Manly Deeds, Womanly Words).
**Flag:** Geometric black-and-gold pattern in top left and bottom right quarters; red and white ornate crosses in other quarters.
**Leading Industries:** Manufacturing (steel, metal products, transportation equipment, appliances, machinery), agriculture (poultry, dairy products, corn, tobacco, soybeans), mining (stone, coal, clay), fishing.
**Climate** (Baltimore): *Normal temperatures:* Jan. high 42° F., low 25° F.; July high 87° F., low 67° F. *Normal yearly precipitation:* 41" (water). *Record snowstorm:* 24.5" in January 1922.
**Recreation Areas:** National seashore, 1; state parks and recreation areas, 49; Atlantic Ocean and Chesapeake Bay resorts.
**Points of Interest:** Fort McHenry National Monument; Harpers Ferry and Chesapeake and Ohio Canal national historical parks; Hampton National Historic Site; Antietam National Battlefield Site and National

Cemetery; U.S. Naval Academy (Annapolis); Assateague Island National Seashore; Catoctin Mountain and Piscataway parks; George Washington Memorial Parkway; Barbara Fritchie House in Frederick; St. Marys City restoration near Leonardtown; USS *Constellation* at Baltimore.

## KEY EVENTS IN MARYLAND

**1608** Chesapeake Bay explored for England by John Smith.
**1631** First English settlement established by William Claiborne of Virginia on Kent Island.
**1632** (June 30) Maryland colony charter granted to Cecil Calvert, 2d Lord Baltimore, by King Charles I.
**1634** (March 25) English Roman Catholics land on St. Clements (now Blakistone) Island, establishing St. Marys City as capital of colony.
**1649** (April 21) Religious freedom granted all Christians in Toleration Act approved by legislature.
**1654–58** Revolt by Puritans led by William Claiborne takes over government, ending toleration.
**1691–1715** Colonial governors appointed by British crown; Church of England established (1692), with Catholics forbidden right to vote or hold office.
**1715** Calvert family regains control of colony under 4th Lord Baltimore, who renounces Catholicism.
**1767** Mason and Dixon Line established as boundary between Maryland and Pennsylvania.
**1774** (Oct. 19) Patriots burn British tea ship *Peggy Stewart* in Annapolis Harbor.
**1776** (Nov. 9) First state constitution adopted.
**1788** (April 28) Maryland becomes 7th U.S. state, ratifying U.S. Constitution.
**1814** (Aug. 24) Battle of Bladensburg: British defeat U.S. forces in War of 1812.
**1814** (Sept. 12–14) British unsuccessfully try to capture Baltimore; bombardment of Fort McHenry inspires Francis Scott Key to write *The Star-Spangled Banner.*
**1828–50** Chesapeake and Ohio Canal built.
**1829** Chesapeake and Delaware Canal completed.
**1844** (May 24) First telegraph line opens between Baltimore and Washington, D.C.
**1845** U.S. Naval Academy founded at Annapolis.
**1861–65** In Civil War, although slave state, Maryland remains in Union; battles include Antietam (Sept. 17, 1862) and Monocacy (July 9, 1864).
**1938** First state income tax adopted.
**1952** Chesapeake Bay Bridge connects eastern and western Maryland; parallel span completed in 1973.
**1977** Gov. Marvin Mandel convicted of fraud; sentenced to 4 years in jail.
**1979** Below average growth rate increases population only 5.7% since 1970.

## MASSACHUSETTS

**Area:** 8,257 square miles; 21,385 sq. km.
**Population:** 5,769,000 (1979); 5,689,170 (1970).
**Capital:** Boston.
**Flower:** Mayflower. **Tree:** American elm.
**Bird:** Chickadee. **Fish:** Cod.
**Song:** *All Hail to Massachusetts.*
**Nickname:** The Bay State.
**Motto:** *Ense Petit Placidam Sub Libertate Quietem* (By the Sword We Seek Peace, but Peace Only Under Liberty).
**Flag:** State coat of arms centered on white field.
**Leading Industries:** Manufacturing (machinery, appliances, printing, metal products), agriculture (dairy products, flowers, shrubs, poultry, beef cattle, hogs, hay, vegetables, tobacco).
**Climate** (Boston): *Normal temperatures:* Jan. high 36° F., low 23° F.; July high 81° F., low 65° F. *Normal yearly precipitation:* 43″ (water). *Record*

*snowstorm:* 19.4″ in February 1958.
**Recreation Areas:** National seashore, 1; state parks and recreation areas, 68.
**Points of Interest:** Adams, Dorchester Heights, John F. Kennedy Birthplace, Longfellow, Salem Maritime, and Saugus Iron Works national historic sites; Minute Man National Historical Park between Lexington and Concord; Bunker Hill Memorial; Cape Cod National Seashore; Nantucket; Martha's Vineyard; Berkshire Music Festival; Salem; reconstruction of first Pilgrim village at Plymouth; Old Sturbridge Village; Basketball Hall of Fame (Springfield); *In Boston:* Old North Church, Old State House, Faneuil Hall, and USS *Constitution.*

## KEY EVENTS IN MASSACHUSETTS

**c.1000** Coast believed explored by Vikings led by Leif Ericson.
**1498** John Cabot explores coast for England.
**1620** (Dec. 26) Pilgrims land, founding Plymouth Colony.
**1628** (Sept. 6) Puritans found Salem under leadership of John Endecott, forerunner of Massachusetts Bay Colony (given royal charter March 14, 1629).
**1630** (Sept. 17) Boston founded; becomes capital of Massachusetts Bay Colony in 1632.
**1636** (Oct. 28) Harvard College founded.
**1636–37** War fought against Pequot Indians.
**1675–78** King Philip's War: Many settlers killed fighting Wampanoag Indians and their allies.
**1684** (Oct. 18) Massachusetts Bay Colony charter annulled by English court.
**1689** (April 18) Revolt in Boston overthrows royal governor of New England Sir Edmund Andros.
**1689–1763** Massachusetts colonists take major role in French and Indian War.
**1691** (Oct. 17) New royal charter for Massachusetts incorporates Plymouth and Maine in colony.
**1692** Witchcraft trials result in execution of 20 persons as witches.
**1775** (April 19) Revolutionary War begins with Battles of Lexington and Concord.
**1775** (June 17) Battle of Bunker Hill: British defeat Massachusetts militia, but with heavy losses.
**1776** (March 17) British evacuate Boston by sea after victorious 9-month siege by Continental Army.
**1780** (June 15) First state constitution, written by John Adams, becomes effective; first ratified by popular referendum.
**1786–87** Shays' Rebellion put down by militia.
**1788** (Feb. 6) Massachusetts becomes 6th U.S. state, ratifying U.S. Constitution.
**1837** (June 29) State board of education established with Horace Mann as secretary.
**1853** (May 17) Labor law adopted reducing hours of work per day from 12 to 10 beginning Oct. 1, 1854.
**1914** Cape Cod Canal opens.
**1919** Gov. Calvin Coolidge calls out national guard to break Boston police strike.
**1966** First black U.S. senator elected in U.S. since Reconstruction era: Edward W. Brooke.
**1977** Islands of Martha's Vineyard and Nantucket vote to secede from state because of redistricting that would eliminate their representation in legislature.
**1979** Low growth rate increases state's population only 1.4% since 1970.
**1980** Voters approve $1.5 billion property tax cut; measure limits property tax to 2.5% of market value.

## MICHIGAN

**Area:** 58,216 square miles; 150,779 sq. km.
**Population:** 9,207,000 (1979); 8,875,083 (1970).
**Capital:** Lansing.
**Flower:** Apple blossom.

## MICHIGAN *(continued)*

**Tree:** White pine.
**Bird:** Robin.
**Stone:** Petoskey stone.
**Gem:** Chlorastrolite.
**Fish:** Trout.
**Song:** *Michigan, My Michigan.*
**Nickname:** The Wolverine State.
**Motto:** *Si Quaeris Peninsulam Amoenam Circumspice* (If You Seek a Pleasant Peninsula, Look About You).
**Flag:** State coat of arms centered on blue field.
**Leading Industries:** Manufacturing (automobiles, machinery, metal products, chemicals), food processing, agriculture (dairy products, beef cattle, hogs, poultry, fruits, vegetables, corn, potatoes, soybeans, sugar beets), mining (iron ore, copper, salt, petroleum, natural gas), tourism.
**Climate** (Detroit): *Normal temperatures:* Jan. high 32° F., low 17° F.; July high 83° F., low 61° F. *Normal yearly precipitation:* 32″ (water). *Record snowstorm:* 19.2″ on Dec. 1–2, 1974.
**Recreation Areas:** National park, 1; national forests, 4; national lakeshores, 2; state parks and recreation areas, 78.
**Points of Interest:** Pictured Rocks and Sleeping Bear Dunes national lakeshore; Isle Royale National Park; Mackinac Island; Greenfield Village (Dearborn); Cook Nuclear Center (Bridgman); Detroit Zoological Park (Royal Oak); automobile plants in Dearborn, Detroit, Flint, Lansing, Pontiac; Soo Canals, Sault Ste. Marie.

### KEY EVENTS IN MICHIGAN

**c.1620  Michigan explored for France** by Étienne Brulé.
**1668  First permanent French settlement** founded at Sault Ste. Marie by Father Jacques Marquette.
**1763  Britain wins region** in French and Indian War.
**1783  U.S. acquires region** in Revolutionary War, but British retain Detroit and other posts until 1796.
**1787  Region becomes part of Northwest Territory;** made part of Indiana Territory in 1800–03.
**1805  (Jan. 11)  Michigan Territory organized.**
**1812  (Aug. 16)  In War of 1812** Detroit and U.S. army of 2,000 surrendered to British by territorial governor, Gen. William Hull; British troops remain on Michigan's Drummond Island until 1828.
**1818  First steamboat on Lake Erie** reaches Detroit.
**1837  (Jan. 26)  Michigan becomes 26th U.S. state.**
**1854  (July 6)  New Republican Party** given name at state convention in Jackson, Mich.
**1855  First Soo Canal** completed at Sault Ste. Marie, linking Lake Superior and Lake Huron.
**1899  First automobile manufacturing company** founded in Detroit by Ransom E. Olds.
**1935–37  United Automobile Workers union** uses sit-down strikes to obtain collective bargaining contracts.
**1957  Straits of Mackinac bridge** opens.
**1967  State income tax** adopted.
**1979  Growth rate slows** as population increases only 3.7% since 1970.
**1980  Slump in auto production** brings state highest unemployment rate in nation with 14.1% jobless.

## MINNESOTA

**Area:** 84,068 square miles; 217,735 sq. km.
**Population:** 4,060,000 (1979); 3,805,069 (1970).
**Capital:** St. Paul.
**Flower:** Pink and white lady's-slipper.
**Tree:** Red pine. **Grain:** Wild rice.
**Bird:** Common loon.
**Gemstone:** Lake Superior agate; **Fish:** lleye.
**Song:** *Hail! Minnesota.*
**Nickname:** The North Star State.
**Motto:** *L'Étoile du Nord* (The Star of the North).

**Flag:** State seal and gold stars on blue field.
**Leading Industries:** Manufacturing (paper, automobiles, printing, lumber), food processing, agriculture (beef cattle, hogs, turkeys, poultry, sheep, dairy products, oats, corn, hay, flaxseed, potatoes, soybeans, sugar beets), mining (iron ore, taconite).
**Climate** (Minneapolis–St. Paul): *Normal temperatures:* Jan. high 21° F., low 3° F.; July high 82° F., low 61° F. *Normal annual precipitation:* 26″ (water). *Record snowstorm:* 16.2″ in November 1940.
**Recreation Areas:** National park, 1; national forests, 2; state parks and recreation areas, 98.
**Points of Interest:** Voyageurs National Park; North Shore Drive; Pipestone and Grand Portage national monuments; St. Croix and Lower St. Croix national scenic riverways; Lumbertown restoration in Brainerd. *In Minneapolis:* Institute of Arts; Walker Art Center; Minnehaha Park; Tyrone Guthrie Theater.

### KEY EVENTS IN MINNESOTA

**1679  Region explored and claimed for France** by Daniel Greysolon, Sieur Duluth.
**1680  Falls of St. Anthony** at present-day Minneapolis named by Belgian missionary Louis Hennepin.
**1762  Spain acquires western Minnesota** from France.
**1763  Britain obtains eastern Minnesota** from France.
**1783  U.S. acquires eastern Minnesota** from Britain.
**1800  France obtains western Minnesota** from Spain.
**1803  U.S. acquires western Minnesota** from France in Louisiana Purchase.
**1805–06  Region explored** by U.S. Lt. Zebulon M. Pike.
**1818  (Oct. 20)  Northern Minnesota** ceded to U.S. by Britain.
**1820–22  Fort Snelling** built by U.S. Army just south of present-day Minneapolis (first called Fort St. Anthony, renamed Fort Snelling in 1825).
**1823  First Mississippi River steamboat** reaches Fort Snelling from St. Louis.
**1832  Lake Itasca,** source of Mississippi River, discovered by Henry R. Schoolcraft.
**1849  (March 3)  Territory of Minnesota** organized.
**1858  (May 11)  Minnesota becomes 32d U.S. state.**
**1862  Sioux Indian uprising** led by Chief Little Crow kills hundreds of settlers.
**1890  Rich iron-ore deposits** discovered in Mesabi Range.
**1894  (Sept. 1)  Forest fire** destroys towns of Hinkley and Sandstone, killing 418 persons.
**1918  (Oct. 13–15)  Forest fire** in Carlton and St. Louis counties kills over 400 persons.
**1955  Taconite processing plant** opens at Silver Bay to extract iron from low-grade taconite ore.
**1979  Growth rate slows** as population increases only 6.7% since 1970.

## MISSISSIPPI

**Area:** 47,716 square miles; 123,584 sq. km.
**Population:** 2,429,000 (1979); 2,216,912 (1970).
**Capital:** Jackson.
**Flower:** Magnolia.
**Tree:** Magnolia.
**Bird:** Mockingbird.
**Song:** *Go, Mississippi.*
**Nickname:** The Magnolia State.
**Motto:** *Virtute et Armis* (By Valor and Arms).
**Flag:** Red, white, and blue stripes, with Confederate flag in upper left.
**Leading Industries:** Manufacturing (clothing, lumber, chemicals, appliances), food processing, agriculture (cotton, rice, soybeans, livestock feed, beef cattle, dairy products, poultry), mining (petroleum, gas).

**Climate** (Jackson): *Normal temperatures:* Jan. high 58°F., low 36°F.; July high 93°F., low 71°F. *Normal annual precipitation:* 49″ (water). *Record snowstorm:* 10.6″ in January 1940.
**Recreation Areas:** National seashore, 1; national forests, 6; state parks and recreation areas, 18.
**Points of Interest:** Gulf Islands National Seashore; Vicksburg National Military Park; Tupelo National Battlefield; Brices Cross Roads National Battlefield Site; Jefferson Davis' homes at *Rosemont* near Woodville and *Beauvoir* at Biloxi; antebellum homes and gardens of Natchez; Old Spanish Trail; Gulf Coast beaches.

## KEY EVENTS IN MISSISSIPPI

**1540–41**  Region explored for Spain by Hernando de Soto, who discovered Mississippi River.
**1682**  (April 9) Region claimed for France.
**1699**  (May) French found first settlement at Old Biloxi (now Ocean Springs).
**1736**  (May) Battle of Ackia: French defeated in attempt to destroy Chickasaw Indian fort in northeastern Mississippi, preventing French conquest of Mississippi Valley.
**1763**  Britain acquires region in French and Indian War.
**1783**  U.S. acquires northern Mississippi in Revolutionary War; Spain obtains southern Mississippi as part of West Florida.
**1795**  U.S. obtains part of Mississippi between 31st and 32d parallels of latitude from Spain.
**1798**  (April 7) Territory of Mississippi organized.
**1810**  (Oct. 27) U.S. annexes West Florida from Spain, including what is now southern Mississippi.
**1817**  (Dec. 10) Mississippi becomes 20th U.S. state.
**1861**  (Jan. 9) Mississippi joins Confederacy.
**1861–65**  In Civil War Biloxi captured by Union Navy on Dec. 31, 1861; Natchez surrenders on Sept. 10, 1862; many battles in state including Vicksburg, which surrendered on July 4, 1863, Brices Cross Roads on June 10, 1864, and Tupelo on July 14, 1864.
**1870**  (Feb. 17) Mississippi readmitted to Union.
**1927**  Mississippi River flood drives 100,000 persons from their homes, causes vast property damage.
**1939**  Petroleum discovered near Tinsley.
**1940–60**  Population declines in Mississippi.
**1969**  First black mayor elected since Reconstruction era, in Fayette: Charles Evers.
**1979**  Population grows 8.5% since 1970.

## MISSOURI

**Area:** 69,686 square miles; 180,486 sq. km.
**Population:** 4,867,000 (1979); 4,677,399 (1970).
**Capital:** Jefferson City.
**Flower:** Hawthorn.
**Tree:** Dogwood.
**Bird:** Bluebird.
**Stone:** Mozarkite.
**Song:** *Missouri Waltz.*
**Nickname:** The Show-Me State.
**Motto:** *Salus Populi Suprema Lex Esto* (The Welfare of the People Shall Be the Supreme Law).
**Flag:** State seal centered on red, white, and blue stripes.
**Leading Industries:** Manufacturing (transportation equipment, chemicals, machinery), food processing, agriculture (dairy products, beef cattle, hogs, sheep, poultry, horses, soybeans, corn, cotton, wheat), mining (lead, clay, barite).
**Climate** (St. Louis): *Normal temperatures:* Jan. high 40°F., low 23°F.; July high 88°F., low 69°F. *Normal yearly precipitation:* 36″ (water). *Record snowstorm:* 20.4″ in March 1890.
**Recreation Areas:** Scenic riverway, 1; national forests,

2; state parks and recreation areas, 53.
**Points of Interest:** Mark Twain's boyhood home and Mark Twain Cave (Hannibal); Harry S. Truman Library and Museum (Independence); house where Jesse James was killed (St. Joseph); George Washington Carver National Monument near Diamond Grove; Winston Churchill Memorial and Library in Fulton; Silver Dollar City reconstruction near Branson; Wilson's Creek National Battlefield; Jefferson National Expansion Memorial National Historic Site (St. Louis); Ozark National Scenic Riverways; Lake of the Ozarks; Meramec Caverns near Stanton.

## KEY EVENTS IN MISSOURI

**1673**  Mouth of Missouri River discovered by French explorers Louis Joliet and Jacques Marquette.
**1682**  (April 9) Missouri region claimed for France.
**1735**  First permanent settlement established at Sainte Genevieve by settlers from Kaskaskia, Ill.
**1762**  Spain acquires region from France.
**1764**  (Feb. 15) St. Louis founded by Pierre Laclede Liguest and René Auguste Chouteau.
**1800**  France regains region from Spain.
**1803**  U.S. acquires Missouri in Louisiana Purchase.
**1812**  (June 4) Territory of Missouri organized.
**1817**  (Aug. 2) Steamboat *General Pike* ascends Mississippi River to St. Louis.
**1821**  Kansas City established as fur trading post.
**1821**  (Aug. 10) Missouri becomes 24th U.S. state.
**1854–65**  Border warfare with Kansas as proslavery Missourians attack antislavery Kansans.
**1859**  First railroad crosses state.
**1861–65**  In Civil War Gov. Claiborne F. Jackson leads state militia in battles with Union forces; Union troops gain control of state in series of battles, but guerrilla warfare continues.
**1874**  (July 4) Eads Bridge opened across Mississippi River at St. Louis, longest steel-arch bridge of day.
**1882**  (April 3) Outlaw Jesse James slain by member of his gang in St. Joseph.
**1904**  World's Fair and Olympic Games held at St. Louis.
**1931**  Bagnell Dam completed, forming Lake of Ozarks.
**1957**  Truman Library opens at Independence.
**1979**  Population grows only 4.1% since 1970.

## MONTANA

**Area:** 147,138 square miles; 381,086 sq. km.
**Population:** 786,000 (1979); 694,409 (1970).
**Capital:** Helena.
**Flower:** Bitterroot.
**Tree:** Ponderosa pine; **Bird:** Western meadowlark.
**Stones:** Sapphire and agate; **Fish:** Blackspotted cutthroat trout; **Grass:** Bluebunch wheatgrass.
**Song:** *Montana.*
**Nicknames:** The Treasure State; Big Sky Country.
**Motto:** *Oro y Plata* (Gold and Silver).
**Flag:** State seal centered on blue field.
**Leading Industries:** Agriculture (beef cattle, sheep, wheat) forestry, food and mineral processing, mining (petroleum, copper, gold, silver), tourism.
**Climate** (Helena): *Normal temperatures:* Jan. high 28°F., low 8°F.; July high 84°F., low 52°F. *Normal yearly precipitation:* 11″ (water). *Record snowstorm:* 21.5″ in November 1959.
**Recreation Areas:** National parks, 2; national forests, 11; national recreation area, 1; state parks and recreation areas, 177.
**Points of Interest:** Glacier National Park; Yellowstone National Park (which extends into Wyoming and Idaho); Custer Battlefield National Monument; Big Hole National Battlefield; Virginia City; Gallery '85 (Billings); Museum of the Plains Indians (Brown-

**MONTANA** (continued)

ing); Fort Union Trading Post and Grant-Kohr's Ranch national historic sites; Bighorn Canyon National Recreation Area.

## KEY EVENTS IN MONTANA

**1742–43 Region explored for France** by François and Louis-Joseph de La Vérendrye.

**1803 U.S. acquires eastern Montana** in Louisiana Purchase.

**1805–06 Region explored for U.S.** by Meriwether Lewis and William Clark.

**c.1807 First trading post** established by Emanuel Lisa at junction of Bighorn and Yellowstone rivers.

**1818 (Oct. 20) Northern boundary of Montana established** in treaty with Britain.

**1829 Fort Union** trading post built for American Fur Company by Kenneth McKenzie near junction of Missouri and Yellowstone rivers.

**1846 First permanent settlement** established at Fort Benton on Missouri River by Alexander Culbertson.

**1846 (Aug. 5) Western Montana obtained from Britain** in Oregon Treaty.

**1852 Gold discovered** in what is now Deer Lodge County by Francis Finlay.

**1860 (July 2) First steamboats reach Fort Benton.**

**1864 (May 26) Territory of Montana** organized.

**1876 (June 25) Massacre of George Custer** and his troops by Sioux Indians in Battle of Little Bighorn.

**1877 (Oct. 5) Chief Joseph surrenders** to Col. Nelson A. Miles, ending Nez Percé War.

**1882 Copper discovered** at Anaconda.

**1883 (Sept. 8) Railroad completed** across Montana.

**1889 (Nov. 8) Montana becomes 41st U.S. state.**

**1916 First woman elected to U.S. Congress:** Jeannette Rankin.

**1940 Fort Peck Dam completed** on Missouri River, largest earth-fill dam in U.S.

**1951 Oil wells begin production** in Williston Basin.

**1975 Libby Dam power project** on Kootenai River begins operation.

**1979 Population grows** 13.2% since 1970.

## NEBRASKA

**Area:** 77,227 square miles; 200,017 sq. km.
**Population:** 1,574,000 (1979); 1,483,791 (1970).
**Capital:** Lincoln.
**Flower:** Goldenrod.
**Tree:** Cottonwood.
**Bird:** Western meadowlark.
**Gemstone:** Blue agate; **Fossil:** Mammoth; **Grass:** Little blue stem; **Insect:** Honeybee; **Rock:** Chalcedony stone.
**Song:** *Beautiful Nebraska.*
**Nickname:** The Cornhusker State.
**Motto:** Equality Before the Law.
**Flag:** State seal centered on blue field.
**Leading Industries:** Agriculture (beef cattle, corn, hogs, wheat), meat-packing, milling, manufacturing.
**Climate** (Omaha): *Normal temperatures:* Jan. high 33° F., low 12° F.; July high 89° F., low 66° F. *Normal yearly precipitation:* 30″ (water). *Record snowstorm:* 29.2″ in March 1912.
**Recreation Areas:** National forests, 2; state parks and recreation areas, 93.
**Points of Interest:** Agate Fossil Beds, Homestead, and Scotts Bluff national monuments; Chimney Rock National Historic Site; re-created pioneer village at Minden; Boys Town near Omaha; Union stockyards in Omaha.

## KEY EVENTS IN NEBRASKA

**1700s French and Spanish explorers** travel through parts of Nebraska.

**1803 U.S. acquires Nebraska** in Louisiana Purchase.

**1804–06 Eastern Nebraska explored** for U.S. by Meriwether Lewis and William Clark.

**1812–13 Oregon Trail pioneered** across Nebraska by fur trader Robert Stuart.

**1819 Fort Atkinson built** by U.S. Army north of present-day Omaha.

**1823 First permanent settlement:** Bellevue.

**1848 Western Nebraska acquired** in Mexican War.

**1854 (May 30) Territory of Nebraska** created.

**1865 Construction of railroad** across state begun.

**1867 (March 1) Nebraska becomes 37th U.S. state.**

**1874–77 Plague of grasshoppers** drives many farmers from state.

**1934 Unicameral legislature** established by amendment to state constitution; first meets in 1937.

**1939 Oil discovered** in southeastern Nebraska.

**1966 Voters abolish state property tax;** replaced with state sales and income taxes in 1967.

**1979 Population increases** 6.0% since 1970.

## NEVADA

**Area:** 110,540 square miles; 286,297 sq. km.
**Population:** 702,000 (1979); 488,738 (1970).
**Capital:** Carson City.
**Flower:** Sagebrush.
**Tree:** Single-leaf piñon.
**Bird:** Mountain bluebird; **Animal:** Desert bighorn sheep; **Mineral:** Silver; **Grass:** Indian rice grass.
**Song:** *Home Means Nevada.*
**Nickname:** The Silver State.
**Motto:** All for Our Country.
**Flag:** Gold and green insignia in upper left on blue field.
**Climate** (Las Vegas): *Normal temperatures:* Jan. high 56° F., low 33° F.; July high 104° F., low 75° F. *Normal yearly precipitation:* 4″ (water). *Record snowstorm:* 9″ on Jan. 4–5, 1974.
**Leading Industries:** Gambling and tourism; mining and processing copper, mercury, gold, and silver; agriculture (beef cattle, sheep).
**Recreation Areas:** National forests, 4; national recreation area, 1; state parks and recreation areas, 16.
**Points of Interest:** Lehman Caves National Monument; Lake Tahoe area; Las Vegas; Reno; Virginia City; Liberty open-pit copper mine (near Ely); Lake Mead National Recreation Area; Hoover Dam.

## KEY EVENTS IN NEVADA

**1775–76 Spanish missionary Francisco Garcés** crosses southern Nevada en route to California.

**1825 Humboldt River discovered** by fur trapper Peter Skeen Ogden of Hudson's Bay Company.

**1830 Old Spanish Trail pioneered** across Nevada from Santa Fe to Los Angeles by William Wolfskill.

**1833 California Trail** from Utah across Sierra Nevada mountains pioneered by Joseph R. Walker.

**1848 U.S. acquires Nevada** in Mexican War.

**1849 First permanent settlement** established at Mormon Station (now Genoa) by H.S. Beatie.

**1850 Nevada included** in new Utah Territory.

**1859 (June 11) Rich Comstock silver lode** discovered near Virginia City, starting rush of prospectors.

**1861 (March 2) Territory of Nevada** created.

**1864 (Oct. 31) Nevada becomes 36th U.S. state.**

**1931 Nevada legalizes gambling;** also reduces residence requirements for divorce to 6 weeks.

**1936 Hoover Dam** on Colorado River completed.

**1951 Atomic weapons** tests begun by U.S. government on Yucca Flats range northwest of Las Vegas.

**1978 Nevada moves ahead of North Dakota** to rank 45th in population.

**1979 Fastest growth rate** among states increases population 43.6% since 1970.

# NEW HAMPSHIRE

**Area:** 9,304 square miles; 24,097 sq. km.
**Population:** 887,000 (1979); 737,681 (1970).
**Capital:** Concord.
**Flower:** Purple lilac.
**Tree:** White birch.
**Bird:** Purple finch.
**Song:** *Old New Hampshire.*
**Nickname:** The Granite State.
**Motto:** Live Free or Die.
**Flag:** State seal centered on blue field.
**Leading Industries:** Manufacturing (machinery, paper, leather products), tourism, food processing, agriculture (dairying, poultry, beef cattle, fruits, vegetables).
**Climate** (Concord): *Normal temperatures:* Jan. high 31° F., low 10° F.; July high 83° F., low 57° F. *Normal yearly precipitation:* 36" (water). *Record snowstorm:* 19" in January 1944.
**Recreation Areas:** National forest, 1; state parks and recreation areas, 67.
**Points of Interest:** Lake Winnipesaukee; White Mountains; North Conway (resort); Portsmouth (old shipbuilding town); Saint-Gaudens National Historic Site (Cornish); President Franklin Pierce's homestead (Hillsboro); Daniel Webster's birthplace (near Salisbury); Mt. Washington cog railway; Profile Mountain at Franconia Notch.

## KEY EVENTS IN NEW HAMPSHIRE

**1603** Mouth of Piscataqua River explored for England by Martin Pring.
**1622 (Aug. 10)** Region of New Hampshire and Maine granted to John Mason and Sir Ferdinando Gorges by England.
**1623** First English settlements established at what are now Rye and Dover.
**1629 (Nov. 7)** Region divided by Mason and Gorges, with Mason keeping New Hampshire.
**1641 (Oct. 9)** New Hampshire settlements unite with Massachusetts.
**1675–76** Many settlers killed by Indian raids in King Philip's War.
**1679 (Sept. 8)** New Hampshire made separate royal colony.
**1689–1763** In French and Indian War New Hampshire's settlements suffer many raids.
**1774 (Dec. 11–12)** Patriots capture British Fort William and Mary in Portsmouth, carrying off 100 barrels of gunpowder and 15 cannon.
**1776 (Jan. 5)** First state constitution adopted.
**1776 (June 15)** New Hampshire assembly votes for independence from Britain; state's delegates receive honor of being first to vote for Declaration of Independence in Continental Congress on July 4.
**1788 (June 21)** New Hampshire becomes 9th U.S. state; ratification puts U.S. Constitution into effect.
**1803** First cotton textile factory in state built at New Ipswich.
**1838** First railroad completed in state.
**1852** State abolishes property ownership qualifications for elected state officials.
**1963** New Hampshire becomes first state to adopt legal lottery as support for public education.
**1978–79** Only state with neither income tax nor sales tax experiences boom as industries move in.
**1979** Fastest growth among New England states increases population 20.2% since 1970.

# NEW JERSEY

**Area:** 7,836 square miles; 20,295 sq. km.
**Population:** 7,332,000 (1979); 7,168,164 (1970).
**Capital:** Trenton.
**Flower:** Purple violet.
**Tree:** Red oak.
**Bird:** Eastern goldfinch.
**Insect:** Honeybee; **Animal:** horse.
**Song** (unofficial): *New Jersey Loyalty Song.*
**Nickname:** The Garden State.
**Motto:** Liberty and Prosperity.
**Flag:** State coat of arms on yellow field.
**Leading Industries:** Chemicals and pharmaceuticals, machinery, food processing, electronics, industrial research, agriculture (vegetables, dairying, poultry), tourism, gambling.
**Climate** (Newark): *Normal temperatures:* Jan. high 39° F., low 24° F.; July high 86° F., low 67° F. *Normal yearly precipitation:* 41" (water). *Record snowstorm:* 26" in December 1947.
**Recreation Areas:** State parks and recreation areas, 104; numerous beach resorts.
**Points of Interest:** Morristown National Historical Park; Edison National Historic Site (West Orange); restored colonial village of Batsto (in Wharton Tract State Forest); Walt Whitman House (Camden); Grover Cleveland Museum (Caldwell); Princeton University; Atlantic City boardwalk; Gateway National Recreation Area; Delaware Water Gap north of Columbia, N.J.

## KEY EVENTS IN NEW JERSEY

**1524** New Jersey coast explored for France by Giovanni da Verrazano.
**1609** Delaware Bay and Sandy Hook Bay explored by Henry Hudson for Netherlands.
**1623** Dutch establish Fort Nassau near present-day Gloucester.
**1660** Dutch build first permanent settlement at Bergen, now in Jersey City.
**1664** Dutch surrender New Jersey to England; English found first permanent settlement at Elizabethtown.
**1665** New Jersey organized as English colony under Gov. Philip Carteret.
**1676** New Jersey divided into two colonies: East Jersey owned by Sir George Carteret and West Jersey owned by William Penn and other Quakers.
**1682** East Jersey also acquired by William Penn and other Quakers, but colony remains divided.
**1702 (April 26)** Proprietors of both Jerseys surrender government control to England's Queen Anne.
**1702–38** New Jersey united with own legislature, but administered by royal governor of New York.
**1738–76** New Jersey separated from New York with its own royal governor.
**1776 (June 17)** Patriots arrest royal Gov. William Franklin, son of Benjamin Franklin.
**1776 (July 2)** First state constitution adopted.
**1776–81** In Revolutionary War many battles fought in New Jersey, including Trenton (1776), Princeton (1777), and Monmouth (1778).
**1787 (Dec. 18)** New Jersey becomes 3d U.S. state, ratifying U.S. Constitution.
**1800** Women first vote in Elizabethtown.
**1807** Law restricts voting rights to men.
**1871** System of free public schools adopted.
**1952** New Jersey Turnpike opens, linking New York City and Philadelphia by superhighway.
**1976** State income tax adopted to finance public schools.
**1978** Legal gambling casino opens in Atlantic City.
**1979** Population grows only 2.2% since 1970.

# NEW MEXICO

**Area:** 121,666 square miles; 315,113 sq. km.
**Population:** 1,241,000 (1979); 1,016,000 (1970).
**Capital:** Santa Fe.
**Flower:** Yucca.

**NEW MEXICO** (continued)
**Tree:** Piñon.
**Bird:** Roadrunner.
**Gem:** Turquoise.
**Animal:** Black bear.
**Fish:** Cutthroat trout.
**Songs:** O, Fair New Mexico and Asi es Nuevo Mejico.
**Nickname:** The Land of Enchantment.
**Motto:** Crescit Eundo (It Grows as It Goes).
**Flag:** Stylized red sun centered on yellow field.
**Leading Industries:** Mining (petroleum, natural gas, uranium, potash, copper), agriculture (beef cattle, sheep, cotton, vegetables, wheat), food processing, atomic research, forestry.
**Climate** (Albuquerque): Normal temperatures: Jan. high 47° F., low 24° F.; July high 92° F., low 65° F. Normal yearly precipitation: 8" water). Record snowstorm: 14.2" in December 1958.
**Recreation Areas:** National park, 1; national forests, 7; state parks and recreation areas, 34.
**Points of Interest:** Carlsbad Caverns National Park; Aztec Ruins, Bandelier, Capulin Mountain, Chaco Canyon, El Morro, Fort Union, Fossil Butte, Gran Quivira, Pecos, White Sands, and Gila Cliff Dwellings national monuments; Taos and Acoma pueblos; Santa Fe; Intertribal Indian Ceremonial (Gallup); Bradbury Science Hall (Los Alamos); Gila Wilderness (near Silver City); Glorieta Battle Site (near Pecos).

## KEY EVENTS IN NEW MEXICO

**c.1528–39  Region explored for Spain** by Álvar Núñez Cabeza de Vaca, Estéban, and Marcos de Niza.
**1540–42  Spanish conquistador Francisco Vásquez de Coronado conquers** Indian pueblos.
**1598  First Spanish settlement** established on Rio Grande River by Juan de Oñate.
**1610  Santa Fe** made capital of New Mexico.
**1680  Revolt of Pueblo Indians** led by Popé drives Spanish settlers out of New Mexico.
**1692–96  Spanish rule restored** by Diego de Vargas.
**1821  Santa Fe Trail** pioneered between New Mexico and Missouri by trader William Becknell.
**1846–48  U.S. occupies and acquires New Mexico** in Mexican War.
**1850  (Sept. 9)  Territory of New Mexico** created.
**1854  Southern New Mexico acquired** from Mexico in Gadsden Purchase.
**1861–62  Confederate troops** from Texas capture New Mexico, but Union forces recapture territory; main battles at Apache Canyon and Glorieta Pass.
**1862–65  Kit Carson** leads New Mexican settlers in subduing Navajo and Apache Indians.
**1867  (March 2)  Peonage abolished** by Congress.
**1876–78  Lincoln County War** among rival cattlemen ends after Gov. Lew Wallace declares martial law.
**1878  (Nov. 30)  Railroad** reaches New Mexico.
**1879–86  Apache Indians** raid and massacre settlers until surrender of Chief Geronimo.
**1881  Outlaw Billy the Kid** killed by Sheriff Pat Garrett near Fort Sumner.
**1912  (Jan. 6)  New Mexico becomes 47th state.**
**1916  (March 9)  Raid by Mexican bandit Pancho Villa** on Columbus kills 17 persons; U.S. troops under Gen. John J. Pershing invade Mexico on March 15 in pursuit of Villa.
**1945  (July 16)  First atomic bomb** successfully tested near Alamogordo.
**1979  High growth rate** increases population 22.1% since 1970.

## NEW YORK

**Area:** 49,576 square miles; 128,401 sq. km.
**Population:** 17,648,000 (1979); 18,241,266 (1970).
**Capital:** Albany.

**Flower:** Rose.
**Tree:** Sugar maple.
**Bird:** Bluebird.
**Animal:** American beaver.
**Fish:** Brook trout.
**Gem:** Garnet.
**Nickname:** The Empire State.
**Motto:** Excelsior (Ever Upward).
**Flag:** State coat of arms centered on blue field.
**Leading Industries:** Manufacturing (leading state), agriculture (dairy products, fruits, vegetables), mining (iron ore, petroleum, salt).
**Climate** (New York City): Normal temperatures: Jan. high 39° F., low 26° F.; July high 85° F., low 68° F. Normal yearly precipitation: 40" (water). Record snowstorm: 26.4" in December 1947.
**Recreation Areas:** National seashore, 1; state parks and recreation areas, 169.
**Points of Interest:** Castle Clinton, Fort Stanwix, and Statue of Liberty national monuments; Niagara Falls; Saratoga National Historical Park; U.S. Military Academy (West Point); national historic sites include homes of F. D. Roosevelt at Hyde Park, of Theodore Roosevelt in Oyster Bay and New York City, Vanderbilt mansion near Hyde Park, and St. Paul's Church; national memorials include General Grant's tomb and Federal Hall in New York City; Fort Ticonderoga; Baseball Hall of Fame (Cooperstown); Finger Lakes, Adirondacks, and Catskill areas; Fire Island National Seashore; Boscobel (Garrison); Gateway National Recreation Area; skyscrapers, museums, theaters, and parks in New York City.

## KEY EVENTS IN NEW YORK

**1524  New York Bay explored** for France by Giovanni da Verrazano.
**1609  (July)  Northern New York explored** and claimed for France by Samuel de Champlain.
**1609  (Sept. 11–Oct. 4)  Hudson River explored** for Dutch by Henry Hudson.
**1614  First Dutch trading post,** Fort Nassau, built on Castle Island at present-day Albany.
**1624  First permanent Dutch settlement** established in New Netherland (New York) at Fort Orange (now Albany).
**1625  New Amsterdam** (New York City) founded by Dutch settlers; Manhattan Island purchased from Indians for about $24 in 1626.
**1664  (Sept. 8)  Dutch surrender New Amsterdam** to English.
**1673–74  Dutch reoccupy New York** but return it to England in exchange for colony of Surinam in South America.
**1683  (Oct. 30)  Charter of liberties adopted;** freedom of religion guaranteed; taxation to be permitted only by consent of voters.
**1689–1763  French and Indian War:** New York is battleground for frequent battles against French and their Indian allies.
**1735  (Aug. 4)  Freedom of press** established in trial of John Peter Zenger on basis that truth is not libel.
**1775–83  In Revolutionary War** British occupy New York City in 1776–83; battles in state include Ticonderoga (1775), Long Island and White Plains (1776), Saratoga (1777), Stony Point (1779).
**1777  (April 20)  First state constitution** adopted; written largely by John Jay.
**1788  (July 26)  New York becomes 11th U.S. state,** ratifying U.S. Constitution.
**1789–90  New York City** serves as first capital of the United States under Constitution.
**1812–14  In War of 1812** many battles fought in state.
**1825  (Oct. 26)  Erie Canal opens,** connecting Hudson River with Great Lakes.
**1827  (July 4)  Slavery abolished** in state.

**1831   First railroad** opens: Albany to Schenectady.
**1832   Cholera** kills 4,000 in New York City.
**1863   (July 13–16)   Riots** in New York City protest Civil War draft, killing about 1,000 persons.
**1883   (May 24)   Brooklyn Bridge opens,** longest suspension bridge of its day, with span of 1,595 feet.
**1904   (Oct. 27)   First subway** completed in New York City.
**1952   UN headquarters** built in New York City.
**1964   Verrazano-Narrows Bridge** opens across New York Harbor from Brooklyn to Staten Island; suspension span, 4,260 feet.
**1974   (April 5)   New York City's highest building** opens: twin-tower 1,353-foot World Trade Center.
**1979   Decline of 3.2%** reduces state's population by more than 592,000 since 1970.

# NORTH CAROLINA

**Area:** 52,586 square miles; 136,197 sq. km.
**Population:** 5,606,000 (1979); 5,082,059 (1970).
**Capital:** Raleigh.
**Flower:** Dogwood.
**Tree:** Pine.
**Bird:** Cardinal.
**Mammal:** Gray squirrel.
**Fish:** Channel bass.
**Song:** *The Old North State.*
**Nickname:** The Tar Heel State.
**Motto:** *Esse Quam Videri* (To Be Rather Than to Seem).
**Flag:** Blue bar to left has letters *NC* (separated by white star) in gold; red and white stripe to right.
**Leading Industries:** Manufacturing (leading state in textiles and tobacco products), agriculture (tobacco, corn, peanuts, soybeans, broiler chickens), forestry.
**Climate** (Charlotte): *Normal temperatures:* Jan. high 52° F., low 32° F.; July high 88° F., low 69° F. *Normal yearly precipitation:* 43″ (water). *Record snowstorm:* 14″ in February 1902.
**Recreation Areas:** National park, 1; national forests, 5; national seashores, 2; state parks and recreation areas, 19.
**Points of Interest:** Great Smoky National Park (partly in Tennessee); the Blue Ridge Parkway; Cape Hatteras National Seashore; Guilford Courthouse and Moores Creek national military parks; Carl Sandburg home (near Hendersonville) and Fort Raleigh national historic sites; Roanoke Island; Wright Brothers National Memorial (Kitty Hawk); Tryon Palace restoration (New Bern); Alamance Battlefield (Burlington); Biltmore Estate (near Asheville); Old Salem restoration (Winston-Salem).

## KEY EVENTS IN NORTH CAROLINA

**1524   Coast explored for France** by Giovanni da Verrazano.
**1585–87   English colonists** sent by Sir Walter Raleigh unsuccessfully attempt twice to settle Roanoke Island.
**1653   First permanent English colonists** settle on Roanoke and Chowan rivers; led from Virginia by Roger Green.
**1663–65   Carolina region** granted to 8 proprietors by England's King Charles II; government established for northern part of region, called Albemarle County, with appointed governor and elected assembly.
**1677–78   Culpeper's Rebellion:** Colonists led by John Culpeper temporarily overthrow proprietary governor.
**1691   Entire Carolina region** begins to be ruled by proprietary governors from Charleston (now in S.C.).
**1711–13   Tuscarora War:** Hundreds of settlers slain in fighting with Tuscarora Indians.
**1712   North Carolina separated from South Carolina** with own governor.
**1718   (Nov. 21)   Pirate Blackbeard** (Edward Teach) killed in battle near Ocracoke Island.

**1729   (July 25)   North Carolina becomes royal colony** as King George II buys out proprietors.
**1771   (May 16)   Battle of Alamance:** Militia led by Gov. William Tryon defeats uprising by western Regulators who protested lack of representation in legislature.
**1775   (May 20)   Mecklenburg Declaration of Independence** said to have been adopted by patriots in Mecklenburg County.
**1776   (April 12)   First colony** to instruct Continental Congress delegates to vote for independence.
**1776   (Dec. 18)   First state constitution** adopted.
**1776–81   In Revolutionary War** major battles in state include Moores Creek Bridge (Feb. 27, 1776) and Guilford Courthouse (March 15, 1781).
**1789   (Nov. 21)   North Carolina becomes 12th U.S. state,** ratifying U.S. Constitution.
**1801–02   Gold discovered** on Meadow Creek in Cabarrus County; state leads in gold production until 1850s.
**1861   (May 20)   State secedes,** joins Confederacy.
**1861–65   In Civil War** many battles fought in state until surrender of Confederate Gen. Joseph E. Johnston to Union Gen. William T. Sherman near Durham (April 26, 1865).
**1868   (June 25)   State readmitted** to Union.
**1890   American Tobacco Company** founded at Durham by James Buchanan Duke; cigarette manufacturing becomes leading industry in state.
**1903   (Dec. 17)   First airplane flight** by Orville and Wilbur Wright at Kitty Hawk.
**1975   North Carolina displaces Indiana** as 11th-ranking state in population.
**1979   Population grows** 10.3% since 1970.

# NORTH DAKOTA

**Area:** 70,665 square miles; 183,021 sq. km.
**Population:** 657,000 (1979); 617,761 (1970).
**Capital:** Bismarck.
**Flower:** Wild prairie rose.
**Tree:** American elm.
**Bird:** Western meadowlark.
**Stone:** Teredo petrified wood.
**Fish:** Northern pike.
**Song:** *North Dakota Hymn.* **March:** *Spirit of the Land.*
**Nicknames:** The Sioux State; The Flickertail State.
**Motto:** Liberty and Union, Now and Forever, One and Inseparable.
**Flag:** Modified Seal of U.S. on blue field.
**Leading Industries:** Agriculture (wheat, flaxseed, barley, rye, beef cattle, sheep, hogs), food processing, mining (petroleum, lignite).
**Climate** (Bismarck): *Normal temperatures:* Jan. high 19° F., low –3° F.; July high 84° F., low 57° F. *Normal yearly precipitation:* 16″ (water). *Record snowstorm:* 15.5″ in March 1966.
**Recreation Areas:** State parks and recreation areas, 20.
**Points of Interest:** International Peace Garden (near Dunseith); Fort Union Trading Post (partly in Montana) National Historic Site; Theodore Roosevelt National Memorial Park; State Capitol (Bismarck); Fort Lincoln State Park (south of Mandan); Fort Abercrombie; Lake Sakakawea; Slant Village restoration (near Mandan); Badlands.

## KEY EVENTS IN NORTH DAKOTA

**1738   Region explored for France** by Pierre Gaultier de Varennes, Sieur de La Vérendrye.
**1803   U.S. acquires** most of North Dakota in Louisiana Purchase from France.
**1804–06   Region explored for U.S.** by Meriwether Lewis and William Clark; Fort Mandan built 1804.
**1812   First settlement established at Pembina** by Scottish and Irish families from Canada.

**NORTH DAKOTA** *(continued)*

**1818**  Northeastern part of state acquired by U.S. by treaty with Britain.

**1823**  (Aug. 8)  U.S. takes possession of Pembina.

**1832**  Missouri River steamboat reaches Fort Union.

**1861**  (March 2)  Territory of Dakota created.

**1863–64**  Battles fought between U.S. troops and Sioux Indians.

**1872**  Bismarck founded.

**1872**  Construction begun on railroad across state.

**1889**  (Nov. 2)  Becomes 39th U.S. state.

**1912**  First presidential preference primary held.

**1914**  Referendum process adopted.

**1920**  Recall procedure adopted.

**1951**  Petroleum discovered near Tioga.

**1960**  Garrison Dam completed, forming Lake Saka-kawea.

**1979**  North Dakota drops to 46th among states in population with increase of only 6.3% since 1970.

## OHIO

**Area:** 41,222 square miles; 106,764 sq. km.
**Population:** 10,731,000 (1979); 10,652,017 (1970).
**Capital:** Columbus.
**Flower:** Scarlet carnation.
**Tree:** Buckeye.
**Bird:** Cardinal.
**Insect:** Ladybug.
**Stone:** Ohio flint.
**Beverage:** Tomato juice.
**Song:** *Beautiful Ohio.*
**Nickname:** The Buckeye State.
**Motto:** With God, All Things Are Possible.
**Flag:** White-bordered red circle and blue stars on blue triangle to left; red and white stripes to right.
**Leading Industries:** Manufacturing (transportation equipment, machinery, metals, rubber products), agriculture (hogs, beef cattle, sheep, dairy products), mining (coal, petroleum).
**Climate** (Cleveland): *Normal temperatures:* Jan. high 33° F., low 20° F.; July high 82° F., low 61° F. *Normal yearly precipitation:* 35″ (water). *Record snowstorm:* 17.4″ in November 1913.
**Recreation Areas:** National forest, 1; state parks and recreation areas, 62.
**Points of Interest:** Mound City Group National Monument (Indian burial grounds); Perry's Victory International Peace Memorial; Presidents' homes: Grant (Point Pleasant), Taft (Cincinnati), Hayes (Fremont), Harding (Marion), and Garfield (Mentor); birthplace of Thomas A. Edison (Milan); Fort Recovery; Campus Martius Museum (Marietta); Pro Football Hall of Fame (Canton); Schoenbrunn village, New Philadelphia.

### KEY EVENTS IN OHIO

**1669–70**  Region explored for France by Robert Cavelier, Sieur de La Salle.

**1763**  Britain wins region in French and Indian War.

**1772**  Moravian settlement at Schoenbrunn near present-day New Philadelphia; abandoned in 1776.

**1780**  (Aug. 6–8)  Shawnee Indian villages of Chilli-cothe and Piqua destroyed by George Rogers Clark.

**1782**  (March 8)  Massacre of 96 Christian Indians by frontiersmen at Gnadenhutten.

**1782**  (June 4–6)  U.S. Col. William Crawford and 480 militia defeated by British and Indians near Upper Sandusky; Crawford tortured to death on June 11.

**1783**  Region acquired by U.S. in Revolutionary War.

**1788**  (April 7)  First permanent settlement established at Marietta, capital of Northwest Territory.

**1790–95**  Severe fighting with Indians; major battle won by Maj. Gen. Anthony Wayne at Fallen Timbers near present-day Maumee (Aug. 20, 1794).

**1803**  (March 1)  Ohio becomes 17th U.S. state.

**1812–14**  In War of 1812 frontier forts withstand sieges; Commodore Oliver H. Perry defeats British in Battle of Lake Erie (Sept. 10, 1813).

**1832**  Ohio and Erie Canal completed.

**1845**  Miami and Erie Canal connects Toledo and Cincinnati.

**1852**  Railroad reaches Cleveland from Pittsburgh.

**1863**  (July 26)  Raiding Confederate Gen. John H. Morgan captured near New Lisbon.

**1913**  (March 25–27)  Floods in Ohio and Indiana kill 732 persons, cause over $180 million in damage.

**1967**  First black mayor elected by major U.S. city: Carl B. Stokes, in Cleveland.

**1971**  State income tax adopted.

**1979**  Low growth rate increases population only 0.7% since 1970.

## OKLAHOMA

**Area:** 69,919 square miles; 181,089 sq. km.
**Population:** 2,892,000 (1979); 2,559,253 (1970).
**Capital:** Oklahoma City.
**Flower:** Mistletoe.
**Tree:** Redbud.
**Bird:** Scissor-tailed flycatcher.
**Fish:** White bass.
**Stone:** Barite rose (rose rock).
**Animal:** American buffalo.
**Reptile:** Mountain boomer lizard.
**Song:** *Oklahoma.*
**Nickname:** The Sooner State.
**Motto:** *Labor Omnia Vincit* (Labor Conquers All Things).
**Flag:** Symbols above "Oklahoma" on blue field.
**Leading Industries:** Manufacturing and food processing, oil refining, agriculture (beef cattle, wheat), oil and natural-gas mining.
**Climate** (Oklahoma City): *Normal temperatures:* Jan. high 48° F., low 26° F.; July high 93° F., low 70° F. *Normal yearly precipitation:* 31″ (water). *Record snowstorm:* 11.3″ in March 1924.
**Recreation Areas:** National park, 1; national forest, 1; national recreation area, 1; state parks and recreation areas, 76.
**Points of Interest:** Lake Texoma recreation area; Philbrook Art Center (Tulsa); Will Rogers Memorial (Claremore); Indian City (Andarko); Fort Sill Military Reservation (Lawton); National Cowboy Hall of Fame and Oklahoma Historical Society (Oklahoma City); Chickasaw National Recreation Area (formerly Platt National Park and Arbuckle National Recreation Area).

### KEY EVENTS IN OKLAHOMA

**1541**  Region explored for Spain by Francisco Vásquez de Coronado.

**1803**  U.S. acquires most of Oklahoma in Louisiana Purchase from France.

**1821**  Santa Fe Trail pioneered across region by American trader William Becknell.

**1823–42**  Eastern Indian tribes forced to move to Oklahoma region, then known as Indian Territory.

**1845**  Western Panhandle region of Oklahoma acquired by U.S. with annexation of Texas.

**1889**  (April 22)  U.S. opens part of Oklahoma to settlement; some 50,000 settlers rush in on first day.

**1890**  (May 2)  Territory of Oklahoma created.

**1893**  (Sept. 16)  Cherokee Outlet opened to settlement; 50,000 to 100,000 settlers rush into area.

**1897**  First major oil well produces at Bartlesville.

**1907**  (Nov. 16)  Oklahoma becomes 46th U.S. state.

**1934–35**  Drought develops "dust bowl"; farmers abandon farms; "Okies" move to California.

**1970**  Arkansas River made navigable, turning Tulsa and Muskogee into important river ports.

**1979**  Population grows 13.0% since 1970.

# OREGON

**Area:** 96,981 square miles; 251,180 sq. km.
**Population:** 2,527,000 (1979); 2,091,385 (1970).
**Capital:** Salem.
**Flower:** Oregon grape.
**Tree:** Douglas fir.
**Bird:** Western meadowlark.
**Stone:** Thunder egg.
**Animal:** Beaver. **Fish:** Chinook salmon.
**Song:** *Oregon, My Oregon.*
**Nickname:** The Beaver State.
**Motto:** The Union.
**Flag:** State seal with "State of Oregon" above it on blue field.
**Leading Industries:** Lumbering and forestry, food processing, manufacturing, agriculture (beef cattle, dairy products, wheat, vegetables, fruits, nuts, flowers).
**Climate** (Portland): *Normal temperatures:* Jan. high 44° F., low 33° F.; July high 79° F., low 55° F. *Normal yearly precipitation:* 38" (water). *Record snowstorm:* 16" in January 1937.
**Recreation Areas:** National park, 1; national forests, 15; state parks and recreation areas, 235.
**Points of Interest:** Crater Lake National Park; Mt. Hood; Oregon Caves National Monument; Oregon Dunes; Cape Perpetua (in Siuslaw National Forest); Columbia River gorge between The Dalles and Troutdale; Bonneville Dam; Hells Canyon; Fort Clatsop National Memorial; McLoughlin House National Historic Site; Picture Gorge and John Day Fossil Beds near Dayville; Sea Lion Caves near Florence.

## KEY EVENTS IN OREGON

**1500s–1600s   Spanish and English sailors** sight coast; Sir Francis Drake in 1579.
**1770s–1780s   U.S. and British ships visit coast,** trading with Indians for furs.
**1792 (May 7)   Columbia River discovered and named** by U.S. Capt. Robert Gray, establishing U.S. claim to area.
**1805   Fort Clatsop** built by Meriwether Lewis and William Clark near mouth of Columbia River.
**1811   Astoria established** as first American settlement by fur trader John Jacob Astor.
**1812–13   Oregon Trail** pioneered to Missouri by fur trader Robert Stuart.
**1818 (Oct. 20)   U.S. and Britain** sign convention agreeing on joint control of Oregon region; renewed in 1827.
**1819 (Feb. 2)   U.S. and Spain** sign Adams-Onís Treaty: Spain gives up claim to Oregon region.
**1825–46   Region controlled** by Hudson's Bay Company's John McLoughlin; becomes known as "Father of Oregon."
**1840s   American settlers** arrive by hundreds along Oregon Trail.
**1846 (Aug. 5)   Oregon Treaty** goes into effect: Britain gives up claims to Oregon region.
**1848 (Aug. 14)   Territory of Oregon** created.
**1851–58   Indian Wars** in eastern Oregon.
**1859 (Feb. 14)   Oregon becomes 33d U.S. state.**
**1877–78   Fighting by settlers** with Nez Percé, Paiute, and Bannock Indians.
**1902 (June 2)   First statewide initiative and referendum** law adopted.
**1908   First statewide recall law** adopted.
**1912   Women given right to vote.**
**1937   Bonneville Dam completed** on Columbia River.
**1964   Worst floods** in state's history.
**1972   First environmental "bottle law"** adopted, outlawing nonreturnable beverage containers.
**1978   Oregon moves ahead of Mississippi** to rank 29th in population among the states.
**1979   State population** grows 20.8% since 1970 despite efforts by state to discourage new residents.

# PENNSYLVANIA

**Area:** 45,333 square miles; 117,412 sq. km.
**Population:** 11,731,000 (1979); 11,793,909 (1970).
**Capital:** Harrisburg.
**Flower:** Mountain laurel.
**Tree:** Hemlock.
**Bird:** Ruffed grouse.
**Dog:** Great Dane.
**Animal:** Whitetail deer.
**Fish:** Brook trout. **Insect:** Firefly.
**Nickname:** The Keystone State.
**Motto:** Virtue, Liberty and Independence.
**Flag:** Gold-bordered blue field with state coat of arms flanked by horse on either side.
**Leading Industries:** Manufacturing (steel, machinery, metal products), agriculture (dairy products, beef cattle, poultry, corn, mushrooms), mining (coal, petroleum, natural gas).
**Climate** (Philadelphia): *Normal temperatures:* Jan. high 40° F., low 24° F.; July high 87° F., low 67° F. *Normal yearly precipitation:* 40" (water). *Record snowstorm:* 21" in December 1909.
**Recreation Areas:** National forest, 1; state parks and recreation areas, 152.
**Points of Interest:** Gettysburg National Military Park; Valley Forge National Historical Park; Independence National Historical Park (in Philadelphia); Delaware Water Gap National Recreation Area; Pennsylvania Dutch region; Fort Necessity National Battlefield; national historic sites include Eisenhower farm near Gettysburg, Gloria Dei Church, Hopewell Village (near Reading); national memorials include Benjamin Franklin, Johnstown Flood, and Thaddeus Kosciusko; Cloisters restoration in Ephrata. Oliver Hazard Perry's flagship *Niagara* from War of 1812 (at Erie); Pennsylvania Farm Museum of Landis Valley (near Lancaster).

## KEY EVENTS IN PENNSYLVANIA

**1609 (Aug. 28)   Delaware Bay explored for Netherlands** by Henry Hudson.
**1643   First Swedish settlements** established on Tinicum Island in Schuylkill River near present-day Philadelphia, and at Upland (now Chester).
**1655   Dutch from New York** capture New Sweden.
**1664   England acquires region** with capture of New York.
**1681   Philadelphia surveyed** and laid out by Thomas Holme as capital of Pennsylvania.
**1681 (March 14)   Pennsylvania granted to William Penn** by King Charles II.
**1682 (Oct. 29)   William Penn** arrives at Upland, renaming it Chester.
**1754–63   French and Indian War:** Begins with skirmish at Great Meadows, Pa., between Lt. Col. George Washington and French on May 28; Washington surrenders Fort Necessity, Pa., to French (July 4, 1754).
**1755 (July 9)   British Maj. Gen. Edward Braddock** killed and army routed by French near Fort Duquesne (Pittsburgh).
**1758 (Nov. 25)   British capture Fort Duquesne;** rename it Fort Pitt.
**1763   Indian Chief Pontiac** wages war on frontier settlers.
**1775–83   In Revolutionary War** Congress meets in Philadelphia for most of period; major battles in state include Brandywine and Germantown (1777); Army winters at Valley Forge (1777–78).
**1776 (Sept. 28)   First state constitution** adopted at convention presided over by Benjamin Franklin.
**1787 (Dec. 12)   Pennsylvania becomes 2d U.S. state,** ratifying U.S. Constitution.
**1790–1800   Philadelphia serves as capital of U.S.**
**1792   State purchases triangle of land** on Lake Erie.
**1794   Whisky Rebellion** in western Pennsylvania as

## PENNSYLVANIA (continued)

farmers protest federal whisky taxes; put down by militia.

**1795   First paved turnpike in U.S.** completed from Philadelphia to Lancaster.

**1811   (Oct. 29)   First Ohio River steamboat** leaves Pittsburgh for New Orleans.

**1829   First railroad** begins operation.

**1859   First successful oil well in U.S.** drilled near Titusville by Edwin Drake.

**1863   (July 1–3)   Battle of Gettysburg:** Turning point of Civil War as Union army defeats invasion of Pennsylvania by Confederate army of Gen. Robert E. Lee.

**1889   (May 31)   Flood** caused by burst dam at Johnstown kills 2,209 persons.

**1957   First full-scale atomic energy plant in U.S.** to produce electricity opens at Shippingport.

**1971   State income tax** adopted.

**1975   State drops from 3d to 4th in population rank** among states.

**1979   Population declines** 0.6% since 1970.

## RHODE ISLAND

**Area:** 1,214 square miles; 3,144 sq. km.
**Population:** 929,000 (1979); 949,723 (1970).
**Capital:** Providence.
**Flower:** Violet.
**Tree:** Red maple.
**Bird:** Rhode Island red.
**Rock:** Cumberlandite.
**Mineral:** Bowenite.
**Song:** *Rhode Island.*
**Nickname:** Little Rhody.
**Motto:** Hope.
**Flag:** White field with gold anchor with state motto underneath, surrounded by 13 gold stars.
**Leading Industries:** Manufacturing (jewelry, silverware, textiles, machinery), food processing, agriculture (dairy products, vegetables, poultry).
**Climate** (Providence): *Normal temperatures:* Jan. high 36° F., low 21° F.; July high 81° F., low 63° F. *Normal yearly precipitation:* 43″ (water). *Record snowstorm:* 18.3″ in February 1961.
**Recreation Areas:** State parks and recreation areas, 85.
**Points of Interest:** Roger Williams National Memorial (Providence); Samuel Slater's Mill (Pawtucket); Touro Synagogue National Historic Site (Newport); Gilbert Stuart birthplace (North Kingstown); Gen. Nathanael Greene homestead (Coventry); Vanderbilt mansions (Newport); Block Island; Narragansett Pier.

### KEY EVENTS IN RHODE ISLAND

**1524   Narragansett Bay explored** for France by Giovanni da Verrazano.

**1614   Explored for Dutch** by Adriaen Block.

**1636   (June)   First English settlement** established at Providence by Roger Williams, providing religious freedom.

**1644   (March 14)   England grants patent for colony** of Providence Plantations; four settlements in Rhode Island unite under this patent in 1647.

**1663   (July 8)   Colony of Rhode Island and Providence Plantations** granted new charter by King Charles II; charter remains state's constitution until 1843.

**1675–76   King Philip's War:** Many settlers killed in fighting with Indians; Wampanoag chief King Philip slain by settlers near present-day Bristol.

**1772   (June 9)   Patriots** destroy British revenue schooner *Gaspée* in Narragansett Bay.

**1776   (May 4)   Independence from Britain** declared by Rhode Island's legislature.

**1776–79   British occupy Newport,** defeating American-French effort to dislodge them in August 1778.

**1787   State refuses to send delegates** to U.S. Consti-

tutional Convention in Philadelphia.

**1790   (May 29)   Rhode Island becomes 13th U.S. state,** ratifying U.S. Constitution by narrow vote of 34 to 32.

**1790   (Dec. 21)   First textile factory in U.S.** begins operation at Pawtucket, built by Samuel Slater.

**1842   Dorr's Rebellion:** Thomas Dorr and followers set up own state government protesting property requirements for voting.

**1870   Imprisonment for debt abolished.**

**1888   Property qualifications for voters abolished.**

**1969   Newport Bridge** built across Narragansett Bay with 1,600-foot suspension span.

**1979   Declining population rate** reduces number of state residents 2.1% since 1970.

## SOUTH CAROLINA

**Area:** 31,055 square miles; 80,432 sq. km.
**Population:** 2,932,000 (1979); 2,590,516 (1970).
**Capital:** Columbia.
**Flower:** Carolina jessamine.
**Tree:** Palmetto.
**Bird:** Carolina wren.
**Stone:** Blue granite.
**Song:** *Carolina.*
**Nickname:** The Palmetto State.
**Mottoes:** *Animis Opibusque Parati* (Prepared in Mind and Resources) and *Dum Spiro Spero* (While I Breathe, I Hope).
**Flag:** Blue field with centered white palmetto and crescent in upper left corner.
**Leading Industries:** Manufacturing (textiles, chemicals, machinery), agriculture (tobacco, soybeans, cotton, beef cattle, hogs), forestry.
**Climate** (Columbia): *Normal temperatures:* Jan. high 57° F., low 34° F.; July high 92° F., low 70° F. *Normal yearly precipitation:* 46″ (water). *Record snowstorm:* 15.7″ in February 1973.
**Recreation Areas:** National forests, 2; state parks and recreation areas, 38; Atlantic beach resorts.
**Points of Interest:** Fort Sumter National Monument, Fort Moultrie, Fort Johnson, and aircraft carrier USS *Yorktown,* in Charlestown Harbor; Cowpens National Battlefield; Kings Mountain National Military Park; Middleton, Magnolia, and Cypress gardens, Charleston; Brookgreen Gardens, Georgetown; Camden and Eutaw Springs battlefields; Hilton Head resorts.

### KEY EVENTS IN SOUTH CAROLINA

**1521   Coast explored for Spain** by Francisco de Gordillo.

**1526–27   Spaniards unsuccessfully try to found colony** near present-day Georgetown; led by Lucas Vásquez de Ayllón.

**1562–64   French Huguenots** unsuccessfully try to colonize Parris Island near Port Royal.

**1566–1650   Spaniards occupy Port Royal** (which they call Santa Elena).

**1663–65   Carolina region** granted to eight proprietors by England's King Charles II.

**1670   First English settlement** established at Albemarle Point on west bank of Ashley River; in 1680 settlement (renamed Charles Town) moves across river; town renamed Charlestown in 1783.

**1706   French-Spanish attack** on Charles Town driven off.

**1711–13   Indian war** between settlers and Tuscaroras.

**1712   South Carolina separated from North Carolina,** each with own governor.

**1715   About 400 settlers killed** in war with Yamassee Indians.

**1719   (Nov. 28)   Rebellion** against proprietary government; colonists choose James Moore as governor.

**1721   (May 29)   New royal governor** takes office.

## SOUTH CAROLINA (continued)

**1729** (July 25) South Carolina becomes royal colony as King George II buys out 7 of 8 proprietors.

**1775** (Sept. 15) Last royal governor flees to British warship.

**1776** (March 26) First temporary constitution adopted; new constitution adopted March 19, 1778.

**1776–81** In Revolutionary War state suffers extensive fighting; British attacks on Charles Town beaten back on June 28, 1776, and May 11–12, 1779; British capture Charles Town on May 12, 1780, after two-month siege; other major battles: Stono Ferry on June 20, 1779, Camden on Aug. 16, 1780, Kings Mountain on Oct. 7, 1780, Cowpens on Jan. 17, 1781, Hobkirk's Hill on April 25, 1781, and Eutaw Springs on Sept. 8, 1781.

**1788** (May 23) South Carolina becomes 8th U.S. state, ratifying U.S. Constitution.

**1832** (Nov. 24) Ordinance of Nullification adopted, forbidding collection of federal tariffs in state; repealed in 1833 after President Andrew Jackson threatens force.

**1860** (Dec. 20) First state to secede from Union.

**1861** (April 12) Civil War begins as South Carolina troops attack federal Fort Sumter in Charleston Harbor.

**1861–65** In Civil War Charleston withstands Union siege from March 1863 to February 1865; in 1865 Union Gen. William T. Sherman marches across state destroying plantations and burning capital city Columbia.

**1868** (June 25) Readmitted to Union.

**1877** (March) Federal troop occupation ends.

**1941** Santee Dam completed, providing hydroelectric power for Charleston area.

**1953** Huge $1.4 billion Savannah River plant near Aiken begins production of atomic materials.

**1975–79** First elected Republican governor since Reconstruction era: James B. Edwards.

**1979** Population increases 13.2% since 1970.

## SOUTH DAKOTA

**Area:** 77,047 square miles; 199,551 sq. km.

**Population:** 689,000 (1979); 666,257 (1970).

**Capital:** Pierre.

**Flower:** Pasqueflower.

**Tree:** Black Hills spruce.

**Bird:** Ringnecked pheasant.

**Stone:** Black Hills gold.

**Animal:** Coyote.

**Song:** Hail, South Dakota.

**Nickname:** The Coyote State.

**Motto:** Under God the People Rule.

**Flag:** Blue field with centered yellow sun encircled by "South Dakota the Sunshine State."

**Leading Industries:** Agriculture (beef cattle, hogs, sheep, wheat, corn, soybeans), food processing, mining (gold, uranium, petroleum), tourism.

**Climate** (Sioux Falls): Normal temperatures: Jan. high 25° F., low 4° F.; July high 85° F., low 62° F. Normal yearly precipitation: 25" (water). Record snowstorm: 26" on Feb. 17–18, 1962.

**Recreation Areas:** National park, 1; national forests, 2; state parks and recreation areas, 1.

**Points of Interest:** Black Hills region (including Wind Cave National Park, Mt. Rushmore National Memorial, and Jewel Cave National Monument); Badlands National Monument near Rapid City; Deadwood; Crazy Horse memorial near Custer; Corn Palace in Mitchell.

### KEY EVENTS IN SOUTH DAKOTA

**1743** (March 30) Region claimed for France by Louis-Joseph and François de La Vérendrye; plant lead plate at present-day Fort Pierre (plate discovered 1913).

**1803** U.S. acquires region in Louisiana Purchase.

**1804–06** Region explored for U.S. by Meriwether Lewis and William Clark.

**1817** Fort Pierre established as fur trading post.

**1831** Missouri River steamboat reaches Fort Pierre.

**1861** (March 2) Territory of Dakota created.

**1873** Railroad reaches capital at Yankton.

**1874–75** Gold discovered in Black Hills.

**1876** Frontiersman Wild Bill Hickok shot to death in Deadwood saloon.

**1889** (Nov. 2) Becomes 40th U.S. state.

**1890** (Dec. 29) Wounded Knee Massacre of 300 captive Sioux Indians by federal troops; last Indian war in West.

**1930–40** Drought, grasshoppers, and depression bankrupt many farmers; about 50,000 leave state.

**1963** Oahe Dam completed on Missouri River at Pierre.

**1972** (June 9–10) Flood at Rapid City kills 242 persons.

**1973** (Feb. 27–May 8) Siege of Wounded Knee: Indians occupy village to protest federal Indian policies.

**1979** Drops in population rank to 45th among U.S. states with only 3.4% increase since 1970.

## TENNESSEE

**Area:** 42,244 square miles; 109,411 sq. km.

**Population:** 4,380,000 (1979); 3,924,164 (1970).

**Capital:** Nashville.

**Flower:** Iris.

**Wildflower:** Passionflower.

**Tree:** Tulip poplar.

**Bird:** Mockingbird.

**Animal:** Raccoon.

**Stone:** Agate; **Rock:** Limestone.

**Songs:** When It's Iris Time in Tennessee; The Tennessee Waltz; My Homeland, Tennessee; and My Tennessee.

**Nickname:** The Volunteer State.

**Motto:** Agriculture and Commerce.

**Flag:** Three white stars in white-bordered blue circle on red field, with narrow white bar and blue bar on right.

**Leading Industries:** Manufacturing (chemicals, electrical equipment, clothing), food processing, agriculture (dairy products, beef cattle, hogs, soybeans, tobacco, corn, cotton), mining (coal, zinc, phosphate).

**Climate** (Memphis): Normal temperatures: Jan. high 49° F., low 32° F.; July high 92° F., low 72° F. Normal yearly precipitation: 49" (water). Record snowstorm: 18" in March 1892.

**Recreation Areas:** National park, 1; national forest, 1; state parks and recreation areas, 37.

**Points of Interest:** Great Smoky Mountains National Park; Cumberland Gap National Historical Park; Rock City Gardens (on Lookout Mountain, near Chattanooga); Chickamauga and Chattanooga, Fort Donelson, and Shiloh national military parks; The Hermitage (home of Andrew Jackson, Nashville); Andrew Johnson National Historic Site (Greeneville); American Museum of Science & Energy (Oak Ridge); Stones River National Battlefield; Parthenon reproduction (Nashville); Grand Ole Opry House and Opryland entertainment park (near Nashville).

### KEY EVENTS IN TENNESSEE

**1540–41** Region explored for Spain by Hernando de Soto, discovering Mississippi River.

**1673** Eastern region explored for Virginia by James Needham and Gabriel Arthur; western part for France by Louis Joliet and Jacques Marquette.

**1682** Region claimed for France by Robert Cavelier, Sieur de La Salle, who builds Fort Prud'homme near present-day Memphis.

**1763** Britain acquires region in French and Indian War, as part of colony of North Carolina.

**1784–87** State of Franklin formed by settlers, electing John Sevier as governor; disbanded when region allowed to elect representatives to North Carolina legislature.

**1790** (May 26) Territory South of the River Ohio

**TENNESSEE** *(continued)*
created; William Blount appointed governor (Aug. 7).
**1796 (June 1) Tennessee becomes 16th U.S. state.**
**1797 (July 7) Tennessee's U.S. Sen. William
Blount** becomes first person impeached (for trying to
stir Indian war against Spain); expelled by U.S.
Senate; impeachment dismissed in 1799.
**1818 (Oct. 19) Western Tennessee purchased** from
Chickasaw Indians in treaty negotiated by Gen.
Andrew Jackson.
**1857 (March 27) Memphis and Charleston Railroad**
completed from Atlantic Ocean to Mississippi River.
**1861 (June 24)** Governor proclaims secession after
people vote June 8 to join Confederacy: east Tennessee
supports Union; U.S. Sen. Andrew Johnson retains seat.
**1861–65** In Civil War many battles fought in state,
including Fort Henry, Fort Donelson, Shiloh, Stones
River, Chattanooga, Franklin, and Nashville.
**1866 (July 24)** Tennessee becomes first Confederate state readmitted to Union.
**1878–79** Yellow-fever epidemic kills over 5,000 persons in Memphis, over fourth of population.
**1933 (May 18) Tennessee Valley Authority (TVA)**
created by Congress, providing cheap electric power.
**1942** Oak Ridge atomic-energy plant built.
**1968 (April 4) Assassination** of black civil-rights
leader Martin Luther King Jr. at Memphis.
**1979** Gov. Ray Blanton removed from office after
pardoning 52 prisoners; aides indicted in pardon-
selling scandal.
**1979** State population grows 11.6% since 1970.

## TEXAS

**Area:** 267,338 square miles; 692,402 sq. km.
**Population:** 13,380,000 (1979); 11,196,730 (1970).
**Capital:** Austin.
**Flower:** Bluebonnet.
**Tree:** Pecan.
**Bird:** Mockingbird.
**Gem:** Topaz; **Stone:** Palmwood; **Grass:** Side oats
grama; **Dish:** Chili.
**Song:** *Texas, Our Texas.*
**Nickname:** The Lone Star State.
**Motto:** Friendship.
**Flag:** Lone star on blue bar on left, with red and
white stripes to right.
**Leading Industries:** Manufacturing (chemicals, trans-
portation equipment, petroleum refining), food proc-
essing, mining (petroleum, natural gas, sulfur, salt),
agriculture (beef cattle, grain, cotton, poultry, dairy
products).
**Climate** (Houston): *Normal temperatures:* Jan. high
63° F., low 42° F.; July high 94° F., low 73° F.
*Normal yearly precipitation:* 48″ (water). *Record
snowstorm:* 20″ on Feb. 14–15, 1895.
**Recreation Areas:** National parks, 2; national forests,
4; national recreation areas, 2; national seashore, 1;
state parks and recreation areas, 75.
**Points of Interest:** Padre Island National Seashore; Big
Bend and Guadalupe Mountains national parks; Gulf
Coast resort area; Alamo (San Antonio); state capital
(Austin); King Ranch (near Kingsville); Lyndon B.
Johnson Space Center (Houston); Amistad and Lake
Meredith national recreation areas; Alibates Quarries
and Texas Panhandle Culture National Monument;
national historic sites include Fort Davis, Lyndon B.
Johnson ranch, San Jose Mission; Chamizal National
Memorial; battleship USS *Texas* in Houston.

### KEY EVENTS IN TEXAS

**1519 Coast explored for Spain** by Alonso Álvarez de
Piñeda.
**1682 First Spanish settlement** established at Ysleta
near present-day El Paso.

**1685 French build Fort St. Louis** at Matagorda Bay.
**1821 Americans led by Stephen F. Austin** settle
along Brazos River in Mexican territory.
**1836 (Feb. 23–March 6) Siege of Alamo:** 187 Texans and frontiersmen fight to death against Mexicans.
**1836 (March 2)** Texas independence declared.
**1836 (April 21) Battle of San Jacinto:** Gen. Sam
Houston defeats Mexicans; captures Mexican Gen.
Antonio López de Santa Anna.
**1836 (Oct. 22) Independent Republic of Texas** installs Sam Houston as president.
**1845 (Dec. 29) Texas becomes 28th U.S. state.**
**1846–48** Mexican War fought by U.S. and Mexico.
**1861 (Feb. 23) Texans vote to secede;** Gov. Sam
Houston, who opposes secession, deposed March 20.
**1861–65** In Civil War several battles fought in state;
last Confederate army under Gen. Kirby Smith
surrenders on May 26, 1865.
**1866 Chisholm Trail** for cattle drives pioneered by
Jesse Chisholm from Texas to Kansas.
**1870 (March 30) Texas readmitted to Union.**
**1900 (Sept. 8) Hurricane and tidal wave** kills 6,000
persons at Galveston.
**1901 Spindletop oil field** opens near Beaumont.
**1962 Space center** built in Houston.
**1963 (Nov. 22) President John F. Kennedy assas-
sinated** in Dallas.
**1979 First Republican governor** in 105 years takes
office: William P. Clements Jr.
**1979 Population grows** 19.5% since 1970; raises
state to 3d in population in U.S.

## UTAH

**Area:** 84,916 square miles; 219,931 sq. km.
**Population:** 1,367,000 (1979); 1,059,273 (1970).
**Capital:** Salt Lake City.
**Flower:** Sego lily.
**Tree:** Blue spruce.
**Bird:** Sea gull.
**Gem:** Topaz.
**Song:** *Utah, We Love Thee.*
**Nickname:** The Beehive State.
**Motto:** Industry.
**Flag:** State seal in gold circle on blue field.
**Leading Industries:** Manufacturing (primary metals,
transportation equipment, machinery), food process-
ing, mining (copper, petroleum, gold, iron, lead, coal,
uranium, zinc), agriculture (beef cattle, dairy prod-
ucts, hay, wheat, sugar beets, fruits, vegetables).
**Climate** (Salt Lake City): *Normal temperatures:* Jan.
high 37° F., low 19° F.; July high 93° F., low
61° F. *Normal yearly precipitation:* 15″ (water). *Record snowstorm:* 18.1″ in December 1972.
**Recreation Areas:** National parks, 5; national forests, 9;
national recreation area, 1; state parks and recreation
areas, 44.
**Points of Interest:** Bryce Canyon, Zion, Canyonlands,
Arches, and Capitol Reef national parks; Cedar
Breaks, Natural Bridges, Rainbow Bridge, Hoven-
weep, Timpanogos Cave, and Dinosaur national
monuments; Mormon Tabernacle (Salt Lake City);
Great Salt Lake; Glen Canyon; Monument Valley;
Flaming Gorge; Golden Spike National Historic Site;
Glen Canyon National Recreation Area.

### KEY EVENTS IN UTAH

**1776 Region explored for Spain** by Franciscan friars
Silvestre Vélez de Escalante and Francisco Atanasio
Domínguez.
**1824–25 Great Salt Lake discovered** by American
frontiersman James Bridger.
**1847 (July 21–24) Mormons reach Great Salt Lake**
under leadership of Brigham Young.

1848   Grasshopper plague wiped out by sea gulls.
1848 (Feb. 2)   U.S. acquires Utah in treaty ending Mexican War.
1849   State of Deseret organized by Mormons.
1850 (Sept. 9)   Territory of Utah created by Congress.
1857–58   Utah War: President Buchanan removes Brigham Young as territorial governor, sends federal troops to take control of Utah from Mormons.
1862 (July 1)   Polygamy practiced by Mormons made crime by act of Congress; much trouble ensues for several decades as federal authorities seek to enforce law.
1869 (May 10)   First transcontinental railroad completed with driving of golden spike at Promontory Point, Utah.
1890 (Oct. 6)   Mormon Church renounces polygamy.
1894 (Sept. 7)   Pardon and restoration of civil rights proclaimed by President Cleveland for persons disfranchised by antipolygamy laws.
1896 (Jan. 4)   Utah becomes 45th U.S. state.
1916   First non-Mormon elected governor: Democrat Simon Bamberger.
1952   Uranium discovered near Moab.
1979   High growth rate increases state population 29.1% since 1970.

## VERMONT

Area: 9,609 square miles; 24,887 sq. km.
Population: 493,000 (1979); 444,732 (1970).
Capital: Montpelier.
Flower: Red clover.
Tree: Sugar maple.
Animal: Morgan horse; Insect: Honeybee.
Bird: Hermit thrush.
Song: Hail, Vermont!
Nickname: The Green Mountain State.
Motto: Freedom and Unity.
Flag: State coat of arms centered on blue field.
Climate (Burlington): Normal temperatures: Jan. high 26°F., low 8°F.; July high 81°F., low 59°F. Normal yearly precipitation: 33" (water). Record snowstorm: 24.2" in January 1934.
Leading Industries: Manufacturing (machinery, paper), food processing, tourism, agriculture (dairy products, poultry, potatoes, apples, maple sugar), mining (granite, marble).
Recreation Areas: National forest, 1; state parks and recreation areas, 72; winter sports areas, 5.
Points of Interest: Green Mountain National Forest; Lake Champlain; Bennington Battle Monument; Calvin Coolidge Homestead (Plymouth); Shelburne Museum; Marble Exhibit (Proctor).

### KEY EVENTS IN VERMONT

1609   Region explored and claimed for France by Samuel de Champlain.
1666   First French settlement established at Fort Sainte Anne on Isle La Motte in Lake Champlain.
1724   First English settlers from Massachusetts establish Fort Dummer at present-day Brattleboro.
1749–64   New Hampshire grants land to settlers.
1763   Britain wins control of region in French and Indian War.
1764 (July 20)   British crown rules New York, controls Vermont region; New York begins trying to force New Hampshire settlers in Vermont to give up land.
1770–75   Green Mountain Boys organize under Ethan Allen to drive out New York settlers.
1775 (May 10)   Fort Ticonderoga captured by Green Mountain Boys led by Ethan Allen.
1777 (Jan. 15)   Vermont settlers declare independence as republic called New Connecticut.

1777 (July 2–8)   First constitution adopted, using name Vermont; abolishes slavery; provides universal male suffrage.
1777 (Aug. 16)   Battle of Bennington: British defeated just west of Bennington in New York.
1790 (Oct. 28)   New York gives up claims to Vermont upon payment of $30,000 by Vermont.
1791 (March 4)   Vermont becomes 14th U.S. state.
1823   Champlain Canal opens, connecting Lake Champlain to Hudson River.
1848   First railroad begins operation in state.
1864 (Oct. 19)   Confederate troops rob St. Albans banks of $200,000 and escape into Canada.
1963   First Democratic governor since 1854 takes office: Philip H. Hoff.
1979   State population grows 10.9% since 1970.

## VIRGINIA

Area: 40,817 square miles; 105,716 sq. km.
Population: 5,197,000 (1979); 4,648,494 (1970).
Capital: Richmond.
Flower: Dogwood.
Tree: Dogwood.
Animal: Foxhound.
Bird: Cardinal.
Shell: Oyster.
Song: Carry Me Back to Old Virginia.
Nickname: The Old Dominion.
Motto: Sic Semper Tyrannis (Thus Always to Tyrants).
Flag: State seal centered on blue field.
Leading Industries: Manufacturing (chemicals, tobacco products, electrical and electronic equipment), food processing, agriculture (tobacco, beef cattle), dairy products, hogs, horses, turkeys, corn, peanuts, soybeans), mining (coal).
Climate (Norfolk): Normal temperatures: Jan. high 49°F., low 32°F.; July high 87°F., low 70°F. Normal yearly precipitation: 45" (water). Record snowstorm: 17.7" in December 1892.
Recreation Areas: National park, 1; national forests, 2; national seashore, 1; state parks and recreation areas, 34.
Points of Interest: Shenandoah National Park; Assateague Island National Seashore; national monuments include Booker T. Washington birthplace (near Roanoke) and George Washington birthplace (in Westmoreland County); Fredericksburg and Spotsylvania National Military Park; Petersburg National Battlefield; Manassas and Richmond National Battlefield Parks; Arlington House, Robert E. Lee National Memorial; national cemeteries at Fredericksburg, Poplar Grove, and Yorktown; Prince William Forest; Wolf Trap Farm; Skyline Drive and Blue Ridge Parkway; Monticello; Williamsburg; Mount Vernon; Appomattox Court House, Cumberland Gap, and Colonial national historical parks (last includes Jamestown and Yorktown); Alexandria; Fredericksburg; Richmond; Stratford Hall; Berkeley Plantation.

### KEY EVENTS IN VIRGINIA

1607 (May 13)   English colony established at Jamestown.
1619   First black slaves in English colonies in America arrive at Jamestown on Dutch ship.
1619 (July 30)   First representative legislature meets in America: Virginia's House of Burgesses.
1622   Indian uprising kills over 300 colonists.
1624   Virginia made royal colony by King James I.
1644   Indian raids massacre about 500 settlers.
1676 (Sept. 19)   Nathaniel Bacon burns Jamestown in rebellion against royal governor.
1693   College of William and Mary chartered.
1754–63   French and Indian War: Virginia's George

**VIRGINIA** (continued)

Washington initiates conflict with French.

**1775 (March 23)** **Patrick Henry appeals to patriots:** "Give me liberty or give me death!"

**1775 (June 8)** **Royal governor** flees to British ship.

**1776 (May 15)** **Virginia directs delegates in Continental Congress** to vote for independence.

**1776 (June 12)** **Declaration of Rights** written by George Mason adopted by Virginia Convention; state constitution adopted on June 29, also written by Mason; Patrick Henry becomes first governor.

**1776–81** **In Revolutionary War** Virginians drive off attacks by British in 1776; British invade Virginia (1780–81) but lose Battle of Yorktown as Gen. Charles Cornwallis' army surrenders (Oct. 19, 1781).

**1788 (June 25)** **Virginia becomes 10th U.S. state**, ratifying U.S. Constitution.

**1798 (Dec. 24)** **Virginia Resolution** by James Madison adopted by legislature, declaring Alien and Sedition Acts unconstitutional.

**1831 (Aug. 13–23)** **Slave uprising led by Nat Turner;** 57 whites and about 100 blacks killed; 20 blacks including Turner executed.

**1861 (April 17)** **Virginia secedes,** joins Confederacy; western Virginians remain loyal to Union, forming separate state of West Virginia in 1863.

**1861–65** **In Civil War** Virginia is major battleground with scores of battles; Richmond serves as Confederate capital (May 1861–April 1865); war ends in Virginia with Lee's surrender to Grant at Appomattox Court House (April 9, 1865).

**1870 (Jan. 16)** **Virginia readmitted** to Union.

**1873** **Railroad built** from Richmond to Ohio River.

**1926** **Colonial Williamsburg restoration** begun by John D. Rockefeller Jr.

**1969** **First Republican elected governor** since 1869: A. Linwood Holton.

**1979** **State population increases 11.8%** since 1970.

# WASHINGTON

**Area:** 68,192 square miles; 176,616 sq. km.
**Population:** 3,926,000 (1979); 3,409,169 (1970).
**Capital:** Olympia.
**Flower:** Western rhododendron; **Tree:** Western hemlock.
**Fish:** Steelhead trout.
**Bird:** Willow goldfinch.
**Gem:** Petrified wood.
**Song:** *Washington, My Home.*
**Nickname:** The Evergreen State.
**Motto:** *Alki* (By and By).
**Flag:** State seal centered on green field.
**Leading Industries:** Manufacturing (aircraft, ships, chemicals, paper, machinery), forestry, food processing, agriculture (wheat, potatoes, sugar beets, apples, beef cattle, dairy products, poultry).
**Climate** (Seattle): *Normal temperatures:* Jan. high 45°F., low 35°F.; July high 76°F., low 56°F. *Normal yearly precipitation:* 36" (water). *Record snowstorm:* 21.5" in February 1916.
**Recreation Areas:** National parks, 3; national forests, 9; national recreation areas, 3; state parks and recreation areas, 187.
**Points of Interest:** Mt. Rainier, Olympic, and North Cascades national parks; Grand Coulee Dam, Ross Lake, and Lake Chelan national recreation areas; Whitman Mission (west of Walla Walla) and Fort Vancouver national historic sites; San Juan Island National Historical Park; Pacific Science Center and Space Needle (Seattle).

## KEY EVENTS IN WASHINGTON

**1774** **Coast explored for Spain** by Juan Pérez.
**1775** **Region claimed for Spain** by Bruno Heceta, who lands near mouth of Quinault River.

**1792 (May 7)** **Columbia River discovered** and named by American Capt. Robert Gray.

**1792–94** **Coast surveyed for Britain** by Capt. George Vancouver.

**1805–06** **Lewis and Clark** explore region along Columbia River and coastal area for U.S.

**1810** **Trading post** built at present-day Spokane by Canadian explorer David Thompson.

**1811** **First American settlement** at Okanogan by David Stuart for Pacific Fur Company.

**1818 (Oct. 20)** **U.S. and Britain** agree to joint control of region; treaty renewed in 1827.

**1819 (Feb. 2)** **Spain gives up claim to region** in Adams-Onís Treaty with U.S.

**1824** **Russia gives up claim to region** in treaty with U.S.; ratified Jan. 12, 1825.

**1825** **Vancouver founded** by Hudson's Bay Company's John McLoughlin, who controls region for next two decades.

**1846 (Aug. 5)** **Britain gives up claim to region** as Oregon Treaty goes into effect.

**1847 (Nov. 29)** **Cayuse Indians** massacre American missionaries Marcus and Narcissa Whitman and 11 other settlers near present-day Walla Walla, touching off Cayuse War; settlers destroy Indian villages.

**1848 (Aug. 14)** **Territory of Oregon** created, including present-day Washington.

**1852** **Seattle founded.**

**1853 (March 2)** **Territory of Washington** created.

**1855–59** **Yakima Indians** war with settlers in effort to protect their land.

**1883** **Northern Pacific Railroad** completed between Washington and eastern United States.

**1889 (Nov. 11)** **Washington becomes 42d U.S. state.**

**1917** **Canal completed** from Puget Sound to Lake Washington.

**1941** **Grand Coulee Dam** begins operation on Columbia River, largest concrete dam and largest hydroelectric power plant in U.S.

**1943** **Hanford Works** atomic-energy plant built.

**1962** **Century 21 World's Fair** held at Seattle.

**1974** **World's first environmental exposition,** Expo '74, held in Spokane.

**1979** **State population increases 15.2%** since 1970.

**1980 (May 18)** **Mount St. Helens erupts;** 66 dead or missing; $1.6 billion in damage.

# WEST VIRGINIA

**Area:** 24,181 square miles; 62,628 sq. km.
**Population:** 1,878,000 (1979); 1,744,237 (1970).
**Capital:** Charleston.
**Flower:** Big rhododendron; **Tree:** Sugar maple.
**Bird:** Cardinal; **Animal:** Black bear.
**Fish:** Brook trout.
**Songs:** *The West Virginia Hills; This Is My West Virginia;* and *West Virginia, My Home Sweet Home* (all official songs).
**Nickname:** The Mountain State.
**Motto:** *Montani Semper Liberi* (Mountaineers Are Always Free).
**Flag:** State coat of arms centered on blue-bordered white field.
**Leading Industries:** Manufacturing (chemicals, iron and steel, nickel, aluminum, glassware, pottery, machinery), mining (coal, natural gas, petroleum), agriculture (beef cattle, dairy products, poultry, fruits, corn).
**Climate** (Charleston): *Normal temperatures:* Jan. high 44°F., low 25°F.; July high 86°F., low 64°F. *Normal yearly precipitation:* 41" (water). *Record snowstorm:* 15.1" in November 1950.
**Recreation Areas:** National forests, 3; state parks and recreation areas, 34.
**Points of Interest:** Harpers Ferry and Chesapeake

and Ohio Canal national historical parks; White Sulphur Springs and Berkeley Springs resorts; National Radio Astronomy Observatory (Green Bank) Blennerhassett Island; scenic railroad at Cass; historic homes at Charles Town.

## KEY EVENTS IN WEST VIRGINIA

**1609–1863**  West Virginia included in Virginia.
**1726  First settler:** Morgan Morgan builds cabin at Bunker Hill.
**1727  German settlers** from Pennsylvania found New Mecklenburg (now Shepherdstown).
**1742  Coal discovered** near present-day Racine.
**1748  Harpers Ferry** begins carrying passengers across Shenandoah River.
**1754–63  French and Indian War:** George Washington commands militia troops on Virginia's frontier, including what is now West Virginia.
**1774 (Oct. 10)  Battle of Point Pleasant:** About 3,000 Virginia militia under Col. Andrew Lewis defeat 1,000 Shawnees led by Chief Cornstalk.
**1775–83  In Revolutionary War** Indians and British loyalists make many raids on settlers; last battle is attack on Fort Henry at present-day Wheeling (Sept. 11–13, 1782).
**1859 (Oct. 16–18)  John Brown** seizes arsenal at Harpers Ferry; hanged at Charles Town on Dec. 2.
**1860  Petroleum** discovered at Burning Springs.
**1861 (April 17)  Opposition to secession** voted by western delegates at Virginia Convention; West Virginians choose governor loyal to union (June 20).
**1861–65  Many Civil War battles** take place.
**1863 (June 20)  Becomes 35th U.S. state.**
**1915  U.S. Supreme Court** rules West Virginia owes Virginia over $12 million as part of state debt before Civil War; debt finally paid in 1939.
**1921  Miners and owners battle** in Logan County.
**1950–70  Poor economic conditions** cause 13% decline in population from 2,005,452 in 1950.
**1965 (March)  Appalachian Regional Redevelopment Act** brings federal aid to revitalize economy.
**1972 (Feb. 26)  Flood** caused by collapse of coal-waste dam at Buffalo Creek kills 118 persons.
**1979  Population increases** 7.7% since 1970.

## WISCONSIN

**Area:** 56,154 square miles; 145,438 sq. km.
**Population:** 4,720,000 (1979); 4,417,933 (1970).
**Capital:** Madison.
**Flower:** Wood violet.
**Tree:** Sugar maple.
**Bird:** Robin.
**Rock:** Red granite.
**Mineral:** Galena.
**Animal:** Badger; **Wildlife Animal:** White-tailed deer.
**Domestic Animal:** Dairy cow.
**Symbol of Peace:** Mourning dove.
**Fish:** Muskellunge.
**Song:** *On, Wisconsin!*
**Nickname:** The Badger State.
**Motto:** Forward.
**Flag:** State coat of arms centered on blue field.
**Leading Industries:** Manufacturing (machinery, automobiles, electrical equipment), food processing, forestry, agriculture (dairy products, beef cattle, hogs, hay, corn, poultry, vegetables, fruits).
**Climate** (Milwaukee): *Normal temperatures:* Jan. high 27°F., low 11°F.; July high 80°F., low 59°F. *Normal yearly precipitation:* 29" (water). *Record snowstorm:* 20.3" in February 1924.
**Recreation Areas:** National forests, 2; national scientific reserve, 1; national lakeshore, 1; state parks and recreation areas, 65.
**Points of Interest:** Apostle Islands National Lake-shore; Ice Age National Scientific Reserve; Wolf, St. Croix, and Lower St. Croix national scenic riverways; Door County resort region; Wisconsin Dells; "Taliesin," Frank Lloyd Wright's home and architectural school (Spring Green); Circus World Museum (Baraboo); Little Norway (near Mt. Horeb).

## KEY EVENTS IN WISCONSIN

**1634  Region explored for France** by Jean Nicolet, landing at Green Bay.
**1660–61  French trading post** and Roman Catholic mission established near present-day Ashland.
**1712–40  War between French and Fox Indians.**
**1763  Britain obtains region** in settlement of French and Indian War.
**1783  U.S. acquires region** in Revolutionary War, but Britain does not turn over outposts to U.S. control until 1796.
**1800–36  Region governed** in turn as part of territories of Indiana, Illinois, and Michigan.
**1820s  American settlers** begin mining lead.
**1832  Black Hawk War:** Settlers end power of Indians in Wisconsin.
**1836 (April 20)  Territory of Wisconsin** created.
**1837  Madison founded;** becomes capital in 1838.
**1848 (May 29)  Wisconsin becomes 30th U.S. state.**
**1851  Railroad** opens, Milwaukee-Waukesha.
**1853  Capital punishment** abolished.
**1854 (Feb. 28)  Formation of Republican Party** first planned at meeting in Ripon.
**1871 (Oct. 8–14)  Forest fire** kills about 800 persons, destroying village of Peshtigo.
**1882  First hydroelectric power plant** built on Fox River at Appleton.
**1884  Ringling Brothers circus** begins at Baraboo.
**1911  First state income tax** adopted.
**1961  State sales tax** adopted.
**1977 (July 3–18)  Illegal 15-day strike** by 23,000 state workers wins higher pay.
**1979  Population grows** 6.8% since 1970.

## WYOMING

**Area:** 97,914 square miles; 253,596 sq. km.
**Population:** 450,000 (1979); 332,416 (1970).
**Capital:** Cheyenne.
**Flower:** Indian paintbrush.
**Tree:** Cottonwood.
**Bird:** Meadowlark.
**Stone:** Jade.
**Song:** *Wyoming.*
**Nickname:** The Equality State.
**Motto:** Equal Rights.
**Flag:** State seal and buffalo centered on red-and-white-bordered blue field.
**Climate** (Cheyenne): *Normal temperatures:* Jan. high 38°F., low 15°F.; July high 84°F., low 55°F. *Normal yearly precipitation:* 15" (water). *Record snowstorm:* 16.5" in April 1955.
**Leading Industries:** Mining (petroleum, natural gas, coal, uranium), agriculture (beef cattle, sheep, beans, hay, sugar beets, wheat), food processing, tourism.
**Recreation Areas:** National parks, 2; national forests, 10; national recreation area, 1; state parks and recreation areas, 11.
**Points of Interest:** Grand Teton and Yellowstone national parks; Fort Laramie National Historic Site; Devils Tower and Fossil Butte national monuments; Buffalo Bill Historic Center (Cody); Flaming Gorge; Bighorn Canyon National Recreation Area.

## KEY EVENTS IN WYOMING

**1742–43  Believed first explored for France** by Louis-Joseph and François de La Vérendrye.
**1803  Region acquired** in Louisiana Purchase.

**WYOMING** *(continued)*

**1807 Yellowstone area explored** by John Colter.

**1833 Petroleum discovered** in Wind River Basin by Capt. Benjamin de Bonneville.

**1834 Fort William (later called Fort Laramie)** built by traders William Sublette and Robert Campbell.

**1846–48 Western Wyoming obtained** by U.S. in Oregon Treaty with Britain and in Mexican War.

**1867 Cheyenne founded;** first passenger train from Omaha reaches Cheyenne (Nov. 13, 1867).

**1868 (July 25) Territory of Wyoming** created.

**1869 (Dec. 10) Women given right to vote** and hold territorial offices.

**1872 (March 1) Yellowstone** becomes first national park in world.

**1890 (July 10) Wyoming becomes 44th U.S. state;** first to give women equal suffrage rights with men.

**1892 Johnson County War:** Cattlemen import gunmen from Texas to kill cattle rustlers.

**1906 Devils Tower** becomes first national monument.

**1924 First woman elected governor in U.S.:** Mrs. Nellie Tayloe Ross.

**1951 Uranium** discovered in Powder River region.

**1960 First intercontinental ballistic missile (ICBM) base** becomes operational near Cheyenne.

**1978–80 Economic boom** brings highest personal income gain in any state and lowest unemployment rate.

**1979 High population growth** of 35.3% since 1970 maintains Wyoming as 49th among states in population.

# U.S. TERRITORIES AND DEPENDENCIES

## DISTRICT OF COLUMBIA (WASHINGTON, D.C.)

**Area:** 67 square miles; 176 sq. km.

**Population:** 656,000 (1979); 756,510 (1970).

**National Capital:** Washington, D.C.

**Flower:** American beauty rose.

**Bird:** Wood thrush.

**Tree:** Scarlet oak.

**Motto:** *Justitia Omnibus* (Justice for All).

**Flag:** Two parallel horizontal red stripes on white field; three red stars above top red stripe.

**Leading Industries:** Government, tourism, service industries, manufacturing (printing and publishing).

**Climate:** *Normal temperatures:* Jan. high 44°F., low 28°F.; July high 88°F., low 69°F. *Normal yearly precipitation:* 39" (water). *Record snowstorm:* 25" in January 1922.

**Points of Interest:** White House, U.S. Capitol, Library of Congress, Supreme Court, U.S. Botanic Garden, Folger Shakespeare Library, Museum of African Art, Smithsonian Building, National Air and Space Museum, National Museum of History and Technology, National Museum of Natural History, National Gallery of Art, Hirshhorn Museum and Sculpture Garden, Freer Gallery of Art, National Collection of Fine Arts, National Portrait Gallery, Washington Monument, Lincoln Memorial, Jefferson Memorial, Ford's Theatre, Kennedy Center for the Performing Arts, National Zoological Park, Corcoran Gallery of Art; *in Arlington, Va.:* Pentagon, Arlington National Cemetery, Marine Corps War Memorial; *in Fairfax County, Va.:* Mount Vernon (George Washington's estate).

### KEY EVENTS IN DISTRICT OF COLUMBIA

**1751 Georgetown laid out** in 80 city lots.

**1788 (Dec. 23) Maryland cedes land** for capital.

**1789 (Dec. 3) Virginia cedes land** for capital.

**1790–91 Congress establishes district** as seat of national government.

**1791 (March 30) President George Washington** proclaims boundaries of federal district.

**1791 (Sept. 9) Washington** chosen as name for city by federal commissioners.

**1791–92 Plan for city** designed by French engineer Pierre Charles L'Enfant.

**1800 (Nov. 1) President John Adams** moves into White House.

**1800 (Nov. 21) Congress first meets** in city.

**1802 (May 3) Washington incorporated** by Congress.

**1814 (Aug. 24–25) In War of 1812** Washington captured and burned by British.

**1820 (May 15) New charter** provides for mayor elected by people.

**1846 (July 9) Congress retrocedes 36 square miles** of district to Virginia because of lack of growth.

**1871 (Feb. 21) Congress repeals charters** of Washington and Georgetown; forms territorial government with officials appointed by President.

**1874 (June 20) Government** by three commissioners appointed by President established by Congress.

**1961 (April 3) Amendment 23** to U.S. Constitution proclaimed; enables residents to vote for President and Vice President; first vote in 1964.

**1967 New district government** established with commissioner (mayor) appointed by President.

**1970 Nonvoting delegate** to represent district in U.S. House of Representatives authorized.

**1974 (May 7) New home-rule charter** approved, giving residents right to elect mayor and council.

**1975 (Jan. 2) First elected government** since 1871 sworn in.

**1976 First subway begins** operation in new $5 billion rapid-transit system.

**1977 Racial composition of population** changes to 75% black from 55% in 1960.

**1978 Congress approves** proposed constitutional amendment to give district voting representation in congress.

**1979 Population decreases** 13.3% since 1970 as district loses over 100,000 residents.

## COMMONWEALTH OF PUERTO RICO

**Area:** 3,435 square miles; 8,896 sq. km.

**Population:** 3,615,598 (1980); 2,712,033 (1970).

**Capital:** San Juan, 516,500.

**Other Cities:** Bayamón, 147,552; Ponce, 128,233.

**Nickname:** Island of Enchantment.

**Motto:** *Joannes Est Nomen Ejus* (John Is His Name)

**Animal:** Lamb.

**Reptile:** Coquí.

**Song:** *La Borinqueña.*

**Flag:** Large white star on blue triangle next to staff; 3 red and 2 white horizontal stripes.

**Leading Industries:** Manufacturing (clothing, chemicals, electrical equipment, machinery), food processing, agriculture (sugarcane, coffee, tobacco, bananas, dairy products, poultry), tourism.

**Climate** (San Juan): *Normal Temperatures:* Jan. high 82°F., low 69°F.; July high 87°F., low 75°F. *Normal yearly precipitation:* 60". *Record rainstorm:* 10.55" in December 1910.

**Points of Interest:** El Morro Fortress (San Juan), Art Museum (Ponce), Caribbean National Forest with El Yunque mountain, Luquillo Beach, Phosphorescent Bay, historic buildings in Old San Juan, beaches.

### KEY EVENTS IN PUERTO RICO

**1493 (Nov. 19) Christopher Columbus** claims Puerto Rico for Spain; names it San Juan Bautista.

**1508 Spanish settlers** colonize island.

**1513 Black slaves** first imported.

**1873 Slavery abolished** by Spain.

**PUERTO RICO** *(continued)*

**1897  Spain grants autonomous government** to Puerto Ricans led by Luis Muñoz Rivera.

**1898 (July 25–Aug. 13)  In Spanish-American War** U.S. troops invade and conquer Spanish defenders.

**1898 (Dec. 10)  Spain cedes Puerto Rico to U.S.**

**1899 (Aug. 8)  Hurricane** kills 3,369 persons.

**1917 (March 2)  Territory of Puerto Rico** created by Jones Act, granting U.S. citizenship to Puerto Ricans.

**1946 (July 25)  First island-born governor:** Jesús Toribio Piñero, appointed by President Truman.

**1948  Luis Muñoz Marin** becomes first elected governor (son of Luis Muñoz Rivera).

**1952 (July 25)  Puerto Rico becomes commonwealth** with own constitution (adopted March 3, 1952).

**1967 (July 23)  Puerto Ricans vote** by 60% majority to retain commonwealth status with U.S.; 39% vote for statehood; less than 1% vote for independence.

**1977 (Jan. 14)  President Ford** asks Congress to grant U.S. statehood to Puerto Rico.

**1979 U.S. Congress passes resolution** favoring a popular vote in Puerto Rico to decide on statehood; referendum planned for 1981.

## U.S. VIRGIN ISLANDS

**Area:** 133 square miles; 344 sq. km.
**Population:** 71,236 (1980); 62,468 (1970).
**Capital:** Charlotte Amalie, 12,220 (on St. Thomas).
**Islands:** St. Thomas, 32 sq. mi.; St. Croix, 82 sq. mi.; St. John, 19 sq. mi.; about 60 small islets.
**Territorial Flower:** Yellow elder or yellow cedar.
**Bird:** Yellow breast.
**Song:** *Virgin Islands March.*
**Flag:** Golden American eagle with shield on white field; eagle between blue letters V and I.
**Leading Industries:** Tourism, manufacturing (rum, refined bauxite, petroleum refining, textiles), agriculture (beef cattle, dairy products, poultry, vegetables, fruits, nuts).
**Normal Temperatures:** Year-round, 78 ° F.
**Normal Yearly Rainfall:** 40–60 inches.
**Points of Interest:** Virgin Islands National Park on St. John; St. Thomas and Christiansted national historic sites; Buck Island Reef National Monument; ruins of castles, forts, and plantations; beaches.

### KEY EVENTS IN U.S. VIRGIN ISLANDS

**1493  Islands discovered** by Christopher Columbus.

**1500s  Spaniards kill or enslave** Carib Indians.

**1672 (May 25)  First permanent settlement** established on St. Croix by Danes led by Jorgen Iverson.

**1716  St. John acquired** by Denmark.

**1733  St. Croix bought** by Denmark from France.

**1848 (July 3)  Slavery abolished** after slave revolt.

**1917 (March 31)  U.S. purchases islands** from Denmark for $25 million; treaty signed Aug. 4, 1916.

**1927  U.S. citizenship granted** to islanders.

**1954  Elected legislature** established by Congress.

**1956  National park** established on St. John.

**1958  First island-born governor:** John D. Merwin, appointed by President Eisenhower.

**1968  Islanders given right** to elect governor.

**1971 (Jan. 4)  First elected governor** takes office: Melvin Herbert Evans.

**1979  (March 6)  Voters reject home rule:** In a 5 to 4 vote, a new constitution was rejected because islanders felt greater autonomy would bring higher taxes.

## AMERICAN SAMOA

**Area:** 76 square miles; 197 sq. km.
**Population:** 35,490 (1980); 27,159 (1970).
**Capital:** Pago Pago, 2,451.
**Islands:** Tutuila and Aunu'u, 53 sq. mi.; Ta'u, 17 sq.

mi.; Ofu and Olosega, 4 sq. mi.; Swain's, 1.9 sq. mi. Rose, 0.4 sq. mi.
**Flower:** Paogo. **Tree.** Moso'oi. **Plant:** Ava.
**Song:** *Amerika Samoa.*
**Motto:** *Samoa—Muamua le Atua* (In Samoa, God Is First).
**Flag:** Blue field; white triangle bordered with red with apex at midpoint of staff; American eagle at right side of triangle.
**Leading Industries:** Tourism, fishing, tuna canning, handicrafts, agriculture (fruits, vegetables).
**Languages:** Samoan and English.
**Normal Temperatures:** Year-round, 70 ° to 86 ° F.
**Normal Yearly Rainfall:** 129 inches.
**Points of Interest:** Villages, beaches.

### KEY EVENTS IN AMERICAN SAMOA

**1722  Discovered** by Dutch explorer Jacob Roggeveen.

**1830  British missionaries** begin converting islanders.

**1839–40  Survey** by U.S. Navy Lt. Charles Wilkes.

**1872  U.S. Navy establishes naval base** at Pago Pago.

**1899 (Dec. 2)  U.S. and Germany agree** to divide Samoan Islands between them; Britain also signs agreement, withdrawing its claims to islands.

**1900–04  Chiefs of islands cede them to U.S.;** formally accepted by U.S. Congress on Feb. 20, 1929.

**1925  Swain's and Rose islands annexed** to American Samoa.

**1900–51  U.S. Navy** administers islands.

**1951  U.S. Department of Interior** takes over administration of islands.

**1966 (Nov. 19)  Constitution** adopted by voters gives elected legislature taxing power.

**1974  Islands declared drought disaster area.**

**1977 (Nov. 22)  Voters for first time elect** Samoaborn governor: Peter T. Coleman.

**1980 Population grows** 31% since 1970.

## GUAM

**Area:** 212 square miles; 549 sq. km.
**Population:** 116,644 (1980); 84,996 (1970).
**Capital:** Agana, 2,119.
**Flower:** *Puti Tai Nobio* (Bougainvillea).
**Bird:** *Toto* (Fruit dove); **Animal:** Iguana.
**Tree:** *Ifit* (Intsiabijuga).
**Stone:** Latte.
**Song:** *Stand Ye Guamanians.*
**Nickname:** Pearl of the Pacific.
**Flag:** Territorial seal on blue field bordered in red.
**Leading Industries:** Military installations, manufacturing (food, beverages, printing, watches, clothing), oil refining, construction, fishing, agriculture (vegetables, fruits, poultry, hogs, beef cattle), tourism.
**Languages:** Chamorro and English.
**Normal Temperatures:** Year-round, 71 ° to 87 ° F.
**Normal Yearly Rainfall:** 80–110 inches (mostly July through November).

### KEY EVENTS IN GUAM

**1521  Portuguese explorer Ferdinand Magellan** believed to have visited Guam.

**1668  Guam colonized** by Spain.

**1898 (Dec. 10)  U.S. acquires Guam.**

**1899–1950  U.S. Navy** administers Guam.

**1941 (Dec. 7–13)  Japan captures Guam.**

**1944 (July 21–Aug. 10)  U.S. recaptures Guam.**

**1950 (Aug. 1)  U.S. Territory of Guam** created under U.S. Department of Interior; islanders become U.S. citizens; given right to elect own legislature.

**1968  Right to elect own governor** given Guam.

**1976  (Sept. 4) Continued status as U.S. territory** approved by voters 10,221 to 7,386.

**1979 (Aug. 4)  Voters reject proposed constitution** by 5 to 1, demanding U.S. military give up much of the island's land to further economic development.

## TRUST TERRITORY OF THE PACIFIC ISLANDS

Including the many islands taken by U.S. military forces from Japan in World War II, the U.S. Trust Territory of the Pacific Islands was formally placed under American administration by the UN in 1947. Until the U.S. gives up administration of the trust as planned in 1981, the territory is divided into four parts: (1) the Northern Marianas, a self-governing U.S. commonwealth; (2) the Federated States of Micronesia, whose capital is at Kolonia on Ponape and includes the island districts of Truk, Yap, and Kosrae of the Caroline group; (3) Palau Island in the western Carolines, with its capital at Koror; and (4) the Marshall Islands, with its capital at Majuro.

### MICRONESIA

**Area:** *Land,* 533 sq. mi. (1,380 sq. km.); *ocean,* 7,772 sq. mi. (20,129 sq. km.)
**Population:** 129,282 (1980); 90,940 (1970).
**Administrative Center:** Saipan in Mariana Islands.
**Islands:** 2,141 atolls and islands (96 inhabited).
**Leading Industries:** Agriculture (vegetables, fruits, poultry, copra), fishing, handicrafts.
**Normal Temperatures:** Year-round, 75° to 89°F.
**Government:** High commissioner appointed by U.S.; congress of Micronesia elected by islanders.

### KEY EVENTS IN MICRONESIA

**1885   Germany annexes** Marshall Islands.
**1899   Germany acquires** Carolines from Spain.
**1914   Japan seizes** Micronesia in World War I.
**1920 (Dec. 17)   Japan receives** League of Nations mandate over German possessions in Micronesia.
**1944–45   U.S. captures** Micronesia from Japan.
**1946–58   U.S. test-explodes 64 nuclear weapons** at Bikini and Enewetak atolls.
**1947 (July 18)   U.S. receives UN trusteeship** over Micronesia.
**1962 (May 7)   U.S. Department of Interior** given administration of entire territory.
**1965   Elective congress of Micronesia** established.
**1975 (Nov. 8)   Constitution for Federated States of Micronesia** adopted.
**1976 (July 14)   UN Trusteeship Council** approves U.S. plan for self-government for Micronesia.
**1978   (Jan. 9)   Northern Marianas** formally separated from Micronesia.
**1978 (July 12)   Micronesians vote to divide into three self-governing states:** In referendum on proposed constitution for Federated States of Micronesia, Palau and Marshall Islands oppose federation.
**1979 (March 1)   Marshall Islands vote to adopt constitution** as separate self-governing nation.
**1979 (July 9)   Palau Islands adopt separate constitution** in 12–1 vote that would ban U.S. military bases and nuclear weapons.
**1979 (Nov. 27–Dec. 3)   Majuro, capital of Marshall Islands,** devastated by storm with 25-foot waves.
**1980 (Jan. 14)   U.S. signs agreement with Marshall Islands** to grant limited independence.
**1980 (April 8)   Enewetak** restored to former residents who were removed for U.S. A-bomb tests in 1940s.

## COMMONWEALTH OF NORTHERN MARIANA ISLANDS

**Area:** *Land,* 184 square miles; 476.6 sq. km.
**Population:** 15,000 (1979); 9,640 (1970).
**Capital:** Susupe, Saipan, 7,967.
**Islands:** Saipan, Tinian, Rota, and 11 islets.
**Legislature:** 23 members.
**Languages:** English and Chamorro.
**Leading Industries:** Agriculture (coconuts); government; fishing.

**Normal Temperatures:** Year-round, 75° to 89°F.
**Government:** Self-governing U.S. commonwealth; governor appointed by U.S.

### KEY EVENTS IN NORTHERN MARIANAS

**1668 Spain** colonizes Mariana Islands.
**1899 Germany** acquires Northern Marianas.
**1947 (July 18)   Northern Marianas** included in U.S. Trust Territory of the Pacific Islands.
**1975 (Feb. 15)   U.S. signs agreement** with representatives of Northern Marianas to make them U.S. commonwealth.
**1976 (March 24)   President Ford signs Northern Marianas Covenant** establishing procedure to separate islands from Micronesia.
**1976 (July 14)   UN Trusteeship Council** approves U.S. plan for Northern Marianas.
**1978 (Jan. 9)   Northern Marianas become U.S. commonwealth;** first elected governor: Carlos S. Camacho.

## OTHER U.S. ISLAND DEPENDENCIES

The United States also occupies or claims several other islands in the Caribbean Sea and the Pacific Ocean. Altogether these islands have an area of about 15 square miles and a total population of less than 5,000 persons. They include:

**BAKER ISLAND** lies in the Pacific Ocean about 1,650 miles southwest of Honolulu. Barren and uninhabited, it has an area of less than 1 square mile. Baker was claimed by the United States in 1857.

**HOWLAND ISLAND,** an uninhabited Pacific island, is about 40 miles north of Baker Island. It has an area of about 1 square mile.

**JARVIS ISLAND,** one of the Line Islands in the central Pacific Ocean, lies about 1,500 miles south of Honolulu. Its area is 2 square miles.

**JOHNSTON AND SAND ISLANDS** have an area of less than ½ square mile. About 800 miles southwest of Honolulu, the islands were claimed by the U.S. in 1934. The U.S. Navy built an airfield on Johnston Island in World War II, and the island was used for atomic-bomb tests in 1962.

**KINGMAN REEF,** a tiny uninhabited island about 150 feet wide, is in the Line Islands about 1,500 miles south of Honolulu.

**MIDWAY ISLANDS,** about 1,200 miles northwest of Honolulu, have a population of about 2,200 and an area of about 2 square miles. The two islands are Sand Island and Eastern Island. Annexed by the U.S. in 1867, the islands are controlled by the U.S. Navy. The Battle of Midway on June 4, 1942, marked the turning point of World War II in the Pacific when a Japanese fleet attempting to capture the islands was defeated by a U.S. fleet.

**NAVASSA ISLAND** lies midway between Jamaica and Haiti in the West Indies. It is in the Jamaica Channel about 100 miles south of Cuba. It has an area of about 2 square miles.

**PALMYRA ISLAND,** one of the northernmost of the Line Islands, is about 1,000 miles south of Honolulu. It has an area of 4 square miles. It was annexed by Hawaii in 1862. It became the private possession of the Fullerd-Leo family of Hawaii. In 1979 the U.S. government reported plans to purchase the island and make it a dumping ground for radioactive waste materials.

**WAKE ISLAND,** about 2,300 miles west of Honolulu, has an area of 3 square miles and a population of 1,647. The U.S. claimed the island in 1899 for use as a station for the transpacific telegraph cable. In World War II, Japan captured Wake Island on Dec. 23, 1941, taking more than 1,600 Americans prisoner. Japan held the island until Sept. 4, 1945.

# Supreme Court

In one of its most notable decisions of 1980, the Supreme Court upheld the right to patent new forms of life created in the laboratory. The case concerned the award of a patent to Dr. Ananda M. Chakrabarty, *right,* a scientist of the General Electric Company, for his development of an "oil-eating" microorganism to be used in cleaning up oil spills. The decision was expected to stimulate greater activity by industrial researchers using the technique of gene-splicing to produce microorganisms for special tasks.

United Press Int'l.

## HIGHLIGHTS: 1980

New attention was focused on the inner working of the Supreme Court in 1980, as Americans read the bestseller *The Brethren.* The book, by investigative reporters Bob Woodward and Scott Armstrong of the *Washington Post,* broke open the traditional secrecy that has surrounded the way the justices arrive at their decisions and their opinions of each other. Much of the book was based on thousands of pages of previously secret documents that were leaked to the reporters by members of the Court's staff.

Although members of the Court did not officially react to the book, their feelings were believed to have been expressed in an opinion handed down in February ordering former CIA agent Frank Snepp to turn over to the government his royalties from his unauthorized book about the spy agency. The justices told Snepp to "disgorge the benefits of his faithlessness . . . to deter those who would place sensitive information at risk."

# MAJOR SUPREME COURT DECISIONS: 1980

## ABORTION

**Limits on federal funding of abortions upheld:** The Court ruled 5–4 on June 30 that federal and state governments are not obligated to pay for abortions for poor women. It was estimated that the ruling would cut off federally funded abortions to more than 250,000 women each year. The Department of Health and Human Services appealed for a rehearing and continued to pay for abortions until the Court denied the rehearing petition on Sept. 17. The ruling in the case of *Harris* v. *McRae* upheld a 1976 congressional ban on Medicaid abortion financing that was sponsored by Rep. Henry J. Hyde (R–Ill.). Although the law forbids federal Medicaid funds to be used for most abortions, it still permits the financing of those needed in cases of rape, incest, or to prevent endangerment of the life of the mother—a number estimated at about 2,000 a year.

The majority opinion written by Justice Potter Stewart said in part: "Regardless of whether the freedom of a woman to choose to terminate her pregnancy for health reasons lies at the core or the periphery of the due process liberty . . . it simply does not follow that a woman's freedom of choice carries with it a constitutional entitlement to the financial resources to avail herself of the full range of protected choices. . . . By subsidizing the medical expenses of indigent women who carry their pregnancies to term while not subsidizing the comparable expenses of women who undergo abortions (except those whose lives are threatened), Congress has established incentives that make childbirth a more attractive alternative than abortion for persons eligible for Medicaid. These incentives bear a direct relationship to the legitimate Congressional interest in protecting potential life. Nor is it irrational that Congress has authorized federal reimbursement for medically necessary services generally, but not for certain medically necessary abortions. Abortion is inherently different from other medical procedures, because no other procedure involves the purposeful termination of a potential life."

## AFFIRMATIVE ACTION

**Congress can set racial quotas to remedy past discrimination:** In a 6–3 decision on July 2, the Court upheld the 1977 Public Works Employment Act in providing that 10% of public-works contracts should be awarded to businesses controlled by racial minority groups. In the case of *Fullilove* v. *Klutznick,* the majority opinion by Chief Justice Burger said that Congress does not have to be "color

blind" and was justified in its action because it "had abundant evidence from which it could conclude that minority business had been denied effective participation in public contracting opportunities by procurement practices that perpetuated the effects of prior discrimination."

## AGRICULTURE

**Big farms in Imperial Valley win water rights:** In a unanimous decision on June 16, the Court overturned a federal appeals-court ruling of 1977 that would have barred farms larger than 160 acres in California's Imperial Valley from having rights to water from federally subsidized irrigation projects. The decision in the case of *Bryant* v. *Yellen* was a defeat for the Carter administration, which had sought to end the spending of federal funds to irrigate huge farms owned by corporations.

## BUSINESS

**Workplaces do not have to be "risk-free":** On July 2 the Court ruled 5–4 that the Labor Department's Occupational Safety and Health Administration (OSHA) had not presented sufficient evidence of risk in ordering the petroleum industry to reduce the permissible exposure of workers to benzene in the air to one part per million. OSHA had issued the order on the basis that exposure to benzene can cause cancer. The petroleum industry had estimated the ruling would cause modifications costing $500 million in plants.
**Patent protection extended to unpatented materials:** In a 5–4 decision on June 27, the Court held that a patent on a process utilizing an unpatented substance extended patent rights to the substance itself. In *Dawson Chemical Co.* v. *Rohm & Haas Co.,* the Court decided that since Rohm & Haas had a patent on a process to use the nonpatented chemical propanil as a weedkiller in rice fields, Dawson should not be allowed to sell propanil to farmers for use as a weedkiller.
**Free-speech rights of corporations extended:** In a 7–2 decision on *Consolidated Edison* v. *Public Service Commission,* the Court held that the electric utility was within its rights to insert materials with its monthly bill that expressed the corporation's position on "controversial matters of public policy."

The Court also decided by 8–1 in *Central Hudson Gas & Electric Co.* v. *Public Service Commission* that the state agency violated the utility's right of free speech by banning it from advertising to promote the use of electricity, even though the intention of the agency was to conserve electricity.

## CRIMINAL JUSTICE

**Police must have a warrant to enter a home for a routine arrest:** In a 6–3 ruling on April 15, the Court invalidated the laws of 23 states that permitted officers to enter homes without a warrant to make an arrest. In the case of *Payton* v. *New York*, the Court said such invasions of privacy were prohibited by the Fourth Amendment's ban on unreasonable search and seizure. The majority opinion, written by Justice John Paul Stevens, said in part:

"The simple language of the amendment applies equally to seizures of persons and to seizures of property. The critical point is that any differences in the intrusiveness of entries to search and entries to arrest are merely ones of degrees than kind.

"The two intrusions share this fundamental characteristic: The breach of the entrance to an individual's home. The Fourth Amendment protects the individual's privacy in a variety of settings. In none is the zone of privacy more clearly defined than when bounded by the unambiguous physical dimensions of an individual's home—a zone that finds its roots in clear and specific constitutional terms: 'the right of the people to be secure in their . . . houses . . . shall not be violated.' "

**Illegally seized evidence can sometimes be used in court:** On May 27 the Court decided 5–4 that illegally obtained evidence could be used to prove that the defendant in a criminal case had lied while under oath. In *United States* v. *Havens,* a Fort Wayne, Ind., attorney, arrested for drug smuggling, had denied knowledge of incriminating evidence found in his luggage, which had been seized without a warrant. However, a government agent testified that the evidence had been found in the luggage. An appeals court had held that the evidence was inadmissible because it had been obtained without a warrant. However, the Supreme Court reversed the ruling of the appeals court.

Also on May 27 the Court ruled 5–4 that evidence obtained in a search of a person being questioned could be used as evidence. This finding was in the case of *United States* v. *Mendenhall.* While questioning a suspected drug courier, government agents obtained her consent to search her. They found two packages of heroin that were used as evidence in convicting her. An appeals court reversed her conviction on the basis that government agents had violated her right to be free from unreasonable search and seizure. The Supreme Court reinstated the conviction. In its majority opinion written by Justice Potter Stewart the Court said: "As long as the person to whom questions are put remains free to disregard the questions and walk away,

there has been no intrusion upon that person's liberty or privacy as would under the Constitution require some particularized and objective justification."

**Pre-arrest silence can be used as basis of cross-examination:** On June 10 the Court ruled 7–2 that questioning a defendant in court about his pre-arrest silence does not violate his constitutional rights. In *Jenkins* v. *Anderson,* it affirmed the conviction for murder of a Michigan man who had testified that he killed his victim in self-defense. He had appealed his conviction on grounds that his constitutional rights were violated when the prosecution questioned him as to why he had not come to the police to explain the circumstances during the two weeks between the slaying and his arrest.

## EDUCATION

**Private universities not required to recognize faculty unions:** On Feb. 20 the Court ruled 5–4 in *NLRB* v. *Yeshiva University* and *Yeshiva University Faculty* v. *Yeshiva University* that faculty members are "managerial employees" and therefore are not entitled to collective bargaining provisions of the National Labor Relations Act. The suit had been initiated by Yeshiva University, which challenged the right of the National Labor Relations Board (NLRB) to certify a union representing the faculty. In the majority opinion of the Court written by Justice Lewis F. Powell Jr. the "managerial" role of the faculty was described: "Their authority in academic matters is absolute. They decide what courses will be offered, when they will be scheduled, and to whom they will be taught."

**Teachers can be fired for refusing to teach patriotism:** On Jan. 7 the Court upheld a court of appeals ruling that a Chicago school teacher could be fired for not carrying out orders to teach the pledge of allegiance, the song "America," and other patriotic material. The teacher, Joethelia Palmer, who was fired in 1977, claimed that as a Jehovah's Witness her religious freedom would have been violated by teaching the required material. The court of appeals ruling stated: "She has no constitutional right to require others to submit to her views and forgo a portion of their education."

## FREEDOM OF THE PRESS

**Criminal trials must be open to press and public:** In a 7–1 decision on July 2, the Court ruled in *Richmond Newspapers Inc.* v. *Commonwealth of Virginia* that a judge acted unconstitutionally under the First Amendment in excluding reporters from a 1978 murder trial in Virginia. The decision written by Chief Justice Burger said: "We hold that the

**MAJOR COURT DECISIONS: 1980** *(continued)*

right to attend criminal trials is implicit in the guarantees of the First Amendment; without the freedom to attend such trials, which people have exercised for centuries, important aspects of freedom of speech and of the press could be eviscerated. . . . To work effectively, it is important that society's criminal process 'satisfy the appearance of justice,' . . . and the appearance of justice can best be provided by allowing people to observe it."

The decision was hailed by news executives as ending months of confusion that had been caused by a Court ruling one year earlier that a New York judge had been justified in excluding the press and public from a pretrial hearing. Many judges had taken that ruling to give them permission to close criminal trials to the public. In the next 12 months the press was barred from all or part of more than 250 criminal proceedings.

### INDIANS

**Sioux win $105 million for land:** In an 8–1 decision on June 30, the Court required the federal government to pay the Sioux Indians $105 million for having illegally taken their land in South Dakota's Black Hills in 1877. The decision upheld a court of claims finding that the land was worth $17 million at the time it was seized and that the Indians were entitled to an additional $88 million in accrued interest. The Sioux began their court efforts to recover the land in 1922. An estimated $10 million of the award was owed for legal fees in the case.

### SCIENCE

**New life forms can be patented:** The Court ruled 5–4 on June 16 that patents can be awarded for new forms of life. In the case of *Diamond* v. *Chakrabarty,* the decision held that a patent should be granted to Dr. Ananda Chakrabarty for a microorganism he had developed through genetic engineering to be used to absorb oil spills. The majority opinion by Chief Justice Burger said in part: "Respondent's microorganism plainly qualifies as patentable subject matter. His claim is not to a hitherto unknown natural phenomenon, but to a nonnaturally occurring manufacture or composition of matter—a product of human ingenuity."

The decision cautioned, however, that "The laws of nature, physical phenomena and abstract ideas have been held not patentable. Thus, a new mineral discovered in the earth or a new plant found in the wild is not patentable subject matter."

### SECRECY

**CIA secrecy rules upheld:** In a 6–3 decision on Feb. 19, the Court upheld the rights of the federal government to restrict its employees' freedom of speech. The ruling was in *Snepp* v. *United States,* a case in which the Central Intelligence Agency (CIA) had won lower-court decisions against a former employee for failing to submit the manuscript of his book *Decent Interval* for CIA review before publishing it. The book described the CIA's activities during the Vietnam War. The courts ordered Snepp to turn over his income from the book to the government and submit any other writings about the agency for approval before publication.

### STATE AND LOCAL GOVERNMENT

**States and localities exposed to new damage suits:** In a 6–3 decision on June 25, the Court ruled that state and local officials can be sued for damages if they withhold federal benefits. The finding came in the case of *Maine* v. *Thiboutot* in which Lionel and Joline Thiboutot and their eight children sued the state of Maine for denying them welfare benefits. State and local officials believed the ruling would open them to a large number of new suits because the Court upheld the right of the plaintiffs to collect attorneys' fees from the state as part of their damages award. The suit was brought under a provision of an 1871 Civil Rights Act that provided for money damages and attorneys' fees for denial of constitutional rights.

Earlier, on April 16, the Court had ruled 5–4 that local governments could be sued for civil-rights violations under the 1871 law. That decision came in a case in which George D. Owen sued the city of Independence, Mo., for violating his civil rights by refusing to explain why he had been dismissed as police chief and by denying him a formal hearing on the matter. The majority opinion written by Justice William J. Brennan said in part: "Many victims of municipal malfeasance would be left remediless" if they did not have the right to sue. "The knowledge that a municipality will be liable for all of its injurious conduct, whether committed in good faith or not, should create an incentive for officials who may harbor doubts about the lawfulness of their intended actions to err on the side of protecting citizens' constitutional rights."

**State taxing powers upheld on international corporations:** In an 8–0 decision on June 10, the Court upheld the right of Wisconsin to tax all of the Exxon Corporation's net income even though it only conducts marketing operations in the state. Earlier, on March 19, the Court ruled 6–1 that Vermont had the right to tax the dividends received by Mobil Oil Corporation from its foreign operations as well as its net income in the United States.

# HISTORIC SUPREME COURT DECISIONS

**1803 Judicial Review**—*Marbury v. Madison:* William Marbury was appointed a justice of the peace a few weeks before President John Adams' term expired. When the next administration refused to deliver his commission, Marbury petitioned the Court for a writ of mandamus to compel Secretary of State James Madison to issue a commission. The Court dismissed the case for lack of jurisdiction. Marbury had based his case on the Judiciary Act of 1789, which authorized the Court to take original jurisdiction over such controversies. Under Article III, Section 2 of the Constitution, Supreme Court jurisdiction over such matters begins at the appellate level. Therefore, the Judiciary Act was unconstitutional and void to the extent that it gave the Court powers implicitly denied by the Constitution.

*Significance:* It established the principle of "judicial review," whereby the Court has jurisdiction to pass on the constitutionality of legislative acts.

**1816 Federal Questions**—*Martin v. Hunter's Lessee:* This case dealt with land ownership in Virginia. The Virginia Court of Appeals ruled against Martin. On appeal to the Supreme Court, that decision was reversed. In 1821 the Supreme Court asserted in *Cohens v. Virginia* that it had power to review final decisions of state courts in criminal proceedings.

*Significance:* The two cases established the Court's appellate power when "federal questions" (involving the Constitution, a congressional statute, or a treaty) are involved. They established that one uniform interpretation will apply for "federal questions."

**1819 Constitutional Interpretation**—*McCulloch v. Maryland:* Congress chartered a federal bank in 1816 to control unregulated issuances of currency by state banks. Maryland then imposed a tax on notes issued by the U.S. Bank's Baltimore branch. The branch refused to pay, and Maryland sued to collect. At the same time it challenged congressional authority to charter a bank. The Court ruled that this was within the implied powers of government, that acts of Congress not expressly authorized are valid so long as they are "necessary and proper" to carrying out express grants of power. It declared further that federal instrumentalities are not subject to state taxes.

*Significance:* The decision sanctioned "loose," or liberal, interpretation of the Constitution.

**1824 Regulation of Commerce**—*Gibbons v. Ogden:* Aaron Ogden, part owner of a steamboat operation monopoly established by New York statute, challenged the right of Thomas Gibbons to operate a rival steamboat service between New Jersey and New York under federal license. The Court declared the New York statute unconstitutional because it clearly came in conflict with congressional power to regulate commerce.

*Significance:* It became the basis for the sweeping exercise of federal controls over commerce. It is significant also for its statement of "pre-emption": when Congress acts within its authorized powers, it can pass legislation to invalidate contradictory laws of the states.

**1852 Local Powers**—*Cooley v. Wardens of the Port of Philadelphia:* The case involved the constitutionality of a Pennsylvania statute regulating navigation in the Port of Philadelphia. Much of the traffic in and out of the harbor was interstate. In its ruling the Court noted that some commerce, although technically interstate, is essentially local in character. U.S. control is not really necessary, and until it is, states and municipalities are free to act according to local needs.

*Significance:* The decision reasserted the authority of the Court over state regulation of commerce, and ensured a national "common market" by stating that some matters are beyond state power.

**1857 Slaves as Property**—*Dred Scott v. Sanford:* Dred Scott, a Missouri slave, was at one time taken into free territory, where an Act of Congress (the Missouri Compromise) prohibited slavery. Several years after his return to Missouri, Scott sued for freedom, claiming he had acquired it through residence in free territory. The decision centered on two principles: first, that Scott, being a Negro, was not a U.S. citizen and therefore could not petition federal courts; second, that the Missouri Compromise was unconstitutional. Slaves were like any other property, the Court said, and under the 5th Amendment Congress could pass no law depriving citizens of their private property.

*Significance:* The decision, acclaimed in the South and bitterly denounced in the North, brought the nation another step closer to civil war.

**1911 Business Regulation**—*Standard Oil Co. of New Jersey v. United States:* The Sherman Act (1890) outlawed "every contract, combination in the form of trust or otherwise, or conspiracy in restraint of trade." In this case the Court said that the "rule of reason" must apply, and that "every" did not mean "all" but only "unreasonable" contracts or combinations or conspiracies in restraint of trade. Later (1932) the Court ruled in *United States v. Swift & Co.* that "mere size" is not an offense against the Sherman Act.

*Significance:* The Court's decisions permitted the growth of huge corporate enterprises in the U.S. by watering down the stringent provisions of the congressional statute.

**1925 Bill of Rights Applied to States**—*Gitlow v. New York:* Gitlow was prosecuted under New York's "criminal anarchy" statute, which made it a crime to advocate or teach the propriety of overthrowing the government by force and violence. The Supreme Court upheld Gitlow's state-court conviction, over objection that it violated Gitlow's rights of freedom of speech and the press. The Court assumed that those 1st Amendment provisions were also limitations on the states because they were "incorporated" in the 14th Amendment's "due process" clause.

*Significance:* For the first time a part of the Bill of Rights of the Constitution was made applicable to the states.

**HISTORIC SUPREME COURT DECISIONS** *(continued)*

**1937 Regulation of Labor—***NLRB v. Jones & Laughlin Steel Corporation:* In upholding the National Labor Relations Board's authority to regulate industrial labor relations, the Court ruled that the U.S. government has jurisdiction over any dispute that will interfere with interstate commerce. The case grew out of a labor dispute in a Pennsylvania steel plant. Iron ore was shipped into the plant from other states, processed, then shipped to warehouses in other cities. A work stoppage in Pennsylvania would directly affect the company's operations in other states. Manufacturing, the Court ruled, was so closely linked to interstate commerce that its control was essential to "protect that commerce from burdens and obstructions."

*Significance:* The decision broadened the definition of interstate commerce to include all activities that would affect its flow, either directly or indirectly, and upheld the power of Congress to regulate industrial relations.

**1954 Racial Segregation—***Brown v. Board of Education of Topeka:* In this case the Court set aside a Kansas statute authorizing segregation in primary schools. The decision declared that the "separate but equal" doctrine, established in *Plessy v. Ferguson* (1896), in fact denied equal protection under the 14th Amendment and was unconstitutional. The verdict directed lower courts to use their authority to implement desegregation of public elementary schools.

*Significance:* This was the first time the Court declared segregation unconstitutional. From the decision evolved a body of legislation and court action aimed at eradicating discrimination in schools, housing, employment, voting, and other areas.

**1962 School Prayers—***Engel v. Vitale:* A nondenominational prayer written by the N.Y. State Board of Regents for voluntary recital in the public schools was ruled unconstitutional as a violation of the 1st Amendment, which provides that Congress "shall make no laws respecting an establishment of religion or prohibiting the free exercise thereof."

A year later, in *School District of Abbington Township v. Schempp,* the Court banned legislation requiring Bible reading and recitation of the Lord's Prayer in public schools on grounds that it tended to establish a state religion.

*Significance:* A state may not require promotion of a specific religion in public schools.

**1962 One Man, One Vote—***Baker et al. v. Carr:* The Court ruled that federal courts have the power to review legislative apportionment. As a result of large population shifts, many legislative districts were unevenly drawn and voters were denied the right to "equal protection" guaranteed by the 14th Amendment. The Baker case led to a number of decisions in 1964 calling for reapportionment on a "one man, one vote" basis. (*Reynolds v. Sims* established this rule for state legislatures, and *Wesberry v. Sanders* did the same for congressional districts.)

*Significance:* Political districts, which often were drawn to favor rural areas, were ordered redrawn to give increased voting strength to city and suburban residents.

**1964 Libel of Officials—***New York Times v.* *Sullivan:* The case revolved around a full-page advertisement placed in the *Times* by Dr. Martin Luther King Jr. and other civil-rights leaders. Many statements in the ad—charging that Negroes in Montgomery, Ala., were being abused—proved false. Sullivan, a Montgomery city official, was subsequently awarded a $500,000 libel judgment. The Court reversed the judgment, ruling that criticism of official conduct cannot be termed libelous without showing actual malice.

*Significance:* The decision gave the news media greater freedom in reporting the news by limiting their liability for libel.

**1966 Rights of Criminal Suspects—***Miranda v. Arizona:* The Court overturned the conviction of an Arizona man charged with rape and kidnapping, on grounds that his voluntary confession was obtained illegally. The decision invalidated any confessions or incriminating admissions unless the suspect is warned that he may remain silent, that anything he says may be held against him, that he has a right to have a lawyer present, and that if he cannot afford one, he is entitled to court-appointed counsel. If the suspect waives counsel and confesses, there is a "heavy burden" on the prosecution to show a waiver of rights.

*Significance:* The decision gives more protection to those accused of crimes.

**1972 Death Penalty—***Furman v. Georgia:* The Supreme Court ruled in a 5–4 decision that the death penalty as it had been imposed by state courts was unconstitutional under the 8th and 14th Amendments.

Subsequently, in 1976, the Court ruled that the death penalty in and of itself was constitutional, upholding newly revised capital-punishment laws that provide separate consideration of sentencing after guilt had been determined.

In 1977 the Court decided that state legislatures cannot make the death penalty mandatory for the slaying of a police officer.

*Significance:* The decisions brought revision of capital-punishment laws to protect defendants' rights.

**1972 Free Legal Counsel—***Argersinger v. Hamlin:* The Court decided that the state must provide free legal counsel for persons accused of crimes for which they may be imprisoned if they cannot afford to pay an attorney.

**1973 Obscenity—***Miller v. California* and *Paris Adult Theatre I v. Slaton:* The Court redefined "obscenity," requiring a defendant prosecuted for obscenity to prove that the work as a whole shows "serious literary, artistic, political or scientific value." In addition, the Court ruled that the work must meet "contemporary community standards."

*Significance:* The decision gave states and local governments greater power to regulate works considered obscene.

**1973 Abortion—***Roe v. Wade* and *Doe v. Bolton:* The Court overturned all state laws banning abortion during the first 6 months of pregnancy on grounds that it is a violation of the right of privacy stemming from the 14th Amendment.

*Significance:* The ruling broadened the rights of women in deciding whether or not to give birth to a child.

# UNITED STATES SUPREME COURT MEMBERS

| JUSTICE (CHIEF JUSTICES IN BOLDFACE TYPE) AND STATE OF RESIDENCE | YEARS ON THE COURT | APPOINTED BY PRESIDENT: | BORN | DIED | POSITIONS BEFORE COURT APPOINTMENT |
|---|---|---|---|---|---|
| 1. **John Jay** (N.Y.) | 1789–95 | Washington | 1745 | 1829 | President of Continental Congress; U.S. Secretary of State |
| 2. John Rutledge (S.C.) [1] | 1789–91 | Washington | 1739 | 1800 | 1st governor of South Carolina |
| 3. William Cushing (Mass.) | 1789–1810 | Washington | 1732 | 1810 | Chief Judge, Supreme Judicial Court (Mass.) |
| 4. James Wilson (Pa.) | 1789–98 | Washington | 1742 | 1798 | Private law practice |
| 5. John Blair (Va.) | 1789–96 | Washington | 1732 | 1800 | State Appeals Court judge |
| 6. James Iredell (N.C.) | 1790–99 | Washington | 1751 | 1799 | North Carolina Council of State |
| 7. Thomas Johnson (Md.) | 1791–93 | Washington | 1732 | 1819 | Chief Judge, General Court of Maryland |
| 8. William Paterson (N.J.) | 1793–1806 | Washington | 1745 | 1806 | Governor of New Jersey |
| 9. **John Rutledge** (S.C.) [1] | 1795 | Washington | 1739 | 1800 | Chief Justice of South Carolina |
| 10. Samuel Chase (Md.) | 1796–1811 | Washington | 1741 | 1811 | Chief Judge, General Court of Maryland |
| 11. **Oliver Ellsworth** (Conn.) | 1796–1800 | Washington | 1745 | 1807 | U.S. Senator; helped write first Judiciary Act |
| 12. Bushrod Washington (Va.) | 1798–1829 | John Adams | 1762 | 1829 | Private law practice |
| 13. Alfred Moore (N.C.) | 1799–1804 | John Adams | 1755 | 1810 | State Superior Court judge |
| 14. **John Marshall** (Va.) | 1801–35 | John Adams | 1755 | 1835 | U.S. Representative; U.S. Secretary of State |
| 15. William Johnson (S.C.) | 1804–34 | Jefferson | 1771 | 1834 | Court of Common Pleas judge |
| 16. Henry Brockholst Livingston (N.Y.) | 1807–23 | Jefferson | 1757 | 1823 | State Supreme Court justice |
| 17. Thomas Todd (Ky.) | 1807–26 | Jefferson | 1765 | 1826 | Chief Justice, Kentucky Court of Appeals |
| 18. Gabriel Duvall (Md.) | 1812–35 | Madison | 1752 | 1844 | Comptroller, U.S. Treasury |
| 19. Joseph Story (Mass.) | 1811–45 | Madison | 1779 | 1845 | Massachusetts legislator |
| 20. Smith Thompson (N.Y.) | 1823–43 | Monroe | 1768 | 1843 | U.S. Secretary of the Navy |
| 21. Robert Trimble (Ky.) | 1826–28 | J.Q. Adams | 1777 | 1828 | U.S. District Court judge |
| 22. John McLean (Ohio) | 1829–61 | Jackson | 1785 | 1861 | U.S. Postmaster General |
| 23. Henry Baldwin (Pa.) | 1830–44 | Jackson | 1780 | 1844 | Private law practice |
| 24. James Moore Wayne (Ga.) | 1835–67 | Jackson | 1790 | 1867 | U.S. Representative |
| 25. **Roger Brooke Taney** (Md.) | 1836–64 | Jackson | 1777 | 1864 | U.S. Attorney General; private law practice |
| 26. Philip Pendleton Barbour (Va.) | 1836–41 | Jackson | 1783 | 1841 | U.S. Circuit Court judge |
| 27. John Catron (Tenn.) | 1837–65 | Jackson | 1786 | 1865 | Private law practice |
| 28. John McKinley (Ala.) | 1837–52 | Van Buren | 1780 | 1852 | U.S. Senator-elect |
| 29. Peter Vivian Daniel (Va.) | 1841–60 | Van Buren | 1784 | 1860 | U.S. District Court judge |
| 30. Samuel Nelson (N.Y.) | 1845–72 | Tyler | 1792 | 1873 | Chief Justice, New York |
| 31. Levi Woodbury (N.H.) | 1845–51 | Polk | 1789 | 1851 | U.S. Senator |
| 32. Robert Cooper Grier (Pa.) | 1846–70 | Polk | 1794 | 1870 | State District Court judge |
| 33. Benjamin Robbins Curtis (Mass.) | 1851–57 | Fillmore | 1809 | 1874 | Private law practice |
| 34. John Archibald Campbell (Ala.) | 1853–61 | Pierce | 1811 | 1889 | Private law practice |
| 35. Nathan Clifford (Maine) | 1858–81 | Buchanan | 1803 | 1881 | Private law practice |
| 36. Noah Haynes Swayne (Ohio) | 1862–81 | Lincoln | 1804 | 1884 | Private law practice |
| 37. Samuel Freeman Miller (Iowa) | 1862–90 | Lincoln | 1816 | 1890 | Private law practice |
| 38. David Davis (Ill.) | 1862–77 | Lincoln | 1815 | 1886 | Judicial Circuit Court judge |
| 39. Stephen Johnson Field (Calif.) | 1863–97 | Lincoln | 1816 | 1899 | State Superior Court judge |
| 40. **Salmon Portland Chase** (Ohio) | 1864–73 | Lincoln | 1808 | 1873 | Governor of Ohio; U.S. Secretary of Treasury |
| 41. William Strong (Pa.) | 1870–80 | Grant | 1808 | 1895 | Private law practice |
| 42. Joseph P. Bradley (N.J.) | 1870–92 | Grant | 1813 | 1892 | Private law practice |
| 43. Ward Hunt (N.Y.) | 1873–82 | Grant | 1810 | 1886 | N.Y. Commissioner of Appeals |
| 44. **Morrison Remick Waite** (Ohio) | 1874–88 | Grant | 1816 | 1888 | President of Ohio Constitutional Convention |
| 45. John Marshall Harlan (Ky.) | 1877–1911 | Hayes | 1833 | 1911 | Member, Louisiana Commission |
| 46. William Burnham Woods (Ga.) | 1881–87 | Hayes | 1824 | 1887 | U.S. Circuit Court judge |
| 47. Stanley Matthews (Ohio) | 1881–89 | Garfield | 1824 | 1889 | Private law practice |
| 48. Horace Gray (Mass.) | 1882–1902 | Arthur | 1828 | 1902 | Chief Judge, Massachusetts |
| 49. Samuel Blatchford (N.Y.) | 1882–93 | Arthur | 1820 | 1893 | U.S. Circuit Court judge |
| 50. Lucius Quintus Cincinnatus Lamar (Miss.) | 1888–93 | Cleveland | 1825 | 1893 | U.S. Secretary of Interior |
| 51. **Melville Weston Fuller** (Ill.) | 1888–1910 | Cleveland | 1833 | 1910 | State legislator; Chicago corporation lawyer |
| 52. David Josiah Brewer (Kan.) | 1890–1910 | B. Harrison | 1837 | 1910 | U.S. Circuit Court judge |

[1] Resigned as associate justice in 1791; was named Chief Justice in 1795, but Senate rejected nomination.

## U.S. SUPREME COURT MEMBERS *(continued)*

| JUSTICE (CHIEF JUSTICES IN BOLDFACE TYPE) AND STATE OF RESIDENCE | YEARS ON THE COURT | APPOINTED BY PRESIDENT: | BORN | DIED | POSITION BEFORE COURT APPOINTMENT |
|---|---|---|---|---|---|
| 53. Henry Billings Brown (Mich.)..... | 1891–1906 | B. Harrison | 1836 | 1913 | U.S. District Court judge |
| 54. George Shiras Jr. (Pa.).......... | 1892–1903 | B. Harrison | 1832 | 1924 | Private law practice |
| 55. Howell Edmunds Jackson (Tenn.) | 1893–95 | B. Harrison | 1832 | 1895 | U.S. Circuit Court judge |
| 56. **Edward Douglass White** [1] (La.)..................... | 1894–1921 | Cleveland | 1845 | 1921 | U.S. Senator |
| 57. Rufus Wheeler Peckham (N.Y.)... | 1896–1909 | Cleveland | 1838 | 1909 | State Appeals Court judge |
| 58. Joseph McKenna (Calif.).......... | 1898–1925 | McKinley | 1843 | 1926 | U.S. Attorney General |
| 59. Oliver Wendell Holmes (Mass.)... | 1902–32 | T. Roosevelt | 1841 | 1935 | Chief Justice, Mass. Supreme Court |
| 60. William Rufus Day (Ohio)........ | 1903–22 | T. Roosevelt | 1849 | 1923 | U.S. Circuit Court judge |
| 61. William Henry Moody (Mass.).... | 1906–10 | T. Roosevelt | 1853 | 1917 | U.S. Attorney General |
| 62. Horace Harmon Lurton (Tenn.).. | 1910–14 | Taft | 1844 | 1914 | U.S. Circuit Court judge |
| 63. Charles Evans Hughes [2] (N.Y.)... | 1910–16 | Taft | 1862 | 1948 | Governor of New York |
| 64. Willis Van Devanter (Wyo.) ...... | 1911–37 | Taft | 1859 | 1941 | U.S. Circuit Court judge |
| 65. Joseph Rucker Lamar (Ga.)...... | 1911–16 | Taft | 1857 | 1916 | Private law practice |
| 66. Mahlon Pitney (N.J.).......... | 1912–22 | Taft | 1858 | 1924 | State Supreme Court judge |
| 67. James Clark McReynolds (Tenn.). | 1914–41 | Wilson | 1862 | 1946 | U.S. Attorney General |
| 68. Louis Dembitz Brandeis (Mass.).. | 1916–39 | Wilson | 1856 | 1941 | Private law practice |
| 69. John Hessin Clarke (Ohio)........ | 1916–22 | Wilson | 1857 | 1945 | U.S. District Court judge |
| 70. **William Howard Taft** (Ohio)..................... | 1921–30 | Harding | 1857 | 1930 | 27th U.S. President |
| 71. George Sutherland (Utah) ....... | 1922–38 | Harding | 1862 | 1942 | Private law practice |
| 72. Pierce Butler (Minn.)............. | 1922–39 | Harding | 1866 | 1939 | Private law practice |
| 73. Edward Terry Sanford (Tenn.) ... | 1923–30 | Harding | 1865 | 1930 | U.S. District Court judge |
| 74. **Harlan Fiske Stone** [1] (N.Y.) ........................ | 1925–46 | Coolidge | 1872 | 1946 | U.S. Attorney General |
| 75. **Charles Evans Hughes** (N.Y.).... | 1930–41 | Hoover | 1862 | 1948 | Judge, Permanent Court of International Justice |
| 76. Owen Josephus Roberts (Pa.)... | 1930–45 | Hoover | 1875 | 1955 | Private law practice |
| 77. Benjamin Nathan Cardozo (N.Y.) . | 1932–38 | Hoover | 1870 | 1938 | State Appeals Court judge |
| 78. Hugo Lafayette Black (Ala.)...... | 1937–71 | F. Roosevelt | 1886 | 1971 | U.S. Senator |
| 79. Stanley Forman Reed (Ky.) ...... | 1938–57 | F. Roosevelt | 1884 | 1980 | U.S. Solicitor General |
| 80. Felix Frankfurter (Mass.) ....... | 1939–62 | F. Roosevelt | 1882 | 1965 | Professor of law |
| 81. William Orville Douglas (Conn.) .. | 1939–75 | F. Roosevelt | 1898 | 1980 | Chairman of the SEC |
| 82. Frank Murphy (Mich.) .......... | 1940–49 | F. Roosevelt | 1890 | 1949 | U.S. Attorney General |
| 83. James Francis Byrnes (S.C.) ..... | 1941–42 | F. Roosevelt | 1879 | 1972 | U.S. Senator |
| 84. Robert Houghwout Jackson (N.Y.) | 1941–54 | F. Roosevelt | 1892 | 1954 | U.S. Attorney General |
| 85. Wiley Blount Rutledge (Iowa) .... | 1943–49 | F. Roosevelt | 1894 | 1949 | U.S. Circuit Court judge |
| 86. Harold Hitz Burton (Ohio) ....... | 1945–58 | Truman | 1888 | 1964 | U.S. Senator |
| 87. **Frederick Moore Vinson** (Ky.) ......................... | 1946–53 | Truman | 1890 | 1953 | U.S. Secretary of Treasury |
| 88. Tom Campbell Clark (Texas)..... | 1949–67 | Truman | 1899 | 1977 | U.S. Attorney General |
| 89. Sherman Minton (Ind.) .......... | 1949–56 | Truman | 1890 | 1965 | U.S. Circuit Court judge |
| 90. **Earl Warren** (Calif.) ....................... | 1953–69 | Eisenhower | 1891 | 1974 | Governor of California |
| 91. John Marshall Harlan (N.Y.) ..... | 1955–71 | Eisenhower | 1899 | 1971 | U.S. Circuit Court judge |
| 92.*William Joseph Brennan Jr. (N.J.) ........................ | 1956– | Eisenhower | 1906 | — | State Supreme Court judge |
| 93. Charles Evans Whittaker (Mo.)... | 1957–62 | Eisenhower | 1901 | 1973 | U.S. Circuit Court judge |
| 94.*Potter Stewart (Ohio) ........................ | 1958– | Eisenhower | 1915 | — | U.S. Circuit Court judge |
| 95.*Byron Raymond White (Colo.) ....................... | 1962– | Kennedy | 1917 | — | Deputy U.S. Attorney General |
| 96. Arthur Joseph Goldberg (Ill.) .... | 1962–65 | Kennedy | 1908 | — | U.S. Secretary of Labor |
| 97. Abe Fortas [3] (D.C.) .............. | 1965–69 | L. Johnson | 1910 | — | Private law practice |
| 98.*Thurgood Marshall (N.Y.) ........................ | 1967– | L. Johnson | 1908 | — | U.S. Solicitor General |
| 99.***Warren Earl Burger** (Minn.) ........................ | 1969– | Nixon | 1907 | — | U.S. Circuit Court judge |
| 100.*Harry Andrew Blackmun (Minn.) ........................ | 1970— | Nixon | 1908 | — | U.S. Circuit Court judge |
| 101.*Lewis Franklin Powell Jr. (Va.) ......................... | 1971– | Nixon | 1907 | — | Private law practice |
| 102.*William Hubbs Rehnquist (Ariz.)........................ | 1971– | Nixon | 1924 | — | Asst. U.S. Attorney General |
| 103.*John Paul Stevens (Ill.) ......... | 1975– | Ford | 1920 | — | U.S. Court of Appeals judge |

*Current Court members. [1] Raised from Associate to Chief Justice: White, 1910 (by President Taft); Stone, 1941 (by President F. D. Roosevelt). [2] Resigned; later named Chief Justice in 1930. [3] Senate rejected nomination as Chief Justice.

# Taxes

Unique work-to-pay-your-taxes program in Hartford, Conn., enables qualified homeowners, such as Mary Haley, *above*, to pay for their property taxes by working part time for city agencies. Persons eligible to participate in the program are limited to those who are unemployed, retired, or whose property taxes exceed 10% of their incomes.

United Press Int'l.

## HIGHLIGHTS: 1980

Although both Democrats and Republicans said they favored reductions in the federal income tax, Congress delayed action on consideration of income tax cuts until 1981. Earlier in the year Congress imposed a windfall-profit tax on corporations that supposedly will save taxpayers about $166 billion in the next 10 years. See page 258.

The Internal Revenue Service (IRS) reported the results of a survey of income tax returns paid in 1980 that showed 60% of the revenues came from persons and families with incomes between $15,000 and $50,000.

The IRS said the tax returns showed that Americans had a total income of $1.4 trillion in 1979 compared with $1.16 trillion in 1977. Although legislation was approved in 1978 to reduce income taxes, the IRS survey revealed that because many taxpayers moved into higher tax brackets the amount of income taken by taxes actually rose from 13.78% in 1977 to 14.79% in 1979.

The IRS said 43.9% of the tax returns were for incomes of less than $10,000, but that they contributed only 4.4% of the tax revenues.

# FILING YOUR FEDERAL INCOME TAX IN 1981

Source: Internal Revenue Service, U.S. Department of the Treasury

## BLUE FORM 1040 AND PINK FORM 1040A

Taxpayers filing 1980 federal income tax returns must use either the blue form 1040 (the long form) or the pink form 1040A (the short form).

You can only use the pink short form if all your income is from salary, wages, tips, other employee compensation, and from dividends and interest of less than $400.

If you have other sources of income or if you list deductions for such expenditures as contributions to religious organizations, you must use the blue long form.

Even though it is simpler to use the short pink form, you can only tell how much money you might save on the blue form by itemizing the deductions that you might claim, and then comparing the results.

## WHAT INCOME IS TAXABLE

The following types of income are taxable: all wages and salaries, tips and gratuities, annuities, alimony, awards, back pay, bonuses, business income, commissions, compensations for personal services, dividends, fees, estate and trust income, gambling winnings, hobby income, illegal income, interest on savings, jury duty fees, partnership income, pensions, prizes, profits from sale or exchange of real estate or other property, rents, retirement pay, rewards, royalties, severance pay, and sick pay.

## INCOME NORMALLY NOT TAXABLE

The following income normally is not taxable and should not be reported on the U.S. tax return: social security or welfare payments; benefits paid by the Veterans Administration; dividends paid on veterans insurance; accident, health, and casualty insurance proceeds; disability and death payments; Federal Employees Compensation Act payments;

## IMPORTANT TAX DATES IN 1981

**February 2**—Employers must provide their employees with a Statement of Wages Earned and Tax Withheld (Form W-2) for 1980.

**February 2**—Individuals should file an income tax return for 1980 and pay the tax due, if the last installment on their 1980 estimated income tax was not paid.

**April 15**—Individuals must file an income tax return for the calendar year 1980. Tax due must be paid in full with the return when filed.

**April 15**—Those required to do so must file a declaration of estimated income tax for 1981 and pay at least 25% of such tax.

**June 15**—Individuals must pay second installment of 1981 estimated income tax.

**September 15**—Individuals must pay third installment of 1981 estimated income tax.

**January 15, 1982**—Individuals must pay fourth installment of 1981 estimated income tax.

gifts; bequests; inheritances; interest on municipal bonds; insurance proceeds paid because of death; mustering-out pay; Railroad Retirement Act pensions; rental allowances of clergymen; certain scholarship and fellowship grants; unemployment compensation; workers' compensation; cost-of-living allowances paid U.S. employees abroad; and Medicare or Medicaid reimbursements.

Taxpayers should obtain IRS booklet *Taxable and Nontaxable Income* (publication 525) for more detailed information on taxable and nontaxable income.

## WHO MUST FILE FEDERAL INCOME TAX RETURNS

No matter how low your income was during the year, you must file a return (1) *to get a refund* if income tax was withheld by your employer, or (2) if you qualify to receive up to $500 as an *earned income credit* (see next page).

No matter how young or how old you are, you must file a federal income tax return if you had as much income as one of the following amounts and meet the other specifications following that amount:

**$400:** if you received this much as net income from self-employment (such as operating your own lawn-mowing business).

**$1,000:** if you can be claimed as a dependent on your parent's return **and** have received this much in taxable dividends, interest, or other unearned income.

**$1,000:** if you are married **and** filing separately or are not living with your spouse at the end of the tax year.

**$1,000:** if you are entitled to exclude income from sources within U.S. possessions.

**$3,300:** if you are under 65 **and** you are single (or legally separated, divorced, or married living apart from your spouse for the entire year with a dependent child).

**$4,300:** if you are 65 or older **and** you are single (or as defined above).

**$4,400:** if you are under 65 **and** you are a qualifying widow or widower with a dependent child.

**$5,400:** if you are 65 or older **and** you are a qualifying widow or widower with a dependent child.

**$5,400:** if you are a married couple filing jointly **and** you both are under 65.

**$6,400:** if you are a married couple filing jointly **and** one of you is 65 or older.

**$7,400:** if you are a married couple filing jointly **and** you both are 65 or older.

## IRS WILL FIGURE OUT YOUR TAX

If you do not feel capable of figuring out how much tax you owe and do not wish to pay someone to do it for you, the Internal Revenue Service (IRS) now will calculate how much tax you owe and (1) send you a refund for overpayment or (2) a bill for underpayment. Most taxpayers qualify for this service, although some do not.

The IRS will figure out your tax for you if you meet all five of these criteria: (1) Your adjusted gross income is $20,000 or less ($40,000 or less if you are married filing a joint return or a qualifying widow or widower). (2) You do not itemize such deductions as medical expenses, taxes, charitable contributions, and so on. (3) All of your income must be from wages, salaries, tips, dividends, interest, pensions, and annuities. (4) You cannot use income averaging to reduce your taxable income. (5) You cannot use an exemption for money earned abroad.

## SIMPLIFIED TAX TABLES

If you do not qualify to have the IRS figure out your tax, you will find that the tax tables that come with your income tax form have been made easier to use in finding how much tax you owe.

The term "standard deduction" was removed from the Internal Revenue Code by Congress when the Tax Reduction and Simplification Act of 1977 was passed. Instead, Congress replaced the term with "zero bracket amount," which is a flat amount of income on which no tax is paid as determined by your filing status.

The zero bracket amount, the personal exemptions, and a general tax credit all have been taken into account in the tax tables so that you *do not* deduct them again in determining your tax.

The tax tables show that you pay **no tax:**

(1) If you file as a single person or head of household with no dependents and have an adjusted gross income of $3,300 or less.

(2) If you are married, file jointly with two exemptions, and have an adjusted gross income of $5,400 or less.

(3) If you are married, file separately with only your own exemption, and have an adjusted gross income of $2,700 or less.

The tax tables have been extended to higher amounts of income to enable more taxpayers to determine how much tax they owe merely by finding the tax in the tables opposite the amount of their adjusted gross income and their number of exemptions.

The maximum incomes included in the tax tables are $20,000 for persons filing separately and $40,000 for married couples filing jointly.

Additional computation using tax rate schedules is necessary for taxpayers with higher incomes or who itemize deductions on Schedule A of blue Form 1040.

## EARNED INCOME CREDIT

You may be entitled to a special payment or credit of up to $500, which you could receive as a refund check or as a credit applied against taxes you owe. You are eligible if you meet all three of these tests: (1) Your adjusted gross income was less than $10,000; (2) Your earned income was more than $1 but was less than $10,000, (3) You paid more than half the cost of keeping up a home in the United States in which you and your dependent child lived.

The credit is equal to 10% of your earned income or your adjusted gross income up to a maximum credit of $500 for an income of $5,000. If your income is larger than $5,000, the credit is scaled down so that you receive a smaller and smaller credit until it reaches zero for an income of $10,000.

If you were married, to be eligible for the earned income credit you must file a joint return (unless you did not live with your spouse at all during the year but did pay over half the cost to maintain the household where the dependent child lived).

If you are eligible for the Earned Income Credit, the IRS also will figure out this credit for you if you write "EIC" and the name of the child that qualifies you for the credit on the line specified on your tax form.

Remember, to receive the credit, you *must* file a federal income tax return, even though your income was so small that otherwise you would not have to file.

## PERSONAL EXEMPTIONS AND DEPENDENTS

You can claim exemptions for yourself and your dependents whether you use the pink short form 1040A or the blue long form 1040. Each exemption reduces by $1,000 the amount of your income on which you are taxed. You do not actually deduct these amounts from your income on the tax form because they have been taken into account in the tax tables provided for use in determining your tax.

**Your Own Exemptions.** Whether you are married or single, you receive at least one

## TAX HOTLINE

If you need special information in preparing your income tax return, you can phone toll-free on your state's IRS hotline. To find out the phone number of your state's IRS hotline, call 800-555-1212 for toll-free directory assistance.

**YOUR FEDERAL INCOME TAX** *(continued)*
exemption for yourself. If you are 65 or older, you can claim a *second* exemption for yourself. And if you are blind, you can claim a *third* exemption for yourself.

To claim the exemption for blindness, you must submit proof with your income tax form. If you are completely blind, submit a statement saying so. If you partially blind, submit a statement from an eye physician or registered optometrist (1) that you cannot see over 20/200 with glasses, or (2) your field of view does not exceed 20 degrees.

**Exemptions for Your Spouse.** If you file a joint return with your spouse, your spouse is entitled to at least one exemption, a *second* exemption if 65 or older, and a *third* exemption if blind. Again, if a blindness exemption for your spouse is claimed, proof should be submitted with the tax form.

If you were legally divorced or separated at the end of the tax year, you cannot take an exemption for your former spouse.

If your spouse died during the year and you did not remarry, you can still claim the exemptions that you could have taken for your spouse on the date of death.

**Exemptions for Dependent Children.** You can claim one additional exemption for each of your dependent children who live with you, listing their first names.

Even if your child who is 19 or younger had income of $1,000 or more and has to file a tax return, you can still claim an exemption if the child lived at your home and you paid over half of his or her support.

Even if your child is 19 or older, earns $1,000 or more, and does not live at home, you can claim him or her as an exemption if the child is enrolled as a full-time student during five months of the year and receives at least half his or her support from you.

**Exemptions for Children of Divorced or Separated Parents.** The parent who has custody of the child during most of the year usually can claim an exemption for the child.

However, the parent who does not have custody can claim the exemption for the child (1) if that parent gave at least $600 toward the child's support during the year and the divorce or separation agreement states he or she can take the exemption, *or* (2) if that parent gave $1,200 or more for the child's support during the year and the parent having custody cannot prove he or she provided more money for the child's support.

**Exemptions for Other Dependents.** You also can claim exemptions for other persons who are related to you or who lived in your home for the full year if you paid more than half their support and they received less than $1,000 income.

You can take an exemption for a dependent who died during the year if he or she met the tests for a dependent while alive.

You can obtain more information about dependent exemptions from the IRS booklet *Exemptions* (publication 501).

**ADJUSTMENTS TO INCOME**
The blue income tax form 1040 provides space where you can deduct certain expenses to determine what is called your *adjusted gross income.*

**Moving Expenses.** If you had to move at least 35 miles during the year for reasons connected with your job or business, you can deduct the cost of moving your family, furniture and other household goods and personal belongings. You also can deduct such related expenses as the cost of hunting for a new home, meals and lodging while living in temporary quarters for up to 30 days, and expenses in selling or renting your old home.

For more information, obtain the IRS booklet *Moving Expenses* (publication 521).

**Employee Business Expenses.** You can deduct the following expenses that were not paid by your employer: (1) *Travel and transportation,* including the cost of using your car in your work. Instead of figuring your actual automobile expenses, you can take a mileage rate of 20¢ a mile for the first 15,000 miles and 11¢ for each mile over 15,000, plus parking fees and tolls. (2) *Meals and lodging* expenses while you were temporarily away overnight on business from the area of your main place of work. (3) *Selling expenses,* if you are an outside salesperson who does all selling away from your employer's place of business. For more information, obtain IRS booklet *Travel, Entertainment, and Gift Expenses* (publication 463).

**Payments to a Retirement Plan.** You can deduct payments to an authorized retirement plan, but you must fill out and attach required forms. You should exercise caution when making such a deduction because the law provides penalties if you fail to provide complete information and fail to file required forms and statements. See IRS booklets *Individual Retirement Arrangements* or *Self-Employed Retirement Plans* (publications 560 and 590).

**Forfeited Interest Penalty.** You can deduct a forfeited interest penalty that you have had to pay because you made a premature withdrawal from a time savings account. To do so, you must have included the interest payment you received as part of your gross income.

**Alimony Paid.** If you are divorced or legally separated from your spouse, you can deduct periodic payments of alimony or separate

maintenance made under a court decree. You also can deduct payments made under a written separation agreement or decree for support entered into since 1954.

You *cannot deduct* lump-sum cash or property settlements, voluntary payments not made under a court order or written separation agreement, or amounts specified as child support.

The person *receiving* the alimony or separation payments must report them as taxable income.

For more information, obtain IRS booklet *Tax Information for Divorced or Separated Individuals* (publication 504).

**Disability Income Exclusion.** If you are under the age of 65 and totally disabled, you may be able to exclude up to $100 a week from your income. You must enclose a physician's certification of your total disability with your return.

For information on how to figure the amount of your disability income exclusion, obtain IRS booklet *Disability Payments* (publication 522).

## TAX CREDITS

You may be eligible for certain tax credits. These are amounts that are deducted directly from the taxes owed on your adjusted gross income.

**Political Contributions.** If you made contributions to political candidates or political organizations, you can claim a tax credit. The amount claimed cannot exceed half the amount you actually contributed and is limited to $50 on a single return or $100 on a joint return.

**Credit for the Elderly.** You may be able to claim this credit and reduce your tax by as much as $375 (if single) or $562.50 (if married filing jointly). To be eligible, you must be (1) 65 or older, *or* (2) under 65 but retired under a public retirement system. For more information, obtain IRS Schedules R and RP, or publication 524, *Credit for the Elderly.*

**Credit for Child and Dependent Care Expenses.** A taxpayer who pays for child care or care of a disabled dependent in order to be gainfully employed is eligible for a credit that can be deducted directly from taxes on blue form 1040. The credit amounts to up to 20% of eligible expenses for such care to a maximum of a $400 credit ($2,000 expenses) for one dependent or $800 for two or more ($4,000 expenses).

A married couple can use this credit if one spouse works full-time and the other works part-time or is a full-time student.

Under certain circumstances payments to relatives for such care can be counted in calculating the tax credit.

For more information, see IRS Form 2441, *Credit for Child Care Expenses.*

**Investment Credit.** You may be eligible for this credit if you have invested in certain trade or business property. For more information, obtain IRS Form 3468, *Computations of Investment Credit.*

**Foreign Tax Credit.** If you paid income tax to a foreign country or U.S. possession, you can claim this credit.

**Work Incentive Credit.** An employer can claim a credit for the salaries and wages paid to employees hired under a Work Incentive (WIN) Program or to federal welfare recipients.

**New Jobs Credit.** This is a credit for business employers who hire additional employees during the year.

**Energy Credits.** You may be allowed a tax credit of as much as $2,500 for energy-saving improvements you have made to your house since April 20, 1977.

## ITEMIZED DEDUCTIONS

If you had certain expenses during the year, such as contributions to a church or large medical expenses, it may be to your advantage to itemize deductions on Schedule A of blue form 1040.

**Medical and Dental Expenses.** Medical and dental expenses that you actually paid during the year can be deducted in part from your income for tax purposes.

You can deduct one-half (up to $150) of the amount you paid for insurance for medical or hospital care.

The medical expenses you claim for deduction can include those for yourself, your spouse, and any dependent who received over half his or her support from you. You may *not* include amounts repaid to you, or repaid to anyone else, by hospital, health, or accident insurance. To qualify as a deduction, your medical expenses must exceed 3% of your adjusted gross income.

**Taxes.** You can deduct state and local income taxes, real estate taxes, sales taxes, and personal property taxes.

You *cannot* deduct federal social security tax, federal excise taxes, fees for hunting and dog licenses, fees for car inspection or drivers' licenses, taxes you paid for another person, water taxes, or taxes on liquor, beer, wine, cigarettes, and tobacco.

**Interest Expenses.** You can deduct interest that you have paid on a mortgage or a loan, on a bank credit-card plan, on charge accounts, and on installment-plan purchases. There are limitations on the amount of interest you can deduct on interest expense paid or accrued on debts related to investment property.

**Contributions.** You can deduct gifts or dona-

**YOUR FEDERAL INCOME TAX** *(continued)*

tions made to organizations operated for religious, charitable, educational, scientific, or literary purposes, or to prevent cruelty to animals and children.

You *cannot* deduct gifts to relatives, friends, or other persons; to social clubs, labor unions, or chambers of commerce; or to foreign organizations, organizations operated for personal profit, or organizations whose purpose is to get people to vote for new laws or for changes in old laws.

For additional information, obtain IRS booklet *Charitable Contributions* (publication 526).

**Casualty or Theft Losses.** You may be able to deduct all or part of your loss if you had property stolen or damaged by fire, storm, automobile accident, shipwreck, and so on. The first $100 of *each* casualty or theft loss of nonbusiness property in excess of insurance reimbursement is *not* deductible.

For more information, obtain IRS booklet *Tax Information on Disasters, Casualty Losses, and Thefts* (publication 547).

**Other Deductions.** A variety of other expenses may be claimed as deductible as follows:

Dues paid to unions, professional organizations, and chambers of commerce.

Expenses for education that helps you keep up or improve skills you must have in your present job, trade, or business. You *cannot* deduct expenses for education to meet the minimum requirements for your job, business, or trade; or for education that is part of a course of study that will lead to your getting a new trade or business.

Gambling losses to the extent of the amount that you won and reported as income.

Cost of safety equipment, small tools, and supplies used in your job.

Expenses relating to business or office use of your home.

Certain costs of business entertainment.

Fees paid to employment agencies.

For more information, obtain IRS booklets *Business Use of Your Home* (publication 587) and *Miscellaneous Deductions and Credits* (publication 529).

## TAX SAVINGS FOR HOMEOWNERS

If you own your own home, you usually can save on your income taxes by itemizing as deductions the interest on your mortgage and the local property taxes you must pay.

Any gain you realize on the sale or exchange of your home is not taxed at the time of sale if within 18 months before or after you buy and occupy another residence whose cost equals or exceeds the price of the old residence. Additional time is allowed if you construct the new residence or if you were on active duty in the U.S. armed forces. The tax is postponed; it is not forgiven.

For additional information, obtain IRS booklets *Tax Information for Homeowners* (publication 530) and *Tax Information on Selling or Buying Your Home* (publication 523).

## INCOME AVERAGING

Certain taxpayers may benefit from a provision that provides for averaging of income. Some persons with fluctuating incomes may be eligible to pay less tax through this provision.

If the income for a given year exceeds one and one-fifth times the average annual income for the four preceding years, and the excess is more than $3,000, the taxpayer may be eligible to use this provision in figuring his tax liability.

For more information, obtain IRS booklet *Income Averaging* (publication 506).

## TAX EFFECT OF CAPITAL GAINS AND LOSSES

Usually, the tax on capital gains is less than the tax on ordinary income.

If the net gains from the sale or exchange of long-term capital assets (those held longer than one year) are greater than the net losses from the sale or exchange of capital assets held for a shorter time, only 40% of the excess is subject to tax.

If the net result of all sales and exchanges of both long-term and short-term capital assets is a loss, you can deduct 50¢ from income for each $1 of loss up to a total of the loss in adjusted gross income or a $3,000 deduction for a $6,000 loss. The balance of the loss may be carried over and deducted in succeeding tax years.

## INCOME FROM DIVIDENDS

Dividends are distributions of cash, property, services, or accommodations by a corporation to its stockholders. They are taxable income to the stockholder. Distributions other than cash are taxed at their fair market value.

The gross amount must be reported. However, the first $100 of qualified dividends may be excluded from income on Form 1040 or 1040A. To qualify for exclusion, dividends must be from taxable domestic corporations.

Husbands and wives are permitted up to $100 exclusions for dividends received by each, regardless of the type of return filed.

In addition to industrial, mercantile, and other commercial corporations, the exclusion applies to dividends on the capital stock of nonexempt cooperatives, stock of the Federal National Mortgage Association, the capi-

tal stock of building and loan associations (as distinct from dividends on deposits and withdrawable accounts), and similar organizations.

Some types of corporations whose dividends do not qualify are: foreign corporations, China Trade Act corporations, exempt farmers' cooperatives, real estate investment trusts, corporations doing business in U.S. possessions (under certain conditions), and a corporation that has elected not to be taxed as a corporation.

## PRESERVE ADEQUATE RECORDS

Maintain proper records to prepare federal income tax returns correctly. These records, if complete, help ensure that you will pay only the proper tax. File and store in a safe place sales slips, invoices, receipts, canceled checks, paid bills, and other documents that are used as evidence of transactions.

Copies of returns filed by the taxpayer should also be kept. These are of help in preparing future returns and if it later becomes necessary to file a claim for refund.

## WHERE TO FILE AND WHEN

Individual federal income tax returns may be filed anytime on or after January 1 of the year following the year of earnings, but no later than midnight April 15, 1981, if the calendar year is the basis for these earnings.

All taxpayers—those entitled to refunds as well as those who are not—should file their returns directly with the Internal Revenue Service center that serves their state (as indicated in the tax form instructions).

If the fiscal year is used, the return is due on or before the 15th day of the fourth month after the close of the particular fiscal or tax year. Returns submitted by mail must be postmarked on or before the due date.

Payment must be made at the time the return is filed. Interest of 12% per year is charged on taxes paid after their due date, even though an extension for filing may have been authorized.

A penalty of ½% a month or part of a month to a maximum of 25% is imposed for failure to pay when due, if for other than reasonable cause.

U.S. citizens abroad on the final filing date are allowed automatic extensions without application to June 15, 1981. Military personnel on duty outside the U.S. and Puerto Rico are allowed the same extension. Statements that the taxpayer was outside the U.S. on the due date must accompany the return.

When filing a return, you should use the preaddressed label (showing your name, address, and Social Security number) that you receive with the form 1040 or 1040A tax packages from IRS at the end of the year. Use of this label expedites processing and the issuance of any refund due.

Before filing your income tax return, make sure it is complete in every detail. It *must* include your complete name, Social Security number, amount of wages from all W-2 forms, total of personal exemptions, deductions (regardless of how computed), and signature (of both husband and wife if a joint return). Any error or omission can result in a processing delay and may slow a tax refund payment.

## ESTIMATED TAX RETURN

In some instances individuals are required to file an estimated tax declaration and pay all estimated tax.

A person must declare and pay an estimated tax if total tax liability is expected to exceed the amount withheld by $100 or more and the taxpayer:

(A) expects to receive more than $500 in income not subject to withholding, or (B) one of the following situations applies:

(1) if the taxpayer is single, head of a household, or a surviving spouse and expects gross income exceeding $20,000;

(2) if the taxpayer is married and entitled to file a joint tax declaration and expects gross income over $20,000, but his spouse will not receive wages;

(3) if the taxpayer is married and entitled to file a joint tax declaration, expects gross income over $10,000, and both he and his spouse will receive wages;

(4) if the taxpayer is married but not entitled to file a joint tax declaration and expects gross income over $5,000.

## HISTORY OF THE U.S. INCOME TAX

The federal government first levied an income tax from 1862 to 1872 to help pay for the Civil War.

A new income tax law passed by Congress in 1894 was declared unconstitutional by the Supreme Court.

In 1909 the first corporate income tax law was approved by Congress.

In 1911 Wisconsin became the first state to levy an income tax on residents.

The 16th Amendment to the U.S. Constitution, adopted in 1913, made possible the present system of federal income taxes.

The first of the new income taxes began to be collected under the Underwood Tariff Act, which became law in October 1913.

Payroll taxes began in 1935, and pay-as-you-go wage deductions in 1944.

Today federal tax returns of all business and individual taxpayers in the U.S. are processed by computers.

## STATE INCOME TAX RATES AND EXEMPTIONS: 1980

Sources: Tax Foundation; Commerce Clearing House

Seven of the 50 states of the United States do not assess any state tax on personal incomes, including Alaska, Florida, Nevada, South Dakota, Texas, Washington, and Wyoming.

| STATE | PERSONAL EXEMPTIONS | | | INDIVIDUAL RATES |
|---|---|---|---|---|
| | Single | Married | Dependent | |
| Alabama | $1,500 | $3,000 | $ 300 | From 1.5% on 1st $1,000 to 5% on income over $5,000 |
| Arizona | $1,000 | $2,000 | $ 600 | From 2% on 1st $1,000 to 8% on income over $6,000 |
| Arkansas | $17.50[1] | $ 35[1] | $ 6[1] | From 1% on 1st $2,999 to 7% on income over $25,000 |
| California | $ 25[1] | $ 50[1] | $ 8[1] | From 1% on 1st $2,000 to 11% on income over $15,500 |
| Colorado[2] | $ 850 | $1,700 | $ 850 | From 3% on 1st $1,000 to 8% on income over $10,000; 2% surtax on intangible income over $15,000 |
| Connecticut[3] | $ 100 | $ 200 | — | 7% on capital gains; on dividends, 1% on 1st $20,000 to 9% on $100,000 or over |
| Delaware | $ 600 | $1,200 | $ 600 | From 1.4% on 1st $1,000 to 13.5% on income over $50,000 |
| Dist. of Col. | $ 750 | $1,500 | $ 750 | From 2% on 1st $1,000 to 11% on income over $25,000 |
| Georgia | $1,500 | $3,000 | $ 700 | From 1% on 1st $1,000 to 6% on income over $10,000 |
| Hawaii | $ 750 | $1,500 | $ 750 | From 2.25% on 1st $500 to 11% on income over $30,000 |
| Idaho | $ 750 | $1,500 | $ 750 | From 2% on 1st $1,000 to 7.5% on income over $5,000; each person (husband and wife filing jointly are deemed one person) filing return pays additional $10 |
| Illinois | $1,000 | $2,000 | $1,000 | 2.5% on net income |
| Indiana | $1,000 | $2,000 | $ 500 | 1.9% on adjusted gross income |
| Iowa | $ 15[1] | $ 30[1] | $ 10[1] | From 0.5% on 1st $1,000 to 13% on income over $75,000 |
| Kansas | $1,000 | $2,000 | $1,000 | From 2% on 1st $2,000 to 9% on income over $25,000 |
| Kentucky | $ 20[1] | $ 40[1] | $ 20[1] | From 2% on 1st $3,000 to 6% on income over $8,000 |
| Louisiana | $2,500 | $5,000 | $ 400 | From 2% on 1st $10,000 to 6% on income over $50,000 |
| Maine | $1,000 | $2,000 | $1,000 | From 1% on 1st $2,000 to 10% on income over $25,000 |
| Maryland | $ 800 | $1,600 | $ 800 | From 2% on 1st $1,000 to 5% on income over $3,000 |
| Massachusetts | $2,000 | $2,600-$4,600 | $ 600 | Interest, dividends, net capital gains, 10%; earned and business income, 5%; additional surtax, 7.5% |
| Michigan | $1,500 | $3,000 | $1,500 | All taxable income, 4.6% |
| Minnesota | $ 60 | $ 120 | $ 60 | From 1.6% on 1st $500 to 17% on income over $40,000 |
| Mississippi[4] | $5,250 | $8,000 | $1,500 | First $5,000, 3%; over $5,000, 4% |
| Missouri | $1,200 | $2,400 | $ 400 | From 1.5% on 1st $1,000 to 6% on income over $9,000 |
| Montana | $ 800 | $1,600 | $ 800 | From 2% on 1st $1,000 to 11% on income over $35,000 |
| Nebraska | $ 750 | $1,500 | $ 750 | 15% of federal income tax liability |
| New Hampshire | $ 600 | $1,200 | — | 5% on income from interest and dividends |
| New Jersey | $1,000 | $2,000 | $1,000 | 2% on 1st $20,000; 2.5% on income over $20,000 |
| New Mexico | $ 750 | $1,500 | $ 750 | 0.8% on 1st $1,000 to 9% on income over $100,000 |
| New York | $ 750 | $1,500 | $ 750 | From 2% on 1st $1,000 to 14% on income over $23,000 |
| North Carolina | $1,100 | $2,200 | $ 700 | From 3% on 1st $2,000 to 7% on income over $10,000 |
| North Dakota | $ 750 | $1,500 | $ 750 | From 1% on 1st $3,000 to 7.5% on income over $30,000 |
| Ohio | $ 650 | $1,300 | $ 650 | From 0.5% on 1st $5,000 to 3.5% on income over $40,000 |
| Oklahoma | $ 750 | $1,500 | $ 750 | From 0.5% on 1st $1,000 to 6% on income over $7,500 |
| Oregon | $ 750 | $1,500 | $ 750 | From 4% on 1st $500 to 10% on income over $5,000 |
| Pennsylvania | — | — | — | 2.2% on all taxable income |
| Rhode Island | $ 750 | $1,500 | $ 750 | 19% of federal income tax liability |
| South Carolina | $ 800 | $1,600 | $ 800 | From 2% on 1st $2,000 to 7% on income over $10,000 |
| Tennessee | — | — | — | On dividends and interest, 6%; on dividends from corporations having 75% of property taxable in state, 4% |
| Utah | $ 750 | $1,500 | $ 750 | From 2.25% on 1st $750 to 7.75% on excess over $4,500 |
| Vermont | $ 750 | $1,500 | $ 750 | 23% of federal income tax liability |
| Virginia | $ 600 | $1,200 | $ 600 | From 2% on 1st $3,000 to 5¾% on income over $12,000 |
| West Virginia | $ 600 | $1,200 | $ 600 | From 2.1% on 1st $2,000 to 9.6% on excess over $200,000 |
| Wisconsin | $ 20 | $ 40 | $ 20 | From 3.4% on 1st $3,000 to 10% on income over $40,000 |

[1] Credit against tax.  [2] For 1980 a credit of 10% of tax is allowed.  [3] Tax applies only to adjusted gross incomes of $20,000 or more; capital gains tax applies to gains of $200 and over for joint returns and $100 or over for singles.  [4] In 1981 exemption for singles increases to $6,000 and for married persons to $9,500.

# STATE CORPORATE INCOME TAXES: 1980[1]

Source: Tax Foundation

Only 5 of the 50 states of the United States do not levy state corporation income taxes. These states are Nevada, South Dakota, Texas, Washington, and Wyoming.

| STATE | RATE | | | SPECIAL CONDITIONS | | | | | |
|---|---|---|---|---|---|---|---|---|---|
| Alabama [2] | | | 5.0% | | | | | | |
| Alaska | | | 5.4% | Additional surtax of 4% | | | | | |
| Arizona [2] | 1st | $ 1,000 | 2.5% | 4th | $ 1,000 | 6.5% | 6th | $ 1,000 | 9.0% |
| | 2d | $ 1,000 | 4.0% | 5th | $ 1,000 | 8.0% | Over | $ 6,000 | 10.5% |
| | 3d | $ 1,000 | 5.0% | | | | | | |
| Arkansas | 1st | $ 3,000 | 1.0% | Next | $14,000 | 5.0% | | | |
| | 2d | $ 3,000 | 2.0% | Over | $25,000 | 6.0% | | | |
| | Next | $ 5,000 | 3.0% | | | | | | |
| California | | | 9.6% | Financial corporations except banks allowed limited offset for personal property taxes and license fees. Minimum tax: $200 | | | | | |
| Colorado | | | 5.0% | | | | | | |
| Connecticut | | | 10.0% | Additional tax of 0.31 mills per dollar of capital stock and surplus to the extent that it exceeds net income tax | | | | | |
| Delaware | | | 8.7% | | | | | | |
| Dist. of Col. | | | 9.0% | Minimum tax: $25; surtax of 10% | | | | | |
| Florida | | | 5.0% | Exemption of $5,000 of net income allowed each corporation | | | | | |
| Georgia | | | 6.0% | | | | | | |
| Hawaii | $25,000 or less | | 5.85% | | | | | | |
| | Over $ 25,000 | | 6.435% | | | | | | |
| Idaho | | | 6.5% | | | | | | |
| Illinois | | | 4.0% | Exemption of $1,000 of net income allowed each corporation | | | | | |
| Indiana | | | 3.0% | Based on adjusted gross income; supplemental 3% based on net income | | | | | |
| Iowa [2] | 1st | $ 25,000 | 6.0% | Financial institutions franchise tax rates range from 5% on 1st $25,000 to 8% on net income over $100,000 | | | | | |
| | Next | $ 75,000 | 8.0% | | | | | | |
| | Over | $100,000 | 10.0% | | | | | | |
| Kansas | | | 4.5% | A 2.25% surtax imposed on taxable income over $25,000 | | | | | |
| Kentucky | $25,000 or less | | 3.0% | Next | $50,000 | 5.0% | | | |
| | Next | $ 25,000 | 4.0% | Over | $100,000 | 6.0% | | | |
| Louisiana [2] | 1st | $ 25,000 | 4.0% | Next | $100,000 | 7.0% | | | |
| | 2d | $ 25,000 | 5.0% | Over | $200,000 | 8.0% | | | |
| | Next | $ 50,000 | 6.0% | | | | | | |
| Maine | $25,000 or less | | 4.95% | | | | | | |
| | Over $ 25,000 | | 6.93% | | | | | | |
| Maryland | Over $ 25,000 | | 7.0% | Domestic corporations deduct franchise tax in excess of $40 | | | | | |
| Massachusetts | | | 8.33% | Net income tax supplemented by a $2.60 per $1,000 levy on tangible property not subject to local taxes, plus 8.33% of net income or $200, whichever is greater. A 14% surtax is also imposed. Interstate corporations not subject to corporate income tax pay 4% of net income plus the 14% surtax | | | | | |
| Michigan | | | 2.35% | Cities are authorized to levy tax (2% in Detroit) | | | | | |
| Minnesota | | | 12.0% | Minimum tax: $100 | | | | | |
| Mississippi | 1st | $5,000 | 3.0% | Over $5,000 | 4.0% | | | | |
| Missouri [2] | | | 5.0% | | | | | | |
| Montana | | | 6.75% | Minimum tax: $50, except $10 for small business corporations | | | | | |
| Nebraska | 1st | $25,000 | 3.75% | Over $25,000 | 4.125% | | | | |
| New Hampshire | | | 8.0% | | | | | | |
| New Jersey | | | 9.0% | Added tax on net worth | | | | | |
| New Mexico | | | 5.0% | Rates on banks and financial corporations is 6% | | | | | |
| New York | | | 10.0% | Alternative computing methods used if tax yield is more. Minimum tax: $250. Surcharge is 20% | | | | | |
| North Carolina | | | 6.0% | | | | | | |
| North Dakota [2] | 1st | $ 3,000 | 3.0% | Additional tax imposed at 1% of net income exceeding $2,000 for privilege of doing business in state | | | | | |
| | Next | $ 5,000 | 4.0% | | | | | | |
| | Next | $ 7,000 | 5.0% | | | | | | |
| | Next | $ 1,000 | 6.0% | | | | | | |
| | Over | $ 25,000 | 8.5% | | | | | | |
| Ohio | $25,000 or less | | 4.0% | Alternative computing methods used if tax yield is more. Minimum tax: $50 | | | | | |
| | Over $25,000 | | 8.0% | | | | | | |
| Oklahoma | | | 4.0% | | | | | | |
| Oregon | | | 7.5% | | | | | | |
| Pennsylvania | | | 10.5% | | | | | | |
| Rhode Island | | | 8.0% | If yield is greater, tax is 40¢ on each $100 of net worth | | | | | |
| South Carolina | | | 6.0% | | | | | | |
| Tennessee | | | 6.0% | Additional tax on dividends and interest | | | | | |
| Utah | | | 4.0% | Minimum tax: $25 | | | | | |
| Vermont | 1st | $ 10,000 | 5.0% | Minimum tax: $50 | | | | | |
| | Next | $ 15,000 | 6.0% | | | | | | |
| | Next | $225,000 | 7.0% | | | | | | |
| | Over | $250,000 | 7.5% | | | | | | |
| Virginia | | | 6.0% | | | | | | |
| West Virginia | | | 6.0% | | | | | | |
| Wisconsin | 1st | $1,000 | 2.3% | 4th | $1,000 | 4.5% | 6th | $1,000 | 6.8% |
| | 2d | $1,000 | 2.8% | 5th | $1,000 | 5.6% | Over | $6,000 | 7.9% |
| | 3d | $1,000 | 3.4% | | | | | | |

[1] All states levy special financial institutions tax based on net income or on value of shares of capital stock.
[2] Federal income tax is deductible in computing state tax.

## STATE TAX COLLECTIONS: WHERE THE MONEY COMES FROM [1]

Source: U.S. Department of Commerce, Bureau of the Census

| STATE | TOTAL | LICENSES | INDI-VIDUAL INCOME | CORPO-RATE INCOME | PROPERTY | DEATH AND GIFT | SEVERANCE | MISC. TAXES [2] |
|---|---|---|---|---|---|---|---|---|
| All states...... | $124,908,123 | $8,214,550 | $32,622,451 | $12,127,524 | $2,490,112 | $1,973,230 | $2,893,148 | $918,757 |
| Alabama ...... | 1,747,350 | 109,331 | 362,929 | 100,610 | 43,417 | 6,666 | 22,281 | 6,477 |
| Alaska........ | 816,710 | 30,651 | 116,049 | 256,986 | 162,151 | 123 | 173,685 | 2,519 |
| Arizona....... | 1,515,826 | 87,685 | 270,265 | 89,352 | 115,022 | 8,429 | — | — |
| Arkansas ..... | 994,560 | 76,084 | 228,681 | 83,608 | 2,419 | 2,938 | 12,502 | 2,718 |
| California .... | 16,351,959 | 588,784 | 4,758,047 | 2,374,712 | 615,679 | 409,478 | 48,093 | — |
| Colorado..... | 1,440,844 | 84,567 | 457,081 | 112,292 | 3,858 | 28,010 | 19,803 | 2,650 |
| Connecticut ... | 1,718,112 | 115,220 | 83,487 | 231,139 | 12 | 52,997 | — | 416 |
| Delaware ..... | 491,906 | 134,165 | 215,847 | 50,091 | — | 6,669 | — | 11,203 |
| Florida ....... | 4,290,975 | 346,241 | — | 314,409 | 77,345 | 55,908 | 91,902 | 198,590 |
| Georgia....... | 2,448,148 | 79,555 | 729,407 | 226,125 | 8,418 | 8,426 | — | 6,301 |
| Hawaii........ | 875,953 | 14,619 | 264,557 | 39,876 | — | 4,141 | — | 1,857 |
| Idaho......... | 466,371 | 58,987 | 143,381 | 39,247 | 165 | 3,495 | 552 | — |
| Illinois....... | 6,322,766 | 430,825 | 1,743,077 | 489,178 | 5,593 | 136,809 | — | 8,104 |
| Indiana ...... | 2,668,557 | 130,534 | 593,572 | 126,876 | 20,883 | 36,802 | 673 | — |
| Iowa.......... | 1,569,348 | 164,774 | 558,879 | 130,074 | — | 40,717 | — | 3,077 |
| Kansas ....... | 1,187,670 | 96,364 | 297,812 | 141,115 | 17,312 | 18,308 | 1,097 | — |
| Kentucky ..... | 2,075,732 | 90,988 | 456,288 | 163,368 | 161,305 | 22,727 | 154,017 | 1,161 |
| Louisiana ..... | 2,240,253 | 143,140 | 240,716 | 214,083 | 53 | 23,728 | 511,589 | — |
| Maine ........ | 554,375 | 42,825 | 112,513 | 41,240 | 12,480 | 10,574 | — | 1,009 |
| Maryland ..... | 2,647,157 | 108,971 | 1,005,631 | 145,571 | 73,144 | 23,818 | — | 32,721 |
| Massachusetts | 3,616,148 | 92,916 | 1,631,384 | 483,281 | 438 | 75,312 | — | 12,415 |
| Michigan...... | 6,017,739 | 322,102 | 1,943,941 | 991,555 | 125,173 | 50,079 | 13,724 | — |
| Minnesota .... | 3,133,761 | 182,013 | 1,255,998 | 356,734 | 3,373 | 40,829 | 71,263 | 25,219 |
| Mississippi .... | 1,196,482 | 73,821 | 193,426 | 58,324 | 4,884 | 4,615 | 32,922 | — |
| Missouri ...... | 2,013,027 | 170,216 | 534,996 | 129,953 | 4,585 | 22,838 | 45 | — |
| Montana ...... | 400,553 | 35,336 | 141,579 | 36,092 | 24,991 | 6,490 | 53,919 | 557 |
| Nebraska ..... | 742,560 | 57,892 | 208,557 | 49,985 | 3,510 | 3,227 | 1,516 | 1,825 |
| Nevada ....... | 462,586 | 60,956 | — | — | 31,376 | — | 54 | 1,872 |
| New Hampshire | 264,107 | 38,406 | 9,207 | 64,018 | 7,518 | 7,528 | 207 | 3,412 |
| New Jersey ... | 3,729,258 | 417,568 | 868,146 | 429,861 | 82,000 | 100,187 | — | 18,247 |
| New Mexico... | 845,391 | 47,156 | 68,550 | 40,514 | 20,687 | 2,522 | 159,431 | — |
| New York ..... | 11,578,978 | 477,870 | 5,057,867 | 1,223,281 | 13,039 | 154,936 | — | 320,780 |
| North Carolina | 2,914,931 | 228,308 | 996,227 | 254,778 | 42,768 | 39,352 | 1,013 | — |
| North Dakota . | 324,791 | 38,821 | 49,218 | 28,871 | 2,487 | 3,613 | 25,503 | — |
| Ohio ......... | 4,619,880 | 436,595 | 868,062 | 505,001 | 132,335 | 42,850 | 4,582 | — |
| Oklahoma..... | 1,515,918 | 162,376 | 334,110 | 94,501 | — | 26,523 | 280,982 | 7,438 |
| Oregon....... | 1,384,493 | 155,197 | 806,928 | 166,034 | 62 | 30,395 | 47,625 | 349 |
| Pennsylvania .. | 6,781,837 | 748,230 | 1,552,159 | 853,715 | 46,467 | 172,827 | — | 94,955 |
| Rhode Island .. | 537,827 | 23,254 | 153,498 | 55,903 | 5,981 | 12,511 | — | 3,077 |
| South Carolina | 1,522,968 | 65,420 | 415,713 | 140,185 | 5,235 | 9,192 | — | 9,242 |
| South Dakota . | 245,535 | 22,869 | — | 2,908 | — | 6,876 | 884 | — |
| Tennessee .... | 1,843,906 | 174,280 | 26,022 | 186,088 | — | 37,827 | 2,155 | 29,282 |
| Texas ........ | 5,738,430 | 632,756 | — | — | 49,249 | 73,748 | 1,025,550 | — |
| Utah ......... | 694,907 | 30,307 | 225,955 | 32,874 | 149 | 1,423 | 8,993 | — |
| Vermont...... | 267,473 | 26,390 | 83,360 | 23,878 | 243 | 2,312 | — | 3,817 |
| Virginia...... | 2,563,713 | 149,752 | 966,627 | 196,220 | 22,593 | 26,276 | 1,003 | 35,281 |
| Washington ... | 2,718,277 | 149,742 | — | — | 423,616 | 50,683 | 37,802 | 7,468 |
| West Virginia.. | 1,150,055 | 68,474 | 217,333 | 25,591 | 1,069 | 10,265 | — | 3,556 |
| Wisconsin..... | 3,260,448 | 151,601 | 1,375,369 | 327,427 | 96,716 | 55,196 | 362 | 5,910 |
| Wyoming ..... | 342,822 | 39,616 | — | — | 20,312 | 2,035 | 87,419 | — |

[1] In $ thousands (add 000) for fiscal year 1979.
[2] Document, stock transfer, and miscellaneous taxes.

| SALES TAXES, AND GROSS RECEIPTS TAXES¹ | | | | | | | INSURANCE TRUST FUND REVENUES² | STATE |
| General Sales Tax | Motor Fuels | Alcoholic Beverages | Tobacco Products | Insurance | Public Utilities | Pari-mutuels | | |
|---|---|---|---|---|---|---|---|---|
| $39,505,479 | $9,980,104 | $2,400,322 | $3,640,466 | $2,937,657 | $2,933,293 | $717,447 | $35,369,897 | .....All states |
| 547,302 | 172,903 | 80,198 | 52,065 | 76,323 | 138,604 | — | 356,687 | .....Alabama |
| — | 22,240 | 7,378 | 4,403 | 10,768 | 1,732 | — | 191,109 | .......Alaska |
| 704,211 | 127,585 | 21,056 | 37,757 | 26,504 | 19,329 | 8,631 | 536,841 | ......Arizona |
| 345,954 | 128,846 | 20,485 | 48,972 | 26,667 | — | 14,686 | 169,617 | .....Arkansas |
| 5,659,322 | 897,698 | 140,075 | 262,004 | 419,326 | 18,154 | 116,321 | 5,965,714 | ....California |
| 515,164 | 114,687 | 24,502 | 33,704 | 34,893 | 989 | 8,420 | 495,846 | .....Colorado |
| 736,119 | 164,042 | 25,423 | 75,163 | 56,353 | 120,873 | 45,966 | 335,936 | ..Connecticut |
| — | 32,252 | 4,585 | 11,998 | 9,841 | 10,918 | 3,249 | 59,937 | .....Delaware |
| 1,946,983 | 430,154 | 268,851 | 239,878 | 105,502 | 80,254 | 97,558 | 982,838 | .......Florida |
| 893,574 | 265,854 | 90,306 | 77,795 | 62,387 | — | — | 504,255 | .......Georgia |
| 430,501 | 35,220 | 20,434 | 11,856 | 18,967 | 33,925 | — | 223,272 | ........Hawaii |
| 129,907 | 58,735 | 7,462 | 7,945 | 14,457 | 1,650 | 388 | 128,510 | ........Idaho |
| 2,195,454 | 424,467 | 76,961 | 179,827 | 87,258 | 434,194 | 76,919 | 1,545,995 | ......Illinois |
| 1,310,321 | 277,007 | 33,435 | 84,119 | 54,236 | — | — | 381,968 | ......Indiana |
| 405,655 | 162,098 | 16,474 | 46,250 | 39,398 | 1,685 | — | 357,931 | .........Iowa |
| 399,103 | 128,163 | 23,769 | 32,065 | 31,526 | 473 | — | 216,861 | .......Kansas |
| 599,296 | 198,907 | 15,855 | 21,274 | 62,048 | — | 13,546 | 375,880 | .....Kentucky |
| 676,630 | 194,028 | 50,157 | 58,557 | 71,063 | 21,415 | 17,653 | 525,908 | ....Louisiana |
| 197,825 | 57,311 | 25,736 | 23,568 | 11,671 | 16,327 | 1,296 | 124,734 | ........Maine |
| 699,140 | 199,599 | 28,979 | 52,765 | 51,302 | 58,820 | 20,482 | 526,125 | .....Maryland |
| 718,287 | 223,738 | 79,980 | 142,272 | 105,433 | — | 28,620 | 656,363 | Massachusetts |
| 1,702,659 | 507,410 | 85,077 | 140,257 | 109,257 | — | 26,415 | 1,316,721 | .....Michigan |
| 607,989 | 216,554 | 53,609 | 85,611 | 59,704 | 78,006 | — | 513,066 | ....Minnesota |
| 603,209 | 126,857 | 31,975 | 32,301 | 33,784 | — | — | 289,578 | ...Mississippi |
| 782,879 | 222,297 | 25,014 | 60,196 | 59,428 | 580 | — | 528,403 | .....Missouri |
| — | 48,359 | 14,497 | 11,364 | 14,367 | 5,140 | — | 151,511 | ......Montana |
| 252,561 | 101,481 | 11,958 | 22,351 | 18,658 | — | 7,236 | 69,682 | .....Nebraska |
| 175,677 | 34,676 | 11,072 | 12,530 | 12,058 | 1,124 | 321 | 312,025 | ......Nevada |
| — | 46,843 | 4,491 | 26,144 | 11,690 | 4,091 | 14,432 | 94,757 | New Hampshire |
| 1,098,124 | 304,371 | 54,463 | 170,274 | 83,074 | 59,350 | 18,516 | 1,504,827 | ...New Jersey |
| 369,824 | 72,462 | 7,591 | 14,101 | 17,312 | 4,474 | 2,470 | 168,914 | ..New Mexico |
| 2,588,732 | 505,589 | 149,689 | 327,947 | 207,904 | 445,264 | 104,953 | 3,919,976 | .....New York |
| 648,293 | 313,471 | 98,279 | 18,826 | 71,233 | 179,335 | — | 725,614 | North Carolina |
| 108,992 | 35,076 | 6,442 | 8,815 | 10,971 | 2,523 | — | 81,207 | .North Dakota |
| 1,427,025 | 422,166 | 74,775 | 203,562 | 119,249 | 357,166 | 26,512 | 3,245,290 | .........Ohio |
| 279,712 | 137,800 | 37,463 | 49,952 | 51,980 | 5,460 | — | 232,293 | ....Oklahoma |
| — | 99,802 | 9,635 | 30,605 | 31,403 | 1,292 | 5,166 | 680,098 | ......Oregon |
| 1,895,499 | 525,564 | 117,198 | 250,525 | 153,933 | 343,535 | 27,086 | 1,814,937 | .Pennsylvania |
| 158,167 | 42,603 | 7,575 | 24,288 | 12,539 | 31,812 | 6,553 | 168,229 | ..Rhode Island |
| 525,858 | 170,852 | 83,012 | 27,539 | 37,007 | 17,521 | — | 389,523 | South Carolina |
| 130,536 | 38,986 | 7,543 | 9,191 | 10,179 | 308 | 2,372 | 52,095 | .South Dakota |
| 942,552 | 228,226 | 48,763 | 72,477 | 59,324 | 13,776 | — | 389,078 | ....Tennessee |
| 2,185,043 | 489,496 | 181,594 | 309,285 | 166,502 | 156,263 | — | 948,225 | ........Texas |
| 290,020 | 74,111 | 5,586 | 8,274 | 16,220 | 995 | — | 244,106 | .........Utah |
| 38,251 | 24,758 | 12,913 | 9,396 | 5,831 | 10,067 | 1,097 | 54,221 | ......Vermont |
| 534,905 | 293,452 | 73,317 | 17,542 | 73,320 | 93,526 | — | 352,821 | ......Virginia |
| 1,524,759 | 248,853 | 78,104 | 64,824 | 40,341 | 85,059 | 7,004 | 1,014,572 | ...Washington |
| 562,477 | 109,815 | 6,005 | 37,101 | 25,947 | — | 13,568 | 331,235 | .West Virginia |
| 819,657 | 183,710 | 39,062 | 85,778 | 42,043 | 77,284 | — | 1,023,020 | ....Wisconsin |
| 141,331 | 38,930 | 1,519 | 5,173 | 6,476 | — | 11 | 91,546 | .....Wyoming |

¹ Does not include miscellaneous selective sales taxes.  ² Includes contributions and earnings on investments for employee retirement, unemployment and workmen's compensation, etc.

## STATE EXPENDITURES: WHERE THE TAX MONEY GOES [1]

Source: U.S. Department of Commerce, Bureau of the Census

| STATE | TOTAL [2] | EDU-CATION | PUBLIC WELFARE | HIGHWAYS | HOSPI-TALS | NATURAL RE-SOURCES | HEALTH | INSUR-ANCE TRUSTS [3] |
|---|---|---|---|---|---|---|---|---|
| United States . | $224,656,920 | $77,722,467 | $38,883,880 | $21,227,502 | $10,298,336 | $3,808,091 | $5,231,148 | $20,107,394 |
| Alabama . . . . . . | 3,558,214 | 1,536,881 | 433,842 | 413,549 | 199,456 | 67,740 | 88,830 | 235,781 |
| Alaska . . . . . . . | 1,466,388 | 454,732 | 101,810 | 143,042 | 12,940 | 84,164 | 32,287 | 118,785 |
| Arizona . . . . . . . | 2,287,937 | 1,055,815 | 117,910 | 300,406 | 75,588 | 34,872 | 63,910 | 148,314 |
| Arkansas . . . . . | 1,896,527 | 681,175 | 307,710 | 299,782 | 84,255 | 52,744 | 38,421 | 123,046 |
| California . . . . . | 28,319,385 | 9,706,001 | 6,946,117 | 1,181,689 | 735,492 | 540,932 | 561,620 | 3,036,880 |
| Colorado . . . . . | 2,517,894 | 1,156,984 | 347,755 | 271,597 | 117,806 | 54,792 | 57,469 | 197,904 |
| Connecticut . . . | 2,963,433 | 739,112 | 569,296 | 210,087 | 185,887 | 23,029 | 50,003 | 291,873 |
| Delaware . . . . . | 762,291 | 310,251 | 84,511 | 62,029 | 26,990 | 9,794 | 19,105 | 53,167 |
| Florida . . . . . . . | 6,461,600 | 2,785,354 | 621,022 | 773,854 | 270,130 | 183,256 | 276,175 | 318,040 |
| Georgia . . . . . . . | 4,346,541 | 1,707,854 | 606,108 | 572,933 | 227,038 | 106,920 | 151,218 | 272,376 |
| Hawaii . . . . . . . . | 1,524,074 | 501,249 | 222,980 | 90,683 | 78,908 | 39,415 | 43,162 | 116,700 |
| Idaho . . . . . . . . . | 891,351 | 298,916 | 94,719 | 134,814 | 16,010 | 46,275 | 29,936 | 79,085 |
| Illinois . . . . . . . . | 10,418,099 | 3,422,788 | 2,305,697 | 1,044,241 | 403,375 | 110,855 | 180,441 | 1,078,545 |
| Indiana . . . . . . . | 4,088,514 | 1,712,156 | 477,975 | 535,660 | 186,896 | 76,045 | 101,367 | 248,074 |
| Iowa . . . . . . . . . | 3,010,871 | 1,175,738 | 407,561 | 477,234 | 171,114 | 68,701 | 28,575 | 187,032 |
| Kansas . . . . . . . | 2,012,395 | 816,802 | 310,930 | 292,092 | 157,309 | 55,130 | 26,853 | 112,051 |
| Kentucky . . . . . | 3,880,372 | 1,419,304 | 519,159 | 745,488 | 96,687 | 82,063 | 88,605 | 269,044 |
| Louisiana . . . . . | 4,123,067 | 1,479,038 | 541,831 | 461,110 | 279,107 | 92,447 | 80,332 | 350,503 |
| Maine . . . . . . . . | 1,182,604 | 351,028 | 224,552 | 133,104 | 29,317 | 38,095 | 22,371 | 126,572 |
| Maryland . . . . . | 4,678,333 | 1,390,715 | 647,282 | 528,539 | 264,169 | 43,007 | 125,372 | 346,553 |
| Massachusetts | 6,377,089 | 1,644,317 | 1,676,826 | 369,780 | 275,467 | 33,579 | 247,573 | 526,647 |
| Michigan . . . . . | 10,507,367 | 3,426,228 | 2,381,860 | 859,161 | 470,619 | 121,828 | 295,245 | 835,762 |
| Minnesota . . . . | 4,778,526 | 1,896,447 | 751,677 | 471,103 | 220,393 | 119,995 | 51,631 | 295,521 |
| Mississippi . . . . | 2,367,447 | 912,062 | 351,579 | 295,657 | 106,820 | 66,457 | 51,228 | 115,703 |
| Missouri . . . . . . | 3,337,485 | 1,204,116 | 551,525 | 491,796 | 209,926 | 82,457 | 85,875 | 251,696 |
| Montana . . . . . . | 900,928 | 278,269 | 85,623 | 131,341 | 24,734 | 38,938 | 26,012 | 95,266 |
| Nebraska . . . . . | 1,249,578 | 385,067 | 179,592 | 224,209 | 72,938 | 50,275 | 31,636 | 34,409 |
| Nevada . . . . . . . | 861,520 | 264,951 | 58,601 | 113,234 | 16,873 | 16,326 | 22,312 | 165,497 |
| New Hampshire | 784,231 | 161,462 | 102,709 | 113,618 | 40,834 | 11,759 | 16,875 | 49,692 |
| New Jersey . . . | 7,718,083 | 2,118,498 | 1,317,478 | 397,181 | 376,916 | 102,421 | 97,179 | 1,178,573 |
| New Mexico . . . | 1,578,199 | 699,575 | 140,474 | 218,072 | 70,316 | 36,765 | 38,463 | 68,664 |
| New York . . . . . | 22,707,937 | 6,028,039 | 4,507,636 | 1,035,196 | 1,281,148 | 89,197 | 518,028 | 2,173,605 |
| North Carolina | 5,249,076 | 2,291,946 | 643,759 | 603,016 | 319,868 | 118,866 | 130,581 | 287,280 |
| North Dakota . | 777,270 | 264,348 | 80,845 | 128,755 | 31,123 | 29,485 | 12,531 | 49,868 |
| Ohio . . . . . . . . . | 9,761,512 | 3,343,254 | 1,345,045 | 914,745 | 506,305 | 101,308 | 265,267 | 1,548,137 |
| Oklahoma . . . . | 2,732,959 | 1,075,826 | 489,630 | 324,866 | 130,467 | 41,939 | 27,761 | 164,466 |
| Oregon . . . . . . . | 2,906,342 | 894,257 | 452,421 | 318,545 | 119,168 | 90,931 | 62,986 | 305,081 |
| Pennsylvania . . | 11,574,943 | 3,468,028 | 2,575,834 | 786,581 | 609,450 | 136,076 | 260,919 | 1,528,476 |
| Rhode Island . . | 1,171,144 | 313,218 | 254,356 | 43,310 | 79,602 | 8,757 | 34,468 | 139,188 |
| South Carolina | 3,007,347 | 1,133,145 | 302,436 | 253,006 | 162,812 | 60,361 | 114,212 | 172,164 |
| South Dakota . | 641,812 | 202,521 | 86,384 | 104,270 | 21,092 | 24,221 | 16,431 | 23,746 |
| Tennessee . . . . | 3,360,630 | 1,263,240 | 530,039 | 500,621 | 155,734 | 59,610 | 73,219 | 253,763 |
| Texas . . . . . . . . | 9,665,072 | 4,541,393 | 1,372,000 | 1,245,664 | 556,361 | 146,951 | 193,868 | 564,850 |
| Utah . . . . . . . . . | 1,464,340 | 661,338 | 182,699 | 155,644 | 70,805 | 37,173 | 34,070 | 97,011 |
| Vermont . . . . . . | 612,297 | 188,896 | 91,008 | 61,395 | 18,445 | 19,962 | 19,804 | 32,258 |
| Virginia . . . . . . . | 4,875,996 | 1,695,986 | 584,709 | 828,455 | 360,204 | 61,338 | 140,256 | 238,312 |
| Washington . . . | 4,859,997 | 1,988,304 | 575,668 | 558,378 | 126,901 | 146,728 | 99,913 | 525,298 |
| West Virginia . | 2,423,711 | 815,314 | 218,028 | 474,271 | 73,691 | 38,405 | 34,124 | 285,856 |
| Wisconsin . . . . | 5,381,001 | 1,691,628 | 1,069,503 | 408,945 | 157,546 | 85,006 | 149,960 | 348,506 |
| Wyoming . . . . . | 633,197 | 168,901 | 35,169 | 124,754 | 13,304 | 20,701 | 12,669 | 41,774 |

[1] In $ thousands for fiscal year 1979.   [2] Includes other expenditures not categorized.   [3] Includes payments for employee retirement, unemployment compensation, workmen's compensation, and disability benefit social insurance programs.

## FEDERAL MONEY GRANTED THE STATES

Source: U.S. Department of Commerce

U.S. aid to the states includes grants for such programs as highways, health, education, and public welfare. These Census Bureau figures are for the fiscal year ending June 30, 1979, except for Alabama and Michigan (ending Sept. 30), New York (March 31), and Texas (Aug. 31).

| STATE | TOTAL AID* | AID PER CAPITA | STATE | TOTAL AID* | AID PER CAPITA | STATE | TOTAL AID* | AID PER CAPITA |
|---|---|---|---|---|---|---|---|---|
| Alabama | $1,072,439 | $284.54 | Louisiana | $1,110,296 | $276.33 | North Dakota | $197,684 | $300.89 |
| Alaska | 283,239 | 697.63 | Maine | 359,027 | 327.28 | Ohio | 2,082,584 | 194.07 |
| Arizona | 479,310 | 195.64 | Maryland | 979,112 | 236.04 | Oklahoma | 680,380 | 235.26 |
| Arkansas | 637,659 | 292.50 | Massachusetts | 1,726,139 | 299.21 | Oregon | 758,722 | 300.25 |
| California | 6,100,424 | 268.81 | Michigan | 2,379,814 | 258.48 | Pennsylvania | 2,611,606 | 222.62 |
| Colorado | 666,831 | 240.56 | Minnesota | 1,048,211 | 258.18 | Rhode Island | 303,017 | 326.18 |
| Connecticut | 720,677 | 231.36 | Mississippi | 753,148 | 310.07 | South Carolina | 785,687 | 267.97 |
| Delaware | 171,477 | 294.63 | Missouri | 944,602 | 194.08 | South Dakota | 219,187 | 318.12 |
| Florida | 1,413,924 | 159.59 | Montana | 294,454 | 374.62 | Tennessee | 1,004,156 | 229.26 |
| Georgia | 1,265,321 | 247.28 | Nebraska | 318,765 | 202.52 | Texas | 2,496,118 | 186.56 |
| Hawaii | 331,852 | 362.68 | Nevada | 179,471 | 255.66 | Utah | 392,865 | 287.39 |
| Idaho | 245,739 | 271.53 | New Hampshire | 204,855 | 230.95 | Vermont | 191,480 | 388.40 |
| Illinois | 2,332,888 | 207.76 | New Jersey | 1,610,116 | 219.60 | Virginia | 1,188,801 | 228.75 |
| Indiana | 917,221 | 169.86 | New Mexico | 424,855 | 342.35 | Washington | 1,111,214 | 283.04 |
| Iowa | 614,084 | 211.61 | New York | 6,004,272 | 340.22 | West Virginia | 611,894 | 325.82 |
| Kansas | 476,981 | 201.34 | North Carolina | 1,344,939 | 239.91 | Wisconsin | 1,329,354 | 281.64 |
| Kentucky | 963,186 | 273.09 | | | | Wyoming | 208,060 | 462.36 |

* In $ thousands (add 000).

## STATE DEBTS

Source: U.S. Department of Commerce

The outstanding gross debt of the 50 states at the end of the 1979 fiscal year reached a new high— $111.7 billion. All but $2.3 billion of this amount was of a long-term nature.

| STATE | TOTAL DEBT* | DEBT PER CAPITA | STATE | TOTAL DEBT* | DEBT PER CAPITA | STATE | TOTAL DEBT* | DEBT PER CAPITA |
|---|---|---|---|---|---|---|---|---|
| Alabama | $1,053,409 | $279.49 | Louisiana | $2,636,921 | $656.28 | North Dakota | $130,792 | $199.07 |
| Alaska | 1,362,526 | 3,355.98 | Maine | 695,558 | 634.05 | Ohio | 3,745,220 | 349.01 |
| Arizona | 96,170 | 39.25 | Maryland | 3,690,228 | 889.64 | Oklahoma | 1,510,966 | 522.46 |
| Arkansas | 244,251 | 112.04 | Massachusetts | 5,414,472 | 938.55 | Oregon | 3,808,764 | 1,507.23 |
| California | 7,676,120 | 338.24 | Michigan | 2,505,461 | 272.13 | Pennsylvania | 6,448,112 | 549.66 |
| Colorado | 426,200 | 153.75 | Minnesota | 1,873,723 | 461.51 | Rhode Island | 1,177,900 | 1,267.92 |
| Connecticut | 3,590,955 | 1,152.79 | Mississippi | 843,131 | 347.11 | South Carolina | 1,590,110 | 542.33 |
| Delaware | 854,958 | 1,469.00 | Missouri | 711,594 | 146.21 | South Dakota | 579,796 | 841.50 |
| Florida | 2,670,982 | 301.47 | Montana | 146,999 | 187.02 | Tennessee | 1,388,633 | 317.04 |
| Georgia | 1,370,711 | 267.87 | Nebraska | 52,672 | 33.46 | Texas | 2,316,852 | 173.16 |
| Hawaii | 1,696,853 | 1,854.48 | Nevada | 374,059 | 532.85 | Utah | 393,057 | 287.53 |
| Idaho | 220,856 | 244.04 | New Hampshire | 738,576 | 832.67 | Vermont | 510,620 | 1,035.74 |
| Illinois | 5,717,915 | 509.21 | New Jersey | 5,382,459 | 734.11 | Virginia | 1,662,758 | 319.95 |
| Indiana | 580,456 | 107.49 | New Mexico | 513,904 | 414.10 | Washington | 1,514,826 | 385.84 |
| Iowa | 372,753 | 128.45 | New York | 22,982,754 | 1,302.29 | West Virginia | 1,636,887 | 871.61 |
| Kansas | 459,143 | 193.81 | North Carolina | 1,107,365 | 197.53 | Wisconsin | 2,233,958 | 473.30 |
| Kentucky | 2,810,488 | 796.85 | | | | Wyoming | 216,070 | 480.16 |

* In $ thousands (add 000).

## STATE RETAIL SALES TAXES: 1980 [1]

Source: Tax Foundation

| STATE | TAX | STATE | TAX | STATE | TAX | STATE | TAX |
|---|---|---|---|---|---|---|---|
| Alabama | 4% | Indiana | 4% | Nebraska | 3% | South Carolina | 4% |
| Alaska | — | Iowa | 3% | Nevada | 3% | South Dakota | 5% |
| Arizona | 4% | Kansas | 3% | New Hampshire | — | Tennessee [3] | 4.5% |
| Arkansas | 3% | Kentucky | 5% | New Jersey | 5% | Texas | 4% |
| California | 4.75% | Louisiana | 3% | New Mexico | 3.75% | Utah | 4% |
| Colorado | 3% | Maine | 5% | New York [2] | 4% | Vermont | 3% |
| Connecticut | 7.5% | Maryland | 5% | North Carolina | 3% | Virginia | 3% |
| Delaware | — | Massachusetts | 5% | North Dakota | 3% | Washington | 4.5% |
| Florida | 4% | Michigan | 4% | Ohio | 4% | West Virginia | 3% |
| Georgia | 3% | Minnesota | 4% | Oklahoma | 2% | Wisconsin | 4% |
| Hawaii | 4% | Mississippi | 5% | Oregon | — | Wyoming | 3% |
| Idaho | 3% | Missouri | 3⅛% | Pennsylvania | 6% | District of | |
| Illinois | 4% | Montana | — | Rhode Island | 6% | Columbia | 6% |

[1] Does not include local sales taxes, which are imposed in 32 states.   [2] In New York City, 8%.   [3] 3% after June 30, 1981.

# CITY INCOME TAXES: 1980

Sources: Tax Foundation

Philadelphia has the distinction of levying the oldest and highest local income tax in effect today. Earlier efforts at such taxation, including one in Charleston, S.C., in the early 1800s, foundered on administrative difficulties.

Since the path-breaking Philadelphia enactment in 1939, however, about 4,000 localities in 10 states have followed suit. And authorizations have been granted (although no locality has acted) in Arkansas and Kansas.

In addition, a related levy has been imposed on employers: the local payroll tax, based on an employer's wage expenses. This has been enacted in Jersey City, Newark, N.J., San Francisco, and four Oregon counties.

Despite first impressions from the table that follows, the local income tax is primarily a big-city phenomenon.

Most of the taxing jurisdictions are small, but this is because many—over 3,800—small towns and school districts in Ohio and Pennsylvania use the levy. Elsewhere the tax is typically used by large jurisdictions.

Nine of the 25 biggest cities in the United States, including Washington, D.C., now impose their own income taxes.

Few of these local taxes are really comparable to state or U.S. taxes, since most apply only to wages and salaries—"earned" income. However, those levied by New York City, Baltimore, and cities in Michigan are closely linked, both in coverage and administration, to overlapping state taxes.

In the District of Columbia, it is similar to a state income tax.

Besides the roughly 40 million residents in localities levying income taxes, countless others who work in them but live elsewhere—commuters in Alabama, Delaware, Kentucky, Missouri, Ohio, and Pennsylvania—are subject to the levy.

Maryland's local taxes apply to residents only, as does the District of Columbia's tax.

Commuters in Michigan pay one-half the resident rates, while those in New York City pay sharply lower rates.

Where many localities in the same area tax income, special arrangements are necessary to avoid unfair treatment of those who work in one jurisdiction but live in another.

As the table below shows, local income taxes are essentially confined to the states in the Northeast and Middle Atlantic regions—with the exception of St. Louis and Kansas City, Mo., and six places in Alabama, including Birmingham and Gadsden.

The table below, compiled by the Tax Foundation from Commerce Clearing House data, lists the rates in effect as of Sept. 1, 1980, for all U.S. localities with income taxes.

## CITY AND LOCAL INCOME TAXES AND RATES [1]

| STATE AND LOCALITY | RATE | STATE AND LOCALITY | RATE | STATE AND LOCALITY | RATE |
|---|---|---|---|---|---|
| **Alabama** | | **Michigan** (continued) | | **Ohio** (continued) | |
| Birmingham | 1.0% | Lansing | 1.0% | Springfield | 2.0% |
| Gadsden | 2.0% | Pontiac | 1.0% | Toledo | 1.5% |
| 3 cities | | Saginaw | 1.0% | Warren | 1.0% |
| under 50,000 | 1.0–2.0% | 10 cities | | Youngstown | 1.5% |
| **Delaware** | | under 50,000 | 1.0% | Over 340 cities | |
| Wilmington | 1.0% | **Missouri** | | and villages | |
| **Indiana** | | Kansas City | 1.0% | under 50,000 | 0.25–2.0% |
| 34 counties | 0.5–1.0% | St. Louis | 1.0% | **Pennsylvania** [6] | |
| **Iowa** | | **New York** | | Abington Township | 1.0% |
| 6 school districts | 1.75–4.0% | New York City [5] | 0.9–4.3% | Allentown | 1.0% |
| **Kentucky** | | **Ohio** | | Altoona | 1.0% |
| Covington | 2.5% | Akron | 1.5% | Bethlehem | 1.0% |
| Lexington | 2.0% | Canton | 1.5% | Chester | 1.0% |
| Louisville [2] | 1.45% | Cincinnati | 2.0% | Erie | 1.0% |
| Owensboro | 1.0% | Cleveland | 1.5% | Harrisburg | 1.0% |
| 42 cities | | Cleveland Heights | 2.0% | Lancaster | 0.5% |
| under 50,000 | 0.25–2.5% | Columbus | 1.5% | Penn Hills | |
| 6 counties | 0.4–2.0% [3] | Dayton | 1.75% | Township | 1.0% |
| **Maryland** | | Elyria | 1.5% | Philadelphia | 4.3125% |
| Baltimore [4] | 50.0% | Euclid | 1.0% | Pittsburgh | 2.25% |
| 24 counties [4] | 20.0–50.0% | Hamilton | 1.5% | Reading | 1.0% |
| **Michigan** | | Kettering | 1.0% | Scranton | 2.6% |
| Detroit | 2.0% | Lakewood | 1.0% | Wilkes-Barre | 1.0% |
| Flint | 1.0% | Lima | 1.0% | Over 3,500 | |
| Grand Rapids | 1.0% | Lorain | 1.0% | other local | |
| | | Mansfield | 1.0% | jurisdictions | Up to 1.0% |
| | | Parma | 1.5% | York | 1.0% |
| | | | | **Washington, D.C.** [5] | 2.0–11.0% |

[1] Rates shown separately for cities of 50,000 or more. Where rates differ for resident and nonresident income, only resident rates are given. In Ohio and Pennsylvania cities, rates are the same.   [2] Additional tax of 0.75% for school purposes is levied by Jefferson County.   [3] Additional tax of 0.2% imposed in Jefferson County outside of Louisville on earnings of employees.   [4] Percent of state income tax.   [5] Resident income taxes are progressive.   [6] Except for Philadelphia and Pittsburgh, the total rate payable by any taxpayer is limited to 1%.

# Travel and Transportation

United Press Int'l.

Chrysler Corporation chairman Lee A. Iacocca prepares to drive off the first of the company's "K" cars, a Plymouth Reliant, produced at Detroit's Jefferson Assembly Plant. Chrysler, which lost a record $1.1 billion in 1979 and received $1.5 billion in federal government loan guarantees in 1980, counts on the lighter-weight, lower mileage "K" cars to restore its competitive edge in 1981 and reverse the trend that brought the company to near bankruptcy.

## AUTOMOBILE HIGHLIGHTS: 1980

### DETROIT FIGHTS FOR SURVIVAL

The automobile industry was hard hit by recession in 1980. The major automakers indicated their losses would be about $3 billion for the year. More than 300,000 auto workers were laid off. Sales of new American-made cars were off about 25% in 1980. Moreover, U.S. automobiles were losing out in their marketing battle with foreign cars, as the U.S. share of domestic auto sales dropped from 66% to 62%. Internationally, Japan produced more cars than the U.S. for the first time in history in 1979.

In the short-term the Big Three automakers were counting on new lighter-weight, higher-mileage small cars—General Motors introduced its "X" cars and planned "J" cars, Chrysler brought out its "K" models, and Ford a "world" car.

But in the long run the automakers were hoping that their plans to rebuild the industry from the ground up would restore American cars to dominance.

In all, the major automakers planned to spend a staggering $80 billion to rebuild and modernize their manufacturing plants. New factories will make full use of automation, with computers controlling production and machine robots manning the assembly lines. Such automation is expected to eliminate about 1 job in 4 for American auto workers.

The auto industry's retooling effort brought a boom to Midwestern machine-tool industries, where skilled craftsmen were working overtime to meet Detroit's needs.

Each of the Big Three said that by the 1985 model year their new cars would exceed the government-required average of 27.5 miles

**AUTOMOBILE HIGHLIGHTS: 1980** *(continued)*
per gallon (mpg). General Motors said its 1985 line would average 31 mpg. But at current rates of inflation these cars are likely to cost $10,000 or more.

## IMPROVED MILEAGE

For the first time three American-made automobiles achieved 30 mpg in fuel economy tests by the Environmental Protection Agency (EPA). The U.S. cars were the Chevrolet Chevette, the Ford Escort, and the Lincoln-Mercury Lynx.

However, in test results announced by the EPA in September 1980, foreign cars remained the most economical in their gas usage. The Volkswagen Rabbit diesel topped the list at 42 mpg. Other cars with the most economical mileages include the Toyota Starlet (39 mpg), the Japanese-built Dodge Colt and Plymouth Champ (37 mpg), the Datsun 210 (36 mpg), the Toyota Corolla Tercel (36 mpg), the Honda Civic (35 mpg), and the Mazda GLC (35 mpg).

After announcing the results of its annual fuel-consumption tests of new models, the EPA reported it was planning to change its procedures in future tests because a Department of Energy survey had shown that its previous estimates of mileage were about 21% too high.

## ELECTRIC CAR BREAKTHROUGH

Hopes for a practical electric automobile were heightened in June 1980 when Gulf and Western Industries announced the development of a powerful new zinc-chloride battery. The company said the battery would enable an electric car to travel 200 miles at speeds up to 55 mph before needing a recharge. The corporation also said the battery could be used by electric utilities to store electricity produced in off-peak periods, providing the potential to save as much as 1 million barrels

# HOW TO FIGURE OUT YOUR CAR'S FUEL ECONOMY

Source: General Services Administration

To check the miles-per-gallon (mpg) fuel economy of your automobile: (1) Fill your car with gasoline. (2) Write down the mileage shown on your car's odometer. (3) The next time you fill your car with gasoline, write down exactly how many gallons it takes. (4) Calculate how many miles you have gone since you last filled it. (5) Then use the following chart to discover how many miles per gallon your car gets. Locate (a) the number of gallons your car used in the row across the top of the table and (b) the number of miles it went in the left-hand column. The intersection of these two columns tells you the number of miles per gallon your car gets. For example, if it went 220 miles and used 15 gallons of gasoline, the table shows your car gets 14.7 mpg.

| MILES | NUMBER OF GALLONS OF GASOLINE USED (top row) | | | | | | | | | | | | | | | | | | | | |
|---|---|---|---|---|---|---|---|---|---|---|---|---|---|---|---|---|---|---|---|---|---|
| | 5 | 6 | 7 | 8 | 9 | 10 | 11 | 12 | 13 | 14 | 15 | 16 | 17 | 18 | 19 | 20 | 21 | 22 | 23 | 24 | 25 |
| 30 | 6.0 | 5.0 | 4.3 | 3.8 | 3.3 | 3.0 | 2.7 | 2.5 | 2.3 | 2.1 | 2.0 | 1.9 | 1.8 | 1.7 | 1.6 | 1.5 | 1.4 | 1.4 | 1.3 | 1.3 | 1.2 |
| 40 | 8.0 | 6.7 | 5.7 | 5.0 | 4.4 | 4.0 | 3.6 | 3.3 | 3.1 | 2.9 | 2.7 | 2.5 | 2.4 | 2.2 | 2.1 | 2.0 | 1.9 | 1.8 | 1.7 | 1.7 | 1.6 |
| 50 | 10.0 | 8.3 | 7.1 | 6.3 | 5.6 | 5.0 | 4.5 | 4.2 | 3.8 | 3.6 | 3.3 | 3.1 | 2.9 | 2.8 | 2.6 | 2.5 | 2.4 | 2.3 | 2.2 | 2.1 | 2.0 |
| 60 | 12.0 | 10.0 | 8.6 | 7.5 | 6.7 | 6.0 | 5.5 | 5.0 | 4.6 | 4.3 | 4.0 | 3.8 | 3.5 | 3.3 | 3.2 | 3.0 | 2.9 | 2.7 | 2.6 | 2.5 | 2.4 |
| 70 | 14.0 | 11.7 | 10.0 | 8.8 | 7.8 | 7.0 | 6.4 | 5.8 | 5.4 | 5.0 | 4.7 | 4.4 | 4.1 | 3.9 | 3.7 | 3.5 | 3.3 | 3.2 | 3.0 | 2.9 | 2.8 |
| 80 | 16.0 | 13.3 | 11.4 | 10.0 | 8.9 | 8.0 | 7.3 | 6.7 | 6.2 | 5.7 | 5.3 | 5.0 | 4.7 | 4.4 | 4.2 | 4.0 | 3.8 | 3.6 | 3.5 | 3.3 | 3.2 |
| 90 | 18.0 | 15.0 | 12.9 | 11.3 | 10.0 | 9.0 | 8.2 | 7.5 | 6.9 | 6.4 | 6.0 | 5.6 | 5.3 | 5.0 | 4.7 | 4.5 | 4.3 | 4.1 | 3.9 | 3.8 | 3.6 |
| 100 | 20.0 | 16.7 | 14.3 | 12.5 | 11.1 | 10.0 | 9.1 | 8.3 | 7.7 | 7.1 | 6.7 | 6.3 | 5.9 | 5.6 | 5.3 | 5.0 | 4.8 | 4.5 | 4.3 | 4.2 | 4.0 |
| 110 | 22.0 | 18.3 | 15.7 | 13.8 | 12.2 | 11.0 | 10.0 | 9.2 | 8.5 | 7.9 | 7.3 | 6.9 | 6.5 | 6.1 | 5.8 | 5.5 | 5.2 | 5.0 | 4.8 | 4.6 | 4.4 |
| 120 | 24.0 | 20.0 | 17.1 | 15.0 | 13.3 | 12.0 | 10.9 | 10.0 | 9.2 | 8.6 | 8.0 | 7.5 | 7.1 | 6.7 | 6.3 | 6.0 | 5.7 | 5.5 | 5.2 | 5.0 | 4.8 |
| 130 | 26.0 | 21.7 | 18.6 | 16.3 | 14.4 | 13.0 | 11.8 | 10.8 | 10.0 | 9.3 | 8.7 | 8.1 | 7.6 | 7.2 | 6.8 | 6.5 | 6.2 | 5.9 | 5.7 | 5.4 | 5.2 |
| 140 | 28.0 | 23.3 | 20.0 | 17.5 | 15.6 | 14.0 | 12.7 | 11.7 | 10.8 | 10.0 | 9.3 | 8.8 | 8.2 | 7.8 | 7.4 | 7.0 | 6.7 | 6.4 | 6.1 | 5.8 | 5.6 |
| 150 | 30.0 | 25.0 | 21.4 | 18.8 | 16.7 | 15.0 | 13.6 | 12.5 | 11.5 | 10.7 | 10.0 | 9.4 | 8.8 | 8.3 | 7.9 | 7.5 | 7.1 | 6.8 | 6.5 | 6.3 | 6.0 |
| 160 | 32.0 | 26.7 | 22.9 | 20.0 | 17.8 | 16.0 | 14.5 | 13.3 | 12.3 | 11.4 | 10.7 | 10.0 | 9.4 | 8.9 | 8.4 | 8.0 | 7.6 | 7.3 | 7.0 | 6.7 | 6.4 |
| 170 | 34.0 | 28.3 | 24.3 | 21.3 | 18.9 | 17.0 | 15.5 | 14.2 | 13.1 | 12.1 | 11.3 | 10.6 | 10.0 | 9.4 | 8.9 | 8.5 | 8.1 | 7.7 | 7.4 | 7.1 | 6.8 |
| 180 | 36.0 | 30.0 | 25.7 | 22.5 | 20.0 | 18.0 | 16.4 | 15.0 | 13.8 | 12.9 | 12.0 | 11.3 | 10.6 | 10.0 | 9.5 | 9.0 | 8.6 | 8.2 | 7.8 | 7.5 | 7.2 |
| 190 | 38.0 | 31.7 | 27.1 | 23.8 | 21.1 | 19.0 | 17.3 | 15.8 | 14.6 | 13.6 | 12.7 | 11.9 | 11.2 | 10.6 | 10.0 | 9.5 | 9.0 | 8.6 | 8.3 | 7.9 | 7.6 |
| 200 | 40.0 | 33.3 | 28.6 | 25.0 | 22.2 | 20.0 | 18.2 | 16.7 | 15.4 | 14.3 | 13.3 | 12.5 | 11.8 | 11.1 | 10.5 | 10.0 | 9.5 | 9.1 | 8.7 | 8.3 | 8.0 |
| 210 | 42.9 | 35.0 | 30.0 | 26.3 | 23.3 | 21.0 | 19.1 | 17.5 | 16.2 | 15.0 | 14.0 | 13.1 | 12.4 | 11.7 | 11.1 | 10.5 | 10.0 | 9.5 | 9.1 | 8.8 | 8.4 |
| 220 | 44.0 | 36.7 | 31.4 | 27.5 | 24.4 | 22.0 | 20.0 | 18.3 | 16.9 | 15.7 | 14.7 | 13.8 | 12.9 | 12.2 | 11.6 | 11.0 | 10.5 | 10.0 | 9.6 | 9.2 | 8.8 |
| 230 | 46.0 | 38.3 | 32.9 | 28.8 | 25.6 | 23.0 | 20.9 | 19.2 | 17.7 | 16.4 | 15.3 | 14.4 | 13.5 | 12.8 | 12.1 | 11.5 | 11.0 | 10.5 | 10.0 | 9.6 | 9.2 |
| 240 | 48.0 | 40.0 | 34.3 | 30.0 | 26.7 | 24.0 | 21.8 | 20.0 | 18.5 | 17.1 | 16.0 | 15.0 | 14.1 | 13.3 | 12.6 | 12.0 | 11.4 | 10.9 | 10.4 | 10.0 | 9.6 |
| 250 | 50.0 | 41.7 | 35.7 | 31.3 | 27.8 | 25.0 | 22.7 | 20.8 | 19.2 | 17.9 | 16.7 | 15.6 | 14.7 | 13.9 | 13.2 | 12.5 | 11.9 | 11.4 | 10.9 | 10.4 | 10.0 |
| 260 | 52.0 | 43.3 | 37.1 | 32.5 | 28.9 | 26.0 | 23.6 | 21.7 | 20.0 | 18.6 | 17.3 | 16.3 | 15.3 | 14.4 | 13.7 | 13.0 | 12.4 | 11.8 | 11.3 | 10.8 | 10.4 |
| 270 | 54.0 | 45.0 | 38.6 | 33.8 | 30.0 | 27.0 | 24.5 | 22.5 | 20.8 | 19.3 | 18.0 | 16.9 | 15.9 | 15.0 | 14.2 | 13.5 | 12.9 | 12.3 | 11.7 | 11.3 | 10.8 |
| 280 | 56.0 | 46.7 | 40.0 | 35.0 | 31.1 | 28.0 | 25.5 | 23.3 | 21.5 | 20.0 | 18.7 | 17.5 | 16.5 | 15.6 | 14.7 | 14.0 | 13.3 | 12.7 | 12.2 | 11.7 | 11.2 |
| 290 | 58.0 | 48.3 | 41.4 | 36.3 | 32.2 | 29.0 | 26.4 | 24.2 | 22.3 | 20.7 | 19.3 | 18.1 | 17.1 | 16.1 | 15.3 | 14.5 | 13.8 | 13.2 | 12.6 | 12.1 | 11.6 |
| 300 | 60.0 | 50.0 | 42.9 | 37.5 | 33.3 | 30.0 | 27.3 | 25.0 | 23.1 | 21.4 | 20.0 | 18.8 | 17.6 | 16.7 | 15.8 | 15.0 | 14.3 | 13.6 | 13.0 | 12.5 | 12.0 |
| 310 | 62.0 | 51.7 | 44.3 | 38.7 | 34.4 | 31.0 | 28.2 | 25.8 | 23.8 | 22.1 | 20.7 | 19.4 | 18.2 | 17.2 | 16.3 | 15.5 | 14.7 | 14.1 | 13.5 | 12.9 | 12.4 |
| 320 | 64.0 | 53.3 | 45.7 | 40.0 | 35.6 | 32.0 | 29.1 | 26.7 | 24.6 | 22.9 | 21.3 | 20.0 | 18.8 | 17.8 | 16.8 | 16.0 | 15.2 | 14.5 | 13.9 | 13.3 | 12.6 |
| 330 | 66.0 | 55.0 | 47.1 | 41.3 | 36.7 | 33.0 | 30.0 | 27.5 | 25.4 | 23.6 | 22.0 | 20.6 | 19.4 | 18.3 | 17.4 | 16.5 | 15.7 | 15.0 | 14.3 | 13.7 | 13.2 |
| 340 | 68.0 | 56.7 | 48.6 | 42.5 | 37.8 | 34.0 | 30.9 | 28.3 | 26.2 | 24.3 | 22.7 | 21.3 | 20.0 | 18.9 | 17.9 | 17.0 | 16.2 | 15.5 | 14.8 | 14.2 | 13.6 |
| 350 | 70.0 | 58.3 | 50.0 | 43.7 | 38.9 | 35.0 | 31.8 | 29.2 | 26.9 | 25.0 | 23.3 | 21.9 | 20.6 | 19.4 | 18.4 | 17.5 | 16.7 | 15.9 | 15.2 | 14.6 | 14.0 |

# POPULATION GROWTH OF THE UNITED STATES: 1790–2000

Source: U.S. Bureau of the Census

In its first census in 1790, the United States reported a population of 3,929,214. The totals for the individual states in 1790 were: Connecticut, 237,946; Delaware, 59,096; Georgia, 82,548; Kentucky, 73,677; Maine, 96,540; Maryland, 319,728; Massachusetts, 378,787; New Hampshire, 141,885; New Jersey, 184,139; New York, 340,120; North Carolina, 393,751; Pennsylvania, 434,373; Rhode Island, 68,825; South Carolina, 249,073; Tennessee, 35,691; Vermont, 82,425; Virginia, 691,737; West Virginia, 55,873. Population growth since 1790 is shown on the chart below.

| | 1850 | 1900 | 1950 | 1970 | 1980[1] | 1990[2] | 2000[2] |
|---|---|---|---|---|---|---|---|
| UNITED STATES . | 23,191,876 | 76,212,168 | 151,325,798 | 203,235,298 | 226,504,825 | 243,004,000 | 259,869,000 |
| Alabama | 771,623 | 1,828,697 | 3,061,743 | 3,444,165 | 3,890,061 | 3,967,000 | 4,148,000 |
| Alaska | — | 63,592 | 128,643 | 302,173 | 400,481 | 441,000 | 474,000 |
| Arizona | — | 122,931 | 749,587 | 1,772,482 | 2,717,866 | 3,031,000 | 3,452,000 |
| Arkansas | 209,897 | 1,311,564 | 1,909,511 | 1,923,295 | 2,285,513 | 2,390,000 | 2,545,000 |
| California | 92,597 | 1,485,053 | 10,586,223 | 19,953,134 | 23,668,562 | 25,588,000 | 28,083,000 |
| Colorado | — | 539,700 | 1,325,089 | 2,207,259 | 2,888,834 | 3,237,000 | 3,615,000 |
| Connecticut | 370,792 | 908,420 | 2,007,280 | 3,032,217 | 3,017,576 | 3,489,000 | 3,713,000 |
| Delaware | 91,532 | 184,735 | 318,085 | 548,104 | 595,225 | 684,000 | 742,000 |
| District of Columbia | 51,687 | 278,718 | 802,178 | 756,510 | 637,651 | 693,000 | 697,000 |
| Florida | 87,445 | 528,542 | 2,771,305 | 6,789,443 | 9,739,992 | 11,305,000 | 12,924,000 |
| Georgia | 906,185 | 2,216,331 | 3,444,578 | 4,589,575 | 5,464,265 | 6,006,000 | 6,625,000 |
| Hawaii | — | 154,001 | 499,794 | 769,913 | 965,000 | 965,000 | 1,157,000 |
| Idaho | — | 161,772 | 588,637 | 713,008 | 943,935 | 982,000 | 1,069,000 |
| Illinois | 851,470 | 4,821,550 | 8,712,176 | 11,113,976 | 11,418,461 | 12,015,000 | 12,491,000 |
| Indiana | 988,416 | 2,516,462 | 3,934,224 | 5,193,669 | 5,490,179 | 5,804,000 | 6,069,000 |
| Iowa | 192,214 | 2,231,853 | 2,621,073 | 2,825,041 | 2,913,387 | 2,988,000 | 3,058,000 |
| Kansas | — | 1,470,495 | 1,905,299 | 2,249,071 | 2,363,208 | 2,429,000 | 2,516,000 |
| Kentucky | 982,405 | 2,147,174 | 2,944,806 | 3,219,311 | 3,661,433 | 3,796,000 | 4,032,000 |
| Louisiana | 517,762 | 1,381,625 | 2,683,516 | 3,643,180 | 4,203,972 | 4,245,000 | 4,471,000 |
| Maine | 583,169 | 694,466 | 913,774 | 993,663 | 1,124,660 | 1,192,000 | 1,273,000 |
| Maryland | 583,034 | 1,188,044 | 2,343,001 | 3,922,399 | 4,216,446 | 5,048,000 | 3,612,000 |
| Massachusetts | 994,514 | 2,805,346 | 4,690,514 | 5,689,170 | 5,737,037 | 6,415,000 | 6,787,000 |
| Michigan | 397,654 | 2,420,982 | 6,371,766 | 8,875,083 | 9,258,344 | 10,302,000 | 10,970,000 |
| Minnesota | 6,077 | 1,751,394 | 2,982,483 | 3,805,069 | 4,077,148 | 4,382,000 | 4,637,000 |
| Mississippi | 606,528 | 1,551,270 | 2,178,914 | 2,216,912 | 2,520,638 | 2,545,000 | 2,653,000 |
| Missouri | 682,044 | 3,106,665 | 3,954,653 | 4,677,399 | 4,917,444 | 5,226,000 | 5,506,000 |
| Montana | — | 243,329 | 591,024 | 694,409 | 786,690 | 821,000 | 862,000 |
| Nebraska | — | 1,066,300 | 1,325,510 | 1,483,791 | 1,570,006 | 1,679,000 | 1,755,000 |
| Nevada | — | 42,335 | 160,083 | 488,738 | 799,184 | 764,000 | 851,000 |
| New Hampshire | 317,976 | 411,588 | 553,242 | 737,681 | 920,610 | 1,007,000 | 1,121,000 |
| New Jersey | 489,555 | 1,883,669 | 4,835,329 | 7,168,164 | 7,364,158 | 8,344,000 | 8,958,000 |
| New Mexico | 61,547 | 195,310 | 681,187 | 1,016,000 | 1,299,968 | 1,322,000 | 1,409,000 |
| New York | 3,097,394 | 7,268,894 | 14,830,192 | 18,241,266 | 17,557,288 | 18,528,000 | 18,816,000 |
| North Carolina | 869,039 | 1,893,810 | 4,061,929 | 5,082,059 | 5,874,429 | 6,332,000 | 6,830,000 |
| North Dakota | — | 319,146 | 619,636 | 617,761 | 652,695 | 633,000 | 631,000 |
| Ohio | 1,980,329 | 4,157,545 | 7,946,627 | 10,652,017 | 10,797,419 | 11,570,000 | 11,999,000 |
| Oklahoma | — | 790,391 | 2,233,351 | 2,559,253 | 3,025,266 | 3,116,000 | 3,347,000 |
| Oregon | 12,093 | 413,536 | 1,521,341 | 2,091,385 | 2,632,663 | 2,781,000 | 3,066,000 |
| Pennsylvania | 2,311,786 | 6,302,115 | 10,498,012 | 11,793,909 | 11,866,728 | 12,272,000 | 12,465,000 |
| Rhode Island | 147,545 | 428,556 | 791,896 | 949,723 | 947,154 | 1,040,000 | 1,107,000 |
| South Carolina | 668,507 | 1,340,316 | 2,117,027 | 2,590,516 | 3,119,208 | 3,346,000 | 3,644,000 |
| South Dakota | — | 401,570 | 652,740 | 666,257 | 690,178 | 679,000 | 679,000 |
| Tennessee | 1,002,717 | 2,020,616 | 3,291,718 | 3,924,164 | 4,590,750 | 4,755,000 | 5,085,000 |
| Texas | 212,592 | 3,048,710 | 7,711,194 | 11,196,730 | 14,228,383 | 15,040,000 | 16,654,000 |
| Utah | 11,380 | 276,749 | 688,862 | 1,059,273 | 1,461,037 | 1,493,000 | 1,643,000 |
| Vermont | 314,120 | 343,641 | 377,747 | 444,732 | 511,456 | 560,000 | 614,000 |
| Virginia | 1,119,348 | 1,854,184 | 3,318,680 | 4,648,494 | 5,346,279 | 5,899,000 | 6,414,000 |
| Washington | 1,201 | 518,103 | 2,378,963 | 3,409,169 | 4,130,163 | 4,312,000 | 4,759,000 |
| West Virginia | 302,313 | 958,800 | 2,005,552 | 1,744,237 | 1,949,644 | 1,869,000 | 1,912,000 |
| Wisconsin | 305,391 | 2,069,042 | 3,434,575 | 4,417,933 | 4,705,335 | 5,156,000 | 5,476,000 |
| Wyoming | — | 92,531 | 290,529 | 332,416 | 470,816 | 425,000 | 450,000 |
| Puerto Rico | — | 950,000 | 2,210,703 | 2,712,033 | 3,187,570 | — | — |

[1] Official 1980 Census, released Dec. 31, 1980.   [2] Estimates based on 1970 census.

## RACIAL POPULATION BY REGION AND STATE

Source: U.S. Census Bureau

| REGION AND STATE | TOTAL | WHITE | BLACK | INDIAN | JAPANESE | CHINESE | FILIPINO | ALL OTHER |
|---|---|---|---|---|---|---|---|---|
| **New England** | 11,841,663 | 11,388,774 | 388,398 | 10,872 | 7,485 | 18,113 | 6,962 | 21,059 |
| Maine | 992,048 | 985,276 | 2,800 | 2,195 | 348 | 206 | 453 | 770 |
| New Hampshire | 737,681 | 733,106 | 2,505 | 361 | 360 | 420 | 157 | 772 |
| Vermont | 444,330 | 442,553 | 761 | 229 | 134 | 173 | 53 | 427 |
| Massachusetts | 5,689,170 | 5,477,624 | 175,817 | 4,475 | 4,393 | 14,012 | 2,361 | 10,488 |
| Rhode Island | 946,725 | 914,757 | 25,338 | 1,390 | 629 | 1,093 | 1,761 | 1,757 |
| Connecticut | 3,031,709 | 2,835,458 | 181,177 | 2,222 | 1,621 | 2,209 | 2,177 | 6,845 |
| **Middle Atlantic** | 37,199,040 | 32,921,730 | 3,955,755 | 38,594 | 31,493 | 97,664 | 24,462 | 129,342 |
| New York | 18,236,967 | 15,834,090 | 2,168,949 | 28,355 | 20,351 | 81,378 | 14,279 | 89,565 |
| New Jersey | 7,168,164 | 6,349,908 | 770,292 | 4,706 | 5,681 | 9,233 | 5,623 | 22,721 |
| Pennsylvania | 11,793,909 | 10,737,732 | 1,016,514 | 5,533 | 5,461 | 7,053 | 4,560 | 17,056 |
| **East North Central** | 40,252,476 | 36,160,135 | 3,872,905 | 57,732 | 33,002 | 31,001 | 22,375 | 75,326 |
| Ohio | 10,652,017 | 9,646,997 | 970,477 | 6,654 | 5,555 | 5,305 | 3,490 | 13,539 |
| Indiana | 5,193,669 | 4,820,324 | 357,464 | 3,887 | 2,279 | 2,115 | 1,365 | 6,235 |
| Illinois | 11,113,976 | 9,600,381 | 1,425,674 | 11,413 | 17,299 | 14,474 | 12,654 | 32,081 |
| Michigan | 8,875,083 | 7,833,474 | 991,066 | 16,854 | 5,221 | 6,407 | 3,657 | 18,404 |
| Wisconsin | 4,417,731 | 4,258,959 | 128,224 | 18,924 | 2,648 | 2,700 | 1,209 | 5,067 |
| **West North Central** | 16,319,187 | 15,481,048 | 698,645 | 93,555 | 9,352 | 8,342 | 5,449 | 22,796 |
| Minnesota | 3,804,971 | 3,736,038 | 34,868 | 23,128 | 2,603 | 2,422 | 1,456 | 4,456 |
| Iowa | 2,824,376 | 2,782,762 | 32,596 | 2,992 | 1,009 | 993 | 614 | 3,410 |
| Missouri | 4,676,501 | 4,177,495 | 480,172 | 5,405 | 2,382 | 2,815 | 2,010 | 6,222 |
| North Dakota | 617,761 | 599,485 | 2,494 | 14,369 | 239 | 165 | 204 | 805 |
| South Dakota | 665,507 | 630,333 | 1,627 | 32,365 | 221 | 163 | 83 | 715 |
| Nebraska | 1,483,493 | 1,432,867 | 39,911 | 6,624 | 1,314 | 551 | 324 | 1,902 |
| Kansas | 2,246,578 | 2,122,068 | 106,977 | 8,672 | 1,584 | 1,233 | 758 | 5,286 |
| **South Atlantic** | 30,671,337 | 24,112,395 | 6,388,496 | 67,126 | 17,467 | 19,332 | 23,914 | 42,607 |
| Delaware | 548,104 | 466,459 | 78,276 | 656 | 359 | 559 | 392 | 1,403 |
| Maryland | 3,922,399 | 3,194,888 | 699,479 | 4,239 | 3,733 | 6,520 | 5,170 | 8,370 |
| District of Columbia | 756,510 | 209,272 | 537,712 | 956 | 651 | 2,582 | 1,662 | 3,675 |
| Virginia | 4,648,494 | 3,761,514 | 861,368 | 4,853 | 3,500 | 2,805 | 7,496 | 6,958 |
| West Virginia | 1,744,237 | 1,673,480 | 67,342 | 751 | 368 | 373 | 722 | 1,201 |
| North Carolina | 5,082,059 | 3,901,767 | 1,126,478 | 44,406 | 2,104 | 1,255 | 905 | 5,144 |
| South Carolina | 2,590,516 | 1,794,430 | 789,041 | 2,241 | 826 | 521 | 1,222 | 2,235 |
| Georgia | 4,589,575 | 3,391,242 | 1,187,149 | 2,347 | 1,836 | 1,584 | 1,253 | 4,164 |
| Florida | 6,789,443 | 5,719,343 | 1,041,651 | 6,677 | 4,090 | 3,133 | 5,092 | 9,457 |
| **East South Central** | 12,803,470 | 10,202,810 | 2,571,291 | 10,363 | 3,795 | 4,235 | 2,473 | 8,503 |
| Kentucky | 3,218,706 | 2,981,786 | 230,793 | 1,531 | 1,095 | 558 | 612 | 2,351 |
| Tennessee | 3,923,687 | 3,293,930 | 621,261 | 2,276 | 1,160 | 1,610 | 846 | 2,604 |
| Alabama | 3,444,165 | 2,533,831 | 903,467 | 2,443 | 1,079 | 626 | 540 | 2,179 |
| Mississippi | 2,216,912 | 1,393,283 | 815,770 | 4,113 | 461 | 1,441 | 475 | 1,369 |
| **West South Central** | 19,320,560 | 16,104,903 | 3,010,174 | 123,733 | 9,655 | 10,717 | 5,592 | 55,786 |
| Arkansas | 1,923,295 | 1,565,915 | 352,445 | 2,014 | 587 | 743 | 289 | 1,302 |
| Louisiana | 3,641,306 | 2,541,498 | 1,086,832 | 5,294 | 1,123 | 1,340 | 1,249 | 3,970 |
| Oklahoma | 2,559,229 | 2,280,362 | 171,892 | 98,468 | 1,408 | 999 | 612 | 5,488 |
| Texas | 11,196,730 | 9,717,128 | 1,399,005 | 17,957 | 6,537 | 7,635 | 3,442 | 45,026 |
| **Mountain** | 8,281,562 | 7,798,087 | 180,382 | 235,439 | 20,360 | 9,245 | 4,466 | 33,583 |
| Montana | 694,409 | 663,043 | 1,995 | 27,130 | 574 | 289 | 236 | 1,142 |
| Idaho | 712,567 | 698,802 | 2,130 | 6,687 | 2,255 | 498 | 206 | 1,989 |
| Wyoming | 332,416 | 323,024 | 2,568 | 4,980 | 566 | 292 | 108 | 878 |
| Colorado | 2,207,259 | 2,112,352 | 66,411 | 8,836 | 7,831 | 1,489 | 1,068 | 9,272 |
| New Mexico | 1,016,000 | 915,815 | 19,555 | 72,788 | 940 | 563 | 386 | 5,953 |
| Arizona | 1,770,900 | 1,604,948 | 53,344 | 95,812 | 2,394 | 3,878 | 1,253 | 9,271 |
| Utah | 1,059,273 | 1,031,926 | 6,617 | 11,273 | 4,713 | 1,281 | 392 | 3,071 |
| Nevada | 488,738 | 448,177 | 27,762 | 7,933 | 1,087 | 955 | 817 | 2,007 |
| **Pacific** | 26,522,631 | 23,579,093 | 1,514,243 | 155,316 | 458,681 | 236,413 | 247,367 | 331,518 |
| Washington | 3,409,169 | 3,251,055 | 71,308 | 33,386 | 20,335 | 9,201 | 11,462 | 12,422 |
| Oregon | 2,091,385 | 2,032,079 | 26,308 | 13,510 | 6,843 | 4,814 | 1,633 | 6,198 |
| California | 19,953,134 | 17,761,032 | 1,400,143 | 91,018 | 213,280 | 170,131 | 138,859 | 178,671 |
| Alaska | 300,382 | 236,767 | 8,911 | 16,276 | 916 | 228 | 1,498 | 35,786 |
| Hawaii | 768,561 | 298,160 | 7,573 | 1,126 | 217,307 | 52,039 | 93,915 | 98,441 |
| **U.S. TOTAL** | 203,211,926 | 177,748,975 | 22,580,289 | 792,730 | 591,290 | 435,062 | 343,060 | 720,520 |

# U.S. FEDERAL BUDGET FOR FISCAL 1980

President Carter submitted to Congress in January 1980 a budget with estimated outlays of $615.8 billion for fiscal year 1981—the period Oct. 1, 1980, to Sept. 30, 1981. The estimated receipts were $600.0 billion, leaving an estimated deficit of $15.8.

The Office of Management and Budget (OMB) issued revised estimates of the 1981 budget in July 1980, indicating outlays of $633.8 billion, receipts of $604.0 billion, and a deficit of $29.8 billion. For details of the revised budget of July broken down into categories of outlays, see pages 966–967.

A comparison of the estimated budget expenditures of the federal government for fiscal year 1981 with those of fiscal year 1980 shows an increase of $55.0 billion.

Since 1970 the expenditures of the federal government have increased by $382 billion—or nearly tripled.

The total debt of the federal government is expected to grow to more than $959 billion by the end of fiscal 1981—or about $4,245 for each person in the United States.

## WHERE THE MONEY COMES FROM

In the fiscal 1981 budget as revised in July 1980, the OMB spelled out where the money for the budget comes from in terms of each dollar of estimated receipts:

Individual income taxes .......................... 44¢
Social insurance receipts (half from employees and half from employers) ..................... 29¢
Corporation income taxes ........................ 10¢
Excise taxes ..................................... 8¢
Borrowing ....................................... 5¢
Other receipts .................................. 4¢

## WHERE THE MONEY GOES

The OMB also indicated the major areas of spending for 1981 in terms of each dollar of estimated outlays:

Direct benefit payments to individuals ............ 44¢
National defense ................................. 25¢
Grants to states and localities ................... 14¢
Net interest on debt ............................. 9¢
Other federal operations ......................... 8¢

## THE FEDERAL BUDGET SYSTEM

Each year's federal budget represents the President's financial plan for operating the government for 12 months. The budget states how much money the President believes the federal government should spend during the fiscal year, where the revenues are to come from, and how much money is to be spent on each government program.

The budget, therefore, is an important tool for determining what the national priorities are to be during the next year.

By increasing or decreasing the amount of taxes to be collected and the amounts of money to be spent on various programs, the government can have an important effect on the entire economy of the nation because of the huge sums involved.

The budget, however, is merely a plan. The amount of money actually spent depends on appropriations and other legislation enacted by Congress. Therefore, whether the plan of the budget really is carried out is determined through the interaction of the President, the executive agencies, and Congress.

Under traditional procedures of the past, Congress did not generally vote on budget outlays directly. Instead, it would enact a variety of bills that permitted or required the government to spend money for specific programs. However, Congress passed budget-reform measures in 1974 to improve congressional control over federal spending.

The federal fiscal year historically was from July 1 to June 30. But beginning with fiscal 1977 the budget year became October 1 to September 30. Thus fiscal 1981 runs from Oct. 1, 1980, to Sept. 30, 1981.

## THE BUDGET CYCLE

The federal budget cycle is a continuous process involving four phases:

**1. Executive Submission:** The President outlines his budget proposals to Congress in January each year, climaxing months of planning and analysis throughout the executive departments and agencies.

**2. Congressional Authorizaton:** Once Congress has the President's recommended budget, it can change programs, eliminate them, or add programs not requested by the President. It can decrease or increase the amounts recommended by the President to finance existing programs and proposed new ones.

Each September Congress is supposed to adopt a budget for the fiscal year that begins in October. Congress then cannot consider any legislation that would increase spending or decrease receipts from the adopted budget. However, Congress can adopt a new revised budget at any time.

**3. Budget Execution and Control:** Once approved, the budget becomes the basis for the operations of each department and agency during the fiscal year. Central control over most of the budget authority made available to the executive branch is maintained through a system of "apportioning" the authority.

**4. Audit.** The final step in the budget process is the audit. This involves the Office of Management and Budget in the executive branch and the General Accounting Office, which is responsible directly to Congress.

## U.S. FEDERAL BUDGET OUTLAYS: FISCAL YEARS 1965–1981

Source: Office of Management and Budget; figures in $ millions (add 000,000).

| | 1965 | 1970 | ACTUAL OUTLAYS 1975 | 1977 | 1978 | 1979 | ESTIMATES [1] 1980 | 1981 |
|---|---|---|---|---|---|---|---|---|
| **NATIONAL DEFENSE:** | | | | | | | | |
| Department of Defense—Military: | | | | | | | | |
| Military personnel.................. | $13,387 | $23,031 | $24,968 | $25,715 | $27,075 | $28,407 | $30,709 | $33,112 |
| Retired military personnel ......... | 1,384 | 2,849 | 6,242 | 8,216 | 9,171 | 10,279 | 11,925 | 13,914 |
| Operation and maintenance........ | 12,349 | 21,609 | 26,297 | 30,587 | 33,578 | 36,424 | 44,531 | 52,550 |
| Procurement ..................... | 11,839 | 21,584 | 16,042 | 18,178 | 19,976 | 25,404 | 29,061 | 33,388 |
| Research and development ........ | 6,236 | 7,166 | 8,866 | 9,795 | 10,508 | 11,152 | 12,721 | 15,332 |
| Military construction and other .... | 928 | 1,059 | 2,486 | 3,065 | 2,734 | 3,347 | 3,652 | 5,584 |
| Atomic defense activities ..... | 1,620 | 1,415 | 1,506 | 1,936 | 2,070 | 2,541 | 2,939 | 3,479 |
| Defense-related activities ........... | −137 | −8 | −850 | −8 | 76 | 129 | 74 | 159 |
| Deductions for offsetting receipts .... | −150 | −151 | −4 | — | −2 | −3 | −3 | −4 |
| **Total outlays** ...................... | **47,456** | **78,553** | **85,552** | **97,501** | **105,186** | **117,681** | **135,611†** | **157,513** |
| **INTERNATIONAL AFFAIRS:** | | | | | | | | |
| Foreign economic and financial assist. | 3,838 | 2,935 | 3,598 | 3,907 | 4,629 | 4,743 | 5,829 | 6,194 |
| Military assistance ................... | 1,205 | 593 | 1,915 | 562 | 484 | 563 | 957 | 881 |
| Conduct of foreign affairs ........... | 335 | 398 | 658 | 981 | 1,128 | 1,310 | 1,345 | 1,507 |
| Foreign information and exchange.... | 224 | 235 | 348 | 386 | 423 | 465 | 535 | 558 |
| International financial programs...... | −242 | 357 | 505 | −914 | −641 | −879 | 2,309 | 1,229 |
| Deductions for offsetting receipts .... | −114 | −223 | −103 | −108 | −100 | −110 | −78 | −79 |
| **Total outlays** ...................... | **5,245** | **4,295** | **6,922** | **4,813** | **5,922** | **6,091** | **10,897** | **10,290** |
| **SCIENCE, SPACE, AND TECHNOLOGY:** | | | | | | | | |
| General science and basic research .. | 789 | 947 | 1,038 | 1,078 | 1,160 | 1,298 | 1,378 | 1,513 |
| Space flight ...................... | 3,756 | 2,340 | 1,661 | 2,252 | 2,260 | 2,217 | 2,668 | 2,940 |
| Space, science, applications, and tech. . | 1,017 | 853 | 958 | 1,006 | 972 | 1,153 | 1,286 | 1,310 |
| Supporting space activities .......... | 261 | 370 | 334 | 343 | 354 | 383 | 398 | 423 |
| Deductions for offsetting receipts .... | −2 | −3 | −2 | −2 | −4 | −10 | −3 | −3 |
| **Total outlays** ...................... | **5,822** | **4,508** | **3,989** | **4,677** | **4,742** | **5,041** | **5,726** | **6,183** |
| **ENERGY:** | | | | | | | | |
| Energy supply ...................... | 573 | 848 | 1,743 | 3,266 | 3,970 | 4,900 | 4,667 | 4,712 |
| Energy conservation ............... | — | — | 48 | 143 | 221 | 252 | 555 | 743 |
| Emergency energy preparedness ..... | — | — | 33 | 123 | 897 | 1,021 | 450 | 618 |
| Energy information, policy, regulation . | 97 | 142 | 389 | 664 | 798 | 742 | 913 | 1,229 |
| Deductions for offsetting receipts .... | — | — | −43 | −23 | −25 | −59 | −72 | −74 |
| **Total outlays** ...................... | **669** | **990** | **2,170** | **4,172** | **5,861** | **6,856** | **6,513** | **7,227** |
| **NATURAL RESOURCES AND ENVIRONMENT:** | | | | | | | | |
| Water resources ................... | 1,607 | 1,564 | 2,633 | 3,241 | 3,468 | 3,897 | 4,340 | 4,154 |
| Conservation and land management .. | 606 | 717 | 1,300 | 1,279 | 1,984 | 1,884 | 2,381 | 2,172 |
| Recreational resources ............. | 219 | 372 | 825 | 1,014 | 1,439 | 1,513 | 1,444 | 1,341 |
| Pollution control and abatement ..... | 134 | 384 | 2,523 | 4,279 | 3,964 | 4,706 | 5,600 | 5,434 |
| Other natural resources ............ | 293 | 432 | 762 | 973 | 1,157 | 1,273 | 1,359 | 1,460 |
| Deductions for offsetting receipts .... | −337 | −467 | −707 | −786 | −1,087 | −1,183 | −1,386 | −1,460 |
| **Total outlays** ...................... | **2,523** | **3,003** | **7,335** | **10,000** | **10,925** | **12,091** | **13,739** | **13,100** |
| **AGRICULTURE:** | | | | | | | | |
| Farm income stabilization ........... | 3,551 | 4,589 | 785 | 4,485 | 6,588 | 4,850 | 4,457 | 748 |
| Agricultural research and services.... | 405 | 579 | 877 | 1,058 | 1,129 | 1,340 | 1,388 | 1,478 |
| Deductions for offsetting receipts .... | −7 | −5 | −2 | −11 | 14 | 48 | −3 | −3 |
| **Total outlays** ...................... | **3,948** | **5,164** | **1,659** | **5,532** | **7,731** | **6,238** | **5,843** | **2,223** |
| **COMMERCE AND HOUSING CREDIT:** | | | | | | | | |
| Mortgage credit and thrift insurance . | −66 | 104 | 2,791 | −3,280 | 210 | −677 | 4,528 | −2,437 |
| Postal service ..................... | 805 | 1,510 | 1,877 | 2,267 | 1,778 | 1,787 | 1,677 | 1,343 |
| Federal financing bank ............. | — | — | — | −143 | — | — | −253 | −188 |
| Other advancement and regulation ... | 462 | 477 | 944 | 1,115 | 1,342 | 1,454 | 2,323 | 1,936 |
| Deductions for offsetting receipts .... | −64 | −14 | −5 | −4 | −5 | — | — | — |
| **Total outlays** ...................... | **1,136** | **2,077** | **5,607** | **−44** | **3,325** | **2,565** | **8,274** | **654** |
| **TRANSPORTATION:** | | | | | | | | |
| Ground transportation.............. | 4,105 | 4,678 | 6,501 | 10,037 | 10,355 | 12,064 | 14,715 | 13,034 |
| Air transportation................. | 944 | 1,422 | 2,408 | 2,816 | 3,277 | 3,392 | 3,743 | 3,853 |
| Water transportation ............... | 730 | 913 | 1,459 | 1,749 | 1,854 | 1,977 | 2,306 | 2,298 |
| Other transportation ............... | 1 | 26 | 74 | 76 | 61 | 93 | 100 | 114 |
| Deductions for offsetting receipts .... | −22 | −26 | −55 | −42 | −102 | −67 | −70 | −55 |
| **Total outlays** ...................... | **5,758** | **7,013** | **10,388** | **14,636** | **15,445** | **17,459** | **20,795** | **19,244** |
| **COMMUNITY AND REGIONAL DEVELOPMENT:** | | | | | | | | |
| Community development ............ | 413 | 1,503 | 2,336 | 3,529 | 3,302 | 3,995 | 4,788 | 4,983 |
| Area and regional development ...... | 597 | 644 | 972 | 2,124 | 4,850 | 3,899 | 2,518 | 2,773 |
| Disaster relief and insurance ....... | 53 | 257 | 398 | 649 | 2,871 | 1,611 | 2,199 | 1,600 |
| Deductions for offsetting receipts .... | −8 | −9 | −17 | −16 | −23 | −23 | −25 | −25 |
| **Total outlays** ...................... | **1,055** | **2,395** | **3,689** | **6,286** | **11,000** | **9,482** | **9,479** | **9,330** |

| | ACTUAL OUTLAYS (in $ millions; add 000,000) | | | | | | ESTIMATES[1] | |
|---|---|---|---|---|---|---|---|---|
| | 1965 | 1970 | 1975 | 1977 | 1978 | 1979 | 1980 | 1981 |
| **EDUCATION, TRAINING, EMPLOYMENT, AND SOCIAL SERVICES:** | | | | | | | | |
| Elementary, secondary, and voc. educ. | $724 | $3,107 | $4,634 | $5,078 | $5,686 | $6,688 | $7,318 | $7,542 |
| Higher education | 412 | 1,385 | 2,050 | 3,104 | 3,486 | 4,528 | 5,241 | 5,255 |
| Research and general educ. aids | 149 | 521 | 947 | 927 | 1,082 | 1,233 | 1,382 | 1,400 |
| Training and employment | 534 | 1,602 | 4,063 | 6,877 | 10,784 | 10,833 | 10,128 | 10,462 |
| Other labor services | 96 | 135 | 259 | 374 | 410 | 488 | 552 | 591 |
| Social services | 230 | 1,884 | 3,923 | 4,632 | 5,027 | 5,923 | 5,279 | 5,676 |
| Deductions for offsetting receipts | -7 | -10 | -5 | -7 | -12 | -8 | -7 | -5 |
| **Total outlays** | **2,138** | **8,624** | **15,870** | **20,985** | **26,463** | **29,685** | **29,893** | **30,921** |
| **HEALTH:** | | | | | | | | |
| Health care services | 881 | 11,142 | 24,242 | 34,524 | 39,103 | 45,121 | 51,992 | 58,281 |
| Health research | 572 | 1,054 | 1,923 | 2,543 | 2,822 | 3,023 | 3,327 | 3,499 |
| Education of health-care workers | 209 | 633 | 856 | 981 | 930 | 583 | 629 | 629 |
| Consumer and occup. health and safety | 130 | 226 | 632 | 747 | 838 | 896 | 974 | 1,009 |
| Deductions for offsetting receipts | -1 | -6 | -5 | -10 | -18 | -10 | -8 | -8 |
| **Total outlays** | **1,791** | **13,049** | **27,648** | **38,785** | **43,676** | **49,614** | **56,913** | **63,411** |
| **INCOME SECURITY:** | | | | | | | | |
| General retirement and disability insurance | 18,124 | 31,303 | 69,382 | 88,642 | 97,257 | 108,492 | 124,453 | 145,104 |
| Fed. employee retirment. and disability | 1,472 | 2,688 | 6,980 | 9,503 | 10,665 | 12,379 | 14,563 | 16,703 |
| Unemployment compensation | 2,787 | 3,364 | 13,459 | 15,258 | 11,769 | 10,742 | 17,988 | 27,232 |
| Housing assistance | — | — | — | 2,968 | 3,677 | 4,367 | 5,302 | 6,663 |
| Food and nutrition assistance | — | — | — | 8,527 | 8,927 | 10,786 | 13,994 | 15,341 |
| Public assistance and other income security | 3,359 | 5,712 | 18,790 | 13,017 | 13,916 | 13,432 | 17,247 | 19,323 |
| **Total outlays** | **25,741** | **43,066** | **108,610** | **137,915** | **146,212** | **160,198** | **193,548** | **230,366** |
| **VETERANS' BENEFITS AND SERVICES:** | | | | | | | | |
| Income security for veterans | 4,215 | 5,546 | 7,860 | 9,216 | 9,745 | 10,780 | 11,566 | 13,054 |
| Veterans' edu., training, and rehabil. | 58 | 1,015 | 4,593 | 3,710 | 3,365 | 2,760 | 2,288 | 2,033 |
| Hospital and med. care for veterans | 1,270 | 1,800 | 3,665 | 4,708 | 5,254 | 5,611 | 6,399 | 6,408 |
| Veterans' housing | — | 54 | 24 | -145 | 28 | 154 | -34 | -374 |
| Other veterans' benefits and serv. | 181 | 263 | 458 | 549 | 585 | 627 | 677 | 652 |
| Deductions for offsetting receipts | -2 | -2 | -2 | -1 | -3 | -4 | -3 | -3 |
| **Total outlays** | **5,722** | **8,677** | **16,597** | **18,038** | **18,974** | **19,928** | **20,893** | **21,770** |
| **ADMINISTRATION OF JUSTICE:** | | | | | | | | |
| Federal law-enforcement activities | 332 | 569 | 1,349 | 1,673 | 1,831 | 1,992 | 2,257 | 2,242 |
| Federal litigative and judicial activities | 141 | 236 | 549 | 842 | 943 | 1,130 | 1,374 | 1,466 |
| Federal correctional activities | 62 | 88 | 200 | 240 | 307 | 337 | 338 | 349 |
| Criminal justice assistance | — | 65 | 853 | 847 | 729 | 710 | 661 | 518 |
| Deductions for offsetting receipts | -5 | -6 | -9 | -2 | -8 | -17 | -12 | -12 |
| **Total outlays** | **529** | **952** | **2,942** | **3,600** | **3,802** | **4,153** | **4,617** | **4,563** |
| **GENERAL GOVERNMENT:** | | | | | | | | |
| Legislative functions | 189 | 303 | 588 | 841 | 900 | 914 | 1,073 | 1,078 |
| Executive direction and management | 17 | 30 | 63 | 76 | 73 | 81 | 102 | 120 |
| Tax collection and fiscal operations | 638 | 934 | 1,752 | 1,947 | 2,124 | 2,330 | 2,748 | 2,757 |
| General property and records manag. | 602 | 616 | 418 | 141 | 214 | 235 | 259 | 333 |
| Central personnel management | 23 | 44 | 88 | 100 | 129 | 127 | 152 | 154 |
| Other general government | 109 | 158 | 472 | 455 | 523 | 586 | 877 | 387 |
| Deductions for offsetting receipts | -117 | -145 | -199 | -186 | -188 | -120 | -197 | -132 |
| **Total outlays** | **1,460** | **1,940** | **3,182** | **3,374** | **3,777** | **4,153** | **5,014** | **4,698** |
| **GENERAL PURPOSE FISCAL ASSISTANCE:** | | | | | | | | |
| General revenue sharing | — | — | 6,130 | 6,762 | 6,830 | 6,854 | 6,869 | 5,151 |
| Other general purpose fiscal assist. | 238 | 536 | 1,057 | 2,737 | 2,772 | 1,518 | 1,764 | 2,114 |
| **Total outlays** | **238** | **536** | **7,187** | **9,499** | **9,601** | **8,372** | **8,632** | **7,264** |
| **INTEREST:** | | | | | | | | |
| Interest on the public debt | 11,346 | 19,304 | 32,665 | 41,900 | 48,695 | 59,837 | 74,800 | 80,400 |
| Other interest | -987 | -992 | -1,754 | -3,891 | -4,729 | -7,281 | -10,516 | -12,760 |
| **Total outlays** | **10,359** | **18,312** | **30,911** | **38,009** | **43,966** | **52,556** | **64,284** | **67,640** |
| **ALLOWANCES:** | | | | | | | | |
| Civilian agency pay raises | — | — | — | — | — | — | — | 1,095 |
| Other | — | — | — | — | — | — | -22 | -198 |
| **Total outlays** | — | — | — | — | — | — | **-22** | **1,400** |
| **UNDISTRIBUTED OFFSETTING RECEIPTS:** | | | | | | | | |
| Employer share, employee retirement. | -1,329 | -2,444 | -3,980 | -4,548 | -4,983 | -5,271 | -5,916 | -6,280 |
| Interest received by trust funds | -1,780 | -3,936 | -7,667 | -8,131 | -8,530 | -9,950 | -11,359 | -12,526 |
| Rents and royalties on the Outer Continental Shelf | -53 | -187 | -2,428 | -2,374 | -2,259 | -3,267 | -4,600 | -5,200 |
| **Total receipts** | **-3,162** | **-6,567** | **-14,075** | **-15,053** | **-15,772** | **-18,488** | **-21,876** | **-24,005** |
| **TOTAL U.S. GOVT. OUTLAYS** | **$118,430** | **$196,588** | **$326,185** | **$402,725** | **$450,836** | **$493,673** | **$578,774** | **$633,791** |

[1] Based on July 1980 revisions to President Carter's budget of January 1980.

## .S. BUDGET AND FEDERAL DEBT: 1789–1981 [1]

Source: Office of Management and Budget; figures are in $ millions (add 000,000).

| FISCAL YEAR | U.S. BUDGET RECEIPTS | U.S. BUDGET OUTLAYS | SURPLUS (+) OR DEFICIT (−) | GROSS DEBT AT END OF YEAR | FISCAL YEAR | U.S. BUDGET RECEIPTS | U.S. BUDGET OUTLAYS | SURPLUS (+) OR DEFICIT (−) | GROSS DEBT AT END OF YEAR |
|---|---|---|---|---|---|---|---|---|---|
| 1789–1849 | $ 1,160 | $ 1,090 | $ + 70 | $ 63 | 1958 | $ 79,636 | $ 82,575 | $ − 2,939 | $279,693 |
| 1850–1900 | 14,462 | 15,453 | − 991 | 1,263 | 1959 | 79,249 | 92,104 | − 12,855 | 287,767 |
| 1905 | 544 | 567 | − 23 | 1,132 | 1960 | 92,492 | 92,223 | + 269 | 290,862 |
| 1910 | 676 | 694 | − 18 | 1,147 | 1961 | 94,389 | 97,795 | − 3,406 | 292,895 |
| 1915 | 683 | 746 | − 63 | 1,191 | 1962 | 99,676 | 106,813 | − 7,137 | 303,291 |
| 1920 | 6,649 | 6,358 | + 291 | 24,299 | 1963 | 106,560 | 111,311 | − 4,751 | 310,807 |
| 1925 | 3,641 | 2,924 | + 717 | 20,516 | 1964 | 112,662 | 118,584 | − 5,922 | 316,763 |
| 1930 | 4,058 | 3,320 | + 738 | 16,185 | 1965 | 116,833 | 118,430 | − 1,596 | 323,154 |
| 1935 | 3,706 | 6,497 | − 2,791 | 28,701 | 1966 | 130,856 | 134,652 | − 3,796 | 329,474 |
| 1936 | 3,997 | 8,422 | − 4,425 | 33,779 | 1967 | 149,552 | 158,254 | − 8,702 | 341,348 |
| 1937 | 4,956 | 7,733 | − 2,777 | 36,425 | 1968 | 153,671 | 178,833 | − 25,161 | 369,769 |
| 1938 | 5,588 | 6,765 | − 1,177 | 37,165 | 1969 | 187,784 | 184,548 | + 3,236 | 367,144 |
| 1939 | 4,979 | 8,841 | − 3,862 | 45,890 | 1970 | 193,743 | 196,588 | − 2,845 | 382,603 |
| 1940 | 6,361 | 9,456 | − 3,095 | 50,696 | 1971 | 188,392 | 211,425 | − 23,033 | 409,467 |
| 1941 | 8,621 | 13,634 | − 5,013 | 57,531 | 1972 | 208,649 | 232,021 | − 23,373 | 437,329 |
| 1942 | 14,350 | 35,114 | − 20,764 | 79,200 | 1973 | 232,225 | 247,074 | − 14,849 | 468,426 |
| 1943 | 23,649 | 78,533 | − 54,884 | 142,648 | 1974 | 264,932 | 269,620 | − 4,688 | 486,247 |
| 1944 | 44,276 | 91,280 | − 47,004 | 204,079 | 1975 | 280,997 | 326,185 | − 45,188 | 544,131 |
| 1945 | 45,216 | 92,690 | − 47,474 | 260,123 | 1976 | 300,005 | 366,439 | − 66,434 | 631,866 |
| 1946 | 39,327 | 55,183 | − 15,856 | 270,991 | TQ [2] | 81,773 | 94,729 | − 12,956 | 646,379 |
| 1948 | 41,774 | 29,773 | + 12,001 | 252,031 | 1977 | 357,762 | 402,725 | − 44,963 | 709,138 |
| 1950 | 39,485 | 42,597 | − 3,112 | 256,853 | 1978 | 401,997 | 450,836 | − 48,839 | 780,425 |
| 1952 | 66,204 | 67,721 | − 1,517 | 259,097 | 1979 [3] | 465,940 | 493,673 | − 27,733 | 833,751 |
| 1954 | 69,719 | 70,890 | − 1,170 | 270,812 | 1980 [3] | 517,892 | 578,774 | − 60,882 | 905,812 |
| 1955 | 65,469 | 68,509 | − 3,041 | 274,366 | 1981 [3] | 604,026 | 633,791 | − 29,765 | 959,357 |
| 1957 | 79,990 | 76,741 | + 3,249 | 272,353 | | | | | |

[1] For 1789–1939, administrative budget. [2] TQ=Transitional Quarter, July 1 to Sept. 30, 1976. [3] July 1980 estimates.

## FEDERAL BUDGET RECEIPTS BY SOURCE: 1940–1981

Source: Office of Management and Budget; figures in $ millions (add 000,000).

| SOURCE | COLLECTIONS | | | | | | | | |
|---|---|---|---|---|---|---|---|---|---|
| | 1940 | 1950 | 1960 | 1970 | 1975 | 1978 | 1979 | 1980 [1] | 1981 [1] |
| Individual Income Taxes . | $1,110 | $15,747 | $40,741 | $90,412 | $122,386 | $180,986 | $217,841 | $240,713 | $278,152 |
| Corporation Income Taxes . | 978 | 10,449 | 21,494 | 32,829 | 40,621 | 59,952 | 65,677 | 65,481 | 66,383 |
| Social Insurance Taxes and Contributions ... | 1,715 | 4,386 | 14,684 | 45,298 | 86,441 | 123,410 | 141,591 | 160,512 | 184,519 |
| Excise Taxes.......... | 1,844 | 7,550 | 11,676 | 15,705 | 16,551 | 18,376 | 18,745 | 25,379 | 48,656 |
| Estate and Gift Taxes . | 353 | 698 | 1,606 | 3,644 | 4,611 | 5,285 | 5,411 | 6,100 | 6,284 |
| Customs Duties ....... | 331 | 407 | 1,105 | 2,430 | 3,676 | 6,573 | 7,439 | 7,050 | 7,510 |
| Miscellaneous Receipts | 30 | 248 | 1,187 | 3,424 | 6,711 | 7,413 | 9,237 | 12,657 | 12,522 |
| TOTAL RECEIPTS | $6,361 | $39,485 | $92,492 | $193,743 | $280,997 | $401,197 | $465,940 | $517,892 | $604,026 |

[1] July 1980 estimates.

## COMPARISON OF FEDERAL RECEIPTS AND EXPENDITURES: 1974–1980 [1]

Source: U.S. Department of Commerce, *Survey of Current Business*; figures in $ billions (add 000,000,000).

| | 1974 | 1975 | 1976 | 1977 | 1978 | 1979 | 1980 Q1 [2] | 1980 Q2 [2] |
|---|---|---|---|---|---|---|---|---|
| **Federal government receipts**............ | **$288.6** | **$286.2** | **$331.4** | **$375.4** | **$432.1** | **$497.6** | **$538.4** | **$531.4** |
| Personal tax and nontax receipts ..... | 131.1 | 125.4 | 146.8 | 169.6 | 194.9 | 230.0 | 246.1 | 249.4 |
| Corporate profits tax accruals......... | 45.9 | 42.8 | 54.8 | 61.8 | 72.0 | 78.2 | 86.8 | 67.3 |
| Indirect business tax and nontax accruals ... | 21.7 | 23.9 | 23.4 | 25.1 | 28.1 | 30.0 | 33.8 | 43.0 |
| Contributions for social insurance .... | 89.9 | 94.2 | 106.4 | 118.9 | 137.0 | 159.3 | 171.7 | 171.8 |
| **Federal government expenditures** ....... | **$299.3** | **$356.8** | **$385.2** | **$421.7** | **$459.8** | **$509.0** | **$561.3** | **$579.5** |
| Purchases of goods and services ..... | 111.1 | 123.1 | 129.9 | 144.4 | 152.6 | 166.6 | 186.2 | 193.3 |
| Transfer payments .................. | 117.6 | 149.1 | 161.6 | 172.7 | 185.4 | 209.8 | 230.0 | 236.3 |
| Grants-in-aid to state and local governments . | 43.9 | 54.6 | 61.1 | 67.5 | 77.3 | 80.4 | 86.0 | 86.0 |
| Net interest paid ................... | 20.9 | 23.2 | 26.8 | 29.0 | 34.8 | 43.1 | 50.2 | 54.0 |
| Subsidies less current surplus of government enterprises............ | 5.3 | 6.8 | 5.8 | 8.1 | 9.7 | 9.1 | 8.9 | 9.8 |
| **Deficit (−)** ........................... | **$−10.7** | **$−70.6** | **$−53.8** | **$−46.3** | **$−27.7** | **$−11.4** | **$−22.9** | **$−48.0** |

[1] Fiscal years. [2] First and second quarters 1980 at annual rates.

# U.S. GOVERNMENT CIVILIAN EMPLOYEES

Source: Office of Personnel Management

| | TOTAL [1] |
|---|---:|
| **TOTAL, ALL BRANCHES** | 2,876,124 |
| | |
| **LEGISLATIVE BRANCH** | **39,670** |
| | |
| Congress | 19,096 |
| Architect of the Capitol | 2,168 |
| Botanic Garden | 56 |
| Cost Accounting Standards Board | 19 |
| General Accounting Office | 5,488 |
| Government Printing Office | 6,767 |
| Library of Congress | 5,487 |
| U.S. Tax Court | 224 |
| Congressional Budget Office | 213 |
| Office of Technology Assessment | 142 |
| Copyright Royalty Tribunal | 10 |
| | |
| **JUDICIAL BRANCH** | **15,178** |
| | |
| United States Courts | 14,847 |
| Supreme Court | 331 |
| | |
| **EXECUTIVE BRANCH** | **2,821,276** |
| **Executive Office of the President:** | **1,799** |
| | |
| White House Office | 406 |
| Office of the Vice President | 16 |
| Office of Management and Budget | 616 |
| Council of Economic Advisers | 35 |
| Council on Environmental Quality | 49 |
| Council on Wage and Price Stability | 215 |
| Domestic Policy Staff | 60 |
| National Security Council | 69 |
| Office of Science and Technology Policy | 40 |
| Office of the U.S. Trade Representative | 127 |
| Office of Administration | 166 |
| | |
| **Executive Departments:** | **1,717,383** |
| | |
| State | 23,497 |
| Treasury | 124,663 |
| Department of Defense, total | 960,529 |
| Defense, Military, total | 927,004 |
| Army | 315,012 |
| Navy | 302,911 |
| Air Force | 233,129 |
| Defense Logistics Agency | 45,840 |
| Other defense activities | 30,112 |
| Defense, Civil, total | 33,525 |
| Army | 33,522 |
| Corps of Engineers | 33,379 |
| Cemeterial expenses | 143 |
| Air Force civil functions | 3 |
| Justice | 56,327 |
| Interior | 77,357 |
| Agriculture | 129,329 |
| Commerce | 48,563 |
| Labor | 23,400 |
| Health and Human Services | 155,662 |
| Housing and Urban Development | 16,964 |
| Transportation | 72,361 |
| Energy | 21,557 |
| Education | 7,364 |
| | |
| **Independent Agencies:** | **1,102,094** |
| | |
| ACTION | 1,837 |
| American Battle Monuments Commission | 385 |

| | TOTAL [1] |
|---|---:|
| **Independent Agencies** (continued) | |
| Arms Control and Disarmament Agency | 221 |
| Board of Governors, Federal Reserve System | 1,498 |
| Civil Aeronautics Board | 734 |
| Commission on Civil Rights | 304 |
| Commodity Futures Trading Commission | 479 |
| Community Services Administration | 1,067 |
| Consumer Product Safety Commission | 921 |
| Environmental Protection Agency | 14,715 |
| Equal Employment Opportunity Comm. | 3,515 |
| Export-Import Bank of the U.S. | 385 |
| Farm Credit Administration | 271 |
| Federal Communications Comm. | 2,244 |
| Federal Deposit Insurance Corp. | 3,520 |
| Federal Election Commission | 265 |
| Federal Emergency Management Agency | 3,427 |
| Federal Home Loan Bank Board | 1,470 |
| Federal Labor Relations Authority | 360 |
| Federal Maritime Commission | 325 |
| Federal Mediation and Conciliation Service | 503 |
| Federal Mine Safety and Health Review Commission | 85 |
| Federal Trade Commission | 1,846 |
| General Services Administration | 37,654 |
| International Communications Agency | 8,138 |
| Inter-American Foundation | 66 |
| International Trade Commission | 424 |
| Interstate Commerce Commission | 1,981 |
| Merit Systems Protection Board | 435 |
| National Aeronautics and Space Administration | 23,714 |
| National Alcohol Fuels Comm. | 45 |
| National Capital Planning Commission | 58 |
| National Commission on Air Quality | 42 |
| National Credit Union Administration | 726 |
| National Endowment for the Arts | 327 |
| National Endowment for the Humanities | 293 |
| National Labor Relations Board | 2,936 |
| National Mediation Board | 68 |
| National Science Foundation | 1,394 |
| National Transportation Safety Board | 384 |
| Nuclear Regulatory Commission | 3,283 |
| Occupational Safety and Health Review Commission | 179 |
| Office of Personnel Management | 8,280 |
| Office of the Federal Inspector for Alaska Natural Gas Transportation System | 103 |
| Panama Canal Commission | 8,700 |
| Pension Benefit Guaranty Corporation | 463 |
| Postal Rate Commission | 71 |
| Railroad Retirement Commission | 1,795 |
| Securities and Exchange Commission | 2,056 |
| Selective Service System | 97 |
| Small Business Administration | 5,804 |
| Smithsonian Institution | 4,403 |
| Soldiers' and Airmen's Home | 994 |
| Tennessee Valley Authority | 51,714 |
| U.S. International Development Cooperation Agency | 6,152 |
| U.S. Postal Service | 660,014 |
| Veterans Administration | 228,285 |
| Water Resources Council | 71 |
| Other boards and agencies | 567 |

[1] On Sept. 30, 1980. Excludes Central Intelligence Agency and National Security Agency.

# U.S. GOVERNMENT AGENCIES AND DEPARTMENTS

The President is the administrative head of the executive branch of the government, which includes cabinet-level executive departments and independent agencies.

The cabinet functions at the pleasure of the President to advise him on matters of importance. The Vice President participates in all cabinet meetings. Others who regularly attend cabinet meetings include the heads of the executive departments, the counsel to the President, the special representative for trade negotiations, the director of the Office of Management and Budget, the U.S. ambassador to the UN, and presidential staff aides.

The President's salary is $200,000 a year plus $50,000 official allowance and $100,000 travel allowance.

## EXECUTIVE OFFICE OF PRESIDENT CARTER

This office consists of the individuals, agencies, and special commissions charged with aiding the President in carrying out the many activities incident to his office.

### THE WHITE HOUSE OFFICE
1600 Pennsylvania Avenue, N.W., and Old Executive Office Building, Washington, D.C. 20500
Phone: (202) 456-1414
*Assistants to the President:* Jack H. Watson Jr. (Chief of Staff); Zbigniew Brzezinski (National Security); Stuart E. Eizenstat (Domestic Affairs and Policy); Hamilton Jordan; Alonzo L. McDonald Jr. (Staff Director); Frank B. Moore (Congressional Liaison); Eugene Eidenberg (Secretary to the Cabinet and Intergovernmental Affairs); Sarah C. Weddington; Anne Wexler
*Counsel to the President:* Lloyd N. Cutler
*Press Secretary:* Joseph L. Powell
*Special Assistants to the President:* Stephen R. Aiello (Ethnic Affairs); Hugh A. Carter Jr. (Administration); Richard M. Harden (Information Management); C. Ray Jenkins, Louis E. Martin; Esther Peterson (Consumer Affairs); Esteban E. Torres (Hispanic Affairs)
*Staff Director for the First Lady:* Edith J. Dobelle
*Special Advisor to the President:* Alfred H. Moses
*Appointments Secretary to the President:* Phillip J. Wise Jr.
*Counselor to the President on Aging:* Harold L. Sheppard
*Deputy Assistants:* David L. Aaron (National Security Affairs); Landon Butler; William H. Cable (Congressional Liaison—House); Bertram W. Carp (Domestic Affairs and Policy); Michael H. Chanin; James M. Copeland Jr. (Congressional Liaison—Legislative Coordination); Bruce Kirschenbaum (Intergovernmental Affairs); David M. Rubinstein (Domestic Affairs and Policy); Danny C. Tate (Congressional Liaison—Senate); Richard Hernandez (Political Liaison); Elizabeth A. Rainwater (Research); William G. Simpson; William E. Albers; Robert Thomson (Congressional Liaison); Bernard Aronson (Labor Liaison); I. Ray Miller Jr. (Minority Affairs)
*Deputy Press Secretaries:* Patricia Y. Bario; Rex L. Granum
*Deputy Counsels:* Michael H. Cardozo V, Joseph N. Onek

*Deputy Appointments Secretaries:* Robert H. Dunn; Frances M. Voorde
*Deputy Secretary to the Cabinet:* Thomas J. Higgins
*Special Assistants for Congressional Liaison:* James C. Free (House); Robert W. Maher (House), Valerie F. Pinson (House); Robert K. Russell Jr.; Terrence D. Straub (House); Ronna Freiberg (Legislative Coordination); Robert M. Schule; Patricia A. DeSouza
*Personal Assistant/Secretary to the President:* Susan S. Clough
*Chief Speechwriter:* Hendrik Hertzberg
*Press Secretary to the First Lady:* Mary Finch Hoyt
*Senior Associate Counsel:* Douglas B. Huron
*Staff Secretary:* Richard G. Hutcheson III
*Director of the Presidential Personnel Office:* Arnie Miller
*Deputy to the Staff Director:* Michael James Rowny
*Associate Assistant:* John Ryor; Jane D. Hartley
*Deputy Special Assistants for Administration:* Marvin L. Beaman Jr. (Military Office); Daniel Malachuk Jr. (White House Operations)
*Personal Assistant to the First Lady:* Madeline F. Macbean
*Social Secretary:* Gretchen Poston
*Deputy Director of the Presidential Personnel Office:* Harley Frankel
*Counsel to the Intelligence Oversight Board:* James V. Dick
*Associate Press Secretaries:* Claudia M. Townsend; Marc T. Henderson
*Associate Director, Presidential Personnel Office:* Peggy E. Rainwater
*Physician to the President:* Rear Adm. William M. Lukash, USNMC
*Chief Usher:* Rex W. Scouten

### CENTRAL INTELLIGENCE AGENCY (CIA)
Washington, D.C. 20505
Director: Adm. Stansfield Turner
*Duties:* To keep National Security Council informed on national-security matters; to coordinate intelligence from government agencies and from its agents in other countries. The CIA has no police or law-enforcement powers and no internal-security functions.

## EXECUTIVE OFFICE OF THE PRESIDENT *(continued)*

### COUNCIL OF ECONOMIC ADVISERS (CEA)

Executive Office Building,
 Washington, D.C. 20506
Established: 1946
Chairman: Charles L. Schultze
Members: Lyle E. Gramley, George C. Eads,
 Charles L. Schultze
*Duties:* To analyze trends in the national econo-
 my; to appraise economic programs and
 policies of the federal government; to assist in
 the preparation of the President's economic
 reports to Congress.

### COUNCIL ON ENVIRONMENTAL QUALITY

722 Jackson Place, N.W.,
 Washington, D.C. 20006
Established: 1969
Chairman: Gustave Speth
*Duties:* To develop and recommend national
 policies to promote environmental quality and
 to administer guidelines for the environmental
 impact statement process.

### COUNCIL ON WAGE AND PRICE STABILITY

Executive Office Building,
 Washington, D.C. 20503
Established: Aug. 24, 1974
Executive Director: Robert Russell
Chairman: Charles L. Schultze
Membership: Eight members; four adviser-
 members
*Purpose:* To monitor the nation's inflation and
 discourage industry and labor from taking
 inflationary actions; to assist the President in
 the development of policies to control and
 reduce inflation.

### DOMESTIC POLICY STAFF

The White House,
 Washington, D.C. 20500
Established: 1977
Director: Stuart E. Eizenstat
*Purpose:* To administer the Presidential Domestic Policy Review System to coordinate the
 work of the departments and agencies in
 developing the administration's position on
 selected key domestic-policy issues.

### INTELLIGENCE OVERSIGHT BOARD

Executive Office Building,
 Washington, D.C. 20500
Established: 1975
Chairman: Thomas L. Farmer
Membership: Thomas L. Farmer, Albert A.
 Gore, William W. Scranton
*Duties:* To review and assess foreign-intelligence
 activities and bring to the President's atten-
 tion any abuses that might occur.

### NATIONAL SECURITY COUNCIL

Executive Office Building,
 Washington, D.C. 20506
Established: 1947
Director: Assistant to the President for National
 Security Affairs Zbigniew Brzezinski

Membership: The President, Vice President,
 Secretary of State, Secretary of Defense
Advisers: Chairman of the Joint Chiefs of Staff and
 director of the Central Intelligence Agency
*Duties:* To advise the President on national-
 security problems, formulating plans to promote the best interests of the United States in
 international relations.

### OFFICE OF ADMINISTRATION

The White House,
 Washington, D.C. 20500
Established: 1977
Director: Richard Harden
*Purpose:* To provide administrative services to
 the components of the Executive Office,
 including accounting and payroll, mail and
 messengers, library facilities, and computer
 facilities; to coordinate the zero-base budget-
 ing system.

### OFFICE OF MANAGEMENT AND BUDGET (OMB)

Executive Office Building,
 Washington, D.C. 20503
Established: 1970
Director: James T. McIntyre Jr.
*Duties:* To aid the President in the preparation
 and administration of the budget and make
 recommendations for the more efficient orga-
 nization of the federal government.

### OFFICE OF SCIENCE AND TECHNOLOGY POLICY

Executive Office Building,
 Washington, D.C. 20503
Established: May 11, 1976
Director: Frank Press
*Duties:* To advise the President on science,
 engineering, and technology; to evaluate the
 overall federal-government efforts in science
 and technology.

### OFFICE OF THE SPECIAL REPRESENTATIVE FOR TRADE NEGOTIATIONS

1800 G Street, N.W.,
 Washington, D.C. 20506
Established: 1963
Special Representative for Trade Negotiations:
 Reubin Askew
*Duties:* To facilitate implementation of the
 trade-agreements program; to assist and advise the President in coordinating international trade policy; and to administer the negotiation and implementation of international trade
 agreements.

### OFFICE OF THE VICE PRESIDENT

Executive Office Building,
 Washington, D.C. 20501
Chief of Staff: Richard Moe
*Executive Functions:* Participation in all cabinet
 meetings and meetings of the National Security Council; member of Board of Regents of
 the Smithsonian Institution; chairs executive
 committee that develops the President's long-
 term agenda.

# CABINET-LEVEL EXECUTIVE DEPARTMENTS

## AGRICULTURE, DEPARTMENT OF
14th Street and Independence Avenue, N.W.,
 Washington, D.C. 20250
Established: 1889 as an executive department
Secretary of Agriculture: Robert S. Bergland
Administrator, Farmers Home Administration:
 Gordon Cavanaugh
*Purpose:* To carry out agricultural research,
 education, conservation, marketing, regulatory
 work, agricultural adjustment, and rural de-
 velopment. It also collects and distributes
 agricultural information.

## COMMERCE, DEPARTMENT OF
14th Street and Constitution Avenue, N.W.,
 Washington, D.C. 20230
Established: 1913
Secretary: Philip M. Klutznick
Director of the Census: Vincent P. Barabba
Director, National Oceanic and Atmospheric
 Administration: Richard A. Frank
*Purpose:* To promote full development of the
 economic resources of the U.S. It conducts
 censuses; disseminates commercial statistics;
 compiles nautical and aeronautical charts;
 establishes weights, measures, and standards;
 issues patents and registers trademarks; pro-
 vides weather forecasting.

## DEFENSE, DEPARTMENT OF
The Pentagon,
 Washington, D.C. 20301
Established: 1949
Secretary: Harold Brown
Deputy Secretary: W. Graham Claytor Jr.
*Functions:* To defend the U.S. against all ene-
 mies; to ensure the security of the U.S. and
 areas vital to its interest.
Secretary of the Army: Clifford L. Alexander Jr.
Secretary of the Navy: Edward Hidalgo
Secretary of the Air Force: Hans M. Mark

## EDUCATION, DEPARTMENT OF
400 Maryland Ave., S.W.,
 Washington, D.C. 20202
Established: 1979
Secretary: Shirley M. Hufstedler
Undersecretary: Steven Alan Minter
*Purpose:* To administer and coordinate federal
 education programs.

## ENERGY, DEPARTMENT OF
1000 Independence Avenue, S.W.,
 Washington, D.C. 20585
Established: 1977
Secretary: Charles W. Duncan Jr.
*Purpose:* To carry out the national energy
 policy, including conservation, resource development and production, research, data management, and environmental protection and
 regulation related to energy.
Chairman, Federal Energy Regulatory Commission: Charles B. Curtis.

## HEALTH AND HUMAN SERVICES, DEPARTMENT OF
200 Independence Avenue, S.W.,
 Washington, D.C. 20201
Established: 1953 as Department of Health,
 Education, and Welfare; name changed 1979.
Secretary: Patricia Roberts Harris
Under Secretary: Nathan Stark
*Purpose:* To administer and coordinate federal
 activities in health and welfare.
Commissioner Food and Drug Administration:
 Dr. Jere Edwin Goyan
Commissioner of Aging: Robert Clyde Benedict
Surgeon General, Public Health Service: Dr.
 Julius B. Richmond
Director, National Institutes of Health: Dr.
 Donald S. Frederickson
Commissioner, Rehabilitation Services Adminis-
 tration: Robert R. Humphreys
Director, National Cancer Institute: Dr. Vincent
 T. DeVita Jr.
Commissioner of Social Security: William J.
 Driver

## HOUSING AND URBAN DEVELOPMENT, DEPARTMENT OF
451 7th Street, N.W.,
 Washington, D.C. 20410
Established: 1965
Secretary: Moon Landrieu
Under Secretary: Victor Marrero
*Purpose:* To administer housing and urban-
 development programs and offer technical aid
 to states, cities, and counties.

## INTERIOR, DEPARTMENT OF THE
18th and C Streets, N.W.,
 Washington, D.C. 20240
Established: 1849
Secretary: Cecil D. Andrus
Under Secretary: James A. Joseph
*Purpose:* To formulate and administer programs
 for the conservation and development of
 natural resources. It supervises the Bureau of
 Mines, Geological Survey, Bureau of Indian
 Affairs, Bureau of Land Management, Na-
 tional Park Service, Fish and Wildlife Service,
 and Water and Power Resources Service.

## JUSTICE, DEPARTMENT OF
Constitution Avenue and 10th Street, N.W.,
 Washington, D.C. 20530
Established: 1870
Attorney General: Benjamin R. Civiletti
Deputy Attorney General: Charles B. Renfrew
Director, Federal Bureau of Investigation: Wil-
 liam Webster
Solicitor General: Wade H. McCree
*Purpose:* To provide means for enforcing federal
 laws, to furnish legal counsel in federal cases,
 and to construe the laws under which other
 departments act.

## LABOR, DEPARTMENT OF

200 Constitution Avenue, N.W.,
Washington, D.C. 20210
Established: 1913
Secretary: F. Ray Marshall
Under Secretary: John Gentry
*Purpose:* To administer and enforce laws designed to advance the public interest by promoting the welfare of U.S. wage earners, improving their working conditions, and advancing their opportunities for profitable employment.

## STATE, DEPARTMENT OF

2201 C Street, N.W.,
Washington, D.C. 20520
Established: 1789
Secretary: Edmund S. Muskie
Deputy Secretary: Warren M. Christopher
Administrator, Agency for International Development (AID): Douglas J. Bennet Jr.
*Purpose:* The President, who has overall responsibility for U.S. foreign policy, looks to the Department of State for primary advice in formulating and executing that policy. The department's primary objective is to promote U.S. interest in international relations.

## TRANSPORTATION, DEPARTMENT OF

400 7th Street, S.W.,
Washington, D.C. 20590
Established: 1966
Secretary: Neil Goldschmidt

Deputy Secretary: William J. Beckham Jr.
Administrator, Federal Aviation Administration: Langhorne McCook Bond
Administrator, Federal Highway Administration: John S. Hassell Jr.
Administrator, Federal Railroad Administration: John M. Sullivan
Administrator, National Highway Safety Administration: Joan B. Claybrook
*Purpose:* To develop national policies to provide fast, safe, efficient, convenient, and economical transportation. It also directs the Federal Aviation Administration, St. Lawrence Seaway Development Corporation, and, in peacetime, the U.S. Coast Guard.

## TREASURY, DEPARTMENT OF THE

15th Street and Pennsylvania Avenue, N.W.,
Washington, D.C. 20220
Established: 1789
Secretary: G. William Miller
Deputy Secretary: Robert Carswell
Treasurer of the U.S.: Azie Taylor Morton
Comptroller of the Currency: John G. Heimann
Commissioner, Internal Revenue Service: Jerome Kurtz
*Purpose:* To manage national finances; provide coined and printed currency; maintain U.S. credit; represent the U.S. in international banking and monetary organizations; collect U.S. taxes through the Internal Revenue Service; and supervise the Secret Service.

# INDEPENDENT AGENCIES OF THE U.S. GOVERNMENT

## ACTION

806 Connecticut Avenue, N.W.,
Washington, D.C. 20525
Established: 1971
Director: Samuel W. Brown Jr.
Deputy Director: Mary King
*Activities:* Coordinates citizen volunteer action programs, including the Peace Corps, VISTA, foster grandparents, and retired volunteers.

## ARMS CONTROL AND DISARMAMENT AGENCY

Department of State Building,
Washington, D.C. 20451
Established: 1961
Director: Ralph Earl II
Deputy Director: Spurgeon M. Keeny Jr.
*Activities:* Participates in nuclear-test-ban and general disarmament negotiations at Geneva and in the United Nations; conducts research on arms control and disarmament.

## BOARD FOR INTERNATIONAL BROADCASTING

Department of State Building,
Washington, D.C. 20451
Established: 1973
Chairman: John A. Gronouski
*Activities:* To provide assistance to Radio Free Europe and Radio Liberty and to encourage a flow of information to people of the communist nations of Europe.

## CIVIL AERONAUTICS BOARD (CAB)

1825 Connecticut Avenue, N.W.,
Washington, D.C. 20428
Established: 1938

Membership: Five members
Chairman: Marvin Cohen
*Activities:* Regulates economic aspects of U.S. air-carrier operations, and of foreign common-carrier operations to and from the U.S.

## COMMISSION OF FINE ARTS

708 Jackson Place, N.W.,
Washington, D.C. 20006
Established: 1910
Membership: Seven expert fine-arts judges
Chairman: J. Carter Brown
*Activities:* Advises, assists on matters relating to art, monuments, and public works.

## COMMISSION ON CIVIL RIGHTS

1121 Vermont Avenue, N.W.,
Washington, D.C. 20425
Established: 1957
Chairman: Arthur S. Flemming
*Activities:* Investigates complaints of persons being deprived of their civil rights because of race, color, religion, sex, or national origin.

## COMMUNITY SERVICES ADMINISTRATION

1200 19th Street, N.W.,
Washington, D.C. 20506
Established: 1974 as successor to Office of Economic Opportunity
Director: Richard John Rios
*Activities:* Seeks to reduce poverty in the United States by helping low-income persons and families attain economic self-sufficiency. Agency guidelines fix the incomes that qualify persons for antipoverty programs.

**INDEPENDENT AGENCIES** *(continued)*

## CONSUMER PRODUCT SAFETY COMMISSION

1111 18th Street, N.W.,
Washington, D.C. 20207
Established: Oct. 27, 1972
Chairman: Susan B. King
Membership: Five members
*Activities:* Studies consumer-product safety; orders unsafe products taken off the market; establishes product-safety standards to reduce risks to consumers.

## ENVIRONMENTAL PROTECTION AGENCY (EPA)

401 M Street, S.W.,
Washington, D.C. 20460
Established: 1970
Administrator: Douglas M. Costle
Deputy Administrator: Barbara Blum
*Activities:* To assure the protection of the environment by monitoring, regulating, abating, and controlling pollution of the environment on a systematic basis.

## EQUAL EMPLOYMENT OPPORTUNITY COMMISSION (EEOC)

2401 E Street, N.W.,
Washington, D.C. 20506
Established: 1965
Membership: Five members, appointed to 5-year terms by the President
Chairperson: Eleanor Holmes Norton
*Activities:* Coordinates federal efforts to end discrimination in employment.

## EXPORT-IMPORT BANK OF THE U.S.

811 Vermont Avenue, N.W.,
Washington, D.C. 20571
Established: 1934
President: John Lovell Moore Jr.
*Activities:* Aids in financing and facilitating trade between the U.S. and foreign countries.

## FARM CREDIT ADMINISTRATION (FCA)

490 L'Enfant Plaza West, S.W.,
Washington, D.C. 20578
Established: 1916
Governor: Donald E. Wilkinson
*Activities:* Supervises and coordinates a cooperative credit system for agriculture, providing long-term and short-term credits to farmers and their cooperative organizations.

## FEDERAL COMMUNICATIONS COMMISSION (FCC)

1919 M Street, N.W.,
Washington, D.C. 20554
Established: 1934
Membership: Seven members, appointed to 7-year terms by the President.
Chairman: Charles D. Ferris
*Activities:* Regulates interstate and foreign commerce in communication by radio and wire to make available a rapid, efficient radio communication service at reasonable cost.

## FEDERAL DEPOSIT INSURANCE CORPORATION (FDIC)

550 17th Street, N.W.,
Washington, D.C. 20429
Established: 1933
Membership: The Board of Directors comprises three members. Two are appointed to 6-year terms by the President. The chairman is one of the presidential appointees. The Comptroller of the Currency serves ex-officio as the third member of the corporation.
Chairman: Irvine Sprague
*Activities:* Insures the deposits of all banks entitled to benefits of insurance under the law, paying depositors of insured banks that close without adequate funds to meet claims against them; acts as a receiver for national banks placed in receivership and, under certain conditions, for state banks placed in receivership.

## FEDERAL ELECTION COMMISSION

1325 K Street, N.W.,
Washington, D.C. 20005
Established: 1975
Chairman: Robert O. Tiernan
*Activities:* Enforces federal laws on election campaign financing.

## FEDERAL EMERGENCY MANAGEMENT AGENCY

1725 Eye St., N.W.
Washington, D.C. 20472
Established: 1979
Director: John W. Macy Jr.
*Purpose:* To oversee federal programs that assist areas and individuals affected by civil emergencies.

## FEDERAL HOME LOAN BANK BOARD

1700 G Street, N.W.,
Washington, D.C. 20552
Established: 1955
Chairman: Jay Janis
*Activities:* Provides credit reserve for savings and home-financing institutions; supervises the Federal Home Loan Bank System, the Federal Savings and Loan System, and the Federal Savings and Loan Insurance Corporation.

## FEDERAL MARITIME COMMISSION

1100 L Street, N.W.,
Washington, D.C. 20573
Established: 1961
Membership: Five members, appointed to 4-year terms by the President.
Chairman: Richard J. Daschback
*Activities:* Regulates rates, fares, charges, classifications, tariffs, regulations, and practices of common carriers engaged in maritime commerce within U.S. jurisdiction.

## FEDERAL MEDIATION AND CONCILIATION SERVICE

2100 K Street, N.W.,
Washington, D.C. 20427
Established: 1947
Director: Wayne L. Horvitz
*Activities:* Assists in the solution of labor disputes affecting interstate commerce by offering conciliation and mediation services to labor and industry.

## FEDERAL RESERVE SYSTEM

Board of Governors of the Federal Reserve System
20th Street and Constitution Avenue, N.W.,
Washington, D.C. 20551
Established: 1913
Membership: The Board of Governors of the Federal Reserve System has seven members appointed by the President.
Chairman: Paul A. Volcker
*Activities:* Provides for establishment of Federal

Reserve Banks to furnish an elastic currency, to afford means of rediscounting commercial paper, and to establish effective supervision of banking in the United States.

## FEDERAL SAVINGS AND LOAN INSURANCE CORPORATION (FSLIC)

1700 G Street, N.W.,
Washington, D.C. 20552
Established: 1934
Director: Samuel Ewing
*Activities:* Insures each depositor's account in approved savings and loan associations; to prevent default of an insured institution, the corporation can make loans or purchase assets of the institution; income is from premiums paid by the insured institutions.

## FEDERAL TRADE COMMISSION (FTC)

Pennsylvania Avenue at 6th Street, N.W.,
Washington, D.C. 20580
Established: 1915
Membership: Five members, appointed to 7-year terms by the President. Not more than three commissioners may be members of the same political party.
Chairman: Michael Pertschuk
*Activities:* Promotes fair and free competition in interstate commerce by prevention of price fixing, boycotts, combinations in restraint of trade, and other practices; safeguards consumers from unfair advertising and sales techniques.

## GENERAL SERVICES ADMINISTRATION (GSA)

18th and F Streets, N.W.,
Washington, D.C. 20405
Established: 1949
Administrator: Rear Adm. Rowland G. Freeman III
*Activities:* Manages government property and records, including the construction and operation of buildings, procurement and distribution of supplies, disposal of surplus property, management of traffic and communications, stockpiling of strategic and critical materials, and care of records.

## INTER-AMERICAN FOUNDATION

1515 Wilson Blvd.,
Rosslyn, Va. 22209
Established: Dec. 30, 1969
Chairman: Peter Jones
*Purpose:* Supports small-scale local social-development projects in Latin America.

## INTERNATIONAL COMMUNICATION AGENCY

1750 Pennsylvania Avenue, N.W.
Washington, D.C. 20547
Established: 1977
Director: John E. Reinhardt
Deputy Director: Charles W. Bray III
*Activities:* Consolidates activities of former U.S. Information Agency (USIA), including Voice of America broadcasts to other countries, and functions formerly exercised by the State Department's Bureau of Educational and Cultural Affairs, including international educational and cultural-exchange activities.

## INTERNATIONAL DEVELOPMENT COOPERATION AGENCY, U.S.

2201 C Street, N.W.,
Washington, D.C. 20520
Established: 1979
Director: Thomas Ehrlich
*Purpose:* To consolidate policy direction of developing agencies and control budgets of various international development agencies.

## INTERNATIONAL TRADE COMMISSION, U.S.

E and 8th Streets, N.W.,
Washington, D.C. 20436
Established: 1916
Chairman: William R. Alberger
*Activities:* Serves Congress and the President as an advisory, fact-finding agency on tariff, commercial policy, and foreign-trade matters.

## INTERSTATE COMMERCE COMMISSION (ICC)

12th Street and Constitution Avenue, N.W.,
Washington, D.C. 20423
Established: 1887
Membership: Eleven members
Chairman: Darius W. Gaskins Jr.
*Activities:* Regulates interstate commerce, and foreign import and export commerce to the extent that it takes place in the United States.

## NATIONAL AERONAUTICS AND SPACE ADMINISTRATION (NASA)

400 Maryland Avenue, S.W.,
Washington, D.C. 20546
Established: 1958
Administrator: Robert A. Frosch
*Activities:* Conducts research on flight within and outside the Earth's atmosphere; develops, constructs, tests, and operates aeronautical and space vehicles.

## NATIONAL CREDIT UNION ADMINISTRATION

2025 M Street, N.W.,
Washington, D.C. 20456
Established: March 10, 1970
Chairman: Lawrence Connell
*Activities:* Regulates credit unions.

## NATIONAL FOUNDATION ON THE ARTS AND HUMANITIES

806 15th Street, N.W.,
Washington, D.C. 20506
Established: 1965
Chairman, National Endowment for the Arts: Livingston L. Biddle Jr.
Chairman, National Endowment for the Humanities: Joseph D. Duffey
*Purpose:* To encourage and support national programs in the humanities and the arts. The Arts Endowment awards grants to groups (and some individuals) engaged in or concerned with the arts, awards grants-in-aid to assist state art agencies, and conducts special studies.

## NATIONAL LABOR RELATIONS BOARD (NLRB)

1717 Pennsylvania Avenue, N.W.,
Washington, D.C. 20570
Established: 1935
Membership: Five members, appointed to 4-year terms by the President
Chairman: John H. Fanning
*Activities:* Prevents, through a variety of powers, unfair labor practices.

**INDEPENDENT AGENCIES** *(continued)*

**NATIONAL MEDIATION BOARD**
1425 K Street, N.W.,
 Washington, D.C. 20572
Established: 1934
Chairman: Robert Harris
*Activities:* Mediates differences between the railroads and airlines on one hand and their employees on the other.

**NATIONAL SCIENCE FOUNDATION (NSF)**
1800 G Street, N.W.,
 Washington, D.C. 20550
Established: 1950
Director: John B. Slaughter
*Purpose:* Strengthens basic research and education in the sciences in the U.S.

**NATIONAL TRANSPORTATION SAFETY BOARD**
800 Independence Avenue, S.W.,
 Washington, D.C. 20594
Established: 1966
Chairman: James B. King
*Activities:* Investigates major accidents in civil aviation, railroads, highways, pipelines, and ships; reports the facts and circumstances of accidents; and makes recommendations for legislation to prevent accidents.

**NUCLEAR REGULATORY COMMISSION (NRC)**
1717 H Street, N.W.,
 Washington, D.C. 20555
Established: Oct. 11, 1974
Chairman: John F. Ahearne
Membership: Five members
*Responsibilities:* Took over duties of former Atomic Energy Commission (AEC) to regulate, license, and supervise the security and safety of peaceful uses of nuclear power.

**OFFICE OF PERSONNEL MANAGEMENT**
1900 E Street, N.W.,
 Washington, D.C. 20415
Established: 1979
Chairman: Alan K. Campbell
*Purpose:* Administration of a merit system for federal-government employees.

**OVERSEAS PRIVATE INVESTMENT CORPORATION**
1129 20th Street, N.W.,
 Washington, D.C. 20527
Established: 1971
President: Bruce Llewellyn
*Purpose:* To provide incentives (including insurance against loss by expropriation) for U.S. private investors in 90 developing nations.

**POSTAL RATE COMMISSION**
2000 L Street, N.W.,
 Washington, D.C. 20268
Established: Aug. 12, 1970
Chairman: A. Lee Fritschler
*Activities:* Holds hearings and submits recommendations to the Postal Service on postage rates, fees, and mail classifications.

**POSTAL SERVICE, UNITED STATES**
475 L'Enfant Plaza, S.W.,
 Washington, D.C. 20260
Established: 1970 (The U.S. Postal Service, which began operations July 1, 1971, replaced the cabinet-level Post Office Department established by Congress in 1872. The first Postal Service was created in 1775.)

Postmaster General: William F. Bolger
*Activities:* To provide postal services.

**RAILROAD RETIREMENT BOARD**
884 Rush Street
 Chicago, Ill. 60611
Established: 1935
Chairman: William P. Adams
*Purpose:* Administers payment of retirement and disability annuities to railroad employees and their families.

**SECURITIES AND EXCHANGE COMMISSION (SEC)**
500 N. Capitol Street, N.W.,
 Washington, D.C. 20549
Established: 1934
Membership: Five members, appointed by the President to 5-year terms. Only three may be members of the same political party.
Chairman: Harold M. Williams
*Activities:* Protects the interests of the public and investors against malpractices in securities and financial markets.

**SMALL BUSINESS ADMINISTRATION (SBA)**
1441 L Street, N.W.,
 Washington, D.C. 20416
Established: 1953
Administrator: A. Vernon Weaver Jr.
*Activities:* Aids, counsels, and protects the interests of small business; ensures that small business concerns receive a fair proportion of government purchases and contracts, and of the sales of government property; makes loans to small business concerns, state and local development companies, and the victims of floods and disasters.

**SMITHSONIAN INSTITUTION**
1000 Jefferson Drive, S.W.,
 Washington, D.C. 20560
Established: 1846
Secretary of the Institution: S. Dillon Ripley
*Activities:* Performs fundamental research; maintains library, theater, and museum facilities; engages in programs of national and international cooperative research.

**TENNESSEE VALLEY AUTHORITY (TVA)**
New Sprankle Building,
 Knoxville, Tenn. 37902
Woodward Building, 15th and H Streets, N.W.,
 Washington, D.C. 20444
Established: 1933
Membership: Three-member Board of Directors appointed by the President.
Chairman: S. David Freeman
*Activities:* Develops the Tennessee River system through construction of a series of dams; conducts forestry programs; assists in flood control; and is an important supplier of electricity to the surrounding region.

**VETERANS ADMINISTRATION (VA)**
Vermont Avenue and H Street, N.W.,
 Washington, D.C. 20420
Established: 1930
Administrator of Veterans Affairs: Joseph Maxwell Cleland
*Activities:* Administers benefits for former members of the armed forces, their eligible dependents and beneficiaries.

# Women's Rights

Wide World

A crowd estimated at 25,000 marches near lakefront in Chicago on May 10 in support of the Equal Rights Amendment. But ERA supporters were unsuccessful in persuading Illinois legislators to vote for ratification.

## HIGHLIGHTS: 1980

The second world conference of the United Nations Decade for Women opened in Copenhagen, Denmark, on July 14 with approximately 1,000 delegates from more than 100 countries in attendance. The intent of the conference was to assess the progress of women's rights midway through the United Nations Decade for Women, which was launched at a world conference in Mexico City in 1975. UN Secretary-General Kurt Waldheim opened the Copenhagen conclave with a plea to change stereotyped attitudes toward women.

Lucille Mair of Jamaica, secretary-general of the conference, suggested in her opening remarks that the status of women had deteriorated since the 1975 meeting.

Although the conference began with high hopes of developing a plan of action to improve the lot of women worldwide, political dissension destroyed the feeling of cooperation. The meeting ended, on July 31, in bitterness and discord.

A plan of action was adopted in the waning hours of the conference, but was rejected by the United States, Israel, Canada, and Australia because of provisions equating Zi-

onism with racism, and a suggestion that UN funds for Palestinian women refugees be channeled through the Palestine Liberation Organization (PLO). The final vote was 94–4, with 22 nations abstaining.

The five-year plan of action called for flexible time schedules for work and study, educational programs, allowances for poor families, mobile schools, and improved job possibilities for women everywhere.

### WOMEN AND THE ELECTIONS

The 1980 congressional elections saw notable gains for women. The number of women in the 97th Congress will be equal to the highest number ever counted in the House and the Senate.

Nineteen women will be members of the House, three more than in the 96th Congress. Fifteen of the sixteen in the 96th were reelected. The sixteenth, Rep. Elizabeth Holtzman (D-N.Y.), waged an unsuccessful battle for a seat in the Senate. The four new women in the House are all Republicans: Claudine Schneider of Rhode Island, Marge Roukema of New Jersey, Lynn Martin of Illinois, and Bobbi Fiedler of California.

**HIGHLIGHTS: 1980** *(continued)*

Republican Paula Hawkins of Florida will join incumbent Sen. Nancy Landon Kassebaum (R-Kan.) on the Senate floor. No more than two women senators have ever served at any one time in history.

## WOMEN IN THE MILITARY

More than 150,000 women were serving in the armed forces in 1980, according to the Defense Department. Of that total about 132,000 were enlisted personnel and 19,000 officers.

In May, the first women graduates of the service academies received their diplomas. The U.S. Military Academy at West Point, N.Y., boasted 62 female graduates, while the U.S. Naval Academy graduated 55 women at Annapolis, Md. Ninety-eight women received their commissions at the Air Force Academy in Colorado Springs, Colo. The Coast Guard Academy in New London, Conn., graduated its first 14 women. The 229 women represented 8% of the 1980 graduates of the service academies.

Although officially barred from combat posts, most of the female graduates looked forward to serving in the various combat-support fields offered to them.

An estimated one-third to one-half of the female graduates planned to be married soon after graduation, and were looking forward to serving with their husbands.

Women in all branches of the military claimed that they experienced sexual harassment and bias, and so testified before the House Armed Services Military Personnel Subcommittee in February.

Capt. Kathleen Wilder claimed sexism denied her the opportunity to become the first woman Green Beret. After completing the 13-week course at Ft. Bragg, N.C., she failed the field exercise portion of the training program and was not allowed to graduate with her class in August. After Capt. Wilder protested, officials said she would be allowed to take the field exercise test again.

## WOMEN IN THE COURTS

A number of sex-discrimination suits were settled during 1980, the largest involving the federal government.

In May, a federal district judge in Washington awarded an estimated $16 million to 324 women bindery workers at the Government Printing Office. The judge found that 28 women in the bindery division made less money than male employees performing equal work, and 296 other women were denied access to higher-paying jobs because these were open only to males. The group of 28 women was awarded the difference between their salaries and the salaries of male bookbinders since 1971, about $3 million.

Sister Carolyn Farrell stands on balcony overlooking Dubuque, Iowa, of which she was elected mayor in 1980. She is believed to be the first Roman Catholic nun to be elected mayor of an American city.

United Press Int'l.

Construction worker Diane Williams, 27, of Brooklyn, N.Y., helping build New York City's Harley Hotel on East 42nd Street, competes successfully for a hardhat job previously limited exclusively to men.

The other 296 women would share $3 million in back pay for being denied better opportunities. Future additional compensation to the women, to be paid until women fill 50% of the bookbinder positions, could amount to as much as $10 million.

Jean Spencer, 57, was awarded $273,387 by the New York Commission on Human Rights for a 6-year-old bias case against Burlington Industries. She claimed that when her job was eliminated in 1974, she was unable to obtain another high-level executive job with the company, although 13 such jobs were filled by men during her job search.

### NEWSWORTHY WOMEN

**Sherry Lansing,** 35, was named president of 20th Century-Fox Productions in January, making her the first woman to head production at a major film studio. The former model was senior production executive on *The China Syndrome* and *Kramer vs. Kramer* for Columbia Pictures.

**Joyce Miller,** 52, became the first woman to serve on the Executive Council of the American Federation of Labor and Congress of Industrial Organizations (AFL-CIO). Previously she was the president of the Coalition of Labor Union Women.

**Marguerite Yourcenar,** 76, a naturalized American novelist, poet, and playwright, was elected in March to the presitigious French Academy, the first woman so honored since its founding in 1635. . . . In January, **Yvonne Choquet-Bruhat** was admitted as a full member of the Academy of Science in Paris, France, the first woman admitted since its creation in 1666.

**Mother Theresa,** winner of the 1979 Nobel Peace Prize, received India's highest civilian award, the Star of India, in March. At the ceremony she announced she would not attend any more functions honoring her, because they took up too much time needed for helping the poor. . . .The headquarters building of the U.S. Department of Labor was dedicated to the late **Frances Perkins,** the first woman U.S. cabinet officer, on the 100th anniversary of her birth. Ms. Perkins was Secretary of Labor in 1933–45.

Former cellist **Marta Istomin** was named artistic director of the Kennedy Center in Washington, D.C. . . . **Shawn Nichols Weatherly,** 21, was crowned Miss Universe in July.

A donation of $500,000 to the National Organization for Women (NOW) Legal Defense and Education Fund was announced by Norman Lear, on behalf of Tandem Productions, which produces the *All in the Family* TV show, now called *Archie Bunker's Place.* The money was to be used to establish an Edith Bunker Memorial Fund, dedicated to causes relating to women's rights, in honor of the role created by actress **Jean Stapleton** on the popular situation comedy series. The character of Edith was written out of the series in 1980 because Miss Stapleton wanted to pursue other acting opportunities.

# IMPORTANT DATES IN THE HISTORY OF AMERICAN WOMEN

**1773** First play by American woman playwright: *The Adulateur,* a satire by Mercy Otis Warren (1728–1814).

**1774–83** First American woman secret agent abroad: Patience Lovell Wright (1725–26), who sent back secret reports while doing wax sculptures of George III and others in London.

**1779** First woman to fight as a uniformed U.S. soldier (disguised as a man): Deborah Sampson (1760–1827), who was wounded twice.

**1790** Publication of first popular novel by an American woman: *Charlotte Temple* by Susanna Haswell Rowson (c.1762–1824).

**1800** Women first vote in local election in Elizabethtown, N.J.

**1821** First college-level school for women: the Troy (N.Y.) Female Seminary, founded by Emma Willard (1787–1870).

**1824** First strike by women workers at Pawtucket, R.I., weaving mill.

**1830** First major women's magazine: *Lady's Book* (later *Godey's Lady's Book*).

**1835** Oberlin College in Ohio admits women, becoming first coeducational college; awards first degrees to women in 1841.

**1836** First American stage actress to become a star: Charlotte Cushman (1816–76) debuts in New York City as Lady Macbeth.

**1836–37** First permanent women's colleges founded: Georgia Female College at Macon, Ga. (later Wesleyan College) and Mt. Holyoke Female Seminary at South Hadley, Mass. (later Mt. Holyoke College).

**1847** First American woman astronomer discovers a comet: Maria Mitchell (1818–89).

**1848** Married women given right to own real estate in own name by New York legislature.

**1848** (July 19–20) First women's rights convention held in Seneca Falls, N.Y.; planned by Elizabeth Cady Stanton (1815–1902) and Lucretia C. Mott (1793–1880).

**1849** First woman doctor granted M.D. degree by medical school at Geneva N.Y.: Elizabeth Blackwell (1821–1910).

**1850** Founding of first school of medicine for women: Women's College of Pennsylvania.

**1852** Publication of first bestselling reform novel by a woman: *Uncle Tom's Cabin* by Harriet Beecher Stowe (1811–96).

**1861** First superintendent of women nurses appointed for Union forces in Civil War: Dorothea Lynde Dix (1802–87).

**1862** An 8-hour-day law for women and children workers enacted by Wisconsin legislature.

**1869** First law giving women right to vote and hold office by Wyoming territorial legislature.

**1869** National American Woman Suffrage Association founded; Susan B. Anthony (1820–1906) served as president from 1892 to 1900.

**1870** (Aug. 1) Women vote in territorial election for first time in Utah.

**1874** National Woman's Christian Temperance Union (WCTU) founded in Cleveland, Ohio.

**1881** American Red Cross organized by Clara Barton (1821–1912).

**1883** First international organization for women, World's Woman's Christian Temperance Union, founded by Frances E. Willard (1839–98).

**1887** First woman mayor elected: Susanna Madora Salter (1860–1961) in Argonia, Kan.

**1889** Woman reporter sets record for trip around the world in 72 days, 6 hours, and 11 minutes: Nellie Bly (1867?–1922).

**1890** Wyoming provides equal voting rights for women in its constitution.

**1895** First American woman interpretive dancer debuts in New York City: Isadora Duncan (1878–1927).

**1910** Congress passes Mann Act: forbids interstate transport of women for immoral purposes.

**1912** First minimum-wage act for women and children enacted in Massachusetts.

**1913** First woman movie star: Pearl White (1889–1938) in the serial *Perils of Pauline.*

**1916** First woman elected to Congress: Jeannette Rankin (1880–1973), U.S. representative from Montana; the only member of Congress to vote against U.S. declarations of war both in World War I and World War II.

**1918** Woman-in-Industry Service established in U.S. Department of Labor as first agency for women; became Women's Bureau in 1920.

**1920** (Aug. 26) Women win right to vote in national elections for first time with proclamation of Amendment 19 to the United States Constitution.

**1922** First woman appointed U.S. senator: Rebecca Latimer Felton (1835–1930; D-Ga.) attended sessions on only two days.

**1924** First woman elected state governor in Wyoming: Nellie Tayloe Ross (1876–1977).

**1931** First American woman to win the Nobel Peace Prize: Jane Addams (1860–1935).

**1932** First woman pilot to solo across the Atlantic Ocean from Newfoundland to Ireland: Amelia Earhart (1897–1937).

**1932** (Jan. 12) First woman elected to U.S. Senate: Hattie Wyatt Caraway (1878–1950) was reelected to full 6-year terms in 1932 and 1938.

**1933** First woman appointed as member of presidential cabinet: Frances Perkins (1882–1965), secretary of labor under President Franklin D. Roosevelt in 1933–45.

**1938** First American woman to win the Nobel Prize for Literature: Pearl S. Buck (1892–1973).

**1955** First American black woman opera star debuts at New York City's Metropolitan Opera: Marian Anderson (born 1902).

**1964** Job discrimination against women forbidden by U.S. Civil Rights Act.

**1966** National Organization for Women (NOW) founded by Betty Friedan as leading organization in women's liberation movement.

**1972** Equal rights for women amendment to U.S. Constitution approved by Congress and sent to states for ratification.

**1973** (Jan. 22) Supreme Court orders repeal of abortion laws in 46 states; rules that women must be allowed to receive abortions on demand during first 6 months of pregnancy.

**1974** (June 3) Supreme Court rules for first time that employers must pay women equal wages for doing the same work as men.

**1978** (Nov. 1) First women report for sea duty aboard U.S. Navy noncombat ships.

**1980** (May) U.S. military service academies graduate women officers for first time.

# Deaths: 1980

Persons who died from Jan. 1 through Dec. 31, 1980, are listed below and on the following pages. Some gained such fame that their names are instantly recognizable. Others are included because of noteworthy activities or achievements in their lifetimes, even though their names are less well known.

**Theodore F. Adams,** 81, president of Baptist World Alliance in 1955–60: in Richmond, Va., on Feb. 27.

**Joy Adamson,** 69, naturalist, wildlife lover who wrote *Born Free* in 1960 about lioness she raised: murdered in her remote northern Kenya camp on Jan. 3.

**Charles Adler Jr.,** 81, inventor granted more than 60 patents for safety devices for trains, planes, and autos: in Baltimore, Md., on Oct. 23.

**Herbert Agar,** 83, writer, editor, winner of 1933 Pulitzer Prize for History: in Sussex, England, on Nov. 24.

**Yigal Allon,** 61, held several Israeli cabinet posts; hero of 1967 Arab-Israeli war: in Tel Aviv, on Feb. 29.

**Mary O'Hara Alsop,** 95, author of *My Friend Flicka:* in Chevy Chase, Md., on Oct. 15.

**Louis Alter,** 78, pianist who composed *Dolores* and *Manhattan Serenade:* in New York City on Nov. 3.

**Andrei Amalrik,** 42, prominent Soviet exile: killed in auto crash near Guadalajara, Spain, on Nov. 11.

**Adalino Amaro da Costa,** 37, defense minister of Portugal: in plane crash in Lisbon, Portugal, on Dec. 4.

**Hamilton S. Amerasinghe,** 67, UN Ambassador from Sri Lanka: in New York City on Dec. 4.

**Jay Anson,** 58, author of *The Amityville Horror:* in Palo Alto, Calif., on March 12.

**Hector Arce,** 44, author, biographer of Hollywood stars: in North Hollywood, Calif., on April 10.

**Horace Armistead,** 82, designer of scenery and costumes for ballet, opera, and theater: in South Miami, Fla., on March 21.

**Elliott Arnold,** 67, author of more than 25 books including *Blood Brother* which later became film *Broken Arrow:* in New York City on May 13.

**Boris Aronson,** 81, stage designer who won six Tony awards: in Nyack, N.Y., on Nov. 16.

**Pierre Arpels,** 61, chief designer for Van Cleef & Arpels jewelers: in Paris, France, on May 26.

**Emmett Ashford,** 66, first black umpire in major league baseball in 1966: in Los Angeles, Calif., on March 1.

**Fred Avery,** 72, cartoon animator; created "Daffy Duck," "Droopy the Dog," and "What's up doc?" salutation: in Burbank, Calif., on Sept. 1.

**Jack Bailey,** 72, actor, radio and TV announcer: in Santa Monica, Calif., on Feb. 1.

**Kenneth Banghart,** 70, former radio and television news broadcaster: in Delray Beach, Fla., on May 26.

**Donald (Red) Barry,** 69, film actor who played Red Ryder in 1940s: suicide in Hollywood, on July 17.

**Roland Barthes,** 64, French writer and literary critic: in Paris, France, on March 25.

**L. C. Bates,** 79, civil-rights activist; key black leader in 1957 desegregation of Central High School in Little Rock, Ark.; publisher of *The Arkansas State Press:* in Little Rock, Ark., on Aug. 22.

**Richard Reeve Baxter,** 59, U.S. judge at International Court of Justice at The Hague since 1979: in Boston, Mass., on Sept. 26.

**Cecil Beaton,** 76, photographer to Britain's royal family, costume designer for such films as *My Fair Lady,* and author: in London, England, on Jan. 18.

**Page Belcher,** 81, U.S. representative (R-Okla.) in 1951–72: in Midwest City, Okla., on Aug. 2.

**Barney Bigard,** 74, jazz clarinetist: in Culver City, Calif., on June 27.

**Salah al-Din Bitar,** 68, prime minister of Syria in 1963–66: assassinated in Paris, France, on July 21.

**John Bonham,** 32, drummer for rock group Led Zeppelin: in Windsor, England, on Sept. 25.

**Giorgio Borg Olivier,** 69, prime minister of Malta for 13 years between 1950 and 1971: in Sliema, Malta, on Oct. 29.

**Prince Boun Oum na Champassak,** 68, prime minister of Laos in 1949–50 and 1960–62: in Paris, France, on March 17.

**Julian Parks Boyd,** 76, historian; editor of *The Papers of Thomas Jefferson:* in Princeton, N.J., on May 28.

**Robert Brackman,** 81, portrait painter of famous people: in New London, Conn., on July 16.

**Millen Brand,** 74, writer, editor, coauthor of *The Snake Pit* movie: in New York City on March 19.

**Alexander Breslow,** 52, pathologist; developed test to diagnose type of skin cancer called melanoma: in Washington, D.C., on July 20.

**Barbara Britton,** 59, film and television actress: in New York City on Jan. 17.

**Alexander Brook,** 81, painter known for landscapes and still-lifes: in Sag Harbor, N.Y., on Feb. 26.

**Manlio Brosio,** 83, secretary-general of NATO in 1964–71: in Turin, Italy, on March 14.

**Rachel F. Brown,** 81, chemist who, in 1950, discovered first antifungal antibiotic for humans (nystatin): in Albany, N.Y., on Jan. 14.

**Edward Bullard,** 72, geophysicist who helped pioneer theory that continents were once joined as a single super-continent: in La Jolla, Calif., on April 3.

**David Burpee,** 87, head of world's largest mail-order seed company; developed hundreds of varieties of flowers and vegetables: in Doylestown, Pa., on June 24.

**Henry Byrd,** 61, New Orleans singer and pianist known as Professor Longhair: in New Orleans, La., on Jan. 30.

**Marcello Caetano,** 74, prime minister of Portugal in 1968–74: in Rio de Janeiro, Brazil, on Oct. 26.

**Tommy Caldwell,** 30, guitarist with Marshall Tucker Band: in Spartanburg, S.C., on April 28.

**Priscilla Lyon Call,** 52, child star of movie series *The Little Rascals:* in Winston-Salem, N.C., on March 7.

**Hector Campora,** 71, president of Argentina in 1973: in Mexico City on Dec. 19.

**Joseph E. Casey,** 81, U.S. representative (D-Mass.) in 1934–42: in Washington, D.C., on Sept. 2.

**Gower Champion,** 59, musical director and choreographer, former dance partner of ex-wife Marge Champion: just six hours before opening of his latest Broadway show *42d Street* in New York City, on Aug. 25.

**John Chapman,** 51, harness-racing driver who won more than 3,900 races: in Westbury, N.Y., on May 2.

**Olga Chekhova,** 83, Russian-born film actress: near Munich, West Germany, on March 29.

**Sheldon Warren Cheney,** 94, author, art historian, theater critic: in Berkeley, Calif., on Oct. 10.

**Clarence (Shorty) Cherock,** 64, jazz trumpeter: in Los Angeles, Calif., on Feb. 26.

**Vulko Chervenkov,** 80, former head of Bulgarian Communist Party who was expelled from party in 1962 for being a Stalinist: in Sofia, Bulgaria, on Oct. 21.

**Harold Clurman,** 78, theater director, critic, author: in New York City on Sept. 9.

## 982   DEATHS

**DEATHS: 1980** *(continued)*

**Jacqueline Cochran,** 70, pilot, first woman, in 1953, to break the sound barrier; set more than 200 aviation records: in Indio, Calif., on Aug. 9.

**Miles Lanier Colean,** 82, economist credited with coining phrase "urban renewal" in 1953: in Washington, D.C., on Sept. 16.

**John Collier,** 78, author known for short stories; wrote film scripts for *The African Queen* and *Paradise Lost:* in Pacific Palisades, Calif., on April 6.

**William Colmer,** 90, U.S. representative (D-Miss.) in 1934–73: in Pascagoula, Miss., on Sept. 9.

**Marc Connelly,** 90, American playwright; *The Green Pastures* won 1930 Pulitzer Prize: in New York City on Dec. 21.

**John Culshaw,** 55, record producer responsible for first stereo version of Wagner's "Ring" operas in 1958: in London, England, on April 27.

**John Davis,** 92, director of NAACP legal defense and educational fund: in Englewood, N.J., on July 12.

**Dorothy Day,** 83, founder of Catholic Worker Movement: in New York City on Nov. 29.

**Hugh DeHaven,** 85, headed Cornell University Automobile Crash Injury Institute in 1942–54: in Lyme, Conn., on Feb. 13.

**Tamara de Lempicka,** age unknown, portraitist in 1920s and 1930s: in Cuernavaca, Mexico, on March 18.

**Alberto Demichelli,** 84, president of Uruguay in 1976: in Montevideo, Uruguay, on Oct. 12.

**Vinicius De Moraes,** 66, Brazilian composer; coauthor of *The Girl from Ipanema:* in Rio de Janeiro, Brazil, on July 9.

**Robert Lee Dennison,** 78, commander in chief of Atlantic fleet in 1960–63: in Bethesda, Md., on March 14.

**Cleveland Denny,** 24, Canadian boxer; as result of June 20 knockout, in Montreal, Canada, on July 7.

**Patrick Depailler,** 35, French auto-racing driver: crashed during training for German Grand Prix in Heidelberg, West Germany, on Aug. 1.

**Adolph Deutsch,** 82, film-score composer of *Annie Get Your Gun, Seven Brides for Seven Brothers:* in Palm Desert, Calif., on Jan. 1.

**Raymond H. Dietrich,** 86, automotive designer of luxury cars in 1920s: in Albuquerque, N.M., on March 19.

**Harold W. Dodds,** 91, president of Princeton University in 1933–57: in Hightstown, N.J., on Oct. 25.

**Karl Doenitz,** 89, commander in chief of German fleet during World War II and successor of Adolf Hitler in 1945; signed surrender to Allies and served 10 years in prison as war criminal: in Hamburg, West Germany, on Dec. 24.

**Forrest C. Donnell,** 95, governor of Missouri in 1940–45; U.S. senator (R-Mo.) in 1945–51: in St. Louis, Mo., on March 3.

**Arthur Donovan,** 89, boxing referee who worked 14 heavyweight title fights: in New York City on Sept. 1.

**Helen Gahagan Douglas,** 79, actress and former U.S. representative (D-Calif.) in 1945-51: in New York City on June 28.

**William O. Douglas,** 81, Supreme Court justice in 1939–75; 36½-year term was longest in Court's history; known for vigorous defense of right to dissent: in Washington, D.C. on Jan. 19.

**Jessica Dragonette,** 75, soprano who brought operetta and semiclassical music to radio in 1920s to 1940s: in New York City on March 18.

**Richard Drew,** 81, inventor of Scotch tape in 1930: in Santa Barbara, Calif., on Dec. 14.

**Anna Duncan,** 85, dancer; adopted daughter and pupil of Isadora Duncan: in New York City on March 7.

**Jimmy Durante,** 86, beloved American comedian known for raspy voice and big nose, and song "Inka, dinka, doo": in Santa Monica, Calif., on Jan 29.

**Roger Duvoisin,** 79, children's book author and illustrator: in Morristown, N.J., on June 30.

**Alexander F. Edouart,** 85, cinematographer responsible for parting of Red Sea in movie *The Ten Commandments:* in Kenwood, Calif., on March 17.

**Ray Eliot,** 74, University of Illinois football coach in 1942–60: in Urbana, Ill., on Feb. 24.

**Grayson M. Enlow,** 63, stage actor, radio announcer known as voice of *The Shadow* on radio in 1940s and 1950s: in Mission, Kan., on May 18.

**Milton H. Erickson,** 79, psychiatrist; authority on hypnosis: in Phoenix, Ariz., on March 25.

**Nihat Erim,** 68, prime minister of Turkey in 1971–72: assassinated in Kartal, Turkey, on July 19.

**George Hyde Fallon,** 77, U.S. representative (D-Md.) in 1944–70: in Baltimore, Md., on March 21.

**Peter Farb,** 50, anthropologist, linguist, naturalist: in Boston, Mass., on April 8.

**Royes Fernandez,** 50, former dancer with American Ballet Theater: in New York City on March 3.

**Thomas K. Finletter,** 86, secretary of Air Force in 1950–53: in New York City on April 24.

**Anne Fogerty,** 60, fashion designer popular in 1950s: in New York City on Jan. 15.

**Jacobus J. Fouché,** 82, president of South Africa in 1968–75: in Cape Town, South Africa, on Sept. 24.

**Virgil Fox,** 68, established modern organ as concert instrument: in West Palm Beach, Fla., on Oct. 25.

**Otto Frank,** 91, father of Anne Frank, whose teenage diary described hiding from Nazis in Amsterdam during World War II: in Basel, Switzerland, on Aug. 19.

**Elizabeth Smith Friedman,** 88, cryptographer who broke enemy codes during World Wars I and II: in Plainfield, N.J., on Oct. 31.

**Jane Froman,** 72, film actress, big-band singer in 1930s and 1940s; in Columbia, Mo., on Apr. 23.

**Erich Fromm,** 79, psychoanalyst, social philosopher, author of *The Art of Loving* (1956): in Muralto, Switzerland, on March 18.

**Julian Funt,** 73, writer of plays and TV serials: in New York City on April 8.

**Robert Fuoss,** 67, editor-in-chief of *The Saturday Evening Post* in 1961–62: in Natick, Mass., on Jan. 27.

**Victor Galindez,** 31, World Boxing Association light-heavyweight champion in 1974–79: in traffic accident in 25 de Mayo, Argentina, on Oct. 26.

**Sanjay Gandhi,** 33, son of Indian prime minister Indira Gandhi and her political heir: in crash of private plane he was piloting near New Delhi, India, on June 23.

**W. Horsley Gantt,** 87, behavioral psychiatrist; promoted work of Pavlov in Western world: in Baltimore, Md., on Feb. 26.

**Ray Garrett Jr.,** 59, chairman of SEC in 1973–75: in Evanston, Ill., on Feb. 3.

**Romain Gary,** 66, French novelist, former diplomat: apparent suicide in Paris, France, on Dec. 2.

**Emile Gauguin,** 80, film director, son of French painter Paul Gauguin: in Panaauia, Tahiti, on Jan. 6.

**Reginald Gardiner,** 77, British-born comedian, character actor: in Westwood, Calif., on July 7.

**Erno Gero,** 82, Hungary's last Stalinist leader before 1956 rebellion: in Budapest, Hungary, on March 12.

**William Gifford,** 60, engineer, expert on low-temperature refrigerators: in Syracuse, N.Y., on March 9.

**V. V. Giri,** 85, president of India in 1969–74: in Madras, India, on June 24.

**Sheldon Glueck,** 83, pioneer criminologist; developed "prediction tables" for detecting potential delinquents as young as age 6: in Cambridge, Mass., on March 10.

**Richard Goldman,** 69, composer, conductor of Goldman Band in 1956–79: in Baltimore, Md., on Jan. 19.

**Babs Gonzales,** 63, jazz singer in 1940s and 1950s: in Newark, N.J., on Jan. 23.

**Michael Gottlieb**, 79, world-renowned contract bridge player: in Burlingame, Calif., on April 8.

**Wanda Grabinska**, 78, first woman judge in Poland in 1929–39, represented Poland at League of Nations: in Albion, N.Y., on June 15.

**Charles N. Granville**, 74, perfume manufacturer notorious for pranks: in Baltimore, Md., on April 28.

**John H. Griffin**, 60, author of *Black Like Me:* in Fort Worth, Tex., on Sept. 9.

**Hugh Griffith**, 67, Welsh character actor, won Academy Award in 1959 as best supporting acting for *Ben-Hur:* in London, England, on May 14.

**David Grubb**, 61, author, known for *The Night of the Hunter:* in New York City on July 24.

**Victor Gruen**, 76, architect; designed suburban shopping malls in 1950s: in Vienna, Austria, on Feb. 14.

**Levi Grunwald**, 87, Hasidic rabbi credited with pushing for establishment of kosher-processing laws in U.S.: in New York City on April 12.

**Robert Gunning**, 71, writing consultant who created *fog index* and *readability yardstick* to test clear writing: in Columbus, Ohio, on Feb. 29.

**Philip Guston**, 66, abstract expressionist painter: in Woodstock, N.Y., on June 7.

**Gus Haenschen**, 90, orchestra conductor for early radio shows in 1920s to 1940s: in Stamford, Conn., on March 27.

**Helen Hagnes**, 30, violinist: murdered after disappearing during intermission at Metropolitan Opera House in New York City on July 24.

**Michael J. Halberstam**, 48, physician, journalist, author of *The Wanting of Levine:* fatally shot by burglar at home in Washington, D.C., on Dec. 5.

**Roy J. Harris**, 77, former reporter for *St. Louis Post-Dispatch* who shared 1949 Pulitzer Prize for public service: in Los Angeles, Calif., on Feb. 20.

**Sam Harris**, 68, prosecutor at Nuremberg war crimes trials; one of original directors of Communications Satellites Corporation (Comsat): in New York City on Nov. 13.

**Mohammed Hatta**, 78, vice president of Indonesia in 1945–56, prime minister and foreign minister in 1948–50: in Jakarta, Indonesia, on March 14.

**Peter Haughton**, 25, harness-racing driver and son of harness driver Billy Haughton: in auto accident near East Rutherford, N.J., on Jan. 25.

**Robert E. Hayden**, 66, poet whose work was based on Afro-American themes; appointed consultant in poetry to Library of Congress in 1976: in Ann Arbor, Mich., on Feb. 25.

**Dick Haymes**, 61, singer with big bands of 1940s: in Los Angeles, Calif., on March 28.

**Hoffman R. Hays**, 76, poet, novelist, playwright, literary critic: in Southampton, N.Y., on Oct. 17.

**Giles G. Healey**, 78, American archaeologist who discovered 1,000-year-old Mayan temples in Central America in 1940s: in Sussex, England, on Feb. 29.

**George W. Healy Jr.**, 75, editor of *New Orleans Times-Picayune* in 1952–72: in New Orleans, La., on Nov. 1.

**Ray Heindorf**, 71, Hollywood film-score composer known for *This Is the Army, The Music Man,* and *Yankee Doodle Dandy:* in Los Angeles, Calif., on Feb. 2.

**Ehrhardt Henry (Ott) Heller**, 70, National Hockey League defenseman with New York Rangers in 1931–33: in Ontario, Canada, on June 16.

**Alfred Hitchcock**, 80, film director known for suspense movies such as *Rebecca, Lifeboat, Spellbound, Rear Window,* and *Psycho:* in Los Angeles, Calif., on April 29.

**Charles B. Hoeven**, 85, U.S. representative (R-Iowa) in 1943–65: in Orange City, Iowa, on Nov. 9.

**Allen Hoskins**, 59, film actor who played Farina in *Our Gang* and *Little Rascals* films in 1920s and 1930s: in Oakland, Calif., on July 26.

**Elston Howard**, 51, catcher for New York Yankees in 1955–67 and Boston Red Sox in 1967–68; American League's Most Valuable Player in 1963: in New York City on Dec. 14.

**José Iturbi**, 84, Spanish-born pianist, conductor, movie actor: in Hollywood, Calif., on June 28.

**Eddie Jackson**, 84, partner of late comedian Jimmy Durante: in Los Angeles, Calif., on July 16.

**Leon Janney**, 63, radio, television, and film actor: in Guadalajara, Mexico, on Oct. 28.

**David Janssen**, 49, TV and movie actor, star of TV series *The Fugitive:* in Malibu, Calif., on Feb. 13.

**Gerald W. Johnson**, 89, author, historian who specialized in Americana: in Baltimore, Md., on March 22.

**Edward Jones**, 71, architect who helped with restoration of White House: in Albany, Ga., on Oct. 1.

**Howard Mumford Jones**, 88, historian of American culture; won 1965 Pulitzer Prize for general nonfiction for *O Strange New World:* in Cambridge, Mass., on May 11.

**Ralph (Shug) Jordan**, 69, Auburn University football coach in 1951–75: in Auburn, Ala., on July 17.

**Dov Joseph**, 80, one of Israel's founding fathers; was military governor of besieged Jerusalem during 1948 Mideast war: in Tel Aviv, Israel, on Jan. 6.

**Bert Kaempfert**, 56, German composer and bandleader; wrote *Spanish Eyes* and *Strangers in the Night:* in Majorca, Spain, on June 22.

**Ida Kaminska**, 80, Polish actress in Yiddish theater, known for role in *The Shop on Main Street* film in 1966: in New York City on May 21.

**Robert W. Kean**, 86, U.S. representative (R-N.J.) in 1939–58: in Livingston, N.J., on Sept. 21.

**Barnaby C. Keeney**, 65, president of Brown University in 1955–66, first chairman of National Endowment and Council on the Humanities in 1966–70: in Providence, R.I., on June 18.

**Pearl L. Kendrick**, 90, microbiologist, developed vaccine leading to eradication of whooping cough in 1939: in Grand Rapids, Mich., on Oct. 8.

**Douglas Kenney**, 33, co-founder of *National Lampoon* magazine: in fall from cliff in Hawaii, on Sept. 1.

**William Kienbusch**, 65, painter known for landscapes of Maine: in New York City on March 23.

**Robert E. Kintner**, 71, president of American Broadcasting Company (ABC) in 1949–56 and National Broadcasting Company (NBC) in 1958–65: in Washington, D.C., on Dec. 20.

**Virginia Kirkus**, 86, founder, in 1933, of book-review service bearing her name: in Danbury, Conn., on Sept. 10.

**Arthur Kleiner**, 77, composer of music for silent films: in Hopkins, Minn., on March 31.

**Oskar Kokoschka**, 93, Austrian expressionist painter and a founder of expressionist drama: in Montreux, Switzerland, on Feb. 22.

**André Kostelanetz**, 78, Russian-American orchestra conductor, known on radio and TV.: in Port-au-Prince, Haiti, on Jan. 13.

**Alexei N. Kosygin**, 76, prime minister of Soviet Union in 1964–80: in Moscow, Soviet Union, on Dec. 18.

**John Kotewala**, 83, prime minister of Sri Lanka in 1953–56: in Colombo, Sri Lanka, on Oct. 2.

**Louis Kronenberger**, 75, critic, anthologist, author of books on 18th century England: in Brookline, Mass., on April 30.

**Edwin Francis Laker**, 70, developer of Pathfinder long-range bombing system: Ijamsville, Md., on March 1.

**Chester A. Lauck**, 78, actor who portrayed Lum on *Lum 'n' Abner* radio show in 1930s and 1940s: in Hot Springs, Ark., on Feb. 21.

**DEATHS: 1980** *(continued)*

**Joël Le Theule,** 50, French defense minister: in Sablé-sur-Sarthe, France, on Dec. 14.

**Jules Léger,** 67, governor-general of Canada in 1974–79: in Ottawa, Canada, on Nov. 22.

**John Lennon,** 40, member of Beatles group that revolutionized rock music in 1960s; Lennon and partner Paul McCartney wrote most of Beatles' hit songs until group broke up in 1970, then went on to write more music with wife, Yoko Ono, in 1970s: slain in New York City on Dec. 8.

**Jean Lesage,** 68, Liberal prime minister of Quebec in 1960–66: in Quebec, Canada, on Dec. 11.

**Sol Lesser,** 90, pioneer filmmaker of such films as *Kon Tiki, Our Town, The Red House,* and *Stage Door Canteen*: in Los Angeles, Calif., on Sept. 19.

**Sam Levene,** 75, stage and screen actor best known for role of Nathan Detroit in *Guys and Dolls*: in New York City about Dec. 27.

**Sam Levenson,** 68, humorist, author, former TV game show host: in Brooklyn, N.Y., on Aug. 27.

**Willard Libby,** 71, atomic scientist, won 1960 Nobel Prize in Chemistry; discovered carbon 14 (radiocarbon) dating in 1947: in Los Angeles, on Sept. 8.

**Fred Lieb,** 92, sports reporter, first writer inducted into Baseball Hall of Fame: in Houston, Tex., on June 3.

**Norman Lloyd,** 70, composer, in 1940s designed new approach to teaching music that changed focus from theory to application: in Greenwich, Conn., on July 31.

**Barbara Loden,** 48, stage and screen actress, director, writer: in New York City on Sept. 5.

**James B. Longley,** 56 governor of Maine in 1975–79: in Lewiston, Me., on Aug. 16.

**Alice Roosevelt Longworth,** 96, last surviving child of President Theodore Roosevelt; reigned over Washington, D.C., society as "Princess Alice" for 80 years: in Washington, D.C., on Feb. 20.

**Allard K. Lowenstein,** 51, U.S. representative (D-N.Y.) in 1969–71; civil rights activist: slain by former co-worker in New York City office on March 14.

**Earle MacAusland,** 90, founder of *Gourmet* magazine in 1941: in Nantucket, Mass., on June 4.

**Rachel MacKenzie,** 70, fiction editor for *The New Yorker* magazine: in New York City on March 28.

**Bernard Mackey,** 70, member of original Ink Spots singing group: in Miami, Fla., on March 5.

**Yakov A. Malik,** 73, Soviet delegate to UN in 1948–52 and 1968–76: in Moscow, Soviet Union, on Feb. 11.

**George Maloof,** 57, owner of Houston Rockets basketball team: in Albuquerque, N.M., on Nov. 29.

**Annunzio Paolo Mantovani,** 74, conductor of popular orchestras, first in 1950s to sell 1 million stereo records: in Tunbridge Wells, England, on March 29.

**Rube Marquard,** 90, major league baseball pitcher in 1908–25, set record of 19 straight victories for N.Y. Giants in 1912: in Baltimore, Md., on June 1.

**John L. Marshall,** 44, team physician of New York Giants football team: in plane crash near Saranac Lake, N.Y., on Feb. 12.

**Strother Martin,** 61, film actor known for role as prison warden in *Cool Hand Luke*: in Thousand Oaks, Calif., on Aug. 1.

**Maria Povera Martinez,** 94, Indian potter: in San Ildefonso Pueblo, N.M., on July 20.

**Bernd T. Matthias,** 62, scientist who discovered elements and compounds with superconducting properties: in La Jolla, Calif., on Oct. 27.

**John W. Mauchly,** 72, co-inventor in 1946 of first electronic computer (Electronic Numerical Integrator and Computer) for U.S. War Department: in Ambler, Pa., on Jan. 8.

**Mary McCarty,** 56, stage and screen actress, won Tony award for 1972 revival of *Anna Christie*: in Westwood, Calif., on April 5.

**John W. McCormack,** 88, U.S. representative (D-Mass.) in 1929–70, Speaker of the House in 1962–70: in Dedham, Mass., on Nov. 22.

**William Moore McCulloch,** 78, U.S. representative (R-Ohio) in 1947–72: in Washington, on Feb. 22.

**James S. McDonnell Jr.,** 81, chairman and cofounder of McDonnell Douglas Corp., known for making fighter planes and spacecraft: in Ladue, Mo., on Aug. 22.

**John McEwen,** 80, prime minister of Australia in 1967–68: in Melbourne, Australia, on Nov. 20.

**Marshall McLuhan,** 69, communications specialist known for phrase "the medium is the message": in Toronto, Ont., on Dec. 31.

**Steve McQueen,** 50, film actor known for adventure-type roles: in Juarez, Mexico, on Nov. 7.

**Cary McWilliams,** 74, editor of *The Nation* in 1955–75: in New York City on June 27.

**George Meany,** 85, first president of AFL-CIO in 1955–79, considered symbol of American labor movement: in Washington, D.C., on Jan. 10.

**Kay Medford,** 59, stage and film comedienne known for roles in *Bye Bye Birdie* and *Funny Girl*: in New York City on April 10.

**Lewis Milestone,** 84, film director; won Oscars for *All Quiet on the Western Front* and *Two Arabian Knights*: in Los Angeles, Calif., on Sept. 25.

**Henry Miller,** 88, American novelist known for *Tropic of Cancer* (1934) and *Tropic of Capricorn* (1939): in Pacific Palisades, Calif., on June 7.

**Hans J. Morgenthau,** 76, author, political scientist known for criticism of U.S. involvement in Vietnam: in New York City on July 19.

**A. S. Mike Moroney,** 77, U.S. senator (D-Okla.) in 1951–69: in Rockville, Md., on Feb. 13.

**Sir Oswald Mosley,** 84, British fascist leader who urged peace with Nazi Germany in World War II: in Orsay, France, on Dec. 2.

**Merrill Mueller,** 64, broadcast and print journalist: in Santa Monica, Calif., on Nov. 30.

**Frederick A. Muhlenberg,** 92, U.S. representative (R-Pa.) in 1946–48: in Reading, Pa., on Jan. 19.

**Luis Muñoz Marín,** 82, first elected governor of Puerto Rico, in 1948–64, who helped raise territory from poverty: in San Juan, Puerto Rico, on April 30.

**Caroline C. Myers,** 92, first woman employed by U.S. Army as teacher in World War I; chairman of board of *Highlights* magazine for children since 1971: in Boyds Mills, Pa., on July 3.

**Harold L. Neal Jr.,** 55, president of ABC Radio in 1972–79: in Darien, Conn., on Feb. 28.

**Pietro Nenni,** 88, Italian political leader of Socialist Party in 1949–69: in Rome, Italy, on Jan. 1.

**Arthur Charles Nielsen,** 83, engineer, devised system of TV ratings: in Chicago, Ill., on June 1.

**John Jacob Niles,** 87, folksinger and folklorist: in Lexington, Ky., on March 1.

**Elliott Nugent,** 83, actor, director, producer, writer of *The Male Animal, The Voice of the Turtle,* and *The Seven-Year Itch*: in New York City on Aug. 9.

**Masayoshi Ohira,** 70, prime minister of Japan since 1978: just 10 days before parliamentary elections: in Tokyo, Japan, on June 12.

**Arthur M. Okun,** 51, chairman of Council of Economic Advisors in 1968–69 and leading economist: in Washington, D.C., on March 23.

**George C. O'Neill,** 59, anthropologist, coauthor with wife of *Open Marriage*: in New York City on Oct. 4.

**Lithgow Osborne,** 87, New York State conservation commissioner in 1933–43 and former U.S. ambassador to Norway: in Auburn, N.Y., on March 10.

**Johnny Owen,** 24, Welsh boxer, in coma since Sept. 19 knockout in world bantamweight title bout: in Los Angeles, Calif., on Nov. 3.

**Jesse Owens,** 66, black track star, won four gold medals in 1936 Munich Olympics and broke numerous world records: in Tucson, Ariz., on March 31.

**Rafael Paasio,** prime minister of Finland in 1966–68, 1972: in Turku, Finland, on March 17.

**Joe Page,** 62, New York Yankees relief pitcher in 1944–50: in Latrobe, Pa., on April 21.

**Mohammed Riza Pahlevi,** 60, shah of Iran, from 1941 until forced to leave country on Jan. 16, 1979, by revolutionaries led by Ayatollah Ruholla Khomeini: of cancer in Cairo, Egypt, on July 27.

**George Pal,** 72, film producer, director, science-fiction specialist; won eight Academy Awards for special effects: in Beverly Hills, Calif., on May 2.

**Justas Paleckis,** 81, president of Soviet Lithuania in 1940–66: in Lithuania on Jan. 26.

**Gail Patrick,** 69, film actress in 1930s and 1940s: in Hollywood, Calif., on July 6.

**Lynn Patrick,** 67, hockey all-star with New York Rangers in 1930s and 1940s: in St. Louis, Mo., on Jan. 26.

**William A. Patterson,** 80, aviation pioneer, headed United Airlines in 1934–66: in Glenview, Ill., on June 13.

**Irwin Pearl,** 35, stage actor who created role of Chico Marx in *Minnie's Boys*: in New York City on Nov. 13.

**Wilfred R. Pehrson,** 53, tribal governor of Penobscot Indians of Maine in 1978–80: in Indian Island, Me., on Oct. 14.

**M. Murray Peshkin,** 88, allergist, originated theory in 1953 that asthma may be caused by emotional factors; founder of Asthma Care Association of America: in New York City on Aug. 17.

**Jean Piaget,** 84, Swiss psychologist noted for study of child development: in Geneva, Switzerland, on Sept. 17.

**George F. Pierrot,** 82, former host of TV travel series: in Detroit, Mich., on Feb. 15.

**Sergio Cardinal Pignedoli,** 70, considered leading contender in 1978 papal elections: in Reggio Emilia, Italy, on June 15.

**James Poe,** 58, screenwriter; won Oscar for *Around the World in 80 Days*: in Malibu, Calif., on Jan. 24.

**Cvjetko Popovic,** 84, one of last-known members of group that assassinated Archduke Franz Ferdinand of Austria in 1914, leading to World War I: in Sarajevo, Yugoslavia, on June 9.

**Katharine Anne Porter,** 90, writer of short stories and novel *Ship of Fools* (1962); won 1966 Pulitzer Prize for fiction for *Collected Stories*: in Silver Spring, Md., on Sept. 18.

**Bob Porterfield,** 56, major league baseball pitcher in 1948–59: in Charlotte, N.C., on April 28.

**Madeleine Porthault,** 73, textile designer: in Paris, France, on April 27.

**John A. (Shorty) Powers,** 57, known as "voice of the astronauts" during 1960s: in Phoenix, Ariz., on Jan. 1.

**Gordon Prange,** 79, historian, author of *Tora, Tora, Tora*: in Baltimore, Md., on May 15.

**John H. Preston,** 74, author known for *Revolution, 1776* that disputed popular beliefs about early U.S. history: in Quebec, Canada, on Nov. 11.

**George Raft,** 85, film actor known for gangster roles: in Hollywood, Calif., on Nov. 24.

**Lillian Randolph,** 65, movie and TV actress: in Arcadia, Calif., on Sept. 12.

**Paul Rappaport,** 58, founder of Solar Energy Research Institute in Golden, Colo.: in Evergreen, Colo., on April 21.

**Charles H. Reed,** 79, commander of tank unit in World War II that helped save Lipizzaner horses of Spanish Riding School of Vienna, Austria: in Richmond, Va., on April 7.

**Stanley Reed,** 95, U.S. Supreme Court associate justice in 1938–57: in Huntington, N.Y., on April 3.

**Robert (Bo) Rein,** 34, Louisiana State football coach: in crash of private plane off Virginia coast, on Jan. 10.

**Duncan Renaldo,** 76, movie, TV actor, played Cisco Kid: in Santa Barbara, Calif., on Sept. 3.

**J. B. Rhine,** 84, psychologist specializing in mysteries of clairvoyance, coined term *extrasensory perception (ESP)*: in Hillsborough, N.C., on Feb. 20.

**Gale Robbins,** 58, actress, singer, and World War II pin-up girl: in Los Angeles, Calif., on Feb. 18.

**Rachel Roberts,** 53, stage and screen actress: in West Los Angeles, Calif., on Nov. 26.

**Richard Roberts,** 69, pioneer in nuclear physics and microbiology; principal contributor to discovery of delayed neutrons as basis for atomic reactors: in Washington, D.C., on April 4.

**Fred Rodell,** 73, law professor at Yale for 41 years; expert on U.S. Constitution: in New Haven, Conn., on June 4.

**Oscar Arnulfo Romero,** 62, archbishop of El Salvador: assassinated by sniper while officiating at mass in San Salvador, El Salvador, on March 24.

**Finn Ronne,** 80, explorer who completed 9 expeditions to Antarctica: in Bethesda, Md., on Jan. 12.

**Lillian Roth,** 69, actress, singer who wrote autobiography *I'll Cry Tomorrow* about her fight against alcoholism: in New York City on May 12.

**Muriel Rukeyser,** 66, poet of social-protest themes: in New York City on Feb. 12.

**Harold Runnels,** 56, U.S. representative (D-N.M.) since 1971: in New York City on Aug. 5.

**Francisco Sá Carneiro,** 46, prime minister of Portugal: in plane crash in Lisbon, Portugal, on Dec. 4.

**Col. Harland Sanders,** 90, founder of Kentucky Fried Chicken restaurants: in Shelbyville, Ky., on Dec. 16.

**Luis (Felipe) Sandrini,** 75, Latin American comedian: in Buenos Aires, Argentina, on July 5.

**Dorothy Sands,** 87, stage actress and mimic: in Croton-on-Hudson, N.Y., on Sept. 11.

**Jean Paul Sartre,** 74, French existentialist philosopher, novelist, playwright known for *Being and Nothingness* (1943), *No Exit* (1944), *Dirty Hands* (1948): in Paris, France, on April 15.

**Louis W. Sauer,** 94, pediatrician, helped develop vaccines against whooping cough, diphtheria, and tetanus: in Coral Gables, Fla., on Feb. 10.

**James Joseph Saxon,** 65, U.S. comptroller of the currency in 1961–67: in Chevy Chase, Md., on Jan. 28.

**W. H. Schaper,** 66, inventor of popular children's game *Cootie*: in Minneapolis, Minn., on Sept. 8.

**Dore Schary,** 74, movie producer and playwright known for *Sunrise at Campobello*: in New York City on July 7.

**John Sebastian,** 65, musician who endeavored to have harmonica treated as classical instrument: in Perigord, France, on Aug. 18.

**August Sebastiani,** 66, head of California wine-making family: in Sonoma, Calif., on Feb. 16.

**Peter Sellers,** 54, British actor, comedian known for roles in *The Pink Panther* and *Dr. Strangelove*: in London, England, on July 24.

**Seretse Khama,** 59, president of Botswana since 1966: in Botswana on July 13.

**Abdul Sharaf,** 41, prime minister of Jordan since 1979: in Amman, Jordan, on July 3.

**Malcolm P. Sharp,** 83, assistant defense counsel at espionage trial of Ethel and Julius Rosenberg in 1953: in Chicago, Ill., on Aug. 14.

**George E. Shea Jr.,** 77, financial editor of *Wall Street Journal* in 1949–67: in New York City on April 27.

**Norman Shelley,** 77, actor known for mimicry of Winston S. Churchill's "We shall never surrender" speech: in London, England, on Aug. 22.

**DEATHS: 1980** *(continued)*

**Allen G. Shenstone,** 86, pioneer in use of atomic spectroscopy to study energy relationships within the atom: in Princeton, N.J., on Feb. 16.

**Henry Knox Sherrill,** 89, presiding bishop of Episcopal Church in 1946–58: in Boxford, Mass., on May 11.

**Ernie Shore,** 89, baseball pitcher who in 1917 pitched perfect game in relief: in Winston-Salem, N.C., on Sept. 24.

**Elizabeth Shoumatoff,** 92, artist; painted portraits of Presidents Franklin Roosevelt and Lyndon Johnson: in Glen Cove, N.Y., on Nov. 30.

**Ahmed Shukairy,** 72, first head of Palestine Liberation Organization (PLO): in Amman, Jordan, on Feb. 26.

**Jay Silverheels,** 62, actor known for role as Tonto in *The Lone Ranger* TV series: in Woodland Hills, Calif., on March 5.

**Frederick D. Sisler,** 63, microbiologist, invented prototype of biochemical fuel cell: in St. Augustine, Fla., on March 2.

**John M. Slack,** 64, U.S. representative (D-W. Va.) since 1959: in Alexandria, Va., on March 17.

**Janet Smith,** 66, mayor of St. Albans, Vt.: shot to death just six days after taking office, in St. Albans, Vt., on March 16.

**Conn Smythe,** 85, former owner of Toronto Maple Leafs hockey team: in Toronto, Canada, on Nov. 17.

**C. P. Snow,** 74, British physicist, playwright, and novelist: in London, England, on July 1.

**Anastasio Somoza Debayle,** 54, ruler of Nicaragua from 1964 until his ouster in July 1979: assassinated in exile in Asunción, Paraguay, on Sept. 17.

**Woodrow Wilson (Red) Sovine,** 61, country music singer: in Nashville, Tenn., on April 4.

**William H. Stein,** 68, co-winner of 1972 Nobel Prize in Chemistry for research on pancreatic enzyme, ribonuclease: in New York City on Feb. 2.

**Elizabeth Stern,** 64, pathologist who discovered relationship of prolonged use of birth-control pills to cervical cancer: in Los Angeles, Calif., on Aug. 9.

**Donald Stewart,** 85, dramatist, humorist, screenwriter known for *The Philadelphia Story*: in London, England, on Aug. 2.

**Clyfford Still,** 75, American abstract expressionist painter; subject of largest one-man exhibition ever devoted to a living artist by Metropolitan Museum of Art in Nov. 1979–Feb. 1980: in Baltimore, Md., on June 23.

**Morris Stoloff,** 81, composer of music for films, won Oscars for *Cover Girl* (1944), *The Jolson Story* (1946), and *Song Without End* (1960): in Woodland Hills, Calif., on April 16.

**Milburn Stone,** 75, actor known for role as Doc Adams in *Gunsmoke* TV show: in La Jolla, Calif., on June 12.

**Dorothy Stratton,** 20, *Playboy* magazine Playmate of the Year: slain in Los Angeles, Calif., on Aug. 14.

**Gladys Guggenheim Straus,** 84, cofounder of *Gourmet* magazine in 1941 and expert on food and nutrition: in New York City on March 13.

**Frank L. Sundstrom,** 79, U.S. representative (R-N.J.) in 1943–49: in Chatham, N.J., on May 23.

**Walter Susskind,** 66, orchestra conductor, music director of St. Louis Symphony in 1968–75: in Berkeley, Calif., on March 25.

**Willie Sutton,** 79, convicted bank robber noted as escape artist: in Spring Hill, Fla., on Nov. 2.

**Henrietta H. Swope,** 78, astronomer; helped develop method of measuring variable stars: in Pasadena, Calif., on Nov. 24.

**Gladys Taber,** 80, author of more than 50 books, including the *Stillmeadow* journals: in Hyannis, Mass., on March 11.

**Ali Akbar Tabatabi,** 49, former press ataché at Iranian Embassy in Washington during regime of Shah Mo-

hammed Riza Pahlevi and outspoken critic of Ayatollah Khomeini: assassinated at home in Washington, D.C., on July 22.

**Herman Tarnower,** 69, physician; author of *The Complete Scarsdale Medical Diet*: killed in dispute with female friend in Purchase, N.Y., home on March 10.

**Clara M. Tead,** 88, head of Briarcliff College in 1942–60: in Washington, D.C., on March 2.

**Edwin Way Teale,** 81, naturalist who won 1966 Pulitzer Prize for general nonfiction for study of winter: in Norwich, Conn., on Oct. 18.

**Billy Thomas,** 49, played Buckwheat character in *Our Gang* comedy movies in 1934–44: in Los Angeles, Calif., on Oct. 10.

**Harry C. Thompson,** 59, publisher of *Newsweek* in 1969–72, former head of Magazine Publishers Assn.: in Wesport, Conn., on April 20.

**Henry M. Tiedemann,** 58, naval architect whose firm developed hydrofoil boats: in Greenwich, Conn., on Jan. 24.

**Josip Broz Tito,** 87, communist leader of Yugoslavia from 1944: in Ljubljana, Yugoslavia, on May 4.

**George Tobias,** 78, film and TV actor: in Hollywood, Calif., on Feb. 27.

**William R. Tolbert Jr.,** 66, president of Liberia since 1971: killed in coup in Monrovia, Liberia, on April 12.

**Ton Duc Thang,** 91, president of Vietnam since 1976: in Vietnam on March 30.

**Ben Travers,** 94, British playwright called "master of theater farce": in London, England, on Dec. 18.

**Kenneth Tynan,** 53, British drama critic: in Santa Monica, Calif., on July 26.

**Bobby Van,** 47, actor, comedian, dancer: in Los Angeles, Calif., on July 31.

**John Van Vleck,** 81, winner of 1977 Nobel Prize in Physics for work explaining magnetic properites of solids: in Cambridge, Mass., on Oct. 27.

**Vladimir Vysotsky,** 46, Soviet satirist, actor, balladeer: in Moscow, on July 24.

**Stella Walsh,** 69, Polish-born track star: won gold medal at 1932 Olympics: in Cleveland, Ohio, on Dec. 4.

**Shields Warren,** 82, pathologist, pioneer in research on biological effects of radiation: in Mashpee, Mass., on July 1.

**George Watts,** 69, chemist who participated in Manhattan Project that produced first atomic bomb: in Austin, Texas, on March 29.

**Mae West,** 87, burlesque, stage, and screen star: in Los Angeles, Calif., on Nov. 22.

**Bell I. Wiley,** 72, Civil War historian; author of *The Life of Johnny Reb*: in Atlanta, Ga., on April 4.

**Wilhelmina (Wilhlemina Behmenburg Cooper),** 40, Dutch-born model and model agency owner: in Cos Cob, Conn., on March 1.

**James Wright,** 52, poet who won 1972 Pulitzer Prize; wrote on poverty and Midwest: in New York City on March 25.

**Patriarch Moran More Ignatiurs Yacoub,** 67, head of Syrian Orthodox Church since 1957: in Damascus, Syria, on June 25.

**Yahya Khan,** 63, military ruler of Pakistan in 1969–71, under house arrest until 1977: in Rawalpindi, Pakistan, on Aug. 8.

**Nathan Yalin-Mor,** 66, former commander of terrorist Stern Gang, fought British army in Palestine in 1940s: in Tel Aviv, Israel, on Feb. 18.

**Jo Ann Yellow Bird,** 32, Sioux Indian activist, won $300,000 civil-rights judgment against city of Gordon, Neb., in 1979: in Martin, S.D., on July 7.

**Dan Zhao,** 66, leading Chinese film actor: in Peking, China, on Oct. 10.

# Index